25⁰⁰ TAB

MODERN WORLD DRAMA

MODERN WORLD DRAMA

AN ENCYCLOPEDIA

BY

MYRON MATLAW

Queens College of
The City University of New York

E. P. Dutton & Co., Inc. | New York | 1972

FIRST EDITION

Published simultaneously in Canada by
Clarke, Irwin & Company Limited, Toronto and Vancouver.

Library of Congress Catalog Card Number: 71-185032
SBN 0-525-15902-9

The material on T. S. Eliot in this book was originally published in another version as "Eliot the Dramatist" in *CLA Journal*, XII (December, 1968), 116–122. It is republished here by permission of The College Language Association.

To Julia

Preface

This book provides English-speaking readers and theatre audiences with a comprehensive reference to modern world drama in one extensively indexed volume containing a single alphabetical listing of plays, playwrights, countries, and technical terms. The national entries are surveys that help to place authors in their native context, just as the playwright entries provide the context for the works that are treated separately. The play entries include, in addition to synopses, encyclopedic information on first publication and production dates, length and setting, as well as notes on philosophical perspectives, dramaturgy, background, and history. The purpose of the synopsis is to familiarize the reader with the plot and perhaps lead him to read or see the play itself, or to recall and revive its original impact if he has already read or seen it. Of course, no summary can possibly reproduce or substitute for the actual play; but I have tried in these synopses to convey some of the tone and flavor of the original.

The presentation and selections from the vast body of drama, literary criticism, and theatrical lore naturally reflect my own tastes and attitudes. However, my emphasis has been on distilling factual material (much of it necessarily based on the studies of specialists in particular areas) in accordance with the anticipated interests and needs of the book's users. I have made every effort to present a balanced and judicious view. Like all readers and audiences, however, an author can perceive history, dramatic literature, and theatrical productions solely through his own understanding and experience. Yet I think that such an individual perspective, while open to disagreement, has some obvious advantages over corporate products.

The precise beginning of the "modern period" cannot be designated by any one particular date. This is especially true in a volume such as this, which describes many diverse cultures that broke with earlier traditions at different times and in somewhat different ways. Nonetheless, Henrik Ibsen (1828–1906), though he wrote all his plays in the nineteenth century, is universally regarded as the father of modern drama. Comparable modern giants like August Strindberg, Anton Chekhov, and Bernard Shaw also wrote their seminal works before the turn of the century. One can say, therefore, that modern drama per se began in the latter half of the nineteenth century, and that within any given country modern drama dates from the time that these and other major European writers began to influence that country's dramatists.

In this encyclopedia of modern world drama I have attempted to cover the work of all major nineteenth-century playwrights who lived into this century, as well as the work of all notable twentieth-century playwrights up to the present time. During this period of well over a hundred years, countless new plays have been published and produced throughout the world. If many of them are dross that is soon and best forgotten, there are many others that are notable (over a thousand separate play entries appear in this book). The modern era has produced as rich a harvest as did the Golden Age of antiquity, the Renaissance, and other illustrious periods—and it usually communicates with greater clarity, urgency, and immediacy to present-day audiences.

During the long process of publication, I attempted to keep this book up to date by noting significant new authors, plays, and studies. Evaluations of some immediately contemporary subjects may nonetheless be modified by subsequent developments.

Occasionally a playwright who once seemed promising or important is later overshadowed by a contemporary who formerly was of little note. Even a playwright whose reputation is securely established may be viewed differently in the light of his latest work—or of the latest critical reappraisals. Thus every book on a living subject is necessarily somewhat tentative in its coverage of recent happenings, which, in this book too, are therefore treated less exhaustively.

The preparation of a volume of this magnitude is immensely dependent on the works of a great many critics, theatre historians, and other scholars. Some of these are cited in the bibliographies, including the "Selective General Bibliography" on page xi. It would be impossible to list the thousands of other books and articles consulted, however, or to acknowledge the assistance of each of the many embassies, consulates, cultural societies, and other institutions, and their many officials in this country and abroad who have responded to my requests for information. Invaluable to my research were the magnificent holdings and the responsive personnel of the Library of Congress and of the New York Public Library, particularly the Theatre Collection of the Library of the Performing Arts at Lincoln Center; and the libraries of the institutions with which I was affiliated during the writing of this book, the University of Hawaii and Queens College of the City University of New York. For their interest, encouragement, and provocative questions I should like to thank my friends, colleagues, and students in both places, including those whose names are among the ones cited below.

The specialists who read this book in manuscript and galleys saved me from many a blunder; their comments were most helpful and informative. It is a pleasure to thank the following: Frank Alberti, Robert Austerlitz, Faubion Bowers, Eugenio Chang-Rodriguez, Rae Dalven, Ahmet Ö. Evin, Malcolm Goldstein, David I. Grossvogel, William L. Hanaway, Jr., Eugene Hanger, William E. Harkins, Robert Hogan, Ante Kadić, Mendel Kohansky, Rosette C. Lamont, Joseph C. Landis, John Gaywood Linn, Fredric M. Litto, Maan Z. Madina, Masahiko Masumoto, Charles A. Moser, Richard Nickson, Martin Nozick, Clinton F. Oliver, Gregory Rabassa, Olga Ragusa, Robert Raphael, Robert K. Sarlos, Harold B. Segel, James A. Sehnert, Rimvydas Šilbajoris, Stavro Skendi, J. W. Smit, Michael S. Tait, Mardi Valgemäe, Richard B. Vowles, and George E. Wellwarth.

I am indebted to many others for their suggestions, ideas, and information. For their helpful responses I should like particularly to thank the following: Denes Agay, Robert H. Ball, Charles S. Bouslog, Thomas R. Buckman, Wendell B. Daniel, Bernard F. Dukore, Lillian Feder, Mirra Ginsburg, Ralph E. Matlaw, James W. McFarlane, Jan M. Meijer, Margaret S. Peden, Ann Saddlemyer, Vera Scriabine, Travis L. Summersgill, Helen A. Topham, Damian S. Wandycz, and Isabel Wilder. Special thanks are due also to the personnel of the Queens College Computer Center for setting up my early working copy of the "General Index."

I have been fortunate with my publisher: President John Macrae III and his staff have been the very model of cooperation. Editor Cyril I. Nelson encouraged my labors quite literally from A to Z, indulging my authorial whims with admirable fortitude and never-flagging support. Margaret E. Ritchie performed her sisyphean task of copy-editing with intelligence and good cheer.

My most profound gratitude is to my wife and children, whose affectionate confidence and patience inspired my undertaking, persistence in, and completion of this work.

New York City
Winter, 1970–71

M.M.

Contents

Selective General Bibliography

For specific bibliographies see individual entries

A History of the Modern Drama (1947), edited by Barrett H. Clark and George Freedley, has essays by twenty-three specialists on different countries covering the European drama from Ibsen to the end of World War II. Notable general histories are those by John Gassner, particularly his *Masters of the Drama* (third edition, 1954); and George Freedley and John A. Reeves's *A History of the Theatre* (third edition, 1968).

Distinguished general critical studies of modern drama can be found in the writings of Eric Bentley, principally in *The Playwright as Thinker* (1946, and subsequently updated editions); in Francis Fergusson's *The Idea of a Theater* (1949); and in the collected theatre reviews of Bentley, Robert Brustein, Martin Esslin, Mary McCarthy, Kenneth Tynan, and Stark Young.

A reference work that merits special mention, though it is general and in a foreign language (Italian), is the vastly informative and lavishly illustrated eleven-volume *Enciclopedia dello spettacolo* (1954–66).

The bibliography *Modern Drama: A Checklist of Critical Literature on 20th Century Plays* (1967), by Irving Adelman and Rita Dworkin, lists books and articles published in English from 1900 to 1965 on about three hundred modern playwrights. It may be supplemented and updated with bibliographies in such scholarly journals as *PMLA* ("Publications of the Modern Language Association of America") and in drama and theatre periodicals.

Among the more important periodicals that regularly discuss new authors, plays, and productions are such journals as *World Theatre* (1951 ff.), *TDR, the Drama Review* (1957 ff., earlier known as the *Tulane Drama Review*), *Modern Drama* (1958 ff.), and *Plays and Players* (1953 ff.), a monthly English magazine similar in format to the American *Theatre Arts* (1916–64).

The annual *Best Plays* volume of the "Burns Mantle Yearbook" series, beginning with *The Best Plays of 1919–20,* contains a wealth of material, including numerous synopses of the season's new plays, American as well as foreign.

Arrangement of Contents

SCOPE: 1. *Geographical entries* summarize the modern drama of individual countries, and in some cases that of whole continents and other large areas, such as LATIN AMERICA and SCANDINAVIA.

2. *Biographical entries* deal with playwrights who have lived in the twentieth century*—some of them more notable in other fields, as are, for instance, D. H. LAWRENCE, ROBERT LOWELL, V. I. NEMIROVICH-DANCHENKO, and MAE WEST.

3. *Dramatic entries* include the synopses of and other information and comments about plays, selected musicals, and drama cycles like O'Neill's A TALE OF POSSESSORS, SELF-DISPOSSESSED, important collections like Strindberg's THE CHAMBER PLAYS, and particularly significant dramatic criticisms like Shaw's THE QUINTESSENCE OF IBSENISM. Play entries cite the year of first publication (including private and translations) as well as of first production (including amateur and foreign).

4. *Technical terms* described are only the modern ones like ABSURD, EXPRESSIONISM, REPRESENTATIONAL; older terms like *comedy, tragedy,* and *masque* are not included.

CROSS REFERENCES: SMALL CAPITALS are used throughout this volume, including the "General Index," to indicate that there is a separate entry for any item thus printed; note that SMALL CAPITALS are used only the *first time* the cross-referenced subject is mentioned in a particular article.

TITLES: An original foreign title followed by an English title indicates that the play has been translated into English under that title.

DATES: Unless otherwise noted, the date following the title of a play is that of its first publication (including private) or production (including amateur), whichever came earlier.

BIBLIOGRAPHIES: Works listed at the end of entries are usually of book length and in English; where no bibliography is given for an author, consult the one listed for that author's native country. See also the "Selective General Bibliography," p. xi.

CHARACTER INDEX: This index lists all characters who are named in the plot synopses as well as many notable historical, legendary, and literary figures who appear as characters in other modern plays mentioned in all entries in this volume, such as Columbus, Hamlet, Jesus, Napoleon, Shakespeare, Zeus, and many others. (See also the headnote to the "Character Index," p. 859.)

GENERAL INDEX: This index covers everything described under SCOPE, above, as well as references to comparable items that have no separate entries, including nineteenth-century playwrights. All subjects are also listed under the alternate names by which they are sometimes known or may have been translated. For example, Giraudoux's *La Guerre de Troie n'aura pas lieu* appears under that title as well as under those of both of its translations, THE TROJAN WAR WILL NOT TAKE PLACE and

* The only exceptions are two authors who died a few months before 1900: HENRY BECQUE, one of the founders of NATURALISM; and AUGUSTIN DALY, a major figure in the generally undistinguished early American period.

Tiger at the Gates. Similarly, authors are listed under possible variant spellings and forms: under each of the composite surnames commonly used by Spanish writers (GARCÍA LORCA, FEDERICO as well as LORCA, FEDERICO GARCÍA), under both given and surnames to allow for the reverse name order commonly followed in Japan (MISHIMA YUKIO as well as YUKIO, MISHIMA), and under standard as well as "last" names of authors known by pseudonymous epithets or other phrases (SHOLEM ALEICHEM as well as ALEICHEM, SHOLEM).

Method of Alphabetizing

By word, not letter:

I Remember Mama
Illumination
In Abraham's Bosom

Punctuation marks are not considered:

Green Goddess, The
Green, Julian
Green Pastures, The
King David and His Wives
King, The
King Ubu

Abbreviations are treated as though they were spelled out:

Dock Brief, The
Dr. Angelus
Doctor Knock
Doctor's Dilemma, The
Dödsdansen
Mississippi
Mr. Pim Passes By
Místico, El
Mrs. Warren's Profession
Molnár, Ferenc

Contractions are treated as words:

Ill Met by Moonlight
I'll Tell You a Story
Illumination
Im Dickicht der Städte
I'm Talking About Jerusalem
Im weissen Rössl

Hyphenated words are considered as two separate words:

Make a Wish
Make-Believe
Make Way for Lucia

Numerals and symbols are treated as though they were spelled out:

Two for the Seesaw
200 Pounds a Year
2 × 2 = 5
Typhoon

Articles are transposed to the end:

Cantatrice chauve, La
Dreigroschenoper, Die
Folkefiende, En
Glass Menagerie, The
Intereses creados, Los

Prepositions are counted as first words:

In the Shadow of the Glen
On Trial
Over the Bridge

Names beginning with *Mac* or *Mc* are alphabetized as *Mac* and *Mc*:

MacLeish, Archibald
Maugham, Somerset
McCullers, Carson

Ligatures, umlauts, accents, and other diacritical marks are not considered:

Glamour
Gläserne Frau, Die
Glastüren
Leçon, La
Léocadia
Naïves hirondelles
Nałkowska, Zofia
Når vi døde vågner
Odysseus und Nausikaa
Œdipe-roi
Oedipus at Colonus

List of Illustrations

MODERN WORLD DRAMA

A

ABBOTT, George (1887–   ), American actor, director, and prolific author and coauthor of plays, many of them musicals. One of his early hits, *Broadway* (1926), a melodrama about prohibition-era cabaret performers and bootleggers, resulted from his collaboration with PHILIP DUNNING. Abbott's *Coquette* (1927; written with a young actress, Ann Preston Bridgers [d.1967], who supplied the original sketch) featured Helen Hayes as an evil girl committing suicide to save her father, who shot a youngster to protect his daughter's reputation. *Three Men on a Horse* (1935), a clever and very successful farce about a poet kidnapped for his uncanny ability to pick winners, was written with JOHN CECIL HOLM, later coauthor of its musical version, *Let It Ride* (1963).

Abbott's many musicals include *The Boys from Syracuse* (1938, music by Richard Rodgers and lyrics by Lorenz Hart), an adaptation of Shakespeare's *The Comedy of Errors; Where's Charley?* (1948), an adaptation with Frank Loesser (1910–69) of Thomas's CHARLEY'S AUNT; *A Tree Grows in Brooklyn* (1951, music by Arthur Schwartz and lyrics by Howard Dietz), an adaptation with Betty Smith (1896–1972) of her best-selling 1943 novel of life in Brooklyn's slums; *The Pajama Game* (1954, music and lyrics by Richard Adler and Jerry Ross), a long-running adaptation with Richard P. Bissell (1913–   ) of the latter's novel, *7½ Cents* (1952), about a romance between a unionist and a pajama factory superintendent eager to increase production; *Damn Yankees* (1955, music and lyrics by Adler and Ross), with Douglass Wallop (1920–   ), based on Wallop's 1954 baseball novel *The Year the Yankees Lost the Pennant; New Girl in Town* (1957, music and lyrics by Bob Merrill), a musical version of O'Neill's ANNA CHRISTIE; and *Fiorello!* (1959, music by Jerry Bock and lyrics by Sheldon Harnick), the Pulitzer Prize-winning musical about New York's peppery Mayor La Guardia, written with Jerome Weidman (1913–   ), who also collaborated on *Tenderloin* (1960, music and lyrics by Bock and Harnick), another Abbott musical about New York.

To celebrate his fiftieth anniversary in the theatre, George Abbott published his autobiography, *"Mister Abbott,"* in 1963.

ABE LINCOLN IN ILLINOIS, a play in three acts by ROBERT E. SHERWOOD, produced in 1938 and published in 1939. Setting: Illinois, 1830–61.

Sherwood's most popular play (and Raymond Massey's most popular performance; he played the title part on both stage and screen) is more episodic than JOHN DRINKWATER's and depicts an earlier period in Lincoln's life. Based on Carl Sandburg's biography and written in the language of its hero's milieu, Sherwood's Pulitzer Prize winner focuses on a character portrayal that utilizes the audience's awareness of Lincoln's subsequent history. Sherwood does not develop other characters or dramatize many historical events. Lincoln is depicted as (rather than how) he changes from an unambitious "failure" to a militant champion of democracy. The play marked Sherwood's first open departure from pacifism.

Act I. Scene 1. Salem's schoolmaster teaches grammar to Lincoln, a twenty-two-year-old backwoodsman, and imbues him with a love of great oratory and poetry. In exemplifying various grammatical moods, Lincoln alludes to his failure as a businessman (he has assumed responsibility for the bankruptcy caused by his alcoholic partner), to his fear of city people, and to his mother's death. He reads Keats's poem "On Death," and remarks, "That sure is good." *Scene 2.* At the Rutledge Tavern on the Fourth of July, a number of young politicians explore Lincoln's potential as a candidate for the State Assembly. He is now the local postmaster, and his deft handling of rowdies about to beat up the governor's son persuades the politicians that Lincoln is their man. The $3-a-day pay, Lincoln suggests, would help pay his debt, and he would be near a library and good lawyers. When the politicians leave, Lincoln sympathizes with Ann Rutledge over her fiancé's jilting her. Though he believes her to be far above him, Lincoln declares his love. When Ann gives him hope, he realizes "this is a land of equal opportunity for all"—and agrees to run for the assembly. *Scene 3.* A year later his friends discuss Lincoln's future. They feel that Ann, "his own romantic ideal of what's beautiful and unattainable," would hinder the lovelorn and not very successful assemblyman. Lincoln comes in: Ann has just died. Broken, Lincoln says: "I've got to die and be with her again, or I'll go crazy!"

Act II. Scene 4. Five years later, Lincoln, a lawyer in Springfield, is now thirty-one, but much aged by Ann's death. Though opposed to slavery after seeing a group of chained Negroes, he is "even more opposed to going to war" and will not support the Abolitionists, "a pack of hell-roaring fanatics." Lincoln assures his friends that he is doing pretty well: he has settled part of his debt, and has even shaken the hand of the President of the United States. He has no desire to "get down into the blood-soaked arena and grapple with all the lions of injustice and oppression" and, as they want him to do, "amount to something." When they call him an "artful dodger" eager to avoid the dictates of his conscience at a time of national stress, Lincoln admits that within him there rages a civil war. To pull Lincoln out of his lethargy, a friend invites him to meet his ambitious sister-in-law, Mary Todd, whose father is the president of the Bank of Kentucky. Lincoln remarks, "They spell their name with two D's—which is pretty impressive when you consider that one was enough for God." *Scene 5.* Half a year later Mary decides to marry Lincoln. Her aristocratic sister is upset because Mary has set her cap for a boor "who is lazy and shiftless and prefers to stop constantly along the way to tell jokes." But Mary is sure Lincoln can be inspired to do great things: "I want the chance to *shape* a new life, for myself and for my husband." *Scene 6.* A few weeks later, on the day of their wedding, a friend tries to dissuade Lincoln from canceling it. Mary's brother-in-law brings Lincoln a wedding gift and urges him to "keep a tight rein on her ambition," for Mary always said her husband would become President. Lincoln's clerk is pleased that someone will goad him to free the slaves. But Lincoln, who as yet has found no ideals worth dying for, goes to cancel the wedding—and leaves town. *Scene 7.* Near Salem two years later, Lincoln meets an old friend heading west with his family. Though he looks forward to building a new life there, his friend recognizes obstacles ahead—for the Dred Scott decision has extended slavery to the West. Lincoln suddenly recognizes the plight of the whole country. "Don't let anything beat you—don't you ever give up," Lincoln exhorts his friend. Then he prays for the friend's sick child: "His people are travelling far, to seek a new home in the wilderness, to do your work, God, to make this earth a good place for your children to live in." And Lincoln entreats God to grant the child and all men their birthrights. *Scene 8.* A few days later he calls on Mary Todd humbly to ask her, again, to be his wife: "The way I must go is the way you have always wanted me to go." He promises to devote the rest of his life to labor for "what is right—as God gives me power to see what is right." Avowing her eternal love, Mary falls into Lincoln's arms.

Act III. Scene 9. On a summer evening in 1858 in an Illinois town, Lincoln and Stephen A. Douglas, rival candidates for the United States Senate, make their concluding speeches in the debate on slavery. *Scene 10.* Lincoln sits in his parlor with his three boys in 1860, as Mary complains bitterly that her oldest son smokes in the house. "Come, come, Mary—you must be

Abe Lincoln in Illinois, Act II, Scene 4. Lincoln (Raymond Massey) and his friends (Arthur Griffin and Calvin Thomas). New York, 1938. (*Culver Pictures*)

respectful to a Harvard man," Lincoln remarks. She is furious because Lincoln has not told her earlier about the imminent arrival of various leaders, coming "to see if I'm fit to be a candidate for President of the United States." But Mary is also aware of her growing irritability: "I've succeeded in nothing—but in breaking myself." The visitors decide that, despite "his curious, primitive way," Lincoln can win. *Scene 11.* As they await the election returns later that year, tension causes Mary and Lincoln to quarrel openly. Even if he wins, she says bitterly as she goes home, "it's ruined, for me. It's too late." Lincoln is elected President. "Yes—we've fought the good fight—in the dirtiest campaign in the history of corrupt politics," he says, feeling the full weight of his responsibilities as he leaves wearily, with a Secret Service escort, to tell Mary he has won the election. *Scene 12.* On February 11, 1861, at the Springfield railroad station, the Secret Service men worry about protecting Lincoln, whom many have sworn to assassinate even before his inauguration. Lincoln has requested that his law-office shingle be kept up until he returns—"if I live." Before the train leaves, Lincoln, wearing "new whiskers—of which I hope you approve," responds to the crowd's request for a speech. There is great danger to freedom, he says, but exhorts all to "cultivate the natural world that is about us, and the intellectual and moral world that is within us, so that we may secure an individual, social and political prosperity, whose course shall be forward, and which, while the earth endures, shall not pass away." The train whistle sounds as the crowd sings: "His soul goes marching on."

ABEL, Lionel (1910–), American poet and playwright, translated modern French drama and wrote philosophical comedies, most of them based on Greek myths and the Bible. They include *The Death of Odysseus* (1953), *Absalom* (1956), and *The Wives* (1965); the last-named is about Herakles's wife, who tries to regain his love and destroys them both. His earlier *The Pretender* (1959) depicts a Negro novelist as a wronged husband who demands vengeance. Most of Abel's dramas have appeared Off-Broadway.

ABELL, Kjeld (1901–61), has been called Denmark's greatest playwright of the twentieth century, and he became his country's most distinguished dramatist after the Nazis murdered KAJ MUNK. To English-speaking audiences Abell's detective drama ANNA SOPHIE HEDVIG (1939) and his fantasy *Dage på en sky* (DAYS ON A CLOUD, 1947) are perhaps the best known of his fifteen plays. They are characteristic of his dramaturgy, which has been likened to that of JEAN GIRAUDOUX. Other playwrights said to have influenced him are ERICH KÄSTNER, NORDAHL GRIEG, and CHRISTOPHER FRY. Abell was deeply concerned with the general erosion of moral responsibility and integrity in the cataclysmic three decades before his death. Like the Swedish playwright PÄR LAGERKVIST, Abell sometimes became excessively philosophic in dramatizing his convictions, which were militantly and rebelliously liberal. But at his best Abell deftly concealed didactic excesses with skillful and imaginative theatricality.

Abell was born in Ribe. He studied economics at the University of Copenhagen, and for a while worked with the Police Identification Bureau as a fingerprint expert. Interested in choreography (he had been associated with George Balanchine at London's Alhambra Theatre in 1931) as well as in art, he was a stage painter for a short time and wrote a ballet, which was produced in 1934. His first play, *Melodien, der blev væk* (*The Melody That Got Lost*) appeared the following year. Immediately captivating audiences with its exuberant irreverence, this witty, EXPRESSIONISTIC drama about a Chaplinesque "little man" searching for meaning (the title's "lost melody") amidst the trivia and commercialism of life expressed Abell's iconoclastic opposition to respectability and authority, and his lifelong conviction that man must be true to his best self.

His next play, the satirical burlesque *Eva aftjener sin barnepligt* (1937), was similarly unconventional. Influenced by Hans Christian Andersen, whom Abell was to feature in a later play, it portrays the biblical Eve restored to life from a museum painting and brought up in a conventional family who are in the end amusingly punished for quelling her natural independence while Adam and Eve must go out into the world to observe and label everything anew. Following his 1938 dramatization of Dickens's *Oliver Twist,* and the anti-Nazi *Anna Sophie Hedvig,* Abell wrote another biblically inspired drama, *Judith* (1940); it is a modern interpretation of the Judith-Holofernes tale in which the heroine's latter-day counterpart as well as the audience are told that "Every woman is a Judith and should be able to act like a Judith," and challenged: "How would *you* act?" This was followed by two plays that again deal obliquely with the Nazi occupation, during which they were composed: *Dronningen går igen* (*The Queen on Tour,* 1943), a murder mystery like *Anna Sophie Hedvig,* and *Silkeborg* (1946), a "resistance" drama which, like the earlier play, exhorts man to battle for liberation from evil. It was written while Abell worked in the underground movement, to which he escaped after publicly protesting the murder of Kaj Munk. Earlier Abell had spent some months as a political hostage in a German concentration camp.

The end of the war and the dawn of the atomic age inspired his next play, *Days on a Cloud.* Though it is an imaginative fantasy that links the Greek gods with a nuclear scientist, the play expresses once again Abell's lifelong protest against human shortcomings and his insistence that men must *act* on their ideals. *Vetsera blomstrer ikke for enhver* (1950), Abell's next play, has been characterized as a CHEKHOVian drama about contemporary terror and despair. It was followed by another imaginative fantasy in which man is urged to reject the death wish and live to fight,

Den blå Pekingeser (1954); this play too is set in a limbo, and its characters consist of the yet-unborn, the living, and the dead—all of whom talk while the invisible title character's bells tinkle. Abell's remaining plays include *Andersen eller Hans livs eventyr* (1955), a tribute to the fellow Dane whose fairly tales had inspired some of Abell's works; *Kameliadamen* (*Camille,* 1959), an adaptation of *La Dame aux Camélias,* in which the novelist Alexander Dumas appears with his fictive creations Marguerite Gautier and Armand Duval, who go on to lead their lives independent of him; and Abell's final and most complex play, *Skriget* (1961). Produced at Copenhagen's Royal Theatre shortly after his death, it is a fantasy acted out on three levels: biblical, contemporary, and anthropomorphic. It is set in the tower of a village church whose Sunday service is interrupted by an innocent sacrificial victim's scream, which is meant symbolically to pierce man's façade and at the same time to express the joy of life; the play, which includes a highly stylized family picnic sequence, also satirizes the sterility of middle-class life, and features speaking animals and the corpse of a drunkard whose spirit rises to reveal his visions.

As his associates testified in the memorial essay collection *En bog om Kjeld Abell* (1961, ed. Sven Møller Kristensen), Abell's character and personality are reflected in his works. His technical virtuosity and his whimsy barely conceal the earnestness of his battle against evil and injustice, and his immense sense of moral responsibility. Abell's dramas are heavily (and obviously) sugar-coated yet intense moralities. In the tradition of Andersen, they are beguiling and fanciful. But they are, at the same time, hortatory. Abell's inventive settings, characterizations, and plots are pegs for expressing an almost obsessive preoccupation with moral integrity in deed more than merely in word or thought. His recurrent theme is rebellion, an admonition to violate the law and commit crimes, if necessary, in order to achieve justice.

Abell's writings include theatre and travel sketches as well as a mystery tale inspired by his 1952 visit to China. Few of his works are available in English. *The Queen on Tour* is one of the translated *Contemporary Danish Plays* (1955), and Abell's two best-known plays were published in two collections: Evert Sprinchorn's *The Genius of the Scandinavian Theater* (1964) and Robert Corrigan's *Masterpieces of the Modern Scandinavian Theatre* (1967); both contain prefatory essays on Abell and bibliographies.

ABIE'S IRISH ROSE, a comedy in three acts by ANNE NICHOLS, produced in 1922 and published in 1924. Setting: New York, early 1920's.

This amusing and unpretentious stereotyped vaudeville portrayal of Jewish and Irish families upset by a mixed marriage became one of the most popular plays ever produced on the American stage. The confident author, who meant to convey "the spirit of tolerance" in the play, borrowed money to keep it going, after a lukewarm reception, until it caught on. Then it broke the previous Broadway record in its five-year run (2,327 consecutive performances). It has been revived periodically, published as a popular novel (1927), and produced on the radio, screen (1928 and 1946), and television.

Act I. As a garrulous neighbor tells of her appendectomy, Solomon Levy waits to hear from his son Abie (Abraham), who has been out of the store all day. Abie finally calls to say he is bringing a girl home for supper. Solomon happily plans to make Abie his partner as soon as he is married, and he looks forward to having grandchildren. Abie comes in with Rose Mary Murphy, a former entertainer whom he met during the war in a military hospital. They have just been married by a Methodist minister, and fear the reaction of both fathers (their mothers are dead). But they are determined to let neither break up their marriage. At first Solomon is cool toward Rose Mary, distressed by her short dress, language ("blarney"), and non-Jewish looks. But when Abie says that she is Rosie Murpheski, the daughter of a clothes "contractor," Solomon beams at her and is so taken with "Rosie" that he arranges for her immediate marriage. "Young man, whose vedding iss dis?" he asks. "It's mine!" the protesting Abie replies—whereupon the father indignantly says: "Den keep *quiet, I'll run it!*"

Act II. On the wedding day a week later, Solomon has decorated the place with real orange trees to make Rose Mary, who comes from California, feel at home. She is eager to get the ceremony over with before her father, Patrick Joseph Murphy, gets there. Arriving with a priest as the ceremony is in progress next door, Patrick fears the oranges indicate that Rose Mary is marrying a Protestant (he has been told the groom's name is Michael Magee). When both fathers discover what has happened, they are ready to assault each other. Then, learning of the original wedding conducted by a Methodist, the fathers decide to have their lawyers declare the marriage illegal. Patrick prepares to take his daughter home, but in the meantime the priest, at the rabbi's suggestion, remarries the couple in a Catholic ceremony. Patrick enters just in time to hear the priest pronouncing Abie and Rose Mary man and wife. "My God! They've done it again!" Patrick exclaims, as Solomon collapses in a chair.

Act III. A year later, Abie and Rose Mary, disowned by both fathers, are poor but happy in their modest apartment. They are preparing for Christmas, and Rose Mary asks Solomon's visiting neighbor (who still talks of her appendectomy) to look after the baked ham while she herself goes to care for her baby. The two fathers sneak in to place their gifts under the tree. They quarrel again, trade insults about the Irish and the Jews, and talk of the grandchild each confidently thinks he has: a boy (says Solomon), a girl (says Patrick). It turns out that Rose Mary

Abie's Irish Rose, Act III. Abie (Harold Shubert) and Rose Mary (Evelyn Nicholas), bending toward the baked ham; the others, left to right, are Solomon Levy (Alfred White), the priest (Harry Bradley), the garrulous neighbor couple (Milton Wallace and Ida Kramer), the rabbi (Jack Bertin), and Patrick Murphy (Andrew Mack). New York, 1923. (*Culver Pictures*)

has had twins: a boy named after Patrick, and a girl named after Solomon's deceased wife. Deeply touched, the grandfathers, holding the infants they now accept wholeheartedly, become reconciled as the Christmas bells ring. "Merry Christmas, Sol!" says Patrick, and Solomon replies: "Goot Yonteff, Patrick!"

ABRAHAM LINCOLN, a play in six scenes by JOHN DRINKWATER, published and produced in 1918. Setting: Springfield, Washington, and Appomattox, 1860–65.

The popularity of this Lincoln play has been rivaled only by Sherwood's ABE LINCOLN IN ILLINOIS. Drinkwater's play has been frequently revived and highly praised on both sides of the Atlantic. In the tradition of the English chronicle play, its six episodic scenes, which freely dramatize history, are separated by verse choruses. Lincoln is idealized—sometimes sentimentalized—as an exemplary and inspiring figure.

Scene 1. Some of his simple neighbors come to congratulate "Abraham" before his nomination for the Presidency. "It makes a man humble to be chosen so," Lincoln tells them, not deluding himself about the difficulties ahead. After promising Mrs. Lincoln to get a new hat, he receives the convention's deputation. Lincoln gravely alludes to the, "shall we say graces, that I lack" and to his stubbornness, and reiterates his intention to resist secession, "with blood if needs be." Hating slavery, he is determined to prevent its extension and to work for its abolition. Then he accepts. Alone, he kneels, "possessed and deliberate, burying his face in his hands."

Scene 2. Ten months later in his Secretary of State's office, President Lincoln surprises the Confederate representatives who persuaded Seward to counsel Lincoln into giving up Fort Sumter. He vainly reasons first with them and later with his Cabinet, called in emergency session. Then he overrides their vote, and decides to hold Fort Sumter.

Scene 3. Almost two years later at a small tea, Lincoln listens to a profiteer's wife who wants to exterminate the rebels, and to a bereaved mother who wants immediate peace. Lincoln is sympathetic to the latter ("she's wrong, but she is noble"), but despises the vengeful profiteer, who dishonors "the hope of love and charity on earth." Then he persuades an elderly Negro preacher, who soon comes to love Lincoln, that it would be wrong to retaliate against and punish Southern atrocities: "It is for us to set a great example, not to follow a wicked one."

Scene 4. Lincoln reads a comic Artemus Ward tale to the members of his Cabinet, to "compose" them. Then he issues the Emancipation Proclamation, though his Cabinet has misgivings about the timing. Afterward, feeling lonesome and "sick at heart," Lincoln reasons, kindly, forgivingly, and unsuccessfully, with a soured, disloyal Cabinet member. Then the tired President asks a secretary to read him a favorite Shakespeare passage from *The Tempest,* and repeats its last words, "We are such stuff / As dreams are made on, and our little life . . ."

Scene 5. In 1865 Lincoln visits General Grant at Appomattox. The President pardons a doomed young soldier and, waiting for the war's end, he spends the night sleeping on two stools. When Lee's surrender comes, Lincoln thanks Grant, commends him for his leadership, and leaves him to receive Lee. The brief and dignified surrender is marked by Grant's generosity to the vanquished Confederate army.

Scene 6. During the intermission, Lincoln is cheered by the theatre audience. He thanks them, rejoices over the abolition of "a great wrong," and looks forward to reunion and reconciliation: "With malice toward none, with charity for all, it is for us to resolve . . . that government of the people, by the people, for the people, shall not perish from the earth." When the play resumes, John Wilkes Booth shoots Lincoln. His loyal maid sobs for her "master" as Stanton comes out of Lincoln's box: "Now he belongs to the ages." The chorus of chroniclers concludes with a tribute to Lincoln's enduring character, "the token sent / Always to man for man's own government."

ABSURD, THEATRE OF THE, a term applied to the avant-garde drama of SAMUEL BECKETT, EUGÈNE IONESCO, ARTHUR ADAMOV, JEAN GENET, EDWARD ALBEE, HAROLD PINTER, and other playwrights of the 1950's and 1960's. As described in Martin Esslin's *The Theatre of the Absurd* (1961, revised in 1968), in which it was first labeled and analyzed, this movement received its impetus from ALBERT CAMUS's *Le Mythe de Sisyphe* (*The Myth of Sisyphus*, 1942). *Absurd* in that essay is used not in the sense of *ridiculous* but, rather, in its original meaning, *out of harmony*. Postwar disillusionment with traditional religions and their substitutes (progress, psychoanalysis, and various political and social systems), Camus wrote, made man a stranger alienated in and out of harmony with a universe now perceived to be meaningless. "Deprived of illusions and light," man suffered the metaphysical anguish portrayed in "absurd" drama.

While such anguish had been dramatized by others, including Camus himself, absurdist playwrights went a step further: they matched form with theme. Eschewing conventional plot, story, and character—and even the didacticism of the EPIC theatre—absurdist playwrights created a dramaturgy that reflected their anguished vision of universal reality through apparently meaningless, illogical, unrelated, and unsequential dialogue and action. Ionesco's THE BALD SOPRANO, Beckett's WAITING FOR GODOT, and other "absurd" plays dramatize the horror of metaphysical irrationality in grotesque dialogue and action. Anguish is heightened by the evocation of timeless perpetuity: both these plays, for example, are repetitive and circular, concluding as they begin and suggesting endless and senseless repetition. But their universal despair is often presented in archetypal symbols that produce a cathartic effect: a reality that had been only vaguely felt before is now clearly perceived for man to face consciously—without nagging doubts, illusions, and self-delusion.

Difficulties in sustaining pure absurdist drama in more than short, usually one-act, plays soon became manifest. Ionesco, Pinter, and others in the movement who continued to write successful drama increasingly utilized conventional plot, allegory, and comedy. But as with other extreme movements (NATURALISM, EXPRESSIONISM, etc.), the "absurd" influenced the development of the art of the theatre and entered the mainstream of modern drama in a modified form.

ACHARD, Marcel [originally Marcel Auguste Ferréol] (1899–), French dramatist, was born in Lyons. He has charmed Parisian as well as Broadway audiences with bubbly comedies and fantasies that are sentimental, ironic, and even tragic. Achard's first success was *Voulez-vous jouer avec moâ?* (1923), a circus play. In *La Vie est belle* (1928) he introduced Charlemagne, the lovable vagabond who appears in other Achard plays. *Jean de la lune* (1929), a long-popular play subsequently filmed, features a similar character, an idealist whose faith in the unfaithful woman he loves ultimately reforms her. Other successes staged also in New York were the romantic *Domino* (1931); *Auprès de ma blonde* (1946), adapted by S. N. BEHRMAN as *I Know My Love; Patate* (1956), also translated as *Rollo; L'Idiote* (1961), adapted by Harry Kurnitz (1908–) as *A Shot in the Dark;* and *Eva ou l'amour est un casse-gueule* (1970), an ironic portrayal of love. Achard's most fanciful depiction of romance is perhaps in *Le Corsaire* (1938), where he dramatizes simultaneously a 1776 romance and its reincarnation by two actors in a Hollywood film.

ADAM THE CREATOR (*Adam stvořitel*), a comedy in six scenes and an epilogue by Josef and KAREL ČAPEK, published and produced in 1927. Setting: a slum, desolation, etc.

The Čapek brothers' last joint work is an EXPRESSIONIST, often comic piece of utopianism. It resembles Josef's 1924 play, *Země mnoha jmen,* and constitutes something of an answer to Shaw's BACK TO METHUSELAH. Its depiction of human evil and its simultaneously sunny conclusion that life is good evidence Karel's ambiguous perspective.

Dissatisfied with the world, Adam destroys it by firing the Cannon of Negation. As punishment, God's voice tells him, "Create it anew yourself!" To see if he can really create, Adam first uses his clay to make fleas. Then he creates a superwoman (Eve), a superman (who, like Eve, disdains Adam and leaves), Lilith (who distracts Adam with her nagging affection), and finally an Alter Ego to talk to. Adam and Alter Ego, however, quarrel. Even the creation of another wife—the most amusing scene in the play—turns out disastrously. Adam and Alter Ego divide the clay and compete as creators. The scientific Alter Ego makes a mold from which he creates many people, "the Mass." Adam produces creative individuals, like poets and artists. Adam's and Alter Ego's camps war perpetually and undecisively. Eventually the two leaders are deposed. They want to start creation anew, find that only a bit of clay is left, and kick it. It becomes Zmetek, a monstrous but generous dwarf teeming with vitality, who independently creates his own progeny: "Saving your presence, sir, a poor man always does have young 'uns, doesn't he?" Adam and Alter Ego decide to appear before their peoples in godly dress "as united creators to a united world." Ready to create a new world themselves, the people reject them. But a Red Messenger, and then a Black Messenger (Communism and Fascism), the supermen, now defeat and tyrannize the people. Adam and Alter Ego curse their world and agree to destroy it. Though they promise the beggar Zmetek that this will put him out of his misery, he wards them off with his pot—made of the Cannon of Negation: "Zmetek ain't got no great ideas; he only wants to be alive. . . . The world's good enough for him." Later all three are driven from the site of creation, on which an enormous temple with a great bell—the Cannon of Negation—is being erected. God's voice summons Adam, who wanted to destroy his creation: "Will you leave it as it is?" Adam says, "Yes! yes! yes!" The voice replies, "So will I!" And the bell peals.

ADAMOV, Arthur (1908–70), Russian-born French playwright, was a leading practitioner in the theatre of the ABSURD. Later he turned from avant-garde works like *La Parodie* (THE PARODY, 1950) and *Le Ping-Pong* (PING PONG, 1955) to EPIC, social-protest drama like PAOLO PAOLI (1957). This change from the absurd to the more traditional paralleled that of his fellow playwright EUGÈNE IONESCO. Both perceived the same breakdown of human communication, but Adamov objectified it without verbal pyrotechnics. Adamov attained less popular and critical success, though he has been praised as a powerful absurdist writer. His metaphysical anguish—which he discussed and analyzed as readily as he did his art—was influenced by AUGUST STRINDBERG (particularly by A DREAM PLAY) and by the novelist Franz Kafka. It was acute, but less nihilistic than that of most existentialist playwrights, for he perceived an ultimate meaning—though one that never could be comprehensible to man. The play Adamov considered his best, *Le Professeur Taranne* (PROFESSOR TARANNE, 1953), dramatized his own most revealing nightmare.

The son of a wealthy Armenian businessman, Adamov was born in Kislovodsk, in the Caucasus. His family left Russia in 1912 and his schooling commenced in Geneva, Switzerland, where Adamov grew up speaking French. Later he attended school in Germany, but he completed his studies in Paris, where he settled in 1924. There he joined SURREALIST groups, for whom he wrote poetry and edited a periodical, *Discontinuité*. These activities ended in 1938 with a mental crisis. He detailed it in *L'Aveu* (*The Confession*, 1946), a masochistic self-revelation of his psychological and existentialist anguish—a quest for self-degradation accompanied by feelings of alienation and despair at the discovery of a godless and absurd universe.

This account—it continues through the years of World War II, which Adamov spent in France, partly in an internment camp—helped exorcise his terrors, as did the plays he began to write in 1947. It also sheds considerable light on these plays. The first of them, *The Parody*, was followed by *L'Invasion* (*The Invasion*, 1950)—the title alludes to the inner "conquest of man"—his second produced play. It is the haunting tragedy of a writer who tries to bring order and meaning to a friend's posthumous works; as he succeeds, he gradually becomes aware of universal disorder and senselessness, gets increasingly confused, withdraws from his family, and dies. *La Grande et la Petite Manœuvre* (1950), Adamov's third play, was the first to be produced; a brutal nightmare drama that like his first play depicts the futility of all action, it is set in a police state where the revolutionary terrorist is no more effective than the passive cripple, the *mutilé* who loses all his limbs and finally his life because he is unable to achieve any real human contact. Adamov dramatized similar obsessions in *Le Sens de la marche* (*The Direction of the March*, 1953), whose protagonist confronts his tyrannical father in a series of surrogates, the last of whom he kills.

Professor Taranne marked a turning point in Adamov's dramaturgy, for here he transformed an actual dream and used real place names. It was the first time, Adamov later noted, "that I emerged from the no-man's-land of poetry and dared to call things by their name." His *Tous contre tous* (1953) deals with a group of persecuted refugees (perhaps Jews) and a protagonist who is both persecutor and victim; he ultimately chooses death, though it is not clear whether as an act of affirmation or one of resignation to existentialist absurdity. The one-act *Comme nous avons été* (*As We Were*, 1953) and *Les Retrouvailles* (1955) are dream plays about mother-dominated men who regress to childhood just before they get married.

With *Ping Pong*, his best-known play, Adamov

transcended what he called his "exploitation of the half-dream and the old family conflict," and created objective, nonautobiographical characters. With *Paolo Paoli,* his next play, Adamov made an almost complete break with the theatre of the absurd. By 1946, when he documented his personal and philosophical crisis, he had already concluded that while universal meaning would remain ever unattainable to man, social action—specifically Marxism—provided a tenable solution. Like BERTOLT BRECHT, whose work began increasingly to influence him, Adamov expressed his left-wing sympathies in sociopolitical epic drama. Nonetheless, elements of the grotesque and fantastic remained in *Paolo Paoli* and in the other later plays. These include a number of short allegorical pieces written during the 1958 campaign against De Gaulle's new constitution; some radio drama; *Le Printemps '71* (*Spring '71,* 1960), a panoramic Brechtian EPIC about the Paris Commune in twenty-six scenes, nine GRAND GUIGNOL interludes that moralize about historical events and characters like Bismarck and Thiers, and an epilogue; and the one-act *La Politique des restes* (1962).

Adamov's other works include a dramatization of Gogol's *Dead Souls;* translations of Dostoevsky, Jung, and Rilke; and adaptations of the drama of Christopher Marlowe, of the early nineteenth-century playwright Georg Büchner, of Strindberg, ANTON CHEKHOV, and of MAXIM GORKY. His analysis of his own drama appears in Adamov's preface to the second volume of the collected plays, which was published in 1955. Parts of *The Confession* were published in English in 1959, and his best-known plays have been translated. A comprehensive chapter on Adamov appears in Martin Esslin's *The Theatre of the Absurd* (1961, revised 1968), which lists writings by and about Adamov.

ADDING MACHINE, THE, a play in seven scenes by ELMER RICE, published and produced in 1923. Setting: New York and various supernatural places, 1920's.

This internationally known play is one of the finest examples of EXPRESSIONISM. Comical and at the same time grimly satiric, it is both a social and a psychological study of a brutalized, worthless human being: Mr. Zero, the barely articulate anti-hero of the world of automation. The half century that has followed his (and his friends') creation has not diminished the portrait's relevance and universality.

Scene 1. Mrs. Zero arranges her hair before retiring. Mr. Zero is already in bed, saying nothing during his wife's monologue. "I'm gettin' sick o' them Westerns," she declares, complaining about the movies, and repeating in angonizing detail her inconsequential gossip. She nags Zero for not taking her to the downtown movies, and complains about her housework and hard life. Sneering at his failure to get ahead after twenty-five years of bookkeeping, she remarks, "I didn't pick much when I picked you, I'll tell the world." Angrily she recalls an "indecent" neighbor girl she made him report to the police. "You'd better not start nothin' with women," she says—and keeps on talking as the curtain falls.

Scene 2. At the office, Zero writes down figures read to him by Daisy Diana Dorothea Devore, another plain, middle-aged clerk. As they monotonously murmur the figures and periodically chide each other ("Aw, you make me sick"—"An' you make me sicker"), Zero and Daisy daydream aloud, revealing their low middle-class character and long-time mutually lustful feelings. Zero deplores his wife's making him report the girl he had enjoyed watching—"the dirty bum. Livin' in a house with respectable people"—regrets that he did not visit her, and expresses his secret attraction to Daisy. Daisy dreams of Zero and wonders "what it feels like to be really kissed. Men—dirty pigs!" Zero hopes his boss remembers that this is his twenty-fifth year as a bookkeeper there, and anticipates a reward. Instead, the boss tells him he is to be replaced by an adding machine, and discharges Zero. As music begins and rises in volume, the floor on which Zero is standing starts to revolve madly. The boss's jaws keep moving soundlessly, while the music and other noises intensify. A peal of thunder is followed by a flash of red, and then all plunges into darkness.

Scene 3. When Zero comes home Mrs. Zero berates him for being late, for they are expecting company. Zero remains silent as he eats. Their friends (Mr. and Mrs. One, Mr. and Mrs. Two, etc.) enter, all identically dressed. The banality of the women's talk is matched by that of their husbands. It ends with a choral curse: "Damn dagoes! Damn Catholics! Damn sheenies! Damn niggers! Jail' em! shoot 'em! hang 'em! lynch 'em! burn 'em!" Then they rise and sing, "My country 'tis of thee." Zero goes to answer the door to admit a policeman. Calmly he accompanies the officer after telling his wife, "I killed the boss this afternoon."

Scene 4. In court before the puppetlike jury, Zero attempts to justify himself in a groping, long, and disconnected speech. "Sure I killed him," Zero admits; "right through the heart with the bill-file, see?" As he recalls it before the twelve jurors, the mention of their number elicits his conditioned response: "Six and six makes twelve. And five is seventeen. . . . Aw, cut it out! Them damn figgers! I can't forget 'em." He recalls his twenty-five years of loyal service, with a few national holidays off, but not the Jewish ones: "The dirty sheenies—always gettin' two to the other bird's one." He remembers the girl he denounced for indecent exposure, daydreams of "just grabbin' women, the way you see 'em do in the pictures," and recalls a Negro's stepping on his foot in a crowded subway: "a nigger's got no right to step on a white man's foot." When he refers to himself as "a regular guy like anybody else. Like you birds now," the jurors indignantly pronounce him "GUILTY!"

Scene 5. At a graveyard, the girl he had de-

The Adding Machine, Scene 4. Zero (Dudley Digges) on the defense stand. New York, 1923. (*Vandamm Photo, Theatre Collection, New York Public Library*)

nounced suggests laughingly to her young man that they cavort on Zero's grave. After they leave Zero arises. An old-timer, the piously puritanical Shrdlu, introduces himself and tells how he for no apparent reason suddenly had cut his mother's throat. Another corpse tells them to be quiet, chases them off, and yawns: "Hohum! Me for the worms!"

Scene 6. At "a pleasant place," a meadow with sweet music and soon identified as heaven, Shrdlu complains to Zero about the immorality of his not being punished. Daisy arrives: she committed suicide shortly after Zero's execution. Shrdlu, who is preoccupied with his guilt, leaves and Daisy admits that she has always yearned for Zero. She has him kiss her passionately, and they dance with abandon. But Zero's conventional puritanism soon is outraged. Shrdlu returns with indignant reports of the "low company" in this place, including Swift and Rabelais, both "much admired for some indecent tales." Zero is shocked: "What kind of a dump is this, anyway?" He leaves, refusing Daisy's plea to sit with her "an' look at the flowers an' listen to the music," which he cannot hear. Daisy is downcast: "Without him I might as well be alive."

Scene 7. Zero is completely absorbed in operating a gigantic adding machine in an office filled with streamers. A middle-aged lieutenant gets Zero to stop so he can be sent back to earth. This is "a sort of cosmic laundry," he explains, where souls are cleaned and sent back to earth for their next corporeal existence. He reviews Zero's previous existences, from the time he was a monkey (and already subservient) through his ever-deteriorating rebirths over the centuries. Zero eagerly welcomes the news that he will again operate an adding machine—"a superb, super-hyper-adding machine, as far from this old piece of junk as you are from God." Though Zero is breathless with wonder, the lieutenant bitterly describes "the culmination of human effort" that makes Zero "a failure. A waste product" with an animal's instincts and appetites, but without its "strength and skill [and] unashamed indulgence." His only hope is sex, an illusory girl whom Zero lustfully pursues. The lieutenant laughs wearily and drains his flask: "Hell, I'll tell the world this is a lousy job!"

ADE, George (1866–1944), American journalist, short-story writer, and playwright, is still remembered for his *Fables in Slang* (1900) and its sequels, the racy stories written in colloquial language and modeled on *Aesop's Fables*. His work reached Broadway with *The Sultan of Sulu* (1902), a long-running musical that was quickly followed by a string of successful farces. The most popular of them (there were almost twenty) was *The College Widow* (1904). One of the first college comedies, it is about a college president's daughter who must use her charms to entice a halfback for their team, and it is highlighted by a thrilling football game; in 1917 the play became a Jerome Kern-GUY BOLTON musical that was revived for a long Off-Broadway run in 1959 as *Leave It to Jane*. Other Ade hits were *The Country Chairman* (1903), featuring a small-town political contest, in which one of the rivals is enamored of the other's daughter; *Just Out of College* (1905), a satire on a college graduate who has nothing to offer the business world; and *Father and the Boys* (1908), a snappy comedy in which a father proves to his sons that he is not the "back number" they take him for.

Ade's farces were hailed as something new when they first appeared at the start of the century. But they are in the tradition of CHARLES H. HOYT, which was subsequently carried on by GEORGE M. COHAN. Ade's satire is gentle, but his characters and situations are the broad exaggerations typical of farces.

ADMIRABLE BASHVILLE, THE; or, CONSTANCY UNREWARDED, "Being the Novel of *Cashel Byron's Profession* Done into a Stage Play in Three Acts and in Blank Verse," by BERNARD SHAW, produced in 1902 and published in 1909. Setting: England, 1882.

In his preface to this burlesque, one of the TRANSLATIONS AND TOMFOOLERIES, Shaw noted his observance of all the established virtues playgoers relish, and explained that he wrote the play in blank verse because it "is so childishly easy and expeditious (hence, by the way, Shakespear's copious output)."

In the park on her estate, Lydia Carew meets and falls in love with Cashel Byron. Though she is shocked when her servant Bashville tells her that Cashel is a prizefighter, she admits him to her home after Bashville, who loves her, trips Cashel with a wrestler's throw. Cashel repudiates gentility and goes off with Lydia to a match. At a melee in the arena, the balcony collapses and Cashel rescues Lydia. Informed by his mother that he is really the son of a nobleman, Cashel proposes to Lydia. She accepts, and Cashel decides to make Bashville a champion fighter.

ADMIRABLE CRICHTON, THE, a comedy in four acts by JAMES M. BARRIE, produced in 1902 and published in 1914. Setting: contemporary Mayfair (London) and a desert island in the Pacific.

This is one of Barrie's most popular plays. Perhaps suggested by LUDWIG FULDA's similar but greatly inferior *Robinsons Eiland* (1896), it has been elaborately produced, frequently revived, and filmed twice (as *Male and Female* in 1921, and as *We're Not Dressing* in 1934). It became a British musical (*Our Man Crichton*, lyrics by Herbert Kretzmer, music by David Lee) in 1964. Also labeled a "fantasy," it satirizes the social order and has sometimes been mistaken for a PROBLEM PLAY or a drama of ideas. But its satire, like the play's resolution, is as gently inoffensive as it is amusing. In the long-delayed published version of the play, Barrie altered his original ending, in which Crichton marries the kitchen maid and opens a public-house (tavern) on Harrow Road, "at the more fashionable end."

Act I. It is the monthly social hour with the servants at the Earl of Loam's. These teas are hated by all but Lord Loam, a ludicrous peer with "advanced ideas." His three daughters and their titled friends are as uncomfortable as the menial "guests." Though Loam insists that "our divisions into classes are artificial," his butler, the loyal Crichton, is deeply pained by such affronts to class distinctions. "They are the natural outcome of a civilised society," he believes and, he tells the haughtiest of the daughters, Lady Mary, "whatever is natural is right." Lord Loam and his family prepare to go on a world cruise, accompanied by two servants—Crichton and *his* social inferior, a kitchen maid on whom the butler nonetheless has "cast a favourable eye."

Act II. All of them have been shipwrecked on a desert island. Under primitive conditions, Crichton's natural abilities immediately become manifest. He saves the castaways and takes charge. The disdainful but helpless lords and ladies soon come to accept his leadership as naturally as he provides it.

Act III. In two years Crichton has built a comfortable and modern home for all. Social inequalities, however, are just as natural on the desert island as they were in England. Now Crichton is a highly respected and absolute monarch. The humbly adoring ladies fight for the honor of serving him. To the incredible joy of the once-haughty Lady Mary, Crichton chooses her: "I have grown to love you; are you afraid to mate with me?" Bewitched, she replies, "You are the most wonderful man I have ever known, and I am not afraid." While the group celebrates the engagement, a ship's gun is heard. Though Lady Mary begs him to ignore it so that their happy island life may continue, he refuses: "Bill Crichton has got to play the game." The rescue party arrives and immediately all roles revert. Crichton's kingly robe and demeanor naturally slip away and he rubs his hands in the humble gesture of a servant.

Act IV. Back in England, one of the lords publishes a fantastic account of their years on the island; it glorifies his own "heroism" and dismisses Crichton with "a glowing tribute in a footnote." Lady Mary resumes her engagement to the young lord who waited for her rescue. But she wants "to play the game" and confess her "extraordinary lapse" to her future husband. Accidentally she is spared by the fiancé's confession of a lapse of his own during their separation. There is another crisis when his suspicious dowager mother questions the others about their doings on the island. This crisis is averted when Crichton, the "perfect butler," assures her that "there was as little equality there as elsewhere." At the end, he announces his intention to leave Lord Loam's service. But in answer to Lady Mary's questions Crichton refuses to entertain the idea that anything may be wrong in a society that does not recognize him as the best of men: "My lady, not even from you can I listen to a word against England."

ADREA, a play in five acts by DAVID BELASCO and JOHN LUTHER LONG, produced in 1904 and published in 1928. Setting: an imaginary island in the Adriatic, late fifth century.

This romantic melodrama features imaginary figures and events, but is based on historical research on the period after the fall of Rome.

The popular Princess Adrea cannot inherit the throne because she is blind. Her younger sister is about to be crowned and married to the ambitious Kaeso of Noricum, Adrea's beloved. She betrays Adrea by having her marry the court jester, an accomplished impersonator who imitates Kaeso. When Adrea discovers the ruse she goes to her death, but is saved when a flash of lightning restores her sight. Ascending the throne and lusting for vengeance, she condemns Kaeso to a public whipping and a brutal death. Adrea relents briefly when he appears to express remorse, but persists when she sees the jester who was the instrument of her humiliation. She herself stabs Kaeso to save him from the worse death she had decreed and the people demand. In "the epilogue in Arcady" fourteen years later, she crowns her sister's son: "May the gods keep thy heart young, thy faith pure, thy soul at peace, O child of Kaeso!" Then, disobeying the prophetic warning at her coronation, she looks directly at the sun: "O Sun, who took my sight at birth, I give thee back . . . thine own." Blinded again, Adrea kneels at the throne: "Long live the King!"

ADVENT, A "MYSTERIUM" (*Advent, ett mysterium*), a miracle play in five acts by AUGUST STRINDBERG, published in 1899. Setting: a vineyard, crossroads, chasm, etc.

Advent was published with CRIMES AND CRIMES under the joint title BEFORE A HIGHER COURT. Partly like a Dickens or an Andersen Christmas story for children, it is primarily a Swedenborgian horror fantasy with autobiographical allusions.

A hypocritical old judge and his equally wicked old wife enslave their daughter, throw out her husband, and punish her little children. The old people have committed many evils, also against each other. Now they are thoroughly scourged by the Devil, while the children are protected by the Christ Child. An infernal ball is followed by a spectral auction and trial. Condemned by their victims, the old couple suffer in hell. At last they repent; it is Christmas Eve, and their eventual salvation is anticipated with a crèche and a "Gloria" chorus.

AFINOGENOV, Aleksandr Nikolaevich (1904–41), was one of the important post-Revolution Russian playwrights. His *Strakh* (FEAR, 1930), produced at the Moscow Art Theatre, was particularly successful and widely discussed.* Killed in Moscow during an air raid, he was thought to have much promise, but he was viewed with some suspicion by the authorities. His name has frequently been coupled with that of NIKOLAI POGODIN, but he lacked the older writer's great theatrical talents. Afinogenov presented more subtle, CHEKHOVian portrayals of people and problems, particularly those of the intelligentsia under the Soviets.

The son of a writer and his village schoolteacher wife, Afinogenov grew up in Yaroslavl on the Volga. He published his first stories when he was fifteen, and by the time he was twenty he had published three volumes of poetry. In 1923 the Moscow Proletcult Theatre produced the first of his fourteen plays, *Robert Tim,* the depiction of weavers' revolt in early nineteenth-century England. His next play was *Po tu storonu shcheli* (1926), based on Jack London's story about a San Francisco strike. Though Afinogenov's popularity rose steadily, neither these nor his other early plays are particularly impressive: *Na perelome* and *V ryady,* both written for the Proletcult Theatre in 1926; *Glyadi v oba* (1927), an exhortation to young Communists to beware of the Soviet's enemies; *Volchya tropa* (1927), about the hunt for an old-regime engineer; *Malinovoe varene* (1928), a comedy with a social message; and *Chudak* (1929), the drama of a misunderstood young Soviet enthusiast (the title's "eccentric") who fights various setbacks at a paper mill and succeeds in accelerating production, and Afinogenov's best-known play after *Fear.*

After *Fear* came *Portret* (1934), the "portrait" being that of a woman with a vile past; *Dalyokoe* (1935, translated as *Remote, Far Taiga,* and *Distant Point,* and produced in Great Britain), in which a dying Red Army general delayed at the small Siberian railroad station of Dalyokoe imbues a group of common Russians with the proper Soviet spirit; *Salyut, Ispaniya* (1936), a spectacle (with music by Dmitri Shostakovich) "Salute to Spain" for her struggle against Fascism; *Vtoroi put* (1939), a sequel to *Dalyokoe; Mat svoikh detei* (1940), whose title ("the mother of her children") refers to Russia; *Mashenka* (1941, produced in New York as *Listen Professor!*), an amusing drama of a girl who kindles her grandfather's interest in the new Russia; and *Nakanune* (*On the Eve*), a play about the outbreak of war and a family's resistance to the German invasion, produced posthumously in 1942.

Afinogenov also wrote a critical study, *Tvorcheski metod teatra* (1931). *Far Taiga* was published in Alexander Bakshy's *Soviet Scene: Six Plays of Russian Life* (1946), *Fear* in Eugene Lyons's *Six Soviet Plays* (1934), and *On the Eve* in H. W. L. Dana's *Seven Soviet Plays* (1946); a brief note on Afinogenov prefaces each play.

AFRICA. Africa's heterogeneous modern drama reflects centuries-long colonization by the British, French, Belgians, Spaniards, and Portuguese—and the political turmoil the continent has undergone since World War II, when a single decade saw some forty new black nations gain their independence. Primary school and chapbook dramatizations of this and earlier history, as well as of the careers of black leaders in various new nations, have proliferated throughout Africa in

* *O "Strakhe" (On "Fear,"* 1931*)* is a collection of essays by twenty-four writers about this play.

English, French, and the vernacular. The prevalent themes have been the changing life in modern Africa and *négritude,* the black aesthetic and mystique launched by the Martinique-born Aimé Césaire (see page 448, *footnote*). Yet few generalizations can be made about African drama. Though European in form, it is distinctively native in setting, atmosphere, and theme; and it often reflects the violence of national liberations as well as internecine struggles. If whites are portrayed at all in black drama, they appear in unflattering guises. The drama most popular with Africans is still that written by whites of European stock, produced in translation as well as in the original.

Though such divisions are not wholly adequate, Africa's drama may best be surveyed regionally: NORTH AFRICA, with much of its drama in ARABIC; the countries in central Africa immediately to the south of the Sahara, which have long been dominated by the theatres of France and Belgium and have produced no new drama of note; EAST AFRICA; SOUTH AFRICA; and WEST AFRICA. It is the last-named region that began to produce the most exciting black African drama—particularly Nigeria, with the continent's first internationally prominent playwrights, JOHN PEPPER CLARK and WOLE SOYINKA.

Extensive collections of African drama in English began to appear in the later 1960's. Cosmo Pieterse's *Ten One-Act Plays* (1968) has notes on the anthologized dramatists, and Fredric M. Litto's *Plays from Black Africa* (1968) includes thumbnail biographies of its half-dozen playwrights in addition to a survey of modern African drama and a critical bibliography. N. B. East's edition of *African Theatre: A Checklist of Critical Materials* (1970), a pamphlet issued by the Africana Publishing Corporation of New York, is an excellent bibliography of African drama and theatre. For other works covering all regions of the continent see *The Afro-Asian Theatre Bulletin* (1965 ff.), which regularly features articles as well as bibliographies of recently published and translated plays, work in progress, and new studies.

AFTER THE FALL, a play in two acts by ARTHUR MILLER, published and produced in 1964. Setting: a three-level stage dominated by the blasted tower of a German concentration camp, 1960's.

This play launched the Repertory Theater of Lincoln Center, but, despite its powerful first act and topical fascination, it had a lukewarm reception. It is a complex and difficult memory kaleidoscope in which people appear and disappear as they come to the consciousness of Quentin, a forty-year-old lawyer. He is a thinly disguised autobiographical figure who, as he reviews his life, agonizes over the meaning of guilt, responsibility, love, and existence.

Quentin comes forward and shakes the hand of an invisible listener—a psychiatrist-confessor and the audience. "Hello! God, it's good to see you again!" he begins, and for the next three hours he simultaneously relates, relives, philosophizes, and attempts to comprehend his life, which emerges in scrambled snatches. There are his failures with various women, notably with his second wife, Maggie (a character based on Miller's second wife, the famous actress Marilyn Monroe, who had just committed suicide in 1962). Other women in the play are his mother, who disillusions the boy Quentin when she abuses his father and lies to Quentin about it; a worshiping young divorcée whom Quentin has helped; his first wife, who insisted on her separate identity; and a girl he is thinking of marrying, a German archaeologist who is guiltily drawn to the concentration camp site because "no one they didn't kill can be innocent again." The men in Quentin's life include his father, his brother, and doomed friends whom he wants to help as they are summoned by a congressional committee to confess and inform—one of whom commits suicide when he feels this help is too burdensome to Quentin. "But who would not rather be the sole survivor of this place than all its finest victims?" Quentin asks, and thus associates all men's actions with the concentration camp horror constantly looming above.

Much of the sometimes tediously pretentious second act is devoted to Quentin's relationship with Maggie, a famous singer and sex symbol who craves love ("all I am is love . . . and sex"). Worshiping Quentin, Maggie tries to subsume her identity in his—and gets just as hateful and resenting of his apparent withdrawal as did his first wife, who flaunted her individuality. As Maggie breaks down, Quentin tells her that, despite her love, she is "full of hatred"; he urges her to "do the hardest thing of all—see your own hatred, and live!" Because he is unwilling to take the responsibility for her life himself ("I am not the Savior and I am not the help") and unable to make Maggie assume it, she takes a fatal dose of pills. Despite their lacerating marriage and her death, Quentin finds "something in me that could dare to love this world again." For "after the fall" of man comes a recognition: "The wish to kill is never killed, but with some gift of courage one may look into its face when it appears, and with a stroke of love—as to an idiot in the house—forgive it." Quentin bids his listener good-bye and greets his German bride, who calls him: "Hello." He takes her hand; all the people in his life whisper, and then they are enveloped in darkness.

AGAMEMNON'S DEATH (*Agamemnons Tod*), a one-act, blank-verse tragedy by GERHART HAUPTMANN, produced in 1947 and published in 1948. Setting: Demeter's temple near ancient Mycenae.

The second play of THE ATRIDES-TETRALOGY, this part of the redramatization of the well-known myth was published and produced together with ELECTRA.

Orestes, Pylades, Electra, and Calchas's old father (his son has in the meantime committed suicide) discuss rumors of Troy's fall and Agamemnon's death. Pylades and Electra reaffirm their love; then he leaves with Orestes to hide from Aegisthus, the tyrannical ruler and Clytemnestra's paramour. Agamemnon returns from the war, and Electra goes joyously to notify the people. Clytemnestra appears, stunned to see Agamemnon. Bitterly she reproaches him for Iphigenia's death, but then beguiles him and accompanies him to his bath. Aegisthus arrives, and soon Agamemnon's death cries are heard. Clytemnestra brandishes the hatchet she drove through Agamemnon's skull to avenge Iphigenia's murder. When the cowardly Aegisthus dissociates himself from the crime, he and Clytemnestra quarrel bitterly—but remain bound to each other. Electra returns with the people. Clytemnestra admits her deed and warns them (in words written, significantly, in 1942): "Accustom yourselves to horror—as the / World already has accustomed itself!" The people's protests are ruthlessly rejected by Aegisthus, who murders Calchas's father and orders the temple burnt down.

AGITPROP (agitation propaganda), a primitive, episodic, and short drama that substituted theme for plot, agitated for Marxism, and could be produced anywhere—even on the street or at a factory gate. Analogous to LIVING NEWSPAPER DRAMA, agitprop is related to EXPRESSIONISM and came to the United States from Russia in the 1920's with MICHAEL GOLD'S *Strike!,* written for *The New Masses* in 1926 after he had seen agitprops during a visit to the Soviet Union. Many of these dramas appeared in *Workers' Theatre,* an American leftist monthly published early in that decade. Agitprop is exemplified by anonymous little pieces of the 1930's like *Tempo, Tempo* and *Unemployed;* a play written by two Group Theatre actors, Art Smith (? – ?) and Elia Kazan's (1909–) *Dimitroff: A Play of Mass Pressure* (1934), which demanded freedom for the still-imprisoned Communist companions of the hero of the unsuccessful Nazi mock trial after the 1933 Reichstag fire; and *Scottsboro Limited* (1932), by LANGSTON HUGHES. Better-known and more artistic American works rooted in this genre are Blitzstein's THE CRADLE WILL ROCK and Odets's WAITING FOR LEFTY.

Agitprop's direct descendant is guerrilla theatre, which began in the late 1960's and reflects radical student and allied movements in contemporary America. Consisting of crude and often obscene sketches produced in the streets, parks, and other public areas, guerrilla theatre exhorts audiences to social and political action against the Vietnamese war, racism, and the Establishment.

AH, WILDERNESS!, a play in four acts by EUGENE O'NEILL, published and produced in 1933. Setting: "a large small-town in Connecticut," 1906.

Nostalgically tender and sentimentally comic, this play, his only comedy, is totally atypical of O'Neill. He characterized it as "a comedy of recollection": that is, "a dream walking" (as he also referred to it) of what O'Neill wished his youth in New London, Connecticut, had been. The autobiographical Richard, passing through painful adolescence; his middle-class, small-town American family; the drunken uncle; the spinster aunt; and even the prostitute—all are comic and nonsymbolic counterparts of *potentially* typical O'Neill characters and situations. GEORGE M. COHAN and later Will Rogers starred as Nat Miller. *Ah, Wilderness!* reappeared as *Take Me Along* (1959), a Bob Merrill musical, book by Joseph Stein (1912–) and others.

The happy family of Nat Miller, the town's shrewd but tender and lovable newspaper owner, is preparing to celebrate the Fourth of July. Of his four children, only the poetic seventeen-year-old Richard feels troubled—by puppy love and other growing pains. He shocks and amuses his family with his Socialist slogans and scandalizes his mother especially with books by such "wicked" writers as BERNARD SHAW, OSCAR WILDE, and Omar Khayyám, whose *Rubáiyát* (" . . . Thou / Beside me singing in the Wilderness— / Oh, Wilderness were Paradise enow!") he recites enthusiastically. But near tragedy descends when the father of Muriel McComber, Richard's sweetheart, storms in with love poetry (Swinburne's "Anactoria") that Richard had copied and sent Muriel. McComber angrily insists that Richard is now proven "dissolute and blasphemous." Though Miller explains that he is "only a fool kid who's just at the stage when he's out to rebel against all authority," McComber forbids further association between his daughter and Richard. The searing love poetry does worry Miller, however, and he has a talk to ascertain his son's intentions. When Richard understands what his father is driving at, he is indignant: "What do you think I am, Pa? I never would! She's not that kind! Why, I—I love her!" Miller is relieved, but Richard is heartbroken when he receives Muriel's letter telling him that she is through with him. After a hilarious holiday family dinner, in which drunken Uncle Sid Davis flirts with the Irish maid and again proposes to spinster Aunt Lilly Miller, and the father again tells the same old stories to his giggling family, Richard goes off to a sordid hotel bar. He gets drunk, but, afraid of and disgusted by the prostitute Belle, he cannot carry out his intention of getting even with Muriel. Later, realizing that her father had forced her to write the letter, he is reconciled with Muriel, and the two sneak out into the moonlight for a tender love scene. Nat Miller has heard about the barroom episode, prepares himself with trepidation, and then tells his son the facts of morality and hygiene, but is again reassured by Richard: "I love Muriel and am going to marry her. I'd die before I'd—!" After the children have gone to sleep, Miller recites the *Rubáiyát* in the moonlight as he embraces his wife: "Well, Spring isn't everything, is it, Essie? There's a lot to be said for Autumn. That's got beauty, too. And Winter—if you're together."

AHLSEN, Leopold (1927–), German dramatist, scored a success in 1956 with his *Philemon und Baukis,* a very popular postwar play about an old couple in the Greek mountains who die for their humanitarianism in sheltering a native partisan as well as a Nazi. Other Ahlsen plays are also parablelike NATURALISTIC works: *Pflicht zur Sünde* (1952), *Wolfszeit* (1954), and *Raskolnikoff* (1960), an adaptation of Dostoevsky's *Crime and Punishment*.

AIGLON, L', a verse drama in six acts by EDMOND ROSTAND, published and produced in 1900. Setting: Austria, 1830–32.

Though Rostand is notable among English-speaking audiences for his CYRANO DE BERGERAC, many French critics consider *L'Aiglon* his greatest play. It is a long, bombastic epic drama about Franz, Duke of Reichstadt—the son of Napoleon and Marie-Louise, Duchess of Parma and the Austrian Emperor's daughter, whom Napoleon married in accord with the Franco-Austrian treaty following the bloody Battle of Wagram (1809). The memory of Napoleon and the efforts of Bonapartists (disguised as servants) to fledge and crown his son, "l'aiglon" ("the eaglet"), inspire Franz to emulate his father. On the other hand, Austria's chancellor, Prince Metternich, nurtures Franz's inherited Hapsburg impotence and indecision, and with the police director Count Sedlinsky keeps him a virtual prisoner at the decadent Austrian court. The eighteen- to twenty-year-old Franz was a favorite role of Sarah Bernhardt (who first played him when she was fifty-six) and, in America, of Maude Adams.

Act I. "Fledgling Wings." Marie-Louise, indifferent to her late husband Napoleon, has set up court at Baden for the sake of her ailing son Franz. At a ball Prince Metternich admits that he rules by controlling Franz, whom he has kept ignorant of his father's glorious history and France's present government. Told about Bonapartist activities and plans for bringing home Napoleon's ashes, Metternich remains confident: "Phoenix may rise, / But not the eagle." While Metternich, Marie-Louise, and the courtiers speculate on his future, the pale young Franz, Duke of Reichstadt, appears. He looks at one of the butterflies arranged for his amusement, fascinated with "The pin by which 'twas killed." A tailor and his fitter, Franz's disguised cousin, conspire to make him emperor. Franz's history lessons, expurgated by Metternich, are supplemented by Fanny Elssler, a patriotic dancer who loves him. Franz confounds his tutors with a fervent account of Napoleon's victories, but when his mother angrily demands his subservience to Metternich, Franz gives in. Later, Fanny Elssler embraces him and continues her clandestine history lessons about Napoleon's victories: "The cannonading was prolonged and hard. / At early daybreak, the Imperial Guard . . ."

Act II. "Fluttering Wings." At the Schönbrunn Palace a year later Franz complains bitterly that Sedlinsky spies on him and keeps him a prisoner. In return for his promise not to flee to Paris without permission from his grandfather, the Hapsburg Emperor of Austria, Franz is allowed to receive a boyhood friend. To him Franz admits his uncertainties: "Can I be Emperor? Am I fit to reign?" The friends enthusiastically play with toy soldiers redecorated in Napoleonic uniforms. As they restage the great Battle of Wagram, Metternich suddenly appears. "I see the army has turned French today. / Where are the Austrians?" he remarks, whereupon Franz promptly replies, "They ran away." Franz is furious when Metternich orders the toy soldiers thrown out, but a lackey makes him pretend obedience to Metternich. Soon this lackey identifies himself as Seraphin Flambeau, a disguised conspirator and a former Napoleonic soldier. He describes his plotting: "Me whispering like a prompter from the wings— / To make you Emperor in spite of kings." Gradually he persuades Napoleon's diffident son to follow his true calling, and commends him for his youthful gaiety. "A little young . . . and gay . . .? That's true," the inspired Franz says and adds, with deep feeling, "Thank you, Flambeau."

Act III. "Spreading Wings." The paternal old Austrian Emperor grants the requests of various petitioners, including that of a young shepherd who wants to return to his father's land. The shepherd unmasks himself as Franz, and persuades his grandfather to let him become emperor. But then Metternich appears and places so many obstacles in the way that Franz gets infuriated. The Emperor, angry at his grandson's proud indignation, retracts his promise. Alone, Franz is ready to gain the French throne. As the signal for the conspiracy he places his father's hat on the table. Flambeau hoodwinks Police Director Sedlinsky and changes into his Napoleonic uniform. Metternich appears and vents his hatred of Napoleon, but is briefly overwhelmed by the vision of the hat and Flambeau's self-confidence. When he alludes to Franz as "the Emperor" Metternich half expects to see Napoleon emerging from the bedroom. But it is only the trembling child-form of Franz, and the illusion is broken. Flambeau escapes, and Metternich leads Franz to the mirror: "Your head's not shaped for action—energy; / That brow means languor, fancies! Look and see!" Point by point he strips Franz's self-confidence and pretensions until, in a frenzy, Franz throws down the mirror. As Metternich leaves victoriously, Franz lies crumpled before the broken mirror: "Help! Help me, Father!"

Act IV. "Bruised Wings." At his masked ball in Schönbrunn, Metternich is confident he has broken Franz's spirit: ". . . I have slain his pride. / He will avoid the ball. He longs to hide." But Franz appears—and participates in the erupting conspiracy. After berating his mother, Marie-Louise, for carrying on with an admirer, he recklessly answers Metternich's taunts ("The little colonel dreams, far from the ball, / Of what, pray?" "Of the little corporal."). Then, while his cousin disguises herself as Franz, Napoleon's son eludes the police and starts his trip to Paris.

Act V. "Broken Wings." Franz and Flambeau arrive at night on the historic field of Wagram. But as Franz envisions his triumphant entry into Paris, he learns of a plot on his life. Fearful for the life of the cousin who is impersonating him, Franz is set to hurry back to Schönbrunn, though it cost his crown, when his cousin, who has escaped the assassins, appears and warns Franz. But it is too late. Sedlinsky enters with his officers and Flambeau stabs himself to avoid falling into their hands. He dies in the arms of Franz, who imagines and vividly describes the progress of the great Napoleonic Battle of Wagram. As its sounds and shapes become increasingly clearer, he gets appalled at the misery and suffering: "All the arms—the bloody arms, I see, / And all the mangled stumps outstretched to me!" Though doubtful of his abilities and worthiness, Franz trembles with enthusiasm as he rallies his phantom armies to charge the Austrian forces. Then he is awakened by reality. Of Napoleon's Grand Army only the dead body of Flambeau remains—and Franz reconciles himself to failure.

Act VI. "Folded Wings." Shortly afterward, Franz is dying in the Schönbrunn Palace, surrounded by his family and the courtiers. "When History tells the story of my life, / No one will see my dreams, fierce, stormy, wild," he realizes. He requests that the story of his grandiose Paris christening be read to him in these last moments of his life. The reading ends with the account of Napoleon's picking up the infant Franz and raising him high so that all might see him: "That evening France seemed all ablaze / With the great splendor and the great delight." Franz dies with his father's name on his lips. Metternich orders that he be buried—in Napoleon's colors: "Bring his uniform.—Of course, the white."

AIKEN, Conrad [Potter] (1889–   ), American writer noted for his poetry, criticism, novels, and short stories. In 1957 he dramatized his popular *Mr. Arcularis* (1931). A short supernatural story with spiritual, philosophical, and psychological overtones, it became a melodrama in the adaptation by Aiken himself and in an earlier one he tried to revise, Diana Hamilton's (1898–1951) *Fear No More* (1946).

AKINS, Zoë (1886–1958), American poet, novelist, and dramatist, is notable for her 1935 Pulitzer Prize winner, *The Old Maid*. It is an adaptation of Edith Wharton's 1924 novella about a heartbroken spinster who puts her illegitimate daughter's happiness first, not revealing her maternity to the girl, who regards her as a quaint nuisance.

Akins was born in Missouri. She became a pioneer in establishing the St. Louis Juvenile Theatre. Her early plays include the somewhat ponderous *The Magical City*, a one-act verse play about a girl ruined by the big city, produced by the Washington Square Players in 1916. Akins's first popular success was *Déclassée* (1919), in which Ethel Barrymore portrayed the decline of an English peeress in America. Her *Daddy's Gone A-Hunting* (1921) depicts (and inconclusively resolves) a bad marriage. These plays were followed by light romances like *The Varying Shores* (1921), which portrays, in reverse chronology, the life and death of a "loose woman"; *A Texas Nightingale* (1922), later produced as *Greatness*, featuring an opera singer reconciled with her second husband; *First Love* (1926), an adaptation of *Pile ou face* (1924), by LOUIS VERNEUIL; *The Greeks Had a Word for It* (1930), a satirical comedy featuring three ruthless girl friends; *O, Evening Star* (1936), depicting an aging actress's successful comeback; and *Happy Days* (1941), an adaptation of *Les Jours heureux* (1938), by CLAUDE-ANDRÉ PUGET. Until 1950 Zoë Akins wrote and adapted other plays as well as films, including EDNA FERBER's *Show Boat*.

ALBANIA did not start producing plays until the twentieth century. Despite a Turkish ban on all Albanian writing, a social drama originally written in Turkey and set in Albania, *Besa* (1901) by Sami Bey Frasheri (pen name of Shemsettin Sami, 1850–1904), was published in Bulgaria and smuggled into Albania, where it remained popular for half a century in Abdyl Ypi Kolonja's translation from the Turkish. Another popular play, also produced in the United States, was *Vdekja e Piros* (1906), a patriotic drama by the novelist Mihal Grameno (1872–1931) about Pyrrhus, the third-century B.C. king of Epirus. Bishop Fan Stylian Noli (1882–1965), who was Albania's Prime Minister but eventually migrated to America, translated some of the dramas of Shakespeare and HENRIK IBSEN, and himself wrote a number of plays, including the political-philosophical *Izraelitë dhe Filistinë* (1907). The poet Gjergj Fishta (1871–1940) wrote many plays, some in verse, like the allegorical *Shqyptari i Gjytetnuem* (about language and religion) and *Juda Makabé*, both of which appeared about the end of the second decade.

By far the most prolific Albanian playwright was Kristo Floqi (1873–1949), a lawyer by profession with a strong inclination to literature, who wrote *Fe e Kombësi* (1912) and many other dramatic sketches, mostly patriotic. Among the playwrights whose work was produced between the two world wars was Et'hem Haxhiademi (1907–?), who dramatized classical themes as in his 1931 trilogy on Ulysses, Achilles, and Alexander the Great (*Ulisi, Akili, Aleksandri*) and wrote other plays like *Pirrua* (1934), *Diomedi* (1936), and *Skënderbeg* (1935), a play about the Albanian national hero and probably Haxhiademi's finest work.

Albania achieved its independence in 1912, but after World War II was incorporated in the Eastern orbit, and came under Communist domination culturally as well as politically. Before World War II the Albanian theatre had a romantic and patriotic revival of histories, including *Trathtija* (1926), another play on Skënderbeg, by Mehdi Frashëri (1872–1963). Since World War II the drama has been of a political-social character, and it has followed the Party line. Among the plays of the 1950's and 1960's are those of Aleks Çaçi (1913?–   ), the title character of whose *Margarita Titulani* is a girl killed during the resistance against Italian Fascists; *Prefekti* by Besim Lëvonja (1918?–   ), an attack on Fascist collaborators during the war; and Fatmir Gjata's (1916?–   ) *Vājza Katundare*, which depicts Albanian girls working in the Stalin Textile Combine.

Albanian drama is discussed in Stuart E. Mann's meager and uneven *Albanian Literature* (1955) and in Koço Bihiku's informative but biased *An Outline of Albanian Literature* (1964).

ALBEE, Edward [Franklin] (1928–), American dramatist, achieved international fame in 1962 with his first full-length play, WHO'S AFRAID OF VIRGINIA WOOLF? Previously he had impressed avant-garde audiences with one-acters that, unlike *Virginia Woolf,* belong to the theatre of the ABSURD. Soon he was acclaimed America's most exciting and promising—some even thought her greatest—playwright. But though he won the 1966 Pulitzer Prize for A DELICATE BALANCE, the plays that followed *Virginia Woolf* have not been as successful commercially. At the same time, his activities—he has also been an enterprising producer—have continued to be of considerable interest, and hopes have remained high that Albee would eventually repeat, or perhaps even surpass, his early achievement.

Born in Washington, D.C., he was adopted as an infant by Reid Albee, the son of the Edward Franklin Albee of the powerful Keith-Albee vaudeville chain. He was brought up in great affluence and sent to select preparatory and military schools. Almost from the beginning he clashed with the strong-minded Mrs. Albee, rebelling against her attempts to make him a success as well as a sportsman and a member of the Larchmont (New York) social set. Instead, he pursued his interests in writing macabre and bitter, usually antifeminine stories and poetry, and kept associating with artists and intellectuals considered objectionable by Mrs. Albee. A large, handsome woman doted upon by her small, silent husband, she inspired Albee's later "Mommy" figures, the females who overpower the ineffectual, sterile "Daddy" of the one-acters—and even the later plays.

Albee left home when he was twenty and moved to New York's Greenwich Village. After using up his paternal grandmother's modest legacy, he took a variety of menial jobs. For a while he and his companions led a dreary and dismal life, some of it devoted to nocturnal "games" portending those of *Virginia Woolf.* THE ZOO STORY (1959) was the first of his writings he felt sufficiently confident about to show in public. New York producers shied away from it, but in 1958 enthusiastic friends promised to have it staged in Germany. Encouraged by the commitment—and by a substantial inheritance that made him independent—Albee began to think of his next play.

After the very successful Berlin premiere of *The Zoo Story*—which soon was produced with equal success in other European cities—he completed his second play, also premiered in Berlin. *The Death of Bessie Smith* (1959) is a one-acter inspired by the Negro blues singer who bled to death in 1937 outside a segregated Tennessee hospital that would not admit her. She never appears onstage, but her agony looms over the play's eight short, cinematic scenes, which counterpoint her death with that of all ideals and decent human relationships; among the characters are her companion, who frantically tries to get her cared for, and a liberal white intern emasculated by the bigoted nurse he loves, who is trapped by Southern life like all the others and at last cries out hysterically, "I am tired of my skin. . . . I WANT OUT!"

In 1959 Albee wrote *The Sandbox*, commissioned by the Spoleto Festival but not performed there. It is a fourteen-minute sketch, soon developed into the slightly longer *The American Dream* (1960), which features the same characters. Both plays are absurdist sketches that vitriolically caricature American values and types, like Mommy, Daddy, and a vacuous but muscular and handsome young man. In the first play the young man continuously performs his calisthenics to keep in shape for an anticipated movie part, while the couple put Grandma—a sympathetic personification of older and more civilized values—in a sandbox to die. The second play's cast is augmented by a "professional woman"; Mommy is even more domineering, Daddy is more emasculated, Grandma waits for a moving van to cart her off, and the young man—the American Dream—explains how he has been drained of all feelings.

As Albee's reputation grew in Europe, his plays at last appeared in America. *The Zoo Story* was produced Off-Broadway with Beckett's KRAPP'S LAST TAPE, and in 1961 *The American Dream* opened with the one-act opera *Bartleby,* Albee's coadaptation (music by William Flanagan) of the Melville tale; when the opera failed, it was replaced by *The Death of Bessie Smith.* It was his first full-length play (*Who's Afraid of Virginia Woolf?*), however, that catapulted Albee into the forefront of contemporary playwrights.

The Ballad of the Sad Café (1963) was a not very successful dramatization of CARSON MCCULLERS's 1951 tragicomic novella about the grotesque triangle of a large woman, a handsome ne'er-do-well, and a homosexual dwarf. Albee's next original work, the mystifying *Tiny Alice* (1964), is a "morality" whose title character, a wealthy woman living in a strange mansion with a butler (her former lover) and her lawyer (her present lover), persuades a cardinal to let her seduce one of his celibate "lay brothers" in return for a vast bequest; when the priest is found wanting, the lawyer shoots the young man, who dies in a crucified position. *Malcolm* (1963), an adaptation of James Purdy's satirical 1959 novel about an innocent young man who dies of sexual overexertion, also failed on the boards. However, with his next work (*A Delicate Balance*) Albee belatedly won the Pulitzer Prize and thus regained some of his earlier prominence.

In 1967 Albee adapted *Everything in the Garden* (1962), a sardonic comedy of middle-class hypocrisy by the English playwright Giles Cooper (1918–66); it portrays suburbanite housewives who, with their husbands' reluctant acquiescence, are part-time prostitutes so that the families can participate in the materialistic rat-race and keep up with the Joneses. More important because of its originality and intensity but criticized by some as being tedious and murky was a twin bill originally presented as *Box-Mao-Box* (1968). It consists of the ten-minute *Box*, a woman's tape-recorded interior monologue on a stage empty except for a large box that is symbolic, perhaps, of a coffin, a womb, the confinement of life, and/or civilization; and *Quotations from Chairman Mao Tse-tung*, set aboard a ship and featuring four characters, three of whom deliver independent monologues that echo snatches from *Box:* a woman tells a smiling and sometimes dozing minister about how she, years ago, fell overboard, an old woman recites corny verses, and the Chinese party chairman delivers his revolutionary aphorisms. Albee's latest play, *All Over* (1971), is in stilted literary language and mixes an experimental, orchestrated style with the earlier NATURALISTIC style of his full-length plays; it depicts a celebrity's wife, mistress, nurse, physician, best friend, daughter, and son—all of whom are nameless—awaiting his imminent death.

In his oft-quoted preface to *The American Dream* Albee characterized that play as an examination of and an attack on social values, "a condemnation of complacency, cruelty, emasculation and vacuity." His full-length plays, conventionally naturalistic (though the characters and settings are of the upper middle class), have pursued the attack in a manner that is more subtle, if equally unrestrained. His characters have changed from mere caricatures into more rounded and frightening personifications of the earlier ogres. Martha and Agnes, for example, are the emasculating Mommy of the one-acters, their husbands are the emasculated Daddy, and the American Dream youngster is the humorless technician go-getter, Nick. The love-hate relationship of *The Zoo Story* is transmogrified into a heterosexual STRINDBERGian battle with similar overtones. Also reappearing in various guises are the earlier plays' animal stories, false pregnancies, and illusory or dismembered (male) or inadequate (female) children. The religious symbolism evident in the very first play recurs and assumes a central (if not very clear) position in the "morality" *Tiny Alice*. Yet there is unmistakable power—and considerable humor—in Albee's dialogue, and in his ability to create dramatic tension and engross audiences. *A Delicate Balance* evidences a perceptible advance in its restraint of language and action. Rather than another extravagant attack on man's shortcomings, it suggests a maturation that presaged new dramaturgical and thematic possibilities in Albee's plays.

Albee's one-acters were collected in 1960 with the earlier-noted preface by the playwright. The full-length works are published separately. Gilbert Debusscher's French study appeared in English as *Edward Albee: Tradition and Renewal* (1967); other books on Albee's life and work include Richard E. Amacher's *Edward Albee* (1969) and Michael E. Rutenberg's *Edward Albee: Playwright in Protest* (1969).

ALBERTI, Rafael (1902–), Spanish writer, is more notable as a versatile poet (often of SURREALIST verse) than as a dramatist, although he wrote a number of lyrical plays. In the early *El hombre deshabitado* (1931) and *Fermín Galán* (1931) he articulated, respectively, his furor against divine injustice and his feelings about a contemporary revolt; in the latter play, which recalls themes of MARIANA PINEDA by his friend FEDERICO GARCÍA LORCA—to whom Alberti bears other resemblances—a blind man introduces each act by singing *romances* (ballads). The founder of a left-wing review that supported the Communist Party, which subsequently expelled him, Alberti fought Franco and exiled himself from Spain after the Civil War—principally to Argentina. The battle against Franco is dramatized in Alberti's *De un momento a otro* (1942). His other plays include a lyric love drama set in the Andalusian mountains, *El Adefesio* (1944); the tragicomedy *El trébol florido* (1950); and *Noche de guerra en el Museo del Prado* (*Night and War in the Prado Museum,* 1956), a fantasy in which victims through the ages materialize out of the Prado's paintings to reenact their defense of Spain as Franco's bombs fall on the museum—suggesting that the people will again overthrow tyranny. This play appears with a note on Alberti in Michael Benedikt and George E. Wellwarth's *Modern Spanish Theatre* (1968).

ALCIBIADES SAVED (*Der gerettete Alkibiades*), a play in three parts by GEORG KAISER, published and produced in 1920. Setting: ancient Athens.

This is the best of Kaiser's early, EXPRESSIONIST dramatizations of the relationship between body and mind. The story of Socrates only vaguely follows tradition. He is presented as a hunchbacked soldier whose delaying action turns Athenian defeat into victory and saves General Alcibiades. But the act is involuntary: Socrates's foot has been injured by a cactus spine, and is excruciatingly painful. Unable to mount the steps, he renounces his golden victory wreath. Though Xanthippe urges that a doctor be called to remove the broken thorn, Socrates refuses: it would reveal the truth and forever ridicule Alcibiades. Socrates resumes making hermae: now that he has experienced the triumph of the flesh, he must tout the sovereignty of the mind—"I had to invent—what should not be invented!!—I had to cover the sky—and wither the earth!!—It was no crime of mine—: Compassion!!—" His intellectual probing disconcerts the Athenians and arouses the resentment of Alcibiades, who smashes the sacred hermae. He escapes, but Socrates is held responsible, tried, and condemned. He cannot accept the proffered escape because of the injured foot. When he drinks the hemlock he is told to walk to hasten the poison's effect. Only then does he have the thorn extracted. He dies, and dawn's sunbeam strikes—his foot.

ALISON'S HOUSE, a play in three acts by SUSAN GLASPELL, published and produced in 1930. Setting: an Iowa homestead on the Mississippi River; December 31, 1899.

This appealing though sentimental play briefly created a furor when it won the Pulitzer Prize. It is a thinly disguised dramatization of the story of Emily Dickinson, who achieved major posthumous fame. The play opens eighteen years after the death of the poet, here called Alison Stanhope. The first two acts depict her still-tremendous spiritual influence on the house and family—and on a young poet, a reporter who wants to see her room before the house is broken up and the family moves. Hitherto unknown poems are discovered, and these reveal Alison's deep but repressed love for a married man. The Stanhopes differ about the manuscript's disposition. Her dying old aunt—a puritan who adored Alison—wants to burn the "confessions of a great but misguided soul." So does the head of the house, Alison's brother, who feels that "she does not have to show her heart to the world." His daughter (who herself created a scandal by running off with a married man) as well as Stanhope's secretary (who falls in love with the reporter) beg Stanhope to release the poems, which they feel Alison had written as if especially for them. His own unhappy marriage finally helps to persuade Stanhope that the poems express his own thoughts too. "She loved to make her little gifts," he says of Alison as he forgives his daughter and hands her the manuscript poems: "If she can make one more, from her century to yours, then she isn't gone. Anything else is—too lonely."

ALL FOR THE BEST (*Tutto per bene*), a comedy in three acts by LUIGI PIRANDELLO, published and produced in 1920. Setting: contemporary Rome.

This bitter comedy is Pirandello's dramatization of a short story he had published in 1910.

Daily for sixteen years Martino Lori, a civil servant, has mourned at his wife's grave and venerated her memory. Oblivious to the world, he now loves only his daughter. But she seems more attached to a wealthy senator, a prominent scientist who has paid for her education and has made possible her marriage with a marquis. Shortly after their wedding Lori discovers what everyone else knew—and thought he knew—all along: his wife had been unfaithful, and the senator is the daughter's real father. Even the daughter knew this; like the others, she has assumed that Lori pretended not to know the truth in order to gain advancement through the senator. Lori is crushed by this discovery, by the loss of his daughter, and by the awareness of how he appears to others. He thinks of killing the senator, of exposing him as a charlatan (Lori has all along had evidence of the plagiarism on which the senator's scientific renown is based), and of committing suicide. When Lori's putative daughter realizes the deception and sees his suffering, she begins to reciprocate his feelings for her. Lori finally wins her affection and she persuades him to accept the situation and say nothing. At the end he comes to see (in the words of Voltaire's Doctor Pangloss) that it was "all for the best."

ALL GOD'S CHILLUN GOT WINGS, a play in two acts by EUGENE O'NEILL, published and produced in 1924. Setting: lower New York, "years ago."

The ineffective time skips (over some sixteen to seventeen years) and the mixture of NATURALISM and EXPRESSIONISM (particularly in the setting) weaken the play, which nonetheless has powerful individual scenes. Though the sensitive portrayals of Jim and Ella make it far more than simply a "race" play, there were concentrated efforts to prevent its New York premiere, and with this play O'Neill first incurred the anger of officialdom.

Act I. Scene 1. At the street corner where the Negro and the white tenements converge, children of both races are playing together. After the Negro boy Jim Harris chases Mickey and the others off for teasing Ella Downey (a white girl) and making her cry, the two shyly hold hands and agree to be each other's "feller" and "girl." *Scene 2.* Nine years later, Jim begs Mickey, now a pug-faced fighter, not to ruin Ella. He is pounced upon by the group for "forgetting your place," "tryin' to buy white," and (by another Negro) for "all dis denyin' you's a nigger." Jim tells Ella, now Mickey's girl and contemptuous of the Negro, that he will always be her "true friend." *Scene 3.* Five years have gone by, in which time Ella has been thrown over by Mickey (the father of her child, who later died), and Jim, panicking at "the white faces," has failed his bar exams. He again offers himself to Ella, who in despair agrees to marry Jim, the only person who has been "white" to her. He kneels in abject gratitude and offers to be her "black slave that adores you as sacred!" *Scene 4.* After the wedding a few weeks later, they leave the church, pass in terror through two bitter, hostile racial lines, and rush off to sail "to the other side of the world—the side where Christ was born—the kind side that takes count of the soul—"

Act II. Scene 1. They return after two unhappy years of marriage, his mother still believing "de white and de black shouldn't mix dat close," and his sister Hattie, a militant Negro, believing "they were cowards to run away." Jim tells them how Ella feared meeting Americans in France, and that they returned because "the reason we felt sort of ashamed was we'd . . . run away from the thing." Ella, who has had a nervous breakdown, is frightened by a beautiful African religious mask, which to her appears stupid and ugly. After her sister-in-law's insulting condescension, Hattie leaves angrily, and Ella, alone for a moment, contemptuously expresses her white supremacy, gets hysterical at the humiliation of her marriage and consequent ostracism, and finally runs out whimpering for Jim. *Scene 2.* Six months later, increasingly hemmed in (suggested by the set's contracted walls and ceiling), Jim is ruining himself with study ("I've got to prove I'm the whitest of the white!") and Ella's breakdown progresses. When Hattie suggests that the raving girl be committed, Jim sends his sister away. As he resumes his studies, Ella insanely sneaks in with a carving knife and, after a moment's sanity, relapses and murderously curses Jim: "You dirty nigger!"

Scene 3. Completely mad six months later, Ella raves at the African mask and flourishes her knife, swearing she will kill Jim if he has passed his bar exam. When he comes home broken by his last failure, she joyfully plunges her knife through the mask, telling Jim that he now need never fear her again. For a moment he turns against both her and God: "Maybe He can forgive what you've done to me; and maybe He can forgive what I've done to you; but I don't see how He's going to forgive—Himself." But he quickly recants, and ecstatically begs God to make him "worthy of the child You send me for the woman You take away!" When Ella, now totally regressed, asks Jim to play with her, he remains on his knees, exalted: "Honey, Honey, I'll play right up to the gates of Heaven with you!"

ALL MY SONS, a play in three acts by ARTHUR MILLER, published and produced in 1947. Setting: a home on the outskirts of an American town, about 1946.

Miller's first success, this is a precursor of DEATH OF A SALESMAN. The two titles suit both plays; *All My Sons,* however, is IBSENite, particularly reminiscent of PILLARS OF SOCIETY. The truth gradually revealed in Miller's play is that Joe Keller, placing family above social obligations, betrayed his partner and saved his business by selling defective airplane parts to the army. Keller's idealistic, almost saintly son Chris cannot bear the discovery of his father's guilt for the resultant casualties: "There's a universe outside and you're responsible to it." Keller maintains that "Nothin' is bigger" than family loyalty, and he also cites the American profit motive: "Nothin's clean. It's dollars and cents [in both] war and peace." Proof comes that Keller's other son, reported missing though his mother believes he must be alive, killed himself when he learned of his father's guilt: he was unable to face his fellow airmen. "I think to him they were all my sons. And I guess they were," Keller concludes—and he goes upstairs and shoots himself.

ÁLVAREZ QUINTERO, the brothers **Serafín** (1871–1938) and **Joaquín** (1873–1944), were among the most prolific and popular Spanish folk dramatists during the early decades of the century. They collaborated on well over two hundred plays, about half of them the short, one-act comic *sainetes.* Many of their plays were produced throughout Europe and America. To English-speaking audiences perhaps the best known were MALVALOCA (1912), *La Consulesa* (THE LADY FROM ALFÁQUEQUE, 1914), and *Mañana de sol* (*A Sunny* [or *Bright*] *Morning,* 1905), a comic one-act sketch (republished in various English anthologies) about an old man and an old woman who meet on a park bench, quarrel, gradually recognize each other as former sweethearts, but reluctantly decline to admit it. Reminiscent in their plays of GREGORIO MARTÍNEZ SIERRA, the Quinteros were dubbed "the professors of happiness" because of their sentimentality and genial Andalusian perspective.

It was in that sunny region of Spain, in Utrera, that the brothers were born, and they grew up in the nearby Andalusian capital, Seville. Apparently influenced by their brother Pedro, Serafín and Joaquín began to write farces very early. In 1889 one of these was produced in a fashionable Seville theatre, whereupon the brothers moved to Madrid. After nearly a decade's struggle they achieved their first success in 1897 with a couple of one-acters, *El ojito derecho* and *La reja.* No more profound but equally entertaining is their *La buena sombra,* a musical comedy that won them considerable popularity in 1898. By the end of the century the brothers had completed over fifty plays.

These and later ones are cheery and picturesque folk pieces that have been characterized as "theatre of kindliness." As HARLEY GRANVILLE-BARKER wrote, "This is not profound drama, but it is alive." Among their few serious plays is *Los galeotes* (1900), a portrayal of ingratitude set in the secondhand bookshop of a good-natured Madrid dealer. In *Don Juan, buena persona* (1918), the Quinteros dramatized the life of the famous lover as a kindly captive of his conquests, whom he escapes when he marries the charmer to whom he has succumbed. Typical of their plays are those adapted by Helen and Harley Granville-Barker in *Four Plays* (1927) and *Four Comedies* (1932). The first volume includes *Puebla de las mujeres* (*The Women's Town,* 1912; also translated as *The Women Have Their Way*), a simple and almost plotless piece in which gossip brings about the romance of a visiting young lawyer and the village belle—"the tragedy of [Echegaray's THE GREAT GALEOTO] turned to laughter," as the Granville-Barker introduction notes; *Papá Juan: Centenario* (*Papa Juan or the Centenarian,* 1909; also translated as *A Hundred Years Old*), whose good-natured hero, over his conservative family's objections, marries off his great-granddaughter to her young freethinking cousin; *Fortunato* (1912), whose good-natured scoundrel is endangered when he joins the act of a catastrophe-prone circus family's sole survivor; and *The Lady from Alfáqueque.* Similarly unpretentious entertainment is provided by the *Four Comedies: El amor que pasa* (*Love Passes By,* 1904), *La Musa Loca* (1905, translated as *Don Abel Wrote a Tragedy*), *La escondida senda* (1908, translated as *Peace and Quiet*), and *Doña Clarines* (1909). See the Granville-Barker prefaces to these volumes and Frank W. Chandler's section on the Quinteros in *Modern Continental Playwrights* (1931).

ALYOSHIN, Samuil (1913-   ), Russian playwright, wrote dramas about workers, technicians, and literary figures like Nikolai Gogol and Shakespeare. Notable are his *Odna* (1956), a play about adultery, and *Palata* (1962), a good example of de-Stalinization drama, set in a hospital ward and depicting four quarreling patients. See Max

Hayward and Edward L. Crowley's essay collection, *Soviet Literature in the Sixties* (1964).

AMÉDÉE OR HOW TO GET RID OF IT (*Amédée ou comment s'en débarrasser*), "a comedy" in three acts by EUGÈNE IONESCO, published and produced in 1954. Setting: contemporary Paris, morning through the next dawn.

Ionesco's first full-length play, this is a partly SURREALIST depiction of the festering, dead love of a mismated couple. It has also been translated simply as *Amédée*.

Act I. Amédée Buccinioni, a forty-five-year-old "petit bourgeois" playwright, nervously snatches something from behind the chair: "A mushroom! Well, really! If they're going to start growing in the dining room!" His cross wife Madeleine (also forty-five) works at a telephone switchboard in the corner of their unpretentious living room, nags, and criticizes his optimism. "It's fifteen years since you had any inspiration," she reminds him. In all that time he has written only the play's first speech. As the hands on the big living-room clock keep moving and Madeleine tries to get the President and other parties, the couple anxiously watch the sprouting mushrooms. What troubles them even more, however, is an enormous corpse rapidly growing in the adjoining bedroom and displacing them and their belongings. Afraid of the police, they do not leave their apartment, they haul food up in a basket, and they accept no letters from the postman. Periodically they look into the bedroom. "He's growing both ends at once," Madeleine says in horror, and soon, after much crackling and banging, as the corpse smashes through the walls, its enormous feet slide in. "He's got geometrical progression," Amédée despairs, "the incurable disease of the dead"; and Madeleine sobs, "It's inhuman, that's what it is, inhuman."

Act II. By three o'clock more of the corpse has entered the living room and giant mushrooms are growing on the walls. "If you don't get rid of him, I'm going to get a divorce," Madeleine insists. She blames Amédée for not reporting the death fifteen years ago, after "you'd killed him in a fit of anger, out of jealousy"—for the corpse is that of her lover. But then Amédée thinks the corpse may be that of the baby a neighbor asked them to look after and never retrieved. Madeleine wonders how that could be possible, but taunts Amédée as a "Murderer! Baby-killer!" As more of the corpse grows into the room, the irresolute Amédée agrees to haul it away that night. In a dream sequence, the married couple appear as they were in their youth. The loving, romantic Amédée is "bursting with song," but the mundane, frigid Madeleine tells him to stop. "Your voice is so piercing!" she complains: "You're . . . hurting me! Don't rend my darkness! S-a-dist!" Their incompatibility is climaxed by the young Amédée's "We love each other. We are happy. In a house of glass, a house of light"—and the already unimaginative Madeleine's correction: "House of brass, house of night!" After their youthful images depart, Amédée desperately tries to save their dull marriage: "If we really loved each other, none of this would be important," he begs her. "Why don't we try to love each other, *please,* Madeleine?" But she rejects him: "Love can't help people get rid of their troubles! You know nothing about real people! When are you going to write an ordinary sort of play?" As the growing corpse drives them into a corner, strange music and a green glow come from the bedroom. Amédée, reluctant and afraid to get rid of the corpse, admires the glowing, blooming acacia trees in the moonlight. But Madeleine insists and helps him to pull the corpse laboriously across the room and out of the window. "Pul-l-l!" she shouts after him as he starts dragging it toward the river. "Go straight there, don't hang abo-o-out. . . ."

Act III. On a city square in front of a bar, Amédée, still pulling the enormous corpse, runs into a drunk American soldier and describes his play: "It's a problem play attacking nihilism and announcing a new form of humanism, more enlightened than the old." The soldier, soon joined by his prostitute and a friend, rolls the corpse around Amédée. There is a loud whistle as the police come after Amédée. However, the part of the corpse already wound around Amédée suddenly opens like a sail and hoists Amédée into the air—to the amazement of the growing crowd. Madeleine rushes up, incredulously shouts after him ("Come down, Amédée, you'll catch a chill"), and apologizes to the police, explaining—as Amédée did before—that she believes in "social realism": "I'm all against dissolution." Amédée keeps rising. "I didn't want to run away from my responsibilities," he apologizes. "It's the wind. . . . Not of my own free will!" Madeleine begs him to return: "Won't you ever be serious? You may have gone up in the world, but you're not going up in *my* estimation!" But buoyant and free of his nagging wife, Amédée floats away. The neighbors assure Madeleine that he will never come back and shut their windows: "The show's over."

AMPHITRYON 38, a comedy in a prologue and three acts by JEAN GIRAUDOUX, published and produced in 1929. Setting: in and about Amphitryon's palace in ancient Greece.

This witty play retells the Jupiter-Alcmena story, purportedly for the thirty-eighth time. S. N. BEHRMAN adapted it for the memorable Alfred Lunt and Lynn Fontanne Broadway production in 1937.

Jupiter, conversing on a cloud with Mercury, is enamored of Alcmena and yearns to possess her as a mortal. The obstacle is her faithful love for her husband, Amphitryon. Mercury suggests he be sent to war and Jupiter assume his form. War is declared and Amphitryon bids tender farewell to his delightful and adoring wife. The two gods arrive, Jupiter struggling to cramp himself into the mortal dimension and frame of mind. He is finally admitted as Amphitryon. By morning he is humbled into conjugal submission. "Come along, Amphitryon, you'll be late for your war!" Alcmena says, refusing to agree that this was their most "divine" night: "of all our nights, [this] was the most—connubial." Jupiter lectures about creation and theology; the intelligent Alcmena listens with rapt wifely devotion, and frustrates his attempted revelations. Jupiter admits to Mercury that "it was impossible for me to be anything but her husband. It was Alcmena who was completely victorious over me." Though Jupiter has impregnated Alcmena with Hercules, he yearns to possess her in his own right—even as a god. Mercury tries to prepare her for Jupiter's arrival—and is surprised to have the god's offer refused. Leda has heard of his imminent visit to Alcmena and comes to talk to her. Learning the particulars about Leda's encounter with Jupiter as a swan, Alcmena persuades her to take her place that night. Leda and Alcmena guess that he will assume Amphitryon's form. Soon the real Amphitryon arrives. Sure that it is Jupiter, Alcmena tricks him into Leda's arms, satisfied to have outwitted the god. Later Alcmena discovers the truth and Amphitryon prepares to battle Jupiter for his wife. Alcmena takes the god aside and charmingly persuades him to accept her friendship rather than force her love. Then she catechizes her new friend: "In a marriage ideally happy, a husband has been unfaithful through no fault of his own—what can you do for him?" And Jupiter replies: "Cause him never to know it." No less a friend, Alcmena agrees to appear "before the whole world as your mistress," and in return Jupiter wipes out Alcmena's suspicion that Jupiter ever assumed the shape of Amphitryon. Jupiter and Alcmena display themselves to the populace and duly establish the legend. Then the god disappears aloft.

ANATHEMA (*Anatema*), a tragedy in seven scenes by LEONID ANDREEV, published and produced in 1909. Setting: before the gates of Heaven, and various parts of Russia in the early twentieth century.

This philosophic and SYMBOLIC play was suppressed during its first run as irreligious and pro-Semitic. It was produced (1910) and revived (1923) in New York, both in Yiddish and in English. Highly praised by some, the play was found meaningless and turgid by others.

The saintly Jew David Leizer is made rich and gives his all—wealth, love, and labor—to the poor. Though he wants to do his good deeds unobserved, he is sought out and idolized. But when his money runs out, the mob turns against him—and stones him. The framework (prologue and epilogue) is set before Heaven's gates. There Anathema seeks to discover and expose God. Barred entrance, he goes to live with his Job-like David. At the end, Anathema returns to the gates. There all remains mysterious. "David has attained immortality," he is told by Heaven's guardian. Laughing scornfully, Anathema vows to return to earth to proclaim how all men "will become murderers and hangmen . . . in the name of David, who brought joy to mankind." For, he adds, looking despairingly at the unreachable inner sanctum, "you have such a bad reputation—of a liar, a deceiver, a murderer. Good-bye."

ANATOL, a cycle of seven one-act plays by ARTHUR SCHNITZLER, published in 1893 and produced in 1910. Setting: Vienna, 1890's.

Schnitzler made his name with this play, still considered by many to be his best. (HARLEY GRANVILLE-BARKER's adaptation further popularized it.) Some of its sketches were first published and performed separately. Though Anatol had been Schnitzler's pseudonym for earlier works, the play's *raisonneur* is Max, the skeptical realist. Anatol (as he himself remarks in the second sketch) is a mixture of frivolity and melancholy, romanticism and cynicism—a Viennese playboy whose affairs constitute the plots of the seven plays. Later Schnitzler portrayed Anatol as a pantaloon—the product of his philandering—in the posthumous one-acter *Anatols Grössenwahn* (*Anatol's Megalomania,* 1932). Introductory verses for *Anatol* were written by HUGO VON HOFMANNSTHAL.

1. "Questioning Fate." Max admires his friend Anatol's hypnotic powers, and suggests he use them to question Anatol's sweetheart. Anatol is cynical about women's constancy, and soon after she appears he hypnotizes her. But though Max encourages him, Anatol cannot bring himself to ask the fatal question—Has she ever been faithless?—because, as Max points out, "your illusion is a thousand times dearer to you than the truth."

2. "Christmas Shopping." On the street, Anatol meets a married woman he once courted. Though she refused to grant him her favors, she mocks his sweet, simple mistress, for whom she helps him shop. But as she leaves in a cab, she asks Anatol to take a bouquet to the mistress and tell her it was sent by "a woman who, perhaps, could love as well as you—but hasn't the courage."

3. "Episode." Anatol discusses his love mementos, particularly one in a packet labeled "episode." It was only a two-hour romance, but "I was all the world to this girl who lay at my feet . . . had thought for nothing but me—and yet for me she was already something past." Max thinks her "just one of a thousand fallen women to whom a dreamer's imagination lends new virginity." When the girl happens to appear, Anatol is crushed by her failure even to remember him, and runs out angrily. Max "avenges" his friend by having the girl tell him of her new lover.

4. 'Milestones." On his wedding day Anatol finds two mementos his fiancée has hidden. She confesses that she kept the ruby because it recalls her first lover, and the diamond because it is rare, "worth a quarter of a million." Disgusted, Anatol calls her a "whore" and leaves.

5. "A Farewell Supper." Somewhat nervous about it but ready to break off his affair with a dancer because he is already in the midst of another one, Anatol has Max stand by to make the parting easier. However, Anatol is unpleasantly surprised to be anticipated: the girl has come to break off their affair because she has found a new lover. Max is greatly amused by their angry squabble, and when she leaves he calmly remarks to Anatol, "There, you see—it was very easy after all."

6. *"Dissolution."* Anatol is waiting for his mistress, a married woman. They are already tired of each other but have not the strength to break up. Their blunted desire to do so is a disease, Anatol tells Max: "There are so many diseases but only one health. . . . One must always be just as healthy as the others—but one can be ill quite differently from anyone else!" The lovers' meeting is unsatisfactory, Anatol kisses her, and she leaves. "It's all so stupid!" he remarks.

7. *"Anatol's Wedding Morning."* Early on the day of his wedding, Anatol is in bed with a mistress. Max is indignant, and Anatol explains how it came about. The men must now go to the wedding, but Anatol has not the courage to confess to his mistress that it is his own wedding. When he finally does, the girl angrily smashes his belongings. Anatol goes off to be married. Max quiets the girl when he remarks that Anatol will soon deceive his bride with her. Consoled, the girl loftily appraises the room before leaving it: "I shall return."

ANATOMIST, THE, a play in three acts by JAMES BRIDIE, produced in 1930 and published in 1931. Setting: Edinburgh, 1828–29.

This is a character study of Dr. Robert Knox (1791–1862), the prominent Scots anatomist who incensed the public with his corpse procurements. "If it illustrates anything," Bridie noted in his preface, "it is the shifts to which men of science are driven when they are ahead of their times." He portrays Knox as a diabolically ruthless but courageous scientist. The events and characters are historical, except for those involved in a romance between the unhappily married Knox and the sister of his assistant's fiancée.

Knox's assistant and disciple defends him against his fiancée's charge that Knox works "hand in glove with the sack-'em-up men. . . . The body-snatchers. The resurrectionists." The couple break up, and the distraught assistant goes to a tavern, where he is comforted by a beautiful but vulgar tart. William Burke and William Hare, two ruffians who sell Knox cadavers for experiments and lectures, kill the tart. The next day the horrified assistant recognizes her corpse—and is sternly castigated by Knox, who refuses to concern himself with where his corpses come from: "I am the apostolic successor of Cuvier, the great naturalist." But word eventually gets out, Burke is hanged, and mobs are out to lynch Knox. He appears at the home of his assistant's fiancée, ready to shoot the "canaille." The mobs are about to tear the house down when Knox, who is coolly determined to deliver his scheduled anatomy lecture, is rescued by his students. The lovers are reconciled, and Knox, then and there, delivers his anatomy lecture—an impassioned one on the heart.

ANCEY, Georges [originally Georges-Marie-Edmond Mathevon de Curnieu] (1860–1917), French dramatist, had his works produced by André Antoine at the Théâtre Libre. Like JEAN JULLIEN, Ancey was particularly expert in *comédie rosse,* viciously ironic, cynical plays like *L'École des veufs* (1889), whose heroine refuses to confine her unfaithfulness to her lover's son, with whom he is willing to share her. Ancey's later play *Ces messieurs* is also notable; banned for its anticlericism in 1901, it was produced in Brussels in 1903.

AND PIPPA DANCES! (*Und Pippa tanzt!*), "a glassworks legend" in four acts by GERHART HAUPTMANN, published and produced in 1906. Setting: Silesian mountains, a winter in the early twentieth century.

This play never achieved the popularity of THE SUNKEN BELL, which it resembles. After a NATURALISTIC first act, the play changes into allegorical fantasy. Its fairy-tale charm is somewhat marred by confused, incoherent SYMBOLISM. Pippa probably represents beauty or the ideal; the manager, capitalism—or civilized human beings; the old glassblower, natural uncivilized lust; the magician, intellect that saves Pippa for the poet—or a Prospero juxtaposed with the glassblower's Caliban; the poet—the only one who believes he wins Pippa—the successful life of the imagination.

In a mountain tavern, Pippa, a young Italian girl, bewitches glassworkers with her dance while her father is caught cheating at cards. He is chased out and eventually killed. During the commotion, the giant old glassblower who made her dance abducts Pippa. She is rescued from his mountain cabin by a young journeyman poet, with whom she falls in love. The glassworks manager, who also loves Pippa and paid to have her dance, visits a mythic figure, an old magician, and solicits his help. Soon Pippa, the poet, and the old glassblower are in the magician's mountain hut. The manager leaves when he sees that Pippa is in love with the poet. The magician subdues the savage old glassblower and warns Pippa to beware of him. But she revives him and accedes to his demand that she dance. When he jubilantly crushes a glass, she dies. The poet at the same time is blinded and imagines Pippa still beside him. In painful renunciation, the old magician supports the poet's happy illusions that he is journeying with her to his dream city in the warm South, "And Pippa dances!"

AND SO IT WILL BE (*Tak i budet*), a comedy in two acts by KONSTANTIN SIMONOV, published and produced in 1944. Setting: a Moscow apartment shortly after the end of World War II.

Produced in America as *The Whole World Over* (1947), this amusing play features a celebrated old Soviet architect, Professor Fyodor Vorontsov.

A strong-minded but lovable eccentric,

Vorontsov presides over the occupants of his increasingly overcrowded apartment. He encourages his daughter to jilt her fiancé, a talented but uninspiring architect, for the apartment's returning owner, a Red Army colonel. Both the colonel and the girl have lost their loved ones in the war, but their growing mutual attraction—amidst the hurly-burly of various visitors—is temporarily impeded by the daughter's fiancé and by a golden-hearted virago of a medical officer who wants to marry the colonel. With the help of Vorontsov, however, the lovers are finally united. As they embrace, Vorontsov drinks a toast to them "and to the world ahead of you—with no more uniforms!"

ANDERSON, Maxwell (1888–1959), American playwright, wrote idealistic verse drama that repeatedly succeeded in the commercial theatres of Broadway. He acclaimed the theatre as democracy's temple, and served it with uncompromising dedication and considerable talent. Critics have always disagreed in their evaluation of Anderson's writings. Unquestionably his plays often are flawed by verbosity—particularly about his pet themes of faith and freedom. Further, Anderson was to modernize older dramatic conventions rather than break new paths. But his accomplishment is nonetheless impressive. Over the years Anderson has retained his distinguished reputation as the author of widely different kinds of plays of lasting appeal.

The son of a Baptist minister, Anderson was born in Pennsylvania. After his schooling there and in the Middle West, he graduated from the University of North Dakota in 1911, married, and became a teacher. Subsequently he attended Stanford University, where he taught until he received his M.A. in 1914. After a year as an English professor at Whittier he turned to newspaper work, partly because of the better pay, and partly because his pacifist views had got him into trouble. His ideals were equally unpopular in journalism, however; in San Francisco he was dismissed by the *Bulletin,* and fared little better with other newspapers, including the *Chronicle.* Then he moved to New York and joined the staffs of the *New Republic* (which had printed some of his poems), the *Globe,* and the *World.*

A newspaper colleague, LAURENCE STALLINGS, steered Anderson to the career in which he soon was to achieve fame. Impressed by Anderson's verse drama WHITE DESERT, Stallings was instrumental in having it produced in 1923. Though it quickly closed, Anderson's first play received a few good notices and kindled his enthusiasm for the theatre. Next he collaborated with Stallings on WHAT PRICE GLORY? Its 1924 success enabled Anderson to give up newspaper work and devote himself entirely to the theatre. He collaborated with Stallings on two more plays, neither of which succeeded. Produced the following year (1925), both are about historical swashbucklers: *First Flight* features Andrew Jackson as a dueling young lover, and *The Buccaneer* melodramatizes the career of the seventeenth-century pirate and later Governor of Jamaica, Sir Henry Morgan.

Anderson's *Outside Looking In* (1925), based on Jim Tully's *Beggars of Life* (1924), a novel about a "sissy" hobo who turns heroic to defend a fugitive prostitute he loves, was a flop. Two years later he won his first solo success, with SATURDAY'S CHILDREN (1927). *Gypsy* (1929), almost a sequel to that play in its Bohemian views, was less successful and less amusing in its NATURALISTIC probing of the downfall of a Greenwich Village nymphomaniac. In collaboration with a Rockland County neighbor, the musician Harold Hickerson (1896–   ), Anderson had created a stir the previous year with GODS OF THE LIGHTNING (1928), about the controversial Sacco-Vanzetti case.

In 1930 Anderson produced one of his finest and most popular plays, ELIZABETH THE QUEEN, the first of many verse histories. *Night over Taos* (1932), the next verse drama, deals with the 1847 defeat of the despot Pablo Montoya by the new order: Mexico's younger generation and greedy invaders from the fledgling American republic that was to annex the territory. Now securely established, Anderson came out with an average of at least one play a year: BOTH YOUR HOUSES (1933), MARY OF SCOTLAND (1933), VALLEY FORGE (1934), WINTERSET (1935)—considered by some to be his greatest play—THE WINGLESS VICTORY (1936), THE MASQUE OF KINGS (1937), and three fantasies: *The Star Wagon* (1937), in which a dissatisfied scientist's invention of a machine to relive one's youth reaffirms the wisdom of his and his wife's original choices; HIGH TOR (1937); and KNICKERBOCKER HOLIDAY (1938). An earlier work that remained unpublished but received a university production in the 1930's was *Sea Wife*, a verse play about a legendary island woman in love with a merman. Anderson also wrote a number of one-act radio plays, some of which were published. Among them are *Second Overture* and *The Feast of Ortolans,* verse plays of the 1930's that M. D. Bailey analyzes in some detail in her book (see below). The first is set in an execution chamber near Moscow in 1918, and the second dramatizes discussions by intellectuals and aristocrats (including Lafayette) on the French Revolution, which is about to begin.

During World War II most of Anderson's work consisted of less distinguished, patriotic drama. First came KEY LARGO (1939) and *Journey to Jerusalem* (1940), a verse play in which the twelve-year-old Jesus (Jeshua), visiting the temple, hears Ishmael's revelation that He is the Messiah who is to suffer and die. (Anderson's introduction stresses the necessity of faith to overcome tyranny.) In *Candle in the Wind* (1941) "victory through faith" and "it's good to fight alone" themes are embodied in a plot that traces the attempts of an American actress to free her French fiancé from Nazi imprisonment. Half of *The Eve of St. Mark* (1942) depicts the simple, touching—and sometimes amusing—home life of an inducted farm boy; the other half shows him on a Pacific island, choosing death to help preserve the ideals and values of American life; the folks at home grieve—but approve of his choice. *Storm Operation* (1944) idealizes a group of fighting GIs, one of whom marries during an air raid.

Truckline Café (1946), a play about the postwar problem of marital infidelity, was so ignominious a failure that Anderson withheld its publication. But the same year he produced the popular Ingrid Bergman vehicle JOAN OF LORRAINE (1946), which was followed by another popular history play, ANNE OF THE THOUSAND DAYS (1948). Anderson returned to the racial theme of *The Wingless Victory* with *Lost in the Stars* (1949, music by Kurt Weill), a dramatization of Alan Paton's South African novel *Cry, the Beloved Country*. *Barefoot in Athens* (1951) depicts the simple, barefooted Socrates with a devoted wife and children, preferring to drink the hemlock in democratic Athens to living in the royal palace of totalitarian Sparta. *The Bad Seed* (1954) is an adaptation of William March's novel about a mother's tragic confrontation with her little girl's inherited criminality. It was Anderson's last Broadway hit, for neither of his last plays fared well. His 1958 dramatization with Brendan Gill (1914–) of the latter's novel, *The Day the Money Stopped,* deals with a family's squabble over the father's will. Anderson's last play, about Augustus's grandchildren, *The Golden Six* (1958), flopped in its Off-Broadway premiere, despite advertisements stressing the seminudity of some of the performers.

Anderson's faith in man's individual responsibility and in democracy, and his distrust of government, permeate all his work. Again and again an often-quoted line from *Elizabeth the Queen* is reechoed: "The rats inherit the earth." This perspective, particularly in the prewar drama, tends to resolve his plots in a spirit of skepticism, with the defeat, or pointless death, of the protagonist. Anderson's affirmative resolutions in these plays, as many commentators have noted, do not reflect and are not always relevant to the events just portrayed. Yet his plays testify to his many and varied gifts as a dramatist: writing in verse as well as prose, he produced histories, romances, fantasies, plays of social protest, tragedies, and comedies.

Aside from these plays, Anderson published a volume of poetry, *You Who Have Dreams* (1925), and collections of critical essays—*Off Broadway* (1947) and others—that reaffirm Aristotelian principles and Anderson's faith that poetry and the theatre are of vital importance to democracy. The most comprehensive study of Anderson's drama is Mabel Driscoll Bailey's *Maxwell Anderson: The Playwright as Prophet* (1957). Barrett H. Clark's *Maxwell Anderson, the Man and His Plays* (1933) is a biography and a study of the earlier plays. Martha Cox's *Maxwell Anderson Bibliography* (1958) lists his works as well as reviews of his plays.

ANDERSON, Robert [Woodruff] (1917–), American playwright, became known with his first work to reach Broadway, TEA AND SYMPATHY (1953). Earlier in 1953 his dramatization of Donald Wetzel's contemporary novel about a divided family, *A Wreath and a Curse,* was produced in Washington as *All Summer Long*, under which title it eventually reached Broadway. Anderson's next original work, *Silent Night, Lonely Night* (1959), portrays an unhappy middle-aged couple who have an affair at Christmas, which enables them to return to and endure their mates. Other domestic dramas are *The Days Between* (1965) and the more autobiographical *I Never Sang for My Father* (1968). His big comic hit was *You Know I Can't Hear You When the Water's Running* (1967), four light one-acters depicting "the seven ages of sex." In a different vein is the double bill *Solitaire—Double Solitaire* (1971), the first being a short science fiction play, and the second a nostalgic study of a disintegrating marriage.

Anderson was born in New York, attended Phillips Exeter Academy, and was graduated from Harvard University, where he also completed his M.A. (1940). He won his first kudos as a dramatist while in the navy (1942–46), when the War Department awarded him its prize for the best play written by a serviceman, *Come Marching Home* (1945). He was given a Rockefeller Fellowship to study playwriting, and subsequently taught at the American Theatre Wing. Anderson has written many one-acters and a number of film scripts, including that of *Tea and Sympathy*. Though his plays are more sophisticated than those of WILLIAM INGE, they also tend to feature sensitive characters whose problems are finally resolved in the bedroom.

ANDORRA, a play in twelve scenes by MAX FRISCH, published in 1961 and produced in 1962. Setting: the mythical state of Andorra, mid-twentieth century.

Originally this was a sketch inspired in early postwar Germany and composed in 1946 under the heading "Thou shalt not make an image unto thyself." The play, one of Frisch's major hits, dramatizes its story retrospectively and combines elements of the medieval morality, EXPRESSIONISM, and EPIC THEATRE. Set in the "model" of "any" European country, it is a harrowing attack on anti-Semitism and on judging men by preconceived "images"—here that of the "Jewish" stereotype (cowardly, rapacious, shrewd, etc.) into which Andri is molded by others and which he himself comes to accept.

Scene 1. Young Barblin is whitewashing the house of her schoolteacher father while a coarse soldier propositions her. She is the only character with a given name—aside from Andri, her putative foster-brother and betrothed. He is the inn's kitchen boy and irritates people because he plays the juke box. Barblin worries about the menacing Blacks in the country across the frontier from which her father had brought Andri, purportedly to save him from anti-Semitic persecution. She shudders as she realizes that, if victorious, the Blacks will kill all Andorran Jews and shave their sweethearts' heads. The teacher apprentices Andri to a carpenter, who like other Andorrans thinks Andri would be happier in a more "Jewish" occupation. The soldier tells Andri he is a coward "Because you're a Jew," and decides to take Barblin. The innkeeper enters an offstage witness box—the first of many guilt-ridden townspeople who step up between scenes to proclaim to the audience their personal innocence in Andri's later martyrdom.

Scenes 2 through 7. After a love scene between Andri and Barblin, the carpenter declares his innocence from the witness box. In his shop, he makes Andri give up carpentry in favor of "wheedling" sales orders. His inept fellow apprentice makes his declaration from the witness box. Examining Andri, a doctor voices crude anti-Semitic sentiments that crush the boy and then remarks: "Never met a Jew yet who could take a joke." When the teacher tries to explain that Andri cannot marry Barblin because they are both his children, Andri does not believe him and is terribly hurt. The equally crushed Barblin, rebellious in her desperation, accepts as her lover the soldier—who then from the witness box admits he always disliked "the Jew" though he is not responsible for what is to happen. The priest urges Andri to think better of himself, for "How can the others accept you, if you don't accept yourself?" Yet he confesses in the witness box that though he meant well, "I too made a graven image of him. . . . I too bound him to the stake."

Scenes 8 through 12. A Black señora visitor saves Andri from sneering rowdies who gang up on him. Later she asks Andri to lead her to the teacher—revealed as her former lover. She reproves him for passing their natural son (Andri) off as a Jew: keeping their indiscretion secret because both feared their peoples, the idealist teacher has used their son to prove his countrymen less bigoted than the Blacks. Upon her departure the señora is stoned to death by Andorrans jittery about an imminent attack by the Blacks. Though obviously innocent, Andri is accused of the murder. One of the townspeople confesses from the witness box that he did not know who threw the stone, and wants to forget Andri's screams. Barblin tries to save her brother, but is cursed as a "Jew's whore." The doctor in the witness box admits it was a "tragic affair," yet notes that Andri's "behavior (there's no concealing the fact) became (let us be quite frank) more and more Jewish." The victorious Blacks conduct a grotesque "Jew inspection" in which, hysterical with fear, everybody is examined by a "Jew Detector." Andri is singled out and carried away screaming after his fingers are hacked off. His execution and the teacher's suicide are announced. Again Barblin is whitewashing the house—but now her head is shorn, and she is insane.

ANDREEV, Leonid [Nikolaevich] (1871–1919), Russian journalist, short-story writer, and dramatist, was among the internationally-renowned authors of his age. Eventually his popularity waned, and for some time he has not been held (as he once was) in the same high esteem as his Russian contemporaries ANTON CHEKHOV, LEO TOLSTOI, and MAXIM GORKY. The first Russian SYMBOLIST in the theatre, however, Andreev is still well remembered particularly for his harrowing anti-capital-punishment novella *Rasskaz o semi poveshennykh* (*The Story of the Seven Who Were Hanged,* 1908) and for *Tot, kto poluchaet poshchochiny* (HE WHO GETS SLAPPED, 1915), which combines the NATURALISTIC and symbolic forms that predominate in his two-dozen plays. These, like Andreev's other works, aim to convey a sense of terror, and they reflect his gloomy and tortured outlook on life.

This outlook was expressed in Andreev's own life no less than in his works. Introspective, discouraged, and bitter, he tried to commit suicide three times: he threw himself under a train, and he sustained knife and gun injuries. Andreev was born in Oryol (about two hundred miles south of Moscow) to a poor, middle-class family. Fascinated with reading and theatricals, he was an intelligent but problem pupil. His father, a surveyor, died while Andreev was still at the *gimnaziya* (roughly equivalent to the American high school). Subsequently he attended Petrograd and Moscow universities. Suffering from intense poverty and too proud to ask for help, Andreev supported himself by painting portraits, and was graduated with a law degree in 1897. After a single and unsuccessful trial he gave up law. He became a court reporter for the *Moscow Courier,* and was soon asked to write *feuilletons* and theatre reviews, which appeared under the pseudonym James Lynch and were collected and republished. Thereafter Andreev devoted himself exclusively to writing. He made his reputation with the first collection of his stories, *Rasskazy* (1901), which sold more than a quarter of a million copies.

Andreev's first play, *K zvozdam* (*To the Stars,* 1905), was refused a production license. It features an astronomer who considers himself above mundane things like the revolution that martyred his son; his counterpart is a revolutionary (based on an actual person) whom Andreev was dissuaded by Gorky from portraying, a character similar to Nil in Gorky's own THE SMUG CITIZENS. The gloominess of *To the Stars* was overshadowed by that of *Savva* (1906), Andreev's next play, whose protagonist is a fanatic nihilist who assails religious superstition. It was *Zhizn cheloveka* (THE LIFE OF MAN, 1906) and *Anatema* (ANATHEMA, 1909) that made Andreev famous as a dramatist. But he was more successful, in Russia at least, with the published rather than the produced versions of his plays. The eighteen thousand copies of the first edition of *Tsar Golod* (*King Hunger,* 1907), for example—a depiction of the misery that helped bring about the 1905 revolution—were sold in a single day.

The plot of *Chornye maski* (*The Black Maskers,*

1908) came from Edgar Allan Poe; its protagonist is modeled on Nietzsche, and its ideas are similar to those of *The Life of Man*. Next came *Dni nashei zhizni* (1908), a naturalistic drama of student life; *Letushchaya mysh* (1908), a farce; *Anfisa* (1909), which is about a brilliant man killed by a discarded mistress; *"Gaudeamus"* (1910), a comedy, also about student life; *Okean* (1911), an allegoric tragedy featuring a Nietzschean superman, a sea captain; and *Chest* (1912), a dramatic parody.

In the atypical comic vein, too, is the SHAVian satire *Prekrasnye Sabinyanki* (*The Sabine Women,* 1912), which, in the guise of the historical event, lampoons the Constitutional-Democratic (opposition) party members. They are embodied in the Sabine husbands, who try to recapture their abducted wives (liberty) from the Romans (the tsar's government); they march two steps forward and one step back: the first two, their leader explains, indicate "the unquenchable fire of our stormy souls, the firm will, the irresistible advance," while the backward step symbolizes "reason, the step of experience and of the mature mind." This farcical work was followed by *Professor Storitsyn* (1912), a naturalistic-symbolic portrayal of an idol who inspires his students but brutalizes his family; *Yekaterina Ivanovna* (1912), whose title character degenerates morally after her husband falsely accuses her of adultery; *Ne ubii* (1913), another character study, this time of a degenerating young man; *Mysl* (*Thought,* 1914; also translated as *A Dilemma*), a dramatization of his earlier story by the same title; *Proisshestvie* (1914), a dramatic scene; *Popugai* (1914), a symbolic one-acter; *Korol, zakon i svoboda* (translated as *The Sorrows of Belgium*), a drama on the German invasion of Belgium, featuring the king as well as a poet modeled on MAURICE MAETERLINCK, and produced in December, 1914; *Mladost* (1914); *Dorogie prizraki* (1916), a lighter play, whose protagonist is the young Fyodor Dostoevsky; and *Rekviem* (1917), a play mourning the end of the Russia that was lost in the Revolution. More important are two posthumous plays, written in 1914: *Sobachi vals* (*The Waltz of the Dogs,* 1922) and *Samson v okovach* (*Samson in Chains,* 1923). The first, which was produced on Broadway in 1928, is a bitter melodrama of love, murder, and abnormal psychology. The second begins after Samson is betrayed and fettered; but his real chains, in this play, are his unshakable carnal drives.

Andreev's congenital gloom was exacerbated when his wife, to whom he had been happily married since 1902, died four years later. Throwing himself into his work, Andreev eventually overcame his grief and remarried. He had supported the earlier revolution, but—unlike his associate Gorky—not the Soviets. From 1906 on he had spent some time in his country house in Finland. After the Soviets came to power he fled to Finland, where he died soon after. It was not so much his opposition to the Soviet government (which allowed the production of some of his plays), however, as a general loss of interest in his drama which gradually drove most of his plays from the boards. His declining popularity was no doubt partly due to Andreev's morbidity and fatalism. Later audiences also rejected his symbolism, which manifested itself in dramatic forms that came from medieval moralities and poetic drama like the second (and theatrically less viable) part of Goethe's *Faust*. Andreev was much influenced by the plays and dramatic theories of Maeterlinck—whose popularity was also short lived. Later, as described in Andreev's *Pisma o teatre* (1913–14), he renounced dramatic symbolism for what he called "panpsychism," the stress on manifesting psychological effects rather than the external actions leading to them. But Andreev's drama was actuated by a philosophic quest for the meaning of life, and it was characterized by almost unremitting despair.

He Who Gets Slapped has been reprinted frequently, and is available in many anthologies. The other plays are less accessible, though most of them were translated and published individually. *Plays by Leonid Andreyeff* (1915), translated by C. L. Meader and F. N. Scott, includes an introductory essay by V. V. Brusyanin on Andreev's symbolism and philosophy, and three plays: *The Black Maskers, The Life of Man,* and *The Sabine Women*. Andreev's plays have been collected and republished in Russia, most recently in 1959. Book-length studies in English are Alexander Kaun's *Leonid Andreyev: A Critical Study* (1924), Maxim Gorky's *Reminiscences of Leonid Andreyev* (translated 1928), and James B. Woodward's *Leonid Andreev* (1970).

ANDROCLES AND THE LION, "A Fable Play" in two acts and a prologue by BERNARD SHAW, produced in 1913 and published in 1916. Setting: Rome and environs in the early days of Christianity.

One of the most interesting sections of Shaw's very long and provocative preface ("On the Prospects of Christianity") to this short, serious, yet farcical and often-revived play is a critical analysis of the Gospel narratives and their differing portrayals of Christ, who emerges as a Shavian superman. Shaw also examined men's two-thousand-year rejection of Christ, whose teachings "are now turning out to be good sense and sound economics."

Prologue. In a jungle Androcles meekly listens to his shrewish wife Megaera's complaints about his addiction to animals and Christianity, which has caused their expulsion from home. Leaving him angrily, she nearly trips over a lion. Though frightened, Androcles chivalrously interposes himself to protect her, but when he sees the lion suffering from a thorn in its paw, he extracts it. He waltzes off with the grateful lion, as Megaera complains of his cowardice.

Act I. A group of joking Christians is being taken to Rome to be killed in the Colosseum. Enamored of the beautiful Christian patrician Lavinia, a Roman captain unsuccessfully urges her and the others to save their lives by simply paying symbolic homage to the gods, if only "as a matter of good taste, to avoid shocking the religious convictions" of the Romans. More Christian prisoners are brought in: Androcles; the powerful warrior Ferrovius, an early Puritan who subdues his aggressive instincts by earnestly proselytizing his tormentors; and the debauched Spintho, who believes that martyrdom will get him to heaven no matter what he does on earth.

Act II. In a panic, the recanting Spintho rushes down a Colosseum passage and is devoured by a lion. Refusing the Emperor's offer to join the Pretorian Guard, Ferrovius is sent to the arena to fight the gladiators, as are the other Christian men—except for Androcles, who is going to be thrown to the lions with Lavinia. The captain once again fails to persuade Lavinia to save herself, though he assures her that educated Romans believe in the stories of the gods no more than she does. The Christians in the arena refuse to fight, but when the Emperor has them goaded with a whip, the enraged Ferrovius single-handedly kills all the gladiators. Delighted, the Emperor awards him a laurel crown and frees the Christians. But to satisfy the masses, Androcles is sent to the arena. About to attack the fearful, praying Androcles, the lion recognizes him as his jungle benefactor, and they again waltz together. Realizing that his own behavior suggests that "the Christian god is not yet," Ferrovius returns to the worship of Mars and joins the Guard; Lavinia will "strive for the coming of the God who is not yet," probably as the captain's wife; and Androcles, refusing an offer in the royal menagerie, walks off unmolested with his lion.

In a terminal note to the play, Shaw pointed to the characteristic nature of the Roman persecution, "an attempt to suppress a propaganda that seemed to threaten the interests involved in the established law and order, organized and maintained in the name of religion and justice by politicians who are pure opportunist Have-and-Holders." And he noted our clergy's acting in wartime as Ferrovius did in the arena, but without the honesty to declare themselves priests of the god Mars.

ANGEL COMES TO BABYLON, AN (*Ein Engel kommt nach Babylon*), "a fragmentary comedy" in three acts by FRIEDRICH DÜRRENMATT, published and produced in 1953. Setting: ancient Babylon.

Freely modernized history and legend, this comedy was meant to be a prelude to a play about the Tower of Babel. The influence of BERTOLT BRECHT is very apparent in Akki, who resembles Azdak of THE CAUCASIAN CHALK CIRCLE, and in the angel's final departure, which resembles that of the gods in THE GOOD WOMAN OF SETZUAN.

An angel brings to earth the beautiful newly created Kurrubi (i.e., Cherub) to be given to the lowliest mortal. King Nebuchadnezzar, involved in a nine-hundred-year power struggle with Babylon's former king, Nimrod, disguises himself as a beggar. He loses a "begging contest" with Akki, an anarchist brimming with vitality—and the kingdom's last surviving beggar. Thus the most wretched of men, Nebuchadnezzar, wins Kurrubi —but swaps her for the imprisoned Nimrod, whom Akki won. Akki takes Kurrubi to his fantastic hovel and protects her from the country's men, all of whom have fallen in love with her. He talks himself out of execution and becomes the royal hangman. Kurrubi cannot love Nebuchadnezzar when she sees him as a king. "I betrayed the maiden for the sake of my power," he now realizes. Heartbroken, Nebuchadnezzar decides to build a tower up to heaven—"and we shall see which is the better: my justice, or the injustice of God." Since the angel has abandoned her to mankind, Kurrubi escapes with Akki to a desert and new troubles but—as the irrepressible Akki adds—also to "a new morning."

ANIMAL KINGDOM, THE, a comedy in three acts by PHILIP BARRY, published in 1931 and produced in 1932. Setting: a country house in Connecticut, and an apartment in New York, 1930–31.

Like HOLIDAY, this once-popular play (it also was filmed) is a triangle drama larded with a moral about the destructive effects of materialism on life, art, and integrity.

Tom Collier, a cheerful young intellectual publisher, has lived for three years with Daisy Sage, an artist. Their affair has ripened into a friendship he thinks they can retain—"it's wicked to give that up . . . for a shabby, lowdown question of convention"—even though he falls in love with and marries a very beautiful girl. Before the marriage Daisy starts to warn Tom that he may be attracted to the girl only sexually because "For all our big talk, we still belong to the animal kingdom." Soon his materialistic wife, using her physical allure, makes Tom betray his artistic ideals, alienate his "smart set" friends, associate with her upper-middle-class crowd, and discharge his butler, a former pugilist and Tom's friend. She almost succeeds in getting him to sell out to a slick firm and compromise his integrity in other ways, but at last Tom realizes that she victimizes him with her seductive wiles, like a mistress. For that reason he leaves her to return to Daisy. It is the mistress who understands and loves Tom for what he is, and therefore she is his "real wife."

ANNA CHRISTIE, a play in four acts by EUGENE O'NEILL, produced in 1921 and published in 1922. Setting: a contemporary New York saloon and a barge.

First produced in 1920 as *Chris Christopherson* (in which the sea-cursed Chris was the hero and Anna was pure), the play closed before reaching Broadway. Another version, *The Ole Devil,* was copyrighted in 1921 but not published. As O'Neill finally rewrote it, the play became very popular (in 1930 Greta Garbo starred in her first speaking role in WALTER HASENCLEVER's film version of the play, and in 1957 GEORGE ABBOTT rewrote it as a musical, *New Girl in Town,* lyrics and music by Bob Merrill) and won O'Neill his second Pulitzer

Prize. But there has been frequent criticism of the imperfectly accomplished shift of emphasis from a character study of Chris to the regeneration of Anna, and of the last act. In a long letter to the *New York Times* (December 16, 1921), O'Neill vigorously attacked the general opinion that the ending is happy, and he wrote the critic George Jean Nathan: "The sea outside—life—waits. The happy ending is merely the comma at the end of a gaudy introductory clause."

Act I. In Johnny-the-Priest's saloon, the barge captain Chris Christopherson is overjoyed with a letter from his daughter Anna that reports her imminent arrival. He has not seen her since he left her to be brought up by her cousins on a Minnesota farm, to keep her from sailors and the sea, which has victimized his family: "It's better Anna live on farm, den she don't know dat ole davil, sea, she don't know fa'der like me." He leaves after telling Marthy Owen, a kindly old slut who lives with him on his barge, that she will have to move out now. Anna Christie's appearance and first words ("Gimme a whiskey—ginger ale on the side. And don't be stingy, baby") leave no doubt as to her profession; as she tells Marthy, "You're me forty years from now." She also tells her how she became a prostitute because she felt "caged in" as a young nurse, and how she hates men, who have always bothered and bossed her. When Chris meets her, however, he notices nothing amiss with the daughter he is so delighted to welcome. To celebrate, "dis one time because ve meet after many year," he thinks she might have some weak port. Lifting his glass, he asks her if she knows the Swedish word "Skoal," and moved as she downs her drink she repeats it: "Guess I know that word, all right, all right!"

Act II. It is a foggy evening ten days later on the stern of Chris's barge. In her new sea life and with her father, Anna appears much softer; she feels clean, and happier than she has ever felt. They talk of the family, Chris telling her how his sailor father and brothers drowned. She and Chris rescue some shipwrecked men, one of whom is a powerful and boasting but decent Irish stoker, Mat Burke. He quickly falls in love with Anna, and Chris, jealous and fearful of her marrying a seaman, shakes his fist at the ocean in a rage: "Not while Ay'm living! No, py God, you don't!"

Act III. About a week later in the barge cabin, Anna relieves Chris's fear that she will marry Burke. Sadly she comments that she has not "the heart to fool him," and she "ain't good enough for him." Later there is a violent argument between the two men and Chris physically attacks Burke. When they fight about her again afterward, each telling her what to do and believe, her face hardens at a scene too reminiscent of her previous life, and she is goaded into revealing her secret. She blames her father for his "bunk about the farm being so fine," even after she wrote him from Minnesota "how rotten it was." She tells how her youngest cousin started her off—though she "hated him worse'n hell and he knew it. But he was big and strong"—and how she ended in "a house—the kind sailors like you and Mat goes to in port—and your nice inland men, too—and all men, God damn 'em!" At last she breaks down and pleads with Burke: "loving you has made me —clean." But he now curses her and rushes off to shore to get drunk and forget her; after a while Chris, blaming their troubles on the sea's "dirty tricks," sadly goes off too.

Act IV. After two days of drinking, Chris returns bedraggled. Anna admits that all of them are "poor nuts, and things happen, and we yust get mixed in wrong, that's all." She is bitter to hear that her father is leaving her again: he has signed up on a ship, and will have his pay sent to her. Bruised after drunken fights on shore, Burke comes back belligerent and insulting, but unable to forget her. When he finally understands that she never loved the men who bought her, he rejoices and makes her swear on his mother's lucky old cross that he is the only man she ever loved. The oath appears meaningless when she admits she is not a Catholic, but he decides to take her "naked word for it and have you anyway, I'm thinking—I'm needing you that bad!" They will marry in the morning, for he has signed up on the same ship, unknowingly, as has Chris. The men become reconciled, and Anna describes the home she will make for both of them. Though Anna and Burke look forward to happiness, the curtain falls to the "muffled, mournful wail of steamers' whistles" and Chris's ominous last words: "Fog, fog, fog, all bloody time. You can't see vhere you vas going, no. Only dat ole davil, sea—she knows!"

ANNA KLEIBER (*Ana Kleiber*), a play in three acts by ALFONSO SASTRE, published in 1952 and produced in 1958. Setting: a contemporary Barcelona hotel and various European cities during the past three decades.

Technically less conventional, and also less preoccupied with social problems than most of Sastre's plays, *Anna Kleiber* depicts the relationship of a demonic woman and her masochistic lover.

Alfonso Sastre is interviewed by the press as a fainting woman asks the desk clerk for a room. After being registered she asks to be awakened early: "I have a very important appointment. I've waited all my life—my meeting tomorrow—" The two men tell the audience that she died of a heart attack in her room that night. At her funeral they met Alfred Merton, whom Sastre accompanies to a café. There Alfred tells of his life with Anna, episodes of which are dramatized. Alfred, a philosophy student, meets Anna as she is about to throw herself into the river after a disgusting night with the director of the troupe in which she acts. A demon inside her forces her into shame, "an animal desire to touch bottom" and pull men into the abyss with her, she confesses. In love with her, Alfred exclaims, "I'll follow you all my life." After a lovers' idyll, she runs away. Alfred finds her, murders her director (a Jew), and to escape prosecution joins the rising Nazi Party. Again the lovers are separated and again they reunite and resume the idyll. But when Alfred goes to war Anna returns to her ignominious life—and taunts him with it when he comes home on leave. He virtually murders her, returns to the front, and after the war tries to forget her. Unable to do so, he tells Sastre how they arranged to meet in Barcelona, and eagerly asks for "the details" of her arrival in the hotel that night. "There were just a few people in the lobby," Sastre says as the hotel settings light up and the fainting Anna comes in, requests a room, and after being registered asks to be awakened early: "I have a very important appointment. I've waited all my life—my meeting tomorrow—"After she leaves, Alfred breaks down. "Life isn't over just because Anna Kleiber has disappeared," Sastre consoles him. Some day Alfred will overcome his guilt feelings and understand what happened, Sastre concludes; "perhaps then you'll decide to live a new life in which Anna Kleiber will only be a human memory. Then you'll never be a coward again. . . ."

ANNA SOPHIE HEDVIG, a play in three acts by KJELD ABELL, published and produced in 1939. Setting: an expensively furnished living room in a Danish town and a provincial schoolhouse, 1930's.

On the surface this is a detective thriller about the murder of a tyrannical new headmistress. To heighten the suspense, Abell uses such theatrical devices as double-frame action and flashbacks. But the play focuses less on the crime than on its significance and its effects on the "practical," worldly people to whom it is revealed. Two fleeting but poignant symbolic tableaux underline the moral implications of the play. Originally concerned with the menace of Nazism, it is universal in its indictment of people's failure to *act* upon their moral indignation. Criminality is thus portrayed as being the passive tolerance of evil.

Act I. In the dark, a young couple mistakenly enter an apartment apparently abandoned except for a body that turns out to be the sleeping maid. As she wakes up and relates how the evening's dinner party suddenly broke off, the scene switches to that afternoon. Anna Sophie Hedvig, an old-maid schoolteacher cousin from the provinces, unexpectedly arrives for a visit. Obviously on edge, she announces that she has quit her job. Her host, preparing for a dinner party that evening with important business associates, gets irritated by his son John's "modern" cynicism. John is gentle with Anna Sophie Hedvig, however. Later he is grimly intrigued by a newspaper photograph of a doomed man standing by a wall, about to be executed. As John bitterly tells the schoolteacher how his parents and their company will soon go through their phony small talk, the guests arrive

Anna Sophie Hedvig, Act I. The title character (Clara Pontoppidan), her hostess (Bodil Ipsen), and the maid (Sigrid Neiiendam). Copenhagen, 1939. (*Teaterhistorisk Museum Kopenhagen*)

and the conversations proceed as he has predicted. All go into the dining room, and soon, over their laughing voices, is heard a roll of drums. The stage darkens, and then a light shines on the doomed man photographed in the newspaper; a short distance away some soldiers play dice.

Act II. Dinner is ending. The businessmen are annoyed by the "flippancy" of John, who castigates them for their hypocrisies and for ignoring the suffering and injustice around them. When he suggests that to fight evil it may sometimes be necessary even to kill, the company is scandalized. But Anna Sophie Hedvig agrees, and begins unfolding her story—into which the scene dissolves. It portrays the old-maid teacher desperate at the thought of a vicious colleague's becoming the new principal. The school's janitor and his wife discuss this appointment; they realize its evil, but they are sure "it can't make any difference to us" and they are unwilling to do more than hope someone—but not they—will protest. A scream is heard. The janitor runs out and discovers that the new principal apparently has fallen down a flight of stairs, and is dead. As the police investigate, Anna Sophie Hedvig, trapped in the room, confesses, to a student victimized by the dead new principal, that she committed the murder. "It was [the new principal] who wanted to assault my world," she tells the girl. "Must I not defend it before she made the assault? Must we not defend our small worlds? Do not they together make up the great world?" The girl gets Anna Sophie Hedvig out of the house and covers up for her. The scene shifts back to the party, where the scandalized businessmen prepare to turn her over to the police. "You might be proud if, in the mass of your so-called legal crimes, you had committed anything as pure as what she has done," John angrily tells the businessmen. "Do you mean to defend her killing?" the latter ask. John replies, "Yes."

Act III. As they wait, John berates the company for spouting pious generalities but leading corrupt lives. In the guise of "humane tolerance," he remarks, we all "look with silent eyes at the result to which our humanity and passivity have led." He praises Anna Sophie Hedvig: "She has broken out of the passivity," while the rest of us "have taken our stand by not taking any stand." John's outburst, however, offends his father's colleague and jeopardizes his business. Angrily he sends John away. The mother, after failing to make it up between them, decides to leave her husband. "I didn't exist any more—like Anna Sophie Hedvig. I was embalmed in my habits—and couldn't give them up. But I *can* give them up—" and she now decides to give up her petty, dishonest way of life. The scene shifts to the young couple and the maid finishing her story. John soon comes in, and tells them that at the police station his parents made it up, after all. He is pleased about Anna Sophie Hedvig. Her life would have been a tragedy "if all this had not happened," for then her epitaph might have been "'Here rests Anna Sophie Hedvig. She never existed.' But you can't write that now." He picks up the newspaper and again sees the picture of the condemned man standing before the wall. "I wonder if the drums will come—if they come after him. Yes, there they are," he suddenly says. The lights fade and then rise on the doomed man. Now Anna Sophie Hedvig stands by him. "You fight for the future," she tells him: "When you die it is to make that possible." And she smiles with him as the soldiers lift their rifles. The lights fade, the drum beats become louder, and, as the stage darkens, there are shots.

ANNE OF THE THOUSAND DAYS, a play in three acts by MAXWELL ANDERSON, published and produced in 1948. Setting: England, 1526–36.

More like ELIZABETH THE QUEEN than MARY OF SCOTLAND, this, the last of Anderson's Tudor plays (filmed in 1969), deals with the conflict of power and sexual passion. But it is a poetic memory play, more stylized and less verbose than the others: a theatrical history characterized by gusto, humor, and tragedy. It begins with Henry VIII's courtship of and determination to win Anne Boleyn, and ends with Queen Anne's mock trial and beheading because she has failed to produce a male heir and Henry has tired of her: "It comes to a thousand days— / out of the years. / Strangely, just a thousand. / And of that thousand— / one— / when we were both in love," Anne muses in the last of the soliloquies which open each act: "Only one / when our loves met, and overlapped and were both mine and his. / When I no longer hated him— / he began to hate me, / except for that day."

ANNIVERSARY, THE (*Yubilei*), "a Jest in One Act" by ANTON CHEKHOV, published in 1892 and produced in 1903. Setting: a contemporary bank president's office.

In 1902 Chekhov completely revised this vaudeville (also translated as *The Celebration*), an exposure of banking practices based on his story "Bezzashchitnoe sushestvo" ("A Helpless Creature," 1887).

Ready to celebrate his bank's fifteenth anniversary, its president is driven to distraction by his chattering wife, by his irritable misogynist cashier, and by an old woman who pesters him for money. A delegation of directors arrives for the formal ceremony just as the cashier hysterically tries to chase the frightened women out.

ANOTHER PART OF THE FOREST, a play in three acts by LILLIAN HELLMAN, produced in 1946 and published in 1947. Setting: Bowden, Alabama; June 1880.

This play was to be the second of the never-completed trilogy that concludes with THE LITTLE FOXES. Set twenty years earlier than the last play, it is equally suspenseful and at times grimly humorous in its portrayal of the predatory Hubbard family (headed by Marcus Hubbard, the father), who roam in "another part of the forest," in the words of the frequent Shakespearean stage direction.

Marcus, a carpetbagger who became rich by

black-marketeering in the Civil War, is hated by the town for his ruthless practices, and indulges his tastes for music and Greek literature. His thoroughly cowed wife attempts to obliterate her dim recollections of their past by going to the Negro church with her servant, with whom she wants to open a Negro school. Marcus treats his wife like a mental patient, and his sons, Oscar and Benjamin, like underpaid hired help. But he dotes on his beautiful daughter, Regina, who shrewdly controls him. She has an affair with a disturbed combat veteran, whose sister, Birdie, attempts to get a loan from the Hubbards to save the family plantation. Ben arranges the loan, but Regina, learning he has arranged also to profit on the deal, foils him. The weak Oscar, who must be bailed out for his Klan escapades, is in love with the local prostitute. He brings her to the Hubbards' party, where Ben gets her drunk. She makes a scene in which she claims that even she is superior to the despised Hubbards. Marcus orders both his sons from the home. Then Ben discovers proof of his father's wartime treason hidden in his mother's Bible. Threatening to expose him and thus have him lynched, Ben takes over his father's business and power, and becomes the new family tyrant. He lets his mother leave with her servant to open a Negro school, and orders Oscar to marry the aristocratic Birdie. As for Regina, he cancels her trip to Chicago, and instructs her to marry a promising Mobile banker, "the only person [who] didn't know you've been sleeping with the warrior." Marcus now is a broken man. Regina ignores him and takes a chair next to the family's new master, Ben, who smiles triumphantly.

ANOUILH, Jean (1910–), after World War II, became one of the most popular French dramatists. Year after year his plays have been produced in Paris—and throughout the world. His work is firmly grounded in the histrionic, improvisational *commedia dell 'arte* tradition, and he was influenced by such earlier masters as Molière, LUIGI PIRANDELLO, and—most immediately—JEAN GIRAUDOUX. Because of his tendency to reuse similar situations and characters in his plays, and because of the unabashed theatricality of his drama, Anouilh has occasionally been denigrated as a mere entertainer. Yet the versatility of his drama is remarkable, and his myth and history plays clearly reveal the seriousness beneath his characteristic farce and caricature. As many critics have suggested, the Gallic-flavored persiflage and romps that have made Anouilh's plays so fashionable and entertaining clothe troubled, pessimistic views of life.

Anouilh was born in Bordeaux, the son of a tailor and his casino-musician wife, whose unglamorous professional career served as a model for many of her son's plays. For a short while he studied law in Paris. He became the secretary of Louis Jouvet, whose company worked closely with Giraudoux: in fact, the sets for the latter's SIEGFRIED furnished the apartment of the impecunious, newly married Anouilh, as its plot suggested that of his first theatrical success. In 1929–30, while working on advertising copy, Anouilh also wrote plays. Aside from some that were not made public, these include *Mandarine,* an unimportant work that appeared in 1933, the year after *L'Hermine* (*The Ermine*), the first of his plays to be produced. *The Ermine* is a WELL-MADE melodrama whose hero, Frantz, a poor youth (the typical Anouilh protagonist), murders for money, which represents worldly nobility and purity to him; but losing the love of the girl for whom he committed the crime, he accepts its consequences and lets himself be captured.

Anouilh continued to work for Jouvet until he achieved financial independence. This came soon, first with Metro-Goldwyn-Mayer's purchase of his unsuccessful play *Y'avait un prisonnier* (1934), the story of a businessman who returns after fifteen years of prison to find he cannot reestablish himself in the depraved society he left, and then with Anouilh's first hit, *Le Voyageur sans bagage* (TRAVELER WITHOUT LUGGAGE, 1937). His collected plays were titled after the (sometimes tenuously) dominant mood of the plays. The early, "black" plays appeared in *Pièces noires* (1942), which includes *The Ermine, La Sauvage* (RESTLESS HEART, 1938), *Traveler Without Luggage,* and his best early play, EURYDICE (1941, also translated as *Legend of Lovers*). Next came the "pink" or lighter plays, *Pièces roses* (1942). These are *Le Bal des voleurs* (THIEVES' CARNIVAL, 1938), one of his most delightful works; *Le Rendez-vous de Senlis* (written in 1937, produced in English as *Dinner with the Family*), in which a young man, to court his beloved, replaces the ugliness of his real life with a rented villa and hired actors who impersonate his family; and LÉOCADIA (1939, also translated as *Time Remembered*).

This collection was followed by a second group of "black" plays, *Nouvelles pièces noires* (1947). It includes *Jézabel* (written in 1932), whose hero assumes the guilt of his criminal mother; *Roméo et Jeannette* (*Romeo und Jeanette,* 1947; also produced as *Jeannette*), whose upper-class "Romeo" falls in love, and finally commits suicide, with the promiscuous sister of his virtuous fiancée; and two critically esteemed classic adaptations: ANTIGONE (1944) and *Médée* (*Medea,* 1946), a one-act version of Euripides's play, ending with the psychopathological title character hurling herself into a fire and Jason resolving to "reconstruct my poor and fragile edifice under the indifferent eyes of the gods [,] . . . give Corinth laws, and without illusions rebuild a world befitting us, in which to wait and die."

Anouilh returned to a lighter vein in his next collection. *Pièces brillantes* (1951) includes *L'Invitation au château* (RING ROUND THE MOON, 1947), COLOMBE (1953), *La Répétition, ou l'amour puni* (THE REHEARSAL, 1950), and *Cécile ou l'école des pères* (*Cecile or the School for Fathers,* 1949), a comic masque in the style of Molière. *Pièces grinçantes* (1956) goes back to the caustic, "grating" mood, and contains four devastating comedies: ARDÈLE (1948), *La Valse des toréadors* (THE

WALTZ OF THE TOREADORS, 1952), *Ornifle, ou le courant d'air* (ORNIFLE, 1955), and *Pauvre Bitos, ou le dîner de têtes* (POOR BITOS, 1956). A collection of history plays, *Pièces costumées* (1960), consists of the successful saints' plays *L'Alouette* (THE LARK, 1953) and *Becket, ou l'honneur de Dieu* (BECKET, OR THE HONOR OF GOD, 1959), and *La Foire d'empoigne* (1959, translated as *Catch as Catch Can*), in which one actor must represent the opposing characters of Louis XVIII and an opportunistic Napoleon who, anticipating his death, bluntly remarks, "I must croak in style."

Anouilh's play on his great seventeenth-century predecessor and his wife, *La Petite Molière* (1959), was followed by *La Grotte* (*The Cavern,* 1961), a variation on Pirandello's SIX CHARACTERS IN SEARCH OF AN AUTHOR, but with a brutalized plot of rape, murder, and other violence; it is a fragmented "play that I have been unable to write," the Author (Anouilh), one of the principal characters, announces in his first speech. Also Pirandellian is the comedy *Cher Antoine* (1969), a play-within-a-play-within-a-play about a popular French dramatist ("Dear Antoine") who has his life re-enacted before assembled guests. Another dramatist named Antoine is featured in Anouilh's next black-and-rose comedy, *Les Poissons rouges* (1970), in which a series of skits dramatizes Antoine's unpleasant memories and past associations; and in the similarly bitter comedy *Ne réveillez pas Madame* (1970) a celebrated Parisian actor-manager relives in flashbacks youthful traumas that still enslave him. An earlier "dark" play is *L'Orchestre* (*The Orchestra,* 1962), whose cast (as in *Restless Heart*) is made up predominantly of third-rate musicians. Anouilh also wrote some curtain raisers, among them *Épisode de la vie d'un auteur* (*Episode in the Life of an Author,* 1948), a farce played with *Ardèle,* and *Le Songe du critique* (1960). Aside from his more than thirty plays, Anouilh has adapted some of Shakespeare's plays, dramatized novels (including Louise de Vilmorin's *Madame de . . .*, produced in 1959 and translated by JOHN WHITING), and written film scripts, including those for his own *Traveler Without Luggage* (1943) and for LEO TOLSTOI's *Anna Karénine* (1947).

Though he wrote tragedies, most of Anouilh's drama is comic. Characteristically it integrates choreography and—almost always—music into the plot. It ranges from vaudevillian farce, through the comic masquerades that heighten the interplay of reality and illusion, to the spicy repartee of comedies of manners. Bitterness and pathos are never far off and color even works of seemingly gay abandon like *Thieves' Carnival* and *Ring Round the Moon.* Anouilh's protagonists usually reject compromise—and therewith life (historical and legendary characters like Antigone, Becket, and Saint Joan no less than the protagonists of *Restless Heart* and *Poor Bitos*). The result is death or escape into an illusory world which eventually becomes untenable. When the plot's resolution is happy, as in *Thieves' Carnival* or *Léocadia,* its fairy-tale artificiality is stressed. Of the lovers, one of the protagonists is inevitably from a poor, often dissolute background, and the other from very wealthy, usually high society. The lovers, who meet and court in a masquerade, are confronted by insurmountable money barriers.

Those plays that do not have young lovers for their protagonists are little different. General Saint-Pé (of *Ardèle* and *The Waltz of the Toreadors*), Poor Bitos, *L'Hurluberlu* (THE FIGHTING COCK, 1959), and "the traveler without luggage" are equally uncompromising. At the end they are more explicitly and totally revealed as individuals surrounded by a corrupt, vicious society. But if Anouilh's world view is tragic, if he finds existence absurd, individual loneliness and social sordidness being the human condition that even money and love finally cannot overcome, his expression of such concepts is gay and playful. A speech in *La Petite Molière* summarizes his philosophy, which is implicit in the dramas. "Of course everything is ugly. Of course everything is sad," Molière remarks, but "the soul must be purged. By laughter. The only virile attitude before the human condition is comedy."

Most of Anouilh's plays have been translated into English and are available in collected and individual editions. There have been numerous studies of his life, art, and theatrical milieu. Edward O. Marsh's *Jean Anouilh, Poet of Pierrot and Pantaloon* (1953), Leonard C. Pronko's *The World of Jean Anouilh* (1961), John Harvey's *Anouilh: A Study in Theatrics* (1964), Philip Thody's *Anouilh* (1968), and Alba Della Fazia's *Jean Anouilh* (1969) are thorough, scholarly works with extensive bibliographies.

ANSKI, S. [Shloyme Zanvil Rappoport] (1863–1920), Yiddish writer, is the author of the most famous Yiddish play, *Der Dibuk* (THE DYBBUK, 1919). First produced, with immense success, shortly after his death, it is his only notable play. Aside from "The Vow," a poem that became the anthem of Poland's Jewish Workers Party, *The Dybbuk* was his only popular work. He wrote some novelettes and short stories, an extended poetic satire, and folk legends. But his primary interest was in folklore, Russian as well as Jewish, and this interest is reflected in his drama.

Anski was born in Vitebsk (some say in Tshashnik), Russia. His mother managed the household as well as the family's inn. Educated in the Talmud, Anski began his career as a blacksmith's apprentice, became involved in politics, and had to escape. In 1894 he settled in Paris, where he became a bookbinder. He also was the secretary (1894–1900) of Pyotr Lavrov, the renowned Russian scholar and revolutionary. Anski spent the years 1911–14 heading an expedition of field-working folklorists in the Ukraine, and he was a member of St. Petersburg's Jewish Historical and Ethnographic Society. During World War I, which interrupted his ethnographic expeditions, Anskí was occupied in relief work. Then, though he remained interested in politics, he retired to Warsaw, where he died.

His dramatic works include the fragment of

another play on a Hassidic theme, *Tog un Nakht,* completed by various writers, among them DAVID PINSKI, and first produced in 1924; and three comedies: *Foter un Zun* (1906), *Der Zeyde* (?), and *In a Conspirativer Dire* (1904). Anski's collected works (1920–28) were published (in Yiddish) in fifteen volumes, the last of which includes his biography. See also Joseph C. Landis's *The Dybbuk and Other Great Yiddish Plays* (1966) and A. A. Roback's *The Story of Yiddish Literature* (1940).

ANTIGONE, a play in one act by JEAN ANOUILH, produced in 1944 and published in 1946. Setting: ancient Thebes.

Anouilh wrote *Antigone* in 1942 and published it as one of his "black" plays. It was immensely popular, especially in its first production—645 consecutive performances during the Occupation—when Frenchmen were confronted by a similar grim choice between practical compromise and unbending idealism.

The plot follows Sophocles's dramatization of the Greek legend of Antigone's rebellion against her Uncle Creon's edict that her brother may not be given proper burial, an act that brings death to herself and tragedy to Creon's family. But the language and atmosphere are modern (there are references to cigarettes and automobiles), and the conflicts are Anouilh's: the chorus speaks in prose and reflects Anouilh's reinterpretation of the classical issues. Though still principally the clash of intransigent individualism and tyrannous government, this conflict is also a psychological one of individuals as well as one of different philosophical concepts. Antigone is an Anouilh protagonist who for the sake of principle alone ("for myself") disobeys Creon's law and thus sacrifices her happiness, a pleasant day-to-day existence—and her life. She personifies an ideal as she declares, "What a person can do, a person ought to do." This assertion of the self is a personal affront as well as a threat to Creon, an intelligent politician concerned with the necessity of maintaining order and administering the law, about whose shortcomings, incidentally, he has no illusions. Presented far more sympathetically than in Sophocles's play, Creon is an able ruler who, despite the need for political expediency, acts conscientiously and perceptively. There is some question about the play's real tragic hero, for both antagonists' viewpoints are equally and disturbingly persuasive.

ANTIGONE OF SOPHOCLES, THE (*Die Antigone des Sophokles*), a play in irregular, unrhymed verse by BERTOLT BRECHT, produced in 1948 and published in 1949. Setting: Berlin in 1945 and ancient Thebes.

This adaptation of Sophocles's *Antigone* largely follows Friedrich Hölderlin's translation. But Brecht's verse changes accentuate the brutal tyranny of Creon, who attacked Argos for its iron ore. A prologue (like Scene I of THE CAUCASIAN CHALK CIRCLE) depicts the contemporary relevance of an old story: near the end of World War II, two sisters find their brother, a deserter, hanged outside their house; should they risk detection by the Nazi SS and cut him down?

In a program note Brecht rejected a classic view, that man is ruled by Fate, for his own view: "Man's fate is man himself."

APOLLINAIRE, Guillaume [Guillaume Albert Wladimir Alexandre Apollinaire de Kostrowitzky] (1880–1918), the avant-garde French poet and artist, wrote few plays and only one that is important: *Les Mamelles de Tirésias* (THE BREASTS OF TIRESIAS, 1917), the first drama of SURREALISM. He was born in Rome, the illegitimate son of a young beauty whose family—lesser Polish nobility—had sought political asylum at the papal court. His father was a prominent officer and the scion of a distinguished Catholic family. Apollinaire eventually performed secretarial jobs in Paris, engaged in amorous affairs, and pursued his artistic and literary proclivities. He became the friend of ALFRED JARRY, Pablo Picasso, and many other experimental artists who subsequently achieved prominence, and had a tempestuous and prolonged affair with Marie Laurencin. Aside from writing the poetry on which his reputation rests, he edited various reviews. But he earned his living by writing and editing pornographic texts. By the end of the century's first decade he was relatively prosperous, and had achieved the reputation of a poet and a flamboyant personality. He became involved in various scandals, was briefly imprisoned for complicity in a series of Louvre thefts, and was finally released for lack of sufficient evidence.

Championing cubist and other avant-garde art, Apollinaire early recognized its finest practitioners and interpreted their work in his reviews. He volunteered for military service when war broke out, went to the front, received a head wound, and eventually returned to Paris. There he resumed his artistic, literary, and journalistic careers, and was hailed as the leader of the post-SYMBOLISTS by *Nord-Sud* (1917), a review that spearheaded the DADA and surrealist movements. But weakened by his injury, he succumbed to influenza and died only a few months after his marriage, and two days before the armistice.

Apollinaire became interested in the theatre early in his career. His first work, the one-act *À la cloche de bois* (written in 1898), was not produced. Subsequently he helped champion such avant-garde drama as Jarry's KING UBU. It was only near the end of his life, however, that he returned to playwriting. At that time he finished his best-known play, its preface (which became a manifesto of surrealism), and the only other plays worth mentioning: *Couleur du temps* (produced in 1918, a few weeks after his death), a three-act verse drama about a fantastic polar expedition; and the *"comédie parodique" Casanova* (1952), a posthumous three-act play he transformed into a comic-opera libretto shortly before his death.

Adrian Henri (? –) and Michael Kustow's (1939–) biographical drama, *I Wonder*, was produced in 1968. The standard biography, Marcel Adéma's *Guillaume Apollinaire le mal-aimé* (1952), was published in English as *Apollinaire* (1955). Other important studies are Francis Steegmuller's *Apollinaire: Poet Among the Painters* (1963); Margaret Davies's *Apollinaire* (1964); and David I. Grossvogel's *20th-Century French Drama* (1961; originally published as *The Self-Conscious Stage in Modern French Drama,* 1958), which has a section dealing exclusively with Apollinaire's drama. All these books have bibliographies.

APPLE CART, THE, "A Political Extravaganza" in two acts and an interlude by BERNARD SHAW, produced in 1929 and published in 1930. Setting: England in the near future.

Despite its loose structure and slight plot, the play succeeds with its wit, characterizations (particularly of the astute philosopher-king and the various ministers), and the charming interlude, which depicts an actual experience of Shaw with Mrs. Patrick Campbell. In his preface Shaw defended his harsh portrayal of democracy, the apple cart upset by the king who wins by threatening to go to democratic polls. He noted that the play "exposes the unreality of both democracy and royalty as our idealists conceive them." Democracy can be improved by modernization, he maintained, and its real conflict is not with monarchy but with plutocracy (represented by Breakages Ltd.), by which it is "bilked."

Act I. Bill Boanerges, newly appointed President of the Board of Trade in the Cabinet, tells the urbane King Magnus that the country must be governed by the ministers, not the King. Through flattery, Magnus quickly calms and charms the aggressive Boanerges, who uses Magnus's own phrases when Prime Minister Proteus and the Cabinet come in. Angry about Magnus's public allusion to his power of the royal veto, Proteus presents him with an ultimatum: he must become a puppet to his ministers, or they will resign. Magnus humors them, and in a long speech deplores their demand: as their scapegoat, the King stands "above the tyranny of popular ignorance"; he is their buffer against the tyranny of the press, run by the country's real ruler, Breakages Ltd., which suppresses inventions that would avert the accidents and breakdowns that make the company's profits. But when the Cabinet ministers insist on their ultimatum, Magnus agrees to give them his decision that afternoon.

Interlude. Magnus visits his platonic mistress, the beautiful and romantic Orinthia. She wants him to divorce his plain wife and marry her: "Heaven is offering you a rose; and you cling to a cabbage." "Some day perhaps Nature will graft the roses on the cabbages," Magnus tells her, but at the moment cabbages are more important. When he wants to leave for his tea appointment with the Queen, she mischievously tries to hold him by force; they are scuffling and rolling on the floor when a royal secretary enters.

Act II. At tea with his Queen, Jemima, Magnus is approached by the American ambassador with his country's offer (suggested by the President of Ireland) to rejoin the British Empire. Though Jemima urges him to accept the offer, Magnus immediately perceives that it would make Britain but a star on the American flag. He meets the Cabinet and announces his decision: he will abdicate, become a commoner, and run for office. They realize that with his abilities he is sure to become prime minister and, "the apple cart" thus upset, Proteus tears up the ultimatum as they depart, thoroughly trounced by Magnus. Before Jemima takes him away for dinner ("you know you will not sleep if you think after seven o'clock"), Magnus, remembering America's offer, shudders at the thought of a future when "London may be outvoted by Tennessee, and all the other places where we still madly teach our children the mentality of an eighteenth-century village school."

ARAB DRAMA is produced in the Near or MIDDLE EAST (ASIA and AFRICA) countries of Algeria, Egypt (or the United Arab Republic), Iraq, Jordan, Lebanon, Libya, Morocco, the Persian Gulf States, Saudi Arabia, Sudan, Syria, Tunisia, and Yemen. Relatively undeveloped and read more than performed, it was influenced by the English in Iraq and Jordan, and by the French in the remainder of the Arabic-speaking world. The Arab theatre was launched in the mid-nineteenth century in Syria, but developed principally in Egypt. It consisted to a large extent of translations of classic Greek and later (including modern) European drama. The first important playwright was a cosmopolitan Cairo Jew, Yaʿqūb ibn Rufāʾīl Ṣanūʿ (1839–1912), or, as he sometimes called himself, James Sanua. He popularized drama by writing in colloquial Arabic; earlier drama, including the many shadow plays, had been written in the esoteric classical style. Most of his plays, in which he himself acted in his Cairo theatre, were political and social comedies like the pro-Turkish *Al-Salāsil al-muḥaṭṭama,* and *Zubayda,* which satirizes Oriental girls' imitation of Western women (both plays were published in 1911). Of some importance is the playwright Rashīd Ksenṭīnī (1887–1944), an Algerian whose comedies created the modern popular theatre in Algeria. The Egyptian-born Lebanese GEORGES SCHEHADÉ is considered a French dramatist.

The three most important modern Arab playwrights are Egyptians. Aḥmad Shawqī (1868–1931), a poet as well as a dramatist, wrote historical verse plays, the most distinguished being *Maṣraʿ Kliyūpātrā* (*The Fall of Cleopatra,* 1929). The Cairo-born Tawfīq al-Ḥakīm (1902–), long considered the leading Arab playwright, wrote fiction and over forty dramas, including *Baʿd al-mawt* (*After Death,* 1937), a misogynist play about a woman-chasing physician's fading youth; *Jinsunā'l-laṭīf* (*Our Gentle Sex,* 1937), a one-act comedy that ridicules women—and was written in response to a feminist leader's request; *Yā Ṭāliʿ al-shajara* (1962), a philosophical murder mystery almost immediately published in English (with a preface) as *The Tree Climber;* and plays based on history and legend: *Muḥammad* (1936, dramatizes the Prophet's life in perhaps the longest Arabic play ever written—the last scene appeared in English translation in 1955); *Ahl al-kahf* (*People of the Cave,* 1933; a historical fantasy based on a Koranic legend); and *Pijmālyūn* (*Pygmalion,* 1942). Maḥmūd Taymūr (1894–), whose short-lived brother Muḥammad Taymūr (1892–1921) also was an accomplished playwright, wrote many social comedies, notably *Al-Makhbaᵓ raqm 13* (*Shelter No. 13,* 1941), which describes a heterogeneous social group forced together in an air-raid shelter; *Ḥaflat shāy* (*A Tea Party,* 1943), a one-act satire of snobbish young Egyptians affecting Western airs; and *Qanābil* (*Bombs,* 1943), a bitter comedy that reveals the hypocritical rationale of townspeople who leave the city to escape bombardment, and then return (with equal hypocrisy) when life in the country becomes troublesome. A popular but controversial play by Egypt's then director of the Voice of the Arabs radio station, Aḥmad Saᶜīd's (? –) *Al-Shabᶜānūn* (*The Satisfied,* 1966), lampoons Communism and political opportunism; it is set in a mythical Baghdad, and it alludes to the late 1950's Iraqi regime of ᶜAbdul Karim Kassim.

Arab drama is little known in the Western world, though many of the above-named plays have appeared in English translation. Jacob M. Landau's scholarly and very readable *Studies in the Arab Theater and Cinema* (1958) includes a checklist of Arabic plays and a bibliography.

ARAGON, Louis (1897–), French novelist, poet, essayist, and playwright, began his career as a DADAIST and SURREALIST. In 1924 he published two relatively conventional plays with surrealist interludes, *L'Armoire à glace un beau soir* (*The Mirror-Wardrobe One Fine Evening*) and *Au pied du mur.* With ANDRÉ BRETON he collaborated on *Le Trésor des Jésuites* (1929), a play that predicted World War II. Later Aragon, whose career exemplifies intellectual-artistic conflicts between the two world wars, embraced Communism and repudiated his early avant-garde ideas.

The first of the above-named interludes—an old-fashioned domestic melodrama with irrational characterizations and action—appears with prefatory comments in Michael Benedikt and George E. Wellwarth's *Modern French Theatre* (1964). *Aragon, Poet of the French Resistance* (1945) is a collection of his poetry with a preface by Hannah Josephson and Malcolm Cowley.

ARBUZOV, Aleksei Nikolaevich (1908–), Russian playwright, gained popularity in the Soviet Union as early as the 1930's. Outside its borders he became known for *Irkutskaya istoriya* (IT HAPPENED IN IRKUTSK, 1960) and *Moi bedny Marat* (THE PROMISE, 1965). The author of over a dozen plays, Arbuzov in 1963 had five of them running simultaneously in some seventy-one Russian theatres.

Born in Moscow, Arbuzov was educated in the Leningrad Theatre School. At fifteen he started to act, becoming a supernumerary in that city. Eventually he turned to directing and, in 1930, to playwriting. He moved to Moscow that year and came out with his first (but unnotable) play, *Klass. Shestero lyubimykh* (1935), his next one, was a light treatment of the early difficulties of collectivization, and was more successful. It was followed by *Dalnyaya doroga* (1935), which portrays the building of Moscow's subway during the first Five Year Plan, and by the very popular *Tanya* (1938). Produced also in England, this play—sometimes called the "Soviet DOLL'S HOUSE"—features a wife who, when her marriage breaks up, is forced to rely on herself, and matures into a wiser, stronger, and happier woman. Arbuzov's later plays were *Gorod na zare* (1940); *Bessmertny* (1942); *Domik na okraine* (1948); *Yevropeiskaya khronika* (1953); *Gody stranstvii* (*The Years of Wandering,* 1954), which features a strange young doctor and deals with the generation that grew up and suffered through the shocks of World War II and evacuation; *Dvenadtsaty chas* (1960), a fantasy about Russia in the 1930's, and a tribute to Meyerhold; and *Potyarenny syn* (1961).

These plays, whose main characters are usually young people, portray everyday life in the Soviet Union. Though faithful to party-line ideals, Arbuzov experimented (however tentatively) with dramatic structure, and he explored (however sentimentally) individual emotions and maturation more thoroughly than have most Soviet dramatists. Arbuzov is noteworthy because of this, which makes his plays atypical of the popular Russian theatrical fare of his age.

Despite Arbuzov's popularity in Russia, few of his works are readily available in English. *The Promise* was published separately; *The Years of Wandering* appears in *Soviet Literature* IX (1954); and *It Happened in Irkutsk* appears in Samuel A. Weiss's collection of *Drama in the Modern World: Plays and Essays* (1964), which also includes an Arbuzov essay on "Soviet Drama" and a bibliography.

ARCHER, William (1856–1924), British drama critic and playwright, is noted for the championing (with his friend BERNARD SHAW) of HENRIK IBSEN, whose works he translated. His version of THE PILLARS OF SOCIETY was the first Ibsen play produced in London, and his twelve-volume *The Collected Works of Henrik Ibsen* (1906–12) long remained the standard and only English translations. Born in Scotland, Archer was educated at Edinburgh University, spent a year in Australia, and eventually became the influential theatre critic of *Figaro,* the *World,* the *Tribune,* the *Manchester Guardian,* and other English newspapers. He also wrote and edited numerous books on modern drama and theatre, for whose artistic integrity he fought vigorously and consistently.

Ironically, his only produced play was THE GREEN GODDESS (1920), a thumping melodrama that was tremendously popular but, as critics slyly remarked, a far cry from Ibsen. Earlier Archer had written

War Is War (1919), an indignant drama about German war atrocities in Belgium; it failed of production when peace was declared. In his last years he wrote a history play, *Martha Washington,* and two blank-verse tragedies based on seventeenth-century plays: *Beatriz-Juana,* after Thomas Middleton and William Rowley's *The Changeling;* and *Lidia,* after Philip Massinger's *The Great Duke of Florence*. They were posthumously published, with a foreword by Bernard Shaw, as *Three Plays* (1927).

See Charles Archer's *William Archer: Life, Work and Friendships* (1931).

ARCHITECT AND THE EMPEROR OF ASSYRIA, THE (*L'Architecte et l'Empereur d'Assyrie*), a play in two acts by FERNANDO ARRABAL, published and produced in 1967. Setting: a tropical island.

Though outwardly REPRESENTATIONAL, this is an ABSURDIST drama. Its structure is circular and, with farcical horror, it explores characteristic Arrabal preoccupations like brutality, sex, and religion. It has but two characters.

"Help me, sir! I am the only survivor of the [airplane] accident," exclaims a gentleman after a tremendous crash is heard and he drops onto an island inhabited only by a savage who lives in a tidy hut. The frightened savage (the "architect") makes inarticulate sounds and the gentleman identifies himself as the Emperor of Assyria. "Civilizing" him, the Emperor tells the Architect stories of his former regal life. The men act out various human relationships: master-slave, priest-worshiper, sadist-masochist, mother-child, and other antipodean parts, in one of which the Emperor simultaneously plays the roles of a childbearing woman and her obstetrician. But suffering guilt for his former life and hatreds, the Emperor insists the Architect execute and then eat him. "How tough he is," the Architect complains as he feasts on the corpse, "a good thing it isn't Friday." Retrieving a bone from under the table, the Architect reappears as the Emperor—with the Emperor dressed as the Architect. Their identities switched, the Architect-Emperor drops from the sky with the exclamation that opened the play, and the frightened savage Emperor-Architect makes inarticulate sounds.

ARDÈLE (*Ardèle ou La Marguerite*), a play in three acts by JEAN ANOUILH, produced in 1948 and published in 1949. Setting: France, "1912 or thereabouts."

Though farcical, this is an intensely bitter portrayal of many love affairs. The play's General is the Saint-Pé of THE WALTZ OF THE TOREADORS. Anouilh labeled both plays "grating."

The General passionately fondles his indifferent young chambermaid while his mad wife calls from her room. Her jealous cries of "Leon! Leon!" resemble those of the mating peacocks outside. "Her voice is just a shade shriller," the General remarks as he justifies himself to his daughter-in-law, who is disgusted by the aging man's philandering. He once loved his wife passionately, but love "has one archenemy," he tells her: "Life." His sister, a Countess, arrives with her urbane husband and her sullen lover. The General informs them that an older sister, the hunchback Ardèle (who is never seen in the play), fell in love with his son's tutor, another hunchback. To avoid ridicule and a scandal, the General stopped the affair. Now they attempt to get the lovesick hunchback to come out of her locked room and end her hunger strike. The Count recognizes in Ardèle's unhappiness that of them all, despite their efforts to keep up appearances. "It is love itself which is on trial," he says, "the demon of love hidden in her hump like a malignant spirit"—just as his wife keeps a lover in a desperate attempt to ward off age, as the Count himself keeps a mistress, and as the General, who has enough love to remain with his insane wife, is reduced to cuddling chambermaids. Even the pure daughter-in-law is tormented—by the sexual gratification she gets from her despised husband, which keeps her from consummating her love with his brother. At night, the various couples are stymied in their trysts, and the desperate hunchbacks commit suicide in Ardèle's room. Then, absurdly clad in their parents' clothing, two children appear. They are the Countess's daughter and the General's young son, who have spied on their elders' doings. Now they mimic and exaggerate them—suggesting that love will continue grotesquely in the next generation.

ARDEN, John (1930–), English playwright born in Barnsley, studied architecture at Cambridge and Edinburgh and produced some juvenilia before he took up drama seriously. Early produced works include *All Fall Down* (1955), put on by fellow students, and a BBC play, *The Life of Man* (1956). His first drama to be accepted by the Royal Court Theatre was *The Waters of Babylon* (1957), a satire of the lottery system, portrayed in a LOWER DEPTHS type of setting. Like SERJEANT MUSGRAVE'S DANCE (1959), with which Arden made his reputation and which is considered his masterpiece, this play exemplifies his characteristic dramaturgy. It resembles that of BERTOLT BRECHT in its use of song and social message, but it is not EPIC and further differs in its frequent use of blank verse, and—more important—in its confusing viewpoint. Arden's protagonists may have admirable ideals and yet be mad (like Musgrave); they may be total scoundrels yet not unsympathetic, like the intruder of *Soldier, Soldier* (1960), who cheats and lies to the family and seduces the wife of a soldier he claims to be saving. For they are like the filthy, degenerate—yet apparently to-be-admired—family who make a municipal housing project unlivable for the respectable lower-class tenants who occupy it in *Live Like Pigs* (1958), a farce with sociological overtones. Arden has been criticized for such confused viewpoints, and his general popularity has suffered accordingly. Yet despite such ambiguities his plots are intensely theatrical and suspenseful, and his admirers praise his ambiguities as attempts to present all sides of every situation, problem, and conflict with fairness.

Arden's other dramas include *The Happy Haven* (1960), a play (with masks) about a scientist who discovers the Fountain of Youth and is transformed into a wailing infant by oldsters who resent being used as guinea pigs; *The Business of Good Government,* "a Christmas Play" (1962); *The Workhouse Donkey* (1963), about municipal corruption, in the manner of farcical vaudeville skits, and featuring the Alderman Charlie Butterthwaite of his first play, of *Soldier, Soldier,* and of *Wet Fish* (a television drama); *Armstrong's Last Goodnight* (1964), set in the style of the writings of one of the play's central characters, Sir David Lindsay, and portraying the famous Scots freebooter who with his band was betrayed and executed in 1530 by order of James V; *Left-Handed Liberty* (1965), another history play, about King John and the Magna Carta; and *The Hero Rises Up* (1968), a play about Lord Nelson, "the last uncontested hero-figure of our time," composed in a mélange of PRESENTATIONAL and EPIC styles.

Arden also wrote *Ironhand* (1963), a free adaptation of Goethe's *Götz von Berlichingen* (1771); a number of television plays; and partly improvisational political allegories, including *Harold Muggins Is a Martyr* (1968), composed with his wife, Margaretta d'Arcy (? –), and large groups of students and actors.

A study of his life and work is Ronald Hayman's *John Arden* (1968).

ARDREY, Robert (1908–), American dramatist born in Chicago. The most successful of his liberal political dramas was the early *Thunder Rock* (1939), a symbolic fantasy that was produced by the Group Theatre and later became a London hit. It features a disillusioned journalist who communicates with ghosts in his lighthouse retreat (Thunder Rock), reviews man's past history, and finally decides he must join the exploding conflict —"not fighting for fighting's sake, but to make a new world of the old." *Sing Me No Lullaby* (1954) portrays an intellectual hounded by the FBI for his Communist past but saved by a friend who will return to politics to make America safe for nonconformity. Ardrey's *Shadow of Heroes* (1958), produced Off-Broadway, deals with the Hungarian revolution of 1956 and features Janos Kadar, at first an admirably undisciplined Communist, achieving personal and national success when he succumbs to the party line—whereupon his disillusioned friend remarks that Communism has ruined "for all eternity more good men than you can mention." Ardrey, who was educated at the University of Chicago, was one of the few relatively successful 1930's playwrights able to revitalize and update his political attitudes and indignations into the late 1950's.

ARENT, Arthur (1905?–), American playwright. An AGITPROP writer for the Federal Theatre Project of the WPA in the 1930's, he is noteworthy for his ONE-THIRD OF A NATION (1938), the best known of the tendentious LIVING NEWSPAPER DRAMAS of that decade. Other such works that he authored in part or whole are *Triple-A Plowed Under* (1936), the first publicly presented living newspaper drama, dealing with the farm depression in twenty-six stylized scenes that culminate with the Supreme Court's ruling the Agricultural Adjustment Administration unconstitutional; *1935* (1936), about justice to criminals, laborers, Negroes, and politicians; *Injunction Granted* (1936), a Marxist presentation of the history of labor; and *Power* (1937), a non-Communist depiction of the TVA. Arent also wrote some of the sketches for a very popular social satire, the ILGWU revue *Pins and Needles* (1937).

ARGENTINA is the center of LATIN AMERICAN theatre, which flourishes in the cosmopolitan capital of Buenos Aires. Early Argentine theatre history is intertwined with that of its River Plate neighbor, URUGUAY: the continent's foremost playwright (FLORENCIO SÁNCHEZ) is claimed by both nations, and its indigenous GAUCHO DRAMA began with a Uruguayan's pantomime in Argentina. Thus, engendered in the circus ring, Argentina's drama evolved slowly from its gaucho origins. Only with its first important modern playwright, SAMUEL EICHELBAUM, did Argentina's still-uninspired drama begin to approach the sophistication of its theatre, which fell into temporary decline during the repressive years (1946–55) of Perón's dictatorship. Nonetheless, Argentina has produced numerous playwrights whose works have achieved a measure of artistic distinction and considerable popularity throughout the Spanish-speaking world.

Because he used national themes, Nemisio Trejo (1862–1916) is called Argentina's first native playwright; he produced topical spectacles, the most popular of which was *Los políticos* (1897). Less popular but more respected was the academician David Peña (1862–1930), who wrote historical drama, notably one on the career of a gaucho governor, *Facundo* (1906). Gringos (foreigners) and criolles (natives) persisted as stock characters in Argentina's dramatic (and other) literature, and Martín Coronado, Roberto Payró, and others noted under GAUCHO DRAMA were the country's major early playwrights. Originally presented as villains, gringos soon were caricatured and became comic figures; but as they prospered and achieved respectability they were portrayed with increasingly more respect. Sánchez's *La gringa* (1904) was the first important such portrayal, and many others were composed by dramatists who viewed the melting pot of New York as a model for their own society.

The following are the more notable Argentine playwrights of the first half of the twentieth century. Gregorio de Laferrère (1867–1913), the Father of River Plate comedy—his *Locos de verano* (1905) is a Latin American YOU CAN'T TAKE IT WITH YOU—also wrote serious drama, including *Las de Barranco* (1908), his masterpiece, which portrays a widow stymied in her efforts to marry off the most ethical of her daughters. Julio Sánchez Gardel (1879–1937) achieved success with *Noche de luna* (1907) and became known abroad with *La montaña de brujas* (*The Witches' Mountain*, 1913), a folk tragedy of jealousy and murder and Argentina's first full-length play to appear in English (in Bierstadt's collection, see below). The French-born Alberto Novión (1881–1937) was the master of immigrant drama, including *Misia Pancha la brava* (1915), something of an answer to *La gringa*. Pedro E. Pico (1882–1945) wrote many poetic but sentimental *sainetes*—notably the NATURALIST portrayal of paupers near a city garbage dump, *Del mismo barro* (*From the Common Clay* 1918)—which were so popular that he was able to make a good living from them; he also collaborated with the less prominent playwright Rodolfo González Pacheco (1881–1949). Armando Discépolo (1887–1952), a director and an admirer of LUIGI PIRANDELLO, was intrigued by the maladjusted and morally crippled, and founded a *grotesco criollo*—a Latin-American GROTESQUE THEATRE—exemplified in his portrayal of a musician who comes to recognize his own inadequacies, *Stéfano* (1928). Juan Fernando Camilo Darthés (1889–) and Carlos S. Damel (1890–1959), the immensely popular "Darthés y Damel" team until Damel's death, produced over fifty slight but amusing plays (many about love and marriage) that were repeatedly performed throughout South America; the most notable among them are *Amparo* (1934), *Los chicos crecen* (1937), *La Hermana Josefina* (*Sister Josephine*, 1938; also translated as *The Quack Doctor*), and *Manuel García* (1946). Francisco Defilippis Novoa (1892–1930) indicted society with his poetic and SYMBOLIC but often cynical drama, some of it avant-garde: the triangle plot of *Tú, yo, y el mundo después* (1929) is depicted in terms of fantasy as well as naturalism. Alberto Vacarezza (1888–1959), notable for his gaucho plays, was equally successful with naturalist drama set in Buenos Aires's slums, as in the popular *El conventillo de la paloma* (1929), featuring a gun moll who foregoes crime for poor but honest tenement life. Conrado Nalé Roxlo (1898–) was a noted poet before he turned to writing fantasy drama (*La cola de la sirena*, 1941), comedy (*Una viuda difícil*, 1944), and a modernization of the Faust legend, *El pacto de Cristina* (1945). Robert Arlt (1900–42), a versatile and experimental writer, mixed farce and tragedy in dramas of ideas that often posit evil fortune as man's nemesis, as in *Saverio el cruel* (1936), which juxtaposes frivolous wealth with miserable poverty in the tragedy of a butter salesman's romance.

Among more recent playwrights are the director Roberto A. Tálice (1902–), who has written well over one hundred technically accomplished plays, including the prize-winning *Noche en los ojos, La llama eterna* (1947); the Russian-born Israel Zeitlin (1906–), who writes under the name César Tiempo and won prizes for his powerful ghetto drama on prejudice, *Pan criollo* (1937); Aurelio Ferretti (1907–), who satirizes morals and customs in farces like the prize-winning *El cajero que fue hasta la esquina* (1958); Malena Sandor (pseudonym of María Elena James de Terza, 1913–), who had the most success with *Una mujer libre* (1938), a play about an emancipated divorcée's affair with her friend's husband, and who later migrated to Spain, where she wrote a hit musical comedy, *Penélope ya no teje* (1946), and other plays; Carlos Gorostiza (1920–), a director who attracted attention with his drama on Argentina's class struggle, *El puente* (1950), and on man's callousness, *Los prójimos* (1966)—the title's "neighbors" being the New Yorkers who saw but ignored the Kitty Genovese murder; Osvaldo Dragún (1929–), a versatile writer concerned with social problems and influenced by the drama of BERTOLT BRECHT, whose MOTHER COURAGE he adapted with a contemporary Argentinian setting as *Heroica de Buenos Aires* (1966); and Abelardo Castillo (? –), whose Edgar Allan Poe drama *Israfel* (1964) was awarded the 1966 UNESCO Prize.

Edward H. Bierstadt's *Three Plays of Argentina* (1920) includes two gaucho plays (Silvero Manco's version of *Juan Moreira* and Bayón Herrera's *Santos Vega*) and *The Witches' Mountain;* Willis Knapp Jones's *Spanish-American Literature in Translation* (1963) has Podestá's *Juan Moreira* sketch and excerpts of plays by Pico, Darthés and Damel, and Eichelbaum; and Jones's *Men and Angels: Three South American Comedies* (1970) reprints Darthés and Damel's *The Quack Doctor*. Among the works listed under LATIN AMERICA, Jones's *Behind Spanish American Footlights* (1966) should be singled out for its six long chapters on Argentina. A notable reference is Tito Livio Foppa's *Diccionario teatral del Río de la Plata* (1961).

ARIA DA CAPO, a one-act verse play by EDNA ST. VINCENT MILLAY, produced in 1919 and published in 1920. Setting: a Harlequinade stage.

A short work popular with amateur groups and made into an opera by Robert Baksa in 1969, the last part of this three-part satire repeats the first, as in a musical "aria da capo."

The harlequins, Pierrot and Columbine, engage in chatter that shows their frivolous self-centeredness. They are interrupted and displaced by Cothurnus, the masque of tragedy, who insists on playing his scene immediately. He presents Corydon and Thyrsis, shepherd friends who first demur that they "cannot act / A tragedy with comic properties," but then sadly admit they are "always ready" to reenact their pastoral tragedy. Weaving a wall of colored paper ribbons between them, they play what soon develops into "an ugly game." It exemplifies human greed that leads to war ("festered pride and a feverish ambition") and ends with the shepherds murdering each other. The harlequins, whose silly chase has been overheard intermittently, return and push the corpses under the table. Columbine resumes the original chatter: "Pierrot, a macaroon,—I cannot *live* / Without a macaroon!" And Pierrot replies, as he did in the beginning: "My only love, / You are *so* intense! . . ."

ARISTOCRATS (*Aristokraty*), a comedy in four acts by NIKOLAI FYODOROVICH POGODIN, published in 1934 and produced in 1935. Setting: Russia, 1931–33.

One of Pogodin's most popular plays, *Aristocrats* was produced also in America, England, and France. It features a group of forced laborers—"aristocrats" of crime like "bandits, thieves, prostitutes, fanatics, *kulaks,* etc."—employed in building the White Sea-Baltic Canal. The criminals are morally "regenerated" (*Aristocrats* was called a modern "miracle play") by this constructive work and by the paternalistic security police (the Cheka). It is an episodic mass drama that inspired with its portrayal of the redemptive powers of Communism, and entertained with its humor and the gangster vernacular. Outstanding among its characters is the exuberant Captain Kostya, a rebellious gangster whose ultimate conversion into a zealous Stakhanovite earns him an official citation.

ARMORED TRAIN 14-69 (*Bronepoezd 14-69*), a play in eight scenes by VSEVOLOD VYACHESLAVOVICH IVANOV, published and produced in 1927. Setting: the Siberian taiga, 1917.

This patriotic melodrama was one of the most popular plays about the Revolution and the Civil War, and long alternated with Pogodin's THE CHIMES OF THE KREMLIN at the Moscow Art Theatre (Vasili Kachalov playing the part of Vershinin). Ivanov's only really successful play, it was the dramatization of his 1922 novella of the same name about an actual event. The play was translated and produced (in altered versions) in France, England, and America.

A disgruntled White officer is jealous of his fiancée and fearful of Red victories. Assisted by the Japanese allies, he commands the armored train (14-69) sent with weapons and ammunition to crush the workers' new republic. His ruthlessness with prisoners is contrasted with the generosity of Vershinin, a reluctant old peasant who joins the Revolution as a partisan leader only after the Whites destroy his farm and kill his sons, and after he has been persuaded of the rightness of the Red cause. Vershinin's men capture a member of the American detachment sent to Vladivostok to crush the Soviets. At the belfry of a run-down church, the peasants prepare to execute him. But when the captured American recognizes and cheers words like "Lenin" and "proletariat," all become comrades. Vershinin realizes that they must stop the armored train. "We must block the line with our bodies. Their wheels shall clog with peasant meat. But there aren't enough of us!" he says desperately, and envisions destruction; yet "It is for the good of truth that Russia is burning." In a tense scene they await the train at an embankment. As the train approaches, the volunteer needed to lie down on the tracks and stop the train falters. To save Vershinin, who is ready to give his own life, a Chinese youth takes his place, and stops the train with his body. The halted train is boarded, the hysterical White officer is shot, and the simple peasant Vershinin is jubilant: "Well, comrades, we've captured the armored train, and I still don't know my multiplication table!" On the outskirts of town, the Communist commissar is treacherously killed. Vershinin and his peasants arrive to take over the harbor. Their joy of victory is marred only by the death of the commissar. His wife cries over his corpse as Vershinin leads the men into the train: "Armored train into battle! Armored Train 14-69!"

ARMS AND THE MAN, a comedy in three acts by BERNARD SHAW, produced in 1894 and published in 1898. Setting: Bulgaria, 1885–86.

This is Shaw's first "pleasant" play, and his first to be produced commercially. Speaking of it in his preface to PLAYS PLEASANT, Shaw stressed his opposition to "idealism, which is only a flattering name for romance in politics and morals, [and] is as obnoxious to me as romance in ethics or religion." While the play, particularly through the practical but unheroic Bluntschli, characterizes war unromantically, its satire is witty and charming throughout. It was adapted as a popular operetta, THE CHOCOLATE SOLDIER.

Act I. Raina is gazing at the snowy Balkans on a beautiful night in November 1885, when Catherine, her mother, rushes in to tell her the news just received from Raina's father, Major Paul Petkoff: the Bulgarians have won a glorious victory at Slivnitza, and her fiancé, Major Sergius Saranoff, was the hero of the main cavalry charge. After the maid Louka advises her to fasten her bedroom shutters, Raina, left alone, rapturously gazes at Sergius's portrait. Bluntschli, a fugitive Serbian captain, climbs in over the balcony, and soon changes Raina's fear into contempt for his unheroic attitudes: a professional Swiss soldier, he admits that he is afraid of death, and he keeps chocolates in his cartridge belt. But remembering that she belongs to a wealthy and refined family to whom a guest must be sacred, Raina hides the fugitive from a searching party. The prosaic Bluntschli attempts to dispel Raina's romantic military notions, and tells her of the comic spectacle of the Bulgarian officer who charged them "like an operatic tenor"; he cannot totally stifle his amusement at Sergius's heroics even when he learns that he is talking of her fiancé. Raina leaves, and when Catherine returns with her to help with Bluntschli's escape, they find the exhausted fugitive fast asleep.

Act II. Four months later, just after the signing of the peace treaty, Sergius, a Byronic "barbarian," visits Petkoff, who has himself just returned home from the war. They discuss a Swiss captain who shrewdly outbargained them in the prisoner exchange, and who had been hidden by two unknown women who then helped him escape. When left alone, Raina and Sergius romantically discuss their "higher love," but as soon as Raina leaves, Sergius tells the maid Louka that this love is a "very fatiguing thing to keep up," and promptly makes advances to her. Louka tells him that he has a rival for Raina, but she will not identify him; angry, Sergius hurts Louka's arm, and staunchly refuses, as a gentleman, to apologize by kissing it. Bluntschli arrives to return Petkoff's coat, in which he had escaped. Though Catherine tries to rush him away, Petkoff sees him and, to the discomfiture of Raina and Catherine, asks him to stay as a guest in their house.

Act III. When she can talk to him in private, Raina scolds Bluntschli for having revealed how he escaped with her help, and is even more concerned about her deception of Sergius, whose relationship with her she considers "the one really beautiful and noble part" of her life. Indignant when he deprecates her sacrificial lies for him, Raina finds her poise shattered as he tells her, "When you get into that noble attitude and speak in that thrilling voice, I admire you; but I find it impossible to believe a single word you say." Completely changed in tone and bearing, she is delighted that he does not despise her for the heroics she has felt were always expected of her, and she begins to be romantically interested in him. Sergius and Louka, in the meantime, continue their flirtation. He tells her that he certainly would dare marry her—if he did not love Raina; when he hears that Raina now loves Bluntschli, Sergius challenges him to a duel. Bluntschli talks his way out of it; but when Raina guesses at Sergius's love affair, their "romance is shattered." Proud to the last, Sergius is maneuvered by Louka into marrying her. Bluntschli, who has just inherited his father's hotel fortune, proposes to Raina, who happily agrees to marry her "chocolate cream soldier."

ARRABAL, Fernando (1932–), avant-garde Spanish-French writer, exiled himself from Fascist Spain, which had imprisoned his father, and moved to Paris in 1954. Most of his works are written in French, and influenced by the ABSURDist theatre of EUGÈNE IONESCO and SAMUEL BECKETT; his drama has been likened also to that of MICHEL DE GHELDERODE, and to the Kafkaesque farce of WITOLD GOMBROWICZ. Nonetheless Arrabal's drama, with its GRAND GUIGNOL and stylized religion and passion, is recognizably Spanish. He has been attacked as blasphemous, obscene, and scatological for his nightmare dramas of human brutality and eroticism, depicted through the innocent viewpoint of children. Though much of Arrabal's drama consists of brief sketches, he first became known for a two-act modern Passion play, *Le Cimetière des voitures* (*The Car Cemetery,* 1958; also translated as *The Automobile Graveyard*). It is set in a car junkyard peopled by crude couples who are serviced by a vicious butler, a kind young prostitute, and three jazz musicians, one of whom is the Christ figure; a "good" man, the latter is betrayed to a grotesque athletic couple, who crucify him on a bicycle and flog him to death while another couple silence and then cuddle their infant. Perhaps more notable is Arrabal's later full-length play, *L'Architecte et l'Empereur d'Assyrie* (THE ARCHITECT AND THE EMPEROR OF ASSYRIA, 1967).

Fernando Arrabal. (*French Cultural Services*)

Arrabal was born in Melilla (Spanish Morocco) and raised in a pious Catholic household. He studied law in Madrid, but turned to writing after settling in Paris. The first volume of his drama appeared in 1958, and the next year saw the first production of one of his plays, the one-act *Pique-nique en campagne* (*Picnic on the Battlefield*); it portrays a soldier, his simple-minded parents, and his prisoner, all of them naïvely oblivious of war's savagery, enjoying a Sunday luncheon at the front until a sudden machine-gun burst wipes them out.

The first collection of Arrabal's drama, translated as *Four Plays* (1962), consists of *The Car Cemetery, Oraison* (*Orison*), *Les Deux Bourreaux* (*The Two Executioners*), and *Fando et Lis* (*Fando and Lis*). *Orison* and *The Two Executioners* are brief sketches: in the first, a childlike couple decide hereafter "to be good" as they sit near a coffin containing their infant, whom they have killed; in the second, a woman denounces her husband, who is thereupon tortured to death while she pours salt and vinegar on his wounds, and then she accepts the apologies of her sons, who embrace her. *Fando and Lis,* for which Arrabal also wrote the screenplay (1969), is a sadomasochistic baby-talk fantasy, in which Fando abuses his crippled beloved to death as they and a group of gentlemen journey to a better place they never can reach.

Subsequent Arrabal drama is similar in style and theme. His second collection (1961, translated in 1967) consists of *Picnic on the Battlefield, Le Tricycle* (*The Tricycle*), *La Bicyclette du condamné* (*The Condemned Man's Bicycle*), *Guernica*, and *Le Labyrinthe* (*The Labyrinth*). The last two were immediately produced by avant-garde groups in France and abroad: *Guernica*, an anti-Franco piece inspired by Picasso's mural about the 1937 bombing, portrays the pitiful attempts at ordinary talk by a doomed peasant couple trapped in the rubble of their home. In *The Labyrinth*, a longer play, a man chained to a toilet howls with thirst until he finally hangs himself, while his friend seeks to escape from the labyrinth of the house. The third collection (1965) of Arrabal's "*théâtre panique*" (alluding to *Pan* more than to *panic*) includes *Le Couronnement, Le Grand Cérémonial* (*The Grand Ceremonial*, a full-length play "about a dupe's ceremonial initiation into truth"), *Concert dans un œuf* (a two-acter subtitled "*cérémonie quichottesque*"), and *Cérémonie pour un noir assassiné*. The short horror play *La Communiante* (*The Solemn Communion*, 1966) counterpoints a young girl's first communion with a necrophiliac rape. Greatly acclaimed in 1969 was a SURREALIST depiction of a famous actress's hallucinations, which range from base humiliations to ecstatic joys, titled after Hieronymus Bosch's painting *Le Jardin des délices* (*The Garden of Delights*).

Arrabal has also written brief dramatic sketches and wordless dramatic spectacles of ballet and movement (*Orchestration théâtrale*, 1959), as well as novels. His drama is discussed in Jacques Guicharnaud's *Modern French Theatre* (revised 1967) and in Martin Esslin's *The Theatre of the Absurd* (revised 1968).

ARTAUD, Antonin (1896–1948), French director and dramatist, completed only one play and is notable principally as the theoretician of the theatre of CRUELTY. His theories, detailed in a number of essays collectively published in 1938 as *Le Théâtre et son double* (*The Theatre and Its Double*), directly influenced the theatre of JEAN GENET, PETER WEISS, and other playwrights and directors of the 1950's and 1960's. The SYMBOLISM and melody of Oriental drama and Balinese dancing interested Artaud far more than dialogue and psychological REALISM. By invoking the incantatory power of myth and ritual in drama he attempted to assault "human sensibilities" and restore to the modern Western theatre an "excruciating, magical relation to reality and danger." Actors as well as audiences were to become "victims burnt at the stake, signaling through the flames"—as in a frenzy-inducing plague that reveals man's true nature. It could be exposed in the theatre, Artaud believed, and "liberate" man from the repressions of civilization. These theories Artaud dramatized in *Les Cenci* (*The Cenci*, 1935), his adaptation of Shelley's verse play and Stendhal's *Chroniques italiennes*. With actor-director disciples like Jean-Louis Barrault and Roger Blin, Artaud produced this play in his short-lived Théâtre de la Cruauté in 1935. Both play and theatre quickly failed.

Artaud was born in Marseilles. His early professional interest was in symbolist and SURREALIST drama, and he wrote the film script of the surrealist *La Coquille et le clergyman* (1926). In his first theatre, founded with ROGER VITRAC in 1927 and named for his precursor ALFRED JARRY, Artaud produced avant-garde works by Vitrac, AUGUST STRINDBERG, PAUL CLAUDEL, and others—including his own short sketch *Le Jet de sang* (*Jet of Blood*, 1927), a gruesome spectacle that includes a whore's eating a young man's eyes and biting God's wrist. After his 1935 failure Artaud traveled to Ireland and Mexico, where he lectured and studied the rituals of lost tribes. He began a drama on Montezuma, but upon his return to France had a mental breakdown and was confined to an insane asylum from 1937 until 1946, shortly before his death.

Artaud's complete works are in six volumes (1956–65), and his productions are discussed in the Artaud-Barrault correspondence published in 1952. *The Cenci* and *Jet of Blood* are readily available, the latter with introductory comments in Michael Benedikt and George E. Wellwarth's *Modern French Theatre* (1964). *The Theatre and Its Double*, Artaud's most influential work, is also available in translation. A book-length study of his theories is Eric Sellin's *The Dramatic Concepts of Antonin Artaud* (1968), a biography is Bettina L. Knapp's *Antonin Artaud: Man of Vision* (1969), and his development as a playwright and poet is explored in Naomi Greene's *Antonin Artaud: Poet Without Words* (1970).

ARTSYBASHEV, Mikhail Petrovich (1878–1927), Russian novelist, essayist, and playwright, first created a sensation with his novel *Sanin* (1907). Its title character embodies and champions the enjoyment of "absolute sexual liberty," as he frankly states, and the book deals with incest and preaches "the doctrine of anarchical individualism," as Artsybashev himself noted. His philosophical convictions—which he claimed were in the tradition of LEO TOLSTOI, although they are precisely the reverse—were based on only two realities, death and sex. The novel *U poslednei cherty* (*The Breaking Point*, 1912), a veritable "hymn to suicide," as it was characterized, celebrated the first reality. More notable and frequently expressed was his espousal of erotic indulgence, which is portrayed also in his plays: *Revnost* (*Jealousy*), *Zakon dikarya* (*The Law of the Savage*), and *Vragi* (*Enemies*, produced in New York as *Lovers and Enemies*, 1927), all notorious stage hits and published in 1913; and *Voina* (*War*, 1915), a wholesale condemnation of marriage, which also was produced in America.

All these plays portray unbridled sensuality, all of them advocate anarchic principles, all of them end tragically—and all of them elicited virulent protest. While they were very actable and demonstrate Artsybashev's skill as a dramatist, they, as well as his fiction, soon disappeared into permanent obscurity. Artsybashev was nonetheless a dominant cultural force in the period between the two revolutions. When the Soviets came to power they banned his works for their "negativism" and scorn of conventional behavior and thought. He was expelled, and spent his last years in Warsaw, where he wrote anti-Soviet articles until his death. Prince D. S. Mirsky's chapter on Artsybashev ends, "At present no one regards him as a significant writer, but only as a curious and, on the whole, regrettable episode in the history of Russian literature" (*Contemporary Russian Literature 1881–1925*, 1926).

AS WELL AS BEFORE, BETTER THAN BEFORE (*Come prima, meglio di prima*), a "comedy" in three acts by LUIGI PIRANDELLO, produced in 1920 and published in 1921. Setting: contemporary Italy.

In this tragicomedy, Fulvia Gelli tries to commit suicide and then returns to her husband and daughter after spending thirteen depraved years with lover after lover. Her husband is a prominent surgeon whose cold rationality has made her feel unworthy of motherhood. Now he reinstates Fulvia, but insists on her appearing as his second wife, for he has told their daughter that her mother is dead. Taught to revere this mother like a saint, the adolescent daughter is resentful of the intruder, who yearns to express her maternal feelings. The tragedy is lightened by a few comic episodes resulting from her supposed death and her role as a second wife. When she gets pregnant, Fulvia finally reveals her true identity to her daughter, whose hostility becomes unbearable. Then Fulvia leaves with an idealistic lover who gives up everything for her. Her husband will not again falsify her image before their child. His blindness to her maternal feelings has killed them for their first child. Fulvia gives the same name to her new baby: this will be "as well as before, better than before" because, she tells her husband, this child will go "with me, alive!—We shall go towards life! Defying fate!"

AS YOU DESIRE ME (*Come tu mi vuoi*), a play in three acts by LUIGI PIRANDELLO, published and produced in 1930. Setting: Berlin and a villa near Udine, Italy; ten years after World War I.

The bizarre plot is a free adaptation of an actual case (the Bruneri-Canella mistaken identity case of 1929) that made Italian headlines. Pirandello's heroine (in real life it was a man), the Strange or Unknown Lady, as in THE NEW COLONY, is presented as an exalted ideal who first appears as "a drunken, baleful slattern" (Brooks Atkinson's 1931 *New York Times* review). In Judith Anderson's American stage production (Greta Garbo starred in the film) the real identities of the heroine and the Demented Lady were blurred, but Pirandello did not intend to mystify audiences about the identity of the flesh-and-blood Cia, Bruno Pieri's wife. He meant the heroine to be the reincarnation of Cia's soul only.

Late at night in Berlin, a beautiful but debauched cabaret dancer in her thirties comes home intoxicated to her German lover, Carl Salter, a sensual middle-aged writer. She is accompanied by raucous drunks and an artist. The latter claims to recognize her as a friend's wife, long given up for dead after her wartime rape and abduction during the sacking of an Italian town. She tantalizes Salter with uncertainty about her real identity. Desperate and disgusted with the "obscene madness" of her life and her unpleasant lover, who now shoots but only wounds himself, she decides to go to the putative husband: "If he can recreate me, if he can give a soul to this body, which is that of his Cia—let him take it, let him take it, and let him build out of his own memories—his own—a beautiful new life...." In Pieri's Italian villa, now recognized as the lost wife, she quickly assumes the noble Cia's identity. But her dignity is degraded by the family's human weaknesses and self-interest. They are concerned with her physical identity in a legal transfer of property and the husband's expression of his love. This concern frustrates her spiritual transformation. Again desperate, she tells Pieri, "I came here; I gave myself to you utterly, utterly; I said to you: 'Here I am; I am yours; there is nothing left in me, nothing of my own; take me and make me, make me over, as you desire me!' ... Being is nothing! Being is becoming! And I have made myself into Cia!—But you understand nothing of all that!" Salter—recuperated from his wound and anxious to have his mistress back—appears with a Demented Lady who, he insists, is the real Cia. Though the family do not recognize the lunatic, telltale marks suggest that she is the real wife. The heroine's attempts to create a new, beautiful life for herself and Pieri fail, and she leaves: "I felt that he was searching for one who could no longer be! One who, as he must know, he could only find alive in me, in order to make her over himself—not as she desired (for she no longer desired anything for herself) but as he desired her!" She returns to her degraded Berlin life with her repulsive lover, as the Demented Lady babbles idiotically.

ASCENT OF F6, THE, a tragedy in two acts by W. H. AUDEN and CHRISTOPHER ISHERWOOD, published in 1936 and produced in 1937. Setting: England, a country inn, and "F6."

This play is an episodic mixture of stylized SYMBOLISM, NATURALISM, satire, and farce. Its language consists of different types of prose and poetry, which ranges from elevated blank verse to pop songs.

Act I. Michael Forsyth ("M. F.") Ransom, a famous mountain climber and a disappointed idealist, sits atop an English hill reading Dante and contemplating life. A lowly clerk and a housewife, Mr. and Mrs. A., reappear periodically to express (in doggerel) lower-middle-class suburban attitudes about their own frustrated lives and the daily news, "The glib justification of the sorry act. / The frantic washing of the grimy fact." Ransom's twin brother, Sir James, a great politician, plans to forestall a hostile power by conquering F6, a border mountain vital in British politics and believed to be haunted. Michael Ransom refuses to head the expedition, because he hates his brother. But when his mother reveals she always loved him most and begs him to be England's savior, he agrees to go. "When the Demon is dead," she says, "You shall be mine, all mine, / You shall have kisses like wine. . . ."

Act II. A great leader, Michael Ransom ably reconciles conflicts within his party, particularly between a carefree playboy and an earnest young climber who idolizes Ransom. In a magic crystal obtained from monks at an F6 monastery, the alpine travelers find their real individual aspirations reflected. The abbot counsels "the complete abnegation of the will" and warns Ransom against yielding to his temptation to be the people's savior; but Ransom proceeds on the expedition nevertheless. All his followers eventually perish: a young botanist is killed by an avalanche, and the earnest climber commits suicide because he is not chosen for the final climb. Only Ransom reaches the summit, where he collapses. In the fantasy episodes that follow, his brother appears in the shape of a dragon. They play chess with life-sized pieces—their respective followers. Michael Ransom wins, but then is condemned by a chorus for the death of his fellow climbers. Patriotic clichés are shouted by the various characters, another avalanche is heard, and then a figure appears: Ransom's mother as a young woman. He falls at her feet and puts his head in her lap. When the lights go on again Ransom is lying dead on F6's summit. The chorus condemns his weakness in succumbing to the temptation to lead the expedition, and various characters, in a chorus of clichés, praise his sacrifice and heroism. Mr. and Mrs. A., gazing at Ransom's monument, have the last words: "He belongs to *us*, now!"

ASCH, Sholem (1880–1957), Yiddish novelist and playwright, is perhaps the most widely known Yiddish writer. His fame rests on his fiction, particularly on *Three Cities* (1930) and the biblical novels: *The Nazarene* (1939), *The Apostle* (1943), *Mary* (1949), *Moses* (1951), and *The Prophet* (1955). His first play, *Tsurik gekumen,* published in 1904 and produced (with Asch in the leading role) in 1907, depicts conflicts between traditional and emancipated Jews. The play that brought him international fame, however, was *Got fun Nekome* (GOD OF VENGEANCE, 1907), and he wrote over twenty others. Many of his novels, too, have been dramatized, Asch himself adapting his *Motke Ganef* (*Motke the Thief,* 1917) and *Der T'hilim Yid* (*Salvation,* 1939) into box-office successes. But after the 1920's Asch stopped writing drama. Though he will be remembered primarily as a popular novelist, and though few of his plays are now known, he achieved considerable fame in the Yiddish theatre, and *God of Vengeance,* SABBATAI ZEVI (1908), and some of his one-acters have been translated.

Asch was born in Kutno, Poland, the son of a

Sholem Asch. (*Culver Pictures*)

tavern owner. His orthodox home and the provincial tradesmen's milieu of his youth left their mark on his writing. His earliest works, romantic tales and sketches, were written in Hebrew. After he went to Warsaw in 1898, where he soon became part of Jewish intellectual life, he wrote in German and Yiddish. Quick financial success enabled him to travel. In 1908 he went to Palestine, and the next year to the United States. There he settled at the beginning of World War I, though he continued to travel widely. In 1954 he moved to Israel, where, at least to some extent, he regained the good will of the Jewish community, whose hostility he had aroused with his "Christian" novels, which suggested to many that Asch had become an apostate.

His religious interests were never parochial. Asch's plays present a motley crew of characters, a cross section not only of his Jewish background, but of the world. They include learned rabbis, respectable middle-class families, laborers, and the riffraff: prostitutes, thieves, drunkards, and paupers. Yet however different they may be, Asch's characters search for a common ideal—or faith. This faith is not confined, even in the early plays, to Judaism. The SYMBOLIC one-acter *Nakht* (*Night,* 1916), for example, presents a group of outcasts achieving a momentary ecstasy of brotherhood as they see a vision of the Virgin Mary. In another intense episodic one-acter, *Der Zindiger* (*The Sinner,* 1910), a rabbi exhorts the reluctant earth to receive the corpse of a Jewish sinner, mourned only by a mysterious, probably Gentile, woman in black.

Characteristic particularly of the young Asch's work was eroticism combined with such spiritual themes. His first great hit (*God of Vengeance*), with its brothel setting and portrayal of lesbianism, created a scandal. Another play, *Yiftakh's Tokhter* (1915), frankly deals with another form of sexual awakening. More muted is the one-act *Um Vinter* (*Winter*, 1906), in which a spinster must give way to her younger sister lest it also be too late for her to marry.

The four Yiddish volumes of Asch's dramatic works published in 1922 include sixteen plays: (I) *Yiftakh's Tokhter, Sabbatai Zevi, Amoon un Tamar* (1909); (II) *Meshiakh's Tsayten* (1906, his second play to appear, a tragedy), *Unzer Gloyben* (1914), *A Shnirl Perl, Der Toyter Mentsh;* (III) *Got fun Nekome, Bund fun di Shvakhe, Motke Ganef, Yikhus* (1909, a satire of the Jewish middle class); (IV) *Di Yorshim, Mitn Shtrom* (1905), *Der Zindiger, Um Vinter, Maranen.* Among his other plays are *A Kholem fun mayn Folk* (1906), which contrasts the older and the newer type of Jew; *Der Landsman* (1910), a tragicomedy on American-Jewish life; *Ver is der Foter?;* and two biblical dramas, *Yoysef-spiel* and *Koyln* (both 1928).

While some seventeen volumes of Asch's fiction are available in English, few of the plays have been translated. *Sabbatai Zevi* was republished (with the novel *Kiddush Ha-Shem*) in 1959, and *God of Vengeance* appears in Joseph C. Landis's *The Dybbuk and Other Great Yiddish Plays* (1966). See also A. A. Roback's *The Story of Yiddish Literature* (1940), Chapter XIII of Sol Liptzin's *The Flowering of Yiddish Literature* (1963), and Charles A. Madison's *Yiddish Literature: Its Scope and Major Writers* (1968).

ASIA despite its many countries, immense size, and heavy population, has a theatre that shares a number of characteristics. Especially in the archipelagoes, dance is often more important and more developed than drama. Much of the latter is based on folklore and myths, most commonly the Hindu, Sanskrit *Mahabharata* and *Ramayana* epics; and despite religious prohibitions against personifying the Buddha, JATAKAS are widely popular. This and other Eastern drama is little known in the West, however. Some classics have been produced in Europe and America, most notably King Shudraka's *Mrcchakatika* (*The Little Clay Cart*) and Kalidasa's *Sakoontalā* (*Shakuntalá*). But though a few modern Japanese and Chinese plays have appeared in the West, only the writings of the Bengali RABINDRANATH TAGORE have been widely translated and produced, and even these draw on mythological or religious sources for their inspiration and settings.

In the Far East, the theatre flourishes in JAPAN, KOREA, and CHINA. Buddha dances, pageantry, and playlets depicting Buddha's life are common in Tibet. Remote Mongolia, influenced in modern times by RUSSIA, founded a state theatre in 1945; it produces Western as well as native plays, but the latter remain unknown abroad. The dance is particularly developed in South and Southeast Asia, but though some of the area's countries are predominantly concerned with dance, there also is drama in BURMA, CAMBODIA, INDONESIA, LAOS, MALAYSIA, the PHILIPPINES, THAILAND, and VIETNAM. In South Asia, INDIA was the progenitor of epics widely dramatized throughout the whole continent, and of its best-known modern writer, Tagore; there also has been drama in CEYLON, but less in PAKISTAN (since Islam forbids theatrical representation) and little in Nepal since its independence in 1947. Afghanistan, despite a rich Persian literary heritage, has produced little modern drama except that of the Tajiks noted under IRAN. Other nations in Southwest Asia, collectively part of the Near or MIDDLE EAST, consist of TURKEY, ISRAEL, and the ARAB countries of Iraq, Jordan, Lebanon, Saudi Arabia, and Syria.

Aside from works noted for individual countries, there are major studies dealing with large areas: Faubion Bowers's *Theatre in the East* (1956), which as its subtitle states is "A Survey of Asian Dance and Drama" as well as opera in a dozen Eastern and Southern countries; and James R. Brandon's *Theatre in Southeast Asia* (1967), which is organized on a topical rather than national basis. The University of Kansas publishes the *Afro-Asian Theatre Bulletin* (1965 ff.), which regularly features articles as well as bibliographies of translated plays, work in progress, and new studies.

ASMODÉE, a play in three acts by FRANÇOIS MAURIAC, published in 1938 and produced in 1939. Setting: a country house on the moors south of Bordeaux, late 1930's.

The best known of Mauriac's plays, *Asmodée* has a CHEKHOVian subtlety of characterization and traces of IBSENite dramaturgy, although the bitter, washed-out priest Blaise Couture is a reincarnation of Molière's Tartuffe.

Tutor at the household of an attractive widow he loves and to whom he makes himself indispensable, Couture dominates the family with his fervent piety, which is the more intense for its underlying—and unconscious—hypocrisy. The arrival of a handsome and innocent young Englishman—the Asmodée, "a demon that lifted the roofs off houses to see what went on inside"—uproots and reveals the family's agonies. Both the widow and her daughter, a devout recluse, fall in love with him. Couture leaves angrily, but then returns to help the daughter marry the Englishman and the widow renounce impossible dreams of youthful bliss. Half despairing, Couture realizes that the widow needs him for "this ignoble help" from fleshly temptation. The two resign themselves to a continuation of their former relationship: the widow's haughty submission to Couture's puritanical despotism.

AT THE EXIT (*All' uscita*), a one-act play by LUIGI PIRANDELLO, published in 1916 and produced in 1922. Setting: a country cemetery, 1916.

This "profane mystery play," as he labeled the fantasy, is a dramatization of a story Pirandello published in 1916. The characters are ghosts who recall their earthly lives.

At the exit of the cemetery a dead philosopher indulges in sophistries with a dead fat man who regrets not having enjoyed his garden enough.

His life was troubled by his unfaithful wife and her terrible laugh: "It boils up from her guts like some raging, destructive frenzy." Her lover had killed her and himself, and the murdered woman now reveals that even in death she did not find the warmth she always yearned for in a kiss. A dead boy is equally frustrated in his lifelong desire for a pomegranate; the wife solicitously feeds him one now and, his desires quenched, the dead boy disappears. As she sobs, "What about my desires? Oh God!" her husband's phantom disappears. A living peasant family passes by, their little girl personifying the dead couple's lifelong tragedy: their childlessness. The murdered wife runs wildly after the little girl. Only the philosopher is left: "I'm afraid I alone will always remain here, still reasoning. . . ."

AT THE HAWK'S WELL, a one-act verse play by WILLIAM BUTLER YEATS, produced in 1916 and published in 1917. Setting: a patterned screen before a wall.

The first of FOUR PLAYS FOR DANCERS and one of the Cuchulain plays depicts the hero while still young and unknown.

For fifty years an old man has sat by a well that is guarded by a hawklike woman. She prevents his drinking of its water, which brings immortality, by lulling him to sleep whenever it flows. Young Cuchulain arrives, desirous of the water. When it gushes forth, he too is entranced by the woman's hawk eyes and her dance. He misses his chance and departs for the fateful battle against "the fierce women of the hills," aroused by the hawklike Guardian of the Well.

ATRIDES-TETRALOGY, THE (*Die Atriden-Tetralogie*), by GERHART HAUPTMANN (*"Atriden"* are "descendants of Atreus"): *Iphigenie in Aulis* (IPHIGENIA IN AULIS), *Agamemnons Tod* (AGAMEMNON'S DEATH), *Elektra* (ELECTRA), and *Iphigenie in Delphi* (IPHIGENIA IN DELPHI). Hauptmann's last dramatic work, this blank-verse modernization of the classic myth was composed in 1940–44, during World War II. *Iphigenia in Delphi* was written first, then *Iphigenia in Aulis,* and finally the one-acters that link the longer Iphigenia plays. Hubert Razinger's German edition (1956) of the tetralogy contains extensive commentary, as does Ralph Fiedler's study, *Die späten Dramen Gerhart Hauptmanns* (1954), in which the tetralogy is interpreted as an "eternally valid characterization of the final consequences of human diabolicalness and the rejection of reason."

AUDEN, W[ystan] H[ugh] (1907–), Anglo-American poet, has also written a number of verse plays and librettos. As a dramatist he is most noted for his collaborations with CHRISTOPHER ISHERWOOD on THE DOG BENEATH THE SKIN (1935), THE ASCENT OF F6 (1936), and *On the Frontier* (1938), an EXPRESSIONIST anticapitalist and antiwar melodrama, which is set in the same mythic and English localities as their earlier plays, and characterized by similar language and dramaturgy.

Auden was born in York and educated at Oxford University. He taught at Malvern, worked with the G.P.O. Film Unit in 1935–36, and was a member of the young British leftist group of avant-garde poets in the 1930's. His *Poems* (1930), and *Spain* (1937), which is based on Auden's experiences in the Spanish Civil War, helped to establish his reputation as a major poet even before 1939, when he moved to and settled in the United States. Auden's drama is distinguished literature that has had only very limited success on the boards. It is as variegated as his poetry: mystic and satiric, formal and pop—and intermediary types of language; the characterization, action, and setting are to some extent influenced by those of BERTOLT BRECHT.

Paid on Both Sides (1933) is a short and difficult "charade" about the spiritual and moral collapse of Western civilization, a theme that recurs in most of Auden's dramatic works. Others are *The Dance of Death* (1933), the religious poetic drama *For the Time Being* (1944), an adaptation of John Webster's seventeenth-century play *The Duchess of Malfi* (1946), a translation of Brecht's THE SEVEN DEADLY SINS OF THE PETTY BOURGEOIS, and a number of librettos: Benjamin Britten's *Paul Bunyan* (1941), Mozart's *The Magic Flute* (1956) and *Don Giovanni* (1961), Igor Stravinsky's *The Rake's Progress* (1951, with Chester Kallman), *Delia, or A Masque of Night* (1953, another libretto with Kallman), and Hans Werner Henze's *Elegy for Young Lovers* (1961). *The Age of Anxiety* (1947), for which Auden won the 1948 Pulitzer Prize, is a dramatic poem, an "eclogue" set in a New York bar, in which four characters discuss man's history, express disillusionment, mourn the death of "lost dad" (God), and seek hope in the discovery of other values. Auden also adapted the lyrics for *No More Peace!* (1937), a play by ERNST TOLLER.

Richard Hoggart's *Auden, an Introductory Essay* (1951), Monroe K. Spears's *The Poetry of W. H. Auden* (1963), and John G. Blair's *The Poetic Art of W. H. Auden* (1965) briefly discuss his drama and contain bibliographies.

AUDIBERTI, Jacques (1899–1965), prolific French author born in Antibes and best known for his fifteen novels and his collected verse, also wrote some twenty avant-garde poetic plays. Most of them are characterized by abstruse logorrhea, pagan settings, and melodramatic actions. These underline Audiberti's existentialist perspectives and ARTAUD-inspired obsession with malignant, primitive powers, principally those of sex.

His most commercially successful play was *Le Mal Court* (1947), a fairy tale about a princess seduced by a pretender shortly before her apparently arranged marriage to the real king, who discovers that she has always been surrounded by evil, and realizes that to survive she must herself become ruthless and evil. Among Audiberti's best plays are two satires of the Church, *La Fête noire* (1948) and *La Hobereaute* (1958). In the first, a monster personifying the protagonist's sexual repressions gorges on women in the countryside and is finally destroyed by the protagonist, who grows rich by selling its relics—though life's horror continues. In *La Hobereaute* the title character, a spirit of nature, is forced by a Druid priest to marry the villain rather than the nobleman she loves—and she ultimately dies with both men.

Other notable Audiberti plays are *Quoat-Quoat* (1946), which features a secret agent falling in love with a ship captain's daughter, sentenced to execution, and rejecting rescue by the stone of the Mexican god Quoat-Quoat, which then destroys the ship; the ironic one-act *Les Femmes du bœuf* (1948), in which a virile butcher's effeminate son gets all "the ox's women"; *Pucelle* (1950), a bizarre dramatization of the Joan of Arc story; *Les Naturels du Bordelais* (1952), about a sadistic Don Juan and other sex-preoccupied characters turned into insects; and *La Logeuse* (written in 1954, produced in 1960), whose title character is a modern Circe.

Audiberti's plays were published in four volumes (1948–61) but are not generally available in English. Studies of Audiberti appear in Leonard C. Pronko's *Avant-Garde* (1962), George E. Wellwarth's *The Theater of Protest and Paradox* (1964), and Jacques Guicharnaud's *Modern French Theatre* (1967).

AUSTRALIA produced little drama of significance before the 1950's, when SUMMER OF THE SEVENTEENTH DOLL by RAY LAWLER became the first Australian play to achieve international renown. Good amateur and little theatre groups had presented classics and foreign plays earlier, but though there was some native drama, the nineteenth-century Australian theatre, like England's and America's, was literarily undistinguished. At the turn of the century some of the younger writers, notably LOUIS ESSON, were interested in the Irish literary movement, and attempted to establish something comparable in Australia. They were unsuccessful, and what Australian drama there was remained provincial, melodramatic, and derivative. During the first decades of the twentieth century, the long-touring and repeatedly filmed *On Our Selection,* based on the *Bulletin* sketches of Steele Rudd (pen name of Arthur Hoey Davis, 1868–1935), was the most popular of the crude farce melodramas. Many writers attempted a literary drama, often in verse: for the most part it was pedestrian and archaic, as in *A Man of His Time* (1927, about Benvenuto Cellini) and other plays by Helen Simpson (1898–1940), and in those by Jack Lindsay (1900–   ); it did not affect the trend of playwriting, which moved steadily toward WELL-MADE and NATURALISTIC drama. The little theatres produced work in this genre by such writers as Vance Palmer (1885–1959), Sydney Tomholt (1890?–1967), Henrietta Drake-Brockman (1901–68), Betty Roland (1903–   ), George Dann (1904–   ), and Alexander Turner (1907–   ), and some of these were published. Since Australians continued to esteem foreign (particularly British) drama and to denigrate their own, Australia's professional writers confined themselves to poetry and fiction, which had possibilities of publication, or—like distinguished native actors and opera stars—they made their careers outside Australia.

In 1955 the government-subsidized Elizabethan Theatre Trust was established, and almost immediately produced Lawler's play. The Trust was eager to encourage more local drama, but despite its efforts and those of the little theatres that remained the most consistent producers of native plays, only a few names have become generally known. Alan Seymour's (1927–   ) *The One Day of the Year* (1962) achieved considerable local popularity; it features a blustering elevator operator who has been called Australia's Archie Rice and Willie Loman.

Particularly esteemed in Australia in the 1960's were Patrick White (1912–   ) and Douglas A. Stewart (1913–   ). White's reputation as a playwright (he was born in London and is better known as a novelist) rests on his *Four Plays* (1965): *The Ham Funeral* (written in 1947, but not produced until 1961), a moving contemporary morality; *The Season at Sarsaparilla* (1961), "a Charade of Suburbia" that evidences White's ability to mix styles and techniques effectively; *A Cheery Soul* (1962), another comedy of the Sydney suburb Sarsaparilla; and *Night on Bald Mountain* (1962), a serious contemporary drama set in New South Wales. The New Zealand-born Stewart is a poet and a verse playwright who made his reputation in 1943 with the widely broadcast *Fire on the Snow,* a blank-verse radio play on Scott's expedition to the South Pole, and he is distinguished for other radio and stage drama, the latter including *Shipwreck* (1947), the Maori legend-play *The Golden Lover* (1958), and the "historical comedy" ballad *Fisher's Ghost* (1960); his best-known drama is *Ned Kelly* (1943), a naturalistic blank-verse depiction of an outlaw from the Australian bush struggling against conformist metropolitan society.

Other playwrights include novelists like Jack McKinney (1893–1966), Sumner Locke-Elliot (1917–   ), Hal Porter (1917–   ), and Ray Mathew (1929–   ). McKinney, who started writing plays only in the last few years of his life, succeeded best with *The Well* (1959), which is, according to its subtitle, a comic "universal folk tale in an Australian idiom," depicting a Romeo and Juliet love story on a poor farm. Locke-Elliot's plays include *Interval* (1942); *Rusty Bugles* (1948), a series of comic military vignettes whose salty language elicited police censorship—and thus popularized the play; and *Buy Me Blue Ribbons,* a farce about the American theatre staged in New York in 1950. Porter, known principally for his stories, also wrote a sinister melodrama, *The Tower* (1963), and *Toda-San* (published as *The Professor,* 1965), a play about Australians in Japan. Among Mathew's plays are *We Find the Bunyip* (1955), a comedy set in a New South Wales pub; and *A Spring Song* (1961), a thoughtful love comedy. These and the many other Australian playwrights active in the past decades have worked in differing styles and dealt with many subjects, with perhaps disproportionately large numbers of plays set in slums. Despite some interesting drama, however, there has as yet been comparatively little of universal interest.

Anthologies include *Three Australian Plays* (1963) in which appears a concise survey of Australian drama by H. G. Kippax together with Stewart's *Ned Kelly,* Seymour's *The One Day of the Year,* and Porter's *The Tower;* and *Three Australian Plays* (1968), with an introduction by Eunice Hanger and Locke-Elliot's *Rusty Bugles,* Mathew's *We Find the Bunyip,* and McKinney's *The Well.* Other collections are the three-volume *Australian One-Act Plays* (1962–67) and *Six Australian One-Act Plays* (1970). *The Literature of Australia* (1964), edited by Geoffrey Dutton, has essays on the drama and on individual writers, with bibliographies. A book-length study is Leslie Rees's *Towards an Australian Drama* (1953). Major works that include important material on drama are the two-volume studies by, respectively, Edmund Morris Miller and Henry M. Green, *Australian Literature from Its Beginnings to 1935* (1940) and *A History of Australian Literature* (1961).

AUSTRIA. Austrian drama developed together with that of Germany, whose language it shares. Many Austrian playwrights—and directors like Max Reinhardt—worked and flourished in Germany. Nonetheless, there is a theatre that is distinctively of the Hapsburgs' Austro-Hungarian empire and, after 1918, of the Austrian republic. Its earliest dramatists were the poet Franz Grillparzer (1791–1872) and the folk playwrights Ferdinand Raimund (1790–1836) and Johann Nestroy (1802–62), one of whose dialect dramas THORNTON WILDER adapted as THE MATCHMAKER. Ludwig Anzengruber (1839–89) promoted NATURALISM with satires of the middle class like *Das vierte Gebot* (1877)—the second German play produced in Berlin's Freie Bühne. HUGO VON HOFMANNSTHAL brought poetry to the modern Austrian theatre, while naturalism and eroticism characterize the plays of ARTHUR SCHNITZLER.

Schnitzler and Hofmannsthal, the major modern Austrian dramatists, belonged to the *Jungwien* (Young Vienna) association of writers that began to dominate Austrian letters in the 1890's. Named by its most articulate spokesman, HERMANN BAHR, this informal group strove to revitalize Austrian literature. These writers followed along the general lines of their distinguished predecessors. Notable verse drama, aside from that of Hofmannsthal, was written by his disciple MAX MELL, by ANTON WILDGANS, and by another *Jungwiener,* RICHARD BEER-HOFMANN. Wildgans linked this movement with naturalism—of which Schnitzler was the outstanding practitioner—and with EXPRESSIONISM, while Beer-Hofmann produced biblical drama from the perspective of Austria's Judaic writers. Among these should be noted Zionism's founder, Theodor Herzl (1860–1904), also a playwright, whose *Das neue Ghetto* (1897) portrays the struggles of assimilated Jews against the Viennese anti-Semitism dramatized in Ferdinand Bronner's *Schmelz, der Nibelunge* (1905).* Austrian expressionist playwrights included the painter OSKAR KOKOSCHKA and Hans Kaltneker (1895–1919), whose "trilogy of redemption" (1919) espouses brotherly love as the universal panacea in *Das Bergwerk* and illustrates it with a criminal redeemed by his death (*Die Opferung*) and with a reformed lesbian (*Die Schwester*). Folk drama was written by KARL SCHÖNHERR and by his fellow-Tyrolean Franz Kranewitter (1860–1938), who portrayed the native heroes *Michel Gaissmayr* (1899) and *Andre Hofer* (1900), and produced a series of one-acters on human passions, *Die sieben Todsünden* (1910–25). Among other reputations established before World War I were those of distinguished story tellers and essayists who also wrote drama: Felix Salten (pseudonym of Siegmund Salzmann, 1869–1945), whose plays include a naturalist soldier tragedy (*Der Gemeine,* 1901), a dramatization of a court scandal (*Luise von Koburg,* 1932), and witty one-acters; and Raoul Auernheimer (1876–1948), who produced Viennese comedies of manners (like *Das Paar nach der Mode,* 1913) and histories, notably one on the great lover, *Casanova in Wien* (1924).

World War I inspired two important pacifist plays: Chlumberg's MIRACLE AT VERDUN, and *Die letzten Tage der Menschheit* by KARL KRAUS. Another bitter antiwar play was *Wer will unter die Soldaten?* (1930) by Hermann Heinz Ortner (1895–1956), who also wrote Catholic miracle plays and portrayed *Beethoven* (1935) and *Isabella von Spanien* (1938), the latter as enamored of a rival of Columbus, who, in turn, is supported by King Ferdinand. Generally popular were the history plays, too, of FERDINAND BRUCKNER; FRANZ CSOKOR; Richard Duschinsky (1897–), the most successful among whose Austrian histories was an episodic biography anticipating Housman's VICTORIA REGINA, *Kaiser Franz Joseph I von Österreich* (1931); and Georg Rendl's (1903–) similar drama on the empress, *Elisabeth, Kaiserin von Österreich* (1937).

Although Vienna's gaiety and charm virtually disappeared with World War I and thus dated Schnitzler, he had notable successors in ALEXANDER LERNET-HOLENIA, FRIEDRICH SCHREYVOGL, and ÖDÖN VON HORVATH. Less acerbic popular Viennese comedies were *Mit der Liebe spielen* (1920, also produced as *Caprice*) by Sil-Vara (pseudonym of Geza Silberer, 1876–1938), and *Kleine Komödie* (*Little Comedy,* 1927; also produced as *By Candle Light* and in P. G. Wodehouse's [1881–] adaptation *Candle-Light*) by Siegfried Geyer (d. 1945). Hans Mueller (1882–1950), most successful with his internationally produced musical comedy *Im weissen Rössl* (*White Horse Inn,* 1930), was a prolific and skillful playwright popular for his romantic and patriotic melodramas, including one on Galileo, *Die Sterne* (1919). Stefan Kamare (1885–1945) wrote romantic comedy hits, including *Leinen aus Irland* (1929), set amidst shady prewar commercial and political huckstering; and *Der*

* Bronner's other writing is noted in the entry on his son, ARNOLT BRONNEN.

Junge Baron Neuhaus (1933), a historical romance set in Maria Theresa's court. A comedy by Hermann Ungar (1893–1929), *Die Gartenlaube* (1929), was praised for its fine characterizations of provincial philistines destroyed by a spiteful servant. Achieving some renown for their drama, too, were the novelists STEFAN ZWEIG, FRANZ WERFEL, and Robert Musil (1880–1942), who wrote an expressionist study of marital problems among intellectuals (*Die Schwärmer,* 1921) and a farce. Finally, if only because of his work in popularizing BERNARD SHAW, must be noted the novelist-playwright SIEGFRIED TREBITSCH.

The 1938 Anschluss ended, until 1945, Austria's independence and made German Nazism Austria's official government. RICHARD BILLINGER had anticipated its fashionable "blood-and-soil" ideology, but the characteristic Austrian Nazi playwright was ERWIN KOLBENHEYER. His and other drama during the Anschluss parallels the period's German productions.

The first important Austrian playwright after World War II, FRITZ HOCHWÄLDER, had started and continued to do his work in Switzerland. Others who began to gain distinction were Franz Hrastnik (1904–), a painter who wrote a play on Van Gogh (*Vincent,* 1945) and whose later plays include *Therese Krones* (1956) and *Das Fräulein vom Kahlenberg* (1958); Elias Canetti (1905–), a Bulgarian-born novelist and poet who wrote a play in 1932 (*Hochzeit*) but produced most of his dramas after the war, notably *Komödie der Eitelkeit* (1950) and *Die Befristeten* (1956), which features characters as "acoustic masks"; Hans Weigel (1908–), a critic and journalist who also wrote musical comedies, satiric reviews, fantasies, and farces; Hans Holt (1909–), an actor-playwright whose hit was the comedy *Der Herzspezialist* (1957); Rudolf Bayr (1919–), a poet and short-story writer who adapted classical Greek plays and wrote poetic dramas based on classical myths; Harald Zusanek (1922–), a poet and short-story writer whose popular plays include *Warum gräbst du, Centurio?* (1949), *Jean von der Tonne* (1954), and *Schloss in Europa* (1960); Kurt Klinger (1928–), a poet and playwright whose dramas include *Odysseus muss wieder reisen* (1954) and an adaptation of Carlo Goldoni's *La casa nova, Die neue Wohnung* (1960); and Peter Handke (1942–), whose first full-length play, *Kaspar* (1967), based on the celebrated "feral foundling" Kaspar Hauser case and presenting his terrifying "education" in simultaneous actions in dramaturgy influenced by the theatre of the ABSURD, was published in English with two "antiplay" sketches, *Publikumsbeschimpfung* (*Offending the Public,* 1966) and *Selbstbezichtigung* (*Self-Accusation,* 1966).

English translations as well as histories and studies of Austrian drama are included in the works noted under GERMANY. Henry Schnitzler, the playwright's son, deals specifically with modern Austrian drama in his essay in *A History of Modern Drama* (1947), edited by Barrett H. Clark and George Freedley.

AUTUMN GARDEN, THE, a play in three acts by LILLIAN HELLMAN, published and produced in 1951. Setting: a summer resort on the Gulf of Mexico, September 1949.

Though this was praised by some as Lillian Hellman's most interesting play and her finest, it failed commercially. A somewhat listless CHEKHOVian derivative, it is set in a Southern "HEARTBREAK HOUSE" temporarily peopled by about a dozen wistful, decadent, empty, or otherwise purposeless characters. The aged matriarch characterizes them as she chides the bounder of the play; attributing his constant touching of people to stifled sensuality, she remarks, "One should have sensuality whole or not at all. Don't you find pecking at it ungratifying?" And she concludes, "There are many of you: the touchers and the leaners. All since the depression, is my theory."

AWAKE AND SING!, a play in three acts by CLIFFORD ODETS, published and produced in 1935. Setting: a Bronx apartment, 1930's.

This was the first success both for Odets and for the Group Theatre, and it had a major New York revival in 1970. Because of its comic-tragic mixture and apparently careless plotting, the play has been likened to those of ANTON CHEKHOV; but as was noted by Harold Clurman, the Group's director, "tenement tenderness" and "improvisatory spontaneousness" make it more akin to the drama of SEAN O'CASEY, particularly to JUNO AND THE PAYCOCK. The title is from Isaiah 26:19.

Act I. Bessie Berger is the spirited and bullying but kindly matriarch in a poor Jewish family. Her husband is a sententious failure who quotes Teddy Roosevelt, and all of them "struggle for life amidst petty conditions." When Bessie tries to break her son Ralph's love for a poor orphan, her father Jacob, a sentimental Marxist dreamer who plays Caruso records, urges Ralph to rebel: "Go out and fight so life shouldn't be printed on dollar bills." Ralph's sister, Hennie, is in love with Moe Axelrod, an embittered war cripple; when Hennie gets pregnant, Bessie makes her marry a meek suitor, a recent immigrant who is hypersensitive but, Bessie thinks, is bound to make "a good living."

Act II. A year later Ralph and Hennie are more depressed than ever. Their lives and the views of old Jacob and Moe Axelrod are contrasted with those of Bessie's brother, a successful and heartless capitalist. When Hennie reveals the truth about her baby's paternity and Ralph acrimoniously blames Bessie for having trapped her daughter's husband, the matriarch angrily smashes her father's records. Old Jacob, crushed but eager to give Ralph a chance in life with his insurance, commits suicide.

Act III. Ralph is inspired by the memory of his grandfather's sacrifice, and he remembers his exhortations to "do" and to "act," to "Awake and sing, ye that dwell in dust," so that "life shouldn't be printed on dollar bills." Hennie is persuaded to desert her family and elope with Moe Axelrod, her proud lover, who urges her, "There's one life to live! Live it!" Ralph renounces the insurance money his mother wants for the whole family: "Did Jake die for us to fight about nickels?" Determined to give up his selfish love and become a radical agitator for a new society, Ralph feels reborn: "I'm one week old! I want the whole city to hear it—fresh blood, arms. We got 'em. We're glad we're living."

AYMÉ, Marcel (1902–67), French writer, though more famous as a novelist, became known as a playwright in the English-speaking world with a delightfully irreverent and risqué satire, CLÉRAMBARD (1950). Born in Joigny, raised by various relatives, and educated haphazardly, Aymé gave up medical school to write. At first he supported himself by selling insurance, clerking, and doing other odd jobs. His early writings were somber peasant studies, but Aymé gradually found his natural style in the biting irony of which *Clérambard* is characteristic. He won recognition with his fourth novel, *La Table aux Crevés* (1929), for which he wrote a screenplay in 1952. His first play, the tragicomedy *Lucienne et le boucher,* was written in 1932 but not produced until 1948. Other plays inc'ude *La Tête des autres* (1952), a satire on law; *Les Quatre Vérités* (1954), a satire of jealousy; *Les Oiseaux de lune* (1956); and *La Mouche bleue* (1957) and *Louisiana* (1961), both anti-American. He adapted Miller's THE CRUCIBLE in 1955.

Clérambard is available in Wallace Fowlie's collection of *Four Modern French Comedies* (1960) with an introduction on Aymé and a bibliography.

B

BAAL, a play by BERTOLT BRECHT, published in 1922 and produced in 1923. Setting: taverns, rooms, dark woods and meadows, etc., in contemporary Germany.

This, Brecht's first play, was written in 1918. It consists of an introductory "Hymn" and twenty-two short, EXPRESSIONISTIC scenes. These feature the activities and songs of the swinish but exuberantly poetic Baal, a primitive Bohemian bum immersed in sensuality and nature. The songs (lyrics and music) are by Brecht. For the Viennese production of *Baal* in 1926, HUGO VON HOFMANNSTHAL introduced Brecht's dramaturgy of violence and shock with a brief prologue-play, "Das Theater des Neuen" ("The Theatre of the New").

Baal sings and plays his guitar in bars and cheap clubs. Despite his coarse, besotted ugliness, he attracts women. He is shown as he seduces, and then cruelly discards and destroys, various women he wants—"no matter which one, but one with a face like that of a woman." Among others are a possible benefactor's wife, a young admirer's seventeen-year-old sweetheart, and a girl Baal simply grabs off the street outside his lodging. Traveling through the country, he drinks, brawls, cheats, whores—and poetically exalts nature. The girl he picked off the street, now pregnant and desperately in love, follows him; when he rejects her brutally, she commits suicide. Even his traveling companion Ekart is appalled by his ruthless selfishness. Baal is in love with Ekart, though he still needs women as well. In a jealous rage when he sees his lover with a waitress on his lap, Baal kills Ekart and escapes. Now a fugitive, he is dying in a forest hut. Baal begs some woodcutters to stay with him, but at last it is his turn to be cruelly discarded. Left alone, he is delirious as he tries to get out: "I'm not a rat. Outside there must be light." Crawling out like a beast, he curses—and thinks of the heavens: "The stars—hm."

BABEL, Isaak [Emmanuilovich] (1894–1941), Russian author, was among the most brilliant Soviet—perhaps international—writers of the 1920's and 1930's. Eventually incurring the displeasure of the authorities, he was published and mentioned with decreasing frequency. Babel was one of the many who simply disappeared: during one of the purges of the late 1930's he was arrested and sent to a concentration camp, where he died—or was killed. The date of his death did not become known until his official posthumous rehabilitation in 1957, when his *Izbrannoe* (*Selected Works*) were published. Best known among his writings are *Konarmiya* (*Red Cavalry,* 1926), a collection of short stories, some of which had made him famous three years earlier; *Yevreiskie rasskazy* (*Jewish Tales,* 1927), which, with other stories, became known as the *Odessa Tales;* and his two plays, *Zakat* (SUNSET, 1928) and MARYA (1935). Like his stories, these plays are tragicomedies with similar settings, and one of them features the naïve but ruthless Robin Hood kind of gangster from the *Odessa Tales,* Benya Krik. The plays reflect Babel's unique and masterful fiction: terse, often truncated dialogue; a penchant for romance and exoticism, but modified by irony and cruelty; and a pervasive effect of both terror and compassion.

Born to a small merchant family in the Moldavanka district of Odessa, Babel studied the Talmud and eventually gained admission to a Russian secondary school. The acceptance of a Jew by the severely restrictive school is narrated in one of Babel's famous autobiographical stories, "Istoriya moei golubyatni" ("The Story of My Dovecote," 1927). At twenty he was in St. Petersburg, where he lived as a poor Bohemian—and in constant danger, because he did not have the residence certificate required of Jews. It was MAXIM GORKY, then the editor of *Letopis,* who published his first stories in 1916. But Gorky declined the many stories he subsequently continued to submit, and advised Babel to "go among the people." Babel thereupon, as he later recalled, "traveled many roads and witnessed many battles." He participated in the revolutionary Civil War, and became a member of Marshal Budyonny's famous cavalry unit that fought against Poland in 1920. Then he returned to Odessa, where he operated a printing press. After the 1923 success of his Cossack stories he devoted himself exclusively to literature. During the enforced silence of his last years Babel wrote another play, which he considered his best. (In fact, he ultimately believed drama to be his métier.) But this play, like his other unpublished manuscripts, was confiscated and disappeared with him.

Sunset was published in *Noonday 3* (1960), and produced in New York in 1966. *Marya* is among the *Three Soviet Plays* (1966) edited by Michael Glenny, and is prefaced by an essay on Babel. See also Natalie Babel's edition of *Isaac Babel: The Lonely Years, 1925–1939* (1964) and the sections on Babel in Gleb Struve's *Soviet Russian Literature 1917–50* (1951), Vera Alexandrova's *A History of Soviet Literature* (1963), and Edward J. Brown's *Russian Literature Since the Revolution* (revised 1969); all contain bibliographies.

BACCHUS, a play in three acts by JEAN COCTEAU, produced in 1951 and published in 1952. Setting:

a castle in a German town near Switzerland, 1523.

Cocteau described this as "a play concerning hard goodness, which I oppose to soft goodness," a play dealing with the "terrible loneliness of youth." Despite its conventional dramaturgy, the play (set at the time of the German Reformation) was criticized as scandalously heretical. Much of the second act consists of theological discussions between a visiting cardinal and the young protagonist.

Hans is a handsome peasant whose mind became unhinged when he (like Pirandello's HENRY IV) was victimized by sporting aristocrats. Regaining his sanity when forced to witness the torture of his friends, Hans has kept up a pretense of feeblemindedness. He is chosen as the absolute king who reigns for seven days during the Bacchus festival—largely through the efforts of the duke's daughter, whose lover Hans becomes. Then he reveals his sanity and executes his program: "To awaken the sleeping strength of love. To abolish fear. To be kind as others are unkind. To love as they hate. To kill hatred." A long debate pits Hans's anarchic idealism against the cardinal's (and the Church's) "hard," orderly goodness. As his reign ends, Hans has aroused everyone's enmity with his program. He refuses to be saved by the cardinal and courts death (saintly martyrdom) by the howling mobs. Shot by an admirer, he escapes the stake, and the cardinal uses a "pious lie" to enable Hans to be buried in holy ground.

BACK TO METHUSELAH, a play cycle in five parts by BERNARD SHAW, published in 1921 and produced in 1922. Setting: Garden of Eden, Mesopotamia, and Britain, 4004 B.C.—A.D. 31920.

The thirty-thousand-word preface to Shaw's ninety-thousand-word play cycle is a scientific-religious explanation of what he called his "Metabiological Pentateuch": only a longer lifespan can give men the impetus, knowledge, and experience needed to save themselves from the destruction they now are capable of wreaking. Shaw expressed his faith that longevity, like other mutations the species had needed and undergone, can be willed, in accord with the creative evolutionary (or vitalist) theories of Jean Lamarck and Samuel Butler. The play illustrates these theories, and is the most explicit dramatization of the convictions that underlie all Shaw's plays. He considered *Back to Methuselah* his masterpiece, but despite its delightful satire and profound examination of men's problems, the scintillating dramatic passages occasionally give way to declamation. Too long to be performed in one evening, the play has been produced infrequently. But it has been widely read for the light it sheds on the mind and drama of Bernard Shaw as well as for its considerable intrinsic merits.

Part I. In the Beginning. Act I. Adam and Eve are troubled at their first confrontation with a dead animal in the Garden of Eden. A beautiful and wise Serpent tells them of Lilith, who with "imagination" and a "mighty will" renewed life by dividing herself into Adam and Eve. They learn of hope, fear, love, and jealousy: Adam's fear and recurring weariness prove stronger than Eve's hope. He rejects immortality and uncertainty, and decides to die after one thousand years. They vow lifetime faithfulness to each other (thus establishing marriage) and the Serpent, knowing that "life must not cease," starts the evolutionary chain by instructing Eve in procreation.

Act II. Over three centuries later in Mesopotamia, Cain, a fighting man of power, attempts to convert the toiling Adam to his way of life. Eve the creator deprecates "Man the destroyer," through whom already "death is gaining on life," but observes that not all her many descendants are toilers or fighters: among them are also an occasional artist, inventor, scientist, and prophet—"always creating either things or wisdom, or at least dreaming of them." She consoles the weary Adam, who is nonetheless determined to live out his one thousand years, that man shall not always live by bread alone: there will be something else. "We do not yet know what it is; but some day we shall find out; and then we will live on that alone; and there shall be no more digging nor spinning, nor fighting nor killing."

Part II. The Gospel of the Brothers Barnabas. Shortly after World War I, the biologist Conrad Barnabas and his brother Franklyn discuss their new theory: in order to attain real knowledge and power, men must use creative evolution and *will* themselves a lifespan of three hundred years. Joined by the young local rector William Haslam, Franklyn's daughter, and the two politicians Joyce Burge and Lubin (caricatures of Lloyd George and Asquith), they engage in a stimulating (and highly satirical) discussion on politics. The Barnabas brothers finally suggest their idea of longevity, and the interested politicians immediately want to adopt the slogan "Back to Methuselah!" to win their next election; but they dismiss the possibility of longevity as absurd when they find that it cannot be attained by an elixir. The brothers nonetheless argue creative evolution: reconstructing the Serpent's secret "of perpetuating life without putting on any single creature the terrible burden of immortality," they insist that the force behind evolution is irresistible: "if it cannot do it through us, it will produce some more capable agents." They are confident that men's souls "will know that they must, if the world is to be saved," will longevity into being, and that soon "the thing will happen."

Part III. The Thing Happens. Some two hundred and fifty years later, in 2170, President Burge-Lubin (a descendant of the politicians) tells Accountant-General Barnabas (a descendant of Conrad) that a new antidrowning invention may throw off his actuarial figures. In a conference with Burge-Lubin, Chief Secretary Confucius attributes the excellent administration of British affairs to the Negresses and Chinese, who now do the actual governing. The flustered Barnabas storms in: he has just learned that the Archbishop of York and four other famous people, who had all been reported drowned in past ages, are all one and the same man. When the Archbishop enters, he turns out to be William Haslam, now two hundred and eighty-three but looking like a well-preserved fifty-year-old. He admits that he staged mock drownings because "I was old enough to know and fear the ferocious hatred with which human animals, like all other animals, turn upon any unhappy individual who has the misfortune to be unlike themselves in every respect." Mrs. Lutestring, the attractive Domestic Minister who appears to be in the prime of her life, is revealed as Franklyn Barnabas's parlormaid of two hundred and fifty years ago. The two talk of the glory—despite the difficulty—of such long lives, and of the childishness of "short-lived" people, particularly the English. Though they have outgrown sensual pleasures, they decide to marry so they can perpetuate their race. Barnabas wants to have them—and other such "privileged" monsters who probably exist now—killed, and the disturbed Burge-Lubin is consoled only when Confucius assures him that while this vital force of evolution was inevitable and is unbeatable, anyone may be "of the elect." Becoming prudent in anticipation of longevity, Burge-Lubin foregoes the risks of an assignation with his attractive Negress Minister of Health.

Part IV. Tragedy of an Elderly Gentleman. Act I. It is now the year 3000. A distinguished Elderly Gentleman from Baghdad, the capital of the British Commonwealth (the British Isles have been appropriated by the longlivers), has come to Ireland with his prime minister and an emperor, who wants to consult the oracle in the land of the longlivers. He is warned that abnormal shortlivers like them are here endangered by "a deadly disease called discouragement" and therefore must always be attended by a nurse. Turned over to the young longliver Zoo, he is repeatedly deflated for his pompous and dated ideas. Though the Elderly Gentleman finally angers Zoo, she takes him to rejoin his friends at the temple in Galway.

Act II. Before the temple, one of the visitors, the arrogant emperor (a Cain-Napoleon man of power), stops the veiled Oracle and demands advice without the usual mummery; but she quickly destroys his bravado, and he rushes away. Zoo brings in the Elderly Gentleman and the rest of the party, and as they await the Oracle they argue about the longlivers' colonization (or extermination) plan.

Act III. Openly contemptuous, Zoo and the Oracle go through the mummery of a show that nonetheless impresses the visitors. The prime minister asks for tactical political advice, as his predecessor had done to win the election, and the Oracle answers as she had answered the predecessor: "Go home, poor fool." The Elderly Gentleman, feeling that he cannot return and live with the lies the prime minister will tell the electorate (as his predecessor had done), begs to be allowed to stay. Pityingly, the Oracle finally looks at him—whereupon he dies: "Poor shortlived thing! What else could I do for you?"

Part V. As Far As Thought Can Reach. The year is 31920, by which time children hatch from eggs as adolescents of seventeen and have but four years to spend on play and love. They then become Ancients, who live for many centuries, without food or sleep, until felled by an accident. They spend all their time in deep contemplation, but "one moment of the ecstasy of [our] life," a passing Ancient tells a group of frolicking youths who deplore such apparent dullness, "would strike you dead." After the hatching of a new adolescent, the youths hold an art festival: one of them (Pygmalion) has sculptured two beautiful living twentieth-century figures (Ozymandias and Cleopatra-Semiramis), who soon quarrel, kill Pygmalion, and must be exterminated by an Ancient. "Art is the magic mirror you make to reflect your invisible dreams in visible pictures," the Ancients explain; because they have "a direct sense of life," they have outgrown art. Instead, the Ancients search for ways of reaching their destiny: immortality as a vortex, thought without body. After they leave, the ghosts of the first living creatures appear and comment on man's progress. The Serpent feels justified in having chosen "wisdom and the knowledge of good and evil; and now there is no evil; and wisdom and good are one." But Lilith, pleased though she is with men's last-minute redemption and subsequent progress, is most pleased that "they are still not satisfied." Men must "press on to the goal of redemption from the flesh, to the vortex freed from matter, to the whirlpool in pure intelligence that, when the world began, was a whirlpool in pure force." She does not know what lies beyond that, but "it is enough that there is a beyond."

BACON, Frank (1864–1922), American actor, achieved his greatest fame with the portrayal of a genial old liar, "Lightnin'" Bill Jones, in LIGHTNIN' (1918). Bacon himself wrote the play, based on his earlier vaudeville sketch *Truthful Jones,* with WINCHELL SMITH, and until shortly before his death starred in its title role. The lovable tippler is a Yankee character in the tradition of Rip Van Winkle; in fact, Bacon modeled his performance on the portrayal of Rip by Joseph Jefferson, whom he resembled physically.

Born in California, Bacon played in vaudeville shows with his wife and children. He wrote and collaborated on a few other plays, none of them very popular.

BADEN-BADEN DIDACTIC PIECE ON ACQUIESCENCE, THE (*Das Badener Lehrstück vom Einverständnis*), an oratorio in eleven short scenes by BERTOLT BRECHT (music by Paul Hindemith), produced (at the Baden-Baden Music Festival) in 1929 and published in 1930. Setting: concert platform with airplane wreckage.

Brecht's and Hindemith's disagreements, detailed in their published "Notes," eventually prevented further performances of this work. It has also been translated as *A Lesson in Acquiescence.*

In response to the pleas for help of four dying airmen, two choruses debate the question: Should one help men? An interlude presents a short film picturing men's cruelty to men, and the knockabout dismemberment of a clown by others. The choruses decide: In this world, the answer to the above question must be "No." The pilot is unwilling to accept this decision—and must die. The others acquiesce, and therefore may live. But they are instructed: "Change the world, change yourselves! / Renounce yourselves!"

BAGNOLD, Enid [Lady Jones] (1889–), English novelist, also wrote a number of plays, the most distinguished of which is THE CHALK GARDEN (1954). She was born in Rochester (Kent) and married the chairman of Reuter's news agency, Sir Roderick Jones. Her first work to be staged was her novel *Serena Blandish* (1924), adapted by S. N. BEHRMAN in 1929. Her own first play was *Lottie Dundass* (1943), whose title character, the descendant of a great homicidal actor, ironically succeeds in realizing her wish to go on the stage. Others are a dramatization of her 1935 novel *National Velvet* (1946, which was filmed), *Poor Judas* (1946, whose protagonist is a writer tortured by his mediocrity), *Gertie* (1952, titled *Little Idiot* in England), *The Last Joke* (1960), and *The Chinese Prime Minister* (1964), a fantasy about aging whose protagonist, a famous septuagenarian actress, wants to end her career and gain the veneration and wisdom accorded retired Chinese statesmen. This play is typical of Enid Bagnold's work: urbane, amusing, intelligent, and gentle. *Call Me Jacky* (1968), her eighth play, features an overly permissive old lady.

Her *Theatre* (1951) consists of *Lottie Dundass* and *Poor Judas,* and the *Four Plays by Enid Bagnold* are *The Chalk Garden, The Last Joke, The Chinese Prime Minister,* and *Call Me Jacky. Enid Bagnold's Autobiography* was published in 1969.

BAHR, Hermann (1863–1934), Austrian playwright, critic, and novelist, was the leading member of the long-dominant *Jungwien* group of his country's greatest writers. Sometimes called a "lesser SCHNITZLER," Bahr strove to modernize and elevate Austrian literature, and experimented with various styles in his fiction, essays, diaries, and some eighty plays. By far the most successful among the plays was his sophisticated four-character comedy *Das Konzert* (*The Concert,* 1909), in which a clever wife, employing jealousy to end the perpetual infidelities of her concert-pianist husband, joins his mountain love nest with a physician, the husband of his latest conquest—who comes to appreciate her husband just as the pianist learns how much he really needs his wife. Many of the prolific Bahr's other plays, though usually derivative of one writer or another, also became popular successes.

Bahr was born in Linz, the son of a notary and his gifted wife, from whom the boy inherited his talents for dialogue. He studied in Paris, traveled widely, and, as a singularly versatile journalist-critic, espoused different literary fashions. Heralding NATURALISM in the 1890's, he almost immediately anticipated the reaction to it and championed such other "isms" as neoromanticism, SYMBOLISM, and, in the following decades, EXPRESSIONISM.

His drama ranged just as widely, from the idealism of his IBSENite first play, *Die neuen Menschen* (1887), which glorifies feelings over impersonal reason, to society comedies like *The Concert.* Among notable other plays are *Die Mutter* (1891), a once-shocking STRINDBERGian portrayal of a neurotically possessive mother; *Josephine* (1897?), an almost SHAVian comedy about the twenty-six-year-old Napoleon preoccupied with passion for his young wife, who, tired of his jealous scenes, manages to have him sent to battle and thus loses the love she then yearns for; *Der Meister* (1904), whose protagonist attempts to master everyone with his cold reason, and thereby loses his wife; *Die Andere* (1905), the tragedy of a woman with a split personality; *Die Kinder* (1910), a comedy suggesting the speciousness of filial blood ties; *Das Tänzchen* (1911), a satire of the German Junkers; and *Das Prinzip* (1912), a popular comic variation of *Der Meister,* featuring a man of principles.

In Berlin in the heyday of naturalism, Bahr edited the literary review of the Freie Bühne, and in 1906 he managed the Berlin Deutsches Theater. He died in Munich. Though a man of the world, he embodied the Austrian spirit. *Theater* (1897), a narrative of Viennese wit and charm, is typical of his novels. Bahr also wrote an autobiography, *Selbstbildnis* (1923). *The Concert* was published in English, and a discussion of others of his plays appears in Henry Schnitzler's essay on Austrian drama in Barrett H. Clark and George Freedley's *A History of Modern Drama* (1947). The bibliography in H. F. Garten's *Modern German Drama* (1964) lists Bahr's books on literary and art criticism.

BALCONY, THE (*Le Balcon*), a play in nine scenes by JEAN GENET, published in 1956 and produced in 1957. Setting: "Le Grand Balcon," a brothel in a modern European country torn by revolution.

This highly theatrical work shocked audiences; it quickly became one of Genet's most successful plays and a popular film. A SYMBOLIC attack on society and its "mirror games" assaults the audience with Genet's view of the human condition as well as of the theatre. Illusion is fused with reality in ritualistic sex fantasies of power. The ceremonial bordello episodes are divided from the rest of the play by the sixth scene. Thereafter, however, the play's symbolism is obfuscated by the intrusion of the real world.

Scene 1. A side mirror pointed at the audience reflects an unmade bed, but the setting represents a sacristy. A provocatively dressed young woman dries her hands as a larger-than-life bishop fervently speculates on her confession: "In truth, the mark of a prelate is not mildness nor unction, but rather the most rigorous intelligence. . . ." A severe older woman, Irma, bluntly interrupts: "An agreement's an agreement." She is the proprietress of this place, a brothel in which the "bishop"—a customer who is actually a gas company employee—now is acting out his fantasies with one of the girls. He is reluctant to end his session and to leave—the more so because civil disorders are making the streets unsafe. Sounds of machine guns and a woman's scream occasionally are heard from offstage. Reassured by the alternately penitent and crudely provocative prostitute that the sins she has confessed are real, he is allowed a few more minutes to act his part. "I never desired the episcopal throne," he declares, preferring the passive illusion of power to its reality: "I wish to be bishop in solitude, for appearance alone," and "to destroy all function, I want to cause a scandal" by crudely taking the prostitute he now reviles. She takes off his ornamental garb while the "bishop" continues to declaim before the mirror.

Scene 2. In another room a beautiful young thief, half naked after being whipped by a muscular "executioner," orders a larger-than-life "judge" to lick her foot. As in the other room, here too a sadistic sex fantasy is enacted between an alternately remorseful and tantalizing whore play-acting for a customer who wants only to act out his illusion and "inhabit that region of exact freedom." The executioner cracks his whip as the "judge" makes the girl confess her crimes and crawls toward her again. "I'm willing to lick your shoes, but tell me you're a thief," he begs. As the lights go out and machine-gun fire is heard from afar, she cries out, "Not yet! Lick! Lick! Lick first!"

The Balcony, Scene 3. The "general" (John S. Dodson) and the girl (Salome Jens). New York, 1960. (*Martha Swope*)

Scene 3. In another room, a "general" worries about the revolution outside. Soon he acts out his fantasies with a girl who plays his horse: "My proud steed! My handsome mare, we've had many a spirited gallop together!" She dresses him in his larger-than-life uniform as he strokes her, makes her go down on her knees, and acts out his death as a war hero.

Scene 4. A little old man, dressed as a tramp, briefly performs his ceremony of being whipped by a beautiful but coarse redhead.

Scene 5. Irma periodically observes the proceedings in her thirty-eight cubicles through closed-circuit television. A sad ex-prostitute who used to act the Virgin now keeps her accounts. Worried about the revolution that might ruin her "severe" and "hellish" brothel, Irma half-woos the girl, who is oppressed by "this world of illusion" and misses her daughter, whom she placed in an institution that, as the ex-prostitute says, has a "real" garden. Irma remarks that "in real life" generals, bishops, and judges are "the props of a display that they have to drag in the mud of the real and commonplace. Here, Comedy and Appearance remain pure, and the Revels intact." The "executioner" of the judge scene, who is Irma's lover, comes to demand his share of the day's take. Then the powerful Chief of Police arrives; he yearns for a customer with a fantasy to represent the Chief of Police. He is Irma's former lover and still is her protector. But he had the executioner become her lover when he himself became impotent. "You were concerned with power, but without fulfilling yourself," Irma remarks; "you relaxed here through [the executioner]." The executioner runs in to announce the rebels' victory. As he describes it, he is felled by a shot from outside.

Scene 6. In a café the revolutionaries are plotting. Members of a real world and thus symbolically opposed to the world of the brothel, they are led by a middle-aged plumber who is beloved by one of Irma's prostitutes. The revolutionaries plan to make the prostitute a symbol to "rouse the people," to "embody the struggle," and to become its martyr. "What you love in her," the plumber is told, "is the very thing you're bent on destroying, the thing that made it possible for her to enter the brothel"—the preference of illusion to reality. Word comes that the palace is destroyed, as is part of the brothel. The plumber dreams of publishing a poem by his beloved whore, "a poem hailing freedom, the people, and their virtue." But another revolutionary rejects such "a heaven of abstractions" where the people would "hang permanently. . . . You've got to leave them in their living reality."

Scene 7. The real rulers are killed or missing and a royal envoy persuades the brothel occupants to enact their parts in public: "The people is awaiting its idol in order to grovel before it." Irma is to be the queen and the customers are to assume publicly the symbols of the power they have heretofore assumed privately. Fearfully the "bishop" and the others agree.

Scene 8. As they appear on the balcony in their enormous ceremonial garments—Irma wearing a crown and ermine cloak—the prostitute symbolizing the revolution is shot and killed.

Scene 9. The customers are amazed at and gratified by the success of their impersonations but confused about their true identity as journalists photograph them. Becoming increasingly confident, the "general," the "bishop," and the "judge" want to take power in earnest, although Irma (as queen) angrily insists that the Chief of Police, who engineered the masquerade (and presumably intended to rule through her), is the real power. Unhappy because no one has yet come to impersonate him, the Chief of Police wants a statue erected presenting him as "a gigantic phallus." As the would-be bishop angrily complains ("you tore us brutally from that delicious, enviable, untroubled state [of passive illusions], but we have since tasted other delights, the bitter delights of action and responsibility"), the Chief of Police squelches the impersonators' attempts to usurp his powers. But illusion is more attractive and wins out, even for the rebels, who found it indispensable when they made the whore into a martyr symbol. Irma, too, recognizes the power of illusion when she tries to hold on to the love of "love and power." Suddenly word comes that at long last a brothel customer seeks to masquerade as the Chief of Police. It is the leader of the unsuccessful rebellion, the plumber. With a prostitute acting as his slave, he impersonates the character of the Chief of Police "to the very limit of his destiny, no, of mine—of merging his destiny with mine," and castrates himself. The Chief of Police, who has watched the masquerade, fearfully examines his own body. Finding himself whole he is content and reassured: "Though my image be castrated in every brothel in the world, I remain intact." Even while another rebellion is breaking out in the city, he disappears into a passive ideal existence—into a mausoleum Irma has prepared in her brothel, where he will await posterity in a charade of his own. Irma dismisses the "bishop," "judge," and "general"; she turns off the lights and gets ready to "distribute roles again" as well as to resume her own. "You must now go home, where everything —you can be quite sure—will be even falser than here," Irma tells the audience. "You'll leave by the right, through the alley," she concludes as a burst of machine-gun fire is heard outside: "It's morning already."

BALD SOPRANO, THE (*La Cantatrice chauve*), a one-act "anti-play" by EUGÈNE IONESCO, produced in 1950 and published in 1953. Setting: a suburban "middle-class English interior" in the late 1940's.

Ionesco's first play depicts man's loss of individuality and his inability to think or communicate. This is dramatized in a farcically illogical, ABSURD dialogue originally inspired by language primers. Because Ionesco intended to portray "the tragedy of language," he was surprised by the play's comic effect. An actor's erroneous reading of a line provided the irrelevant title, which was translated in England as *The Bald Prima Donna.*

Mr. Smith—"an Englishman, seated in his English armchair and wearing English slippers, is smoking his English pipe and reading an English newspaper," etc.—clicks his tongue while his wife—"an Englishwoman . . . darning some English socks"—tells him about the meal they just ate, their family, and such other things as yogurt, which is "excellent for the stomach, the kidneys, the appendicitis, and apotheosis." Mr. Smith finally breaks her monologue, wondering about the newspapers' failure to give the ages of the newly born. The Smiths soon get involved in a confusing discussion about a Bobby Watson—he died two years ago, the funeral was a year and a half ago, his death was announced three years ago, and his body is still warm—and his large family, every one of whom is named Bobby Watson. The maid announces the arrival of Mr. and Mrs. Martin. The Martins look familiar to each other, and try to determine where they met before. Eventually Mr. Martin discovers that they "live in the same room and we sleep in the same bed, dear lady. It is perhaps there that we have met!" They embrace expressionlessly and fall asleep after they realize both have the same two-year-old daughter with "a white eye and a red eye." But the maid determines that despite such airtight reasoning, they are not who they think they are. A fire chief joins the party and the inane talk continues. Various pointless stories are told and morals are drawn. "If you catch a cold, you should get yourself a colt," Martin says, and Smith adds, "It's a useless precaution, but absolutely necessary." The maid embraces her sweetheart, the fire chief, who reveals that "it was she who extinguished my first fires." His allusion to "the bald soprano" embarrasses everybody, and he leaves. The others recite various maxims: "He who sells an ox today, will have an egg tomorrow"; "In real life, one must look out of the window"; "The car goes very fast, but the cook beats batter better"; etc. As these gradually collapse into total meaninglessness ("A, e, i, o, . . . B, c, d, f, g," etc.), the couples' nervousness and hostility grow, as they scream sounds at each other furiously. The lights go out and they all repeat, with increasing speed, the phrases: "It's not that way, it's over here." When the lights go on, the Martins are seated as the Smiths were at the start of the play, reciting the play's inane opening speeches as the curtain falls.

BALDERSTON, John Lloyd (1889–1954), American dramatist, is best known for his romantic fantasy BERKELEY SQUARE (1926), an adaptation (with JOHN COLLINGS SQUIRE) of an unfinished tale by HENRY JAMES. Notable too is Balderston's melodrama *Dracula* (1927), his adaptation (with Hamilton Deane, d. 1958) of Bram Stoker's 1897 horror novel. Aside from these two hits, Balderston had scant success. His *The Genius of the Marne* (1919), a war drama, though published with a preface by GEORGE MOORE, remained unproduced —as did his *A Morality for the Leisure Class* (1924), *Tongo* (1924), and *Frankenstein* (1932; written with Peggy Webling, ? – ?). *Red Planet* (1932; written with J. E. Hoare, 1886–) appeared on Broadway but failed.

A Philadelphian of British descent, Balderston was educated at Columbia University. He moved to England, where he edited *The Outlook* (1920–23) and served as chief London correspondent of the *New York World* (1923–31). After his return to America, Balderston wrote film scripts.

BALDWIN, James (1924–), American writer, achieved national fame with his searing portrayals of the deep-seated sense of his and his fellow blacks' anguish over their history of slavery and oppression in a predominantly white society. After the success of his novels, beginning with *Go Tell It on the Mountain* (1953), and essay collections like *Notes of a Native Son* (1955) and *The Fire Next Time* (1963), he became an important leader and an active worker and spokesman in early civil rights movements. In 1964 he achieved his first success as a playwright with the Broadway production of BLUES FOR MISTER CHARLIE.

Baldwin was born in the Harlem ghetto of New York, the oldest of a Holy Roller lay preacher's nine children. Until he began to publish his writings, Baldwin struggled at various odd jobs to help support the large family. A sensitive person deeply affected by the daily humiliations of blacks in the city, he expressed his feelings in brilliant and moving prose that gradually brought him fame. Though he won numerous prizes and fellowships, he considered his stay in Paris (1948–57) the most important part of his salvation.

Baldwin received his theatrical apprenticeship as an assistant to the director Elia Kazan. His first play, *The Amen Corner*, is about a Harlem storefront church and its congregation's various reactions to ghetto-life pressures. Staged by Howard University in 1955, its professional production in California almost a decade later helped inspire Baldwin to finish his first Broadway play. Originally *Blues for Mister Charlie* was suggested by the 1955 murder in Mississippi of a northern Negro boy, Emmett Till; it was dedicated to Baldwin's recently slain friend, the civil rights leader Medgar Evers, and to the children bombed in a Birmingham church. Baldwin also dramatized his novel *Giovanni's Room* (1956) for the Actors Studio workshop, in 1957.

Baldwin has expressed himself most powerfully and effectively in his essays, though his novels and plays have achieved moderate success. Believing racial hatred to be as harmful to whites as to blacks, Baldwin at the start of his career rejected propagandistic oversimplifications as lies that he himself was determined to avoid in all his writings.

BAŁUCKI, Michael (1837–1901), was the best and most popular writer of satiric comedy in Poland in the second half of the nineteenth century. He achieved his first success with *Radcy pana radcy* (1867), which depicts a kindly but incompetent municipal official. Frequently revived later hits were *Grube ryby* (1881), a satire on the loves of the nouveaux riches, and *Dom otwarty* (1883). Bałucki's other comedies include *Gęsi i gąski* (1884), *Klub kawalerów* (1890), and *Blagierzy* (1900). When this last play failed, Bałucki committed suicide.

BANKRUPTCY, A (*En fallit*), a play in four acts by BJØRNSTJERNE BJØRNSON, published and produced in 1874. Setting: Norway, 1870's.

Bjørnson's most popular play—it was performed throughout Scandinavia and then the rest of Europe—this was also Norway's first play about money and "social reform," and the first to depict family life NATURALISTICally. Its great success encouraged HENRIK IBSEN to continue writing social plays, including the two works most comparable to *A Bankruptcy*, PILLARS OF SOCIETY and A DOLL'S HOUSE. But Bjørnson's characteristic sentimentally "happy" resolution weakens the attack, which is made on behalf of—not against—society and the family. His frequently voiced ideals of family solidarity are expressed at the end of Act III.

Act I. Though the merchant Henning Tjælde seems to be prosperous, he is in reality desperate and is juggling accounts to avoid bankruptcy. Oblivious to the true state of affairs, his daughters continue to expect their lavish allowances. The bored older girl is engaged to a harebrained officer concerned only with horses, while the younger, Valborg, coldly remarks that she would disown her father were he ever to become bankrupt like the father of one of their friends. Tjælde's ailing wife, in the meantime, struggles to keep up a good table. A distinguished old lawyer comes to check up on Tjælde, who thereupon decides to have a banquet, to which he will invite useful guests—both to demonstrate and to assure his continued solvency. Vowing never again to leave himself vulnerable, he sighs, "If only I could get safely out of my difficulties without anyone's suspecting it!"

Act II. The banquet (in which various pillars of society are satirized) is a success, despite the older daughter's fiancé's bungling and the strain on Tjælde. Afterward the lawyer arrives to examine Tjælde's books—and soon demonstrates their fraudulence. Though Tjælde protests that he is honest, the lawyer exposes him as a crooked and ruined speculator. He begs to be allowed to manipulate his finances in order to save his business, and, when refused, he threatens to shoot himself. "A man who has for so long shivered with falsehood and terror in his innermost heart has lots of schemes but no courage," the lawyer replies. He persuades the desperate merchant to face his shameful situation, confess it to his family, and try to resolve it honestly: "The man who has enjoyed a respect that he did not deserve must someday undergo the humiliation that he has deserved." Tjælde, now a broken man, signs the bankruptcy papers and agrees to talk to his wife.

Act III. Mrs. Tjælde has known of her husband's true state of affairs all along. As the lawyer guessed, it was she who "slaved to prepare these banquets that were to conceal the nakedness of the land." After giving him the money she has saved, she tries to help her husband escape. But it is too late. Receivers strip Tjælde of his belongings, angry creditors stone his house, and the older daughter's fiancé deserts the family. Remaining with Tjælde are only his wife and his loyal secretary, who is in love with the proud and insulting younger daughter, Valborg. He offers his savings to Tjælde, and finally persuades Valborg to stand by her father. "Look forward," Valborg thereupon encourages the wretched Tjælde: "A united family is invincible!"

Act IV. It is three years later, and the family lives in more modest circumstances. Tjælde is much aged, and his wife is invalided. But with the help of the loyal secretary, Tjælde has finally discharged his bankruptcy. The family is poor, but as Mrs. Tjælde remarks, "the honorable name you will leave to your children will be well worth it." They are saddened only by the imminent departure of the secretary, who is most responsible for Tjælde's success and his regeneration. When Valborg at last persuades the secretary that she really loves him, however, he joyfully agrees to remain and marry her. "My dear, God has blessed our house now!" Tjælde whispers to his wife as he starts to wheel her into the dining room. "My dear man!" she replies affectionately.

BARABBAS, a play in three acts by MICHEL DE GHELDERODE, produced in 1929 and published in 1931. Setting: Palestine at the time of the Crucifixion.

Commissioned by the Flemish Popular Theatre for production during Holy Week, this imaginative reconstruction of the biblical account of the Crucifixion has remained popular over the years. It dramatizes the Passion from the viewpoint of Barabbas and the common people, but features the principal actors, including a silent Christ.

The play opens in prison, where the blustering criminal Barabbas, who cannot hide his fear of death, confronts the silent, suffering Christ. Later on the street before his palace, Pilate talks with Herod and Caiaphas, and Christ's doom is sealed. Given the choice to release one of the two condemned prisoners before them, the crowd cheers Barabbas and reviles Christ. During the Crucifixion, at a fairground in the shadow of Calvary, the apostles hide fearfully, Judas quarrels with his wife Yochabeth and goes to hang himself, and Mary Magdalene weeps as she experiences Christ's dying. Barabbas more and more identifies himself with Christ, whom he rowdily tries to avenge; but he is stabbed in the back. "Hey! Jesus! I too am bleeding. Sacrificed the same day," he says as he collapses; "but you died for something. I am dying for nothing. Nevertheless it's because of you—for you . . . Jesus—my brother." Looking toward Calvary, he dies.

BARLACH, Ernst (1870–1938), German EXPRESSIONIST sculptor, graphic artist, and author of a number of novels and plays. His writings are mystic visionary works influenced by the later drama of AUGUST STRINDBERG. They enjoyed considerable distinction in the 1920's and 1930's, and were often revived in the postwar decades. Yet Barlach never gained much popularity with audiences and he remained little known outside Germany. Only as an artist did Barlach establish a major reputation, though German directors continued to produce his eight plays. Barlach's lack of success in the theatre notwithstanding, some have ranked him as an important German dramatist; he is, in any case, unique for his accomplishments and versatility as a prolific artist and writer.

Barlach was born in Wedel, northern Germany, the son of a physician who died when the boy was fourteen. He was educated in Germany and Paris, where he pursued his interest in art. In the 1920's Barlach was a leader in the German expressionist movement and produced his major sculpture, graphic art, novels, and plays. His prominence continued into the 1930's, when the Nazis, objecting to his antiwar themes, removed his art from display, confiscating and eventually destroying much of it, and then officially declared it "decadent." Controversial as an artist, Barlach was victimized by the Nazis as well as by what he called "the irresistible force of a united mediocrity."

Barlach's drama is less blatantly expressionistic than that of GEORG KAISER, ERNST TOLLER, and other contemporaries. His first work, *Der tote Tag* (1912), is an obscure three-character play that is in part autobiographical and ends with the suicide of a blind adolescent who attempted to break away from the domination of his mother—modeled on the woman with whom Barlach had an unfortunate liaison and whose son, Nikolaus, later became very important to Barlach. In this play there is already a strong search for God—for the father the boy seeks turns out to be the divine spirit. This religious theme is more pronounced in Barlach's next play, *Der arme Vetter,* finished in 1912 but not published until 1918 and produced the following year. Sometimes praised as among his finest, this play too is characterized by obscurity and features a young man who seeks God and finally despairs and commits suicide; but here the act brings about a worldly girl's break from her former life.

Subsequent plays similarly dramatize spiritual quests. *Die echten Sedemunds* (*The Genuine Sedemunds,* 1920), Barlach's only comedy despite the tragic lives of the title characters, satirizes small-town life in its colorful secondary characters and episodes. *Der Findling* (1922) is an allegorical verse play characterized by metaphysical obscurity and physical horrors, including cannibalism. Barlach's most important drama is the biblical prize winner *Die Sündflut* (THE FLOOD, 1924). His last significant play, *Der blaue Boll* (*The Blue Boll,* 1926; also translated as *Squire Blue Boll*), features a country squire whose life is transformed from preoccupation with the material to the spiritual. Barlach's other plays are a ten-act mystery, *Die gute Zeit* (1929), and *Der Graf von Ratzeburg* (1951), a posthumous work set in the Middle Ages; both treat the same spiritual themes in the same poetic, brooding, and nebulous manner.

Alex Page's translation, *Three Plays by Ernst Barlach* (1964), consists of *The Flood, The Genuine Sedemunds,* and *The Blue Boll,* as well as an informative introduction. Edson M. Chick's *Ernst Barlach* (1967) is a comprehensive study of Barlach's life and works; its bibliography lists other publications, including Barlach's correspondence and memoirs.

BARRETTS OF WIMPOLE STREET, THE, a play in five acts by RUDOLF BESIER, published and produced in 1930. Setting: Elizabeth Barrett's bed-sitting room at 50 Wimpole Street, London; 1845.

This play depicts Elizabeth's father, Edward Moulton-Barrett—here a sadistic, incestuous, and pious tyrant—more than her romance with Robert Browning, and is in part based on both poets' letters. Rejected by almost thirty producers before Katharine Cornell accepted the play, it became her greatest success. It was produced throughout the world, notably during World War II, when she toured with it among the troops. The tour is described in Margalo Gillmore and Patricia Collinge's *The Barretts of Wimpole Street* (1945). In 1964 the play was revived as a musical, *Robert and Elizabeth* by Ronald Millar (1919–   ).

Act I. "Porter in a Tankard." The invalided Elizabeth Barrett lies on her sofa, her dog Flush asleep in his basket near her. She persuades the doctor to substitute something for the prescribed porter—"horrible to look at, more horrible to smell, and most horrible to drink." After supper, her six brothers come by, like robots, to say good night to "Ba," as they call her. Elizabeth's youngest sister, Henrietta, complains about their ruined dinner. Papa was in a dark mood because of the impending visit of a cousin who is getting married—something he would never allow any of them to do. An uneasy silence falls as Barrett comes in. He insists she drink the porter, and commands the momentarily defiant Henrietta to fetch the tankard. Changing his tactics, he then lets Elizabeth decide: "You shall never know by deed or word, or hint, of mine how much you have grieved and wounded your father by refusing to do the little thing he asked." She empties the tankard, he kneels beside her and prays, and then leaves. Alone, Elizabeth bursts into tears.

Act II. "Mr. Robert Browning." Elizabeth remarks on her brothers' lifelessness. "We're all of us wholly dependent on Papa, and must obey, or be broken," they admit. The visiting cousin arrives—a pretty, vivacious, and affected girl. Alone with Elizabeth later, Henrietta confesses that her admirer has just asked for her hand; although she loves him, she despairs because Papa would never allow it. At last, though Elizabeth nervously tries to avoid meeting the persistent poet face to face, Robert Browning is allowed to visit. He is an intense, handsome young man who

The Barretts of Wimpole Street. Robert Browning (Brian Aherne) and Elizabeth Barrett (Katharine Cornell). New York, 1931. (*Vandamm Photo, Theatre Collection, New York Public Library*)

admires Elizabeth's poetry. She tries to resist him: "I am a dying woman." But he stops her: "I've more life than is good for one man—it seethes and races in me." And he repeats what he wrote her: "I love your books with all my heart—and I love you too." After he departs, Elizabeth's face is still alive with excitement and happiness. She gets up and, for the first time in many years, walks again.

Act III. "Robert." It is some months later, and the doctors are amazed at her recovery, which they attribute to her sudden will to live. Her doctors encourage her plan to go to Italy. When Barrett learns of it, he is incensed. He comes to her room, where his repressed incestuous lust emerges and frightens the "pwetty" cousin, who flirts with him. Then he castigates Elizabeth, his favorite daughter, for her "underhand conduct"—planning to enjoy herself in Italy while her father would be left "utterly alone." Later Browning proposes to her: "I love you now more than words can tell—and I shall love you to the end, and beyond." Though Elizabeth feebly tries to resist and to talk him out of burdening himself with "the pale ghost of a woman," she soon falls into his arms and confesses her love. "Here's life—*life*—offering us the best that life can give," Browning exclaims as he plans to share his future with her.

Act IV. "Henrietta." A few weeks later Barrett decides to isolate his family in the country. Browning asks Elizabeth to marry him at once and escape to Italy. Still obsessed with her duty to her father, she pleads for time to consider her answer. While Henrietta introduces Elizabeth to her admirer, an officer just honored by the queen, Barrett appears unexpectedly. With insane fury and brutality he castigates Henrietta, throws her down, and threatens to send her into the street penniless unless she will swear on a Bible never to see the officer again. This ugly scene persuades Elizabeth that she must leave, and she sends her answer to Browning.

Act V. "Papa." It is shortly before Elizabeth's flight with Browning, whom she has married secretly a week earlier. Since his outburst Elizabeth has not seen her father, who is waiting for her to apologize for her "complicity" in Henrietta's love affair. Suddenly he comes in, unable any longer to bear the separation from his favorite daughter. He reveals to her the "reality" of love, as he talks of his wife's fear of him and her early death. "Do you suppose I should have guarded my house like a dragon from this so-called love if I hadn't known, from my own life, all it entails of cruelty and loathing and degradation and remorse?" Proud that he has been, with God's help, able to strangle love in himself, Barrett has sworn to "keep it away from those I was given to protect and care for," and draws Elizabeth into his arms. She extricates herself and he goes out to pray. Now Elizabeth has no further doubts about her course, and leaves. A little later the family discover their individual farewell letters. Henrietta hands Papa his. He reads it, and then orders Elizabeth's pet destroyed. Unable to conceal her triumph, Henrietta says: "In her letter to me Ba writes that she has taken Flush with her." Barrett stares ahead, mechanically tearing up Elizabeth's letter.

BARRIE, [Sir] **James M[atthew]** (1860–1937), British playwright and novelist, was one of the most famous and beloved writers of his age. Like his novels, most of his plays are sentimental, whimsical comedies and fantasies. He produced some forty-odd plays, the most popular of which have been THE LITTLE MINISTER (1897), THE ADMIRABLE CRICHTON (1902), WHAT EVERY WOMAN KNOWS (1908), THE TWELVE-POUND LOOK (1910), A KISS FOR CINDERELLA (1916), and DEAR BRUTUS (1917). But their popularity is completely overshadowed by that of PETER PAN (1904), one of the best-known of all modern plays. Though the sugar coating is thick, a "problem" or an "idea" usually underlies Barrie's work. He was well aware of troublesome reality, but preferred to engage in charming illusions. Chronologically his work parallels that of BERNARD SHAW. Both playwrights revitalized English drama and both were and have remained extremely popular. Both, too, were first-rate theatrical craftsmen and businessmen who appealed also to the reading public—Barrie by publishing his plays long after their production, with an extensive narrative and description that makes them as readable as his novels. But if Shaw stimulated audiences with uneasy thoughts, Barrie reassured and beguiled them with pleasant sentiments, lovable humor, and charming romance.

The son of poor weavers, Barrie was born in the village of Kirriemuir ("Thrums"), Scotland. He was educated at Dumfries Academy and Edinburgh University, whose chancellor he later became. After finishing his studies (1882) he turned to journalism, first in Nottingham and then in London. He started his literary career as a novelist, his earliest success being *Auld Licht Idylls* (1888). From the beginning he was interested in the theatre. He failed in his first attempt, *Richard Savage* (1891), a collaboration with the novelist H. B. M. Watson and produced at the authors' expense. Next came a burlesque of Ibsen's HEDDA GABLER, *Ibsen's Ghost* (1891), which was applauded at Toole's Theatre. Barrie's first real theatrical successes were the comedies *Walker, London* (1892) and *The Professor's Love Story* (1894). But it was *The Little Minister,* the dramatization of a novel he had published in 1891, that solidly established his fame and wealth.

Barrie had two failures in 1893: *Becky Sharp,* a one-act adaptation of Thackeray's conclusion to *Vanity Fair,* and a comic opera written with Arthur Conan Doyle (1859–1930), *Jane Annie, or The Good Conduct Prize.* Thereafter his plays charmed English and American audiences. Many of them are light, short pieces, often one-acters: *Pantaloon* (1905); *Josephine* (1906); *Punch* (1906); *The Twelve-Pound Look,* his most famous one-act play; *Old Friends* (1910); *Rosalind* (1912); *The Will* (1913); *Half an Hour* (1913), a popular melodrama; *"Der Tag"* (1914), subtitled "The Tragic Man," a patriotic war piece on the rape of Belgium that ends with Culture's assurance to the Emperor: "If God is with the Allies, Germany will not be destroyed"; *The New World* (1915); *The Fatal Typist* (1915); *Shakespeare's Legacy* (1916), a joke on the Bacon controversy; the five war playlets *A Slice of Life* (1916), *The Old Lady Shows Her Medals* (1917, a popular bittersweet piece about an old charwoman who again finds romance by "adopting" a soldier eventually killed in action), *La Politesse* (1918), *Barbara's Wedding* (1918), and *A Well-Remembered Voice* (1918, introducing the supernatural); *The Real Thing at Last* (1920); *The Truth About the Russian Dancers* (1920), a comic ballet; and the grotesque detective work *Shall We Join the Ladies?* (1921), the popular and often-performed first part of a never-completed four-act play.

His full-length plays, aside from the popular ones already alluded to, are *The Wedding Guest* (1900), an IBSENite PROBLEM PLAY about a man with a past—a former mistress who is carrying his child; *Quality Street* (1902), a popular period piece in which a lover's proposal after returning from the Napoleonic Wars rejuvenates the long-waiting "Phoebe of the ringlets" ("Sir, the dictates of my heart enjoin me to accept your too flattering offer"); the joke play *Little Mary* (1903), whose surprise panacea is an exhortation against overeating; *Alice Sit-by-the-Fire* (1905), a parody of problem plays; *The Adored One, A Legend of the Old Bailey* (1913, successfully produced in America as *The Legend of Leonora*), a murder comedy hissed off the boards in England, subsequently revised, and later made into the one-act *Seven Women* (1917); the musical review *Rosy Rapture* (1915); MARY ROSE (1920), one of his very popular works; and finally, after fifteen years without a new play, the interesting biblical drama written for Elisabeth Bergner and barely completed before his death, THE BOY DAVID (1936).

Critics have attacked Barrie's works for their whimsical unreality and their cloying sentimentality, but his plays still continue to charm and delight people. His fantasy is expressed with humor and consummate artistry. Though he loved children, he had none of his own. His 1894 marriage to the actress Mary Ansell ended in divorce fifteen years later. In 1913 Barrie was created a baronet. His plays, many of them produced by Charles Frohman, were vehicles for the great actors and actresses of his time, and among his friends were the famous writers of his age. MAURICE MAETERLINCK inscribed his tribute to the "grandfather" of his own THE BLUE BIRD on Barrie's living-room wall: "Hommage d'admiration au père de 'Peter Pan,' grandpère de 'l'oiseau bleu.'"

The "definitive edition" of Barrie's *Plays* appeared in 1942. H. M. Walbrook's *J. M. Barrie and the Theatre,* though published in 1922, deals with all but Barrie's last play. The most comprehensive account of his life and work is Denis Mackail's *Barrie: The Story of J. M. B.* (1941); its "Author's Note" and the "Bibliographical Notes" to R. L. Green's book on *Peter Pan* list other works by and about Barrie. Janet Dunbar's biography, *J. M. Barrie: The Man Behind the Image* (1970), includes many hitherto unpublished Barrie journals and letters. A good concise study is Harry M. Geduld's *James Barrie* (1971).

BARRY, Philip [James Quinn] (1896–1949), was one of America's leading playwrights in the twenty-five years before his death. Thereafter his work has been for the most part forgotten, though some twenty-one of his plays had been produced on Broadway—many of them successfully. Only THE PHILADELPHIA STORY (1939), his best play, has retained a measure of popularity—particularly in the movies and on television. Like his other most popular works—particularly PARIS BOUND (1927), HOLIDAY (1928), and THE ANIMAL KINGDOM (1931)—it is a modern comedy of manners. Barry excelled in this genre, though even here one notes a strong, serious undercurrent. The grave side of his nature—his concern with metaphysics, religion, and psychology—was brought to the fore in biblical and other noncomedic plays, which fared less well with the public and the critics alike. The best known of his attempts in that genre are HOTEL UNIVERSE (1930) and the artistically more successful HERE COME THE CLOWNS (1938). But Barry is better remembered for his drawing-room comedies, which depict the sophisticated society of the 1920's and 1930's.

The youngest child of Irish-Catholic parents—his father was a businessman—Barry was born in Rochester, New York. He attended parochial schools and Yale University, where he indulged his literary proclivities. Rejected by the army because of deficient eyesight, Barry did code work in Washington and London during World War I. His first publication was a story that had appeared before he was nine, and at thirteen he started writing a play about reincarnation, *No Thoroughfare.* Later he used the same title for his first completed drama, a play about psychoanalysis that Barry tried unsuccessfully to have produced shortly after the war. However, Yale University, where he returned to complete his degree in 1919, did produce, in that year, his *Autonomy,* a one-act satire of President Wilson's international ideals. The same year, too, Barry enrolled in Professor George Pierce Baker's Workshop 47 at Harvard, where he wrote *A Punch for Judy.* A farcical love-triangle drama, it was produced in 1921—at Harvard, in New York City, and on national tour.

Now committed to playwriting, Barry left the advertising firm for which he worked and returned to Harvard's Workshop 47. There he completed *The Jilts,* a comedy that deals with the conflict of art and marriage; retitled *You and I,* it was his first play to reach Broadway (1923). The next year Broadway featured his *The Youngest* (1922), an autobiographical comedy about the conflict of the generations ("a man's greatest victory is over his own family") that appeared also under the titles *Poor Richard, God Bless Our Home,* and *The New Freedom.* The next play was *In a Garden* (1925), a witty comedy about a playwright's construction of a psychodrama of his wife's first love affair, to purge its memory—which results, instead, in the wife's leaving her manipulating husband; despite its poor run, it was the first Barry play to be heralded by important critics. More significant was his next comedy, *White Wings* (1926). Again a commercial failure, but praised widely for its charm, it is a fantasy about the old horse-barrels-and-brushes New York streetcleaners (the "white wings"), one of whom resists motorization and proudly vows to remain in his profession until the last horse is gone; thereupon the equally determined automobile-maker's daughter he loves shoots the last horse.

In his next play, the religious tragedy *John* (1927), Barry attempted for the first time to dramatize serious problems that troubled him; retelling the biblical story of Herod, Herodias, and Salome, *John* focuses on the Baptist's struggle against sinners. It too failed, but Barry was slightly more fortunate with *Cock Robin* (1928), a comic mystery play written with ELMER RICE. Barry first enraptured Broadway audiences with *Paris Bound,* and consolidated his popularity with other earlier-mentioned hits. Less successful but praised by some commentators was *Tomorrow and Tomorrow* (1931), a biblical story (that of Elisha and the Shunammite woman) which Barry changed into a modern triangle of love and adultery; the "facts" of a child's paternity in Barry's characteristic resolution become less important than the "truth" of the marriage.

Barry's other plays include three Broadway failures: *The Joyous Season* (1934), a Christmas mystery featuring a nun; *Bright Star* (1935), a character study about an idealist who suffers from "the inability to love"; and *Spring Dance* (1936), a college comedy by two Vassar students (Eleanor Golden and Eloise Barrington), revised by Barry. *Here Come the Clowns,* Barry's dramatization of his only novel and his next work to reach Broadway, had a mixed reception and a relatively short run; despite its flaws, it is his best serious play. There was no question of the critical as well as popular success of his next work, *The Philadelphia Story*. Barry's remaining plays, however, are relatively unimportant: *Liberty Jones* (1941), "An Allegory with Music for City Children" was an amplification of the earlier and unproduced *The Wild Harps Playing* (1936), an allegory on totalitarianism; *Without Love* (1942), a comedy that aimed to goad the Irish into doing more for the Allied war effort, was a vehicle for the star of *The Philadelphia Story,* Katharine Hepburn, who also starred in the film version of both plays; *Foolish Notion* (1945) is a comedy about four fantasies on, and the actual return of, a war veteran; and *My Name Is Aquilon* (1949), "a sophisticated sex comedy," was adapted from Jean-Pierre Aumont's (1911–) Parisian hit, *L'Empereur de Chine* (1948). Barry's posthumous *Second Threshold* (1951) is a serious play about a psychic father-daughter relationship; it was prepared for production by Barry's friend, ROBERT E. SHERWOOD.

The family as well as psychiatry are recurrent Barry themes. Father-daughter relationships occupy a subsidiary role in a number of his important plays (*The Philadelphia Story, Hotel Universe,* and others). Even more often Barry focused on the relationship of husband and wife: in play after play he sought to reconcile marital love with sex, art, integrity, self-realization and fulfillment—and temporal compromise. Only rarely did Barry succeed fully in his dramatizations of these and related themes: tradition and progress, the meaning of life, of good and evil, of God, etc. Frequently characters become unbelievable, situations pathetic and sentimental, symbols trite or murky, dialogue forced in its raciness and sophistication, and the humor flat. But at their best, Barry's whimsy and wit coalesce with his innate seriousness; the resultant plays are amusing as well as penetrating portrayals of man and life.

Barry was one of the playwrights of The Theatre Guild, which he saved from financial ruin with *The Philadelphia Story*. He was married and had two sons (a daughter died in infancy). In the 1930's the family spent much time in their villa in Cannes. Barry died suddenly in New York of a heart attack. His plays were published individually, and some were reprinted in anthologies of the 1930's, 1940's, and 1950's. Thereafter he was rarely mentioned, and few studies of the drama have devoted much space to his work. Notable exceptions are the extensive homage in W. David Sievers's *Freud on Broadway* (1955); and Joseph Patrick Roppolo's *Philip Barry* (1965), a study of the playwright's life and work. The latter book has a comprehensive Barry bibliography.

BATAILLE, Henry [Félix] (1872–1922), French poet and playwright, achieved considerable native popularity in the early years of the century. His plays feature morbid, love-obsessed women whose passions, whether gratified or frustrated, bring about tragedy—usually suicide or attempted suicide. A poet influenced by the drama of GEORGES DE PORTO-RICHE, Bataille in 1894 produced *La Belle au bois dormant* (written with Robert d'Humières, 1868–1915), a fairy play. It was hissed off the boards, but two years later Bataille had moderate success with a couple of verse tragedies based on legend, *Ton Sang* and *La Lépreuse*. With his subsequent plays Bataille heightened and sustained his fame until World War I. His most popular plays were *Maman Colibri* (1904), whose protagonist falls in love with her son's friend; *La Marche nuptiale* (1905), in which a young wife's temptation causes the downfall of a provincial couple in Paris; *Poliche* (1906), whose plot and characterizations recall those of Donnay's LOVERS; *La Femme nue* (1908), the tragedy of a successful artist's desertion of his ardent wife (modeled on the life of Claude Debussy); and three further plays on similar themes, *Le Scandale* (*The Scandal,* 1909), *L'Enfant de l'amour* (*The Love Child,* 1911), and *La Tendresse* (1921), all of which were produced on Broadway, the last-named under its French title. Other Bataille plays include *Résurrection* (*Resurrection,* 1902), a dramatization of the novel by LEO TOLSTOI; and *Le Phalène* (1913), a sensation-causing drama inspired by the life of the nineteenth-century Russian painter and diarist Marie Bashkirtsev. All these once-effective portrayals and Bataille's so-called *théâtre de la femme* now appear considerably dated and display little of the "psychological insight" and lyricism they once were thought to possess.

Bataille's works were published in twelve volumes (1922–29). Barrett H. Clark's chapter on Bataille in *Contemporary French Dramatists* (1916) includes extensive excerpts from *La Femme nue* and a bibliography of works by and about Bataille.

BEAR, THE (*Medved*), "A Jest in One Act" by ANTON CHEKHOV, published and produced in 1888. Setting: the drawing room of a country house, late nineteenth century.

Though they deplored its "triviality," the censors soon lifted their original ban of the play for its "peculiar theme" and its "coarseness and impropriety of the tone throughout." Also known as *The Boor,* this popular vaudeville became an excellent source of income for Chekhov.

A gruff middle-aged creditor bullies a young widow who has sworn eternal mourning. When they become exasperated with each other, he challenges her to shoot it out, and she readily agrees. But the creditor, now in love, proposes. When the servants arrive to throw the ruffian out, they are amazed to find him and the widow in a passionate embrace.

BEAUTIFUL DESPOT, THE (*Krasivy despot*), "the last act of a drama" in one act by NIKOLAI NIKOLAEVICH YEVREINOV, published and produced in 1906. Setting: a luxurious room in 1904, but furnished in an earlier style.

Yevreinov's first important play features a disillusioned liberal who has forsaken his ideals: "Better beautiful and wrong than right and ugly." He now lives in a household modeled (as in Pirandello's HENRY IV) on an earlier age, 1808. A friend arrives, the two debate the advantages of the past and the present, and the friend is almost persuaded to give up the real present for the charming but illusory past.

BEAVER COAT, THE (*Der Biberpelz*), "a Thieves' Comedy" in four acts by GERHART HAUPTMANN, published and produced in 1893. Setting: a village near Berlin, 1880's.

This outstanding folk comedy has always been popular in Germany, though it failed to captivate American audiences. In its satire of militant but stupidly bungling officialdom—personified by von Wehrhahn ("Fighting Cock")—it is a precursor of Zuckmayer's THE CAPTAIN OF KÖPENICK; its impudent but shrewd and energetic washerwoman, the thieving Mrs. Wolff (generally acclaimed as a masterful portrayal), cheerfully enunciates the Peachum philosophy of Brecht's THE THREEPENNY OPERA and is a recent ancestress of Brecht's MOTHER COURAGE. Hauptmann's NATURALISM makes the play a character comedy and contributes effectively to its farcical humor. The two principal comic characters reappear in Hauptmann's sequel to this play, THE RED COCK.

Act I. Returning with a poached deer to her kitchen at night, Mrs. Wolff finds her older daughter asleep. She has left her landlord employer because she considers herself overworked, having been asked to carry firewood into the house. Mrs. Wolff ridicules her daughter's complaints and threats, and quickly puts her to work. When Mrs. Wolff's laborer husband comes home, she manages him as deftly, though he threatens to flog the girl. Ambitious for her family, Mother Wolff is proud of having had her daughters educated, and expects the older, at least, to become a famous actress. She scolds her younger girl for hanging around at the "lousy" shoemaker's (a procurer and informer she herself marries in *The Red Cock*), puts her and the husband to work, and questions the older daughter about her employer's firewood. After some shrewd bargaining, she sells the deer to a boatman, who expresses his yearning for a beaver coat. An unemployed forester blackmails her with snares found outside the house, and she willingly pays to keep his goodwill. Finally, though her stolid husband grumbles about the danger of being jailed, she prepares to steal the firewood. The rich old landlord will not really miss it, and she must provide for her family: "Once y're rich and sit in yer carriage no one'll ask ya where ya got yer money from." She even has a slow-witted constable help them take out the sled.

Act II. Next morning at his office, magistrate von Wehrhahn pompously blusters over the inefficiency of his predecessor and the troublesome elements he must ferret out—"doubtful characters, political criminals, dangerous to king and country." The unemployed forester arrives, anxious to denounce the landlord, who has evicted him for nonpayment of rent. He also denounces an intellectual young doctor who lives in his house and, he claims, associates with Democrats and mocks "people in high places." Although this case is of far greater interest to von Wehrhahn, who is obsessed with national security, he must deal first with the almost deaf old landlord, who comes complaining about the theft of his wood and the disappearance of his servant girl. Von Wehrhahn summons his washerwoman, Mrs. Wolff, "who works as hard as four men." Respectful but adamant, Mrs. Wolff insists that her daughter will not return to such a slave driver. When the landlord holds her responsible for her daughter's negligence in leaving the wood outside, she angrily decides to quit doing his laundry and other chores. The magistrate tries to calm her and attempts to get to the wood theft. When asked, she and the slow-witted constable assure him that they did not pass a sled carrying wood last night. Mrs. Wolff furthermore succeeds in getting the landlord and von Wehrhahn to argue with each other. The magistrate finally dismisses the landlord angrily and sighs about his troubles. But then, "one must fight for the supreme welfare of the nation."

Act III. Back in her kitchen, Mrs. Wolff is counting a large sum of money and sends her husband to the tavern when he starts worrying about the boatman's new beaver coat. Having lost her own little son, she sentimentally pets the young doctor's boy, and then warns the father to be careful and beware of the forester informer. When he tells her that the landlord has been robbed again—this time of a beaver coat—she expresses amazement; the place seems unsafe to live in and she herself is thinking of moving: "Tsk! tsk! Such people! It's unbelievable! . . . To steal—naw, it's better to work till ya drop." The unhappy landlord himself soon comes, doubly upset because his new washerwoman is not nearly as good or efficient. He apologizes to and rehires Mrs. Wolff, and raises her daughter's wages. Mrs. Wolff encourages his returning to von Wehrhahn to complain about the second theft. He unhappily remembers his "good, expensive wood, like yours there." Angrily waving one of the logs, he vows to catch the thieves, and Mrs. Wolff remarks, "That would be a blessin'. Honest to God!"

Act IV. Back at the magistrate's office, total confusion reigns. Mrs. Wolff has a package that may help "solve" the beaver coat theft. The boatman arrives to register his newborn child. The doctor comes to report having seen an unknown boatman wearing an expensive beaver coat. Von Wehrhahn, preoccupied with thoughts about enemies of the fatherland, is confused by all these goings-on, and is unable to finish pursuing a single one of them. The landlord insists he examine the evidence relating to his beaver coat. The magistrate is completely satisfied that the boatman has refuted the doctor's evidence when the boatman blandly insists that many boatmen have expensive coats—why, even he has one! The doctor also presents an affidavit proving von Wehrhahn's pet informer a scoundrel who solicits false evidence. Seeing Mrs. Wolff's package persuades von Wehrhahn that the coat must have been taken to Berlin. There is an angry argument with the landlord, who departs after insisting that von Wehrhahn examine the matter more carefully. After the others leave, von Wehrhahn, trusting her completely, tells Mrs. Wolff that she is too gullible: "You look at people's outside. Men like me look a little deeper." He puts his hand on her shoulder and assures her that he knows what he is doing: "As sure as it's true when I say: Mrs. Wolff is an honest soul, so I say with the same certainty: your doctor . . . he's an extremely dangerous fellow." Mrs. Wolff shakes her head resignedly: "Well, I don't know about that . . ."

BECHER, Johannes Robert (1891–1958), German writer, was an important poet and novelist between the world wars. He distinguished himself first with *Verfall und Triumph* (1914), an EXPRESSIONIST collection of verse and prose whose cacophonous style reflects the world as Becher saw it. A radical, he joined the Communist Party and emigrated to Moscow in 1933. Among his writings are oratorios and other quasi-dramatic works about the Soviet Union, its workers, and its soldiers. His only significant writing for the theatre was *Arbeiter, Bauern, Soldaten* (1921), a utopian pageant in verse and music, produced for mass audiences and featuring large groups of workers, peasants, and soldiers.

After the war Becher moved to East Berlin, where he became president of the East German Cultural Union. His work was published in some two dozen volumes.

BECKET, OR THE HONOR OF GOD (*Becket, ou l'honneur de Dieu*), a play in four acts by JEAN ANOUILH, published and produced in 1959. Setting: twelfth-century England and France.

Though to some extent stylized, like Eliot's MURDER IN THE CATHEDRAL, this is a very different, distinctly Gallic, reinterpretation of history. In many, fast-changing scenes it depicts a deep friendship between King Henry II and a Saxon Thomas à Becket, who seeks honor. He finds it in his archbishopric, which destroys his bond with the king.

Act I. In the cathedral where Becket, already canonized, is entombed, King Henry strips himself. "Well, Thomas Becket, are you satisfied?" he asks, as he prepares to be scourged by four monks in order to win over the Saxons. He recalls Becket, and the scene flashes back to their youthful companionship. Before his council, Henry names Becket chancellor, and Becket helps collect taxes from the clergy. Hunting, the king and Becket seek shelter in the hovel of a poor Saxon whose daughter Henry wants to seduce. Becket is wounded by her brother, and asks the king to leave him the girl. Cunningly Henry agrees, in return for Becket's promise of "favor for favor." And soon, at his chancellor's party, Henry collects his favor: Becket's mistress. The king is terrified when the girl stabs herself in his bed. Frightened, he insists on

Becket, or The Honor of God. Becket (Laurence Olivier) and the king (Anthony Quinn, right). New York, 1960. *(Zodiac Photographers)*

sharing Becket's bed that night. As Henry is racked by nightmares, Becket ponders his confused loyalties as a Saxon among the conquerors, and his loyalty to the king: "So long as Becket is obliged to improvise his honor, he will serve you. And if one day he meets it face to face"—Becket pauses, and sighs as he goes to bed: "But where is Becket's honor?"

Act II. In a French forest Becket prepares the English troops and Henry, who is wenching in his tent, for a triumphant entry into a defeated city. He cautions the king against the clergy's growing power. In the French cathedral Henry suddenly decides to have his own man appointed archbishop. Unaware of what Henry is driving at, Becket remarks that "once the Primate's miter is on their heads, [archbishops] grow dizzy with power." He is horrified when he realizes it is to be himself. "If I become Archbishop, I can no longer be your friend," he warns Henry: "This is madness, my Lord. Don't do it. I could not serve both God and you." But Henry remains adamant. Later, Becket gives away his worldly goods. "I wish there had been something I had regretted parting with, so I could offer it to You," he says before the crucifix: "Lord, are You sure You are not tempting me? It all seems far too easy."

Act III. Henry quarrels with his mother and his wife, and ridicules his eldest son, "Henry III": "Not yet, Sir! Number II is in the best of health." He is hurt by Becket's resignation of the chancellorship: "I loved you and you didn't love me." But he adds, "I shall learn to be alone." Becket refuses to rescind his excommunication of the king's friends who interfered with matters under the archbishop's jurisdiction: "The Kingdom of God must be defended like any other Kingdom." As Henry watches through a curtain, the council tries Becket on trumped-up charges. But the archbishop silences them with a gesture and strides out. Henry cannot help admiring him, though he rages, "I am surrounded by fools and the only intelligent man in my Kingdom is against me!" In the French court, where Becket has gone for refuge, King Louis VI warns him that the Pope will sell him. A grubby-looking Pope (Alexander III) and an equally grubby cardinal discuss Henry's price for Becket and pursue their schemes. Sheltered in a convent, Becket prays and decides, "I shall take up the miter and the golden cope again." He will return, face Henry, and "do what I believe is my life's work. For the rest, Your will be done."

Act IV. King Louis arranges a peace meeting between Henry and Becket. They confer on a cold, wind-splashed plain. Henry is racked with love for Becket, and pleads that his archbishop act logically. Becket disagrees: "We must only do—absurdly—what we have been given to do." And he tells Henry how he found honor "—the honor of God. A frail, incomprehensible honor, vulnerable as a boy-King fleeing from danger." Although they reach an agreement, Henry and Becket part coldly after the king cries out, "I should never have seen you again! It hurts too much." Becket replies, "I know I shall never see you again." In his palace Henry furiously throws his family out of the room. When he is told of Becket's safe return to England, he cries out before his barons, "Will no one rid me of him? A priest! A priest who jeers at me and does me injury!" The stupid barons at last understand. To the accompaniment of tom-toms echoing Henry's heartbeats, they go to slay Becket. In his cathedral, they hack the archbishop down. The scene changes into the first one, the gestures of the killer barons changing into those of the scourging priests. The crowds now acclaim both Henry and Becket. "With a touch of hypocritical majesty beneath his slightly loutish manner," the king determines that Becket's killers be found—by the barons themselves, "so that no one will be in any doubt as to our Royal desire to defend the honor of God and the memory of our friend from this day forward."

BECKETT, Samuel [Barclay] (1906–   ), Irish-French writer, is one of the most important contemporary dramatists and novelists. Writing sometimes in English and sometimes in French, he brought out his best-known plays—*En attendant Godot* (WAITING FOR GODOT, 1952) and *Fin de partie* (ENDGAME, 1957)—in French, and later himself translated them into English. Beckett's ABSURDist drama, even more than his fiction (novels like *Murphy, Watt, Molloy, Malone meurt,* and *L'Innommable*), is lucid yet opaque, full of obscenities and literary and biblical allusions, comic yet despairing, a blend of slapstick comedy and metaphysical introspection. His portrayal of man absurdly trapped, going through a life of absurd routines in an absurd universe—and occasionally and unsuccessfully questioning his condition—has fascinated a worldwide audience. He is the literary heir of JAMES JOYCE, whose companion and "disciple" he was; but Beckett's work—certainly his drama—has attained wider general popularity and quicker esteem than that of the older expatriate Irishman, and in 1969 Beckett was awarded the Nobel Prize for literature.

The son of a surveyor, Beckett was born at Foxrock, near Dublin, to a well-to-do Protestant family. At fourteen he was sent to Portora Royal, the Irish boarding school OSCAR WILDE once attended. In 1923 Beckett went to Trinity College, Dublin. A brilliant scholar, he received his B.A. in French and Italian four years later, and spent the next two years as a lecturer in English at the École Normale Supérieure, in Paris. There he first met Joyce, and became part of his avant-garde circle. He began to publish poetry, criticism, and fiction, and in 1930 won a prize for *Whoroscope,* a long poetic soliloquy by an "Irished" René Descartes. Briefly Beckett returned to Trinity as a lecturer in French. He received his master's degree in 1931, the year he published a study on Marcel Proust.

Soon he left the routine of academic life, and during the years 1932–36 wandered through England, France, and Germany. He wrote and took odd jobs during those years, and published a collection of short stories, *More Pricks Than Kicks* (1934). In 1937 he settled in Paris. During the war he joined a French resistance group; when he was forced to escape to the unoccupied zone in 1942, he did some farming, and wrote. In 1945 Beckett returned to Paris. He briefly visited Ireland and joined a Red Cross unit at St. Lô. He remained in France, where he has spent most of his subsequent life, and began to write his plays.

The first of these, *Eleutheria,* remained unpublished, though Beckett has made it accessible to scholars. It is a play of many characters with a divided stage and alternating plots, and it is, to some extent, autobiographical. Its apathetic protagonist remains in bed, and is discussed (on the other part of the stage) by his family and friends—characters bearing names like Krap, Piouk, Skunk, and Meck. During 1947–49 Beckett also wrote *Waiting for Godot,* the first and most important of his plays to appear. Its modest premiere in a small, now-defunct house (the Théâtre de Babylone) created a sensation that soon became international, and the play was translated into many languages. It secured the reputation Beckett began to make for himself upon the publication of *Molloy* in 1951.

His next play, *Endgame,* was also first produced in French (though the premiere was in London) and it is, as Beckett himself noted, "more inhuman than *Godot*"—and even more evocative. It too features two sets of characters, and mixes low comedy with the cosmic quest, pantomime, and fragmentary dialogue. In all Beckett's plays the ignominious pratfalls and other positions his characters assume symbolize the human condition, man's impossible striving for dignity, meaning, and

Samuel Beckett in 1957. (*P. Brassai from Rapho Guillumette*)

communication with other men or with God. His work has been likened to that of Franz Kafka and Fyodor Dostoevsky, as well as Joyce. But his drama is unique and original. It invariably is pared down to essentials, even in its frequent repetitions.* These, like many of the speeches, often are elliptical. They are highly suggestive, as are the pauses and the tableaux that begin and end his plays. The humor is Rabelaisian. Beckett's settings too are sparse: usually they insinuate a dying earth. But the form of his plays cannot be isolated, for it is integral to and inseparable from the meaning of his plays. Beckett persistently refused to "explain" the meaning of his works, though he denied their containing any hidden, secret keys. When asked about the identity of Godot, for example, he responded, "If I knew, I would have said so in the play."

On the 1957 bill with *Endgame* was *Acte sans paroles* (*Act Without Words I*), the first of two mimes. They are not among Beckett's major works, but they present the Beckettian man with complete clarity. In a desert and in dazzling light, he for a while responds to mysterious whistles and grasps at various objects that are dangled before him. Unable quite to reach them, he tries to leave—but is always hurled back from the wings to the stage. At the end, a carafe is dangled in front of him, the whistle blows, the various objects are pulled away by the same unseen forces—but now, at last, he remains immobile, staring at his hands. An equally clear mime of human existence is the second *Acte sans paroles* (1959). It depicts two players who come out of sacks† and perform various routines of life—eating, dressing, praying, etc.; one goes through them slowly and despairingly, the other busily and senselessly.

Similar perspectives of life are reflected in Beckett's other dramatic works: KRAPP'S LAST TAPE (1958); HAPPY DAYS (1961); *Comédie* (*Play,* 1963; a one-acter filmed in 1966), in which the heads of three ghosts appear above their funeral urns to resume the squabbles resulting from their lifetime adulteries; and *Come and Go* (1966), a very short work, written in English, in which three women on a park bench whisper unmentionables to and about each other. For radio productions he wrote *All That Fall* (1957), *Embers* (1959), and *Words and Music* (1962), commissioned and broadcast by the BBC; and *Cascando,* broadcast by RTF (Paris, 1963). The first, a tragicomedy titled after David's praise of the Lord in Psalm 145, dramatizes an old Irishwoman's trip to a railroad station to meet her blind husband; it projects Beckett's characteristic despair and desire for cosmic enlightenment and human contact and, in the person of her husband, man's inherent viciousness and cruelty: "Did you ever wish to kill a child," the husband, who himself admits to such feelings, asks her, "nip some young doom in the bud?" *Embers* presents similar themes in an old man's reminiscences (as in *Krapp's Last Tape*) and in his ramblings with his wife. Beckett also wrote a solo mime for Buster Keaton, *Film,* which won kudos at the 1965 Venice Film Festival. Some of his fiction, too, has been dramatized.

All That Fall, Embers, and the two *Act Without Words* mimes are reprinted in Beckett's *Krapp's Last Tape and Other Dramatic Pieces* (1960). *Cascando and Other Short Dramatic Pieces* (1969) is a collection of radio, film, and television scripts, including the TV monologue *Eh, Joe* and the *"dramaticule" Come and Go*. Critical and scholarly examinations of Beckett and his works continue to proliferate. Book-length studies are Hugh Kenner's *Samuel Beckett: A Critical Study* (1961), Ruby Cohn's *Samuel Beckett: The Comic Gamut* (1962), Frederick J. Hoffman's *Samuel Beckett: The Language of Self* (1962), John Fletcher's *Samuel Beckett's Art* (1967), and Michael Robinson's *The Long Sonata of the Dead* (1969); good collections of essays on Beckett by many other writers are Melvin J. Friedman's *Samuel Beckett* (1964), Martin Esslin's *Samuel Beckett* (1965), and the Beckett issue of *Modern Drama* (December, 1966). A bibliography of works by and studies of Beckett is James T. F. Tanner and J. Don Vann's *Samuel Beckett: A Checklist of Criticism* (1969).

* Hence the writing in French: the discipline of using a foreign language, Beckett felt, would avert flights into stylistic embellishments.

† Beckett suffered from "a terrible memory of life in his mother's womb," according to Peggy Guggenheim's autobiography, *Confessions of an Art Addict* (1960). His characters frequently assume the fetal position.

BECQUE, Henry [-Francois] (1837–99), French playwright, was one of the founders of NATURALISM. He was not a very prolific writer, completing a mere dozen plays. Most of them are one-acters and only two—*Les Corbeaux* (THE VULTURES, 1882) and *La Parisienne* (THE PARISIAN WOMAN, 1885)—are still notable. Yet he was important not only for these and other plays once controversial, highly esteemed by critics, and produced with some popular success at the most distinguished Parisian theatres, the Comédie-Français and the Vieux-Colombier. Contemptuous of the inanities and sentimentalities of the popular younger Dumas and VICTORIEN SARDOU drama of the late nineteenth century, Becque along with ÉMILE ZOLA (whose more important work was as a novelist and pamphleteer) succeeded in infusing new REALISM into the theatre of his age. He had little fondness for Zola ("an excellent lawmaker who wrote superb programs and miserable plays"), though the two men's ideals and ultimate reforms were quite similar. Becque too became a founding spirit of André Antoine's Théâtre-Libre and was (according to James Huneker) "the true father of the latter-day movement in French dramatic literature."

Becque was a sharp-tongued misanthrope whose subsequent career accentuated his waspishness. He was the son of a clerk and a Parisian by birth and lifelong residence. His interest in the theatre was stimulated by an uncle who had himself written and produced farces. Becque soon left his job as a railroad clerk and pursued his literary inclinations, reading voraciously and writing poetry, as he continued to do for the rest of his life. He became the tutor and private secretary of a Polish diplomat who introduced him to Victorien Joncières, a young composer for whom Becque, in 1865, wrote his first dramatic work, a libretto for the opera *Sardanapale;* almost immediately produced and published (1867), it is a slight work imitative of Byron. Becque subsequently ignored the opera, and he thereafter devoted his time and efforts principally to drama and the theatre. He started publishing newspaper criticisms (periodically he was to eke out his living from journalism) and wrote his first play, *L'Enfant prodigue,* a slight if witty vaudeville. The influential drama critic Francisque Sarcey refused to help get it produced —he was later to attack Becque, and in turn was attacked even more vitriolically by Becque; but Sardou assisted in getting the farce produced and published (1868), thereby winning Becque's lifelong admiration—though Sardou's own drama was precisely the type Becque despised and sought to supplant.

Becque's next play, *Michel Pauper* (1870), a brutal romantic melodrama about a hero destroyed by his monstrous wife, excoriates cupidity—the same theme that he later treated in *The Vultures. Michel Pauper* was roundly rejected—thus starting Becque's lifelong struggle with managers—and the playwright rashly produced it himself. Even the sympathetic Huneker characterized it as "an indigestible mess," and audiences ridiculed it off the stage: "to laugh as one did at *Michel Pauper*" became a fashionable *bon mot.* Becque's next work, *L'Enlèvement* (1871), a domestic play whose thesis resembles that of Ibsen's A DOLL'S HOUSE but whose dramaturgy is that of the younger Dumas, fared little better. Increasingly embittered and financially ruined, Becque left the theatre to work in a stockbroker's office and write newspaper articles. His mordant wit and quarrelsomeness accentuated his difficulties, and he returned to try his luck once again as a playwright. But though his masterpiece (*The Vultures*) was completed by 1877, five years were to pass before he won his struggle with managers to have it produced exactly as he had written it.

In the meantime Becque did gain some success, if little income, with the production of two one-acters: *La Navette* (*The Merry-Go-Round,* 1878; also translated as *The Gadfly*), a short precursor of *The Parisian Woman* that features a flirt who plays "shuttlecock" (a more literal translation of the title) with various lovers; and *Les Honnêtes Femmes* (1880), an atypical comedy—it became one of Becque's most popular plays and long remained in the repertory of the Comédie-Française—about a married woman who disposes of an importunate suitor by having him marry her goddaughter. With the next two plays—*The Vultures* and *The Parisian Woman*—Becque established his stature as a major playwright. His remaining output consists of short pieces: *Veuve!* (1897), the sequel to *The Parisian Woman; Le Domino à quatre* (1897), a farce; *Le Départ* (1897), a Zolaesque portrayal of a working girl whose virtue becomes her undoing; *Une Exécution* (1897), another farce; and *Madeleine* (1896), one act of the uncompleted *Les Polichinelles.* A militant exposé of the world of finance, this play was finished by Henri de Noussanne (1865–1936) and published in 1910. Though he was elected to the Legion of Honor in 1886 after the appearance of his greatest works, popular esteem continued to elude Becque except, curiously, in Italy. He became increasingly splenetic, consoling himself with the knowledge that he had always aimed only "to satisfy myself." An impecunious and lonesome man, he died in a sanatorium.

Becque has been praised most for his merciless depiction of contemporary society's immorality and for the naturalness of his characterization and dialogue, which he strove to perfect by articulating written lines before his mirror. A comparison with the dialogue of fashionable contemporary plays shows how he managed in his best works to avoid melodramatic excesses. Only *The Parisian Woman* is still effective, however—and no little because of its wit and the *coup de théâtre* at the end of the first scene. Otherwise Becque's plays have dated hopelessly, despite his eschewing traditionally mechanical plotting, "big" scenes, and declamations. ("I have never entertained much liking for assassins, hysterical and alcoholic characters, or for martyrs of heredity and victims of evolution," Becque wrote.) They are not redeemed today even by his deeply felt indignation against moral turpitude, or by the irony with which characters themselves unwittingly reveal their own immorality in platitudinous would-be justifications. Yet the influence of Becque on the modern drama should not be underestimated. In 1882 he drew up a series of articles to guide the government if it should decide to assist theatre artists. These articles, which expressed Becque's artistic ideals on the writing as well as the production of plays, became the germ of Antoine's Théâtre-Libre—the theatre that was to help reform modern drama along the lines proposed by both Becque and Zola and with their support.

Becque's plays were published in three volumes in 1898, and his seven-volume complete works appeared 1924–26. Becque's autobiography is *Souvenirs d'un auteur dramatique* (1885). *The Vultures* and *The Parisian Woman* (along with *The Merry-Go-Round*) are published in *Three Plays by Henry Becque* (1913), edited by Freeman Tilden, which has an informative introduction; they also appear in various anthologies. Other appraisals of Becque's work appear in James Huneker's *Iconoclasts* (1905) and in studies of Zola and of the Théâtre-Libre, notably in Samuel M. Waxman's *Antoine and The Théâtre-Libre* (1926).

BEDBUG, THE (*Klop*), "a fantasy in nine scenes" by VLADIMIR VLADIMIROVICH MAYAKOVSKY, published and produced in 1929. Setting: Russia in 1929 and in 1979.

Originally a failure but frequently performed in Soviet Russia (with music by Dmitri Shostakovich) after its successful revival in 1955, Mayakovsky's best-known work has also appeared in the West. It is an extravagant, fast-paced satire of Soviet bureaucracy—hence it was banned for some years—and of the bourgeoisie, of which there were still uneradicated traces in 1929. Mayakovsky portrays them as curious historical specimens fifty years in the future.

Scene I. Vendors hawk their wares in a department store. Former worker and Party member Prisypkin ("fried fish"), a philistine with social ambitions, comes in with the mother of his new fiancée and with Oleg Bayan, "a man of natural talents from a family of landlords." Prisypkin buys fur-lined brassieres, which he mistakes for caps, for his future children: "My home has got to be a place of plenty." Bayan is amused at Prisypkin, who is "of ancient, unsullied proletarian stock," and who proclaims that "Our Red family must have no bourgeois ways in it"—as he buys fancy goods. An ignorant boor, he constantly misunderstands the sophisticated Bayan. Prisypkin's former betrothed appears, grief-stricken at being jilted. "Citizen! Our love is liquidated," Prisypkin tells her; "don't interfere with free civil sentiment."

Scene II. In his dormitory, Prisypkin's associates are amused to see that he has changed his name to the aristocratic-sounding "Pierre Skripkin." Along with Bayan, they chaff him. But when they hear that his jilted former fiancée has tried to commit suicide, they throw him out. "You sure are busting out of your class with a bang, pal!" the janitor says as he picks him up. Prisypkin ignores him, hails a cab, and moves to his new home.

Scenes III and IV. Prisypkin has a rowdy, drunken wedding. It culminates in a brawl during which the stove is turned over, and the place goes up in flames like a powder keg. "Why shouldn't it burn? Cobwebs and liquor," the fire chief says as his men flood the house with water that soon freezes.

Scene V. Fifty years later a digging squad discovers a block of ice in the basement. It contains the frozen figure of a man. "Radioscopy showed that on the creature's hands there were calluses, formerly, half a century ago, the sign of a workingman," the president of the Institute of Human Resurrection announces. The international vote (for the whole world now is Soviet) is to "resurrect" this "individuum."

Scene VI. The process is observed with interest by the scientists. "The movements are normal, he's scratching—evidently certain parasites pertaining to such individuums are coming alive," a professor remarks. Revealed is a bewildered and disheveled Prisypkin, with a guitar. He scratches, and a bedbug crawls out of his collar.

Scene VII. Reporters discuss the spreading epidemic caused by "this resurrected mammal." Smoking, drinking, and even dancing are breaking out everywhere, they reveal: "the doctors say that people bitten by such beasts acquire all the basic traits of this toadyism epidemic." They hunt and finally catch the escaped bedbug. "Our city can well be proud," the director says. "Here, in my hands, lies the only living *bedbugus normalis*."

Scenes VIII and IX. The filthy Prisypkin, bottles and cigarette butts littered around his bed, repulses everybody. He is displayed at the zoo together with the bug, after the chairman delivers a long address. "There are two of them—of different sizes but essentially identical," he explains; "they are the famous *bedbugus normalis* and—the *inhabitantus vulgaris*. Both are to be found in the rotten mattresses of time." The cage is uncovered and the curiosities are displayed. Prisypkin is let out, starts to talk to the horrified audience, and is quickly put back and covered. Attendants ventilate the area and the director explains, "The noise and all the lights made him have hallucinations. . . . Don't worry. There's nothing to it. . . . Go home quietly, now, citizens."

BEER-HOFMANN, Richard (1866–1945), Austrian novelist, poet, and dramatist, was an important member of the *Jungwien* group that dominated the Austrian literary scene at the turn of the century. More like HUGO VON HOFMANNSTHAL than ARTHUR SCHNITZLER, its other principal members, Beer-Hofmann was a religious dramatic poet, and he was inspired chiefly by Goethe, Shakespeare, and—most of all—the Bible. He wrote much but published very little, for he carefully reworked everything. DIE HISTORIE VON KÖNIG DAVID (1933), his ambitious major work, remained uncompleted. But its prelude, *Jaakobs Traum* (JACOB'S DREAM, 1918), was produced in theatres throughout the world after World War I. The play's continuing importance was stressed by THORNTON WILDER'S introduction to the American translation published after World War II.

The sole heir of a patrician Jewish family, Beer-Hofmann earned a jurisprudence doctorate at the university of his native Vienna in 1890. His first publication, the short-story collection *Novellen* (1893), was praised for its psychological insight. In these stories Beer-Hofmann deals with the theological and moral themes he was to portray in his later works. Even more popular was his "Schlaflied für Miriam" (1898), a much-anthologized poem that was originally a lullaby to his daughter. After the publication of *Der Tod Georgs* (1900), his only novel, came his first and other important stage work, *Der Graf von Charolais* (1904), an impressionistic *Volks-Schillerpreis*-winning adaptation of Philip Massinger and Nathan Field's *The Fatal Dowry* (1632). Beer-Hofmann freely altered its original plot and characterization to stress the irresistible power of fate; he invented the Shylock-like Jewish creditor, who bitterly explains how the wrongs inflicted on his race prevent his being as "all human beings should / Be kind unto each other," and he changed the adulterous wife from a lustful hussy to a decent woman momentarily overcome by temptation, the uncontrollable force that "drove us—drives us. It! Not I—nor you!"

Similar ideas about divine omnipotence and the need for human brotherhood were developed more lyrically and with greater complexity in the trilogy in which Beer-Hofmann interpreted and universalized Judaic history and myth. He had spent six years on the prelude, and the trilogy's first play

(*Der Junge David,* 1933) was not to appear until nearly two decades later, when the Nazis came to power. Their rule helped impede the completion of the trilogy. At the very last moment, after the Anschluss and the pogroms that followed, his friends rescued Beer-Hofmann. In 1939, at the outbreak of World War II, he emigrated to New York. There he spent his last years.

Ida Bension Wynn's translation of *Jacob's Dream* (1946) has, aside from Wilder's introduction, a bibliography and an extensive biographical-analytical essay by Solomon Liptzin, who had earlier published a book-length study in English, *Richard Beer-Hofmann* (1936).

BEERBOHM, Sir **Max** (1872–1956), English writer and caricaturist, was famous as a wit, novelist (*Zuleika Dobson,* 1911), the successor of BERNARD SHAW as the *Saturday Review*'s drama critic (1898–1910), and the personification of the man-about-town at the turn of the century. He also dabbled in drama, producing a total of four plays. *The Happy Hypocrite* (1900), a one-act curtain raiser and originally a story (1897), was based on his romance with the music-hall actress Marie Cecilia "Cissie" Loftus; later it was made into a three-act play by CLEMENCE DANE. *Caesar's Wife* (1920) is an adaptation (written with Frank Harris, 1855–1931) from the French, and *The Fly on the Wheel* (1904) is a comedy written with Murray Carson (1865–1917). While all these were produced, none was as popular as his last work, *A Social Success* (1913), a one-act comedy written in the style of OSCAR WILDE. These plays are discussed in David Cecil's biography, *Max* (1965). His dramatic criticisms were republished in the two-volume *Around Theatres* (1930) and in *Last Theatres, 1904–1910* (1970).

BEFORE A HIGHER COURT, or, **ECSTASY** (*Vid högre rätt, eller, Rus*), is the inclusive title under which Strindberg's *Advent, ett mysterium* (ADVENT) and *Brott och brott* (CRIMES AND CRIMES) were published in 1899.

BEFORE BREAKFAST, a one-act play by EUGENE O'NEILL, published and produced in 1916. Setting: a dingy contemporary flat on Christopher Street in New York City.

In his "last appearance on any stage" O'Neill played the offstage Alfred, his favorite role, in this otherwise little notable play. O'Neill's father, who volunteered suggestions for the monologue, was glad to see his son finally receive some recognition, but is reported to have remarked, "My boy, why don't you write pleasanter plays?"

Preparing breakfast, Mrs. Rowland nags and bitterly complains about her marriage and her husband Alfred, an unsuccessful writer who is in the adjoining room. The monologue (modeled on Strindberg's THE STRONGER) is interrupted only by the husband's "sensitive hand" reaching into the kitchen for shaving water, and by his groan—for, as Mrs. Rowland finally discovers to her horror, Alfred has just slashed his throat.

BEFORE SUNRISE (*Vor Sonnenaufgang*), a "social drama" in five acts by GERHART HAUPTMANN, published and produced in 1889. Setting: a wealthy farmhouse in a contemporary Silesian coal-mining district.

This historically important play, also translated as *Before Dawn,* launched German NATURALIST drama as well as the career of Germany's first great modern playwright. Its representation of depravity created a furor when the play was produced by Otto Brahm's Freie Bühne, which had opened a month earlier with Ibsen's GHOSTS. Hauptmann's first play, stressing man's victimization by heredity and environment, is a doctrinaire apprentice work. Yet it has some power, particularly in its speeches in different dialects. The unsavory naturalism is relieved, too, by the hero's idealism and the lyrical love scenes. Hauptmann's defense of the "unnaturalism" of these scenes was: "Can I help it if nature is also beautiful?"

Alfred Loth, a young Socialist, prepares to study the condition of coal miners. He visits his college friend, who controls the mines. The latter, once an idealist, is now an opportunistic, ruthless engineer living in the house of wealthy peasants, whose daughter he has married. Loth falls in love with her sister, Helene Krause, the only one not degraded by the family's suddenly acquired wealth. The father is a depraved alcoholic, the vicious stepmother has an affair with an equally vicious fop, who is to marry Helene, and the engineer (her brother-in-law) tries to seduce her. Helene soon falls in love with the visiting young idealist. Though a bit smug—in his abstention from liquor, tobacco, and gorging like her nouveau riche, philistine family—Loth is cultivated and full of ardor to end human "sickness and want, servitude and spiritual meanness." The engineer fears that Loth will stir up the poverty-stricken miners, and tries to bribe him to forgo his investigation. Helene—who is yearning to escape from her despicable environment—confesses her love to Loth, and they prepare to elope. Just then, her sister (the engineer's wife) is revealed to be an alcoholic, whose first child died of alcoholism at the age of three and whose second child now is stillborn. As her physician, another old, corrupted friend of Loth's, tells the appalled idealist, "There's nothing but drunkenness, gluttony, inbreeding, and, in consequence, degeneration along the whole line." Having all along stressed the necessity of physical and mental health "before the sunrise" of a new life, Loth renounces his plans and leaves. When she discovers his escape, Helene commits suicide. Her drunken father stumbles home from the tavern, singing lasciviously, "Ain' I got me a couple o' purty daughters?"

BEFORE SUNSET (*Vor Sonnenuntergang*), a play in five acts by GERHART HAUPTMANN, published and produced in 1932. Setting: a large city in contemporary Germany.

Hauptmann's last full-length prose drama, written when he was seventy, consciously alludes to the title of his first produced drama, BEFORE SUNRISE.

Matthias Clausen is a rich, cultivated industrialist celebrating his seventieth birthday. Having mourned for his wife for some time, he is regaining his interest in life. He falls in love with his gardener's young daughter and prepares to marry her. But his adult children, afraid of being disinherited, have him declared senile. Thwarted and broken, Clausen commits suicide.

BEGGAR ON HORSEBACK, a play in two parts by GEORGE S. KAUFMAN and MARC CONNELLY (music by Deems Taylor), produced in 1924 and published in 1925. Setting: an American apartment on a spring afternoon.

Kaufman's sharp wit and Connelly's whimsy made this the only commercially successful EXPRESSIONIST drama in New York, where it had a major revival in 1970. A zany fantasy in the form of a dream play, it spoofs America's business-oriented, money-worshiping society, and pleads for artistic integrity. It is a thoroughly American pendant to Paul Apel's comedy *Hans Sonnenstössers Höllenfahrt* (1912). The title comes from Robert Greene's proverbial sentence, "Set a beggar on horseback and they say he will never light" (*Orpharion,* 1599).

Part I. Neil McRae's job, orchestrating cheap tunes, leaves him no time for his symphony. The overworked composer is visited by the vulgar Gladys Cady, who wants to marry him, and by her equally vulgar but wealthy family. When they finally leave, the attractive girl next door, though she loves Neil, decides he should take the opportunity to have the Cadys subsidize his genius, and advises him to marry Gladys. Feeling rebuffed by the girl he loves, the overtired Neil angrily proposes when Gladys calls him up. Then he falls asleep and has a dream.

The Dream. Neil and Gladys marry and move to an extravagant house. Never getting the chance to compose, Neil is miserable among ever-growing numbers of butlers, Gladys (who loves cheap music), her father (in golf clothes and with a telephone attached to his chest), her mother (with a rocking chair attached to her seat), and her faceless relatives and friends. He is equally miserable in Cady's "widget" industry, where he fills out endless requisition forms and participates in a ridiculous conference. At supper, Gladys insists on dancing. Neil is desperately unhappy and thinks of the poor but happy life he might have had with the girl next door. He kills Gladys and her family, and is instantly surrounded by reporters.

Part II (Dream continues). Judge Cady presides over a comic-opera trial. Neil presents "A Kiss in Xanadu," a delightfully romantic pantomime he composed with the girl next door. But the court rules it "highbrow," pronounces him guilty, and sentences him to the "Cady Consolidated Art Factory." There various great artists produce machine art in their cells. Neil composes "mammies, sweeties, and fruit songs," and "a pathetic": "You've broken my heart like you broke my heart, / So why should you break it again?" He wants to escape, but Cady will not allow it: "We pay the piper and we tell him what to play. / You sold your soul and you can't get away." But as Neil shakes his cage door, it opens. He walks out in happy amazement: "It was never locked!"—and awakes.

Gladys's request to postpone their engagement for a week to "sort of play around" with a visiting boyfriend gives Neil the opportunity to break their engagement—and to marry the girl next door.

BEGGAR, THE (*Der Bettler*), a drama in five acts by REINHARD JOHANNES SORGE, published in 1912 and produced in 1917. Setting: Germany, c. 1911.

Sorge won the Kleist Prize for this autobiographical play, his only notable one. Subtitled *"Eine dramatische Sendung"* ("a dramatic mission"), it has been credited with introducing EXPRESSIONIST drama to Germany. Characteristic of the genre are this play's almost interchangeable unnamed characters and the tableaux (or "stations") in which they appear, an apparent formlessness heightened by fantasy scenes, theatricalized "stream of consciousness" achieved by floodlighting the scene segment that occupies the hero's mind, and the father-son conflict. The family scenes (Acts II and III) have a romantic spring setting and are predominantly NATURALISTIC.

The Poet excoriates tradition. He seeks to dramatize his fantasy of "a higher life . . . in glorious sublimity," he tells his friend, though this statement alienates a potential backer of his play. In cafés habituated by newspaper readers, fliers, and prostitutes, the Poet declaims his ideals. Only a Girl, who is troubled by worry about her illegitimate child, follows him. At home the Poet (now the Son) plays out his domestic tragedy. His Father, representing the Establishment, is an insane engineer who dreams of technological projects to create a utopia for mankind. More dismayed than hostile, the Son—whose idea of utopia is spiritual and moral—grants the Father's wish and poisons him (and incidentally his Mother as well) as they drink to the future. Later, after a brief stint as a journalist, the Poet again declines to alter his play to get it produced. The Girl gives up her illegitimate child when she conceives the Poet's child, which symbolizes the eternity for which he craves. Thus redeemed, she and the Poet are mystically united as vistas of the future beckon them with a hymn.

BEHAN, Brendan [Francis] (1923–64), Irish playwright, had a brief but flamboyant career. Repeatedly serving prison terms for activities with the secret Irish Republican Army (I.R.A.), he was noted for his drunken roistering (his appearance on the stage to argue with the actors performing his plays, he claimed, was good for the box office) and for the writings (many of them originally in Gaelic) based on his experiences. The most important of his works are *Borstal Boy* (1958), an anecdotal account of his three-year term in a Borstal reformatory, and dramatized in 1967 by Frank McMahon (? –) into a record-breaking

Brendan Behan. (*Irish Tourist Board*)

hit at the Abbey Theatre, and his two best plays, THE QUARE FELLOW (1954) and *An Giall* (THE HOSTAGE, 1958).

Behan was born in the slums of Dublin to a family of rebellious nationalists. At the time, his father, a housepainter, was serving a prison term for political crimes. His brother Dominic (1928-), who wrote a number of books about the family, also wrote an antipatriotic play, *Posterity Be Damned* (1959); and his uncle, Peader Kearney, wrote "The Soldier's Song," Ireland's national anthem. Brendan Behan was educated by the French Sisters of Charity (1928–34) and at the Irish Christian Brothers School, whence he was expelled. He learned his father's trade, joined the I.R.A., and was arrested in England while on a mission to blow up a battleship. He was sent to Borstal for three years; back in Dublin, he was sentenced to a fourteen-year term for political offenses. After almost six years he was released during the general amnesty of 1946, but subsequently he was rearrested twice, and deported to France in 1952.

His prison experiences inspired *The Quare Fellow,* which made his name famous when Joan Littlewood produced it with her Theatre Workshop at the Theatre Royal in Stratford (East London), two years after its Dublin production by Alan Simpson. *The Hostage* had a similar but even more notable history, though its spirited bawdiness and irreverent satire occasionally caused it to be banned in Canada and in the United States. Behan's *Moving Out* and *The Garden Party,* slight comic sketches about displaced Dublin families (actually about the relocation of the Behans), were written for the radio (as *The Quare Fellow* originally had been) and produced in 1952 by Radio Éireann, and subsequently played over other European airwaves as well as on Dublin's stages. A similar sketch is *The Big House,* which first appeared in the miscellany collection *Brendan Behan's Island: An Irish Sketchbook* (1962). A final play, *Richard's Cork Leg,* was completed but remained unproduced at the time of Behan's death—from various infirmities, all of them aggravated by his heavy drinking.

Behan's drama has many vaudeville features and is highly theatrical. Therefore, however, it is not particularly amusing on the printed page. It is also shapeless, according to many critics, though others have vigorously refuted that charge. Joan Littlewood has been credited for reworking his two famous plays into the form in which they were produced and published. At the same time, these plays are highly entertaining and they reveal fine powers of observation and satire. Critics have disagreed about Behan's work: some have denigrated it as talented wisecracking that is totally dependent on creative direction; others have hailed it as witty and brilliant (if occasionally undisciplined) playwriting.

Apart from the works already cited, Behan wrote sensitive Gaelic poetry; *The Scarperer* (1964), a posthumously published novel that had been serialized in a Dublin newspaper in Behan's lifetime; *Hold Your Hour and Have Another* (1964), a collection of essays on pub-touring in Dublin, illustrated by his wife; *Brendan Behan's New York* (1964), another miscellany; and the posthumous tape-recorded second autobiography, *Confessions of an Irish Rebel* (1965). See also Alan Simpson's account of the first productions of Behan's plays at the Pike Theatre in Dublin, *Beckett and Behan and a Theatre in Dublin* (1962). Book-length studies of the playwright and his work include Dominic Behan's *My Brother Brendan* (1965), Sean McCann's collection of essays on *The World of Brendan Behan* (1965), Rae Jeffs's *Brendan Behan: Man and Showman* (1966), Ted E. Boyle's *Brendan Behan* (1969), and Ulric O'Connor's *Brendan* (1970).

BEHRMAN, S[amuel] N[athaniel] (1893-), American dramatist, between the 1920's and the 1960's wrote some thirty plays, many of them adaptations and translations. His best and most original work appeared in the dozen years before World War II, and consists of drawing-room comedies like THE SECOND MAN (1927), BIOGRAPHY (1932), RAIN FROM HEAVEN (1934), and END OF SUMMER (1936). Increasingly dominant in these comedies was Behrman's concern with the menace of Fascism and the need for humanitarianism and tolerance. Such concern with contemporary social problems changed his plays from conventional high comedy into a more earnest type of drama. But if Behrman's plays are comedies of ideas, they are in the tradition of Congreve and Molière rather than in the tradition of BERNARD SHAW. Portrayed and explored and resolved are drawing-room characters and situations, not ideas—though the plays *are* heavily freighted with ideas. Nonetheless, Behrman felt ambivalent about producing even serious comedies during the tragic 1930's, a feeling that he dramatized in the dilemma of the playwright-protagonist of NO TIME FOR COMEDY (1939).

Behrman was born in Worcester, Massachusetts, and grew up in a markedly different setting from that of his salon comedies. In *The New Yorker* autobiographical sketches he later republished as *The Worcester Account* (1954) and dramatized in *The Cold Wind and the Warm* (1958), Behrman depicts his small-town, Jewish middle-class boyhood. He was early attracted to the theatre by a local stock company, wrote short plays, and did some acting. He was sent to Clark University and then Harvard University (where he studied in Professor George Pierce Baker's 47 Workshop), and in 1918 he completed his M.A. at Columbia University. Throughout these and later years, Behrman's interest in the theatre persisted. He wrote plays and, to support himself, magazine and newspaper articles. Briefly he worked as a theatre press agent.

After some undistinguished collaborations (with OWEN DAVIS and others), Behrman achieved immediate success in 1927 with his *The Second Man.* It was followed by *Serena Blandish* (1929), his dramatization of ENID BAGNOLD's then-popular but anonymous satirical novel about English society; *Meteor* (1929), a character comedy that features a ruthless financier; and *Brief Moment* (1931), a less popular comedy about an enervated playboy who marries a lusty cabaret singer. Between *Biography,* his finest comedy, and his earlier-mentioned hits of the 1930's, came *A Love Story* (1933), a flop; AMPHITRYON 38 (1937), a popular adaptation of Giraudoux's comedy; and *Wine of Choice* (1938), an antitotalitarian drawing-room comedy whose villain is a ruthless American Communist.

Behrman's high reputation as a major comic dramatist led critics and reviewers to expect further distinguished work from him. But they waited in vain. Behrman's later works include few original plays—another two anti-Fascist comedies, *The Talley Method* (1941) and *Dunnigan's Daughter* (1945), followed the formula of the earlier ones—and a number of translations and adaptations: *The Pirate* (1942), which features a mountebank in the West Indies and is based on *Die Seeräuber* (1911), a romantic drama by the German playwright LUDWIG FULDA; JACOBOWSKY AND THE COLONEL (1944), an adaptation of *Jacobowsky und der Oberst* by FRANZ WERFEL; *Jane* (1946), a dramatization of SOMERSET MAUGHAM's story; *I Know My Love* (1949), a sentimental romance based on *Auprès de ma blonde* by MARCEL ACHARD; *Fanny* (1954), a musical (written with JOSHUA LOGAN) adaptation of MARCEL PAGNOL's trilogy; *The Cold Wind and the Warm,* the already-cited dramatization of Behrman's autobiography; and *Lord Pengo* (1962), his adaptation of his biography of the famous art dealer *Duveen* (1952). Behrman's last notable play was the "serious comedy" *But for Whom Charlie* (1964), a social satire about a foundation whose insensitive executive officer (Charlie) awards grants without regard to the applying authors' talents. Featured in the Lincoln Center Repertory Company's opening season, the play failed dismally: it was a tired replica of Behrman's 1930's comedies of manners.

Most of Behrman's comedies follow this formula: A famous sophisticated (often liberal and/or idealistic) man or woman, surrounded by two or more suitors, agonizes over his (or her) choice; this agonizing is replete with much witty self-analysis, confrontation with a diametrically opposed social viewpoint personified by a doctor or a financier who is a totalitarian egomaniac, and is resolved in favor of the genial protagonist's detached comfort. Ideas and social criticisms, important though they were in raising (or seeming to raise) Behrman's drama above the merely commercial and entertaining, are subsidiary to the drawing-room personalities and to the particular situation, and they usually evaporate in a stalemate and a cavalier reaffirmation of virtues like decency and tolerance. Granting Behrman's limitations as a dramatist, however, he was nonetheless a fine craftsman, marvelously adept at creating entertaining drawing-room situations (though rarely much plot), witty dialogue, and charming worldly characters that provided excellent parts for stars like Alfred Lunt, Lynn Fontanne, Ina Claire, Katharine Cornell, and Laurence Olivier. Behrman was thus one of the important playwrights during the first two decades of his creativity, and one of the very few successful American practitioners of "high comedy."

Behrman also wrote film scenarios and a biography of MAX BEERBOHM, *Portrait of Max* (1960). Significant discussions of his work may be found in Joseph Wood Krutch's *The American Drama Since 1918* (1957), Gerald Rabkin's *Drama and Commitment* (1964), and Allan Lewis's *American Plays and Playwrights of the Contemporary Theatre* (revised, 1970).

BEIN, Albert (1902–), American novelist and playwright, was one of the proletarian authors of the 1930's. The most successful of his social protest dramas are *Let Freedom Ring* (1935), an adaptation of Grace Lumpkin's novel about a North Carolina mill strike, *To Make My Bread* (1932); and *Heavenly Express* (1940), a poetic fantasy (with much local color and singing) about the hereafter as imagined by hoboes, who see their old patroness picked up by the heavenly express after she is selected by the Almighty Vagabond to "mudder du boys an' make 'em hot meals." Bein's *Land of Fame* (1943; written with Mary Bein, ? -) is an anti-Nazi play about Greece's fight to regain her independence. His fiction includes an autobiographical novel about a brutal reform school, *Youth in Hell* (1930).

BELASCO, David (1859–1931), American producer and playwright, was the outstanding personality of the theatre of his time. His career lasted from the 1870's until shortly before his death, thus linking the mid-nineteenth-century age of Dion Boucicault with that of EUGENE O'NEILL and the postwar writers. Belasco is notable for his ultimately victorious struggle with the powerful Klaw-Erlanger syndicate; for the meticulous care he devoted to the discovery and training of great actors like Mrs. Leslie Carter, David Warfield, Ina Claire, and Fanny Brice; for his exotic stage productions, which became world-famous for their lavishness and scenic REALISM; and, finally, for the plays that he wrote and adapted by himself and in collaboration. Belasco had a hand in the composition of countless plays, at least fifteen of which were produced before he was thirteen years old. His more popular plays (some of them written with JOHN LUTHER LONG) during the twentieth century include DU BARRY (1901), THE DARLING OF THE GODS (1902), ADREA (1904), and THE RETURN OF PETER GRIMM (1911). But even better remembered, because of Giacomo Puccini's subsequent operas, are Belasco's MADAME BUTTERFLY (1900) and THE GIRL OF THE GOLDEN WEST (1905).

The son of English Jews who were connected with the theatre, Belasco was born in San Francisco. Part of his early education was in a monastery, which influenced the later "Bishop of Broadway's" mode of dress. Interested in the theatre almost from infancy, Belasco played children's parts and adapted popular novels, poems, and other plays for productions in which he acted and which he helped stage. He played with various companies, including that of his first important collaborator, JAMES A. HERNE. Their most significant joint work, *Hearts of Oak* (1879), was a melodrama of the rivalry of a father and his foster son for the love of the foster daughter; first produced as *Chums*, it was based on Henry J. Leslie's *The Mariner's Compass*, an English play that had briefly appeared in New York in 1865. After a quarrel, Belasco sold his rights to Herne, who made a fortune out of the play and later rewrote it again. Belasco soon moved to New York, where he became stage manager of the Madison Square Theatre in 1884. *May Blossom* (1884), his first and most popular play there, is a variation on the plot of *Hearts of Oak;* it features a girl who marries the man she loves upon receiving false reports of her husband's death.

Next Belasco teamed up with the otherwise unnotable playwright Henry C. De Mille (1850–93) to produce four plays: the most popular of them were *The Wife* (1887), a derivative of *The Banker's Daughter* by BRONSON HOWARD; and *Lord Chumley* (1888), a domestic drama featuring an Englishman who bears some likeness to Lord Dundreary of Tom Taylor's *Our American Cousin* (1858). With Franklyn Fyles (1847–1911), the well-known drama critic, Belasco wrote a popular Indian melodrama set at an army post in Sioux country, *The Girl I Left Behind Me* (1893). Another hit was Belasco's *The Heart of Maryland* (1895), a Civil War play based on Rose Hartwick Thorpe's poem "Curfew Must Not Ring Tonight!" (1867) and featuring Mrs. Leslie Carter as Maryland Calvert, who saves her Northern lover by swinging on the curfew bell clapper to deaden the sound that would signal his execution. Of historical interest is Belasco's "naughty" *Zaza* (1898), an adaptation from the French that was made into an opera by Ruggiero Leoncavallo in 1900. It was the already-cited works that followed, however, which Belasco wrote in his characteristic exotic style, with which he made his most notable contribution to world drama. Belasco's last important play was *The Return of Peter Grimm,* whose plot is based on a suggestion by his old collaborator's son, the movie director Cecil B. De Mille. He succeeded neither with *Van Der Decken* (1915), based on the Flying Dutchman myth, nor with *The Son Daughter* (1919), a Chinese melodrama written with George Scarborough (1875–1951).

Though Belasco continued to write—adapting foreign plays—his major efforts thereafter went into producing and managing. Aside from bringing to the American stage exotically lavish and photographically realistic as well as imaginative settings, Belasco encouraged native writers, producing hundreds of their plays in the Broadway theatre he took over and named after himself. His own plays were, for the most part, collaborations and adaptations that today read like the claptrap sentimentality and melodrama of a bygone age. But they were never meant to be read. Penned for the living stage, they long entertained great masses of theatregoers in America and England, and they have provided drama for opera lovers to this day.

Belasco's plays were collected in *Six Plays* (1928) and in Volumes XVII and XVIII of *America's Lost Plays* (1941, republished 1963–65). *Six Plays,* with an introduction by Belasco and notes by Montrose J. Moses, includes *Madame Butterfly, Du Barry, The Darling of the Gods, Adrea, The Girl of the Golden West,* and *The Return of Peter Grimm.* Volume XVII of *America's Lost Plays* (also with an introduction and notes) includes Belasco's collaborations with Henry C. De Mille, and was edited by Robert H. Ball; Volume XVIII includes *The Girl I Left Behind Me* and *The Heart of Maryland,* and was edited by Glenn Hughes and George Savage. Belasco's autobiography is *The Theatre Through the Stage Door* (1919). William Winter's adulatory two-volume biography, *The Life of David Belasco* (1918), has been superseded by Craig Timberlake's *Life and Work of David Belasco, Bishop of Broadway* (1954), which has bibliographies.

BELGIUM. Like the rest of the country's cultural and social life, Belgian drama is bilingual. Its most renowned author, MAURICE MAETERLINCK, wrote in French for the Parisian theatres—like the majority of his confreres (notably FERNAND CROMMELYNCK), whose work was absorbed by and usually is considered as belonging to the French. Flemish-language playwrights, though almost unknown elsewhere, are produced in both Belgium and HOLLAND, for in twentieth-century literature and theatre the national boundary is irrelevant. Belgium's other major playwright, MICHEL DE

GHELDERODE, composed some of his plays in Flemish and was first produced by the Vlaamse Volkstoneel, the popular troupe founded by Oskar de Gruyter in 1920 that gave birth to the modern Flemish theatre. Both the Flemish and the French dramas reflect their authors' heritage, shared with the peasants, the merchants, and the artisans immortalized by native painters and transmitted in the still-popular medieval religious and folk legends. The early modern Belgian and the Flemish drama is poetic, SYMBOLIC, mystic, and gothic; and particularly in the comedies, it reflects the canvases of its great masters—the droll settings and folk of Breughel the elder, the sensuousness of Rubens, and the frightening grotesqueries of Hieronymus Bosch.

The modern Belgian drama received a belated start with *La Jeune Belgique,* a literary review founded in 1881 by a group of students who sought to revive native literature. The self-styled *Les Jeunes Belgiques* included Maeterlinck as well as great poets like EMILE VERHAEREN; CHARLES VAN LERBERGHE, whose mood drama anticipated Maeterlinck's; Georges Rodenbach (1855–98), who dramatized one of his own novels; Iwan Gilkin (1858–1924), a disciple of Charles Baudelaire and the author of grandiose tragedies about student rebellions in the tsarist capital, *Les Étudiants Russes* (1906) and *Savonarole* (1906), whose protagonist agonizes between religious and political aspirations; Paul Spaak (1870–1936), whose great hit was *Kaatje* (1908), the title heroine of which reveals the beauty of Belgium to her lover, an artist returning from Italy after being thrown over by his previous mistress; Count Albert Du Bois (1875–1940), whose many plays focused on biblical characters and other figures like Homer, Lord Byron, and Don Quixote; and Edmond Picard (1836–1924), a lawyer-playwright who in 1880 founded *Les Jeunes Belgiques'* first review and whose most distinguished play was *Ambidextre journaliste* (1904).

Other early Belgian writers of French plays were the novelist of Antwerp life Georges Eekhoud (1854–1927), who also translated English Elizabethan drama and wrote a play about a medieval Flemish adventurer, *L'Imposteur magnanime* (1902); Gustave Vanzype (1869–1955), "the Belgian CUREL," the titles of whose NATURALIST plays, some of which have appeared in English, suggest their theses: *La Souveraine* (1899, translated as *Mother Nature*), *L'Aumône* (1901, translated as *Charity*), and *Les Étapes* (1907, translated as *Progress*); and the collaborators Jean-François Fonson (1870–1924) and Fernand Wicheler (1874–1935), whose boulevard comedy satires *Le Mariage de Mademoiselle Beulemans* (1910) and *La Demoiselle de magasin* (1913) were produced on Broadway respectively as *Suzanne* and *Along Came Ruth.* In the years around the turn of the century, however, Maeterlinck was the reigning Belgian playwright.

Flemish-language drama during this period for the most part consisted of heroic and religious verse plays. Notable were Alfred Hegenscheidt's (1866–1964) *Hamlet*-like *Starkadd* (1898), Raf (Raphaël) Verhulst's (1866–1941) Passion drama *Jezus de Nazarener* (1904), and the nationalistic and biblical plays of the poet-priest Cyriel Verschaeve (1874–1949). The development of farce in Belgium was stimulated by other Flemish-language writers, beginning with the dialect comedies of CYRIEL BUYSSE. Of later importance in Flemish drama was HERMAN TEIRLINCK, who introduced EXPRESSIONISM into the Belgian theatre; he had a prolific but less accomplished disciple in the playwright-critic Willem Putman (1900–54). Other significant writers of Flemish drama in the 1920's and 1930's were ANTON VAN DE VELDE and PAUL DE MONT.

In the years between the two world wars much of Belgium's French-language drama was absorbed by Parisian theatres. By far the most important playwright was Ghelderode, but his work did not become widely known until the late 1940's. Another important playwright of the age was Crommelynck, whose work also appeared abroad. Other notable Belgian writers of the period were HERMAN CLOSSON, whose reputation rests on his portrayals of historical figures; and HENRI SOUMAGNE, the unconventional lawyer-playwright.

Wartime and postwar playwrights of note are the Flemish author of light popular plays GASTON MARTENS and the more serious CHARLES BERTIN; JOHAN DAISNE; HERWIG HENSEN; and Charles Cordier (1911–), who adapted Roman plays and dramatized legends and history. There has been continued interest in dramatizations of legend (classic and medieval) and folklore (Renard the Fox, Tyl Uylenspiegel, etc.), history and national heroes (Godefroy de Bouillon and others), and the Bible. Younger or newly discovered mid-century Flemish-language dramatists of particular interest include HUGO CLAUS; the prolific Tone Brulin (1921–), whose hits include the anticolonialist *De Honden* (1961); and Jozef van Hoeck (1922–), who distinguished himself with *Voorlopig Vonnis* (1957), a drama that explores the problems of a conscience-stricken nuclear scientist. French-language dramatists are GEORGES SION; JEAN MOGIN; FÉLICIEN MARCEAU; Paul Willems (1912–), one of whose poetic dramatizations of folk legends, *Le Bon Vin de Monsieur Nuche* (*The Good Wine of Mr. Nuche,* 1950), was produced in New York; and José-André Lacour (1919–), who wrote a popular play about postwar adolescents, *L'Année du Bac* (1958).

The work of Maeterlinck and Ghelderode is readily available in translation, and there are a number of English studies of both authors' lives and work. Relatively few other Belgian plays have been translated, and discussion of Belgian writers is usually confined to books on French literature, drama, and theatre. Devoted entirely to the modern Belgian drama is a handsome pamphlet by the playwright SUZANNE LILAR, *The Belgian Theater Since 1890* (3d edition, 1962), first published in translation by the Belgian Government Information Center in 1950. Much of its content reappears in Vernon Mallinson's *Modern Belgian*

Literature 1830–1960 (1966), though the pamphlet is not cited in Mallinson's bibliography.

BELL, BOOK AND CANDLE, a comedy in three acts by JOHN VAN DRUTEN, published in 1949 and produced in 1950. Setting: a fashionable Murray Hill apartment in New York City, 1950.

This popular light piece features a beautiful modern witch, Gillian Holroyd. She becomes interested in the handsome young publisher living on the floor above. By casting a spell on him she wins him away from his fiancée, whom she had known and disliked during her schooldays. But when Gillian really falls in love with him, she loses her magic powers. Now an ordinary mortal, Gillian can live happily ever after with her publisher.

BELLAVITA, a one-act comedy by LUIGI PIRANDELLO, produced in 1927 and published in 1928. Setting: a small town in south Italy, 1927.

After his wife's death, the café proprietor Bellavita revenges himself on her lover. Bellavita follows him everywhere and publicly makes the lover appear so ridiculous that he rushes away furiously, spluttering in impotent rage.

BELLIDO [Cormenzana], **José María** (1922–), Spanish playwright, emerged in the 1960's with a number of political allegories. The first of them, *Fútbol* (*Football,* 1963), evaded censorship though it transparently satirizes the aftermath of the Spanish Civil War with its crushed soccer team hoping for a better day, its strutting victors, and its caricatures of an American, a Russian, an impotent Christ, and the Church. Bellido's next plays are similar allegories, but they were banned and first appeared in translation: *Tren a f . . .* (*Train to H . . . ,* 1970) portrays the passenger-shareholders of a rickety train en route to a destination that might be happiness; and *El pan y el arroz o geometría en amarillo* (*Bread and Rice or Geometry in Yellow,* 1970) depicts a group of brutal exploiters scheming to conquer the world but defeated by the passive resistance of multiplying numbers of smiling children. In these works, though they are abstract, Bellido presents his viewpoint and moral clearly and effectively.

A trained lawyer and a linguist, Bellido was born and raised in the Bay of Biscay border town of San Sebastián, where he became the owner of a resort hotel. Brief discussions of his work may be found in Michael Benedikt and George E. Wellwarth's *Modern Spanish Theatre* (1968), which includes *Football;* and in Wellwarth's *The New Wave Spanish Drama* (1970), in which *Bread and Rice or Geometry in Yellow* and *Train to H . . .* first appeared.

BENAVENTE [y Martínez], **Jacinto** (1866–1954), was Spain's foremost modern dramatist. Immensely prolific, he wrote some 170 plays—as well as poetry, essays, and newspaper articles. Outside Spain and South America, whose stages his plays dominated for half a century, his name is less well known today than that of his countryman FEDERICO GARCÍA LORCA, who only lived long enough to produce a handful of plays. Benavente's works display an acute intelligence and great virtuosity. They include all types of drama: romances, fantasies, comedies and farces, tragedies and melodramas, philosophical and psychological (and psychoanalytic) drama, drama of ideas, plays of SYMBOLISM and NATURALISM, moralities, pastorals, satires, librettos, monologues, and translations and adaptations. Thoroughly familiar with the work of contemporary European artists, Benavente wrote plays that were frequently iconoclastic and consistently entertaining to his enormous public. They were moving and meaningful, qualities that are recognizable in his best early plays to this day. In 1913 he was elected to the Spanish Royal Academy, and in 1922 he won the Nobel Prize—primarily for his greatest international hits, *Los intereses creados* (THE BONDS OF INTEREST, 1907) and *La malquerida* (THE PASSION FLOWER, 1913).

Benavente was born in Madrid, the son of a pediatrician. He studied law, but he left the University of Madrid before finishing his degree and devoted himself to literature. The first drama he published was *Teatro fantástico* (1892), four short and romantic sketches, including *El encanto de una hora* (*The Magic of an Hour*); it portrays porcelain figures that come to life for an hour, experience human passions, and finally return to their inanimate states. Next Benavente published a volume of poetry, and *Cartas de mujeres* (*Women's Letters,* 1893), which foreshadows his fascination with sympathy for and knowledge of women, who were so often to become the suffering and lonely protagonists of his serious plays. Early in his career he immersed himself not only in writing drama but in all aspects of production, particularly as a director and as a promoter of children's and art theatres. "The true playwright must have passed his life in the theatre," he wrote; "he must have seen all the plays and all the actors within his reach, and he must have acted himself." Leading a life devoted to his dramaturgy to the exclusion of almost everything else, Benavente expressed regrets at not having been a great actor.

His first produced plays, *El nido ajeno* (*Another's Nest,* 1894) and *Gente conocida* (*People of Importance,* 1896), are in the naturalistic SLICE-OF-LIFE style, and constituted a break with the WELL-MADE romanticism of the popular Spanish theatre of JOSÉ ECHEGARAY. The intensity of passions and the recurrent preoccupation with religion and honor in Benavente's drama, however, are typically and indigenously Spanish. These plays, too, reflect the influence of HENRIK IBSEN in their attacks on social conventions and hypocrisies. They satirize the fashionable theatre and the milieu of his audiences, and Benavente was abused. "I make the public for my plays, not my plays for the public," he remarked, and persisted in dramatizing his liberal *fin de siècle* ideas.

At the same time, he realized the necessity for

achieving popularity in order to be heard. His technical mastery and the appeal of his folk drama, pageantry, low comedy, and searing tragedy soon gained him a vast and appreciative public. For the next half century he produced play after play for this public. The satire in his early works was incorporated in the plays of his second and greatest period, beginning at the turn of the century and ending during World War I. During that time he wrote his two masterpieces and such other works as *La noche del sábado* (SATURDAY NIGHT, 1903; also translated as *The Witches' Sabbath*), *Los malhechores del bien* (THE EVIL DOERS OF GOOD, 1903), SEÑORA AMA (1908), *El principe que todo lo aprendió en los libros* (THE PRINCE WHO LEARNED EVERYTHING OUT OF BOOKS, 1909), and *Campo de armiño* (FIELD OF ERMINE, 1916). These plays demonstrate the variety of his talents as a dramatist, and with them he reached the peak of his career. He was little heard of during the Spanish Civil War years, but subsequently reappeared in public. He remained a notable figure, and some of his plays were internationally produced. Yet his excellence as a dramatist had for some time lagged far behind his unabated productivity.

Now most of his plays are little known outside Spain. They consist also of translations and adaptations of the works of Shakespeare and Molière; and of the younger Dumas, Edward Bulwer-Lytton, and other novelists, including the Abbé Marcel Prévost (*Manon Lescaut,* 1905); a number of Don Juan plays; and librettos. The 150-odd original plays he wrote in the years 1892–1953 include *La Gobernadora* (*The Governor's Wife,* 1901), *No fumadores* (*No Smoking,* 1904), *Rosas de otoño* (*Autumnal Roses,* 1905), *La princesa Bebé* (*Princess Bebé,* 1906), *El marido de su viuda* (*His Widow's Husband,* 1908), *Por las nubes* (*In the Clouds,* 1909), *La escuela de las princesas* (*The School for Princesses,* 1909), *La señorita se aburre* (1909, based on Tennyson's "Lady Clara Vere de Vere"), *La verdad* (*The Truth,* 1915), *La ciudad alegre y confiada* (THE CITY OF JOY AND CONFIDENCE, 1916; the sequel to *The Bonds of Interest*), *Una señora* (*A Lady,* 1920), and *Cuando los hijos de Eva no son los hijos de Adán* (1931, an adaptation of Kennedy and Dean's THE CONSTANT NYMPH).

Almost all of these and some of the earlier-mentioned plays are collected in John Garrett Underhill's extensive four-volume translation, *Plays by Jacinto Benavente* (1917–24), each volume prefaced by commentaries on Benavente and his drama. All of Benavente's plays were published in a number of editions in Spanish, notably the eleven volumes published from 1950 through 1958. His collected writings on theatre and the drama were published in Spanish in 1909. Book-length studies in English, with bibliographies, are Walter Starkie's *Jacinto Benavente* (1924) and Marcelino C. Peñuelas's *Jacinto Benavente* (1968).

BENELLI, Sem (1877–1949), Italian playwright, authored poetic dramas like those of GABRIELE D'ANNUNZIO. His greatest hit was *La cena delle beffe* (1909), a blank-verse melodrama set in the Renaissance and depicting a weakling's terrible revenge—ending in fratricide and madness—on the powerful man who stole his mistress; in 1919 John and Lionel Barrymore starred in an adaptation by EDWARD SHELDON in New York, where it was produced both as *The Jest* and as *The Jester's Supper*. Most of Benelli's other plays are also poetic melodramas, though in his later works—especially after combat experience in World War I —Benelli was more subdued and began to stress SYMBOLISM and didacticism. Thus, though he was D'Annunzio's most prominent disciple, Benelli changed the "superman" drama into more humane portrayals of individual pathos.

Benelli's first significant play was *Tignola* (1908), a prose comedy, the "bookworm" of whose title, a librarian, returns to the security of his desk after briefly living his dream of dangerous adventure. This play was followed by two precursors of the GROTESQUE theatre of LUIGI CHIARELLI and LUIGI PIRANDELLO, *La maschera di Bruto* (1908) and *L'amore dei tre re* (*The Love of the Three Kings,* 1910). The first dramatizes the murder of Alessandro by Lorenzo de Medici, his weak and effeminate cousin who assumes "the mask of Brutus" but fails to elevate his personality accordingly, even in death. *The Love of Three Kings,* subtitled "a tragic poem" and made into an opera by Italo Montemezzi, is a melodrama of adultery, murder, and suicide; it is set in the tenth century, after the barbarian invasion of Italy.

These four remained Benelli's best-known plays, though he wrote until his death. In the late 1920's he began to manage a company of his own, for which he wrote his last important play, *Orfeo e Proserpina* (1928). Other early plays include such historical works as *Il mantellaccio* (*The Mantellaccio Society of Poets,* 1911), about competing literary societies in the sixteenth century; and further dramatizations of myth and history, including *Rosmunda* (*Rosmunda, Queen of the Lombards,* 1911), *La Gorgona* (1913), *Le nozze dei centauri* (1915), *L'arzigogolo* (*The Enigma,* 1922), *Adamo e Eva* (1932), and *Caterina Sforza* (1934). Weaker are three studies of frustrated idealism: *Ali* (*Wings,* 1921),* *La santa primavera* (1923), and *L'amorosa tragedia* (1925). Among his last works are *Il ragno* (1935) and *L'elefante* (1937), character studies; and, finally, *Paura* (1947).

Benelli's best-known plays were translated but are no longer readily available. A discussion of his work appears in the second volume of Joseph S. Kennard's *The Italian Theatre* (1932).

BENNETT, Arnold [Enoch] (1867–1931), English writer, is remembered principally for *The Old Wives' Tale* (1908), a modern classic, and other novels about the inhabitants of the "Five Towns," the North Staffordshire manufacturing district where Bennett grew up. He was the son of a lawyer, and educated for the same profession, but

* Extensively analyzed in Isaac Goldberg's chapter on Benelli in *The Drama of Transition* (1922).

gave it up in 1893. An immensely prolific writer and a major English novelist, Bennett started as a journalist and later became an editor. He also wrote about a dozen plays, but the only notable ones are MILESTONES (1912, written with EDWARD KNOBLOCK) and *The Great Adventure* (1913), a dramatization of his novel *Buried Alive* (filmed as *Holy Matrimony* in 1943), which became a Jule Styne musical, *Darling of the Day* (1968). Other plays include *Cupid and Commonsense* (1908), *What the Public Wants* (1909), *The Honeymoon* (1911), *Rivals for Rosamund* (1914), *The Title* (1918, a comedy), *Judith* (1919, a modern version of the biblical tale), *Sacred and Profane Love* (1919), *The Love Match* and *Body and Soul* (1922), and two more plays written with Knoblock, *London Life* (1924, a spectacle) and *Mr. Prohack* (1928, a comedy).

His comprehensive posthumous *Journals* cover Bennett's life from 1896 on, and Reginald Pound's *Arnold Bennett: A Biography* (1959) includes many of his letters. A study of his work is James G. Hepburn's *The Art of Arnold Bennett* (1963).

BERGMAN, Hjalmar [Fredrik Elgérus] (1883–1931), Swedish novelist and playwright, is one of the "portal figures" in contemporary Swedish literature. The only major native novelist and (to a lesser degree) dramatist between AUGUST STRINDBERG and PÄR LAGERKVIST, he has been called the "Swedish Dickens" as well as Strindberg's successor. His writing, which is characterized by a fatalistic mysticism, was influenced by his great predecessor as well as by HENRIK IBSEN and MAURICE MAETERLINCK. Bergman first gained popularity relatively late in his career as a novelist, in 1919, with *Markurells i Wadköping* (*Markurells of Wadköping*, also translated as *God's Orchid*), a comic work he later dramatized, which features an inhuman scoundrel redeemed only by his love for his son. His first play, *Maria, Jesu moder*, was published in 1905; it was unsuccessful, as was an IBSENite PROBLEM PLAY, *Familjens renhet* (1907). Bergman achieved critical praise for Maeterlinckian drama like *Det underbara leendet* (1907) and the collected *Marionettspel* (1917), including *Herr Sleeman kommer* (MR. SLEEMAN IS COMING, 1917). Yet, though he had written over a dozen plays by 1925, he did not make his reputation as a dramatist until—as he had earlier done with his fiction—he turned from the somberly poetic to the comic, in *Swedenhielms* (THE SWEDENHIELMS, 1925). Produced in many countries and praised as Sweden's greatest comedy, it has remained his most popular play.

Bergman was born in Örebro, Sweden, into the wealthy and affectionate family of a banker. An extremely sensitive child, he reacted defensively against his environment. He studied at the University of Uppsala and then in Italy. Bergman spent most of his adult life abroad; constantly on the move, he would return to Sweden only in the summer, when he worked on a small island in the Stockholm archipelago. His sensitivity gradually evolved into acute neuroses (he suffered, too, from

Hjalmar Bergman, 1924. (*Drottningholms Teatermuseum*)

poor eyesight) which only his wife, Stina, who came from a prominent theatrical family, was able to alleviate.

Bergman's first mature work was *Hans nåds testamente* (*His Grace's Last Testament*, 1910), a comic novel that he later dramatized and in which he created the great comic figure of a golden-hearted tyrant. Also translated as *The Baron's Will*, it is set in the imaginary Bergslagen foundry and mining region of central Sweden, whose eccentric middle- and upper-class inhabitants, characterized with Freudian perception, became the subjects of many Bergman novels. These have been praised as brilliant works whose psychological insight and sometimes macabre humor and irony do not conceal Bergman's terror of the tragic meaninglessness of human life and fate.

Such perspectives also characterize his early plays. The impressive *Mr. Sleeman Is Coming*, published in 1917 with such other Maeterlinckian pieces as *Dödens Arlekin* and *En skugga*, were no more appreciated by the public than the distinctive, occasionally EXPRESSIONIST plays that followed: *Ett experiment* (1918), *Lodolezzi sjunger* (1919), and the short plays published in 1923—*Vävaren i Bagdad, Spelhuset,* and *Porten*. These plays, because of their mordancy, did not appeal to the public that eagerly bought his novels. Bergman thereupon changed the style of his drama, as he had done earlier with his fiction—and with *The Swedenhielms* found the public he had sought.

His major status as the great Swedish writer who straddles the age of Strindberg and the contemporary age of Lagerkvist is due precisely to these comic, sometimes grotesque novels and plays he wrote to achieve popularity. *The Swedenhielms* was followed by another successful drama, *Patrasket* (1928), a comedy vaguely based on *The Merchant of Venice* and featuring a wealthy German-Jewish antiquarian who in desperation abandons his business and the housekeeper he has lived with for many years, when her impoverished family appear; and the dramatizations of his earlier-cited popular novels, *God's Orchid* (1929, the ninth in the Bergslagen series) and *His Grace's Last Testament* (1931). If his best-known plays are more conventional in structure and characterization than those of Strindberg and Lagerkvist, they are distinguished by a comic and trenchant (but not vicious) satire that barely hides Bergman's sense of terror and tragic mysticism. His anguish was heightened by self-condemnation, portrayed in his last novel, *Clownen Jac* (1930). Originally a radio serial read (in part) by Bergman over the national station shortly before his death, its broken autobiographical protagonist exploits his own dread by exhibiting it to the paying, amused public. "I was born a human being," he declares; but "I lived as a clown—I sold my heart—I shall die poor...." Bergman's discouragement by what he considered improperly achieved and insufficiently popular acclaim hastened his premature death on January 1, 1931, in a Berlin hotel room.

Bergman wrote some thirty plays, as many film scripts (he worked briefly in Hollywood, which he despised and quickly escaped), and a dozen radio plays. His complete works are readily available in Swedish, in which language there are many book-length studies and monographs (including some by his wife) on his life and work. The *Four Plays by Hjalmar Bergman* (1968) collection consists of *Markurells of Wadköping, The Baron's Will, Swedenhielms,* and *Mr. Sleeman Is Coming;* edited by Walter Johnson, it has introductions by Stina Bergman.

BERKELEY SQUARE, a play in three acts by JOHN LLOYD BALDERSTON and JOHN COLLINGS SQUIRE, produced in 1926 and published in 1928. Setting: a house in Berkeley Square, London; October 1784 and 1928.

Suggested by *The Sense of the Past* (1917), an incomplete novel by HENRY JAMES, this is a fantasy about a twentieth-century American who exchanges his being with that of an eighteenth-century ancestor. A. A. Brill, Freud's translator and interpreter, saw the play as a clinical portrayal of schizophrenia, while Karl Menninger saw it as a dramatization of *déjà vu.* But it was its romance, comedy, and suspense that made this play—like ALAN JAY LERNER's musical on a similar theme, *Brigadoon* (1947)—popular in both England and America.

In 1784 the Pettigrews—an English matron ambitious for her wastrel son and two daughters, Kate and Helen—are a titled but impoverished family. They eagerly await the arrival of a wealthy American cousin, Peter Standish, who is to marry Kate. In the same setting in 1928, Peter Standish, an American who has recently inherited the house from his ancestors, becomes increasingly fascinated with their history. More and more he identifies with his eighteenth-century namesake, until he literally overcomes time and merges into the being of this ancestor. In that guise in 1784 he blunders because of his foreknowledge of everything, including his eventual marriage to Kate. At a grand ball Peter amazes the company with his clairvoyance, and impresses them with OSCAR WILDE witticisms. But Peter gets increasingly disgusted with the filth and viciousness of eighteenth-century life—its smells, public whippings, and executions. "God, how the Eighteenth Century stinks!" Peter exclaims, and bitterly remembers his earlier fondness for the past, "this filthy little pigsty of a world!" He is in love with Kate's sister Helen, who, through her love for him, can for a moment share his transcendent vision—and see, too, horrors of twentieth-century warfare. Realizing that Peter's loathing of eighteenth-century reality exceeds his love of its art and architecture, she gives him up. Back in 1928, his fiancée and friends worry about the missing Peter. He sadly comes in, an exile of both centuries. With a breaking voice he reads the epitaph on the tombstone of Helen, "who departed this life June the fifteenth, 1787, aged twenty-three years—"

BERNANOS, Georges (1888–1948), French poet, shortly before his death adapted Gertrude von Le Fort's novel about the execution of twelve Carmelite nuns in the French Revolution, *Die Letzte am Schafott* (1934), into *Dialogues des Carmélites* (*Dialogues of the Carmelites,* 1948; also translated as *The Carmelites*). Originally a film script, its 1951 stage version by Albert Béguin (1898–1957) and Marcelle Tassencourt (1914–) features a young aristocrat who tries to overcome her congenital fears by joining the Carmelite Order, deserts it during the persecutions, but finally gains courage and rejoins the sisters at the guillotine. Except for the drama of PAUL CLAUDEL, Wallace Fowlie wrote in *Dionysus in Paris* (1960), this is "the most moving play of the century." In 1955 Francis Poulenc made it into an opera, *Les Carmélites,* and it was filmed in 1960.

BERNARD, Jean-Jacques (1888–), French dramatist, was the son of TRISTAN BERNARD but wrote in a very different vein. His "dramas of silence" were inspired by those of MAURICE MAETERLINCK and deal with the disillusionment of love. Characteristic is *Le Printemps des autres* (*The Springtime of Others,* 1924), in which a woman mistakes a man's interest in her daughter for an interest in herself; gradually and almost unwittingly but silently, in accord with Bernard's "art of the unexpressed," she destroys the happiness of the man and her daughter, until the two women look at each other mutely—and understand. Similarly, *Le Feu qui reprend mal* (*The Sulky Fire,* 1921) portrays a soldier returning from war to find a wife whose love has grown cold but who remains with him out of pity. In *Martine* (1922), a peasant girl never forgets the city charmer who, after a sentimental acquaintance, married another girl; *L'Invitation au voyage* (*Invitation to a Voyage*, 1924) is about a prosperous wife who idealizes an unremarkable young man while he is away, and then sees him for what he is; and in the tragic *L'Âme en peine* (*The Unquiet Spirit*, 1926) two soul mates, a man and a woman, are meant for—though they never recognize—each other.

These five plays—he wrote others, including one on *Marie Stuart, Reine d'Écosse* (1941) and such variations on *Martine* and *Invitation to a Voyage* as *National 6* (1935) and *Le Jardinier d'Ispahan* (1939)—were translated and collected, with an introduction, in John L. Frith's *The Sulky Fire* (1939).

BERNARD, Tristan [pen name of Paul Bernard] (1866–1947), French novelist and playwright, like GEORGES COURTELINE was notable for his light comedies. The most popular of them was the melodramatic farce about a dawdler confused by his friends' advice about getting married, *Triplepatte* (1905), written with André Godfernaux (1864–1906) and adapted by CLYDE FITCH as *Toddles* (1906). His son, JEAN-JACQUES BERNARD, wrote his biography, *Mon père Tristan Bernard* (1955).

BERNSTEIN, Henry [Léon Gustave Charles] (1876–1953), French playwright, achieved popularity in the first two decades of the century with a number of sensational plays, particularly *Le Voleur* (THE THIEF, 1906). His career began with the Théâtre-Libre production of *Le Marché* in 1900, and his success grew with *Frère Jacques* (*Brother Jacques*, 1904), a comedy written with Pierre Eugène Veber (1869–1942) and adapted for Broadway by CLYDE FITCH. Bernstein's subsequent plays portray human passions, often lust. He appeared to dissect characters with the scalpel of the NATURALIST; but the intrigue and the inevitable *scène à faire* in his skillfully constructed and highly theatrical works—not to mention his dramatizing of themes that happened to be currently fashionable—place Bernstein in the tradition of VICTORIEN SARDOU and Alexandre Dumas fils.

His emphasis on character studies began with *La Rafale* (*The Whirlwind*, 1905; also produced as *Baccarat*), and continued with *La Griffe* (*The Claw*, 1906), the portrayal of an unscrupulous woman. Of Bernstein's many later plays, the best known in Europe and America were *Israël* (1908), a depiction of anti-Semitism in polite society, like Galsworthy's later LOYALTIES; *Samson* (1908), the drama of a husband's terrible vengeance following his wife's adultery; *Après moi* (*After Me*, 1911), a domestic drama memorable for the anti-Semitic riots following its production at the Comédie-Française, which had to withdraw it; *L'Assaut* (*The Attack*, 1912); *Le Secret* (*The Secret*, 1913), featuring a sadistic woman; *L'Élévation* (1917); *Judith* (1922), a biblical play; *La Galerie des glaces* (1924), the portrayal of an inferiority complex; and *Mélo* (1929) and *Espoir* (*Promise*, 1936), both of which also were produced in English.

Born in Paris, Bernstein was the grandson of a wealthy Jewish New York banker. He attended Cambridge University and inherited a fortune after his mother's death. During World War II Bernstein fled Paris—his anti-Nazi *Elvira* (1940) was playing there until the city fell—and worked against the Vichy government from the United States. After the war he returned to Paris, where he spent the remainder of his life. His plays continued to appear until the year before his death.

In his later works he attempted to deal less sensationally with social and psychological problems. But Bernstein became increasingly heavy-handed and lost popularity in the boulevard theatres whose audiences had once applauded his entertaining depictions of passion. *The Thief* and a few of his other plays are available in English. Barrett H. Clark's *Contemporary French Dramatists* (1916) has a chapter on Bernstein and a bibliography.

BERTIN, Charles (1919–   ), French-writing Belgian novelist and poet, first succeeded as a dramatist with his adaptation into a modern situation of Odysseus's return from the wars, *Les Prétendants* (1947), a play produced in England as *Love in a Labyrinth* (1950). It was followed by *Don Juan* (1948), which depicts the legendary lover as a debaucher whose love for Doña Ana ultimately becomes real and therefore tragic. Bertin's 1953 prizewinning radio play *Christophe Colomb* (*Christopher Columbus*), a poetic-religious portrayal of Columbus overcoming various temptations aboard the *Santa Maria*, was first produced at the Brussels World Exhibition in 1958. Another play, *Le Roi Bonheur* (1966), despite its comic and happy ending, is something of a pendant to Camus's CALIGULA.

William Jay Smith published the first English translations of his drama, *Two Plays by Charles Bertin* (1970), *Don Juan* and *Christopher Columbus*.

BESIER, Rudolf (1878–1942), English dramatist, is remembered for a single play, THE BARRETTS OF WIMPOLE STREET (1930). Born in Java, educated in Guernsey and Heidelberg, and employed as a journalist for a while, he became a playwright in 1906, when his poetic drama *The Virgin Goddess* was produced in London. It was followed by *Olive Latimer's Husband* (1908) and, the next year, by *Don*, a briefly popular comedy about a frustrated idealist—a modern Don Quixote. Talented as a writer of strong acting vehicles, Besier also translated and adapted plays from the French, and collaborated with H. G. Wells (1866–1946) on dramatizing the latter's novel *Kipps* (1912); and with May Edginton (d. 1957) on writing three sentimental plays: *The Prude's Fall* (1920), *The Ninth Earl* (1921), and *Secrets* (1922). Besier's other plays include *Lady Patricia* (1911), *Kings and Queens* (1915), *Kultur at Home* (1916), and *A Run for His Money* (1916).

BETROTHAL, THE (*Les Fiançailles*), "a fairy play" in five acts by MAURICE MAETERLINCK, produced in 1918 and published in 1922. Setting: a woodcutter's cottage and assorted dream scenes.

This sequel to *L'Oiseau bleu* (THE BLUE BIRD), though it has the same characters and format, failed to duplicate the earlier play's success. It portrays the dream adventures of an older Tyltyl, searching for a wife. Destiny and Light lead him through the Land of Ancestors and to the Milky Way. There, among the yet-unborn children, he meets his bride—the neighbor girl to whom he gave the Blue Bird.

BETTI, Ugo (1892–1953), Italian writer and jurist, was esteemed by his countrymen as their leading modern dramatist, the successor of and perhaps even greater than LUIGI PIRANDELLO. Outside Italy Betti has remained little known, though his drama has occasionally been produced and published in translation. His first important play, *Frana allo Scalo Nord* (LANDSLIDE AT NORTH STATION, 1935), appeared in English—as did others, including *Corruzione al Palazzo di giustizia* (CORRUPTION IN THE PALACE OF JUSTICE, 1949), *Delitto all'isola delle capre* (CRIME ON GOAT ISLAND, 1950), *La regina e gli insorti* (THE QUEEN AND THE REBELS, 1951), and *L'aiuola bruciata* (THE BURNT FLOWER-BED, 1953). Ranging from NATURALISM through SYMBOLISM, EXPRESSIONISM, and even light farce, his twenty-seven plays reflect Betti's lyric talents and artistic versality no less than his ambivalence about authority and his preoccupation with justice, morality, religion, and sex—all of which are the subject of virtually every Betti play. His protagonists are sinners redeemed after an anguished existentialist quest for identity and responsibility. Like the protagonists of *Landslide at North Station* and *Corruption in the Palace of Justice,* some of them are high-court judges—as was Betti himself.

The son of a country doctor who became head of Parma's municipal hospital, Betti was born in Camerino, a small hilltop city in central Italy. He wanted to study literature, but his practical father had him study law at the University of Parma. There he completed his doctorate with a thesis on revolution in which he justified warfare. Front-line and prison-camp experiences in World War I changed Betti's attitudes; in 1922, when he published his first work, a collection of poetry, Betti revealed the humanistic bias that characterizes his later work.

After the war he began his career as a municipal judge in small towns; eventually he was transferred to the higher court of Parma and ultimately Rome. There he served throughout the regime of the Fascists, to whom, however, he paid little more than lip service. He was exonerated in a post-World War II investigation, became the Justice Department librarian, and, finally, the legal consultant to the national association of writers and publishers. These later positions he requested to give him more time to write—something he had done throughout his career as a judge. Though he never used courtroom experiences directly, they strongly influenced his perspective and insight. To the question of what the benefits of his legal profession were to his fiction and drama, Betti replied, "Nothing in particular, everything in general."

Ugo Betti. (*Italian Cultural Institute*)

Betti's early plays are derivative experiments. The strong and attractive but cynical protagonist of his prize-winning first play, the naturalistic *La padrona* (1929), symbolizes "Life" and is stymied in her identity struggle by family bonds. Similarly inhibited by heredity and environment are the protagonists of *La casa sull'acqua* (1929) and other early plays. Only with his sixth play, *Landslide at North Station,* was Betti first recognized as an important new dramatist. It was followed by *Il cacciatore d'anitre* (written in 1937 and produced in 1940), an attempt at symbolic naturalism reminiscent of the late HENRIK IBSEN plays, and *Una bella domenica di settembre* (1937), a light comedy. Perhaps most successful in this latter genre was *Il paese delle vacanze* (1942, produced in English as *Summertime*), a farce about a resourceful girl who plots to marry her doltish childhood friend.

More characteristic of Betti's drama is his next work, *Notte in casa del ricco* (1942), a tragedy about an ex-convict killed by his wealthy former associate; now a pillar of society, the latter thus destroys incriminating evidence but is in turn ruined by the death of his daughter, who becomes his scapegoat. *Il diluvio* (1943) features a tragicomic husband who (like Corvino in Ben Jonson's *Volpone*) prostitutes his wife to a much fawned-upon millionaire—a satire of Fascist Italy and its contemptible parasites, all doomed, Betti suggests, in "the deluge" to come.

Betti's postwar plays include *Il vento notturno*

(1945); *Ispezione* (*The Inquiry,* 1947, also translated as *Island Investigations*), a Kafkaesque unmasking of society's moral corruption and guilt, as reflected in an ordinary family who, after the "investigation," resume their trivial and sordid lives; *Marito e moglie* (1947); and the plays already noted above. Another prominent late play is *Lotta fino all'alba* (*Struggle Till Dawn,* 1949), which recalls Zola's THÉRÈSE RAQUIN and foreshadows Betti's own *Crime on Goat Island* with its stark portrayal of remorse and repentance following promiscuity: its haunted hero returns to southern Italy after World War II to expiate the cuckolding of his now-vengeful friend, but kills him and then dies himself as his loyal wife and his sensual mistress "struggle till dawn" for his soul—like the Good and Bad Angels in a medieval work.

Betti's final plays (some of them posthumous) include these further ones: *Irene innocente* (1950, adapted in America as *Time of Vengeance*); *Spiritismo nell'antica casa* (1950); *Il giocatore* (*The Gambler,* 1951), a theological study of a gambler's mounting awareness of his inescapable responsibility to God for his wife's death—and of man's existentialist need to rebel; *Inquisizione* (1952); and *La fuggitiva* (*The Fugitive,* 1953), a semiexpressionistic portrayal of a thoroughly unpleasant woman who commits murder (like the protagonist of Treadwell's MACHINAL), her uxorious husband, and a Mephistopheles who manipulates them until the wife gains divine grace in death. Betti wrote his last work, *Il fratello protegge e ama,* also titled *Acqua turbate* (1955), while dying of cancer; it is an exploration of psychological and moral problems presented as a melodrama of passion, prostitution, and incest.

Betti's drama is characterized by his concern with guilt, justice, and the other earlier-noted universal themes of spirituality, morality, and sensuality. These are dramatized in lyrical and theatrical terms that sometimes employ ballet and chorus and reflect such disparate traditions as classical starkness, medieval moralities and iconography, romanticism, and modern expressionism. Betti's occasionally mannered style, as well as the intensity and earnestness of his quest for salvation, may account for his lesser success with foreign audiences.

Betti published many volumes of poetry, fiction, and essays as well as drama. His complete plays (with a prefatory essay) were published in Italian in 1955. Edited English collections of his plays, with prefatory discussions of his life and work, include Henry Reed's *Three Plays by Ugo Betti* (1956): *The Queen and the Rebels, The Burnt Flower-Bed, Summertime;* G. H. McWilliam's *Three Plays on Justice* (1964): *Landslide, Struggle Till Dawn, The Fugitive;* and Gino Rizzo's *Ugo Betti: Three Plays* (1966): *The Inquiry, Goat Island, The Gambler.*

BEYOND HUMAN POWER I (*Over ævne, første stykke*), a play in two acts by BJØRNSTJERNE BJØRNSON, published in 1883 and produced in 1899. Setting: a cottage in northern Norway, early 1880's.

Bjørnson's masterpiece, this is a lyrical religious drama, classic in form and theme. It features a joy-spreading and miracle-performing idealist, Pastor Adolf Sang, whose zeal exemplifies the danger of striving "beyond human power." His fanaticism, combined with his sensitive altruism and purity, manifests traits of HENRIK IBSEN's Brand and Rosmer. One of the great Scandinavian religious plays—Munk's THE WORD was a direct reply to it and FERDINAND BRUCKNER explored its resolution in yet another play—*Beyond Human Power I* is devoted to long and earnest but satiric theological disputations among a choruslike assembly of pastors. One of them reappeared in 1895 as the antagonist of Sang's son in Bjørnson's second play by the same name: amidst grim destitution caused by a long strike, *Beyond Human Power II* depicts the conflict between capital and labor as well as that between fighters for social justice and proponents of blessed submission, poverty, and peace.

Act I. The invalided Clara Sang, long unable to sleep or rise from her bed, tells her visiting sister of the wonders performed by her beloved husband, the "miracle priest" who is "always beaming with the gladness of Sunday" and is irresistible for his "sheer goodness," self-sacrifice, and childlike faith. Clara spent her health in bringing up their children and providing for the family's necessities in the face of her husband's generosity. The only reason for Clara's failure to be cured by Sang—who has cured so many others—is her inability to share his unquestioning faith. Pastor Sang returns from his morning walk, full of joy and love. Unable to make himself pluck the newly sprouted "wonderful vegetation," Sang could not bring home any flowers. He asks his grown-up children, just returned from a trip, to join him in prayers for Clara that evening. They no longer share his faith and belief in miracles, for, on going into the world, they have found only their father to be a true Christian: all others make their religion "a compromise." Secure in his faith, Sang comforts them and his wife, and departs for his church to pray for the miracle to cure Clara: "I shall not come from there until I have procured from God's hands sleep for your mother, and after sleep, health; so that she may arise and walk among us." As soon as he is gone, the family are amazed to discover that Clara, for the first time in months, is asleep. This miracle is almost immediately duplicated by a more sensational one outside: a mountainslide, about to destroy the church in which Sang is praying, veers aside, sparing both the church and its pastor. Clara goes on sleeping soundly throughout the uproar.

Act II. As Sang continues to pray in his church, crowds who have heard of this latest miracle gather in the churchyard. His still-doubting children fear that now their mother "no longer has any strength left to resist. And he will urge her on" to perform his miracle. A group of pastors and a bishop arrive to decide upon the position the Church will take. They debate the validity of Sang's miracles. "The fact alone of these hundreds kneeling in prayer about the church, and he inside, and

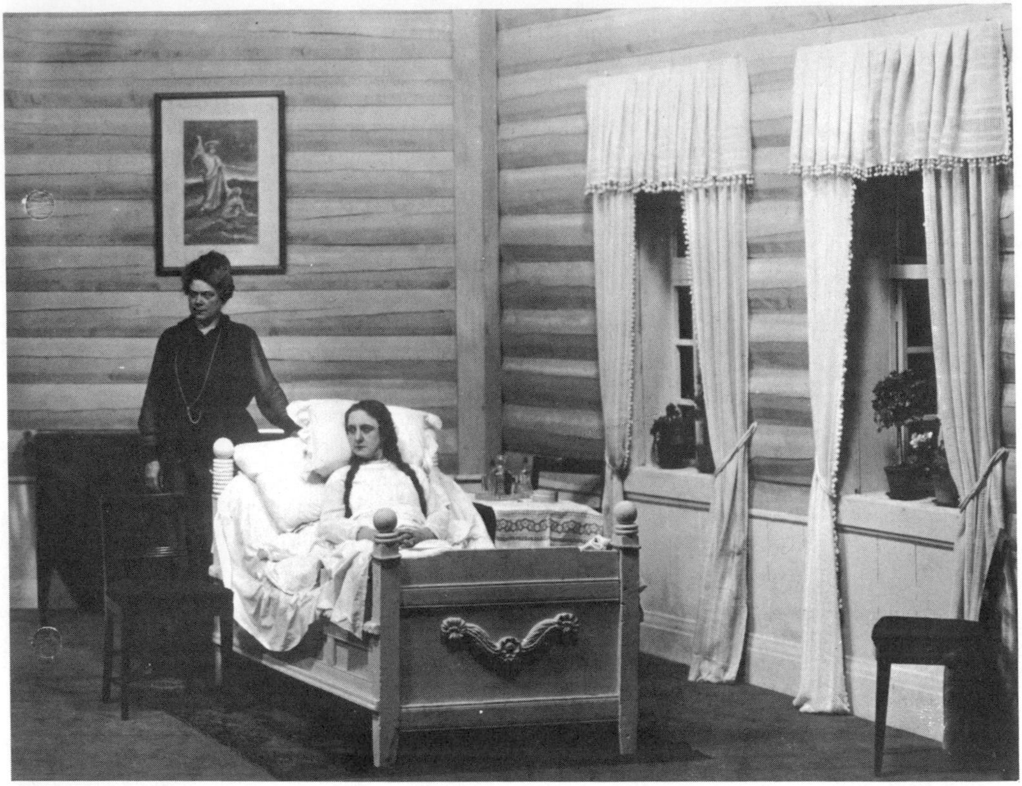

Beyond Human Power I, Act I. Clara (Johanne Dybwad, in bed) and a friend (Schibsted Hansson). Christiania (Oslo), 1899. (*National Theatret archives, Oslo*)

knowing nothing about it! I cannot think of anything more beautiful!" a pastor remarks. The bishop gently chides him: "I noticed that you had overexerted yourself and were sick. But they all become so who follow Pastor Sang." Yet another pastor, overwhelmed by Sang's influence, abjectly renounces any doubts he ever had about the miracles: "His love and his faith ought to have humbled me. I accuse myself, and in the depths of my heart beg him for forgiveness!" Without exception all the pastors join him, anticipating the imminent occurrence of another miracle—"because all the people need it sorely!" As the crowds outside sing a "Hallelujah," Clara makes the superhuman effort to accomplish her husband's miracle. She rises from her sickbed, and enters the room. The pastors thereupon join the "Hallelujah" singing and the church bell peals. At the height of the mighty music Pastor Sang enters, stretches out his hands toward his wife, and embraces her. "Oh, glorious—when you came—my beloved!" Clara says, gazing at him—and then sinks to the ground, and dies. Puzzled, Pastor Sang looks up at heaven: "But this was not my intention—? Or?—or?" And he collapses—also dead. The pastors wonder what he meant by that "Or," and the church bell keeps pealing.

BEYOND THE HORIZON, a play in three acts by EUGENE O'NEILL, published and produced in 1920. Setting: a contemporary American farm.

This was O'Neill's first-performed full-length play, his first play on Broadway, and his first play to win him a Pulitzer Prize. Symbolically, each act has an expansive outdoor (suggesting longing) and a confined indoor (suggesting loss) scene, but in performance the last scene of the play was incorporated into the first scene of that act.

Act I. Scene 1. Ready to ship out with his uncle in the morning, the intellectual and sensitive young Robert Mayo, sitting on a farm-road fence at sunset, tells his prosaic brother Andrew romantic dreams of sailing "beyond the horizon." He elaborates on them to their neighbor, Ruth Atkins—his brother's girl, whom he also loves—and is surprised and overjoyed to learn that it is really him and not Andrew she loves. Persuaded that this "is sweeter than any distant dream," he agrees to forgo his trip and marry her. *Scene 2.* In the farmhouse, his mother is delighted to hear that he is staying home. After the shock wears off, Andrew congratulates him and decides to sail in his stead, which relieves the uncle, who has feared his crew would think that he had prepared the cabin for a woman who had then jilted him. The furious father—who had counted on Andrew, a "born farmer," to take over—warns him not to run "against your own nature," and heaps scorn and curses on him when he remains adamant. A farewell in which Andrew confesses that he is leaving to forget Ruth cements the brothers' love for each other.

Act II. Scene 1. Three years later, because Robert is totally unsuited for farming, the place is going to seed. The father has died, Ruth's nagging invalid mother has moved in, and Robert and Ruth have a sickly daughter, Robert's only joy. He envies his brother's travels and curses the distant hills, "walls of a narrow prison yard shutting me in from all the freedom and wonder of life!" Unable to contain herself when he deprecates Andrew's prosaic accounts of his travels, Ruth castigates Robert for his incompetence and defiantly tells him she loves Andrew, who is due to come home that day: "He'll show what a man can do! I don't need you." *Scene 2.* The next day Andrew, who has suffered from betraying *his* nature, with a life of travel and business, tells Robert and Ruth separately that he quickly got over his passion for Ruth. He departs after one day, leaving Ruth without any further hope.

Act III. Scene 1. Five years later, the farm is in debt and almost total decay, Ruth has "aged horribly," Robert's mother and daughter are dead, and he is dying of consumption. In response to Ruth's telegram, Andrew returns from Argentina. High-strung and hardened, he tells her that he lost a fortune speculating on grain and has to go to recoup his business, though he is "sick of it all." Robert concludes that although Ruth and he are failures, "we can both justly lay some of the blame for our stumbling on God. But you're the deepest-dyed failure of the three, Andy. You've spent eight years running away from yourself . . . gambling with [grain,] the thing you used to love to create." He asks Andrew to marry Ruth after his death, but Andrew "brutally" tells her later that he does not love her and demands that she go to comfort his dying brother, even by lying to him, and thus undo the suffering she has caused him. *Scene 2.* Robert has escaped from his bed to the farm road, where he dies "exultantly," still the dreamer, vainly hoping for a happy union between Ruth and Andrew and the long-awaited travel for himself: "This time I'm going! It isn't the end. It's a free beginning—the start of my voyage! I've won . . . my trip—the right of release—beyond the horizon!"

BIEDERMANN AND THE FIREBUGS (*Biedermann und die Brandstifter*), a play in six scenes and an epilogue by MAX FRISCH, published and produced in 1958. Setting: "Europe, today."

Subtitled *"ein Lehrstück ohne Lehre"* ("a morality without a moral") and translated also as *The Firebugs* and *The Fire Raisers,* this was Frisch's first international hit. It was inspired by the Communist overthrow of Eduard Beneš's democratic Czechoslovakian government. Originally a prose sketch (1948) reworked into a radio play (1953), it allegorizes good-natured citizens' temporizing with evil—and thus inviting catastrophe. Derived from THORNTON WILDER and BERTOLT BRECHT are various PRESENTATIONAL devices, including the chorus and simultaneous living-room and attic setting. The grotesquely comic epilogue, which Frisch wrote for German audiences, often is deleted in productions.

[Prelude.] A match is struck in the dark and its flare illuminates a face. "One can't even light a cigar nowadays without thinking of fire!—It's revolting," Gottlieb Biedermann says as helmeted firemen step forward. "Looking, / Listening, / Full of goodwill toward the well-intentioned citizens," they chant of their eagerness to guard their city. "Much can be avoided / By common sense," they note. As the hour strikes, they sit down: "Our watch has begun."

Scene 1. Biedermann indignantly reads news of "another 'harmless' peddler settling in an attic," and thus another fire: "They ought to be strung up." As his maid reports that the peddler who called an hour ago still insists on seeing Biedermann, he walks in, introducing himself as Joseph Schmitz, an unemployed wrestler. Deferentially insolent, he accepts a snack, "if it's no trouble." He eats heartily, all the while discussing the fires and alluding to God's judgments. Biedermann loses his temper when an employee from his hair tonic firm, dismissed because he had asked for a share in the profits from his own invention, appeals to be reinstated. Biedermann is indeed a kind man, Schmitz reassures him—else "you wouldn't be giving me shelter tonight . . . even if it's only in the attic." Then he laughs when Biedermann asks, "Will you promise me that you're really not a firebug?" Biedermann promised to check the attic nightly, his fearful wife Babette tells the audience. Though also disturbed by the visitor, the firemen note that "No harm has come to our sleeping town. / Not yet."

Scene 2. Biedermann leaves for the office the next morning, irritable because he has spent a sleepless night but reassured because there was no fire. Schmitz familiarly greets him and his wife, and wolfs down the huge breakfast that he had ordered submissively. Instilling Babette with remorse because she has commented on his boorish table manners, Schmitz invites in his friend Willie Eisenring, a former waiter at a hotel recently burned down. The firemen, worried because two suspicious characters now occupy the attic, deplore "faint-hearted" Biedermann's hospitality. "Disarmed, tired out with terror, / Yet hoping somehow to avoid it," they remark, "With open arms he invites it! / Woe!"

Scene 3. Schmitz and the equally sinister but well-dressed Eisenring roll barrels of gasoline into the attic. Biedermann orders both men out just as a policeman comes to report the suicide of Biedermann's discharged employee. As Schmitz and Eisenring chime in helpfully, the guilt-ridden Biedermann assures the policeman that the barrels contain only harmless hair tonic. The chorus castigates Biedermann for permitting gasoline in his house. Biedermann proclaims his "sacred property rights" to do as he likes. He had intended to expel the men, he admits, but has never gotten around to it—and then he denies that there is a smell of

Biedermann and the Firebugs, Scene 6. Left to right: Schmitz (Ernst Schröder), Babette (Elsbeth von Lüdinghausen), the maid (Targot Trooger), Biedermann (Gustav Knuth), Eisenring (Boy Gobert). Zurich, 1958. (*Bernhard Obrecht*)

gasoline. The chorus remarks, "He who dreads change / More than disaster, / How can he fight / When disaster impends?"

Scene 4. Rather than antagonize his guests by reporting them to the police, Biedermann invites them to a roast goose supper. In the attic he obligingly holds the detonating fuse while they make their measurements. When he goes downstairs, a third accomplice comes out of hiding—an idealistic Ph.D. who wants to reform the world. The firemen prepare to man the pumps and ladders, convinced that Biedermann's good nature will be calamitous.

Scene 5. Biedermann dismisses the supplicating widow of his dead employee and prepares the feast. The setting and the dress are to be especially simple so as to make the guests feel at home: "What we need is humanity, brotherhood." As the firebugs upstairs look for matches, Biedermann turns to the audience. Things sneak up on you slowly, he says, and being suspicious means nothing for "one is always suspicious." Defensively he asks, "What would you have done in my place, damn it all, and at what point?"

Scene 6. At the feast Biedermann and his guests laugh and joke about preparing the fuse, though Babette is fearful and the simple maid is scandalized. To accommodate the men, Biedermann has the fanciest settings and other valuables brought out. Schmitz and Eisenring relate their criminal past and, putting the tablecloth and napkins over their heads, play theatre. "EVERYMAN! EVERYMAN! BIEDERMANN! BIEDERMANN!" they chant, and frighten Babette by invoking the ghost of Biedermann's dismissed dead employee. As they carouse and Biedermann himself leads the fun, fire sirens are heard. The two look at their watches and tell Biedermann that, being firebugs, they must get to work. "As a sign of trust" they ask him to supply the matches. Begging them to stop joking, Biedermann nonetheless obliges, while the Ph.D. comes in to read his own proclamation, which dissociates him from the firebugs' imminent action. After the guests go upstairs, Biedermann reassures his frightened wife: "If they really were firebugs, do you think they wouldn't have matches?" Darkness falls, there are explosions and a sea of flames, and sirens and other noises start. The firemen step forward. "Long foreseen, disaster / Has reached us at last," they chant as gas tanks explode throughout the city; "Woe to us! Woe to us! Woe!"

Epilogue. In a noisy hell ready to strike for more sinners and peopled by a talking monkey, a policeman, Schmitz (as Beelzebub), Eisenring (as Satan), and others, Biedermann and his wife defend themselves and ask for reparations. A chorus sings of the new, miraculously rebuilt city: "Finer than ever, / Richer than ever." "Do you think we are saved?" Babette wonders. "It looks like it,"

Biedermann replies as both kneel to the accompaniment of rising organ music.

BILL-BELOTSERKOVSKY, Vladimir Naumovich (1884–), Russian playwright, acquired his hyphenated name from a twelve-year stay in the United States, where he worked as a stevedore, got material for his earliest and unimportant NATURALIST plays, and wrote a book of stories. The son of a laborer, Bill-Belotserkovsky became a sailor. He returned to Russia in 1917, in time to participate in the Revolution, and became an active Party worker. He expressed the ideas and ideals of the Bolsheviks, whom he supported wholeheartedly, and produced a number of popular, crude propaganda plays.

By far his biggest hit was *Shtorm* (1925), a pageant (with a cast of fifty) depicting the bittersweet story of a selfless, iron-willed Bolshevik leader, his assistant (a lame sailor), and a village experiencing the difficulties of implementing Socialist directives. Rabid in its abuse of the intelligentsia, the play, according to Nikolai A. Gorchakov's *The Theater in Soviet Russia* (1957), "was the first authentically Bolshevik Party play." Further noteworthy Bill-Belotserkovsky plays are *Shtil* (1927) and *Luna sleva* (1927). The first features the hero of *Shtorm* and depicts post-Civil War stagnation—the return of private enterprise and speculation during the period of NEP (New Economic Policy): "The Revolution that shook the entire world and all the thrones in it is expiring under the dirty heel of the petite bourgeoisie," one "heartsick" Bolshevik exclaims. *Luna sleva* is a semiautobiographical cloak-and-dagger comedy that features a Communist who fears (needlessly, it turns out) that his passion for his wife may interfere with his passion for the Revolution.

Bill-Belotserkovsky's other plays include *Ekho* (1924, set in America); *Levo rulya* (1926), in which a revolt stops the delivery of arms to the White Guards; *Golos nedr* (1929); *Zapad nervnichaet* (1931); *Zhizn zovyot* (*Life Is Calling*, 1934), a domestic triangle drama (published in English in 1938) resolved by the father, an old scholar, who persuades the three that social duty—the building of a new society—transcends their personal problems; and *Tsvet kozhi* (1947), an anti-American play loosely based on the career of Jack Johnson, the Negro prizefighter who appears in the play as Jack Morrison.

Bill-Belotserkovsky's life and work are discussed briefly in Peter Yershov's *Comedy in the Soviet Theater* (1956).

BILLETDOUX, François (1927–), French dramatist born in Paris. After a SUCCÈS D'ESTIME with the one-act *À la nuit la nuit* (1955), he achieved his greatest renown with *Tchin-Tchin* (1959). A play about two deserted spouses who become lovers and alcoholics, it was adapted in the United States by SIDNEY MICHAELS and in England by WILLIS HALL. Billetdoux's later plays are more didactic and pretentious, focusing increasingly on man's exploitation of his fellowman and on his use as a mere commercial object. In *Le Comportement des époux Bredburry* (1960), for example, a wife offers her husband for sale, whereas *Va donc chez Törpe* (*Chez Torpe*, 1961) is a macabre comedy set in a hellish paradise where men try to escape exploitation. The plays that followed are melodramatic spectacles on the same theme. *Comment va le Monde, Môssieu? Il tourne, Môssieu!* (1964) is a crude BRECHTian work set at the end of World War II and featuring many characters, only two of whom speak. *Il faut passer par les nuages* (1964) also has operatic qualities and dramatizes the epic revenge of a bourgeois woman enslaved by her children's dependence.

Billetdoux's collected plays started to appear in 1961. In English, his *Two Plays* (1964) are *Tchin-Tchin* and *Chez Torpe*. His work is discussed in Jacques Guicharnaud's *Modern French Theatre* (1967).

BILLINGER, Richard (1890–), Austrian poet and dramatist, was the most distinguished native "blood-and-soil" writer to achieve prominence before the rise of Nazism. His peasant plays feature hosts of vividly realized characters and an authentic atmosphere of village and farm life. They stress conflicts of country and city, and—even more important—of Christian and pagan passions. A mixture of NATURALISM and poetic mysticism, they are intense but have flashes of earthy humor. The best of these plays appeared in the 1930's, though Billinger continued to write in the same vein through World War II and the postwar period.

Billinger came of peasant stock that had lived on the German border in Upper Austria near Schärding since the twelfth century. He prepared for the priesthood but gave up his studies when he achieved success with his poetry and his first stage hit, *Das Perchtenspiel* (1928), notably produced by Max Reinhardt. It portrays a characteristic struggle between superstition and Christianity in a married peasant's love for a "pagan Perchten" girl; her people burn down his farm and kill all but his illegitimate child before forces representing the Catholic Church protect other peasants from further destruction by the Perchten demons.

Later hits were *Rauhnacht* (1931), in which the traditional pagan orgy of the title (December 23) provides the backdrop for a frenzied peasant's African dances before a young girl he ultimately rapes and kills; *Die Hexe von Passau* (1935), whose protagonist, an actress performing Mary Magdalene in a Passion play, so moves a nobleman that he pardons convicted rebels and leads peasants in the Thirty Years' War—though she is burnt at the stake for having "bewitched" him; and *Der Gigant* (1937), the "giant" being Prague, which lures and ruins a farmer's daughter who returns broken and despised to die on the soil whose uncanny powers transcend the evil ones of the city for, as the girl is told, "If you are unfaithful to the plot of land on which you are born as a peasant you will dry up, wither away, and be cut off."

Such ideas inform all Billinger's plays. Others

include *Rosse* (1931), in which a farmhand murders a farm machinery salesman before committing suicide near his beloved horses; *Das Verlöbnis* (1932), a violent sex tragedy; *Lob des Landes* (1933), a comedy juxtaposing the peasant and the townfolk; *Stille Gäste* (1933), whose "silent guests" are the ancestral spirits that alone can inspire true emotions; and similar postwar plays, including *Der Plumpsack* (1954), *Bauernpassion* (1960), and *Die Schafschur* (1963). Lacking artistic distinction and popular appeal, the last plays failed to sustain the reputation of their author; he was dismissed by contemporary critics and historians as "the once highly promising Richard Billinger."

BIOGRAPHY, a play in three acts by S. N. BEHRMAN, produced in 1932 and published in 1933. Setting: a New York studio apartment, 1932.

Behrman's most accomplished comedy of manners, *Biography* in its underlying theme and its vivacious heroine presents a tolerant, detached compromise with worldlinesss.

Act I. Richard Kurt, an angry young man, is waiting for Marion Froude, an artist famous for her portraits of and affairs with international celebrities. Arriving late but radiant, she asks him to postpone their appointment: she is overjoyed to greet her dear old Viennese composer friend, who is frequently mistaken for his dead brother, a famous composer and once Marion's lover. A later visitor is the pompous, Babbitt-like Leander Nolan, her Tennessee childhood sweetheart "Bunny," now engaged to the daughter of a wealthy publisher, and running for senator. He is appalled by Marion's "promiscuous" life with "foreigners," but also feels personally responsible: "It was I with whom this woman first sinned before God." Affectionate and indulgent, Marion promises to paint his portrait, and Nolan departs after a disagreeable scene with Kurt. This fanatic young man, contemptuous of the "stuffed shirt—flatulent and pompous—perfect legislator" Nolan, is an editor. He wants Marion to write her autobiography for his magazine. Her need for the money and his sneer when she hesitates ("padded episodes hovering on the edge of amour—") finally persuade her: "I'm going to write the damn thing just to show you." She happily waves the advance check after he leaves, and, as the curtain falls, starts to brood over her past.

Act II. Marion is working on Nolan's portrait. Unsettled by a conceited movie idol who is visiting Marion and watching, and concerned with his election, Nolan demands that Marion leave him out of her biography. Marion thinks he takes the whole matter too seriously, but finally realizes that his blustering is caused in part by his revived passion for her. Nolan offers to buy Kurt off and then threatens to have him fired, so as to quash the biography. Furious, Kurt is the more determined to fight Nolan and his backers, and castigates Marion for being irresponsibly detached. She deplores his vindictiveness: "You simplify unduly. It is a defect of the radical and the young." Kurt tells her how his father, a miner, was shot

Biography, Act II. Marion (Ina Claire) and her German maid (Helen Westley). New York, 1933. (*Vandamm Photo, Theatre Collection, New York Public Library*)

during a strike, and reveals not only the cause of his hatred of the system but also his repressed love for her. Overcome with compassion, Marion embraces him: "Dickie . . . Why have you been afraid to love me?"

Act III. Nolan, his fiancée (a high-spirited flapper), and her father (a muscular health addict) visit Marion, who quickly and wittily charms the old publisher. She suggests to Kurt that they give up the biography. While Kurt is out she declines Nolan's proposal to give up his career and marry her. Though in love with Kurt, whose mistress she now is, Marion is frightened by his hatreds, and burns her manuscript. As he leaves her, Kurt bitterly reflects that social injustices "go on—year after year—century after century—without change—because—as they grow older—people become—*tolerant!*" He hates her detached tolerance and, as Marion realizes, thereby hates her "essential quality—the thing that is me." Similarly, she realizes, to change his uncompromising idealism "should destroy what makes me love you." Though heartbroken at giving up Kurt, Marion regains her warmth and exuberance when she receives a telegram from her Viennese composer. He has obtained commissions for her to paint Academy Award winners, and invites her to Hollywood. Marion happily starts packing and eagerly tells the German maid of her plans for further travels.

BIOGRAPHY (*Biografie*), a play in two parts by MAX FRISCH, published and produced in 1968. Setting: a German theatre stage, 1968.

Frisch called this a *comedy* (and it was translated also as *Biography: A Game*), in LUIGI

PIRANDELLO's sense of the term. Its protagonist reenacts episodes from his life, much as do the SIX CHARACTERS IN SEARCH OF AN AUTHOR. But Frisch's theme parallels Barrie's in DEAR BRUTUS and Lord Dunsany's in IF.

A professor repeatedly interrupts the action and replays autobiographical scenes. He is given the opportunity to do so by a "Registrar" with an objective account of the past. Within the rules of their game, he allows the professor to change former events and reshape his life's course. The professor again marries and thus causes his first wife's suicide, and he again associates with Communists and thus jeopardizes his career. Principally, however, he is concerned with his unhappy second marriage. Beginning with the night on which he met the girl seven years before, he declines to change happenings significantly—for though she betrays him, he still loves her. In a surprise ending *she* alters the first encounter, thus forestalling their continued affair and everything that followed—but not his suddenly revealed future.

BIRABEAU, André (1890–), French dramatist, wrote many boulevard comedies and farces, some of which were hits in the United States: *Un Déjeuner de soleil* (1925), produced as the Broadway musical *Lovely Lady* (1927); *Dame nature* (1936), the love story of two innocents who become parents, adapted by the Irish actress Patricia Collinge (1894–) under the same title in 1938; *Fisten* (1936), a political farce; and *Pamplemousse* (1937), translated as *Little Dark Horse* (1941), a tragicomic play about a mulatto boy concealed by his white father until the wife unwittingly brings him to their home.

BIRD IN HAND, a comedy in three acts by JOHN DRINKWATER, published and produced in 1927. Setting: an inn in the English Midlands in the summer.

Drinkwater's only comic-drama success is about a modern daughter of the (to her, old-fashioned) proprietor of the "Bird in Hand" Inn. She is in love with a squire's son who, her father fears, is out only to seduce her. The father-daughter quarrel is resolved with the advice of some guests, after the squire has his son propose marriage to the girl.

BIRTHDAY PARTY, THE, a play in three acts by HAROLD PINTER, produced in 1958 and published in 1959. Setting: the living room of a seaside boardinghouse, 1950's.

Pinter's first full-length play is a Kafkaesque horror farce, a modern allegory that bears some resemblance to Beckett's WAITING FOR GODOT. It has been variously interpreted as a depiction of man's (or the artist's) straitjacketing into deadly conformity, and as a depiction of man's being wrenched from his womblike shelter by death.

Act I. Stanley Webber is the sole roomer in the boardinghouse of a laconic old deck-chair attendant and his wife. A one-time concert pianist retreating from the world, Stanley tells the almost incestuously mothering old woman how he once gave a successful concert—and then "they carved me up." Sure that "they want me to crawl down on my bended knees," Stanley feels "they" are after him. He never goes out, but vaguely asks a neighbor girl to go away with him—though he admits "there's nowhere to go." Then come two visitors, Nat Goldberg and Seamus McCann. Though the former is ingratiating and full of clichés, both men are sinister, clearly on a mission to get Stanley. The half-senile old woman tells them it is Stanley's birthday, and Goldberg and McCann insist on a party.

Act II. First they brainwash and terrify Stanley. "Why did the chicken cross the road?" they finally ask him. Stanley, by then broken down, cannot answer. "Which came first? Which came first? Which came first?" Stanley screams, kicks Goldberg, is subdued—and remains inarticulate for the remainder of the play. There is an increasingly rowdy birthday party, during which all play blindman's buff, Goldberg seduces the neighbor girl, and Stanley remains oblivious. At the end, blindfolded, he is made to fall over a toy drum. He tries to throttle the old proprietress, who is enjoying the party, unaware of what is really going on.

Act III. The next morning, Goldberg and McCann report that Stanley has had a nervous breakdown. They are taking him away in Goldberg's big, black car. Clean-shaven and natty for the first time, Stanley comes down with them—dressed in striped trousers, black jacket, white collar, and carrying a bowler hat. Echoing their stichomythic barrage, which had broken him down, they now recite what they will do for Stanley. "You'll be adjusted," says Goldberg. "You'll be a success," McCann adds. The old proprietor attempts to save him: "Stan, don't let them tell you what to do!" But the proprietor cowers before their veiled threat, and stands aside. After they leave, he sits down. The play's opening small talk—comic and half senile—resumes when his old wife appears. "Wasn't it a lovely party last night?" she asks. "I was the belle of the ball," she remembers; "I know I was."

BISHOP'S BONFIRE, THE, "A Sad Play Within the Tune of a Polka" in three acts by SEAN O'CASEY, published and produced in 1955. Setting: contemporary Ballyoonagh, Ireland.

This play, a mixture of farce, fantasy, tragedy, and melodrama, is similar in theme to COCK-A-DOODLE DANDY. (After the tempestuous Dublin premiere, one irate reviewer attacked it as "Cock-a-snoot anticlericalism.") It consists of many characters and episodes, and two plots: (1) the hectic preparations for the visit of a bishop, which are thoroughly (and comically) bungled by a few villagers' cavorting, arguing, and drinking; and (2) the love affairs of the wealthy host's daughters, thwarted by their canon's and father's fanatic—and lucrative—pietism. A young priest, the play's *raisonneur,* vows "never [to] turn my back on a beautiful world, nor on the beautiful flesh of humanity, asparkle with vigour, intelligence, and health." But though he characterizes the devil as "truth who has at last mustered the courage to speak it," and declares that we "ourselves are the saints" who must solve our own problems, he fails to persuade the young to revolt against Ballyoonagh's puritan joylessness, which is as deadly as that of *Cock-a-Doodle Dandy's* Nyadnanave, and ends in the melodramatic shooting of one of the daughters.

BJØRNSON, Bjørnstjerne [Martinius] (1832–1910), Norwegian political leader, poet, novelist, and dramatist, was second among his country's major authors only to HENRIK IBSEN, his one-time friend and lifetime rival. (Though they became irritated with each other, Bjørnson later championed Ibsen.) In political and social commitment as well as in artistic development, the two were idealists whose writings had much in common. But their different personalities manifested themselves in their drama, however similar were their subjects and themes. A bitter youth in a dark and cold land left its imprint on Ibsen's plays, whereas the plays of Bjørnson, who had a pleasant childhood in a sunny climate, often mirror his cheerful and optimistic personality—the complete reverse also of AUGUST STRINDBERG, though Bjørnson was embroiled in as many controversies as was that other great Scandinavian. Though his plays were the first to deal critically with social problems soon dramatized by Ibsen, many of Bjørnson's plays (he wrote over twenty), despite their immediate impact, are superficial and more limited in appeal. But Bjørnson's work was of tremendous importance in the development of modern literature; he achieved immense popularity with his peasant tales, lyric poetry, and songs (including Norway's national anthem), and in 1903 was rewarded—as Ibsen never was—with the Nobel Prize.

The son of a pastor, Bjørnson was born in Kvikne, northern Norway. In 1837 his father was transferred to the Nesset pastorate, a lovely rural spot at the mouth of the Romsdal, where Bjørnson spent the remainder of his childhood and which became the setting for much of his fiction. Yet this early life was not wholly idyllic. Even as a youth he was active in politics, and by the time he was sent to Christiania (Oslo), from whose university he graduated in 1852, he was fired by the ambition to be a great poet. One of his first plays was accepted for production—but finding it artistically inadequate, Bjørnson withdrew it. While yet a student, he met Ibsen, the novelist Jonas Lie, and other later notables. At that time, too, he became a journalist, writing articles on politics and the theatre as well as short stories and poems. His first significant play, *Mellem slagene* (1857), is about King Sverre, the twelfth-century title character of a play Bjørnson was to produce in 1861. While involved in various political and nationalistic battles, he was also the stage director of the Bergen Theatre, one of whose actresses (Karoline Reimers) he married in 1858.

In the more than a dozen years that followed, Bjørnson wrote poetic sagas, the popular series of peasant novels beginning with *Synnøve solbakken*

Bjørnstjerne Bjørnson. (*Norwegian Embassy Information Service*)

(*Sunny Hill,* 1857), history dramas, and peasant tales that were to imbue his countrymen with a feeling for their heritage and emphasize their kinship with Norway's heroic past. The verse plays *Halte-Hulda* (1858) and *Kong Sverre* (1861) were panned; but they were followed by his masterpiece in the genre, *Sigurd Slembe* (SIGURD THE BASTARD, 1862), which established Bjørnson as one of the foremost verse dramatists; and by *Maria Stuart i Skotland* (1864), a lyrical Renaissance drama that, like the earlier plays, has excellent crowd scenes as well as interesting portrayals of John Knox and other historical figures. Though it was not published until 1872, *Sigurd Jorsalfar* belongs with these heroic saga plays; it became one of Bjørnson's most popular works in Norway.

In the early 1860's Bjørnson traveled extensively in Europe, and in 1865 he became the director of the Christiania Theatre, a post he occupied successfully for two years. During that period he also edited a newspaper and played a leading role in the Liberal Party, campaigning for aid to Denmark in its struggle against Prussia (though he was a lifelong advocate of pan-Germanism). He became a proponent of the synthesis of Christianity and Nationalism espoused by the Danish poet and divine Nikolai Grundtvig, and increasingly deviated from religious as well as political orthodoxy. Bjørnson's new convictions were expressed in his social plays, some of them conceived during his self-imposed exile, which soon became popular (and notorious)—and antedated Ibsen's plays on the same topics. The most commercially successful of them was *En fallit* (A BANKRUPTCY, 1874), the most esteemed critically was *Over ævne, første stykke* (BEYOND HUMAN POWER I, 1883), and the most controversial was *En hanske* (A GAUNTLET, 1883). Others were *De nygifte* (THE NEWLY-MARRIED COUPLE, 1865); *Redaktøren* (*The Editor,* 1874), an attack on unprincipled journalism; *Kongen* (*The King,* 1877), a criticism of traditional royalism as well as hypocrisy in Christianity, which, as the sensitive and noble king remarks, "has laid aside its ideals [and] is living on dogmas and formulas instead"; *Det ny system* (*The New System,* 1879), which like Ibsen's AN ENEMY OF THE PEOPLE lashes out not only at social hypocrisy but also at Church and clergy, government, and respect for traditional authority; and—marking Bjørnson's complete conversion to modernism—*Leonarda* (1879), which portrays an older woman's passion for her adopted daughter's lover, and a bishop's ultimately admitting the Church's wrongs in the face of the "unbeliever's" nobility. This last play adumbrated the controversial theme of divorce—but it was overshadowed, as Bjørnson's plays often were, by an Ibsen drama on the same theme, A DOLL'S HOUSE. Bjørnson's remaining plays are *Geografi og kjærlighed* (LOVE AND GEOGRAPHY, 1885); *Paul Lange og Tora Parsberg* (PAUL LANGE AND TORA PARSBERG, 1898); *Laboremus* (1901) and *På Storhove* (1904), both of which portray an emancipated woman's deleterious effect on marriage; *Daglannet* (1904), expressing Bjørnson's concern with education and the "continuity of tradition"; and his last play (which both echoes and answers Ibsen's last play), *Når den ny vin blomstrer* (WHEN THE NEW WINE BLOOMS, 1909).

During most of these years Bjørnson was engaged in such heated political controversy that for a while he had to take refuge in Germany. He spent much of his later life in Paris, where he died. Immensely enthusiastic and energetic, he interspersed his persuasive lecturing, pamphleteering, and other political activities with the writing of many stories, novels, poems, and songs. His development as a dramatist paralleled Ibsen's: early romantic and historical drama was followed by NATURALISTIC social plays, and, finally, by spiritual drama—notably the *Beyond Human Power* plays. Bjørnson was, furthermore, an innovator, among the first to explore and represent modern life on the stage. But as critics have often remarked, in any comparison with Ibsen it is Bjørnson who suffers, and GUNNAR HEIBERG viciously attacked Bjørnson's zeal as a reformer. Skillful as a constructor of plays, Bjørnson only rarely transcended the sentimentally happy resolutions that are symptomatic of his cheerful optimism and his unswerving faith in a benevolent deity and the innate human goodness that must overcome the social ills depicted in the drama. Such characteristically superficial (if not simplistic) attitudes pervade and vitiate Bjørnson's drama. They have been responsible more than anything else for the steady decline of his reputation: modern thought and art seem more attuned to the brooding intensity and the depths of the drama of Ibsen—and of Strindberg.

Most of Bjørnson's plays are available in translation. R. Farquharson Sharp's collections of *Three Comedies* and *Three Dramas* (1912, 1914) have informative prefaces and include, respectively: *The Newly-Married Couple, Leonarda,* and *A Gauntlet;* and *A Bankruptcy, The Editor,* and *The King.* Modern literature and drama books devote sections to Bjørnson's work, as does Harald Beyer's *Norsk Litteraturhistorie* (1952), published in translation as *A History of Norwegian Literature* (1956). In English, the most comprehensive work is Harold Larson's *Bjørnstjerne Bjørnson; a Study in Norwegian Nationalism* (1944).

BLACK GLOVE, THE (*Svarta handsken*), Opus V of THE CHAMBER PLAYS, "a lyrical fantasy" in five acts by AUGUST STRINDBERG, published in 1909 and produced in 1911. Setting: an apartment house in Stockholm, early twentieth century.

This Dickensian Christmas fantasy—also performed under the alternate title *Jul* (*Christmas*)—was the last play Strindberg wrote for his Intima Teatern. But it was not performed there, and it belongs to a different period and mood. It combines poetry and prose as well as NATURALISM and fantasy.

On Christmas, Saint Nicholas punishes an ill-tempered wife who browbeats her child and accuses others of having stolen her ring. She is temporarily deprived of her child so that she may learn to appreciate it, and the ring is found in a glove, where she herself had misplaced it. Her consequently improved disposition and new ability to love bring happiness to a charitable old taxidermist who is living in the attic and turns out to be her father, and allow him to die happily.

BLACK MASK, THE (*Die schwarze Maske*), a one-act play by GERHART HAUPTMANN, produced in 1929 and published in 1930. Setting: Bolkenhain, Silesia; February 1662.

This play was published and produced with *Hexenritt* (WITCH'S RIDE) under the joint title *Spuk* (*Spectre*).

A mixed gathering of people and their conversations in Mayor Silvanus Schuller's house exhibit various facets of seventeenth-century life. Schuller's cultivated, wealthy wife, Benigna, has lately felt terrified, guilt-ridden, and tormented by carnal passions. Long before she had been the mistress of a Negro, whose child she bore and who has continued to pursue and blackmail her. Now she senses his frightening presence under what is taken as "the black mask" of an intruder in the house, and commits suicide. (It is not clear whether she does so because of guilt or because of her delirium from the black plague, which has just broken out.) Friends try to console her husband, a kind man who is overwhelmed by his inexplicable misfortune.

BLACKS THE, (*Les Nègres*), a *"Clownerie"* ("Clown Show") by JEAN GENET, published in 1958 and produced in 1959. Setting: a two-level stage with black velvet curtains and a green screen.

Genet insisted that this successfully produced grotesquerie be performed by Negroes before an audience of whites or Negroes wearing white masks, and "if the blacks refuse the masks, then let a dummy be used." Characteristic Genet outcasts, the blacks, led by Archibald, the master of ceremonies, perform their ceremonial crime in a series of almost plotless and EXPRESSIONISTically dancelike rituals. The complexity of the rituals is heightened by the play's "mirrors game" of multiple realities that are transformed into artifacts and stress rather than obscure theatre make-believe. On an upper stage there is an audience court of "whites": Negroes wearing white masks and consisting of THE BALCONY characters of queen, judge, bishop, and general. Their behavior accords with the resentful blacks' concept of the dominant whites as they watch the blacks enact their sometimes grisly rituals and behave according to the whites' supposed concepts of Negroes—violent yet childlike, smelly yet exotic, etc.

The curtain is drawn manually and reveals four Negro couples in evening dress dancing to a Mozart minuet around a white-draped catafalque. The court members (in white masks) enter on the upper stage. One of the dancers steps forth to address them. "Ladies and gentlemen," he begins: "My name is Archibald Absalom Wellington." He bows and introduces his colleagues. They include Deodatus Village, who is in love with the prostitute Virtue (Stephanie Virtue Secret-rose Diop), and a priest. The "white" audience-court wonder if the blacks have murdered someone, whereupon the Negroes burst into shrill laughter. The general (he is also the governor) decides to "stamp out the Blacks!" as Archibald announces that "this evening we've come again to round out your grief." Archibald explains how the Negroes will act out their play and "increase the distance that separates us—a distance that is basic—by our pomp, our manners, our insolence—for we are also actors." Then he reveals their crime. "We have killed this white woman," he begins, pointing at the catafalque: "Only *we* could have done it the way we did it—savagely!" In stylized detail the Negroes portray the murder, for they seek to "deserve [the whites'] reprobation and get them to deliver the judgment that will condemn us." But from time to time the Negro actors object to playing their parts, and the "white court" attempts to control the progress of their performance. Village has supposedly committed the crime, whose victim (supposedly) was an old white woman. Later she is identified as a buxom white girl seduced by the Negroes' supposed superior virility, and then raped and strangled by the priest. Transvested, this priest gives birth to a bunch of eighteen-inch, but full-grown, white dolls; pinned on the stage and on the verge of being raped, they appear petrified as they face the audience they symbolize. Suddenly news comes that the blacks all over the world are rising in a plot against the whites: this production of *The Blacks* is merely a diversionary decoy, a screen. The "whites" on the upper stage descend to exterminate the blacks, but instead they themselves are trapped and killed, and their missionary bishop is castrated. "How well you hate!" the "white" queen says as she dies, "choked by my desire for a Big Black Buck." As the play ends and the "whites" get up to join the other actors, Archibald thanks all the actors for their performance. He regrets "the time has not yet come for presenting dramas about noble matters. But perhaps they [white audiences] suspect what lies behind this architecture of emptiness and words," Archibald continues: "We are what they want us to be. We shall therefore be it to the very end, absurdly." He has the actors don their white masks and orders them escorted to Hell. Only Village and Virtue remain on stage. Now, in another world, their love is possible. Then all the Negro actors, now without masks, appear about the white-draped catafalque at the back of the stage. The *Don Giovanni* minuet is played as Village and Virtue walk toward them hand in hand, away from and with their backs to the (real white) audience.

BLANCHETTE, a comedy in three acts by EUGÈNE BRIEUX, published and produced in 1892. Setting: the French provinces, 1892.

The premiere of this play (on a double bill with Curel's A FALSE SAINT) at André Antoine's Théâtre Libre established Brieux as an important playwright. It became one of the most popular and most-often revived of Antoine's productions, and in 1903 was added to the Comédie-Française repertory, where it remained for decades. It is an attack on the educational system as well as on the attempts of people to rise above their station.

At considerable sacrifice her peasant family has sent Blanchette to study for her teacher's certificate. She returns with grandiose notions and contempt for her provincial background. Her government post fails to materialize, for there are too many applicants who have been promised such employment. Nonetheless impressed with Blanchette, her parents reject the blacksmith's son: "We did not educate our daughter to give her to a laborer like ourselves." Misapplying her education, Blanchette ruins her father's crops, and he finally tells her to do menial work like everybody else or "leave this house." She leaves, but returns a year later. In Paris she discovered that the few available openings force the many girls with teacher's certificates to take up prostitution or do menial work for starvation wages. Now Blanchette can find happiness in the province with the blacksmith's son. When her father wonders whether "it is wrong to educate one's children" she replies, "No. But one should show them how to make use of their education."

BLIND, THE (*Les Aveugles*), a one-act play by MAURICE MAETERLINCK, published in 1890 and produced in 1891. Setting: an ancient Norland forest at night.

This short, SYMBOLIC play is among Maeterlinck's most effective ones. It depicts twelve blind people, six men and six women (one with her infant), lost on an island. They are unaware that in their midst sits the dead old priest who led them out into the elements—the leader for whose return they are waiting anxiously. As their fears from unseen dangers grow, a dog leads them to the corpse. Their terror is climaxed by footsteps that approach and stop among them. "Who are you?" one of the blind asks the invisible stranger (Death), and another begs, "Have pity on us!" But there is no answer—and the infant weeps louder.

BLITHE SPIRIT, "an improbable farce" in three acts by NOËL COWARD, published and produced in 1941. Setting: a living room in Kent, England; c. 1940.

Blithe Spirit is probably Coward's best play, his most popular work (its Madame Arcati is a masterful comic creation), and England's wittiest comedy about the dead. It broke London production records, and it was performed by British and American touring companies at the time of and long after Pearl Harbor. Subsequently *Blithe Spirit* was filmed (1945), televised (1956), and made into the musical *High Spirits* (1964), and Coward wrote a ballet version of the play for his revue *Sigh No More* (1945).

Act I. Ruth and Charles Condomine, a writer, prepare for a séance, which is to furnish material for his next novel. As their breathless new maid rushes in and out, Ruth jealously questions her husband about his first wife, who died seven years ago. "I remember her physical attractiveness, which was tremendous," Charles says, "and her spiritual integrity which was nil." The guests arrive: a doctor and his wife, and the spiritualist, Madame Arcati—a hearty and barbarically dressed spinster who bicycles, spouts penny-novel clichés, and overwhelms them all with her bizarre speech and stories. "Heigho, to work we go," she exclaims after a few martinis and dinner, and prepares to summon her medium, a child who died long ago and now suffers from a cold. They put on a dance record and the table thumps in reply to Madame Arcati's questions. After she emits a scream, Madame Arcati falls into a trance. A voice is heard—that of Elvira, Charles's first wife—but only by him (and the audience), though Madame Arcati, when she is brought to with brandy, feels something "psychic" in the air. After she cycles away and the other guests leave, Elvira appears—visible only to Charles (and the audience). Ruth thinks he is insulting her when he tells Elvira to shut up and behave, and she goes out. Elvira sweetly remarks, "To hell with Ruth."

Act II. At breakfast the next morning, Ruth is still angry, but Charles, though disturbed by last

Blithe Spirit, Act III. Madame Arcati (Mildred Natwick), the maid (Doreen Lang), Charles (Clifton Webb), Elvira (Leonora Corbet), and Ruth (Peggy Wood). New York, 1941. (*Vandamm Photo, Theatre Collection, New York Public Library*)

night's "hallucinations," is cheerful. Soon they bicker, Ruth accusing Charles of drinking too much and not understanding women: "Just because you've always been dominated by them it doesn't necessarily follow that you know anything about them"; Charles thereupon accuses Ruth of trying to dominate him, and complains, "I've been imploring your sympathy and all I got was a sterile temperance lecture." Ruth suggests a psychiatrist, but Charles refuses "to endure months of expensive humiliation only to be told at the end of it that at the age of four I was in love with my rocking horse." Suddenly Elvira reappears and Ruth, worried about Charles's apparently mad talk and believing him to be sick, suggests that Charles go to bed. ("The way that woman harps on bed is nothing short of erotic," Elvira remarks.) To prove to Ruth that he is not crazy, Charles has Elvira move some objects around. At last Ruth realizes that she is really there, and when Elvira smashes an expensive vase she runs out screaming. Later she summons Madame Arcati to exorcise Elvira. Madame Arcati is absolutely thrilled by her professional success in summoning Elvira, but admits that she is unable to get rid of her. When Ruth angrily reveals that Madame Arcati had been invited merely to provide material for Charles's next novel, the spiritualist leaves in a huff. Charles comes in, much cheered. He is beginning to enjoy being what Ruth calls "a sort of astral bigamist." But Ruth is furious, especially because she realizes that Charles, in communicating Elvira's catty answers to her questions, is "editing" them. A few days later, both Charles and the maid are injured by accidents (caused by Elvira). After explaining to Charles that Elvira is trying to kill him so as to get him back for herself, the desperate Ruth leaves to try her luck again with Madame Arcati. When Elvira hears that Ruth has driven off she gets hysterical: expecting Charles to be the next driver of the car, she has tampered with it. The telephone rings, and Charles is informed that Ruth has just had a fatal car accident. Suddenly Elvira is retreating from something. "Of all the filthy, low-down tricks," she yells as she shields her head: "Ow—stop it—Ruth—let go—"

Act III. A few days later, Madame Arcati, terribly conscience-stricken ("I threw up the sponge instead of throwing down the gauntlet") calls on Charles, who is in deep mourning. Now she thinks she has found the formula to "dematerialize" Elvira. She is enchanted with a demonstration of the supernatural when Elvira blows into her ear: "I can sense the vibrations—this is magnificent." Elvira tells Charles she wants to be sent back: now that Ruth has joined her she is unhappy. Charles and Elvira bicker jealously and rehash old quarrels. When he accuses her of being a wife who was interested only in enjoying herself, Elvira replies, "Why shouldn't I have fun? I died young, didn't I?" Madame Arcati continues her gushing and finally tries exorcizing Elvira with a pepper-and-salt formula. It does not work. ("Merlin does all this sort of thing at parties and bores us all stiff with it," Elvira comments.) Then Madame Arcati falls into a trance: "Now first the music and away we go!" The table bumps, but instead of Elvira's vanishing, Ruth now appears, visible to her husband: "Once and for all, Charles, what the hell does this mean?" Some hours later, Madame Arcati is asleep, and the room is cluttered with her crystal, birch branches, a Ouija board, cards, sandwiches, and empty beer mugs. Elvira and Ruth are bickering, frustrated at the spiritualist's failure, after five séances and flinging herself in and out of trances. Madame Arcati awakes refreshed, eats more sandwiches, shakes her crystal ball, sees a white bandage, and suddenly understands the situation. She waves the branches: the hypnotized maid appears, a bandage around her injured head. Despite her denial, it is clear that she was the medium who had materialized the wives. Madame Arcati helps her exorcise them, and Elvira and Ruth gradually "dematerialize." Refreshing herself with a final sandwich, the spiritualist pedals home. Charles sends the still-dazed maid back to bed and gives her a pound note, which horrifies her: "Oh, sir, whatever for?" Then Charles tells his now invisible and inaudible wives that he will travel far away. He treats them to some unflattering comments, and—as the noises of poltergeist activities start and mount, he dashes out—"just as the overmantel crashes to the floor and the curtain pole comes tumbling down."

BLITZSTEIN, Marc (1905–64), American composer, carved a niche for himself in theatre histories with his musical drama THE CRADLE WILL ROCK (1937), a "proletarian" work he dedicated to BERTOLT BRECHT. Blitzstein was associated with the group of liberal and left-wing writers of the Federal Theatre Project of the Works Progress Administration, and was a proponent of "socially significant" art. Primarily a composer, he was most successful with his adaptation of Brecht's THE THREEPENNY OPERA (1952), which two years later started a record Off-Broadway run of 2,611 performances—the first time a Brecht play became a hit in New York. Less successful adaptations were *Regina* (1949), an operatic version of Hellman's THE LITTLE FOXES, and *Juno* (1959), a musical based on O'Casey's JUNO AND THE PAYCOCK. Blitzstein also contributed some of the sketches of *Pins and Needles* (1937), the long-running satiric ILGWU revue. When Blitzstein died—he was killed by sailors in Martinique—he was working on an opera about Sacco and Vanzetti.

BLOK, Aleksandr [Aleksandrovich] (1880–1921), the Russian SYMBOLIST, is better known for his poems and essays than for his plays, all of which are in verse. Most of them are stylized and static, like Yeats's FOUR PLAYS FOR DANCERS. This is particularly true of *Balaganchik* (THE PUPPET SHOW, 1906). It and *Roza i krest* (THE ROSE AND THE CROSS, 1916) are considered his best plays, though both are closet dramas. The first (available in Volume II of F. D. Reeve's *Anthology of*

Russian Plays, 1963) created a stir in St. Petersburg (Leningrad), where opponents attacked Blok as an apostate mystic and a blasphemer; others hailed the play as a lyric work that established Blok as a leading Russian poet. His other dramas are *Korol na ploshchadi* (*The King in the Square*, written in 1906 but unproduced); *Neznakomka* (written in 1906 and produced in 1913), an allegory about a poet-astrologer who finds out too late that the falling-star-turned-human is the woman (the title's "unknown lady") he has been seeking all along; and *Pesnya sudby* (*The Song of Fate*, rejected by Konstantin Stanislavsky, but published in 1909), a patriotic, diffuse, and abstract play.

Blok was the son of a brilliant but emotionally unstable professor of public law, whose wife separated from him even before the poet's birth in St. Petersburg. Blok attended the University of Petrograd, married a distinguished Russian chemist's daughter who became an actress, separated from her, and then traveled in Western Europe. He became something of a romantic legend even during his life. Disappointed by the 1905 Revolution, Blok served in World War I and supported the 1917 Revolution. *Dvenadtsat* (*The Twelve*, 1918), his and the Revolution's most famous poem, depicts twelve workers as if they were the Apostles. His poetry is characterized by disillusionment and irony, despite its enthusiasm and mastery of lyricism. Some of these qualities appear in his plays. The momentous events in which he participated during his brief lifetime inspired all his writing.

While not all his dramas are available in English, there are several studies of his life, dramatic works, and poetry; these include Sir Cecil Kisch's *Alexander Blok: Prophet of Revolution* (1960) and F. D. Reeve's *Aleksandr Blok: Between Image and Idea* (1962), which has an extensive bibliography.

BLOOD WEDDING (*Bodas de sangre*), a tragedy in three acts by FEDERICO GARCÍA LORCA, published and produced in 1933. Setting: the hills of Andalusia, early twentieth-century Spain.

Also presented as *Bitter Oleander*, this is perhaps Lorca's best-known play and the first of his trilogy of "rural tragedies" (the others are YERMA and THE HOUSE OF BERNARDA ALBA). *Blood Wedding* is full of rich and varied folk poetry, symbolism, and powerful elemental passions that victimize and doom everyone in the play. But these passions are restrained by a stark, ritualistic plot that bears only a superficial resemblance to the sensational newspaper account that inspired it. An even stronger influence on the play's composition was Synge's RIDERS TO THE SEA, which (in Juan Ramón Jiménez's translation) had particularly impressed Lorca. According to his brother, Lorca thought about it for a year and then wrote the play in one week. Except for Leonardo, the characters are nameless.

Act I. Scene 1. Though suspicious of her son's beloved, the Mother knows his Bride to be good and hard working. But the girl once loved Leonardo Félix, whose family killed the Mother's husband and her other son in a blood feud.

Blood Wedding, Act III, Scene 1. The Bride (Adele Lamont) and Leonardo (Daniel Sirvent). New York, 1958. (*Avery Willard*)

Leonardo himself, innocent of the killings, is now married to the Bride's cousin; but the Mother is obsessed with hatred for the killers and their family. She agrees to the wedding, however, for she yearns for descendants—"as many as you want, since your father didn't live to give them to me." *Scene 2.* Leonardo's wife and mother are lullabying his baby. Soon Leonardo arrives on his exhausted horse. Bitter about the imminent wedding, he speaks angrily to the women. His wife weeps as she sings to the baby. *Scene 3.* Mother and Groom visit the Bride and her Father in their "wasteland" farm. Even though there is no water, "your father would have covered it with trees," the Mother tells her son: "in the three years we were married he planted ten cherry trees." The financial arrangements are made laconically and quickly, and the wedding date is set. But when the visitors leave, the Bride angrily bites her hand and refuses to have the wedding presents opened. When her servant tells her of a rider who appeared the night before, the Bride furiously silences her. Just then the rider is heard again. It is Leonardo.

Act II. Scene 1. On her wedding morning, the Bride is bitter and tense. She recalls her dead mother, who came from "fertile country" but "wasted away here." A servant heartens her as she helps her dress. Voices sing the bridal song in the distance, and the first guest arrives: Leonardo. The Bride, proud and angry, tries to send him off, but she has difficulty tearing herself away from him: "It's as though I'd drunk a bottle of anise and fallen asleep wrapped in a quilt of roses. . . . I know I'm drowning—but I go on down." As the wedding party and song progress, the Bride desperately urges the Groom to speed their marriage: "I want to be your wife right now so that I can be with you alone, not hearing any voice but yours." Leonardo's wife arrives, and pitifully insists that her rejecting husband accompany her to church. *Scene 2.* The marriage is over and the party festivities begin. But there are ominous forebodings. The Mother recalls the murder of her men, and her obsessive hatred of Leonardo grows as he slinks in the background. The Bride becomes increasingly tense and unyielding to the Groom, and finally goes out to rest. It is Leonardo's wife who discovers the Bride's escape with her husband. The disconcerted Mother first hesitates; but then, though she senses impending tragedy, she sends her son after them: "Those people kill quickly and well—but yes, run, and I'll follow!" Then she remarks bitterly, "Decent women throw themselves in the water; not that one! But now she's my son's wife." As the chase begins, the Mother realizes that "the hour of blood has come again."

Act III. Scene 1. In the forest, woodcutters discuss Leonardo's escape with the Bride. "They were deceiving themselves but at the last blood was stronger," they agree. "Better dead with the blood drained away than alive with it rotting." The Moon and Death appear: "Light up the vest and open the buttons, / and then the knife will know its way," says the latter, personified as a Beggar Woman, and then she leads the Groom to the escaped lovers. These now arrive, lamenting yet accepting their passion: "Glass splinters are stuck in my tongue," Leonardo says, echoing the Bride's earlier statement; "the fault is the earth's." The scene becomes "violent, full of great sensuality." The pursuers approach. "It's fitting that I should die here, / with water over my feet, / with thorns upon my head," the Bride says: "And fitting the leaves should mourn me, / a woman lost and virgin." They embrace, ready to die together, and go deeper into the woods. Then shrieks are heard, the music stops, and the Moon and the Beggar Woman reappear, silently. *Scene 2.* In a simple dwelling suggestive of a church, the women come to mourn. The Beggar Woman describes the killing, "like two torrents / still at last, among the great boulders, / two men at the horse's feet," and the Bride's return, "with bloodstains on her skirt and hair." Now that her last son is dead, the Mother can "sleep without terror of guns or knives." The Bride seeks death, but she wants the Mother to know that "I'm clean, that I may be crazy, but that they can bury me without a single man ever having seen himself in the whiteness of my breasts." Though the Mother no longer cares, the Bride justifies herself: "I was a woman burning with desire, full of sores inside and out, and your son was a little bit of water from which I hoped for children, land, health; but the other one was a dark river, choked with brush, that brought near me the undertone of its rushes and its whispered song." She requests an ordeal by fire to prove her innocence. The Mother turns a deaf ear; she controls her vengeance and blesses "the wheat stalks, because my sons are under them; blessed be the rain, because it wets the face of the dead. Blessed be God, who stretches us out together to rest." In a final chorus, the Mother laments the victims of a little knife that "slides in clean / through the astonished flesh / and stops there, at the place / where trembles enmeshed / the dark root of a scream."

BLUE BIRD, THE (*L'Oiseau bleu*), a fairy play in six acts by MAURICE MAETERLINCK, published and produced in 1908. Setting: a woodcutter's cottage, and assorted dream scenes.

This, Maeterlinck's best-known play, has been popular with adults as well as children. Originally produced by Stanislavsky in Russia, it has been frequently played and revived throughout the whole world. Its "beauty," "wisdom," and "loftiness" were praised by MAX BEERBOHM, Léon Blum, and many others. Maeterlinck acknowledged his indebtedness to JAMES M. BARRIE, *"père de 'Peter Pan,' grandpère de 'l'oiseau bleu.'"* But beyond the fairy-tale charm it has in common with PETER PAN, *The Blue Bird* is also Maeterlinck's allegorical portrayal of the universe's mysteries and of man's quest for happiness. Act IV was written and added later, and there is a sequel to the play, THE BETROTHAL.

Act I. Tyltyl and Mytyl, a sleeping little boy and girl, are tucked in by Mummy and Daddy Tyl, a

The Blue Bird, Act II. At the Fairy's Palace, left to right: Water (Gwendoline Valentine), Fire (Pedro de Cordoba), Bread (Robert E. Homans), Sugar (Georgio Maveroni), Milk (Elizabeth Van Sell), Cat (Cecil Yapp), Dog (Jacob Wendell), Light (Margaret Wycherly), Mytyl (Irene Brown), Tyltyl (Gladys Hulette), the Fairy (Louise Closser). London, 1910. (*Culver Pictures*)

woodcutter. After the parents go out the children seem to awake. (It is their dream that constitutes the body of the play.) They bemoan their poverty as they observe a wealthy neighbor's Christmas party. An old fairy enters, seeking the Blue Bird for her sick little daughter. She gives the children a hat with a magic diamond that can open the eyes of humans, who, "since the death of the fairies, see nothing at all." The cottage suddenly becomes beautiful and alive with fairies: the souls of the faithful dog (Tylô) and treacherous cat (Tylette), and of the children's other companions—Milk, Fire, Water, Light, Bread, and Sugar, who gives the children one of her candystick fingers whenever they are hungry. Transformed into enchanted beings who must die at the end of the journey, they all agree to accompany the children on their search for the Blue Bird. As Tyltyl and Mytyl and the others leave noisily, Mummy and Daddy Tyl worriedly rush in. But everything seems magically restored and the parents find their children "sleeping quite quietly."

Act II. Scene 1. At the Fairy's Palace, the cat conspires to prevent the children from finding the Blue Bird, even if they should have to be harmed. The dog, who adores his "little gods," angrily rejects this idea. As other "animals, things, and elements" join in the debate, the Fairy arrives and deputizes Light as the leader in the quest for the Blue Bird. The children are first to go to the Land of Memory. *Scene 2.* In the Land of Memory Tyltyl and Mytyl have a joyful reunion with their grandparents, who—like all dead people—are alive whenever remembered by the living. They also meet their dead brothers and sisters, and all spend happy moments together. Discovering the grandparents' caged blackbird to be blue, Tyltyl and Mytyl take it with them, but it soon turns black again.

Act III. Scene 1. At her palace, Night refuses to help Tyltyl and Mytyl: "I have the keeping of all Nature's secrets and I am absolutely forbidden to deliver them." Aided by their magic diamond, however, the children and their friends enter her realms. They repulse Ghosts, Sicknesses, and other Terrors, and they admire Stars, Dews, and other delightful figures. In the abode of the "perpetually and harmoniously" hovering "blue birds of the dreams that live on the rays of the moon" they joyfully capture many and carry them out. But they miss the real Blue Bird, and weep as the other birds expire at daylight. *Scene 2.* At the Forest, the trees debate on ways to resist the children's quest for the Blue Bird, "the great secret of things and of happiness" that would enable man to "make our servitude still harder." Helped by the treachery of the cat, many animals and trees viciously attack the children. They are saved only by the valor of Tyltyl and the dog, and by Light's intervention. The cat again traduces the dog and ingratiates itself with Mytyl.

Act IV. Scene 1. Light explains the nature of Joys, Miseries, and Fate. She then sends the children to the Palace of Happiness. *Scene 2.* At the Palace they are tempted by various Luxuries, frightened by Miseries, and delighted by Happinesses and Joys, including that of Maternal Love: Mummy Tyl, looking younger and more beautiful because of their love. But they do not find the Blue Bird. The time is not ripe for the revelation of "the last truths and the last happinesses."

Act V. Scenes 1 and 2. Pursuing their quest in the graveyard at night, Tyltyl and Mytyl tensely await the rising of the dead. By dawn they still see no one, the graveyard is revealed to be a garden, and they realize that "There are no dead." *Scene 3.* In the Kingdom of the Future, Tyltyl and Mytyl meet hordes of as yet Unborn Children, including their own brother-to-be. They find no happiness; but they learn much about the future, and think they have found the Blue Bird.

Act VI. Scene 1. Back in their house, the children are sad to discover the bird has turned pink. The hour for their awakening comes. All their companions bid the children farewell, the cat and dog fighting until the last moment. *Scene 2.* The children wake up, worrying their parents with apparently delirious talk about their adventures. A neighbor looking like the Fairy asks for Tyltyl's bird for her sick daughter. As he fetches it, Tyltyl notices that it is blue: "That's the Blue Bird we were looking for! We went so far and he was here all the time!" The neighbor soon returns with her daughter, who has been miraculously cured by the Blue Bird. But their joy is brief, for it flies off. Tyltyl begs the audience, "If any of you should find him, would you be so very kind as to give him back to us? We need him for our happiness, later on."

BLUES FOR MISTER CHARLIE, a play in three acts by JAMES BALDWIN, published and produced in 1964. Setting: a small Southern town, early 1960's.

This protest play is remotely based on the 1955 Mississippi murder of Emmett Till, a fourteen-year-old Negro boy. Inflammatory in the AGITPROP tradition, with stereotyped "Whitetown" and "Blacktown" characters, it portrays racial oppression and hatred as due to white envy of supposed black sexual superiority. The play's skeletal stage setting and fluid, kaleidoscopic form with constant shifts between present and past action closely resemble those of Miller's AFTER THE FALL, which appeared in the same year.

A shot is heard, and a white man drops a black boy's corpse to the ground: "And may every nigger like this nigger end like this nigger—face down in the weeds." The victim, son of the local minister and leader of the nonviolent civil rights movement, has recently returned South from New York. His militant resentment of white intimidation "unsettles" both sides, whose suppressed anger flares into the open after the murder and during the trial. The minister hides his son's gun under the Bible. At the trial, the religious grandmother lies to protect the slain youth's reputation and to condemn his murderer; and a juke-joint owner, a lifelong "Uncle Tom," turns on the murderer. "*All* white men are Mister Charlie!" the minister tells the wealthy newspaper editor, a liberal who befriends the Negroes but finally weakens and helps ultimately to absolve the murderer. Other whites are the murderer's anemic wife, who gives a perjured account of the victim's conduct, and the couple's various Negro-hating friends. A final scene portrays the murder. The youth goads the white man: "You can't eat because none of your sad-assed chicks can cook." Then, riddled with bullets, he dies glorying in the black man's phallic supremacy. "I had to kill him then, I'm a white man! Can't nobody talk that way to *me*!" the murderer later remarks—and the blacks start marching.

BLUME, Bernhard (1901–), German dramatist, wrote politically oriented plays in the 1920's and 1930's. His first hit was *Fahrt nach der Südsee* (1924), in which political prisoners mutiny aboard a ship they are unable to steer. His epic *Bonaparte* (1926) in many fast-moving scenes portrays Napoleon's relentless quest for power. Other Blume plays are *Treibjagd* (1927), about the suffering of the victims of the Bolshevist Revolution; *Im Namen des Volkes* (1929), on the Sacco-Vanzetti case; and a number of comedies. In 1936 Blume migrated to the United States, where he taught German literature in various universities. He also published a novel and studies of Thomas Mann and Goethe.

BOLIVIA became independent only in 1825 and its theatre long remained derivative of Spain's. It presented romantic history plays—many of them in verse and all in the century's declamatory-romantic fashion—Indian plays, conquistador drama, and COSTUMBRISMO. Notable authors were Félix Reyes Ortiz (1828–82) and José Bustamante (1821–86), both of whom wrote comedies, and Nataniel Aguirre (1843–88), Bolivia's first major novelist. Early twentieth-century writers were Ricardo Jaimes Freyre (1868–1933), the author of patriotic and biblical drama and the son of Carolina Freyre de Jaimes, a playwright prominent in PERU; the poet Gregorio Reynolds (1882–1948); and Federico More (1889–), whose SYMBOLIC *Interludio* (*Interlude*) was the earliest Bolivian drama to appear in English.* Among more recent playwrights are Mario Flores (1901–), whose first success was the comedy *Cruz Diablo* (1920) but who subsequently moved to ARGENTINA to write popular comedies and political satires; and Joaquín Gantier (1903–), who produced a rural comedy partly in Quechua, *El molino* (1943), and the drama of a father penalized for his divorce, *Divorcio* (1946). Both playwrights had difficulties finding actors to perform their work—a major Bolivian problem that was to be rectified by the Festivals del Teatro launched in 1961.

For studies, see LATIN AMERICA.

BOLT, Robert [Oxton] (1924–), English dramatist, became known for his Thomas More play, A MAN FOR ALL SEASONS (1960). He was born near Manchester, whose Grammar School and University he attended, and he served in the army and the air force during World War II. Then he completed his studies at Manchester and Exeter universities (1946–50), and supported himself as an English teacher for the next eight years.

A playwright whose work is traditional and not related to the "angry" drama of his contemporaries

* In Frank Shay and Pierre Loving's *Fifty Contemporary One-Act Plays* (1920).

(JOHN OSBORNE, ARNOLD WESKER, etc.), Bolt has written sensitive, competent acting vehicles. Many of them have modern settings and are "uneasily straddled," Bolt himself noted, "between NATURALISM and non-naturalism." *The Critic and the Heart* (produced at the Oxford Playhouse in 1957) was followed by Ralph Richardson's London production of *Flowering Cherry* (1958), which, with its unsuccessful-insurance-man protagonist, has been compared to Miller's DEATH OF A SALESMAN. The play's success enabled Bolt thereafter to devote full time to his writing, which continued with *The Tiger and the Horse* (1960), *Gentle Jack* (1963), *The Thwarting of Baron Bolligrew* (1965, a fairy-tale comedy about a dragon-slaying duke), and *Vivat! Vivat Regina!* (1970, a dramatization of the counterpoise of Elizabeth I and Mary, Queen of Scots).

An anti-Establishment liberal once imprisoned for his political activities, Bolt nonetheless works within the Establishment. He has written a number of radio and television dramas, and screenplays like those for *Lawrence of Arabia* (1962) and *Doctor Zhivago* (1965), for which he won an Academy Award.

A study of his life and work is Ronald Hayman's *Robert Bolt* (1969).

BOLTON, Guy (1886–), American playwright and novelist, wrote many dramas and musicals by himself and in collaboration. His most popular play was his 1954 adaptation of Marcelle Maurette's (1903–) *Anastasia* (1951), the drama of a sick girl who is used by a gang of crooks plotting to steal the imperial Russian fortune banked after the Revolution; after persuading various people (including, in the climactic scene, the stern and suspicious Dowager Empress) of her identity as the Tsar Nicolas's daughter Anastasia, she is betrothed to a prince she does not love—but she ultimately vanishes.

Other Bolton plays include *Leave It to Jane* (1917), based on GEORGE ADE's *The College Widow;* numerous collaborations with George Middleton (1880–1968), with the English novelist P. G. Wodehouse (1881–), with OSCAR HAMMERSTEIN II, and with others, including musicals like *Lady, Be Good!* (1924) and *Rio Rita* (1927), both written with Fred Thompson (1884–1949), and *Oh, Kay!* (1928, with Wodehouse). Further popular Bolton plays were *Girl Crazy* (1930), written with John McCowan (? – ?); *Anything Goes* (1934), with Wodehouse; *Theatre* (1941), based on the SOMERSET MAUGHAM novel and produced as *Larger Than Life* in England; and *Child of Fortune* (1956), a dramatization of HENRY JAMES's novel *Wings of the Dove.* Bolton also wrote many screenplays and novels.

BOND, THE (*Bandet*), a one-act tragedy by AUGUST STRINDBERG, published in 1893 and produced in 1902. Setting: a Swedish village circuit court, in the 1890's.

This courtroom drama, a powerful dramatization of his and Siri Strindberg's divorce and custody proceedings, has also been translated as *The Link.*

Forced by arbitrary legalisms to condemn an honest man and reward the thief, a Judge is confronted with the day's main case: the divorce suit of the Baron and Baroness. They privately agree to avoid recriminations in the crowded courtroom. But soon they are driven to shameless battle and sordid accusations to gain custody of their child, "the embodiment of our love, . . . the bond that links our souls together." The Judge is appalled by the savage spectacle of their bloody clawing. "Such is love," the Pastor remarks; "hate is the lining inside the garment." The court finally deprives both parents of custody. Grief-stricken, the Baron attributes their catastrophe to "Nature, which drove us to hate each other," while the Baroness, weeping hysterically, wants to hide and "scream myself tired against God who has allowed this fiendish love to come into the world as a torment to us human beings."

BONDS OF INTEREST, THE (*Los intereses creados*), a comedy in three acts and a prologue by JACINTO BENAVENTE, produced in 1907 and published in 1908. Setting: an imaginary country at the beginning of the seventeenth century.

Benavente's acknowledged masterpiece (it launched New York's Theatre Guild in 1919), this play uses the traditional characters of the *commedia dell'arte.* Its masks conceal life's nakedness, as Benavente saw it; but revealed is the mixture of good and evil in human nature, man's preoccupation with ideals no less than with sordid reality. Though he also manifests the virtuous ideal that is personified by Leander, it is the practical appraisal of the world that characterizes Crispin, the clever rogue-protagonist and artificer of the romance who voices many of the satiric commentaries on life. The play's sequel is THE CITY OF JOY AND CONFIDENCE.

Prologue. Crispin reviews the origin, spread, and development of comedy. But "our farce," he continues, "is a little play of puppets, impossible in theme, without any reality at all." It is a show of marionettes wearing masks and moved by visible wires, a "primitive spectacle"—for art cannot reconcile itself to growing old—"to entertain you with child's play."

Act I. Leander and Crispin, a self-acknowledged "subject of the Kingdom of Roguery," have escaped their creditors and arrive penniless in a city. They must conquer it with "effrontery," Crispin tells the despondent Leander, an unworldly idealist. He persuades Leander to say nothing: Crispin, his servant, will "call attention to his merits." For "men are like merchandise: they are worth more or less according to the skill of the salesman who markets them." Crispin arrogantly demands lodging for his master, whom he describes as a nobleman on a secret mission. The innkeeper interprets Leander's timidity as lordly disdain, and prepares his best rooms for the shabby travelers. Crispin insists that similar credit be extended to a penniless captain and to Harlequin, a poet. He beats the servants, orders a feast, and even has the innkeeper lend them money. "Now poesy and arms

The Bonds of Interest. The Theatre Guild production, with EDNA ST. VINCENT MILLAY as Columbine (center) and Helen Westley as Doña Sirena (left). New York, 1919. (*Vandamm Photo, Theatre Collection, New York Public Library*)

are ours," Crispin tells the worried Leander: "We shall achieve the conquest of the world!"

Act II. Doña Sirena, a matchmaker and an impecunious widow, is chagrined. She chides Columbine, her beautiful young confidante, who loves the poet Harlequin, for not having a wealthy adorer with whom she could arrange a marriage. The servants and tradesmen refuse to extend credit for Sirena's fete, to which she has invited the wealthy Polichinelle. She expects to complete her lucrative matchmaking for his daughter Silvia. Crispin too has his eyes on the heiress, and persuades Columbine to get an invitation for Leander. He describes his master's lofty nature and his own baseness; there are advantages, he says, in dividing such qualities, "usually found confused clumsily and joined in one." But he adds, "There is something in me that redeems me and elevates me in my own eyes. It is the loyalty of my service, this loyalty which humiliates and abases itself that another may fly, that he may always be the lord of the towering thoughts, of the lofty, beautiful ideals." Promising that Leander will bring the musicians and attendants needed for the fete, Crispin offers a handsome sum for Sirena's help in arranging the match. At first Sirena is indignant, but Crispin persuades her that "whatever may happen hereafter will be the work of chance and love." At the party, Silvia and Leander quickly fall in love. Crispin reveals himself to her father Polichinelle, once his companion and a galley slave who by murder and other crimes acquired his present wealth and respectability. He suggests that Polichinelle forbid his daughter to see Leander. When Leander grieves, Crispin explains, "If Polichinelle opposes it, that will be enough to make his wife take the opposite side, and the daughter will love you madly." He is delighted that Leander has really fallen in love with Silvia: that will serve even better than pretense. As for his timidity, it "always makes the woman bolder." At the end of their long love scene Leander and Silvia embrace. They do not notice the pleased Crispin. "Poesy and night and madness of love," the plotter remarks: "Who shall overcome us when love beats the drum?"

Act III. Ruffians have attacked Leander, and Crispin has spread word that they were Polichinelle's hirelings. People are indignant at the rich merchant who is thwarting love. Leander, in turn, is indignant with Crispin, who hired the ruffians so the city would turn against the father, and resolves to lose Silvia rather than win her by trickery, for he will be what she thinks he is. When he is her husband, Crispin replies; deceit is only a temporary means for Leander, but common elsewhere. Only because of Crispin could Leander afford "the luxury of being honest." Now he can no longer afford it because the happiness of many depends on his marriage to Silvia. Their own salvation lies in "the bonds of interest": their own interests now intertwine with those of their creditors. Soon this is dramatized. Sirena comes with the distraught Silvia, who is eager to comfort her wounded beloved, and brings word that the prosecutor they have fled is coming for Leander and Crispin. She herself would settle for half her fee if she can have it now. Leander reveals the truth to Silvia, confesses to being a "nameless outcast, a fugitive from justice," and urges her to forget him. But this only inflames Silvia's love. Various creditors appear with the prosecutor and with Polichinelle, and Silvia is quickly hidden. Crispin persuades them that it will be to their best interest to have the penniless Leander marry Silvia. Eager to be paid, the prosecutor himself rationalizes the justice of Crispin's arguments. The creditors readily agree, and only Polichinelle remains to be convinced. "Let them marry!" the others keep chanting. When his daughter appears from Leander's chambers and the family is thus threatened with shame, Polichinelle submits. But Crispin must leave Leander's service. Crispin agrees, "I can be of no further use to you." He remarks, "The ties of love are as nothing to the bonds of interest," and when Leander protests Crispin replies, "I have always given due credit to the ideal and I count upon it always. With this the farce ends." Silvia turns to the audience and explains the meaning of the play: like men, the puppets were moved by various obvious interests, but also by the less obvious ideals; all is not a farce, "for there is in our life something divine, an eternal truth, which cannot end when the play ends."

BONTEMPELLI, Massimo (1878–1960), Italian novelist, journalist, and playwright, was influenced by LUIGI PIRANDELLO as well as by FUTURISM. Nonetheless Bontempelli developed along independent lines and made his reputation with a number of plays that like his novels are charged with intellect and stress the power of the imagination. His most notable play, *La guardia della luna* (1920), is a lyrical portrayal of a woman who loses her mind after her baby daughter's death; she wanders among strangers, climbs a mountain to kill the moon she blames for her sorrow, and dies of exhaustion. *Siepe a nord-ovest* (1923), *Nostra Dea* (1925), and *Minnie, la candida* (1929) portray

Pirandellian mask-and-face, reality-and-illusion themes. The first resembles Pirandello's SIX CHARACTERS IN SEARCH OF AN AUTHOR with its scenes by "actors" before "puppets" and "marionettes"; Dea in the second play personifies the automaton with her personality changes, which accompany and match her changes of dress; while Minnie of the third play is unable to distinguish between real men and marionettes. With less success Bontempelli continued writing plays until shortly before his death.

Bontempelli was born in Como and began his career as a teacher. His first novel appeared in 1904, but most of his important work came in the 1920's. Bontempelli's contemporaries esteemed his intellect and irony; the many distinctions bestowed upon him included election to the Italian Academy.

BOOK OF CHRISTOPHER COLUMBUS, THE (*Le Livre de Christophe Colomb*), a lyrical drama in two parts and an entr'acte by PAUL CLAUDEL, published and produced in 1930. Setting: the earth, the heavens, etc.

This is a vast SYMBOLIC spectacle (with music by Darius Milhaud), a dramatized narrative in which events portrayed on the stage are simultaneously universalized on giant screen projections. Its 1953 revival by Jean-Louis Barrault was a notable example of THÉÂTRE TOTAL.

The opening prayer is followed by successive choral and ballet interpretations and episodes, while the narrator "reads" the story of Columbus. He is a saintly hero who must give up the temporal to be united in heaven with Queen Isabella. Santiago reminds her of the ringed dove she released, and Isabella thereupon helps Columbus overcome his hardships and men's scorn. He sails to the New World but, after overcoming many troubles, becomes increasingly embroiled in cruelty to the Indians. The expected wealth from the New World does not materialize, and Columbus is sent home in chains. Over the sea storm come the verses of Saint John: "There was a man whose name was John!" Repeating them, Columbus realizes that he is merely a forerunner, like John—the continent he discovered will not even bear his name. "Out of the depths I have cried unto thee, O Lord!" the dying discoverer weeps. In the paradise of ideas, Isabella kneels to pray: "How can I enter heaven without my brother Christopher!" The dove she released flies on, as the chorus sings an alleluia.

BOOTHE, Clare (1903–), American author active as a politician under her married name, Clare Boothe Luce, was born in New York and began her career as a magazine writer and editor. Then, after a stint at journalism, she wrote satirical comedies. *Abide With Me* (1935) failed on Broadway, but subsequent plays (all of which she published under her maiden name) succeeded with the public—despite the critics' reservations about their merit. Her greatest hit was *The Women* (1936), a cynical and viperish all-female exposé of wealthy and philandering New York matrons; it ran for over a year and was filmed in 1939 and again (as *The Opposite Sex*) in 1956. *Kiss the Boys Goodbye* (1938), satirizing the Hollywood talent hunt for a *Gone With the Wind* star and itself eventually filmed, was meant by the author to be a denunciation of native Fascism; while *Margin for Error* (1939), a melodrama, became the first anti-Nazi Broadway hit.

Mrs. Luce became interested in other things before further developing her gifts as a satiric playwright. In 1940 she turned to politics, serving in Congress (1943–47), and later becoming America's ambassador to Italy (1953–56). After an unsuccessful first marriage, Clare Boothe married the publishing tycoon Henry Luce in 1935. She was the model for a character in Stein's YES IS FOR A VERY YOUNG MAN. In 1970, Mrs. Luce came out with *Slam the Door Softly,* an amusing one-act women's liberation play inspired by HENRIK IBSEN and originally entitled *A Doll's House 1970*.

Margaret Case Harriman's *Blessed Are the Debonair* (1956) and Stephen Shadegg's *Claire Boothe Luce* (1970) are accounts of her often-controversial career.

BORCHERT, Wolfgang (1921–47), German writer, became known posthumously for his only play, *Draussen vor der Tür* (THE MAN OUTSIDE, 1947). Its great success and repeated revival was in part due to its author's poignant personal experiences. He was only twenty-six when he died in Switzerland of a disease resembling malaria, and the tragedy of so early a death was ironically heightened by its timing: the day before his play had its triumphant premiere in Borchert's native Hamburg. A book salesman and later an actor, Borchert grew up during the Nazi regime. Nonetheless he came to oppose it. He was tried, convicted, and condemned to death. This sentence was commuted because of his youth, and he was assigned to a punishment battalion on the Eastern front. After being imprisoned by the Russians in Siberia, he returned a fatally sick man.

Borchert also wrote poems and sketches, most of them bitter and about the war. The play and his fiction appeared with a biographical-critical introduction by STEPHEN SPENDER in the English collection of Borchert's prose, *The Man Outside* (1952).

BOSS, THE, a play in four acts by EDWARD SHELDON, produced in 1911 and published in 1917. Setting: one of the Eastern lake-ports, 1911.

This crude but powerful melodrama portrays the career of a political boss and business tycoon suggested by William James ("Fingy") Connors of Buffalo.

Michael Regan, though vulgar and ruthless, is basically honorable. His rival's daughter, whom he loves, marries him to save her father. Though the marriage is to be in name only, Regan's love and her admiration of his strength finally bring the couple together in fact as well as name.

BOTH YOUR HOUSES, a play in three acts by MAXWELL ANDERSON, published and produced in

1933. Setting: House Office Building, Washington, D.C.; early 1930's.

Anderson's spirited indictment of Congress—"a plague o' both your houses," in Shakespeare's words—won the 1933 Pulitzer Prize. For all its cynicism about democratic government in action, the play entertainingly presents the corrupt legislators as likable human beings.

Alan McClean, an idealistic freshman congressman, attempts to kill pork-barrel legislation in committee. He discovers the committeemen's graft and resorts to playing their own game to defeat them. Loading the bill with extravagant appropriations, he thinks now "it's a monstrosity and no one will dare sponsor it!" But it passes and he is hailed by his delighted colleagues. "Our system is every man for himself—and the nation be damned!" the committee chairman remarks, while a tippling old congressman adds, "And it works! It works when you give it a chance." This is the Depression, but "Graft, gigantic graft brought us our prosperity in the past and will lift us out of the present depths of parsimony and despair!" McClean leaves bewildered but determined to broadcast the truth about "this charlatan's sanctuary you've built for yourselves. You think the sacred and senseless legend poured into the people of this country from childhood will protect you. It won't." But though they admit to themselves that they are "a bunch of crooks" who may be caught some day, the congressmen are completely confident that this particular scandal will blow over and do them no damage.

BOUND EAST FOR CARDIFF, a one-act play by EUGENE O'NEILL, published and produced in 1916. Setting: the crowded seamen's forecastle on the steamer *Glencairn,* in one of the years preceding World War I.

O'Neill's first mature play (written in 1914 and originally titled and copyrighted as *Children of the Sea*), and his first ever produced, was also probably the most impressive one-acter yet written in the United States. It is the final part of the S.S. GLENCAIRN cycle, and was republished in THE MOON OF THE CARIBBEES, AND SIX OTHER PLAYS OF THE SEA.

The whistle of the steamer, en route to Cardiff on a foggy night, blasts at minute intervals. As his companions deride the bragging Cocky and then gripe about their hard and hopeless sea life, Yank is dying in his bunk from internal injuries received in a fall. The captain can do nothing for him, and the seamen sympathize perfunctorily, but his friend Driscoll desperately tries to comfort him. The two talk of their experiences and their dreams of buying a farm. Yank fears death—though "I know whatever it is what comes after it can't be no worser'n this"—particularly on "a rotten night like this with that damned whistle blowin' and people snorin' all round." As the grieving Driscoll watches helplessly, death appears to Yank in the form of "a pretty lady dressed in black." Coming in to announce that the heavy fog has finally lifted, Cocky mocks Driscoll's crossing himself, but when he sees the reason he is awed: "Gawd blimey!"

BOURDET, Édouard (1887–1945), administrator of the Comédie-Française (1936–40) and French playwright popular in Paris as well as abroad, wrote gay social satires and serious dramatic studies of moral problems. Among the former are *Le Rubicon* (*The Rubicon,* 1910), in which champagne cures a bride's initial shyness; and *La Fleur des pois* (1932), a light treatment of homosexuality. Bourdet handled the theme seriously in the successful *La Prisonnière* (*The Captive,* 1926), a psychological study of a lesbian. The history play *Margot* (1935) suggests incest in the love-hate relation of Henri III and his sister Marguerite, wife of Henri of Navarre. Other often picturesque and ironic Bourdet plays include *Vient de paraître* (1927, translated as *Best Sellers*), a satire of writers and publishers; *Le Sexe faible* (1929, translated as *The Sex Fable*), a slashing portrait of the corruption of fashionable Parisian life; and *Les Temps difficiles* (1934), a satire of middle-class venality reminiscent of Becque's THE VULTURES and adapted by Louis Bromfield (1896–1956) as *Times Have Changed* (1935).

Bourdet's plays were republished in French in five volumes in 1961.

BOW OF ODYSSEUS, THE (*Der Bogen des Odysseus*), a drama in five acts by GERHART HAUPTMANN, published and produced in 1914. Setting: legendary Ithaca.

This blank-verse reinterpretation of Homer's story deals with Odysseus's arrival in Ithaca. Odysseus is tormented by the discrepancy between his beggarly appearance and the reality of his tempered wisdom and heroism, and confounded by the enigma of Penelope. Most of the play is given to his Hamlet-like perplexities and Lear-like anguish. Penelope herself never appears; but she is a constant topic of speculation by her family, her suitors, and the herdsmen. In the last act Odysseus assumes his power and, as in the legend, uses his bow to kill the suitors. The play ends as Odysseus wonders, "What will thy mother say, O Telemach, / That I her favorite playthings broke so soon?"

BOY DAVID, THE, a play in three acts by JAMES M. BARRIE, produced in 1936 and published in 1938. Setting: biblical Israel.

Barrie's last work was written for Elisabeth Bergner, who acted the partly autobiographical title role. After many obstacles the play was successfully produced in Edinburgh, but failed in London. It contains individual scenes of considerable power, as well as typical Barrie touches. The play is discussed in HARLEY GRANVILLE-BARKER'S introduction to the published text and in Cynthia Asquith's *Portrait of Barrie* (1954).

In this retelling of the First Book of Samuel, David is an appealingly artless twelve-year-old boy. He is sometimes frightened, yet he performs great and heroic feats when exalted. He leaves home after his anointment by the prophet Samuel, and goes to Israel's camp. There he meets and becomes the friend of King Saul, whom he mistakes for a simple shepherd. In battle, David slays Goliath, and later plays music before the king. Fearing the shepherd boy will supplant him, Saul attempts to kill David. At home again with his parents and brothers, David goes to sleep. His future now appears in numerous dream visions. The Witch of Endor summons the ghost of Samuel, who prophesies Saul's and Jonathan's deaths in battle, where David soon is seen mourning for them. In the last scene the boys David and Jonathan conclude an eternal friendship covenant.

BRACCO, Roberto (1861–1943), Italian dramatist who, like MARCO PRAGA, wrote NATURALISTIC plays about love, was among Italy's most popular early twentieth-century playwrights. Even more than those of his contemporary, Bracco's are IBSENite "dramas of ideas" that explore the underworld of his native Naples and the subconscious of his characters. Probably his best play is *Il piccolo santo* (*The Little Saint,* 1909); its title character, a priest, finds his long-ago love for a woman rekindled when her daughter comes to seek his help. Other notable Bracco plays are *Don Pietro Caruso* (1895), a one-acter whose unadmirable title character is redeemed by his love for his daughter and his suicide when she becomes the mistress of one of the politicians he served; *Sperduti nel buio* (1901), portraying a blind man who loses the girl he loves; *La piccola fonte* (1905), a play that, with its poet hero who is inspired by his wife, is similar in plot to—though it expresses contrary themes from those of—D'Annunzio's LA GIOCONDA; and *I fantasmi* (1906), whose protagonist is prevented from achieving happiness with the man she loves because of the promise extorted by her husband on his deathbed.

Bracco began his career as a journalist and then turned to writing poems, sketches, and music and drama criticism. He served as a deputy in parliament, but was persecuted for his anti-Fascist convictions, had his works banned, and died in poverty. His drama, published in eleven volumes in 1927, has been praised for its psychological insight, humor, and compassion. Bracco and his work are discussed in Lander MacClintock's *The Contemporary Drama of Italy* (1920).

BRAND, a verse drama in five acts by HENRIK IBSEN, published in 1866 and produced in 1885. Setting: a village and mountains on the west coast of Norway, mid-nineteenth century.

Brand (Norwegian for "fire" and "sword"), a SYMBOLIC poem in rhymed octosyllables, became one of Ibsen's most popular plays in SCANDINAVIA. He composed it after he had exiled himself to protest Norway's failure to support Denmark against the invading Prussian army in 1864. Though Ibsen probably intended the protagonist to be a heroic, ideal Norwegian antitype ("Brand is myself in my best moments"), the priest's character became rounded and individualized: his stern idealism, as the play's final words suggest, is flawed by its disregard of divine love. Kierkegaard's "Either/Or" becomes a tragic "All or Nothing" for Brand, a man as determined in his refusal to compromise as is the hero of the companion poem, PEER GYNT (published the following year), in his comic propensity to compromise.

Act I. Pastor Brand is braving the icy mountain wilds to solace a dying girl. Her father refuses to risk his life, and Brand goes on alone. He meets two dancing lovers, the painter Einar and his bride Agnes, and chides them for their frivolity. Near his childhood village he is accosted by the screaming Gerd, a Gypsy girl who is frightened by an ugly hawk and urges Brand to seek shelter in the unsafe mountain Ice Church. To Brand, these encounters typify human sickness, the "triple enemy" of man's salvation—dull-heartedness, lightheartedness, and wild-heartedness—which Brand determines to battle and slay "for the heirs of Heaven!"

Act II. Brand will not help the villagers, who are suffering from a famine: "A living people," he says, "sucks strength from sorrow." Though he gains their respect when he braves the stormy fjord to console a dying murderer, he resists a petition that he become their pastor. Later his avaricious mother offers him her savings, but when Brand refuses to promise to keep the money in the family, and urges her to renounce her earthly goods and repent of their acquisition, she goes home, resolving to keep her wealth as long as possible. Determined to pay for his mother's sins, Brand finally agrees to remain in the village and become the local pastor. "There is a higher purpose than the glory of battle," he decides: "To hallow daily toil to the praise of God." Einar demands back his bride, but Agnes, having followed Brand and glimpsed his vision, chooses to stay, though Brand warns her: "Remember, I am stern / In my demands. I require All or Nothing."

Act III. Brand has married Agnes, they have a child, and Brand's next three years are easy. Then his mother dies; the doctor goes to tend to her, but Brand refuses to go unless she calls him with an offer of all her worldly goods for the sacrament—which she never does. His child falls ill, and the doctor tells Brand that, to save it, they must move away from the cold, misty village to a place of sunshine and light. Brand agrees, but when the doctor remarks on his being less stern with himself than he has been with others, and when the Gypsy Gerd talks madly of trolls and demons that come when "the parson's flown away," Brand wavers, and then despairs. He begs Agnes to choose their path, but she refuses. Brand himself must make the choice. He decides to stay, though it means the death of their child.

Act IV. At Christmas in the parsonage, Agnes is mourning for their child. Brand insists that she accept its death as God's will and cease grieving. He will build a larger church and asks for her continuing support and encouragement. The village mayor, who had opposed Brand but now recognizes his power over the people, decides it will be politically expedient to help with the building. Seeing Agnes cling to their child's clothes, Brand forces her to give them to a needy Gypsy. It must be "All or Nothing," and he succeeds in making her part joyfully with the last mementos of their child; but his victory will kill her. Brand remains steadfast in his faith before the coming blow of her death: "Only that which is lost remains eternal."

Act V. Six months later the new church is ready to be consecrated, but Brand is tired and lonesome without Agnes. The hypocrisy of high Church authorities and the zeal of Einar, now a missionary, renew Brand's vigor. Rejecting the new church as inadequate, he calls it a compromise, and "Compromise is the way of Satan!" He inspires the crowds, who enthusiastically follow him to worship on the mountain. But soon they tire of the hardships. Brand promises eventual victory—but for later generations ("The only road to Canaan lies through a desert"). When the authorities trick them with lies, the people reject and stone Brand. Alone on the mountain, he resists the temptation to compromise offered by a vision of Agnes. The Gypsy Gerd mistakes the bloodstained Brand for Christ. As he weeps at the sight of the Ice Church, she fires at and finally kills the apparition of the ugly hawk that has always haunted her. But the shot loosens an avalanche that buries them. With his final breath Brand asks, "If not by Will, how can Man be redeemed?" And a voice from the thunder announces: by "The God of Love."

BRANDSTAETTER, Roman (1906–), Polish playwright, lived in the Middle East during World War II. He wrote about twenty dramas, some in verse and many of them histories and biographies. Among his early works are *Powrót syna marnotrawnego* (*The Return of the Prodigal Son,* 1947), a romantic drama inspired by the life of Rembrandt, and *Noce narodowe* (1949), a play depicting an episode in the life of the poet Adam Mickiewicz, who is also the hero of a STANISŁAW WYSPIAŃSKI drama. Brandstaetter's later plays include *Król i aktor* (1952, about the eighteenth-century Polish theatrical entrepreneur Wojciech Bogusławski), and dramatizations of the lives of such other figures as Odysseus, Medea, Copernicus (*Kopernik,* 1953), and Sułkowski (*Bonaparte i Sułkowski,* 1953), Napoleon's adjutant who is the subject also of one of the plays of STEFAN ŻEROMSKI. Other notable Brandstaetter plays are *Milczenie* (*Silence,* 1956), which criticizes Stalinist Poland and carried its author's name beyond his native land; *Dzień gniewu* (*Day of Wrath,* 1962), a drama that resembles Eliot's MURDER IN THE CATHEDRAL and deals with an SS major who cannot get himself to kill a Jew hiding in a monastery; and *Zmierzch demonów* (*Twilight of the Demons,* 1964), "an inhuman [verse] comedy in four acts" set in Hitler's bunker during the last days of the Nazis.

BRAZIL proclaimed its independence from PORTUGAL in 1822, but the mother country's influence—and then that of SPAIN—diminished only gradually. By the mid-twentieth century, however, Brazil's Portuguese was a different language and its principal literary influence was that of FRANCE. Brazil's theatre was launched in 1838 with plays by the romantic poet Domingos José Gonçalves de Magalhães (1811–82) and by [Luís Carlos] Martins Pena (1815–48), the founder of Brazil's theatre and the author of nearly thirty plays, most of them comedies of manners. As important during the nineteenth century was the novelist José Mariniano de Alencar (1829–77), who wrote thesis plays about fallen women, prejudice, and slavery.

In the early part of the twentieth century popular playwrights were Artur Azevedo (1855–1908), a journalist and poet who aspired to serious drama but succeeded with comedies and musicals, many written in collaboration; and Cláudio de Souza (1876–), whose great hit was a sentimental drama about "the good old days," *Flores na Sombra* (1916).* The later Brazilian theatre, in both Rio de Janeiro and São Paulo, aside from distinguished children's productions has boasted notable dramatists and drama including *Deus lhe Pague* (1932), a very popular, light, social-protest drama by Joracy Camargo (1898–); Nélson Rodrigues (1912–), a journalist who wrote classically inspired verse drama with choruses on domestic and psychological themes like adultery and jealousy (*A Mulher sem Pecado,* 1941) and an EXPRESSIONISTIC multilevel portrayal of a woman's hallucinations (*Vestido de Noiva,* 1943); Guilherme Figueiredo (1915–), who dramatized legends beginning with *Lady Godiva* (1948) and two prize winners: *Um Deus Dormiu là em Casa* (1949), in which Jupiter is the title god who "slept there at [the] home" of Alcmene and Amphitryon, and *A Rapôsa e as Uvas* (1952), the title echoing one of the fables ("Sour Grapes") of Aesop, whose life the play dramatizes; Jorge Andrade (1922–), who wrote numerous commercially successful serious plays on social and personal issues; Gianfrancesco Guarnieri (1936–), an Italian-born actor-playwright who effectively portrayed the poor and the downtrodden, beginning with *Êles Não Usam Black-tie* (1958) and *Gimba* (1959), the latter of which has been compared to *Orfeu Negro* (*Black Orpheus,* 1959), a film which was based on Vinícius de Morais's (1913–) *Orfeu da Conceição* (1956); Augusto Boal (1931–), who adapted Spanish classics and wrote comedies as well as social and political protest drama, and who became the leader of the Teatro Arena of São Paulo, which has had successful tours in the United States; and Alfredo Dias Gomes (1924–), whose popular satires and social drama include the prize-winning and later filmed tragedy of a peasant victimized in his quest to save a friend, *O Pagador de Promessas* (*The Given Word,* 1960), and a similar play whose protagonist resembles Joan of Arc, *O Santo Inquérito* (1966).

Perhaps the best modern Brazilian play was written by Ariano Suassuna (1927–), a Catholic convert: *Auto da Compadecida* (*The*

* A description of Cláudio de Souza's plays constitutes all of the "Brazil" chapter in Isaac Goldberg's *The Drama of Transition* (1922).

Rogues' Trial, 1956), an anti-Establishment and anticlerical poetic fantasy based on folklore. Native black consciousness was stimulated by the playwright Abdias do Nascimento (1914–) with his founding of the Teatro Experimental do Negro and the publication of his anthology of plays by black Brazilians, *Dramas para Negros e Prólogo para Brancos* (1961), including his own *Sortilégio.* By far the most active theatre in Brazil in recent times has been the "show," a kind of intimate performance, usually with music, done in cabarets and small theatres. However, national military rule and its accompanying censorship have stifled all creative theatrical activity.

The annual volume of the University of Florida's extensively annotated *Handbook of Latin American Studies* (1935 ff.) and the *Latin American Theatre Review* journal (1967 ff.) both cover Brazil. A useful study available in English translation is Manuel Bandeira's *Brief History of Brazilian Literature* (1958). *An Introduction to Literature in Brazil* (1969), Afrânio Coutinho's one-volume collection of the introductions to his four-volume *A Literatura no Brasil* (1955–59), has been translated by Gregory Rabassa and has extensively augmented bibliographies, including one on the Brazilian theatre.

BREAK OF NOON (*Partage de midi*), a verse play in three acts by PAUL CLAUDEL, published in 1906 and produced in 1916. Setting: a ship in the Indian Ocean, a Hong Kong cemetery, and a Confucian temple in a small Chinese port; early twentieth century.

Claudel rewrote this very personal drama for Jean-Louis Barrault's revival in 1948. A characteristic poetic-theological quest for spirituality, the play resembles Strindberg's contemporaneous TO DAMASCUS. Claudel's title suggests the turning points in the lives of the play's four characters, particularly those of Ysé (from the Greek *isos,* "equality") and Mesa ("the half"), whose long, lyric monologue fills much of Act III.

The beautiful Ysé de Ciz, en route to China, meets a former French lover and Mesa, a returning thirty-year-old Chinese whose "strength is diminished" by God's long silence before his offer of devotion. Ysé considers her marriage inadequate. "Do you think I am good only for having children," she asks her husband, a businessman: "Is it for nothing that I am beautiful?" She arouses the sexuality of both her husband and her former lover, but it soon becomes evident that she herself is most captivated by Mesa, who in his weakened condition quickly succumbs to her. To him she reveals herself and emphasizes her identity: "Mesa, I am Ysé, it is I!" In a Hong Kong cemetery they submit to their passions after Ysé's husband goes on a dangerous business trip in which he is to die. But Ysé can find fulfillment with Mesa neither in adultery nor in marriage. Conceiving his child, she abandons Mesa and marries her former lover. During a Chinese uprising they are besieged and doomed. Preparing to dynamite their place, they are ready to die in it. Suddenly Mesa comes through the enemy lines. In his monologue before the wordless Ysé he reveals that he still loves her, despite Ysé's betrayal and failure to answer his pleading letters. Her present husband seriously wounds him and knocks him out; then he takes Mesa's pass, which will let them get through the enemy lines, and rushes off with Ysé. But soon she returns—to be united with Mesa in death. His cross and his redemption, Ysé professes her love for Mesa as he helps her prepare for their only possible but eternal reunion: "How long now, O woman, tell me, fruit of the vine, / Before I drink thee new in the Kingdom of God?" They await the fatal explosion, enveloped in each other's love. Mesa raises his hand as the lights go out and Ysé sinks down at his feet. "Remember me for one moment in this darkness," Ysé concludes; "I was once your vine."

BREASTS OF TIRESIAS, THE (*Les Mamelles de Tirésias*), "a surrealist drama in two acts and a prologue" by GUILLAUME APOLLINAIRE, produced in 1917 and published in 1918. Setting: a mythic "present-day Zanzibar."

The term SURREALISM was first used here, in Apollinaire's subtitle and preface. It indeed characterizes this comic, nonsensical verse skit, which Apollinaire started writing as early as 1903. Partly influenced by ALFRED JARRY, the play purports to deal with "the female problem" and with overpopulation. It was produced with cubist sets, and later made into an opera by Francis Poulenc.

In a prologue, the director proclaims anti-NATURALISTIC principles: a play should aim at producing the essential theatrical element of surprise, not at "photographing the so-called SLICE OF LIFE / But to bring forth life itself in all its truth." In the Zanzibar marketplace are a dicebox-shaped megaphone, a dancing kiosk, and "the collective speechless person who represents the people of Zanzibar." Blue-faced Thérèse appears and shouts over the orchestra, "No Mister husband / You won't make me do what you want." A rebelling feminist, she opens her blouse; her breasts emerge, "fly off like toy balloons," and explode when she strikes a lighter. A beard and mustache sprout on her face and she shouts into the megaphone, "I feel as virile as the devil." Thus newly recreated, Tiresias overpowers the husband and exchanges clothes with him. Various placards are put up ("Since the scene's at Zanzibar / Just as the Seine's at Paris"), and Thérèse-Tiresias goes off to be manly in Paris. "Long live Tiresias / No more children no more children," the voices of women chant. Amidst much horseplay, the husband worries about the need for children and seeks ways to attain "progeny without a woman." Between the two acts of the play he succeeds in instant and liberal procreation: "Ah! what a thrill being a father / 40,049 children in one day alone," he remarks, standing amidst many cradles and incessant infant wailing. "Willpower sir that's the whole secret," he explains to an inquiring reporter: "The child is the wealth of the family / It's worth more than cash and a legacy." One of his sons, rocking a cradle, reveals news from the outside world: ". . . Mister Picasso's / New picture can move / As this cradle does." To feed the many children becomes a grave problem in Zanzibar. After various farcical-brutal episodes, Thérèse-Tiresias comes back to be her husband's Thérèse again. She throws balloons at the audience: "Fly away birds of my frailty / Go and feed all the children / Of the new population." "The People of Zanzibar dance jingling bells" and join in a chorus: ". . . Luck is a game win or lose / Just keep your eye on the play."

BRECHT, Bertolt [Eugen Berthold Friedrich] (1898–1956), was modern Germany's greatest playwright after GERHART HAUPTMANN. Many of his dramas expound Marxism and all are written in a colloquial yet poetic language that loses much in translation. Despite these obstacles, his international reputation has steadily grown. Russia, ironically, is one of the few European countries where his dramas have not been widely produced. Brecht also was unable to conquer Broadway's commercial theatres, but his popularity in American university and Off-Broadway theatres is high. As his foremost champion in the United States (Eric Bentley) noted, Brecht has posthumously become "a chic celebrity."

"Bert" Brecht was born in Augsberg, Bavaria—neither in the city jungle nor as the proletarian he later pictured himself. His father was the prosperous manager of a paper mill, a Catholic who married a Protestant. Young Brecht was christened in his mother's faith, and the Bible was to remain the book exerting the most powerful influence on him. But he soon rebelled against his background, rejecting his given names as well as his religion. Though strongly pacifist, he was drafted and, having studied medicine, was made a hospital orderly. The horrors he experienced during World War I accentuated his lifelong pacifism and always haunted him. These feelings permeate his moving ballad "Legende vom toten Soldaten" ("The Legend of a Dead Soldier"), which later caused the Nazis to place Brecht high on their blacklist. In 1918 he participated in the revolutionary Communist uprising in Bavaria, but he soon returned to his studies and a Bohemian life in Munich.

There he almost immediately began his theatrical career. His first play, BAAL (1922), is nihilistic and violently turbulent. Since it had little chance of immediate production, he wrote a second one, *Trommeln in der Nacht* (DRUMS IN THE NIGHT, 1922), and asked the already-established LION FEUCHTWANGER for help in getting it produced. This took a few years, and in the meantime Brecht supported

Bertolt Brecht with the actor (and Brecht's collaborator on LIFE OF GALILEO) Charles Laughton and the artist George Grosz. 1946. (*Culver Pictures*)

himself by playing the guitar and singing racy ballads in taverns and cafés. He dissipated, argued, captivated girls, and met such later friends as ARNOLT BRONNEN and Peter Suhrkamp, who was to become his publisher.

While yet a student, Brecht became drama critic for Augsburg's socialist newspaper, and *Dramaturg* (i.e., playreader and adapter) in Munich. In 1922 *Drums in the Night* was produced, won the Kleist Prize, and launched Brecht's career in the theatre. Other early plays followed quickly: *Im Dickicht der Städte* (IN THE JUNGLE OF THE CITIES, 1923), *Leben Eduards des Zweiten von England* (LIFE OF EDWARD II OF ENGLAND, 1924; written with Feuchtwanger), *Mann ist Mann* (A MAN'S A MAN, 1926), and MAHAGONNY (1927). In 1919 Brecht wrote five farces that until 1966 remained unpublished and, except for one, unproduced.*

In 1924 Brecht moved to Berlin, where he immersed himself in the capital's theatrical activity—including that of such important producer-directors as Max Reinhardt, Leopold Jessner, and Erwin Piscator. Brecht became *Dramaturg* of the Deutsches Theater and was involved in tempestuous literary and theatrical disputes and scandals that were meant to (and did) shock the middle class. He also was the center of a large circle that included such well-known fellow workers as the artist George Grosz, the stage designer Caspar Neher, and various actors and composers. Important further activities of his Berlin period were the reading of Marx's *Das Kapital,* the publication of his *Hauspostille* (*Domestic Breviary,* 1927) poems, and his collaboration with the composer Kurt Weill, which immediately brought them both worldwide fame with *Die Dreigroschenoper* (THE THREEPENNY OPERA, 1928). Brecht divorced his first wife (Marianne Zoff) and in 1928 married Helene Weigel, a distinguished actress who starred in almost all his works and continued to direct his Berliner Ensemble after his death. They had two children.

During his Berlin period Brecht wrote the lyrics for HAPPY END (1929) by his secretary Elisabeth Hauptmann (? –), who was to edit his posthumous works; collaborated with Feuchtwanger on *Kalkutta, 4. Mai* (CALCUTTA, MAY 4, 1927); with Weill, adapted *Mahagonny* as an "operatic cantata" and subsequently as an opera, *Aufstieg und Fall der Stadt Mahagonny* (RISE AND FALL OF THE CITY OF MAHAGONNY, 1929); and wrote *Die Mutter* (THE MOTHER, 1932), *Die heilige Johanna der Schlachthöfe* (SAINT JOAN OF THE STOCKYARDS, 1932; the best of his plays on Joan of Arc), and a series of *Lehrstücke*. These oratorio-like "didactic pieces" were intended as Marxist propaganda. But their ideological stance was criticized by the Communists, and their form and language, meant to be coldly argumentative, became unexpectedly dramatic and lyrical. The finest of them is *Die Massnahme* (THE MEASURES TAKEN, 1930); others are *Lindberghflug* (LINDBERGH'S FLIGHT, 1929), *Das Badener Lehrstück vom Einverständnis* (THE BADEN-BADEN DIDACTIC PIECE ON ACQUIESCENCE, 1929), *Der Jasager* (HE WHO SAYS YES, 1930) and *Der Neinsager* (HE WHO SAYS NO, 1930), *Die Ausnahme und die Regel* (THE EXCEPTION AND THE RULE, 1937), and *Die Horatier und die Kuratier* (THE HORATII AND THE CURIATII, 1938). In Berlin, Brecht also participated in adapting Jaroslav Hašek's novel *The Good Soldier Schweik* for Piscator's 1928 production, won a short-story competition, and wrote a film, *Kuhle Wampe* (featured in the United States as *Whither Germany?*). Finally, he began composing his anecdotes about Keuner (*Geschichten vom Herrn Keuner*), who, like the Good Soldier Schweik, personifies many of the paradoxical characteristics of Brecht and his art.

When Hitler came to power in 1933, Brecht escaped from Germany and began his exile. After living in Scandinavia, he came to the United States in 1941. Settling in California, he struggled, with little success, to make his name in America. He was able to sell Hollywood but one movie story, *Hangmen Also Die* (1942). After the war—and right after his 1947 appearance before the House Committee on Un-American Activities—he returned to Europe and stayed in Switzerland, where many of his plays had been first produced. Despite the disappointments of his exile, he had in those fourteen years written the plays that were to establish his reputation: *Furcht und Elend des Dritten Reiches* (FEAR AND MISERY OF THE THIRD REICH, 1938; also known as *The Private Life of the Master Race*); *Mutter Courage und ihre Kinder* (MOTHER COURAGE, 1941); *Leben des Galilei* (LIFE OF GALILEO, 1943); *Der gute Mensch von Sezuan* (THE GOOD WOMAN OF SETZUAN, 1943); and *Der kaukasische Kreidekreis* (THE CAUCASIAN CHALK CIRCLE, 1948). Other plays written in that period were *Die Rundköpfe und Spitzköpfe* (THE ROUNDHEADS AND THE PEAKHEADS, 1936), *Die sieben Todsünden der Kleinbürger* (THE SEVEN DEADLY SINS OF THE PETTY BOURGEOIS, 1933), *Die Gewehre der Frau Carrar* (SEÑORA CARRAR'S RIFLES, 1937), *Herr Puntila und sein Knecht Matti* (HERR PUNTILA AND HIS SERVANT MATTI, 1948), *Das Verhör des Lukullus* (THE TRIAL OF LUCULLUS, 1940), *Der aufhaltsame Aufstieg des Arturo Ui* (THE RESISTIBLE RISE OF ARTURO UI, 1957), *Die Gesichte der Simone Machard* (THE VISIONS OF SIMONE MACHARD, 1956; with Feuchtwanger), and *Schweyk im zweiten Weltkrieg* (SCHWEYK IN THE SECOND WORLD WAR, 1957).

In 1949 Brecht accepted the Communists' offer of a theatre and a company of his own, and settled in East Berlin. There he founded his soon

* *Die Kleinbürgerhochzeit* (staged as *Die Hochzeit* in 1926 and translated as *The Wedding*), a Bavarian slapstick portrayal of the collapsing genteel veneer of middle-class domesticity; *Der Bettler oder der tote Hund (The Beggar, or the Dead Dog),* a dialogue between a beggar and a king who is disconcerted by the ordinary people's disgust for upperclass extravagances; *Er treibt einen Teufel aus (He Drives Out a Devil),* a Bavarian folk skit of lovers' wooing amidst parental interruptions; *Der Fischzug (The Catch),* a lugubrious farce about a drunken fisherman who publicly traps his wife and her lover in his net; and *Lux in tenebris,* a satire of sex hypocrisy, featuring an "educational" venereal disease exhibit that actually is a brothel frequented by pillars of society.

world-famous Berliner Ensemble at the Theater am Schiffbauerdamm, and worked until his death of a coronary thrombosis in 1956. His last plays were *Die Antigone des Sophokles* (THE ANTIGONE OF SOPHOCLES, 1948), *Die Tage der Commune* (THE DAYS OF THE COMMUNE, 1956), *Der Hofmeister* (THE PRIVATE TUTOR, 1950), *Herrnburger Bericht* (REPORT ON HERRNBURG, 1951), *Der Prozess der Jeanne D'Arc zu Rouen 1431* (*The Trial of Joan of Arc at Rouen 1431*, 1952; a Berliner Ensemble adaptation of Anna Segher's radio dramatization of the trial records), *Don Juan* (1953, an adaptation of Molière's play), *Pauken und Trompeten* (*Drums and Trumpets*, 1956; an adaptation of George Farquhar's late Restoration comedy *The Recruiting Officer*, with the setting shifted to the time of the American Revolution and with interpolated anti-imperialist sentiments and songs), and the unproduced propaganda piece *Turandot oder der Kongress der Weisswäscher* (*Turandot*, 1954; an allegorical attack, with music by Hanns Eisler, on intellectuals who "whitewash" capitalism). He also left a number of unfinished works, some of which long remained unpublished. The most important of them are *Der Brotladen* (*The Breadshop*, 1958), a work anticipating *Saint Joan of the Stockyards; Untergang des Egoisten Johann Fatzer* (*The Decline of the Egoist Johannes Fatzer*, 1930), two verse scenes featuring army deserters in quest of black market food; an adaptation of Selma Lagerlöf's novel *Gösta Berling;* one scene of *Hannibal* (1922); one scene of *Leben des Konfutse* (*Life of Confucius*, 1958), a children's play featuring a young Confucius; and *Coriolan* (1957), an adaptation of Shakespeare's *Coriolanus* on which Brecht worked during the last years of his life, and which became the basis of Brecht's devastating personification in Grass's THE PLEBEIANS REHEARSE THE UPRISING (1966).

Brecht's work is in many ways unique. Like Shakespeare, he frequently used other writers' plots and even dialogue. His *The Threepenny Opera* is the most famous—but not the only—example of this practice. Further, almost all of his plays in their final form are the product of teamwork. But Brecht was the undisputed master; he even wrote music and participated in preparing the scores of such composers as Weill, Hanns Eisler, and Paul Dessau. Though Brecht faithfully gave credit by-lines to "collaborators" with whom he worked out the composition of the plays, his was the final word. A poet of the people and a dramatist of the living stage, Brecht did not work in ivory-tower isolation. He created amidst the hustle and bustle of discussion, argument, and the trappings of the theatre—a model of which he always kept nearby to remind him of his purpose. And because of this concern with the theatricality of drama, he would not publish his plays before they had gone through the test and revisions of stage productions he himself usually supervised.

His cavalier attitude toward plot originality came from his concept of the function of theatre. Even more than BERNARD SHAW, Brecht believed in the didactic purpose of drama—and like Shaw, he succeeded least in this purpose. A dedicated propagandist of Marxism, Brecht ran afoul of the Communist Party line with his plays. Though he received the Stalin Peace Prize (1955), he succeeded most with non-Communist audiences, who (Brecht believed) misunderstood or missed the social-revolutionary "message" of his plays. His EPIC THEATRE—of which he was also an articulate theorist—was meant to diminish, and if possible completely do away with, traditional theatrical effects. He attempted to destroy any illusion that would induce identification with a character and produce Aristotelian effects of catharsis, pity, and fear. He fictionalized and parodied his Oriental and Western settings as well as his sources, and distorted traditional (thereby creating new) forms like the musical comedy and the cantata. And he employed various devices—movie projections, masks, flat characterization, fragmentary episodes, narration, chants, etc.—to dispel illusion. Instead, he created a distinguished body of drama that defies conventional labels like REALISM or EXPRESSIONISM.

Brecht did not succeed in creating the emotional distance he strove for in order to elicit rational, intellectual judgment. His art presents what all art worthy of its name presents: a new, meaningful, and deeply moving insight into reality. His Galileo, Mother Courage, and Herr Puntila fail as the villains Brecht meant them to be because he was too fine a poet and artist to create flat mouthpieces. Even the ideological didacticism misfired, for his plays do not teach Marxism. Rather, they "teach" non-Marxist verities of the complexity and ambiguity of life, of human nature, and of conduct. They are masterful for their rich variety and satiric, often broadly comic, manner of performing the primary, age-old purpose of drama—to entertain.

Brecht's twenty-volume collected works (1967) were published in German, but even these are incomplete, and much of Brecht's work is not yet available in English. But all his important plays have been—and others are in the process of being—translated. Eric Bentley's translations of *Seven Plays by Bertolt Brecht* (1961) has an introduction, as do Bentley's subsequent editions of individual Brecht plays. The first volume of Ralph Mannheim and John Willett's projected nine volumes of Brecht's *Collected Plays* was published in 1970; it includes "definitive" texts, Brecht's comments, variant readings, and editorial notes and comments. Book-length studies in English, with further bibliographies, include Willett's *The Theatre of Bertolt Brecht* (1959), Ronald Gray's *Brecht* (1961), Martin Esslin's *Brecht, A Choice of Evils* (1959; reprinted in 1960 and revised in 1971 as *Brecht: The Man and His Work*), Frederic Ewen's *Bertolt Brecht: His Life, His Art and His Times* (1967), and Charles R. Lyons's *Bertolt Brecht: The Despair and the Polemic* (1968). The first volume of an annual *Brecht Yearbook* was scheduled for publication in 1971.

BRETON, André (1896–1966), French poet and playwright, was the founder and theoretician of

SURREALISM. Formerly a medical student, he admired Freud and practiced psychiatry during World War I. These interests prompted his espousal of spontaneous, "automatic writing," unimpeded by intellectual restrictions, in surrealist art: "A dictation of thought without any control of reason, outside all aesthetic or moral preoccupation." Originally he was a follower of TRISTAN TZARA and DADAISM. He hastened that movement's demise when he proclaimed its successor, surrealism, to which many of the Dadaists flocked. In 1938 he met Leon Trotsky, with whom he set up an international anti-Stalinist artists' association. During World War II he was active in America. He returned to France in 1946, publishing and organizing exhibitions until the end of his life.

Breton wrote a number of "automatic" plays with PHILIPPE SOUPAULT, including *Les Champs magnétiques* (1920) and *S'il vous plaît* (IF YOU PLEASE, 1920), and he collaborated with LOUIS ARAGON on a play that prophesied the next war, *Le Trésor des Jésuites* (1929). He published manifestoes on surrealism in 1924, 1930, and 1934 (the last entitled *Qu'est-ce que le surréalisme?*); and a successful autobiographical novel, *Nadja* (1928). The translated *Manifestoes of Surrealism* appeared in 1969, and book-length studies are J. H. Matthews's *André Breton* (1967), Clifford Browder's *André Breton, Arbiter of Surréalisme* (1967), and Anna Balakian's *André Breton: Magus of Surrealism* (1971).

BRIDIE, James (1888–1951), Scottish playwright and physician, led a double life. As Dr. Osborne Henry Mavor he was active as a prominent doctor, Honorable Consulting Physician to the Victoria Infirmary of Glasgow. At the same time he was a prolific and versatile dramatist (a career he began in middle age) and Scotland's most important playwright and theatrical force. He encouraged younger playwrights, and produced many original plays. These were praised by contemporary colleagues like BERNARD SHAW (to whom Bridie was occasionally likened), and were popular in Scotland and England. But Bridie remained practically unknown in the United States, and his popularity in Great Britain did not equal, in the opinion of many critics, his great gifts as a playwright. He was influenced by Shaw as well as by HENRIK IBSEN, but his work was distinctive. Bridie wrote comedies, domestic dramas, plays on biblical themes, and a number of experimental plays. All demonstrate his concern with morality, ethics, and religion—as well as his wit, and language that occasionally sparkles in dazzling dialogue. Yet Bridie frequently did not develop strong situations satisfactorily because, as another colleague with whom he was compared remarked, he aimed higher than most playwrights. Like a tailor with small scissors cutting "rich brocade," J. B. PRIESTLEY wrote, Bridie was "trying to cram a large loose mind and a large loose play into the narrow space of our convention." But though he often failed—particularly with American audiences—Bridie still has enthusiastic admirers; he provided strong roles for major British actors, and he was an important influence on the theatre of his time.

The son of an engineer, Bridie was born and educated in Glasgow. While he prepared for his career in medicine he dabbled in writing and sketching, and he was fascinated by the theatre. He became a successful general practitioner; during World War I he served as a British medical officer in Asia and Russia, and then returned to Glasgow to practice medicine. Eventually he was drawn into the theatre life of Scotland and began writing plays. His first play was *The Sunlight Sonata* (1928), a "farce-morality" on middle-class sin in which—as so often in Bridie's plays—the Devil appears. It was produced under the name of Mary Henderson, and dedicated to Tyrone Guthrie, who directed it and was to influence Bridie's later grandiose and NONNATURALISTIC drama. Writing under the name Bridie thereafter, he next came out with his first critical success, *The Switchback* (1929); it depicts the ruin of a doctor whose discovery of a cure for tuberculosis causes his exploitation by profiteers and by his shallow wife. After *What It Is to Be Young* (1929) came perhaps his best-known play and the first to be produced in London, THE ANATOMIST (1930). A comedy, *The Girl Who Did Not Want to Go to Kuala Lumpur* (1930), was followed by his first biblical drama, TOBIAS AND THE ANGEL (1930).

Writing quickly and with apparent ease, Bridie subsequently produced some forty-two plays. These include *The Dancing Bear* (1931), a satire of the snobbish pseudo literati who surround a rural poet; *Jonah and the Whale* (1932), a morality that appeared in various other forms; A SLEEPING CLERGYMAN (1933), one of his major plays; *Marriage Is No Joke* (1934), a comic melodrama about an adventurous divinity student, with settings that reflect Bridie's wartime travels; *Colonel Witherspoon* (1934), a comedy; *Mary Read* (1934; written with the producer Claud Gurney, 1897–1946), based on Charles Johnson's account in *General Histories of the Robberies and Murders of the Most Notorious Pirates* (1724) of the adventures of an illegitimate eighteenth-century pirate, the play's title heroine, who was brought up as the legitimate male heir to a fortune; *Storm over Patsy* (1936, originally produced as *Storm in a Teacup*), an adaptation of a play by BRUNO FRANK; *Susannah and the Elders* (1937), another free dramatization of a story from the Apocrypha; and *The King of Nowhere* (1938), a play—with overtones about contemporary dictators—featuring a paranoid matinee idol who is sent to an institution where he imagines himself king.

Others include *Babes in the Woods* (1938), a domestic comedy; *The Last Trump*, a drama written for the 1938 Malvern Festival; *The Golden Legend of Shults* (1939), a Scottish play; *Holy Isle* (1942), which is set in King Arthur's time; *The Dragon and the Dove* and *A Change for the Worse* (1942), two playlets on medieval themes; *Mr. Bolfry* (1943), another play about the Devil, a force of evil in a necessary conflict with God for, as Bolfry (the Devil) says, "We cannot conceive the

Universe except as a pattern of reciprocating opposites"; *It Depends What You Mean* (1944), a play about marriage subtitled "an improvisation for the glockenspiel"; *The Forrigan Reel* (1944), a frolic; *Lancelot* (1945), based on Sir Thomas Malory's tales; *The Pyrate's Den* (1946), a comic pantomime written under the pseudonym A. P. Kellock; *Dr. Angelus* (1947), a witty characterization of a criminal charlatan; *John Knox* (1947), featuring the Scottish Calvinist and Queen Mary; *Gog and Magog* (1948), whose hero suggests the tramp poet McGonagall of Dundee; DAPHNE LAUREOLA (1949), another major play; the experimental *The Queen's Comedy* (1950), a Trojan War drama set on a tripartite stage representing heaven, earth, and the bottom of the sea; and *Mr. Gillie* (1950), a highly praised drama about an obscure village schoolmaster, with a prologue in heaven. Significant posthumous plays are *The Baikie Charivari, or, The Seven Prophets* (1952), a miracle play that has been likened to Eliot's THE COCKTAIL PARTY and that features an ex-Governor of India, a reincarnated Pontius Pilate whose brilliant guests cannot supply a satisfactory blueprint for modern times; and *Meeting at Night* (1954), an entertaining suspense comedy revised by Archibald Batty (1887–1961).

Bridie became a medical officer again during World War II, but continued to write plays and subsequently returned to Glasgow, where with PAUL VINCENT CARROLL and others he helped establish its Citizens' Theatre and in 1950 founded Scotland's first officially recognized College of Drama. His plays (including unproduced ones not listed above) have appeared singly and in many collections. He also wrote film scripts, *The British Drama* (1945), and an autobiography, *One Way of Living* (1939). His preoccupation with theological themes is discussed at some length in Gerald Weales's *Religion in Modern English Drama* (1961). Book-length studies of Bridie's life and work include Winifred Bannister's *James Bridie and His Theatre* (1955), which discusses the plays seriatim; and Helen L. Luyben's *James Bridie: Clown and Philosopher* (1965), which contains a bibliography.

BRIEUX, Eugène (1858–1932), French NATURALIST playwright, first became notable with BLANCHETTE (1892). He achieved international renown when BERNARD SHAW wrote an extravagant preface for *Three Plays by Brieux* (1911): *Maternité* (MATERNITY, 1903; translated by Mrs. Shaw); *Les Trois Filles de M. Dupont* (THE THREE DAUGHTERS OF M. DUPONT, 1894; translated by ST. JOHN HANKIN); and *Les Avariés* (DAMAGED GOODS, 1902), whose concern with venereal disease made it a SUCCÈS DE SCANDALE. More esteemed than these plays was *La Robe rouge* (THE RED ROBE, 1900), which, like most of Brieux's works, deals with a particular social abuse. It was his fiery concern with contemporary social problems that appealed to Shaw, who in his preface called Brieux "the most important dramatist" of Europe after the death of HENRIK IBSEN, and "incomparably the greatest writer France has produced since Molière." Shaw's enthusiasm for Brieux's plays now seems incredible, their didacticism and occasional flashes of life notwithstanding. Yet though unable to attract large audiences, Brieux won considerable respect in his day. He was made a Chevalier of the Legion of Honor, and in 1910 was elected to the French Academy.

Brieux was born in Paris, the son of a carpenter. Orphaned by the time he was fifteen, he went to work but continued on his own to study the classics and soon started writing plays. The first to be produced was a one-act verse drama (written with Gaston Salandri [1856– ?] and performed only once, in 1879) about the sixteenth-century discoverer of enamel, *Bernard Palissy.* Immediately giving up his clerk's job, Brieux tried to approach the career of playwriting by becoming a journalist. While doing newspaper work in Dieppe and Rouen for the next seven years he continued writing plays. He failed to secure a hearing or even a reading of his scripts by prominent critics and playwrights to whom he appealed. Finally in 1890 André Antoine accepted and produced at the Théâtre-Libre Brieux's *Ménages d'artistes,* a serious three-act comedy exposing artistic poses as mere egotism that flaunts ordinary human decencies. After Antoine produced *Blanchette,* two years later, Brieux left the provinces, where he had learned much about the life he was soon to dramatize, and returned to Paris, where he continued for some years to support himself as a journalist for *Figaro* and other newspapers.

Characteristically, *Blanchette* is a didactic presentation of a particular contemporary issue (teacher education and social mobility) whose dramatic resolution has little to do with the plot. Until his last produced play, *Puisque je t'aime* (1929), Brieux dealt in similar ways with other problems: in *The Three Daughters of M. Dupont* with arranged marriages; in *The Red Robe* with legal injustice; in *Damaged Goods* with syphilis; and in *Maternity* with hypocrisy in the encouragement of rising birth rates. Other Brieux plays include *L'Engrenage* (1894), a political satire exposing bribery as well as the fickleness of the masses; *L'Évasion* (*The Escape,* 1896), a satire of the medical profession and science; *Les Bienfaiteurs* (1896), a satire both of organized charity and of its beneficiaries; *Les Remplaçantes* (1901), an attack on the system and the recruitment of wet nurses; *Simone* (1908) and *Suzette* (1909), pleas for the rights of the children of divorced parents; *La Foi* (*False Gods,* 1909), a spectacle—set in ancient Egypt and elaborately produced in London with music by Camille Saint-Saëns—that suggests that even a false religion is better than none; and *La Femme seule* (*Woman on Her Own,* 1912), a drama that deplores the economic dependence of married women.

These and other social issues were dramatized, examined, and discussed in Brieux's plays. "I wish through the theatre not only to make people think, to modify habits and facts, but still more to bring about laws which appear to me desirable," Brieux said in his 1914 address to the American

Academy of Arts and Letters; stressing his eagerness to improve the human lot, he was gratified to note that his attacks on particular evils "have helped to save the lives of some and to make the lives of others less burdensome." But such didactic intentions to ameliorate immediate problems not only lessened the plays' theatrical effect for contemporary audiences; they also made them decidedly uninteresting to later ones. Brieux's integrity in exposing and combating the evils of his day was indisputable. Yet there is much truth to H. L. Mencken's observation in his preface to *Two Plays by Brieux* (1913, *Blanchette* and *The Escape*) that Brieux's own viewpoints were as middle class, platitudinously pious, and often false as the viewpoints he attacked. In that sense as well as in their excessive sermonizing his plays differ from those of the writers who most influenced Brieux, Émile Augier (1820–89), ÉMILE ZOLA, and Ibsen.

Most of his thirty-odd plays were collected in nine volumes (1921–30). Translated collections include the above-noted editions prefaced by Shaw and Mencken as well as *Three Plays by Brieux* (1916), which includes *Woman on Her Own* (translated by Mrs. Shaw), *False Gods, The Red Robe,* and an introduction by Brieux. Book-length studies in English of his life and work are P. V. Thomas's *The Plays of Eugène Brieux* (1915) and William H. Scheifley's *Brieux and Contemporary French Society* (1917).

BRIGHOUSE, Harold (1882–1958), English novelist and playwright, belonged to the Manchester School of STANLEY HOUGHTON, whose *Works* (1914) he edited, with whom he collaborated on a play, *The Hillarys* (1915), and whose HINDLE WAKES he made into a novel in 1927. Brighouse was born in Eccles (Lancashire) and wrote over fifty one-act plays. Most popular, however, was his full-length *Hobson's Choice* (1915), a play about a domestic tyrant who is subdued by his daughter; it was filmed in 1954 (with Charles Laughton) and revived in the 1960's. Brighouse's first play was *Dealing in Futures* (1909), a study of the capital-labor conflict. Others include *The Price of Coal* (1909), *The Northerners* (1914, a grim drama that has been likened to Toller's THE MACHINE WRECKERS and deals with the same subject), *Zack* (1916), *Garside's Career* (1919, a political comedy), *Mary's John* (1924), and *Sporting Rights* (1943), a one-act comedy.

BROADHURST, George H[owells] (1866–1952), Anglo-American journalist and playwright, was born in London but did most of his work in America, where he migrated at the age of twenty. He had a number of Broadway hits, the best of which is *The Man of the Hour* (1907), about political corruption. The melodramatic *Bought and Paid For* (1911), later a successful film, is about marriage and its problems; at its climax a drunken husband, insisting on his marital rights, breaks down the bedroom door. Broadhurst is most notable for his popular farces and a horse-racing play for Lillian Russell, *Wildfire* (1908). Also a theatre manager who began that career in the American provinces in the 1880's, he in 1914 opened his own Broadhurst Theatre on Broadway; since then, hits have played there for well over half a century.

BROADWAY JONES, a comedy in four acts by GEORGE M. COHAN, produced in 1912 and published in 1923. Setting: New York City and Jonesville, Connecticut; 1912.

Cohan made this popular comedy into a musical, *Billie,* in 1928. Its title character, a gay spendthrift, inherits a million-dollar business, and with it acquires responsibility and maturity.

BRONNEN, Arnolt (1895–1959), Austrian-born German playwright, created a sensation with his *Vatermord* (*Parricide,* 1920). Its depiction of incest and a father-son fight over the naked mother who beckons her son to bed after the parricide were staged NATURALISTICally. But the play is EXPRESSIONISTIC with its theme of youth's rebellion ("You are old, I am young," the son says, rejecting his lecherous mother and gloating, "No one above me—my father—dead!") and its subjective projection of Bronnen's dreams and sufferings, as he confessed in his autobiography.

Born in Vienna, Bronnen was the son of Ferdinand Bronner (1867–1948), who under the pseudonym Franz Adamus wrote plays including *Familie Wawroch* (1899), an Austrian equivalent of Hauptmann's THE WEAVERS. His son, altering his family name, fought in World War I and early in his career joined Berlin art circles. Originally an expressionist, he followed in the footsteps of FRANK WEDEKIND in portraying erotic themes. In 1914 he wrote *Geburt der Jugend,* a play that appeared in 1922 and deals with youthful revolts in an even more sadistic manner than the play that had first made him famous. With his friend BERTOLT BRECHT he was the most produced German playwright of the 1920's. It is no surprise, however, that Bronnen became an enthusiastic Nazi, for his later plays rely increasingly on brutality and the lurid: *Die Exzesse* (1923), a crude farce about sex-obsessed youngsters; *Anarchie in Sillian* (1924), *Katalaunische Schlacht* (1924), and *Rheinische Rebellen* (1925), sensational sex plays set, respectively, in a Tyrolean power station, battlefront trenches, and the post-World War I Rhineland; *Ostpolzug* (1926), a one-act drama whose star portrays Alexander the Great as well as a contemporary waiter who embodies his namesake's energies and leads an expedition to Mount Everest; and *Reparationen* (1926), an allegory attacking the consequences of the Versailles Treaty.

Despite his success in pre-Nazi Germany, Bronnen's work remained virtually unknown in the English-speaking world. Though he supported the Nazis, he wrote little while they were in power. After the war he became a Communist and resided in East Berlin for the remainder of his life. His later plays include one on Napoleon, *N* (1951), and *Die jüngste Nacht* (1958), a comedy about Americans in Germany.

His autobiography is *Arnolt Bronnen Gibt zu Protokoll* (1954).

BROSZKIEWICZ, Jerzy (1922–), Polish novelist, music critic, and playwright, in the 1960's made a reputation for himself with experimental, sometimes SURREALISTIC dramas. His career as a playwright began early but he became known only in 1956, with *Imiona władzy* (*The Names of Power*), three one-acters—*Claudius, Philip,* and *114*—that explore the moral problems of tyranny and resistance in ancient Rome, in the dying Philip II's Spain, and in the mid-twentieth century. Other philosophic plays that stress the conflicts of the individual and society include *Dwie przygody Lemuela Gullivera* (*The Adventures of Lemuel Gulliver,* 1961), a two-act monologue by Swift's famous character to a Lilliputian and to a Brobdingnagian, illustrating the transposed relations of strong and weak; and *Bar Wszystkich Świetych* (*All Saints' Café,* 1961?), a SYMBOLIC drama set in a shady bar and portraying the victimization of a pair of lovers.

Of Broszkiewicz's nearly thirty plays these three, though not readily available, have been translated. Broszkiewicz achieved considerable popularity also with a biographical novel on Chopin, *Opowieść o Chopinie* (1950).

BROWNE, Maurice (1881–1955), English producer, director, and actor, is particularly notable as a pioneer (with his American wife Ellen Van Volkenburg) in the little theatre movement in America, where he founded and directed the Chicago Little Theatre (1912–18). He also wrote a number of plays, including *The King of the Jews* (1916) and *The Mother of Gregory* (1923), the latter a long one-acter based on a legend. But Browne's claim to notice as a dramatist rests on the play he coauthored with ROBERT M. B. NICHOLS, WINGS OVER EUROPE (1928).

Browne was born in Reading, educated at Cambridge, and served in the South African War in 1900. He became a successful London producer in 1927. He also wrote poetry and an autobiography, *Too Late to Lament* (1955).

BROWNING VERSION, THE, a one-act play by TERENCE RATTIGAN, produced in 1948 and published in 1949. Setting: southern England, the sitting room of a public school apartment on a July evening in the 1940's.

This long one-act character play is an affecting and masterly study of a failure. It was produced, as *Playbill,* with *Harlequinade,* "a soufflé designed to end a meal of which *The Browning Version* was the main course" (Rattigan).

It is the last day of school. The master of the Lower Fifth, Andrew Crocker-Harris, is forced by illness to leave for a lesser post. A once-brilliant classical scholar, "the Crock" is now feared and disliked by his pupils, patronized by the headmaster, and hated by his frustrated wife, who has seduced and tries to hold on to a younger schoolmaster. A pupil who has come for his last private lesson remarks that Crocker-Harris is "all shrivelled up inside like a nut and he seems to hate people to like him." The headmaster comes to tell him that he will not, after all, qualify for a pension, and asks him to give up his privileged spot at the farewell ceremonies to a junior but more popular colleague. With cold serenity, Crocker-Harris bears these indignities. Then his successor comes by with his wife, to examine their new apartment. He lets slip Crocker-Harris's other nickname, "the Himmler of the Lower Fifth." This blow ("an utter failure as a schoolmaster," he remarks, "I hadn't realized that I was also feared") intensifies his reaction when his pupil returns to give him a farewell present, an inscribed copy of Robert Browning's version of their favorite play, *Agamemnon.* Such an unexpected act of kindness causes Crocker-Harris to break down for the first time. But his wife demolishes him by insinuating that "the artful little beast" did it only to get a passing grade. Her reluctant lover is horrified at this cruelty, and at her comment: "You can't hurt Andrew. He's dead." Though she pleads desperately for his love, he breaks with her. Then he tries to persuade Crocker-Harris that the pupil really loves him, and is staggered to learn that Crocker-Harris has known about his wife's adultery. She has always made it a point to inform him of her betrayals! "Nothing is ever too horrible to think of," Crocker-Harris says; "it is simply a question of facing facts," and he describes the pathetic, unfulfilled lives of both himself and his wife. His wife later sneers that though her former lover plans to visit her husband in their new home, he will be coming to her. "The likeliest contingency is, that he's not going to either of us," Crocker-Harris remarks, at last finding the strength to confront humiliation. Politely he excuses himself when the headmaster calls, and insists on exercising his privilege after all: "I am now seeing the matter in a different light." And then he has his wife serve their meal: "Come along, my dear. We mustn't let our dinner get cold."

BRUCKNER, Ferdinand (1891–1958), Austrian playwright, first became prominent under his given name, **Theodor TAGGER,** as an EXPRESSIONIST poet and as a Berlin theatre director. As Tagger, too, he wrote *Te deum* (1929), a mystic one-acter exploring the resolution of Bjørnson's BEYOND HUMAN POWER I. Subsequently he achieved lasting fame as the pseudonymous playwright "Ferdinand Bruckner" (whose true identity long remained unrevealed), beginning with his own production of *Krankheit der Jugend* in 1926. A portrait of cynical postwar disillusionment among Berlin medical students and their girl friends, the play created a sensation with its blatant eroticism, sexual perversions, suicide, and murder. Thereafter Bruckner wrote many other popular though less sensational plays that range from contemporary REALISM to stylized history. It was with the latter, in the chronicle *Elisabeth von England* (ELIZABETH OF ENGLAND, 1930), that Bruckner became known to international audiences.

Ferdinand Bruckner (originally Theodor Tagger) in 1946. (*Bildarchiv der Österreichischen National Bibliothek*)

The son of an Austrian merchant and his French wife, Bruckner was born in Vienna but grew up in Graz. He studied music, medicine, and law in Vienna, Paris, and Berlin, where in 1923 he founded the theatre he was to direct until 1927. In 1933 Bruckner returned to Vienna, but soon emigrated—first to France and then, in 1936, to the United States. He became an American citizen and lived in New York until 1951.

The multiple settings Bruckner was soon to employ so effectively in his Elizabeth play he first used in *Die Verbrecher* (*The Criminals,* 1928), a courtroom drama given a spectacular production by Max Reinhardt in 1929; on three stage levels are presented simultaneously criminals from various social circles tried and wrongly condemned —for, according to Bruckner, individual conscience is the only proper judge and, as the *raisonneur* says, "we have set up a retributive authority [only] in order to relieve our conscience, and . . . in this [fearful] escape from ourselves lies the indestructible power of public jurisdiction."

Die Kreatur (1929), a STRINDBERGian marriage play, was followed the next year by the hit *Elizabeth of England.* In 1931 Bruckner modernized Shakespeare's language and psychological motivation in *Timon,* and two years later did the same with Heinrich von Kleist's story, *Die Marquise von O.* In a contemporary original tragedy, *Die Rassen* (*Races,* 1933), Bruckner poignantly depicts a university community's succumbing to Nazi racial (i.e., anti-Semitic) laws. During the years that followed, Bruckner produced historical dramas which continued to stress ethical values: *Napoleon I* (1937), on the conflict between the emperor's power struggle and his passion for Josephine; *Simon Bolivar* (1945), a panoramic work in two parts; and *Heroische Komödie* (1946), on Madame de Staël.

During his exile Bruckner also wrote war plays, but neither these nor his adaptations of classic tragedy (like *Pyrrhus und Andromache,* 1952) were particularly successful. His last plays, like those of T. S. ELIOT, are in verse and disguise classical themes with modern plots: *Der Tod einer Puppe* (1956) and *Der Kampf mit dem Engel* (1957) both feature widows who fervently try to make up for previous deprivations. Bruckner's final work was *Das irdene Wägelchen* (1957), an adaptation of King Shudraka's Indian classic *Mrcchakatika* (*The Little Clay Cart*).

From the time of his initial dramatizations of psychopathology and legal injustice, Bruckner continued to produce theatrically effective portrayals of the age's moral confusion. Perhaps most successful were his modernizations of historical characters. Bruckner achieved striking effects with vast simultaneous actions on multistages as well as with classically circumscribed domestic plays, but whatever the plot or form, he expressed his concern with ethics and morals.

After the defeat of the Nazis, Bruckner (like CARL ZUCKMAYER) was among the few to return from exile and resume playwriting. In 1951 he settled in Berlin, where he worked as a *Dramaturg* until his death. H. F. Garten's *Modern German Drama* (1964), which has a bibliography, discusses Bruckner's work.

BRUES, Otto (1897–1967), German dramatist, wrote predominantly religious plays from the 1920's through the 1950's. In the tragedy *Die Heilandsflur* (1921) military orders stop men from settling down to peaceful country life, while *Der Prophet von Lochau* (1923) features a fanatical priest whose vision of Judgment Day almost wrecks his community. Later plays include the patriotic comedy *Der alte Wrangel* (1936), *Johanna in den Zelten* (1956), and works composed for special occasions.

BRUST, Alfred (1891–1934), German playwright, like HANS HENNY JAHNN in his later works, was preoccupied with the conflicting passions of sensuality and asceticism. After producing his *Der ewige Mensch* (1919), a dramatic celebration of love, Max Reinhardt in 1922 produced Brust's *Der singende Fisch,* a pious legend-play set in the Baltic regions and depicting the divorce of a man's spirit from his body, as experienced through the sensibilities of his fearful bride. Such conflicts were expressed most notably in Brust's trilogy of one-acters produced jointly as *Tolkening* (1924), a legendary IBSENite drama set in primitive Eastern Europe and depicting extreme passions: *Die Wölfe* (*The Wolves*) features a libidinous clergyman's wife who is killed as she commits sodomy with a wolf; in *Die Würmer* the clergyman's second marriage is portrayed amidst similarly animalistic, but more sadistic, passions; in *Der*

Phönix, the final and most symbolic play of the trilogy, evil sensuality is defeated by the spirit as the redeemed clergyman battles for the soul of a peasant girl who dances before a gigantic cross.

Brust, an East Prussian, also wrote a number of comedies, the most successful of which was *Ostrom* (1920). *Kaufmann Christleit* (1933), his last play, appeared as Hitler and the Nazis came to power; ironically, it celebrates the existence of the divine love that brings salvation to mankind.

The Wolves was published with an introduction in James M. Ritchie and Hugh F. Garten's *Seven Expressionist Plays: Kokoschka to Barlach* (1968).

BUERO VALLEJO, Antonio (1916–), is one of the leading post-World War II playwrights in Spain (ALFONSO SASTRE is the other). He first achieved prominence in 1949 when he won the important Lope de Vega and Amigos de los Quintero prizes for, respectively, *Historia de una escalera* and *Las palabras en la arena*. The first traces the similar hopes and disillusionments of a house's four families over the generations; the second, a NATURALISTIC one-acter, is a drama of adultery. *La tejedora de sueños* (THE DREAM WEAVER, 1952), the first of Buero Vallejo's works published in an English anthology, freely dramatizes a Homeric tale. Though virtually unknown abroad and little produced in Franco's Spain, Buero Vallejo was acclaimed by native critics as the most important Spanish dramatist of the 1950's and 1960's—and possibly a writer of major stature. He was elected to the Royal Spanish Academy in 1971.

Born in Guadalajara, Buero Vallejo began his career as a painter—and was considered to be an excellent artist. During the Civil War he served as a medical aide for the Republicans, was captured, and upon the Falangist victory remained imprisoned until 1945. When he was finally released Buero Vallejo resumed his painting and in 1946 wrote his second full-length play, *En la ardiente oscuridad* (*In the Burning Darkness*, 1950); poetic and with SYMBOLIC overtones, it too depicts shattered ideals—here in an asylum for the blind, whose happiness is destroyed by a rebellious newcomer who refuses to accept illusions and, before his mysterious death, compels the others to face unpleasant realities.

Further Buero Vallejo plays include *La señal que se espera* (1952), in which a harpmaker's sweetheart, not his just-completed instrument, provides the longed-for inspiration; *Casi un cuento de hadas* (1953), portraying the love of a beautiful princess and an ugly prince; *Madrugada* (1953), depicting the petty scheming for an artist's inheritance; *Irene o el tesoro* (1954), another play on illusion, here that of a miserable servant girl who finds happiness in fantasy; *Hoy es fiesta* (1956), a naturalistic lower-class drama that, like his early prize-winning one-acter, has been likened to Rice's STREET SCENE and other American naturalist drama; *Las cartas boca abajo* (1957), which depicts five characters frustrated by life—not unlike those of Miller's DEATH OF A SALESMAN; *Un soñador para un pueblo* (1958), a historical play set at the time of Carlos III and depicting the Marchese di Squillace's ideal and often unsuccessful quests to modernize Spain; *Las Meninas* (1960); *El concierto de San Ovidio* (*The Concert at Saint Ovide*, 1962), in which blind Parisian paupers cared for by nuns during the French Revolution are hired by the wealthy ostensibly as musicians—but actually to be laughed at; *La doble historia del Dr. Valmy* (*The Double Case History of Dr. Valmy*, 1967), depicting violent police-state methods; and *Sueño de la razón* (1970), featuring the seventy-six-year-old Goya just before his flight from Spanish tyranny.

Buero Vallejo, who has also written film scripts, often deals with the anguished and the downtrodden, and with their yearning to find solace in illusions and love. The fantasy and the poetic quality of his writing, combined with naturalist depictions, recall the drama of GERHART HAUPTMANN.

J. E. Lyon and K. S. B. Croft's text edition (1964) of *Hoy es fiesta* has an informative introduction in English, and a bibliography. A note on Buero Vallejo and a short bibliography appear in Robert W. Corrigan's *Masterpieces of the Modern Spanish Theatre* (1967), which includes *The Dream Weaver* as well as Buero Vallejo's comments "About Theatre," which stress the REALISTIC and didactic qualities of drama no less than the evocative and poetic ones. *The Concert at Saint Ovide* was published, with further notes on Buero Vallejo, in Marion Holt's *The Modern Spanish Stage: Four Plays* (1970).

BULGAKOV, Mikhail Afanasyevich (1891–1940), Russian novelist and playwright, became best known for his controversial *Dni Turbinykh* (THE DAYS OF THE TURBINS, 1926). Its popularity and that of the novel on which it is based, however, subjected him to lifelong slander, harassment, and censorship, though he was more than rehabilitated posthumously with *Master i Margarita* (*The Master and Margarita*), an allegorical novel published in 1966–67 and hailed as a masterpiece of the Stalin era, during which it had been banned. Eventually Bulgakov's satirical tales and dramas ceased to be published. He became a literary consultant—first at the Moscow Art Theatre, and then at the Bolshoi.

The son of a theology professor, Bulgakov was born in Kiev. There he spent the turbulent days of the Revolution, when the city changed hands ten times. Like ANTON CHEKHOV, he became a doctor, graduating (with distinction) from the Kiev College of Medicine. Like Chekhov, too, he found writing more congenial than medicine. He composed his first story on a train, and submitted it to a newspaper in the city to which he was traveling on a case. It was published in 1919, and Bulgakov thereupon gave up medicine for journalism and literature. His first important work was a partly autobiographical novel which he soon dramatized as *The Days of the Turbins*.

Bulgakov is said to have written well over twenty plays, most of which were banned and are currently

Mikhail Afanasyevich Bulgakov. (Sovfoto)

unavailable even in manuscript. His eleven extant plays include a satire on the morality of various government functionaries, *Zoikina kvartira* (1926); an allegory on Russian censorship, *Bugrovy ostrov* (1928); and a sequel to *The Days of the Turbins*, *Beg* (*Flight*, 1929), a play about émigré life that also depicts the flight and disintegration of White officers after their defeat by the Red armies in southern Russia. Then Bulgakov became a *Dramaturg*, in which position he in 1932 prepared for the Moscow Art Theatre an adaptation of Gogol's masterpiece, *Dead Souls*. Bulgakov's *Blazhenstvo* (*Bliss*), a pessimistic satire linking the past, present, and future, was written in 1934 but barred from production and not published until 1966; it dramatizes the life of a time machine inventor plagued by bureaucrats in each of his trips. *Ivan Vasilevich*, a variation on this theme, was prepared for performance in 1936; it was ultimately banned, and remained unpublished until 1965. The production of Bulgakov's dramatization of the life of *Molière* (1936), which also appeared as *Kabala svyatosh*, caused bitter disputes that resulted in Bulgakov's break with the Moscow Art Theatre and its directors. Bulgakov's last works were a dramatization of Cervantes's *Don Quixote* (1940); and a play about the duel and death of the poet Pushkin, *Poslednye dni*, produced posthumously (in 1943) by the Moscow Art Theatre.

Bulgakov's death of uremia at the age of forty-nine was not reported in the Soviet newspapers. His *Teatralny roman* (*Theatrical Novel*), first published in 1966 and translated as *Black Snow* (1968), is an autobiographical *roman à clef* that depicts his encounters with censorship and portrays demonic but frightened and demoralized directors —thinly veiled satires of the aging Konstantin Stanislavsky and of VLADIMIR NEMIROVICH-DANCHENKO.

The Days of the Turbins is reprinted in Volume II of F. D. Reeve's *An Anthology of Russian Plays* (1963) and in Eugene Lyons's edition of *Six Soviet Plays* (1934), which includes an essay on Bulgakov, as does Mirra Ginsburg's translation of *Flight* (1969).

BULGARIA. The country's drama, like the rest of Bulgarian literature, is relatively undeveloped and little known abroad. In 1865, a dozen years before national liberation, a theatre troupe was organized by Dobri Voinikov (1833–78), the author of melodramatic history plays and of *Krivorazbranata tsivilizatsiia* (1871), a comedy that satirizes the fashionable deprecation of native in favor of French living. Perhaps the best early Bulgarian play is *Ivanko ubietsut na Asenia I* (1872), a historical drama by Voinikov's rival, Vasil Drumev (1840?–1901).

Bulgaria's drama began to develop with the founding of the National Theatre, in 1907. Its most popular playwright was the country's first major poet and novelist, Ivan Vazov (1850–1921). For the most part melodramatic and sentimental, his plays often are dramatizations of his novels and include comedies like *Sluzhbogontsi* (1903), a satire of the title's careerist "jobseekers." He also wrote history plays dealing with the immediate past, as in *Pod igoto* (1910), about the 1876 uprising against the Turks; as well as with remote times, as in *Ivailo* (1914), featuring the thirteenth-century peasant revolutionary who briefly reigned as king.

Lesser works were written by Petko Todorov (1879–1916), the author of folk drama like *Zmeiova svatba* (1911), a fusion of fantasy and NATURALISM. The first Bulgarian verse drama, *Boyan Magesnikut* (1914), is a patriotic piece by the poet Kiril Khristov (1875–1944). Important Western drama influenced Ana Karima (1871–1949) and Ivan Kirilov (1876–1935); the former portrayed, in *Probuzhdane* (1903), a HEDDA GABLER type who, however, adjusts to her environment; and Kirilov's *Chuchuliga* (1906), with its mountain scalers who strive to reach ecstatic heights, echoes other HENRIK IBSEN plays. The poet Peio Yavorov (1878–1914) in the latter part of his life became *Dramaturg* of the National Theatre and wrote two domestic tragedies in the vein of Ibsen and ANTON CHEKHOV: the autobiographical *V polite na Vitosha* (1911) and *Kogato grum udari—kak ekhoto zaglukhva* (1912). Stefan L. Kostov (1879–1939) created effective characters in social satires like *Zlatnata mina* (1925) and *Golemanov* (1927). Similar comedies of manners were written by the short-story writer Yordan Yovkov (1880–1937), who also produced a more serious domestic drama, *Albena* (1929). Though Yovkov was the only notable playwright of the period between the two world wars, much of the drama that continued to be produced was historical, such as *Zlatnata chasha* (1922), a SYMBOLIC study of medieval history by Ivan Grozev (1872–1957).

After World War II Bulgarian drama, like the

rest of Bulgarian life, was controlled by the Soviet Union. The most distinguished playwright since the war has been Kamen Zidarov (1902–), a writer of historical drama; his *Tsarska milost* (1949) is a bitter portrayal of Ferdinand I, while the poetic *Ivan Shishman* (1959, republished in a revised version under this title in 1962) depicts Bulgaria in the late fourteenth century, shortly before its defeat by the Ottomans. Other noteworthy postwar plays include Audrey Gulyashki's (1914–) *Obeshtanie* (1949), whose hero brings about the successful fulfillment of production norms: and Georgi Dzhagarov's (1925–) *Prokurorut* (*The Public Prosecutor,* 1964), a popular anti-Stalinist courtroom drama set in 1955–56 provincial Bulgaria and adapted by the English writers C. P. Snow (1905–) and Pamela Hansford Johnson (1912–).

A tendentious and comprehensive but not always accurate study is Clarence A. Manning and Roman Smal-Stocki's *The History of Modern Bulgarian Literature* (1960).

BUOYANT BILLIONS, "A Comedy of No Manners" in four acts by BERNARD SHAW, produced in 1948 and published in 1949. Setting: Panama and London in the late 1940's.

In his "prefacette," Shaw called this play, written in his nineties, a "trivial" comedy "with some hope in it."

Junius Smith, a "world betterer" who wants to help man's evolution and the "scientific political reconstruction" of a world threatened by class war, goes to Panama to study ways of using atomic energy to rid the world of noxious insects. In a jungle clearing he meets Clemmy, a recluse with whom he argues about Karl Marx, vegetarianism, love, and modern life; and her native servant, with whom he argues about education and the native god Hoochlipoochli. In a London drawing room converted into a Chinese temple to solace the financier Bastable Buoyant, Clemmy's family are discussing their impractical upbringing and other topics with the solicitor Sir Ferdinand Flopper. Buoyant's daughter Clemmy unexpectedly arrives; she has fallen in love with Junius and is escaping him, because she believes love to be unreal and transitory. Physically attracted to her and wanting to marry her for her money, Junius follows and finds her. The play ends, after a number of long discussions, when Clemmy agrees to take her father's advice that she marry Junius, whose intelligence and frankness have impressed Buoyant.

BURMA was greatly admired among colonized countries for its *zat pwe,* the classical native dance drama, and other entertainments. Its most distinguished playwright was U Pon Nya (1807?–66), a court poet executed after political and romantic intrigues, whose masterpiece was *Wizaya* (1872), his adaptation of a Ceylonese JATAKA that he made entirely Burmese in feeling and intent. Excerpts from it as well as further plays by Pon Nya and others were translated in Maung Htin Aung's *Burmese Drama* (1937), a study that also discusses the playwrights' lives and work in some detail.

Burma's twentieth-century drama is not generally available in the West. It consists principally of *zat,* a mixture of legend and contemporary themes and characters from all social classes; and *pya zat,* which deals with contemporary themes, characters, and speech, and excludes nobility and courtly language. The present-day theatre in both the capitals of Rangoon and Mandalay has suffered considerably because of Burma's economic decline.

For the later period see Kenneth (Maung Khe) Sein and Joseph A. Withey's *The Great Po Sein* (1965), a biography of the family head of "the Barrymores of Burma" as well as "a Chronicle of the Burmese Theater"; it has a glossary and a bibliography.

BURNING GLASS, THE, a play in three acts by CHARLES MORGAN, produced in 1953 and published in 1954. Setting: England, "soon."

As its preface, "On Power Over Nature," reiterates, Morgan's last play deals with the urgent problem of saving man from the destructive consequences of his own scientific precociousness. Its suspense and portrayal of high-level affairs helped make it Morgan's most popular play.

Christopher Terriford has discovered a way to harness the sun's rays, focus them on selected regions, and thus burn the globe at will. He tells the Prime Minister, a wise man and a former admirer of Christopher's mother, of his "burning glass." But knowing man's weakness, he refuses to reveal his machine's setting—even for beneficial means. Only in case of war will he set the combination, now known only—and only partially—to two others, one of them being his brilliant and beautiful wife, Mary. The enemy kidnaps Christopher, and Mary agrees to demonstrate "the burning glass" to the enemy. He is released, and war is averted. His assistant, a bitter man who loves Mary, has become familiar with the machine's setting during the demonstration. Realizing the danger of his knowledge and his own unreliability, he commits suicide. Christopher persists in his refusal to reveal the setting and the Prime Minister, alluding to the suicide, finally remarks, "To see an evil power not exercised—by young men—gives me even now a little hope for the future of the world."

BURNT FLOWER-BED, THE (*L'aiuola bruciata*), a play in three acts by UGO BETTI, published and produced in 1953. Setting: a mountain retreat near a border in the "present time."

Political in plot like THE QUEEN AND THE REBELS, this suspenseful play deals with nonpolitical themes of individual and collective guilt—like Betti's first success, LANDSLIDE AT NORTH STATION.

Act I. Former colleagues visit Giovanni, their country's deposed ruler who now lives alone with his slightly deranged wife. Cynical about his former activities, Giovanni wonders why he is wanted again. His retirement followed his fifteen-year-old son's fall from an apartment window to the flower bed below, to a death which Giovanni has tried to understand and to come to terms with ever since. His colleagues want him to head their efforts to negotiate secretly with an emissary of their hostile neighbor, and thus force both governments to agree to peace. Among the conspirators is Nicola, Giovanni's former rival and now a dying man lovingly cared for by Rosa, a nurse whose father was shot in a political uprising. She does not know that it was the leader Giovanni, needing an incident at the time, who ordered the haphazard shooting into the crowd that resulted in her father's death. Nicola agrees with the others that Giovanni must lead them, but Giovanni starts explaining why he thinks their undertaking is a mistake.

Act II. Disillusioned, Giovanni dismisses the conspirators' ideals because he thinks that men are now dissatisfied with the concept "that all that progress means is merely dying fatter, cleaner, better dressed." The conspirators leave Nicola to persuade Giovanni, and in their talk Nicola confesses to and describes the terror of his approaching death, while Giovanni recalls how his son took his hand as they walked and then asked, "Papa, where are you taking me?" Now he wishes he had taken more notice of the boy, and while pursuing these admittedly "sentimental" and symbolic memories decides to join the conspirators' plan—for "why shouldn't it happen, sooner or later; the Great Thaw, the Recovery?" Rosa worries about Nicola as she and Giovanni's wife talk of their dead father and son. And indeed, soon word comes that Nicola is dead. Rosa warns Giovanni: with his dying breath Nicola revealed that, like her father, Giovanni is to be sacrificed in an incident meant to trigger a cataclysm: "He said you will also tip the scales, in the same way, only with much more noise." Giovanni runs off, for however difficult the escape, "it'll be better than sacrificing oneself to *this!*" His wife feels betrayed at being left alone to ponder the mystery of their son's death in "that dreadful flower bed." Angrily she taxes Giovanni with responsibility for the boy's death and denounces him. Before the plotters can search for him, Giovanni reappears.

Act III. Almost sadly the plotters admit that Giovanni is to be shot when he goes out to meet the other emissary. They admit too that they killed Nicola, who was himself too weak either to take on the job or to warn Giovanni. Mankind being what it is, they insist that it is pointless really to come to an agreement with their neighbor. The conspiracy is too far advanced; they themselves are powerless to stop it; and in the final analysis, they submit cynically, all "action is a dream." Giovanni confesses that his son's death was a suicide—despair of the world that his father and others had made for him, a world that is "diseased. It's one vast, blighted flower bed." To atone for his responsibility for his son's despair Giovanni is now ready to die and cause the death of others, for "there is not a living soul among them." But Rosa persuades him he is wrong, that men must have faith, and that Giovanni must lead them. "I do not believe that they will really shoot. I don't believe that people want to kill. They do it because they are truly, truly in a dream," she says as she runs out—and intercepts the fatal bullet. Giovanni lifts up her corpse. "We will go up there and say what has to be said, and they will listen to us," Giovanni concludes as he walks out, and the bugle calls for the negotiation sound joyfully.

BURNT HOUSE, THE (*Brända tomten*), a play in two scenes by AUGUST STRINDBERG, published and produced in 1907. Setting: a fire-gutted Swedish house and the adjacent orchard, early twentieth century.

This is Opus II of THE CHAMBER PLAYS.

After thirty years a Stranger from abroad visits his childhood home—the morning after it has burned down. His proximity to death after hanging himself when he was a boy gave him clairvoyant powers. With these he now cynically untangles the grim truths revealed under the home's façade, and demonstrates supernatural justice in the "world weaver's" complex and mysterious—but meaningful—design that is life. The respected, wealthy parents were scoundrel smugglers, and everything in the house was counterfeit. His brother, a dyer who occupied the house, tries to pin an arson charge on their young boarder, a student who is his wife's lover—and probably the Stranger's illegitimate son. But the dyer's plan may be foiled by someone whom he once injured. Others are implicated, until a tangled network of crime and injustice that involves everybody is traceable in the ashes of the probably accidental fire. The orchard, in the meantime, has prematurely bloomed because of the fire's heat. At the end, the dyer is deservedly ruined because his insurance premium arrived too late, and the Stranger places the wreath meant for his parents' grave on their burnt house, "my childhood's home! And now, Wanderer, resume thy pilgrimage!"

BURROWS, Abe (1910–   ), American director and playwright, coauthored many Broadway hits, most of them musicals. They include the award-winning dramatization of DAMON RUNYON tales, *Guys and Dolls* (1950), written with Jo Swerling (1897–   ), music by Frank Loesser; *Silk Stockings* (1955), written with GEORGE S. KAUFMAN and Leueen McGrath (1914–   ), the Cole Porter musical based on *Ninotchka* (1939), the Ernst Lubitsch film adaptation of a story by MENYHÉRT LENGYEL; *Say, Darling* (1958), written with Richard P. Bissell (1913–   ) and his wife Marian, about an author who transforms a novel into a hit musical—as Bissell did with GEORGE ABBOTT in *The Pajama Game* (1954); the Pulitzer Prize-winning satirical musical *How to Succeed in Business Without Really Trying* (1961), music by Loesser; and a popular comedy about an amorous dentist and his secretary, *Cactus Flower* (1965).

Born in New York, Burrows was once an accountant and broker, and a writer for radio and television.

BURTE [pseudonym of Strübe], **Hermann** (1879–1960), German writer, prefigured National Socialism in works like *Wiltfeber, der ewige Deutsche* (1912), a philosophic novel that won the Kleist Prize; and *Mensch mit uns* (1936), a play that similarly propounds Nietzschean and racial ideals, and features the Germanic hero Siegfried. Already in Burte's early *Drei Einakter* (1907) collection he celebrated the physical power he was to stress in later plays. These include *Herzog Utz* (1913), whose medieval prince foresakes romantic love and rises to a life of duty; *Katte* (1914), on the conflict between Friedrich Wilhelm I and his son, Frederick the Great; *Simson* (1917), embodying chauvinistic racism in the biblical Samson; *Krist vor Gericht* (1930), a modernization of the trial of Jesus; and *Prometheus* (1932), a verse interpretation of the title hero as a superman forerunner of Christ. Burte, who also published collections of poetry, came of south German peasant and artisan stock. Interested in aesthetics, he studied art in France and England.

BURY THE DEAD, a one-act play by IRWIN SHAW, published and produced in 1936. Setting: an almost empty two-level stage with props representing a battlefield in "the second year of the war that is to begin tomorrow night."

The New Theatre League's next important play after Odets's WAITING FOR LEFTY, this is another long one-acter with some AGITPROP features. It is an antiwar drama suggested by Chlumberg's MIRACLE AT VERDUN, and a fantasy after the NATURALISTIC opening scene. Some of the play's power is vitiated by excessive shrillness, repetition, and explanation.

A weary front-line digging detail is burying six fallen comrades. Suddenly the corpses rise and refuse to be buried. In subsequent episodes spotlights focus on groups of generals, businessmen, and priests. Getting increasingly panicky, they exhort the dead soldiers to submit patriotically to a quiet burial. Even the pleas of their mothers, sisters, wives, and sweethearts—all hastily summoned to the burial place—fail to move the recalcitrant young dead. They are eager to savor life: "Joy and pain—to each man in his own way, a full seventy years, to be ended by an unhurried fate, not by a colored pin on a General's map." Voices chanting "Bury the dead!" grow, and a priest tries to exorcise the six. When his soldiers refuse to obey him, a general himself machine-guns the dead. Slowly these walk over his slumping figure, and the living soldiers follow them out. The last soldier flicks his cigarette butt at the now dead general, whose silent gun still points at the empty grave.

BUS STOP, a play in three acts by WILLIAM INGE, published and produced in 1955. Setting: a roadside café in a small Kansas town; a night in March, early 1950's.

This popular play, which became an even more popular film the following year, is an expansion of *People in the Wind,* a one-acter written in the early 1950's and published with *Summer Brave and Eleven Short Plays* (1962). The characters are obvious and cliché-ridden, but amusing. Inge described them as "a composite picture of varying kinds of love," and they also portray varying yearnings.

Thrown together in a drab rest stop when their bus is delayed by a blizzard are Cherie, an uneducated and amoral chanteuse trying to escape a rough and dumb but lovable cowboy who insists on marrying "Cherry," as he calls her, because they were "familiar" with each other; a depraved, alcoholic professor who plans to seduce an innocent high-school girl, the café's waitress; her divorced older companion, an earthy girl who takes the occasion to make love with the bus driver; and a wise and strong but humble sheriff who protects the girls and chastens the cowboy. By daybreak, Cherie agrees to marry the penitent ruffian, the professor gives up his planned seduction, and the bus continues on its journey.

BUTTER AND EGG MAN, THE, a play in three acts by GEORGE S. KAUFMAN, published and produced in 1925. Setting: New York City and Syracuse, New York; 1920's.

Kaufman's only full-length play written without a collaborator, this is a farce about a young "butter and egg man" (or "angel") from Chillicothe, Ohio. He is enticed by shady theatre producers to invest his inheritance in a sure flop—Kaufman's parody of contemporary hits. The naïve youth beats the city sharpers at their own game, both during the tryouts and on Broadway, and ends up marrying their attractive secretary.

BUTTERFLY'S EVIL SPELL, THE (*El maleficio de la mariposa*), a play by FEDERICO GARCÍA LORCA, produced in 1920. Setting: an Andalusian field.

This was García Lorca's first play and its manuscript survived only in an incomplete version (without the final pages), translated in *Five Plays* (1963). Though premiered by GREGORIO MARTÍNEZ SIERRA, with sets by Salvador Dalí, it was not a success. Anticipating the Čapeks' FROM THE LIFE OF INSECTS, it is a parable in the form of a short, poetic fantasy: a cockroach learns all about a visiting butterfly's life; when it leaves, the roach is disoriented and keeps yearning for the butterfly's enchanting world.

BUYSSE, Cyriel (1859–1932), Belgian novelist and playwright, brought an authentic Flemish note into his native theatre. Most popular among his dozen plays were his dialect comedies, beginning with his first and probably best one, *De Plaatsvervangende Vrederechter* (1895), a GEORGES FEYDEAU-like intrigue about a "substitute magistrate." Also notable are his more somber play about the struggle of peasants and nobility, *Het Gezin van Paemel* (1903); and a satire of materialism, *Susususut* (1929). An account of his work appears in SUZANNE LILAR's *The Belgian Theatre Since 1890* (third edition, 1962).

C

CAESAR AND CLEOPATRA, "A History" in five acts by BERNARD SHAW, produced in 1899 and published in 1901. Setting: Egypt; October, 48 B.C. to March, 47 B.C.

Devoting a part of his preface to THREE PLAYS FOR PURITANS, of which this is the most impressive play, to the question of "Better than Shakespeare?" Shaw noted the superiority of his "real" characters over Shakespeare's "love-obsessed" ones. Even more important, he stressed a conception of history in terms of his own modern philosophy, which in time, he admitted, was likely to become as dated as has Shakespeare's "knightly conception." These ideas are echoed in the Ra Prologue (which Shaw wrote later, for a 1912 production; the "alternative" is the play's original prologue) and in the "Notes" to the play, where he calls Caesar a "naturally great" man whose striking mark is originality, giving him "an air of frankness, generosity, and magnanimity by enabling him to estimate the value of truth, money, or success in any particular instance quite independently of convention and moral generalization"—a portrayal realized masterfully in this, Shaw's first dramatization of the Superman. It was adapted by Ervin Drake (1919–   ) as a musical, *Her First Roman* (1968).

Prologue. In a monologue, the Egyptian god Ra satirically presents the political-military background of Rome and of the story of the "great man" Caesar and the sixteen-year-old Cleopatra, stressing one of the play's themes: "men twenty centuries ago were already just such as you." In *"An Alternative to the Prologue,"* a messenger tells the guards in Cleopatra's palace, near the Syrian border, of Caesar's recent victory and imminent arrival. Cleopatra's chief nurse, the "huge grim" Ftatateeta, announces Cleopatra's flight from the palace, probably to the desert to consult the Sphinx.

Act I. Caesar hails the Sphinx, symbol of his own genius: "part brute, part woman, and part god." A frightened and superstitious Cleopatra calls him, and Caesar, at first believing that he is dreaming, tells her that she can avoid being eaten by Caesar only if she faces him like a queen, not a child. Though scared when he tells her that he is a Roman, she comes to like this nice "old gentleman." She leads him to her palace and is quickly emboldened by Caesar, who tries to coach her in the art of ruling, to assert herself with feline ferocity over the domineering Ftatateeta. But when she mounts her throne to await the arrival of Caesar she is white with terror. The Roman troops enter; when they hail him, she finally realizes who he is and, sobbing with relief, falls into Caesar's arms.

Act II. On his throne in Alexandria, the boy-king Ptolemy dutifully delivers a proclamation to his guardian Pothinus, his tutor Theodotus, and his general Achillas, who is commander of the Roman occupation troops that have been stationed in Alexandria since Mark Antony's conquest some years earlier. They are now on the side of Ptolemy, who recites by rote his refusal to allow Cleopatra, aided by Caesar, to take the throne from him. Caesar enters with his secretary, the loyal but moralistic "islander" Britannus, and the bluff officer Rufio, whereupon a long conference follows. Over the objections of Rufio, who repeatedly mistakes Caesar's humanity and political wisdom for weakness, Caesar allows Achillas and Pothinus to leave. Alone with him, Cleopatra asks Caesar to send the "beautiful young" Mark Antony to her from Rome. When Caesar gets word of the revolt in town against his soldiers, he has his west harbor boats burned and orders the seizure of the Alexandrian lighthouse. Pothinus enters with an ultimatum and, to the indignation of Rufio, Caesar permits the frantic Theodotus to use Achillas's soldiers to put out the fire raging in the famous Library of Alexandria. Thus occupied, they cannot interfere with Caesar's capture of the lighthouse. He puts on his armor, and orders Cleopatra, who is amused to find a bald spot under his crowning wreath, to watch the battle.

Act III. The dashing young aesthete Apollodorus, with the help of the "venerable grotesque" Ftatateeta, succeeds in passing the Roman sentinels to present Cleopatra with a beautiful carpet. The sentinels refuse to let Cleopatra leave the palace grounds to visit Caesar at the lighthouse; but they allow Apollodorus to row out with the carpet, in which Cleopatra has, in the meantime, stowed herself. Britannus is scandalized when they arrive and the carpet is unrolled: "She cannot stay here, Caesar, without the companionship of some matron." Egyptian troops suddenly surround the quay and cut off the lighthouse; Apollodorus dives into the sea to swim to the Roman ships in the east harbor. Pitching the screaming Cleopatra into the sea for Caesar to carry on his back, Rufio follows Caesar into the water, while Britannus, who cannot swim, cheers.

Act IV. Some six months later, Cleopatra's growing maturity gains the grudging respect of Pothinus, who has come to invite her to plot against Caesar but now does not dare; he tells

Ftatateeta, however, that since Cleopatra is "a woman with a Roman heart," she shall not rule Egypt. At a palace roof banquet he warns Caesar that Cleopatra is a traitor who, once she has her crown, will not care what happens to him. With his customary sagacity, Caesar accepts this as perfectly natural and orders his release, but the furious Cleopatra secretly orders his execution. When Pothinus's death is reported, Caesar is horrified: "And so, to the end of history, murder shall breed murder, always in the name of right and honor and peace, until the gods are tired of blood and create a race that can understand." Soon enough he is proven right, for the city mobs are up in arms about the murder. Caesar hears that reinforcements are about to cross the Nile, and he works out a route to join them. Rufio finds out that Ftatateeta was the one who killed Pothinus and, fearing further treachery, he kills her.

Act V. Ready to depart for Rome after having defeated Ptolemy's troops, Caesar has appointed Rufio as governor. Cleopatra, dressed in mourning, demands punishment for Ftatateeta's murder, but when Rufio explains that he killed her as he would a wild beast, without moral judgment or vengeance, Caesar approves. Cleopatra stops sulking when Caesar makes her laugh and promises to send her Mark Antony. She weeps as he sails away.

CALCUTTA, MAY 4 (*Kalkutta, 4. Mai*), "a colonial history" in four acts by LION FEUCHTWANGER and BERTOLT BRECHT, published and produced in 1927. Setting: India, 1775.

Feuchtwanger based this play on his earlier novel and originally published it as *Warren Hastings, Gouverneur von Indien* (1916). It portrays the man who won India for the British (and became its first governor-general) in his conflicts with and execution of the Bengali Brahman Nuncomar. In the main the plot follows Macaulay's celebrated essay on Hastings, here characterized as a cruel but idealistic political superman triumphing over unimaginative bureaucracy. In the later collaborative version Brecht's touch is evident principally in the "Surabaya Johnny" sung by Hastings's mistress, Lady Marjorie Hike. (This song is used again in HAPPY END.)

CALIGULA, a play in four acts by ALBERT CAMUS, published in 1944 and produced in 1945. Setting: the imperial Roman palace, A.D. 38–41.

This, the most famous of Camus's plays, dramatizes the views of his seminal essay, *Le Mythe de Sisyphe* (*The Myth of Sisyphus,* 1942). Of the different versions of the play Camus produced between 1938 and 1958, the 1944 version is the one commonly used and the one he preferred. He followed Suetonius's account (in *Lives of the Twelve Caesars*) of the brief reign of Caligula, though the play's ideas, like its setting and language, are modern. It is, Camus wrote in his preface, "a tragedy of the intelligence" and portrays "the passion for the impossible, . . . illustrating the havoc it wreaks, bringing out its failure."

Act I. The patricians worry about Caligula: he disappeared three days ago, after the death of his beloved sister and mistress, Drusilla. Asked, when he left, what was amiss, his only answer was "Nothing." Soon Caligula comes in, looks into the mirror, and mutters. Then he tells his friend and aide Helicon that he wants "the impossible": "This world of ours, the scheme of things, as they call it, is quite intolerable. That's why I want the moon, or happiness, or eternal life." Through his grief he has discovered a great truth, which he will reveal to all: "Men die; and they are not happy." When one of the intendants alludes to the Treasury, Caligula decrees that all patricians shall will their money to the state: "As the need arises, we shall have these people die." Decided hereafter to eliminate lies and follow logic to its ultimate conclusions, Caligula explains, "If the Treasury has paramount importance, human life has none." To a former mistress, Caesonia, he confides his new "truth about love; it's nothing, nothing!" Therefore he will present a show wherein he, "the one free man in the Roman Empire," can express his convictions. Madly he hammers the gong and summons the staff, as the half-crazed Caesonia, who loves Caligula, agrees to stand by him. He stares at his image in the mirror and summons all to observe it: "An end of memories; no more masks."

Act II. It is three years later. The once decent Caligula now reigns with ruthless brutality. He decrees famine for the masses, and his killing and rapine extend freely among the humiliated patricians—including his former friends. One of them, Cherea, rallies the opposition. He recognizes Caligula's real evil: "He's putting his power at the service of a loftier, deadlier passion"—the promulgation of life's meaninglessness. Caligula's view —however logical it may seem—must be defeated to make life and happiness possible. Wantonly rude at dinner, Caligula quickly exhibits incredible cruelty. He jeers at a grieving patrician whose son he has just killed, and then debauches another patrician's wife in an adjoining room. "One is always free at someone else's expense. Absurd perhaps, but so it is," he tells the patrician. After pointlessly executing another patrician, he is still able to regain his young friend Scipio's love—though he has tortured and killed this poet's father. Caligula admits his lack of nobility—but claims "a keen appetite for life" and the solace of scorn.

Act III. Grotesquely costumed as Venus, Caligula commands sacrilegious public worship. Later he explains, "There's no understanding fate; therefore I choose to play the part of fate, I wear the foolish, unintelligible face of a professional god." When Helicon warns him about the conspiracy, Caligula reiterates his desire for the moon—the only thing he really wants. He summons the plot's ringleader, Cherea, and the one-time friends frankly voice their opposition. Cherea refuses to live in a topsy-turvy world that "pushes the absurd to its logical conclusion"; he seeks a life of happiness and security. Caligula answers, "Security and logic don't go together." As courageous as Cherea, however, he destroys the treasonable evidence and lets the surprised conspirator go free.

Act IV. Scipio cannot bring himself to join the plot: "Something inside me is akin to him." Caligula's teaching Scipio despair, says Cherea, is "the foulest of the crimes he has committed." At a poetry contest, a dozen poets step in to await and hear Caligula's command: "Subject: death. Time limit: one minute." They scribble furiously, and then, one by one, start reciting. But Caligula stops each with a whistle blast. Then he calls on Scipio, the only poet without a tablet, and the only one whose lines affect Caligula: "Pursuit of happiness that purifies the heart, / Skies rippling with light, / O wild, sweet, festal joys, frenzy without hope!" Alone with his mistress Caesonia, Caligula realizes that he has chosen a false happiness, "the murderous kind. . . . I know now that nothing, *nothing* lasts," he tells Caesonia, and strangles his unresisting mistress with "the ruthless logic that crushes out human lives." He looks into the mirror and is distressed with a new knowledge. He can never have the moon, and he himself is afraid—as afraid as were those he slew. He anticipates "that emptiness beyond all understanding, in which the heart has rest," and screams at his own reflection. It is the only thing he has ever found, and he has come to loathe it: "I have chosen a wrong path, a path that leads to nothing. My freedom isn't the right one." He hurls a stool at the mirror, and shatters it. The conspirators rush in and stab him to death. Gasping, choking, and laughing, he shrieks with his last breath, "I'm still alive!"

CALVARY, a one-act verse play by WILLIAM BUTLER YEATS, published in 1921 and produced in ?. Setting: a bare stage.

In the introduction to this last of the FOUR PLAYS FOR DANCERS, Yeats explains Christ's inability to save Lazarus and Judas, "types of that intellectual despair that lay beyond His sympathy"; the Roman gamblers, he notes, "suggest a form of objectivity that lay beyond His help."

The choral musician intones, "God has not died for the white heron." Christ encounters Lazarus and Judas. Both seek freedom: Lazarus in the solitude of death, Judas in independence from an all-powerful God. Before dicing for His cloak, three Roman soldiers express their contentment with chance; then they dance.

CALVO SOTELO, Joaquín (1905–   ), Spanish playwright, lawyer and lecturer, has also written short stories and has won a number of prizes for his many plays. Most of these dramatize the daily problems of ordinary Spaniards, and touch on such themes as morality, politics, and international relations. Mostly thesis plays, they are serious in intent as well as tone, though Calvo Sotelo has also written some sentimental pieces and farces. His drama first appeared in 1932, though he did not become important as a playwright until the 1950's. His most frequently performed and republished play is *La muralla* (1954), which has been likened to *O locura o santidad* by JOSÉ ECHEGARAY and which depicts the agonies and repentance of a conscience-stricken man who wrongfully acquired a hacienda but is prevented from returning it by his "sensible" family and friends.

Among other notable Calvo Sotelo plays are the prize-winning *La visita que no tocó el timbre* (1950), in which two brothers find an abandoned infant; *Criminal de guerra* (1951), about an American occupation army officer—ironically the title character—who helps the suicide of the father of the girl he loves, a German general discovered, too late, to have been innocent and pardoned; *El jefe* (1953), depicting a group of criminals on an island who themselves establish the kind of brutal, law-and-order society they earlier rebelled against; *Historia de un resentido* (1956), dramatizing the self-torture of a common modern type, an envious failure seething with hostility; *Una muchachita de Valladolid* (1957), a light comedy about a philandering diplomat and his young wife; and *La herencia* (1957), whose "inheritance" —the Civil War hatreds—is transmitted to the next generation and overcome only by love.

Calvo Sotelo's work is discussed in Richard E. Chandler and Kessel Schwartz's *A New History of Spanish Literature* (1961).

CAMBODIA. Since this small country became an independent kingdom in 1955, it has continued to emphasize and excel in the dance, most notably in the productions of the Royal Cambodian Ballet. Popular drama consists of JATAKAS and *lakon bassac,* the ancient Cambodian theatricals in forty to fifty scenes of romantic comedy, farce, dance, music, and song. After France's rule Cambodian drama remained influenced by the French who had introduced the modern theatre in Cambodia. Its many VIETNAMese shopkeepers and traders have their own theatre in Cambodia.

See the chapter on Cambodia in Faubion Bowers's *Theatre in the East* (1956) and James R. Brandon's *Theatre in Southeast Asia* (1967).

CAMINO REAL, a play in a Prologue and sixteen "Blocks" by TENNESSEE WILLIAMS, published and produced in 1953. Setting: an unspecified Latin American country.

This EXPRESSIONIST phantasmagoria, a theatrical allegory that appeared in different versions and partakes of the traditions of the masque and burlesque, is atypical of Williams's drama. Most audiences and critics have found its plot, symbolism, and poetry murky; but the play has had stalwart champions, and its 1960 and 1970 New York revivals were comparative successes. The ambiguous Spanish title alludes to the "Royal" or "Real Highway" of a brutal wasteland, an Inferno world of cruelty and squalor.

"Nothing wild or honest is tolerated" in this place, one of the characters notes. But Jacques

Casanova, king of the cuckolds at the festival of the virgin, is hopeful: "The violets in the mountains can break the rocks if you believe in them and allow them to grow." Other historical and legendary figures are Don Quixote, who first appears with Sancho Panza at the dry fountain that divides the village's rich and poor sections; Lord Byron, who recounts Shelley's cremation; Esmeralda (of Victor Hugo's *The Hunchback of Notre Dame*), who delivers a paean to the world's misfits, "all two-time losers who're likely to lose once more"; and an aging and desperate Marguerite Gautier (Camille), the sentimental courtesan popularized by Dumas fils. The principal character is America's mythical World War II figure, Kilroy, a down-and-out former "champ" with golden gloves and a heart of gold. He tries to escape, but after a wild chase is degraded by the villain, outfitted in a circus patsy's costume and a flashing nose, and finally stuffed into the street cleaners' can. Instead of dying, he snatches his heart out of the hands of the medical students, and races out. Esmeralda's mother ignominiously douses Kilroy: "Stewed, screwed, and tattooed on the Camino Real! Baptized, finally, with the contents of a slop-jar!" But Don Quixote urges him, "*Don't! Pity! Your! Self!*" The fountain begins to flow. *"The violets in the mountains have broken the rocks!"* Don Quixote exclaims, and walks out with Kilroy through the Triumphal Arch.

CAMUS, Albert (1913–1960), Algerian-born French philosopher and novelist, playwright, actor, and director, was concerned with drama more than is popularly recognized. He is best known as the Nobel Prize (1957) author of such influential works as *L'Étranger* (*The Stranger,* 1942), *La Peste* (*The Plague,* 1947), and *Le Mythe de Sisyphe* (*The Myth of Sisyphus,* 1942), whose philosophy was to label the theatre of the ABSURD. Of his four plays, only CALIGULA (1944) is generally known, although some of his adaptations became popular. But from as early as 1935 until the sudden end of his life, in an automobile accident that ironically illustrated his own vision of life's "absurdity," Camus loved and was deeply committed to the theatre. He dissociated himself from the philosophy of existentialism that popularly links his name with that of JEAN-PAUL SARTRE. Yet the thoughts that animate his drama—highly ideational and poetic drama, despite its theatricality—are concerned with the existentialist concept of cosmic meaninglessness, and with death. Camus's heroes recognize and rebel against these forces. It is this conflict and the quest for human decency and ethics that constitute the essence of Camus's drama.

Of French and Spanish extraction, Camus was born in Mondovi (near Constantine) and spent his first twenty-seven years in Algiers. His father, a day laborer, was killed in World War I when Camus was a year old. The child and his older brother lived in great poverty in an apartment with their illiterate mother, a partly paralyzed uncle, and a domineering, cancer-ridden grandmother. Tuberculosis temporarily checked Camus's energy in 1930, but immobilization in the clinic's public ward apparently stimulated his human awareness and his intellect. Helped by teachers, he eventually was able to study philosophy at the University of Algiers, where he completed a thesis in 1936 on Plotinus and Saint Augustine. During the 1930's he held odd jobs, married a physician's daughter, and joined the Communist Party; both attachments proved disappointing and short-lived. He remarried later, and out of his political work came the establishment of the Workers' Theatre (Le Théâtre du travail, 1935), of which he was the guiding light. For it he helped write the "collective" amateur play *La Révolte dans les Asturies* (1936), his first dramatic venture, an experimental, ritualistic work that portrayed a recent miners' revolt in Oviedo. Until the dissolution of the Workers' Theatre in 1939 (long after it broke away from the Party), Camus was its leading writer and adapter as well as the director and an actor. At that time he also completed the first version of his best play, *Caligula.*

In 1940 Camus went to France, where he was active in the underground newspaper *Combat* throughout World War II. *The Stranger,* which appeared at that time, was soon to gain him international fame. His four plays—aside from *Caligula* there are *Le Malentendu* (THE MISUNDERSTANDING, also produced as *Cross Purpose*), *L'État de siège* (STATE OF SIEGE), and *Les Justes* (THE JUST)—came out in the years 1944–49. But more popular on the boards than most of his own plays were his adaptations, particularly those of Faulkner's *Requiem for a Nun* (*Requiem pour une nonne,* 1956) and Dostoevsky's *The Possessed* (*Les Possédés,* 1959). Other adaptations include one of Pierre de Larivey's sixteenth-century comedy *Les Esprits* (1953, written while Camus was still in Algiers), Calderón's *La devoción de la cruz* (*La Dévotion à la croix,* 1953), and Lope de Vega's *El caballero de Olmedo* (*Le Chevalier d'Olmedo,* posthumously published in Camus's complete works, 1962).

These adaptations—particularly the first two mentioned—reflect Camus's philosophical perspective as much as do his original plays. Like them, the adaptations are strongly charged with ideas. The form of Camus's drama, however, does not match the originality of his thoughts, and its distinction falls below that of his fiction and his other writing. Aside from *Caligula,* Camus's plays—despite the operatic spectacle of a work like *State of Siege* and the harrowing, stark melodrama of the other plays—have proved to be more successful in the study than on the stage. Intellectual and philosophical, they are singularly disembodied and lifeless, considering Camus's grasp and experience of and interest in the details of practical theatre production. Nonetheless, his *Caligula* as well as his adaptations of Faulkner and Dostoevsky suggest Camus's potential as a dramatist. At the time of his death he was writing a drama on Don Juan, a theme with which he had been long preoccupied and one to which he might have given artistically successful expression, as he had done to *The Myth of Sisyphus.*

His plays are readily available in English translation in *Caligula and Three Other Plays* (1958). Albert Maquet's *Albert Camus: The Invincible Summer* (1958) and Germaine Brée's *Camus* (revised edition, 1961) are among the many studies of his life and work. These and other books on Camus have bibliographies, but the most comprehensive listing of works by and about Camus is Robert F. Roeming's *Camus: A Bibliography* (1968).

CANADA. The development of a Canadian theatre has been impeded by the country's vastness and its sparse population, composed of different national stocks. Because of Canada's bilingual (English and French) tradition, there are two distinct theatres and dramas. Canadian drama, which is generally unknown abroad, has been more commonly produced by amateur and community groups (many affiliated with universities) than in professional theatres, though these existed long before the renowned Stratford (Ontario) Festival was launched in 1953. Other festivals have featured work by native dramatists who have won competitions for the annual Dominion Drama Festivals (DDF) that began in 1932. But Canada's proximity to Broadway has tended to siphon off native playwriting as well as performing talent (numerous famous "English" and "American" stars have been native Canadians), and much of the professional theatrical activity consists of visiting French, English, and United States companies.

Native drama, nonetheless, has appeared in the twentieth century. After World War I, the rise of the little theatre movement prompted a spate of original plays. In the 1920's and 1930's many of them were written for production in Hart House Theatre, at the University of Toronto, and elsewhere. Among recent English-Canadian playwrights, the most impressive has been James Reaney (1926–), a poet turned dramatist; the imagery and atmosphere of his pastoral comedies are particularly evocative, though their farcical structure sometimes negates the terrifying events on which his plots are based, as in his finest work, *The Killdeer* (1960), a portrayal of youths passing from innocence through experience to wisdom. Also acclaimed in mid-century were the Indian-born Lister Sinclair (1921–) and Robertson Davies (1913–). The former's *The Blood Is Strong* (1956) satirizes reactionary old-time Scots settlers in the Maritime provinces, but Sinclair is better known for his ambitious dramatization of the life and death of *Socrates* (1957) and for *A Play on Words and Other Radio Plays* (1948). Davies, a popular novelist, was equally successful with a collection of witty, farcical one-act satires of Canadian life (*Eros at Breakfast,* 1949), the best known of which, *Overlaid,* is set in backwoods Ontario; with *Fortune, My Foe* (1948), a serious play about a Canadian professor lured to the United States, which, despite its attractions, is shown as a less desirable place; and with another full-length drama, *At My Heart's Core* (1950), set in 1837 in Upper Canada and featuring a mysterious protagonist who fails to persuade three wives to abandon their husbands and barren environment in order to realize their individual potentials.

Older English-Canadian dramatists include Merrill Denison (1893–), who before settling in the United States produced light and mostly one-act comedies like those collected as *The Unheroic North* (1923): *From Their Own Place, The Weather Breeder, Marsh Hay,* and *Brothers in Arms,* a satire of middle-class values; and the Irish-born John Coulter (1888–), distinguished for his character portrayals and spirited dialogue, as in the Irish Civil War drama *The Drums Are Out* (1951) and in *Riel* (1962), a play about the Canadian Northwest Rebellion and its leader, Louis Riel, which has been hailed as Canada's finest historical drama. A few plays by Canadians have reached Broadway and English stages, notably Bruce Marshall's (1899–) adaptation in 1936 of Brian Doherty's sentimental comic novel, *Father Malachy's Miracle* (1931); and more recently, John Herbert's (1928–) *Fortune and Men's Eyes* (1967), a depiction of penal viciousness and homosexuality, based on Herbert's own experiences in a reformatory.

French Canada's theatre began only recently. It was launched with *Tit-Coq* (1948), a popular and soon-filmed romantic comedy about a soldier ashamed of his illegitimacy, by Gratien Gélinas (1909–), Canada's outstanding French actor-manager-playwright, and director of the Théâtre de la Comédie Canadienne; however, the play failed when it was produced (in English) in New York. French Canada's most prolific playwright in mid-century, Marcel Dubé (1930–), portrays socially alienated characters like the protagonist of his comedy *Un Simple Soldat* (1958).

Canada on Stage (1960) is a good collection of one-act plays: it has a brief introduction on Canadian drama by Stanley Richards. Among other collections are the two-volume *Plays from Hart House Theatre* (1926–27), introduced by Vincent Massey. Malcolm Ross's handsome collection, *The Arts in Canada* (1958), has chapters on drama and theatre, as does *Literary History of Canada* (1965), edited by Carl F. Klinck, which includes a bibliography. While Desmond Pacey considered Canadian drama too "negligible" to warrant separate sections in his *Creative Writing in Canada* (revised 1961), he describes what drama there is in some detail, and the book has a very extensive bibliography.

CANDIDA, a play in three acts by BERNARD SHAW, produced in 1895 and published in 1898. Setting: London, an October day in 1894.

One of the "pleasant" plays, *Candida* has fascinated audiences and readers with its enigmatic heroine and the poet's "secret," which Shaw suggested is his final understanding and rejection of the "greasy fool's paradise" of every-day marriage (letter to James Huneker, 1904). Though the play contains a searching analysis of conventional morality and marriage (as in Ibsen's LOVE'S COMEDY, whose heroine, like Candida, must choose), the analysis is integral to the plot, and the play ends with marriage emerging victorious. Stephen S. Stanton's *A Casebook on Candida* (1962) is a handy collection of source material, criticisms, and interpretations of the play.

Act I. The Reverend James Mavor Morell, a suave and successful Christian Socialist, is visited by his father-in-law, the coarse merchant Burgess. He comes to make up after a quarrel with Morell, who caused him to lose a contract by denouncing the sweat conditions in his shop. To the jealous annoyance of the secretary Proserpine ("Prossy") Garnett, a spinster who adores Morell, his beautiful wife Candida unexpectedly returns from a holiday; with her is the effeminate and shy Eugene Marchbanks, an eighteen-year-old poet whom Morell has befriended. Though badly frightened, Marchbanks tells Morell, when Candida leaves the room, that he loves her; he finally succeeds in angering the complacent Morell by telling him that Candida, "a great soul, craving for reality, truth, freedom," must despise her husband for his eternal "metaphors, sermons, stale perorations, mere rhetoric." When Morell orders him out of the house, Marchbanks, though almost frightening himself "into a fit," accuses Morell of cowardice: "You are driving me out of the house because you darent let her choose between your ideas and mine. You are afraid to let me see her again." Morell is badly shaken when Candida returns and asks Marchbanks to stay for lunch.

Act II. Marchbanks is disconcerted to learn from the conventionally scandalized Prossy that women can, indeed, love Morell. In an attempt to cheer him up, Candida guilelessly tells Morell that he owes his great success in part to the many women who come not for moral edification but to hear and see him, all of them suffering from "Prossy's complaint"—infatuation with Morell. She expresses her hope that Marchbanks, who is ready for love, will some day forgive her for not having been the one who taught him about it. Her love for Morell restrains her from doing so, not her "goodness and purity" and the other fancy "phrases" he always uses. When Marchbanks comes in, he is upset to see the husband's great suffering. But to test Candida, Morell decides to deliver the public address he had canceled when he heard of Candida's unexpected return, and he insists that Marchbanks stay with her: "I shall shew him how much afraid I am by leaving him here in your custody." Marchbanks is overwhelmed with Morell's poetic gesture: "Thats brave. Thats beautiful."

Act III. Marchbanks, placed on his honor, stops reading sonnets to Candida, and is worshipfully repeating her name, when Morell returns. He tells the frantic husband that they must both give her up: "Why should she have to choose between a wretched little nervous disease like me, and a pig-headed parson like you?" Following an interruption by Prossy, Burgess, and others who have been celebrating after Morell's address, the two ask Candida to choose between them. Morell offers "my strength for your defence, my honesty for your surety, my ability and industry for your livelihood, and my authority and position for your dignity"; Marchbanks offers "My weakness. My desolation. My heart's need." Candida decides to give herself "to the weaker of the two" —Morell. In a speech in which she details the banalities of her domestic chores, she tells Marchbanks how she is Morell's "mother and three sisters and wife and mother to his children all in one," and how she is building "a castle of comfort and indulgence and love for him." Morell is overcome with new insight, and so, perhaps, is Marchbanks, who leaves them, walking out into the night; but (according to the final stage direction) "they do not know the secret in the poet's heart."

CAP AND BELLS (*Il berretto a sonagli*), a comedy in three acts by LUIGI PIRANDELLO, produced in 1917 and published in 1920. Setting: a small town in contemporary Sicily.

This bitter comedy suggests that truth is possible only to the mad, and that the sane are doomed to misery. The protagonist, Ciampa, is Pirandello's mouthpiece in much the same way as is Toti in JUST THINK, GIACOMINO!

A malicious friend goads Beatrice Fiorica to punish her husband's adultery with the wife of Ciampa, his ugly old bookkeeper. During Ciampa's absence Beatrice has the lovers surprised and arrested. Ciampa is crushed: he knew of his wife's adultery, but by ignoring it had maintained the respectable front that is now destroyed. He feels ruined by the scandal, which he does not want to resolve by killing his wife and her lover. A way out is suddenly discovered by Ciampa and Beatrice's family, who are reluctant to have her return to live with them. They decide to declare Beatrice temporarily insane and send her to an asylum for a few months. It will be easy to act mad, Ciampa tells her: "It is enough for you to shout out the truth. Nobody will believe and all will take you for mad." In fact, he envies her the chance "to snatch completely open the mad switch, to put on, down to [one's] ears, the cap and bells of madness." Beatrice shrieks hysterically and is carried out. Ciampa remains alone, "breaking forth into a horrible laughter of rage, of cruel pleasure, of desperation."

ČAPEK, Karel (1890–1938), Czechoslovakian novelist and playwright, is best known for his utopian fiction and drama. The most popular of his works have been a novel, *Válka s mloky* (*The War with the Newts,* 1936), and two plays: *Ze života hmyzu* (FROM THE LIFE OF INSECTS, 1920, also translated under many other titles) and R.U.R. (1920). The first of these plays was written with

Karel's brother, Josef,* a frequent collaborator whose career was intertwined with his own and to whom he was very close. Almost all of Čapek's works are fantasies. In the guise of the marvelous he set forth his philosophic speculations about technology, warfare, totalitarianism, and their effect on individuals in a democracy. Although not discursive "discussion" dramas, his plays are no less probingly ideational than those of BERNARD SHAW, who called Čapek "a prolific and terrific playwright."

Čapek was born in Malé Svatoňovice, a Czech village near the German border. He was the third child (there was also a girl, Helena Čapková, who became a minor writer) of a country doctor and an intellectual but sickly mother from whom Čapek probably inherited his own physical frailty. The family moved to Prague in 1907, and after studying there, in Berlin, and in France, Karel wrote a dissertation on aesthetics and received his doctor's degree in 1915. He had been publishing stories, some together with Josef, since 1908. They wrote their first drama in 1910: *Lásky hra osudná* (1916), a one-act spoof of SYMBOLIST art and the *commedia dell'arte*. Physically unable to serve during World War I, Karel became a tutor on an estate, then turned to journalism (a profession he pursued throughout his life), and translated French symbolist poetry. His first full-length play was *Loupežník* (1920), a comedy of love frustrated by parental interference; it is written in prose and verse, and is a mixture of NATURALISM and symbolism, as well as farce, melodrama, and tragedy.

In about 1920 began his long friendship with and love of Olga Scheinpflugová, an actress who later became prominent; he did not marry her until 1935, when he was informed that his spinal disease was quiescent. Following the production of his two most famous plays he became the director of the Prague City Theatre (1921–23), where he staged, among other plays, *Věc Makropulos* (THE MAKROPULOS SECRET, 1922). It was followed by the last drama written jointly with his brother Josef, *Adam stvořitel* (ADAM THE CREATOR, 1927). Its relative failure ended Josef's career as a playwright completely, and stopped Karel's for ten years. He continued his journalistic work, wrote novels, pursued his nature studies and other hobbies, and traveled. His interest in politics was stimulated by a close friendship with Czechoslovakia's President Tomáš Masaryk, about whom Čapek wrote a number of books (1928–35).

Karel Čapek in 1935. (*East Photo*)

A Czech patriot, socialist, and democrat who worked for the Republic, Čapek became increasingly disturbed by the rise of Fascism. But despite his apparently total political involvement, he wrote and published in the crucial years 1933–34 the trilogy critics have hailed as his masterpiece—the novels *Hordubal, Povětroň* (*Meteor*), and *Obyčejný život* (*An Ordinary Life*).

Čapek's ambivalent feelings about war appear to have diminished as the totalitarian threat grew. His writing aroused the fury of Czech rightists, and was said to have cost Čapek the Nobel Prize because of Sweden's presumed reluctance to antagonize Germany. Increased depression after the Munich Pact aggravated his illness, and he died of lung inflammation on Christmas Day, 1938. When the Nazis entered Prague three months later, his widow hurriedly destroyed many of his papers, especially his extensive correspondence.

Karel Čapek's last two plays were EXPRESSIONIST antiwar tragedies. *Bílá nemoc* (*The White Plague*, 1937; produced in England as *Power and Glory*) depicts people over forty (the noncombatant, managerial class) being decimated by a fatal disease; only one doctor can cure them, but he refuses to treat patients who decline to work for peace. In *Matka* (*The Mother*, 1938), the title's unnamed protagonist loses her sons in battle: they reappear as ghosts, and justify to the uncomprehending mother the defense of their ideals which led to their deaths; when an enemy invades the country, the mother is able to send the remaining son to war. Čapek was undoubtedly affected

* Josef Čapek (1887-1945) was also a journalist, and he wrote essays, stories, and three plays: *Zemé mnoha jmen* (*Land of Many Names*, 1923); *Dobré to dopadlo aneb Tlustý pradedeček, lupiči a detektývové* (1932), a dramatization of his children's story with a similar title; and *Jak pejsek s kočičkou slavili 28. říjen* (1933), a puppet play about the Czech independence day. But Josef Čapek was most notable as a leading Czech painter of the Cubist school. When the Nazis took over Czechoslovakia in 1939, he was sent to a concentration camp, where he died a few weeks before the end of World War II.

by the contemporary threat of Nazism in thus resolving the painful problems adumbrated in his play.

Čapek was an immensely productive writer, though he completed only eight plays (three of them with his brother Josef). Even these few, however, have established his position among important modern dramatists. The plays may have achieved popularity for the wrong reasons. But their science-fiction plots do not negate their theatrical power—or the significance of their content. A more valid criticism is that Čapek's characters are often nonhuman. His people are no more developed or rounded than his insects and his robots, for the most part. (The protagonist of *The Makropulos Secret* is one of the few exceptions.) The philosophic ambiguities that so often confuse his themes (as do the resolutions of his most famous plays) are thus reflected in a final paradox: Čapek's concern with individuals—who are portrayed without individuality. Yet his awareness of the relativity of values and his agonizing exploration of these values invested his theatre and spectacle with a meaning that has made his drama increasingly relevant in a post-Čapek age.

Čapek's plays are generally available in English. Comprehensive studies of his life, work, and ideas are William E. Harkins's *Karel Čapek* (1962) and Alexander Matuška's *Karel Čapek, Man Against Destruction: An Essay* (1964); both books include bibliographies.

CAPOTE, Truman (1924–), American novelist, dramatized his *The Grass Harp* (1951) the following year and helped make it into a musical, *Yellow Drum,* in 1968. Like the wistful novel, the play depicts the private, romantic tree-house world of sensitive souls who ultimately return to the world of reality. The Louisiana-born Capote also wrote a musical comedy set in a West Indies brothel, *The House of Flowers* (1954). A lavish musical production of *Breakfast at Tiffany's* (1958), his novel about a zany girl camping out in New York, though it was successfully filmed, was canceled just before opening on Broadway in 1966.

CAPTAIN BRASSBOUND'S CONVERSION, "An Adventure" in three acts by BERNARD SHAW, produced in 1899 and published in 1901. Setting: Morocco, 1890's.

In his "Notes" to this, the most exotic of the THREE PLAYS FOR PURITANS, Shaw acknowledged Cunninghame Graham as his source for the Eastern scenery and tribesmen, and discussed his orthography (there being no "phonetic alphabet") for the various dialects, particularly Drinkwater's Cockney speech. Interesting accounts of the play appear in Shaw's correspondence with Ellen Terry.

Lady Cicely Waynflete, arriving in Morocco with Sir Howard Hallam, her brother-in-law and a prominent judge, insists on visiting the nearby mountains, though they are full of dangerous native tribes. At the suggestion of the Cockney scoundrel Felix Drinkwater, they hire for their escort a grim young brigand, Captain Brassbound. In a Moorish castle in the mountains, Brassbound has Hallam arrested: he is Brassbound's uncle, who many years ago had appropriated his father's estate and caused his mother's death. In a delightful comic scene, the persuasive Lady Cicely gets Brassbound to give up his romantic notions of vengeance. The sheik, who was to have Hallam for a slave, is willing to give him up for ransom and for the charming Lady Cicely. But they are all taken into custody by an expedition headed by a cadi sent by Hamlin Kearney, an American gunboat captain, to rescue the English travelers. Brassbound wonders whether Lady Cicely will be able to persuade Hallam, who now has him in his power, to spare him, as she had persuaded him to spare Hallam earlier. Before Brassbound's trial for abducting them begins, Lady Cicely prevails upon Hallam to let her do the talking. At the inquiry held by Kearney, she deftly but truthfully tells what happened and gets Brassbound exonerated. Talking to him in private, she induces Brassbound to destroy the documents he had kept to spur his vengeance. In turn, she is mesmerized by his new power; he asks her to marry him and she is about to accept him, when a broadside from his ship breaks the spell. He thanks her "for a man's power and purpose restored and righted," and dashes away to the pirate ship. She too is relieved by the outcome: "How glorious! And what an escape!"

CAPTAIN JINKS OF THE HORSE MARINES, "A Fantastic Comedy" in three acts by CLYDE FITCH, produced in 1901 and published in 1902. Setting: New York, early 1870's.

This once-popular play, republished in Volume 4 of Eric Bentley's *The Modern Theatre* (1956), provided Ethel Barrymore with one of her first starring roles. In 1925 it was made into a musical comedy that featured the 1880's song hit "Shoo, Fly, Don't Bodder Me." A frothy but still amusing period piece with numerous zany characters, the play has a slight plot that centers on the romance of an idealized young opera singer and the title hero, a dandy. Her love reforms him, but his former indiscretions with evil companions threaten their union. All misunderstandings are cleared up after the heroine's triumphant debut, and the lovers are united.

CAPTAIN OF KÖPENICK, THE (*Der Hauptmann von Köpenick*), "a German fairy tale in three acts" by CARL ZUCKMAYER, published in 1930 and produced in 1931. Setting: Berlin and environs, early twentieth century.

An actual occurrence that became a national joke inspired the plot of this popular folk comedy. Filmed, translated, and revived periodically, it has been compared to Hauptmann's THE BEAVER COAT and praised as one of Germany's finest modern comedies. In twenty-one fast-moving scenes Zuckmayer ridicules narrow-minded Prussian bureaucracy and veneration of

Captain Jinks of the Horse Marines. Right to left: Captain Jinks (H. Reeves Smith), the opera singer (Ethel Barrymore), and two ladies (Sidney Cowell and Fanny A. Pitt). New York, 1901. (*Culver Pictures*)

the military. Voigt, the victimized "little man," rebels and becomes the impudent protagonist of rollicking merriment as he outwits officialdom and its eternal and stupid red tape.

Act I. Wilhelm Voigt, a forty-six-year-old cobbler timidly entering a Potsdam shop, is driven away by the tailor, who is fitting a captain for a new uniform. Voigt tries to get a residence permit but is turned down when the police note his fifteen-year prison record for forgery committed as a boy. Since that record will forever prevent his getting work, Voigt asks for a passport to leave Prussia, but is told passports are handled by another office. In a café, Voigt and a friend fight with a couple of soldiers over some girls. The captain, whose new uniform is not yet ready, intervenes and is arrested along with the common soldiers—for in civilian dress his claims to being an officer are not recognized. "See," Voigt concludes, "you're judged by how you look." The humiliated captain resigns his commission and returns the uniform. As Voigt can get no work without papers, he decides, while lodged in a flophouse, to destroy his files and steal work and residence papers. The tailor reads newspaper accounts of an unsuccessful break into the police station, and then waits on a smug newly commissioned lieutenant eager to buy the captain's uniform.

Act II. In the ten years that have followed, the imprisoned Voigt has studied an army manual. His knowledge of military details impresses the prison governor, who celebrates the anniversary of a battle by having the prisoners reenact it. After his release, Voigt visits his married sister in Rixdorf but soon is ordered to leave the municipality for lack of the residence papers he tries to, but cannot, procure. In nearby Köpenick the mayor and his wife anxiously await a new uniform from the Potsdam tailor. When it arrives, the mayor's wife sends the old captain's uniform away. It gets soiled and ruined at a banquet attended by the tailor, who decides to sell it to a second-hand clothes dealer. Voigt in the meantime despairs about his papers, and is deeply upset by the death of a sick little child to whom he read fairy tales, including the Grimm brothers' with the line Voigt stresses: "One can always find something better than death." Returning from the funeral he says, "One day each of us kicks the bucket and stands before God and He'll ask you: 'Wilhelm Voigt, what did you do with your life?'" Realizing that he has been nothing but a doormat all his life, Voigt concludes that God will say, "For that I didn't give you life." And so Voigt decides to let himself be pushed around no more.

Act III. Voigt buys the old captain's uniform and, when he appears in it, readily persuades some veterans that he is an officer, and intimidates a lieutenant in a railway-station rest room. Then he proceeds to the town hall in nearby Köpenick and orders some soldiers to arrest the mayor and the town treasurer. Fawned upon by local officials,

Voigt collects the town funds and has the leading officials imprisoned in the New Fortress in Berlin. Then he gives the soldiers money and orders them to report to the New Fortress. Two weeks later Voigt is lying in a drunken stupor in a beer hall. He hears customers laugh at news reports of an impostor who got away with the Köpenick funds. The merriment continues over the "practical joker" for whose arrest there is a reward. Voigt sadly mutters, "If they only knew . . ." He offers to reveal the impostor's identity in exchange for a passport. When his offer is accepted, Voigt surrenders himself as the bogus captain. He does not know how he can prove it to the Berlin police: "You got to do that, I ain't no educated criminal." As they fetch the uniform with the railroad luggage check he gives them, Voigt explains how he arrested the mayor by mistake: he was after a passport, but got to the wrong municipality. Now he is willing to serve another prison sentence, for "that passes, I'm used to that. But this running around without papers, hiding, and all that stuff—that I can't take anymore." Amused by the joke and by Voigt's attitude, the police ply him with wine as he explains how easy it was to pull off his trick: "Any kid knows that with us one can do anything with the military act." Voigt becomes cockier as he keeps drinking. He returns all the money he requisitioned except a small sum he duly accounts for, and assures the police he never stole. "All I want is peace and freedom," he says; "and the only one I ever had to fight was the authorities." But he does want to see just what he looks like in the old uniform with which he bamboozled a whole town. He puts it on and stands before the mirror, wineglass in hand. Looking at himself as "the captain" for the first time, Voigt starts laughing until tears roll down his cheeks. His laughter explodes into a single word: "Incredible!!"

CAPUS, [Vincent Marie] **Alfred** (1858–1922), French novelist, journalist, and playwright, was popular in Paris at the turn of the century for his amusing dramas of contemporary life. JULES LEMAÎTRE praised the originality and keen perception that underlay Capus's indulgent optimism, considering him "vastly more significant than the great mass of Parisian goods and psychological studies of greater renown." But even Lemaître did not credit Capus with brilliance, and he is little remembered today though some of his plays were translated and appeared on Broadway.

Born in Aix-en-Provence, Capus studied mine engineering but soon turned to writing. After publishing stories and sketches he became interested in the theatre. The Gallic wit of his novels and journalistic pieces brought him popularity and, eventually, the coeditorship of the *Figaro*. But he fared less well with his first plays. *Brignol et sa fille* (*Brignol and His Daughter,* 1894) ran only a week, though it was successfully revived later. It is typical of his subsequent plays: the daughter of its carefree title character, a scoundrel, confirms his belief that "everything will turn out all right in the end" by marrying the nephew of his creditor, thus averting ruin. Among Capus's most popular plays was *La Veine* (1901), a charming little illustration of the validity of trusting in one's "luck." His other plays are *La Petite Fonctionnaire* (1901), whose poor heroine scandalizes the town by attracting admirers and eventually a husband to support her—a theme treated more seriously by EUGÈNE BRIEUX; and *Les Deux Écoles* (*The Two Schools,* 1902), a popular light piece on divorce and the economic subservience of wives—a topic that served for another Brieux PROBLEM PLAY. Capus was more serious but less successful in such sentimental and didactic pieces as *La Châtelaine* (1902, produced in America as *The Brighter Side*), *L'Attentat* (1906; written with Lucien Descaves, 1861–1949), and *L'Aventurier* (*The Adventurer,* 1910). Light comedy and intrigue drama were more in Capus's line. His genial, indulgent cynicism provided happy resolutions that subordinate idealism to man's practical needs. Such plays and the appealing scoundrels that people them brought Capus distinction, climaxed by his election to the French Academy in 1914.

Of his plays, only *Brignol and His Daughter* is accessible in English; Barrett H. Clark's *Contemporary French Dramatists* (1916) has a chapter on Capus and a bibliography.

CARETAKER, THE, a play in three acts by HAROLD PINTER, published and produced in 1960. Setting: the dilapidated and cluttered room of a house in west London; winter, c. 1960.

This was the first popular success achieved by Pinter, who also wrote the film version (1962). The play presents characteristic settings, themes, and farce-tragedy—as in the earlier THE DUMB WAITER and THE BIRTHDAY PARTY—but in a more REPRESENTATIONAL, less Kafkaesque manner. Nonetheless highly suggestive as well as amusing, it has been variously interpreted, like his previous full-length play, *The Birthday Party*. It may portray the common man (Davies) or the more perceptive or rebellious man (Aston) being destroyed by society, or the viciousness of a man unwittingly causing the reconciliation of brothers, or a study of fraternal jealousy. According to still other views, the room is a refuge from the world to all three—and the tramp's final ejection "assumes almost the cosmic proportions of Adam's expulsion from Paradise" (Martin Esslin's *The Theatre of the Absurd,* 1961).

Act I. Mick, a young man wearing a leather jacket, leaves the room as he hears his older brother come into the house. The laconic Aston is accompanied by Mac Davies, a dirty and malicious old cadger he befriended and invited home when the latter was fired from his job after a quarrel. Irascibly muttering about the "Greeks," "Poles," and the "blacks" who live next door, Davies vaguely talks of his intention to get his identity papers from Sidcup as soon as he has proper shoes and the weather improves. "They prove who I am," says the old man, who has lost

The Caretaker. Alan Bates (left) and Donald Pleasance, reenacting their stage roles of Mick and Davies in the film, 1962. (*Janus Film Library*)

his identity since he changed his name; "I'm stuck without them." Aston in the meantime tries to repair an electric plug. He gives Davies his own bed, but the old man—comic with his boasts, cringing, and cussedness—becomes increasingly demanding and inconsiderate. When Aston goes out the next morning, Davies starts rummaging around. Mick quietly enters, observes him, and frightens Davies with a mock assault. Then he sits down without any expression and watches the old man for a while. Finally he asks, "What's the game?"

Act II. A few seconds later he demands, "Well?" Then Mick alternately humors, bullies, and confuses him, recalling—at length—various people Davies reminds him of. Aston returns with a suitcase for Davies, from whom Mick keeps grabbing it. After a few words to Aston about redecorating the house, Mick leaves. He is Aston's brother and owns the place but lives elsewhere, Aston tells Davies and offers to make Davies the caretaker of the house. Later, in the dark, Mick frightens Davies with a vacuum cleaner. After suggesting that Aston is a slow worker, Mick, too, offers Davies the caretaker's job. Asked for references, Davies tells Mick about the papers he is waiting to pick up at Sidcup. The next morning, however, when Aston wakes him up, Davies decides the weather is not right. He complains about the open window and asks about the wood outside. It is for a shed he is building, Aston explains. Then, in a long, halting monologue, Aston talks about his past. He "used to have kind of hallucinations. . . . I used to get the feeling I could see things . . . very clearly." He was taken to a hospital, and eventually forced into electric shock treatment. Though he struggled, "big pincers, with wires on," were put on his head. After that "my thoughts . . . had become very slow. . . . I couldn't look to the right or the left, I had to look straight in front of me." Aston concludes, remembering the doctor, "I've often thought of going back and trying to find the man who did that to me. But I want to do something first. I want to build that shed out in the garden."

Act III. Two weeks later Davies is complaining to Mick about Aston. Mick ruminates about his dream to turn the place into a penthouse. Describing his ideas in detail, he concludes it could be made into a palace for his brother and himself. He asks Davies to talk to Aston about it, but Davies hedges. After Mick leaves, Aston comes with shoes for Davies. The old tramp criticizes them, and gradually becomes abusive. He warns Aston that his brother is now his friend, and has his eyes on Aston: "So don't you start mucking me about." Then, feeling superior when he remembers Aston's monologue, he viciously alludes to it: "Treating me like a bloody animal! I never been inside a nuthouse!" When he pulls his knife out, Aston suggests that Davies find himself another place, and offers him money to help him get to Sidcup. Davies sneers about the unbuilt shed and angrily goes to fetch Mick. But his hopes from that quarter quickly fade. "You're the only man I've told . . . about my deepest wishes," Mick says, and discards Davies as a stinking liar and a troublemaker. Aston returns, and the brothers briefly smile at each other before Mick goes out. Desperately Davies tries to reestablish himself with Aston: "I'll be your man, you say the word," offering to take either bed, begging not to be thrown out. "I've got that shed to get up. If I don't get it up now it'll never go up. Until it's up I can't get started," Aston remarks, and turns away from Davies: "You make too much noise." The undeserving old scamp falters pitifully: "Listen . . . if I . . . got down . . . if I was to . . . get my papers . . . would you . . . would you let . . . would you . . . if I got down . . . and got my. . . ."

CAROUSEL, a musical comedy in two acts by Richard Rodgers and OSCAR HAMMERSTEIN II, produced in 1945 and published in 1946. Setting: a New England coastal town, 1873.

This musical version (score by Hammerstein's frequent composer-collaborator, Richard Rodgers) of Benjamin F. Glazer's (1887–1956) adaptation of Molnár's LILIOM was filmed in 1956 and has been frequently revived. It follows Molnár's play closely, except that the original Hungarian locale is changed to an American one. Idiom and general flavor are changed accordingly: the characters are native types—the protagonists are the small-town girl Julie Jordan and the Yankee amusement-park barker Billy Bigelow—and there are such other American features as a clambake and Virginia creepers.

CARRION (*Neveyle*), a play in four acts by PERETZ HIRSHBEIN, published in 1905 and produced in 1908. Setting: an East European province, early twentieth century.

This early Hirshbein play is the most important of those produced by his company in Odessa. Its browbeaten heroine yearns for the richness life might offer. Because he smells of the carcasses with which he deals, she rejects one of her suitors. Losing her and resentful of his heritage, the lover goes mad and butchers his father.

CARROLL, Paul Vincent (1900–68), Irish dramatist, established his reputation with one of the important plays produced at the Abbey Theatre, SHADOW AND SUBSTANCE (1937). It was followed —but not at the Abbey—by his much-praised THE WHITE STEED (1939). Carroll has been likened to SEAN O'CASEY. But though Carroll, too, castigates the Irish clergy for its repressive zeal, his subject matter is different, and the artistry of his drama falls considerably below that of O'Casey's work, and his dialogue lacks the sustained, poetic power. Though he continued to produce plays in the next decades, none of Carroll's later works achieved either the artistic or the popular success of his two best-known works.

Carroll was born in County Louth, Ireland, the setting of many of his plays. He became a schoolmaster, like his father, after he completed his education in St. Patrick's Training College for Teachers, in Dublin. There he frequently visited the Abbey Theatre, and was inspired by its possibilities for reviving Irish culture. He lived through the upheavals of the Irish revolution that constitutes the setting of O'Casey's famous plays. But these events hardly ever appear in Carroll's drama.

In 1921 he took a teaching position in Glasgow, Scotland, where such employment did not have to be humbly solicited from the local priest, as in Ireland. He started to write plays that were, at first, promptly rejected and sent back to him by the Abbey directors. It was not until 1930 that his first play, *The Watched Pot,* was staged, at the Abbey's experimental wing, the Peacock Theatre. At the time, Carroll wrote under the influence of LEO TOLSTOI; the play was so gloomy that, the author later noted, it elicited laughs. Carroll came under the influence of HENRIK IBSEN, and wrote the social criticisms that one finds in his other plays. His debut at the Abbey proper was with *Things That Are Caesar's* (1932), a strong play whose anticlerical bias (in its portrayal of one bigoted and one liberal parent's struggle over their daughter) was handled with sufficient delicacy to make it inoffensive—and the play was a hit.

Carroll returned to Scotland to resume his teaching, determined eventually to make playwriting his career. It was five years before he could do so, after the production of his masterpiece, *Shadow and Substance.* It was followed by the one-act *The Coggerers,* on the Easter Rebellion, later that year. Carroll was disappointed and surprised when his next major play, *The White Steed,* was rejected by the Abbey. When it failed to take New York by storm, he returned to the Abbey in 1939 with *Kindred,* a play in six scenes. Its failure harmed the future of Carroll as much as that of the Abbey Theatre. Only one more play of his was to be produced there, *The Wise Have Not Spoken* (1944).

Of Carroll's plays, two others are notable: *The Strings, My Lord, Are False* (1942) and THE WAYWARD SAINT (1955). The former is a spectacle that presents a kindly canon ministering to a group of men and women who seek refuge in the church from German bombardments of Scotland in 1941; they find strength in the horror and the courage displayed amidst the carnage, and finally succeed in picking up their lives and resolving their various affairs. Most of Carroll's plays, however, deal with small-town life and the middle class, usually with schoolmasters and clergymen. Generally he portrays two types of the latter: intolerant stultifiers of life—like the later O'Casey's priests—whom he bluntly characterizes as fascists; and the intellectual and cultivated, or the lovable and tolerant priests, the canon-protagonists of his best plays. It is these and the crusading liberal intellectuals, frequently appearing as schoolmasters, whom he would like to see unite to save Ireland; for Carroll, who was born into it, accepted Catholicism, though he rejected what he considered some of its dangerous reactionary manifestations in Ireland.

In 1943 Carroll (with JAMES BRIDIE and others) helped found the Glasgow Citizens' Theatre, of which Carroll subsequently became a director. His other works include *Plays for My Children* (six one-act plays, 1939), *The Old Foolishness* (1940), *The Chuckeyhead Story* (retitled *The Devil Came from Dublin,* 1950; "a satirical extravaganza"), *Green Cars Go East* (1951), *Farewell to Greatness!* (1966; another minor Carroll play, about Jonathan Swift, originally produced on television in the 1950's), and a number of film scripts, including the popular *Saints and Sinners* (1949). Some of his works were published as *Irish Stories and Plays* (1958). See also Peter Kavanagh's *The Story of the Abbey Theatre* (1950) and Robert Hogan's *After the Irish Renaissance* (1967).

CASE OF REBELLIOUS SUSAN, THE, a comedy in three acts by HENRY ARTHUR JONES, produced in 1894 and published in 1897. Setting: London, 1890's.

This play was the first of its time successfully to portray a "sinning" woman who is, at the end, happily reconciled with her husband. Though Jones's preface (dedicated to "Mrs. Grundy") left no doubt as to the wife's adultery, its dramatization was so tactful and amusing that it gave no offense to Victorian audiences.

Lady Susan Harabin is incensed to learn of her husband's infidelity and, though he is contrite, she vows revenge. Her friends advise her to be reasonable, and her worldly-wise uncle assures her that different standards apply to men and women; in fact, "there is no gander sauce." Nonetheless, she goes to Egypt "to find a little romance, and introduce it into our married life." When she returns, it transpires that she has fallen in love with a young diplomat. The kindly uncle prevents the affair from progressing and becoming known. Without confessing everything, Lady Susan finally returns to her jealous but penitent husband.

CASONA, Alejandro [pseudonym of Alejandro Rodríguez Álvarez] (1903–65), Spanish dramatist, was a poet before he turned to the theatre. A friend of FEDERICO GARCÍA LORCA and a leading contender for his preeminence as a dramatist after García Lorca's death, Casona wrote about thirty wistfully lyric plays, which were sometimes called *teatro de evasión*. Their philosophic whimsicality is reminiscent of PHILIP BARRY's, and is exemplified in Casona's *Prohibido suicidarse en primavera* (SUICIDE PROHIBITED IN THE SPRINGTIME, 1913?) with its themes of love, despair, and self-destruction, and the achievement of joy and redemption not through illusion but by the confronting of reality. This and his other dramas influenced Spanish writers from the 1930's on, when they first appeared. Throughout the 1950's and after, they were produced with particular success in Eastern Europe.

Casona was born in the Asturian village of Besullo. Following in the footsteps of both his parents, he became a schoolteacher and, with his wife, settled in a Pyrenees village. In 1931 he was appointed to organize and direct the Teatro del Pueblo (Theatre of the People), for which he wrote farces that were later published. The thesis Casona completed in 1936 on "The Devil in Literature and Art" documented his interest in fantasy and the Devil, who appears in a number of his plays. The first to be produced was the three-act comedy *El crimen de Lord Arturo* (1929), an adaptation of an OSCAR WILDE story, "Lord Arthur Savile's Crime." In 1933 Casona won the prestigious Lope de Vega Prize for *La sirena varada,* whose title character, a madwoman with a sordid past, falls in love with and reclaims the despairing founder of a home for the disillusioned from his fantasy world; together, in anticipating the birth of their child, they start a new life of hope. This play was followed by the symbolic fantasy *Otra vez el diablo* (1935), a three-character morality in which a student battles and defeats the Devil.

One of Casona's best-known and typical plays is *La dama del alba* (*The Lady of the Dawn,* 1944), which employs ballad and folklore, and whose title character—Death—visits an unhappy young man whose wife has run off with another man but is thought by all to have drowned; the husband rescues a desperate young woman with whom he finds happiness after Death persuades the returning wife to accompany her. A less successful drama on the life of *María Curie, Biografía escénica* (1940; written with Francisco Madrid, 1889–1942) was followed by the more popular *Las tres perfectas casadas* (1941), based on an ARTHUR SCHNITZLER story; then by another popular Casona play, *La barca sin pescador* (*The Boat Without a Fisherman,* 1945), whose protagonist, a ruined financier, enters into a pact with the Devil but is transformed and redeemed when he falls in love with his victim's widow, recants, gives up his wealth, and thus foils the Devil; and by *Los árboles mueren de pie* (*Trees Die Standing,* 1949), in which an old lady (later played by Ida Kaminska in a Yiddish adaptation) after discovering that she has been deceived keeps silent so as not to disappoint those who thought their deception would help her. Casona's *Nuestra Natacha* (*Our Natacha,* 1936), a great popular success whose protagonist—an educator who is unable to reform the wrongs in her reformatory—personifies young Spain fighting intolerance, offended the rising Falangists. Casona soon fled with his family to Buenos Aires, where he lived from 1939 until 1962. Then he was able to return to Madrid, witness the successful production of his plays, and spend his remaining few years there.

Casona also wrote film scripts, including those of his plays. Some of the latter were translated into English. *Suicide Prohibited in the Springtime* appears in Michael Benedikt and George E. Wellwarth's *Modern Spanish Theatre* (1968), and *The Boat Without a Fisherman* is in Marion Holt's *The Modern Spanish Stage: Four Plays* (1970). The editorial comments in these collections may be supplemented with José A. Balseiro and J. Riis Owre's text edition (1955) of *La barca sin pescador,* which has an informative introduction in English and a bibliography; and Eduardo Betoret-Paris's bibliographical-biographical-critical article, "Alejandro Casona: 1903–1965," *Drama Critique* IX:2 (1966).

CAT ON A HOT TIN ROOF, a play in three acts by TENNESSEE WILLIAMS, published and produced in 1955: Setting: the bed-sitting room of a plantation home in the Mississippi Delta, 1950's.

This popular but controversial play won the Pulitzer Prize as well as the Drama Critics' Circle Award, and was filmed. It is a typical Williams play in its setting, emphasis on sex and violence, SYMBOLISM, and concern with illusions and ideals. New are the charm and vitality of both the Rabelaisian father figure, Big Daddy Pollitt, and the high-strung and frustrated Maggie, who claws her way to sexual and material victory. In response to pressure by his director (Elia Kazan), Williams altered the last act—which exists in two versions—to have Big Daddy reappear onstage and to depict a change in Brick's character. The play's action is continuous.

Act I. "One of those no-neck monsters hit me with a hot buttered biscuit so I have t' change!" Maggie (Margaret) shouts as she enters the room. Her husband, Brick, makes an occasional perfunctory reply from the adjoining bathroom as Maggie complains about his brother's five obnoxious children, come to celebrate the sixty-fifth birthday of Big Daddy. Brick appears with a crutch, his broken ankle in a plaster cast; he is a one-time football star and sports announcer, handsome and charming, but detached from life and interested only in alcoholic oblivion. In what is virtually an act-long monologue, in which Maggie's nervousness and "bitchy" humor increase with his curt, if polite, rejection of her, Brick's pretty wife talks of Big Daddy's dying of cancer, which only he and Big Mama do not know. She is irritated with Brick's brother and pregnant wife, who are scheming for the old man's huge estate. Maggie loves Big Daddy and has no intention of losing the inheritance. Though Big Daddy favors him, Brick may lose out because of his drinking and irresponsibility—and Maggie's childlessness. When she complains about Brick's hateful indifference toward her and speaks of her love and need for him, Brick suggests that she take a lover. But Maggie refuses to give up trying to regain her husband. Only her talking of "Skipper," a forbidden subject, arouses Brick. There is a short, catty interlude with her sister-in-law, and a talk with Big Mama, a silly woman who adores both her son and Big Daddy, and is elated at the thought that he may not, after all, have cancer. When they leave, Maggie resumes her monologue. She insists on talking of Skipper, the football hero whose friendship with Brick threatened their marriage. She had accused him of unnatural feelings for Brick, and, after a night of drinking, gave him the chance to prove his heterosexuality with her. When he failed, Skipper disintegrated on liquor and drugs, and soon died. Furious at Maggie's "dirtying" his friendship with Skipper, the "one great true thing," Brick throws his crutch at her, and falls. One of their nieces barges in, taunting them for being childless. Maggie begs Brick to make love to her, for this is her time to conceive. "How in hell on earth do you imagine—that you're going to have a child by a man that can't stand you?" Brick asks. Maggie replies, "That's a problem that I will have to work out."

Act II. Big Daddy comes in with the family. He is a large and coarse one-time farmer, now a millionaire. Relieved to think he is not dying of cancer after all, he is disgusted with the catty rivalries and the celebration put on for him by his scheming son's family, and clears the place to talk with Brick. Brick keeps drinking and trying to get out as Big Daddy snatches his crutch away and demands to know why he turned to liquor. Despite their mutual love, their talk threatens to end as inconclusively as earlier talks did. But Big Daddy keeps probing Brick's need for the "click" of alcoholic oblivion. It is because of his disgust with the world's mendacity, Brick replies, evasively. But when Big Daddy casually traces the beginning of his alcoholism to Skipper's death, Brick is outraged: "Oh, *you* think so, too, you call me your son and a queer." Maintaining that their friendship "was a pure an' true thing an' that's not normal" in a mendacious world, Brick finally reveals that just before his death Skipper called him long distance and made a drunken confession—upon which Brick hung up on his friend. Thus Brick's disgust "is disgust with yourself," Big Daddy remarks. It is Skipper's truth, Brick insists. "His truth, okay! But you wouldn't face it with him!" Big Daddy replies. "Who can face truth? Can *you?*" Brick asks. "Being friends is telling each other the truth," Brick continues, stung at being forced to face his guilt, and reveals Big Daddy's imminent death of cancer: "You told *me!* I told *you!*" Overwhelmed with horror, Big Daddy goes out cursing "all lying dying liars!"

Act III. Now the family reveal the cancer diagnosis to Big Mama. Brick's brother and his wife have prepared a trusteeship for the estate; but Big Mama, on the verge of collapse from the news, summons up unexpected strength. Her silliness vanishes as she turns to Brick and ignores her other son and his scheming and squabbling family. She tells Maggie how proud Big Daddy would be if "you gave him a child of yours." Thereupon Maggie announces: "Brick and I are going to—*have a child!*" Although her sister-in-law screams that this is a lie—for she has overheard Maggie's arguments with Brick—Big Mama joyfully rushes out to tell Big Daddy. There is an agonizing cry from the dying man, whose pains are starting: Margaret throws out Brick's crutch and liquor bottles. "Tonight we're going to make the lie true, and when that's done, I'll bring the liquor back here and we'll get drunk together, here, tonight, in this place that death has come into." Powerless, Brick submits. "Oh, you weak people, you weak, beautiful people! —who give up. —What you want is someone to— take hold of you. —Gently, gently, with love!" Maggie says, telling Brick of her great love for him. As his father had responded earlier to Big Mama's protestations to him, Brick replies sadly, "Wouldn't it be funny if that was true?"

(*Act III, alternate version,* used in the Broadway production). Big Daddy comes into the room and twits his other son, who quickly puts aside the bulging briefcase containing the prepared trusteeship papers. Maggie kneels before Big Daddy to announce his birthday present: "A child is coming, sired by Brick, and out of Maggie the Cat!" Brick backs her story, and is more agreeable to resuming their marriage. "I admire you, Maggie," he tells her after she throws away his crutch and liquor. She turns out the light, kneels beside him at the foot of the bed, and tenderly proclaims that she will save him, return his life to him, with love. "I'm determined to do it—and nothing's more determined than a cat on a tin roof—is there? Is there, baby?" she concludes, gently touching his cheek as the curtain falls.

CATHLEEN NI HOULIHAN, a one-act play by WILLIAM BUTLER YEATS, published and produced in 1902. Setting: a cottage near Killala, Ireland; 1798.

This very short play (LADY GREGORY also had

a hand in its composition) is one of Yeats's most popular ones. The name was originally spelled Kathleen, and the play was among those given on the Abbey Theatre's opening bill. Yeats spent sleepless nights wondering about the effects of its patriotic exhortations: "Did that play of mine send out / Certain men the English shot?"

Peter Gillane and his family are getting ready for the marriage of his son, Michael, when an old woman comes in. It is Cathleen, the daughter of Houlihan (the personification of Ireland). She talks of the beautiful fields she has lost to strangers, and of the men who died for her. "It is a hard service they take that help me," she says. "They that have red cheeks will have pale cheeks for my sake, and for all that, they will think they are well paid." Her stirring words and songs, and the cheering outside as "the French are landing at Killala!" inspire Michael to forget his bride and follow Cathleen. After he leaves, the father asks his younger boy, Patrick: "Did you see an old woman going down the path?" And Patrick answers: "I did not: but I saw a young girl, and she had the walk of a queen."

CATILINE (*Catilina*), a blank verse tragedy in three acts by HENRIK IBSEN, published in 1850 and produced in 1881. Setting: Rome and vicinity, and Etruria, 63–62 B.C.

Unable to get Ibsen's first play performed, a friend paid for its practically unnoticed publication under the pseudonym Brynjolf Bjarme. Lifeless and declamatory, it focuses on the inner conflict of a heroic Catiline, who, influenced by two contrasting women, rebels against pillars of society like Cicero. It also foreshadows Ibsen's preoccupation with other later characteristic themes such as the ghosts of past misdeeds and "the contradiction between ability and desire," as Ibsen noted in his preface of 1875, when he revised and republished the play.

Lucius Catiline's gentle wife Aurelia urges him to retire from political strife, but his "wild and passionate" mistress, the Vestal Furia, who loves yet hates him for raping her sister, spurs him on to seek vengeance and overthrow the Senate. Catiline insists that "Civic freedom, / The welfare of the state—these were my aims. / Men have misjudged, appearances belied me." His followers are interested only in loot, however, and he and his army are betrayed. Slain by Furia, Catiline finds peace in death with his wife, Aurelia, whom he stabs: "The gods of dawn are smiling in atonement from above; / All the powers of darkness you have conquered with your love."

CAUCASIAN CHALK CIRCLE, THE (*Der kaukasische Kreidekreis*), a play in six prose and verse scenes by BERTOLT BRECHT (music by Paul Dessau), produced in 1948 and published in 1949. Setting: Georgia (Russia) in 1945 and in feudal times.

The first version to be published and produced was Eric Bentley's English translation, consisting of a prologue (Scene 1) and two parts (Scenes 2 through 4, and Scenes 5 and 6). Grusche, personifying "the temptation of kindness," is ultimately more fortunate than Shen Te, the good woman of Setzuan. The most memorable figure of this play, however, is the scoundrel judge Azdak —an autobiographically colored character reminiscent of Brecht's Puntila and Galileo. Here Brecht was inspired by an adaptation of an old Chinese play by KLABUND, *Kreidekreis* (*Chalk Circle*, 1925). *The Caucasian Chalk Circle* is the last and most EPIC of Brecht's major works—as well as the one most complex in structure and eclectic in form: "The plot and some of the language are Biblical; the 'Song of Chaos' Egyptian; the technique of narration and comment Japanese; the construction cinematic; the conclusion didactic; the wedding scene a reflection of the Marx brothers' *A Night at the Opera;* the soldiers an apparent recollection of *Mann ist Mann* [A MAN'S A MAN]; the atmosphere a cross between Brueghel and the pseudo-Chinese; the framework a commonsense, non-political issue debated in modern Georgia" (J. Willett, *The Theatre of Bertolt Brecht*).

Scene 1. Amidst the ruins of war, two groups of Caucasian villagers meet to decide who should get a disputed valley: the original owners, a collective of goat herders who abandoned it before the Nazi advance; or a collective of fruit growers, who defended it, and developed it with modern techniques. After some discussion, the latter is awarded the valley. The winning collective provides a communal feast and, to the recurrent accompaniment and commentary of a professional storyteller (or singer), performs an adaptation of "a very old Chinese play that has a bearing on our problem."

Scenes 2 through 4. The wealthy and cruel governor of an ancient town is overthrown by his feudal nobles, and eventually beheaded. His wife, preoccupied with her wardrobe and jewels, escapes in panic, leaving her baby behind her. The kitchen maid Grusche Vachnadze, in a tender but very formal love scene, bids farewell to Simon Chachava, an army paymaster going to battle, and promises to wait for him "until the last soldier has returned / And longer." Her fellow servants urge her not to risk her life by harboring the governor's heir. Grusche hesitates, but by dawn cannot resist saving the baby, which seems to implore her help. "Terrible is the seductive power of goodness," the Story Teller says. She flees into the mountains, where she experiences terrible hardships and dangers. Grusche must knock out one of the pursuing soldiers, cross a rotting bridge over a deep abyss, and seek shelter with her brother's inhospitable, miserly wife. To conceal the little boy's identity, she "legitimatizes" him by marrying a wealthy peasant who is on his deathbed; but the war ends and he turns out to be a healthy draft dodger. Her reunion with Simon is tender, no less so for their comically formal exchanges across a river. Simon misunderstands the situation when he sees the child, and as the Story Teller reveals the "many words left unsaid" by Grusche and Simon, he leaves. Soldiers sent by the governor's widow seize the child; Grusche follows them, determined to go to court to fight for the child.

Scenes 5 and 6. In order to clarify Grusche's coming trial before a grotesque judge, the story flashes back to the night of the nobles' revolt. A crude, drunken village scribe, Azdak, shelters a fugitive. When he later learns that it was the Grand Duke, Azdak denounces himself and wants to be tried. The judge has been hanged during the insurrection, and the comic, big-mouthed Azdak so amuses the troops that they elect him the new judge. Cunningly he seeks bribes, but his judgments favor the poor and are invariably bizarre. A callipygian plaintiff, for example, loses her suit: "You have raped that unfortunate man. Do you imagine you can run around with a behind like that and get away with it in court? This is a case of intentional assault with a dangerous weapon!" And he concludes lecherously, "You must come with me to the stable so the Court may inspect the scene of the crime." He celebrates the times in the "Song of Chaos," an age where only the poor get justice. But after two years the old social order is being restored, and Azdak quakes in cowardly fear: "I'll beg on my knees for mercy. Spittle will slobber down my chin." He is manhandled and about to be hanged when the grateful Grand Duke saves him—by appointing him judge. Azdak must adjudicate the governor's widow's claim for her child, in whose name (incidentally) all her estates are tied up. Grusche claims it as hers, and angrily rejects the arguments that riches might be better for the child. To her mind, riches would only harden his heart. Azdak finally applies the chalk test: the true mother is she who can pull the child out of the chalkmarked circle. Not wishing to harm the boy, Grusche (not the natural mother, as in the biblical test of Solomon) is the one who lets go. Azdak rules Grusche the true mother; he makes it possible for her to marry Simon, and disappears forever during the dancing that follows. The Story Teller concludes the tale. Azdak's judgeship was long remembered "as a brief golden age / Almost an age of justice." He exhorts the audience to "note what men of old concluded: / That what there is shall go to those who are good for it." For that reason, children are awarded "to the motherly, so that they may thrive," and the valley goes to the fruit growers, "so that it may bring forth fruit."

CAVALCADE, a play in three parts by NOËL COWARD, published and produced in 1931. Setting: England, 1899–1930.

This popular patriotic spectacle, filmed a number of times in England and America, dramatizes in twenty-two brief scenes the lives of an English family and their friends.

John and Jane Marryot usher in the new century with their children. Then he leaves on a troopship, amidst cheers, to fight in the Boer War. He returns with a Victoria Cross and participates in Queen Victoria's funeral processions. ("She must have been a very little lady," his boy says as the coffin passes.) The years pass, and the children and their friends grow up. On his honeymoon, the older Marryot son and his bride wonder how long the raptures of love last; it is 1912, and they are aboard the doomed *SS Titanic*. Two years later John drinks to the defeat of Germany. Soldiers are seen marching, endlessly, "out of darkness into darkness," as the years pass and the orchestra plays World War I songs. The remaining Marryot son, after an affair with a neighbor girl that temporarily estranges their mothers, is killed in battle. On Armistice Night, Jane wends her way through Trafalgar Square, cheering with the crowds and weeping, as the band plays. At the end of another decade, Jane and her neighbor friend—who has aged less gracefully—toast the 1930's. Then Jane toasts her husband John—"loyal and loving always"—and the future of England, "this country of ours, which we love so much." Finally there is "Chaos," a series of visions accompanied by the noise of industry, loudspeakers, and jazz bands. Amidst the silent darkness that follows, a Union Jack begins to glow, and the company sings "God Save the King."

CECÈ, a one-act play by LUIGI PIRANDELLO, produced in 1920 and published in 1926. Setting: a room in a first-class hotel in Rome, 1920.

In this brief comic sketch (also translated as *Chee-Chee*) a playboy nicknamed Cecè tricks his new mistress out of the IOU's with which he won her affection. He asks a friend to defame him before her, to tell her the IOU's are worthless, and to get them back for a fraction of their value. Cecè then convinces the girl that she gave the IOU's to a notorious extortionist who now has Cecè at his mercy. She must make it up to Cecè with her kisses.

CEYLON. Ceylon's most popular modern plays are *nadagams,* folk dramas that are usually episodic spectacles with song and slight plots based on native history and folktales, and first introduced in the nineteenth century. However, the dance is the far more distinguished and popular theatre in Ceylon: *Kolam* dance dramas, derived from the Sinhalese devil dance performed to exorcise evil spirits, in which carved wooden masks are worn to represent stock characters; and the classically derived and partly religious *Kandyan* dance, praised as one of Ceylon's purest forms of national expression. A survey of these appears in Faubion Bowers's *Theatre in the East* (1956).

CHAIRS, THE (*Les Chaises*), a one-act "tragic farce" by EUGÈNE IONESCO, produced in 1952 and published in 1954. Setting: a large, almost empty circular room with many doors, atop a tower surrounded by water.

Though many invisible and inaudible characters people the play, the only ones to appear physically on stage are a senile couple and (at the end) a

The Chairs. The Old Man (Jacques Mauclair) and the Old Woman (Tsilla Chelton). Paris, 1957. (*Agnes Varda*)

mute Orator. The empty chairs that finally crowd the stage poignantly dramatize Ionesco's vision of life's materialistic "nothingness." This ABSURD long one-acter also dramatizes human failure and illusion—and man's quest for a meaning.

A ninety-five-year-old handyman and his ninety-four-year-old wife, Semiramis, await visitors to their tower, which is surrounded by water. They reminisce, and when the Old Man weeps for his mama on the Old Woman's lap, she affectionately comforts him: "My pet, my orphan, dworfan, worfan, morphan, . . . my little general"—for he is the tower's general factotum. Consoled, he tells her of the Orator he hired for his "message to communicate to humanity, to mankind." The Old Woman wonders if he invited everybody for the occasion: "The janitors? the bishops? . . . the building? the pen holders? the chromosomes? . . . the alienists and their alienated?" Soon they note a boat landing outside, and their first invisible and inaudible visitor arrives. They talk with her for a while, and then usher in the second visitor, a colonel whose invisible doings with the first guest shock them. The next visitors are a photoengraver and his wife—the Old Man's childhood sweetheart. As he talks with her, the Old Woman talks with the photoengraver. Suddenly the Old Woman reveals her "hidden personality" with grotesquely obscene gestures, those of an old prostitute at work. Simultaneously the Old Man waxes maudlin with his former sweetheart. Later the Old Woman tells the photoengraver of her husband's great filial love and of their son, the Old Man simultaneously telling his childhood sweetheart how cruel he was to his parents and how he regrets he never had a son. Doors begin to open and shut, more invisible guests arrive, and the increasingly harried old couple bring in more and more chairs. Then there is an intensive light: "It's His Majesty the Emperor!" As they alternately honor him and bemoan their hard lives, the old couple anxiously await the Orator. "He will come," they keep repeating; and then, "He is coming, he is here." A real person, looking very unreal in his nineteenth-century artist's getup, appears onstage. Overjoyed, the old couple express gratitude to their guests. "Our existence can come to an end in this apotheosis. . . . My mission is accomplished. I will not have lived in vain, since my message will be revealed to the world," the Old Man confidently asserts while the Orator signs autographs for the invisible guests; "as for me and my faithful helpmeet, after our long years of labor in behalf of the progress of humanity during which we fought the good fight, nothing remains for us but to withdraw." Together they make the "supreme sacrifice"—and jump out of the tower window into the water below. Now the Orator starts his oration. But he is a deaf-mute, and can emit only meaningless guttural sounds. So he writes on the blackboard: "ANGELFOOD"; then, "NNAA NNM NWNWNW V"; and finally, "ΛADIEU ΛDIEU ΛPΛ." But when this fails to produce the desired effect his smile disappears; he bows to the audience, and leaves. All that remains is a stage full of chairs. Suddenly, for the first time, the many invisible people's voices are audible—as the curtain falls. (In the first productions the curtain fell during the Orator's mumbling, and no blackboard was used.)

CHALK GARDEN, THE, a play in three acts by ENID BAGNOLD, produced in 1954 and published in 1956. Setting: a Sussex, England, manor house; 1950's.

Enid Bagnold's most esteemed and evocative play (it was filmed in 1964), this is a genteel comic thriller with philosophic and SYMBOLIC overtones about religion and the topsy-turvy nature of life. The play's conflicts and themes are projected in terms of the central symbol, the garden.

A mysterious Miss Madrigal is employed as governess by the eccentric Mrs. St. Maugham. Disappointed in her daughter, the old lady has been bringing up her self-styled "sixteen but backward" granddaughter in her own image, as her "little immortality." The precocious girl is a pathological liar who claims to have been a rape victim at twelve and a witness to her father's suicide. Neither she nor the manservant can fathom the strange if congenial Miss Madrigal, the first person to oppose the old butler whose instructions have always dominated house and garden, even as he is now dying upstairs. Then a visiting judge identifies Miss Madrigal as a murderess he long ago condemned. Ultimately Miss Madrigal persuades the granddaughter, whom she herself resembled as a girl, to give up her fantasies and return to the mother she has been jealous of and hated. "You have not a green thumb, Mrs. St. Maugham, with a plant or a girl," Miss Madrigal tells the old lady. Rather than be left alone, Mrs. St. Maugham invites Miss Madrigal to stay with her, and asks whether she was indeed guilty of murder. Chastened and wise through suffering (she had served a fifteen-year prison term), Miss Madrigal refuses to answer. But she offers to help Mrs. St. Maugham to plant her chalk garden. "If *I* stay with you," she says, thinking of one of the plants that has not flourished in the chalky soil, "and we work together . . . with potash—and a little granular peat . . . We can *make* it do so."

CHAMBER PLAYS, THE (*Kammarspel*), five plays by AUGUST STRINDBERG: *Oväder* (THE STORM, 1907), *Brända tomten* (THE BURNT HOUSE, 1907), *Spöksonaten* (THE GHOST SONATA, 1907), *Pelikanen* (THE PELICAN, 1907), and *Svarta handsken* (THE BLACK GLOVE, 1909). All but the last-named were written for and performed in the small experimental Intima Teatern in Stockholm that Strindberg opened with the young actor August Falck in 1907. Influenced by Max Reinhardt's recent work in the Kammerspielhaus, Strindberg, in *Öppna brev till Intima Teatern* (OPEN LETTERS TO THE INTIMATE THEATRE, 1911–21), defined his new genre as "the idea of chamber music transferred to the drama: intimate approach, significant theme, careful treatment." Strindberg wrote two further *Chamber Plays: Den blödande handen* (1907), which he found too self-defensive and destroyed; and *Toten-Insel, eller, Hades* (ISLE OF THE DEAD, 1918).

CHANDALIKA, a play in two acts by RABINDRANATH TAGORE, published and produced in 1933. Setting: a village in India, fifth century B.C.

This short work is considered the best of Tagore's later drama. It is based on the Buddhist legend of a chandalika (a girl of the untouchable caste) who falls in love with Buddha's ascetic disciple Ananda and persuades her mother to cast a magic spell on him. Overcome by shame at her house, Ananda prays to Buddha, who breaks the magic spell. In Tagore's play the girl's humanity—which transcends caste—is awakened when (at the end of the play) the monk enters. Eager to give herself not to the lust-ridden man but to the hero whose "light and radiance, shining purity, and heavenly glow" aroused her womanhood, she begs the monk's forgiveness and has the mother revoke the spell though it costs the old woman's life. The girl is redeemed by her understanding and remorse as Ananda chants his homage to Buddha.

CHANTICLEER (*Chantecler*), a verse play in four acts by EDMOND ROSTAND, published and produced in 1910. Setting: a French farmyard and environs, early twentieth century.

Because of the difficulties of making this poetic animal fable appear believable on the stage, it did not achieve the popularity of Rostand's other major plays. The Gallic cock Chanticleer (created for the actor Constant Coquelin) is a Rostandian poet-idealist confronting reality and disillusionment, while the Pheasant Hen is an "emancipated, independent, domineering" female, Rostand wrote, who is "jealous of the male's high task"; their love affair provides the universal conflict of "will and feeling at war with each other." Among the many other anthropomorphic farm and forest beasts are a cynical blackbird, a rough but loyal hunting dog, and a stupid guinea hen—a fussy society female preoccupied with her "at homes."

A book-length study of the play is Marco F. Liberma's *The Story of Chantecler* (1910).

Chanticleer is adored by a bevy of hens for his beauty and his daily clarion call—"Cocorico!"—which summons dawn and the sun. After blessing the rising sun, Chanticleer struts around, protecting and ruling his roost. He falls in love with a golden Pheasant Hen from the forest, who is smitten with him but resists until he tells her his secret—which is that, though it is he who makes the sun rise, "I find myself unworthy of my gift. / Why am I chosen this great orb to lift?" During her stay at the barnyard she overhears his enemies plotting to do away with him. After he battles them, she takes Chanticleer to the forest. There she demands that he prove he loves her best by forgoing—just for once—his morning call to the sun. Chanticleer refuses, but seduced by a nightingale's song and the Pheasant Hen's blandishments, he misses his moment. The sun rises anyway, and the Pheasant Hen is triumphant: "You see that Dawn can come without you!" Chanticleer is momentarily crushed, but his love and idealism renew his faith: He will proclaim—if not produce—the sun. Envisioning himself the "Cock of yet more distant Suns," he declaims, "Can I forget the noble, verdant spot, / That taught me this: who loses the Great Dream / Must die, or rise and conquer in its beam!" Though the Pheasant Hen loves him above all, she refuses to take second place to his dream—and Chanticleer must give her up: "I adore you. Therefore I / But ill could serve the Great Cause I adore / Near one who values any creature more." The Pheasant Hen bemoans the loss of her beloved, and when he is in danger of being shot by a hunter she sacrifices her life to save him: "Light, whom I dared dispute, O please forgive! / Shine in the hunter's eyes, and let him live!" The animals rejoice as Chanticleer's voice is again heard in the distance: "Cocorico!"

CHAPIN, Harold (1886–1915), English playwright born in Brooklyn, New York, was active in England's repertory theatre. A skillful dramatist, he wrote a number of comic and sentimental plays, including *The Marriage of Columbine* (1910), *Augustus in Search of a Father* (1911), *Art and Opportunity* (1912), and *It's the Poor That Helps the Poor* (1915). He was killed in World War I.

CHARLEMAGNE'S HOSTAGE (*Kaiser Karls Geisel*), a verse "legend play" in four acts by GERHART HAUPTMANN, published and produced in 1908. Setting: Aix-la-Chapelle and vicinity, ninth century.

Unlike THE SUNKEN BELL, this play depicts pagan passions as completely evil.

The aged Charlemagne is infatuated with a beautiful Saxon hostage, the fifteen-year-old Gersuind. Though warned that she is "worm-eaten—and corrupted at the core," he gives her complete freedom to do as she likes. Her total depravity horrifies the Emperor—and yet he remains enthralled by Gersuind. Only after his chancellor poisons her can Charlemagne return to his duties. The crowds cheer their revitalized Emperor and the chancellor rejoices: "Hail! He is raising his sword!"

CHARLES XII (*Carl XII*), a historical play in five acts by AUGUST STRINDBERG, published in 1901 and produced in 1902. Setting: Sweden and Norway, 1715–18.

This haunting work is one of Strindberg's minor chronicle plays. An impressionistic "classical tragedy of fate and catastrophe," as Strindberg called it, it depicts "the end of a life that was a big mistake" (quoted in Walter Johnson's edition).

After fifteen years of wars, Charles returns to Sweden. The countryside is desolated by poverty and destruction. Only a withered tree stands, "with a rotten apple on top." It should be shaken down—like their villain king—the people mutter impotently. Arrogantly taciturn, Charles terrorizes his subjects with his cruelty. He is sick and senses his doom, but insists on royal absolutism, and employs a shrewd Holsteiner to manipulate his currency to finance his wars. Intermittently broken by the saraband of Bach ("the King of the Land of Sorrows and Pain") is the everlasting, "terrible silence." Charles complains, "The whole city says nothing; the whole country says nothing! A silence as of death is beginning to close about us! (*Pause.*) And besides I am sick! (*Pause.*) The streets are empty; no one comes to call! No one protests! . . . No one says anything! (*Pause.*)"—and he despairs before his stern Lutheran God. Always avoiding women, whom he fears, he angrily rejects the seductive bride of his friend Emanuel Swedenborg. The currency schemes become a public scandal and, warring in Norway, Charles is doomed. Courageous as always, he is seen in the trenches and is soon killed. The shot came "from up *there*," says Swedenborg, who had mystically foretold the king's death a moment earlier, and he points to heaven. "And if it didn't, it should have come from there!"

CHARLEY'S AUNT, a comedy in three acts by BRANDON THOMAS, published and produced in 1892. Setting: Oxford, late nineteenth century.

Perhaps the most popular farce ever written, *Charley's Aunt* was translated into many languages. It has been widely and successfully produced from the very start, consistently and profitably revived throughout the twentieth century, and made into *Where's Charley?* (1948), a musical hit by GEORGE ABBOTT and Frank Loesser (1910–69) that was subsequently filmed.

Charley Wykeham, an Oxford student, is expecting his wealthy and recently widowed aunt from Brazil. Her chaperoning would make it possible for him and his friend to invite their girls, to whom they want to propose before the girls leave on a trip. The aunt is delayed and their plans threaten to fail. The boys get another undergraduate to impersonate the missing aunt—"Babbs," Lord Fancourt Babberley, who is rehearsing for a show in which he plays an old

Victorian lady. Many comic confusions follow after Babbs introduces himself as "Charley's aunt from Brazil, where the nuts come from." The real aunt, an attractive young widow, arrives and under an assumed name observes things and mischievously plagues Babbs. The masquerading Babbs fondles the girls and engages in female chitchat, is caught smoking a cigar, and is proposed to by the girls' suspicious and mercenary old guardian. If he will allow them to marry, Babbs hints, "she" may give in. But unwilling to win his girl fraudulently, Charley reveals the masquerade. All ends happily: the young lovers are united; so are the aunt and her poor but honest and sincere admirer, and Babbs and his dream girl.

CHASE, Mary Coyle (1907–), American playwright, received much praise for her imaginative, comic drama about a giant invisible rabbit, *Harvey* (1944), which won the Pulitzer Prize in 1945 and was revived on Broadway in 1970. Her other Broadway hits were the fantasy *Mrs. McThing* (1952), about a witch who uses magic to make an arrogant mother accept her little boy on his own terms; and *Bernadine* (1952), a depiction of defensive adolescent fantasies.

CHAYEFSKY, Paddy [originally Sidney] (1923–), American playwright, made his name with *Marty* (1953), a television romance (adapted into an Academy Award-winning film two years later) about two of the kind of plain people he grew up with in the Bronx during the Depression. After writing other successful television plays, Chayefsky turned to the stage. His first play was *Middle of the Night* (1956), another love story of simple, unattractive people: an old manufacturer ("Even a few years of happiness you don't throw away") and an unhappily married girl ("Maybe there's something wrong with loving an older man, but any love is better than none"). These quotations suggest Chayefsky's wistfully NATURALISTIC style. His concerns with loneliness and amatory panaceas resemble those of WILLIAM INGE, but Chayefsky added fantasy and a religious (or pseudoreligious) theme, as in his most popular plays, THE TENTH MAN (1959) and GIDEON (1961). His venture into EPIC THEATRE with *The Passion of Josef D.* (1964), about Lenin and Stalin (*né* Dzhugashvili), was a failure. The satiric *The Latent Heterosexual* (1968) fared better; as its protagonist summarizes it before committing suicide, he "got married [to the town's prostitute] to get the benefit of the joint declaration, got divorced to maintain his Lichtenstein tax status, and finally killed himself on the advice of his accountant."

Chayefsky graduated from the College of the City of New York and served in World War II as a machine gunner. Aside from many television dramas, he has also written screenplay adaptations and an original film case study of a movie star, *The Goddess* (1958).

CHEKHOV,* Anton [Pavlovich] (1860–1904), the great Russian writer, once remarked that he considered fiction his "legal wife" and drama his "noisy, impudent, and tiresome mistress." His towering stature as the prolific master short-story writer has remained unsurpassed. Writing drama came less easily to him and his reputation rests on only four plays, his last ones: *Chaika* (THE SEAGULL, 1896), *Dyadya Vanya* (UNCLE VANYA, 1897), *Tri sestry* (THE THREE SISTERS, 1901), and *Vishnyovy sad* (THE CHERRY ORCHARD, 1904). Despite his limited dramatic corpus and his remark, he was, from the very beginning of his career, seriously occupied with the theatre. His early dramatic works are of interest primarily because of his later ones; it is therefore a telling comment on his genius that those last plays alone assure his inclusion among the ranks of giant modern dramatists.

The son of a former serf, Chekhov was born in the South Russian town of Taganrog. His industrious and shrewd grandfather had amassed enough capital at forty-two to purchase his own and his family's freedom. His father (Pavel Yegorovich Chekhov) acquired a grocery store in which young "Antosha" had to work many miserable hours. Though there was an artistic side to him and though he thought he was doing his best for his six children, Pavel's own hard youth had developed his least attractive features; Chekhov flinched at memories of paternal beatings and humiliations for the rest of his life. His mother (Yevgeniya), from whom he inherited his gentleness, was powerless to make his childhood easier.

His father's bankruptcy left Chekhov to his own resources early in life. He finished school and then went to Moscow to study medicine. Although these studies, which were to affect his literary attitudes, earned him a degree (1884), he practiced medicine only intermittently. Writing was more lucrative and soon took up much of the doctor's time. The publication of his earliest works—short comic sketches—had already helped pay his way through the university. In 1886 he published the first collection of his tales, and Chekhov quickly became and remained a leading figure—along with LEO TOLSTOI, MAXIM GORKY, and others—in Russia's literary world.

While still at the university Chekhov also wrote plays. His theatrical career, however, was launched with considerably less éclat than his literary one. Except for *Na bolshoi doroge* (ON THE HIGHWAY, banned in 1885), the comic *Tatyana Repina* (1889) —a sequel to Aleksei Suvorin's (1834–1912) play by that name—and the unfinished dramatization of Chekhov's 1886 story *Noch pered sudom* (*The Night Before the Trial,* 1890), his early dramatic writings, too, were comic sketches—horseplay or "jests" and "vaudevilles," as they were called: *O vrede tabaka* (ON THE HARMFULNESS OF TOBACCO, 1886), *Lebedinnaya pesnya* (THE SWAN SONG, 1887), *Medved* (THE BEAR, 1888), *Predlozhenie* (THE PROPOSAL, 1888), *Svadba* (THE WEDDING, 1889), *Yubilei* (THE ANNIVERSARY, 1892), and *Tragik ponevole* (A TRAGEDIAN IN SPITE OF HIMSELF, 1889). They evidence Chekhov's gifts as a skillful farceur who knew and dissected, and yet sympathized with, human pathos—a subtle combination that

*Illustration on page 665.

characterizes all of Chekhov's works. (In this connection, a comparison of his early and late versions of *On the Harmfulness of Tobacco* is revealing.) Some of these short pieces, particularly *The Bear,* were quite popular, and he found their composition effortless. But his major attempts—full-length plays—proved to be considerably more troublesome, both to write and to produce.

The first of these, PLATONOV (written in about 1881), was rejected by a Moscow theatre and not heard of again until long after Chekhov's death; for years it was confused with *Bezotsovshchina* (*Without Fathers*), a lost play he had written as a student. Next came IVANOV (1887), whose premiere, poorly staged though moderately successful, created an uproar. *Ivanov* made a reputation for Chekhov as a playwright, but he remained totally dissatisfied with this work. His next full-length venture was *Leshi* (THE WOOD DEMON, 1889). This was the first of his "plays of indirect action," as David Magarshack aptly terms Chekhov's unique dramatic handling of REPRESENTATIONALISM. He had not yet mastered his elusive form, however, and the production left much to be desired. *The Wood Demon* was roundly panned; Chekhov withdrew it and temporarily put it aside, to be reworked later.

His next play had an even less auspicious beginning. Its St. Petersburg premiere was so disastrous and the play was attacked so unmercifully that Chekhov vowed never again to write for the theatre. The failure this time, however, was entirely due to the performance and the audience. The play itself is one of Chekhov's finest —*The Seagull.* Its full possibilities were revealed in a notable production two years later. The novelist-playwright VLADIMIR NEMIROVICH-DANCHENKO persuaded Chekhov to allow a second production of the play, this time by the group Nemirovich-Danchenko had recently founded with Konstantin Stanislavsky. The success of this group —the Moscow Art Theatre, which was to revolutionize the theatre of the whole Western world in fact began with Chekhov's *The Seagull* in 1898. So did Chekhov's important relationship with the Moscow Art Theatre. He now reworked *The Wood Demon* into *Uncle Vanya* and then wrote his other great plays, *The Three Sisters* and *The Cherry Orchard.* All these were produced by the group with Stanislavsky directing as well as acting in them. Chekhov also fell in love with one of the group's leading actresses, Olga Knipper—the Irina of *The Seagull* revival, and the original Yelena, Masha, and Lyubov in the other plays. (She still performed Lyubov in 1943, at the three-hundredth performance of the play.) They married in 1901, but as he had feared, Chekhov was not fated to enjoy this union (and his association with the Moscow Art Theatre) for long. Soon he succumbed to the ill health that had forced his frequent banishment from Moscow and plagued his whole life. He died of tuberculosis in Germany at the age of forty-four.

Chekhov's four plays assure his immortality as much as do his many hundreds of stories (some of which have been dramatized). Like them, the plays diagnose and portray human beings with masterful subtlety and consummate art. His characters are, for the most part, frail, frustrated failures—attrition personified; ineffectual and lonely, they cannot even communicate with each other. Their wasted lives presage the passing of an old order. But though Chekhov foresaw its doom clearly, he foresaw with equal clarity the inevitable imperfections of the brave new world that was to come. A gentle (though not a soft) man, he depicted his findings with compassion for men's weaknesses and miseries, and showed their eternal longings for nobility and beauty.

However, that is only one side of the story, and the side too often exaggerated, sentimentalized, and misrepresented as tragedy. Despite notable exceptions, productions of his plays—particularly challenging because of Chekhov's subtle orchestration—have thus misrepresented his drama and done little really to popularize Chekhov in the English-speaking world. Even at its premiere *The Cherry Orchard* was presented as a tragedy, and the dying Chekhov complained, "Stanislavsky has ruined my play." Chekhov was a scientist, trained to probe with a doctor's scalpel—and he was a first-rate farceur. His humor and propensity for horseplay are ever present in his plays. These may not always be the "comedies" or even "farces" he called them, and they are basically serious (as is all great comedy); but they are not tragedies.

They defy conventional labels, for Chekhov's genius was that of an innovator who created new dimensions in the theatre. His plays communicate the illusion—but only the illusion—of everyday life. The tragic and the sentimental are intermingled with the comic and farcical. Talk is punctuated by the hesitations and pauses (an integral part of Chekhov's dialogue), unanswered speeches, and irrelevancies characteristic of everyday speech. The dynamically meaningful, artistic depiction of boredom and other meaningless REALISM is perhaps the most difficult of all literary and theatrical representations. It has been attempted by many artists after Chekhov, most recently in the mid-century ABSURD dramatizations of human failure and noncommunication. Together with the "methods" propounded and practiced by the Moscow Art Theatre, therefore, Chekhov's viewpoints and techniques exerted a decisive influence on the direction modern drama was to take.

Chekhov's plays, including his one-act farces, are readily available in English translations, notably in the first three volumes of Ronald Hingley's *The Oxford Chekhov* (1964–68). Comprehensive English studies of Chekhov's plays are David Magarshack's *Chekhov the Dramatist* (1952) and Maurice Valency's *The Breaking String: The Plays of Anton Chekhov* (1966). For Chekhov's life see Magarshack's *Chekhov: A Life* (1952), whose "Bibliographical Index" lists the title of every one of Chekhov's individual works, with the date of first Russian publication, as well as the translator, the publisher, and the date of English publication; and Ernest J. Simmons's *Chekhov: a Biography* (1962), whose "Bibliographical Survey" describes the important editions of Chekhov's writings (and archive material) and lists Russian and English works about Chekhov.

CHERRY ORCHARD, THE (*Vishnyovy sad*), a comedy in four acts by ANTON CHEKHOV, published and produced in 1904. Setting: a Russian estate, early twentieth century.

In his masterful last play Chekhov's dramaturgy was perfected to the point where, as he noted, he could even dispense with melodramatic pistol shots. He called the play "a comedy, and in places even a farce." But beginning with its successful premiere (a gala occasion honoring the author a few months before his death)* it has often been misrepresented as a tragedy. Lyubov's cherry orchard symbolizes an old culture that was doomed, like Shaw's in HEARTBREAK HOUSE. There are other serious undercurrents beneath the comic action and speeches of the ineffectual, sometimes charming characters that, despite their ludicrousness, Chekhov depicted with understanding and sympathy. The play was censored in 1906 and "Americanized" in Logan's THE WISTERIA TREES (1950).

Act I. Madame Lyubov Ranevsky, a widow, and her seventeen-year-old daughter are returning to her estate after Lyubov's five-year absence. Various people welcome her: her brother, Leonid Gaev, an elegant but impractical gentleman; Yermolai Lopakhin, a wealthy merchant whose father was a serf; Lyubov's adopted daughter, Varya, a tearful girl who manages the estate and is expected to marry Lopakhin; Pyotr Trofimov, a radical student expelled from the university, and formerly tutor to Lyubov's son, who drowned; and a landowner who frequently falls asleep while he talks. The domestics include an accident-prone clerk, a simpering maid whom he loves, a conceited servant whom the maid adores, a superannuated deaf butler, and a charming governess who performs magic tricks. While Lyubov reminisces sentimentally, her daughter tells Varya of their poverty and her generous mother's extravagances. Varya is appalled to learn that the mortgage has not been paid. Lopakhin (who according to Varya has been too busy to propose to her) recommends a simple way of saving the estate from the auction block: convert the now-useless cherry orchard into summer rental villas. Lyubov and Gaev will not even consider such an idea. Gaev munches his candy drops, makes billiard motions ("Cannon off the red . . ."), and sententiously apostrophizes the old bookcase. The aged butler mutters about the past, the landowner asks for a loan, and Lyubov looks out and cries, "Oh, my childhood, my innocence! I slept in this nursery and looked out on the orchard from here. . . ." Deciding to ask a rich aunt for a loan, Gaev cheers up: "The estate shall not be sold!" Later Varya relates her household troubles; but Lyubov's daughter soon falls asleep, and Trofimov gazes at her tenderly.

* It is described in Konstantin Stanislavsky's *Moya zhizn v iskustve* (*My Life in Art*, 1924), as is Chekov's original ending of Act II, a lyrical scene between the governess and the superannuated butler, deleted by Stanislavsky (who played Gaev) and the Moscow Art Theatre.

The Cherry Orchard. Gaev (Joseph Schildkraut) and Lyubov (Eva Le Gallienne). New York, 1944. (*Culver Pictures*)

Act II. Outdoors at sunset, the foolish maid, the clerk, and the servant are individually preoccupied with their love triangle. Later, Lopakhin deplores Lyubov's and Gaev's "frivolous" attitudes; but they scornfully reject the commercial plan that would save their estate: "Summer cottages and summer residents—it is so vulgar," Lyubov remarks. She feels grief-stricken at the thought of her lover, who dropped her after she had given him her money, but now wants her back in Paris because he is ill. Lopakhin sadly regrets his own intellectual and artistic inadequacies. The "perennial student" Trofimov bitterly describes contemporary social conditions: "One must work and must help with all one's might," he maintains. An ominous distant sound and a drunken beggar eventually cause the departure of all but the student and Lyubov's daughter. "We are above love," Trofimov tells her as she wonders why she no longer cares about the cherry orchard. "All Russia is our orchard," he declaims, exultantly envisioning the future. But first the past must be wiped out and atoned for, through "suffering" and "incessant work." Annoyed when Varya calls them, they leave, Trofimov still talking of future happiness.

Act III. While Gaev is away at the auction, trying to save the estate, Lyubov is giving a ball. There is dancing and drinking, and the governess is performing tricks. Trofimov's lectures amuse Lyubov, but when he criticizes her lover she angrily ridicules him: "Imagine, at your age, not having a mistress!" He rushes out furiously—and falls down a flight of stairs. The ball is at its high point when Lopakhin comes in, catching a blow Varya had just aimed at the impertinent clerk. Overwhelmed with embarrassment and incredulous joy, Lopakhin finally announces, "The cherry orchard is mine now. Mine!" He bought the estate "where grandfather and father were slaves," and plans to build it up for the needs of the future. At the same time he tearfully reproaches Lyubov for not having listened to his plan to save the estate: "Oh, if this could all be over soon, if somehow our awkward unhappy life would be changed!" He leaves after calling for music: "Here comes the new squire, the owner of the cherry orchard!" Her daughter consoles Lyubov, who is weeping bitterly: ". . . don't cry, Mama, you've your life still left you. . . ."

Act IV. Lyubov is ready to leave the estate, which is being closed up, and to return to Paris. As he keeps looking for his galoshes, Trofimov is full of hope: "Humanity is moving toward the loftiest truth, toward the loftiest happiness that is possible on earth, and I am in the front ranks." Gaev has found a job in the bank and is momentarily happy: "I am a financier now—Yellow ball into the side pocket—anyway, Lyuba, you look better, no doubt about that." While the domestics drink, discuss their affairs, and take out the luggage, the others conclude their emotional farewells. Lyubov embraces Gaev tearfully and in despair: "Oh, my dear, my lovely, beautiful orchard! My life, my youth, my happiness, goodbye!" Finally everybody is gone. And then the superannuated butler, forgotten and now locked in, enters the empty room, looks around, weakly lies down, and mutters to himself, ". . . nothing is left, nothing— Oh, you—good-for-nothing—" From the distance comes the sound of an ax cutting down the cherry orchard.

CHIARELLI, Luigi (1880–1947), Italian playwright, was the progenitor of the theatre of the GROTESQUE, the type of drama more notably produced by his countryman LUIGI PIRANDELLO. It was Chiarelli's best-known work, *La maschera e il volto* (THE MASK AND THE FACE, 1916), that launched the grotesque movement. His other plays, which similarly satirize the ritualistic social conventions that mask people's real "faces," did not achieve the same popularity. Like his masterpiece, however, many of them are witty as well as incisive in their observations and criticisms of life.

Born in Trani, Chiarelli worked originally as a journalist. Soon, however, he turned to the theatre, for which he was to write some two dozen plays. The first was a one-acter, *Una notte d'amore* (1912), which, like the next half-dozen plays, aroused little interest. It was not until the production of *The Mask and the Face* that Chiarelli became prominent. Thereafter he went on to depict society's corruption, in "grotesque" play after play, with verve, wit, and considerable dexterity in plot construction—and occasional sentimentality.

Among Chiarelli's more popular other plays were *La scala di seta* (1917), in which social corruption enables a stupid but ambitious dancer to win success as a politician; *Chimere* (1920), an exposition of self-proclaimed idealists as nothing but gross opportunists—here personified by a puritan (like Paolo Grazia) who, however, readily agrees, when convenient, to prostitute his wife; *La morte degli amanti* (1921), a spoof of the "grand passion" of a romantic housewife who tries to commit suicide with her lover but is saved by her prosaic husband, whose jealousy she was trying to arouse; *Fuochi d'artificio* (1923), a satire of social position whose plot resembles that of Benavente's THE BONDS OF INTEREST and was produced in England as *Money, Money!* (1927); *Una più due* (1935), another sophisticated comedy; *Il cerchio magico* (1937), a more whimsical drama; and his last works, *Pulcinella* (1939) and *Il teatro in fiamme* (1945).

Only a few of these appeared in England and America. With *The Mask and the Face* alone did Chiarelli reach notable heights and international renown. It was republished with a brief introduction on Chiarelli and a bibliography of his work in Anthony Dent's collection of *International Modern Plays* (1950).

CHICKEN SOUP WITH BARLEY, a play in three acts by ARNOLD WESKER, produced in 1958 and published in 1959. Setting: the East End of London, 1936–56.

The first of *The Wesker Trilogy* (ROOTS and I'M TALKING ABOUT JERUSALEM followed), *Chicken Soup With Barley* dramatizes the saga of the Kahns, a Jewish working-class family who gradually lose their Socialist ideals. Their son, Ronnie, the unseen hero of the next play, here is a nebulous poetic—and autobiographical—figure.

The matriarch Sarah Kahn, a crusading Communist, fusses with her weak husband, Harry. Trying to escape participating in her political demonstrations, he usually runs off or simply goes to sleep. Their daughter Ada is a dedicated organizer. But in 1946, after years of office work with "lip-sticked, giggling morons," and her husband's Spanish Civil War experiences with ignorant men who "behaved like animals," both have lost their illusions "about the splendid and heroic working class," and decide to withdraw to an idyllic country life (see I'M TALKING ABOUT JERUSALEM). By 1946, too, the father has had a stroke, sleeps most of the time, and is out of work even during national prosperity. Ronnie, now fifteen, is full of ideals and will not believe his father's "You can't alter people, Ronnie. You can only give them some love and hope they'll take it." But in 1956, by which time Harry Kahn is paralyzed, Ronnie is sympathetic with his father's views—and well on the way to following in his footsteps. Ronnie has worked in a Paris kitchen, where he learned that "earning an honest penny is all my eye," and has realized that all men are simply "terrified of old age, hoping for the football pools to come home." What has totally disillusioned him is the Soviet action in Hungary. "You're a

Chicken Soup with Barley. Sarah (Kathleen Michael) and Ronnie (David Saire). London, 1960. (*British Theatre Museum*)

pathological case, Mother," he tells Sarah, the only one who remains unchanged. "You're still a *communist!*" She lashes out at Ronnie's defense of his father, who did not care to work—or care, in general. He was out eating delicatessen on his relief check while the sick infant Ada was starving, Sarah reveals, saved only by a neighbor's feeding her chicken soup with barley. Desperately Sarah fights Ronnie's denial of her values: "You've got to care, you've got to care or you'll die." Brokenly he goes to his room. "I can't, not now, it's too big," he mumbles, as Sarah shouts, "Ronnie, if you don't care you'll die."

CHILDREN OF DARKNESS, a tragicomedy in three acts by EDWIN JUSTUS MAYER, published in 1929 and produced in 1930. Setting: the jailer's lodgings adjoining Newgate Prison, London; 1725.

A long-praised SUCCÈS D'ESTIME, this play features the thief Jonathan Wild (also the subject of works by Daniel Defoe and Henry Fielding) and other eighteenth-century criminals, noble and ignoble. The play's characters, settings, and attitudes are reminiscent of such works as Brecht's THE THREEPENNY OPERA, the plays of BRENDAN BEHAN, and (in its cynical polished wit) the comedies of the English Restoration.

Mr. Snap gives special privileges to those of his prisoners who can pay him well. Lodging with him and his buxom and carnal daughter, Laetitia, are her lover, La Ruse, a worldly-wise and witty count imprisoned for debt; an idealistic young poet, another debtor; the boisterous Jonathan Wild, fearfully awaiting his execution; and an old nobleman imprisoned for poisoning "my wife and a few of her intimate friends" because he could no longer stand their "cant." Desperate to keep her lover, La Ruse, whose child she is carrying (she reveals at the end), Laetitia tries to arouse his jealousy by taking up with the young poet. But La Ruse, eager to escape, under the pretense of buying Jonathan Wild's pardon swindles him and pockets the money as Wild is dragged out to be hanged. Then, feeling compassion for the poet and despairing about his own reform, La Ruse gives the money to free the poet, and he himself commits suicide. Laetitia is left to the cold passion of the cant-hating old nobleman she fears, hates, and swore to repel until he succeeds in what she is sure he can never do, "gain ingress over my threshold." As she collapses hysterically, the old poisoner calmly helps her father pick her up: "Pray, Mr. Snap, show me into her room—I must have ingress into her room."

CHILDREN'S HOUR, THE, a play in three acts by LILLIAN HELLMAN, published and produced in 1934. Setting: New England, 1930's.

The theme of lesbianism made this play a sensation: both in the original production and in the 1952 revival prominent actresses turned down the leading roles for fear of damaging their public image, and attempts were made to suppress the play. It was filmed in 1936 without the homosexual theme and refilmed more frankly but less successfully in 1962. The author observed that a more important concern of the play (suggested by an early nineteenth-century Scottish court case) was with lying. "The bigger the lie the better, as always," she remarked pointedly, and added that it was lies that made the originally neurotic child "the utterly malignant creature which audiences see in her."

Act I. As some girls study during an April day in a farmhouse recently converted into a boarding school, Mary Tilford, a sullen fourteen-year-old, appears. Karen Wright, a teacher who helped establish the school, tries to reason with the unpleasant and troublesome child. Mary persists in her lies and has to be punished—whereupon she complains of heart trouble aggravated by her "persecution," and faints. Karen confers with her friend and colleague, Martha Dobie, who is also troubled by her foolish old aunt, a former actress and a bad influence on the girls, and by Karen's imminent marriage, which, she fears, will cause Karen to lose interest in their school. When she urges her aunt to go to Europe, the aunt indignantly accuses Martha of jealousy because Karen is getting married. "It's unnatural, just as unnatural as it can be," she says. "You were always like that even as a child. If you had a little girl friend, you always got mad when she liked anybody else." A couple of girls overhear the squabble and are sent upstairs. Mary soon learns about it and forces the girls to tell her exactly what they heard. Then she smiles mysteriously, decides to run away from school, and, brutally twisting a girl's arm until she screams, Mary extorts her savings so she can travel home.

Act II. At home, Mary tries to persuade Amelia Tilford, her grandmother, to let her stay away from school. When she realizes that her grandmother is shocked by the overheard squabble, Mary quickly embellishes it, inventing horrendous lies about "strange" relations between her teachers, Karen and Martha. Thereupon the gulled Mrs. Tilford calls her friends, who immediately withdraw their children from the school. She also summons Karen's fiancé, the local doctor. He, Karen, and Martha are dazed and appalled by what is suddenly happening to them. They try to reason with the intractable Mrs. Tilford: "We're human beings, see? It's our lives you're fooling with." The doctor demands to question the child. Quickly he exposes Mary's lies, but Mary cunningly presses on. "Everybody is yelling at me," she cries; "I don't know what I'm saying with everybody mixing me all up." Recently she had blackmailed a girl who had borrowed a bracelet without permission, and she had forced her to make an oath to be Mary's vassal. Now she calls this girl as a witness. She denies any knowledge of what Mary is talking about. But when Mary reminds her of her oath and threatens to tell about the bracelet and have her languish in prison, the frightened girl "corroborates" Mary's accusations of Karen and Martha. "Yes. Yes. I did see it. I told Mary," she cries out hysterically. "What Mary said was right. I said it, I said it—"

Act III. Seven months later, Karen and Martha sit listlessly in the neglected living room of their one-time schoolhouse. A delivery boy stares and giggles at them, and aware of the hostile townspeople, they are afraid to go out for a walk. Martha's aunt returns from Europe, and they angrily remind her that it was her failure to come and testify that lost their libel suit. Karen's fiancé, intent on marrying her, gives up his practice and urges Martha to accompany them to Vienna, where he has found a position. Later Karen gets him to admit he is not quite sure whether she was completely innocent. Thereupon she bids him good-bye. "We'd be hounded by it all our lives," she tells him; "it's no good now, for either of us." Martha gradually comes to believe in her guilt: "I love you that way—maybe the way they said I loved you." Though Karen refuses to believe her, Martha blames herself for ruining their lives: "Suddenly a child gets bored and lies—and there you are, seeing it for the first time." She goes into the adjoining room—and shoots herself. A few minutes later Mrs. Tilford comes in: she has just discovered the truth. An old woman, broken by the knowledge of the human destruction she has caused and burdened with a monstrous grandchild, Mrs. Tilford offers all she has to undo the wrong, and begs Karen to make something of her broken life, to get married. After castigating her bitterly, Karen promises to write Mrs. Tilford, "If I ever have anything to say." The old woman leaves. Karen looks out of the window, and then waves to her.

CHILE. Native drama was stimulated in the post-World War II era by the temporary decline of Argentina's during Perón's suppressive dictatorship (1946–55). Before it thus achieved temporary leadership in LATIN AMERICA, Chile's theatrical activity was considerable—1890–1930 was its golden age of COSTUMBRISMO—but it produced few important dramatists. Its earliest notable ones were Daniel Barros Grez (1834–1904) and Juan Rafael Allende (1850–1909). Barros Grez, the foremost *costumbrista,* was a prolific folk playwright who dramatized proverbs with great success; his *Cada oveja con su pareja* (1879) deals with a situation resembling that of Coward's PRIVATE LIVES, while *Ir por lana* (1880) is one of his recurrent May-December romances. "The poet of the people," Allende wrote seventeen verse dramas, patriotic plays, and sentimental melodramas on native themes, superimposing local characteristics on SPAIN's *género chico*—an importation whose popularity reached its height in 1917—to portray and entertain Chile's lower classes. The most popular play in the late nineteenth century was *Don Lucas Gómez* (1885), a comedy by Mateo Martínez Quevedo (1848–1923) about the discomforts of a *huaso* (rustic) amidst snobbish city folk, which was produced until the early years of the twentieth century.

The modern impetus to Chile's theatre came in 1911 with the production of a number of hits and the establishment of a second theatre company. Actors, poets, and others were inspired to write for the stage thereafter, and three of them achieved prominence in the early modern period. The first was the left-winger Antonio Acevedo Hernández (1886–1962), who wrote NATURALIST drama that forcefully portrayed Chile's social problems and whose stated purpose it was "to reform through revolution." Outstanding among Acevedo Hernández's fifty plays are *Cardo negro* (1913), depicting a Chilean village; *La canción rota* (1921), portraying an abusive administrator of farm hands; *Caín* (1928), a protest against God's having favored Abel over his hardworking brother; *El árbol viejo* (1928), about an aged patriarch who protects his family; and *Chañarcillo* (1933), which was revived in the 1950's and dramatizes a nineteenth-century California bandit's quest for silver in Chilean mines. The country's next important playwright was Armando Moock (1894–1942), whose many genial comedies, noted for their sprightly plots and clever characterizations, were among the most widely produced of those by any Latin American playwright; particularly popular were the romantic skit *Cuando venga el amor* (1920), the small-town comedy *Mocosita* (*The Youngster,* 1929), the tragicomic portrayal of a henpecked husband in *Rigoberto* (1935), as well as a drama of ideas, *La serpiente* (1920), and a largely autobiographical tragedy, *Monsieur Ferdinand Pontac* (1922). Last in the trio of early modern playwrights was Germán Luco Cruchaga (1894–1936), an aristocrat *costumbrista* who distinguished himself with character portrayals; most impressive was his later-revived *Viuda de Apablaza* (1928), featuring a tough old widow farmer in the Cordilleras who commits suicide after realizing that the boy she loves, her husband's natural son, is enamored of her visiting niece.

Little of note appeared until the 1940's, when the Chilean theatre was stimulated by (and flourished at) the universities. Among its most successful dramatists have been Pedro de la Barra (1912–), a director whose writings include *Viento de proa* (1948), a national play produced in England as *Headwind* (1951); María Asunción Requena (1915–), a dentist who has written history plays like the prize-winning *El camino más largo* (1959), about Chile's first female doctor (Ernestina Pérez), and depicted lower-class problems in another prize winner, *Pan caliente* (1958); Roberto Sarah (1918–), a physician who has sometimes written plays under the pen name Andrés Terbay and whose *Algún día* (*Some Day,* 1949), a drama on an immigrant family's unrealized hopes over a period of thirty years, won prizes and was produced abroad; Isidora ("Nene") Aguirre (1919–), who has portrayed Chilean themes and characters in one-act comedies like *Carolina* (1955; translated as *Express for Santiago* in *The Best Short Plays 1959–1960*) and in tragedies like *Las tres Pascualas* (*The Three Pascualas,* 1957), based on the Chilean legend of three women's suicide for a man; Miguel Frank (1920–), another author of comedies, including *El hombre del siglo* (*The Man of the Century,* 1958); and Gabriela Roepke (1920–), another woman writer and the country's "psychological dramatist," represented in the same *Short Plays* collection with *Mariposa blanca* (*The White Butterfly,* 1957).

Others are Sergio Vodánovic (1926–), the author of light comedies like *La cigüeña también espera* (1955) and a drama (later filmed, as was the comedy) of a man who witnesses his son following in his footsteps by betraying integrity to make money, *Deja que los perros ladren* (1960); Egon Raúl Wolff (1926–), who has written satires and psychological drama like *La niña madre* (1960), his masterpiece, which was produced in English as *A Touch of Blue* and which features a prostitute yearning for respectability in a world resembling the one envisioned by ABSURD playwrights; Luis Alberto Heiremans (1928–64), who in his short productive life acted and wrote musicals, dramas, and a modern Christmas fantasy that was successful on a European tour in 1960, *Versos de ciego;* Jorge Díaz Gutiérrez (1930–), an avant-garde playwright who attracted interest first with his portrayal of the Chilean revolutionary *Manuel Rodríguez* (1957) and even more with the experimental Teatro ICTUS group's introduction of his SURREALIST works, notably *El velero en la botella* (1962) and *El cepillo de dientes* (1961, revised 1965); and Alejandro Sieveking (1934–), one of Chile's "angry young men" whose drama has been likened to that of TENNESSEE WILLIAMS and whose early successes were *El paraíso semi-perdido* (1958) and *Parecido a la felicidad* (1959), the latter about a middle-class girl's romantic problems.

Willis Knapp Jones's *Spanish-American Literature in Translation* (1963) has excerpts of plays by Acevedo Hernández, Moock, and Mrs. Aguirre; and his *Men and Angels: Three South American Comedies* (1970) includes Frank's *The Man of the Century*. Chile's drama is discussed in both collections as well as in other works listed under LATIN AMERICA; another bibliography is Walter Rela's *Contribución a la bibliografía del teatro Chileno, 1804–1960* (1962).

CHIMES OF THE KREMLIN, THE (*Kremlyovskie kuranti*), a play in three acts by NIKOLAI FYODOROVICH POGODIN, produced in 1940 and published in 1941. Setting: Moscow and the countryside, 1920.

This is the second in Pogodin's Lenin cycle. Still immensely popular in Russia decades later, it was the first Soviet play to be incorporated into the repertoire of the Moscow Art Theatre. The play has also appeared as *Kremlin Chimes* and exists in differing versions; in one of these—produced after Khrushchev's denunciation of the dead dictator—the once-important character of Stalin is completely eliminated.

The Civil War is over, and Russia is devastated. At Iverskaya Chapel near Red Square, profiteers exchange food for gold, religious relics, and pornography. An old peddlar with a tray chants, "Matches, prewar matches." It is Zabelin, once a prominent electrical engineer, but now a bitter and introspective old-guardist who holds the Revolution responsible for Russia's ills. His degradation is heightened by his daughter's going to the Metropole Hotel with a sailor. But this sailor deeply loves the girl, and he is Lenin's companion. Soon Lenin appears in a rustic setting, laughing with children and worshiped by old women. Later, on a moonlit night, as he walks with the sailor on the embankment by the Kremlin wall, he dreams of Russian electrification. There is a comic encounter with a peasant woman who, not recognizing Lenin, blames him for "ruining Russia." Old Zabelin. in the meanwhile, is summoned to the Kremlin, After taking leave of his fearful family who are sure that he will be arrested, Zabelin is bewildered and inspired by Lenin's abrupt question: "Sabotage or work?" and his ridicule of Zabelin's "prewar matches." Flattered by confidences and exalted by the knowledge that he is needed, the "Hamlet of Iverskaya Chapel" agrees to help Lenin and again become an engineer. "I have just seen a man of genius in the Kremlin," Zabelin tells his daughter, and he then reforms spiritually. In the presence of other Soviet greats like Felix Dzherzhinsky (the first Cheka director) and (originally) Stalin, Lenin next asks a humorous Jewish watchmaker to restore the chimes on the Kremlin's Spassky Tower, "the main clock of the state." Soon they sound the "Internationale." After trying to indoctrinate a "philistine" Englishman (a caricature of H. G. Wells) in the Communist faith, Lenin completes plans for Russia's electrification: "Our country stands like an enormous rock in the ocean of bourgeois states. Wave after wave rolls up against it, threatening to engulf it and to erode it.

And the rock stands firm. We will not yield, believe me, we will not yield."

CHINA has produced great actors and some drama of distinction since it became a republic in 1912.* Little of it, however, has appeared in the West. China's theatre was propelled by Western social protest drama like that of HENRIK IBSEN, JOHN GALSWORTHY, and BERNARD SHAW, and is a product of political revolution. Even before 1949 most modern Chinese drama was written by left-wing sympathizers and supporters of the Communist Party, which thereafter stimulated the theatre with state subsidies—with not apparently distinguished results, for the plays of protest and struggle were more theatrical than those written after the Revolution had been achieved. NATURALISTIC street plays on topical subjects—*hwo pao ju,* or LIVING NEWSPAPER DRAMA—presented by students and other troupes supporting sociopolitical changes became popular in the villages, especially after the Japanese invasion (1931) and the war that followed. Such theatre was exploited by the Kuomintang and later governments. In recent times these have been virtually discontinued as incommensurate with a progressive present and an idealistic future. The great and long popular Peking Opera and China's music-permeated classic theatre fares (aspects of which were adapted and popularized in Brecht's THE CAUCASIAN CHALK CIRCLE, and elsewhere), are known in the West also in adaptations like *Lady Precious Stream* (1935); the *Wang Pao Ch'man* modernization by Hsiung S[hi-i]. I. (1902–   ), who wrote another play in English, *The Professor from Peking* (1939). These employ stylized techniques and dress, and the archaic language that was the sole permissible public expression until a "literary revolution" in 1919 forced the authorities to legitimatize the vernacular.†

Modern Chinese drama began in 1907 with adaptations of *Uncle Tom's Cabin* and *La Dame aux camélias,* which appeared in the new genre of *hua chü* (talking drama) rather than with the hitherto customary music and singing. They were followed by other adaptations from the West, whose dress, techniques, and conventions (including the use of female performers) paved the way for a new theatre—first an ephemeral one founded by zealous students of literature (notably "The Spring Willow Dramatic Society," in 1915), then the popular commercial one for which Shanghai businessmen hired hacks to write vulgar comedies and melodramas. The 1920's saw the founding of Peking's drama school and the first drama periodicals. Modern China's foremost dramatist was TS'AO YÜ, but credited with being the first modern Chinese playwright was the physicist Ting Hsi-lin (1893–   ), the author of Ibsenite one-act PROBLEM PLAYS (collected in 1925) that, like subsequent *hua chü,* advocated such Western concepts as female emancipation and the freedom to choose one's own marriage partner.

T'ien Han (1898–   ), the doyen of Communist Chinese playwrights, was a prolific translator and author of the words of Communist China's national anthem as well as of works that include a twenty-one-act didactic tragedy with slides and films, and domestic dramas that portray the clash of old and new ways of life; after having fallen into disfavor for his *Hsieh Yao-Huan* (1961), whose fictitious protagonist loses her life for petitioning a T'ang dynasty empress for political reforms, T'ien Han was victimized by the 1966–67 Red Guard movement. It launched the Cultural Revolution and the ensuing crackdown on all modern plays and the extinction of the classical Peking Opera. Responsible for inadvertently unleashing it and the Red Guards was Peking's former deputy mayor, the playwright Wu Han (1909?–   ), when in his play *Hai Jui pa-kuan* (*Hai Jui's Dismissal from Office,* 1961) he suggested that the morality of the past is instructive and not incommensurate with the present. Hung Shen (1893–1955), a graduate of George Pierce Baker's Harvard Workshop, is credited with fashioning the new language used not only in his own plays, which sympathetically portray peasants (as in *Hsiang-tao-mi,* 1933), but as well in those produced by the theatre companies and schools of drama he founded; he also helped develop Chinese cinema. Another very prolific author, the intellectual leader, statesman, and President of the Chinese Academy of Sciences, Kuo Mo-jo (1892–   ), wrote historical tragedies, including one on the ancient poet-statesman *Chu Yuan* (translated in 1953). Hsiung Fo-hsi (1900–65) was a leading popular (as opposed to literary) dramatist whose plays were written to educate the peasantry. The critic and short-story writer Li Chien-wu (1906–   ) is also the author of amusing if moralistic farces (recently out of favor) for a theatre that has otherwise tended to confine itself to serious polemics.

Currently produced are new operas (with piano accompaniment instead of the former raucous band music) and modernized versions of the classics that have up-to-date themes meant to promote the continuing revolution and to stir the people to greater patriotic efforts. Many theatrical forms of China's past have been lost and refound, notably the *kun-ch'ü* resurrected by the great actor (and scholar-director) Mei Lan-fang. In Taiwan, instead of modern theatre it is the classical Peking Opera that is encouraged and frequently sent abroad, particularly whenever Communist China sends out its theatrical representatives.

* A second Republic of China was established on Taiwan in 1949 by Nationalists who escaped from Mainland China, which the ruling Chinese Communist Party thereupon proclaimed as the People's Republic of China.

† One of the important figures of the Literary Revolution was a prominent intellectual and ambassador to the United States (1938–42), the American-educated Hu Shih (1891–1962), who also wrote drama; his farcical playlet *The Greatest Event in Life* was published in A. E. Zucker's *The Chinese Theatre.*

The *Three Famous Chinese Plays* (1946?) collected without English commentary are Ts'ao Yü's *Thunder and Rain,* T'ien Han's one-act *A West Lake Tragedy,* and the internationally popular writer Lin Yütang's (1895–) one-act tragicomic *Confucius Saw Nancy* (1937). Propaganda *hwo pao ju* playlets and a few other dramas were published in translations by the Peking Foreign Languages Press beginning in the 1950's, and Walter J. and Ruth I. Meserve's collection of *Modern Drama from Communist China* (1970) has an extensive introduction. Peiping's Catholic University Press publication, *1500 Modern Chinese Novels and Plays* (1948), compiled by Joseph Schyns and others, is tendentious but has a wealth of material, including an introductory essay, short biographies of playwrights, and synopses. A chapter on modern Chinese drama appears in Faubion Bowers's *Theatre in the East* (1956). L. C. Arlington's beautifully illustrated and comprehensive guide to the theatre, *The Chinese Drama from the Earliest Times Until Today* (1930, republished 1966), deals with classical but not with modern Chinese drama. Notable among the older studies of modern drama are A. E. Zucker's authoritative if chatty *The Chinese Theatre* (1925), which has a critical bibliography; and Jack Chen's *The Chinese Theatre* (1949).

CHINESE WALL, THE (*Die chinesische Mauer*), "a farce" in twenty-four scenes by MAX FRISCH, produced in 1946 and published in 1947. Setting: a twentieth-century stage.

Totally revised in 1955 into the version appearing in Frisch's collected plays, this experimental fantasy has been called a "pessimistic counterpart of Wilder's THE SKIN OF OUR TEETH." It is set in 200 B.C. (at the time of the building of the Great Wall)—and simultaneously in the present-day atomic age, in which the Wall's construction seems the more absurd. The intellectual Contemporary is a major participant in the action, as well as Frisch's *raisonneur*. Moving through jumbled Einsteinian time and disjointed episodes are notable historical and fictitious characters.

The Contemporary has considerable license to speak his mind at the court of China's tyrant, Emperor Tsin She Hwang Ti. Among others who comment about what is important to them are "maskers" like Romeo and Juliet, Napoleon, Columbus, Pontius Pilate, Don Juan, Brutus, Cleopatra, and Mary Stuart. Emperor Hwang Ti, who delivers Hitlerian tirades and is cheered with "heils," is unaware of time's relativity. His daughter, however, by rejecting her princely suitor transcends time and falls in love with the Contemporary. He becomes the people's voice—and the Emperor's sole remaining enemy. "The more we become able to do (thanks to technology), the more nakedly we stand, like Adam and Eve, before the primal question: 'What do we want?' —before what is ultimately a moral decision," he tells the Emperor; "your way of making history is no longer of any importance. We can no longer tolerate a civilization which considers war unavoidable." An innocent mute becomes the tyrant's scapegoat while (ironically) the Contemporary is awarded the poet's prize for demonstrating "what would happen to the world if it should dare rebel against the Emperor." The Contemporary announces the play's conclusion, but the universal farce resumes its cycle, for "again we must repeat it—" Romeo and Juliet replay their scene, which opened the play. The maskers leave, and all that remains is the princess —prostrated before, and professing her love to, the now-mute and despairing Contemporary.

CHIPS WITH EVERYTHING, a play in two acts by ARNOLD WESKER, published and produced in 1962. Setting: a Royal Air Force base somewhere in England, c. 1960.

His first major success, this sometimes brutal play made Wesker's name known beyond England. It consists of twenty-three short but suggestive scenes, and marks a departure from the NATURALISM of Wesker's earlier plays. But his anti-Establishment attitudes and major themes remain unchanged. The play's greatest effects are produced in wordless action scenes and tableaux.

Act I (11 scenes). A corporal introduces himself to some new RAF conscripts: "I'm not a very happy man. I don't know why. I never smile and I never joke—you'll soon see that," and he imbues them with the importance of doing their best for him. Among the conscripts is a rebellious aristocrat, Pip Thompson, who insisted on joining the ranks. He tells the other conscripts of his past, and of how, when he was once in London's East End, he was appalled by its shabbiness. Pip recalls going to a restaurant whose stained menu read "Chips with everything." The workers deprive themselves of all that is beautiful, he feels, and he mutters, "Chips with every damn thing. You breed babies and you eat chips with everything." The men are drilled into shape so that they will lose all individuality. Effeminate and snobbish officers lecture them about physical fitness: "I want you like Greek Gods. You heard of the Greeks? You ignorant troupe of anaemics, you were brought up on tinned beans and television sets, weren't you?" Later an officer subtly propositions the orderly and, when turned down, warns him "not to be fooled by good nature, we slum for our own convenience." Pip slowly wins his working-class fellow conscripts over with tales of his aristocratic background and the French Revolution, implying that the future lies not with royalty but with the revolutionary working classes. At a Christmas party, the officers' contempt for the men shows in their expressions. At the party the wing commander learns of Pip's identity, and starts a campaign to have the young aristocrat won away from the plebeians and back to his own class. First the commander tries to get the men to act as inferiors should, inciting them to have fun with "a dirty recitation, or a pop song." In an effective countergesture, however, Pip gets them to sing an old revolutionary folksong, "The Cutty Wren." Pip's mates are still suspicious of the aristocrat's attempts to be one of them. "I've known a lot of people like you, Pip," one of the men says. "They come drinking in the pub and talk to us as though we were the salt of the earth, and then, one day, for no reason any of us can see, they go off, drop us as though that was another game they was tired of." Pip asks, "I don't have to drop my aitches in order to prove friendship, do I?" But when accused of being a prig, he remarks, "a snob perhaps, but nothing as common as a prig, please." He gains his mates' confidence, however, when he proposes and then (in a wordless climactic scene) leads the men in a successful raid on a wire-netted and guarded yard, from which they steal soft drink bottles.

Act II (12 scenes). The dehumanizing drills of the men continue. An unfortunate conscript whose congenital expression suggests a smile is tormented by the corporal: "You're like an old Jew—you know what happens to Jews? They go to gas chambers." Then he is sent to the guardroom and tormented by sadistic Air Force police. At the same time Pip, too, is being broken—though in different ways. When he refuses to be recommended for officer training, mass reprisals are exercised on his mates. The interrogating officer also uses flattery and ridicule, and then impresses on Pip the hopelessness of his rebellion. Pip's "courage and idealism," the officer tells him, "goes right through us. We listen but we do not hear. . . . We will tolerate and ignore you." At bayonet practice, Pip refuses to obey the corporal's orders to charge the straw dummy. His mates are not impressed by or grateful for Pip's rebellion against their brutalization. Again the officer works on Pip. "Your mates are morons, Thompson, morons," he remarks. "You cannot fight us from the outside. Relent boy, at least we understand long sentences." And then he gets through to Pip with the suggestion that Pip's motives are not particularly admirable: Pip is merely seeking power. "Among your own people," the officer says, "the competition was too great, but here, among lesser men—here among the yobs, among the good-natured yobs, you could be king." And this breaks Pip, for "No man survives whose motive is discovered, no man." Now Pip obeys the bayonet-charge order. The system wins, and the rebellion is over. The unfortunate smiler, who is briefly seen on the road trying desperately to escape from the camp, returns—bloody and defeated. His mates stand by him and threaten mass rebellion. It is Pip who quells it. Before their very eyes he pulls out an officer's uniform. As he changes into it and takes on his role as a member of the Establishment, he coaxes the men into obedience and loyalty: "Don't think ill of us, the stories you read, the tales you hear. We are good, honest, hard-working like yourselves." In a stunningly sarcastic finale, the conscripts parade in mechanical perfection—as the national anthem blares forth.

CHLUMBERG, Hans (1897–1930), Austrian dramatist, was one of his country's promising writers when he died prematurely from head injuries suffered in an accidental plunge into a Leipzig theatre orchestra pit during the dress rehearsal of his masterpiece, *Wunder um Verdun* (MIRACLE AT VERDUN, 1930). Born in Vienna as Hans Bardach, Edler von Chlumberg, he was the son of an army officer who had received his title of nobility for heroism in the Austro-Prussian war of 1866. Chlumberg himself was educated at a military academy near Vienna. He hated its rigorous discipline and expressed his feelings in clandestinely written poems and stories that he submitted under a pseudonym. During World War I he served in the Austrian cavalry and was profoundly shaken by the wholesale slaughter he witnessed at the battles of Isonzo. Their impact on his sensitivities permeates the tone and themes of *Miracle at Verdun.*

After the war Chlumberg joined a group of radical intellectuals and artists, but could find employment only as an office clerk. He persisted in his writing, and in 1926 Vienna's Deutsches Volkstheater produced his first play, *Eines Tages,* a NATURALISTIC portrayal of the mundane hardships that erode and finally destroy the love of a poor young couple. It was followed by the comedy *Das Blaue vom Himmel* (*Out of a Blue Sky,* 1928), a PIRANDELLian play-within-a-play in which theatre-audience volunteers performing in place of the absent resident company act the parts of the scheduled play's lovers—and thus can continue their real-life affair before the eyes of the lady's unsuspecting husband, who is sitting in the audience. Though *Out of a Blue Sky* ran only a few days on Broadway, it was a hit in various European countries and enabled Chlumberg henceforth to devote his full time to writing. He sketched out plans for a novel and a number of plays, but dropped them to write the only work for which he was to be remembered. Told of its success as he lay dying, Chlumberg is said to have gasped, "I know that I must die. The dead soldiers are wreaking their revenge because I have brought them back into this terrible world. Now they are taking me with them to the grave."

A sketch of Chlumberg's life and work appears in the preface to *Miracle at Verdun* in Frank W. Chandler and Richard A. Cordell's anthology of *Twentieth Century Plays* (1934).

CHOCOLATE SOLDIER, THE (*Der tapfere Soldat;* literally: "the gallant soldier"), an operetta in three acts by Rudolf Bernauer (1880–1953) and Leopold Jacobson (1878–?), music by Oscar Straus; published in 1908 and produced in 1909.

This musical version of ARMS AND THE MAN closely follows the plot of BERNARD SHAW's play, though there are "comic variations" characteristic of the romantic musical genre, and the names of all the characters—and even of the historic battle of Slivnitza—are different. Immensely successful in many translations, the operetta has been frequently revived all over the world. At the 1910 London premiere of the English version, by Stanislaus Stange (1861–1917), the program printed "apologies to Mr. Bernard Shaw for an unauthorised parody of one of his comedies." Shaw had vigorously attempted to prevent its production, as well as the use of any part of his own play in the 1927 film version of Straus's operetta.* The 1914 film of *The Chocolate Soldier,* despite its use of the operetta's title, music, and lyrics, curiously enough is based on Molnár's THE GUARDSMAN.

CHODOROV, Edward (1904–), American director and playwright (and brother of JEROME CHODOROV), was stage manager for Nichols's ABIE'S IRISH ROSE before he was twenty. His first play, *Wonder Boy* (1931; with Arthur Barton, 1904–36), was a satire of Hollywood, where he spent much of his time. The most popular and widely acclaimed of his plays is *Kind Lady* (1934), a chilling psychological melodrama about a woman kidnaped in her own home. Another mystery play is *Listen to the Mocking Bird* (1959), his adaptation of a detective novel. Chodorov's other drama includes a lighter play, *Oh Men! Oh Women!* (1953), and many films (including the screen version of Kelly's CRAIG'S WIFE) and television scripts.

CHODOROV, Jerome (1911–), American director and playwright (and brother of EDWARD CHODOROV), collaborated with JOSEPH FIELDS on light plays and musicals. Their most popular works were such dramatizations as that of Ruth McKenney's comic Greenwich Village novel *My Sister Eileen* (1940), which they—and Betty Comden (1919–) and Adolph Green (1918–) converted into the award-winning Leonard Bernstein musical *Wonderful Town* (1953); and that of Sally Benson's *New Yorker* stories of an obstreperous thirteen-year-old, *Junior Miss* (1942). Other notable Chodorov-Fields collaborations are the marital comedy *Anniversary Waltz* (1954) and a dramatization of Eudora Welty's farcical 1953 novella about an old eccentric charged with murder, *The Ponder Heart* (1956). Later collaborations include *Dumas and Son* (1967), with Robert Wright (1914–) and George Forrest (1915–).

CHRONICLES OF HELL (*Fastes d'enfer*), a one-act tragedy *bouffe* by MICHEL DE GHELDERODE, published in 1943 and produced in 1949. Setting: the hall of a decaying episcopal palace in ancient Flanders.

This wildly noisy, sometimes obscure play was written in 1929. Its Paris premiere scandalized the fashionable audience and first popularized Ghelderode's name. An obscene mock epic, it became his most notorious work.

A sumptuously laden table stands in the center and a chaplain gorges himself: "Yum—yum—I'm nibbling ... Mutton! Good! Veal! Lovely! Yum—yum ..." In an adjoining room lies the body of Jan in Eremo, Bishop of Lapideopolis. Angry crowds outside suspect foul play against Jan, who many years before had become Bishop after exorcizing the plague. Various priests rush in and out, and a storm and the noise grow. Though happy to be rid of the herculean Bishop, the priests are fearful and raucous. Their leader is Simon Laquedeem, the equally herculean auxiliary bishop. It turns out that he was the Bishop's chief enemy, and that he poisoned him with a consecrated wafer. When Laquedeem now relates the Bishop's career, he is questioned and protests that he had no part in the Bishop's death: "May a thunderbolt—if I am lying—fall at once on our heads." The first of a number of thunderbolts thereupon crashes near them. The dead Bishop arises and, automatonlike, walks to the table. He tries to extricate something from his mouth, battles with Laquedeem, is pulled away, and finally has the poisoned wafer dislodged. Then he is made to return to his funeral couch, and dies again. After further havoc in the hall, ten giant butchers bear away his corpse. Laquedeem is convulsed with joy. But he suffers from bowel trouble, and the hall soon begins to stink. The priests laugh wildly and sniff each other like dogs. "Dung! Dung!" they howl, and Laquedeem shouts, "The pigs—They've filled their cassocks with dung!" He himself "crouches—gown tucked up—his rabbinical face expressing demonic bliss—while the curtain comes slowly down on these chronicles of Hell."

CIRCLE, THE, a comedy in three acts by SOMERSET MAUGHAM, published in 1920 and produced in 1921. Setting: a summer day and evening in Dorset, 1920.

Generally acclaimed as Maugham's finest play, this high comedy abounds in wit and striking characterizations. Serious observations about life and human nature are implicit beneath the spirited action. The first audiences were shocked by the unconventional ending, and booed the heroine's flight with her lover. The play was filmed in 1925 and again, as *Strictly Unconventional,* in 1930.

Act I. Elizabeth Champion-Cheney has persuaded her husband Arnold, a likable M.P. but a prig, to invite and become reconciled with his mother, Lady Kitty (Catherine). He is still bitter about her having left him and his father (Clive) thirty years before. Since then she has lived with Lord Hughie Porteous, a once-handsome and promising young statesman whose career was ruined by the scandal that followed his and Kitty's desertions of their spouses. Now Elizabeth has arranged a party and, to make the reunion between mother and son less awkward, has invited a few guests. One of them is Edward Luton, a young businessman on leave from Malaya. Unexpectedly Champion-Cheney, Arnold's urbane father, also arrives. He tells Elizabeth, who romanticizes Lady Kitty's infidelity and subse-

* The story of Shaw's epistolary and legal opposition is detailed in Archibald Henderson's *George Bernard Shaw: Man of the Century* (1956).

quent life as a social outcast ("she gave up everything for love"), that he is curious whether his wife has ever regretted her action. Alone, Elizabeth and young Luton confess their mutual love. Just then the principal guests arrive. Lady Kitty is an absurd elderly woman, overdressed, heavily painted, vain, and empty-headed. Lord Porteous is an irritable, unpleasantly gruff old man with ill-fitting false teeth. To the discomfiture of all but his wife, old Champion-Cheney appears from his cottage to join them for lunch.

Act II. It is the end of an acrimonious game of bridge, punctuated by Porteous's and Kitty's bickering. Elizabeth blames Champion-Cheney for aggravating an already tense situation. Guessing her feelings for Luton, Elizabeth's father-in-law sums up Lady Kitty's life. He remembers his wife's youthful animation and "charming impulsiveness," and deplores their transformation into frivolity and "ridiculous affectation." "Don't let pure humbug obscure your common sense," he tells the protesting Elizabeth; "she's a silly worthless woman because she's led a silly worthless life." Nonetheless, Elizabeth decides to desert her husband and go with Luton when the latter again declares his love for her and envisions their "ripping" future together in Malaya. But unlike Lady Kitty, who merely left a note before running away, Elizabeth intends to talk to her husband first. When Lady Kitty and Porteous reappear with Champion-Cheney, the old lovers exchange bitter recriminations, blaming each other for their failure. Lady Kitty's offer to return to him is declined by Champion-Cheney, who relishes his present life of "old wine, old friends and old books, but . . . young women." When Elizabeth confesses to her husband, he is appalled to learn that she intends to emulate his mother. Arnold refuses to release her and tells Luton, "I can't prevent my wife from going off with you if she's determined to make a damned fool of herself, but this I tell you: nothing will induce me to divorce her." And then he angrily shows Luton the door.

Act III. Observing "that the most useful thing about a principle is that it can always be sacrificed to expediency," Champion-Cheney persuades his reluctant son to pretend to release Elizabeth. He is sure that, given her freedom, Elizabeth will find romance less enticing and choose to remain

The Circle, Act III. Edward (John Halliday), Elizabeth (Estelle Winwood), Porteous (John Drew), and Kitty (Mrs. Leslie Carter). New York, 1921. (*White Collection, New York Public Library*)

married. Then he conditions her by exhibiting photographs of the now-absurd Kitty at the height of her beauty and social success. All was lost when she deserted him and became a social outcast, dependent on her lover. "When you come down to bedrock it's the man who pays the piper who calls the tune. Woman will only be the equal of man when she earns her living in the same way that he does," Kitty tells Elizabeth. "It breaks my heart to think that you're going to make the same pitiful mistake that I made," she continues, and describes her progressively degenerating life with Porteous. It started with love, but social ostracism accentuated her utter dependence on the lover—whose passions naturally waned. "I didn't dare make a scene as I should have done if I'd been married," she notes as she remembers his affairs. "One sacrifices one's life for love and then one finds that love doesn't last. . . . The tragedy of love is indifference." Following his father's advice, Arnold tells Elizabeth that he loves but is willing to release her, though the scandal will ruin his career. He even offers to give her money if she should decide to accompany the not very successful Luton. Later, Porteous and Kitty counsel both lovers against running off and repeating their mistake. "We're members of a herd. If we break the herd's laws we suffer for it," Porteous tells them. "We suffer damnably," and Kitty adds, "Don't go. It's not worth it." Still, their love proves irresistible and the young couple run off together. "No one can learn by the experience of another because no circumstances are quite the same," Porteous tells Kitty, and adds hopefully, "If we made rather a hash of things perhaps it was because we were rather trivial people." Oblivious of Elizabeth's desertion and confident of success in his stratagem to prevent a repetition ("the circle") of Kitty's mistake, Champion-Cheney notes that Elizabeth was shaken up: "I'm willing to bet five hundred pounds to a penny that she won't bolt." He calls himself "A downy old bird, eh? Downy's the word. Downy," and smugly starts laughing. Amused, Porteous and Kitty also laugh, and the curtain falls as "they are all three in fits of laughter."

CITIZENS OF CALAIS, THE (*Die Bürger von Calais*), a play in three acts by GEORG KAISER, published in 1914 and produced in 1917. Setting: Calais, 1347.

Kaiser became established with the production of this SYMBOLIC antiwar play, delayed at first by the outbreak of World War I. Translated also as *The Burghers of Calais,* it is loosely based (like Shaw's THE SIX OF CALAIS) on Jean Froissart's *Chronicles.*

Eustache de Saint-Pierre succeeds in persuading the townsmen to save Calais by accepting the English king's ultimatum, and offers himself as one of the six required hostage-victims. But since two brothers offer themselves simultaneously, there is an extra volunteer. Which of the seven should be spared? All take leave of their families, and at a feast at which "we divide the same meal" (as in the Last Supper) they throw lots. These are so controlled that all are elected to go, for all have come to recognize the need for self-sacrifice. Eustache thereupon proposes that the last to appear in the morning will be saved. When he himself fails to appear, the enraged citizens think him guilty of cowardice. But he has merely anticipated the self-sacrifice, and committed suicide during the night. His corpse is brought by his blind father, who rejoices: "I have seen the New Man—he was born on this night!" But then the message of the king's pardon arrives, for that night his queen bore him a son. The citizens place Eustache's body at the altar. As they await the king, the corpse suddenly rises. With amazement, they watch the Ascension.

CITY OF JOY AND CONFIDENCE, THE (*La ciudad alegre y confiada*), a comedy in three acts and a prologue by JACINTO BENAVENTE, published and produced in 1916. Setting: an imaginary city in seventeenth-century Italy.

This is a relatively unsuccessful sequel to THE BONDS OF INTEREST. Crispin, "El Magnífico," is the ruler of a sinful city; other characters from the earlier play reappear, aged and flabby. But the soul of Leander awakes, and with it that of the city. Crispin then becomes its scapegoat, and is killed.

CITY, THE, "A Modern Play of American Life" in three acts by CLYDE FITCH, produced in 1909 and published in 1915. Setting: Middlebury (New York) and New York City, early twentieth century.

Considerably dated in its melodrama, this once-popular and occasionally reprinted posthumous play was Fitch's last, and according to many his best work. Though it condemns the city, it does not wholly attribute the tragedy to it.

Rand is a respected small-town citizen. When he is blackmailed by his illegitimate son, the villainous George Frederick Hannock, who does not suspect Rand's paternity but knows of his shady business deals, Rand dies of a stroke. His death enables his son George and the rest of the family to fulfill their dreams and move to New York. Some years later George Rand is about to reap the fruits of his overweening ambitions, the governorship. Though he has compromised his business and professional integrity as much as had his father (whose reputation remained unblemished), Rand is ready to proclaim his clean record to clinch the nomination. Then he learns that his sister has fallen in love with and secretly married Hannock. He tells Hannock that they are related and must annul the marriage. The deranged Hannock thereupon shoots the girl and tries to commit suicide. Rand is shaken into a realization of his own questionable behavior—and his own responsibility for it, for "What the City does is to bring out what's strongest in us." He confesses his dishonest dealings, though this will ruin his career and his impending marriage. His owning up to his errors at the cost of his happiness, and his striving to reestablish his integrity, however, so impress his fiancée that she stays with him: "Your real self has triumphed! *To-day* you *are* the man I loved yesterday!"

CLARK, John Pepper (1935–), Nigerian author, was among the first major AFRICAN writers. His plays are written in English and, like WOLE SOYINKA's, are a mixture of bush country and Western civilization. Clark has been less influenced than Soyinka by contemporary European theatre and has manifested his academic background in heavily SYMBOLIC drama with classical choruses and sometimes declamatory verse but little action. *Song of a Goat* (1961), his best play, deals with society's pressure to procreate and the concomitant impotence of a fisherman; his wife is driven to commit adultery with her brother-in-law, which brings about the tragedy of her miscarriage and the doom of all the principals, the symbolic sacrificial goats. Clark's study of Ijaw folk drama is reflected in *Ozidi* (1965), which is based on legend and marks his first dramatic use of drums and masks.

Clark was born in Kiagbodo and educated at various WEST AFRICAN colleges. He completed his degree at the University of Ibadan and was awarded a postgraduate fellowship at Princeton University. A journalist and film-maker as well as a lecturer at the University of Lagos, Clark is a major African poet whose other books include monographs and an autobiography critical of the United States, *America, Their America* (1964). With *Masquerade* and *The Raft*, a symbolic drama of four men on the Niger Delta, *Song of a Goat* appears in Clark's *Three Plays* (1964) and was republished with a thumbnail biography in Fredric M. Litto's *Plays from Black Africa* (1968).

CLAUDEL, Paul [-Louis-Charles-Marie] (1868–1955), French playwright, poet, and diplomat, was the outstanding Catholic dramatist of his age. *L'Annonce faite à Marie* (THE TIDINGS BROUGHT TO MARY, 1912), a religious verse drama that first brought him international acclaim, became his best-known and most frequently produced play. Almost equally important, however, is his epic Renaissance spectacle *Le Soulier de satin* (THE SATIN SLIPPER, 1924), a self-acknowledged summation of Claudel's spiritual fulfillment and his life's work. Highly praised among his other drama is the first of his "Papal trilogy," *L'Otage* (THE HOSTAGE, 1911). The actor-director Jean-Louis Barrault persuaded him to release for revised production another important earlier play, *Partage de midi* (BREAK OF NOON, 1906), as well as a musical-narrative, *Le Livre de Christophe Colomb* (THE BOOK OF CHRISTOPHER COLUMBUS, 1930). All these are poetic dramatizations of Claudel's profound Catholic convictions. Widely produced and frequently revived, they celebrate man's ultimate salvation, through self-abnegation, within the all-embracing symbol of the cross.

The son of a minor civil servant of peasant stock, Claudel was born in Villeneuve-sur-Père, an austere place in Champagne that he was to liken to the setting of Emily Brontë's *Wuthering Heights*. In 1882 the family moved to Paris, where Claudel attended a lycée. He was a diligent and promising student, though his adolescence was marked by great bitterness. Like many cultivated people in the late nineteenth century he lost his faith, believing that "whatever was notable in the arts, science, and literature was irreligious." The turning point of his life came in 1886 when he discovered the poetry of Arthur Rimbaud—and through it perceived an existence of the supernatural. Attending a Christmas Mass at the cathedral of Notre Dame later that year, Claudel was suddenly and instantly transformed from a sophisticated but moody young aesthete into a firm believer. Amidst the "throbbing of my whole being," he later recorded in *Contacts et circonstances* (1940), "I had suddenly experienced the excruciating consciousness of the Innocence, of the eternal childhood of God—an ineffable revelation." This experience brought him back into the Catholic fold—and found expression in all his future writings.

In 1890 Claudel joined the diplomatic service, in which he served with distinction in many parts of the world for nearly half a century. As consul, minister, and ambassador, he held posts in the United States, China, Japan, Brazil, and in a number of European capitals. In 1906 he took his bride along to his post in Peking, where he was the ministerial secretary, and their first child was born the following year in Tientsin.

It was during his government service that Claudel produced most of his plays. The first of them, *Tête d'or* (1890), deals—as do all his plays—with the emptiness of a life lacking spiritual guidance. In much poetry but little drama, Claudel here portrays the vanity of human wishes, as his protagonist, victorious in conquering the world, can save neither his friend nor his beloved from death. Claudel's next verse play, *La Ville* (*The City*, 1893), while still static, reflects Claudel's spiritual development and personifies himself as a poet who alone achieves salvation and is saved in a city damned and destroyed because of its preoccupation with material values.

While he was the acting consul in Boston in 1893 Claudel wrote *L'Échange* (*The Exchange*, 1901). Again spiritually autobiographical but less static than the earlier works, this play is set in the United States and features a young husband who sells his wife to a businessman with whose actress wife he enters into a liaison; the husband's breakdown and eventual repentance stress Claudel's conviction that God's will cannot be transgressed with impunity. While in China Claudel dramatized further spiritual themes in *Le Repos du septième jour* (1896), a static verse mystery about a Chinese emperor who journeys through nether regions as a scapegoat for his subjects, is wasted away by purgatorial leprosy, and finally delivers the message of redemption through Christ. The first Claudel translation of Aeschylus's *Oresteia*, *L'Agamemnon d'Eschyle*, appeared in 1896. More important at the time, however, were *Break of Noon* and his work on *La Jeune Fille Violaine,* the play that gradually evolved into *The Tidings Brought to Mary.* These were followed by his much-praised *The Hostage,* which he had begun to write in Tientsin in 1908 but did not conclude until he was transferred to Prague in 1912. It was produced in 1914, the year in which Claudel started on the remaining plays of the "Papal trilogy," *Le Pain dur* (*Crusts*) and *Le Père humilié* (*The Humiliation of the Father;* for both, see THE HOSTAGE). *Protée, drame satirique* (1920), a lyrical farce, portrays Menelaus and Helen on a lonely island during the return trip from Troy. Music for this play was composed by Darius Milhaud, who also wrote the score for *The Book of Christopher Columbus.*

Soon after Claudel became France's ambassador to Japan in 1921 he began to write what he considered his masterpiece, *The Satin Slipper.* Along with his other belongings he lost its manuscript during the earthquake that laid Tokyo waste in 1923. With his wife he worked zealously to help its victims. Claudel's prestige kept growing, and he was appointed ambassador to Washington in 1928. He retired from government service in 1935, and returned to his birthplace. In 1947 he joined the ranks of the Immortals of the Académie Française, and three years later he was honored by Pope Pius XII in an unprecedented public ceremony. The most notable among his remaining stage works are *Jeanne au bücher* (*Joan at the Stake,* 1939), a play also produced as an opera-oratorio with music by Arthur Honegger; and a free adaptation of the Book of Tobias, *L'Histoire de Tobie et de Sara* (1942, translated as *Tobias and Sara*). Claudel also wrote about a dozen volumes of poetry, as many volumes of prose, and nearly twenty religious books, including interpretations of, and commentaries on, the Bible.

Claudel's drama is not entirely restricted to Catholic audiences, though it is distinctly if unconventionally sectarian in appeal and theme. All his plays are predicated on a Christian concept of salvation, and without exception they depict a conflict between the worldly or physical and the spiritual. Claudel's heroes and heroines are usually errant beings who become purified through a life of self-abnegation. A calvary prepares them for paradise or, as in the case of the heroine of *The Tidings Brought to Mary,* for sainthood. It delivers their souls from the prison of the material world, in the terminology of the concluding speech of *The Satin Slipper.* Elaborately and sometimes tortuously poetic—Claudel was a descendant of the SYMBOLIST writers—these plays are weighted by long, stylized speeches and scant action. Yet there is entertainment in their spectacle, for Claudel's texts call for mighty and magnificent stagings to reflect his cosmic themes. Especially when produced with the imagination of a Barrault, who found them ideal vehicles for his THÉÂTRE TOTAL, these plays are highly theatrical despite their poetic-theological didacticism and discursiveness.

Claudel consistently rewrote his plays, which often appear in different versions. A revised two-volume edition of his collected plays was published in Paris in 1965, and there are many French studies of his life and work. Most of Claudel's plays are available in English, and *The Tidings Brought to Mary* appears in a number of drama anthologies. Other Claudel writings include a memoir (with others) of GEORGES DUHAMEL, *Duhamel et nous* (1937). Louis Chaigne's biography, *Vie de Paul Claudel* (1961), appeared simultaneously in English translation as *Paul Claudel: The Man and the Mystic.* Among book-length studies in English are Mary Ryan's *Introduction to Paul Claudel* (1951), Ernest Beaumont's *The Theme of Beatrice in the Plays of Claudel* (1954), Joseph Chiari's *The Poetic Drama of Paul Claudel* (1954), Wallace Fowlie's *Paul Claudel* (1957), Richard Berchan's *The Inner Stage* (1966), and Harold A. Waters's *Paul Claudel* (1970).

CLAUS, Hugo [Maurice Julien] (1929–), Belgian novelist, poet, and playwright, won prizes for his first novel at nineteen and five years later for *Een Bruid in de Morgen* (1953). Portraying an incestuous relationship as an example of pure love, it is characteristic of Claus's coarse NATURALISTIC, Flemish peasant drama, and it was the first of the plays that made this experimental nonconformist the most notable of the new Flemish dramatists.

Claus was born in Bruges into the family of a printer. He attended an art and theatre academy in Paris (1951–53), traveled in Europe, and visited the United States before settling down in Ghent.

Some of his later plays Claus directed himself. They include *Suiker* (1958), which depicts the romance of a worker in the rough sugar beet harvest and a prostitute who is trying to liberate herself; *Thyestes* (1965), which Claus directed in a much acclaimed style influenced by Eastern dance and the Kabuki theatre; *Vrijdag* (1970), a domestic drama about working-class Belgians; and *De Spaanse Hoer* (1970), "the Spanish bawd" of the title being a female Falstaff, an eighty-six-year-old prostitute who reminisces wistfully with a one-time colleague in a Goyaesque world of violence and death.

Claus's experimental poetry as well as his novels and plays have been translated into French and German, but thus far only his novels have appeared in English.

CLÉRAMBARD, a play in four acts by MARCEL AYMÉ, published and produced in 1950. Setting: a dilapidated castle in modern France.

This biting comedy, denounced by FRANÇOIS MAURIAC as "frivolous impiety," entertained audiences on both sides of the Atlantic in the 1950's. Its title character is an impoverished and eccentric nobleman whose family (the long-suffering wife, the intrepid mother-in-law, and his idiotic son) must slave at knitting machines to subsist. A false vision of Saint Francis of Assisi changes the nobleman from a frenzied killer and devourer of cats and dogs to an extravagant lover of all creation, from "sister spider" to his fellow-man. Though temporarily disillusioned, he remains unshaken in his new faith. He decides to have his son marry the earthy village whore ("an admirable daughter of joy") rather than the ugly daughter of rich burghers, sells his castle, and with his family, neighbors, the streetwalker, and his animals sets out in a wagon—mendicants "eager [for] the joy of possessing nothing [and eager] to walk in the ways of the Lord." Now the true vision of Saint Francis appears to all except the worldly priest, who is unable to see "a blessed thing" and wonders, as the inspired but grotesque caravan sets out, "what the mixture will have produced at the end of a month."

CLOSSON, Herman (1901–), Belgian dramatist, was notable for a number of plays popular in the 1930's and 1940's. Almost all of them portray famous men's quests for greatness, which, ironically, they themselves recognize as merely transient and futile though historians naïvely recount them and thus immortalize "heroes." Only Shakespeare in *William ou La Comédie de l'aventure* (1938) can resist sacrificing his art (a play he is writing) when carnally tempted in the fantastic setting of a gangster hideout, brothels, and slums. Closson's most notable play is *Godefroid de Bouillon* (1933), which in fifteen theatrically spectacular tableaux recounts the eleventh-century crusade of Godefroy de Bouillon from Belgium to Jerusalem. It shocked audiences with its portrayal of a national hero with clay feet. Other Closson plays featuring personages thus humanized are *L'Epreuve du feu* (1945), about a false Joan of Arc; and *Borgia* (1947), in which Cesare foregoes an easy seduction of Lucrezia in her bedroom. Closson's preoccupation with sensuality is given a modern setting in *Faux-Jour* (1941), in which three men fail to consummate their plans after inviting a beautiful model to their jungle retreat.

The grandiose settings and poetic language of Closson's plays reveal the influence of MAURICE MAETERLINCK as well as the Elizabethans, and his single farce, *La Farce des deux nues* (1935), shows the influence of Crommelynck's THE MAGNIFICENT CUCKOLD. Another atypical yet popular Closson play is a patriotic piece written and performed during the Nazi occupation but finally banned in 1941, *Le Jeu des quatre fils Aymon;* it retells the old legend of four outlaw brothers who regain Charlemagne's grace with their noble behavior and great deeds.

The Brussels-born Closson's work is discussed in David I. Grossvogel's *The Self-Conscious Stage in Modern French Drama* (1958, republished in 1961 as *20th Century French Drama*) and in Vernon Mallinson's *Modern Belgian Literature 1830–1960* (1966).

COCK-A-DOODLE DANDY, a play in three scenes by SEAN O'CASEY, published and produced in 1949. Setting: the garden of a house in Nyadnanave, Ireland.

O'Casey considered this comic fantasy by far his best, "most cockeyed" play, and "a ball from start to finish." It is a morality, a paean to the joy and life force symbolized by a rooster. For a while, at least, his magic defeats the comic yet sinister forces of evil—puritan joylessness and superstition characterized by the priest and other inhabitants of "Nyadnanave" (a Gaelicism, O'Casey explained, meaning "Nest of Saints" as well as "Nest of Rogues—or Knaves"). But the ending is savage, recalling that of another Irishman's bitter satire, Swift's *Gulliver's Travels.*

Scene 1. There is a brief dance by a handsome Cock with the face of a "cynical jester." Then Michael Marthraun and Sailor Mahan come into Marthraun's garden. The elderly men argue about the wicked magic in the house since the arrival of Marthraun's first wife's attractive daughter, Loreleen. When she walks by, "an invisible wind" turns the holy pictures to the wall, and his second wife "is mixin' herself with th' disordher," prettying herself. When Mahan suggests "there's nothin' evil in a pretty face, or in a pair of lurin' legs," Marthraun disagrees: "your religion should tell you th' biggest fight th' holy saints ever had was with temptations from good-lookin' women." The old friends also argue about a business transaction. Then Loreleen appears as a cock crows lustily, and Marthraun is persuaded by two superstitious young workers that she has transformed herself into a fowl. His belief in "th' sthrange dodges of unseen powers" is supported by a religious old quack who professes expertise at identifying an evil spirit ("*Daemones posteriora non habent*—they have no behinds") and exorcising it with his faulty Latin: "Th' Latin downs her. She tangles herself in a helluva disordher. She busts asundher, an' disappears in a quick column of black an' blue smoke, a thrue ear ketchin' a screech of agony from its centre!" Immediately a tremendous commotion breaks out inside. Marion, the maid, excitedly reports that a strange flying thing is wrecking the house. Just then her lover, the messenger Robin Adair, arrives, embraces Marion, and tells her and Marthraun's pretty young wife that they have scared the bird: "if only you'd given him your lily-white hand, he'd have led you through a wistful an' wondherful dance." He leads the Cock off, and the women now admire it. But the men are frightened and the old quack, after trying to exorcise it, warns them against "th' circumnambulatory nature of a woman's form [which] often has a detonatin' effect on a man's idle thoughts." Then he cautions them "against any unfamiliar motion or peculiar conspicuosity or quasimodical addendum ... but don't, for th' love of God, notice it!" Marthraun is deeply moved by the old quack, but Mahan characterizes him as a "Latin-lustrous oul' cod of a prayer-blower"—and a menace to society. Marion brings drinks, and the old men start cuddling her. The Cock magically places horns over her head, frightening the men and reaffirming Marthraun's belief in the evil of beautiful women. His second wife's sister is carried to Lourdes, to be cured of her disease by a miracle. She is enthusiastically sent off by Father Domineer, a hard, puritanical clergyman who has faith in God's miracles: "Forward, in th' name o' God and of Mary, ever Virgin, ever blessed, always bending to help poor, banished children of Eve!"

Scene 2. Marthraun is sure God will answer their call. But Mahan thinks God has more important people to listen to: "Are you goin' to pit our palthry penances an' haltin' hummin' o' hymns against th' piercin' pipin' of th' rosary be Bing Bang Crosby an' other great film stars, who side-stepped from published greatness for a holy minute or two to send a blessed blast over th' wireless, callin' all Catholics to perpetuatin' prayer!" Various magic happenings now disconcert the friends, though they try to ignore them as instructed by the quack. Their chairs collapse under them, and their bottles get "bewitched" ("You'd think good whiskey would be exempt from injury even be th' lowest of th' low," Mahan says indignantly). A new hat Marthraun ordered has a bullet hole in it, for the town's constabulary, mobilized by Father Domineer to find and kill the Cock, are shooting wildly. A police sergeant explains that they were outfoxed by magic: "the demonised Cock [changed] himself into a silken glossified tall-hat!" Suddenly darkness falls, there is a flash, the Cock appears in place of the hat, and then both disappear. The men fall down and tremble. As they work up the courage to call Father Domineer, the bellman announces the Cock's appearance in the shape of a woman and warns the men to lock themselves in their houses. Soon the beautiful women come—Loreleen amidst a golden light, and then Marthraun's wife, and their maid Marion, both gaily costumed for the evening's ball. Though warned, the women drink the "bewitched" whiskey and raise their glasses to "Th' Cock-a-doodle Dandy!" The police sergeant, Marthraun, and Mahan eventually join in the drinking and dancing. But the mischievous Cock again makes the devil-horns grow atop the women's heads. In the midst of the dancing there is a peal of thunder and the Cock crows. Father Domineer hysterically comes to "stop that devil's dance!" He curses the modern poison of "films, plays, an' books," and though the women refuse to be penitent, the men kneel. Father Domineer demands that Mahan dismiss one of his lorry drivers, a man "livin' in sin." When that man appears, Domineer angrily strikes him so vicious a blow that the man is killed.

Scene 3. At dusk the hunt for the Cock is in full swing; vigilantes are terrorizing the countryside, hounding out the pretty women. Father Domineer and a half-blind idiotic assistant come to cast the evil spirits from Marthraun's house, which shakes during the "battle." "They're terrible powerful spirits," the assistant reports; "knocked th' bell outa me hand, blew out th' candle, an' tore th' book to threads! Thousands of them there are, led be th' bigger ones—Kissalass, Velvethighs, Reedabuck, Dancesolong, an' Same-again." Victorious at last, Father Domineer prepares to burn the books—particularly one "about Voltaire" and another called "Ullisississies, or something." Now the Cock reappears, pirouetting around the garden. Amidst thunder, lightning, and darkness, the Cock snatches Father Domineer and shoots the men with cigar-shaped bullets (unharmed, the men later pull them out). When he departs, the Cock looses a wind that whips the trousers off the men. But he is finally exorcised, and Father Domineer miraculously returns on a white duck. He commands the men's assault against the "onward rush of paganism"; "We know where we're goin', an' we know who's goin' with us." Loreleen, caught with Mahan, who tried to help her, is beaten up by vigilantes, and Father Domineer expels the girl, the "shuttle-cock of sin," from Nyadnanave. "When you condemn a fair face, you sneer at God's good handiwork," Loreleen tells him; "you are layin' your curse, sir, not upon a sin, but on a joy." But like the Cock, the women are defeated. Marthraun's wife and Marion leave with Loreleen; Marion cannot even kiss Robin here, for "a whisper of love in this place bites away some of th' soul!" The invalided sister returns from Lourdes—uncured. But the believers in miracles who had earlier cheered her trip avoid her now and celebrate the victory over the Cock. Robin follows his love Marion "to a place where life resembles life more than it does here." Deserted by everybody, Marthraun asks him what to do. "Die," Robin tells him; "there is little else left useful for the likes of you to do." Accompanying himself on his accordian, Robin leaves, singing of happiness where "lads follow lasses out nutting in May, / For ever and ever and ever!"

COCKTAIL PARTY, THE, a verse comedy in three acts by T. S. ELIOT, produced in 1949 and published in 1950. Setting: contemporary London.

This was Eliot's greatest popular success. It is written in conversational, unobtrusive verse. He later revealed that it is based on Euripides's *Alcestis,* but R. H. Robbins in *The T. S. Eliot Myth* (1951) suggests Charles Williams's novel *Descent into Hell* (1937) as the more immediate source. In this pervasively symbolic play Eliot blended Christian morality and miracle drama didacticism with drawing-room humor. A book-length chronicle of its composition and production is E. Martin Browne's *The Making of a Play* (1966).

Act I. Scene 1. Despite comic chitchat, Edward Chamberlayne's cocktail party is strained because of the hostess's absence. He explains that his wife Lavinia is visiting a sick aunt in the country. But Edward, a middle-aged lawyer, is not taken seriously by the guests, particularly by a shrewd and amusingly meddlesome elderly woman, Julia Shuttlethwaite. The other guests are Alexander (Alex) MacColgie Gibbs, a traveler who tells exotic tales; Celia Coplestone, an attractive young woman; Peter Quilpe, a young film writer; and a mysterious stranger who drinks gin. Relieved when the guests depart, Edward asks the unidentified man to stay, and tells him that his wife Lavinia has deserted him. Unaccountably he wants her back, though the mysterious guest appears to attempt to dissuade him. Then, suggesting that the experience may lead "To finding out / What you really are," he promises to have Lavinia return, on the condition that Edward not question her. He leaves after singing a song about "One-Eyed Riley." Now Edward is repeatedly disturbed by visitors and telephone calls. Julia keeps coming back and calling for things she forgot; Alex returns to prepare Edward a meal; and Peter arrives to ask Edward to find out why Celia, with whom he is in love, has lost her interest in him. *Scene 2.* After they leave, Celia enters. She realizes that Lavinia has deserted, and expects that she and Edward can now get married. But Celia is soon disillusioned in finding Edward fainthearted and wanting his wife back. "I listened to your voice, that had always thrilled me," she says, and it now is "only the noise of an insect, / Dry, endless, meaningless, inhuman." Then Celia asks his forgiveness: she had used him, mistakenly projecting him into "Something that I desperately wanted to exist." Before she leaves they have a last drink together. *Scene 3.* The next afternoon the unidentified guest comes back to confirm Lavinia's return. He knows Edward will change his mind, but it is too late. Figuratively speaking, Lavinia is brought back from the dead, since "we die to each other daily." The stranger leaves, and soon the guests of the previous day appear, summoned by mysterious telegrams. Lavinia herself arrives, equally puzzled by the telegrams. After the guests depart Edward and Lavinia bicker and insult each other at length. She criticizes his indecisiveness and suggests that he is near a nervous breakdown. Edward blames her overbearing nature and regrets having wanted her back—"you / The angel of destruction."

Act II. Several weeks later, in his consulting room, Sir Henry Harcourt-Reilly (the unidentified guest, who is a psychiatrist) brings together Lavinia and Edward, who has moved to his club because married life has again become unbearable. In the confrontation before the psychiatrist not only Edward's former affair with Celia is revealed, but also Lavinia's with Peter. Reilly helps Edward and Lavinia expose and perhaps learn to live with this "mutual treachery" and their faults: Edward's inability to love, and Lavinia's inability to be loved. He helps them recognize that their making "The best of a bad job is all any of us make of it— / Except of course, the saints." When they leave, Julia, revealed as Reilly's aide, announces that she has persuaded Celia to come. After her disillusionment with Edward, Celia has suffered from a sense

The Cocktail Party, Act II. The libation: Alex (Ernest Clark), Reilly (Alec Guiness), and Julia (Cathleen Nesbitt). New York, 1950. (*Culver Pictures*)

of sin and the need to atone. She is unwilling to settle for "the human condition," as Reilly describes marriage to her: "Two people who know they do not understand each other, / Breeding children whom they do not understand / And who will never understand them." Yet, he adds, "... In a world of lunacy, / Violence, stupidity, greed ... it is a good life." Celia chooses another, more difficult way. Reilly says, "Both ways avoid the final desolation / Of solitude in the phantasmal world / Of imagination, shuffling memories and desires." Celia decides to seek the other more unusual and mysterious way, in which one cannot even forget one's loneliness. "Work out your salvation with diligence," Reilly bids her, but later wonders with Julia about "the terrors of the journey" en route to "illumination." Reilly, Julia, and Alex, "guardians" over the confused lives of their acquaintances, drink a libation to the Chamberlaynes and to Celia. Though Peter cannot yet be included, Alex is confident that the time will come: "You know, I have connections—even in California."

Act III. Two years later the Chamberlaynes, now leading a mundanely happy life of mutual tolerance and affection, are ready for another cocktail party. Before it starts, Julia appears with Alex, who has just returned from Kinkanja, "An island that you won't have heard of / Yet." Reilly too appears, and Alex tells of the heathen natives who venerate monkeys, the converted Christian natives who eat them, and the foreign agitators who fan political troubles on the island. These agitators have brought about some natives' "relapse into heathendom. So, instead of eating monkeys / They are eating Christians." Alex is interrupted when Peter, now a successful film writer, returns from California. When he asks about Celia, whom he seeks for a film, Alex reveals that she is dead. She joined a Christian nursing order, helped plague-stricken natives, and in the Kinkanja troubles was "crucified / Very near an ant-hill." Edward and the others are appalled at the waste of her life, but Reilly is satisfied that Celia's violent death "was her destiny": while "she suffered all that we should suffer / In fear and pain and loathing," the consequence of her choice also made her life "triumphant" and brought her spiritual fulfillment. "And now the consequence of the Chamberlaynes' choice / Is a cocktail party," Julia remarks cheerfully. Alone for a few minutes, Edward and Lavinia amicably await the arrival of their other party guests. Lavinia is relieved when the doorbell rings: "Oh, I'm glad. It's begun."

COCTEAU,* Jean [-Maurice] (1889–1963), French writer, stage designer, and actor, was best known as an avant-garde playwright whose dramatic masterpieces are ORPHÉE (1926) and *La Machine infernale* (THE INFERNAL MACHINE, 1934). He also wrote novels, poetry, essays, and film scripts. His most popular novel was *Les Enfants terribles* (1929); he filmed it (1950) as well as some of his plays, and produced such outstanding other motion pictures as *Le Sang d'un poète* (*The Blood of a Poet,* 1932) and *La Belle et la bête* (*Beauty and the Beast,* 1945). His drama synthesizes ballet, music, pantomime, and poetry. Immensely versatile, Cocteau was involved in all the physical aspects of production. "Astound me!" he was exhorted by Sergei Diaghilev, whose Ballets Russes performed Cocteau's first work. In response, he created the startling, spirited, fantastic, irreverent works that made him France's *enfant terrible*. Between the two world wars he was also one of her leading playwrights, and in 1955 he once more astounded people by agreeing to become one of the forty Immortals of the French Academy; this capitulation to respectability, he remarked, was one of the few remaining unconventional acts left him.

The son of an attorney, Cocteau was born in the Maisons-Laffitte summer residence of a Parisian family immersed in the arts, particularly music, painting, and the theatre. These interests and Cocteau's love of the fun and horseplay of the circus characterize all his drama. They already were manifested in his first produced work, the *"ballet réaliste" Parade*. It consists only of choreographic and scenic notes; but its 1917 production so scandalized those whose philistinism it satirized that Cocteau and his collaborators—the painter Pablo Picasso and the composer Erik Satie—had to be rescued from outraged matrons flourishing hatpins. This and later works are associated with the French experimental movements already set in motion by ALFRED JARRY, Cocteau's friend GUILLAUME APOLLINAIRE, and others—though Cocteau stressed his own strong opposition to SURREALISM.

Cocteau frequently acted and collaborated with the great artists of his age in producing the poetically subjective. With Darius Milhaud and Raoul Dufy he brought out *Le Bœuf sur le toit ou "The Nothing-Doing bar"* (1920), a pantomime-ballet for the Fratellini clowns; set in a speakeasy, it reaches its climax with a raid in which a policeman is decapitated by a fan and then has his head restored. Though it was popular, it is less important than is *Les Mariés de la Tour Eiffel* (*The Wedding on the Eiffel Tower,* 1921; with music by Milhaud, Francis Poulenc, Arthur Honegger, and others of *Les Six*): two narrators costumed as phonographs narrate the fantasies pantomimed by a weird but banal wedding party, dominated by a poetic photographer whose camera subsumes them all. Cocteau wrote other theatrical ballets and condensed versions of classical plays, such as *Antigone* (1922, opera by Honegger in 1942), *Roméo et Juliette* (1924), *Œdipe-roi* (1928), *Phèdre* (1950), and *Un Tramway nommé Désir* (1949; i.e., A STREETCAR NAMED DESIRE). His oratorio librettos range from Igor Stravinsky's *Oedipus-Rex* (1927) to Paul Hindemith's *Patmos* (1962).

Always experimenting in his thirty-odd stage works (including ballets), Cocteau consistently dramatized, with remarkably daring histrionics, poetic creativity in an essentially alien and hostile environment. His protagonists are invariably poets or figures imbued with poetic temperaments, which

*Illustration on page 574.

he defined with the term *angélisme*. The philistine bacchantes who lynch—and then venerate—Orpheus immortalize the hatpin-brandishing matrons of 1917, and are a recurring Cocteau theme. His frequent use of classical legend suggests other themes that recur in his plays, particularly the inevitable working of destiny amidst man's illusive self-deception or blindness. And there are repeated echoes of his preoccupation with the Catholicism in which he grew up, described in his philosophic essay *Lettre à Jacques Maritain* (1926) and revealed in poetry like *L'Ange Heurtebise* (1925). Themes like these permeate his acknowledged masterpieces—*Orphée* and *The Infernal Machine*—no less than *Les Chevaliers de la Table Ronde* (THE KNIGHTS OF THE ROUND TABLE, 1937), *Les Parents terribles* (1938; translated as INTIMATE RELATIONS), *L'Aigle à deux têtes* (THE EAGLE HAS TWO HEADS, 1946), and BACCHUS (1951).

His other plays include *Le Gendarme incompris* (1921); *Le Pauvre Matelot* (1927); the one-act *La Voix humaine* (1930, filmed with Roberto Rossellini in 1947), a shocking departure from boulevard theatre in which a jilted girl's telephone monologue concludes with her suicide; *L'École des veuves* (1936); *Les Monstres sacrés* (1940), a serious comedy about the theatre that explores the paradox of reality and illusion in terms of the story of a famous actress, one of the "sacred monsters" who are Cocteau's artist-heroes; *Le Bel Indifférent* (1940), written for the chanteuse Edith Piaf; *La Machine à écrire* (1941), a NATURALISTIC thriller about a provincial hunt for a writer of diabolical letters anonymously signed "the typewriter"; and his sole verse play—and love story *Renaud et Armide* (1943), a three-act tragedy inspired by a sixteenth-century epic poem, Tasso's *Gerusalemme Liberata*.

Almost from the beginning of his career, Cocteau moved in high life and among the world's great artists, many of whom were his close friends. Yet his works reflect a strong consciousness of alienation—that of the homosexual as well as the poet. These attitudes are reflected also in the appeal of death—of suicide resisted with the opium to which he became addicted. His *Opium: Journal d'une désintoxication* (1930) describes these experiences.

His autobiography *La Difficulté d'être* (1947) was translated in 1967 as *The Difficulty of Being*. His collected plays appeared in two volumes in 1957; most of them have been translated. Biographies in English include Margaret Crosland's *Jean Cocteau* (1956), Elizabeth Sprigge and Jean J. Kihm's *Jean Cocteau: The Man and the Mirror* (1968), Frederick Brown's unsympathetic *An Impersonation of Angels* (1968), and Francis Steegmuller's distinguished *Cocteau: A Biography* (1970). English-language studies of the man as well as his drama include Neal Oxenhandler's *Scandal & Parade: The Theater of Jean Cocteau* (1957) and Wallace Fowlie's *Jean Cocteau* (1966).

COHAN, George M[ichael] (1878–1942), American actor, producer, and song writer, also wrote hundreds of vaudeville sketches and over forty plays and musical comedies. An apostle of Americanism, his comedies are in the tradition of the farces of CHARLES H. HOYT and GEORGE ADE. His plays are slight but entertaining, and his immense stature as a showman makes him memorable beyond his own age.

When a child, Cohan joined his parents and sisters in "The Four Cohans," one of America's star vaudeville attractions. He took his family into the legitimate theatre with his first Broadway play, *The Governor's Son* (1901). Typical of Cohan's plays are comedies like BROADWAY JONES (1912) and SEVEN KEYS TO BALDPATE (1913), an adaptation like most of his works. Among the other plays he wrote and starred in are farces like *Forty-Five Minutes From Broadway* (1906), a musical; *Get-Rich-Quick Wallingford* (1910), a dramatization of the stories of George Randolph Chester about the proverbially dishonest and scheming title character, who barely escapes being caught but concludes piously, "What a fool a man is to be a crook!"; and *The Song and Dance Man* (1923), about a second-rate variety actor, ably created (both in the script and onstage) by Cohan, who was by then America's most popular variety actor.

In 1904 Cohan and Sam H. Harris began their important partnership, which in fifteen years produced numerous plays and controlled five theatres at one time. Among Cohan's popular songs were the World War I favorite, "Over There," and such other still-famous songs as "Give My Regards to Broadway," the patriotic "I'm a Yankee Doodle Dandy," and "Grand Old Flag." Cohan's most highly praised acting was as the father in O'Neill's AH, WILDERNESS!, and he came out of retirement to play President Franklin D. Roosevelt in the farce *I'd Rather Be Right* (1937), by GEORGE S. KAUFMAN and MOSS HART.

Cohan's autobiography, *Twenty Years on Broadway and the Years It Took to Get There,* was published in 1925. Ward Morehouse's biography is *George M. Cohan, Prince of the American Theatre* (1943). His life was made into a movie (*Yankee Doodle Dandy,* 1942), and into *George M!* (1968), a musical by Michael Stewart (1929–) and John (? –) and Fran Pascal (? –). In 1940 Cohan was awarded a special Congressional Medal for his patriotic services.

COLLEAGUE CRAMPTON (*Kollege Crampton*), a comedy in five acts by GERHART HAUPTMANN, published and produced in 1892. Setting: a large city in Silesia, late nineteenth century.

This early and not very successful work was Hauptmann's first comedy.

Professor Crampton, a dissipated, Micawber-like painter who is considerably more gifted than his philistine colleagues, loses his position at the Art Academy. His wife leaves him, and Crampton becomes increasingly seedy. A grateful pupil, wealthy but also misunderstood by society, becomes engaged to Crampton's beloved daughter, and they delightedly prepare a place for him in their home. Overjoyed and ready to move in, Crampton at once resumes bullying his pupil and future son-in-law: "Such a blockhead!"

COLOMBE, a play in four acts by JEAN ANOUILH, published in 1953 and produced in 1954. Setting: a Parisian theatre, c. 1900.

This play was written in 1950, published among the *"pièces brillantes,"* and appeared in English also as *Mademoiselle Colombe*. It is unusual in that the untemporizing character here is a poor and angrily defiant young *man,* Julien. When he insists on joining the army, his wife, Colombe, enters the hypocritical and licentious theatre world of his mother, a famous actress. There Colombe finds fulfillment, easily accommodates herself to men's attentions, and becomes the mistress of Julien's cynical half-brother. An ironic last scene dramatizes Julien's and Colombe's first meeting, at which they exchanged vows of eternal love and happiness.

COLOMBIA still proudly claims Bogotá as the "Athens of America" and enjoys cultural prestige in LATIN AMERICA. Its drama is less distinguished. After nineteenth-century historical romanticism derivative of SPAIN's cloak-and-sword plays, Colombian drama employed native themes in its COSTUMBRISMO. There were many early-modern playwrights, the most successful among them being Antonio Alvarez Lleras (1892–1956). He was influenced by JOSÉ ECHEGARAY and JACINTO BENAVENTE as well as HENRIK IBSEN, and his most popular plays were the NATURALISTIC *El zarpazo* (1927), the children's play *Alma de ahora* (1941), and the much-praised *El Virrey Solís* (1948), a historical tragedy about an eighteenth-century colonial governor's romance, retirement, and repentance.

The playwright of greatest later significance was Luis Enrique Osorio (1896–), the director and author of experimental drama and many comedies in both Spanish and French that sometimes satirize Colombian foibles, as did the popular *El Doctor Manzanillo* (1943). He became a political exile in the 1950's, the theatre he had founded was turned into a movie house, and Colombian drama fell into decline. Though repeated attempts have been made to raise Colombia's theatre to the level of its other arts, its best drama in mid-century was that written for the radio.

For further studies see LATIN AMERICA.

COLUM, Padraic (1881–1972), Irish-American writer born in Longford, Ireland, was one of the leading early dramatists of the Abbey Theatre. His NATURALISTIC "peasant" drama influenced the Abbey's development. After a number of early plays (*The Kingdom of Youth, The Foleys,* and *The Saxon Shillin',* 1903), came *Broken Soil* (1903), his best and his first produced play, revised in 1907 as *The Fiddler's House*. It depicts a father who remains on his farm, though he yearns to wander and pursue his artistic bent. *The Land* (1905), too, depicts such a conflict, as well as the conflict of the generations. *Thomas Muskerry* (1910), his last important play, is about small-town society and evidences the influence of HENRIK IBSEN.

In 1912 Colum married the writer Mary Maguire, with whom he settled in the United States in 1914. He virtually gave up playwriting but became very prominent as a poet and an author of children's stories based on Irish legend. Among his remaining plays are *Mogu, The Wanderer* (1917); *The Grasshopper* (1922); *Balloon* (1929), a comedy revised and performed in 1946; *Moytura* (1963), a poetic Noh drama about the nineteenth-century surgeon Sir William Wilde; and *Carricknabauna* (1967), a musical folk play loosely adapting his earlier-published poems. A book-length study is Zack Bowen's *Padraic Colum: A Biographical-Critical Introduction* (1970).

COME BACK, LITTLE SHEBA, a play in two acts by WILLIAM INGE, produced in 1949 and published in 1950. Setting: the run-down section of a Midwestern city, late 1940's.

This "pathetic comedy," as Inge called it, was the first and best of his four consecutive Broadway hits. It portrays the "lives of quiet desperation" of the chiropractor Doc Delaney and his wife Lola, a once-beautiful girl whose former youth and present immaturity are symbolized by her dreams about Sheba, her long-lost dog.

Act I. Scene 1. Doc makes his breakfast and chats with their boarder, Marie Buckholder, an attractive art student. His fat and slovenly wife, Lola, sharply contrasts with the youthful Marie and the neat Doc. Lola tells Doc about her latest dream about Sheba. "I miss her so," Lola says. "She was such a cute little puppy. I hated to see her grow old." Doc agrees: "Little Sheba should have stayed young forever. Some things should never grow old." A reformed alcoholic, he prays for strength, and Lola praises him for his year-long abstinence. After he goes to his office, the bored Lola tries to detain Marie and various passersby, including the mailman, the milkman, and a hard-working neighbor. To each she talks of her past, her marriage twenty years ago, at eighteen, to Doc (the first boy her father allowed her to go out with), the loss of their baby, and Doc's alcoholism and reform. She offers the use of her house to Marie and her boyfriend, a muscular javelin thrower. Doc comes home for lunch and angrily chides Lola for encouraging the boyfriend's visiting Marie, whose purity he extols. *Scene 2.* Later Doc gets engrossed in a soprano's rendition of "Ave Maria" on the radio. Lola reminisces about their courtship, Doc's shyness, and his long-delayed first kiss. Doc replies, "Baby, you've got to forget those things. That was twenty years ago." Lola replies, "Those years have just vanished—vanished into thin air." Eagerly she insists, as she remembers how they had to get married quickly, "You *were* the first one, Daddy, the *only* one." Doc gave up his medical studies, she repeats, and the baby died, probably because of the inadequate midwife who delivered it, because Lola was ashamed to go to a doctor. "You've got to forget it and live for the present," Doc tells Lola; "I might be a big M.D.

Come Back, Little Sheba. Lola (Shirley Booth) and Doc (Sidney Blackmer). New York, 1950. (*Vandamm Photo, Theatre Collection, New York Public Library*)

today, instead of a chiropractor; we might have had a family to raise and be with us now; I might still have a lot of money if I'd used my head." But it is pointless to dwell on the past: "We gotta keep on living, don't we?" Later, when Marie's boyfriend returns, Doc again gets very resentful, and leaves. Playfully the athlete persuades Marie to make love that night, though he is in training. They fondle each other as Lola secretly and happily watches the young lovers from the adjoining room. After they leave, however, Lola cries out plaintively, "Little Sheba . . . Come back . . . Come back, Little Sheba. Come back."

Act II. Scene 1. The next morning Doc catches the boy leaving Marie's room. Doc's long-suppressed frustrations explode. He pockets the whiskey he has resisted for a year, and leaves. *Scene 2.* Lola does not notice, for she is excited about the arrival of Marie's well-to-do fiancé and is preparing a festive dinner. But she is disillusioned with Marie, who calls her a sentimentalist when Lola mentions the athlete, whom Marie admits liking but "wouldn't think of marrying." *Scene 3.* Doc returns early in the morning, drunk and berserk. "I suppose you tucked them in bed together and peeked through the keyhole and applauded," he says when Lola mentions Marie's fiancé; "he probably *has* to marry her, the poor bastard . . . Just like I had to marry *you*." Castigating Lola for her sloppiness, Doc rips off the tablecloth, breaks all the dishes, and then chases Lola with a hatchet. "Scream your head off, you fat slut," he yells, threatening to chop off Marie's "pretty ankles" and "fix" her lover. As his terrified wife reminds him of their courtship he collapses: "Lola . . . my pretty Lola." AA companions come and take Doc to the city hospital, though he resists frantically. Alone and desperate, Lola calls her mother. "Do you think Dad would let me come home for a while?" she asks. "No, I guess it wouldn't do any good for you to come here," she says. "That's all, Mom. Thanks. Tell Daddy hello." *Scene 4.* A week later Doc returns from the brutal cure. "Honey, don't ever leave me," he begs penitently. "Daddy! Why, of course I'll never leave you," she replies, caressing him. "You're all I've got. You're all I ever had." As Lola prepares his breakfast, Doc decides to get "a sad-looking old bird dog," and she tells him of her latest dream: in the school stadium her father has disqualified Marie's athlete. "You picked the javelin up real careful," she continues, and "threw it, Daddy, clear, *clear* up into the sky. And it never came down again." Lola then sought her dog. "All of a sudden I saw Little Sheba," she goes on, "lying in the middle of the field . . . dead . . . her curly white fur all smeared with mud, and no one to stop and take care of her . . ." In the dream Doc would not let her tend to Sheba. "We can't stay here, honey; we gotta go on," he kept telling her. Lola concludes, "I don't think Little Sheba's ever coming back, Doc. I'm not going to call her any more." Doc agrees, "Not much point in it, Baby. I guess she's gone for good." Lola embraces him, and goes to the stove; Doc sips his fruit juice.

COMMEMORATION MASQUE (*Festspiel in deutschen Reimen;* literally: "festival play in German rhymes"), a verse puppet play by GERHART HAUPTMANN, published and produced in 1913. Setting: three stages.

As its subtitle states, this pageant was written "To commemorate the spirit of the Wars of Liberation in 1813, 1814, and 1815," and "performed at the Centennial in Breslau, 1913." Germany's uprising against Napoleon—further quickened by memories of Louis XIV's seizure of Strasbourg one hundred years earlier—is reinterpreted in this "cosmic puppet play" (Ludwig Lewisohn's introduction to Volume VII of *The Dramatic Works of Gerhart Hauptmann*). The authorities expected the conventional, patriotic, anti-French sentiments. They were disappointed by (and rejected) the work's ironic attack on war and its glorification of peace, declaimed by historical personages.

COMPLAISANT LOVER, THE, a comedy in two acts by GRAHAM GREENE, published and produced in 1959. Setting: London and Amsterdam, 1950's.

The comic dialogue, situation, and resolution of this middle-aged love triangle do not obscure its serious implications or Greene's preoccupation with moral problems.

Mary Rhodes's husband, Victor, is a dentist addicted to practical jokes. She has an affair with Clive Root, a bookseller. "Love and marriage don't go together," she tells him, and enumerates the practical aspects of rearing her children and running her household. Children's music lessons and dinner plans—"that's the sort of talk that kills desire. Only kindness grows in that soil." Mary and Clive have a secret holiday in Amsterdam, at the end of which the still-unsuspecting husband arrives from a convention. "He's not satisfied with moving into our room and our bed," Clive complains. "He has to make it a cheap farce with his Dutch manufacturer of dental instruments." At last the husband does discover the affair. Distraught, he implores Mary not to leave him: "The trouble about marriage is, it's a damned boring condition even with a lover." Then he goes to the garage to commit suicide—but returns, for the fashionable district seems "wrong for tragedy." When Mary begs him, "why can't we sometimes, just once, have our cake and eat it?" he generously agrees. Clive is less generous: "You can be a complaisant husband if you like, I'm not going to be a complaisant lover." But when the husband finds the strength to invite him home, Clive "sadly accepts his fate" and replies: "I expect I'll come."

COMRADES (*Kamraterna*), a comedy in four acts by AUGUST STRINDBERG, published in 1888 and produced in 1905. Setting: an artist's studio in Paris, late nineteenth century.

A complete revamping of MARAUDERS, this is a bitter antifeminist satire. Originally it may have been planned as a sequel to THE FATHER, whose doctor and daughter reappear with the same names and similar backgrounds. Harriet Bosse (Strindberg's third wife) acted Bertha in the German film (1919).

Axel and Bertha Alberg have a modern marriage: they are comrades. She intrigues and cajoles her talented husband to help get her painting accepted in the salon. Shamelessly overbearing when she succeeds and Axel's painting is rejected, the mannish Bertha attempts to unman her uxorious mate totally. To humiliate him, she has a big party and triumphantly displays the losing entry. It is revealed to be the untalented Bertha's painting, which Axel had chivalrously switched with his own. He finally rebels against her ruthless competitiveness and greed. Though she capitulates, he insists on a divorce and turns her out of the house. A young lady is announced. Axel denies that she is his "new comrade"—she is his new mistress, and he may marry her: "I want to see my comrades at the café—but at home I want to have a wife!" Bertha wonders if they will ever meet again. "Why not," Axel replies. "But at the café!— Good-bye!"

CONDEMNED OF ALTONA, THE (*Les Séquestrés d'Altona*), a play in five acts by JEAN-PAUL SARTRE, produced in 1959 and published in 1960. Setting: Altona, an industrial suburb of Hamburg, Germany; 1959.

Loser Wins, the other English title of this ambitious, over four-hour-long play, stresses its universal theme of personal and collective guilt. It is specifically applied to France (the protagonist is Franz) after its fall and during the contemporary Algerian War, which Sartre protested against. But the play is less didactic than theatrical with its scenes of madness, incest, brutality, and suicide. As in NO EXIT, individuals are "sequestered" and trapped into mutual and self-judgments. The play resembles THE FLIES not only with its incest but also with the pervasive and symbolic little creatures; here they are crabs—humanity's posterity and its court of judgment. The crimes, like the plot's complexities, are incremental and are revealed gradually, in flashbacks.

The powerful shipbuilder von Gerlach, a family autocrat now dying of throat cancer, asks his son to give up his law practice, take over the firm, and never leave the family mansion. The weak son is ready to obey and take his oath on the family Bible; but his reluctant wife, Johanna, a former actress, discovers and wants to know more about the family skeleton. It is Franz, the older and favorite son, who since 1946—for thirteen years—has been living alone upstairs in a windowless and bolted room, dressed in his tattered army uniform. (Like "the corpse of murdered Germany, I shall stink like a bad conscience.") He is cared for and seen only by his sister, Leni, who nurtures their incest ("my law and fate," she laughs. "It's my way of strengthening the family ties"), keeps him ignorant of Germany's revival, and fails to transmit their father's messages to him. Flashbacks help dramatize the unfolding past. Franz had a "Luther dominated" conscience and resembles his once-adored father, who despised the Nazis—"the scum of the earth on the throne; but they make war in order to find us markets." But unwilling "to quarrel with them over a piece of land," the father sold it to them for a concentration-camp site. Appalled, Franz sheltered an escaped Polish rabbi and is in danger of being denounced; Gerlach used his influence to save his son, who was forced to watch the rabbi being butchered. Immediately thereafter Franz joined the German army and fought heroically, unsuccessfully seeking expiation and death. Only later is it revealed that he tortured and executed several Russian peasants who were suspected partisans. Upon his return to a destroyed Germany, Franz again gets in trouble with the authorities and is again saved by his father's influence. He attacked an American officer who had tried to rape his sister Leni after she sexually provoked and then insultingly rejected him. Gerlach obtains permission for Franz to leave for Argentina but Franz sequesters himself in his room forever. "Leni had won," Gerlach tells his daughter-in-law, Johanna. Later flashbacks reveal how Gerlach used his influence yet again to obtain an Argentinian death certificate for Franz.

Gerlach persuades Johanna to gain entrance into Franz's room to inform him of the father's imminent death and his desire to see his favorite son once more. In his room Franz declaims before the invisible "Tribunal of the Crabs" while Leni cleans up the oyster shells he throws at Hitler's portrait: "My century was a rummage sale in which the liquidation of the human species was decided upon in the highest places." Franz continues, "Man is dead, and I am his witness. Centuries, I shall tell you the taste of my century and you will acquit us." When Johanna appears, beautifully made up as she has been instructed by old Gerlach, Franz's madness slowly gives way. He eats his medals—which are made of chocolate. At the same time Johanna, becoming aware that the "only" truth is "the horror of living," is fascinated by his world of madness and seduced by his proclamation of her beauty, in which she never before could believe. Insisting that she judge him, Franz reveals his past to her—but only in part: "I will give up my cult of illusion when I love you more than I love my lies and you love me in spite of my truth." She believes his incomplete story, but when the jealous Leni reveals his wartime atrocities Johanna rejects him with loathing.

Franz's illusion of a prostrated Germany in which he can drown his personal guilt is destroyed when he learns of Germany's present prosperity. Then he agrees to meet his father. To him Franz confesses his brutality and self-recognition as "Hitler's wife," one who "condemned the Nazis in spirit to hide the fact that he was serving them in the flesh." "Loser takes all," Gerlach insists, and shows his son how Germany's—as well as his own and all—power stems from defeat. Franz finally faces his own guilt. His single free act, committed when not directly under his father's domination, stemmed from an inherited quest for power and was an act of gratuitous brutality: his torture of the suspected partisans. Franz also understands another lie he has lived: "I pretended that I was locking myself up so that I shouldn't witness Germany's agony," the ruins and starvation; but the truth was, "I wanted my country to die, and I shut myself up so that I shouldn't be a witness to its resurrection." His father refuses to judge him, but Franz persuades him to commit suicide with him in a car accident. Thereupon Leni condemns herself to her beloved brother's room. Johanna plays the tape Franz has left her, his "defense speech" to the crabs. "Centuries of the future, here is my century, solitary and misshapen," it begins. Soon Johanna and her husband leave the house of Gerlach for a doubtful future as the tape continues on the empty stage: "Oh, tribunal of the night—you who were, who will be, and who are—I have been!" And it ends, begging acquittal for the century's crimes: "I, Franz von Gerlach, here in this room, have taken the century upon my shoulders and have said: 'I will answer for it. This day and forever.' What do you say?"

CONDEMNED, THE (*Den Dödsdömde*), a play in four acts by STIG DAGERMAN, produced in 1947 and published in 1948. Setting: the prison and a restaurant in a Swedish town, late 1940's.

This was Dagerman's first and most effective drama. Like the novels of Franz Kafka and Strindberg's CHAMBER PLAYS, its action and dialogue are fragmentary, suggestive—even gothic in their evocative portrayal of the limitations of justice and of human callousness, cruelty, and stupidity.

Act I. An old lawyer relates a weird and frightening park experience to the prison doorkeeper, who, in turn, explains the buttons he pushes to admit condemned convicts and their guards. Reporters come to interview such a convict, who was miraculously saved by the last-minute illness of the executioner. Thinking him safely dead, the real murderer has confessed that he killed the Condemned Man's wife, whose lover he was. The doorkeeper describes how he once beat up the Condemned Man when he tried to escape—"for you can't just let anything go on in a place like this." But, he adds, "Cruelty certainly has a limit here like every other place." When the Condemned Man appears, he is unable to respond satisfactorily to the reporters' questions on what it feels like to be released: "Wouldn't it be sufficient if I said that I am very, very tired but very, very happy?" He then agrees to let the reporters accompany him to the "Rescued Men's Club," whose members have invited him to celebrate his release.

Act II. The club's members are an explorer, "a

man who was almost crucified," a duelist, and a rapids-shooter. They drink and describe how they were saved from death, their conversation becoming increasingly bizarre. The Condemned Man, too, must tell his story. He describes the "ocean of silence," the "merciless" world he perceived as he entered the execution chamber. His companions admit that they had no sympathy for him during the trial; they were, in fact, revolted by the crime they thought he had committed. The Condemned Man is both puzzled and disgusted by their ability "to hate and detest a man one second and the next to pour your sympathy over him without the man having changed in the least. How do you think one could depend on your kindheartedness when one cannot even depend on your hardheartedness?" Rejecting their sympathy, he conceives of life as "a series of misconceptions, misconceptions of what one ought to have done and of what one ought not to have done. I have been in a place where it does not serve any purpose to curse, to rebel, to hope, because the law takes its course and nothing can be changed." Now he is indifferent both to the people, who condemned him, and to fortune, which is blind. As the club members continue to joke and drink, a girl (a prostitute) invites the Condemned Man to accompany her to a private room upstairs.

Act III. Throughout this act, the girl lies on a sofa, while the Condemned Man stands leaning against the door. She asks him to come to her, but he is unable to do so. "There's something wrong here," he keeps insisting, though the girl is attractive. He declines to kiss her: "There's nothing wrong with your lips. It's just that I don't want to." Trying to understand what keeps him from going to her, he concludes that there is "something in the room that hurled me back, down into eternity." But then he begins to reason his way out of "the darkness," to make himself "go toward the terrible things that are waiting." He confuses the girl with his wife—whom he had frequently imagined in his cell, whereupon he "fell on an empty bed with my desire and my hate." As the girl continues to talk seductively, he pulls out a revolver and shoots her. The stage darkens, and he is heard walking across the room to the sofa.

Act IV. The old lawyer and the doorkeeper are talking; the members of the Rescued Men's Club castigate the Condemned Man for spoiling their party; and the journalists ask inane questions and prepare to write about the new murder. The Condemned Man explains that it was his wife he shot, though the dead woman has turned out to be someone else. He calls himself a dead man, for "a condemned man does not die when the ax falls. He has died long before that"—when sentence is pronounced, for then "he has nothing more to hope for." Life is hope, but "You demanded too much of me," he says, for "it was just a dead man that you turned loose." He is bitterly amused: "First you force us to accept death. Then suddenly you force us to accept life. A man cannot be condemned to death in the

The Condemned, Act III. The Condemned Man (Olaf Widgren) and the girl (Eva Dahlbeck). Stockholm, 1947. (*Drottningholms Teatermuseum*)

morning, and condemned to life in the evening." And he denies the existence of courage and cowardice: "There is only being awake and being asleep." He goes out after describing the corridors he will have to pass on his road to eternity. Understanding nothing, the reporters eagerly try to record the story and transmit it to their papers. After they and the club members leave, the old lawyer finally also must depart, to the "cold and foggy" outside.

CONFIDENTIAL CLERK, THE, a verse play in three acts by T. S. ELIOT, produced in 1953 and published in 1954. Setting: contemporary London.

This is a farce about confused parents and their illegitimate and misplaced offspring. Though witty, it displays the thematic preoccupation with Christian theology of Eliot's other plays. The verse is conversational, and the plot was inspired by Euripides's *Ion*.

Sir Claude Mulhammer hires as his private secretary (confidential clerk) Colby Simpkins, whom he believes to be his illegitimate son. He plans eventually to adopt Colby, and therefore hopes his eccentric wife will take to this unacknowledged son. (He also has an illegitimate daughter, whom, however, he has reluctantly acknowledged.) All of them have yearnings: Colby to be a musician, the financier Sir Claude to be a potter, and his wife to inspire an artist. She once bore an illegitimate son to a guardsman who wrote poems. The man died, and the baby was placed with someone whose name she has forgotten. Sir Claude's charming illegitimate daughter and Colby are attracted to each other, but when he is disturbed to learn of her parentage she mistakes his disappointment at their consanguinity for scorn of her illegitimacy. Hurt, she returns to her fiancé, whom Sir Claude's wife dislikes. In a heart-to-heart talk with young Colby, Sir Claude's wife recognizes the name Mrs. Guzzard of Teddington, Colby's foster-mother, as the one she "misplaced." She is sure Colby is her son, and when Sir Claude insists that Colby is *his* son, Mrs. Guzzard is summoned. There is a long interview, presided over by Sir Claude's retired confidential clerk. Mrs. Guzzard, a formidable woman, identifies the "misplaced" son of Sir Claude's wife as the brash fiancé, and Colby as the son of neither claimant—he is her own son. Sir Claude's mistress—Mrs. Guzzard's sister—died before the child's birth, and Sir Claude mistook the Guzzards' child as his. Colby is now free to retire to the "secret garden" of his "inner world": to spiritual fulfillment as the organist—eventually perhaps the canon—in the retired confidential clerk's church. Dazed by his loss, Sir Claude is comforted by his wife, who says, "We've got to try to understand our children." It is the illegitimate children whom they have spurned, Sir Claude's daughter and her fiancé, who now ask their shaken parents to allow them to "mean something to you . . . if you'd let us; / And we'd take the responsibility of meaning it."

CONKLE, E[llsworth] P[routy] (1899–   ), American playwright and academician, was a drama professor at the University of Iowa, where he also directed the progressive University Theatre. His Broadway play *200 Were Chosen* (1936) deals with Depression farmers relocated from the Midwest to Alaska by the government. *Prologue to Glory* (1938), portraying the young Lincoln and his romance with Ann Rutledge, received a very successful Federal Theatre production; though it is only mildly political, a few sensitive politicians attacked it as a sinister piece of Marxism. Conkle also wrote many one-acters, most of them dealing with and set in the Middle West.

CONNECTION, THE, a play in two acts by JACK GELBER, produced in 1959 and published in 1960. Setting: a stage and a city pad, late 1950's.

This controversial hippy SLICE OF LIFE frankly portrays drug addiction. It assaults the audience with obscene language, the improvisations of the characters and a jazz combo, and a PIRANDELLian blending of levels of make-believe in which characters (filming a supposed drama on addiction performed by real addicts) panhandle among the audience. In the first act the junkies await "the connection" bringing their fix. "The people who work every day, the people who worry so much about the next dollar," one of them remarks about the "squares" in the street, "those people are hooked worse than me." When the connection arrives, in the second act, each of the addicts gets his shot in the (visible) toilet. They achieve their euphoria, although the owner of the pad is almost killed by an overdose.

CONNELLY, Marc[us Cook] (1890–   ), American dramatist and producer, had his earliest success together with GEORGE S. KAUFMAN. Their collaboration produced about half a dozen plays. It began with DULCY (1921), which popularized Franklin P. Adams's character for a decade and made Lynn Fontanne a star; and it ended with their best work, BEGGAR ON HORSEBACK (1924). Subsequently Connelly was to collaborate with others and to write plays by himself. With one significant exception, however, none of his later works succeeded to any marked degree. The exception was THE GREEN PASTURES (1930). It was with this morality, performed by an all-Negro cast, that Connelly's name became and has remained important in the annals of the American drama.

Connelly was born in Pennsylvania. He began his career as a journalist in Pittsburgh, and then went to New York. There he continued his newspaper work, and began writing lyrics for the theatre. His friendship with Kaufman led to their collaboration—and their first hits. Their second work, *To the Ladies* (1922), was a comedy featuring a wife who is as intelligent as Dulcy is stupid. Their most appealing other play was *Merton of the Movies* (1922), a comedy based on HARRY LEON WILSON's satiric novel about Hollywood, and featuring a film-struck drygoods clerk who wins fame because of his unconscious burlesque of a serious role.

Of Connelly's other collaborations, the most notable is *The Farmer Takes a Wife* (1934), an adaptation with Frank B. Elser (1885?–1935) of Walter D. Edmonds's novel *Rome Haul* (1929). Further collaborations were *The Wild Man of Borneo* (1927), with the film script writer Herman J. Mankiewicz (1897?–1953); and *Everywhere I Roam* (1938), with Arnold Sundgaard (1909–). The first of Connelly's solo plays was *The Wisdom Tooth* (1926), a wistful dream comedy about a clerk beset by an inferiority complex. Other plays —none of them important—include *The Flower of Virtue* (1942), *A Story for Strangers* (1948, a parable about a talking horse), and *Hunter's Moon* (1958).

All these plays suggest a penchant for wit and whimsy that could well have continued Connelly's success indefinitely—had he continued collaborating with Kaufman. But though the remainder of Connelly's career as a dramatist was, on the whole, anticlimactic, *The Green Pastures* secures his position as a significant American playwright. After World War II Connelly taught playwriting at Yale University. There he hoped to imbue his students with the importance of writing for the world, he remarked, "not just for Broadway." His memoirs appeared as *Voices Offstage* (1968). The first book-length study of his work was Paul T. Nolan's *Marc Connelly* (1969).

CONQUERING HERO, THE, a play in four acts by ALLAN MONKHOUSE, published and produced in 1923. Setting: England and France during World War I.

This ironically titled antiwar play was much praised in the 1920's.

Colonel Rokeby's sons are cruelly jeered for their opposition to war and their failure to enlist. One of them, a parson, considers war unchristian; the writer Chris (Christopher), another son, espouses civilized values. "Some of us have to keep the eternal going," he tells his sister, whose husband is going to the front; it is not only soldiers we need, but "the idea" of them, and "I can give you that." But his sister's and his fiancée's sneers and growing war hysteria finally enmesh him. A brief war episode manifests the dreadful dehumanization of Chris, as well as that of a fellow prisoner and their German captor. Back in England Chris is cheered as "the conquering hero" by his proud family and neighbors. But he is crushed. "This war is very hard on men like me," he tells the fiancée, sends her away, and breaks down weeping before his father: "We've both done our best, Daddy."

CONRAD, Joseph [Josef Teodor Konrad Nalecz Korzeniowski] (1857–1924), the renowned Polish-born English novelist, made three stage adaptations of his fiction: *One Day More* (1905), a one-act dramatization of his short story "Tomorrow"; *Laughing Anne* (1920), a slight play based on his equally slight tale "Because of the Dollar"; and *The Secret Agent,* a drama in four acts produced in 1922 and published the following year. The most successful stage adaptation of Conrad was *Victory* (1919), by Basil Macdonald Hastings (1882–1928), a minor English playwright. The Polish physicist-playwright Bruno Winawer (1883–1944) sent Conrad, whom he did not know, a copy of his just-published and produced portrayal of the post-World War I degradation of a Warsaw scientist, *Księga Hioba* (1921); intrigued with the play, Conrad translated it, and it was published in London as *The Book of Job* in 1931. Another Conrad item of relevance to the drama is Lvov's Teatr Ludowy's 1963 production of *Panna Mężatka,* a comedy by Conrad's father, Apollo Korzeniowski (1820–69).

One Day More and *Laughing Anne* were jointly published in 1924, with an introduction by JOHN GALSWORTHY; *One Day More* was republished, with notes by Eric Bentley, in Volume 3 of *The Modern Theatre* (1955).

CONSTANT NYMPH, THE, a play in three acts by MARGARET KENNEDY and BASIL DEAN, published and produced in 1926. Setting: contemporary Switzerland, England, and Brussels.

Margaret Kennedy's popular romantic novel of love among artists, on which this play is based, was also adapted by JEAN GIRAUDOUX and by JACINTO BENAVENTE. Equally successful as a drama in England, and filmed a number of times, it fared less well in America. Like the novel, it portrays the sensitive and gifted, unconventional Sanger family of musicians defeated by society. The title character is the capricious Teresa, a precocious fifteen-year-old. She falls in love with her father's arrogant disciple, the talented musician Lewis Dodd. He, however, falls in love with and marries a domineering relative of Teresa's. Later, back in England, when he discovers his wife's real nature, Dodd persuades Teresa to elope with him. On their way to Europe Teresa falls ill, and she dies in Brussels.

CONSTANT WIFE, THE, a comedy in three acts by SOMERSET MAUGHAM, produced in 1926 and published in 1927. Setting: a contemporary Harley Street (London) residence.

This has been one of Maugham's more successful plays. It was filmed in 1929 (as *Charming Sinner*), and the role of the title character has been played by Ethel Barrymore and Katharine Cornell. Like OUR BETTERS, its spirit is wittily amoral, akin to that of Restoration comedy. But like THE CIRCLE (one of whose key sentences it duplicates), it has serious implications, specifically in its heroine's attitudes, which echo those of Ibsen's A DOLL'S HOUSE, and in its challenge to double standards in sex.

Act I. Constance's husband, the distinguished surgeon John Middleton, is having an affair with her pretty but empty-headed friend, Marie-Louise Durham. Everybody knows about it except, apparently, Constance, a handsome thirty-six-year-old woman who has been happily married for fifteen years. Adroitly she parries her family's and friends' insinuations and their attempts to reveal the liaison. She ignores Marie-Louise's transparent stratagem to see Middleton privately,

The Constant Wife. Constance (Katharine Cornell), her mother (Grace George), and Middleton (Brian Aherne). New York, 1951. *(Vandamm Photo, Theatre Collection, New York Public Library)*

declines a friend's solicitous offer of economic security as her partner in an interior-decorating business, and assures her mother, who presses Constance to confide in her, that she loves her husband. Then Constance is visited by Bernard Kersal, a successful silk merchant returning from Japan. He is her one-time suitor who, Constance immediately discovers, is as attractive as he had been fifteen years before when she last saw him. Respectfully but ardently he expresses his unflagging love for Constance. Intending to meet Marie-Louise, Middleton tells Constance he must be out for an emergency operation that evening. He amiably suggests that she dine with Kersal, who is delighted to oblige.

Act II. Marie-Louise's husband has discovered Middleton's cigarette case under his wife's pillow, and angrily accuses her of adultery. The clever Constance persuades him that he is mistaken and gets him penitently to buy Marie-Louise jewelry, in a scene that is witnessed by her family and friends. Constance then admits she has known of their affair all along: "I've been spending the last six months in a desperate effort to prevent my friends and relations from telling me your ghastly secret." They fail to understand Constance, who is grateful for the first five years of love she shared with her husband. Then she realized that their mutual passion had turned to "genuine affection." This, Constance explains, accounts for their happy and perfect marriage. "There are some things that two people may know very well, but which it's much more tactful for them to pretend they don't." However, now that she has been forced openly to acknowledge the situation, she must act. She considers accepting her interior-decorator friend's offer. "I'm tired of being the modern wife," Constance remarks, "a prostitute who doesn't deliver the goods." To Kersal she explains why she cannot complain about her husband's adultery: "He bought a toy, and if he no longer wants to play with it, why should he? . . . It all comes down to the economic situation. He has bought my fidelity and I should be worse than a harlot if I took the price he paid and did not deliver the goods." Then she calls up her friend to accept the partnership: "I want to earn my own living."

Act III. A year later, Marie-Louise is back from a long trip with her husband, and in love with "a perfectly divine young man" she met on the boat. In the meantime Middleton has tired of her and asks Constance to tell Marie-Louise gently that their affair is over. Privately she asks Constance to give Middleton a similar message. His big shock comes when Constance gives him the money she has earned and tells him she is taking a six-week vacation with Kersal before he returns to Japan. Having paid her own way, she has gained the "one freedom that is really important and that is economic freedom, for in the long run the man who pays the piper calls the tune." Middleton's incredulity and anger do not shake her. When he observes that a man's infidelity is not comparable with a woman's, she suggests that he rid himself of conventional prejudices like her mother's: "Men were meant by nature to be wicked and delightful and deceive their wives, and women were meant to be virtuous and forgiving and to suffer verbosely." And when he complains that Kersal is "a drivelling idiot," Constance remarks that "perhaps it's natural that a man and his wife should differ in their estimate of her prospective lover." She turns down her husband's offer to take her on a second honeymoon. It would not be the same: "Once more before it's too late I want to feel about me the arms of a man who adores the ground I walk on," to do all the silly things new lovers do. But she assures her husband of her everlasting affection: "I may be unfaithful, but I am constant." He blusters as she starts to leave, but Constance knows that as a gentleman, "you could never bring yourself to divorce me for doing no more than you did yourself." And he finally agrees: "You are the most maddening, wilful, capricious, wrong-headed, delightful and enchanting woman man was ever cursed with having for a wife. Yes, damn you, come back." Constance blows him a kiss as she "slips out, slamming the door behind her."

COOK, George Cram (1873–1924), American producer and dramatist born in Iowa, is most notable as the founder and director of the Provincetown Players. "Jig," as he was known, was closely assisted in this history-making achievement (including the production of all of EUGENE O'NEILL's early work) by his wife, SUSAN GLASPELL, with whom he also collaborated on two one-act plays, SUPPRESSED DESIRES (1915) and *Tickless Time* (1918). Cook himself wrote other one-acters: *Change Your Style* (1915), an attack on various art schools; and *The Spring* (1921), a SYMBOLIC drama. He also wrote a full-length antiwar play, *The Athenian Women* (1918). The biography of Cook constitutes part of Glaspell's *The Road to the Temple* (1927).

COPEAU, Jacques (1878–1949), French writer and theatre man, is more notable for his work as critic-director-producer than for his acting and for the few plays he wrote: *Les Frères Karamazov* (*The Brothers Karamazov,* 1911), an adaptation (written with Jean Croué, ? – ?) of Dostoevsky's novel; *La Maison natale* (1923); and *Le Petit Pauvre* (*The Little Poor Man,* 1946), a lyrical and devout portrayal of Saint Francis of Assisi.

Copeau's manifesto calling for the establishment of a new art theatre was published in 1908, in the *Nouvelle Revue Française,* which he founded with ANDRÉ GIDE. Opposed to fashionable NATURALISTIC and WELL-MADE drama, Copeau conceived of the director-actor as being a priest. He favored poetic stage art: emphasis on mime and speech and minimally naturalistic but austerely simple acting, setting, and decor. To accomplish these ideals he trained a company of young, later notable actors like Louis Jouvet and Charles Dullin, and launched the Vieux-Colombier art theatre in 1913. Upon the outbreak of World War I he moved his company to New York, where for two seasons he produced some fifty classical and modern plays. Returning to Paris in 1919, Copeau at the Vieux-Colombier spearheaded a movement of stage art that continued to stress "pure theatre," the unadorned poetic and imaginative. Disillusioned with its failure—despite some artistic successes—in 1924, Copeau and company returned to his native Burgundy. There *Les Copiaux* "renewed contact with the soil," perfected their art, and performed before peasant audiences. His nephew Michel Saint-Denis in 1931 reorganized the group into the Compagnie des Quinze, and Copeau returned to Paris. In 1936 Copeau became director of the Comédie-Française, where for four years he staged Shakespeare and the French classics.

Copeau's memoirs were published as *Souvenirs du Vieux-Colombier* (1931). *The Little Poor Man* appears in Richard Hayes's collection *Port-Royal and Other Plays* (1962), with an introduction and a bibliography.

COPPÉE, François [Joachim Édouard] (1842–1908), French short-story writer, poet, and dramatist, wrote verse history plays, among the more notable of which are *Severo Torelli* (1883), a fifteenth-century melodrama about a man saved from parricide by his mother's stabbing her lover; and *Pour la couronne* (1895), another drama about parricide. Sarah Bernhardt played in Coppée's *Le Passant* (1869), a one-acter. Exemplifying the romantic literary tradition of Victor Hugo, Coppée's drama was praised for its eloquence but was eclipsed by the drama of EDMOND ROSTAND.

Coppée's collected works appeared in seventeen volumes (1885–1909).

CORAL, THE (*Die Koralle*), a play in five acts by GEORG KAISER, published and produced in 1917. Setting: an industrialized country, 1917.

Though an independent work, this became the first part of the GAS trilogy. *The Coral,* too, is EXPRESSIONISTIC, and none of the characters is named.

Acts I through III. It is "Open Thursday" in the Billionaire's factory. On that day the needy are given charity (conscience money) by his secretary—his secret double, distinguishable from the Billionaire only by the coral he wears on his watch chain. One petitioner has an odd request: a Socialist intellectual eager for reform, he asks the Billionaire to declare capitalism "the most monstrous of evils." The Billionaire accidentally is there himself instead of the secretary who usually insulates him from the sight of poverty. He relates how he came from an impoverished family victimized by the system and was driven by fear to destroy his childhood memories and "keep the distance ever wider between the horror and myself." His is also "*the* cosmic plan." Universal chaos, he tells the horrified Socialist, already is here: "therefore let whoever can, save himself on the first spot of firm ground he can find." The Billionaire's son is to immortalize this quest for him. But the son rebels against his wealthy background and injustice. Returning from a world cruise, he becomes a stoker. With his daughter, the Billionaire meets him in his private yacht. There the son's ministering to a collapsed stoker inspires his sister. The Billionaire's ruthless coping with a factory disaster sends the daughter to care for the victimized workers, and the son into open rebellion. The Billionaire staggers under the blow of his children's desertion and the consequent destruction of his insulation from the horrors of poverty. "Will no one help me now out of the darkness of my past?" he asks. "I'll give my life in exchange for any other man's." Seeking one in whom he could "sink myself and lose this fear," he discovers that his secretary had a happy childhood. The Billionaire shoots him and just before the entry of the guards—the only ones who know the secret—slips the dead secretary's coral on his own watch chain.

Acts IV and V. Arrested as the secretary who murdered the Billionaire, he claims for a while to be the Billionaire. Then he eagerly acknowledges the secretary's childhood as his own, and is condemned to death for the murder. Before his execution he is visited by the Socialist, his son, and a priest. The Socialist is the only one to recognize him as the Billionaire. Now a successful capitalist, he is grateful because he had his eyes opened and can carry on the Billionaire's secret of salvation: ruthlessly to trample down the weak and leave chaos behind. The son sympathizes with the supposed secretary who rid the world of a tyrant, something he himself had wanted to do. He offers to save the Billionaire if he will join in his crusade: "in our untiring zeal we shall be bound together as father and son." The Billionaire agrees—but only if he were to be the son his father wished him to be and return to luxury, "back again to the bank where the sun is shining." After the son departs, the priest offers the comforts of the cross. "We are all driven from our paradise of tranquility," the Billionaire tells him; "pieces broken from the glimmering coral tree—bearing a wound from our first day that never heals, but burns and burns. It is the terrible pain that drives us on our way!" The Billionaire looks at the crucifix: "That only dulls the pain." Then he looks at the coral piece: "This delivers from sorrow!" Seeking quiescence—like that of the sea-sheltered coral tree—he walks steadfastly to his execution.

CORN IS GREEN, THE, a play in three acts by EMLYN WILLIAMS, published and produced in 1938. Setting: the living room of a house in a remote Welsh village, late nineteenth century.

Williams made his reputation as a dramatist with this autobiographical play. He starred in it (with Sybil Thorndike) in London, it was produced in New York (with Ethel Barrymore), and it was subsequently filmed. Colorful with its host of Welsh characters, and moving despite patches of sentimentality and melodrama, it has been called tenderly comic as well as tragic.

Act I. A kindly no-nonsense English spinster of forty, Miss Moffat ("I've never felt that Lily Christabel really suited me") settles in the small village of Glansarno. She is accompanied by a cockney servant and the latter's teen-age daughter. When she hears about the illiteracy of the villagers, who cannot even speak English and, at twelve, "are sent away over the hills to the mine, and in one week they are old men," Miss Moffat decides to use her money to start a school. "These nippers are to be cut off from all that, for ever, are they?" she asks, pointing at her many books, "because they happen to be born penniless in an uncivilised countryside, coining gold down there in that stinking dungeon for some beef-headed old miser!" For her school she enlists the help of a frustrated spinster and a salvationist clerk. "When I've finished with you," she tells them, "*you* won't have time to think about snapping up a husband, and *you* won't have time to be so pleased that you're saved!" After six weeks she is stymied by a squire, the vain coal-mine owner who is not

The Corn Is Green, Act I. Miss Moffat (Ethel Barrymore) with the squire (Edmond Breon), the clerk (Rhys Williams), and the cockney servant (Rosalind Ivan) and her daughter (Thelma Schnee). New York, 1939. (*Vandamm Photo, Theatre Collection, New York Public Library*)

having "any of this damned hanky-panky in my village." She loses her temper with the "stupid, conceited, greedy, good-for-nothing, addle-headed nincompoop," and gives up. But then she reads the laboriously written exercise of a young boy named Morgan Evans. "The mine is dark," it begins, and in groping words envisions the appearance of light and nature, "where the corn is green." Struck by his incipient genius, Miss Moffat decides to persevere. "I am going to get those youngsters out of that mine. . . . We are going on with the school," she tells her assistants, and rereads Morgan's essay.

Act II. After two years Miss Moffat, a natural teacher, has made marvelous progress with the village. Her servant's teen-age daughter—"Guttersnipe species—if there is such a fish," Miss Moffat remarks—ridicules Morgan's studies and obedience. Considering him "the most brilliantly receptive brain I've ever come across," Miss Moffat plans to enter him for a scholarship competition at Oxford, and sweet-talks the foolish squire into helping her. But Morgan, exercised by the servant girl's taunts, rebels at being "the schoolmistress's little dog." He gets drunk and tells Miss Moffat, "I don't want to be thankful to no strange woman—for anything!" Yet three months later he is back at his work, and the girl is gone. The Oxford examination is about to be administered by Miss Moffat and the squire when the girl returns to see Morgan: "He'll have to marry me, or I'll show him up, 'cause I must give the [expected] little stranger a name." Furiously Miss Moffat forces her to hide in the kitchen until after Morgan finishes his examination. As he starts writing, she looks toward the kitchen, and then watches him steadfastly.

Act III. It is seven months later. Morgan anxiously returns from his Oxford interviews. "Since the day I was born, I have been a prisoner behind a stone wall, and now somebody has given me a leg-up to have a look at the other side," he says to Miss Moffat; "they cannot drag me back again." He tells her of walking up the streets of Oxford, looking at the colleges, and suddenly "everything I have ever learnt from those books, and from you, was lighted up—like a magic lantern: . . . Everything had a meaning." As the town's excitement about the imminent scholarship announcement grows, the servant girl, now a flashy tart, comes back. She has had her baby, and expects Morgan to marry her. He despises her, but insists on doing "what any fellow with any guts in him must do!" Just then comes the news that he has won the scholarship. "I want you to change suddenly from a boy to a man," Miss Moffat tells him. She persuades him that his duty is "to the world," since he has it in him to become great and "free these children" from the coal mines. He goes out to the village celebration, and Miss Moffat, though she will therefore never see her protégé again, adopts the infant Morgan fathered so that he can go on to pursue his studies. As the cheering and singing come from the distance, she looks down at the infant's birth certificate. "Moffat, my girl, you mustn't be clumsy this time," she tells herself, and walks to the kitchen.

CORRUPTION IN THE PALACE OF JUSTICE (*Corruzione al Palazzo di giustizia*), a play in three acts by UGO BETTI, published and produced in 1949. Setting: "a large severe room in the Palace of Justice of a foreign city" at "the present time."

This suspenseful and SYMBOLIC drama focuses more NATURALISTICALLY than LANDSLIDE AT NORTH STATION on similar themes of the limitations of human justice and man's inner need to be judged.

Following the suicide of a distinguished racketeer, a state investigator seeks among the justices for his accomplice, the "little red pustule of leprosy—Corruption." Though all of them squirm culpably, the greatest guilt is experienced by three: the weak President of the Court, who tries unsuccessfully to conceal his recent association with the suicide; the very aged and diabolical Chief Justice, ambitious to be the next president; and his major rival, Judge Cust. Cust implicates the President, who, visibly shaken, is persuaded by Cust to make a partial confession and write out a full account of his shady dealings. As the investigation threatens to implicate him, Cust suggests that the record archives be examined for "the flavor of corruption." He is saved momentarily from the Chief Justice's innuendos by the breakdown of the President, who wrote the requested account. The President's adoring daughter attributes his unbelievable confessions to his breakdown. With vivid intensity Cust, who begrudges the President the wife and daughter Cust himself never had, details her father's very human venality. Totally disillusioned and ashamed to look at her father, the girl commits suicide. The written account seems to the Chief Justice to point clearly to Cust as the "leper," though he considers all guilty: "We judges are all hypocrites, all of us stuffed with stale, rancid sausage-meat." He summons the investigator and the now totally unhinged President to reveal the tantalizing secret of the culprit's identity—and thus win the coveted presidency. When the investigator returns from their meeting he reports the Chief Justice's death and his fiendish last words that consign his enemy to lifelong, solitary remorse: "the person responsible for the corruption in these courts was —himself," the President and all the others being innocent, "mainly, he observed, because they hadn't the brains to be anything else." Now his rival, Cust, is nominated to be the next President. But Cust, who was prepared for humiliation and punishment rather than elevation to the coveted high position, feels overwhelmed by guilt and fear. "There is no argument on earth that would let me shut my eyes in peace tonight," he says, ready to "confess the truth." He declines the old records clerk's kindly offer to accompany him: "I'm a bit frightened. But I know there is no one who can help me." Then he opens the hitherto-closed door to the "Lord High Chancellor," passes its portals, and slowly ascends a long and steep staircase.

COSTA RICA. Costa Rica's theatre *"no existe,"* Fernando Borges Pérez noted in his *La historia del teatro en Costa Rica* (1942), though he discussed it for some one hundred pages. Other writers agree that Costa Rica's drama has been inferior to its fiction and poetry. Among the few notable Costa Rican playwrights and plays are Eduardo Calsamiglia (1880–1918), whose best work is *Bronces de antaño,* a posthumous (1919) poetic tragedy set in fifteenth-century Spain; the prolific Italian-educated José Fabio Garnier (1884–1956), particularly praised for his love tragedy, *A la sombra del amor* (1921), and a NATURALIST domestic tragedy, *Con toda el alma* (1933); Marizancene (pen name of Héctor Alfredo Castro Fernández, 1889–   ), influenced by Freud, Marcel Proust, and existentialism, who produced drama (some of it in French) that deals with the vagaries of love, jealousy, and adultery in psychoanalytic terms, as in *Le Vitrail* (1937); and Manuel G. Escalante Durán (1905–   ), noted especially for his metaphysical romance *Bruma* (1948). Most of Costa Rica's novelists have occasionally written plays, but with indifferent success.

For works in English see under LATIN AMERICA.

COSTUMBRISMO, a LATIN AMERICAN literary term, in the theatre refers to plays, usually light comedies, that focus on the customs and manners of a particular region. A writer of such plays is known as a *costumbrista.* The greatest *costumbrista* was Daniel Barros Grez (1834–1904), who flourished at the start of CHILE's golden age of *costumbrismo* (1890–1930). Typical of the genre is his *Como en Santiago,* which became very popular in mid-twentieth-century Chile though it was forgotten after its original production in 1875; it is a *sainete* about a city slicker's deception of a girl in her impoverished but pretentious town, which is wittily satirized with stock characters like the henpecked husband and a forthright peasant.

COUNSELLOR-AT-LAW, a play in three acts by ELMER RICE, published and produced in 1931. Setting: a suite of law offices in New York, c. 1931.

As in STREET SCENE, the melodramatic plot of this play (later filmed) is overshadowed by a large gallery of amusing characters. The play was very popular when first produced, as well as in its 1942 revival. Paul Muni made his name as an American actor as George Simon, the former poor immigrant, now a great lawyer. Ruthless yet warmhearted, Simon is portrayed in various roles: affectionate with his mother, a simple old Jewess; an efficient executive with his associates, clients, staff, and adoring secretary; a selfless friend to people he knew when a poor boy; and an uxorious husband to his snobbish socialite wife. A shady transaction of long ago threatens Simon's ruin. At the last minute Simon discovers the unsavory past of the bluestocking lawyer out to disbar him. Though this discovery saves him, Simon's jubilation is cut short when he realizes the contempt and probable unfaithfulness of the wife he worships. Only his loyal secretary and the lure of a challenging new case prevent Simon from committing suicide.

COUNT OEDERLAND (*Graf Oederland*), a play in ten scenes by MAX FRISCH, published and produced in 1951. Setting: a twentieth-century study, prison, woods, hotel, palace, etc.

Originally a prose sketch, this fantasy was produced in another form in 1956 before it appeared in its "final" 1961 version as a twelve-scene *Moritat* ("crime story"; literally, "horror ballad"). Frisch remained long preoccupied with his depiction of social chaos in this partly EXPRESSIONIST play, which has general resemblances to Kaiser's FROM MORN TO MIDNIGHT.

A prominent judge emotionally identifies himself with an ordinary man on trial for a pointless murder. Breaking with routine, the judge abandons his home and adulterous wife. After axing three policemen to death he takes to the woods, and as "Count Oederland" (literally, "Wasteland") heads a group of outlaws. Nightmarish episodes portray his life with the fairylike reembodiment of his maid, and his leadership of a revolution from subterranean city sewers. Victorious, he is offered the country's premiership. Back in his study exactly as in the play's first scene, he thinks it all was a nightmare. Then he notices his muddy boots and hears rifle shots in the distance. "I am a dream—" he says; "Wake up. Now—quick; now; wake up—wake up—wake up!—" Stupefied, he remains seated.

COUNTESS CATHLEEN, THE, a verse play in five scenes by WILLIAM BUTLER YEATS, published in 1892 and produced in 1899. Setting: "in Ireland and in old times."

Aside from two juvenile works deleted from his *Collected Plays,* this is Yeats's first drama (though THE LAND OF HEART'S DESIRE was produced earlier). Produced in Dublin's "Antient Concert Rooms," the play also launched the Irish Literary Theatre that was eventually to move to the Abbey Theatre. It did so in characteristic style, for the police had to restrain irate auditors who resented the depiction of Irishmen selling their souls. This short, part-NATURALISTIC part-fantastic play was one of Yeats's own favorites, and he frequently revised it. The objective and subjective ways of life are personified by the countess's action and the poet's dreams.

A starving peasant family bemoan the great famine raging about them. The mother retains her faith in God, but father and son despair: "What can we do but live on sorrel and dock, / And dandelion, till our mouths are green?" The Countess Cathleen enters with her foster mother and the poet Aleel, all of whom have gotten lost in the woods. She gives the peasants what money she has, and the poet sings before they leave. But father and son, still dissatisfied, summon evil spirits. Two "merchants" enter, seeking to buy souls for "so good a price that all may live / In mirth and comfort till the famine's done." To make Cathleen forget the misery about them,

Aleel sings to her in the woods. Told that famished peasants have looted her castle, the countess does not consider it a sin. But she is horrified to learn of the demon merchants' quest for souls. She tells her steward to sell her lands and distribute the proceeds to the famished. Aleel begs her to flee to "music and the light / Of waters, till the evil days are done." Though she reciprocates his love, Cathleen has vowed to help the people, and sends him away. The demon merchants, angry because Cathleen's charity is losing them souls, rob her treasure room. Though desolate, she does not lose her faith. At the peasant hut, the demon merchants haggle for the peasants' souls. Cathleen arrives and stops their trading by selling her own precious soul in exchange for those of the peasants, and then dies. But in a vision, the grief-stricken Aleel learns from an angel that Cathleen is saved: "The Light of Lights / Looks always on the motive, not the deed."

COUNTRY GIRL, THE, a play in two acts by CLIFFORD ODETS, published in 1949 and produced in 1950. Setting: New York and Boston, 1949.

Rewritten a number of times, produced in England as *Winter Journey,* made into a popular film in 1954, and revived in New York in 1968, this was Odets's only play to eschew undisguised social protest. It is set in a theatre milieu and features Frank Elgin, a once-famous actor who has become a drunkard, and his much younger but maternal wife, Georgie, "the country girl." Their portrayal is harrowing and moving, though neither Elgin's earlier fall nor his final redemption is adequately motivated.

Elgin is offered his chance for a comeback, as the star of a new play, by a dynamic young director who subsequently falls in love with Georgie. Covering his introversion and tremendous insecurity with joviality before others, Elgin attributes his alcoholism, suicide attempt, and other shortcomings to Georgie. ("He doesn't like to make the slightest remark that might lose him people's regard or affection," she explains.) In time, he himself comes to believe his lies. Only Georgie knows the truth, and she constantly buttresses his bruised ego. At a particularly stressing time during the play's tryout Elgin goes on a bender. The simmering conflict between the young director and Georgie explodes—and ends with a kiss. At the New York opening of the play Elgin regains his confidence and makes a sensational comeback. The director takes his farewell from the loyal Georgie. "Stay unregenerate," she tells the director. "Life knocks the sauciness out of us soon enough." Then she tears up one of the congratulatory telegrams she herself had sent to bolster her husband's self-confidence, and puts up Elgin's robe.

COURT SINGER, THE (*Der Kammersänger*), a one-act play by FRANK WEDEKIND, published in 1897 and produced in 1899. Setting: a flower-strewn hotel room in an Austrian city, 1890's.

Wedekind described this once-popular, still anthologized play (also translated as *The Tenor*) as "the collision of a brutal intelligence with blind passion." In three amusing scenes it portrays Oscar Gerardo, a famous Wagnerian tenor, smugly resisting emotional involvements with various admirers. Repeatedly interrupted as he tries to practice his aria and prepares to leave, he ushers out a starry-eyed girl, who offers herself to him: "You rob Art of its dignity, my child." Then he dismisses an unsuccessful old composer: "The measure of a man's worth is the world's opinion of him. . . . There are no misunderstood geniuses"; artists "are merely a luxury for the use of the bourgeoisie . . . good for business. . . . [Art] keeps money circulating; it keeps blood running. It gets girls engaged, spinsters married, wives tempted." His beautiful mistress, a married woman with children, implores him to take her along. He resists her charms: "I am an artist first and a man next. . . . Love is a beastly bourgeois virtue." When she shoots herself before his eyes, the tenor is momentarily disconcerted. Then he picks up his score and rushes out to catch his train: "I must sing Tristan in Brussels tomorrow night."

COURTELINE, Georges [pen name of Georges Victor-Marcel Moinaux] (1858–1929), French writer, produced satiric verse, fiction, and the twenty-eight farces and comedies on which his reputation rests. These were collected and republished, and remained popular through the 1960's, when three of them played concurrently in Paris. Sometimes gross in the NATURALISTIC satire of the foibles of officials and other people—often women—their depiction and tight construction recall the comedies of Molière.

Courteline was introduced at the Théâtre-Libre in 1891 with a dramatization of one of his popular sketches of military life, *Lidoire*. Two years later he became well known with his most popular work, *Boubouroche,* a farce with wistful overtones about an unfaithful mistress and a gullible lover that has been likened to Becque's THE PARISIAN WOMAN and that became part of the Comédie-Française repertory. Among the short pieces that launched the GRAND GUIGNOL theatre in 1897 was Courteline's farcical *Hortense, couche-toi!* (*Hold on, Hortense!*). Other popular short Courteline plays include *La Peur des coups* (*Afraid to Fight,* 1894), *Monsieur Badin* (1897, translated as *Badin the Bold*), *Une Lettre chargée* (*The Registered Letter,* 1897), *Les Boulingrin* (*These Cornfields,* 1898), *Le Gendarme est sans pitié* (*The Pitiless Policeman,* 1899), and *Le Commissaire est bon enfant* (*The Commissioner Has a Big Heart,* 1899), written with Jules Lévy (1857–1903), and translated also as *The Commissioner*. His popular *L'Article 330* (*Article 330,* 1900), an exposition of France's judicial system, features a character who became known as "the friend of the law" for his outsmarting of legal officers, and was described as "a hero of nonconformity" by GEORGES DUHAMEL. *La Paix chez soi* (1903, translated as *Peace at Home*) was produced in New York as *A Private Account.*

Courteline's complete plays were republished in 1963. Volume I of *The Plays of Courteline* (1961), edited and introduced by Albert Bermel, has *Article 330, Badin the Bold, Hold on, Hortense!, Afraid to Fight,* and *Boubouroche. These Cornfields* is included in Eric Bentley's collection *Let's Get a Divorce! and Other Plays* (1958), and *The Commissioner* appears in Wallace Fowlie's collection *Four Modern French Comedies* (1960). All have introductions and a bibliography.

COWARD,* [Sir] **Noël** [Pierce] (1899–), English playwright and actor, and master technician of the theatre. He wrote many popular songs—sentimental, satiric, and nonsensical; acted, sang, and danced in his plays and in those of others; produced and directed his drama, films, and television shows; and for his costars acquired (among other notables) the Lunts, Laurence Olivier, Beatrice Lillie, John Gielgud, and Gertrude Lawrence, for whom he wrote numerous parts. Many of Coward's sixty-odd plays were resounding hits, particularly the sentimental and patriotic pieces, and the witty drawing-room comedies in which he excelled. Most critics, while acknowledging his energy, versatility, and craftsmanship, consider his drama amusingly clever at times but innately "mindless," and unlikely to retain its luster. Tapping a similar vein as did SOMERSET MAUGHAM, Coward lacks the bite, the genius for yarn telling, and the epigrammatic wit of Maugham—not to mention those of classic dramatists like William Congreve and modern ones like OSCAR WILDE. Yet there is no denying Coward's adroit playwriting in comedies like PRIVATE LIVES (1930) and BLITHE SPIRIT (1941), the nationalistic extravaganza CAVALCADE (1931), the twice-filmed romantic operetta *Bitter-Sweet* (1929), and the film *"In Which We Serve"* (1942).

The son of musical parents (his father was a piano salesman whose poverty Coward was determined to avoid), Coward was born in Teddington, Middlesex. He was educated first at Croydon, and then "informally." Eager to achieve wealth, he became an actor at eleven, touring in the seventeenth-century burlesque *The Knight of the Burning Pestle,* Barrie's PETER PAN, Hauptmann's HANNELE, and other plays until 1918. Injured during military training, he spent some time in the hospital, and wrote songs and plays. Most of the early ones were comedies, including *"I'll Leave It to You"* (1920), his first produced play; *The Young Idea* (1921); and *The Better Half* (1922), a one-act play. But Coward made his name in 1924, both in England and America, with THE VORTEX. Thereafter his reputation suffered only one setback, when *Sirocco,* a serious play written in 1921, was hissed off the stage in 1927. Otherwise his success was fantastic. Several of his plays often ran concurrently in London in the 1920's and 1930's. Typical of them is *Fallen Angels* (1924), in which two wives are distraught at the reappearance of their one-time lover; they finally accompany him to his newly rented flat upstairs, while their husbands below have a drink. The play is witty, titillating, in good taste—and dated after the theatre of the ABSURD and the "angry" postwar English drama.

In the decades of the 1920's, 1930's, and 1940's, however, Coward and his plays were very much in vogue, and other successes followed: HAY FEVER (1925); *Easy Virtue* (1925), characterized by a reviewer as "a sort of SECOND MRS. TANQUERAY"; *"This Was a Man"* (1926), a trifling play, banned in England as immoral, whose protagonist finally divorces his adulterous wife; *The Rat Trap* (1926), his first play, a "psychological" drama written in 1918; *The Queen Was in the Parlour* (1926), a romantic melodrama; *The Marquise* and *Home Chat* (1927); *This Year of Grace!* (1928), a successful revue; *Post-Mortem* (1931), an unproduced "angry little vilification of war," Coward commented, "strongly affected by [Sherriff's] JOURNEY'S END"; DESIGN FOR LIVING (1933), one of his major successes; *Conversation Piece* (1934), a romantic musical comedy; *Point Valaine* (1934), a torrid love drama set in the British West Indies; the ten one-acters that comprise TO-NIGHT AT 8:30 (1935–36); a nostalgic musical, *Operette* (1938); one of Coward's revues for Beatrice Lillie, *Set to Music* (1938); *This Happy Breed* (1942), a play (later filmed) chronicling the lives of a suburban family between the two world wars, and *Present Laughter* (1942), a comedy portraying a series of whirling love affairs among the members of a theatrical firm—both of which were concurrently popular during World War II; *Sigh No More* (1945), a successful revue; *Pacific 1860* (1946), a musical romance; *Peace in Our Time* (1947), a speculative thriller about the German occupation of Britain; *Ace of Clubs* (1950), a musical; *Island Fling* (1951), a light comedy, triggered by the Empire's loss of India, that was produced as *South Sea Bubble* in England; *Relative Values* (1951), a light comedy; *Quadrille* (1952), a romantic comedy along the lines of *Private Lives; After the Ball* (1954), a musical based on Wilde's LADY WINDERMERE'S FAN; NUDE WITH VIOLIN (1956); *Look After Lulu* (1959), an adaptation of GEORGES FEYDEAU; *Waiting in the Wings* (1960), a play set in a home for retired famous but impoverished actresses; *Sail Away!* (1961), a musical; and the triple bill *Suite in Three Keys* (1966), consisting of two one-acters—*Shadows of the Evening* and *Come Into the Garden, Maud*—and the full-length *A Song at Twilight,* a study of homosexuality focused on a famous, recently deceased writer who bears some resemblances to Maugham. *Noel Coward's Sweet Potato* (1968), a musical revue, was based on his works.

His drawing-room plays often deal with sex among the upper classes in Coward's characteristically sophisticated manner. As in his treatment of cockney and middle-class people, the superficiality occasionally alternates with profundity and REALISM. But Coward did not usually explore these, being content to confine himself to

*Illustration on page 626.

inoffensive satire, sentimentality, and patriotism. If these limitations reduce his stature as a dramatist, they have aided his popular success. He amused the English-speaking world during the grimmest days of World War II, and created roles for its most distinguished stars. And if his occasional forays into the meaningful and serious (in comedy as well as drama) were not crowned with wild success, they at least were not, as a rule, disastrous failures.

Coward was knighted in 1970. His immense versatility extended beyond the theatre. Aside from his plays—which were published individually and in numerous collections, including the *Play Parade* volumes (1933 ff.)—he wrote satires, short stories, a novel, and assorted nonfiction, including two autobiographies, *Present Indicative* (1937) and *Future Indefinite* (1954). The most comprehensive survey of Coward's activities to 1957, including photographs of productions and films, synopses of all the plays, revues, and musicals, and invaluable reference data, is Raymond Mander and Joe Mitchenson's *Theatrical Companion to Coward* (1957). Later book-length studies include Milton Levin's *Noel Coward* (1968) and Sheridan Morley's *A Talent to Amuse* (1969).

CRADLE SONG, THE (*Canción de cuna*), a comedy in two acts with a verse interlude by GREGORIO MARTÍNEZ SIERRA, published and produced in 1911. Setting: a Dominican convent in Spain, late nineteenth and early twentieth centuries.

For over three decades audiences throughout the world were moved to floods of tears and a few smiles by this tenderly sentimental portrayal of convent life. Virtually without action, it exposes in small but emotional incidents the feminine—particularly the maternal—yearnings of cloistered nuns. An interlude marks the almost imperceptible passage of eighteen years. Martínez Sierra's wife, María, contributed more than usual to this play, which was his greatest success.

Act I. Young nuns are celebrating the birthday of their prioress. She allows Sister Joanna of the Cross to read a poem the eighteen-year-old nun has composed for the occasion, though the novices' mistress and the ever-vigilant vicaress worry that it may lead to pride. A wise woman, the prioress understands that though her "tender lambs . . . perhaps do frisk a little in the pastures of the Lord," there is no harm in this and other birthday offerings. A canary sent the prioress by the mayor's wife so delights the nuns that they beg permission to chat until prayer time. Their old doctor comes to examine them. He commends a "well-rounded" young nun's looks and prescribes, "for melancholia at eighteen, matrimony or cold water." Sister Joanna of the Cross wistfully recalls how she took care of her baby brother; she adds, "whenever I take Communion I try to think I am receiving our Lord as a little child, and I take and press him like this to my heart." Another present is brought the prioress: an abandoned infant. Though the vicaress objects, the nuns beg to keep it. To legalize it, the doctor offers to adopt the child and have it brought up in the convent. Sister Joanna of the Cross eagerly offers practical suggestions to enable them to keep the child. The prioress agrees, and puts the infant in the care of Sister Joanna of the Cross. After the others leave, the young nun passionately embraces the infant: "Little one! Whom do you love?"

Interlude. "Being women, you are lovers, nuns," the poet says, narrating how the infant Teresa enabled them to be "mothers without being wives," and how they "poured all the honey of your souls" into the child, who has grown up gay, though devout. Thus eighteen years have passed, and "the curtain rises on a soul in flower."

Act II. As the nuns finish a fancy trousseau for Teresa, the girl's happy singing in the garden continually interrupts their meditations. The nuns are heavy-hearted, for they know Teresa will leave them soon. The most refractory of the nuns is caught with a forbidden mirror; she has used it to reflect sunbeams that cheer her up, she explains, by pretending to herself that they are free birds or butterflies. Bubbling with cheer, Teresa cannot be subdued by the nuns, though she is grateful for them and sad about leaving. Alone with Sister Joanna of the Cross, whom Teresa has always thought of as her mother, she rejoices to hear the nun admit that she has looked upon Teresa as her particular child. Teresa's fiancé arrives and promises always to care well for her. Reluctant to see her go, the nuns outline detailed instructions for her care. When the old doctor comes to drive her to the station, Teresa tearfully apologizes for all the trouble her gaiety has caused and promises that though she could not join the order, "I will never forget you!" She embraces every one of them, and leaves. The overwrought nuns slowly go to their choir, the vicaress trying hard to control herself by issuing strict instructions. Sister Joanna of the Cross remains alone, falls on her knees, and weeps.

CRADLE WILL ROCK, THE, a musical drama in ten scenes by MARC BLITZSTEIN, produced in 1937 and published in 1938. Setting: a bare stage.

This occasionally revived "proletarian" work, written in the episodic style of AGITPROP, became famous with its premiere. Originally prepared as a Federal Theatre Project, its performance was canceled by Washington, for political reasons. Thereupon the actor-producer Orson Welles asked the first-night audience to accompany the cast to another theatre that the group had just rented. Using various subterfuges against production bans, they performed the play there (as it later was on Broadway) in pantomime, without costume or scenery, in the front orchestra rows; Blitzstein played the piano and introduced the characters and episodes.

In night court in a contemporary "Steeltown, U.S.A." during a union drive, a girl is tried for prostitution. Flashbacks then present various respectable citizens, caricatured as far greater prostitutes. Selling their souls to Mr. Mister, the corrupt and corrupting mill-owner, are the local Liberty Committee he has appointed to combat radicalism, consisting of a newspaper editor, a minister, a college president, a physician, and others. Mr. Mister tries to bribe and then to assassinate the incorruptible union organizer, but is finally overwhelmed by his henchmen. "There's a storm that's going to last until / The final wind blows," the organizer warns. "And when the wind blows . . . / The cradle will rock!"

CRAIG'S WIFE, a play in three acts by GEORGE KELLY, produced in 1925 and published in 1926. Setting: a contemporary New York living room, from five-thirty in the afternoon to nine the next morning.

The title character of this Pulitzer Prize winner, a WELL-MADE PLAY with a thesis, is a materialistic wife who is ruthless in her quest for security and in her obsessive housekeeping. ALEXANDER WOOLLCOTT aptly described her as "a woman who would rather have her husband smoke in hell than in her living room." The play was filmed and twice revived on Broadway in the 1940's.

Act I. Harriet Craig chides the servants for bringing flowers into her house, because "the petals'll be all over the room." Attempting to assure her security by controlling her husband, Walter ("that is the independence of authority," she instructs her young niece; "authority—*over* the man I married"), she is coldly calculating as she spies on his innocent activities and alienates all who come into the house, including a kindly widow who lives next door. Craig's elderly aunt finally decides she can no longer remain in the immaculate but sterile house, from which Mrs. Craig excludes even her husband's friends. She would remove her husband, too, but "he's necessary to the upkeep here," the aunt says. "People who live to themselves, Harriet, are generally left to themselves," she tells Mrs. Craig, and she warns Craig about his wife. Her way of life is "very ridiculous, and incredibly selfish," and is undoing him socially as well as professionally, his aunt says. Craig is further upset when he learns that the man with whom he had played cards the previous night was found shot to death.

Act II. To avoid scandal and hide her spying on her husband, Mrs. Craig does not tell the police it was she who made the mysterious call they are investigating. Later she insists that Craig not report he was the unknown man seen to leave the house of the dead man. She conceals from Craig the police's real reason for coming: their desire to trace the mysterious telephone call. Wanting to save herself, she is willing even to risk his becoming implicated as a murder suspect. Finally Craig sees his wife's true personality, and understands how she has exploited him. She readily admits that she drove away his friends and is interested only in preserving her house. "I saw what happened to my own mother, and I made up my mind it 'ud never happen to me," she explains. "She was one of those 'I will follow thee, my husband' women . . . and all the time

Craig's Wife, Act I. Craig (Charles Trowbridge) is being warned about his wife (Chrystal Herne, left) by his aunt (Anne Sutherland). New York, 1926. (*Culver Pictures*)

he was mortgaging her home over her head for another woman." Craig is furious to hear his wife's brazen claims of superiority. "I married a romantic fool!" she tells him. "I don't know what 'ud become of you if I didn't [understand you]." He smashes her favorite ornament, and starts smoking in the living room.

Act III. Craig has spent the whole night in the living room, leaving cigarette butts all over the floor. By dawn the police have solved the murder mystery; but Craig, deeply wounded by his wife's contempt for his manhood, as well as by her egotism and dishonesty, leaves her. "You neither loved nor honored me," he tells her; "You married a house . . . [and] I'll see that you have it." The other inhabitants—the aunt, the servants, and the visiting niece, whose engagement Mrs. Craig has tried to break off—also leave that morning. Harriet Craig remains in her house alone. Petals fall all over the floor as she clutches a bunch of roses left by the spurned neighbor, "her eyes wide and despairing."

CREDITORS (*Fordringsägare*), "a tragicomedy" in one act by AUGUST STRINDBERG, produced in 1889 and published in 1890. Setting: the sitting room of a hotel in a contemporary Swedish watering place.

This psychological thriller, highly esteemed by the author and many critics, is transparently autobiographical. Adolf (also the name of THE FATHER) and Gustav (also the name of Siri Strindberg's former husband) are the "creditors" of the charming vampire wife.

The sick artist Adolf tells Gustav, an avowed "teacher of dead languages and a widower," how he has made his wife Tekla a successful author. Gaining hypnotic power over Adolf, Gustav mentally tortures him and extracts intimate details of their marriage. He persuades Adolf that he is epileptic and dying, the superficial Tekla having drained his strength for herself. She is now unfaithful, Gustav declares. To prove it, he arranges two interviews with her: the first with Adolf, and the second with himself. Adolf will "watch me dissecting a human soul and exposing its entrails on the table." Tekla returns from a trip. The scene with her husband dramatizes her charm, egotism, and power over him. In the second interview, which Adolf must overhear, the tables are turned. Gustav, revealed as the first husband seeking revenge for her scandalously libelous book, soon has the amoral Tekla consent to an assignation. Adolf emerges and collapses, dead of an epileptic fit. Tekla penitently throws herself over Adolf's body and caresses it, weeping for forgiveness. "She really does love him too. Poor creature!" Gustav remarks.

CRIME ON GOAT ISLAND (*Delitto all'isola delle capre*), a play in three acts by UGO BETTI, published and produced in 1950. Setting: a barren Italian heathland, c. 1950.

Produced in New York as *Island of Goats,* this is a classically taut, ironic drama of passion and poetry. Its isolated characters are three frustrated women and a diabolic yet angelic visiting male. Their quest for rational self-knowledge is overpowered by animalistic instincts, which parallel those of the "island's" goats. The final tableau has been likened to that of Pirandello's HENRY IV.

The loquacious friend of a military prison-camp casualty who had revealed all his marital intimacies visits his widow. She lives in a lonely house with her daughter and her sister. Soon the friend becomes the lover of all three women and masters their lives. Apparently as a joke but then in earnest, the widow traps and lets him languish in the well. Shaken up by the guilty realization of her past wifely inadequacy, as well as her lust, she says of the visitor, "It was as though he'd discovered for each one of us—a sort of root between us and the earth: a piece of gut, a bloody navel cord; and he twisted it round his fist and dragged us along by it." Her daughter and sister leave hysterically as the man dies. The widow sits by the well, trapping herself forever with his corpse and contemplating her expiatory murder: "We shall go on calling to each other and fighting with each other through all eternity."

CRIMES AND CRIMES (*Brott och brott*), a comedy in four acts by AUGUST STRINDBERG, published in 1899 and produced in 1900. Setting: Paris, 1890's.

This sin-and-redemption play (also translated as *Crime and Crime* and *There Are Crimes and Crimes*) was published, by design, with the occult *Advent, ett mysterium* (ADVENT) under the joint title *Vid högre rätt, eller, Rus* (BEFORE A HIGHER COURT). Strindberg called this autobiographical work, filmed in German (1917, by Ernst Lubitsch) and Swedish (1928), his "boulevard play." Though it is deceptively simple and apparently derivative, it is an original, haunting mixture of comedy and tragedy, prosaic REALISM and poetic SYMBOLISM, naïveté and sophistication.

Act I. Jeanne has waited humbly for two hours in the cemetery for the playwright Maurice Gérard, her lover. She is tortured by premonitions, and their little daughter is getting hungry. An Abbé and then her brother, a common laborer, console them. Maurice finally arrives, penitent but optimistic about their future. His play is opening tonight, and he is confident of great success and of victory over his rivals, at last. After affectionate words with mistress and child, Maurice leaves. Alone with her child, Jeanne awaits their fate: *"O crux! Ave spes unica!"* Later, in a café, Maurice for the first time meets Henriette Mauclerc, the mistress of Adolphe, an artist and his best friend. Maurice is smitten with Henriette, a sculptress who is drawn to him and at the same time exerts an almost supernatural effect on him. "What an infernal woman!" he exclaims.

Act II. Late that night, Maurice and Henriette celebrate his great success as a playwright. Though reveling in victory, Maurice is conscience-stricken about his waiting friends in the café, and his self-sacrificing mistress at home. Henriette ridicules

Jeanne and crowns Maurice with a laurel wreath. Her evil "entices me with the irresistible charm of novelty," Maurice admits as she glories in a crime she refuses to discuss. When he suggests that they celebrate with a sunrise breakfast in the Bois de Boulogne, Henriette enthusiastically agrees to invite Adolphe ("We may need an ass to pull the triumphal chariot"), and then throws herself into Maurice's arms. In the morning Maurice, tormented by his passion and guilt, proposes joint suicide. Henriette thinks the suggestion insane: "Now I want to begin to live!" Adolphe arrives and soon departs sadly, after telling Maurice of Jeanne's unhappiness. The child stands between Henriette's and Maurice's love and should be destroyed, Henriette declares—and Maurice is horrified, but deeply stirred. They agree to leave Paris, and he goes to bid his child and his friends farewell.

Act III. That evening the child is dead. Henriette and Maurice's conversation having been overheard, he is believed to have murdered the child. Distraught by guilty thoughts, Maurice implicates himself and is taken to the police with Henriette. The following day the scandal has made newspaper headlines. His play is withdrawn and he is ruined, though released for lack of evidence. Adolphe, who in the meantime has quietly gained great artistic success, suggests to the conscienceless Henriette that there are "crimes and crimes." Some—for instance, wishing for someone's death—are not in the Criminal Code. But these are the worst, "crimes we ourselves must punish—and no judge is as severe as oneself!" Henriette and Maurice are shadowed by detectives, humiliated, and expelled from the restaurant where they had celebrated his triumph two nights before. "What is left for us now but to seek the river?" Henriette asks, and Maurice, taking her hand as they leave, agrees, "The river, yes!"

Act IV. Like Adam and Eve after the expulsion, Maurice and Henriette loathe and blame each other for the murder of the child. Since society has ostracized them, however, they see no alternative to their getting married. Adolphe declares them both "psychopathic cases . . . in the clutches of the demons of dread and mistrust," each feeling guilty and revolted by the evil within himself. Henriette leaves Paris, persuaded to attempt repentance. Maurice too is chastened, ready to reject worldly things and devote himself solely to religious asceticism. Suddenly word comes of his public rehabilitation: now his play is being restaged, and his fortune is restored. The curtain is at eight—and the church service at nine! Maurice hesitates. Then, remembering the wish he once harbored to do away with his daughter, he tells the Abbé: "I shall meet you this evening in church and settle my accounts. And tomorrow I shall go to the theatre." The Abbé approves of the compromise solution, "the right answer."

CROMMELYNCK, Fernand (1885?–1970), Belgian dramatist, achieved world fame in 1920 with his "lyric farce" *Le Cocu magnifique* (THE MAGNIFICENT CUCKOLD, 1920). A major playwright in the period between the world wars, he came out with only about a dozen plays. Like *The Magnificent Cuckold* these depict characters who become increasingly obsessed, usually by sex. The brutality of the dramatizations as well as their elevated poetic language recall Ben Jonson's seventeenth-century "comedies of humour." But Crommelynck's plays have more REPRESENTATIONAL settings and details, an air of mystery, and crowd scenes that reflect the paintings of Pieter Breughel the elder—and sometimes those of Hieronymus Bosch.

A Fleming by ancestry as well as temperament, Crommelynck was born in Brussels* to a middle-class family. His father worked in the theatre, and young Crommelynck early learned much about the stage. He became an actor and wrote plays in his mother's native tongue, French. *Nous n'irons plus au bois,* a light and ephemeral short piece, was his first work to be published and produced, in Brussels in 1906. Earlier he had written the sensuous *Le Sculpteur de masques* (1908, revised in 1911), whose title character is a Flemish dealer in antique masks; his dreams of beauty and passion interrupted by drunken orgiastic revelers, he despairs after his beloved (the sister of his dead wife) becomes enamored of a leper, and is destroyed by his horrible masks. Less under the morbid influence of Belgium's most famous playwright, MAURICE MAETERLINCK, was Crommelynck's next play, *Le Marchand de regrets* (1913); its satiric plot about an antiquarian deserted by his neglected young wife ends with a more tragic irony than that of *The Magnificent Cuckold,* Crommelynck's next play and his generally acknowledged masterpiece, which was first produced in Lugné-Poë's art theatre in Paris.

Les Amants puérils (1921), the play that followed *The Magnificent Cuckold,* is a simultaneously poetic and lusty farce that deals with the failure of people to communicate. It was less of a hit. *Tripes d'or* (1925), on the other hand, has been much praised and was produced successfully in Moscow. Like Molière's *L'Avare,* its protagonist is avarice personified: becoming so obsessed with the wealth he inherits that he is advised by a veterinary friend to eat it, he consumes his gold in powdered form, gets constipated ("I can hold out no longer. The microbes are waging, with modern weapons, an intestine war"), and grotesquely dies, still admiring the beauty of his beloved, who is waiting outside and whom he will not admit to his wealth-stacked room. Other Crommelynck satires are *Carine, ou La Jeune Fille folle de son âme* (1929), whose pure-minded protagonist, innocently oblivious of human coarseness and brutality and believing in the possibility of total candor, destroys both her husband and herself; *Une Femme qu'a le cœur trop petit* (1934), portraying a similar situation more farcically, and featuring a woman whose excessive prudery causes a general saturnalia; and *Chaud et froid, ou L'Idée de Monsieur Dom* (1934), a multiplotted satire about a town's sudden deification of

* Some authorities cite Paris.

an insignificant dead man whose wife, learning that he adored another woman who inspired him to amazing lyrical outbursts, pathetically triumphs over him by forcing her own lover on her rival.

The success of *The Magnificent Cuckold* had made it possible for Crommelynck to give up acting in the early 1920's. With his family he thereupon settled near Paris, where he devoted himself to his writing. Aside from publishing a Shakespeare adaptation, *Le Chevalier à la lune, ou Sir John Falstaff* (1954), Crommelynck remained virtually unheard from after World War II. The interwar plays, on which his reputation rests, are a mixture of grotesqueness, satire, folk drama, and bitter tragedy. They are distinguished for their lyricism, language whose poetry is sustained even through the coarse, Rabelaisian action. Crommelynck's demented, carnally obsessed protagonists strive for human certainty, for ideals of beauty and purity. Enigmatic, almost supernaturally evil creatures, like Bruno's secretary in *The Magnificent Cuckold,* provide tragic undercurrents of mysticism and malignity. These, as well as the Breughel country folk and lifelike details of setting and action, constitute a "mask" that elevates Crommelynck's farce into a drama of metaphysics reminiscent of some of LUIGI PIRANDELLO's plays.

The Magnificent Cuckold was published, with an introduction by Jan-Albert Goris, in *Two Great Belgian Plays, about Love* (1966). A comprehensive essay on Crommelynck and a bibliography appear in David I. Grossvogel's *The Self-Conscious Stage in Modern French Drama* (1958, republished in 1961 as *Twentieth Century French Drama*).

CROTHERS, Rachel (1878–1958), American playwright, was particularly interested in woman's position in modern society. Her many popular dramas, though apparently daring in their day, are liberally seasoned with sentimentality and are resolved in a manner readily acceptable to matinee audiences. Adept at writing clever dialogue, Crothers was the leading female American dramatist of the first three decades of the century. Most successful was one of her last plays, *Susan and God* (1937); its title character, busily espousing a new religion of "Love—love—*love* for other people—*not* for yourself," neglects her child and husband—whom she almost loses because of her selfishness.

Crothers's first hit was *The Three of Us* (1906), a Nevada mining-camp drama that resembles Moody's THE GREAT DIVIDE. *A Man's World* (1909), the first of Crothers's plays to deal with the woman topic that subsequently preoccupied her, is concerned with double standards in sex. *He and She* (1911), another popular play, portrays a competing artistic couple; the wife, ultimately realizing and accepting her family responsibilities, surrenders to her husband the lucrative commission she has won. Notable among Crothers's other works—she wrote nearly fifty plays, some of them one-acters—are *Ourselves* (1913), about cultivated women's responsibilities for society's morals; *A Little Journey* (1918), a skillfully wrought comedy; *Nice People* (1920), also a clever (if dated) comedy, about the post-World War I "lost generation"; *Mary the Third* (1923), another play about youth, revealing three generations' attitudes about marriage; and social-problem comedies like *Expressing Willie* (1924) and *Let Us Be Gay* (1929).

Born in Bloomington, Illinois, Crothers was the daughter of Dr. Eli Kirk Crothers, a friend of Abraham Lincoln. She directed and staged all her own plays, and occasionally acted in them. For a résumé of her life and an analysis of her plays, see Volume II of Arthur H. Quinn's *A History of the American Drama from the Civil War to the Present Day* (1936).

CROUSE, Russel (1893–1966), American journalist, actor, playwright, and director, did his most notable work with HOWARD LINDSAY.* Their collaborations include LIFE WITH FATHER (1939), STATE OF THE UNION (1945), and over a dozen other plays, some of them musicals, most of them Broadway hits. By the time they began their collaboration with a revision of Cole Porter's *Anything Goes* (1934), Crouse had spent some twenty years as a writer. Born in Ohio, he became a journalist in the Midwest. After World War I, in which he served as a sailor, he worked on New York newspapers (including the *Evening Post,* for which he wrote a humorous column) with other journalists who were also disillusioned veterans destined to become playwrights, notably MAXWELL ANDERSON. Crouse made a name for himself with two nineteenth-century histories (*Mr. Currier and Mr. Ives,* 1930; and *It Seems Like Yesterday,* 1931), and did some undistinguished acting and playwriting before he met Lindsay. Aside from their successful collaborations as playwrights and directors (their most popular directing venture was JOSEPH O. KESSELRING's *Arsenic and Old Lace*), Crouse was as active as Lindsay in many artistic and literary causes, wrote some half dozen other volumes of history, and in 1943–45 was President of the Authors League of America.

CROWN-BRIDE, THE (*Kronbruden*), a folk-play in six scenes by AUGUST STRINDBERG, published in 1902 and produced in 1907. Setting: Dalarna province, Sweden; 1860's.

This tragedy is an admixture of NATURALISM and fantasy; of Swedish folk songs and lore; of Christian as well as pagan superstitions (and supernatural characters); and of the family-enmity motif of *Romeo and Juliet*. Ture Rangström used Strindberg's script, verbatim, for his operatic version of *Kronbruden* (1919).

Because of their baby and the animosity between their families, Kersti Hansdaughter and Mats Larsson hallow their union in a private, secret betrothal. Kersti, however, is so eager to be married properly that she gives in to temptation. She lets a witch have her baby in return for the

* See the entry on Lindsay for further details of their joint work.

bridal crown that will make possible a wedding and symbolize her chastity: "What no one sees and no one knows does not exist." The families reluctantly agree to the wedding, but the festivities soon turn into horror: the bridal crown drops into a millrace, and Mats's vindictive sister, announcing the existence—and the drowning—of the baby, has the bride arrested. The families' hostilities resume as the grief-stricken Mats, bearing the child's coffin, is turned against Kersti: "No clergyman can read him into his grave—because of you!" At last the penitent bride is redeemed by her faith in the apparition of Christ. She is able to resist the evil spirit, and receives a royal pardon. Doing her yearly public penance at Easter, she stands on an icy river between the feuding families. But the ice cracks, and Kersti drowns. The dead girl is carried out solemnly, and pronounced a crown bride and the divine sacrifice for reconciliation. The families join Mats and his once-vindictive sister in kneeling by Kersti's corpse, and sing Luther's "Hymn of Praise."

CRUCIBLE, THE, a play in four acts by ARTHUR MILLER, published and produced in 1953. Setting: Salem, Massachusetts; 1692.

This is the most impressive of a number of dramatizations of the Salem witch-hunt, which Miller intended and many recognized as a parallel of the early-1950's "McCarthyism." But the play transcends mere topicality and has had many later productions, including a film adaptation by JEAN-PAUL SARTRE. Dealing with individual and social guilt unleashed and accentuated by mass hysteria, as Miller noted in his preface, it portrays public pressure divesting man of conscience. Unlike Willy Loman in the earlier DEATH OF A SALESMAN, however, John Proctor is a man of awareness. Because of the play's historical notes and its scenes of trial, confession, recantation, and martyrdom, it has been likened to Shaw's SAINT JOAN. Both present the recurrent conflict between social order and individual freedom—but Miller portrays antagonists of unmitigated viciousness.

Act I. Salem's minister prays at his sick daughter's bedside. The night before he had surprised her and some other girls, including his beautiful young niece Abigail Williams, "dancing like heathen in the forest." Now he is frightened—for people are talking of witchcraft. He urges Abigail to tell him whether, led by his Negro slave, Tituba, they had done unnatural things. A vindictive neighbor couple report that their daughter, who participated in the dancing, is also bewitched. To escape being whipped for her dancing, Abigail soon "confesses" that the girls had trafficked with spirits, and she threatens the other (younger) girls into corroborating her story. She then tries to entice John Proctor—a young farmer at whose house she had lived as a servant girl until his wife, Elizabeth, discovered their affair—to be her lover again. But Proctor, deeply penitent, rejects her once and for all. The minister's sick little girl cries out when psalm words are heard from the parlor,

The Crucible. Left to right: Elizabeth (Beatrice Straight), Proctor (Arthur Kennedy), and the Salem minister (E. G. Marshall); Danforth (Walter Hampden) is on the right. New York, 1953. (*Fred Fehl*)

but an old and widely respected grandmother quiets the child. Next appears the neighboring minister, summoned for his knowledge of demonology. Proctor's protests are discounted, for he rarely attends church: he cannot abide the Salem minister, who is generally disliked for his hellfire and damnation sermons. The demonologist examines the children and the terrified Negro slave Tituba, who, to save her life, confesses to "conjuring." As though suddenly touched by God, Abigail cries out a "confession" and names those she saw "with the Devil." The sick child ecstatically participates in the accusations, as the minister shouts a prayer of thanksgiving and the town marshall is summoned.

Act II. At home a week later, Elizabeth Proctor tells her husband that their new servant girl has spent another day in the town court, which is now trying witches. To check the growing madness, she urges Proctor to report Abigail's statement that the girls were dancing innocently that night. His hesitation makes it appear that he is still attracted to Abigail. Angrily Proctor castigates the puritanical Elizabeth for not forgiving his lapse: "Your justice would freeze beer!" Their servant returns with a rag doll she has sewed in court and with news of many new convictions. When Proctor chides her for aiding the hysteria, the girl reveals that she has saved Elizabeth from an anonymous accuser. The demonologist, who has come to question them, is shaken by Proctor's remark about the many witchcraft confessions: "And why not, if they must hang for denyin' it?" All are appalled by the news of further arrests: the wife of an irascible old-timer, and the much-respected old grandmother. If she "be tainted," the now-troubled demonologist declares, "then nothing's left to stop the whole green world from burning." Then the court clerk comes to arrest Elizabeth: the evidence of her witchcraft is the rag doll, which has a needle in it. Abigail (who watched the servant girl sewing it) has had a fit and pulled a needle out of her own flesh—claiming that Elizabeth's "familiar spirit pushed it in." Frantically Proctor tears up the warrant and tries to resist his wife's arrest. After she is chained and taken away, Proctor tells the servant girl she must tell the court the truth about the doll. "She'll kill me for sayin' that!" the girl cries, and adds: "Abby'll charge lechery on you." Realizing that Abigail schemes to supplant Elizabeth, Proctor vows, "My wife will never die for me!" He catches the servant girl by her throat to force her to testify, as she keeps sobbing, "I cannot."

Act III. In the court's anteroom, accusations and denials of witchcraft are heard. The old-timer, after disrupting his wife's trial, is brought in, and Deputy Governor Danforth comes to examine Proctor and his servant girl, who has signed a recantation. Danforth announces that because Elizabeth is pregnant she cannot be sentenced, and he urges Proctor to drop his fraud charges against the court. But backed by ninety-one signatures testifying to the other accused women's characters, Proctor refuses. Danforth orders the arrest of the signers and of the old-timer, who reveals that a man coached his daughter to denounce a neighbor whose land he craved. When the demonologist objects to the ruthless proceedings, Danforth explains that because "witchcraft is *ipso facto,* on its face and by its nature, an invisible crime," it is impossible to hear other witnesses than the children. Abigail comes in with the girls and denies Proctor's maid's account that "it was only a sport." When Abigail pretends to be bewitched, Proctor, deeply shamed to blacken his own name, pulls her by the hair and discloses their affair. "She thinks to dance with me on my wife's grave!" he tells Danforth; "it is a whore's vengeance, and you must see it." To test the truth of Proctor's statement, Elizabeth, who has never been known to lie, is brought in. But to protect her husband's name, she denies his adultery. Now Abigail pretends to fend off an attacking bird. As if transfixed, she begs the Proctors' maid, in the form of the bird, not to attack her: "This is a black art to change your shape. No, I cannot, I cannot stop my mouth; it's God's work I do." As the maid cries for her to stop, Abigail and the others mimic her cries until, whimpering hysterically, the servant girl starts to scream with them. She accuses Proctor of being the devil's agent who made her sign a lie. "Will you confess yourself befouled with Hell?" Danforth demands of Proctor, threatening to hang him. "I say—God is dead!" Proctor replies, and warns of a fire "for them that quail to bring men out of ignorance, as I have quailed, and as you quail now when you know in all your black hearts that this be fraud." He is arrested, but the disillusioned demonologist resigns: "I denounce these proceedings, I quit this court!"

Act IV. In the Salem jail cell, it is just before the hanging of Proctor and the others accused. Salem's minister is now full of doubts and horror: his daughter and Abigail have stolen his money and run off. The demonologist urges Danforth to pardon the doomed, who refuse to confess: "There are orphans wandering from house to house; abandoned cattle bellow on the highroads, the stink of rotting crops hangs everywhere, and no man knows when the harlots' cry will end his life." But Danforth remains adamant, eager only for Proctor's confession. He has Elizabeth talk to Proctor. In a touching interview, when Proctor asks for his wife's forgiveness, Elizabeth admits her own guilt ("It needs a cold wife to prompt lechery") but refuses to counsel him. Though it humiliates Proctor, he decides to "confess," and the old grandmother, doomed to hang, is brought in to witness his confession. But he refuses to give up his good name. When he realizes his signed confession will be exhibited, he tears it up: "I do think I see some shred of goodness in John Proctor. Not enough to weave a banner with, but white enough to keep it from such dogs." After Elizabeth embraces him passionately, he goes out to be hanged. Frantically the minister begs her to run and save Proctor. "He have his goodness now, God forbid I take it from him!" his wife weeps, as the drumrolls crash outside.

CRUELTY, THEATRE OF, a type of drama promulgated and practiced by ANTONIN ARTAUD in his attempt to eschew psychological REALISM and revive ritual and catharsis in the modern Western theatre. As described in his essays collected in 1938 as *Le Théâtre et son double* (*The Theatre and Its Double*), "cruelty" is to be understood in its "broad sense," alluding not so much to physical punishment as to "rigor, implacable intention and decision, irreversible and absolute determination." Artaud considered a "rigid control and submission to necessity" to be revealing of the essence of life, of "the cruel necessity of creation," of "the face within"—which is evil. While Artaud was not successful with his own drama, the mid-century theatre of cruelty he espoused achieved both popular and critical acclaim with the works of playwrights like JEAN GENET and PETER WEISS, particularly with the latter's MARAT/SADE.

CSOKOR, Franz Theodor (1885–1969), Austrian playwright, started as an EXPRESSIONIST with *Die rote Strasse* (1918), a fantasy on the battle of the sexes and a condemnation of materialism; and *Ballade von der Stadt* (1922), an attack on city life concluding with a vision of utopia. Subsequently Csokor wrote more traditional plays: *Gesellschaft der Menschenrechte* (1926), a twelve-scene biography of the revolutionary, early-modern German playwright Georg Büchner (1813–37); *Gewesene Menschen* (1932), a tragedy about Russian émigrés; and *Gottes General* (1938), about Loyola. Probably his best play is *3. November 1918* (1936), which depicts the dissolution of the Hapsburg army with prescient assumptions of the historical consequences of Austria-Hungary's fall. This play is the first of Csokor's "European Trilogy," which concludes with the earlier-composed *Besetztes Gebiet* (1930), set in an occupied Rhineland town; and *Der verlorene Sohn* (1946), dealing with a partisan family and reminiscent of LEOPOLD AHLSEN's later hit, *Philemon und Baukis*. Csokor wrote another trilogy, a historical "idea drama" ranging from antiquity to the rise of Christendom: *Kalypso* (1946), *Caesars Witwe* (1952), and *Pilatus* (1952). His last play was *Das Zeichen an der Wand* (1963).

CUBA as early as the sixteenth century had flourishing productions of comedy and romantic drama. After Cuba achieved independence in 1902, its theatre declined and the most popular entertainment became the *bufo,* comic sketches that often featured a shrewd Negro outwitting Galician immigrant exploiters. The foremost *bufo* author was Federico Villoch (1866–1954), and his greatest hit, *La casita criolla* (1928), had significant political repercussions. The "Solitary Star of the Cuban Theatre" was José Antonio Ramos (1885–1946), a social reformer who also labored for a Cuban National Theatre and served as consul in Spain, Mexico, and the United States. His masterpiece was a prize-winning NATURALIST thesis drama portraying the clash between colonialism and progress (and the problem of native wealth and sovereignty squandered and sold out to foreigners) on a sugar plantation, *Tembladera* (1918). Other of his plays praised for their SYMBOLISM and psychological insight include a one-act tragedy about the revolutionary Cuban officer Juan García, whose son supported the Spaniards, *El traidor* (*The Traitor,* 1915)*.

Others whose plays appeared in the teens and twenties include the poet Gustavo Sánchez Galarraga (1893–1934), a disciple of JACINTO BENAVENTE —and almost as prolific; Ramón Sánchez Varona (1883–), who won much honor for his domestic and patriotic tragedies but could make a living only by producing radio sketches; and Luis A. Baralt (1892–), who wrote symbolic and philosophic plays.

Thereafter little noteworthy Cuban drama appeared until after World War II. The most prominent later playwright was the versatile Virgilio Piñera (1912–), a social critic whose drama was influenced by EUGENE O'NEILL as well as by EUGÈNE IONESCO. Others include Carlos Felipe (pseudonym of Carlos Fernández, 1914–), who had a Freudian bias and won prizes for his *El travieso Jimmy* (1949); and Eduardo Manet (1927–), who settled in Paris and wrote in French, also focusing on psychology and producing poetic fantasies (*Scherzo,* 1948) and GRAND GUIGNOL, one of which is a four-character drama of the 1791 Haitian slave revolt, *Les Nonnes* (*The Nuns,* 1969), which has been produced in Europe and America.

A "new wave" of playwrights appeared shortly before Castro's regime and in the 1960's continued to produce works that though politically slanted were less party-line dramas than portrayals of human and social problems. The most promising among these newer playwrights are Rolando Ferrer (1925–), who writes psychologically oriented drama; Abelardo Estorino (1925–), whose *El robo del cochino* (1961) was especially praised as a naturalistic portrayal of rural family life; Manuel Reguera Saumell (1928–), notable for his avant-garde portrayal of an aging dancer in *Recuerdos de tulipa* (1962); José Triana (1932–), who under Piñera's influence has employed myth to depict irrational ordinary life, as in *La muerte del Ñeque* (1963) and *La noche de los asesinos* (1965), an internationally produced (in America as *The Criminals*) play that has been likened to Genet's THE MAIDS and that depicts the attic charades of three adolescents who may or may not have killed their parents; and Antón Arrufat (1935–), who, similarly affected by

* A truncated version of this play appears in Willis Knapp Jones's *Spanish-American Literature in Translation* (1963). Ramos's early drama is analyzed in Isaac Goldberg's *The Drama of Transition* (1922).

contemporary ABSURD currents, distinguished himself with a zany parody of the fear of death, *El vivo al pollo* (1961).

The work of the newer Cuban playwrights is described in Frank Dauster's "Cuban Drama Today," *Modern Drama,* IX: 2 (1966). In addition to the studies listed under LATIN AMERICA, a useful work on Cuba that also discusses its theatre is Ruby H. Phillips's *Cuba, Island of Paradox* (1959).

CUMMINGS, E[dward] E[stlin] (1894–1962), American poet, was also a diarist, dramatist, essayist, and painter. He was most famous for his often lyrical but always typographically eccentric verse, signed "e. e. cummings." Characterized by odd run-ons as well as broken words and lines, unusual punctuation, noncapitalization, grammatical shifts, and the frequent use of gross language, Cummings's very personal style nonetheless was rooted both in nineteenth-century poetic and in DADAIST traditions. A leading imaginative writer, he attracted immediate attention with his first published work, *The Enormous Room* (1922), an autobiographical journal of his World War I experiences in a French prison. Aside from other autobiographical writings, lectures (*i: six nonlectures,* 1953), and volume after volume of poetry, Cummings published drama. One of his plays, HIM (1928), enjoyed a moderate success with avant-garde theatre audiences.

Born in Cambridge, Massachusetts, Cummings received his B.A. and M.A. degrees from Harvard University, and then volunteered for ambulance-corps work in France during World War I. Interned for treason charges that were eventually dismissed, Cummings lived in Paris for a while, and then returned to America. He settled in New York's Greenwich Village and in New Hampshire, and devoted himself to the poetry on which his reputation rests—and to painting. After *Him*, Cummings published *Anthropos* (1930), a skit about the manipulation of the masses by slogans; *Tom* (1935), a ballet scenario based on *Uncle Tom's Cabin;* and *Santa Claus* (1946), a poetic morality play in which the title character, when his gifts are spurned, exchanges masks with Death, poses as a scientist, and finds that the phony wares he sells to an eager public become real: the people's empty wishes come true and kill them.

Cummings's plays are a typical, although—aside from *Him*—unimportant part of his writings. His often-unpopular ideas as well as his literary techniques made his work highly controversial. He was idolized by many college students for his ideas and the often-erotic lyricism of the poems, as well as for his unconventional manner of writing. Though some critics deplored what they considered his merely clever idiosyncracies, affected inanities, and occasional social viciousness, Cummings won growing acclaim from many critics and fellow poets—an esteem expressed in the Academy of American Poets Award for 1951.

His *Three Plays and a Ballet* (1966) includes *Him, Anthropos, Santa Claus,* and *Tom,* as well as an introduction by George J. Firmage. Cummings's *A Miscellany* (1958) has three brief selections from unfinished plays and a couple of essays on the theatre. A revealing collection of polemical as well as informative criticisms of Cummings's work is S. V. Baum's *E. E. Cummings and the Critics* (1962), which has extensive bibliographies. Book-length studies of the poet are Charles Norman's *The Magic Maker: E. E. Cummings* (revised 1964) and Norman Friedman's *E. E. Cummings: The Growth of a Writer* (1964).

CUREL, François de (1854–1928), French NATURALIST playwright whose outstanding work appeared at the *fin de siècle,* was called a "dramatist's dramatist." He achieved real popular success only with a now little-known comedy, *L'Âme en folie* (1919). But Curel, for whom writing was an avocation, has impressed critics with many of his sixteen plays—most notably with *Les Fossiles* (THE FOSSILS, 1892) and *L'Envers d'une sainte* (A FALSE SAINT, 1892), whose production on a double bill with Brieux's BLANCHETTE at the Théâtre Libre launched the careers of both EUGÈNE BRIEUX and Curel.

Viscount François de Curel was the scion of wealthy aristocrats. Born in Metz, he was educated at the local Jesuit college and then at Nancy's École Centrale des Arts et Manufactures. His aristocratic, religious, and scientific backgrounds are reflected in his plays, however much these may focus on character abnormality. After publishing some novels Curel was advised to write for the stage. His first plays (*Sauvé des eaux* and *La Figurante*) were rejected by fashionable Parisian theatres, one of whose readers suggested that Curel study the work of successful manufacturers of the WELL-MADE PLAY like Eugène Scribe. Thereupon Curel, in 1891, submitted these and a third play—each under a different pseudonym—to the founder of the Théâtre-Libre, André Antoine. Antoine accepted all three. Upon discovering their single authorship, he chose to produce *A False Saint*—the least likely to achieve popular acclaim but, he assured Curel, the one that would "at once win [Curel] a reputation as a writer, a thing not to be despised."

The prediction proved as accurate with this play as with the next Curel drama Antoine produced, *The Fossils.* Francisque Sarcey's and JULES LEMAÎTRE's acclaim thereupon moved the Comédie-Française to solicit a Curel play. He obliged with *L'Invitée* (1893), a psychological study of a woman reunited with her children many years after abandoning them because of her husband's infidelity; because reservations were again expressed, Curel had the play produced elsewhere, but submitted yet another script to the Comédie-Française. A revision of the earlier-rejected *Sauvé des eaux,* now retitled *L'Amour brode,* was produced there in 1893 but proved a failure. However, it impressed Sarah Bernhardt, who offered Curel her theatre, where, in 1896, the third of Curel's early plays, *La Figurante,* was produced. This is another psychological study of a woman, the dancer of the title, who ultimately succeeds in winning her politician-husband's love despite their original agreement to keep the marriage nominal and not have it interfere with his long-time liaison.

In succeeding plays Curel turned to larger social issues, often expressed in polemical, NATURALISTIC, and idealistic terms. But he continued to focus on psychological analysis, usually that of aberrant characters. Other notable plays with such characters are *Les Repas du lion, La Nouvelle Idole,* and *La Fille sauvage.* The first, produced by the Théâtre-Libre in 1897, features a religious orator (modeled on the statesman-philosopher Albert de Mun), who, to atone for a childhood misdeed, temporarily deserts his industrialist class to fight for the workers; the play was marred by long debates on Christian socialism and by the hero's melodramatic death, but Curel persisted and in 1920 produced a successful revision. *La Nouvelle Idole* (published in 1895 but not produced until 1899) deals with the conflicts of religion and science, "the new idol": the imminent death of a scientist who has lost some of his faith in science is accompanied by his final perception of a soul and suggests that the conflicts are reconcilable in a faith that may transcend both medicine and Christianity. *La Fille sauvage* (1902) features a captured African girl who is driven back to her "savage" tribal state, brokenhearted by Europe's emotional and intellectual civilization, which ultimately cannot cope with and may destroy natural instincts.

Curel dramatized other psychologically slanted problems of society, morality, and philosophy in sometimes diffuse and SYMBOLIC ways in *Le Coup d'aile* (1906); *La Danse devant le miroir* (1914), yet another revision of the early *Sauvé des eaux* that here portrays the tragic futility and loneliness of a love that ends with suicide because each lover sees not what is there but only what he seeks in the beloved; *L'Âme en folie* (1919), an arbitrarily resolved comedy and, as noted above, Curel's only real popular success, dealing satirically with human passions that "drive the soul insane" by contrasting them with the animal kingdom and suggesting stoicism and humility as means of salvation; *L'Ivresse du sage* (1922), which has been likened to Ibsen's WHEN WE DEAD AWAKEN; *Terre inhumaine* (1922), dramatizing conflicts of patriotism and love; and *Orage mystique* (1927), Curel's last play, which deals with passions, life's mystery, and attempts to communicate with the dead.

Curel's is a mixture of thesis drama, naturalistic tragedy, and contemporary symbolism. But he was principally interested in analyzing and depicting passions. These almost always victimize the heroines and elevate the heroes, who dramatize Curel's preoccupation with and his ambivalent attitudes about social and moral problems. Though impressive for his artistic integrity and his carefully structured drama, Curel was an uneven craftsman whose plays usually foundered because he failed to make complexly conceived characters and situations clear and vivid.

There are many studies of his life and work, including the chapter on Curel in Barrett H. Clark's *Contemporary French Dramatists* (1915); Archibald Henderson's introduction to *A False Saint* (1916); and the preface in E. Bradlee Watson and Benfield Pressey's *Contemporary Drama European Plays I* (1931), which includes *The Fossils.*

CURTMANTLE, a blank-verse play in three acts and a prologue by CHRISTOPHER FRY, published and produced in 1961. Setting: England, 1160–89.

This is a dramatization of the reign of Henry II, nicknamed "Curtmantle" after his short and plain cloak. The play focuses on the characters of the king, his wife (Eleanor of Aquitaine), and Thomas Becket, dramatizing the conflict and death of both men. Unlike JEAN ANOUILH's and T. S. ELIOT's themes in their Becket plays, Fry's avowed themes are the interplay of human and divine laws; and Henry's search for reality, symbolized in the early "Where is the King" and the final, unresolved "He was dead when they came to him."

CWOJDZIŃSKI, Antoni (1896–), Polish dramatist, in the 1930's wrote extremely popular pseudoscientific comedies in the tradition of BERNARD SHAW. Cwojdziński was particularly successful with *Teoria względności* (*Theory of Relativity,* 1934), also known as *Teoria Einsteina* (*The Einstein Theory*), which is set in a university professor's home and elucidates the theory as well as its philosophic implications; and with *Freuda teoria snów* (*Freud's Theory of Dreams,* 1937), a comedy about a theatre director and an actress who interpret and comment on Freud's theories—and discover they are in love with each other. Cwojdziński's other plays include *Niemiec* (*The German,* 1944), which illustrates the theory of conditioned reflexes with the behavior of Luftwaffe fliers shot down in blitzed Coventry; and *Życie i sny* (*Life and Dreams,* ?), another comedy about the theories of Einstein, featuring the venality of his followers in America.

Though translated, these plays are not easily available in English. After World War II, Cwojdziński migrated to America. Later he settled in London.

CYMBELINE REFINISHED, "A Variation on Shakespear's Ending" by BERNARD SHAW, produced in 1937 and published in 1946. Setting: a rocky defile.

In his "Foreword" to this version of the ending of Shakespeare's drama, Shaw remarked that "Cymbeline, though one of the finest of Shakespear's later plays now on the stage, goes to pieces in the last act." He decided "to rewrite the act as Shakespear might have written it if he had been post-IBSEN and post-Shaw instead of post-Marlowe." Retaining 89 of Shakespeare's 836 lines, Shaw wrote 213 additional blank-verse lines. Without changing the basic plot, he attempted to heighten the plausibility, "humanize" the characters (particularly Imogen), and delete the archaic devices of revelation. Of course, there are Shavian touches in these alterations. Shaw defended "the propriety of meddling with masterpieces" by citing many precedents, among them Shakespeare's own alterations of *Hamlet.*

CYRANO DE BERGERAC, "an heroic comedy" in five acts by EDMOND ROSTAND, produced in 1897 and published in 1898. Setting: Paris and a battlefield near Arras, France; 1640 and 1655.

This romantic verse drama was one of the most popular successes of all times in the theatres of Europe and America, and Rostand's best-loved play—though some French critics prefer his L'AIGLON. Cyrano is loosely modeled on a Gascon soldier-poet who lived from 1619 to 1655. A choice role for actors—he was originally created for Constant Coquelin, as Roxane was for Sarah Bernhardt—the self-sacrificing, long-nosed idealist Cyrano embodies the play's torrential and passionate poetry, its bombast and wit, as well as its concern with heroics and honor. Yet beneath these musketeer-heroics there is Cyrano's wistfully quixotic striving for the ideal. A powerful reaction to contemporary NATURALISM and frequently revived to this day, the play has been made into operas (including one by Walter Damrosch and William J. Henderson, 1913) and musical comedies (by Victor Herbert and others).

Act I. "A Performance at the Hotel de Bourgogne." Cavaliers and commoners await the start of a theatrical production. Among them is Baron Christian de Neuvillette, a handsome but dull-witted officer in love with Roxane (Madeleine Robin), a beauty he has observed from afar but has not dared to address. Soon joined by Ragueneau, a poet whose bakery is frequented by hungry poets, Christian hears about the planned murder of a companion by one hundred hirelings of a wealthy old count who lusts for Roxane. Though loath to leave Roxane's presence, Christian goes off to warn the endangered man. The play starts, but its star is immediately interrupted: "Wretch, Have I not forbade you these three weeks?" It is his enemy Cyrano de Bergerac, Roxane's swashbuckling cousin, a "Poet—Swordsman—Musician—Philosopher" disfigured by an enormous nose. He kicks out the hated actor, thus defying the disappointed audience. Though he reimburses the owner by grandly throwing him a full purse, Cyrano challenges the angry audience, demolishes and boots out a meddler, and even braves the count himself. When the latter alludes to the nose, Cyrano in a witty long speech suggests how variously his nose might be described. "AGGRESSIVE: I, sir, if that nose were mine, / I'd have it amputated—on the spot! / FRIENDLY: How do you drink with such a nose?" he begins. He cites examples for a score of other such possibilities, and finally ridicules the count for lacking wit. Then he contemptuously duels with an insulting nobleman—composing a ballad during the swordplay and finishing both his ballad and his opponent with a grand lunge. Alone, Cyrano reveals that the purse he so grandly tossed the proprietor was his month's allowance. "What a fool!" a friend remarks; Cyrano replies, "But—what a gesture!" Equally nonchalant about the enemies he has made by exposing fraud and hypocrisy, Cyrano admits, "I have my bitter days, / Knowing myself so ugly, so alone." But he never weeps: "That would be too grotesque—tears trickling down / All the long way along this nose of mine." Then he confesses to loving his cousin Roxane. He dares not tell her about it, fearing she will laugh at so ugly a suitor. When her duenna delivers a message that Roxane wishes to talk privately with him, Cyrano is overjoyed. Before meeting her, he undertakes to rescue the man who is to be murdered: Cyrano will fight and defeat the hundred hirelings "Alone, with glory fluttering over me."

Act II. "The Bakery of the Poets." Early the next morning, hungry poets help themselves to the impractical Ragueneau's goods as he apostrophizes them and is chided by his flirtatious wife. Cyrano, slightly wounded after defeating the would-be assassins, is ready to meet Roxane, and the poets and the duenna are sent out. Roxane recalls their childhood games and confides to Cyrano that she is deeply in love with "A big boy who loves me too, / And is afraid of me, and keeps away, / And never says a word." For a moment Cyrano's hopes rise. But it is Christian Roxane loves, and she elicits from the heartbroken Cyrano the promise that he will protect Christian and have him write her of his love. After she departs the crowds congratulate Cyrano on his heroism. Cyrano proudly rejects the count and, discovering him to be the hirer of the hundred cutthroats, insults him. "Have you read *Don Quixote?*" the count asks. "I have—and found myself the hero," Cyrano replies. When a friend urges him to "stop trying to be Three Musketeers in one," Cyrano reaffirms his determination to remain true to himself. "I am too proud to be a parasite," he declares; "I stand, not high it may be—but alone!" Christian, as a new cadet, must prove his manhood. Immediately he finds his chance as Cyrano starts telling a story: "It was so dark, . . . you could not

Walter Hampden as Cyrano de Bergerac. New York, 1923. *(Brown Brothers)*

see beyond—" "Your nose," Christian interrupts. When he learns that the insult comes from the man he has promised to protect, Cyrano pales and continues. But as Christian persists with similar insults, Cyrano clears the room. He identifies himself as Roxane's cousin and Christian's friend, and proposes, when Christian deplores his inability to speak or write finely, to help with the letters to Roxane: "Come, shall we win her both together? Take / The soul within this leathern jack of mine, / And breathe it into you?" The cadets, who expected to see Christian demolished by the sensitive Cyrano, are amazed, instead, to find them friends: "Here's our devil—Christianized! / Offend one nostril, and he turns the other!"

Act III. "Roxane's Kiss." Roxane is thrilled with Christian's "beautiful" letters, although Cyrano (their real author) criticizes them. As night falls, Christian visits Roxane. "Speak of love in your own words— / Improvise! Rhapsodize! Be eloquent!" she demands. Christian is eager to speak for himself, but is so inept he is about to lose her. Beneath her balcony Cyrano starts prompting him, and then impatiently pushes him aside and in a muffled voice rhapsodizes his love for Roxane: "Let me enjoy / The one moment I ever—my one chance / To speak to you—unseen!" As the invisible lover opens his heart to her, Christian eagerly has him request a kiss. "Climb up, animal!" Cyrano says, pushing the young man to the balcony. Christian takes Roxane in his arms while Cyrano sadly likens himself to Lazarus: "Yet—I have something here that is mine now / And was not mine before I spoke the words / That won her—not for me!" And as Roxane and Christian still embrace, Cyrano concludes, "kissing my words / My words, upon your lips!" A Capuchin sent by the lustful count delivers a note asking Roxane to meet him. Dissimulating cleverly, Roxane has the Capuchin marry her at once to Christian. The count himself appears but Cyrano, pretending to be a madman, delays him with wild antics (including an account of "six ways to violate the virgin sky") until the ceremony is over. When the couple appears and the count realizes he has been duped he takes instant revenge. As their new commander, he orders both men to battle. Roxane entreats Cyrano to protect Christian, "to keep him dry and warm . . . and faithful," and to "have him write to me / Every single day!" Cyrano replies, "That, I promise you!"

Act IV. "The Cadets of Gascoyne." Though his company is hopelessly outnumbered and besieged by the Spaniards, Cyrano daily mails his letter (written in Christian's name) to Roxane. "I promised he should write / Every single day," he tells a comrade who resents Cyrano's risking his valuable life thus. Cyrano encourages his starving, doomed companions. "Let me die so," he declaims, "for a good cause!" The cadets conceal their anguish before the despised commander, the count who is committing them to the massacre. Cyrano hands Christian a farewell letter he has written for him to Roxane—spotted with a tear. As the drums roll, a coach appears. Out steps Roxane, who has come through the Spanish lines and cheerfully dispenses provisions that are voraciously consumed. Heartened, the doomed men use her handkerchief for a banner, and even the count becomes courageous. Before the battle Roxane tells Christian she now loves him—not frivolously, for his looks, but for the soul revealed in his daily letters. Now she would love him though he were "less charming—ugly even." Bitterly Christian is about to reveal the truth and have her choose between him and Cyrano. But before he can do so he is hit by a bullet, and dies. "I cannot ever / Tell her, now—ever," Cyrano says as Roxane finds her blood-spattered farewell letter in Christian's breast pocket. As Roxane grieves, Cyrano concludes: "I am dead, and my love mourns for me / And does not know." In despair, Cyrano leads the cadets against the Spanish hordes and declaims amidst a hail of bullets, "Free fighters, free lovers, free spenders—"

Act V. "Cyrano's Gazette." It is fifteen years later, in the park of the convent to which Roxane retired to nurture her eternal love for Christian. Every Saturday Cyrano comes to bring Roxane news of the world. His persistent satires have made him many enemies: now he is impoverished —and he has just been fatally wounded by a hired assassin. Unaware of this, Roxane wonders why Cyrano is late—for the first time. But soon he appears, and she does not notice his paleness and the bandages covered by his hat. Cyrano tries to be amusing as he recites the weekly news. Obviously suffering, he asks now to see "Christian's" last letter, as she promised he might some day. "Farewell Roxane, because today I die—" he starts reading, and continues, though darkness falls rapidly. Roxane finally realizes that he is reciting by heart, in a voice "I remember hearing—long ago." And though he still denies it, she exclaims, "It was you . . . I understand everything now." His friends rush in, revealing that Cyrano has hastened death by leaving his bed. But Cyrano concludes his "Gazette": "An hour or so / Before dinner, Monsieur de Bergerac / Died, foully murdered" by "a lackey, with a log of wood" thrown from a window. He despairs because he was cheated even of an ideal heroic death. But when Roxane confesses, "I never loved but one man in my life, / And I have lost him—twice," the brief ecstasy of this discovery of her love redeems Cyrano's whole life of emptiness. Deliriously he lunges at all his enemies, "Falsehood—Prejudice—Compromise—Cowardice—Vanity." As Roxane kisses him, the dying Cyrano smiles up at her and proudly envisions his imminent appearance before God, bearing with him his unstained ideal, "My white panache . . ."

CZECHOSLOVAKIA. Czech drama attained international fame with the works of KAREL ČAPEK. His fantasies, particularly R.U.R. (1920) and *Ze života hmyzu* (FROM THE LIFE OF INSECTS [1920], written with his brother Josef), and one or two dramas of FRANTIŠEK LANGER, were the only generally known Czech plays until recently, when the works of VÁCLAV HAVEL and other new writers appeared abroad. Only a few dramatists wrote in Slovak, and plays written by German Czechs are subsumed in Germany's drama.

In modern times, the first major stimulus to Czech drama was the work of Josef Jiří Kolár (1812–96), an actor-dramatist who translated Shakespeare, Goethe, and Schiller, and wrote historical tragedies, including *Pražský žid* (1871) and *Primátor* (1883). Contemporaneous with him were writers of Scribean drama and popular farces, playwrights like Emanuel Bozděch (1841–91) and František Ferdinand Šamberk (1838–1904). More serious work was produced by the distinguished poets Julius Zeyer (1841–1901) and Jaroslav Vrchlický (1853–1912).

NATURALISM and social criticism appeared with the work of Jaroslav Hilbert (1871–1936), who was strongly influenced by HENRIK IBSEN; Gabriela Preissová (1862–1946), whose *Její pastorkyňa* (1891) Leoš Janáček made into his best-known opera, *Její pastorkyňa* (1904, often performed as *Jenufa*); and other writers. Viktor Dyk (1877–1931) became a leading dramatist with a historical trilogy written in 1907–09 (*Revoluční trilogie*) and a Don Quixote drama portraying the conflict of the mundane and the ideal (*Zmoudření dona Quijota,* 1914). Fráňa Srámek (1877–1952) wrote lyrical SYMBOLIC drama, some of it (like *Léto,* 1915) influenced by FRANK WEDEKIND. Soon after the establishment of the independent Republic of Czechoslovakia in 1918, ideals of social reform burgeoned in *Husité* (1919) by Arnošt Dvořák (1881–1933), a prominent dramatist whose *Václav IV* (1910) was praised as the finest Czech history play. Notable also are the poetic dramas of Otokar Fischer (1883–1938), the brutal tragedies of Jiří Mahen (1882–1939), the comedies of Vilém Werner (1892–)—particularly his *Právo na hřích* (1931)—and Edmund Konrád (1889–1957), as well as this writer's attack on technology in his play about Edison, *Čaroděj z Menlo aneb pokolení prvních věcí* (*The Wizard of Menlo,* 1934).

Čapek stimulated a group of Czech "pragmatists" including Zdeněk Němeček (1894–1957), Josef Kopta (1894–1962), and most notably Langer. George Voskovec (*né* Jiří Wachsmann, 1905–), later an American character actor, and Jan Werich (1905–), comedians who directed Prague's progressive "The Unfettered Theatre" until the Munich Pact, wrote over twenty plays like the popular *Balada z hadrů* (1935), many of them anti-Nazi satires. F. X. Šalda (1867–1937) after some decades as a critic turned to writing plays of social protest, and Jan Bartoš (1893–1946) produced EXPRESSIONIST and GROTESQUE drama. Among other playwrights of the period between the wars were Lev Blatný (1894–1930); Alfred Radok (1914–); Vladislav Vančura (1891–1942), who wrote literary tragedies; and the Slovak Július Barč-Ivan (1909–55), who portrayed social problems resolved in a manner reflecting his religious viewpoints, as in *3000 l'udí* (1934). The major Slovakian playwright during this period was Ivan Stodola (1888–), a government official who participated in the World War II national rebellion against the Nazi armies; the most popular of his many comedies was *Jožko Púčik a jeho kariéra* (1931), satirizing false philanthropy that here improves the lot of a lowly clerk.

The impetus given to literature by national independence in 1918 was stifled—first by the Nazi occupation (1939–45), which paralyzed all art, and later by the Soviet cultural directives in control since 1948. The first noteworthy postwar drama was a comic satire about the return of a soldier to his hometown, *Na dosah ruky* (1948) by Jaroslav Klíma (1916–), a playwright who two decades later satirized contemporary life even more sharply in *Porota* (1969), which features a jury bullied to condemn an already-beheaded accused. The surrealist poet Vítězslav Nezval (1900–58) wrote among other experimental plays the ambitious literary drama *Dnes ještě zapadá slunce nad Atlantidou* (1956), which was subsequently incorporated into the predominantly classical and foreign repertoires of Czech theatres.

New writers mentioned in the 1950's were Jan Drda (1915–), Vojtěch Cach (1914–), František Hrubín (1910–), and Miloslav Stehlík (1916–), who wrote a drama on the Nazi occupation, *Mordová rokle* (1949), the tragicomic *Selská láska* (1956), and later plays like *Tygří kožich* (1960) and *O korunu a lásku* (1961). Communist ideology permeates the fiction and drama of the brilliant Slovakian official, critic, and editor Peter Karvaš (1920–): his plays include *Polnocná omsa* (1959), which glorifies the post-World War II uprising in which he participated; and the notable comedy *Veľka parochna* (1964), which under the guise of conflicts between hairy and bald people satirizes sociopolitical hypocrisy.

Aside from Havel, notable dramatists emerging in the 1960's include Josef Topol (1935–) and Ladislav Smoček (1932–), the popularity of whose black comedies and farces extended beyond Czech borders. Topol, "a realist with the tongue of a poet" according to a Czech critic, made his name with the existentialist drama *Konec masopustu* (1963), in which a traditional village masque results in tragedy; and with the mordant love drama *Kočka na kolejích* (1965). *Platkovina* (1969), a malicious sex satire by the novelist Milan Kundera (1929–), portrays the seduction of a minor politician's mistress comically but with political overtones applauded by Czechs the year after the Russian occupation.

Except for Čapek's work, translated Czech drama is still not easily accessible. English studies and historical accounts of Czechoslovak drama and theatre are equally rare. A collection of miscellaneous informative essays edited by Jindřich Honzl was translated and published as *The Czechoslovak Theatre* (1948); it includes lists of Czech playwrights and their plays, as well as articles on variety theatre, ballet, and opera. For other studies see the bibliographies in Harkins's and Matuška's books on Čapek.

D

DADAISM, a bizarre movement in literature and the arts, was founded in Zürich, Switzerland, in 1916, and soon spread across Europe. It began with a group headed by ROGER VITRAC and by TRISTAN TZARA, who eventually moved to Paris. The movement's name was picked at random from a French dictionary, the founders maintained, but it suggests both the masculinity and the childishness ("hobbyhorse") they sought. Innately nihilistic, Dadaism was defined by Tzara as "a protest with the fists of its whole being engaged in destructive action." It protested against World War I, and attempted to match the war's carnage and the demonstrated meaninglessness of "civilized" values. Its art and poetry reflect these aspirations, as did its drama, which for the most part has been lost.

Performed before unruly audiences in cabarets, some of Dada's best plays (for example Tzara's THE GAS HEART) proved to be stimulating experiments in the deliberate portrayal of monotony and illogic. Because Dadaism is negative and pointless by definition and by intent, it waned rapidly and was virtually dead by 1922—only to reappear in another form, as HAPPENINGS, four decades later. Some Dada artists formed and joined the rising movement of SURREALISM. Dada reviews and anthologies between 1916 and 1921 were *Cabaret Voltaire, Dada,* and *Littérature.* For the movement's history *see* Hans Richter's *Dada: Art and Anti-Art* (1966). Such distinctively Dada drama as Tzara's *The Gas Heart* is included in Michael Benedikt and George E. Wellwarth's collection, *Modern French Theatre: The Avant-Garde, Dada, and Surrealism* (1964), whose informative introduction refers to other studies on the subject.

DAGERMAN, Stig (1923–54), Swedish novelist and playwright, had a brilliant but short-lived career. He first made his name with the symbolic novel *Ormen* (*The Serpent,* 1945), which was soon followed by such other EXPRESSIONIST novels as *De dömdas ö* (*The Isle of the Damned,* 1946) and *Bränt barn* (*A Burnt Child,* 1948). Of his four plays, all of which were produced in Stockholm with varying success, the most impressive is the first, *Den Dödsömde* (THE CONDEMNED, 1947). To a larger extent than the others, it, like his novels, was influenced by the fiction of Franz Kafka and WILLIAM FAULKNER as well as by the drama of his great fellow Swedes, AUGUST STRINDBERG and PÄR LAGERKVIST. At the same time Dagerman manifested considerable originality in his depiction of the ever-present evil that he believed man has to

Stig Dagerman. (*Swedish Information Service*)

recognize and acknowledge before conquering. He attributed suffering not to the flaws inherent in a man himself but to the limitations of his fellowmen. Politically, Dagerman was allied with the syndicalist movement, to which his wife's family, emigrants from Germany, belonged. (His second marriage was to the distinguished Swedish actress Anita Björk.) Dagerman fully shared the syndicalists' rejection of political compromise and expediency and their idealistic quest to accomplish the impossible.

Dagerman was less successful in dramatizing these views in his later plays. *Skuggan av Mart* (1948) is a psychological drama about a man whose life is frustrated by the eternal "shadow" of his heroic brother's martyrdom in the underground, during World War II; ultimately he shoots his mother, who has tried to interfere with his love for his brother's widow. *Ingen går fri* (1949), another psychological study and Dagerman's dramatization of his *A Burnt Child,* explores a young man's Oedipal fixation. *Streber* (1949), Dagerman's last play, is an IBSENite drama that features a go-getter whose villainy destroys a business venture; the play has been praised for the fidelity with which it portrays the working-class milieu, though it has been criticized for its simplistic bias.

Dagerman displayed considerable power in articulating man's anguish in modern society. But he was unable to continue satisfying the public's expectations and demands after the big splash made by his early fiction and drama. The 1950's found him increasingly less productive, and he finally succeeded in committing suicide, never having fulfilled the high promise of his brilliant youth.

The Condemned, with a prefatory essay by Alrik Gustafson, appears in the third series of *Scandinavian Plays of the Twentieth Century* (1951). Gustafson's *A History of Swedish Literature* (1961) has an expanded version of this essay, as well as a bibliography of Swedish books and articles on Dagerman.

DAISNE, Johan [originally Herman Thiery] (1912–), Belgian poet, novelist, and playwright, in the 1940's produced a number of notable Flemish plays. They deal with the divine nature of Platonic love, most symbolically dramatized by the sword laid between Tristan and Isolde in Daisne's *Het Zwaard van Tristan* (1942). This play is the first of a trilogy that concludes with *Tine van Berken* (1945) and *Veva* (1945).

DALY, [John] **Augustin** (1838–99), American producer and playwright, was the outstanding theatre manager before DAVID BELASCO and for most of the late nineteenth century. After a brief stint as a newspaper critic, Daly started adapting popular novels and foreign plays. Premières in his theatres (also in England) were major social events and featured the greatest stars of the age. But Daly disapproved of the star system, and rigorously controlled his own company as an ensemble—with a sensitive but dictatorial hand that became proverbial. A master technician, Daly strove for scenic REALISM in plays like *Horizon* (1871), one of his many "frontier" dramas. In all, Daly wrote and reworked about one hundred plays, almost all of them melodramas. They include an adaptation of Salomon Hermann Mosenthal's (1821–77) German play about anti-Semitism *Deborah* (1849) as *Leah the Forsaken* (1862), a play greeted with particular enthusiasm by American northerners for its timely analogy with anti-Negro prejudice in the South; and one of the most famous of all melodramas, the still revived *Under the Gaslight* (1867), which originated the vogue for railroad-track rescue scenes in the theatre. For an exhaustive study of the man and his work see Marvin Felheim's *The Theater of Augustin Daly* (1956).

DAMAGED GOODS (*Les Avariés*), a play in three acts by EUGÈNE BRIEUX, published and produced in 1902. Setting: Paris, c. 1901.

This thesis play about venereal disease was banned in André Antoine's Théâtre-Libre in 1901 and created a minor sensation in England and America, where it was performed before the United States Congress and the President. BERNARD SHAW enthusiastically endorsed it in his long preface to *Three Plays by Brieux* (1911), and Antoine and Brieux himself, who gave it a public reading in 1901, made impassioned pleas on behalf of this "study of syphilis in its bearing on marriage" and the need to publicize the evil of the disease and pass health laws to protect the innocent. The play is undramatic, however; the last act entirely jettisons any pretense of plot for debate and lecture.

George Dupont breaks down pitifully when he learns that his one "lark" had infected him. The doctor consoles George with the assurance that science can probably cure him. But he insists that, despite all protests, George must delay his marriage for at least three years. It would be criminal to expose his unsuspecting bride and future children to syphilis, which the doctor describes graphically. Nonetheless, George (the "damaged goods" of the title) soon marries and has a child—who now develops telltale symptoms. George's doting but still unsuspecting mother ruthlessly intends to save the sick infant by retaining the wet nurse who, the doctor warns, must be protected from further danger of infection. The nurse learns the truth and as she leaves indignantly shouts it out. George's wife collapses in a fit of disgust and hatred, shrieking at her husband, "Don't touch me!" Her father, a prominent politician, demands a certificate of George's disease so that she can divorce him. The doctor refuses. Syphilis is a misfortune most men expose themselves to, he explains, and lectures on the need for health laws. The truth about syphilis must be made known to all, he continues, though we envelop sex "in a gigantic conspiracy of silence." It would be best to save the marriage and cure George, who may yet have healthy children, the doctor argues, demonstrating his lecture with the case study of a syphilitic young prostitute. "If you give a thought or two to what you have just learned when you sit in the Chamber," the doctor concludes as the politician departs, "we shall not have wasted our time."

DANCE OF DEATH, THE (*Dödsdansen*), a drama in two parts by AUGUST STRINDBERG, published in 1901 and produced in 1905. Setting: an island fortress off Sweden's coast, 1890's.

This partly autobiographical portrayal of a love-hate relationship is considerably longer and more vicious and tragically farcical than that of THE FATHER; and the fault is here more evenly distributed between husband and wife. Though predominantly NATURALISTIC, it is in part EXPRESSIONISTIC and reflects the medieval iconography suggested in the title. Many later plays directly derive from it, particularly Albee's WHO'S AFRAID OF VIRGINIA WOOLF? Only Part I is usually produced. Much of Part II deals with the romance of the youngsters ("To think that flowers can grow out of filth!" the wife remarks). Though unable to stand by itself, it is integral to the play, and both parts were presented together by Laurence Olivier

The Dance of Death. Alice (Geraldine McEwan), Kurt (Robert Stephens), and the Captain (Laurence Olivier). London, 1967. (*Dominic Photography*)

and the National Theatre in 1967. The play was transformed by FRIEDRICH DÜRRENMATT into an avant garde farce, *Play Strindberg* (1969).

Part I. Act I. Artillery Captain Edgar and his wife Alice, a former actress, wearily talk in their living room. Their mutual hatred is expressed in tired but still-lacerating dialogue. After twenty-five years of passionate loathing, they are isolated and friendless because of their repulsive conduct in "Little Hell," as the island is nicknamed. "Everyone is scum," says the Captain, who has despaired of promotion and sits in his tattered uniform. They are relieved by a visit from Kurt, the new quarantine officer and Alice's cousin, whom each tries to win over. Kurt is reluctant to stay in the house, whose "very walls smell of poison . . . and such hatred that one can scarcely breathe." The Captain, suffering from a weak heart, collapses in a deadly faint. Alice remarks that she hates him "so utterly that the day he dies, I'd laugh aloud. . . . But we are welded together—we can't escape." Then she weeps at their unhappiness: they have not even food in the house. After performing a sword dance to Alice's piano playing, the Captain collapses again. The doctors whom Kurt calls refuse to treat him. Sitting by his side all night, Kurt comforts the arrogant and insulting Captain, who has more nearly fatal seizures. But he goes on duty in the morning. Alice, cursing him, tells Kurt that the Captain once had an affair with Kurt's wife and has caused Kurt to be deprived of his children's custody. However, Kurt forgives the Captain.

Act II. After two days the dying Captain seems chastened. Alice is nonetheless convinced the "vampire" is still planning evil. He soon appears. Sadistically he announces that he has had Kurt's son, a cadet, transferred to the island; and he taunts Alice by telling her that he is divorcing her to marry someone who is pretty. Kurt is appalled by the threat of the Captain's mastery of him through his son. Alice, telling him that the Captain is an embezzler who once tried to drown her, plays the piano, dances madly, and seduces the weak, now-sympathetic Kurt. Thus entrapped in their evil, he is soon disgusted with himself as well as with Alice, the more so when she shamelessly humiliates him and the Captain brokenly talks of his approaching death. Alice flaunts her liaison before the maddened husband, who rushes her with a sword and collapses when he misses. Her joy—"Hurrah! He's dead!"—is brief, however, for he quickly recovers. They beg Kurt to stay but, pushing Alice aside, he leaves them: "Go to the hell from which you came! Good-bye forever!" As soon as Kurt goes out their mood changes completely. Though they accept their apparent destiny "to torment one another," they become reconciled and, as Alice giggles appreciatively, the Captain plans the celebration of their silver wedding: "They'll laugh at us, but what does that matter? We'll laugh with them—or else be serious—just as we choose . . . . Cancel out and pass on! So—let us pass on!"

Part II (two acts). It is the following summer in "Little Hell." Kurt's son is in love with the Captain's favorite daughter, who torments him by flirting with others. Alice's wit is sharpened by her hatred of the recuperated and now-prosperous Captain. She strives to frustrate his plans of promoting himself by marrying his daughter off to the old colonel, and she observes his systematic ruin of Kurt: the loss of his house to the Captain, his displacement (by the Captain) as a parliamentary candidate, and the ignominious transfer of his son to a remote assignment. The Captain boasts of having won "through perseverance, attention to duty, energy, and—integrity." Kurt submits meekly: "This man-eater has left my soul untouched: that he could not devour." But encouraged by Alice, the daughter at last perceives her own great love for Kurt's son, and foils the Captain's plans. When he hears that she has insulted the colonel, the Captain has his last stroke. Alice sneers over the body of her dying husband, who is speechless and can but spit at her. Jubilantly she boxes his ears and pulls his beard: "Out with the carcass! Out with it and throw everything open! The place must be aired." Later, word comes that his last words were, "Forgive them, for they know not what they do." Alice can finally speak well of him. She feels her life dissolving in the peace that follows the end of their dance of death, and now remembers how once she had loved the Captain—"*And* hated him. May he rest in peace!"

DANE, Clemence (1888?–1965), English actress, novelist, and dramatist, née Winifred Ashton, wrote over thirty plays. She was born in Blackheath (England), taught French in Switzerland when she was sixteen, returned to England to study painting, resumed teaching, and in 1913 became an actress under the stage name Diana Cortis. Clemence Dane established her reputation as a writer with her third novel, *Legend* (1919). With her first and most successful play, *Bill of Divorcement*

(1921), the story of the intertwined love lives of a devoted mother and her daughter for which she also wrote the film scenario, Clemence Dane became a popular dramatist. *Bill of Divorcement* was republished in the *Collected Plays* (1961), with her short preface and four other dramas: *Scandal at Coventry* (1958), *Granite* (1926), *Wild Decembers* (1932, a play featuring the Brontë sisters), and *Till Time Shall End* (1958, a play about Queen Elizabeth I). Among her other plays are *Will Shakespeare* (1921), "an invention in four acts" in which the bard discusses his life and work with Christopher Marlowe and others; *Come of Age* (1934), an imaginative and controversial play (with music by Richard S. Addinsell) about the eighteenth-century poet Thomas Chatterton; and an adaptation of *The Happy Hypocrite* (1936) by MAX BEERBOHM. Two of her novels deal with the theatre: *Broome Stages* (1931), which is also an account of the Plantagenets, and *The Flower Girls* (1954). Clemence Dane also wrote television, radio, and film scripts, including those for *Anna Karenina* (1935) and *Vacation from Marriage* (1946), for which she won an Academy Award. Shortly before her death she published *London Has a Garden* (1964), reminiscences about herself and about Covent Garden; this book includes a bibliography.

DANGEROUS CORNER, a play in three acts by J. B. PRIESTLEY, published and produced in 1932. Setting: the living room of an English country home, early 1930's.

This is a deftly constructed drama of suspense, murder, and passion. Its continuous action produces surprise after surprise.

After dinner, a number of publishers, their wives, a novelist, and the firm's secretary discuss the proverb "Let sleeping dogs lie." They disagree about its wisdom as regards truth. "Telling the truth's about as healthy as skidding round a corner at sixty," says a publisher, and the wife of another adds, "and life's got a lot of dangerous corners." Nonetheless, they start probing each other, and learn much that is unpleasant. One partner has embezzled company funds, another had not committed suicide but was killed by one of the women, and had had an affair with another of them. All are adulterous, disillusioned, and unhappy bounders. Their conversation and movements suddenly begin to duplicate the early ones. In identical words, they again discuss the proverb. Then, however, the conversation stops short of the probing. Instead, they turn on some music, and the couples dance and chat amiably.

D'ANNUNZIO, Gabriele (1863–1938), Italian writer, patriot, and adventurer, was one of the most flamboyant and controversial figures of his age. His heroics as well as his love affairs, looks, dress, and habits made him a living legend—like OSCAR WILDE. D'Annunzio's poetic drama, much of it written for the actress Eleonora Duse, has been likened to that of EMILE VERHAEREN and EDMUND ROSTAND. It is as simple as it is bombastic and theatrical, full of violence and torrential passions and elaborate settings carefully described by its archaeologically oriented author. Even the most successful of D'Annunzio's plays—LA GIOCONDA (1899), FRANCESCA DA RIMINI (1901), and *La figlia di Jorio* (THE DAUGHTER OF JORIO, 1904), which is generally considered his best—are rarely performed today, though they and a dozen others once enthralled worldwide audiences.

D'Annunzio was born in Pescara, a small central Italian town on the Adriatic coast. Confusion about his antecedents was encouraged by D'Annunzio's romantic accounts, but apparently he was the son of the lustful and subsequently bankrupt former mayor, who had changed his name from Rapagnetta to that of his wife's brother-in-law, D'Annunzio—the symbolic name which Gabriele made famous.

A handsome youth who early captivated women, D'Annunzio distinguished himself as an academy student and at the University of Rome. While yet a penniless poet in 1883, he eloped with and then married an aristocrat who bore him three sons; the second of them, Gabriellino (1890–1945), later became a minor dramatist in his own right. After achieving some reputation for his poetry and fiction, D'Annunzio turned to the theatre in 1897, at the time of the most famous of his many liaisons, with Duse. She inspired his novel *Il fuoco* (*The Flame of Life,* 1900) as well as most of his dramas. Shortly after the turn of the century he escaped his creditors by emigrating to France. There he continued his career as a poet-dramatist, writing in French—and thus establishing his niche in French letters—until World War I, when he returned to Italy. An arrant nationalist and glorifier of warfare, he helped enlist Italy on the Allied side and became a military aviator. He defied the Versailles Treaty as well as his own government in 1919 by leading an expedition (ultimately unsuccessful) to restore Fiume to Italy. His adventures inspired Mussolini's march on Rome and the victory of the Fascists, who adopted for their uniform the black shirts worn by D'Annunzio's Fiume legionnaires. In 1924 a grateful government bestowed upon him the title Prince of Montenevoso, but he spent the final years of his life in relative solitude.

Always searching for novel ways to portray sensual experiences—the "new shudder"—D'Annunzio was a worshiper of unbridled instincts no less than of Friedrich Nietzsche's superman theories. In his writings as in his life D'Annunzio identified himself with the superman-artist-genius, the hero of plays like *La Gioconda* and *La gloria* (*Glory,* 1899), whose superman is a politician enamored of an old prostitute who once was his rival's mistress. D'Annunzio's first important play, *La città morta* (*The Dead City,* 1898), already featured such a superman, as well as D'Annunzio's preoccupation with lust, in a plot of incest and adultery, and a fusion of present and past heroism: an archaeologist working in the Atride tombs at Mycenae falls in love with his sister and jealously murders her when he discovers that she is loved also by his friend, whose wife is blind. History and legend reappear in *Francesca da Rimini,* as does an emphasis on primitive passions and superstitions, particularly pronounced in the two plays that followed, *The Daughter of Jorio* and *La fiaccola sotto il moggio* (*The Light Under the Bushel,* 1905). Both were praised for their lyric beauty; the latter, also set in the Abruzzi, deals with the rivalry of two brothers over a maid and with her rise in a dynasty that parallels that of Aeschylus's *Oresteia.* Notable among D'Annunzio's remaining plays are *La nave* (1908), a verse tragedy that portrays the founding of Venice and its collective degeneracy; and *Fedra* (1909), the lust of whose protagonist (Phaedra) epitomizes and symbolizes the tragedy of all Greece. The most important of his three French plays is *Le Martyre de Saint Sébastien* (1911), a mystery that typically stresses eroticism and is still performed because of Claude Debussy's score. D'Annunzio's last work for the theatre includes a sequel to *Francesca da Rimini* titled *Parisina* (1913), for which Pietro Mascagni composed the music.

Despite the carnality, horror, and brutality of these works, D'Annunzio's plays are predominantly static. There is virtually no characterization or development: the focus is on the "shudder," articulated in poetry that testifies to D'Annunzio's considerable rhetorical skills. His plays' popularity was enhanced by Duse's promotion of and acting in them—as well as by the reputation of the star and the author. Artistically the plays are inferior to D'Annunzio's poetry, fiction, and essays.

D'Annunzio's complete writings were collected in forty-nine volumes (1927–36), and there are numerous translations as well as studies of his life and art. In English, these include Frances Winwar's dual biography of D'Annunzio and Duse, *Wingless Victory* (1956), and Anthony Rhodes's *D'Annunzio: The Poet as Superman* (1960); both have bibliographies.

DAPHNE LAUREOLA, a play in four acts by JAMES BRIDIE, published and produced in 1949. Setting: London, 1940's.

In this play Bridie achieved his most accomplished full-length portrayal of a woman in the characterization of Lady Pitts (Katherine), a complex, brilliant, middle-aged wife frustrated at being the collector's item (the "Daphne Laureola") of a wise old millionaire who rescued her from a difficult life.

Lady Pitt becomes an alcoholic to relieve her inhibitions: "My loneliness finds expression only in drunkenness or in delirium. At other times I say: Keep off; keep far away from me." After her husband's death she marries the chauffeur, and thus horrifies a Polish admirer whom the old millionaire had restrained earlier from pressing his suit. Disillusioned by life and love, Lady Pitt defies him. "The pigs are at least honest with themselves and with us," she says in explanation of her marriage and in memory of her former life among prostitutes; "that's why I've settled down in a nice clean pigsty."

DARK AT THE TOP OF THE STAIRS, THE, a play in three acts by WILLIAM INGE, produced in 1957 and published in 1958. Setting: a small Oklahoma town, early 1920's.

A reworking of his first play, *Farther Off From Heaven* (produced in 1947), this is an at times comic, often wistful, and heavily SYMBOLIC portrayal of a cliché-spouting lower middle-class family who suffer from various psychological difficulties. The prim mother is preoccupied with her Oedipal son, who is afraid to go upstairs where it is dark because "you can't see what's in front of you. And it might be something awful." The others are equally fearful of "climbing life's staircase." The father, beneath his bravado, resents being bossed by his wife. Her sister and brother-in-law have marital problems of their own. Their shy daughter, a high-school girl, is jarred out of her self-centered sensitivity when at a critical moment she deserts her escort, a Jewish cadet who commits suicide after being insulted at a country-club dance. The parents eventually reach understanding and adjustment. Their son looks accusingly at his mother as she goes upstairs "like a shy maiden" to her waiting husband, whose "naked feet [are] standing in the warm light at the top" of the staircase.

DARK IS LIGHT ENOUGH, THE, a blank-verse "winter comedy" in three acts by CHRISTOPHER FRY, published and produced in 1954. Setting: an Austrian country house near the Hungarian border, winter 1848–49.

This is a solemn though epigrammatic play with religious overtones. Its elderly protagonist, the Countess Rosmarin Ostenburg, is an almost divine yet human figure of selfless love and generosity. Generally adored, she is hospitable to Austrian soldiers as well as Hungarian revolutionaries. Under her pervasive spell, embittered and embattled individuals are appeased and become friends. "How apparently undemandingly / She moves among us; and yet / Lives make and remake themselves in her neighbourhood / As nowhere else," remarks a guest. Other characters include her children, an ineffectual son and a contrary daughter. The latter is drawn again to her cowardly former husband, Richard Gettner. He is a wastrel Hungarian officer, a deserter not only from the army but from all humanity. The only one who seems unaffected by the countess's beneficient influence, he is transformed in the last scene. As Austrian soldiers hammer at the door and he prepares to hide, Gettner sees that Countess Rosmarin has just died. Somehow her courage now enters him. "This isn't how I meant that you should love me!" he remarks—and then, standing beside her corpse, he awaits the enemy.

DARK LADY OF THE SONNETS, THE, "An Interlude" by BERNARD SHAW, produced in 1910 and published in 1914. Setting: Whitehall Palace, London; 1590's.

Written as a money raiser for the projected

National Theatre, this playlet is prefaced by an essay on Shakespeare which, Shaw claimed, shows "that trivial as this little play of mine is, its sketch of Shakespear is more complete than its levity suggests." The preface also gives Shaw's reasons for making Mary Fitton, one of Elizabeth's maids of honor, the Dark Lady of Shakespeare's sonnets.

Instead of Mary Fitton, the Dark Lady for whom Shakespear is waiting, a muffled lady (Queen Elizabeth I) appears on the palace terrace. His amatory advances to her are interrupted by the furiously jealous Mary, who becomes terrified when the lady reveals herself as Queen Elizabeth. Shakespear impudently charms the angry Queen into forgiveness, and asks her to endow a national theatre, a proposal she declines as impractical for England until it has first been tried by other countries.

DARKNESS (*Die Finsternisse*), a "requiem" in five scenes by GERHART HAUPTMANN, published in 1947. Setting: a small Silesian town, 1934.

In 1937 Hauptmann wrote this short but moving tribute to his friend Max Pinkus, a Jewish industrialist. Though he had to hide the manuscript, Hauptmann and his wife were the only Gentiles in Nazi Germany who dared attend the distinguished philanthropist's funeral in 1934. The play dramatizes their visit in terms of a religious fantasy.

A mourning family is portrayed as the playwright and his wife arrive. The industrialist's death mask is cast, there is a séancelike dinner, and the dead man appears supernaturally in the company of Ahasuerus, Elijah, and Saint John. The tragedy of Germany's anti-Semitic persecutions is expressed in the intensity of this religious vision. Ghostliness is balanced by reason through Hauptmann's grieving prototype, who concludes that the Nazi horror victimizes not only his Jewish friends: "It hits us all."

DARLING OF THE GODS, THE, a play in five acts by DAVID BELASCO and JOHN LUTHER LONG, produced in 1902 and published in 1928. Setting: Japan during the Samurai period.

The plot of this popular exotic romance, lavishly produced in America and Europe, was inspired by the heroism of a Japanese leader in the Satsuma rebellion of 1868.

Princess Yo-San, "the darling of the gods," does not want to marry her intended betrothed. She therefore sets him the difficult task of capturing a notorious outlaw, Prince Kara, not knowing he is the stranger she fell in love with when he saved her life. As he then promised, he now visits her. But he is wounded by the men of Zakkuri, the fiendish war minister. Yo-San hides Kara, and blandly denies knowing his whereabouts: "It is better to lie a little than to be unhappy much." Eventually Zakkuri discovers and captures Kara. Eager to learn the hiding place of his followers, Zakkuri forces Yo-San to watch through a trapdoor as Kara is tortured until she reveals the secret. "Whisper that you forgive," Yo-San begs Kara, when he honorably commits suicide among his fallen Samurai; "that you will wait for me at the edge of the First White Heaven beyond the Meido where I shall come to meet you pure and white . . . in one long thousand years." The dying Kara asks the gods to "be gentle with her . . . remembering it was for love." Amidst ghostly intermezzo music, the soul of the purged Yo-San floats by, calling to Kara, "It is a thousand years. . . . Have you forgot? . . . Which is the way to the First White Heaven?" There their forms soon meet joyfully and ascend to the next heaven.

DAUGHTER OF JORIO, THE (*La figlia di Jorio*), a verse drama in three acts by GABRIELE D'ANNUNZIO, published and produced in 1904. Setting: the Abruzzi in Italy, "many years ago."

This play, generally considered D'Annunzio's best, was inspired by a friend's painting of a village scene they had both witnessed years before: a group of drunken peasants chasing a disheveled woman. Symbolic as well as psychological and moralistic, the play, with its florid, precious language, depicts primitive superstitions and passions in an archaic pastoral setting in which violence and self-sacrifice mingle.

Act I. The mother and sisters of Aligi, a shepherd artist about to be married, are performing the mystic wedding rituals and conjurations. As villagers place offerings before the couple, a distraught woman rushes in, imploring protection from a group of drunken reapers "brutal with lust and with cursing" who "would seize me—me—/ The creature of Christ." She is Mila di Codra, the daughter of the sorcerer Jorio. As she crouches fearfully on the sacred hearth, all want to cast her out, fearing she may bring "bad fortune" and evil magic upon them. Only one of Aligi's sisters helps her, barring the door before the raging peasants who clamor for "the harlot." "No! It is not true!" Mila protests. "Do not believe what such dogs say!" Aligi raises his arm to strike Mila when suddenly he sees an angel hovering above her. Repentant, he burns his hand, lays a crucifix on the threshold, and orders the reapers to leave: "You may not sin against this gentle / Lamb of Christ who here finds refuge." Awed, they depart. Outside, Aligi's father guiltily falls on his knees.

Act II. In a mountain cave where a votive lamp burns before the Virgin's image, Mila and Aligi live in holy love. Mila now is purified, for "born anew then was I when love was born in me." Caring only for Aligi's safety, she wants him to return home though he wants to stay with his beloved Mila, "who weeps unheard." He seeks advice of other holy fugitives who live in the cave, and then starts to leave. In her agony of prayerful self-sacrifice, Mila forgets to refuel the votive lamp. It goes out and in the darkness, as it storms outside, Aligi's father appears, lustful and determined to take Mila. Aligi returns and pleads with him, but is bound and taken away. Again the father seizes Mila, who cries for help. Aligi rushes in and in a blind fury murders his father.

Act III. Back home, the weeping women prepare

for the ritual of the parricide's torture. In a stately procession Aligi is brought in and, amidst lamentations before his father's corpse, drinks the proffered potion that will bring him oblivion. Suddenly Mila appears, proclaiming Aligi "innocent. But he knows it not," for she bewitched him: "I have upset his reason, / I have confused his memory. / I am the Sorcerer's daughter. . . ." She craves the punishment the crowds are all too eager to administer: "Let the sorceress be led to the stake." The drugged and bewildered Aligi himself urges them on and curses her. "Aligi, Aligi, not you! / Oh, you cannot, you must not," she cries out. Only his sister pities Mila: "My sister in Jesus! / I kiss your feet that bear you away! Heaven is for thee!" Purified by her sacrifice which atones for her erstwhile life of shame, Mila exults as she embraces the fire: *"La fiamma è bella!"* ("The flame is beautiful!")

DAUGHTER OF THE CATHEDRAL, THE (*Die Tochter der Kathedrale*), a "dramatic poem" in five acts by GERHART HAUPTMANN, published and produced in 1939. Setting: the medieval dukedom of Andorra and vicinity.

Based on a French legend, this verse-and-prose play dramatizes the enmity and reconciliation of the ducal Andorra and Foix families and their children's courtships. The feud between the families had begun when Andorra's duchess gave birth to twin boys and Foix's duchess enviously remarked that the twin birth was a sign of their mother's marital infidelity. Subsequently the Foix duchess herself was delivered of twins (girls); fearful of the scandal that would result because of her own words, she has abandoned one of the girls at the Cathedral of Andorra. That child has become "the daughter of the Cathedral," now a beautiful maiden. The Andorra twins fall in love with the Foix twins, and the abandoned girl's origin is eventually revealed. With the dying Foix duchess's blessing, the two families are united by their children's double betrothal.

DAVIS, Owen (1874–1956), American dramatist, wrote almost three hundred plays, most of them very profitable but ephemeral melodramas. He also adapted such novels as F. Scott Fitzgerald's *The Great Gatsby* (1926), Pearl Buck's *The Good Earth* (1932), Edith Wharton's *Ethan Frome* (1936; written with his son, and the most successful of Davis's many adaptations), and Frances and Richard Lockridge's *Mr. and Mrs. North* (1941) stories. He collaborated with S. N. BEHRMAN and others, but his most distinguished work consists of two NATURALISTIC portrayals of American life, THE DETOUR (1921) and ICEBOUND (1923); the latter won the Pulitzer Prize. Critics and theatre historians deplored Davis's inability to follow these with equally impressive serious works, though his adaptations (including that of Čapek's FROM THE LIFE OF INSECTS as *The World We Live In*, 1922) have considerable merit.

Davis was born in Portland, Maine, grew up in Kentucky, attended the University of Tennessee, and graduated from Harvard University in 1893. A learned and intelligent man, he failed with his first play, a verse tragedy. Thereupon he studied the structure of melodramas, evolved his own formulas for westerns, light comedies, and sex plays, and wrote the stage potboilers that made him famous and wealthy—notably the long-running melodrama *Nellie, The Beautiful Cloak Model* (1906) and the farce *The Nervous Wreck* (1923), an adaptation of E. J. Rath's novel. His other writings include two autobiographies, *I'd Like to Do It Again* (1931) and *My First Fifty Years in the Theatre* (1950).

DAYS OF THE COMMUNE, THE (*Die Tage der Commune*), a play in fourteen scenes by BERTOLT BRECHT (music by Hanns Eisler), produced in 1956 and published in 1957. Setting: Paris and Versailles, January–April 1871.

This was the last play completed by Brecht, though it was not produced in his lifetime; because he did not prepare manuscripts for publication before incorporating changes made during production, Brecht left this play unpublished. In a note, he stated that it was written in 1948–49 after NORDAHL GRIEG's *Nederlaget:* "Some of its features and characters have been used, though on the whole *The Days of the Commune* is an answer to it." Brecht's play depicts the workers' defeat by a cautiously liberal bourgeoisie and the reactionary ruling aristocracy. It views the Commune as an abortive dry-run of the coming world revolution. Though didactically tendentious, the play has moving and picturesque NATURALISTIC scenes.

The Paris Commune is seen principally from the vantage point of a group of the Montmartre poor, including a soldier, a worker, a seamstress, a teacher, etc. The war has "exhausted all possibilities for business," a fat bourgeois remarks. But it has intensified the misery of these simple workers, who finally rise above their squabbles. They help take over the City Council, and in their revolutionary fervor even vulgar preoccupation with sex and possessions gives way to ardent concern for the community. "*We,*" says the schoolteacher, "is not *you* and *me;* I said *us. We* is much more than *you and I!*" Nonetheless, the revolutionary forces are split and weakened by their leaders' respect for law and reluctance to use violent means to impose discipline and to vanquish their opponents. They are therefore defeated by the enemies of the Commune, including the Prussian leader, Otto von Bismarck. From the walls of Versailles the bourgeoisie and the aristocrats observe and applaud the death of the men on the barricades of the burning city of Paris. They congratulate their president, Louis Adolphe Thiers, on the fall of the Commune: "You have restored Paris to its rightful master, France." Thiers bows and smiles at them: "France, that is—yourselves, Mesdames et Messieurs."

DAYS OF THE TURBINS, THE (*Dni Turbinykh*), a play in four acts by MIKHAIL AFANASYEVICH BULGAKOV, published (?) and produced in 1926. Setting: Kiev, the winter of 1918–19.

This has been called the best Soviet portrayal of the Civil War and the Communist Revolution (although the Reds do not appear on stage), one of the few depictions of the Whites as more than stage villains. Bulgakov's dramatization of his *Belaya gvardiya* (*The White Guard,* 1925), the play created a furor that abetted its popularity. Because the treatment of a White family was regarded as being too sympathetic, both the play and its author were attacked as "counter-revolutionary," and Bulgakov was harassed by suspicion for the remainder of his life. In 1926 Konstantin Stanislavsky asked Stalin to lift the censor's ban (later the play was again temporarily banned and again cleared by Stalin); doing so, the dictator explained, "The play shows an intelligent and powerful enemy. That is good. We must show the enemy as he is."* Between 1926 and 1941, despite various bans, the play was presented 987 times by the Moscow Art Theatre. It became part of the K. S. Stanislavsky Theatre repertoire in 1954, and was republished in 1955.

Kiev is in control of the Germans, who dominate the Ukrainian puppet regime of Hetman (i.e., Commander-in-Chief) Skoropadsky. Colonel Aleksei Vasilevich Turbin and his younger brother Nikolai are among the White Guard tsarist officers in Kiev who help the Hetman fight off Petlura's ultra-nationalistic Cossacks. The Germans abandon the Ukraine; Hetman Skoropadsky, too weak to hold the city, smuggles himself out to safety with them, and many of the White Guard leaders also turn tail. Among them is the cowardly husband of the Turbins' sister. Admired by many and toasted at a party of her family and friends, she eventually marries a former officer who has become an opera singer. The nationalist forces of Petlura are supported by the peasants, and the position of the Whites becomes hopeless. Colonel Turbin courageously fights to cover the retreat of the Whites, realizing, as he falls, that the Whites are finished: "The people aren't with us. They're against us. That means it's done!" His brother Nikolai has been crippled in the fighting and later, as the Reds approach to the strains of the "International," he observes, "This evening is a great prologue to a new historical drama." A White Russian officer replies, "For some, the prologue; for others, the epilogue."

DAYS ON A CLOUD (*Dage på en sky*), a play in three acts by KJELD ABELL, published and produced in 1947. Setting: a large cloud inhabited by Greek deities.

This imaginative play, like Abell's ANNA SOPHIE HEDVIG, deals with the crime of social passivity. Its sole male character, an Icarus and professional descendant of Aesculapius, is an atomic-age scientist who has compromised his idealism for safe, law-abiding cliché spouting. He plans to commit suicide while on a flying mission. His past is gradually revealed in the play, which features the deities and takes place just before he decides after all to pull the parachute cord, the moment during which he relives his whole life.

The goddesses fight for the scientist's soul when he is magically wafted to their cloud. Anadyomene immediately is infatuated with him. Representing youthful love and idealism, she is the daughter of Aphrodite, who stands for mature love; both are contrasted with Kokyta, a bawdy old servant who embodies the spirit of human compromise and denial. The scientist has decided to commit suicide after becoming aware that he has betrayed his ideal, which once had inspired a particular man to join the Resistance—and die. Now he recalls that man's sister's reply to the detached intellectual's "We can't change the world—at least not by force": "Can one ever get anywhere near achieving justice if one is so fearful of doing an injustice that one dare not move at all—dare not set sail for fear of underwater rocks? Is it possible to live on Mount Olympus?" The scientist also has a vision of his disappointed wife. "You made no conditions when the order came," she tells her husband, who had helped to make the atom bomb; "You gave away the weapon, the knowledge, everything—and showed us that freedom, freedom without restraint, can lead straight to the suicide of man." Men's battle between ideal and expediency is refought by the Greek gods. It is the idealistic young Anadyomene who, by sacrificing herself, inspires the scientist to choose life—and resume his fight. Because he let her live "in the thoughts and the divine aspirations of men"—which is the only existence of the gods—"the parachute will open" now, she tells him. And as he is about to return to that instant at which the play began, he realizes his spirit is saved: "Even should I founder again—it doesn't matter. I know now that I am a drop in the ocean on which mankind shall one day sail free." Kokyta sneers that all will be as before, that the "old Adam" will continue to run the world. But Hera determines to help the "new Adam": "Your image of the ancient man—if no one else can stamp it out—then I shall!"

DAYS WITHOUT END, a play in four acts by EUGENE O'NEILL, published and produced in 1934. Setting: New York, Spring 1932.

This in part EXPRESSIONISTIC play is the last one in which O'Neill was to use masks. He agonized over the ending of this "modern miracle play," as he called it, and later was bitter for having allowed himself to be dissuaded by Jesuit priests from letting the protagonist commit suicide. According to his wife Carlotta, "He felt he had ruined the play and that he was a traitor to himself as a writer. He always said the last act was a phony and he never forgave himself for it" (Barbara and Arthur Gelb's *O'Neill*). The play, reflecting O'Neill's apparently sole attempt to return to Catholicism, is generally considered one of his least effective ones.

* For a fuller account, see Nikolai A. Gorchakov's *The Theater in Soviet Russia* (1957) and Bulgakov's autobiographical novel *Teatralny roman,* translated as *Black Snow* (1968).

John Loving is divided into two beings: the novel-writing businessman John and his Mephistophelean *doppelgänger* Loving, visible only to the audience and to John, whose scornful death mask he wears. John tells his uncle, Father Matthew Baird, the plot of his autobiographical novel. John's life is revealed in this narrative and also in his arguments with Loving. He had turned against his parents' Catholic God when they died, but he has kept searching for a faith, without success, in Eastern religions and in social and scientific dogmas. Though he accepts Loving's belief that "we are all the slaves of meaningless chance—electricity or something, which whirls us—on to Hercules!" and that ours is a world without ends that are worthwhile, John seeks to find a meaning in life, a "new savior" to teach us "to create new goals for ourselves, ends for our days!" He has found a god in his love for Elsa, his wife, but impelled by the complex drives personified in Loving, he has committed adultery to free himself from this new faith. As John narrates the remainder of the novel's plot and asks his wife's opinion on the ending, she realizes what he has done. He has been her god, and his adultery so horrifies her that she seeks death as Loving has hoped she would. Broken because she will not forgive him, John struggles to resolve his problems: Loving urges suicide, but John finally rushes out and finds himself in his parents' church. At that moment Elsa is able to forgive him, and simultaneously regains her will to live. John repents before the Cross, the light of dawn animates the face of the life-sized Christ, and Loving crumples up, a corpse. When Father Baird comes to tell him of Elsa's recovery, John Loving (now an integrated, whole being) replies in exaltation, "I know! Love lives forever! Death is dead! . . . Life laughs with God's love again! Life laughs with love!"

DE FILIPPO, Eduardo (1900–), Italian playwright, actor, and director, began writing for the theatre in 1926 but did not achieve prominence until after World War II. Like his most popular work, FILUMENA MARTURANO (1946), most of de Filippo's plays are grounded in the tradition of the *commedia dell'arte,* melodrama, and sex farces, and they frequently posit the reality-and-illusion themes characteristic of the theatre of the GROTESQUE. Despite such derivations and their descent also from the work of LUIGI PIRANDELLO, they have considerable originality and sometimes affectingly painful humor. Invariably they are set in Naples and flavored with de Filippo's Neapolitan heritage.

He was the illegitimate son of the actor Eduardo Scarpetta and the brother of the actor-playwrights Titina (1898–1963) and Peppino de Filippo (1903–). Performers from their early youth, the three de Filippos toured throughout the 1920's, founded a company of their own, and in 1931 opened their popular Teatro San Ferdinando in Naples. For this theatre they wrote *commedia dell'arte* types of sketches, scenarios, and the longer works with which Eduardo became famous. It was for this company that he produced his three most successful plays: *Filomena Marturano; Napoli milionaria* (1945), the depiction of the Neapolitan life that persists regardless of changing political regimes; and *Questi fantasmi* (1946), a comedy about a deceived husband who believes his house to be haunted. Notable among de Filippo's many plays are another and more Pirandellian portrayal of a deceived husband, *La grande magia* (1949); *Le voci di dentro* (1948); *La paura numero uno* (1950); *Bene mio, coro mio* (1955); *La fortune va in cerca di tasche* (1958); *Sindaco del rione Sanità* (1960), the tragedy of a gangster who becomes exalted in death; and *Il figlio die Pulcinella* (1962). This last play was meant to demonstrate that Pulcinella's persona is unchanged since his inception in the sixteenth century, "for our weaknesses remain exactly the same: we still overrate our unimportant selves and underrate our neighbor," de Filippo wrote of it: "Pulcinella must not die, for he embodies human conscience."

De Filippo's immense popularity as a *capocomico* (actor-playwright-director-manager) did not spread to the English-speaking world, where he became known only for *Marriage, Italian Style* (1964), his film script of *Filumena Marturano*. This play is republished with an essay on de Filippo and a bibliography in Robert W. Corrigan's collection of *Masterpieces of the Modern Italian Theatre* (1967). An earlier essay, "Son of Pulcinella," appears in Eric Bentley's *In Search of Theater* (1953).

DEAD END, a play in three acts by SIDNEY KINGSLEY, produced in 1935 and published in 1936. Setting: a dead-end slum street in the rear of an East River luxury apartment house; New York, 1930's.

In 1937 this powerful NATURALIST drama was made into an equally popular film that featured the six "Dead End Kids" of the original production. Evidencing keen observation, Kingsley in his comic dialogue in the frequent SLICE OF LIFE scenes duplicates the speech of slum children. The social themes transcend the Depression era and the occasionally melodramatic action. For his epigraph, Kingsley quotes Thomas Paine: "The contrast of affluence and wretchedness is like dead and living bodies chained together."

Act I. A group of boys dive into, and swim and cavort in the sewerage of the East River. They joke, argue, grapple for pennies, make horse-manure cigarettes, and try to emulate their tubercular friend's feat of spitting blood. Wealthy people from the adjacent luxury building periodically pass by. The gang sneer when a wealthy boy answers his French governess with a "Oui, oui" (thereafter they call him "Wee-wee"), and brutally initiate a new neighborhood youngster. But they respond to the maternal affection of the older sister of Tommy McGrath, the gang's leader, though they resist her and swear at each other ("Ah, yuh mudduh's chooch!" "Ah, yuh fadduh's doop!"). Gimpty Pete, an unemployed

Dead End. The "Dead End Kids," with the contiguous luxury and slum buildings in the background. New York, 1935. (*White Collection, Theatre Collection, New York Public Library*)

young architect crippled by rickets, recognizes an expensively dressed newcomer as a boy who grew up with him on the dead-end street. Now he is a notorious gangster, returning to see his mother and his first sweetheart. Gimpty thinks of him as he stresses the importance of environment ("It can give you a chance to grow, or it can twist you") and envisions Evolution's asking men, to whom it gave feeling, reason, dignity, and a sense of beauty and wonder, "Now let's see what you're going to do with them." An attractive girl from the luxury apartment house is fond of him, but is unwilling to give up her wealthy lover to share Gimpty's poverty. As Tommy's sister tries to get him home to be deloused, "Gimpty's goil fren" follows the architect to his slum apartment.

Act II. The boys play a game of poker, and accept a challenge from a rival gang. The gangster advises them to disregard rules and fight dirty: "When yuh fight, dee idee is tuh win. It don' cut no ice how." The boys lure "Wee-wee" into their midst, "cockalize" him, and take his watch. "Gimpty's goil fren" is shocked by the poverty she has seen when visiting him: she admits loving him, but is determined not to ruin their lives by getting married. The gangster's reunions prove disillusioning: his mother calls him a murderer, slaps his face, rejects his money, and warns him to "leave us alone"; his childhood sweetheart is now a hardened, visibly diseased prostitute. "Wee-wee's" father indignantly grabs Tommy and calls the police. Frantic, Tommy pulls out a knife, jabs the man's wrist, and runs off. In the meantime, Gimpty, disgusted with the gangster, who has brutally kicked his crippled foot, and thinking of the reward money that would make it possible for him to marry, denounces him to the police. G-men close in on the gangster and, after he shoots the arresting officer, riddle him with bullets. During the search for the gang's leader, one of the boys, to save his own skin, betrays Tommy.

Act III. Tommy is hiding, eager to find and punish the boy who "snitched" on him. "Gimpty's goil fren" sadly decides to leave with her wealthy lover: Gimpty's reward money would last only a short while, and then poverty would stalk them. Tommy is stopped from carving up his betrayer's face with a knife, and then gives himself up—though his sister tries to get him to escape. She pleads with "Wee-wee's" father not to press charges. But he remains adamant, even after Gimpty's well-documented assurance that reform school will make Tommy a gangster. As the police take Tommy away, a friend refers his sister to "a guy at rifawm school" who "knows a lot of swell rackets fuh Tommy when ee gits out." Gimpty consoles the distraught girl by promising to get Tommy the best lawyer his money can buy. The gang tell reform-school anecdotes, curse the doorman, and sing funereally as a tramp steamer hoots on the East River.

DEAN, Basil (1888–), English writer, actor, film and theatre director, became noted primarily for his collaboration on THE CONSTANT NYMPH (1926). His other plays include a dramatization of P. C. Wren's 1924 novel *Beau Geste* (1929). He acted with the Manchester Repertory Company from its inception in 1907 to 1911, and in many London productions thereafter. Also a prominent director, Dean wrote other works, including the official history of E.N.S.A. (*The Theatre at War,* 1955) and *The Changing Theatre* (1965).

DEAR BRUTUS, a play in three acts by JAMES M. BARRIE, produced in 1917 and published in 1922. Setting: England on a midsummer evening.

The title and theme of this popular fantasy are from Shakespeare's *Julius Caesar:* "The fault, dear Brutus, is not in our stars, / But in ourselves, that we are underlings" (I, ii, 139–140). This depiction of a second chance at life differs from both Dunsany's IF and Frisch's BIOGRAPHY. There is something of Barrie himself in the puckish host and conjurer of the enchanted setting, Mr. Lob (Puck in *A Midsummer Night's Dream* is called a "lob of spirits"). The scene that has charmed audiences most is that of the artist and the daughter he has always yearned for, Margaret.

Act I. The wizened old Mr. Lob has invited some guests to his country house. They include a philandering husband with his wife and paramour, an artist whose life and career are ruined by drink, and an affectionate elderly couple. The butler is caught stealing, but blames his dishonesty on a "wrong turning" in his youth. He puzzles the guests by cautioning them against visiting an enchanted forest Lob may conjure. The philandering husband, surprised by his wife, complains about the unfairness of being "battered for ever just because I once took the wrong turning." The drunken artist does not at all resent his wife's contempt. He admits his failure as a man and as a painter: "Perhaps if we had had children—Pity!" His wife coldly assures him he would make no more of neglected opportunities if he had them again. Though the guests have been cautioned, Lob's invitation to the magic woods is irresistible when he tells them that they may there get "what nearly everybody here is longing for—a second chance."

Act II. In the woods they all have that chance. One of the unhappy ladies is no happier with a distinguished financier—the butler, who is no less a crook in his alternate career. The philanderer is now married to his paramour—and philandering with his wife. The painter, however, is "ablaze in happiness and health and a daughter." Margaret "is as lovely as you think she is, and she is aged the moment when you like your daughter best." Their happiness with each other, expressed in a long and poignant scene, is interrupted by an unhappy vagrant, the artist's wife. Strangely affected by the unknown woman, the artist feels sorry for one who probably has had a difficult time, for which no doubt "some man is to blame." To get food for her, he goes off to a house he spots in the distance. Margaret, who begins to disappear, begs her beloved "Daddikins" not to leave her: "I don't want to be a might-have-been."

Act III. Back in Lob's rooms, the ancient host is asleep on his chair, a peculiar look on his face. The guests gradually return, magically reawake, and recognize the futility of their original yearnings. As the philanderer remarks, life is not Kismet: "What really plays the dickens with us is something in ourselves. Something that makes us go on doing the same sort of fool things, however many chances we get." The loving elderly couple is reunited when the husband—as happy and cheerful by nature when a bachelor in the enchanted woods—proposes to the girl of his dreams he does not yet recognize as his wife: after thirty years of marriage, he "had a second chance, and [chose] her, again!" The seedy artist, grateful for his hour of joy with the daughter he always wanted, returns to his empty life with the wife who perhaps realizes now that, as another guest remarks, "there is nothing the matter with her except that she would always choose the wrong man." (In some of the productions, however, the reconciled couple depart arm in arm, the dream child walking behind them.) The morning's sunlight shines and old Lob magically disappears from his chair. "The garden has returned, and our queer little hero is busy at work among his flowers."

DEATH AND DEVIL (*Tod und Teufel*), "a death dance in three scenes" by FRANK WEDEKIND, published in 1905 and produced in 1906. Setting: a contemporary brothel.

Also translated as *Damnation* and *The Dance of Death* (*Totentanz*), this macabre play features Marquis Casti-Piani—the procurer of PANDORA'S BOX—and a spinster reformer from the International Society for the Suppression of the White Slave Traffic. Eventually he persuades her that prostitution is natural and her crusade is inverted sexuality. When they secretly observe a girl entertaining her client—this scene is in verse—the "sanctity of sensual pleasure" is revealed to the sex-starved missionary. But the lifelong advocate of fleshly joys is totally disillusioned by what he has just witnessed: "Even sensual pleasure is nothing but satanic slaughter . . . in the dreadful midnight martyrdom of human existence"—and shoots himself. The aroused spinster passionately kisses the dead man's lips, sobbing about the final irony "that a *virgin* should close your eyes in death!"

DEATH AND THE FOOL (*Der Tor und der Tod*), a one-act lyric drama by HUGO VON HOFMANNSTHAL, published in 1894 and produced in 1898. Setting: a luxurious study in the 1820's.

Written in 1892, this is one of Hofmannsthal's earliest and best-known plays. It is a short morality with little action but rich poetry that suggestively expresses his preoccupation with aesthetics. Here, Hofmannsthal exhorts the oneness of art and of being, the need to participate in life in order to experience its beauty.

Young Claudio is meditating about human existence as he watches the sunset. He deplores his ignorance of life: "True, I appeared to stand inside it, / But, at the most, I studied it, / Never was caught, but held aloof, / Never lost myself but, alien, eyed it." Cloistered with his artworks and books, and controlling his natural emotions, he has escaped ugliness and pain. But "faith was gone and bliss an empty word. / And suffering, too! All shredded, torn, devoured / With too much thinking, faded, wrung, and scoured!" His servant reports the appearance of strange beings in the garden. Soon music is heard, and an urbane gentleman with a violin enters. He is Death, the self-styled "great god of the soul." He castigates Claudio for frivolously substituting art and ideas for the beauties and sensibilities of life: "You fool! Pernicious fool, I'll teach you yet / To honor life—before you part with it." He evokes the figures of the dead who loved him: his mother, his sweetheart, and his friend. They reveal how, juggling with their love for him and "reducing sweet and enigmatic charm / To nothing with abominable art," Claudio has never experienced human feelings. Now Claudio realizes that he has lived "without conviction, strength or worth." It is only in death that he experiences life's ecstasy and mystically discovers the meaning of existence: "So from the dream of life I now may wake, / Cloyed with emotion, to death's wakefulness." As Claudio expires before him, Death speculates about the strange creatures who fathom the unfathomable, who "Knit and command the tangled mystery / And in the eternal dark yet find a way."

DEATH OF A SALESMAN, "Certain Private Conversations in Two Acts and a Requiem" by ARTHUR MILLER, published and produced in 1949. Setting: New York and Boston, the present and the past.

Miller's masterpiece and one of the most important American plays, *Death of a Salesman* won many honors (including the Pulitzer Prize) and had a long Broadway run. Its enormous emotional impact has persisted for decades: the play has been revived again and again, filmed, televised, and studied as a profoundly SYMBOLIC criticism of the worship of material success. Considerable disputation has centered on the play's qualification as genuine tragedy, as opposed to social drama. The sixty-three-year-old protagonist Willy Loman ("low man"), a rounded and psychologically motivated individual as well as a familiar American Babbitt and even a universal type, embodies the stupidity, immorality, self-delusion, and failure of middle-class values Miller portrays as being sterile and vicious. At the same time Willy's love of his delinquent sons, however harmful and wrongly expressed, has made him (in John Gassner's apt phrase) "a King Lear in mufti." The transparent skeletal settings may be altered instantaneously; they modify NATURALISM into an EXPRESSIONISTIC and dream-like dramatization of Willy's free association (the play was originally to be titled *The Inside of His Head*), shifting between and confusing the present, the past, and the hallucinatory. All these converge on Willy's tortured consciousness during the last two days of his life. Gerald Weales's edition of the play's *Text and Criticism* (1967) contains many reviews and essays, and a comprehensive bibliography.

Act I. It is night, and flute playing is heard. Willy enters his Brooklyn apartment, weighted down by two large sample cases. "I'm tired to the death," he tells his devoted and worried wife. "I just couldn't make it, Linda." He complains irritably about the car, which he soon confuses with one he had owned years ago. Though he claims to be "vital in New England," he agrees to request a transfer from road travel to the New York office. Willy is also agitated about his son Biff, who has just returned home after tramping around the country. "Not finding yourself at the age of thirty-four is a disgrace!" he tells Linda. "Biff is a lazy bum!" Soon contradicting himself he continues, "In the greatest country in the world a young man with such—personal attractiveness, gets lost. And such a hard worker. There's one thing about Biff—he's not lazy." As Willy and Linda reminisce about the beautiful elms that grew outside before "they boxed us in here," Biff and his brother Happy sit up on the beds in their room. Happy is concerned about his father's driving and about his brother's instability. "All I've done is to waste my life," Biff replies; he deplores the jobs he took when all he really wanted was "to be outdoors," and he admits being "mixed up very bad." Happy is pleased to have his "own apartment, a car, and plenty of women. And still, goddammit, I'm lonely." For a moment he welcomes Biff's suggestion to give up the commercial rat race. But soon Happy reverts to his determination to rise to the top and "show some of those pompous, self-important executives over there that Hap Loman can make the grade." He persuades Biff to ask his former boss for a loan—though Biff wonders whether they know that he had stolen some of the firm's basketballs. The scene shifts to the past. Willy praises the eager boys for their car polishing, and laughs about Biff's theft of a football. The coach will praise his "initiative," Willy remarks, "because he likes you"—which does not apply to their neighbor Charley's son, a studious boy who is "liked, but he's not—well liked." Willy exhorts his boys, "Be liked and you will never want." He brags about his business success on the road, and listens proudly to Happy's account of the school's adulation of Biff, their football hero. Willy's swaggering about his earnings ends with Linda's computations of payments due on the

Death of a Salesman, Act I. Jo Mielziner's design for the original production. New York, 1949. (*Peter A. Juley & Son*)

refrigerator and other merchandise that is already wearing out. She comforts and encourages Willy, who confesses self-doubts. "You're the handsomest man in the world," she tells him; "few men are idolized by their children the way you are." But when he starts to embrace her, a woman's laughter intrudes as Willy remembers (and starts re-enacting) an escapade in a hotel room. When that woman thanks him for the stockings he has given her, Willy's consciousness is recalled to Linda, who is mending her stockings. Angrily he yells, "I won't have you mending stockings in this house!" His neighbor Charley, realizing Willy's desperation, offers him a job. But Willy acts insulted: "I got a good job." Increasingly upset, Willy finds it difficult to concentrate on Charley's kindly talk. More and more Willy thinks of his brother Ben, a successful prospector who died a few weeks before. Ben becomes so real to the raving Willy that Charley disgustedly walks out. Now Willy's memory completely takes over. Ben arrives on a long-ago visit en route to Africa. To teach Biff a lesson, Uncle Ben tricks the youngster in a game: "Never fight fair with a stranger, boy. You'll never get out of the jungle that way." Charley warns Willy about his boys' "pranks," but Ben commends Biff for stealing. The insecure Willy listens eagerly, reassured that he is raising his boys properly: "That's just the spirit I want to imbue them with! To walk into a jungle! I was right!" Then the scene returns to the present. Worriedly Linda questions the evasive Biff about his and his father's mutual hatefulness. As Happy joins the discussion, Linda gets increasingly upset. "I don't say he's a great man," she says of their father. "But he's a human being, and a terrible thing is happening to him." She adds, "He's not to be allowed to fall into his grave like an old dog. Attention, attention must be finally paid to such a person." She tells them how Willy, "who never worked a day but for your benefit," no longer receives a salary; he borrows money, pretending to her it is his commission, and furtively is preparing to commit suicide with a rubber tube connected to the gas pipe on the water heater. Shamed, the sons decide to make it up to him. Willy comes in and starts arguing with Biff. But soon he gets caught up in the excitement of Biff's willingness to ask his former boss to "stake" him to a sporting goods store. When Willy eagerly gives Biff contradictory advice, they flare up at each other again. Then the boys decide to take their father out the next evening. As Willy dreams about Biff's future ("he'll be great yet!"), Linda timidly asks, "Willy dear, what has he got against you?" Evading the question, Willy stares out the window: "Gee, look at the moon moving between the buildings!" Elsewhere in the house, Biff sees the rubber tube Willy has prepared; horrified, he takes it away.

Act II. The next morning Willy promises Linda to ask for an advance to make all of the necessary time payments. He is elated about the planned evening dinner with his boys, and Linda too feels things will change. At the office, Willy tries to make his request, as the young boss, enthralled with a new recording machine, plays his child's endless recitation of state capitals. When he gently turns down Willy's request, Willy angrily cites the many years he has worked for the firm. "It's business, kid, and everybody's gotta pull his own weight," the boss replies. Willy recalls the career of a successful salesman who, at eighty-four, still pursued his business, right from his hotel room.

"Selling was the greatest career a man could want," Willy concludes, and notes how hundreds of salesmen and buyers went to that old timer's funeral. Though sympathetic, the boss—as he has intended to do for some time—fires Willy. Stupefied, Willy now relives the day of Biff's big football game, as he goes to Charley's office. There he meets his neighbor's once-despised son, now a prominent lawyer ready to appear before the Supreme Court. "What's the secret?" Willy asks him. He gets furious when the lawyer recalls that Biff seemed beaten when he returned from Boston, where he had gone on an impulse to ask for Willy's intercession with the mathematics teacher who had failed him: "What happened in Boston, Willy?" Broken, Willy does not reply. Gruffly Charley gives him some money, as Willy, still incredulous, reveals that he was fired. "The only thing you got in this world is what you can sell," Charley tells him, rejecting Willy's assertion that being liked is what matters. Though Willy realizes Charley is his only friend, he will not accept a job from him, and stumbles out. In the restaurant, Happy picks up a model, who also finds a date for Biff. Biff, however, insists on telling what has happened to him: after waiting all day, he was not even remembered by the man he had counted on; in desperation Biff thereupon stole his fountain pen and ran out. Willy appears, washed out and unwilling to listen to any of Biff's truths: he demands a success story. As they argue, Willy's mind wanders to the past, the Boston hotel room episode. He staggers to the washroom, where he collapses. "You've just seen a prince walk by," Biff tells the pickups; but he is unable to help, and Happy, denying Willy ("that's not my father. He's just a guy"), shepherds them all out to have a good time. Alone, Willy fully relives the terrible moment when young Biff, seeking his help, finds him with the woman in the Boston hotel room. This traumatizes and breaks Young Biff. "You—you gave her Mama's stockings!" he cries out as he leaves, weeping angrily at the father he had worshiped: "You phony little fake!" Back in the present, at home late that night, Linda excoriates her sons for having left their father in the restaurant. Outside, Willy is planting a garden with seeds he bought on the way home, and talks to Ben. Biff, ready to leave the house forever, tries to make up with Willy. As Willy angrily accuses him of jeopardizing his future "for spite," Biff breaks down and sobs in his father's arms, "I'm nothing, Pop. Can't you understand that? There's no spite in it any more." Willy is astonished: "Isn't that remarkable? Biff—he likes me!'" Determined his "boy is going to be magnificent" with the insurance money to back him ("Ben, he'll worship me for it!"), Willy rushes out and commits suicide. A death march starts as Linda and her sons, and Charley and his son, attend Willy's funeral.

Requiem. "Nobody dast blame this man," Charley says at the graveside of the salesman, "a man way out there in the blue, riding on a smile and a shoeshine. . . . A salesman is got to dream." Biff gets ready to leave, for he has had enough. "I know who I am, kid," he tells Happy, who is sure their father "did not die in vain. He had a good dream. It's the only dream you can have—to come out number-one man." Linda sits alone by the grave, puzzled. "I made the last payment on the house today," she says. "Today, dear. And there'll be nobody home." Biff comes to lift her up as she sobs over Willy's grave, "We're free . . . We're free . . ." The flute plays, darkness falls, and "the hard towers of the apartment buildings rise into sharp focus."

DEATH OF CUCHULAIN, THE, a one-act verse play by WILLIAM BUTLER YEATS, published in 1939 and produced in 1949. Setting: a bare stage.

This is Yeats's last play. It is stylized and based on the same source as the first of his five Cuchulain plays, ON BAILE'S STRAND.

After an old man's cantankerous prologue, Cuchulain's mistress, temporarily bewitched by the war goddess, delivers a false message from the elderly Cuchulain's wife, Emer. Cuchulain realizes the mistake and reads the true message. He thinks his mistress tired of him, and goes off to battle: "We have faced great odds before, a straw decided." Fatally wounded, he is about to be killed by his antagonist, "the mother of my son. We met / AT THE HAWK'S WELL under the withered trees. / I killed him upon Baile's Strand. . . ." She helps bind Cuchulain to a stone so that he may die on his feet. They are interrupted by a blind man, who "stood between a Fool and the sea at Baile's Strand / When you went mad." He has been offered twelve pennies for Cuchulain's head. As the blind man decapitates him, Cuchulain talks of his soul, a bird: "And is not that a strange shape for the soul / Of a great fighting-man? . . . / I say it is about to sing." The war goddess places his head and those of his slayers on the ground, and arranges the death dance that Emer now performs about them. A harlot sings the epilogue.

DEATHWATCH (*Haute Surveillance*), a one-act play by JEAN GENET, published and produced in 1949. Setting: a prison cell in France, 1940's.

Genet's first play, this long and at least spiritually autobiographical one-acter resembles THE MAIDS, which had been produced two years earlier. In an as yet conventional theatrical form but already allusive and ritualistic, it features Genet's "religion of evil," characteristic criminal and homosexual relationships, and his preoccupation with illusion and reality.

A condemned Negro murderer who never appears on stage provides a divine aura and an ideal to three prisoners who yearn for similar criminal glory. The cellmates are the "very beautiful" condemned killer of a young girl; a "tall, beautiful" tough, who in his letters to the killer's wife prepares for her eventual seduction; and a "small, handsome," and effeminate youngster. Their agonized love-hate and jealousy relationships culminate with the tough's killing the youngster. But it is to no avail. "Don't you realize it's impossible to overshadow me?" the "very beautiful" killer sneers—and the tough, also doomed now, realizes that "I really am all alone."

DEBIT AND CREDIT (*Debet och kredit*), a one-act play by AUGUST STRINDBERG, published in 1893 and produced in 1915. Setting: a contemporary hotel room.

The hero of this slight Strindberg drama is an ironic self-portrait and a caricature of the superman.

Having achieved success by using his brother, mistress, and friends, the great man is now implored by them to meet his obligations to them. When he skips out, one of his victims remarks, "I would have done just as he did!—And so would you, perhaps?"

DEEP BLUE SEA, THE, a play in three acts by TERENCE RATTIGAN, published and produced in 1952. Setting: a contemporary furnished flat in London on a September day.

This once-popular play features Hester Collyer, who has left her husband for a young former Royal Air Force flier who has taken to drink. Aware of his moral and intellectual inferiority but unable to overcome her physical passion for him, she tries to commit suicide: "When you're between any kind of devil and the deep blue sea, the deep blue sea sometimes looks very inviting." The flier, shaken by the suicide attempt and conscious of his limited capacity for love, decides to leave Hester: "I don't enjoy causing other people misery. I'm not a ruddy sadist." Hester's husband, a distinguished judge who is still in love with her, tries to help. But heartbroken, she refuses to go back to him and prepares to turn the gas on again. A fellow tenant who has also suffered much talks her out of it. He gives Hester the strength to face life—"without hope" but also "without despair"—and to regain her self-respect.

DEIRDRE, a one-act verse play by WILLIAM BUTLER YEATS, produced in 1906 and published in 1907. Setting: a guest house in a wood in legendary Ireland.

Unlike J. M. SYNGE, who dramatized the complete legend in his DEIRDRE OF THE SORROWS, Yeats (assisted by LADY GREGORY) in this heroic tragedy focused on the final episode and on the noble Deirdre, a "wild bird in a cage." The play is indebted to the Japanese No drama; its static nature as well as the central imagery (hunting and chess) mirror the lovers' entrapment.

Musicians retell the famous story before the arrival of Naoise and Deirdre, at old King Conchubar's invitation. He has promised his guests full pardon, but the musicians know that "An old man's love / Who casts no second line is hard to cure; / His jealousy is like his love." When the lovers enter, Deirdre senses their impending betrayal and doom. But Naoise and Conchubar's old councilor friend, trusting in Conchubar's good faith, reject all omens and await a messenger to reassure them of the king's intention to keep his promise. "This king / Will murder Naoise, and keep me alive," Deirdre realizes, and she is certain of it when she learns that Conchubar has prepared a bridal chamber. Naoise will not believe her, and Deirdre tries to get him away and save him by arousing his jealousy. When that fails, she plans to repel Conchubar by disfiguring herself; but Naoise submits to fate: "Leave the gods' handiwork unblotched, and wait / For their decision, our decision is past." Like earlier legendary lovers who played chess while awaiting their death, Deirdre and Naoise sit at the ominously prepared chess table. Soon Conchubar's treachery is revealed, and Naoise rushes out to fight him. While Deirdre succeeds in attaining a knife, Naoise is trapped. Conchubar offers to spare him if Deirdre will be his. She tries to save Naoise by agreeing to submit, by imploring Conchubar's pardon for their elopement, and by assuming sole guilt for it. Despite her efforts Naoise is taken out and executed. Once he is dead Deirdre assumes various masks in order to shape her own final destiny. She persuades Conchubar that he is beginning to stir her passions. Then—by ridicule, seductive words, and natural dignity—she elicits his permission to perform the final rites for Naoise. "Now strike the wire, and sing to it a while, / Knowing that all is happy," she tells Conchubar as she goes to kill herself behind the curtain. And she concludes, with tragic irony: "You know / Within what bride-bed I shall lie this night, / And by what man, and lie close up to him, / For the bed's narrow, and there outsleep the cockcrow." When he realizes that she has killed herself, Conchubar is momentarily overwhelmed; but though rebellion brews, he reaffirms his rightness "In choosing her most fitting to be Queen, / And letting no boy lover take the sway."

DEIRDRE OF THE SORROWS, a play in three acts by J. M. SYNGE, published and produced in 1910. Setting: legendary Ireland and Scotland.

The legend of Deirdre, Naisi (also Naise or Naoise), and Conchubor (or Conchubar), which resembles that of Tristram and Isolde as well as Shakespeare's *Antony and Cleopatra,* is perhaps Ireland's greatest and most famous one. It has been dramatized frequently, notably by WILLIAM BUTLER YEATS and GEORGE WILLIAM RUSSELL (Æ), but this is the legend's outstanding dramatization. Synge based his play on LADY GREGORY's retelling of the Irish sagas in *Cuchulain of Muirthemne* (1902).It was Synge's last work. He rewrote it during his final illness, but did not live to complete his revision. Melodious and moving prose is spoken by Synge's peasant as well as noble characters.

Act I. Deirdre's nurse tries to dissuade old Conchubor, the High King of Ulster, from marrying the young foundling he has raised. Out "picking flowers or nuts, or sticks itself," Deirdre now returns from the fields. She rejects Conchubor's annoyed criticism, "it's that way you're picking up the manners will fit you to be Queen of Ulster?" Bluntly she tells him that she does not want to be queen; she wants a mate "with his hair like the raven, maybe, and his skin like the snow and his lips like blood spilt on it." But Conchubor insists on having her; he promises her expensive gifts and orders her to his castle in Emain Macha, the capital, the next day. He rejects as coyness her pleas to stay at her nurse's house, and leaves. Terrified and desperate, Deirdre decides to assume "the right of a queen who is a master, taking her own choice." While she is out, Naisi and his brothers, "the Sons of Usna," come in. They are looking for the mysterious and beautiful girl they met in the woods that day. She has invited them, and Naisi therefore exuberantly dismisses the nurse's attempts to make him leave: "At your age you should know there are nights when a king like Conchubor would spit upon his arm ring, and queens will stick their tongues out at the rising moon." Deirdre enters, royally dressed and beautiful: "Do not leave me, Naisi. I am Deirdre of the Sorrows." Naisi is awed. He has heard the prophesy that she will ruin him and his brothers, but Deirdre woos him, and expresses her aversion to the old, if wealthy, king. She wants to live her life fully: "Isn't it a small thing is foretold about the ruin of ourselves, Naisi, when all men have age coming and great ruin in the end?" Naisi responds to her dangerous suggestions: "The stars will be our lamps many nights and we abroad in Alban, and taking our journeys among the little islands in the sea. There has never been the like of the joy we'll have, Deirdre, you and I, having our fill of love." In a simple ceremony, Naisi and Deirdre join hands and are wed.

Act II. Deirdre and Naisi are in Alba, after seven glorious years of love. Conchubor sends them an offer of peace if they and Naisi's brothers return to Emain. Worrying about the mutability of their love, Deirdre wonders whether it is "a game worth playing, living on until you're dried and old, and our joy is gone forever." Her nurse tells her of the joys of old age, but soon Deirdre's fears are accentuated. The king's attendant and spy predicts that she will see Naisi "getting a harshness in his two sheep's eyes" and pictures her getting old, with her "nose reaching down to scrape her chin." Deirdre is brokenhearted as she realizes that Naisi too dreads wearying of her some day. She decides to return to Ireland, though she has no faith in Conchubor's promise. "There is no way to keep life, or love with it, a short space only," she tells Naisi. And he gives in: "It should be a poor thing to see great lovers and they sleepy and old." They return to Ireland, "facing death, maybe, and death should be a poor, untidy thing, though it's a queen that dies."

Act III. In a shabby tent prepared for them outside Emain, old Conchubor impatiently waves aside the nurse's pleas and waits to possess Deirdre. He goes out before she arrives with Naisi. They discover a newly dug grave and realize they are trapped. Yet when Conchubor enters, Deirdre tries to make peace: "So near that grave we seem three lonesome people, and by a new-made grave there's no man will keep brooding on a woman's lips, or on the man he hates." She almost succeeds. Just then, Naisi's brothers are attacked outside and Conchubor leaves: "I was near won this night, but death's between us now." Naisi wants to help his brothers, but Deirdre clings to him and begs him not to leave her. "The hardness of death has come between us," Deirdre remarks as they quarrel bitterly before he goes out to his doom. She is terrified and wild with sorrow when Conchubor, oblivious in his passion even to the burning of his capital, comes to claim her. She laments at the grave of Naisi and his brothers: "It's you three will not see age or death coming," she weeps, and rejects her nurse's urgings to live out the many years still left her. Gradually Deirdre's keening becomes triumphant. Choosing to stay "young forever," she spurns Conchubor, a mighty king but here "an old man and a fool only." She remembers her life with Naisi: "Little moon of Alban, it's lonesome you'll be this night" and forever, looking for "the two lovers who slept so sweetly with each other." And she concludes, "It is not a small thing to be rid of grey hairs, and the loosening of the teeth. . . . It's a pitiful thing, Conchubor, you have done this night in Emain; yet a thing will be a joy and triumph to the ends of life and time." Before they can stop her, Deirdre plunges Naisi's knife into her heart and sinks into his grave. With pity the nurse leads a broken, old Conchubor off: "Deirdre is dead, and Naisi is dead; and if the oaks and stars could die for sorrow, it's a dark sky and a hard and naked earth we'd have this night in Emain."

DELANEY, Shelagh (1939–   ), English playwright, created something of a sensation because her first play, A TASTE OF HONEY (1958), was produced and became popular when she was but nineteen. Born in Salford, Lancashire, Shelagh Delaney left school at sixteen, worked at various odd jobs, and soon decided that she could write plays as good as those she saw and characterized (in the dialogue of *A Taste of Honey*) as "all mauling and muttering, can't hear what they're saying half the time and when you do it's not worth listening to." She succeeded particularly in catching speech rhythms—though her play does not read very well, and her plotting, themes, and dramaturgy are confused. Joan Littlewood, the experimental theatre director, whipped the script into shape without, apparently, changing the original unduly. After writing the screenplay for this play, Miss Delaney came out with *The Lion in Love** (1960), which also deals with loneliness and a mother-daughter relationship. The focus this time is on the mother, and the play has many more characters and a more complex plot—and it was not particularly successful. Delaney has written film scripts and published her autobiography, *Sweetly Sings the Donkey,* in 1963. Her life and

* The title comes from Aesop's Fable CIX, whose moral the play dramatizes: "Nothing can be more fatal to peace than the ill-assorted marriages into which rash love may lead."

work are also discussed in John Russell Taylor's *Anger and After* (1962, revised in 1969 and retitled *The Angry Theatre* in America).

DELICATE BALANCE, A, a play in three acts by EDWARD ALBEE, published and produced in 1966. Setting: a "well-appointed" American suburban house on a weekend in 1966.

Albee was awarded the Pulitzer Prize for this play, perhaps to compensate for the board's failure to act on WHO'S AFRAID OF VIRGINIA WOOLF? *A Delicate Balance* is a less dynamic but more subtle and frightening portrayal of the emasculating "Mommy" and the emasculated "Daddy," and of pervasive emptiness and fear. It is reminiscent of similar evocations by HAROLD PINTER, though not perhaps quite as terrifying.

Agnes garrulously speculates on the attraction of going mad. She is the bored but intelligent and charming elderly wife of Tobias, a well-to-do retired gentleman. He prepares drinks and says little—even in reply to Agnes's suspicions of an affair with her alcoholic and witty sister, who lives with them. But he becomes expansive as he tells the story of a harrowing experience: because his cat would not love him, he finally had it killed. Suddenly there appear an elderly couple, their neighbors and best friends. "WE WERE FRIGHTENED . . . AND THERE WAS NOTHING," they explain, requesting that they be allowed to stay overnight. Their visit precipitates family squabbles, which reach a crisis with the arrival of Tobias and Agnes's angular daughter. Hysterical, she has come home for refuge after the failure of her fourth marriage, and is resentful to find her room occupied by the neighbors. These two, in turn, are panic-stricken at the thought of returning home, and intend to board here permanently. Tobias tries to maintain the "delicate balance" between obligation to friends and to family privacy. Sobbing and laughing, he finally tells his friend: "So bring your wife, and bring your terror, bring your plague." Then he shouts his admission: "I DON'T WANT YOU HERE! . . . BUT BY GOD . . . YOU STAY!!" After they leave, Tobias tries to persuade himself he has been both honest and neighborly. Agnes repeats the play's opening speech: "What I find most astonishing . . . [is] that I might very easily—as they say—lose my mind one day. . . ." Then she sighs, "Well, they're safely gone . . . and we'll forget . . . quite soon."

DELIVERER, THE, a one-act play by LADY GREGORY, produced in 1911 and published in 1912. Setting: biblical Egypt.

This is a free dramatization of Moses's discovery of his origin, his killing of an Egyptian oppressor of the Jews, and his determination to lead them to freedom in their homeland. But the focus is on the downtrodden mob and its fickleness, its vicious betrayal of the leader who sacrifices his well-being for them. This story of Moses, "the King's Nurseling," is made suggestively to parallel that of Charles Stewart Parnell.

DENMARK, unlike most Scandinavian countries, started to produce plays in the Middle Ages. Danish drama followed the same general development through neoclassicism and romanticism as did other European literature. Yet Denmark achieved little comparable distinction in the modern drama. Though the early eighteenth century witnessed the extraordinary energy of Ludvig Holberg, a writer of comedies that rivaled those of Molière, the modern period has produced neither a HENRIK IBSEN nor an AUGUST STRINDBERG. Denmark's only dramatists to achieve even minimal international renown, to date, have been KAJ MUNK, the leading Danish playwright of the first half of this century; KJELD ABELL, Denmark's most distinguished modern dramatist; and the "bad boy of Danish drama," CARL ERIK SOYA.

Georg Brandes (1842–1927), a seminal modern literary critic and an exponent of NATURALISM, was a guiding spirit also of the dramatic revival of the late nineteenth century. His brother Edvard Brandes (1847–1931), a minor playwright, was the most influential Danish drama critic of his age. Among those belonging to the Brandes brothers' literary circle was a poet who often scandalized his contemporaries with satiric social and erotic verse, Holger Drachmann (1846–1908); also a dramatist, Drachmann wrote a number of popular operettas, notably *Der var engang* (1885, with music by P. E. Lange-Müller), which has been frequently revived in the twentieth century. Another early modern dramatist is Otto Benzon (1856–1926), whose *En skandale* (1884) deals with contemporary problems. The most important playwright of the naturalist period that ended at the turn of the century was the comic novelist Gustav Wied (1858–1914), who because of his eccentric characterizations was sometimes likened to Strindberg; he wrote witty and exuberant "satyr-dramas" for the closet and a number of comedies that were successfully produced, including the sophisticated *Ranke Viljer* (1906, translated as *2 × 2 = 5*).

Other early playwrights of note include Hjalmar Bergström (1868–1914), Henri Nathansen (1868–1944), the prolific and versatile Einar Christiansen (1861–1939, Director of the Royal Theatre from 1899 to 1911), and Helge Rode (1870–1937), a poet who produced some verse drama on distinctively Danish themes. Bergström wrote Ibsensite PROBLEM PLAYS, the best known of which are *Lyngaard & Co.* (1905), which depicts a conflict between capital and labor; *Karen Bornemann* (1907), whose passionate title heroine refuses to marry a former lover she no longer cares for and who pities her religious father for breaking down when he learns of her "sinful" past ("How can I help it that I am a child of a time you don't understand?"); and *Dame-Te* (*Ladies' Tea*, 1910; also translated as *The Birthday Party*), an almost plotless sketch in which a number of women relate the tragicomic reasons for their spinsterhood. Nathansen, a Jewish lawyer, novelist, theatre historian, and playwright, commited suicide after escaping from the Nazis;

he was best known for his half-dozen plays on modern Jewish themes, notably *Indenfor Murene* (1912), an exhortation that Danish Jews retain their heritage and resist assimilation.

Recent times have brought only slightly more notable activity to the Danish drama. The Nobel Prize novelist Johannes V. Jensen (1873–1950) also wrote drama, but with undistinguished results. Svend Borberg (1888–1947), whose reputation declined in part because of his pro-Nazi sympathies, produced the only successful Danish play about World War I, *Ingen* (1920)—a tense psychological drama about a returning soldier and the strange alter ego who kills his wife—and another play about the complexity of man's personality, *Circus Juris* (1935). The most important plays of the imaginative poet, essayist, and law professor Sven Clausen (1893–1961) are the experimental *Naevningen* (1929) and *Paladsrevolution* (1923, revised in 1948), a dramatization of Queen Caroline Mathilda's late eighteenth-century love affair. The outstanding mid-century Danish author Hans Christian Branner (1903–66), principally noted for his psychoanalytical novels and short stories, dramatized the novella that made him famous, *Rytteren* (*The Riding Master,* 1949; also translated as *The Mistress,* 1953), and became an important playwright with the three-act *Søskende* (1952, translated as *The Judge*). Another Danish novelist-playwright was Leck Fischer (1904–56), who often depicted family life with great objectivity; the best known of his few plays are *Barnet* (1936), a double tragedy about abortion-seeking lovers and a childless married couple, and the atypical *Jordens Salt* (1954), a portrayal of a Christian idealist who becomes a murderer. More recently, Bruun Olsen (1923–   ) attracted notice with his *agitprop* sequel to Ibsen's A DOLL'S HOUSE, *Hvor gik Nora hen, da hun gik ud* (1968), whose heroine joins the labor movement.

Few of these writers have aroused interest outside of Scandinavia. Only Munk, Abell, and (to a lesser degree) Soya became at all known to non-Scandinavian audiences, and even these prominent native writers have had very limited success beyond their own borders. *Contemporary Danish Plays* (1955), with an introduction by Elias Bredsdorff, is the only extensive English collection (nine plays by as many writers) of modern Denmark's drama; general collections occasionally include a play by Munk or Abell. P. M. Mitchell's comprehensive *A History of Danish Literature* (1957) discusses the more important Danish playwrights and includes a selective bibliography. Bredsdorff's *Danish Literature in English Translation* (1950) includes an extensive bibliography of Danish literature as well as discussions of it in English books and articles.

DENNIS, Nigel (1912–   ), English novelist, critic, and playwright. An individualist and a witty, intellectual writer, he made his name with *Cards of Identity* (1955), a comic novel he dramatized the following year. It was published in *Two Plays and a Preface* (1958), with *The Making of Moo* (1957), an attack on the stifling dogmatism of religion. Dennis's next play, *August for the People* (1961), like his other works, is a caustic satire of the malleability of robotlike man in mid-century Western society.

After his father's death in World War I, Dennis was moved from England, first to South Africa and then to Europe. In 1934 Dennis went to the United States, where he became a book reviewer for *Time* magazine and, among other writings, translated the works of the psychologist Alfred Adler. Upon his return to England fifteen years later, Dennis became the drama critic for *Encounter*. His reviews are collected in *Dramatic Essays* (1962).

DEPUTY, THE (*Der Stellvertreter*), a verse play in five acts by ROLF HOCHHUTH, published and produced in 1963. Setting: Berlin (Germany), Rome (Italy), and Auschwitz (Poland); 1942–44.

This long and controversial play was produced throughout the world (as *The Representative* in England) in variously cut versions—and amidst picketing and riots. Its dramatization of Pius XII (God's "Deputy") and the Church's failure to protest Germany's systematic murder of millions of Jews was documented in Hochhuth's sixty-five-page historical postscript and vehemently debated in thousands of articles by outstanding thinkers and world figures. It aroused *"almost certainly the largest storm ever raised by a play in the whole history of the drama,"** though the play, despite the power of its theme, was generally criticized for its pedestrian free verse, excessive dramatization of atrocities, and the diffusion of an epic canvas and a multitude of shadowy, one-dimensional characters. Many of them—like the martyred idealist hero, Riccardo, modeled on Father Maximilian Kolbe—are fictitious; the historical figures in the play are the Pope, the Nuncio (Cesare Orsenigo), Kurt Gerstein, August Hirt, and Adolf Eichmann.

Act I. The Mission. Scene 1. Father Riccardo Fontana, a young Italian Jesuit priest, urges the Papal Nuncio in Berlin to denounce Germany's slaughter of Jews. He is joined by Kurt Gerstein, an SS officer who secretly sabotages Nazi extermination projects. Gerstein is beside himself with horror as he describes in detail the atrocities committed daily on thousands of Jewish families, and he demands that this information be transmitted so that the Pope may act. The Nuncio refuses, though he promises to "pray for the victims." *Scene 2.* Near Berlin Eichmann, a colorless bureaucrat, is giving a party. His guests include Professor Hirt, a repulsive skull-collecting anatomist; the fiendish Doctor of Auschwitz, who selects gas-chamber victims, embarrasses the

* Eric Bentley (ed.), *The Storm Over The Deputy* (1964). Another collection of articles on this play is *The Deputy Reader* (1965), edited by Dolores and Earl R. Schmidt; both books have extensive bibliographies of further works on the subject.

company with a macabre pornographic song, and seduces and dominates a blond girl engaged to an Auschwitz officer; and Gerstein, reporting to Eichmann on "the final solution" project. *Scene 3*. In his apartment Gerstein is helping a Jew to escape Germany. After a brief visit by the diabolical Doctor, Riccardo comes to assure Gerstein, who has been ordered to assemble extermination gas, that the Pope will speak out. He helps the Jew's escape by donating his passport. Sadly Riccardo then examines the yellow star the Jew has had to wear and has given Riccardo in exchange. Holding it over his heart, Riccardo asks, "Here?"

Act II. The Bells of Saint Peter's. Riccardo visits Count Fontana, his wealthy father and the Pope's friend. Riccardo insists that the Church denounce Nazi atrocities, but the father supports the Pope's policy of neutrality. Riccardo scoffs at Rome's concern for "its power / over banks, industries, and ministers," but is assured by his father and a jovial cardinal that the Pope "will not / expose himself to danger for the Jews." Yet Riccardo remains confident, for the appointment of Weizsäcker as the new German ambassador to the Vatican demonstrates Hitler's fear of a papal protest.

Act III. The Visitation. Scene 1. In late 1943 an SS sergeant and Fascist militia arrest a baptized Jewess and her Catholic family, whose apartment window affords "a reassuring view of the papal palace." *Scene 2*. The jovial cardinal is disappointed that Germans are arresting Italians in the very shadow of the papal palace. He assures Riccardo and Gerstein that though extermination of the Jews is blinding them to the need of defending the West against Russia, Nazi excesses will now prompt the Pope to speak out. Riccardo vows that unless this happens, he himself will join the Jews on the cattle trains: "Since the Pope, although only a man, / can actually represent God on earth, / I . . . a poor priest . . . if need be / can also represent the Pope—*there* / where the Pope ought to be standing today." In their desperation Gerstein and Riccardo even consider seizing the Vatican's radio station—and assassinating the Pope, to "save him from—complete perdition." *Scene 3*. An SS lieutenant in Rome's Gestapo headquarters sadistically questions and dooms Italian-Jewish prisoners. Gerstein frightens him by suggesting that extermination policies may soon be ended by a papal protest.

Act IV. Il gran rifiuto. Pope Pius endorses checks as he discusses the Church's financial holdings with Count Fontana and the jovial cardinal. Riccardo appears, and in their bitter confrontation tries, with his father's help, to have Pius protest Nazi atrocities. "Hitler alone, dear Count, is now defending Europe" against the Russians, the Pope replies, adding that Germany's viability must be sustained "also to hold the balance of power" that safeguards the Church's wealth.

The Deputy, Act IV. Pope Pius (EMLYN WILLIAMS), the cardinal (Fred Stewart), Riccardo (Jeremy Brett), Count Fontana (Carl Low). New York, 1964. (*Friedman-Abeles*)

When asked to break his silence about the murder of the Jews, the embarrassed Pope says he will indeed not "permit this sacrilege beneath Our very windows." A scribe is summoned and Pius dictates a proclamation. But it is in such general and temporizing terms that the proclamation is totally ineffectual. Thereupon Riccardo pulls out the yellow cloth Star of David and pins it to his cassock. Quivering with mortification and rage, the Pope drops the pen with which he is signing the proclamation, and lifts his ink-stained hands. Then he rejects Riccardo's final plea: "We cannot—will not—write to Hitler," who would "only be antagonized and outraged." Riccardo departs: "God shall not destroy His Church / only because a Pope shrinks from His summons." Temporarily stunned, the Pope soon regains his composure: "Whatever *has been granted Us to do was done.* / We are—God knows it—blameless of the blood / now being spilled." Then he leads his friends in prayer for the "heavenly comfort" of the Jews being slaughtered outside.

Act V. Auschwitz, or Where Are You, God? Scene 1. In a misty light scarcely distinguishable deportees arrive at the concentration camp, their thoughts articulated in monologues above the sound of a moving freight train. *Scene 2.* At Auschwitz, the diabolical Doctor continues his macabre liaison with the blond to whom he describes his seduction of a Jewish mother whose children he had ordered gassed. Riccardo, now a prisoner, appears with a child whose father has just been beaten to death. The Doctor taunts him, describing concentration camp atrocities and assuring him that "Auschwitz refutes / creator, creation, and the creature." When Riccardo maintains that "Since / the devil exists, God also exists," the amused Doctor expresses his delight with their "debate." *Scene 3.* A week later Gerstein comes with fake orders for Riccardo's release. Just then the Jew whom Gerstein had harbored in Berlin appears in the priest's guise, in which he was arrested. Riccardo insists that the Jew continue to pretend he is the priest and escape in his place, for "What would I have on my conscience if I weren't here?" But the Doctor's arrival foils their plan. He has Gerstein imprisoned, and laughs about the atrocities of the camp. When he taunts and finally kills a Jewess, Riccardo tries to kill him. Thereupon SS guards shoot Riccardo and carry him out to be burned alive in the crematorium. The glow of its fires sinks in the background as a loudspeaker announcement quotes Weizsäcker's report to Berlin on the innocuous papal proclamation: "There is no need to raise objections to its publication." And as the stage darkens, an unemotional voice tells how, until the end of the war, "the gas chambers continued to work [on their] so-called daily quota of exterminations . . ."

DESIGN FOR LIVING, a comedy in three acts by NOËL COWARD, published and produced in 1933. Setting: Paris, London, and New York, early 1930's.

This once-popular comedy was adapted for the screen by BEN HECHT and Ernst Lubitsch in 1934.

Gilda, an interior decorator, is in love with both Otto Sylvus, a painter, and Leo Mercuré, a playwright. Though they are great friends, Otto and Leo are hurt and jealous when the other one lives with Gilda. To escape these love-hate complications, Gilda marries a conventional art dealer with whom she goes off to settle in New York. But when Otto and Leo impudently show up in her apartment after two years, Gilda cannot resist resuming their Bohemian association. The husband stomps out indignantly—and falls over his canvases. Gilda, Otto, and Leo collapse in uproarious laughter.

DESIRE UNDER THE ELMS, a play in three parts by EUGENE O'NEILL, produced in 1924 and published in 1925. Setting: a New England farmhouse with two huge elms that suggest "exhausted women resting their sagging breasts and hands and hair on its roof," 1850–51.

Though now acknowledged as one of O'Neill's most powerful plays and frequently revived, *Desire Under the Elms*—with its stark NATURALISTIC presentation of greed, lust, murder, vengeance, adultery, and incest—at first ran into major censorship difficulties in America and was banned in England for many years. It prefigures O'Neill's MOURNING BECOMES ELECTRA in its dramatization of Freudian psychology and its modernization of classical myths (the *Oresteia,* Medea, and Hippolytus and Phaedra).

Part I. Scene 1. Twenty-five-year-old Eben and his older half-brothers admire the "purty" sunset. Simeon and Peter laconically yearn for the treasures of the "Golden West" and curse their old slave-driving father, Ephraim Cabot, whose farm and stone walls fence them in. He left two months ago, and Eben frankly wishes him dead. *Scene 2.* At supper, though his country-bumpkin brothers assert he is the "dead spit an' image" of Cabot, Eben fiercely claims to be like his dead "Maw." He bitterly blames Cabot for having stolen her land and then slaved her to death. The farm is rightly his, Eben insists, and goes off to the local prostitute, whose softness and warmth he craves—even though his father (as Eben discovers furiously) had her before him. *Scene 3.* He returns at dawn with the news that Cabot has just married again. Convinced that his new wife will inherit everything, Peter and Simeon decide to quit slaving for Cabot and to head for California, and Eben offers them six hundred dollars for their share of the farm. *Scene 4.* The brothers sign their inheritance claims over to Eben, who steals the money from Cabot's hiding place. Cabot, a hard, proud, and powerful seventy-five-year-old Puritan, appears with his new wife, Abbie Putnam, a buxom and sensual thirty-five-year-old woman, full of vitality, who gloats over her new home. Peter and Simeon contemptuously insult both of them and leave. Abbie and Eben immediately feel attracted to each other, but Eben angrily accuses her of stealing his farm; she decides complacently that he is "nice," and proudly begins washing *her* dishes.

Part II. Scene 1. As Eben goes off to his prostitute, two months later, still hating Abbie, she seductively assures him that "Nature'll beat ye, Eben. Ye might's well own up t' it fust 's last." But they argue fiercely after he taunts her for having sold herself for the farm "like any other old whore." Cabot, feeling that he is "gittin' ripe on the bough," assures Abbie he would leave the farm to her if she had a son. When she suddenly suggests that they may, he fervently drops on his knees and starts praying for one. She watches him with "scorn and triumph." *Scene 2.* In their bedroom, Cabot tells Abbie how he built his farm out of fields of stone, and how lonesome he has always been. Meanwhile Abbie, paying no attention to him, gazes passionately at the wall, on the other side of which Eben, in his bedroom, similarly seems to watch her. When Cabot senses her not understanding him, he bitterly goes off to the barn to sleep with the cows. Desire finally drives Abbie to Eben's room. She kisses him ardently, and though he tries to resist, she compels him to follow her to the parlor, which has remained closed since his mother's death. *Scene 3.* Abbie's ardor, at first a mixture of maternal love and lust, persuades Eben that his mother's spirit demands vengeance on Cabot, and he gives full sway to his pent-up desires. *Scene 4.* When he meets Cabot returning from the barn at dawn, Eben wants to shake hands: "Yew 'n' me is quits. . . . [Maw] kin rest now an' sleep content."

Part III. Scene 1. The following spring, Cabot is celebrating the birth of a son. At the dance, as Abbie keeps asking for and later joins Eben, who is watching the infant upstairs, the townspeople snicker about "the old skunk gittin' fooled," but Cabot pays no attention and joyfully outdances them all. *Scene 2.* Furious when Cabot tells him that Abbie wanted a son to get the farm away from him, Eben wants to kill her, but Cabot easily fights him down. Abbie cannot persuade her heartbroken lover that while what Cabot told him had been true in the beginning, she now cares only for him. He blames the baby for his sorrow, and determines to go away. Panicky at the thought of losing him, Abbie vows to regain his love by proving that "I wa'n't schemin' t' steal from ye." *Scene 3.* At dawn she hysterically tells Eben she has proven her love to him: she just killed their baby. Horrified, Eben rushes off to report the crime. *Scene 4.* Cabot is equally horrified. Hearing that the baby was Eben's, however, he looks forward to her hanging, though he despises Eben: "I'd never told no Sheriff on ye no matter what ye did, if they was t' brile me alive!" He decides to leave his hard and lonely life on the farm, but when he discovers that his money has been stolen by Eben, he interprets it as a sign from his Puritan God: "Mebbe they's easy gold in the West but it hain't God's gold. It hain't fur me. I kin hear His voice warnin' me agen t' be hard an' stay on my farm. . . . Waal—what d'ye want? God's lonesome, hain't he? God's hard an' lonesome!" Eben returns penitent, truly loving Abbie, feeling his complicity in her guilt, and insists on sharing her punishment. When the sheriff comes, the now-serene and happy lovers kiss and leave for jail hand in hand, devoutly admiring the "purty" sunrise. The curtain falls as the sheriff looks around enviously: "It's a jim-dandy farm, no denyin'. Wished I owned it!"

DETOUR, THE, a play in three acts by OWEN DAVIS, produced in 1921 and published in 1922. Setting: a farmhouse near Northport, Long Island; 1921.

This grim yet amusing play about American country life depicts the difficult lives of the truck-farming Hardy family. When she fell in love and married Hardy twenty years ago, Helen gave up her dreams of being an artist "somewhere's where bein' born an' bein' dead wasn't the only things that ever happened." She has transferred all her ambitions to her daughter, painfully saving her pennies. Now there is enough money to send her to a New York art school, but Hardy demands the money for the farm. Helen is about to leave him, when the daughter realizes that she has no real talent. Thereupon she gives the money to her father and decides to marry the neighbor boy she loves—thus repeating her mother's life. Immediately Helen starts a new fund, for her grandchild. "For the baby that ain't even born yet," her husband laughs, as Helen happily thinks of the future, "her heart swelling with eternal hope."

DEVAL [originally Boularan], **Jacques** (1890–), French novelist and playwright, is the author of many romantically bittersweet but clever comedies. His greatest success was *Tovaritch* (1933), a comedy on the plight of White Russians in Paris after the Revolution; adapted by ROBERT E. SHERWOOD as *Tovarich* (1936), it was made into a musical comedy (by David Shaw, ? – ?) in 1963. Popular too was Deval's *Dans sa candeur naïve* (1926), almost immediately adapted by Valerie Wingate (? - ?) and P. G. Wodehouse (1881–) as *Her Cardboard Lover,* a comedy about a divorcée who hires a "cardboard lover," who is to save her from yielding to her pursuing ex-husband but succeeds, instead, in winning her himself; his kiss elicits her curtain line: "That's not so cardboard!"

The son of a writer, Deval was born in Paris. His first play, *Une Faible Femme* (*A Weak Woman,* 1920), is appropriately titled after the typical Deval heroine, who like the divorcée ultimately succumbs. Other early plays include *Etienne* (1930, produced in New York as *Another Love*), *Mademoiselle* (1932), the atypically sociological *Prière pour les vivants* (1933), the tragicomic adolescent love drama *L'Age de Juliette* (1934), and the dramatization (with music by Kurt Weill) of his 1931 novel *Marie Galante* (1934).

Deval traveled to the United States in the 1930's, served in the American Army during World War II, and translated English and American plays into French. A number of his own plays appeared originally in English, including *Lorelei* (1938), *Behold the Bride* (1939), *Oh, Brother!* (1945), and *Bathsheba* (1947). Subsequently Deval returned to France and continued writing comedies, including *Corrida* (1957) and *La Vénus de Milo* (1962).

DEVIL AND THE GOOD LORD, THE (*Le Diable et le bon Dieu*), a play in three acts by JEAN-PAUL SARTRE, published and produced in 1951. Setting: Worms, Germany, and vicinity; a year and a day in the sixteenth century.

A long, savage mass-drama also translated as *Lucifer and the Lord,* this play consists of much philosophizing (including monologues with an absent God) and hocus-pocus. Like THE FLIES, it ends with an existentialist as well as a Nietzschean vision of a godless universe. It dramatizes and rejects as escapist Christian charity and love—and urges humanists to use "DIRTY HANDS" to fight pervasive evil—as does Goetz, the tormented hero alienated in the world of the early Reformation. Anti-Christian, the play shocked theatre audiences with the line: "The Church is a whore: she sells her favors to the rich."

Act I. Goetz, the bastard nobleman and the incarnation of evil, is besieging Worms. A shifty priest escapes and presents Goetz with the key to the city—to massacre the rebellious peasants and thus save the imprisoned clergy. He persuades Goetz that there is no distinction in doing evil, for everyone is doing it and "the world itself is iniquity." Goetz takes this as a challenge to do good. He bets that he can become goodness incarnate within a year and a day: "I was a criminal—I will reform. I turn my coat and wager that I can become a saint." To get God's approval for his decision, he throws dice with his whore—and cheats to elicit the "divine" omen.

Act II. Goetz distributes to the poor the land he inherited by betrayal, though the leader of the peasants urges him to donate it to the revolution. Goetz declines, however, "to do good by installment." Eager to bring about immediate "happiness, love, and virtue," he wants to use the land for his Christian utopia—a "City of the Sun" rather than a war site. But Goetz soon finds his peasants more interested in the indulgence-selling monk Tetzel, especially after a leper prefers Tetzel's wares to Goetz's "useless" kiss of charity. Later the suffering peasants huddle in a church, cared for and consoled by a saintly Christian girl they adore. She reveals to Goetz, who is jealous of the peasants' love he himself has failed to win, that his whore is dying. He brings her final happiness by piercing his palms for her, a gesture that convinces her of his love. "You have shed your blood for me," she exclaims, and dies. The superstitious peasants accept the "stigmata" and now obey him. Goetz is jubilant: "They are mine, at last."

Act III. Goetz has built the "City of the Sun" and tries to prevent its inhabitants from joining the Peasant Revolt. But they ignore Goetz's exhortations. He curses them and goes into the forest to mortify his flesh. His model city is destroyed, and its peasants are slaughtered in the premature rebellion. The once-saintly Christian girl answers Goetz's "God is dead" with her own discovery of His irrelevance to practical moral problems. Now that Goetz's year and one day are up, the shifty priest reappears, accompanied by the Devil. Goetz admits that he has lost: whether evil or saintly, he has brought only suffering and death, and his supplications to Heaven have gone unanswered. "You see this emptiness over our heads? That is God," he says. "Silence is God. Absence is God. God is the loneliness of man." The final "colossal joke" is that "God doesn't exist. . . . There is nothing left but mankind." Goetz kills the priest, who has attacked him, and is then captured by the peasants. Their leader urges him to become their commander, but Goetz declines a position of lonely leadership, for he needs "men all around me . . . to hide the sky from me." But then he submits: "Suffering, anguish, remorse are all very well for me," but if the men fall, "the last candle goes out." He takes command of the army, "vows to be relentless"—and immediately stabs a mutinous officer. "The kingdom of men is beginning," he says, ready to be "hangman and butcher." He will lead the peasants: "I shall give them orders, since I have no other way of obeying. I shall remain alone with this empty sky over my head, since I have no other way of being among men."

DEVIL, THE (*Az ördög*), a play in three acts by FERENC MOLNÁR, published and produced in 1907. Setting: Vienna, early twentieth century.

Molnár's first international success, this witty play originally appeared in America in four simultaneous productions (1908), and has been revived through the 1960's.*

The attractive young Olga Zanden is to have her portrait painted by Karl Mahler, her childhood sweetheart. Her dense husband, a rich banker, leaves the couple alone, and they discuss their early love. Karl decorously goes out while she takes off her blouse—for her husband wants a décolleté portrait. Suddenly a fashionably dressed Devil appears. "Pardon, madame," he remarks, handing back the blouse, "I think you dropped something." And then the cynical Devil, personifying their yearnings, proceeds systematically to inflame the couple's repressed love. "A life that has not been squandered—has not been lived," he remarks cheerfully, and so arranges things that night at the Zandens' ball that Karl spurns the pert heiress he is to marry, and becomes crazed with jealousy when he thinks Olga is about to be escorted by the Devil, nude beneath her cloak "like a classic goddess—like a modern Mona Vanna." Intending to avert an affair with Karl, Olga instead writes him a passionate love letter—at the Devil's dictation. She insists Karl burn it without looking at it—and when he does so she is

* See Edmund Wilson's article on Hungary in *The New Yorker,* June 4, 1966.

relieved, though sad. Then the Devil reappears—and salvages it. "Karl! My letter! I have my letter—" Olga cries, and runs into his study. The Devil smiles, listens at the door, joyfully rubs his hands, and exclaims, "Voilà!"

DEVIL'S DISCIPLE, THE, "A Melodrama" in three acts by BERNARD SHAW, produced in 1897 and published in 1901. Setting: Websterbridge, New Hampshire; 1777.

In the preface to THREE PLAYS FOR PURITANS, of which this is the first, Shaw ridiculed the critics for calling the play advanced: it is hackneyed in structure and plot, Shaw insisted, the play's novelty being its REALISTIC presentation of character. Dick Dudgeon, a Puritan appearing, "like all genuinely religious men, a reprobate and an outcast," acts as he does not for romantic reasons, but for no particular reason, as men often act. Mrs. Dudgeon (like Mrs. Clennam in Dickens's *Little Dorrit*) seems religious only because she is "detestably disagreeable." In his "Notes" to the play, Shaw paid homage to General Burgoyne, who was also a fellow-playwright.

Act I. The vindictively pious Mrs. Dudgeon, whose husband has just died, bullies Essie, the "irregular child" of his brother, who was hanged by the British in one of their attempts to crush the American Revolution. Mrs. Dudgeon is annoyed when the genial minister Anthony Anderson tells her that, before he died, Dudgeon made a new will, which the family has come to hear. The profligate son Dick outrages them by his arrival and his arrogance to all except the despised Essie, but, to his mother's fury, he turns out to be the heir. As the others also turn away from him, he welcomes Essie into his house, and tells her that he has become the "devil's disciple" in reaction to the spirit-breaking sanctimony around him.

Act II. That evening, at his home, Anderson is waiting for Dick. The minister's pretty wife Judith is unhappy that he has invited "a blasphemer and a villain" whom she hates, and is piously severe when Dick appears. Quickly Dick comes to respect Anderson, who is called away during their interview. In his absence, British soldiers arrive and arrest Dick, mistaking him for Anderson. As Judith watches in terror, Dick takes Anderson's coat and coolly agrees to go with them; surreptitiously he warns her to get Anderson to escape and, to allay the soldiers' suspicion about his identity, she kisses him farewell. When Anderson returns and finds out what has happened, he takes Dick's coat, some pistols, and money, and gallops away. Judith tells Essie, "He has gone to save himself. Richard must die."

Act III. Judith is permitted an interview the following morning, and tells Dick that she now loves him for his heroism and despises her husband for having run away. Dick refuses to allow her to save him by revealing his true identity, and disappoints her by saying that he acted as he did not because he loves her, but simply because he could not take his "neck out of the noose and put another man's into it." At the trial, openly scornful of the English, Dick is quickly condemned. Judith cannot contain her agony, and despite her earlier promise not to do so, she reveals that Dick is not her husband; he must nevertheless hang. The suave General Burgoyne tells the presiding major, whom he soon gives up for a hopeless fool, that the rebel troops in the area have beaten the English, who must now grant safe-conduct to the victorious American officer coming to arrange evacuation terms for them. With the noose already around Dick's neck, Anderson appears and saves him: he is the victorious officer, having found, in the "hour of trial," that it was his "destiny to be a man of action." He will make the army his career, and predicts that the idealist Dick "will start presently as the Reverend Richard Dudgeon, and wag his pow in my old pulpit, and give good advice to this silly sentimental little wife of mine." A "fool" in his own eyes but a "hero" to the townsfolk and to Judith, who is now ashamed of having doubted her husband, Dick promises her that he will never reveal her romantic avowal to him.

DEVIL'S GENERAL, THE (*Des Teufels General*), a drama in three acts by CARL ZUCKMAYER, published and produced in 1946. Setting: Berlin, shortly before America's entry into the war (late 1941).

This became the most successful drama about the Nazi military, and it established Zuckmayer as West Germany's leading postwar playwright. Replete with many strong characterizations and theatrically powerful despite some sentimentality and garrulity, it was performed throughout the world and made into a major film. The play aroused controversy because of the inconclusive resolution of the hero's dilemma and the sympathetic portrayal of the popular daredevil Luftwaffe General Harras, modeled after the German World War I ace Ernst Udet, who also served the Nazis loyally though he expressed his opposition to and contempt for them with daring witticisms. Hedda Zinner's (1905–) dramatization of Martha Dodd's novel *General Landt* in 1957 presented a popular East German counter-portrayal of an officer bestialized by Nazism.

Act I. "The Infernal Machine." Youthful General Harras is charming, cheerful, and hard-drinking, as usual, at his party for a fighter squadron leader on leave from the front. But Harras shows signs of nervous tension, knowing that the Gestapo suspects him and that "their snuffle-hounds are leering around every hydrant." His principal antagonist, the Minister of Culture, "translates" Harras's heretical jokes into orthodox sentiments ("What the General is really saying . . ."), but Harras's frankness shocks an industrialist. "The minute I start being careful they'll think my pants are full and they can spit on my head," Harras explains, blaming the industrialist and his friends who "financed these bums" to power. When asked why he himself works for the Nazis, Harras admits he joined the "gang" only because "I'm a fool about flying. Air combat without me—naw, I couldn't stand that." As the festivities go on he also argues against a young pilot's blind nationalistic idealism. With his adjutant and his weather-beaten old chauffeur, both of whom revere him, Harras secretly helps an opera singer, an old flame of his, to save Jewish friends. At the party, too, Harras falls in love with a young actress. He resists the blandishments of the industrialist's daughter, who is attractive but a rabid Nazi. After Harras leaves, a waiter defends his reporting on Harras to the Gestapo. "You want to land in a concentration camp?" he asks, and adds, "Show me a guy who isn't a son of a bitch around here!"

Act II. "Stay of Execution, or The Hand." Harras's worried adjutant and chauffeur await his release by the Gestapo. At last he appears in his apartment, soon followed by the Minister of Culture. The latter gives him ten days to find the saboteurs responsible for the increasing number of defective Luftwaffe planes mysteriously exploding in the air. A tender scene with the young actress inspires Harras and gives him new purpose in life. But he gets increasingly angry as his adjutant is arrested and as he learns of the suicide of the Jews he had tried to help. When the industrialist's daughter comes to seduce the unwilling Harras and threatens to expose him for helping Jews, he kicks her out. Then he and his chief engineer continue their search for the saboteurs.

Act III. "Damnation." Only a few hours remain to find the saboteurs. Preparing for his probable arrest, Harras provides for his chauffeur's future. He is unable to persuade the suspected workers to admit to him that they are in the underground, which would enable Harras to save them from the Gestapo. The idealistic young pilot of the party returns from a visit to the occupied countries, appalled by the atrocities of Extermination Commandos and totally disillusioned about Germany. Then the wife of his squadron leader, who has just been killed in a sabotaged plane, bitterly blames Harras for sending men out to die in a cause Harras himself never believed in. At last Harras discovers the saboteur: it is his friend the chief engineer—working with a whole network of people ashamed of Hitler's Germany. "If Germany wins this war—then Germany is lost. Then the world is lost," the engineer says. Harras accepts this conclusion, declining to denounce his friend and thus save himself or to attempt another escape offered him. "I've been the Devil's General on earth too long," he says, alluding to Hitler. "I'm going to fly an advance mission for him in hell too—in preparation for his imminent arrival." He runs out to one of the defective planes and flies it up—and almost at once it explodes. Delighted with this perfect solution of an awkward case, his enemy, the Minister of Culture, calls Headquarters: "Case closed perfectly. General Harras this moment killed accidentally in the performance of his duties to the Führer and the Third Reich." And he concludes: "Yes, certainly. State funeral, with full military honors."

DEVILS, THE, a play in three acts by JOHN WHITING, published and produced in 1961. Setting: Loudun and Paris, 1623–34.

While based on ALDOUS HUXLEY's historical novel *The Devils of Loudon* (1952), the characters, themes, and even the actions are considerably altered in this play. It consists of short, nervous episodes, many of them barbaric and carnal. They are matched by the sketchy dialogue, which, however, periodically waxes eloquent.

The handsome priest, Urbain Grandier, consciously destroys himself to find God: "My sin, my presumption, my vanity, my love, my hate, my lust. And last I gave myself and so made God." Secretly he marries a young virgin, and he declines the written invitation of Sister Jeanne of the Angels to be the spiritual adviser of St. Ursula's Convent. The hunchbacked prioress, racked by lust for him, becomes possessed by devils—as do the other nuns. They are subdued and the devils are exorcised from their bodies, privately and then publicly. Grandier is envied by the priests for his eloquent sermons, disapproved of by the parishioners for his sensuousness and urbanity, and feared by Richelieu for his political influence. He is condemned for instigating the devils, brutally tortured, and sentenced to burn at the stake. Grandier and Jeanne meet for the first time as the mutilated, shaven priest is taken to his death. "They always spoke of your beauty," Jeanne says, staring at him. "Now I see it with my own eyes and I know it to be true." Grandier replies, "Look at this thing which I am, and learn the meaning of love."

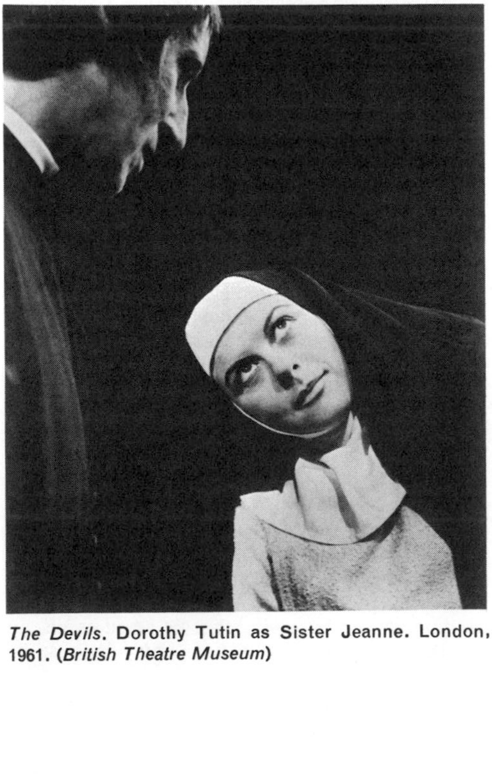

The Devils. Dorothy Tutin as Sister Jeanne. London, 1961. (*British Theatre Museum*)

As the crowds snatch bits of his corpse to use as charms, Jeanne cries out for him, "Grandier! Grandier!"

DIANA AND TUDA (*Diana e la Tuda*), a drama in three acts by LUIGI PIRANDELLO, produced in 1926 and published in 1927. Setting: contemporary Italy.

In this drama of aesthetic polemics Pirandello's spokesman is Nono Giuncano, an old sculptor who has become dissatisfied with his statues because they are death-like in their fixity. His pupil, Sirio Dossi, is obsessed by opposite frustrations: the eternal mutability that prevents his capturing and immortalizing life in his statues.

Tuda, a beautiful model, poses for Dossi's statue of Diana. She loves him and wants to be considered more than a mere model: "Alive! eyes, mouth, arms, fingers, legs—look at them. I move them, and this is flesh; feel it: warm." To Dossi, "What counts is the statue—not you. Marble: it's matter; not your flesh." In order to retain her as a model she forces him to marry her. But Dossi makes her suffer. He continues relations with a mistress and Tuda, who yearns for his love, becomes haggard. She offers herself to Dossi's noble master, Giuncano, who loves but refuses her, and she tells Dossi that she can no longer pose for him. During a final debate, Dossi thinks Tuda is about to harm his statue of Diana—and threatens her. Enraged at all Dossi has done to her, Giuncano leaps at him and strangles him. Tuda falls weeping over Dossi's corpse, her life finally emptied of all meaning: now she is neither model nor wife.

DIARY OF ANNE FRANK, THE, a play in two acts by Frances Goodrich and ALBERT HACKETT, produced in 1955 and published in 1956. Setting: a warehouse and office building in Amsterdam, 1942–45.

This dramatization by Albert Hackett and his wife of Anne Frank's *Het Achterhuis* (1947), published in English as *The Diary of a Young Girl* (1952), won the Pulitzer Prize and many other awards. Anne Frank, born in 1929, perished with her family in a Nazi concentration camp shortly after their capture; only her father survived. The play, like the diary, has moved audiences all over the world. Both works are bittersweet portrayals of a Jewish adolescent under stress, the more poignant because of audiences' awareness of the cataclysmic events outside the warehouse and the gruesome aftermath.

Ready to leave Amsterdam after the war, Mr. Frank reveals his daughter's diary. The scene shifts to the hiding place the Franks occupied from July 1942 to August 1944. Arriving in their upstairs hideout, where they can make no noise whatever during the day, Anne decides to think of it as a strange summer resort. She is strongly attached to her father, argues incessantly with her mother, and has a youthful romance with the shy son of the family hiding them. There are joys and heartbreaks, festivities and fights. Just before the hideout is discovered by the Nazis, Anne describes to her young boyfriend the lovely day she sees through the skylight.

DIETZ, Howard (1896–   ), American librettist and press agent, wrote and collaborated on some of the most popular musical stage and screen hits of his time. Notable among the former are *Dear Sir* (1924), with music by Jerome Kern; *The Band Wagon* (1931), an extravaganza written with GEORGE S. KAUFMAN that satirizes musical comedy; *Sadie Thompson* (1944), a musical version, written with the Russian-born director Rouben Mamoulian (1898–   ; music by Vernon Duke) of John B. Colton (1874–1960) and Clemence Randolph's (1881–1970) adaptation of SOMERSET MAUGHAM's *Rain;* and *Inside U.S.A.* (1948), a musical revue suggested by John Gunther's book by the same name, and with sketches contributed by others, including MOSS HART. Dietz has also adapted foreign operas and operettas.

DIFFICULT HOUR, THE (*Den svåra stunden*), a trilogy of one-act plays by PÄR LAGERKVIST, published in 1918 and produced in 1919. Setting: a darkened stage, occasional grotesque forms.

These simply set but bizarre episodes portray climactic moments in the minds of characters just before or after death, and (particularly in III) visions of the land of the dead. Brief, EXPRESSIONISTIC, nightmarish moralities with violent emotion but scant plot, they convey a sense of life's meaninglessness and brutality. The trilogy's premiere—the first production of a Lagerkvist drama—took place in Düsseldorf: it enraged the audience, who attacked the director outside the theatre.

I. A Man in Tails excitedly describes a car accident and explains to a hunchback how he could not help stealing his girl: "I was young and all the rest of it. . . . And you . . . well, there was that matter of the hump." Smugly confident of winning the girl tonight, he nevertheless feels strange. He attributes the feeling to the accident, which he continues to describe. One of his fellow passengers "got it right in the stomach so that his eyes stuck way out of his head!" he laughs: "I thought I'd split!" Continuing in a monologue punctuated by the hunchback's laconic comments, the Man in Tails belligerently justifies taking the girl away from his companion, who has loved her for years though she made fun of him: "My God, everyone wants to live . . . and you . . . well, you were so frail," explains the Man in Tails. But he becomes increasingly guilt-ridden over what he has done. "Oh, it's dreadful, dreadful! . . . It was I . . . *I* who was responsible for it," he exclaims: "I drove you to your death!" Suddenly he draws back, terrified by a new realization. "Help! Help! You're dead!" he screams. The hunchback laughs: "He, he, he!—And you are too." As the Man in Tails collapses, the hunchback walks into the darkness, tapping his cane: "Well, I'll be on my way again . . ."

II. An elderly man lies motionless on a hospital bed while two old gentlemen quietly chat about him. "They say he'll die at nine o'clock," one tells his companion; when the other suggests that "a little later, say eleven o'clock" might be better, the first is adamant: "It's been decided once and for all. AND IT CANNOT BE CHANGED!" As they discuss his life, it is dramatized in fragments. He tells a woman that he is going to die, and begs her to reciprocate his love. Nonchalantly she agrees, but demands he get her fancy kitchen supplies. "But I'm going to die. . . . At nine o'clock, nine o'clock!" he protests, to which she replies, "That's none of my business!" A stationmaster blows a shrill whistle. The two old gentlemen realize that the elderly man probably is dead now. "Kind-hearted boy, downright kind-hearted," one of them remarks: "Perhaps, a little too soft and a little too concerned about himself, but such a kind heart." When his companion remarks that death is "dreadful," he disagrees: "At all odds it must be an experience." A laborer finally succeeds in repairing a cable, and retrieves an important telegram. "It only said: The canary bird died, you swindler!" he tells the old gentleman, who wonders what it can mean. "I can't make heads or tails of it," the laborer says. Then they go out.

III. A desperate little boy, wondering where he should go in the darkness, seeks advice from a bickering old couple. "We just sit here and sicken each other," these two, both of them dead, tell the boy. "We're happy together in a way." The howling of their pet monkey further frightens the boy. "Was it better down there—living?" they ask him. "It was all so wonderful," the child exclaims, reminiscing about his joyful life and the mother he loved. "I was out in the woods every day and I had a mill wheel," he recalls: "And the whole garden was full of flowers. . . . And the birds sang all evening." The old people corrupt the naïve boy. "It's hell," the old man says when the boy asks where he is; "heaven is even worse, a thousand times worse, even, because it's just nothingness!" The old woman persuades the child that she is his grandmother; eager to be with her always, the ensnared boy gives his candle to their yelping monkey—and descends into the darkness.

DIFF'RENT, a play in two acts by EUGENE O'NEILL, produced in 1920 and published in 1921. Setting: a New England seaport village, 1890 and 1920.

Though there was an official attempt to have it banned in New York, this NATURALISTIC play—a favorite of O'Neill's, who regarded it as "a tale of the eternal, romantic idealist who is in all of us," as quoted in Barbara and Arthur Gelb's *O'Neill*—was a success neither with critics nor with audiences.

Emma Crosby is appalled to find out that her fiancé, Captain Caleb Williams, was once seduced by a South Sea Island native. Everyone in town regards that episode as a big joke on Caleb, including Emma's family, who accuse her of "makin' a durned creepin'-Jesus out of him! What d'you want to marry, anyhow—a man or a sky-pilot?" But Emma stubbornly breaks off their engagement because Caleb has not lived up to her ideal: "What you done is just what any other man would have done—and being like them is exactly what'll keep you from ever seeing my meaning. . . . I've always had the idea that you was—diff'rent. . . . You've busted something way down inside me—and I can't love you no more." A sexually repressed Puritan spinster thirty years later, Emma suddenly lusts for Caleb's rotten young nephew. She absurdly primps herself and simpers for the young wastrel, who, to get her money, encourages Emma's pathetically passionate lovemaking and promises to marry her. Having courted her faithfully for almost a lifetime, Caleb goes disgustedly to the barn to hang himself: "Folks be all crazy and rotten to the core and I'm done with the whole kit and caboodle of 'em." When the nephew remarks that he could not possibly love such an old woman, "And I'll say you look it, too!" Emma realizes that the nephew has made a fool of her. Grief-stricken and like a sleepwalker, she follows in Caleb's footsteps: "Wait, Caleb, I'm going down to the barn."

DINNER AT EIGHT, a play in three acts by GEORGE S. KAUFMAN and EDNA FERBER, published and produced in 1932. Setting: New York, a week in the early 1930's.

This popular play, filmed in 1933 and revived on Broadway in 1966, is a multiepisodic melodrama of New York life behind the scenes.

Millicent Jordan, a fashionable matron, has invited to dinner an English lord and lady and various other people she considers suitable company for them. The insipid Mrs. Jordan, who does not know that her husband suffers from a serious heart condition and that the family business is on the verge of ruin, is equally unaware of the crises faced by her guests. An aging actress, a beauty once adored by Jordan, is bankrupt and wants him to buy back the stock she owns in his business; Jordan's wealthy "associate," a brash and uncouth operator, secretly has bought the stock and is about to take over Jordan's company; the associate's coarse, gum-chewing blond wife excoriates him for his crooked deals, and is having an affair with Jordan's doctor—who is tired of her; the Jordans' daughter is infatuated with a washed-up movie idol, a drunkard glad to accept Mrs. Jordan's dinner invitation—but he commits suicide that same afternoon. Oblivious to all these things, the foolish Mrs. Jordan is distraught when the guests of honor at the last minute break their promises to attend. A substitute couple is hurriedly summoned. As the curtain falls, the company chatter and laugh as they go into the Jordan dining room.

DIRTY HANDS (*Les Mains sales*), a play in seven scenes by JEAN-PAUL SARTRE, published and

Dinner at Eight. The crooked operator (Paul Harvey) with his wife (Judith Wood) and their maid (Janet Fox). New York 1932. (*Culver Pictures*)

produced in 1948. Setting: the imaginary Balkan country of Illyria, 1943 and 1945.

Also translated as *Red Gloves* and as *Crime Passionnel,* this suspenseful play within a play was Sartre's most popular success on the stage, as a film, and as a best seller. Hugo becomes the existentialist hero when he makes his assassination of Hoederer meaningful with his final gesture, but it is Hoederer who is the most magnetic and interesting character. Sartre's ideal political man, he dramatizes the relation of means and ends. This was the play's principal theme according to Sartre, though the play was generally interpreted as an attack on Communism.

Scene 1. Hugo Barine, a bitter young intellectual of a well-to-do family, has just been released from prison and visits Olga Lorame, a Party worker formerly in love with him. Gunmen come to wipe out the "undisciplined bourgeois intellectual," Hugo, but Olga cites his former service to the Party: Hugo "shot down Hoederer despite his bodyguards and managed to disguise a political assassination as a *crime passionnel*." But Hugo's real motives are not yet clear, and Olga persuades the gunmen to give her three hours to discover them and determine if Hugo is still "salvageable." After the gunmen leave Hugo tells his story. "The fact is that I pulled the trigger," he begins. "But what it means, that's something else again."

Scene 2. It is two years earlier. The Party's newspaper editor, Hugo, is dissatisfied with his desk job. "You talk too much," Olga cautions him as he discusses his family and his general disaffections, and questions her on Hoederer, a high Party official. One of the revolutionaries is incensed by Hoederer's plan for a coalition with the fascist Royalists and the bourgeois Liberals. Considering this a betrayal of the workers, the outvoted revolutionary agrees to let Hugo, who is similarly incensed and is eager to prove himself, become Hoederer's secretary and in that position find the opportunity to kill the well-protected leader.

Scene 3. Hugo and his frivolous wife, Jessica, settle at Hoederer's country house. As they play "pretend" games about the Revolution, Hoederer's guards come to search them. Fearful that they will find his pistol, Hugo refuses, standing on his "human dignity." The guards sneer at the well-bred Communist and call Hoederer. Immediately and completely in authority, Hoederer reconciles the squabblers and agrees to take Hugo's word that he has no weapons. But Jessica thereupon invites a search. A tense scene follows, but nothing is found. After Hoederer leaves, Jessica laughingly betrays her attraction to him and remarks that this is the first time she has seen her husband "at grips with real men." She laughs at Hugo: "My poor little darling, if you want to convince me that you're going to become a murderer, you should start by convincing yourself." They scuffle in semiearnest for the pistol, which she has hidden in her dress. "Careful!" Jessica cries out as Hugo seizes it: "It'll go off!"

Scene 4. Jessica curiously examines Hoederer's office and flirts with him. Waiting for the Royalist and Liberal emissaries, Hoederer remarks to Hugo that this would be a good time for his enemies to kill him. He admits that "in principle, I have no objection to political assassination." Hugo starts to drink heavily, working up the courage to shoot Hoederer. Before he can do so the emissaries arrive. Negotiations follow, Hoederer insisting that his party be given equal power in a new central committee—a demand Hoederer wins because the Communists will be vital to the government when the Soviet Union occupies Illyria after the expected defeat of Germany. Furious at Hoederer's "treason to the workers," Hugo is about to shoot him when a bomb explodes in the room—but without hurting anyone. Jessica runs in: "Was Hoederer killed?" Hoederer dryly replies: "Your husband is all right," and ushers his visitors out. Increasingly drunk, Hugo talks wildly and almost reveals his intended assassination of Hoederer—which he feels he has botched. Jessica covers up for him. "You don't know him," she assures the suspicious guards. "Nothing he says really means anything."

Scene 5. Olga, who threw the bomb, warns Hugo that unless he immediately performs his task the Party will consider him a traitor and send someone else to assassinate Hoederer. Later Jessica asks Hugo to reason with and persuade—rather than kill—Hoederer. As they argue, Hoederer himself appears, dejected and lonesome. He explains how "revolutionary parties are organized to take power," and that his is the most practical policy to achieve the party's ultimate aim. Hugo disagrees, "It has only one goal: to make our ideas . . . victorious," and he protests lying to the rank-and-file. Hoederer stresses the need of "using every means at hand to abolish classes." When Hugo objects to the Party's befouling itself by collaborating, Hoederer describes the impossibility of being pure in practical politics. "I have dirty hands," he says. "I've plunged them in excrement and blood." He scornfully dismisses Hugo's willingness to do the same as an aristocratic gesture confined to "red gloves, that's elegant. It's the rest that scares you." Though he wants to help them, Hoederer has no illusions about men: "I love them for what they are." Hugo, he knows, "detest[s] men because you detest yourself"; he is a "destroyer" whose purity is sterile: "You don't want to change the world, you want to blow it up." Again wrought up, Hugo is about to shoot Hoederer when the bodyguards come in.

Scene 6. Jessica reveals to Hoederer her husband's intention to kill him. Instead of having Hugo disarmed and humiliated, Hoederer courageously demonstrates Hugo's inability to murder a man merely because he disagrees with him. Hugo admits his impotence as a killer—as well as his admiration for Hoederer. Disconsolate, he goes to the garden to ponder Hoederer's offer of help and his proposal that they continue to work together. Jessica comes out of hiding and tries to seduce Hoederer. Hugo happens to return just as they kiss. He snatches the pistol: "You see, Hoederer, I am looking you straight in the eyes and I'm aiming and my hand's not shaking and I don't give a bloody damn for what's going on in your head." He shoots Hoederer, who lies to save Hugo from the bodyguards: "I've been sleeping with his wife." And he adds, dying, "What a goddamn waste!"

Scene 7. Hugo finishes his story. He still agonizes over his real reason for shooting Hoederer: chance helped, but was his act one of jealousy or was it political passion triggered by "a little jolt needed to make my task easier?" He knows that he "loved Hoederer more than I ever loved anyone in the world," recalls the magnetic "reality" of the man, is tortured by the nagging awareness of Hoederer's death, and persuaded of his own inadequacies as a revolutionary. Olga is satisfied that Hugo is salvageable. But he must play a new role because while he was in prison the Communist Party had changed its policy: it entered the alliances envisioned by Hoederer—who therefore is now considered a martyr. Hugo is horrified to hear Olga use Hoederer's phrases to explain his plans, even the need to lie: "One doesn't give the troops a play-by-play description of the battle." He laughs bitterly when she asks him to forget his Party cover-name of Raskolnikov—the assassin of Hoederer whom, the Party later announced, they had executed. Hugo can now make his choice. Though he still worships Hoederer and still does not know exactly why he shot him, he knows now "why it was right to kill him: because his policy was wrong." Hugo refuses to "dishonor" himself by fulfilling the requirements of a changed Party line. "A man like Hoederer doesn't die by accident. He dies for his ideas, for his political program; he's responsible for his death," he tells Olga: "If I openly claim my crime and declare myself Raskolnikov and am willing to pay the necessary price, then he will have the death he deserves." Only now can Hugo really act with responsibility. He kicks open the door and defiantly shouts at the gunmen returning for their answer, "Unsalvageable!"

DISRAELI, a play in four acts by LOUIS NAPOLEON PARKER, published and produced in 1911. Setting: England, early 1870's.

Presented as a portrayal of "some of the racial, social, and political prejudices [Disraeli] fought against and conquered," this deft melodrama, an immensely popular vehicle for George Arliss (also filmed), depicts Disraeli's maneuvers against Russian spies (his secretary and a beautiful lady) conniving to beat England to the Suez Canal purchase. The Bank of England refuses to finance the purchase, and a cooperative Jewish banker loses his fortune at the critical moment. The suave but ruthless Disraeli threatens to smash the Bank of England unless it underwrites the credit essential to the nation. Its director angrily submits to force, but a charming girl, whose romance the Prime Minister is assisting, exclaims, "Oh, Mr. Disraeli; thank God you have such power." In the third act curtain that made the play, Disraeli replies, "I haven't, dear child; but he doesn't know that." At a reception, the successful Disraeli is hailed for making Victoria Empress of India, the romantic match is approved, the groom and both bankers receive royal honors, and his ailing wife appears, as Disraeli, the worried husband, still clutches the telegram he has been afraid to open.

DIVINE WORDS (*Divinas palabras*), a "tragicomedy of village life" in three acts by RAMÓN MARÍA DEL VALLE-INCLÁN, published in 1920 and produced in 1933. Setting: the parish of Viana del Prior in Galicia (northwest Spain), early twentieth century.

Written in 1913, this many-charactered and episodic folkplay juxtaposes an idyllic setting with a plot of horrendous barbarism. Fusing Valle-Inclán's *comedia bárbara* (savage comedy) and ESPERPENTO, it was far ahead of its time with its nudity and black humor.

Before the church, a variously named vagabond sneers at his mistress and their child, and at the old sexton. The latter's sister, a pauper, pulls the cart on which lies her idiot child, a hydrocephalic dwarf. After the sister's agonizing death, Mary Gaila, the sexton's fair and lustful wife, preempts the idiot for profit. Plying him with liquor to make him swear and display his enormous sex organ, Mary travels about and collects offerings from the country folk. She frequents the taverns, shamelessly cavorts with the men, and has a passionate affair with the vagabond. Her humiliated and distraught husband gets drunk at home and tries to seduce their dull-witted daughter. When the monster dies in a tavern, Mary Gaila angrily wails that God "took away my living and left me with misery." She transports the corpse home—romping lasciviously with goblins en route—and then forces her daughter to take it to the house of her sister-in-law. There hogs gnaw off half the corpse's face before they are chased away. Mary Gaila, discovered copulating in the fields, is abused by an irate mob, who strip her and transport her naked atop a wagon to her husband's church. The sexton attempts to commit suicide; he fails, and then takes the hand of his naked adulterous wife. Frightened, the crowds disperse, as a vision of the idiot's huge head appears in the form of an angel. The sexton leads Mary into the resplendent sanctuary, whose religious prestige, "in that superstitious world of rustic souls, is conjured up by the incomprehensible Latin of the DIVINE WORDS."

DOCK BRIEF, THE, a play in two scenes by JOHN MORTIMER, published and produced in 1958. Setting: an English prison cell, 1950's.

Originally produced as a radio play in 1957, this comedy has a cast of two pathetic characters.

Wilfred Morgenhall, a seedy old lawyer who has waited hopefully all his life to be chosen for a dock brief (charity case), finally gets his chance. The defendant is a simple bird-fancier who has murdered his irritating wife. Morgenhall dreams of the brilliant defense that will make him famous, as the prisoner obligingly acts out various parts in the coming trial. Later it is revealed that Morgenhall has bungled his chance—in fact, he did not say a word in court. As with the girl he once loved, at the big moment "a tremendous exhaustion" overcame him. "I was tired out by the long wait, and when the opportunity came—all I could think of was sleep," he explains. "I had lived through that moment so many times. . . . When it came, I was tired of it," he concludes: "I wanted to be alone in my room, in the darkness, with a soft pillow round my ears. . . . So I failed." He is crushed to learn that his client has been freed: the defense was judged so incompetent that the case was not even sent to the jury. But the prisoner persuades the disheartened Morgenhall that he had made a brilliant defense. "Your artfulness saved me," he says, calling it "the dumb tactics." The two leave happily as Morgenhall, whistling and dancing, builds up new illusory hopes: "As your legal adviser I will follow at a discreet distance, to straighten out such little tangles as you may hope to leave in your wake."

DOCTOR KNOCK (*Knock ou le triomphe de la médecine*), a comedy in three acts by JULES ROMAINS, produced in 1923 and published in 1924. Setting: the French provinces, early 1920's.

This became Romains's most popular play. Almost immediately it was translated and produced by HARLEY GRANVILLE-BARKER, and it brought Romains international fame as a playwright. Louis Jouvet, who acted Knock for twenty-five years, called it *"un chef-d'œuvre dramatique."* Like Sganarelle in Molière's *Le Médecin malgré lui,* Knock is a charlatan. However, Romains primarily satirized not medical humbug but—in accord with his concept of *unanimisme*—collective social gullibility.

Act I. Dr. Knock is a forty-year-old quack. He has just bought the practice of Dr. Parpalaid, who, with his wife, is driving Knock in an ancient automobile. As it stalls, Knock is surprised to learn how unprofitable Parpalaid's practice has been, but is satisfied that the townspeople are not addicted to adultery, drugs, "queer religions, superstitions, Orders of Druids," and other potential rival cults. "You have made a mess of a most magnificent opportunity," he tells Parpalaid and, as they try to get the automobile moving, Knock makes his plans: "The medical age now can start."

Act II. Knock has the town crier announce a free weekly consultation hour "to help check the alarming increase of diseases," expresses amazement at his predecessor's cavalier dismissal of patients' minor complaints, and persuades the town crier that he is seriously ill. With equal psychological cunning he enlists the aid of the druggist and the schoolmaster. Shocked that hitherto "those wretched folks have been left to their own devices—hygienically—prophylactically!" Knock arranges for illustrated lectures on disease. Then he tends to those gathered for his free consultation, adeptly bilking and frightening them with suggestions of serious illness. The village idiots who come to laugh at him run off in panic as other waiting-room occupants are awed into respectful—and terrified—silence.

Act III. Some months later the local hotel is a hospital and the town a disease-obsessed society. "To rescue and resolve each one of them into a scientific individuality, into a medical existence"—that is Knock's self-proclaimed task. To the visiting old Dr. Parpalaid Knock glories in the vision of his clients, "250 clinical thermometers lifted in unison and gently placed and held beneath 250 silent tongues" every morning. Knock himself is overwhelmed by his powers, he realizes with trepidation. "Almost unconsciously" he starts to diagnose anybody he sees—"so much so that lately, d'you know, I've had to stop looking at myself in the mirror." Parpalaid now wonders if the observations he has made about himself perhaps "fit in, so to speak, with this automatic diagnosis of yours." Knock's face lights up as he invites his predecessor to lunch—and to his consulting room to see "whatever may need to be done about the state of your health."

DOCTOR'S DILEMMA, THE, "A Tragedy" in five acts by BERNARD SHAW, produced in 1906 and published in 1911. Setting: England, 1903.

In a "Preface on Doctors" to this tragicomedy of a dishonorable genius and of medical ignorance and cupidity, Shaw discussed vivisection and various other medical "infamies" of private practice and their human, economic, and historical roots. Because of the great necessity for doctors, Shaw concluded, the profession must be socialized —that is, brought under effective public control. The play itself exposes professional pomposity in its doctors gallery of Dickensian characters who are confronted by a flamboyant artist and his strong-willed wife.

Act I. The newly knighted Sir Colenso Ridgeon, the discoverer of an inoculation that must be given only when the patient's "opsonin index" is in its proper phase, is visited by various colleagues who have come to congratulate him and discuss their own pet theories, among them the loquacious Sir Ralph Bloomfield Bonington ("B.B."), who is responsible for Ridgeon's knighthood because of his accidentally successful use of Ridgeon's opsonin on the prince. After they leave, Ridgeon finally consents to see Jennifer Dubedat, who begs him to cure her tubercular husband. Reluctant because he has room for only one more patient for his special treatment, Ridgeon soon becomes interested in Jennifer, and after she shows him Dubedat's drawings, he agrees to have her bring her husband to a dinner where his worthiness to be saved will be judged by himself and his colleagues.

Act II. After the dinner, Jennifer is assured that Louis Dubedat, who has charmed the company, will be taken on. When the couple has left, however, the doctors discover that a maid in the hotel is Dubedat's deserted wife, that he has shamelessly touched each of them (including an almost destitute general practitioner, Blenkinsop) for a loan, and that he has made off with a gold cigaret case. As they reconsider Dubedat's position, Blenkinsop reveals that he too is tubercular. Who, now, should be the one to be cured, "that honest decent man Blenkinsop, or that rotten blackguard of an artist"? "If I let Blenkinsop die, at least nobody can say I did it because I wanted to marry his widow," says Ridgeon; but he decides to resolve his dilemma by curing Blenkinsop and entrusting Dubedat to Bonington's care.

Act III. The doctors arrive in Dubedat's studio, and in a long, amusing scene they are shocked by his brazen proposals for further loans and blackmail, an announcement that his marriage with the hotel maid was mutually bigamous, his views on science, religion, and morals, and his claim to be "a disciple of Bernard Shaw." Though they admire his brilliant drawings, they give him up as a hopeless scoundrel. However, Bonington agrees to take his case, and Ridgeon reassures the disappointed Jennifer, who tells him how she idolizes Dubedat, that "the one chance of preserving the hero" lies in Bonington's treatment.

Act IV. The doctors are discussing Dubedat's imminent death, which Ridgeon attributes to Bonington's inoculating in the improper phase of the "opsonin index." An inept reporter is allowed to join them as Dubedat is wheeled into his studio. Courageous but histrionic, he makes the most of his death scene, exhorting Jennifer to remarry and always look beautiful. Then he utters his creed: "I believe in Michael Angelo, Velasquez, and Rembrandt; in the might of design, the mystery of color, the redemption of all things by Beauty everlasting, and the message of Art that has made these hands blessed. Amen. Amen." Thereupon he dies—"splendidly," as Bonington says. Jennifer at once leaves to change into beautiful clothes, as Dubedat had bidden her to do, and returns to shake the hands of all the doctors but Ridgeon.

Act V. At a Bond Street gallery, Ridgeon looks at Jennifer's biography of Dubedat, *The Story of a King of Men,* and admires the exhibition of his pictures. Overhearing Ridgeon's comment of "clever brute," Jennifer congratulates him on his cure of Blenkinsop and reproaches him for having killed Dubedat. He tells her that he did it because he loves her, but is quickly chastened by her "You! an elderly man!" and by her contempt for his heartlessness and inability to understand Dubedat, about whom he attempts to disillusion her. When she reveals that, in accord with Dubedat's last wishes, she has remarried, he departs: "Then I have committed a purely disinterested murder!"

DOCTOR'S DUTY, THE (*Il dovere del medico*), a one-act play by LUIGI PIRANDELLO, published in

1912 and produced in 1913. Setting: a city in contemporary southern Italy.

Pirandello's third play was originally a short story he had published in 1910.

An otherwise admirable family man has been seduced by a tramp, caught, and shot at by her worthless husband. He has killed the husband in self-defense, and then, humiliated and guilt-ridden, has shot and almost succeeded in killing himself. Now his forgiving wife reveals that he will be tried and perhaps condemned, despite his self-punishment and expiation. He bitterly attacks the doctor for having saved him for such degradation, proving to him that it was wrong to do so. He also proves to the lawyer that he has already punished himself by attempting suicide and that the law therefore has no further hold on him. In a rage he tears at himself until his wounds reopen. He is dying, but the doctor will not again do his duty: "He's right. Didn't you hear him? I can't! I mustn't!"

DOG BENEATH THE SKIN, THE; OR, WHERE IS FRANCIS? a play in three acts by W. H. AUDEN and CHRISTOPHER ISHERWOOD, published in 1935 and produced in 1936. Setting: various imaginary places in Europe and Great Britain.

This is a raucous verse satire in the tradition of GILBERT and Sullivan and of BERTOLT BRECHT, loosely episodic and with musical choruses.

Alan Norman, a young man of Pressan Ambo, goes to seek a missing heir, Sir Francis Crewe. Accompanied by an intelligent local dog, Alan has many adventures. With two journalists he meets on a ship, he arrives at Ostnia during public executions ("He can't have been more than nineteen, I should say. / He must have been full of Vitamin A," remarks a court lady), goes through the red-light district where "Plato's halves are at last united," is rescued from a Westland lunatic asylum (reminiscent of a scene in Ibsen's PEER GYNT), visits a hospital, and then a hotel, where he falls into the clutches of a cheap cabaret performer. The missing Francis Crewe finally is revealed, disguised beneath the dog's skin whence he has observed the "obscene, cruel, hypocritical, mean, vulgar" degeneracy of Pressan Ambo's inhabitants. At their return, the vicar delivers a hysterical long prose sermon. Publicly Francis sheds his dog's skin and leaves to find and fight for a better land, while the pillars of the town turn into animals.

DOLL'S HOUSE, A (*Et dukkehjem*), a play in three acts by HENRIK IBSEN, published and produced in 1879. Setting: a contemporary Norwegian residence, December 24–26.

If not Ibsen's greatest play, *A Doll's House* certainly spread his fame furthest. It was begun (and is often cited) as a propaganda piece for women's rights, which has had renewed appeal in recent years, and stimulated a production of a sequel in DENMARK. But the dramatic poet in Ibsen prevailed and wrought a less tendentious and a more human and universal work. Its characters are subtly rounded, and its themes of individuality, freedom, and responsibility transcend specific, dated issues. Nora has been played by many European and American stars. In 1883 and 1884 it was performed in America by Helena Modjeska and others as *The Child Wife* and under other titles, and in England as *Creditors* (1889). As early as 1884 it had appeared there in HENRY ARTHUR JONES's free adaptation *Breaking a Butterfly*, in which Nora repents of her rebellion. The final sound of the closing door reverberated throughout Europe, where Nora's action became a major debating topic. To forestall someone else's "barbaric deed of violence," Ibsen himself reluctantly drafted an alternate "happy" ending, in which Nora stays for the sake of her children. He did not, however, publish it, nor has it ever been performed with any success.

Act I. Nora Helmer happily comes home after Christmas shopping for her husband Torvald and their three children. She overtips the porter and munches some macaroons, but hides the confections bag when her husband comes in. Sternly but gently he chides his "little spendthrift," whom he babies affectionately. As Torvald expects his "little lark" and "squirrel" to do, she manages charmingly to wheedle money from him. She is visited by her old schoolfriend Kristine Linde, who has recently been widowed and, feeling lonesome and empty, has come to town to seek employment. Nora promises to get her a job in the bank whose president Torvald will become on the first of the year, and then tells her of their former tribulations. Years ago, Torvald's life had depended on his being taken to Italy for a rest, and Nora herself had to raise the money for the trip. Because Torvald would not allow borrowing, she had told him that the money came from her father, who died shortly thereafter. To date, she has secretly worked at odd jobs and used part of her allowance to pay up the debt. Now Nora rejoices in seeing her difficulties soon ended by Torvald's raise, and in thoughts of redecorating her home and spending more time with her children. After Torvald promises Mrs. Linde a job in his bank, they leave with Dr. Rank, an old and sick family friend. Nora plays with her children, but is suddenly interrupted by Nils Krogstad, a bank employee whom Torvald is firing and who turns out to be Nora's creditor. He insists that she must save his job: if not, he will tell Torvald not only that she borrowed money, but also that she had forged her father's name to the note. Because she did it to spare her dying father and save her husband's life, Nora can see nothing morally or legally wrong in her action. But her confidence falters when her husband refuses to listen to her request to retain Krogstad, a widower with children. Torvald condemns him for having once committed forgery and then lied, and deplores the morally debilitating effect on children of guilty, dishonest parents. Alone at last, Nora echoes his words and applies them to herself in terror: "Harm my children!—Corrupt my home! . . . It could never, never be true!"

Act II. It is Christmas Day, and the tree now

stands in the corner, stripped. Despite Nora's pleas, Torvald sends off the dismissal letter and, mistaking the cause of her terror of Krogstad, reassures her, "I have strength and courage for us both. My shoulders are broad—I'll bear the burden." Now sure that Torvald will sacrifice himself for her and take the blame once he learns the truth, Nora vows that "he mustn't—never, never! Anything but that!" She starts telling her secret to Dr. Rank, the cynical old friend who suffers mortally from a congenital disease inherited through his father's gay "exploits." But when Dr. Rank tells her that he loves her, Nora is unable to ask him for the money, as she had intended to do. In response to Torvald's letter, Krogstad comes to blackmail him for a new and higher position. Though Nora vows that she will kill herself, he leaves in Torvald's mailbox a letter revealing Nora's loan and forgery. She confesses the full story to Mrs. Linde, insisting that she must not allow the "wonderful thing" that is sure to happen —her husband's sacrifice for her. Mrs. Linde goes to appeal to Krogstad, who, it turns out, once loved her; and Nora hysterically dances a tarantella to distract Torvald, and obtains his promise not to open his mailbox until after the dress ball the next night. "I've thirty-one hours left to live," Nora tells herself.

Act III. Though Krogstad is now willing, for Mrs. Linde's sake, to withdraw his charges, she insists he not retrieve his letter: "This wretched business must no longer be kept secret; it's time those two came to a thorough understanding." Torvald returns from the ball with Nora. His ardor had been inflamed by liquor and her dance, and he can spare nothing more than a few pat phrases for Dr. Rank, whose death is now unexpectedly imminent. Nora insists that Torvald go to read his mail. She is about to leave and commit suicide when Torvald rushes in. Dramatically she insists, "I won't have you suffer for it! I won't have you take the blame!" But Torvald quickly reveals his true nature to her. Enraged, he accuses her of being totally unprincipled—"no religion, no moral code, no sense of duty"—and bemoans the inevitable scandal and his endangered position. As Nora goes to the adjoining room to change from her party costume to an everyday dress, he tells her that though they must continue to keep up appearances, she "won't be allowed to bring up the children. . . . There [also] can be no further thought of happiness between us." Just then comes a remorseful note from Krogstad, who returns the forged I.O.U. Jubilantly announcing that "I'm saved!," Torvald now is willing to forgive Nora and take her back: "I'll cherish you as if you were a little dove I'd rescued from the claws of some dreadful hawk." Instead, she insists on their having a "serious talk"—the first they have ever had. In the climactic scene of the play, she tells him that she has been no more than a doll wife in his house, and will now leave him. Torvald lost her love when the "wonderful thing" that she "hoped for with such terror" did not happen, and she dismisses his claim that "one doesn't sacrifice one's honor for love's sake": "Millions of women have done so." Also dismissing his enumeration of her "sacred" duties, she is determined first of all to do her duty to herself, to educate herself and find out who is right, she or society and its laws. She returns his ring, demands back hers, and leaves, never to return unless some day both of them should change so miraculously that their "life together might truly be a marriage." The curtain falls to the sound of the closing of the outside door after her.

DOMINICAN REPUBLIC, THE, emerged independently out of Santo Domingo in 1844, its culture Hispanic but tempered by the legacy of the African slaves imported in colonial times. The "father" of the Dominican Republic's drama was Felix María del Monte (1819–99), author of the national anthem and a number of plays, including a dramatization of a national catastrophe, *El General Antonio Duvergé o Las víctimas del once de abril* (1856). Ulises Heureaux, Jr. (1876–1938), son of the Negro dictator, wrote over a dozen produced plays, some of them histories, including *De director a ministro* (1926). The occupation of the United States Marines (1916–24) inspired dramatic activity, some of it nationalist. So too did the dictatorship of Trujillo (1930–61); the triumph of his wife María Martínez de Trujillo's *Falsa amistad* (1946) resulted in the establishment of the Teatro Escuela de Arte Nacional. It encouraged the formation of other theatre groups and the activity of native dramatists. Notable are Franklin Domínguez (1913–), author of puppet plays and biblical and metaphysical dramas, as well as a distinguished domestic tragedy, *Espigas maduras* (1960); and Máximo Avilés Blonda Acosta (1931–), a poet and critic who became director of the University theatre and turned to the drama with *Las manos vacías* (1960), a shattering play about an amnesiac priest and a German concentration camp officer.

For further information see LATIN AMERICA.

DOÑA ROSITA, THE SPINSTER, OR THE LANGUAGE OF THE FLOWERS (*Doña Rosita la soltera, o el lenguaje de las flores*), a play in three acts by FEDERICO GARCÍA LORCA, produced in 1935 and published in 1938. Setting: a Spanish parlor overlooking a hothouse, 1890–1910.

Subtitled "a poem of Granada in 1900, divided into various 'gardens' with scenes of singing and dancing," this is the last play staged during García Lorca's lifetime. Its central symbol is the "rosa mutabile" poem Rosita sings at night. The lyrically evoked atmosphere of melancholy and boredom that pervades the actions suggests ANTON CHEKHOV's influence.

Vowing to return to her, Rosita's betrothed departs for Peru to make his fortune. She is still waiting confidently fifteen years later, and will not consider another suitor. Finally he writes, suggesting that because he can not yet return they marry by proxy. Though the lusty housekeeper cannot understand it—"And at night, what?"—Rosita happily agrees. More years pass and Rosita is wasting away. She knows he is untrue to her and married to someone else, but she keeps her dreams. It is the interference of others that makes her admit her situation and retreat into illusion: "Now the only thing left me is my dignity. What I have within I keep for myself alone." She is like a rose: "In the morning unfolding," then "wide open and hard as coral." Finally, at night, she sings about the end of the rose: "It turns white, white as a cheek of salt," and "its petals begin to fall."

DONLEAVY, J. P. (1926–), American novelist, in 1959 dramatized *The Ginger Man,* his popular novel about a zany young American abroad. Donleavy himself has long resided in England, and was educated at Trinity College, Dublin. In 1964 he dramatized *A Singular Man,* his novel about a confused American tycoon. Original Donleavy plays include *Tales of New York* (1960), a satire.

DONNAY, Maurice [-Charles] (1859–1945), French playwright, has been likened to both ARTHUR SCHNITZLER and to GEORGES DE PORTO-RICHE for his *théâtre d'amour.* As in *Amants* (LOVERS, 1895), the play for which he is remembered and that JULES LEMAÎTRE considered "probably a masterpiece," so in Donnay's other plays passions are depicted with little sentimentality but with sophistication as well as compassion. "A play is a love story," Donnay explained; "since that story is laid in various places, we are led to believe that plays differ." Few of his twenty plays are notable today, though his characterizations and dramatizations of love and adultery exemplify the better popular French comedy at the turn of the century.

Parisian-born and of a well-to-do family, Donnay became a civil engineer. Then he turned to composing cabaret monologues and launched his playwriting with the farcical one-acter *Eux!* (*They!,* 1889) and an original adaptation of Aristophanes's *Lysistrata* (1892). Soon thereafter *Lovers* brought him fame. The plays that followed portray similar passions: *La Douloureuse* (1897) and *L'Affranchie* (*The Free Woman,* 1898) are somber comedies that focus on heroines whose loves are blighted by lies; the more tragic *Le Torrent* (1899) ends with suicide and comments on adultery and marriage laws; *L'Autre Danger* (*The Other Danger,* 1902), another and even more "unpleasant" thesis play, features a woman who marries her daughter off to her lover; *Le Retour de Jérusalem* (*The Return From Jerusalem,* 1903), an ambitious PROBLEM PLAY, depicts racial incompatibility as the force that breaks up a Gentile's marriage with a Jewess; and *Le Ménage de Molière* (1912), a verse comedy, features Molière, to whom Donnay expresses his tribute and admiration. Less notable are some thesis plays written with Lucien Descaves (1861–1949).

Donnay's *Théâtre* was published in eight volumes (1908–27). *Lovers, The Free Woman, They* (1915) appear in a collection with an introduction by Barrett Clark. Clark also provided an informative essay on Donnay and a bibliography for *Three Modern Plays From the French* (1914), which includes Donnay's *The Other Danger.*

DOROTHEA ANGERMANN, a play in five acts by GERHART HAUPTMANN, published and produced in 1926. Setting: various parts of Germany and Meriden, Connecticut; 1890's.

The play failed to duplicate the success of ROSE BERND, though some of its scenes are effective. Despite its middle-class milieu, it strongly resembles the earlier play.

Pastor Angermann's daughter, Dorothea, is sensitive and demure, yet vivacious and hot-blooded. One afternoon she gives in to her passions with a despised cook. Her narrow-minded, hypocritical father forces her and the cook to marry and to depart for America. There they sink into poverty and crime, and the cook eventually deserts Dorothea. A professor whom she loved has followed her to America and still wants Dorothea to be his wife. As they become happily reconciled, the cook returns, and she decides to remain with him. Later the cook dies of an overdose of morphine. Dorothea, debased and broken, returns to Germany. After a chilling interview with her self-righteous father, she commits suicide.

DORST, Tankred (1925–), German dramatist, has written dramatic parables that in a lightly amusing and semistyled manner present the horrors of an existentialist or Kafkaesque world in microcosm. His first play, *Gesellschaft im Herbst* (1959), portrays the ruin of a castle by speculators while its owner, an old countess, waits in vain for the family treasure she thinks is being excavated. Much praised was Dorst's *Grosse Schmährede an der Stadtmauer* (1961), which has a BRECHTian parable plot about a poor Chinese woman who tries to reclaim a husband from the war and is defeated before the SYMBOLIC town wall where she speaks her diatribe against the emperor. In the long one-act *Die Kurve* (*The Curve,* 1960) two brothers vainly protest the absence of signs warning motorists of a deadly mountain curve; when the highway commissioner happens to pass by they kill him—to protect their source of income, the wrecked cars they sell—and write his successor to protest the danger of the unmarked curve. The shorter *Freiheit für Clemens* (*Freedom for Clemens,* 1962) features a prisoner who gradually loses his desire to be released and is happy to tap messages to the warden's daughter. Dorst also wrote the comedy *Der tote Oberst* (1961) and essays on drama and theatre in which he himself noted the characteristic and symbolic *Ortslosigkeit* (delocalization) of his plays.

Freedom for Clemens and *The Curve* appear with introduction in, respectively, Michael Benedikt and George E. Wellwarth's *Postwar German Theatre* (1967) and Robert W. Corrigan's *The New Theatre of Europe 3* (1968).

DOS PASSOS, John [Roderigo] (1896–1970), American novelist, also wrote "social protest" drama collected as *Three Plays* in 1934. The first was an EXPRESSIONIST satire, *The Garbage Man* (1925), "A Parade with Shouting" about a couple defeated by socioeconomic forces and published as *The Moon Is a Gong; Airways, Inc.* (1928), a NATURALISTIC drama, is about a down-and-out family whose sole success, an aircraft designer and pilot, is crippled in an accident; and *Fortune Heights* (1933) portrays a real-estate boom and collapse. In 1959 Dos Passos (with Paul Shyre, 1927–) dramatized his best-known work, the panoramic trilogy of novels *U.S.A.* (1938). Dos Passos's plays were generally unsuccessful, although, like his popular early novels, they are experimental portrayals of social problems. See George A. Knox and Herbert M. Stahl's *Dos Passos and "The Revolting Playwrights"* (1964), edited by S. B. Liljegren.

DOSTIGAEV AND THE OTHERS (*Dostigaev i drugie*), a play in three acts by MAXIM GORKY, published and produced in 1933. Setting: a provincial Russian town, 1917.

This sequel to YEGOR BULYCHOV AND THE OTHERS, while reintroducing most of the same characters, features a contemptible protagonist. More tendentious than the earlier play—and more scathingly satiric of anti-Bolsheviks—it has some effective comic scenes. It portrays the period between the fall of the Tsar and the victory of the Soviets.

Dostigaev schemes to profit from increasingly chaotic political and military events. (Kerensky's government is tottering, and the Bolsheviks' threat grows.) The abbess and priest become more virulent while various industrialists and politicians double-cross each other as they jockey for profits and power. The fiery Shura forces her suitor to propose to her and seeks to join the revolutionaries. But her friend, Dostigaev's daughter, feels useless and is unable to think matters out. She commits suicide—propitiously, for just then the late Bulychov's godson, Yakov Laptev, arrives with Communist soldiers, who surround and occupy Dostigaev's house. Admittedly concerned only with his own safety, Dostigaev effectively uses his daughter's suicide to escape arrest. He reassures his wife as he adjusts to the new political situation: "It was a near thing. It wouldn't have worked if it hadn't been for—" and they remember their dead daughter.

DRAGON, THE (*Drakon*), a satiric fable in three acts by YEVGENI LVOVICH SHVARTS, produced in 1943 and published in 1960. Setting: a mythical city.

Banned after the first few productions, this fairy tale, a transparent attack on totalitarianism, was revived in Russia and produced in the United States in the 1960's.

The city is well adjusted and accommodated to the four-hundred-year-old rule of a three-headed dragon who assumes different human shapes. It prepares for his annual devouring of a virgin when the visiting brave knight Launcelot ("a distant connection"), ever ready to fight for people's rights and enamored of the beautiful victim, challenges the dragon. The people resent Launcelot's upsetting the routine—"everything was running smoothly"—and try to foil him. But with the help of a cat who gets him weapons and a helmet of invisibility, Launcelot is armed. The beautiful and hitherto acquiescent victim falls in love with Launcelot, and refuses to obey the dragon and murder the challenger. After a sky battle, during which the populace is given misleading bulletins, the dragon is defeated. But Launcelot is badly wounded and disappears. A year later the Burgomaster is in firm control. He takes credit for killing the dragon and he terrorizes the population—just as the dragon did. He is about to marry the only person who does not kowtow to his regime, the rescued damsel. Launcelot again saves her, exposes the toadying opportunists, and imprisons the Burgomaster and his equally vicious son. Matured by his suffering and his realization of the difficulties ahead, Launcelot takes the hand of his beloved. "My friends, I love you all," he tells the people. "And after all our trials and tribulations we're going to be happy, very happy at last!"

DRAYMAN HENSCHEL (*Fuhrmann Henschel*), a play in five acts by GERHART HAUPTMANN, produced in 1898 and published in 1899. Setting: hotel in a Silesian resort, 1860's.

This NATURALISTIC tragedy of the ruin of the hotel's simple drayman by his second wife is one of Hauptmann's finest works.

Act I. Wilhelm Henschel's ill wife is exasperated by the rude unkindness of the maid, Hanne Schäl. She knows that she is dying, and fears Hanne is waiting to get Henschel for herself. Half-delirious, she believes they both want her to die quickly, and she vows to take her infant girl with her: "I'd rather choke her than leave her to that damn bitch." Her husband comes home; he has had all sorts of bad luck of late, and his trusting generosity is often abused. He brings an apron the maid has asked for, and Mrs. Henschel now is convinced her suspicions are well founded. She begs her husband not to marry Hanne after she dies and Henschel—who has never thought much about the maid—readily agrees: "Sure, I promise. . . . Now leave me in peace with such stuff."

Act II. His wife has died. The grieving Henschel is left with an infant and the necessity of changing his occupation because of expanding rail services and industrialization. Though she thinks him stupid and slow, the ambitious Hanne needs a husband, and schemes to marry him. She denies having an illegitimate daughter, but Henschel, who has found out about it, does not mind: "She didn't even know me then. A hot-blooded girl she is and that has to come out somehow. . . . No, that don't bother me none." His real concern is with the promise he made his wife. He seeks a sign at her grave and talks to a friend, the hotel's owner, who advises him to remarry. When Hanne tells him she must leave because of the gossip, she ensnares him into proposing. As soon as he is out of earshot, she reveals her delight and mutters to herself, "I'll show all of you! Just you watch me!"

Act III. Avaricious and ruthless, Hanne quickly alienates Henschel's friends and takes a dandified hotel waiter for a lover. Henschel's baby dies, and when he good-naturedly brings home her neglected illegitimate child to take its place, Hanne is furious. She does not want to "slave" over another child, and most of all, she does not want people to know (although they already do) of its existence. Henschel patiently endures Hanne's outburst: "We're alone. Why shouldn't we take care of the kid? That's the way I feel and I ain't even her father." But he begins to despair of his shrewish wife: "You trying to drive me out o' the house?—I always think some day things'll improve, but they just get worse!"

Act IV. Things come to a climax at the hotel's taproom. The bankrupt hotel owner is leaving, and Henschel is expected to take over the taproom from an old onetime actor, his friend. All Henschel's friends, long insulted and driven away by Hanne, gradually voice their accumulated resentments: "Ye used to have nuttin' but friends, and now—now not a soul comes to see ye and even if they wanted to come to see ye, they stay away because of the wife." In their mounting anger they accuse Hanne of having caused Henschel's first wife's and the infant's death, and then they reveal her adultery. At first Henschel controls himself, but finally he becomes enraged. He throws out one man and, holding another in his powerful grip, calls for Hanne to confront her accuser. When she can only reply weakly, "damned lies," and rush out, Henschel collapses, a broken man.

Act V. A few nights later Henschel is unable to sleep. The neighbors come to console him. He cannot fathom the collapse of his world and blames his misfortunes on the broken promise to his dying wife. He acknowledges the justice of his friends' coolness toward him. "I know you're right," he tells them. "I'm really not very proud of myself now." They try to persuade him that he need not feel guilty. "It's not a question of sin or guilt," one of them remarks, just "a man's particular fate." They appear to succeed in calming him. He even makes up with Hanne: "If you did something wrong, let the good Lord be the judge of that. I don't want to damn you about that anymore." After the others leave, however, Hanne's shrewishness resumes. Henschel goes to his room. Shortly later, Hanne rushes out of the house, screaming hysterically that he has killed himself.

DREAM (BUT PERHAPS NOT) (*Sogno* [*ma forse no*]), a one-act play by LUIGI PIRANDELLO, published in 1929 and produced in 1931. Setting: a room in a large city.

This partly SURREALIST sketch (also translated as *I'm Dreaming, But Am I?*) depicts a young lady's nightmare of her lover's fury when she casts him off for a richer lover; she awakes, and soon the same situation begins, more subtly, in reality.

DREAM GIRL, a comedy in two acts by ELMER RICE, produced in 1945 and published in 1946. Setting: New York, 1940's.

Rice's last major success, both in America and in England, is this light EXPRESSIONISTIC vehicle (transformed into the musical *Skyscraper* in 1965) that has been compared to James Thurber's story "The Secret Life of Walter Mitty" (1939)—for the action constantly shifts into the heroine's romantic cliché dream world.

Twenty-three-year-old Georgina Allerton, a whimsically wistful and idealistic proprietor of a money-losing bookstore, is the author of a bad, unpublishable romantic novel. She is infatuated with her useless brother-in-law, and wonders whether she ought to accompany a married admirer to Mexico or to elope with her brother-in-law before she goes "through middle age, on to senility, never experiencing anything." A wisecracking reporter takes Georgina to dinner and a play. During the course of the evening he makes her face reality—and they get married that same night.

DREAM OF PETER MANN, THE, a play in three acts by BERNARD KOPS, published and produced in 1960. Setting: a London market place, 1960.

This is a semiEXPRESSIONIST fantasy with songs; the young peddler, its title hero, is an Everyman, a spirited visionary who wants to search for uranium and is persuaded by a tramp to rifle his mother's safe. Most of the play consists of his dream.

A safe falls and knocks Peter out. In a dream, he returns years later, unsuccessful, and finds everybody digging for uranium. Not recognized, Peter is about to be executed by the villain when his mother saves him. His sales ability eventually makes him the wealthy boss of all shroud factories. He argues against the use of the Bomb, but it finally is dropped. Peter alone is saved in his shelter. Then he awakes, marries the girl who has always loved him, and goes off to hunt for uranium with her. He tells the other peddlers, "You can always make money, but you can't always make merry. You're saving up for nothing, going nowhere, hoarding nothing, losing—everything." Life, Peter says, is "a great opportunity never to be repeated . . . so make the most of it before it's gone!" But after he leaves the merchants keep chanting, "MONEY IS TIME AND TIME IS MONEY—"

DREAM PLAY, A (*Ett drömspel*), a drama without act or scene designations by AUGUST STRINDBERG, published in 1902 and produced in 1907. Setting: clouds, growing castle, etc.

Here, "anything can happen . . . time and space do not exist," Strindberg wrote in his brief preface to this very influential avant-garde work, a favorite of his and one that has had many important productions. "The characters split, double, multiply, vanish, intensify, diffuse, and disperse." But there is a "motivated" logic that unifies the play and gives it form: the consciousness of the dreamer. The author appears in various guises among the principal male characters. Endlessly suggestive—and elusive—in its lyrical SYMBOLISM, the play's depiction of the human condition (the divine heroine soon discovers and repeatedly reaffirms that "life is a misery! Men are to be pitied!") in part anticipates the alienation and despair common in mid-century literature and theatre. Like some other critics, Maurice Valency considered this "the most exasperating and also the most impressive piece of dramatic writing of our time" (*The Flower of the Castle*). As he remarked in his detailed study, "seldom has a plot had less relation to a play."

Indra's Daughter decides to descend to earth and examine the reason for men's discontent. First she appears before a castle growing out of manure and crowned by a flower bud. She enters it and liberates the imprisoned Officer. At home, his parents deplore their tormenting of each other; the Mother then shows the Officer how a childhood injustice he suffered is balanced by an injustice he himself has caused. Next the Officer, carrying a bunch of roses, is at the opera's stage door. He confidently expects the bride for whom he has already waited seven years, but he is mystified by what may be behind a door with an air hole shaped like a four-leaf clover. (This door remains onstage throughout the remainder of the play.) To see if life is really as hard as people complain it is, Indra's Daughter becomes the stage-door portress. The Officer, now old and white but still waiting for his bride, tries to break open the mysterious door. When the Policeman interferes, the Officer goes to the Lawyer for an injunction. The Lawyer deplores the stench and ugliness he has absorbed from his clients' crimes. Unjustly, he is now denied his doctor's degree during a convocation; Indra's Daughter, with compassion and love—and to experience the joys and agonies of life—marries him.

Their marriage quickly degenerates into suffocating squalor and bickering, and Indra's Daughter gladly leaves her husband and daughter. With the rejuvenated Officer, she travels to the seashore. They meet the black-faced Quarantine Master, who fumigates two lovers (one is the Officer's elusive bride), and the Poet, who wallows in skin-hardening mud but "is forever flitting about in the loftier regions." Soon the Officer is seen as a humiliated schoolboy, and Indra's Daughter wearily retraces her steps. Dutifully she returns to her Lawyer-husband, with whom she visits a beautiful beach that has been made hellish by society. Witnessing a shipwreck at Fingal's Cave, Indra's Daughter recites the Poet's long complaint to God in the music of the wind. Back in the alley outside the opera, Indra's Daughter has summoned all for the opening of the mysterious door. After angry disputations among the learned faculties, the door is opened, and reveals—Nothing. Outside the growing castle, Indra's Daughter, having been threatened with flogging, bids an anguished farewell to the Lawyer and the Poet. To the latter she explains his "dream of truth," but she does not answer his ultimate questions. Preparing to ascend after a procession at which all throw their little possessions into the fire, Indra's Daughter enters the castle, feeling "the whole of life's pain" —the needless remorse, the "conflict, indecision, and uncertainty." She promises humanity: "I shall never forget them where I go—and I shall bring their lamentations to God's throne. Farewell!" As the castle burns up, the bud on its roof bursts into a giant chrysanthemum.

DREAM WEAVER, THE (*La tejedora de sueños*), a play in three acts by ANTONIO BUERO VALLEJO, published and produced in 1952. Setting: Odysseus's palace in Ithaca, after the Trojan War.

This free dramatization of the Homeric legend of Odysseus's homecoming universalizes Penelope's problems and anguish after prolonged absence from the husband gone to war.

Her slave girls chant as Penelope weaves a shroud for Odysseus's aged father, which she secretly unravels to cheat the suitors who impoverish her household and debauch her slaves. Cursing Helen, who twenty years ago caused the war that took away her man, Penelope weeps before the old nurse Euriclea. Penelope is attracted to only one suitor (as is also a slave girl, who is loved by but despises Penelope's son, Telemachus). Arriving as an unrecognized stranger, Odysseus overhears Penelope tell this suitor of the dreams she embroiders but "must unravel at night in order that, someday, I may realize them." The disguised Odysseus proposes a bow contest, at which he kills the suitors. "We want peace, a husband, and children," Penelope grieves after the heroic death of the suitor she has come to love, "and you give us wars, you thrust us into the danger of adultery and"—alluding to Orestes—"turn our sons into our murderers." Odysseus accuses her of "sterile dreaming and weaving" instead of managing his household. "You didn't dare trust me," she counters, because Odysseus came disguised, fearful of finding her aged; she calls him a "miserable reasoner," a cruel "sly, hypocritical, cowardly clown" who "destroyed all my hopes" and dreams. All that is left to the despised Odysseus, Penelope concludes, "is the appearance, the laughable shell of marriage." Now she no longer cares whether he examines the secret dreams she has embroidered. Odysseus declines: "They don't exist. You dreamt of Odysseus! That shroud will be burned tomorrow"—together with her fallen suitor's corpse. Penelope turns to the corpse, yearning for the day when there will be no more wars, only love and courage. "The chamber of my soul is empty," she weeps. But she consoles herself with the memory of the slain suitor: "I envy you. The dead are fortunate!" Odysseus sits dejected as the slave women resume their chant.

DREAMING OF THE BONES, THE, a one-act verse play by WILLIAM BUTLER YEATS, published in

1919 and produced in 1931. Setting: a patterned screen before a wall.

The third of FOUR PLAYS FOR DANCERS is a patriotic ghost play that merges ancient and recent history. It depicts an encounter between an Irish soldier of the Easter Rebellion and the shades of two lovers who betrayed Ireland to the Normans seven hundred years earlier. As punishment, they are kept from each other's arms until someone is willing to pardon their crime. But though the remorseful couple's tale moves the soldier, he refuses: "O, never, never / Shall Diarmuid and Dervorgilla be forgiven." The yearning lovers gaze at each other passionately, dance their dance of agony, and disappear.

DREAMY KID, THE, a one-act play by EUGENE O'NEILL, produced in 1919 and published in 1920. Setting: a bedroom in New York on a winter night.

An unimpressive dialect melodrama, *The Dreamy Kid* anticipates THE EMPEROR JONES.

Though sought for murder, Dreamy, a tough young Negro, chances a visit to his dying grandmother. The police net tightens and his girl friend almost persuades him to escape, but the grandmother (unaware of Dreamy's position) begs him to stay by her deathbed: "If yo' leave me now, yo' ain't gwine git no bit er luck s'long's yo' live." Fearful of incurring "her dyin' curse," he decides that his "game's up." At the curtain, he readies his revolver when he hears the police, and grimly vows not to be caught alive, "Lawd Jesus, no suh!" The dying woman mistakes the oath for piety: "Dat's right—yo' pray—Lawd Jesus—Lawd Jesus—"

DREISER, Theodore [Herman Albert] (1871–1945), American novelist, published a collection of *Plays of the Natural and the Supernatural** (1916) and an unsuccessfully produced drama of sexual perversion, *The Hand of the Potter* (1918). He was a major writer of NATURALISTIC novels, notably *Sister Carrie* (1900) and *An American Tragedy* (1925). *An American Tragedy,* inspired by the Gillette-Brown murder case of 1906, was filmed (1931 and 1951) and also dramatized twice (1926 and 1936). The first was a straight dramatization by Patrick Kearney (1894–1933). The 1936 drama, a Marxian thesis play produced by the Group Theatre as *The Case of Clyde Griffiths,* was by Erwin Piscator (1893–1966; written with Lena Goldschmidt, ? – ?), the distinguished German producer who during his exile headed the Dramatic Workshop of the New School for Social Research in New York.

DREYER, Max (1862–1946), German playwright of the pre-World War I period, had his greatest success with *Der Probekandidat* (1899, translated as *On Probation*), a NATURALISTIC drama about a young teacher who, because he refuses to declare the findings of religion superior to those of science, loses his job and his girl friend and—at the much-cheered curtain—is ironically advised by a friend to go to Prussia "where everyone may express himself freely." A disciple of GERHART HAUPTMANN and HENRIK IBSEN, Dreyer wrote other plays in the same vein, including adolescent love dramas like *Drei* (1893), about a marital triangle, and *Die Siebzehnjährigen* (1904), which recalls Wedekind's SPRING'S AWAKENING. Dreyer also wrote comedies, of which the most successful was *Das Tal des Lebens* (1902), a frequently produced and ultimately filmed trifle about a lusty soldier who guards an impotent governor's quarters and impregnates his wife with the much-desired heir.

Born in Mecklenburg, Dreyer taught after receiving his doctorate, but eventually turned to free-lance writing. His works include a number of novels and a volume of poetry.

* *The Girl in the Coffin, Laughing Gas, The Spring Recital, The Light in the Window, The Blue Sphere, In the Dark,* and *"Old Ragpicker."*

DRINKWATER, John (1882–1937), was an English poet, playwright, and actor. Though credited as a popularizer of verse drama, his only successful plays were in prose: ABRAHAM LINCOLN (1918) and BIRD IN HAND (1927). Born in Leytonstone, Essex, and educated at the Oxford high school, Drinkwater worked as an insurance clerk for a dozen years before he began his professional career. With Sir Barry Jackson he founded and became the producer of the Pilgrim Players. When this group became the Birmingham Repertory Theatre, Drinkwater was its general manager for a while and acted in the company (he performed in the American as well as English productions of *Abraham Lincoln*). His first play was a verse one-acter, *Cophetua* (1911). But it was not until the end of World War I that Drinkwater achieved fame as a dramatist, with his Lincoln play.

A series of less successful biographical dramas followed: *Mary Stuart* (1921), *Oliver Cromwell* (1921; in which Cromwell is overshadowed by his mother, whose epitaph for Charles I is "Poor, silly King"), *Robert E. Lee* (1923,) *Robert Burns* (1925), and *Napoleon, The Hundred Days* (1932; an adaptation of GIOVACCHINO FORZANO). While these plays were respectfully greeted by critics, Drinkwater succeeded with the public again only with the comic *Bird in Hand.*

The Collected Plays (1925) were published in two volumes; among them are the poetic *Rebellion* (1914), *The Storm* (1915, a one-acter), *The God of Quiet* (1916), and *X = 0: A Night of the Trojan War* (1917), a one act pacifist play in verse on a classic episode. Drinkwater's other publications include a few volumes of poetry; critical studies of William Morris, Algernon Charles Swinburne, Shakespeare, Lord Byron, Samuel Pepys, and others; editions of Sir Philip Sidney's poetry and the drama of ST. JOHN HANKIN; and two autobiographical works, *Inheritance* (1931) and *Discovery* (1932).

DROVERS, THE, a one-act play by LOUIS ESSON, produced in 1919 and published in 1920. Setting:

a droving camp on the edge of the Barklay Tableland (the Australian bush country), early twentieth century.

Esson's best-known play has been compared to O'Neill's BOUND EAST FOR CARDIFF as well as Synge's RIDERS TO THE SEA. Very short and stark, it portrays the intrepid death of Esson's protagonist, the cattle drover "Briglow" Bill.

Briglow has just been injured in a stampede. Because the other drovers must proceed and he is too hurt to be moved, Briglow calmly reconciles himself to staying behind—and dying. "Well, it's been a good life. I'm satisfied," he tells his somber mates: "No man can dodge his fate." Only a young aborigine is able to stay with him. When Briglow is dead the boy builds a grass mound to keep off bush spirits. "Debbil-debbil can't catch-im Briglow now," he chants, and clicks his sticks.

DRUMS IN THE NIGHT (*Trommeln in der Nacht*), a drama in five acts by BERTOLT BRECHT, produced in 1922 and published in 1923. Setting: Berlin immediately after the end of World War I, during the abortive Spartacist uprising by insurgent veterans.

In 1922 Brecht won the Kleist Prize, awarded annually to the best young dramatist, for this, his second play. A red moon hung over the stage, and antiromantic slogans were posted in the auditorium. Later Brecht labeled the play a "comedy."

Because her soldier-fiancé, Andreas Kragler, has been missing for four years, her bourgeois parents persuade Anna Balicke to forget him and marry her lover, an obnoxious war profiteer. That evening he takes them all out to celebrate the engagement, and Kragler, who has been a war prisoner in Africa, returns ghostlike for his bride Anna. He finds her and the others drinking in the Piccadilly Bar, while the Spartacists start their revolution in the streets. Kragler argues with her smug parents and repulsive lover, who insult and ridicule the soldier as a vagabond and a pauper. Anna still loves Kragler, but she is deeply ashamed of her disloyalty—and pregnancy. She sends him away, but soon changes her mind and runs out to find him. Kragler, in the meantime, has gotten drunk and exaltedly starts leading a group of revolutionaries. On the way Anna meets him, and confesses her love as well as her shameful disloyalty, and its consequence. Though Kragler reproaches her bitterly, he finally discards ideals for the sake of comfort. He deserts his friends: "Should my flesh become rotting garbage to carry your ideals to heaven? . . . I'm a swine, and the swine is going home . . . to bed!" He echoes Anna's parents as he ridicules the revolutionaries as hoodlums. Then, angrily chiding the audience for its romantic attitudes, he tears down the moon and other props—all unreal theatricality: "But the slaughterhouses behind them are very real." As the battle noises are heard in the back, he puts his arms around Anna and tenderly takes her out: "It's been four years."

DRUMS OF FATHER NED, THE, a play in three acts and a "prerumble" by SEAN O'CASEY, published and produced in 1959. Setting: Doonavale, contemporary Ireland.

This is O'Casey's last full-length play. Its world premiere was scheduled for production by the International Theatre Festival at Dublin's 1958 Tostal (spring celebration), but the archbishop pressured its cancellation—whereupon O'Casey forbade all further performances of his dramas in Ireland. But as he noted (in a letter to David Krause quoted in *Sean O'Casey: The Man and His Work*), it had been THE BISHOP'S BONFIRE "that soured his archiepiscopal soul." *The Drums of Father Ned* is a good-natured romp depicting a village's festive preparations for a tostal. The feuding elders, dour representatives of sterile but expedient piety, are ludicrous—and ultimately harmless. Youth's joyful love and vitality, abetted (and symbolized) by the offstage Father Ned and his audible roll drums, are victorious.

DU BARRY, a play in five acts by DAVID BELASCO, produced in 1901 and published in 1928. Setting: eighteenth-century Paris and Versailles.

This episodic extravaganza was originally composed by JEAN RICHEPIN and failed in England. Belasco rewrote it into a great success in America. It was published in Belasco's *Six Plays* (1928), and a popular burlesque of the play, *Du Hurry,* was produced at the Weber and Fields in 1902. Notable scenes include the famous courtesan's hiding her lover in her bed as Louis XV searches for him, and the spectacle of the Revolution, with Du Barry being carted off ("Yes, yes, I will be brave") to the guillotine amidst a howling mob.

DUBILLARD, Roland (1923–), French actor (under the stage name Grégoire) and dramatist, like MARGUERITE DURAS has written ABSURD plays in a NATURALISTIC style. The first important one was *Naïves hirondelles* (1961, translated as *The Swallows*), depicting often farcical doings in a shop rented from his aunt by a young man, who eventually disappears with a maid, and an older man who is left with the aunt. *La Maison d'os* (1962), an allegory on the demise of the body's various organs, features an old man dying in a fantastic house occupied by forty servants and professionals, including a doctor and a priest.

Dubillard's dialogue is original in its almost poetic articulation of the difficulties of human expression. His characters are anguished by problems that are absurd as well as pathetic, simultaneously comic and tragic.

The work of Dubillard is discussed in Jacques Guicharnaud's *Modern French Theatre* (1967).

DUCHESS OF PADUA, THE, a drama in five acts by OSCAR WILDE, privately printed in 1883 and produced in 1891. Setting: Padua, last half of the sixteenth century.

Wilde wrote this, his second play, for the actress Mary Anderson. She had given him an advance for it, but then rejected the completed play. Later

Wilde called it his only work "unfit for publication," though it was published, in verse as well as prose. A bombastic revenge drama first produced in New York as *Guido Ferranti,* it features a hero who falls in love with the wife of his father's murderer, the Duke of Padua; she slays her husband, the lovers share the guilt, and both eventually commit suicide.

DUEL OF ANGELS (*Pour Lucrèce*), a play in three acts by JEAN GIRAUDOUX, published and produced in 1953. Setting: Aix-en-Provence, about 1868.

Giraudoux's last play was completed in three variant manuscripts shortly before his death and was translated by CHRISTOPHER FRY. It echoes the oft-retold story of Tarquin's rape of Lucrece (here Lucile).

The "duel" is between Paola, a placid personification of worldly amorality, and Lucile, a personification of uncompromising virtue and purity. Lucile and her husband, the new public attorney, ruthlessly combat the town's licentiousness. She exposes the adulteries of Paola, who soon revenges herself. She drugs Lucile and then persuades her that while unconscious she was raped by the town roué (one of Paola's former lovers)—and relished it. The "rape" is avenged by Paola's husband, who duels and kills the roué. Though she was duped, Lucile's husband is outraged and expels her. Paola reveals the hoax, but Lucile is disgusted with humanity and commits suicide. Unlike Paola, who cannot remember shame, Lucile could never forget it. The bawd who assisted in Paola's revenge blesses Lucile as an angel killed by the wicked stupidity and coarseness of men.

DUHAMEL, Georges (1884–1966), French writer and physician, became best known abroad for his novels and essays, many of which were based on his experiences as a wartime surgeon. Humanist and poet as well as playwright, Duhamel with a group that included CHARLES VILDRAC, later his brother-in-law and coauthor of *Notes sur la technique poétique* (1911), in 1906–07 founded an experimental community-living house for artists. The plays he wrote, like those of ROMAIN ROLLAND, were to popularize art theories, though their elevated poetry and SYMBOLISM made such plays relatively inaccessible to the masses. His plays include *La Lumière* (*The Light,* 1911), a romance about blind lovers whose perceptions transcend the physical sight they have lost; *Le Combat* (*The Combat,* 1913), a much-praised verse drama about a rich invalid who dies forgotten after saving a community from natural disaster; *Dans l'ombre des statues* (*In the Shadow of Statues,* 1914), a humorous poetic drama; *L'Œuvre des athlètes* (1920), which satirizes a literary club; and a comedy, *La Journée des aveux* (1923).

Duhamel's wife Blanche Albane starred in his plays and was a protégée of Sarah Bernhardt. His critical writings include a study of PAUL CLAUDEL, who, with others, wrote a memoir, *Duhamel et nous* (1937). There is an extensive discussion of Duhamel's drama in Isaac Goldberg's *The Drama of Transition* (1922), with reference to other sources.

DULCY, a comedy in three acts by GEORGE S. KAUFMAN and MARC CONNELLY, published and produced in 1921. Setting: a Westchester (New York) suburb; late summer, 1921.

This comedy features a character created in Franklin P. Adams's newspaper column, the bromidic, cliché-spouting Dulcinea. A beautiful and well-meaning but dull and dull-witted young matron, "Dulcy" Smith nearly wrecks her husband's career when she invites a business associate, his family, and others to the Smith home. During the hectic weekend, her stupid meddling causes calamity after calamity, but all turns out well at the end.

DUMB WAITER, THE, a one-act play by HAROLD PINTER, published and produced in 1960. Setting: a basement room in Birmingham, 1950's.

Pinter's characteristic early play, a mixture of farce and terror, is set in a room occupied by two people, hired killers.

Two men are awaiting instructions for the next job. Nervously and in monosyllabic clichés they read the newspaper, talk of football, argue about trivialities, and wish they had some tea. Mysteriously an envelope is slipped under the door: it contains twelve matches, but lacking a coin for the gas meter, they cannot light the kettle. ("How can you light a kettle?" one gunman argues angrily; you "put on a kettle.") The room used to be the kitchen of a supposedly deserted upstairs restaurant, but suddenly a dumb waiter transmits orders for increasingly exotic dishes. Desperately the gunmen scurry around and send up the few things they have. They discover a speaking tube and learn that what they have sent up was unsatisfactory. Then they rehearse their job instructions. When another food order comes, one of the gunmen screams, "We've got nothing left! Nothing! Do you understand?" He goes to the lavatory, the speaking tube signals, and the other gunman repeats its instructions: the victim "will be coming in straight away. The normal method to be employed." He calls his companion, who stumbles in from the main door—stripped—obviously the designated victim. They stare at each other.

DUNCAN, Ronald [Frederick Henry] (1914–), is a prolific British poet, novelist, biographer, literary critic, and librettist. He has also produced a number of plays, most of them in verse and many on religious themes. They include *This Way to the Tomb* (1945, a masque), *Nothing Up My Sleeve* (1950), *Our Lady's Tumbler* (1951), *Don Juan* (1952), *The Death of Satan* (1954; a verse comedy set in Hell and contemporary Spain, and portraying Don Juan and three writers—Lord Byron, OSCAR WILDE, and BERNARD SHAW—who play poker with their reputations), *The Catalyst* (1958, an originally banned drama on homosexuality), and *Abelard and Heloise* (1960, "a correspondence for the stage"). He also adapted and translated plays by JEAN GIRAUDOUX, JEAN COCTEAU, JEAN ANOUILH, and others.

Duncan was born in Salisbury, Rhodesia, and educated in Switzerland and at Cambridge University. He founded the Devon Festival of the Arts in 1953, and The English Stage Company in 1955. His opera librettos include *The Rape of Lucretia* (1946, for Benjamin Britten) and *Christopher Sly* (1962, for Thomas Eastwood). Among his many other works are an edition of the writings of Mahatma Gandhi and an autobiography, *All Men Are Islands* (1964). An analysis of his drama is Max W. Haueter's *Ronald Duncan: The Metaphysical Content of His Plays* (1969).

DUNNING, Philip [Hart] (1890–1968), American actor and producer, was also the coauthor of numerous plays, many of them boisterous comedies. He was most successful in his collaborations with GEORGE ABBOTT, particularly with their *Broadway* (1926); their later *Lily Turner* (1932), like his other plays, was less notable. In 1931 Dunning went to Hollywood, where he became a film writer-director. Shortly before his death he completed a courtroom melodrama about President Kennedy's assassin, Lee Harvey Oswald, *A Fantastic Chain of Events*.

DUNSANY, Lord (18th Baron) [Edward John Moreton Drax Plunkett] (1878–1957), Irish writer, is best known for his one-act fantasies, though he also produced full-length plays, poetry, sketches, stories, and novels. Dunsany's own life was almost as exotic as his imaginative writings. Born on the family estate in County Meath, East Ireland, he attended Eton, prepared at Sandhurst for an army career, served with the Coldstream Guards in the South African War, and then with the Royal Inniskilling Fusiliers during World War I. A giant (6 feet 4 inches) outdoors man and a frequent world traveler, he was also poetic and imaginative; at the age of sixty-two he entered the academic profession as Byron Professor of English Literature at the University of Athens.

In 1909 WILLIAM BUTLER YEATS was instrumental in having him write THE GLITTERING GATE (1909), one of his best plays, for the Abbey Theatre. Thus started Dunsany's career as a playwright. His drama is highly theatrical, dependent on physical (often supernatural) effects and surprise. It is characterized by fantasy and romance, linked in spirit to Dunsany's Celtic heritage. Sometimes, as in his popular A NIGHT AT AN INN (1916), the predominant atmosphere is a Poe-like horror. Most of Dunsany's settings are oriental never-never lands because, Dunsany commented, "the kind of drama that we most need today seems to me to be the kind that will build new worlds for the fancy, for the spirit as much as the body sometimes needs a change of scene." His plays, though not very successful on the commercial stage, have intrigued repertory groups—and readers.

Lord Dunsany wrote only a few full-length plays, notably IF (1921), *The Gods of the Mountain* (1911, whose green-jade title characters punish some beggars who have been impersonating the gods in order to rule a city), and *The Queen's Enemies* (1916). His many other one-acters were published in various collections. *Plays of Near and Far* (1923) contains *The Compromise of the King of the Golden Isles, The Flight of the Queen, Cheezo, A Good Bargain, If Shakespeare Lived To-day,* and *Fame and the Poet; Plays of Gods and Men* (1923) contains *The Tents of the Arabs, The Laughter of the Gods, The Queen's Enemies,* and *A Night at an Inn; Plays for Earth and Air* (1937) contains *Fame Comes Late, A Matter of Honour, Mr. Sliggen's Hour, The Pumpkin, The Use of Man, The Bureau de Change, The Seventh Symphony, Golden Dragon City, Time's Joke,* and *Atmospherics. Patches of Sunlight* (1938) is his autobiography, and Hazel L. Smith's *Lord Dunsany: King of Dreams* (1959) is a study of his life and work.

DURAS [originally Donnadieu], **Marguerite** (1914–), French novelist and playwright born in Indochina, has written ABSURD plays, often one-act adaptations of her fiction, in an almost NATURALISTIC manner though in slightly stylized language. Most of her protagonists are women who are lonely and weary, and dream of some form of escape—whether through romance or crime. In *Le Square* (*The Square,* 1956) a bitter young maid chats with a dispirited old salesman in the park; in *Les Viaducs de la Seine-et-Oise* (*The Viaducts of Seine-et-Oise,* 1960) two old people almost commit the perfect crime by dismembering a corpse and throwing its pieces from a bridge onto passing freight trains—an actual episode Duras again dramatized in *L'Amante anglaise* (1968, produced in New York as *A Place Without Doors* and in London as *Lovers of Viorne*), a suspenseful three-character play in two parts: the interrogation first of the husband and then of the wife; *La Musica* (1965), a two-character play (Duras co-directed its 1966 film) about a divorcing couple, mirror images whose characters and felonious pasts are revealed as they experience a rekindling of their now impossible love; and in *Des Journées entières dans les arbres* (*Days in the Trees,* 1965) an old mother tries to reestablish contact with her wastrel son. Even in *Les Eaux et forêts* (1965), a farce about a man bitten by a dog, desperation is conveyed—here in the dialogue of two women. Despair, too, permeates *Suzanna Andler* (1968), which depicts general moral bankruptcy in the upper-class adulteries pursued in St. Tropez. In 1963 Duras adapted a HENRY JAMES story, *La Bête dans la jungle*. She wrote the script for a distinguished film, *Hiroshima, mon amour* (1959).

The first volume of Duras's collected plays was published in 1965. The translated *Three Plays* (1967) are *The Square, Days in the Trees,* and *The Viaducts of Seine-et-Oise*. A book-length study of her life and work is Alfred Cismaru's *Marguerite Duras* (1971).

DURRELL, Lawrence (1912–), British poet and novelist noted particularly for his *Alexandria*

Quartet (*Justine, Balthazar, Mountolive,* and *Clea,* 1957–1960). He has also written a few verse dramas: *Sappho* (1950), a complexly plotted play about wars and the amorous doings of the poetess of Lesbos; *Acte* (1961), a romantic play about Petronius and Nero and his captive, the blinded Scythian princess Acte; and *An Irish Faustus* (1964), "a morality" with the traditional characters and plot, but set in Ireland (the palace of Queen Katherine of Galway, Princess Margaret's aunt) and depicting a Faust who wants to divest himself of black magic and save others from its destructive powers.

DÜRRENMATT, Friedrich (1921–), Swiss novelist and playwright, after the war along with MAX FRISCH became the major new dramatist writing in German. *Der Besuch der alten Dame* (THE VISIT, 1956), which brought Dürrenmatt international fame, is his most notable play, though *Die Physiker* (THE PHYSICISTS, 1962) has been almost as successful. Like his other plays and his fiction and literary criticism, both dramas express Dürrenmatt's intense concern with contemporary moral and political bankruptcy—and the religious orientation of a pastor's son who early in life became interested in the writings of Kierkegaard and Kafka. At the same time a cynical, sardonic detachment informs Dürrenmatt's imaginative and chilling plots. His dramaturgy is rooted in the classicism of Aristophanes and the AUSTRIAN Johann Nestroy (1801–62), and in the PRESENTATIONAL drama of FRANK WEDEKIND, LUIGI PIRANDELLO, and THORNTON WILDER. Even stronger and more apparent are the influences of BERTOLT BRECHT and the Zurich cabarets—and the art of painters like Hieronymus Bosch, George Rouault, and the EXPRESSIONISTS ERNST BARLACH and OSKAR KOKOSCHKA. Dürrenmatt's drama nevertheless is distinctively original in its characteristic and very theatrical suspense, horror—and comedy.

Born in Konolfingen, a village in Canton Berne, Switzerland, where his father—the son of a popular satirist once jailed for a libelous political poem—served as pastor, Dürrenmatt studied in Bern and attended Bern's as well as Zurich's university. He majored in literature and philosophy, but did not complete his degree and began his career as a painter. (Later he illustrated some of the editions of his plays.) In 1943 he wrote a comedy and some fiction, none of which was published. He supported himself as a free-lance writer in the years 1946–48, during which time he got married and composed his first play, *Es steht geschrieben;* it had its premiere in Zurich in 1947 though it remained unpublished until 1959. A historical-religious spectacle loosely based on the fanatic and abortive Münster Anabaptist uprising of 1533–36, it features a poor Leyden tailor who exploits the movement for his own advancement (and in his limited reign is more animated than Charles V) and a rich alderman who accepts its holy ideals literally and gives away all his and his family's wealth; after a weird reconciliation dance on the rooftop before Münster's fall, both men are broken

Friedrich Dürrenmatt. (*Swiss National Tourist Office*)

on the wheel, the tailor confirmed in his cynical despair and the alderman in his new faith—a characteristic Dürrenmatt hero: the passive, brave martyr who is also somewhat absurd, the fool in Christ.

This first play with its ironies, grotesqueries, and religio-moral quests is typical of the later ones that brought Dürrenmatt renown. His second play, *Der Blinde* (produced 1948, published 1960), is set in the Thirty Years' War; it is a stark parable about the defeat of an unscrupulous impostor-tempter by a Job-like blind duke who piously accepts the loss of his family and the ruin of the lands he thought were flourishing. It was with the "unhistorical historical comedy" *Romulus der Grosse* (ROMULUS THE GREAT, 1948) that Dürrenmatt produced his first important work. Less SHAVian was the next "comedy"—as he invariably has labeled his dramas—*Die Ehe des Herrn Mississippi* (THE MARRIAGE OF MISTER MISSISSIPPI, 1952), his first play to be staged in England and America. It was followed by *Ein Engel kommt nach Babylon* (AN ANGEL COMES TO BABYLON, 1953) and by the two plays that established his international reputation, *The Visit* and *The Physicists.* Between these came the less successful *Frank der Fünfte* (1959, revised 1964), an "Opera of a Private Bank" set to music by Paul Burkhard; a melodrama modeled on Brecht's THE THREEPENNY OPERA, it portrays the criminal administration of the bank of Frank the Fifth, later killed by his son and heir to the dynasty, who is determined to restore its bank's greatness by "brutal honesty." *Die Wiedertäufer* (1967), a play-within-a-play about a theatre director, bishops, and princes, is a new version of *Es steht geschrieben;* it is another drama that because of its EPIC characteristics has been likened to the works of Brecht, with whose theories Dürrenmatt has reluctantly continued to be preoccupied. Even more anti-illusionist is *Play Strindberg* (1969), Dürrenmatt's self-styled "attempt to clarify [AUGUST STRINDBERG's] theatrical vision to modern audiences" by turning THE DANCE OF DEATH into a virtually stichomythic black farce in twelve "rounds" (of a boxing match).

Slighter Dürrenmatt plays are similarly invested with moral and theological implications. Some are radio dramas that were subsequently staged, among them *Abendstunde im Spätherbst* (*An Evening in Late Fall,* 1959), about a Nobel Prize author who openly commits the murders he then transcribes into his best sellers; *Herkules und der Stall des Augias* (1954), reworked in 1963 as a stage play that suggestively dramatizes the legend of Hercules and the Augean Stables as a modern political-religious satire; and *Der Meteor* (*The Meteor,* 1966), a bitter comedy about a latter-day Lazarus, a laureate writer who, despairing of death, destroys those around him. James Yaffe (1927–) dramatized as *The Deadly Game* (1960) Dürrenmatt's suspense novel (*Die Panne,* 1956) about an American salesman trapped in the Swiss mountains into a parlor game that gradually exposes his moral culpability and costs him his life. Dürrenmatt also adapted Shakespeare's *King John,* as *König Johann* (1968).

His further works include novels, stories, and essays. Important among the last-named is "Theaterprobleme" ("Problems of the Theatre"), originally a lecture delivered (1954–55) in various European cities, in which Dürrenmatt discussed the evolution of classical tragedy into modern tragicomedy: "Our world has led to the grotesque as well as to the atom bomb, and so it is a world like that of Hieronymus Bosch whose apocalyptic paintings are also grotesque. But the grotesque is only a way of expressing in a tangible manner . . . the form of the unformed, the face of a world without a face"—since "guilt" and "responsibility" are no longer individual but collective and universal. Thus traditional classic tragedy is no longer possible, according to Dürrenmatt, and writers are "challenged" to express contemporary problems in new "poetic" styles. Dürrenmatt's own plays express this "apocalyptic" vision and reflect his preoccupation with sin and redemption in apparently allegorical terms. At the same time they do not propound specific solutions or theologies, for Dürrenmatt believed that art could not be made "to teach a lesson" nor indeed "to prove anything." His plots are resolved with thematic ambiguity and with ironies that cancel each other out. The appeal of his plays—whose language alternates between the colloquial, the rhetorical, and the stylized poetic and choric—lies in their immense and versatile theatricality: a master craftsman who continuously experiments, he has remained intrigued by the possibilities of staging. Dürrenmatt imaginatively dramatizes his age's black humor, horror, and nihilistic *Zeitgeist* in fantastic mystery thrillers. These exemplify his own tentative answer to the problems of producing art in a world whose consumers are educated and literate: "Perhaps the writer can best exist by writing detective stories, by creating art where it is least suspected."

Most of Dürrenmatt's plays are available in English. *Four Plays* (1965) is prefaced by his "Problems of the Theatre," and consists of *Romulus the Great, The Marriage of Mister Mississippi, An Angel Comes to Babylon,* and *The Physicists.* The first book-length study in English, with a bibliography, was Murray B. Peppard's *Friedrich Dürrenmatt* (1969).

DUTCHMAN, THE (*Holländarn*), a fragment (three acts) by AUGUST STRINDBERG, written in 1902 and published in 1918. Setting: a modern seaport.

This EXPRESSIONISTIC work, praised by Martin Lamm (*Strindbergs dramer*) as Strindberg's "poetically finest portrayal of the love-hate complex," was produced over the radio by Ingmar Bergman in 1947 and 1953. The principals are modernized mythical figures. (As recounted in A DREAM PLAY, the Flying Dutchman is punished because he has had seven unfaithful wives.)

A painter (the Dutchman) tells his mother, who provides him with illusionary greatness, of his six unsuccessful marriages. Despite the warnings of his apprentice, he allows the demonic Lilith into his house, and then with her enters into his seventh unhappy marriage. To his relief she soon leaves him, and the apprentice remarks that all the men in town have known her.

DYBBUK, THE (*Der Dibuk*), a "dramatic legend" in four acts by S. ANSKI, published in 1918 and produced in 1920. Setting: the towns of Brinnitz and Miropolye, before World War I.

The most widely known of all Yiddish dramas, this "realistic play about mystical people," as Anski described it, has been filmed, televised, made into a number of operas, and repeatedly produced throughout the world. The plot portrays the exorcism of a dybbuk, a dead man's spirit entering a living person, here that of his beloved. The Russo-Polish setting of Hassidic pietism and mysticism poignantly underlines the play's morality, Anski's faith in man's innate potential for good, in his obligations to his fellow men, and in celestial justice. Anski wrote the play in 1914 in Russian for Konstantin Stanislavsky, but the censor banned it. Incorporating Stanislavsky's suggestions, Anski enlarged and translated it into the Yiddish *Tsvishn Tsvey Veltn: Der Dibuk* (*Between Two Worlds: The Dybbuk*). The poet Chaim Nachman Bialik translated it into Hebrew, in which language it was first published as *Bney Schney Olamot: Ha'Dibuk*. Anski amplified and retranslated it into the Yiddish play which had its world premiere in Warsaw a month after his death.

Act I. It is dark. "Why did the soul / From its exalted height / Fall into abysmal depths?" a chorus sings, and concludes: "Within itself, the Fall / Contains the Resurrection." In the old Brinnitz synagogue, professional prayermen tell each other wondrous tales. When a young yeshiva student, Khonnon, goes out, they talk about him. Originally a stranger in Brinnitz but long a brilliant student at the local yeshiva, Khonnon has changed lately: now he fasts and meditates constantly, and appears to be involved in cabalistic studies. The prayermen discuss Reb Sender, at

The Dybbuk, Act II. The dance of the beggars, Leah (Mary Ellis) at right. Habima production in New York, 1925. (*Culver Pictures*)

whose house Khonnon once lived. He is a wealthy and pious man who keeps breaking off financially unsuitable matches arranged for his only daughter, Leah. Later Khonnon returns. His and Leah's names, he remarks, have the same sum: "'Leah' also spells 'not God.' Not through God." He shudders: "What a thought—and how I am drawn to it." But he justifies his studies: "Cabala tears one's soul from the earth! It raises man to the most exalted holiness—to Paradise!" Then he shocks the others by declaring that sin contains holiness—since God creates everything: "Sin must be purified of its uncleanness until only holiness remains." Leah appears with her aged nurse and a friend. Khonnon stares at the beautiful girl, but does not talk as she passes him and kisses the holy scrolls passionately. To his frightened friend, Khonnon reveals that to win Leah he must get money, by whatever means, "for him who can count only coins." Reb Sender comes in to announce the betrothal of his daughter Leah. Khonnon is distraught: "So they were useless! All the fasts, all the ablutions, all that harrowing of flesh, all those spells—were wasted!" He falls to the ground. A mysterious Messenger who earlier had discussed the transmigration of souls remarks: "the candle has burnt out. A new one must be lit." When the engagement celebration begins, the dancers realize to their horror that Khonnon is dead. The Messenger concludes: "The harm has been done."

Act II. On the Brinnitz square three months later, the festivities preceding Leah's wedding are in full swing. There is a feast for the poor, and Leah dances with beggar women. As if in a dream, however, Leah feels the souls of the dead about her, particularly those who have died before their time. The Messenger tells her of the "wandering souls that find no rest. They enter the living body of another as a dybbuk and thereby attain purity." But though she trembles, Leah goes to the cemetery to visit her mother's grave. She intends to invite her and other family souls to her wedding—and also that of one who "was like one of us." As Reb Sender talks with the bridegroom, and as the beggars discuss the wedding, Leah is brought back from the cemetery. Her frightened nurse refuses to reveal what happened. But Leah, tearing her veil from her face, rejects the bridegroom, calls his father a "murderer," and cries out wildly in strange, masculine tones, "I have returned to my destined bride, and I will not leave her." The excited bystanders think she is mad, but the Messenger announces: "The bride has been possessed by a dybbuk."

Act III. A few days later, old Rabbi Azrielke of Miropolye wearily preaches of man's unrealized spiritual potential, of the divine, and of individual human sins, each of which brings universal destruction. Even exalted souls may fall, he concludes: "And the more exalted it was, the deeper is the abyss into which it falls. And when such a soul falls, a world is destroyed." Reb Sender arrives with Leah and begs Azrielke's help. He tells the rabbi he cannot recall any sin, and thus cannot explain his daughter's possession by a dybbuk. Rabbi Azrielke questions Leah, who (in the dybbuk's voice) defends his cabalistic studies and insists: "I am her destined bridegroom." He will not obey the rabbi's command "to leave the body of this girl so that a living branch of the eternal tree of Israel may not wither and die." Azrielke threatens to excommunicate the dybbuk, and seeks the Rabbi of Miropolye's leave to do so. Both rabbis question Sender. Khonnon's dead father has appeared before him in a dream, the Miropolye Rabbi reveals, and cited an unrealized claim against Sender. Before any excommunication, the rabbi decrees a trial of the deceased and of Sender, to examine the claim. Though staggered by the turn of events, Sender submits to the rabbis' summons.

Act IV. After incantations and the drawing of magic circles, the trial of Reb Sender and Khonnon's dead father begins. Miropolye's Rabbi narrates the dead man's claims. They were once friends and pledged to have their children marry each other. Though their children eventually fell in love, Khonnon was poor, "and you turned your gaze from him and sought other matches." This plunged Khonnon into despair, causing him to die before his time, "and his soul wandered homelessly until it entered as a dybbuk into the body of its destined bride." The rabbis decree that while it is true Sender did not know Khonnon was his friend's son, he perceived it deep in his heart, and therefore did not inquire. To be forgiven, Sender must give half his wealth to the poor and recite prayers for the dead men as if they were his own family. Though Sender submits to this decree, Khonnon's father does not, and will not forgive. Now Rabbi Azrielke again exhorts the dybbuk to leave Leah's body. The dybbuk resists with all his strength. The rams' horns are blown as the incantations are pronounced, and he weakens. Finally, when the excommunication formula is spoken, the dybbuk submits. The excommunication is thereupon revoked, and all go out to welcome the bridegroom's party, arrived for the wedding that may now take place. Left with only her nurse, Leah hears Khonnon's voice. He and Leah reaffirm their mutual love. "You returned and in my heart bloomed a life of death and a joy of sorrow," Leah says: "Why have you forsaken me again?" Khonnon recounts his struggle against the rabbi's commands: "When the last spark of my strength was burned out, I departed from your body to return to your soul." As the wedding march is heard outside, the lovers call to each other. Leah goes to the white spot that is Khonnon, "and her figure blends with his." The crowds enter, and Leah's voice is heard as from afar: "I am joined with you, my destined bridegroom. Together we will soar higher, higher, higher." Darkness falls, and Rabbi Azrielke realizes they are too late. "Blessed be the True Judge," says the Messenger, and in the distance there is singing: "Why did the soul / From its exalted height / Fall into abysmal depths? / Within itself, the Fall / Contains the Resurrection."

DYMOV, Ossip [Joseph Pearlman] (1878–1959), Yiddish playwright, first wrote in his native Russian. His plays range from comedy through poetic SYMBOLISM, the two most successful ones being a tragedy and a fantasy. The first, *Nyu, Oder Alle Tog* (1907), later became famous as *Nju* and was filmed with Elisabeth Bergner; its restless title character leaves her husband for an artistic libertine, and when he discards her and her child, she eventually ends in prison. The second, *Bronx Express* (1919), is a Yiddish precursor of Kaufman and Connelly's BEGGAR ON HORSEBACK. The Habima theatre of Israel achieved its first success with Dymov's *Shema Yisrael,* with which, beginning in 1913, it toured in Vienna before the Eleventh Zionist Congress and in many East European communities. Another notable production of a Dymov play was that of the historical *Der Eybiker Vanderer* (1913) in New York. Dymov's other plays include *Shklafn fun Folk* (1918) and *Mentshn-Shtoyb* (1927).

DYNAMO, a play in three acts by EUGENE O'NEILL, published and produced in 1929. Setting: a small Connecticut town and a nearby hydroelectric power plant, late 1920's.

Though the abstract, lifeless characters help make this one of his least appealing plays, they most explicitly express O'Neill's pervasive theme of "the roots of the sickness of today." As he defined this sickness in a frequently quoted letter to George Jean Nathan, it is "the death of the old God and the failure of science and materialism to give any satisfying new one for the surviving primitive religious instinct to find a meaning for life in, and to comfort its fears of death with." The play is the first of a trilogy that was never continued; it uses asides in the manner of STRANGE INTERLUDE.

Reuben, the shy son of the Fundamentalist Reverend Hutchins Light, loves Ada, the daughter of his militantly atheist neighbor, Ramsay Fife. Playing a practical joke on the Lights, Fife exposes the fanatic minister's vicious stupidity. He incidentally brings out also Mrs. Light's jealousy of Ada, which is so strong that she vindictively betrays Reuben, who has always adored her. Broken by this betrayal and disillusioned with his father, Reuben renounces God as well as his parents, and leaves home. He returns fifteen months later, the hardened preacher of a new religion: science, whose godhead is electricity. The bovine and fleshy May Fife, Ada's sentimental mother, who loves the humming of dynamos, stupidly encourages this new religious fanaticism and what is now his lust for Ada. Reuben's mother is dead, but he is comforted to learn that she sought his forgiveness and that she rejected God with her dying words. Considering it as "sinful" to his new god as it would have been to his father's Jehovah, Reuben soon begins to feel guilty over his love-making with Ada, whom his mother hated. He experiences a growing need to worship, and he approaches the dynamo in the power plant:

"It's like a great dark idol . . . round like a woman's [body,] . . . a great, dark mother!" He kneels and prays before this "Mother-God." Some months later, having "given up the flesh and purified myself," and expecting to be men's new savior, he awaits a revelation from his God: "the Great Mother of Eternal Life, Electricity, and Dynamo is her Divine Image on earth!" As a final act of contrition and purification from fleshly sin he kills Ada. In anguish and fear he then embraces the dynamo and is instantly electrocuted. He dies "in a moan that is a mingling of pain and loving consummation."

DYNASTS, THE, "an epic-drama of the war with Napoleon in three parts, nineteen acts, and one hundred and thirty scenes" by THOMAS HARDY, published in 1904 (Part I), 1906 (Part II), and 1908 (Part III), and produced in 1914 (abridged). Setting: Europe, 1805–15.

This poetic history play, Hardy's most ambitious work, is in blank verse alternating with other meter and with prose. Resembling LEO TOLSTOI'S panoramic novel *War and Peace* in scope, its protagonist is Napoleon, but there are hundreds of other historical as well as supernatural characters, plus "crowds" and "armies." Hardy noted in his preface that "*The Dynasts* is intended simply for mental performance, and not for the stage," and the introduction to the text's 1965 republication stresses its cinematic qualities, particularly evident in the descriptive "dumb shows" and stage directions, the structure, and the epic canvas. Though adapted for stage production by HARLEY GRANVILLE-BARKER and others, *The Dynasts* is a closet drama. It has received very mixed critical appraisals. See A. Chakravarty's *The Dynasts and the Post-War Age in Poetry* (1938), J. O. Bailey's *Thomas Hardy and the Cosmic Mind: A New Reading of The Dynasts* (1956), and Harold Orel's *Thomas Hardy's Epic-Drama: A Study of The Dynasts* (1963).

Part I portrays the House of Commons coping with the threat of invasion, Napoleon's coronation in Milan, various battles (Ulm, Austerlitz, Trafalgar), and the deaths of Nelson and of Pitt. *Part II* portrays the Jena victory, Napoleon's meeting with the Emperor Alexander I, the defeat of Spain and its king's abdication, and Napoleon's divorce from Josephine and marriage to Marie Louise. *Part III* portrays the Russian campaign, British victories, the Leipzig battle, and Napoleon's abdication, his return from Elba, and Waterloo. His final realization is that "Great men are meteors that consume themselves / To light the earth. This is my burnt out hour." All human events, the "Spirit Ironic" chants, are controlled by a "dark, dumb Thing / That turns the handle of this idle Show!"

These grand historical events are interspersed with ordinary episodes among common people, and with speeches by "Phantom Intelligences." The latter are contrasting spirits and choral groups of supernatural characters ruled by an Immanent Will—the force that (according to Hardy's fatalism) destroys men and governs the cosmos.

E

EACH IN HIS OWN WAY (*Ciascuno a suo modo*), "a comedy in two or three acts with choral interludes" by LUIGI PIRANDELLO, published and produced in 1924. Setting: contemporary aristocratic homes and a theatre lobby.

This is the second play in the trilogy that begins with SIX CHARACTERS IN SEARCH OF AN AUTHOR. It is, like *Six Characters,* a play-within-a-play, but here the conflict is portrayed on three levels of reality: the "play," the "audience" in the "lobby" during the interludes, and the two "real" people in that audience on whose lives the "play" is based. The "play" is a cerebral melodrama, but one of the characters—Pirandello's spokesman Diego Cinci—portrays the tragic torment that seethes beneath the "play."

Act I. At a tea party some guests discuss opinions. The most eloquent speaker—Diego Cinci—says that one cannot possibly have any opinions, because they constantly change along with the people and situations on which they are based. Further, Diego maintains that individual conscience is nothing but public opinion. This negation of the rational is reflected in the guests' speculations about the behavior of their hostess's son and his friend on the previous evening. The young men had quarreled publicly about a notoriously promiscuous actress whose fiancé committed suicide when he found her unfaithful. One friend charged that she had killed her suitor with her treachery, while the other idealized her act as intentional kindness to the fiancé, an artist she knew would be ruined if he married her. The friends soon are eager to apologize: each has been persuaded by the other's arguments. Thus, still as far apart as ever, they quarrel again and arrange to fight a duel. The actress, Delia Morello, appears to thank her (former) defender, whose remarks explained and revealed her true self to her. Her beauty and her exultant acceptance of his earlier rationale change his mind about her once more. A tormented and confused soul, Delia tells him that she gave herself to the artist's brother-in-law, Michele Rocca, because the artist prized only her beauty and because his family would not accept her. Her defender now sneers smugly at his opponent's initial attacks on her "cheap game" to advance herself and humiliate the artist's family. But he is crushed when—impressed by that version of her behavior—Delia says, "Who knows that those weren't the reasons?"

Interlude I. In the theatre lobby during the intermission, spectators are discussing the first act. Some are puzzled. Pirandello's supporters argue with his opponents, and newspaper critics cagily express tentative opinions. The "play" is gradually revealed to be a dramatization of a real contemporary scandal. An elderly baron and a young actress—Rocca and Delia in the "play"—are among the audience and both are enraged at the insult. The actress wants to go backstage, but as the second act is starting, she returns to her box to watch it. The ushers are sure there will be trouble later.

Act II. Diego tells a friend about Delia's grateful visit and the consequent confusion: "After we have witnessed the farce of our own absurd changes of opinion, we have before us the tragedy of a bewildered spirit, gone astray and unable to find its way again." He is talking not only of Delia but also of Rocca, who has returned from Naples to challenge one of the friends. Having fathomed his own despair, Diego suggests that the two quarreling young men also recognize their "filth and muck and smallness," and forego the duel brought on by their self-delusions: "Shake yourself free from the manikin you create out of a false interpretation of what you do and what you feel." Rocca arrives with his challenge: he claims that he spent the night with Delia on a wager, proving her perfidy in order to save the artist. Just then Delia appears. Their sudden confrontation reveals the self-deception with which Rocca and Delia have consistently masked their mutual passion, and a new reality that neither they nor the others had perceived before emerges. They fly into each other's arms; then, sharing the guilt for the artist's suicide, they rush out together to "drown in his blood." "Two lunatics!" cries one of the two young men. Diego answers, "You don't see yourself!" His comments suggest that these events illustrate the tragedy that follows delusion —the failure of men to face their own reality, "each in his own way."

Interlude II. In the theatre lobby, unusual noises are heard from backstage. The real Delia has slapped the leading lady, and bedlam breaks out. The actors leave in anger, while the baron indignantly complains about being ridiculed in public. Then the young actress appears, disheveled and weeping. Their sudden confrontation reveals the self-deception with which the baron and the young actress have masked *their* mutual passion. Like their prototypes in the "play," they fly into each other's arms; but feeling guilty about the artist's suicide, they rush out together to "drown in his blood." A spectator remarks, "They rebelled because they saw themselves there, as in a mirror, forced into a situation that has the eternity of art! . . . They have done, here before our eyes and quite involuntarily, something that the author had foreseen!"

Act III does not begin. The stage manager announces that because of the backstage disturbances the evening's performance cannot be concluded.

EAGLE HAS TWO HEADS, THE (*L'Aigle à deux têtes*), a play in three acts by JEAN COCTEAU, published and produced in 1946. Setting: Krantz Castle.

The plot of this gothic melodrama (filmed by Cocteau in 1948) is vaguely based on the 1898 assassination of the Empress Elizabeth of Austria. In the play neither queen nor country is named.

The queen holds a ghostly celebration of the tenth anniversary of her marriage and widowhood, for her husband was assassinated on the day she was going to start living as a married woman. Since then she has felt dead. She is surprised by a would-be assassin, the anarchist Stanislas, who under the name *Azraël* has written treasonable poems that she admires. The queen intends to make him the instrument of her wished-for death, but he remarkably resembles her husband, and she falls in love with him. Poetic in temperament, they share their solitude and become lovers—like the two-headed eagle on her coat of arms: "If one head is cut off, the eagle dies." Court intrigue soon convinces Stanislas that the world is debased, and their happiness is thus impossible. He takes poison, and the queen, heartbroken, taunts him into stabbing her so that they may die together.

EARL OF BJÄLBO, THE (*Bjälbo-Jarlen*), a historical play in five acts by AUGUST STRINDBERG, published and produced in 1909. Setting: Sweden during Birger's regency, 1248–66.

In his last chronicle play, the aging and lonely Strindberg painted an autobiographically colored portrait of his protagonist. In the thirteenth century, Earl Birger schemed ruthlessly to unify a loose confederacy, introduce justice and law, and make Sweden a great power. The culmination of the dynasty he established is dramatized in Strindberg's spectacular earlier play THE FOLKUNG SAGA.

Earl Birger has almost achieved his goals, but he is troubled by his family and his failure to gain the crown. Despite the fact that he himself has introduced Christianity and many popular reforms, he is contemptuous of both the Church and the people. Arrogant and bitter, he believes only in himself: "This! My fist!" Eventually his various schemes collapse. His second son, displaying unsuspected courage and ability, takes the crown from his disgraced elder brother, and stands up to and defeats the earl, who is humbled at last: "Be master and ruler. My son, I forgive what you have done to your father this hour. My king, I hail thee!" But the new king assures his weary father, "Foremost in the list of Swedish kings, though not a king, shall be the name that you have made as ruler!"

EARTH-SPIRIT (*Erdgeist*), a tragedy in a verse prologue and four acts by FRANK WEDEKIND, published in 1895 and produced in 1898. Setting: studio, theatre dressing-room, and drawing rooms; *fin de siècle* Germany.

This is the first part of the "Lulu monster tragedy" that concludes with PANDORA'S BOX. Its clipped dialogue anticipated EXPRESSIONISM, and its daring portrayal of sexuality ("earth-spirit") shocked many audiences. Lulu is a "Pandora's box" for the illusive happiness of men: each of her lovers gives her a different name. But she is really their amoral destroyer—soulless and lustful Woman, portrayed in the prologue as a beautiful serpent in the menagerie that is mankind. At first these interdependent plays were conceived as a five-act tragedy, but Wedekind kept reworking its structure as well as Lulu's character. Accompanied by one of the original scenes, these changes are described by his daughter, Kadidja Wedekind-Biel, in *Modern Drama IV: 1* (May 1961).

Acts I and II. Lulu's doting husband, an elderly physician, brings her to an artist's studio to have her portrait painted. Her provocative attitude is criticized by Dr. Ludwig Schön, a powerful editor. When alone with the artist, Lulu seduces him. Her husband unexpectedly returns, realizes what has happened, and dies of apoplexy. The cold-blooded, rich widow then marries the painter, who soon becomes a great success. Lulu admits to her father, Schilgoch—who was her former lover and subsequently becomes her pimp—that she is an animal. She lusts for Schön, who wants to marry an innocent young society girl and warns Lulu to leave him alone and stay with her painter. But she is jealous of Schön's fiancée and bored with her doting husband, whom she asks Schön to destroy: "You must lead him astray. You're an expert in such things. Bring him into bad company." To protect himself, Schön tells the painter to keep closer watch on his wife and reveals how he had arranged this as well as Lulu's previous marriage, in order to have her under "safekeeping." "You married half a million. Today you're one of our leading artists. One doesn't get as far as that without money," he tells Lulu's husband and notes, "You're not the one to sit in judgment on her." When he understands that Lulu is Schön's mistress, the husband cuts his throat. Schön's son Alwa, a young dramatist who grew up with Lulu, blames the death on his father for not marrying Lulu. Coolly wiping off her husband's blood stains, Lulu assures Schön, "You'll marry me in the end."

Acts III and IV. Again a widow and aided by Schön, Lulu is now a famous ballet dancer starring in Alwa's play. She tells a prince who pays her court in the dressing room that she never notices the audience. But during her skirt dance she sees Schön with his fiancée, and collapses. In a stormy session, Lulu finally vanquishes Schön and dictates a note from him to his fiancée: "I have been trying to break away for three years; I have not the strength. I am writing to you at the side of the woman who dominates me. You must forget me." Soon married to Lulu and bitterly suspicious, Schön pretends one day to be out of the house. He observes the people who visit her—and then hide—in tandem: her lesbian friend, Countess Martha Geschwitz; the depraved old Schigolch; a powerful acrobat, the common Rodrigo Quast; a young student; and finally his own son, Alwa. Lulu glories in her body: "When I looked at myself in the mirror I wished I were a man—my own husband!" She provokes even the butler, and Alwa finally confesses his "unsiblinglike" love. While telling Alwa that she poisoned his mother (Schön's wife), Lulu sees her husband. Schön curses her as a "wretched creature, dragging me through the gutter to a martyr's death," and hands her a pistol: she must kill herself—or him. After melodramatic exchanges, Lulu shoots Schön, "The only man I ever loved!" Lulu feeds him champagne as he writhes in agony and tells his son Alwa, "You are the next one." When Schön is dead, Lulu implores Alwa, "You can ask what you please. Don't let me fall into the hands of the law. It would be such a pity!" She throws herself at him—"Look at me, Alwa, look at me, man! Look at me!"—as the police knock on the door.

EASIEST WAY, THE, a play in four acts by EUGENE WALTER, published and produced in 1908. Setting: Colorado Springs and New York City, early twentieth century.

This popular "sinning woman" play, published with elaborate character analyses, has been praised by some as a skillful and uncompromising portrayal of reality. Yet the play also has been criticized for its inconsistent characterization and contrived melodrama. Walter himself later dismissed the play as "rather devilishly clever."

Laura Murdock, the lavishly kept mistress of a wealthy elderly man, falls in love with a poor journalist. As an actress, she tries to live a pure and independent life, but finds sordid poverty too difficult. She returns to her wealthy lover, again choosing "the easiest way." Laura does not reveal her relapse to the journalist she loves, who returns for her after making his fortune. When her elderly lover learns that she has not kept her promise to write the journalist about her choice, he informs the latter of Laura's "fall." Desperately she tries to justify her action. But the young man leaves her: "Laura, you're not immoral, you're just unmoral, kind o' all out of shape, and I'm afraid there isn't a particle of hope for you." Hysterical, she tries to shoot herself, and then recklessly decides to have a gay evening. "Dress up my body and paint my face," she bids her maid: "I'm going to Rector's to make a hit—and to hell with the rest!" But the sounds of a hurdy-gurdy from the street, playing the suggestive song "Bon-Bon Buddie, My Chocolate Drop," make her realize the inevitable consequences of her "questionable career." Grief-stricken, she totters to the bedroom.

EAST AFRICA has produced scant literature except poetry, though numerous modern plays began to appear in Ethiopia after World War II. Tsegaye Gabre-Medhin (1935–), director of the new Haile Selassie Theatre, wrote some twenty plays in Amharic and his *Oda Oak Oracle, A Legend of Black Peoples . . .* (1965) has appeared in English. Other modern Ethiopian playwrights are Berhanu Denqé (? –), whose poetic *Negest Akeb* (1951) depicts the Queen of Sheba's visit to King Solomon; Katchew Bitwoded Makonnen (1927–), Ethiopia's former Prime Minister and the author of historical dramas including one about King David, *Salsawi Dawit* (1951); Mikael Kabbada (? –), whose verse plays include *Ya-tinbit qutaro* (*Fulfillment of Prophecy,* 1946); and Takla-Hawaryat Germanchew (? -), whose poetic drama *Tiēwodros* (1950) features Emperor Theodore II (Negus), who committed suicide after battling the English.

Other East African nations also produced some drama shortly after the mid-century, some of it written by young black playwrights. Tanzania's President Mwalimu Julius K. Nyerere (1922–) prepared a frequently performed Swahili version of Shakespeare's *Julius Caesar* (published in 1963). In Kenya, Rebecca Njau (1932–) was acclaimed for *The Scar* (1965), a poetic tragedy; and the journalist and short-story writer James Ngugi (1938–) has written a notable play about an educated native torn between the tribal and the modern ways of life, *The Black Hermit* (1962). In Malagasy (formerly Madagascar) the poet-playwright Jacques Rabemananjara (1913–) has written popular plays in French.

David Cook and Miles Lee's *Short East African Plays in English* (1968) includes ten one-acters originally produced in the vernacular by traveling theatres, by amateur groups, and over the radio. Its prefatory essay on East African drama may be supplemented with works listed under AFRICA.

EASTER (*Påsk*), a play in three acts by AUGUST STRINDBERG, published and produced in 1901. Setting: a small-town home in southern Sweden at the turn of the century.

Sanctimonious and atypical of Strindberg in its subdued tone and its presentation of woman as the agent of domestic peace, *Easter* is a NATURALISTIC yet mystical exemplum, like CRIMES AND CRIMES. The gentle Eleonora, a clairvoyant whose language is highly lyrical, was created for Harriet Bosse, the young actress who became Strindberg's third wife. Each act is introduced by music from a corresponding movement of Haydn's *The Seven Last Words of Christ.*

Act I. Maundy Thursday. Elis Heyst, a teacher, talks to his fiancée about his guilt and shame for his family—his father, an imprisoned embezzler, and his feeble-minded sixteen-year-old sister Eleonora, whom he helped commit to an asylum. Elis resents an ungrateful friend and is bitter about the family's main creditor, Lindkvist, whose threatening proximity looms over the house. His suffering grows when his best pupil fails the Latin examination, thus threatening Elis's professional ruin. Later his sister arrives, having escaped from the asylum. Deeply religious and sensitive to the pain of others, Eleonora has taken their guilt upon herself. With her extrasensory vision she had perceived the sorrow of some flowers in a store window; on her way home she broke into the shop and took them, leaving her card and money. Elis is overwhelmed when he hears of Eleonora's escape and arrival: "She is so unhappy herself—yet she brings joy to others. May God give me strength!"

Act II. Good Friday. The family is frightened by the threatened arrival of Lindkvist, who, however, fails to come. But Elis's relief is shattered when his fiancée prepares to go to a concert with his ungrateful friend. Sure now that he has lost her, Elis is a broken man. The flowershop "burglary" is being investigated because the money Eleonora left has been overlooked. But the family's trouble "will straighten itself out when Good Friday is over," she declares: "Today the rod, tomorrow the Easter eggs. Today snow, tomorrow thaw! Today death, tomorrow the Resurrection!"

Act III. Easter Eve. There is coldness in the house, particularly between the jealous Elis and his fiancée. Elis is further humiliated when his mother reveals her complicity in his father's downfall, and justifies it as due to his "arrogance—presumption—by which we all fall!" The discovery of Eleonora's innocence when the money is found produces only momentary solace, for Lindkvist at last does come. He is a Dickensian character, who is, at the same time, the play's *raisonneur* and all-knowing *deus ex machina.* His menacing threats are instruments for scourging Elis: "I am bent on squeezing all your false pride, your haughtiness, and maliciousness out of you!" When Elis finally humbles himself, Lindkvist displays "a kind of charity that conflicts with justice—and that goes *beyond* justice—and that is—mercy!" He reveals that he has also been the father's debtor for an old kindness. The ungrateful friend, whose meeting with Elis's fiancée was totally innocent, is discovered also to have done the family a good turn. Happily Eleonora calls for a thanksgiving prayer, "for now there are no more clouds . . . and so it can be heard up there."

ECHEGARAY [y Eizaguirre], **José** (1832–1916), was Spain's first important modern dramatist. Achieving early prominence as a mathematician and then as a statesman, Echegaray turned to the theatre at forty-two. His plays are hopelessly dated romantic thesis melodramas in the tradition of Castilian chivalry (principally the seventeenth-century plays of Calderón) and of late nineteenth-century NATURALISTIC thesis drama (principally that of HENRIK IBSEN). Yet from the 1870's through the first decade of this century, Echegaray dominated stages with his nearly seventy plays—many of them hits, the most pronounced and best-known being *El Gran Galeoto* (THE GREAT GALEOTO, 1881). Echegaray also was the first modern Spaniard to gain major foreign recognition; jointly with the poet Frédéric Mistral he was awarded the 1904 Nobel Prize for literature.

Echegaray was born in Madrid. As a student he excelled in mathematics, and he headed the list of graduating engineers. In his early twenties he was appointed professor of mathematics at Madrid's School of Civil Engineering; soon he published two authoritative technical books and began to propagate freer trade doctrines. During the Revolution of 1868 he was appointed the interim minister of education and finance. After the restoration of the Bourbons, Echegaray became a dramatist, following in the footsteps of his brother Miguel (1848–1927), the author of many comedy hits.

As early as 1867 José Echegaray had written two plays. These—*La última noche* (1875) and *Para tal culpa tal pena* (1877)—appeared only after he became famous as a playwright. He made his debut as a dramatist in 1874 with *El libro talonario,* a clever one-act verse comedy, and a yet more successful romantic drama, *La esposa del vengador.* Both were characteristic of his mathematically constructed plots and extravagance, and they launched him on his career in the theatre. Echegaray's popularity was sealed the following year with an even greater hit, the romantic melodrama *En el puño de la espada* (1875). In the next three decades appeared a steady stream of popular Echegaray plays.

Most notable after *The Great Galeoto,* especially abroad, were *O locura o santidad* (1876, translated as both *Folly or Saintliness* and *Madman or Saint*), *Mariana* (1892), and *El hijo de Don Juan* (*The Son of Don Juan,* 1892). The first, which marks the start of Ibsen's influence (in this case that of BRAND) on Echegaray, features a man ever more madly pursuing his "duty" to restore his fortune to its rightful owner; when his efforts conflict with his daughter's happiness in a projected marriage, which he considers ignoble, his family ends the honorable pursuit by having him committed. The protagonist of *Mariana* gives up the man she loves because his father had wronged her mother, and marries a middle-aged general because she knows he will punish her if she yields to her lover; she does yield, then promptly summons her husband ("Your honor calls you!") to kill her, and he complies before dueling with his rival. *The Son of Don Juan* was praised by BERNARD SHAW for Echegaray's "original treatment" of the theme of Ibsen's GHOSTS: it attacks a father's immorality and dramatizes his son's problem of honor (whether the son should ignore duty and seek happiness in marriage); though congenitally syphilitic, he decides to marry the girl he loves and needs, but is stopped by his father and collapses (like Oswald in *Ghosts*)—asking for the sun. Among other Echegaray plays that appeared in English is *El loco dios* (*The Madman Divine,* 1900), whose insane protagonist wants to marry a young widow but is stopped by her relatives; the play is so bad that some considered it a parody of Ibsen's symbolic dramas. Echegaray's last play was *A fuerza de arrastrarse* (1905), "a comic farce" about a ruthless upstart.

In his preface to an early social play, *Cómo*

empieza y cómo acaba (1876), which is part of a trilogy on the heritage of evil, Echegaray wrote of his concern with fate and "the logic of fatality" that "dominates when moral liberty cedes to passion its place in the human soul." He seriously pursued this theme—and seriousness is precisely one of the weaknesses of Echegaray's plays, for they consistently lack humor. He was deficient too in characterization, and his dialogue—verse as well as prose—is undistinguished. But Echegaray was immensely prolific, highly imaginative, and a master technician of the theatre. His inevitable concern with the *punto de honor,* the Castilian "point of honor" and its esteem for men's passionate defense of women's ethereal purity, would today seem peculiarly anachronistic to Anglo-American audiences. At the time, however, Echegaray's histrionics had an appeal even to them. In his collected *Dramatic Opinions and Essays* (1916) Shaw, who considered Echegaray "extremely readable," praised *The Son of Don Juan,* though he had less use for another play popular in England, *Mariana.*

Readily available among the translations of Echegaray's plays is *The Great Galeoto,* which appears in Angel Flores's collection of *Spanish Drama* (1962). Its prefatory note and bibliography may be supplemented with the chapters on Echegaray in Isaac Goldberg's *The Drama of Transition* (1922) and Frank W. Chandler's *Modern Continental Playwrights* (1931).

ECUADOR, whose theatre is negligible, has produced few playwrights and little drama. Notable are Enrique Avellán Ferrés (1908–), a prolific dramatist whose first play, the antidivorce tragedy *Como los árboles* (1927), was praised for its character portrayals and suspense, but who gave up playwriting in the 1940's to become a lawyer; Luis A. Moscoso Vega (1909–), whose best play, *Conscripción* (1941), deals with the mistreatment of the Indians; Demetrio Aguilera Malta (1909–), who wrote many plays, beginning with an often-produced tragedy about a schoolteacher, *Lázaro* (1941), but finding native theatre inadequate migrated to BRAZIL and then to MEXICO; and Francisco Tobar García (1928–), a professor who has written over a dozen anguished tragedies as well as some comedies, most popular among them being *La noche no es para dormir* (1960)—which was influenced by HENRY JAMES and CHRISTOPHER FRY—the Sophocles-inspired *Las llave del abismo* (1961), and a "burlesque detective play," *En alguien muere la víspera* (1962).

For studies in English see LATIN AMERICA.

EICHELBAUM, Samuel (1894–1967), was the leading mid-twentieth-century Argentine playwright. Influenced by HENRIK IBSEN as well as AUGUST STRINDBERG and ANTON CHEKHOV, Eichelbaum created often unpleasant, tormented characters in NATURALISTIC settings. Though his plots and language are of little distinction, he excelled in subtle depictions of character and family life. Most notable is his *Un guapo del 900* (1940), his first "universal" drama and the first to bring him financial success: the title's "twentieth-century bully," a politician's bodyguard, kills the rival who betrayed his patron's honor by seducing the latter's wife; at the play's climax, his mother begs the bully to hide his crime so that he will remain free later to perform a son's last rites for her. Among Eichelbaum's other plays are *La mala sed* (1920), which traces the transmission of evil—excessive sexuality—from father to children, ending with a suicide; *Cuando tengas un hijo* (1929), a moving psychological melodrama dealing with three lonely people; *Pájaro de barro* (1940), again about lonely people, here a woman who proudly refuses to marry her sculptor-lover after their child's birth because he is interested only in his clay; and *Un tal servando Gómez* (1942), an atypically "pleasant drama" in which a son reunites his parents. Because of their cerebral qualities and abstract psychology, these and Eichelbaum's later plays appeared more effective in print than on the stage.

The son of Russian Jewish immigrants, Eichelbaum began writing plays when he was seven. He managed a stock company with which he toured Argentina and neighboring countries, and he organized and directed other companies. As a leading Spanish American playwright, his work is discussed in LATIN AMERICAN studies. The climactic scene of *Un guapo del 900* appears in Willis K. Jones's *Spanish-American Literature in Translation* (1963).

EITHER OF ONE OR OF NO ONE (*O di uno o di nessuno*), a play in three acts by LUIGI PIRANDELLO, published and produced in 1929. Setting: contemporary Italy.

As in THE NEW COLONY, motherhood purifies and redeems the prostitute heroine, here called Melina Franco.

Two clerks invite Melina from their hometown to live in Rome with them. They enjoy a happy life for a while, and Melina flourishes. Then nature trips them up: Melina becomes pregnant and, much as they try, the clerks cannot determine which of them is the father. Deciding that the baby will be "either of one or of no one," they ask Melina to give it up. But radiant at her impending motherhood, she absolutely refuses: "The child will be born and I shall bring him up—keep him with me—he's my child." They quarrel and leave her; when it is born, Melina gives the child her own family name and tries to care for it herself. But she is sick and soon dies. Pirandello's spokesman is a sarcastic lawyer who understands better than the clerks do that they invited Melina because of their sentimentality and homesickness. He laughs at "the buffoonery of nature"; yet he is the one who is by Melina's side when she dies. Her baby is left to a mother who has just lost her child and changes the new baby's family name to her own.

EL SALVADOR, the smallest of Central America's republics, has been very active culturally. Though its theatre has remained relatively undeveloped because cheaper movies could attract more of its impoverished populace, El Salvador has produced some notable playwrights. Their precursor was the poet Francisco Antonio Gavidia (1864–1955), who for over half a century wrote elaborate and massively cast plays—romantic as well as SYMBOLIC—on native themes: *Jupiter esclavo o Blanca Celis* (1895), his best drama and a plea for education and liberty, exemplifies his symbolism in the Negro Jupiter's personification of the people; *Cuento de marino* (1947), a colonial Erl-king verse drama, is among Gavidia's finer romances. Other early moderns include Joaquín Emilio Aragón (1887–1938), a romanticist whose *Los contrabandistas* (1911) was much admired; and the GUATEMALA-born José Llerena (1895–1943), who wrote a number of comedies that express his fears of North America's growing influence. Llerena also brought NATURALISM to the drama of El Salvador.

Among promising later playwrights are Waldo Chávez Velasco (1922–), a poet praised as El Salvador's leading contemporary dramatist and a prize winner for his *Fábrica de sueños* (1957) and *Un poco de silencio en la tormenta* (1958); and Walter Béneke (1928–), once an ambassador to Germany and known abroad for *El paraíso de los imprudentes* (1956), a multiple love-affair drama with existentialist overtones and set in Paris, and the poetic *Funeral Home* (1958), portraying an American Christmas Eve celebration as a widow watches by her husband's corpse and a fearful murderer commits suicide at midnight.

For studies in English see LATIN AMERICA.

ELDER STATESMAN, THE, a verse play in three acts by T. S. ELIOT, produced in 1958 and published in 1959. Setting: London and Badgley Court, contemporary England.

Eliot's last play, loosely based on Sophocles's *Oedipus at Colonus,* celebrates human love. The title character, Lord Claverton, is a retired executive. Because he is terrified by loneliness, his daughter postpones her marriage. Lord Claverton is tormented by the reappearance of a man and a woman he had wronged in his youth. Eventually he recognizes them as "merely ghosts" who were always with him. After confessing his disreputable past, Lord Claverton finds himself "emerging / From my spectral existence into something like reality." He goes off to die, content with newfound love and forgiveness, while his daughter and her fiancé reaffirm their mutual love.

ELECTRA (*Electre*), a play in two acts and an interlude by JEAN GIRAUDOUX, published and produced in 1937. Setting: ancient Greece.

This is a somewhat diffuse but original modernization of the Greek legend: Orestes's furies are little girls, Electra is about to marry a gardener, an ironic beggar (originally played by Louis Jouvet) is the choral *raisonneur,* etc. Electra only gradually discovers that her mother and Aegisthus are guilty of Agamemnon's murder, although she has instinctively always hated Clytemnestra. Private vengeance now is complicated by Aegisthus's capable and beneficial rule. Further, the town is besieged and is doomed without him. Nonetheless, and despite Aegisthus's eloquent defense of practical expedience, Electra chooses ruin over a national weal based on lies. She insists on punishing Aegisthus and Clytemnestra. They are killed, the city is aflame, and casualties mount. Electra is satisfied: "I have my conscience, I have Orestes, I have justice, I have everything."

ELECTRA (*Elektra*), a one-act blank-verse tragedy by GERHART HAUPTMANN, produced in 1947 and published in 1948. Setting: the ruins of Demeter's temple near Mycenae, ancient Greece.

The third play of THE ATRIDES-TETRALOGY, it was published and produced together with AGAMEMNON'S DEATH.

Orestes has fled in horror from the Delphic oracle. Now he yearns for his mother's love; but a greatly changed Electra appears and calls for the revenge of Agamemnon's murder, as she has done for years. Sensitive and contemplative, Orestes shudders and collapses before the coming task. Fate, in the form of a thunderstorm, drives Clytemnestra and Aegisthus to shelter at the site of Agamemnon's murder. Electra presents Clytemnestra's blood-encrusted hatchet to Orestes and spurs him to action. He begs for the love that Clytemnestra contemptuously withholds until, realizing her doom, she attempts to beguile him with it and his father's crown. Threatening to interfere, Aegisthus is stabbed by Pylades. Clytemnestra curses her two children and attacks Orestes, who drags her to the bath where she slew his father. Screams are heard and Orestes returns with the hatchet: "Delphi's oracle has been fulfilled!"

ELECTRA (*Elektra*), a one-act verse tragedy by HUGO VON HOFMANNSTHAL, produced in 1903 and published in 1904. Setting: the inner court of the palace, ancient Greece.

Electra, Hofmannsthal's first popular success, subsequently became the libretto for Richard Strauss's opera (1909). The plot is freely adapted from Sophocles, but the tone resembles that of Wilde's SALOMÉ.

Electra's suggestively libidinous preoccupation with her dead father Agamemnon and with blood and revenge are contrasted with her sister Chrysothemis's yearnings for wife- and motherhood. She fails to persuade Chrysothemis to kill Clytemnestra and Aegisthus, but easily persuades the returning Orestes. Her frenzy reaches its climax after Orestes kills Clytemnestra and Aegisthus. Maenad-like, Electra triumphantly dances a "nameless dance," at the end of which she collapses lifeless.

ELGA, a play in six scenes by GERHART HAUPTMANN, published and produced in 1905. Setting: the medieval principality of Sendomir.

A once-popular but unimpressive dramatization of Franz Grillparzer's novella *Das Kloster bei Sendomir* (*The Cloister of Sendomir*, 1828), the play depicts a knight's dream of an ancestor's revenge on his adulterous wife (Elga) and her lover.

ELIOT, T[homas] S[tearns] (1888–1965), Anglo-American poet, critic, and playwright. Eliot's fame as the leading modern poet in England and America was rivaled only by that of WILLIAM BUTLER YEATS. Further, as the century's most influential literary critic, Eliot for decades shaped and dominated standards of taste. His importance as a dramatist, on the other hand, is decidedly minor, though in his later life he became increasingly interested and moderately successful in the theatre. His reputation as dramatist rests on five verse plays: MURDER IN THE CATHEDRAL (1935), THE FAMILY REUNION (1939), THE COCKTAIL PARTY (1949, his most popular play), THE CONFIDENTIAL CLERK (1953), and THE ELDER STATESMAN (1958).

Eliot was born in St. Louis, attended Harvard University as an undergraduate, and continued his studies there and in Europe. At the outbreak of World War I he left Germany for England, where he married (he remarried in 1957, ten years after his first wife's death) and lived most of his life. In 1927 he assumed British citizenship and was confirmed in the Church of England. It was in England that he met the poet Ezra Pound (who was to influence Eliot's work), reviewed books, taught, worked in a bank, edited books, lectured, and eventually joined the publishing firm of Faber & Faber. In England, too, he wrote the works that made him famous: such poems as "The Love Song of J. Alfred Prufrock" (1915), *The Waste Land* (1922), "The Hollow Men" (1925), and *Four Quartets* (1943); and the collections of criticisms published in *Selected Essays* (1932), *The Use of Poetry and the Use of Criticism* (1933), *On Poetry and Poets* (1957), and others.

Eliot's plays are prefigured in these poems and essays. In his early drama, the verse is rich in symbol, sound, and rhythm; effectively varied; and modulated to reflect different speakers and moods. In his later plays, on the other hand, the verse is hardly distinguishable from prose. The themes reflect Eliot's avowed convictions of "an Anglo-Catholic in religion, a classicist in literature, and a royalist in politics"; particularly they urge the reassertion of traditional Christian values amidst what Eliot portrays as the hollowness of modern life.

His first dramatic efforts were fragmentary. SWEENEY AGONISTES (1932), though highly praised by some critics, is felt by others to be very sketchy and incomplete; and *The Rock* (1934), written for the scenario by E. Martin Browne (who was to produce Eliot's later plays) for a liturgical pageant, consists mostly of nondramatic choral verses. His next play, the much-admired *Murder in the Cathedral*, portrays Thomas à Becket's martyrdom both as a medieval Christian drama with classic (Aeschylean) choruses and as a contemporary presentation with at times a shockingly modern perspective. Eliot felt encouraged by his success to continue writing verse drama. But since he considered this play a special case—it was written for the atypical religious audience at the Canterbury Festival—he changed his approach. To appeal to general theatre audiences, Eliot next used modern settings, middle-class characters, and predominantly prose dialogue that appears as verse only on the printed page. At the same time, the Christian themes explicitly presented in *Murder in the Cathedral* are implicit in and motivate the plots of the later plays. The protagonist of *The Family Reunion,* pursued Orestes-like by the furies of his conscience, gains blessed peace through expiation; Celia and Colby, the saintly figures of classic plots transformed into the drawing-room comedies *The Cocktail Party* and *The Confidential Clerk,* reach comparable goals; and the partly autobiographical, Oedipus-like Lord Claverton in *The Elder Statesman* through confession gains the human love that is celebrated in this final Eliot play.

Perhaps because he tried to popularize unpopular views and poetic theatre among mass audiences stealthily, Eliot produced drama that is often obscure in plot and rarely sustains the wit of first-rate drawing-room comedy. The characterizations are too flat and the situations too vague to be impressive as spiritual examples; and the ubiquitous liturgical overtones frequently detract from the comedy. Similarly, the language, when it does occasionally become unmistakably poetic, is embarrassingly out of place—as in the runic chorus of *The Family Reunion* and the litanies of *The Cocktail Party*. It is ironic but not surprising that Eliot was most successful as a dramatist when he least concealed poetry, ritual, and theology: in *Murder in the Cathedral*. Of his other works, only *The Cocktail Party* was popular as a play, and *its* success was primarily due to the appeal of the sparkling Broadway production and the distinction of Eliot's name as poet and literary critic—a distinction which had been rewarded the previous year (1948) with the Nobel Prize.

No less for his fine poetry than for the unabashed conservatism that permeates all his writings, Eliot has elicited a mass of polemical commentary. Among the many books devoted to him, the following deal particularly with Eliot the dramatist: Grover Smith's *T. S. Eliot's Poetry and Plays* (1956); F. O. Matthiessen's *The Achievement of T. S. Eliot* (3rd edition, 1959); David E. Jones's *The Plays of T. S. Eliot* (1960); Carol H. Smith's *T. S. Eliot's Dramatic Theory and Practice* (1963); and E. Martin Browne's *The Making of T. S. Eliot's Plays* (1969). These contain extensive bibliographies. His five full-length dramas were published as *The Complete Plays of T. S. Eliot* (1969).

ELIZABETH OF ENGLAND (*Elisabeth von England*), a play in five acts by FERDINAND BRUCKNER, published and produced in 1930. Setting: England and Spain, c. 1601.

This chronicle play features simultaneous actions in different settings on a divided stage and interprets history in modern terms. The psychology of the aging queen is explored in her almost STRINDBERGian sex duels with a ruthless young Essex and (from afar) with Philip II of Spain. The latter's still-reactionary Catholic theocracy is contrasted with a Protestant England already blessed by the enlightenment embodied in the peace-loving Elizabeth, in Lord Cecil, and even in the unscrupulous Francis Bacon.

Concerned only with power, Essex seeks to obtain from Elizabeth advancement for his equally ruthless friend Bacon. Despite her passion for him, the queen resists his blandishments. Essex chances to see her without makeup and, angry because she refuses to promote Bacon, insults her as an "old witch," thus incurring her hatred. Elizabeth also resists her counselors' demands that she declare war against Spain. Essex leads an uprising that collapses when Elizabeth eludes arrest. Now fully in control of her feelings, she vows to think only of war against Philip, the fanatic leader of Catholic Spain. Learning of the failure of Essex's plot, Philip orders the Armada out against England. Elizabeth condemns Essex to death despite Lord Cecil's counsel of clemency; she realizes that the alternative lifelong imprisonment would be worse for Essex, whom despite his treason she still loves. Inside St. Paul's and in a Spanish church, Elizabeth and Philip simultaneously pray for victory in identical words. Simultaneously too both monarchs faint: Philip when he learns of the Armada's defeat, Elizabeth when she hears the sounds of Essex's execution. Bacon turns Elizabeth's counselors against her. Only Cecil remains loyal, and he persuades Elizabeth to yield her royal monopolies and thus save England and the crown. He reassures her too about the exemplary life she has led. As Philip is dying, Elizabeth wonders if they were not both right in their differing reigns: "He with his senseless bigotry, I with my senseless prudence." Yet she realizes that Philip "leaves his people ruins, and they will weep for him. I leave my people possessions, and they will cry for more." In an adjoining hall an organ plays and monks sing. Tired and drained, Queen Elizabeth finds consolation by reading Petrarch's *Del dolor e della ragione* (*On Pain and Prudence*).

Elizabeth of England. Essex (O. W. Fischer) and Elizabeth (Maria Eis). Vienna, 1949. (*Bildarchiv der Österreichischen National Bibliothek*)

ELIZABETH THE QUEEN, a verse play in three acts by MAXWELL ANDERSON, published and produced in 1930. Setting: England, 1599–1601.

The popular success of this historical poetic tragedy—the first and one of the few such successes in modern American stage history—was due in part to the original Theatre Guild production. Alfred Lunt and Lynn Fontanne starred as the doomed lovers of the play, earlier titled *Elizabeth and Essex*. It is written in very loose blank verse mixed with prose, and it is peppered with court repartee, a fool's wit, and other Shakespearean touches that are as modern, however, as are the characterizations. This is Anderson's earliest historical drama and one of his most moving works.

Act I. Scene 1. Sir Walter Raleigh is jealous of his rival Essex, the favorite of the people and of Queen Elizabeth. He plots against him with Sir Robert Cecil, the queen's secretary of state. The Earl of Essex is cautioned by his friend Francis Bacon about his military and even regal ambitions: though the queen loves him, "she will not suffer / A subject to eclipse her." Essex promises to "walk softly." *Scene 2.* When the lovers meet, their mutual passion soon gives way to strife. The proud queen is fearful of losing the younger man's love, and Essex, just as fervently in love with Elizabeth, is driven by his lust for power. Their personal feelings are intertwined with their aspirations for England: Essex urges bold action—the conquest of Spain; Elizabeth wants peace and prosperity. In any case, she begs Essex not to request a new battle command, ". . . not because I think you reckless / With men and money, though I do think that, / Not because you might return in too much triumph / And take my kingdom from me, which I can imagine, / And not because I want to keep you here / And hate to risk you, though that's also true," but because she considers her lover "more a poet than general." *Scene 3.* Nonetheless, in council Raleigh and Cecil succeed in baiting Essex to take command of a hopeless expedition against Ireland. Sadly Elizabeth gives him her father's ring: if ever the need, she will forgive anything when he presents it. Though Essex remarks, "Darling, if ever / You're angry rings won't help," Elizabeth promises, "I'd think of you as you are now, and it would."

Act II. Scene 1. There is a brief exchange between the queen's fool and her lady-in-waiting, who also loves Essex. Then Cecil and Raleigh attempt to win Essex's friend, the crafty Bacon, to their side. Bacon knows they have intercepted the lovers' mail, but does not reveal this treachery. Elizabeth is distraught by Essex's apparent failure to reply to her love letters. Her pride hurt, she curtly orders his return—but secretly commands he always be allowed to see her. *Scene 2.* The queen's courier brings Essex Elizabeth's peremptory command—the first word from her to reach him. Furious, he decides to capture London and usurp the throne: "By right of name / And power and popular voice this is my kingdom," he declares; "This England under my feet, more mine than hers, / As she shall learn"—and he tears up her order. *Scene 3.* After extensive court banter, Essex's return is announced. Despite the popular uprisings in favor of Essex, the Queen calmly allows a performance of William Shakespeare's *Richard II* with it topically suggestive deposition scene. Essex himself appears, his troops now in command of the palace. The lovers quickly discover the treachery that has caused their misunderstanding and subsequent anger, and their passion, never really dead, rekindles. But they still have their pride, and Essex is still ambitious. He offers to rule jointly with Elizabeth, but the queen does not allow herself to be threatened. By her promise of sharing the throne and to prove his love, Essex is inveigled to dismiss his army. Immediately Elizabeth arrests him for treason and sends him to the tower: "I have found that he who would rule must be / Quite friendless, without mercy, without love."

Act III. Elizabeth keeps waiting for Essex to present the ring and beg forgiveness. It is an hour before his execution, and the queen and her retinue are exhausted. She seeks distraction in a performance of favorite Falstaff scenes, but in vain. Her and Essex's enemies have won: "The snake-in-the-grass / Endures, and those who are noble, free of soul, / Valiant and admirable . . . they go down in the prime, / Always they go down," she tells Cecil: "The rats inherit the earth." Finally Elizabeth herself takes the first step and summons Essex. But even when she demands the ring he will not ask for her pardon. He loves her but, he says, "if I had / Another chance I think I'd play and win." Yet he realizes that Elizabeth is better for England: he would leave "debts and bloodshed after me. You will leave / Peace, happiness, something secure." Essex is willing to take life only if he can have her throne. "There's been an empire between us!" he says. "There's nothing I'm very loath / To leave save you. Yet if I live I'll be / Your death or you'll be mine." When he starts to go, Elizabeth breaks down. Faced with losing her lover, she is willing to give up her queenship of "emptiness and death" at last: "Take my kingdom. It is yours!" she cries after him. But Essex continues walking forward to his execution.

EMPEROR AND GALILEAN (*Keiser og Galilæer*), "a world-historic drama" in two parts (ten acts) by HENRIK IBSEN, published in 1873 and produced (in six acts) in 1896. Setting: the Roman Empire, A.D. 351–363.

Ibsen always considered this long, philosophical, and highly complex work with an enormous cast his masterpiece. Though it was his first play to be translated into English (1876), it is generally little known and has rarely been performed (never, apparently, in its entirety). The struggle of the partly autobiographical Julian is, in Ibsen's words, "between two irreconcilable powers in the life of the world, something which will in all ages repeat itself"; he suggests a "third empire" that would synthesize the joyful freedom of paganism and the moral idealism of Christianity. Although he claimed to have "kept strictly to history," Ibsen freely altered real figures and events, and invented others; his portrayal of Julian maligns an enlightened and just emperor.

Part I: Caesar's Apostasy (*Cæsars Frafald*). *Act I.* It is Easter night in Constantinople. Renowned from boyhood as an eloquent advocate of Christianity, young Prince Julian longs to escape from the corrupt Christian court of his weak cousin, the Emperor Constantius, whose heir all assume Julian to be: "Christ is deserting me; I grow evil here." Unexpectedly Constantius names Gallus, Julian's half brother, as Caesar (i.e., heir to the throne), and grants Julian his request to study philosophy abroad. *Act II.* In Athens, Julian is disgusted with the corruption and hypocrisy of the philosophers. When he hears accounts of Gallus's bloody reign in Antioch, he cries, "A Christian murderer, a Christian adulteress, a Christian . . ." However, he disregards the pleas of his Christian friends and fellow students, Gregory of Nazianzus and Basil of Caesarea, to overthrow the tyrant and seeks the philosopher-magician, Maximus. *Act III.* At Ephesus, Julian rejoices in Maximus's revelations of truth, which reinforce Julian's belief that he is the chosen man of his age. Maximus expounds to Julian his philosophy of the three empires, founded "on the tree of knowledge, . . . on the tree of the cross, . . . [and the empire that] shall be founded on the tree of knowledge and the tree of the cross together." In an elaborate magical symposium, Maximus conjures the spirit of the third empire and the shades of Cain and Judas, whose ways Julian is to follow in establishing the empire. Julian protests that he will not serve such a cause. However, when the Emperor's messenger announces that he has been named Caesar, successor to the murdered Gallus, Julian accepts the purple robe and the hand of the Emperor's sister, Princess Helena. *Act IV.* In Gaul, Julian gloriously defeats the barbarians despite the machinations of the Emperor, whose emissary arrives to disband Julian's army and imprison him. Helena, poisoned by the Emperor's orders, dies ranting of her love affair with a priest. Julian rallies the army and marches on Vienna. *Act V.* With Maximus, Julian withdraws from his army in Vienna as he struggles to free himself from Christianity and set himself on the throne—to choose between "Emperor and Galilean." Hearing the priests proclaim Helena's corpse miraculous, he discards Christianity, undergoes the ritual of blood sacrifice, and emerges with the cry, "Mine is the army, mine is the treasure, mine is the throne! . . . Mine is the kingdom!"

Part II: The Emperor Julian (*Keiser Julian*). *Act I.* Emperor Julian greets the late Constantius's funeral barge with a public sacrifice to Apollo. He announces that although he has returned to the old gods, he will not interfere with Christian worship. Despite Julian's protestations of justice and charity, Christian courtiers are imprisoned and executed, including the wise and just treasurer, Ursulus. Julian heeds the most abject flatterers and announces his own semidivinity. *Acts II and III.* In his palace in Antioch, the courtiers and the populace become disgusted with Julian's excesses—his earnest polemics, his tattered clothing, his Spartan life, and his innumerable sacrifices to the gods. In his intense struggle to overcome the Galileans, Julian orders scriptures burned, houses ransacked, and men (including old friends) tortured and killed. But to his dismay he sees the Christians grow in number and spirit. Disapproving of his course, Maximus chides Julian, "Oh fool, drawing your sword against what shall be—against the third empire, where he who is two in one shall rule!" Later, Julian sets forth to battle the Persians: "I will possess the world!" *Act IV.* In the mountains Julian struggles against the Galileans in his army, and orders his soldiers to throw incense before his busts. Upon learning of widespread conversions at home, Julian seeks a quick victory. He heeds the advice of a Persian deserter and burns his supply ships—learning too late that the deserter was a spy. *Act V.* On the Persian plain the army is dangerously dispirited. Julian falters, seeking advice from oracles that remain silent. His aides fear for his sanity, and he contemplates suicide. Still believing Julian is to establish the third empire, Maximus urges him on. Julian is mortally wounded in battle. "Thou hast conquered, Galilean!" he says and dies, looking at the sun: "Beautiful earth—beautiful life—Oh, Helios, Helios—why didst thou deceive me?" Maximus mourns the friend he has unwittingly misled: "The world-will shall answer for Julian's soul. . . . The third empire shall come! The spirit of man shall reclaim its heritage." The devout Christian Basil and his sister Macrina, reconciled to Julian's life and death, kneel over his corpse in prayer: "The Emperor Julian was a rod of chastisement—not for our death, but for our resurrection."

EMPEROR JONES, THE, a play in eight scenes by EUGENE O'NEILL, produced in 1920 and published in 1921. Setting: "An island in the West Indies as yet not self-determined by white marines."

The most striking device (originated by AUSTIN STRONG) in this famous EXPRESSIONISTIC monodrama (Scenes 2–7) set in a REPRESENTATIONAL framework (Scenes 1 and 8) is the persistent and nerve-racking drum beat. The forces that bring about the defeat of Brutus Jones, who symbolically emerges as modern man, break down his ego and strip him psychically as the jungle, ripping his uniform, strips him physically. His individual memories are subsumed by his racial and finally his human (mankind's) past, expressing the "collective unconscious" of Jung, in whose psychoanalytic theories O'Neill was particularly interested.

Scene 1. In the palace, the shiftless Cockney trader Henry Smithers gloats at the thought that Brutus Jones is at the end of his reign. A shrewd and impressive American Negro, Jones rose "from stowaway to Emperor in two years" by emulating the whites he observed when he was a Pullman porter: "For de little stealin' dey gits you in jail soon or late. For de big stealin' dey makes you Emperor and puts you in de Hall o' Fame when you croaks." Now the natives whom Jones has exploited are in revolt, but he has faith that his Baptist religion will protect him against their heathen tricks, though "I'se after de coin, an' I lays my Jesus on de shelf for de time bein'." Coolly he "cashes in and resigns de job of Emperor right dis minute": he has stowed away supplies in the jungle, through which he intends to make his escape and sail to Martinique for his stolen fortune. He does not worry about being shot, since he has convinced the natives that only a silver bullet can kill him. The last bullet in his own gun is silver, just in case things do not work out, "'cause I'm de on'y man in de world big enuff to git me." The native tom-tom thump of the chase begins "at a rate exactly corresponding to normal pulse beat—72 to the minute—and continues at a gradually accelerating rate from this point uninterruptedly to the very end of the play." Jones regally saunters off to the jungle, where he soon loses his way and encounters various phantoms.

Scenes 2 through 7. (*2*) When he cannot find the place of his stowed-away food, there appear mocking "little formless fears," and Jones shoots his first bullet at them. Later (*3*) he sees Jeff, the fellow porter he once killed; he shoots at Jeff's ghost and wildly plunges on. Next (*4*) there is a reenactment of his murder of a prison guard, at whom he shoots in terrified rage. Then (*5*) Jones is auctioned off at a southern slave market, and he uses two bullets to exorcise the Auctioneer and the Planter who buys him. In the fantasy that follows (*6*), Jones is among naked Negroes wailing on a slave transport. Finally (*7*), as Jones kneels before an altar, a Congo Witch Doctor motions him to be the sacrifice, and Jones squirms toward a huge crocodile; moaning in terror to "Lawd Jesus," Jones remembers his silver bullet and fires at the crocodile.

Scene 8. At the place where Jones had entered the jungle and they expect him to circle back after getting lost, the natives, led by old Lem and armed with silver bullets they have forged from money, are waiting for the Emperor. Four shots are heard and, as Lem had predicted to the skeptical Smithers, "We cotch him. Him dead." As the body is brought in, Smithers cannot help an admiring exclamation, "Silver bullets! Gawd Blimey, but yer died in the 'eighth o' style, any'ow!"

END OF SUMMER, a play in three acts by S. N. BEHRMAN, published and produced in 1936. Setting: an estate in northern Maine, 1936.

Like RAIN FROM HEAVEN, this is a drawing-room comedy about contemporary problems—in this case, the plight of Depression youngsters and the end of the security of inherited wealth. Its charming protagonist is a flighty middle-aged beauty, the wealthy hostess to young radicals, to a Russian refugee with an Oedipus complex, and to a psychiatrist who "gave up tonsillectomy for the soul [because] the poor have tonsils but only the rich have souls." She falls in love with the psychiatrist, but sends him off when the ruthless cad proposes to her daughter. The slight plot concludes as she wistfully agrees to finance the revolutionary magazine of a young radical, who consoles her with the thought that "come the Revolution—you'll have a friend in high office."

ENDGAME (*Fin de partie*), a one-act play by SAMUEL BECKETT, published and produced in 1957. Setting: a bare, gray-lit interior with two windows and a door.

This is one of the "plays of inaction" written in French and translated by Beckett himself. The limbolike setting, four characters, "undramatic" plot, and particularly the dialogue (with its puns and literary and biblical allusions)—all are sparse, elliptic, and SYMBOLIC. The protagonist is Hamm, whose name echoes, among other things, an actor and William Shakespeare's most famous character. The play has been variously interpreted as a chess game (the title is also a chess term), as morality theatre, and even as a monodrama: the setting could suggest a skull, a womb—or outer space. But the infinite meanings are subsumed in the pervasive overall picture of a sinister, dying—or already dead—world. Bell Gale Chevigny edited *Twentieth Century Interpretations of "Endgame": A Collection of Critical Essays* (1969).

Clov is the menial of Hamm, a blind old invalid in an armchair. In an opening tableau, Clov stares at Hamm. Then he removes the sheet that covers Hamm, and another sheet that covers two ashbins. "Finished, it's finished, nearly finished, it must be nearly finished," he remarks, pauses, and waits for Hamm's summoning whistle: "I can't be punished any more." Hamm wakes up and removes the handkerchief from his very red face: "Me—(*he yawns*)—to play." Then he clears his throat: "Can there be misery—(*he yawns*)—loftier than mine?" From the ashbins his white-faced, crippled parents arise periodically. As the day progresses, there are quarrels, talk, sudden fury, and vain appeals for sustenance and relief from discomfort and pain. Instructed by Hamm, to whom he is bound and whom he has tried to leave "since I was whelped," Clov shifts the armchair so that it rests in the dead center of the room and goes through other apparently pointless motions. "Why this farce, day after day?" he asks, and Hamm replies: "Routine." Clov looks out the window with a telescope and he reports: "Zero" water and earth, "there's no more nature." Except for the elegiac ashbin mother, who remembers the past and listens to the father's joke, all the characters are cruel. For a moment Hamm yearns to go far away with Clov, to join "other . . . mammals!" Then, collecting himself, he tells Clov to set his toy dog before the armchair, "begging me for a bone . . . imploring me." He tells the story of "a madman who thought the end of the world had come," complains of Clov's "stink," promises his father—whom he curses for engendering him—a sugarplum if he listen to a story he is composing, and then cruelly breaks his promise. The story remains unfinished: it is about a poor man "crawling on his belly, whining for bread" for his starving son. Later Hamm tells Clov to see if his father still lives. "He's crying," Clov reports. "Then he's living," Hamm replies, and subsequently orders both ashcan lids sealed. When it is time for Hamm's pain killer, none is left, and there also are no more coffins. The ashbin occupants, whose sand has remained unchanged, presumably die. Hamm again has Clov look out the window. He reports seeing a small boy. "A potential procreator?" Hamm asks. "If he exists he'll die there or come here." Then, "It's the end, Clov, we've come to the end. I don't need you any more." Clov prepares to leave: "I say to myself—sometimes, Clov, you must learn to suffer better than that if you want them to weary of punishing you—one day." Silently he remains standing at the door and observes Hamm, who—not seeing him—calls in vain. Then Hamm concludes: "No? Good." He unfolds his bloody handkerchief: "Old stancher! (*Pause*) You . . . remain." Hamm puts the handkerchief over his face and remains motionless in a closing tableau.

ENEMY OF THE PEOPLE, AN (*En folkefiende*), a play in five acts by HENRIK IBSEN, published in 1882 and produced in 1883. Setting: a coastal resort town in contemporary southern Norway.

After the abusive reception of GHOSTS, Ibsen wrote this popular play, modernized by ARTHUR MILLER, to show that the democratic majority (led by a hypocritical, liberal middle class) is always wrong, and that the strongest man is the solitary idealist. Despite such themes the play is a comedy, especially in the protagonist's depicted naïveté and exuberant love of battle. Dr. Stockmann, a reckless champion of truth, is partly modeled on BJØRNESTJERNE BJØRNSON. Even more, however, he represents the views of Ibsen, though "the Doctor is more muddle-headed than I am."

Act I. The townsmen are gratified with the prosperity brought about by their mineral baths. The baths were made possible by the visionary energy of Thomas Stockmann, a provincial doctor who is now the sanitary inspector. Liberal newspapermen and other friends are enjoying his hospitality, when his brother Peter, the town's powerful conservative mayor, appears. Though the talk is of harmony and prosperity, there are undercurrents of economic and political frictions, and the jealous mayor criticizes his brother's personal extravagance and official impetuousness. After the mayor's departure, a long-awaited report arrives. It confirms Dr. Stockmann's suspicions that commercial refuse pollutes the cheaply constructed baths. He sends off his already-prepared report and guilelessly rejoices in the support of his friends and in anticipated rewards for his diligence.

Act II. Eager to attack conservative officialdom by publishing Dr. Stockmann's findings, the newspapermen (including the printer Aslaksan of THE LEAGUE OF YOUTH, now an influential burgher) assure him of the support of the solid middle-class majority. But the mayor, envisioning financial ruin for the vested interests—as well as the town—because of the report, demands that his brother deny it publicly: "The matter in this instance is by no means a purely scientific one; it is a combination of technical and economic factors." His brother refuses to consider denying the report. Ordered to obey or be fired, Dr. Stockmann loses his temper. He insists that he has right on his side and must disobey the authorities: "I want to be able to look my boys in the face when they grow up into free men." His wife breaks into desperate sobs, but his daughter is proud: "Father's grand! He'll never give in."

Act III. At the newspaper office, the report is about to be printed. Still in a temper and supported by the editors, the doctor wants to replace the officials with younger, honest men. But after he leaves, the mayor adroitly wins over the newspapermen: publishing the report, he persuades them, would be the ruin of their vested interests—and those of their readers. Ignorant of the new turn of events when he returns, the doctor struts around and disports with the mayor's emblems of office. He is finally made to understand how he has lost all support: "It's public opinion, the educated public, the ratepayers and all the others—these are the people who control the press." Suddenly muzzled (he is even refused a hall for a public meeting), he decides to march around town with a drummer and proclaim the truth: "We'll see whether you and your shabby tricks can stop an honest citizen who wants to clean up the town."

Act IV. Dr. Stockmann is ready to proclaim his findings in a friend's home, before a curious crowd, inflamed by the press. His enemies maneuvre a public meeting; they elect a chairman and then prevent the doctor, by a democratically passed resolution, from reading his report. Suddenly inspired with something like divine wrath, Dr. Stockmann delivers a long oration on his discovery of a greater pollution than that of the baths: "The worst enemy of truth and freedom in our society is the compact majority"; by worshiping truths only when they are so old that they have become decrepit, the public—mongrels, merely "the raw material from which a people is made"—"is the thing that's polluting the sources of our spiritual life and infecting the very ground we stand on." Heckled and officially branded "an enemy of the people," an angry Dr. Stockmann escapes from the violent mob.

Act V. Stoned, threatened, and about to be evicted, Dr. Stockmann decides to leave town. The mayor comes to offer his eventual reinstatement if he recants, but then, finding a way to discredit him by misrepresentation, the mayor makes the dismissal irrevocable. Next his wife's wealthy foster father arrives; he has bought up deflated bath shares, and now—on the pain of disinheriting his family—he wants the doctor to clear the baths in order to inflate the value of his shares. Finally, the newspapermen come with their business proposal: in return for part of his expected profits after whitewashing the authorities later, they will support his present attack, thus depressing the shares' value still further. In a fury at their effrontery, Dr. Stockmann chases them all out with his umbrella. He decides to remain in town and by himself fight and enlighten rotten society. For he has made yet another great discovery: "The strongest man in the world is the man who stands alone."

ENGELBREKT, a historical play in five acts by AUGUST STRINDBERG, published and produced in 1901. Setting: fifteenth-century Sweden.

Engelbrekt Engelbrektsson is a folk hero. Strindberg considered him "one of Sweden's most beautiful memories" and was deeply disappointed at the play's failure with audiences.

Despite the shabby treatment of Sweden in the union with Denmark and Norway, Engelbrekt remains loyal to the union's king. When he witnesses the exploitation of the Swedes at a castle banquet, however, he is finally aroused and attempts to stop the reelection of the union king. Though he fails, he becomes the liberator and temporary ruler of the Swedes. For a while it looks as if he will be elected regent, and eventually king. He is aged by responsibilities and dissensions at home that end in his family's separation from him. Losing the election, Engelbrekt is soon mortally wounded by his enemy's son. He dies happily as he sees his children returning to him with his wife: "In the days of joy she was gone, but in times of need she was always there. . . ."

ENGLAND, SCOTLAND, and WALES. Modern British drama* began in the late nineteenth century with a Norwegian whose plays were introduced to England by a Scot and an Irishman. The work of HENRIK IBSEN, championed by WILLIAM ARCHER and BERNARD SHAW, started to extricate British drama from the disrepute into which it had fallen since Elizabethan and Stuart times. Except for Restoration Comedy and its sentimentalized, watered-down reincarnation by Oliver Goldsmith

* See also IRELAND.

and R. B. Sheridan one hundred years later, English theatrical activities until the late nineteenth century consisted of abortive poetic drama, melodramatic thrillers and tearjerkers, and grand spectacles. The theatre was very much alive and popular, but it was increasingly shunned by discriminating audiences. In fact, Matthew Arnold declared in the *Nineteenth Century Review* for August 1879: "In England we have no modern drama at all."

The first writer credited with English drama's rebirth was Thomas William Robertson (1829–71). The youthful Shaw's excessive respect for his work suggests the bankruptcy into which English drama had fallen—and Robertson's real innovations. His refreshingly brief titles immediately signaled something new: *Society, Ours, Caste, Play,* and *School.* Produced at the Prince of Wales's Theatre in the years 1865–69, these plays satirize contemporary materialism, female inequality, and snobbery. Robertson's portrayal of ordinary people and current "problems," his attempts to replace fustian with dialogue that at the time appeared natural, and the verisimilitude of his sets (the use, for example, of actual instead of painted doorknobs)—these earned Robertson's plays the "cup-and-saucer" label. But despite the label's echo in a later sobriquet, his plays are a far cry from England's "kitchen drama" of the 1950's and 1960's.

Robertson's work was followed by the delightfully irreverent operettas of W. S. GILBERT and Arthur Sullivan and by the drama of two playwrights who achieved great popularity and critical esteem. ARTHUR WING PINERO and HENRY ARTHUR JONES were heralded by some as "advanced" writers, and they shocked and titillated English audiences. But though they conveyed something of Ibsen's spirit and seriousness to the English drama, their break with the past was as spurious as were the "ideas" of their plays. Pinero and Jones worked primarily in the tradition of popular entertainers like the immensely prolific Henry J. Byron (1834–84), whose comedy drama *Our Boys* (1875) enjoyed a historic and record-breaking run; Dion Boucicault (1822?–90), the Irish-born dramatist-actor-impresario who divided his career between England and America; the French masters of WELL-MADE PLAYS; and other, less successful potboiler-makers. They adhered, for the most part, to the formulas of sentimental melodramas, and they skirted moral issues (often attitudes toward sex) they only *seemed* to raise. Ibsen was the one who really brought such issues to the theatre—and when they appeared in England, his plays were recognized as something quite new. Though hailed by some, they were viciously attacked by many others: the distinguished critic of *The Daily Telegraph,* Clement Scott, was a spokesman for those who fulminated against "the gross and almost putrid indecorum" of GHOSTS.

Ibsen's heir and greatest champion in England was Shaw, who became the towering figure of modern British drama. Though it is as difficult to pinpoint Shaw's specific influence on individual playwrights as it is to assess its exact scope, there is no question of Shaw's overwhelming effect on the whole subsequent course of the drama. As critic and as playwright, he exposed the pretentious and illustrated the genuine in dramatic art. Chronologically, his work spanned most of the period of modern British drama: Shaw started his first play in 1885, and wrote his last one in 1950—only six years before the epoch-marking production of Osborne's LOOK BACK IN ANGER. Among other important playwrights active before and at the turn of the century were OSCAR WILDE, whose most brilliant comedy has become a modern classic; JAMES M. BARRIE, the immensely popular author of whimsical, sentimental comedies; and JOHN GALSWORTHY, a very successful NATURALIST and, in a way, a social crusader. In the Edwardian period, too, SOMERSET MAUGHAM's comedies became popular and HARLEY GRANVILLE-BARKER produced his best dramas.

Managements like Granville-Barker's (with J. E. Vedrenne) of the Court Theatre (1904–07) and various experimental companies gave important new writers their early hearings. J. T. Grein's Independent Theatre opened in 1891 with the controversial *Ghosts,* and it was the first to stage the works of Shaw. It was followed by the Stage Society (1899), which produced plays (including Shaw's and those of new Continental writers) considered commercially unviable and objectionable to the Lord Chamberlain (the government censor). In the early years of the century various repertory companies made possible the careers of writers like HAROLD CHAPIN and JOHN DRINKWATER. Particularly distinguished in connection with such organizations was Annie E. F. Horniman, who supported the founding of two theatres that were to produce important dramatists, the Abbey in Dublin and the Gaiety in Manchester. The Gaiety established a group of post-Ibsenites, the Manchester School, which included STANLEY HOUGHTON, HAROLD BRIGHOUSE, ALLAN MONKHOUSE, and others. Along with their naturalistic portrayals of lower-class life should be noted such similar plays as Elizabeth Baker's (1876?–1962) *Chains* (1909) and Githa Sowerby's (? – ?) *Rutherford and Son* (1912), both of which were praised for their harrowing but honest depictions.

While some writers—notably the short-lived ST. JOHN HANKIN—out-Ibsened Ibsen with drama of social protest, many others turned to the commercial theatre to entertain audiences with lighter fare and to make money. The most talented craftsmen among them succeeded on London's Broadway, the West End—writers like ALFRED SUTRO, FREDERICK LONSDALE, A. A. MILNE, CLEMENCE DANE, IVOR NOVELLO, NOËL COWARD, BENN W. LEVY, JOHN VAN DRUTEN, PATRICK HAMILTON, DOUGLAS HOME, PETER USTINOV, and WILLIS HALL. Some are remembered only for a single success: Thomas's CHARLEY'S AUNT, McCarthy's IF I WERE KING, Jerome's THE PASSING OF THE THIRD FLOOR BACK, Parker's DISRAELI, Knoblock's KISMET, Vane's OUTWARD BOUND, Dean and Kennedy's THE CONSTANT NYMPH, Browne and Nichols's WINGS OVER

EUROPE, Sherriff's JOURNEY'S END, Besier's THE BARRETTS OF WIMPOLE STREET, and Shairp's THE GREEN BAY TREE. To these might be added such musical hits as *Chu Chin Chow* (1916), the phenomenally successful drama by Oscar Asche (1871–1936) about the *Arabian Nights'* Ali Baba; L. Arthur Rose (1887–1958) and Douglas Furber's (1885–1961) comic *Me and My Girl* (1938); Sandy Wilson's (1924–) burlesque of the 1920's, *The Boy Friend* (1954); Dorothy Reynolds (1913–) and Julian Slade's (1930–) cross between a musical and a revue, *Salad Days* (1957); and Lionel Bart's (1930–) adaptation of Dickens's *Oliver Twist* into *Oliver!* (1960).

Other famous hits were the posthumous verse drama *Hassan* (1923) by James Elroy Flecker (1884–1915), produced with music by Delius; *The Farmer's Wife* (1916), a comedy by the Devon novelist Eden Phillpotts (1862–1960); the play about Samuel Pepys, *And So To Bed* (1926), by James B. Fagan (1873–1933); *The Mousetrap,* Agatha Christie's (1891–) record-breaking thriller that opened in 1952 and continued running into the 1970's; and long-running comedies like Hugh Hastings's (1917–) *Seagulls over Sorrento* (1950), R. F. Delderfield's (1912–) *Worm's Eye View* (1954), Ray Cooney (? –) and Tony Hilton's (? –) farcical *One for the Pot* (1961), and Beverley Cross's (1931–) 1962 adaptation of Marc Camoletti's (? –) French comedy about a roué with three air-hostess mistresses, *Boeing-Boeing* (1961).

Authors notable in other branches of literature attempted playwriting, but usually with indifferent success: THOMAS HARDY, JOSEPH CONRAD, ARNOLD BENNETT, MAX BEERBOHM, D. H. LAWRENCE, ALDOUS HUXLEY, WILLIAM GOLDING, and LAWRENCE DURRELL. And there were those whose efforts were both popular and of artistic stature, playwrights like ENID BAGNOLD, J. B. PRIESTLEY, and TERENCE RATTIGAN.

While most of these writers are English, Scotland and Wales—not to mention IRELAND—produced a number who made their mark on English, American, and even international stages. Scotland was the birthplace of Barrie, Archer, ERIC LINKLATER, and a playwright much esteemed in Britain though little known elsewhere, JAMES BRIDIE. From Wales came the poet DYLAN THOMAS and the actor-playwright EMLYN WILLIAMS, among others. The West Indies' first notable native dramatist was ERROL JOHN. Some playwrights from the Midlands and other parts of Britain used local settings and characters for their plays. Anglo-Jewish drama (as distinguished from YIDDISH DRAMA) set in Jewish milieus outside the ghetto started before the turn of the century with ISRAEL ZANGWILL and reappeared in the mainstream of British drama in the work of mid-century authors like ARNOLD WESKER and BERNARD KOPS.

British verse often went together with historical religious drama. Important religious prose writers include the popular GRAHAM GREENE and the prolific LAURENCE HOUSMAN—whose great hit, however, was the nonreligious VICTORIA REGINA; other religious prose writers include CHARLES MORGAN and JAMES FORSYTH. Most of the great nineteenth-century poets wrote verse drama, but none—not even Shelley or Lord Byron—succeeded in the theatre. In the late nineteenth century some of the plays of Tennyson, Browning, and Swinburne (including his trilogy on Mary, Queen of Scots) were produced commercially; they made little impression on theatre audiences. The first modern poet-dramatist to attain any theatrical prominence was STEPHEN PHILLIPS, and it was short lived. JOHN MASEFIELD appealed more with his prose plays, and the poets of the left who essayed the drama—notably W. H. AUDEN (collaborating with CHRISTOPHER ISHERWOOD) and STEPHEN SPENDER—had no popular success whatever, despite their use of colloquial, even jazzy, language. T. S. ELIOT's religious poetic drama, because of the distinction of its author, reached a wider audience; and such drama also was produced (although with less popular acclaim) by DOROTHY SAYERS, CHARLES WILLIAMS, RONALD DUNCAN, and others. Even before Eliot's later religious drama (disguised as drawing-room comedy) became fashionable, CHRISTOPHER FRY achieved popularity with a different and startling type of verse drama. His and Eliot's work was hailed as the beginning of a long-awaited renaissance of poetic drama. But Eliot's later plays failed commercially as well as artistically, and Fry turned to translating and to writing scripts for Hollywood extravaganzas.

The robust artistic activities that had ushered in twentieth-century British theatre gradually languished. Shaw became a respectable West End and international success. He remained the giant of British drama until his death, despite the acknowledged falling off in his later plays. No playwright appeared even remotely able to step into his boots, and the theatre resumed its nineteenth-century placidity. Then a movement arose that did in mid-century what Shaw had done at the end of the previous century: it rebelled at conventions and presented new attitudes and artistic approaches. The emotional keynote was delivered by JOHN OSBORNE, whose "anger" provided the movement's name and a wedge into the commercial theatre.

The New British Drama, as it was called, was not only "angry": influenced by the French (as the popular nineteenth-century drama had been) ABSURD playwrights as well as by such great modern innovators as ANTON CHEKHOV, AUGUST STRINDBERG, LUIGI PIRANDELLO, and BERTOLT BRECHT, British writers began to articulate post-World War II life and attitudes in dramatic terms. They presented their "welfare state" milieu and the pervasive psychological impact of The Bomb. Like women's rights and slum housing in the drama of Ibsen and Shaw, however, these external forces or "problems" merely particularized timeless, universal dilemmas. Whether they dealt with immediate issues or with more esoteric ones, some of these writers were presenting the human condition in vivid new terms. The best known among them are JOHN ARDEN, N. F. SIMPSON, ROBERT

BOLT, PETER SHAFFER, JOHN WHITING, and the already-mentioned Kops, Wesker, and Osborne. Others include NIGEL DENNIS, ANN JELLICOE, DORIS LESSING, HENRY LIVINGS, CHRISTOPHER LOGUE, JOHN MORTIMER, JOE ORTON, TOM STOPPARD, FRANK NORMAN, and SHELAGH DELANEY. These last two, as well as the Irishman BRENDAN BEHAN, were the products of an experimental movement. It resembled the classic *commedia dell'arte* more than Grein's and Granville-Barker's projects. But Joan Littlewood's Theatre Workshop, which began shortly after World War II and moved to the Theatre Royal in Stratford (East London) in 1953, carried on the tradition of these earlier groups by presenting original works and new playwrights. Among the Theatre Workshop's successful ensemble productions was a grand musical "entertainment" replete with caustic trench humor, *Oh What a Lovely War* (1963, filmed in 1969), a grimly comic portrayal of 1914–18 in a *commedia dell'arte* framework.

The most promising among recent British playwrights has been HAROLD PINTER; his "comedies of menace" reflect the *Zeitgeist* and contemporary life in a distinctively terrifying yet comic manner. Other writers who have become notable in recent years are the Irish-born Bill [William John] Naughton (1910–   ), whose conventional but appealing regional drama, domestic comedies set in Bolton (northern England), became famous in the 1960's, especially with the 1965 filming of his *Alfie* (1963), the portrayal of a Cockney lecher; the Welsh-born physician-poet Dannie Abse (1923–   ), whose *House of Cowards* (1960), a hit in London's "Off-Broadway," presents a domestic situation and characters paralleling those of O'Neill's THE ICEMAN COMETH; David Mercer (1928–   ), whose preoccupation with individual psychology and left-wing politics is reflected in plays like the 1966–67 London hit about a neurotic intellectual, *Belcher's Luck;* Peter Nichols (1928–   ), whose *A Day in the Death of Joe Egg* (1968) farcically depicts a spastic child and its parents' stultified marriage; the German-born Frank Marcus (1928–   ), whose greatest hit has been a drama (subsequently filmed) about a lesbian soap-opera star, *The Killing of Sister George* (1965); Peter Terson (1932–   ), originally a regional writer whose *The Mighty Reservoy* (1966) and other plays poetically—and with colloquial language and humor—dramatize life in Worcestershire and London; Charles [Gerald] Wood (1932–   ), who has succeeded best with *Dingo* (1967) and other theatre of CRUELTY depictions of military life, attitudes, and idiom; the novelist-playwright David Storey (1933–   ), whose dramas, likened by some to those of Chekhov, include *The Contractor* (1969), an evocative symbol of uneasiness in contemporary England suggested in a simple plot about the erection of a tent for a wedding, and *Home* (1970), a comic yet compassionate drama of life in a mental home; and Edward Bond (1935–   ), whose *Saved* (1965), a powerful drama of almost inarticulate London proletarians that created a sensation with its depiction of the wanton gang-murder of an infant, was followed by *Early Morning* (1968), a historical nightmare fantasy of present and past which portrays, among others, Queen Victoria as a lesbian enamored of Florence Nightingale. Recent hit plays, some of them even better known as films, include *Staircase* (1966), a drama of two middle-aged homosexual barbers' love-hate relationship, by Charles Dyer (1928–   ); *The Man in the Glass Booth* (1967), the actor Robert Shaw's (1927–   ) dramatization of his fanciful novelistic treatment (also 1967) of the career and trial of the Nazi Adolf Eichmann; and Peter Luke's (1919–   ) *Hadrian VII* (1968), a dramatization of the semiautobiographical novel by that intriguing Victorian figure, Frederick William Rolfe, alias Baron Corvo.

To summarize all modern British drama adequately is well-nigh impossible, for it is far too variegated in form and subject matter. The only thing British playwrights have in common is language—and sometimes even that similarity is tenuous. Some students of the drama consider the British strongest in comedy. The light comic fare of earlier-mentioned dramatists has, indeed, often dominated British theatres—along with suspense thrillers (like those of Christie) and other frothy entertainment. At the same time, many of the British playwrights here mentioned have dealt seriously with social and psychological issues. The postwar dramatists especially have attempted to transcend the forms of conventional naturalism and SYMBOLISM. It is too early to evaluate recent ferments in the British drama, but they set the stage, at least, for the emergence of new writers. Though the twentieth century has so far produced no new native dramatists of major international stature, the British theatre has shown signs of life, health, and renewed vigor.

There are many works about modern British drama, including collected reviews by writers like Shaw, Beerbohm, Dennis, Whiting, Desmond MacCarthy, James Agate, and Kenneth Tynan. Volume V of Allardyce Nicoll's *A History of English Drama, 1660–1900* (1959) contains the most comprehensive account of the 1850–1900 period. Albert E. Wilson's *Edwardian Theatre* (1951) is a useful compendium that contains much first-hand information. Nicoll's *British Drama* (revised edition, 1962) is a handy survey, as is Ernest Reynolds's *Modern English Drama* (1949). Among studies dealing with specialized topics are Denis Donoghue's *The Third Voice: Modern British and American Verse Drama* (1959), Gerald Weales's *Religion in Modern English Drama* (1961), Glynne Wickham's *Drama in a World of Science* (1962) lectures, and John Russell Taylor's *The Rise and Fall of the Well-Made Play* (1967), a study of British well-made drama from the 1870's to the 1960's. Taylor's *Anger and After* (1962, revised and expanded 1969 and retitled *The Angry Theatre* in America) is an invaluable and comprehensive guide to mid-century British drama; good collections of essays on the same subject are "Stratford-Upon-Avon Studies" (*Contempor-*

ary Theatre 4, 1962) and William A. Armstrong's *Experimental Drama* (1963).

ENTER SOLLY GOLD, a comedy in five scenes by BERNARD KOPS, published in 1961 and produced in 1962. Setting: contemporary London.

The protagonist of this wildly comic play is an exuberant sharper determined to avoid work. In a poor Jewish neighborhood he bargains with a prostitute, cons a tailor out of money, almost seduces the tailor's fat wife (fat women are his special weakness), and cheats a recently bereaved widow of money, her chickens, and her late husband's rabbinical clothes. Posing as a distinguished rabbi celebrating the Rabbinical Chicken Sunday proclaimed by the American Reform Orthodox Proxy Rabbi's Association, Solly bamboozles a Jewish millionaire and his family with his gibberish prayers: "That's the new semantic Semitic based on the emetic antics of the yigdal incorporating the Aztectoltec Ashkenazim. We're branching out." He settles in the palatial residence, dislocates the family, proclaims its millionaire the Messiah, and manages to embezzle a fortune and seduce the fat daughter. When he is unmasked Solly admits, "I'm a liar, a lobos, a gonif. . . . But I'm the best con man in the business." Finally, however, he loses both fortune and fat heiress. Solly contemplates his next move as he picks up a cigarette butt: "I'm bloody fed up. You can't con an honest coin these days. . . ."

ENTERTAINER, THE, a play in thirteen "numbers" by JOHN OSBORNE, produced in 1957 and published in 1958. Setting: a large English coastal resort, 1950's.

This loud, brassy play—a tour de force in which Laurence Olivier created the lead, as he did in the film version—portrays a family of three generations of music-hall entertainers, the Rices, in alternating domestic and music-hall scenes. The brash and vulgar Archie sings most of the music-hall numbers and badgers his old father (a sentimental embodiment of Edwardian England) and his second wife. Archie plans to throw over this wife for a girl his daughter's age, and remarks how nothing matters: "I'm dead, just like the whole inert shoddy lot out there" before whom he performs. When told of his son's death, Archie sings the blues—and then the squabbles resume. Before he dies, Archie's father reveals Archie's shoddy character to the parents of his bride-to-be. Foiled, Archie Rice continues to sing the blues—"Why should I care"—until the stage darkens.

EPIC THEATRE or **EPIC DRAMA,** BERTOLT BRECHT's espousal and practice of didactic dramaturgy. It strives to induce audiences as well as actors to analyze characters and action intellectually (critically) rather than to be affected by and to identify with them emotionally. Thus *epic* signifies the opposite of REALISTIC, *dramatic, conventional, Aristotelian.* Like the director-producer Erwin Piscator, Brecht sought to destroy theatrical illusion and suspense and to establish "distance" (*Verfremdung*) between the audience and the fictitious characters and the action. Therefore he dispensed with conventional act and scene divisions, attempted to portray types rather than rounded individuals, and used songs, narrative, projected titles, and other devices. Brecht discussed his epic theories in many places, and all but his earliest plays exemplify them. See Brecht's later statement in *Kleines Organon für das Theater* (*Little Organon for the Theatre,* 1948), the studies of Martin Esslin and John Willett, Eric Bentley's *In Search of Theater* (1947), and Max Spalter's *Brecht's Tradition* (1967).

EPITAPH FOR GEORGE DILLON, a play in three acts by JOHN OSBORNE and Anthony Creighton, published and produced in 1958. Setting: a home outside London in the 1950's.

Written with a fellow actor some years before LOOK BACK IN ANGER made Osborne famous, this play dramatizes the story of an untalented but ambitious playwright.

George stays with and bamboozles money and love from a middle-class family he despises. When his serious play is rejected, he vulgarizes it and sells out. Trapped as a honky-tonk success, he prepares to marry the family's stupid, animalistic daughter. He recites his epitaph to her sister, a disillusioned intellectual to whom he had earlier admitted doubts of his artistry: "George Dillon . . . who thought, who hoped, he was that mysterious, ridiculous being called an artist. He never allowed himself one day of peace. He worshipped the physical things of this world, and was betrayed by his own body." And George adds, "He was a bit of a bore, and, frankly, rather useless. But the germs loved him."

ERDMAN, Nikolai Robertovich (1902–), Russian playwright, and a keen satirist whom MAXIM GORKY called "our new Gogol." His *Mandat* (1925), a very popular raucous comedy of manners, satirizes the old regime overtly—but covertly it ridicules the new one. Gorky persuaded Stalin to permit the production of Erdman's second play, *Samoubiitsa,* and it was rehearsed in 1936, but the production was ultimately banned. Revived in 1969 and later in West European countries, it is a comedy about a Soviet philistine who is encouraged by the "former people" of the title to carry out his decision to commit suicide—as the only way to escape the realities of Soviet life. Like Vsevolod Meyerhold, who put on both plays, Erdman soon was arrested, and disappeared. But unlike the great producer, Erdman reappeared in the 1950's, apparently a broken man. His plays and life are discussed in Peter Yershov's *Comedy in the Soviet Theater* (1956) and in Nikolai A. Gorchakov's *The Theater in Soviet Russia* (1957).

ERIK XIV, a historical play in four acts by AUGUST STRINDBERG, published and produced in 1899. Setting: Sweden, 1567–68.

The sequel to GUSTAV VASA and last in the Vasa trilogy, this popular play focuses on a Renaissance king who particularly fascinates Scandinavians. The action is exciting and the characterizations, especially those of the king and the procurator, are superb. Gustav's son Erik was emotionally unbalanced to the point of madness, and Strindberg identified him with Hamlet—and with himself.

Erik is spying on his mistress, Karin Månsdotter. He hurls down objects at Göran Persson, his close friend and secretary, who is temporarily in disfavor. When he learns that England's Queen Elizabeth has rejected his suit, he storms and then seeks Göran's help. "You use that word 'hate' so often you'll finally imagine yourself the enemy of the human race," Göran remarks after Erik's paranoiac outbursts, and suggests marriage with the Polish princess Erik has just permitted his brother to wed. Erik belatedly rescinds that permission ("everything I touch becomes stupid and twisted") and appoints the indispensable friend as procurator, for "Göran alone knows all the secret ways in my soul." At home, Göran tells his mother of his close bond with Erik. Born to rule, Göran can do so only through the king: "When that sun sets, I'll be extinguished, and that will be that!" He checks the lords' usurpation of power, and when Erik's brother rebels against royal orders, Göran advises the duke's execution. Erik is reluctant to use such strong tactics, but the procurator insists, "As long as I can, I'll defend your crown against your enemies." After a visit from Karin's common and indignant father, Göran advises the king to marry Karin. Göran arrests the rebelling lords, but Erik ruins the trial and they are acquitted. In the meantime, Karin has fearfully escaped with their children. Unhinged by sorrow, Erik permits and even watches the massacre of the lords—and then goes temporarily insane. After his recovery he marries Karin and has her crowned. Göran has succeeded in legalizing the mass execution, but Erik now reveals that in his remorseful grief he had impulsively apologized and publicly decreed the victims innocent. Already half-broken by the perfidy of a woman, Göran now loses his will and power to rectify the royal blunders. Erik too has lost his will to fight, though he swears madly at the absence of the nobles and his brothers, an absence he blames on Karin. In a frenzy he opens the banquet doors to the riffraff from the street and calls out, "We won't wait for the bride, for she has just gone into labor!" Then, forgiving Karin, he goes out to seek her, for "in her presence I feel calmer and less inclined to evil." His two brothers appear and news of Erik's arrest and imprisonment quickly spreads. At the curtain, one of his brothers, cheated of the kingdom by the other brother, smilingly remarks, "The struggles of life are never over!"

ERNST, Otto (1862–1926), German playwright and novelist, was a humorist of NATURALISM who wrote one of the many "school plays" inspired by Wedekind's SPRING'S AWAKENING, *Flachsmann als Erzieher* (*Flachsmann as Teacher,* 1899; also translated as *Master Flachsmann*); it presents the distorted if popular view of the schoolmaster as a crafty and pedantic hypocrite. Earlier, in *Jugend von Heute* (1900), Ernst had satirized youth, whose immorality he blamed on Nietzsche. Ernst's other plays include *Die Gerechtigkeit* (1902), a satire of journalists.

Born in Ottensen and originally named Otto Ernst Schmidt, he lived in Hamburg, and was a schoolteacher before he turned to writing. His other works include children's books in Low German dialect, and largely autobiographical *Bildungsromane*, notably *Asmus Sempers Jugendland* (1905).

ERNST, Paul (1866–1933), German writer, was a very prolific religious and social philosopher—and a precursor of Nazism. Novelist, poet, and essayist, he also wrote some twenty-three dramas, beginning with NATURALISTIC plays. His *Lumpenbagasch* (1898), a one-acter about two village paupers, was produced at Die Freie Bühne in Berlin. After a trip to Italy, Ernst turned from naturalism to neoclassicism, of which he became the leading spirit among German playwrights. He propounded his new literary theories of "redemptive-" and "meta-tragedy" in numerous studies and exemplified his ideals of neoclassic and neoromantic tragedy in various dramatizations of history and myth. They include *Canossa* (1908), in which the German Emperor Henry IV because of his flexibility is able to defeat Pope Gregory VII, vulnerable in his intransigent loyalty to God alone; *Brunhild* (1909), a contrast of good and evil; classical legends like *Ariadne auf Naxos* (1912) and *Kassandra* (1915); *Preussengeist* (1915), about Frederick the Great; *Yorck* (1917), on the Prussian military hero of the Napoleonic war, Count Ludvig Yorck von Wartenburg; and *Chriemhild* (1922), dealing with the protagonist's vengeance of Siegfried's murder. Ernst's comedies, which are less exclusively talkative though also thought-provoking, include Italian-flavored plays like *Eine Nacht in Florenz* (1905), whose plot resembles that of Shakespeare's *Romeo and Juliet;* and *Pantalon und seine Söhne* (1916), which features *commedia dell'arte* characters.

Though Ernst was highly esteemed by academicians and philosophers, and most influential on WILHELM VON SCHOLZ and HANS FRANCK and other German playwrights, he could not attract general audiences. His failure to gain wide recognition was not overcome posthumously by Nazi attempts to popularize him as an Aryan genius and pioneer National Socialist man of the theatre.

ERVINE, St. John* [Greer] (1883–1971), Irish dramatist, critic, novelist, and biographer, was an Ulster Protestant who spent most of his life in England; but his association with the Abbey Theatre, which he managed in 1916 and where

* Pronounced "Sin-jn."

some of his plays were produced, places him among the Irish dramatists. Immensely prolific, he wrote fiction; critical biographies of public figures (Charles Stewart Parnell, General William Booth, and Sir Edward Carson) and of writers (Shelley, BERNARD SHAW, and OSCAR WILDE); books on the theatre and the drama; criticisms for the *Morning Post,* the *London Observer,* the *New York World,* and other newspapers on which he served as drama critic; and twenty-odd plays. The later ones are of little importance. But JOHN FERGUSON (1915) is a major drama, JANE CLEGG (1913) has been rated almost as highly. MIXED MARRIAGE (1911, his first produced work) is a significant PROBLEM PLAY, and his sprightly comedies—plays like THE FIRST MRS. FRASER (1929)—were popular and still make good reading.

Ervine was born in Belfast. He went to London when he was seventeen. While working as an insurance clerk there, he published two novels and began writing plays. The first one, *The Magnanimous Lover,* deals with religious hypocrisy and remained unproduced until 1912, the year after *Mixed Marriage* made his name known. These plus *The Orangeman* and *The Critics* (1913, which lambasted the reviewers of his second produced play) were published as *Four Irish Plays* in 1914. His next two works, *Jane Clegg* and *John Ferguson,* established him as a major Irish playwright, though he was never again to equal such accomplishments.

His other serious drama includes *Robert's Wife* (1937), whose heroine's work in a birth-control clinic upsets her stodgy and bigoted clergyman husband. More popular were some of his comedies, particularly the already noted *The First Mrs. Fraser; Mary, Mary, Quite Contrary* (1923); and *Anthony and Anna* (1926). Ervine's serious plays are respectably moralistic and often employ stock devices of melodrama. Yet the topics were at the time provocative, and Ervine succeeded in investing his better plays with strong characterizations and admirable protagonists so that, as he wrote of *John Ferguson,* "the audience should leave a theatre . . . proud that they are human and of the same species as the tragic figures."

Following his directorship of the Abbey Theatre, Ervine in World War I served at the front, where he was seriously wounded and lost a leg. Subsequently Ervine wrote his controversial and astringent criticisms and his other works. He received many academic and national honors and became president of the League of British Dramatists in 1937.

Among Ervine's other plays are *The Island of Saints and How to Get Out of It* (1920), *The Wonderful Visit* (1921, written with H. G. Wells, 1866–1946), *The Ship* (1922), *The Lady of Belmont* (1925, a comic sequel to *The Merchant of Venice*), *Old George Comes to Tea* and *She Was No Lady* (1927), *Boyd's Shop* and *People of Our Class* (1936), *The Christies* (1939), *William John Mawhinney* (1940), *Friends and Relations* (1941), *Private Enterprise* (1947), *My Brother Tom* (1952), and *Esperanza* (1957).

ESCAPE, "an episodic play in a prologue and two parts" by JOHN GALSWORTHY, published and produced in 1926. Setting: Hyde Park (London) and Devonshire in the 1920's.

One of Galsworthy's last and most popular plays, this is a fast-moving, loosely knit work that combines urbane geniality with suspense. Various people are portrayed as reacting in different ways to the plight of the gentle fugitive. The sentimental touch is offset by humor and picturesque dialogue, and the total effect suggests innate human decency.

Matt Denant, an army captain during the war, kindly intercedes for a streetwalker about to be hauled off. In a scuffle, he accidentally kills a policeman. Next seen in prison, Matt finds confinement unbearable and escapes during a dense fog. He confronts a number of people who discover his identity; a few are vindictive, but most of them turn out to be charitable and courageously helpful. They include a lady surprised in her bedchamber, a retired judge, picnickers, hunters, laborers, a farmer, maiden ladies, and a parson. In the last episode, in a church, the conflict between duty and compassion reaches its climax. The parson shelters Matt, and when the pursuers arrive, he is even ready to perjure himself. But Matt emerges from hiding to spare the parson's conscience, and surrenders. As he is led off he remarks, "It's one's decent *self* one can't escape."

ESPERPENTO is a style—or, rather, a deformation of style—conceived by RAMÓN DEL VALLE-INCLÁN and employed in many of his works, including a dramatic tetralogy. The *raisonneur* in one of them, *Luces de Bohemia* (1924), remarks that "the tragic sense of Spanish life can only be expressed with a systematically deformed aesthetic," and observes, "My present aesthetic is to transform, with the mathematics of a concave mirror, the classic norms." In fact, the word *esperpento* (Spanish for *nonsense, absurdity, ridiculousness*) derives from the fun-house mirrors that distort images. Valle-Inclán employed *esperpento* to ridicule and reject society by presenting his characters as parodies of heroic figures.

ESSIG, Hermann (1878–1918), German playwright, was influenced by FRANK WEDEKIND particularly in his best-known work, the EXPRESSIONIST *Überteufel* (1912). A play about incest, parricide, and other passions, written in 1906 and produced in 1923, its title's "superdevil" is a bestial middle-class wife who destroys her family. Similarly brutal is his *Mariä Heimsuchung* (1909), but Essig, the son of a Swabian pastor, was artistically more successful with comedies like *Die Glückskuh* (1910), the first of his plays to be produced.

ESSON, [Thomas] **Louis** [Buvelot] (1879–1943), Australian playwright, has been called the Father of Australian Drama. Though born in Edinburgh, Scotland, he spent all his life in Australia. He was educated at the University of Melbourne (but did not complete his degree), became a journalist, lived in the bush country for a while, and traveled abroad. He met and was greatly impressed by the writers of the Irish Revival, particularly J. M. SYNGE and WILLIAM BUTLER YEATS, who advised him to "keep within your own borders," i.e., to dramatize the life and people he knew best. Thereupon Esson returned to Australia, and wrote for the Adelaide Repertory Company. With Vance Palmer (1885–1959) he founded the Pioneer Players (1921–23), whom he (and Palmer) also supplied with plays.

Esson was not so much interested in "events," he said, as in "the lyric and dramatic, a vivid impression, a twist of thought, a crisis, a glimpse of beauty." His best plays are one-acters like *Dead Timber* (produced in 1911 and set in the bush country) and THE DROVERS (1919); and *The Southern Cross* (completed in 1927), a four-act chronicle play, about the 1854–55 Eureka Stockade revolt, that won a competition but remained unproduced.

Esson's plays were collected in *Dead Timber and Other Plays* (1920) and in *The Southern Cross and Other Plays* (1946), the introduction to which contains memoirs of Esson and the Pioneer Players. See also Vance Palmer's *Louis Esson and the Australian Theatre* (1948), a slim volume that consists mostly of Esson's revealing letters to the author.

ESTONIA was part of the Russian Empire until 1918, when, like its neighbors Latvia and Lithuania, it became independent. This was a short-lived state, for in 1940 Estonia was occupied by Russian troops, and (after being overrun by the Germans and then reoccupied by Russia) in 1944 it was incorporated into the Soviet Union.

The first significant native drama was *Saaremaa onupoeg* (1870), a comedy adapted from the German by Lydia Koidula (1843–86), a seminal figure in Estonian literature, whose most popular play was the original comedy *Säärane mulk* (1871). The leading playwright before independence, August Kitzberg (1856–1927), wrote dramas about rural life. His *Libahunt* (1911), a folk tragedy, has been widely translated; the "werewolf" of the title of that play, a spirited girl thus stigmatized in a drama of medieval superstitions, suggests more contemporary evils. Eduard Vilde (1865–1933) is the author of *Pisuhänd* (1913), the best-known Estonian comedy; it satirizes the artistic pretensions of writers who capitalize on the debased popular taste for patriotic literature.

In the brief period of Estonia's independence appeared the history plays *Juudit* (1921) and *Kuningal on külm* (1936) by the country's foremost novelist, A. H. Tammsaare (pen name of Anton Hansen, 1878–1940), as well as the social satires of Hugo Raudsepp (1883–1952), including *Sinimandria* (1927), *Mikumärdi* (1929), and *Vedelvorst* (1932). Since 1945, Estonian drama has languished in exile or has been forced into the rigid mold of SOCIALIST REALISM at home. Significant exceptions to the latter trend are the ABSURDist allegories of the 1960's, the most outstanding of which is Paul-Eerik Rummo's (1942–) *Tuhkatriinumäng* (*The Cinderella Game*, 1969).

See Howard E. Harris's "The Estonian Theatre," *Life and Letters To-Day* (August 1939); the literature and theatre essays in Villibald Raud's compilation *Estonia: A Reference Book* (1953); and Mardi Valgemäe's "Recent Developments in Soviet Estonian Drama," *Bulletin* (September 1969) of the Institute for the Study of the USSR.

EULENBERG, Herbert (1876–1949), German dramatist, wrote most of his many oft-performed plays before World War I. Because of their focus on extreme passions, they have been likened to the Elizabethan as well as the *Sturm und Drang* drama. Frequently dealing with history and legend, Eulenberg repeatedly presented the individual (often female) destroyed by intense yearnings, usually lust. Typical is his early well-known play *Anna Walewska* (1899), which portrays the incestuous passions of a Polish count and his daughter.

Born in the Rhineland town of Mülheim, Eulenberg studied law but soon turned to the stage and became the *Dramaturg* of the Düsseldorf theatre. Among his more important plays are *Münchhausen* (1900), which portrays the legendary baron as another Cyrano; *Leidenschaft* (1901), the title's "passion" being that of a middle-class girl who gives herself to an officer and later commits suicide; *Ein halber Held* (1903), juxtaposing a man of reason and a man of feelings; *Kassandra* (1903), whose title heroine is enervated by the fall of Troy and yearns only for death; *Ritter Blaubart* (1905), a symbolic fairy play made into an opera by Emil von Reznièek in 1920; *Ulrich, Fürst von Waldeck* (1906), whose protagonist escapes worldly intrigues by moving to the woods and living with animals; *Der natürliche Vater* (1907), a comedy about a girl who chooses the son rather than his father; *Alles um Liebe* (1910), a marriage comedy; the prize-winning *Belinde* (1912), an Enoch Arden tragedy of a woman in love with her husband, who has gone to make their fortune, as well as with her young lover, who upon the husband's return duels him, loses, and commits suicide—as does the guilt- and grief-stricken Belinde; and *Die Insel* (1917), a variation of Shakespeare's *The Tempest*.

In his later plays, including a depiction of the machine age (*Industrie*, 1930), Eulenberg's flair for dramatizing grotesque behavior failed. He was more successful with his fiction and with his autobiography, *So war mein Leben* (1948).

EURYDICE, a play in four acts by JEAN ANOUILH, produced in 1941 and published in 1942. Setting: a French provincial railway station and a hotel bedroom.

Unlike Anouilh's other modernizations of classic themes, this dramatization of the Orpheus and Eurydice legend (which in English appeared also under the title *Legend of Lovers*) has modern settings and characters. But like the other Anouilh plays, its tragedy is portrayed as resulting from men's refusal to compromise their ideals. Though predominantly NATURALISTIC, it is in parts poetic fantasy.

Acts I and II. Orphée is an itinerant accordianist traveling with his father, a ruined harpist. At a railway station restaurant Orphée meets Eurydice, an actress traveling with a provincial troupe that includes her vulgar mother and the mother's lover. Orphée and Eurydice are immediately drawn to each other, swear eternal love, and leave their companions. They spend a blissful night in a hotel. Though Eurydice confesses that she once had a lover, she does not tell Orphée that she is the mistress of the troupe's coarse manager, who now sends her a note through the hotel waiter. She leaves without enlightening Orphée, who learns the truth from the manager himself. As Orphée recoils from this discovery of her immediate past, the waiter brings news that Eurydice has been killed in a bus accident.

Acts III and IV. Back at the railway station, a mysterious young man, the emissary of death, has compassion on the grieving Orphée. Though he believes their brief affair is all life can offer, the emissary agrees to bring Eurydice back from death if Orphée will not look at her until dawn. Orphée believes passionately in life with all its "mistakes, and failures, the despair, the fresh starts, the shame," and gives his word. Eurydice returns, but Orphée is uncompromising and eager to determine the truth of her love for him. Though she implores him to wait so that they may live together, he breaks his promise: "Live! Like your mother and her lover, perhaps, with baby talk, smiles, and indulgences, and then a good meal, a little love-making, and everything's all right. Ah, no! I love you too much to live!" Only by looking into her eyes can he believe her profession of love for him. Eurydice admits her affair with the manager: she ran away from Orphée because she was ashamed, afraid he would never understand and therefore would stop loving her. Orphée begs her forgiveness, but having looked at her it is too late and she returns to the dead. His old father revels in voluptuous thoughts and then starts snoring. Death's emissary attempts to persuade Orphée that life and all love inevitably degenerate into the stupidity and ugliness of old age, but Orphée refuses to accept love's transience. He is willing to pay any price—even to die—to have Eurydice again. Then Eurydice clasps him in her arms: "My darling, what a long time you've been!" The lovers are united, at last, in death.

EVERYMAN (*Jedermann*), a one-act verse play by HUGO VON HOFMANNSTHAL, published and produced in 1911. Setting: outside a house, a banquet, etc.

This rhymed modernization of the classic English morality (c. 1450) is Hofmannsthal's most popular play. Though they parallel those of the simple original, the episodes are modernized and amplified. Max Reinhardt's production of the play as a vast outdoor spectacle in 1920 on the town's cathedral square launched the Salzburg Festivals, which feature *Everyman* annually. Hofmannsthal's essays on the play and the Festivals are collected in *Festspiele in Salzburg* (1952), and

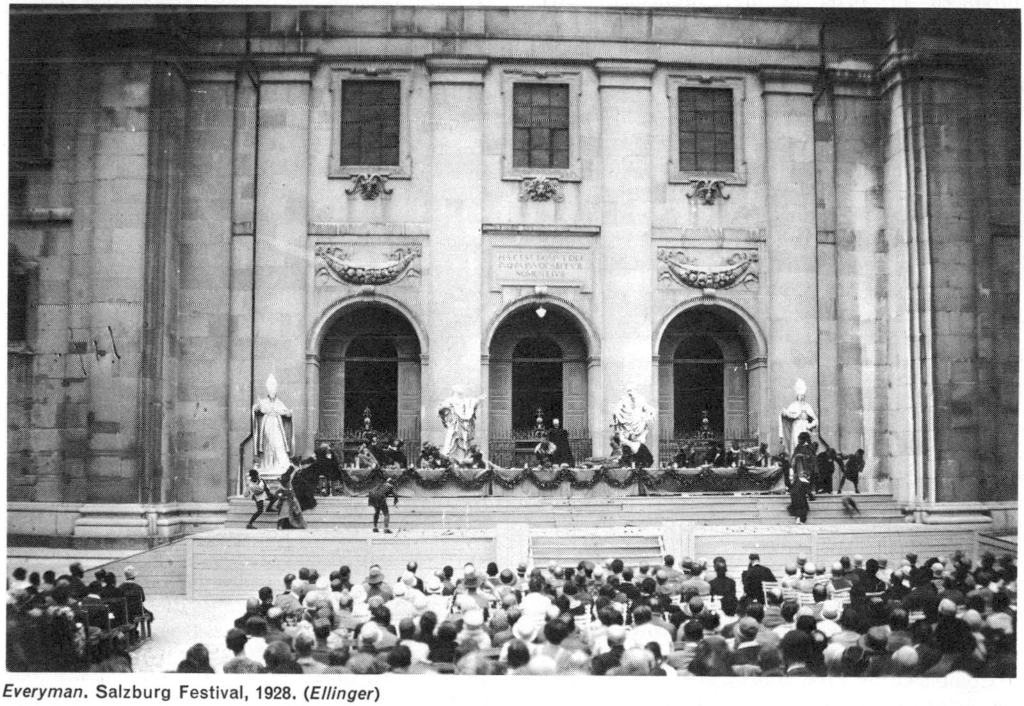

Everyman. Salzburg Festival, 1928. (*Ellinger*)

the play has appeared in English also under its German title and as *The Play of Everyman.*

In a picturesque banquet scene Everyman carouses with his mistress and guests when God's messenger, Death, appears. Everyman gradually learns that no one is willing to accompany him to his final Judgment. Then he understands the transience of earthly life and the importance of the larger world of Eternity, repents, and regains his faith. To the intense vexation of the Devil, Everyman is saved. He calmly steps into his grave, assisted by Faith and Good Deeds.

EVIL DOERS OF GOOD, THE (*Los malhechores del bien*), a comedy in two acts by JACINTO BENAVENTE, published in 1903 and produced in 1905. Setting: a small Spanish seaport, 1905.

A satire on hypocritical philanthropy, this amusing but verbose play depicts an old lady tyrannizing her dependents. Surrounded by her scandalmonger friends, she has forced her young niece to marry an ugly old man, browbeats her lovable brother, and treats her grown son like a child. Her victims manage to frustrate her attempt to separate a young couple who are in love, and help them escape. Though the family incur the old lady's wrath, they are satisfied. "Suppose they did eat your bread," the brother says; "we have given them something that is better than life—liberty and love."

EXCEPTION AND THE RULE, THE (*Die Ausnahme und die Regel*), a play by BERTOLT BRECHT (music by Paul Dessau), published in 1937 and produced in 1938. Setting: Mongolia, early twentieth century.

This "didactic piece" consists of nine short prose sections and a verse prologue and epilogue. It was written in 1930.

A cruel merchant races through the desert to win an oil concession. Suspicious and fearful, he fires his guide and mistreats his coolie. When they run short of water, the coolie kindly offers him his own flask. Mistaking the mute gesture for an attack, the merchant shoots him. He is subsequently hailed to court. The judge finds that the coolie's gesture was, indeed, not an attack, though the coolie had every reason to hate the merchant. Murdering his oppressor would have been sensible and the expected thing—the rule—in our society, while repaying evil with kindness is the exception. Therefore the merchant really acted in self-defense, and is acquitted. The epilogue exhorts the audience: "Consider everything usual, unusual! / What is customary, consider puzzling!" And lastly, "Whatever is the rule, consider injurious / And where you recognize the injurious / Remedy it!"

EXILES, a play in three acts by JAMES JOYCE, published in 1918 and produced in 1919. Setting: Dublin suburbs; summer 1912.

Completed by 1915, shortly after *A Portrait of the Artist as a Young Man,* Joyce's only play was rejected the following year by the Stage Society (because it was considered obscene by BERNARD SHAW, of whose CANDIDA it is a morbid variation), and was first produced in Germany. It is a disquisitional, IBSENite PROBLEM PLAY, neatly patterned into duologues—a love quadrangle weighted with psychology and cerebration. Doubts and guilt torture Richard, the same autobiographical hero who appears in Joyce's novels as Stephen Dedalus—just as Bertha prefigures Molly Bloom of *Ulysses,* his next work. Though abstruse and unsuccessful on the boards until its 1970–71 revival under HAROLD PINTER's direction—and without the striking originality and challenging suggestiveness of his novels—the play has been praised for its rich SYMBOLISM.

Act I. After living in exile with his common-law wife Bertha and their eight-year-old son, Richard Rowan has achieved some success as a writer, and the family has returned to Ireland. There they have met old friends: the journalist Robert Hand and his cousin and one-time fiancée, Beatrice Justice, now Richard's son's music teacher. She confesses that Richard's intellectual appeal has caused her to break with the superficial journalist. Robert, in turn, has become attracted to the simple Bertha. Alone, they kiss and he elicits her tentative agreement to visit him that night. Later he reaffirms his friendship with Richard and urges him to accept the professorship that now may be offered him. After Robert leaves, Richard closely questions Bertha about the physical details of Robert's wooing. She is jealous of Beatrice, but frankly tells Richard all—as she has done ever since Robert first approached her. Though excited, Richard denies being jealous; and though Bertha begs him to do so, he absolutely refuses to forbid her to keep her tryst. As he insists on his own freedom, so she too must be allowed complete freedom: "Decide yourself."

Act II. That night Richard visits the waiting Robert's cottage to tell the journalist he knows all about the affair but cannot and will not interfere. If he did, he would be guilty of "having taken all for myself because I would not suffer her to give to another what was hers and not mine to give, because I accepted from her her loyalty and made her life poorer in love." Richard admits that "in the very core of my ignoble heart I longed to be betrayed by you and by her—. . . I longed for that passionately and ignobly, to be dishonoured for ever in love and in lust." Robert offers to duel, but Richard rejects this as the kind of romanticism he has outgrown. When she does appear, Bertha is confused by Richard's presence. Then she implores him, "Dick, my God, tell me what you wish me to do?" Again he refuses, and leaves. Robert asks Bertha to deliver Richard from his torments of guilt and shame, as he wants them to: "Every chain but one he has broken and that one we are to break."

Act III. The next morning it is not quite clear what has really happened. After a sleepless night, Bertha is reassured by Beatrice's innocence and tells her of her own unhappiness. She does not understand Richard's work, Bertha confesses: "I don't even understand half of what he says to me sometimes!" And then, bitterly, "I am only a thing he got entangled with and my son is—the nice name they give those children." When Richard returns from a solitary walk, Bertha reassures him of her love: nothing happened between her and Robert. Richard maintains that he will never really know. Angrily she accuses him of making her unhappy—as he has made Beatrice unhappy, "and as you made your dead mother unhappy and killed her. Woman-killer!" He accuses her of wanting the freedom to meet her lover, and when she passionately agrees, he tells her that she is free. Later, after being reassured of Bertha's faithfulness by the departing Robert, Richard tells Bertha, "You were my bride in exile," but "I have wounded my soul for you—a deep wound of doubt which can never be healed." Wearied by this wound, he lies down, and Bertha holds his hand. Softly she yearns for her lover: "To meet him, to go to him, to give myself to him. You, Dick. O, my strange wild lover, come back to me again!"

EXIT THE KING (*Le Roi se meurt*), a one-act play by EUGÈNE IONESCO, produced in 1962 and published in 1963. Setting: a "vaguely Gothic" throne room in an unnamed country at an unspecified but suggestively modern time.

Also translated, more literally, as *The King Dies,* this long one-act Bérenger play marks a departure from Ionesco's total ABSURDist style. Much of the dialogue is conventional—although Ionesco employs chants and stylized gestures. The play is an extended dramatic nightmare, the death of the title character, who is a human yet mythic figure incorporating classical, medieval, renaissance, and modern heroes and writers.

The ageless King Bérenger I cannot believe he is to die shortly, but his doctor insists, "You will have no breakfast tomorrow morning." His entire kingdom and nature itself is expiring with Bérenger as he himself gradually experiences the feeling and looks of death. "Teach me what I must do to acquire disgust for life. Teach me lassitude," the suffering king implores those who have died by their own hands. His young wife tells him the beautiful things he wants to hear, but his older wife constantly keeps reality before him ("You are going to die at the end of the show"). Ultimately the older queen leads Bérenger to his death. Like everyone else in the play, she is herself incorporated into final nothingness. Bérenger remains alone on his throne but then, together with his throne and his room, he is enveloped by and disappears into a shadowy mist.

EXPRESSIONISM in drama refers to a particular and extreme reaction—aesthetic, ethical, social, and even political—to NATURALISM. Though expressionism covers many divergent practices, all its plays distort external, photographic, objective reality in order to express a subjective *inner* reality. In the Fifth Avenue scene of O'Neill's THE HAIRY APE, for example, the wealthy parishioners' imperviousness to Yank is conveyed by their failure even to be jarred when he viciously rams into them; it is Yank who recoils from the collisions. Similarly, stage settings are distorted, as in the dream in Kaufman and Connelly's BEGGAR ON HORSEBACK and in Rice's THE ADDING MACHINE, in which walls close in and the floor spins. Dialogue, too, is distorted, and characterization is flat rather than rounded—the portraits often being of masses rather than of individuals. Because they are types, characters in expressionist drama usually remain nameless, as in Kaiser's GAS trilogy and FROM MORN TO MIDNIGHT.

The works of FRANK WEDEKIND and the late drama of Strindberg (A DREAM PLAY, THE GHOST SONATA, and the TO DAMASCUS trilogy) foreshadowed the movement, and psychoanalytic writings (particularly Freud's) gave it a powerful impetus. Introduced by OSKAR KOKOSCHKA, and in Germany with Sorge's THE BEGGAR, it flowered there in the 1920's—particularly with the works of GEORG KAISER—and spread to the United States and elsewhere. At first experimental, its influence has persisted long after its heyday. Expressionist drama has been allied to other avant-garde arts and literatures, and to other movements like SURREALISM, cubism, FUTURISM, EPIC DRAMA, and the theatres of CRUELTY and the ABSURD.

Since the movement flourished in Germany, studies tend to focus on that country. Particularly notable among the English studies is Richard Samuel and R. Hinton Thomas's *Expressionism in German Life, Literature and the Theatre (1919–1924)* (1939). Claude Hill and Ralph Ley's *The Drama of German Expressionism: A German-English Bibliography* (1960) lists many books on the subject; Martin Esslin's *The Theatre of the Absurd* (revised edition, 1968) contains further bibliography and an informative essay, as do such collections as Walter H. Sokel's *An Anthology of German Expressionist Drama* (1963), James M. Ritchie and Hugh F. Garten's *Seven Expressionist Plays: Kokoschka to Barlach* (1968), and Ritchie's *Vision and Aftermath: Four Expressionist War Plays* (1969).

F

FABBRI, Diego (1911–), Italian dramatist, has written on religious topics and has been called a poet of the theatre and the successor of both LUIGI PIRANDELLO and UGO BETTI. Though his plays have been performed throughout Europe and South America, Fabbri is little known to English-speaking audiences. His most successful plays have been *Inquisizione* (1950), a parallel study of two priests who counsel an unhappily married couple; *Processo di famiglia* (1953), a sharp satire of domestic life; and *Processo a Gesù* (1955, translated as *Between Two Thieves*), a play-within-a-play that explores race prejudice and features itinerant German-Jewish actors who stage improvisations of Christ's trial. Other notable Fabbri plays are *Paludi* (1942), the revision of his earlier play censored by the Fascists; *Il seduttore* (1951), whose title character is torn by his love for three women and whose suicide in the original version prompted the Catholic Church's demand that Fabbri revise the ending; *Veglia d'armi* (1956), which portrays a crisis among a group of Jesuits; *La bugiarda* (1956); and two adaptations of Dostoevsky, published as *I demoni* (1961).

Fabbri was born in Forlì to a devout Catholic family. He studied law but soon turned to writing and teaching. After participating in amateur theatricals, he devoted all his energies to the drama, considering it his life's mission to express his concept of "tragic Christianity" and the need of man to accept his responsibilities.

FACING DEATH (*Inför döden*), a one-act play by AUGUST STRINDBERG, published in 1893 and produced in 1910. Setting: a diningroom in French Switzerland in the 1880's.

This short tragedy, also translated as *In the Face of Death,* features a latter-day King Lear, a scapegoat for his vicious family.

Exactly as his wife used to do, so his three extravagant daughters now humiliate and insult an indigent old widower. Still loving and provident, he finally burns down the house for the insurance money and commits suicide.

FAITH HEALER, THE, a play in three (originally four) acts by WILLIAM VAUGHN MOODY, published and produced in 1909. Setting: a Midwestern farmhouse, early twentieth century.

Moody's last work, this play was conceived long before it appeared. A. H. Quinn in *A History of the American Drama* quotes from Moody's 1895 letter: "I am losing sleep over a play dealing with a character and a situation which seem to me intensely significant and eloquent, that of Slatter, the 'New Mexico Messiah,' who has been doing things in Denver of late." A first draft had been completed by 1900. The play, which was eventually filmed, portrays well-conceived characters who personify two conflicts: that of divine faith and scientific skepticism, and the claims of love and mission. Both conflicts are somehow reconciled in the denouement.

Young Ulrich Michaelis, a famous faith healer, miraculously cures a crippled woman. When he falls in love with her niece, he loses his self-confidence. As the worshiping crowds outside wait for another miracle, he is unable to heal a dying child. The cripple relapses, and Michaelis is opposed not only by her skeptical husband, an admirer of Darwin and Spencer, but also by a dogmatic young minister and a young doctor, who is revealed to be the niece's previous lover. Now reformed, she confesses her sin to Michaelis, to "set you free. I have given you back your mission." Her story rejuvenates them both. Michaelis triumphs over her seducer and heals the crippled and dying. It is Easter morning, and a choir sings a hymn "of martial and joyous rhythm" as Michaelis reveals how her confession and his love have saved them both: "You needed what the whole world needs —healing, healing, and as I rose to meet that need, the power that I had lost poured back into my soul." He concludes, as they look at each other, that they "shall be delivered. By faith which makes all things possible, which brings all things to pass."

FALSE SAINT, A (*L'Envers d'une sainte*), a play in three acts by FRANÇOIS DE CUREL, published and produced in 1892. Setting: a small-town country home in France, 1892.

This play, Curel's first, premiered at André Antoine's Théâtre-Libre on a double bill with another playwright's first, Brieux's BLANCHETTE. Less successful with audiences than with critics, Curel's play is an IBSENite character study.

Julie Renaudin returns from eighteen years of self-imposed seclusion in a convent after her attempt in a fit of insane jealousy to kill the wife for whom her lover had jilted her. Now Julie learns that his wife revealed to him before he died the terrible secret of Julie's attack. Foiled in her pose as a martyr for love, Julie avenges herself on her former lover's daughter by driving her to a convent. In time Julie learns that her lover had repented the jilting, never forgot Julie, and died thinking of her. This obviates the need for vengeance, and Julie stops the daughter's going to the convent, returning to it herself. Releasing her murderous instincts by crushing a bird ("It would be cruel and brutal to put it in a cage, poor little bird! So long as it lived, *that* would be wrong"), she concludes, as she leaves, "Now that I can't manage my will, the responsibility is driving me mad." If not the "false saint" of the past eighteen years, perhaps the nun can now become more genuinely pious.

FAMILY REUNION, THE, a verse play in two parts by T. S. ELIOT, published and produced in 1939. Setting: a contemporary North England country house, a day late in March.

In this modernization of the Orestes legend Eliot focused on the hero's brooding conscience and experimented by juxtaposing drawing-room REALISM with ghosts and ritualism (particularly choral incantations). Audiences and Eliot himself found the mixture intractable and the plot too obscure, though the play has been praised by some critics as an advance in poetic drama.

Harry, Lord Monchensey, returns home after many years for a family reunion on the occasion of his aged mother's birthday. Harry murdered (or thinks he murdered) his wife and is pursued by the Furies: "Can't you see them? *You* don't see them, but I see them, / And they see me. . . ." As he talks with a cousin to whom he is momentarily attracted, he again sees the Furies. He feels revolted by the "diseased" world and is reluctant to remain at home. His uncles and aunts, who periodically chant as a chorus, invite a doctor to probe his sanity. Eventually Harry discovers his past: Long ago his most sympathetic aunt, Agatha, was in love with his father but prevented him from killing Harry's dominating mother. Ready to expiate his father's murderous thought, Harry accepts his destiny to "follow the Furies." When he leaves in his car, his mother dies of a heart attack. The play ends with Agatha and Harry's cousin chanting a rune as they file around the birthday cake, blowing out candles at each revolution: "This way the pilgrimage / Of expiation / Round and round the circle." It is totally dark when they reach the last words, about the departed: "May they rest in peace."

FANNY'S FIRST PLAY, "An Easy Play for a Little Theatre by Xxxxxxx Xxxx"—i.e., BERNARD SHAW—produced in 1912 and published in 1914. Setting: England, early 1900's.

This is a three-act play-within-a-play, a domestic comedy with a framework that consists of an Induction and an Epilogue. In a brief preface Shaw, who did not acknowledge his authorship of the play until its publication, castigated the English for inculcating the young with their soulless morality: "I hate to see dead people walking about: it is unnatural. And our respectable middle class people are all as dead as mutton." He also apologized impishly to those critics whom he had not been able to fit into the satire of the Epilogue of this play, which became Shaw's first commercial success.

Induction. Count O'Dowda, who prefers the "beautiful realities" of the eighteenth century to present-day England, which he considers "ugly and Philistine," has set up his country house for a private theatrical performance of a play written by his daughter, Fanny. As part of her birthday gift she has asked for "real critics," who are not to be told who the author is; after they arrive, Fanny's play begins. (In 1916, Shaw provided an alternate to the Induction, a Prologue spoken by Fanny O'Dowda, who "acts" Margaret Knox in the "play".)

Play. Bobby Gilbey and Margaret Knox, strictly brought up by their middle-class families and pressed by them into an engagement, have disappeared. Independently, they have gone off on sprees that ended in brawls and landed them in jail. The two scandalized families are shown, separately, as they learn that Bobby has been keeping company with the common "Darling Dora" Delaney, while Margaret, off to a dance hall after prayers, had picked up a married French officer. Bobby and Margaret break their engagement; Bobby marries the gay Darling Dora, and Margaret marries Juggins, the Gilbeys' footman, to whom she has long felt attracted and who turns out to be a duke's brother.

Epilogue. Fanny's father, who had expected a pastoral masque from his once-sheltered daughter, is shocked by the modernity of the play. The drama critics (all caricatures of contemporaries) debate its merits and authorship: one considers it "the most ordinary sort of old-fashioned IBSENite drivel"; another refuses to discuss its merits until he knows who the author is, for "if it's by a good author, it's a good play, naturally"; a third senses in Darling Dora a latent passion that proves that Shaw ("a giant brain . . . but no heart") could not have been the author. The critics having bandied about the names of prominent playwrights as the likely author, Fanny is naturally proud of her success.

FANTASTICKS, THE (*Les Romanesques*), a verse comedy in three acts by EDMOND ROSTAND, published and produced in 1894. Setting: "The action [is set in a park] and may take place anywhere, provided the costumes are pretty"; late nineteenth century.

This was Rostand's first produced play. Curiously—because of his later success with romances—this is a slight if charming satire of the genre. The play also appeared in English as *The Romancers* and *Romantics,* and as Tom Jones's (1928–) Off-Broadway musical *The Fantasticks* (music by Harvey Schmidt), which opened in 1960 and continued its run into the next decade, setting the record for New York's longest-running play.

"Sir Percinet, how beautiful and wise!" Sylvette exclaims at the reading of her equally starry-eyed companion, who answers: "Is it not? Hear what Romeo replies . . ." and continues the play. The youngsters, separated by the wall bordering their homes, imagine themselves to be Shakespeare's lovers and plan to elope. Humoring the romance, their fathers simulate being mortal enemies and hire a braggadocio who is to pretend he wants to kidnap Sylvette. Percinet "fells" him and the lovers escape. Later they discover the deception and get angry at their fathers—who also have failed in their own attempts to substitute illusion for a humdrum life. The lovers part, each seeking but failing to find romance separately. Weary at last, they come together again. Percinet finds he loves Sylvette as much as ever. When she complains that their fathers deceived them, "only pretended to be mortal enemies," Percinet points out that this made their romance no less real: "Did *we* pretend that we loved each other?" And when Sylvette regrets that their danger was "only imaginary," Percinet finds it too no less "real, because we thought it so." Now Sylvette as well as Percinet realizes the foolishness of evading reality with pretended attitudes and phrases: "Poetry, love, but we were crazy, dear, / To seek it elsewhere. It was always here!"

FAR-OFF HILLS, THE, a comedy in three acts by LENNOX ROBINSON, published and produced in 1928. Setting: Ireland, 1920's.

This popular comedy centers around Marian Clancy, the serious, domineering eldest daughter, who manages the family after her mother's death. She gets rid of a doleful old suitor by threatening actually to marry him. But after her father escapes her tyranny by remarrying, she succumbs to an ambitious younger suitor whom she will help with her managerial talents.

FARFETCHED FABLES, six "fables" by BERNARD SHAW, published and produced in 1950. Setting: London and the Isle of Wight, now and in the future.

The first two of these six debates, which take place in a park and in the War Office and are thinly disguised as "childish fables," reveal a poison-gas catastrophe and demonstrate how nonatomic war resumes after the banning of atomic war. The remaining science-fiction "fables" illustrate the discussion in Shaw's last extensive preface, which, appropriately, recapitulates the beliefs—in the Life Force and in Creative Evolution, and in political, economic, and social reforms—enunciated in his other prefaces and plays.

FASHIONS FOR MEN (*Úri divat,* literally: *Clothes for the Quality*), a play in three acts by FERENC MOLNÁR, published and produced in 1914. Setting: Budapest and a Hungarian estate, early twentieth century.

This play—EDMUND WILSON called it "something of a comic masterpiece" (*The New Yorker,* June 4, 1966)—features a saintly hero, Peter Juhasz. Much of its humor is in the portrayal of various customers and in their continuous interruption of domestic and amorous affairs.

Peter owns a fashionable clothing shop, but his guilelessness is exploited by all. His bankruptcy is final when his wife steals his savings and elopes with his clerk. Peter's pretty young cashier accompanies him to the estate of his benefactor, an elderly count who makes Peter his manager. The cashier's real aim is not to stay with the protective Peter but to gain wealth by ensnaring the count. Peter is sent back to his shop by the count, who wants to make the cashier his mistress. At the end the cashier, overcome by Peter's incorrigible saintliness, returns to take over the management of the store and to marry him.

FATHER, THE (*Fadren*), a tragedy in three acts by AUGUST STRINDBERG, published and produced in 1887. Setting: a contemporary Swedish living room.

One of Strindberg's most famous plays, *The Father* won immediate success, notoriety, and special praise from ÉMILE ZOLA. Still overpowering, it is classic in its modernized Agamemnon theme, its starkness, and its observance of the unities of time, place, and action. The NATURALISTIC, searing, bitter sex duel is autobiographical, dramatizing Strindberg's own suffering at the time his first marriage broke up. Strindberg may have intended COMRADES to be a sequel to this play; it deals with the marriage of Bertha, an untalented painter in both plays.

Act I. The Captain (Adolf) confronts a difficulty in disciplining a cavalryman: it is impossible to be sure that the rogue fathered the kitchen maid's child. Later the Captain talks to the pastor, his wife Laura's brother, about his daughter Bertha, whom he wants to remove from his female-dominated home. Alone, the Captain and Laura soon start arguing. Though Laura objects to having Bertha study and board in town with "freethinkers" like him, the Captain insists that a mother has no say in such matters. Laura wonders why fathers have such powers if, as the Captain earlier remarked, paternity can never be established. Later, while the Captain is out, Laura welcomes the new country doctor. Sobbing bitterly, she tells him that her husband is losing his mind and enumerates various symptoms. Though he withholds judgment, the doctor cautions her against upsetting her disturbed husband. The Captain returns, meets the doctor, and dispels Laura's false charges. But he harangues about booksellers who, ignoring his orders and urgent communications, seem to conspire to keep him from concluding and publishing his scientific discoveries. Later Bertha rushes in. She is hysterically afraid of her grandmother, who makes her participate in séances. Unhappy in her parents' gloomy house, she tells her father that she wants to move to town. Even though this supports his own case, the Captain will not allow Bertha's preference to enter into his discussions with Laura: "I will not let anyone, neither woman nor child, encroach upon my rights!" Insisting that she will not lose her influence over her daughter, Laura remarks, "I have never been able to look at a man without feeling myself his superior." She wantonly suggests that the Captain may not be

Bertha's father. The Captain dismisses the affectionate but pietistic old nursemaid and angrily calls for his sleigh: "To hell with you, you hags! . . . Don't expect me home before midnight!"

Act II. As they await the Captain's return at midnight, Laura admits to the doctor that she has intercepted the Captain's mail to protect them from "ruin and disgrace." She nonetheless wins the doctor over, revealing that the Captain himself once wrote that he feared for his sanity. When the Captain returns, he excitedly proves to the doctor the scientific impossibility of establishing paternity. He also insists that women are brazenly inconstant, as he himself had learned in his youth. The Captain later confronts Laura with her rumor-spreading about his insanity and her interception of the mail dealing with work she knows would have gained him fame, and thus "exposed your own inferiority." In a long talk, he bitterly reviews his seventeen years of love and slavery for her. He asks that she cease struggling for power—and begs her to confess the illegitimacy of their child. Such a confession would at least stop the gnawing uncertainty she has caused and now denies. When he weeps in despair Laura becomes maternally tender: "The mother was your friend, you see, but the woman was your enemy; and love between the sexes produces strife, dissension, conflict." Insisting that she is the stronger one, however, she reveals her plan to have him committed—on the strength of his own confession of approaching insanity in a letter she has appropriated. "Now you have fulfilled your destiny as a father and family supporter—a function that unfortunately is a necessary one," she tells him: "You are no longer needed. . . . Since you don't want to stay and acknowledge . . . that my intellect is as strong as my will, you must be gotten rid of." Goaded into fury, he provides her with the necessary medical grounds for his commitment: he hurls the burning lamp after her as she backs through the door.

Act III. Even the pastor is amazed at—though he admires—his sister's clever ruthlessness, her "unconscious crime," while preparations are being made to commit the Captain. When he bursts in, the Captain ridicules the pastor and doctor—both of whom have been cuckolded. He grieves for the loss of his child, "my conception of a life after death." A broken man, he is ready to shoot Bertha—and himself. But the old nursemaid skillfully soothes him and, believing that she is doing what is best for him, craftily slips a straitjacket over him and ties him to the sofa. Beaten by women, the Captain bemoans man's once "healthy, sensuous love." "You did not wish it to become like this, nor did I—and yet it has," he tells Laura, as he rapturously recalls the early years of their love. Then he rages impotently: "Omphale! Rude strength has given way before weakness fortified by treachery. A curse on you, woman of Satan, and may all your sex be damned!" When Laura asks him if he wants to see his child, the Captain declines: "A man has no children!" Almost immediately after he collapses, dead of an apoplectic fit. Bertha rushes in, weeping, and as the curtain falls, Laura comforts her: "My child! My own child!"

FAUCHOIS, René (1882–1962), French actor and dramatist, wrote allegorical poems and numerous plays, the best-known of which is *Prenez garde à la peinture* (1932), adapted by both EMLYN WILLIAMS and SIDNEY HOWARD as THE LATE CHRISTOPHER BEAN. Fauchois's other works include plays about Pilate's daughter (*La Fille de Pilate,* 1908), *Beethoven* (1909), Napoleon (*Rivoli,* 1911; portraying him after Josephine's deception), *Rossini* (1913), *Penelope* (1913), and *Mozart* (1925).

FAULKNER, William (1897–1962), major American novelist and short-story writer. His only venture into drama was with *Requiem for a Nun* (1951), "written not to be a play, but as what seemed to me the best way to tell the story in a novel." Published originally in three acts with very long prose sections providing the background, the drama (written in collaboration with the actress Ruth Ford, 1920–)* presents Temple Drake's suffering self-recognition and spiritual redemption through the trial of her child's killer, her "guiltless-accused" Negress-nun servant Nancy Manningoe. An unsuccessful experimental play, it appeared in London in 1957, and on Broadway (and as a published play) in 1959. Some of Faulkner's fiction has been dramatized by others, notably Jean-Louis Barrault's (1910–) version of *As I Lay Dying* (1935).

FEAR (*Strakh*), a play in four acts by ALEKSANDR NIKOLAEVICH AFINOGENOV, published in 1930 and produced in 1931. Setting: Moscow, 1931.

The popularity of this, Afinogenov's best-known and most daring play, extended beyond Russia's borders. The anguished dilemma of its protagonist Borodin symbolized that of all Soviet artists and scholars blocked by party interference. Like Olesha in his A LIST OF ASSETS, Afinogenov temporized by resolving the problem with party slogans and Borodin's "regeneration," and the play is further marred by diffusiveness. But Afinogenov courageously raised a major problem and presented it forcefully.

Professor Ivan Ilich Borodin, "an old 'intellectual,'" is the scientific director of the Institute of Physiological Stimuli. Believing all human behavior to be conditioned by "love, fear, rage, and hunger," Borodin thinks his government is founded exclusively on fear. Proletarian graduate students take over, elderly professors are dismissed, and the Institute shifts its focus from the study of rabbits to the more practical one of human behavior. The Soviet aim admittedly is "to transform

* For a book-length history and study of the play, see Barbara Izard and Clara Hieronymous's illustrated *"Requiem for a Nun": On Stage and Off* (1970).

people": to kill off "withering feelings" like jealousy, anger, and fear; and to cultivate other innate feelings like "collectivity, enthusiasm, [and] the joy of life." Borodin courageously attempts to fight the Bolshevik takeover, which even his son-in-law joins. Honest but gullible, the suffering Borodin is supported by his daughter, friends, and assistants. In a public lecture he reveals his findings, that the "Soviet system of administration does not suit people at all" and that 80 percent of those he has investigated are motivated by fear: "Fear compels the repudiation of mothers, the falsifying of social origins, and the wriggling into high positions. . . . Destroy fear—destroy everything that occasions fear—and you will see with what a rich creative life our country will blossom forth!" An old Communist factory worker readily shows the errors of Borodin's teachings. Workers and peasants experienced fear under the tsar, she demonstrates in her reply, but their fear "gave birth to fearlessness! The fearlessness of the oppressed who have nothing to lose, the fearlessness of proletarians—of revolutionists—of Bolsheviks." And she concludes with an exhortation to "prepare yourselves for the new advances of the enemy, and strike with all the might of which the powerful arms of the working class are capable!" It is only when he is arraigned before the G.P.U. (the secret police) that Borodin learns the "monstrous" truth: his associates, motivated by fear, were scoundrels, saboteurs, and the tools of foreign powers, and Borodin himself was their unwitting tool. Persuaded of his gullibility and the error of his ways, Borodin wants to give up science: "I have been too seriously mistaken in people and in my conclusions." But he is allowed to recant and happily prepares to do so: "I will tell how I joyously greeted every manifestation of fear and how I failed to notice fearlessness. . . . I did not understand real life. And life penalizes those who shun it." He eagerly returns to work under the new management: "I can still be useful. I'll show them how to call me an old overshoe!"

FEAR AND MISERY OF THE THIRD REICH (*Furcht und Elend des Dritten Reiches*), twenty-four sketches by BERTOLT BRECHT (music by Paul Dessau), published and produced in 1938 (second version, with music by Hanns Eisler, in 1945). Setting: Nazi Germany.

Appearing in France as *99%* and in America as *The Private Life of the Master Race,* these twenty-four sketches (there are unpublished others) are introduced and linked by a poem and the framework of a roaring, troop-carrying Panzer (armored tank) rolling through Europe, soldiers' singing, and a menacing voice periodically declaiming from the dark. Perhaps best known is the ninth episode ("The Jewish Wife") which, like the tenth ("The Informer"), has been produced separately. Though the individual scenes are NATURALISTIC, their episodic brevity provides typically Brechtian "distance" and EPIC THEATRE.

(*1*) "National Unity": On the night of January 30, 1933, drunken SS men express their confidence in Hitler, "now that we're on top." In sudden fear of Communists, they riddle the street with bullets. (*2*) "The Betrayal": A terrified couple stand on the stairway, having just heard a neighbor they denounced beaten senseless and dragged out. (*3*) "The Chalk Mark": A worker, teased by a friendly but brutalized SA man into acting out his true feelings about Nazi Germany, is half-jokingly chalk-marked with a cross. (*4*) "Marsh-Soldiers": The inmates of a concentration camp squabble about one another's culpability for Hitler and are soon disciplined by the guard. (*5*) "National Service": An exhausted guard whips a concentration camp inmate. (*6*) "In Search of Justice": Fearful for himself and his family, a judge despairs as he seeks to discover the approved Nazi solution of a case he must try. (*7*) "Occupational Disease": Making his hospital rounds, a physician explains the importance of learning a man's background in order to diagnose occupational diseases. The next patient is from a concentration camp: mutilated, he is also "occupationally diseased." (*8*) "Physicist": At Göttingen, two scientists softly discuss gravity problems. Terrified of having been overheard when they inadvertently allude to Einstein's work, they shout, "typical Jewish sophistry!" (*9*) "The Jewish Wife": To save her prominent husband's position, a Jewish wife decides to emigrate. She packs and telephones friends to bid them farewell. Then she rehearses a speech to her decent but humanly frail husband. Everything, she knows, is a question of time—even character: "It lasts as long as a glove. Good ones last longer. But none lasts forever." When he comes in, her husband goes through the charade of preparing for a short separation. Just as she had anticipated, as he helps her pack the fur coat she will not need until winter, he remarks, "It's only for a couple of weeks."

(*10*) "The Informer": A husband and wife, having made slighting remarks about Nazi Germany, are terrified to discover their little son gone. Sure that he is denouncing them, the father is ready to be dragged to a concentration camp. The boy returns—he had merely bought some candy. But: "Is that really all he did?" (*11*) "The Black Shoes": A mother is willing to have her daughter's pretty shoes repaired, but will not contribute to the corrupting Hitler Youth. (*12*) "Servitude" portrays bribery and disaffection in a labor camp. (*13*) "The Worker's Hour": A radio announcer interviews workers, who slip a few truthful observations into his patriotic promptings. (*14*) "The Box": SA men bring a widow a box containing the mutilated corpse of her husband, who had criticized the government. (*15*) "Discharged": A worker released from a concentration camp finds reemployment difficult. (*16*) "Winter Relief": An old woman and her pregnant daughter receive a food contribution, which the mother throws up when the daughter is arrested for a stray comment. (*17*) "Two Bakers": In prison, a baker tells a new inmate he was arrested for mixing bran and potatoes into his dough two years before. The newcomer has been arrested for *not* doing the same. (*18*) "The Peasant Feeds His Sow": Despite Nazi orders to surrender all grain, a farmer risks his life and refuses to let his sows starve. (*19*) "The Old Warrior": After his long service to the party, an old man does some protesting; his son is arrested, and the old Nazi finally hangs himself, a sign around his neck: "I voted for Hitler!" (*20*) "The Sermon on the Mount": A dying man asks the attending pastor whether Christianity is still meaningful in anti-Christian Germany. The hesitating pastor finally replies: "Render therefore unto Caesar the things which are Caesar's." (*21*) "The Exhortation": A boy is picked on by his Hitler Youth leader because he has no gas mask. (*22*) "The Barracks Hear of the Attack on Almeria" (February, 1937): Two boys sneaking food out of a barracks discuss the soldiers' reaction to the German attack on Spain. (*23*) "Providing Jobs": A woman inconsolably refuses to ignore the real cause of her brother's death: the Spanish war. Jobs are plentiful only because of rearmament. Her outspokenness risks her husband's job, but when she is told that such an attitude will not help, she cries out, "What will help? Tell me!" (*24*) "Plebiscite" (March, 1938): As the radio loudly transmits Hitler's triumphant entry into Vienna, some Hamburg workers decide, despite all danger, to distribute leaflets before the national plebiscite. These will simply read: "No!"

FEAST AT SOLHOUG, THE (*Gildet på Solhaug*), a play in three acts by HENRIK IBSEN, published and produced in 1856. Setting: Solhaug, Norway; fourteenth century.

This play, Ibsen's earliest popular success, was the first to bring him fame outside Norway. Partly in verse, it is based on medieval Norwegian ballads and owes something to *Svend dyrings hus* (1837), a dramatic adaptation of heroic ballads by the Danish poet Henrik Hertz. Though he disowned his Scribean thriller in 1870, Ibsen defended it in 1883 as an original "lyric drama."

Margit Gauteson is the proud wife of a wealthy but weak and foolish man. She is shaken by the sudden return of her beloved kinsman, Gudmund Alfson, who left home "a penniless swain" and later became a famous knight. Now, having incurred the king's unjust anger, he is a hunted outlaw. Though Margit tells him of her unhappy marriage ("My heart's content I have bartered for gold") and all but declares her passion for him, Gudmund falls in love with her vivacious younger sister, Signe. For some time Margit mistakingly believes herself to be the object of his love. During a big feast, however, she discovers the truth. Heartbroken, she concludes that Gudmund prefers her sister only because she herself is not free. She decides to poison her husband: "Doubly alluring methinks is the goal / I must reach through blood, with the wreck of my soul." Her plan accidentally fails, but her husband is killed in combat. Gudmund's name is cleared; he is reinstated in the king's favor and joyfully returns to court with Signe. Margit, having "felt the remorse, the terror I know, / Of those who wantonly peril their soul," decides to enter a convent.

FEAST OF RECONCILIATION, THE (*Das Friedensfest*), "a family catastrophe" in three acts by GERHART HAUPTMANN, published and produced in 1890. Setting: a German home on Christmas Eve in the 1880's.

Like Hauptmann's first play, this (his second, also translated as *The Reconciliation* and as *The Coming of Peace*) is a NATURALISTIC portrayal of man's victimization by heredity and environment. Its ending is hopeful, however, despite the irony of the title and the IBSENite unfolding of the family's rotten past. The plot was suggested to Hauptmann by FRANK WEDEKIND's real life experience.

Years before, a dissension-ridden family had broken up after violent quarreling that culminated in the son's striking his father. Now that son, ennobled by the kindly neighbor's daughter, penitently returns home to his embittered mother, cynical brother, and shrewish old-maid sister. Unexpectedly the father, an arrogant but broken old doctor, returns the same night. The family's "feast of reconciliation" soon collapses in angry recriminations. After a few drinks, the father imagines that his son is about to hit him again, and he collapses with a stroke. Unnerved, his son fears being doomed to perpetuate the family's viciousness and decides to leave. But the neighbor's daughter insists on standing by him and gives him the courage to stay with her: "It will be different! It will be better!" As his father dies, she comforts her distraught lover: "Have faith . . . then I'll be able to help you."

FERBER, Edna (1887–1968), American writer, was best known for her fiction, principally *So Big* (1924, her Pulitzer Prize-winning first success), *Cimmaron* (1930), *Saratoga Trunk* (1941, presented on Broadway in 1960 as a musical adaptation, *Saratoga*), and her novel about the floating theatres on the Mississippi River, *Show Boat* (1926). The following year Jerome Kern and OSCAR HAMMERSTEIN II made *Show Boat* into an operetta, which was filmed (screenplay by ZOË AKINS) and has been frequently revived.

As early as 1915 Ferber tried her hand at playwriting, but she succeeded as a dramatist only in her collaborations with GEORGE S. KAUFMAN. *Minick* (1924), a comedy based on her short story "Old Man Minick," was followed by their THE ROYAL FAMILY (1927), DINNER AT EIGHT (1932), and STAGE DOOR (1936). Other Kaufman-Ferber collaborations are *The Land Is Bright* (1941), a drama about political and economic problems; and *Bravo!* (1948), an optimistic pitch for the return of romantic drama, in a plot featuring a European couple (a playwright and a star) who find a new home in the United States.

Ferber wrote two autobiographies, *A Peculiar Treasure* (1939, revised 1960) and *Kind of Magic* (1963).

FERDINAND, Roger (1898–1967), French dramatist who published under the name Roger-Ferdinand, wrote comedies like *La Foire aux sentiments* (1928) and *Les Croulants se portent bien* (1959). Among his hits about young people was one on the wartime black market, *Les J3 ou la nouvelle école* (1943). Ferdinand also translated popular American plays.

FESTIVAL OF OUR LORD OF THE SHIP, THE (*La Sagra del Signore della nave*), a one-act comedy by LUIGI PIRANDELLO, published in 1924 and produced in 1925. Setting: the space in front of an Italian country church on a warm autumn day.

This play, also translated as *In a Sanctuary,* dramatizes a short story Pirandello published in 1916. Its production launched his Art Theatre in Rome on April 4, 1925. A thanksgiving festival commemorating a miraculous sea rescue becomes an orgy of food, drink, and lust. The saturnalia, depicted NATURALISTICALLY, is the main part of the play. An argument provides a slight plot.

A fat man and his family are disconsolate over the slaughter of their pet pig, while an idealistic young teacher deprecates the dumb beast and exalts the divinity of human intelligence and sensitivity. Surrounding these characters, human bestiality rages with growing frenzy. "There's your humanity!" the fat man jeers as the teacher collapses with horror. But when the religious procession to the famous Christ effigy starts, the teacher feels vindicated: "Yes, they were drunk, they became animals, but look at them now! Look at them weeping behind their blood-stained Christ! Could any tragedy be more tragic than this one?"

FEUCHTWANGER, Lion (1884–1958), German writer, is more notable for his novels and essays than his two dozen plays. The latter include adaptations of the classics and collaborations with BERTOLT BRECHT: *Leben Eduards des Zweitens* (THE LIFE OF EDWARD II OF ENGLAND, 1924), *Die Gesichte der Simone Machard* (THE VISIONS OF SIMONE MACHARD, 1956), and *Kalkutta, 4. Mai* (CALCUTTA, MAY 4; 1927), the reworking of an original Feuchtwanger novel and play. Like his most distinguished novels—*Jud Süss* (*Jew Süss,* 1925) and others, and his satire of American life, *Pep* (published under the pseudonym J. L. Wetcheek and translated by Dorothy Thompson as *Pep; American Songbook,* 1929)—they deal with the historical (often Jewish) topics Feuchtwanger was especially interested in and successful in depicting.

Son of a wealthy businessman, Feuchtwanger was born in Munich, at whose university he earned his Ph.D. Turning to literature for his profession, he edited a journal of criticism and adapted plays by Aeschylus, Aristophanes, and the classic Indian dramatists Śūdraka and Kālidāsa. Feuchtwanger's original plays began with the biblical *König Saul* (1905). His *Die Kriegsgefangenen* (*Prisoners of War,* 1918), a once popular though often banned drama, portrays the romance and jealousy that destroy a French prisoner of war beloved by a number of German girls. Feuchtwanger's next work, *Thomas Wendt* (1919, also titled—and translated as—*1918*), is a long "dramatic novel" in which the action is slowed down and suspended to dramatize "epic" scenes of German history and the motivations of its protagonist, a playwright turned revolutionary leader and frustrated by problems in both his occupations. More popular as stage works were *Die Petroleuminseln* (1927), whose protagonist's energy and intelligence compensate for her extreme homeliness and enable her to become a tycoon, buy power and love, and vanquish her antagonist; *Wird Hill amnestiert?* (1927), a comedy about a political prisoner and his girl friend's attempts to free him; and *Der holländische Kaufmann* (*The Dutch Merchant,* 1923), a fantasy "in chiaroscuro" about yet another business baron.

Feuchtwanger achieved much greater popularity, however, with his fiction, his satires, and accounts of his exile after his dramatic escapes from Hitler's Germany and France to the United States, where he spent his later years and where he died. Among his most effective dramas were the collaborations with Brecht. Feuchtwanger's later plays include *Wahn oder der Teufel in Boston* (1948), about Cotton Mather, whose fanatic witch-hunting is finally ended by a rationalist compatriot; and *Die Witwe Capet* (1956), originally (1955) a radio play about Marie Antoinette.

Feuchtwanger's *Three Plays* (1934) contains *Prisoners of War, 1918,* and *The Dutch Merchant.* His memoirs include *Moskau 1937* (*Moscow, 1937;* 1937) and *Unholdes Frankreich* (1942), which was first published in English as *The Devil in France* (1941).

FEYDEAU, Georges [Léon Jules Marie] (1862–1921), French playwright, was the author of over sixty popular bedroom farces. The son of a distinguished Second Empire novelist and himself a notorious wit, Feydeau began his career in 1880 with a one-act comedy, *Par la fenêtre* (translated as *Wooed and Viewed*), and became known three years later with a comic SUCCÈS D'ESTIME, *Amour et piano* (1883). His subsequent triumphs remained in the Comédie-Française repertoire long after the heyday of his popularity in the early decades of the century, and they have been revived successfully to the present time. They include *Le Mariage de Barillon* (1890, translated as *On the Marry-Go-Wrong*), a characteristic madcap written in collaboration with his friend Maurice Desvallières (1856–1926); *Un Fil à la patte* (1894, translated as *The Lady from Lobster Square* and as *Not by Bed Alone,** and adapted in 1969 as *Cat Among the Pigeons!* by JOHN MORTIMER), whose 1964 Comédie-Française production featured Feydeau's grandson; *Le Dindon* (1896); *L'Hôtel du libre échangé* (1896, written with Desvallières), which regained English and American fame in 1957 (and

* The original title is not literally translatable into English. It refers to the thread that ties the hero to his mistress.

was filmed in 1966) as *Hotel Paradiso; La Dame de chez Maxim* (1899), produced in England and America as *The Girl from Maxim's* and as *The Girl from Montmartre;* the farce that became his masterpiece, *Occupe-toi d'Amélie* (1908), filmed in 1949 (and distributed in America as *Oh, Amelia!*) and produced in English as *Keep an Eye on Amelia!, Breakfast in Bed,* and, in a less successful 1959 adaptation by NOËL COWARD, as *Look After Lulu;* and *La Puce à l'oreille* (*A Flea in Her Ear,* 1910), another popular bedroom farce, translated by Mortimer and made into a major film in 1968.

These light, fast-paced, spicy works are notable for their masterful craftsmanship and Feydeau's humor, which has continued to convulse audiences. Though they all deal comically with sex, Feydeau's farces subtly changed with time. The early ones, including *L'Hôtel du libre échange,* feature middle-class wives who (Feydeau remarked) "breathe virtue and are forthwith out of breath," dream of adultery, and deplore the fact that "one cannot take a lover without deceiving one's husband." Later comedies (including *Occupe-toi d'Amélie!*) are dominated by less reticent and more sportive trollops, ladies concerned principally with jewelry but kind to their lovers, whom they console with the explanation: "Look, I had that diamond he gave me set into a ring just for you." Feydeau's last comedies, mostly one-act farces like *On purge bébé* (*Going to Pot,* 1910), feature couples: weak and stupid men united by lifelong habit with ruthless shrews. *Cent millions qui tombent* (1923), Feydeau's last play, was produced posthumously.

Keep an Eye on Amélie! was republished in Eric Bentley's collection *Let's Get a Divorce! and Other Plays* (1958) with a translation of MARCEL ACHARD's amusing biographical introduction to Feydeau's *Théâtre complet* (1948). Norman R. Shapiro's edition of *Four Farces by Georges Feydeau* (1970) includes *Wooed and Viewed, On the Marry-Go-Wrong, Not by Bed Alone, Going to Pot,* and an informative essay on Feydeau's drama.

FIELD OF ERMINE (*Campo de armiño*), a drama in three acts by JACINTO BENAVENTE, published and produced in 1916. Setting: contemporary Madrid, Spain.

Despite its relative failure in New York and elsewhere, this play has been highly praised by critics. It portrays two groups, aristocrats and social dregs.

Irene, Marchioness of Montalbán, is gulled into thinking a poor child her illegitimate nephew. When she discovers the deception of his scheming mother, a prostitute, she discards the boy. Then, despite society's sneering and scandalmongering, Irene's love and generosity prevail over her "pride of race." When the boy returns, calls her "Mother," and asks for help, she adopts him. Irene feels purified as if by "a spiritual fire, in whose brightness a son has been born in my soul. It glows in my soul like a mystery of love and redemption." Rather than a mark of shame, the boy becomes her badge of glory: "Upon my field of ermine I shall place a lily as a new charge, whiter than the ermine."

FIELDS, Joseph (1895–1966), American playwright, was best known for his collaboration with JEROME CHODOROV. (For their plays, see the article on Chodorov.) Aside from Chodorov, Fields collaborated with Anita Loos (1893–) on a musical version of her 1925 novel about a moronic flapper in the gay 1920's, *Gentlemen Prefer Blondes* (1949), originally dramatized in 1926; with Peter de Vries (1910–) on a dramatization of the latter's 1954 comic sex novel, *The Tunnel of Love* (1957); and with JOSHUA LOGAN on the Richard Rodgers and OSCAR HAMMERSTEIN II musical based on C. Y. Lee's novel about San Francisco's Chinatown, *Flower Drum Song* (1958). His brother and sister, Herbert Fields (1895–1966) and Dorothy Fields (1905–), were successful librettists who wrote the books for many musical hits, including *Annie Get Your Gun* (1946), the long-running comedy about Annie Oakley, the famous sharpshooter and performer in Buffalo Bill's Wild West Show.

FIGHTING COCK, THE (*L'Hurluberlu ou le réactionnaire amoureux*), a play in four acts by JEAN ANOUILH, published and produced in 1959. Setting: a French country house, 1950's.

The comedy's title character is a retired, young, spirited general with a very young wife and very old-fashioned ideas. He plots to restore "honor" to France and rails against the "maggots" who undermine life: "I want life to become difficult again; I want us to pay for everything[,] . . . not to have them for the asking by simply filling out a form!" A pert young man enlightens him about the mid-century world and human nature. The general learns to accept them and view things less tragically.

FILUMENA MARTURANO, a comedy in three acts by EDUARDO DE FILIPPO, produced in 1946 and published in 1947. Setting: Naples, "not long ago."

Subtitled "A Mother's a Mother," this is de Filippo's most popular and probably his best play. It was filmed under its original title in 1950 and in the 1960's became popular in another movie version, *Marriage, Italian Style* (1964).

Twenty-five years ago Domenico Soriano made an honest woman of the former prostitute Filumena by setting her up as his mistress. Before the play opens she has pretended to be dying and has tricked him into marrying her. Furious when he discovers the deception, Domenico threatens to annul the marriage—even when Filumena reveals that she had tricked him for the sake of her three now-adult sons, of whose existence he has been unaware and whom she wants legitimized. Later she upsets Domenico with another revelation: one of the men is his own son. Domenico proceeds with the annulment nonetheless, but ten months later he is about to remarry Filumena. "I am fifty-two, you are forty-eight. We are two mature souls in duty bound to understand what they are about—ruthlessly and to the depths," he admits, ready to assume "full responsibility." But he is tortured by the uncertainty as to which of the three is his son. To preclude favoritism, Filumena refuses to tell him. She loves them as well as she loves Domenico, and he must "decide whether you want them"—all three. "You've got to be a gentleman and not ask [which one is yours], or I might give way in a moment of weakness, and that would be the end." Domenico accepts all three as his sons—as they accept him as their "papa." Filumena, who never in her life could weep, finally does—"and, oh, how *sweet* it is to cry!" Domenico embraces her affectionately, recalling the hard life she has led. "And now it's time for a rest," he concludes. "A mother's a mother, and sons are sons, Filumena Soriano."

FINLAND. Finnish drama is a recent phenomenon and of negligible international significance. Finland proclaimed its independence in 1917, until which time it had been a Grand Duchy in the Russian Empire. It resisted the Russian invasion of 1939–40, a struggle celebrated in Sherwood's THERE SHALL BE NO NIGHT. Culturally, Finland has been dominated by Sweden, and Finnish literature, including drama, was written in Swedish until the mid-nineteenth century. Because of the Swedish minority residing in Finland, some native drama is still written in Swedish.

Noteworthy Finns who wrote in Swedish were [Karl] Mikael Lybeck (1864–1925) and [Ernst] Runar Schildt (1888–1925). Lybeck's plays, which reveal the influence of HENRIK IBSEN, include *Dynastin Peterberg* (1913), a popular nationalistic satire of tsarist statesmen, and *Bror och syster* (1915), a lyrical portrayal of nobility and probably his finest work. The short-lived Schildt wrote three NATURALISTIC-SYMBOLIC plays about the redeeming power of a woman's love, including the one-act *Galgamannen: en midvintersaga* (*The Gallows Man: A Midwinter Story,** 1922), and *Lyckoriddaren* (1923). A later Swedish-Finnish playwright (and novelist) of importance is Walentin Chorell (1912–), whose drama ranges from farce to tragedy and, like many of EUGENE O'NEILL's, deals with the illusions of down-and-outers: in *Madame* (1952) illusions of an elderly prima donna; in *Systrarna* (*The Sisters,* 1955) illusions of two girls; and in the prize-winning incest drama *Gräset* (1958), illusions of a young man.

The first great Finnish writer was Aleksis Kivi (Finnicized name of A. Stenvall, 1834–72), a novelist and playwright who was dubbed the Father of Finnish Drama for his popular tragedy *Kullervo* (1860); its title character (a dim-witted Hercules) and its plot were inspired by Finnish folklore. Kivi's miracle play *Lea* was the first native drama to be produced—on May 10, 1869, in Helsinki. The best known of his other plays is *Nummisuutarit* (*The Heath Cobblers,* 1864; also translated as *The Country Cobblers*), a romantic-naturalistic peasant comedy. The next important native playwright (and novelist) was Minna Canth (1844–97), born Wilhelmina Johnsson. The mother of seven children and widowed at thirty-five, she became a businesswoman and a zealous temperance agitator. Her first play, *Murtovarkaus* (1882), portraying the victim of an unjust accusation, became a success, and she thereafter turned to expressing her humane and feminist ideals in didactic but very popular naturalistic plays like *Työmiehen vaimo* (1885), *Kovan onnen lapsia* (1888), *Papin perhe* (1891), and a TOLSTOIan drama of redemption, *Anna Liisa* (1895). Among Finnish poets, Juhana Henrik Erkko (1849–1906) wrote plays based on the Bible and on Finnish folklore, and Eino Leino (originally Armas Eino Leopold Lönnbohm, 1878–1926) wrote a historical trilogy that ends with *Alkibiades* (1909).

Dramatists who became prominent in independent Finland include Maria Jotuni (also known as Haggrén and as Tarkiainen, 1880–1943), who wrote comedies like *Tohvelisankarin rouva* (1924), and a tragedy, *Olen syyllinen* (1929), on the theme of Saul and David; Erkki Kivijärvi (1882–1942), who wrote sophisticated comedies like *Eva* (1925); Hella [Maria] Wuolijoki, née Murrik (1886–1954), who first wrote in her native Estonian and also used male pseudonyms like Juhani Tervapää and Felix Tuli, a translator of MAXIM GORKY and LEONID ANDREEV, directress of the Finnish radio, distinguished author of *The Niskavuori* cycle (1936–53) and of such tragedies as *Justina* (1937) and *Vihreä kulta* (1938), and the comedy *Juurakon Hulda* (1937), and memorable for her share in Brecht's HERR PUNTILA AND HIS SERVANT MATTI; Matti Kurikka (1863–1915), a theosophic-socialist journalist whose *Viimeinen ponnistus* (1884) was republished well into the twentieth century; and Lauri Haarla (1890–1944), whose many plays, including *Juudas* (1927) and the prize-winning *Sukeltaja* (1938), were influenced by earlier Finnish poetic playwrights as well as by German EXPRESSIONISTS.

See Ilmari Havu's prefaces to his collection of readings, *An Introduction to Finnish Literature* (1952); and the Summer 1959 issue of *World Theatre*.

FIRST MAN, THE, a play in four acts by EUGENE O'NEILL, published and produced in 1922. Setting: a contemporary home in Bridgetown, Connecticut.

Unsuccessful artistically as well as commercially, this NATURALISTIC play apparently echoes O'Neill's own feelings at the time about marriage and fatherhood. It was originally titled *The Oldest Man*.

Curtis Jayson, a prominent and dedicated anthropologist, is preparing to go on an excavating expedition for "the first man." He is appalled when Martha, his wife, who was to accompany him and help him with his work, reveals that she is pregnant: "I love you! And I love the things

* Published with a prefatory note on Schildt in Alrik Gustafson's *Scandinavian Plays of the Twentieth Century* (First Series, 1944).

you love—your work—because it's a part of you. And that's what I want you to do—to reciprocate—to love the creator in me—to desire that I, too, should complete myself with the thing nearest my heart!" But he refuses: "Can you expect me to be glad when you propose to introduce a stranger who will steal away your love, your interest—who will separate us and deprive me of you!" She dies in childbirth (after shrieking audibly offstage), but the grieving Curtis triumphs in her final thought of him: "she loved me again—only me—I saw it in her eyes! She had forgotten—*it*." Ready to depart without even looking at the infant, he finally understands that his many relatives (whose small-town-society nastiness and suspicions compose much of the play) are insisting that he visit the infant because they believe its father to be another man and are anxious to avoid scandalous talk. Furious at the "swarm of poisonous flies," he determines that he will teach his son "to know and love a big, free life. . . . Martha shall live again for me in him." After he has left, the hypocritical relatives are relieved: "He did acknowledge the kid—before witnesses, too."

FIRST MRS. FRASER, THE, a comedy in three acts by ST. JOHN ERVINE, published and produced in 1929. Setting: London, 1929.

Marie Tempest played the title role of this popular comedy for two years. It was revived in New York in 1947.

James Fraser asks Janet, his charming and sensible middle-aged first wife, to extricate him from difficulties with his impossible young second wife. Janet succeeds, as their adult offspring keep volunteering advice. At the end she rejects his hoped-for proposal for remarriage because it is too selfish and matter-of-fact. But when Fraser is jealous of another beau and sends her a gift, she is delighted: "He's beginning to court me all over again . . . and I rather like it. . . ."

FIRST WARNING, THE (*Första varningen*), a one-act comedy by AUGUST STRINDBERG, published in 1893 and produced in 1910. Setting: a German dining room, about 1890.

Strindberg originally called this comedy, based on an incident in his marriage with Siri, *The First Tooth.*

A husband, jealous of his aging but coquettish wife, is ready to leave home. The wife, just having broken a front tooth and jealous of a schoolgirl who is infatuated with her husband, becomes afraid that he will leave her because she is now old and ugly. When he discovers her jealousy they are reconciled. "Oh, you child!" he exclaims; "with pain comes the first tooth, and with pain the first one goes."

FIRSTBORN, THE, a blank-verse play in three acts by CHRISTOPHER FRY, published in 1946 and produced in 1948. Setting: Tanis, Egypt; pharaoh's palace; and the tent of Miriam (Moses's sister); the summer of 1200 B.C.

Fry repeatedly revised this play about Moses's growth to maturity and his unleashing uncontrollable forces to emancipate the Jews. He rejects the offers of Seti II, a selfless but ruthless pharaoh. The death of Seti's generous son Rameses in the Plague of the Death of the Firstborn, which frees the Israelites, temporarily weakens Moses: "I followed a light into a blindness." But his greatness is presaged in his recognition of the need to discover individual meaning "until we meet in the meaning of the world."

FITCH, [William] **Clyde** (1865–1909), was the most popular American playwright of his time and the first to achieve international acclaim. He was praised for his REALISTIC dialogue, his keen powers of observation, his consummate satire of American society, and his skillful plot construction. An immensely successful man of the theatre during the Broadway reign of Charles Frohman, Fitch tended to compromise artistic truth in order to gratify audience expectations. Consequently he merited his "popular, prolific, and prosperous" epithet. The pressures of commercial theatre prevented him from developing his considerable talents and from producing superior drama of more lasting interest. Still, Fitch's work was by and large the best written for the American theatre until then, however melodramatic and contrived it now appears. Twenty-two of Fitch's plays are adaptations of fiction (including Edith Wharton's *The House of Mirth,* 1906) and drama by VICTORIEN SARDOU and other French and German writers. Of Fitch's thirty-six original plays, a few are worth remembering: CAPTAIN JINKS OF THE HORSE MARINES (1901, made into a musical in the 1920's), THE GIRL WITH THE GREEN EYES (1902), THE CITY (1909), and THE TRUTH (1906), which made his name known in Europe.

Born in Elmira, New York, Fitch pursued his childhood interest in theatricals throughout college (Amherst). He went to New York, where the actor Richard Mansfield soon commissioned him to write a play. His successful depiction of the life of the Georgian dandy *Beau Brummell* (1890) launched Fitch's career and revealed his distinctive dramaturgy: characters flawed by a particular weakness (like Ben Jonson's "humour"), keenly observed social milieus, witty dialogue, and a happy ending—however inappropriate. With *A Modern Match* (1892), the portrayal of a selfish and flippant wife, Fitch began his plays about contemporary society, in a setting he used again in *Her Great Match* (1905), the love story of an American girl and a German crown prince that contrasted manners on both sides of the Atlantic.

Notable among the other plays are *Mistress Betty* (1895), a romantic comedy written for Helena Modjeska and revived as *The Toast of the Town* in 1905; *The Moth and the Flame* (1898), a powerful melodrama; *The Climbers* (1901), set in New York and excoriating the new century as "the Era of Egotism"; and *Toddles* (1906), the popular adaptation of a farce by TRISTAN BERNARD. The same focus on social manners and individual "humours" characterizes Fitch's loose dramatizations of American history: *Nathan Hale* (1898), *Major André* (1903), and *Barbara Frietchie* (1899), a Civil War romance that celebrated his parents' courtship and was made into a Sigmund Romberg operetta, *My Maryland* (1927).

Fitch was eager to portray the "truth." His plays had a serious purpose, and they include—beyond Fitch's insistence on "realistic" scenery—often accurate and satiric portrayals of society and individuals. But Fitch was a part of the commercial theatre, and his plays are too flawed by turn-of-the-century sentimentality and melodrama to interest later generations—however much they impressed the American and European audiences of the time. Fitch worked himself feverishly and literally to a premature death, which occurred during one of his many European trips.

A dozen of his most important plays were collected in *Plays* (four volumes, 1915). Biographies are Archie Bell's *The Clyde Fitch I Knew* (1909) and Montrose J. Moses and Virginia Gerson's *Clyde Fitch and His Letters* (1924). Arthur H. Quinn's *A History of the American Drama from the Civil War to the Present Day* (1936) includes a detailed discussion of Fitch's work; it also has a comprehensive bibliography of Fitch's drama and a listing of works about Fitch.

FITZMAURICE, George (1877–1963),* Irish dramatist, was almost unknown throughout his entire life, although PADRAIC COLUM and a few other Irish poets consistently hailed him as a genius. A pioneer Abbey Theatre playwright, Fitzmaurice was quickly forgotten after a 1907 success, and most of his subsequent work remained unproduced. Occasionally one of his plays appeared in the *Dublin Magazine,* whose editor was one of his few friends. Shy and somewhat eccentric as well as plagued by illness, Fitzmaurice lived in seclusion and kept writing, though he received virtually no encouragement. Since his death, however, his reputation has begun to grow, and though his plays are still little known, some critics and historians of the 1960's proclaimed Fitzmaurice as a major Irish playwright.

He was born in County Kerry, one of the twelve children of a Church of Ireland minister and a Catholic twenty years his junior. Fitzmaurice briefly worked for a Cork bank, served in France with the British in World War I, and then settled in Dublin, where he was employed by the Land Commission and then the Department of Agriculture. Frequently absent from work, he continued to write. He left some twenty one-act and full-length folk plays.

The first produced and still best known of these, *The Country Dressmaker* (1907), is a racy comedy about Irish peasant matchmaking; though WILLIAM BUTLER YEATS, who admired it, thought its portrayal of the Irish unflattering enough to rekindle the riots that had greeted Synge's THE PLAYBOY OF THE WESTERN WORLD earlier that year, the play became one of the Abbey's first hits and popular plays. Fitzmaurice's unique style—a mixture of fantasy and REPRESENTATIONALISM, of exuberance and grimness or wry resignation—also characterizes other plays that have been especially praised: *The Pie-Dish* (1908), a tragicomic one-acter about a dying man's frantic attempts to stave off death until he finishes the ornamental pie dish he has been fashioning for two decades; *The Dandy Dolls* (1908), a dark, evocative, short fantasy that has been ranked with masterpieces of the same genre by Yeats, J. M. SYNGE, and SEAN O'CASEY; *The Magic Glasses* (1913), another dark fantasy, about a man ultimately killed because of (or by) the glasses that have enchanted him with beautiful sights: *'Twixt the Giltinans and the Carmodys* (1923), a farce parable on idealism (and Fitzmaurice's last play to be staged by the Abbey) in which a would-be heir must choose a wife; and *The Enchanted Land* (1957), a satiric children's fairy tale with elements of romanticism and Celtic myth.

The first volume of *The Plays of George Fitzmaurice* was published in 1967; it has an informative introduction, as have subsequent volumes, edited by Howard K. Slaughter. See also Robert Hogan's *After the Irish Renaissance* (1967).

FIVE FINGER EXERCISE, a play in two acts by PETER SHAFFER, published and produced in 1958. Setting: a weekend cottage in Suffolk, England; late 1950's.

Shaffer's first hit, this is a sensitive study of five characters.

Walter Langer, a young German tutor, is hired by the Stanley Harrington family: a prosperous and stodgy furniture manufacturer, his scatterbrained and culture-loving wife, and their children—the confused nineteen-year-old Clive, who is scared of his father and dominated by his mother, and an exuberant fourteen-year-old daughter. Walter's presence accentuates their individual failures and inability to communicate—the broken family relationships beneath the respectable façade. Harrington can talk to the mysterious young Walter as he never can to Clive; Mrs. Harrington sees Walter as a possible lover; and Clive finds, in Walter, a friend. When the tutor reveals no more than filial interest in Mrs. Harrington, she dismisses him, rationalizing that the dismissal is for her daughter's well-being and suggesting that Clive has a homosexual attachment to him. Clive confronts his parents with all his new insights. At the end, frightened, he prays for "courage. For all of us. Oh, God—give it."

FLAVIN, Martin (1883–1967), American author, began his career as a businessman and then turned to writing fiction and drama. His first hit, *Children of the Moon* (1923), is set in Flavin's birthplace, San Francisco; it is a once-praised, weird, and

* Not to be confused with the identically named Paris-born Hollywood director (1885–1940) of films starring Rudolph Valentino, Greta Garbo (in Pirandello's AS YOU DESIRE ME), and others; and also the author of *The Perils of Pauline* serial.

Five Finger Exercise. Left to right: Mr. Harrington (Roland Culver), Mrs. Harrington (Jessica Tandy), Walter (Michael Bryant), Clive (Brian Bedford), Miss Harrington (Juliet Mills). New York, 1959. (*Zodiac Photographers*)

poetic study of family insanity. *Lady of the Rose* (1925) is a tragic dream romance, while *The Criminal Code* (1929) and *Amaco* (1933) are protest dramas, the first about the penal code, the second about the machine's effect on man. Flavin's fiction includes *Journey in the Dark* (1943), which won the Pulitzer Prize.

FLERS, Robert de (1872–1927), French playwright, is notable primarily for his charming, sentimental yet satirical dramas about society in the Third Republic, written in collaboration with another French playwright, Gaston-Armand de Caillavet (1869–1915). Particularly amusing also to Americans were the pair's *L'Amour veille* (*Love Watches,* 1907), whose heroine attempts to make her husband jealous; and *L'Âne de Buridan* (1909, produced on Broadway as *Inconstant George*), the portrait of a ladies' man. More satiric but less successful Flers-Caillavet collaborations that also appeared abroad were *Le Roi* (*The King,* 1908) and *Le Bois sacré* (1910), a satire of Parliament produced in New York as *Decorating Clementine*.

Born Robert de Pellevé de la Motte Ango, the Marquis de Flers married the daughter of VICTORIEN SARDOU. Though he took various diplomatic posts, Flers devoted his life primarily to the theatre. He was the drama critic of the *Figaro,* and was elected to the French Academy (1920), which he and Caillavet had satirized in their popular comedy *L'Habit vert* (1912). After Caillavet's death in World War I, Flers collaborated with the Belgian-born playwright Francis de Croisset (pseudonym of Frantz Wiener, 1877–1937), their most successful work being the operetta *Ciboulette* (1923). Croisset wrote one of the Flers biographies, *Le Souvenir de Robert de Flers* (1929).

FLIES, THE (*Les Mouches*), a play in three acts by JEAN-PAUL SARTRE, published and produced in 1943. Setting: ancient Argos.

Sartre's first play, this modernization of Aeschylus's *Oresteia* was originally produced in occupied France. The Nazis were oblivious to its thinly veiled attack on Vichy collaborators and its call for freedom from tyranny. A philosophical drama, it is marred by many long and abstract speeches but distinguished for its ideas. Orestes becomes the existentialist man who achieves freedom by being "responsible" and "engaged" in social action. The divine and psychological antagonists he rejects ultimately appear to be imaginary: Zeus, guilty remorse, and the Furies, who are represented by swarms of oppressive, disgusting flies.

Act I. Old women squealing with terror make libations to the blood-smeared and fly-covered statue of Zeus in the public square, while an idiot boy squats in the background. Orestes arrives with his tutor. They are unaware of the identity of another traveler—the bearded Zeus—who explains that the loathsome flies all about them were drawn to Argos fifteen years ago by the murder of King Agamemnon. Shrieks from the palace announce the yearly ceremony of "Dead Men's Day" as Zeus blames Agamemnon's murder on the people, who relish brutality: "Each was gloating in imagination of the picture of a huge corpse with a shattered face." One of the old women describes her family's exquisite terror of and preoccupation with "original sin." The Tutor urges Orestes not to give up his detached irony and skepticism. "You are free to turn your hand to anything," the Tutor says, cautioning Orestes against getting involved with his native city; "but you know better than to commit yourself—and there lies your strength." Reluctantly Orestes agrees, though he deplores his rootlessness. Electra comes from the palace to sneer at Zeus's statue and present her offering: a pail of garbage. As she talks of the brother she is waiting for to expose and destroy Zeus, Orestes steps forth. Eagerly curious about people's lives elsewhere, Electra describes her own degrading life with her hated mother and the king, and the Argos rituals of confession and remorse. Clytemnestra comes to remonstrate with the rebellious Electra. Clytemnestra glories in her abject contrition, but Electra dismisses it as mere indulgence "in our national pastime." Still cloaking his true identity, Orestes decides to stay for the festival. Zeus magically removes the pervasive flies and accompanies Orestes to an inn.

The Flies, Act I. Orestes (Dan Matthews) and his tutor (Nehemiah Persoff); the disguised Zeus (Jack Burkhart) is on the other side of the god's gigantic and blood-smeared statue. Erwin Piscator's production at the New School for Social Research; New York, 1947. (*Balcombe*)

Act II. Scene 1. Before a mountain cavern blocked by a boulder, "Dead Men's Day" is about to start. Writhing in deliciously fearful suspense, the crowds wallow in penitence and anticipate the agonies to come. The high priest rolls away the boulder and evokes the dead, who are vividly envisioned by their guilt-ridden families as Aegisthus confesses his own crimes and catalogues those of his subjects. At the height of the orgy Electra appears in a white dress and denounces the superstitious rites with a joyful dance. She sways the crowds until Zeus magically rolls the boulder across the stage to enforce divine rule. Thereupon the frightened people resume castigating themselves and turn against Electra. Now Orestes reveals himself as her brother. He wants to help her, but still feels "a mere shadow of a man," one who has always lacked "the solid passions of the living." Overjoyed as she is to find her brother, Electra ridicules his appeal to the gods for guidance. When Zeus obligingly gives a magic sign, however, Orestes rejects eternal submission, for suddenly he is changed. "Until now I felt something warm and living around me," but now he perceives only "endless emptiness, as far as the eye can reach." Now he can decide—and act. Jubilantly anticipating their bloody vengeance, Electra passionately embraces Orestes. *Scene 2.* In the throne room Zeus cautions Aegisthus against Orestes, but the king is "too tired" to protect himself. Zeus reveals "the bane of gods and kings," who must conceal even from themselves the knowledge that "once freedom lights its beacon in a man's heart, the gods are powerless against him." Orestes has discovered this secret. Now he slays Aegisthus and his mother, Clytemnestra, whose screams are heard from the adjoining room. "Take me in your arms, beloved," Electra exclaims when her brother returns, proud and joyful. But Electra's resolution weakens as she sees the huge swarms of ever-growing flies, "the goddesses of remorse." To shelter themselves from these Furies and from the populace, Orestes and Electra escape to Apollo's shrine.

Act III. At the shrine dancing Furies surround the sleeping couple. "We shall settle on your rotten hearts like flies on butter," they sing: "All your life we will be with you, / Until we make you over to the worms." Soon assisted by Zeus, the Furies try to get Orestes and Electra to repent. Orestes is invulnerable, for he is free: "You have no power to make me atone for an act I don't regard as a crime." As the temple walls part to reveal the firmament, Zeus rises to supernatural heights to proclaim his divinity. "You are a mite in the scheme of things," he thunders through a loudspeaker: "Know your sin, abhor it. . . . Or else—" Orestes replies, "I *am* my freedom. No sooner had you created me than I ceased to be yours." Zeus is impotent as Orestes perceives existentialist reality: "You are God and I am free; each of us is alone, and our anguish is akin." Beaten,

Zeus sadly admits Orestes's world view, but he does win the weak and fearful Electra. "Save me from the flies, from my brother, from myself!" she begs: "Do not leave me lonely and I will give up my whole life to atonement. I repent, Zeus. I bitterly repent." The flies leave her and surround Orestes. The vengeful crowd rushes in. He confronts them, exhorts them to "reshape your lives" as he has reshaped his, and proclaims himself their king—ready to assume their sins and remorse. Followed by the Furies, he departs into the light, "a king without a kingdom, without subjects."

FLOOD, THE (*Die Sündflut*), a drama in five acts by ERNST BARLACH, published in 1924 and produced in 1925. Setting: the biblical period of the Flood.

Upon publication this quasi-EXPRESSIONIST work won the much-coveted Kleist Prize. It is considered Barlach's most distinctive and best known play. Though it vaguely follows the sixth chapter of Genesis, most of its episodes and characters are invented to enhance what is primarily a dialogue about God between the submissive Noah and his powerful antagonist.

Noah is troubled by his sons' and wife's often impious demands, and then by Calan. This strong and imaginative man successfully challenges Noah, as well as God, whom Noah exhorts to prevent Calan's cruel deed: having an innocent shepherd's hands chopped off. Yet Calan is also kind. In accordance with a vow, he gives Noah his favorite wife and materially helps him and his family. Amidst the comings and going of a hunchbacked leper who denounces God, various embodiments of a god and angels, and a sensuous woman who perceives God ecstatically, Calan proclaims his own divine potential. The flood reaffirms the power of Noah's God. Calan is bound to the leper, to drown with him—for the shepherd who could have untied them is the one whose hands Calan had chopped off. Yet to the end Calan proclaims his freedom and superiority over Noah's God "of floods and flesh." Calan conceives of God as "smaller than nothing," a formless "spark" in which all begins and ends: "He creates and his creation creates him anew." Noah meekly intones, "God is my shepherd. . . ." But the dying Calan joyfully unites with the divine: "God becomes Calan, and Calan God—he in my lowliness, I in his splendor—one indivisible." As the waters rise Noah is pulled to the ark by his son: "Live, Father, live lest God's wrath bury you with the lost!"

FLORIAN GEYER, a historical drama in a prologue and five acts by GERHART HAUPTMANN, published and produced in 1896. Setting: Germany, 1525–26.

This crowded and long play is subtitled "The Tragedy of the Peasant War." It portrays the aggrieved peasantry in their partly religious struggle against the nobility. Like THE WEAVERS, it is a NATURALISTIC "mass drama" that is almost devoid of conventional action and plot. Instead, the events are mirrored in discussions and debates held in archaic language; hosts of minor characters and episodes are interwoven into a colorful and panoramic view of the age of Luther, whose condemnation of the peasants helped defeat them. Diffuse as well as confused, the play was originally a failure. It became popular after World War I, when it was found to have considerable twentieth-century relevance as well as the impact of gripping tragedy.

The noblemen are bitter at the promulgation of the twelve Articles of Memmingen, the peasant demands for social, economic, and religious reform. But many knights join the peasants, most notably Götz von Berlichingen and Florian Geyer, the idealistic "black knight." As these leaders confer, their divergent—often selfish—aims become apparent and presage eventual disaster. Soon disorder and disunity in the peasant forces begin to bring about defeat. Disobeying their leader Florian Geyer, who is away seeking the necessary cannons, the peasants attack the Würzburg castle and are repulsed. Disorder spreads, and the knights are deserting. The final battle is lost through the treachery of Berlichingen, who had joined the uprising for selfish reasons (unlike Goethe's *Götz von Berlichingen*, who is a lover of freedom and an idealist pitted against materialistic society). The remaining peasant leaders escape to save themselves, but Geyer declines the refuge offered him. Wounded, he is betrayed by his own relatives in their castle. When his mistress is stabbed, he emerges out of hiding and contemptuously rejects the roistering knights' demand for his abject surrender. A religious fanatic who is eager to settle a personal account and collect the reward shoots Geyer from the rear as he is calling for freedom. The knights pick up his sword and read out its inscription: *Nulla crux, nulla corona* (no cross, no crown). A fanfare is heard from the courtyard after a knight shouts down the news: "Florian Geyer is dead."

FLOWERING PEACH, THE, a play in eight scenes and an epilogue by CLIFFORD ODETS, produced in 1954 and published (abridged) in 1955. Setting: the biblical period of the Flood.

This is a free retelling—in the modern Jewish-American idiom, situation, and costume—of the Genesis story of Noah and the Ark. It is an allegorical drama of ideas about the mid-twentieth-century world. In 1970 Peter Stone (1930–   ) made it into a musical, *Two by Two* (music by Richard Rodgers).

Noah awakes from a dream in which God has revealed coming universal destruction. Deeply pious and obedient, the aged Noah follows God's instructions despite his fears of inadequacy and his family's skepticism. Divine signs confirm the dream: Noah is miraculously transformed into a vigorous "young man of fifty, with eagle-bright eyes and reddish hair," and the animal pairs by themselves gather about. Noah's principal conflict is with his son Japheth, who wants to remain behind and die "to protest such an avenging, destructive God." Noah forces him into the ark.

where they clash again later, when Japheth insists on building a rudder. Though God gave no such instructions, Noah is forced to submit because Japheth is the only one who can handle the damaged ark. Another son, Shem, is an opportunistic businessman; when he and his wife hoard manure for "briquettes" to be sold later, Noah is appalled: "On the Holy Ark he's makin' business! Manure! With manure you want to begin a new world!" Ham, the playboy son, craves the girl brought along for Japheth, who is in love with Ham's wife. With her last breath his aged wife persuades the reluctant Noah to countenance their "ungodly" behavior and marry the couples according to their inclinations: "The children, their happiness . . . is my last promised land." A blossoming young tree is at the ark's gangplank when it comes to rest. "It's a flowering peach, Poppa," Japheth remarks. The family disembark—all three daughters-in-law are pregnant now—and Noah asks for a divine sign that God will not again destroy the world. A rainbow appears in the sky. "Yes, I hear You, God," Noah says: "Now it's in man's hands to make or destroy the world."

FOG, a one-act play by EUGENE O'NEILL, published in 1914 and produced in 1916. Setting: a drifting lifeboat, 1914.

More of a parable than a REPRESENTATIONAL drama of action, *Fog* consists of ethical and social discussions conducted in a SYMBOLIC and mystical setting. It was originally published in THIRST AND OTHER ONE-ACT PLAYS.

Enveloped by heavy fog, a poet and a businessman discuss their fellow passenger's grief over her child's death. The Babbitt businessman feels superior to the poet, who considers early death fortunate for one born in "poverty—the most deadly and prevalent of all diseases," and who insists on men's responsibility for social injustice. Just as they discover their proximity to an iceberg, they hear a rescue ship. The businessman loses his bearing after the poet courageously prevents his shouting for help, which would jeopardize the ship. When the fog lifts they are saved, the rescue party claiming to have been guided by the cries of the child—who has been dead for twenty-four hours.

FOLKUNG SAGA, THE (*Folkungasagan*), a historical play in five acts by AUGUST STRINDBERG, published in 1899 and produced in 1901. Setting: fourteenth-century Sweden.

Like THE EARL OF BJÄLBO, this play deals with the Folkung dynasty (1248–1364), which unified Sweden. Its last king, Magnus II (Eriksson), here is a good man who must atone for his ancestors' bloody reigns. Strindberg's "classical and Christian" play abounds in characterizations and spectacle.

The corruption of Magnus's court is common gossip: the queen is having an affair with the king's best friend, and the king's mother, Dowager Duchess Ingeborg, is the mistress of a powerful duke, Knut Porse. Amidst his unfaithful and disloyal retinue, Magnus presides over a picturesque pageant in which his achievements are illustrated. He rejects the gratitude of those he has benefited, but his foolish generosity and his thanks to God for his good fortune soon backfire. A military defeat is announced, and a madwoman shouts the truth about his family from a balcony. Though sickened, Magnus does not believe the evil words. A wily bishop who considers himself God's scourge gets ready to excommunicate the king: "The country may not be ruled by fools who . . . undermine the strength of the crown and authority." While Ingeborg and Porse give rein to their mutual passion and plot for power, the queen dallies with her lover. Magnus is excommunicated and, humbly accepting his penance, is humiliated by the people when he appears among them bearing his huge cross. In a spectacular medieval pageant the Church litany is accompanied by a dance of frenzied flagellants. Finally Ingeborg tricks the young co-king into having his father Magnus arrested. A plague-girl with bloody hands and face appears. As she chalks crosses on the doors of the doomed, the crowd's horror grows. The queen's lover is beaten to death, the madwoman (revealed as his wife) is shot, and the flagellants resume their dance. Soon the square is full of corpses, victims of the plague. To assure their political power, Ingeborg and Porse marry, only to find that their schemes have failed. Thereupon they depart with vicious outbursts of mutual hate. At the end, Magnus quietly sits with his wife before the palace fireplace and narrates the long and bloody tale of the Folkung dynasty. His son and his beloved daughter-in-law are brought in, dying of the plague, and his German successor is announced. Magnus is resigned to providence: "It is fulfilled!"

FOR SERVICES RENDERED, a play in three acts by SOMERSET MAUGHAM, published and produced in 1932. Setting: a small town in Kent, England; 1932.

A bitter attack on romantic glorifications of war, this play portrays war's long-range effects on a family and their neighbors. The son was blinded during World War I; a daughter lost her fiancé in that war, turned into a frustrated spinster, and is going mad; another daughter made an unhappy war marriage. The youngest daughter, who is twenty-six, is fearful of following her sisters' examples, but there are no suitable young men in the small town. The spinster proposes to and is rejected by an ex-officer, who has failed as a garage owner and shoots himself when his creditors are about to have him imprisoned. The mother is dying while the father, an insensitive businessman oblivious of the harsh realities around him, confidently looks forward to the future: "This old England of ours isn't done yet and I for one believe in it and all it stands for." His spinster daughter, now completely mad, sings "God save our gracious King," and her youngest sister rushes off with a married, old, and lecherous war profiteer in order to experience something of love before it is too late.

FORBES, JAMES (1871–1938), American playwright, began his career as an author of New York farces. His greatest hit was *The Famous Mrs. Fair* (1919), whose title character, returning from war work in France, finds her family disintegrating. Like most of his other plays (he wrote a score of them), it begins as a clever comedy and culminates as social drama.

During World War I, Forbes was instrumental in having actors sent to the front to entertain American soldiers. *The Famous Mrs. Fair* was republished in Montrose J. Moses's *Representative American Dramas* (1925), which has an essay on the life and work of Forbes.

FORMALISM, a Russian literary-artistic theory first enunciated during World War I, was ultimately rejected by the Soviets as incompatible with SOCIALIST REALISM. After being suppressed in 1930, the charge of "formalism" was used to reprimand or to purge creative experimentalist playwrights and artists like the stage director Vsevolod Meyerhold. The principal tenet of formalism is that art must be evaluated only by "formal" or impersonal and objective ("scientific") aesthetic standards, such as linguistics. It rules out as irrelevant the author's biography and other extraliterary considerations like utilitarianism, didacticism, and subjective impressionism. The formalists included divergent theoreticians, who, together with their theories and the movement's history, are discussed in Gleb Struve's *Soviet Russian Literature 1917–50* (1951), in Victor Erlich's *Russian Formalism: History-Doctrine* (second edition, 1965), and in Edward J. Brown's *Russian Literature Since the Revolution* (revised 1969).

FORSAKEN NOOK, A (*A Farvorfn Vinkl*), a play in four acts by PERETZ HIRSHBEIN, published in 1915 and produced in 1918. Setting: a contemporary Lithuanian province.

Written in 1912–13, this play was enormously successful in Maurice Schwartz's 1918 production. It has been credited with restoring serious drama to the American Yiddish theatre. Despite its happy ending, the multicharactered play—with its Romeo and Juliet plot transposed to the *shtetl*—depicts the bitterness and obstinate rivalries of the older generation, which almost destroy the happiness of the young.

The "forsaken nook" is the cemetery-corner home of a gravedigger. His daughter loves the son of a nearby miller, her father's enemy. The hatred of the fathers, exacerbated by economic rivalries (the gravedigger plans to build a competing mill), temporarily drives the lovers apart. But with the help of a wise old grandfather, youth eventually prevails, the quarrels are resolved, the lovers are reunited, and the play ends with reciprocal shouts of congratulatory *"Mazel tov!"*

FORSYTH, James (1913–   ), British painter, poet, and author of a number of dramas, usually on religious themes. He was born in Glasgow, Scotland, educated in that city's School of Art, and became dramatist-in-residence of the Old Vic Company. Most notable is his *Héloïse* (1951), a prose drama about the famous twelfth-century lovers. His other plays include *The Medicine Man* (1950), *The Other Heart* (1952, a play about François Villon), *The Pier* (1958), *The Road to Emmaus* (1958, "a play for Eastertide"), *Trog* (1959), *Emmanuel* (1960, a nativity play), *Fifteen Strings of Money* (1961, based on an old Chinese play), a new version of *Everyman* (1962), and *If My Wings Heal* (1968, about Saint Francis). Forsyth also wrote radio, television, and film scripts, and a dramatization of C. S. Lewis's *The Screwtape Letters* (1942) as *Dear Wormwood* (1961).

FORZANO, Giovacchino (1883–1970), Italian writer, was one of the most commercially successful dramatists of the Fascist regime. He specialized in light comedies, like *Un colpo di vento* (1930); and in history plays, some of which—including *Campo di maggio* (1930, adapted in 1932 by JOHN DRINKWATER as *Napoleon, The Hundred Days*) and *Cesare* (1939, about Julius Caesar)—were suggested by Benito Mussolini (1883–1945). Mussolini was Forzano's collaborator in these and in another work, *Villa Franca,* a play about Italy's unification written in 1932 and premiered with great pomp in Berlin in 1940. Other notable Forzano plays are *Sly* (1920), a portrayal of Christopher Sly, the drunken tinker in the prologue of Shakespeare's *The Taming of the Shrew,* who is here transformed into a poetic lover; *Gianni Schicchi* (1918), based on an episode of Dante's *Inferno* and made into an opera by Puccini; and a series of French Revolution dramas.

Forzano was born at Borgo San Lorenzo, near Florence. He had a variegated career in medicine, law, journalism, film and stage directing (including at La Scala in Milan), and singing. Aside from Puccini, for whom he also wrote the one-act *Suor Angelica* (1918), Forzano worked as a librettist for Mascagni, Leoncavallo, and other opera and operetta composers. Equally important and successful was Forzano's work as a dramatist who has occasionally been likened to VICTORIEN SARDOU. A section on Forzano, dealing almost exclusively with *Sly,* appears in Isaac Golberg's *The Drama of Transition* (1922).

FOSSILS, THE (*Les Fossiles*), a play in four acts by FRANÇOIS DE CUREL, published and produced in 1892. Setting: a large country house in the Ardennes and a villa near Nice, France; late nineteenth century.

Curel's second play established his reputation as a dramatist. Like A FALSE SAINT, it also premiered at the Théâtre-Libre and it subsequently became part of the repertory of the Comédie-Française. Eloquent and lyrical, the play features the decayed aristocracy ("the fossils") that desperately tried to survive in the French republic.

Young Robert de Chantemelle is ailing and will probably die soon. He reveals his liaison with a commoner, and the family, to save and perpetuate their noble old family, decide to adopt his illegitimate child. But its mother has also been the mistress of the Duke de Chantemelle, Robert's father. Robert's sister reveals this shocking secret, whereupon father and son grimly agree that one of them must die. Robert deliberately exposes himself to a cold climate and thus hastens his death. His will is read at the coffin. It specifies that the child's name, "transmitted by means of a terrible crime, should be borne with superhuman dignity." In its desperate quest to survive, the nobility must not become inhuman: "The future Duke de Chantemelle must be educated with the idea that his rank is not an excuse to dispense with personal merit."

FOUNTAIN, THE a play in eleven scenes (three parts) by EUGENE O'NEILL, produced in 1925 and published in 1926. Setting: Spain, Columbus's flagship, and the New World; 1492–c. 1514.

O'Neill's reach exceeded his grasp in this at-times poignant spiritual quest. Particularly effective are the climactic tenth scene, devoted to Juan's visions, and a recurrent "Fountain Song." But the language is often bombastic, and some of the scenes and character portrayals are simplistic.

Young and noble, but hard and patriotic, Juan Ponce de Leon rejects the love of an older woman who warns him, "You will go far, soldier of iron—and dreamer. God pity you if those two selves should ever clash!" They soon do. He hears a legend about a sacred grove in the Far East, where there is a Fountain of Youth, where nature is in pristine harmony, where men are at peace, and where gold is plentiful. But Juan seeks only wealth and power for Spain and joins in the second New World journey of Columbus, who seeks only wealth and power for the Church. Twenty years later, Juan is governor of Porto Rico, having succeeded in his youthful quests, but now old and disillusioned. His spirit revives at the arrival of Beatriz de Cordova, daughter of the woman he had rejected. He falls in love with her, and, wanting to regain his youth in order to win her, he becomes obsessed with locating the Fountain: "There is no God but Love—no heaven but youth!" He tortures an Indian prisoner to discover the site of the legendary Fountain, undertakes a long journey, and is finally shot by some Florida Indians, who are horrified by Christian cruelty and cupidity. In extended delirious visions the mortally wounded Juan discovers the cyclical unity of nature and his being: "Age—Youth—They are the same rhythm of eternal life!" Through these visions he learns to accept age, mortality, and, finally, even Beatriz's new lover—his own nephew, the youthful Juan. Having discovered that "One must accept, absorb, give back, become oneself a symbol!" he dies ecstatically: "I have found my Fountain! O Fountain of Eternity, take back this drop, my soul!"

FOUR PLAYS FOR DANCERS (1921), WILLIAM BUTLER YEATS'S AT THE HAWK'S WELL, THE ONLY JEALOUSY OF EMER, THE DREAMING OF THE BONES, and CALVARY. These are very short, SYMBOLIC plays whose form is derived from ancient Japanese No drama. But Yeats claimed to have established a new form, "distinguished, indirect and symbolic, and having no need of mob or press to pay its way—an aristocratic form." The plays are anti-REPRESENTATIONAL and purposely distanced from life. In them Yeats conjoins poetry, song, music, narrative, mime, and dance; stresses audience intimacy by calling for small auditoriums, preferably "a friend's drawing-room"; and achieves aesthetic distance and effect with extreme but simple stylization (including masks and chorus) in setting and performance.

FRANCE.* French drama in modern times has been of major international importance. Though there has emerged no single towering native playwright comparable to Italy's LUIGI PIRANDELLO or Britain's BERNARD SHAW, the modern French theatre has been the focus of seminal drama movements. NATURALISM and SYMBOLISM flourished in Paris's avant-garde theatres in the late nineteenth century, and religious spectacle and SURREALISM in the early twentieth century. These and other genres paved the way for the native and naturalized French playwrights who were to launch mid-century movements like the theatre of the ABSURD and the theatre of CRUELTY. Of great importance too—despite their subliterary quality—are the GRAND GUIGNOLS and the Gallic intrigues and farces still profitably imported by New York's Broadway and London's West End from the Parisian boulevard.

In the nineteenth century, particularly successful fare of this sort was written by Eugène Scribe (1791–1861) and Alexandre Dumas *fils* (1824–95). Scribe, the author of some four hundred works for the theatre, was the originator of the WELL-MADE PLAY subsequently produced by VICTORIEN SARDOU and other fashionable early modern playwrights: Eugène Labiche (1815–87), among whose great farces (most of them written with various collaborators) was *Le Chapeau de paille d'Italie* (*The Italian Straw Hat,* 1851; also adapted as *The Wedding March* and as *Horse Eats Hat*); Edouard Pailleron (1834–99), whose masterpiece is a satire on pseudoculture and pedanticism, *Le Monde où l'on s'ennuie* (1881); and Émile Augier (1820–89), the most successful writer of early-modern French satire, whose social criticisms were dramatized in plays like *Le Mariage d'Olympe* (*Olympe's Marriage,* 1855), a naturalistic refutation of *La Dame aux camélias* (1852, best known as *Camille*). Dumas *fils,* author of this frequently revived romance of a "fallen woman," later wrote intensely didactic and moralistic works, including *Le Fils naturel* (1858), a dramatization

* For other important drama in French, see BELGIUM.

of the "natural son's attitudes about his illegitimacy."* Other notable boulevard playwrights were LUDOVIC HALÉVY, GEORGES COURTELINE, GEORGES FEYDEAU, and HENRI LAVEDAN. The poetic fustian of nineteenth-century romantic drama made its sensational appearance with Victor Hugo's (1802–85) *Hernani* (1830) and reached another high point with Alfred de Musset's (1810–57) *Lorenzaccio* (1834); but the greatest romantic playwright was EDMOND ROSTAND, the protagonist of whose CYRANO DE BERGERAC became the most coveted role after Hamlet. Other early modern playwrights who wrote romantic verse drama were his son MAURICE ROSTAND and FRANÇOIS COPPÉE.

More significant in the development of drama was ÉMILE ZOLA, whose work helped bring about the Théâtre-Libre, founded by André Antoine. Featuring naturalistic drama already produced by HENRY BECQUE—SLICE-OF-LIFE drama, as characterized by JEAN JULLIEN—this short-lived theatre (1887–94) introduced to the world the work of HENRIK IBSEN, AUGUST STRINDBERG, and GERHART HAUPTMANN; launched the careers of native playwrights like EUGÈNE BRIEUX and FRANÇOIS DE CUREL; and paved the way for later movements like JACQUES COPEAU's art theatre and its successors. Among other writers of naturalistic and thesis drama were GEORGES ANCEY, PAUL HERVIEU, OCTAVE MIRBEAU, JEAN RICHEPIN, and the critic JULES LEMAÎTRE, whose studies of love were only tangentially related to the *théâtre d'amour* of GEORGES DE PORTO-RICHE, PAUL GÉRALDY, and MAURICE DONNAY. Other notable early director-producers include Aurélien-Marie Lugné-Poë; principally interested in symbolist drama, he introduced the works of MAURICE MAETERLINCK and influential French writers like ALFRED JARRY, PAUL CLAUDEL, and ARMAND SALACROU.

Boulevard comedy remained popular at the turn of the century and beyond—with the work of ALFRED CAPUS, JULES RENARD, ROBERT DE FLERS, and TRISTAN BERNARD. Equally popular but less amusing was the intrigue drama of HENRY BERNSTEIN and HENRY BATAILLE. Of greater importance to the later drama was the work of the avant-garde, surrealists and DADAISTS like ANDRÉ BRETON, PHILIPPE SOUPAULT, GUILLAUME APOLLINAIRE, GEORGES RIBEMONT-DESSAIGNES, LOUIS ARAGON, and, later, JEAN COCTEAU. In 1927 Jarry's *fin de siècle* work was acknowledged with the founding of the Théâtre Alfred-Jarry by ROGER VITRAC and ANTONIN ARTAUD, the theoretician of the theatre of cruelty. Other avant-gardists of the period included the eccentric novelist Raymond Roussel (1877–1933), who wrote complex "anti-plays" (*L'Étoile au front,* 1924, and *La Poussière de soleils,* 1926) later extolled by the PATAPHYSICIANS; and Robert Desnos (1900–45), the surrealist poet-film writer murdered by the Nazis, who in 1927 wrote the posthumously published *"antipoème," La Place de l'Étoile,* a dreamlike romance.

Early in the new century appeared the symbolic history cycles of the Nobel Prize novelist ROMAIN ROLLAND and the ambitious poetic-religious spectacles of Claudel. These continued to be presented in the period between the two world wars, along with similar drama by GEORGES DUHAMEL, HENRI GHÉON, and JULES SUPERVIELLE. PAUL RAYNAL and ANDRÉ OBEY wrote adaptations of the classics, while the critic GABRIEL MARCEL and HENRI-RENÉ LENORMAND wrote esoteric philosophic drama. Denys Amiel (1884–) first achieved success collaborating with Obey, and went on to depict feminine psychology and emotions in many of his own plays, including *Trois et une* (*Three and One,* 1932), adapted as a comedy in New York the following year. Another Nobel Prize novelist, Roger Martin du Gard (1881–1958), wrote two sardonic peasant farces satirizing man's bestiality, *Le Testament du Père Leleu* (1914) and *La Gonfle* (1928), as well as a naturalistic drama about sex perversion, *Un Taciturne* (1931).

Boulevard drama continued to flourish, particularly with the work of SACHA GUITRY, the leading playwright of his age, and with that of MARCEL ACHARD, ANDRÉ BIRABEAU, EDOUARD BOURDET, JACQUES DEVAL, RENÉ FAUCHOIS, ROGER FERDINAND, CLAUDE-ANDRÉ PUGET, and LOUIS VERNEUIL. The novelist JULES ROMAINS wrote internationally successful comedies, while more serious work was produced by JEAN-JACQUES BERNARD, the laureate ANDRÉ GIDE, JEAN GIONO, STÈVE PASSEUR, JEAN SARMENT, and CHARLES VILDRAC. During the period between the wars—and indeed for some years after his death in 1944—the leading French playwright was JEAN GIRAUDOUX.

The variegated drama that had proliferated on French stages in the period before World War II continued, in the main, thereafter. Popular postwar playwrights have been the boulevardier wits ANDRÉ ROUSSIN and FRANÇOIS BILLETDOUX (who have subsequently written Brechtian EPIC DRAMA) and the satirist MARCEL AYMÉ. Poetic drama has been written by HENRI PICHETTE; the novelists FRANÇOIS MAURIAC and HENRY DE MONTHERLANT and the poet GEORGES BERNANOS have made their mark as playwrights as well. The film-maker MARCEL PAGNOL achieved international acclaim with the film trilogy of *Marius, Fanny,* and *César*—two of which were first presented in the theatre. The writer-statesman André Malraux (1901–) dramatized (with Thierry Maulnier, 1909–) his novel about the Chinese Civil War, *La Condition humaine* (1954).

Leading postwar playwrights have been JEAN ANOUILH and—though practically unknown in the English-speaking world—ARMAND SALACROU. Neither, however, has been especially associated with the new dominant movements that have spread from France to the rest of the world—the avant-garde drama that has particularly engrossed critics and social historians. Even during the war philosopher-novelists like JEAN-PAUL SARTRE and ALBERT CAMUS had begun to dramatize the

* His father, Alexandre Dumas *père* (1803–70), now remembered principally as a novelist, was a successful playwright particularly noted for his historical romances.

existentialist agony eventually given artistic expression in what became known as the theatre of the absurd and the theatre of cruelty. Its major practitioners are the Rumanian-born EUGÈNE IONESCO, the French-writing Irish expatriate SAMUEL BECKETT, and JEAN GENET; others include ARTHUR ADAMOV, JACQUES AUDIBERTI, GEORGES SCHEHADÉ, JEAN TARDIEU, JEAN VAUTHIER, and BORIS VIAN. Georges Neveux (1900–), who wrote the poetic-surrealist *Juliette* in 1929, has continued with similar works: *Voyage de Thésée* (1943) and *La Voleuse de Londres* (1960). Younger experimental playwrights in the 1960's include ROLAND DUBILLARD, MARGUERITE DURAS, ARMAND GATTI, RENÉ DE OBALDIA, ROBERT PINGET, and the French-writing exiled Spaniard FERNANDO ARRABAL.

Modern French drama has been uniquely indebted to director- and actor-producers. Notable aside from Antoine, Copeau, and Lugné-Poë are Georges Pitoeff, whose art theatre introduced Lenormand and important foreign playwrights; Louis Jouvet, the actor-director long associated with Giraudoux; and Jean-Louis Barrault, the actor-mime who, after directing the Comédie-Française, has presented THÉÂTRE-TOTAL productions of classics and modern plays like *The Trial* (with Gide) and the works of Claudel, Obey, and others.

The many useful English studies of modern French drama include, for the early period, Barrett H. Clark's *Contemporary French Dramatists* (1915) and Frank W. Chandler's *The Contemporary Drama of France* (1925); for the period between the world wars, Dorothy Knowles's *French Drama in the Inter-War Years 1918–1939* (1968); for the avant-garde and other more recent drama, Martin Esslin's *The Theatre of the Absurd* (revised edition, 1968); David I. Grossvogel's *The Self-Conscious Stage in Modern French Drama* (1958, republished in 1961 as *20th Century French Drama*), and Jacques Guicharnaud's *Modern French Theatre from Giraudoux to Genet* (revised edition, 1967). Their bibliographies list other general as well as more specialized studies.

Eleanore Duse as Francesca di Rimini. Rome, 1902. (*Culver Pictures*)

FRANCESCA DA RIMINI, a blank-verse drama in five acts by GABRIELE D'ANNUNZIO, produced in 1901 and published in 1902. Setting: Ravenna and Rimini, Italy; thirteenth century.

This is among the most popular dramatizations of Dante's fifth-canto episode of the *Divine Comedy* and one of D'Annunzio's most successful works. (In 1914 it was made into an opera by Riccardo Zandonai.) Characteristically violent and brutal and lyrical, it is a play whose pageantry and spectacular setting approximate historical authenticity. D'Annunzio embellished Dante's story with a lustful third brother, and characterized Francesca as a beautiful, fiery intriguer. The play is the first of a trilogy (*I Malatesti*) to which belongs one of D'Annunzio's last works, the opera *Parisina* (1913, music by Pietro Mascagni).

Francesca's women celebrate her coming wedding to Malatesta's son Giovanni (Gianciotto). They rejoice as they mistake the handsome Paolo, his brother and envoy, for the crippled Gianciotto. From a sarcophagus the deceived Francesca picks a red rose, which she hands to Paolo; her bloodied bastard brother, wounded by the legitimate son, watches the scene from a barred window. Later, on the tower during a battle, Francesca reproaches Paolo for the deceit that has made her Gianciotto's wife. His youngest brother is brought in with one of his eyes gouged, and Paolo shoots at the enemy while Francesca calls on "the judgment of God [to] / Make proof of you / Now by the arrow / That it touch you not"—in which case Paolo's deceit will be pardoned "with all love." Later she and Paolo read the Lancelot story—and kiss. Because of the deceitful way in which Gianciotto won her, Francesca feels little guilt about her adultery. But she is terrified by the brutality around her and by a recurrent dream in which she is chased "by two mastiffs at her heels / That bite her cruelly when they overtake her." When Francesca repulses the advances of the lustful youngest brother, he betrays her affair to Gianciotto, who surprises the guilty pair. Paolo tries to escape but is caught in a trapdoor. The crippled Gianciotto stabs Francesca and Paolo to death and, painfully bending his knee, breaks the blood-stained sword.

FRANCK, Hans (1879–1964), German novelist, poet, and playwright, was a neoclassic disciple of PAUL ERNST. As a glorifier of the mystique of

German soil, Franck was a precursor of national-socialist art. His first success, *Freie Knechte* (1918), dramatizes the conflict of a peasant mother who has lost two sons in battle and struggles to save the last one from a similar fate—though her husband proclaims the need of self-sacrifice for the fatherland. Influenced also by the philosophical drama of Friedrich Hebbel (1830–63), Franck was particularly interested in the conflict of the spirit and the flesh—a conflict that appears in various guises in all his works.

A north German from Mecklenburg, Franck served as *Dramaturg* at the Düsseldorf Schauspielhaus. His works usually deal with history and the peasants. *Der Herzog von Reichstadt* (1910), like Rostand's L'AIGLON, portrays Napoleon's weak son, Franz. The most interesting of Franck's later plays include *Godiva* (1919), in which the legend is dramatized as a marital struggle over differing notions of purity; *Geschlagen* (1923), about the political strife between Frederick the Great and his brother; *Klaus Michel* (1925), the tragedy of a peasant who "betrays" his heritage by becoming a famous surgeon, and then expiates his betrayal and sacrifices his life for his son and his country; and *Kleist* (1933), a drama presenting the poet-playwright Heinrich von Kleist in his struggle against Napoleon—and for the identification of poetry with national interests. Franck's subsequent works are similarly chauvinistic.

FRANK, Bruno (1887–1945), German poet, novelist, and playwright, achieved early success with his fiction and the drama *Die Schwestern und der Fremde* (1917). His fame spread as he turned from EXPRESSIONISM and discovered audience-pleasing formulas for his writing, including lively plots and psychologically motivated historical figures. Most successful among his plays were *Zwölftausend* (*Twelve Thousand,* 1927), about a nobleman who sells his subjects into British conscription to fight against the rebelling American colonists; and *Sturm im Wasserglas* (1930, translated as *Storm over Patsy*), which satirizes bureaucracy. Other plays include *Das Weib auf dem Tiere* (1921), a social protest drama dealing with prostitution; *Perlenkomödie* (1929), a comedy; *Nina* (1931), about a film star and her *Doppelgänger;* and *Der General und das Gold* (1932), about Johann A. Sutter, the German-American who lost his fortune when squatters overran his land during the 1848 California gold rush.

Born in Stuttgart, Frank settled in Munich after he received his Ph.D. He became a close friend of Thomas Mann, who was to influence his writings. Many of Frank's novels, including one on Cervantes, have appeared in English. In 1933 he left Germany and settled in California, where he wrote film scenarios until his death.

FRANK, Leonhard (1882–1961), German writer, is best known for his fiction, some of which he dramatized. Most notable is his 1927 dramatization of his novel *Karl und Anna* (*Karl and Anna,* 1926), an Enoch Arden tale of a soldier returning from the war; he looks like and impersonates his closest comrade, thus winning the latter's wife, whom he had heard so much about at the front. Another important Frank dramatization (1928) was of his novel *Die Ursache* (1916, translated as *The Cause of the Crime*), which depicts a man's vengeance against a teacher who had maltreated him in school long before. *Das Männerquartett* (1958) dramatizes parts of *Das Ochsenfurter Männerquartett* (1925, translated as *The Singers*), the sequel to the novel that first made Frank famous, *Die Räuberbande* (*The Robber Band,* 1914); it depicts the escapades of a gang of adolescents emulating the Wild West adventures of Karl May's novels, the sequel portraying them as middle-aged and dispirited after World War I. Other Frank plays are *Der Aussenseiter* (1937), a satire he revised twenty years later as *Die Kurve,* which was published in 1959 together with *Ruth,* another dramatization of a novel, this one about the post-Nazi sufferings of a Jewess.

Born in Würzburg into a laborer's family, Frank worked at various menial jobs before he became a successful author. He went to Switzerland during World War I, joined a group of antiwar writers, and published *Der Mensch ist gut* (1917), a frightening novelistic tract on the horrors of war that was credited with having weakened homefront morale. Frank again left Germany when Hitler came to power, and his writings were officially banned and burned. He lived in France, the United States, and England until 1951, when he returned to Munich. Some of Frank's works with their rapidly changing scenes are almost EXPRESSIONISTIC, and the influence of Freud manifests itself in his psychological probings. Much of Frank's fiction has been translated into English, including his autobiographical novel *Links wo das Herz ist* (*Heart on the Left,* 1952).

FRANKEN, Rose (1895–), American novelist famous for her sentimental Claudia novels about a girl's happy domestic life, also wrote popular plays. Most praised among them are *Another Language* (1932), a comedy of domestic life darkened by parental tyranny, and such other family dramas as *Claudia* (1941, an adaptation of her fiction) and *Outrageous Fortune* (1943), a play about a wealthy Jewish family's problems.

FRATTI, Mario (1927–), has been one of the few Italian post-World War II playwrights to arouse interest abroad. He lives in New York, from where he has reported on the theatre for Italian newspapers. Many of his plays (including television dramas) were first produced in America. They are characterized by their theatricality as well as their intellectual impact. Yet Fratti has eschewed the characteristic intellectual agonizing of the modern Italian drama of the GROTESQUE and the obscurity of the theatre of the ABSURD. Typical among Fratti's plays are one-acters like *Il ritorno* (*The Return,* 1963) and *L'accademia* (*The Academy,* 1963). Both begin with NATURALISTIC simplicity in, respectively, an Italian adult-education class and a home; gradually bizarre situations are unveiled (the young men are "educated" to seduce and fleece wealthy American matrons; the ashes of a concentration-camp victim are being returned to his mother and his former bride), and the plays are resolved with yet another bizarre twist. Fratti's intention is to disclose reality in such a manner. "By writing plays I hope to communicate my awareness," he wrote, "because I believe in man, man notwithstanding."

He was born in L'Aquila, studied in Venice, and earned a doctorate in languages and literature. His first work, *Il campanello* (*The Doorbell*), appeared in 1958. Among his many other plays are *La menzogna* (*The Lie*, 1959), *La partita* (*The Match*, 1960), *Il suicidio* (*The Suicide*, 1962), *La gabbia* (*The Cage*, 1964), *I frigoriferi* (*The Refrigerators*, 1964), *Il rifiuto* (*The Refusal*, 1965), *Eleonora Duse* (1967), and *"Che" Guevara* (1968). Most of these are available in English, and *The Return* and *The Academy* were published with a bibliography and a preface on Fratti, and an essay on the theatre by Fratti, in Robert W. Corrigan's collection of *Masterpieces of the Modern Italian Theatre* (1967).

FREETHINKER, THE (*Fritänkaren*), a play in three acts by AUGUST STRINDBERG, published in 1870. Setting: a Swedish village, 1860's.

Strindberg's earliest extant play was written the year before its publication under the pseudonym Härved Ulf. It is transparently autobiographical and shows the influence of HENRIK IBSEN's early drama. Strindberg's apprentice work received one notice—in which the play was ridiculed mercilessly.

An earnest young schoolteacher decides to follow the dictates of his conscience and refuses to make the necessary social compromises. When he is consequently fired and his fiancée and his family turn against him, he goes to preach Unitarianism in America: "The last link that still held me has been broken. Now I stand alone in the fight, but with the Lord as my shield."

FRENCH WITHOUT TEARS, a comedy in three acts by TERENCE RATTIGAN, produced in 1936 and published in 1937. Setting: a seaside villa in southern France during a summer in the 1930's.

In this popular comedy a pretty English girl learning French upsets fellow students who are in training for the diplomatic service by flirting with and then jilting them. They conspire to get even, and use similar tactics on her. She is pained and, to assuage her feelings, plans to ensnare a lord whose arrival is imminent. He turns out to be a little schoolboy.

FRIEL, Brian (1929–   ), Irish playwright, made his name with *Philadelphia, Here I Come!* (1964), a play featuring the two selves (played by two actors, as in O'Neill's DAYS WITHOUT END) of a young Irishman on the eve of his leaving family and friends to emigrate to the United States. It set a record as the longest-running Irish play on Broadway, passing the mark of such classics as Carroll's SHADOW AND SUBSTANCE and Synge's THE PLAYBOY OF THE WESTERN WORLD. This was Friel's first play to reach America, though three of his works had already been produced at the Abbey and in other Dublin theatres: *This Doubtful Paradise* (1959), *The Enemy Within* (1962), and *The Blind Mice* (1963). Like his later plays, they are melodious and bittersweet, set in Ireland but suggesting universal themes. His next play, *The Loves of Cass McGuire* (1966), is set in an Irish old folks' home populated with dreamers and a hard-boiled old woman who is dismayed to discover that she too has lived with an illusion. It was followed by the plaintive *Winners* and the farcical *Weepers*, one-acters presented jointly as *Lovers* (1967); both are romances, the first (reminiscent of Wilder's OUR TOWN) about young lovers who will soon die, the second about a middle-aged couple whose love-making is periodically interrupted by a sick mother upstairs. *Crystal and Fox* (1968) is in a more melodramatic vein; it portrays the catastrophe of a married couple, former itinerant players, when the husband becomes obsessed with the need to work by himself again, as he did before his wife joined the act. *The Mundy Scheme* (1969) is a comedy that depicts the corruption of national ideals by scheming politicians of newly emerging countries.

Friel was born in County Tyrone and raised in Derry, northern Ireland, where he became a schoolteacher. Turned free-lance writer, he published short stories in *The New Yorker* before he achieved success as a dramatist in America.

FRISCH, Max (1911–   ), Swiss writer, was prominent as a novelist and essayist in the 1930's. After World War II, along with FRIEDRICH DÜRRENMATT, Frisch became the major new dramatist writing in German. It was then that he achieved his first success in the theatre with *Die chinesische Mauer* (THE CHINESE WALL, 1946). After another play, *Graf Oederland* (COUNT OEDERLAND, 1951), Frisch became internationally known for his *Biedermann und die Brandstifter* (BIEDERMANN AND THE FIREBUGS, 1958) and ANDORRA (1961). In 1968 Frisch produced his fascinating if derivative PIRANDELLian comedy, *Biografie* (BIOGRAPHY).

The youngest of an architect's three children, Frisch was born in Zurich. He studied philology and art at the local university until 1933. His father's death that year forced Frisch to interrupt his studies and he became a free-lance journalist. Until 1936 he traveled—and also published the first of his novels. Then Frisch resumed his studies, finishing his degree in architecture in 1940 after serving briefly in the Swiss army. Frisch worked as an architect until the end of the decade, winning a competition for the construction of a major project outside Zurich. Its profits enabled Frisch to give up his profession and devote full time to the writing he had pursued throughout these years, though he subsequently continued to engage in polemics on urban planning. In 1951 he

Max Frisch. (*Swiss National Tourist Office*)

traveled in America on a Rockefeller Foundation grant, and in the late 1950's moved to Rome, where he resided for a decade before returning to live in Switzerland.

As a sixteen-year-old boy Frisch, already influenced by his reading of HENRIK IBSEN, had composed a number of plays including *Stahl,* which is set atop a skyscraper and is climaxed by the hero's jumping off it as the metropolis is destroyed by a chemical catastrophe. Max Reinhardt's Berlin theatre rejected the manuscript, but asked the youngster to submit his future works. Later Frisch destroyed all his unpublished juvenilia and nearly twenty years passed before he returned to playwriting, in 1944, with *Santa Cruz, "eine Romanze"* (a sentimental lyrical piece) produced two years later. Fluctuating between past and present, it poetically explores the conflicting yearnings for excitement and domestic stability of a couple and an adventurer once close to them both. Frisch's next play—his first to appear on the boards or in print—was *Nun singen sie wieder: Versuch eines Requiems* (1945), whose subtitle expresses its elegiac quality; World War II horror episodes reminiscent of Brecht's FEAR AND MISERY OF THE THIRD REICH and fantasy scenes derivative of Wilder's OUR TOWN suggest that the survivors have not learned from the dead with whom they appear, and the climax is a despairing cry that reality is "nothing."

Frisch reworked his next play, *The Chinese Wall,* repeatedly in subsequent years. More conventional despite its EPIC devices is *Als der Krieg zuende war* (*When the War Was Over,* 1949), a drama about a woman (who is both a participant in and an objective commentator on the play) in postwar Berlin who to save her husband sleeps with the Russian officer billeted in her home and becomes emotionally involved with him; when her husband is exposed as a war criminal who encouraged her adultery to save his life, she commits suicide. Frisch's *Don Juan oder Die Liebe zur Geometrie* (*Don Juan, or The Love of Geometry,* 1953) is a romantic comedy personifying the legendary Don as a lover of mathematical treatises and a misogynist whose scientific detachment attracts women; seduced by them and involved in unwelcome erotic entanglements, he escapes into marriage. Also among Frisch's works for the theatre is the short afterpiece produced at the premiere of *Biedermann and the Firebugs, Die Grosse Wut des Philipp Hotz* (*The Great Rage of Philip Hotz,* 1958), a Brechtian farce about a man who constantly fans his dying rage so that he be taken seriously by his wife.

A Swiss intellectual, Frisch has been preoccupied with the moral and political problems of his times. He has deplored his country's self-righteous assumptions that Switzerland—like his mythical Andorra—differs generically from its Fascist neighbors. Frisch has been plagued by people's Biedermann-like moral flabbiness, which, he believes, invites catastrophes like totalitarianism and The Bomb; and by their tendency to have rigid preconceived—and therefore false—notions about each other, which usually brings about personal catastrophes. These convictions Frisch expresses in a sparse type of drama that is much influenced by BERTOLT BRECHT, THORNTON WILDER—and the Zurich cabaret. Its skits, songs, parodies, burlesques, and fragmentary narratives have long been popular in Zurich, where, in fact, during World War II it was with cabaret audiences that movements like DADA had originated. Other anti-illusionist elements in Frisch stem from Brecht, whose acquaintance Frisch had made in 1948 and many of whose plays had had their world premieres in Zurich during the war. But while Brecht's "alienation" effects have greatly influenced Frisch's plays, perhaps even more important has been the influence of Wilder, whose work had originally revived Frisch's interest in the drama. Wilder's handling of time has particularly intrigued Frisch, who has been preoccupied with the flux of theatre, including elements like gesture and movement. Loathing the stasis of a completed work, Frisch has rewritten and revised his plays incessantly—in that respect presenting textual problems akin to those of Brecht.

Many consider Frisch more successful artistically with his essays and fiction than with his drama (most of which has originally appeared as sketches). The best known of his novels is *Stiller* (1954, translated as *I'm Not Stiller*), which reflects Frisch's own ambivalence toward society in its portrayal of a sculptor with a dual personality. Also important among Frisch's nondramatic writings are his journals, *Tagebuch*

1946–1949 (1950). Most of his plays are readily available in various translations. Michael Bullock's *Three Plays* (1962) collection consists of *Biedermann and the Firebugs* (here translated as *The Fire Raisers*), *Count Oederland,* and *Andorra;* J. L. Rosenberg's translation of Frisch's *Three Plays* (1967) consists of *Don Juan, or The Love of Geometry, The Great Rage of Philip Hotz,* and *When the War Was Over*. A book-length study in English, with bibliographies, is Ulrich Weisstein's *Max Frisch* (1967).

FROM MORN TO MIDNIGHT (*Von Morgens bis Mitternachts*), a play in two parts by GEORG KAISER, published in 1916 and produced in 1917. Setting: a small town and a city in Germany, c. 1912.

This is Kaiser's best-known play. Max Reinhardt premiered it in Berlin, and the Theatre Guild produced it in New York in 1922. A typical though early EXPRESSIONIST drama (Kaiser wrote it in 1912), it is divided into seven short "stations." These symbolize modern man's martyrdom by externalizing a bank cashier's feelings during one harrowing day, "from morn to midnight."

Part I. (1) Silently, like an automaton, the provincial bank's Cashier performs his tasks. The wordly manager and a fat, jovial customer speculate about a well-dressed, exotic visitor who wishes to cash her check but whose credit letter from Florence has not been received by the bank. The manager and the customer joke coarsely about the lady, whom they take for a Monte Carlo adventuress. The fat gentleman deposits sixty thousand marks and leaves. The Cashier is mesmerized by the lady: he pockets the sixty thousand marks and escapes. (2) In the hotel, the lady meets her son, an art historian who has brought her to the town because he is seeking a painting there. The excited Cashier arrives, offers the lady money, and asks her to "bolt" with him: "Hurry up—take it. No time for lovemaking." He is shattered to discover that instead of the adventuress his manager took her for, she is a respectable woman. "Your scent hung on the air," he stammers; "you glistened and rustled—you put your naked hand in mine—your breath came warm across the counter—" She advises him to go back to the bank, return the money, and plead a momentary lapse. But he refuses and escapes: "I've delivered myself into your hands, destroyed my livelihood. I've burned my bridges behind me." (3) Alone in a snow-covered field, he takes stock of his situation: "This morning a trusted employee.... At noon an out-and-out scoundrel." But he is grateful to the lady, who has "electrified me—set me free." Now he will use the money. He addresses a bare tree, which looks like a skeleton: "Does your rather well-ventilated appearance suggest the final truth—emptiness?" It would be easy to accept this truth, he says, "but I prefer complications." And he walks on, though "I really carry you about me now." (4) He returns home, where he sees his mother, wife, and daughters go through banal motions and speeches: "Warm and cozy, this nest; I won't deny its good points; but it doesn't stand the final test." His routine-breaking departure before dinner kills his mother and drives his wife to hysteria. She screams at her daughters and then collapses: "My husband has left me."

Part II. (5) In the big city, at the bicycle races run by identical-looking men wearing dinner jackets, silk hats, and binoculars, the Cashier offers immense money prizes to see the crowds whipped into a frenzy of excitement: "Passion rules.... No restraint, no modesty, no motherhood, no childhood—nothing but passion! There's the real thing. That's worth the search!" A man is thrown over the balcony railing and killed as the excitement mounts. But when royalty arrives and the crowds hush in respectful silence, the Cashier withdraws his offer: he refuses to "throw one single penny under the snouts of these groveling dogs, these crooked lackeys!" (6) In a cabaret's private room, the Cashier orders a sumptuous feast and brings in various masked girls. One by one, they disappoint him with their drunkenness and ugliness. Disgusted, he insults them and chases them out. Then he puts a thousand-mark note on the table and leaves. The girls' debauched escorts find the bank note and decide to use it for an orgy. They ridicule the consumptive waiter who is liable for the bill and hurl him under the table. (7) The Cashier is led to a Salvation Army hall by one of its girls, who had earlier asked him for a donation. Various people confess to sins that recall different parts of the Cashier's life. Finally, he himself is ready to confess: "I won't weary you with the halting places that wearied me. None of them were worth my break with the old life." His discovery is that "you can buy nothing worth having, even with all the money of all the banks in the world. You get less than you pay, every time. The more you spend, the less the goods are worth." He scatters his remaining banknotes around. The repentant sinners fight for them, but the Salvation Army lass fetches a policeman so she can collect the reward for the Cashier's capture. As the policeman prepares to arrest him, the Cashier blows a trumpet. "My forces are spent." he announces; "I've made the path hard, where it might have been easy." He remembers the skeletal tree in the field that morning: "You should have been more pressing in your invitation. One spark of enlightenment would have helped me and spared me all the trouble. . . . From morn to midnight, I rage in a circle." Now he sees his proper path, and shoots himself. As he falls, his arms are stretched out, "his husky gasp is like an *'Ecce,'* his heavy sigh like a *'Homo.'*" The lights explode, and in the ensuing darkness the policeman comments, "There must be a short circuit in the main."

FROM THE LIFE OF INSECTS (*Ze života hmyzu*), a comedy in three acts with prelude and epilogue by Josef and KAREL ČAPEK, published in 1920 and produced in 1922. Setting: various parts of a forest.

This prose and verse morality in the form of an insect fable is also known as *The Insect Comedy,*

The World We Live In (as adapted by OWEN DAVIS), and *And So Ad Infinitum*. Its tramp is an Everyman who dreams various episodes that mordantly portray human evil. The Čapeks denied the play's pessimism, but its thematic ambiguity is heightened by a variant ending they supplied later. The play has been colorfully and spectacularly produced all over the world.

Prelude and *Act I. The Butterflies*. A drunken Tramp staggers in, loquaciously insists he is sober, and explains why he just fell: "I was performing—the fall—of man." A lepidopterist runs in with a net and tells the Tramp the butterflies are mating, not playing: theirs is "the way of nature. The eternal contest of love." He collects them because he loves nature, and laughingly runs off. The Tramp mumbles about love, falls asleep, and has a dream that takes place in the butterfly world. The poet Felix (all the insects wear human clothes), a would-be rake, is pursued by various females. Iris is peeved when she fails to seduce him. "There is no true love except in the unapproachable," Felix remarks and admits his virginity. She insults a rival and starts playing tag with a new lover. Though she proclaims her adoration of poetry, the rival soon tires of Felix's recitations and flirts with another lover. Noticing the Tramp, she propositions him, but he chases the "hussy" off. Iris returns, amused with what has happened to her new lover: "He kept running after me like mad, and suddenly, ha, ha, ha, a bird flew along and ate him up... oh, the look in his eyes, all on fire, and then, ha, ha, ha—" The rivals fly off seeking new mates, and Felix, still reciting poetry though his audience has left, starts to declaim to the Tramp. He flies off reciting amorous verses, and the Tramp laughs: "Ha, ha, ha, butterflies!"

Act II. The Marauders. A chrysalis (throughout this and the next act) struggles to be born and keeps promising to astound the world with something momentous: "Something great is at hand." The Tramp observes two beetles. Excitedly they push up their treasure, a ball of dung. "To think how we've saved and scraped, toiled and moiled, denied ourselves," Mr. Beetle declares, and seeks yet another treasure for them. Momentarily distracted, the wife does not notice a strange beetle, who steals the pile. She accuses the Tramp, who tells her "a surly chap with crooked feet, a vulgar, conceited person" took the pile. Sure "that's my husband," Mrs. Beetle follows him. "Stinginess is a virtue, when it's for the family," the Tramp reflects. An Ichneumon Fly brings a cricket to his larva offspring; proudly he tells the Tramp of her cleverness in eating "only the tenderest parts, while they're still alive." Mr. Beetle, discovering the disappearance of his treasure, angrily searches for it: "I don't care what he did with my wife. But where's my pile?" Mr. Cricket solicitously ushers his pregnant wife into their new home. They laugh about the previous occupant, a cricket caught by Fly and impaled on a thorn. While the husband is out, Mrs. Cricket chats with Mrs. Beetle, and then laughs about her neighbor's troubles and the comic wriggle of the impaled cricket. Just then, to the horror of the Tramp and the delight of the larva, Fly stabs Mrs. Cricket and, when he returns, her husband. An oily parasite agrees with the Tramp that it is shocking. It is wrong for some to have so much when he, himself, lacks the means of killing and must take what he can from his host. The Tramp angrily reflects and then decides, "It is only a tiny drama between blades of grass, / Nothing but insect war, nothing but beetle behavior." But "Man does not crave merely to devour, he craves to create and build. / He indeed has some aim, and raises his pile," Bloated, hiccuping and laughing, the parasite returns; he has just eaten the crickets as well as the larva: "The table of nature is spread for all. Hup, hup, hup."

Act III. The Ants. Reflecting on the insects' greed and cruelty, the Tramp decides that selfish individualism must give way to communal—"call it nation, mankind, or state"—ideals of personal sacrifice. As the chrysalis continues its birth struggle and promise of great things, an ant colony appears. A blind ant keeps time and orders an increasingly quicker work tempo, though many ants drop of exhaustion. The ants believe themselves to be the masters of the earth and laugh at the Tramp's statement that humans make similar claims. The "democracy of ants" consists of beings who live for the state. Soon there is a brutal war between this colony and the adjoining yellow one. The Yellow State wins. Its leader announces, "The world belongs to us Yellows. I proclaim myself ruler of the world." As the Tramp reels among the battlefield corpses, the leader continues, "Most righteous God, thou knowest that we fight only for justice. Our history, our national honor, our commercial interest..." Contemptuously the Tramp crushes the leader under his boot.

Epilogue. Life and Death. The Tramp is frightened as noises of the various insects come from the darkness. Suddenly there is light. Moths appear, dance ecstatically for a moment, and die. At last the chrysalis bursts and the newborn moth prepares to deliver its long-promised message. But before it can even start, it, too, falls dead. The Tramp despairs: "Wherefore this fearful lack of meaning?" Now he himself is attacked by death. His struggle is in vain, though he pleads, "There's still so much for me to say. Now—I—know—*how* to live." Two lisping snails observe his death, are amused by the spectacle, blithely comment on it, and regret the inedibility of the dead moths. Dawn comes, and a woman is taking a baby to baptism. She and a woodcutter notice the Tramp's corpse. "One is born and one dies." the woodcutter says, and the woman adds, "And always there are people enough."

[This ending appeared cynical to audiences. But the Čapeks meant it to be optimistic—life goes on—and so they wrote an alternate one:] After the snails leave, the Tramp awakes and finds he has merely dreamed his death. The woodcutter offers him a job as his helper. Delighted, the Tramp goes to work.

FRONT, THE (*Front*), a play in three acts by ALEKSANDR YEVDOKIMOVICH KORNEICHUK, published and produced in 1942. Setting: the Russo-German front, 1942.

One of the most popular and important World War II plays in Russia, *The Front* is an attack on Russian military leadership during the early fighting, when the Soviet Union suffered defeat after defeat. The play was immediately published in *Pravda* and aroused much discussion. Its author was publicly hailed—which suggests that he may have been officially encouraged to level the kind of criticism that eventually caused the replacement of, among others, Red Army Marshals S. M. Budyonny and K. Y. Voroshilov.

Commander of the Front Ivan Gorlov, a much-decorated bluff and old-fashioned veteran of the civil war, believes that "what's important about a military leader is his soul. If he's brave, gallant, tenacious, then nothing scares him." He is fond of recalling the old days of the Revolution, surrounds himself with sycophantic followers and fellow officers from those campaigns, and sneers at and represses younger commanders and critics, "Blabbermouths [who] were still wetting their diapers while we were fighting fourteen nations. We'll crush any enemy. Not with radio communications but by heroism and valor." Particularly opposed to his conduct of the war is Army Commander Volodya Ognev, a talented young officer. But Gorlov's methods are also opposed by his family: his brother, an important director of airplane production, sent by Moscow to study captured German planes; and his son, a young Guards lieutenant. "Bravery alone won't win wars for you," his brother tells Gorlov: "You must learn modern warfare. Civil war experiences are not enough these days." Ultimately Gorlov is replaced as Commander of the Front—by Ognev. "How is this possible? I'm so young . . ." the incredulous youthful general asks. "Stalin says that it's necessary to advance young, talented military commanders to leading positions," he is told, "to work together with the older men to conduct war along modern lines and not in the old-fashioned way."

FRONT PAGE, THE, a play in three acts by BEN HECHT and CHARLES MACARTHUR, published and produced in 1928. Setting: the press room in the Chicago Criminal Courts Building on a Friday night, 1927.

This popular farce (also filmed, televised, and revived on Broadway in 1969–70) is the first important dramatization of modern journalism. It is an earthy, hard-boiled madcap that takes swipes at social cynicism and political corruption and incompetence.

A reporter is ready to depart and get married when Chicago's stupid sheriff, who has pledged "to reform the Reds with a rope," inadvertently lets escape an anarchist convict who is to hang at dawn. The journalists' antics are abetted by a half-witted policeman, the fiancée's termagant mother, a "ham gunman," an idiotic scrubwoman, a soft-hearted prostitute, and a blockhead messenger delivering the governor's last-minute reprieve, which the sheriff and the mayor try to conceal in order to win an election. A newspaper editor, apparently reconciled to losing his star journalist, presents the reporter with a gold watch —and then, in the curtain line, wires ahead to have him taken off the train: "The son of a bitch stole my watch!"

FRUITS OF ENLIGHTENMENT, THE (*Plody prosveshcheniya*), a comedy in four acts by LEO TOLSTOI, published and produced in 1889. Setting: a wealthy contemporary Moscow home.

Also translated as *Fruits of Culture,* this play was originally composed for the private amusement of Tolstoi's family, but it proved very popular in professional productions. It farcically depicts the capers of a wealthy landowner-spiritualist, his germ-obsessed wife, and their children, assorted friends, and servants. The comic climax is a séance during which a clever and charming chambermaid tricks the master into signing a land deed for a group of petitioning peasants. Their poverty and the empty lives of the rich suggest an underlying seriousness that prompted BERNARD SHAW's relating the play to his own HEARTBREAK HOUSE.

FRY [originally Harris], **Christopher** (1907–   ), English verse dramatist, for a while was acclaimed as a neo-Elizabethan playwright who, with T. S. ELIOT, would revitalize and repopularize English poetic drama. These hopes soon evaporated—as they had half a century before, at the time of STEPHEN PHILLIPS. But the plays that made Fry famous—A PHOENIX TOO FREQUENT (1946) and, even more, THE LADY'S NOT FOR BURNING (1948)—are comedies whose striking dialogue best illustrates Fry's inimitable talents. The latter is an outstanding example of verse drama in the tradition of the lusty Elizabethans, to whom Fry has been likened. Aside from verse comedy Fry has also written religious drama—notably A SLEEP OF PRISONERS (1951)—and a chronicle play (though he denied it this label) about Henry II and Thomas à Becket, CURTMANTLE (1961).

He was born in Bristol, the son of an architect and Anglican lay preacher named Charles John Harris. After his father's death in 1910, Christopher adopted his maternal grandmother's surname and his mother's Quaker inclinations. Though the family was financially pressed, Fry was sent to private school. He finished when he was eighteen, by which time he had already written *Youth and the Peregrines,* a comedy subtitled "a fantastic triviality," which he produced in 1934. Earning his living first as a schoolmaster, Fry soon joined different provincial repertory companies as an actor and an odd-jobs man. One such job was secretary to a songwriter; musical himself, Fry composed a revue, *She Shall Have Music,* which was later (1935) produced in London. Encouraged in 1932 by his poet-friend Robert

Gittings (the dedication to *A Sleep of Prisoners* describes the circumstances), Fry began writing the verse plays on which his reputation is based.

At the same time he secured the post of theatre director, first of the Tunbridge Wells Repertory Players, and then of the Oxford Playhouse. It was in the former that he premiered his own *Youth and the Peregrines,* as well as BERNARD SHAW's latest play, VILLAGE WOOING—in which Fry, replete with a Shavian beard, played "A." His other early works include *Open Door,* a commissioned dramatization of the life of the founder of Dr. Barnardo's homes, which he toured for a couple of years; a number of religious pageant plays, including *The Tower* and *Thursday's Child* (both produced in 1939, but unpublished); and children's plays for the BBC. He got married in 1936, and during World War II, being a Quaker, served in the noncombatant Pioneer Corps.

It was before then that his first published play appeared. This was the blank-verse *The Boy with a Cart* (1939), a drama about Saint Cuthman of Sussex. A pastoral adventure play, it depicts Cuthman frolicking as a shepherd boy; when his father dies, the boy builds a cart and transports his mother to a new home, where they build a church. At the time war broke out Fry was also at work on his Moses play, THE FIRSTBORN (1946); but like most of his plays, it was long in the writing. After the war Fry returned to directing, until he made his name as a playwright with *A Phoenix Too Frequent* and *The Lady's Not for Burning*. The verse plays that followed had only moderate success. After VENUS OBSERVED (1949) Fry returned to serious, usually religious drama. His most notable achievements in that genre are *A Sleep of Prisoners* and THE DARK IS LIGHT ENOUGH (1954), the "winter play" of the "seasonal quartet"—*The Lady's Not for Burning* (spring), *Venus Observed* (autumn)—completed with *A Yard of Sun* (1970), a "summer comedy" set in Siena on a hot July day in 1964. Earlier appeared a blank-verse drama of violence and passion written for the 1948 Canterbury Festival, *Thor, With Angels,* whose setting is a Jutish farmstead at the time of Augustine's mission to Britain. In this play, a captive Christian who is finally crucified converts a Jutish father from the gods of Norse mythology (Thor, among others) and presages the dawn of Christianity in England.

There is a religious strain in all of Fry's drama. In that respect too he resembles Eliot, the writer with whose name his own is invariably coupled. Unlike Eliot, however, Fry flaunted the poetry of his comedies, and his mastery of articulation made them great box office successes (in 1950, four Fry plays ran concurrently in London). Their flowery verbosity, the juxtaposition of Elizabethan-sounding words and modern colloquialisms, the innuendo, punning, and occasional epigram, and most of all the stunning verbal pyrotechnics—all these have intrigued great actors and mass audiences alike. The compliment that is said to have flattered Fry most came after a radio broadcast of *The Lady's Not for Burning:* "It's the liberation of the English language!" exclaimed a taxidriver. But the later plays are less impressive. They are more indistinct and, despite occasional flashes of the earlier brilliance, less interesting.

His most notable later works have been his adaptations of modern French plays, particularly Giraudoux's THE TROJAN WAR WILL NOT TAKE PLACE (which he translated as *Tiger at the Gates*) and DUEL OF ANGELS, and Anouilh's RING ROUND THE MOON and THE LARK. Fry has also collaborated on such biblical motion picture scripts as *Ben Hur* (1959), *Barabbas* (1962), *The Bible* (1966), and others.

Aside from his plays, Fry has published *An Experience of Critics* (1963), a book in which he analyzes the creative process and wittily discusses the criticisms of his plays. See also Derek Stanford's *Christopher Fry: An Appreciation* (1951), *Christopher Fry Album* (1952), and Emil Roy's *Christopher Fry* (1968).

FUKUDA Tsuneari (1912–   ), Japanese playwright, director, and critic, has been one of his country's important post-World War II theatre figures. In 1963 he headed the disaffected group that went on to found the aesthetically oriented *Kumo* drama movement. Notable among Fukuda's plays is *Kitty Taifū* (1950), a metaphysical comedy depicting a postwar reunion during a typhoon as various people try to overcome the psychic damage incurred by the war and, after a death and a suicide, realize that most of them are battling phantoms. Fukuda's other plays include *Yurei Yashikiri* (1951), a ghost drama; *Ryu wo Nadeta Otoko* (1952); and *Meian* (1956), a verse drama about the family difficulties of a blind man whose sight is restored.

Born in Tokyo, Fukuda studied English literature at Tokyo University, from which he graduated in 1936. For a short time he was a preparatory school teacher before his appointment as a professor at Tokyo's Women's College. Among his other accomplishments are distinguished translations and productions of Shakespeare's drama.

FULDA, Ludwig (1862–1939), German dramatist, was more successful with his translations of the classics than with his sixty-odd plays. He was a director of the Freie Bühne and a great admirer of HENRIK IBSEN, and his own writings had touches of the PROBLEM and NATURALISTIC drama. Yet his plays followed the claptrap style of the popular nineteenth-century German and French theatres. The most notable of his plays are *Das verlorene Paradies* (*The Lost Paradise,* 1890) and *Der Talisman* (1893). The former anticipated Hauptmann's THE WEAVERS with its sympathetic portrayals of poverty-ridden workers, whose threatened strike is averted by the compassionate daughter of one of the wealthy absentee bosses. *Der Talisman,* a verse play based on Hans Christian Andersen's "The Emperor's Clothes," was the most popular in the fairy-play genre that Fulda introduced—

and EVGENI SHVARTS was to adapt in his brilliant Soviet satires. Other Fulda hits were the naturalistic *Die Sklavin* (1892), which features a character somewhat like Nora of Ibsen's A DOLL'S HOUSE; *Die Kameraden* (1894), a prize-winning satire of the "new woman"; and *Robinsons Eiland* (1896), a precursor of Barrie's THE ADMIRABLE CRICHTON, in which a minor Berlin official becomes the leader of a shipwrecked group of his social superiors, but reverts to his lowly status upon their rescue. Fulda's romantic *Die Seeräuber* (1911) was adapted by S. N. BEHRMAN as *The Pirate* (1942).

Fulda was born in Frankfurt and educated at the universities of Heidelberg, Munich, and Berlin. His own shortcomings as a playwright—despite his intelligence and keen sensibilities—are symbolized in his biographical drama of the eighteenth-century German poet *Christian Günther* (1882).

FUTURE IS IN EGGS, OR IT TAKES ALL SORTS TO MAKE A WORLD, THE (*L'Avenir est dans les œufs, ou il faut de tout pour faire un monde*), a one-act play by EUGÈNE IONESCO, produced in 1957 and published in 1958. Setting: "a messy room."

The sequel to JACK, OR THE SUBMISSION, this play opens with the embracing lovers still squatting amidst their dancing families, as they did at the earlier play's curtain. After many attempts to obey their families' exhortations to produce children, the lovers succeed in laying and hatching innumerable eggs—future "bankers and pigs . . . federalists and spiritualists . . . stairs and shoes . . ." etc. Jacques is still dissatisfied, yearning for "a fountain of light," but the two families are happy and chant, "Long live production! Long live the white race!"

FUTURISM, a short-lived movement in the arts and in politics, was founded by FILIPPO TOMMASO MARINETTI and proclaimed in a *Figaro* manifesto on February 20, 1909. Extravagantly coarse and nihilistic, it called for a variety theatre that would present all forms of entertainment with total abandon and in violation of all traditions and inhibitions. In 1915 Marinetti and others signed a second manifesto, which stressed the need for their drama's harmonious and almost instantaneously brief and improvisational synthesis of feeling, ideas, actions, speech, etc. Nonetheless, rejecting all humanistic thoughts and feelings, the movement defied and repudiated civilization itself. Analogous to DADAISM and as short lived, it was a glorification of ruthless power and the machine age—a romantic reaction to the reactionary romanticism of GABRIELE D'ANNUNZIO. While principally Italian and French, the movement spread across Europe as far as Russia, where its practitioners included VLADIMIR MAYAKOVSKY. Michael Kirby's study of *Futurist Performance* (1971) includes photographs, scripts, and manifestos. Futurism is also discussed in the chapter on Marinetti in Isaac Goldberg's *The Drama of Transition* (1922) and in R. T. Clough's *Futurism: The Story of a Modern Art Movement* (1961).

G

GABRIEL SCHILLING'S FLIGHT (*Gabriel Schillings Flucht*), a drama in five acts by GERHART HAUPTMANN, published and produced in 1912. Setting: a Baltic island, c. 1900.

Though this play was completed by 1906, Hauptmann would not allow its production for six years. In a mixture of REPRESENTATIONALISM and dreamlike unreality, it freely dramatizes the fate of a close friend who had died in 1899. The setting, here called Fischmeisters Oye, is Hiddensee, the small island that became Hauptmann's summer home and final burial site. Ludwig Lewisohn ("Introduction" to Volume VI of *The Dramatic Works of Gerhart Hauptmann*) considered the play of "rare exquisiteness in both its spiritual and stylistic texture," and Margaret Sinden (*Gerhart Hauptmann: The Prose Plays*) commended and analyzed the play at length; most later writers, however, have not shared their enthusiasm.

Gabriel Schilling is a once-great painter who has been unable to work for years. Overly sensitive, he is helplessly victimized by the destructive love of two women: his common, whining wife, and his vampiric Russian mistress. He seeks refuge on an island with two famous artist friends, a couple whose healthy affair, like the outdoor setting and the fishermen, is symmetrically contrasted to Schilling's debility. His women come after him; their venomous quarrels scandalize the community and hasten his end. He escapes them by throwing himself into the ocean. As his corpse is recovered from the water, one of his friends concludes, "If Schilling has really fled—no, don't let's go after him like hounds!"

GALE, Zona (1874–1938), American author, suffragette, and pacifist, wrote autobiographies, short stories, novels, poetry, and plays. Her most successful work was NATURALISTIC sentimental fiction set in the Midwest, principally her best-selling novel about a scorned but rebellious spinster rehabilitated by romance, *Miss Lulu Bett* (1920). Likened to SINCLAIR LEWIS's *Main Street* (1920), it was dramatized by Zona Gale—with two different endings—the year the novel was published and won the Pulitzer Prize. Her other stage works are also adaptations of her novels: *Mr. Pitt* (1924), whose title hero is a paper hanger longing for a better life and character, is an adaptation of *Birth* (1918); and *Faint Perfume* (1933) is a dramatization of the 1923 novel by the same name, about a sensitive small-town heroine in a crass middle-class environment sweetened only by the "faint perfume" of a forbidden romance.

Zona Gale was born in Portage, Wisconsin, where she lived most of her life. She graduated from the state university in 1895, and spent a few years working as a reporter in New York. Studies of her life and work are August Derleth's *Still Small Voice: The Biography of Zona Gale* (1940), and Harold P. Simonson's *Zona Gale* (1962), which includes a bibliography.

GALSWORTHY, John (1867–1933), English dramatist, was already established as a novelist when he began writing for the theatre, and his reputation rests on his fiction as much as on his drama. The first volume of his monumental double trilogy, *The Forsyte Saga,* was published in 1906, the year in which his first play was written and produced. He was one of the most important and popular writers of his time, winning the Nobel Prize the year before his death. His drama (he completed some twenty-seven plays) is for the most part NATURALISTIC, and deals with social problems. Like his fiction, it has dated to some extent. Yet because of the fine sense of theatre with which he expressed his irony, insight, and compassion, some of his plays have remained effective.

Galsworthy was born into an old and well-to-do Devon family in Coombe, Surrey. Educated for the law at Harrow and at Oxford, he was called to the bar in 1890, but soon gave up practice for traveling and writing. After his successful publication of stories and novels, Edward Garnett induced him to write for the theatre. Galsworthy was further encouraged along this path by his wife. His first play, THE SILVER BOX (1906), was written in a few weeks, and quickly accepted for production by HARLEY GRANVILLE-BARKER. It was followed by *Joy* (1907), a situation comedy about an adolescent girl whose jealousy of her mother stops when she herself falls in love; depicting the stories of a number of people, it stresses the subjective nature of morality (the subtitle is "A Play on the Letter I"). It was less of a hit than his first play, but Galsworthy's next two works, STRIFE (1909) and JUSTICE (1910), firmly established his reputation as a playwright.

Though most of Galsworthy's plays are as naturalistic as his two early masterpieces, *The Little Dream* (1911) is a delicate poetic allegory about the soul's search for happiness. This play was followed, for the most part, by his more characteristic drama. In *The Eldest Son* (1912) the double-standard theme of *The Silver Box* is presented in terms of an affair between a wealthy heir and a servant girl; but here the poor are the moral victors: "I'll have no *charity marriage* in my family," her father tells the discomfited landowners. The year after

Galsworthy's popular THE PIGEON came *The Fugitive* (1913), the story of an appealing and proud woman who attracts men but can find fulfillment neither with her husband nor with a lover; a "fugitive" from men's lust and unable to fend for herself without compromising her pride, she commits suicide. In *The Mob* (1914), a statesman fails to stem patriotic militarism, is killed by the mob, but triumphs in spirit. *A Bit o' Love* (1915) is a lyrical portrayal of an idealistic clergyman rejected by his parishioners but saved from suicide by a child's "bit o' love." *The Foundations* (1917) of the title are those of human society, depicted in a farcical comedy about a future, post-World War I England.

Most of these plays enjoyed only moderate popularity, but Galsworthy was soon to scale the heights of fame again with two plays, THE SKIN GAME (1920) and one of his finest works, LOYALTIES (1922). With the exception of ESCAPE (1926), the remaining plays declined in quality as well as popularity. *A Family Man* (1921) depicts a conservative and tempestuous domestic tyrant who finally is chastened; *Windows* (1922) is a family drama that symbolizes the difference between theoretical ideals and the actual reality beyond the windowed rooms; *The Forest* (1924) juxtaposes an African jungle with the financial "jungle" of London; *Old English* (1924) is Galsworthy's dramatization of "A Stoic" (*Five Tales,* 1918), his comic character sketch of an intemperate octogenarian; *The Show* (1925) depicts the miseries brought about by the sensational investigation (the show) of a suicide; *Exiled* (1929) is a sentimental comedy about "evolution and the present state of England," in Galsworthy's words; and *The Roof* (1929), his last completed play, is an episodic portrayal of differing reactions by various characters, like *Escape* but almost entirely plotless. Galsworthy also wrote six short one-act plays, the best known of which are *The Little Man* (1913), a farce, and *The First and the Last* (1917), a dramatization of a story in *Five Tales;* the others are *Hall Marked* (1913), *Defeat* (1916), *The Sun* (1919), and *Punch and Go* (1920).

Galsworthy's plays are noted for the objectivity with which they probe social problems. Despite their theatricality and affinity to the WELL-MADE PLAY genre, there is a remarkable absence of heroes and villains, and a reserve that is supposed to be characteristic of the English. Yet this objectivity vanishes when Galsworthy turns from individuals to society and institutions. His attack on penal practices was so vehement and effective that *Justice* helped bring about speedy prison-law reforms.

What popularized Galsworthy's drama, however, was not thesis but entertainment. He himself commented: "It might be said of [BERNARD] SHAW's plays that he creates characters who express feelings which they have not got. It might be said of mine, that I create characters who have feelings which they cannot express." But if his dialogue lacks the polemical skill of Shaw's dialogue, Galsworthy did effectively reproduce ordinary speech and dialect. Further, he occasionally created drama without resorting to any language: some of his most powerful scenes are wordless, and constitute something like a Galsworthy trademark. The solitary-confinement scene in *Justice* is the best-known instance; but most of his plays contain silent and motionless episodes, usually at the play's climax—such as the confrontations of the antagonists in *Strife* and *Loyalties.*

His plays were commended (or attacked) for their subdued endings, for an absence of a resolution; his curtains, it was remarked, hesitate to fall. But this hesitation pertains only to the thesis: Galsworthy presents problems, not their solutions. The *dramatic* resolution is there, however, and it is usually very theatrical—like the suicides that end *Justice* and *Loyalties.* The conflict often is between an individual and the society about him. Galsworthy balances, sometimes excessively (as in the parallelism of scenes in *Strife*), labor and capital, rich and poor, the charitable and the vindictive, and, perhaps most persistently, the ideal and the real. Another theme of many Galsworthy plays is the decline of English gentility, to which Galsworthy himself belonged and which constitutes the subject of his great novels.

Galsworthy's plays are available singly and collectively. His essay on drama, "Some Platitudes Concerning the Drama," appears in *The Inn of Tranquillity* (1912). H. V. Marrot published the monumental biography, *The Life and Letters of John Galsworthy* (1936), as well as a bibliography (1928). Other book-length studies of his life and work include Leon Schalit's *John Galsworthy: A Survey* (1929), *John Galsworthy* (1934) by the playwright HERMON OULD, and Dudley Barker's *The Man of Principle: A View of John Galsworthy* (1963). Though Schalit's book appeared before *Exiled* and *The Roof,* it contains detailed discussions of the other Galsworthy plays.

GAOL GATE, THE, a one-act play by LADY GREGORY, produced in 1906 and published in 1909. Setting: outside the gate of Galway Gaol just before dawn; early twentieth century.

Lady Gregory's finest short tragedy portrays two illiterate peasants, a prisoner's wife and his mother. The prisoner has been arrested for a murder that was committed, as everyone knows, by one of his companions. Now it is rumored that he has informed on his companion. In response to an official letter his illiterate women cannot read, they arrive at the jail gate after a night's trip. The wife, who only wants him back, sees "no wrong in it at all" if he did disclose what all know anyway. But despite her love, the mother disagrees. If he bought his life at that price, then "he must live in some other place." The prison gatekeeper comes out and reveals that the man is dead. His mother keens in despair: "To have died with his name under blemish, and left a great shame on his child! Better for him to have killed the whole world than to give any witness at all!" His wife's long keening expresses her misery and her solitude: "My heart is broken you to have died with the hard word upon you! My grief you to be alone now that spent so many nights in company! What way will I be going back through Gort and through Kilbecanty? . . ." Then the women learn that he was hanged, while his companions were released for lack of evidence. His wife curses "them that did not let you die on the pillow!" But the mother rejoices that he did not save his life at the price of his name: "They brought him drink in the gaol, and gold, to swear away the life of his neighbour!" He could have been free, but "he would never be an informer." She calls on the grieving wife to help her shout out his praise so that "all Ireland will have a welcome before him," for her boy "died for his neighbour!"

GARCÍA LORCA, Federico (1898–1936), the Spanish poet and dramatist, might well have become one of the century's greatest playwrights. His creative genius was flowering when he was shot by a Falangist (Fascist) squad at the age of thirty-eight. The posthumous *La casa de Bernarda Alba* (THE HOUSE OF BERNARDA ALBA, 1945), which he completed shortly before his sudden death, is the third of his "rural tragedies" trilogy and is considered by many to be his greatest play, though *Bodas de sangre* (BLOOD WEDDING, 1933) is the more famous one. (YERMA [1934] is the second in the trilogy.) García Lorca left only a dozen dramas, but they comprise an impressive monument to his developing genius as playwright and poet. Lorca's poetry is genuinely popular, earthy folk (as distinguished from cultish highbrow) language like that of another noted playwright who died very young, J. M. SYNGE.

Lorca was born in the town of Fuente Vaqueros, province of Granada. His father, Federico García Rodríguez, was a successful farmer; his mother, Vicenta Lorca, was a cultivated schoolteacher who encouraged her son to develop his artistic talents. These proceeded to flourish amidst the picturesque and hybrid culture of southern Spain. García Lorca began writing when he was a child, and he published his first work (an article in tribute to the poet José Zorrilla y Moral) in 1917. But his interests and gifts were by no means confined to literature. A student of Manuel de Falla and a friend of Salvador Dalí (both of whom helped stage his plays), Lorca was an excellent pianist and a lifelong painter (his work was exhibited first in Barcelona in 1927). These accomplishments—and his poetry and songs—all shaped his drama, which is distinctive for the art, music, and verse that are integral parts of it. Equally integral are the Andalusian folk traditions of balladry and dance incorporated in Lorca's plays.

He studied law at the University of Granada but soon changed to philosophy and letters, which he continued to study at the University of Madrid in 1919. There he also continued to read the Spanish classics as well as the works of established contemporaries like Juan Ramón Jiménez and MIGUEL DE UNAMUNO. At the university-connected *Residencia* Lorca had appreciative audiences for his readings: his fellow students, who recited his poetry and made it popular even before it was published. Soon he joined leading intellectual and artistic circles GREGORIO MARTÍNEZ SIERRA's production of Lorca's first play, *El maleficio de la mariposa* (THE BUTTERFLY'S EVIL SPELL, 1920), was followed the next year by the publication of his *Libro de poemas* (*Book of Poems,* 1921). By the time he left for America in 1929 Lorca was a leading figure in Spanish letters. His year's stay in New York (spent partly at Columbia University) inspired such distinguished verse as *Poeta en Nueva York* (*Poet in New York,* 1940), which includes his ode on Walt Whitman (he also composed one on Dalí).

Lorca's development as a dramatist, as his brother Francisco emphasized, also began in adolescence. His second play was produced in 1923: *La niña que riega la albahaca y el príncipe preguntón* (*The Girl Who Waters the Sweet Basil Flower and the Inquisitive Prince*), an unpublished puppet show in whose production de Falla participated at the piano and whose manuscript has apparently been lost. A similar extant play, written about the same time and also featuring the traditional Spanish puppet character Don Cristóbal, is *Los Títeres de Cachiporra* (*The Billy-Club Puppets*). Other sketches and playlets include *El paseo de Buster Keaton* (1926?), ludicrous variations on Keaton's films; and *El público* (*The Audience,* 1933), a SURREALIST fragment. Lorca's first success as a playwright came in 1927, when MARIANA PINEDA was produced in Barcelona. Shortly afterwards he wrote the surrealist posthumous play *Así que pasen cinco años* (IF FIVE YEARS PASS, 1937), and produced his short masterpiece, *Amor de Don Perlimplín con Belisa en su jardín* (THE LOVE OF DON PERLIMPLÍN AND BELISA IN THE GARDEN, 1928). *Retablillo de Don Cristóbal* (*In the Frame of Don Cristóbal,* 1931), a "puppet farce" prefaced by a dispute between poet and director, resembles *Don Perlimplín* particularly in its eroticism.

After Lorca returned to Spain in 1930 he devoted most of his energies to the theatre. At the end of that year the delightful *La zapatera prodigiosa* (THE SHOEMAKER'S PRODIGIOUS WIFE, 1930) was first produced. The following year, under the new and liberal regime, he organized and became codirector of the government-sponsored "La Barraca," a theatre troupe. Traveling throughout the Spanish provinces (and also to South America, where some sixty thousand people attended one of his productions), Lorca and his troupe presented before enthusiastic peasant audiences not only such native classics as the plays of Lope de Vega and Calderón but also his own works. It was during those years of intense theatrical activity that he wrote his great "rural trilogy." The earlier *Doña Rosita la soltera, o el lenguaje de las flores* (DOÑA ROSITA, THE SPINSTER, 1935) was the last of his plays produced during Lorca's lifetime. His subsequent sudden arrest and almost immediate execution by the Falangists has remained something of a mystery, for Lorca had always eschewed politics. He was a proud Spaniard who, however, espoused the brotherhood of all men and opposed abstract, blind nationalism.

Lorca's dramas are remarkable for their intensity, earthiness, theatricality, and poetry in all but the last play, where he turned to NATURALISTIC prose. Despite his plays' diversity, one theme appears in all of them and dominates the tragedies: the quest for fulfillment in a life thwarted by barrenness, particularly by old codes and customs. The resulting conflict is personified in Lorca's sensitively portrayed heroines. With emotional fervor they believe in such traditional concepts as the Castilian code of honor and Catholicism. At the same time, they find themselves frustrated and destroyed by these codes, and therefore they rebel against them. The conflict is heightened by the characters' ardent religious feelings, which are instinctive, primitive, and occasionally (as in *Yerma*) frankly pagan. It is a clash of universal and dichotomous forces: instinct and convention, fecundity and sterility, joy and sorrow, life and death.

Most of Lorca's plays are available in translation: *Three Tragedies* (1947), which consists of the "rural trilogy," has an informative introduction by the playwright's brother, Francisco; so has *Five Plays: Comedies and Tragicomedies* (1963), which includes *The Shoemaker's Prodigious Wife, The Love of Don Perlimplín and Belisa in the Garden, Doña Rosita, the Spinster, The Billy-Club Puppets,* and *The Butterfly's Evil Spell.* Edwin Honig's *García Lorca* (1944), Robert Lima's *The Theatre of García Lorca* (1963), and Carl W. Cobb's *García Lorca* (1967) are English biographies that also contain bibliographies and extensive analyses of the plays; Manuel Durán's *Lorca: A Collection of Critical Essays* (1962) is a handy compilation.

GAS I, a play in five acts by GEORG KAISER, published and produced in 1918. Setting: a factory.

Second in the trilogy that begins with THE CORAL and concludes with GAS II, this is a notable EXPRESSIONIST play. The chief character is *The Coral* Billionaire's idealistic son, now a still-idealistic sixty-year-old director of a profit-sharing industry from which he himself earns no more than any of his workers. His antagonists are the Engineer and the nameless other dehumanized "slaves of the machine." Stylized in form and charged with the urgency of social problems accentuated by World War I, *Gas I* was first produced shortly after the armistice. The play's final words echo those of the "Don Juan in Hell" scene in Shaw's MAN AND SUPERMAN.

Act I. The clerk proudly tells a mysterious white figure how the factory in which he works produces a new source of energy—Gas that "feeds the industry of the entire world"—and how "profit-sharing according to age" makes the factory men work harder than other workers. The white figure personifies disaster: the clerk runs out screaming when he realizes that there will shortly be a gas explosion. The Billionaire's Son, at his daughter's wedding, sends the guests off to safety. He informs his son-in-law that the girl's fortune was the mother's, for he himself has no wealth: "I cannot follow you in your world—a world of fallacies." Then he questions the plant Engineer, who insists that though there is no mistake in the chemical formula, the sight tubes are changing color and an explosion is imminent. It occurs, toppling the smokestacks, shattering the glass, and causing an "immense radius of devastation." A workman, stripped of his clothes by the explosion, totters in and briefly describes the havoc: "Report from Shed 8—Central—white cat burst—red eyes torn open . . . the white cat has—exploded!" He collapses, and the Billionaire's Son bends over his corpse, grieving: "O man! O mankind!"

Act II. After seventeen days the workers are ready again to work with the same dangerous formula. "The whole world is in urgent need of Gas—the demand is imperative," the clerk tells the incredulous Billionaire's Son. Like the workers who are enslaved to their habits, so the clerk insists on continuing in his "calling." A workers' delegation demands that the Billionaire's Son rebuild the factory, reuse the formula, but fire the Engineer—their scapegoat. He refuses. "The machines might be stopped—but not men," he sadly tells the Engineer, yet they must be stopped from exposing themselves to a second holocaust. He seeks the Engineer's help in creating an agricultural settlement for them, but finds the Engineer tied to his routine like the others. The Billionaire's Son rejects his resignation: "No! *that* would bring back the others . . . they would come storming back, and build up their hell again—and the fever will continue to rage." Again he asks for the Engineer's help, is refused, and decides: "Then I must force, must force you—every one of you!"

Act III. The son-in-law of the Billionaire's Son has gambled away his wife's fortune and incurred debts of honor. Also facing military disgrace, he comes for financial help. Instead, the Billionaire's Son seeks his help in the cause. He urges his son-in-law to confess his guilt and decline allegiance to an unnatural code of honor. Five identical marionette-like business tycoons dressed in black appear. They oppose the methods of the Billionaire's Son: "This sharing of profits with everybody causes unrest in all the other syndicates." Their workers are on a sympathy strike, and the industrialists have come to demand that he fire the Engineer and reopen his factory, on whose product they depend. In tandem they protest, "We are—to do without—Gas?" The Billionaire's Son interjects, "Without human sacrifices!" But they conclude, "We are set up—for Gas." The Billionaire's Son is adamant: "Man is the measure for me—and the needs that uphold him," and he tells of his plan for the agricultural settlement. In unison, the tycoons express their indignation, repeat their demands, threaten to call in the government if refused, and then leave. A shot is heard: the son-in-law has been unable to face disgrace and has acted in accord with the code of honor. The Billionaire's Son is momentarily dazed: "The world is out of joint—let others force it back again!"

Act IV. The workers are holding a mass meeting to demand the Engineer's dismissal. A sister, a mother, and a wife mount the platform and tell of their men's death. Then various workers speak, and the frenzied crowd shouts, "No Gas—if this Engineer remains!" The Billionaire's Son has stood among the crowds unrecognized. Now, in a long speech frequently interrupted by the crowd, he tells them to "Be human, human, human!" He recalls the sacrifices they have already made, and presses them to give up industry, the bondage of profit making: "Walk upon the new homesteads—take measure of the land! . . . Come into the open!' The Engineer too has stood unrecognized in the crowd. Willing to give his own life, he now urges the workers' return to the factory: "Would you leave your kingdom and enter a sheepfold? . . . Here you are rulers—there you are—peasants!" The appeal of "Gas" wins. The Billionaire's Son, standing alone in the hall, again vows to protect man against himself.

Act V. The workers have attacked the Billionaire's Son with rocks and forced him to seek military protection. A government commissioner arrives and demands the reopening of the factory, even though the Billionaire's Son tells him that the catastrophe is certain to reoccur. "Future eventualities cannot be accepted as evidence," the commissioner replies, and industrial paralysis is intolerable; war is impending, and the factory is needed. The workers are howling, ready to clash with the military guards. The Billionaire's Son, capitulates. He remains alone—"like all men who wish to give themselves to all men." "Where can I find Man?" he despairingly asks his widowed daughter. "When will he understand himself? And plant the Tree of his Knowledge of Himself? When will he rid himself of the primal curse?" His daughter drops on her knees before him, promising such a man: "I will give him birth."

GAS II, a play in three acts by GEORG KAISER, published and produced in 1920. Setting: that of GAS I, a generation later.

The final part of the *Gas* trilogy reflects contemporary defeated Germany and ends with a prophetic tableau of mass annihilation. Even the speeches are mechanized.

Figures in Blue sit like automatons and read the machines' flashing lights: "Report from third fighting sector—enemy concentration preparing." Another flash reveals dropping gas production and eventual military defeat. The Chief Engineer, "aged in petrification of fanatical working energy" (probably the Engineer of *Gas I*), has a Figure in Blue summon the Billionaire Worker (the great-grandson of THE CORAL Billionaire). He is to fan the workers' energy: "Fanaticize them. . . . Hate and pride can kindle a fever to heat the coldest veins for once." But the Billionaire Worker refuses to exert his moral leadership; unless the factory is free as "my mother and my mother's father demanded," he is merely a worker. Increased production loads create havoc, and the workers revolt: "No Gas!" They haltingly seek fulfillment. The Billionaire Worker clarifies their yearnings: "You have come home again—out of bondage—returned to the ultimate duties of life." They shout their agreement: "No Gas!" But when the universal message of brotherhood is sent out, there is no reply. Instead, the enemy Yellow Figures occupy the dismantled factory, and force the Blue Figures to produce gas for them. They manipulate the machines as the Blue Figures did before. Again production lags: the Chief Engineer has invented the ultimate Poison Gas, and urges the Blue Figures to destroy the enemy. The Billionaire Worker urges them to reject force: "Your Kingdom is not of this world. . . . Be your Kingdom." As in *Gas I,* the masses are exhorted contrapuntally; the Billionaire Worker: "Found the Kingdom!" and the Chief Engineer: "Ignite the gas that kills!" Again the crowd opts for materialism: "The gas that kills!" Now the Billionaire Worker bitterly accepts defeat: "Our voices could wake the wilderness—men's ears are deaf. I am vindicated!" He exercises his right to fire the Poison Gas. There is a gigantic explosion. A Figure in Yellow inspects the shambles, amidst which "the skeletons of the workers, already bleached, jut out." He wildly telephones: "Turn your bullets on yourselves—exterminate yourselves—the dead crowd out of their graves—day of judgment—*dies irae—solvet—in favil* . . ." His last words are stopped by his own bullet. In the distance bombs burst, portraying the army, "vivid in self-extermination."

GAS HEART, THE (*Le Coeur à gaz*), a play in three acts by TRISTAN TZARA, produced in 1920 and published in 1938. Setting: a stage.

This very short play was produced before DADAISM's usual rowdy, jeering cabaret audiences. "The only and greatest three-act hoax of the century," Tzara noted in the first stage direction. The play consists of nonsensical and banal speeches that are unrelated to the biological identities of the characters—various parts of the head (Eye, Mouth, Eyebrow, etc.). It opens with a manifold repetition of the phrases "Statues jewels roasts" and "cigar pimple nose," and ends with each of the characters repeating the incantation: "Go lie down."

GATTI, Armand [Dante Armando] (1924–), French dramatist. After his burlesque of dictatorship in *Le Crapaud-buffle* (1959), Gatti began in the 1960's to produce SYMBOLIC avant-garde plays distinguished for their elaborate and complex structures. In order to present the totality of an experience, Gatti imaginatively telescopes time and place in multifarious spectacles. The concentration camp deportees of *L'Enfant-Rat* (1960) are labeled by impersonal numbers. In his *La Vie imaginaire de l'éboueur Auguste Geai* (1962) the different parts of a dying striker's life are relived simultaneously—on various parts of the stage. *La Deuxième Existence du camp de Tattenberg* (1962) portrays the fairground meeting of a concentration camp survivor and a murder victim's widow, and simultaneously depicts their pasts; characters used include, among others, concentration camp inmates and giant puppets from a parade. In *Chant public devant deux chaises électriques* (1966), a play-within-a-play about the Sacco-Vanzetti case, simultaneous "performances" in different cities before fictitious "audiences" also depict numerous individuals reexperiencing the trial. *V comme Vietnam* (1966), an anti-American drama on the contemporary Vietnamese war is set in a Pentagon-like military-political-civilian complex.

Gatti was born in Monaco of Italian-Russian parentage. He served in the French Underground during World War II and, when captured by the Nazis, he escaped from a labor camp. Gatti has been a journalist and has also written and directed films. A discussion of his work appears in Jacques Guicharnaud's *Modern French Theatre* (1967).

GAUCHO DRAMA, indigenous LATIN AMERICAN melodrama embellished with dances and guitar-accompanied singing, originated in URUGUAY and ARGENTINA in the late nineteenth century. It features a noble outlaw, the "gaucho" or creole cowboy adept with knife and lasso—a composite of Buffalo Bill, Daniel Boone, and Robin Hood. Though he appeared on stages earlier, 1884 marks the start of gaucho theatre. That year the most notable of a Uruguayan circus family, José J. Podestá (1856?–1937), concluded his turns with a pantomime by Eduardo Gutiérrez (1853–90), *Juan Moreira,* a famous adventure novel serialized in *La Patria Argentina* in 1879–80. In 1886 Podestá added dialogue from the novel to the pantomime and thus produced the play. In it the idealized Moreira—historically a filthy and treacherous criminal who was executed in 1874—attempts to recover a debt from a gringo (Italian) shopkeeper but is turned down by the judge, who has Moreira beaten up; later Moreira kills the shopkeeper, becomes an outlaw, and, after adventurous escapes, is trapped by soldiers and fatally stabbed in the back. This crude play launched the genre that supplied Spanish American drama with stock gaucho and gringo characters—its other popular hero was the mythical gaucho minstrel Santos Vega—and for decades to come achieved considerable literary stature.

Authors of gaucho drama included the most distinguished South American playwright, FLORENCIO SÁNCHEZ, as well as ERNESTO HERRERA and indeed most of the dramatists of the River Plate and other Latin American regions. Further notables in the genre were Martín Coronado (1850–1915), a poet whose many popular gaucho plays stress romance and whose great hit was *Piedra de escándalo* (1899); Roberto Payró (1867–1928), a novelist and newspaperman whose *Sobre las ruinas* (1904) depicts a less nomadic gaucho facing problems of a more settled society; Enrique García Velloso (1880–1938), whose *Jesús nazareno* (1902) presents Christ's life and death in gaucho terms; and Alberto Vacarezza (1896–1959), the most prolific of the gaucho playwrights, whose biggest hit was the sentimental *Lo que pasó a Reynoso* (1936). The virtual disappearance of gauchos and the rise of a new socioeconomic order and its concomitant problems diminished serious authors' interest in the gaucho. But gaucho theatre, like western novels in the United States, have continued to remain popular as folk entertainments.

Podestá's version of *Juan Moreira* was published in Willis Knapp Jones's *Spanish-American Literature in Translation* (1963). A fuller version by Silvero Manco (? – ?), as well as a 1913 *Santos Vega* play (a "poetic evocation" by Luis Bayón Herrera [? – ?]), were published in *Three Plays of Argentina* (1920) with an essay on the gaucho drama by Edward H. Bierstadt. There are chapters on gaucho literature and theatre in Isaac Goldberg's *The Drama of Transition* (1922) and in the studies listed under LATIN AMERICA, ARGENTINA, and URUGUAY.

GAUNTLET, A (*En hanske*), a play in three acts by BJØRNSTJERNE BJØRNSON, published and produced in 1883. Setting: Christiana (Oslo), early 1880's.

This PROBLEM PLAY, like Ibsen's earlier A DOLL'S HOUSE, attacks sexual double standards. Though Bjørnson's resolution is sentimentally happy, the play's moralizing for high standards of purity for both sexes (further accentuated by Bjørnson in a revised version and a series of lectures on "Monogomy and Polygamy") appalled liberals, who attacked the play vociferously.

When Svava Riis, a moral idealist who believes in marriage "for the sake of our own self-development," discovers her beloved fiancé to have a past less pure than her own, she is crushed. Her fiancé's belief that "a woman owes a man both her past and her future while a man owes a woman only his future" enrages Svava, and she flings her glove (the title's "gauntlet") in his face. "It is *before* marriage that a marriage is marred," she insists to their two families, who believe she is acting too "high and mighty" over what is merely a socially acceptable lapse. Then Svava learns that the dandified father she admires also has "a past." Though heartbroken and oblivious to pressures exerted by her fiancé's powerful family, she gives him hope that she will eventually forgive and marry him.

GAY LORD QUEX, THE, a comedy in four acts by ARTHUR WING PINERO, produced in 1899 and published in 1900. Setting: London, 1890's.

The bedroom scene in the deftly constructed third act of this comedy has been likened to the "screen scene" in Richard Brinsley Sheridan's *The School for Scandal* (1777).

A pert but humble manicurist surprises the title character, an old roué, in the boudoir of a former mistress. Though he is innocent, the manicurist plans to denounce him, but he cleverly outwits her. Then she foils his designs on her innocent foster-sister by bravely risking her own reputation and happiness. Impressed by her pluck, Lord Quex is reformed, and, with the help of the manicurist, wins the hand of her foster-sister.

GELBER, Jack (1932–), American playwright, became famous with his controversial first play, THE CONNECTION (1959), one of the successful social protest plays written by young writers in the 1950's. Some of Gelber's later plays, following the jazzy and PIRANDELLian format of his first play, have been less well received. They include *The Apple* (1961), an antic piece about actors and the morbid characters they improvise; *Square in the Eye* (1965), featuring the troubles of a pop artist; and *The Cuban Thing* (1968), a domestic drama dealing with the impact of Fidel Castro's revolution on a liberal middle-class family.

Gelber, who was born in Chicago, received a journalism degree at the University of Illinois. He has also written fiction as well as the screenplay for *The Connection*.

GENET, Jean (1910–), French novelist, poet, and playwright, in the late 1940's started to shock audiences with bizarre works that reflect an equally bizarre life led by the writer. Arrested at the age of ten, Genet gloried in becoming a social outcast, a criminal, and a pederast. He spent most of his early life in reformatories and then in prison. After his tenth conviction in 1948, Genet was saved from serving a life sentence only upon an appeal to the President of the French Republic by a group of distinguished men of letters that included PAUL CLAUDEL, JEAN COCTEAU, ANDRÉ GIDE, and JEAN-PAUL SARTRE. It was during one of his many prison sentences in the early 1940's that Genet wrote his first and most successful novels, *Notre-Dame-des-Fleurs* (*Our Lady of the Flowers,* 1944) and *Miracle de la rose* (*Miracle of the Rose,* 1946). His earliest play was *Haute Surveillance* (DEATHWATCH, 1949), but the first of his plays to appear in public was *Les Bonnes* (THE MAIDS, 1947), produced in 1947 by Louis Jouvet. These plays, as Sartre has shown in his monumental study of Genet, are similar not only in their thinly disguised autobiographical nature but also in their religious symbolism. A major practitioner of the theatre of ANTONIN ARTAUD, Genet has produced drama of ritual and CRUELTY in a decidedly original and increasingly complex and symbolic manner. Examples of this style are such later plays as *Le Balcon* (THE BALCONY, 1956) and *Les Nègres* (THE BLACKS, 1958), both of which have had long and successful runs. *Les Paravents* (THE SCREENS, 1961), a mass drama set in the contemporary Algerian War, is even more allusive, but was less popular. All of these are often obscene rituals of evil, crime, and hate. They are portrayals in multiple refractions that stress rather than conceal theatricality, plays that depict a world of loneliness, emptiness, and nihilism. To Sartre, this vision of the world made Genet the prototype of modern existentialist man.

Born out of wedlock in Paris, Genet was immediately abandoned by his mother, Gabrielle Genet (his father is unknown). A foundling society placed him with Moravian peasants, and he was considered a good, gentle boy. But when he was ten years old he was caught stealing and put into a reformatory at Mettray, from which he escaped. Thereafter Genet strove to be what he felt society considered him to be—a criminal outsider, a pariah. As he put it in his autobiography, "I decisively repudiated a world that had repudiated me." To collect the bonus for a five-year hitch in the Foreign Legion, he signed up—and deserted a few days later. Amidst other outlaws and perverts Genet led the life of a vagabond as he traveled throughout Europe. He begged, stole, forged, smuggled narcotics, became a male prostitute, and served prison terms until he was granted presidential amnesty in response to the writers' appeal. Then Genet settled down in Paris as a book dealer and an important if notorious dramatist.

As a writer Genet has been likened to other social outcasts like Arthur Rimbaud and the Marquis de Sade. Genet's drama, however, is in the tradition not only of cruelty but also of the ABSURD. Blatantly theatrical, it is rooted in psychology as well as religion and philosophy. Sartre has described Genet's metaphysics, the existentialist horror of Genet's characterization and embodiment of twentieth-century man, and shown the inverted religion, which is most obvious in *Deathwatch.* There the "beautiful men" personify the hierarchical universe of Genet's "black mass": the invisible Negro murderer is the divine idol, the white killer is the Christ (or anti-Christ) figure, and the tough is a priest who seeks unsuccessfully to emulate his idol by murdering the sacrificial victim. The tough is the autobiographical figure; he represents Genet's own readily acknowledged admiration of criminals and homosexuals like his lovers, whom he described in his autobiography. The tough's ultimate failure dramatizes the failure of Genet himself—despite his success as a writer.

Genet's writing—the prose as well as the verse—is poetic despite its scatology and despite its preoccupation with the ugly, violent, pornographic, and evil. These elements provide a cathartic outlet for Genet's daydreams, his preoccupation with his loneliness and hatreds of a society that has rejected him and which in turn he has rejected. Even in his plays, which are less blatantly personal, this preoccupation finds constant expression. Like Genet himself, his heroes are pariah-saints who glory in their outcast states and their evil, and strive (like Saïd in *The Screens*) to plumb the depths of degradation before sinking into nothingness. Genet's individual solitude, as well as universal nihilism, are stressed especially in the plays' resolutions.

However intriguing the metaphysics, what has most impressed audiences about Genet's drama is its theatricality. It is flamboyant in its inverted religious ritual and in the "mirror games" in which reality and illusion (except for the first play) are blended as subtly and completely as in the drama of LUIGI PIRANDELLO. Distinctions between fact and artifact, between face and mask, diminish progressively as Genet's ultimate visions and experience of horror and doom assault the audience with an overwhelming directness.

Genet wrote a film, *Mademoiselle,* which was released in 1966. His plays and other writings are readily available in English translation. The autobiography *Journal du voleur* (*A Thief's Journal,* 1948) and Sartre's philosophical-psychological biography *Saint Genet, comédien et martyr* (1952), published as the first volume of Genet's *Œuvres complètes* and translated as *Saint Genet: Actor and Martyr* (1963), make fascinating reading; the latter has an important and frequently cited analysis of the plays written up to the time of publication, *Deathwatch* and *The Maids*. Separately published studies in English with further bibliographies include Joseph H. McMahon's *The Imagination of Jean Genet* (1963), Richard N. Coe's *The Vision of Jean Genet* (1968) and his "Casebook" edition of essays on *The Theater of Jean Genet* (1970), Bettina L. Knapp's *Jean Genet* (1968), and Philip Thody's *Jean Genet: A Critical Appraisal* (1968, published in the United States as *Jean Genet: A Study of His Novels and Plays*).

GENEVA, "Another Political Extravaganza" in four acts by BERNARD SHAW, produced in 1938 and published in 1939 (and with a new act in 1946). Setting: Geneva and The Hague before World War II.

Shaw's preface was written seven years after the play—when he was eighty-nine, in 1945. It discusses World War II, the atom bomb, democracy, and dictators. Reiterating his belief in the need for the longevity portrayed in BACK TO METHUSELAH, which would enable man to learn to govern himself in the complex modern state, Shaw was hopeful that such an evolution is possible. Since atomic war would destroy mankind, he thought it "conceivable even that the next great invention may create an overwhelming interest in pacific civilization and wipe out war. You never can tell." The satire is keen and entertaining, but presenting dictators at their "best" (despite the impressive character of Sir Orpheus) did not appeal to audiences, particularly when war broke out.

Various complainants at the International Committee for Intellectual Co-operation in Geneva tell their stories to the typist Begonia Brown. Among them are an elderly English bishop and a Soviet commissar—each of whom claims that agents of the other power are undermining his household—a Jewish refugee, and an anti-Semitic widow of an assassinated president. After Begonia sends letters to the Court of International Justice at The Hague, its senior judge orders a trial and summons the dictators—though Sir Orpheus Midlander, the British Foreign Secretary, thinks the gesture will be futile. In a seriocomic interlude (Act III, written later in response to changing international events, particularly Mussolini's anti-Semitism) it is revealed that the typist who started the worldwide furor, an ordinary, sincere, and "cheerful person with absolutely no mind," has won a Parliament seat and is now Dame Begonia. The Secretary of the League of Nations expresses his disgust with the selfishness of individual nations and his own conversion to internationalism. The judge, deploring man's patriotism, ignorance, and pride, is certain that though he cannot force them to come, the dictators will be attracted by the spotlight. And they do come for the climactic *scène à faire:* Bombardone (Mussolini), Battler (Hitler), and finally General Flanco (Franco). After long histrionic confrontations among the characters, the judge, discouraged by the militant attitudes of all the powers, is ready to adjourn when he receives a report of an imminent world catastrophe that is to be caused by the "quantrum theory." Since "Science cannot be wrong" (although Flanco and the Soviet commissar go off to consult, respectively, the Vatican and the Kremlin), man's annihilation is accepted bravely by all but Battler, who breaks down at the thought of the death of his "little doggie" Blonda. When they are left alone, the Secretary of the League of Nations admits that nonsense though it was, the report at least "broke up this farce of a trial"; but the judge disagrees: "Not a farce, my friend. They came, these fellows. They blustered: they defied us. But they came. They came."

GENTLE PEOPLE, THE, a play in three acts by IRWIN SHAW, published and produced in 1939. Setting: Brooklyn's Steeplechase Pier and vicinity, late 1930's.

This wistfully comic melodrama, labeled "a Brooklyn Fable," allegorically suggested the only possible way to deal with the contemporary menace of Fascism.

Two elderly friends, a Jew and a Greek, troubled by their women, plan to buy a boat to go fishing in the Gulf Stream. These harmless men are shaken down by a gangster who also turns the head of the Jew's daughter. His philosophy is simple: "The superior people make the inferior people work for them. That is the law of nature." His extortion grows increasingly larger as he brutally beats them to enforce his demands. The old men's attempts to appease him and to gain legal redress fail. They realize at last that to have "peace and gentleness, you got to take violence out of the hands of [criminals]," for reason is futile here: "Can you convince airplanes with bombs and men with guns in their pockets?" Luring the hoodlum into their boat, they fell him, dump the body into Sheepshead Bay—and remain undetected, able to resume their gentle, bittersweet lives.

GÉRALDY [originally Le Fèvre], **Paul** (1885–), French poet and playwright, was the successor of GEORGES DE PORTO-RICHE as the author of sex plays. The most notable of them is *Aimer* (1921), a three-character study of a wife tempted to leave her husband for a lover. A similar study of a marriage (this time featuring only the couple) is *Robert et Marianne* (1925). In both plays the suspense is created not so much by whether the wife will resist temptation but rather by how husband and wife will continue their joint lives. Other notable plays are the "WELL-MADE" *Les Noces d'argent* (1922, translated as *Nest*) and *Christine* (1932). In 1955 Géraldy adapted NOËL COWARD's comedy *Quadrille*.

John Palmer's *Studies in the Contemporary Theatre* (1927) has a chapter on Géraldy.

GERMANY.* German drama held a preeminent position in world literature from its eighteenth-century beginnings with Lessing through the late

* For other important German-language drama see AUSTRIA and SWITZERLAND.

eighteenth and early nineteenth centuries, when Goethe and Schiller produced their masterpieces. The importance of Heinrich von Kleist (1777–1811) and Georg Büchner (1813–37) was recognized only after their deaths, the latter's *Dantons Tod* (*Danton's Death*) and *Woyzeck* remaining unstaged until 1902 and 1913, respectively. But significant other premoderns were esteemed in their own lifetimes: Friedrich Hebbel (1813–63), whose *Maria Magdalena* (1844) anticipated the NATURALIST movement by a quarter of a century; Karl Gutzkow (1811–78), whose *Uriel Acosta* (1847) was the most important work of the *Junges Deutschland* movement and long remained popular with German and YIDDISH audiences; and of course Richard Wagner (1813–83), whose operatic glorifications of mythology had a spectacular impact on the romantic theatre.

Its once-fashionable high-flown drama was displaced by productions of HENRIK IBSEN and the great French and Russian naturalists at Otto Brahm's Freie Bühne. There, in 1889, modern German drama had its start with *Vor Sonnenaufgang* (BEFORE SUNRISE). The distinction of its author, GERHART HAUPTMANN, as a world-renowned and Germany's foremost playwright was equaled only by that of BERTOLT BRECHT, the second giant of modern German drama, for even FRANK WEDEKIND could not rival Hauptmann's enormous influence on later playwrights, and CARL ZUCKMAYER never achieved universal prestige. The plays of ERNST VON WILDENBRUCH linked the old romanticism with the new style, whose other early practitioners include GEORG HIRSCHFELD, JOHANNES SCHLAF, and ARNO HOLZ. The most prominent naturalist writers after Hauptmann were HERMANN SUDERMANN and MAX HALBE; among Hauptmann's innumerable other disciples were MAX DREYER, OTTO HARTLEBEN, JOSEF RUEDERER, OTTO ERNST, and LUDWIG THOMA—the last two leavening naturalist grimness with satiric comedy.

Romanticism did not entirely disappear, for its flavor in drama on mythological, historical, and literary themes remained popular. Max Reinhardt's twenty-eight-year directorship of the Deutsches Theater, which he took over from Brahm in 1905, constituted a magnificent era of imaginative productions, world-famous for their lavish spectacles as well as for the more intimate poetic performances. Among the poets, novelists, and playwrights of such drama were WILHELM SCHMIDTBONN; HERBERT EULENBERG; KARL VOLLMOELLER; ERNST HARDT; the neoromantic poet Eduard Stucken (1865–1936), whose eight-play Arthurian cycle appeared in 1902–16; the widely traveled novelist and poet Max[imilian] Dauthendey (1867–1918), whose *Spielereien einer Kaiserin* (*Caprices of an Empress,* 1910) portrays Catherine I of Russia; Alfred Mombert (1872–1942), whose verse "symphonic dramas" develop the "myth" of his complex philosophy in the *Aeon* trilogy (1907–11); and the well-known Bohemian Jewish writer Else Lasker-Schüler (1876–1945), whose 1909 Kleist Prize winner, *Die Wupper,* presents a series of portraits that anticipated the next major movement, EXPRESSIONISM.

It is difficult to overestimate the importance of the work of Wedekind, though he is little known today and his dramatization of eroticism has been superseded by even more graphic and explicit portrayals. A precursor of expressionism as well as other postnaturalistic drama, Wedekind's SPRING'S AWAKENING (more than his notorious "Lulu plays") spawned a host of imitations. His many disciples included HERMANN ESSIG, and he influenced countless others in their portrayals of child sexuality. Among those were Anton Dietzenschmidt (1893–1955) in plays like *Kleine Sklavin* (1918) and *Verfolgung* (1923); and *Gestern und Heute* (1930), a play by Christa Winsloe (Baroness Hatvany, ? – ?) produced also as *Children in Uniform* and made world-famous in the film *Mädchen in Uniform* (1932).

Though World War I affected subsequent German drama more noticeably than that of the victorious allies, the war years themselves produced little drama of distinction. Patriotic plays were conventionally REPRESENTATIONAL and featured historical heroes, most often Frederick the Great, sometimes Bismarck. Emerging from postwar despair and expressionistic excesses, Max Mohr (1891–1944) wrote *Improvisationen im Juni* (1922), an optimistically resolved comedy about a millionaire's attempt to purchase an old German castle. An important war play was written by CARL HAUPTMANN, the older brother of the great dramatist, and the first expressionist antiwar plays appeared even before the armistice. In the period that followed, the effects of that conflict were dramatized in many ways. A German equivalent of Sheriff's JOURNEY'S END and Anderson and Stallings's WHAT PRICE GLORY? was produced concurrently in Germany (see SIGMUND GRAFF). Perhaps most popular were the *Heimkehrerdrama* portraying the returning soldier and his problems, as in Brecht's DRUMS IN THE NIGHT and GERHARD MENZEL's *Toboggan.* Expressionists repeatedly dramatized the horrors of war and depicted youthful rebellion, most shockingly in ARNOLT BRONNEN'S staging of parricide and incest. Standing in the forefront of the social (as well as aesthetic) revolution, the most successful German expressionists were GEORG KAISER, ERNST BARLACH, and ERNST TOLLER; only slightly less well remembered are CARL STERNHEIM, WALTER HASENCLEVER, and FRITZ VON UNRUH, and also notable are ROLF LAUCKNER, REINHARD GOERING, PAUL KORNFELD, REINHARD SORGE, AUGUST STRAMM, Julius Maria Becker (1887–1949), and Leo Weismantel (1888–). Becker wrote mystery plays on spiritual struggles (*Das Letzte Gericht,* 1919; and *Der Brückengeist,* 1929) and dramatizations of the careers of the spy *Mata Hari* (1931) and Bavaria's insane monarch *Ludwig II* (1932), while Weismantel depicted the Last Judgment (*Der Totentanz,* 1921) from the Roman Catholic viewpoint that informs his other religious and history plays. More radical were the theoretician YVAN GOLL, JOHANNES BECHER, FRIEDRICH WOLF, and Peter Martin Lampel (1894–1962), who attacked rearmament (*Giftgas über Berlin,* 1929) and, in his best known play (*Revolte im Erziehungshaus,* 1928), the brutality of state reformatories.

Much of Germany's left-wing drama was produced in the Volksbühne, in which Erwin Piscator, Reinhardt's disciple, developed with Brecht the EPIC techniques for which both became famous. Political subjects were treated also in the drama of BERNHARD BLUME, ALFONS PAQUET, and ERNST PENZOLDT, while the popular topical dramas were those of LUDWIG FULDA and HANS REHFISCH. The latter wrote one of the many 1930's protest plays against antiabortion laws. The already-mentioned Graff and Wolf also wrote on this theme, as did Walter Erich Schäfer (1901–) in his *Schwarzmann und die Magd* (1933); later Schäfer dramatized the unsuccessful generals' plot to assassinate Hitler (*Die Verschwörung,* 1949) and the life of Friedrich Wilhelm I (*Aus Abend und Morgen,* 1952). Other notable prewar writers are ALFRED BRUST and HANS JAHNN, who depicted conflicts of asceticism and sensuality; OTTO BRUES, who was concerned with religious problems; Max Alsberg (1877–1933), a lawyer who in the last years of his life explored legal ethics in his popular courtrooms dramas; and Walter Mehring (1896–), whose spectacle about an Eastern Jew in postwar Berlin, *Der Kaufmann von Berlin* (1929), was produced by Piscator. Romantic dramatizations of history were made by the already-cited Paquet and Penzoldt as well as by HANS REHBERG (its most successful practitioner), WOLFGANG GOETZ, ALFRED NEUMANN, BERNT VON HEISELER (who thus carried on the work of his father, HENRY VON HEISELER), and Joachim von der Goltz (1892–), whose *Vater und Sohn* (1921) is one of the popular Frederick the Great plays.

Among prominent novelists and poets whose works also appeared on the stage are LION FEUCHTWANGER, the MANN family, ERICH KÄSTNER, ARNOLD ZWEIG, KLABUND, HERMANN KESTEN, THEODOR PLIEVIER, BRUNO FRANK, and LEONHARD FRANK. Others include Paul Zech (1881–1946), whose *Das trunkene Schiff* (1924), an expressionistic "scenic ballet" with film clips, dramatizes the life of Arthur Rimbaud amidst an African revolt; René Schickele (1883–1940), whose popular *Hans im Schnackenloch* (1915) portrays a lusty Strasbourg farmer who vacillates between his German wife and his French mistress—as well as in his allegiance to the two countries; and Peter Huchel (1903–), the post-World War II East German lyric poet and editor, who early in his career wrote literary drama like *Doktor Faustens Teufelspakt und Höllenfahrt* (1934).

Thereafter, excepting in the unique case of Hauptmann, personal integrity or Jewish antecedents exiled those writers who escaped murder or the concentration camps. During the Nazi period creativity in the drama was as sterile as in the other arts, though abroad the country's major playwright, Brecht, was composing his masterpieces. In Germany itself, nationalistic plays like Friedrich Bethge's (1891–) *Reims* (1929) and particularly Heinrich Zerkaulen's (1892–1954) *Jugend von Langemarck* (1933) exploited World War I themes and linked future hopes with the new movement that was consolidating its power. Nazism's most characteristic drama had been presaged by the *Blut und Boden* (blood and soil) literature of HERMANN BURTE, PAUL ERNST, and the latter's disciples, including WILHELM VON SCHOLZ and HANS FRANCK. Other such playwrights were FRIEDRICH GRIESE and August Hinrichs (1879–1956), whose later-filmed hit, the farce *Krach um Jolanthe* (1939), features a pig. But the most notable Hitlerite dramatist was HANNS JOHST, and the most notable Nazi theatrical entertainment was the THINGSPIEL, whose masters included KURT HEYNICKE and EBERHARD MÖLLER.

Germany's postwar artistic and literary emergence from the ruins was slower and more painful (and less sensational) than its economic-industrial revival. The most important writers in the German-speaking theatre after Brecht have been the Swiss dramatists MAX FRISCH and FRIEDRICH DÜRRENMATT. A few popular playwrights from but not identified with the Nazi era—including FRIEDRICH MICHAEL and the already-cited Rehberg—have continued to attract audiences with their uncontroversial plays. Zuckmayer returned to become West Germany's leading postwar dramatist, and GÜNTHER WEISENBORN, WOLFGANG HILDESHEIMER and others also came back from their exile to begin (or resume) playwriting. War drama has been written by WOLFGANG BORCHERT and CLAUS HUBALEK. Reinhold Schneider (1903–58) produced Catholic history drama, notably *Innozenz und Franziskus* (1953), a contrast of Pope Innocent III and Saint Francis of Assisi. Hans-Joachim Haecker (1910–) wrote plays on biblical and classical themes as early as the 1930's, but was more successful with his one-act *Dreht euch nicht um* (1961), a haunting portrait of two concentration camp survivors (sisters) and their former tormentor. Naturalist drama was modernized in the 1950's by younger playwrights like GERD OELSCHLEGEL and LEOPOLD AHLSEN, while KARL WITTLINGER has written popular comedies and the novelist Hans Erich Nossack (1901–) became known for his biblical play *Die Rotte Kain* (1949), a lyrical romance about the aged Cain and the family's descendants.

As elsewhere in the Western world, ABSURD and Kafkaesque drama emerged in the 1950's and 1960's in Germany—with the plays of TANKRED DORST, HERMANN MOERS, and GÜNTER GRASS. More conventional plays have been written by HANS MICHELSEN and MARTIN WALSER. The conscience of the world was shaken with Hochhuth's THE DEPUTY. Equally shocking and nearly as controversial was the MARAT/SADE of PETER WEISS, who repopularized the theatre of CRUELTY, while HEINAR KIPPHARDT is among the less well-known polemicists. Further new playwrights in the 1960's include Siegfried Lenz (1926–), a novelist but also the author of *Zeit der Schuldlosen* (1961), originally a *Hörspiel* (radio play) that explores the topic of collective guilt—which ERWIN SYLVANUS had dramatized powerfully a few years earlier; Konrad Wünsche (1928–), whose *Der Unbelehrbare* (1964) resembles *Hamlet* and has an "unteachable" protagonist too weak to avenge his mother's poisoning of his professor father; Richard Hey (1926–), who in a number of semiabsurdist yet romantic plays starting with *Thymian und Drachentod* (1956), the portrayal of an East-West refugee who fits nowhere and dies, dramatizes contemporary problems in no-man's-land settings or, as in *Weh dem der nicht lügt* (1962), in a collapsing house; Mattias Braun (1933–), who has modernized Greek legends; and Martin Sperr (1944–), whose *Jagdszenen aus Niederbayern* (1966) was originally (1962) a six-hour play about a "pansy" killed by fellow villagers when he demonstrates his "normality," and who next produced a Romeo and Juliet variant, *Landshuter Erzählungen* (1967).

Soviet-dominated East Germany has had less to offer since Brecht's death. Jochen Ziem (1932–) and Hartmut Lange (1936–) have provided a link with the West, to which they migrated. Ziem, beginning with *Die Einladung* (1967), has employed cliché to indict his characters; and Lange, a Brecht disciple, the hero of whose *Marski* (1967) is modeled on Brecht's title character Herr Puntila and who wrote in a verse form parodying the classics, has subsequently produced dialectic studies of Stalinism. Among other playwrights who began to appear in the East in the 1950's are PETER HACKS; Fritz Kuhn (1918–), with his popular play *Venezianisches Glas* (1958); Heiner Müller (1928–), the success of whose *Spartakus* in 1959 was topped the following year with *Die Umsiedlerin;* Hedda Zinner (1905–), who has written popular history plays on such topics as the Reichstag fire (*Der Teufelskreis,* 1953), an answer to Zuckmayer's THE DEVIL'S GENERAL (*General Landt,* 1957), and another dramatization of the recent past, *Ravensbrücker Ballade* (1961); and Helmut Baierl (1926–), author of *Die Feststellung* (1958), portraying the trial and exoneration of a returned fugitive from a peasant collective, and *Frau Flinz* (1961), a popular Brechtian comedy that has been called an answer to MOTHER COURAGE AND HER CHILDREN. A great hit in East Berlin in 1969 was Günther Rücker's satire *Der Herr Schmidt,* "a German Spectacle with Police and Music" that in quasi-documentary fashion dramatizes Friedrich Wilhelm IV's "conspiracy" to extradite Karl Marx—who never appears onstage.

Translated collections of German plays with introductions and bibliographies include Walter H. Sokel's *An Anthology of German Expressionist Drama* (1963), Michael Benedikt and George E. Wellwarth's *Postwar German Theatre* (1967), and Wellwarth's *German Drama Between the Wars* (1971). A comprehensive survey in English is H. F. Garten's *Modern German Drama* (enlarged edition, 1964), and its bibliography lists many general and specialized works. Peter Bauland's *The Hooded Eagle* (1968) deals exhaustively with the subject summarized in its subtitle, "Modern German Drama on the New York Stage."

GETTING MARRIED, "A Disquisitory Play" by BERNARD SHAW, produced in 1908 and published in 1911. Setting: London, 1908.

Shaw's preface to this satire is a comprehensive study of marriage, viewed in economic, historical, anthropological, moral, and biological terms. He concluded that "to make the sexual relations between men and women decent and honorable," men and women must be economically independent of each other, and divorces must be granted for the asking. Without conventional breaks or dramatic action, this full-length play consists of extensive discussions of the total impracticability of marriage laws as they affect various characters. The discussions take place in the palatial kitchen of the Bishop of Chelsea (Alfred Bridgenorth) on the morning of his daughter Edith's marriage to Cecil Sykes.

Delays in the marriage occur as Sykes is appalled to learn that he would be legally responsible for any libel action incurred by the sharp-tongued Edith, "though all her property is protected against me"; Edith, for her part, is equally appalled to discover that according to the marriage law she could not divorce Sykes if he were to commit crimes—a "wicked contract" that binds people for better or worse, she feels, simply encouraging wickedness. They finally do get married, after taking out insurance policies against libel actions and agreeing to divorce if Cecil should commit crimes.

Throughout, the bishop, who deplores the unreasonableness of the laws, sympathizes with its victims. He is writing a history of marriage and has repeatedly (and futilely) warned the government that "unless the law of marriage were first made human, it could never become divine." He believes in giving the devil fair play and, though he agrees that it is a mistake to get married, he thinks "it's a much bigger mistake not to get married."

Among other characters agonizing over their problems with the marriage laws are the bishop's two brothers. One of them, the pompous "sentimental noodle" General Bridgenorth ("Boxer"), has for twenty years been proposing to the bishop's wife's sister, Lesbia Grantham, who wants children but does not want to be bothered with a husband around the house—and therefore must remain a spinster. The bishop's second brother, Reginald, has just been divorced by his young wife Leo for adultery. Everyone is shocked to find that the adultery was really a sham—collusion done for the sake of Leo, who is in love with the dashing young St. John Hotchkiss as well as with her husband, and wants to be married to both men. Their affairs are finally settled when Leo rescinds her divorce after discovering that Hotchkiss is in love with the amorous clairvoyant Mrs. George Collins, the mayoress and something of a *deus ex machina* in the play.

GHELDERODE, [Adolphe Adhémar Louis] **Michel de** (1898–1962), Belgian playwright, wrote over fifty dramas in French and Flemish. Despite this productivity and a flurry of recognition after World War II, he remained little known. His work has been hailed by a distinguished coterie; but though it is similar to that of the playwrights of the theatres of CRUELTY and of the ABSURD, it is even further off the beaten track of playwriting.

Occasionally flawed by stasis and obscurity, his drama is highly imaginative and poetic. It is characterized by the grotesque, fantastic, and macabre; and by sometimes excessive sadism, ribaldry, and scatology. His plays are based on history, folklore, and the Bible; reflecting Ghelderode's Catholicism, they are nonetheless neither didactic nor conventionally theological. Many of them are set in "Flanders, in olden times," and influenced by the paintings of his countrymen Pieter Breughel the elder and Hieronymus Bosch —and by Edgar Allan Poe.

The son of an Archives Générales clerk, Ghelderode was born in Elsene (near Brussels) and himself was an archivist for a long time in the small Brussels suburb Schaerbeek, where he lived. Though Ghelderode became the official playwright of Antwerp's Flemish theatre, he was a hermit, an invalid who lived in seclusion with his wife. He led the life of a scholar and gentleman in an eighteenth-century Brussels house full of masks and the puppets for which he wrote many plays. Never courting publication or success, he was pleased but confused by the moderate popularity and critical acclaim he received toward the end of his life.

Ghelderode was haunted by death and God. Both subjects as well as the erotic—and indeed all sensual experience—are central themes that recur in his plays, including his best-known, typical ones: BARABBAS (1929), PANTAGLEIZE (1939, probably his finest drama), *Fastes d'enfer* (CHRONICLES OF HELL, 1943; the SUCCÈS DE SCANDALE that launched his reputation), *Magie rouge* (RED MAGIC, 1934), HOP, SIGNOR! (1938), and *Mademoiselle Jaïre* (*Miss Jairus,* 1942), a "mystery" that Ghelderode considered his "climactic work." Other plays that achieved a measure of fame are *La Mort du Docteur Faust* (*The Death of Doctor Faust,* 1926; a PIRANDELLian dramatization of the production of a Faust play), *Escurial* (1928; a harrowing one-acter featuring a king who, as his wife dies offstage from the poison he has administered, taunts and finally kills his crippled jester, who may have been her lover), *Les Femmes au tombeau* (*The Women at the Tomb,* 1934; another one-acter, written in 1928, depicting biblical women discussing the Crucifixion, and ending with the aged Virgin Mary sweeping Judas's home), and *Sire Halewyn* (*Lord Halewyn,* originally in Flemish translation, *Sire Halewijn,* 1936; a gothic dramatization of the Flemish medieval ballad).

Ghelderode's remaining plays are about similar topics, as some of the titles suggest. They include *Un Soir de pitié* (*A Night of Pity,* 1929), *Trois Acteurs, un drame* (*Three Actors and Their Drama,* 1929; a parody of Pirandello's SIX CHARACTERS IN SEARCH OF AN AUTHOR), *Beeldekens uit het leven van Sint Fransiskus* (1927), *Christophe Colomb* (*Christopher Columbus,* 1928; a vaudevillian retelling, with much mocking of society, of Columbus's trip and his frustrated quest for an "ideal sphere"), *Vénus* (1927), *Don-Juan* (1928), *La Tentation de Saint Antoine* (1929), *Sortie de l'acteur* (1942, a play about the theatre), *Duveloor* (1931, a spoof of the devil), *Les Aveugles* (*The Blind Men,* 1936; the dramatization of a Breughel painting), *La Balade du Grand Macabre* (1935; whose hero, Death, is about to exterminate a town), *Le Singulier Trépas de Messire Ulenspiegel* (originally in Flemish translation, *De Dood van Ulenspiegel,* 1937–38), *L'École des bouffons* (*School for Buffoons,* 1942; the victimization of whose monstrous title characters reveals modern social and political horrors), *Le Soleil se couche* (1942, on the last days of Charles V), and the miracle play *Marie la misérable* (1952).

Michel de Ghelderode. (*Belgian Government Information Center*)

Most of these plays have been translated. The first of George Hauger's two volumes of collected translations (*Seven Plays,* 1960 and 1964) contains selections from *The Ostend Interviews* (1951), in which Ghelderode revealed much of his life and thought. David I. Grossvogel's *20th Century French Drama* (1961; originally *The Self-Conscious Stage in Modern French Drama,* 1958) contains an extensive bibliography and analysis of Ghelderode's works. Samuel Draper's collected translation of Ghelderode's *The Strange Rider and Seven Other Plays* (1964) has a bibliography and a Ghelderode chronology.

GHÉON, Henri [born Henri Léon Vangeon] (1875–1944), French dramatist, wrote over one hundred plays as well as novels and poetry. His plays are simple and in lyrical prose, and they dramatize Catholic themes. They were intended to make religious drama popular, as it had been in the Middle Ages. Therefore Ghéon wrote not for the commercial theatre but for the masses—and for young people. Successful especially with amateur and school groups, his religious plays are less impressive than those of PAUL CLAUDEL.

JACQUES COPEAU admired them and produced some at the Vieux-Colombier—notably *Le Pauvre sous l'escalier* (1921): considered his best work, it is a typical mixture of comedy and tragedy; it dramatizes the story of Saint Alexis, the fourth-century Roman who disappeared on his wedding night to spend the rest of his life in humility to expiate mankind's sins.

Ghéon wrote a number of other notable plays. *L'Histoire du jeune Bernard de Menthon* (1925, which was lavishly produced as *The Marvelous History of St. Bernard* at the 1926 Malvern Festival) is a dramatization of the *Acta Sanctorum* tale of Saint Bernard de Menthon's defeat of the Devil and the Deadly Sins who kill passing pilgrims. In *Le Comédien et la grâce* (1925, translated as *The Comedian*) a bored old third-century emperor, Diocletian, orders his playwright to prepare a drama on a Christian martyr, who is then portrayed by the emperor's favorite but reluctant actor—the actor himself ultimately becoming a Christian martyr. *La Vie profonde de Saint-François* (1926), translated as *The Marriage of St. Francis,* is another religious drama that was successfully produced. *Le Noël sur la place* (*Christmas in the Market Place,* 1935) is a religious show very popular with amateur provincial troupes. This and Ghéon's other medieval mystery and miracle plays were often produced in cathedrals by Les Compagnons de Notre-Dame, a troupe he founded in 1925.

Many of Ghéon's plays were never published, and relatively few are available in English. *The Comedian, The Marriage of St. Francis,* and *The Marvelous History of St. Bernard* were collected in *Three Plays* (1937), translated by Alan Bland et al. Other translated collections are *St. Anne and The Gouty Rector, and Other Plays* (1950) and *Secrets of the Saints* (1944), consisting of four saint plays. Ghéon's theories on drama and the theatre were translated as *The Art of the Theatre* (1961). Joseph Chiari's *The Contemporary French Theatre* (1958) has a chapter on Ghéon and a short bibliography. Other studies of Ghéon with bibliographies appear in *Drama Critique,* IX:3 (Fall 1966).

GHOST SONATA, THE (*Spöksonaten*), a play in three scenes by AUGUST STRINDBERG, published in 1907 and produced in 1908. Setting: contemporary Stockholm.

The best (and best-known) of THE CHAMBER PLAYS, of which it is Opus III, this play is considered by many critics to be a masterpiece. Despite its complexity, the play, with its mixture of macabre NATURALISM and EXPRESSIONISTIC fantasy, exerts an immediate and powerful grip over audiences and readers.

Scene 1. On the street, a student (Arkenholtz) asks a milkmaid for water and tells her of his rescue work at a collapsed house. A sinister old man in a wheelchair—Jacob Hummel—cannot see the milkmaid, a specter (it later turns out) visible to the Student only because he is a "Sunday child." Hummel shows the Student a newspaper story and photograph of the latter's heroism at the rescue. He also recognizes him as the son of a man Hummel claims to have helped long ago. Now he asks the Student to attend that night's performance of *Die Walküre* so that he can meet a colonel and his daughter (the Young Lady) who live in the adjoining house. Hummel tells the Student about other tenants in that house, including the Colonel's wife, "a mummy worshiping her own statute"; an old woman, once Hummel's fiancée; and a Lady in Black, who is the Superintendent's putative daughter and who mourns her natural father, the Consul who lived upstairs and has just died. When Hummel grasps him with his withering hand, the Student tries to extricate himself: "You are drawing all my strength from me—you're freezing me to death!" The Colonel's daughter enters the house and, seeing her, the Student immediately falls in love. Calling it a "devil's bargain," he agrees to accept Hummel's help to win the Young Lady. The dead Consul appears in a winding sheet and surveys the mourning arrangements made for him. Though Hummel's servant tells the Student that his master, once reputed a Don Juan, has a diabolic hold over people, the Student decides to stay and go to the opera as requested. The milkmaid reappears and stares at Hummel, who (apparently seeing her this time) becomes terrified.

Scene 2. Inside the house a few evenings later, in the Colonel's salon, Hummel arrives uninvited. Coming out of the closet where she has sat and clucked parrotlike for decades, the Mummy (the Colonel's wife) first startles Hummel. Their talk soon reveals that Hummel, in revenge for the seduction of his fiancée, cuckolded the Colonel and is himself the Young Lady's father. To further his vengeance he plans to make the Student his heir and have him marry the Young Lady. The Mummy talks of the supper soon to begin and of the various guests: the tenants, who are all mutually bound in old guilt and crimes. Having bought up the Colonel's obligations, Hummel now strips him of all his belongings, false titles, and claims. The ghost supper takes place while the Student talks with the Young Lady in her Hyacinth Room. Amidst pointed silences, Hummel makes a speech. He discusses the guilty secrets, including his paternity of and plans for the delicate Young Lady, who is "withering away because of the air in this house, which reeks of crime, deception, and falseness of every kind." As he threatens and prepares to expose and punish each of the ghostly visitors, the Mummy suddenly intervenes. She denounces Hummel as the first sinner, a "stealer of souls" and a murderer. He collapses when he is branded as the vampirelike ex-servant who let his masters starve, ruined the Student's father, murdered the Consul, and drowned a milkmaid who had discovered one of his crimes. Hypnotizing him, the Mummy makes him turn over all incriminating papers, cluck like a bird, and finally go to her closet and hang himself. A death screen is put before the door, the Young Lady plays the harp, and the Student paraphrases verses of "The

Song of the Sun" from the *Elder Edda:* "Man reaps as he sows."

Scene 3. A few days later in the Young Lady's bizarre room, which is decorated with a Buddha and myriads of hyacinths, the Young Lady makes the courting Student rhapsodize over the flowers. When he talks of marriage, the bloated Cook appears. She extracts the nourishment from her employers' food and is starving them ("You suck the sap from us, and we from you," she explains). Now the Young Lady changes. Her lassitude increases at the very thought of "the drudgery of keeping oneself above the dirt of life. . . . Imagine, if on top of it all one had a nursery and a baby crib!" Rejecting marriage, she asks, "Is life really worth so much trouble?" The Student bitterly tells her of the behind-the-scenes squalor and his disillusionment with Hummel and his funeral, and then recalls a dinner party at which his father (as Hummel had intended to do at the ghost dinner) told his guests the truth about themselves, after which he was committed. Now totally disenchanted to discover the rottenness beneath the façade of the house he once thought was paradise, the Student talks himself into something like a frenzy. He begs her to continue the idyll interrupted by the Cook: "Try just once again to pluck fire and brightness from the golden harp." But the harp is silent. "Why would you not become my bride?" he asks and suddenly perceives the reason: "Because you are sick, infected at the very core of life—Now I can see that vampire in the kitchen begin to suck the blood from me." He feels impelled to continue his tirade, and the Young Lady collapses. Her strength drains away and she rings for the death screen. The Student prays to the Buddha, the harp begins to play, and light pours into the room as he repeats the verses from "The Song of the Sun." A death moan comes from behind the screen, and he bids the Young Lady farewell: "Child of this world of illusion and guilt and suffering and death—this world of eternal change, disappointment, and pain! May the Lord of Heaven have mercy on you as you journey forth." As the room vanishes, a vision of beauty—Arnold Böcklin's "Isle of the Dead" painting—appears, with music "soft, sweet, and melancholy."

GHOSTS (*Gengangere*), a domestic drama in three acts by HENRIK IBSEN, published in 1881 and produced in 1882. Setting: a Norwegian country estate, late nineteenth century.

This major Ibsen play launched Germany's and England's important experimental art theatres: Otto Brahm's Die Freie Bühne in 1889, and J. T. Grein's Independent Theatre in 1891. Despite its WELL-MADE PLAY trappings, *Ghosts* is an intense and austere tragedy of fate, a classic Greek drama in nineteenth-century dress. The Darwinian and NATURALISTIC representation of Nemesis—particularly Oswald's congenital syphilis and the sympathetic allusions to such other taboos as incest and euthanasia—shocked even Ibsen's liberal contemporaries, and the play was viciously attacked everywhere. An answer to critics of his A DOLL'S HOUSE, it portrays a wife who *did* remain with her worthless husband and it dramatizes the answer Nora had left home to find: society's ideals are a harmful, rotten façade. The failure of this wife, Mrs. Alving, to defy convention is immoral; her conventional ideals and her loveless marriage become retributive "ghosts" as much as do the profligacy and disease of her late husband.

Act I. Regine Engstrand, Mrs. Alving's maid, refuses to accompany her rascally old father, the carpenter Jacob Engstrand, and become a hostess in the "sailors' hotel" he wants to open. The local pastor, Manders, arrives. Unctuously he tells Regine that it is her duty as a daughter to go with the alcoholic Engstrand, but she prefers finding a position in some wealthy gentleman's house in town. Manders has come to discuss with Helene Alving the orphanage she has just built in memory of her late husband. He persuades her that it should not be insured against fire: influential people might think that they lack "proper faith in Divine Providence," and be offended. Mrs. Alving rejoices at the recent return of her son Oswald, an artist, who startles Manders with his amazing resemblance to the late Alving—which Mrs. Alving denies. Oswald, who was brought up away from home, has but one memory of the father Mrs. Alving had taught him to idealize: a painful trick he played on him when Oswald was a child. Manders is scandalized when he hears of the "illicit"—though decent—family lives of Oswald's Parisian friends who cannot afford marriage, and he is shocked to find Mrs. Alving agreeing with the unconventional views of her son after Oswald has gone out. As they talk, Mrs. Alving's past begins to unfold. Her marriage of convenience to the wealthy Lieutenant (later Captain and Chamberlain) Alving had been arranged by her mother and aunts. Soon she discovered and then could not stand his dissipation, and ran away to seek refuge with Manders. He still insists that she had to bear her cross with humility and not cause a scandal, and congratulates himself for having had the strength to lead her "back into the path of duty." (Manders's act of "strength" she later calls "a crime against us both.") Mrs. Alving soon reveals the truth to Manders: her husband had remained dissolute until his death, which was caused by his debauchery. When he got her maid with child, Mrs. Alving took over the management of the estate; to shield Oswald and keep up appearances, she sent her son away from the poisoned home atmosphere. Bitterly she remembers overhearing her maid's remonstrates at Alving's first advances. Now she is terrified to hear, after a scuffle in the adjoining room, Regine's almost identical remonstrances against Oswald's advances. Revealing that Regine is the maid's daughter (and therefore Oswald's half-sister), Mrs. Alving cries out, "Ghosts! Those two in the conservatory . . . come back to haunt us."

Act II. The same evening, Manders is scandalized by Mrs. Alving's revelation that Engstrand had married "a fallen woman" (as Manders refers to the maid) for three hundred dollars; he cannot understand Mrs. Alving's likening it to her own marriage to "a fallen man" (as she refers to Alving) for a comfortable fortune. Mrs. Alving deplores her lifelong cowardice in adhering to ideals of "law and order," and outrages Manders by suggesting that she tell Oswald the unvarnished truth about his father. "Don't you feel your mother's heart prompting you not to shatter your son's ideals?" he insists. "But what about the truth?" asks Mrs. Alving; we are haunted by ideals (lies), ghosts of "all kinds of old defunct theories, all sorts of old defunct beliefs ... we cannot get rid of. ... And here we are, all of us, abysmally afraid of the light." Engstrand now appears, and with his hypocritical cant quickly bamboozles Manders into commending him for having married Regine's mother. As twilight falls over the mist-laden landscape, Oswald becomes bored, restless, and totally unable to work. He tells his horrified mother that he suffers from a disease that his doctor has pronounced congenital, though from what Oswald knows of his father he cannot, of course, credit that. Increasingly depressed by the eternal cloudiness and rain, he insists that his only salvation is Regine, who is "full of the joy of life." Mrs. Alving is ready to agree even to such a marriage, if it will make him happy and if he still wants it after learning of her true parentage. She is about to reveal it when they are interrupted by shouts of fire. "A flaming judgment on this house of iniquity," Manders declares as all hasten out to the burning orphanage, and then he clasps his hands desperately: "And not insured!"

Act III. It is still night, and the orphanage has burned to the ground. Though Engstrand is responsible for the fire, he blames Manders, assures him that that is what others will believe, and then sanctimoniously offers to avert the scandal Manders fears: "It's not the first time somebody I know has taken the blame for somebody else." Just as he took Regine's pregnant mother, so he agrees to take the blame for the fire—in return for the self-righteous Manders's support of the "sailors' hotel." Mrs. Alving reveals to Oswald his father's past debauches, his disease, and the paternity of Regine. When she learns of this paternity, Regine is indignant at her servant upbringing. Declaring that she has inherited Alving's "joy of life" (Manders's euphemism for Alving's debauchery), she walks out on Oswald: "No, you don't catch me staying out here in the country, working myself to death looking after invalids." Mrs. Alving promises the despondent Oswald that the sun will rise soon. He tells her that his brain has been affected by the disease. Preparing for his next, probably fatal, attack, Oswald has obtained lethal pills. He makes his mother promise to administer them to him before his suffering should begin. Suddenly the attack is upon him. As he dully and tonelessly begs for the sun, Mrs. Alving, pills in hand, shrinks back and screams in horror: "No, no, no! ... Yes! ... No, no!" (Asked whether, after the curtain, Mrs. Alving will give her son the lethal pills, Ibsen replied, "I should never dream of deciding such a difficult question. Now, what do *you* think?")

GIACOSA, Giuseppe (1847–1906), Italian playwright, was a practitioner of VERISM. Despite his considerable popularity in the theatre of his age, he is remembered now principally as the colibrettist of such Giacomo Puccini operas as *La Bohème* (1896), *Tosca* (1899), and *Madama Butterfly* (1903). Born in industrialized northern Italy, Giacosa was originally a lawyer. But he soon was able to abandon his legal career with the success of his one-act *Una partita a scacchi* (1872; translated as *The Wager*), a medieval tale about a chess game in which a young page stakes his life against a night with the daughter of the house. The most successful of Giacosa's nearly thirty plays were *Il fratello d'armi* (1877), a romantic drama; *Tristi amori* (*Unhappy Love,* 1887), a drama of adultery and its agonizing consequences; *La Signora di Challant* (*The Lady of Challant,* 1891), a tragedy whose title character (played by Eleanora Duse as well as Sarah Bernhardt) seeks fulfillment with a series of lovers, the last of whom alone proves worthy; *Diritti dell'anima* (1894), "the rights of the soul" violated being those of a faithful wife whose husband's relentless probings precipitate disaster; *Come le foglie* (*As the Leaves,* 1900), depicting a family scattered by adversity into the gutter, "like fallen leaves"; and *Il più forte* (1904), which portrays the conflict between an unscrupulous businessman and his artist son. Some of these were popular comedies but most deal with social and family problems while illustrating the proverbs alluded to in their titles.

Giacosa's dramaturgy has been praised for its psychological insight, language, restraint, and humor. A brief study of his work appears in the second volume of Joseph S. Kennard's *The Italian Theatre* (1932).

GIBSON, William (1914–   ), American playwright, started his career as a novelist. His first success on the Broadway stage came in 1958 with *Two for the Seesaw,* a two-character play about a troubled Bronx girl and a married Nebraska lawyer whose affair with the girl gives him the strength to return to his wife. After an Off-Broadway fantasy, *Dinny and the Witches* (1959), Gibson came out with his greatest hit, *The Miracle Worker* (1959). A portrayal of Anne Sullivan's heroic struggles with the recalcitrant blind, deaf-mute child Helen Keller that culminated in understanding and paved the way for Miss Keller's later greatness, the play was criticized by some for its sentimentality and slickness. Gibson had originally (1957) written it as a television play, and later he prepared the script for the 1962 film. *A Cry of Players* (1968), the refurbished version of a play Gibson had written twenty years before, portrays the troubled life of young Shakespeare (identified only as "Will") with his older wife ("Anne") and ends with his joining a troupe of players and running off to London. Gibson also collaborated on the musical version of Odets's

GOLDEN BOY, and he gave a fascinating account of the pre-Broadway trials and tribulations of his first hit in *The Seesaw Log* (1959). He wrote an autobiography, *A Mass for the Dead* (1968).

GIDE, André (1869–1951), French novelist and one of the most influential authors to emerge between the two world wars, also wrote a number of plays. A SYMBOLIST early in his career and one of the founders of *La Nouvelle Revue française* in 1909, Gide exerted considerable power as a critic. Aside from novels like *L'Immoraliste* (*The Immoralist,* 1902), *La Symphonie pastorale* (*Symphony Pastorale,* 1919), and *Les Faux Monnayeurs* (*The Counterfeiters,* 1925), Gide wrote about his government and foreign service work. Some of the resulting books brought about reforms in French colonial administration. His political and social attitudes, including his defense of homosexuality (*Corydon,* 1924) and his renunciation of Communism (1936), made him enemies and deprived him of various honors. But at last, in 1947, he was awarded the Nobel Prize for literature.

Gide came of Cevennes Huguenot and Norman Catholic parentage, a mixture to which he attributed the agonizing contradictions in his feelings and thoughts. His father died when Gide was a child, and he was brought up by austere females. A delicate boy, Gide became very ill during his subsequent travels. He occupied various government posts in North Africa and in France before settling down to full-time writing. His works—the philosophical treatises as well as his novels and plays—reflect the influence of writers like Henri Bergson, Friedrich Nietzsche, and Fyodor Dostoevsky. Even more strongly they reflect Gide's soul, tormented by the contradictions that provide the themes of his novels and plays: God and the Devil, skepticism and fervor, mysticism and sensualism, freedom and authority, self-assertion and self-abnegation.

The most widely performed of Gide's stage works has been *Le Procès* (*The Trial,* 1947; produced in New York as *The Scapegoat*), a dramatization with the actor-director Jean-Louis Barrault (1910–   ) of Kafka's novel about a man's experience with bureaucracy; nightmare episodes portray him as he is kept ignorant about his supposed crime, sees others in similar predicaments, fails to secure his acquittal, denounces the court, is pronounced guilty, and finally submits to his execution "like a dog!"* Another notable dramatic work is Gide's modernization of Sophocles, *Oedipe* (*Oedipus,* 1930); this anticlerical version stresses Oedipus's rationalism and quest for individuality, juxtaposed with Tiresias's sternness, Jocasta's hypocrisy, and other attitudes depicted in contemporary guises.

* The novelist Franz Kafka (1883–1924) in 1916 wrote the fragment of a drama, *Der Gruftwächter (Guardian of the Tomb)*: a grotesque question-and-answer confrontation between a prince and a watchman, it was published in James M. Ritchie and Hugh F. Garten's *Seven Expressionist Plays: Kokoschka to Barlach* (1968).

Most of Gide's dramas are adaptations of classical plays and legends. *Philoctète ou le traité des trois morales* (*Philoctetes or The Treatise on Three Ethics,* 1898), a short three-character play based on Sophocles's version of the legend, portrays Philoctetes as a philosopher whose final submission is an *"acte gratuit"* that stems from a sense of man's innate virtue, Ulysses as an authoritarian antagonist representing the state's collective will, and Neoptolemus as an emotional young idealist; the play consists of many MAURICE MAETERLINCK-like silences—Act V, for instance, comprising only a single two-line speech.

Later Gide plays include *Le Roi Candaule* (*King Candaules,* 1899), a verse tragedy about the legend narrated by Herodotus and Plato, here a psychological study of the Lydian monarch who urges his courtier Gyges to observe the queen in her bedchamber, and then is slain by Gyges. One of Gide's earliest dramas was the biblical *Saül* (*Saul,* 1902; produced by JACQUES COPEAU in 1922), a study of the pathological degeneration of a Saul driven by the demon of his passion for David. Another biblical work is Gide's *Bethsabé* (*Bathsheba,* 1909), a verse play in which the lonely, old King David is attracted to but finally resists the temptation to possess the title character, who never appears in the play. As a result of a prolonged religious debate with PAUL CLAUDEL Gide reinterpreted the New Testament story of *Le Retour de l'enfant prodigue* (*The Return of the Prodigal,* 1907) to dramatize the problem of moral authority. Gide's *Perséphone* (*Persephone,* 1934), an opera libretto for which Igor Stravinsky composed the music, is based on Homer's narration of the classic legend.

Gide wrote two original but not very impressive plays, the one-act farce *Le Treizième Arbre* (1935) and *Robert ou l'Interêt général* (1945), a study of social conflict personified in a father-son crisis. Gide's 1914 translation of Tagore's THE POST OFFICE was produced in 1928 as *Amal et la lettre du roi.* Also produced were his translations of Shakespeare's *Antony and Cleopatra* (1920) and *Hamlet* (1946), the latter played by Barrault and responsible for launching the famous company founded in 1946 by the actor-producer and his wife, Madeleine Renaud. After an unsatisfactory stage version of *Les Caves du Vatican* (*The Vatican Swindle,* 1925) appeared in 1933, Gide himself dramatized his novel the same year. *The Immoralist* was adapted for the stage by Ruth (1912–   ) and Augustus Goetz (1901–57) in 1954.

Most of Gide's works are readily available in English. Jackson Mathews's translations, *My Theater* (1952), consists of five plays (*Saul, Bathsheba, Philoctetes, King Candaules,* and *Persephone*) and an essay on "The Evolution of the Theater." Gide's lifelong record, *Journal* (1889–1949), provides the best account of his life and work, though many volumes in various languages have been written on the subject: the bibliography of Wallace Fowlie's *André Gide: His Life and Art* (1965) notes eight books in English. Some of these as well as Gide's own works are listed in the bibliography of James C. McLaren's book-length study of his drama, *The Theatre of André Gide* (1953).

GIDEON, a play in two acts by PADDY CHAYEFSKY, produced in 1961 and published in 1962. Setting: biblical Palestine, 1100 B.C.

Like MacLeish's J.B., this play modernizes an Old Testament tale and traditional religious beliefs.

God, appearing in the form of an angel, tries to use the oafish peasant Gideon as His messenger on earth, and raises him to leadership in the Israelites' victory over the Midianites. Gideon eventually rejects His demand for blind obedience. "I shall betray you many times," he tells God: "I do not love you, Lord." For Gideon has discovered that "I must believe in my own self" and in man, and explains his victories as resulting from causes that are "historical, economic, sociopsychological, and cultural." "God no more believes it odd / That man cannot believe in God," the angel concludes laughingly. "Man believes the best he can, / Which means, it seems, belief in man" as a god. He bows to the audience: "Well, let him try it anyway. / With this conceit, we end the play."

GIEROW, Karl Ragnar Kunt (1904–   ), Swedish poet, dramatist, and theatre director, was once likened to T. S. ELIOT and MAXWELL ANDERSON for his attempts to revitalize poetic drama. The results are plays like *Rovdjuret* (1941), a somewhat ponderously philosophical blank-verse personification of good and evil, laden with symbolism and grisly in its depiction of medieval cruelty. Gierow has also written lighter works, such as the comic satire *Av hjärtans lust* (1945) and *Cembalo* (1961).

Dr. Gierow was a product of the academic community at Lund, whence came other distinguished Swedish poets as well as essayists and novelists. His most important theatrical feat came while he was the director of Sweden's Royal Dramatic Theatre (1951–63): he prepared the uncompleted manuscript and extant notes of EUGENE O'NEILL for the production of MORE STATELY MANSIONS, and in 1962 gave the play its world premiere in the same theatre in which other O'Neill plays had been first produced.

GILBERT, Sir **W[illiam] S[chwen(c)k]** (1836–1911), English playwright, authored a number of once-popular dramas that have been long forgotten. But his name was immortalized with the comic operas he wrote with the composer Sir Arthur Sullivan. Before he began his association with Sullivan in 1871, Gilbert had made something of a reputation for himself with the comic verses subsequently published as *Bab Ballads* (1869) and with several dramatic sketches and plays. His first dramatic work, written at the suggestion of the playwright Thomas William Robertson, was *Dulcamara* (1866), a successful burlesque. It was followed by *The Palace of Truth* (1870), a fairy

Gilbert and Sullivan's *The Mikado,* Act II finale. The D'Oyly Carte Company; London, 1964. (*Houston Rogers*)

comedy in blank verse. Next came his "mythological comedy" *Pygmalion and Galatea* (1871), a frequently performed but artificial dramatization of the famous legend. Other Gilbert plays include *Sweethearts* (1874), *Tom Cobb* and *Broken Hearts* (both 1875), *Dan'l Druce* (1876, inspired by George Eliot's novel *Silas Marner*), *Charity* and *Engaged* (both 1877), *Gretchen* (1879, a poetic drama), and minor sketches like *Rosenkrantz and Guildenstern* (1891), a burlesque of *Hamlet*. Though frothy, these plays are clever, amusing, and sentimental, and some of them enjoyed considerable if short-lived popularity.

Gilbert was born in London, the son of a novelist. After obtaining a B.A. from the University of London (1856) he joined the civil service; then he studied and briefly practiced law. Over the signature of "Bab," he contributed verses to the comic journal *Fun* when it was founded in 1861.

In the fall of 1871 he started his momentous and later tempestuous collaboration with Sullivan, which lasted twenty-five years. It began with *Thespis; or, The Gods Grown Old* (1871) and *Trial by Jury* (1875), a spoof on a breach-of-promise suit, and their first joint success. The most popular of their works was *The Mikado; or, The Town of Titipu* (1885), a satire of England set in a storybook Japan. Other perennial hits are *The Sorcerer* (1877), their first operetta produced by Richard D'Oyly Carte, depicting a couple who so rejoice in romance that they employ a sorcerer to spread love around—which creates some ludicrous matches; *H.M.S. Pinafore; or, The Lass That Loved a Sailor* (1878), the immensely popular burlesque of nautical melodrama and politics by which Queen Victoria was "not amused"; *The Pirates of Penzance; or, The Slave of Duty* (1879), whose hero, born on Feburary 29 (leap year), is apprenticed to pirates until his twenty-first birthday—for sixty-two more years; *Patience; or, Bunthorne's Bride* (1881), the satire of OSCAR WILDE and the aesthetes of the age; *Iolanthe; or, The Peer and the Peri* (1882), a fairy play and a satire of politics and law; and *The Gondoliers; or, The King of Barataria* (1889), Gilbert and Sullivan's last successful collaboration, which ended—after a separation caused by financial quarrels—with the now-forgotten *The Grand Duke; or, The Statutory Duel* (1896).

Their Savoy operas (produced at the Savoy Theatre) were their most famous works, though both men collaborated with others. Gilbert, whose knighthood was deferred because Queen Victoria took umbrage at his spoofing, was noted for his autocratic and waspish temperament. A century later, however, his brilliantly clever librettos still delight audiences all over the world. He died by drowning, on his estate, while trying to rescue a lady. *The Hooligan,* his last play, was produced shortly before his death.

Gilbert's dramatic works were collected in *Original Plays* (four series, 1876–1911). The comic operas have been frequently republished. Comprehensive recent books about them are Raymond Mander and Joe Mitchenson's *A Pictorial History of Gilbert and Sullivan* (1962) and Frank L. Moore's *The Handbook of Gilbert and Sullivan* (1962). For biographical, critical, and bibliographical accounts of Gilbert, see also Townley Searle's *Sir William Schwenck Gilbert* (1931) and Hesketh Pearson's *Gilbert, His Life and Strife* (1957).

GILLETTE, William (1855–1937), American actor and dramatist, wrote over a dozen plays and a number of adaptations. Born in Connecticut and the son of a United States Senator, Gillette was a studious actor and writer, attending the College of the City of New York while playing at the New York Park Theatre, and Harvard and Boston universities as well as the Massachusetts Institute of Technology when in Boston. His dramatization of a story by Frances Hodgson Burnett (the author of *Little Lord Fauntleroy*) as *Esmeralda* in 1881 became very popular, but Gillette's great acting vehicle was his adaptation of Sir Arthur Conan Doyle stories, *Sherlock Holmes* (1899). Gillette revived both these plays throughout his career. Gillette also wrote the best nineteenth-century Civil War plays aside from BRONSON HOWARD's *Shenandoah: Held by the Enemy* (1886) and *Secret Service* (1895), two melodramas that celebrate the gallant heroism of espionage agents. The roles were dashingly acted by Gillette himself, who also starred in Shakespearean and other plays.

GILROY, Frank D. (1925–), American playwright, became prominent with *The Subject Was Roses* (1964), a Pulitzer Prize-winning drama about a returning World War II soldier's troubled relations with his Irish-American parents in the Bronx. Gilroy's first play, on a similar theme, was *Who'll Save the Plowboy?* (1962), an Off-Broadway success that won the Obie Award as the best American play of the year. Gilroy's *That Summer* (1967), a modernized version of the Hippolytus-Phaedra story set in New York, failed. It was followed by a frothy sex comedy, *The Only Game in Town* (1968).

Gilroy was born in the Bronx and served in the infantry during World War II. He attended Dartmouth College and the Yale Drama School.

GIOCONDA, LA,* a play in four acts by GABRIELE D'ANNUNZIO, published and produced in 1899. Setting: Florence and the Pisa coast "at the present time."

Dedicated to "Eleonora Duse of the beautiful hands," this popular romantic triangle play focuses on Silvia, the wife of the sculptor Lucio Settala—an autobiographically conceived Nietzschean genius torn between the love of Silvia and the inspirational passion for his model, Gioconda Dianti. The play was highly praised by the French statesman Léon Blum for its musical and other qualities.

Silvia rejoices at the apparent recovery of Lucio

* Not to be confused with Ponchielli's 1876 opera by the same name, which is based on Victor Hugo's play about seventeenth-century Venice, *Angelo* (1835).

who attempted to commit suicide for the love of Gioconda. Though her tender forgiveness and Lucio's repentance seem to reunite the couple, Lucio soon confesses to a friend that life with the devoted Silvia is deadly to him as an artist. Gioconda, on the other hand, "is always varied. . . . Every motion of her body destroys one harmony and creates another even more beáutiful." Even as Silvia nurtured his body back to life, so Gioconda nourished the clay of his sculpture during his absence. Lucio justifies his continuing passion by his genius. "Goodness! Do you think that light and life are likely to come to me out of goodness?" he cries out: "I am no longer under law, I am beyond Good and Evil." In a confrontation between the women, Silvia, desperate after being taunted by the mistress, finally lies: "Lucio has lost the memory of what has been" and no longer loves his model. Gioconda furiously cries out, "Tell him I take with me all that was his—power, joy, life," and she goes behind the curtains to smash Lucio's masterpiece, for which she had posed. Silvia runs after her, shrieks, and comes out fainting, her hands crushed by the statue she strove to protect: "It . . . is safe!" Nonetheless Lucio leaves her and follows Gioconda. The couple's little daughter returns to her crippled mother and a fairylike servant, and all weep at Silvia's pain.

GIONO, Jean (1895–1970), French novelist, was also a minor playwright. He became internationally famous because of the films based on his stories, particularly *La Femme du boulanger* (*The Baker's Wife,* 1935), screened in 1938. The immense success of Giono's fiction was not equaled in his plays, some of which are dramatizations of his novels. Poetic in mood, these include *Le Lanceur des grains* (1932), which contrasts lovers with exploiters of nature; and *Le Bout de la route* (*The End of the Road,* 1941), a poignant but simple romance about a stranger in a village.

Giono was born and died in the small village of Manosque in Provence, which provides the setting for his works. A pacifist who was not particularly interested in social problems, Giono was concerned with individualism and he opposed everything that hampers it. Because of his views he was ignored in literary circles after World War II, and it was not until 1954 that he became a member of the Goncourt Academy. See Maxwell A. Smith's *Jean Giono* (1966) and W. D. Redfern's *The Private World of Jean Giono* (1967).

GIRAUDOUX, [Hippolyte-] **Jean** (1882–1944), French novelist and playwright, was by profession a diplomat. He eventually became the foreign ministry's press chief and, when World War II broke out, Minister of Information (propaganda). Giraudoux achieved success as a writer as early as 1909 with *Provinciales,* a collection of short stories. This book was followed by volume after volume of sophisticated fiction. Though he was to become the most famous French dramatist of the first half of the century, it was not until he was in his late forties that he began to write plays.

The son of a civil servant, Giraudoux was born in Bellac, a small town in south-central France. He became interested in German literature, which he studied at the Sorbonne, and upon winning a scholarship he continued his schooling in Munich (1905–06). After extensive travel, including a year in the United States as a Harvard exchange student, Giraudoux became a journalist in 1908. At the same time he started writing his stories and novels, a successful avocation which he continued after his appointment to the consular service in 1910. Assignments in Germany provided material for his novels. These reflect Giraudoux's growing concern with Franco-German relations and his indictment of a new Germany that he felt was betraying its greatness and heading for disaster. Such subjects, among others, permeate a novel that long preoccupied him, *Siegfried et le Limousin* (1922). His dramatization of that novel into SIEGFRIED (1928), his first play, brought about his collaboration with the famous actor-director Louis Jouvet, and it immediately established Giraudoux's reputation as a dramatist. Jouvet's part in Giraudoux's career was of great importance. As producer for all but the last, posthumous play, Jouvet also starred in most of them, providing the dramatist with invaluable practical advice and the constant stimulus of a first-rate theatre company eager to perform his work.

Giraudoux's stature as a playwright increased with his popular second drama, AMPHITRYON 38 (1929); it declined briefly with his biblical tragedy JUDITH (1931); it grew with INTERMEZZO (1933) and with *Tessa* (1934), his adaptation of Kennedy and Dean's THE CONSTANT NYMPH, and with one of his best-known works, *La Guerre de Troie n'aura pas lieu* (THE TROJAN WAR WILL NOT TAKE PLACE, 1935; translated by CHRISTOPHER FRY as *Tiger at the Gates*). For this last work he wrote two curtain raisers: *Supplément au voyage de Cook* (*Supplement to Captain Cook's Voyage,* 1935; also translated as *The Virtuous Island*) is a satire that depicts a zealous English deacon and his wife amazing uninhibited Tahitian natives with Christian morality; for the 1937 revival of the Trojan play, Giraudoux wrote *L'Impromptu de Paris* (*The Impromptu of Paris*), a sketch inspired by Molière, in which Giraudoux's views of the theatre are amusingly dramatized in the guise of a government representative's discussions with the rehearsing troupe, including Jouvet. Another Giraudoux curtain raiser is *Cantique des Cantiques* (*Song of Songs,* 1938), a modernization of the story of King Solomon in which a distinguished minister's Sulamite leaves him for her oafish but more youthful lover.

One of Giraudoux's most charming works, ONDINE (1939), was produced shortly before the outbreak of World War II. Earlier, in *Electre* (ELECTRA, 1937), the playwright had once more turned to an oft-dramatized Greek myth, and again he gave it a characteristic modern twist; its resolution anticipates that of Giraudoux's last biblical play, *Sodome et Gomorrhe* (SODOM AND GOMORRAH, 1943), which reflects the European holocaust during which it was written. His modern one-act farce, *L'Apollon de Bellac* (*The Apollo of Bellac*), set in his native town and first produced in Argentina in 1942 as *L'Apollon de Marsac,* depicts a girl's learning to overcome shyness by employing flattery as her formula for success. During the war Giraudoux also wrote two films: *La Duchesse de Langeais* (*The Duchess of Langeais,* 1942), a free adaptation of Balzac's novella; and *Les Anges du péché* (*The Angels of Sin,* 1943), a stark melodrama set in the Béthanie convent. Giraudoux's finest play, *La Folle de Chaillot* (THE MADWOMAN OF CHAILLOT, 1945), was produced posthumously. It was the last of his plays to be presented by Jouvet and the troupe that they had worked with for so long. The second posthumously produced work, *Pour Lucrèce* (DUEL OF ANGELS, 1953), was translated by Fry and produced by Jean-Louis Barrault.

Giraudoux's plays, often based on myth and legend, are usually witty and enchanting. Their popularity was abetted by a reaction to the NATURALIST social drama and the derivative melodramas and farces that constituted most of the French drama written in the first three decades of the century. Giraudoux's drama, furthermore, is original and distinctive in style and particularly rich in such qualities as whimsy, cleverness, and charm. Like the plays of BERNARD SHAW, Giraudoux's works abound in verbal pyrotechnics. But they are not disquisitory, and fantasy has a part in all of them—often a decisive one. This is not to say, however, that his comedies are frivolous. A recurrent serious motif in Giraudoux's portrayal of human follies—and all his plays depict human folly—is the conflict between the absolute and the practical, the ideal and the real. In most of the early works, the ideal somehow prevails (as, for example, does the virtue of Amphitryon's wife, despite the god's doings). But in the later plays the dynamic ideal, usually represented by women (like Ondine), is more polarized, intransigent—and doomed.

Survived by his wife and son, Giraudoux died in Paris during the German occupation. Though he briefly served as director of historical monuments for the Vichy government, he was also engaged in resistance activities. He wrote his plays in what time he could spare from his official duties in the many government positions he held during his life.

Most of Giraudoux's plays are available in English translation. There is a book-length biography in English, Laurent LeSage's *Jean Giraudoux: His Life and Works* (1959); its last chapter is a survey of international scholarship and criticism. Extensive studies of the plays are Donald Inskip's *Jean Giraudoux: The Making of a Dramatist* (1958), Agnes G. Raymond's *Jean Giraudoux: The Theatre of Victory and Defeat* (1966), and Robert Cohen's *Giraudoux: Three Faces of Destiny* (1968); all these contain biographical sketches and bibliographies.

GIRL OF THE GOLDEN WEST, THE, a play in four acts by DAVID BELASCO, produced in 1905 and published in 1925. Setting: "the steep snow tipped Sierras" in California, 1849.

In this popular western romance Belasco dealt with what he knew at first hand, including the "traveling camp minstrel" who entertains the salon habitués. Almost immediately Giacomo Puccini chose the play for his *La fanciulla del west* (1910), the first grand opera on an American theme. Its Metropolitan Opera House production, with the greatest singers of the age (headed by Enrico Caruso) and with Arturo Toscanini conducting, was also directed by Belasco.

"The Girl" (Minnie) is an angelically pure, friendly, and heroic saloon keeper and schoolmistress for the rough miners, who adore her. She fends them all off, but falls in love with a gentleman stranger, at first not knowing that he is the bandit Dick Johnson, alias Ramerrez the road agent. Their idyllic love scene is ended by a blizzard that traps Johnson. The sheriff wounds the escaping outlaw, who seeks refuge in Minnie's cabin. She hides him in the loft and almost succeeds in fooling the sheriff. In the climactic scene, blood drips down on the sheriff from the loft, Johnson is discovered, and The Girl challenges the sheriff to a game of poker. "If you're lucky, you git him an' me; but if you lose, this man . . . is mine," she offers. "Hatin' the sight of you—it's the nearest chance you'll ever git for me." The sheriff, a born gambler and long smitten with The Girl, cannot resist: "You and the cards have got into my blood." In a tense game The Girl—though she has to cheat—wins, and the sheriff leaves. Later Johnson is captured and about to be hanged. But realizing how The Girl whom all of them adore and respect loves Johnson, the miners release him. Setting out for another part of the country, the lovers watch the rising sun. "Oh, my lovely West—my Sierras!—I'm leaving you!" The Girl cries, and then falls into Johnson's arms.

GIRL WITH THE GREEN EYES, THE, a play in four acts by CLYDE FITCH, produced in 1902 and published in 1905. Setting: New York and the Vatican, early twentieth century.

The title figure of this once-popular play personifies jealousy. Amusing minor characters provide comedy and satirize New York society and European tourism. Fitch provided a "happy ending" in deference to popular taste.

Even as she marries Jack Austin, Jinny displays the jealousy inherited from her parents. Both suffering from the same weakness, the parents understand each other; but Austin, who is never jealous, cannot sympathize with Jinny's outbursts. Jinny's jealousy is aroused as Austin tries to straighten out her brother's difficulties. "I want to be Brunhilde, and I'm only Frou Frou!" she admits every time Austin castigates her "green eyes" of jealousy. When Jinny finally perceives Austin's innocence it is too late. Disgusted with her jealousy, he leaves her. She turns on the gas and almost succeeds in committing suicide. In the nick of time Austin returns and saves her. "There's one thing stronger

The Girl of the Golden West as opera: Enrico Caruso (tenor) as the outlaw, Emmy Destinn (soprano) as The Girl, and Pasquale Amato (baritone) as the sheriff. The Metropolitan Opera in New York, 1910. (*Brown Brothers*)

even than jealousy," he says, "and that's LOVE!"

GLASPELL, Susan (1882–1948), American novelist and playwright born in Iowa, was one of the founders (with her husband, GEORGE CRAM COOK) of the Provincetown Players. From 1914, the year after they married, until 1922, when they left America shortly before "Jig's" death, the Cooks' lives were bound to that group, whose leading playwrights included Glaspell herself and EUGENE O'NEILL. Thus she was credited, too, with having been a founder of modern American drama, though she lacked O'Neill's sustaining genius for theatricality. Glaspell's gifts for portraying situation, dialogue, and—especially—ideas, however, are impressive, particularly in her finest works: unpretentious but effective sketches like SUPPRESSED DESIRES (1915) and TRIFLES (1916), and her most notable full-length work, the Pulitzer Prize-winning play about Emily Dickinson, ALISON'S HOUSE (1930).

Glaspell was successful with Provincetown audiences with her other one-acters. *The People* (1917), *Tickless Time* (1918, with Cook), and *Woman's Honor* (1918) are mixtures of the comic and serious, but *The Outside* (1917) is a wholly serious one-acter about a servant girl seeking self-realization. Glaspell's first full-length play, *Bernice* (1919), is a mood piece whose heroine—like other Glaspell heroines she never appears—reforms her husband by having a servant tell him after her death that she has committed suicide because of his philandering. Other full-length plays are *Inheritors* (1921), a drama of ideas set in a Midwestern college and exploring the American pioneer heritage; the once highly praised *The Verge* (1921), an idealistic SYMBOLIC tragedy about a sensitive woman on the verge of insanity; and *Chains of Dew* (1922), a serious comedy about a priggish poet and his self-sacrificing wife.

After her husband's death, Glaspell returned to Provincetown. She married the writer Norman H. Matson (1893–1965), who collaborated on her three-act comedy *The Comic Artist* (1927). Thereafter, as before the Provincetown period, she published many undistinguished Midwestern novels and short stories.

Glaspell's *Plays* (1920) includes *Bernice* and five one-acters; most of her other plays were published separately. She also wrote *The Road to the Temple* (1927), which is an autobiography, a biography of Cook, and an account of both the Provincetown Players and the Cooks' year-and-a-half stay in the ancient mountain village of Delphi, Greece. A book-length account of her life and work is Arthur E. Waterman's *Susan Glaspell* (1966); it includes a bibliography.

GLASS MENAGERIE, THE, a play in seven scenes by TENNESSEE WILLIAMS, produced in 1944 and published in 1945. Setting: an alley apartment in St. Louis, "Now and the Past."

Originally planned as a film script, *The Gentleman Caller,* this play became a hit in Chicago before its successful runs on Broadway (where it won the New York Drama Critics' Circle Award) and elsewhere in America and abroad. A wistful "memory play," it was Williams's first triumph. It is autobiographical and PRESENTATIONAL. The author, thinly disguised as the narrator Tom, dramatizes the loneliness and failures of the Williams' lives in the 1930's in vignettes whose emotion is heightened by suggestive music, lighting, and pantomime. (Another device, screens with legends, was omitted in production.) This is the least violent and most lyrical—and considered by some to be the best—of Williams's major plays.

Part I: Preparation for a Gentleman Caller. Scene 1. The rear wall of a tenement, flanked by alleys and fire escapes, is transparent and soon reveals the interior of an apartment. Tom Wingfield, dressed as a merchant sailor, enters. "I give you truth in the pleasant disguise of illusion," he tells the audience, describing the impending action and the characters: Amanda, his mother; Laura, his sister; and Jim O'Connor, a gentleman caller and "the most realistic character" in this "memory play." Then Tom points to a large photograph of his father, who long ago deserted the family. Amanda and Laura appear and Tom joins them in a pantomime dinner. "Honey, don't *push* with your *fingers,*" Amanda corrects Tom, and continues to instruct him until, exasperated, he stops eating. She also exhorts Laura to "stay fresh and pretty—for gentlemen callers!" Though Laura expects none, Amanda persists. "Sometimes they come when they are least expected," she remarks, and glowingly reminisces about her youth, when in a single day she received "*seventeen*—gentlemen callers!" Laura replies, "I'm just not popular like you were in Blue Mountain," and turns to the groaning Tom: "Mother's afraid I'm going to be an old maid." *Scene 2.* Laura is cleaning her collection of glass animals as Amanda appears melodramatically: "Deception? Deception?" She tears up Laura's typewriting and shorthand charts, for she has just learned that Laura, after getting sick to her stomach at a speed typing test six weeks earlier, had never returned to secretarial school. Unable to face the class again, Laura has taken walks during school hours. Weary and despairing, Amanda wonders what will happen to her daughter. When Amanda asks, "Haven't you ever liked some boy?" Laura talks of Jim, a high school hero she had a crush on. Amanda decides Laura must get married, but the girl fearfully alludes to her crippled leg. It is merely "a little defect—hardly noticeable," Amanda replies, urging her to develop "vivacity

The Glass Menagerie, Scene 6. Tom (Eddie Dowling) before the tenement wall (a painted scrim); behind it, Laura (Julie Haydon) and Amanda (Laurette Taylor). New York, 1945. (*George Krager* from "Pix")

—and—*charm!*" *Scene 3.* Tom tells the audience of Amanda's determination to get a gentleman caller for Laura. "To properly feather the nest and plume the bird," Amanda tries to sell magazine subscriptions over the telephone, but her prospect hangs up on her. Tom and Amanda quarrel about his reading, and he finally loses his temper. Tired of getting up every morning for his shoe-warehouse job to Amanda's cheerful "Rise and Shine!" Tom explodes: "You'll go up, up on a broomstick, over Blue Mountain with seventeen gentleman callers! You ugly—babbling old—*witch,*" and he accidentally breaks some of Laura's glass animals. The women and Tom himself are stunned by his outburst. *Scene 4.* At dawn, Tom returns half drunk. He tells Laura about all the movies he went to see. Amanda awakes, calling for Laura to "go tell your brother to rise and shine!" Laura begs Tom to apologize to their mother. When Tom finally does so, Amanda weeps: "My devotion has made me a witch." Soon she resumes her platitudinous exhortations. Tom objects: "Man is by instinct a lover, a hunter, a fighter, and none of those instincts are given much play at the warehouse." But Amanda replies, "Instinct is something that people have got away from! It belongs to animals! Christian adults don't want it!" She implores him not to leave them until Laura is married, and she wonders if there are eligible suitors at the warehouse. As Tom leaves, agreeing in exasperation to find out, Amanda returns to the telephone to hustle magazine subscriptions. *Scene 5.* Several evenings later, Tom watches a dance hall from the apartment's fire-escape landing. He tells Amanda he has invited a gentleman caller for tomorrow's supper. Immediately Amanda is full of questions, bustle, and plans. Though his friend is merely a shipping clerk, Amanda is undaunted by the prospect: "The future becomes the present, the present the past, and the past turns into everlasting regret if you don't plan for it!" Tom cautions her that the crippled Laura lives in a private world of glass animals and old, worn-out phonograph records: "Those things make her seem a little peculiar to people outside the house." He goes to the movies and Amanda, in a tearful, trembling voice, tells Laura to look at the moon and make a wish for "Happiness! Good fortune!"

Part II: The Gentleman Calls. Scene 6. "And so the following evening I brought Jim home to dinner," Tom begins, and describes Jim, an all-around high school hero who did not live up to his great promise. Amanda adjusts Laura's new dress and then, looking absurd in girlish clothes and carrying jonquils, excitedly relives the legend of her youth. Laura is terrified to learn the caller is the boy she liked in high school. She panics when the doorbell rings, but Jim does not remember her. Sitting on the fire escape, Jim tells Tom of his ambitions and suggests that "Shakespeare" (for Tom writes poems on shoeboxes) pay more attention to his work. But Tom dreams of leaving the hated business world for a life of adventure. Amanda appears, girlishly exuding Southern charm and fluttering and talking incessantly. Laura is too terrified to eat. "Standing over the hot stove made her ill," Amanda explains to Jim. She has Laura rest on the couch, and asks Tom to say the blessing. *Scene 7.* As dinner ends, the lights go out—for Tom has used the electricity money to pay his Merchant Seamen union bill. Amanda insists Tom help with the dishes, and tells Jim to go to Laura. He talks to her gently, and soon Laura reminds him of their high school acquaintance, when Jim used to call her Blue Roses because he mistook the name of her sickness, pleurosis. Laura recalls, too, his beautiful voice. Basking in her adoration though he feels himself to be a failure, Jim starts preening and, carefully disposing of his chewing gum, he lectures about her inferiority complex and urges her to be confident. Laura tells him of her glass menagerie, and Jim has her dance with him. Accidentally they break the horn off her glass unicorn, but Laura, elated for the first time, does not mind. "The horn was removed to make him feel less—freakish," she says: "Now he will feel more at home with the other horses." Jim kisses her, but immediately apologizes, for he is engaged and "not in a situation to—do the right thing." Totally crushed, Laura hands him the broken unicorn as a souvenir. When Amanda learns of his engagement, she too keeps up a brave front. But as soon as Jim is gone she berates Tom for the gaffe: "You live in a dream; you manufacture illusions!" Tom departs to the movies as Amanda angrily continues, "Go, then! Then go to the moon—you selfish dreamer!" During Tom's closing narration Amanda is seen in a dumb show, consoling Laura. Inaudible, Amanda no longer seems foolish; now "she has dignity and tragic beauty." Tom tells how he left home, traveling "to find in motion what was lost in space." But always he has remembered home. "Oh, Laura, Laura, I tried to leave you behind me, but I am more faithful than I intended to be!" And he concludes, "nowadays the world is lit by lightning! Blow out your candles, Laura—and so good-bye. . . ."

GLASS SLIPPER, THE (*Az üvegcipö*), a play in three acts by FERENC MOLNÁR, published and produced in 1923. Setting: an outlying district of Budapest during a summer in the 1920's.

Very reminiscent of Barrie's A KISS FOR CINDERELLA, this play, Molnár stated, was based on his early relationship with his last wife. It is one of his most popular bittersweet comedies.

Irma Szabó, a pathetic but pert young drudge in a boarding house, worships an elderly cabinetmaker there. "The brokenest blossom in all Budapest," as the extravagantly sentimental and romantic Irma calls herself, kisses his drinking glass, caresses his pillow, and lovingly touches the various objects of her "darling, angry one," who brusquely orders her about. But the landlady, a wicked shrew who really yearns for decency, is set on marrying the cabinetmaker, though she is unfaithful to him with a younger boarder who thus avoids paying the rent. The cabinetmaker ignores the warning of Irma, who gets drunk at his wedding. Then the heartbroken, lovesick girl enters a house of prostitution. "If I had jumped into the Danube and they had found my beautiful pale corpse in the morning, I wouldn't have been able to cry for myself anymore. This way I could always have cried for my pure love and young soul," she explains after she is picked up in a raid the very first night. Her purity immediately becomes self-evident in the police station, where she finally wins the heart of her Prince Charming, who has quickly become disenchanted with the landlady. As she leaves with him, Irma exuberantly recites the verse she composed during her unhappiness: "Faded flower of the Spring, / Beaten blossom in the rain, / All the leaves are whispering, / That my heart is full of pain."

GLEBOV, Anatoli Glebovich (1899–   ), Russian playwright, was also an active political organizer for the Soviets. This commitment is reflected in his twenty-odd plays, including *Rost* (1926), *Vlast* (1927), *Zoloto i mozg* (1929), and *Galstuk* (1930). Most notable among his dramas are *Zagmuk* (1925) and *Inga* (1929). The first deals with a subject dramatized in Lagerkvist's THE KING, and is set in the Babylon of the eighth century B.C., during the annual festival (*Zagmuk*) in which the slaves became the rulers for a week. Its depiction of the slaves' attempts to perpetuate their rule and overcome their cruel masters is typical of the many Soviet plays in which, notes Nikolai A. Gorchakov in his discussion of *Zagmuk* in *The Theater in Soviet Russia* (1957), "the heroes are condemned to death. Inevitably they break out in moving soliloquies: though we are condemned to death, our cause will not fail; in the future the Bolsheviks will come to complete our work." Glebov's other important play, *Inga*, had a long run in Moscow and in the 1930's was produced as *Frau in Front* in Erwin Piscator's "political theatre" in Berlin. Set in a clothing factory at the time of the first Five-Year Plan, *Inga* portrays women's conflicts and their problems of love, family, and daily living in a collective society; its theme, Glebov noted, is "The Soviet woman: the old in the new and the new in the old." The play was published in English, with an introductory note on Glebov's life and work, in Eugene Lyons's edition of *Six Soviet Plays* (1934).

GLITTERING GATE, THE, a one-act play by LORD DUNSANY, produced in 1909 and published in 1914. Setting: "a lonely place" at the "present" time.

Lord Dunsany's very short first play was written —reluctantly—in one afternoon, at the suggestion of WILLIAM BUTLER YEATS, for the Abbey Theatre. It has only two characters, dead burglars. Similar to this play are some of SAMUEL BECKETT's, especially his WAITING FOR GODOT.

A convict who has been hanged examines numberless empty beer bottles, while one who has been shot tries and finally succeeds in jimmying the heavenly gates. But beyond it are only "empty nights and stars." The shot criminal staggers: "Blooming great stars. There *ain't* no Heaven"; and the hanged one replies, "That's like them. That's very like them. Yes, they'd do that!" The curtain falls as the offstage laughter heard throughout the play "howls on."

GOAT SONG (*Bocksgesang*), a drama in five acts by FRANZ WERFEL, published in 1921 and produced in 1922. Setting: a Slavic countryside, 1790's.

Produced throughout Europe and in America (by the Theatre Guild), this eerie and part-EXPRESSIONIST play aroused considerable controversy with its SYMBOLISM. The title alludes to the origin of tragedy (the Greek *tragōidia* means "goat song") and the goat-footed god Dionysius—and more generally to primitive scapegoat ritual. Though he never appears on stage, the terrifying monster pervades the play. Elevated to sainthood, he embodies the human bestiality perpetuated in the resolution.

Act I. Stevan Milic, a gospodar (squire), arranges the marriage of his son Mirko to their wealthy neighbor's daughter, Stanja Veselic. The young couple are neither consulted nor much interested. Later Mirko's parents bemoan a secret shame: their firstborn, a goatlike monster they have kept hidden in a locked shed since his birth. Never again seen by them, he is cared for by the servant who suckled him. Their physician suggests that this "bio-anatomical-morphophysiological wonder" be institutionalized. They refuse, for his mother nonetheless loves him, and Stevan will not have his shameful secret revealed by registering the monster's patronym. For their peace of mind and for Mirko's sake, Stevan goes to shoot their abomination—but finds the shed unlocked and the monster escaped.

Act II. That same evening the landowners' council hears a delegation of destitute vagabonds and gypsies petition for help. Stevan, who is to preside at the council, comes late and is still preoccupied with the monster's escape. "Oh, you outcasts who call nothing your own, if you knew how happy you are," he tells the delegation, and chases them off. The landowners huddle in frightened confusion, convinced that the frenzied Stevan has become a madman.

Act III. Juvan, a student, incites the desperate vagabonds to plunder and kill the landowners. At an inn he meets Mirko and Stanja, to whom he is drawn, as she is to him. But they are enemies, and Juvan insults her. Mirko prepares to fight Juvan just as panic-stricken mobs report seeing a monster. Juvan, who knows of Stevan's secret, glories in his new power over the superstitious mobs, provided by the monster's appearance: "Now has the secret given itself into my hands."

Act IV. Juvan has had the caged monster placed behind the church's altar and has worked the idolatrous mob into frenzies of murder and arson. Drunk, they now demand to see the monster whom they believe to have been sent because of their sins and who has been appeased by murdering their fellows. As Juvan prepares the ghoulish exhibition ceremony, Mirko appears with Stanja and his parents. Stevan tries to bargain with Juvan, who, however, forces Stevan to acknowledge publicly that the monster is his son, and agrees to release him only if Stanja cuts his bonds and leads him out. Horrified, Mirko's parents urge her to flee, but the proud Stanja takes a knife and goes into the cage. Furious, Mirko attacks Juvan and is killed by a guard. Now Juvan tries to save Stanja but the frenzied chanting mobs hold him back. A wild cry is heard from behind the altar. There is a tremendous flash—and a gigantic shadow. The mob prostrate themselves: "We see him!"

Act V. The rebels have been driven off by soldiers, Juvan is to be executed, and the monster is reported dead. Though bereaved and poor, Stevan and his wife are strangely happy together now. They let Stanja stay with them, for the girl considers herself Mirko's widow and refuses to return to her home. On his way to the gallows, Juvan confesses his love to Stanja and tells her how it and her self-sacrifice in unfettering the monster have transformed Juvan's "lust for ruin" to a joyous appreciation of universal beauty. Reciprocating his love, Stanja offers to die with Juvan. But he insists she "live still in the world like light and like warmth," a part of himself—and goes to his execution. Later the hangman tells of the unsinged corpse of the monster found in the charred forest. His mother cries out her grief that there will be no trace of the secret of her womb. "You are wrong, Mother," Stanja replies with icy self-control. "I am carrying his child."

GOD, MAN, AND DEVIL (*Got, Mentsh un Tayvl*), a play in four acts and a prologue by JACOB GORDIN, published and produced in 1903. Setting: Heaven and the town of Dubrovna at the turn of the century.

Goat Song. Stanja (Lynn Fontanne, right) and Mirko's mother (Blanche Yurka). New York, 1926. (*Vandamm Photo, Theatre Collection, New York Public Library*).

This play, inspired by the Book of Job as well as by Goethe's *Faust,* has been hailed as Gordin's finest play, and was frequently revived.

The Devil wagers that he can win a pious soul. "Truth is eternal, eternal and one. The good and the beautiful are the truth," the angels chant. Then Satan, disguised as one Uriel Mazik, makes the poor scribe Hershele wealthy. He tempts Hershele to leave his wife for a younger woman and set up house with her, to found a prayer-shawl factory, and to exploit his neighbors. When he finally realizes his sins and the harm he has done, Hershele hangs himself with a shawl splattered with the blood of his friend's son, who died at the factory loom.

GOD OF VENGEANCE (*Got fun Nekome*), a play in three acts by SHOLEM ASCH, published and produced in 1907. Setting: a cellar brothel and the apartment above in a large Polish town, early 1900's.

Asch's best-known play has been compared to O'Neill's ANNA CHRISTIE and Shaw's MRS. WARREN'S PROFESSION. But Asch's is a tragedy of self-deception, of delusions destroyed by a God of Vengeance manifested in the retribution of worldly reality. The protagonist, a vulgar brothelkeeper, is also a self-sacrificing father who naïvely tries to separate his pious contrition and his daughter's purity from his business life. The play, frequently banned because of its setting and the portrayal of lesbianism, has been produced in many countries and languages. Asch reworked it for Rudolph Schildkraut's highly praised characterization—in German in Max Reinhardt productions, in English at New York's Provincetown Playhouse and on Broadway.

Act I. Yekel (Yankel) Chapchovich, the proprietor of the basement brothel, is eager to bring his pretty young daughter Rivkele up to be wholesome and pure. All admire Rivkele's virtue, the more amazing because of her surroundings. "Let the whole town know it. What I am, I am," Yekel says. Pointing to his wife, a former prostitute, he continues, "What she is, she is. It's all true, all of it. But they better not whisper a word against my child. If they do, I'll crack their skulls with this bottle." His wife rationalizes their respectability: "You're in business. Everybody is in business." But Yekel is very conscious of sinfulness, and he insists, "My home must be kept separate, do you hear, the way kosher food is kept separate from forbidden food." He points to the cellar: "Downstairs is a house, and up here lives a pure bride-to-be, you hear?" He attacks a procurer, the lover of one of his employees, who mentions Rivkele. Yekel prepares to purchase a Torah scroll. "We've already given our souls over to the devil," he tells the matchmaker and the scribe who is to copy it; "it's for her, Rebbe. I'll put the Holy Scroll in her room. Let her take care of it. As for us—we're forbidden to." Later, while her mother tells Rivkele from the adjoining room about her groom-to-be, one of the young prostitutes tiptoes in. Coquettishly the girls wink at each other, Rivkele falls into her arms, and the prostitute kisses her passionately.

Act II. In the large cellar room, with cubicles for the girls, the procurer quarrels with his prostitute. Then he persuades her to lure Rivkele to a rival house he intends to open. "The daughters of such mothers later become just like their mothers," one of the prostitutes remarks; "they're drawn to it." The girls discuss their lives and, when Rivkele sneaks down, they go out to play in the rain. Fondling her, Rivkele's prostitute gets Rivkele to run away with her to the new house: "You'll see how good it will be. Young men will come, officers. We'll be alone the entire day." When Yekel discovers Rivkele's disappearance, he is frantic. He drags his wife down by her hair: "Your daughter! Where is your daughter?"

Act III. His wife counsels Yekel to be calm, pay off the procurer, and thus get Rivkele back. But Yekel, who has prayed for his child before his Torah scroll, is inconsolable, though the marriage broker too urges common sense: "God helps. Troubles pass. The main thing is: nobody knows . . . you make believe nothing happened." But Yekel hears nothing. He attributes the tragedy to his sinful life, for sins pass "from generation to generation." He asks for a miracle, and when nothing happens, vents his fury on God: "You are vengeful! You are like a man!" His wife succeeds in buying Rivkele back from the procurer. "Are you still a chaste Jewish girl?" Yekel asks her. "I don't know," she replies, and then defiantly asks about her parents' life. The matchmaker brings in his clients, a father with his son, who is a rabbinical student ready to marry Rivkele. The distraught Yekel humiliates Rivkele and her mother before them, and then sends his daughter to the cellar, to become a prostitute. "Down to the house!" he shouts. And when they all leave, he tells the matchmaker, "Take the Torah scroll with you. I don't need it anymore!"

GODS OF THE LIGHTNING, a play in three acts by MAXWELL ANDERSON and Harold Hickerson, published and produced in 1928. Setting: "a city on the eastern seaboard in the 1920's."

This play was intensely topical in 1928: it is an anguished, indignant protest by Anderson and his neighbor Hickerson (1896–   ), a musician, against the 1927 execution of Sacco and Vanzetti in Massachusetts. Highly theatrical though completely one-sided in its dramatization of the very controversial case, it depicts the arrest and trial of two radicals, a gentle foreign anarchist and an idealistic I.W.W. organizer, Capraro and Macready. Though they are unquestionably innocent, "capitalist society" ruthlessly condemns them by use of blackmail and all possible legal chicanery. The sinister and cynical *raisonneur,* Suvorin, expresses the futility of their martyrdom and of the struggle against "class justice." Anderson's WINTERSET is a less propagandistic sequel to this play.

The restaurant owner Michael Suvorin pays and sends off his henchman, who has bungled a robbery by shooting the paymaster. Oblivious of this episode, Dante Capraro and James Macready are preoccupied with their unsuccessful strike activities when they are arrested, and then tried, for the murder. The prosecutor, aware of their innocence, blackmails witnesses; the presiding judge's rulings constantly assist the prosecutor's case; and the jury is out to "burn" the "red" agitators. When Suvorin unexpectedly proves their innocence with his confession, his testimony is thrown out because he is an escaped convict. Capraro and Macready are condemned. Later, Suvorin's daughter—Macready's fiancée—and their friends await the governor's pardon, but apprehensive tensions mount as the last minutes pass. One of the men whispers the news: Capraro and Macready have been electrocuted. At the curtain, Suvorin's daughter weeps: "Shout it! Cry out! Run and cry! Only—it won't do any good—now."

GOERING, Reinhard (1887–1936), German playwright, is memorable for his first work, *Seeschlacht* (*Naval Encounter,* 1917), an EXPRESSIONISTIC one-acter notably produced by Max Reinhardt in 1919. In choppy free-verse lines it dramatizes the differing memories, thoughts, and feelings of seven sailors doomed in their ship's armored turret during the Jutland battle (1916); it begins with a scream, traces the sailors' progressive awareness of and preparation for death (". . . O dear Fatherland! / We are swine / Waiting for the butcher . . ."), and ends when even their notions of possible mutiny are crushed. *Scapa Flow* (1919), its epilogue, tragically portrays the scuttling of the fleet and laments Germany's defeat. Both plays are interesting for Goering's eschewing conventional depictions of war in terms that suggest either romantic heroism or sentimental pacifism. In Goering's drama, his concept of war is like his concept of life: a murderous challenge that must be met with manliness.

A physician, Goering was born in a castle near Fulda, in Hesse. His other works include *Der Erste* (1918) and *Der Zweite* (1919), tragedies about the entangled love relationships of, respectively, a priest and two married couples. His last work, *Die Südpolexpedition des Kapitäns Scott* (1930), is a hortatory verse dramatization (with choruses) of Robert Falcon Scott's last expedition. Goering won the Kleist Prize for it—as he had for *Seeschlacht.*

Naval Encounter was published with an introduction in James M. Ritchie's *Vision and Aftermath: Four Expressionist War Plays* (1969). Goering's drama is analyzed in Richard Samuel and R. Hinton Thomas's *Expressionism in German Life, Literature and the Theatre (1919–1924)* (1939).

GOETZ, Wolfgang (1885–1955), German playwright, achieved his greatest success with *Neidhardt von Gneisenau* (1925), a portrayal of Napoleon's Prussian antagonist as an artistic, proud, vain, and intelligent leader struggling against—and ultimately defeating—personal shortcomings and the resistance of his own followers. Other Goetz successes were also romantic histories. They include *Robert Emmet* (1927), dramatizing Georg Brandes's account of the Irish leader's fall because his love for Sara Curran is stronger than his patriotism; *Kavaliere* (1930), a raucous portrayal of Lola Montez and her adventures during and after her expulsion from Munich; and *Der Ministerpräsident* (1936), a drama of intrigue about the son who gives up romance and the woman he wants to marry so that Otto von Bismarck may retain his chancellorship.

GOLD, a play in four acts by EUGENE O'NEILL, published and produced in 1921. Setting: a barren coral island, later Bartlett's place on the California coast, c. 1920.

Artistically this melodrama is one of the weakest works in the O'Neill canon, and he ultimately came to deplore it. The last—and best—act had appeared earlier as a one-act play, WHERE THE CROSS IS MADE.

Almost mad with thirst and the tropical sun, the shipwrecked Captain Isaiah Bartlett and his men find a box of brass and imitation jewelry on a desert island. All but the cook and the cabin boy are persuaded that the treasure is genuine. When a rescue ship appears, Bartlett has the box buried and tacitly causes the murder of the doubters. At home six months later, Bartlett is ready to sail back to the island. He is gradually losing his sanity because of his greed for the "gold" and his growing guilt feeling over the murder, although, having "spoke[n] no word," he keeps persuading himself of his innocence. Talking in his sleep, he is overheard by his sick and religiously obsessed wife. She urges him not to return to the island, and to confess and repent. Nonetheless ready to leave, he is persuaded to visit her deathbed, and his daughter Sue uses his absence from the schooner to have her fiancé sail it away. In the final act, which takes place a year later, the now totally mad Captain awaits the return of the schooner, which is known to have sunk. Falling more and more under Bartlett's spell, his son Nat approves of the island murder and finally shares the captain's hallucination of the returning ship and crew. When Sue fiercely insists that Bartlett save his son from madness by telling him that "it's all a lie," Bartlett's love for Nat at last enables him to face reality: "I gave the word—in my mind—to kill them two. I murdered 'em in cold blood." He also admits that the treasure, in which he "*had* to believe," was probably worthless, and shows Nat a sample he had "been afeerd to show" before. Confirming that "it's brass, of course! The cheapest kind of junk," Nat bitterly blames himself for having been "a damned fool." Bartlett tears up the map of the island, and dies.

GOLD, Michael [Irving Granich] (1894–1967), American novelist and journalist, also wrote a few plays. They include *Fiesta* (1927) and *Battle Hymn* (1936), a social-protest drama written with Michael Blankfort (1907–   ) and produced in the Federal Theatre Project's first season. A stylized NATURALISTIC account of John Brown's career, it was to exemplify the type of "proletarian realism" Gold advocated for literature and the theatre.

Gold was an influential critic and the editor of left-wing magazines like *The Masses* and *The New Masses,* for which he wrote the AGITPROP *Strike!* in 1926. His other writings include *Jews Without Money* (1930), autobiographical "proletarian" sketches of Lower East Side New York life, and "Wilder: Prophet of the Genteel Christ" (1930), a controversial *New Republic* article that attacked the work of THORNTON WILDER.

GOLDEN BOY, a play in three acts by CLIFFORD ODETS, published and produced in 1937. Setting: New York, 1936–37.

Odets's most popular play, *Golden Boy* has been interpreted both as an indictment of America's business-oriented society and as a contemporary *Faust* (Odets subtitled an early draft "a modern allegory"). Because the protagonist sacrifices art and sensitivity for a (literal) fight for material success, it also is something of an autobiographical purgation for Odets's Hollywood "sellout," as his friends had termed it. *Golden Boy* was filmed in 1939 and was made into a musical by Odets and WILLIAM GIBSON (lyrics by Lee Adams, music by Charles Strouse) in 1964.

Act I. Scene 1. While a fight manager argues with Lorna Moon, the girl he loves and wants to marry when his wife agrees to divorce him, a brash young Italian-American comes in to announce that the manager's best boxer, whose fight is scheduled for that evening, has just broken his hand in the gym. The young man identifies himself as Joe Bonaparte and offers to take the injured boxer's place. The manager is furious when he learns that the sparring partner who broke his boxer's hand is Joe. But impressed by Joe's confidence, the desperate manager agrees to let Joe fight that night. *Scene 2.* At the Bonaparte home, Joe's father good-naturedly declines to buy his amusing Jewish son-in-law the cab he wants, while his daughter cheerfully calls her husband back to bed. Mr. Bonaparte has bought an expensive violin for Joe's twenty-first birthday, which is the next day—for Joe is a talented violinist. Soon Joe's brother brings in a newspaper, which has in it a picture of Joe, the "new cock-eyed wonder." Joe comes home and admits that he was in a prize fight: "I want to do what I want. I proved it tonight I'm good—I went out to earn some money and I earned!" His disappointed father sadly puts the violin away. *Scene 3.* Two months later, his manager, his trainer, and a partner are puzzled by Joe: he fights well, but seems to be holding back. Bonaparte comes in to inquire whether Joe's "hand coulda get hurt," and proudly tells them that "My boy'sa besta violin' in New York." Now they understand Joe's hesitation in the ring. Because Joe's success will give his manager the money to marry Lorna Moon, the manager urges her to get him to fight. *Scene 4.* A few evenings later, on a park bench, Joe tells Lorna how music has afforded him solace during his loneliness. Hurt by the lifelong indignities suffered because of his odd name and strabismic eyes, Joe remarks, "You can't get even with people by playing the fiddle. If music shot bullets I'd like

Golden Boy, Act I, Scene 2. In the center, Mr. Bonaparte (Morris Carnovsky) and Joe (Luther Adler); the others are Joe's brother (John O'Malley) and a Jewish neighbor (Lee J. Cobb, seated). New York, 1938. (*Theatre Collection, New York Public Library*)

it better—artists and people like that are freaks today." Lorna persuades him that boxing will bring him "fame and fortune," and taunts him with fearing to reach out for what he really wants: "Your arm in *gelt* [money] up to the elbow . . . fame so people won't laugh or scorn your face." This decides Joe to become the champion—and buy the fast car he yearns to have. *Scene 5*. The next week he packs up to go on a boxing tour. Bonaparte gives him the violin, and Joe briefly plays on it. Then he hands it back. "Return it, poppa," he says, and begs his father's approval for his new career. But Bonaparte cries out his refusal: "*No. No word!* You gonna fight? All right! Okay! But I don't gonna give no word! No!"

Act II. Scene 1. Six months later Joe is ready for big fights. A notorious gangster decides to buy a share of him, but Joe's manager stalls by complaining of Joe's dangerous driving. Coarsened and arrogant, Joe demands better fights and publicity. The manager again asks Lorna to use her wiles on Joe, to keep him out of trouble. *Scene 2*. On the same park bench a few nights later, Joe tells Lorna he loves her. She admits staying with the manager only out of gratitude for what he has done for her, "a tramp from Newark." Weeping, she confesses that she loves Joe. *Scene 3*. The next day the manager is upset by the gangster's insistence on a share of Joe, and by Lorna's evading the question of marrying him now that he has his divorce. Joe belligerently reveals that Lorna loves him. To spare the manager's feelings, Lorna denies it—but alone with the manager, she admits loving Joe. *Scene 4*. Six weeks later in the dressing room before an important bout, Bonaparte visits his son Joe. He realizes "is'a too late for music," and sadly gives his approval of Joe's career: "The men musta be free an' happy for music . . . not like-a you. . . . I sorry for you." Hurt by his father's attitude and Lorna's intention to marry the manager, Joe fights viciously. He breaks his fist in knocking out his opponent, and rejoices—for now he can no longer play the violin and is committed to boxing: "Hallelujah!! It's the beginning of the world!"

Act III. Scene 1. Six months later Joe, successful and bellicose, irritates reporters with his arrogance. Now the gangster's friend, Joe frightens well-wishers with his hatred. When he scornfully congratulates Lorna on her imminent wedding, she remarks on his "getting to be a killer!" But the gangster approves: "Now he wears the best, eats the best, sleeps the best. He walks down the street respected—the golden boy!" *Scene 2*. The next night Joe is fighting his only remaining contender for the championship bout. "I gave him the fury of a lifetime in that final punch!" he says when he returns victoriously, and bitterly adds: "I'd like to go outside my weight and beat up the whole damn world!" Soon word comes that his opponent has died from Joe's punch. Joe is stunned: "I murdered myself, too! I've been running around in circles. Now I'm smashed!" Only Lorna remains to comfort him, to remind him that his real self is "that kid in the park" who opened his heart to her: "And now, tonight, here, this minute—finding yourself again—that's what makes you a champ." She urges him to give up fighting and take up music again: "We'll find some city where poverty's no shame—where music is no crime!—where there's no war in the streets—where a man is glad to be himself, to live and make his woman herself!" Together they rush off for a ride in his car, to "speed through the night . . . burn up the night!" *Scene 3.* His manager, friends, and family await Joe at home. His brother, a union organizer recently injured in a strike, is poor. "But I get what Joe don't," he remarks: "The pleasure of acting as you think! The satisfaction of staying where you belong, being what you are . . . at harmony with millions of others!" The telephone rings: Joe and Lorna have been killed in a car smashup. "What waste!" his brother says sadly, and joins the grieving father, who prepares to "bring-a him [Joe] home . . . where he belong . . ."

GOLDEN HARP, THE (*Die goldene Harfe*), a play in fifteen scenes by GERHART HAUPTMANN, published and produced in 1933. Setting: a wealthy estate, 1820's.

The mixture of allegory and poetic suggestion that succeeds in AND PIPPA DANCES! does not in this play, which is permeated with music, provided even for the intermissions.

Two counts, twin brothers, return from the Napoleonic wars. They visit a fallen comrade's sensitive sister, who, still prostrated by grief, sadly plays her golden harp. Their growing passion reawakens her zest for life, but breaks up the brothers' deep mutual attachment. She hesitates in making her choice between the cheerful stronger and the thoughtful weaker brother. The latter nobly departs, at last, to a heroic death in battle.

GOLDFADEN, Abraham (1840–1908), was the founder of the Yiddish theatre, as the epitaph over his New York City grave states. He was also a dramatist, an impresario, a poet, and a songwriter. Early in life he made his name as a poet, and in 1869(?) he published two comedies, *Tsvey Shkheynes* and *Di Mume Sosye*. It was in the beginning of October 1876, at Simon Mark's large tavern in Jassy, Rumania, that Goldfaden presented a two-act musical sketch. This historic production was a great success. Goldfaden thereupon trained other performers, assembled large troupes, wrote longer plays, and organized extensive tours. His and competing troupes of actors who left Goldfaden soon spread throughout eastern Europe, and then the West.

Goldfaden, a watchmaker's son, was born in Old Constantine, Russia. To avoid his being impressed as a child into the Russian army, his parents sent him to a government rather than a Jewish school. Later he attended a rabbinical academy—and wrote songs. *Dos Yidele* (1866) was followed by the publication of other well-known collections of songs. These were performed by *"Broder Zinger,"* Jewish entertainers who were also costumed impersonators and monologists. Goldfaden traveled from place to place, unsuccessfully working as a teacher, a shopkeeper in Odessa (where he married), a medical student (in Munich), and a journalist. Finally, in Jassy, the success two *"Broder Zinger"* had had there suggested dramatic possibilities to Goldfaden. He hired them to perform his sketch—and the Yiddish theatre was born.

Goldfaden composed innumerable popular Yiddish songs, and he wrote and adapted hundreds of plays, many of them musical comedies and all of them literarily crude but vastly entertaining. Some of Goldfaden's plays were popular because of their comforting (though rarely compromising) morality and didacticism, but most of all because they were so amusing. His most famous early play was *Shmendrik* (1877), the name of whose title character became the proverbial designation for a fool who is neither lovable nor vicious. Other comedies are equally good-natured in their satire, their simple characterizations and action, and their mixture of farce and sentimentality. Best remembered among these are *Di beyde Kuni-Lemls* (published in 1887), which bears some resemblance to Shakespeare's *Comedy of Errors,* and *Kabzensohn et Hungerman,* which was influenced by Molière.

Following the Russian pogroms of the 1880's, Goldfaden's plays became more serious. *Doctor Almasado* (an operetta produced in 1882) and *Moshiakhs Tsayten* (a panoramic six-act drama written in 1891) dramatize the suffering of the Jews. His later plays, including some his best-known works, reflect Goldfaden's Zionist aspirations. *Shulamith* (published in 1886), a musical drama that has been hailed as Goldfaden's masterpiece, is based on the Talmudic legend of a jilted shepherdess who remains faithful until her lover returns to her. *Bar-Kokhba* (published in 1887) features the warrior who refused to submit until the coming of the Messiah, led the Jews' revolt against the Romans (in 132–135), and, after the defeat, was denounced as the false Messiah of force. Other plays are the musical comedy *Lo Tachmod* (1887, written in 1882 and known as *The Tenth Commandment*), based on Goethe's *Faust* but featuring a devil of Talmudic lore, Ashmoday; and *Di Kishefmakherin* (1879). Goldfaden's last play, *Ben-Ami,* was inspired by George Eliot's last novel, *Daniel Deronda* (1876); *Ben-Ami* was produced in New York a few days before Goldfaden's death there.

After launching the Yiddish theatre, Goldfaden toured Rumania, Russia, and Poland. Then he went to France, England, and (in 1887) to the United States. Finding a Yiddish theatre already established in America, he returned to Europe, where he remained, poor, ill, and disillusioned, until 1903. He then returned to New York, where he opened an actors' school. His funeral was attended by seventy-five thousand people.

Despite their one-time popularity, Goldfaden's plays are not easily available. *Shulamith* alone appears to have been translated, and it was revived in New York in 1951. For information on Goldfaden's life and work see Isaac Goldberg's *The Drama of Transition* (1922), Sol Liptzin's *The Flowering of Yiddish Literature* (1963), and David S. Lifson's *The Yiddish Theatre in America* (1965).

GOLDING, William [Gerald] (1911–   ), English novelist who became world famous with *Lord of the Flies* (1954) and later novels, wrote less notable drama. *The Brass Butterfly* (1958), based on his novella *Envoy Extraordinary* (1956), is a philosophical farce about Caesar and a third-century genius whose inventions appear at the wrong time.

GOLEM, THE (*Der Golem*), a dramatic poem in eight scenes by H. LEIVICK, published in 1921 and produced in 1925. Setting: seventeenth-century Prague.

Leivick's most famous work is based on Jewish legend. Frequently produced in Hebrew translation by the Habima Theatre of Israel, which presented its premiere, *The Golem* also has been filmed and set to music. Its title character is the legendary monster believed to have been fashioned out of clay by Judah Loew (1512–1609), the Rabbi of Prague, known as "the Maharal." Brought to life by this cabalist to save Prague's Jews from destruction, the Golem Joseph (according to legend, Ben Joseph is the unholy Messiah of force), like the robots of Čapek's R.U.R., eventually gets out of control. This SYMBOLIC play also features the holy Messiah, Elijah, and Jesus. Profoundly philosophical as well as theological, it is a morality about human suffering and redemption, and the use of force against evil. Leivick wrote a sequel, *Di Geule-Komedie: Der Goylem Kholemt* (1934), in which the inanimate Golem, yearning to reawaken, envisions the far-off future: the bloody struggles of the Ages of Gog and Magog, followed by the final triumph of the long-suffering Ben David, the true Messiah.

Scene 1. "Clay." Outside Prague the aged Maharal kneads a clay figure—the Golem. Its spirit warns him: "Create me not! / . . . where my foot will tread, / A blight will grow." But though aware of the dangers and fearful omens, the Maharal prays to God and continues work on his creation.

Scene 2. "Walls." Now alive, the mindless Golem almost wrecks the Maharal's study. His looks and bearing frighten the rabbi's wife and his granddaughter, of whom the Golem instantly becomes enamored. The Maharal is able to enforce obedience, but later shudders as he watches the sleeping Golem, "the man I dreamt into existence." Puzzled, he looks at the huge frame: ". . . So much body? / So much still sorrow?"

Scene 3. "Through Darkness." The Maharal becomes increasingly worried about his powerful, childlike creature. But though "Helpless himself—he must bring help to us. / Himself in darkness—he must bring us light." Deeply disturbed by his doings, the Maharal yet reassures his people, who are frightened by the Golem. Only in him does the Maharal see salvation from the plotting of their enemies. Upset by human emotions he cannot control, the Golem is calmed by the Maharal. Together they trace the enemies' plot to commit a murder that is to be blamed on the Jews as part of their "Passover ritual."

Scene 4. "Beggars." In the tower, in a large room containing sacred objects and now desecrated and in shambles, are crowded poor and sick Jews. Two beggars arrive: the older is Elijah the Prophet and the younger is the Messiah. The Maharal sends them away. ". . . *Their* time / Has not yet come. This is *your* time," the Maharal tells the Golem, who wants to join them. For now comes their chief enemy, Thaddeus, accompanied by a monk. Always ready to crucify opponents, Thaddeus is infuriated by the Jews' tenacity, by their passive resistance to worldly violence. "You sit upon your conscience and our brain," he admits. Growing increasingly angry, he taunts and expels the Jews. But then the Golem goes to work, spiritedly beating up Thaddeus and hurling him out. Alone, the frightened Golem calls the Maharal: "It is so dark!"

Scene 5. "Unbidden." In a field outside Prague, Elijah and the Messiah bemoan the people's suffering. The Maharal sends them further away: the night ahead is a bloody one, and the time for the Messiah has not yet come.

Scene 6. "Revelations." In the tower, the Golem reveals himself to the Maharal's frightened wife and granddaughter: he yearns for love, and he aches to ruin their enemies. Then he leads the women to safety. Later he tells the Maharal of a dream in which the rabbi asked to be saved from the cross, and finally buried the Golem. Together the Maharal and the Golem go out to do their task.

Scene 7. "In the Cave." Aided by a monk, Thaddeus conceals bottles of human blood in the tower's catacombs, cursing the Jews: "Those crucifiers never will deprive / Or rob us of the sanctity of knives." After they leave, the Maharal brings in the Golem. Alone, the Golem must battle many powerful spirits. At last he discovers the concealed bottles. Later the Golem, Elijah, and "The Man with the Cross"—the three redeemers—meet. Cave spirits dance around these suffering, rejected outcasts, who huddle in a magic circle. When the Maharal later sees the bottles of blood, he urges the dispirited Golem to complete his mission of saving the Jews.

Scene 8. "The Last Mission." In the anteroom of the synagogue, the Golem, having saved the Jews, begs the Maharal to stay with him. The Maharal sees that the Golem is becoming increasingly human, racked by hatred and fears. He begs the Golem to pray. But the Golem smashes a window and jumps out to the street. Soon word comes of his bloody attacks—this time against the Jews. The Maharal is in agony. Tired of his people's suffering, he had meant to create an instrument of justice and liberation. It became, instead, a monster of injustice and new oppression. Suffering, it would appear, is the necessary human condition. As the "final task," he has the Golem lie down, and then destroys him: "Breathe out your final breath. Amen." Then the Maharal bids the congregation "sing again / From the beginning the Psalm of Sabbath praise."

GOLL, Yvan (1891–1950), Franco-German poet, novelist, playwright, and theoretician, wrote drama that has been labeled EXPRESSIONIST, SURREALIST, DADA, and ABSURD. His plays are less original and notable than his prefaces to them, which propound a "total" theatre that seeks to approximate classic Greek effects by expressing essential, subsurface REALISM in a shocking, antirealistic manner. These theories are adumbrated in his preface to *Die Unsterblichen* (1920), two plays subtitled *Überdramen* (superdramas). The title character of the first, the short two-act *Der Unsterbliche* (*The Immortal One*), is a musician whose mistress floats out of the window to betray him and who becomes immortal when his soul is filmed; the second, *Der Ungestorbene*, is a similarly avant-garde dramatization, with film projections, of an idealistic philosopher.

Born in the Vosges of Alsatian parents, Goll was educated in German-controlled Metz. He finished his doctorate at the University of Strasbourg and went to Switzerland to escape conscription at the outbreak of World War I. There he became the friend of pacifists like FRANZ WERFEL and STEFAN ZWEIG, and of members of the Dadaist movement. In Switzerland he also met his future wife Claire, a poet. In 1919 they moved to Paris, where Goll worked with JAMES JOYCE on the German translation of *Ulysses*. One of Goll's first original works was *Die Chaplinade* (1920), a "film poem" fantasy that features Charlie Chaplin's tramp. Goll used film devices in his other plays, notably in *Methusalem, oder Der ewige Bürger* (*Methusalem, or The Eternal Bourgeois*, 1922), which was produced with masks designed by Georg Grosz, who also illustrated the published play. It is a satire of the middle class, personified by a businessman who has a telephone mouth, coin eyes, and a typewriter-and-radio-antenna head; also prefaced by an essay on theory, the fantasy is about an idealistic student who ultimately becomes conventionally bourgeois. In 1924 Goll helped the surrealist movement by founding *Surréalisme*, a periodical of which only the first issue ever appeared.

After the fall of France the Golls fled to New York, where he worked with ANDRÉ BRETON, founded a French-American magazine, and befriended many American writers. In 1947 the Golls returned to Paris, where Goll died of leukemia three years later.

Goll's plays were hailed by BERTOLT BRECHT when first published in 1920. Together with his poetry—for which he is far more distinguished and which has been translated by major poets and illustrated by major artists—the plays were republished in 1960. *The Immortal One* and *Methusalem* appear with their prefaces and with commentaries in, respectively, Walter H. Sokel's *An Anthology of German Expressionist Drama* (1963) and in *Plays for a New Theater* (New Directions Playbook 2, 1966). Goll's life and work are discussed in Martin Esslin's *The Theatre of the Absurd* (revised edition, 1968), which has a bibliography.

GOMBROWICZ, Witold (1904–69), Polish novelist and playwright, became important in Poland as an avant-garde figure with the publication of his novel *Ferdydurke* (1937). Two years later, at the outbreak of World War II, Gombrowicz was in Argentina, where he remained for the next twenty-five years. He continued to write there and in France, where he lived for the rest of his life. In the 1950's his work began to attract general attention. It increasingly appeared in translation and exerted a significant influence on younger writers and film directors.

Gombrowicz's drama with its nightmare ritual has been likened to that of JEAN GENET. *Iwona, Księżniczka Burgunda* (*Ivona, Princess of Burgundia*, 1938; also translated as *Princess Iwona*), Gombrowicz's first play, is a tragic, Kafkaesque farce; it is set in a grotesque fairy-tale world. Gombrowicz's other and better known play is *Ślub* (*The Marriage*, 1948; also translated as *The Wedding Ceremony*), written in 1946 and produced in 1964; it dramatizes a modern French soldier's nightmare in which he, his family, fiancée, and friend are transformed into actors of multiple archtypal roles like Father-King, Friend-Courtier-Rival, and Servant-Betrothed-Princess. In part a parody of Shakespearean tragedy, the drama portrays PIRANDELLian illusion-and-reality concepts and in tone recalls Jarry's KING UBU.

The English translation of *The Marriage* (1969) has an informative introduction by Jan Kott.

GOOD HOPE, THE (*Op Hoop van Zegen*), "a drama of the sea" in four acts by HERMAN HEIJERMANS, produced in 1900 and published in 1901. Setting: a North Sea fishing village in Holland, 1900.

Heijermans's widely translated masterpiece has been likened to Synge's RIDERS TO THE SEA. But though their settings and tragic poignancy are comparable, *The Good Hope's* social criticism and its portrayal of defiance and earthy humor make the play more comparable to Hauptmann's THE WEAVERS. Heijermans's depiction of the wretched plight of Dutch fishermen was credited with arousing the popular indignation that culminated in the industry's reform.

In the cottage of Kniertje, the shipowner's old scrubwoman, paupered old fishermen joke and exchange tales with the women who struggle to eke out an existence while they await their men's return. Kniertje, who has lost her husband and two sons to the sea, has a youngster who is afraid to sail and an older son who has been imprisoned for shipboard insubordination. Released, he frightens his mother and his spirited sweetheart with bitter accounts of the brutal shipmasters and his determination to be submissive no longer. Ships return with news of more lost lives, and Kniertje's younger son, discovering that *The Good Hope,* which he has reluctantly signed up on, is unseaworthy, braves taunts of cowardice and deserts rather than board her. Kniertje's misery increases as her older son again defies the arrogant shipowner, and as the coast guard pick up her frantic youngster in the cottage and force him to board ship. "The fish are dearly paid for," the women grieve as they await overdue ships and recall the sea's many victims. *The Good Hope* sinks in a storm and the shipowner, who had been warned of her structural deficiencies, angrily calculates his losses. His daughter finally perceives his evil and heartlessness, and the sweetheart of Kniertje's son hysterically taxes him with murder. When the shipowner learns that she is pregnant, he piously remarks that the family's "immorality" and "ungodliness" may lose them their pittance from the Widow's and Orphan's Fund. Kniertje brokenly recalls how she herself helped deliver her sons to the "floating coffin," and stumbles out of the shipowner's office in dazed despair.

GOOD WOMAN OF SETZUAN, THE (*Der gute Mensch* [literally, "person"] *von Sezuan*), a "parable play" in ten prose and verse scenes (plus prologue, interludes, and verse epilogue) by BERTOLT BRECHT (music by Paul Dessau), produced in 1943 and published in 1948. Setting: the "half Europeanized" capital of Szechwan province in modern China.

Brecht noted the universality of his theme in the setting, "symbolizing all the places where man is exploited by other men." Beyond the setting, the influence of Chinese theatre is reflected in stylized dialogue and the use of masks. Shen Te's transformations into "Shui Ta" again portray a split personality (as in THE SEVEN DEADLY SINS OF THE PETTY BOURGEOIS and HERR PUNTILA AND HIS SERVANT MATTI)—and the dichotomous problem of goodness in an evil world.

Prologue and Scenes 1 through 3. A water seller addresses the audience: "I am a water seller in this capital of Setzuan. My work is very difficult." Then he announces the arrival of three gods. To save the world and justify their own existence, they must find one good person. The water seller seeks shelter for them, but the city's inhabitants are hard-hearted and unwilling to be troubled with the gods. Finally a poor but kind young prostitute, Shen Te, gives up a customer to provide shelter for them. When they leave, the gods thank her and grandly exhort her to "be good." Shen Te wants to know: "How can I, when everything is so expensive?" So the gods decide to give money to the one good person they have met. With it, Shen Te opens a tobacco shop. "Now I hope to do much good," she tells the audience. Immediately, however, she is invaded by hordes of parasitic needy and debtors. As they swarm over her shop, she declaims: "The little lifeboat / Soon is pulled under: / Too many drowning ones / Greedily grab it." She disguises herself as a hard male cousin, "Shui Ta," kicks them out, sets order in the shop, and ruthlessly builds up a business. As Shen Te, she meets an unemployed and desperate young aviator who is about to hang himself. Though it is raining, she buys him water from the needy water seller, but the aviator in the meantime falls asleep. In love, Shen Te laughs happily: "Despair and rain and I have worn him out!" The gods are glad to hear of her kindnesses, but are disturbed over her ruthless "cousin," and became progressively disillusioned with mankind.

Scenes 4 through 7. Shen Te returns from the aviator's house, deeply in love and enraptured with the early-morning beauty of the world. But soon she is saddened by the human misery she encounters at her shop. She tries to cope with it, but must again don "Shui Ta's" mask: "The good / Cannot help themselves, and the gods are defenseless." As her hard cousin "Shui Ta," she has to listen to the crude aviator brag that he is interested only in Shen Te's money and intends to desert her. But though the wealthy barber next door loves and wants to marry her—and "Shui Ta" arranges the match—Shen Te is stopped by the aviator, who readily confesses being low and bad: "That's why I need you." Shen Te now remains true to her heart: "I want to go with the man I love"—however senseless and costly that may be. The wedding does not, finally, take place, for "Shui Ta" cannot bring the money needed by the aviator. Angry and bitterly disappointed, he sings "The Song of Saint Nevercome's Day." Shen Te tenderly admits that "When I saw his cunning laugh I was afraid, but / When I saw the holes in his shoes, I loved him dearly." Now she finds herself pregnant—and rejoices at the thought. Happily she envisions life with her child, for whose sake, however, she must once more change into the ruthless "Shui Ta."

Scenes 8 through 10. "Shui Ta" runs Shen Te's tobacco factory like a sweetshop, and becomes "fat" and wealthy. To avoid being jailed for breach of promise, the aviator must slave there too, but soon becomes a ruthless foreman. Now he is again interested in marrying Shen Te. She has not been around for some time, and when she cannot be found, he suspects "Shui Ta" of having murdered her and has "him" arrested. The judges are the three gods, appearing incognito. Before them, the "fat" businessman "Shui Ta" is given excellent character references by the rich and cursed by the poor. Finally, "he" reveals "his" true identity as the pregnant Shen Te to the gods. She pleads her inability to follow the gods' injunction to "be good"—and yet live. "Like lightning, it cleft me in two," she tells them: "To be good to others / As well as to myself was impossible." She acknowledges—indeed stresses—having been bad and heartless as "Shui Ta," but pleads that her crime was "to help my neighbor, / Love my lover, and / Save my little son from want." The impotent, foolish gods ignore her dilemma and pompously praise her goodness, declaim their optimistic clichés, and repeat their exhortation: "Continue to be good. . . . / Blessed be, blessed be / The good woman of Setzuan!" They float away smiling fatuously at Shen Te, who desperately implores them: "Help!"

GORDIN, Jacob (1853–1909), Yiddish dramatist, brought literary integrity to New York's Yiddish theatre, then dominated by the musicals of ABRAHAM GOLDFADEN's tawdry imitators and the mass-produced (often in part plagiarized) sensationalist pieces of JOSEPH LATEINER and MOSHE HURWITZ. Born in the Ukraine of well-to-do merchants, Gordin began his career as a liberal journalist. In 1880 he founded a Jewish Bible Brotherhood that, according to religious principles inspired by LEO TOLSTOI, was to replace mercantilism with an agricultural mystique that would guide its settlement members' lives. Pogroms and the hostility of fellow Jews, who continued to suffer persecution despite the change from money-making to land-tilling, drove Gordin to America in 1891. Though he had intended to establish his Brotherhood there, the needs of his growing family (eventually there were fourteen children) turned him to writing for New York City's Yiddish theatre. His plays became a permanent and the most important part of the theatre's repertoire in the years 1895–1908.

Gordin completed over seventy plays, many of them adaptations and translations of the works of classic and contemporary Western playwrights from Euripides through GERHART HAUPTMANN and AUGUST STRINDBERG. His first play, *Siberia* (1891), the tragedy of an innocent convict, had some success, and *Der Yidisher Kenig Lear* (1892), an adaptation of Shakespeare's tragedy into a Jewish milieu, established Gordin's reputation. Six years later he made Shakespeare's theme wholly his own with *Mirele Efros* (subsequently filmed), the tragedy of a businesswoman whose sons turn against her. Perhaps even more distinguished is *Got, Mentsh, un Tayvl* (GOD, MAN, AND DEVIL, 1903). His play on the second-century Palestinian heretic *Elisha ben Abuya* (1906) to some extent portrays Gordin's own early activities in Russia. His dramatization of Tolstoi's novel, *The Kreutzer Sonata,* was adapted by LANGDON MITCHELL in 1906.

Though Gordin was sometimes deficient in his characterizations, and though he forced happy endings and succumbed occasionally to the tricks of melodrama and vaudeville, he rescued the Yiddish theatre from triviality and falseness. Gordin replaced stilted with NATURALISTIC dialogue and action, and unlike most other Yiddish dramatists of his time, opposed improvisation and insisted that his scripts be followed. He brought not only artistic integrity to the theatre but also—however tentatively at times—contemporary problems of family life and religion. Almost from the start Gordin articulated his conviction that playwriting is a meaningful occupation. He wrote in 1897: "The Yiddish theatre will never be in a position to undergo normal development as long as the intellectual Jews continue to disregard a problem so important to the masses as the upbuilding of a literary, serious stage."

Isaac Goldberg's *The Drama of Transition* (1922) and Sol Liptzin's *The Flowering of Yiddish Literature* (1963) include sections on Gordin.

GORKY, Maxim [Aleksei Maksimovich Peshkov] (1868–1936), Russian novelist and dramatist, is best known for his short stories, autobiographies, and only one play—*Na dne* (THE LOWER DEPTHS, 1902). Though he is usually ranked among his country's major modern dramatists, most of his remaining seventeen plays are inferior and little known outside Russia. There, however, many of them succeeded because of their topical interest; later Gorky's work was accorded classic stature, and his plays have been produced regularly. One of the greatest practitioners of NATURALISM at a time when SYMBOLISM was becoming increasingly fashionable, Gorky bridged the old and the new. He achieved international fame in both Tsarist and Soviet Russia—and was the only important writer to do so.

He was born in Nizhni Novgorod (subsequently renamed Gorky) to Varvara and Maksim Peshkov, an artisan. His youth was appallingly hard. Orphaned at an early age, the boy was sent by his grandfather to fend for himself before he was eleven. He became a wanderer and a tramp, experienced much brutality, and absorbed the milieu he was to immortalize in his writings. He picked up odd jobs, but somehow also managed to educate himself and muster the strength to rise from the lowest depths of society. Seeking beauty and the ideal, Gorky became increasingly embittered and discouraged by his experiences. At nineteen he shot himself, but succeeded only in permanently injuring his lung. Then, in 1892, he published his first story and adopted an appropriate pen name: *Gorky*—"the bitter." His first novel, *Foma Gordeev* (1899), was repeatedly dramatized: he had become famous the previous year with his collected sketches and tales. However, it was his dramatic masterpiece, *The Lower Depths,* which carried Gorky's reputation beyond Russia.

It was ANTON CHEKHOV who brought together Gorky and the Moscow Art Theatre. Its directors, VLADIMIR NEMIROVICH-DANCHENKO and Konstantin Stanislavsky, urged Gorky to write plays for them. Their production of his first attempt, *Meshtchane* (THE SMUG CITIZENS, 1902), created a stir, but Gorky was dissatisfied with his play. Later that year he came out with *The Lower Depths.* In the next four years he produced as many new plays, none of them even nearly as successful as the first two: *Dachniki* (*Summer Folk,* 1904), an attack on the intelligentsia; *Deti solntsa* (1905), a domestic tragicomedy that voices an ideal ("We are the Children of the Sun, radiant source of life") but portrays the contemporary chasm between the intellectuals and the masses; *Varvary (Barbarians,* 1906), a tragedy in which a group of sophisticated engineers confronts the primitive inhabitants of an isolated Russian town; and *Vragi* (*Enemies,* 1906),

Maxim Gorky in 1901. (*Sovfoto*)

a drama about strikebreaking, whose performance was banned by the censor. These were followed by *Poslednie* (1908), featuring—as do many of Gorky's plays—a divided family; *Chudaki* (*Queer People,* 1910; translated also as *Odd People*), a comedy of manners, produced in the United States in 1970 as *Country People,* dealing with adultery and connubial love and portraying the intelligentsia more favorably than do Gorky's earlier plays; VASSA ZHELEZNOVA (1910), a play he was to return to later; *Dobro pozhalovat* (1910), a Chekhovian one-act comedy; *Deti* (1912), in which flatterers try to buy a prince's forest; *Zykovy* (*The Zykovs,* 1914), a character study of a merchant; *Falshivaya moneta* (*The False Coin,* 1913), portraying the corruption of a poor jeweler; *Starik* (*The Old Man,* 1919; also translated as *The Judge*), another character study, and one that portrays (as Gorky remarked) "how unpleasant it is when a man becomes totally absorbed in his troubles and gradually comes to the belief that he has the right to torture others because of it"; and *Rabotyaga Slovotikov* (1920), a vaudeville sketch satirizing Soviet bureaucracy.

Gorky's outspoken championing of freedom and opposition to cruelty made him suspect in the tsarist police state. Imprisoned for revolutionary activities, he was eventually banished. It was abroad that he met and became the friend of Lenin, whose leadership he supported though he frequently opposed Bolshevik excesses. After the Revolution Gorky returned to Russia. Despite long stays abroad (1921–28, mostly spent in Italy), he was hailed as and remained the leading Soviet writer, and the benefactor of many younger writers, whom he discovered and assisted, and on whose behalf he periodically interceded with the authorities. As was true of his drama during the reign of the tsars, however, he wrote but one really notable play under the Soviets, *Yegor Bulychov i drugie* (YEGOR BULYCHOV AND THE OTHERS, 1932; the projected trilogy's second work is *Dostigaev i drugie* DOSTIGAEV AND THE OTHERS [1933]). Two plays appeared posthumously: *Yakov Bogomolov* (1941), an uncompleted work resembling and considered superior to *Queer People;* and *Somov i drugie* (1941), which depicts an attempt by villainous engineers to sabotage the Soviet economy. Many of his short stories, too, have been dramatized.

Gorky's plays, like his other writings, usually portray down-and-outers or the isolation of the intelligentsia. The plays particularly are distinguished by Gorky's vitality and great gifts of characterization and dialogue. They clearly express his passionate moral commitments: compassion for suffering, anger at human cruelty, and undying faith and exaltation in the power of man and the improvability of his lot. At the same time, his plays are flawed by discursiveness and intrusive preaching. Gorky himself deplored the moral didacticism in his plays—but was unable always to control it.

With the help of the Russian Embassy, which reflected his country's hostility to the revolutionary writer, Gorky's trip to the United States in 1906 turned into a fiasco. He was thrown out of hotels with his companion, whom he had registered as his wife. Gorky had married in 1890, but was soon divorced. There was a son, who died a year before his father. His son's death, like Gorky's own, has remained a mystery unlikely ever to be solved. A year and a half after Gorky's impressive state funeral (Stalin was one of the pallbearers) the Kremlin announced that Gorky had been poisoned, the victim of a Trotskyite plot.

Gorky's life can best be studied in his celebrated autobiographies. His works were collected and published in Russia in thirty volumes, 1949–55. Many of his plays have been translated (as have his autobiographies, letters, and fiction), notably by Alexander Bakshy in *Seven Plays of Maxim Gorky* (1945);* its introduction surveys Gorky's career as a dramatist. Igor Gouzenko's *The Fall of a Titan* (1954) is a fictionalized account of Gorky's last years and death. More recent book-length studies of his life and writing include Richard Hare's *Maxim Gorky, Romantic Realist and Conservative Revolutionary* (1962), Dan Levin's *Stormy Petrel: The Life and Work of Maxim Gorky* (1965), Irwin Weil's *Gorky, His Literary Development and Influence on Soviet Intellectual Life* (1966), and F. M. Borras's *Maxim Gorky, the Writer: An Interpretation* (1967). These all refer to other pertinent studies.

* The plays are *The Lower Depths, Barbarians, Enemies, Queer People, Vassa Zheleznova (Mother), The Zykovs,* and *Yegor Bulychov and the Others.*

GRAFF, Sigmund (1898–), German playwright, coauthored with another combat veteran, Carl Ernst Hintze (1899–1931), the most successful German World War I drama, *Die endlose Strasse* (*The Endless Road,* 1926). Modeled on Sherriff's JOURNEY'S END, it features as its mass hero a German company on leave near the western front and NATURALISTICALLY portrays their loyalty, humor, and endurance when they must resume their "endless road" to combat. Graff's subsequent plays include a protest against antiabortion laws, *Mary und Lisa* (1931); a characterization of August von Kotzebue's assassin, Karl Ludwig Sand, as a mad fanatic, *Die einsame Tat* (1930); and two returning-soldier plays, *Die vier Musketiere* (1932) and *Die Heimkehr des Matthias Bruck* (1933). The latter is a variation on the Enoch Arden theme popular in these dramas, but it stresses the blood-and-soil sentiments that increasingly preoccupied Graff, an enthusiastic Nazi supporter.

GRAFTING (*L'innesto*), a comedy in three acts by LUIGI PIRANDELLO, produced in 1919 and published in 1921. Setting: Italy, 1919.

In this tragicomedy a happily married woman, Laura Banti, is brutally attacked and raped. Her husband Giorgio, who has always loved her with a possessive passion, reacts less with compassion than with jealous hatred. The abyss between them deepens when Laura is found to be pregnant (their marriage has heretofore been childless). Giorgio insists on an abortion, but to Laura the new life stirring inside her not only arouses her maternal feelings but heightens her great love for Giorgio. She considers the child Giorgio's and finds an analogy to her experience and feelings in grafting, which succeeds only when the plant is in sap. A gardener explains to her that the plant, after being cut open for the insertion of the scion, "must be in love, that is, it must desire to have the fruit that it cannot have by itself." Giorgio, however, remains adamant, even when Laura confronts him with a parallel case in which he himself, as a youth, seduced an engaged peasant girl. Only when Laura prepares to leave him does Giorgio yield. She has succeeded in raising his feelings above the purely physical and, as she happily exclaims, their "love has triumphed."

GRAND GUIGNOL are short, sensational plays that titillate and terrify audiences with a bloodcurdling focal scene of ghostly horror or frightening violence, such as murder, suicide, torture, insanity, rape, etc.—and a surprise ending. Plays of the genre flourished in small Parisian theatres in Montmartre at the turn of the century and then spread to England and America, where they reappeared in the early 1920's. The term originated in French Punch-and-Judy shows with a late eighteenth-century puppet named Guignol. Later, *Guignol* referred to decadent Parisian cabarets of the sort that eventually were performed at the Théâtre du Grand Guignol. As the showplace for plays of the genre, this theatre was launched in 1897 by Oscar Méténier (1859–1913), a Théâtre-Libre charter member whose underworld drama *En famille* (1897), aptly characterized as "a monologue on the guillotine," is a prototype of the Grand Guignol. The theatre's opening bill consisted of seven playlets, including one by GEORGES COURTELINE and three by Méténier, most notably his long-popular dramatization of de Maupassant's story *Mademoiselle Fifi.* Occasionally Grand Guignol plays were written by better dramatists (including OCTAVE MIRBEAU and HENRI-RENÉ LENORMAND) and depicted something akin to the SLICE OF LIFE.

GRANIA, a play in three acts by LADY GREGORY, published in 1912. Setting: legendary Ireland.

This is the best known of Lady Gregory's Irish folk tragedies. It has been highly praised—but has apparently remained unproduced. Lady Gregory was fascinated by the dramatic possibilities of this Finn Cycle legend (as WILLIAM BUTLER YEATS and GEORGE MOORE had been in their *Diarmuid and Grania*) more than by those of similar, oft-dramatized legend of DEIRDRE. She confined her play to the loves and jealousies of the three principal characters, focusing on the psychology that motivates the intriguing *volte-face* of Grania.

The beautiful young Princess Grania, about to wed old King Finn, falls in love with Finn's handsome young kinsman, Diarmuid O'Duibhne. She seduces Diarmuid, first into fleeing with her, and then into breaking his chastity vow. The angry Finn eventually brings about Diarmuid's death. At the last, Diarmuid totally forgets Grania in his love for the king. King Finn, mourning his beloved kinsman, releases Grania from her original vows. But furious at her lover's failure even to remember her at his death, Grania now insists on becoming Finn's queen. The armies outside laugh mockingly, but her terrible determination silences them as soon as she emerges: "There is not since an hour ago any sound would matter at all, or be more to me than the squeaking of bats in the rafters, or the screaming of wild geese overhead!"

GRANVILLE-BARKER, Harley (1877–1946), is more often remembered as an English critic-scholar, producer-director, and actor than he is as a dramatist. His *Prefaces to Shakespeare* (1927–47) are studies of major importance. His management of the Court Theatre (1904–07) with J. E. Vedrenne constitutes one of the most significant chapters in modern English theatrical history; many old and new playwrights were produced there, notably BERNARD SHAW, who himself was active in its premieres of his plays. As an actor, Granville-Barker performed in many plays by Shakespeare, HENRIK IBSEN, and others, and he created the Shavian roles of Jack Tanner in MAN AND SUPERMAN, Adolphus Cusins in MAJOR BARBARA, Louis Dubedat in THE DOCTOR'S DILEMMA, and others. As a dramatist, his reputation has been less distinguished. He wrote about a dozen original plays, and collaborated on, adapted, and translated many others. Outstanding among the former are THE

VOYSEY INHERITANCE (1905), WASTE (1907), and THE MADRAS HOUSE (1910). They were popular for a time, esteemed by the most perceptive critics of the age, and praised by later critics. Shaw called Granville-Barker a "first class" dramatist, and noted (in 1946), "His original contributions to our dramatic literature are treasures to be preserved."

Harley Granville Barker (he adopted the hyphenated form only after 1917) was born in London, the son of Albert James Barker, an architect, and his wife, Mary Elisabeth Bozzi-Granville, a professional reciter and bird mimic. Most of Granville-Barker's education apparently came from her, and he made his first stage appearance when he was thirteen. Subsequently he became friendly with important London figures: the classics scholar Gilbert Murray, WILLIAM ARCHER, and the leading theatre people and dramatists. Even before he created the role of the poet in CANDIDA at the Stage Society, he met Shaw, with whose career his own was for some time intertwined.

His biographer, C. B. Purdom, notes that Granville-Barker became, as he had planned, an actor for ten years (1894–1904), a producer for ten years (1904–14), and a writer thereafter—but that these activities overlapped. His playwriting began before 1895. Together with another actor, Herbert Thomas, he wrote *A Comedy of Fools,* which was rejected in 1895 and subsequently destroyed; *The Family of the Oldroyds,* written in 1869 and his earliest extant play, which also remained unproduced; a variation on Ibsen's A DOLL'S HOUSE titled *The Weather-Hen,* a comedy produced in 1899; and another extant, unproduced play, *Our Visitor to "Work-a-Day."* By himself he wrote *Agnes Colander* (which remained unpublished) in 1901, and a one-act verse play, *A Miracle,* a pseudomedieval allegory written about 1902 and produced in 1907. Then came his first play to be published (in 1909), *The Marrying of Ann Leete.*

It was also Granville-Barker's first significant play. Produced in 1902, it is set in England at the time of the French Revolution, and depicts a ruthlessly ambitious politician and his children's marriages, one of them among the lower classes. A similar politician is portrayed in *Waste;* and an examination of marriages and moneymaking are the bases of his other important plays, *The Madras House* and *The Voysey Inheritance.* These themes also appear in his remaining dramas: the one-act pieces published in 1917, *Vote by Ballot, Farewell to the Theatre,* and *Rococo* (produced in 1911); *The Morris Dance,* a dramatization of Robert Louis Stevenson and Lloyd Osbourne's *The Wrong Box,* produced in 1917; and his last plays, *The Secret Life* (1923) and *His Majesty* (1928). The former is about middle-aged lovers and features an English politician who goes to America. *His Majesty,* which has been compared with Shaw's THE APPLE CART, is a Ruritanian fantasy in which a king abdicates his throne for romantic reasons. Granville-Barker also collaborated on a number of other plays, notably PRUNELLA (1904), with LAURENCE HOUSMAN; and he translated and adapted plays by ARTHUR SCHNITZLER, SACHA GUITRY, JULES ROMAINS, and (with his wife Helen) plays by GREGORIO MARTÍNEZ SIERRA and the ÁLVAREZ QUINTERO brothers.

Granville-Barker the dramatist has been classified as a minor Shaw. While there are similarities in the subjects of their plays, this comparison is neither fair nor accurate. The two men worked together for years, and in their plays occasionally (and directly) even alluded to one another's drama. Both published their scripts with long, novelistic stage directions. But that was a common practice, and even on this superficial level they differed: the preciousness of the younger man's stage directions makes them resemble those of JAMES M. BARRIE more than those of Shaw. Granville-Barker's drama, though it deals wittily with topics wittily treated by Shaw, is concerned almost exclusively with portraying themes. He usually eschews the conventional plot and action that characterize even Shaw's plays, with all their ideas and conversation. It is only with Shaw's blatantly disquisitory plays (principally GETTING MARRIED) that their dramaturgical similarity is notable. Granville-Barker's subjects are almost always moneymaking, politics, and marriage. But basically his drama deals with the quest for a meaning in life—or with the portrayal of people whose lives are meaningless. The autobiographical element in these plays is suggested by their frequent irresolutions, and is confirmed by Granville-Barker's own final dissatisfaction with his life: he came to consider it useless, despite his immense productivity and success in so many areas.

In 1906 he married Lillah McCarthy (later Lady Keeble), who became a famous English stage star. They were divorced in 1917, and the next year he married a writer previously married to one of the Huntington millionaires, Helen *née* Gates, who outlived him by four years. During World War I he served with the Red Cross in France, and with British Intelligence (partly in America); during World War II he headed a section of the British Library of Information in New York.

He was addicted to constant revising and rewriting, and his plays consequently were published in variant editions. *The Marrying of Ann Leete, The Voysey Inheritance,* and *Waste* were collected in *Three Plays* (1909), and also published separately, as were his other plays. *The Madras House* has appeared in a number of modern drama anthologies. C. B. Purdom's *Harley Granville Barker: Man of the Theatre, Dramatist and Scholar* (1955) is a biography that contains a wealth of correspondence, production and performance tables, and extensive bibliographical material. Margery M. Morgan's *A Drama of Political Man: A Study in the Plays of Harley Granville Barker* (1961) is a sympathetic and exhaustive study of all his drama.

GRASS, Günter (1927–), German writer, in the 1950's started to publish poems and produce plays but achieved international fame with his novels, particularly with *Die Blechtrommel* (*The*

Tin Drum, 1959). A leading European man of letters, Grass has become an active and often polemical exponent of his liberal social and intellectual commitments. Though these are expressed too in his drama, he has failed to establish himself as a major playwright even with his controversial drama about BERTÓLT BRECHT, *Die Plebejer proben den Aufstand* (THE PLEBEIANS REHEARSE THE UPRISING, 1966). Generally unsuccessful, Grass's plays nonetheless are a significant and characteristic expression of one of his age's important writers.

Born in Danzig and the son of a grocer, Grass was conscripted into the German army at seventeen, captured by the American army, and released shortly after the end of World War II. He worked as a laborer and began his professional career as a promising painter and sculptor in Paris. Turning to writing, he published his first work, a volume of poetry, in 1956. This was followed by the production of a number of his plays. The first, *Hochwasser* (*Flood,* 1957), is a bizarre modernization of the biblical story, here depicting a Noah and his strange family and their friends, driven by the rising waters to a roof inhabited by philosophizing rats; when the waters recede, all reluctantly return to their earlier unexciting and corrupt fantasy lives.

Yet more grotesque is *Onkel, Onkel* (1958; translated as *Mister, Mister*), whose protagonist's determination to murder is frustrated by his would-be victims: unafraid of him, a sick little girl has him read to her, a gamekeeper continues his nature lesson, a prima donna tries to seduce him, and two children pester him—and finally murder him. Another work of interest, *Die bösen Köche* (*The Wicked Cooks,* 1957), is an ABSURDIST allegory: a group of cooks (representing the tycoons of modern society) seek a recipe known only to a mysterious "count" whom they entice with an attractive nurse; love makes the count forget the secret and, unable after their idyll to fulfill his obligation to the menacing cooks, the lovers kill themselves. The more recent *Davor* (1969, translated as *Uptight*) is a parable drama of antiwar student activists in conflict with a liberal professor who has outgrown his own youthful pacifist extremism. Grass has also written brief curtain raisers, farces like *Noch zehn Minuten bis Buffalo* (*Ten Minutes to Buffalo,* 1957), *Beritten hin und zurück* (*Rocking Back and Forth,* 1960), and *Zweiunddreissig Zähne* (1961, translated as *Demisemiquaver Teeth*).

Even the farces, like Grass's longer plays and, indeed, his novels, are "black comedies." Grotesque vignettes, they often suggest human degradation, especially in Hitler and postwar Germany. Almost nauseating viciousness and carnality are the substance of Grass's comedy and characterize the themes of his work. His intellectual and artistic seriousness, however, have helped to keep them from sensationalism. Grass's lyricism clarifies and controls the chaotic exuberance of his novels. Yet it rarely appears in the necessarily more compressed and often obscure plays, and no appropriate production style has successfully expressed his ideals and his artistry in the theatre.

Grass's *Four Plays* (1967) has an introduction by Martin Esslin and includes *Flood; Mister, Mister; Only Ten Minutes to Buffalo;* and *The Wicked Cooks.* Book-length studies in English are Norris Yates's *Günter Grass* (1967) and W. Gordon Cunliffe's *Günter Grass* (1969).

GRAU [Delgado], **Jacinto** (1877–1958), has been considered by some critics to be the foremost modern Spanish playwright because of his intellectual and poetic sensitivities, his dynamic style, his characterizations, and his humanism. Grau's struggle against commercialization and for artistic dignity in the theatre aroused the hostility of producers and helped keep Grau's works off native stages, though they were produced abroad. Beginning in 1899, Grau strove for four decades to revamp the Spanish stage with the vitality yet classic restraint of his own plays. But they never gained much popularity. After the Spanish Civil War Grau became an exile in Buenos Aires, where, for the remainder of his life, he continued to write and republish his drama and essays on Spanish theatre and literature.

Grau was born in Barcelona of Catalonian as well as Andalusian extraction. His plays suggest the complexities of love and of man's quest to transcend his organic limitations. Their principal recurrent themes deal with reality and the ideal, love and sex, and such more specifically contemporary topics as SYMBOLISM and existentialism. Notable plays in which these ideas are expressed include *El Conde Alarcos* (1917), a poetic drama based on a medieval ballad about the power of demonic love; *El hijo pródigo* (1918), a biblical tragedy about the Prodigal Son; *Don Juan de Carillana* (1913) and *El burlador que no se burla* (1930), differing characterizations of Don Juan, the first presenting the aging hero in love with a mysterious woman who turns out to be his daughter, the second an existentialist celebration of natural love that shows how, after the Don surrenders to enigmatic death, his women nostalgically and gratefully remember him as the man who dominated them; *El señor de Pigmalión* (1921), a once-controversial allegory resembling Čapek's R.U.R., in which the title character is destroyed by the puppets he creates to improve the human race; and *La casa del diablo* (1942), whose criminal protagonist is forgiven by God because he really loved, while his wife and other victims must return to earth and suffer until they learn to love. Grau's other works include a literary study, *Unamuno y la España de su tiempo* (1943).

Translations of Grau's dramatic and literary writings are not generally available, and little has been written about him in English. William Giuliano's 1952 text edition of *El señor de Pigmalión* has an informative introduction in English, and there is a brief section on Grau in Richard E. Chandler and Kessel Schwartz's *A New History of Spanish Literature* (1961).

GREAT CATHERINE (Whom Glory Still Adores), "A Thumbnail Sketch of Russian Court Life in the XVIII Century" in four scenes by BERNARD SHAW, produced in 1913 and published in 1919. Setting: St. Petersburg, 1776.

In his preface Shaw discussed the writing of plays for particular actors, as he wrote this "seeming tomfoolery" for Gertrude Kingston. As for Catherine—"plenty of character and (as we should say) no morals"—Shaw claimed that "what Byron said was all there really is to say that is worth saying": "In Catherine's reign, whom Glory still adores, / As greatest of all sovereigns and w—s" (*Don Juan* VI, xcii). The playlet was made into an opera (music by Ignatz Lillien) in 1932 and was filmed in 1968.

The English Captain Edstaston asks Queen Catherine's ugly and disgusting counselor and one-time lover, Prince Patiomkin, for an audience with the queen. Patiomkin, after much rude behavior, carries the protesting Edstaston to the bored but vivacious queen, who is surrounded by her fawning retinue, and dumps him on her bed. To escape her indignant fury, Patiomkin pretends drunkenness, but Catherine soon becomes enamored of Edstaston. He escapes to his English fiancée Claire, but is kidnapped and returned to the palace, where Catherine has him trussed to a pole and tickles him while she reads Voltaire. Thinking his howls are caused by torture, Claire rushes in to save him. Claire is jealous when she surveys the scene but is finally pacified by Catherine, who lets them leave, amidst her courtiers' insistence that Edstaston kiss Claire "till she swoons." Catherine is speechless when the departing Edstaston smugly tells her that "Russian extravagance" is improper and that she should "marry some good man who will be a strength and a support to your old age." After he leaves she clenches her fists: "If I could only have had him for my—" "lover?" Patiomkin jealously asks. With "an ineffable smile" Catherine replies, "No: for my museum."

GREAT DIVIDE, THE, a play in three acts by WILLIAM VAUGHN MOODY, produced in 1906 and published in 1911. Setting: a cabin in the Arizona desert, a home in the Cordilleras Mountains, and a house in Milford Corners, Massachusetts; early twentieth century.

Originally conceived in blank verse and first produced as *The Sabine Woman,* this was probably the most successful American play to date; it was filmed twice (1917 and 1924), was hailed as a pioneering masterpiece of REALISM as late as 1920, and was characterized (in *Theatre Magazine*) as "the best play written by an American." Somewhat old-fashioned in ideas as well as in action and speech—which are both melodramatic and sentimental—the play still evidences insight in its contrast of puritanism with natural freedom.

Act I. Nineteen-year-old Ruth Jordan is a mixture of her New England background and the romance and freedom of her present setting. In the Arizona desert with her brother and his wife, she tries to recoup the family wealth by establishing a cactus-fiber industry. Gently she rejects the suit of a childhood friend, a young doctor who is too "finished" for her. She yearns for a romance with "a sublime abstraction—of the glorious unfulfilled —of the West—the Desert." Alone in the cabin, she is about to be raped by three drunkards. Resisting desperately, Ruth finally appeals to one of them, Stephen Ghent, offering to marry him if he will save her. Ghent accepts: he buys off his Mexican companion with a string of gold nuggets, and defeats the other man (who wounds Ghent slightly) in "a square stand-up shoot" for Ruth. Then he places his pistol in her reach. Afraid to kill herself and eager to have him suffer for his sin, Ruth decides he too must live. Solicitously she tends to his wound, composes a farewell note for her brother, kisses her mother's picture, and leaves with Ghent.

Act II. About a year later Ghent is a prosperous partner in a Cordilleras gold mine. He is a model husband and has built a beautiful new home for Ruth. But she is too proud to forget the sordidness of their first meeting and remains cold to him. "My price has risen!" she remarks bitterly as she refuses to accept his presents. Now her brother, his wife, and the young doctor arrive, all of whom have sought her since her mysterious departure. Before them Ruth pretends her marriage is happy, and she reproves her brother for insulting Ghent. After they leave, she tells Ghent that she almost fell in love with him when they married. As they rode through the majestic West, she recalls, "it seemed as if you were leading me out of a world of little codes and customs into a great new world." But though struggling to forget, Ruth always sees Ghent as he first appeared before her, "the human beast, that goes to its horrible pleasure as not even a wild animal will go—*in pack, in pack!*" Therefore she has refused to accept even her keep: like a poor Navajo squaw, she has sold rugs and baskets that she had made herself. Then she repurchased the string of gold nuggets from the Mexican, which she now returns to Ghent. Though he protests, she demands her freedom—and that of her expected child. She vows never to be Ghent's: "Not yours! By everything my people have held sacred!" Her returning brother overhears them, and takes Ruth back to Massachusetts.

Act III. In Massachusetts, some months later, Ruth is near a physical and emotional breakdown from her self-imposed penance for her sinful marriage. She now realizes that her marriage and subsequent departure from Arizona have destroyed the cactus-fiber enterprise and ruined her family. Unknown to Ruth, Ghent has followed her and is in hiding nearby. For some months he has saved the family from ruin, and he secretly visits his infant son. Ghent offers to repurchase for the family the enterprise lost because of him. When Ruth learns of his presence and his generosity to her family, she angrily reveals the true story of her marriage. They are shocked. "You ought to have —died—first!" Ruth's mother exclaims, and her

The Great Divide, Act II. Right to left: Ghent (Henry Miller) facing Ruth (Gladys Hanson), her sister-in-law (Alice Lindahl), the doctor (Charles Gotthold), and Ruth's brother (Byron Beasley). New York, 1906. (*Culver Pictures*)

enraged brother tries to assault Ghent. Alone with him, Ruth apologizes for revealing their story: "God forgive me! You never can." Ghent, now reluctantly ready to leave her, gives back the gold chain. He tells Ruth that he is a new man, ennobled by his love for her—a love that "burned away all that was bad in our meeting" and has made life "pure good—pure joy." Pointing at the family portraits on her wall, he attacks the puritanism that wards him off: "It's these fellows are fooling you! It's they who keep your head set on the wages of sin, and all that rubbish." He paid for her, he adds, not only with the chain of gold nuggets "but with the heart in my breast." Finally he implores her, "If you can't see it my way, give me another chance to live it out in yours." Since she does not answer, Ghent concludes "it's been a losing game with you from the first!— You belong here, and I belong out yonder—beyond the Rockies, beyond—the Great Divide!" But as he leaves, Ruth finally confesses the love for him she has repressed all along to cleanse them both of sin. "You have taken the good of our life and grown strong," she now realizes, and "I have taken the evil and grown weak, weak unto death." Voluntarily putting the nugget chain about her neck and acknowledging Ghent's moral growth, Ruth decides to accompany him: "Teach me to live as you do!" Joyfully Ghent vows to make a good life for their "little rooster." Ruth holds out her arms to him and adds happily, "And for us! For us!"

GREAT GALEOTO, THE (*El Gran Galeoto*), a play in three acts and a prologue by JOSÉ ECHEGARAY, published and produced in 1881. Setting: contemporary Madrid.

Echegaray's masterpiece despite its old-fashioned declamations and chivalric attitudes, this play (also produced as *Calumny* and as *The World and His Wife*) was often revived. Its prologue emphasizes the difficulty of dramatizing group motivation, here that of the "everybody" to whom the play is dedicated. The populace never appears on stage but its slander—to which the principals eventually succumb—is vividly communicated by the play's few characters.

Prologue. Young Ernesto struggles over his play, unable to find a title or to dramatize his ideas of "everyday events" motivated by a "chief personage" who cannot appear on stage. He is consoled by his patron Don Julian, a wealthy middle-aged businessman once saved by Ernesto's father. Alone, Ernesto is inspired by Dante's *Inferno*. He starts writing feverishly, beginning with his title: *The Great Galeoto*.*

Act I. Watching the sunset with his young wife Teodora, Don Julian worries that his benefactor's son, Ernesto, will not accept even the little he is doing for him. Ernesto soon joins them and, since he declines "charity," Don Julian makes him his secretary. Afraid that his living there might cause gossip, Ernesto demurs; but upon the couple's eager insistence that he remain as Don Julian's son and Teodora's brother, he agrees. Don Julian's meddlesome brother and his wife warn them that the whole town is already discussing Ernesto and Teodora's "affair." Angry at the slander, Don Julian insists the more that Ernesto live with them. Yet he suddenly finds himself being suspicious: "I've caught your madness. Ah, how sure a thing is calumny! It pierces straight to the heart."

Act II. To end the gossip Ernesto has moved to a garret. He is momentarily out when Don Julian comes to invite him back to his house. Awaiting his return, Don Julian tells his brother he blames himself for his own cowardice and baser instincts, and worries too that repeating the slander "may eventually drive them to the fact." His nephew brings news that Ernesto will duel a nobleman who has repeated the slander. Immediately Don Julian rushes out to defend his wife's honor. His nephew, a busybody like his parents, feels confirmed in his suspicions when he sees love verses on Ernesto's desk. Taxed with them, Ernesto angrily explains Dante's story and adds that every case "has its own special go-between. Sometimes it is the entire social mass that is Galeoto." Teodora appears in the garret: she has just learned that Ernesto intends to sail away forever, and sadly bids him farewell. She is disturbed to hear of the impending duel for she believes that her husband, not Ernesto, is the one to defend her honor. As they argue, Don Julian is brought in—he has been seriously wounded in the duel. Teodora, who has quickly hidden in Ernesto's bedroom, is discovered, thus seeming to confirm the ugly gossip—and Don Julian faints.

Act III. Don Julian's family discuss the latest developments: Ernesto has killed the slandering count in a second duel and Don Julian is still in critical condition. His brother and his family are scandalized when Ernesto comes to bid farewell to Don Julian and Teodora, and will not admit him. Ernesto tells them exactly what happened in his garret. When they refuse to believe the innocent truth he concludes bitterly, "You may see what reputation remains for an innocent woman and two honest men when the town takes to jabbering about them." Brutally they question Teodora, trying to make her confess to an affair with Ernesto. "Why should you strive to convince me that little by little I am ceasing to love my husband, and that more and more I am imbued with an impure tenderness?" the harrowed Teodora asks. Lying, they tell her that Ernesto has confessed his love, and therefore, when he returns, she asks him to leave the house. But when he sees the brother manhandling Teodora, Ernesto forces him to kneel and apologize. The commotion brings Don Julian from his sickbed. Believing the calumny, Don Julian slaps Ernesto. Then he collapses, is carried back to his bed, and dies. "This woman must not remain in my house—turn her out at once," his brother commands, furious at the scandal Teodora has brought to their house. "You impel me with the current," Ernesto says; "the world has so desired it, and its decision . . . has driven her to my arms." He blames "the stupid chatter of busybodies," pandering society, "the great Galeoto." Defiantly he takes Teodora in his arms: "She belongs to me, and let heaven choose its day to judge between you and me."

GREAT GOD BROWN, THE, a play in four acts, a prologue, and an epilogue, by EUGENE O'NEILL, published and produced in 1926. Setting: a twentieth-century Casino Pier and an office and residential rooms, over a period of eighteen years.

Interpretations of this difficult but rewarding play must start with a long, frequently quoted letter in the New York *Evening Post* (February 13, 1926) in which O'Neill noted that Dion[ysus] [St.] Anthony embodies "creative pagan acceptance of life, fighting eternal war with the masochistic, life-denying spirit of Christianity"; Brown, the empty and "visionless demigod of our new materialistic myth," envies Dion's "creative life force"; Margaret is "the eternal girl-woman," whose sole purpose is to maintain the race; and the Earth Mother Cybel[e] is "doomed to segregation as a pariah in a world of unnatural laws." The masks are an EXPRESSIONISTIC device externalizing changes and conflicts within these characters. Highly experimental and SYMBOLIC, this is also one of O'Neill's most lyrical plays.

Prologue. At their commencement on the Casino Pier, the well-adjusted Billy Brown obediently promises his parents to study architecture; Dion Anthony, wearing a mask of Pan over his sensitive "spiritual and poetic" face, ironically thanks his father for the same "splendid opportunity to create myself"; and Margaret, in a mask that abstracts her features, rejects Billy for Dion, who is different—artistic and "just like a baby sometimes." Dion rejoices in her love and takes off his mask, thus frightening Margaret and becoming a stranger to her. Bitterly he puts on his mask and promises to marry her: "I'll never let you see again. By proxy, I love you."

Act I. Scene 1. Seven years later in their ugly home, which mirrors the philistine society that is defeating him, Dion's face has aged and his mask, showing signs of dissipation, is becoming Mephistophelean. He has squandered his money and the tenderly loving Margaret suggests that he work for his friend Billy, now the successful businessman

* At the end of Canto V of *The Inferno* Francesca talks of the Arthurian romance Paolo read her "that day" and remarks, *"Galeotto fu il libro e chi lo scrisse"* (a pander was the book and he who wrote it); Galeotto (pander) is also the name of Lancelot and Guinevere's intermediary.

William A. Brown. Dion derisively sends her to get the job for him. *Scene 2.* Though he sees through Margaret's loyal falsehoods about Dion's success as artist and father, Brown agrees to take him on as chief draftsman in his contracting business. *Scene 3.* The sensual young Cybel shelters Dion, who has drunkenly fallen asleep on her steps. She accepts him without his mask, removes her own hard-prostitute mask, and becomes his comforting and maternal "Miss Earth." When Brown finds him, Dion talks wildly of his past and finally agrees "to foreswear my quest for Him and go in for the Omnipresent Successful Serious One, the Great God Mr. Brown, instead!"

Act II. Scene 1. Seven more years have passed. Martyred by self-torture and pain, Dion thanks Cybel for having given him the strength to live all these years. She assures him, "You're not weak. You were born with ghosts in your eyes and you were brave enough to go looking into your own dark." Later Brown visits Cybel but does not recognize her without her mask. He begs her not to see Dion, and having already sensed Dion's approaching death, she sadly promises it. *Scene 2.* Hiding the brave mask she now wears before the world, Margaret visits Dion in the office. He shows her the dying "life-denying Christian slave you have so nobly ignored" by tearing off his mask, and she faints. Lovingly and with understanding he kisses her mask and her face. *Scene 3.* After long and bitter recriminations, Dion mockingly wills Brown his mask and then dies, praying at his feet. Brown puts on Dion's mask, and in it is taken for Dion by Margaret.

Act III. Scene 1. Brown's face now becomes ravaged with suffering and in his office he must wear a mask of his successful businessman's face of a month ago. He realizes that "it's the Dion you buried in your garden who killed you." *Scene 2.* Unable to continue his double life as Dion and Brown, he prepares to dispose of "Brown." He hopes eventually to win Margaret's love for "what is beneath—me!" *Scene 3.* As Dion, he weeps when Margaret tells him of her and her boys' growing happiness with him, and then resumes his drafting in the cynical spirit of Dion's commercial work.

Act IV. Scene 1. Before Margaret and the committee who have come for the new Capitol plans, Brown madly tears up his work and then, having changed to Dion's mask, announces Brown's death and rushes off. After solemnly carrying Brown's mask as if it were his corpse, the committee, convinced that he was murdered, send out to arrest "Anthony." *Scene 2.* Cybel comes to Brown's house to warn "Dion Brown" of the police, but he is too tired to escape, and is shot. Margaret mourns over Dion's mask, while Cybel comforts him as he dies. When Cybel tells the inquiring police captain that the name of the corpse is "Man!" the officer asks, "How d'yuh spell it?"

Epilogue. The Anthony boys' commencement and courting four years later echo the prologue; Margaret kisses the mask of Dion, who lives and sleeps "forever under my heart."

GREAT HIGHWAY, THE (*Stora landsvägen*), "A Wayfaring Drama with Seven Stations" (i.e., in seven scenes) by AUGUST STRINDBERG, published in 1909 and produced in 1910. Setting: mountains, etc.

The Great Highway was Strindberg's last play. Like TO DAMASCUS (whose title is echoed in the subtitle), it is a spiritual autobiography dramatized as a SYMBOLIC fantasy. But here there is no repetition of Strindberg's "Inferno" struggles; there is only a review of his travels over the great highway that is life. There is also almost no action whatsoever: the play consists primarily of poetic monologues by the Hunter and other embodiments of Strindberg himself that express his lifelong suffering, compassion, and ideals.

(*1*) In the mountains, the Hunter observes a two-armed signpost pointing up and down. "Where have I arrived, and how far have I come?" he asks: "Yes, there the track leads up, and there it goes down. Descent is the common way: I want to rise!" Seeing a vision of the Country of Desire and seeking the self that he has lost, the Hunter starts on his journey with another traveler. Their first two stops are at the idyllic yet unsatisfactory (*2*) Place of the Windmills and (*3*) at Eselsdorf, where they clown and argue with various inhabitants (including a schoolmaster who must act insane to avoid being locked up), reluctantly get involved, and are nearly crushed. (*4*) At Tophet (Hell) the mood becomes more somber (and, incidentally, weirdly prophetic): the Hunter meets a Japanese who is about to commit hara-kiri ("I have traveled, and sinned, and suffered under the name of 'Hiroshima,' after my native town") and a murderer whom the Hunter counsels, "Execute yourself, as I did—as I had to do—when you turned me into a scapegoat." (*5*) At a crematorium, while the Japanese waits for the furnace to heat, the murderer and the Hunter discuss the bitterness of life.

The vision of the Country of Desire reappears and the Hunter next (*6*) visits his former home. There, at "the Last Gate," he talks with a sweet little girl who does not recognize him as her father; he remembers her mother ("a vanishing but lovely image") and envisions her life with her new husband: "a summer day in the woods near the ocean; a birthday table and a cradle; a ray of sunshine from a child's eyes; a gift from a child's hands." Quickly he leaves, and is next (*7*) seen lost in a Dark Wood where he meets a blind woman and then a tempter who offers riches if the Hunter will conduct himself "like an ordinary human being." The Hunter blames the woman for having blackened him, who "coughed up first his lungs and finally his heart," and he rejects the tempter. Alone at last, he prays to God for the return of the vision of the Country of Desire. Calling himself the wandering Ishmael, the Hunter now prepares for the final rest after his battles against God. "Defeated by His Almighty Goodness," the Hunter asks for divine blessing: "[My] deepest suffering—the deepest of all human suffering—was this: I could not be the one I longed to be!"

GREECE. Greek drama in modern times hardly reflects the glories of its golden age. Intimidated by their classical heritage, and hampered by political and social upheavals, modern Greek dramatists have produced few notable plays. A further deterrent to a Greek renaissance has been the stultifying effect of the mannered purist (Katharevusa) language, which was long considered the only respectable literary medium; it was not until relatively recent times that playwrights began to use *demotiki,* the modern vernacular. Nonetheless, throughout the nineteenth century there was sporadically popular theatrical activity. Early playwrights who made reputations for themselves were Demetrios Vernardakis (1833–1907) and Spiridon Vassiliadis (1845–74)—Vernardakis with *Maria Doxapatri* (1865, a verse tragedy written in 1858 and set at the time of the Crusades) and *Fausta* (1893, inspired by Euripides's *Hippolytus* and based on the career of Constantine the Great), and Vassiliadis with a romantic dramatization of the Pygmalion legend (*Galatea,* 1873) and with historical plays written in less stilted language.

In 1901 the Royal Theatre opened in Athens, and among its offerings were a number of works by new native playwrights. Costis Palamas (1859–1943), one of Greece's major poets, in 1903 wrote his only play, the distinguished verse drama *Trisevgene.* More notable is Georgios Xenopoulos (1867–1951), a novelist-playwright who achieved his greatest success as a dramatist with a sentimental and symbolic portrayal of a father-daughter struggle, *Stella Violanty* (1903, filmed in 1931), and whose many other plays include character studies like *Psychosabbato* (1911, about a murderess) and *Monakrivi* (1912, about a child), and folklore comedies like *O Peirasmos* (1910) and *To Phiori tou Levanti* (1914). Xenopoulos greatly influenced the development of Greek REPRESENTATIONAL and social drama with his writings as well as with his directorship of the state-subsidized National Theatre—established in 1932—and he became known as Father of the Contemporary Athenian Theatre.

The pervasive influence of HENRIK IBSEN, the NATURALISTIC folk plays of GERHART HAUPTMANN, and popular French comic fare appeared also in the works of early modern Greek playwrights. Pantelis Horn (1881–1941) is particularly notable for his folklore drama, outstanding of which is the naturalistic portrayal of lower-middle-class life, *Fintanaki* (1921). Spyros Melas (1882–1966) wrote topical as well as historical plays: finest among the former is *O Babbas Ekpaidevetai* (1935), a very popular satire of mores; Melas's histories include *Papaphlessas* (1937, about the friar-revolutionary of the Greek rebellion of 1821), *Judas* (1934, portraying Judas sympathetically as Christ's revolutionary compatriot), *O Basileus kai O Skylos* (1953; a comedy about Alexander the Great and Diogenes, "the king and the dog" of the title), and *Rhegas Velestinlis* (1962, featuring a hero of the 1821 rebellion in Greece). These and other dramatists achieved considerable popularity in Greece, but their work is little known elsewhere. Though the verse dramas of Anghelos Sikelianos (1884–1951) are undistinguished, this poet-playwright and his American wife (Eva Palmer) are important for their Delphic productions of the Greek classics translated into the demotic (*demotiki*), beginning in 1927—productions that strove to fuse the ancient with the modern impulse, attracted audiences from all over Europe, and ultimately inspired the establishment of the National Theatre. Since 1942, Karolos Errikou Koun and his Art Theatre have stimulated the work of contemporary playwrights with productions of the classics as well as European and American avant-garde drama.

Best known in English-speaking countries is the poet-novelist Nikos Kazantzakis (1885–1957), whose most popular novel, *Tou Alexi Zorba* (*Zorba the Greek,* 1946), Joseph Stein (1912–) made into the American musical *Zorba* (1968, music by John Kander); Kazantzakis's less important plays, like his novels, reinterpret classical and biblical themes—as in the posthumous verse drama *Sodoma kai Gomora* (*Sodom and Gomorrah,* also translated as *Burn Me to Ashes,* originally produced in New York in 1965) and in the *Three Plays by Nikos Kazantzakis* (1969) on history and Greek legend: *Melissa* (1939), *Christopher Columbus* (1954), and *Kouros.* His novel *O Christos Xanastavronetai* (1956, translated and filmed as *He Who Must Die*) was dramatized by Notis Peryalis (1920–), a leading Greek playwright. Peryalis has also written a drama about the unemployed, *To Koritsi Me To Kordellaki* (1954); *Maskes gia Angelous* (*Masks of Angels,* 1959), a short play about two characters who painfully strive to accept their own identities—and each other; and *Antigone tis Katochis* (1961), a play set in Nazi-occupied Greece. Other major contemporary playwrights are Anghelos Demetriou Terzakis (1907–) and Iakovos Stephanos Kambanellis (1922–). The novelist-playwright Terzakis has written historical and biblical dramas in a lofty style, notably *Theophano* (1956, written in 1946), a tragedy about the tenth-century Roman empress, and an original play on man's guilt complex and divine justice, *O Progonos* (*The Ancestor,* 1970). The more popular Kambanellis has written naturalistic plays on contemporary themes—best known among which is *Avli ton Thavmaton* (1957), the second in a trilogy—and such hits as *Odyssea, Yirisi Spiti* (1966), which deals with the exploitation of a hero and satirizes contemporary life as well as the government. Such political satire, however, has become impossible in recent years; the junta's repressive rule and censorship, in effect since 1967, have effectively controlled all intellectual and artistic activities in Greece.

Very little modern Greek drama has appeared in English. Readily available, aside from the Kazantzakis collection of plays, is Peryalis's *Masks of Angels,* included in Robert W. Corrigan's anthology, *The New Theatre of Europe* (1962). See also the International Theater Institute's study of *The Modern Greek Theater* (1957).

GREEN BAY TREE, THE, a play in three acts by MORDAUNT SHAIRP, published and produced in 1933. Setting: London, early 1930's.

This sophisticated portrayal of homosexuality created a wild sensation in London and then in New York, with Laurence Olivier in the cast. The play depicts the battle between a wealthy, middle-aged homosexual dilettante, Mr. Dulcimer, and a beautiful young woman over his adopted son, Julian.

The charming Julian vacillates between his love of the woman and of the decadent luxury in which "Dulcie" has raised him. Julian's natural father, an alcoholic turned preacher, castigates his son in the Psalmist's words ("I myself have seen the wicked in great power and spreading himself like a green bay tree") and shoots the evil Dulcimer when Julian, giving up study and work, returns to effete idleness. But Dulcimer's hold persists beyond the grave. In the end, with Dulcie's death mask smiling down from the wall, Julian opts for sybaritic bachelorhood. As Mr. Dulcimer did at the beginning of the play, Julian arranges the *fleurs du mal,* the irises handed him by the same butler.

GREEN COCKATOO, THE (*Der grüne Kakadu*), "a grotesque in one act" by ARTHUR SCHNITZLER, published and produced in 1899. Setting: the taproom of "The Green Cockatoo," Paris; July 14, 1789.

This colorful, philosophic melodrama is set on the eve of the French Revolution. It portrays Schnitzler's characteristic preoccupation with sex. But it also represents ironically men's obliviousness to the great contemporary happenings around them, and the frequent interchangeability of reality and illusion.

The tavern proprietor, Prospère, is a former theatre manager. With his troupe he prepares an entertainment for his customers, noblemen who come to be amused by low-life. Prospère's companions gossip about the shouting mobs outside and about each other's affairs. The troupe's star, Henri, has just married a popular but notoriously promiscuous actress he has courted for seven years. One of her lovers is a handsome duke, now in the audience. In the entertainment, Henri plays the part of a husband who finds his wife in the arms of a duke. "There is an undercurrent—that's what makes it so fascinating—bits of the real flashing through," a poet in the audience observes to his mistress, the lascivious wife of a nobleman. When Henri declaims of killing his wife's lover, other people's comments on the resemblance of the play to the actual situation reveal the truth to him—and he really kills the duke. Just then the fall of the Bastille is announced, the crowd's excitement mounts, and, as the tavern's philosopher remarks, Henri will not be arrested. It is the common folk who make the laws now: "He who wipes out a duke is a friend of the people. *Vive la liberté!*"

GREEN FIELDS (*Grine Felder*), a play in three acts by PERETZ HIRSHBEIN, published in 1916 and produced in 1918. Setting: a Jewish farm in pre-World War I Russia.

This bucolic idyll charmingly blends romance and gentle folk comedy. Credited by some with having launched New York's Yiddish art theatre, it is one of the few Yiddish plays ever filmed.

The appearance of Levi-Yitskhok, a traveling young rabbinical student, disturbs the equilibrium of two neighboring farms. The farmers' daughters fancy him, and since a learned man is a good catch, both sets of parents are eager for the match—and quarrel. The more daring and ebullient girl, Tsine, persuades Levi-Yitskhok to stay with them a bit longer—"There's always food on a farm"—when the earnest student tries to get away, and she eventually succeeds in getting him to reciprocate her love. Tsine's shy and stubborn brother is in love with the neighbor's girl. Despite her father's efforts to break their engagement because he would prefer Levi-Yitskhok for a son-in-law, the lovers are happily reunited. Tsine can marry the rabbinical student, and the families make up—as is always done before the High Holy Days. "You'll have a fine Jewish girl," the neighbor tells Levi-Yitskhok, congratulating him, "even though she did grow up among the peasants, out in the field." And his wife embraces Tsine's mother and congratulates her on her son-in-law: "You see, even in the country, God provides. . . ."

GREEN GODDESS, THE, a play in four acts by WILLIAM ARCHER, produced in 1920 and published in 1921. Setting: Rukh, a remote region behind the Himalayas, c. 1920.

This romantic melodrama was a great hit in England and America. George Arliss played the suave, westernized Raja of savage Rukh. A conventional thriller, it is spiked by philosophic reflections on Western "civilization," and literary allusions like the Raja's "BERNARD SHAW, I suppose he's quite a back number; but I confess his impudence entertains me."

An English doctor has made a forced aircraft landing with his passengers, the unhappily married Lucilla and Antony Crespin, the latter a bumptious and hard-drinking major. Entertained in splendor by Rukh's Raja, the Englishmen learn of the priests' determination to sacrifice them to the green goddess. Lucilla indignantly refuses the Raja's offer to spare her if she will enter his harem. Her husband and the doctor kill the Raja's servant, a Cockney criminal, and capture the wireless set. Crespin manages to telegraph for help before the Raja shoots him. As the sacrifice is about to begin, Lucilla and the doctor confess their mutual love. They are saved at the last moment by a British air squadron. The Raja lights his cigarette, wishes Lucilla a happy reunion with her children, and remarks, as the lovers depart, "Well, well—she'd probably have been a deuce of a nuisance."

GREEN GROW THE LILACS, a folk play in six scenes by LYNN RIGGS, produced in 1930 and published in 1931. Setting: the Indian Territory shortly before it became part of Oklahoma, 1900.

Most famous as the source of Rodgers and Hammerstein's OKLAHOMA!, the original play has the same characters and plot. In his preface Riggs described his play as a "nostalgic" attempt to recapture in dramatic dialogue as well as singing "the great range of mood which characterized the old folk songs and ballads." Riggs's first success, this colorful cowboy play has many rural characters as well as a Syrian peddler whose cunning provides some of the comedy.

Handsome Kansas-born Curly McClain is a "Cowpuncher by trade and by profession. I break broncs, mean uns. I bull-dog steers." But however tough, Curly has a self-acknowledged "good disposition," likes to sing, and is in love with the pretty but spoiled Laurey Williams. Orphaned, she lives with her comic old aunt, who realizes that her niece reciprocates Curly's feelings, though Laurey lets on that she despises "the braggin', saddle-awk'ard, wish-'t-he-had-a-sweetheart bum!" She goes to a "play-party," instead, with their ugly and criminal hired hand, whom Curly warns to watch his step. There Laurey repulses and fires this sinister suitor and agrees to marry Curly. Their wedding night is spoiled by the traditional bawdy "shivaree," during which the vengeful criminal returns to murder Curly. Instead, he himself is accidentally killed as he struggles with Curly, who is thereupon imprisoned. The trial is bound to exonerate Curly, and he plans to give up his old way of life for farming. "Quit a-thinkin' about dehornin' and brandin' and th'owin' the rope, and start in to git my hands blistered a new way!" he says, recognizing that "things is changin' right and left! Buy up mowin' machines, cut down the prairies! . . . Country a-changin', got to change with it!" Desperate to see Laurey, he escapes from prison, and the sly old aunt persuades the sympathetic deputies to allow Curly to spend the night before the trial with Laurey. The newlyweds go to the bedroom, and soon Curly is heard singing the title song, as the delighted aunt remarks, "Listen to that fool cowpuncher! His weddin' night—and there he is singin'!"

GREEN HELMET, THE, a one-act "heroic farce" in verse by WILLIAM BUTLER YEATS, published and produced in 1910. Setting: legendary Ireland.

First published and produced in a version entitled *The Golden Helmet* (1908), this play depicts King Cuchulain as a jovial hero. Despite his wife Emer's pleas, Cuchulain offers his head, as demanded by the Red Man with the green helmet, for the sake of the nation's weal and peace. But because of Cuchulain's fearless gaiety, he is instead dubbed champion and wins the golden helmet.

GREEN, Julian [or Julien] (1900–), French-born American novelist who studied at the University of Virginia but returned to France, where he published his works on American life in French and wrote a few controversial but undistinguished psychological tragedies. They include *Sud* (*South,* 1953), a Civil War drama about an officer becoming aware of his homosexuality; and *L'Ennemi* (*The Enemy,* 1954), a drama about the conflict between the forces of lust and divine grace.

GREEN PASTURES, THE, "a fable" play in two parts by MARC CONNELLY, published and produced in 1930. Setting: a Louisiana Negro Sunday School; heaven; earth.

Based on Roark Bradford's Bible stories, *Ol' Man Adam an' His Chillun* (1928), this Pulitzer Prize folk drama attempted, "in the terms of its believers," in Connelly's words, "to reflect a simple, unsophisticated faith, visualized in graphic form" and Negro spirituals. The humorous but reverent play strongly moved American as well as European audiences, though some charged condescension in the portrayal of a naïve, anthropomorphic religion and a Negro-preacher "Lawd" troubled by mankind's sins. In his *Voices Offstage* (1968) Connelly extensively discussed and illustrated the play's history, and reprinted the text of "Little David," a deleted scene which ends with the slaying of Goliath.

Part I (*10 scenes*). (*1*) A Louisiana Negro preacher reads and interprets Genesis in Sunday School. Angels, he tells the children, "had fish frys, wid b'iled custard and ten cent seegars for de adults," and God looks like an old preacher. (*2*) Just such a heaven now appears, and soon Gabriel, shouting "Gangway! Gangway for de Lawd God Jehovah!"* announces the arrival of such a God—a tall Negro in a Prince Albert coat. After the angels sing of their redemption, the fry continues, God accepts a "ten cent seegar," and orders more firmament for the custard. Then he creates the world and man, "one of de most impo'tant miracles of all." (*3*) In Eden, God tells Adam and Eve to "enjoy yo'selves"; then, in darkness, the Sunday School preacher's voice is heard narrating the loss of Eden. (*4 and 5*) Cain, who has just killed Abel, meets his "gal," a flashily dressed chippy. Observing them, God "don' like de way things is goin' *a*tall." (*6*) In his office (resembling that of a Southern Negro lawyer) hundreds of years later, God stops Gabriel from blowing his horn, and decides to visit earth. (*7*) He is disgusted by the sinning he encounters, but heartened when he meets Noah, a pious country preacher, (*8*) at whose home God plans the Flood. He tells Noah to build an ark, and allows him to take along but one keg of liquor. (*9*) While his neighbors sneer and sin, Noah and his family build the ark and load it; the rain begins. (*10*) It is forty days later, and Noah's wife is complaining of her husband's heavy drinking as the flood ends. Feeling "solemn an' serious," the Lawd, starting all over with man ("quite a proposition"), remarks to Gabriel, "Well, it's did. . . . I only hope it's goin' to work out all right."

Part II (*8 scenes*). (*1*) In God's office, cleaning women deplore "de scum" on earth who are

* Brooks Atkinson called this "the greatest entrance cue in modern drama."

The Green Pastures, Part II, Scene 3. Aaron (McKinley Reeves) demonstrates his magic powers to Pharoah (George Randol). New York, 1930. (*Picture Collection, New York Public Library*)

worrying "de Lawd." Though displeased with His creation, God decides, "Man is a kind of pet of mine." He tells Abraham, Isaac, and Jacob that he is "gonter be lookin' out fo' yo' descendants only." They recommend Canaan as "de choice piece of property" for the Jews and Moses as the leader. God prepares to try again: "Dis time my scheme's *got* to wukk." (*2*) He appears before Moses and his wife Zipporah, performs miracles, and tells Moses to lead his people out of bondage; Aaron is to help "wid de Exodus." (*3*) In his throne room (resembling a Negro lodge), Pharoah is bored with his magicians. Moses and Aaron impress him with their magic and, by visiting the plagues on him, force the release of the Jews, whom he is tormenting. (*4*) The Chosen People are marching on a treadmill near Canaan forty years later. Moses, old and dying, is allowed only to watch as Joshua fights the Battle of Jericho, and then takes the people into the Promised Land. (*5*) Debauchery even by the High Priest in a Babylonian cabaret (resembling a Negro nightclub) finally breaks God's forebearance: "I repent of dese people dat I have made and I will deliver dem no more." (*6*) Daily petitioned by the patriarchs ("bein' Gawd ain't a bed of roses"), God at last visits earth. (*7*) He is impressed by the valorous defenders of Jerusalem. Though the odds are hopeless, they are inspired by the faith of Hosea, who has found mercy through suffering. (*8*) God sits pensively at a fish fry. Still preoccupied with what he has learned about Hosea, he suddenly realizes "dat even God must suffer." He envisions the Crucifixion—and then smiles gently. Relieved, the angels burst into song: "Hallelujah, King Jesus."

GREEN, Paul [Eliot] (1894–), is America's first and perhaps best folk playwright. His numerous plays, usually set in his native North Carolina, include both regional and pageant drama. Depicting Negroes as well as whites, Green has been most successful with regional dramas like IN ABRAHAM'S BOSOM (1926), featuring a Negro would-be Moses, and THE HOUSE OF CONNELLY (1931), a play that portrays a disintegrating aristocratic family and was responsible for launching The Group Theatre. Another tragedy about Southern whites—this time common whites—that was produced on Broadway is *The Field God* (1927). Its protagonist is a farmer whose invalid wife, a religious fanatic, dies when she discovers that he is in love with her niece; the lovers marry, but their fortunes fail and they are hounded by the intolerant scripture-quoting townspeople until their pride is gone and they appeal to God for salvation. Another Green tragedy of superstition and religious fanaticism among the uneducated Southern whites is *Shroud My Body Down* (1935). Green's most popular "symphonic drama," as he called his pageants, is the annually produced THE LOST COLONY (1937). Others include *The Highland Call* (1939), commemorating the Scots settlement in North Carolina; *The Common Glory* (1947), portraying Jefferson and Virginia's role in the American Revolution; *Faith of Our Fathers* (1950), which features George Washington; *The Founders*

(1957), which deals with the Jamestown Colony; and *Stephen Foster* (1959).

Born on a North Carolina farm where he stayed until he was twenty-two, Green started his career as a country-school teacher. After serving in France during World War I, he returned to the University of North Carolina. He studied philosophy there and soon was appointed to the faculty. As a freshman he began writing drama and (like THOMAS WOLFE) he came under the influence of Professor Frederick Koch, whose Carolina Playmakers produced Green's early one-acters. Three collections of his plays were published in quick order: *The Lord's Will and Other Carolina Plays* (1925), *The Lonesome Road: Six Plays for the Negro Theatre* (1926), and *In the Valley* (1928). These include farces as well as poignant one-acters like *The Last of the Lowries* (1920) and *White Dresses* (1926). The first, resembling Synge's RIDERS TO THE SEA, focuses on a woman whose outlaw family are killed, the last son shooting himself to avoid capture; *White Dresses* features a mulatto who fails to escape her Negro environment: her grandmother burns the dress given her by their white landlord's son—together with the faded dress his father once gave the girl's mother. Other one-acters popular with little theatres are *Fixin's* (1924; written with Erma Green, ? –), whose heroine yearns for some of the finer things of life ("fixin's") hopelessly—until she leaves her hard and dull husband; and the lighter *The No 'Count Boy* (1924). *Hymn to the Rising Sun* (1930), a short chain-gang drama, however, is deeply serious. It stresses the social criticism that permeates most of Green's plays.

Potter's Field (1931), which combines music, pantomine, and poetry, was rewritten as *Roll Sweet Chariot* (1934) and was presented on Broadway with indifferent success; "a symbolic play of the Negro people" portraying a day in a Southern slum, it fuses SYMBOLISM and REPRESENTATIONALISM. All these elements are combined more effectively in *Johnny Johnson* (1936), an anti-war play written by Green with the composer Kurt Weill and produced by the Group Theatre. Unsuccessfully revived on Broadway in 1971, it is a biting caricature of patriotism and war, which its naïve title character considers "about the lowest-darnedest thing the human race could indulge in"; but persuaded that World War I will end all wars, he enlists, experiences the madness of warfare, and ends up selling toys. Another Green play produced on Broadway is his dramatization of *Native Son* (1941), Richard Wright's novel about a Negro driven to crime by his hostile environment, and finally executed.

Green has always been conscious of the social ills about him and has never forgotten the gratuitous brutal blow he once saw administered to an innocent Negro teacher. Green has succeeded admirably in portraying common people—particularly the manners and speech of Southern Negroes. These are depicted with compassion, whether the scenes are humorous, satiric, or tragic. The intensity of Green's tragedies occasionally becomes excessive and his points tend to be repetitive. But Green did not compromise or pander to Broadway audiences. When his plays failed with them, he wrote for others: amateur little theatre groups, with whom his one-acters are still popular; and the regional outdoor theatre audiences that still flock to see his pageants. Since Green is weak in dramatic structure but strong in episodes and narrative, his talents are best displayed in these one-acters and in his vast pageant drama.

In the 1930's Green spent some time in Hollywood, preparing screen scripts. Then he returned to his university teaching and other writings, including fiction, an adaptation of Ibsen's PEER GYNT (1951), and numerous lectures and essays—some autobiographical, some about the theatre and society. The latter were reprinted in *Dramatic Heritage* (1953), *Drama and the Weather* (1958), and *Plough and Furrow* (1963). His drama has been published in the already-cited collections and in individual editions. Green's *Five Plays of the South* (1963) includes *Johnny Johnson, In Abraham's Bosom, Hymn to the Rising Sun, The House of Connelly,* and *White Dresses:* the volume's introduction by John Gassner is a biographical sketch and a critical assessment of Green's drama. A book-length study is Agatha Adams's *Paul Green of Chapel Hill* (1951).

GREENE, Graham (1904–), English novelist and playwright, became popular with his "entertainments"—fiction thrillers like *The Confidential Agent* (1939), *The Ministry of Fear* (1943), and *Our Man in Havana* (1958)—and the novels that portray his interest in psychology and Catholicism, to which he converted after a flirtation with Communism. Particularly popular among the novels—some later filmed and dramatized—are *The Power and the Glory* (1940), *The Heart of the Matter* (1948), *The End of the Affair* (1951), *The Quiet American* (1955), and *A Burnt-Out Case* (1961). Greene turned to drama relatively late in his career. His first play, THE LIVING ROOM, appeared in 1953. It was followed by THE POTTING SHED (1957), THE COMPLAISANT LOVER (1959), and *Carving a Statue* (1964), a tragicomedy featuring an unsuccessful sculptor (vaguely based on the painter Benjamin Robert Haydon) obsessed with his gigantic statue of God.

The son of the local school's headmaster, Greene was born in Berkhampstead, Hertfordshire. He had a turbulent adolescence, described in his autobiographical writings and reflected in his fiction and drama. There were a number of suicide attempts, an escape from home and school, and early (at sixteen) psychiatric treatment. He was educated at Balliol College (Oxford), and employed at various times as subeditor for the London *Times,* film critic for *The Spectator,* and director of a number of publishing houses.

Greene's plays resemble his novels. But they were never as popular, nor are they artistically as satisfying. His characters tend to be unattractive. Usually featured are a psychiatrist and a priest whose faith is, at best, shaky. Except in *The Complaisant*

Graham Greene in the late 1940's. (*Culver Pictures*)

Lover, his comic and most successful play, there are always suicides or other deaths. The characters invariably are unable to face their past and other unpleasant realities. Most important is their (and their author's) preoccupation with sin and faith. Considering the theological explorations that propel Greene's plays, it is noteworthy that he sustains dramatic interest even in patent failures like *Carving a Statue.* As Greene noted in that play's "Epitaph," however, "I earn my living in another field."

Greene novels converted into plays include *The End of the Affair, The Power and the Glory,* and *The Heart of the Matter* (1950), dramatized by Greene and BASIL DEAN. Greene also wrote screen scripts and the autobiographical *The Lost Childhood* (1951) and *A Sort of Life* (1971). His plays are analyzed in Robert O. Evans's collection, *Graham Greene: Some Critical Considerations* (1963); see also A. A. DeVitis's *Graham Greene* (1964). Both studies refer to other works about Greene.

GREGORY, Lady [Isabella Augusta Persse] (1852–1932), Irish playwright, was one of the founders of the Irish Literary Theatre (1899) and then codirector of the Abbey Theatre with WILLIAM BUTLER YEATS and J. M. SYNGE. An attractive and wealthy gentlewoman, she was the hostess and financial contributor to the fledgling Irish Literary Revival, which could not have survived without her. Among her most notable nonliterary accomplishments were defying the censorship of THE SHEWING-UP OF BLANCO POSNET (which earned her BERNARD SHAW's lifelong friendship) and leading the Abbey troupe during its triumphant American tour (1911), when she saw to it that Synge's THE PLAYBOY OF THE WESTERN WORLD remained on the boards despite opposition by indignant and rowdy Irish-Americans. As Yeats's secretary, Lady Gregory collaborated in writing a number of his dramas.* At the age of fifty she began to practice playwriting and soon mastered her art. Aside from translations and collaborations (also with DOUGLAS HYDE, a number of whose Gaelic plays she translated), she produced thirty plays of her own, most of them one-acters or short three-acters. Though she wrote many fantasy, legend, and history plays, her fame rests chiefly on her one-act peasant drama—the tragic THE GAOL GATE (1906) and the farcical SPREADING THE NEWS (1904), HYACINTH HALVEY (1906), and THE WORKHOUSE WARD (1908).

Lady Gregory was the twelfth child of Dudley Persse, a gentleman farmer descended from a long line of Irish Protestants. In 1880 she married the cultivated, sixty-three-year-old retired governor of Ceylon, Sir William Gregory of Coole. They lived together happily for twelve years and had a son. After Sir William's death in 1892, she edited and published his *Autobiography* and letters. About 1895 Lady Gregory met Yeats, whose *The Celtic Twilight* (1893) had sparked her interest in folklore. She invited him to her Coole estate (where he was to do much of his writing), and helped him financially as well as professionally. With GEORGE MOORE and EDWARD MARTYN, they planned and then launched the movement that eventually culminated in the National Theatre.

Her first important writings were *Cuchulain of Muirthemne* (1902) and *Gods and Fighting Men* (1904), celebrated prose retellings of Irish legends that furnished material for many plays, including those of Yeats and Synge. Her own first play (though her biographer assigns *Cathleen Ni Houlihan* that position), the one-act *Twenty-Five,* was produced in 1903; later she repudiated it as "sentimental and weak in construction," and refused to have it included among her collected plays.† It is about "a boy of Kilbecanty that saved his old sweetheart from being evicted," she wrote in her note to *The Jackdaw* (1907), another short play, in which she devises an alternate method of deceit to help a needy female. Lady Gregory's first collection, *Seven Short Plays* (1909), includes her most popular works: *Spreading the News, Hyacinth Halvey,* THE RISING OF THE MOON (1907), *The Jackdaw, The Workhouse Ward* (1908; her reworking of a one-act comedy written with Hyde, *The Poorhouse,* 1907), *The Travelling Man* (a miracle play), and *The Gaol Gate.* All these were successfully produced at the Abbey Theatre.

Similarly popular, if less well known today, were

*CATHLEEN NI HOULIHAN, DEIRDRE, THE HOUR-GLASS (prose version), *King Oedipus, The King's Threshold,* ON BAILE'S STRAND, *The Pot of Broth, The Unicorn from the Stars,* and *Where There Is Nothing.*

† It was discovered in the December 1902 issue of *The Gael* (published by the American Gaelic League) under the title *A Losing Game,* and republished in Robert Hogan and James Kilroy's collection of *Lost Plays of the Irish Renaissance* (1970).

the *New Comedies* (1913): *The Bogie Men* (1912, a farce about two chimney sweeps), *The Full Moon* (1910, a sequel to *Hyacinth Halvey*), *Coats* (1910, in which an unintentional exchange of garments proves mutually revealing), *Damer's Gold* (1912, a two-act comedy featuring an Irish miser à la Molière, a number of whose plays Lady Gregory translated into Irish dialect), and *McDonough's Wife* (1912), in which an Orphic poet uses his gifts to summon mourners for the funeral of his beloved but unpopular wife. All these exemplify Lady Gregory's talents for creating farcical situations, colorful peasant characters, and rich, colloquial speech.

Though in a different vein, her *Irish Folk-History Plays* (1912, two volumes) reflect the same talents. Most of these dramatizations of Gaelic legends and history are short three-act plays: GRANIA (1912); *Kincora* (1905), which depicts Brian, King of Munster and unifier of Ireland, betrayed to the Danes by his ambitious wife Gormleith; *Dervorgilla,* a one-act tragedy about a legend Yeats dramatized in THE DREAMING OF THE BONES; *The Canavans* (1906), a comedy set in Ireland during the reign of Queen Elizabeth I, whose reputation there was "awful"; the frequently praised THE WHITE COCKADE (1905); and the Moses–Charles Stewart Parnell play, THE DELIVERER (1911). The title play of *The Image and Other Plays* (1922), produced in 1909 and published in 1910, is a three-act comedy about the erection of a statue to an imaginary hero. The other plays in the collection are *Hanrahan's Oath* (1918), a one-act peasant comedy; *Shanwalla* (1915), a three-act ghost play; and *The Wrens* (written in 1914), a comic one-act "folk history" that supposes the opposite outcome of the vote on the 1799 Union Bill in Dublin. The *Three Wonder Plays* (1922) are *The Dragon* (1919), whose title character seeks a princess for his victim; *Aristotle's Bellows* (1921), another Irish fantasy; and *The Jester* (1918), a school play. An earlier fantasy, *The Golden Apple,* was published in 1916 (produced 1920). Lady Gregory's *Three Last Plays* (1928) are *Sancho's Master* (1927), a three-act adaptation of *Don Quixote;* the one-act *Dave* (1927), a story, with religious implications, about an orphan; and her last translation of Molière, *The Would-Be Gentleman.*

Though Lady Gregory's accomplishments are dwarfed by those of Yeats, Synge, and SEAN O'CASEY, she has earned her respectable reputation. She was a master of the short play, exploiting its possibilities of situation, character, and—particularly—language. Only when she tried to stretch slight episodes into longer plays did she fail. Her importance as a playwright is subsumed in her total contributions to the Irish literary renaissance. These are acknowledged and described by many writers, notably by Yeats in his *Dramatis Personae* (1936). Lady Gregory herself chronicled the movement's history in *Our Irish Theatre* (1913), her autobiography. Her "Collected Plays" constitute the last four volumes of *The Coole Edition of the Collected Works of Lady Gregory* (Volumes I–VIII, 1970), edited by T. R. Henn and Colin Smythe. O'Casey introduced *Lady Gregory: Selected Plays* (1963), edited by Elizabeth Coxhead. The latter's *Lady Gregory: A Literary Portrait* (1961), a biography and discussion of her works, includes a bibliography. Another useful study is Ann Saddlemyer's *In Defence of Lady Gregory, Playwright* (1966).

GREVENIUS, Herbert (1901–   ), Swedish playwright, came from a working-class family, but nonetheless attended the University of Stockholm. Upon concluding his studies he turned to journalism, where his ideas on the theatre were expressed in drama reviews and essays eventually published in three books (1940–51). It was Grevenius's journalism, too, that motivated his writing lively plays on topical themes, and with local color. Most successful was his *Som folk är mest* (1941), which sketches groups of simple people facing ordinary problems of life. Also popular have been working-class dramas like *Sonja* (1927) and *Första maj* (1935); *Tåg 56* (1936), which deals with the birthrate crisis made topical the previous year by Alva and Gunnar Myrdal's work; *Krigsmans erinran* (1947), a military comedy; and *Lunchrasten* (1952), which, like Grevenius's most popular play, depicts the ordinary Stockholm milieu.

GRIEG, [Johan] **Nordahl** [Brun] (1902–43), Norwegian journalist, novelist, poet, and playwright. His promising career was cut short when he was killed in a World War II bombing raid over Berlin. Grieg wrote a half dozen plays of which two became known outside Norway: *Vår ære og vår makt* (1935), a powerful attack on wartime profiteering by Norwegian merchant-ship owners insensitive to human life; and *Nederlaget* (*The Defeat,* 1937), a four-act mass drama (reworked in Brecht's THE DAYS OF THE COMMUNE) about the Paris Commune uprising of 1871 and the need to guard freedom with unrelenting vigilance. These left-wing plays were written after Grieg's extensive visit to the Soviet Union, whose theatre—like its society and government—deeply impressed him. Though a fervent nationalist who did not become a Communist Party member, Grieg's proletarian sympathies were as great as was his distrust of capitalism.

Primarily, however, Grieg was a writer of lyric poetry. His earlier plays include *En ung manns kjærlighet* (1927), which explores the choice between decency and violence; and *Barabbas* (1927), in which a similar problem is personified by Jesus and the title character. Educated in Norway as well as at Oxford and Cambridge, Grieg (who was distantly related to the composer Edvard Grieg) became a foreign correspondent during the Chinese and Spanish civil wars. When Germany invaded Norway, he joined the government in exile, enlisted in the armed forces, and devoted all his literary talents to encouraging his occupied countrymen with radio addresses and fervent verse.

Though most of Grieg's poetry, novels, and journalistic accounts have been translated, few of his plays are available in English. *The Defeat* appears in Robert W. Corrigan's collection,

Masterpieces of the Modern Scandinavian Theatre (1967), along with a brief account of Grieg's life and work, and a bibliography.

GRIESE, Friedrich (1890–), German novelist and playwright, is notable principally for powerful peasant stories published between the world wars. His plays deal with similar subjects; *Mensch aus Erde gemacht* (1932), for instance, portrays two men's bitterly passionate struggle over a farm girl. The same kinds of characters and settings are found in Griese's comedies, as in *Die Schafschur* (1934).

A former schoolmaster, Griese became increasingly immersed in the blood-and-soil ideology fashionable under Nazism, throughout which regime he continued to write in Germany. His later plays include *Der heimliche König* (1940) and *Wenn der Schein zerfällt* (1956).

GRISELDA, a comedy in twelve scenes by GERHART HAUPTMANN, published and produced in 1909. Setting: medieval Germany and Italy.

The story of a suffering wife, made famous by Boccaccio and Chaucer, is dramatized in an unsuccessful fusion of comedy and abnormal psychology—neither of which is here effective.

A wild Italian lord, Ulrich, falls in love with, pursues, and finally marries a robust German peasant girl, Griselda Helmbrecht. He becomes pathologically jealous when she is confined, and banishes their infant immediately after his birth. When Griselda asks about her baby, Ulrich deserts her. Griselda goes back to her parents' farm, but is at length prevailed upon to return to Ulrich. During their tearful reconciliation he asks how he can expiate. Griselda replies, "You must love me less, beloved!"

Later Hauptmann allowed two discarded scenes to be appended to provide more comedy.

GROTESQUE, THEATRE OF THE, is a term applied to the tragicomic Italian drama that criticized society's shortcomings and contradictions by stressing their grotesqueness. A reaction against NATURALISM, this drama (its authors were called *i grotteschi*) denounced society by means of irony and laughter. Portraying the conflict between illusion and reality, the mask and the face, *teatro del grottesco* was named and launched in 1916 with Chiarelli's THE MASK AND THE FACE, and flourished with the drama of LUIGI PIRANDELLO. Sometimes its bizarre plots—though not its actions—suggest the GRAND GUIGNOL. A mid-century descendant of the grotesque movement was the theatre of the ABSURD.

GUARDSMAN, THE (*A testőr*), a play in three acts by FERENCE MOLNÁR, published and produced in 1911. Setting: early twentieth-century Vienna.

This popular comedy, translated also as *Where Ignorance Is Bliss,* was the first profitable production (1924) of the Theatre Guild. In it, Alfred Lunt and Lynn Fontanne made their initial joint and successful appearance (the play had been a failure before); in 1931 they made *The Guardsman* into their only motion picture. The 1941 film THE CHOCOLATE SOLDIER combines the music and lyrics of the operetta with the plot of *The Guardsman.*

A recently married prominent stage couple quarrel bitterly. Madly in love with his flirtatious wife and eager to test her questionable fidelity, the husband pays court to her in a disguise he thinks will appeal to her, that of an Austrian (a Russian, in Lunt and Fontanne's production) guardsman. This masquerade is a test of his manhood as well as of his professional worth. When in the last act he reveals his true identity, the actress wife looks up and slowly begins to smile. The play's climax is the final ambiguity about who has really been deceived as she continues artlessly in the manner in which she has flirted with the guardsman, and then tells the exasperated husband, "I'm going on with our little comedy from where we left off last night—the comedy that I've been playing for your sake since yesterday afternoon."

GUATEMALA has produced little important drama and the work of its most notable playwright, CARLOS SOLÓRZANO, belongs to the theatre history of MEXICO. Early moderns in Guatemala, who wrote the then-fashionable romantic tragedies, include Vicenta Laparra de la Cerda (1834–1905), a pioneer in Guatemala's theatre and the first of her country's numerous female playwrights; Miguel Angel Urrutia (1852–1931), some of whose now equally dated dramas are in verse; and Ismael Cerna (1856–1901) and Manuel Valle (1861–1913), both of them members of talented playwriting families. Among later dramatists, Miguel Marsicovétere y Durán (1913–), a poet and a founder of a theatre group, wrote fifteen fantasies and *El espectro acróbata* (1953), a "grotesque in five cartoons" that in the printed version become a "tragedy of masks" when turned upside down and read backwards. Manuel Galich (1913–), a versatile playwright whose career spans the pre- and post-Ubico dictatorship years (1931–44), wrote COSTUMBRISMO comedies; grimly NATURALISTIC social and political protest drama; history plays that include a trilogy (*Ida y vuelta*) on Guatemalan poverty and military carnage in the nineteenth century, which won the Central American Drama Competition in 1948; and the satire *El pescado indigesto*, which won first prize at the Pan American drama competition in 1961.

Among the works listed under LATIN AMERICA, Willis Knapp Jones's *Behind Spanish American Footlights* (1966) includes a comprehensive survey of Guatemala's drama.

GUITRY, Sacha [Alexandre-Georges-Pierre] (1885–1957), French actor and playwright, was a leading theatre figure between the two world wars. He was born in Leningrad (then St. Petersburg), Russia, where he made his first stage appearances under the management of his father, the prominent actor-playwright Lucien-Germain Guitry (1860–1925). The younger Guitry's earliest successful play was *Nono* (1905), a comedy in which he again starred later with the second of his five wives, the actress Yvonne Printemps. Well over one hundred plays and musical reviews (plus about thirty film scripts) flowed from Guitry's versatile pen, most of them light, witty comedies not unlike those of NOËL COWARD. Guitry skillfully produced popular fare that includes sentiment as well as bawdiness, romance as well as cynicism.

Very popular were his intimate dramatic biographies, particularly *Deburau** (1918), *Pasteur* (1919), *Mozart* (1925), *Frans Hals ou "L'Admiration"* (1931)—and the autobiographical *Quand jouons-nous la comédie?* (1935). Other notable Guitry plays are fantasies like *Faisons un rêve* (1916, produced in America as *Sleeping Partners*) and *L'Illusioniste* (1917), a long-time hit performed by Guitry with Yvonne Printemps; comedies like *Le Grand Duc* (*The Grand Duke*, 1921); and the more serious *Le Nouveau Testament* (1934), produced in English as *Where There's a Will.* Guitry liked to star as the "great lover" in his own plays, and he also appeared in and directed many films. After World War II he was tried and acquitted of pro-Nazi sympathies.

Guitry's plays are collected in fifteen volumes (1959–64); his autobiography, *Memoires d'un tricheur* (*Memoirs of a Cheat*, 1935), was translated also under various other titles. James Harding's *Sacha Guitry: The Last Boulevardier* (1968) is a biography.

GUSTAV ADOLF, a historical play in five acts by AUGUST STRINDBERG, published in 1900 and produced in 1912. Setting: Germany, 1630–32.

Strindberg considered his massive canvas of the Thirty Years' War, and King Gustav II's part in it, his *Nathan the Wise*. Like Lessing's play, *Gustav Adolf* deals with religious tolerance and is more suitable to the study than the boards. Its sixty-odd characters, seven-hour length, and immense complexity make it theatrically unwieldy. But the play excels in fine scenes and characterizations, particularly in the rounded portrait of the admirable Gustav.

The people are suffering from the terrible brutalities of the war that has been devastating Germany. Their hopes rest with Sweden, and indeed, Gustav's proclamation and advance troops promise relief, order, justice, and religious tolerance. To Gustav, admired by his people and his commanders, his task is clear and simple: a Lutheran crusade against the hated Catholics. But as the war progresses and religious intolerance is seen to be more complex than it first appeared, Gustav confronts many difficulties. He is forced to compromise, break promises, solicit the help of Jewish financiers, and ally himself with Catholic France. His idealistic young chamberlain, the keeper of his conscience, finally becomes too troublesome. But though Gustav is victorious and achieves his aim, to secure freedom of worship for Protestants, his ambitions for power grow. His advisers try to dissuade him from seeking to emulate Alexander the Great. But his eyes are opened only when he is wounded in battle: "I thought . . . that I was the chosen one, but then I had to learn better. My time has not yet come, but I'm grateful for the warning." His personal tolerance now develops to the point where he accepts the basic similarity of all monotheistic religions, and he even punishes Protestant intolerance of Catholicism. His humility, too, grows. He becomes increasingly troubled by the suffering and brutalization of his own army, by his blood guilt for his ancestors' crimes, by doubts about the legitimacy of his throne, and by his concern about Sweden's future. Finally he resigns himself to being "a poor sinner"—no longer "the anointed of the Lord" he earlier had proclaimed himself to be—and gives up his dreams "to collect a wagonload of crowns." Humbled and chastened, he goes to his last battle. In the final scene, a subdued funeral service celebrates Gustav's victory in death.

GUSTAV III, a historical play in four acts by AUGUST STRINDBERG, published in 1903 and produced in 1916. Setting: Sweden, 1788.

Strindberg's charming and witty chronicle play matches the complex character of its protagonist. Highly gifted, Gustav III was an enlightened despot as well as a consummate actor and playwright. His reforms brought Sweden the freedom spirit of the contemporaneous American and French revolutions, and his reign stimulated Sweden's most impressive cultural flowering. The play successfully fuses history, Eugène Scribe-like intrigue, fine characterizations, and high comedy.

It is the eve of Gustav's assembly of the Estates, whose meeting is to grant almost absolute power to the king and extend that of the commoners. Gustav's reforms have antagonized and impoverished some of the aristocrats. Waiting for the king, numerous conspirators and some supporters discuss the difficulties of Gustav's unconstitutional but necessary war. Later, as Gustav deals with various people (including the conspirators, whose plans he discovered), he expresses his ideals: "I am the radical, the democrat, the one who hates the nobility, the first citizen in a free country! The man of the people and the defender of the oppressed! I am the disciple of Rousseau . . . and of Voltaire! . . . George Washington is my friend! Franklin my ideal!" He begs his unimaginative, conventional queen to bear their unhappy marriage courageously, for the sake of the country as well as their child. Then, as he plans his campaign against the conspirators, his arrogant but loyal favorite remarks, "That's not badly put together! Considered as a play!" The king answers, "Who knows? Perhaps the whole thing is a play." As for the last act, "it will come of itself!" At their assembly the conspirators plan the overthrow of Gustav, who theatrically appears in their midst and invites them to a

* About the famous early-nineteenth-century pantomimist Jean-Gaspard Deburau and his affair with Marie Duplessis, Dumas *fils*'s model for Camille —whose lover, Armand, Guitry's father played at his stage debut (1878), in *La Dame aux Camélias*. A tragicomedy in verse, Sacha Guitry's *Deburau* was adapted by HARLEY GRANVILLE-BARKER.

fete. There, he confronts his most hated enemy (later his assassin), and narrowly foils the conspirators' plans. Alone, he is thrown into helpless misery by a scurrilous lampoon on the queen's rumored adultery: "They have stolen my son ... How can he be successor to the throne after this?" Gustav is about to be shot by his concealed enemy when the queen enters, inadvertently saving his life by blocking the assassin's aim. Sensing his danger and her providential intercession, Gustav asks her to stay with him this evening: "I was born with a caul and with Caesar's luck." He leads her out histrionically, laughing at her reply: "'Wasn't there someone called Brutus?'—that is superb! Superb! Madame!"

An important subplot deals with Gustav's loyal state secretary and his less loyal and promiscuous—but attractive and witty—wife.

GUSTAV VASA, a historical play in five acts by AUGUST STRINDBERG, published and produced in 1899. Setting: Sweden, 1543–44.

Written some twenty years after the trilogy's first play, MASTER OLOF, *Gustav Vasa* focuses on the historical events occurring about a generation later. Olof is now a skillful and loyal servant to the king, and an upright if disillusioned man. (His marriage, in the meantime, has degenerated from a love relationship to a DANCE OF DEATH relationship.) Towering above him and all others, however, is Gustav I, now at the height of his power and threatened by rebellion. The play is a character study of this complex "practical but idealistic realist,"* who is admirable despite his many shortcomings. Though he does not appear in the first two acts, Odin-like Gustav dominates even them. Many consider *Gustav Vasa* the finest historical drama since those of Shakespeare.

Acts I and II. The mine owners of Dalarna nervously await the arrival of the king. Gustav has forgiven their previous insubordination because they had been the first to help the young king. But though they admire him, they still resent paying the taxes needed to settle Sweden's debts. They discuss foreign plots and the growing insurrection in Småland province. Master Olof arrives with Herman Israel, Lübeck's representative and Gustav's old friend. The mine owners' fears grow after Olof announces the king's orders: they must stay home and await the royal summons. Olof shrewdly questions them while individual Dalesmen are summoned out (and, as is soon revealed, killed). When the tension reaches its high point, the bloody coats of the executed mine owners are thrown in. The others, frightened and trapped by their own words, are permitted to leave for Stockholm. (Olof and Israel characterize the Dalesmen as "a stiff-necked people, faithful as gold. ... But a little naïve.") In Stockholm, the emotionally disturbed Crown Prince Erik slurs his royal father, whom he hates, and complains, "Lovelessness ... has become a fire that is consuming me." Israel sadly deplores the events that force Lübeck to help those who oppose his royal friend. But he presciently warns his son, who worships Gustav, against treason: "My country first, then my family!" While roistering in a tavern with his equally dissolute secretary Göran Persson, Prince Erik is arrested by order of the king: "Always this giant hand, which one never sees, only feels."

Acts III–V. In his study, Gustav gently rejects his beloved queen's mercy pleas for the Dalesmen, and then angrily castigates his besotted son Erik. Negotiating with his old friend Israel to wipe out all debts with Lübeck and make Sweden totally independent, the king confesses to agonies over his necessarily ruthless political actions. Gustav is further tried by his Catholic mother-in-law and Olof's criticisms for waiving religious laws for her. Exasperated, he sends Olof out: "Here *I* do the thundering!" After begging divine guidance in dealing justly with the traitors, he finally and swiftly condemns them—and then buries his face in anguish. At a tavern, his son Erik falls in love with the beautiful flower girl Karin Månsdotter, and begins to reform. The king disguises himself, mingles with the commoners, and is confronted with the unhappy effects of his policies. Despairing as the rebellion grows, he seeks Olof's advice. When Olof frankly catalogues Gustav's offenses and censures his pride, the enraged king asks him who he thinks he is. Olof replies, "A humble instrument of God made to serve what is great: the great miracle man of the Lord" who united Sweden. He counsels Gustav to humble himself and negotiate. The king does so, but his offer is contemptuously rejected. No longer believing himself to be God's chosen instrument and admitting the justice of his punishment, Gustav is ready to abdicate and flee when the troops are heard. A drunken soldier appears, and the king learns that the Dalesmen have come—to help *him,* not the Småland rebels. Gustav embraces his queen and then achieves his greatest victory, the one over himself: "O God, Thou hast punished me, and I thank Thee!"

Also important in the plot are numerous parallel domestic scenes and relationships, including those of Gustav, Israel, and Olof with their sons; Gustav and Olof with their wives; and young Israel and Erik with their sweethearts.

GUY DOMVILLE, a play in three acts by HENRY JAMES, produced in 1895 and published in 1949. Setting: England, 1780.

This is James's best-known play because of the near-riot at its memorable premiere in London on January 5, 1895. The sensitivity and subtlety for which it was praised by the discriminating did not appeal to the hooting pit and gallery. Nevertheless, it ran for five weeks, at the end of which James wrote, "It has been a great relief to feel that one of the most detestable incidents of my life has closed." Though the play was considered promising, it is dated because of its sentimental dialogue and stock melodrama, strained motivation, and excessive reliance on chance. Leon Edel's edition of the play (in *The Complete Plays of Henry James,* 1949) was

* Walter Johnson's introduction to his translation of *The Vasa Trilogy* (1959), which ends with ERIC IV.

republished separately in 1960, together with its comprehensive history, pertinent parts of James's biography, and the contemporary reviews of BERNARD SHAW, ARNOLD BENNETT, and H. G. Wells.

Guy Domville, tutor to the son of a beautiful young widow, is about to enter Holy Orders. Lord Devenish (the scheming villain of the plot) persuades him to carry on the tradition of the Domville family, whose only other remaining male has just been killed. Guy goes to London, where he experiences worldly evil. In the nick of time he is saved from marrying Lord Devenish's illegitimate daughter, who is betrothed to a naval officer; in a famous scene the men have a drinking bout, and Guy then helps the lovers escape. Guy returns to marry the widow, to whom he could not earlier confess his love because his friend, too, loves her. Lord Devenish again enters at the crucial moment, armed with new schemes. Though the widow loves him and his friend is willing to step aside, Guy now decides otherwise: "I'm the *last,* my lord, of the Domvilles!"* He will join the monastery "if the Church will *take* again an erring son!" And Guy leaves, after bidding farewell to the widow and to his friend: "Be kind to him. . . . Be good to her."

* At this point of the premiere, a voice from the gallery shouted: "It's a bloody good thing y'are!"

H

HACKETT, Albert (1900–), American playwright, was a young New York actor in 1927 when he started collaborating on plays with a young New Jersey-born actress, Frances Goodrich (1891?–). She soon divorced her husband, the notable historian Hendrik Willem Van Loon, and married Hackett. Together the Hacketts wrote a number of popular film scripts like *The Thin Man* (1934), and a few plays. But their only memorable drama, on which they spent years of research and writing, is their skillful adaptation of *Anne Frank: The Diary of a Young Girl* (1947), the moving account of an adolescent Jewish girl who was murdered in a Nazi concentration camp after hiding in an Amsterdam warehouse and office building for two years, as THE DIARY OF ANNE FRANK (1955).

HACKS, Peter (1928–), East German dramatist, made his name in the 1950's. The following decade his plays—satiric comedies written in the vein of BERTOLT BRECHT—were criticized for political unorthodoxy, and Hacks repeatedly revised them. This was the fate of *Moritz Tassow,* the 1965 Berlin Festival play, whose title character, an anti-Nazi swineherd, demands a Marxist paradise but succeeds only in eliciting the peasants' greed. Though Hacks maintained that Tassow is a villain and tried to rewrite the play accordingly, he was unsuccessful with the arguments that had worked for Brecht in the analogous MOTHER COURAGE. *Moritz Tassow* was taken off the boards, and Hacks turned to other writings.

He was born in Breslau, studied in Munich, and received his Ph.D. in 1951. Four years later he joined the Berliner Ensemble, and soon made his reputation as a playwright with *Eröffnung des indischen Zeitalters* (*Opening of the Indian Era,* 1955), an EPIC drama that portrays Columbus, like Brecht's Galileo, sacrificing his discoveries to power-hungry and avaricious rulers; *Die Schlacht bei Lobositz* (1957), which won the Lessing Prize, a comic depiction of an anti-hero of the Seven Years' War, shown to be an officers' conspiracy against humanity; and *Der Müller von Sans-souci* (1958), a comedy based on Brecht's idea for the dramatization of an anecdote about Frederick the Great's attempt to prove that he is not a despot.

These are *Lehrstücke,* Brechtian historical parables. Then, however, Hacks turned to dramatizing contemporary themes—and encountered the difficulties that were to trouble him thereafter. Learning of complaints made by steel workers in Senftenberg, Hacks went to live with the miners and wrote a play about them. It was criticized for its negative attitudes, the original production was canceled, and workers were assigned to discuss the play's ideology with Hacks. He ultimately rewrote the play as *Die Sorgen und die Macht,* and it was produced at the Berlin Festival of 1961. The play was the festival's major contribution, and both it and Hacks were criticized for exhibiting "decadent" values.

After *Moritz Tassow* was similarly criticized, Hacks supported himself by writing children's plays, adapting operettas, and translating theatre classics.

HAINES, William W[ister] (1908–), American writer, gained prominence as a dramatist with *Command Decision,* which in 1947 became a Broadway hit, was published as a novel, and made into a film. Dramatizing the tribulations of a commanding general of an American bombardment division stationed in England in 1944, this war play graphically depicts a life once led by Haines, a former combat air officer. Haines's other writing has consisted of short stories and novels.

HAIRY APE, THE, "A Comedy of Ancient and Modern Life" in eight scenes by EUGENE O'NEILL, published and produced in 1922. Setting: a ship and various parts of contemporary New York City.

Particularly in its ship, prison, and Fifth Avenue scenes, this play is even more EXPRESSIONISTIC and SYMBOLIC than THE EMPEROR JONES, which it resembles in design and theme. "[Man] has lost his old harmony with nature, the harmony which he used to have as an animal and has not yet acquired in a spiritual way," O'Neill wrote to the New York *Herald Tribune* (November 16, 1924); "The subject here . . . is man and his struggle with his own fate. The struggle used to be with the gods, but is now with himself, his own past, his attempt 'to belong.' " Despite its at first luke-warm reviews, this play has remained an O'Neill favorite. It is one of his major plays and in 1944 was made into what O'Neill considered a distorted film version.

In the cramped and prisonlike forecastle of a transatlantic liner, Yank glories in his obvious superiority over the other stokers, in "belonging," in being part of the steel and machinery that run the ship. He disparages Long's Marxist-Christian harangue ("nix on dat Salvation Army-Socialist bull") and Paddy's nostalgic reminiscences of sailing in the glorious past, when "a ship was part of the sea, and a man was part of a ship,

The Hairy Ape, Scene 5 ("Fifth Avenue Scene"). Yank (Louis Wolheim) and Long (Harold West), at right. New York, 1922. (*Theatre Collection, New York Public Library*)

and the sea joined all together and made it one." Yank brags, "I'm de end! I'm de start!" and concludes that both the "rich guys dat tink dey're somep'n" and his griping mates simply "don't belong." But Yank's complacence is shattered by the decadent Mildred Douglas, a millionaire's daughter traveling with her aunt. Both women are hateful and incongruous, artificial, disharmonious figures in the midst of nature's ocean and sunshine. A dabbler in social work, Mildred visits the stokehole, sees the cursing Yank, and faints in horror at "the filthy beast." To his mates' grotesque laughter and cynical accompanying chants ("Think!" "Love!" "Law!" "Governments!" "God!"), back in the forecastle, Yank broods—assuming the position of Rodin's "The Thinker." His fury reaches its high point when Paddy describes Mildred's looking at him as if he were a "hairy ape." In a frenzy, Yank vows to get even with her. Three weeks later with Long on Fifth Avenue (grotesquely commercial and disharmonious with nature), Yank attacks an impervious "procession of gaudy marionettes" leaving a church after absurdly platitudinous chatter. He is clubbed and sent to jail, where he hears about the I.W.W. Eager to join them and get his revenge by dynamiting the Douglas Steel Works, Yank is contemptuously kicked out as "a brainless ape." He finally goes to the zoo, where he admires a gorilla which seems so much better off. "I kin make a bluff at talkin' and tinkin'—a'most git away wit it—a'most!—and dat's where de joker comes in. I ain't on oith and I ain't in heaven, get me?" he tells the gorilla: "I'm in de middle tryin' to separate 'em, takin' all de woist punches from bot' of 'em. Maybe dat's what they call hell, huh? But you, yuh're at de bottom. You belong!" Forcing the lock and offering to shake its hand, he is crushed by the gorilla, which throws him into the steel cage and leaves. Yank dies as the monkeys start wailing. "And, perhaps, the Hairy Ape at last belongs."

HAITI. The country's official language is French, but the Creole patois used by three quarters of the population is also the language of much of Haiti's literature. Romanticism and SYMBOLISM were succeeded by indigenous themes flavored with anti-Yankee sentiments during the United States occupation of Haiti (1915–34), and then by NATURALISTIC depictions of social concerns. Though there has been some Haitian drama throughout Haiti's history, little of it is notable and the theatre has presented mostly classic (particularly French) and modern European drama.

HALBE, Max (1865–1944), German playwright and novelist, comes after GERHART HAUPTMANN and HERMANN SUDERMANN in the triumvirate of his country's principal NATURALISTS. His greatest popular success was the early *Jugend* (*Youth,* 1893; translated also as *When Love Is Young*), a poetic drama of adolescent love set amidst fanatic Catholicism and Polish-German antagonisms in West Prussia, the locale of most of Halbe's work; *Jugend* depicts the affair of an illegitimate girl and her cousin, and ends when her demented half-brother jealously shoots her as she throws herself in front of her lover. Halbe's other plays, some of which have been translated into English, include histories and comedies. Though similarly praised for conveying turn-of-the-century feelings, they were less successful. Halbe never achieved the high distinction for which he had originally appeared destined.

Born of Catholic parents near Danzig in northeast Germany, Halbe left home to study law, languages, and history at various German universities. In Berlin he met Hauptmann and came under his influence as well as that of other German naturalists and HENRIK IBSEN. Halbe's first produced play, *Eisgang* (1892), is a psychological portrayal of the conflicts between humanistic and business orientations. After *Youth* came the play that has been called his greatest artistic success, *Mutter Erde* (*Mother Earth,* 1897); also set in the east German borderland, it too is a love tragedy and features a couple whose union, prevented by the man's unfortunate marriage to a sophisticated city girl, is achieved only through the regenerative powers of "mother earth"—when the lovers commit suicide together.

Other notable Halbe plays are *Haus Rosenhagen* (1901, translated as *The Rosenhagens*), on a similar theme; and *Der Strom* (1903), depicting the passions of three brothers for the same woman. Halbe's history plays include *Das wahre Gesicht* (1907), in which three friends compete for the rule of Danzig as well as the love of a doomed woman whose "true face" is seen only by the artist who paints her portrait. The influence of FRANK WEDEKIND, a member of a group Halbe joined in Munich at the turn of the century, is notable in such plays as *Die Insel der Seligen* (1905, about a utopian troupe), *Blaue Berge* (1909), and the comedy *Kikeriki* (1921). Halbe's later plays, like Ibsen's, veer toward mysticism and include the atypical superman drama *Schloss Zeitvorbei* (1917) and *Die Traumgesichte des Adam Thor* (1929), whose nightmare episodes portray recurrent relationships between a teacher's former and present pupils.

Halbe wrote until the end of his life, his last play, *Die Friedeninsel,* appearing in 1944. His novels have been praised for their superior mastery of style. Other activities he ventured into were the short-lived turn-of-the-century Intimate Theatre for Dramatic Experiments and a People's Theatre. Halbe's collected works were published in 1917–23. *Jahrhundertwende: Geschichte meines Lebens, 1893–1914* (1935), his autobiography, is significant also for its discussions of naturalism.

HALÉVY, Ludovic (1833–1908), French short-story writer and dramatist, collaborated with others, particularly with Henri Meilhac (1831–97), with whom he wrote librettos for Jacques Offenbach's operettas and many long-popular vaudevilles and light comedies. Among the most successful Halévy-Meilhac collaborations was the comedy *Frou-Frou* (1869). Their plays were published in eight volumes (1900–02).

HALL, Willis (1929–), English playwright, has produced about one hundred radio and television scripts and numerous films. His first and most notable stage play was *The Long and the Short and the Tall* (1959), a popular World War II drama in which a group of English soldiers and their Japanese prisoner are surrounded and finally decimated in the Malayan jungle. Though influenced by JOHN OSBORNE and the other "angry young men," Hall subsequently turned to light comedy: *Last Day in Dreamland* and *A Glimpse of the Sea,* two 1959 one-acters about marital infidelity; an adaptation of FRANÇOIS BILLETDOUX's *Tchin-Tchin* as *Chin-Chin* (1960); and many works in collaboration with Keith Waterhouse (1929–). The adaptation (also as a film) of Waterhouse's comic *Billy Liar* (1960) was their most successful venture; others include *England, Our England* (1962, a revue); two one-act comedies on adultery, *Squat Betty* and *The Sponge Room* (1962); and a full-length farce on the same subject, originally titled *Help Stamp Out Marriage!* (1966) and also produced as *Say Who You Are.*

HALLSTRÖM, Per (1866–1960), Swedish author, was distinguished at the turn of the century as a master of the short story. Although he was also a poet, novelist, essayist, and playwright, his work in these other genres is of lesser importance. Most of his score of plays are of more literary interest rather than theatrical. But in *Erotikon* (1908) and *Nessusdräkten* (*The Mantle of Nessus,* 1919), satires of hypocrisy in sex and politics, Hallström touched on provocative contemporary issues. Of lesser popular success, though praised by the critics, were two historical plays, *Karl XI* and *Gustaf III* (both 1918). He also wrote tragedies like *Bianco Capello* (1900), comedies like *En veneziansk komedi* (*A Venetian Comedy,* 1901), and dramatizations of a number of legends and sagas. His pro-German sympathies during World War I isolated him from the intellectual community and caused a sharp decline in his subsequent productivity. Hallström's only significant later work consisted of his translation of Shakespeare's plays in the 1920's.

HAMILTON, Patrick (1904–62), English novelist and playwright, was born in Sussex. He made his name with *Twopence Coloured* (1928), a novel with a theatre setting and characteristic Dickensian touches, particularly in characterization. Hamilton became fascinated with melodrama when he worked with various theatre groups. His first play was *Rope* (1929), which later appeared as *Rope's End* and was filmed. He became known with his play *Angel Street* (1938), which was originally produced—and subsequently filmed—as *Gaslight*. A "good Victorian thriller," this melodrama is included in Burns Mantle's *Best Plays of 1941–42*. Hamilton's dramatic works include such other macabre thrillers as *The Duke in Darkness* (1942) and *The Governness* (1945), and some radio plays. His sister Diana Hamilton (1898–1951), an actress and playwright, was the wife of SUTTON VANE.

HAMLET IN WITTENBERG, a "dramatic poem" in five acts by GERHART HAUPTMANN, published and produced in 1935. Setting: sixteenth-century Wittenberg and environs.

Hauptmann's preoccupation with *Hamlet* dates to long before his *Hamlet in Wittenberg*. His translation of Shakespeare's play was produced in 1927 and published the following year; in it he added a few scenes of his own and made minor changes, most notably transposing the "To be or not to be" soliloquy to Act V and giving some speeches of Laertes to Hamlet. The wholly original *Hamlet in Wittenberg* was written in "humble homage" (*"demutsvolle Huldigung"*) to Shakespeare, Hauptmann noted in his preface. It presents a meditative, infatuated nineteen-year-old prince amidst his student companions and others. The play is lively and has many characters (but aside from Hamlet himself, only Horatio, Rosencrantz, and Guildenstern are from Shakespeare). There are frequent verbal echoes of Shakespeare's lines, and the play's convivial bustle has a tragic undertone.

Hamlet falls in love with a worthless gypsy girl, defends her from a seducer, and even seeks the advice of the elderly Philipp Melanchthon, Luther's fellow reformer, about marrying her. Her unfaithfulness is discovered by Hamlet's friends, who arrest her; but Hamlet sadly releases her and sends her off. Throughout the play the prince is preoccupied with resentment of his mother's messages urging his return; of his uncle, who is keeping her company; and of his father's seeming indifference to him. At a banquet, Hamlet goes temporarily mad as he senses the news just before messengers arrive with word of his father's death.

HAMLET OF STEPNEY GREEN, THE, "a sad comedy with some songs" in three acts by BERNARD KOPS, produced in 1958 and published in 1959. Setting: Stepney Green (London), late 1950's.

Kops's first play is a jazzy, sentimental analogue (sometimes parody) of Shakespeare's play. The hero is David Levy, a dreamer who wants to be a great crooner instead of a pickled-herring peddler like his father Sam: "I want to hear my voice blaring from the record shops as I whizz by in my Jaguar. . . . I want to make people happy." David misunderstands his dying father's ramblings, thinks he was murdered, and assumes a Hamlet pose. Sam returns as an amiable ghost and eventually persuades David that all was for the best—even his mother's remarriage. Finally David's reason returns. He decides to follow in his father's footsteps: he will be a singing peddler, and marry the girl he loves. The ghost departs happily, exhorting him to "make the most" of youth and life, "because life is a holiday from the dark." He concludes, "the world is a wedding" (subsequently the title of Kops's autobiography), "so— Let the wedding continue—"

HAMMERSTEIN, Oscar, II (1895–1961), American lyricist and playwright, collaborated on many highly successful operettas and musicals, including *Rose Marie* (1924), *The Desert Song* (1926), *Show Boat* (1927, a dramatization of the EDNA FERBER novel), OKLAHOMA! (1943), CAROUSEL (1945), SOUTH PACIFIC (1949), *The King and I* (1951, a dramatization of Margaret Landon's *Anna and the King of Siam*), *Pipe Dream* (1955, a dramatization of a JOHN STEINBECK novel), *Flower Drum Song* (1958), and *The Sound of Music* (1959).

HANDS AROUND (*Reigen*), "Ten Dialogues" by ARTHUR SCHNITZLER, privately printed in 1900 and produced in 1912. Setting: Vienna, 1890's.

This, the most popular of Schnitzler's plays, has also appeared in various film and stage productions under such titles as *Merry-Go-Round, La Ronde,* and *Circle of Love*. It is a fast-moving comedy consisting of ten amorous and symmetrically interrelated dramatic sketches. The play was banned as subversive and obscene when published in 1903, and driven off the Berlin boards in 1920 at its first authorized production, by Max Reinhardt. (The premiere had taken place in Budapest, Schnitzler being unable to prevent it because the play was not copyrighted in Hungary.) A sprightly erotic round-dance of a chain of partners, the comedy satirizes, in ten copulation scenes, the moral looseness of *fin de siècle* Vienna and ten foolish people's illusive quest for human contact and happiness.

(*1*) A prostitute urges a soldier who has little time to take her right there, on the ground and for free; afterwards, when he refuses to tip her, she curses him. (*2*) The soldier seduces a maid in the amusement park, but then lets the clinging girl cool her heels while he goes off to dance again. (*3*) After ringing for this maid, who is writing her lover, a bored young gentleman easily seduces (or perhaps is seduced by) her and then leaves—and she steals one of his cigars. (*4*) When the young gentleman gets a young wife to come to an assignation and to bed, the young gentleman is impotent. "I must be too much in love with you," he tells her, and recounts tales of true love in which the participants spent nights together doing nothing except weep with happiness. But finally he succeeds. When they get dressed, the wife remarks that "it's much better that we didn't just cry"; and after she leaves he smiles with satisfaction at having an affair with a real and respectable woman. (*5*) The young wife is cautioned by her smug husband not to associate with loose married women; after their lovemaking, he rejoices that the two of them after five years can still remember their honeymoon. (*6*) In a restaurant's private dining room, the husband briefly worries about disease after he seduces a pickup. But entranced with her youth and sweetness, he suggests that "if you want to love me—only me—we can fix things up." (*7*) Charmed by this young miss despite her ignorance, a conceited poet, after they sleep together, wonders how she will react to his new play. (*8*) The poet and an actress just jilted by her lover start an affair in a country inn. (*9*) The actress seduces a visiting count in her bedroom in the morning. (*10*) The count awakes in a brothel, next to the common whore of the first "dialogue." Solicitously he questions her about her life, romanticizing her and his own gallant behavior. But when she tells him he was drunk when they came in last night, dropped on the couch with her, and "fell asleep right afterwards," he leaves with a disillusioned "Good morning."

HANGMAN, THE (*Bödeln*), a one-act play by PÄR LAGERKVIST, published and produced in 1934. Setting: a medieval tavern and a modern nightclub.

Adapted from his 1933 novella by the same name, this became Lagerkvist's most successful theatre piece and the most sensational Scandinavian play of the decade. It transcends its immediate protest against Fascism and vividly embodies, in the obtrusive, terrifying title character who sits silent until almost the end, man's unchanging, persistent cruelty. An extended, partly NATURALIST and partly EXPRESSIONIST one-acter, it is a mass drama with episodic visions. By means of lighting and other devices it is divided into two parts: a medieval tavern suddenly is transformed into a horrendous modern nightclub.

The awesome and gigantic Hangman, draped in a blood-red robe and branded on his forehead, sits alone at a table. Observing him with frightened fascination, half-drunken craftsmen shout and laugh and drink ale that is rumored to be exceptionally good because the tavernkeeper "pinched a poacher's finger" from the gallows and put it in the barrel: "There's nothing like a finger from the gallows to give the ale a musty smack, y'know!" A carpenter relates a tale—which is soon dramatized—that demonstrates the Hangman's supernatural power: Though his wife has objected, the Hangman gives in to a mother's pleas and lifts the curse off a doomed boy. "Sure the headsman's good sometimes, too," one of the men admits, and an old shoemaker adds that "he can suffer like the rest of us" and "feels the ill of what he does. And it's well known that he always asks the victim's pardon before he takes off his head." They laugh boisterously as a butcher's helper urges the women to go to the gallows and look at a recently hanged man whose clothes were stolen "and all the Lord's work and wonders are there to see. Womenfolk have trudged from far off since morning to see the splendor." Amidst other coarse joking they relate the story—some of which is soon dramatized—of the Hangman's marriage to a girl he could not persuade himself to execute; but when she strangled their child, who inherited the gallows marks with which she was branded, the Hangman ultimately had to execute her. The craftsmen become increasingly raucous as they relate their cruel medieval practices and superstitions. A disfigured criminal tells how he picked a mandrake root from under the very corpses on the gallows. Shaking the stumps of his amputated hands, he rages, screams, and finally collapses. The tavern darkens, except for the spotlight that continues to play on the motionless Hangman.

More people enter, there is laughing, and soon a larger interior is visible. It is occupied by festive people in modern evening dress, eating, drinking, and dancing to the Negro jazz-band music. The wealthy customers are thrilled to see the Hangman, and salute him by extending an arm: "Heil!" Awed though intrigued by him, the women lasciviously speculate on "what it's like with a hangman, hmn?" The men discuss mass liquidations and agree that there is "no harm in that. After all, there are lots of people in the world," and an officer remarks, "Order is an excellent thing." Another man adds that "violence is the highest expression of humanity's physical and spiritual powers!" while yet another insists that they "demand absolutely that those who think in any other way shall be castrated." Ignoring occasional beggars, who are quickly ejected, they become increasingly raucous and belligerent, convinced that their "glorious people" are united as never before: "The world has never seen anything like it!" In the meantime a radiant woman, dressed as a beggar but with a halo of light about her, sits by the Hangman. Suddenly the crowds become enraged at the Negro musicians. First they curse at them, and then they beat and shoot them until the defeated Negroes surrender. They must play faster and louder, while the whites dance in a growing orgy of sex and violence. Then the crowd hails the Hangman: "His mighty figure fills us with confidence and courage! It shall lead us—the only one we intend to follow!" At last the Hangman rises. "Since the beginning of time I have looked to my task, and it seems I shall not have finished with it yet a while," he begins. Then he details his journey, "spattered with blood," generation after generation. "I have ravaged and laid waste kingdoms. Done everything you have asked of me," he continues, bemoaning what men have done to the earth, symbolized by the radiant woman seated beside him, a vision of immortal, boundless love—"a

The Hangman, Gösta Ekman playing the title character. Göteborg, 1935. (*Drottningholms Teatermuseum*)

prisoner, as I am, in our common home." But the Hangman must pursue his destiny. He recalls executing Christ, whose voice is soon heard from the distance. "But I, I am your Christ, I live!" the Hangman continues, though he longs to die as a sacrifice. "And me you'll not crucify, not me!"—not so long as men shall live. He envisions a final "eternal darkness with my broadax thrown down on the barren earth in memory of the breed that live here!" The woman comforts him: "I kiss your burning forehead and wipe the blood from your hand. You know that I wait for you!" He looks at her, smiles sorrowfully, and as a roll of drums is heard outside, "adjusts his belt and goes out into the raw light of dawn."

HANKIN, St. John [Emile Clavering] (1869–1909), English dramatist, was among those who strove to emancipate the English theatre from sentimentality and commercial dross. He wrote dramas of ideas that bear some resemblance to those of BERNARD SHAW and HARLEY GRANVILLE-BARKER, the latter of whom first produced Hankin's plays. They are cynical and somewhat mechanically plotted to advance "modern" ideas, and they depict man almost exclusively as a social animal. But they are witty satires of the English society of the time, and they enjoyed popularity with the intelligent Court Theatre audiences.

Born in Southampton and educated at Oxford, Hankin was a successful journalist. Often sick and succumbing to neurasthenia, he committed suicide by drowning in the Ithon River. He turned to playwriting only in the last seven years of his short life, when he produced as many plays. The first of them, *The Two Mr. Wetherbys* (1902), presents the dual personality of the protagonist husband: his conventional attempt to keep his wife from leaving him and his difficulty in living up to an undeserved good reputation when she wants to come back. THE RETURN OF THE PRODIGAL (1905), a delightful comedy, was followed by *The Charity That Began at Home* (1906), a satire of thoughtless philanthropy; the popular *The Cassilis Engagement* (1907), a cynical portrayal of a would-be match between a gentleman and a lower-class girl who, accompanied by her vulgar mother, soon gets bored with society; two one-acters, *The Burglar Who Failed* and *The Constant Lover* (1908); and the translation of Brieux's THE THREE DAUGHTERS OF M. DUPONT. His final plays were THE LAST OF THE DE MULLINS (1908), an IBSENite drama; and *Thompson,* an unfinished play that appeared posthumously.

The Dramatic Works of St. John Hankin was published in 1912 with an introduction by JOHN DRINKWATER.

HANLEY, William (1931–   ), American playwright, first attracted attention with his off-Broadway one-acter *Mrs. Dally Has a Lover* (1962). Expanded into a full-length Broadway version, *Mrs. Dally* (1965), of which *Mrs. Dalley Has a Lover* constitutes the first half, this one-act play is the wistful portrayal of an affair between an eighteen-year-old and a married woman. Similarly wistful is his first Broadway play, *Slow Dance on the Killing Ground* (1964), in which a Negro fugitive and a homely girl seeking an abortionist find brief refuge from the world's "killing ground" in the Brooklyn shop of a guilt-ridden former Nazi victim.

Hanley was born in Ohio, but has spent most of his life in New York.

HANNELE'S JOURNEY TO HEAVEN (*Hanneles Himmelfahrt*), "a Dream Poem" in two acts by GERHART HAUPTMANN, produced in 1893 and published in 1894. Setting: a poorhouse in a contemporary German mountain village on a stormy winter night.

Often simply called by its original title, *Hannele,* this play is Hauptmann's first—and best-known—departure from pure NATURALISM. It is written in prose and verse, and his earlier naturalistic style is here blended with fantasy. In the child Hannele's visions, people she knows appear as characters out of popular folk and religious tales; the conscious gives way to the subconscious as her heavenly dreams compensate for and soon overcome the wretchedness of real life. The naturalistic setting provides a framework that controls what otherwise would be excessively sentimental.

Act I. There are some rowdy scenes among the paupers in the shabby poorhouse. Then the village teacher Gottwald carries in Hannele Mattern, a fourteen-year-old girl who whimpers: "I'm so afraid! . . . I'm so afraid that my father will come." Frequently beaten by her drunken stepfather, she has tried to drown herself in the almost-frozen village pond. The paupers' squabbles occasionally are heard as Gottwald and a kind deaconess, followed by the magistrate and a doctor, try to comfort the girl. Refusing to take medicine because she wants to die, Hannele tells Gottwald that Jesus is calling her. But, she then says to the deaconess, she fears having sinned. Alone for a moment, she is terrified by the apparition of her scoundrel stepfather. When the deaconess returns, Hannele's delirium increases. She mistakes the deaconess for her dead mother and talks of marrying "handsome Mr. Gottwald," who soon melts into her vision of Christ. Lullabying Hannele, the deaconess turns into an apparition of her mother, who gives Hannele a primrose. The setting is now entirely Hannele's vision. Accompanied by music, angels review Hannele's earthly suffering, and they promise her ample recompense in the delights of paradise.

Act II. Hannele awakes exalted, and "shows" the deaconess her heavenly primrose. The scene again shifts to her fantasies. Hannele meets the angel of death and her mother, who gives her courage when she falters. Then Hannele envisions herself as dead. The village tailor decks her in white silk and tiny glass slippers. Lying dead, she sees Gottwald weeping over her; his pupils beg her forgiveness for evils they all have done her. The village women admire her crystal coffin and Hannele now is revealed as and proclaimed a saint. A holy stranger sternly chastises her evil stepfather, who finally rushes out to hang himself. Looking like Gottwald, the stranger is Christ. He raises Hannele from the dead and, as she buries her head in his breast, he purifies her. Angels and harp music surround them while he describes heaven and Hannele's imminent ascent. After the angels sing a final chorus, the scene shifts to the poorhouse. The doctor bends over the body of Hannele and examines her. Sadly he then nods to the deaconess: "Dead."

HANSBERRY, Lorraine (1930–65), American playwright, became notable for her first Broadway play, A RAISIN IN THE SUN (1959). Soon filmed, it was followed by *The Sign in Sidney Brustein's Window* (1964), whose Jewish title character is a Greenwich Village intellectual restored to integrity and social involvement. "I care about it all. It takes too much energy *not* to care," he says in words expressing the author's own commitment; "the 'why' of why we are here is an intrigue for adolescents; the 'how' is what must command the living." The play was enthusiastically praised by a number of people, who succeeded in keeping it on Broadway for almost three months, despite mixed reviews and poor sales, until Hansberry's premature death of cancer on January 12, 1965. Her incompleted *Les Blancs,* an allegorical fantasy on race relations, was produced posthumously in 1970; it features a liberal white American journalist and a London-educated African come home for the funeral of his tribal-chief father.

Lorraine Hansberry was born to a prosperous Negro family in Chicago, where her father was a prominent banker and real estate investor—and a slum landlord. She attended public school and then studied painting at the Chicago Art Institute, the University of Wisconsin, and the University of Guadalajara (Mexico). In 1950 she moved to New York, where she worked at odd jobs, attended the New School for Social Research, and turned from painting to writing.

Although she was deeply concerned with civil rights, her first play transcends the portrayal of the problems encountered by Negroes: there is in Walter Lee Younger the same frustration in his quest for the mythical American success story that there is in Miller's Willy Loman (DEATH OF A SALESMAN). Hansberry's second play is set in the predominantly white New York milieu into which she had settled. She was married to, but a year before her death divorced, the writer Robert Nemiroff (? –), who in 1969 adapted selections from her letters, novels, and plays as *To Be Young, Gifted and Black,* a biographical drama.

HAPPENINGS, a nonliterary form of theatre that originated among abstract EXPRESSIONIST artists in New York, and flourished there and in other American cities in the 1960's. Though Happenings were not improvisations, they were created for only a single or a very few "performances," usually before limited, esoteric audiences. In Happenings,

18 Happenings in 6 Parts, Part IV, Room 1. The orchestra (Allan Kaprow, center); seated spectators are visible through the plastic wall between Kaprow and the violinist. New York, 1959. (Rehearsal photograph, *Fred McDarrah*)

cacophonous noises and verbal effects like grunts, humming, and laughter were substituted for dialogue; images or events for plot; and activities for action. The primary emphasis was on the visual—on objects and human motions. Hence scenario took the place of script. Instead of drama's traditional single focus, Happenings had a multifocus, and dispensed with themes, set meanings, and a resolution. Spatially, there was little or no distinction between auditorium and stage (which consisted of places like lofts, ball courts, parking lots, etc.), or audience and performers. Audiences, in fact, sometimes were altogether dispensed with, and when there, often participated in the Happening.

Happenings derived from the theories of ANTONIN ARTAUD, DADAISM, and SURREALISM. There are some stylistic similarities among these three theatrical forms: events progress by free associations, and proliferating objects and sounds are important. But Happenings were unique in that their progression was determined solely by chance or mechanical means. Further, being nonverbal and, as it were, inanimate and nonreferential, Happenings consisted *only* of objects, noises, and activities.

Discussions and "scenarios" of Happenings are collected in the *Tulane Drama Review,* X:2 (Winter 1965) and in Michael Kirby's collection *Happenings* (1965), whose copious introduction reviews the history and development of the movement. Another noteworthy collection is *Assemblage, Environments, & Happenings* (1966), by Allan Kaprow (1927–   ), one of the leading creators of the form as well as author of an early production that gave the genre its name, *18 Happenings in 6 Parts* (1959). Both Kirby's and Kaprow's books describe and illustrate the productions, and refer to other relevant studies.

HAPPY DAYS, a play in two acts by SAMUEL BECKETT, published and produced in 1961. Setting: an expanse of scorched grass, blazing light, "pompier trompe-l'oeil backcloth."

This ironically titled two-character play, translated by Beckett into the French as *Oh les beaux jours* (1963), is a tragicomedy like WAITING FOR GODOT and ENDGAME. For the most part it is a monologue by Winnie, an optimistic bourgeois wife embedded in a mound of sand—in the first act to above her waist, in the second up to her neck.

Winnie, a middle-aged, buxom blond, is sleeping. Behind her to the right, and hidden by the mound, lies her husband Willie—also asleep. Next to her is her black bag. When a piercing bell rings Winnie wakes up and gazes at the zenith: "Another heavenly day." She says her prayer and then goes through her morning routine: she brushes her teeth, polishes her spectacles, and wakes up Willie, who reads want ads and obituaries in a yellowed newspaper. She also unpacks her revolver and a music box that plays sentimental love songs. And she waits for the whistle that will send her back to sleep. Later, the pistol is "conspicuous" on the mound near her. The bell wakes her again. "Hail, holy light," Winnie says, smiling, happy at the thought that someone may hear her. Now she can move none of her limbs and reach none of her belongings. She calls for Willie. When he does not answer or come, she tells a story about a little girl frightened by a mouse. Suddenly Willie crawls up, "dressed to kill," like a dandy. With a "happy expression" on her face Winnie says, "Oh this *is* a happy day, this will have been another happy day!" Then she sings the music-box love song. She looks at Willie (who is still on his hands and knees) and smiles. Then she stops smiling. "They look at each other. Long pause." And the curtain falls.

HAPPY END, a musical play in three acts by BERTOLT BRECHT and Elisabeth Hauptmann (? –   , music by Kurt Weill), produced in 1929 and published in 1971. Setting: Chicago, 1929.

Brecht later disowned this play, for which he admitted having written the lyrics, by noting that his SAINT JOAN OF THE STOCKYARDS "is derived from Elisabeth Hauptmann's play *Happy End.*" She was his secretary, friend, and frequent literary collaborator. The play is replete with jazz music and lyrics, and its plot resembles a later DAMON RUNYON story, "The Idyll of Sarah Brown" (1933). Billed as the dramatization of a nonexistent American story by a "Dorothy Lane" and produced the year following the hit run of THE THREEPENNY OPERA, *Happy End* was totally unsuccessful, and was first published in an English translation.

A gangster falls in love with a Salvation Army lieutenant, the gang's planned robbery fails, and both are expelled from their group. All ends happily when the gangsters join the Salvation Army.

HAPPY JOURNEY TO TRENTON AND CAMDEN, THE, a one-act play by THORNTON WILDER, published and produced in 1931. Setting: New Jersey, c. 1930.

Often produced by amateurs, this short PRESENTATIONAL play (performed on a bare stage, with four chairs representing a car) portrays an average family driving to visit an older, married daughter. The dialogue is full of fussy, homely humor as they depart from home, observe roadside signs, chat with the stage manager doubling as a gas station attendant, and finally reach their destination. Particularly affecting are the married daughter's tearful greeting ("Are you glad I'm still alive, pa?") and her chat with her mother, whose matter-of-fact attitude and middle-class clichés cannot conceal her deep love of her family.

HAPPY VINEYARD, THE (*Der fröhliche Weinberg*), a comedy in three acts by CARL ZUCKMAYER, produced in 1925 and published in 1926. Setting: a Rhineland vineyard in Hessen, fall 1921.

Zuckmayer's first hit, this Rabelaisian folk comedy won him the Kleist Prize—and the enmity of the Nazis. Their rioting, provoked by Zuckmayer's ridicule of anti-Semitism and chauvinism, helped publicize and popularize the play. Simple country folk with their vineyard and tavern life—their harvesting, brawls, and lovemaking—are contrasted with city people. These are represented by Knuzius, the pompous and pedantic suitor of the pretty Klärchen Gunderloch. Her father, the vineyard owner, will not approve the marriage until Knuzius proves his ability to make her pregnant. But Klärchen outwits her father and her suitor and wins the sailor she loves. The play ends as the celebrating guests sing and laugh at Knuzius, who awakes stupidly drunk atop a pile of manure.

HARDT, Ernst (1876–1947), German writer, like KARL VOLLMOELLER was a neoromanticist disciple of HUGO VON HOFMANNSTHAL and similarly had a greater effect on the Austrian than on German theatre. His stage success was *Tantris der Narr* (*Tantris the Fool,* 1907; also translated as *Tristram the Jester*), in which the unrecognized Tristram attempts again to court Isolde at Mark's court; its most spectacular scene is the jealous king's delivery of the naked Isolde to lepers. Hardt's only other notable plays are also based on legend: *Gudrun* (1911), a tragedy; and *Schirin und Gertraude* (1913), a travesty of the legend of the count permitted by the pope to keep a second wife.

Hardt, a West Prussian who traveled widely and became the director of Weimar's theatre (1919–24), also published volumes of verse and fiction, as well as translations from the French. He stopped writing shortly after World War I.

HARDY, Thomas (1840–1928), is almost exclusively remembered as an English poet and novelist. Yet his most ambitious work and the one he would have liked most to be remembered for was a drama, THE DYNASTS (1904)—an epic (featuring Napoleon and a cast of thousands) that was meant for the closet but has, in fact, been adapted for performance. Its low-life scenes occur in the Wessex setting of his novels and poems. There is also a privately printed edition of Hardy's *The Play of "Saint George"* (1921). Another Hardy drama is based on the legends of King Mark, Tristram, and Isolde: *The Famous Tragedy of the Queen of Cornwall,* which was produced in 1923 and revised for publication the following year. Some of Hardy's novels have been successfully dramatized. See Marguerite Roberts's *Tess in the Theatre: Two Dramatizations of Tess of the D'Urbervilles . . .* (1950); and Roberts's study of *Hardy's Poetic Drama and the Theatre* (1965).

HARRIGAN, Edward (1845–1911), American actor, producer, lyricist, and playwright, was a notable variety entertainer. Though his popular acts burlesqued various racial types, he was most successful with his "Dan Mulligan" sketches. The "Mulligan Guard" plays featured an Irish immigrant and his wife, played by Harrigan's partner Anthony Cannon, better known as Tony Hart. The theme song of the first, *The Mulligan Guard Picnic* (1878), became world famous. In 1884 the popular Harrigan and Hart partnership broke up, but Harrigan continued writing until 1903, completing a total of almost a hundred sketches and at least thirty-five plays. Only marginal as drama—he wrote for audiences that resembled the low-life characters he portrayed—Harrigan's farces and sentimental pieces are picturesque revelations of life on New York's Lower East Side.

Harrigan published *The Mulligans* as a novel in 1901. The first of these plays to be published, *The Mulligan Guard Ball* (1879), is in Richard Moody's *Dramas from the American Theatre 1762–1909* (1966), which includes an informative preface and bibliographies. A delightful biographical and historical account is E. J. Kahn, Jr.'s *The Merry Partners: The Age and Stage of Harrigan and Hart* (1955).

HART,* Moss (1904–61), American playwright, librettist, and director, achieved his earliest and most sustained success with the comedies written with GEORGE S. KAUFMAN. Most popular among these were ONCE IN A LIFETIME (1930), YOU CAN'T TAKE IT WITH YOU (1936), and THE MAN WHO CAME TO DINNER (1939). Hart's greatest later hit was the musical LADY IN THE DARK (1941). As a director, he distinguished himself both with his own plays

* Illustration on page 426.

and with those of others, particularly with MY FAIR LADY. And he was equally successful as a scriptwriter for movies, notably *Gentlemen's Agreement* (1947).

Born in New York, the grandson of a cigarmaker who (Hart recalled in his autobiography) was the friend, benchmate, and rival of the A.F. of L.'s Samuel Gompers, Hart grew up in poverty. He began his career in the office of the theatre manager Augustus Pitou. After unsuccessful solitary attempts at playwriting, he joined forces with the older Kaufman. Among their other works are *Merrily We Roll Along* (1934), the depiction of a playwright's disintegration; *I'd Rather Be Right* (1937), a satire of the Roosevelt administration, starring GEORGE M. COHAN, who came out of retirement to play the President; *The Fabulous Invalid* (1938), an unsuccessful play about the theatre; *The American Way* (1939), a patriotic piece; and their final work, *George Washington Slept Here* (1940), an only moderately popular satire of city people who redo their country houses. With DOROTHY HEYWARD Hart wrote a musical comedy, *Jonica* (1930). He also wrote the books for *Face the Music* (1932) and *As Thousands Cheer* (1933), both with lyrics and music by Irving Berlin; and for *Jubilee* (1935), with lyrics and music by Cole Porter.

In his own plays, Hart twice repeated formulas he had exploited with Kaufman: *Winged Victory* (1943), a patriotic play about the Army Air Force; and *Light Up the Sky* (1948), a comedy whose characters suggest various Broadway personalities of the time. But in two other plays, both of them double-plotted dramas, Hart attempted something more original: *Christopher Blake* (1946), a divorce drama featuring a couple's son, consists of fantasy scenes that recall *Lady in the Dark;* and *The Climate of Eden* (1952), an adaptation of Edgar Mittelhölzer's novel *Shadows Move Among Them,* deals with maturation and guilt in British Guiana. Neither drama was successful on the boards, though the latter received some critical praise.

Hart's plays were published individually as well as in Kaufman and Hart's *Six Plays* (1942). Hart, who was married to the actress Kitty Carlisle, wrote the best seller *Act One* (1959), an amusing autobiography that is particularly informative about the beginning of his career, including his early association with Kaufman.

HARTLEBEN, Otto Erich (1864–1905), German NATURALIST writer influenced by de Maupassant, was the author of verse, short stories, and drama. Of Hartleben's plays, the most notable is the portrayal of arrogant Prussian militarism in *Rosenmontag* (1900, translated as *Love's Carnival*), a tragic drama of the romance of a lower-class woman and an officer. Artistically Hartleben was more successful with *Hanna Jagert* (1893), a play about the growth and development of a working girl.

Born in the Harz Mountains and orphaned at an early age, Hartleben studied law but became a free-lance writer. He built a villa that was to become a poetry center, but he died at an early age after considerable dissipation.

HASENCLEVER, Walter (1890–1940), German playwright and poet, was one of the first EXPRESSIONISTS. His most notable works are the revolutionary *Der Sohn* (1914), a "rebellious son" play; and an adaptation of *Antigone* (1917), one of his pacifist dramas. These and his other serious plays are only of historical interest now. But Hasenclever also wrote popular light comedies like *Ein besserer Herr* (1927), an amusing depiction of a matrimonial confidence man that is still occasionally performed in Germany.

Hasenclever was born in Aachen and studied at universities in Leipzig, Oxford, and Lausanne. After publishing some hedonistic verse, he became famous with *Der Sohn,* which, despite its link to the *Sturm and Drang* drama of Schiller, employs new expressionistic devices like nameless characters to vent revolutionary fervor: its twenty-year-old title hero, failing his school examinations and thereafter supervised the more strictly by his middle-class father, escapes "the desert of this house" to experience "ecstasy" and incite others to revolt against their parents; brought home by the police and threatened with a whipping, he brandishes a pistol—causing the father's fatal stroke, which saves the son from parricide.

World War I, in which Hasenclever served as "interpreter, purchaser, and kitchen-boy" before he was wounded, intensified his pacifist fervor. It is expressed in *Der Retter* (1915), a dramatic poem whose protagonist (a poet personifying intellect, love, and human brotherhood) fails to overcome the army and the state (the powers of force). Similar sentiments are enunciated in Hasenclever's masterpiece, his version of Sophocles's *Antigone,* which was hailed as a revolutionary manifesto after Max Reinhardt produced it in 1920. In Hasenclever's play Creon resembles the German Kaiser—a ruthless dictator forcing his reluctant and repressed subjects to war, for "only the strong will conquer the world"—and Antigone represents the powers of human love, which, after the tragedy, cause Creon to abdicate and peace and freedom to be established by the humble masses as they proclaim the dawn of "the new world." Hasenclever's most expressionistic play, *Die Menschen* (1918, translated as *Humanity*), recalls early silent art films like *The Cabinet of Dr. Caligari* (1919), and consists principally of SYMBOLIC mime and stage directions, and periodic interjections by the many characters: a corpse, who rises from a grave to expiate his murderer's crime, is himself accused of it, condemned to death, and executed; when the corpse is reburied, the real murderer is converted, spreads out his arms, and exclaims, "I love."

Hasenclever's remaining serious plays are *Jenseits* (*Beyond,* 1920), a two-character ghost tragedy; and *Mord* (1926), an indictment of the judiciary and society in general. This play, though still in part expressionistic, already veers toward NATURALISM. The plays that followed are not only in conventional REPRESENTATIONAL styles but, in fact, completely in the more popular comic genre. The already-cited *Ein besserer Herr,* the first and most popular of them, was followed by *Ehen werden im Himmel geschlossen* (1928), *Bourgeois bleibt Bourgeois* (1929, written with ERNST TOLLER), *Napoleon greift ein* (1930), *Kommt ein Vogel geflogen* (1931), *Kulissen* (1932), and *Münchhausen* (1947). Aside from these and other plays, Hasenclever published poetry and wrote filmscripts, including the 1930 version of O'Neill's ANNA CHRISTIE, which featured Greta Garbo in her first speaking role.

Hasenclever won the Kleist Prize in 1917. In the 1920's he was one of the more interesting international playwrights who had strong social and artistic commitments and who reacted in extreme ways against political as well as aesthetic conventions. But like others among these dramatists—particularly the expressionists with whom he is especially identified—he is little remembered today. When the Nazis came to power in 1933, Hasenclever, who was partly Jewish, had to flee Germany. Interned in France, he committed suicide there in 1940.

A few of Hasenclever's plays are available in English: *Humanity* appears in Walter H. Sokel's *An Anthology of German Expressionist Drama* (1963); *Antigone* in James M. Ritchie's *Vision and Aftermath: Four Expressionist War Plays* (1969); and *Christoph Columbus . . .* (*Christopher Columbus,* 1932), a parable written with (and reflecting the style of) the cabaret satirist Kurt Tucholsky (1890–1935) and portraying Europeans as the corrupters of civilized and urbane American Indians, in George E. Wellwarth's *German Drama Between the Wars* (1971). Hasenclever's life and work are discussed in Isaac Goldberg's *The Drama of Transition* (1922) and in H. F. Garten's *Modern German Drama* (1964).

HAUNTED INN, THE (*Di Puste Kretshme*), a drama in four acts by PERETZ HIRSHBEIN, produced in 1913 and published in 1914. Setting: a contemporary East European farmhouse and surroundings.

In 1919 this play (also presented as *The Idle Inn*) inaugurated Emanuel Reicher's Jewish Art Theatre in New York. Both the play and Jacob Ben-Ami's performance as Itsik were so resounding a success that they were moved to Broadway for an English production. Not Hirshbein's best work, *The Haunted Inn* is nevertheless a very theatrical mixture of rural romance, fantasy, and spectacle.

A provincial horse dealer arranges a marriage for his daughter, Meta, and decides to give the couple his abandoned inn, which is supposed to be haunted. The rebellious Meta, however, loves her crude cousin Itsik. At the wedding feast, a group of passing merchants join the celebration. Even as she is under her wedding canopy, Itsik runs off with Meta. The merchants are taken for haunted spirits, and Meta's frightened father, accompanied by relatives and neighbors, searches the grounds for his daughter. Itsik and Meta quarrel passionately, and her father takes her home. Later Itsik returns, as Meta's superstitious father, convinced that its evil spirits are in league against him, burns down the inn—and then his own house. Meta, who finally confesses her love, wants to jump into the flames. But romance wins out as Itsik carries her off: "Now you'll never run away from me again!"

HAUPTMANN, Carl (1858–1921), German writer, was the older brother of GERHART HAUPTMANN. If not for that relationship, he would be as well remembered for his plays as he still is for his novels—which escaped the inevitable comparisons with his famous brother. Despite such comparisons, drama critics and historians have treated his plays with considerable respect.

Born in Silesia, Hauptmann early became interested in the natural sciences, in which he took a doctorate at Jena. But impressed by his brother's success as a playwright, Carl too essayed the drama with a number of NATURALISTIC plays: *Marianne* (1894), *Waldleute* (1895), and *Ephraims Breite* (1900, translated as *Brigitte*). In his later work he demonstrated considerable versatility as a dramatist: *Die Bergschmiede* (1902), his most successful play, is SYMBOLIC; *Die lange Jule* (*Lanky Julia,* 1913) and *Die armseligen Besenbinder* (1913) are fantasies; *Bürger Napoleon* (1910) and *Kaiser Napoleon* (1911), histories that are considered by some to be his finest achievement, portray the emperor as a hero of the French Revolution who failed only when his idealism was debased by personal ambition; and Hauptmann's EXPRESSIONISTIC works, the war play *Der abtrünnige Zar* (1919) and *Die goldenen Strassen* trilogy, tragicomedies portraying the dramas of a wealthy and brilliant cripple (*Tobias Bundschuh,* 1916), an epicure (*Gaukler, Tod und Juwelier,* 1917), and an artist (*Musik,* 1919).

Hauptmann's most notable play is *Krieg* (*War,* 1914), a powerful semiexpressionistic prophecy of the impending world cataclysm; it begins with a party of international guests (figures with animal heads) arguing their countries' claims, then portrays war allegorically in the person of Napoleon in a chariot pulled by the hysterical masses, and finally depicts postwar desolation in the hovels of the earth—though a glimmer of hope is represented by a temple-building hermit and child-bearing women who pray as they envision a "new morrow . . . for this poor, beautiful earth."

Aside from his novels, Hauptmann published collections of short stories and poetry. His fiction, often set in his native Silesia, is concerned with social as well as ethical problems, while his poetry reflects another strain in Hauptmann's thinking and writing, that of mysticism. His works are diversified in type and style, and of substantial artistic merit. Had it not been for the overshadowing reputation of his brother—whose outlook he shared to a considerable degree—Carl Hauptmann would occupy a more important niche among early modern German playwrights.

Book-length studies of Carl Hauptmann have

appeared in German, the most important among them being listed in the bibliography of H. F. Garten's *Modern German Drama* (1964); this study's discussion of Hauptmann is focused on the play *War*. As *War, a Te Deum,* this drama was republished with an introduction in James M. Ritchie's *Vision and Aftermath: Four Expressionist War Plays* (1969).

HAUPTMANN, Gerhart [Gerhard Johann Robert] (1862–1946), was Germany's leading early modern playwright. His reputation tarnished in his old age, when he failed to join the other prominent writers and artists who left Germany after Hitler came to power. Further, his plays are usually in verse or dialect, neither of which yields easily to graceful translation (Hauptmann's post-1920 drama is virtually unknown in England and America). Nonetheless, his stature as one of the great modern playwrights has remained unchallenged. It rests almost entirely on the predominantly NATURALIST dramas of the years 1892–1903—particularly on his most famous play, *Die Weber* (THE WEAVERS, 1892), for which he was awarded the Nobel Prize in 1912. But his contribution to literature goes considerably beyond one play (he finished forty-six others). It also goes beyond the theatrical naturalism of which he was Germany's central figure (some of his early plays already reveal his genius for comedy and farce, lyricism, and fantasy). His contribution even goes beyond drama, for his writing was as diversified as it was prolific. He composed aphorisms as well as a considerable body of poetry, some of which is excellent; fiction that includes such distinguished novels as *Der Narr in Christo Emanuel Quint* (*The Fool in Christ Emanuel Quint*, 1910), *Der Ketzer von Soana* (*The Heretic of Soana,* 1918), and *Die Insel der grossen Mutter* (*The Isle of the Great Mother*, 1924); and, finally, he wrote a number of autobiographies, the most important of which are *Das Abenteuer meiner Jugend* (1937) and *Der grosse Traum* (*The Big Dream*), an epic poem (modeled on Dante's *Divine Comedy*) that was completed by 1932 but not published until ten years later.

He was the youngest of four children, of whom another, CARL HAUPTMANN, was also to achieve prominence as a writer. Gerhart Hauptmann was born in Silesia, whose dialect predominates in many of his plays. His grandfather, a former weaver, acquired the mountain resort hotel in Salzbrunn that the writer's father (Robert Hauptmann) inherited, and where he spent his childhood. There Hauptmann was exposed to the Moravian pietism and love of romance and nature that may be traced in his writings. In 1874 he was sent to board and school in Breslau with an older brother. Introverted and sensitive, he did not do well in the Prussian-spirited environment of the *Realschule* he attended. At sixteen he was sent to learn agricultural management at an uncle's estate, where he worked with the peasants. But the following year he decided to become an artist. He went to Breslau to study sculpture, and also considered becoming a painter and a musician. He traveled ceaselessly to find his proper vocation in life. At the University of Jena he attended lectures on art, literature, philosophy, and science. His student career took him to Dresden, Rome (where he worked as a sculptor), and Berlin (where he studied acting). By 1885 he had chosen literature as his profession. He had already done some writing, though he had not yet settled on drama.

That year he married Marie Thienemann, a wealthy heiress who was two years older than the writer. She supported both of them during his early and lean apprentice years. Like Hauptmann, she was given to periods of profound depression. She was a good wife and proud of Hauptmann's work, though she understood little of it. As early as 1889 he became intrigued with Margarete Marschalk, then fourteen years old. A vivacious and charming yet strong-willed girl, she eventually became an artist. She adored Hauptmann, and was interested in and understood his work. Hauptmann was torn between his love for both women, a conflict he dramatized in such plays as *Einsame Menschen* (LONELY LIVES, 1891) and *Die versunkene Glocke* (THE SUNKEN BELL, 1896). After a number of separations, his divorce from Marie became final in 1904. She took their four sons with her and Hauptmann married Margarete, who had already borne their child. His marriage to her was a lifelong and happy one. (She outlived him by ten years.) That his love for Marie, whose sisters had married his two brothers, was still profound, is suggested by such a work as *Die Jungfern vom Bischofsberg* (THE MAIDENS OF BISCHOFSBERG, 1907), written in 1905.

In the early years of his first marriage Hauptmann continued his social and scientific studies. A liberal and a romanticist, he was interested in social problems as well as literature. Success after the publication of his naturalistic story *Bahnwärter Thiel* (*Flagman Thiel,* 1888) led to his association with Berlin's leading young artists and writers, most of them political and social (and Socialist) idealists. Stimulated by the naturalism of ÉMILE ZOLA, Gustave Flaubert, and others, and by the drama of HENRIK IBSEN, Hauptmann turned to playwriting. That career, in which he quickly gained international fame, began in 1889, though he had earlier written some now-lost historical dramas. He was encouraged by the naturalist theoretician and dramatist ARNO HOLZ (who may have supplied the title and some of the ideas) to write *Vor Sonnenaufgang* (BEFORE SUNRISE, 1889) for Otto Brahm's recently established Freie Bühne.

That play launched German naturalism as well as Hauptmann's career. Its grim stage REALISM created a popular sensation that immediately made the young writer famous. Hauptmann's reputation grew with the plays that followed in quick succession: *Das Friedensfest* (THE FEAST OF RECONCILIATION, 1890), *Lonely Lives,* and *Kollege Crampton* (COLLEAGUE CRAMPTON, 1892). It spread beyond Germany in 1893, when he produced three of his best-known plays: *The Weavers, Der Biberpelz* (THE BEAVER COAT, 1893), and *Hanneles Himmelfahrt* (HANNELE'S JOURNEY TO HEAVEN, 1893). These

Gerhart Hauptmann in 1932. (*Wide World*)

works well illustrate Hauptmann's naturalism, comedy, and poetic SYMBOLISM.

In his naturalistic plays he depicted vividly and sympathetically the pain and suffering of human beings overwhelmed by powers beyond their control—and even their understanding: the social and economic forces that crush the weavers, and the forces of nature and the uncontrollable impulses that ruin the protagonists of *Fuhrman Henschel* (DRAYMAN HENSCHEL, 1898), ROSE BERND, (1903), and DOROTHEA ANGERMANN (1926). Hauptmann's humanitarianism, however, is not confined to his naturalist dramas. It also appears in virtually all of his comedies, as it does in *The Beaver Coat.* His gift for comedy and farce is displayed in almost untranslatable idiom and dialect and in striking characterizations that reveal tragic depths beneath the surface comedy.

Though *Hannele's Journey to Heaven* has a naturalistic framework, it is a poetic fantasy. Such drama, often romantic and symbolic, tended to predominate in Hauptmann's later writings. The most famous play of that type—and one that long rivaled the popularity of *The Weavers*—is *The Sunken Bell.* It was in such plays, usually written in verse, and based on legend or history, that Hauptmann gave the freest reign to his religious and romantic proclivities. It was in them, too, that he indulged his fancy for the depiction of dreams and hallucinations—as consistent a trademark of Hauptmann's drama as the suicide that so often concludes his plays.

For a few years after the tremendous accomplishments of 1893 there were no new Hauptmann productions. Then came FLORIAN GEYER (1896), a historical drama whose failure in 1896 grievously disappointed Hauptmann. The same year, however, came the phenomenally successful *The Sunken Bell.* Thereafter, until the 1930's, new Hauptmann plays were produced at an average rate of one a year: the afore-mentioned *Drayman Henschel, Schluck und Jau* (SCHLUCK AND JAU, 1900), MICHAEL KRAMER (1900), *Der rote Hahn* (THE RED COCK, 1901; *The Beaver Coat's* less-successful sequel), *Der arme Heinrich* (POOR HENRY, 1902), *Rose Bernd,* ELGA (1905), *Und Pippa tanzt!* (AND PIPPA DANCES!, 1906), *Das Hirtenlied* (*The Herdsmen's Song,* a two-act fragment about an artist, published in 1904 and produced in 1906), the earlier-mentioned *The Maidens of Bischofsberg, Kaiser Karls Geisel* (CHARLEMAGNE'S HOSTAGE, 1908), GRISELDA (1909), *Die Ratten* (THE RATS, 1911; a naturalistic tragicomedy often considered his last important play and among his greatest works), *Gabriel Schillings Flucht* (GABRIEL SCHILLING'S FLIGHT, 1912), *Helios* (1899, a fragment about the clash of paganism and Christianity, produced in 1912), *Festspiel in deutschen Reimen* (COMMEMORATION MASQUE, 1913), *Der Bogen des Odysseus* (THE BOW OF ODYSSEUS, 1914), MAGNUS GARBE (1942), *Winterballade* (A WINTER BALLAD, 1917), *Der weisse Heiland* (THE WHITE SAVIOR, 1920; depicting Montezuma's defeat by Cortez), PETER BRAUER (1921), INDIPOHDI (1920), *Till Eulenspiegel* (1922, a serious scene in verse), *Kaiser Maxens Brautfahrt* (1922, a short verse idyll), *Festakus* (1925, a short verse drama written for the opening of the Munich Museum), VELAND (1925), *Dorothea Angermann,* and the two one-acters that appeared jointly as *Spuk* (*Spectre*): *Die schwarze Maske* (THE BLACK MASK, 1929) and *Hexenritt* (WITCH'S RIDE, 1929).

During the 1930's Hauptmann's productivity decreased sharply. Unwilling, perhaps unable, to tear himself from native roots in his old age, the once-outspoken liberal humanitarian remained in Nazi Germany and, therefore, could not speak out against its atrocities. Though his subsequent writings did not vitiate his propaganda value to the Nazis, Hauptmann's bitterness and horror are reflected in private protests and some of his later plays: *Vor Sonnenuntergang* (BEFORE SUNSET, 1932), *Die goldene Harfe* (THE GOLDEN HARP, 1933), HAMLET IN WITTENBERG (1958; the second *Hamlet* play, his earlier one having been an edited translation), *Die Tochter der Kathedrale* (THE DAUGHTER OF THE CATHEDRAL, 1939), ULRICH VON LICHENSTEIN (1939), and *Die Atriden-Tetralogie* (THE ATRIDES TETRALOGY, 1940-44), his impressive last work. Two fragments were published in the 1940's: twelve scenes of *Der Dom* (1942) and one act of *Jubilate!* (1948). And there appeared two posthumous plays: *Die Finsternisse* (DARKNESS, 1947) and *Herbert Engelmann.* The latter is a four-act drama that portrays the deleterious psychological effects of World War I; written and discarded by Hauptmann in 1942, it was adapted by CARL ZUCKMAYER in 1952.

Though Hauptmann's plays were published in various collected German editions before and after his death, many of them—almost all of his later ones—are not yet available in English. Ludwig Lewisohn's nine-volume *The Dramatic Works of Gerhart Hauptmann* (1912–29) contains his first twenty-eight plays and two fragments that reflect his conflicting attractions to paganism and rationalism, art and the sciences: the afore-mentioned *Helios,* which is set in ancient times and concludes with the laughing entrance of the title hero, a "slender, golden-cinctured boy"; and *Das Hirtenlied* (*Pastoral,* 1898), featuring the visit of a "virile" angel to a sick artist. However convenient, the set lacks the later works, and the translations (not all by Lewisohn) are uneven. John Gassner's collection, *Five Plays by Gerhart Hauptmann* (1961), contains Theodore H. Lustig's translations of *The Weavers, Rose Bernd, Drayman Henschel, The Beaver Coat,* and *Hannele's Journey to Heaven,* as well as biographical, critical, and bibliographical (English and German) information.

Critical and biographical Hauptmann studies in English, beyond essays in standard general works, are equally scant—more so than those for any other major world dramatist. Hugh F. Garten's concise *Gerhart Hauptmann* (1954) contains a biography, a survey of his writings, and a bibliography. In English, the most comprehensive study of Hauptmann's plays—but excluding his many verse dramas—is Margaret Sinden's *Gerhart Hauptmann: The Prose Plays* (1957).

HAVEL, Václav (1936–), Czech essayist and poet, became his country's leading dramatist in the mid-1960's. He was the resident playwright of Prague's avant-garde Theatre on the Balustrade, and his satires have appeared in Central Europe and in Scandinavia, and, eventually, also in the English-speaking world. They are characteristic of the contemporary theatre of the ABSURD. In his early dramas Havel was particularly preoccupied —like the English novelist-essayist George Orwell —with the dehumanizing effects of language. After an early but unimportant collaboration, Havel by himself wrote his popular first play, *Zahradní slavnost* (*The Garden Party,* 1963). It deals with de-Stalinization and a foolish young man who wanders among and thoroughly confuses various bureaucratic organizations, but the play's real protagonist is a cliché that comes to dominate all the characters.

Havel developed this theme in his next and even more popular and grimly amusing satire, *Vyrozumění* (*The Memorandum,* 1965): instruction in Ptydepe, a new nonconnotative, scientific language, paralyzes but does not essentially change the lives of those who conform or of the antihero, who tries to resist contemporary society's pervasive authoritarianism, under which (as he sadly concludes), "Manipulated, automatized, made into a fetish, Man loses the experience of his own totality; horrified, he stares as a stranger at himself, unable not to be what he is not, nor to be what he is." *Ztížená možnost soustředení* (*The Increased Difficulty of Concentration,* 1969), a similar satire, features a social scientist whose work and complicated sex life—with a demanding mistress, his slovenly wife, and a reluctant secretary —are aggravated when he is chosen as A Random Sample and questioned by a computer and its weird attendants.

The Memorandum was published in the *Tulane Drama Review,* T35 (1967), which also contains "A Preface to Havel" by Jan Grossman.

HAY FEVER, a comedy in three acts by NOËL COWARD, published and produced in 1925. Setting: a contemporary country house in Cookham on a June weekend.

A favorite in stock-company productions, *Hay Fever* features the eccentric Bliss family—a writer, his actress wife, and their two grown-up children—modeled, according to Coward, on the family of the American actress Laurette Taylor.

Without telling the others, each family member has invited a singularly inappropriate weekend guest. The visitors are confused by the family, who ignore them; nonetheless, couples soon pair off and flirt. The next morning there is a dismaying breakfast; "This haddock's disgusting," one of the guests comments, and another tries a wild cure to relieve his hiccups. While the family argue about Parisian street locations in Bliss's new novel, their guests steal away from what they consider a madhouse. "How very rude!" the Blisses declare: "People really do behave in the most extraordinary manner these days—."

HÁY, Gyula (1900–), Hungarian playwright, became one of his country's leading post-World War II dramatists. Active in the evanescent Hungarian Soviet Republic, he had to emigrate to Germany in 1919 for a few years. From 1935–45 he worked in the Soviet Union. Then he returned to Hungary, where in 1951 he became Professor of Dramaturgy at the Academy of Theatrical Art. He participated in the 1956 Revolution, was arrested and imprisoned as a leader of the "writers' rebellion," and upon his release in 1960 emigrated to Switzerland. Since then his plays have been produced throughout Europe.

Isten, császár, paraszt (1932), his first and perhaps best play, depicts a confrontation between King Sigismund and Jan Hus, and received a lavish production at Max Reinhardt's theatre. Later plays include *Tiszazug* (completed in 1936, produced in 1945), an attack on Hungarian land hunger, based on a series of shocking murders of peasants by their young wives in the 1920's; *Az élet hídja* (1950), a Kossuth Prize-winning drama of postwar reconstruction; *A barbár* (1964), a short play on Mithridates's defeat by the Romans he admired and attempted to conquer; *A ló* (completed in 1961, produced in 1964), an anti-totalitarian comedy about Caligula's horse; and *Attila éjszakái* (1964), a tragedy that features an admirable Attila, whose love for a young princess brings about his early death and the dissolution of the Hun empire.

HE WHO GETS SLAPPED (*Tot, kto poluchaet poshchochiny*), a "dramatic presentation" in four acts by LEONID ANDREEV, produced in 1915 and published in 1916. Setting: the anteroom of a circus in a large French city, early twentieth century.

Andreev's best-known play, produced in England as *The Painted Laugh,* is an uneven but theatrical, NATURALISTIC yet at times SYMBOLIC and dreamlike work. It has been criticized for its despairing attitudes, but found intriguing and therefore revived periodically and reprinted in many anthologies. The title's agonized, philosophizing "He" is the author's spokesman, who attempts to communicate to the simple circus folk the artist's complex emotions about the human predicament, the perils of sensuality and cold reason, and the importance of feeling.

Act I. Circus troupers are rehearsing in the adjoining hall. Count Mancini, a lustful and seedy but graceful old cadger, tries to borrow money from the circus's manager, "Papa" Louis Briquet. Mancini threatens—as usual, it turns out—to take away his daughter, half of whose salary he pockets. She is Consuelo ("Consolation," from a novel by George Sand, Mancini explains), "The Equestrian Tango Queen" and the circus's main attraction. The troupe begin filing in, among them Briquet's common-law wife, the "burningly beautiful" and love-starved lion tamer. A cultivated but very strange middle-aged gentleman appears and begs to join the circus. When asked his name, he replies, "I don't quite know myself—yet"; and he admits he can do nothing—"Isn't that funny! I can't do a thing!" He is charmed (as all are) by the simple and angelic Consuelo, and finally decides: "Here, with you, I'll be He Who Gets Slapped. . . . I'll be called 'He.'" Amused, they agree. Compelled to register, "He" mysteriously begs the manager and his wife not to reveal his identity. Later "He" overhears the lion tamer begging for the love of a reluctant young equestrian, Consuelo's fellow performer. After the equestrian goes out, "He" tells the lion tamer, "I feel as dizzy as a young girl at her first ball. It is so nice here—slap me, I want to play my part. Perhaps it will awaken love in my heart, too." The lion tamer asks him: "'He!' What can I do to make my animals love me?"

Act II. During a performance, while "He" makes another successful appearance as a clown, a lustful baron casts "bulging, spidery eyes" at Consuelo. He hates her father, who insists he must first marry her, and he falls on his knees and pleads his love. "Get up, please, it's disgusting—you're so fat," Consuelo says just as the intermission starts and the performers come in. "He" is praised for his success but asked not to philosophize to the audience. Mancini confides to "He" that he plans to give Consuelo to the fat baron for a good price. Inadvertently Mancini reveals, too, that she is not really his daughter but a Corsican of mixed, lowly parentage. When Consuelo tells "He" that the baron will probably marry her, "He" poses as a palm reader. Mesmerizing her with his fantasies, "He" warns her that such a marriage will kill her, and suggests that she really loves the young equestrian, who also loves her. "'He' is an old god in disguise, who came down to earth only to love you, foolish little Consuelo," "He" says, and commands the hypnotized girl: "Remember—Consuelo!" Then "He" tells her of his love for her, but when she slaps him, he tells her that it is part of the play: "Didn't you understand that you are a queen, and I a fool who is in love with his queen?" Later "He" has a gentleman visitor—a former friend who eloped with "He's" wife and thus caused "He" to escape from the world.

Act III. In a morning interview, "He" castigates the visitor. The visitor is a writer who has also appropriated and popularized "He's" philosophical theories, thus becoming famous—while "He" has remained betrayed and unknown: "With the art of a great vulgarizer, a tailor of ideas, you dressed my Apollo in a barber's jacket, turned my Venus into a whore, pinned ass ears on my bright hero—and your career is made." But "He" reassures the uneasy and shamed visitor that "He" will not return to his wife and the world. "He's" next battle is in the greasepaint

He Who Gets Slapped, Act IV. Center group, left to right: "He" (Dennis King), Consuelo (Susan Douglas), Briquet (Wolfe Barzell), and the costumed lion tamer (Stella Adler). New York, 1946. (*Vandamm Photo, Theater Collection, New York Public Library*)

circus world. Mancini warns Consuelo against "He," who implores her not to marry the baron. But when she angrily berates "He" as a fool, "He" grovels before Consuelo, his ideal: "Forgive me. Give me back the image of my beautiful, piteous goddess." After she goes out, "He" begs the young equestrian to "save her from the spider" baron, "a defiler of love."

Act IV. It is just before the benefit performance for Consuelo, who is to marry the baron. The baron has provided a truckload of roses to carpet the arena in her honor: she is to perform for the last time by galloping on "hymeneal roses." The lion tamer consoles the unhappy "He": "If this one does not buy her, another will." Consuelo and the baron enter arm in arm. Mancini happily starts the party as the other circus people join them, and "He" once more urges Consuelo not to marry the baron. When she tells him that it is "too late," "He" asks her to have a drink with him. Desperate, "He" has poisoned the drink and empties the glass after she drinks half of it. Consuelo dies, made happy by his final reassurance that she is not dying, but will live eternally. The beautiful lion tamer is envious: "'He' was a man, and he loved. Happy Consuelo!" Foiled, the lustful baron shoots himself. "You loved her so much, Baron?" the dying "He" asks: "And you want to be ahead of me there, too? No! I'm coming! We shall fight it out there, whose she is to be—forever. . . ." And "He" falls dead, amidst the agitated circus people.

HE WHO LIVED HIS LIFE OVER AGAIN (*Han som fick leva om sitt liv*), a play in three acts by PÄR LAGERKVIST, published and produced in 1928. Setting: a contemporary Swedish shoemaker's shop.

Lagerkvist's first popular success and his first REPRESENTATIONAL drama, this play features a man who is granted the opportunity to relive his life.

Daniel is in his shoemaker's shop, happily married and with fine children. But repressed evil—a consuming passion for life that destroyed Daniel's earlier existence—again surges forth. He interferes in his son's love affair, whereupon the son shoots himself. A personification of the past recounts Daniel's previous fall, when he knifed a girl "because I loved her." Daniel's crime is a rebellion against reason, which would have man restrain his fervor to know and experience life: "Cursed life that gave us passions—to smother us. We have to be burned up by them to find ourselves as we really are."

HE WHO SAYS NO (*Der Neinsager*), a "school opera" by BERTOLT BRECHT (music by Kurt Weill), published in 1930 and produced in 1958. Setting: two rooms, chairs.

In response to student criticisms (published in the notes to the play) after a performance of HE WHO SAYS YES, Brecht reworked the ending of that play. Until the sick boy is asked the customary question, the script remains unchanged. Then:

"No. . . . I want you to take me home, in accord with the new situation," the sick boy replies, violating one custom and enunciating another one: "To think anew in every new situation." His logic persuades the other members of the expedition, and the chorus concludes the story: with a new custom established, the expedition has brought the boy home and it has braved ridicule, each student "no more cowardly than his neighbor."

HE WHO SAYS YES (*Der Jasager*), a "school opera" by Bertolt Brecht (music by Kurt Weill), published and produced in 1930. Setting: two rooms, chairs.

Based on Arthur Waley's translation of the fifteenth-century Japanese No play *Taniko,* this short, didactic prose and verse piece, also translated as *The Yea-Sayer,* "should, if possible, always be performed together" with HE WHO SAYS NO, according to Brecht.

The opening chorus exalts "The great importance of acquiescence. / Many say Yes, yet it is not acquiescence." A teacher leads a mountain expedition seeking medicine to combat an epidemic. A boy whose mother is sick joins them, and himself falls ill. According to custom, he says "Yes" when asked if he should be left behind to die so that the expedition can proceed for the public good. Frightened of dying alone, however, he asks to be hurled to his death by the others. The chorus concludes the story: custom satisfied, the expedition members sadly continue their trip, each student "no one more guilty than his neighbor."

HEARTBREAK HOUSE, "A Fantasia in the Russian Manner on English Themes" in three acts by BERNARD SHAW, published in 1919 and produced in 1920. Setting: Sussex (England) at the outbreak of World War I.

One of his major and most elusive plays, *Heartbreak House* was begun in 1913 but took Shaw six years to complete. The frivolity of wartime theatres made him withhold this play for a while, and it was given its world premiere by the New York Theatre Guild (which was to present the premieres of four more Shaw plays). An atypical atmosphere of sadness permeates this CHEKHOVian comic tragedy of "cultured, leisured Europe before the war," in a moral vacuum consisting of futile personal and economic discourses or Ariadne's alternative: hunting and other pleasures. Shaw's long and bitter preface discussed these alternatives. In war and the "blockader's house," Shaw wrote, "there are many mansions; but I am afraid they do not include either Heartbreak House or [Ariadne's] Horseback Hall." He deplored the neglect of political science by men of action, and the neglect of action by thinkers, and the total madness of the war and its effects on people. Seeking to combine wisdom and power, the madly sane Captain Shotover, something of a self-portrayal, echoes Shaw's prophetic warnings about the need for intellect and daring if the world is to survive: "Learn [navigation] and live; or leave it and be damned."

Act I. Captain Shotover, an eccentric eighty-eight-year-old man, lives in his house (built to resemble a ship) with his daughter Hesione Hushabye and her family. A number of visitors arrive and engage in fruitless discussions and flirtations. Among them are Hesione's attractive young friend Ellie Dunn and the middle-aged "Boss" Alfred Mangan, an industrial magnate she intends to marry out of gratitude for his help to her father, Mazzini Dunn, an ineffectual old-time liberal and a failure in business, who is also visiting the house. Hesione disapproves of the match, the more so when Ellie tells her that she has fallen in love with a romantic stranger. To Ellie's intense disillusionment, he now turns out to be Hesione's husband, Hector, a congenital liar and lady's man, but something of a hero. Other arrivals are Shotover's second daughter, Lady Ariadne Utterword, and her elegant but spiritless brother-in-law Randall, who is in love with her. Lady Ariadne had left home twenty-three years before and moved to the colonies governed by her empire-building husband. Hurt by her family's cool reception, Lady Ariadne is soon consoled by Hector, who starts a flirtation with her. Shotover himself dashes in and out of "the Poop," firing off curt observations and unsuccessfully trying to achieve "the seventh degree of concentration." He hoards dynamite "to blow up the human race if it goes too far," and is working on a "mind ray" to kill "hogs to whom the universe is nothing but a machine for greasing their bristles and filling their snouts." Because they need more money than Shotover gets for "life-saving inventions," Hesione asks him to "think of something that will murder half Europe at one bang." As dusk falls, Shotover asks for "deeper darkness. Money is not made in the light."

Act II. Having become infatuated with Hesione, Boss Mangan bluntly tells Ellie after dinner that she need not feel bound to him for his kindness to her sentimental father: he had actually ruined, not saved, him. But Ellie, now disillusioned about romantic love, is determined to "make a domestic convenience" of Mangan. She gets him into a hypnotic sleep in which he overhears Hesione's contemptuous comments about him. After he is awakened he shames her, though he becomes increasingly confused in the strange house. When a burglar is caught, begs to be jailed so he can repent, and then takes up a collection (his usual way of operating), the exasperated Mangan notes that "the very burglars cant behave naturally in this house." Hesione takes Mangan out for a walk, and Ellie has a long talk with Shotover. She wants money to "keep" her soul with "music and pictures," beautiful things, and nice people, but he advises her not to marry for security: "At your age I looked for hardship, danger, horror, and death, that I might feel the life in me more intensely." He warns her that if she lets "the fear of poverty govern" her life, her "reward will be that you will eat, but you will not live." For the first time since her arrival, Ellie feels happy. But for his West Indian Negress wife, she would marry Shotover, though he reveals that his strength now is sustained by rum. After they leave, Randall, who is jealous of Hector, is sent to bed by Ariadne after she has goaded him to tears.

Act III. Later at night in the garden, the company discuss their aimless lives. Mangan is maddened by the talk and the soul stripping. Preferring horseback riding (the other occupation of good society) to neurotic talk, Ariadne finds the atmosphere of the house as depressing as ever. Ellie, who now considers herself Shotover's spiritual wife, calls his strange place "Heartbreak House." Shotover predicts that since its "crew is gambling in the forecastle, [the vessel] will strike and sink and split" unless they learn to navigate, but Mazzini Dunn insists that this is not true in politics, where nothing ever happens. Suddenly, at that point, an air raid begins. "The judgment has come. Courage will not save you; but it will shew that your souls are still alive," says Shotover as the women, radiantly excited, await the bomb. It falls, but it kills only Boss Mangan and the burglar—"the two practical men of business," who had sought cover in the pit containing Shotover's dynamite.

HECHT, Ben (1894–1964), American writer, began his career as a Midwestern journalist, gained prominence with his short stories and novels, and achieved fame with THE FRONT PAGE (1928). It was written with CHARLES MACARTHUR, with whom he collaborated on a number of other plays, notably *Twentieth Century* (1932), a comic satire of Hollywood; *Jumbo* (1935), a Richard Rodgers and Lorenz Hart musical extravanganza; *Ladies and Gentlemen* (1939); and *Swan Song* (1946). Hecht's other plays include *The Great Magoo* (1932; written with Gene Fowler, 1890–1960), "a dramatic cartoon"; *To Quito and Back* (1937), a serious play that was inspired by the Spanish Civil War and received critical acclaim, but failed commercially; and *Winkelberg* (1958), a *drame à clef* about the New York poet and novelist Maxwell Bodenheim, who was murdered in 1954.

Aside from fiction and film scripts (including that of Coward's DESIGN FOR LIVING), Hecht wrote studies of Israel; reminiscences of Chicago; an autobiography, *A Child of the Century* (1954); and a biography of MacArthur (*Charlie; The Impossible Life and Times of Charles MacArthur,* 1957). The collaborators are personified as two prankster screenwriters in *Boy Meets Girl* (1935), a Hollywood satire by SAM and BELLA SPEWACK.

HEDBERG, Tor [Harald] (1862–1931), Swedish author and director, was born in Stockholm, the son of Franz Hedberg, another successful playwright. Tor Hedberg began his career as a drama critic, novelist, and short-story writer. In 1886 he turned to drama, producing a total of some twenty plays of various types. His masterpiece was *Johan Ulvstjerna* (1907), an imaginative account of the assassination of the Russian tyrant

Nikolai Bobrikov in 1904 by the poet-patriot Eugen Schauman. The protagonist in Hedberg's psychoanalytical dramatization is a once-famous but now seedy poet who suffers from a martyr complex and sacrifices his life to regain his self-respect and improve life for the next generation; "I must die so that you may live," he tells his grieving son.

Hedberg's other plays include the comedy *Nattrocken* (1893); *Judas* (1895), another psychological drama, in which Judas resolves his problems by betraying Christ; and the tragedy *Borga gård* (1915), depicting life in a Swedish manor. Hedberg became director of the Royal Theatre (1910–22) and a distinguished critic, one of the first to perceive and proclaim the importance of AUGUST STRINDBERG's late plays.

HEDDA GABLER, a play in four acts by HENRIK IBSEN, published in 1890 and produced in 1891. Setting: a villa in west Oslo, late nineteenth century.

This late Ibsen play—one of his best and most popular ones—is less a PROBLEM PLAY than a character study of a complex woman. Hedda has been variously interpreted as demonic, neurotic, spiritually barren, or the "new woman" destroyed by philistine society. Ibsen wrote of the play: "What I principally wanted to do was to depict human beings, human emotions, and human destinies." As BERNARD SHAW noted in THE QUINTESSENCE OF IBSENISM, however, the play also dramatizes, as most of Ibsen's plays do, the evil of ideals in a world of reality.

Act I. Jørgen (or George) Tesman, a pedantic scholar, returns from his honeymoon with Hedda. He is smug about his marriage to General Gabler's aristocratic daughter: "I wouldn't be surprised if some of my friends were a bit jealous of me—eh?" When she comes in, Hedda coldly insults his affectionate maiden aunt, and is contemptuous of her husband and exasperated with his naïve allusions to her "rounded" figure. She extricates herself from the embraces of the aunt, who leaves after promising to see her daily. Alone, Hedda clenches her hands in despair. The pretty Mrs. Thea Elvsted, Hedda's one-time schoolmate, comes in. Thea asks Tesman to keep an eye on his friend Eilert Løvborg, a brilliant scholar whose last book is a sensation, and who has just come to town. Under Hedda's private questioning, Thea reveals how she has reformed the once-dissipating Løvborg and inspired him to write an even greater book; now, though there is an unknown woman's shadow between them, Thea and Løvborg are trusting "comrades." But worrying about the city's temptations for Løvborg, Thea—oblivious of a possible scandal—has left her husband and followed Løvborg. Judge Brack, who had handled the purchase of Tesman's home, invites Tesman to a stag party. Brack also tells Tesman that he will have to economize: his professorial appointment has been deferred and must now be won in a competition, with Løvborg. Since he has married on the expectation of this

Hedda Gabler. Left to right: Tesman (Roy Shuman), Løvborg (Donald Madden), Hedda (Claire Bloom), and Judge Brack (Robert Gerringer). New York, 1970. (*Samuel J. Friedman*)

appointment, Tesman is very upset; but Hedda, mimicking his expressions ("Fancy!" "Just think!"), looks forward to the "sporting" competition and is angry at having to economize and do without the luxuries she had married for. But, she coldly announces, she has one amusement left: General Gabler's pistols. As she leaves disdainfully, Tesman begs her not to play with "those dangerous things. For my sake, Hedda, eh?"

Act II. Hedda playfully shoots at Brack, who is returning in the afternoon by way of Tesman's garden. She complains of boredom with her life and her husband. Disgustedly she rejects the idea that love ("that revolting word") can make her marriage more endurable, and she angrily rejects the thought of motherhood. Hedda hates even the house, which to her smells of Tesman's stuffy middle class and his tiresome old aunts. It would be a welcome relief, she agrees with the flirting Brack, to have a third person join their lives as an entertaining friend. Løvborg comes in. He amazes the unimaginative Tesman with the topic of his new work, a history of the future. As Tesman and Brack talk in the inner room, Løvborg and Hedda discuss their former relationship. She had always made him tell her of all his wild escapades, and now blames the still-passionate Løvborg for having "wanted to spoil our intimacy—to drag it down to reality." Admitting that she had not shot him as she had threatened because she feared the scandal, she confesses that she had also lacked the courage to make their relationship real. When the mousy Thea joins them, happy and proud of her love for the reformed Løvborg, Hedda taunts him to relapse to drink. She succeeds only when, abusing Thea's confidence, she reveals that his "comrade" had been anxious about him. Angry that Thea lacked faith in him, Løvborg now accepts Brack's invitation to the stag party. After the men's departure, Hedda tells the distraught Thea why she had acted so horridly: "For once in my life I want the power to shape a human destiny." But she assures Thea that Løvborg will keep his promise and come back by ten to take her home. Romantically, Hedda envisions his heroic return "with vine leaves in his hair. Flushed and fearless!"

Act III. Daylight is breaking and the men have still not returned. Hedda, who has slept soundly all night, gets the restless Thea to go to bed, promising to call her when there is word of Løvborg. Tesman returns from the party, and tells Hedda how Løvborg, after reading parts of his remarkable book to Tesman, got drunk and lost his manuscript on the street, where Tesman found it. Keeping it when Tesman goes off to visit his dying aunt, Hedda refuses to accompany him: "I'll have nothing to do with sickness or death. I loathe anything ugly." Brack comes in and reveals that Løvborg went to a disreputable house after the party, started a brawl, and was hauled away by the police. Wishing to be the "cock-of-the-walk" in Hedda's household, Brack suggests that she not welcome the "undesirable and superfluous" Løvborg to her home anymore. When he appears later, Hedda does not mention the manuscript, and Thea leaves in utter despair after Løvborg tells her that he no longer has the manuscript, which they have considered their "child." When Løvborg talks of ending his life, Hedda, irked "that that pretty little fool should have influenced a man's destiny," gives him one of her pistols: "Use it now! But let it be—beautiful." After he leaves, she throws his manuscript into the lit stove: "I'm burning your child, Thea. I'm burning it—burning it—"

Act IV. That night Hedda tells Tesman what she has done with Løvborg's manuscript—and why: "I couldn't bear the thought of anyone putting you in the shade." This lie and the discovery of her pregnancy so delight Tesman that his initial horror at her destructive act vanishes. Brack comes in and reveals that Løvborg is dying of a self-inflicted shot in the heart. Thea's grief is assuaged when she discovers Løvborg's notes, and she goes off with Tesman to reconstruct the book. Hedda, in the meantime, rejoices over Løvborg's courageous act, but Brack quickly dispels her "beautiful illusion": the sordid truth is that Løvborg returned to the disreputable house, where the pistol discharged—into his bowels. Brack persuades Hedda that she need not fear a court scandal: he alone knows whose pistol it is. Now in Brack's power, Hedda's despair deepens ("Everything I touch becomes ludicrous and despicable"). Tesman, deeply engrossed with Thea in reconstructing Løvborg's book, asks the delighted Brack to entertain Hedda in the months ahead. But a shot is heard from the adjoining room, and when Tesman opens the door, Hedda's body is seen on the couch. "Shot herself in the temple! Think of that!" he cries, as the urbane Brack for once is discomposed: "Good God—but—people don't *do* such things!"

HEIBERG, Gunnar (1857–1929), was the leading Norwegian dramatist after HENRIK IBSEN, by whom he was influenced and whose work he greatly admired. But he was repelled by BJØRNSTJERNE BJØRNSON, whose writings, reformatory zeal, and person he satirized viciously in a controversial play, *Kong Midas* (1890).

An experimental playwright distinguished for his often lyrical satires, the Oslo-born Heiberg began his career as an essayist and a poet. His first play, *Tante Ulrikke* (1883), is an Ibsenite PROBLEM PLAY about justice. More daring in conception and theme are his next two plays, the witty and lyrical "conversations" *Kunstnere* (1893) and *Gerts have* (1894). Heiberg's best plays are *Balkonen* (*The Balcony,* 1894) and *Kjærlighetens tragedie* (*The Tragedy of Love,* 1904), both erotic in theme, though sex constitutes only part of the female protagonists' grand passion. *The Balcony* portrays a woman's relations with three men: her materialistic and gross husband, an idealistic lover who wants to transform love into an altruistic abstraction, and a healthy and ardent lover who is attracted to the idealistic concept. In the less lyrical but psychologically more profound *The Tragedy of Love* the hero is exhorted to "be proud" and "paint a cross above your door. A bloody cross. For love has visited your house"; when his wife perceives that his initial ardor is gradually subordinated to his work, her life becomes meaningless to her and she commits suicide.

Heiberg's attitudes (reminiscent of Ibsen's BRAND and Bjørnson's BEYOND HUMAN POWER I) are equally uncompromising in other areas. *Det store lod* (1895) excoriates a labor leader who loses his idealistic zeal as he becomes wealthy; *Hans Majestæt* (1896) attacks the Swedish monarchy, while *Folkerådet* (1897) lampoons the cautious Norwegian parliament. Other plays dealing with contemporary problems are *Harald Svans mor* (1899), an Aristophanic comedy satirizing modern journalism; *Kjærlighet til næsten* (1902), a satire of hypocritical idealism; and *Jeg vil værge mit land* (1912), the most scornful of these plays, dealing with the 1905 break between Sweden and Norway. Heiberg's last play, *Paradesengen* (1913), is a portrayal of a great man's children haggling outside his sickroom for the movie rights to his death scene; the notorious satire was apparently directed at Bjørnson's descendants, though his son Bjørn Bjørnson directed the play when it was finally produced at Oslo's National Theatre in 1924. All of these are witty, often sardonic comedies that, at the same time, burn with moral indignation.

Notable among the other writings of Heiberg, who was also director of the Bergen Theatre, are his essays. They include a series on the Dreyfus Affair and many others about drama and the theatre, like *Ibsen og Bjørnson på scenen* (1918). Though some of Heiberg's plays have been translated, they are not generally available in English. Harald Beyer's *Norsk Litteraturhistorie* (1952), translated as *A History of Norwegian Literature* (1956), has a section on Heiberg and a bibliography.

HEIJERMANS, Herman (1864–1924), Dutch journalist, novelist, and Holland's outstanding modern playwright, became internationally famous with his drama, *Op Hoop van Zegen* (THE GOOD HOPE, 1900). Perhaps inspired by the works of HENRIK IBSEN and GERHART HAUPTMANN, Heijermans wrote plays of social protest, NATURALISM, and SYMBOLISM. His drama was distinguished for its often comic and detailed portrayal of Dutch characters and life—and for its depiction of social ills. The effectiveness of his criticisms was such that his *The Good Hope*, for example, launched the drive that culminated in governmental reform of the fishing trade. As an expression of gratitude, the Dutch merchant marine established a fund for Heijermans's widow and orphans, who had been left impoverished by the bankruptcy of his theatrical company.

Born in Rotterdam to an old Dutch-Jewish family, Heijermans was trained for business but turned to journalism—and the theatre. His first drama, *Dora Kremer* (1893), which portrays a rural, middle-class marriage, was panned by the critics. To get back at his critics Heijermans capitalized on the appeal of foreign plays and brought out his next work, the one-act *Ahasverus* (1893), as a "translation" from the Russian of "Ivan Jelakowitch." The play, depicting a Jewish family during Russian pogroms, was a great hit.

Thereafter Heijermans presented his drama under his own name. Both in the Netherlands and abroad his success continued with such plays as *Ghetto* (1898), an indictment of fanatic religious orthodoxy as well as a portrayal of life in the Jewish ghetto; *Het Zevende Gebod* (*The Seventh Commandment,* 1899), a satire of middle-class morality; psychological studies of disturbed characters like *De Meid* (*The Hired Servant,* 1905) and *Eva Bonheur* (1917); *De rijzende Zon* (*The Rising Sun,* 1911), the study of a failing businessman and his relationship with his daughter; the witty and incisive social satire featuring a tomcat, *Die wijze Kater* (1918); and the symbolic *Uitkomst* (1907), which, like Hauptmann's HANNELE'S JOURNEY TO HEAVEN, features a sick child and her visions. Produced in London in 1908 were the one-act *De Brand in de Jonge Jan* (as *A Case of Arson*) and *Schakels* (*Links*); both originally appeared in 1904, Henri de Vries notably impersonating all seven witnesses in the one-acter. Heijermans also wrote some twenty volumes of popular and long-republished short stories.

Many Heijermans plays have appeared in English, and the much-produced *The Good Hope* has been included in a number of anthologies. A scholarly book-length study is Seymour L. Flaxman's *Herman Heijermans and His Dramas* (1954).

HEISELER, Bernt von (1907–), German playwright and HENRY VON HEISELER'S son, is notable principally for his historical dramas. In the most successful of them, *Cäsar* (1941), the conflict between Caesar and Brutus—both righteous men—is tragic because the latter unjustly takes the law into his own hands; chided by Mark Antony, Brutus then confronts and (in Heiseler's version) is killed by the angry masses. Another success, *Hohenstaufentrilogie* (1939–45), consists of three romantic tragedies about the medieval House of Hohenstaufen, principally Frederick II. Heiseler has also been praised for his play about a mythical Assyrian queen, *Semiramis* (1943), a free adaptation from Calderón—like the comedy *Das laute Geheimnis* (1931). Later Heiseler wrote *Ländliche Winterkomödie* (1948) and other topical comedies, as well as religious drama like *Das Haller Spiel von der Passion* (1954).

HEISELER, Henry von (1875–1928), German author born in St. Petersburg, Russia, wrote historical tragedies on Russian subjects like the struggle of Tsar Peter I and his son, whom Peter killed, *Peter und Alexej* (1912); *Die Kinder Godunófs* (1929), on Tsar Boris Godunov and his heirs; and *Die magische Laterne* (1919), on Ivan the Terrible. *Der junge Parzival* (1927) and the posthumous *Die Rückkehr der Alkestis* (1929) are among others of his plays based on history and myth. He was the father of BERNT VON HEISELER. André von Gronicka's *Henry von Heiseler, A Russo-German Writer* (1944) is a study of his unusual career.

HELL-BENT FER HEAVEN, a play in three acts by HATCHER HUGHES, published and produced in 1924. Setting: North Carolina mountains near Asheville, early 1920's.

This often-comic Pulitzer Prize-winning folk drama features Rufe Pryor, a religious fanatic "hell-bent fer heaven." In love with a girl who is engaged to a returning veteran, and the son of a neighboring family with whom the girl's family has long feuded, Rufe tries to prevent the marriage. He uses various ruses and hypocritical religious exhortations, rekindles the slumbering feud, and finally tries to murder the veteran. Rufe gets God's "order" to blow up the dam to drown his "blaspheming" rival, but is caught in his own trap. Though Rufe cannot swim, the others refuse to take him along as the water rises. They tell him to call for God's help, and then row away. Rufe starts praying, but as the water gets close, he curses God—and screams hysterically for help.

(The ironic ending was later changed so that Rufe is rescued.)

HELLMAN, Lillian (1905–), American playwright, was the country's first important dramatist of the 1930's. Her two best-known works appeared in that decade: THE CHILDREN'S HOUR (1934) and THE LITTLE FOXES (1939). Like most of her other plays, both are chilling depictions of evil, thrillers that are also compelling as character studies. Her most notable later works include THE AUTUMN GARDEN (1951), her adaptation of Anouilh's *L'Alouette* (THE LARK, 1955), and the book for *Candide* (1956), a "comic operetta based on Voltaire's satire" that, despite its commercial failure, is considered by many to be a distinguished American musical. Hellman's other post-1930's drama has for the most part, however, been undistinguished. It is too marred by self-acknowledged artistic limitations, including the excessive pushing of the moral, which, even in her best plays, has resulted in tacked-on, false endings. Nonetheless, in the major Hellman plays the deep concern with individual decency and social justice reflected in all her drama is powerfully expressed in harrowing characterizations and plots that make first-rate theatre. Many of her plays have been filmed and have been given major revivals.

Born into a New Orleans Jewish middle-class family, Lillian Hellman was the daughter of a traveling salesman who semiannually shuttled his family from Louisiana to New York City, until they finally settled in New York when she was sixteen. After attending New York University and Columbia University, Hellman worked for a publisher, wrote short stories, and became a book reviewer for the *New York Herald Tribune*. Interested in the theatre, she worked as a press agent and, briefly, as a script reader in Hollywood. Back in New York in 1932, and after the breakup of her six-year marriage to ARTHUR KOBER, she became a play reader for the Broadway producer Herman Shumlin, who was to present most of her plays. She collaborated on a stillborn farce with the essayist Louis Kronenberger (1904–), and came under the enduring influence of Dashiell Hammett, the author of *The Maltese Falcon* (1930), *The Thin Man* (1932), and other "hard-boiled" detective novels. It was he who steered Hellman to a book on obscure lawsuits, and suggested she dramatize the early nineteenth-century Scottish "Great Drumsheugh Case." Hellman transformed it into *The Children's Hour,* which Shumlin immediately produced.

Her success with this play, to some extent heightened by the protests it elicited because of its lesbian theme, was not immediately repeated. *Days to Come* (1936), a melodrama about contemporary labor strife, was too confused to be effective. After it closed, Hellman traveled to the Soviet Union and Western Europe. She was profoundly affected by the Spanish Civil War, and returned to the United States firmly committed to combating Fascism as well as social problems. Both these commitments inform the plays that followed. Her interest in social problems, dramatized in a less contemporary situation than the one that had helped make *Days to Come* a failure, was implied in *The Little Foxes,* a play in the tradition of Becque's THE VULTURES. Hellman's concern with the evil of Fascism found expression in *Watch on the Rhine* (1941), probably the best wartime American anti-Nazi play; dramatizing the country's complacency shortly before Pearl Harbor, it features a refugee undercover agent who, after killing a blackmailing Nazi agent, must leave his affectionate wife and precocious children in the United States and return to Europe to fight the Fascists. The play, soon filmed, was very popular, but like Sherwood's THERE SHALL BE NO NIGHT and most other wartime plays, it rapidly became dated.

More interesting is ANOTHER PART OF THE FOREST (1946), which features "the little foxes" twenty years earlier (Hellman at one time intended to write a trilogy about the Hubbards). Aside from other previously mentioned writings, she adapted the Algerian Emmanuel Roblès's *Montserrat* (1948), the dramatization of an early-nineteenth-century Venezuelan struggle in which a young idealist must make a grim choice that eventually dooms six innocent people. She wrote two further original works, *The Autumn Garden* (which some consider among her finest dramas) and TOYS IN THE ATTIC (1960). Her *My Mother, My Father and Me* (1963) is a stylized dramatization of Burt Blechman's novel *How Much?,* a travesty on a middle-class Bronx family; it is an interesting but unsuccessful departure from her characteristic drama.

Hellman's work has occasionally been criticized as GRAND GUIGNOL and as following the WELL-MADE PLAY formulas of the nineteenth century. While there is justice in the charge, the plays may also, by the same token, be likened to those of HENRIK IBSEN: thrillers whose contrivance is muted by an exciting plot that meaningfully portrays the problems of society and of the individual. Though born in the South, Lillian Hellman has not been associated with the Southern or, for that matter, any regional American playwrights. The Southern setting of her most famous play is almost irrelevant: its protagonists might just as well have been Northerners, as are the protagonists of her first play. What is distinctive in Hellman's drama is the pervasive depiction of evil—societal and, to a far greater extent, individual evil. Such evil is personified by the predatory Hubbards and the neurotic little girl in *The Children's Hour,* just as the wasting and the decay of human decency are displayed in *The Autumn Garden* and *Toys in the Attic*. Hellman anatomized the various human characteristics that kill love in relentless depictions of the perversions of those who are brutal and of those who squandered their lives, and also in sympathetic portrayals of the victimized and the lost. Some of her creations, it is true, veer toward caricature, but Hellman has succeeded in producing an impressive number of psychological studies in plays that became and to some extent have remained popular, as well as critical, successes.

The *Six Plays by Lillian Hellman* (1960) are *The Children's Hour, Days to Come, The Little Foxes, Watch on the Rhine, Another Part of the Forest,* and *The Autumn Garden*. Hellman's introduction to the volume is a revealing self-evaluation, in which she also deals with critics' charges that her plays are "well made" and melodramatic, and admits to being "a moral writer, often too moral a writer." *An Unfinished Woman* (1969) is her autobiography. Studies of her life and work include a chapter in Jean Gould's *Modern American Playwrights* (1966) and a section in Allan Lewis's *American Plays and Playwrights of the Contemporary Theatre* (1965), both of which refer to other discussions.

HELLO OUT THERE, a one-act play by WILLIAM SAROYAN, produced in 1941 and published in 1942. Setting: a small-town Texas jail, c. 1940.

In this much-praised, short Saroyan play a traveling young gambler taps on his jail cell's floor with a spoon: "Hello—out there!" The young girl who cooks whenever there is a prisoner answers his call. Both are trapped in their environment, scared, and "as lonely as a coyote." They quickly fall in love, and he urges her to "get the hell to San Francisco, where you'll have a chance." She fetches a gun to protect him from a lynch mob. The gambler is in jail because a woman first led him on, later demanded money, and then charged him with rape when he left, disgusted. Her husband shoots the gambler to avoid facing his wife's infidelity. The young girl weeps and whispers after the dead youngster: "Hello—out there!"

HEMINGWAY, Ernest [Miller] (1899–1961), major American novelist and short-story writer, essayed the drama only once—and unsuccessfully—with *The Fifth Column,* a play about love and violence in the Spanish Civil War. The title work of a Hemingway collection of short stories published in 1938, the play was adapted by Benjamin Glazer (1885–1956) and produced in 1940. DORÉ SCHARY's *Brightower* (1970) is a loose dramatization of Hemingway's life and death.

HENRY IV (*Enrico IV*), a tragedy in three acts by LUIGI PIRANDELLO, published and produced in 1922. Setting: an Italian villa in "our own time."

Enrico IV (which has been translated into English under its Italian title) and SIX CHARACTERS IN SEARCH OF AN AUTHOR are Pirandello's most popular works and his finest dramatizations of the conflicts of reality and illusion, the rational and the irrational, and the conscious and the subconscious. This play presents a few difficulties at first (despite the long exposition in Act I) because of the only gradually unfolding revelation of the protagonist's past, the mixture of periods, and the historical details. Henry IV—he has no other name in the play—has been called a modern Hamlet, and this tragic figure indeed resembles Shakespeare's prince in, among other things, his introspection, his disgust with men, and his bitter wit.

Act I. A new servant, dressed as a courtier, is brought into Henry IV's salon. It is elaborately furnished as the emperor's throne room, but the mood created by the stately setting and costumes is quickly destroyed by colloquial modern speech. The newcomer is upset when he realizes that he has studied the history of the wrong king. This "Henry IV" believes himself to be the eleventh-century German emperor, the enemy of Pope Gregory VII. After the "courtiers" gaily explain these matters and provide further historical information to their new colleague, some light is shed on Henry's strange behavior by a group of visitors. They are Matilda Spina, a still-handsome, forty-five-year-old marchesa with whom Henry was in love; Tito Belcredi, a brilliant but cynical baron, Henry's former rival and now Matilda's lover—and yet the butt of her angry ridicule; Matilda's nineteen-year-old daughter, the image of her mother as a young woman; the daughter's fiancé; and a pretentious doctor, a psychiatrist who will attempt to cure Henry's madness. The madness is the result of an accident twenty years earlier: at a pageant the protagonist had been masked as Henry IV of Germany and Matilda had been impersonating her historical namesake, Henry IV's enemy, who welcomed the pope at Canossa. "Henry," thrown from his horse, had knocked his head against a rock and lost consciousness. When he came to, he believed he actually was the historical emperor whose reign he had studied before impersonating him in the pageant. Rather than send him to an asylum, his wealthy relatives humored his madness: they set up and maintained for him a palace complete with retinue in authentic costumes. The only modern objects are oil paintings of Henry and Matilda in their pageant masquerade. To Henry, these are two mirrors in which he sees the frozen, unaging past. Matilda, now a widow, regrets having treated him as contemptuously as she had all her suitors; she confesses that he was different, and that she really felt afraid of him. The visitors are soon costumed in eleventh-century dress, and at last Henry IV appears. A wreck of a fifty-year-old man, he wears a penitent's sackcloth over his royal garments, and his hair and cheeks are grotesquely tinted to suggest youth. Though Belcredi masquerades as a monk, Henry IV immediately looks upon him with hatred, insisting he is his enemy Peter Damiani. Henry ironically but earnestly talks to Matilda—who is masquerading as the emperor's mother-in-law—about everyone's need to mask his fleeting youth, and seems almost to reproach her. After flaring up at Belcredi again, Henry expresses full penitence following his excommunication by the pope; he suggests that their roles may change, and he remarks, "But woe to him who doesn't know how to wear his mask, be he king or pope!" He implores Matilda to intercede for him with the pope, and to beg the pope to free Henry from the oil portrait of his youth: "Let me live wholly and freely my miserable life." Profoundly moved, Matilda weeps when he leaves.

Act II. Though the doctor pompously expatiates on Henry's particular type of madness, Matilda thinks her former suitor recognized her and flared up at Belcredi because he is her lover: "And then his speech seemed to me full of regret for his and my youth—for the horrible thing that happened to him, that has held him in that disguise from which he has never been able to free himself, and from which he longs to be free." The doctor prepares to restore Henry's "sensation of the distance of time" and his mental balance by a trick: the joint appearance of the older and the younger woman, Matilda and her daughter, dressed exactly alike in the costume Matilda wore on the fateful day of the pageant. The shock of simultaneously seeing his beloved as she was then and as she is now will "set him going again, like a watch which has stopped at a certain hour," the doctor believes; "let's hope it'll tell the time again after its long stop." Later they take their leave of Henry. As soon as they go out, Henry drops his twenty-year demeanor. He is enraged by "the impudence" of Matilda, "come here along with her lover" under the guise of pity, "so as not to infuriate a poor devil already out of the world, out of time, out of life!" In this anguish, which causes him to drop his mask, he chides his servants for their failure to enjoy the fantasy they have been paid to enact: while the servants have lived an immutable life "fixed forever" in perfect historical logic and coherence, "the men of the twentieth century are torturing themselves in ceaseless anxiety to know how their fates and fortunes will work out." Angrily he insists that his pose is his truth, not a jest. The servants are now moved by the beauty of the illusory spell, but it is already breaking for Henry.

Act III. The doctor's scheme is carried out: Matilda's daughter, in her mother's costume and in the niche formerly occupied by her portrait, calls to Henry. Her sudden live appearance overpowers him, and for a few moments Henry really doubts his sanity. Then the visitors emerge, he understands their trick, and begins meditating on revenge. Belcredi, who has discovered Henry's deceptive pose from the servants, mocks him. Now Henry angrily tells his story. He really was mad for twelve years after his injury; when his sanity returned, he saw "how my friends deceived me, how my place was taken by another, and all the rest of it!" Everything had passed him by and was finished for him: to return to life would be "to arrive hungry as a wolf, at a banquet which had already been cleared away." And so he decided to make his former delusion "a reality, the reality of a real madness." His costume is a symbol, "the evident, involuntary caricature of that other continuous, everlasting masquerade, of which we are the involuntary puppets." All men wear masks but "I am cured, gentlemen: because I can act the madman to perfection, here." He exposes Belcredi as his rival, one of his enemies who at the pageant treacherously pricked his horse to make it throw and injure Henry. Then, castigating Matilda for her perfidy, he embraces and claims her daughter, the dream of his beloved now come alive: "You're mine, mine, mine, in my own right!" Belcredi tells him that he is sane and therefore should control himself. "I'm not mad, eh? Take that, you!" Henry exclaims, and drives his sword into Belcredi. Then Henry gathers his servant-courtiers around him, terrified by the trap of his mask of madness, to which, as a murderer, he is now doomed: "Now, yes . . . we'll have to . . . here we are . . . together . . . forever!"

HENSEN, Herwig [originally Florent Constant Albert Mielants] (1917–), Belgian mathematician, poet, and playwright born in Antwerp, achieved considerable popularity in the 1940's with Flemish dramatizations of legends. Typical of his transformations of them is his *Lady Godiva* (1946), whose heroine rides naked through the streets of Coventry not so much for the sake of the oppressed populace for whom she has interceded with her brutal husband but, rather, out of pride; and the act's consequences are dramatized: her husband becomes sentimental, her young admirer stops loving her, the townspeople joke coarsely, and Lady Godiva herself succumbs to cynicism and despair.

Hensen's first play was the Shakespearean romance *Antonio* (1942). It was followed by *Don Juan* (1943), *Polycrates* (1946), and *Koningin Christina* (1946). In *Alkestis* (1953) Hensen portrays Hercules as a brash liar; *Agamemnon* (1953) depicts the title hero as merely feigning his daughter's sacrifice; and *Tarquinius* (1953) dramatizes the danger of the supernatural to human freedom. Hensen also wrote a lively comedy, *Niets zonder de proef* (1947).

A first-rate craftsman, Hensen brought classic restraint and universal themes to the Flemish theatre. He has also intrigued audiences with his existentialist ideas and his poetic language. An account of his work appears in SUZANNE LILAR's *The Belgian Theatre Since 1890* (third edition, 1962).

HERBERT, Zbigniew (1924–), Polish poet, wrote an intriguing dramatization of the death of Socrates, *Jaskinia filozofów* (*The Philosophers' Den,* 1956). Appearing with the thaw that followed years of moral and intellectual coercion by the Communist Party, the play features a Socrates who expresses Herbert's lyricism and philosophic attitudes: he is courageous but not rebellious, escapist but not affirmative. Herbert's later plays include *Drugi pokój* (*The Other Room*, 1958), a one-acter about a young couple waiting for a neighbor to die so that they can have his room; and *Lalek* (1961), "a play for voices" expressing moral and cultural depravity in a village's threnody for the title character. *The Philosophers' Den* is included, with a note on Herbert, in Pawel

Mayewski's collection of contemporary Polish literature, *The Broken Mirror* (1958).

HERE COME THE CLOWNS, a play in three acts by PHILIP BARRY, produced in 1938 and published in 1939. Setting: the back room of a café next to the Globe, a theatre in "an American city on a Saturday night in late March, several years ago."

Barry's dramatization of his only novel, *War in Heaven* (1938), this is a more successful religious-psychological allegory than the earlier HOTEL UNIVERSE. Here, too, the action is continuous and there are a number of psychodramas. Like O'Neill's THE ICEMAN COMETH, *Here Come the Clowns* is an astringent portrayal of grotesques forced to shed their illusions. Barry noted that his characters represent "all forms of human wretchedness, congenital and imposed." They include the café's proprietor, a hermaphrodite; a lesbian whose husband is a ventriloquist; a midget who cannot forget his dead wife, "the Vest-pocket Venus"; a dwarf-hating dancer who, because he is a foundling, fears to marry his partner; an alcoholic press agent; and a down-and-out stagehand, Dan Clancy, who still mourns the death of his long-lost baby daughter and the disappearance of his wife.

A German illusionist, Max Pabst, gets these "clowns" to face reality. In a series of psychodramas he makes the ventriloquist articulate his wife's duplicity through his dummy, and for a while Pabst frightens both dwarf and dancer with the possibility that they are father and son. Clancy learns that his wife deserted him: she never loved him, and the child he adored was her lover's. Agonizing to discover why "if it's Good that rules over us, [it is] Evil that always seems to have the upper hand," Clancy angrily summons God. A mysterious figure appears and gives conventional answers. "There must be persecution . . . to fortify man's faith in heaven," he says, counseling resignation: "All must be left to the Almighty Will." The figure defends the creation of freaks like the hermaphrodite and the dwarf: "Would you deny Him a sense of humor?" Angrily Clancy objects—and the divine figure is unmasked as Pabst.

Furious at the destroyer of illusions, the drunken press agent shoots Pabst—but Clancy intercepts the bullet. "It's no will of God things are as they are—no, nor Devil's will neither," Clancy realizes. Through his free will man himself makes his own good and evil. "For it's a fine instrument, the free will of man is, and can as easy be turned to Good as to Bad," Clancy concludes as he dies happily, in the arms of his wife's sister, who loves him: "It can rise over anything, anything!"

HERMIONE, a historical play in five acts by AUGUST STRINDBERG, published in 1960. Setting: Athens, 343 B.C.

Strindberg's third play, the poetic drama originally titled *Det sjunkande Hellas,* was rejected by Stockholm's Royal Theatre in 1870. He expanded it into this Schiller-like blank-verse tragedy and submitted it to the Swedish Academy of Literature. It was commended but did not win a prize. The plot depicts the betrayal of Demosthenes by his people while Athens is being conquered by Philip of Macedonia.

HERNE, James A. [originally James Ahern] (1839–1901), American dramatist, actor, and manager, made his debut in *Uncle Tom's Cabin* in Troy, New York, in 1859. He married the actress Helen Western in 1866, and after their separation was leading man to her sister Lucille. In 1874 he began his association with DAVID BELASCO, then a bit player in Herne's version of *Rip Van Winkle* (c. 1874); they collaborated on a number of plays, including *Marriage by Moonlight* (later called *Hap-Hazard,* 1879), *Within an Inch of His Life* (1879), and the long-popular *Hearts of Oak* (1878), a domestic melodrama first titled *Chums* and adapted with Belasco from an older English play. Earlier, Herne had become the stage manager and leading actor at San Francisco's Baldwin Theatre. There he met and in 1878 married Katharine Corcoran, who inspired his writing and thereafter played the lead in most of his plays.

Herne's work was strongly influenced by HENRIK IBSEN and Charles Dickens, whose *Oliver Twist* he dramatized in 1874. Becoming active in art movements advocating REALISM, Herne formulated his theories in the significantly titled essay "Art for Truth's Sake in the Drama," published in *Arena* (February 1897). His MARGARET FLEMING (1890) was hailed by a cultivated minority, but *Shore Acres* (1892), a melodrama and sentimental character study of the lovable Uncle Nat, was more attuned to mass tastes and made Herne's fortune. Among other plays that dramatized with some realism the common American and in which Herne starred with his wife are his *The Minute Men of 1774–75* (1886), *Drifting Apart* (1888), *The Reverend Griffith Davenport* (1899, a Civil War drama later produced as *Griffith Davenport*), and *Sag Harbor* (1899), a very popular revamping of his earlier *Hearts of Oak,* the original characters of the foster father and son being replaced by two brothers as rivals in the romance.

Herne's plays were published in *Shore Acres and Other Plays* (1928) and in *The Early Plays of James A. Herne* (1940); the biography by Herbert J. Edwards and Julie A. Herne, *James A. Herne: The Rise of Realism in the American Drama* (1964), has a complete bibliography.

HERNE'S EGG, THE, a verse play in six scenes by WILLIAM BUTLER YEATS, published in 1938. Setting: mist and rocks, banqueting hall, etc.

Yeats called this stylized, SYMBOLIC farce "the strangest wildest thing I have ever written."

After his fiftieth "perfect" and even battle with Tara, King Congal of Connacht steals herne eggs for the peace celebration. To the priestess Attracta, bride of the bird-god, these eggs are sacred. The unbelieving Congal attributes her worship of the bird-god to sexual frustration, but Attracta maintains that "I burn / Not in the flesh but in the mind." Congal and his men try but fail to kill the great herne, which they take for only an angry bird. The bird priestess, Attracta, sows discord by substituting a hen's egg for Congal's sacred one, and in a drunken fit of anger at the feast Congal kills his enemy-friend, the King of Tara, with a table leg. To revenge himself against the bird-god, Congal pronounces a "pleasant" and "legal" judgment on the god's bride, one that will also "do her a great good." As Congal and six of his men rape her, Attracta sings of her mystic union with the herne. Afraid of the god, Congal's men later deny their act, and Attracta herself remembers it only as a holy sacrament: "My husband came to me in that night." For their cowardice the men are to be transformed into animals. Congal alone refuses to deny his act or himself. Despite the god's curse, Congal cannot believe that his fate is to die at the hands of the grotesque fool who tries to kill him. He proclaims his victory because of the multiple rape of the god's priestess-wife and because he falls over the fool's spit "at my own will": "I have beaten you, Great Herne, / In spite of your kitchen spit—seven men—" Now compassionate, Attracta tries to save Congal from a dreadful reincarnation by giving herself to a servant. But the servant is too slow, and Congal will be reincarnated as a beast, "Nothing but just another donkey."

HERR PUNTILA AND HIS SERVANT MATTI (*Herr Puntila und sein Knecht Matti*), a folk play in twelve scenes by BERTOLT BRECHT (music by Paul Dessau), produced in 1948 and published in 1950. Setting: pre-World War II Finland.

Brecht's comedy is "based on the folk tales and an outline for a play by Hella Wuolijoki," the Finnish playwright (1886–1954) whose guest he was in 1940, when he wrote the play. It is full of earthy humor, and in theme resembles the film *City Lights* (1931). But unlike Charlie Chaplin's Tramp, Brecht's Matti is more critical of the mercurial moods of his wealthy companion (Puntila), the play's Gargantuan protagonist. In the late 1950's Paul Dessau expanded his original incidental music for the play into an operatic score, which was first produced in 1966. The play was filmed (its script prepared with Brecht's advice) in Vienna in 1955. It has also been translated as *Puntila and Matti, His Hired Hand.*

At the end of three days of drinking, estate-owner Puntila befriends his chauffeur, Matti Altonen. Comradely and lovable when drunk, Puntila is surly and mean when sober—and he alternates between these two states. Drunk, he proposes to four village girls whom he asks to his estate, and goes to the market to "invite" (hire) farmhands; he wants to cancel his daughter Eva's engagement to a diplomat and asks her to marry his friend, the chauffeur Matti. Sober, Puntila abuses his servants, throws out the village girls, and insists on Eva's more suitable marriage to her fiancé. Puntila's shifts in mood are as amusing to observe as they are baffling and irritating to those who must cope with them.

Matti never can forget the difference in their social positions. But when Eva—who is attracted to him—has Matti compromise her before her fiancé, and the drunken Puntila finally throws the diplomat out, Matti agrees to give her a test that will determine the possibility of her becoming a worker's wife. Eva's bourgeois education and her love for Matti prove insufficient to survive the hardships of a proletarian wife, and she fails the test. On a magnificent drunken spree, Puntila scales an imaginary mountain (made of smashed furniture) that Matti helps him to build in his library. Puntila is exalted, and vows to share his wealth with Matti. But the next morning Matti leaves the estate. He fears Puntila's sober awakening and has had enough of their unstable relationship. "Water and oil don't mix," the servant Matti remarks, going out hurriedly: "A good master can be found faster / Only if you are your own master."

HERRERA, Ernesto (1886–1917), Uruguayan playwright, was the successor of FLORENCIO SÁNCHEZ, his first play, the incest-and-suicide melodrama *El estanque* (1910), appearing the year of Sánchez's death. Herrera's drama is NATURALISTIC, influenced particularly by MAXIM GORKY and dealing with middle-class and (often) rural families. His masterpiece, *El león ciego* (1911), portrays an unsuccessful old gaucho revolutionary ("the blind lion") and was praised as "a highpoint in Uruguayan drama" that also helped to avert senseless political violence. His other important plays are *La moral de Misia Paca* (1912), a drama of ideas about a mismated Creole girl; and *El pan nuestro* (1912), depicting the breakup of a family because of the wife's self-sac ifice.

The illegitimate offspring of a prominent family, Herrera was nonetheless self-made and lived among the poor and lowly. Like Sánchez, he started as a newspaperman, wrote plays at record-breaking speed, went abroad after achieving success, and died early of tuberculosis, which was aggravated by his irregular living. Though his plays have not been published in English, Herrera is considered a major New World figure and is discussed at length in LATIN AMERICAN studies. All of his plays, as well as a biography, appear in Herrera's *Obras completas* (1917).

HERVIEU, Paul Ernest (1857–1915), French playwright, began his writing career as a novelist. He became famous as a dramatist with *La Course de flambeau* (THE PASSING OF THE TORCH, 1901), and most of his dozen plays became part of the Comédie-Française repertory. Like EUGÈNE BRIEUX, Hervieu wrote thesis plays. But Hervieu, who was a member of the bar, focused on legal impediments to family happiness. Hervieu portrayed the upper classes and was given less to sermonizing than to forcing plots and resolutions to demonstrate his theses. Because he was concerned more with his age's law and morals than with psychological "truth," and with theatrical effect rather than dramatic REALISM, Hervieu's drama has become hopelessly dated. His contemporary reputation, however, was considerable. He was elected to the French Academy, became president of the Society of Dramatic Authors, and received many honors. In his *Iconoclasts* (1905), James Huneker praised Hervieu's "real artistry" and called him "the present master-psychologist of the French stage."

Hervieu was born in Neuilly and graduated from law school in Paris in 1881. He was employed as a minor diplomat, but soon began to write (as Éliacin) and make a reputation with articles, stories, and novels. His first play, an adaptation of Vincent Denon's story *Point de lendemain,* was produced in 1890. His next play was *Les Paroles restent* (*Words Remain,* 1892), a romantic melodrama about a man who traduces a girl with whom he subsequently falls in love. More important is *Les Tenailles* (*The Chains,* 1895, also translated as *In Chains*), his first success at the Comédie-Française; it was also his first play about the divorce laws' inadequacy, here the laws' failure to resolve the problems of a couple who, although they have had a child conceived in adultery, are nonetheless both trapped by their marriage "chains."

Other Hervieu plays dealing with family problems of divorce, honor, and children are *La Loi de l'homme* (*Man's Law,* 1895) and *Le Dédale* (*The Labyrinth,* 1903). In the latter, one of Hervieu's great hits, the illness of a child brings about the heroine's agonizing realization that she can now live with neither her divorced husband nor her second husband, both of whom (therefore) are killed. Hervieu's remaining plays include *L'Énigme* (*The Enigma,* 1901), a play about infidelity produced in England as *Cæsar's Wife; Théroigne de Méricourt* (1902), a long—and his only—historical drama, acted by Sarah Bernhardt; *Connais-toi* (*Know Thyself,* 1909), in which the moralistic protagonist is paralyzed upon discovering his wife in the arms of another man, but forgives her because he realizes that no man "knows himself" how he might act; and *Le Destin est maître* (*Destiny Is Master,* 1914), another domestic tragedy, first produced in Spain in a translation by JACINTO BENAVENTE.

Hervieu's plays appeared in four volumes (1910–22), and most of them are available in English. To French studies, Huneker's *Iconoclasts,* and Hulet H. Cook's learned monograph *Paul Hervieu and French Classicism* (1945), may be added Barrett H. Clark's *Contemporary French Dramatists* (1916), which has a chapter on Hervieu's life and work as well as a bibliography.

HEYNICKE, Kurt (1891–   ), German poet and dramatist, came of Silesian laborer stock and began his career by publishing EXPRESSIONIST verse, IBSENite plays like *Das Meer* (1925), comedies like *Wer gewinnt Lisette?* (1928), and spectacles like *Neurode* (1934), whose mass choirs glorify the indomitable spirit of coal miners who continue working against all odds. He became most successful with his Nazi-established THINGSPIELE.

HEYWARD, Dorothy (1890–1961), American novelist and playwright, is best known for PORGY (1927) and for her 1939 dramatization of her husband DUBOSE HEYWARD's other notable novel, *Mamba's Daughters* (1929). Née Dorothy Hartzell Kuhns, in Ohio, Mrs. Heyward studied playwriting at Harvard, where her first drama, *Nancy Ann,* was produced in 1924. Her other plays include *Jonica* (1930, with MOSS HART); *South Pacific* (1943; with Howard Rigsby, 1909–   ), which, despite its title, war setting, and antiracist theme has no relation to Richard Rodgers and OSCAR HAMMERSTEIN II's popular 1949 musical; and *Set My People Free* (1948), a play about an early slave rebellion, produced by the Theatre Guild, which also had produced the Heywards' *Porgy.*

HEYWARD, DuBose (1885–1940), American poet, novelist, and playwright, will be remembered longest for PORGY, his first novel (1925), which he dramatized in 1927 and which George Gershwin made into the folk opera *Porgy and Bess* (1935). A native of South Carolina, Heyward was very familiar with the waterfront as well as the Gullah Negroes featured in his masterpiece. As a poor youth he had worked side by side with such people on the Charleston docks. He was a kindly man who loved the people he portrayed, and took it as a compliment when *Porgy* was thought to have been written by a Negro.

Another play he wrote is *Brass Ankle* (1931), featuring a white supremacist who kills his wife and her baby when he discovers she has Negro blood. Heyward's other notable novel is *Mamba's Daughters* (1929). DOROTHY HEYWARD, his wife, who had collaborated on the play *Porgy,* in 1939 dramatized *Mamba's Daughters* into a melodramatic folk drama; an account of the misfortunes of a Negro woman, memorably portrayed by Ethel Waters, it has a Charleston setting similar to that of *Porgy.*

Heyward was a direct descendent of the patriot Thomas Heyward, Jr., a signer of the Declaration of Independence. With the novelist Hervey Allen, with whom in 1920 he had founded the Poetry Society of South Carolina, Heyward wrote *Carolina Chansons* (1922). Aside from other poetry collections and novels, Heyward also published a Civil War chronicle. His biography is Frank Durham's *DuBose Heyward: The Man Who Wrote "Porgy"* (1954).

HIDALLA, OR KARL HETMANN, THE MIDGET-GIANT (*Hidalla, oder Karl Hetmann der Zwerg-Riese*), a play in five acts by FRANK WEDEKIND, published in 1904 and produced in 1905. Setting: early twentieth-century Germany.

This, one of Wedekind's popular plays during his life, is patently autobiographical and resembles THE MARQUIS OF KEITH in its protagonist.

The deformed philosopher Hetmann too is embued with brains, vitality, and sensuality. To breed beautiful, superior people, he establishes a promiscuous "International Society for the Founding of Thoroughbreeds." But his utopian ideas are generally misunderstood and he himself is denied membership, and is imprisoned. When released, Hetmann is offered work in a circus, and commits suicide.

HIGH TOR, a play in three acts by MAXWELL ANDERSON, produced in 1936 and published in 1937. Setting: a mountain top—High Tor—overlooking the Hudson River.

This poetic fantasy is a gossamer of the present and the long-ago past. Like Shakespeare's *A Midsummer Night's Dream,* it is a compound of the real and the unreal, of romance and farce. The play glorifies nature and the past over the industrialized and materialistic present. But many apparently contradictory lines suggest further meanings, and the play provoked much critical controversy. Nonetheless, Mabel D. Bailey remarked in *Maxwell Anderson: The Playwright as Prophet* (1957): "It is a free fantasy with no better object and no greater merit than its sheer fun."

Van Van Dorn wants to continue his carefree life of nature, hunting and fishing for his food. He refuses to imprison himself in an industrial job, or to sell High Tor for commercial razing and development. His girlfriend wants a regular American home and therefore leaves him. Night falls, and various people appear on High Tor: an old Indian seeking a site for his grave, two crooked officials who want to purchase the mountain, a gang of bank robbers with their loot, and the ghost crew of a seventeenth-century Dutch ship. Among the adventures of the night are a love idyll between Van and the ghost captain's wife, and the arrest of the officials for bank robbery, after they have spent a precarious and uncomfortable night hanging over the precipice in a steam shovel. At the end, the ghost crew leaves and his girlfriend rejoins Van, who plans to "move out farther west / where a man's land's his own." The Indian has persuaded him to sell High Tor because "there's no hill worth a man's peace. . . . / Nothing is made by men / but makes, in the end, good ruins." Van replies: "Well, that's something. / But I can hardly wait."

HILDESHEIMER, Wolfgang (1916–   ), German dramatist, was originally a painter. In the 1950's he turned to playwriting. His first works were radio dramas, including one staged as *Der Drachenthron* (1955), a satirical contemporary variation of the eighteenth-century play by Carlo Gozzi on which Puccini's opera *Turandot* is based. Hildesheimer's plays—most of them one-acters—resemble SAMUEL BECKETT's type of ABSURDist theatre. *Nachtstück* (*Nightpiece,* 1962), for example, portrays a compulsive's elaborately ritualistic precautions before going to sleep and his encounter with a burglar, who has easily entered and then extricates himself from the complex system of knots in which he is fettered by the compulsive. The latter's monologue, which constitutes most of the play, invests the action with a SYMBOLISM suggesting the humanist's victimization by forces of universal and all-pervasive evil. Other Hildesheimer plays similarly dramatize such themes, sometimes with verbal assaults on cliché reminiscent of the early EUGÈNE IONESCO.

Born in Hamburg, Hildesheimer went to school in Germany. When the Nazis came to power he fled, first to Palestine, where he studied interior decorating (1933–36), and then to England, where he studied painting and stage design (1937–39). He was a British Army liaison officer in Palestine during World War II, and an interpreter at the Nuremberg trials of Nazi war criminals. Subsequently he settled in Bavaria, where he began his writing career. Among his plays are *Spiele in denen es dunkel wird* (1958), a collection of one-acters; and *Die Verspätung* (1961), which depicts a disintegrating village where an old professor dies brokenhearted when the fantastic bird he has awaited turns out to be the wrong one. *Nightpiece* appears in Michael Benedikt and George E. Wellwarth's *Postwar German Theatre* (1967).

HIM, a play in three acts by E. E. CUMMINGS, published in 1927 and produced in 1928. Setting: a stage with rocking chairs, a room, etc.; c. 1920's.

This avant-garde drama, written in the tradition of EXPRESSIONISM and SURREALISM, was produced by the Provincetown Players and revived in the same Greenwich Village theatre in 1948. Cummings's program "warning" was that "this PLAY isn't 'about,' it simply is. Don't try to despise it, let it try to despise you. . . . Don't try to understand it, let it try to understand you." The play suggests problems of artistic creation, self-identity, and the relativity of reality. Some critics have praised its "brilliant" experimental daring, other critics have deplored what they consider its banality and excesses—and the public has ignored it.

A backdrop painting through which protrude two living heads portrays a doctor anesthetizing a woman (who may be dreaming the play, for the doctor constantly reappears, in many guises). Periodically three weird old figures rock, knit, and chat nonsensically before the painting. The title protagonist (Him) and his beloved, Me ("him" backwards—"mih"), talk in their room. She faces the audience, primping before an imaginary mirror hanging on the invisible fourth wall. Him questions Me's love, and despairs over a play he is writing: "But why die now? the morn's on the thorn, the snail's on the wing, the play's on the way; and who knows?" Both question the identity of their real selves. Upon her request, Him shows Me scenes from his other play, the popular one she wants him to write. The various skits—vaudeville in form and often bawdy—include a drunk scene with an intrigued maiden lady, a Negro "Frankie and Johnnie" song-and-dance interrupted by a representative of the Society for the Contraception of Vice, the burning of Rome as Benito Mussolini boasts to adoring homosexuals that he is burning

Communists, a Paris dive with sleeping whores, etc. At the end, the various characters of the play attend a freak show. The barker (played by the doctor) introduces "duh Princess Anankay [who] is about tuh purform fur duh benefit uv duh Oreye-entul Ee-lectrickully Lighted Orphunts' Home un duh boys in genrul uh hiddurto strickly sacred Oo-pee-lah ur Spasmwriggle." She is a draped white female, holding a newborn baby. The three weirds disgustedly shout, "It's all done with mirrors!" When the woman is revealed as Me, Him shrieks in terror. Back in their room, Me informs Him that there are people beyond the invisible wall facing the audience: "They're pretending that this room and you and I are real." Him whispers, "I wish I could believe this." But he says he cannot, "Because this is true."

HINDLE WAKES, a play in three acts by STANLEY HOUGHTON, published and produced in 1912. Setting: a small Lancashire town, early twentieth century.

In part influenced by the drama of HENRIK IBSEN, this protest against the double standard is nonetheless typical of Houghton's interest in portraying the clash between generations. This play, considered his best, was immensely popular for some time and made Houghton famous. HAROLD BRIGHOUSE transformed it into a novel in 1927.

Alan Jeffcote, the weak-willed son of the town's highly principled mill owner, spends a weekend with Fanny Hawthorn. Hers is in part a rebellious gesture against a dull environment, and she shocks all concerned when Alan submits to the demands of both their families that they get married—and she refuses. "You're a man, and I was your little fancy. Well, I'm a woman and *you* were *my* little fancy. You wouldn't prevent a woman enjoying herself as well as a man, if she takes it into her head?" she asks the incredulous Alan, who replies, "It sounds so jolly immoral. I never thought of a girl looking at a chap like that!"

HINKEMANN, "a German tragedy" in three acts by ERNST TOLLER, published in 1922 and produced in 1924. Setting: a German town, c. 1922.

Translated also as *Brockenbrow,* this NATURALISTIC drama of post-World War I disillusionment features a veteran who was emasculated on the battlefield.

Eugene Hinkemann is powerfully built, simple, and confused, but sensitive and kindhearted to the point where, as his wife remarks, "he wouldn't let me set mouse traps in the kitchen because it's wicked to torture animals." Despairing because he is broke and fears that his beloved wife now may scorn him all the more because of his maimed body, he takes the only job available: that of a peepshow performer who "devours live rats and mice before the very eyes of our esteemed public" —for, as the showman cynically remarks, "The public likes *blood.* Plenty of it. Christians or no Christians!" Disgusted and bitter after the performance, Hinkemann is crushed to learn of his wife's unfaithfulness. He staggers into a Walpurgis Night street scene. His repentant wife returns but Hinkemann can never forgive her laughing at him. "I'm fit to laugh at, yes, and so is everything else in our times—as miserable and ridiculous as I am," he tells her: "The world has lost its soul and I have lost my sex. What's the difference?" Her pleas for their reunion do not overcome his despair, for "A man who has no strength for dreams has lost the strength to live." She commits suicide and Hinkemann remains alone, puzzled about the meaning of existence: "Any day the kingdom of heaven may arise, any night the great flood may come and swallow up the earth."

HIRSCHFELD, Georg (1873–1942), German novelist and playwright, was a disciple of GERHART HAUPTMANN. His big hit was *Die Mütter* (*The Mothers,* 1895), a NATURALISTIC play about a young composer who quarrels with his father, leaves home, and has a liaison with a lower-class girl; he returns to his comfortable home after his father dies, though his mother declines to accept the girl—who thereupon consoles herself with their child. Hirschfeld's less theatrical *Agnes Jordan* (1897) chronicles the lifelong drab marriage of a woman to an inferior man. In a lighter vein, *Mieze und Maria* (1907) portrays the unsuccessful attempts of a natural father to transform his fourteen-year-old daughter from her proletarian Berlin upbringing.

Ludwig Lewisohn's translation of *The Mothers* was published in 1916.

HIRSHBEIN, Peretz (1880–1948), Yiddish playwright and novelist, wrote over fifty plays, many of them one-acters. More than the works of any other dramatist, these stimulated the development and growth of the Yiddish art theatre. For a time, Hirshbein was also well known beyond the Yiddish theatre world, because of the popularity of *A Farvorfn Vinkl* (A FORSAKEN NOOK, 1915) and *Di Puste Kretshme* (THE HAUNTED INN, 1913). But he is best remembered for some of his short symbolic pieces, and for charming dramatic idylls like *Grine Felder* GREEN FIELDS, 1916).

Born to a miller's family in Grodno, Russia, Hirshbein is unique among Yiddish playwrights in having grown up on a farm. This bucolic background, which is exquisitely recounted in the autobiography *Mayne Kinderyoren* (1932), characterizes the countryside setting and spirit of many of his fifty-odd plays. When he turned to writing after an education in the yeshivas of Brest-Litovsk and Vilna, however, Hirshbein first depicted the life of the city poor. His earliest play, *Miriam* (1905), is a NATURALISTIC tragedy about a Jewish prostitute. Like his other early work, including his next play, *Der Inteligent* (1907), it was originally written in Hebrew. It was published in *Hazman,* a periodical Hirshbein helped to found in 1905. A number of other plays, including *Eynzame Veltn* (*Lonely Worlds,* 1906), were translated into and published in Russian. Some are naturalistic, but SYMBOLISM became increasingly pronounced in his plays, which have been likened to the static mood drama of MAURICE MAETERLINCK. The haunting little one-act *In der Finster* (*In the Dark,* 1906), for instance, portrays a girl, in the family's basement hovel, yearning for love and life; but poverty makes her future so hopeless that she despairs and hangs herself in the presence of her blind old grandmother. Plays of this sort earned Hirshbein the sobriquet "poet of the cellar folk."

Encouraged by the poet Chaim Nachman Bialik, Hirshbein in 1908 organized a group of Yiddish actors, amateur and professional, into a company (The Hirshbein Troupe) in Odessa, and toured it across Russia. Its members later joined the important art theatres of Vilna and New York, and The Hirshbein Troupe, though it lasted only two years, had an enormous effect on the Yiddish stage. Hirshbein produced the work of SHOLEM ASCH, YITSKHOK LEYBUSH PERETZ, JACOB GORDIN, and SHOLEM ALEICHEM, as well as his own plays, the most important being *Neveyle* (CARRION, 1905). Among his other early plays—he soon wrote in Yiddish rather than Hebrew—are *Di Erd* (1907) and *Tkias Kaf* (1907), the latter the tragedy of a Jewish girl whose parentally arranged betrothal keeps her from the man she loves—a common plot in Hirshbein's plays, but one that he later resolved happily, with the victory going to youth and true love.

The difficulties of producing Yiddish drama under the tsar eventually prompted Hirshbein to leave Russia. In 1911 he came to New York, where he soon completed *The Haunted Inn* and *A Forsaken Nook*. But it was years before these popular plays were to find a producer—and to make him famous. In the meantime, Hirshbein traveled through North as well as South America, and published books about his travels. During World War I he wrote a series of one-act plays subsequently translated into English (*Raisins and Almonds, On the Threshold, Bebele*—an idyll about an ecstatic Jewish bride and her self-sacrificing mother—*The Snowstorm,* and *When the Dew Falleth*), as well as *A Leben far a Leben, Green Fields*—considered by many to be his finest work—*In Shotn fun Doyres,* and *Dem Schmid's Tekhter* (produced in 1919), which in plot and popularity resemble his two most successful plays.

It is in these later works that his unique dramatic talent best manifests itself. They have been likened to the plays of LADY GREGORY, and there is indeed a resemblance. Hirshbein depicts East European Jewish country folk, succeeding admirably in fusing comedy and farce, romance, and folklore. Always perceptible in these comedies is his awareness of life's tragedies, of the struggle between generations, of the individual's difficult quest for self-realization and dignity, and of man's aggressive and erotic instincts. This awareness, as well as his gift for creating memorable characters and situations, prevents the plays' turning saccharine or sentimental—though Hirshbein opted for compromise, for decency, and for compassion and happiness. At first the actor-manager Maurice Schwartz did not want to produce these "amateur" plays in New York; when he finally agreed to put on *A Forsaken Nook* in 1918, the success of Schwartz's theatre and Hirshbein's reputation were made.

Hirshbein soon resumed his travels and his books about them. He finally returned to live in the United States, but it is these travel books and his novels that are the most important of his later works—particularly his travel books on Palestine and India (where he met Mahatma Gandhi and RABINDRANATH TAGORE) and his novels *Royte Felder* (1935) and *Bovel* (1942).

Five volumes of Hirshbein's collected works came out in 1951. *The Haunted Inn* was published in English in 1921, and various anthologies contain other translated plays, among them the one-acters written during World War I as well as *In the Dark, Lonely Worlds,* and *Green Fields.* Hirshbein's work is discussed in Isaac Goldberg's *The Drama of Transition* (1922); in Sol Liptzin's *The Flowering of Yiddish Literature* (1963); in David S. Lifson's *The Yiddish Theatre in America* (1965); and in Charles A. Madison's *Yiddish Literature: Its Scope and Major Writers* (1968).

HIS HOUSE IN ORDER, a comedy in four acts by ARTHUR WING PINERO, produced in 1906 and published in 1907. Setting: a countryhouse in the English Midlands, early 1900's.

This was one of Pinero's most popular plays. Like Mrs. Tanqueray (in THE SECOND MRS. TANQUERAY), the protagonist is a second and lower-class wife. But here the husband makes her miserable by constantly and unfavorably comparing her to his paragon of a first wife. When she discovers evidence of her predecessor's infidelity, the *raisonneur* talks her out of using it: "The happy people I've come across have never been the people who, possessing power, have employed it malevolently or uncharitably." He himself must finally reveal the truth to the abusive husband, who thereupon becomes affectionate.

HISTORIE VON KÖNIG DAVID, DIE, a projected biblical trilogy by RICHARD BEER-HOFMANN, like the Greeks' and Goethe's dramatized myths of their peoples, was to personify Judaism in the legends about King David. Its emphasis on the Hebraic precepts of human brotherhood contrast sharply with the contemporary Fascist ideologies of nationalism and racism. Beer-Hofmann completed the prelude, *Jáakobs Traum* (JACOB'S DREAM, 1918), and the trilogy's first play, *Der Junge David* (1933). Linked by poetic language and the evocation of David's ancestress Ruth, the latter drama portrays the aging Saul's fall and the rise of Jacob's descendant David, climaxed by David's coronation. *König David,* the second play, according to extant fragments (including *Vorspiel auf dem Theater zu König David,* 1936) and outlines, was to feature Absalom's revolt and David stripped of royal accouterments, reverting to youthful simplicity, goodness, and piety. Of the final play, *Davids Tod,* Beer-Hofmann completed only a single lyrical passage.

HOCHHUTH, Rolf (1931–   ), German playwright, achieved international fame with his first play, *Der Stellvertreter* (THE DEPUTY, 1963)—a SUCCÈS DE SCANDALE that attacked Pope Pius XII; many publishers, though they were profoundly shaken by it, feared to print the drama. Hochhuth's next play, *Soldaten* (SOLDIERS, 1967), with its portrayal of Winston Churchill, proved to be equally controversial, but it aroused considerably less fanfare. It was followed by yet another long (220 fine-print pages of dialectical documentation) play, *Guerillas* (1970), which features an idealistic United States senator killed by the Central Intelligence Agency for attempting to fulfill the ideals of the American Constitution by setting up a revolutionary pro-youth but non-Communist government. These works exemplify Hochhuth's talent for the polemic that unmasks and publicizes contemporary issues, and for the idealism articulated by such protagonists as the fictitious Riccardo Fontana in *The Deputy* and the historical Bishop Bell in *Soldiers*.

Hochhuth was born to a Protestant family in Eschwege/Werra, a Hessian town a few miles west of what later became the border between East and West Germany. His father, an officer in both world wars, was a shoe manufacturer who was ruined in the Depression and became an accountant. Young Hochhuth spent the first thirty-one years of his life in the provinces. He served in the Hitler *Jugend*—for his parents led an "ordinary" German life, though they risked their lives by helping Jews and some of their less fortunate distant relatives, who were victimized by the Nazis. One of Hochhuth's first jobs—the only political one he ever held—was as a city hall runner: his uncle, a retired army officer, had been appointed by the United States as Eschwege's first post-Nazi mayor. Hochhuth attended the universities of Marburg, Munich, and Heidelberg; he read widely, published short stories, and wrote a novel. In time he became a reader and editor for a publishing company specializing in school texts and children's literature. Hochhuth was particularly successful in editing for this firm a collection of children's stories, for which he was rewarded with a three-months paid leave of absence.

This provided him with the opportunity to study at first hand a problem in which he had become increasingly interested: the Vatican's reaction to the Nazi extermination of the Jews. He went to Rome, where he pursued the subject intensively. Irritated by the worldwide veneration of Pope Pius XII upon his death in 1958, Hochhuth decided to publish his conclusions on the Pope's failure to denounce Nazi mass murders, for, Hochhuth remarked, "the record should be put in perspective."

His own publisher, like the others to whom he subsequently offered the finished play, was unwilling to risk bringing out anything so controversial. (It was finally published by the Rowohlt firm.) The famous director Erwin Piscator, who had recently returned from the United States, where he had spent the Nazi years, offered to produce it. He considered *The Deputy* "a historical drama in Schiller's sense . . . an epic play for epic 'political' theatre, the theatre for which I have fought for more than thirty years." It was to Piscator that Hochhuth consequently dedicated his second play, *Soldiers*.

Established as a documentary playwright, Hochhuth has been widely hailed as a fervent and fearless idealist who has brought vital issues into the fashionable and commercial theatre. The powerful effect of his drama—invariably composed in verse—is undeniable. He has brought to life prominent figures and issues with personifications and scenes that have aroused worldwide audiences—and have incited riots and picketing wherever his plays are produced. Yet Hochhuth's artistry, as is readily admitted even by his more enthusiastic supporters, is vitiated by his pedestrian verse and his inability to confine his drama to the requirements of the stage. Long, novelistic books—the novelist Thomas Mann exerted the most profound influence on him, Hochhuth has noted repeatedly—his plays necessarily have had to be produced in fragmented form. Since each director makes cuts according to his own tastes, Hochhuth's plays have appeared in totally differing versions.

Eschewing personal publicity, Hochhuth, whose face was slightly disfigured by a nervous illness, has continued to lead an obscure life. After the success of *The Deputy* he settled with his wife and children in Basel, Switzerland. He has also written fiction in which he explores the political crimes of his fellow Germans in Nazi times, as in the novella *Die Berliner Antigone* (1965).

The books listed under THE DEPUTY discuss Hochhuth's work from many perspectives.

HOCHWÄLDER, Fritz (1911–), Austrian playwright, was his country's first important post-World War II dramatist—though he has spent most of his life in Switzerland, to which he escaped in 1938 shortly before the outbreak of the war, and where his major works have originally appeared. Principal among his plays is *Das heilige Experiment* (THE HOLY EXPERIMENT, 1943; also translated as *The Strong Are Lonely*), which, like most of Hochwälder's other plays, deals with historical themes in a dramaturgically conventional manner but with a stress on modern intellectual and moral values.

Born in Vienna, Hochwälder started his career as a craftsman, working as a carpenter and an upholsterer. In Switzerland he met and became the friend of GEORG KAISER. Hochwälder adapted a scenario that Kaiser had prepared shortly before his death as *Der Flüchtling* (1945), a three-character dramatic parable about a fugitive and a border guard and his wife in a totalitarian country. Hochwälder's comedy *Hôtel du Commerce,* an adaptation of Guy de Maupassant's *Boule de suif,* also appeared in 1945. More characteristic of Hochwälder's plays is *Meier Helmbrecht* (1946), the drama of a medieval peasant turned criminal, and *Der öffentliche Anklager* (*The Public Prosecutor,* 1949); the latter features Robespierre's successor, Antoine Quentin Fouquier-Tinville, unwittingly concluding the Reign of Terror when he seeks to find and guillotine the "enemy of the people"—

Fritz Hochwälder in 1963. (*Otto Breiska, Bildarchiv der Österreichischen National Bibliothek*)

who turns out to be Fouquier-Tinville himself, brought to his just end by the retribution of the "Madonna of the August Rebellion," Jeanne Marie Ignace Thérésa Tallien. As early as 1940 Hochwälder had allegorically portrayed the rise and fall of Nazism in an adaptation of the biblical tale of *Esther,* Mordecai, and Haman, here Hitler's prototype.

Later Hochwälder plays include *Der Unschuldige* (1949, revised in 1956), a moral comedy in which a skeleton is found in a garden whose owner is proved innocent but gains awareness of the criminal potentialities within him; *Donadieu* (1953), based on Conrad Ferdinand Meyer's ballad about the French Huguenot war, and dramatizing a man's internal conflict before he foregoes vengeance on the enemy in his power; *Die Herberge* (1956), another parable, in which the investigation of a robbery at an inn reveals more serious crimes; *Donnerstag* (1959), a mystery play suggestive of the Faust legend, written for the Salzburg Festival; the two-character *1003* (1963), a PIRANDELLian sequel to *Donnerstag* that makes use of tape recordings and other modern devices and in which a literary character becomes more real than his creator; and *Der Himbeerpflücker* (*The Raspberry Picker,* 1965) and *Der Befehl* (1966), both dealing with the effect of Nazism, thirty years later, on the Austrian mentality.

Hochwälder continued his residence in Switzerland after the war ended. Yet he has retained his Austrian citizenship, and his work has continued to reflect the influence and traditions of Viennese folk drama. *The Raspberry Picker* was published in Martin Esslin's collection, *The New Theatre of Europe 4* (1970), with comments on this play and on Hochwälder. Other discussions of his work appear in H. F. Garten's *Modern German Drama* (1964) and George E. Wellwarth's *The Theater of Protest and Paradox* (1964).

HOFMANNSTHAL, Hugo von (1874–1929), Austrian poet and dramatist, is best known as the librettist of *Der Rosenkavalier* (*The Cavalier of the Rose,* 1911) and other Richard Strauss operas.* He was one of the founders of the Salzburg Festival along with his two collaborators: Max Reinhardt, who produced Hofmannsthal's plays, and Strauss. A precocious poet as well as a playwright, Hofmannsthal wrote the first of his thirty-odd dramas at the age of sixteen. The son of an Austrian banker and of mixed antecedents (German, Jewish, and Italian), he was converted to Catholicism in later life. Except for some travels he spent his entire life in or near Vienna, whose culture strongly affected his work. The dissertation for his doctorate (1898) was on Victor Hugo. He married in 1901 and had three children.

Hofmannsthal's richly poetic plays, particularly the early "lyric dramas," were influenced by the SYMBOLISM and aestheticism (including decadence) that flourished in the late nineteenth century. These short, dramatically static plays consist of extensive interior monologues. Like *Der Tor und der Tod* (DEATH AND THE FOOL, 1894), the most famous of them, all are concerned with the relation between art and life. The protagonist of his first play, *Gestern* (*Yesterday,* 1891), finds that life and time—the past, "yesterday"—cannot be ignored in one's quest to experience the immediate. And so with *Der Tod des Tizian* (*The Death of Titian,* 1892), *Der weisse Fächer* (1897), *Der Kaiser und die Hexe* (*The Emperor and the Witch,* 1897), and *Das kleine Welttheater* (*The Little Theatre of the World,* 1897). Other early poetic plays are *Die Frau im Fenster* (1897, translated as *Madonna Dianora*), *Das Bergwerk zu Falun* (*The Mine at Falun,* 1899; his first full-length play, which he suppressed except for the first act); *Die Hochzeit der Sobeide* (*The Marriage of Zobeide,* 1899); and *Der Abenteurer und die Sängerin* (1899).

Though many of Hofmannsthal's plays are adaptations, he transformed them into wholly original works. In the Greek plays—*Ödipus und die Sphinx* (1905) and *Electra*—classic restraint is changed into a violence expressive of Freudian abnormal psychology and of Hofmannsthal's preoccupation with the horror of chaos. Aside from his frequently performed *Jedermann* (EVERYMAN, 1911), he also adapted an English Restoration tragedy, Thomas Otway's *Venice Preserv'd* (*Das gerettete Venedig,* 1905), Molière's *Le Bourgeois Gentilhomme* (*Der Bürger als Edelmann,* 1918), and three plays based on Calderón: *La Dame duende* (*Dame Kobold,* 1920), *Das Salzburger grosse Welttheater* (THE SALZBURG GREAT THEATRE OF THE WORLD, 1922), and *Der Turm* (THE TOWER, 1925). These late mystic works center on human suffering and redemption.

His other plays include *Cristinas Heimreise* (*Cristina's Journey Home,* 1910), an eighteenth-

* *Ariadne auf Naxos* (1912), *Die Frau ohne Schatten* (1919), *Die aegyptische Helene* (1928), and the posthumous *Arabella* (1933). The collaboration began with *Elektra* (ELECTRA, 1903), Hofmannsthal's earliest success.

century Venice comedy suggested by Casanova's *Memoirs; Der Schwierige* (*The Difficult Man*, 1920), a comedy about a cultivated Viennese gentleman whose reticent sensitivity is misunderstood and ridiculed; *Der Unbestechliche* (1923), another Viennese comedy; and a number of pantomimes and fragments, one being another adaptation from Calderón, *Semiramis und die beiden Götter* (1933). He also wrote many prose works, including an uncompleted novel and *Die Frau ohne Schatten* (1919), a reworking of the fairy-tale libretto for Strauss's opera.

The Bollingen Foundation's three-volume *Selected Writings of Hugo von Hofmannsthal* (1952–63) was edited and has extensive introductions by Michael Hamburger; Volume II (*Poems and Verse Plays*, 1961) includes *Death and the Fool, The Emperor and the Witch, The Little Theatre of the World*, the first act of *The Mine at Falun*, and *The Marriage of Zobeide;* Volume III (*Selected Plays and Libretti*, 1963) includes *The Salzburg Great Theatre of the World, The Tower*, and *The Difficult Man*, as well as the librettos of *Electra, The Cavalier of the Rose*, and *Arabella*. Brian Coghlan's study of *Hofmannsthal's Festival Dramas* (1964) analyzes *The Salzburg Great Theatre of the World, The Tower*, and *Everyman;* it has biographical, textual, and bibliographical notes, as has an earlier English study of Hofmannsthal's work, A. H. A. Hammelmann's *Hugo von Hofmannsthal* (1957).

HOLIDAY, a comedy in three acts by PHILIP BARRY, produced in 1928 and published in 1929. Setting: a New York mansion, 1927–28.

Originally titled *The Dollar*, this once-popular play features an appealing young man who "can't quite believe that a life devoted to piling up money is all it's cracked up to be." Johnny Case finds he is well-enough off to quit work and enjoy life. His determination to do so—and perhaps settle down to work when he is much older—shocks his fiancée and her affluent, money-grubbing father. She tries to persuade him that "there's no such thrill in the world as making money," and her father "consider[s] his whole attitude deliberately un-American." But Johnny is backed by her brother, a tippler enervated by the family's wealth and eternal preoccupation with money; by her sister, who is stronger but equally miserable in the cold mansion and who falls in love with Johnny; and by a delightful young couple who lead the kind of life Johnny envisions. When he discovers that despite his concessions his fiancée means to keep him trapped in a business career, Johnny breaks their engagement and bolts. Her sister, too, breaks with the family, and follows Johnny.

HOLLAND. Dutch drama in modern times has been of minor importance.* A single playwright of the Netherlands, HERMAN HEIJERMANS, has achieved more than passing or regional fame. Like the rest of Holland's modern literature, its drama originated with *De Nieuwe Gids* (The New Guide), a literary reform movement led by a group of rebellious young Amsterdam writers. It was founded in the latter part of the nineteenth century and reached its peak in 1880—and hence became known as the movement of the "Eightiers." Only two of its members were interested in the theatre, however. The poet-critic Albert Verwey (1865–1937), striving to revive Dutch poetic drama, wrote two historical plays, *Johan van Oldenbarnevelt* (1895) and *Jacoba van Beieren* (1902). His brother-in-law Frederick Willem van Eeden (1860–1932) was even more interested in the theatre; a poet and novelist who began his career as a physician, van Eeden was a versatile playwright whose greatest work is the unproduced *De Broeders; Tragedie van het Recht* (*The Brothers; a Tragedy of Justice*, 1894), a poetic tragedy soon retitled *De Broederveete* (*The Brothers' Feud*), but whose other plays, ranging from farce through tragedy (such as that of a woman's guilty love and the ambiguities of fidelity experienced by a Viking king's wife, *Lioba*, 1897), were successfully produced: *Ijsbrand* (1908), *In Kenterend Getij* (1910), *De Heks van Haarlem* (1915)—a dramatization of the seventeenth-century history of "the witch of Harlem"—and others.

Much of the later drama of the Netherlands was lyrical, like that of Henriette Roland Holst (née Henriette van der Schalk, 1869–1952), particularly her *Thomas More* (1912) and *Wij willen niet* (1931). NATURALISTIC drama was written by Josine Adriana Simons-Mees (1863–1948), notably *Vóór het diner* (1892), *De Veroveraar* (1906) and its sequel *Atie's huwelijk* (1907), and *Geloof* (1924). More romantic are the plays of Jan Fabricius (1871–1966), whose dramatization of the breakdown of a man on a desert island, *Eenzaam* (1907), was long performed. During the 1960's Holland had a remarkable increase in the production of modern—mainly avant-garde—plays, including those of Lodewijk de Boer (1938–), whose one-act horror drama *Lykensynode* (*The Corpse Synod*, 1968) depicts a dead pope's trial and mutilation by his ninth-century successor.

Plays in Dutch have also appeared in SOUTH AFRICA, and Flemish-written Belgian drama is regularly produced in Holland. Little of it is available in English, however, and there have been few studies of it.

* For Flemish drama, much of which is produced also in Holland, see BELGIUM.

HOLM, John Cecil (1904–), American actor and playwright, had his most notable success with *Three Men on a Horse* (1935), a farce he wrote with GEORGE ABBOTT and helped make into a musical, *Let It Ride* (1963). Holm's other works include the book for the musical comedy *Best Foot Forward* (1941), which he revised in 1963. He also wrote a number of books, including an autobiography, *Sunday Best* (1942).

HOLY EXPERIMENT, THE (*Das heilige Experiment*), a play in five acts by FRITZ HOCHWÄLDER, produced in 1943 and published in 1947. Setting: the Jesuit College in Buenos Aires; July 16, 1767.

The Holy Experiment. Miura (Albin Skoda) and Father Provincial Alfonso Fernandez (Ewald Balser). Vienna, 1947. (*Bildarchiv der Österreichischen National Bibliothek*)

Hochwälder's first international success, this play was a hit in London as well as in Paris (as *Sur la terre comme au ciel*), and has also been translated as *The Strong Are Lonely* and as *Faith Is Not Enough*. It portrays the last day of a Jesuit commune that had flourished since 1609 and gave natives not only Christianity but a means of livelihood and human dignity. Such a "holy experiment" upset the interests of the Church, the local bishop, and imperialist Spanish exploiters—and therefore was destroyed.

A commission arrives from Madrid to investigate the community, whose very existence exposes the injustices of society everywhere else. Commissioner Don Pedro de Miura notifies its director, Father Provincial Alfonso Fernandez, that the experiment must end. To defend and maintain it, the commune's inhabitants take up arms, and the priests implore the Father Provincial to resist and disobey superior orders. Gradually, however, he is compelled to realize that the larger interests of the Church require that he give in, and Miura's dissolution of the commune also helps break the resistance of the priests and the natives. When the Father Provincial himself goes out to command that his people stop firing, he intercepts a bullet. Agonized by his divided loyalties between human charity and ecclesiastic obedience, he dies despondent because he himself had to order the destruction of his handiwork, "God's kingdom on earth." Miura signs the many death warrants and deportation orders, and then remains alone as darkness falls. "For what is a man profited, if he shall gain the whole world, and lose his own soul," he says quietly; "that voice too is in my heart, Alfonso Fernandez . . . I confess—"

HOLZ, Arno (1863–1929), German writer, was among the founders of NATURALISM. He inspired GERHART HAUPTMANN with the *Papa Hamlet* sketches he published in 1889 with JOHANNES SCHLAF. Also with Schlaf, Holz wrote the naturalistic drama *Familie Selicke* (1890). Though historically less important, Holz's *Traumulus* (1904; with Oskar Jerschke, 1861–1928) was more popular; filmed and frequently revived, it depicts the tragedy of an innovative and kind schoolmaster abused by his undisciplined pupils. In another play, *Sonnenfinsternis* (1908), Holz portrayed the tragedy of a great artist destroyed by his marriage to a beautiful actress who is incestuously tied to her father. Earlier Holz had produced a comedy about an artist, *Sozialaristokraten* (1896).

Born in East Prussia and brought up in Berlin, Holz was principally a poet and a literary theorist whose aesthetics excluded subjectivity from art and based NATURALISM on logic and objectivity. The defense of his "new free verse" techniques, which stress the "natural," as well as his poetry and drama, was published in his seven-volume collected works (1961–64).

HOME, William Douglas (1912–   ), Scottish dramatist, was born in Edinburgh, the son of the thirteenth Earl of Home. He became an actor in

1937, and that year produced his first play, *Great Possessions. The Plays of William Douglas Home* (1958) includes his very popular play, *The Reluctant Debutante* (1955), a light family comedy. The other plays in the volume are *"Now Barabbas . . ."* (1947), a play on prison life; *The Chiltern Hundreds* (1947), a political comedy about the class system—still from the perspective of Barrie's THE ADMIRABLE CRICHTON; *The Thistle and the Rose* (1949), a historical tragedy on King James IV of Scotland; and *The Bad Samaritan* (1952). Later plays include *The Bad Soldier Smith* (1961); *The Reluctant Peer* (1964); *A Friend Indeed* (1966), a comedy about two politicians; and *The Secretary Bird* (1968), a comedy about a middle-aged novelist and his young wife, who is attracted to a philandering stockbroker. Home also wrote an autobiography, *Half-term Report* (1954).

HOMECOMING, THE, a play in two acts by HAROLD PINTER, published and produced in 1965. Setting: an old house in North London, 1960's.

This is a sinister NATURALISTIC comedy, punctuated by many pauses, repetitions, and ritualistic groupings. The portrayal of an ambiguous and bizarre family situation caused a sensation and elicited numerous interpretations, some of which have been republished in John Lahr's *Casebook on Harold Pinter's "The Homecoming"* (1971).

The head of the family, a retired butcher and a seedy loudmouth, argues with his two sons and his dull brother, a chauffeur. Unexpectedly the family is visited by the third son, who is a doctor of philosophy at an American university, and his wife. Eventually the brothers (one is a pugilist, the other an aggressive pimp) paw and embrace the cool but encouraging wife, even in the presence of her apparently indifferent husband. The family decide to keep her around as a whore, and she readily agrees to pay her own way by renting herself out periodically in an apartment that is to be set up for her. As the play ends, the husband returns to their three children in America, the wife starts to pet the pugilist, and the father—shouting that he is not yet too old—sinks to his knees before her and hoarsely demands, "Kiss me!"

HONDURAS has produced virtually no modern drama. A short discussion of its theatre, including a description of its few plays and a bibliography, appears in Willis Knapp Jones's *Behind Spanish American Footlights* (1966).

HOP, SIGNOR! a one-act play by MICHEL DE GHELDERODE, published in 1938 and produced in 1949. Setting: Flanders, in olden times.

Though Ghelderode called this "a drama of impotence," it is among his most bacchanalian works and is peopled with pornographic monsters. Among these is the lustful virgin wife Marguerite Harstein, a historical figure who was executed in the sixteenth century. She rejoices as a lynch mob tosses her husband in a blanket until he is dead, and she joins in their shouts: "Hop, Signor!" Two of her would-be lovers then quarrel over her as she calls to them from her bed. Finally the almost-naked widow thrusts herself at her enemy, a hysterically ascetic monk who succumbs to her sensuality and then denounces her. Condemned, she is taken to the rose-chewing executioner, to whom she has been attracted all along.

HOPPLA! SUCH IS LIFE! (*Hoppla, wir leben!*), a play in a prologue and five acts by ERNST TOLLER, published and produced in 1927. Setting: Germany, 1919 and 1927.

This play was translated by HERMON OULD and produced in England as *Hoopla!* NATURALISTIC scenes are framed by EXPRESSIONISTIC split staging, loudspeakers, and newsreels linking the plot with contemporary affairs. Toller's disillusionment is manifested in the cynical title and a descriptive remark ("the action of the play passes in many countries . . ."), in the idealistic protagonist's suicide, and in portrayals of Germany's social, political, and economic decadence at the advent of Nazism.

A number of prisoners awaiting execution after their abortive political revolt are reprieved. Eight years later one of them, Karl Thomas, is released from a lunatic asylum. His opportunistic comrade, now the nation's minister of the interior, dismisses him with platitudes. Thomas becomes increasingly discouraged as he watches the blatant corruption of an election and the continued abortive revolutionary work of his sweetheart, who refuses to settle down (or escape) with him. Realizing how she has changed during his eight years as an asylum inmate, Thomas understands that "I belong to a generation that has disappeared." While working as a waiter Thomas witnesses the vile behavior of the minister and the people around him. Thomas is about to shoot the minister but then finds him too contemptible to be worth the bother. A reactionary nationalist, however, does shoot him and escapes. Thomas is arrested as the assassin. In prison, he despairs and hangs himself—shortly before the real killer confesses. In adjoining cells other prisoners—the comrades with whom Thomas shared a cell eight years ago—knock messages of their imminent release on the walls, but "Karl doesn't answer." The knocking continues as darkness falls.

HOPWOOD, Avery (1882–1928), American journalist and playwright, began his playwriting career with *Clothes* (1906), a drama written with CHANNING POLLOCK. He achieved his greatest success with one of his four collaborations with MARY ROBERTS RINEHART, which began with their farce *Seven Days* (1910). Their *The Bat* (1920), which is based on a Rinehart mystery tale, became a phenomenal Broadway hit. Other Hopwood successes include a number of farces, notably *Getting Gertie's Garter* (1921; with Wilson Collison, 1894–1941) and *Why Men Leave Home* (1922).

Born in Ohio, Hopwood attended the University of Michigan. After his death, a distinguished literary prize was established at the University in his name, and promising authors have published their books with these awards.

HORATII AND THE CURIATII, THE (*Die Horatier und die Kuriatier*), a "school piece" by BERTOLT BRECHT (music by Kurt Schwaen), published in 1938 and produced in 1958. Setting: a platform.

This short "didactic play for children about dialectics" was written in 1934. It consists of an introduction and three episodes that are mostly in free verse.

Marxist dialectics and tactics are demonstrated by choruses and by a stylized battle. As in classic Chinese drama, both sides are represented by a few actors; each stands for a military unit whose strength is noted on the pennant he carries. The mighty attackers, the "Curiatii," are finally defeated by the stratagems of the weaker "Horatii."

HORVÁTH, Ödön von (1901–38), Austrian novelist and playwright, gave promise of a distinguished career before his sudden and premature death. His drama is lyrical as well as amusing (often in Viennese dialect), yet perceptive as social satire and cynically fatalistic. He was one of the post-World War I left-wing writers, though his works were radical neither in content nor in form. Instead, he produced what he himself called "folk plays" that depict common men whose *Gemütlichkeit* transparently masks repulsive banality and, even worse, horrendous bestiality.

The son of a Hungarian diplomat, Horváth was born in Fiume and educated in Vienna and Munich. His first play was *Revolte auf Côte 3018* (1927), a comedy published later as *Die Bergbahn,* which portrays the construction of a mountain railway. It was followed by a number of other comedies and political satires, culminating in his first hit, *Italienische Nacht* (1930). Characterizing folk at a beer garden party, it appears to be a "comfortable" comedy, but it reveals ominous undercurrents in its satire of the guests—smug republicans and the already-emerging Nazis. It was followed by *Geschichten aus dem Wiener Wald* (1931), Horváth's most carefully wrought work, which in fifteen "pictures" portrays a destructive love affair that ruthlessly exposes the inferno of a war-torn Vienna and its depraved and vicious burghers. Upon the nomination of CARL ZUCKMAYER, Horváth was awarded the Kleist Prize that year (1931). The following year appeared *Kasimir und Karoline* and *Glaube, Liebe, Hoffnung*. The first, portraying Munich festivities, again satirizes smugness in the face of looming catastrophe; the second, subtitled "a small dance of death," dramatizes an actual case of judicial error and attempts to prove that (as ARTHUR MILLER was to insist later) the "little man" is the proper subject of modern tragedy.

When the Nazis came to power in 1933 Horváth fled to Austria, where he compulsively wrote play after play. His hurried, often sketchy works include *Die Unbekannte aus der Seine* (1933), whose angellike "stranger from the Seine" assumes the guilt of a community that continues its foul lives; *Don Juan kommt aus dem Krieg,* a characteristic dramatization (composed in 1937, produced in 1952) of the Don Juan legend; *Figaro lässt sich scheiden* (1937), an adaptation of Beaumarchais's 1784 comedy; and *Pompeji* (1937), "an Earthquake Comedy." At the time of the Anschluss in 1938 Horváth again had to flee, and he emigrated to Paris. There he was killed in a freak accident during a storm.

His work is not readily available in translation, although his plays, like his novels, enjoyed European popularity.

HOSTAGE, THE (*An Giall*), a play in three acts by BRENDAN BEHAN, published and produced in 1958. Setting: a Dublin lodging house, 1958.

Originally produced in Gaelic, this play is a frenetically comic, bawdy romp. It is interlaced with song (like Brecht's THE THREEPENNY OPERA), and the plot is slight. The play's success lies in its stage depiction of a madcap potpourri of sex perversions, Irish jingoism, and general (and blatantly irreverent) political and social satire.

Act I. When the curtain rises, the "whole company dances an Irish Jig after two figures in which two whores and two queers have danced together." A lodger in this "brockel—that's English for a whorehouse" dances with Miss Gilchrist, an absurd, gospel-singing social worker. Its owner, Monsewer, is an Englishman who has become more Irish than the Irish; he makes hideous noises with his bagpipes, which he deludes himself into thinking he plays well—just as he imagines the riffraff in his place to be Irish Republican Army heroes. His one-time fellow fighter in the I.R.A., the one-legged lecher Pat, is the caretaker of the place. Pat argues with the "perverts," reminisces in word and song, and squabbles with Meg Dillon, an old bawd who helps him and is "nearly" his wife. The maid is Teresa, an innocent, pretty country girl just out of convent school. She and Meg discuss the imminent hanging of an old I.R.A. man who shot a British policeman. The I.R.A. has kidnapped a British soldier, is holding him as a hostage, and decides to hide him in the "brockel." He is brought in just as the girls are dancing to radio music. Completely at ease, the soldier—Leslie A. Williams—sings one of Pat's favorite songs, "There's no place on earth like the world." It ends: "The South and the North Poles they are parted, / Perhaps it is all for the best, / Till the H-bomb will bring them together— / And there we will let matters rest."

Act II. Teresa and Leslie immediately fall in love, and she sneaks a cup of tea into his guarded room. A procession denouncing the British passes by. Miss Gilchrist tries to cheer Leslie up by reading him an article from the *Daily Express*

The Hostage. The two homosexuals (Dudley Sutton and Melvin Stewart) argue; the others are, left to right: the lodger (Aubrey Morris), Teresa (Celia Salkeld), Meg (Avis Bunnage), a whore (Anita Dangler), and Pat (Warren O'Connell). New York, 1960. (*Zodiac Photographers*)

about the royal family, and then she joins in a song, "Nobody Loves You Like Yourself." Teresa and Leslie's brief tryst is interrupted by the bagpipe-playing Monsewer, who sings a nostalgic song, "The Captains and the Kings." Pat checks up on these doings, but Teresa and Leslie finally are left alone. They tell each other about their orphaned childhoods, and, though Teresa is shy, they soon dance and sing. After the final refrain of "If you'll marry me" they join in the last verse, "But first I think that we should see / If we fit each other. Yes, I agree." They leap into bed, the light goes out, and Miss Gilchrist runs into the spotlight to sing a sentimental song with bawdy overtones. Then Leslie sees a newspaper clipping about his capture and, for the first time, worries about what may happen to him.

Act III. Pat, Miss Gilchrist, and Meg are drinking and quarreling. Pat sneers about today's I.R.A. youngsters, Meg sneers about Pat, and Miss Gilchrist becomes increasingly drunk and maudlin —and lustful. She sings a hymn for Leslie, a plea to various statesmen: "Don't muck about with the moon." The homosexuals, whores, and other inhabitants object to the planned execution of Leslie, which, as the time for the I.R.A. man's hanging approaches, is imminent. Pat believes the I.R.A. is only bluffing, and Teresa therefore does not try to help Leslie. Since this angers Leslie, she goes out to get him some chips. Suddenly the British police raid the place. They are led by two of the boarders—informers. In the confusion Leslie is shot and killed; Pat, Monsewer, and Meg are arrested. Teresa returns, sees Leslie lying dead, and weeps over his corpse. Astonishingly, he sits up and sings: "The bells of hell / Go ting-a-ling-a-ling / For you but not for me. / Oh death where is thy / Sting-a-ling-a-ling / Or grave thy victory? / If you meet the undertaker / Or the young man from the Pru, / Get a pint with what's left over. / Now I'll say goodbye to you."

HOSTAGE, THE (*L'Otage*), a drama in three acts by PAUL CLAUDEL, published in 1911 and produced in 1914. Setting: France, early nineteenth century.

This is the first and best known of Claudel's pseudohistorical "Papal" trilogy. Although a departure from his earlier, static drama like THE TIDINGS BROUGHT TO MARY, THE SATIN SLIPPER, and BREAK OF NOON, it deals with the same religious themes.

Sygne de Coûfontaine and her cousin Georges, aristocrats who lost their family and possessions in the Revolution, exchange lovers' vows. Georges is unable to perceive the end of the old feudal world and battles for the monarchy's restoration. Sygne, devoutly religious, is sheltering Pope Pius VII. Georges urges the Pope to go into exile with the French king, whom Georges rescued from Napoleon's soldiers. The Pope refuses to do so, holding his proper place to be Rome. Napoleon's prefect, Toussaint Turelure, the peasant become revolutionary, is in love with Sygne and, incidentally, eager to become an aristocrat. Therefore he seeks to marry Sygne, a plan aided by the fact that the fugitive Pope, "the hostage," is at his mercy. A priest tries to persuade Sygne to marry Turelure, the hated enemy of her people. To save the Pope is her sole reason for existence, the priest tells her, and he suggests that her beloved Georges, too, is in Turelure's power. God demands this sacrifice of her, the priest insists, but it must be voluntary: "You alone must do it of your own free will." The pious Sygne thereupon makes her choice: she breaks her pledge to Georges and marries Turelure. They have a child, but her sacrifice is deficient: she is able to give him only her body, not her heart and soul, which, it is suggested, Turelure needs for his salvation. She is condemned by Turelure as well as by Georges, who reproaches her for her betrayal. Both Georges and Sygne are shot, Sygne praying for forgiveness and divine mercy as she dies. The dead lovers are placed side by side. Their symbolic union is differently portrayed in a variant ending that denies that union and suggests, instead, Georges's eternal rejection—or, perhaps, Sygne's error in choosing to betray their love.

The second "panel of the triptych," as the trilogy has been characterized, is *Le Pain dur* (*Crusts,* 1917). Here Turelure, now Louis Philippe's minister, has a Jewish mistress. However, she loves his and Sygne's son, and with the help of the boy's Polish mistress gets the boy to murder his father. Ultimately she is converted and marries Turelure's son.

The last of the trilogy is *Le Père humilié* (*The Humiliation of the Father,* 1920). Set in the Rome of 1869–71, it features a later descendant of the Turelure-Sygne marriage, a blind but divinely beautiful girl who achieves spiritual redemption. She defends Pope Pius IX, consummates her love with his nephew, who is soon killed in battle, and then, to legitimatize their child, marries the Pope's other nephew.

HOTEL UNIVERSE, a one-act play by PHILIP BARRY, published and produced in 1930. Setting: the terrace of a château in southern France on an early July evening, 1929.

This two-hour play is a complex, often pretentious psychiatric parable about some members of the "lost generation," whose will to live is depleted. They are the sophisticated guests of Ann Field and her father, Stephen Field, a brilliant old scientist and a mystic, omnipotent figure—reminiscent of the enchanter in James M. Barrie's DEAR BRUTUS, a play which *Hotel Universe* resembles also in other respects. All of the characters express their disillusionment and periodically act out their early lives in a series of trances, or Freudian psychodramas.

The man Ann loves has "a date with a mountain": he wants to commit suicide, as did his beloved. Other visitors are an actress still suffering from an Electra complex for her dead father, a ham actor and a drunkard; a Catholic who feels sinful for having lost his religion, and his wife who neglects him in her preoccupation with motherhood; a wealthy Jew who has also lost his zest for life, and a dispirited girl who loves him. Under the guidance of Field these characters eventually are cured and find the meaning in life that Field has discovered. It consists of adjustment to three worlds—the temporal, the spiritual, and the universally timeless: "The life of chairs and tables, of getting up and sitting down. . . . The life one lives in one's imagining, in which one wishes, dreams, remembers. [And thirdly] the life past death, which in itself contains the others." Field dies, but his message—"Wherever there is an end . . . From it the beginning springs"—is echoed by Ann and her beloved, as Field's pet, a white cock heralding another dawn, crows exultantly.

HOUGHTON, [William] **Stanley** (1881–1913), English playwright, was the most important member of the Manchester school of NATURALIST playwrights (others included HAROLD BRIGHOUSE and ALLAN MONKHOUSE) supported by Miss Annie E. F. Horniman, the wealthy Englishwoman who also was an important patroness of IRELAND's theatre. Though Houghton entered his father's cotton business, his own interest was in the theatre. In his spare time he wrote drama criticisms for the *Manchester Guardian* (1905 ff.) and plays that were produced at Manchester's Gaiety Theatre. His first dramas were *The Dear Departed* (1908), *Independent Means* (1909), *The Master of the House* (1910), and *The Younger Generation* (1910). The last-named was revived in London as well as in many amateur productions, and portrays a well-intentioned but conservative father who is appalled by his son's wild-oats sowing—something he finally realizes he too did as a youth.

Houghton was able to give up business and devote himself exclusively to writing and the theatre when his most famous play, HINDLE WAKES (1912), had an immediate and successful production in London. His career became more promising than ever in the last year of his short life, when two more plays were produced in London, *Trust the People* and *The Perfect Cure* (both in 1913). Writing in the naturalist tradition of HENRIK IBSEN, Houghton also echoed the wit of his greater Anglo-Irish contemporaries, BERNARD SHAW and OSCAR WILDE. Houghton was given to portraying the conflict between the generations, but he eschewed political and social PROBLEM PLAYS. His other dramas are the one-act *Fancy-Free* and *Partners* (1911, the latter a full-length version of the original one-acter), *Phipps*

(1912), *Pearls* (1912), *Ginger* (1913), and *The Old Testament and the New* (written in 1905, produced in 1914).

For an account of Houghton's Manchester productions see Rex Pogson's *Miss Horniman and the Gaiety Theatre, Manchester* (1952). His fellow dramatist Brighouse (who collaborated on his posthumous play, *The Hillarys,* 1915) edited Houghton's *Works* (1914), for which he supplied an informative introduction.

HOUR-GLASS, THE, a one-act play by WILLIAM BUTLER YEATS, published and produced in 1903. Setting: a room.

In 1912 Yeats produced a poetic version of this modern morality play, a mystic fantasy originally written with LADY GREGORY.

A Wise Man has persuaded his pupils and the villagers that unseen things do not exist. Only the Fool still believes, and he uses the pennies he begs to cut the nets the unbelievers cast for angels. An angel comes to announce that the Wise Man will die when the sand in his hourglass runs out. But if he can find one believer during that hour, he will be spared the fires of hell. The frantic Wise Man searches in vain: the villagers have learned his lesson well and faith has been abolished. In his terror the Wise Man discovers the truth: "We perish into God and sink away / Into reality—the rest's a dream," and "our speculation [is] but as the wind." He dies; the Fool proclaims the reality of unseen things like the wind and the growing of grass: "I know. / But I will not speak, I will run away."

HOUSE OF BERNARDA ALBA, THE (*La casa de Bernarda Alba*), a play in three acts by FEDERICO GARCÍA LORCA, published and produced in 1945. Setting: the whitewashed rooms of a Spanish countryhouse; summer.

García Lorca's final, posthumous play, completed shortly before his death in 1936, is subtitled "a drama about women in the villages of Spain"—and only women appear in it. It is the third of his "rural tragedies" (the others are BLOOD WEDDING and YERMA), and the most objective. "Not a drop of poetry! Reality! Realism!" Lorca is reported (in Arturo Barea's *Lorca, The Poet and His People,* 1949) to have exclaimed proudly, and he added a footnote to the play: "The writer states that these three acts are intended as a photographic document." Like Lorca's other rural dramas, it portrays a sterile honor code and its tragic consequences to Bernarda and her passionate daughters, drawn to a man who is never seen but whose sexual attraction infuses the play.

Act I. The bells toll for Bernarda Alba's husband, who has just died. His proud sixty-year-old widow has five daughters and, as the lusty old family servant, Poncia, observes, she is "a tyrant over everyone around her." Leaning on a cane, Bernarda enters with the mourners, whom she soon angers with her sanctimonious, sharp tongue. When they leave, Bernarda imperiously orders her daughters to observe eight years of mourning: they are to see no men, and "not a breath of air will get in this house from the street." The youngest daughter, twenty-year-old Adela, starts to rebel; another daughter, a frustrated hunchback, angers Bernarda by watching men through the door's cracks. But Bernarda rejects the suggestion that her daughters need husbands: "None of them has ever had a beau and they've never needed one! they get along very well." Besides, she asserts proudly, the men in this area are not good enough for her family. The sheltered sisters are bewildered by their natural longings. The hunchback says she fears men: once she stood at her window in her nightgown all night, vainly waiting for the one man who courted her—but (unbeknown to her) he was driven away by Bernarda. The sisters talk of the handsome young man who is betrothed to the oldest, Bernarda's thirty-nine-year-old daughter by a first husband, whose money the girl has now inherited. Both the hunchback and Adela love him, and Adela knows he returns her passion. As one of the sisters says, he is marrying for money: "We know she's old and sickly, and always has been the least attractive one of us!" Adela is enraged: "I will not get used to it! I can't be locked up." Bernarda's mad eighty-year-old mother escapes from her room: "I want to get married to a beautiful manly man from the shore of the sea," she cries: "I don't want to see these single women, longing for marriage, turning their hearts to dust."

Act II. Adela is restless—"as if a lizard were between her breasts," Poncia remarks. It appears that on the previous night after the betrothed couple's traditional chat on opposite sides of the window bars, the man went to Adela's window and talked passionately with her until dawn. Poncia cautions Adela: though she sympathizes with her, "I want to live in a decent house." But Adela is desperate: "I'd leap not over you, just a servant, but over my mother to put out this fire I feel in my legs and my mouth." The passionate intensity of the sisters grows as Poncia talks of young reapers who have just arrived, and of the fun they are having with a whore. The sisters fight viciously when it is discovered that the hunchback has stolen the betrothed daughter's picture of her fiancé, but Bernarda sends them out: "I have five chains for you." Only two of the girls seem to have a chance of surviving: one because she is totally brainless, the other because she is cynically resigned to her fate. Though Poncia tries to warn the mother—"You've never given your daughters any freedom"—Bernarda proudly rejects advice. Adela and her hunchback sister openly quarrel over their sister's fiancé. Just then a girl is being dragged through the streets: the villagers have found the corpse of her illegitimate infant. Bernarda is self-righteous. "Finish her before the guards come! Hot coals in the place where she sinned!" she shouts: "Kill her! Kill her!"

Act III. It is a hot night. As Bernarda talks to a friend, a stallion frisks in his stall until Bernarda angrily orders him released: "Lock the mares in the corral, but let him run free or he may kick down the walls." Now Bernarda is keeping close watch over her daughters, but Poncia knows they are not bad: "They're women without men, that's all. And in such matters even blood is forgotten." Later, spying on her sister, the hunchback catches Adela defiantly returning from a tryst. The sisters' bitter quarrel culminates in the hunchback's angry denunciation of Adela to their mother: "She was with him. Look at those skirts covered with straw!" Adela breaks Bernarda's cane, and rebelliously tells her that he is in the yard: "I'm his. Know that . . . and tell him." Appalled, Bernarda runs out with a gun. A shot is heard. Distraught when the jealous hunchback tells her that her lover is dead, Adela rushes out and hangs herself. But he has escaped—Bernarda missed her shot. Though Bernarda shrieks when she discovers Adela's suicide, she soon controls herself. Bernarda will not have her house disgraced; Adela's corpse must be dressed as though she died a virgin. "And I want no weeping," she tells her daughters: "Tears when you're alone! We'll drown ourselves in a sea of mourning." As for outsiders, Adela "died a virgin. Did you hear me? Silence, silence, I said. Silence!"

HOUSE OF CONNELLY, THE, "A Drama of the Old South and the New" in two acts by PAUL GREEN, published and produced in 1931. Setting: an old Southern mansion, early twentieth century.

Green's best drama of Southern whites, this play launched The Group Theatre. A vivid and at times moving portrait of the postbellum South, the play features the aristocratic Connelly family. They dream of the days of yore, though they are on the verge of bankruptcy and extinction. Will (William Byrd) Connelly, the son and the family's hope for rescue, realizes that his mother and sisters live in the dead past, but he is too weak to stand up to them. But when the Connelly women try to save themselves from ruin by marrying Will to a wealthy aristocrat, he summons the strength to rebel and marry the girl he loves, Patsy Tate. The determined daughter of their tenant farmer, Patsy is a lively girl who loves the land and would restore vigor to the decadent Connelly stock. She realizes the cruelty of pushing the others out of the way, but knows that "It's our life or theirs. It can't be both."

In one version of the play Patsy is victorious in making herself the mistress of the house. But in another version, Will weakens when his sisters leave and the two old Negro field women, who thoughout the play have commented on the family's weaknesses and functioned as a ribald chorus, rebel; they strangle Patsy to death, thus avenging the mansion's former mistress, old Mrs. Connelly.

HOUSMAN, Laurence (1865–1959), English writer and artist, was the author of hundreds of books, including novels, poetry, satires, and fairy tales. Many of them were illustrated by himself, and he first made his name as a book illustrator. In 1900 his anonymous *An Englishwoman's Love Letters,* not recognized for the fiction it was, created a sensation and brought him unexpected wealth.

More important are his plays, notably VICTORIA REGINA (1935), the forty-five LITTLE PLAYS OF ST. FRANCIS (1922–35), and PRUNELLA (1904, written with HARLEY GRANVILLE-BARKER). Housman wrote well over one hundred plays, ranging from short through full-length dramas and play cycles, and from children's fantasies through historical, romantic, and religious drama, much of it biographical. Occasionally his work was censored because of his familiar portrayal of religious and royal figures: his most popular play, *Victoria Regina* (which is composed of ten of the fifty-four one-acters of his Queen Victoria cycle), was at first banned in England. His plays are simple, often sentimental and romantic, occasionally moving.

Housman's dramas and drama cycles have been published singly and in collection (some of the collections duplicating others, in part); they include *Bethlehem* (1902, a Nativity play), *The Chinese Lantern* (1908), *Pains and Penalties: The Defence of Queen Caroline* (1911, banned by the Censor), *The Lord of the Harvest* (1916, a one-act morality play), *Bird in Hand* (1916, a one-act play), *Angels and Ministers* (1922), *Dethronements* (1923; imaginary dialogues of Charles Stewart Parnell, Joseph Chamberlain, and Woodrow Wilson), *A Likely Story* (1928, a collection of one-acters), *The New Hangman* (1930), *Palace Plays* (1930, a series of Queen Victoria one-acters), *Palace Scenes* and *The Golden Sovereign* (both 1937; further Victoria one-acters), *Palestine Plays* (1942, a series of Old Testament plays), and *The Family Honour* (1947). Important as well as informative accounts are his autobiography, *The Unexpected Years* (1936), and *A. E. H.* (1937), his biography of his brother, the poet A. E. Housman.

HOW HE LIED TO HER HUSBAND, a one-act comedy by BERNARD SHAW, produced in 1904 and published in 1909. Setting: a contemporary flat in Cromwell Road, London.

About his first play to be filmed (1930) and televised (1937) Shaw claimed in his prefatory note to have converted a hackneyed situation into an "original play, . . . trifling as it is."

A husband angrily confronts a poet with incriminating love poems to "Aurora," but is insulted when the poet denies that they were written to his wife. The husband is later delighted and flattered when the poet confesses that the wife had, in fact, inspired the poems, and he decides to publish them himself as "To Aurora." The poet suggests another title for the book: "I should call it How He Lied to Her Husband."

HOWARD, Bronson [Crocker] (1842–1908), American journalist and playwright, was "the first American dramatist of his day," according to AUGUSTUS THOMAS. The founder of the American Dramatists Club in 1891, Howard was influential in having copyright laws improved and thus raised the stature of his profession, which he dignified even further by being the first American dramatist to make his living entirely from playwriting. Concerned with the craft of writing for the theatre, he stressed the need to gauge and gratify audience expectations, and "divorce" literary considerations. He was a master craftsman, always cognizant of audience demands and adept at constructing suspenseful and amusing yet serious plays.

Howard was born in Detroit, studied at Yale University, and became a drama critic, eventually, for New York's *Tribune* and *Post*. Beginning with *Saratoga* (presented by AUGUSTIN DALY in 1870), a comedy produced in England as *Brighton*, Howard wrote about twenty plays. The most popular of them were *The Henrietta* (1887), a melodramatic satire of Wall Street that netted Howard almost half a million dollars; *Shenandoah* (1888), the still anthologized and most successful Civil War play of the nineteenth century; and *Lillian's Last Love* (1873), revised as *The Banker's Daughter* (1878).

This last play is in some ways his most memorable work, for it became the subject of his "The Autobiography of a Play," originally a Harvard University address (1886). In this "Autobiography," Howard traced the extensive development and revisions of the play (for the British as well as for the American productions), and enunciated the "laws of dramatic construction"—contingent on audience expectations rather than artistic considerations—that turn a play into a hit. Published in 1914, the essay appears in *Papers on Playmaking* (1957), edited by Brander Matthews.

Bronson's *The Banker's Daughter and Other Plays* was edited, with an introduction and notes by Allan G. Halline, as Volume X of *America's Lost Plays* (1941 and 1964).

HOWARD, Sidney [Coe] (1891–1939), one of the important American NATURALIST playwrights of the 1920's, was particularly successful with the daring THEY KNEW WHAT THEY WANTED (1924); with his Freudian attack on momism, THE SILVER CORD (1926); and with the melodramatic NED MCCOBB'S DAUGHTER (1926). Howard was praised also for his portrayal of American business values in the ironically titled LUCKY SAM MCCARVER (1925), which failed on the boards. Always stressing the importance of the actor, Howard considered it the playwright's job to provide acting vehicles. This concern with the actor manifests itself in his published plays, which abound in descriptions of characters' actions, feelings, and thoughts. To provide effective vehicles, Howard often adapted the works of others—most successfully RENÉ FAUCHOIS's *Prenez garde à la peinture* into THE LATE CHRISTOPHER BEAN (1932), and the Walter Reed chapter of Paul de Kruif's *Microbe Hunters* into YELLOW JACK (1934). Howard usually followed the traditions of the nineteenth century, resolving situations artificially, in accord with audience expectations. Yet he succeeded in portraying colorful local idioms, effective characterizations, entertaining spectacles, and interesting, often gripping plots.

Coming of pioneer stock, Howard was born and raised in California. In 1915 he graduated from the University of California, where he wrote poetry as well as drama. He attended George Pierce Baker's 47 Workshop at Harvard, and then served on the western front in World War I. After the war he became a radical reporter, quickly gaining prominence for his articles on industrial spying—which he later rewrote as a novel. But Howard soon returned to his primary interest, the theatre.

His first professional venture was *Swords* (1921), a blank-verse drama about the struggle between the Guelphs and the Ghibellines. It was followed by translations, adaptations, and collaborations. He adapted plays by CHARLES VILDRAC (*S.S. Tenacity*, 1922; and *Michel Auclair*, 1925), MENYHÉRT LENGYEL (*Sancho Panza*, 1923), EDMOND ROSTAND (*The Last Night of Don Juan*, 1925), FERENC MOLNÁR (*Olympia*, 1928), and MARCEL PAGNOL (*Marseilles*, 1930); as well as novels like SINCLAIR LEWIS's *Dodsworth* (1934) and Humphrey Cobb's *Paths of Glory* (1935). He collaborated most notably with EDWARD SHELDON on *Bewitched* (1924), a romance set in postwar France; and with CHARLES MACARTHUR on *Salvation* (1928), which features an evangelist. *Lute Song*, a musical adaptation by Howard and Will Irwin (1907–   ) of the classic fourteenth-century Chinese love play *Pi-Pa-Ki*, was sumptuously produced on Broadway in 1945. Aside from the earlier-mentioned hits, Howard's original plays include *Half Gods* (1929); *Alien Corn* (1933), set in a small Midwestern college town; *The Ghost of Yankee Doodle* (1937), which speculates about America's ability to keep out of a European war; and his last play, the posthumously produced Faust fantasy *Madam, Will You Walk?* (1954).

Howard's principal attribute as a playwright was his craftsmanship. He wrote over two dozen plays, as well as numerous film scripts (including those for *The Silver Cord* and *The Late Christopher Bean*). With their strong roles, his plays attracted the prominent actors of his time, which helped to establish and sustain Howard's popularity. If he was not an original playwright or an experimenter, Howard nonetheless had considerable technical skill and courage. His plays sought to entertain and were for the most part devoid of the "thesis" so fashionable in the thirties. Nevertheless they display social consciousness and responsibility.

Howard's first wife was Clare Eames, the star for whom he had written *Swords*. After her death in 1930, he married the daughter of the noted conductor and composer Walter Damrosch. Howard died in a tractor accident while farming in Massachusetts.

Arthur Hobson Quinn's *A History of the American Drama From the Civil War to the Present Day* (1936) discusses Howard's works and includes a bibliography of them; other evaluations appear in Joseph Wood Krutch's *The American Drama Since 1918* (1957) and in Walter J. Meserve's "Sidney Howard and the Social Drama of the Twenties," *Modern Drama,* VI (1963).

HOWELLS, William Dean (1837–1920), American writer and editor, was a major novelist and a champion of REALISM in his time. He was also devoted to the theatre, and wrote knowledgeably of contemporary drama. Because of their realism, he inordinately praised EDWARD HARRIGAN's New York vaudeville sketches and the plays of JAMES A. HERNE, the foremost American dramatist in Howells's opinion. He himself produced some thirty-six plays, including dramatizations of his famous novels, *The Rise of Silas Lapham* and *A Hazard of New Fortunes*. But his plays had only limited success in his time, and were soon forgotten. His *A Counterfeit Presentment* (1877) and *Colonel Sellers as a Scientist* were fairly well-known comedies. The latter was written in 1883* with Mark Twain (1835–1910), from whose *The Gilded Age* came the absurdly comic protagonist.

Howells's first play (*Samson,* 1874) is a verse translation from the Italian, and he wrote other serious dramas. But his best plays are the many polite farces relished by his *Atlantic Monthly, Harper's Weekly,* and *Harper's Magazine* readers; two of them, *The Mouse Trap* (1885) and *The Garroters* (1886, also produced as *A Dangerous Ruffian*), were often performed in England and America. There are some twenty-five amusing one-acters, of which a dozen feature two Boston couples and —like his other comedies—portray manners and social values.

Walter J. Meserve's scholarly edition of *The Complete Plays of W. D. Howells* (1960) includes notes, a bibliography, and a study of Howells as a dramatist.

HOYT, Charles Hale (1859–1900), American playwright, was his country's most popular farce writer in the late nineteenth century, and provided the lyrics for many popular songs. Combining his often plotless slapstick with satirical portrayals of different American regions, character types, and topical subjects like women's suffrage and politics, he produced some sixteen plays in as many years, beginning in 1883. The most popular of the plays, *A Trip to Chinatown* (1891), held the record for consecutive performances (657) until Smith and Bacon's LIGHTNIN' (1918), and featured the song "After the Ball." Other popular Hoyt works were *A Texas Steer* (1890), which pokes fun at a Lone Star State congressman, and *A Temperance Town* (1893), which, aside from entertainment, aimed, Hoyt noted, "to expose the inquisitorial cruelty of the law and its unjust interference with personal liberty."

Some of Hoyt's drama was collected in *Five Plays* (Volume IX of *America's Lost Plays,* 1941 and 1964), edited by Douglas L. Hunt, who also wrote a book on the *Life and Work of Charles H. Hoyt* (1945).

*It was first produced in 1887 as *The American Claimant or Mulberry Sellers Ten Years Later,* and first published in 1960.

HUBALEK, Claus (1926–), German dramatist, in the 1950's wrote a number of war plays like *Der Hauptmann und sein Held* (1953), a tragicomedy that was filmed in 1955; *Keine fallen für die Füchse* (1957), a comedy about divided post-World War II Berlin; and *Die Festung* (1958), portraying the experiences of a German army officer from June 30, 1934, through April 7, 1945. Later plays by the Berlin-born Hubalek include *Die Stunde der Antigone* (1960), an application of the classic myth to the last days of Nazism; and *Stalingrad* (1961), a dramatization of THEODOR PLIEVIER's novel.

HUGHES, Hatcher (1881–1945), American scholar and playwright. In 1921 he collaborated with ELMER RICE on a play for Minnie Maddern Fiske, *Wake Up, Jonathan.* A North Carolinian by birth, Hughes wrote a number of other plays, the best of which—the Pulitzer Prize-winning HELL-BENT FER HEAVEN (1924)—portrays the mountaineer types of his native region. *Ruint* (1925) also presents the isolated, hard-drinking, religiously fanatic and fundamentalist characters of the mid-Appalachian area. The last notable play by Hughes was *The Lord Blesses the Bishop* (1932). Most of Hughes's career he served as Professor of Drama at Columbia University.

HUGHES, [James] **Langston** (1902–67), "the Poet Laureate of Harlem" and the most distinguished midcentury black American writer, published almost thirty volumes (including anthologies) of poetry, fiction, journalism, opera librettos, and plays. It is for his poetry and his stories of Simple, a genial character who freely expressed the thoughts of many urban blacks, that Hughes is best known. He adapted some of these popular stories into his most popular play, the romantic musical comedy *Simply Heavenly* (1957, music by David Martin). In these stories, as in his other writing, Hughes reproduces Negro folk speech and expresses deeply felt resentments against racial discrimination. But he does so humorously, in a satirical, wry manner: "White folks is the cause of a lot of inconvenience in my life," remarks Simple.

Part Cherokee Indian, Hughes was born in Joplin, Missouri, and raised first by his grandmother in Kansas and then by his mother in Illinois and Ohio. After graduating from high school, he spent a few uncongenial months with his father in Mexico, and then went to New York, where he attended Columbia University. Seeking out life directly, he became a vagabond as he traveled in Africa and western Europe, doing odd jobs and eventually working his way back as a sailor. He completed his education when he took a degree at Lincoln University (Pennsylvania) in 1929. Subsequently he returned to New York, and settled in Harlem.

Though Hughes is less distinguished for his drama than for his fiction and poetry—which first gained him fame in the 1920's—*Simply Heavenly* and his other plays are notable. In the 1930's he wrote two AGITPROPS: *Scottsboro Limited* (1932), dramatizing the notorious Alabama case of 1931; and *Don't You Want to Be Free?* (1936), which had a long run in Hughes's improvised Suitcase Theatre in Harlem in 1936–37. His other dramatic writings include *Little Ham* (1935), a folk comedy about the roaring twenties; *Soul Gone Home* (1937), a NATURALIST fantasy about white repression of blacks; *Tambourines to Glory* (1949, gospel music by Jobe Huntley), a musical melodrama set in Harlem and dealing with Faustian themes of good, evil, and redemption; and lyrics for the musical versions of Rice's STREET SCENE and for his own drama on the problems of mulattoes, *The Barrier* (1950, music by Jan Meyerowitz), based on his earlier play *Mulatto* (1935), which was performed in New York but banned elsewhere for its portrayal of miscegenation.

Five Plays by Langston Hughes (1963) includes *Mulatto, Soul Gone Home, Little Ham, Simply Heavenly,* and *Tambourines to Glory*. He also wrote two autobiographies, *The Big Sea* (1940) and *I Wonder as I Wander* (1956). Studies of his life and work are Donald C. Dickinson's *A Bio-bibliography of Langston Hughes: 1902–1967* (1967) and James A. Emanuel's *Langston Hughes* (1968).

HUGHIE, a one-act play by EUGENE O'NEILL, produced in 1958 and published in 1959. Setting: a hotel lobby in midtown New York before dawn, 1928.

Written about 1941, *Hughie* is the only extant and completed part of *By Way of Obit,* a projected cycle of eight one-act plays. Although *Hughie* has been successfully produced, it is less a play than a sensitive two-character sketch: the personality of Erie is revealed in a long monologue; and the night clerk, the second character, in extensive (and often poetic) stage directions and unspoken soliloquies. The city night noises furnish the background for this dramatization of illusion and love pitted against human despair and isolation, themes that preoccupied O'Neill particularly in his late and posthumous plays.

"Erie" Smith, a small-time gambler, returns from an extended spree following the funeral of Hughie, the former night clerk of his shabby hotel. Pathetically boastful, he tells the new night clerk his life story, talking mostly of his relationship with Hughie, the "sucker" Erie loved. Lonesome and insecure beneath his Broadway-sport façade, Erie needed Hughie's admiration, as Hughie, leading a drab family life, needed Erie's "glamor." But the new night clerk is not listening: preoccupied with illusions (stimulated by outside noises) and his own wretched existence, he is as dead within as is Erie; in listless despair he wonders, when he hears an ambulance, "Will he die, Doctor, or isn't he lucky?" The two men at last establish the contact that Erie has ached for. Now "purged of grief, his confidence restored," he decides to "quit carryin' the torch for Hughie. . . . He's gone. Like we all gotta go . . . and who cares, and what's the difference? It's all in the racket, huh?" Happily he starts rolling dice with the new night clerk (coincidentally also named Hughes), as he formerly did with Hughie.

HUNGARY. Hungarian drama, which gained worldwide fame with the plays of FERENC MOLNÁR, became noteworthy only in the nineteenth century. Among early modern playwrights were József Katona (1791–1830), famous for his still-produced drama of the popular nationalistic theme of Hungary's thirteenth-century King Endre II and his palatine, *Bánk Bán* (1820); Mihály Vörösmarty (1800–55), whose romantic masterpiece is *Csongor és Tünde* (1831), a poetic and philosophic fairy-tale drama; the immensely prolific Ede Szigligeti (1814–78), who wrote well over one hundred folk plays (*népszinmü:* idealized portrayals of village life, some of them sketches and vaudevilles) including *Liliomfi* (1849), a comedy about itinerant actors that features a clever, rascally libertine; Imre Madách (1823–64), whose much-translated philosophical verse drama, *Az ember tragédiája* (*The Tragedy of Man,* 1862), which has remained in native repertoires since its first production in 1883, features Lucifer, Adam, and Eve in a dream fantasy on the struggle of good and evil and on man's fate, traced from man's creation to the future; Gergely Csiky (1842–91), who wrote romantic dramas and quasi-REPRESENTATIONAL satires in the vein of VICTORIEN SARDOU; Jenö Rákosi (1842–1928), a poet, novelist, and translator of Shakespeare, whose best stage works are symbolic fairy plays like the early *Aesop* (1866); Lajos Dóczy (1845–1918), a popular playwright who wrote similarly romantic dramas, of which the most popular was a comedy, *Csók* (1874); the poet and novelist Sándor Bródy (1863–1924), who also wrote influential NATURALIST tragedies, including *A dada* (1902), featuring a dishonored peasant girl, and *A tanitónö* (1908), for which he provided an alternate happy ending to a doomed romance; and Jenö Heltai (1871–1957), the best of whose romantic dramas, *A néma levente* (*The Silent Knight,* 1936), has been produced abroad.

The heyday of Hungarian drama came between the two world wars—i.e., from the time Hungary became independent until 1946, when it became a "people's republic" in the Soviet orbit. Molnár's best-known drama and some of the witty melodramatic plays of MENYHÉRT LENGYEL appeared earlier, but the bulk of their work as well as that of other notable Hungarian playwrights came during that period. It was then that Ferenc Herczeg (1863–1954) brought out his many comedies of manners, notably *Kék róka* (1917) and *Az ezüst róka* (1921), and his historical tragedies, the most distinguished of which is *A híd* (1925), featuring the leader of the 1848 Revolution, Lajos Kossuth; but Herczeg's dramatization of his popular, amusing story *Gyurkovics lányok* appeared in 1899, and many of his distinguished tragedies, including the allegorical *Bizánc* (1904), came before World

War I. Less important but also known outside Hungary was the satirist Lajos Biró (1880–1948), who became famous with an attack on the aristocracy, *Sárga liliom* (1910). He collaborated on some of Lengyel's hits, moved to London during World War II, and wrote in English: *Patricia's Seven Houses* (1942), a comedy not unlike Shaw's WIDOWERS' HOUSES; *School for Slavery* (1942), a play set in occupied Poland; and *Our Katie*, produced in London in 1946.

Other well-known dramatists (most of them also wrote in other genres) in the period between the wars were Zsigmond Móricz (1879–1942), Hungary's most outstanding novelist, whose drama, which inspired other Hungarians to write on native themes, includes unidealized portrayals of peasants in *Sári biró* (1910), *Buzakalász* (1924), and *Uri muri* (1928), which satirizes declining feudalism in a mixture of suspense and grotesquerie; Lajos Zilahy (1891–), who wrote novels and plays about contemporary Hungarian problems after World War I and a very successful comedy about women's rights, *Tüzmadár* (*The Firebird*, 1932), protested the anti-Semitic policies that exiled or silenced many Hungarian writers in the 1930's, donated his considerable fortune to help these writers, and in 1947 migrated to the United States, where he wrote in English (*The Wooden Towers* appeared in 1948); Ernö Vajda (1887–), who wrote historical plays but became known outside Hungary for his portrayal of the disillusionment of first love, *Fata Morgana* (1915); and László Bus-Fekete (1898–), some of whose many plays appeared in English, notably CHARLES MACARTHUR and BEN HECHT's adaptation of his *Ladies and Gentlemen* (1938) and his 1944 dramatization of a FRANZ WERFEL novel, *Der veruntreute Himmel* (*Embezzled Heaven*, 1938).

Hungary's leading post-World War II dramatists are GYULA HAY—whose work, though it appeared for the most part at an earlier period, won increasing popularity throughout Europe in the 1960's—László Németh (1901–), and Gyula Illyés (1902–). Németh, a physician as well as a distinguished philosopher, novelist, and playwright, has written disquisitory dramas on historical figures (Jan Hus, Galileo, Pope Gregory VII) who are portrayed as opposing an ignorant public, one of these plays (*Galilei*) being premiered in 1956 only after many delays caused by authorities who feared the implied analogy between past and present; Németh also succeeded with a father-son conflict drama about two prominent nineteenth-century mathematicians, *A két Bólyai* (1961), and with *Utazás* (1962), a contemporary play about a professor who offends Communists as well as "reactionaries" with his objective comments about the Soviet Union. Illyés, one of Hungary's great poets, has also written novels and plays: *Ozorai példa* (1952), on patriotism; *Fáklyaláng* (1953), dramatizing a cerebral confrontation between the 1848–49 antagonists Kossuth and Arthur von Görgey; and *Dózsa* (1956), featuring the leader of the abortive peasant rebellion of 1514. Other playwrights to appear in Hungary recently include Miklós Hubay (1918–), who has written musicals as well as a cycle of one-act satires of tyranny (*Néró játszik*, 1968); and Ferenc Karinthy (1921–), whose *Négykezes* (1966) consists of two tragicomic one-acters each of which depicts the loneliness of two people.

A detailed study on Hungarian drama is the translated *History of Hungarian Literature* (1964) by Tibor Klaniczay and others—but this book is highly slanted; see also Emro J. Gergely's account of *Hungarian Drama in New York: American Adaptations, 1908–1940* (1947).

HUNTER, Kermit (1910–), American playwright, was strongly influenced by the pageant drama of PAUL GREEN and Frederick Koch's North Carolina Playmakers. The most successful of his own dozen "symphonic" plays has been the annually produced UNTO THESE HILLS (1950).

Born in West Virginia, Hunter graduated from Ohio State University in 1931. He did his graduate work at the University of North Carolina; there he wrote *Unto These Hills* as his master's thesis, and completed his Ph.D. in 1955. He taught English and drama in a number of colleges and universities, and subsequently became dean of the School of Arts at Southern Methodist University. A frequent lecturer especially in conjunction with regional pageants, Hunter has continued writing historical outdoor spectacles.

HURWITZ, Moshe (1844–1910), Yiddish playwright born in Stanislawow, Galicia, and self-titled "Professor," like his rival JOSEPH LATEINER wrote potboilers for immigrant audiences after he came to New York. Among his ninety plays, hodgepodge constructs of older plays that are effectively staged to evoke tears and laughter, are *Tissa Eslar* (1886), the dramatization of a famous contemporary trial; and *King Solomon* (1887), the first of Hurwitz's "historical cycle."

HUXLEY, Aldous [Leonard] (1894–1963), the prominent English novelist and essayist, also tried his hand at drama. Only one insignificant play, *The World of Light*, however, was original (it received a matinee performance in 1931). He adapted his story "The Gioconda Smile" into a play by the same name and into a film (*A Woman's Vengeance*, both in 1948), and dramatized his novel *The Genius and the Goddess* in 1958. Huxley also wrote and collaborated on screen plays, notably *Pride and Prejudice* (1940), *Madame Curie* (1944), and *Jane Eyre* (1944). George Campbell Dixon (1896–1960) dramatized *Point Counterpoint* (as *This Way to Paradise*, 1930), and Whiting's THE DEVILS is a dramatization of Huxley's *The Devils of Loudon* (1952).

HYACINTH HALVEY, a one-act play by LADY GREGORY, produced in 1906 and published in 1909. Setting: the little town of Cloon in contemporary Ireland.

This Molière-like comedy is about a very simple young Sub-Sanitary Inspector, Hyacinth

Halvey, who is new at his job. Armed with a bag of laudatory character references from his mother's friends and relatives, he is soon plagued by the burdensome admiration of a busybody postmistress, a dishonest butcher, a loutish telegraph boy, and other villagers. Halvey's every effort to blacken his own reputation boomerangs. At the end he is cheered as a veritable saint and presented as a model to the town's youth.

A one-act sequel, *The Full Moon* (1910), continues the hero's adventures and also features characters from SPREADING THE NEWS and *The Jackdaw* (1907), another one-acter; but *The Full Moon* was not very successful.

HYDE, Douglas (1860–1949), Irish writer and statesman, is especially notable as a dramatist because his *Casadh an t-Sugain* (*The Twisting of the Rope,* 1901), a one-act comedy based on Irish folklore, was the first Gaelic play produced in a Dublin theatre. (It opened the Irish Literary Theatre's third season, with Hyde himself playing the leading role of Hanrahan.) His other one-act plays include *Teach na mBocht* (1903, translated by LADY GREGORY as *The Poorhouse* and ultimately revised as THE WORKHOUSE WARD), *An Tincear Agus an tSideog* (*The Tinker and the Fairy,* 1902), *An Posadh* (*The Marriage,* 1902), *Drama Breite Criosta* (*The Nativity Play,* 1902), *Ar Naom ar Iarraid* (*The Lost Saint,* 1902), *Pleusgadh na Bulgoide, or The Bursting of the Bubble* (1903, a bilingual play), *Rig Seumas* (1903, translated as *King James* by Lady Gregory, whose THE WHITE COCKADE dramatizes the same legend), and *An Magistir Sgoile* (*The Schoolmaster,* 1904). Most of these were translated by Lady Gregory and published in her *Poets and Dreamers* (1903).

Hyde, who wrote under the pseudonym "An Craoibhin Aoibhinn" ("The Delightful Branch") and strove to revive ancient Gaelic, also published *A Literary History of Ireland* (1899), and—though a Protestant—was Eire's first President (1938–45). See Diarmid Coffey's *Douglas Hyde, President of Ireland* (1938).

I

I AM A CAMERA, a play in three acts by JOHN VAN DRUTEN, produced in 1951 and published in 1952. Setting: Berlin, 1930.

This is a popular adaptation of CHRISTOPHER ISHERWOOD short stories (particularly "Sally Bowles") collected in *Goodbye to Berlin* (1939). Isherwood referred to the protagonist Sally Bowles as "a little girl who has listened to what the grown-ups had said about tarts, and who was trying to copy those things." The semiautobiographical hero, who is also named Christopher Isherwood, is a writer who sees much but has not yet interpreted it. The play was filmed (1955) and made into a musical hit by Joe Masteroff (1919–), *Cabaret* (1966, music by John Kander).

Isherwood and the amoral Sally, who has just had an abortion, fall in love. But neither will admit it, for this would give meaning to these young sophisticates' lives. However, Isherwood becomes emotionally entangled with Sally as well as with the horror of the Nazi rise to power. At the end Sally blithely goes off, promising to write him postcards. Love is not enough to hold them together. "The camera's taken all its pictures, and now it's going away to develop them," Isherwood says: "I wonder how Sally will look. . . ." And as she goes "into the photograph" he calls after her: "Don't forget those postcards, Sally."

I REMEMBER MAMA, a play in two acts by JOHN VAN DRUTEN, produced in 1944 and published in 1945. Setting: San Francisco, 1910.

Based on *Mama's Bank Account* (1943), Kathryn Forbes's sketches about a Norwegian-American family, this play subsequently was transformed into a television series. In various daily episodes recollected by Katrin, the oldest daughter, it depicts the devoted Mama bringing up her children. She is assisted by Papa, her carpenter husband, and the ferocious but golden-hearted Uncle Chris, "the head of the family." Other characters include three aunts (two of them unpleasant, the third a lovable spinster who at last finds happiness with an undertaker), an aging British actor, and a famous lady writer.

IBSEN, Henrik [Johan] (1828–1906), Norwegian playwright, is generally credited with being the "father of modern drama," and most studies of the modern theatre start with his works. Ibsen's early plays were produced in the 1850's, and his last play was published before the twentieth century began; but despite dated theatrical conventions and (occasionally) subject matter, his range, powerful imagination, and vitality have kept Ibsen's plays alive to this day. He is credited with providing modern drama with REALISM, lyricism, masterful plot construction, and discussion—particularly of social issues in the PROBLEM PLAYS, for which he is best known; yet when praising him for any one of these contributions, different critics have denied him some or all of the others. The very preoccupation of critics and theatre historians with his plays, however, as well as continued worldwide production of his works, evidence Ibsen's undiminishing stature as a modern dramatist. His considerable influence on other playwrights—beginning with BERNARD SHAW—is the more striking when one remembers that Ibsen, like his great fellow-Scandinavian, AUGUST STRINDBERG, wrote in a language known but to few Westerners. (JAMES JOYCE was so impressed with Ibsen's work that he learned Norwegian in order to read it in the original.)

Ibsen was born in the port town of Skien, Norway. In 1836 his family lost their wealth and, impoverished and ostracized, moved to a cottage at the edge of town. Because of his father's preoccupation with his business failures and his mother's dogmatic religious beliefs, Ibsen was close only to his sister Hedvig. His schooling was poor, and he became introverted and bitter. In 1843, the fifteen-year-old boy left Skien and went to Grimstad, another small coastal town, where be became a pharmacist's apprentice. Ibsen spent seven years there, drudging for a pittance. As the result of an affair with an older servant, he fathered a child that he supported for some fourteen years. He also read avidly—particularly romantic and chivalric poetry, and Norse history—and began writing poetry. Participating in local politics, he attacked provincial hypocrisies and espoused Scandinavian nationalism as a defense against Prussian expansionism. The revolutionary atmosphere of the late 1840's, as well as his reading, influenced the writing of his first play, *Catalina* (CATILINE), published under the pseudonym Brynjolf Bjarme in 1850.

That year Ibsen left Grimstad for the University at Christiania (now Oslo). In 1851 he became assistant manager of the Bergen Theatre, and received a travel grant to study stage production in Denmark and Germany. After his return he stage-managed productions at Bergen's and later at Christiania's National Theatre. He gained much practical theatre experience from the productions of the WELL-MADE PLAYS of Eugène Scribe and his followers, which constituted the most popular theatrical fare at the time. Their influence on his own dramas, some of which he produced during that period, is unmistakable. Like *Catiline,* all his

Henrik Ibsen in 1905. (*Norwegian Embassy Information Service*)

early works—*Kjæmpehøjen* (WARRIOR'S BARROW, 1850), *Sancthansnatten* (ST. JOHN'S NIGHT, 1853), *Fru Inger til Østråt* (LADY INGER OF ØSTRÅT, 1855), *Gildet på Solhoug* (THE FEAST AT SOLHAUG, 1856), OLAF LILJEKRANS (1857), and *Hær mændene på Helgeland* (THE VIKINGS AT HELGELAND, 1858)—are romantic verse dramas based on Norwegian ballads and history.* They are typical of the melodrama popular in the nineteenth-century theatre. But though artificial and for the most part lifeless, they have the characteristic Ibsen touches associated with the later and greater plays: the reappearance of "ghosts" from the past, the conflict between idealism and reality, recurrent mysticism, a concern with social problems, and—perhaps most important—rounded characterizations of protagonists who struggle in their quest for individual "freedom under responsibility," as *Fruen fra hauet* (THE LADY FROM THE SEA, 1888) terms it.

Ibsen's first major popular success did not come until 1877, with *Samfundets støtter* (PILLARS OF SOCIETY). But he had achieved some popularity with *The Feast at Solhaug* in 1855, and had written two notable minor works—*Kjærlighedens komedie* (LOVE'S COMEDY, 1862) and *Kongsemnerne* (THE PRETENDERS, 1863)—before leaving Norway in 1864. He received a grant, supplemented by money raised by his friend and later rival, BJØRNSTJERNE BJØRNSON, and began his travels with his family.† Although he always remained fiercely preoccupied with Norway's social and national problems, he was to spend most of the remainder of his life in Italy and Germany. The publication in 1866 of his first major work, BRAND, brought him acclaim and money (from royalties and a government pension); these ended the artistic self-doubts and financial worries that had plagued Ibsen until then.

The publication and production of the dramas that made him famous soon followed. With almost monotonous regularity, Ibsen first thought out his play, wrote his notes and drafts, and then had the manuscript ready for publication every other December (for the Christmas trade); production usually followed in January. After PEER GYNT (1867), his next play, he gave up history, legend, and verse—except for *Keiser og Galilæer* (EMPEROR AND GALILEAN, 1873), an impossibly long and confused play that was his own favorite and occupies a niche in Ibsen's corpus not unlike that of BACK TO METHUSELAH in Shaw's. Ibsen now presented contemporary problems NATURALISTICally, if often melodramatically: *De unges forbund* (THE LEAGUE OF YOUTH, 1869), followed by the already noted *Emperor and Galilean* and *Pillars of Society, Et dukkehjem* (A DOLL'S HOUSE, 1879), *Gengangere* (GHOSTS, 1881), *En folkefunde* (AN ENEMY OF THE PEOPLE, 1882), *Vildanden* (THE WILD DUCK, 1884), ROSMERSHOLM (1886), the earlier-noted *The Lady from the Sea,* and HEDDA GABLER (1890).

These major problem plays, usually depicting small-town life, are meaningful beyond their portrayal of contemporary issues of marriage and female emancipation, religious and moral fanaticism, parochial hypocrisy, and corruption. They no longer shock present-day audiences as *Ghosts* and *A Doll's House,* particularly, shocked and incensed their first audiences; the immediate problems are now, if not totally resolved, at least considered respectable topics of discussion. But there is much more to Ibsen's plays. They grapple with and reveal human problems that are as relevant to our age as to Ibsen's. The characters are complex and universal; one can still identify with their struggles for self-understanding and self-realization. Yet the brooding and the classical starkness of many of these dramas are punctuated by humor—an ever-present quality that some critics would deny Ibsen.

In 1891, Ibsen finally returned to settle in his native Norway. There he wrote his last plays: *Bygmester Solness* (THE MASTER BUILDER, 1892), *Lille Eyolf* (LITTLE EYOLF, 1894), JOHN GABRIEL BORKMAN (1896), and *Når vi døde vågner* (WHEN WE DEAD AWAKEN, 1899). In these works Ibsen deals with the guilty introspection of artists and businessmen, and goes back, as it were, to the poetry of his first plays—though the last plays, allusive and poetic as they may be, are written in prose. Beginning with the earlier *The Wild Duck,* Ibsen increasingly turned from problem plays and from the societal to the individual, the SYMBOLIC, and the mystical. These last plays are difficult, enigmatic, and highly metaphorical. In them, as in his earlier plays, it is not the "realism" or the choice of the particular situation or problem that constitutes Ibsen's artistry. It is, rather, the striking dramatization of his poetic vision of the human enigma that, finally, puts Ibsen in the forefront of modern literature and makes him the father of the modern drama and theatre.

There are excellent English translations by Eva LeGallienne, Michael Meyer, and others of many of the individual plays. The standard translations, William Archer's twelve-volume *The Collected Works of Henrik Ibsen* (1906 ff.), with their now dated English, convey a misleading picture of Ibsen's dialogue, which in its day introduced contemporary idiomatic speech into modern drama. A new series, James W. McFarlane's *The Oxford Ibsen,* began publication in 1960; it contains not only fresher translations of the plays but also Ibsen's comments and drafts, invaluable notes, and extensive bibliographies that list the many critical and biographical works on Ibsen that have been—and continue to be—published. McFarlane's *Henrik Ibsen: A Critical Anthology* (1970) is a collection of criticisms by and of Ibsen. Because of their special value and interest, particular mention should be made of Shaw's THE QUINTESSENCE OF IBSENISM (1891, 1913) and the

* He also wrote a parody of Vincenzo Bellini's opera *Norma* (1831), *Norma eller en politikers kjærlighed (Norma, or A Politician's Love,* 1851*),* in which he satirized opportunistic politicians.

† Ibsen was married in 1858. His son, Sigurd Ibsen (1859–1930), became a dramatist in his own right with *Robert Frank* (1914), which achieved a measure of success in Norway; it depicts a premier who settles a syndicalist strike and safeguards modern industrial society by establishing a profit-sharing arrangement.

book-length studies by M. C. Bradbrook, Brian W. Downs, Janko Lavrin, F. L. Lucas (*The Drama of Ibsen and Strindberg,* 1962), J. R. Northam, P. F. D. Tennant, Maurice Valency (*The Flower and the Castle,* 1963), and Hermann J. Weigand. Adolph E. Zucker's *Ibsen, The Master Builder* (1930) and Halvdan Koht's *Life of Ibsen* (revised 1954) have been superseded by Michael Meyer's monumental *Ibsen, a Biography* (1971).

ICEBOUND, a play in three acts by OWEN DAVIS, published and produced in 1923. Setting: a homestead near Veazie, Maine; 1922–23.

In this grim, NATURALISTIC play Davis depicts the speech and folkways of his native New England. *Icebound* won the 1923 Pulitzer Prize.

The Jordan family members are gathered at the homestead, bickering as they wait for the death of the old mother. Mother Jordan wants to see only her youngest son, Ben, a ne'er-do-well who escaped prison years ago when he was indicted for arson. She loves him though he is a "bad man" because he was "my baby so long after all the others had forgotten how to love me." After waiting for the mother's death, the family are chagrined to find that the old lady has left the bulk of the estate to Jane Crosby, the poor relative who tended her and whom they dislike and had planned to send packing. Now they fawn on her. Jane sets out to captivate the dissolute Ben, whom she loves. She makes him work for her, and succeeds in having the charges against him dropped. Then Jane gives the inheritance to Ben as, she says, his mother would have wished. He proves worthy of Jane by breaking the "icy" Jordan character and asking her to marry him. Though his reformation and their lasting happiness are uncertain, Jane will try to fulfill the injunction of the mother: "There's only just one chance to save my boy—through a woman who will hold out her heart to him and let him trample on it as he has on mine"—she had written in the letter that left Jane the Jordan property—"Who'd work, and pray, and live for him, until as age comes on and maybe he gets a little tired, he'll turn to her."

ICELAND. Icelandic drama dates back to the eighteenth century. In 1897 a dramatic society was founded in Reykjavík, then a small village. The great Icelandic poet and translator Matthías Jochumsson (1835–1920), who also wrote history plays and lyrical dramas, became famous with the still-popular *Útilegumennirnir* (1864, later titled *Skugga-Sveinn*), his country's first romantic play. Another of Iceland's successful playwrights was the neoromanticist Jóhan Sigurjónsson (1880–1919), whose best-known work, *Fjalla-Eyvindur* (*Eyvind of the Hills,* 1911), a domestic tragedy originally written in Danish and titled *Bjærg-Ejvind og hans hustru* (*Eyvind of the Hills and His Wife*), was performed in England and America; based on eighteenth-century history, it dramatizes the love of a widow for a criminal fugitive, with whom she escapes, and her suicide after years of hardship and despair when he no longer loves her. Sigurjónsson's *Galdra-Loftur* (1915), simultaneously appearing in Danish as *Ønsket* (*The Wish*), is also based on legend, this time on a Faustian quest for knowledge. Another Danish-writing Icelander was Guđmundur Kamban (1888–1945), a novelist-playwright whose social satires achieved popularity in Scandinavia and Germany, and whose *Hadda-Padda* (1914) appeared in English. The prolific poet Davið Stefánsson (1895–1964) also wrote widely read novels and a few plays, including *Gullna hliðið* (*The Golden Gate,* 1941), a lusty folktale about a scoundrel whose soul is saved from damnation by a good wife.

Iceland's Nobel Prize novelist Halldór Kiljan Laxness (1902–   ) has written a few dramas; however, except for *Silfurtunglið* (*The Silver Moon,* 1954)—a protest against his government's granting America permission to establish and keep air bases in his country—which was produced also in Moscow, his plays have remained unknown outside Iceland. His *Snæfriður Íslandssól* and Tryggvi Sveinbjörnsson's (1891–   ) *Bishop Jón Arason* were presented after the National Theatre opened in Reykjavík in 1950; the latter play, one of the many native dramatizations of the life of Iceland's sixteenth-century patriot, won the 1950 national playwriting contest. The National Theatre was launched with *Nýjársnóttin* (1872), an Icelandic folklore drama resembling Shakespeare's *A Midsummer Night's Dream,* by Indriði Einarsson (1851–1939), his nation's first author to devote all his energies to drama and to the establishment of a national theatre. Although most of the National Theatre's production are of popular foreign plays, nearly a quarter are devoted to native dramas, like those of the more contemporary Agnar Þórđarson (1917–   ), a British-educated and widely traveled novelist and prolific playwright. Þórđarson's historical as well as modern dramas include *Kjarnorka og kvenhylli* (*Atoms and Madams,* 1955), a satire of a corrupt politician and his wife, rejected by their daughter for a moral farmer uncontaminated by post-World War II affluence and its generally depraving effects; and *Glaukskluhkan* (1958), a drama set in contemporary Reykjavík.

Einar Haugen's *Fire and Ice: Three Icelandic Plays* (1967) includes *The Wish, The Golden Gate,* and *Atoms and Madams;* it has extensive bibliographies and essays on the represented playwrights, as well as on other Icelandic drama. Stefán Einarsson's *A History of Icelandic Literature* (1957) also covers Icelandic drama and theatre.

ICEMAN COMETH, THE, a play in four acts by EUGENE O'NEILL, published and produced in 1946. Setting: bar and back room of a New York flophouse, summer 1912.

Though in some ways reminiscent of Ibsen's THE WILD DUCK and Gorky's THE LOWER DEPTHS, *The Iceman Cometh* is original in theme and execution. Written in 1939, it is one of O'Neill's most distinguished and finest plays, despite its inordinate length. Differing interpretations of the play are possible, but there is no question about its concern—in highly theatrical, probing, and suggestive terms—with such general concepts as reality versus idealism and illusion, and the relationship of all of these to man's destiny. The play's spiritual post-Christian despair—echoed in the title's allusion to Jesus (Matthew 25:6: "the bridegroom cometh")—is depicted SYMBOLICally as well as NATURALISTICally, but relieved by much humor. Most of the characterizations (even that of Larry, the autobiographically transformed *raisonneur*) are based on people O'Neill met at "Jimmy the Priest's," the waterfront dive where he lived in 1912 and which he used also in ANNA CHRISTIE. Book-length studies are Winifred D. Frazer's *Love as Death in "The Iceman Cometh": A Modern Treatment of an Ancient Theme* (1967) and John H. Raleigh's collection of essays, *The Iceman Cometh: Twentieth Century Interpretations* (1968).

Act I. Harry Hope's saloon is occupied by some fifteen derelicts who indulge themselves and each other in dreams of former and future glory. Among them are the testy but soft-hearted proprietor himself, a one-time wardheeler who has not set foot outdoors for twenty years; his two cronies, one a former circus con man and the other a former police lieutenant; a Harvard Law School alumnus; a Negro, Joe Mott, the one-time proprietor of a gambling house; two former military officers who fought on opposing sides in the Boer War, and a former correspondent in that war; and Hugo Kalmar, a one-time anarchist editor who occasionally awakes from his drunken stupor to curse capitalists and solicit drinks. Larry Slade, a former syndicalist-anarchist and now a detached and cynically tolerant drunkard, observes the scene philosophically. "To hell with the truth! As the history of the world proves, the truth has no bearing on anything," he says; "the lie of a pipe dream is what gives life to the whole misbegotten mad lot of us, drunk or sober." He is disturbed by the arrival of young Don Parritt, whose mother has recently been denounced and arrested with other anarchists. Parritt insists on telling his problems to Larry, her former lover, who gets increasingly uneasy and does not want to become involved with Parritt. All are awaiting the entertaining and generous Hickey (Theodore Hickman), a traveling salesman who periodically treats the habitués to a lavish bender. Rocky Pioggi, who refuses to admit that he is a pimp, looks forward to Hickey's working up "dat gag about his wife, when he's cockeyed, cryin' over her picture and den springin' it on yuh all of a sudden dat he left her in de hay wid de iceman." The establishment's streetwalkers (Pearl, Margie, and Cora, whose illusion is that they are "tarts," not "whores") and Chuck Morello, the day bartender, join the group, and finally Hickey himself appears. The derelicts' joy at his arrival quickly fades: Hickey has changed. Though he is still the glib kidder, he no longer drinks, and he soon begins to sermonize. Tearing the veil off the derelicts' illusions, he announces that he has "finally had the guts to face myself and throw overboard the damned lying pipe dream that'd been making me miserable"; for their own happiness, he insists they do the same. As they stare at him in amazed resentment, he encourages them to enjoy their bender as always: "Don't let me be a wet blanket—all I want is to see you happy."

Act II. Late that night everything is being readied for a big party, but all are edgy. Hickey has been persuading them, individually, to go out the next day and do what they have always deluded themselves they would do someday. Larry, puzzled and worried about this "Nihilist [starting] a movement that'll blow up the world," also is approached by Hickey, who assures him that Larry will be grateful once he can "admit, without feeling ashamed, that all the grandstand foolosopher bunk and the waiting for the Big Sleep stuff is a pipe dream. You'll say to yourself, I'm just an old man who is scared of life, but even more scared of dying. . . . [Then] you won't be scared of either life or death any more. You simply won't give a damn! Any more than I do!" The party preparations are completed—"Be God, it's a second feast of Belshazzar, with Hickey to do the writing on the wall," Larry remarks—while Parritt insists on confessing to Larry that he betrayed his mother, and various friendships among the derelicts break up under Hickey's persistent, ruthless unveiling of "pipe dreams." As their resentment grows, Hickey confesses at last, "I was a damned busybody who was not only interfering in your private business, but even sicking some of you on to nag at each other. . . . I had to—for your own good! I had to make you help me with each other. I saw I couldn't do what I was after alone." Driven to fury, they insist on knowing what has caused his own conversion. They jeeringly decide that his wife must in fact have played him for a fool with the iceman, and they are stunned by his unexpected, calm announcement: "I'm sorry to tell you that my dearly beloved wife is dead."

Act III. Hickey has "his Reform Wave goin' strong" the next morning. The bartenders and Joe Mott are stopped from knifing and shooting each other only by Larry's sardonic laugh: "That's it! Murder each other, you damned loons, with Hickey's blessing! Didn't I tell you he'd brought death with him?" and Joe angrily departs to open a new gambling house. "Death was the Iceman Hickey called to his home!" Larry concludes prophetically. Hickey brings down Harry Hope and "Jimmy Tomorrow" (James Cameron), the former correspondent, both looking (Cora remarks) "like dey was goin' to de electric chair." As they had always said they would do, Hope must now take that walk and renew his ward connections, and Jimmy, cursing Hickey, goes to get a newspaper job. Similarly, the Boer War officers go for jobs to earn their passage home, Hope's cronies are off to resume their old professions, Cora and Chuck leave to marry and buy their Jersey farm ("imagine a whore hustlin' de cows home," Rocky remarks), and the Harvard lawyer goes for an appointment with the district attorney. Just before Hope bolts back from the outside world in terror, Hickey confidently predicts, "Of course, he's coming back. So are all the others. By tonight

The Iceman Cometh, Act IV. Left to right: Larry (Carl Benton Reid), Hugo (Leo Chazel), Parritt (Paul Crabtree), Hickey (James Barton), Cora (Marcella Markham), Chuck (Joe Marr), the former British infantry commander (Nicholas Joy), the Harvard Law School alumnus (E. G. Marshall), the former police lieutenant (Al McGranary), Joe Mott (John Marriott), the former Boer Commander (Frank Tweddell), Rocky (Tom Pedi, wearing suspenders), Harry Hope (Dudley Digges), the former circus con man (Morton L. Stevens), the former war correspondent (Russell Collins); standing in back are the police detectives (Michael Wyler and Charles Hart, wearing bowler hats). New York, 1946. (*Vandamm Photo, Theatre Collection, New York Public Library*)

they'll all be here again''—cured of their delusions—"that's the whole point." Broken, Hope listlessly refers to the wife he had idolized since her death as "that nagging bitch," and vainly tries to get drunk. Larry bitterly reproaches Hickey for his interference and vengefully speculates that he drove his own wife to suicide. Hickey's quiet reply horrifies him: "No, I'm sorry to have to tell you my poor wife was killed." As Hope keeps whining ("Bejees, what did you do to the booze, Hickey? There's no damned life left in it"), Hickey begins to lose his self-confidence: "It's time you began to feel happy—"

Act IV. By midnight the bums have crawled back unmasked, "one by one," as Rocky describes it, "lookin' like pooches wid deir tails between deir legs." Hickey, slowly breaking down, has telephoned the police, who arrive while he tells his life story (in some fifteen minutes, constituting one of the longest speeches in modern drama). His loving wife eternally forgave his debauchery, even when he came home looking "like something they threw out of the D.T. ward in Bellevue along with the garbage, something that ought to be dead and isn't!" Her unshakable confidence in his imminent reform and her perfect love and goodness (his jokes about her being "in the hay with the iceman" were really wishful thoughts) made him hate and finally shoot her. He deludes himself into believing the killing was done for love, to free her and bring her peace. But inadvertently he voices his real motive: "I couldn't forgive her for forgiving me. I even caught myself hating her for making me hate myself so much. There's a limit to the guilt you can feel and the forgiveness and the pity you can take!" Now Hickey persuades himself that he has no illusions left, although he is puzzled by his laugh and comment to the corpse of his beloved wife after the murder: "Well, you know what you can do with your pipe dream now, you damned bitch!" He convinces himself that he was insane when he said that. The others, as he is led off, seize this new illusion to regain their own peace: they are now convinced that they knew all along that he was mad, and that they were only humoring him. Parritt and Larry alone are unable to resume their illusions. Antiphonally with Hickey's self-revelation, Parritt confesses that his betrayal was done neither for patriotism nor for money, but because he hates his mother; he is grateful when Larry at last tells him to relieve his guilt by committing suicide. When Larry finally hears Parritt jumping to death from the fire escape, he can face his own complete—no longer philosophically detached—desperation: "I'm the only real convert to death Hickey made here. From the bottom of my coward's heart I mean that now!" As the curtain falls, the others bless the liquor's returning "kick," and laughingly join Hugo, the anarchist editor, in his habitual drunk declamation: "The days grow hot, O Babylon! 'Tis cool beneath thy willow trees!"

IDEAL HUSBAND, AN, a drama in four acts by OSCAR WILDE, produced in 1895 and published in 1899. Setting: London, 1895.

In one of his first reviews BERNARD SHAW highly praised this, the best of Wilde's three seriocomic plays. Though it was modeled on a VICTORIEN SARDOU melodrama (*Dora*) and echoes the Victorian touches of LADY WINDERMERE'S FAN, it scintillates with wit. The idealized character of the "flawless dandy" Lord Goring, as Wilde himself stressed, contains "a great deal of the real Oscar."

Act I. One of the guests at Lady Chiltern's party introduces Mrs. Cheveley, "a genius in the daytime and a beauty at night." She is anxious to meet Sir Robert Chiltern, a young statesman. Soon she demands that he suppress his imminent censure of a dishonest scheme in which she has invested heavily. She reveals her possession of a letter he wrote at the start of his career. It establishes the basis of Chiltern's wealth and position to be his sale of a state secret. Unwilling to face public disgrace and expose clay feet to his worshiping and idealistic wife, Chiltern submits. Lady Chiltern, who had known and disliked Mrs. Cheveley as a scheming and dishonest schoolmate, finds out about his intention to change his official report. She insists he not do so: "You have brought into the political life of our time a nobler atmosphere, a finer attitude towards life, a freer air of purer aims and higher ideals—I know it, and for that I love you." Though crushed, he submits helplessly to her demand.

Act II. He seeks the advice of his best friend, Viscount Goring. This witty dandy, whose levity masks inner strength and wisdom, is courting Chiltern's vivacious young sister. Goring urges Chiltern to confess the truth to his wife. Though the statesman justifies his lapse ("I fought the century with its own weapons and won"), Goring does not approve. But he agrees that Mrs. Cheveley, whom he knew "so little that I got engaged to be married to her once," must now be fought. Then he tries to persuade Lady Chiltern to be less priggish: "Life cannot be understood without much charity, cannot be lived without much charity." But she remains intransigent, unable to conceive of her husband's ever having done anything foolish or wrong. It is Mrs. Cheveley, returning for some jewelry she lost at the party, who is goaded by Lady Chiltern's zealous virtue to reveal the truth. Overwhelmed, Lady Chiltern thrusts her husband away when he returns. He bitterly turns on her. "Let women make no more ideals of men!" he says: "Let them not put them on altars and bow before them, or they may ruin other lives as completely as you—you whom I have so wildly loved—have ruined mine!"

Act III. Herself confused now, Lady Chiltern plans to seek Goring's help and writes him a note. He awaits her when, instead, his father appears. In a comic scene, the old politician castigates his son for his idleness and bachelorhood. While they are in another room, Mrs. Cheveley arrives, eager to resume her one-time intimacy with Goring. When Goring finally gets rid of his father, Chiltern unexpectedly comes for advice. He rushes out angrily when he discovers Mrs. Cheveley, not believing the innocent Goring's protestations. She begs Goring to marry her; for that, she offers to relinquish Chiltern's incriminating letter. Goring attempts to reason her out of it. He fails, but when he confronts her with the theft of lost jewelry and threatens to have her arrested, she hands over the letter. Yet she has the last laugh, for she leaves with Lady Chiltern's carelessly phrased note to Goring; mistaking it for a love declaration, she vows to use it to ruin Chiltern.

Act IV. Chiltern's sister happily agrees to marry Goring, which surprises and delights Goring's father. Then Goring tells Lady Chiltern of Mrs. Cheveley's intention to use her note to him, and urges her to tell her husband about it. She cannot bring herself to confess having sought help elsewhere; but fortunately her note had no salutation, and when Chiltern receives it he takes it as his wife's forgiveness. Now comes word of his appointment to the cabinet. Chiltern's happiness is short-lived, for his wife insists that even though his professional misconduct has remained secret, he must resign from the government. Goring pleads with her not to "condemn him to sterile failure" but to forgive him: "If he has fallen from his altar, do not thrust him into the mire." Chastened by her experience, she finally agrees and also tells him about her note to Goring. Goring leaves with his bride, contented and quite ready never to be "an ideal husband." The Chilterns embrace, secure now in their love and future.

IDIOT'S DELIGHT, a play in three acts by ROBERT E. SHERWOOD, published and produced in 1936. Setting: a hotel in the Italian Alps on the Swiss and Austrian frontiers, a winter of "any imminent year."

This Pulitzer Prize winner, Sherwood's strongest antiwar play, is a "dark comedy"—or vaudeville—in which he nonetheless expresses his optimism about human nature. A great hit both of stage (with Alfred Lunt and Lynn Fontanne) and screen (1939, with Norma Shearer and Clark Gable), the play's dramatic tension was heightened by that of the international situation, just before the outbreak of World War II.

Act I. Various guests arrive at the almost-vacant hotel atop the mountains. They are delayed there because the imminence of war has caused a temporary sealing of the borders. The hotel's social director and the older guests, a French Communist and a German doctor, greet the newcomers: a honeymooning English couple; a munitions manufacturer and his White Russian mistress, Irene; and Harry Van, an American "hoofer," and "Les

Blondes," the bevy of chorus girls in his touring show. Irene finds the hotel's setting suggestive of "an amusing kind of horror." She tells incredible tales of her escapes from the Soviets and her other escapades, and she looks vaguely familiar to Van. The German doctor is eager to get to Switzerland, for he is experimenting on a cure for cancer. He is briefly riled when Van tells him that among other shady deals, he "once sold a remedy for it." "I've been selling phony goods to people of meagre intelligence and great faith" for a long time, Van remarks; but rather than making him contemptuous, "it has given *me* Faith . . . that no matter how much the meek may be bulldozed or gypped they *will* eventually inherit the earth."

Act II. War is declared. Van offers to put on a show with "Les Blondes," and Irene tries to cheer up the English couple. But she is bitter when her munitions manufacturer calls himself God's instrument. "Poor, dear God. Playing Idiot's Delight. The game that never means anything, and never ends," Irene remarks. Vividly she envisions the falling of bombs, the death of the Englishman on the front and of his wife in a cellar, "the embryo from her womb . . . splattered against the face of a dead bishop." Irene adds, "It makes me so proud to think that I am so close to you—who make all this possible." The munitions maker remarks that those who buy and use weapons are guiltier: he merely gives them "what they want"—the "illusion of power" they vote for, cheer for, and glorify. When news comes that Paris has been bombed, the Communist is beside himself with rage at the stupidity of war. Interrupting Van's show, he shouts, "Down with Fascism!" He is taken out by the officers who have joined the festivities and are enjoying the company of the chorus girls. The party continues and Van dances with Irene. Suddenly he remembers where he met her: it was in an Omaha show in which he played. Irene was in another act and, greatly impressed by her, Van had invited her to his room: "No matter how much you may lie, you can't deny the fact that you slept with me in the Governor Bryan Hotel in Omaha in the fall of 1925." He has never forgotten her—"womanhood at its most desirable—and most unreliable." But though Van assures her he is still "crazy about her," she denies being that girl, and leaves to join the manufacturer, who suffers from insomnia. "It is something on his mind," Irene says: "He is like Macbeth." And still denying Van's discovery, she bids him good night: "And thank you for making me laugh so much—to-night."

Act III. The following afternoon Van's troupe, chewing gum, seriously discuss those "awfully sweet boys, those Wops" they danced with. But when the girls hear that they have shot the Communist, they are indignant. Now that war is declared, the honeymooning couple sadly prepare to return home, for the Englishman—an artist who remembers Leonardo da Vinci's calling war "bestial frenzy"—is ready "to do his bit, manning the guns, for civilization." The passports are stamped, but the doctor, instead of going on to Switzerland to conclude his experiments, decides to help the war effort and returns to Germany: "I'll be a maniac, too." Because she has criticized him, the munitions maker sees to it that Irene is detained—and thus faces almost certain death, for the nearby airfield is about to be bombed. As Van talks with Irene, his blonds keep calling him to the waiting bus ("Can you imagine? He stops everything to make another pass at that Russian"). Saying good-bye, Irene admits to Van that "I did know you, slightly, in Omaha!" Alone, she accepts the officer's apology for her detention. When, alluding to his being polite, he asks, "Under these tragic circumstances—what else can I do?" she replies deliberately: "You can refuse to fight! Have you ever thought of that possibility?" Suddenly Van comes in. Irene is touched at his returning "to aid and comfort a damsel in distress," at the cost of his own life. She has always realized, she tells him when he questions her about herself, that "it is no use telling the truth to people whose whole life is a lie." But "you are different. You are an honest man." The bombardment starts. "Let them be idiotic if they wish," Irene says, and suggests they sing. "You know, babe—you look better blonde," Van notes. He starts playing a hymn—in furious jazz-time. As the bombs fall, Irene and Van sing "Onward, Christian Soldiers"—

> Marching as to war—
> With the Cross of Jesus
> Going on before. . . .

IF, a play in four acts by LORD DUNSANY, produced in 1921 and published in 1922. Setting: a London suburb and the wilds of Persia; "ten years ago, three years ago, and the present."

Perhaps the most successful of Dunsany's few full-length plays, this is something like an answer to Barrie's DEAR BRUTUS. In a plot as fantastic as that of Dunsany's one-acters, *If* suggests that mere chance—not character—determines the course of our lives.

An insignificant London clerk lives a contented, suburban life. But offered a magic crystal with which he can relive his past, he catches a commuter train he had missed ten years earlier. That small act leads him into the mountains of Persia. There he becomes a great ruler who experiences fantastic adventures, breaks idols, kills monarchs, and is surrounded by exotic beauties. At the end he is defeated and returns to England a beggar. There everything is magically transformed back into his customary, humdrum, happy life.

IF FIVE YEARS PASS (*Así que pasen cinco años*), a play in three acts by FEDERICO GARCÍA LORCA, published in 1937. Setting: library, forest, etc.

Subtitled "a legend of the times," this posthumous work was written in 1929–30. It is a long and difficult SURREALIST play, in part lyrical. Its characters are designated by type rather than proper name, and its atmosphere, according to Angel del Río, is one "of dreams, with masks, mannequins, clowns, or real people like the rugby player or the card players dehumanized in the manner of the characters of Gómez de la Serna, to whose influence this work is largely indebted" (*Federico García Lorca, 1899–1936*).

A Young Man has agreed to wait five years for his Fiancée. In his library, he does not take the advice of various visitors (including a dead child and his cat) representing abstractions like age, friends, the future, and the present. When the five years are up, the Fiancée, enamored of an athlete, puts the Young Man off. He is regretful over his "lost treasure: my love without an object." A Mannequin urges him to return to the present, represented by a Stenographer. In a forest, there is a play-within-a-play: masked figures discuss time, truth, etc. The Young Man falls in love with the delighted Stenographer, who promises to accompany him "if five years pass." In a card game, gamblers shoot an arrow into a huge ace of hearts —and the Young Man dies: "There are no human beings here."

IF I WERE KING, a play in four acts by JUSTIN HUNTLY MCCARTHY, produced in 1901 and published in 1902. Setting: fifteenth-century France.

This popular romantic drama, dealing with a legendary episode in the life of François Villon, was adapted by Brian Hooker (1880–1946) and William H. Post (? – ?) as *The Vagabond King* (1925, music by Rudolf Friml), one of Friml's most famous operettas, and was made into a film (1938). The play was launched in America, became E. H. Sothern's first great hit as an actor, and featured "Cissy" Loftus, who had just recently divorced McCarthy.

Roistering in a tavern, François Villon is overheard by the incognito Louis XI as he insults the monarch and boasts about what he would do were *he* the king. After Villon fights the (treacherous) Grand Constable, the king gives Villon the opportunity to act on his boasts. For a week he is to have virtually unlimited powers; but unless he in that time wins the love of a royal kinswoman, Katherine de Vaucelles, he must forfeit his life. The swashbuckling Villon defeats the king's enemies, finally wins Katherine's love—and is free to seek his happiness with her. He sings of his love to her: "I could not give you any goodlier thing / If I were king."

IF NOT THUS (*Se non così*), a comedy in three acts by LUIGI PIRANDELLO, produced in 1915 and published (in revised form, as *La ragione degli altri* [*The Rights of Others*]) in 1921. Setting: Italy.

Pirandello's preface is in the form of a letter to the wife, the only character not ruled by passion or sentimentality. Her belief, quoted below, constitutes a favorite theme in Pirandello's writings.

A wife is willing to give up her husband to a mistress who has borne him a child. But the mistress has tired of him, and the wife, believing that "where children are, there is the home," will take him back only if the mistress gives the child to her. The husband is torn between his love for both women, and the mistress is torn between possessive love for her child and the realization that it would be better off with the wealthy couple. The wife's logic wins out; at the end, the mistress sits alone sadly, having given up her child.

IF YOU PLEASE (*S'il vous plaît*), a play in four acts by ANDRÉ BRETON and PHILIPPE SOUPAULT, published in 1920. Setting: a drawing room, an office, a café—all during the afternoon.

An early SURREALIST attempt at automatic writing, this play features mostly irrational dialogue and three different situations and groups of characters. The first act (an evocative love scene like the third act) ends with a wife being shot by her lover; the second features complex doings in a multi-business office; and the third depicts a haunting encounter between a diseased whore and a new client. The fourth act consists only of a brief note by the authors, who proclaim that they "do not want the fourth act printed."

ILE, a one-act play by EUGENE O'NEILL, produced in 1917 and published in 1918. Setting: the Captain's cabin on a steam whaler; early twentieth century, in one of the years preceding World War I.

A revised text of this play was published in THE MOON OF THE CARIBBEES, AND SIX OTHER PLAYS OF THE SEA. Based on a true story, this grim play prefigures such more developed O'Neill characters as Cabot (DESIRE UNDER THE ELMS) and Mary (LONG DAY'S JOURNEY INTO NIGHT).

At the end of a two-year trip, Captain Keeney, "as hard a man as ever sailed the seas," is determined to remain on the icy Arctic Ocean until he fills his quota of whale oil ("ile"). He ruthlessly quells the crew's incipient mutiny, and rejects his wife's request to sail home before she is driven mad by the trip's "brutality and cold and horror." He explains that it is not for money or reputation (other "skippers would never dare sneer to my face"), but "I've always done it . . . and—it don't seem right not to—somehow. I been always first whalin' skipper out o' Homeport." When she finally succeeds in touching his deepest affection and solicitude for her, he agrees to sail home, but just then comes the fateful announcement of a break in the ice. "Dazedly—trying to collect his thoughts," Captain Keeney returns to his earlier determination to get the oil "in spite of all hell, and by God, I ain't agoin' home till I do git it!" As he grimly departs, Mrs. Keeney's sanity snaps. The curtain falls as she plays the organ "wildly and discordantly."

ILENKOV, Vasili Pavlovich (1897–), Russian novelist, wrote one play, *Ploshchad tsvetov* (*The Square of the Flowers,* 1944). A war drama, its title alludes to the Roman square where Giordano Bruno was burned at the stake, thus suggesting a parallel with the play's collective protagonist, the brave Russians who suffered at the hands of the invading Nazis. With a brief preface on Ilenkov, it was published in Alexander Bakshy's collection, *Soviet Scene: Six Plays of Russian Life* (1946).

I'M TALKING ABOUT JERUSALEM, a play in three acts by ARNOLD WESKER, published and produced in 1960. Setting: Norfolk, England; 1946–59.

The protagonists of this play, the last of *The Wesker Trilogy* that begins with CHICKEN SOUP WITH BARLEY, are Ada Kahn and her husband, Dave Simmonds. It traces their life in a William Morris idyll, their "new Jerusalem." Their escape from urban society and mechanization into rusticity and creative craftsmanship fails. Dave finally says: "Machinery and modern techniques have come about to make me the odd man out. . . . I don't count. . . . Maybe Sarah's right, maybe you can't build on your own."

IMBECILE, THE (*L'imbecille*), a one-act play by LUIGI PIRANDELLO, produced in 1922 and published in 1926. Setting: a newspaper office in a provincial town in early twentieth-century Italy.

Pirandello's dramatization of a short story he published in 1912 depicts a dying consumptive, Luca Fazio, as he outwits the feuding politicians who want to use him. One of them, the editor, calls a recent suicide "an imbecile": having nothing to lose, he should have shot the editor's political enemy before hanging himself. Fazio, himself about to commit suicide, has been sent on just such an errand by the editor's enemy. Faced with death, Fazio becomes disgusted with the selfish pettiness and hypocrisy of politicians. He makes the editor cringe before his gun and then write out an admission that it is not imbecility but "loathing and pity for my cowardice" that has stopped Fazio from killing him. Then Fazio goes out "to do something a little more difficult than anything you've had to do here this evening."

IMPORTANCE OF BEING EARNEST, THE, a drama in three acts by OSCAR WILDE, produced in 1895 and published in 1899. Setting: London and an English country house, 1895.

Subtitled "a trivial comedy for serious people," this play is generally acknowledged to be Wilde's masterpiece and among the finest of English comedies. As Wilde himself said, the play is "a delicate bubble of fancy"; but he noted, though perhaps facetiously, that the play does have a philosophy: "We should treat all the trivial things of life seriously, and all the serious things of life with sincere and studied triviality." Throughout, Wilde parodies the WELL-MADE PLAY and satirizes Victorian earnestness: the first act ends with Algernon's statement that nobody ever talks anything but nonsense. However lightly and absurdly, Wilde's comedy skims almost every conceivable topic of importance. A mad, witty farce peppered with epigrams, an *Alice in Wonderland* drawing-room comedy that is inimitably Wildean, it was immediately hailed by audiences and critics—with the notable exception of BERNARD SHAW.

Act I. Algernon (Algy) Moncrieff, a playboy, is visited by a friend who wants to marry Algy's cousin, Gwendolen Fairfax. The friend's name is supposed to be Ernest, but Algy finds his cigarette case affectionately inscribed "from little Cecily" to "Uncle Jack." John (Jack) Worthing soon con-

The Importance of Being Earnest. Left to right: Algy (Robert Flemyng), Cecily (Jane Baxter), Gwendolyn (Pamela Brown), Jack (John Gielgud). New York, 1947. (*Vandamm Photo, Theatre Collection, New York Public Library*)

fesses that his name is "Ernest in town and Jack in the country," where he has a pretty young ward, Cecily Cardew. Before her he must adopt a high moral tone. To get away to town, he pretends to look after a debauched brother named Ernest. Algy calls such a double life "Bunburying," something he does himself: he pretends to have an out-of-town invalid friend, Bunbury, whom he uses as a pretext for his out-of-town escapades. Soon Gwendolen arrives for tea with her mother, Lady Bracknell. Though his aunt is quite formidable, Algy adroitly steers her out in order to leave the lovers by themselves. Gwendolen helps Jack to propose to her: "I think it only fair to tell you quite frankly beforehand that I am fully determined to accept you." She has always wanted to love someone named Ernest, and he now cannot persuade her that any other name would do as well—for instance Jack: "It does not thrill. It produces absolutely no vibrations." When Lady Bracknell is informed of the engagement, she interviews Jack: "I have always been of opinion that a man who desires to get married should know either everything or nothing. Which do you know?" His negative answer pleases her: "I do not approve of anything that tampers with natural ignorance. Ignorance is like a delicate fruit; touch it, and the bloom is gone." She adds, "The whole theory of modern education is radically unsound. Fortunately in England, at any rate, education produces no effect whatsoever." Jack's qualifications seem adequate until he confesses to being a foundling left in a handbag in the cloakroom at Victoria Station. Considering this "to display a contempt for the ordinary decencies of family life that reminds one of the worst excesses of the French Revolution," Lady Bracknell insists that to be an eligible suitor he must produce at least one parent, and sweeps out after Gwendolen. The girl briefly returns to vow eternal love to "Ernest" and gets Jack's country address. Algy notes it unobtrusively: he is curious about Jack's ward and has therefore been eager to discover the country address.

Act II. In the country, Cecily is discussing Uncle Jack's wicked brother Ernest with Miss Prism, her spinster governess, but the elderly local rector exhorts Cecily to be more attentive to her studies: "Were I fortunate enough to be Miss Prism's pupil, I would hang upon her lips"; when the spinster glares at him he quickly adds, "I spoke metaphorically." Miss Prism and the rector go for a stroll and Algy arrives, posing as Uncle Jack's bad brother. He and Cecily immediately fall in love. Just after they walk off together Jack appears in deep mourning. Lugubriously he tells the rector and Miss Prism, when they return from their walk, that his brother Ernest has just died. "What a lesson for him! I trust he will profit by it," Miss Prism remarks. For Gwendolen's sake, Jack makes arrangements to be christened "Ernest" later in the day, and then is appalled to hear Cecily's happy news of "Ernest's" arrival. Algy blandly promises his "brother" to reform in the future. As soon as they are alone Jack insists on Algy's immediate departure. Algy's farewell to Cecily turns into a prolonged and amusing love scene. Cecily admits that she has long been fascinated by the thought of Jack's wicked brother. She had always hoped to marry someone named Ernest and therefore had worked out their engagement some weeks before. Her diary entries confirm it—and she has also written his love letters to herself: "The three you wrote me after I had broken off the engagement are so beautiful, and so badly spelled, that even now I can hardly read them without crying a little." Just as Gwendolen has insisted with Jack, so Cecily insists that Algy's name is an important part of her love. Another name—for instance Algy—would not do: "I might respect you, Ernest, I might admire your character, but I fear that I should not be able to give you my undivided attention." No sooner is Algy off to arrange for his rechristening when the confusion is heightened by the appearance of Gwendolen. The girls at once become affectionate friends, but when it turns out that both are engaged to "Ernest" their friendship turns to indignant hostility. Jack and Algy's return clears up this misunderstanding. But when the girls discover that neither man's name is really Ernest, they embrace tenderly and, now reunited in their sorrow, they leave the men. The aggrieved men eat up all the muffins. When troubled, Algy says, "I refuse everything except food and drink."

Act III. Cecily and Gwendolen soon return for an explanation. They immediately accept the men's ardent protestations, for, as Gwendolen says, "In matters of grave importance, style, not sincerity, is the vital thing." The names do, however, remain a barrier, until Jack and Algy reveal their intention to be christened "Ernest" this very day. Then the redoubtable Lady Bracknell appears, somewhat disconcerted by the many engagements, "considerably above the proper average that statistics have laid down for our guidance." Her coolness toward Cecily vanishes when she learns of the girl's wealth. But Jack refuses to give his consent for her marriage to Algy unless he is allowed to marry Gwendolen. Being refused, Jack surmises that "a passionate celibacy is all that any of us can look forward to." Someone mentions the governess's name, and Lady Bracknell starts: "Is this Miss Prism a female of repellent aspect, remotely connected with education?" Prism turns out to be the governess who once lost a baby, Lady Bracknell's nephew, in a handbag. For a moment Jack—mistakenly but gallantly—embraces the spinster: "Mother, I forgive you." When he realizes that he actually is Algy's elder brother Ernest, he apologizes: "It is a terrible thing for a man to find out suddenly that all his life he has been speaking nothing but the truth." The couples (including Prism and the rector) embrace happily and Lady Bracknell criticizes their levity; but Jack concludes, "I've now realized for the first time in my life the vital Importance of Being Earnest."

IMPROVISATION, OR THE SHEPHERD'S CHAMELEON (*L'Impromptu de l'Alma, ou le caméléon du berger*), a one-act play by EUGÈNE IONESCO, produced in 1956 and published in 1958. Setting: the author's study, 1950's.

The title echoes *L'Impromptu de Versailles* (1663) and *L'Impromptu de Paris* (1937), plays in which, repectively, Molière and JEAN GIRAUDOUX dramatized their theories of art and ridiculed others. Ionesco does the same here.

Asleep over his table, a ball-point pen in hand, Eugène Ionesco is visited by three "doctors in theatrology," all named Bartholomeus. In the play-within-a-play he is writing (dramatizing what has just occurred), Ionesco attempts to portray his ideas on playwriting. The Bartholomeuses set forth to teach him "costumology, historicization, decorology, and audiencology," and urge him to become existentialist and adapt the alienation techniques of BERTOLT BRECHT. As their speech and antics become more extravagant, Ionesco becomes increasingly rattled and finally starts braying like a donkey. He is saved by his no-nonsense charwoman, who chases out the doctors. Then Ionesco starts addressing the audience on his own theories of drama: "For me, the theatre is the projection onto the stage of the world within: it is in my dreams, my anguish, my dark desires, my inner contradictions that I reserve the right to find the stuff of my plays." He becomes more pedantic and the charwoman throws a doctor's gown over him. Ionesco realizes that he has fallen into his own trap: "I'm sorry, I won't do it again, this is the exception—" but the charwoman (punning on the title of Brecht's THE EXCEPTION AND THE RULE) interjects: "Not the rule!"

IN ABRAHAM'S BOSOM, "The Tragedy of a Southern Negro" in seven scenes by PAUL GREEN, produced in 1926 and published in 1927. Setting: North Carolina, 1885–1906.

Green's most powerful folk drama—the 1927 Pulitzer Prize winner—features "a latter-day Moses," Abraham ("Abe") McCranie. An

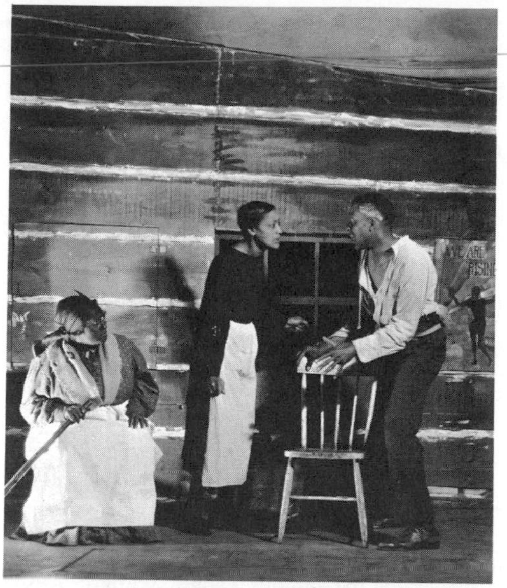

In Abraham's Bosom. Abe (Julius Bledsoe), his wife (Rose McClendon), and Muh Mack (Abbie Mitchell). New York, 1927. (*Culver Pictures*)

utterly selfless visionary, he is defeated not only by the hostile white environment but also by the Negroes he is trying to help—and by his own human shortcomings. The common Negroes, including Abe's shiftless guitar-playing son and his old aunt Muh Mack, provide a comic note in the grim tragic action. The play was moved uptown after its initial Provincetown Players production, and has been revived frequently.

Scene 1. Negro workers joke and sing at their lunch break in the turpentine woods of Colonel McCranie, a Southern gentleman. They respect Abe, who is reading, for his strength, intelligence, and intensity, but they also resent him: "Trouble 'bout de nigger, wanter rise him up wid eddication—fact!" They blame "de white blood in him coming to de top," for Abe is a mulatto—and the Colonel's bastard son. Abe persists in asking the Colonel for a schoolhouse so he "kin teach de colored boys and gals." The Colonel's legitimate son, objecting to Abe's "sass," strikes Abe—who strikes the white man back. Thereupon the Colonel must whip Abe, who weeps: "I yo' son too, you my daddy." Abe's girl gently washes his welts, and takes him to the woods to "love you, make you fohgit." Thereupon the others start dancing erotically and sing, "'Way, 'way up in de Rock of Ages, / In God's bosom gwine be my pillow."

Scene 2. It is three years later and Abe's wife has had a baby. Abe's old aunt Muh Mack deplores his persistent studying and his pride. His wife agrees, but comforts and encourages Abe. The Colonel comes to see the baby, and deeds Abe the house and surrounding land. After commending Abe—"you the first nigger I ever see so determined," he had remarked earlier—and complaining of his white son, the Colonel further surprises Abe by getting him the schoolhouse. "I fohgives him all," the overjoyed Abe says, and vows to be a new man: "I gwine lead." He picks up his baby: "I gwine raise him up a light unto peoples. He be a new Moses, he bring de chillun out of bondage, out'n sin and ign'ance."

Scene 3. In time most of Abe's pupils drop out of the school. One of the Negro board members comes to the schoolhouse to tell Abe it is being closed, for Abe has whipped a student and the community "ain't gwine stand foh no nigger beating deir young 'uns." The boy stole and lied, Abe protests, and furiously chases the board member out: "You know I trying do right. You weak, coward, no backbone."

Scene 4. Abe and his family are impoverished and starving fifteen years later. His pride has cost him their property and, as Muh Mack complains, he was run out by whites and blacks there as well as elsewhere. "He gwine be a big man yit," says his loyal wife, who now takes in washing. Their son has turned out worthless, but is doted upon by Muh Mack, who dances and sings with him. Abe comes home: talking back to the whites, he has lost his job. Almost broken, he agrees to return to the country, although the Colonel is now dead: "Dere at last I knows I'm going to build up and lead!"

Scene 5. Abe is completing a speech, three years later, to urge the founding of a school that will bring Negroes "freedom of the mind." Ignoring his recitation, Muh Mack berates him for causing trouble "wid yo' schooling and mess," and for forbidding his son the house. "They ain't no man, flesh of my flesh or not, going to lie rotten with liquor and crooks around me," Abe says, and continues his speech. To himself he admits doubts and fears: "You're right, I'm none of yours, nor my own mother either."

Scene 6. Abe has been chased off by the crowds. On a country road, his white half-brother chides him for neglecting the fields. In a fury Abe kills him. Hysterical, he has visions of the future and the past: a lynching party, and his father and mother going off to the bushes. "Stop dat, Mammy, Colonel Mack!" he screams; "Stop dat, I tell you, dat's me! Dat's me!"

Scene 7. Meanwhile his son, who has spent time in a chain gang for assault, comes into Abe's shack. Soon he plays, sings, and dances with Muh Mack. Abe returns, bruised and swaying, and tells his family to run away. He discovers that it was his own son who had egged the crowds on to run him off. As the lynch mob approaches, only his wife remains with Abe. "I've tried to walk de path, but I'm po' and sinful," Abe prays: "Give me peace, rest—rest in yo' bosom—if it is dy will." Then he walks out and is shot by the lynchers. His wife falls down beside his body, weeping.

"IN GOOD KING CHARLES'S GOLDEN DAYS," "A True History That Never Happened" in two acts by BERNARD SHAW, published and produced in 1939. Setting: England, 1680.

In contrast with his other "dramas of my

dotage" (as Shaw called his later works), this last full-length play by Shaw is a pleasant intellectual romp that contains no apocalyptic visions or implications. There also is next to no plot: the dramatic conflict consists of lively and highly entertaining arguments on government, science, art, religion, and related topics. His preface explains the characterization of Charles, whose "reputation as a Solomonic polygamist has not only obscured his political ability, but eclipsed the fact that he was the best of husbands," and Shaw's interest in creating a hypothetical confrontation of great Restoration figures. The title of the play comes from a famous eighteenth-century song, "The Vicar of Bray." The very long first act is usually performed in two parts.

Act I. In his library, Isaac Newton is visited by King Charles II, incognito as Mr. Rowley; George Fox, the zealous Quaker founder; James, the Duke of York—"that very disagreeable character[,] a man of principle," as his brother Charles calls him; the artist Godfrey Kneller; and three of Charles's beautiful mistresses: the witty and earthy —but genial—Nell Gwynn; Barbara Villiers, Duchess of Cleveland, who is unpleasant and whose temper repeatedly flares; and the charming and clever Louise de Kéroualle, Duchess of Portsmouth, who has come to buy a love charm. Newton himself, brilliant though somewhat literal-minded, immediately assures the jealous Barbara, mathematically, that Charles could not possibly have been unfaithful to her 100,000 times. The men's intellectual discussions are periodically interrupted by the women's entertaining catty outbursts, and there is a wrestling bout when Newton attempts to throw out the "Popish blockhead" James after he insults the name of Galileo ("the arch infidel") and threatens the Royal Society ("a club of damnable heretics"). Charles and James discuss modern kingship, Catholicism, and the Popish Plot; in contrast to the wise and witty Charles, who lacks military ambition and cruelty, James projects a strong monarchy, and Charles predicts that he will be beheaded like their father. Newton asks to be left alone to work on his studies of the prophesies in the Book of Daniel and his world chronology, but what started as a morning's interruption threatens to discredit his life's work when Fox, fulminating against clergy and churches ("They stand between Man and his Maker"), ridicules Newton's naïve acceptance of Archbishop Ussher's date of the Creation at 4004 B.C. Kneller, who believes that "the world must learn from its artists because God made the world as an artist," further unsettles Newton: for Newton's law of motion (and gravitation) in a straight line, Kneller aggressively substitutes his own belief that "motion in a curve is the law of nature." The discussions end with the call and departure for dinner, as Newton wonders "what is amiss with the perihelion of Mercury."

Act II. Late that afternoon Charles is napping in the boudoir of Queen Catherine of Braganza, his loving and pious wife, who soon awakens him. Considering him "the very best husband that ever lived," she does not resent his infidelities with "the servants of your common pleasures," which have set her "free to be something more" to him. They discuss the ungovernable English—hence Charles's success as a king: "I enjoy myself and let the people see me doing it, and leave things as they are." Since the Catholic Catherine will not be safe in England, Charles begs her to return to Portugal after his death. He speculates on the eternal problem of civilization—"how to choose a ruler" —and then promises Catherine that he will convert to Catholicism for her before his death. Tenderly, she helps him dress and he leaves for a council meeting.

IN ROME (*I Rom*), a historical play in one act by AUGUST STRINDBERG, published and produced in 1870. Setting: a studio in eighteenth-century Rome.

This rhymed-verse drama, though flatulent and unsuccessful, was the first Strindberg play to reach the boards (eleven performances in Stockholm's Royal Theatre). *In Rome* dramatizes the early struggles of the famous Danish sculptor Albert Thorvaldsen, whose centenary was celebrated that year (1870). Strindberg identified his hero with Ibsen's BRAND—and even more with himself. He portrayed the young Thorvaldsen in his studio, almost compelled to yield to his father's demand that he foresake art for business, and ready to smash his great sculpture.

IN THE JUNGLE OF THE CITIES (*Im Dickicht der Städte*), a play in eleven scenes by BERTOLT BRECHT, produced in 1923 and published in 1927. Setting: Chicago, 1912–15.

Brecht's third play, a complex and enigmatic fantasy set in a mythical Chicago, was originally titled *Im Dickicht* (*In the Swamp;* literally, "In the Thicket") and subtitled "The Fight of Two Men in the Giant City of Chicago." In a brief prefatory note, Brecht commented about the "inexplicable ring-fight of two men" (a struggle that is homosexual, metaphysical, and moral): "Do not rack your brains over the motives of this fight, but participate in the human stakes, impartially judge the opponents' style, and direct your interest to the finish."

Scene 1. Shlink, a middle-aged Malayan lumber dealer, wants to dominate over and therefore picks a quarrel with George Garga, an impoverished but idealistic assistant in a rental library. Garga's sweetheart has already been seduced by one of Shlink's animal-nicknamed, gangsterlike henchmen. Even her remonstrations and his own family's poverty do not move Garga, and he refuses to sell Shlink his unimportant opinion of an unimportant book. Furiously rejecting economic security for freedom, Garga sacrifices his girl, throws away most of his clothes, and runs off. Shlink's gang is delighted: "We finally got under his skin."

Scenes 2 through 9. The battle between Garga and Shlink has begun. When Garga comes to Shlink's office, he discovers his sister there, in love with Shlink. Garga is ready to fight, and the wealthy Shlink happily gives him his home and his lumber business to make their fight fairer. Immediately Garga makes a fraudulent deal in Shlink's name. Shlink moves to the house of Garga's parents, whom he helps support. But he does not reciprocate the sister's love for him. Eventually, she and Garga's sweetheart become prostitutes. The battle between the men continues; Garga marries his soiled sweetheart, and Shlink sleeps with the sister. Garga's fraudulent deal comes to light, and he decides to go to prison in Shlink's place. At the same time, however, he prepares a document in which he denounces Shlink to the police as his sister's rapist and his wife's molester. Shlink is reestablished in his business three years later, when Garga returns from prison. Garga's wife goes off with her lover (one of Shlink's henchmen) and his sister admits she still loves Shlink. Garga awaits the total destruction of his enemy: he has just produced the denunciation of Shlink, whose lynching is imminent.

Scenes 10 and 11. At an abandoned site along Lake Michigan, Garga and Shlink have their last talk. Shlink tells Garga he loves him, and then deplores man's eternal solitude: "Love, physical love, is man's only redemption." But fleshly contact provides insufficient communication for people: "If you crammed a ship to its bursting point with human bodies, man would still freeze in loneliness. . . . So great is our isolation that even conflict is impossible. The jungle, this is whence mankind comes." Garga declares himself the winner of their match, though he concedes the absence of a resolution and an understanding. Ideals are so much drivel to him now, and he runs off—feeling young and alive, and safe. Just before the lynch mob arrives, Shlink dies. His last words are to Garga's sister: "Throw a rag over my face, have compassion." A week later, Garga's abandoned family seek shelter in "the jungle of the city." Callously, Garga himself intends to go to New York and sells the lumber business, which now lies in ashes. "To be alone is a good thing," he remarks as he clutches the money he has just received from the sale: "Chaos is used up now. It was the best time."

IN THE SHADOW OF THE GLEN, a one-act play by J. M. SYNGE, produced in 1903 and published in 1904. Setting: evening in a cottage at the head of a Wicklow (Ireland) glen.

Synge's short first play, loosely based on Irish folklore, is a somber comedy. Though innocent enough, this story of marital incompatibility offended its first audiences. WILLIAM BUTLER YEATS described Nora, "of the glens, as melancholy as a curlew, driven to distraction by her own sensitiveness, her own fineness." Synge himself is reflected in the portrayal of the Tramp.

Nora Burke is lighting candles as a Tramp knocks and seeks shelter. Kindly she provides him with drink and a pipe, and tells him how her husband, now lying covered with a sheet, died that day, "the time the shadow was going up through the glen." She goes out to find a neighboring young farmer to announce her husband's death. No sooner is she gone than the "corpse" comes to life. Old Dan Burke has feigned death to spy on his young wife. Now he has a drink, arms himself, and, as Nora returns with the farmer, lies down again and demands the Tramp's silence. Expecting to marry Nora, the young farmer counts the money Burke has left. She admits "it's a hard woman I am to please." Her husband, whom she married for security, has turned out to be a sour, insensitive old man. In her loneliness and the desolation of the glen, where she saw "nothing but the mists rolling down the bog," she has talked to and sought affection from passing men. Very conscious of life's brevity, she thinks of people she knows, "the young growing behind me and the old passing." As she describes her husband "sitting up there in his bed with no teeth in him, and a rough word in his mouth," he does indeed sit up—and sneeze. Angrily he casts her out. The young farmer, a coward who wanted to marry her for her money, remains silent. The Tramp, however, offers to take Nora: "You'll be hearing the herons crying out over the black lakes, and you'll be hearing the grouse and the owls with them, and the larks and the big thrushes when the days are warm; and it's not from the like of them you'll be hearing a tale of getting old." Nora feels compassion for her hard husband as she leaves with the Tramp. The young farmer and old Dan Burke sit down to have a drink.

IN THE ZONE, a one-act play, by EUGENE O'NEILL, produced in 1917 and published in 1919. Setting: a ship's forecastle, 1915.

This is the second of O'Neill's S.S. GLENCAIRN cycle and was first published in THE MOON OF THE CARIBBEES, AND SIX OTHER PLAYS OF THE SEA.

Aboard a British ammunition-carrying steamer entering the enemy submarine zone, the nervous crewmen become suspicious of their wistful and more cultivated mate Smitty, whom they hysterically take for a German spy. They immerse in water a black box he has hidden under his mattress, and when he comes in they bind and gag him. Carefully opening the box, they find love letters, but are not persuaded of their authenticity until they read the last one, in which Smitty's fiancée rejects him because, as she has written, he prefers drunkenness to her love and faith in him. "A bit av a dried-up flower,—a rose, maybe," falls out of the packet, and, now thoroughly shamed, they untie Smitty. As he noiselessly weeps, they crawl into their bunks and go to sleep.

INADMISSIBLE EVIDENCE, a play in two acts by JOHN OSBORNE, produced in 1964 and published in 1965. Setting: a solicitor's office in London, 1964.

This is a partly EXPRESSIONIST portrayal of Bill Maitland, a middle-aged failure. In an opening sequence Bill, the head of a small law firm, dreams of his own trial and sees himself for what he is.

Subsequent episodes with his colleagues and clients depict simultaneously external happenings and Bill's painful thoughts. He is revealed as an unpleasant but pathetic man, obsessed by sex and gradually deserted by those around him.

INCIDENT AT VICHY, a one-act play by ARTHUR MILLER, produced in 1964 and published in 1965. Setting: a detention room in Vichy, France; 1942.

Like Miller's earlier AFTER THE FALL, whose looming symbol also is Nazi bestiality, this long one-acter deals with man's guilt and redemption. Fredric Wertham's *A Sign for Cain: An Exploration of Human Violence* (1966) includes an extended discussion of the play.

A group of men and a boy, all suspected of being Jews, await Nazi interrogation. Their terror mounts as they are individually summoned out and realize that they will be slaughtered. The last two are an Austrian nobleman who will be released (a detached liberal who has rejected Nazism because it is vulgar) and a Jewish doctor. The latter persuades the protesting nobleman that he, like everyone else, "has his Jew" to hate: his only salvation is to "face your own complicity with this . . . your own humanity." The nobleman finally accepts his guilt for the Nazi murders, but the doctor persists: "It is not your guilt I want, it's your responsibility." When the nobleman comes back from his interrogation he gives the doctor his pass, thus sacrificing himself to free the doctor.

INDIA, whose classical treatises on dance and drama are the ultimate source of all Asian theatrical expression, completely integrated drama, music, and dance. In modern times Indian drama has been best known for the work of RABINDRANATH TAGORE. The most professionally polished theatres were those of the actor-producer Prithvi Raj [Kapoor], who starred in plays written for him from 1944 until his physical collapse in 1960. Much of India's twentieth-century drama is based on history and on tales of the Hindu, Sanskrit religious epics *Ramayana* and *Mahabharata*. It is modernized and Westernized yet endemic with its vestiges of ancient folk dance and ritual. The modern theatrical center is New Delhi, and modern plays often deal with contemporary topics that are so controversial that their authors are jailed. English and Hindi remained India's principal languages even after Independence (1947); but there are some sixty others in as many provinces, in addition to countless dialects. Different modern drama appears in all of the provinces, the most important of which are Bengal, Madras, Andrah, and Bombay, which in 1960 was divided into Maharashtra and Gujarat but remained the home of the Gujarat-speaking Parsis as well as of Hindi and English theatres.

Britain introduced the new Western drama to India in the nineteenth century. Ironically it there manifested itself with anticolonial and other political-protest plays that were frequently banned by the authorities. Though not characteristic of the pioneer Bengali poet and playwright Michael Madhusadana Dutt (1824–73) and of its greatest writer, Tagore, such drama was important in Bengal's professional theatre. This theatre was founded by the actor-director-playwright Girish Chandra Gosh* (1844–1912) and launched with Dinabandhu Mitra's (1829–73) "oriental *Uncle Tom's Cabin*" (as the play was characterized) about impoverished peasants and a brutal plantation overseer, *Neeldarpana* (*Nil Durpan,* 1861). Gosh disguised his own nationalistic drama as mythological or historical tragedy, as in *Vilwamangal* (translated in 1956) and his play on *Sirajuddaulah,* Bengal's last Indian ruler, who was betrayed to the British in 1757. Another early writer, Dwijendra Lal Roy (1864–1913), after a series of farces wrote fashionable and still-produced nationalistic history plays: *Mewar Patan* (*The Fall of Mevar,* 1908); *Shah Jehan* (1909); and a powerful portrayal of the Hindu monarch of antiquity, *Chandragupta* (1911).

Early Marathi playwrights in Bombay include Bhargavaram Vitthol Warerkar (1883–), among whose nearly two hundred works are NATURALISTIC dramas of social protest; Ram Ganesh Gadkari (1885–1919), who achieved distinction with his five tragicomic social problem plays; and Purushottam Lakshman Deshpande (1919–), who has been widely praised for his characterizations, such as that of a liberal reformer in *Tuze Ahe Tujpashi* (1957). The commercial Parsi theatre flourished in Bombay in the late nineteenth and early twentieth centuries, each company hiring its own resident playmaker. The theatre of the Gujarati was founded by Vishnudas Bhave (1820–1901), author of some fifty plays, many of them based on the epics. Among later Gujarati playwrights are Dayabhai Dholshaji (1877–1902), whose drama employs contemporary settings; the scholar and politician Kanaialad Maneklal Munshi (1887–), the author of over seventy novels, histories, and plays that satirize social conventions, protest against political injustice, and plead for reforms and female emancipation, as in his masterpiece *Kakani Shashi* (1928); and Chandravadan Mehta (1901–), who distinguished himself with *Ag-gadi* (1932), a melodrama about contemporary railway workers, and also wrote a number of comedies.

Particularly popular in modern Madras have been the mythological pageants produced by the Rajamanickam troupe. In the neighboring state of Andhra, the pioneer Telugu dramatist was K. Veerasalingam Pantulu (1848–1919). Other playwrights of note were G. Appa Rao (1861–1915), who early in his career produced significant social drama; and Adya Rangacharya (1904–), who, in the Kannada-speaking southern state of Mysore, after early social-message drama like *Harijanwar* (1932), turned to writing experimental plays. Notable Urdu playwrights include Rajinder

*Also spelled Ghosh and Ghose, and not to be confused with the poet-playwright Aurobindo Ghose (1872-1950), who wrote verse drama based on Hindu and Greek legends.

Singh Bedi (1915–), who has depicted passions in sometimes turgid drama like *Bejan Chizan* (1943). Hindi theatre achieved stature with the historical drama of the successful 1940's novelist Jayshankar Prasad (? – ?), especially with his *Skandagupta* (1928) and *Chandragupta* (1931), both of which exemplify his rich style and complex characterization. More recent plays popular in the Hindustani theatre are those of the aforementioned Prithvi Raj and those of the left-wing novelist-historian-journalist Khawaja Ahmed Abbas (1914–), which advocate harmony between post-partition India and PAKISTAN, and which depict Muslim peasant life in documentaries that resemble LIVING NEWSPAPER DRAMA.

In North India, the award-winning Punjab State Dramatist of the Year (1959) was the short-story writer, critic, and scholar Balwant Gargi (1918–); he himself translated his *Kanak di Balli* (*The Mango Tree,* 1954), a drama of ill-starred lovers, which has been frequently performed in the Soviet Union. Gargi also published the comprehensive original surveys of *Theatre in India* (1962) and *Folk Theater of India* (1966), both of which have bibliographies of the relatively few works on the subject. Also authoritative and readily accessible is the India chapter of Faubion Bowers's *Theatre in the East* (1956).

INDIPOHDI, a blank-verse "dramatic poem" in five acts by GERHART HAUPTMANN, published in 1920 and produced in 1922. Setting: a remote island.

First produced as *Das Opfer* (*The Sacrifice*), this play resembles Shakespeare's *The Tempest.* Even more, however, its exotic setting (the natives are Indians) and abnegating hero (though he is named after Shakespeare's character) resemble those of THE WHITE SAVIOR.

The natives have long honored Prospero, a magician cast upon their island, as a divine leader. His son is shipwrecked there, falls in love with Prospero's daughter, and (together with a jealous native) wars against his unrecognized father. He is defeated by Prospero's magic and is doomed as a sacrifice to the volcanic demon. When he sees his children's deep love for each other, however, Prospero countenances it, frees his son, and prepares instead to hurl himself into the volcanic crater. In his final soliloquy he bids farewell to the world and seeks the unknown nothingness ("Indipohdi") of man's origin and destination: "I feel thee, I am sinking into thee! Nothingness!" —and all vanishes in mist.

INDONESIA—the thousands of islands including the Sunda chain of Sumatra, Java, Bali, Borneo, and Celebes—is more notable for its music and dance than for its drama. As in neighboring MALAYSIA, many types of puppet and shadow plays, as well as Western-type modern entertainments, are produced throughout the area. Particularly in Java the indigenous modern *ketoprak* and *ludruk* flourished in the 1920's; both are REPRESENTATIONAL and use improvised dialogue and action, but in the *ludruk*, popular farce and melodrama, dancing and music occur only between scenes. A Sundanese genre that originated in modern west Java is *sandiwara,* musical comedy romances performed by troupes on festive private occasions like marriages, births, etc., when whole villages or *kampong* (town districts) participate as audience.

Modern Indonesian drama began with the subsequently prominent writer Sanusi Pané (1905–); his *Air Langga* (1928) portrays eleventh-century Javanese history. Pané wrote other plays in Dutch, and a later drama about social problems in modern India, *Manusia Baru* (1940). During and after World War II nationalism stimulated the Indonesian theatre—especially during the Japanese occupation. It was then that another playwright of the 1930's, Armijn Pané (1908–), wrote propaganda comedy; afterwards he produced a play about an idealistic flirt, *Djinak-djinak Merpati* (1944), the title work of his collected drama (1953). Usmar Ismail (1921–), an important dramatist though his plays have never been popular, began to write during the occupation; his domestic plays, collected as *Sedih dan Gembira* (1948), probe man's responsibility to man—as in *Api,* in which a selfish scientist is destroyed by his own military invention while his colleague is praised for finding a cure for malaria. The more popular one-act plays constitute most of the published native drama, greatly stimulated by the Indonesian Dramatic Academy workshops and The Performing Arts Theatre of Jakarta.

Major studies with extensive bibliographies are A. Teeuw's *Modern Indonesian Literature* (1967) and James L. Peacock's anthropological analysis of *ludruk* theatre, *Rites of Modernization: Symbolic and Social Aspects of Indonesian Proletarian Drama* (1968).

INFERNAL MACHINE, THE (*La Machine infernale*), a play in four acts by JEAN COCTEAU, published and produced in 1934. Setting: legendary Thebes and vicinity.

This histrionic, tragicomic modernization of the myth of Oedipus conceives the universe as a destructive, "infernal machine." For the last act, Cocteau refurbished his versions of Sophocles's play previously made for Igor Stravinsky's opera-oratorio *Oedipus-rex* (1927) and his own play *Œdipe-roi* (1928). Otherwise *The Infernal Machine* —with its Sphinx, its ghost of Laius, and its idiomatically farcical remarks on the myth's significance —is original. Francis Fergusson (*The Idea of a Theater,* 1949) considered it "a masterpiece of the modern theater."

Act I: "The Ghost." A Voice summarizes the story of Oedipus, and exhorts the audience to observe the unraveling of its plot, "one of the most perfect machines devised by the infernal gods for the mathematical destruction of a mortal." On the ramparts of Thebes at night, two worried guards speculate on the identity of the Sphinx threatening the city. They report the appearance of the ghost of their recently slain king, Laius, who anticipated dreadful punishment because he discovered

The Infernal Machine, Act II. Oedipus (Jean Marais) and the Sphinx (Jeanne Moreau). Paris, 1954. (*French Cultural Service*)

forbidden secrets, and begged them to warn Queen Jocasta. Soon the queen ascends the ramparts, accompanied by the high priest, Tiresias. As he accidentally treads on her scarf, the vain, foolish Jocasta, in her "international accent of royalty," cries out, "Zizi! You're walking on my scarf," and complains that "always this scarf is strangling me. . . . It will be the death of me." She is excited by the younger guard, whose legs she admires, and she questions him about the ghost. As they talk the ghost appears and pleads with them, but without being seen or heard by anybody. After Jocasta and Tiresias leave, disappointed at his failure to appear, the guards can see the ghost. He starts to warn them about the coming of Oedipus. Before he can finish he vanishes, screaming: "Mercy! They've got me! Help! Ended! . . ."

Act II: "The Sphinx." That same night, on a hill overlooking Thebes, the Sphinx—Nemesis in the form of a young girl—talks with jackal-headed Anubis, the Egyptian god of the dead. Though the Sphinx is tired of killing young Thebans, Anubis insists on their obeying orders: "We have our gods and they have theirs. That's what is called infinity." After an interlude with a Theban gossip, young Oedipus appears. He is ambitious and fearless despite the dread oracle and his slaying of a man at the crossroad: "The thing is to clear all obstacles, to wear blinkers, and not to give way to self-pity." Failing to entice him as a girl, the Sphinx reveals herself, and overpowers him with a long incantation. But she falls in love with him, and reveals the riddle's answer. Oedipus runs away victoriously, and the Sphinx despairs at his ingratitude. Soon he returns to carry off the Sphinx's earthly body, his trophy, "Over my shoulder! Like a demigod!" He jubilantly anticipates marrying Jocasta, while veiled Nemesis grieves about mankind. Murmurs envelop the gigantic veiled divinities, but the oblivious Oedipus rejoices: "I shall be king!"

Act III: "The Wedding Night." The Voice describes the bedroom-farce act that follows, how, "in spite of a few hints and civilities on the part of destiny, sleep will prevent [Oedipus and Jocasta] from seeing the trap which is closing on them forever." In the bedroom, "which is as red as a little butcher's shop," is the cradle, which Jocasta had never removed. They are ready to retire after the coronation and marriage ceremonies. Tiresias's coming to bestow the customary blessing arouses Oedipus's arrogance and anger. As Jocasta did earlier, so he too defends the marriage of the older woman and the younger man: "I have always dreamed of such a love, an almost motherly love." He is momentarily blinded and in pain as he looks into the crystal-ball eyes of Tiresias. Later, sleepy and haunted by suggestive nightmares, Oedipus and Jocasta periodically doze off. Jocasta starts when she sees Oedipus's pierced feet. Without admitting herself to be the mother, she reveals the story of the child cursed by a prophecy and cast away with pierced feet. Oedipus talks of his past, too, and of the prophesies that made him leave home—"but the nearer I came to Thebes, the more I felt I was returning home." He falls asleep while Jocasta massages her wrinkled cheeks before the mirror. Outside, a drunkard sings of the queen's marrying a green youth.

Act IV: "Oedipus Rex." The Voice announces the passage of seventeen years: "After delusive good fortune the king is to know true misfortune, the supreme consecration, which, in the [infernal machine] of the cruel gods, finally makes of this playing-card king a man." When Oedipus rejoices at the Corinthian messenger's seeming good news, he discovers the prophecy's truth: Oedipus had slain his father and married his mother. Jocasta hangs herself with her scarf. Little Antigone shrieks at the carnage: her mother is dead and her "father is writhing over her body and stabbing at his eyes with her big golden brooch." The dead Jocasta appears, and with Antigone leads Oedipus away. Tiresias prevents Creon from stopping them, for they no longer come under his authority. Now they belong "to the people, poets, and unspoiled souls," and they will be admitted to "glory." Creon says, "You mean rather dishonor, shame." Tiresias answers, "Who knows?"

INGE, William [Motter] (1913–), was one of the major American playwrights of the 1950's. COME BACK, LITTLE SHEBA (1949), PICNIC (1953), BUS STOP (1955), and THE DARK AT THE TOP OF THE STAIRS (1957)—his first plays to be presented in New York—were all hits on Broadway as well as on the screen, and the second won him the Pulitzer Prize. In these four plays Inge portrayed lower middle-class Midwesterners, their banal lives, cliché ideas and speech, personal frustrations that explode in crises, and their ultimate acceptance of the limitations of reality. Catering to popular concepts of psychology, Inge provided resolutions that tended to be spurious or pat. His later work has been rejected by the public and the critics alike. Nevertheless, in his early works Inge excelled in entertaining, sometimes touchingly tender depictions of "little people."

Inge was born in Independence, Kansas, the youngest of five children of a small-town traveling merchant and his wife, a descendant of theatre people. Particularly close to his mother, Inge dramatized his adolescent problems in the most autobiographical and psychological of his hits, *The Dark at the Top of the Stairs;* like the boy in that play, Inge tried to escape reality by collecting the photographs of film stars. Intent on becoming an actor, he majored in acting and speech at the state university, and he performed in campus theatre productions and, after graduation (1935), in summer tent and stock shows. But he was unable to obtain enough money to go on to New York, and instead accepted a graduate scholarship at the Peabody Teachers College in Tennessee. Subsequently he worked as a news announcer; taught high school in Columbus, Kansas; completed his M.A. (1938) with a thesis on DAVID BELASCO; and then joined the faculty of Stephens College (Columbia, Missouri), whose drama department was headed by a distinguished retired actress, Maude Adams. During World War II Inge became the art, music, book, and drama critic for the St. Louis *Star-Times;* when the war ended and the regular critic returned, Inge taught English at Washington University in St. Louis.

It was through his newspaper work that he met TENNESSEE WILLIAMS, who was then becoming famous with THE GLASS MENAGERIE. Inge interviewed Williams in 1944, became friendly with him, and went to see the play in Chicago. Deeply moved and feeling "a little ashamed for having led an unproductive life" heretofore, Inge told Williams that "being a successful playwright was what he most wanted in the world for himself." He wrote his first play, *Farther Off from Heaven*—later reshaped into *The Dark at the Top of the Stairs*—and Williams helped to get it produced in 1947 by Margo Jones's Little Theatre Group in Dallas, Texas. Encouraged by Williams, Inge continued playwriting. Two years and four scripts later he sent Williams *Come Back, Little Sheba,* which soon made Inge prominent.

His record of successful Broadway productions was broken in 1959 with a play in which Inge had great faith, *A Loss of Roses.* Again autobiographical, it is set in the tent-show world in which he began his theatrical career, and it focuses on the mother-son relationship of the previous play. Inge was deeply disturbed by the play's failure, repeated in such later attempts to recapture Broadway as *Natural Affection* (1963), a study of sexual depravity and of despair; and in *Where's Daddy?* (1966), another drama about the personal problems of a young actor, produced originally as *Family Things, Etc.* in summer stock in 1965. Inge's only subsequent success has been an Academy Award screen play about adolescent love, *Splendor in the Grass* (1961), though his one-act *The Disposal* was published in the *Best Short Plays of the World Theatre: 1958–1967* (1968), and a full-length drama set on Death Row, *The Last Path* (1970), was produced Off-Broadway. He also wrote a novel, *Good Luck, Miss Wyckoff* (1970).

Inge's seriousness about his craft is documented in his essays on the drama. Repeatedly stressing artistic integrity, he has claimed to be concerned not with story and theme but, rather, with the portrayal of human nature, with "the deep inner life that exists privately behind the life that is publicly presented," as Inge wrote in *Theatre Arts* (April 1954). He succeeded in presenting the troublesome "inner lives" of ordinary people, most effectively those of women. But he succumbed to a superficial depiction of popular psychology, to the portrayal of what pretends to be intellectual and what audiences imagine to be true—rather than what is artistically valid. Inge resolves problems through what one critic (Gerald Weales) dubbed "phallic romanticism." His characters learn to face and live with personal shortcomings—their own as well as those of the people they love—through the panacea of sexuality; Inge's final curtain invariably suggests that all will be well, that his characters will bed and therefore live happily ever after.

His hits were collected in *Four Plays by William*

Inge (1959), which has a preface by Inge, as does his second collection, *Summer Brave and Eleven Short Plays* (1962). Tennessee Williams's introduction to *The Dark at the Top of the Stairs* (1958) recounts their association and the younger man's start as a playwright. Gerald Weales's *American Drama Since World War II* (1962) has a stimulating analysis of Inge, described as the chief of "the new Pineros." R. Baird Shuman's *William Inge* (1965), a book-length study, includes a bibliography.

INSPECTOR CALLS, AN, a play in three acts by J. B. PRIESTLEY, published and produced in 1947. Setting: an industrial city in the English North Midlands, 1912.

A suspense drama as well as a morality, this play was popular in many countries—particularly in Russia—and bears some affinity to Gogol's *The Government Inspector* (1836). The play's action is continuous.

A police inspector questions a factory owner, Arthur Birling, and his family about a girl who has just committed suicide. Gradually all admit their share in the tragedy and every family member is morally exposed. When the inspector leaves, the son and the daughter are profoundly disturbed, but the parents are worried only about a possible scandal. They are unmoved by the inspector's remark that there are "millions and millions and millions" of such victimized girls, "still left with us, with their lives, their hopes and fears, their suffering, and chance of happiness, all intertwined with our lives, with what we think and say and do. We don't live alone. We are members of one body." Then the Birlings discover the strange inspector to be unknown to the police. Quickly dismissing the whole affair as a hoax and resuming their smug lives, the Birlings are soon shaken by a phone call: the girl has just committed suicide, and an inspector is coming to question them.

INTERMEZZO, a comedy in three acts by JEAN GIRAUDOUX, published and produced (with music by Francis Poulenc) in 1933. Setting: a small French town, spring.

This whimsical fantasy has also been translated as *The Enchanted.*

A pretty schoolteacher flirts with a ghost who delightfully upsets life's—and the town's—equilibrium. Ultimately the teacher opts for the attractive Inspector of Public Weights and Measures (one of Louis Jouvet's favorite roles). He makes life's routine itself poetic—and ends her romantic "intermezzo" with the ghost.

INTIMATE RELATIONS (*Les Parents terribles;* literally, "the terrible parents"), a play in three acts by JEAN COCTEAU, published and produced in 1938. Setting: Paris, 1938.

This work follows the traditions of NATURALISM and the WELL-MADE PLAY. Its production (filmed by Cocteau in 1948 and shown in America as *The Storm Within*) achieved popular success because of the scandal caused by its portrayal of incest, and it has been praised by many critics. The character of Yvonne, the mother, dominates the play. But Jean Marais won stardom for his performance as the son, Michel.

Upset because her son has not come home, Yvonne almost kills herself with an overdose of insulin. Her sister Léonie (Léo), whose rational but impure orderliness (as Cocteau also stressed in his preface) contrasts vividly with those of Yvonne and her son, opens Yvonne's eyes to what is going on: Michel has spent the night with his sweetheart, and his father, neglected by Yvonne because of her exclusive love for her son, has taken a mistress. The spinster Léo, who has lived with the family in their "caravan" for over twenty years, has always loved her sister's husband. Now Yvonne goes to pieces about her boy's "unfaithfulness" to her. He comes home and kisses her as she lies in bed: "My darling, you're not angry with me, are you?" She pouts, but when he tells her that he has fallen in love, she becomes hysterical. Later his father discovers to his horror that Michel's sweetheart is his own mistress, and seeks Léo's advice. Amused, she arranges to break off the young people's romance, and persuades Yvonne to join the family in visiting Michel's sweetheart. The girl turns out to be charming, orderly, and deeply in love with Michel. She tells Michel about the "older man": she was fond of him, but not really his mistress. Now the jealous father blackmails her into pretending to Michel that she has a third lover. Crushed, Michel rejects her and returns to his mother's protective arms. But Léo, who planned the intrigue, is charmed by the girl. She decides to clear up the "disorder" the parents have made of Michel's life, and persuades the father to allow the marriage. Yvonne is again hysterical, and this time her suicide attempt succeeds. Michel throws himself over the body of his mother, "the best friend I ever had," and madly kisses it. His sweetheart pulls him away, and he is utterly bewildered as she holds him in her arms. The doorbell rings. "It was the cleaning woman," Léo reports when she comes back: "I told her there is nothing for her to do, that everything is in order."

INTRUDER, THE (*L'Intruse*), a one-act play by MAURICE MAETERLINCK, published in 1890 and produced in 1891. Setting: an old Flemish countryhouse on a Saturday night in the nineteenth century.

This was the first Maeterlinck play to reach the boards, at a Paris benefit for Paul Verlaine and Paul Gauguin. Though very short, it is one of Maeterlinck's most accomplished works, and one that approaches his ideal of SYMBOLIC "static" drama.

In a dimly lit room with a large Dutch clock, a blind old grandfather worries about his sick daughter. The rest of the family think she is recovering, but tension grows as an inexplicable presence nears the house. Perceived only by the terrified blind grandfather, the invisible intruder is soon amidst the family. It is Death, come for the sick woman.

INVESTIGATION, THE (*Die Ermittlung*), a verse play in "eleven songs" by PETER WEISS, published and produced in 1965. Setting: a German courtroom, 1964–65.

Performed both in Iron Curtain and in Western countries, this play distills the Frankfurt-am-Main court testimony actually given by nine witnesses against eighteen concentration camp officials who had murdered four million people at Auschwitz. In unemotional tones the witnesses—all anonymous and most of them surviving prisoners, male and female—describe the technical details of gas chamber and crematorium operations, starvations, beatings, and other atrocities, including "medical experimentations," and conclude that "what they did / could not have been carried out / without the support / of millions of others." But the accused—all bearing their real names—feel no guilt whatever, for they merely obeyed orders. "All of us / I want to make that very clear," one of them remarks, "did nothing but our duty." Now that the war is over "we ought to concern ourselves with other things" than those "that should be thought of / as long since atoned for," he concludes—to the "loud approbation from the [other] accused."

IONESCO, Eugène (1912–), French dramatist, became world famous in the 1950's as a leading writer for the theatre of the ABSURD. Originally produced in small halls before sparse audiences, his early one-act plays seemed more formless and nonsensical than the SURREALIST drama that they resemble and in which they are rooted. Upon closer examination, however, those early plays (like Ionesco's later ones) were found to have a rigid if untraditional form beneath the surface nonsense. Soon distinguished enthusiasts like JEAN ANOUILH praised him as a playwright superior to AUGUST STRINDBERG, and used the word *classical* to describe Ionesco's apparently grotesque drama—his tragicomic characters and his strange dialogue, settings, and action. As his plays attracted larger audiences Ionesco, characterized by some as a "hoaxer" and a mere curiosity, became more controversial. An attack by a prominent critic (Kenneth Tynan) provoked replies by the playwright and by others in the London *Observer* in 1958 that revealed Ionesco to be an important artist meriting the seriousness he himself devoted to his craft. His later plays, though less extravagant, have established Ionesco as a mid-century avant-garde metaphysical farce writer of major international significance. In 1969 he was awarded Le Prix National du Théâtre, and he was elected to the French Academy in 1970.

Like the French-writing DADAIST TRISTAN TZARA, Ionesco was born in Rumania. But his mother was French, and shortly after Ionesco's birth the family settled in Paris. Paris, where he spent his first thirteen years, provided Ionesco with his earliest memories—particularly of the enthralling Punch and Judy shows at the Luxembourg Gardens. When the family returned to Rumania in 1925 Ionesco was traumatized by a casual street scene of human

Eugène Ionesco, joining the French Academy. Paris, 1970. (*French Embassy Press & Information Division*)

brutality—an episode that prefigured the world he was to perceive hereafter, he noted in 1959: "Vain and sordid fury, cries suddenly stifled by silence, shadows engulfed forever in the night." He wrote poetry and criticism, learned Rumanian, studied at the University of Bucharest, and taught French at the metropolitan *lycée*. Iron Guard Fascism as well as the growing native sympathy for Nazism in the 1930's revolted him. When the government awarded him a grant for literary study in France in 1938, Ionesco and his family (their daughter was born in 1944) settled there permanently.

In France Ionesco worked in a publishing house and did some writing before he started on his first play, at the age of thirty-six. He disliked the theatre, and his becoming a dramatist was a fortuitous accident. It was brought about by his study of English conversation under the *Assimil* method: laboriously writing out the primer's sentences for easier memorization, Ionesco was struck by the universal absurdity of the dialogue of the Smiths—and converted it into his parody "anti-play," *La Cantatrice chauve* (THE BALD SOPRANO, 1950). He described it as a "tragedy of language"—a dramatization of the lack of human communication, of the terrifying banality and emptiness that he envisioned to be modern life. This dramaturgy was developed in the plays that followed in the next few years: *La Leçon* (THE LESSON, 1951), *Les Chaises* (THE CHAIRS, 1952), *Jacques, ou la soumission* (JACK, OR THE SUBMISSION, 1953) and its sequel *L'Avenir est dans les œufs* (THE FUTURE IS IN EGGS, 1957), *Victimes du devoir* (VICTIMS OF DUTY, 1953), and his first full-length play, *Amédée ou comment s'en débarrasser* (AMÉDÉE OR HOW TO GET RID OF IT, 1954). The characters in these plays are caricatures, but their dialogue is not confined merely to absurd talk that collapses into often belligerent vocables. In these plays in particular, the dialogue is, rather, a brilliant mélange of puns, incongruous analogies, non sequiturs, and sundry perversions of rational discourse. Wittily phrased and juxtaposed in sound as well as distorted logic, their very form of expression mirrors the plays' subjects—Ionesco's perception of an absurd reality that audiences are meant not merely to think about but, rather, to feel and experience.

Similar in dramatic form and content are Ionesco's portrayals of what Rosette C. Lamont has aptly termed "The Proliferation of Matter in Ionesco's Plays" (*L'Esprit Créateur,* Winter, 1962)—the endless amassing of objects, of things that invade and soon overwhelm the human environment, thus gradually paralyzing and destroying man—as in *The Chairs* (where multiplying seats are visibly real, though humans are not) and in *Amédée or How to Get Rid of It* ("It" being a gigantic, ever-growing corpse), and in *Le Nouveau Locataire* (*The New Tenant,* 1955), where the stage gradually is inundated by furniture that buries the mild gentleman tenant as it also is inundating and paralyzing the whole city. Similarly evocative absurdities are portrayed in Ionesco's seven short sketches with trick endings, produced in 1953, that satirize politics, love, the family, etc. They include *Le Salon de l'automobile* (*The Motor Show*), in which a young man drives away a new car that turns out to be a girl; *La Jeune Fille à marier* (*Maid to Marry*), whose title character turns out to be a man; and *Le Maître* (*The Leader*), whose protagonist ultimately is revealed to the excited audience to be a headless figure.

Ionesco did not immediately include in his collected plays an unsuccessfully produced "guignolade," *Le Tableau* (*The Picture,* 1955), which appeared with *Les Salutations* (*Salutations,* 1950) and other short plays in 1963. More important, however, is *L'Impromptu de l'Alma, ou le caméléon du berger* (IMPROVISATION, OR THE SHEPHERD'S CHAMELEON, 1956), a theatrical presentation of his artistic credo, and *Tueur sans gages* (THE KILLER, 1958). This latter work is the first of Ionesco's plays to feature Bérenger, a Chaplinesque figure who appears in *Rhinocéros* (RHINOCEROS, 1959)—Ionesco's commercially most successful play—in *Le Piéton de l'air* (THE PEDESTRIAN IN THE AIR, 1963), in *Le Roi se meurt* (EXIT THE KING, 1962), and in *La Soif et la faim* (*Thirst and Hunger,* 1966; also translated as *Hunger and Thirst*), where, renamed Jean, Ionesco's alter-ego escapes in his imagination from a basement apartment sinking into slimy soil into a region of the mind, a platform high in the mountains, where he expects to meet the ideal woman of his dreams. *Délire à deux* (*Frenzy for Two, or More,* 1963) is a one-act farce about a married couple who assault each other in a room while an equally chaotic revolution rages outside. *La Lacune* (*The Gap,* 1966), another brief comic tragedy, depicts the demise from *hubris* of an academician who is discovered never to have passed a section of the baccalaureate examination, which invalidates all his doctorates. In *Jeux de massacre* (1970, produced in America as *Wipe-Out Games*), inspired by Daniel Defoe's *A Journal of the Plague Year* (1722), Ionesco denounces "the scandal of death" in numerous episodes that portray the death of many different people by a mysterious "scourge."

In his later, full-length plays, Ionesco has more closely approximated conventional dramaturgy, although he still incorporates the grotesque in both action and speech. The early plays are circular—the end repeating the beginning, as in *The Bald Soprano* and *The Lesson*—and consist of bizarre characters and episodes like the three-nosed heroine who lays eggs, in the Jacques plays. Later plays, it is true, include stylized scenes, as in *The Killer;* elements of fantasy, as in *Rhinoceros;* and liturgy and dreamlike sequences, as in *Exit the King*. But these plays in their plot development and characterization more closely approximate the conventional. Ionesco's dramaturgy has remained distinctly original, however, and his world vision and the attitudes of the early plays have persisted.

This vision is an anguished perception of an existentialist, absurd cosmos. Ionesco juxtaposes the hideous, frightening totalitarian mass-man—brutal, banal, thick-skinned—with the little man, the victim-hero who voices his creator's hopes, perception, and fears. In that, Ionesco resembles BERTOLT BRECHT, but unlike Brecht, he believes neither in the didacticism of stage "alienation" ("the theatre cannot be EPIC ... because it is dramatic," Ionesco wrote in 1960) nor in a mimetic confrontation of simple good and evil. Always suspicious of political ideology and slogans no less than of progress in a mechanical, indifferent society, Ionesco has rejected both the *boulevard* and the social drama popular with the "bourgeoisie" featured in his plays, often as husband and wife. Made ridiculous because of their inability to communicate—since language, like other forms of expression, when it disintegrates reveals the bankruptcy of man's feelings and thought, and the inadequacy of human banality in the face of cosmic absurdity—human beings face each other like puppets of the shows Ionesco had admired in childhood. Only Bérenger retains his humanity. A spokesman for the decent, an enemy of the powers of darkness—especially in his later manifestations—he is nevertheless far from a simple, idealized "little man." His final breast beating in *Rhinoceros* is comic as well as tragic: if he could, Bérenger would join the animals; his individualistic, humanistic proclamations are embarrassingly, foolishly impotent. Increasingly rounded, Bérenger as the dying king becomes a genuinely tragic figure. His final silence, though one of an awareness of "the world . . . [of] life seeping away," is still akin, however, to the inarticulateness of Ionesco's earliest characters, like the Smiths in *The Bald Soprano* and the Orator in *The Chairs*. But Ionesco expresses all these visions, his animus and his despair, in an often amusing and always flamboyant theatrical manner, imaginatively reshaping the Punch and Judy farces he admired as a child.

Ionesco's other dramas include such trifles as *Impromptu pour la Duchesse de Windsor,* a party joke with allusions to Ionesco's dramaturgy, privately presented before the Duke and Duchess of Windsor in 1957; and *Scène à quatre* (*Foursome*), a characteristically farcical sketch about a political summit meeting, presented at the Spoleto Festival in 1959. In 1962 Ionesco published his *Notes et contre-notes* (*Notes and Counter Notes*), an important statement of his theories of drama. Most of his plays appeared first as short stories, published in *La Photo du colonel* (1962), whose title story is the original of *The Killer*.

Volumes of Ionesco's collected plays have been published since 1954 and (like his essays) translated into many languages. Notable among the many extensive studies of his works are Richard N. Coe's *Eugène Ionesco* (1961), Leonard C. Pronko's *Eugène Ionesco* (1965), and Martin Esslin's *The Theatre of the Absurd* (revised edition, 1968), all of which contain extensive bibliographies.

IPHIGENIA IN AULIS (*Iphigenie in Aulis*), a blank-verse tragedy in five acts by GERHART HAUPTMANN, produced in 1943 and published in 1944. Setting: ancient Aulis and Mycenae.

This is the first play of THE ATRIDES-TETRALOGY. Here, Calchas (a rejected suitor of Iphigenia) and Odysseus are Agamemnon's enemies and fan the Greeks' discontent; Achilles and Iphigenia are inflamed by erotic passions; and Aegisthus is a bitter rejected suitor of both Iphigenia and Clytemnestra.

Because Agamemnon has killed a stag sacred to the goddess Artemis, a windless calm delays the Greek ships at Aulis. The people's restlessness becomes increasingly menacing, and the wily priest Calchas demands that Agamemnon sacrifice his daughter Iphigenia to appease the goddess. The king hesitates in his difficult decision, summoning and then sending away his beloved Iphigenia and his wife, Clytemnestra. Sensing danger to the daughter she dotes upon, Clytemnestra tries desperately to protect Iphigenia. The girl herself agrees to be sacrificed, however, for she yearns to be united forever with Achilles. At the end, Hecate's priestesses abduct Iphigenia and place a stag on the altar in her place. As in a dream, Agamemnon sacrifices it, and neither he nor the people become aware of the substitution. The winds rise and the Greeks enthusiastically depart for Troy.

IPHIGENIA IN DELPHI (*Iphigenie in Delphi*), a blank-verse tragedy in three acts by GERHART HAUPTMANN, published and produced in 1941. Setting: Apollo's temple in Delphi, ancient Greece.

This is the last part of THE ATRIDES-TETRALOGY, though it was the first written of the four plays. It is a somber drama of atonement and reconciliation.

Separately Electra and Orestes undergo their expiation. Electra has brought the hatchet that slew Agamemnon and Clytemnestra, and Orestes has been ordered to deliver Artemis's portrait to the "terrible priestess" who offers human sacrifices. Unknown to each other, Electra and Orestes observe a procession. Electra is feverish and, believing that her brother has been sacrificed, attacks the high priestess. Only Pylades's interference stops Electra from using the hatchet on the priestess. Sickened with humanity, the priestess comes to offer prayers to Artemis, her divine mother. Electra apologizes to her, and in a moving scene the women are revealed as sisters. Iphigenia's soul begins to heal; she admits her identity and tells Electra that she spared Orestes, implying incestuous passions as the reason for her clemency. Considering herself thrice killed, Iphigenia renounces the world and insists on remaining a priestess. But Electra and Pylades finally unite and plan to start life anew. Orestes has dreamed that his mother gave him a wreath; now he is fully released from his curse and hailed as the ruler of Argos, Mycenae, Arcadia, and Sparta. Then a priest rushes in with a dreadful announcement: Iphigenia has hurled herself to death from a cliff. The high priest proclaims her a semidivinity whose self-sacrificial death is the final episode in the fate-ridden House of Atreus.

IRAN, formerly known as Persia, has no theatrical history comparable to that of its rich literary heritage. Though stymied by rigid censorship, its theatre in modern times has remained lively if undistinguished. Teheran now has a permanent professional company that produces plays by contemporary Iranian playwrights in its new theatre.

Persia's literary theatre began in the mid-nineteenth century with translations of European plays. Among the early dramatists was Mirza Malkom Khan (1833–1905), who in 1908 published three satirical comedies. Social and historical dramas were written in the 1920's, but for lack of a tradition they found little popular support.

Despite the absence of a heritage of literary Persian drama, a popular form of theatre arose in the late eighteenth and early nineteenth centuries. Known as the *ta'ziya,* it is something of a Persian-Islamic counterpart of the medieval passion play. It seemed about to develop into a significant modern dramatic form, but then it was banned from production in the 1930's and it is now rarely performed. Other early modern folk theatre included shadow and puppet plays.

Among notable contemporary playwrights are Bahman Forsi (? –), Bahrām Beyzā'i (? –), Gholāmhoseyn Sā'edi (? –), and Ali Nasiriyan (1934–), the last of whom achieved considerable success with *Sharāre, chand dāstān* (1950), a legend drama. But despite their plays and the many Tajik productions, drama has lagged considerably behind the nation's other literature.

Distinct from the Persian tradition is the Tajik drama. Inspired by native Iranian materials as well as by the Russian theatre and by Shakespeare, Tajik drama began in 1929. It developed rapidly under Russian guidance and produced popular light comedies, although its content has been heavily influenced by the Soviet political scene. Notable Tajik writers are Abdushukur Pirmuhammadzoda (1914–42), who was killed in World War II after distinguishing himself with a dramatization of a popular epic poem, *Rustam va Sūhrob* (1936); and the prominent novelist and essayist Sotim Ulughzoda (1911–), who has also written plays, including the first Tajik biographical drama, *Rūdakī* (1958, about the tenth-century poet), and a prize-winning comic satire of village foibles, *Gavhari shabchirog* (1962).

There is no satisfactory work in English on Iranian drama since World War II. See Volume IV of E. G. Browne's *A Literary History of Persia* (1924) for Persian drama to the early 1920's; and Jan Rypka's (et al.) *History of Iranian Literature* (1968) for the Tajik drama.

IRELAND. Irish drama remained derivative and unnoteworthy for almost three hundred years. A distinctively native drama began only with the Irish Literary Movement, at the very end of the nineteenth century. It flourished for a few decades, and in its heyday produced some of the great masterpieces of modern drama. Of particular renown are the poetic plays of WILLIAM BUTLER YEATS, the peasant comedies of LADY GREGORY (Yeats's co-director at the Abbey Theatre), and the works of the leading Irish playwrights, J. M. SYNGE and SEAN O'CASEY.

Other dramatists—some of them major—were born in Ireland. But many found their homeland economically unrewarding and culturally stultifying, and they quickly emigrated—as had other Irish writers of modern as well as earlier times. They are not usually grouped among the Irish dramatists: BERNARD SHAW lived in England, and though some of his plays appeared at the Abbey, most of them became and remained popular in England; OSCAR WILDE similarly left Ireland to take his place in England's literary and theatrical life; and JAMES JOYCE did not even bother to send his play to Ireland. More recently, BRENDAN BEHAN—a characteristically Irish dramatist—was turned down by the Abbey company and found fame in England (though after his death a dramatization of his *Borstal Boy* became a record-breaking hit at the Abbey in 1967), while SAMUEL BECKETT settled in France and even used another language to write his best-known plays.

The history of modern Irish drama in its first quarter of a century, like that of the Irish Literary Revival as a whole, is intimately associated with the career of Yeats, who participated in the discovery and production of many of its playwrights. In 1898, with Lady Gregory, GEORGE MOORE, and EDWARD MARTYN, he conceived the plans for the Irish Literary Theatre. Their Manifesto (1899) called for the production of "certain Celtic and Irish plays" that were to constitute a native dramatic literature reflecting "the deeper thoughts and emotions of Ireland." On May 8, 1899, at the Antient Concert Rooms in Brunswick (later Pearse) Street, the Irish Literary Theatre was launched with Yeats's THE COUNTESS CATHLEEN. The following season the Theatre moved to another house, the Gaiety, where it produced three plays. In 1901, it merged with an Irish group of actors led by the brothers Frank and William Fay, and became the Irish National Theatre Society, with Yeats as its president. That year it produced the first Gaelic play ever staged in a legitimate theatre, *Casadh an t-Sugain* (*The Twisting of the Rope*), by DOUGLAS HYDE.

Indigenous Irish—Gaelic—drama is little known. Hyde, who in 1893 helped found the Gaelic League, was its most important writer. Others who produced Gaelic plays that were popular in Ireland include MICHEÁL MAC LIAMMÓIR, who helped found and directed the Dublin Gate Theatre. To produce native drama, Mac Liammóir established the Taibhdhearc na Gaillimhe (Galway Theatre) in 1928, and featured original Gaelic plays as well as translations of Shaw and other dramatists. The theatre was launched with Mac Liammóir's play *Diarmuid agus Gráinne,* the popular Finn Cycle legend also dramatized by Yeats, Moore, and Lady Gregory. Mac Liammóir's and Hyde's are among the few Gaelic plays translated into English, of which the best known is *An Giall* (THE HOSTAGE, 1958) by Behan, a later Gaelic writer.

When Yeats's newly merged Society toured London in 1903 its success was so great that the benefactress of Manchester playwrights like STANLEY HOUGHTON, Miss Annie E. F. Horniman, became its patroness and presented it with the little house that was to become world-renowned, the Abbey Theatre. It opened on December 27, 1904, with a triple bill: Yeats's CATHLEEN NI HOULIHAN and ON BAILE'S STRAND, and Lady Gregory's SPREADING THE NEWS. Its history, thereafter, is an important part of the history of Irish drama. It includes the shameful (though exciting) stories of the rioting that greeted masterpieces like Synge's THE PLAYBOY OF THE WESTERN WORLD and O'Casey's THE PLOUGH AND THE STARS. More important is its roll of playwrights, for these include most of the modern Irish dramatists. ST. JOHN ERVINE and GEORGE SHIELS were associated also with the Ulster Theatre, which began as the Ulster Literary Theatre in 1902. A few other dramatists were produced at the Dublin Gate Theatre, which began in 1928 to produce primarily foreign plays, as Mac Liammóir noted in his professional autobiography, *All for Hecuba* (1946); but it also introduced important native writers like DENIS JOHNSTON and Donagh MacDonagh (1912–), the author of *Happy as Larry* (1946), of a verse drama on the Deirdre legend (*Lady Spider,* 1959), and of low comedy like *Step-in-the-Hollow* (1959). A post-World War II avant-garde playhouse is Dublin's Pike Theatre, whose stormy history is discussed by its director, Alan Simpson, in *Beckett and Behan and a Theatre in Dublin* (1962).

Irish drama is distinctive particularly for its sound. In seeking to create a native drama of beauty, Yeats called for fresh, poetic language. Gaelic would have served excellently, but few dramatists were sufficiently well-versed in it. The idiom subsequently used by most Irish playwrights approximated the peasant dialect of western Ireland. Such is the language that predominates in the drama of Lady Gregory—and of Synge, who heeded Yeats's advice to study the speech of the Aran islanders. At their best, these adaptations of peasant dialects have the vividness and cadence of fine poetry.

The Irish plays best known to the world are the masterpieces of Synge and O'Casey. They are distinguished by what are considered typically Irish characters, and by their picturesque, flavorful language. Yeats also wanted a literary drama that would find its inspiration and subject matter in native history and folklore, and eschew the polemics of politics and "theses." Many of the plays were, indeed, based on Irish legend. Yet the impact of HENRIK IBSEN made itself felt almost from the very beginning: the second work produced by the Irish Literary Theatre was Martyn's *The Heather Field,* which, like most of his drama, was strongly influenced by Ibsen as well as by MAURICE MAETERLINCK.

"Thesis" and PROBLEM PLAYS were written by LENNOX ROBINSON, another important Irish playwright, who was also one of the guiding figures in the administration of the Abbey Theatre. Other playwrights of note during the golden age of Irish drama include T. C. MURRAY; BRINSLEY MACNAMARA; GEORGE WILLIAM RUSSELL (Æ), who primarily contributed ideas to other dramatists, but did produce a fine literary drama of his own; PADRAIC COLUM, who later emigrated to the United States and turned to other genres, but whose early NATURALISTIC drama was important and influential in the development of the Abbey Theatre; LORD DUNSANY, who became a prolific and popular writer of fantasies; and PAUL VINCENT CARROLL, one of the most distinguished of Irish dramatists. In 1951, after a fire at the Abbey Theatre, the company moved across the Liffey River to another house, where it continued its productions until 1966, when the new Abbey Theatre opened on the original site.

There were many writers of farce and light comedy who, though little known outside of Ireland, provided popular staple for the great actors of the Irish theatre—playwrights like William Boyle (1853–1922), notable for *The Building Fund* (1905) and *The Eloquent Dempsy* (1906). Other Irish playwrights relatively unfamiliar to the rest of the world include the important pioneer Abbey dramatist GEORGE FITZMAURICE, whose reputation has grown impressively since his almost unnoticed death in 1963; the actor-playwright Rutherford Mayne (pen name of Samuel John Waddell, 1878–   ), who distinguished himself particularly with *The Drone* (1908) and the one-act *Red Turf* (1911), both of which portray the difficult lives of the northern Irish; Seumas O'Kelly (1881–1918), a prominent theatre critic who achieved some popularity with his tragedy of a vagabond mother, *The Shuiler's Child* (1910); James Thomas ("Frank") Harris (1856–1931), notorious for his autobiography and biographies, but also the author of several minor plays, the most successful

The Old Abbey Theatre, Dublin. (*Irish Tourist Board*)

being his reworking of an Oscar Wilde scenario into *Mr. and Mrs. Daventry* (1899); the poet Austin Clarke (1896–   ), among whose religious verse plays is *The Moment Next to Nothing* (1958); Walter Macken (1915–67), better known as an actor and as a widely read novelist, who managed the Abbey in 1965–66 and wrote plays that have been likened to those of the early O'Casey: *Mungo's Mansion* (1946, his first drama, depicting slum life), *Home Is the Hero* (1952, which has been filmed, and whose family resembles that of O'Casey's JUNO AND THE PAYCOCK), *Twilight of a Warrior* (1956, featuring a dominant personality in a crumbling society), and others; and the Waterford playwright Teresa Deevy (1903–63), who wrote a number of moving plays, notably the whimsical *Katie Roche* (1936), which one critic praised as displaying "[J. M.] BARRIE's charm without sentimentality." Among prominent Irishmen who occasionally wrote for the Abbey were its founder's brother, the painter Jack B. Yeats (1871–1957), whose *La La Noo* was produced in 1942; and the short-story writer Frank O'Connor (pseudonym of Michael O'Donovan, 1903–66), one of the theatre's directors (1935–39), who wrote *Time's Pocket* (1938) for the Abbey and collaborated on a number of other plays.

Since the 1950's the annual Dublin Theatre Festival has provided considerable impetus to the Irish theatre. It has brought about revivals of the classics, participation by prominent guest artists like Tyrone Guthrie and Siobhan McKenna, and encouragement of new dramatists at the Gate, the Abbey, and other theatres. The Abbey produced the work of Michael J. Molloy (1917–   ), who was hailed as another Synge upon the appearance of his first work, *The King of Friday's Men* (1948), a play set in eighteenth-century Ireland that rises above its melodramatic plot through its characterizations and evocations of the past; Molloy has continued, but with somewhat less success, to deal with vanishing traditions in contemporary Ireland in *The Wood of the Whispering* (1953), a wistful comedy set in more recent times, and *Daughter from over the Water* (1962), "a religious problem play." The Ulster theatre and the Southern Theatre group in Cork also have been active. Ulster playwrights of note are Sam Thompson (1916–65), particularly significant for his documentaries and his controversial depiction of religious hostilities in contemporary Belfast in *Over the Bridge* (1957); and the actor-novelist Joseph Tomelty (1911–), who wrote naturalistic tragedies like *All Souls' Night* (1948), which bears some resemblance to Synge's RIDERS TO THE SEA, and a very popular drama about a clergyman's life, *Is the Priest at Home?* (1954). The Cork group has produced an important new playwright, John B. Keane (1928–), who has been called "a latterday Boucicault"; his *Sive* (1959), one of the most popular recent Irish works, is a folkplay that Keane has followed with dramatizations of modern life, like his portrayal of a disaffected football player in *The Man from Clare* (1962), and with musical dramas.

Widely successful in recent years has been BRIAN FRIEL, but mention also should be made of others, some of whom are equally well known in Ireland. Probably the most commercially successful playwright—certainly of the Festival—has been Hugh Leonard (pseudonym of John Keyes Byrne, 1926–); aside from his notable adaptations of Joyce —particularly *Stephen D* (1962)—Leonard's plays include two psychological melodramas, *A Walk on the Water* (1960) and *The Poker Session* (1963), and *All the Nice People* (originally titled *Mick and Mick,* 1966), a dramatic indictment of middle-class Dubliners. Other notable playwrights are Seamus Byrne (1904–), the 1950 premiere of whose naturalistic *Design for a Headstone,* set in a prison and portraying the Church's conflict with Republicanism, touched off public demonstrations; Padraic Fallon (1906–), who has written poetic drama like *The Seventh Step* (1954), a tragedy that is classic in form though contemporary in its Irish setting, but who is even more distinguished for his extravagantly praised 1953 verse radio plays of myth and legend, *Diarmuid and Grainne* and *The Vision of Mac Conglinne;* Bryan Michael MacMahon (1909–), who employed fiction's picaresque style in his tragicomedy of contemporary Irish life, *The Honey Spike* (1961); the Irish scholar-statesman Conor Cruise O'Brien (1917–), who stirred up international controversy with *Murderous Angels* (1968), a ROLF HOCHHUTH type of play subtitled "a political tragedy and comedy in black and white" and portraying United Nations Secretary General Dag Hammarskjöld as responsible for the 1961 murder of Patrice Lumumba; John Purcell O'Donovan (1921–), an authority on Shaw—whose family O'Donovan dramatized in *The Shaws of Synge Street* (1960) and whose influence (particularly that of THE APPLE CART) is perceptible in O'Donovan's most successful play, *The Less We Are Together* (1957); Maurice Meldon (1926–54), an experimental playwright notable for his *Aisling* (1953), "A Dream Analysis" (subtitle) of recent Irish history that has been likened to Johnston's THE OLD LADY SAYS "NO!"; James Douglas (1929–), whose *The Ice Goddess* (1964) and other plays (some of them written for television) are modern parables of social protest that portray man's anguish in a manner approaching that of the ABSURD; and Thomas Murphy (1936–), who created a sensation with *Whistle in the Dark* (1961), a much-praised and subsequently filmed portrayal of the violence of Irish immigrants in Coventry, England.

There are many anthologies of Irish drama, and these supplement individual editions of the minor writers. In addition to the Gate and the Pike theatre histories already alluded to, Irish dramatists and productions are listed and discussed in books on the Abbey Theatre, principally Lennox Robinson's *Ireland's Abbey Theatre: A History 1899–1951* (1951, the "official history"), Gerard Fay's *The Abbey Theatre: Cradle of Genius* (1958), and Peter Kavanagh's *The Story of the Abbey Theatre* (1950). Of great interest and basic importance are the accounts by its founders, Yeats's "The Irish Dramatic Movement" (in *Plays and Controversies,* 1923) and Lady Gregory's *Our Irish Theatre* (1913); O'Casey's autobiographies also contain much useful (occasionally polemical) material. Perhaps the most profound study of the subject is Una Ellis-Fermor's *The Irish Dramatic Movement* (2nd edition, 1954), but Andrew E. Malone's *The Irish Drama* (1929) is more comprehensive. Later studies include Robert Hogan's *After the Irish Renaissance: A Critical History of Irish Drama Since "The Plough and the Stars"* (1967).

IRIS, a drama in five acts by ARTHUR WING PINERO, produced in 1901 and published in 1902. Setting: London and Italy, c. 1900.

The actresses who played the leading part in this drama were unequal to the demanding role of the weak-willed protagonist, a woman defeated by material adversity. *Iris* was esteemed but not successful, in part because of its harrowing though effective ending. Lowered curtains to denote time passage within an act were first used in this play.

Her late husband's will prevents Iris Bellamy from remarrying without losing her fortune. An attractive young widow idolized by her friends, she loves a poor man. To save herself from marrying him, she accepts the ardent proposal of Frederick Maldonado, a Jewish tycoon. Then she reneges and, too dependent on luxury to marry the poor man, takes him for her lover: "I hadn't the recklessness on the one hand nor the power of self-denial on the other." Her fortune is stolen, and her friends scorn Iris because of her affair. Generous and used to a comfortable life, she accepts Maldonado's money. Once she is in his power Maldonado makes Iris his mistress. His passion for her is such that he still wants to marry her, though she scorns him. Her lover returns but rejects her when he learns of her infidelity. Maldonado discovers their meeting, turns Iris out on the streets, and then breaks down in a rage of despair.

ISAAC SHEFTEL, a drama in three acts by DAVID PINSKI, published in 1907 and produced in 1909. Setting: "a large city of the Jewish pale" in Russia, early 1890's.

The title character of this NATURALISTIC work, Pinski's first significant play (it was written in 1899), is a creative but slow-witted lacemaker. He has invented two simple machines, for which his employer paid him a pittance. Now Sheftel is obsessed with an idea for a new invention, able neither to eat nor sleep as he silently struggles with it at home. He is nagged by his impoverished family, who resent their breadwinner's losing time, and being threatened with dismissal by the boss who exploited him. Because Sheftel's intelligence is too limited to realize his vision, he is unable to make his contrivance work, gets frustrated, and smashes it. He is derided by his fellow workers, who then try to cheer him up with food and drink. Quickly getting drunk, Sheftel goes berserk and wrecks the shop. After he has wandered around all day he returns home and, exhausted and despairing, swallows rat poison. But as it takes its effect, he changes his mind and starts to shriek: "I don't want to die!"

ISHERWOOD, Christopher [William Bradshaw-] (1904–), English writer, is best known as a novelist. Perhaps most famous is his *Goodbye to Berlin* (1939), the semiautobiographical collection of stories dramatized in Van Druten's I AM A CAMERA. Isherwood wrote a number of plays with W. H. AUDEN: THE DOG BENEATH THE SKIN (1935), THE ASCENT OF F6 (1936), and *On the Frontier* (1938), an EXPRESSIONIST anticapitalist and antiwar melodrama; the play is set in the same mythical and English localities as the duo's earlier plays and is characterized by similar language and dramaturgy, which was to some extent influenced by that of BERTOLT BRECHT. In 1960, with the actor Charles Laughton, Isherwood worked on a dramatization of Plato's dialogues; and in 1969 he dramatized BERNARD SHAW's satire, *The Adventures of the Black Girl in Her Search for God.* With Don Bachardy (? –) he wrote *A Meeting by the River* (1970), a dramatization of Isherwood's 1967 novel about the tragicomic struggle of two London-born brothers in India.

Isherwood was born in Disley, Cheshire, attended Corpus Christi College in Cambridge, and studied medicine. Then he went to Germany, where he joined his friend Auden. The two men traveled to China and wrote *Journey to a War* (1939), which includes poems and a diary of the trip. Isherwood has spent much of his later life in the United States. Notable among his novels is *The Last of Mr. Norris* (1935, published in Britain as *Mr. Norris Changes Trains*); like the Berlin stories, it is something of a study in abnormal sex and is about expatriate characters in Berlin on the eve of the Nazi takeover. Isherwood also has written an autobiography, *Lions and Shadows* (1938).

ISLE OF THE DEAD (*Toten-Insel, eller, Hades*), a two-scene fragment by AUGUST STRINDBERG, published in 1918. Setting: Hades.

This EXPRESSIONISTIC work, written in 1907, was planned as the fourth of THE CHAMBER PLAYS and the sequel to THE GHOST SONATA. The title refers to the painting, by the Swiss romantic symbolist Arnold Böcklin, that appears at the end of *The Ghost Sonata* and is reproduced on a backdrop for this play.

A teacher arrives in Hades, but is unaware of his death. He discusses with a supernatural Instructor his dreary earthly preoccupations—mainly his nagging wife and his tedious life—and the reality and meaning of his identity. The Instructor gives him hope of eventual beauty and light.

ISRAEL, the homeland of Hebrew—as distinct from YIDDISH—drama, became an independent republic in 1948. Though part of the MIDDLE EAST, Israel is anomalously European in its culture. As early as 1926, the Ohel Theatre was founded in what was then Palestine, and it survived until 1969. The famous Habima theatre visited Palestine in 1928, and settled there permanently four years later. It had begun in 1918 in Moscow, where Konstantin Stanislavsky was its adviser and Yevgeni Vakhtangov trained its company and directed its most influential production, that of Anski's THE DYBBUK. This and another early offering, Leivick's THE GOLEM, long remained staples of the Habima and are still performed on Habima's foreign tours.

Drama in Hebrew was presented in Palestine as early as 1894, but it was not until 1936 that the first original Hebrew play was produced there. That year Habima presented *Be'Layil Zeh*, a dramatization of the Jewish struggle against Rome at the time of the destruction of the Second Temple; the play depicts the Zealot commander, who is willing to sacrifice the population for political redemption, in conflict with his peace-counseling uncle, who embodies humanism and spirituality. The play was written by Nathan Bystrytzky (1896–), who in *Yerushalayim Ve'Romi* (1941) again presented the same antagonists but featured the Jewish traitor Josephus Flavius, and who in *Sabbatai Zevi* (1936) turned to the intriguing figure also portrayed by DAVID PINSKI and SHOLEM ASCH. Another early Israeli playwright whose works became popular is the Ukrainian-born Aaron Ashman (1896–). His *Mihal Bat Shaul* (1941) focuses on psychological motivations in dramatizing the story of the title character, the daughter of Saul who married King David; and his *Ha'Adanah Hazot* (1942) is an idealized and sometimes sentimental portrayal of the *halutzim,* Israel's pioneers.

The first theatrical hit of independent Israel was *Hu Halakh Ba'Shadot* (*He Walked Through the*

Fields, 1948), Moshe Shamir's (1921–) 1948 dramatization of his novel about the *kibbutz* and the struggle for independence and freedom. Featuring the *sabras* (native-born Israelis), the play was successfully revived in 1956 by Israel's third theatre, the Cameri, and stimulated the production of other Hebrew plays on contemporary themes. Notable War of Independence dramas were Igal Mossinson's (1917–) *Ba Arvot Ha'Negev* (1949), which is based on a historical incident; and Nathan Shaham's (1925–) *Hem Yagiuh Makhar* (1950), a searing NATURALISTIC portrayal of the 1948 war.

Other Israeli plays on topical themes have been written by the Polish-born novelist-playwright Aaron Megged (1920–); his *Ba'Derekh Le'Eilat* (1951) deals with the search for water in the Negev Desert and recalls Soviet SOCIALIST REALISM drama, *Be'Reshit* (1962) is a modern interpretation of Genesis, and *Ha'Onah Ha'Boeret* (1967) is a treatment of the Nazi holocaust in terms of the story of Job. Mossinson's *Casablan* (1954), remade into a hit musical in 1967, features a resentful young Moroccan hero of the War of Independence, now troubled in Jaffa's slums and underworld. Shamir has continued to dramatize his fiction and has written original plays on the problems of the *kibbutz* (*Bet Hillel,* 1950), older immigrants (*Agadot Lod,* 1958), and the morality of receiving German indemnities (*Ha'Yoresh,* 1963); he has also written a modernization of the biblical story of Ruth (*Ha'Lailah L'Ish,* 1963) and a family comedy (*Bayit Be'Matsav Tov,* 1962).

There have been attempts to depict Israel's problems symbolically. Nissim Aloni (1926–) became particularly distinguished for his portrayal of a Jeroboam who tries to make the Judeans rise above narrow patriotism, *Akhsar Mi'kol Ha'Melekh* (1953); and for *Bigdeh Ha'Melekh* (1961), which in the guise of a sequel to Andersen's story by the same name (*The Emperor's Clothes*) satirizes modern society and was hailed as the first important Israeli play to deal with universal problems in the Western idiom. Less experimental but more poetic is the drama of the Polish-born translator and poet Nathan Alterman (1910–70), whose *Kineret, Kineret . . .* (1961), a portrayal of early Israeli pioneers, was the first modern native verse play; Alterman's *Pundak Ha'Rukhot* (1962) deals sensitively with the contemporary as well as the timeless problems of the artist. The Hungarian-born humorist Ephraim Kishon (1924–), starting with *Shmo Holekh Le'Fanav* (1951), a lampoon of bureaucracy, has satirized various domestic issues and has particularly succeeded with a romantic family comedy, *Ha'Ketubah* (1958).

The establishment of a Jewish state with geographic boundaries and a modernized Hebrew language and culture did not immediately generate original native drama of international significance. It did, however, greatly stimulate the development and growth of the Hebrew theatre. Most popular in the first few decades of the nation's independence have been translations of the classics (Western as well as Yiddish) and of popular modern drama, European and American.

The first book-length work to describe the new Israeli theatre and to discuss native plays in some detail was Mendel Kohansky's *The Hebrew Theatre: Its First Fifty Years* (1969).

IT HAPPENED IN IRKUTSK (*Irkutskaya istoriya;* literally, "Irkutsk story"), a play in two parts by ALEKSEI NIKOLAEVICH ARBUZOV, published and produced in 1960. Setting: Irkutsk, Siberia; 1950's.

The great Moscow hit of the 1960 season, this play carried Arbuzov's name beyond the borders of Russia. Its setting is the construction site of a hydroelectric station, and its perspective—with its "positive hero," optimism, and SOCIALIST REALISM—is in accord with Communist dogma. But Arbuzov's structural experimentation (fluid scenes, chorus, and narration) and even more his depiction of emotional development, individual growth, and love transcend the conventional Soviet drama. The play was characterized (by Norris Houghton) as "an only slightly vulgarized Communist OUR TOWN."

Valya is an attractive young grocery store cashier. Though innocent, she is wildly flirtatious, models herself on Carmen, and has thus acquired the reputation of a hussy, "Good-Time Valya." A foreman in the local plant takes her to see an Italian film—he prefers Italian pictures to Soviet pictures, which mostly "try to convince me of things I've taken for granted for a long time. And that's boring. I don't need convincing. I could convince others." He falls in love with Valya and marries her—despite her reputation and her hesitation, for she is unsure of her feelings and herself. "His love has saved me," Valya soon realizes, as she becomes aware of her love for him, of the great capacities for feeling he has released in her. Then he is drowned while saving some children. His friend, who is also Valya's former beau and a once-superficial electrician whose love for Valya became apparent only after he lost her, is made the new foreman. The workers and the chief foreman, who is needled for falling in love with Valya's older friend, all agree to help the widowed Valya and her infant twins. The new foreman resumes his courtship, and urges Valya to join the construction workers. Gradually Valya agrees, as she gains a new and deeper insight into life. "People must be happy in this world, . . . especially those who are building Communism," the chorus advises her, defining happiness as "the satisfaction of knowing one's doing a worthwhile job, that one's part of something bigger than oneself." The drama's opening scene is replayed at the end. Valya gently stops the now-matured new foreman from proposing to her. "With tears in her eyes and a smile on her lips she runs off the bridge into the night," the foreman says, wondering if she will ever be his; "but that's another story, another tale. This one ends with me standing on the road, looking after her and thinking how dearly I love her."

IT IS REALLY NOT SERIOUS (*Ma non è una cosa seria*), a comedy in three acts by LUIGI

PIRANDELLO, produced in 1918 and published in 1919. Setting: a contemporary northern Italian city and the surrounding countryside.

This dramatization of a short story Pirandello published in 1912 presents the converse of IF NOT THUS: logic is defeated by emotion, and pretense becomes reality.

At twenty-seven, Gasparina Torretta is a worn-out drudge. She runs a boarding house, some of whose motley (and highly picturesque) clientele take advantage of her self-effacing goodness by not paying their debts. Memmo Speranza, a young dandy, returns from the hospital after a duel brought about by his latest love affair. He likens himself to a straw: "I catch fire immediately, I am a big flame, then I am drowned in smoke. Marriage is not for me. Love, yes. Marriage, no." As a joke but also to protect himself from marriage, he asks the bedraggled Gasparina to marry him, in name only: no one will take it seriously, and he will be able to pursue his affairs with no danger of being ensnared by matrimony. He promises to set her up in a house in the country, "with a nice allowance and entirely free to do as you wish." Gasparina finally gives in, accepts the bargain, and marries him: "It is really not serious." The calm and healthy life in the country soon bring out her innate attractions. Memmo in the meantime continues his intrigues in the city, but he is becoming less of a dandy. A widowed boarder who has always been kind to Gasparina now entreats her to end her arrangement with Memmo and marry him. She asks Memmo to dissolve their unconsummated marriage, though she is in fact beginning to fall in love with him. Memmo, struck by her good looks, refuses to give her up to the widower. Gradually he falls in love with her—and the mock marriage becomes a real one.

ITALY. Italian drama, except for that of LUIGI PIRANDELLO, has been of lesser originality and consequence than that of almost any other European country. Yet the Italian theatre has remained as lively and popular as it was in the days of the *commedia dell'arte* and Carlo Goldoni. However, few outsiders know of any modern Italian playwrights other than Pirandello—and perhaps the flamboyant GABRIELE D'ANNUNZIO and the outstanding more recent dramatist, UGO BETTI. In the last quarter of the nineteenth century French romanticism and IBSENITE NATURALISM provided the mold for much of the Italian drama. Even then and in the early years of the twentieth century there were distinctive native literary movements.

The most important of these movements was the theatre of the GROTESQUE. Launched with Chiarelli's aptly titled *La maschera e il volto* (THE MASK AND THE FACE, 1916), the *grottesco* (or *grotteschi*) tragicomically and with characteristic Italian volatility presented conflicts between reality and illusion. Pirandello explored this theme in play after play—as did LUIGI CHIARELLI and others, including PIER MARIA ROSSO DI SAN SECONDO, Luigi Antonelli (1882–1942), and Enrico Cavacchioli (1885–1954). Antonelli succeeded particularly with *L'uomo che incontrò se stesso* (1918), which in theme resembles Barrie's DEAR BRUTUS, and with other satiric Pirandellian comedies like *L'isola delle scimmie* (1922) and *Il maestro* (1933); while Cavacchioli, who was a notable technical innovator, focused on dichotomies of feeling and intellect in plays like *L'uccello del paradiso* (1919), his first hit, and *La danza del ventre* (1921). Earlier movements that strove to bring serious purpose to the Italian theatre are the TWILIGHT or *crepuscolari,* whose principal exponent was FAUSTO MARIA MARTINI; VERISM, a form of naturalism whose major practitioners were GIOVANNI VERGA (of *Cavalleria rusticana* fame) and GUISEPPE GIACOSA (better remembered as Puccini's librettist); and FUTURISM, an anarchic movement launched by FILIPPO TOMMASO MARINETTI.

Early modern Italian dramas derivative of the PROBLEM PLAYS of HENRIK IBSEN include studies of eroticism by ROBERTO BRACCO and MARCO PRAGA; the Milanese dialect sketches of Carlo Bertolazzi (1870–1916), whose *L'egoista* (1900), *Lulù* (1903), and other plays were revived in midcentury and esteemed (belatedly) for their naturalistic portrayals of the middle class; and Enrico Annibale Butti's (1868–1912) studies of euthanasia (*L'utopia,* 1894), agnosticism (*Lucifero,* 1900), and spiritual redemption (*Fiamme nell'ombra,* 1904). The novelist-playwright Gerolamo Rovetta (1851–1910) too was a verist; his most popular play, *Romanticismo* (1901), is an antiheroic historical drama of the 1850's independence struggle, set in Lombardy-Venetia. The wild and decadent romanticism that reached its pinnacle with D'Annunzio and his celebration of the superman was also expressed in the work of others, including SEM BENELLI (particularly in *The Jest*), ERCOLE LUIGI MORSELLI, and GIOVACCHINO FORZANO, Fascism's most popular playwright, with whom Mussolini himself collaborated. On the opposite ideological side during Mussolini's regime was Leo Ferrero (1903–33), known principally for a posthumous anti-Fascist allegory, *Angelica* (1936).

More recently romanticism has been represented by Cesare Meano (1899–1957), with plays like *Nascita di Salomé* (1937) and *Melisana per me* (1940), and by Luigi Squarzina (1922–). The latter, an immensely prolific writer, has authored successful murder mysteries like *La sua parte di storia* (1958) and quasi-historical plays like *Romagnola* (1959), has adapted the works of numerous foreign authors, and has collaborated with Alberto Moravia (1907–) on *Gli indifferenti* (1948). One of Italy's major modern writers, Moravia (born Pincherle) has dramatized some of his own popular novels and has written original plays like *Beatrice Cenci* (1955), a Renaissance tragedy (also the subject of Shelley's poetic drama) whose title character is raped by her bored father, Francesco; and *Il Dio Kurt* (1968), a modernized *Oedipus Rex* set in a Nazi concentration camp whose commander, "the God Kurt," arranges for the real life incest and expiation of two inmates. The novelist Natalia Ginzburg (1916–) won the 1968 Marzotto Prize for European drama for

L'inserzione (*The Advertisement*, 1968; her tragicomedy about a loquacious deserted wife. Another major novelist, Secondo Tranquilli, better known as Ignazio Silone (1900–   ), dramatized his *Pane e vino* (*Bread and Wine*, 1937) as *Ed egli si nascose* (*And He Did Hide Himself*, 1945); subsequently he wrote an impressive original play, *L'avventura d'un tovero cristiano* (*The Story of a Humble Christian*, 1968), a study of the conflicts of morality and administration as personified by Saint Clement V, who abdicated the papacy in 1294. Earlier novelists who occasionally essayed the drama with success include MASSIMO BONTEMPELLI, Riccardo Bacchelli (1891–   ), Curzio Malaparte (1898–1957), and Dino Buzzati (1906–   ). Bacchelli retold the Hamlet story in *Amleto* (1918) and wrote a tragicomedy on the fall of Troy, *Il Figlio di Ettore e Nostos* (1957); Malaparte, whose original name was Kurt Eric Suckert, dramatized the lives of Marcel Proust (*Du Côté de chez Proust*, 1948) and Karl Marx (*Das Kapital*, 1949), and wrote a play on post-World War II Vienna (*Anche le donne hanno perso la guerra*, 1954); and Buzzati is notable principally for his Kafkaesque drama of a businessman's gradual destruction in an institution, *Un caso clinico* (1953).

While Betti has been the most notable Italian playwright in recent decades, three others have achieved considerable native prominence and a measure of recognition abroad: EDUARDO DE FILIPPO, the most successful of a famous Neapolitan theatre family; DIEGO FABBRI, the author of distinguished Catholic plays; and MARIO FRATTI, who early emigrated to New York to continue his career. Other practicing Italian playwrights have not succeeded sufficiently to become known outside their homeland: Gherardo Gherardi (1891–1949), Valentino Bompiani (1898–   ), Cesare Zavattini (1902–   ), Federico Zardi (1912–   ), Leopoldo Trieste (1917–   ), and Paolo Levi (1919–   ). Of these, Zardi has distinguished himself with satirical social comedies like *I tromboni* (1956) and history plays like *I Giacobini* (1957), while Levi has succeeded with a religious play in a war setting, *Gli dei di pietra* (1958).

Some of these and some of the earlier-mentioned dramatists have also written film scripts. It is in that genre, indeed, that modern Italian drama has become world renowned. The most authentic expression of native stage drama was perhaps in dialect plays—particularly Sicilian—such as those of Pirandello's collaborator Nino Martoglio (1870–1921) and of Luigi Capuana (1839–1915), the theorist of verism who wrote a comic masterpiece about a matchmaking old soldier, *Lu paraninfu* (1914). In the native tradition also is Dario Fo (1926–   ), a left-wing actor-dramatist who has written and performed anti-Establishment sketches that gained considerable popularity in the 1960's.

Lander MacClintock's exhaustive and scholarly study of modern Italian drama, *The Age of Pirandello* (1951), may be supplemented with the introductions and bibliographies in such collections as Eric Bentley's *The Genius of the Italian Theater* (1964), Robert W. Corrigan's *Masterpieces of the Modern Italian Theatre* (1967), and Felicity Firth's *Three Plays* [by Pirandello] (1969).

IVANOV, a drama in four acts by ANTON CHEKHOV, published and produced in 1887. Setting: a central province in contemporary Russia.

Chekhov's first major play created a tremendous stir and immediately established his reputation as a playwright. But he was dissatisfied with what he called "a dramatic miscarriage" and continued rewriting it (his seventh version appeared in 1901). The hero is a disillusioned Russian Hamlet who suffers from the inner emptiness Chekhov observed among the educated. Although less melodramatic than PLATONOV, *Ivanov* still displays the popular theatrical conventions Chekhov was soon to discard.

Nikolai Ivanov feels guilty because he no longer loves his adoring wife, an ailing Jewess who defied and then was disowned by her wealthy parents when she married him. Castigated by Yevgeni Lvov, a self-righteous young doctor, Ivanov complains of fatigue: "Don't marry a Jewess or a bluestocking or a woman who is queer in any way," he remarks; "do not try to fight alone against thousands." His wife cannot persuade Ivanov to spend the evening with her, but defends him to Lvov as "a wonderful man" despite his current depression. Then, unable to bear his neglect, she decides to follow him to the home of his friend Lebedev. There Sasha, the daughter, is bored with the dull company. She defends Ivanov when her miserly mother and some of the guests gossip about him. Confessing her love when they are alone, she begs Ivanov to run away with her. They embrace passionately as his wife enters. Wallowing in guilt, shame, and self-pity, Ivanov is driven wild by his despairing wife's accusations that he married her for her money, and has turned Sasha's head to get out of his debts to Lebedev. Furious, he shrieks at her, "Hold your tongue, Jewess!" Worse, he cruelly reveals that she is dying, though he is immediately remorseful. About a year later she has died and it is the day of Ivanov's wedding to Sasha. Crushed by his guilt and self-contempt, he angrily arrives to reject the "new life" and call off the wedding. When Lvov again denounces him as a scoundrel, Ivanov shoots himself.

The play's many fine minor characterizations include those of Sasha's parents, Ivanov's titled but poor uncle, and a distant relative, one of whose many schemes is to marry the uncle off to a wealthy local widow.

IVANOV, Vsevolod Vyacheslavovich (1895 or 1896–1963). Russian novelist and playwright, was more successful with his fiction than with his drama. But one of his plays—the immensely popular *Bronepoezd 14–69* (ARMORED TRAIN 14–69, 1927)—made up for the relative failure of the others. This play, like all Ivanov's writing, is characterized by high-flown dialectic speeches, an episodic style, and melodrama that is reminiscent of American westerns and—in its portrayal of cruelty and horror—the fiction of Ambrose Bierce.

Ivanov was born in the village of Lbyazhen, Siberia, on the border of the steppe near the Irtysh River. His father, Ivanov wrote in an autobiographical note, was "the bastard son of the Governor-General of Turkestan and his housekeeper." Ivanov ran away from home before he completed his schooling and joined a traveling circus as a clown. After a short while he quit and attended an agricultural school for a year. From 1912 to the Russian Revolution, he worked in a printing shop, although he traveled with circuses in the summer. He read much but was perpetually plagued by boredom. After having a story accepted in a Siberian newspaper in 1916, Ivanov sent his next story to MAXIM GORKY. Gorky liked it, and wrote Ivanov a letter telling him so. Receiving this letter in his dingy printing shop was the happiest event in Ivanov's life. But when he wrote some twenty other stories in the next two weeks and sent those to Gorky, Gorky replied (much as he did to ISAAC BABEL) that Ivanov needed to study more before writing again.

At the time of the Revolution Ivanov was so unpolitical that he joined both the Socialist Revolutionary and the Social Democratic parties. Though he was criticized in the 1920's for "political blindness," he soon became more knowledgeable. First he fought for the Whites, and subsequently, after being imprisoned and very nearly executed, he fought on the side of the Soviet partisans. He became Secretary of the Committee of Public Safety, and helped defend Omsk against the Czechs. According to his own account, he became frightened and hid. Then he was wounded and contracted typhoid fever. In 1920 Gorky helped to get Ivanov to Lenigrad, and subsequently helped set him up there. Ivanov was a Red Army instructor 1920–41, a front-line reporter during World War II, a contributor to the journals *Krasnaya Nov* and *Novy Mir,* and *Izvestiya's* correspondent during the Nuremberg trials.

His first major work was the novel *Partizany* (*Partisans,* 1921), an account of his experiences during the Revolution. It was followed the next year by a story on the same subject, *Armored Train 14–69;* adapted for the stage, it became his most famous play. His fifteen plays include *Blokada* (1929), about the Kronstadt uprising of 1921; *Kompromis Naib-Khana* (1931); *Golubi mira* (1938), about the civil war battles in Vladivostok; *Kantsler* (1945); and *Lomonosov* (1953), about Russia's foremost eighteenth-century scholar. Notable among his many novels is *Pokhozhdeniya fakira* (*The Adventures of a Fakir,* 1935), a semi-autobiographical work also translated as *Patched Breeches,* and *I Live a Queer Life.*

The first volume of Ivanov's collected works appeared in 1958. A brief autobiography prefaces the English edition of *Armored Train 14–69* (1933). See also Gleb Struve's *Soviet Russian Literature 1917–50* (1951).

IWASZKIEWICZ, Jarosław (1894–   ), Polish novelist, poet, and essayist, also wrote a number of plays. His biggest hit was *Lato w Nohant* (*Summer in Nohant,* 1936), a dramatization of Frédéric Chopin and George Sand's affair. Other Iwaszkiewicz stage works include a play about Pushkin, *Maskarada* (*Masquerade,* 1938); *Gospodarstwo* (1941); and *Wesele pana Balzaka* (*The Wedding of Balzac,* 1959), dramatizing the great novelist's romance with the countess Evelina Hanska.

In 1948 Iwaszkiewicz won the Olympic Literary Competiton. He also edited his country's leading literary monthly and served as president of the Association of Polish Writers.

J

J.B., a verse play in a prologue and eleven scenes by ARCHIBALD MACLEISH, published and produced in 1958. Setting: interior of a huge and once-splendid but now tattered traveling circus; the present.

This philosophic modernization of the biblical story of Job is one of the few modern American religious-poetic dramas to succeed on Broadway (only Eliot's THE COCKTAIL PARTY fared similarly well). Presented as a play-within-a-play, it has been translated and produced in many countries, and won MacLeish a number of awards, including his third Pulitzer Prize.

The Prologue. "This is it. . . . Where they play the play," Mr. Zuss, a balloon vendor, tells his younger companion Nickles, a popcorn vendor. Themselves actors, they will play the story of Job. The platform is to represent heaven, the floor earth. Mr. Zuss will play God. As for Job—"Oh, there's always / Someone playing Job," Mr. Zuss says and Nickles agrees, "Millions and millions of mankind / Burned, crushed, broken, mutilated, / . . . / Questioning everything. . . ." Nickles is to play God's "opposite," the "Father of lies." He quotes suffering man crying on his dung heap: "If God is God He is not good, / If God is good He is not God." They examine their masks: God's is huge, white, and beautiful; Satan's is dark and small. When Mr. Zuss calls it evil, Nickles demurs: "Look at those lips: they've tasted something / Bitter as a broth of blood / And spat the sup out. Was that evil?" The grin is one of "anguish," the eyes suffer, yet Nickles declares, "I'd rather wear this look of loathing / Night after night than wear that other / Once—that cold complacence." They put on their masks, and in the dark recite verses from the Book of Job. There is rising laughter, which Nickles, his face in agony, swears did not come from him: "If you had seen what I have seen / You'd never laugh again!" His mask eyes can see, and "Hell is now—to *see*." The two resume their recitations: *"Hast thou considered my servant Job. . . ."*

Scene 1. After a short blessing, J.B. and his family have their traditional Thanksgiving dinner. He is a handsome and successful businessman in his mid thirties; his slightly younger wife, Sarah, is an attractive New England woman, and their five beautiful children are happy and lively. People call him lucky, but "It isn't luck when God is good to you," J.B. says; "I've always known that God was with me." Sarah, fearful because things seem to be going too well for them, attributes J.B.'s success solely to his deserving it. J.B. disagrees: "Nobody *deserves* it, Sarah: / Not the world that God has given us." They are well off because God is eternally just, J.B. maintains. *Scene 2.* On the platform the cynical Nickles scoffs at J.B.'s performance ("lousy actor"), optimism ("Best thing you can teach your children / Next to never drawing breath / Is choking on it"), and gratitude ("A rich man's piety stinks"). Mr. Zuss is confident that "God will show [J.B.] what God *is*"—infinite perfection. Nickles replies cynically, "Suffering teaches! Suffering's good for us!" He predicts J.B. will curse God from the ash heap. Mr. Zuss is sure J.B. will trust God, and he answers Nickles's sneer, "It's from the ash heap God is seen / Always! . . . / Every saint and martyr knew that." Through their masks they continue to confront each other with biblical words. The God-mask agrees to have Job thoroughly tried: "*Only / Upon himself / Put not forth thy hand!*"

Scene 3. Two drunken soldiers appear at J.B.'s house. After some roistering they express surprise that the army has failed to notify J.B. and Sarah of their son's death—just at the end of the war. As Sarah grieves pitifully, Nickles leers. *Scene 4.* An attractive girl is made to distract J.B. and Sarah, who are returning from an evening out. Then a reporter and a photographer minutely record the afflicted parents' reactions as they are told of their son's and daughter's deaths in a drunken-driving accident. J.B. curses the reporters and chases them off. But the grief-stricken Sarah blames God, and when J.B. asks, "Shall we . . . / Take the good and not the evil?" and tries to console her, she bitterly turns away: "Don't touch me!" *Scene 5.* Mr. Zuss and Nickles comment on what is to follow. Policemen question J.B. and Sarah—and identify a girl, found raped and killed by a boy "hopped to the eyes," as their daughter. With a broken voice, as Mr. Zuss from above whispers encouragement, J.B. starts intoning: "The Lord giveth . . . the / Lord taketh away!" He stands silently over his dead child's parasol, as Mr. Zuss and Nickles go out into the darkness toward a far-off star. *Scene 6.* Blackness and crashes are followed by sirens: it is an air raid, and Sarah is brought in, calling for her daughter. J.B.'s last child, his bank, and his millions were all blown to bits. Broken, J.B. asks Sarah to pray with him: "The Lord / Giveth . . . / The Lord taketh away. . . ." But she shrieks "Kills! Kills!" as J.B. concludes, "Blessed be the name of the Lord." *Scene 7.* Nickles is disgusted with J.B.'s failure to despair. Putting on his mask, he disputes with the masked Mr. Zuss, and urges that J.B. be tried with personal pain—"*And he will curse thee to thy face.*" The God-mask agrees to

J. B. Nickles (Christopher Plummer) and Mr. Zuss (Raymond Massey, right). New York, 1958. (*Zodiac Photographers*)

the trial though he adds: "*but . . . / Save his life!*"

Scene 8. J.B. is in torn clothes, his skin horribly scorched with burns after an atomic attack. Women walk around him as J.B. begs for death. Sarah taunts him, angry at what she considers J.B.'s betrayal of their dead children: "I will not stay here if you lie— / Connive in your destruction, cringe to it." Then she shouts, "*Curse God and die,*" and leaves her suffering husband. J.B. continues searching in himself for the cause of his misfortunes: "God is unthinkable if we are innocent." One of the women remarks, "And he's alone now." Ignoring them, J.B. raises his arms and cries out, *"Show me my guilt, O God!"* and bitterly asks for comforters. *Scene 9*. Agonizing to discover his guilt and demanding an answer, J.B. is visited by the three comforters: a priest, a psychiatrist, and a social historian. "Why should God reply to *you* / From the blue depths of His Eternity?" the priest asks—a question echoed by the psychiatrist (from the "Blind depths of His Unconsciousness") and the historian (from the "Blank depths of His Necessity"). Individually the tempters intone their unsatisfactory explanations: "God is far above in Mystery. / God is far below in Mindlessness. / God is far within in History." J.B. argues with them, insisting that he be shown his transgression, which alone could warrant his heavy punishment: "Speak of the sin I must have sinned / To suffer what you see me suffer." Ultimately he rejects their pat traditional and modern scientific conclusions. As J.B. cries out, *"God, my God, my God, answer me!"* the Whirlwind Voice proclaims the limitless power and glory of God. With resigned acceptance, J.B. repeats his prototype's biblical prayer: *"But now . . . mine eye seeth thee! Wherefore / I abhor myself . . . and repent. . . ." Scene 10*. Arguing, Nickles declares J.B. a "Pious, contemptible, goddam sheep," while Mr. Zuss is exalted by J.B.'s victory. He insists that they end the play properly. J.B.'s errant wife is to be restored, and eventually they will have more children. "He wouldn't touch her," Nickles predicts, and no man, given the chance, would live his degraded life again. "He does, though," Mr. Zuss replies—as does every man, "time and again," in "Every blessed generation." Nickles visits J.B., tells him what is in store for him, and suggests that he commit suicide. But despite Nickles's raging, J.B. answers the door. *Scene 11*. It is Sarah. She shows him a broken twig with a few petals—which she has found growing in the ashes. J.B. roughly asks why she left him. "You wanted justice and there was none— / Only love," Sarah replies, and tells him of how she sought to die. Softly J.B. drops beside his wife and embraces her: "It's too dark to see." "Then blow on the coal of the heart, my darling," Sarah tells J.B.: "Blow on the coal of the heart and we'll know. . . ." The daylight grows as they begin to straighten up the room.

JACK, OR THE SUBMISSION (*Jacques, ou la soumission*), a one-act "NATURALISTIC comedy" by EUGÈNE IONESCO, published in 1953 and produced in 1955. Setting: "a messy room."

This ABSURDist play (also translated as *Jacques, or Obedience*) about individualism and conformity to bourgeois values features Jacques and his family: Mother Jacques, Father Jacques, Jacqueline, Grandmother Jacques, and Grandfather Jacques. They gradually get him to express the obligatory love for the family potato dish (*"les pommes de terre au lard"*). But he resists their urgings that he marry Roberta, the Robert family's two-nosed daughter. The Roberts thereupon present him with Roberta II, their other "only daughter"—who has three noses. After a lewd conversation he succumbs to her attractions. As the embracing lovers squat, their families perform erotic dances and the darkened stage is filled with animal noises.

The sequel to this play is THE FUTURE IS IN EGGS, OR IT TAKES ALL SORTS TO MAKE A WORLD.

JACOBOWSKY AND THE COLONEL (*Jacobowsky und der Oberst*), "a comedy of a tragedy" in three acts by FRANZ WERFEL, published and produced in 1944. Setting: Paris and the French coastline, June 1940.

Originally this play appeared in a popular American adaptation by S. N. BEHRMAN, who stressed its comedic elements. In 1945 Werfel published his own more serious German version of what is a sometimes autobiographical depiction of a Jewish refugee's escape. It was filmed as *Me and the Colonel* (1959), and made into an opera score by Giselher Klebe (*Jacobowsky und der Oberst*, 1965).

As France is falling during World War II, a Polish Jew who has fled Hitler through all Europe joins forces with a conventionally anti-Semitic Polish officer to escape Paris and transmit secret papers to England. Against the somber backdrop of Nazi conquest and vignettes of people's different reactions to stress, this unlikely pair make their journey in a car that the resourceful Jew acquires. They are menaced by a comic Gestapo officer, and accompanied by the orderly and the mistress of the Polish officer. A decadent and stubborn but courageous man, the officer learns much about suffering from the kindly, optimistic, and amusing Jacobowsky who alone, it is decided when they reach the Allied lines, deserves to be given passage to escape and begin a new life.

JACOB'S DREAM (*Jaákobs Traum*), a verse drama in two acts by RICHARD BEER-HOFMANN, published in 1918 and produced in 1919. Setting: a Beersheba courtyard and the mountain Beth-el, at the biblical time of the Patriarchs.

Conceived as a prelude to DIE HISTORIE VON KÖNIG DAVID, *Jacob's Dream* had major productions throughout the world—including in New York, where in 1927 Habima presented an EXPRESSIONIST version of the play in its repertoire. The play is neoromantically transcendental in its poetic dramatization of the Bible and its panegyric of Judaism.

Act I. His wives are waiting as Edom (Esau) returns from the hunt. He is infuriated with his mother for tricking him out of the paternal blessing. "Am I not your son, your flesh?" the proud and powerful yet God-fearing first-born asks, deeply hurt. "Your pleasures are of the earth! So take your earthly portion!" Rebecca replies, giving him the farm and all the family's holdings. She contrasts his practicality and lust for life with his brother Jacob's daily "wrestling with God," Jacob's eternal quest, and his forefathers' "doubts and dreams and longings." With growing ecstasy, Rebecca envisions Jacob as the bearer of Israel's fate, his glorious "blessing—*and* the blessing's burden." Edom rushes out with his hunting dogs, vowing to "tear to pieces, him—my brother." Rebecca forces Edom's wives to kneel and join in her prayer: "Blessed is he who blesses Jacob! Cursed— / Accursed he who curses him!"

Act II. With limitless compassion, Jacob perceives all men and beasts, even the rocks and the brooks. How can he "Know of all suffering—you, boy—who told you / What it means to be old?" his amazed slave asks as Jacob reveals the man's long-forgotten secret feelings. When the bloodthirsty Edom tracks him down and shoots, the arrow is intercepted by the lamb Jacob is cradling. Jacob then pacifies his angry brother with gentle love, reconciles him to their mother, and reassures him that he is not inferior though Jacob has prevailed: "God wants me THUS, and wants you OTHERWISE!" Alone, Jacob in his dream has agonizing debates with the archangels and with Satan, who expresses the curse that accompanies the blessing. The Voice of God confirms it: "Mercy—I grant thee not!" But the Voice adds, "I wish My guilt toward thee, My son, to be so great / That—as atonement—above all I set thee high!" Awakening, Jacob accepts eternal woe with eternal life, though he asks, humble yet proud, that each of the chosen ones be helped: "Lord—do it not for his sake—but for THINE!" Then he anoints the rock on which he slept. As day breaks and he is called from the valley, he sings out his new name: "No, not 'Jacob'! Down / To thee comes—who with God strove—Yisro-El!"

JAHNN, Hans Henny (1894–1959), German novelist and playwright, began as an EXPRESSIONIST but gradually and less PRESENTATIONALly depicted psychological studies of passion and perversion in the manner of ALFRED BRUST. Jahnn first achieved success with the drama *Pastor Ephraim Magnus* (1919), a very long tragic disquisition about a despairing clergyman who enshrines the headless corpse of his executed brother, yearns to be crucified, and gouges out his own eyes. Characteristically agonizing over the relationship of man to his body at the expense of his soul, it ends with Jahnn's most pervasive belief: "He who has only flesh is doomed." *Die Krönung Richards III* (1921) dramatizes English history with similar emphases on passion and erotic murder, juxtaposing Richard III with the even more evil widow of Edward IV, Queen Elizabeth. Also in verse and in a like manner, Jahnn aroused considerable controversy at the Berlin State Theatre in 1926 with his bestial *Medea,* here a fat, aging Negress whose sons by Jason are rejected as half-castes; the play received very popular German productions in the 1960's in a revised version Jahnn had prepared only months before his death. His other hits include *Armut, Reichtum, Mensch und Tier* (1948), a mystic peasant tragedy; and *Thomas Chatterton* (1955), a dramatized biography of the eighteenth-century poet-forger who at eighteen committed suicide.

Born in a Hamburg suburb, Jahnn wrote distinguished but complex novels that evidence the influence of Freud and JAMES JOYCE. Jahnn was a pacifist who lived in Norway during World War I and whose works were later banned by the Nazis. In his last years, he wrote *Denkspiele* (idea plays) on race and the atomic bomb. Appearing posthumously, these plays include *Die Trümmer des Gewissens* (1961), the tragedy of a nuclear scientist and a plea to ban the bomb, produced as *Der staubige Regenbogen.*

JAMES, Henry (1843–1916), Anglo-American writer, is distinguished for his novels, short stories, and essays. His only play to achieve fame was GUY DOMVILLE (1895) and its catastrophic reception kept James from developing his talents as a dramatist. Nonetheless, a very significant part of his life was devoted to the stage. He frequently went to the theatre, published perceptive dramatic criticism, and completed twelve plays. Some of these were moderately successful, but they never brought him the wealth for which he yearned and kept writing. The only real hit connected with his work is BERKELEY SQUARE, Balderston and Squire's dramatic adaptation of James's incompleted tale, *The Sense of the Past*. Also popular was Ruth (1912–) and Augustus Goetz's (1901–57) dramatization of James's *Washington Square* as *The Heiress* (1947). GUY BOLTON's dramatization of *The Wings of the Dove* as *Child of Fortune* (1956) and MARGUERITE DURAS's adaptation of *The Beast in the Jungle* fared less well.

In his earlier plays James tried to match the lightness of OSCAR WILDE, whom he referred to as the "unspeakable one." These include three experimental comic sketches published between 1869 and 1872: *Pyramus and Thisbe, Still Waters,* and *A Change of Heart*. The first work he seriously intended for the stage was a dramatization of his earliest and greatest popular success, *Daisy Miller*. He transformed the novella into an artificial comedy with a happy ending. When it was turned down for production, James had it printed (1882). His dramatization of his novel *The American* was more successful; also given a happy ending, it was produced in 1891 and enjoyed some popularity, but failed to bring James the fortune he dreamed of. Nonetheless, he was inspired to write and publish four comedies in 1894–95: *Tenants, Disengaged* (based on his story "The Solution"), *The Album,* and *The Reprobate* (produced posthumously). These were followed by the harrowing *Guy Domville* experience.

Contrary to his announced determination, however, *Guy Domville* did not end James's relation with the theatre. The same year he wrote *Summersoft* for Ellen Terry; a one-act play, it depicts a charming American widow's attempts to rescue a country estate from capitalist exploitation. When Terry failed to produce it, James made it into a short story, "Covering End"; and at the request of Sir Johnston Forbes-Robertson thirteen years later, he reworked it into his most popular stage work, the three-act comedy *The High Bid,* produced in 1908. Its success encouraged James to complete his dramatization of "Owen Wingrave" as *The Saloon,* produced in 1911. In 1908 he dramatized his novel *The Other House,* originally intended as an IBSENite murder drama; it remained unproduced until 1968. James was one of the literary notables invited to write a play for Charles Frohman's London repertory. He completed a three-act comedy, *The Outcry,* about an American collector's attempted raiding of English art holdings; when Frohman's project collapsed in 1910, James converted *The Outcry* into a novel. It was his last play.

James was unable to reproduce for the theatre the intense but subtly wrought drama of the novels that make him one of the great modern writers. Suffering cruelly from the rebuffs common in the world of the theatre, he fulminated against the theatre's grossness and escaped—somewhat like his Guy Domville—into a literary priesthood. Yet his passion for the theatre and his insight into the art of drama are well demonstrated in his reviews. Collected and edited by Allan Wade, James's *The Scenic Art* (1948) is a finely etched picture of the French, English, and American theatrical scene from 1872 to 1901. The monumental collection of *The Complete Plays of Henry James* (1949) was edited by Leon Edel; it contains comprehensive notes as well as the biography of James the dramatist.

JANE CLEGG, a play in three acts by ST. JOHN ERVINE, produced in 1913 and published in 1914. Setting: contemporary Ireland.

This play has a NATURALISTic urban setting, and, like JOHN FERGUSON, features a strong protagonist struggling nobly against adversity. As with *John Ferguson,* the 1920 American production of this tragedy (which had opened in England at Manchester's Gaiety Theatre) was so successful that it assured the continuation of the New York Theatre Guild.

For a dozen years Jane Clegg has lived in poverty with her scoundrel husband Henry, a liar and a philanderer. She has always been affectionate and tried hard to raise and educate her young children properly. Henry, it is true, loves Jane and admires her nobility; but he is weak, has always been spoiled by his fussy mother (who lives with them), is not very intelligent, and, himself coarse, feels more at ease with a common mistress. When a small inheritance comes Jane's way, she stands up to Henry. But he embezzles money to pay the bookie who controls him, and the inheritance may have to be used to save him from prison. Then Jane discovers that Henry has used the money for tickets to Canada for himself and his mistress. Jane determinately tells him to leave for good. He begs to be allowed to stay and deplores her morality: she should tear his mistress to bits, instead of "condoning the offense" by sending him back to his mistress. But when Jane insists that he leave, and refuses to kiss him good-bye (it would be "a sin," now), he goes out slowly, puzzled and unable to understand her.

JAPAN. Japanese drama became known to the modern Western world largely because of WILLIAM BUTLER YEATS's popularization of the No drama. In Japan itself, however, there had been earlier attempts to update the classics, even by the great Kabuki dramatist Kawatake Mokuami (1816–93)* and the stars for whom he wrote. Modern Japanese theatre—which is the best in all of Asia—began in the Meija era (1868–1912) at a time when Western civilization, including its drama, made its first impact on the hitherto-insular nation. Various theatre societies were founded and with them originated Shimpa. This new drama school, the first departure from Japan's classic modes, reached its height in 1904–09 and its principal figures were Sudō Sadanori (1867–1909) and the oft-imprisoned Kawakami Otojirō (1864–1911). Beginning with a drama about a martyred leader, *Itagaki-Kun Sōnan Jikki* (1891), Sudō and Kawakami wrote (as well as directed and acted in)

* The Japanese follow a reverse name order from that of Westerners, citing family names (surnames) first, individual (or given) names next; this order is followed here.

popular liberal political satires and thrillers like Kawakami's *Igai* (1894) and its sequels. When the Sino-Japanese war broke out, their patriotic and military spectacles flourished. All these productions were so REALISTIC that the audiences, who had been accustomed to stylized theatre, became confused by the make-believe and the employment of women performers; on one occasion their stupefaction apparently caused them to kill an actor who played the villain.

Shimpa, much of which was melodramatic and sentimental hack work, consisted of more dramatized novels and translated European works than original plays. It was but the precursor of the New Theatre—Shingeki—that was launched in 1906 by TSUBOUCHI SHŌYŌ. Its movements began to parallel those of the Occident, and they were influenced particularly by the NATURALISM of HENRIK IBSEN and the SYMBOLISM and stylization of MAURICE MAETERLINCK and HUGO VON HOFMANNSTHAL. Although he was a second-rate playwright, Osanai Kaoru (1881–1928) is particularly important in the history of the Shingeki: in 1909 he cofounded the Jiyu Gekijo (Free Theatre), which for ten years introduced modern European plays to Japan; and from 1924 until his death, as director of the short-lived Tsukiji Shogekijo (Tsukiji little theatre), he brought that company everlasting distinction with his productions of modern Western as well as native drama.

Other early modern Japanese writers of note include NAKAMURA KICHIZŌ, KIKUCHI HIROSHI, and MUSHANOKŌJI SANEATSU. Religious drama was written by Kurata Hyakuzō (1891–1943), whose play on the life of the thirteenth-century Buddhist Shinran, *Shukke to sono Deshi* (*The Priest and His Disciple,* 1916), was praised by ROMAIN ROLLAND as one of the world's great modern religious dramas. Seto Eiichi's (1892–1934) plays enjoyed considerable popular success, particularly the romantic tragedy of a business failure and his geisha, *Futasuji-michi* (1931). The novelist-playwright Yamamoto Yūzō (1887–), who translated AUGUST STRINDBERG and ARTHUR SCHNITZLER, was a popular dramatist of the 1920's.* Also popular was the sentimental drama of Kawaguchi Matsutarō (1899–), especially his chronicle of the family proprietors of an eating establishment, *Furyu Fukagawa-uta* (1936). In the 1920's and 1930's foreign as well as domestic left-wing proletarian drama flourished; among its major figures was Tokunaga Sunao (1899–1958), whose hit was his dramatized autobiographical "worker's novel" (published also in French, German, and Russian) on the mass strike he helped lead against Japanese publishers, *Taiyō-no-nai Machi* (1930). This and other drama of social criticism—and with it much of the new Westernized Japanese drama—was increasingly suppressed after the China Incident of 1937. It was altogether banned by the outbreak of World War II, though the left-wing theatre was to reappear in the 1950's.

After World War II Japanese drama, like that of the West, developed in various directions. Important postwar writers are FUKUDA TSUNEARI, KINOSHITA JUNJI, and Japan's best-known modern playwright (and novelist), MISHIMA YUKIO. Another dramatist of note is the Nagasaki-born Tanaka Chikao (1905–), whose moving play about a returning war veteran, *Kumo no Hate* (1947), established the *Bungakuza* (Literary Theatre). Hotta Kiyomi's (1922–) *Shima* (1957) attracted mass audiences because it was the first dramatization of the atom bomb's effects on individuals. A major hit was *Dorei-gari* (1955), which attacked immoral profiteering on vivisection and militarism; it was written by the physician Abe Kōbō (1924–), who subsequently wrote a musical fantasy on similar themes, *Yurei wa Kokoni Iru* (1958), and the drama *Tomodachi* (*Friends,* 1967) about a young man destroyed by a family who cheerfully move into his home; Abe Kōbō became world-famous in 1964 when his novel *Suna no Onna* (*The Woman in the Dunes*) was filmed and published in English. Kikuta Kazuo (1908–) wrote musical comedy and other hits in the 1940's and 1950's.

Most popular of all were the "New Kabuki" writers Hōjō Hideji (1902–), whose "Later Shimpa" hits dealing with his native Osaka include the domestic drama *Okami* (1952), the courtesan drama *Kottai San* (1955), and a three-part play about the pauper who became a great *shogi* (Japanese chess) player, *Ōshō* (1947–51); and Funabashi Seiichi (1904–), a writer of erotically charged novels and dramas, one of them on Samurai use of a geisha to distract Townsend Harris from helping to modernize Japan. Hōjō and Funabashi have employed a modern style, but their plots are derived from Lady Murasaki's *The Tale of Genji* and other classics and history, not unlike the Akutagawa Ryūnosuke (1892–1927) story popularized by the movie and Fay [Mitchell] (1915?–) and Michael Kanin's (1910–) American stage version, *Rashomon* (1959).

Though humor and satire are relished less by Japanese theatre audiences than emotionalism, an exception is the drama of Iizawa Tadasu (1909–), a popular comic playwright; his very successful *Mō-hitori-no* (1970), set at the end of World War II, lampoons fanaticism and the military in its portrayal of a humble shoemaker's refusing to go along with a mad general's plot to make the shoemaker Emperor of Japan. Avant-garde drama since the 1960's has included a Japanese equivalent of the theatre of the ABSURD; it mixed old Shimpa plots, the *yose* (Japanese variety turns that originated in the late nineteenth century), and techniques of popular fiction and movies. A leading playwright among the SURREALISTS is Terayama Shuji (1936–), whose works suggest the influence of FERNANDO ARRABAL and JEAN

* Glen W. Shaw's translation of his trilogy on feudal, transitional (featuring Townsend Harris), and modern Japan, *Three Plays* (1935), consists of *Sakazaki Dewa no Kami* (*Sakazaki, Lord Dewa,* 1921), *Nyonin-aishi, Tōjin Okichi monogatari* (*The Story of Chink Okichi,* 1930), *Seimei no kammuri* (*The Crown of Life* 1920), and an introduction by the translator.

GENET; first to be translated into English was *La Marie Vison* (*Mink Marie,* 1967), his French-titled Japanese drama about a homosexual living in a libidinous imaginary world and, as part of a bizarre revenge, mothering a little boy.

Little modern Japanese drama is readily available in English aside from the translations noted under individual playwrights. Both of the collections by Yozan T. Iwasaki and Glenn Hughes have prefatory essays: *Three Modern Japanese Plays* (1923) includes drama by Nakamura and Kikuchi, while *New Plays from Japan* (1930) has a play by Mushanokōji, as well as the anticipatory autobiographical (and STRINDBERGian) *Death* by the nobleman-scholar Arishima Takeo, who in 1923 committed suicide with his married inamorata, and *Burning Alive* (1921), an almost immediately banned one-acter by the popular reviewer-dramatist Suzuki Senzaburo (1893–1924). Religious drama by Mushanokōji (as well as religious poetry and fiction) appear in Umeyo Hirano's *Buddhist Plays from Japanese Literature* (1962).

There are extensive discussions of the modern drama in the latter chapters of Faubion Bowers's *Japanese Theatre* (1952), in V. H. Viglielmo's translation of Okazaki Yoshie's *Japanese Literature in the Meiji Era* (1955), in the Japanese National Commission for UNESCO's *Theatre in Japan* (1963), in Frank A. Lombard's *An Outline History of Japanese Drama* (1966), and in Peter Arnott's *The Theatres of Japan* (1969). An interesting study of the early modern drama is Osman Edwards's *Japanese Plays and Playfellows* (1901). In 1970 appeared the first number of *Concerned Theatre Japan,* an illustrated English-language quarterly that features articles as well as playscripts.

JAR, THE (*La giara*), a one-act comedy by LUIGI PIRANDELLO, produced in 1917 and published in 1925. Setting: the Sicilian countryside on an October day.

First published as a short story in 1909, this play was originally produced in Sicilian dialect.

An irascible farmer with a penchant for lawsuits is infuriated at the breaking of his brand new olive-oil jar—a huge, veritable "Mother Superior of a jar!" The masterful local tinker mends it—but then cannot get out of it. Joined by the lawyer, they argue and shout amidst the laughter of the farmhands. The old tinker refuses to pay for the jar, which will have to be broken if he is to get out, and calmly lights his pipe. The farmer retires for the night, and the tinker starts a party with the farmhands. Unable to bear the noisy singing, the enraged farmer rushes out shouting, and kicks the jar down the slope. It smashes into a tree and the tinker emerges triumphantly: "I win! I win!"

JARDIEL PONCELA, Enrique (1901–52), Spanish novelist, playwright, and journalist, wrote some forty popular light dramas, many of them in collaboration with others. Though he produced mysteries, romances, and melodramas, he was particularly praised for his fantastic and extravagant humor, influenced in part by LUIGI PIRANDELLO. Notable among his own plays are *Angelina, o el honor de un brigadier* (1934), a parody verse play; *Eloisa está debajo de un almendro* (1943); and *El pañuelo de la dama errante* (1945).

JARRY, Alfred [-Henry] (1873–1907), French playwright, novelist, and essayist, is famous for his SUCCÈS DE SCANDALE, *Ubu roi* (KING UBU, 1896), also translated as *Ubu Rex.* For a while after his short, ultra-Bohemian life, he was forgotten. Then his reputation as a precursor of SURREALISM and avant-garde drama in general began to grow. In 1927 ANTONIN ARTAUD founded the Théâtre Alfred-Jarry, and by the time of the mid-century theatre of the ABSURD Jarry's importance as a seminal modern dramatist was no longer questioned.

Jarry was born in Laval, the son of a cloth manufacturer. A brilliant but unruly student at the Lycée in Rennes, he frequently disorganized classes—particularly those of one M. Hébert, the incarnation of all Jarry considered hateful in the middle class, and the prototype of Father Ubu. In 1888, with other schoolboys, Jarry wrote and performed his first (now lost) Ubu play, *Les Polonais.* He continued his studies in Paris, under Henri Bergson, and soon began to write and publish in reviews that he himself founded. Before the production of his first and most famous work, he published two SYMBOLIST plays—*Les Minutes de sable mémorial* (1894) and *César Antéchrist* (1895)—in both of which the figure of Ubu appears. Jarry chose to protest against the cosmic senselessness he perceived by leading a completely dissolute life. He assumed an eccentric "Ubuesque" pose, roomed in incredible squalor, and literally drank himself to death with alcohol and ether.

He expressed his view of life in the Ubu plays. To his anti- and non-intellectual rebellion against middle-class morality and cosmic absurdity he gave the ironically pompous title PATAPHYISICS. His protest—expressed with Rabelaisian obscenity—assumes a deceptively simple form: that of the children's fairy tale and of the puppet show. He wrote about a dozen plays in all. These include *Les Paralipomènes d'Ubu* (1896); *Ubu cocu* (*Ubu Cockolded,* written in 1897 or 1898 and translated also as *Turd Cuckolded*), which features Ubu as a maliciously destructive commoner; *L'Amour en visites* (1898); *Par la taille* (1906, written about 1898); *Ubu enchaîné* (*Ubu Enchained,* 1900; translated also as *King Turd Enslaved*), which parodies human nature and depicts the Ubus in France, with Father Ubu seeking slavery to achieve the only possible freedom in a "free society"; *Ubu sur la butte* (1901); the opera libretto for *Pantagruel* (1911, written c. 1903); and *Le Moutardier du pape* (1907).

Jarry's success in having Lugné-Poë stage *King Ubu* gained him immediate fame. In the frequently reprinted letter he wrote Lugné-Poë, Jarry listed specific instructions for the play's staging. These summarize his artistic views. Jarry strove to break with NATURALISM (the only contemporary play he admired was Ibsen's PEER GYNT) and to return to the primitive and stylized: masks, plain backdrops, token crowds, and idiosyncratic speech for the protagonist. Later Artaud was to use, modify, and systematize the implications of Jarry's practices and notes into a coherent philosophy of drama. But it was the utterance by Fermin Gémier (as Ubu) of *King Ubu*'s opening scatological expletive which helped to inaugurate the many types of modern drama that subsequently tried to shock audiences out of their smugness.

Cyril Connelly and Simon W. Taylor's translation of *The Ubu Plays* (1968) has an introduction. *King Ubu* has been anthologized and published separately, and others in the "Ubu Cycle" (*Ubu cocu* and *Ubu colonialist*) appear, along with Jarry's fiction and essays on drama and the theatre, in Roger Shattuck and Simon W. Taylor's *Selected Works of Alfred Jarry* (1965), a volume that also contains an informative introduction and a bibliography. See also Shattuck's *The Banquet Years* (1958).

JATAKAS are dramatized stories about the birth of Gautama Buddha and one of his many lives. Though Buddhist law prohibits his representation on stage, *jatakas* have remained a popular staple of the folk theatres in twentieth-century Asia, particularly in BURMA, CAMBODIA, LAOS, and THAILAND.

See James R. Brandon's *Theatre in Southeast Asia* (1967).

JEFFERS, [John] **Robinson** (1887–1962), American poet, wrote a popular theatrical adaptation of Euripides's *Medea* (1946), a *tour de force* in its (and Judith Anderson's) portrayal of Medea's violent hatred. His second adaptation from Euripides, that of *Hippolytus* as *The Cretan Woman* (1954), fared less well in the theatre: his Phaedra is a demanding woman, and the tragedy is in part triggered by Hippolytus's homosexuality. Also produced were some of Jeffers's longer dramatic poems, notably *Dear Judas* (1929), an unorthodox retelling of the Gospel story, produced in 1947; and in 1950 *The Tower Beyond Tragedy* (1924), an adaptation (primarily in narrative form) of the first two parts of Aeschylus's *Oresteia* in which Jeffers stressed Cassandra's prophetic powers, Electra's incestuous feelings, and Orestes's development into an ideal hero—and which features Clytemnestra doing a striptease to distract the soldiers.

JELLICOE, Ann (1928–), English director and dramatist, has written a number of plays in which she has attempted to portray "incoherent people" who are unable to analyze (much less articulate) the emotions, fears, and insecurities that drive them. Because she eschews traditional appeals to the audience's intellect, her dialogue is for the most part meaningless. The audience, she has noted, must allow itself "to be excited by the visual action and the gradual crescendo of noise underlining this" in her plays; then it may "begin to appreciate what it's about." When Jellicoe adhered less rigidly to her method, she produced a popular success: her *The Knack* (1958), a comedy staged in 1961 and filmed, is a hilarious depiction of three men and a girl, all obsessed with sex.

Her first play, *The Sport of My Mad Mother* (1956), is a semiEXPRESSIONISTIC depiction of fear among a group of Teddy boys; they are inspired by a girl who corresponds to the Hindu war goddess (the title comes from a hymn to that goddess: "All creation is the sport of my mad mother Kali"). Jellicoe's next work, *The Rising Generation* (1960), a spectacular feminist youth pageant, was even less successful: it was rejected by the Girl Guides' Association which had commissioned it. Her *Shelley* (1965) is an atypically straightforward dramatization of the poet's last eleven years. It was followed by a comedy, *The Give-away* (1969).

Jellicoe was born in Middlesborough and studied at the Central School of Speech and Drama, whose staff she later joined. With considerable distinction she has directed many plays, including her own adaptations of ANTON CHEKHOV and HENRIK IBSEN. See John Russell Taylor's *Anger and After* (titled *The Angry Theatre* in the United States; revised edition, 1969).

JEROME, Jerome K[lapka] (1859–1927), English writer and actor born in Walsall, Staffordshire, became well known in England and America with amusing novels and accounts: *On the Stage—and Off* (1888), *Idle Thoughts of an Idle Fellow* (1889), *Three Men in a Boat* (1889), and others. He was a drama critic (for the London *Times*), a magazine editor, and the author of a number of plays, some no longer extant. His importance as a dramatist rests on THE PASSING OF THE THIRD FLOOR BACK (1908), in which Sir Johnston Forbes-Robertson was a great hit, and which was frequently revived.

See Alfred Moss's *Jerome K. Jerome: His Life and His Works* (1929).

JEWISH WIDOW, THE (*Die jüdische Witwe*), a play in five acts by GEORG KAISER, published in 1911 and produced in 1921. Setting: biblical Bethulia and the Assyrian Camp.

Written in 1904 and revised in 1908, this was Kaiser's first published play, and the first to bring him some recognition. It is an imaginative dramatization of the apocryphal Judith's slaying of Holofernes. But here Judith, like FRANK WEDKIND's Lulu, embodies ruthless sexuality. Forced to marry an old man, the unsatisfied twelve-year-old Judith kills her senile husband and seeks gratification in the woman-starved enemy camp. She decapitates the brutal Holofernes because she is enamored of the king, Nebuchadnezzar. He, in turn, flees with his armies, and the frustrated Judith, now a heroine to her people, is dedicated a priestess. Her resistance to apparent lifelong virginity stops when she sees the virile young High Priest. "Caressing her thighs with trembling fingers, her body tensing," she goes with him into the inner sanctuary—and at last is gratified.

JITTA'S ATONEMENT (*Frau Gitta's Sühne*), a play in three acts by SIEGFRIED TREBITSCH and revised by BERNARD SHAW, produced in 1920 and published in 1923. Setting: Danzig, 1920.

Shaw's translation of this play was published in 1923, in his TRANSLATIONS AND TOMFOOLERIES, and in the later editions of Shaw's *Complete* and *Collected Plays*. In his "Translator's Note" Shaw paid grateful homage to Trebitsch and explained his changes of setting and tone, which transform the original tragedy into "almost a comedy": "In real life the consequences of conjugal infidelity are seldom either so serious as they are assumed to be in romantic tragedy or so trivial as in farcical comedy."

Professor Bruno Haldenstedt dies in a rented flat during a meeting with his mistress, Mrs. Jitta Lenkheim, who hurriedly leaves the compromising situation. Attempts to identify the mistress result in the widow's relief at Jitta's assurance to her that it was not she; in the marriage of his daughter, who admires Jitta and is therefore happy when Jitta confesses that it *was* she; and in a reconciliation with her husband, Haldenstedt's executor and literary heir, after Jitta's repentance.

JOAN OF LORRAINE, a play in two acts by MAXWELL ANDERSON, produced in 1946 and published in 1947. Setting: the stage of a New York theatre, 1946.

This play's Broadway success was greatly helped by Ingrid Bergman's appearance in the title rôle. The film (1948, with the same star) omitted the play's modern framework, which is juxtaposed with the lyrical (though prose) play-within-a-play and supplies the dramatic tension—and Anderson's viewpoints, which are voiced by the Director.

The rehearsal of a new play about Saint Joan is interrupted by "interludes" in which the Director argues with his cast—primarily with the star, Mary Grey. She is increasingly disturbed by the "desecration of Joan" in the author's changes: "The way the play's being re-written it's in favor of compromise and getting along as well as you can with what you have." The Director, harassed with practical problems that require constant compromise if the play is to open at all, believes this interpretation of Joan to be realistic and true to life. "Nearly always the crooks are in control," he says; they "were running the earth when she was alive," and if Joan was to accomplish anything, she had to work with them—"just as we have to decide whether we'll keep an eye on the United Nations or give up and look the other way." To put on their idealistic play, for instance, the Director must deal with and bail out the swindling theatre renter. After their lunch break, the cast ask the Director to explain why faith is needed at all, and what his faith is. Everyone has faith in something, he tells them: "I believe in democracy, and I believe the theatre is the temple of democracy." When the rehearsal continues, Mary balks again, unable to understand how Joan "can decide so deliberately to give her blessing to corruption." The question of faith, the central one of the play-within-the-play as the Director sees it, is the focal one in Joan's trial scene: "Why do you believe what you believe?" After her recantation, Joan prays in prison, and her voices speak to her. Suddenly Joan regains her faith and with it the courage to face the stake. And Joan's words suddenly make Mary understand: "It's true that she would compromise in little things—but it's also true that she would not compromise her belief—her own soul." Now Mary will act in the play, though the author has changed the portrait of Joan to some extent: "It doesn't matter what we try to say about her. Nobody can use her for an alien purpose. Her own meaning will always come through, and all the rest will be forgotten." And she plays the last scene: Joan walking before the executioner, ready to "follow my faith, even to the fire."

JOHN BULL'S OTHER ISLAND, a play in four acts by BERNARD SHAW, produced in 1904 and published in 1909. Setting: London and Rosscullen, Ireland; 1904.

In a "Preface for Politicians" Shaw had "a good deal more to say about the relations between the Irish and the English [and about imperialism] than will be found in my play," which is more of a platform for witty polemics and a presentation of stage Irishmen than a dramatic story. Written at the request of WILLIAM BUTLER YEATS for the Irish Literary Theatre, it was beyond that theatre's resources, and was first produced in England. The play, which amusingly inverts and thus explores Irish and English characteristics, succeeded with English audiences for its presentation of irresponsible Irishmen, and with the Irish for the sympathetic presentation of their problems and for the satiric portrayal of the English "hero."

Thomas Broadbent, an English babbitt, and his Irish business partner, Larry Doyle, decide to visit the latter's home town. Doyle has not been to Ireland for eighteen years and is worried about seeing both his father, whose religious and political attitudes he opposes, and Nora Reilly, who is still in love with him. When the townspeople want him to run for election to Parliament, Doyle shocks them with his "scandalous" views on the disestablished church, free trade, absentee landownership, and home rule. The clever and effusive Broadbent, on the other hand, impresses them with his practicality, money, and conventional views; and he amuses them with the good-natured stupidity with which he conducts his campaign, which features an almost catastrophic car ride with a pig and makes him a laughingstock—but endears him to the town. Broadbent wins the nomination and even succeeds, in one day, in winning Nora on the rebound from Doyle. He tells Doyle and the unfrocked priest Keegan, an unsentimental idealist who talks to a grasshopper and is thought to be half crazy, of his plans to make the town prosper by replacing the small tenant farms with a hotel and a golf course. Before Broadbent goes off to choose the site, Keegan tells of his own dream of heaven: a trinity of state-church-people, work-play-life, priest-worshiper-worshiped—"a godhead in which all life is human and all humanity divine: three in one and one in three. It is, in short, the dream of a madman."

JOHN, Errol (1925?–), West Indian actor and playwright, became known with his prize-winning *Moon on a Rainbow Shawl* (1957). Appearing in the United States, England, and a number of European countries, it is a study of slum life among the Negroes of John's native Port-of-Spain, Trinidad. John has also written a filmscript, *The Dispossessed,* and has played major roles in English and American productions.

JOHN FERGUSON, a tragedy in four acts by ST. JOHN ERVINE, published and produced in 1915. Setting: the kitchen of a farmhouse in County Down, Ireland; summer 1885.

Ervine's masterpiece features a simple family of North Irish Protestants. The aged title character undergoes harrowing trials but never loses his faith in God. Despite its dependence on stock melodramatic devices, it is an effective "play of the soil" that has repeatedly moved audiences. Noteworthy among its revivals after the Abbey Theatre premiere were a very successful production that saved the newly founded New York Theatre Guild in 1919 and a television performance in 1947.

Act I. John Ferguson, an invalided old farmer, is sitting with his Bible as his wife knits. "Weeping may endure for a night, but joy cometh in the morning," he reads. Their son Andrew is not much of a farmer, and their farm mortgage is about to be foreclosed by Henry Witherow, a coarse neighbor. Only a check from Ferguson's American brother can save them. Kindly about everyone, Ferguson excuses the lateness of the mail, the wicked mortgage holder, and an importuning, whistle-blowing beggar who is a shrewd half-wit in saying: "I can't see God's purpose, but I know well there is one. His hand never makes a mistake." Hope rises again when the grocer, James Caesar, wants to marry Ferguson's beloved daughter Hannah. He is willing to pay the mortgage, but Hannah despises him as a spiritless "old collie." Caesar has a streak of meanness in him, and constantly blusters about what he will do to Witherow, who has injured him, too; but he is too cowardly ever to do anything. When Witherow comes in and hectors everyone, Hannah slaps him. But as the check has failed to come and they face being dispossessed, Hannah, urged on by her mother and eager to help the father she adores, at last agrees to marry Caesar. They go out together. Soon Hannah returns, unable to face marrying a man who so repels her. Ferguson trusts in divine providence, and agrees to let Hannah go and tell Witherow to foreclose. Then he asks for his Bible.

Act II. When Caesar comes back a little later and learns that the wedding is off, he is furious. "Would you marry a woman that doesn't want you?" Hannah's brother Andrew asks. "I want her, don't I? What does it matter to me whether she wants me or not so long as I'm married to her?" Caesar replies, and whines about his love for her, though he "knew she was only consenting to have me to save your farm." Suddenly Hannah runs in hysterically. In broken snatches she tells her horrified family that Witherow has raped her. Caesar swears this time to kill the man, and Andrew encourages him. But Ferguson, though hit hard by this new calamity, objects when Andrew quotes, "An eye for an eye, da, and a tooth for a tooth!" "That's not the spirit that lives now, son!" Ferguson replies; "you have your own work to do in the world, and you must leave God to do His; it's His work to judge, not ours!" Though Hannah needs him to comfort her, Ferguson goes out to stop Caesar. The whistle-playing half-wit knows Caesar will be too cowardly, anyway: "If I was Hannah's brother, I'd make sure!" Andrew finally takes his gun and goes out.

Act III. In the morning Ferguson still defends his view, glad he was able to resist the temptation to harm Witherow: "God's Word says I must love my enemies." Andrew is incredulous at such forbearance. "Witherow will have to make his answer to God," Ferguson explains: "He just gives knowledge to you so that you can see yourself as He sees you, and that's your punishment, Andrew, if you've done wrong. It's knowing yourself as God knows you that hurts you harder nor anything else in the world." Caesar comes in, full of self-loathing. Despite his passionate hate of Witherow and his intention to shoot him, he was too fearful, and cowered in the fields all night. But word soon comes that Witherow was, indeed, shot. Now Caesar starts quaking and tries to hide, fearful he will be blamed for the murder. "I'd be proud if you had done it, Jimmy!" Hannah says, and stands by the panicky Caesar as the constables arrest him.

Act IV. Though Caesar keeps denying it, Hannah is sure he killed Witherow, and for the first time is kind to him. Ferguson remains adamant in condemning the killing: "Nothing can extenuate a murder." He is somewhat jolted when the check from America comes—two weeks too late because his brother had missed the earlier mail. "One man's dead and another's in jail in danger of his life because my uncle Andrew forgot the mail day," Hannah remarks bitterly. Her brother Andrew, increasingly conscience-stricken at Caesar's suffering for his own act, confesses that it was he who had killed Witherow. At last Ferguson is shaken to his innermost being. Momentarily he thinks of hiding his son, though he abhors the crime. Andrew's mother, too, wants him to escape. But Andrew insists on giving himself up: "Oh, don't you mind what my da said to Jimmy: 'You can't hide from yourself'? There's nothing truer nor that." And he leaves, accompanied by Hannah. Alone with his weeping wife, Ferguson opens the Bible. "And the king was much moved, and went up to the chamber over the gate, and wept: and as he went"—Ferguson reads from II Samuel 18, but finally collapses, sobbing—"thus he said, O my son Absalom, my son, my son Absalom! Would God I had died for thee, O Absalom, my son . . . my son."

JOHN GABRIEL BORKMAN, a drama in four acts by HENRIK IBSEN, published in 1896 and produced in 1897. Setting: a night in a mansion outside Oslo, and on a mountain; late nineteenth century.

An exposed crooked tycoon, Borkman, like Bernick in PILLARS OF SOCIETY, had expediently married the sister of the woman he really loved. But in this late play Ibsen focused on "the coldness of the heart": Borkman's proud self-delusions, the relation among the three old people, and the relation between them and youth. The action is continuous, the SYMBOLISM of the last scene rising to affecting lyrical heights.

Acts I and II. Bitterly proud, old Mrs. Borkman dreams of the day her son Erhart will redeem her ex-convict husband's name. John Gabriel Borkman stalks in his upstairs room (as he has since his release eight years before) like "a sick wolf pacing his cage," while his wife talks to Ella Rentheim, her twin sister, on whose estate they live. As the sisters once battled for Borkman, so they now battle for his son Erhart, whom Ella has raised. In Borkman's upstairs room, Saint-Saëns's "Danse Macabre" is being played on the piano. The elderly, distinguished-looking Borkman assumes a regal position when he hears a knock. But it is only his one friend, the washed-out clerk Vilhelm Foldal, who imagines himself a great poet. Borkman supports this illusion, and in return Foldal supports Borkman's unceasing expectation that the leading bankers will come to beg for the return of Borkman, the Napoleon of finance. He ruthlessly dismisses Foldal when, crushed by Borkman's contempt for his poetry, he questions Borkman's illusions. For the first time in many years Ella visits Borkman. Though grateful for her financial help, he reminds Ella that his love made her wealthy: in his manipulations he had spared only her securities. He justifies bartering her for what nearly gave him "a kingdom for myself, and prosperity for thousands." But she refuses to forgive him: his choice has murdered their souls, and it has "created this emptiness and sterility." Having learned that she must soon die, Ella offers to leave Erhart her fortune. Mrs. Borkman, who has not spoken to her husband for eight years, comes up and vows to keep her son.

Acts III and IV. Persuaded by Ella to attempt to reach an understanding with his wife, Borkman insists that he was justified in having sacrificed everything for power—including her and the thousands he swindled. He wants to resume his quest, and seeks Erhart's help. Mrs. Borkman, who considers only her husband's name yet alive, asks Erhart to clear it. Ella, finally, asks Erhart to spend the remaining months of her life with her. Erhart rejects all of them: "I want happiness! . . . I'm young! I'm suffocating in this house! . . . I don't want to work! I just want to live—to live—live!"—and he departs with the sophisticated divorcée whom he has been courting. Borkman too leaves the house—for the first time—and Ella follows him up to the wilds and "back to freedom and life and humanity," where they view the vast landscape. There Borkman apostrophizes his kingdom—the millions he tried to release from the mountain ores: "I love you, treasures that crave for life, with your glittering retinue of power and glory. I love you—love you—love you!" The icy night air kills him, and the sisters can finally join hands: "We twin sisters—over the man we both loved. We two shadows—over the dead man."

JOHNSON OVER JORDAN, a play in three acts by J. B. PRIESTLEY, published and produced in 1939. Setting: an English suburb, a bar, an office, etc., in the 1930's.

Priestley characterized this EXPRESSIONISTIC fantasy (with masks, music, and ballet) as "a biographical-morality play in which the usual chronological treatment is abandoned for a timeless-dream examination of a man's life." It begins with the funeral of Richard Johnson, a business executive. He is then seen in various objectified manifestations of his life and thoughts—and of Europe's collapsing civilization: Johnson's rise in the firm, his cavorting in bars and nightclubs, and his association with a number of family members (living and dead), friends, and teachers. Periodically the setting shifts back to his recently bereaved home. The last scene, with his wife, recalls their first meeting: "We'll see the beginning again but now we shall know everything that came out of it," Johnson tells her; "we'll be ourselves as we were then but we'll also be all the selves we've been since, so that we'll have *everything*." And then Johnson, suddenly small and alone, walks into the eternity of the universe.

JOHNSTON, [William] **Denis** (1901–   ), Irish dramatist, is best known for his first two plays, THE OLD LADY SAYS "NO!" (1929) and THE MOON IN THE YELLOW RIVER (1931). A lawyer as well as a radio, television, and film writer, Johnston has lived in Dublin (where he was born), London, and the United States. During World War II he was a BBC correspondent (his *Nine Rivers from Jordan* is a much-praised account of that experience). In America he has served on various college faculties. He also was on the Board of Directors of Dublin's Gate Theatre and directed the Smith College Theatre.

Johnston's drama has been praised for its excellence and—though some of it reflects the influence of the German EXPRESSIONISTS—the variety of techniques and subjects, which are often historical. Produced mainly in repertory, his plays include *A Bride for the Unicorn* (1933), which carries expressionism beyond his first work; *Storm Song* (1934), a satire on documentary film-making; *Blind Man's Buff* (1937), an adaptation of *Die Blinde Göttin* by ERNST TOLLER; *The Golden Cuckoo* (1939), which features a modern Diogenes; *The Dreaming Dust* (1940, originally *Weep for the Cyclops*; completely revised and produced under its present title in 1954), a "speculative story" about Jonathan Swift (with Stella and Vanessa) and the Seven Deadly Sins; *A Fourth for Bridge*, a comic one-act antiwar comedy published among his collected plays; *"Strange Occurrence on Ireland's Eye"* (1956), which is based on the 1852 murder trial of William Burke Kirwan, an artist convicted not because he was guilty but because he was considered obnoxious; and *The Scythe and the Sunset* (1958), an Easter Rebellion "anti-melodrama" whose title (though not the play itself) parodies O'Casey's THE PLOUGH AND THE STARS.

Many of these plays are collected in *The Old Lady Says "No!" and Other Plays* (1960), which includes Johnston's introduction and prefaces to each of the plays. See also Robert Hogan's *After the Irish Renaissance* (1967), which has a chapter on Johnston and a bibliography.

JOHST, Hanns (1890–), German writer, was the most notable Nazi dramatist. Originally an EXPRESSIONIST, he first produced a one-act antiwar play (*Die Stunde des Sterbenden*, 1914) and a NATURALISTIC comedy on war profiteering (*Stroh*, 1915). He followed these with *Der junge Mensch* (1916), a one-act autobiographical "ecstatic scenario" about a rebellious youth, derivative of AUGUST STRINDBERG and FRANK WEDEKIND. It was with his next play that Johst found his characteristic style: reshaping historical material to express his philosophy. *Der Einsame* (1917) is a heroic portrait of the dissipated early nineteenth-century playwright Christian Dietrich Grabbe, here actuated by grief over the loss of his beloved to drink himself to an early death after flaunting all standards of decency. This, as a "German genius," he may do with impunity—for as Grabbe declares in his opening soliloquy, "I am the cosmos!"

Born in Saxony to the family of a schoolteacher, Johst studied theology, medicine, philology, and art history. In his writings, he substituted for expressionism's humanitarian perspectives a call for nationalism and ethnic consciousness. *Der König* (1920), for example, features a king who fails because of his liberal ideas, for, as Johst's spokesman in the play remarks, "He who believes in the people the people will chastise, but he who chastises the people—in him will they believe." Johst's Luther play, *Propheten* (1923), stresses its hero's nationalistic aspirations ("Germany takes her heaven by storm!") and portrays Jews as blaspheming usurers who should be butchered. It was followed by other dramas and comedies that increasingly stressed anti-Semitism and other Fascist propensities.

Thomas Paine (1927), Johst's most popular work, depicts the title hero as the inspirer of the American Revolution and George Washington as a good Nazi who leads storm-trooperlike volunteers and tells merchants that "The State . . . demands blood!" With *Schlageter* (1933), dedicated to "Hitler, in affectionate veneration and unchanging loyalty," Johst explicitly dramatized his Nazi ideology; the play portrays "the last soldier of the Great War and the first soldier of the Third Reich"—a saboteur in the French-occupied Ruhr whose sentiments are expressed by "When I hear '*Kultur*' I loosen the safety catch on my revolver" and who becomes the martyred hero of a new Germany as he marches to his execution crying out, "Germany! A final word! A demand! A command!! Germany!!! Awake! Inflame! Burn enormously!"

This was Johst's most important play in the Nazi period—and his last notable work, though he was naturally much honored by the Nazis, becoming, among other things, an SS brigade leader. He presented a fictionalized account of his youth in his first novel, *Der Anfang* (1917), and described his development from a "humanitarian" to a "conscious German" in *Ich glaube* (1928). H. F. Garten's *Modern German Drama* (1964) discusses Johst's drama.

JONES, Henry Arthur (1851–1929), English dramatist, like ARTHUR WING PINERO was a pioneer in the renaissance of the English theatre. He enjoyed great popularity during the last decades of the nineteenth and the first decade of the twentieth centuries. A moralist as well as an experienced man of the theatre, Jones introduced seriousness and social criticism into English theatres—before his contemporary and long-time friend BERNARD SHAW did so with his plays. Particularly audacious were Jones's depiction of religious topics (as in SAINTS AND SINNERS, 1884) and his dramatizations of passions and of "sinning women," who are treated with unusual sympathy—and in THE CASE OF REBELLIOUS SUSAN (1894) are even restored socially. As moral fashions changed, other playwrights went beyond Jones, whose daring now seems modest, though at the time it shocked audiences. Time has made increasingly evident his reliance on melodrama and his limitations as a comic writer, though his comedies long amused large audiences on both sides of the Atlantic. As a social critic he was vastly overshadowed by Shaw; and his social comedies were eventually eclipsed by those of SOMERSET MAUGHAM, who became more fashionable, and by OSCAR WILDE, the age's greatest wit. Of Jones's many plays (he wrote over eighty), only MICHAEL AND HIS LOST ANGEL (1896) and THE LIARS (1897) are generally remembered now. Yet his historical importance is considerable, his popularity was genuine, and his best plays possess intrinsic merits.

Jones was born in Buckinghamshire, the oldest of the five children of tenant farmers. His formal education went only as far as grammar school, and when he was twelve, he became an apprentice in his uncle's draper's shop. Later Jones worked in a London warehouse and then he became a commercial traveler. Mostly self-educated, he had done some writing before he became intrigued with the theatre. In London he would return to see the popular plays again and again to study their construction. A number of his own plays were rejected before a one-acter, *It's Only Round the Corner,* was produced in 1878. It was followed by *Hearts of Oak, Elopement,* and *A Clerical Error* the following year; *An Old Master* in 1880; *His Wife* and *Home Again* in 1881; and *A Bed of Roses* in 1882.

It was his next work that year that made him famous and sufficiently wealthy to gain him independence. *The Silver King,* a four-act play (written with apparently minor contributions by Henry Herman, 1832–94) that WILLIAM ARCHER hailed as the greatest modern English melodrama, suspensefully dramatizes the story of a man (one of Wilson Barrett's most popular parts) wrongfully accused of a murder that he himself believes he has committed; it reaches a high point with his agonized cry, "O God! put back Thy universe and give me yesterday!" This melodrama was followed two years later by *Breaking a Butterfly* (a free adaptation of Ibsen's A DOLL'S HOUSE that ends with Nora's repenting of her rebellion—and a play that Jones later repented having written), *Chatterton* (1884, written with Herman), and one of his best-remembered plays, *Saints and Sinners.*

Hoodman Blind was produced in 1885, *The Lord Harry* and *A Noble Vagabond* in 1886, *Hard Hit* and *Heart of Hearts* in 1887, and *Wealth* in 1889. That year, too, appeared *The Middleman,* a very successful and possibly Jones's best melodrama. With his next play, *Judah* (1890), characterization assumed greater importance and Jones's dramaturgy started to become something more than farce and pure melodrama. *Sweet Will* and *The Deacon* were followed by the popular society drama *The Dancing Girl* (1891), in which an independent woman who wants to lead her own life flaunts society and ruins a dissolute nobleman (played by Beerbohm Tree). It was followed by *The Crusaders* (1891), *The Bauble Shop* (1893), *The Tempter* (1893, Jones's only verse tragedy); and by *The Masqueraders* (1894), a melodramatic PROBLEM PLAY about marriage. After *The Case of Rebellious Susan* came *Grace Mary* (1895) and *The Triumph of the Philistines* (1895), a satire of the middle class that was praised by many important critics but fared less well with audiences. The next play, *Michael and His Lost Angel,* also fared badly with them, though later critics agreed with Jones, who considered it his finest work. After *The Rogue's Comedy* (1896) and *The Physician* (1897) came *The Liars,* usually considered his best comedy, *The Manœuvres of Jane* (1898), *Carnac Sahib* (1899), and *The Lackey's Carnival* (1900).

Though he remained prolific to the end of his life, Jones wrote few other significant works. He published three books on drama and the theatre: *The Renascence of the English Drama* (1895), *The Foundations of a National Drama* (1913), and *The Theatre of Ideas* (1915); and four film scenarios. Of his remaining plays, *Dolly Reforming Herself* (1908) and *Mary Goes First* (1913) have been praised as skillfully constructed comedies; *The Lie* (1914), a melodramatic love triangle, was his last hit. Aside from numerous unpublished and unproduced plays, Jones also wrote the following, with decreasing popular and critical success: *The Princess's Nose* (1902), *Chance the Idol* (1902), *Whitewashing Julia* (1903), *Joseph Entangled* (1904), *The Chevaleer* (1904), *The Heroic Stubbs* (1906), *The Hypocrites* (1906), *The Evangelist* (1907), *The Knife* (1909), *Fall in Rookies* (1910), *We Can't Be as Bad as All That* (1910), *The Ogre* (1911), *Lydia Gilmore* (1912), *The Divine Gift* (1912), *Her Tongue* (1912, published 1915), *The Goal* (1914), *Cock o' the Walk* (1915), and *The Pacifists* (1917).

In his last years Jones wasted much creative energy in feuds with H. G. Wells and Bernard Shaw. His patriotic diatribes against their social and political theories were published in *My Dear Wells* (1921) and in the unfinished book on Shaw, *What Is Capital?* (1925). That same year he wrote an even fiercer attack on his one-time friend Shaw, *Mr. Mayor of Shakespeare's Town.*

MRS. DANE'S DEFENCE (1900) embodies the characters and situations typical of many of Jones's plays: a young lady, often a widow, is wooed and won by an elderly *raisonneur,* an experienced man of the world who understands the unfairness of social customs, but realizing their necessity, upholds them and urges potential or actual transgressors to compromise and comply with them. It was such conservatism that enabled Jones to get away with portraying the daring ideas, passions, and actions of his protagonists. The *raisonneur* parts were written for and performed by Charles Wyndham, and other great actors of his time appeared in Jones's plays. Mrs. Patrick Campbell's withdrawing from the cast of *Michael and His Lost Angel* because of its audacity suggests how advanced Jones's ideas were. Yet, though he is considered, with Pinero and Shaw, as the pioneer who brought the spirit of HENRIK IBSEN to modern English drama, Jones's earnestness now looks more like priggishness. It is ironic that his moral fervor and his theatrical gifts were precisely the qualities that helped date his drama. Further, his theatricality was firmly rooted in the melodrama with which he first made his name and whose influence he never was quite able to shake off. Yet at their best his dramas—noted for their excellent construction and characterizations—are still moving, and his comedy, while it lacks the epigrammatic brilliance of a Wilde, is still amusing.

Jones's plays were published individually, and seventeen of them were collected in the four-volume *Representative Plays by Henry Arthur Jones* (1925), edited and with introductions by Clayton Hamilton. Jones's youngest daughter, Doris Arthur Jones, published the most comprehensive biography, *The Life and Letters of Henry Arthur Jones* (1930), including an exhaustive bibliography of her father's publications. Richard A. Cordell's *Henry Arthur Jones and the Modern*

Drama (1932) is a detailed critical and scholarly study of all Jones's work, viewed in the context of his age.

JONES, LeRoi (1934–), American black militant novelist, poet, and playwright, graduated from Howard University at the age of nineteen, won a John Hay Whitney fellowship for poetry and fiction in 1962, and a Guggenheim award in 1965. Proclaiming his hatred of white people and the violence he would use to defeat them, Jones changed his name to Imamu Amiri Baraka after he achieved fame as a dramatist with his *Dutchman* (1964), a long one-act play (subsequently filmed) about a crude and provocative white girl who entices, baits, and finally murders an educated young Negro in the New York subway, which Jones characterizes as "heaped in modern myth."

Other long one-acters similarly portray racial antagonisms with symbolic and mythic overtones, and employ the violence and increasingly obscene language that has made Jones notorious and frequently caused the banning of his plays. In *The Slave* (1964) a Negro menaces his former wife, a white woman now married to a professor and soon killed with her mulatto daughters in their collapsing house. *The Toilet* (1964) portrays a group of Negro boys beating up a white schoolmate in a lavatory; the play was published jointly with *The Baptism,* a more comic one-act satire of contemporary society. *Slaveship* (1969) consists of vignettes, some of them portraying Africans transported to America and other blacks who moan and cry for revolution and the destruction of "whitey."

Four Black Revolutionary Plays (1969) is a collection of one-acters Jones wrote for the Spirit House Theatre he organized in Newark after the collapse of the Black Arts Theatre Jones had founded in Harlem in 1965 which, despite its brief (seven months), stormy history has been credited with having launched the Black Renaissance.

JOSEPHSON, Ragnar (1891–), Swedish academician, poet, and dramatist, taught art history at the University of Lund, whence have come many Swedish men of letters. Though he is principally a verse playwright, Josephson has gained most popularity with tragicomic prose dramas in which he explored the psyches of men coping with moral dilemmas. His *Kanske en diktare* (*Perhaps a Poet,* 1932) furnished the Swedish star Gösta Ekman with a major part: that of a simple man whose drab life is changed when, in order to make his existence more meaningful than his unsuccessful poetry could, he assumes the guilt for a murder committed by a kindly acquaintance; realizing that even this act is based on illusion, he commits suicide.

More interested in psychology than in ethical and social problems, Josephson succeeded also with such later and less effective plays as *Leopold, luftkonstnär* (1934) and *Farlig oskuld* (1939). *Perhaps a Poet* was published in the first volume of *Scandinavian Plays of the Twentieth Century* (1944), with Alrik Gustafson's introductory comments on Josephson.

JOURNEY'S END, a play in three acts by R. C. SHERRIFF, produced in 1928 and published in 1929. Setting: the British trenches before Saint-Quentin, France; March 1918.

This was the most popular English antiwar play to appear after World War I. More reserved than the American WHAT PRICE GLORY? (by Anderson and Stallings), it was first produced professionally by MAURICE BROWNE, and has been frequently revived in the United States and in England. There is little focus on a developing plot: effect is achieved by the powerful portrayal of the officer-protagonists' shattered nerves as they do their duties; and by an evocation of the atmosphere of their fears, courage, and impending doom.

Act I. A major German attack is expected momentarily. Lieutenant Osborne, an elderly former schoolmaster and the company's second-in-command, mentions their captain's increasing addiction to drink. Young Captain Dennis Stanhope came to the front right out of school, and is much respected; but after three years without a rest "his nerves have got battered to bits." Osborne welcomes a new officer, young Lieutenant James Raleigh. He is a former schoolmate of Stanhope's; in fact, Raleigh got himself assigned to this company because he idolizes Stanhope. Osborne tries to warn Raleigh that Stanhope has changed after years on the battlefield, which "tells on a man—rather badly—" The now cynical Stanhope, who can bear the daily horrors only by consuming immense quantities of whiskey, is unpleasantly surprised to find Raleigh assigned to him, but says little. The tension is temporarily lightened at supper by an unimaginative fellow officer's concern with food. "War's bad enough with pepper," he remarks sadly when the orderly forgets it; "but war without pepper—it's—it's bloody awful!" Alone with Osborne, Stanhope expresses his anger at a cowardly lieutenant who plans to shirk battle. Then Stanhope reveals his bitterness about Raleigh's appearance. Not only will Raleigh be disillusioned by his hero, Stanhope fears, but he will communicate with his sister, Stanhope's fiancée. "She doesn't know that if I went up those steps into the front line—without being doped with whisky—I'd go mad with fright," he tells Osborne, who feels the same front-line strain: "You know he'll write and tell her I reek of whisky all day." Increasingly drunk and exhausted, he determines to censor Raleigh's letters to his sister. "Hero-worship be damned!" Stanhope exclaims; she will never find out what became of him: the German attack will come, "and she goes on thinking I'm a fine fellow forever—and ever—and ever." That too will punish Raleigh for forcing his way into the company, Stanhope mutters. Finally he collapses into bed, and asks Osborne to cover him up.

Act II. Early the next morning at breakfast, an officer reminisces and passes around photos of his

Journey's End, Act II. Stanhope (Colin Clive), right, demands that Raleigh (Maurice Evans) submit his letter for censorship. London, 1929. *(British Theatre Museum)*

"fine 'olly'ocks out the back" of his house. Laughing, they remember a gas alarm called because of the appearance of a sweet smell—which turned out to be a blooming, "blinkin' may-tree!" Chatting, Osborne and Raleigh become friendly. The older officer recalls how the Germans once told them to carry back their wounded comrade—and the "next day we blew each other's trenches to blazes." Raleigh wonders: "It all seems rather—*silly,* doesn't it?" Later Stanhope announces that the German attack is expected in two days; the company has been ordered "to stick it"—regardless of the consequences. When Raleigh prepares to mail a letter, Stanhope hysterically orders him to submit it for censorship. Then, breaking down when alone with Osborne, Stanhope cannot face reading the letter. Osborne does it for him. Raleigh's letter to his sister is full of praise for Stanhope and concludes, "I'm awfully proud to think he's my friend." In the afternoon come new orders from above: a raid to capture some Germans needed for interrogation. Though Stanhope is reluctant to let either of them go, Osborne and Raleigh are detailed to this dangerous mission. Just then the cowardly officer announces his determination to go on sick leave. Stanhope first reasons with him, then threatens him with a gun, and finally, when the officer submits, consoles him by admitting to similar fears. But, Stanhope tells him, they cannot betray their companions: "Don't you think it worth standing in with men like that?—when you know they all feel like you do—in their hearts—and just go on sticking it because they know it's—it's the only thing a decent man can do." When Osborne and Raleigh are told of their assignments, Raleigh is full of excitement. Osborne realizes the horror of what is before them, and is more subdued. From his copy of *Alice's Adventures in Wonderland* he reads about the crocodile: "How cheerfully he seems to grin / And neatly spread his claws, / And welcomes little fishes in / With gently smiling jaws!" The fellow officer, who retains equilibrium with his total lack of imagination, remarks, "I don't see no point in that." Osborne replies, "Exactly, that's just the point."

Act III. At dusk the next day, though the Germans are prepared for the raid, it must nevertheless take place. The colonel has promised Osborne and Raleigh a Military Cross if they succeed. The two officers have a cigarette and a cup of coffee, Osborne trying to take Raleigh's mind off their mission during the last few moments. They recite nonsense rhymes from *Alice in Wonderland,* and reminisce about the woods in England. Then they go on their mission. There is a lot of firing, and almost immediately a young prisoner is brought in and questioned. The colonel is gratified with the information he has obtained. But Stanhope answers bitterly, in a dead voice, for Osborne and six of the ten men sent on the mission have been killed. Raleigh returns, dazed by his baptism of fire, and drops on the nearest bed. As Stanhope goes out, his voice remains dead: "Must you sit on Osborne's bed?" That night the success of the raid is celebrated with a chicken dinner and champagne. The officers' drunken jollity is spoiled by Raleigh's absence: he has stayed with the men. When he returns, Stanhope greets him with a cold fury that Raleigh does not understand: "How *can* I sit down and eat that—when . . . —when Osborne's—lying—out—there—" At this point Stanhope's hysteria rises to a climax: "You bloody little swine! You think I don't care—" His voice breaks as he remembers his best friend, "the one man I could talk to as man to man." And when Raleigh asks him how, then, he could celebrate, Stanhope replies: "To forget, you little fool—to forget! D'you understand? To forget! You think there's no limit to what a man can bear?" The next dawn the German attack starts. Again the cowardly officer malingers, but Stanhope gets him out. And then, almost immediately, Raleigh is brought down, shot in the spine. Stanhope comforts him, the two talking, for the first time since their reunion, like the old friends they used to be. A few minutes later Raleigh is dead. Stanhope, summoned by the enemy's attack, runs his fingers over Raleigh's hair and stiffly goes out. The shells shriek, the dugout begins to collapse under the bombardment, rifle fire spatters feverishly, and the red dawn glows.

JOYCE, James [Augustine] (1882–1941), Irish writer who lived in Zurich and Paris during most of his adult life, was primarily a novelist. His *Dubliners* (1914), *A Portrait of the Artist as a Young Man* (1916), *Ulysses* (1922), and *Finnegans Wake*

(1939) are among the most influential literary works of the century. Also a poet, he wrote but one play, EXILES (1918). It manifests the influence of the later HENRIK IBSEN, whom Joyce greatly admired.* Joyce's most effective drama is in his novels. And these have, in fact, been adapted for the stage, most successfully in Marjorie Barkentin's (? –) *Ulysses in Nighttown* (1958) and in *Stephen D* (1962), a distinguished dramatization of *A Portrait of the Artist as a Young Man* by the Irish playwright Hugh Leonard (1926–), who also adapted some of Joyce's *Dubliners* stories as *Dublin One* (1963). Other adaptations are *Passages from Finnegans Wake* (produced in 1955 and published as *The Voices of Shem*) by Mary Manning (Mrs. Mark de Wolfe Howe, Jr., 1910–); and *The Coach with the Six Insides* (1962), an acting and ballet version of *Finnegans Wake* by the dancer Jean Erdman (1914?–) and her company.

Of the many studies of Joyce, the most comprehensive is Richard Ellmann's biography, *James Joyce* (1959). The 1951 edition of *Exiles* contains Joyce's notes to that play; William York Tindall's *A Reader's Guide to James Joyce* (1959) devotes a chapter to the play and appends a bibliography.

JUDITH, a tragedy in three acts by JEAN GIRAUDOUX, published and produced in 1931. Setting: biblical Bethulia and the Assyrian camp.

Like Giraudoux's previous play, AMPHITRYON 38, this tragedy (the only one of his works so labeled) interprets a much-dramatized legend, the Apocryphal Book of Judith. The play was praised by some critics; but it failed, probably because of its complexity.

The people—led by the High Priest, the prophets, and the army officers—demand that Judith sacrifice herself to save them. A beautiful young aristocrat and a virgin, Judith is persuaded to visit the enemy commander's tent at night and beg him not to sack the Jewish city. After being humiliated by his coarse underlings, Judith meets Holofernes. Unlike any of the other Assyrians or Jews, he is heroic and noble, and Judith gives herself to him. In the morning she beheads him in his sleep—for love: "Having to choose between her people and Holofernes[, I] chose love, chose Holofernes," Judith tells the shocked assemblage; "and since then [my] only wish is to find him again in death." But an angel convinces her that she must yield to destiny. She agrees to lie, to say what all want to hear: that she slew the enemy of God and her people. At the end she tells the High Priest, "Your procession can move off. Judith the saint is ready."

JULLIEN, Jean [-Thomas-Édouard] (1854–1919), French playwright, was associated with André Antoine in the Théâtre-Libre, and is notable principally for having coined the phrase *tranche de vie* (SLICE OF LIFE). Though his NATURALISTIC ideas derived from ÉMILE ZOLA, Jullien dispensed with that writer's emphasis on science. He particularly admired the plays of HENRY BECQUE, and he advocated the removal of footlights to reproduce a more REALISTIC light from above. Preferring classical and foreign to contemporary native drama, Jullien himself wrote a dozen *comédie rosse*—viciously ironic naturalistic plays like *La Sérénade* (1887), a quadrangle in which a man's wife and daughter become the family tutor's mistresses; *Le Maître* (1890), in which a tramp seduces and leaves with the daughter of the invalid farmer who took him in; and the later *L'Oasis* (1903), in which a nun marries her Muslim abductor and helps establish a desert utopia. Jullien's work is discussed in Samuel M. Waxman's *Antoine and the Théâtre-Libre* (1926).

JUNO AND THE PAYCOCK, a tragedy in three acts by SEAN O'CASEY, produced in 1924 and published in 1925. Setting: a Dublin tenement apartment, 1922.

This is among O'Casey's finest dramas, and perhaps his most popular one (in 1959 MARK BLITZSTEIN made it into a musical, *Juno*). The play is set in the period of the internecine struggle that terrorized newly independent Ireland. The musical prose rises to elegiac heights in the repeated maternal lament, and the contrapuntal tragic understatement and comedy reach their climax in the masterful tragicomic finale. The indomitable mother, the family mainstay, is nicknamed after the Roman goddess because significant events in her life transpired in June. But unlike the classic heroine's peacocks, Juno Boyle's "paycock" is her parasitic husband, a strutting, mock-heroic windbag.

Act I. The Boyles' attractive daughter, out of work because of a strike, reads the newspaper account of the slaying of their neighbor's son. Her brother Johnny, crippled "for Ireland" by a wounded hip and a lost arm, is sick and very edgy. Their mother, Juno, once handsome, at forty-five has a harassed, anxious look. To her children's proud "a principle's a principle," for which they strike and become maimed, she replies that money and an arm are the best principles, and the only ones useful to a workingman. She is exasperated with her husband, "Captain" Jack Boyle, who she knows is bar-hopping with his mooching crony, Joxer Daly: "He wore out the Health Insurance long ago, he's afther wearin' out the unemployment dole, an', now, he's thryin' to wear out me!" When word of a construction job comes, she is sure he will dodge it: "I killin' meself workin', an' he sthruttin' about from mornin' till night like a paycock!" Almost immediately Boyle is heard singing outside. He is followed by Joxer, and prepares to get his one bit of "comfort," a cup of tea. "Ah, a cup o' tay's a darlin' thing, a daaarlin' thing," his fawning crony says, and starts to mouth a platitude. Juno's appearance stops both men. In answer to Boyle's pretended eagerness for work, Juno tells him of the

* A comprehensive study of Joyce's indebtedness to Ibsen is Bjørn J. Tysdahl's *Joyce and Ibsen* (1968).

job. Her irony becomes more bitter when he angrily rejects the job, pleading sudden leg cramps. She threatens to stop supporting him, but offers to prepare his breakfast before leaving for work. Boyle proudly refuses—"it ud choke me afther all that's been said"—but when she goes out he stealthily starts preparing it himself. Joxer obsequiously sympathizes as Boyle complains about his wife and the priest who found the construction job for him: "Let him give his job to wan of his hymn-singin', prayer-spoutin', craw-thumpin' Confraternity men!" Then he nostalgically recounts an exotic past as a sea captain, though in reality he made but one trip—on a collier to Liverpool. While the wastrels prate of past and future glory, they are suddenly frightened out of their wits by Juno's return, and Joxer hides on the roof. But Juno has good news. She introduces an English schoolteacher who tells Boyle of an inheritance from a wealthy relative. Envisioning a glorious future, Boyle says a prayer for the relative, whom he has just cursed, and promises to have nothing further to do with the good-for-nothing Joxer. Angrily Joxer climbs back into the apartment, ridicules Boyle's pretensions, and leaves. "He'll never blow the froth off a pint o' mine agen, that's a sure thing," Boyle vows. He promises to be "a new man from this out," and amorously serenades his Juno.

Act II. Two days later the apartment is vulgarly but amply furnished. Boyle has borrowed heavily against the inheritance, and has made up with Joxer. Juno brings a new gramophone, and the English teacher, their daughter's new suitor, discusses his theosophist philosophy and ghosts. Suddenly their son Johnny screams in terror, imagining that he sees the bullet-ridden corpse of their slain neighbor: "Oh, why did he look at me like that? . . . it wasn't my fault that he was done in. . . . Mother o' God, keep him away from me!" Later the Boyles and their friends celebrate with drink, song, and reminiscences. Outside, the funeral of the slain neighbor is about to begin. The victim's grieving mother cannot be comforted by political ideals or religion: they "won't bring me darlin' boy from the grave." But the Boyles want to continue their celebration, and are not very sympathetic. "No use o' them squealin' when they meet a soldier's fate," Boyle remarks grandly, and the oily Joxer declaims, "Let me like a soldier fall—me breast expandin' to th' ball!" They continue their singing and poetic recitations, and play the gramophone just as the procession starts. When chastised for it, Juno says that "it's nearly time we had a little less respect for the dead, an' a little more regard for the livin'." But they watch from the window with interest—"a darlin' funeral, a daarlin' funeral," as Joxer remarks—and eventually follow it. No sooner is Johnny left alone than a young man enters and orders his

Juno and the Paycock, Act II. Juno (Sara Allgood) and Boyle (Barry Fitzgerald) with their children (Aideen O'Connor and Harry Young). New York, 1940. (*Vandamm Photo, Theatre Collection, New York Public Library*)

coming to a meeting later. He is suspected of knowing about the betrayal of the fallen neighbor. Johnny begs to be left alone: "I've lost me arm, an' me hip's desthroyed so that I'll never be able to walk right agen! Good God, haven't I done enough for Ireland?" But the young man answers that "no man can do enough for Ireland," and leaves.

Act III. It is two months later. Boyle's daughter has been abandoned by her English suitor and seems to be sick. Creditors are hounding the still-swaggering Boyle, finally repossessing his suit and the gramophone. Joxer angrily leaves him, and Juno comes in with the further bad news that their daughter is pregnant. Compassionate, she insists that he say nothing to the daughter: "Ever since she left school she's earned her livin', an' your fatherly care never throubled the poor girl." Yet Boyle blusters melodramatically about the disgrace. Now he finally reveals that the inheritance has fallen through because of a legal technicality, and the crushed Juno understands why her daughter's lover disappeared. As their son Johnny becomes hysterical over the hopeless situation, Boyle angrily warns Juno not to bring their daughter back. He calls Joxer, who is delighted to accept an invitation to go drinking with Boyle. As Juno wonders how she will continue keeping her home together, movers start repossessing the furniture. A former suitor declines the daughter's hand when he hears of her "fall." Alone, Johnny is visited by two Irregulars, who drag him off to avenge the betrayal of the ambushed neighbor. A few minutes later, Juno and her daughter are in the empty flat. They are called to identify a corpse found outside—Johnny's. And now Juno echoes the agony of her neighbor, equally unable to accept consolation: "What was the pain I suffered, Johnny, bringin' you into the world to carry you to your cradle, to the pains I'll suffer carryin' you out o' the world to bring you to your grave!" And like her neighbor she asks, "Blessed Virgin, where were you when me darlin' son was riddled with bullets?" Then she leaves, in tragic dignity, to start life anew with her pregnant daughter. The stage is empty. Suddenly Boyle and Joxer shuffle in, full of bravado and stone drunk. Boyle drops his last coin, both wallow in patriotic slogans, and Boyle, babbling drunkenly on the floor, concludes, "I'm telling you . . . Joxer . . . th' whole worl's . . . in a terr . . . ible state o' . . . chassis!"

JUST, THE (*Les Justes*), a play in five acts by ALBERT CAMUS, produced in 1949 and published in 1950. Setting: Russia, 1905.

As Camus noted in his preface, the play (also translated as *The Just Assassins*) follows historical fact. In dramatizing the socialists' assassination of the Grand Duke Sergei Aleksandrovich, Camus stressed the ethical responsibility of the heroes—particularly Ivan ("Yanek") Kaliayev. Despite his conviction about the righteousness of his act, he recognizes its limitations, the culpability of murder. First Kaliayev is unable to bring himself to throw the bomb because there are children in the carriage, but he succeeds in killing the Grand Duke two days later. Kaliayev refuses the Grand Duchess, Elizabeth Fedorovna, who begs him in prison to repent and thus obtain the state's pardon: "In dying, I shall keep the agreement I made with those I love ... and it would be betraying them to pray."

JUST THINK, GIACOMINO! (*Pensaci, Giacomino!*), a comedy in three acts by LUIGI PIRANDELLO, produced in 1916 and published in 1918. Setting: Sicily, before World War I.

This dramatization of a short story he published in 1912 was Pirandello's fourth produced play. It was the first to achieve a modicum of success. The play has also been translated as *Think it Over, Giacomino!*

Professor Agestino Toti, an old schoolmaster, is a butt of ridicule who is constantly berated for his inability to maintain discipline. But he is compassionate and has a sense of humor. Out of kindness and for companionship in his old age, he marries a pregnant young girl; this will also help him to get back at the government by making it pay a family pension for a long time. He braves popular ridicule and scandal and insists that his wife and her young lover, Giacomino Delisi, whom he helps to get a job, continue their relationship. He loves his wife and her baby as if both were his own children. Despite his ludicrous violation of apparent logic and popular (but superficial) morality, it is really Toti who is logical, kind, and moral: he saves the girl from disgrace, provides for her future, and is himself happy. When Giacomino is pressured by society to desert the *ménage*, Professor Toti successfully pleads with him to return: "Is it right to so ruin a home, a family, to break the heart of a poor old man, of a poor mother, and to leave without help and guidance a poor little innocent child, like this one, Giacomino, like this one! Don't you see? Have you no heart?"

JUSTICE, a tragedy in four acts by JOHN GALSWORTHY, published and produced in 1910. Setting: a contemporary English law office, court, and prison.

The only one of Galsworthy's plays labeled "tragedy," *Justice* created a sensation when first produced, particularly with the brief and wordless solitary-confinement scene on which the third act closes. Galsworthy's indictment of legal justice stirred the British Home Secretary, Winston Churchill, to effect immediate penal reforms. The United States, where the play was equally successful, soon did likewise.

Act I. A forgery is detected in a law office, and suspicion falls on William Falder. He is a junior clerk whose behavior has always been above reproach. But he confesses his guilt, a crime he committed in a weak moment of desperation: the money was to help Ruth Honeywill, a young woman maltreated by her brutal husband. Old Robert Cokeson, the kindly office manager (a Dickensian character who provides comic relief),

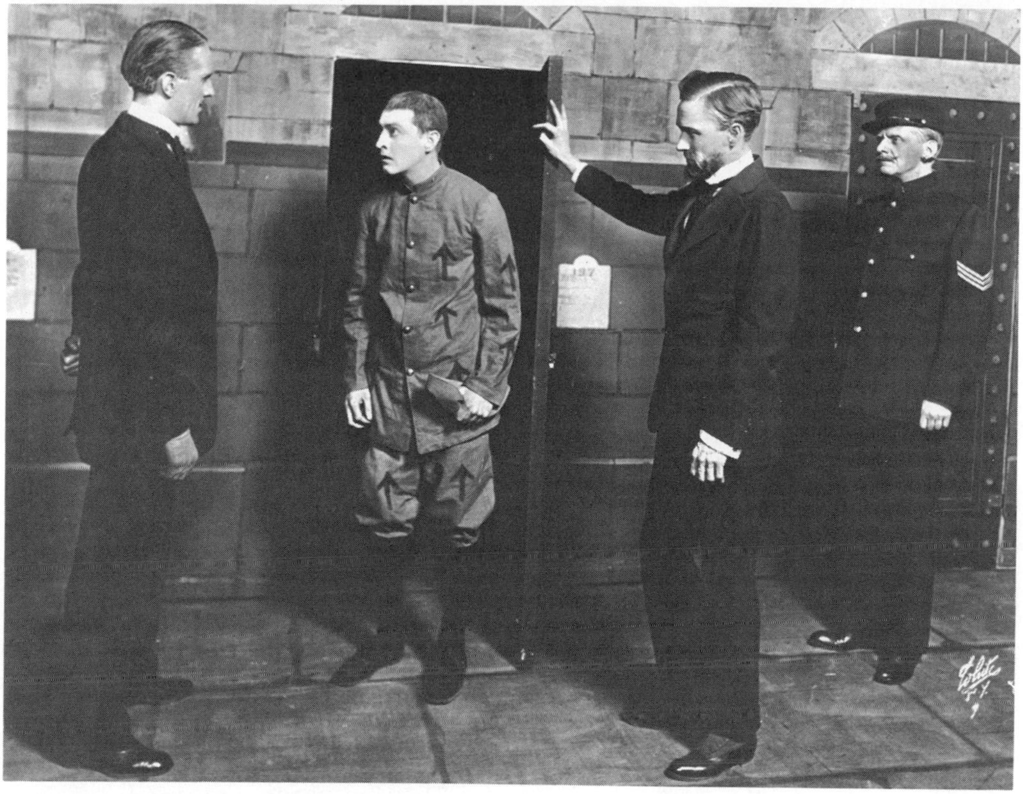

Justice, Act III. John Barrymore as Falder (second from left). New York, 1916. (*Culver Pictures*)

begs his employer to spare Falder. But the old lawyer is adamant. People like Falder, he says, must be kept out of harm's way: "One must think of society." And so Falder is arrested just as he is ready to leave the country with Ruth Honeywill and her children.

Act II. At the trial, Falder's lawyer pleads temporary insanity because of his anguish over the danger to the woman he loves. Ruth's testimony confirms her husband's brutality and her and her children's total dependence on Falder if she is not to go to the poorhouse or walk the streets. Though she and Falder have "not yet" been intimate, they are deeply in love and want to start a new life together. Falder's own testimony reveals the extent of his desperation. His lawyer eloquently states Falder's position, and begs the court not to ruin him for his innate weakness. "Justice is a machine that, when some one has once given it the starting push, rolls on of itself. Is this young man to be ground to pieces under this machine?" he asks, and then admonishes the court: "Imprison him as a criminal, and I affirm to you that he will be lost. . . . The rolling of the chariot-wheels of Justice over this boy began when it was decided to prosecute him." The prosecution ridicules the defense of "temporary insanity" and what it calls a suggestion of "romantic glamour" in the case. Prejudiced too by the accused's attachment to a married woman, the judge and the jury condemn Falder. The law, says the judge, is "a majestic edifice, sheltering all of us, each stone of which rests on another." Therefore he imposes the maximum prison sentence on Falder.

Act III. Scene 1. On Christmas Eve, old Cokeson visits the prison governor to request Falder's release from the three-months' solitary confinement with which all prisoners must start their sentence, and which is breaking him. Though the governor is sympathetic, he must refuse the request. The chaplain defends such confinement as the proper way to impress sinning humans with a sense of right and wrong, and the doctor says that although Falder is nervous, confinement has not damaged him physically. Cokeson's request that the prisoner be allowed to see Ruth Honeywill is also denied. *Scene 2.* Making his rounds and talking to various prisoners, the kindly governor admonishes Falder to "take a good hold of yourself." He has him examined again, and when the doctor repeats his diagnosis asks if Falder's state "doesn't amount to melancholia." "I can report on him if you like; but if I do I ought to report on others," the doctor replies. The governor sadly remarks, "The poor devil must just stick it then." *Scene 3* shows Falder alone in a small cell, like an animal. Eventually he participates, as the prisoners—desperate for a sound—hammer on their doors.

Act IV. Back in the law office two years later, Ruth begs Cokeson to give Falder another chance with the firm. After his release he has been shunned by his relatives as an ex-convict, and has lost his job. Cokeson remarks that she looks fairly prosperous and suggests that she might help him until he gets settled. "I could have—but not *now*," she confesses. She had to leave her brutal husband and tried to earn a living as a seamstress. But unable thus to support her children, she was forced to give herself to her employer. Falder, crushed by society, begs for another chance. His former employer is finally persuaded to take him on again—if he gives up his illicit relationship with Ruth. When Falder refuses, the lawyer offers to help Ruth get a divorce. But then Cokeson whispers that "she's not been quite what she ought to ha' been. . . . She's lost her chance." Falder eventually understands the truth. When a detective comes to arrest him for failure to report to the police and for forging a reference to get a job, he throws himself over the bannister and breaks his neck. "No one'll touch him now! Never again!" the compassionate, if old-fashioned, Cokeson says. He comforts the broken Ruth, who cries over the corpse of Falder, who is now "safe with gentle Jesus!"

K

KAISER, Georg (1878–1945), leading German EXPRESSIONIST playwright, was immensely prolific. Aside from two novels, many poems and essays, and lost or incompleted stage works, he left over sixty plays. For decades these were performed more frequently in Germany than those of any but GERHART HAUPTMANN's—thirteen in the 1917–18 season alone. Except for the Nazi period, when Kaiser's plays were banned, they have remained popular. Outside Germany his plays are less well known. But the GAS trilogy—*Die Koralle* (THE CORAL, 1917), GAS I (1918), and GAS II (1920)—and *Von Morgen bis Mitternachts* (FROM MORN TO MIDNIGHT, 1916), in particular, have been produced internationally. They have strongly influenced not only fellow German but also American playwrights like EUGENE O'NEILL, ELMER RICE, and others, and have indelibly affected subsequent modern drama.

The son of a Magdeburg businessman, Kaiser also entered the commercial world. He spent some years in South America, contracted malaria, and returned to Europe, where he remained in ill health for years. It was not until about the time of his marriage, in 1908, that he began to write professionally. Once started, however, his dedication to art assumed monomaniacal intensity. He sold furnishings from the house he rented for his family, was arrested (1920), and was sentenced to six months' imprisonment. His defense was that he needed luxurious quarters, and society cannot afford to hamper productive creators in their work. Artists, he maintained, stand outside the civil law: "One does not bring a Heinrich von Kleist or a Büchner to court; that is unfair." Though naïve as well as arrogant, his attitude was sincere: upon release from prison he quietly returned to his work with the same intensity, until the advent of Hitler, whose government banned and burned his books for their humanism and antimilitarism. Again Kaiser faced ruin, for he was dependent on royalties. He barely managed to escape Nazi Germany, and exiled himself to Switzerland in 1938. There he worked until his death.

His early plays have been characterized as "flesh dramas." These deal not only with sex but also with the relationship between body and spirit, most successfully in his Socrates play, *Der gerettete Alkibiades* (ALCIBIADES SAVED, 1920). *Rektor Kleist,* generally considered his first play, appeared in 1918 but had been written about thirteen years earlier. It resembles Wedekind's SPRING'S AWAKENING in form, in its portrayal of callous adults causing an adolescent's suicide, and in its concern not so much with sex as with the body. Kaiser's second play, however, was preoccupied with sex. The first to be published and to bring him fame, *Die jüdische Witwe* (THE JEWISH WIDOW, 1911) is the earliest of his imaginative interpretations of the Bible and Greek mythology. It was followed by other "flesh dramas": *Der Geist der Antike* (1923, written 1905 and also titled *Die Falle*), *Der Zentaur* (1916, a five-act comedy about a pedagogue, written in 1906; also titled *Konstantin Strobel* and revised as *Margarine*), his Tristan-Isolde-Marke play *König Hahnrei* (1913), and the comic modernization of Zeus's abduction of *Europa* (1915), thematically analogous to *The Jewish Widow.*

But in the majority of plays on the "flesh" theme the mind predominates. These—most of them centering on love, often redeeming wifely love—include the nonbiblical *David und Goliath* (1920, written in 1906 and published as *Grossbürger Möller,* 1914), *Die Sorina* (1917, written in 1909), *Die Versuchung* (1917, written in 1910), *Der mutige Seefahrer* (1926, written in 1907), *Das Frauenopfer* (1918), *Der Brand im Opernhaus* (*Fire in the Opera House,* 1918; a popular drama set in historical France, like many Kaiser plays), *Der Präsident* (1905, a revised version of *Der Kongress*), *Oktobertag* (1928, translated as *The Phantom Lover*), *Hellseherei* (1929), *Adrienne Ambrossat* (1935, based on de Maupassant's story "La Parure"), *Der Gärtner von Toulouse* (1938), *Der Schuss in die Öffentlichkeit* (1939), *Rosamunde Floris* (1940), *Alain und Elise* (1940), *Der englische Sender* (an anti-Nazi play written in 1940, produced over the BBC in 1947), *Die Spieldose* (1943), and two Napoleon plays written in 1938, *Napoleon in New Orleans* (1948) and *Pferdewechsel* (1954).

Kaiser's dichotomy of body and mind often evolved into a portrayal of the ideal "New Man" celebrated in the *Gas* trilogy, *Die Bürger von Calais* (THE CITIZENS OF CALAIS, 1914), and *Der Soldat Tanaka* (SOLDIER TANAKA, 1940). Other plays that feature such a hero are three one-acters produced in 1918 (*Claudius* and *Friedrich und Anna,* written in 1911, and *Juana*), *Hölle Weg Erde* (1919), *Kanzlist Krehler* (1922), *Gilles und Jeanne* (1923, which appeared the same year as Shaw's SAINT JOAN but consists of a ghoulish plot dominated by Gilles de Rais's lust for Joan), *Nebeneinander* (1923, presenting three parallel plots on a tripartite stage), *Kolportage* (1924), *Gats* (1925, a "birth control" play), *Die Lederköpfe* (1928), *Zwei Krawatten* (1929, a comic revue), *Mississippi* (1930), *Der Silbersee* (1933), *Das Los des Ossian Balvesen* (1936), and *Das Floss der Medusa* (*The Raft of the Medusa,* 1945), a poignant antiwar tragedy written in 1943 and (like WILLIAM GOLDING's 1955 novel *Lord of the Flies*) enacted by children isolated in a lifeboat: their evil (a murder of the weakest among them) is recognized and resisted by only one child (the "New Man"), who finally assumes their guilt and becomes the martyr.

In other plays Kaiser depicted similar themes in terms of the artist. The one-act *Der Protagonist* (*The Protagonist,* 1921) and *Zweimal Oliver* (1926) feature an actor. *Noli me tangere* (1922), portraying Saint Paul as a creative artist, Christ, and Judas (the sixteen characters in this prison play are referred to only by numbers), explicitly interprets their story. *Die Flucht nach Venedig* (1923), similarly imaginative, depicts the love affair of Alfred de Musset and George Sand. The hero of the comedy *Papiermühle* (1926) is a poet, tracked down by a critic. Kaiser's remaining artist plays appeared posthumously. *Klawitter* (written in 1940) is a bitterly autobiographical play about a writer whose work is banned by the Nazis. The Greek trilogy (written in 1943–44), his last dramatic work, consists of *Zweimal Amphitryon,* in which Zeus condemns Amphitryon but enables his eventual regeneration through Alcmena's love; PYGMALION; and Kaiser's self-styled "swan song" *Bellerophon,* the innocent idealist who is saved from worldly evil by Apollo. Among Kaiser's other works are two further posthumous plays (*Agnete* and *Vincent verkauft ein Bild*) and an opera buffa with music by Kurt Weill, *Der Zar lässt sich photographieren* (1927).

Different and uneven though these many plays are, their grouping (suggested by critics like B. J. Kenworthy) reveals Kaiser's interest in related themes. These center about love, the power of the imagination, and the conflict of the mundane and the ideal. Kaiser's preoccupation with and usually bitter portrayal of such ideas and his militant pacifism earned him the label "Denkspieler" or "playwright of ideas," a German BERNARD SHAW. (He was in fact greatly impressed with Shaw, echoes of whose works recur in Kaiser.) But the German's plays are totally different. As Kaiser himself noted, he was directly influenced by the early nineteenth-century poet and playwright Georg Büchner, whose dramaturgical innovations he developed and popularized. Kaiser's distinctively fragmentary, sketchy, telegraphic dialogue became one of the trademarks of expressionism. His action is divided into scenes that omit traditional continuity and feature only highpoints—instead of acts, the "stations" of his *Stationsdrama.* Kaiser's symbolism, particularly the religious symbolism, at times is grotesque and crude—again in the traditionally unsubtle ways of expressionism. There is little or no individual characterization. But Kaiser was a master at portraying crowd scenes, and in creating memorable theatre with stylized, halting talk—often with dramatic silence.

Although Kaiser's plays are readily available in the original, only a few have been translated. Aside from studies exclusively concerned with Kaiser, works dealing with German drama and with expressionism in the theatre devote much space to him. B. J. Kenworthy's *Georg Kaiser* (1957) is a comprehensive study in English. It contains a biographical sketch and an extensive bibliography.

KANIN, Garson (1912–   ), American actor, director, and writer, has been particularly successful with *Born Yesterday* (1946), his long-running comedy about an ex-chorus girl who is educated by a liberal reporter to understand and defeat the tycoon junk dealer—a menace to democracy—who is keeping her. After departing together victoriously, the girl and the reporter are described (in the words of a lawyer who has been corrupted by the junk dealer) as "all the dumb chumps and all the crazy broads, past, present, and future—who thirst for knowledge—and search for truth——who fight for justice—and civilize each other—and make it so tough for sons-of-bitches like you—and you—and me."

Kanin's other plays, also comedies with liberal sentiments, have been less successful. They include *The Smile of the World* (1949); *The Rat Race* (1949), the story of a dancer and a saxophonist; and *The Live Wire* (1950), about a ruthless show business operator. Kanin has directed many Broadway hits and the 1950 Metropolitan Opera production of Johann Strauss's *Die Fledermaus,* whose libretto he adapted. In Hollywood, Kanin has written screenplays with his wife, the actress and dramatist Ruth Gordon (1896–   ), as well as many stories and a novel, *Blow Up a Storm* (1959).

KASPROWICZ, Jan (1860–1926), an important and influential late nineteenth-century Polish poet, wrote only a few plays: *Bunt Napierskiego* (1899), a verse drama about the sixteenth-century uprising in the Tatras, Kasprowicz's beloved mountains, at whose foot he is buried; *Uczta Herodjady* (1905), a biblical play on the Salomé motif; and *Marcholt* (1907), a legend drama. The son of a peasant, Kasprowicz became a radical and the leading literary figure of Lvov, at whose university he occupied the comparative literature chair.

KÄSTNER, Erich (1899–   ), German novelist and poet, and one of his country's most delightful humorists, became popular with his juvenile novels, particularly with *Emil und die Detektive* (*Emil and the Detectives,* 1928) and its sequel *Emil und die drei Zwillinge* (*Emil and the Three Twins,* 1934), and with *Pünktchen und Anton* (1931), all of which he has dramatized (1930, 1961, and 1932, respectively). Also notable is *Die Schule der Diktatoren* (1956), a tragicomic political satire. His other plays are less impressive. They include *Zu treuen Händen* (1950), a comedy published under the pseudonym Melchior Kurtz. His autobiography is *Als ich ein kleiner Junge war* (*When I Was a Little Boy,* 1957).

KATAEV, Valentin Petrovich (1897–   ), Soviet novelist and playwright, has been called "the NOËL

COWARD of Russia." Best known for his popular comedy *Kvadratura kruga* (SQUARING THE CIRCLE, 1928), he has written more than fifteen plays, some of them dramatizations of his novels. His playwriting talents flowered during the period of relative artistic freedom that existed in Russia in the late 1920's and early 1930's; at that time Kataev's flair for satire was given wide scope. Kataev was a *"poputchik,"* i.e., a Communist sympathizer who did not join the party but is considered a "fellow traveler." Though he has made fun of the shortcomings of his society, he has never questioned—and his criticisms and satires have never attacked—the essence of Communism and Soviet life. They have ridiculed only some of its superficial elements, and in a style that, particularly in his most famous plays, bears close resemblance to that of Coward's light comedies.

Kataev was born in Odessa, the son of a schoolmaster. His younger brother, Yevgeni Petrov (1903–42), was a noted humorist who was killed during the defense of Sevastapol in World War II. As a child Kataev wrote poetry, some of which was published when he was sixteen. He volunteered for artillery service during World War I, in which he was wounded and gassed. Then he fought for the Reds, and spent the early and turbulent post-revolutionary days in the Ukraine, a background he later used in his drama and fiction. Despite his Communist sympathies, however, he was briefly imprisoned by the Cheka.

His first notable success was *Rastratchiki* (*The Embezzlers,* 1928), Kataev's dramatization of his satiric novel about speculation and dishonesty among employees of the new Soviet government. It was followed by his masterpiece, *Squaring the Circle,* and by *Univermag* (1929), a satiric verse comedy. *Avangard,* which appeared the same year, is a comedy set on a collective farm, depicting the tribulations of its pioneering settlers. *Million terzanii* (1931), a satire of the intelligentsia, was followed by Kataev's dramatization of his novel *Vremya, vperyod!* (*Time, Forward!,* 1932; also translated as *Forward, Oh Time!*), a satire on the speed demanded of contemporary industrial workers in Soviet Russia, depicted more earnestly in Pogodin's TEMPO; *Doroga tsvetov* (*The Path of Flowers,* 1934; also translated as *The Primrose Path*), a comedy about dilletantism; *Pod kryshei tsirka* (1934), a musical written with his brother Yevgeni Petrov, and with the latter's newspaper colleague Ilia Ilf (pseudonym of Ilya Arnoldovich Faynzilberg, 1897–1937); *Bogataya nevesta* (1936), a farce; *Beleet parus odinoki* (1937, translated in England as *A Lonely White Sail Gleams* and in America as *Peace Is Where the Tempests Blow*), the later-filmed dramatization of his semi-autobiographical novel about Odessa children through whose eyes are portrayed the 1905 Revolution and its backgrounds; a dramatization of his novella *Ya, syn trudovogo naroda* (1938), a depiction of the battle against the German invaders of the Ukraine in 1918 (the title is the first line of the oath of allegiance to the Red Army); and *Shol soldat s fronta* (1938), which was added to the repertoire of Soviet productions.

Kataev's other plays include *Sini platochek* (1943), a popular wartime farce produced near the Russian front; *Syn polka* (1945), a Stalin Prize-winning children's play about a boy who fights the Nazis; *Otchi dom* (1945), depicting the rebuilding of homes destroyed by the Nazi invaders; and *Den otdykha* (1945). A number of these, as well as some of his novels and short stories, have been filmed in Russia.

Squaring the Circle has been reprinted in a number of anthologies, including Eugene Lyons's *Six Soviet Plays* (1934) and Harlan Hatcher's *Modern Drama* (1948), both with prefatory comments. Comprehensive English studies of Kataev's work are Gleb Struve's *Soviet Russian Literature 1917–1950* (1951) and Edward J. Brown's *Russian Literature Since the Revolution* (revised 1969).

KAUFMAN, George S[imon] (1889–1961), American journalist and playwright, was the author of many Broadway hits. Beginning with his first play, *Someone in the House* (1918), written with Larry Evans (? –1925) and Walter Percival (1888–1934), almost all were collaborations. With MARC CONNELLY Kaufman produced his first big hit, DULCY (1921), as well as BEGGAR ON HORSEBACK (1924) and half a dozen other comedies. (For other joint plays, see entries on Kaufman's individual collaborators.) Kaufman's most successful collaborations were with MOSS HART, particularly in hits like ONCE IN A LIFETIME (1930), YOU CAN'T TAKE IT WITH YOU (1936), and THE MAN WHO CAME TO DINNER (1939). His other important collaborators were EDNA FERBER and MORRIE RYSKIND. The half-dozen plays written with Ferber include THE ROYAL FAMILY (1927), DINNER AT EIGHT (1932), and STAGE DOOR (1936). He collaborated with Ryskind on as many plays, the most notable being the book for the musical OF THEE I SING (1931). And he helped JOHN STEINBECK stage OF MICE AND MEN. By himself, Kaufman wrote only a few one-acters and two full-length plays: *The Cocoanuts* (1925), a musical (songs by Irving Berlin), and THE BUTTER AND EGG MAN (1925).

Kaufman was born in Pittsburgh, where he began his career as a newspaperman; eventually he succeeded Franklin P. Adams as a columnist on the New York *World;* he then became a theatre critic for the New York *Tribune* and, later, for *The New York Times.* Kaufman continued in this work long after he had established himself as one of the most successful playwrights of the 1920's and 1930's, and, indeed, one of the New York theatre's major figures.

Most of Kaufman's collaborators did little significant playwriting of their own. Except for a few slight sketches, the great humorist Ring Lardner (1885–1933) did not again essay the drama after *June Moon* (1929), their amusing spoof of Tin Pan Alley song writers. Other Kaufman collaborators included ALEXANDER WOOLLCOTT, HOWARD DIETZ, and John P. Marquand (1893–1960), whose novel about old Boston society, *The*

George S. Kaufman with MOSS HART (left). (*Culver Pictures*)

Late George Apley (1937), the two men dramatized in 1944. Other Kaufman plays are *First Lady* (1935), a satirical comedy about Washington society, written with Katharine Dayton (? – 1945); *The Solid Gold Cadillac* (1953), a comedy about a little-old-lady stockholder who takes over a large corporation, written with Howard Teichmann (1916–); and three plays written with the actress Leueen MacGrath (1914–), Kaufman's London-born wife: *The Small Hours* (1951), *Fancy Meeting You Again* (1952), and *Silk Stockings* (1955), a musical (score by Cole Porter, book by Kaufman, Leueen MacGrath, and ABE BURROWS) based on the MENYHÉRT LENGYEL-Ernst Lubitsch film *Ninotchka* (1940).

Kaufman's plays are conventional in plot and usually devoid of theme. His distinctive touch in his collaborations is "the destructive wisecrack" —"the verbal ricochet"—as Brooks Atkinson noted in his introduction to the Kaufman and Hart collection *Six Plays* (1942); Atkinson aptly catalogued Kaufman's comic devices: "The fury of the gags, the bitterness and speed of the attacks upon stupidity, the loudness of the humor, the precision of the phrasing." These qualities made Kaufman's works popular and carried their appeal beyond the usually ephemeral life on Broadway.

Aside from playwriting, directing, "play-doctoring," and journalism, Kaufman also acted on occasion. Almost all of his fifty-odd plays were published, many of them in anthologies. An extensive—and delightful—account of Kaufman appears in Moss Hart's autobiography, *Act One* (1959).

KELLY, George [Edward] (1887–), American actor and playwright, became famous in the 1920's with two hits: THE SHOW-OFF (1924) and CRAIG'S WIFE (1925). He had already made a reputation for himself with numerous popular vaudeville sketches, and he continued writing for the legitimate stage for twenty years thereafter. But he was unable to repeat his success. The plays that followed received short shrift from the public and the critics, whom Kelly ignored. Though *The Show-Off* and *Craig's Wife* have been repeatedly revived, Kelly was soon forgotten—his name overshadowed by that of his niece Grace, a famous actress and the later Princess of Monaco.

Kelly was born in Philadelphia and began his career as a juvenile actor. He played in vaudeville, for which he started writing the popular one-acters collected in *The Flattering Word and Other One-Act Plays* (1925). Notable among these are the title play, which satirizes most actors' irrepressible conviction that they have talent; *Poor Aubrey,* an early sketch of *The Show-Off;* and *Smarty's Party,* something of a precursor of *Craig's Wife*. Kelly's first full-length play was *The Torch Bearers* (1922), a satire of the social and artistic pretensions of amateur ("little theatre") players. It was followed by his two big hits. In his next plays, *Daisy Mayme* (1926) and *Behold the Bridegroom* (1927), Kelly failed to sustain his art and popularity, though *Behold the Bridegroom* has been praised by some critics; its heroine's girlhood indiscretions make her unworthy for the right man when he comes along. A similar attack on middle-class morality appears in *Maggie the Magnificent* (1929), whose title character strives to rise above the vulgarity of her mother and emulate her artist father.

Although notable actresses starred in them, relatively little notice was accorded Kelly's later plays: *Philip Goes Forth* (1931) satirizes a young man who tries to become a playwright because he wants publicity; *Reflected Glory* (1936) is about an actress unable to give up the stage; and *The Deep Mrs. Sykes* (1945) is a pendant to *Craig's Wife*. Only in his last play, *The Fatal Weakness* (1946), did Kelly portray a more congenial heroine, a helplessly sentimental woman who likes weddings; she loses her husband to another woman—but cannot resist attending even their wedding.

Kelly's dramaturgy is wholly traditional. What distinguishes his plays are the broad characterizations of types (notably the selfish and predatory American female personified by Harriet Craig, and the beef-witted and noisy Rotarian featured in *The Show-Off*) and situations, and his excoriation of middle-class manners and morality. These qualities manifest both his strengths and his weaknesses. The truthfulness of Kelly's characters and situations gave him the reputation of an important REALIST and "thesis" playwright of the 1920's. But they also limited his scope. His characterizations are often exaggerated into caricatures and set off by a gallery of dull minor characters. Kelly's moral satire, which is pseudo-IBSEN, is hardly distinguishable from bitterness, and brings about predetermined and unbelievable dramatic resolutions. Even Kelly's comedy is grim, and his "realism" is too often a NATURALISTIC preoccupation with "things"—external details, stage props (telephones, cigarettes, coffee cups) that seem to be more important than character and plot. Only at the peak of his accomplishment was Kelly able to transcend, or perhaps almost transcend, these shortcomings.

Arthur Wills's "The Kelly Play," *Modern Drama* VI (1963), surveys his playwriting and refers to other studies. For Kelly's early plays, see Joseph Wood Krutch's *The American Drama Since 1918* (1957); interesting observations on Kelly's later plays are included in Mary McCarthy's *Sights and Spectacles* (1956), republished in *Mary McCarthy's Theatre Chronicles 1937–1962* (1963).

KENNEDY, Margaret (1896–1967), English novelist, became a successful playwright when she and BASIL DEAN dramatized her popular novel THE CONSTANT NYMPH (1926). Her other play on the Sanger family was *Escape Me Never!* (1935), which was filmed and became one of the actress Elisabeth Bergner's great hits. Kennedy wrote many novels, books of literary criticism, and a biography, *Jane Austen* (1950). Born in London, she was educated at Cheltenham Ladies' College and Somerville College of Oxford University, where she received an M.A. in history. She was the wife of a distinguished lawyer, Sir David Davies.

KESSELRING, Joseph O. (1902–67), American dramatist, wrote a dozen plays, from 1933 (*Aggie Appleby, Maker of Men*) to 1963 (*Mother of That Wisdom*), only one of which, however, is really notable. *Arsenic and Old Lace* (1941), a delightful comedy, produced by HOWARD LINDSAY and RUSSEL CROUSE, ran on Broadway for almost four years; it portrays two kindly old ladies who systematically poison lonely elderly men. Kesselring, a one-time music professor in Kansas, was born in New York City. He also wrote a number of film scripts, including that of *Arsenic and Old Lace* (1944).

KESTEN, Hermann (1900–), German writer, was known chiefly for his novels, some of them anti-Nazi. With ERNST TOLLER he wrote *Wunder in Amerika* (*Miracle in America,* 1931), a play about the founder of Christian Science, that appeared also as *Mary Baker Eddy*. Kesten's half-dozen other plays were produced before he had to flee Hitler's Germany; they include *Admet* (1928), a dramatization of the Alcestis legend.

KEY LARGO, a play in a prologue and two acts by MAXWELL ANDERSON, published and produced in 1939. Setting: Spain and Key Largo, Florida; 1938–39.

This somewhat verbose poetic drama has been esteemed as one of Anderson's clearest and most positive affirmations of human integrity.

Prologue. During the last days of the Spanish Civil War, King McCloud becomes disillusioned when he discovers that his group of American volunteers is being sacrificed in the hopeless Loyalists' cause, and he prepares to desert. But the others decide to die fighting, inspired by Victor d'Alcala's words: "... If I went with you / I'd never know whether the race was turning / down again, to the dinosaurs—this way / I keep my faith. In myself and what men are. / And in what we may be."

Act I. In Key Largo, some gangsters have paid off the sheriff and commandeered a cabin in the tourist camp of Victor's blind father and his sister. After visiting all his fallen comrades' families and explaining what has happened in Spain, King arrives in Key Largo. Though he knows he had done the right thing in choosing life over pointless death, he is tormented by guilt. He further confesses that after leaving his doomed friends he was captured and then fought with Franco's army: "I was willing to eat dirt and be damned / if I could live. I ate dirt, and I'm damned." He seeks forgiveness from Victor's sister, Alegre—with whom he has fallen in love. Though they despise King's desertion, Alegre and her father ask him to stay; he might help protect them from the gangsters. King is pleased to be of some use, but he admits that "If it comes to dying I don't trust my brain, / my busy, treacherous, casuistic brain, / presenting me with scientific facts / and cunning reasons." And indeed, confronted with the gangster chief, he soon quails and gives in.

Act II. The gangster has murdered a man the previous night and sunk his body in the gulf. To get rid of the intruders, D'Alcala has two fugitive Indians who are grateful for his help release the corpse and float it into the open water. It will force the sheriff, D'Alcala hopes, to arrest the gangster. In the meantime, King is passed off as D'Alcala's son, to keep the gangster from moving into the D'Alcala apartment and assaulting Alegre. When the corpse is discovered, the sheriff pins the murder on the fugitive Indians—or if they are not found, on D'Alcala's "son," against whom there is an old charge. Alegre reveals the whereabouts of the fugitive Indians, thus forcing King to make the choice between their lives and his. In agony he demands, "Show me one thing secure / among these names of virtues—justice and honor / and love and friendship—and I'll die for it gladly." As his pessimism grows, Alegre begins to despair: "Answer him, father, answer, / because it sounds like truth—but if it were true / one couldn't live!" D'Alcala's long answer suggests the hopeful ideal, though "Over and over again the human race / climbs up out of the mud" merely to sink down once more. By the time the Indians are captured, however, King has decided. He saves them by assuming the guilt for the murder, and shoots the gangster, though he himself is killed—as he knew he would be. Given a second chance, he has realized that "A man must die / for what he believes—if he's unfortunate / enough to have to face it in his time— / and if he won't then he'll end up believing / in nothing at all—and that's death, too."

KEYS OF HEAVEN, THE (*Himmelrikets nycklar*), a fantasy in five acts by AUGUST STRINDBERG, published in 1892 and produced in 1962 (radio production in 1929). Setting: smithy, woods, Schlaraffenland, Rome, etc.

Though this verse drama has the structure of a fairy tale, its harsh grotesquery as well as its autobiography and SYMBOLISM make the play more akin to TO DAMASCUS.

A heartbroken smith searching for his dead children accompanies an aging and forgetful Saint Peter searching for the keys of heaven. During their adventurous pilgrimage they have many visions. They meet Don Quixote as well as other legendary figures. Finally Saint Peter dies of weariness. But despite repeated disillusionment and despair, the smith rejoices when he sees his children —above Jacob's Ladder, inside the ruins of the Tower of Babylon.

KIKUCHI Hiroshi [Kan] (1888–1948), Japanese writer and editor, wrote popular plays, novels, and short stories. Best known in English is his repeatedly anthologized short one-acter *Okujō no Kyōjin* (*The Madman on the Roof,* 1916; also translated as *The Housetop Madman*) about a crippled half-wit who likes to climb atop his house and whose superstitious family agrees to a religious quack's treatment; the educated other son ultimately sends off the "priestess" and affectionately joins his brother on the roof. Kikuchi's other plays, some influenced by BERNARD SHAW and JOHN GALSWORTHY, are similarly based on observations of common life, and tend to portray moralistically the ultimate defeat of evil or its conversion to good.

Kikuchi was born in Takamatsu, Shikoku. He was expelled from two high schools for his Bohemianism but nonetheless graduated from Kyoto University, where he studied English. Subsequently he became a newspaperman and founded the successful literary magazine *Bungei Shunju* (in 1923) and others. While still a student he wrote a number of plays that later became popular; three years after his graduation (1916) appeared his successful dramatic biography of the seventeenth-century actor Tōjūrū Sakata, *Tōjūrō no Koi* (*Tōjūrō's Love,* 1919). Kikuchi's other plays include *Katakiuchi Ijō* (*Better than Revenge,* 1920), a dramatization of his short story on the building of a tunnel; *Chichi Kaeru* (*The Father Returns,* 1917), another popular and moving play that, like *The Madman on the Roof,* depicts everyday life; and *Kiseki* (*The Miracle,* 1916), a farce. These were translated, with a preface by Glenn W. Shaw, as *Tōjūrō's Love and Four Other Plays* (1925).

KILLER, THE (*Tueur sans gages;* literally: "killer without wages" or "remorse"), a play in three acts by EUGÈNE IONESCO, published in 1958 and produced in 1959. Setting: a day in contemporary Paris.

Praised as one of Ionesco's finest plays, this is the first to feature Bérenger. In this play this "average, middle-aged citizen" is a little Chaplinesque figure whose euphoric idealism turns to despair before the dramatized nightmare of human existence. The final scene, with the Killer (a symbol of inevitable death as well as the absurdity of life), is a "short act in itself," according to Ionesco's initial stage direction; its long monologue should "bring out the gradual breaking-down of Bérenger, his falling apart, and the vacuity of his own rather commonplace morality, which collapses like a leaking balloon." The play is based on a short story Ionesco wrote in 1955, "La Photo du colonel."

Act I. "Amazing! It's extraordinary! As far as I can see it's a miracle," Bérenger exclaims as he examines a "radiant city within a city"—a housing project depicted on an empty stage by gray lighting only. He marvels at the "sunny streets and avenues bathed in light," for as the Architect explains, it never rains here. The Architect, an "ageless, bureaucratic" figure carrying a heavy briefcase (like those in the other acts, symbolizing their owners' share in the evil they do not oppose), reveals that though the district is ruled by various specialists, he himself has many positions, including that of commissioner. He has a dossier on everyone (including Bérenger), and periodically administers his departments with a pocket telephone. As Bérenger rhapsodizes on the district's superiority to the "gray city" outside, the Architect dryly implies that the district, whose beauty and light are artificial, may be less than perfect. Though it is dangerous to leave "our organization," his young secretary, with whom Bérenger immediately falls in love, resigns to regain her freedom. All the other inhabitants, the Architect admits, are equally eager to leave—for they are afraid of a mass killer who cannot be caught. Bérenger is appalled, but the Architect seems unperturbed by the Killer. "We've all got to die," he observes, and as for other calamities, "that's how journalists earn their daily bread. Everything has its bright side." He describes the Killer's method: he lures victims with the photograph of a colonel, and then pushes them into the pool to drown. Just then there is a commotion outside: the Killer has struck again—drowning the secretary who just resigned. Heartbroken, Bérenger rushes off: "It can't go on! We must *do* something! We must, we must, we must!"

Act II. A friend is waiting in Bérenger's ugly and heavily furnished apartment. He is invisible in the dark for half the act, until Bérenger's entrance. In the meantime there are only sounds, snatches of the gray city's noises, of the mechanized, absurd, and vacuous life outside: the philosophizing of a platitudinous, self-pitying, prejudiced concierge; two old men's talk of lost former days; a teacher's nonsensical history lesson; and an efficiency expert's calculations for saving time by having employees bunch their restroom visits into one monthly trip ("After all, *camels* store up water"). When the upset Bérenger enters he tells his friend, a tubercular youth with a withered arm, of his disillusionment with the "radiant city." He is astounded that his friend, like everybody else, knows all about the Killer "who terrorizes and kills everyone." The friend keeps whining about his illness and dismisses the murders as "the way of the world." Bérenger is disgusted by such general indifference to evil. Getting ready for a walk, the sick youth drops his large briefcase. Out of it spill the colonel's photograph and the unknown Killer's other accouterments—including boxes within boxes, the Killer's calling card, even a map with his itinerary and an address book listing future victims. Gradually Bérenger's friend remembers where he got all these things: the Killer sent them to be published, before he decided actually to carry out his crimes. "Literature can lead anywhere," Bérenger thereupon remarks, insisting that writers and poets must be stopped. Eagerly he collects the evidence and makes his friend accompany him to the police, for "there comes a time when one can no longer accept all the horrible things that happen." As they go out and he turns off the light, his friend leaves behind the briefcase containing the evidence.

Act III. In the street there is a mass meeting. A female demagogue spouting totalitarian slogans promises to change everything—though beneath the new names things will remain the same: "Tyranny restored will be called discipline and liberty. The misfortune of one is the happiness of all." Her harangue is interspersed with the heckling of a liberal drunk who prefers science and art to politics. It is Einstein, Picasso, and other geniuses, he says, who are "extending our field of knowledge, renewing our vision of the world." The liberal drunk is finally knocked out. In the meantime, Bérenger, discovering the loss of his friend's briefcase, snatches briefcases from various people, including a Parisian seeking the Danube. They turn out to be the wrong ones, and his friend goes off to find his own. Two gigantic traffic policemen, instead of helping to catch the Killer, insist on directing traffic and bully Bérenger—who thereupon decides to go to the police station.

Suddenly alone on a darkening road as the sun sets, Bérenger is confident: "Once he's arrested, bound hand and foot, out of harm's way, the spring will come back for ever, and every city will be radiant." But as he walks on through ploughed fields and deserted streets, Bérenger becomes increasingly anxious and less determined: "Another victim here or there, what's it matter in the state we're in. . . . There's no harm putting it off. . . . The Superintendent will arrest him tomorrow." Just as he decides to go home, he is confronted by the Killer—a one-eyed, degenerate, shabbily dressed, puny dwarf. At first unafraid, Bérenger tries to reason with him. Idiotic chuckles are his only response to the platitudes with which Bérenger attempts to understand and reform him by appealing to his reason, morality, religion, self-interest, and idealism. "Perhaps you kill all these people out of kindness! To save them from suffering!" Bérenger speculates, but the Killer merely chuckles idiotically. Gradually Bérenger loses his self-assurance: "There must be one thing in common, a common language— What is it?" He tries ridicule: "There's the idiot going by, there's the idiot! Ha! Ha! Ha! — Who believes in crime for its own sake! Ha! Ha!" Still chuckling, the Killer slowly pulls out a knife. "You filthy dirty moronic imbecile!" Bérenger exclaims, taking two pistols from his pocket. But "how weak my strength is against your cold determination, your ruthlessness!" Bérenger realizes. Impotent, he finally drops his pistols: "Oh God! There's nothing we can do. What can we do—What can we do . . ." The Killer draws nearer and raises his knife, still chuckling.

KING DAVID AND HIS WIVES (*Dovid Hamelekh un zayne Vayber*), five scenes by DAVID PINSKI, published in 1919. Setting: the days of David in biblical times.

This is a series of one-acters written from 1913 to 1915. Together they constitute a play that portrays David's development from idealism, through blatant sensualism, to a final realization that man's exaltation lies not in the achievement of but in the search for the ideal. Imaginative dramatizations of a few Old Testament verses in simple but lyrical prose, these episodes have been characterized as "a biblical version of Schnitzler's ANATOL." The play has apparently remained unproduced.

Mikhal (I Samuel 17–18). Though he loves King Saul's daughter Mikhal, young David refuses to claim her as his just reward for defeating Goliath because he did it for God: "Only the love of God gave strength to my arm." Neither proud Mikhal's confession of her love nor Jonathan's insistence that David won her swerves him from this religious ideal. When the maddened king ridicules him, however, David seizes the chance to fight for Mikhal alone and thus win her. Joyfully he goes off to slay twice the number of Philistines Saul demands. "He'll never return," Saul laughs, but Mikhal is exalted: "He—loves—me. He will conquer!"

Abigail (I Samuel 25). As David and his exhausted men prepare to punish Nabal for his cruelty and affronts, Nabal's beautiful wife Abigail secretly comes with supplies for them. David immediately falls in love with her. Abigail admits her husband's wickedness, but though she does not love him, she will not dishonor her marriage vow. Nabal soon appears. While insulting her as well as David and his men, he has a sudden, fatal stroke. "Blessed be the Lord who has pleaded the cause of my insult from Nabal and has kept me from evil," David says. Then he takes Abigail in his arms.

Bathsheba (II Samuel 11–12). Smitten with Bathsheba when he sees her bathing, King David has her forcefully brought to him. Though warned by his prophet and by Bathsheba, who vows eternal fidelity to Uriah, her adored husband, David insists on possessing her: "I am ready to break God's word, His Commandment, His laws. I am drunk with you. Let Him punish me. . . . But I must have you." Uriah refuses to disobey his king, willingly preparing to give his beloved wife to David and go to his own death. Bathsheba begs him to kill David, or her, and tears up the king's orders. When Uriah persists in humble obedience to his king, Bathsheba dismisses him as a despicable worm and walks toward David: "He shall cleanse me of my stain. . . . He shall make me chaste. Oh, I loved a slave. Now I shall love a king!"

In the Harem. After their return to Jerusalem, King David's wives quarrel among themselves. They mourn the sons they have lost, and argue about the royal succession. The old king bitterly notes how his wives have aged: "Every one of you was the beginning of a new life for me; every new love, a new spring, full of song and renewal." Now they are—only mothers. When reminded of his own age, he rises up: "I am not yet stiff and frozen. My heart and blood still boil with flaming fires, and passions of all kinds still roar within me." But he sends out not only his wives but also his young concubines: "I feel cold."

Abishag (I Kings I: 1–4). The most beautiful of women, Abishag, is found for the seventy-year-old King David. When she comes to him, adoring and ready to wed him, David realizes that only desire can give his life meaning: "If you were to be my wife, then you would become a riddle solved. What would then keep King David warm?" He concludes, "You must remain my great longing, never to be fulfilled." He will marry her, but never consummate his love. Abishag dances a wild, passionate dance. "Pour hot coals into me with the movement of your young limbs," King David urges her, and breathes deeply as the dance gets wilder. At last he understands his quest for the ideal: "For this I thank thee, God, and to Thy name do I sing praise!"

KING NICOLO, OR SUCH IS LIFE (*König Nicolo, oder So ist das Leben*), a play in five acts and a prologue by FRANK WEDEKIND, published and produced in 1902. Setting: Perugia, the capital of Umbria, Italy; 1499.

This is Wedekind's last important play. It is a poetic, comically grotesque, inconsistently SYMBOLIC, and autobiographical fairy tale about a sensual king who is eventually dethroned and exiled with his daughter. After wandering and serving as a laborer he returns in disguise, remains unrecognized, and becomes the jester in the court of the usurper, a commoner. At Nicolo's death he reveals his true identity, for his daughter has fallen in love with the new prince. No one believes Nicolo, but the usurper orders his interment in the royal tomb: "History shall never say that I made a king my court jester!"

KING OF THE GREAT CLOCK TOWER, THE, a one-act play by WILLIAM BUTLER YEATS, published and produced in 1934. Setting: a screened stage.

In 1935, Yeats published this play in verse, as well as in another poetic version, *A Full Moon in March*. Though based on Celtic legend and characteristically Yeatsian, like FOUR PLAYS FOR DANCERS, its theme resembles that of Wilde's SALOMÉ. The unnamed Orphic hero anticipates his ritualistic impregnation of the queen, a SYMBOLIC consummation of profane and sacred love that echoes the lunar myths Yeats adumbrated in his *A Vision* (1925).

Before "the King of the Great Clock Tower" and his disdainfully silent queen there appears a common "stroller and a fool." He has made poems about the queen's beauty, wants to see her, and asks that she dance for and kiss him. The king executes the stroller for his impertinence. Then the stroller's severed head sings, and the queen dances with and finally kisses it.

In the second version there is no king: only an aloof queen, "cruel as the winter of virginity." A swineherd courts her during the spring equinox, "a full moon in March," and promises she will "bring forth her farrow in the dung." His triumph is foreshadowed by her removal of her veil before his beheading.

KING, THE (*Konungen*), a play in three acts be PÄR LAGERKVIST, published in 1932 and produced in 1950. Setting: an unidentified kingdom in ancient times.

This is a dramatic protest, in the form of a philosophical disquisition, against the rise of Fascism. It was inspired by and partly follows J. G. Frazer's description in *The Golden Bough* of a Babylonian scapegoat ritual in which the king is replaced briefly by a condemned criminal. His temporary reign is accompanied by a national bacchanalia and customarily ends with his execution.

The temporarily deposed king, now a despised beggar, reveals himself in a series of dialogues as a philosopher who believes in mankind, discovers "love and humanity," and is able to transmit his ideals to his favorite wife and to the young disciple who refuses to leave him. In the meantime the scapegoat king, a criminal sobered by his new position, transcends the orgiastic revels about him and determines "not to be sacrificed! Not this time! Now we shall live instead—finally!" He wins his battle against reaction, represented by the convention-bound priests. The dying old king is brought in. "You must believe again," he exhorts his grieving disciple. Placing the youngster's hand in that of his favorite wife, he dies, confident that "you shall believe again." The new king saves the disciple from the priests, who want to kill him as an "unclean" blasphemer. "There are no longer any divine laws," the new king declares: "And therefore he shall not be banished. Not if he will serve us." He accepts the disciple's reply that he will "serve mankind." "That is right," the new king says, taking his hand. "And all of us are men." The crowds cheer: "Hail to thee! — Our king! — Hail to thee!"

KING UBU (*Ubu roi*), a play in five acts by ALFRED JARRY, published and produced in 1896. Setting: "timeless and spaceless" Poland, the Ukraine, etc.

This play, which has also been translated as *Ubu Rex,* is a landmark in avant-garde drama. The premiere took place on December 10, at Lugné-Poë's Théatre de l'Oeuvre in Paris, and is described in WILLIAM BUTLER YEATS's *Autobiographies;* pandemonium broke out with the opening expletive (to which Jarry added a letter), which is repeated throughout the play. The bestial and avaricious Ubu was meant to mirror the middle-class audience's true self; despite his comic stupidity, he is a frightening personification of senseless cosmic evil (Cyril Connolly called him the "Santa Claus of the Atomic Age"). But on the surface the play is like a scatological children's puppet show—a bizarre and Rabelaisian fairy tale, with corresponding sets and masks. Subsequently Jarry wrote other, less noteworthy Ubu plays.

Act I. "Merdre!" fat and pear-shape-headed Father Ubu exclaims when his wife urges him to kill the Polish king; "aren't I Captain of the Dragoons, confidential adviser to King Wenceslas . . . and ex-King of Aragon—what more do you want?" In a parody of Shakespeare's *Macbeth,* Mother Ubu calls him "a pig-headed ass," tempts him with the royal accouterments, and succeeds in rousing him. He invites Captain Bordure and his followers to a gargantuan dinner, into which he throws a toilet brush. Encouraged to taste the brush, many die. Bordure is promised a dukedom and agrees to support Ubu's plot. Summoned by Wenceslas, Ubu accuses his wife when he fears discovery. But instead, Wenceslas honors him, presents him with a toy whistle, and invites him to a parade. On that occasion Ubu intends to murder the king. His fellow conspirators overrule Ubu's cowardly plan to poison the king; Bordure is to kill him with the sword at Ubu's signal: *"Merdre!"*

Act II. Though warned by his fearful queen, Wenceslas attends the parade. The plot to kill him succeeds. Prince Bougrelas, after stabbing Ubu's paunch protector, escapes to the mountains with his mother. She dies, and his ancestors' shades give him the sword with which he can avenge his parents. In the meantime the stingy Ubu is persuaded by his wife to follow tradition and distribute gold and food.

Act III. Ubu decides to double-cross Bordure, though Mother Ubu urges him to do what is right. "Doesn't the wrong always get you more than the right?" Ubu asks, and chases her away. He "disembrains" and kills the nobles for their money, has the magistrates support themselves with the fines they impose, and invokes many brutal measures. Though cowardly, Ubu himself enforces his ruthless taxation and supervises the slaughter of grumblers. The peasants who escape rally around Bordure, who flees to Russia and implores the tsar's aid in fighting Ubu. Ubu agrees to fight after his "Phynancial Advisers" and Mother Ubu urge him to: "By my green candle, let's wage war, since you're so excited about it, but let's not spend a penny." His underfed nag is dying of starvation, but Ubu gets another horse and works up the courage to leave. "Now that that big fat booby has gone," Mother Ubu remarks, "let's look to our own affairs, kill Bougrelas, and grab the treasure."

Act IV. While Mother Ubu ransacks the royal tombs, Prince Bougrelas recaptures Warsaw. Mother Ubu barely escapes. In the Ukraine, the Russians start attacking. Ubu blusters belligerently, but soon panics and runs away. He is next seen in a Lithuanian cave with two of his men, where a bear attacks them. The fat Ubu clambers atop a rock and recites a Paternoster, while the men fight and kill the bear. Ubu takes credit for saving them and defeating the bear. Disgusted with him, the men leave Ubu when he is asleep.

Act V. Mother Ubu enters the cave and finds her sleepy husband "even stupider than when he left." While he is still frightened, she makes him promise to forgive her "for having side-tracked some of the funds." Angrily, Ubu throws the bear at her, tells her that "despite my incontestable valor, everybody beat me up," and devises ways to torture her: "Twisting of the nose, tearing out of the hair, penetration of the little bit of wood into the earens, extraction of the brains by the heels," etc. But as "he begins to tear her to pieces," Prince Bougrelas enters with his soldiers. Father and Mother Ubu both fight them, aided by Ubu's followers, who suddenly appear. They all manage to battle their way out and escape Bougrelas. "I don't envy him that crown," Ubu remarks, and with his followers he boards a ship on the Baltic. "We must be making at least a million knots an hour, and these knots have been tied so well that once tied they cannot be untied," Ubu says happily. The others pity the "pathetic imbecile," but Ubu looks forward to being appointed Minister of Finances in Paris. After the ship passes Elsinore Castle, Mother Ubu remarks on the beauty of Germany. "Ah! Gentlemen!" says Ubu: "Beautiful as it may be, it cannot compare with Poland. For if there were no Poland, there would be no Poles!"

KINGDOM OF GOD, THE (*El reino de Dios*), a play in three acts by GREGORIO MARTÍNEZ SIERRA, published and produced in 1915. Setting: an asylum for old paupers, a maternity home, and an orphanage in Spain; nineteenth and twentieth centuries.

HARLEY GRANVILLE-BARKER called this "in some ways the most considerable" of Martínez Sierra's work, and praised the "variety, fidelity, vitality of the sketched characters with which it is so economically filled." The role of the play's protagonist, a beatific character whose life is traced from youth to old age, was given notable performance by Ethel Barrymore.

Sister Gracia, a nineteen-year-old nun, ministers cheerfully to the asylum's tiresome old men, humoring the obstreperous and the sick and the frightened, who all adore her. "I've nothing to give away except my happiness," she says, determined to renew her yearly vow and refusing to return home with her visiting family. A decade later, Sister Gracia is equally beloved and generous among "fallen" women, some of them cynical, some desperate, some hysterical. A handsome doctor wants to take Sister Gracia away from the misery that is overwhelming her. "You dare to speak to me of love—here—where we see how it all ends?" she exclaims, rejecting marriage for the holy love to which she has pledged her life "once and for all. . . . I live for that love and I will die in it." In the final act Sister Gracia, now the indomitable seventy-year-old director of an orphanage, settles fights and accepts a trophy from one of her charges: the bloody ear of the first bull he ever killed. Because their meals are inadequate the hungry orphans threaten to mob the authorities outside. Sister Gracia quells the riot and urges the revolutionaries to fight injustice with love: "Help to build on earth the Kingdom of God." After convincing them that rebellion would be futile she comforts the ringleader. "Don't cry," she concludes gently; "men don't cry, you know. And they don't complain. They suffer—but they work and hope."

KINGSLEY, Sidney (1906–), American dramatist, gained fame with his first two professionally produced plays, MEN IN WHITE (1933) and DEAD END (1935). Both demonstrate amply his talent to depict local color, particularly in big-city life. Kingsley has used similar milieus in most of his later work. A writer with social consciousness, he strove to deal with serious problems. But invariably he has succumbed to pat contrivance and melodrama.

Kingsley was born in New York, and graduated from Cornell University, where he wrote a few short plays. Later he appeared in minor roles in stock companies and married the well-known actress Madge Evans. After his success as a playwright, Kingsley regularly produced his own works.

The most popular of his subsequent plays was *Detective Story* (1949, filmed in 1951), a police-department melodrama starring a storybook hero whose tragic flaw is his uncompromising adherence to prescribed morality: the harm of overzealousness constitutes Kingsley's social message. His other plays consist of a couple of war dramas, including *The World We Make* (1939), an adaptation of Millen Brand's novel about mental instability; *The Outward Room* (1937); *The Patriots* (1943), a portrayal of George Washington, Thomas Jefferson, and (to a lesser degree) Alexander Hamilton; *Darkness at Noon* (1951), a dramatization of Arthur Koestler's well-known 1941 novel about a purged Soviet leader who confesses to crimes he did not commit; *Lunatics and Lovers* (1954), a farce about shady habitués of the Times Square area; and *Night Life* (1962), a multicharacter lust-and-intrigue melodrama set in a nightclub, which presents its social message through a little man's courage in defying and being shot by a mobster, a would-be dictator.

Though these later plays recall *Dead End,* they neither equal the power and artistry of that imposing early work, nor have they achieved anything like its popularity. Despite his seriousness, Kingsley has been faulted for his timidity in developing problems he appeared to confront, and for his penchant for artistic compromise. These flaws have finally precluded his becoming the important playwright he seemed to be developing into in the 1930's.

KINOSHITA Junji (1914–) is representative of Japan's better post-World War II playwrights. He became known abroad with the one-act *Yūzuru* (*Twilight Crane,* 1949), the folktale of a crane that assumes human form to reward the man who released her from a snare, marries him, and makes him rich by secretly weaving valuable cloth out of her own feathers; but when he greedily compels her to weave incessantly though it makes her waste away, and break the rule by looking into the secret chamber where she works for him, the crane resumes her natural form and flies away forever. *Yūzuru* was also produced as No, Kabuki, and opera—in Japan as well as in Europe.

Kinoshita studied English literature at Tokyo University. During World War II, he started to write *minwa-geki,* i.e., plays based on folk tales; most of these were performed by the *Budo no Kai* (Grapes Club), a drama study group that used Konstantin Stanislavsky's methods. The year it was founded (1947) Kinoshita produced another prize-winning play, *Fūrō.* His later drama includes a left-wing portrayal of the conflict between nationalism and socialism, *Otto to yobareru nihonjin* (1962). Kinoshita has also written radio plays and has translated Shakespeare and SOMERSET MAUGHAM into Japanese.

A. C. Scott's translation of *Twilight Crane* appears in *Playbook* (1956).

KIPPHARDT, Heinar (1922–), German playwright, achieved international renown with *In der Sache J. Robert Oppenheimer* (*In the Matter of J. Robert Oppenheimer,* 1964), a historical courtroom drama based on the proceedings of the 1954 Atomic Energy Commission hearings. Originally a radio play, this controversial hit (produced in Berlin by Erwin Piscator) depicts Dr. Oppenheimer as an opponent of the hydrogen bomb project who unsuccessfully fights his dismissal as a security risk, supported by friendly witnesses, but opposed by extremists like Edward Teller, the noted physicist who developed the H-bomb.

Kipphardt was born in Heidersdorf, Silesia. His father, a dentist, spent five years in a Nazi concentration camp as a political prisoner. Kipphardt studied medicine and was sent to the Russian front as a Wehrmacht conscript. After the war he completed his studies and worked in various hospitals as a psychiatrist. In 1951 he gave up medicine to become a producer at East Berlin's Deutsches Theater. At the same time he started his writing career. His first produced play was *Shakespeare dringend gesucht* (1953), a satiric comedy about censorship behind the Iron Curtain. It was followed by *Der Aufstieg des Alois Piontek* (1956), a farce, and *Die Stühle des Herrn Szmil* (1961), a satire of local bureaucracy that was produced after Kipphardt had moved to West Germany in 1959.

There he soon achieved distinction as a documentary dramatist employing EPIC THEATRE devices, as in the Oppenheimer play. His other works include the original television drama *Der Hund des General* (1961), about a now-affluent burgher who during World War II had sent an entire regiment to their death because one of its soldiers had inadvertently killed his pet dog; *Joel Brand, die Geschichte eines Geschäfts* (1965), a documentary portrayal of the abortive Eichmann plan to exchange a million Jewish lives for ten thousand trucks; and *Die Nacht, in der der Chef geschlachtet wurde* (1967), a nightmare portrayal of modern technocracy.

KIRKLAND, Jack [John M.] (1902–69), American dramatist and producer, wrote a dozen plays, most of them adaptations of novels. His greatest success was his adaptation of Erskine Caldwell's TOBACCO ROAD (1933), which made millions of dollars for Kirkland.

Born in St. Louis, Missouri, Kirkland began as a newspaperman and had written an earlier play, *Frankie and Johnnie* (1928). Later he also adapted other novels for the stage, including JOHN STEINBECK's *Tortilla Flat* (1938), Erskine Caldwell's *Georgia Boy* (1945), and Nelson Algren's *The Man with the Golden Arm* (1956). Shortly before his death he began rewriting *Tobacco Road* as a "folk musical" libretto.

KIRSHON, Vladimir Mikhailovich (1902–38?), Russian playwright, was born in Leningrad. He fought on the Caucasian front with the Reds during the Civil War, studied at Sverdlovsk University, was one of the founders of RAPP (the Russian Association of Proletarian Writers), and then became a member of the Presidium of the Union of Soviet Writers. He was an exponent of the principle that drama must depict valid contemporary political views, but his party activities as well as his ideologically orthodox plays did not save him from the grim fate of many Soviet intellectuals. In 1937 he was arrested as a Trotskyite "enemy of the people," his plays were banned, and he soon perished mysteriously. Like many others, too, he was posthumously "rehabilitated" in 1956.

Particularly notable among his plays are two that had immense if ephemeral popularity: *Khleb* (*Bread,* 1930) and *Chudesny splav* (1934). The first, produced at the Moscow Art Theatre and throughout Russia, portrays the defeat of the kulaks; two of these wealthy farmers, represented as powerful and menacing starvers of the people, are contrasted with two Party members who work for collectivization. *Chudesny splav* is a farce about the discovery of a "miraculous alloy" that makes Soviet planes superior to those of the capitalist countries; the comedy for the most part is provided by the antics of some of the workers when a beautiful new colleague joins the group and inadvertently turns the men's heads.

Kirshon's first play, written with A. V. Uspensky (? – ?), was *Konstantin Terekhin: rzhavchina* (*Konstantin Terekhin: Rust,* 1927), a play that was also produced in the United States, England, and France. The plot is based on a sensational contemporary murder case involving a degenerate Communist ("Terekhin" is his fictitious name) and the question, widely discussed at the time, of whether the criminal's past entitled him to a pardon and possible rehabilitation as a useful Communist. The play was produced in 1929 by the New York Theatre Guild Studio as *Red Rust,* the "rust" being that of the corruption of youths after the Russian civil war. Its foreign productions stressed the work's sensuality and melodrama. The play was later attacked by the Soviets—as were all Kirshon's works—as superficial.

Kirshon's *Relsy gudyat* (*The Rails Are Humming,* 1928), which he later made into an opera libretto, was also produced in New York and London, and widely translated; it deals with problems caused by industrial saboteurs. His other plays are *Gorod vetrov* (1929), which deals with the 1918 Baku revolt and features the martyrdom of twenty-six executed Communists, and was also made into an opera libretto; *Sud* (1933), set in Germany and depicting the struggle of the Reds and the Social Democrats; and *Bolshoi den* (1937), which predicted the Nazi invasion of Soviet Russia, and its heroic defense. Aside from the opera librettos, Kirshon also wrote film scenarios.

Bread appears in Eugene Lyons's edition of *Six Soviet Plays* (1934), where it is prefaced by a brief introduction on Kirshon.

KISMET, an "Arabian night" in three acts by EDWARD KNOBLOCK, produced in 1911 and published in 1912. Setting: ancient Baghdad.

This popular oriental spectacle was filmed twice, adapted by Charles Lederer (1911–   ) and Luther Davis (1916–   ) into a musical (music adapted from Aleksandr Borodin) in 1953, and gave Otis Skinner one of his greatest roles, that of the "gay and gaudy adventurer" and "gorgeous rogue," Haji the Beggar. In a single day, he cheats and robs, tries to kill the Caliph and is imprisoned, strangles his enemy (a sheikh) to death, and escapes from a dungeon. Later Haji saves his daughter from the harem of a wazir, whom he then drowns. Finally, when he is banished, Haji decides to make a pilgrimage to Mecca, and falls asleep on the steps of the same mosque where he awoke that morning.

KISS FOR CINDERELLA, A, a play in three acts by JAMES M. BARRIE, produced in 1916 and published in 1920. Setting: contemporary London and a seaside hospital.

This modernization of the fairy tale, immensely popular during World War I, was produced as a musical by William Roy (1928–   ), *Penny Friend* (1966).

"Cinderella" is a young charwoman who shelters war orphans in her penny establishment. She falls asleep on the street in front of her house, and dreams of an elaborate if fantastic ball; it is attended by equally fantastic royalty, including her prince—the policeman who is investigating her curious behavior. When she wakes up she is recuperating from pneumonia. The policeman visits her and proposes and, instead of an engagement ring, presents her with glass slippers. The happy girl exclaims, "They're like two kisses."

KLABUND [pen name of Alfred Henschke] (1890–1928), German writer, became most popular with his novellas. Of his plays, the romantic adaptation from the anonymous thirteenth- or fourteenth-century Chinese parable play *Hoei lan kia* that subsequently inspired BERTOLT BRECHT, *Der Kreidekreis* (*The Circle of Chalk,* 1924), was a hit in Berlin as well as New York. Even more romantic is *Das lasterhafte Leben des Christoph Wagner* (1925), a dramatization of the folktale of Wagner the sorcerer. Other plays, like *Die Nachtwandler* (1920) and *Brennende Erde* (1926), are more EXPRESSIONISTIC; Klabund also wrote a social comedy, *X Y Z* (1927).

Born in Crossen on the Oder, Klabund was the son of an apothecary. Consumption forced him to spend much of his brief life in sanatoriums. He was discovered by the critic Alfred Kerr, and he remarried after the early death of his first wife, for whom he wrote the much-praised poem "Totenklage" (1918–19). The public was often shocked by Klabund's poetry, which ranges from the vulgar and patriotic to the lyric, religious, and pacifist—and like his fiction includes many translations and imaginative adaptations of Oriental works.

KNICKERBOCKER HOLIDAY, a musical comedy in two acts by MAXWELL ANDERSON (music by Kurt Weill), published and produced in 1938. Setting: New Amsterdam, 1640's.

In this pseudohistorical slapstick, Washington Irving, writing his Knickerbocker *History of New York,* is the impresario. Anderson's "Preface to the Politics" of the play reaffirmed his fear of efficient government-planning and dictatorship, and his preference for minimal governing by inept democracy.

Governor Pieter Stuyvesant, a Chaplinesque seventeenth-century Fascist dictator, saves the young hero, Brom Broeck, from a festive hanging in the governor's honor. But Stuyvesant soon threatens to execute Broeck, who cannot take orders and is in love with a councilman's daughter whom the governor himself intends to marry. After various episodes, including a comic prison love scene, Broeck courageously repels an Indian attack and then rejects Stuyvesant's friendship: "All governments are crooked, . . . vicious and corrupt, but a democracy has the immense advantage of being incompetent in villainy and clumsy in corruption." Therefore he incites the council to regain its petty and corrupt power: "Let's keep the government small and funny, and maybe it'll give us less discipline and more entertainment!" Irving persuades Stuyvesant to give in for the sake of his reputation with the posterity that is already watching him.

KNIGHTS OF THE ROUND TABLE, THE (*Les Chevaliers de la Table Ronde*), a play in three acts by JEAN COCTEAU, published and produced in 1937. Setting: legendary Camelot and an enchanted castle.

The most striking of the many innovations in Cocteau's suggestive version is the invisible scamp Ginifer, Merlin's helper, who assumes the shape of various characters in the play. The primary character in the play according to Cocteau, Ginifer confounds his master Merlin as well as King Arthur and his court.

Act I. King Arthur is enchanted by the False Gawain—really Ginifer, who, when taken to task by Merlin, justifies his frolicking: "Do you think it's fun never being oneself, never living inside one's own skin? I used to be such a nice young demon, so young, so quiet." The whole castle seems bewitched: the flowers no longer grow, nor do the birds sing. Though this has occurred since Merlin came, the court blames it on the Holy Grail. After eighteen years Launcelot wants to end his secret adultery. "I haven't got that facility which women seem to have of inventing happiness whenever they want it," he tells Guinevere; "I want a real happiness, a real love. . . ." Galahad appears at the Round Table, submits himself to the "siege perilous," and is revealed as the "pure one" who will free the land. Merlin tricks the knights into a false quest for the Grail. But Galahad recognizes and challenges Merlin as "the power of negation" whose "one desire is to destroy, to turn life into death." A flower tape-records his incantations as the magician flies off with Ginifer to destroy the knights in an enchanted castle.

Act II. In the enchanted castle, the fatigued Launcelot defeats an invisible devil in an eerie chess game. Ginifer, now in the shape of Guinevere, horrifies Launcelot as she becomes increasingly drunk and vulgar. Galahad arrives in time to reveal Merlin's machinations. The real Gawain is released and, because Ginifer has double-crossed Merlin by leaving the flower open to record their departure, Launcelot can now use the magic formula himself and return to Camelot. Using a new formula, Merlin mounts Ginifer (still in the shape of the queen) and rides her back to Arthur's court as she screams in pain: "Have mercy! Help!"

Act III. Arthur discovers that Launcelot and Guinevere have been lovers. He kills Launcelot in an alcove bed. Guinevere lies beside his corpse to die and, as the alcove curtains close, the elves' voices chant of the union of Launcelot and Guinevere. When Merlin tries again to defeat Arthur, Galahad exposes him and the king banishes him: "I wish life to return to Camelot." Merlin sneers, pointing to the alcove. But Arthur replies, "I would rather have real deaths than a false life." Now there is a miracle: out of the alcove come Guinevere's children, looking like Launcelot and the queen, whose corpses have been made invisible by the elves. Merlin leaves, nature (life) reawakes, and the Grail appears in a wonderful blaze to all but the departing Galahad: "It is within you. Each of you sees it as soon as he is in harmony with himself. . . . I shall never see it. I am the one who makes it visible to others. . . . Everyone must always pay, pay in his person and in his actions." His final revelation is that "I am only a poet." And the birds sing again: "You must pay . . . pay, pay, pay . . ."

KNOBLOCK, Edward (1874–1945), Anglo-American playwright, was born in New York, attended George Pierce Baker's 47 Workshop at Harvard University, and then settled in England. In 1911 he made his reputation and wealth with KISMET (1911). Though he is said to have had a hand in some ninety productions (forty of them stillborn), he was even more successful in helping to work out other people's ideas than with his own plays. He collaborated with ARNOLD BENNETT (notably on MILESTONES), J. B. PRIESTLEY, and others; adapted a number of stories; and was a much sought-after "play doctor." See Baker's introduction to Knoblock's *The Lullaby and Other Plays* (1924) and Knoblock's autobiography, *Round the Room* (1939).

KOBER, Arthur (1900–), American producer and writer, has specialized in dialect short stories. From these came a comedy about husband-hunting vacationers in a Jewish summer camp in the Berkshires, *"Having Wonderful Time"* (1937), and its popular musical version, *Wish You Were Here* (1952, music by Harold Rome), written with JOSHUA LOGAN. Born in Poland, Kober was at one time married to LILLIAN HELLMAN.

KOKOSCHKA, Oskar (1886–), Austrian painter and writer, is famous for his canvases and lithographs rather than for his plays, which are considerably more experimental. Invariably portraying the battle of the sexes, they have been credited with starting EXPRESSIONIST drama. *Sphinx und Strohmann,* produced originally in 1907, ten years later launched a new DADA theatre in Zurich. Kokoschka's *Mörder, Hoffnung der Frauen* (*Murderer the Women's Hope,* 1913) is an early expressionist drama, a one-acter written in 1907 and made into an opera by Paul Hindemith in 1921; it portrays a bloody battle of the sexes that ends with the near death by stabbing of a caged man, his grotesque revival, and his slaughter of all females. In *Der brennende Dornbusch* (1911), whose 1919 premiere production by Max Reinhardt created a scandal, choruses accompany the ecstatic duologues of a couple. A new and longer three-act version of *Sphinx und Strohmann* is *Hiob* (*Job,* 1917); its title character, an intellectual whose head is (literally) turned by his wife Anima who loves a satanic "rubberman," is revived when the old gardener Adam neatly replaces his head and Anima proclaims herself to be Eve. Kokoschka redramatized the legend of *Orpheus und Eurydike* (1919) in similarly bizarre, erotic, and violent ways.

Interesting as curios, these short pieces are extreme examples of expressionism, whose obscurity, as Isaac Goldberg noted in his chapter on Kokoschka in *The Drama of Transition* (1922), "reduces the theory to absurdity." *Murderer the Women's Hope* and *Job* were published in Walter H. Sokel's *An Anthology of German Expressionist Drama* (1963). W. I. Lucas's essay on Kokoschka's life and work, with bibliographies, appears in Volume III of Alex Natan's *German Men of Letters* (1964).

KOLBENHEYER, Erwin Guido (1878–1962), a leading Austrian Nazi writer born in Budapest of Sudeten German descent, as early as his *Giordano Bruno* (1903), a play he revised as *Heroische Leidenschaften* in 1928, celebrated the Nordic superman—here as the philosopher struggling against the sixteenth-century Catholic Church. Strongly nationalistic, Kolbenheyer developed his "biological" theories in many essays and propagandized them in novels and in such other plays as *Die Brücke* (1929), whose title's "bridge" symbolizes the understanding youth must develop for the older generation's accomplishments; *Jagt ihn—ein Mensch!* (1929), an attack on both capital and labor; and *Das Gesetz in Dir* (1931), in which a man creates his own ethical rules and assumes collective guilt.

The Nazi philosophy Kolbenheyer had anticipated in these plays he expressed explicitly when Hitler came to power. Kolbenheyer welcomed Nazism with enthusiastic choral speeches in *Deutsches Bekenntnis* (1933) and in his dedication ("To the resurgent German spirit") of *Gregor und Heinrich* (1934), a dramatization of the struggle of Pope Gregory VII and Henry IV of Germany, who even at his Canossa defeat proclaims his ideal of the "Reich." More popular than these plays, however, were Kolbenheyer's novels, particularly his trilogy on Paracelsus (1917–25).

KOPIT, Arthur (1938–), American playwright, won early fame with *Oh Dad, Poor Dad, Mamma's Hung You in the Closet and I'm Feelin' So Sad* (1960). A soon-filmed ABSURDist "Pseudo-classical Tragifarce in a Bastard French Tradition" that ridicules cliché and popular notions about psychology in life and art, the play features a domineering mother, her emasculated son, and the sensuous girl he murders when she tries to seduce him as his father's corpse drops out of the closet.

An honors graduate of Harvard University in 1959, Kopit started out as an engineer. He won a prize at Harvard with his first play, *The Questioning of Nick* (1957), and has made the theatre his career. But his subsequent plays have been less successful. *The Day the Whores Came Out to Play Tennis* (1964), another comedy, portrays the vulgarity of wealthy country-club members whose cardboard world finally collapses; it was published in 1965 with Kopit's Harvard prize winner and other short plays, including the lyrical and nostalgic *Sing to Me Through Open Windows,* the curtain-raiser in the preview productions of *Oh Dad, Poor Dad.* Kopit turned to a PIRANDELLian style with his next full-length play, *Indians* (1968), a pageant indicting America's exploitation of the Indians and featuring Buffalo Bill Cody as a well-intentioned but bungling liberal.

KOPS, Bernard (1926–), English dramatist, has written fantasies in settings that, like those of ARNOLD WESKER, are often Jewish and feature rebellious poet-dreamers who deplore mechanization and The Bomb. Though pretentious as a philosopher, Kops has established himself as an entertaining playwright whose best work consists of jazzy and comic plays with interpolated songs.

The son of a shoemaker, Kops was born in London's poor Jewish quarter. He left school at thirteen, worked at odd jobs, and wrote poems, a novel, and radio scripts before he took up drama. In 1956, he wrote his first play, THE HAMLET OF STEPNEY GREEN (1958). It was followed by the less successful *Goodbye, World* (1959) and by THE DREAM OF PETER MANN (1960), which was written during his term as the Old Vic's resident dramatist and particularly impressed critics. Kops's penchant for humor was given freer reign in *Change for the Angel* (1960), a fantasy about a disintegrating city baker and his family, and in ENTER SOLLY GOLD (1961), which some consider his best play. It and *The Hamlet of Stepney Green* were collected in 1964, with Kops's preface and two other plays: *Home Sweet Honeycomb* (1963), an Orwellian nightmare Kops described as "devoid of love and feeling," and *The Lemmings* (1963), a pessimistic ČAPEK-like fantasy in which mankind destroys itself by drowning.

Kops's works include radio plays, novels, and an autobiography, *The World Is a Wedding* (1963). See also John Russell Taylor's *Anger and After* (titled *The Angry Theatre* in America; revised edition, 1969).

KOREA. The country's first national theatre was founded in 1908 and went on to launch modern drama with its productions of translated Japanese plays and dramatizations of Korean novels. More recently, Korea's leading dramatist, Yu Chi'i-jin (1905–), wrote IBSENite plays on social injustice in the 1930's and continued dramatizing contemporary themes through the 1960's. Beginning in 1931 he founded some of the many Korean theatre and research societies that encouraged the work of native playwrights, and he became director of the South Korean Drama Center when it was founded in 1962. Commercial and experimental troupes flourished, despite repressive censorship, until after World War II. The country's ideological struggles have subsequently been reflected also in its drama and theatre, which was crippled by the divisive Korean war (1950–53) and by the stalemate between the two sections of the country. Thereafter new theatrical groups stimulated the production of native drama, which, however, has remained little known abroad. These groups have also produced translations of Western drama, which is popular with the increasingly sophisticated audiences.

John Kardoss's *An Outline History of Korean Drama* (1966) was republished as one of the supplementary chapters in the enlarged third edition of George Freedley and John A. Reeves's *A History of the Theatre* (1968).

KORNEICHUK [or Korniychuk], **Aleksandr Yevdokimovich** (1905–), Soviet playwright and politician, was born in Khristinovka, Ukraine. He graduated from the Kiev Institute of Public Education in 1929, and married the well-known Polish author Wanda Wasilewska. During the 1930's and 1940's, Korneichuk became one of the most prominent Soviet playwrights, creating something of a sensation with his wartime drama *Front* (THE FRONT, 1942). Most of his plays focus on military and political problems more than on characterization and domestic situations. Some of his plays have been very successful with the public as well as with the Soviet authorities. Korneichuk won the Stalin Prize a number of times, became the Ukraine's People's Commissar for Foreign Affairs, and eventually was named its Chairman of the Committee on Art Affairs.

Korneichuk has written over twenty plays, beginning with *Kamenny ostrov* (1929), an attack on the Ukrainian bourgeoisie, and *Shturm* (1931), a drama that celebrates working-class solidarity. His first important play was *Gibel eskadry* (1934); a Stalin Prize winner, it depicts courageous Red sailors, who, with their idealized Communist leaders, scuttle their ships to keep them from being seized by the Whites. Even more important was *Platon Krechet* (1934), a widely produced play; its title protagonist is a young doctor who—like Ognev in *The Front*—fights the old-fashioned and represents the new Soviet leadership, this time in medicine. Subsequent plays dramatize similar themes. *Bankir* (1936) features the new, socially minded Soviet financier; *Pravda* (1937), a eulogy of Lenin and Stalin produced at the twentieth celebration of the Revolution, is set at the period just preceding the Revolution; another historical drama, *Bogdan Khmelnitsky* (1938), portrays the seventeenth-century Ukrainian people's revolt led by the title character against the nobility; *V stepyakh Ukrainy* (1941), another Stalin Prize winner, portrays Marshal S. M. Budyonny helping a group of Ukrainian peasants, veterans of the Civil War, with their domestic problems; its sequel is *Partizany v stepyakh Ukrainy* (*Guerrillas of the Ukrainian Steppes,* 1942), in which the peasants burn down their collective farm as part of the scorched-earth tactics before the Nazi onslaught; *Misya Mistera Perkinsa v stranu Bolshevikov* (1944), an anti-American satire; *Priyezzhaite v Zvonkoe* (1945), depicting a Ukrainian soldier's return to his destroyed home town; *Makar Dubrova* (1948); *Kalinovaya roshcha* (1950); *Krylya* (1953); *Pochemu ulybalis zvyozdy* (1956), a comedy; and *Nad Dneprom* (1960).

Most of these plays were originally written in Ukrainian and then translated into Russian. Aside from drama, Korneichuk has written short stories, screen plays, and opera librettos. Of his many works, only *The Front* and *Guerillas of the Ukrainian Steppes* are readily available in English. Together with brief prefaces summarizing Korneichuk's life and work, both appear in *Four Soviet War Plays* (1944). *The Front* appears also in H. W. L. Dana's collection of *Seven Soviet Plays* (1946).

KORNFELD, Paul (1889–1942), German dramatist and literary theoretician, was an EXPRESSIONIST who later turned to writing comedies. The most successful of his early tragedies were *Die Verführung* (1917) and *Himmel und Hölle* (1919); in the former the despairing and significantly named Bitterlich murders an innocent man who to him embodies the age's "stupidity" and "vulgarity," is imprisoned, is then "seduced" (hence the title) to life and love by a girl, and finally is poisoned by her brother, whom, in turn, he persuades to commit suicide—as does the girl. Equally gory and melodramatic is the second play, which depicts an unhappy marriage that brings about crimes and pervasive guilt, but is resolved in a poetic celebration of divine redemptive love. Kornfeld's most popular comedies were *Der ewige Traum* (1922), a bitter satire of pseudointellectuals; *Palme, oder Der Gekränkte* (1924), a Molière-like depiction of an easily affronted neurotic; and *Kilian, oder Die gelbe Rose* (1926), a farce again ridiculing pseudo-intellectualism.

Kornfeld was born in Prague, Czechoslovakia, but spent most of his life in Germany, where he wrote and also served as Max Reinhardt's *Dramaturg*. He formulated his expressionist doctrines on objectifying the "souls" of his characters in "Der beseelte und der psychologische Mensch," an essay first published in 1918. In 1933, Kornfeld escaped to Prague. He was arrested when the Nazis conquered Czechoslovakia and was killed in a concentration camp in Poland.

KRAMM, Joseph (1907–), American actor who grew up in Philadelphia, became known as a playwright with *The Shrike* (1952), a harrowing Pulitzer Prize melodrama set in a municipal hospital and featuring a mental patient's systematic destruction by his wife.

Originally a journalist, Kramm turned to acting in 1928 and achieved moderate success in that profession. After serving in the United States Army during World War II, he directed productions in America and in England. Among his few other writings is his second play, *Giants, Sons of Giants* (1962).

KRAPP'S LAST TAPE, a one-act play by SAMUEL BECKETT, published and produced in 1958. Setting: a den on "a late evening in the future."

This is a monologue by Krapp, "a wearish old man" (as Beckett describes him) who finds it hard to walk, is almost deaf and blind, has a cracked voice, and mimes as he listens to and comments about a tape he recorded thirty years earlier. The monodrama created considerable interest when it was produced Off-Broadway in 1960.

Krapp fishes bananas out of his desk, gazes vacuously, and slips on a peel. Then he examines a ledger, reads various descriptions ("Mother at rest at last . . . The dark nurse . . . Slight improvement in bowel condition . . . Memorable equinox") and selects a tape: "Farewell to—(*he turns the page*)—love." Intermittently going backstage for a drink, he plays the tape he recorded on his thirty-ninth birthday. His younger voice discusses various impressions in a disjointed manner. The thing that most interests Krapp now is the description and dissolution of a love affair. Krapp clears his throat and records a new entry: "Just been listening to that stupid bastard I took myself for thirty years ago." Then he describes his present failure as an author, his miserable life, and lovemaking with a "bony old ghost of a whore." He replays the lovemaking description of thirty years ago, and the reel ends: "Perhaps my best years are gone. When there was a chance of happiness. But I wouldn't want them back. Not with the fire in me now. No, I wouldn't want them back." The tape runs on silently as Krapp sits motionless, staring ahead.

KRAUS, Karl (1875–1936), Austrian journalist and critic born in Czechoslovakia, became famous with an eight-hundred-page "tragedy of mankind" that remained unproduced, *Die letzten Tage der Menschheit* (*The Last Days of Mankind*, 1918). A cataclysmic epic featuring hundreds of historical and fictitious characters, the play is a mixture of NATURALISM and LIVING NEWSPAPER DRAMA that documents the horror of the 1914–18 period, indicts the society responsible for it, and concludes with the Voice of God: "I did not want this to happen" (purportedly the Austrian emperor's words upon the outbreak of World War I). In an EXPRESSIONIST epilogue, *Die letzte Nacht* (1922), Kraus presented a verse summary of the epic and concluded with an apocalyptic vision of humanity's doom.

A satirist who in his periodical *Die Fackel* waged a constant battle against public corruption and literary hypocrisy, Kraus dramatized his indignation in other, less notable plays, including anti-commercial poetic curtain-raisers, a free adaptation of Aristophanes's *The Birds* (*Wolkenkuckucksheim,* 1923), and translations of Shakespeare. These he recited before spellbound audiences at the "Theatre of Poetry" that he had founded in opposition to the naturalist theatre. His *Literatur* (1921) parodies FRANZ WERFEL's *Spiegelmensch.* Kraus was most notable, however, as "the good conscience of Austria."

An excerpt from *The Last Days of Mankind* and introductory comments on Kraus and the play appear in George E. Wellwarth's *German Drama Between the Wars* (1971).

KRISTINA, a historical play in four acts by AUGUST STRINDBERG, published in 1903 and produced in 1908. Setting: Stockholm, 1653–54.

Strindberg characterized Queen Kristina—the daughter of GUSTAV ADOLF, about whom he had written his most ambitious historical play—as "a woman reared to be a man, fighting for her self-existence, against her feminine nature and succumbing to it. . . . So genuine a woman that she was a woman hater" (quoted in Walter Johnson's edition of the play). *Kristina,* popular in Sweden and Germany, presents a fascinating portrayal of this ruler.

Kristina—"little Kerstin," as the tempestuous twenty-seven-year-old queen calls herself—appoints her latest lover, Baron Klas Tott, chamberlain to the *king:* "I am not queen to any king. I was proclaimed king!" Her illusion that governing is a game and that she is beloved by all her subjects is suddenly shattered. She is mercilessly attacked in a pamphlet, and a former lover tells her the reason for the attack: "You have played with the destinies of men as if you had been playing with dolls." Immediately arresting the authors of the pamphlet, Kristina soon suffers the consequences. Their trial threatens to air her mismanagement and frivolous waste, though the able old chancellor finally gives in to her cajoling and agrees to help her. Displaying her total ignorance of finances, she begs advice from her cousin and, dangling the succession to the throne before him, alternately threatens and wheedles money from him. The trial and new diplomatic mismanagements worsen her position and turn her subjects completely against her. At a masked ball she announces her decision to abdicate. "Receive my sacrifice, the greatest and the only man I have ever seen, the man who has made me a woman!" she tells Tott. But though he reciprocates her passionate love, Tott now feels compelled to hurt and reject her. "You have soiled my soul," he says, having just called her a whore: "Farewell, my bride, my one great love, Queen of my heart!" Blamed for her "unlawful acts, embezzlements, scandals, and favorites," Kristina reveals her hatred of Sweden: "I am a German as my mother is." She had wanted to end the Thirty Years' War: "I tried to educate this crude nation and awaken its interests in something other than war!" When she leaves her court, no longer play-acting or deceiving even herself, she admits that she is thinking of becoming a Catholic. Though her father gave his life in a Protestant crusade, it was one "for freedom of faith, for tolerance!" And now, at last fully mature, Kristina bids farewell, and departs with dignity.

KRLEŽA, Miroslav (1893–), Yugoslavia's leading writer, was a major Croatian dramatist from the 1920's through the 1950's. A fervent pacifist who bitterly attacked reactionary authoritarianism in the army and the government, he became Yugoslavia's most popular poet and novelist shortly after the end of World War I. His plays were rejected at first because of their revolutionary socialism as well as their difficult staging requirements. But in 1920 Krleža at last succeeded with *Galicija,* the first in a trilogy that unfavorably depicts the war and its later effects on soldiers, workers, and the intelligentsia. Fearfully withdrawn hours before its scheduled premiere but ultimately produced as *U logoru,* it protests against man's inhumanity and features a Croatian officer who overcomes his moral scruples about executing a peasant woman for a minor offense. With the remaining plays in the trilogy, *Golgota* (1922, set in a shipyard) and *Vučjak* (1923, set in the title's "Wolf Village"), Krleža's success as a dramatist was assured.

The son of a civil servant, Krleža was imbued with a hatred of reactionary authority while attending the Hungarian military school his father had sent him to. This attitude was reinforced by his service during World War I. His Catholic education similarly left its imprint although, after his readings of Darwin, Nietzsche, and others converted him to atheism and materialism, he persisted in attacking the church with almost fanatical hatred. Krleža started to write at the beginning of World War I and was greatly inspired in 1917 by the Russian Revolution—especially by Lenin, who came to replace Christ as Krleža's idol. He founded the left-wing literary review *Plamen* in 1919 and its successor, *Književna republika,* in 1924, and published many poems and bitter criticisms of the Croat bureaucracy and the ruling classes.

Krleža's first plays are EXPRESSIONIST studies of historical figures, idealists who are ultimately disillusioned with their vision as well as with their followers. These *Legende*, as he called them, include depictions of Jesus, John the Baptist, Columbus, and Michelangelo. *Legenda* (1914) is an erotic triangle drama of Christ, Judas, and Lazarus's sister Mary—and the Sjena (Shadow), an earthly alter ego as well as tempter of Christ. *Saloma*, rejected in 1914 by the Croatian theatre as unproducible (it was published in 1963), though its eroticism is closer to OSCAR WILDE's play than the Bible, portrays the Evangelist as a fanatic fool succumbing to the temptations of Salomé, who is disillusioned and disgusted with him after a night of love. *Cristoval Colon* (1918, produced in Belgrade as *Christopher Columbus* in 1955) features a visionary who is crucified on the mast of his ship by his crew, who want to make the New World a replica of the corrupt and greedy old one. The more poetic *Michelangelo* (1919) portrays a sensitive artist frustrated by the Church (including the keenly satirized Pope), which causes his self-betrayal. Interesting as they are, these plays are literarily uneven and present difficulties in staging which in some cases delayed their production for many years.

But Krleža's persistence ultimately gained him a hearing, popularity, and esteem as a dramatist. His most frequently revived plays, the social dramas of the *Glembays* trilogy, started to appear in 1928. IBSENite dissections of the upper bourgeoisie, they consist of the title play, *Gospoda Glembajevi* (1929); of *U agoniji* (1928), a two-acter portraying a disillusioned officer who commits suicide and his wife who also kills herself after being disillusioned—by another man who proves unworthy of her love; and of *Leda* (1930), which concludes the portrayal of the decay of nobility in Croatia under the Austro-Hungarian rule. Krleža continued to attack provincialism and ruthless political authoritarianism in as late a play as *Aretej* (1959), a fantasy in five scenes.

Krleža fearlessly and passionately criticized social injustice also in his novels. An individualist, despite his adherence to Communist ideology, he did not join the Partisans during World War II, and he rejected Communist Party encroachments on artistic expression, including his own. Krleža strove to raise the literary and cultural standards of his country and, indeed, of all the Balkans. After World War II he recouped his predominant position in Yugoslav letters with his fiction and verse. In 1952 he created a sensation and became the leading spokesman of younger Yugoslav artists when he publicly attacked SOCIALIST REALISM and Stalinist aesthetics with a call "for freedom of artistic expression, for simultaneous existence of differing schools and styles, for liberty and independence of moral and political convictions."

A Croatian edition of his collected works appeared in 1953–55, but his plays are not generally available in English. They are discussed in Ante Kadić's "Krleža's Tormented Visionaries," *The Slavonic and East European Review* XLV: 104 (1967).

KROG, Helge (1889–1962), Norwegian playwright and essayist, achieved fame with *Det store Vi* (1919), an IBSENite attack on the press and on the exploitation of garment workers. After a few other social plays he wrote comedies that were slightly less indebted to his great Norwegian predecessor, advocate female emancipation, and display Krog's insight into human psychology, particularly that of women in love.

The most erotic of these plays, *Konkylien* (*The Sounding Shell,* 1929; also translated as *Happily Ever After?*), depicts a woman in love with love. His most popular play was *Opbrudd* (*Break-up,* 1936), portraying a triangle in which a woman breaks up her marriage and her love affair to lead an independent life. Also very successful was *Underveis* (*On The Way,* 1931), whose Communist doctor heroine has a child but turns down marriage. Krog followed these plays with frothy high comedies whose dialogue sparkles with epigrammatic wit. Popular in Norway in their time, they include *På solsiden* (*On Life's Sunny Side,* 1927), *Blåpapiret* (1928), and *Trekland* (*Triad,* 1933). Krog's other writings include incisive literary criticisms. His drama was translated in Roy Campbell's collection, *Three Plays by Helge Krog* (1934), and in *Break-up and Two Other Plays* (1939).

KRUCZKOWSKI, Leon (1900–62), Polish novelist and playwright, became particularly prominent as a SOCIAL REALIST after World War II. His *Niemcy* (1949), featuring a scientist who is wrenched out of his comfortable ivory-tower neutrality, was the first Polish dramatic exploration of honest Germans' problems under Nazism. Other Kruczkowski plays include *Grzech* (1951), an adaptation with a new final act of a play by STEFAN ŻEROMSKI; *Juliusz i Ethel* (1954), a tendentious dramatization of the case of the Rosenbergs, the condemned American spy couple; *Pierwszy dzień wolności* (1959), the depiction of a group of Polish soldiers at the end of World War II; and *Śmierć gubernatora* (1960), the dramatization of a story by LEONID ANDREEV,

Chairman of the Cultural Commission of the Communist Party's Central Committee until his death, Kruczkowski was feared by fellow writers as a rigid and authoritarian enforcer of the party line. Before World War II, which he spent in a German prison camp, he was famous for his historical novels. His subsequent works were polemical. The Lenin Prize was awarded him in 1953.

L

LABURNUM GROVE, "an immoral comedy" in three acts by J. B. PRIESTLEY, published and produced in 1933. Setting: Laburnum Grove, a suburb of North London; c. 1933.

This comedy, which established Priestley's reputation as a playwright, features George Radfern, an apparently dull and unimaginative but pleasant family man who likes to potter in his greenhouse. Sponging in-laws and his daughter's opportunist fiancé leave when he tells them his respectable business is merely a front for a lucrative forgery racket. His family soon realize that he must be pulling their leg. Radfern is indeed, however, the crook he has said he is. The police are after him, but have not yet gathered enough evidence to arrest him. As soon as the inspector leaves, Radfern calls his associates and has the presses and plates sunk. His family still think it is all a great joke. They are thrilled to learn they will leave their uneventful suburban life for a while and take a long vacation cruise. But they are surprised at Radfern's sudden energy. "Have to assert myself sometimes, Mother," he tells his wife, who insists: "You needn't tell me you haven't been up to *something*." He grins at her and his daughter: "All right, Mother. I needn't tell you."

LADY FREDERICK, a comedy in three acts by SOMERSET MAUGHAM, produced in 1907 and published in 1912. Setting: Monte Carlo, 1890.

The first of Maugham's works to be produced in London's West End, this sophisticated and still-amusing play made his fortune and his reputation as a dramatist. Despite the makeup scene, Maugham (as he revealed in his preface) strove to attract a star actress with the title part: "the adventuress with a heart of gold; ... the charming spendthrift and the wanton of impeccable virtue; the clever manager who twists all and sundry round her little finger and the kindly and applauded wit."

Lady Frederick Berolles, a most attractive Irishwoman in her thirties, is courted by a wealthy lord much her junior. His mother is horrified at the thought of her boy's marrying an old "abandoned creature." Though Lady Frederick is overwhelmed by debts, she rejects her ruthless creditor's importunities, magnanimously spares the insulting mother whom she could ruin, and gently turns down her young suitor by revealing herself to him most unromantically in the morning light as she undergoes the "horrible mysteries of my toilette." Instead, she agrees to marry one of her older suitors—the lord's uncle, an urbane gentleman who knows "that behind that very artificial complexion there's a dear little woman called Betsy who's genuine to the bottom of her soul."

LADY FROM ALFÁQUEQUE, THE (*La Consulesa;* i.e., "The Lady Consul"), a comedy in two acts by SERAFÍN and JOAQUÍN ÁLVAREZ QUINTERO, published and produced in 1914. Setting: a Madrid home, early twentieth century.

This sentimental comedy, one of the authors' most widely performed plays, features a small-town matron who, even after twenty years in the metropolis, staunchly persists in her provincial fashions and customs. With amused tolerance her husband suffers the many visitors who ingratiate themselves in their house with real or pretended gossip from Alfáqueque, her home town. A poet bearing gifts—which later will have to be paid for by the recipients—easily worms himself into her graces by claiming an Alfáqueque background. Unmasked as a pretender and a scoundrel, the poet is expelled after he seduces the lady's and her neighbor's daughters. But when he launches into new verses, the "consul" lets him stay. "Hush, it's a poem about Alfáqueque," she tells her husband, who resignedly remarks, "God's will be done!" The poet keeps reciting the glories of Alfáqueque.

LADY FROM THE SEA, THE (*Fruen fra havet*), a play in five acts by HENRIK IBSEN, published in 1888 and produced in 1889. Setting: a small contemporary Norwegian town by a fjord, summer.

Though this lyrical and psychological study of Ellida (named after the mythical Frithjof's magic vessel) resembles those of Rebecca West in ROSMERSHOLM and of HEDDA GABLER, it resolves the problem of A DOLL'S HOUSE: here, finally, the "miracle" occurs and the wife returns to her husband. There are subplots and minor characters: one, the tubercular artist Lyngstrand, is a reincarnation of the egotistical hero of LOVE'S COMEDY; another, Hilde, reappears as a major character in THE MASTER BUILDER. One of Ibsen's last plays, *The Lady from the Sea* has also been translated as *The Mermaid.*

Acts I and II. Though Ellida Wangel is fond of her kindly husband, a widowed elderly doctor, she feels stifled and distracted in the small town. She grew up by the sea, which still attracts her so greatly that the townsfolk call her "the lady from the sea." A stranger even to her stepdaughters—Hilde, a hostile adolescent, and Bolette, who runs the house—Ellida's only occupation is her daily swim. Dr. Wangel decides to move his family to the seashore, for her sake. Touched by this devotion and miserable because it cannot help her, Ellida finally reveals the cause of her morbidity. Ten years ago she had loved a strange sailor who completely hypnotized her. But he had been guilty of murder, and escaped after their symbolic betrothal by the sea. Ellida had forgotten the sailor but she had begun to feel his spell again three years ago, when her child was born. Though Wangel thinks it was merely Ellida's imagination, she insists that their child (who soon died) had eyes that changed with the sea. Agonized, Ellida suggests to Wangel the "unspeakable" reason "why I never dared live with you as your wife again": "The child had the Stranger's eyes!" (In his drafts Ibsen wrote: "It is really with him she is living in marriage.")

Act III. Ellida is spellbound with horror by the sudden reappearance of the Stranger—whom, however, she fails to recognize at first. He claims her on the strength of their "sea wedding." Wangel denies him all legal rights and protests against his "childish tricks," which he cannot force her to honor now. The Stranger agrees: "I have no rights—the way you mean.... She must come of her own free will." He leaves after promising to return for her final decision the next day. His reference to "free will" leaves a strong impression on the terrified Ellida, who begs Wangel to save her from that man, who is "like the sea."

Act IV. Convinced that "there are aspects of this case that cannot be explained," Wangel refuses to cancel immediately "the bargain" of their marriage, into which Ellida now feels she had sold herself to be supported. But she begs Wangel to let her be fully "free to choose" between him and the demonic Stranger, from whose returning fascination she wants her husband to save her. When Bolette tells her that Hilde's hostility is caused by her yearning for Ellida's love, her confusion mounts: "Could there be a place for me in this house?"

Act V. Earlier, Bolette had envied the wild fish in the fjord, and pitied the tame carp who know nothing of life beyond their pond. Now, longing for travel as well as security, she accepts the proposal of an elderly schoolmaster, which will liberate her from small-town spinsterhood: "To come out into—all that's strange. Not to have to worry about the future—that, too, is good." At the confrontation with the Stranger, Ellida tremblingly begs Wangel for the freedom "which I was born for—and which you have locked me away from." Despairing of her, Wangel agrees to "cancel the bargain": "Now you can choose—freely—on your own responsibility." This phrase at once vanquishes the Stranger's appeal and power over her. Cured, Ellida opts for "my dear, faithful Wangel. Now I come to you freely, of my own choice." She begins to win over the daughters, delighting Hilde with her first affectionate word. The town's jack-of-all-trades, an unsuccessful artist, approvingly reiterates his temporizing credo: "Acclimatize!"; but Ellida echoes Wangel's words: "Free and responsible!"

LADY IN THE DARK, a musical play in two acts by MOSS HART (lyrics by Ira Gershwin; music by Kurt Weill), published and produced in 1941. Setting: New York, 1941.

This popular musical (it was soon filmed) features Liza Elliott, a fashion magazine's dynamic editor-in-chief—the "lady in the dark" about herself. A visit to the psychiatrist triggers her self-discovery in a series of musical dream sequences. Then she rejects both her elderly publisher and a movie idol, who want to marry her for her strength, and becomes partners in editing the magazine with the able but ruthlessly outspoken editor she once secretly feared.

LADY INGER OF ØSTRÅT (*Fru Inger til Østråt*), a historical play in five acts by HENRIK IBSEN, produced in 1855 and published in 1857. Setting: Castle Østråt on the Trondheim Fjord, Norway; a night in 1528.

The intrigue (derivative of Eugène Scribe) in the plot of this early, unsuccessful Ibsen tragedy is overly complex and not always clear. A historical figure, Inger Gyldenløve is idealized into a heroic but self-doubting leader in Norway's patriotic aspirations, a schemer who willed more than she could accomplish. Her battle of wits with Nils Lykke, another historical figure, is complicated by the love of her daughter Elina (inspired by a girl Ibsen courted in 1853) for this dashing, unscrupulous Danish knight.

The patrician Lady Inger hesitates and then decides to gamble for Norway's freedom when she is informed of the secret arrival of a Danish envoy. Postponing the signal for an uprising against the Danes, she will attempt to outwit the envoy. This courtly diplomat, Nils Lykke, intends to foil her plans to crown the popular Count Sture. The unexpected arrival of Nils Stensson, whom Lykke knows to be the count's half-brother, gives him an opportunity to further his schemes for checkmating Lady Inger. While a number of mysterious visitors come and leave during the moonlit night and discuss various intrigues, Lady Inger's proud daughter Elina eventually succumbs to the charms of Lykke, the knight of her dreams. Her passionate love turns to horror, however, when she discovers him to be the hated seducer of her dead sister, whose betrayal she had sworn to avenge. Lykke is repentant and, for the first time, sincere in his love. As the intrigues come to a head, he tries to save Stensson, who is Lady Inger's illegitimate son, and who is generally mistaken for the aspirant to the crown, Count Sture. But Lady Inger, not knowing either man and now believing his death essential to save her illegitimate son's life, has Stensson killed. She discovers Stensson's identity too late: having kept her intentions and secrets hidden, she has unwittingly murdered her own son. She shrieks with grief, calls for "another coffin, and a grave beside my child," and, as Lykke leaves, drops senseless on Stensson's coffin.

LADY WINDERMERE'S FAN, a drama in four acts by OSCAR WILDE, produced in 1892 and published in 1893. Setting: London, 1892.

Wilde's first popular play is a serious comedy. The situation and sentimentality are Victorian. But the epigrammatic dialogue is in the comic tradition of the Restoration, and the sympathetic modern portrayal of a "fallen woman" anticipates (a year before Pinero's THE SECOND MRS. TANQUERAY) a topic popular with later dramatists. Though Mrs. Erlynne's identity was originally withheld in the play, Wilde was persuaded to reveal it almost at once. The author's nonchalant curtain call with a cigarette and his response ("... a *delightful* play...") to the immense ovation amused the first-night audience but offended the critics. NOËL COWARD adapted Wilde's play into a musical, *After the Ball* (1954).

Act I. It is just before the party for her twenty-first birthday, and Lady Windermere chastizes a young gallant, Lord Darlington, for courting her. She is a meticulous moralist who considers life "a sacrament," knows the difference between "what is right and what is wrong," and will allow no compromise. Darlington, on the other hand, considers "life far too important a thing ever to talk seriously about." A foolish old duchess soon reveals something to Lady Windermere that the rest of society has known for some time: her husband is in constant attendance on a Mrs. Erlynne, a woman of questionable reputation to whom he gives large sums of money. Lady Windermere is further pained when her husband not only admits it, but insists that Mrs. Erlynne be invited to the birthday party. He assures his wife that there are good reasons, which he cannot reveal. But Lady Windermere vows that if that woman dares show her face at her house she will strike it with her new fan, Windermere's birthday present.

Act II. When the beautiful Mrs. Erlynne arrives, Lady Windermere lacks the courage to strike her. Though her guests are scandalized by her presence, Mrs. Erlynne soon succeeds in charming them. Lady Windermere feels increasingly humiliated, but when Darlington begs her to leave Windermere and become his, she hesitates. A private talk between Windermere and Mrs. Erlynne unmasks her as Lady Windermere's mother. A fallen woman, she abandoned her husband and baby daughter for a lover who subsequently left her. Now she is in effect blackmailing Windermere for the money needed to reestablish herself in society. Her aplomb vanishes when she discovers a letter Lady Windermere has just left for her husband. Anguished, she hides the letter after reading it: "The same words that twenty years ago I wrote to her father!"

Act III. Lady Windermere has escaped to Lord Darlington's rooms. Ready now to be his, she is nervously waiting for his return from the party. Mrs. Erlynne suddenly rushes in. Despite the younger woman's contempt for her, Mrs. Erlynne succeeds finally in persuading her to return to her husband and child. Just then the men—including Windermere—are heard coming in. The two women barely manage to hide. Among the men is Mrs. Erlynne's suitor, who expresses his preference for "women with a past. They're always so demmed amusing to talk to." Windermere calls the men cynical, which Darlington defines as the quality of "a man who knows the price of everything and the value of nothing." Suddenly they notice Lady Windermere's fan, which she had carelessly dropped on the sofa. Mrs. Erlynne manages to get her away unnoticed; then, to avert a suspicion that would blight her daughter's life as hers has been blighted by a youthful rashness, she emerges from hiding and herself faces humiliation. "I'm afraid I took your wife's fan in mistake for my own," she tells the contemptuous Windermere, as the other men smile knowingly at one another.

Act IV. Back home, the penitent Lady Windermere is ready to confess her near fall to her husband. Mrs. Erlynne soon arrives, demanding of the grateful Lady Windermere only that she not spoil her husband's love by confessing her visit to Darlington's rooms. Alone with him for a moment, Mrs. Erlynne promises Windermere never to reveal her identity to her daughter, but she conceals from him her recent maternal sacrifice. His contempt for her having been found in Darlington's rooms costs her the money Windermere would have given her. But she easily mollifies her elderly suitor. He will marry her and they will leave England, Mrs. Erlynne taking as a present the momentous fan, inscribed with the name "Margaret"—which happens also to be her name. "Well," Windermere says to the suitor, "you are certainly marrying a very clever women!" Lady Windermere adds: "You're marrying a very good woman!"

LADY'S NOT FOR BURNING, THE, a blank-verse comedy in three acts by CHRISTOPHER FRY, produced in 1948 and published in 1949. Setting: the small English market town of Cool Clary, c. 1450.

Fry became renowned with this witty play, which is suffused with brilliant poetic pyrotechnics and delightful characters. The protagonist's sentiments are echoed in the play's epigraph, a convict's false murder confession made in 1947: "In the past I wanted to be hung. It was worth while being hung to be a hero, seeing that life was not really worth living." But in this comedy love finally makes life tolerable.

Act I. Thomas Mendip, a discharged soldier, startles the mayor's orphaned clerk by demanding to be hanged for no apparent crime. The conversation is interrupted by the appearance of a seventeen-year-old girl who is to marry one of the mayor's two nephews. Fighting over her, one has knocked the other out—fatally, he now claims extravagantly. Their mother has him picked up and brought in. When the mayor finally arrives,

The Lady's Not for Burning. Jennet (Pamela Brown), the mayor's orphaned clerk (Richard Burton), and Mendip (John Gielgud). London, 1949. (*Culver Pictures*)

Mendip repeats his request to be hanged: "You're about to become my gateway to eternal / Rest." But the mayor, considering the request "Incompatible with good citizenship," absolutely refuses. Thereupon Mendip claims he murdered the local rag-and-bone merchant as well as another man. Just then enters a beautiful young woman, Jennet Jourdemayne. Accused of being a witch, she seeks the mayor's protection. Jennet is sure he too will laugh at the people's absurd accusations, beginning with the charge that she transformed the ragman into a dog. But the mayor is indignant at her "Terrible frivolity, terrible blasphemy, / Awful unorthodoxy." He arrests Jennet, who is incredulous. "Does everyone still knuckle / And suckle at the big breast of irrational fears?" she asks; "Can they think and then think like this?" In the meantime Mendip looks out the window at "a world / So festering with damnation" and, furious at being ignored, importunes the mayor to hang him: "You bubble-mouthing, fog-blathering, / Chin-chuntering, chap-flapping, liturgical, / Turgidical, base old man! What about my murders?" Unable to find the bodies of the supposed victims, the people charge Mendip with being the devil who has Jennet, a witch, in his toils. Mendip readily agrees, and furthermore proclaims the imminent end of the world. Jennet appeals to reason, but the mayor has them both incarcerated as Mendip pleads, "For God's sake hang me, before I love that woman!"

Act II. An hour later, the town's justice is disappointed with his examination of the prisoners: Jennet has admitted nothing, and Mendip "won't stop admitting." A kindly chaplain who is astonished by everything, most of all himself, has a suggestion: release Mendip for the evening's festivities to "bibulate," as the justice puts it, "from glass to glass"—which may put him in a better mind to retract his confession. The mayor is eager to have the wealthy Jennet condemned, for her property would go to the town. He suggests to the justice that they eavesdrop on the prisoners after they are brought together. When Mendip and Jennet are alone with each other, Mendip still claims to be the devil, and the unbelieving Jennet talks of her dead father. His alchemy drove her to reality: "My father broke on the wheel of a dream; he was lost / In a search. And so, for me, the actual! / What I touch, what I see, what I know; the essential fact"—which Mendip calls "the bare untruth." He scolds her for rejecting the glories of "paradox and mystery." Gradually drawn to him, Jennet confesses her love. "You may be decay and a platitude / Of flesh," she tells him, "corrupt as ancient apples" and hell itself. But "if so / Hell is my home, and my days of good were a holiday." Interpreting her words as a confession of witchery, the mayor emerges from hiding and condemns Jennet to burn the next day. But Mendip, who has confessed to crimes only because he is sick of life, is sentenced (as the chaplain suggested) to participate in the night's celebration of the nephew's marriage. Mendip insists that Jennet be permitted to share this punishment: "Shall we not / Suffer as wittily as we can?"

Act III. Later, escaping the festivities, Mendip encounters the mayor's nephews. Both have fallen out of love with the bride and are enamored of Jennet. Expecting to be burned the next day, she now longs to live her remaining night imaginatively. The mayor chides his nephews for leaving the party, and they escort Jennet back. Alone with him, Mendip accuses the mayor of punishing Jennet because he himself has a rotten soul. The mayor weeps, and then urges his colleagues to burn the disconcerting Jennet immediately, "before she destroys our reason." In the meantime, the disillusioned would-be bride and the mayor's clerk declare their mutual love, and prepare to elope. One of the nephews offers to save Jennet if she will give herself to him. Mendip climbs in through the window, disgusted with what he has just overheard and ready to fight the nephew. Mendip admits he is most angry because he is in love with Jennet, who appeared in his life just when he "was nicely tucked up for the night / Of eternity." Cynically she reminds him of his death wish: "Am I to understand that your tongue-tied dust / Will slip a ring on the finger of my ashes / And we'll both die happily ever after?" He suggests she accept the nephew's offer and save her life. Just then the rag-and-bone merchant appears—alive and untransformed, but very drunk. This absolves Jennet of witchery and the authorities therefore allow her to escape. Though Mendip still loathes the world, he goes with her. He admits Jennet is an "inconvenience" as "inevitably as original sin," but "I shall be loath to forgo one day of you, / Even for the sake of my ultimate friendly death."

LAGERKVIST, Pär [Fabian] (1891–), Swedish novelist, poet, and dramatist, is his country's most important writer after AUGUST STRINDBERG. He is known abroad primarily for the fiction and verse that won him a Nobel Prize in 1951, but in Sweden he is an important figure in the theatre as well. He electrified readers with his stimulating essay, *Modern teater: synpunkter och angrepp* (*Modern Theatre: Points of View and Attacks*, 1918). In that work, Lagerkvist rejected the NATURALISM of HENRIK IBSEN as dated and unviable in a modern world, and he championed Strindberg as the seminal playwright whose post-Inferno works had set the path for modern and future drama. At the same time, Lagerkvist started

Pär Lagerkvist. (*Swedish Information Service*)

writing EXPRESSIONIST plays, thus following in Strindberg's footsteps. Most of these plays are directly concerned with the political cataclysms of the period between the world wars, though Lagerkvist ultimately dealt with larger intellectual-philosophical problems (hence the quasi-exotic setting of his drama, whose time and place invariably remain unspecified). Lagerkvist's plays touch on such universal themes as decency, love, and responsibility. But most of the portrayals are of evil—particularly of human brutality and injustice—and Lagerkvist's resolutions are mystic. His *Bödeln* (THE HANGMAN, 1934) created a sensation throughout Scandinavia for almost a decade, though *De vises sten* (THE PHILOSOPHER'S STONE, 1947) became the most popular of his dozen plays.

Lagerkvist was born in Växjö, a small town in southern Sweden, the son of a retired railroad foreman. His parents were pious Christians of peasant stock, but the boy was raised also amidst the less gentle Fundamentalism of his grandfather. By the time he left the *gymnasium* Lagerkvist had rejected all conventional religious beliefs. Soon he was to replace them with a belief in evolution, and with an enthusiasm for radical politics, literature, and art.

Lagerkvist attended the University of Uppsala in 1911, but left after the first semester to study independently. His career as an author began with the publication of revolutionary poems and songs. These quickly made Lagerkvist known, and his reputation soared with two provocative essays, *Ordkonst och bildkonst* (*Word Art and Pictorial Art*, 1913) and the already-cited *Modern Theatre*.

Almost shrill in its polemicism, this latter essay was published with his first notable drama, *Den* *svåra stunden* (THE DIFFICULT HOUR, 1918).* *Modern Theatre* proclaimed the bankruptcy of naturalism and argued the necessity for expressing contemporary reality in an aesthetic manner approximating the abstract and PRESENTATIONAL the visual arts. *The Difficult Hours* playlets exemplify some of these ideals, which were further illustrated in Lagerkvist's next work, *Himlens hemlighet* (THE SECRET OF HEAVEN, 1919).

Beginning with the less successful *Den osynlige* (1923), Lagerkvist's dramatic works are tempered in their expressionism and follow more traditional dramatic modes. Nonetheless, the presentational appears in all Lagerkvist's plays; the later ones in particular are characterized by a dependence on the strange and the marvelous and the philosophical—barely controlled by the REPRESENTATIONAL. This is particularly true of the powerful drama *The Hangman*, but to lesser or greater degrees applies to the other Lagerkvist plays of the 1920's and 1930's: *Han som fick leva om sitt liv* (HE WHO LIVED HIS LIFE OVER AGAIN, 1928), *Konungen* (THE KING, 1932), *Mannen utan själ* (THE MAN WITHOUT A SOUL, 1936), and *Seger i mörker* (1939), in which the same themes recur in a conflict personified by twin brothers—with the good ultimately triumphant.

Lagerkvist's next drama, *Midsommardröm i fattighuset* (*Midsummer Dream in the Poorhouse,* 1941), is a half-naturalistic Fairy play in which a blind institutionalized pauper, in telling a young girl his unhappy love story, reshapes it into a joyful tale that promises happiness for her life. After the very successful *The Philosopher's Stone* Lagerkvist wrote but one other notable play, *Låt människan leva* (*Let Man Live,* 1949), an oratorio-like one-acter in which fourteen figures (including Socrates, Christ, Judas, Giordano Bruno, Joan of Arc, an American Negro, and a World War II underground fighter) step up, one by one, to tell of their victimization by man; in the finale, Paolo Malatesta and Francesca da Rimini, who belong to the same group, nevertheless reaffirm the beauty of life and declaim the words of the title. Lagerkvist's last work for the stage (he also wrote its filmscript) was an adaptation of the widely translated 1950 novel that increased his international renown, *Barabbas* (1953); a variation of *The Hangman,* this work's title character (whose place Christ took on the cross) until he dies is unable to believe in Christ.

In these later plays, too, the influence of the post-Inferno Strindberg is quite notable. Lagerkvist's early concern with love-hate relationships and his depiction of a nightmare atmosphere are transmuted, in these later plays, into SYMBOL, pantomime, and philosophical discourse. Despite the modified expressionism, Lagerkvist's preoccupation with the nature of evil and his penchant for mysticism remain unchanged. His gloomy despair was accentuated by the rise of Fascism, which Lagerkvist portrayed obliquely but vividly. Yet he was even more preoccupied with questions of the responsibility of the individual, particularly the artist, the scientist, and the philosopher. Lagerkvist went to sometimes tedious lengths to dramatize such preoccupations, though his daring dramaturgy and exotic plots, replete with violence and sex, are sufficiently dramatic not only to interest theatregoers but, in fact, to make Lagerkvist a major playwright.

Lagerkvist's volumes of verse range from the pessimistic early, expressionist *Ångest* (*Anguish,* 1916) to the mature, contemplative *Aftonland* (*Evening Land,* 1953), the latter one more powerful because of its restraint. His most successful fiction aside from *Barabbas* includes the novels *Det eviga leendet* (*The Eternal Smile,* 1921), *Dvärgen* (*The Dwarf,* 1944), *Sibyllan* (*The Sybil,* 1956), and many collections of short stories. Lagerkvist's works have been collected in various Swedish editions. Aside from individual plays included in English anthologies, seven Lagerkvist plays and his celebrated theatre essay were collected in Thomas R. Buckman's *Modern Theatre* (1966), with an introduction and a bibliographical note by Buckman. Little else has been written about Lagerkvist's life; the most revealing account is his own sketch of his childhood and youth, *Gäst hos verkligheten* (*Guest of Reality,* 1925). Alrik Gustafson's *A History of Swedish Literature* (1961) devotes a section to Lagerkvist and has an extensive descriptive bibliography.

LAND OF HEART'S DESIRE, THE, a one-act verse play by WILLIAM BUTLER YEATS, published and produced in 1894. Setting: Ireland, "in the Barony of Kilmacowen, in the County of Sligo, and at a remote time."

Yeats's first produced play, this short poetic fantasy appeared on a double bill with another new play, Shaw's ARMS AND THE MAN. Its romantic simplicity made it a great favorite, especially in the amateur theatre; this embarrassed the older Yeats, who, despite its depiction of characteristic Yeatsean themes, considered the play a "vague and sentimental trifle."

In a simple peasant house, the hard-working mother complains to a visiting priest and to her easy-going husband and her son. She is irritated by her daughter-in-law, Mary Bruin. Dissatisfied with the dullness and hard work of everyday life, Mary yearns for freedom and summons spirits to take her along to their glorious dance. "Unholy powers," the "maddening freedom and bewildering light" represented by a Faery Child, trick the priest into removing the crucifix. Though powerless now, the priest proclaims God's love and warns Mary that "only the soul's choice can save her." But she is still tempted by the evil spirits' "Land of Heart's Desire." She dies, her young husband holding in his arms but "a drift

* Lagerkvist's little-known first play, *Sista mänskan,* had been published a year earlier. It portrays the title's "the last man" on the frozen earth, blinded by the woman to whom he is bound in a Strindbergian love-hate relationship. Almost totally expressionistic, it consists in large part of repetitive screams of the words "love" and "death."

of leaves, / Or bole of an ash-tree changed into her image." Because she, like others, left the old ways, Mary was snatched by the spirits of evil. Outside, dancing figures sing: "The wind blows over the lonely of heart, / And the lonely of heart is withered away."

LAND OF PROMISE, THE, a comedy in four acts by SOMERSET MAUGHAM, published and produced in 1913. Setting: Tunbridge Wells (England) and rural Canada, 1912.

Maugham considered this the most lasting of his early plays.

A deceased old lady's companion, Norah Marsh, is unexpectedly ignored in the will. Destitute, she moves to her brother's primitive farm in Manitoba, Canada. There she is humiliated by his wife. To escape, the proud Norah marries a rough farmhand. In his prairie cabin he bullies her and breaks her pride. But he is basically decent, and Norah gradually comes to love him and their hard life. She belatedly gets a bequest from the inheritance as well as the chance to return to England and gentility. Instead, she remains with her husband, gives him her money, and saves him from ruin.

LANDSLIDE AT NORTH STATION (*Frana allo Scalo Nord*), a play in three acts by UGO BETTI, published in 1935 and produced in 1936. Setting: "a foreign city, . . . the present."

Betti's first major critical success, this play appeared in English also as *Landslide*. A courtroom drama about guilt, justice, and mercy, it is partly NATURALISTIC and partly a fantasy with suggestions of EXPRESSIONISM.

A judge, who becomes increasingly troubled and introspective, examines an industrial disaster, a landslide that took three lives. Townspeople and workers testify that the project's mean-tempered and avaricious entrepreneur was responsible. The entrepreneur, with his meek wife alongside him, desperately denies the charge, and tries to defend himself against the crowd's hostility. Later he attempts to commit suicide and eagerly accepts his guilt: "I've been an unprincipled cheat and a scoundrel." A mysterious and tenacious witness, however, insists that the guilty one is the industrialist who controls the region's works. The judge wonders what to do about the case when suddenly three spectral figures appear in a mist: the victims of the landslide. Later the industrialist comes to court: he is the father of the mysterious witness, his accuser. But the industrialist rejects responsibility for the disaster, and points his finger at the courtroom audience: "You are responsible!" Gradually the townspeople recognize their selfishness, accept their collective guilt, and seek judgment. They clamor increasingly for punishment as the judge refuses to deliver his verdict—for "Nothing is more dear to them than their own suffering." Like all human beings, "they want to suffer," the judge adds; "they themselves pronounced their just and proper sentence. They pronounce it every day, in the lives that they lead and the torments that they suffer." For that reason the judge must give them "something higher." In subdued voices the crowds echo his last word: "Compassion."

LANGER, František (1888–1965), Czech writer, was noted both for his fiction and his drama. Born in Prague of Jewish ancestry, Langer spent many years as a surgeon in the Austrian and Czech armies. He retired with the rank of general in 1948. One of the members of the Czech "pragmatist" group inspired by KAREL ČAPEK, Langer stressed individual integrity and social responsibilities in his tragedies as well as in his comedies. These were successfully produced abroad even after World War II. His later works, however, were criticized as being superficial and commercially oriented.

Langer's greatest hit was *Velbloud uchem jehly* (*The Camel Through the Needle's Eye*, 1923), a NATURALIST comedy that lauds health and common sense. Other successes were *Periférie* (*The Outskirts*, 1925; also translated as *The Ragged Edge*), a psychological study of a penitent murderer written in a cinematic style and given an alternate happy ending to gratify Langer's public; *Grand Hotel Nevada* (1927), a comedy featuring a couple of Czech immigrants shrewdly exploiting American capitalist follies; *Andělé mezi námi* (1931), a fantasy that dramatizes the problems of euthanasia; *Jízdní hlídka* (1935), a play based on Langer's experience as a military prisoner during the Russian Revolution and celebrating the valor of the Czech army; and *Jiskra v popelu—Pocta Shakespearovi* (1948), a genial comedy in praise of life as well as the theatre. Aside from farces and sentimental pieces, Langer's other popular stage works include children's puppet plays.

LANGNER, Lawrence (1890–1962), Welsh-born American producer and playwright, founded the Theatre Guild in 1918, and as its director premiered major plays of BERNARD SHAW, EUGENE O'NEILL, and other important dramatists. Langner himself wrote and adapted about twenty plays, some of them with his Oklahoma-born wife, Armina Marshall (1899–). Their most successful dramatic collaborations were two comedies: *The Pursuit of Happiness* (1934), a play about colonial times, whose highpoint is a "bundling" scene; and *Suzanna and the Elders* (1939), a story about life in the experimental communist Oneida colony. A successful patent lawyer, Langner also helped found the Washington Square Players (1914) and the American Shakespeare Festival Theatre and Academy at Stratford, Connecticut (1951). He produced radio and television plays and wrote important books on drama and the theatre. These include a fascinating professional autobiography, *The Magic Curtain* (1951), and reminiscences of his association with Shaw, *G.B.S. and the Lunatic* (1963).

LAOS, a small and isolated Asian kingdom (until it became a battlefront in recent years), like CAMBODIA has a theatre devoted principally to the dance. Popular in modern times have been JATAKAS and, since 1924, the *mohlam luong*, stories that are acted, sung, and danced, in Laos as well as in neighboring THAILAND. There is no indigenous Laotian theatre.

See James R. Brandon's *Theatre in Southeast Asia* (1967).

LARK, THE (*L'Alouette*), a play in two acts by JEAN ANOUILH, published and produced in 1953. Setting: the trial of Joan of Arc—bare stage with some fifteenth-century props.

In adapting this play about Saint Joan (which was strongly influenced by Shaw's SAINT JOAN) for English and American productions, CHRISTOPHER FRY and LILLIAN HELLMAN, in their versions, muted Anouilh's ironies—particularly those dealing with sex and religion.

Act I. Though the British Earl of Warwick is eager for Joan's trial and execution, Bishop Cauchon insists that her story be played out. Periodic flashbacks portray Joan's family life and her departure from Domrémy; her charming of Beaudricourt into giving her a horse and an escort; and finally, her persuading the Dauphin—seen with his mistress, his wife, and his mother-in-law, as well as the court—to be courageous and give Joan command of the army. At the end of that scene, Warwick remarks that in real life it did not work out as theatrically: "Desperate, frightened, with nothing to lose, they decided to dress the girl in battle flags and let her go forth as a symbol of something or other. It worked well. A simple girl inspired simple people to get themselves killed for simple ideals."

Act II. Warwick urges the court to "get on with the trial. The lark has been captured." In her defense, Joan glorifies man, who is capable of heroism as well as bestiality: "He has done both good and evil, and thus twice acted like a man. That makes God happy because God made him for just this contradiction." She agrees to follow the Church in matters of faith: "But what I am, I will not denounce. What I have done, I will not deny." The Inquisitor recognizes in Joan "our enemy . . . natural man . . . the symbol of that which is most to be feared." By assuring her that it is God's will, Cauchon persuades Joan to recant. But in prison she bemoans her being able to look forward only to old age and shame for what she did. The visiting Warwick assures her that "we all try to save a little honor, of course, but the main thing is to be here." Now Joan realizes her mistake, and withdraws her recantation. She is tied to the stake and is about to be burned when Beaudricourt reappears to insist on a reenactment of the coronation scene. King Charles agrees on this "true conclusion . . . that of a lark in the free sky; it is Joan at Reims in all her glory. . . . Joan's story has a happy end." Joan's father—still crude but proud of her now—forgets his former abuse and beatings: "I have always said, I did, that this little girl had a great future in store for her." There is a coronation tableau: Joan leans on her standard, "smiling upward, like a statue of her," and

The Lark, Act II. Cauchon (Boris Karloff) and Joan (Julie Harris). New York, 1955. (*Theatre Collection, New York Public Library*)

"the curtain falls slowly on this pretty picture, this illustration from a school prize book."

LAST KNIGHT, THE (*Sistæ riddaren*), a historical play in five acts by AUGUST STRINDBERG, published and produced in 1909. Setting: Sweden, 1512–20.

Among Strindberg's last chronicle plays, this is a companion piece to THE REGENT.

Young Sten Sture, the last knight, succeeds in having himself elected regent. He leads the Swedes most ably, but his unswerving dedication to chivalric codes and his naïve idealism—contrasted with the practical realism of his loyal supporter Vasa (later King Gustav I)—finally enables a Machiavellian archbishop, the rapacious Gustav Trolle, to bring about Sten Sture's excommunication and fatal defeat by the Danes.

LAST OF THE DE MULLINS, THE, a play in three acts by ST. JOHN HANKIN, produced in 1908 and published in 1909. Setting: Dorset, England; early 1900's.

Hankin's last completed full-length play is more serious than his others. It features an IBSENite new woman, Janet De Mullin, who has left her convention-stifled village, earned her own living, and had a child. She shocks her family, particularly her father, who worships his squire ancestors and yearns to make his illegitimate grandson "worthy of the race from which he is descended," and her sister, who is doomed to sterile spinsterhood. Her father sadly bows his head when Janet returns to London with her child, "the last of the De Mullins!"

LATE CHRISTOPHER BEAN, THE (*Prenez garde à la peinture*), a play in three acts by RENÉ FAUCHOIS, published and produced in 1932. Setting: vicinity of Boston (in Howard's version) or in Wales (Williams's version), early 1930's.

Successfully adapted within the same year as the French production by SIDNEY HOWARD and also by EMLYN WILLIAMS, this comedy is vaguely based on the destiny of the painter Vincent Van Gogh. In the original, Mavrier is the dead artist, the name of the village doctor whose family is featured in the play is Odilon Gadarin, and the setting is Liserac, near Avignon.

A friend of Dr. Milton Haggett's young patient Christopher Bean—who had died penniless ten years before—suddenly appears to pay Bean's medical bill. All the friend asks in return is a memento of Bean, some of his paintings. The Haggetts, who have never thought much of them, rescue what is left from the chicken coop and the attic, where the paintings have been used to plug up leaks. But soon more strangers arrive from New York, as well as telegrams and telephone calls: Christopher Bean has just been hailed as a genius and his paintings are worth a fortune. The simple doctor's greed is aroused, as is that of his "citified" wife and foolish daughter. Together with visiting art dealers, critics, and speculators, they tussle for a large portrait of their servant, with which the servant does not want to part. This pitiful drudge soon reveals she has saved seventeen paintings that Mrs. Haggett had thrown away to be burned. Recalling her affection for the poor boy to whom nobody paid much attention, the servant explains that "he was the only man ever asked me to marry him." The others are speechless when she adds, "He was so sick, I couldn't refuse him nothing." And though Mrs. Haggett tries to hold onto the now-valuable paintings, Christopher Bean's widow smilingly takes them, and leaves.

LATEINER, Joseph (1853–1935), Yiddish playwright born in Jassy, Rumania, like his rival MOSHE HURWITZ wrote potboilers for immigrant audiences after he came to New York. Among his one hundred and fifty plays, often confusing concoctions of other plays but successful in eliciting laughter and tears, are *Joseph and His Brethren* (1884), *The Immigration to America* (1885), *Hinke Pinke* (1907), and two plays for the actress Molly Picon: *Plenty* (1928) and *The Comedienne* (1930).

LATIN AMERICA* has flourishing cultural centers in various capitals, but pervasive illiteracy and poverty, and the absence of leisure-oriented populations, have impeded the development of a major theatre. Relatively little momentous drama has been produced in either South or Central America, and few important playwrights have appeared there—though there are more of both than is generally assumed. Latin America's theatre was nurtured by the traditions of both the Spaniards and the Indians—and in some countries by that of Africa, because of the slaves imported in colonial times. The natives retained little power after European settlers took over early in the sixteenth century, and Spain's political rule was overthrown in country after country between the 1820's and the 1880's. However, the Indian and the Spanish cultures—native spectacles and pageants, and Iberian religious and secular mores—left their ineradicable marks on the drama and theatre south of the Rio Grande.

It is as difficult to categorize Latin America's drama as it is that of any continent. A common cultural heritage, however, flowered similarly in the South and the Central American countries. Nineteenth-century European movements like romanticism and SYMBOLISM spread from the theatres of Madrid to those of Latin America. Late in the century the best-known modern indigenous drama began, that of the GAUCHO, as well as the COSTUMBRISMO; in vogue for many years, both were literarily esteemed and produced by such writers as FLORENCIO SÁNCHEZ—Latin America's first great playwright—and his successor, ERNESTO HERRERA. In the present century Latin American drama has increasingly mirrored that of Europe, though NATURALISM has focused on the local problems accentuated by revolutions, and protest drama was occasionally very anti-United States. In some cases native and North American themes have been coupled with naturalism and *costumbrismo*—as in the plays of Puerto Rico's RENÉ MARQUÉS. Though even more completely indebted to Western writers in their approach, other major Latin American playwrights have dramatized national themes: Argentina's SAMUEL EICHELBAUM and the often-experimental Mexicans RODOLFO USIGLI and CARLOS SOLÓRZANO.

The most comprehensive account of Latin America's theatre is Willis Knapp Jones's *Behind Spanish American Footlights* (1966). Jones's collections of modern *Spanish-American Literature in Translation* (1963, including excerpts from the drama of seven countries) and *Men and Angels: Three South American Comedies* (1970) have informative introductions. *TDR, The Drama Review* XIV: 2 (Winter 1970), the "Latin American Theatre" issue, includes the texts of a play (José Triana's *The Criminals*) and various skits, as well

* Including the following Spanish-speaking countries: ARGENTINA, BOLIVIA, CHILE, COLOMBIA, COSTA RICA, CUBA, THE DOMINICAN REPUBLIC, ECUADOR, EL SALVADOR, GUATAMALA, HONDURAS, MEXICO, NICARAGUA, PANAMA, PARAGUAY, PERU, PUERTO RICO, URUGUAY, and VENEZUELA. HAITI's official language is French and BRAZIL's is Portuguese. The geographically contiguous West Indies, famous for their calypso music, have also produced the dramatist ERROL JOHN; and the Martinique-born Parisian poet-playwright-politician Aimé Césaire (1913–), who launched the *négritude* movement, wrote the 1964 Salzburg Festival play about Henri Christophe, the early-nineteenth-century ex-slave and later Haitian king, *La Tragédie du Roi Christophe (The Tragedy of King Christophe,* 1963), and glorified the modern African statesman Patrice Lumumba in the epic drama *Une Saison au Congo* (*A Season in the Congo,* 1966).

as a bibliography. Another major study is John V. Falconieri's translation of Enrique Anderson-Imbert's *Spanish-American Literature: A History* (1963). The bibliographies in these works are supplemented by Frank P. Hebblethwaite's *A Bibliographical Guide to the Spanish American Theater* (1969), the annual volumes of the University of Florida's extensively annotated *Handbook of Latin American Studies* (1935 ff.), and the *Latin American Theatre Review* (1967 ff.). Specialized studies are listed under individual countries.

LATVIA, like it neighbors LITHUANIA and ESTONIA, was part of the Russian Empire until 1918, when it proclaimed its independence. Because all writing until the mid-nineteenth century had been in Russian or German, Latvian (or Lettish) drama did not even begin until then. The theatre director Ādolfs Alunāns (1848–1912) became known as the "father" of the Latvian theatre because of his organizational work and his successful efforts to bring up a generation of Latvian actors; he also wrote popular but artistically unimportant historical tragedies and rustic comedies. More significant was the drama of Rūdolfs Blaumanis (1863–1908), a rural gentleman whose early plays were comedies, but whose finest works are *Indrāni* (1904), a domestic tragedy, and *Ugani* (1906), another serious drama.

In urban centers, noted local playwrights included the patriot Anna Brigadere (1861–1933), whose dramas consist of folklore adaptation like *Tom Thumb* (1903), children's plays like *Maija un Paija* (1922), and PROBLEM PLAYS. The most important literary figures at the time of World War I were the poets Rainis (1865–1929) and his wife Aspazija (1868–1945), whose real names were Jānis and Elza (née Rozenberge) Pliekšāns. Rainis's verse plays include his first distinguished drama, *Uguns un nakts* (1905), and legendary and historical dramatizations such as *Ilja Mūromietis* (1922) and *Jāzeps un viņa brāli* (*The Sons of Jacob*, 1919); Aspazija wrote plays that reflect her ardent espousal of feminism, including *Neaizsniegts mērkis* (1894), a drama that heralded the revolution to come; *Sidraba šķidrauts* (1904); and *Vaidelote* (1894), a tragedy of pagan Lithuania and Aspazija's first literary success.

Among the playwrights who were popular in independent Latvia are Andrejs Upīts (or Upītis, 1877–1970), remembered for his Saint Joan tragedy *Žanna d'Ark* (1930) and for a number of comedies, notably *Peldētāja Zuzanna* (1922); Julius Pētersons (1880–1945), the last of whose well-known plays was *Cilvēki, kas paši bēg no sevis* (1929); and Eduards Vulfs (1886–1918), whose most successful work was the satirical comedy *Meli* (1913). Even more notable is Martiņš Zīverts (1903–), particularly for the historical tragedy *Vara* (1944). Subsequent Lettish drama has been unnoteworthy. In 1934 the theatre was enlisted by the newly established nationalistic dictatorship and featured patriotic pageantry as well as the conventional dramatic fluff. In 1940 Latvia, like its neighbors, was incorporated into the Soviet Union, under whose total control its drama thereafter came.

Jānis Andrups and Vitauts Kalve's handsomely illustrated *Latvian Literature* (1954) occasionally alludes to the drama and contains a bibliography. William K. Matthews's collection of Latvian verse, *The Tricolour Sun* (1936), has brief essays on the anthologized poets, some of whom were also playwrights.

LAUCKNER, Rolf (1887–1954), German playwright, was the stepson of HERMANN SUDERMANN and one of the first post-World War I EXPRESSIONISTS. He focused on individual tragedies, as in his *Wahnschaffe* (1920), a long and ambitious five-act play that features a weak but idealistic enthusiast—alternately an author and a physician—who struggles impotently against the chaos of his age, to which the play is Lauckner's tribute. A similar portrayal is that of an ultimately crooked faithhealer in *Der Sturz des Apostels Paulus* (1917), who remains a believer though a failure. *Predigt in Litauen* (1919) is a domestic tragedy about a strict parson who threatens to whip his scoundrel son, who thereupon pulls out a gun—and shoots himself. Other domestic tragedies include *Christa die Tante* (1919), in which an aging spinster desperately seeking something from life, lusts after her young nephew, and becomes a humiliated failure; and *Krisis* (1928), a love triangle in which a man is deserted by two women. Lauckner's plays about legend and history include *Die Reise gegen Gott* (1923), portraying the torments of a painter (suggesting Paul Gauguin) after he leaves his homeland; *Matumbo* (1924), a play about the Negro in Europe; *Bernhard von Weimar* (1933), about the Thirty Years' War general; *Das Leben für den Staat* (1936), about Frederick the Great; *Die Flucht des Michel Angelo* (1944); *Cäsar und Cicero* (1947); and a Job drama, *Hiob* (1949). Lauckner's comedies include *Die Entkleidung des Antonio Carossa* (1925), the portrait of a swindler who is exposed; and the very successful *Der Hakim weiss es* (1936), which reveals a mysterious stranger in a province to be an ordinary man.

Lauckner was born in Königsberg and died in Bayreuth. He studied at various German universities, earning his doctorate from Würzburg. His expressionism is closely linked with NATURALISM, with which, indeed, it sometimes alternates. Though he dramatized social protest and the struggle of the generations, he did so in a form that approximates domestic tragedy and tragicomedy. His concern was with individuals and their affairs as much as with the abstract characters more typical of expressionist drama. The blend of these forms may be seen in the eerie "Legend of the Periphery" vignette from his one-act *Schrei aus der Strasse* (*Cry in the Street*, 1922). It appears in Walter H. Sokel's *An Anthology of German Expressionist Drama* (1963). Although Lauckner's nearly thirty plays were published in six volumes in 1953, few are available in translation.

LAURENTS, Arthur (1920–), American playwright, has won success particularly with his books for a number of hit musicals, notably *West Side Story* (1957, music by Leonard Bernstein), the Romeo and Juliet story transferred to the slum gang fights of New York City; and *Gypsy* (1959, music by Jule Styne), a biography of the stripteaser Gypsy Rose Lee and her driving, go-getting mother. Laurents initially gained notice with *Home of the Brave* (1945), a war play in flashbacks about racial and religious prejudice: the protagonist (a Jew in the play, a Negro in the 1949 film), who breaks down under the pressures of war and bigotry, is cured of his paralysis when a psychiatrist proves that despite his ancestry he does not differ in his human limitations from all other people. All Laurents's nonmusical drama is psychiatrically oriented and features characters wistfully searching for happiness; he customarily employs PRESENTATIONAL devices like fantasy and flashbacks.

The Bird Cage (1950) has a symbolically skeletal setting and features a dictatorial nightclub owner whose employees finally defy and leave him. The most conventional of Laurents's plays is *The Time of the Cuckoo* (1952), a play about a puritanical American schoolteacher's bittersweet and futile search for romance in Venice, filmed as *Summertime* (1955) and adapted by Laurents for a Richard Rodgers musical, *Do I Hear A Waltz?* (1965). His *A Clearing in the Woods* (1956) depicts an American woman as she really is and also as she envisions herself in the different stages of her fantasy—as sweetheart, wife, mother—from girlhood to middle age. Like Laurents's other protagonists, she yearns "to rise in the air just a little, to climb, to reach a branch, even the lowest"—and finally comes to accept her limitations as "an imperfect human being." *Invitation to a March* (1960), an amusing modernization of the Sleeping Beauty legend, has the heroine constantly falling asleep—a psychological rejection of the conventional marriage planned for her—until she is awakened by a nonconforming plumber with whom she dances away, declining the "invitation to the march" of humdrum life. Here Laurents's usually affirmative resolution gives way to fantasy.

Laurents, who was born in Brooklyn and graduated from Cornell University, also has directed and has written other musicals as well as a number of film scripts, notably those for *The Snake Pit* (1948) and for GUY BOLTON's play *Anastasia* (1956).

LAVEDAN, Henri [-Léon-Émile] (1859–1940), French playwright, portrayed social problems in a number of once-popular comedies and PROBLEM PLAYS. The most famous of them, *Le Prince d'Aurec* (THE PRINCE D'AUREC, 1892), is concerned with anti-Semitism as well as with the decline of the aristocracy after 1871. Other Lavedan plays that were produced also in the United States are *Catherine* (1898), an insipid comedy featuring a little bourgeois music teacher; *Le Duel* (*The Duel,* 1905), a WELL-MADE PLAY in which two brothers (a priest and an atheist) clash over a married woman torn by conflicts of "body and soul"; and *Sire* (1909), a romantic intrigue about a young man who pretends to be the lost son of Louis XVI.

Born in Orléans, educated in Paris, and originally a lawyer, Lavedan soon turned to writing. After some of his QUARTS D'HEURE appeared at the Théâtre-Libre, the Comédie-Française produced his first play, *Une Famille* (1891), a series of trifling but clever conversations. Lavedan's other plays include *Le Nouveau Jeu* (1898), an episodic comedy featuring the antics of a boulevardier and his equally amoral wife; *Le Marquis de Priola* (1902), portaying a sinister Don Juan; *Le Goût du Vice* (1911), another comedy of manners; and *Servir* (1913), a domestic drama in which a father and his son clash in their ideas on military service. All these plays exemplify competent if uneven craftsmanship that excelled in characterization.

The Prince d'Aurec was published in *Three Modern Plays from the French* (1914), which includes Barrett H. Clark's study and bibliography of Lavedan.

LAVERY, Emmet [Godfrey] (1902–), American lawyer and journalist, was attracted to his later profession by the Federal Theatre Project of the 1930's. He became an actor, and then went to Hollywood as a script writer and organizer of Catholic drama groups. He turned to playwriting with *The First Legion* (1934), a drama about schisms among the Jesuits; and *Second Spring* (1938), a biography of Cardinal Newman. Lavery's most successful play was *The Magnificent Yankee* (1946), an episodic biography of Justice Oliver Wendell Holmes.

LAVRENEV [or Lavrenyov], **Boris Andreevich** (1892–1959), Russian poet, novelist, and playwright, was an officer under the tsar. He neither joined nor opposed the Soviets, but achieved a prominent position in Soviet literature with his fiction and drama. A romanticist concerned with plot ("Literature must excite and captivate . . . must master *above all* the plot"), his predominant theme was that of the officer's honor, regardless of the cause he serves.

Popular early plays were revolutionary pieces like *Myatezh* (1925, later retitled *Dym*), which depicts the revolt of a former White Guard officer; and *Prostaya veshch* (1927), which deals with a Soviet commissar hiding from the Whites. Next came *Razlom* (1927), whose naval officer protagonist is prompted by honor finally to transfer his allegiance to the Soviets aboard a cruiser modeled on the *Aurora,* which first fired on the Winter Palace. *Vragi* (1929) is a play about two pilot brothers, one of whom opposes the Soviets. *Za tekh, kto v more* (1947), another war play, portrays an officer who seeks personal glory, an attitude that dooms him; the play's stated moral is "The successes of each individual are basically the successes of the collective that nurtured him." Among Lavrenev's other plays is an anti-American diatribe, *Golos Ameriki* (1949), which won the Stalin Prize.

Lavrenev's life and nondramatic writings are discussed in Gleb Struve's *Soviet Russian Literature 1917–50* (1951). For his plays, see Martha Bradshaw's anthology, *Soviet Theaters 1917–41* (1954), and Nikolai A. Gorchakov's *The Theater in Soviet Russia* (1957).

LAWLER,* Ray (1921–), Australian actor and playwright, became that continent's first internationally known dramatist with his SUMMER OF THE SEVENTEENTH DOLL (1956), in which he himself acted the part of Barney. His other plays, about a dozen, have not fared as well. The only one known abroad is *The Piccadilly Bushman* (published in 1961), which features a successful actor returning from England to make a film, who is repulsed by his native Australia; his wife is torn between patriotic loyalty and the obligations she feels toward her crumbling marriage. The play's satire of "overseas crawling" (Australian deference to foreign cultures) was too strong for fashionable local audiences.

Lawler was born in Footscray, an industrial suburb of Melbourne, and educated at a State school. At thirteen, he began working in factories and eventually as a ghost-writer. Then he turned to acting and directing. He stage-managed theatres in Brisbane and Melbourne, and was associated with the Union Theatre Repertory Company of Australia and, subsequently, the Australian Elizabethan Trust's Drama Company.

Lawler has a fine gift for creating situations and characters, and a good ear for speech. His drama is not wholly free of sentimentality and plot artifice. But it transcends—especially in his best-known work—the local and immediate, and effectively presents universal issues. Lawler's other plays include *Cradle of Thunder* (1949), *The Unshaven Cheek* (1963), and several children's shows.

LAWRENCE, D[avid] H[erbert] (1885–1930), English writer, is best known as an essayist, poet, and the author of short stories and many novels, including *Sons and Lovers* (1913) and the long-banned *Lady Chatterley's Lover* (1928). But he also wrote ten plays (eight of them full length), some of which were produced—unsuccessfully. They are interesting as Lawrence's attempts to reformulate his ideas and art for the theatre, and some of them had major revivals in London in 1968. Best are his three plays published in the first collection (1933): *The Widowing of Mrs. Holroyd* (written 1914, produced 1920), whose plot resembles that of Lawrence's short story "Odour of Chrysanthemums," though the miner's wife here is attracted to another man and despairingly blames herself later, as she washes her husband's corpse ("Oh dear, oh, dear! ... I *would* have loved you—I tried hard"); *Touch and Go* (1920), which depicts, though in significantly different ways, the industrial problems and the characters of his novel *Women in Love* (1920); and the biblical *David* (produced 1927, also titled *Saul*), sixteen short "cinemagraphic" scenes based on I Samuel 15–20. *A Collier's Friday Night* (1906), his first play, is something of an early draft for *Sons and Lovers*. Most of Lawrence's other plays were written in 1912, and all of them were published posthumously: *The Married Man, The Merry-Go-Round*, and the fragment *Altitude*, all comedies; *The Fight for Barbara* (first published as *Keeping Barbara*), a dramatization of Lawrence's life with Frieda after she deserted her husband; *The Daughter-In-Law*, a four-act play; and *Noah's Flood*, a fragment written about 1925.

All of these are collected in *The Complete Plays of D. H. Lawrence* (1966). They are briefly alluded to in many of the countless books and articles on Lawrence, and are the subject of Arthur E. Waterman's "The Plays of D. H. Lawrence," *Modern Drama*, II (February 1960). Lawrence had a significant influence on TENNESSEE WILLIAMS, who dramatized Lawrence's life as well as his fiction.

LAWRENCE, Jerome (1915–), American playwright, has done most of his work in collaboration with ROBERT E. LEE. Their biggest hits have been *Inherit the Wind* (1955) and *Auntie Mame* (1956). The former, a fictionalized dramatization of the John T. Scopes "monkey" trial of 1925, features the debate between the thinly disguised William Jennings Bryan and Clarence Darrow, and also presents a newspaperman whose character is based on the writer H. L. Mencken. *Auntie Mame* is a dramatization of Patrick Dennis's 1955 farcical novel about a frenetically unconventional female and her orphaned nephew, which Lawrence, Lee, and the composer Jerry Herman made into the popular musical *Mame* (1966).

Further collaborations of Lawrence and Lee include another fictionalized dramatization of history, *The Gang's All Here* (1959, with MORRIE RYSKIND), a portrayal of President Harding as a mediocre man duped by crooked politicians; a dramatization of Harry Golden's book *Only in America* (1959); *The Night Thoreau Spent in Jail* (1970), performed widely and successfully because of the immediacy to contemporary audiences of Henry David Thoreau's concerns; and musicals like *Look Ma, I'm Dancing* (1948), *Shangri-La* (1956; based on James Hilton's novel *Lost Horizon*, 1933), and *Dear World* (1969, based on Giraudoux's THE MADWOMAN OF CHAILLOT).

LAWSON, John Howard (1895–), American social critic and dramatist, has been called (by Gerald Rabkin) "the dean of the revolutionary movement in the theatre." He became famous in the 1920's with a number of experimental plays, chiefly PROCESSIONAL (1925). A cofounder of such precursors of the social theatre of the 1930's as the Workers' Drama League (1926) and the New Playwrights (1927), Lawson was also associated briefly with the Group Theatre, whose most notable playwright was CLIFFORD ODETS. Lawson considered art a weapon for bringing about the

* Illustration on page 735.

revolution, and he was intransigent in his Marxist commitment. Investigated by the House Un-American Activities Committee in 1947, Lawson angrily refused to answer its questions—and was imprisoned for contempt of Congress. Many literary and theatre critics considered Lawson a playwright of great potential, Harold Clurman looking upon him as "the hope of our theatre." Despite Lawson's vitality and the integrity of his commitments, however, this potential was never realized, and after the 1930's he slipped into obscurity.

Lawson was born in New York, and was graduated from Williams College in 1914. He served with the Volunteer Ambulance Corps during World War I, and two of his plays were produced in America before the war's end. But it was with *Roger Bloomer* (1923) that he first became notable. The earliest native American EXPRESSIONIST play (Rice's THE ADDING MACHINE opened a few days later), its title character is a sex-obsessed adolescent, the suicide of whose frigid girl friend brings about his arrest and the Freudian dream that constitutes most of the play: it reviews his life, ultimately cures his obsessions, and brings about his maturation. It was with *Processional* that Lawson reached the peak of his achievement as a playwright.

In later drama Lawson continued to express his social-political commitments. After *Nirvana* (1926), *Loud Speaker* (1927), and *The International* (1928), Lawson's experimental drama—variations of expressionism, LIVING NEWSPAPER DRAMA, and vaudevillian farce—gave way to more traditional NATURALISM, in which melodrama often predominates: *Success Story* (1932), which features a Jew who disavows his youthful radicalism in an obsessive drive for money and power; *The Pure in Heart* (1934); and *Gentlewoman* (1934), whose protagonist gives up her lover (without revealing to him that she is carrying his child) to free him for his proletarian destiny, which it is too late for her to achieve.

The failure of these plays brought about Lawson's "intensive reevaluation of my work as an artist." He joined the Communist Party and became active in many of its causes. In his *Theory and Technique of Playwriting* (1936, revised in 1949) he discussed the deficiency of bourgeois drama, and in his *Marching Song* (1937), a proletarian play about a strike, he attempted to produce an artistic revolutionary drama whose title song expresses Lawson's moral: "Step by step the longest march / Can be won, can be won; / Single stones will form an arch / One by one. . . ." The Group Theatre rejected this as well as his next work, *Parlor Magic* (1940), a play about Fascism in England. His Hollywood films, while commercially successful, were not distinguished artistically, and did little to advance his commitment to Marxism.

Even Lawson's masterpiece, *Processional*, is now only of historical interest: it and his other plays are artistically flawed by their strident ideological tendentiousness. A later book that expresses his ideas is *Film in the Battle of Ideas* (1953). Gerald Rabkin's *Drama and Commitment* (1964) has an extensive analysis of Lawson's work and includes a bibliography. See also Harold Clurman's *The Fervent Years* (1945).

LAZARUS (*Lazzaro*), a play in three acts by LUIGI PIRANDELLO, produced in 1929 and published in 1930. Setting: Italy, 1929.

This play, like THE LIFE I GAVE YOU, dramatizes Pirandello's philosophy of the interrelationships of life and death. Critics have differed about the play's meaning—as well as its importance. While Eric Bentley found evidence of "a definitely fascist mentality" in its "miracle mongering" (though Pirandello depicts miracles in a number of plays), others have found it to represent "humanitarian liberal" (Lander MacClintock), ethical, or deeply religious viewpoints.

Diego Spina has neurotically Fundamentalist convictions. "A huge black cross bearing a depressing, painted, bleeding figure of Christ" dominates his courtyard—and his unbending, sacrificial mode of life. He has sent his children to a seminary and a convent, and has refused the pleas of his beautiful wife Sara to bring them back to their healthy country life. Legally powerless, she has left Spina and eventually became the common-law wife of one of his farmers, whose children she has borne. Sara and her second family have flourished in a simple, natural peasant life. Spina's daughter has become a cripple, and now lives with the father. His son has just returned from the seminary, and Sara comes (after years of separation) to tell him of their son's determination not to become a priest. She begs Spina to relent, but he rushes out furiously, is run over by a car, and is certified as dead. A doctor injects adrenaline into his heart and revives Spina, who is oblivious to what happened after the accident. When he learns the truth he is crushed to realize that—though he was dead—he saw neither God nor the afterlife he has believed in so fanatically. In a crazed frenzy at the loss of his faith, he now rejects all moral restraints and is ready to kill, for "there's nothing on the other side! I *know!*" His son, on the contrary, regains his wish to become a priest. He helps calm down his father. "If our soul is God within us, what else would you call his science and a miracle achieved by means of it, if not one of His miracles, wrought when He would have it accomplished?" he asks his father, concluding: "What can you possibly know of death if there is no death in God? And if He is now once again to be found in you, as He is still to be found in all of us here . . . Eternal, in this moment of our life which only in Him is life without end?" Spina gains a more humane faith as the son, in divine exaltation, bids his crippled sister to rise from her wheelchair and walk again. She does, and the people are dumbfounded with joy at this divine miracle.

LAZARUS LAUGHED, a play in four acts by EUGENE O'NEILL, published in 1927 and produced in 1928. Setting: Bethany, Athens, and Rome; after Lazarus's resurrection (John 11).

A spectacular poetic pageant that employs elaborate settings and masked crowds by the hundreds, the play is rarely performed. O'Neill highly esteemed it as a "Play for an Imaginative Theatre," though most critics do not share this view. In this work O'Neill affirms a Dionysian vitality—defeated in THE GREAT GOD BROWN—a joyful immortality and love, manifested in persistent choral chants and laughter.

The head of Lazarus (the only character not wearing a mask) is haloed, his body illumined, and his former sorrow turned into joy and almost constant laughter. With him is his quickly aging wife Miriam, a symbol of motherhood. When asked about the beyond, Lazarus replies, "There is only life! I heard the heart of Jesus laughing in my heart; 'There is Eternal Life in No,' it said, and there is the same Eternal Life in Yes!' Lazarus continues: "'Death is the fear between!' And my heart reborn to love of life cried 'Yes!' and I laughed in the laughter of God!" The crowd, infected by his laughter, exultantly joins in it and chants that "Death is dead! / There is only laughter." Fearless and becoming ever younger, Lazarus is shown as he goes to his martyrdom, converting some and almost converting others among the multitudes of Jews, Christians, Greeks, and Romans, all of whom fear life because they fear death and alternately worship and lust to kill Lazarus. Individuals similarly affected by his mysticism and ecstasy include the bestial Gaius Caligula, who embodies fear and pride; Tiberius Caesar (soon killed by Caligula), a cruel and lonely old lecher who tells Lazarus how his mother made him Caesar and the "most swinish" of men; and Tiberius's beautiful mistress Pompeia, who jealously poisons Miriam, but finds Lazarus loves not only her but all mankind. When Lazarus is burned at the stake in the amphitheatre, his dying laughter draws Pompeia to throw herself into the flames with him, and Caligula to grovel in fear and remorse: "Forgive me, Lazarus! Men forget!"

LEAGUE OF YOUTH, THE (*De unges forbund*), a comedy in five acts by HENRIK IBSEN, published and produced in 1869. Setting: a small town in southern Norway, 1860's.

Ibsen's earliest attempt to depict everyday speech, this light melodrama was Norway's first important prose comedy. Its political satire outraged liberals, who rioted at the premiere. The protagonist, Stensgård, a rounded PEER GYNT (and a caricature that deeply offended BJØRNSTJERNE BJØRNSON), is an unprincipled, self-deluding idealist—"a disintegrated attitudinizer," as Ibsen later characterized this politician, and "a split personality."

Against the background of "de lokale forhold" ("the local situation") of corruption, Stensgård, an ambitious lawyer, seeks election to Parliament. The crowd is inflamed by his liberal oratory: "God be with us! For we are going about His work, with youth and faith to help us." He founds a league of youth to replace the old ruling order, which consists of a chamberlain, a leading landowner, and the town's wealthy financier. At the same time, he intrigues to ingratiate himself with and invade the ranks of these capitalists, courting their daughters as well as a rich and amorous widow. He rejoices in his love for his fellow creatures ("I feel as if I could clasp them all in one embrace, and weep, and beg their forgiveness because God has been so partial as to give me more than them"), but he pitilessly forces a newspaperman to support him ("What are your bedridden wives and deformed brats to me?") and blackmails the chamberlain. At last his various intrigues are revealed to all, and he is thrown out. Still, the landowner understands him: "Squalor at home, high pressure at school; soul, temperament, will, talents, all pulling in different ways—what could it lead to but disintegration of character?" However, the landowner predicts that in ten to fifteen years "Stensgård will either be in Parliament or in the Ministry—perhaps in both at once." For the moment, the town has been saved by the angels; if these were only "middling" ones, "that," as the newspaperman remarks, "comes of the local situation."

The newspaperman is the printer Aslaksen, who reappears as a solid burgher in AN ENEMY OF THE PEOPLE. Among the many other characters appearing in the complex plot is the chamberlain's daughter-in-law, who foreshadows Nora of A DOLL'S HOUSE, and the bankrupt but sharp-witted Daniel Heire, a Dickensian portrayal of Ibsen's father.

LEE, Robert E[dwin] (1918–), American playwright, has collaborated with his fellow Ohioan JEROME LAWRENCE on such hits as *Inherit the Wind* (1955), *Auntie Mame* (1956), and many other plays and musicals (for which see LAWRENCE). Among their later and less successful productions was one on Soviet-American relations, *A Call on Kuprin* (1961); and a drama about a dictator and his wife (modeled on Argentina's Juan and Eva Perón), *Diamond Orchid* (1965). Lee and Lawrence have also written many radio and television scripts. Lee was a one-time astronomer and the cofounder (with Lawrence) of the Armed Forces Radio Service.

LEIVICK, H. [Leivick Halper] (1888–1962), Yiddish poet, playwright, and essayist, is best remembered for *Der Goylem* (THE GOLEM, 1921). But though he wrote some twenty other plays, it is his poetry that made him the outstanding Yiddish literary figure of his time, perhaps the greatest of all Yiddish poets. Leivick's verse, like his drama, portrays his deep personal awareness of suffering and his anguished yearning for the Messiah who would liberate not only the Jews but all humanity.

Leivick was born to a poor family in Ihumen, Russia, the oldest of nine children. Originally named Leivick Halper, he later transposed his names when Moyshe Leyb Halpern, an established

Yiddish poet, objected to what he thought was the younger man's capitalizing on a well-known similar name. Leivick was thrown on his own resources at the age of ten and was sent off to attend the Berezin yeshiva. After four years he earned his living as a private tutor—and wrote poetry. The 1905 revolts inspired his joining the Jewish labor movement. Quickly involved in political activities, Leivick was arrested, tried, and convicted (1906). Eventually he was banished to Siberia, and in 1912 began his harrowing trek among a brutalized chain gang that was literally whipped across the snow-covered prairies. These experiences indelibly affected his whole life and outlook, and colored all his writings. In the poem "A Lid Vegn Sikh" ("A Song About Myself") he recalled the horrors of those years and their effect on his later work and thought.

Somehow he was able to escape, working his way—alone—back to Russia and at last, in 1913, to the United States. There he was welcomed by *Di Yunge,* a group of young Yiddish poets who knew some of the poems Leivick had written in prison. Though he had already published some of his writings, it was in America that Leivick was to produce most of his important work. At first he earned his living as a factory hand and a wall-paper hanger, but soon he won recognition with *Hintern Shloss* (*Locked In*, 1918) and *Lidr* (*Songs*, 1919), both volumes of poetry. Then came his masterpiece, *The Golem*, the most popular of his "messianic trilogy," which begins with *Di Keyten fun Moshiakh* (written in 1908 and published in 1939) and concludes with *Di Geula-Komedie: Der Goylem Kholemt* (1934). The former depicts Azriel, alone among the angels, revolting against God's command to forge the chains of the Messiah, since earth is not yet ready for him; Azriel renounces his celestial state and, along with the prophet Elijah, joins suffering humanity, ministering to it until the coming of the liberating Messiah.

Leivick's other plays, many of them produced by Maurice Schwartz in New York, include *Shmattes* (1921) and *Bettler* (1923), two social dramas, and *Shop* (1926), a revolutionary drama; all were successful in the theatre. The historical *Hirsh Lekert* (1927, produced in 1933 as *Heroic Years*) is a dramatic poem about a shoemaker who attempted to assassinate Vilna's ruthless governor, succeeded only in wounding him, and then behaved so courageously in refusing to expose his fellow conspirators that he became the people's hero after his execution by hanging. Another historical play is the "dramatic poem" *Abélard and Héloise* (1936). *Di Akeyde* (1935, on the Sacrifice of Isaac) and *Sdom* (1937) are biblical dramas. *Ver Iz Ver* (*Who's Who*, 1938; later changed to *Dr. Schelling*) is the tragedy of a Nobel Prize winner who sues a Jewish publication for (correctly) identifying him as a Jew. *Der Nes in Getto,* an epic on the Warsaw ghetto, was written in 1940, and *Maharam fun Rothenburg* appeared in 1945. Leivick further dramatized the harrowing events of the 1940's in *Di Khasene in Fernvald* (1949), which portrays the marriage of widowed concentration-camp survivors, and presents a vision of the start of new life after the debacle. In *In di Teg fun Iyev* (1953), published shortly before MacLeish's J.B., Job as well as the biblical Isaac (who according to a Talmudic passage may have lived in Job's time) questions God's infliction of misery on humanity; the figure of Satan finally bows before God—and Job, Isaac, and Abraham bind their wounds and start to build anew. Among Leivick's other plays are *Dort, Vu di Frayhayt* (written in Siberia in 1912, published in 1952) and *Der Poet iz Gevorn Blind* (1938).

Leivick was long hospitalized in Denver's Jewish tubercular sanitarium during the 1930's, debilitated by illness for most of his later life, and totally paralyzed in his last four years. He literally embodied his people's suffering, which he felt so acutely. But in his last years, the cataclysmic horrors of Nazism notwithstanding, Leivick's drama and poetry expressed hope for eventual liberation. Of his plays, only *The Golem* is readily available in translation, in Joseph C. Landis's *The Dybbuk and Other Great Yiddish Plays* (1966). See also Sol Liptzin's *The Flowering of Yiddish Literature* (1963) and Charles A. Madison's *Yiddish Literature: Its Scope and Major Writers* (1968).

LEMAÎTRE, Jules [-François-Hélie] (1854–1914), French critic and dramatist, was more distinguished for his subsequently collected theatre reviews and literary criticisms than for his dozen dramas. The best of the latter is *Le Pardon* (*Forgiveness,* 1895), a short three-character play about a couple whose respective adulteries end with mutual understanding and forgiveness. Perhaps his most popular play was the dramatization of his novel *Les Rois* (1893), a psychological study of a young prince who copes with revolution and two women, one of whom ultimately assassinates him. These and some of Lemaître's other plays have occasionally effective characters and situations, but they appear too dated to be of much interest now.

Few of Lemaître's plays have been translated into English. *Forgiveness* is one of the *Three Modern Plays From the French* (1914), which includes Barrett H. Clark's study and bibliography of Lemaître.

LENGYEL, Menyhért [or Melchior] (1880–), Hungarian playwright, an able craftsman who, like his more famous countryman FERENC MOLNÁR, began his career as a journalist. Lengyel received worldwide acclaim for *Tájfun* (*Typhoon,* 1909), a romantic thriller featuring Japanese agents in Paris, and contrasting (as the final stage direction emphasizes) the "conflicting life standards of two continents." Another play produced outside Hungary was *A cárnö* (1912), a witty drama about Catherine the Great, written in collaboration with Lajos Biró (1880–1948). Lengyel's *Antónia* (1925), a play with music, also achieved considerable popularity, and he wrote the scenario for Béla Bartók's once-banned ballet *A csodálatos mandarin* (*The Miraculous Mandarin,* 1919). The most successful of Lengyel's writings was a story made into the Ernst Lubitsch film *Ninotchka* (1939) and remade into *Silk Stockings* (1955), a Cole Porter musical by GEORGE S. KAUFMAN, ABE BURROWS, and Leueen MacGrath (1914–).

LENORMAND, Henri-René (1882–1951), French playwright, is best known in the English-speaking world for *Le Temps est un songe* (TIME IS A DREAM, 1918), a characteristically philosophical tragedy about the mystery and inexorability of time. Called "the EUGENE O'NEILL of the French stage," Lenormand probed—often in a dreamlike manner, as in the serious drama of PHILIP BARRY—the agonizing effects of the unconscious and other mysterious powers that are shown to be pervasive and destructive. A host of tortured, psychopathic characters like the protagonists of *Time Is a Dream* appear in Lenormand's two dozen plays, some of them GRAND GUIGNOL. These characters as well as their torments are analyzed from psychological, moral, mystical, and philosophical perspectives; they are portrayed as the playthings of fate, victims of forces they only dimly perceive and are unable to control.

In his often exotic settings Lenormand reflected the interest of his father, a prominent writer-composer who was intrigued by Eastern art and thought. After attending the Sorbonne, Lenormand published a volume of prose poems. In 1905 his *La Folie blanche* was produced at the Grand Guignol; the title's "white madness" is the Alpine snow that brings death to two young lovers, climbers joined by a rope, who agonize over their probable reaction were one of them to slip and thus jeopardize the other's life. Lenormand's first important play was *Les Possédés* (1909), the study of genius sacrificing itself and others to fulfill creative destiny. Subsequent works were also praised by critics, but popular success came to Lenormand only in 1919, when Georges Pitoëff produced *Time Is a Dream* in his art theatre.

This play was followed by *Les Rates* (*The Failures*, 1920), which depicts the moral as well as physical disintegration of a playwright and his actress wife. The play introduced Lenormand's drama to New York in 1923, a year before the American production of *Time Is a Dream*. Lenormand's other tragedies include *Le Simoun* (1920), which portrays in an African setting a father's incestuous passion for his daughter; *Le Mangeur de rêves* (*The Dream Doctor*, 1922; also translated as *The Devourer of Dreams*), whose protagonist relishes "women's morbid or criminal dreams" and thus causes a patient's suicide; *La Dent rouge* (1922) and *À l'Ombre du mal* (1924), both dealing with superstition, the latter with a chain of evil that devours innocents in a primitive outpost; *L'Homme et ses fantômes* (1924), featuring Don Juan as a magician who is defeated by his inability to subjugate women and who finds in love the self-knowledge that had always eluded him; and *Les Trois Chambres* (1931), a haunting tragedy about a man, his wife, and his mistress. Lenormand's later plays similarly probe "the flower of evil"—as in *Pacifique* (1937), in which flight from civilization to Polynesia and love fails ultimately to bring the protagonist happiness.

Lenormand also wrote poetry, fiction, and essays on the theory of drama, including the autobiographical two-volume *Confessions d'un auteur dramatique* (1949). *Time Is a Dream* appears in Harlan Hatcher's collection of *Modern Continental Dramas* (1941) with an essay on Lenormand and a bibliography.

LÉOCADIA, a play in five acts by JEAN ANOUILH, produced in 1939 and published in 1942. Setting: a French château and park, 1930's.

One of the *"pièces roses,"* this play also appeared in English as *Time Remembered.*

Léocadia was a ballerina who captivated a prince a few days before her sudden death. The prince has kept her alive in his memory by setting up elaborate props amongst which he relives each moment with her. To break the spell, an old duchess, his aunt, hires Amanda, a little milliner who looks like Léocadia, to impersonate the dead ballerina. Eventually the prince falls in love with her, Amanda's reality overcoming his self-deceptive illusions.

LEONOV, Leonid Maksimovich (1899–), Russian novelist and playwright hailed by MAXIM GORKY in the 1920's as their country's most important young writer, first gained prominence with *Barsuki* (*The Badgers*, 1925). It is a novel, dramatized two years later, about partisans who hid like badgers during the Revolution, and it features two brothers who end up on opposing sides. Like his other novels—the most significant ones are *Vor* (*The Thief*, 1927; revised in 1959) and *Sot* (1931, published in English as *The Soviet River*)—it reflects Leonov's pessimism and his propensity for depicting horror, and evidences the profound influence of Dostoevsky. More important as a novelist than as a playwright, Leonov was concerned with psychological rather than the social and political developments usually portrayed by Soviet artists. This psychological emphasis is perceptible, too, in Leonov's plays, most particularly in *Polovchanskie sady* (THE ORCHARDS OF POLOVCHANSK, 1938) and *Nashestvie* (*Invasion*, 1942), his best dramas. *Invasion* (which won the Stalin Prize and was filmed and also made into an opera) is outstanding among the many Russian plays depicting the German attack on the Soviet Union. It features an introspective, sullen, Dostoevskian figure who, after prison and torture by the Russian NKVD, atones for his guilt with heroic partisan activities that ultimately lead to his capture by the German Gestapo and to his death. Leonov's superior artistry and his original manner of hewing to the Communist Party line set him apart from and above most Soviet writers.

The son of a peasant who became a poet and a journalist, Leonov was born and educated in Moscow. He joined the Red Army during the Civil War, and then lived and worked with his uncle, a locksmith. After his first play, the dramatization of *The Badgers,* came *Untilovsk* (1928), set in a primitive Siberian town peopled by "useless, harmful, and superfluous people," as *Pravda* (February 21, 1928) reviewed the Moscow Art Theatre's production of Leonov's satire of the evils he deplored. Other Leonov plays are *Provintsialnaya istoriya* (1928); *Usmirenie Badadoshkina* (1929); *Skutarevsky* (1934), Leonov's dramatization of his melodramatic 1932 novel about an aging scientist whose reactionary family plot against the Soviet Union and Skutarevsky, after he gains social consciousness; *Volk* (1938), also known as *Begstvo Sandukova; Lyonushka* (1943), a Stalin Prize war play, and *Obyknovenny chelovek* (1945), both full of Nazi horrors and Soviet heroism; *Vzyatie velikoshumsk* (*Chariot of Wrath,* 1944), a drama about a tank and its crew, revived in a new version at the Moscow Art Theatre in 1958; *Zolotaya kareta* (1957), a domestic drama about a mother who meets her lover of long ago, with whom she had once hoped to ride off in "a golden coach of love"; *Russki les* (*The Russian Forest,* 1959), Leonov's dramatization of his 1954 novel about the many facets of Russian life; *Begstvo mistera Mak-Kinly* (1961), a script adapted for the stage the same year and filmed in 1963; and *Metel* (1963), a new version of a play that first appeared in 1940.

Originally a "fellow traveler," Leonov eventually joined the Congress of Soviet Writers and became an officer in the State Literary Publishing House. *The Orchards of Polovchansk* was published in H. W. L. Dana's collection of *Seven Soviet Plays* (1946), and *Invasion* is one of the *Four Soviet War Plays* (1944). Brief prefaces there deal with Leonov's work and life, as do Gleb Struve's *Russian Literature 1917–1950* (1951), Vera Alexandrova's *A History of Soviet Literature* (1963), and Edward J. Brown's *Russian Literature Since the Revolution* (revised 1969).

LERBERGHE, Charles van (1861–1907), Belgian poet and playwright, with his mysterious SYMBOLIST drama about death, *Les Flaireurs* (1889), anticipated and may have helped inspire the drama of his Ghent classmate MAURICE MAETERLINCK. Lerberghe's other play—he was principally a poet—*Pan* (1906), is a "fantasy in the mood of Breughel." A farcical pantheistic satire, it portrays the god and his dancing pagan creatures in conflict with organized society represented by officials and clerics out to destroy them. Joyous and lively, the play was criticized as anticlerical and was seldom produced.

LERNER, Alan Jay (1918–), American producer, film-script writer, and lyricist, has authored a number of highly successful musicals, most notably MY FAIR LADY (1956), an adaptation of Shaw's PYGMALION. Another hit with music by Frederick Loewe was the Scottish fantasy *Brigadoon* (1947), but their *Camelot* (1960) was a disappointment.

LERNET-HOLENIA, Alexander (1897–), Austrian novelist and poet, and also a dramatist whose cynical farces portray the dissolution of the upper classes and the general breakdown of moral standards after World War I. His first play, *Demetrius* (1926), is historical: set in an atmosphere of brutality and horror, it depicts the career of the Polish usurper who reigned briefly after Boris Godunov's death. More characteristic are Lernet-Holenia's comedies. The most important of them is the Kleist Prize winner *Österreichische Komödie* (1927); it is set in an old castle whose inhabitants' depravity threatens to become a public scandal, which is only barely averted. Others are the farce *Ollapotrida* (1926), whose title "hotch-potch" refers to a series of adulteries portrayed in theatre and other settings; and *Glastüren* (1937), in which a young man discovers disturbing things in his fiancée's past, decides to bolt, but gains enough insight and humanity to agree to marry her and thus provide the play's final affirmative "yes."

Of ancient French-Belgian stock on his father's side, Lernet-Holenia grew up in Vienna. He lived also in South America as well as in St. Wolfgang (Salzkammergut), where he eventually settled down. He served as an officer in the cavalry during World War I and as *Dramaturg* of a military film company in World War II, in which he was wounded. Versatile and prolific in many forms of literature (including essays, biographies, and translations), Lernet-Holenia was influenced as a dramatist by the German classics and the *Jungwien* playwrights HERMANN BAHR, ARTHUR SCHNITZLER, and HUGO VON HOFMANNSTHAL. Other Lernet-Holenia's plays, all of which were noted for their theatricality, include the comedies *Die Frau des Potiphar* (1934), *Spanische Komödie* (1948), and *Finanzamt* (1955).

LESSING, Doris [May] (1919–), the Iranian-born English novelist who spent much of her life in Rhodesia, SOUTH AFRICA, turned to playwriting with *Mr. Dollinger* (1958). Like the plays that followed, it is an "angry" JOHN OSBORNE or ARNOLD WESKER kind of drama, with a female spokesman. It was followed by *Each His Own Wilderness* (1958), featuring a middle-aged radical who is disgusted with her "little petty-bourgeois" son, a supposedly typical, security-conscious, modern young man: "My God, the irony of it—that *we* should have given birth to a generation of little office-boys and clerks. . . . Little people who count their pensions before they're out of school"; but the futility of her own life of social protest and free love is suggested in the title. *The Truth About Billy Newton* (1960) echoes the title of Milne's THE TRUTH ABOUT BLAYDS; here, the old man whose life upsets his family is an angry scientist. *Play with a Tiger* (1962) resembles Mrs. Lessing's novel *The Golden Notebook* (1962); its heroine (again) is an older woman, an intellectual pitted against an attractive but oblivious American.

A study of her work is Dorothy Brewster's *Doris Lessing* (1965).

LESSON, THE (*La Leçon*), a one-act "comic drama" by EUGÈNE IONESCO, produced in 1951 and published in 1953. Setting: an apartment office-dining room in a small French town, c. 1950.

A circular "tragedy of language" like THE BALD SOPRANO, this is also a satiric dramatization of pedagogy, pendanticism, and the quest for ruthless domination.

The doorbell rings and the maid admits a lively and gay eighteen-year-old girl coming for her lesson. The timid, elderly Professor at first deferentially commends his Pupil, who is preparing for the "total doctorate," for her knowledge of geography (she correctly guesses that Paris is the capital of France). Gradually the lewd gleam in his eyes becomes more pronounced and his voice becomes more authoritative as he progresses with his bewildering mathematics lesson. "It's not enough to integrate, you must also disintegrate. That's the way life is," he insists as he tries to teach her to subtract. He rejects her astounding ability to multiply astronomical sums instantaneously—because she does it by rote: "The thing that counts is, above all, understanding." Then, becoming increasingly aggressive as his Pupil becomes increasingly passive and morose, the Professor launches into a philology lesson. He illustrates the subtle differences in the "neo-Spanish languages," showing how despite their "extraordinary resemblance" words in different languages differ because of their meanings to the speaker. The words "my grandmother" sound the same, but mean something else to every person. "When a Spaniard says 'I reside in the capital,' the word 'capital' does not mean at all the same thing that a Portuguese means when he says 'I reside in the capital,'" the Professor concludes, getting increasingly angry as the Pupil persists in her complaints about a violent toothache that is preventing her from following his instructions. Grabbing a large (but invisible) knife, he circles around his now languid Pupil "in a sort of scalp dance"—and finally plunges his knife into her. Both he and his victim simultaneously shout an orgasmic "Aaah!" The Pupil "flops onto the chair, her legs spread wide," while the Professor stands over her, his back to the audience. Breathing hard, the Professor finally comes to himself and in a panic shouts for the maid: "What have I done!" Sternly she recalls warning him that "Arithmetic leads to philology, and philology leads to crime " This is his fortieth victim today, she reveals, and angrily disarms him when he tries to knife her: "Little murderer! Bastard! You're disgusting! You wanted to do that to me? I'm not one of your pupils." But then the domineering maid indulgently agrees to get rid of the penitent Professor's forty corpses. To assuage his fears, she pins a swastika insignia on him ("That's good politics") and they go into the apartment, taking the corpse with them. Soon the doorbell rings. The maid returns and opens the door. "You are the new pupil? You have come for the lesson?" she asks the girl who comes in. And then, as she did in the beginning of the play, she adds: "The Professor is expecting you. I'll go tell him that you've come."

LEVY, Benn W[olfe] (1900–), English playwright and theatre director, was born in London, attended Oxford University, served in both world wars, became a managing director of a publishing house (Jarrolds), and was a Socialist member of Parliament from 1945 to 1950. His first play, *This Woman Business,* appeared in 1925. It was followed by many other popular but trifling plays, adaptations, and collaborations produced in both England and the United States. They include the popular farce *Springtime for Henry* (1931); *Hollywood Holiday* (1931, written with JOHN VAN DRUTEN); *Clutterbuck* (1946); *Return to Tyassi* (1950); *The Rape of the Belt* (1957), a slick comedy about Hercules's attempts to get the Amazon queen's belt, while the statuesque Hera and Zeus symbolize marital infidelity; *The Tumbler* (1960), a prolix and symbolic verse drama of sex and murder; and *Public and Confidential* (1966), a drama of hypocrisy in officialdom, subsequently produced as *The Member for Gaza.*

LEWIS, [Harry] Sinclair (1885–1951), major American novelist, helped dramatize some of his best-known fiction: *Dodsworth* (1934, with SIDNEY HOWARD), his 1929 novel (filmed in 1936) about a Midwestern businessman's European visit with his wife; and *It Can't Happen Here* (1936; with John C. Moffitt, ? –), his 1935 novel describing a Fascist anti-Utopia in the United States. Lewis also collaborated on *Jayhawker* (1934; with Lloyd Lewis, 1891–1949), an original but unimportant history play about Kansas.

LIARS, THE, a comedy in four acts by HENRY ARTHUR JONES, produced in 1897 and published in 1904. Setting: England, 1890's.

Jones's most successful play, *The Liars* for many years was esteemed in England as the greatest comedy of manners since the works of Sheridan. The climactic third act exemplifies Jones's comic dialogue and fine characterizations in a plot that has serious undertones. However, the *raisonneur's* attitudes now seem excessively Victorian, and his concluding sermon brings about an unbelievable resolution.

Act I. The attractive Lady Jessica Nepean, married to an elderly boor, is flirting with Edward Falkner. "A Puritan Don Quixote, mounted on Pegasus," Falkner has distinguished himself fighting slave traders in Africa, and now is lionized by society. A party of friends and relatives fear that the frivolous Lady Jessica will go too far with Falkner, who is deeply in love with her. Though her husband angrily warns her before he leaves, and though Falkner's elderly friend begs him to give up a hopeless and dishonorable quest, Lady Jessica coquettishly arranges an assignation with Falkner at a "delightful little riverside hotel" renowned for its French cooking.

Act II. The assignation turns out to be catastrophic. Shortly after they meet and before they start on the sumptuous dinner Falkner has ordered, her husband's brother sees the innocent couple and threatens to tell all. Lady Jessica panics: "I can't face it. I can't give up my world, my friends. Oh, what can I do?" When her sister happens by with her foolish husband, Lady Jessica implores her to testify that they were at the completely harmless dinner party.

Act III. The next day Lady Jessica and her friends rehearse elaborate alibis before her husband and his brother arrive to listen to the explanation. Their story becomes increasingly confused as more people must be drawn into the conspiracy. The women are exasperated by the men's incompetence, and the reluctant men, in turn, are overwhelmed by the women's facility in lying. When Falkner appears with a story that has since altered, Lady Jessica instructs him to tell the truth. He does so. Hers was no more "than a passing folly and amusement at my expense," his nothing less than "the deepest, deepest, deepest love and worship," he tells the husband. And he assures Lady Jessica, "I am at your service—always!"

Act IV. Moved by his love and fed up with her husband, Lady Jessica writes Falkner that she will be his. Falkner's elderly companion is preparing to return to Africa and rejoices in the love of a young widow who has at last accepted his suit. He cannot get Falkner to give Lady Jessica up, but he persuades her husband to try kindness with his wife. When Lady Jessica herself appears, he ultimately persuades her to return to her husband. "I've nothing to say in the abstract against running away with another man's wife," he tells her and Falkner; "but it has this one fatal defect in our country today—it won't work!" And he describes the inevitable scandal, social ostracism, and misery that would follow. Wistfully, Lady Jessica bids farewell to Falkner, who reluctantly agrees to return to Africa, and she goes to dinner with her repentant husband.

LICENSE, THE (*La patente*), a one-act play by LUIGI PIRANDELLO, published in 1918 and produced in 1919. Setting: a provincial town in southern Italy, early twentieth century.

This bitterly ironic comedy, originally produced in Sicilian dialect, dramatizes a short story Pirandello published in 1911.

Knowing the man will lose his case, a compassionate judge asks an embittered pauper to withdraw his suit against two influential townspeople. The plaintiff eloquently explains that, having gained the reputation of a sorcerer, he cannot get work and his family is now destitute. Losing his slander suit will officially certify his evil reputation and give him the "license" he now needs to make a living. He will use it to make people pay, as he does immediately by threatening some of the judge's colleagues with his "evil eye." Triumphantly he shows their money to the judge: "You see? And I don't even have my license yet! Get on with the trial! I'm rich! I'm rich!"

LIFE I GAVE YOU, THE (*La vita che ti diedi*), a tragedy in three acts by LUIGI PIRANDELLO, produced in 1923 and published in 1924. Setting: a lonely villa in the Tuscan countryside, 1923.

Written for Eleonora Duse and originally entitled *La madre,* this highly theatrical play is Pirandello's adaptation of a story he published in 1916. It and LAZARUS dramatize his philosophy of life and death.

Donn' Anna Luna's son, just come home after many years, dies. He returned completely different from the image she had carried in her mind since he had left as a boy. Now she finds solace in ignoring his death: "God wants my son to continue to live. Not, of course, the life that He gave him here, but that which I have always given him"—in her mind; that life "cannot be taken away from him as long as life endures in me." Her son had been passionately in love with a married woman, who reciprocated his feelings. Donn' Anna, imitating his handwriting, encourages the woman to leave her family and visit him. When the wife comes and reveals that she is carrying his child, the mother does not tell her of his death. She pretends that he has gone on a trip and will return: "I will teach you how not to go crazy, as I did for such a long time, as long as he was there with you. I used to feel him near me because I held him in my heart," she says, and tells the wife, "Never seek anything that does not come from within you." But when the wife's mother comes after her the following day, Donn' Anna's illusion is destroyed: "Now *I* am dying." As soon as her grandchild is born, she realizes in her despair, it too will start dying: it will change, and its life will be in the mother's memory. Though the wife would stay with her, Donn' Anna sends her away: "Go out into your life! So that you too may be consumed! You too are but suffering flesh and blood. For that, that is the real meaning of death." Life is perpetual change, and all change is death: "We are the poor, busy dead.—To torture ourselves—to console ourselves—to quiet ourselves—this is truly death."

LIFE OF EDWARD II OF ENGLAND (*Leben Eduards des Zweiten von England*), a history play in twenty-one scenes by BERTOLT BRECHT (with LION FEUCHTWANGER), published and produced in 1924. Setting: England, 1307–27.

This very free adaptation in irregular blank verse of Christopher Marlowe's *Edward II* (1590?) is a modernization that anticipated Brecht's later EPIC THEATRE. The collaboration of the authors has been described thus: "Brecht would bring him his version, and Feuchtwanger would tighten the construction and roughen the verse when it ran too smoothly" (Martin Esslin). The main plot follows Marlowe's; but it is simplified, and the motives and the viewpoint are altered.

When he becomes king, Edward II summons his favorite, Gaveston. Their friendship—almost openly homosexual—causes the power conflict between monarchy and nobility. The Church's and the queen's opposition to the king helps the nobles to effect the murder of Gaveston and the imprisonment of Edward. In their struggle, Earl Roger Mortimer is supported by Parliament and the barons. Edward, supported by the soldiers, spiritedly refuses to abdicate and finally is executed. His young son (later Edward III) avenges him by hanging Mortimer and imprisoning his own mother, the queen: "May God have mercy on them in this hour / So our generation need not atone for this sin. / As for us, may God / Not make corrupt our generation / From its mother's womb."

LIFE OF GALILEO (*Leben des Galilei*), a play in fifteen scenes by BERTOLT BRECHT (music by Hanns Eisler), produced in 1943 and published in 1955. Setting: Italy, 1609–37.

The first of the three extant versions of this play—one of Brecht's finest—was written in Denmark in 1938–39. In 1945–46 Brecht collaborated on an American adaptation (published in 1952) with Charles Laughton (1899–1962), its star in the 1947–48 productions. Brecht wrote his final version, based on the adaptation, in East Berlin shortly before his death. The principal difference among the three texts is the progressive attempt "to bring out the criminal element in the hero," Brecht told his Berliner Ensemble. In many short and quick-moving biographical scenes, Brecht stressed Galileo's betrayal, of science as well as of society, which was to culminate in the atom bomb. The characters and events are very freely adapted from history; in the story of Galileo, a comfort-loving glutton, Brecht reflected his own life. The scientist's very human sensuality provides the play's dramatic tension—and the hero's weakness as well as genius. The play has appeared also as *Galileo*.

Scenes 1 through 7. Galileo Galilei is washing himself in his Padua study. He demonstrates to his housekeeper's son, Andrea Sarti, how the earth revolves around the sun: "The millennium of faith is ended—this is the millennium of doubt." A Dutch invention of the telescope provides the discontented Galileo with funds, for he palms it off as his own invention. This fraud he justifies with his need for books and money to support his daughter: "And what about my appetite? I don't think well unless I eat well. Can I help it if I get my best ideas over a good meal and a bottle of wine?" But he improves the pirated telescope and uses it to make discoveries that displace the earth from the center of the universe. He is confident that he can prove his theories, and as for God's location in the new universe, Galileo believes Him to be "within ourselves, or nowhere." In Venice Galileo can work in relative freedom; yet he leaves for Florence, where he may be censored—but will be paid better. He demeans himself before the nine-year-old Prince Cosimo de Medici. "The only way a man like me can land a good job is by crawling on his stomach," he remarks; "I have no patience with a man who doesn't use his brains to fill his belly." At his fine house in Florence, Galileo flatters the nobility but shocks the Aristotelian court philosophers with his discoveries. Even the plague does not stop his labors, however, and he finally persuades the papal astronomer himself with his proofs. Nonetheless, the Church forbids Galileo to pursue or disseminate theories that question the cosmic order, and pronounces them heretical.

Scenes 8 through 13. An earnest young monk begs Galileo not to rob poor people of the "comforts of the Holy Scriptures," the only thing that gives meaning to their miserable lives. But the scientist's hard answers and passionate hunger for truth overwhelm the monk. Galileo wonders how long he can obey the Church and remain silent: "I have to boast about every new discovery like a lover, like a drunkard, like a traitor." And after eight years he finally disobeys. Even though the people publicly vulgarize his theories and his daughter's chance of marriage is ruined, Galileo persists: "My intention is not to prove that I was right but to find out whether I was right." The new pope is expected to be open-minded, for he is a mathematician, a cardinal who has been sympathetic to Galileo. Each layer of papal raiment now placed upon this new pope weakens his objections to the Grand Inquisitor's urgings to stop Galileo's work; when fully robed, Pope Urban VIII helplessly accedes: "Let it be clearly understood: he is not to be tortured. (*Pause.*) At the very most, he may be shown the instruments." Galileo's daughter, his assistants, and his friends tensely await the outcome of the trial. Especially the monk and Andrea Sarti, now an adult, cannot believe that Galileo will betray them, science, and humanity. When his recantation is publicly announced they are crushed. Galileo shuffles in and Andrea becomes hysterical: "Wino! Glutton! Have you saved your precious skin? Unhappy the land that breeds no hero!" Galileo answers quietly, "Unhappy the land that needs a hero!"

Scenes 14 and *15*. Imprisoned by the Inquisition in a comfortable house near Florence, the aging and almost blind Galileo is living with his daughter, now a nagging old maid who makes him compose repentant pious tracts. Still angry, Andrea visits Galileo before leaving Italy. Gradually he learns that Galileo has been writing the *Discorsi*, which the Inquisition has been confiscating as each page is completed. But Galileo has rewritten it every night, and now offers Andrea the hidden manuscript. As in a trance, Andrea takes it. "This will be the foundation of a new physics," he realizes. Shamefacedly he confesses having unjustly calumniated Galileo, who has outsmarted the authorities. But Galileo does not accept this whitewash of his cowardice. "Had one man put up a fight it could have had wide repercussions," he now knows. His own opportunity was unique, but "I surrendered my knowledge to the authorities, to use it, no, to abuse it, as it suits their ends. I have betrayed my profession," Galileo adds: "Any man who does what I have done must not be tolerated in the ranks of science." He also has betrayed what could have been an age of enlightenment, and therefore the generations to come: "This age of ours turned out to be a whore, spattered with blood. Maybe new ages look like blood-spattered whores." Finished with his self-denunciation, Galileo becomes preoccupied with devouring a goose. Later, at an Italian customs house, Andrea fails to persuade some children that a neighbor woman cannot be a witch. But he succeeds in smuggling Galileo's book across the border.

LIFE OF MAN, THE (*Zhizn cheloveka*), a drama in five scenes and a prologue by LEONID ANDREEV, published in 1906 and produced in 1907. Setting: dark rooms, a hall, a tavern.

This "was the first SYMBOLIC drama written in Russia," according to V. V. Brusyanin in Andreev's *Plays* (1915), and Konstantin Stanislavsky describes its production in *My Life in Art* (1924). It is a gloomy allegory in which Man (none of the characters has a name) is depicted from his birth to his death.

An omniscient but coldly indifferent Gray Figure (God or Fate) in the prologue comments on Man's limitations, and reappears throughout with a shrinking candle that symbolizes Man's life. Old women cackle maliciously as Man is born. Subsequent scenes portray him, with his wife, as a poor young man impudently challenging the mysterious Gray Figure, and dreaming of wealth and fame; achieving these, as depicted in a sumptuous but lifeless ball attended by Guests, Friends, and Enemies; falling from pride and wealth into poverty; experiencing tragedy when his son dies, and impotently assaulting the Gray Figure, who melts into space; and finally drinking himself into a forgetful stupor and dying, amidst a bacchanal of misshapen drunkards. In an alternate last scene, Man dies amidst his eagerly waiting Heirs.

LIFE WITH FATHER, a play in three acts by HOWARD LINDSAY and RUSSEL CROUSE, produced in 1939 and published in 1940. Setting: the morning room of a Madison Avenue residence in New York, a summer in the late 1880's.

This still-amusing dramatization of Clarence Day's 1935 classic collection of humorous sketches played in New York until 1947 for over 3,200 consecutive performances (the longest recorded Broadway run), and had a major revival in 1967. The same authors' less successful *Life with Mother* ran in the 1948–49 season. Both plays genially portray Day's mercurial father, forever outsmarted by his clever but affectionate wife. It is a nostalgic storybook portrait of a Victorian family.

Vinnie Day breaks in the newest of their ever-changing maids as Father (Clarence Day, Sr.) complains about his tailor, city politics, and his wife's expenditures—which he would not mind so much if she would only keep proper accounts. He raps on

Life With Father. Vinnie (Dorothy Stickney) and "Father" (HOWARD LINDSAY). New York, 1939. (*Brown Brothers*)

the floor, summoning the cook to be praised for a dish, and later to be scolded for her coffee ("slops"). After breakfast with their four red-haired boys, Father's temper flares up again when Vinnie invites house guests, and he tries to fend off her and the rector's appeal for a sizable contribution to the church. Incidentally Father reveals that he was never baptized. Though this horrifies Vinnie, who begins to wonder about the validity of their wedding, Father has no intention of doing anything about it: "Damn it Vinnie, we have four children! If we're not married now we never will be!" His oldest son, in the meantime, has fallen in love, and Father gives him a lecture about women. Despite its length, it disappointingly adds up merely to an exhortation: "Be firm!" When the boy wears his inherited suit, he finds himself assuming Father's attitudes—thus offending the girl. To get money for a new suit he sells patent medicine, some of which he slips into his mother's tea—whereupon she gets seriously ill. Father is deeply moved by his wife's sickness and promises to be baptized. Later he reneges: "We all thought you were dying, so naturally I said that to make you feel better"; since it was his gesture that cured her, "it seems to me pretty ungrateful of you to press this matter any further." But Vinnie quietly makes preparations. "I never had any trouble with God until you stirred Him up!" Father complains, as Vinnie gets him ready. Leaving, they pass their son, dressed in his new suit and kneeling before his beloved. "Going to the office, Father?" the embarrassed boy asks. "No! I'm going to be baptized, damn it!" Father replies, and stalks out. Vinnie nods triumphantly, and follows.

LIGHT-O'-LOVE (*Liebelei*), a play in three acts by ARTHUR SCHNITZLER, produced in 1895 and published in 1896. Setting: Vienna, 1890's.

One of Schnitzler's most popular plays and made into an opera (music by Franz Neumann) in 1910, this play has also been translated as *Amours,* as *Game of Love,* as *The Reckoning*, and as *Playing with Love*. Despite a superficial sentimentality, it is as trenchant a dissection of contemporary Viennese morality as HANDS AROUND. Christine is the best of Schnitzler's many portrayals of a "*süsse Mädel*" ("sweet young girl").

Act I. Young Fritz Loheimer has two affairs. One, with a society matron (who never appears on stage), is tempestuous and melodramatic. The other is with Christine Vyring, a poor violinist's daughter. Fritz tells his friend how he "longed for such an affection as hers, so sweet and quiet, that would hover about me and soothe me, and help me to recover from these everlasting irritations and torments." Soon Christine and his friend's sweetheart visit them, and the couples have a party. Christine tells Fritz that he is everything to her: "I can't imagine an hour ever coming when I wouldn't want to see you. As long as I live." But when he begs her not to say such things she sadly says, "Have no fear, Fritz—I know this can't be for always." Though timid, she keeps asking Fritz who the other woman is for whom he so often deserts her. The party is interrupted by an ominous caller. Sending the others out of the room, Fritz talks with and is scornfully challenged by the husband of his mistress. Later, oblivious of the interview, the others merrily leave, and Fritz remains behind, troubled.

Act II. An interfering neighbor tries to persuade Christine to give up Fritz. But Christine's father wants her to enjoy her youth, and she leaves for her date with Fritz. Soon she returns: Fritz has stood her up. Her friend is irritated with Christine's putting up with such treatment and taking her first love affair so seriously: "He's a man like the rest, and the whole manpack isn't worth a single bad hour." But Fritz soon arrives, and in a tender scene savors Christine's love and the cozy simplicity of her room—her pictures, her books, the view from her window. Full of emotion he tells her how sheltered he feels with her, and that he really loves her. Though he refuses to confide in her and soon tears himself away, she is overjoyed: "I've been happy for once, and that's all I ask of life. I only want you to know that and to believe that I never—loved any man before you, and that I never shall love any man—when you get tired of me—" Deeply moved, he begs her, "Don't say it, don't say it—it sounds—so sweet." Then his friend takes him home; he must prepare for a duel she knows nothing about. Fritz leaves full of premonitions, and tells his friend: "I'm almost ready to believe that my happiness is here."

Act III. A few days pass, Fritz has not returned, and Christine is heartbroken. Her father knows that he has been killed. He tries to prepare Christine, telling her that her love was not happy and that she has much to live for: "Just think how beautiful, how wonderful life is. Just think how many things there are to give you joy, how much youth and how much happiness still lies before you." Christine is totally overcome when she learns that Fritz was killed in a duel over another woman. And she is not consoled when her friends say that he loved her: "Love? He? I was nothing to him but a pastime—and he died for another woman! And I—I worshiped him! Didn't he know that ... I gave him everything I could give, that I would have died for him—that he was my God and my bliss of Heaven?" Her father cannot console her, and her friends, unable to understand such love, try to prevent her visiting Fritz's grave until she is calmer. "Tomorrow? When I shall be calmer? And in a month completely consoled, eh? And in six months I can laugh again, can I?" She laughs shrilly, refusing to play the conventional "game of love": "And then when will the next lover come?" Wildly she rushes out to his grave, and "I won't pray there—no." Her father sinks to the floor, sobbing, "She won't come back!"

LIGHT SHINES IN DARKNESS, THE (*I svet vo tme svetit*), a play in five acts by LEO TOLSTOI, published in 1911. Setting: a Russian country house and various places in Moscow at the end of the nineteenth century.

Tolstoi conceived this posthumously produced play in the 1880's, continued to work on it in 1900 and 1902, but never completed it. Expressly autobiographical ("my struggle, my faith, my sufferings," Tolstoi wrote a friend), this play has greatly fascinated his readers, though some have found it wanting as drama. BERNARD SHAW called it "Tolstoi's masterpiece," a play in which "he turns his deadly touch suicidally on himself" (*London Mercury*, May 1921). But Tolstoi meant his prototype Nikolai to represent the rightness of his beliefs. This is suggested too by the title from John 1:5 ("The light shineth in darkness and the darkness comprehendeth it not"), which echoes Tolstoi's earlier play, THE POWER OF DARKNESS.

Act I. The family of Nikolai Ivanovich Saryntsov, a wealthy landowner, are increasingly perturbed by his actions and attitudes. Appalled by unchristian social inequalities and injustice, Nikolai is thinking of giving up his lands and urges his son to be a ploughman rather than a government official or an army officer. His wife Marya Ivanovna loves Nikolai but worries about her children's future. Her sister fans Marya's opposition to Nikolai, who is persuading even the young local priest that man should deny the worldly Church and live by the Gospels and the Sermon on the Mount. Nikolai tries to free needy peasants convicted for cutting trees off his land. "Land belongs to everyone," he insists, and if in need he would act as a condemned peasant did; "as I wish to do to others as I wish them to do to me, I cannot condemn him, but do what I can to save him." One should give everything away: "Therein lies the whole teaching of Christ." Man need not worry about his animal needs, he continues; "the flesh draws him to live for itself, while the spirit of light draws him to live for God and for others." He argues for faith, not in the compromising Church, not "in what other people tell us, but faith in what we arrive at ourselves, by our own thought, our own reason—faith in God," in "the teaching of love and truth," and against the "absurdities and meannesses" preached by the Church. His wife does not know what to do about the various problems arising from his new course of life. But she refuses to take over the estate, which Nikolai offers her so that he himself, at least, will not be responsible for injustice.

Acts II and III. Nikolai suggests to his wife that they give their land to the peasants, retaining for themselves only enough to work and subsist on. "I do not think that Christianity calls upon us to ruin our families," a visiting princess remarks. Nikolai converts the princess's son Boris, who is to marry Nikolai's daughter, publicly bests a high churchman in a theological disputation, and turns his estate over to his wife. In Moscow, he tries to work as a carpenter. He is followed by the young priest, who has gotten into trouble with the Church because of Nikolai's influence on him, and the princess. She angrily tells Nikolai that he has ruined her son, for, inducted into the army, Boris refused to serve and was arrested: "What cursed Christianity it is that makes people suffer and perish! I hate this Christianity of yours." In the army, Boris adamantly sticks by his pacifist convictions, confounding a general, a military priest, and a doctor. Though the visiting Nikolai suggests that he obey his mother—if he can—Boris persists. He is disciplined by confinement to a lunatic ward.

Act IV. In Moscow a year later, Nikolai's wife is giving an engagement party for their daughter, who has reluctantly given up Boris for a more worldly man. Nikolai has failed as a laborer and is ashamed of his present life of luxury (which he considers depravity) in his wife's house. He is ready to leave again, but Marya, who loves him though she cannot understand him, begs him to remain. The princess arrives, beside herself with anger and grief: Boris is being removed to the Disciplinary Battalion. Nikolai promises to try to help her. Alone and realizing how all his followers except Boris have recanted, he wonders: "Can it be that I have been mistaken? Mistaken in believing in Thee? No! Father, help me!"

Act V was never written. Tolstoi's notes for it sketch out a NATURALISTIC scene in the Disciplinary Battalion, where Boris explains the Gospels and is led off to be flogged after his mother tries to visit him. She unsuccessfully petitions the tsar for his release, and Boris dies. Dispirited, Nikolai doubts himself and deplores his weakness: "Evidently God does not wish me to be his servant. He has many other servants—and can accomplish His will without me, and he who realizes this is at peace." As he prays, the princess rushes in and shoots him. He tells the assembling crowds that he shot himself. The presence of pacifist dissenters makes him rejoice, in death, "that the fraud of the Church is exposed, and that he has understood the meaning of life."

LIGHTNIN', a play in a prologue and three acts by WINCHELL SMITH and FRANK BACON, published and produced in 1918. Setting: Nevada, and the Nevada-California state line; early twentieth century.

This multicharactered "pleasant Western, minus cowboys, miners, or shooting," as John Chapman described it in *S.R.O.: The Most Successful Plays of the American Stage* (1944), was a record-breaking Broadway success. Until his death, Frank Bacon himself played the amusing title character. Inspired by Rip Van Winkle, he is a homespun scamp nicknamed "Lightnin'" for his slow speech and movement.

Foiled in his attempts to arrest a young log chopper, the Nevada sheriff runs into him in Lightnin' Bill Jones's hotel. It is situated right on the state line, and the youth again evades arrest by going to the other side of the room, which is in California. Lightnin', a genial old loafer fond of lying and liquor, gets into trouble with his wife, who is running the place. A crook has talked her into selling the hotel, whose Nevada part is thriving with guests awaiting their divorces. The young log chopper, who is in love with Lightnin's adopted daughter, warns him against the swindler by whom he too has been cheated. But the hard-working Mrs. Jones and the daughter trust the villain. Indignant at Lightnin's defiance of her, Mrs. Jones sues Lightnin' for a divorce on the grounds of "failure to provide, habitual intoxication and intolerable cruelty." At court, the crook is not able to prove Lightnin' a liar when he boasts: "I drove a swarm of bees across the plains in the dead of winter. And never lost a bee. Got stung twice." The log chopper, handling the defense, saves the day by exposing the villain. He reconciles Lightnin' and his wife, and wins their daughter. As the young couple embrace, Lightnin' blithely takes personal credit for the happy outcome: "I fixed that."

LILAR, Suzanne (1901–), Belgian playwright, achieved success in 1947 with the Paris premiere of her *Le Burlador* (*The Burlador*). Its title's "mocker" (or "joker") is Don Juan, here characterized as deceiving and punishing himself no less than the women he conquers, but becoming heroic, finally, when able to be really faithful—thus vitiating his essential legendary character and inviting death. Mystical implications also underlie Lilar's *Tous les chemins mènent au ciel* (1947), whose protagonist is a nun in fourteenth-century Ghent; and *Le Roi lépreux* (1951), a play-within-a-play about a group of actors performing a play about Baudouin IV of Jerusalem, a king who died of leprosy at twenty-five.

Lilar was born in Ghent and practiced law before turning to playwriting. She and her husband, a notable barrister who repeatedly served as Belgium's Minister of Justice, had a daughter, the prominent novelist Françoise Mallet-Joris. Suzanne Lilar published a study of drama that appeared in English, *The Belgian Theater Since 1890* (3rd edition, 1962); it has a note on its author's life and work by the translator, Jan-Albert Goris. The latter also wrote an introduction to *The Burlador,* published with Lilar's comments on it in *Two Great Belgian Plays, about Love* (1966).

LILIOM, "A Legend in Seven Scenes and a Prologue" by FERENC MOLNÁR, published and produced in 1909. Setting: Budapest and "the Beyond," early twentieth century.

Molnár's best-known play, *Liliom* is a sophisticated justification of a temper fit during which, his first wife charged, Molnár slapped their daughter. The love of Liliom and Julie, which resembles that of Ibsen's PEER GYNT and Solveig, is as real as it is inarticulate and unconventional. Molnár portrays the ambiguity of human feelings with humor and pathos, sentimentality and cynicism, brutality and romance. But the most striking

Liliom, Scene 1. Policemen (Joseph Macauley and Francis De Sales) warn Julie (Ingrid Bergman) about Liliom (Burgess Meredith). New York, 1940. (*Vandamm Photo. Theatre Collection, New York Public Library*)

dramaturgical shift is from NATURALISM to fantasy (with touches of EXPRESSIONISM), in the depiction of the incorrigible Liliom's concept of the hereafter. Frequently revived after an unsuccessful premiere, *Liliom* was originally produced in England as *The Daisy* (1920), and made into a musical, Rodgers and Hammerstein's CAROUSEL (1945).

Prologue. Before the merry-go-round in a cheap amusement park, the barker Andreas Zavocki, nicknamed Liliom ("Lily" is Hungarian slang for a roughneck and a ne'er-do-well), swaggers, cuddles the girls, and threatens their protesting escorts.

Scene 1. The circus proprietress has noticed that Liliom fondled Julie Zeller, a naïve servant who came with her friend, an even simpler girl from the provinces. Furious, the jealous proprietress forbids Julie ever to return. But Liliom, understanding the reason for her anger and attracted to Julie, stands up for her and is fired. While he collects his things, her friend realizes that Julie is in love with Liliom. "Now you have a lover—and I'm free to speak," the country girl confesses, and Julie laughs at her artless description of her own "uniformed lover," a porter. Liliom returns and, irritated because he lost his job, gruffly asks, "What do you suppose I want with two of you?" Julie alone remains with him, and they sit down on a bench as night falls. Julie too is now jobless, because of her failure to return at the appointed hour. "God, you're dumb! I don't need to be alone. I can have all the girls I want. Not only servant girls like you," Liliom tells her. "I know, Mister Liliom," Julie replies gently: "I stayed because you've been so good to me." Policemen warn her that Liliom is a seducer and a fleecer of servant girls. But Julie chooses to stay with him. When Liliom asks her if she is not afraid he will take her money, she replies, "I haven't got any. But if I had—I'd—I'd give it to you—I'd give it all to you." No, she does not love him, she says; but when Liliom asks why she stays on, Julie can only reply, "Um—nothing." She will never get married, though she would marry him—"if I loved you." Amidst many silences, Liliom remarks, "I think—that even a low-down good-for-nothing—can make a man of himself." His boss would take him back, but Julie quietly urges him, "Don't go back—to her—"

Scene 2. A few months later Julie and Liliom, now married, live in her aunt's house. After Julie's friend tells her of the progress of her own love affair with the porter, she asks about Julie's life. Liliom has not been working, but he has been swaggering around, the aunt grumbles. "He's unhappy because he isn't working," Julie explains: "That's really why he hit me on Monday." The friend is indignant: "Liliom doesn't support you, and he beats you—he thinks he can do whatever he likes just because he's Liliom. He's a bad one." But Julie thinks "he's not really bad." The circus proprietress comes to offer Liliom his old job—"the only thing you're fit for. You are an artist, not a respectable married man." Her blandishments almost persuade Liliom—until Julie shyly tells him that she is going to have a baby. Overwhelmed by the thought of fatherhood, Liliom summarily rebuffs the proprietress. But he approaches a disreputable companion about a planned robbery: "This scheme—about the cashier of the leather factory—there's money in it—" Then, alone and desperate, he shouts, "I'm going to be a father!"

Scene 3. Liliom and his companion discuss the projected holdup, pretending to learn a new song whenever the suspicious Julie comes by. "O God, what a dirty life I'm leading—God, God!" Liliom suddenly exclaims, and decides to go through with the job. However, he worries about "the next world—when I come up before the Lord God—what'll I say then?" He pockets a big kitchen knife and they go out, though Julie tries to search and obstruct him. While Julie is preoccupied with her fear for Liliom, her friend comes to introduce her fiancé, amidst much bashfulness and many awkward silences.

Scene 4. On a railroad embankment Liliom and his companion await their victim. They play cards, and Liliom loses his share of the expected loot. As he starts arguing, the cashier appears. Their robbery fails; his companion escapes, but Liliom, determined not to be caught and sent to prison, laughs madly, utters Julie's name, and plunges the knife into his chest.

Scene 5. "I beat you . . . only because I can't bear to see any one crying," he gasps to Julie as he is brought in on a stretcher. Dying, he explains that he tried to do something for Julie. "Tell the baby—I wasn't much good—" He advises her to marry the elderly carpenter who had proposed to her, and he insists he was right to beat Julie, though he adds: "Nobody's right—but they all think they're right— A lot they know!" Then Liliom asks Julie to hold his hand tight—and he dies. Her aunt, her friend, the policemen—all present tell Julie she is well rid of him. She does not contradict them. Alone with the dead Liliom, however, she caresses him tenderly. "Now I'll tell you—you bad, quick-tempered, rough, unhappy, wicked—*dear* boy," she says, and continues, in broken snatches, until she concludes with great love in her voice: "It was wicked of you to beat me—on the breast and on the head and face—but you're gone now . . . sleep peacefully, Liliom . . . I love you—I never told you before—I was ashamed—but now I've told you—I love you." She gently declines the carpenter's suit, and leaves. Music starts, and two solemn men arrive. "We are God's police," they announce, and then order Liliom to rise and go with them: "These people suppose that when they die all their difficulties are solved."

Scene 6. In a celestial police court, Liliom is tried along with other suicides. When his case comes up, Liliom is ashamed to say he loved Julie, but he admits he hit her "because she was right [and] I couldn't answer her—and I got mad." He refuses to say he is sorry, and insists he would not act differently if he had another chance. He is sentenced to burn for sixteen years, "until your child is full grown. By that time your pride and your stubbornness will have been burnt out of you."

Scene 7. Sixteen years later, in a small tumble-down house, Julie and her daughter chat with her old friend and the latter's husband, now prosperous and pompous. After they leave, Liliom appears, followed by the celestial police. Taken for a beggar, he accepts some soup. He tells the daughter that he used to know her father—a bully who "even hit your dear little mother." "That's a lie," Julie exclaims, and angrily castigates the "beggar" for slandering the girl's father: "He was always good to me." Liliom gives his daughter a star he stole for her from heaven, but the frightened women send him off. Liliom begs his daughter: "Miss—please, Miss—I've got to do something good—a good deed—" When she peremptorily extends her hand and tells him to get out, Liliom sharply slaps her hand. She is bewildered, for—amazingly—it does not hurt. Julie sends her indoors and asks Liliom who he is. "A poor, tired beggar," he replies. Julie is deeply shaken as he turns away. The girl comes out again, still puzzled about how it was possible to be hit hard and yet not be hurt. "It is possible, dear," Julie explains, "that someone may beat you and beat you and beat you—and not hurt you at all.—"

LINDBERGH'S FLIGHT (*Lindberghflug*, also titled *Flug des Lindberghs*), a didactic radio play for boys and girls, in seventeen sections, by BERTOLT BRECHT (music by Kurt Weill and Paul Hindemith), produced in 1929 and published in 1930. Setting: concert platform.

This is one of the *Lehrstücke* (didactic pieces) performed at the post-World War I Baden-Baden festivals, and one of Brecht's early collaborations with Weill. Because of Charles Lindbergh's later politics, Brecht deleted the flyer's name and changed the title to *Der Ozeanflug* (*The Flight over the Ocean*).

A chorus describes Lindbergh's preparation for his 1927 transatlantic flight. Reports of his flight come from land and sea. Fog, Snowstorm, and Fatigue try to defeat him. Lindbergh battles against and reflects about these obstacles of the Primitive and the evil unknown (God). His arrival marks the triumphant victory of scientific progress, "our ingenuity of steel."

LINDSAY,* Howard (1889–1968), American playwright, actor, and director, did his most notable work with RUSSEL CROUSE. Their collaboration—which ended only with Crouse's death in 1966—reached its high point in LIFE WITH FATHER (1939), in which Lindsay and his wife, Dorothy Stickney, starred for five years. Another collaboration with Crouse, STATE OF THE UNION (1945), was awarded the Pulitzer Prize. In 1959 both authors won a special joint Antoinette Perry ("Tony") Award for their twenty-five-year "distinguished achievement in the theater" and for their "long, successful collaboration in playwriting."

* Illustration on page 460.

Lindsay, the team's older member, was born in Waterford, New York. He grew up with his mother's family, for the father was a charming drifter. Briefly Lindsay attended Harvard University but, despising it, he transferred to the American Academy of Dramatic Art in New York. After graduation he began touring the vaudeville circuits and various road companies. He acted, directed such hits as Kaufman and Connelly's DULCY, and himself wrote plays, of which the most notable is the comedy *Young Uncle Dudley* (1929). He had become moderately successful—his *A Slight Case of Murder* (1935), written with DAMON RUNYON, was to become a popular hit—when he teamed up with Crouse, whose work he had for some time admired.

Both men, already in their forties and established, worked well together. They preferred to write comedy with a bite, but however amusing, their satire was too genial to be offensive. Beginning with their revision of a Cole Porter musical, *Anything Goes* (1934), they collaborated on some fifteen plays and codirected a number of others. Their hits include *Call Me Madam* (1950), the Irving Berlin musical spoof of Perle Mesta, whom President Truman had appointed minister to Luxembourg; *The Great Sebastians* (1955), a "melodramatic comedy" featuring a pair of vaudevillians (played by Alfred Lunt and Lynn Fontanne) amidst postwar Communist intrigue in Prague; and the immensely popular—if cloying—musical about the Trapp family of singers, *The Sound of Music* (1959, with Richard Rodgers and OSCAR HAMMERSTEIN II). Lindsay and Crouse also established the New Dramatists Committee to assist promising playwrights as well as the Dramatists' Play Service, which makes bound playscripts easily available for rehearsal use; and they were active in many other important causes.

Lindsay and Crouse's was the longest and most successful of American playwrights' collaborations.

LINKLATER, Eric (1899–   ), the versatile Scottish writer, is better known as a novelist, biographer, and historian than as a playwright. But he wrote a few dramas which manifest his characteristic wit and gift for satire and fantasy: *Crisis in Heaven* (1944), *Love in Albania* (1949), *The Mortimer Touch* (1952), and *Breakspear in Gascony* (1959). Linklater was born in Dounby, Orkney Islands (Scotland), and traveled frequently and widely. Two of Linklater's books are autobiographical, *The Man on My Back* (1941) and *A Year of Space* (1953).

LIOLÀ, a "country comedy" in three acts by LUIGI PIRANDELLO, produced in 1916 and published in 1917. Setting: the Sicilian countryside, near Agrigento, 1916.

This dialect play was published simultaneously in its original Sicilian and in Italian translation. Though typically Pirandellian in its preoccupation with reality and illusion (Simone's fluctuating views on his paternity), it is atypical in its spirited comic treatment of this theme.

Act I. Peasant girls are singing happily as they shell almonds for rich old Uncle Simone Palumbo, young Mita's husband. Stingy and sour, he is particularly nasty to Mita, whom he blames for their being childless. Soon Nico Schillaci—known as Liolà—comes home from work, singing as usual. This gay, rustic Don Juan lives contentedly with his mother, who takes care of the children of various girls who could not resist his charms. One of his conquests is Tuzza Azzara, the daughter of Simone's cousin. Tuzza envies Simone's wife Mita her wealthy husband as well as Liolà's continuing interest in her: "Must the little guttersnipe have all those things? Wasn't a rich husband enough? Without a gallant lover?" Pregnant with Liolà's child, Tuzza is angry when, for once conscience-stricken, he asks her mother for her hand. Instead, she and her mother scheme to ruin Mita and get her husband's money: Tuzza persuades Simone to claim paternity of her child (thus proving his virility) and eventually make it his heir.

Act II. Though no one really believes Simone, the scheme works. Mita, humiliated and maltreated by her husband, is threatened with being supplanted by Tuzza and the child in her own home. Liolà tells her that confessing his paternity of Tuzza's child would not help: "Who will believe it? Well, possibly they all will. Except [Simone]. He'll never believe it—for the good reason that he doesn't wish to." However, he shrewdly uses the opportunity to win Mita and get back at Tuzza and her mother for scheming at his expense: "No: this outrage must not stand, Mita. *You* shall punish them. God himself bids you do so. The wretch mustn't make use of me to bring about your ruin!" Simone's timely appearance with boasts and insults to his wife drives Mita to yield to Liolà.

Act III. Tuzza and her mother crow about Mita's eventually total defeat: "The home is where the children are." However, Simone soon brings news that Mita is now pregnant. Preparing for the birth of his "legitimate" son, he retracts his paternity claim of Tuzza's child: "What I did was charity, that's all. But with my wife, I was in on it, I was in on it!" Their taunts that he has been deceived by Liolà do not move him or Mita, who answers the angry Tuzza's sneer, that it took her a long time to have a child, with: "I tarried, it is true; but I was not found wanting. You went ahead; I followed after." Upon suggesting that Tuzza have Liolà take care of his child, Simone is momentarily stunned by her question, "Which child?" Mita calmly replies for him: "Why yours, my dear! Which do you think? I have my husband who cannot doubt me." But Liolà refuses to marry Tuzza now: "I did want her once, it's true. It was my conscience, nothing else. I knew that, marrying her, all the songs would die in my heart. —Then Tuzza didn't want me . . . [and] now you've lost the game." He does offer to have the child eventually join those his mother already takes care of for him. When the furious Tuzza attacks him, he laughingly wards her off and breaks into a new song.

LION AND THE JEWEL, THE, a play in three parts by WOLE SOYINKA, published and produced in 1963. Setting: a contemporary Nigerian village.

This is a light but lively and delightful satire, in poetry and prose and with folk music and dance, of both the old and the new Africa. It was produced at London's Royal Court Theatre.

The tragicomic young village schoolmaster is eager to marry "the jewel" Sidi, the pert and vain local belle. But determined on Westernizing society, he will not pay the traditional bride price for Sidi, who ridicules his new ways, including his "strange unhealthy mouthing," the "licking of my lips with yours." Large photographs of Sidi appear in a magazine and make her more renowned than the village chief. Piqued, this wily old man ("the lion") attempts to seduce Sidi, who turns down his invitation. But when his head wife tells Sidi that the aged chieftain is impotent Sidi goes to tease him. On her visit the old man tricks her. A bit shamefacedly Sidi announces the next morning that she will marry without bride money after all. "Out of my way, book-nourished shrimp," she exclaims, shoving the teacher away, and asks the village maidens to "Come, sing to me of seeds / Of children, sired of the lion stock."

LIST OF ASSETS, A (*Spisok blagodeyanni*), a play in eight scenes by YURI KARLOVICH OLESHA, published and produced in 1931. Setting: Soviet Russia and Paris at the end of the first Five Year Plan, early 1930's.

Like Afinogenov's FEAR, this widely discussed play is a portrayal of the intelligentsia's dilemma during the early years of Communism, their allegiance wavering between the new and the traditional society and values. Olesha's play is a mixture of NATURALISM, conventional Soviet exhortation and melodrama, and SYMBOLISM—including such characteristic Olesha symbols as Charlie Chaplin, Hans Christian Andersen's Ugly Duckling, and Hamlet. The two performances of the recorder scene of Shakespeare's *Hamlet* reflect the actress-protagonist's ambivalent attitude toward the new regime and her eventual acceptance of it. The failure of Lola (Lyolya in Russian), the playwright's spokesman and alter ego, reflects that of Olesha himself.

The famous Russian actress Lola Goncharova has just completed a performance of *Hamlet,* and a discussion of the play follows. In response to critical questions from the audience, Lola declares —while the manager blows his whistle to stop her —that Soviet plays are "sketchy, false, devoid of imagination, heavy-handedly obvious"; that she finds it "very difficult to be a citizen of the new world"; and that—like Hamlet—"an artist must keep thinking slowly." The audience requests that she replay the scene in which Guildenstern is goaded to play the recorder (the obvious message being that though the state "would pluck out the heart of my mystery," the artist, like Hamlet, is not a pipe—"you cannot play upon me"). There is no applause. To a final question Lola replies that she definitely intends to return after her projected trip to France. At her farewell party, Lola confesses to a friend that she is "a woman from the old world engaged in a debate with myself": she yearns for such old concepts as "friendship" and "glory," and looks forward to seeing Chaplin films again; on the other hand, she recognizes the blessings of the new society, and she keeps a notebook that contains "the whole truth": a list of Soviet "crimes against the individual"—as well as "a list of assets."

In the Paris she so eagerly wished to see, Lola discovers "the ancient stones of Europe" she had yearned for. But gradually she also discovers the cancer in the capitalist world. An émigré editor is amazed at the freedom allowed her: "She produced *Hamlet*... in a country where art has been reduced to the level of propaganda for breeding pigs or digging silage ditches. The Soviet regime has treated her as its pet." He sees to it that she is tempted into buying a beautiful dress on credit to attend a banker's ball, steals her notebook, and publishes its compromising part, her list of Soviet "crimes." To pay for the dress, Lola auditions for a capitalist music-hall manager for a part, and suggests that she act the Hamlet-Guildenstern scene. The manager offers to let her do it alone, by playing the recorder and thereupon swallowing it. Then, to titillate the audience, he proposes that she turn around and "start blowing [something cheerful] into the recorder from what we might call your [bared] reverse end." Disgusted and disheartened as she walks out, Lola gives money to a tramp who looks exactly like Chaplin. Various émigré plots almost succeed, but Lola now comes to understand the beauty of the Soviet world. She confesses her errors to a Soviet delegation, and helps foil the émigrés. Finally, on a Paris street, as she shields a Communist from the shots of a mad émigré, Lola is mortally wounded. "Comrades, tell them that I understood everything at the end and that I'm sorry," she gasps as she dies. She begs that her body be covered with the Red flag; but, taken for a whore shot by a jealous lover, she is left on the road, uncovered. "The mounted police are coming! Raise your flags, Comrades," the Party leader says as the unemployed move on: "Let's march to meet them!"

LITHUANIA, like its neighbors ESTONIA and LATVIA, was part of the Russian Empire until 1918; that year it became independent, but in 1940 it was reincorporated into the Russian state. The "father" of his country's drama was Vydūnas (pen name of Vilius Storasta, 1868–1953), a Tilsit mystic and a poet-philosopher. His most important plays are *Amžina ugnis* (1912–13), a trilogy; and *Pasaulio gaisras* (1928), a five-act tragedy.

There were also later Lithuanian playwrights of note. Vincas Krėvė-Mickevičius (1882–1954), the major literary figure of modern Lithuania, who in 1944 exiled himself to the United States, where he died, wrote comedies as well as historical and legendary plays like *Šarūnas* (1911), *Skirgaila* (1925), and *Karaliaus Mindaugo mirtis* (1935), whose historical title hero was the earliest unifier of Lithuania. Most of the plays by Petras Vaičiūnas (1890–1959) are comedies; his best-known works are a political satire, *Patriotai* (1927), and a popular dramatization of a fairy tale, *Laimės gėlė* (1929). Balys Sruoga (1896–1947) wrote distinguished historical dramas, notably *Milžino paunksmė* (1932, in verse) and *Kazimieras Sapiega* (1947). As an old man Maironis (pen name of Jonas Mačiulis-Mačiulevičius, 1862–1932), well known and esteemed for his patriotic poetry, wrote a trilogy dramatizing (and idealizing) early Lithuanian kings, *Kęstučio mirtis, Vytautas pas kryžiuočius,* and *Vytautas karalius* (1922–30).

In the post-World War II period, Juozas Grušas (1903–) has been the most important of the Soviet-Lithuanian playwrights; his *Herkus Mantas* (1957) deals with a medieval Lithuanian uprising in East Prussia. Significant though little-known Lithuanian drama has been written by the exiles Antanas Škėma (1911–61), Algirdas Landsbergis (1924–), and Kostas Ostrauskas (1926–). Škėma's plays, dramatic variations on biblical stories, depict life in Soviet-occupied Lithuania, as in *Žvakidė* (1957, Cain and Abel) and in *Kalėdų vaizdelis* (1961, Judas's betrayal of Christ). Landsbergis, a few of whose plays have appeared in English, wrote a comedy on the Horatio Alger theme, *Meilės mokykla* (*The School of Love*, 1965); and a drama on the destruction of Lithuanian guerrillas after World War II, *Penki stulpai turgaus aikštėje* (*Five Posts in the Market Place*, 1966). Some of the avant-garde drama of Ostrauskas has also been translated: *Duobkasiai* (*Gravediggers*, 1967) is an ABSURDist depiction (with ironic counterpoints to Shakespeare's *Hamlet*) of two gravediggers who literally bury themselves at the behest of Death, a mysterious and slightly vulgar woman.

These and other works are discussed in Rimvydas Šilbajoris's *The Perfection of Exile: Fourteen Contemporary Lithuanian Writers* (1970). See also Antanas Vaičiulaitis's *Outline History of Lithuanian Literature* (1942); and *Lituanus*, an English-language quarterly that includes articles on Lithuanian theatre and drama, as well as translations of plays.

LITTLE EYOLF (*Lille Eyolf*), a play in three acts by HENRIK IBSEN, published in 1894 and produced in 1895. Setting: a Norwegian estate near a fjord, late nineteenth century.

This late Ibsen play attempts to present a livable alternative to the resolutions of ROSMERSHOLM and THE MASTER BUILDER. But though Allmers shares their protagonists' "sickly conscience," he is subtly portrayed as a basically vain, egotistical idealist and charlatan.

Act I. Rita is overjoyed at the homecoming of her husband, Alfred Allmers. Discontented with his "life's work," a "great solid book on human responsibility" that Rita's wealth has been giving him the leisure to work on, he had gone for a trip to the mountains—his first separation from Rita in their ten-year marriage. He amazes her with his decision to give up writing and devote himself exclusively to their crippled son, Eyolf—build up his "instinct for happiness," make him an athlete, perhaps even pass his life's work on to him. Rita demands that she have Allmers "just as I had you in those first lovely, glorious days," and resents sharing him with his sister Asta and even with their nine-year-old son, who is "only half my own. But *you* shall be mine only! All mine!" In a passion of jealousy, she raves of her son's "evil eyes ' and almost expresses a wish for his death. A passing "Rat Wife" had earlier offered to exterminate "anything here gnawing and biting," and now there is a commotion from the fjord. They hear the words "The crutch is floating" and learn that Eyolf has followed the Rat Wife, and drowned. Grief-stricken, Rita shrieks and Allmers is stunned with their loss: "Such a precious life! Such a precious life!"

Act II. The next day Allmers is comforted by and reminisces with his beloved sister Asta, whom he used to call Eyolf. He tells her that he already catches himself forgetting the drowned Eyolf: "In the midst of my misery I caught myself wondering what we should have for lunch today." Later he and Rita bitterly reproach each other for Eyolf's affliction, because in their sexual passion they had neglected their then-infant son, who fell off a table and became crippled. Allmers considers Eyolf's death a retribution: "We let ourselves shrink from him while he was alive, in secret, craven remorse." Their "grief and bereavement" is really "the gnawing of conscience," and even Rita's possessive love is selfish. Though an atheist, Allmers holds their only "resurrection" to lie in atonement for their common guilt. Rita castigates his vanity and, though grief-stricken, refuses, as "a warm-blooded human animal," to spend her life in perpetual remorse. Allmers admits he married her for her wealth—"the gold and the green forests" —but claims he did it to support his sister. Shrinking back from memories of his passion for Rita, he now wants to leave with Asta, yearning for the sister's love that is "not subject to the law of change." He is horrified to learn that they are not, in fact, brother and sister. Soon, however, he declares that it does not matter. Asta reminds him that now their relationship, too, is subject to "the law of change," and leads him back to Rita.

Act III. Dreading their future, Rita joins her husband in imploring Asta to stay with them. But Asta leaves Allmers forever—in "flight from you —and from myself." Allmers decides to leave Rita. He tells of his revelation while traveling in the mountains: he got lost, and it was when he felt death walking at his side that he resolved to devote his life to Eyolf. Rita, haunted by visions of Eyolf's staring eyes and floating crutch, decides to fill her now-empty life with love for the poor fjord urchins, whom she will board in her home. Allmers offers to remain and help her, and she holds out her hand to him gratefully. Together, they may transcend their earthbound natures and, as Allmers says, look "Upwards—to the mountain tops. To the stars. And to the great stillness."

LITTLE FOXES, THE, a play in three acts by LILLIAN HELLMAN, published and produced in 1939. Setting: a small Southern town, Spring 1900.

Hellman's masterpiece, this play depicts the predatory Hubbards—"the little foxes," of the Song of Solomon (2:15), "that spoil the vineyards"—twenty years after ANOTHER PART OF THE FOREST. Though meant to be a "truthful and realistic" portrait of evil, this is a sardonic and well-constructed melodrama. The most greedy and vicious of the burgeoning Southern-industrialist family is Regina, memorably portrayed by Tallulah Bankhead in a long stage run, and by Bette Davis in Hellman's 1941 film version. In 1949 MARC BLITZSTEIN made the play into an opera, *Regina.*

Act I. After concluding the big deal to build a cotton mill with a Chicago businessman, Ben and Oscar Hubbard and their sister Regina relish thoughts of the wealth it will bring them. Oscar sadistically silences his genteel, browbeaten wife Birdie, and dreams of grander hunting (though he forbids hunting by the hungry Negroes). Ben questions Regina about her still-missing third of the capital, which they must soon produce. Her husband, Horace Giddens, recuperating from a heart ailment in Baltimore, has consistently failed to answer their proposals. Shrewdly Regina suggests that, since his money is essential, she be given a larger share of the partnership. After crafty bargaining, Ben agrees to her demand: the extra percentage will come from Oscar, who objects furiously but impotently. He is pacified only by Regina's vague promise to think about letting her daughter marry his worthless son, Leo. Then Regina persuades her daughter to travel to Baltimore to bring back her father, Horace. Birdie whispers a warning of the Hubbards' plot to marry her off to Leo. Though she is his mother, Birdie wants to save the girl from being trapped in as unhappy a life as her own. When the girl leaves, Oscar, who has overheard them, viciously slaps Birdie across the face.

Act II. A week later Oscar worriedly awaits the return of Horace. He admonishes Leo to give up women and work more conscientiously at his job in Horace's bank, for he must marry his cousin—and make his family's fortune. Inadvertently Leo discloses that he has examined Horace's safe-deposit box, which contains $88,000 in negotiable bonds—and Oscar suggests that Leo might "borrow" these. Finally Horace arrives with his daughter. He is obviously ill and fatigued, and depends on medicines to keep him alive. From a trusted old Negro servant he learns why his wife and her brothers were so eager for his return. Regina coldly rejects his plea for harmony, and sneers about his "fancy women" of former days. Sharply Horace recalls how Regina "has not wanted me in bed with her." Though he is exhausted, Regina insists he discuss the business proposition immediately. Ben explains how they will make their fortune because of the cheap local waterpower and labor: "Why, there ain't a

The Little Foxes, Act II. Regina (Tallulah Bankhead), Horace (Frank Conroy), Leo (Dan Duryea), Ben (Charles Dingle), and Oscar (Carl Benton Reid). New York, 1939. (*Vandamm Photo. Theatre Collection, New York Public Library*)

mountain white or a town nigger but wouldn't give his right arm for three silver dollars every week, eh, Horace?" Disgusted, Horace refuses to join the partnership: "We've got enough money, Regina. We'll just sit by and watch the boys grow rich." Regina is furious. She follows him upstairs and her angry voice can be heard below. There Oscar reveals Leo's discovery, and Ben sends him off to steal the bonds. When Regina returns she is mystified by Ben's announcement that he can now conclude the business deal without her. Infuriated at being deprived of her share, Regina taunts Horace with his imminent death. Horace persists in refusing to give her the money. "You wreck the town, you and your brothers, *you* wreck the town and live on it," he says, ready himself to die "without making the world any worse. I leave that to you." Regina looks at him: "I hope you die soon." Their daughter shrieks for him not to listen as Regina continues, smiling, "I'll be waiting for you to die."

Act III. Horace discovers the theft and, two weeks later, sits in his wheelchair, the safe-deposit box and a medicine bottle beside him. Birdie, getting increasingly drunker, talks of the brutality of the Hubbards, including her husband and her son, and their exploitation of the townspeople, particularly the Negroes. She and Horace warn his daughter to get away before she ends up as miserably as Birdie, whom Oscar married for her family's cotton fields. When Regina enters Horace tells her that Leo, "this fine gentleman, to whom you were willing to marry your daughter," has stolen the bonds and invested them in the projected mill. But he amazes Regina with his determination to do nothing about it. He has decided to make a new will, leaving to Regina the bonds, which he knows her brothers will shortly return. The rest of Horace's money is to go to their daughter. Regina is livid when she realizes this will deprive her of the business's millions and she taunts Horace until he suffers a heart attack. He drops and breaks his medicine bottle, but Regina ignores him as he frantically starts up the stairs to get more medicine, and collapses. When he is taken to his room, she confronts her brothers with the theft. As soon as Horace is dead, Regina blackmails them for a 75 percent share. Oscar rages, for the extra share will come out of his pocket, but Ben remains urbane. "The century's turning, the world is open. Open for people like you and me . . . and they will own this country some day," he tells Regina, confident that they will get along—and obliquely counterthreatening her with his suspicions about her part in Horace's death. Regina happily anticipates going to Chicago. But her daughter refuses to accompany her, or to remain with the Hubbards. She recalls the Negro servant's comment on "people who ate the earth and other people who stood around and watched them do it"

—and decides not to be in either group. When Regina asks her if she would like to spend the night in Regina's room, her daughter faces her: "Are you afraid, Mama?" Regina slowly goes out.

LITTLE MINISTER, THE, a play in three acts by JAMES M. BARRIE, produced in 1897 and published in 1942. Setting: "Thrums," Scotland; "eighty years ago."

Barrie's immensely successful dramatization of his popular novel established him as a playwright (and Maud Adams, who played Babbie, as a star) and started his long association with the American producer Charles Frohman. From his novel Barrie extracted a comedy and a sentimental romance set against a Puritan background of poor weavers in conflict with English soldiers.

Young Reverend Gavin Dishart ("the little minister") falls in love with an enticing gypsy who leads the weavers in a revolt. Dishart tries to prevent them from resisting the law, but Babbie, the gypsy, tricks him. All ends happily with the scandalized villagers' becoming reconciled to the marriage when the gypsy turns out to be Lord Rintoul's daughter, Lady Babbie.

LITTLE PLAYS OF ST. FRANCIS, a cycle of one-act plays by LAURENCE HOUSMAN, published and produced in 1922–35. Setting: twelfth- and thirteenth-century Italy.

Various episodes in the life of Saint Francis of Assisi are depicted in this cycle of forty-five plays. Housman noted in his introduction to the complete three-volume collection (1935) that Brother Juniper was given a prominent role as a foil to "the gay and serene character of Francis." These one-acters also were published individually and in a number of series, and they have been especially popular in amateur productions.

LIVE CORPSE, THE (*Zhivoi trup*), a drama in six acts by LEO TOLSTOI, published and produced in 1911. Setting: a Russian city, early twentieth century.

Written in 1900 and never quite completed, this episodic posthumous tragedy appeared also under the English titles *The Living Corpse, Reparation,* and *Redemption.* It was based on an actual case narrated to Tolstoi. His play attacks the inadequacy of official justice: divorce laws that invite degrading perjury and ruthless legal intrusion into private lives. The challenging role of the degenerating aristocrat Fedya was successfully performed throughout the world by Ivan Moskvin, Alexander Moissi, and John Barrymore. The play is still produced in the Soviet Union.

Acts I and II. Fedya (Fyodor Vasilevich Protasov) left his wife Liza (Yelizaveta Andreevna) after the birth of their son. Her mother cannot understand why Liza still loves a husband guilty of "drunkenness, deception, and infidelity, . . . a broken reed." But Liza sends their friend Viktor Mikhailovich Karenin to ask her husband to come back. Viktor and Liza are both virtuous and conceal their deeper feelings toward each other even from themselves. The dissolute husband, carousing with an attractive gypsy who loves him, refuses to return home. He knows that he will only relapse again, and he suggests that Liza would be happier with Viktor who is "so much better than I am." Superfluous in Liza's life and aware that she is "an honest, moral woman," he points to himself as he says of Liza and Viktor, "She loves, and will love him when this obstacle is removed; and I will remove it, and they shall be happy! . . . I shall not return, but shall give them their freedom."

Acts III and IV. Liza and Viktor have acknowledged their mutual love. Her goodness eventually wins over his mother, a "grande dame" who first objects to Viktor's marrying an "impure" woman. Fedya's gypsy, whose love ennobles him, is taken away by her parents, who are angered by what they mistake as a base liaison ruinous to their daughter. Fedya assures a visiting nobleman that since he is a wastrel too weak to prevent his own ruin, he will not stand in the way of a marriage between Liza and Viktor, "an excellent, honorable, moral man" who has always loved her. Yet he cannot get himself "to lie, and do all the dirty work necessary to get a divorce." Unwilling to have them suffer any longer, he prepares to commit suicide. But his gypsy returns and persuades him that a pretended drowning would serve as well. The deception succeeds, and when they receive his farewell letter, Liza and Viktor grieve over his death. Later, when the suicide appears verified, they get married.

Acts V and VI. Some time later in a low-class restaurant, the drunk and ravaged Fedya tells his life story to a companion. He became a wastrel, he says, because the careers open to noblemen all increase "social abominations" and he was not heroic enough to take the alternate path and fight evil. His only way was "to forget it all by going on a spree, drinking and singing." The revelation that he pretended suicide to enable his wife to remarry is overheard by a scoundrel, a would-be blackmailer who has Fedya arrested. Amidst their happy family life, Liza and Viktor are informed of Fedya's deception and arrest. All three are tried for collusion and bigamy. Liza and Viktor behave with great dignity, and the broken Fedya castigates the stupid magistrate, who neither understands nor believes them. He is interfering in their complex relationships, "a struggle between good and evil," Fedya says, "a spiritual struggle such as you know nothing of," and one that ended well with his own disappearance and their consequent happiness. Then Fedya learns that they all may be exiled, that in any case the second marriage will be annulled and they will have to do church penance. Realizing that he can be redeemed and help the others only by becoming a real corpse, Fedya shoots himself. "Forgive me that I could not . . . free you any other way," he tells Liza; "it's not for you . . . it's best for me." And as his beloved gypsy arrives, Fedya dies, weeping happily: "This time you're too late. . . . How good I feel . . . how good!"

LIVING NEWSPAPER DRAMA, like AGITPROP, substituted theme for plot and sought to channel audiences' social and political attitudes toward liberal commitments. Produced by the Federal Theatre in the 1930's, this episodic kind of drama portrayed contemporary problems, as in Arnold Sundgaard's (1909–) living newspaper international survey of syphilis, *Spirochete* (1938). Commonly used living newspaper drama props were loudspeakers, projections, bare spotlights, personified articulate objects, etc. Perhaps the best-known living newspaper dramas were those authored and coauthored by ARTHUR ARENT, particularly those on the agricultural depression (*Triple-A Plowed Under,* 1936) and on housing, ONE-THIRD OF A NATION (1938).

LIVING ROOM, THE, a play in two acts by GRAHAM GREENE, published and produced in 1953. Setting: the converted upstairs living room of a London house, a winter in the 1950's.

Greene's first play, it resembles in theme and characters his Catholic novels and THE POTTING SHED.

Young Rose Pemberton joins the household of her pious old great-aunts and their brother James Browne, a crippled priest. After her mother's funeral Rose became the mistress of an elderly married psychologist, with whom she wants to run away. Obstructed by her aunts, who try to break up the "sinful" romance, Rose bitterly complains about the abnormality of their lives—for fear of death has made the women shut off every room in the house in which anyone has died, leaving only the living room open. When her lover's wife comes to weep for the return of her husband, and Rose actually sees them as man and wretched wife, she is shaken. "Tell me what to do, Father!" she implores James. The priest can give her no help: "We always have to choose between suffering our own pain or suffering other people's. We can't *not* suffer." He can offer only hope, and exhorts prayer. Rose finds herself unable to pray and she commits suicide in "the living room."

LIVINGS, Henry (1929–), English playwright, began making a name for himself in the 1960's with a number of wildly farcical television and radio plays. Born in Prestwich (England) to a working-class family, he attended Liverpool University for two years, served in the Royal Air Force, and subsequently became a cook and an actor. Among the plays he acted in were those of BRENDAN BEHAN, which were to influence his own. Livings's first play, *Jack's Horrible Luck,* was originally produced on television, in 1961. Like the plays that soon followed, it suggests metaphysical dilemmas beneath the rowdy external action, here that of a sailor's night out in Liverpool. Livings's first produced stage play, *Stop It, Whoever You Are* (1961), dramatizes the bizarre adventures of a lavatory attendant who is beaten up, caught by the police with a nymphet, dies, and sneers at his wife from the hereafter—the play ending as the setting blows up. Then came *Big Soft Nellie* (1961, originally called *Thacred Nit*), an almost plotless comedy about a sissy who tries to assert himself before his fellow workers; *The Quick and the Dead* (1961), a history play about François Villon; *Nil Carborundum* (1962), a play about the RAF produced right after Wesker's CHIPS WITH EVERYTHING, but depicting the military as an escape from—rather than an exemplum of—society; and a number of television dramas.

Kelly's Eye (1963), a new kind of play for Livings, is a melodramatic parable about a fugitive murderer who takes up with an inexperienced girl and is finally tracked down by a reporter; his sensational end is overshadowed by the outbreak of a bigger horror, World War II, and a blind narrator concludes that though the murderer is "hollow, inferior and evil," what "recommend[s] him to us is his humanity, which we share and so must love." *Eh?* (1964), a wildly comic farce with metaphysical implications, praised as "Livings's masterpiece" and "probably the best English farce since the death of [BERNARD] SHAW" (by L. D. Giannetti), is in the style of Livings's early television and radio plays and features an eccentric employee in a dyeing-factory boiler room. *The Little Mrs. Foster* (1966) is a bizarre play-revue about an Englishman captured in black Africa and nursed by the title character. *Good Grief* (1967) is a collection of dramatic sketches on such topics as a person whose limbs change in size as he talks, and a ventriloquist who changes places with his dummy. *Honor and Offer* (1968, subtitled *Or inefficiency, lack of organisation and self-indulgence alone cannot overcome the sexual, financial and political power of capital*) in a similarly uninhibited manner portrays a virile husband and his envious wife outsmarting their lustful boarder by parlaying his worthless check into a fortune. *The Finest Family in the Land* (1970) is described as "an outrageous farce on the seamier side of life in a council flat."

Kelly's Eye and Other Plays (1964) includes *Big Soft Nellie* and the not unsimilar television drama *There's No Room for You Here for a Start* (1963). John Russell Taylor's *Anger and After* (titled *The Angry Theatre* in America; revised edition, 1969) has an extensive discussion of Livings's drama. See also Louis D. Giannetti's "Henry Livings: A Neglected Voice in the New Drama," *Modern Drama,* XII: 1 (May 1969).

LOAVES AND FISHES, a satire in four acts by SOMERSET MAUGHAM, produced in 1911 and published in 1924. Setting: a contemporary English vicarage drawing room.

This comedy shocked reviewers and was not very successful with audiences "because the public of that day was uneasy at seeing a clergyman made fun of," Maugham suggested in *The Summing Up* (1938), where he noted that his play "is written somewhat extravagantly, so that it suggests farce rather than comedy, but it has some amusing scenes in it." Written in 1903, it was not included in Maugham's *Collected Plays.* Instead, he made it into a novel, *The Bishop's Apron* (1906).

Canon Theodore Spratte is a hypocrite on the make. He courts a wealthy widow, maneuvers successfully for a bishopric, and ultimately manages to win an attractive heiress.

LOGAN, Joshua (1908–), American producer and director, wrote THE WISTERIA TREES (1950), an adaptation of Chekhov's THE CHERRY ORCHARD, and coauthored a number of popular comedies and musicals: *Mister Roberts* (1948), the boisterous World War II tale of a U.S. Navy cargo ship, dramatized with the novel's author, Thomas Heggen (1919-49); SOUTH PACIFIC (1949); *Wish You Were Here* (1952), with ARTHUR KOBER; *Fanny* (1954), with S. N. BEHRMAN; and *Flower Drum Song* (1958), with JOSEPH FIELDS and OSCAR HAMMERSTEIN II.

Born in Texas, Logan was educated at the Culver Military Academy and at Princeton University. He studied acting on a scholarship at Stanislavsky's Moscow Art Academy, and married the daughter of EDWARD HARRIGAN. Though he collaborated on the hits listed above, Logan is perhaps more notable as a theatre as well as a film director and producer.

LOGUE, Christopher (1926–), English poet and playwright, has succeeded in arousing some controversy with his Marxian productions. After army service in World War II and various odd jobs, he edited anthologies of erotica. His short plays *Cob and Leach* (1959) and *Antigone* (1960) were performed jointly as *Trials by Logue*. The first depicts a respectable female whose frustrations bring about her arrest for indecent public behavior; the arguments of the second, an adaptation of Sophocles, suggest an apologia (voiced by Creon) for Russia's 1956 suppression of Hungary. Logue wrote *The Lily-White Boys* (1960), a musical featuring London's low life, as a protest drama.

LONELY LIVES (*Einsame Menschen;* literally, "lonely people"), a drama in five acts by GERHART HAUPTMANN, published and produced in 1891. Setting: a country house near Berlin, 1890's.

Hauptmann's third drama was dedicated to "those who have lived it," deals with marriage, and is in part autobiographical. A psychological study whose plot is reminiscent of Ibsen's ROSMERSHOLM, *Lonely Lives* first carried Hauptmann's name beyond the borders of Germany.

Johannes Vockerat is a young scholar who believes in modern scientific ideas. A decent person, he is nonetheless irritated by his family: an uneducated but good and self-effacing wife, who fears she is not good enough for him; and pious and meddling but kindly middle-class parents who deplore what they consider his freethinking. Into this milieu comes an emancipated university student, Anna Mahr. Vockerat is inspired by her interest in his work, and happy in what both believe will remain a Platonic friendship. But this friendship puts an increasing strain on Vockerat's suffering and scandalized family. Despite their fondness for the girl, they insist on Anna's leaving. Vockerat loves his devoted wife and his old parents. At the same time, he becomes aware of his true feelings for Anna, who reciprocates them but departs. Vockerat is too weak to resolve his conflicting passions and to defy convention. As his terrified wife wrings her hands and vows "to do anything he likes" to save him, he commits suicide in the nearby lake.

LONELY WAY, THE (*Der einsame Weg*), a drama in five acts by ARTHUR SCHNITZLER, published and produced in 1904. Setting: contemporary Vienna, c. 1903.

Schnitzler spent much time revising this play to unify its various plots. Though he did not quite succeed, it has been praised for its autumnal atmosphere and sensitive portrayal of man's "lonely way" to the grave. Particularly striking is the character of Sala, who is sentimental as well as sarcastic, and whose great zest for life is not quenched by his awareness of its sadness and transience.

Johanna Wegrath, the daughter of the Art Academy's director, is attracted to the middle-aged Stephen von Sala, a widowed neighbor who does not realize how close he is to dying of a heart ailment. Johanna's brother Felix, an officer, comes home on leave to visit their dying mother. Julian Fichtner, an elderly, once-successful artist, is shaken by her death. Lonely and full of self-pity, Fichtner reveals himself as Felix's natural father and solicits filial love. He admits that he ran away from marriage because he wanted "to take life wholly and enjoy it to the full, to live according to my destiny, [to] have absolute freedom and absence of care." He fails to win Felix, who does not want to leave Wegrath, a conscientious worker and affectionate paterfamilias oblivious of his son's true parentage. But Professor Wegrath refuses to let Felix give up his plans in order to stay with him now that Wegrath's wife is dead and he is alone. "Sooner or later we always get over everything," he tells Felix: "But if we sin against our inmost being we've got to pay for it till the end of our lives." The stoic Sala refuses to sympathize with Fichtner's self-pity, his "practising his scales . . . on a cracked violin." Fichtner never loved, never gave himself, Sala tells him, and he would be lonely even if there were wife, "children and grandchildren . . . money and fame and genius—Even in the very midst of the dance the lonely way stretched ahead for us—for us who have never belonged to anyone but ourselves." Sala wants to live his own life to the full, though he may have little time left. In a tender scene Johanna professes her love for Sala, but he now understands from her near hysteria that he is closer to death than he thought. Though he proposes to her, their union is not to be. The melancholy girl drowns herself, and Sala, unwilling to spin out the little time left him, goes off to put an end to it all. He is proud of Felix: "Somehow, I feel it's a better race that's growing up now—perhaps not quite so brilliant—but with more poise." Then he stops Fichtner from accompanying him as he leaves to die: "Any messages for—up there?" When Professor Wegrath enters, Felix embraces him affectionately. "My father!" he exclaims, and the rejected Fichtner walks off slowly.

LONG CHRISTMAS DINNER, THE, a one-act play by THORNTON WILDER, published and produced in 1931. Setting: the dining room of a Midwestern home, over a span of ninety years.

In his introduction to Wilder's one-acters, John Gassner called this "the most beautiful one-act play in English prose." Wilder made it into a libretto for which Paul Hindemith wrote the score (the opera was first produced in 1961). The half-hour play takes place on a simple stage set of a table, chairs, and two doorways through which three generations of family members enter and leave. The many Christmas dinners, beginning with that of the house's first occupants, merge gently into one prolonged dinner that conveys the repetitive flux of life—of birth, marriage, old age, and death. A bereaved daughter cries out, "I never told her how wonderful she was. We all treated her as though she were just a friend in the house. I thought she'd be here forever." Such griefs are balanced by the joys of warm family love, murmured at the end by the house's "immensely old" last resident.

LONG DAY'S JOURNEY INTO NIGHT, a tragedy in four acts by EUGENE O'NEILL, published and produced in 1956. Setting: a (Connecticut) summer home on a day in August, 1912.

Despite its prolixity and some repetition, this elegiac but harrowing portrayal of a family's love-hate conflicts is among O'Neill's—and America's—greatest plays. At the moving, powerful finale, at least some of the characters are stripped of their illusions and hopes, but they gain insight and compassion. NATURALISTIC and almost completely autobiographical, the play tortured the author ("Edmund") throughout its composition. As his wife Carlotta described it, "He would come out of his study at the end of a day gaunt, his eyes red from weeping. Sometimes he looked ten years older than when he went in in the morning" (Barbara and Arthur Gelb's *O'Neill*). In 1941 O'Neill presented and inscribed the completed manuscript to his wife Carlotta, who "gave me the faith in love that enabled me to face my dead at last and write this play—write it with deep pity and understanding and forgiveness for *all* the four haunted Tyrones." The play, written in 1940–41 but withheld from publication for fifteen years because of its personal nature, won the Pulitzer Prize and raised O'Neill's posthumous stature and fame enormously.

Act I. After breakfast, the famous stage star James Tyrone playfully flatters his wife: "You're a fine armful now, Mary." She is fifty-four, white-haired, and attractive; but her most striking characteristic is nervousness, evinced by her over-active and uncontrollable hands. Tyrone is sixty-five, earthy, healthy, handsome but unpretentious and carelessly dressed. She teases him affectionately but self-consciously about his hearty eating, his loud snoring which drowns out the foghorn outside, and his eternal real-estate speculations. Tyrone just as affectionately tries to dispel her sensitivity (though he is obviously worried about her) by complimenting her improvement since her recent return from the hospital. He complains about their son James Jr. (Jamie), who is "forever making sneering fun of somebody" and at thirty-three has not succeeded at anything, while she worries about the coughing of their sickly younger son, Edmund. The boys enter. Jamie, looking cynical and dissipated, resembles his father, whose vitality and bearing, however, he lacks. The twenty-three-year-old Edmund takes more after his mother—particularly in his hypersensitiveness—and looks quite ill. He tells an amusing story about one of Tyrone's tenants (an episode dramatized in A MOON FOR THE MISBEGOTTEN), but leaves after repeated bickerings between his father and brother. In a private talk, Jamie blames Tyrone for going to cheap quacks, aggravating Edmund's probable consumption, and of encouraging Mary in her delusion that it is only a cold. Tyrone blames Jamie for being a ne'er-do-well and a bad influence on Edmund, which Jamie considers "a rotten accusation." Though father and son worry about the danger to Mary of Edmund's sickness, they soon resume their bitter arguments, now about the cause and possible relapse of Mary's sickness—dope addiction. When she returns, they unwittingly increase her uneasiness by asking her to be careful. In a talk with Edmund, Mary expresses her hatred of their cheap summer home, and is upset when he too begs her to be careful and admits their worries and suspicions about a possible relapse—goading her to comment resentfully that "It would serve all of you right if it was true!" She resignedly admits, however, that none of them can help remembering the past, and when left alone, she is "seized by a fit of nervous panic" in which her knotted fingers are "driven by an insistent life of their own, without her consent."

Act II. Scene 1. Around noon Jamie joins his brother in a drink from Tyrone's bottle, brought by the maid Cathleen, and then refills it with water "to cover up from his eagle eye." Jamie is appalled to hear that Mary had been left alone, and dismisses the usual promise "on her sacred word of honor" as meaningless. When Mary comes in, it is clear that she has indeed relapsed into addiction. In a detached way she talks of "the things life has done to us" that make one lose the "true self forever." Jamie bitterly reproaches his mother for her relapse, and she leaves after denying his accusation. Tyrone has a drink with his sons when Mary returns, excitedly blaming him for not having "remained a bachelor and lived in second-rate hotels and entertained your friends in barrooms! Then nothing would ever have happened." She scolds him for giving Edmund a drink that might kill him, as it had her consumptive father; but then, terrified, she stammers, "But, of course, there's no comparison at all. I don't know why I—" Broken by her relapse, Tyrone

Long Day's Journey Into Night, last scene. Mary (Florence Eldridge); in background, left to right: Edmund (Bradford Dillman), Jamie (Jason Robards), Tyrone (Frederic March). New York, 1956. (*Theatre Collection, New York Public Library*)

begins to walk away, and Mary for one moment faces reality: "James! I tried so hard! I tried so hard! Please believe—!" But when her grief-stricken husband asks her, "For the love of God, why couldn't you have the strength to keep on?" she reverts to her usual delusive denials: "I don't know what you're talking about. Have the strength to keep on what?" And Tyrone gives up: "Never mind. It's no use now." *Scene 2.* After lunch, the doctor telephones for Edmund to see him that afternoon. The worried Mary refers to the doctor as "an ignorant fool" and recalls her suffering and humiliation when she begged him for morphine. She goes off for "another shot in the arm," as Jamie brutally observes. Tyrone castigates his sons for having flouted religion for their "rotten" philosophies—Jamie's "learned from Broadway loafers" and Edmund's learned "from his books." He reveals to Jamie the doctor's confirmation of Edmund's tuberculosis, and Jamie bitterly insists that his father this time not economize on the cure for the sake of his property purchases. Afraid to remain alone, Mary begs Tyrone to stay with her for a while, and then reluctantly agrees to be driven (to the drugstore) in the expensive "bargain" car he bought her. She reverts to her past, talks of their early life, their dead son Eugene, the painful birth of Edmund and the morphine administered by the cheap hotel doctor, which started her addiction. When Tyrone asks her to forget the past she objects: "Why? How can I? The past is the present, isn't it? It's the future, too. We all try to lie out of that but life won't let us." Before Tyrone and Edmund leave to see the doctor, Mary hopelessly tries to persuade Edmund (and herself) that she is not using his illness as an excuse for her relapse. Frightened and then "glad they're gone," Mary laughs in despair: "Then Mother of God, why do I feel so lonely?"

Act III. Mary has returned from the drugstore with Cathleen, whom she detains by feeding her drinks. Welcoming the fog, which "hides you from the world," and resenting the foghorn, which "keeps reminding you, and warning you, and calling you back," Mary reverts to past dreams of becoming a concert pianist, of her convent days, and of her first meeting and falling in love with Tyrone, then a famous matinee idol. Tyrone returns with Edmund, both flushed with drink after having seen the doctor, and they bitterly listen to Mary's morphine-stimulated chatter. She recalls Tyrone's periodic drunkenness and her having to wait for him in cheap hotels (which now infuriates Edmund), and the beautiful wedding gown her father had bought her. She does not inquire about the doctor's diagnosis, and, highly resentful, Edmund finally tells her that "It's pretty hard to take at times, having a dope fiend for a mother!" and goes out, feeling terribly guilty. Mary starts to leave and Tyrone harshly comments that after taking "more of that God-damned poison" she will "be like a mad ghost before the night's over!" But Mary blankly escapes into her self-delusions: "I don't know what you're talking about, James. You say such mean, bitter things when you've drunk too much. You're as bad as Jamie or Edmund."

Act IV. Around midnight, as the fog appears denser and the foghorn sounds, Edmund returns home drunk. He refuses to turn out the hall light, and Tyrone, who is also drunk, melodramatically turns on three bulbs: "The poorhouse is the end of the road, and it might as well be sooner as later!" For a long time they drink and listlessly play cards, rehashing their frustrations and expressing their love-and-hate feelings toward each other. Particularly resentful of his father's latest bargain-hunting, Edmund angrily refuses to go to the state sanatorium. Tyrone justifies his miserliness by the abject poverty of his youth, and then grandly offers to send his son to "Any place you like—within reason." For the first time, he talks of his ruined artistic career, prostituted for a secure fortune made year after year on one easy box-office success. Edmund talks of his own dreams, and Tyrone admits that his son has the makings of a poet, though a morbid one. But Edmund says he can never really express his deepest feelings: "Stammering is the native eloquence of us fog people," those who are unwanted, unable "to belong," and always "a little in love with death." Jamie, very drunk, comes home and tells Edmund of his brothel escapades. In their long talk he warns Edmund that though he loves him, he also hates his guts and is jealously trying to ruin him by dissipation. Tyrone and his sons are at last on the verge of falling asleep when suddenly piano playing is heard. And then Mary appears. Totally oblivious of her surroundings, she holds her old wedding gown in her arms. "The Mad Scene. Enter Ophelia!" Jamie says bitterly. Both men turn fiercely on him, and Edmund slaps his face. Then he tries to get through Mary's somnambulism with his bewildered and hurt cry of "Mama! it isn't a summer cold! I've got consumption!"; but it is no use, as Tyrone notes, while Jamie recites Swinburne. Passing the bottle they watch hopelessly and listen to her convent-day memories, the boys remaining motionless but Tyrone stirring as the curtain falls after she sadly finishes her dreamy recollections: "Then in the spring something happened to me. Yes, I remember. I fell in love with James Tyrone and was so happy for a time."

LONG, John Luther (1861–1927), American lawyer and writer, became famous as the collaborator of DAVID BELASCO after the latter read Long's MADAME BUTTERFLY in the *Century* magazine (January 1898) and dramatized it. Long's penchant for the exotic perfectly suited Belasco, and they collaborated on two great hits, THE DARLING OF THE GODS (1902) and ADREA (1904). The plays Long wrote by himself were less successful. *Dolce* (1906), his dramatization of a nostalgic short story he had published earlier, provided Minnie Maddern Fiske with a good part, as did *Kassa* (1909); his *Crowns* (1922), a romantic tragedy, portrays two Palestinian heirs at the time of Christ. Long also wrote novels, and practiced law throughout his playwriting career.

LONG VOYAGE HOME, THE, a one-act play by EUGENE O'NEILL, published and produced in 1917. Setting: a London waterfront bar, in one of the years preceding World War I.

The third in the S. S. GLENCAIRN cycle, this play's revised text was published in THE MOON OF THE CARIBBEES, AND SIX OTHER PLAYS OF THE SEA.

After being paid for their two-year hitch, a number of seamen go to a "low dive" London bar. Olson is the only one not drinking. He happily looks forward to sailing home to Sweden as a passenger, and buying and settling on a farm there. He had never succeeded in accomplishing this before because he always got drunk and broke when in port. This time he is about to succeed, but he is tricked by a barmaid into taking a doctored drink, and is shanghaied to a departing ship that needs more crew members. When his mates return to the bar, they are told that he has left with the barmaid. The curtain falls as one of the mates, impressed by Olson ("Who'd think Ollie'd be sich a divil wid the wimin?"), calls for another "whiskey, *Irish* whiskey!"

LONSDALE, Frederick [Leonard] (1881–1954), English playwright born in Jersey, Channel Islands, wrote drawing-room comedies that were popular through the 1930's but dated rapidly, though he continued producing them until 1950. He considered his comedy "tragedy averted," and began with the plots' serious implications. London saw his first three plays simultaneously in 1908: *The Early Worm, The King of Cadonia,* and *The Best People.* During the war, *The Maid of the Mountains* (1916) was a great favorite with soldiers on leave, and another popular and characteristically sprightly comedy was *Aren't We All?* (1923).

Lonsdale's best-known work was *The Last of Mrs. Cheyney* (1925), a "crook play" (filmed in 1929 and again in 1937) whose title character, when foiled in a theft and ready to admit everything, discovers the fashionable company more disreputable than herself; offered a ten-thousand-pound bribe to keep silent, she rehabilitates herself socially by destroying the check. Among Lonsdale's other plays are *Monsieur Beaucaire* (1919, an adaptation of BOOTH TARKINGTON'S novel), *On Approval* (1927), *Once Is Enough* (1938), *But for the Grace of God* (1946), and *The Way Things Go* (1950), his last play.

LOOK BACK IN ANGER, a play in three acts by JOHN OSBORNE, produced in 1956 and published in 1957. Setting: an English Midlands town in the 1950's.

This was the decade's most important—though certainly not the best—British play. Its premiere on May 8 signaled a turning point in the history of English drama, made its young author famous, and provided a name and a spokesman for that generation's "angry young men." Though the play is conventionally structured, its misanthropic hero's stream of anti-Establishment invective jolted native dramatists out of the doldrums as no play had done since those of BERNARD SHAW. Indeed, Jimmy Porter's rantings resemble those of Shaw's Jack Tanner in MAN AND SUPERMAN (and, incidentally, those of AUGUST STRINDBERG'S sex duelists). And his attempts to escape the "cruel steel traps" the atomic age and the welfare state set for his generation also resemble those of CLIFFORD ODETS'S spokesmen for the 1930's generation in America. John Russell Taylor collected reviews and studies of the play, as well as five articles by the playwright, in *John Osborne: "Look Back in Anger": A Casebook* (1968).

Act I. On an April evening in their one-room attic flat, Jimmy Porter and Cliff Lewis are reading the Sunday papers. Jimmy's wife Alison, wearing one of his shirts, is ironing. The friends banter and tussle. With increasing viciousness, Jimmy taunts his apparently unperturbed young wife. He is a State-college-educated snob who keeps a sweet-stall (candy shop) with Cliff and resents the "posh crowd" and his wife's upper-class background. Bored and disgusted with his life, he lashes out in a perpetual tirade: "Nobody thinks, nobody cares. No beliefs, no convictions and no enthusiasm." Alison tries to remain calm even when he ridicules her family—her parents and her brother, whom he calls "the Platitude from Outer Space"—and herself, "Lady Pusillanimous." Again the friends tussle; they knock over the ironing board and

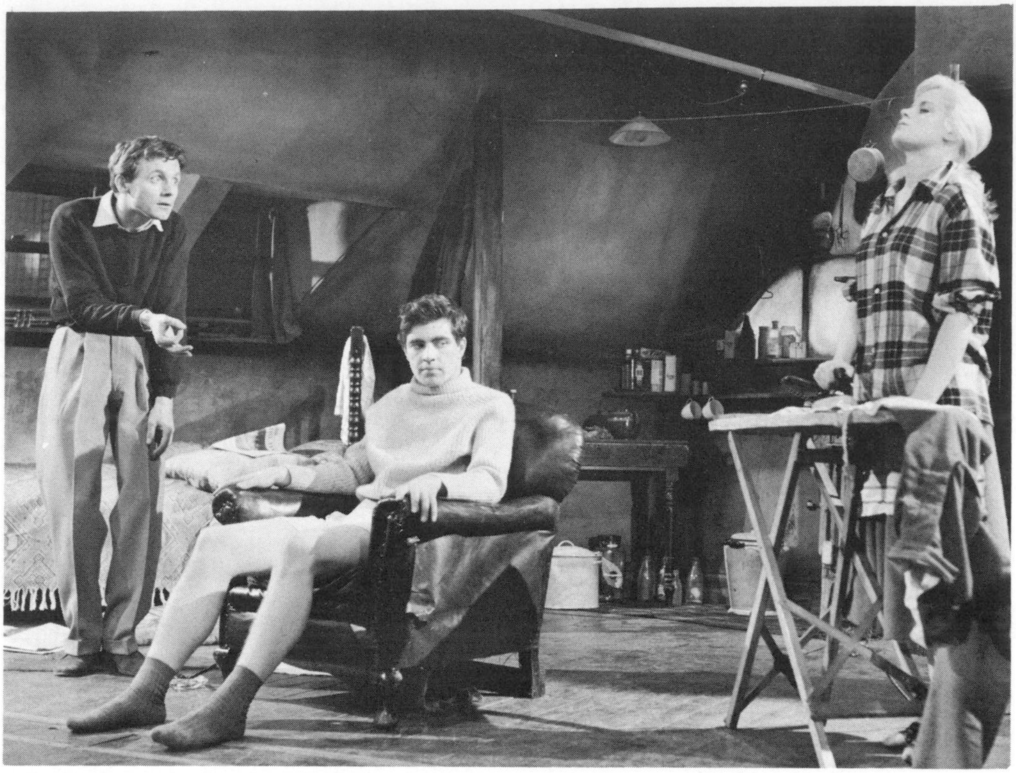

Look Back in Anger, Act I. Jimmy (Kenneth Haigh), Cliff (Alan Bates), Alison (Mary Ure). London, 1956. (*Houston Rogers*)

Alison's arm is slightly burned. Jimmy goes out, and Cliff ("a no-man's-land between" Jimmy and Alison, as he later characterizes himself) comforts the unhappy Alison. She tells him she is pregnant, and is afraid that Jimmy would be angry if he knew. When he returns the couple make up and play their favorite game: Jimmy pretends he is a bear and Alison is his little squirrel. Their fun ends when Alison receives a call from Helena Charles and invites her to stay with them. Helena is an actress friend Jimmy detests, and he angrily berates Alison again: "If only something—something would happen to you, and wake you out of your beauty sleep!" And he adds, venomously, "If you could have a child, and it would die. . . . Please—if only I could watch you face that."

Act II. It is two weeks later. Alison has been ill and Helena has stayed on to help her keep house. Jimmy spends much time in Cliff's room, playing the trumpet to annoy Helena. Alison tells Helena how she met Jimmy, who wanted to marry her because her parents disapproved of him; how Jimmy and a friend had used her to crash dinner parties; and how she and Jimmy play at being stuffed animals, games, "a silly symphony for people who couldn't bear the pain of being human beings any longer." When the men come in for tea, Jimmy insults both women. He gets furious when Alison plans to go to church with Helena, who threatens to slap his face. "I've no public school scruples about hitting girls," Jimmy tells her, and then talks about death, how he grew up when he watched his father die after his return from the Spanish Civil War. A call from London informs Jimmy that his friend's mother is dying. While Jimmy is out, Helena reveals that she has sent for Alison's father to take Alison home. Jimmy returns, upset about the call, and asks Alison to go to London with him. She however ignores him and leaves for church with Helena. Jimmy throws the stuffed bear on the floor, falls on the bed, and buries his face in the cover. The next evening Alison is packing. She is watched by her father, a retired colonel whom Jimmy has characterized as "one of those sturdy old plants left over from the Edwardian Wilderness." He cannot understand why the educated Jimmy can find nothing better to do than run a sweetstall. Alison leaves a note for Jimmy and departs. Staying over for an important job interview, Helena gives the note to Jimmy when he returns from London, and tells him about Alison's pregnancy. Still in a daze after having watched his friend's mother die, Jimmy bursts into invective and orders Helena to "*get out,* you evil-minded little virgin." She slaps his face; then she kisses him ardently and pulls him to the bed.

Act III. An evening several months later, Jimmy Porter and Cliff Lewis are reading the Sunday papers. Then they banter and scuffle, and Jimmy taunts his woman, who is wearing his shirt and is ironing. It is a replay of the opening scene, except that the woman now is Helena. Cliff tells Jimmy he intends to move and leave the sweetstall business. Jimmy sneers at his friend's likely end—in a respectable middle-class marriage, being "bled to death" by a woman. He deplores the absence of worthwhile causes for which men can bleed, as in former decades. Now, "if the big bang does come, and we all get killed off, it won't be in aid of the old-fashioned, grand design," Jimmy complains: "It'll just be for the Brave New-nothing-very-much-thank-you. About as pointless and inglorious as stepping in front of a bus." And he adds, "No, there's nothing left for it, me boy, but to let yourself be butchered by the women." Suddenly Alison comes in, looking sick. "Friend of yours to see you," Jimmy tells Helena, and goes out. While he angrily blows his trumpet in Cliffs' room, Alison tells Helena that she lost her baby. Now she feels foolish and vulgar for having returned, as she does not wish to break up their affair. It is Helena who insists. "When you came in at that door, ill and tired and hurt, it was all over for me," she tells Alison, shocked by the miscarriage: "It's like a judgment on us." She tells Jimmy that she is leaving him: "I can't take part—in all this suffering." Jimmy sadly questions his own beliefs in the "burning virility of mind and spirit" in man, "the old bear, following his own breath in the dark forest" with "no warm pack, no herd to comfort him." Alison weeps: "I was wrong! I don't want to be neutral, I don't want to be a saint"—for that is the only alternative, Jimmy has said, to being a human being who must dirty his hands if he loves. Alison describes the pain and humiliation of losing her baby, and her awareness throughout of how Jimmy would have relished the experience. "This is what he's been longing for me to feel," she remembers thinking, "this is what he wanted from me!" Alison collapses: "I'm in the mud at last! I'm groveling! I'm crawling!" Jimmy embraces her: "We'll be together in our bear's cave, and our squirrel's drey." But they must be careful, for "there are cruel steel traps lying about everywhere." And "pathetically" he remarks, "Poor squirrels!" Looking tenderly at him, Alison adds: "Oh, poor, poor bears!"

LÓPEZ RUBIO, José (1903–), Spanish writer, became a distinguished and prize-winning dramatist in mid-century. An early full-length play, written with JARDIEL PONCELA in the 1920's, was not produced, but López Rubio succeeded better with a collaboration with Eduardo Ugarte (? - ?), *De la noche a la mañana* (1929). Thereafter López Rubio translated, adapted, and collaborated on numerous plays; wrote short stories, novels, and newspaper articles; and for nearly two decades did film work in Spain, the United States, Mexico, and Cuba. Subsequently he returned to Spain and in the 1950's was established as an important dramatist. Like ALEJANDRO CASONA's, López Rubio's plays dramatize the ideal in conflict with reality—which López Rubio evades or, sometimes, interprets. The play that first brought him prominence was *Alberto* (1949), an intellectual comedy about a group of boardinghouse guests, who, upon the departure of their landlady, create an imaginary guest who embodies their fantasies. Among the plays that followed are *Celos del aire* (1950), a marriage intrigue drama; *La venda en los ojos* (*The Blindfold,* 1954), in which a deserted wife pretends that her husband is still with her and when he returns sends him off so that she can persist in her illusory life; *En la otra orilla* (1954), in which ghosts discuss their *crimes passionnels;* and *Las manos son inocentes* (1958), portraying remorse for an intended crime that was fortuitously aborted.

The Blindfold appears in Marion Holt's *The Modern Spanish Stage: Four Plays* (1970). López Rubio's work is discussed (in English) in Anthony M. Pasquariello and John V. Falconieri's introduction to the 1958 text edition of *En la otra orilla,* and in Richard E. Chandler and Kessel Schwartz's *A New History of Spanish Literature* (1961).

LOST COLONY, THE, a play in two acts by PAUL GREEN, published and produced in 1937. Setting: England and Roanoke Island, North Carolina; late sixteenth century.

Annually produced at Roanoke's Waterside Theatre, this vast historical-religious pageant was written to honor the three-hundred-and-fiftieth anniversary of Sir Walter Raleigh's colony. It is "an outdoor play with music, dance and pantomime" (subtitle) that features Raleigh, Queen Elizabeth, William Shakespeare, and other figures.

A narrator-historian recites and an enormous cast dramatizes the story of the group that in 1587 sailed from England under the leadership of Governor John White. In Roanoke they make friends with the Indians, and settle down. White's grandchild is the first English child to be born in America. White must briefly go back to England. Upon his return to Roanoke he finds the colony abandoned. Its only trace is a word carved on a tree: "Croatoan," their destination when forced out by the Spaniards. "And thus the Lost Colony disappeared into the vast unknown," the narrator concludes, and the chorus sings a final hymn to God.

LOST PLAYS OF EUGENE O'NEILL (1950). These five of EUGENE O'NEILL's earliest plays were not "lost" but purposely discarded by O'Neill and published without his consent when their copyright expired. Aside from O'Neill's first one-acter (A WIFE FOR A LIFE) and his first full-length play (SERVITUDE), they consist of *Abortion* (a melodrama) and *The Movie Man* (a farce), both written in 1914 and unproduced until 1959, and *The Sniper*. Produced by the Provincetown Players in 1917, *The Sniper* is a one-act antiwar play that features a Belgian peasant who shoots Germans when he learns that his family was killed, and defies "God who allows such things to happen!" All these were republished, together with those of O'Neill's THIRST

AND OTHER ONE-ACT PLAYS, as *Ten "Lost" Plays* (1964).

LOVE AND GEOGRAPHY (*Geografi og kjærlighed*), a play in three acts by BJØRNSTJERNE BJØRNSON, published and produced in 1885. Setting: a Norwegian home, 1880's.

This still-produced domestic comedy is something of a self-satire and has been likened to Shaw's MAN AND SUPERMAN.

A professor is so absorbed in geography that he not only neglects his wife and child but also nearly drives them out of their home with his maps. His wife finally makes him surrender his individual freedom and development to the claims of domesticity.

LOVE IN IDLENESS, a comedy in three acts by TERENCE RATTIGAN, produced in 1944 and published in 1945. Setting: London, 1944.

This popular Alfred Lunt and Lynn Fontanne vehicle was produced in the United States as *O Mistress Mine*.

The eighteen-year-old son of a separated cabinet minister's mistress is a political radical but a moral prig "with an Oedipus complex and a passion for self-dramatization." He compels his mother to move out of the lavish home she has shared with her lover, and take a drab flat with him instead. Later the son himself falls in love; after helping him with similar problems, the cabinet minister marries the mother.

LOVE OF DON PERLIMPLÍN AND BELISA IN THE GARDEN, THE (*Amor de Don Perlimplín con Belisa en su jardín*), "an erotic allelujah [i.e., cartoon]" in four scenes by FEDERICO GARCÍA LORCA, produced in 1928 and published in 1938. Setting: eighteenth-century Spain.

This short masterpiece in a prologue and an "only act" in three scenes is a lyrical, highly stylized tragic farce. Its stage directions stress the distorted spatial relations of the settings, the dramatic color schemes, the music, and movements like the recurrent flights of black paper birds. When a prominent officer acted the role of the cuckolded Perlimplín in 1928, the play was promptly banned as an insult to the army.

His old servant urges Perlimplín, a well-to-do bachelor of fifty, to marry. Perlimplín fears marriage and would rather stick with his books, but he is quickly persuaded that "marriage holds great charms." On a nearby balcony the young, scantily clad Belisa sings a naïvely erotic song. Urged on and prompted by his servant, Perlimplín proposes. Belisa's mother, eager to have her marry a rich man, at once arranges for the wedding. Perlimplín thrills to Belisa's beauty, but he is timorous. On their wedding night he trembles while Belisa is coy and ironic. At

Love in Idleness. **Alfred Lunt, Lynn Fontanne, and Dick Van Patten in the play renamed *O Mistress Mine.* New York, 1946. (*Culver Pictures*)**

dawn the doors to five balconies are open and Perlimplín has enormous gilded horns. Later he learns that she had five visitors on the wedding night, representatives of the human races, and is in love with a mysterious young man. Delighted, the elderly husband tells her that he loves her like a father now and urges her to confide in him. She reveals that the young man's letters, unlike those of her other lovers, ask not for her soul but for her "white and soft trembling body." Perlimplín promises to help her: "I am already beyond the world and the ridiculous morals of its people." At a rendezvous in the garden at night, Belisa waits for her lover. Perlimplín ascertains that Belisa loves the youth "more than her own body"; then he tells her that he will kill her lover to make him completely hers: "He will love you with the infinite love of the dead, and I will be free of this dark little nightmare of your magnificent body." He rushes off as she frantically calls for help. The mysterious, red-caped lover stumbles in. He uncovers himself and is revealed as Perlimplín. "Your husband has just killed me with this emerald dagger," he tells Belisa: "He killed me because he knew I loved you as no one else" and, he adds, "while he wounded me he shouted: 'Belisa has a soul now!'" With his last breath he says, "Don't you understand? I am my soul and you are your body." His imagination has finally given Belisa a soul, but she does not seem to quite understand. She loves Perlimplín now, "with all the strength of my flesh and my soul—but where is the young man in the red cape?"

LOVE OF FOUR COLONELS, THE, a play in three acts by PETER USTINOV, published and produced in 1951. Setting: Herzogenburg, "a village in the Harz mountains disputed by Britain, France, America, and Russia after the Great War of 1939–45."

Ustinov's most successful play, which made him internationally famous, is this witty fantasy. Confusing in plot but rich in comic dialogue, its most masterly parts are the four parodic love scenes.

The colonels of the title are likable stereotypes of the countries they represent. As they argue about a nearby castle (the "realist" Russian periodically leaving in protest), a wicked fairy appears. After establishing his credentials, this fairy is joined by a good fairy, in the shape of a comely army girl. Together they transport the colonels to the castle, which turns out to be that of the Sleeping Beauty. The colonels are challenged to make her fall in love with them. Each is given the opportunity to be transformed into—and court the Sleeping Beauty in the form of—his ideal. The Frenchman does so in the guise of a Restoration gallant ("Untruss, ma'am, untruss!"). The English colonel chooses an Elizabethan setting, and

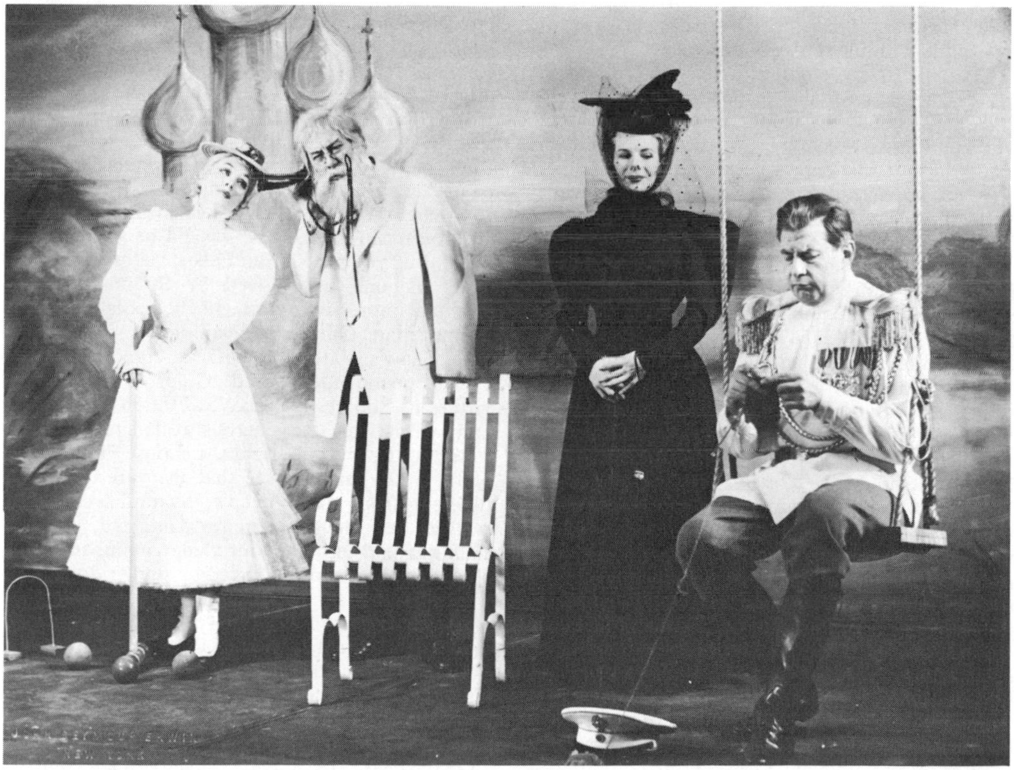

The Love of Four Colonels. Left to right: Sleeping Beauty (Lilli Palmer), the wicked fairy (Rex Harrison), the good fairy (Leueen MacGrath), and the Russian (Stefan Schnabel). New York, 1953. (*John Erwin Photos*)

courts her in Shakespearean verse ("For when a man is bent on sin / His conscience does fly out, his lewdness in!"). The American envisions himself in a honky-tonk as a fighting priest ("The guy that started Girls' Town") rescuing a gun moll and saving her soul, but finally tempted by "old man nature" and marrying her. The Russian colonel, in the shape of an elderly uncle who knits, evokes a languorous CHEKHOVian idyll—abortive because he refuses to seduce his stout, maternal ideal. Because the fairies have interfered throughout, the other colonels have not succeeded, either. Then they overhear their wives' frank revelations, some of covert desires and acts. Given the opportunity to return to them or to continue pursuing their ideal, the dog-loving Englishman and the Russian choose to return. The French and the American colonels choose otherwise, and lie down near the Sleeping Beauty. Before going on the long sleep that precedes their pursuit, the American wonders if they have chosen wisely. The Frenchman considers the question useless. The other colonels "at this precise moment," he says, "are asking themselves if they were wrong not to stay."

LOVERS (*Amants*), a comedy in five acts by MAURICE DONNAY, produced in 1895 and published in 1897. Setting: Paris and the shores of an Italian lake, 1890's.

Donnay's most popular play, *Lovers* is free of didacticism and typical in its urbane portrayal of love and of adulterous establishments.

Claudine Rozay, a retired actress, like others in her circle is comfortably settled with her married lover and their child. She falls in love with Georges Vétheuil and becomes his mistress. Though madly in love, she cannot because of her daughter give up her "respectable" establishment, while Vétheuil, enslaved by passion, resents the loss of his freedom. They bicker jealously and, to prevent their affair from deteriorating in the usual Parisian fashion, Vétheuil ends it during an idyllic interlude. Some eighteen months later he returns from extensive travels. "Cured" of passion though still affectionate, he is getting married—as is Claudine, for the father of her child is freed by his wife's elopement with her latest lover. With their spouses, Vétheuil and Claudine will leave "this city of trouble and suggestiveness," Vétheuil remarks. Here "we should again be tempted to have an adventure before the flame flickered for the last time"—she with a youngster, he "with some child who would lead me a merry chase" at fifty. A group of celebrants separate them and end their farewells as Vétheuil speculates about "happiness, or at least what most nearly approaches it . . ."

LOVE'S COMEDY (*Kjærlighedens komedie*), a verse play in three acts by HENRIK IBSEN, published in 1862 and produced in 1873. Setting: a villa outside Oslo, nineteenth century.

Ibsen wrote Edmund Gosse in 1872 that this satire, on which he had been working since 1858, "is actually to be regarded as a forerunner to *Brand,* in that I described there the conflict that prevails in our social conditions between reality and the claims of idealism in everything that concerns love and marriage." Though he considered it "among the best things I have done," it was originally condemned as an attack on marriage and the clergy, and later overshadowed by Ibsen's NATURALISTIC dramas. Its plot was inspired by a Norwegian novel, Jacobine Camilla Collett's *Amtmandens døttre* (*The Sheriff's Daughters,* 1855); but many of its ideas—including those embodied in the partly autobiographical Falk and the conflicts among aesthetic, ethical, and religious forces—stem from Søren Kierkegaard's works, particularly *Enten-Eller* (*Either/Or,* 1843).

Amidst engaged and married couples and their approving aunts and mothers is Falk, a young poet who offers his love to Svanhild, and eventually discovers that he has a rival in the elderly businessman Guldstad. All about him Falk sees how marriage—and even engagement—kills romantic love and artistic propensities. For example Pastor Stråmand, once an idealist, is now a model family man—and a comic, "living drama of degeneration": a pompous political cleric, an uxorious husband, and the provident father of twelve girls. Convinced that "marriage has no more to do with love / than mathematics has," Falk intends to escape this fate. He offers to defy convention by loving Svanhild freely, and having her inspire his work. But believing him capable of greater deeds, Svanhild rejects the role of his poetic muse; she knows that in that role he would soon cast her off—as he does a bird, which he kills after it finishes its song. Falk therefore decides to "write poetry in deeds." Ridiculing the petty, stultifying, and often hypocritical conventions of Philistine love and marriage, his eloquent rhetoric routs the company in a debate at tea. Now Svanhild admiringly throws herself into his arms: "If you mean to fight the lie / I'll be your squire, faithful at your side." But Falk's victory is short-lived. Though not moved by Stråmand's surprisingly impressive arguments, he is bested by the businessman Guldstad. Svanhild is confronted (like Shaw's CANDIDA) with a choice between Falk's poetic ideals and Guldstad's practical virtues of "domestic peace": affection, solicitude, and wealth (which he generously offers to bequeath to the young lovers, should she choose Falk). Both of them are made to see that they are really no different from other people. Svanhild therefore realizes that she must marry Guldstad, so that Falk's love, "Our love, our glad, triumphant love, shall never / be paled by age and riddled by disease." They agree to part, Svanhild now willing to become his inspiration: "I've filled your soul with light and poetry! / Fly up! I've kindled you to victory." Falk departs for the mountains, to write poetry: "the winged steed is saddled; / I know you have ennobled my whole life."

LOVING WOMAN, THE (*Amoureuse*), a comedy in three acts by GEORGES DE PORTO-RICHE, published and produced in 1891. Setting: Paris, 1891.

This drama of passion and marital incompatibility is a NATURALISTIC study that dissects love without resorting excessively to fashionable melodramatics or sentimentality. Originally titled *Bien aimé* and *L'Ennemie* and performed in New York as *The Tyranny of Love* (1921), it was praised as epoch making.

After eight years of marriage Étienne Fériaud, a prominent scientist, can no longer bear—but yet is unable to resist—the passions he himself has aroused in his young wife, Germaine. He admits that he wanted to be loved, but "not so much as I have been," which overtaxes his energies and hampers his research. Germaine replies: "Poor man! I love him too much, and he loves me too little. That is my crime." But Étienne adds, "Our misery!" Departing for Italy, he advises a friend who is infatuated with Germaine to "console her." Thereupon the angered Germaine has a brief affair with him. On his return Étienne discovers it and, certain he no longer loves Germaine, tells her to leave his house. But he cannot after all let her go. "We have fought like mortal enemies," he weeps, "and yet here I am. We are bound together by the evil we have done." Germaine too weeps as they reconsider their separation. "There is no justice, thank God!"—no externally imposed punishment for the adultery, only the suffering of a couple inextricably bound by their unequal passions. "Think, Étienne, you will be very unhappy," Germaine warns him, and starts to leave him. But he stops her: "What difference does that make?"

LOWELL, Robert [Traill Spence, Jr.] (1917–), distinguished American poet, wrote a drama trilogy, *The Old Glory* (1964): *Benito Cereno; My Kinsman, Major Molineux;* and *Endecott and the Red Cross.* Verse adaptations of a novella by Herman Melville and two short stories by Nathaniel Hawthorne, this SUCCÈS D'ESTIME is unified by the symbol of the American flag.

LOWER DEPTHS, THE (*Na dne;* literally, "at the bottom"), a play in four acts by MAXIM GORKY, published and produced in 1902. Setting: a flophouse in a Volga town, c. 1900.

Gorky's frequently revived masterpiece, one of the great NATURALIST plays, has little plot and no central figure. But it is rich in the depiction of characters, and in action and dialogue revealing their miseries, secret yearnings, and interrelationships—and is thus a *Lumpen Proletariat* analogue of Chekhov's THE CHERRY ORCHARD. It resembles Ibsen's THE WILD DUCK and O'Neill's THE ICEMAN COMETH, though the outsider, old Luka, is a more perplexing and ambiguous character than either Gregers or Hickey. The play was originally translated as *At the Bottom of Life*, and has also been translated as *The Night's Lodging;* it was adapted by Walter Carroll (1922–) and Randolph Goodman (1908–) as a Negro play set in North Carolina, *A Long Way from Home* (1948).

Act I. On a spring morning a group of unfortunates huddle in the cavelike basement lodging of the despicable Mikhail Ivanovich Kostylyov, a buyer of stolen goods. His hard young wife, Vasilisa Karpovna, is having an affair with one of the lodgers, Vasili Pepel, a fatalistically cheerful youth doomed to thievery because his father was a thief. But he is tiring of his landlady and is interested in her younger sister. There is also a baron, a conceited young embezzler supported by the earnings of a young streetwalker who imagines she has had romances like those of the sentimental novels over which she weeps. Others include a dour locksmith who beats his tubercular wife and waits for her to die so he can be free; a sarcastic capmaker, whose wife ran off with his employer; an unsuccessful actor ruined by drink; the realist Satin, a card sharper; a corrupt policeman who wants to marry a dumpling vendor; a gossip-mongering young cobbler; and two longshoremen, one of them a Tatar devoted to the Koran. Into this milieu comes a new lodger, Luka. He is a sixty-year-old pilgrim who brings understanding

The Lower Depths. The streetwalker (played by ANTON CHEKHOV's wife, Olga Knipper), the baron (Vassili Kachalov), and Satin (Konstantin Stanislavsky). Moscow, 1902. (*Sovfoto*)

and pity to all these lost dregs of humanity: "To my way of thinking, every flea is a good flea—they're all dark and all good jumpers." All are human beings who want something better in life, he knows, and all are—like himself—pilgrims: "The earth itself is a pilgrim in the heavens." Pepel makes the baron get down and bark for a drink, and Vasilisa, irritated at the tale-bearing young cobbler as she looks for her lover, orders the lodgers about. "So many different people order others around on this earth," Luka observes, "but still there's no order in life—no cleanliness"; and he begins to sweep up the place. Later, the muffled noises of a fight are heard: the jealous Vasilisa is beating her sister. The locksmith's dying wife is touched by Luka's kindness. "I've been through the wringer," he tells her; "that's why I'm soft."

Act II. It is evening. Luka sits by the dying woman's bed, and a card game is in progress nearby. Satin ridicules the baron for muffing an attempt to cheat at cards, and the actor tries to recite. When he sadly complains that he is through because his "organism" is "poisoned with alcohol," Luka offers encouragement by telling of a free clinic that cures alcoholics. Then he comforts the dying woman: "You'll have nothing to fear—nothing at all. There'll be peace and quiet. . . . Death quiets everything. It's kind to us humans." As for God, "If you believe in Him, He exists. If you don't, He doesn't." Alone with Pepel, Vasilisa begs him to release her from her husband: she would even let him marry her sister then. "Very neat," Pepel remarks; "the husband packed off into the grave, the lover to Siberia . . ." But she stops him: "You don't have to do it yourself—you can get others." She recalls how her husband informed on him, and how she herself cannot help tormenting her sister, whom he loves. Kostylyov breaks in angrily, and is saved from Pepel's grip when Luka, who has accidentally overheard the talk, interferes. He cautions Pepel against Vasilisa, and urges him to leave with her sister and settle down. The locksmith's wife dies just then. Soon the lodgers come in. The locksmith worries about the burial fee and the others comment on death and the meaning of life. The actor enthusiastically plans to go to another town for his cure at the clinic, though Satin tells him that "the old man lied to you. There's nothing! No town, no people—nothing!" And as the actor starts reciting over the corpse and Luka reappears, Satin cries out: "Shout—yell—corpses don't hear."

Act III. It is early spring now. In the littered yard, the baron sneers at the streetwalker, who relates her imaginary romantic experiences. Luka chastises him: "It doesn't matter what's said, but why it's said." And when others too ridicule her, he tells the girl, "Yours is the truth, not theirs. If you believe you had a real love, then you did have it—you certainly did." The capmaker is puzzled about Luka: "He lies an awful lot—gets nothing out of it. And he's already an old man." But the baron understands that "all human beings have gray little souls—and they all want to rouge them up." And Luka himself later explains that one must sympathize with people, try to teach them to do good. Illustrating his point with a story, he says that "it isn't always truth that's good for what ails a man—you can't always cure the soul with truth." He plans to leave soon, and suggests that Pepel marry Vasilisa's sister and come along. The couple agree, but Vasilisa eggs Pepel into a brawl with her husband after maiming her sister by dumping scalding water on her feet. Pepel accidentally kills Kostylyov and is taken away. The suffering sister, who was ready to marry Pepel, thinks he did it for Vasilisa and denounces them both: "That one, my sister, taught—got him—her lover—there he is, damn him—they killed the man! Arrest them—try them. Take me too—to jail! For Christ's sake, take me to jail!"

Act IV. During the brawl Luka had left the flophouse. Pepel will be tried for murder, Vasilisa is likely to talk herself out of jail, and her sister has disappeared from the hospital. Now it is night and over some drinks the others are discussing Luka. Satin speaks eloquently and at length. Luka lied out of pity for them, the card sharper says, and they needed his lies because they are weak: "Lies are the religion of slaves and bosses" who use them as a screen, while "truth is the god of the free man." He remembers Luka's telling him that "everybody lives for something better to come. That's why we have to be considerate"—particularly of children: for anyone may turn out to help man rise from the lower depths. The baron again jeers at the prostitute, who angrily replies that he is "living off me like a worm off an apple." The policeman comes in drunk, married to the dumpling vendor. The actor, disillusioned because Luka did not give him the address of the free clinic that was to help him start life anew, goes out after asking the Tatar to pray for him. As the derelicts start to play and sing, the baron comes in and announces that the actor has just hanged himself. The singing stops and Satin quietly remarks, "Ah, spoiled the song—the fool!"

LOYALTIES, a drama in three acts by JOHN GALSWORTHY, published and produced in 1922. Setting: contemporary London and a country estate near Newmarket.

One of Galsworthy's best, least dated, and most successful plays depicts anti-Semitism in polite society. Stressed above all else, loyalties soon are found to transcend caste, to conflict with each other, and finally to be inadequate as an ideal. The play's popularity was originally due in large part to its excellence as a simple crime (or "crook") drama.

Act I. Scene 1. At night at a country estate, a perturbed "young, rich, and new" guest, the wealthy Jew Ferdinand De Levis, reports a theft. While he was taking his bath a few minutes earlier, nearly a thousand pounds was stolen from under his pillow. His host reluctantly agrees to call the police, questions the butler, and discusses the awkward situation with his friend, a socially prominent, elderly general. Put increasingly ill at ease by their coldness, De Levis defensively persists: "I suppose it's natural to want my money back." After he goes to his room to await the police, the aristocrats and their facetious wives are openly hostile about the Jew. They admit that they also would report a theft, but they resent his ways. "How quaint!" one of them remarks upon hearing that he has locked his door: "Just like an hotel. Does he put his boots out?" *Scene 2.* A comically bumptious detective questions De Levis and examines the room. After he departs De Levis excitedly tells the general that he himself has discovered the culprit. Examining his balcony, he noticed evidence of someone's having made a daring jump from the adjoining balcony. That room is occupied by Captain Ronald Dancy, a war hero recently married, in financial difficulties, and known to bear De Levis (a fellow member of his social club) a grudge. The general is appalled at an accusation against "a gallant fellow, with a fine record as a soldier." At his and the estate owner's hostile condescension, De Levis's anger rises. "You think I've no feelers, but I've felt the atmosphere here," he tells the general, and sneers at the host's complaint about the way he repays hospitality: "Hospitality that skins my feelings and costs me a thousand pounds!" In a markedly kinder way the general again questions Dancy. But when they are alone, the general tells their host that Dancy's sleeve was wet: Dancy has denied going outside, but it was raining at the time of the theft. Yet the friends refuse to entertain suspicion against someone in their set: "Dash it, General, we must do as we'd be done by. It hits us all—it hits us all. The thing's intolerable." And the general agrees. When De Levis returns, the general coldly tells him: "Young Dancy was an officer and is a gentleman; this insinuation is pure supposition, and you must not make it." He subtly threatens to blackball De Levis's application to another social club, thus forcing De Levis reluctantly to quash his charge. "Good. We have implicit faith in Dancy," the general says, leaving with their host. De Levis looks after them and remarks: "Rats!"

Act II. Scene 1. Some weeks later, De Levis's membership application to the other club is turned down. Angry, he publicly accuses Dancy in their London club. The general summons De Levis for an accounting. Bitterly denouncing their anti-Semitism, De Levis repeats the accusation against Dancy and produces further evidence. When Dancy is summoned, he calls De Levis a "damned Jew"; the enraged De Levis counters with "Thief!" and refuses his challenge: "You're very smart—dead men tell no tales. No! Bring your action, and we shall see." Told that his membership in the club is suspended, De Levis resigns angrily: "My race was old when you were all savages." Dancy is reluctant to bring suit, and the club members begin to have some slight question of his innocence. But whatever the facts, they agree to stick by him, "an old school-fellow, a brother officer, and a pal." *Scene 2.* In Dancy's flat the next day, his adoring young wife chats with a friend who suggests that Dancy likes to court danger, and that the general was rather silent during the confrontation at the club. "I hate half-hearted friends. Loyalty comes before everything," Dancy's wife says. "Ye-es; but loyalties cut up against each other sometimes," the friend replies. Dancy enters, and suggests to his amazed wife that they get away from society's "rotten menagerie" and leave the country. She insists that they ought to see it through. De Levis now appears: Dancy has called on him to sign a retraction. Their mutual antagonism threatens to end in blows, but Dancy's wife interposes and her husband yells furiously at him, "Get out of here, you swine." After De Levis's departure, Dancy's wife has a momentary doubt of her husband's innocence. But she overcomes it, loyally sticks by him, and persuades him to fight it out in court.

Act III. Scene 1. A distinguished law firm is handling Dancy's libel action and the senior partner discusses the case in his office. It is going well, and though the general is slated to testify, the matter of Dancy's wet sleeve will not create difficulties. Then comes a garrulous grocer who wants to help them: "I don't like—well, not to put too fine a point upon it—'Ebrews. They work harder; they're more sober; they're honest; and they're everywhere. I've nothing against them, but the fact is—they get *on* so." The fact is, too, that he has one of the stolen bank notes, whose numbers were published. The note is traced to an Italian, the father of Dancy's former mistress. He soon reveals that, just before his marriage, Dancy paid her off with about one thousand pounds. Though the law partners sympathize with Dancy, they must now give up the case: "There's duty to our profession," and "professional honour comes first." *Scene 2.* Dancy does not flinch when confronted with the notes. The lawyers, knowing he may be arrested now that the theft is proven, advise Dancy to leave the country. His friends offer help and rebuke the attorneys for their disloyalty to a client. De Levis comes in to tell Dancy of the warrant out against him—it was not his doing—but Dancy says nothing. De Levis proudly remarks: "I didn't come because I feel Christian. I am a Jew. I will take no money—not even that which was stolen. Give it to a charity." He continues, "I'm proved right. And now I'm done with the damned thing." They look at each other, but Dancy still says nothing. De Levis shrugs his shoulders and leaves. *Scene 3.* In his flat, Dancy must tell his wife of his crime. Though overwhelmed, she remains loyal to him, whatever is to come. The police knock, and Dancy disappears while she delays them. Then there is a shot. Dancy's suicide note is read: "This is the only decent thing I can do. . . . It's only another jump. A pistol keeps faith." One of the sophisticated society ladies shouts out hysterically, "Keeps faith! We've all done that. It's not enough."

LUCKY PEHR'S JOURNEY (*Lycko-Pers resa*), a drama in five acts by AUGUST STRINDBERG, published in 1882 and produced in 1883. Setting:

church tower, forest, palace, etc., in medieval times.

This early Strindberg play is an allegorical fantasy that resembles Ibsen's PEER GYNT. Probably at the suggestion of producers, Strindberg changed his original ending—Pehr's final disillusionment—into a happy one. The play has also been translated as *Lucky Peter's Journey*.

Pehr is a secluded fifteen-year-old boy living in a church tower. One Christmas a fairy gives him a magic ring that he uses to seek happiness. Granted such wishes as freedom, power, wealth, and a life amidst nature, Pehr has many adventures. But his quest is always frustrated by the ways of the world and his own self-love. Happiness comes, finally, when Pehr expresses the wish "to free myself from myself," and thus realizes true love for the girl who has devotedly guided him all along.

LUCKY SAM MCCARVER, a play in three acts by SIDNEY HOWARD, produced in 1925 and published in 1926. Setting: New York and Venice, Italy; 1924–25.

In an introduction to the published play Howard elaborated on his characters' "false values" and on their complex motivations. "Four Episodes in the Rise of a New Yorker," as this ambitious but unsuccessful work is subtitled, consists of a series of tableaux.

Sam McCarver is a nightclub proprietor, a self-made man who worships success. He saves the reputation of Carlotta Ashe, a somewhat shallow society woman who gets involved in a murder. They fall in love and marry, but neither can accept the other's world. They separate and return to their individual lives. When Carlotta again needs him, Sam comes to help her. But it is too late, for she dies that night.

LUNACHARSKY, Anatoli Vasilevich (1875?–1933), Russian politician, literary critic, and playwright, was primarily a reformer of the Russian theatre. He was the Soviet Union's first Commissar of Education, an important post he held for ten years. A highly cultivated man and a friend of Lenin, he was responsible for preserving classic Russian plays and encouraging a Soviet drama that portrayed the Revolution as an integral universal phenomenon rooted in the literary and historical past.

As something of an example, he himself wrote over a dozen plays, many of them set in history and legend: *Izkushenie* (1896), about a socialist-preaching monk; *Korolevski bradobrei* (1906); *Faust i gorod* (*Faust and the City*, 1910–16), in which the legendary philosopher, dismissing Mephistopheles, turns his power over to the people; *Magi* (*The Magi*, 1918) about a reincarnated slain chief of Wise Men (the Magi); *Vasilisa Premudraya* (*Vasilisa the Wise*, 1919), in which sacrifices are made for the sake of a better new generation; *Ivan v rayu* (1919); *Kantsler i slesar* (1921), about a workers' revolt; *Oliver Kromvel* (1921), in which the Puritan Revolution is paralleled with that of the Soviets; *Foma Kampanella* (1920–21), a two-part drama (*Narod* and *Gertsog*) about Campanella, the seventeenth-century Italian philosopher of the ideal commonwealth, who was imprisoned by the Inquisition; *Osvobozhdonny Don-Kikhot* (1922), wherein Don Quixote rescues revolutionaries and is then saved by them—though he deplores their violence; *Medvezhya svadba* (1924), a dramatization of Prosper Mérimée's story of a vampiric count, *Lokis; Yad* (1925), an atypically melodramatic play aimed to attract general, uncultivated audiences; *Barkhat i lokhmotya* (1927); and *Nashestvie Napoleona* (1931), an adaptation of *Napoleon greift ein* (1930) by WALTER HASENCLEVER, in which a reincarnated Napoleon enters the contemporary political scene.

These plays were only occasionally successful, and they present historical events from a philosophical and distinctly Soviet, though occasionally unorthodox,* perspective. They reflect, however, Lunacharsky's cultivation, his dynamic effect as a force in the Russian theatre, and his theories on the drama. These were articulated in *Teatr i revolyutsiya* (1924), a collection of his articles, and in a number of other volumes. Translations of *The Magi, Vasilisa the Wise,* and *Faust and the City* were published in *Three Plays of A. V. Lunacharski* (1923).

LUSATIAN DRAMA is written in the dialect falling between Czech and Polish. It is produced by the small Slavic group—known as Lusatians, Sorbs, or Wends—occupying that part of Germany called Lausitz, which is located between the Oder and the Elbe and Saale rivers. Despite attempts to absorb Lusatians into the national culture, they have continued to retain their dialect. Lusatian drama began relatively late, with the plays of its people's finest poet, the priest Ćišinski (pen name of Jakub Bart, 1856–1909). His earliest play was *Na hrodźišću* (1880), the often-produced first part of a never-completed trilogy about the struggle between paganism and Christianity in the ninth century. Ćišinski's work was continued by Józef Nowak (1895–   ), a priest who wrote the trilogy's second play, *Wjelesław,* as well as other SYMBOLIC-lyrical plays, sometimes under the pseudonym Wotrowski; the most popular of them were *Posledni kral* (1916) and further plays about Lusatian history. Other Lusatian dramatists are Kupščan (pen name of Jurij Wjela or Wehle, 1893–1969), the author of historical plays about peasants; Jurij Słodeńk (also known as Georg Melzer, 1873–1945), who wrote a play about Napoleon; and Marja Kubašec or Kubasch (1890–   ), whose folk dramas include the much-praised medieval drama *Khodojta* (1926). Lusatian playwrights have also translated many other European dramas.

After World War II Lusatia was absorbed into the Soviet Russian orbit. In the postwar period

* See, for example, Nikolai A. Gorchakov's account, in *Theater in Soviet Russia* (1957), of Lunacharsky's *Oliver Kromvel.*

the most prominent playwright has been Jurij Brězan (1916–), whose greatest play, *Marja Jančowa* (1958), deals with the transition of the Lusatian peasants from a capitalist to a socialist society.

See Józef Gołabek's "Sorb-Lusatian Literature" in the *Slavonic and East European Review* XIX (1940); Clarence A. Manning's addendum on Lusatia in William E. Harkins and Klement Šimončič's *Czech and Slovak Literature* (1950); and James A. Sehnert's bibliography on the Sorbians in Paul L. Horecky's edition of *East Central Europe; A Guide to Basic Publications* (1969).

LUTHER, a play in three acts by JOHN OSBORNE, published and produced in 1961. Setting: Germany and Italy, 1506–30.

Many of Luther's actual words are used in this historical drama which, like the plays of BERTOLT BRECHT, consists of numerous brief scenes. Luther's concern with his painful constipation—here portrayed as motivating some of his actions—is also historical. Constantly questioning God and fighting "ungodly" men, Luther is one of Osborne's "angry young men."

Act I. Martin Luther's father witnesses the ceremony of his son's reception into the Augustinian Order in Erfurt. Then Luther is seen performing lowly duties, castigating himself, and suffering from chronic constipation. He rejects his father's skepticism about the vision that induced Luther to become a monk. Alone, however, Luther expresses his doubts: "But—but what if it isn't true?"

Act II. At Juterbög in 1517 the famed Dominican monk Johann Tetzel hawks indulgences to the crowds. The reputation of Luther is rising. He is commended for his scholarship, cautioned against self-mortification, and urged to be prudent in criticizing indulgence sales like Tetzel's. Suffering from his chronic ailment ("I'm like a ripe stool in the world's straining anus, and at any moment we're about to let each other go"), Luther replies, "Who knows? If I break wind in Wittenberg, they might smell it in Rome." In Wittenberg on October 31, 1517, he preaches against indulgences and nails his ninety-five theses to the church door. He refuses the papal legate's demand to retract these—unless scriptural proof of his error be shown. Pope Leo X finally orders his excommunication. Luther scornfully burns the decree of the pope, "an overindulged jakes' attendant to Satan himself, a glittering worm in excrement." Then he prays, "Lord, I'm afraid. I am a child, the lost body of a child. . . . Give me life."

Act III. Before the Diet of Worms in 1521, Luther is urged to reconsider his position. Luther still refuses, unless his error be proven scripturally: "Here I stand; God help me; I can do no more." After the Bundschuh uprising in 1525, Luther is blamed for inciting the slaughter of the peasants. But Luther remains steadfast in his interpretation of God's words: "The peasants rebelled against that Word." In 1530, Luther and his wife, a former nun, live with their child in a vacated cloister in Wittenberg. The visiting vicar-general of the Augustinian Order expresses his approval of most of Luther's work: Luther has taken "Christ away from the low mumblings and soft voices and jewelled gowns and the tiaras and put Him back where He belongs. In each man's soul." Luther admits to persisting doubts: "Oh, Lord, I believe. I believe. I do believe. Only help my unbelief." Then he takes the sleeping infant his wife brings in. At Worms Luther was like this child, he remembers, "come to set a man against his father"—and they listened to him. Luther carries his child to bed: "A little while, and you *shall* see me. Christ said that, my son. I hope that'll be the way of it again. I hope so. Let's just hope so, eh? Eh? Let's just hope so."

M

MAC LIAMMÓIR, Micheál (1899–), Irish director, designer, actor, and playwright, founded two theatres in 1928. The first was Dublin's Gate Studio (founded with Hilton Edwards), which was to present both the classics and new Irish plays that did not fit the Abbey Theatre's style; eminently successful, this theatre has produced ancient as well as modern classics, and has introduced new writers like DENIS JOHNSTON. Mac Liammóir's second house, *Taibhdhearc na Gaillimhe* (the Galway Gaelic Theatre), has featured such stars as Siobhan McKenna and presented plays of the Irish actor-novelist Walter Macken (1915–67) and translations of the plays of BERNARD SHAW, ANTON CHEKHOV, and others. Until 1931 this theatre, under Mac Liammóir's direction, produced some twenty plays. The theatre was launched with his own best-known drama, *Diarmuid agus Gráinne* (1928), which reinterprets the legend also dramatized by WILLIAM BUTLER YEATS and GEORGE MOORE, and in Lady Gregory's GRANIA.

Mac Liammóir's plays, produced with much success in English as well as Gaelic, are characterized by a peculiar blend of charm, wit, melodrama, and Irish legend. They include *Where Stars Walk* (1940), *Dancing Shadows* (1941), *Ill Met by Moonlight* (1946, a comic melodrama), *Portrait of Miriam* (1947), *The Mountains Look Different* (1948), *Home for Christmas* (1950), *A Slipper for the Moon* (1954), and dramatic monologues like *The Importance of Being Oscar,* which heightened his fame in the 1960's. In 1968 he published *An Oscar of No Importance,* an account of his international tours with this production of OSCAR WILDE's works.

For Mac Liammóir's life and extensive theatrical activities see his autobiographies, *All for Hecuba* (1946) and *Each Actor on His Ass* (1960). He also wrote a short history of the *Theatre in Ireland* (2nd edition, 1964).

Machinal. The Young Woman (Zita Johann) and the outlaw (Clark Gable). New York, 1928. (*Culver Pictures*)

MACARTHUR, Charles (1895–1956), American writer and producer, was born in Pennsylvania, began his journalistic career in Chicago, and continued to pursue it in New York from 1914 to 1923. He collaborated with BEN HECHT on a number of plays, notably THE FRONT PAGE (1928); *Twentieth Century* (1933), an amusing satire of Hollywood; *Jumbo* (1925), a Richard Rodgers and Lorenz Hart musical extravaganza; *Ladies and Gentlemen* (1939); and *Swan Song* (1946). His other plays were also collaborations: *Lulu Belle* (1926, written with EDWARD SHELDON), a melodrama about a Negro prostitute; and *Salvation* (1927, written with SIDNEY HOWARD), about a female evangelist. Then MacArthur turned to writing and producing films, and beginning in 1948 he edited *Theatre Arts Magazine.* He was married to the actress Helen Hayes. Ben Hecht wrote his biography, *Charlie; The Impossible Life and Times of Charles MacArthur* (1957). Hecht and MacArthur are caricatured as two prankster screenwriters in *Boy Meets Girl* (1935), a Hollywood satire by SAM and BELLA SPEWACK.

MACHINAL, a play in nine episodes by SOPHIE TREADWELL, produced in 1928 and published in 1929. Setting: New York and a seaside hotel, 1920's.

Suggested by a notorious contemporary murder case, this very effective EXPRESSIONISTIC play (also produced as *The Life Machine*) aroused considerable attention in Russia. Its heroine, referred to as the Young Woman, is stultified by a banal society and a mechanized world, represented by a profusion of offstage sounds. The role of the lover was played on Broadway by the then-unknown Clark Gable.

Amidst office noises, fellow workers tease the Young Woman secretary about the unattractive, Babbitt-like boss. She thinks, "Marry me—wants to marry me— . . . you have such pretty little hands—thin—bald—don't touch me." But to escape her drab home and mother, she marries him. The honeymoon terrifies her, and she comes to loathe her earthy husband and her baby when it is born. An affair with a young outlaw she meets in a speakeasy gives her the only happiness she has ever known. At her trial, she confesses that she murdered her husband "to be free." She resists having her head shaved for her execution: "I won't submit! Not now!" Her "sin of love," she tells the priest, "was all I ever knew of Heaven." To the reporters she seems very small as she is led to the electric chair.

MACHINE-WRECKERS, THE (*Die Maschinenstürmer*), "A Drama of the English Luddites in a prologue and five acts" by ERNST TOLLER, published and produced in 1922. Setting: London and Nottingham, c. 1812–15.

Like MASSES AND MAN, *The Machine-Wreckers* was written during Toller's imprisonment, and deals with materialism and the masses' betrayal of their idealistic leader. Though partly in verse, this is a NATURALIST mass drama, comparable to Hauptmann's THE WEAVERS. Toller's play, too, is partly historical. The prologue in the House of Lords is followed by a dramatization of the English Chartists' revolts against the manufacturers and their new machines, which reduced the weavers to mechanical assembly-line workers and threatened their livelihood.

In the House of Lords debate on a bill "to render the destruction of machinery punishable by death," Lord Byron, in his maiden speech, defends the weavers. Citing their misery, he asks, "Is hanging medicine / For hunger and despair?" But the arguments of Lord Castlereagh prevail, and the bill is passed.

Suffering and starvation are rampant in Nottingham because of the new machines. Men are replaced by women and children who slave sixteen hours a day for a pittance. Jimmy Cobbett's brother has worked his way up to the position of foreman in Ure's factory. Fearing the loss of his job if Ure learns that the agitator Jimmy is his brother, the cruel foreman plots with John Wibley, a villainous weaver, to get Jimmy away. Wibley urges the men to destroy the works: "Death to the machine! War to the tyrant steam!" But Jimmy exhorts them to enlist the machine in their cause: "The commonwealth shall be our master, not Mammon! Men shall rule, not machinery!" He sees the suffering of the weavers and visits the industrialist Ure. In their long discussion he fervently urges the capitalist to run his works in a spirit of brotherhood and godliness. "Young man, the dreams you dream are dangerous," Ure replies: "He who survives, survives by Nature's law / Which must remain unfathom'd by our minds." Jimmy asks him to "lift the Scriptural curse of toil, / And what is now our scourge, our brand of bondage / Shall be again our holy, happy task!" Moved, Ure offers him an important position, but Jimmy declines. "We fight against you, and yet on your side," he tells Ure: "The light of justice flames upon our banner!" Amidst further scenes of misery, Wibley traduces Jimmy before the workers and gets them to destroy the machines. Frenzied, they break into the works, smash them, and attempt to murder the engineer. When Jimmy tries to stop them, Wibley inflames the mob against him: "Would you leave the traitor's tongue, the traitor's eyes, to live?" As he is struck down Jimmy tells them they are fighting the wrong enemy and urges them to join "the workers of the world in fellowship, / To build the house of human brotherhood." Though too cowardly to look at blood, Wibley gets the mobs to beat Jimmy to death: "Pull his tongue from his mouth! Tear his eyes from their sockets!" A beggar who has come to warn the workers of the police is appalled to see what they have done to Jimmy, "who forsook place and name for your sake." Singing defiantly, the peasants march out to be arrested as an old weaver prays and weeps over Jimmy's torn body: "Ah, poor dear Son! We must bury him. We must be good to one another."

MACKAYE, Percy [Wallace] (1875–1956), American poet and playwright, was a pioneer in producing enormous pageant drama and the author of many plays. He was the son of notable parents—the distinguished stage innovator, producer, and dramatist Steele MacKaye (1842–94), who is still remembered for his immensely successful and long-popular domestic drama *Hazel Kirke* (1880), and of Mary Medbery MacKaye (1845–1924), who in 1877 dramatized Jane Austen's *Pride and Prejudice* (1813). Percy MacKaye, born in New York and educated at Harvard University and in Europe, began his career as a teacher in a private school in New York. He lectured in major American universities, and he spent much of his time writing often ambitious plays. Most of them were meant for regional rather than commercial theatres, although some of them appeared on Broadway. But even the nonpoetic, more conventional plays—notably THE SCARECROW (1908)—are singularly imaginative and highly dependent on spectacle. He was successful also with two comedies: *Anti-Matrimony* (1910), which spoofs a younger generation "liberated" by the drama of HENRIK IBSEN and BERNARD SHAW; and a Kentucky-mountain folk comedy in dialect, *This Fine-Pretty World* (1923).

Outstanding among his verse plays are *The Canterbury Pilgrims* (1903), a portrayal of the journey, including a sentimental episode between the Prioress and Geoffrey Chaucer who, in turn, is pursued by the lusty Wife of Bath and saved by Richard II's ruling that she marry the Miller; *Jeanne d'Arc* (1906), a retelling of that popular story, but with an emphasis on Joan's battles and a dramatization of her visions; *Sappho and Phaon* (1907), a tragedy depicting the Greek poet's love for a slave; and *A Thousand Years Ago* (1913), a romantic fantasy based on Carlo Gozzi's *Turandot* (1762), the Italian comedy which also is the basis of Giacomo Puccini's opera.

Among MacKaye's productions of his own mass spectacles were *The Gloucester Pageant* (1909), a version of *The Canterbury Pilgrims* with fifteen hundred extras, presented in honor of President Taft; *Saint Louis: A Civic Masque* (1914), a dramatization of the city's history; *Caliban, by the Yellow Sands* (1916), "a Community Masque of the Art of the Theatre" commemorating the tercentenary of Shakespeare's death with a twenty-five-hundred-character extravaganza sequel to *The Tempest* in which Caliban, representing "that passionate child-curious part of us all," is regenerated by Miranda and Prospero; and *Washington, the Man Who Made Us* (1918), an episodic biographical drama, which like some of MacKaye's other works used the "participatory technique" that made production possible by large community as well as small professional casts. His *The Canterbury Pilgrims,* which appeared in the mass-spectacle format in 1909, was presented at the Metropolitan Opera House in 1917 as an opera, with music by Reginald de Koven, who collaborated with MacKaye on another opera, *Rip Van Winkle* (1919).

MacKaye's trips to Kentucky inspired his writing of numerous plays about that area, including the above-mentioned folk comedy and the one-act *Kentucky Mountain Fantasies* (1928). The most ambitious of MacKaye's dramatic writings is *The Mystery of Hamlet, King of Denmark—or What We Will* (1949), a verse tetralogy on the characters of Shakespeare's play—including Hamlet as a child, his father, Yorick, the jealous Claudius, and others.

MacKaye was one of the prime progenitors of the American little- or community-theatre movement. His ambition to create a native poetic folk drama is reflected also in his many books on the theatre. His two-volume *Poems and Plays* (1916) includes the early verse plays; his other drama was published in numerous individual and collected volumes. MacKaye also edited the tenth volume of *America's Lost Plays* (1941 and 1964), devoted to his father's drama, and he wrote the two-volume *Epoch, the Life of Steele MacKaye* (1927). His career and drama are described in Volume II of Arthur Hobson Quinn's *The History of the American Drama from the Civil War to the Present Day* (1936).

MACLEISH, Archibald (1892–), American poet and dramatist, and also an educator and a public official. He became best known for his poetry, for which he won two Pulitzer Prizes, the Bollingen and National Book awards, and many other distinctions. MacLeish began writing plays early in his career, and eventually succeeded with that rarest of all Broadway hits, a religious verse play. His most famous work, J.B. (1958) is the only modern American play to achieve such a popular success. Like Eliot's religious verse play THE COCKTAIL PARTY, *J.B.* is an attempted fusion of verse, of the depiction of a spiritual quest, and of diverting theatre. And like the earlier play, its long New York run (364 performances) was abetted by a good production and theatre audiences' willingness to follow intellectual fashion and hail a major poet. MacLeish's other plays have fared less well, and his next major one, *Scratch* (1971), failed on Broadway; a free adaptation of Stephen Vincent Benét's short story "The Devil and Daniel Webster" (1937), the play stresses morality and politics in the struggle between Webster and the Devil (Scratch). Also a pioneer author of radio verse plays, he wrote *The Fall of the City* (1937), an effective portrayal of Franklin D. Roosevelt's proclamation that "the only thing we have to fear is fear itself," which dramatizes a city's succumbing to an empty threat. Like his next radio play, *Air Raid* (1938), it was written in the form of a news broadcast.

MacLeish was born in Glencoe, Illinois. After graduating from Yale University in 1915, he enlisted in the army as a private and, by the end of World War I, he had attained the rank of captain. Returning to his studies, he soon graduated from the Harvard Law School. Then he turned to teaching and writing, and moved to Paris with his family in the 1920's. There he met important expatriate poets of the time, including Eliot. One of the profound influences on his work was Ezra Pound, who introduced him to Oriental poetry, which became important in MacLeish's later writings. In these years he published a number of volumes of lyric poetry and his first drama, *Nobodaddy* (1926), a philosophical verse play about Adam and Eve.

It was his second play, *Panic* (1935), that actually reached the commercial theatre and determined the verse form MacLeish was to use in his dramas. Depicting the irresistible mob hysteria that followed the 1929 stock market crash, the play, a sophisticated AGITPROP, was prefaced by an essay in which MacLeish explained his preference for drama in accentual meter (a count of stresses rather than syllables), which more closely approximates American speech, over blank verse. The play was scheduled for and had a three-day run in New York.

MacLeish's stature as a poet and a man of letters grew steadily. In recognition of his distinction he was appointed Librarian of Congress (1939–44). An important and often controversial figure in the inner circle of President Roosevelt and often attacked for his liberalism, MacLeish held other prestigious public positions during and after World War II, when he was Assistant Secretary of State and headed the American delegation that drew up the UNESCO constitution. In 1949 MacLeish returned to his earlier literary and academic life, becoming the Boylston Professor of Rhetoric and Oratory at Harvard University. Following the implications of his most famous line, "A poem should not mean / But be" (*Ars Poetica*), his lectures and writings in support of the appreciation of literature stressed the compatibility of science and poetry. MacLeish's critical theories of that period were collected in *Poetry and Experience* (1961).

Aside from *J.B.*, MacLeish's most successful dramatic work was for the radio, which is "perhaps the best medium for the verse play," he remarked, "for it requires the ear alone." *The American Story* (1944), a collection of ten radio scripts, is a dramatized narrative pageant of the birth and rise of America from the time of Columbus to the time of George Washington. MacLeish also wrote a ballet and other verse plays. His *This Music Crept By Me Upon the Waters* (1953), first produced on the radio, is a one-act mood piece set on an Antilles island. *Herakles,* another verse drama combining a modern setting with ancient myth, was produced on the stage in 1965. *An Evening's Journey to Conway, Mass.*, a play about a boy who yearns to leave his small hometown, appeared on television in 1967.

Except for *J.B.*, however, MacLeish's drama is of minor significance. He is notable as a poet and a critic—a distinguished gentleman of letters and a public servant whose rarefied drama is of interest almost exclusively to his audience of liberal and cultivated poetry readers, whom he has so well represented. Even *J.B.* soon lost its popular appeal.

His many prose and verse books include a prize-winning epic poem on the conquest and his own explorations of Mexico, *Conquistador* (1932). MacLeish was also one of the original editors of *Fortune* magazine and a president of the American Academy of Arts and Letters. A book-length study of his life and work is Signi L. Falk's *Archibald MacLeish* (1965).

MACNAMARA, Brinsley [John Weldon] (1890–1963), Irish writer and actor, is better known as a novelist than as a dramatist. But he was, with SEAN O'CASEY and GEORGE SHIELS, one of the "new pillars who supported the [Abbey] Theatre" between 1918 and 1924, according to the account of LENNOX ROBINSON. He effectively depicted small town society (as in *Look at the Heffernans!*, 1926) and political agitators and turmoils. *The Rebellion in Balleycullen* (1919), his first play, satirizes Irish chauvinism; in *The Land for the People* (1920) he lashed out at profiteering land agitators. *The Glorious Uncertainty* (1923), which deals with track betting, was an especially popular comedy, and he wrote some half-dozen other plays, the last of them *Marks and Mabel* (1945), a comedy that features the Heffernans of his 1926 play. His strongest and best play is *Margaret Gillan* (1933), an intense domestic drama of passion and intrigue that excels in the portrayal of the title character.

MacNamara's denunciation of O'Casey's THE SILVER TASSIE in 1935 was so rabid that WILLIAM BUTLER YEATS—who himself had rejected the play seven years earlier—was obliged to ask for MacNamara's resignation from his theatre's board of directors. See Peter Kavanagh's *The Story of The Abbey Theatre* (1950) and Robert Hogan and Michael J. O'Neill's edition of *Joseph Holloway's Abbey Theatre* (1967).

MADAME BUTTERFLY, a one-act play by DAVID BELASCO, produced in 1900 and published in 1917. Setting: a little house near a Japanese harbor, late nineteenth century.

Based on JOHN LUTHER LONG's 1898 story, this play in 1904 was made into one of Giacomo Puccini's great operas. Outstandingly successful in the play was the representation of an entire night in fourteen silent minutes: Belasco sustained audience interest by the experimental use of lights and evocatively painted curtains.

Cho-Cho-San, or Madame Butterfly, as the American Lieutenant Pinkerton she married called her, is awaiting his return. "I goin' back to my own country and here's moaney—an' don' worry 'bout me," she recalls his saying when he left two years before; "I come back w'en 'Robins nes' again!" The American consul tries to tell her Pinkerton is returning with an American wife. But Madame Butterfly insists that she herself is "Mrs. Lef-ten-ant B. F. Pik-ker-ton," and rejects a wealthy Japanese suitor who also warns her that the marriage to Pinkerton was meaningless. "I am jus' waitin'," she says, "sometimes cryin', sometimes watchin', but always waitin'." For "Loave don' forget some thin's or wha's use of loave?" She has not written to Pinkerton of the baby she bore him, and now excitedly prepares the child for its father's arrival, lullabying it with a song Pinkerton taught her: "Rog'—a—bye, bebby, / Off in Japan, / You jus' a picture, / Off of a fan." Joined by her servant, who soon falls asleep, Cho-Cho-San waits all night for Pinkerton. In the morning she is still hopeful and goes to watch "from liddle look out place." Pinkerton arrives. "Poor little devil," he remarks; "I thought when I left this house, the few tears, sobs, little polite regrets, would be over as I crossed the threshold." Unable to face her, he gives the consul some money for her, and leaves. Pinkerton's wife pities the girl: "Why, you poor little thing . . . you pretty little plaything." But Madame Butterfly softly replies, "No playthin' . . . I am Mrs. Lef-ten-ant B. F. —No—No—now I am, only—Cho-Cho-San, but no playthin'." With dignity she bids the American wife farewell and promises her crying servant that "when you see me again, I pray you look whether I be not beautiful again . . . as a bride." Madame Butterfly takes down her father's hara-kiri sword and goes behind a screen. Reappearing deathly pale, she clasps her child just as Pinkerton comes in. He draws her and the baby toward him as Madame Butterfly dies, saying: "Too bad those robins didn' nes' again."

MADRAS HOUSE, THE, a comedy in four acts by HARLEY GRANVILLE-BARKER, produced in 1910 and published in 1911. Setting: London, early twentieth century.

Revised and republished in 1925, this is a "disquisitory" play like Shaw's GETTING MARRIED and MISALLIANCE. *The Madras House* is a subtle examination and comic depiction of sexual repression and frustration. The caricatures and amusing dialogue portray the debilitating effects of Western sex mores, both on wealthy suburbanites and on the "boarding" employees of the Madras and Huxtable drapery emporium.

Act I. It is Sunday morning at the plush Denmark Hill residence of Henry Huxtable, the semiretired partner of the drapery establishment. His nephew, Philip Madras, and the latter's friend and associate await Huxtable when he returns from church with his wife and their six unmarried daughters. Madras apprises Huxtable of the next day's negotiations for the sale of the establishment to an American millionaire. To the consternation of the Huxtables, present will be Madras's father, the emporium's director and a Don Juan who long ago had left his wife (Huxtable's sister) and gone abroad. There is much repetitive small talk that reveals the triviality of their lives: the six daughters' frustrations, not relieved by sketching, charity, gardening, and other work; the sterile propriety of Mrs. Huxtable and of Madras's mother, the "deserted" wife; the confusion of the genial Huxtable, recovering from an illness and no longer as sure of the ways of the world as he used to be; and the sententiousness of Madras, who wants to give up business so that he can become a reformer.

Act II. At the office, Madras adjudicates a crisis among his employees. Males as well as females there participate in the company's "living-in system," which is economically profitable but stifling and psychologically devastating. The housekeeper, shocked to discover one of her spinster charges pregnant, has observed her kissing a timid married employee, and has spread the rumor that he is the father. Now this employee and his hysterical wife accuse the housekeeper of slander. The latter, in turn, is indignant about the affront to respectability by the pregnant girl, who exclaims, "I took the risk. I knew what I was about. I wanted to have my fling. And it was fun for a bit." Later Madras's wife, Jessica, arrives and flirts with his friend. She is a beautiful, cultivated, but bored young lady. After she leaves, Madras's friend, embarrassed by acting like a cad, asks Madras to see to it that his wife stops flirting with him, for, married himself, he does not want to fall in love with her.

Act III. At the showroom of the emporium, the partners meet with the American to discuss the sale. Mannequinlike models strut around vacuously in adornments copied from French cocottes—a continuous parade that exposes the exploitation of sex. The loquacious American, who has made his millions on canned peaches and ready-made skirts, rationalizes his business in terms of grandiose ideals and culture: to provide every woman with clothes "to dazzle and conquer," as is her right in the "march of civilization" toward the economic emancipation of the female. He is particularly interested in cultivating the middle class, "one of the greatest money-spending machines the world has ever seen." But the most imposing figure, from the moment of his entrance, is Constantine Madras, Philip's father. Repulsed by the notions of the American and his own associates, he reveals his conversion to Muhammadanism. "Europe in its attitude toward women is mad" and unmanning, he declares. And while the modeling proceeds and his associates comment, he elaborates his views: "The well-kept women you flatter and aestheticize till they won't give you children, and the free women you work at market rates till they can't give you children." Good-naturedly he then grants the American his wish to dream about women and how to dress them, "their bodies in silks and their virtues in phrases." Constantine Madras himself opts for libertinism, and he charms Huxtable, his brother-in-law, who has refused to speak to him for thirty years, into expressing his reluctant admiration. He even invites Huxtable to return with him to Arabia, where his views are sanctioned by the religion he has adopted to accommodate his propensities.

Act IV. At the fashionable home of Philip Madras, his father, for the first time since he deserted her, meets his wife. Though she tries to have him take her back—"You're mine in the sight of God, Constantine, and you can't deny it"—he dismisses her. Then he reveals to his son, the product of "a quarrelsome marriage," that he is the father of the little employee's illegitimate child: but that the girl had sent him away, and "I never felt so degraded in my life." After Constantine Madras leaves, there is a confrontation between young Madras and his wife, Jessica, whom he chides for flirting. They diagnose his cold intellectuality and her empty respectability, which even a love of culture and beauty cannot make into a meaningful life. He admits his coldness, though he has always tried to overcome it—"But I do so hate that farmyard world of sex." They become reconciled, and he will try to make the world better by getting elected to the County Council: "That's how these great spiritual revolutions work out in practice, to begin with." They cannot really resolve their problems, but they stand together, looking at their fireplace, temporarily contented.

MADWOMAN OF CHAILLOT, THE (*La Folle de Chaillot*), a play in two acts by JEAN GIRAUDOUX, published and produced in 1945. Setting: Paris, a day "in the Spring of next year."

This posthumous work was first performed in gala triumph before an audience that included General de Gaulle. It was completed shortly before Giraudoux's death and is perhaps his best-known—and best—play. Not unlike *Alice in Wonderland,* it is a lyric madcap resolved by a captivating paean to life, nature, and joy. Giraudoux inverts the sane and the insane, depicting a predatory, dehumanizing modern society that is roundly defeated by the fantastic machinations of the mad and the humble. The character of the title protagonist was suggested by a real Parisian madwoman. The play was filmed and was made into a musical, *Dear World* (1969), with the book by JEROME LAWRENCE and ROBERT E. LEE, and music by Jerry Herman.

Act I. Ruthless financiers conspire in a Parisian café in the Chaillot quarter. They are preparing

The Madwoman of Chaillot. The Madwoman (Marguerite Moreno) surrounded by her friends; the ragpicker (Louis Jouvet) is on the right. Jouvet's production in Paris, 1945. (*French Cultural Service*)

to wreck Paris in order to get at oil they believe is flowing in the subsoil beneath the city. Their talk is constantly interrupted by noises of the happy street life and the people around them—a ragpicker, a flower girl, a singer, a juggler, a peddler, etc. The most annoying interruption is by a fantastically got-up old woman—Countess Aurelia, the Madwoman of Chaillot. Dressed in the high fashion of the 1880's, she pulls a bell from the bosom of her gown, rings it, and asks the waitress, "Are my bones ready?" Then she asks the doorman whether he has found the feather boa she lost five years before. One of the financiers is irked by the respectful care lavished on her. Angry to hear that she cannot be gotten rid of because she owns the café, he storms against the anarchy all about him: "The only safeguard of order and discipline in the modern world is a standardized worker with interchangeable parts," he says, envisioning the beauty of "one composite drudge grunting and sweating all over the world." A prospector in the group is listening for an explosion, which he has arranged to browbeat the authorities into letting him drill for oil. But instead of lighting the dynamite, his desperate young agent has tried to throw himself into the river. Now he is brought to the café, and as soon as he regains consciousness he falls in love with the waitress. The Madwoman tells the policeman not to take down his name: he should instead console the attempted suicide and praise life, to convince him that it is worth living. The policeman fails, but the Madwoman succeeds. "To be alive is to be fortunate," she tells the young man. "Of course, in the morning, when you first awake, it does not always seem so very gay," she admits—especially "when you take your hair out of the drawer and your teeth out of the glass." But things become "pure delight" as soon as one fixes oneself up and reads the morning paper—an old and happy one, of course, not "these current sheets full of lies and vulgarity." She describes her mad life, an imaginative preoccupation with long-past gaieties. When the blackmailing prospector returns for the young man, the Madwoman protects him by squirting soda at the prospector and then bashing him over the head with the siphon. Later the Madwoman learns that they intend to ruin the city by drilling for oil. She is sure that "these horrible men" cannot change the beauty and happiness of the world. But others soon open her eyes to what the world is like now, with the financiers in control. "Little by little, the pimps have taken over the world," the ragpicker tells her; "they don't do anything, they don't make anything—they just stand there and take their cut." He and the other paupers persuade her that the world is no longer happy, that "pimps" control everything, that the mad and the riffraff "are the last of the free." The Madwoman decides to rid the world of this blight. She writes notes to inform leading financiers that she has discovered an oil well beneath her house. Then she summons some friends—madwomen from other parts of Paris—to a conference on "the future of humanity." Alone, the waitress, who has never before told any man that she loves him, whispers it after the departing young man.

Act II. In the basement of her house, a sewer man reveals to the Madwoman the mysteries of Parisian underground (i.e., sewer) life. Then he shows her how to move a secret stone that opens a trap staircase deep into the earth. Soon the other madwomen arrive. They, too, are fantastically got up in bizarre costumes of the past, and they, too, live happy lives of illusion. In their discussion and frequent digressions, it takes the Madwoman a while to get to her point. At last she reveals that, having discovered the human "rats" who poison contemporary life, she has devised a trap into which they will soon fall. But first the doomed financiers must be tried—in absentia. The assorted street people are invited to sit in judgment. The ragpicker, under the guise of defending them, denounces the parasites who batten on humanity and deprive the world of beauty and happiness. "I mix morals with mink," he tells them; "to have money is to be virtuous, honest, beautiful, and witty. And to be without it is to be ugly and boring and stupid and useless." If he were to find subterranean oil, he would make war and conquer the world. He—and the other "accused"—are quickly pronounced guilty. Now the Madwoman happily awaits their arrival, imagining in the meantime that the young man saved from drowning himself is her long-lost lover. Word of the Madwoman's notes about the oil well has spread quickly, and financiers, prospectors, and newspapermen all hasten in. They fall over each other in their hurry to get down the staircase and examine the "oil well." When they are gone, the Madwoman shuts the trap. Slowly light begins to suffuse the setting "with the quiet radiance of universal joy." The air becomes purer, strangers become friendly, and beautiful, unearthly music is heard. A voice comes out of that music. It thanks the Madwoman—in the name of humanity, animals, and flowers. The long-lost lover of the Madwoman appears—in fact, there is a whole group of them, all identical in face and dress. But it is too late for her, and she waves them away. It is not too late for the waitress and the young man, however. Knowing they are in love, the Madwoman begs them to kiss each other quickly, to have the courage to do what she failed to do many years before. Now the world is saved—and it was simple: "Nothing is ever so wrong in this world that a sensible woman can't set it right in the course of an afternoon." And she returns to more important things. Again she asks for bones and gizzard: "My poor cats must be starved. What a bore for them if humanity had to be saved every afternoon. They don't think much of it, as it is."

MAETERLINCK, Maurice [Mauritius Polydorus Maria Bernardus] (1862–1949), Belgian dramatist, poet, and essayist, was the most successful SYMBOLIST playwright and one of the most important writers at the turn of the century because of his theories of the drama of atmosphere and "stasis." The 1911 Nobel Prize and two of his plays, *Pelléas et Mélisande* (PELLÉAS AND MÉLISANDE, 1892) and *L'Oiseau bleu* (THE BLUE BIRD, 1908), made him internationally famous. After World War I his importance waned—so much so that his death in 1949 came as a surprise: it was generally thought that he had already died long before. But if Maeterlinck did not deserve his inflated reputation, he also did not deserve oblivion. His plays—aside from their originality and occasional intrinsic merit—demonstrated the possibilities in symbolism eventually realized and incorporated into the mainstream of modern drama. The words of Maeterlinck's Nobel Prize citation are still valid: his plays "are outstanding for their richness of imagination and for poetic realism, which sometimes in the dim form of the play of legend display a deep intimacy of feeling, and also in a mysterious way appeal to the reader's sentiment and sense of foreboding."

Born in Ghent, Maeterlinck was educated in a Jesuit college and in his hometown's university. His father, a retired notary, encouraged his studying law, and Maeterlinck was admitted to the bar in 1885. But he was a singularly unsuccessful lawyer. Primarily eager to pursue his literary bent, Maeterlinck persuaded his parents to send him to Paris. There he settled that same year (1885) and met various writers. The most influential of these was Villiers de L'Isle-Adam, the prominent French symbolist. Later Maeterlinck met the poet Paul Verlaine, but the two remained unimpressed with each other. For almost a year Maeterlinck devoted most of his time to writing. Then he returned to Ghent, where he lived on a generous allowance from his father and practiced law half-heartedly. Poems that had been published separately were collected in 1889 in *Serres chaudes* (*Hothouses*), his first book. It went unnoticed.

Maurice Maeterlinck. (*Belgian Consulate General*)

The same year he also published his first play, *La Princesse Maleine* (*Princess Maleine*). It attracted the attention of the dramatist-journalist OCTAVE MIRBEAU. His extravagant review in the Paris *Le Figaro* (August 24, 1890) and his calling the author "a Belgian Shakespeare" made Maeterlinck famous overnight and inspired Strindberg's SWANWHITE. But the play remained unacted. It is a crude and bloody mixture of Edgar Allan Poe and Shakespeare (Maeterlinck himself called it "a mere *Shakspiterie*") in which endless sequences of lust, horrors, and multiple murders are piled up in a confused, disjointed, medieval plot. The play is characteristically Maeterlinckian in atmosphere and symbolism.

These characteristics appear in their purest form in a trio of one-acters about death: *L'Intruse* (THE INTRUDER, 1890), *Les Aveugles* (THE BLIND, 1890), and *L'Intérieur* (*Interior,* 1894), which portrays people bearing home a drowned girl. Punctuated by silences, apparent indirection of dialogue, and settings and atmosphere pregnant with terror, these plays are typical of the interior drama, the static theatre of mood, associated with Maeterlinck's symbolism and, incidentally, occasionally ridiculed in parody. He derived his aesthetics from a medieval inscription ("Within me there is more") and detailed them in *Le Trésor des humbles* (*The Treasure of the Humble,* 1896), particularly in its opening chapter on silence. Maeterlinck believed drama as well as a metaphysical type of tragedy to lie in silences that reveal the inexpressible mysteries of man's soul and the universe, admiring, as he did, the transcendentalism of Ralph Waldo Emerson and of Novalis. Some of Maeterlinck's early plays, for that reason, were intended to be played by marionettes.

He almost realized such "stasis" in the three one-acters and in *Les Sept Princesses* (*The Seven Princesses,* 1891), which followed. But soon he was compelled to discard it for more externalized dramatization of conflict, as in *Pelléas and Mélisande* and, even more, in *The Blue Bird.* In time, his stature diminished as his drama became more conventional, spiritually uplifting—and banal. With the exception of *The Blue Bird,* it failed to impress his admirers as his earlier plays had, despite its exotically historic or legendary settings. Those that immediately followed—*Alladine et Palomides* (1894), *Le Mort de Tintagiles* (*The Death of Tintagiles,* 1894), and *Aglavaine et Sélysette* (1896)—are now forgotten. Only slightly less obscure are *Ariane et Barbe-blue* and *Soeur Béatrice,* three-act verse dramas written as librettos and published in 1902; the first reinterprets the Bluebeard and other legends, and the second, a miracle play set in thirteenth-century France, depicts the Virgin's taking the place of an errant nun who is finally ruined. The once-popular MONNA VANNA (1902) dispenses entirely with Maeterlinckian silences, and is no more suggestive in its atmosphere than other dramas.

The optimistic *Joyzelle* (1903), an allegory of love ("*The Tempest* rewritten") in which the magician Merlin is foiled, was followed by *Le Miracle de Saint-Antoine* (1903), *Le Malheur passe* (completed in 1904), *Marie-Victoire* (completed in 1907), and his most popular play, *The Blue Bird.* A biblical drama that explores Maeterlinck's metaphysics of love was his reinterpretation of the story of *Marie-Magdaleine* (MARY MAGDALENE, 1910), which was followed by his last significant plays, *Le Bourgmestre de Stilemonde* (*The Mayor of Stilemonde,* 1918) and *The Blue Bird*'s sequel, *Les Fiançailles* (THE BETROTHAL, 1918); the former is a violent antiwar play in which German soldiers execute an innocent Flemish villager and the mayor who defends him. Maeterlinck's remaining dramatic works (he wrote thirty of them) are *Berniquel* (1923), *La Puissance des morts* (*The Power of the Dead,* 1926), the fragment *Juda de Kérioth* (1929), *La Princesse Isabelle* (written for and performed by his wife in 1935), *Jeanne d'Arc* (completed in 1940), *L'Abbé Sétubal* (1940), *Les Trois Justiciers* (written c. 1942), *L'Enfant qui ne veut pas naître* (a sketch in which his wife acted her part in English in the summer of 1942 in New York), *Le Jugement dernier* (written c. 1944), and his last work, *Le Miracle des mères,* written shortly before his death.

Though he loved children, he never had any. For twenty-three years he lived with but never married Georgette Leblanc, the actress and singer who appeared in many of his plays and who was his artistic collaborator. Subsequently he broke with her and married a minor actress, Renée Dahon. Because of his later anti-Catholicism, his fatherland was long cool to its greatest playwright; but in 1932 Belgium made Maeterlinck a count, the highest honor it could bestow. During World War II he lived in the United States. In 1947 he returned to France, where he had spent much of his life. He died in his villa near Nice.

Maeterlinck wrote many essays on quasi-scientific, metaphysical, and occult subjects, as well as a memoir. His most famous nondramatic work is *La Vie des abeilles* (*The Life of the Bees,* 1901), available in translation, like many of the plays. W. D. Halls's *Maurice Maeterlinck: A Study of His Life and Thought* (1960) is a reliable biography and criticism, and contains an extensive bibliography. See also Jethro Bithell's *Life and Writings of Maurice Maeterlinck* (1930) and the works listed under SYMBOLISM.

MAGDA (*Heimat;* literally, "home"), a play in four acts by HERMANN SUDERMANN, published and produced in 1893. Setting: a provincial town, 1890's.

Sudermann's most successful play, this was a popular vehicle for many great actresses of the age, Sarah Bernhardt's and Eleonora Duse's competing 1895 London performances prompting a particularly interesting comparative review by BERNARD SHAW. Though it deals with a "problem"—the challenge of rigid, old-fashioned family morality by the title character—its cant and contrivance are characteristic of the WELL-MADE PLAY.

The pensioned-off army officer Leopold Schwartze is a stuffy patriarch. Eleven years ago he had disowned his daughter, Magda, when she refused to marry the man of his choice, now the local pastor. Unknown to the family, Magda has become a famous singer, Maddalene dall' Orto, now come to participate in a local music festival. When her identity is discovered, the pastor persuades her father to receive the "erring soul." Magda becomes the family's benefactor by providing a dowry for her sister. But though she loves her family and is touched by their love for her, Magda is increasingly troubled by the "yoke of paternal authority" and reluctant to "grovel in the dust in full consciousness of all my sins." Dr. von Keller, a respectable local councillor, visits her and (in the play's big scene) is identified as her seducer of eleven years before. Magda now thanks him, for "through you I became a woman," and informs him that she bore his child. Contemptuous of the narrow conventions of respectable society, she chastises his "cowardly dignity—unwilling to take upon you the slightest consequence of your doings," while she "sank through your love to be a pariah and an outcast." When her father learns of their old affair, he prepares to duel the doctor, "to bring back your honor." But von Keller readily agrees to marry Magda and she reluctantly submits, for her father's sake. Von Keller, however, has no intention of jeopardizing his career by acknowledging their child, whereupon Magda dismisses him disdainfully. Schwartze is determined to have his daughter marry von Keller. Blaming her obstinacy on "the spirit of rebellion abroad in the world," he threatens to kill her as well as himself. "See how much the family with its morality demands from us! It throws us on our own resources, it gives us neither shelter nor happiness, and yet, in our loneliness, we must live according to the laws which it has planned for itself alone," Magda says, growing increasingly more excited as she recalls how he had expelled her: "If you give us freedom, don't be surprised if we use it." When her father persists in his demand that she marry von Keller, Magda becomes desperate. "Are you sure," she asks, "that, according to your standards, I am altogether worthy of him?"—and more explicitly, "that he was the only one in my life?" Overwhelmed by the full discovery of his daughter's "depravity," Schwartze raises his pistol to shoot her—but collapses with an apoplectic stroke and dies amidst his weeping family and the consoling pastor. "His life was the cost of my coming," Magda weeps as she "spreads out her arms in agony."

MAGNIFICENT CUCKOLD, THE (*Le Cocu magnifique*), a "lyric farce" in three acts by FERNAND CROMMELYNCK, produced in 1920 and published in 1921. Setting: a contemporary Belgian village.

Crommelynck's masterpiece, this outlandish portrayal of love and jealousy was produced both as farce (in Aurélien-Marie Lugné-Poë's Paris art theatre premiere) and as tragedy. Bruno's agonizing for human certainty is ridiculous yet pitiful. Mock sublimity of language and comic characterization (also of the Breughel-like townsfolk) are balanced by Bruno's secretary, an alter ego and latter-day Iago whose silences, like Stella's increasingly hysterical indulgence of Bruno's bizarre whim, accentuate the play's terror.

Act I. Stella eagerly awaits the return of her husband, the village scribe. "I was born to love Bruno," the young wife exclaims to her flowers and birds as neighbors pass by. An infatuated cowhand tries to abduct Stella, but her nurse clouts him on the head; another admirer who has heard of her beauty, whose intimate details the proud husband has freely described in public, pays her court. At last Bruno appears. "Stellakins!" he shouts, she joyfully rushes into his arms ("My manekins, snookykins, oh!"), and they exchange caresses and endearments. Later Bruno barely listens to the mayor's business. Instead, he regales the pompously dishonest official with descriptions of Stella's grace and beauty ("her breasts are small . . .") and rhapsodizes, "I carry her in my heart like the kangaroo carries her little ones in her pouch. . . . I love her madly." He urges a visitor, Stella's cousin and childhood friend, to kiss her, and proudly has Stella display her breast, "a swollen pearl." Suddenly Bruno slaps the cousin hard. "I thought I saw a flame in his eyes," he later tells his silent secretary, becoming increasingly wilder, convinced that "I am a cuckold." Madly he questions Stella, is momentarily reassured, and angrily sends out his secretary, who "brought me to the point of doubting myself and Stella." As she bursts into tears ("Oh you bad man," she says to the secretary; "what have you been up to?"), Bruno gets suspicious and shouts at her: "For whom are you weeping?"

Act II. Disheveled and run down three months later, Bruno alternately complains and blusters as he begs his mute secretary to tell him about Stella's infidelities, of which he is now convinced. He demands to know the name of her lover and instructs his secretary to discover and reveal "more details about her debauchery." Then he calls Stella, whom he has hooded with a black cloak and covered with a grotesque paper mask: "Here, you witch. Here, you frog. Sow-bitch. . . ." Meekly the innocent wife appears: "Here I am, my Love." As Bruno curses her and cajoles her to name her lover, she passively indulges him by agreeing with all he says. Briefly penitent, Bruno soon tries to trap her with a young man, suspect because he knows intimate details of her body and movements because Bruno has fondly revealed them to all. Bruno realizes his madness: "My color is dull, bile chokes me, my intestine sleeps in terrible nightmares, my hair falls out," he admits: "If that uneasiness gnaws at me much longer I'll soon die." Eager to help, Stella is horrified by Bruno's proposed cure. "In order not to doubt your fidelity any longer, let me be certain of your infidelity," he concludes, ordering her to sleep with her cousin: "Ridicule and suffering are born out of ignorance and doubt. . . . I will be a cuckold this very day or I will be dead. The horns or the rope. Choose for me." Adamant, Bruno asks the cousin to "plant such horns on my brow that their shadow will obscure the whole countryside," and forces Stella to beg him to agree to his plan. But then Bruno refuses to believe the scandalized report of his secretary, whom he instructs to watch through the bedroom keyhole. "You lie," he shouts, and chases the secretary off. He tells the mayor and the villagers of his wife's adultery as she blushingly returns with the cousin. Subsequently, however, Bruno rejects the evidence of his eyes. "Don't think that you can deceive me. I don't believe a thing." Stella despairs: "Oh Bruno, has my sacrifice been in vain?" As the laughing crowds leave, Bruno's tortured uncertainty returns. Her cousin and Stella have tricked him, Bruno is sure; but if her cousin is not her lover, "who is it then?"

Act III. Stella laughs hysterically amidst a crowd of young men, but Bruno deprecates his secretary's protests: "She pretends, she plays around with these upstarts . . . to put my justified suspicions to sleep." He is sure he will catch her lover now that he has ordered her to let "all the men of the village from fifteen to sixty . . . have their will with you." Stella tears herself away and rushes to her husband: "Leave me alone, you rakes! Bruno, save me from them!" But Bruno confidently insists that she is pretending. When the indignant cowhand refuses to share her "with those pigs," Bruno orders him to, and the frightened Stella begs him, "Bruno, don't get upset. If he refuses to come, I'll go and call for him." The mayor comes to complain about the scandal of Stella's forced promiscuity with almost all the village males. Stella assures Bruno, "Oh! My Love, soon you will have nothing more to wish for." But Bruno is still troubled; he does not believe any of it and considers himself fooled by "the other one for whom she detours the natural course of my suspicions," whom he is sure she sees secretly. Disguised, Bruno visits and courts Stella—and wins her. "I am as cuckolded as one can be," he shouts, "with me myself, if I had wanted it." But again Bruno decides she has deceived him: "She played quite a good comedy for me and . . . the other one is still there." Outraged village matrons angrily bear Stella off, but the cowhand saves her. The wholesale adulteries she has committed for Bruno have finally killed Stella's love for him, but now her soul is regained. She throws herself at the cowhand and kisses him. "It's him, so it's him!" Bruno exclaims, ready to shoot him. Yet as Stella departs with the cowhand, Bruno again refuses to perceive reality and will not believe that she is gone forever. "Oh no, no, I'm not that stupid!" he guffaws, as he sits down unconcerned: "That's again one of her tricks. You'll not deceive me anymore."

MAGNUS GARBE, a tragedy in three acts by GERHART HAUPTMANN, published in 1942 and produced in 1956. Setting: a German free city, sixteenth century.

This diffuse play was conceived as early as 1898 and completed by 1915. It remained unpublished until World War II, perhaps because of its ruthless depiction of the horrors of the Catholic Inquisition.

The highly esteemed mayor, Magnus Garbe, has resisted Rome's inquisitional excesses in his city. As a result, the Church manages to turn the fickle masses, who are threatened by drought and disease, against him. Persuaded that she is a witch, they drag out his beloved wife, Felicia, and torture her even while she undergoes labor pains. During these events, the mayor is away at a vineyard retreat. When informed of them, he has a stroke. Later he visits his horribly mutilated wife in prison, to die with her, minutes before she is to be burned at the stake.

MAHAGONNY, an operatic cantata by BERTOLT BRECHT (music by Kurt Weill), published and produced in 1927.

The "Mahagonny Songs" section of *Bertolt Brechts Hauspostille* (*Domestic Breviary,* 1927), the poetry collection he had just published, is the basis of this forty-five minute musical skit of six songs and orchestral interludes. Produced at the 1927 Baden-Baden modern music festival, it launched the collaborations of Brecht and Weill. Eventually they reworked this skit into *Aufstieg und Fall der Stadt Mahagonny* (RISE AND FALL OF THE CITY OF MAHAGONNY).

MAIDENS OF BISCHOFSBERG, THE (*Die Jungfern vom Bischofsberg*), a comedy in five acts by GERHART HAUPTMANN, published and produced in 1907. Setting: an estate on the Elbe, late nineteenth century.

Passion and illusion compensate for life's transitory briefness in this nostalgic dramatization (also translated as *The Maidens of the Mount*) of the youthful romances of Hauptmann and his brothers with four sisters. The heroine is saved from marriage to a pedantic cousin by an irresponsible, if more interesting, traveler. One of her sisters expresses their final realization: "The dream of life is its best part."

MAIDS, THE (*Les Bonnes*), a one-act play by JEAN GENET, published and produced in 1947. Setting: a Louis XV bedroom in France, 1940's.

This was the first of Genet's plays to be produced. Its three characters portray his world of human evil and corruption in a typical "mirrors game." To stress the confusing make-believe, Genet wanted male actors to play the maids, sisters who alternately act out other parts. In the revised version of the play (1954) Genet diminished the older sister's (Solange's) feelings for the lover, who never appears onstage, but made more explicit the sisters' lesbianism as well as their symbolic roles.

Claire is attended by the maid Solange, whom she calls Claire. She wants her white dress, but the maid insists, "I'm sorry, Madame will wear the scarlet velvet dress this evening." The maid is alternately affectionate, respectful, domineering, and resentful. "Madame should be in mourning," she remarks—for the maid Claire has secretly denounced Madame's lover to the police and he is now imprisoned. They argue about "Solange's" love affair with the milkman and about other things when an alarm clock suddenly rings. Thereupon the two "actresses" huddle together in fright: they are unmasked as sisters, Claire and Solange Lemercier, the maids of Madame, toward whom they have the same love-hate ambivalence they have toward each other. Now, as Madame is about to return, they fearfully remove the traces of their game. Solange admits that she expresses her hatred of both Madame and her sister in these impersonations. Though their mistress is kind, she lives in another world and loves them "like her pink enamel toilet-seat," Solange says; "and we can't love one another. Filth . . . doesn't love filth." She will not put up with it, "and if I have to stop spitting on someone who calls me Claire, I'll simply choke! My spurt of saliva is my spray of diamonds!" A telephone call interrupts their quarrel: it is the lover, unexpectedly released on bail. Afraid their denunciation will now be disclosed, the sisters, alternately quarreling and affectionate with each other, decide to murder their mistress by putting an overdose of sleeping pills in her tea. She comes in, preoccupied with getting her lover released. She is kind and affectionate to her maids, but lives the pseudoaristocratic life created by her maids, whom, in turn, she does not actually understand either. "You are really lucky, you and Claire, to be alone in the world," she remarks with questionable tact as she criticizes their lavish flower arrangements: "The lowliness of your situation spares you all kinds of misfortune." Mournful about her doomed lover, she gives the maids her fine clothes. Then she notices the telephone receiver off the hook, and the maids inadvertently reveal her lover's call. Excitedly rushing out, their mistress declines the (poisoned) tea prepared for her. After she leaves, the maids bitterly resume their game. "Hurry up! Let's drop the preliminaries and get on with it," Solange urges: "I'm quivering, I'm shuddering with pleasure." As she ecstatically praises Claire's beauty, her younger sister invites "the insults." Impersonating her mistress, Claire speaks of her loathsome, inhuman servants: "They're a foul effluvium drifting through our rooms and hallways, seeping into us, entering our mouths, corrupting us. I vomit you!" Alternately amorous and frenzied, Solange strikes back viciously at Claire and refuses to stop the game. Claire is broken by her rage, gets sick, and is led to the kitchen. Soon Solange returns. "At last! Madame is dead!—laid out on the linoleum," she announces in a long soliloquy about the murder that will avenge all maids. Solange imitates the hated mistress and envisions her own hanging and rise to celestial nobility. Suddenly and unexpectedly Claire reappears from the kitchen. Though Solange begs her to stop their "idiotic game," Claire insists the "maid" pour her a cup of tea: "Nothing exists but the altar where one of the two maids is about to immolate herself." Then she forces Solange to hand her the poisoned cup and make her drink it. Solange concludes her oration: "The orchestra is playing brilliantly . . . as Madame is descending the stairs." Solange envisions her mistress's evening party and its aftermath—as Claire drinks the poisoned tea. "Madame is dead. Her two maids are alive: they've just risen up, free, from Madame's icy form," Solange continues. They represent the multitudes of maids, of all social outcasts, she concludes: "All that remains of them to float about Madame's airy corpse is the delicate perfume of the holy maidens which they were in secret. We are beautiful, joyous, drunk, and free!"

MAJOR BARBARA, "A Discussion" in three acts by BERNARD SHAW, produced in 1905 and published in 1909. Setting: England, 1906.

Shaw's brilliant wit and effective theatrical touches (particularly in the Salvation Army scene), despite perhaps excessive Socialist preaching, made this one of his most popular as well as one of his most intriguing and challenging plays for critics. In his long preface Shaw reviewed the English source for the "modern ideas" in his other plays, and then explicated this play: money "represents health, strength, honor, generosity and beauty as conspicuously and undeniably as the want of it represents illness, weakness, disgrace, meanness and ugliness," as the energetic and mystic Undershaft, a Shavian Superman and a personification of the Life Force (and the most compelling character in the play) knows; the Salvation Army has to (and does) accept tainted money—its error lies in its practice of "Crosstianity,"which punishes by confession, rather than in a practice of real religion (like Barbara's rejecting bribery and forcing Bill Walker to recognize and attempt to overcome his moral inferiority), which all creeds must emulate to cope with the world's Bill Walkers, rich and poor. He concluded that human salvation is possible only when wealth is divided among the workers, punishment is abolished, and religions become "intellectually honest." Shaw helped to make the play into a major film (1941). Rose Zimbardo edited a collection of *Twentieth Century Interpretations of "Major Barbara"* (1970).

Act I. Lady Britomart tells her stuffy son, Stephen, that she has invited her husband to their home. He is the powerful munitions maker Andrew Undershaft, from whom she has been separated for many years. She needs money for Stephen and her daughters: one is marrying a fool who will inherit money only later; the other, Barbara, has joined the Salvation Army and will marry a professor of Greek, Adolphus Cusins. Stephen will be disowned for some qualified foundling, for by tradition a foundling inherits the Undershaft name and empire. Meeting the uneasy family for the first time, Undershaft quickly takes to the militantly proselytizing Barbara, whose Salvation Shelter he agrees to visit if she in turn will visit his cannon works. With Barbara and the others, all of whom—to the annoyance of Stephen and the proper and forceful Lady Britomart—his charm has conquered, he goes to the drawing room to sing hymns and play the trombone.

Act II. In the Salvation Army shelter, the ruffian Bill Walker, angry because the Army has lured away his girl, hectors the beggars in the shelter and hits a young Salvation girl. Major Barbara succeeds in humiliating him and tells him that his girl has taken up with another convert, a former wrestler. Undershaft pays his promised visit, cheerfully answers an indignant pauper that "I wouldn't have your income, not for all your conscience," and has a talk with Cusins that leads to mutual liking and respect. Cusins quotes Euripides and admits that he joined the Salvation Army for the love of Barbara, whom he is determined to marry, although he sincerely rejoices in "drumming dithyrambs" for "honor, justice, truth, love, mercy"; Undershaft considers these "the graces and luxuries of a rich, strong, and safe life" attainable only through "money and gunpowder." Returning after a drubbing from his girl's new "blowk," who sat on him during hymn singing and prayed for his soul, Bill Walker gruffly offers his money (a sovereign) as a donation to make up for having struck the Salvationist, but Barbara refuses it: "the Army is not to be bought. We want your soul." A Salvation Army Commissioner jubilantly announces a sizable donation by a millionaire distiller, which will enable them to continue operating their shelters, and Undershaft offers to match the sum. Barbara alone is horrified at the Army's acceptance of "Drunkenness and Murder" money, and bitterly resigns. Cusins hands

Major Barbara, Act II. Left to right: the young Salvation Army girl (Nancy Malone), Undershaft (Charles Laughton), Walker (Eli Wallach), Cusins (Burgess Meredith), and Barbara (Glynis Johns). New York, 1956. (*Zodiac Photographers*)

Undershaft a trombone and leads him and the others to a thanksgiving prayer meeting. The heartbroken Barbara is heckled by a now cynical Walker, who had been just on the brink of conversion: "Wot prawce selvytion nah?"

Act III. Scene 1. At Lady Britomart's the next morning, Cusins tells the family, including the unhappy Barbara, who no longer wears a uniform, of the successful prayer meeting: there were many conversions, and "The Prince of Darkness played his trombone like a madman." Undershaft and Lady Britomart discuss Stephen's future with him, and Undershaft finally sees it: "He knows nothing and he thinks he knows everything. That points clearly to a political career." Undershaft is able to restore Barbara's faith and courage, and all go off to visit his "factory of death." *Scene 2.* It turns out to be a model town that stupefies everyone with its perfection. "It needs only a cathedral to be a heavenly city," says Cusins. Undershaft tells Barbara that bribing starved converts with bread is "cheap"; his own work is justified by this town, which keeps its happy dwellers from poverty (the "worst of crimes") and the seven deadly sins ("Food, clothing, firing, rent, taxes, respectability and children"). Cusins unexpectedly qualifies as a foundling and, after driving a hard bargain with him, is finally persuaded by Undershaft to join him, since Cusins now sees that the poor can be made to do more for themselves than social workers can do for them. Barbara decides to spread her gospel among the well fed, agrees to marry Cusins, and enthusiastically goes to choose a home in the model town.

MAKROPULOS SECRET, THE (*Věc Makropulos*), a comedy in three acts by KAREL ČAPEK, published and produced in 1922. Setting: twentieth-century Vienna.

Commonly regarded as a rebuttal to BACK TO METHUSELAH, this play actually was written before Čapek knew Shaw's play. In a complex but intriguing plot *The Makropulos Secret* portrays the horrors of longevity. Like ADAM THE CREATOR, this play suggests that wisdom consists in accepting life as it is. Leoš Janáček made the play into an opera in 1926.

Emilia Marty is a beautiful but mysterious opera singer. Disputes about an inheritance and an old manuscript bring about lawsuits, and Emilia's mystery gradually is solved. She is Elena Makropulos, the daughter of a sixteenth-century physician who had discovered a rejuvenation formula that has kept her alive for three hundred years. In a succession of existences and affairs under different names, Emilia has become increasingly bored and disgusted. Now she is horrified to see her great-great-grandson, who does not know who she is, falling in love with her. Fearing death, she intends to reapply the formula. However, she comes to fear eternal life even more. "No man can love three hundred years," she tells visitors seeking her formula, "nor hope, nor create, nor even watch three hundred years. Everything will disgust him," will lose its meaning: "In fact there is nothing. Nothing exists. Neither sin, nor pain, nor earth—nothing." The formula is destroyed, and Emilia is content to die—like a human being.

MALATESTA, a play in four acts by HENRY DE MONTHERLANT, published in 1946 and produced in 1950. Setting: Rimini and Rome, 1468.

This is an animated Renaissance spectacle as well as a portrait of Sigismondo Pandolfo Malatesta, the lusty, swashbuckling Lord of Rimini. Based on history, it dramatizes Malatesta's crude ruthlessness, his journey to and prolonged stay in Rome, his struggle with Pope Paul II, and his attempt to murder him. Then Malatesta returns to Rimini, where the scribe hired to chronicle Malatesta's "magnificent life" treacherously poisons him. As Malatesta dies he sees specters of former great conquerors and begs them to reassure him "that my name will go on pulsing by the side of yours! Say to me that I am not going to cease to exist, that would be horrible!" Malatesta collapses as the visions fade: "Then let me, too, fade." His "hired literary man" comes out of hiding and, page by page, burns his *Vita Magnifici et Clarissimi Sigismondi de Malatestis.*

MALAYSIA. Malaysia's sole distinctive drama in modern times has been the *bangsawan* (modern theatre), action plays on historical or contemporary themes whose dialogue is interspersed with song and dance. As in the neighboring INDONESIAN islands, other stage entertainments on the peninsula and in Singapore are puppet and shadow plays as well as Western-style drama.

See James R. Brandon's *Theatre in Southeast Asia* (1967).

MALTZ, Albert (1908–), American writer, was a dramatist for the Theatre Union, a leftist venture founded in 1933. He collaborated on *Merry-Go-Round* (1932) and *Peace on Earth* (1933) with GEORGE SKLAR (for which see SKLAR). Maltz succeeded with two other plays, which he wrote alone: *Black Pit* (1935) and *Private Hicks* (1936). The first, a Marxian "tragedy of a stool pigeon" —a mine strikebreaker who betrays his class—is defeatist despite the shout of ultimate proletarian triumph: "By God, miner gone raise head oop in sun. . . . Holler out loud 'Jesus Chris' miner got blow whistle . . . not boss blow . . . miner blow' . . . Jesus Chris I nevair gone die. . . . I gone sit here wait for dat time!" Private Hicks, the title hero of the frequently performed one-acter, is a National Guardsman who, rather than shoot strikers, proudly goes to prison. Maltz also wrote many short stories and novels, as well as popular patriotic films such as *Destination Tokyo* (1943), which the United States armed forces used as a training film, and *The Pride of the Marines* (1945).

MALVALOCA, a drama in three acts by SERAFÍN and JOAQUÍN ÁLVAREZ QUINTERO, published and produced in 1912. Setting: the Andalusian village of Las Canteras, early twentieth century.

This Spanish Academy prize winner, probably the best known of the Quinteros' plays, was produced in many countries, and republished in Thomas H. Dickinson's *Chief Contemporary Dramatists, Third Series* (1930). Characteristically gentle, it portrays and resolves more sentimentally but less cataclysmically a situation analogous to those of O'Neill's ANNA CHRISTIE and Howard's THEY KNEW WHAT THEY WANTED.

Named after a flower, Malvaloca is a pretty, graceful, and vivacious lower-class girl. Visiting a friend—"I have been a tiny bit more than that, but that's a thing of the past"—who is recuperating from an injury incurred at his brass foundry, she and the friend's partner, Leonardo, fall in love. Immensely generous to the poor ("Sometimes I think there is nothing but heart in my head"), Malvaloca heretofore has been philosophical about her promiscuity and her scoundrelly family. Now she bitterly regrets her past, which prevents her marrying Leonardo. "If *he* had been the first, I should have been different altogether," she says, wishing that, like the damaged convent bell, she could be recast in the foundry. Equally unhappy about their plight, Leonardo cannot even introduce her to his sister. When his partner sees how his very presence painfully recalls Malvaloca's past to Leonardo, he generously leaves. During a religious procession their misery and passion overwhelm the lovers. As the newly recast bell starts to peal, Leonardo exclaims, "I will also recast your life by the warmth of my kisses, by the fire of this wild love of mine, which is as great even as your misfortune!" They embrace as the chimes rise to a happy and victorious crescendo.

MAN AND SUPERMAN, "A Comedy and a Philosophy" in four acts by BERNARD SHAW, published and produced in 1903. Setting: contemporary England and Spain, and Hell.

Shaw's first major treatment of the theme of "creative evolution" (the Life Force), this brilliantly witty and popular philosophical comedy, one of Shaw's greatest plays, was written in response to the critic Arthur Bingham Walkley's request for a play on Don Juan. In his preface, addressed to Walkley, Shaw discussed the Don Juan legend as treated by others and as relating to the present, and explained his hero (a "political pamphleteer") and his heroine (an Everywoman, mother, vehicle of the Life Force, whose "business" is "fecundity"). The "Don Juan in Hell" scene, usually performed separately, dramatizes the idea of an unorthodox Heaven (a place of creative thought and will) and Hell (a place of fun), and a Tanner idealized from the somewhat ludicrous windbag he is in the play into an unorthodox Don Juan: a spiritual seeker who has spent his life escaping amorous women. The published play is followed by "The Revolutionist's Handbook and Pocket Companion" mentioned in Act I: an essay on modern society and the need for the Superman, and a collection of Shavian aphorisms.

Act I. The "advanced" thinker Roebuck Ramsden fulminates against a scandalous work, *The Revolutionist's Handbook* by John Tanner, M.I.R.C. (Member of the Idle Rich Class). Tanner, very angry at finding himself named as Ann Whitefield's coguardian with Ramsden, "an old man with obsolete ideas," shocks Ramsden and the poet Octavius Robinson, who worships Ann, by predicting that she will "commit every crime a respectable woman can; and she'll justify every one of them by saying that it was the wish of her guardians." Ann comes in with her mother, and with a sweet helplessness that cloaks her strength and shrewdness she quickly gets the men to agree to the joint guardianship. Tanner warns the incredulous Octavius, her "Ricky-ticky-tavy," that he is endangered by Ann in the "treacherous and remorseless . . . struggle between the artist man and the mother woman." Privately Tanner lectures Ann about his important work—"I shatter creeds and demolish idols"—and her designs on Octavius, thus amazing Ann by his failure to perceive her real prey—Tanner himself. A report that Octavius's sister, Violet, is pregnant scandalizes all but Tanner, who commends the "fulfilment of her highest purpose and greatest function"; but when he congratulates her, Violet indignantly announces that she is respectably married, though she refuses to identify her husband.

Act II. The "New Man" Henry ("Enry") Straker, Tanner's Cockney chauffeur, is amused at Tanner's ignorance of Ann's actual designs when Tanner tells Octavius, come to ask him for Ann's hand, that Octavius really is the pursued, not the pursuer. Ann inveigles Tanner into asking her to go with him on a Continental motor tour; Hector Malone, a young American visitor, suggests that they all go, and asks to escort Violet. In a private talk Hector, Violet's previously unnamed husband, objects to keeping their marriage secret. But Violet, knowing his father would stop his allowance if he knew of their marriage, insists: "You can be as romantic as you please about love, Hector; but you mustn't be romantic about money." When Straker tells Tanner that he, not Octavius, is Ann's "marked down victim," Tanner, in a panic, leaves for the Continent with Straker.

Act III. Motoring in the Sierra Nevada, Tanner and Straker are captured by brigands led by a former London waiter, Mendoza, who introduces himself by telling Tanner, "I live by robbing the rich." Tanner replies, "I live by robbing the poor. Shake hands." By the fireside, Mendoza tells the story of his life, mooning over his hopeless love for a girl who rejected him. As he reads his love poems, everyone falls asleep and Tanner has the following dream:

"Don Juan in Hell"

Don Juan (Tanner) greets a new arrival, Doña Ana (Ann), who is indignant at being in Hell, at meeting Don Juan, and then at her father, The Statue (Ramsden), who is bored with Heaven and has come for a visit. The remainder of the scene consists of long debates, primarily between Don Juan and The Devil (Mendoza), on the Life Force. Don Juan decides to move to Heaven, "the home of the masters of reality," where he can serve man's "real purpose." The Statue decides to remain in Hell, the home of "love and beauty" for "seekers for happiness." When Doña Ana hears that the Superman has not yet been created, she rushes off with a cry for "a father for the Superman."

When they awake, Violet, Hector, Ramsden, and Octavius arrive with Ann, who has assiduously tracked Tanner's route.

Act IV. At a villa in Granada, the elder Malone is furious at the discovery of his son's marriage to a commoner and vows to cut him off without a penny. Violet stands up to him, quickly wins his respect, and, though Hector nobly insists on being a worker, she privately assures the grateful father that she will get Hector to accept his money. Ann refuses Octavius: she could never live up to his ideal, and (she claims) her mother wants her to marry Tanner. When Octavius is shocked by her planning to marry an "unwilling man," she shocks him even more: "There's no such thing as

Man and Superman, last scene. Ann (Frances Rowe) and Tanner (Maurice Evans). New York, 1947. (*Graphic House*)

a willing man when you really go for him." She corners Tanner, who resists stubbornly, but when she "faints" in his arms, he surrenders. In a long and sarcastic speech, he agrees "to renounce happiness, renounce freedom, renounce tranquillity, above all, renounce the romantic possibilities of an unknown future, for the cares of a household and a family." To the amusement of the others, Ann affectionately bids him: "Go on talking."

MAN, BEAST, AND VIRTUE (*L'uomo, la bestia e la virtù*), an "apologue" in three acts by LUIGI PIRANDELLO, produced in 1919 and published in 1922. Setting: a contemporary Italian port town.

This work, a dramatization of a short story Pirandello published in 1912, was produced in America in 1926 as *Say It with Flowers*. Written in the Renaissance tradition of as lusty a work as Machiavelli's *La mandragola* (1524), it has been played both as comedy and as farce. It is a broad, harsh satire with a strange moral: the beast in man can save morality; or, virtue is the mask for wholesome instinct.

Paolino, a nervous schoolmaster who eloquently rants against hypocrisy, is in love with Signora Pinella, a demure woman. Her terrible husband, a sea captain, has a mistress, rarely comes home, and never sleeps with his wife. His adultery has caused the neglected wife to find solace with Paolino, and now she is pregnant. The lovers' only hope for avoiding detection lies in getting the captain for once to sleep with his wife. So Paolino (the "man" of the title) must pander Signora Pinella ("virtue") to her husband (the "beast"). The lovers prepare a cake containing a powerful aphrodisiac, and the usually modest wife dresses seductively. If successful, she is to signal her lover by placing a flower pot on the balcony. Though the dinner at first does not go at all well and the captain ridicules his wife, he eats the cake and her virtue is finally saved. The next morning Paolino, looking at her balcony, sees five flower pots.

MAN FOR ALL SEASONS, A, a play in two acts by ROBERT BOLT, published and produced in 1960. Setting: sixteenth-century England.

This dramatization of Sir Thomas More's later career stresses the conscience and the integrity (also his wisdom, humor, and geniality) that caused More's downfall. The play, in which Bolt achieved his first and major success, was staged in semi-impressionistic episodes, a roguish Common Man (deleted from the 1966 film version) acting as commentator as well as stage manager. The title comes from Robert Whittinton's characterization of More.

"The Sixteenth Century is the Century of the Common Man," says the personifier of this man —"Like all the other centuries." Then follow More's struggles with the mercurial young (not Hans Holbein's bearded) Henry VIII, a ruthless and vulgar Thomas Cromwell, and others. More's tenderness with his wife and daughter is climaxed by an agonizing farewell when he goes to the block, his conscience not allowing him to sanction the king's divorce and establishment of a new church. "I do no harm," More says before his condemnation; "I think none harm. And if this be not enough to keep a man alive, in good faith I long not to live." After More's execution the Common Man reappears. "It isn't difficult to keep alive, friends—just don't *make* trouble," he tells the audience. "Well, I don't need to tell you that," he concludes: "If we should bump into one another, recognize me."

MAN OF DESTINY, THE, "A Trifle" in one act by BERNARD SHAW, produced in 1897 and published in 1898. Setting: Italy, the evening of May 12, 1796.

This is one of Shaw's "pleasant" plays. In his preface to PLAYS PLEASANT he called it "hardly more than a bravura piece to display the virtuosity of the two principal performers." Extensive stage directions and a long speech by Napoleon at the end of the play gave Shaw the chance to voice his opinions of Napoleon and the English.

At an inn in Tavazzano, the twenty-seven-year-old Napoleon is waiting for his dispatches and letters. His lieutenant finally arrives and reports that a youth has tricked him out of them. Napoleon quickly perceives that a Lady at the inn is the "youth." Alone with Napoleon she admits it, but, after he succeeds in regaining the packet from her, she implores him to return one of the letters. Eventually she makes it clear to him that the letter reveals an intrigue between his wife and Director Barras. She refuses to accept the packet Napoleon now wishes her to take back so he can avoid official knowledge of the letter, which would force him into a duel and a scandal that might wreck his career. To establish the loss of the letter, he calls the lieutenant and orders him to find the "youth" and the packet or face public degradation. The Lady, transforming herself into the "youth," forces Napoleon to acknowledge receipt of the packet, but makes the frightened innkeeper and lieutenant believe she is a witch. This gives Napoleon the opportunity to have the "bewitched" packet (and letter) burned.

MAN OUTSIDE, THE (*Draussen vor der Tür;* literally, "outside the door"), a play in five scenes and a prologue by WOLFGANG BORCHERT, published and produced in 1947. Setting: Hamburg, Germany; c. 1946.

This powerful and widely performed play, also translated as *The Outsider,* is the autobiographical cry of outrage of a returning war veteran. Partly EXPRESSIONIST and partly NATURALIST, it has some grotesque theatrical satire. SYMBOLICally it portrays God as a forgotten old beggar and Death as an undertaker and street cleaner.

Beckmann, a crippled German sergeant just returned from Siberian imprisonment, throws himself into the Elbe but is rejected by the river, personified as an old hag. Displaced in his home by his wife's lover, Beckmann follows a friendly young woman but is then frightened away by the apparition of her husband, a war casualty. Beckmann is left "outside the door" wherever he goes. His former commander feels no guilt (as Beckmann does) about his men's death, a cabaret producer will not employ him, and new tenants in his parents' home coldly relate how his parents committed suicide in the kitchen. All are unsympathetic to Beckmann's inability to readjust to civilian and peacetime life, though his alter ego keeps trying to bolster his courage. In a concluding outburst that summarizes his recent experiences, Beckmann curses his existence as he shouts in vain for answers to his despairing questions. "Where is the old man who went around calling himself God?" Beckmann finally cries out: "Will no one answer? *Is* there no answer at all?"

MAN WHO CAME TO DINNER, THE, a play in three acts by GEORGE S. KAUFMAN and MOSS HART, published and produced in 1939. Setting: a small Ohio town, late December in the 1930's.

This aptly termed "comedy of bad manners" features Sheridan Whiteside, a famous lecturer modeled on ALEXANDER WOOLLCOTT. The ruthlessly ill-mannered and insolent tyrant so delighted Woollcott that he himself played Whiteside on tour. (Hart, too, played the role.) Perhaps the most uproariously comic play produced by Kaufman and Hart, it was filmed in 1941 and converted into *Sherry!* (1967), a musical by James Lipton (1926–   ; music by Lawrence Rosenthal).

An accident immobilizes the overbearing Whiteside at a small-town house. Immediately he takes it over, insulting and displacing its owners and meddling with their children's lives. When his secretary falls in love with a local newspaperman, Whiteside schemes to break up the romance so as to retain her services. The madcap includes actual and phony transatlantic calls with contemporary celebrities, a shipment of live penguins, a mummy case into which is locked a loose-moraled movie star who has been summoned to seduce the newspaperman, and a Christmas broadcast—all presided over by the scurrilous Whiteside.

The Man Who Came to Dinner. Whiteside (Monty Woolley) and the film star (Carol Goodner). New York, 1939. (*Culver Pictures*)

MAN WITH A FLOWER IN HIS MOUTH, THE (*L'uomo dal fiore in bocca*), a one-act play by LUIGI PIRANDELLO, produced in 1923 and published in 1926. Setting: a present-day café in a large city, late at night.

Pirandello's dramatization of a short story he published in 1918 soon becomes a haunting monologue by a man dying of "a flower in his mouth"—cancer.

A sick man reveals himself to a stranded commuter who is upset about having missed his train because of all the errands he had to run for his troublesome wife and daughters. Having little time left before he will die, the sick man is afraid to stay home. His solicitous and grief-stricken wife wants to follow him as he wanders through the city. The man tries to distract himself by observing everything minutely and by imaginatively entering the lives of strangers he sees and talks to, "clinging like this—I mean, in my imagination—to life." He asks the now-frightened commuter to look at a tuft of grass when he gets to his village: "As many blades as you can count, that's the number of days I still have to live." And then he departs with a laugh: "Be sure you pick me a nice fat one."

MAN WITHOUT A SOUL, THE (*Mannen utan själ*), a play in five acts by PÄR LAGERKVIST, published in 1936 and produced in 1938. Setting: an unnamed country resembling Nazi Germany.

Like Lagerkvist's earlier THE HANGMAN, this is a protest against growing Fascism and its dehumanizing effects. It is similarly preoccupied with brutality and is resolved in mysticism. The play's stark, skeletal action and dialogue resemble those of Kaiser's FROM MORN TO MIDNIGHT and other EXPRESSIONIST drama. None of the characters has a name.

A young man rushes into a barroom, sits by a woman, and tells her not to call for help. "One lives only when something is happening!" he says as policemen search for an assassin; "when there is action, one feels the excitement, the tension, like a wild joy within one!" And he informs a salvationist, "I haven't got a soul!" He persuades the Woman, who considers life meaningless and has gotten up, to let him accompany her. They spend the night together, and he learns that she is carrying the child of the man he murdered. Pariahs both, the Man and the Woman fall in love and begin to find meaning and beauty in life. But the Woman, cared for only by the mother of the assassin's victim (the unborn child's father), dies in childbirth, and the Man is arrested for deserting his political-activist companions. "I have got new orders to obey. . . . I have other powers above me . . . greater powers," he pleads. But they do not understand his changed attitudes and his anguish. Condemned to death, the Man has vague intimations of the human potential. "I have only . . . restlessness and anxiety . . . something burning . . . without flame, without light," he tells the prison's priest, who suggests these may be divinely purposeful. "Yes . . . yes . . . perhaps there is a meaning in it. . . . Yes, yes . . . I would like so much to believe that," the Man affirms. Then, ready to be executed, he walks into the increasingly radiant light outside, "his head lifted."

MANN, Heinrich (1871–1950), German novelist, also wrote plays. The most important of them was a French Revolution drama, *Madame Legros* (1913); in part satiric, it portrays the title character, a latter-day Antigone, becoming famous after setting off the Revolution by interceding with the queen for the release of an innocent prisoner, but then losing faith in herself. Mann's other plays include *Schauspielerin* (1911), a character study of an actress; *Der Weg zur Macht* (1919), an EXPRESSIONISTIC portrayal of the young Napoleon as an opportunist; *Das gastliche Haus* (1924), a comedy; and *Bibi* (1929), a topical music drama about youth. Among Mann's many novels, *Professor Unrat* (1905) was translated and made into the classic film *Der blaue Engel* (*The Blue Angel,* 1930).

His better-known brother, the novelist Thomas Mann (1875–1955), wrote one play, a dramatization of the life of Lorenzo de Medici, *Fiorenza* (1904); and Thomas Mann's son, Klaus (1906–49), also known principally as a novelist, wrote a few comedies and the first important postwar "school play" about adolescents, *Anja und Esther* (1925).

MANNERS, J[ohn] Hartley (1870–1928), British-born American actor, director, and playwright, was a performer of some note before 1902, when he came to America with Lily Langtry's company. He settled in the United States, eventually associated himself with the New York theatre, and became a dramatist. He wrote some thirty plays but only one of them is notable. Written for his wife, Laurette Taylor, in the year they were married, PEG O' MY HEART (1912) was one of the most popular plays of its time. It was translated into several languages and toured season after season in Europe and America. It was his wife's greatest hit until her memorable return to the stage, shortly before her death, to launch Tennessee Williams's THE GLASS MENAGERIE with her portrayal of Amanda.

Further information about Manners may be found in his wife's biography, Marguerite Courtney's *Laurette* (1955).

MAN'S A MAN, A (*Mann ist Mann*), a comedy in eleven scenes by BERTOLT BRECHT, produced in 1926 and published in 1927. Setting: India, 1925.

The play has also been translated under such other titles as *Man Equals Man* and *Man Is Man,* and is subtitled "The Transformation of the Porter Galy Gay in the Kilkoa Military Barracks in 1925." The British soldiers and India (language, characterization, topography, and various details) here represented are fantastic knockabout parodies of Kipling. As he did with his other early works, Brecht later revised this play to make it more Marxist. It is considered his first characteristically didactic, EPIC DRAMA, and portrays the depersonalization of machine-age man. Brecht wrote a SURREALIST farce, *Das Elefantenkalb* (*The Baby Elephant,* 1927), for production during the intermission; its title character (played by Galy Gay) is accused of matricide and convicted, despite proving that he is not the child of the murdered elephant—who is, in fact, alive.

Scenes 1 through 8. The meek porter Galy Gay sets out to buy a little fish for supper. A drunken machine-gun squad loses one of its men in an attempt to rob a pagoda. Terrified of roll call by the ferocious Sergeant Bloody Five, the remaining three soldiers are delighted to meet Galy Gay, who obviously cannot say no, and is overheard being unable to withstand the importunities of the widow Leocadia Begbick, owner of the traveling canteen. Soon the soldiers persuade him to impersonate their missing gunner at roll call. The wily Chinaman in charge of the pagoda, in the meantime, has transformed the missing gunner into a lucrative miracle-working divinity and refuses to release him. The squad must make Galy Gay's impersonation more permanent. Because of their flattery and promises, the simpleminded porter repudiates and refuses even to recognize his wife, who has waited for the fish and comes looking for her husband. Orders are issued to break camp and prepare to board troop trains before dawn. "One man is just like any other man," the gunners conclude, and they start their machinations. Before the metamorphosis of Galy Gay, the Widow Begbick recites a poem: "Mr. Bertolt Brecht claims: a man's a man. / Anyone may say so; he proves one can, / In any way, at will, transform a man."

Scenes 9 through 11. As her canteen is being dismantled for the expedition and the Widow Begbick sings "The Song of Things That Pass," the gunners build a big fake elephant, which they trick Galy Gay into selling to the Widow. When the deal is concluded, the fraud is revealed and Galy Gay is hailed before a mock military court. Frightened and utterly confused, the porter finally repudiates his identity: "I'm a man who doesn't know who he is. But I'm not Galy Gay, that I know." Still, he must face the firing squad. He faints before they fire their mock bullets, but they shoot anyway: "At least he must hear that he's dead." Galy Gay, "the last man of character in 1925," finally even agrees to deliver an oration over his coffin: "In the morning he went to buy a little fish, in the evening he had a large elephant, and that night he was shot." Sergeant Bloody Five, his ferocious lust aroused by the rain, arrives to sleep with Widow Begbick's three daughters.

Appearing, as instructed, in tails and bowler hat, he is ridiculed and humiliated by his soldiers. The next morning on the train Sergeant Bloody Five bemoans the loss of his reputation and yearns to have his honorable nickname restored. To prevent future humiliations because of his sensuality, he takes a pistol and castrates himself. Galy Gay remarks, "It's good that I saw it, for now I see where stubbornness leads to, and what a bloody thing it is when a man is dissatisfied with himself and fusses over the importance of his name." The missing gunner returns to his squad, but is sent away, unrecognized without his identity card. Galy Gay now has it and, integrated into the army, he quickly becomes a model soldier. Single-handed he destroys a Tibetan fortress, and is admired and acclaimed by the other soldiers as "a human battle machine." Galy Gay becomes the leader of his squad, swaggering: "On the double: now we'll cross the icebound border of Tibet."

MARAT/SADE, a verse play in two acts by PETER WEISS, published and produced in 1964. Setting: communal bath hall of a mental institution in Charenton, France; 1808.

The complete title of this highly theatrical play, which brought Weiss international acclaim, summarizes its plot: *Die Verfolgung und Ermordung Jean Paul Marats dargestellt durch die Schauspielgruppe des Hospizes zu Charenton unter Anleitung des Herrn de Sade* (*The Persecution and Assassination of Jean-Paul Marat as Performed by the Inmates of the Asylum of Charenton Under the Direction of the Marquis De Sade*). It is a play within a play that teems with historical characters. Soaking in the tub in which he will be assassinated (1793), Marat argues about revolution with De Sade, the play's author—as the inmates, including those acting in his play, sprawl about apathetically or writhe and scream hysterically. The play assaulted the senses of worldwide theatre and film audiences with its pandemonium—blaring music, the spattering of blood, and mass and individual violence such as whippings performed in styles that ranged from the REPRESENTATIONAL to the EXPRESSIONISTIC. Fused with other styles, such as the EPIC, *Marat/Sade* is a notable manifestation of the theatre of CRUELTY.

Act I. A bell rings and the patients—a few of them political prisoners—walk in or are led in by attendants. The corpulent and asthmatic De Sade, a sixty-eight-year-old inmate, prepares the stage

Marat/Sade. Left to right: Simonne (Susan Williamson), Sade (Patrick Magee), Corday (Glenda Jackson), Marat (Ian Richardson), and two patients (Guy Gordon and Carol Raymond). New York, 1965. (*Morris Newcombe*)

for his play about Marat and motions the spectators, the asylum's director and his family, to take their seats. A herald introduces the inmate-actors: the fifty-year-old Marat, who sits in a bathtub to soothe his painfully diseased skin; his solicitous mistress-nurse, Simonne Evrard; his beautiful twenty-four-year-old assassin, Charlotte Corday, a somnambulist; her Girondist lover, Duperret, an erotomaniac; and the rabble-rousing priest Jacques Roux, straitjacketed to control his violence. The chanters, three former alcoholics and a prostitute, gather around the tub and sing their "Homage to Marat." It is four years after the Revolution, but Marat still writes denunciations of the rulers, and the people are still unhappy ("Marat we're poor and the poor stay poor / Marat don't make us wait any more") and want "our revolution NOW." When Roux incites them, the asylum's director has the attendants push them back and the nursing sisters sing a tranquilizing litany. Corday is awakened and announces that, though she believes in change too, Marat's ways are too bloody "and so I say no / and I go / to murder you Marat and free all mankind." Tended by Simonne in his tub, he tyrannically calls for more "bloodbaths": "I am the Revolution." De Sade interrupts the action: "Not yet Corday / You have to come to his door three times." The patients mime the singers' narrative of Corday's arrival in Paris amidst executions and mutilations, which Marat defends as "the people's justified revenge against their exploiters." Though the asylum's director protests the expression of such sentiments, De Sade has the scene continued and then begins his running debate with Marat. Despising the indifference of nature, "this passionless spectator this unbreakable iceberg-face," he insists that men kill with passion and minutely describes the four-hour torture killing of Damiens "while the crowd goggled." Marat replies that by acting against nature's indifference he invents a meaning: "The important thing / is to pull yourself up by your own hair / to turn yourself inside out / and see the whole world with fresh eyes." Then, over the objections of the asylum's director, Marat leads the patients in a "liturgy" detailing the Church's exploitation of the people. It is interrupted by a patient who prays to "Our Satan which art in hell . . ." and declares man to be a mad animal. When De Sade proclaims "imagination" as the only reality, Marat demurs. He deplores the "dead ideas" that hamper the Revolution, while the quartet and chorus demand "our Revolution NOW." The patients playing Corday and Duperret are led in; she seeks his support against Marat, but Duperret is intent only on fondling her. As the scene ends, De Sade scorns patriotism and idealists: "I believe only in myself." Marat admits that the Revolution succeeded merely in establishing the bourgeoisie, and the rabble-rousing Roux, attacking the new authorities, is strapped down. Then De Sade invites Corday to "beat me / while I talk to you about the Revolution." He strips, and as she whips him to the ground, De Sade expatiates on his inability to participate in the revolutionary orgy he had hoped for: all men's brutality "was inhuman, it was dull," and led to the "withering of the individual man / and a slow merging into uniformity." Depressed, Marat starts writing, and the quartet sings "Poor Old Marat" and again demands the revolution "NOW." Again aroused from her sleep with difficulty, Corday declaims on man's ideal future and fends off Duperret's increasingly frenetic fondling. Marat rises from his bathtub and orates on economic inequities. As the quartet chants he is seized by attendants and returned to the tub. A second time Corday, trying to see Marat, is barred by Simonne. De Sade cynically lists the material benefits people expect from the Revolution he considers futile, and the quartet mocks Marat. His visions of his bloody past are narrated by his schoolmaster and his parents. Voltaire and Lavoisier come to ridicule Marat's theories: "No wonder [Marat] sits there in his bath" hatching revolution, for "the more you scratch the more you itch." But Roux defends Marat as the chorus continues calling for revolution—and the herald announces an intermission.

Act II. From his bathtub and in his imagination, Marat addresses the National Assembly, accusing the Revolution's leaders of corruption and treason. Again the asylum's director objects to the seditious comments, and the patients become noisy and scream while the quartet sings "Poor Old Marat." De Sade suggests that Marat stop his futile writings, for the state he envisions will "rule you / to control the words you write." The herald calls for the third visit: "Charlotte Corday awake and stand / Take the dagger in your hand." She imagines herself at the guillotine but, remembering the Book of Judith and identifying with its heroine, turns down Duperret's plea to leave with him. The herald narrates her approach and De Sade points out to Marat the beauty of the "untouched virgin [who] stands before you and offers herself to you. . . . Perhaps . . . she carries a knife / to intensify the love-play," he remarks, and the chorus repeats his comment: "And what's the point of a revolution / without general copulation." Corday stands before Marat, caresses him, and raises her dagger. But the herald interrupts so the singers may describe how, year by year, "the world will go after his death." Then the cast resume their positions—and Corday stabs Marat. The patients scream, Corday crumples, and Marat lies dead in the position of David's portrait. "Today we live in far different times / We have no oppressors no violent crimes," the asylum's director says as the quartet sings about "how much nearer our goal we have got." But the patients become increasingly unruly, marching and shouting for "Napoleon . . . Nation . . . Revolution . . . Copulation." The director's family flee, De Sade smiles, the shouts grow louder, and the inmates overcome the attendants and reach the front of the stage. The straitjacketed Roux tries to force them back: "When will you learn to see / When will you learn to take sides." He disappears as the patients go completely berserk. To stop them, the director incites the attendants to violence. De Sade stands on his chair and laughs triumphantly as the director signals for the curtain.

MARAUDERS (*Marodörer*), a comedy in five acts by AUGUST STRINDBERG, privately printed in 1886 and subsequently rewritten as COMRADES.

Strindberg revised this play, which his publisher had rejected, and collaborated with the Swedish novelist Axel Lundegård (1861–1930) on yet another revision. His deteriorating first marriage helped make the satire more bitter, but did not improve it. Act I (deleted in *Comrades*) portrays the Albergs' courtship. At the end of the play a less brutal Axel tells Bertha, "It's strange how you want to maraud and plunder what we have battled for while you were at your cooking!"

MARCEAU, Félicien [originally Louis Carette] (1913–), Belgian-born French dramatist and Goncourt Prize-winning novelist, first produced serious plays, such as *Caterina* (1954). Then he turned to light comedy, the most successful of which was *L'Oeuf* (*The Egg,* 1956), an episodic farce about a scoundrel who penetrates "the eggshell" of others to join the human race and system, thus prospering on his way from charming youth through middle-aged cynicism and crime. Another internationally-known cynical comedy, *La Bonne Soupe* (*The Good Soup,* 1958), features a kept woman. Other popular Marceau drama includes a Nero play (*L'Étouffe-chrétien,* 1960), a witty drama espousing romantic pluralism (*La Preuve par quatre,* 1964), and another social satire (*Le Babour,* 1969).

MARCEL, Gabriel (1887–1964), French critic and dramatist, has been likened to FRANÇOIS DE CUREL for the esotericism of his plays and to JEAN-PAUL SARTRE for their philosophical bent. Self-styled "drama of the soul in exile," Marcel's plays communicate the problems of conscience Marcel examined in his many treatises. A Christian existentialist, he believed (in direct opposition to Sartre's famous line in NO EXIT) that "There is only one suffering, it is to be alone," as a character exclaims in *Le Coeur des autres* (1921). Marcel dramatized his antinomic views on self-knowledge, the ambiguity of the soul, and communion and salvation in this and in others of his two dozen plays, which were published but rarely produced.

Considered best among them are those published in America as *Three Plays* (1958): *Un homme de Dieu* (*A Man of God,* 1925), portraying a pastor and his wife's agonizing reexamination of the long-past forgiveness of her adultery; *La Chapelle ardente* (*The Funeral Pyre,* 1931; later translated as *The Votive Candle*), about a woman's meddlesome destruction of the life of her dead son's fiancée; and *Le Chemin de Crête* (1936, translated as *Ariadne*), a study of despair caused by the protagonist's selflessness toward her husband and his mistress. Other notable Marcel plays are the domestic tragedy *La Soif* (1938, republished in 1952 as *Les Coeurs avides*) and *Rome n'est plus dans Rome* (1951), whose professor protagonist flees Communism, discovers academic freedom is equally threatened by a fanatic clergy, but ultimately finds the true church and a platform from which to oppose Communism.

Marcel was born in Paris, where he also died. In addition to plays, he wrote philosophy tracts as well as music and theatre criticisms; the latter were collected as *L'heure théâtrale* (1959). His plays are discussed in the preface to *Three Plays* and in Kenneth T. Gallagher's comprehensive analysis of *The Philosophy of Gabriel Marcel* (1962), which has bibliographies.

MARCO MILLIONS, a play in three acts, a prologue, and an epilogue by EUGENE O'NEILL, published in 1927 and produced in 1928. Setting: Venice and Asia in the thirteenth century.

This exotic and picaresque (and occasionally lyrical, yet comical) drama satirizes the American babbitt businessman in the guise of Marco Polo, and confronts him with the mystic wisdom and pride, in the guise of Kublai Kaan, of the medieval Orient. O'Neill had completed the play in early 1925, but because DAVID BELASCO and other producers hesitated to risk the necessary expenses, the play was not put on until the Theatre Guild decided to undertake its lavish production.

Prologue. In Persia, from her coffin being transported to Cathay, Queen Kukachin's voice sends a message to Venice of her love, death, and forgiveness.

Act I. Scene 1. In Venice twenty-three years earlier, Marco Polo (aged fifteen) and Donata (aged twelve) agree to marry when Marco returns from his travels. *Scene 2.* The Syrian papal legate (soon Pope Gregory X) predicts that Marco will shed his poetic aspirations, successfully follow the crass merchant ways of his father and uncle, and "set an example of virtuous Western manhood" that will drive the Kublai Kaan "to seek spiritual salvation somewhere!" *Scenes 3 through 5.* In Persia, India, and Mongolia, the Polos go through almost identical stylized scenes, each of which dramatizes Marco's declining sensitivity and growing callousness and materialism over a period of twenty months. *Scene 6.* In his Cathay palace, Kublai Kaan is impressed by the indignant courage with which Marco stands up for his Christian and mercantile platitudes, and he accepts him in his kingdom: "This [fool] Marco touches me, as a child might, but at the same time there is something warped, deformed—"

Act II. Scene 1. After fifteen years Kublai has become disgusted by "Marco's spiritual hump"—ruthless cupidity—and is incredulous to hear that he is loved by Kukachin, his beautiful granddaughter, who is to marry the Khan of Persia. Brazenly explaining his tyrannical "reforms," Marco forces Kublai to buy his inventions, including gunpowder and paper money: "You conquer the world with this—and you pay for it with this." Kukachin, who shares his confidence in his "immortal soul," asks that Marco command the fleet and attend her on her long voyage to Persia.

Kublai stares at them in "weary amazement": "Life is so stupid, it is mysterious!" *Scene 2.* Kublai sadly bids Kukachin farewell. His sage, hoping that perhaps some good will come of it, bids Marco to look deeply into Kukachin's eyes daily. Under Marco's noisy and ruthless command, the vessel departs. *Scene 3.* Though Marco repeatedly risks his life to save Kukachin during the voyage, he lacks the imagination to perceive her love, and at last she realizes that he has no soul. When they get to Persia, she throws gold at this "idol of stuffed self-satisfaction": "Here! Guzzle! Grunt! Wallow for our amusement!"

Act III. Scene 1. Grief-stricken at Kukachin's imminent death of a broken heart a year later, Kublai is ready to fight the West. He stares into his crystal and observes Venice's voluptuous welcoming festivities for Marco and his millions. Kublai's bitter conclusion that "God is only an infinite, insane energy" seems verified: "The Word became their flesh, they say. Now all is flesh! And can their flesh become the Word again?" *Scene 2.* At Kukachin's lavish burial ceremony, the Eastern priests cannot satisfy the grieving Kublai: "Against Death all Gods are powerless." He knows that "the living of life can be noble," and weeps over Kukachin's corpse.

Epilogue. A man in the first row of the theatre gets up and goes out, somewhat disturbed by the play. But by the time he gets into his limousine, he is again self-satisfied. It is Marco Polo.

MARGARET FLEMING, a play in four acts by JAMES A. HERNE, produced in 1890 and published in 1930. Setting: Canton, Massachusetts; 1890.

A milestone in the development of REALISM in American drama, *Margaret Fleming* is an IBSENite PROBLEM PLAY that deals frankly with adultery. It was considered too daring in theme and treatment, was denied a hearing in the regular theatres, and failed to appeal to the public. But it was hailed by WILLIAM DEAN HOWELLS and Hamlin Garland. With their support, Herne's revisions, and Mrs. Herne's acting, it became a SUCCÈS D'ESTIME.

Despite his philandering, Philip Fleming is devoted to his wife, Margaret, and their year-old daughter. Their nursemaid's sister is dying after having given birth to an illegitimate child fathered by Fleming, and asks to see Margaret. By the time she arrives at the cottage the woman is dead, and Margaret learns of her husband's adultery. Her agony is heightened by the infant's wails, and at the climactic curtain she begins to nurse it, as Fleming enters. He runs away in shame, and her suffering causes Margaret's blindness from glaucoma. Later she adopts the infant and forgives Fleming when he returns.

MARIANA PINEDA, a historical play in three scenes by FEDERICO GARCÍA LORCA, published in 1925 and produced in 1927. Setting: Spain, 1820's.

García Lorca subtitled his first full-length play a "Popular Ballad in Three Prints." It is a stylized, poetic retelling of a well-known Spanish legend. Mariana Pineda, the Betsy Ross of Granada, was a widow who perished in the revolt against Ferdinand VII. The play's 1927 sets were designed by Salvador Dalí.

Mariana Pineda is sewing a flag for the liberal conspirators whose leader, Don Pedro Sotomayor, she loves. When the uprising fails, Pedro escapes with his men, leaving Mariana behind. She protects her honor against the advances of the king's constable, decides not to escape when she hears her children cry, and is arrested for treason. Persuaded of her martyrdom, Mariana refuses to divulge the names of the conspirators and is hanged. Her last words identify her love for Pedro with her love for freedom: "I am Liberty because love willed it so. / Pedro: the Liberty for which you left me. / I am the Liberty wounded by mankind! / Love, love, love, and eternal solitude!"

MARINETTI, Filippo Tommaso (1876–1944), Italian poet and playwright, was the founder of the FUTURIST movement, which his plays exemplify. His *Re Baldoria* (1909), originally *Le roi Bombance* (1905), is a satire of parliamentarian government; set in the Middle Ages, the play had an eventful 1909 production in Lugné-Poë's Théâtre de l'Œuvre—like Jarry's KING UBU, which it resembles. The title play of Marinetti's *Elettricità sessuale* (1909) collection is a more conventional satire of marriage and sex—as are the other short pieces in the volume, published in 1920.

Marinetti experienced difficulties with the authorities and emigrated to France, where he wrote in French and where he later espoused Fascism. A chapter on Marinetti appears in Isaac Goldberg's *The Drama of Transition* (1922).

MARQUÉS, René (1919–), Puerto Rican playwright, became known to American audiences with the island's "national play," *La carreta* (*The Little Cart*), which was originally produced in New York in 1950 and—as *The Ox Cart*—was featured there in 1960's mobile outdoor productions. A tragedy about an old *jibaro* (Puerto Rican farmer) and his family (three generations), it portrays with pathos, humor, and considerable local color their uprooting and their move to San Juan and then to the Bronx, their dreams gradually lost amidst slum life, violence, rape, prison, and death.

Marqués, who first achieved prominence as a short-story writer, studied at the University of Madrid, where he was influenced by the philosophy of MIGUEL DE UNAMUNO and in 1947 wrote his first play, *El sol y los Macdonald.* It was premiered in 1950 by a troupe of Puerto Rican students recruited by Marqués, and deals with one of his principal interests, racial problems. In 1958 Marqués consolidated his reputation with the hit of the Puerto Rican Drama Festival, *Los soles truncos,* based on his nationalistic short story about three old sisters, survivors of an ancient family whose decline amidst changing social orders is dramatized through flashbacks.* *Un niño azul*

* The play also appeared under the story's title, *Purificación en la Calle de Cristo,* and an excerpt in English, *The House of the Setting Sun,* appears in Willis Knapp Jones's *Spanish-American Literature in Translation* (1963).

para esa sombra, a patriotic drama of rebellion and suicide for principles, won Marqués the Ateneo Prize in 1959. His other plays include *El hombre y sus sueños* (1948), dramatizing man's tragic quest for immortality; *Palm Sunday* (1949), a controversial anti-American interpretation of the 1937 Ponce Easter Massacre, written in English for a Columbia University playwriting class Marqués attended on a Rockefeller grant and premiered under his direction in 1956; *La muerte no entrará en palacio* (1957), featuring a local despot supported by "a country up north" and assassinated by his own daughter for betraying his people; and *La casa sin reloj* (1962), a partly ABSURD "antipoetic comedy."

A major LATIN AMERICAN postwar dramatist who has also written prize-winning film scripts, Marqués and his work are discussed, in addition to general studies, in Charles Pilditch's introduction to *The Ox Cart* (1969).

MARQUIS OF KEITH, THE (*Der Marquis von Keith*), a play in five acts by FRANK WEDEKIND, published in 1900 and produced in 1901. Setting: Munich, late summer of 1899.

This play, considered by Wedekind and others as his best, satirizes the success morality of the middle class. The character of the swindler protagonist, a lusty, cynical gambler and racketeer with irrepressible vitality, was inspired by a daring forger and art dealer Wedekind had met in Paris, as well as by Casanova and others.

Act I. The self-styled Marquis of Keith, a twenty-seven-year-old upstart who has gained some power as an art dealer, a concert manager, and a newspaper writer, is about to bring off a coup. He intends to found a monumental concert center that will gain him wealth and respectability. At the moment, however, he is broke. He lives with Molly Griesinger, his adoring common-law wife, who at fifteen accompanied him to America and other refuges when he had to abscond. His acquaintance Ernst Scholz, who has renounced his title and feels morally culpable and confused, places himself under the "guidance" of Keith, "although I detest your entire conception of life." Keith rejects Molly's pleas to lead a simple life with her. He wants to observe how the wealthy, ethical Scholz will "turn himself into an epicurean."

Acts II and III. After a tryst Keith has arranged for him, Scholz is further confused and amazed by his "fallen girl's" exuberant joy of life. "The happiness of these creatures would never be so despised were it not the most unprofitable of all businesses imaginable," Keith tells him; "sin is a mythological name for bad business. Good business always works its way into the existing social order! No one knows this better than I." Keith introduces various rich merchants he is swindling to his mistress, a beautiful countess, and announces a "founders' party" at her villa. "I use every mortal according to his talents," he later tells her, but denies her accusation: "I thought you wanted to use me as a whore for your friend" Scholz. Passionately he describes the concert dress in which she is to make her debut as a singer. To assure his success, he forges a congratulatory telegram from the most influential merchant and displays fireworks at the party. Unsuccessful in her plea for a simple life, Molly embraces Keith fervently and runs away. And Scholz, intoxicated by the festivities and enamored of Keith's countess, momentarily becomes a changed, jubilant person: "I have overcome the evil spirits; happiness lies before me; I belong to life!"

Acts IV and V. Keith's ruthless comments about various unfortunate associates appall Scholz. Cynically Keith ridicules his moralizing: "Why should anyone even *want* to become a useful member of society?" The missing Molly, he thinks, is probably "reveling in an ocean of petit bourgeois sentimentality," and "love of God" is every man's "summary and symbolic way of expressing love of oneself." But Keith's fortunes are rapidly turning; Molly's disappearance bodes evil, and he begins to despair: "Am I to be driven like an outcast again from country to country?" Then he quickly formulates new and more daring plans. But his mistress, who has succeeded brilliantly in her debut, staggers him with the news that she will marry the city's wealthiest merchant, and jilts Keith. Desperate, he begs Scholz for money. Scholz wants to "settle his account with reality" by escaping life, and tempts Keith to accompany him to a sanatorium. Keith rejects the temptation and the philosophy it represents, and gets on his knees to implore Scholz's help—and Scholz refuses and leaves. Now come Keith's creditors, accompanied by the angry bearers of the corpse of Molly, who has drowned herself. He is told to leave the city and is given some money to do so at once. Alone, Keith picks up a revolver, with which he intends to shoot himself. He recoils in horror, turns from it to the money, puts away the revolver, and grins: "Life is a slippery business . . ."

MARRIAGE OF MISTER MISSISSIPPI, THE (*Die Ehe des Herrn Mississippi*), a comedy in two parts by FRIEDRICH DÜRRENMATT, published and produced in 1952. Setting: a gradually disintegrating room, "always five years before the present."

This partly EXPRESSIONIST and metaphysical parody of melodrama evidences influences of BERTOLT BRECHT, THORNTON WILDER, FRANK WEDEKIND, and the Zürich cabaret. Produced also as *Fools Are Passing Through,* Dürrenmatt revised it in 1957.

A Communist revolutionary leader is executed. Then he informs the audience that this was the end of the play about to start. As others periodically do later, he discusses the play's characters, plot, and setting. He is one of four lovers of Anastasia, who, like Wedekind's Lulu, is a "woman who consumes an immoderate quantity of men." Her other men are his friend Florestan Mississippi, a public prosecutor fanatical about reestablishing "the Mosaic law" by condemning hundreds to death, who compels Anastasia to marry him so both may atone for having poisoned their adulterous spouses; the country's Minister of Justice, Mississippi's friend and an opportunistic politician; and a quixotic count who has loved her since childhood. After much social violence and private plotting Anastasia and Mississippi poison each other, leaving only the count alive. A self-proclaimed disillusioned fool, he apostrophizes the "eternal comedy" of God's infinity: "Let His glory blaze forth, / fed by our helpless futility."

MARSHAK, Samuil Yakovlevich (1887–1964), Russian writer and translator, and originally a protégé of MAXIM GORKY, was actively engaged in making the works of English poets known in Russia. He also wrote children's and satirical works, and a play based on Slovak and Czech folk tales, *Dvenadstat mesyatsev* (*Twelve Months*), for which he won a Stalin Prize in 1946. With a brief preface on Marshak, it was published in Alexander Bakshy's collection *Soviet Scene: Six Plays of Russian Life* (1946).

MARTENS, Gaston [Marie] (1883–1967), Belgian dramatist, wrote popular Flemish folk comedies and satires set in his native Lys Valley. The most successful of them, *Paradijsvogels* (1932), he adapted with ANDRÉ OBEY as the Paris hit and later film *Les Gueux du Paradis* (1945, translated as *The Hopeful Traveller*).

MARTÍNEZ SIERRA, Gregorio (1881–1947), Spanish writer, was immensely prolific in many genres but became notable especially for his numerous plays. Ranging over all types, the best among them are gently emotional dramas that substitute simple, pedestrian episodes for strong plot, and feature sensitive and pious yet strong characters. The most popular of these plays were the filmed and internationally produced *Canción de cuna* (THE CRADLE SONG, 1911) and, to a lesser degree, *El reino de Dios* (THE KINGDOM OF GOD, 1915). Especially the first of these evidences more than do Martínez Sierra's other plays the contribution of María de la O Lejárraga, the poetess he married in 1899. She collaborated in all his writings and (as Underhill notes) his name really denotes their joint pen name.

Born in Madrid, where he attended the university, Martínez Sierra started his career as a poet. JACINTO BENAVENTE, to whom *The Cradle Song* is dedicated, encouraged the young man and arranged for his first publication, *El poema del trabajo* (1898). These verses were followed by stories and novels. When Benavente founded the Madrid Art Theatre at the end of the century, Martínez Sierra became one of its gifted young actors. He translated some one-acters by MAURICE MAETERLINCK, and his own first published dramas were four dialogues that resemble the Belgian's dreamlike plays and, in fact, were entitled *Teatro de ensueño* (1905). Martínez Sierra did not really begin his own career as a playwright until he collaborated with SANTIAGO RUSIÑOL on a comedy, *Vida y dulzura* (1907). Martínez Sierra's *Hechizo de amor* (*Love Magic*, 1908), a Pierrot-Columbine-Harlequin trifle, was his first play to appear in English. In 1909 he achieved success with the comedy *La sombra del padre*, and two years later he established his reputation with his masterpiece, *The Cradle Song*.

Similarly gentle and sentimental is *Los pastores* (1913, translated as *The Two Shepherds*), a play about a doctor and a priest who are good shepherds to their village flock but, being out of step with modern times, cannot pass the new science and theology examinations and therefore are replaced by men who are more knowledgeable if less wise. Other full-length comedies by Martínez Sierra are *El ama de la casa* (1910), whose characteristically virtuous heroine demonstrates to the troublesome children of the widower she marries how a good woman's love is indispensable to family life; *Primavera en otoño* (1911), in which a daughter reunites her long-separated parents; *Madame Pepita* (1912), whose dressmaker heroine marries a friend who has long protected her from a cheating count, whose noble and artistic son then marries Pepita's daughter; *La mujer del héroe* (*Wife to a Famous Man*, 1914), a tribute to Spanish women, here the wife and the mother-in-law of an aviator who is a bit of a scoundrel; and *Sueño de una noche de agosto* (1918, produced in English as *The Romantic Young Lady*), in which the title character finds adventure and love with a novelist hero who courts her by throwing his straw hat into her window and proposes while the sprightly old grandmother pretends to nap. Even more trifling pieces to appear in English include the one-acters *El pobrecito Juan* (*Poor John*, 1912) and *El enamorado* (*The Lover*, 1913); the first portrays a bumbler who fails even at committing suicide, while the hero of *The Lover* is a manufacturer who gives up everything to follow the queen he worships.

There is considerable tenderness, charm, and optimism—and sometimes sentimentality—in Martínez Sierra's drama, but little depth of characterization, profundity of ideas, or social or philosophical commitment. His drama portrays the virtues of piety as well as the pathos and comedy of everyday life, romantic daydreams, and homely whimsicalities. Aside from scores of such original plays, librettos for musicals, and adaptations of his fiction, he translated well over fifty plays by Shakespeare, Maeterlinck, EUGÈNE BRIEUX, BJØRNSTJERNE BJØRNSON, HENRIK IBSEN, JAMES M. BARRIE, BERNARD SHAW, and others. In 1916 Martínez Sierra became director of Madrid's Eslava Theatre, where in 1920 he premiered FEDERICO GARCÍA LORCA's first play (THE BUTTERFLY'S EVIL SPELL) and for which he organized a stock company that performed modern plays in Europe and America. Spending much of his later life outside Spain, Martínez Sierra traveled widely. He practiced journalism, founded and directed two publishing ventures, and edited the World's Classics in Translation. His poetry, fiction, and books of essays—many on feminism, to which his wife contributed extensively—appear in over forty volumes.

The translated dramas noted above are collected in *The Cradle Song and Other Plays* (1922) and *The Kingdom of God and Other Plays* (1922), with introductions by John G. Underhill and Helen and HARLEY GRANVILLE-BARKER, respectively. The former is reprinted as the introduction to *The Cradle Song* in Robert W. Corrigan's collection of *Masterpieces of the Modern Spanish Theatre* (1967); to the latter's bibliography may be added Frank W. Chandler's *Modern Continental Playwrights* (1931), which has an extensive section on Martínez Sierra, and Patricia W. O'Connor's *Women in the Theater of Gregorio Martínez Sierra* (1967).

MARTINI, Fausto Maria (1886–1931), Italian novelist, poet, and playwright of the dreamlike *Crepuscolari* or TWILIGHT school of writers, is best remembered for his drama, particularly the one-act *Ridi, pagliaccio!* (1919), which as *Laugh, Clown, Laugh* received a lavish DAVID BELASCO production in New York in 1923–24. A typical and very successful drama of disillusionment inspired by Ruggiero Leoncavallo's opera and characterized also as a GROTESQUE drama, it features two neurotics who view everything in opposite ways, one reacting with incessant and uncontrollable mirth, the other with baleful tears; they meet in a psychiatrist's office and become rivals in love, and the play ends in tragedy.

Martini's other plays similarly reflect despairing post-World War I disillusionment in PIRANDELLian "masks and faces." In *Il fiore sotto gli occhi* (1921), a couple tries to escape a humdrum marriage through erotic fantasy; in a similar vein, the heroine of *L'altra Nanetta* (1922) commits suicide when her husband composes a vivid and too evocative poem on her earlier life; and the couple of *La sera del 30* (1926) becomes embittered when badly treated at a dance. In all these plays Martini espouses the antiromantic virtues of the well-ordered and respectable bourgeois life in which he himself grew up (later he became a journalist, and he was seriously wounded in World War I). He expounded his theories in his *Teatro breve* (*Dramatic Sketches*, 1929).

MARTYN, Edward (1859–1923), Irish novelist and playwright, was one of the original founders and a major financial supporter of the Irish Literary Theatre. His *The Heather Field* (1899) was its second production: it dramatizes a man's sacrificing everything for his dream—to reclaim his submerged field—and emerging with his spirit unvanquished though his ideals are shattered. *The Heather Field* and *Maeve* (1900), featuring a girl ultimately killed by her vision of a Celtic fairyland, in both of whose composition GEORGE MOORE had a hand, are considered his best plays. They are SYMBOLIC, poetic works that reflect Martyn's love of nature. So is his next play, *The Enchanted Sea* (1902). Beginning with *The Tale of a Town* (1902), which Moore rewrote as *The Bending of the Bough* and which deals with provincial society, Martyn's plays became increasingly bitter satires, influenced by the social drama of HENRIK IBSEN.

In 1901 Martyn broke with the Irish Literary Theatre, disagreeing with WILLIAM BUTLER YEATS over its basic policies. Martyn became the president of Sinn Fein (1904–08) and founded the Irish Theatre in Dublin in 1914. His other plays include *Grangecolman* (1912) and *The Dream Physician* (1918), a lampoon on Moore, Yeats, and JAMES JOYCE. Martyn also wrote satiric prose.

A book-length study of his career is Denis Gwynn's *Edward Martyn and the Irish Revival* (1930). Una Ellis-Fermor's *The Irish Dramatic Movement* (1954) contains an extensive analysis of his drama. See also Sister Marie-Therese Courtney's *Edward Martyn and the Irish Theatre* (1956) and Jan Setterquist's *Ibsen and the Beginnings of Anglo-Irish Drama: II. Edward Martyn* (1961).

MARY MAGDALENE (*Marie-Magdeleine*), a play in three acts by MAURICE MAETERLINCK, produced in 1910 and published in 1913. Setting: Bethany and Arimathea in Christ's time.

In this "free adaptation" of a work by the German writer Paul Heyse (1830–1914), Mary Magdalene rejects a Roman officer's proposition to free Christ in return for her body. She loves the officer, but her divine love for Christ prevents her yielding to shameful surrender. Cursed by all for her refusal, she experiences ecstasy as Christ passes her house on His way to Crucifixion.

MARY OF SCOTLAND, a play in three acts by MAXWELL ANDERSON, produced in 1933 and published in 1934. Setting: Scotland and England, 1561–67.

In this prose-and-verse history play Mary Stuart is portrayed as a beautiful, gracious idealist victimized by the shrewd machinations of a jealous rival, Queen Elizabeth. Love and integrity defeat Mary as a ruler—but glorify her as a woman. The absence of these qualities gives Elizabeth victory; but her success is depicted as being sterile—as in ELIZABETH THE QUEEN.

Act I. Scene 1. Queen Mary returns from France to rule Scotland. Young, attractive, and espousing "tolerance and mercy," she quickly charms even the fanatic old Protestant reformer John Knox, who has come to curse the Catholic Mary as "the whore of Babylon—the leprous and cankerous evangel of the Beast!" Her outspoken admirer James Hepburn, the Earl of Bothwell, counsels war against her Protestant opponents, but Mary plans to "win in a woman's way, not by the sword." *Scene 2.* In the meantime Queen Elizabeth cunningly and ruthlessly spins her web of intrigue. Mary has a legitimate claim to the English crown and, as Elizabeth's heir, poses a further threat. Queen Elizabeth therefore plans to destroy her—but not by war. Believing that "we are not what we are, but what is said of us and what we read in others' eyes," she plans to spread scandals that will ruin Mary's reputation. She also plans to bring about her rival's marriage to a weak fool, Lord Henry Darnley; though a Catholic, he will serve Elizabeth's purpose, for "a woman's mind and spirit are no better than those of the man she lies under in the night." *Scene 3.* Mary falls into the trap. She rejects the suit of the man she truly loves—and her strongest supporter—the forthright and militant Bothwell, because she wants "to rule gently." Led to believe that Elizabeth fears him most, she accepts Darnley, "a punk" (as Bothwell characterizes him) whose coarse drunkenness repulses her.

Act II (three scenes). Mary soon comes to rue her error. Darnley, now crowned, is a disgusting sot. He becomes the rebelling earls' tool, assists in murdering Mary's loyal private secretary, and is finally himself murdered. Bothwell returns from exile to help the queen. They marry, but it is too late, and they enjoy only brief happiness. Soon Elizabeth's machinations come to full fruition: the scandalous rumors she has spread about Bothwell and Mary help Knox rally the Scottish armies against Mary. Bothwell's agreement to relinquish his earldom and leave Scotland do not finally save Mary; the earls treacherously imprison her, though Bothwell succeeds in fighting his way out.

Act III. Mary has escaped to England, but is held captive there. At last Queen Elizabeth visits her, and Mary learns the truth. In a highly dramatic encounter between the queens, Elizabeth admits her longtime plots—and her jealous fear: "I am all women I must be. One's a young girl, / Young and harrowed as you are—one who could weep / To see you here—and one's a bitterness / At what I have lost and can never have, and one's / The basilisk you saw. This last stands guard / And I obey it." She offers Mary her freedom if she will give up the dangerous Bothwell and abdicate in favor of her and Darnley's son, James. Mary refuses, though it means solitary, lifelong imprisonment: history will restore her reputation. Elizabeth soon disillusions her; history, she says, is not truth but what people believe, and she has taken care to shape these beliefs: "It will be said of me that I governed well, / And wisely, but of you, cousin, that your life, / Shot through with ill-loves, battened on lechery, made you / An ensign of evil, that men tore down and trampled." Suddenly Mary perceives her true situation; though it appears hopeless, "Still, STILL I win! I have been / A woman, and I have loved as a woman loves, / Lost as a woman loses. I have borne a son, / And he will rule Scotland—and England. You have no heir! / A devil has no children." Now Mary can unhesitatingly reject Elizabeth's offer and accept her own doom: "My pride is stronger than yours, and my heart beats blood / Such as yours has never known. And in this dungeon, / I win here, alone." The curtain falls as Mary looks into the darkness outside, alone.

MARY ROSE, a play in three acts by JAMES M. BARRIE, produced in 1920 and published in 1924. Setting: Sussex and a Hebrides island.

For a long time among Barrie's most popular plays, this is his best-known "ghost" fantasy. It is a variation of PETER PAN, for though Mary Rose becomes a mother, she also does not grow up and she retains her child's heart.

A soldier is shown through an old manor house. He is the son of Mary Rose, whose ghost still haunts the rooms in which he grew up. As a girl, Mary Rose mysteriously disappeared for a few days on a little "Island that likes to be visited," but remembered nothing of the episode. Her puzzled parents tell her suitor of this strange episode. During a picnic some years later with her husband, on the same island, she is called by supernatural voices and again disappears. This time she stays away twenty-five years. Suddenly she returns, as youthful as ever, and asks for her baby. In the meantime he has grown up and her aged parents and her husband have lost touch with him. The shock kills her and the framework now merges into the conclusion. The soldier "releases" the ghostly Mary Rose by giving his mother, who does not recognize him, the one thing she seeks before returning to the lovely other land: she yearns for the time when her son "is a man and takes me on his knee instead of my taking him on mine." The celestial call comes again, and Mary Rose, her wish granted, "walks out through the window into the empyrean."

MARYA, a play in eight scenes by ISAAK BABEL, published in 1935 and produced in 1964. Setting: Petrograd (Leningrad), 1920.

One of the last works published during Babel's life, *Marya* reached the rehearsal stage—but ultimately remained unproduced in Russia. (Its premiere was in Italy, with music by Shostakovich.) It is the first of a projected trilogy and portrays the inability of the old order to adjust to the new Soviet life, primarily in the home of a speculator and that of a general's frivolous daughter. Her admirable sister—the title character—never appears in the play: Marya's absence and her letter to her home underline the contrast between the new and the old way of life.

Isaak Markovich Dymshits, a Jewish speculator, questions the crippled soldiers who smuggle in the goods he sells: business is falling off because they have increasing difficulty evading search at the roadblocks of the besieged city. Dymshits keeps company with Lyudmila Mukovnin, a girl of easy virtue who leads him on but resists his advances. In a brawl, one of her other suitors—who has seduced her despite his venereal infection—is shot and Lyudmila is arrested. Her father, an elderly former general, hears about this and learns that Marya's visit, which he has looked forward to, has been canceled. Thereupon he dies of a heart attack. The Mukovnin apartment goes to new tenants, a working couple. A laborer tells the pregnant wife, "Kids being born today are going to have a marvelous life when they grow up," and a friend sings raucously in anticipation of the housewarming party.

MASEFIELD, John (1878–1967), English Poet Laureate, also wrote novels and dramas. The most successful of his prose plays was THE TRAGEDY OF NAN (1908). It and a few of his other prose dramas have poetic power in their simple folk speech. They were popular for a short while, but soon dated and were rarely performed after the 1940's. His verse drama includes a number of biblical plays. These were esteemed by specialized audiences, but never achieved any general popularity. Masefield's stature as a playwright, despite his productivity in that genre, is considerably below his stature as a poet.

He was born in Ledbury, Herefordshire, the son of a provincial lawyer. At thirteen he became a seaman and served on the merchant ship *Conway*. In the mid-1890's he took odd jobs in New York and London, and began his writing career with *Salt-Water Ballads* (1902), simple verses that include his well-known "Sea Fever." Though Masefield reacted against Victorianism, he himself in time became conservative. His diction is rustic, in the tradition of the poetry of Wordsworth. Very prolific, Masefield published literary studies, fiction, many volumes of poetry (including verse narrative in the convention of Chaucer, like *Reynard the Fox* (1919), and about twenty plays.

The first of these was *The Campden Wonder* (1907), a short prose play based on a Gloucestershire fable. So was the next of his *Prose Plays* (1925), *Mrs. Harrison* (written in 1906). *The Sweeps of Ninety-Eight* (1916), another one-acter, was followed by *The Locked Chest* (1916), a dramatization of an Icelandic (*Laxdaelasaga*) tale. *The Tragedy of Nan,* the most important play in the collection, was his first full-length drama. *The Tragedy of Pompey the Great* (1910), based on Sir Thomas North's translation of Plutarch, dramatizes events of 50–48 B.C. and portrays Pompey as a wise ruler who is "miserably killed." *The Faithful* (1915) is an early eighteenth-century Japanese pageant depicting the tragedy of the forty-seven Ronin. *Melloney Holtspur, or, The Pangs of Love* (1923), an experimental play, deals with the supernatural in a modern setting: the ghosts of the title character and her faithless sweetheart appear during the courtship of contemporary lovers and strive to pass on (as in Aeschylus's *Oresteia*) the evil and vengeance of previous generations.

There are occasional flashes of fine poetry in Masefield's *Verse Plays* (1925). The best of them is probably *Good Friday: A Dramatic Poem* (1916), whose protagonist-chorus is a madman who experiences and expresses the meaning of the Crucifixion as it occurs offstage. Other plays in that collection are *Philip the King* (1914), a one-act portrayal of the religious imperialism of Philip II of Spain; Racine's *Esther* and *Berenice,* the first an adaptation, the second a translation; and *A King's Daughter* (1923), a play about Ahab's wife, Jezebel.

Masefield's other plays include *The Witch* (1910), an adaptation of a Norwegian tragedy; *The Trial of Jesus* (1925), a verse drama; *Tristan and Isolt* (1927); *The Coming of Christ* (1928); *Easter: A Play for Singers* (1929); *End and Beginning* (1933); *The Empress of Rome* (1937), an adaptation of a French miracle play; and *A Play of St. George* (1948), which is set in Lydda during the reign of Diocletian: after defeating the dragon, a young pirate, George is killed by centurions because he refuses to deny his God in return for worldly power.

Masefield also wrote a book about *A Macbeth Production* (1945) and an autobiography, *So Long to Learn* (1952). Later studies of his life and work are L. A. G. Strong's *John Masefield* (1952), Margery T. Fisher's *John Masefield* (1963), and Corlis Lamont's *Remembering John Masefield* (1971).

MASK AND THE FACE, THE (*La maschera e il volto*), "a grotesque comedy" in three acts by LUIGI CHIARELLI, produced in 1916 and published in 1917. Setting: Lake Como, early twentieth century.

This biting comedy labeled and launched the theatre of the GROTESQUE that paved the way for the drama of LUIGI PIRANDELLO. Chiarelli wrote it in 1913 but could not get it produced for some time. The play's corrupt society and its protagonist, Paolo, personify a Pirandellian contrast between illusion and reality—the mask of convention that obscures reality and often destroys true feeling and happiness.

Act I. The fashionable guests of Count Paolo Grazia discuss infidelity. An elderly banker ruefully reconciles himself to his young wife's adulteries, but Paolo declares that "at the very first symptom of anything of the sort I should have been without mercy. . . . I know myself, and I know that I would kill her." Among the company's many affairs is that of an engaged young lawyer with Paolo's wife, Savina. When Paolo hears about it, he frantically breaks down the door to his wife's room but fails to catch or even identify her paramour. In his rage he tries to throttle his repentant wife, who submits but begs him to save their marriage and not be "a slave to your words and to your conventional ideas." Unable to bring himself to kill her, Paolo insists that she now is dead for him and, to put up a proper front, makes her go abroad into permanent hiding. Then he meets his lawyer friend (her paramour) and tells him that Savina has betrayed him with an unknown lover. Haltingly Paolo describes how he thereupon killed her and dumped her body into the lake. To avoid suspicion of his own guilt, the reluctant lawyer agrees to handle Paolo's defense.

Act II. Ten months later Paolo returns from prison, acquitted because he had acted to protect his honor. The town welcomes him as a hero with great festivities, women shamelessly offering themselves to him. The disillusioned Paolo becomes increasingly bitter, also because his lawyer friend, whose wife too offers herself to Paolo, obtained his acquittal by defaming Savina. A corpse is fished out of the lake and identified as

Savina's. "This is the last straw!" Paolo exclaims when he is alone—upon which Savina suddenly appears: "I thought that on this day of your rejoicing it would be nice for you, in the midst of so much homage to receive also—the pardon of your victim." Still in love with her, Paolo quickly hides her—whereupon the repentant lawyer comes to confess that it was he who was Savina's lover. Paolo throws him out contemptuously, but cannot muster the strength to send Savina away and decides to wait until the next morning. "I shall wait for you," Savina says as she retires to her room—almost immediately followed by her agitated husband.

Act III. It is the afternoon of "Savina's" funeral. The elderly banker takes back his repentant wife, who has tired of her adulteries. Paolo confesses that after their night together his love for Savina is as great as ever and that, appearances notwithstanding, they somehow must resume their joint lives. Savina confounds the lawyer, who is thunderstruck to see and hear his supposedly dead mistress bitingly read the peroration of his defamatory defense speech. When Savina's presence becomes known, Paolo is threatened with prosecution for perjury. "I killed her and was acquitted," he observes incredulously; "I did not kill her, and I am sent to prison!" Realizing that there is no solution but to flee, which the old banker advises him to do, Paolo and Savina leave to hide abroad. "I have no longer the slightest desire to render an account of my life to anyone," Paolo concludes: "not to society, nor to my friends, nor to the law, nor to anyone." They run off as the funeral march is heard in the distance.

MASQUE OF KINGS, THE, a verse play in three acts by MAXWELL ANDERSON, published and produced in 1937. Setting: Vienna and Mayerling, 1889.

Anderson articulates characteristic and timely ideas in this dramatization of the Hapsburg tragedy. Archduke Rudolph is portrayed as an idealistic liberal disillusioned when he becomes aware of political realities. However, personal integrity and nobility ultimately restore his idealism.

The Crown Prince, Archduke Rudolph, plots against his autocratic old father, Emperor Franz Joseph. To bring freedom to the people, he participates in a conspiracy and stages a palace revolution. But that very night Rudolph himself must be ruthless and brutal. With growing disillusionment he sees how as emperor he will be as oppressive as the astute Franz Joseph—for power and freedom are incompatible. His despair overwhelms him when he learns that the mistress he adores and would marry, Baroness Mary Vetsera, was his father's spy when she met Rudolph. Though she became loyal as soon as they fell in love, his faith in love, too, now dies. He retires to his hunting lodge at Mayerling. Mary follows him and, distraught by his contempt, commits suicide. Now Rudolph regains faith. "I thought, indeed, / of going back with you, but I'll die young / and pleasanter to remember," he tells his parents, who have come to him to compromise: "We are all ghosts, we three, / walking the halls of Europe in a dream / that's ended, a long masquerade of kings / that crossed the stage and stumbled into dark / before we came." Then he shoots himself. The old emperor resumes his burdens sadly: he recognizes the truth in Rudolph's vision of their dying old order, "that same darkness / he prophesies—"

MASSES AND MAN (*Masse-Mensch*), a verse play in seven "pictures" by ERNST TOLLER, produced in 1920 and published in 1921. Setting: a workmen's tavern, a meeting hall, open space, etc.; 1918–19.

Also translated as *Man and Masses,* this is an EXPRESSIONIST drama in four "visionary abstracts of reality" and three alternating dream interludes. Toller composed this revolutionary work in two nights, while he was in prison. It transcends proletarian art and became his best-known play. Brilliantly premiered in Berlin, it received notable productions throughout the world. Three characters emerge from the anonymous masses: the Woman (Sonia Irene L.), symbolizing man's idealistic humanism; her husband, representing the established order; and the Nameless One, embodying the equally materialistic and ruthless masses of the revolution.

First Picture. In the back room of a tavern the workers' executive board proclaims a strike and the Woman fervently agrees to lead "the armies of humanity" to world peace. The workers depart upon the entry of her husband, a government official. Because it threatens his honor and position, he urges her to give up revolutionary work and express her idealism in conventional charitable works. "This is treason / To the State!" he maintains, but the Woman replies that the "State makes war," "betrays the people," and "robs, squeezes, and oppresses." Yet she yearns for her husband and, though tomorrow she will "attack the State / To which you have sworn loyalty," she begs to spend a last night with him—and follows him passionately.

Second Picture (*Dream*). On a high stool at the stock exchange sits a clerk who resembles the Woman's husband. Bankers are bidding on military contracts, but the war may be lost because "the masses / Require [the] incentive" of love. Thereupon the bankers found a "Convalescent Home / For strengthening the will to victory"—brothels for officers, noncoms, and the ranks. A national bond issue for such an establishment soon finds bidders. A figure resembling the Woman leads in the Woman and warns the bankers that "There's a flaw in your system: / Human nature." The Woman softly cautions them against their mechanism: it consists of human beings, *"men* and *women."* News of disaster prompts the bankers to conduct a "charitable entertainment." To the accompaniment of music resembling the clink of coins, the bankers in their top hats perform a fantastic dance around the exchange.

Third Picture. In a large hall masses of workers decide to destroy the machines. "Down with the factories!" they shout as they catalogue their grievances and determine to strike. The Nameless One emerges and calls for "a last, most ruthless fight!"—a revolution. The Woman first opposes violence: "I will not have fresh murder." But as the Nameless One proclaims himself speaker for "the Masses! / Masses are fate," the Woman succumbs to his and the workers' rhetoric: "Whoever stands across our path, / Be trodden down! / Masses are deeds!"

Fourth Picture (*Dream*). In a courtyard surrounded by high walls the Nameless One appears amidst the downtrodden, playing a concertina. A condemned man with a rope around his neck gets others to join him in a wild dance, lit by colored and flickering spotlights. The Woman suddenly recognizes a condemned prisoner as her husband and begs the sentries to let him go. "Only the Masses count," the sentry says. But the Woman replies, "Only Man counts," and offers herself up "To mankind." When the sentries jeer, she stands beside her husband: "Then shoot me! / I renounce."

Fifth Picture. The Woman and the Nameless One debate across a long table as workers rush in with bad news about the progress of the revolt. It is failing and the armies are near. "The Masses are revenge!" the Nameless One insists and, supported by the workers, turns against the Woman, who considers all men brothers—including the captured soldiers. As the armies approach, the doomed workers defiantly sing the "Marseillaise" (or the "Internationale"). There is gunfire, and then the soldiers enter. They order all to raise their arms, and they handcuff the Woman.

Sixth Picture (*Dream*). A prisoner with the face of the Woman is crouching in a cage. Shadows of the killed workers circle about her. They accuse the Woman of their death because she was silent—thus acquiescent—when they went to battle. She admits her guilt and then accuses God. Masses of prisoners join in her accusation. When the warder says that God is within her, the Woman vows to "overcome this God," and summons Him. The prisoners vanish and the warder releases her from the cage. "I am free?" she asks. He replies, "Unfree! / Free!"

Seventh Picture. The Woman sits in her prison cell. Her husband comes to save her, considering her guiltless of the killings of the workmen—for her principles were noble. But the Woman decides both of them are guilty: "I, the accused, I am the judge, / I prosecute, I pronounce guilty / And I absolve." As he leaves, she calls him her "brother." The Nameless One, too, comes to save her, but when she hears that they must strike down a guard "for the Cause," she refuses: "The warder is a man," and "To be a man is plain, is primal." She rejects the Nameless One's contention that "only the Masses are holy": "No man may kill men for a cause. / Unholy every cause that needs to kill." She accepts a priest's exhortations but sends him off, too: "I believe!!! / But I am cold . . . go, now, / Go!" When the officer comes to lead her to her execution she accompanies him calmly: "I am ready." Two female prisoners steal into her empty cell and start to rifle her belongings. But when they hear the firing squad's shots, they guiltily put back what they have taken and cower in fright. "Sister, why do we do such things?" one of them asks, and the other breaks down, crying.

MASTER BUILDER, THE (*Bygmester Solness*), a play in three acts by HENRIK IBSEN, published in 1892 and produced in 1893. Setting: contemporary Norway.

This late Ibsen drama, a NATURALISTIC yet also a SYMBOLIC and lyrical work, has been variously interpreted: as a modern morality play, as a study of abnormal psychology, and as an autobiography. Though Solness has been identified with BJØRNSTJERNE BJØRNSON and such statesmen as Gladstone and Bismarck, Ibsen publicly acknowledged his own resemblance to Solness; Hilde Wangel (a minor character in THE LADY FROM THE SEA) is at least in part modeled on an eighteen-year-old with whom Ibsen, then sixty-one, kept company in 1889.

Act I. Halvard Solness, a vigorous but aging master builder, is tired of constructing villas. Yet he refuses to give an assignment to his draftsman apprentice, who has drawn up the plans. He is obsessed by fears of youth replacing him, as he himself once had ruthlessly displaced others to reach the top: "Make way for the young! . . . Not of my own free will. Never, never!" Exploiting his hypnotic power over her, he uses a young bookkeeper to hold the draftsman, her fiancé, in his employ. His wife, Aline, is suspicious of his relation with the bookkeeper—and of his sanity. But Solness, bored with pretending to love the girl, admits to the family doctor that "it does me good to suffer Aline to do me an injustice"; it relieves his guilt. He is bitter about his success, achieved at the expense of his wife's ancestral home. He had wished it destroyed so he could build developments there, and its accidental burning—and then the death of their children—broke her. Hilde Wangel arrives. Solness had met her ten years earlier, when he built a church tower in her home town. Hanging a wreath on its top, he had almost lost his footing when the then thirteen-year-old Hilde shouted and waved excitedly. Half-teasingly she recalls how he flirted with her at the banquet that night and kissed her "many times"; he then promised to return "like a troll," carry her off, and buy her a kingdom. Under his spell, she has now come "to collect." When she hears that he is building a new home, she asks him for a spire "so high it makes you giddy!" Despite his fears of youths, Solness welcomes her: "You are the one I've been wanting." Hilde rejoices: "Then I have my kingdom!"

Act II. With her usual plaintiveness, Aline tells Solness that their lives will remain empty: "You'll never be able to build a real home for me again." But she amazes him by confessing guilt feelings of her own for not having fulfilled her duty to him and the children: "I shouldn't have let grief and fear overwhelm me." The naturally exuberant Hilde is impatient with "that nasty, beastly word," *duty:* "It sounds so cold and sharp, like a knife." Solness unburdens himself to Hilde. He tells her how, feverish after the fire that destroyed her home, Aline insisted it was her duty to nurse their twins, who thereupon died from her infected milk. Aline's talent for motherhood has since lain "waste and barren, like the charred ruins left after a fire." Solness himself has stopped building churches. He has become a great builder of "homes for people," but success is painful: "It feels as though the skin has been flayed from my breast." He is sure that he has demonic powers—powers that caused the fire he willed, as well as Hilde's visit in response to his silent call for her youth. She too, he believes, has demons in her, and these make her the "wild bird" she is. At the end of their strange but tender lovers' talk, she insists that he be "great" for her: he must give up the apprentice and let him become independent, and he must hoist a wreath atop the spire of his new home. Aline is terrified, for she knows Solness suffers from vertigo. When Hilde learns this, she excitedly whispers to herself: ". . . frightfully thrilling!"

Act III. Opening her heart to Hilde, Aline tells of the destruction of her home and belongings, including her beautiful dolls—"little unborn children." Now Hilde wants to leave the Solness house: "I can't hurt someone I *know.* I can't take what belongs to her." But Solness tells her that she must stay; Aline is really dead: "The trolls in me have sucked her blood. It was done for my happiness. And for my sake she died. And I am chained to the corpse." Hilde decides to assume a "robust Viking conscience" and seize happiness. She demands of Solness what he had promised her, and he agrees: "The princess shall have her castle." Since people cannot be happy in homes, he will build castles in the air—but "on a true foundation." Only once had he dared climb a tower. Now he will challenge God and do so again. As the townsfolk watch, he reaches the top. Hilde waves and shouts as she did ten years before, but this time he does lose his footing and plunges to his death. "In quiet, crazed triumph," Hilde glories over his heroism: "I heard harps in the air!" She waves up at the empty tower again and "cries wildly and ecstatically: *My—my* Master Builder!"

MASTER OF SANTIAGO, THE (*Le Maître de Santiago*), a play in three acts by HENRY DE MONTHERLANT, published in 1947 and produced in 1948. Setting: Alvaro's house in Avila, Spain; January 1519.

This self-styled *"auto sacramentale"* features the exalted Don Alvaro Dabo, a forty-seven-year-old knight of the Order of Santiago (Saint James). Despite his renunciation the old Castilian is not a model Christian, Montherlant asserted in his "Notes" to the play. Short, stark, and static, its only dramatic action is the third-act conversion, Mariana's giving up of the lover who never appears on stage. The characters and the plot, while based on history, are fictitious.

Act I. Alvaro's house is dilapidated, but "the Master of Santiago" does not care because, as his daughter Mariana says, "For my father, the only important thing, or rather the only essential, or rather the only real thing is what goes on in the inside of the soul." Proudly content to watch the snow and contemplate, Alvaro declines his fellow knights' urgings to accompany them to the New World and reap its immense wealth—although they assure him that they are concerned with perpetuating "the glory of the Order . . . and of Spain." Alvaro scornfully rejects fame, wealth, or comfort—as well as the ideals mouthed by his friends. "Spain is my greatest humiliation," he says, and catalogues its moral bankruptcy and degeneration. And Alvaro rejects as well the proposal that the Order go to the New World: "The Order is the reliquary of all remaining magnanimity and integrity in Spain."

Act II. Alvaro is not moved to change his mind and acquire wealth even for his daughter's happiness when he learns of her desire to marry and her need for a dowry. "I love Spain in proportion to its merits, exactly as I would a foreign country," he remarks: "In the same way, Mariana's being my daughter will never make me go too far in her favor." His friends argue against but then reluctantly bow to Alvaro's absolute conviction that though the Order is dead for others, "if it existed in only a single heart, the Order would still exist." Mariana, though she is heartbroken, refuses to implore her father to change his mind. She will not participate in his friends' ruse to make him accompany them by exploiting Alvaro's loyalty to the king. So long as her beloved is nearby, she admits, "I shall pray on my knees before the crucifix that my father let himself be persuaded"; but she will gladly sacrifice love and happiness for the sake of her father. "No," she declares, realizing the hopelessness of Alvaro's changing his mind; "I do not want to be happy."

Act III. Mariana reads an old romance and, admiring her father, castigates herself for thinking of leaving him, stern though he is. A courtier arrives with a (false) message that the king wishes Alvaro to lead the expedition to the New World. Opposing the expedition and reluctant to give up his pious solitude, Alvaro nonetheless is prepared to obey his king. But Mariana bursts into the room and exposes his friends' ruse. After the courtier leaves, Mariana reveals to Alvaro how, as she was praying before the cross, "suddenly it was you I saw, in the place of the Crucified One." This vision convinced her that she must stand by her father. Alvaro kneels before Mariana and begs her to join him in giving up "the things of the earth. Let us enter again into reality. Oh, how I have always aspired to that!" He persuades Mariana to sacrifice her affections and forgo "the contamination of a man's love. No blood will come to mix with our blood," he continues, "no children, nobody to defile me."

Inspired by Alvaro's ecstasy for the *"Nada"* of Christian renunciation, Mariana agrees to cloister herself with him in a convent as the darkness and silence of the falling snow engulf them. "All is saved and all is accomplished, for I am aware of a steadfast-gazing Being, who gazes upon me with an unendurable gaze," Mariana concludes. "All is well!" they agree: *"Unum, Domine!"*

MASTER OLOF (*Mäster Olof*), a historical play in five acts by AUGUST STRINDBERG, published and produced in 1881. Setting: Stockholm and nearby Strängnäs, 1524–40.

Though Strindberg's earliest work and Sweden's best-known historical drama, *Master Olof* was rejected at first (1872). After prolonged and extensive revision, Strindberg completed a verse play under the same title. It was immediately (1878) published in that form with an *Efterspel* (epilogue), a short and bitter miracle play he later repudiated; but the verse play remained unproduced until 1890. Strindberg's long discussion of the play in the posthumous autobiographical novel *I röda rummet* (*In the Red Room*) reveals his identification with the Luther of Sweden, Olaus Petri, or Master (i.e., Magister) Olof. Strindberg also identifies with the other major figures: "In Olaus Petri [Strindberg] would appear as the idealist, in Gustav Vasa as the realist, and in the Anabaptist Gert as the communard," an uncompromising visionary. In this drama of ideas, which stresses the relativity of truth (one of its tentative titles had been *What Is Truth?*), "no one [would] be wrong." Except for the fictitious Gert, the characters and events are in the main portrayed with what was then accepted as historical fact—as in Shakespeare's chronicle plays, to which Strindberg admitted indebtedness. The play is the first in a trilogy that concludes with GUSTAV VASA and ERIC XIV.

Acts I and II. Olof is with his pupils when Gert Bookprinter, the excommunicated Anabaptist printer of Luther's tracts, spurs him to action against papal abuses. Defiantly Olof rings the vesper bells and conducts mass in the vernacular. He is saved from immediate punishment only by King Gustav I (Gustav Vasa), to whom antipapal activities are politically expedient. Gustav appoints Olof as a high civil administrator—"my right hand on the condition that the left doesn't know for the time being what the right is doing"—and Olof leaves his pupils to battle for his beliefs. In Stockholm, Olof tears up his excommunication, refuses his devoutly Catholic mother's pleas to recant and, despite a warning, preaches Luther's doctrines in the Great Church. Abused and stoned, he is at first disheartened. But when Kristina, Gert's daughter, reveals her love for and faith in him, his confidence returns. Despite his priesthood, he decides to marry her.

Act III. Some years later the king moves to destroy the pope's power in Sweden. Olof agrees to help and, despite Gert's arguments, does not perceive that the King is merely using him as a tool. At home bitter fights between his outraged mother and his adoring but simple wife complicate and sadden Olof's life. The victorious king awards him the rectorship of the Great Church, and Olof rejoices, though he regrets his battles' end. When he finally realizes that the Church's control has merely shifted from pope to king, he decides to fight Gustav.

Acts IV and V. At his mother's bedside during the plague Olof temporarily compromises his religious convictions for her sake after she curses him with her dying breath. But following Gert's urgings, he insists on taking over spiritual leadership: "I'll cleanse the temple of the Lord even if the pope and the king don't want it!" He joins a plot against the king: "Let him die that all may live!" Betrayed, the conspirators are captured and condemned. Gert joyfully anticipates martyrdom and eventual victory for the cause. He exhorts Olof, "Believe your heart if you have the courage! The day you deny yourself, you're dead." But pilloried before his congregation and facing death, Olof's will falters; he is persuaded to retract his attacks on the king and to serve him. Freed, he is crushed and collapses when he hears Gert's curse from afar: "Renegade!"

MATCHMAKER, THE, a play in four acts by THORNTON WILDER, produced in 1954 and published in 1957. Setting: Yonkers and New York, the early 1880's.

This is a revised version of *The Merchant of Yonkers,* Wilder's satire of conventional stock-company drama. It was based on Johann Nestroy's *Einen Jux will er sich machen* (1842), a Viennese comedy which, in turn, had been adapted from a British operatic farce, John Oxenford's *A Day Well Spent* (1836). Directed by Max Reinhardt in 1938, Wilder's farce was a failure. In 1954 he revised it slightly and retitled it, focusing on the matchmaker, Dolly Levi, Wilder's most original contribution to the play. Under Tyrone Guthrie's direction it became a rousing hit in this form. It became an even more sensational hit as Michael Stewart's (1929–) *Hello Dolly!* (1964, music by Jerry Herman), which topped MY FAIR LADY's record to become Broadway's longest-running musical (2844 performances). A fast-moving farce, *The Matchmaker,* Wilder noted in his preface, depicts "the aspirations of the young (and not only of the young) for a fuller, freer participation in life."

The underpaid clerks of a misanthropic merchant of Yonkers sneak off to New York to have some fun. There they have various ludicrous adventures as they try to have a good meal and kiss a pretty girl—and hide from the merchant. All ends happily as a result of the machinations of the comical and fun-loving Mrs. Levi, "a woman who arranges things" and ensnares the wealthy merchant for herself.

MATERNITY (*Maternité*), a play in three acts by EUGÈNE BRIEUX, published and produced in 1903. Setting: the French provinces, early twentieth century.

This PROBLEM PLAY deals with birth control and

abortion in a society that hypocritically advocates higher birth rates. BERNARD SHAW introduced his wife's translation in *Three Plays by Brieux* (1911), where, together with THE THREE DAUGHTERS OF M. DUPONT and DAMAGED GOODS, *Maternity* appears in two versions.

A provincial prefect's and his colleagues' hypocrisy about raising the French birth rate is fully revealed when his wife's young sister is rejected by her weak fiancé and his opportunistic family. Appalled by the prefect's cruel insistence that the pregnant girl be abandoned to save his own reputation and that his wife continue, despite her abhorrence of him, to submit to his demands for more children, she deserts him and goes with her sister. The last act is set in court, where it is revealed that the desperate sister had gone to a Paris midwife for an abortion that proved fatal. The midwife and her other clients, all indigent defendants, are tried for infanticide. They vividly demonstrate society's heartless hypocrisy and the mockery of the law, now upheld by two-faced judges. The counsel pleads for the day when everyone may have "none but the children he wants! That will indeed be a victory over nature, that cruel nature which sows with criminal profusion the life that she watches die with indifference." The trial ends with an indignant, passionate outburst by the condemned victims: "It's the men that are guilty! All men!" they shout, as the judges adjourn the court and walk out.

MAUGHAM, [William] **Somerset** (1874–1965), English novelist and playwright, was one of the most popular writers of the twentieth century. Particularly notable among his many prose works are his novels *Of Human Bondage* (1915), *The Moon and Sixpence* (1919), and *Cakes and Ale* (1930); his short story *Miss Thompson* (1921, later known as *Rain*) and *The Casuarina Tree* collection (1926, including *The Outstation* and *The Letter*); and his memoirs and literary criticisms, *The Summing Up* (1937). When he gave up drama in 1933, he had produced twenty-nine original plays. Many of them were popular successes, and at least two —THE CIRCLE (1920) and THE CONSTANT WIFE (1926) —are acknowledged masterpieces of English comedy. Maugham's reputation as a playwright rests on these and other drawing-room comedies, though he also excelled in less popular types of drama.

His father was a cultivated, well-to-do solicitor, and his mother was a beautiful society lady. Maugham was born in Paris, where he spent his first ten years. Then his parents died, and the boy was brought up by an uncle, a stern Kent vicar. He was schooled in Canterbury, eventually studied medicine at the University of Heidelberg, and received his doctor's training at St. Thomas's Hospital in London. It was during his internship that he wrote his first novel, *Liza of Lambeth* (1897). Though qualified as a physician, he became a writer. But disappointed by the royalties from his first novel, Maugham turned to drama. In that genre he achieved the desired goal.

But not immediately. Before he suddenly and quickly made his name in 1907–08, he had written ten plays in more than a decade. His first play, *Schiffbrüchig* (*Shipwrecked,* 1902; also translated as *Marriages Are Made in Heaven*), written in the 1890's in German, is a cheerful precursor of Pinero's THE SECOND MRS. TANQUERAY. It was followed by another one-acter, the farce *Mademoiselle Zampa* (1904). The next play, his first to be produced, was *A Man of Honour,* a bitter four-act drama about the tragic consequences of the honorable behavior of a man who marries beneath his station; it ran two nights at the experimental Stage Society in 1903. Maugham's first hit came in 1907 with LADY FREDERICK, and the following year he reached the pinnacle of success when *Lady Frederick* appeared in the West End concurrently with three further plays: *Jack Straw,* featuring an archduke (a role played by John Barrymore) disguised as a waiter to woo a commoner; MRS. DOT; and *The Explorer* (rewritten and published as a novel the same year, 1908), whose hero is traduced for the death of his sweetheart's brother, a cad. These successes were followed with two similar ones the next year: in *Penelope,* the clever title character ends her husband's affair and regains his love by bringing him together with his mistress; the hero of *Smith* returns from Rhodesia and, unable to find a suitable wife in "flippant and frivolous and inane" English society, marries the title character, a servant. In 1909, too, Maugham translated from the French of Ernest Grenet-Dancourt (1858–1913) a three-act Victorian farce, *The Noble Spaniard.* The next year he came out with the more serious but less successful *The Tenth Man* and *Landed Gentry* (later called *Grace*); these were followed by LOAVES AND FISHES (1911), THE LAND OF PROMISE (1913), and a translation of Molière's *Le Bourgeois Gentilhomme, The Perfect Gentleman* (1913).

During World War I Maugham served with the Red Cross and then as a British secret agent in Geneva. The *Ashenden: or, The British Agent* stories came later (1928), but at the time, for relaxation and as a smoke screen for his cloak-and-dagger work, he wrote comedies, notably THE UNATTAINABLE (1916, originally produced as *Caroline*). Then came his well-known OUR BETTERS (1917), followed by *Love in a Cottage* (1918); *Caesar's Wife* (1919), suggested by Madame de Lafayette's novel *La Princesse de Clèves* and portraying an elderly English consul in Egypt, strong yet kind with his young wife when she falls in love; *Home and Beauty* (1919, produced in America as *Too Many Husbands*), a popular, biting farce about a selfish woman whom both husbands try to divorce when the second one reappears after having been reported missing in action; and *The Circle,* generally acclaimed as Maugham's best play. His most successful work in the theatre, however, was John B. Colton (1886–1946) and Clemence Randolph's (1881–1970) 1922 dramatization of *Rain* (made into a musical by HOWARD DIETZ), Maugham's South Seas story of a zealous Puritan missionary whose passion for Sadie

Thompson, the prostitute, brings about his downfall. Other adaptations of Maugham's fiction include Edith Ellis's (1874–1960) *The Moon and Sixpence* (1925, filmed in 1942), Bartlett Cormack's (? –1942) *The Painted Veil* (1931; a different version was filmed in 1934), George Campbell Dixon's (1896–1960) *Ashenden* (1933, unproduced but filmed in 1936 as *Secret Agent*), GUY BOLTON's *Theatre* (1941, titled *Larger than Life* in England), S. N. BEHRMAN's *Jane* (1946), and Rodney Ackland's (1908–) *Before the Party* (1949).

Beginning with THE UNKNOWN (1920), Maugham's last original plays are, for the most part, more serious and astringent. *East of Suez* (1922) is a spectacular melodrama of adultery dealing with miscegenation in Peking. It was followed by *The Camel's Back* (1923) and *The Road Uphill*, a script written in 1924 and discovered by Mander and Mitchenson (and described in their book) thirty years later. Then came *The Constant Wife*, one of his most popular plays; *The Letter* (1927), Maugham's dramatization (subsequently filmed) of his popular short story of adultery and murder in Singapore; THE SACRED FLAME (1928); *The Breadwinner* (1930), a one-act comedy about a middle-aged man who deserts his humdrum family and middle-class life; FOR SERVICES RENDERED (1932); a translation (1933) of Chiarelli's THE MASK AND THE FACE; and his striking last play, SHEPPEY (1933).

Maugham's dramas share the popular appeal of his novels, and they have been criticized on the same grounds. His frank desire for fame and wealth alienated critics and intellectuals; to which Maugham replied disarmingly, "It is not immediately obvious why a play that people do not want to see is more artistic than one they do." His plays exemplify particularly the "competent technique" he himself espoused, his flair for spinning sophisticated yarns, and his keen, often epigrammatic wit. His plots are not tightly constructed, but this is not uncommon in high comedy, and the loose construction provides the opportunity for amusing situations and polished dialogue—as well as the shrewd observations characteristic of drama of ideas and the situations characteristic of thesis drama. Though tart and even sardonic, Maugham's plays are not as cynical as they were often said to be. Despite his avowed intention "to please," he rejected romanticized views of love, marriage, and human relationships. The more impressive, therefore, was his genuine appeal to audiences conditioned to the saccharine. His drama's abiding vogue is evidenced by continued revivals and adaptations for television. There and in the movies, his plays, like his fiction, have been extremely popular. Most critics' dismissal of Maugham as a "serious" writer has obscured the recognition of his artistic success also in his less popular works, the last plays. And when the public did not respond to them as it had to the comedies, Maugham gave up drama in 1933. "I grew conscious that I was no longer in touch with the public that patronises the theatre," he wrote in the preface to the last volume of his plays. "This happens in the end to most dramatists and they are wise to accept the warning."

Maugham was married to a prominent interior decorator for eleven years and had a daughter. After their divorce in 1927 he lived and traveled alone, eventually settling in a luxurious villa on the French Riviera. The protagonist of NÖEL COWARD's *A Song at Twilight* (1966), a play about a prominent homosexual author, is to some extent a portrayal of Maugham.

The Collected Plays (eighteen) were republished in three volumes in 1952. The prefaces to these volumes and Sections 30 to 42 of *The Summing Up* provide Maugham's own commentary on his drama. His later-dramatized novel *Theatre* (1937) reveals the London setting in which he worked as a playwright, and much of his other fiction and *The Travel Books* collection (1955) are highly autobiographical. Notable among the many works on Maugham's life and writing are Richard A. Cordell's *Somerset Maugham: A Biographical and Critical Study* (1961; updated in 1969 with a new subtitle, *A Writer for All Seasons*), Laurence Brander's *Somerset Maugham: A Guide* (1963), and Ronald E. Barnes's *The Dramatic Comedy of William Somerset Maugham* (1968). Charles Sanders compiled and edited *W. Somerset Maugham: An Annoted Bibliography of Writings About Him* (1970). The most comprehensive survey of Maugham's drama, including photographs of productions and filmings, synopses of all the plays, and invaluable reference data, is Raymond Mander and Joe Mitchenson's *Theatrical Companion to Maugham* (1955).

MAURIAC, François (1885–1970), French writer and the 1952 Nobel Prize laureate, is famous principally for his novels, though he began his career as a poet and also wrote a number of plays. The most distinguished of these is ASMODÉE (1938), which, like his other writings, subtly but dramatically psychoanalyzes men's anguished struggles between human and divine love and the manifestations of sin and grace. Mauriac's remaining plays also deal with such religiously oriented topics: *Les Mal aimés* (1945), depicting the destruction of a girl's love by her domineering and unloved father, to whom she is thereafter bound; *Le Passage du malin* (1947), a similar play, set in a girls' school; and *Le Feu sur la terre* (1951), in which a girl destroys the marriage of her beloved brother. Mauriac wrote biographies of Racine and Jesus, criticisms, and (under the name Forez) resistance articles during World War II. His novels include *Le Baiser au lépreux* (1922) and *Genitrix* (1923), jointly translated as *The Family* (1930). Substantial extracts of his *Journal* were published periodically, beginning in 1934.

Asmodée appears with an introduction in Richard Hayes's collection, *Port-Royal and Other Plays* (1962). Among book-length studies, Cecil Jenkins's *Mauriac* (1965) is a concise and handy survey of his writings, including his plays; it has a bibliography.

MAYAKOVSKY, Vladimir [Vladimirovich] (1893–1930), Russian artist, writer, and dramatist, was the "Poet of the Revolution" and the leader of the FUTURISTS. As a playwright he celebrated the victorious Revolution with his grandiose pageant, *Mysteriya-buff* (MYSTERY-BOUFFE, 1918). A romantic finally disillusioned with love and with the failure of the brave new world to materialize as he had hoped (and possibly tired of AGITPROP art and depressed by declining popularity), Mayakovsky committed suicide shortly after the production of what later became his most famous play, *Klop* (THE BEDBUG, 1929).

Mayakovsky was born in the village of Bagdady (subsequently renamed Mayakovsky), Georgia, the son of a forester who died in 1906. Thereupon the family moved to Moscow, where Mayakovsky attended but failed to graduate from the *gymnasium.* While still a child he joined the Bolshevik Party, was arrested, and at fifteen served almost a year in solitary confinement. At a Moscow art school he attended, Mayakovsky met and joined a group of young painters and poets, futurists and cubists. He soon (1912) published his first futurist poems and "Cubo-Futurist" manifesto. Despite its unorthodoxy and SURREALISM, Mayakovsky's art is grounded in romantic subjects and themes.

He supported the Revolution wholeheartedly, producing posters and verse that soon made him an official Soviet spokesman. From Red Square he declaimed his poems to the marching workers, and he was the director of propaganda for ROSTA, the Soviet wire service, from 1919 to 1922. In 1926 he visited the United States and Latin America. Though changes in the Party line helped lessen his popularity and obscure his work for a while, Mayakovsky was never officially discredited and banned, and he has remained a model of a revolutionary poet.

While much of his poetry is declamatory propaganda, some of it is vivid in its imagery—notably the poem *150,000,000* (1920; the title refers to the Russian population) which contrasts the common Ivan with Woodrow Wilson, who here controls the capitalist puppets of the world. Mayakovsky also wrote film scripts and pageants. His first play, a SYMBOLIC monodrama produced in 1913, was titled *Vladimir Mayakovsky* because the censor confused the names of the play and its young author. Other plays were *Radio Oktyabrya* (1926, written with Osip M. Brik, 1888–1945); *Banya* (*The Bath House,* 1929; "a drama in six acts with circus and fireworks"), a satiric and futuristic fantasy similar to *The Bedbug;* and *Moskva gorit* (1930), another massive circus spectacle like *Mystery-Bouffe,* celebrating the Revolution's twenty-fifth anniversary and produced the week after its author's suicide.

A controversial and highly theatrical dramatization of his life by the director of the Taganka Theatre, Nikolas M. Lyubimov's (1912–) *Poslushaite!* (1967), presents a heroic portrait of Mayakovsky as an artist tormented and driven to his death by a sterile and servile bureaucracy. *Vladimir Mayakovsky, The Bedbug, The Bath House,* and *Mystery-Bouffe* appeared as *The Complete Plays of Vladimir Mayakovsky* (1968) with an introduction by Robert Payne. Mayakovsky's works are also available in English in Patricia Blake's *The Bedbug and Selected Poetry* (1960, translated by Max Hayward and George Reavey), which has a long and informative introduction; and in Herbert Marshall's *Mayakovsky* (1965), translations and reproductions of poetry, posters, letters, colleagues' memoirs, and brief autobiographical notes, with introductions by the editor. Lawrence L. Stahlberger's *The Symbolic System of Majakovskij* (1964) includes a chapter on the first play, "Vladimir Majakovskij, a Tragedy," and a bibliography of English studies.

Vladimir Mayakovsky preparing THE BEDBUG production; seated: the composer Dmitri Shostakovich and the director Vsevolod Yemilevich Meyerhold. Moscow, 1929. (*Sovfoto*)

MAYER, Edwin Justus (1896 or 1897–1960), American dramatist, was praised by critics like Joseph Wood Krutch and John Gassner for his witty tragedy about Jonathan Wild, CHILDREN OF DARKNESS (1929). Revived Off-Broadway in 1958 and characterized as a neglected American masterpiece, neither it nor Mayer's other plays succeeded with the general public.

Mayer was a New York reporter, a stage and film press agent, and an actor before the production of his first play, *The Firebrand* (1924), a Renaissance fantasy about Benvenuto Cellini and the Duke Cosimo de Medici. It was written in the same witty black-humorous vein as Mayer's most notable work; it was filmed as *The Affairs of Cellini* (1934), and was made into an unsuccessful Broadway musical, *The Firebrand of Florence* (1945; lyrics by Ira Gershwin and music by Kurt Weill). Among Mayer's other plays are *Sunrise in My Pocket,* "an American Saga" about Davy Crockett that was repeatedly announced for production in New York but never made it (it was put on in

Texas in 1940) and was finally published in 1941; *A Night at Mme. Tussaud's* (1952), a thriller; and *The Last Love of Don Juan* (1955), "a travesty with a moral." Mayer also wrote numerous film scripts and an autobiography, *A Preface to Life* (1923).

MCCARTHY, Justin Huntly (1860–1936), English playwright and novelist, is best remembered for his 1891 novel IF I WERE KING, which was dramatized by him immediately and later became a popular operetta. The son of Justin McCarthy, the distinguished Irish politician and author of many histories, the younger McCarthy was born and educated in England. He spent most of his life there—though he traveled widely—and during 1884–92 was a Member of Parliament. For a few years (1894–1899) he was married to the famous music-hall actress Marie Cecilia ("Cissie") Loftus, who, although they were by then divorced, starred in the first production of McCarthy's best-known play. He wrote over a dozen others, some twenty novels (many of them historical), and a number of histories.

MCCULLERS, Carson [Smith] (1919–67), American novelist, in 1950 dramatized her successful novel *The Member of the Wedding* (1946) into the even more successful Drama Critics' Circle Award winner, filmed in 1953. It is a wistfully comic, CHEKHOVian evocation of her own youth, and its production was distinguished by Julie Harris's twelve-year-old motherless adolescent and Ethel Waters's Negro cook. *The Square Root of Wonderful* (1957) was McCullers's second but this time unsuccessful Broadway play. Again autobiographical, it dramatizes her turbulent marriage (and remarriage) with a dashing army ranger who committed suicide in 1953. Among her other well-known writings are her first novel, *The Heart Is a Lonely Hunter* (1940), and *The Ballad of the Sad Café* (1951), a novella dramatized by EDWARD ALBEE in 1963; it portrays a grotesque triangle featuring a giantess, a good-looking wastrel, and a homosexual dwarf. A Southerner, Mrs. McCullers's many artist and writer friends included TENNESSEE WILLIAMS, who encouraged her to dramatize *The Member of the Wedding*. Oliver Evans's *The Ballad of Carson McCullers* (1965) is a sympathetic biography that evaluates her writings and alludes to other studies.

MEASURES TAKEN, THE (*Die Massnahme*), a didactic piece in eight sections by BERTOLT BRECHT (music by Hanns Eisler), produced in 1930 and published in 1932. Setting: a concert platform.

This stark dramatic cantata in prose and verse is an apologia for (and incidentally a prediction of) Marxist political executions; however, it was not totally approved of by Communist ideologists. It elicited particular attention during Brecht's testimony before the House Committee on Un-American Activities in 1947, where the play was confused with HE WHO SAYS YES.

Before a Control Chorus that represents the Communist Party, four agitators defend their killing of a comrade while on a mission in China. They act out and discuss their story. The victim was a fervent Communist, but he committed four errors: (1) overcome by sympathy for some coolies, he alleviated immediate suffering—and thus delayed the revolution; (2) opposing a worker's unjust arrest, he delayed victory over the larger injustice of strikebreaking; (3) repelled by a capitalist's dishonorable methods, he broke off negotiations that would have enlisted the capitalist's help in the struggle against imperialism; (4) unable to bear the suffering of the unemployed, he began a premature revolution that was doomed to failure, disobeyed Party instructions, and endangered the others by exposing their identity. Their only hope was to kill and bury him in quicklime, which would obliterate his features. Himself finally aware of his errors, he agreed to his execution. The Control Chorus praises the agitators for their work and the measures they had taken against their comrade: "Only if instructed by reality can we / Alter reality."

MELL, Max (1882–), Austrian poet, novelist, and playwright, wrote Christian folk drama in verse. His most popular play was the internationally produced *Das Apostelspiel* (*The Apostle Play*, 1923), a portrayal of two evil tramps who break into a mountain hut on a winter night and are transformed into apostles by the peasants' childlike faith in their holiness. Often produced, too, were Mell's many legend plays. Most of them are on religious topics, though during World War II he broached the fashionable Nazi theme of "blood and soil": in *Das Spiel von den deutschen Ahnen* (1935) a discouraged family are reminded by their ancestors' apparitions of their affinity and responsibilities to the land, and are dissuaded from selling the farm. The two world wars increased the poignancy of Mell's religious message. His later works are *Jeanne d'Arc* (1956), which focuses on the final phase of Joan's trial and suggests that, though the world is terrible, "it cannot prevent saints from growing in it"; and *Paracelsus* (1965), a new, humanistic interpretation of the life of the alchemist.

Mell was born in Styria at Marburg. When his father became director of a state institute, the family resettled in Vienna. There Mell grew up and earned his Ph.D., after which he devoted all his time to writing. He published a collection of stories and a book of poems, and then had his first successes as a playwright. It was in that capacity that Mell became best known. Among his other important plays—all of which are in verse—are *Das Wiener Kripperl von 1919* (1921), a miracle play set in a streetcar terminal where a vision of the manger appears to a cross section of oppressed and despairing Viennese; *Das Schutzengelspiel* (1923), in which a proud girl becomes humble and is rewarded; *Das Nachfolge-Christi-Spiel* (1927), featuring the "imitation of Christ" by a seventeenth-century nobleman "who has seen the world from above" before he dies and forgives the robbers who crucified him; *Die*

Sieben gegen Theben (1931), a modernized version in strictly classical form of the Oedipus-Antigone cycle; and *Die Nibelungen Not* (1944–51), a two-part Christianized reinterpretation of the legend of Siegfried.

Major productions were accorded these plays in Austria: *Die Nibelungen Not* was produced at Vienna's Burgtheater, and *Paracelsus* reopened the Graz Schauspielhaus in 1965. All of the plays of Mell, a disciple of HUGO VON HOFMANNSTHAL, who highly praised Mell's work, portray an appealingly pious and simple medieval faith.

MELTING-POT, THE, a drama in four acts by ISRAEL ZANGWILL, produced in 1908 and published in 1909. Setting: New York, early twentieth century.

The catchy title of Zangwill's most famous and controversial play became synonymous with "America." A melodrama without artistic pretensions, it is an emotional plea for racial tolerance and a wishful dramatization of the democratic crucible in action. At the world premiere in Washington President Theodore Roosevelt shouted across the theatre, "That's a great play, Mr. Zangwill!"—and many (including Clarence Darrow and AUGUSTUS THOMAS) agreed. The English critic A. B. Walkley represented others, who thought the play "romantic claptrap" and Roosevelt's comment "stupendous naïveté." Absent from the play's early draft was the vivid evocation of the 1903 Kishinev pogrom.

Act I. At the Quixano home, the Irish maid gets exasperated by the immigrants' strange ways and threatens to quit. Vera Revendal, a beautiful settlement worker, comes to ask David Quixano to play for the crippled children. She is taken aback to learn that David, a brilliant violinist and composer, is a Jew: "He had such charming manners." Soon she conquers her instinctive repugnance, however; though she is of aristocratic blood, she too had left Russia, as a revolutionary about to be imprisoned. David rejoices in America, "God's Crucible, the great Melting-Pot where all the races of Europe are melting and re-forming!" But when Vera mentions her birthplace, Kishinev, David becomes hysterical and runs out. His uncle explains that David is a pogrom orphan, his family's sole survivor of the Kishinev massacre.

Act II. The pacified Irish maid, now converted and chatting a mixture of Yiddish and brogue, happily participates in Purim festivities. To help David, Vera introduces him to Quincy Davenport, a supercilious millionaire who wants to divorce his wife and marry Vera. His private orchestra leader declares David a genius, but when David indignantly turns from the rich "animals" who ruin America by partying while the poor starve (in his box, Roosevelt exclaimed, "You're right; I've been warning the people against these Quincy Davenports!"), Davenport gets angry at the "Jew-immigrant," fires his orchestra leader, and leaves. Later Vera and David avow their love. But then the uncle sadly tells David that his marrying a gentile would kill the uncle's aged mother, and David must leave the house.

Act III. Davenport brings Vera's father from Russia to stop her marrying David. Baron Revendal (arriving with his foolish second wife) is ready to shoot the "Jew vermin" at once. But he is so delighted to see Vera, for whom he would do anything, that he finally agrees to have her "mate with an unbaptized dog." When David sees the baron, however, he recognizes him as the instigator of the Kishinev pogrom and totters back in horror: "The face!" Brokenly he describes the murderous terrors of that day, and then rushes away from Vera, "the butcher's daughter."

Act IV. Some time later, on the Fourth of July, David's symphony "America" is performed at a rooftop concert. Its great success before an audience of immigrants and others reunites him with Vera, despite the painful memories of Kishinev. "Yes, cling to me, despite them all," he tells her, "cling to me till all these ghosts are exorcised, cling to me till our love triumphs over death." And then, with Vera nestling to him, he raises his hands over the city at sunset, as "My Country, 'Tis of Thee" is heard from below: "Peace, peace to all ye unborn millions, fated to fill this giant continent—the God of our *children* give you Peace."

MEMORY OF TWO MONDAYS, A, a one-act play by ARTHUR MILLER, published and produced in 1955. Setting: the shipping room of an auto-parts warehouse, New York; early 1930's.

Miller characterized this "pathetic comedy," produced with A VIEW FROM THE BRIDGE, as his favorite, a play "not of obsession but of rent and hunger and the need for a little poetry in life." Dramatizing his own experience during the Depression, it is a tragicomic portrayal, almost plotless but wistfully humorous, of people defeated by their "endless, timeless, will-less environment." In the second half, a lusty old-timer dies, and the others are aged and deteriorated. Only the autobiographical youngster escapes, to college. The others hardly notice his departure.

MEN IN WHITE, a play in three acts by SIDNEY KINGSLEY, published and produced in 1933. Setting: a hospital in a large American city, 1930's.

The Pulitzer Prize winner (though the overruled judges' unanimous recommendation was for Anderson's MARY OF SCOTLAND) for 1934, when it was also filmed, this is a sentimental melodrama with a hackneyed plot. It was superbly produced by the Group Theatre—particularly in the portrayals of teeming hospital life and in a long-rehearsed operating-room scene. The idealized characterizations of the "men in white" naturally charmed the American Medical Association: its *Journal* lauded the play, and its members flocked to see it. The play was originally entitled *Crisis*.

A handsome young intern's fiancée resents his wholehearted devotion to his profession and his intention to sacrifice personal comfort to years of further study with a great scientist. Peeved, the overworked intern fleetingly gets involved with a nurse, who subsequently must be operated upon by him. She dies, but the fiancée gets a deeper insight into doctors' selfless and uncompromising adherence to the Hippocratic oath.

MENDELE MOKHER SFORIM [Sholem Yankev Abramovitch] (1836–1917) is the "Grandfather of Yiddish Literature." The publication of his satire *Dos Kleyne Mentshele* (*The Mannikin,* also translated as *The Parasite*) in 1864 marks the beginning of modern Yiddish literature. It appeared under his later-famous *nom de plume* ("Mendele the Bookseller"), as did his other works: novels, prose and verse epics, poems, and satires exposing the moral and material evils besetting his fellow Jews in Russia. Only one drama is associated with his name, and it is characteristically satiric: *Di Takse* (1869), an exposure of corrupt Jewish representatives who profited, at the expense of the poor and the pious, from the hated meat and candle taxes imposed on Jews. Its main character has been called "a Yiddish minor Tartuffe." See Isaac Goldberg's *The Drama of Transition* (1922), Sol Liptzin's *The Flowering of Yiddish Literature* (1963), and Charles A. Madison's *Yiddish Literature: Its Scope and Major Writers* (1968).

MENZEL, Gerhard (1894–), German playwright, was best known for his "returning soldier" play *Toboggan* (1928). Its protagonist, given up for dead on the battlefield, is rejected by everyone when he comes back, and commits suicide when the woman he loves also turns from him in horror. Other Menzel plays include *Fern-Ost* (1929), a dramatization of China's revolt against imperial Europeans that has been likened to *Roar China!* by SERGEI TRETYAKOV. Menzel became an ardent Nazi and wrote no further works of note.

MERRY DEATH, A (*Vesyolaya smert*), a harlequinade by NIKOLAI NIKOLAEVICH YEVREINOV, produced in 1909 and published in 1914. Setting: Harlequin's house.

Like Blok's THE PUPPET SHOW, this is a harlequinade that uses masks of the *commedia dell'arte.* It was one of Yevreinov's own favorite works.

Harlequin is determined to meet Death merrily at midnight and has invited Pierrot and his faithless wife, Columbine, for supper. Fearing that Harlequin will take his wife, Pierrot advances the clock to hurry Death. The sick Harlequin wakes up and soon enjoys himself with Columbine, who castigates her husband while she kisses her lover. When Death comes, Harlequin invites her to dance: "Here one can laugh at all that's tragic, even your gestures." Harlequin kisses Columbine, sneers at Pierrot's cowardice, and dies. Pierrot impudently admits his cowardly role and quotes Rabelais's last words, "Let down the curtain; the farce is over." Then Pierrot returns before the curtain to announce the author's scorn for the audience's reactions to the play.

MEXICO. The Mexican theatre is among the more flourishing in LATIN AMERICA, and the fame of some of its playwrights—notably RODOLFO USIGLI and CARLOS SOLÓRZANO—spread abroad. Independent theatres were established in nineteenth-century Mexico, and among contributing writers were poets and Yucatán romanticists such as José Peón Contreras (1843–1907), who was proclaimed as "Restorer of the Mexican Theatre" and whose masterpiece is *La hija del rey* (1876), a tragedy about Philip II's illegitimate daughter. Among the poets was Manuel José Othón (1858–1906), author of a number of plays including one on Cervantes and Don Quixote, *El último capítulo* (1905). Serious twentieth-century drama was impeded by the popularity of the *carpas,* comic skits descended from the Italian *commedia dell'arte* and performed in tents and on the streets; in them were started the careers of many later-famous stage and screen stars, including Cantinflas.

A number of Mexico's successful twentieth-century playwrights other than Usigli abandoned the theatre for diplomacy, beginning with the novelist-dramatist Federico Gamboa (1864–1939), whose best work was a tragedy of two brothers' romantic rivalry, *Entre hermanos* (1928). The first notable play of the century was *Así pasan . . .* (1908), the portrayal of an actress's life by Marcelino Dávalos (1871–1932), who started as a romanticist but then turned to NATURALISM and social problems whose portrayal eventually caused his expulsion and emigration to the United States. Much praised for his nationalist poetic drama during the first years of the century was Antonio Médiz Bolio (1884–1957), a diplomat who wrote a play on the Indians published in his native Yucatán, *La flecha del sol* (1918). Julio Jiménez Rueda (1898–1960), a lawyer and director who also wrote farces and a play about Maximilian (*Miramar,* 1932), stimulated social-PROBLEM drama with his own tragedy on madness and suicide, *Caída de flores* (1923). The novelist-playwright María Luisa Ocampo (1907–), one of many Mexican women writers, also dramatized social problems from the 1920's through midcentury.

A group of Mexican writers in the 1920's published a manifesto urging a revival of native drama. For the occasion one of them, José Joaquín Gamboa (1878–1931), wrote the short farce *Un cuento viejo* (*An Old Yarn,* 1925); Gamboa, who became a diplomat, shortly before his death produced his masterpiece, *El caballero, la muerte y el diablo* (1931), an allegorical struggle of Death and the Devil. Another member of the group was Victor Manuel Diez Barroso (1890–1930), a prolific prober of the subconscious whose SYMBOLIC *El y su cuerpo,* dramatizing the possible return of a lost flier hero, appeared posthumously. The first really popular serious Mexican play was *Padre Mercader* (1929), a portrayal of "three generations from shirtsleeves to shirtsleeves" by the aged poet Carlos Díaz Dufoo (1861–1941).

During the 1930's the amateur Teatro Orientación stimulated Mexican drama with its productions of BERTOLT BRECHT and other European playwrights. It was founded by Celestino Gorostiza (1904–66), who later was to win awards for his drama attacking race prejudice (*El color de nuestra piel,* 1951) and to write other hits, such as the comedy *Columna social* (1952) and the history play *La leña está verde* (1958), featuring Cortés's son and the latter's Indian mother, Malinche, after whom the play was later retitled. In the following decades many professional groups emerged—and with them new playwrights, of whom a number achieved prominence. Francisco Navarro (1902–), whose play about Judas's suicide (*La muerte en el bosque*, ?) was produced in Stockholm while he served as Ambassador to Sweden, wrote other drama including *La ciudad* (*The City,* 1935), the first in a naturalist trilogy on Mexico. Xavier Villaurrutia (1903–50), a poet and an associate of Gorostiza, wrote existential mysteries and comedies of which the most successful was *La hiedra* (1941). Salvador Novo (1904–), cofounder with Villaurrutia of a theatre and also a poet and translator, wrote children's plays, satires, and the prize-winning *Yocasta o casi* (1960).

Federico Schroeder Inclán (1910–) was educated in the United States and at the age of forty started dramatizing native themes in plays that launched a number of Mexican theatres; he won prizes for his play on a director's attempts to stage *Romeo and Juliet* (*Cada noche muere Julieta,* 1959) and the following year wrote a hit, *Cuartelazo*. Rafael Solana (1915–), an unusually prolific novelist and poet whose comedies show the influence of TENNESSEE WILLIAMS, won prizes for *A su imagen y semejanza* (1957), about a conductor who derides his critics by creating a puppet to do his work. Sergio Magaña (1924–), who was trained by Jesuits and influenced by JEAN-PAUL SARTRE, had unexpected popular success with a bitter portrayal of lowlife, *Los signos del zodíaco* (1951), and won distinction for *Montezuma II* (1953), depicting the Aztec emperor's last day of power. The versatile Emilio Carballido (1925–), a frequent prize-winner whose first published play was *La zona intermedia* (*The Intermediate Zone,* 1948), is the author of such other drama as *La hebra de oro* (*The Golden Thread,* 1957), a part-naturalistic, part-fantasy play on dead souls in transit; *El espejo* (*The Mirror,* 1957), a one-act farce; *El lugar y la hora* (*The Time and the Place*, 1957), a trilogy of one-act horror plays; *El relojero de Córdoba* (*The Clockmaker from Cordoba,* 1960), a satiric and poetic mixture of naturalism and fantasy inspired by a Chinese short story; and *Teseo* (*Theseus,* 1962), a modernization of the legend. Héctor Mendoza (1932–) won drama prizes as a youth and was particularly successful with *Las cosas simples* (1952), a drama about "simple things" in everyday life; and with *Olor de santidad* (1961), a comedy about vice and religion.

Willis Knapp Jones's *Spanish-American Literature in Translation* (1963) includes *An Old Yarn* and selections from Navarro's and Usigli's plays. Those of Carballido were translated as *"The Golden Thread" and Other Plays by Emilio Carballido* (1970) by Margaret Sayers Peden, whose introduction also describes other Mexican drama. The works noted under LATIN AMERICA have sections on Mexico.

MICHAEL, Friedrich (1892–), German dramatist, wrote comedies—notably *Der blaue Strohhut* (1942), reminiscent of Eugène Labiche; and *Ausflug mit Damen* (1944). The latter, a sequel to the many Amphitryon plays (including JEAN GIRAUDOUX's), occurs on the twentieth birthday of Hercules; again longing for Alcmena, Jupiter visits her, accompanied by Mercury, Juno, and Iris.

Born in Ilmenau (Thuringia), Germany, Michael earlier had made his reputation as a novelist.

MICHAEL AND HIS LOST ANGEL, a play in five acts by HENRY ARTHUR JONES, published and produced in 1896. Setting: England and Italy, nineteenth century.

Jones considered this play his masterpiece, and despite its occasional bathos, later critics have shared this judgment. But the play was a failure on the boards. The church setting of a love scene scandalized audiences, and the reviewers (BERNARD SHAW excepted) condemned the play. While the portrayal of the minister's fall through an unholy attachment recalls works by HENRIK IBSEN (particularly ROSMERSHOLM), AUGUST STRINDBERG, and other insurgent nineteenth-century playwrights, the situation and the treatment are more analogous to those in Hawthorne's novel *The Scarlet Letter*. Shaw found Jones's protagonist unheroic, lacking in tragic stature; but, like subsequent writers, Shaw praised the drama as an outstanding one in contemporary England: "A genuinely sincere and moving play, feelingly imagined, written with knowledge as to the man and insight as to the woman."

Act I. The Reverend Michael Feversham of Cleveheddon returns to his vicarage after a public confession by the daughter of his clerk, Andrew Gibbard. Because both have lied to him about her sin and her child, Michael has sternly insisted on the humiliating performance. "Would you rather that she held up her head in deceit and defiance, or that she held it down in grief and penitence?" he asks the father. Though Andrew is indebted to the minister, who is full of compassion and provides for the girl, he finds it difficult to forgive him: "Ah, sir, it's easy for you to talk. You aren't likely to be tempted, so you aren't likely to fall." Alone, Michael reverently studies his dead mother's portrait. He is interrupted by the appearance of a wealthy parishioner, Audrie Lesden. Repelled by her "frivolity and insincerity," Michael is also attracted to this handsome young woman, who is said to be a widow and who teases and flirts with him. "You come neither as a penitent, nor as a woman of the world," he tells her when she offers gifts and money for the church; "you come like—like some bad angel, to mock, and hint, and question, and suggest." She wants to become worthy of Michael and yet cannot relinquish her love of worldly pleasures. "You may do me good, but I am far more likely to do you harm," Audrie warns him. Seductively she mesmerizes Michael into letting her kiss the portrait of "your good angel," his mother.

Act II. Some months later Andrew observes that Michael is increasingly overcome by the same passions he had so sternly rebuked in the clerk's daughter. He is in his Bristol Channel island retreat, racked by his feelings. Suddenly Audrie appears. She admits that she originally strove to gain power over "this sculptured saint," Michael, but now lacks the strength to leave him. "We are choosing heaven or hell for both our souls this night!" Michael says after they avow their mutual love: "Help me to choose heaven for you, and I'll help you to choose heaven for me." He girds himself to accompany her to the bay, but by chance there is no boat. Alone on the island all night, they succumb to their passions.

Act III. Ashamed of his lying but wishing to protect Audrie, Michael works out elaborate deceptions. Andrew discovers the truth and, though resentful of the vicar's treatment of his daughter, promises not to reveal the secret. Michael is almost broken. Now he realizes how harsh he had been to the clerk's daughter, and he bitterly castigates himself. Audrie horrifies Michael with the revelation that they have committed adultery, since her husband is alive. Her marriage was unhappy and she gave him money to leave England, but he is returning. Telling her to rejoin her husband, Michael begs Audrie to keep him from further sin: "Won't you be my better angel, now I've lost her [Mother]?" After she leaves, Andrew grimly tells Michael to "mete out to yourself the same measure you meted to others."

Act IV. It is a year later. Through an anonymous donation (obviously by Audrie, who is leading a wild life in London), the Cleveheddon church is restored. Michael has resolved to confess his sin publicly at the dedication the next morning and has summoned Andrew's daughter to witness it. Unexpectedly Audrie returns, and in a passionate scene in the chancel Michael refuses her pleas: "You are the holiest thing on earth to me. I will keep you white and stainless from me." Her heart broken, Audrie throws a rose on the altar steps and leaves. Michael spends all night in the church. In the morning, as the dedication ceremonies are to begin, he makes his public confession: "My own life has been polluted with deceit and with deadly sin. . . ." He asks the congregation to pray for him, resigns his position, and leaves.

Act V. Almost a year later, in an Italian monastery where Michael prepares to join an order, Audrie arrives. She is very ill: "Pay—coachman (*taking out purse feebly*)—outside— No, perhaps —better—wait—or bring another sort—of—carriage. But no mutes—no feathers—no mummery." Even before he realizes that she has arrived, Michael admits his "pretended peace is no peace! There is no peace for me without her, either in this world or the next!" Although overjoyed to see her, he knows that it is too late for them, though her husband is now dead. She looks at his mother's portrait, confident of forgiveness: "But I'm your angel—I'm leading you—" Then: "You won't keep me waiting too long? Hold my hand— Tight! tight! Oh! don't look so solemn—" and she dies, laughing. Michael kisses her, throws himself over her body, and calls for death: "Do what you please with me! I'll believe all, do all, suffer all— only—only persuade me that I shall meet her again!"

MICHAEL KRAMER, a drama in four acts by GERHART HAUPTMANN, published and produced in 1900. Setting: a provincial capital in contemporary Germany.

A number of "lonely lives" (as Hauptmann had titled an earlier play) strive for artistic and spiritual fulfillment in a Philistine environment: Michael Kramer, an ungifted but exalted artist; his daughter, equally ungifted and productive, though quietly frustrated; his rebellious son, Arnold, sensitive and talented but deformed and despised; and a former student, frustrated and fretful, but unable to rebel like Arnold or endure "heroically" like the others. The characters and environment are at times repulsive—and yet affecting. NATURALISM occasionally gives way to mystic dialogue, particularly in Kramer's long speeches in the last act.

Acts I and II. Kramer's daughter, Michaline, an art teacher, defends the father she esteems. His disciplining her brother, Arnold, she tells her nagging mother, was just: he had forged his father's signature; though wretched, he should strive to better himself. She leaves with a former student and admirer of Kramer, Ernst Lachmann. The deformed and slovenly Arnold appears. He mocks her and his anxiously reproachful mother. When she questions him about a girl she considers low, and threatens to tell his father about her, Arnold is furious. "You can't help me," he says, and he warns her that he will not listen to his father's "moral preachments." At his studio Kramer sermonizes to Lachmann on fortitude, industry, and the seriousness of art. Almost ecstatically, however, he talks of two things: the birth of his son, who—he had hoped—would have the artistic genius he himself lacks; and his own unfinished portrait of Christ. A girl comes to complain about Arnold's making a nuisance of himself nightly at her father's restaurant. When Arnold appears, Kramer tries to establish a closer relationship with him. His platitudes irritate Arnold, and father and son part more angrily estranged than ever.

Acts III and IV. At the restaurant, Arnold pathetically woos the girl. Then a number of successful habitués arrive and ridicule the arrogant but poor and deformed artist. While their boorish roistering goes on next door, Michaline and Lachmann discuss their own personal and artistic frustrations. (They were once in love, but he is now reduced to hackwork to support a vulgar wife.) An increasingly tense situation reaches its climax as Arnold pulls out a pistol, is ignominiously disarmed, and is chased out. A few days later Kramer is working in his studio. Arnold's body lies in the background: humiliated and surrounded by enemies, he has committed suicide. Michaline, Lachmann, the restaurant girl—all attempt to explain what happened. Kramer alone is exalted. He is struck by Arnold's bitter yet obviously artistic drawings, and now etches his son's portrait as a dead knight in armor. Life, he remarks, no longer can give him joy or dread. Almost reverentially he describes the divine beauty of Arnold's face. He associates it with Beethoven's death mask, and Arnold's death with that of Christ. He apostrophizes Death, "the mildest form of life: the masterpiece of Eternal Love." Yet, he wonders, what does death really mean, "what will be, at the end?"

MICHAELS, Sidney (1927–), American playwright, has written light-comedy hits and an episodic play about DYLAN THOMAS, *Dylan* (1964), which Alec Guinness made popular with his portrayal of the Welsh poet's self-destructive agonies in various drunken scenes. Michaels's first Broadway hit came in 1962 with an adaptation of FRANÇOIS BILLETDOUX's comedy of adultery, *Tchin Tchin* (1959). His earlier works include a drama, *The Plastic Bambino* (1960); and *Ben Franklin in Paris* (1964, music by Mark Sandrich, Jr.), which features the American statesman's amatory capers and his attempts to gain Louis XVI's recognition of the United States.

Born in New York but raised in Boston, Michaels has written many scripts for the movies and for television.

MICHELSEN, Hans Günter (1920–), German dramatist, became notable in the 1960's for a number of philosophical-psychological plays, notably in 1965 with *Helm* and *Drei Akte;* the former, like his first play, *Stienz* (1963), is about an officer who attempts to justify an unsuccessful military act, the latter about the confused doings at a party for an old man reluctant to face another birthday. Other plays by Michelsen, who was born in Hamburg, include *Lappschiess* (1963) and *Feierabend 1 und 2* (1963).

MID-CHANNEL, a play in four acts by ARTHUR WING PINERO, produced in 1909 and published in 1910. Setting: London, an afternoon in January and a day in the following June.

This frequently anthologized Pinero play resembles his best-known work, THE SECOND MRS. TANQUERAY—and Ibsen's HEDDA GABLER. It is more successful than his earlier play in construction and characterization, particularly of the neurotic protagonist, whose marriage is floundering—and sinking—in "mid-channel."

Act I. Zoe Blundell, an attractive woman in her thirties, shocks visitors with her remark that "when I put an end to myself, it will be in the winter time." Again she has quarreled with her husband, who is angered by her gadding about with her coterie of unattached young men, whom she calls "my tame robins." She tells Peter Mottram, her husband's brokerage partner, that after fourteen years of marriage they get "on each other's nerves. . . . He's getting so stodgy and pompous and flat-footed," and she knows that her "little jokes and pranks, that used to amuse him so—they annoy him now." Mottram tries to reconcile them. Married people often undergo a crisis midway, he tells them: "However successful the first half of their journey may be, there's the rough-and-tumble of mid-Channel to negotiate." Though placated, they soon squabble again, and the husband angrily leaves the house.

Act II. Half a year later Zoe is back from a trip to Italy. She looks ill and haggard. Soon it comes out that one of her "tame robins" has become her lover. Her husband, in the meantime, has moved to other luxurious quarters and has taken up with an adventuress. Again Mottram persuades each of them to make it up. Zoe learns that before she summoned him to Italy, her "robin" had seriously paid court to an innocent girl who became heartbroken by his subsequent neglect; thereupon Zoe ends her affair with him.

Act III. Her husband is tired of his "brainless, mercenary, little trull," and pays her off. Zoe arrives, and a reconciliation appears to be imminent. But when she confesses her affair, Zoe's husband refuses to forgive as she has forgiven. Their anger mounts, and Zoe blames their broken marriage on their determination not to have children, for "everything in the earlier years of our marriage was sacrificed to coining money." With growing bitterness she adds, "Oh, yes, we were happy in those climbing days—greedily, feverishly happy; but we didn't look to the time when we should need another interest in life to bind us together." If not for their "cursed selfishness," she says, "we should have crossed that Ridge [in mid-channel] safely enough." But her husband will not take her back. Her lover must marry her: "it 'ud save you from going utterly to the bad." Though Zoe does not want to marry him, her husband's taunts that she has been "chucked" by her lover goad her into submission.

Act IV. Zoe visits her lover, who, when Zoe cast him off, had immediately returned to the other girl. After she leaves with her mother, Zoe learns that he has become engaged to the girl. She hides on the balcony when her husband and Mottram are announced, ready to verify her lover's willingness to marry Zoe. While they talk, the desperate Zoe jumps to her death. Stunned, Mottram recalls, "She told me once it would be in the *winter* time—!"

MIDDLE EAST [or Near East] **DRAMA** is that of IRAN, ISRAEL, and TURKEY; and of the following ARAB-language countries of ASIA and AFRICA: Egypt, Iraq, Jordan, Lebanon, Libya, Morocco, the Persian Gulf States, Saudi Arabia, Sudan, Syria, Tunisia, and Yemen. See the individual above-noted entries.

MIDSUMMER (*Midsommar*), a "serious comedy" in six "pictures" by AUGUST STRINDBERG, published and produced in 1901. Setting: contemporary Sweden.

This slight, late Strindberg drama portrays a cruelly arrogant and cynical youth who travels around Sweden. Through suffering he learns about human goodness and finally reforms.

MIHURA, Miguel (1903–), Spanish playwright, has also been a painter, an editor of humor magazines, and a film scenarist. Among the popular post-World War II writers freely produced in Franco's Spain, Mihura has authored a number of satires of modern man's enslavement to routine and convention. In style they resemble ABSURDism —especially EUGÈNE IONESCO's, whose trenchancy, however, they lack. Best known among them is *Tres sombreros de copa* (*Three Top Hats*), which originally appeared in 1932 and was revised in 1952; its middle-aged protagonist carouses with a motley Bohemian ballet troupe before he shuffles off in the morning to marry his ugly fiancée and lead a life of dull respectability and routine.

Other successful Mihura plays are *El caso de la mujer asesinadita* (1946; with Alvaro de Laiglesia, ? –); *A media luz los tres* (1953); *Sublime decisión* (1955); *Mi adorado Juan* (1956); *Carlota* (1957), a crime comedy; *Melocotón en almíbar* (*Peach in Syrup,* 1958), a comedy about jewel thieves foiled by a nun; and *Maribel y la extraña familia* (1959), a contrast of naïve provincial and sophisticated urban life.

John V. Falconieri and Anthony M. Pasquariello's 1964 text edition of *Mi adorado Juan* has an essay on "Miguel Mihura's Dramatic Formula" and a bibliography. *Three Top Hats* appears with a brief prefatory note on Mihura in Michael Benedikt and George E. Wellwarth's *Modern Spanish Theatre* (1968).

MIKHALKOV, Sergei Vladimirovich (1913–), Russian writer, is best known for his children's stories, poems, and plays. His first important work was a clever apolitical comedy, an adaptation of Carlo Gozzi's *Gli amore delle tre melarance* (*The Love of Three Oranges,* 1761): *Vesyoloe snovidenie* (1945), originally titled *Smekh i slyozy*. Mikhalkov's *Ilya Golovin* (1948) is a propaganda play about the repentance of a "formalist" artist apparently modeled on Dmitri Shostakovich. This play was followed by *Raki* (1952), a broadly farcical satire about a group of naïvely trusting people who are swindled by a confidence man.

The *Detski teatre v klube* (1950) collection includes Mikhalkov's best-known children's play, the anti-Western diatribe *Ya khochu domoi* (1949), a sentimental drama about Soviet children who languish in camps for displaced persons because "English and American warmongers" refuse to repatriate them. Further children's plays in that collection are *Krasny galstuk* (1947), which enunciates the proper qualities for Soviet youths; and *Osoboe zadanie,* a three-act exhortation to "vigilance, adroitness, resourcefulness, ability to serve as informant and reconnaissance scout, and loyalty to the native land." Other drama by Mikhalkov includes *Ostorozhno listopad* (1960), more children's plays, and film scripts. For a discussion of Mikhalkov, particularly of his *Raki,* see Peter Yershov's *Comedy in the Soviet Theater* (1956).

MILESTONES, a play in three acts by ARNOLD BENNETT and EDWARD KNOBLOCK, published and produced in 1912. Setting: a London drawing room in 1860, 1885, and 1912.

This play about three generations of two families, partners in a shipbuilding firm, was immensely popular for a long time and has been frequently revived. An extensive study of the collaboration is Wilbur D. Dunkel's *The Genesis of "Milestones"* (1952).

In 1860 the forward-looking John Rhead breaks with Samuel Sibley, his friend and old-fashioned partner who refuses to believe iron will replace wood as shipbuilding material. Their disagreement breaks up a match between Sibley and Rhead's sister, Gertrude (who subsequently becomes an old maid), and threatens the match of Sibley's sister, Rose, with John Rhead. Nonetheless, twenty-five years later, they are a happily married couple. Tremendously successful because he anticipated the advent of iron, Rhead now is as conservative about steel as his erstwhile partner once was about iron. At the Rheads' golden anniversary in 1912, the problems of the two families' children recur with the grandchildren. Old John Rhead, now a reactionary tyrant, must give way to the new at last. He sits by the fire with Rose, his loving wife, who with her ancient voice serenades him as she did back in 1860.

MILLAY,* Edna St. Vincent (1892–1950), American poet, also wrote a few verse dramas. Her most successful play was the one-act antiwar satire ARIA DA CAPO (1919), presented by the Provincetown Players. Millay herself directed this production and also acted with the Provincetown Players, who produced her other one-act moralistic fantasies, *The Princess Marries the Page* (1918) and *Two Slatterns and a King* (1921). For a Vassar commencement she later wrote a five-act medieval verse drama about the deep friendship of two girls, *The Lamp and the Bell* (1921). In 1923 Millay adapted a FERENC MOLNÁR tragedy, *Heavenly and Earthly Love* (1919), into a Pauline Lord vehicle, *Launzi*. Her only other notable dramatic work was the libretto for Deems Taylor's opera *The King's Henchman* (1927), a tragedy loosely based on the *Anglo-Saxon Chronicle* love-triangle tale of King Eadgar, his thane, and his betrothed; its language and mores reflect the play's tenth-century English setting.

Millay participated in launching the Theatre Guild and acted in its opening bill of Benavente's THE BONDS OF INTEREST. Her most memorable work, however, was her poetry. Expressing the spirit of rebellion and emancipation of the 1920's,

* Illustration on page 98.

it made her one of the most popular poets of her age. Recognition for her many volumes of verse came with the Pulitzer Prize for *The Harp-Weaver and Other Poems* (1923) and with the Poetry Society of America Award in 1943.

Norman A. Brittin's and James Gray's studies, both titled *Edna St. Vincent Millay,* were published in 1967; a biography is Jean Gould's *The Poet and Her Book* (1969).

MILLER, Arthur (1915–), American playwright, novelist, and essayist, is most notable for his searing drama of personal and societal failure, DEATH OF A SALESMAN (1949). Though he has written relatively few later plays, Miller has been considered one of America's foremost dramatists. His first hit was ALL MY SONS (1947), and, after the masterpiece that gained him world fame, he almost duplicated this success with THE CRUCIBLE (1953). This and his next play, A VIEW FROM THE BRIDGE (1955), despite their initial lukewarm reception, have won increasing popular and critical acclaim. Following a long hiatus, Miller came out with AFTER THE FALL (1964) and with INCIDENT AT VICHY (1964). Though interesting, both plays were disappointing: the first was a SUCCÈS DE SCANDALE that won few kudos, although some theatre historians have devoted considerable attention to it; *Incident at Vichy* deals with similar themes of individual guilt and commitment, but found even fewer admirers. In the later THE PRICE (1968) Miller dramatized the same themes but in a more anachronistic manner. It is his earlier works that have continued to have the most deeply stirring effect on audiences as well as readers.

The son of a businessman, Miller was born in New York and grew up in a Jewish middle-class Brooklyn home. He became a tall, gaunt, high-school football star, prevented from going to college because of the Depression, which affected his father's business. Instead, Miller worked as a clerk in an automobile warehouse for over two years, an experience he dramatized in A MEMORY OF TWO MONDAYS (1955). Like the autobiographical character in that one-acter, Miller read through *War and Peace* while commuting on the subway, and saved enough from his job to go to Ann Arbor. The University of Michigan, which he had always wanted to attend, became the more appealing when he read one of its professors' books on playwriting. At Michigan he almost immediately wrote dramas that won local and, subsequently, national awards.

When he graduated in 1938, Miller worked for the Federal Theater Project. Among his scripts was *Montezuma,* a play on the conquest of Mexico. It found no takers, but Miller did succeed with radio plays, and upon the dissolution of the project he became a radio scriptwriter. Rejected for military service because of a football injury, he worked during World War II on *The Story of G.I. Joe* (1945), a documentary film based on Ernie Pyle's front-line newspaper columns. Miller's diaries on research in army camps were published as *Situation Normal* (1944). This book was followed by his first popular success, *Focus* (1945), a novel about anti-Semitism.

By then Miller had written some nine plays. The first to be produced on Broadway (it ran only four days) was *The Man Who Had All the Luck* (1944). It is a tyro's forerunner of his maturer plays; the title character, guilt-ridden with "all the luck" that befalls him and racked with forebodings, embodies the moral problems that were to predominate in the Miller hits that soon followed. *All My Sons,* three years later, though in the tradition of the contrived nineteenth-century WELL-MADE PLAY and not very impressive in retrospect, won the Drama Critics' Circle Award as the best American play for that season (which, incidentally, also saw the premiere of O'Neill's THE ICEMAN COMETH). This established Miller as a recognized playwright; two years later came the phenomenal success of *Death of a Salesman.*

But Miller's career soon was impaired by personal and social upheavals. In 1950 he adapted Ibsen's AN ENEMY OF THE PEOPLE, but he wrote nothing new for Broadway for a decade (1955–64). His growing concern about the witch hunt unleashed by McCarthyism in the 1950's (reflected in *The Crucible*) was climaxed with Miller's own subpoena in 1956 by the House Committee on Un-American Activities. His refusal to inform on other writers and artists—though he readily testified about his own activities and beliefs—resulted in a contempt citation and a fine. Miller's appeal was upheld on a technicality, and he was acquitted. But he was lacerated by the hearings (many of whose legal aspects he handled himself) as well as by the inevitable publicity. Agonized soul searching is reflected in his speeches and articles, during that time, on censorship and artistic freedom, and on political hypocrisy.

There were also personal upheavals. His fifteen-year marriage broke up (the Millers had two children)—a particularly harrowing failure to a writer so committed to family loyalties. In 1956 he married the movie star Marilyn Monroe, America's sex symbol and to Miller, apparently, a symbol of admirably naïve innocence in a world of complexity and corruption. The marriage was dissolved in 1960, two years before her suicide and Miller's third marriage to the Austrian photographer Inge Morath, with whom he collaborated on the picture book *In Russia* (1969). The tempestuous Miller-Monroe relationship, which brought more of the publicity so deleterious to the writer, is reflected in some of his fiction and in *After the Fall.* Miller wrote no plays during those years, but he reworked a short story into a successful film script for Marilyn Monroe, *The Misfits* (1961).*

During these years Miller's next play gradually began to formulate in his mind. The intensely personal *After the Fall,* however questionable its success as a work of art, chronicles Miller's anguish of that time. The play launched New York's Repertory Theatre of Lincoln Center, and the autobiographical revelations—particularly

* See James Goode's *The Story of the Misfits* (1963). Also featured in the film were Clark Gable and Montgomery Clift.

Arthur Miller, 1967. (*Inge Morath from Magnum*)

those concerned with Marilyn Monroe—made it an even more newsworthy production. Yet neither this play nor the next (*Incident at Vichy*) achieved the popular or critical acclaim of Miller's earlier work.

The merit of that earlier work, nonetheless, justifies Miller's reputation as a major midcentury American—perhaps international—dramatist. He has written at least three first-rate plays, one of them an established modern classic. *Death of a Salesman,* like the less successful *After the Fall,* is distinguished, among other things, for Miller's original technique. To dramatize the protagonist's state of mind vividly and suspensefully, he expertly fused form and idea, adapting and reshaping PRESENTATIONAL devices such as EXPRESSIONISM. The fluidity of a skeletal setting made possible quick transitions in time and place. These were necessary to dramatize the protagonist's agonized unblocking of his guilty memories and his increasing inability to distinguish between illusion and reality—an evil confusion of values that Miller blames on all of American society. Miller has further universalized all of his drama with carefully wrought dialogue that strives for and occasionally achieves poetic heights—without, however, falsifying the prose appropriate to the speakers. Particularly notable in this respect are the echoes of seventeenth-century Salem in the modern speeches of *The Crucible,* and Linda's characterizations of the Brooklyn salesman—and the requiem in *Death of a Salesman.* Usually grounded in the environment with which he is most familiar, Miller's plays have struck responsive chords in people everywhere—testifying to his drama's essentially universal quality. As uniquely American a babbitt character as the salesman, stooped by his two sample cases, seemed recognizable in other Western—and even in Eastern—societies. The close family relationships (particularly between father and son) stemming from Miller's own background transcend his Brooklyn locales and portray the relationships in other families.

The themes that have preoccupied Miller are equally universal, timeless—and timely. It is true that Miller seemed to be especially affected by the Nazi holocaust (whose frightening consequences became the more vivid when he attended some of the Nazi criminal trials) and by the anti-Communist McCarthyist hysteria that forced him to reexamine his own convictions. But Miller's preoccupation with individual and social morality antedated these personal experiences, and it is very evident in the plays that preceded them. Indeed, his first two Broadway hits are interchangeable in theme: both protagonists die for their sons because they have predicated their lives on the profit-and-success values of society, values Miller excoriated even when pursued wholly for the sake of the family; both Joe Keller and Willy Loman commit suicide because, by adhering to social morality, they have affronted moral decency. Later Miller characters are more explicitly concerned with individual integrity, with preserving the honor of their names. The protagonists of *The Crucible* and of *Incident at Vichy* die to preserve this honor, as does even the bestial longshoreman of *A View from the Bridge.* They all find that they cannot dissociate themselves from guilt, wherever it occurs. Salvation is possible only through a recognition of the individual's personal involvement in society, and his acceptance of a share in social evil. Final expiation—usually through death—comes with such a recognition. Only Quentin (in *After the Fall*) chooses life: willing to accept his share of guilt, he is able to commit himself to life and face a future still possible for man, Miller suggests, "after the fall."

If these themes are in the tradition of Greek tragedy, that is no accident. Miller, an intellectual who has painstakingly crafted and evaluated his works, is concerned with creating tragic drama in the age of the common man. In essay after essay Miller has explored the classical basis and artistic ramifications of bourgeois tragedy; he has consciously sought to apply classical and universal concepts to the drama of his age—even before his own masterpiece became the focal exhibit in debates about and studies of modern tragedy. Miller's attempts to redefine tragedy in modern terms has transcended mere academicism because he has grappled with vital contemporary issues. In his essays as in his plays, Miller has dealt with such issues, from universal guilt in the Nazi genocide and the atomic bomb to questions of artistic freedom and industrial morality, and the sometimes conflicting claims of family loyalty and individual integrity.

Particularly important among his essays are "On Social Plays," the introduction to the 1955 version of *A View from the Bridge,* and the fifty-two-page introduction to his *Collected Plays* (1957). Miller's stories were collected in *I Don't*

Need You Any More (1967). Tetsumaro Hayashi's *Arthur Miller Criticism (1930–1967)* (1969) includes a compilation of all Miller's published and unpublished work, but is often unreliable. Robert W. Corrigan's *Arthur Miller: A Collection of Critical Essays* (1969) presents a wide selection of critical approaches as well as bibliographies that list the many book-length studies of Miller's work.

MILLIONAIRESS, THE, "a Jonsonian Comedy in Four Acts" by BERNARD SHAW, published and produced in 1936. Setting: England, 1935.

In "Preface on Bosses," the introductory essay to the published version of this relatively unsuccessful farce, Shaw provided a provocative analysis of Hitler's and Mussolini's careers, dealt with the danger of born leaders whose talents are devoted to moneymaking (when "the world's welfare depends on operations by which no individual can make money"), treated the question "What safeguards have the weaponless great against the great who have myrmidons at their call?" and considered the problems of dealing with naturally dominant people who are valuable as well as dangerous to society. Shaw's answer to this last problem was: "By all means dominate: it is up to us to so order our institutions that you shall not oppress us. . . ."

A number of people assemble in a solicitor's office: the domineering and tempestuous—but unhappy—millionairess Epifania Fitzfassenden (*née* Ognisanti di Parerga); her husband, Alastair, who keeps her under control by punching her, and who wants a separation; his affectionate and placid paramour; and Epifania's cultivated "Sunday husband," Adrian Blenderbland. After providing entertaining reviews of their various histories, Epifania and Adrian go to an inn. Disgruntled with the meal, Adrian infuriates Epifania with his deprecation of money and her father, and she kicks him down a flight of stairs. She feigns convulsions as an Egyptian doctor appears, but his bluntness and his refusal to be awed by her money and bullying intrigue her and she decides to marry him. About to tell him of her father's marriage test, she is confronted by the test his mother enjoined *him* to put to a prospective wife: to earn her own living for six months. Epifania begins as a scullery maid and by ruthlessly efficient management soon becomes the owner of a fashionable inn where the people from the solicitor's office eventually reassemble. Adrian, limping and bandaged, wants to sue Epifania for assault, and she threatens a countersuit. She still intends to marry the humanitarian but reluctant Egyptian doctor: "Shall I, the healer, the helper, the guardian of life and the counsellor of health, unite with the exploiter of misery?" After Epifania extols marriage eloquently and at length, however, the doctor finally gives in: "There is no wit and no wisdom like that of a woman ensnaring the mate chosen for her by Allah."

MILNE, A[lan] A[lexander] (1882–1956), English writer, became world famous with children's poetry such as *When We Were Very Young* (1924) and the series of stories beginning with *Winnie-the-Pooh* (1926). But he also wrote essays and novels for adults, and some thirty plays. The best known among them are MR. PIM PASSES BY (1920, which is typical of Milne's drama) and the more biting THE TRUTH ABOUT BLAYDS (1921). Most of his plays are short, whimsical comedies, slight but amusing. Milne acknowledged his gratitude to JAMES M. BARRIE, who gave him a "first chance" and—though Milne did not say so—a model for the genial sentimentality and humor for children of all ages that he, too, was to excel in. Also like Barrie, Milne was much concerned with the craft of playwriting. His drama was particularly popular with amateur groups, though some of it was very successful in professional London and New York productions.

Milne was born in London, attended Trinity College, Cambridge, and then edited and contributed to *Punch* until he entered the army in 1915. There, he later remarked, he could write plays, a "luxury" not afforded the journalist. His first play was a sketch written for the troops and later expanded into a novel, *Once on a Time* (1917). Its success prompted him to write for the professional stage, and the production of WURZEL-FLUMMERY in 1917 started his career as a playwright. It was followed by the other works published in *First Plays* (1920): *The Lucky One,* which later reappeared as *Let's All Talk About Gerald; The Boy Comes Home,* a one-act comedy about a returning veteran, later produced as *Hallo, America!; Belinda,* a romantic "April folly in three acts" (produced in 1918) about a supposed widow who introduces her daughter as her niece and keeps two suitors around until her husband returns; and a one-act operetta, *The Red Feathers.*

That collection was followed by *Second Plays* (1922): *Make-Believe* (a children's play), *Mr. Pim Passes By, The Camberley Triangle, The Romantic Age* (a popular three-act comedy about a girl who dreams of epic tales and finds romance with a stockbroker), and *The Stepmother.* Then came *Three Plays* (1922): *The Dover Road* (a middle-age romance of runaway couples, successfully produced in 1921), *The Truth About Blayds,* and *The Great Broxopp. Four Plays* (1926) includes *To Have the Honour* (1925, produced in America as *Meet the Prince*), *Ariadne; or, Business First* (1925), *Portrait of a Gentleman in Slippers,* and *Success* (1923, produced in New York as *Give Me Yesterday*). A later *Four Plays* (1932) collection includes *Michael and Mary* (1930) and a mystery play, *The Fourth Wall* (produced in America as *The Perfect Alibi*). Milne's other plays are *The Man in the Bowler Hat* (1924), a burlesque melodrama whose title character is a stage manager watching a rehearsal while two innocents mistake the exciting goings-on for a real adventure; *The Ivory Door* (1928), a comic-romantic fantasy; *The Wind in the Willows* (1929), a dramatization of Kenneth Grahame's novel, also produced as *Toad of Toad Hall; Other People's Lives* (1935), produced in America as *They Don't Mean Any Harm;*

Miss Elizabeth Bennet (1936), a dramatization of Jane Austen's *Pride and Prejudice; Miss Marlow at Play* (1937); *Sarah Simple* (1937); *Gentleman Unknown* (1938); *The Ugly Duckling* (1940); and *Before the Flood* (1951), a one-act comedy.

For further information, see Milne's prefaces to his early play collections and Chapters 14 through 16 of his *Autobiography* (1939), simultaneously published in England as *It's Too Late Now*.

MIRACLE AT VERDUN (*Wunder um Verdun*), a play in thirteen scenes by HANS CHLUMBERG, produced in 1930 and published in 1931. Setting: the French-German military cemetery near Verdun, August 1939.

This EXPRESSIONIST antiwar fantasy, a precursor of Irwin Shaw's BURY THE DEAD, haunted worldwide audiences. It is set in the future, on the anniversary of the outbreak of World War I—and by a grim coincidence at the very time World War II was to begin. The play consists of short, telegraphic scenes and occasional film clips.

A group of tourists visit and examine the cemetery. When they depart, one of them, a German veteran of the Battle of Verdun, remains behind. The cemetery's old caretaker, a French army veteran, tells him about the next day's scheduled anniversary celebration, when there is to be a prayer for the glorious resurrection of the dead. The two veterans envision the memorials in France and Germany, and hear the biblical summons of the dead (Ezekiel 37).

The dead now arise from their graves, pick up their crosses, and start to return to their homes. They interrupt their march to rest in a cornfield, and reminisce about their past lives. Then they continue and soon clash against the reality of a world that has forgotten them and no longer wants them—nor can use them. Their resurrection inconveniences and appalls the French premier and his mistress, a German burgher and his wife, a pipe-smoking Englishman, and many others. One of the resurrected dead finds his former wife happily married to another, who threatens him with a gun. The great powers confer and quarrel in Paris, worry about the possibilities of unemployment, and urge the dead to return to their graves. "Bear your fate," a committee of religious leaders urges them: "Your return would bring not faith but confusion and the destruction of the Church. Return to your graves." As the clergymen and politicians debate, the resurrected soldiers, realizing that their military heroism and their deaths were in vain, scornfully return to their graves.

The tourists leave the cemetery memorial after tipping the old caretaker. He and the German veteran, who makes his donation before rejoining his fellow tourists, are the only ones who have been truly resurrected.

MIRBEAU, Octave [Henri Marie] (1850–1917), French novelist and playwright, was a journalist and a revolutionary artist before he started writing his violently satiric, NATURALISTIC social-protest plays. The most successful of these were *Les Mauvais Bergers* (1897), a labor-strike drama; *Les Affaires sont les affaires* (*Business Is Business*, 1903), an indictment of industry and the businessman; *Le Foyer* (1908), a satire of philanthropic institutions; a number of one-acters satirizing social injustice and provincial life; and some GRAND GUIGNOL plays.

Mirbeau's most memorable accomplishment was an enthusiastic review in *Le Figaro* in 1890, which made MAURICE MAETERLINCK famous overnight. Mirbeau was also active, with ROMAIN ROLLAND, in trying to found a "people's theatre" at the end of the nineteenth century. His own drama was published in three volumes.

MISALLIANCE, "A Debate in One Sitting" by BERNARD SHAW, produced in 1910 and published in 1914. Setting: England, 1909.

This comedy consists for the most part of extensive conversations among individualized characters, of whom the most delightful are Tarleton and Lina. Shaw's long preface, an essay on "Parents and Children," discusses the wrong ways in which children are usually brought up and educated, and suggests various remedies.

In his father's garden pavilion in which the continuous action of the play occurs, Johnny Tarleton is exasperated by the antics of Bentley Summerhays, a neurotic weakling. Lord Summerhays comes in, guesses at once that only his son Bentley could have driven anyone to such anger, and has Johnny smash a punchbowl to relieve his feelings. Having comforted the weeping Bentley, Johnny's sister, Hypatia, tells her mother that though she fears that his family may consider it a misalliance, she will probably marry the "little squit of a thing" because he is smart and comes from a good family. Later she humiliates Lord Summerhays by recalling and ridiculing his earlier marriage proposal to her. She wants to be the "glorious young beast" he called her, and she yearns for excitement. John Tarleton, a charming and wealthy old rake and underwear manufacturer who takes every occasion to cite his favorite authors ("Joy of life. Read Ibsen." "The superman's an idea. I believe in ideas. Read Whatshisname."), says that his daughter, Hypatia, "wants adventures to drop out of the sky"—which directly happens when an airplane crashes into his garden.

Its occupants are Joseph Percival and Lina Szczepanowska, a beautiful Polish acrobat. Hypatia quickly falls in love with the handsome Percival and shamelessly makes advances to him, which are overheard by a hidden gunman who has come to kill Tarleton for having seduced his mother years before. After indignant Socialist speeches (influenced by books from the Free Libraries Tarleton has been opening), the nervous gunman is disarmed by Lina. In a comic scene, Percival makes him retract his accusations against Hypatia on her forwardness, but the gunman is protected from further bullying when Mrs. Tarleton recognizes him as her friend's son. Hypatia decides to marry Percival, and asks Tarleton to "buy the brute" for her. Lina takes Bentley, who has another fit, for exercises in the gymnasium. He falls in love with her and, though frightened to death, is willing to accompany her in the plane. Eager to leave the unhealthy house where every man has propositioned her within an hour of her arrival, Lina is finally persuaded to postpone her departure until the next day. Tarleton, who is not impressed with Percival, deplores Hypatia's independence and wants to go off and read *King Lear,* but is finally reconciled and has nothing further to say.

MISHIMA Yukio [originally Hiraoka Kimitake] (1925–70), Japanese writer, became known abroad for his fiction and plays as well as for some of his other activities. An enormously versatile and charismatic figure who was considered Japan's outstanding writer after World War II, Mishima was also a screen star, a lecturer, a swordsman, and a bon vivant. He wrote about his Japanese countrymen and their legends; but he transcended national concerns since he dealt with human love, hate, and the problems of our times. Such universal themes permeate his immensely successful novels as well as his plays. Outstanding among the latter are the widely translated free adaptations of the classics (*Kindai Nōgakushū*), published in English as *Five Modern Nō Plays* (1957).

The son of a high civil servant, Mishima was born in Tokyo. A brilliant but physically frail student, he proceeded on a vigorous body-building regimen (including karate and fencing) until he became a muscular athlete. He was intimately familiar with and strongly influenced by Western culture: his Tokyo villa was crammed with baroque and rococo art objects, and his wife studied Western cooking. But Mishima deplored his country's increasing Westernization, which he felt corrupted and enfeebled Japan's samurai tradition, her essential ethics and aesthetics. In 1948 he became a government official, joining the Japanese Finance Ministry. A patriot characterized by some as a right-winger, Mishima in 1968 organized a private army, the Tate no Kai (Shield Society). Two years later he died in a characteristically spectacular manner: attempting to overthrow the government in order to restore Japan to its former glory under the Emperor, he led his army in a raid on Japan's Self-Defense headquarters, captured its commanding general, and, after haranguing crowds of soldiers from the balcony, committed suicide by *seuppku* (hara-kiri).

Mishima Yukio, 1970. Practising *Iai* (the art of sword handling) shortly before his death. (*Eiji Miyazawa*, from "Black Star")

Mishima's novels began to be published in 1944. *Shiosai* (1954), the best known among them in the English-speaking world, where it was translated as *The Sound of Waves* (1956), is based on the Greek romance of Daphnis and Chloë. Mishima has also been acclaimed for his travel books, operettas, and the plays which he (like FUKUDA TSUNEARI) began to contribute to the newly formed Dramatic Research Institute in 1950.

Mishima's No plays are erotically suggestive, but even more evocative is their lyric SYMBOLISM, which fuses Oriental and Occidental themes and styles. Much as Western playwrights have modernized Greek legends, Mishima redramatized the five fifteenth-century No plays with contemporary settings and characters: *Aoi-No-Ue* (*The Lady Aoi,* 1954) is destroyed by a *femme fatale* in love with her handsome husband in a hospital specializing in cases of sexual repressions (modernized demons); *Sotoba Komachi* (1952) similarly modernizes the supernatural, as a cigarette-butt-collecting hag in a park kills a young poet by reliving her youth as a heartless beauty; in *Aya-No-Tuzumi* (*Damask Drum,* 1951), another fantasy with ghosts, yet another woman incapable of love goads her aged admirer to suicide; in *Kantan* (1950) an idle youth dreams of being a tycoon, much as his No prototype dreamed of being the Emperor; and *Hanjo* (1955) portrays a lonely woman holding in her power a girl who does not recognize and therefore sends away the returning lover whose desertion caused her to go mad.

Mishima's other plays include *Yoru No Himawari* (*Twilight Sunflower,* 1953), which dramatizes the end of World War II; *Wakodo Yo Yomigaere* (*Young Man Back to Life,* 1954), which describes a schoolboy's crush; and *Rokumeikan* (1956), the 1962 hit melodramatizing a tale of nineteenth-century Japanese-Western political intrigue. Even more interesting, perhaps, is the later *Sado Kōshaku Fujin* (*Madame de Sade,* 1965), a play about the Marquis de Sade, who, however, does not appear in this all-female "Sade seen through women's eyes" drama; it interprets the reasons for the title character's abandonment of her husband the moment he was released from prison, though she had remained devoted to him throughout his notorious adventures and his incarceration.

The first collection of Mishima's plays and librettos appeared in 1962. In English his drama is discussed in Donald Keene's prefaces to *Five Modern Nō Plays* (1957) and *Madame de Sade* (1967).

MISS JULIE (*Fröken Julie*), "A Naturalistic Tragedy in One Act" by AUGUST STRINDBERG, published in 1888 and produced in 1889. Setting: contemporary Norway; the count's kitchen on Midsummer Night's Eve.

Miss Julie (or *Countess Julia*) is one of Strindberg's most popular works, and was made into a ballet in 1950, a film in 1951, and an opera (by Ned Rorem) in 1966. The play was a by-product of his marriage with Siri von Essen, who was also the first to act the decadent young countess. The bitter sex duel between Julie and the coarse butler-valet Jean is exacerbated by their class and other environmental and hereditary backgrounds. The preface to the play, perhaps Strindberg's most important essay on drama, elaborates on this "multiplicity of motives." It also defends the play's NATURALISTIC stress on "social Darwinism" and the Nietzschean power struggle, as well as its REPRESENTATIONAL innovations in setting, dialogue, and technical matters of staging. Because of these daring approaches, the play was at first banned, but it was a favorite of the experimental theatres. The continuous one-and-a-half-hour action is divided by a dramatic ballet interlude.

"Now Miss Julie's mad again—absolutely mad!" the valet, Jean, remarks to the cook, Kristin, to whom he is engaged. He tells her that their mistress, Julie, keeps insisting on being his partner at the holiday festivities in the barn. He also reveals that her fiancé had angrily left when she whipped him while training him to jump over her riding crop. Soon Julie comes to the kitchen after Jean and, despite his servile but impertinent remonstrations, coquettishly leads him back to the dance. They shortly return. The overtired Kristin falls asleep and Julie, insisting on their having a drink together, continues her flirtation. Jean, who has picked up some fashionable airs, confesses childhood miseries and aspirations. Eventually he claims that as a boy he loved Julie: "You represented to me the hopelessness of ever rising above the social level to which I was born." She slaps him when he makes advances, and refuses to heed his warning against her staying with him at so late an hour. But her excitement mounts, and when the dancing peasants are about to enter, she quickly agrees to flee into his room, to escape discovery.

When the dance is over, Jean and Julie return, visibly changed. The seduction completed, Jean has coarsened. He suggests that Julie help him open a hotel in Switzerland. Breaking into hysterical remorse, Julie wonders what drew her to him: the intoxication of the festival night? "The attraction of the weak to the strong, the ones on the decline to the ones rising?" Jean is sleepy and ridicules her crudely. But though she loathes him, she cannot leave, and insists on talking about her family's sordid past and her upbringing as a man hater: "But occasionally—when my weakness comes over me—oh, the shame of it!" She prepares to leave with Jean and steals money from the absent count. Refusing to be burdened with her luggage, Jean brutally slaughters her little bird. Now Julie loses all her self-control; she raves about her hatred of men, gloating as she envisions her father's stroke upon discovering her doings. Kristin is appalled when she learns of Julie's affair ("She—who was about to have her [bitch] Diana shot just because she was running after the gatekeeper's pug dog!"), theft, and plans. Though Julie begs her to join them, and though Kristin is herself a petty thief, she self-righteously goes to church, refusing to "demean" herself by remaining in "a place where one can't respect one's employers." The count's bell unexpectedly rings for Jean. Suddenly totally servile and bereft of will power, he is ready to polish the count's boots. Julie begs him to order her to cut her throat: "I'll obey like a dog!" When the bell rings again, Jean quails. But finally he turns to her: "It's horrible! But it's the only way to end it!— Go!" Holding the razor he had put in her hand, Julie walks out to the barn.

Miss Julie. Jean (Anders Soh) and Julie (Ingrid Thulin). Stockholm, 1960. (*Swedish Information Service*)

MR. PIM PASSES BY, a comedy in three acts by A. A. MILNE, produced in 1920 and published in 1922. Setting: contemporary Buckinghamshire.

This popular trifle features Carraway Pim, a "wistful, kindly, gentle, little" man whose forgetfulness of names creates the play's comic confusions.

Mr. Pim, who has come from Australia, visits George Marden, an English country gentleman to whom he has a letter of introduction. Marden's

Mr. Pim Passes By. Left to right: Lady Marden (Helen Westley), George Marden (Dudley Digges), Mr. Pim (Erskine Sanford), Olivia (Laura Hope Crewes). New York, 1921. (*Culver Pictures*)

vivacious young niece (Dinah) tells Mr. Pim about her charming aunt, Olivia: she first "married the Telworthy man and went to Australia with him, and he drank himself to death in the bush"; then she returned to England and married Dinah's old-fashioned Uncle George. The latter refuses to allow his niece to marry her indigent young "futuristic" artist, and objects to the gay curtains Olivia wants for the house: "I don't want any of these new-fangled ideas . . . the house of my fathers and forefathers is good enough for me." Absent-minded old Mr. Pim tells them all about an Australian he met on the boat, "a bad fellow" whose name he finally remembers is Telworthy. The Mardens are appalled to realize they have therefore committed bigamy. There is a painful supper with a straitlaced old aunt, and an even more painful interview between Marden and Olivia. He is anxious to do the legally correct thing, while Olivia waits for him to say, simply: "You're *mine,* and let this other damned fellow come and take you from me if he can." Mr. Pim passes by again and eases their worries by revealing that Telworthy died when they landed. Now Marden is eager to marry Olivia properly. With growing amusement as Marden's discomfiture grows, Olivia exacts his romantic proposal, and his approval of the curtains and his niece's marriage to the poor artist. Mr. Pim again comes by and reveals to Olivia that he was mistaken about the name—it was not *Telworthy* but *Polwittle,* although Mr. Pim is not sure about the first name. Olivia does not enlighten Marden about the turn of events that has made their remarriage unnecessary. As both couples leave to get married and start their honeymoons, Mr. Pim passes by again. Happily he *whispers* to Olivia, "I've just remembered. His name was *Ernest* Polwittle—*not* Henry."

MR. SLEEMAN IS COMING (*Herr Sleeman kommer*), a one-act play in three scenes by HJALMAR BERGMAN, published and produced in 1917. Setting: an attic room near a forest in Sweden, early twentieth century.

This captivating short drama was among the three *"Marionettspel"* written by Bergman in 1915 and 1916. It resembles a fairy tale and—with its brooding fatalism, only briefly interrupted by flashes of humor and a scene of wild abandon—the evocative mood pieces of MAURICE MAETERLINCK.

Two elderly spinster sisters agree to have their innocent and attractive young ward taken off their hands by marrying her to the old, crippled, and lecherous but wealthy title character. This breaks the girl's heart, which belongs to a dashing forester. As the clock, signifying Sleeman's approach, ticks away, the young couple spend a final evening together and recklessly go off once more into the woods they love. The next day the girl obediently but mechanically greets and accepts old Sleeman, as she is bidden to do by the simpering sisters. When he expresses his love for her in the same plain words as did the forester, she replies just as she had to her lover—but changes her original *unhappy* to *happy:* "I am so happy. But if I begin to cry I'll never stop." The pleased spinsters congratulate the couple, though they are troubled by the girl's weeping. "Keep calm, ladies," Sleeman reassures them: "Joy too has tears."

MRS. DANE'S DEFENCE, a play in four acts by HENRY ARTHUR JONES, produced in 1900 and published in 1905. Setting: Sunningwater (near London), c. 1900.

The masterly third-act interrogation that breaks the title character assured the success of this suspenseful drama. It is "an excellent example of

Mr. Sleeman Is Coming. Mr. Sleeman (Carl Browallius), his bride (Mona Martenson), and the spinster sisters (Ellen Borländer on the left and Tyra Dörum on the right). Stockholm, 1922. (*Drottningholms Teatermuseum*)

the WELL-MADE PLAY, but with enough warmth and reality to make the framework subsidiary," as Richard A. Cordell noted (*Henry Jones and the Modern Drama*). Like THE LIARS, its resolution is disappointingly Victorian: the judge is a sermonizing, elder *raisonneur* who, like the *raisonneur* of the earlier comedy, breaks up a "sinful" love but succeeds in his own romantic quest.

Mrs. Lucy Dane, an attractive young woman, is in love with and loved by the adopted son of a distinguished jurist, Sir Daniel Carteret. A malicious townswoman learns of her resemblance to a governess who some years earlier had created a scandal in Vienna: the mistress of her employer, she had escaped after the liaison was discovered, the wife committed suicide, and the man lost his sanity. Though the rumor appears to be false, the townswoman persists in scandalmongering. Sir Daniel examines Mrs. Dane at length and is almost persuaded of her innocence until he inadvertently stumbles on the truth. "Woman, you're lying!" he thunders at her. (These climactic words, from an actual case Jones had read about, were the play's germ.) Though Mrs. Dane begs that her youthful indiscretion be forgiven, and though the love-struck boy persists in wanting to marry her, Sir Daniel remains adamant. Even the young woman he is courting objects to his sternness: "Don't we all have one code on our lips and another in our hearts, one set of rules to admonish our neighbours, and another to guide our own conduct?" The judge, however, insists, "We can't help ourselves. But at any rate the outside of the platter must be clean." And though he himself has been guilty of occasional indiscretions, the same standards do not apply to women: "Whatever I've done, whatever I've been myself, I'm quite resolved my son sha'n't marry another man's mistress." His lady friend sees to it that the scandalmonger, who is unaware of the truth of her charges, signs the apology that Sir Daniel had earlier prepared for her. Then, revealing that he and the boy's mother were in love but "gave each other up" because she was married, Sir Daniel persuades his adopted son to give up Mrs. Dane. She leaves with the realization that "we mustn't get found out. I'm afraid I've broken that part of the law." Calmed down with a pill, the heartbroken boy falls asleep. The young Scottish girl he loved before Mrs. Dane appeared in town kisses him tenderly.

MRS. DOT, a farce in three acts by SOMERSET MAUGHAM, produced in 1908 and published in 1912. Setting: London, 1905.

Mrs. Dot (Mrs. Worthley), the widowed, very spirited young heroine, is "even more virtuous" (Maugham noted) than the protagonist of his just-completed LADY FREDERICK. Her machinations for bringing about her marriage to the hero, who loves her, are complicated by his unexpected inheritance of a title and a fortune. These temporarily threaten to prevent his breaking an old and mutually undesired engagement with the daughter of a scheming dowager.

MRS. WARREN'S PROFESSION, a play in four acts by BERNARD SHAW, published in 1898 and produced in 1902. Setting: Surrey and London, 1890's.

This is the last of Shaw's three "unpleasant" plays about "social horrors," here that of prostitution. In his preface to PLAYS UNPLEASANT Shaw noted, "Rich men without conviction are more dangerous in modern society than poor women without chastity." The title page bears these lines from William Blake: "The harlot's cry from street to street / Shall weave old England's winding sheet." Written in 1894, the play was denied a license until 1902, when it had a private performance; it had a stormy public premiere in Arnold Daly's American production in 1905. Shaw discussed the censorship of this play in a long "Apology" (1902).

Act I. The attractive and practical Vivie Warren, who has been educated away from home and intends to enter the law in London, is on a holiday in Surrey. She is visited by her mother, "a genial and fairly presentable old blackguard" whom she hardly knows, and her mother's friends: Mr. Praed, a naïve artist who inadvertently reveals that there is a mystery about Mrs. Warren's life; and Sir George Crofts, a scoundrel who soon becomes interested in Vivie. Vivie herself is interested in the pleasant young ne'er-do-well Frank, son of the local Reverend Samuel Gardner, a pretentious windbag who warns Frank about compromising himself with women, as he himself had once done in his youth with a barmaid. When Mrs. Warren sees Gardner, she recognizes him as a former lover.

Act II. In the cottage in the evening, Mrs. Warren rejects both Frank and Crofts as Vivie's suitors. Mrs. Warren, alone with Vivie, is shocked by her unfilial coldness. Admitting that she is not certain who Vivie's father is, Mrs. Warren tells her why she had chosen a disreputable career. Her respectable half-sister died of lead poisoning in a factory, and her own sole alternative was hard work at starvation wages for the rest of her life; in such slavery, "how could you keep your self-respect?" Instead, she chose to profit from her looks, save her money, and then open her own establishment—one that was better than the factory for her young women. Mrs. Warren concludes that in our society "the only way for a woman to provide for herself decently is for her to be good to some man that can afford to be good to her." Vivie, who assumes that this part of her mother's life is over, is impressed; though she had intended otherwise, she now wants to become her friend.

Act III. The next morning, in the rectory garden, Frank and Vivie's embraces are interrupted by Crofts, who has come to propose to her. He reveals that he is her mother's partner in a still-thriving chain "hotel" business. Vivie is shocked—also at Crofts, who has not been driven by necessity as was her mother—but he sees nothing wrong with good business, from which she herself has benefited: "If you're going to pick and choose your acquaintances on moral principles, you'd better clear out of this country, unless you want to cut yourself out of all decent society." When she summons Frank, Crofts angrily tells her that her father is Gardner, and that she is thus Frank's half-sister. After a melodramatic scene with Frank, the disgusted Vivie at once leaves for London.

Act IV. A few days later, Frank and Praed appear in Vivie's office. She declines Frank's "love's young dream" and Praed's "romance and beauty" of foreign travel, and then reveals to them her mother's profession. Frank bows out—he cannot now bring himself to touch Mrs. Warren's money. In a final interview, Vivie reproaches her mother for continuing her business, but Mrs. Warren explains that, like Vivie, she must work. Vivie understands, but when Mrs. Warren lapses into maternal and moral attitudes, Vivie finally rejects her mother: "I might have done as you did; but I should not have lived one life and believed in another. You are a conventional woman at heart." Mrs. Warren leaves, and Vivie quickly and happily becomes absorbed in her work.

MISUNDERSTANDING, THE (*Le Malentendu*), a play in three acts by ALBERT CAMUS, published and produced in 1944. Setting: an inn in central Czechoslovakia, 1930's.

This play, also produced as *Cross Purpose,* is a folktale retold in an episode of Camus's novel *The Stranger*. Here, he notes in his preface, it is "an attempt to create a modern tragedy" which reveals "that in an unjust or indifferent world man can save himself, and save others, by practicing the most basic sincerity and pronouncing the most appropriate word."

A poor mother and her daughter yearn to escape their isolated inn, "this land of shadows." A wealthy traveler puts up for the night. He is their son and brother, returning after many years, during which he made his fortune. But he does not immediately reveal himself, for he wants to surprise them and share his happiness and wealth with them. Ignorant of his true identity, they murder him and anticipate the joy his money will help to bring them. Then they discover who he was. By the time his wife appears in the morning, despair has driven the mother to suicide. "In the normal order of things no one is ever recognized . . . we're cheated," the hardened daughter, before she too kills herself, tells the horrified wife. Heartbroken, the wife implores divine compassion. When an old manservant appears, she begs him, "Be kind and say that you will help me." Clearly and firmly he replies, "No."

MITCHELL, Langdon [Elwyn] (1862–1935), American short-story writer, poet, and playwright, adapted novels for the stage and wrote a number of original dramas. The most popular of them was THE NEW YORK IDEA (1906), an outstanding American comedy of its time that followed the models of HENRY ARTHUR JONES and ARTHUR WING PINERO. Mitchell's earliest play was a romantic tragedy, *Sylvian* (1885); but his first success was *Becky Sharp* (1899), a dramatization for Minnie Maddern Fiske of Thackeray's *Vanity Fair*. After adapting JACOB GORDIN's Yiddish dramatization of LEO TOLSTOI's novel *The Kreutzer Sonata* in 1906, Mitchell turned to comedy with his masterpiece, which again starred Mrs. Fiske. But though some called him an "American Shaw," except for another Thackeray dramatization, *Major Pendennis* (1916), Mitchell was unable to repeat his earlier successes.

Mitchell was born in Philadelphia, the son of the prominent physician and writer S. Weir Mitchell, some of whose work he adapted for the stage. He was admitted to the New York bar, but turned to writing, lectured at George Washington University from 1918 to 1920, and became a professor of playwriting at the University of Pennsylvania in 1928. His wife was Marion Lea, an English actress who gained fame in HENRIK IBSEN's plays.

A volume of Mitchell's critical essays, *Understanding America,* was published in 1927. Some of his work appeared under the pseudonym John Philip Varley. For a discussion of his work and a bibliography see Volume II of Arthur H. Quinn's *A History of the American Drama from the Civil War to the Present Day* (1936).

MIXED MARRIAGE, a play in four acts by ST. JOHN ERVINE, published and produced in 1911. Setting: contemporary Belfast.

This tragedy, Ervine's first produced work, immediately established his reputation. It is a PROBLEM PLAY about religious bigotry and the class struggle. Loosely based on history, it dramatizes contemporary conflicts between Catholics and Protestants, and their necessary union to win a labor dispute. The dispute is lost when a bigoted Orangeman discovers that his liberal son plans to marry one of the hated "Papists." They argue bitterly about such a mixed marriage. It is tragically averted during the riots when the girl (as was her historic counterpart) is accidentally killed.

MOBERG, Vilhelm (1898–), Swedish author, was one of the major novelists of his age but was considered only a minor playwright. Yet almost from the beginning of his career he wrote all types of drama, ranging from comedy through PROBLEM PLAYS, folk tragedy, and biblical drama. Highly honored in Sweden, Moberg had most of his plays produced by the National Radio and in the Swedish theatres. *Hustrun* (1929) and *Mans kvinna* (1941) are generally considered his finest stage works. The first is a peasant tragedy; the second, the dramatization of his 1933 novel by the same name and translated as *Fulfillment,* a problem play about marriage and sex that suggests larger conflicts between individual fulfillment and conventional conformity. Other notable Moberg plays are *Våld* (1932), an intense problem play that bears similarities to the works of both HENRIK IBSEN and AUGUST STRINDBERG, and *Vår ofödde son* (1946), a SYMBOLIC work that deals with the devastating consequences of an illegal abortion. Moberg also dramatized novels such as his *De knutna händerna* (1930) and *Rid i natt!* (*Ride This Night!,* 1941); the former deals with peasant life in Moberg's native Småland, while the latter (dramatized in 1942) is a historical play about the seventeenth century. He dramatized his novel about a contemplative elderly American Swede, *Din stund på jorden* (1963), in 1967.

Some of Moberg's novels have appeared in English, but few of his plays are known outside Sweden. Alrik Gustafson's *A History of Swedish Literature* (1961) has a section on Moberg's fiction and drama as well as an extensive bibliography of Swedish books and articles on the writer and his works.

MOELLER, Philip (1880–1958), American playwright and director born in New York, adapted Hungarian plays and wrote comic satires of myth and history for the Washington Square Players, which he helped found. His plays include *Helena's Husband* (1916), a one-acter about Helen's abduction by Paris; *Madame Sand* (1917), a romantic tragedy about George Sand's love affairs; and *Molière* and *Sophie* (both 1919), biographical comedies about the French playwright and the eighteenth-century French opera singer Sophie Arnould. Moeller spent most of his later life as a director and was a leading member of the Theatre Guild. A collection of his drama is *Five Somewhat Historical Plays* (1918).

MOERS, Hermann (1930–), German dramatist, first became popular with *Zur Zeit der Distelblüte* (1959), a Kafkaesque one-acter about prison life. His other works include *Beginn der Badesaison* (1961), a comedy; and *Der kleine Herr Nagel* (1965), a melodrama set in a totalitarian state and featuring a released convict out to revenge himself against the man who denounced him—and now owns his firm. Moers has also written many successful radio plays.

MOGIN, Jean [Georges Elie Fernand] (1921–), Belgian poet and dramatist, achieved prominence with his prize-winning first play, *À Chacun selon sa faim.* Premiered in 1950 at the Théâtre du Vieux-Colombier in Paris, it portrays the revolt of a Spanish abbess whose quest for direct communion with God and absolute purity becomes a fixation. Among Mogin's later plays that portray similar obsessions for purity is *La Fille à la Fontaine* (1955), a peasant love tragedy.

Mogin was born in Brussels and writes in French. In mid-century he was considered to be perhaps the most promising of the young Belgian playwrights.

MÖLLER, Eberhard Wolfgang (1906–), German playwright, authored the most successful of the Nazi-established THINGSPIELE, *Das Frankenburger Würfelspiel* (1936), an ambitious allegorical pageant on the Peasant War and featuring Ferdinand II and his princes, all of whom are condemned for their betrayal of the freedom-loving German peasants. Möller's earlier hit was an agonizing "returning soldier" modernization of the classics, *Douaumont oder Die Heimkehr des Soldaten Odysseus* (*Douaumont, or The Return of the Soldier Odysseus,* 1929), about a survivor of Fort Douaumont who is at first rejected by his wife but becomes reconciled with her after he defeats her suitors.

Later Möller plays are histories presented with a Nazi bias. They include *Kalifornische Tragödie* (1930), about Johann A. Sutter, like BRUNO FRANK's play; *Panamaskandal* (1930), portraying Ferdinand de Lesseps's destruction by speculators; *Rothschild siegt bei Waterloo* (1934), an anti-Semitic dramatization of Nathan Rothschild's success in getting the news of Napoleon's defeat; and *Der Untergang Karthagos* (1938), a verse play showing a disciplined Scipio defeating the corrupt and materialistic Carthaginians. This characteristic attack on the Weimar Republic and the Western democracies he hoped to see destroyed was the last significant play of Möller, whose work stopped with the fall of Hitler.

MOLNÁR [originally Neumann], **Ferenc** (1878–1952), Hungarian playwright and director, was perhaps even better known in his native land as a novelist—particularly for *A Pál-uccai fiúk* (*The Paul Street Boys,* 1907), a novel about adolescents. But his international fame came with his plays. Undoubtedly his greatest hit was LILIOM (1909, later made into the Rodgers and HAMMERSTEIN musical CAROUSEL), although Molnár was enormously successful also with such other drama as *Az ördög* (THE DEVIL, 1907), *A testör* (THE GUARDSMAN, 1911), *Úri divat* (FASHIONS FOR MEN, 1914), *A hattyú* (THE SWAN, 1918), *A vörös malom* (THE RED MILL, 1922; also produced as *Mima*), *Az üvegcipö* (THE GLASS SLIPPER, 1923), and *Játék a kastélyban* (THE PLAY'S THE THING, 1924). Molnár's greatest popularity came in the period between the two world wars, and it rested on his sophisticated, cynical yet sentimental, and often bittersweet comedies. Though his writing is facile, his plays are witty and charming, and they often rise above mere clever stagecraft and dialogue. But Molnár himself stressed his primary aim, in which he succeeded admirably: to entertain audiences and "perhaps induce a tear or two."

The son of a successful Jewish physician, Molnár (Hungarian for "Miller") was born in Budapest. He changed his name for patriotic—not assimilative—reasons, for there was a strong pressure toward Germanization in the Austro-Hungarian Empire, and the future writer wanted Hungarian literature to appear under a Hungarian name. He went to law school and, after completing his course at the Royal University, continued his legal studies in Geneva. But he never practiced the profession. Instead, he turned to journalism, writing sketches and fiction, and went back to Budapest. In that gay city Molnár led an exciting life. He soon became known—no less for his writing than for his love affairs and his personality. His celebrated charm and banter (he had a reputation as a wit and raconteur) quickly made him the center of a circle of admiring artists, writers, and theatre people—including contemporary playwrights. He had written a drama when he was fourteen—a serious juvenile work about alchemy that was produced in a neighbor's basement—but his first professional playwriting consisted of a farce in the French manner, *A doktor úr* (*The Lawyer*), published and produced in Budapest in 1902. It was followed by *Józsi* (1904), which deals with spoiled children and the trouble they cause. But it was his next play, *The Devil,* that made his fame international—a fame that grew with *Liliom,* with which Molnár reached his pinnacle as a dramatist.

Then came *The Guardsman* and the not unsimilar *A farkas* (*The Wolf,* 1913), also produced in English as *The Tale of the Wolf* and as *The Phantom Rival;* presented in America by DAVID BELASCO, this play depicts a wife's dream of her first lover, who now reappears in the various guises in which he once swore romantically to return to her—but he proves singularly unromantic now, a mere "phantom rival" to her jealous husband. Molnár's cynicism is muted in his next play, *Fashions for Men* (which nonetheless contains some delicious satire), and it is modified in a fantasy about casualties in World War I, *A fehér felhö* (*The White Cloud,* 1915); a satire on sham heroics, patriotism, and the birth of myths, this play was written in an army headquarters while Molnár was a war correspondent. His other wartime play, *Farsang* (*Carnival,* 1916), is a cynical love-triangle drama written for his second wife.

Molnár's first postwar play was his popular comedy about royalty, *The Swan.* It was followed by the tragic *Égi és földi szerelem* (*Heavenly and Earthly Love,* 1919), adapted by EDNA ST. VINCENT MILLAY as *Launzi* (1923), under which title it was produced in the United States. Originally it was a novel, and Molnár wrote the dramatization as a vehicle for his third wife; like Hauptmann's THE SUNKEN BELL, it portrays the conflict between prosaic marital and divinely inspired love, Launzi resembling the heroine of Hauptmann's HANNELE'S JOURNEY TO HEAVEN. This was followed by a trio of sardonic one-act comedies that portray adulterous theatre people and deal with conflicts of reality and illusion; they were performed under the collective title *Szinház* (*Theater,* 1921): *Elöjáték Lear Királyhoz* (*A Prologue to "King Lear"*), *Marsall* (*Marshal*), and *Ibolya* (*The Violet*).

After Molnár's spectacular second "devil" play, *The Red Mill,* came two equally notable works, *The Glass Slipper* and *The Play's the Thing.* These were followed by the less successful *Csendélet* (*Still Life,* 1925) and *Riviera* (1926); and by another biting comedy about royalty, *Olympia* (1927), whose princess scorns honorable love with a social inferior, but when blackmailed all too readily agrees to an intrigue with him.

Except for *Józsi* all these plays—some of them important vehicles for Europe's and America's great stars—appeared in *The Plays of Ferenc Molnár* (1929); it was republished in a deluxe edition in 1937 as *All the Plays of Molnár,* with a foreword by DAVID BELASCO—who successfully produced a number of Molnár's plays, as did such other great directors as Max Reinhardt—and a more extensive introduction by Louis Rittenberg. Other plays appeared in his translated collection, *Molnar's Romantic Comedies* (1952): *Actor from Vienna* (a revision of an earlier one-act play);

President, a one-act caricature that originally appeared as *Egy, kettö, három* (*One, Two, Three,* 1926), and satirizes the speed of American business —here personified in a desperate banker who must (almost in a flash) transform a cabdriver into a prominent executive and a nobleman; *Panoptikum* (1944, translated as *Waxworks*), a fantasy-farce set in turn-of-the-century Austria-Hungary; the comedy *Arthur,* originally produced as *Valaki* (*Someone,* 1932); *Blue Danube,* "a sentimental love-story" originally produced as *Delilah* (1937); *A jó tündér* (*The Good Fairy,* 1930), a comedy that was made into a musical by Preston Sturges (1898–1959), *Make a Wish* (1951; music by Hugh Martin); *Anniversary Dinner,* a one-act comedy that appeared originally as *Souper;* and *Game of Hearts,* a three-act comedy written in America, English text by P. G. Wodehouse (1881–). Molnár's other plays include *Harmónia* (*Harmony,* 1932), *A cukrászné* (*A Street in the Suburbs,* 1933), *Az ismeretlen leány* (*The Harbor Girl,* 1934), *Nagy szerelem* (*A Great Love,* 1935), and *Delicate Story* (1940), which first appeared in America. Molnár himself directed the New York production of his last play, also written in the United States, *Miracle in the Mountains* (1947); it was not a success.

Shortly before World War II Molnár emigrated to New York, where he spent the rest of his life. His first marriage was brief, stormy, and unhappy —notable only for the birth of his only child, a daughter who inadvertently inspired the writing of *Liliom.* Molnár's second marriage, equally tempestuous, was to Sári Fedák, a great singer and actress who later became a fanatic Nazi and was imprisoned by the Hungarian government after the war. His final marriage was with another famous actress, the much younger Lili Darvas; though they later lived separately, they maintained amiable relations until he died.

Most of Molnár's plays are available in English in the above-mentioned collections. His autobiography, *Companion in Exile,* was published in 1950, and a series of 1946 *New Yorker* profiles by S. N. BEHRMAN was republished in Behrman's *The Suspended Drawing Room* (1965). Molnár's plays (he wrote about forty) are discussed seriatim in Frank W. Chandler's *Modern Continental Playwrights* (1931) and in Rittenberg's aforementioned introduction; EDMUND WILSON's *New Yorker* piece on Hungary (June 4, 1966) includes extensive commentaries on 1960's productions of Molnár's plays, specifically those of *The Devil* and *Fashions for Men.*

MONKHOUSE, Allan [Noble] (1858–1938), English novelist and dramatist, belonged to the Manchester school, whose most distinguished playwright was STANLEY HOUGHTON. He wrote some twenty plays, which evidence his versatility, but only a few of them were successful. These include his antiwar drama THE CONQUERING HERO (1923); *Sons and Fathers* (1926), which portrays a frustrated idealist in industry; and *The Grand Cham's Diamond* (1918), a comic one-act fantasy about a woman's romantic—if brief—dreams when a diamond is hurled into her house: "Well, I 'ad my bit o' fun for onct," she concludes. Monkhouse's first plays were collected as *Four Tragedies* (1913): *Reaping the Whirlwind, Resentment, The Stricklands,* and *The Hayling.* His masterpiece is foreshadowed in his three *War Plays* (1916): *Shamed Life, Night Watches,* and *The Choice.*

MONNA VANNA, a play in three acts by MAURICE MAETERLINCK, published and produced in 1902. Setting: Pisa and a camp outside, at the end of the fifteenth century.

Though full of passion and intensity, this once-popular play lacks Maeterlinck's characteristic stress on atmosphere and SYMBOLISM. He is more concerned, in this variation on the apocalyptic Judith-Holofernes story, with such moral and philosophical problems as the sacrificing of the individual for social good and the meaning of life, love, and honor.

Pisa is besieged and desperate. Prinzivalle, the commander of the Florentines, offers to save the city if Monna Vanna (Giovanna), the Pisan commander's beautiful wife, will visit him that night— "alone, and clad only in her mantle." Over the objections of her appalled husband, but supported by his old father, she accepts the offer. In his tent Prinzivalle is revealed as a cultivated mercenary about to be deposed in a Florentine conspiracy— as well as Monna Vanna's childhood sweetheart. Without molesting her, he tells her of his lifelong adoration of her. At dawn she takes him to Pisa to save him from the Florentine conspirators. But her maddened husband refuses to believe in her innocence. Infuriated by his father's understanding trust in her and by the presence of Prinzivalle, he orders the latter's execution. Monna Vanna, repelled by her husband's distrust and touched by Prinzivalle's constancy, decides to escape with him. Making the "confession" her hysterical husband demands, she obtains Prinzivalle's prison-cell keys by vowing to kill him herself. "Yes, it has been a bad dream," she tells the unsuspecting husband, with whom she is now disillusioned; "but the beautiful one will begin. The beautiful one will begin . . ."

MONT, Paul de (1895–1950), Belgian playwright, was a significant contributor to the Flemish theatre in the 1920's. His attack on false patriotism in the war drama *Nuances* (1925) was the more poignant because he himself had been crippled in battle. Also successful was his modern Passion play *Het Geding Van Ons Heer* (1925).

MONTHERLANT, Henry de (1896–), French writer, was a famous novelist, essayist, and poet before he made his reputation as a playwright. It was with *La Reine morte* (QUEEN AFTER DEATH, 1942) that Montherlant at forty-six became a prominent dramatist—soon France's most important post-World War II dramatist in the estimation of some critics, most of whom reacted strongly to his traditionally structured but stimulating

Henry de Montherlant. *(French Cultural Services)*

and provocatively inconsistent plays. Though they have remained little known in the English-speaking world, his plays have been regularly produced in France. They are stark and discursive, in the seventeenth-century manner of Racine, rather than action-packed, as might be supposed from their historical (usually Renaissance) settings and Montherlant's own versatile life and activities, which ranged from politics to athletics. Though his writings appear static and conservative, they have outraged his readers—yet have continued to fascinate Parisian audiences. In 1960 Montherlant was elected to the French Academy.

He was born in Paris to a family that traced its ancestry to Catalonian aristocracy. At the age of eight he completed his first novel. He was intrigued by the Roman age, whose ideals of valor and magnanimity appealed more to him than the Christian ones of self-abnegation and pacifism. Early in life he rejected Catholicism, but remained as fascinated by it as by classical and medieval ritual. In 1912 Montherlant was expelled from school because of a passionate friendship with another adolescent boy. Soon thereafter he was introduced to bullfighting, a major interest expressed in his 1926 novel *Les Bestiaires* (translated as both *The Matador* and *The Bullfighters*) and in the rhythm of much of his drama. He read voraciously, and in 1916, as soon as his parents died, he enlisted in the army. Refusing an officer's commission, he served as a private and was seriously wounded. Nonetheless he was eager to return to the front, but did not recuperate in time. In the years following the armistice Montherlant devoted his energies to sports—and to the memory of his army comrades, by helping in the construction of the Douaumont War Cemetery. The publication in 1924 of his books on both these subjects (*Les Olympiques* and *Chant funèbre pour les morts de Verdun*) made him famous. But disliking celebrity, Montherlant spent much of the next decade traveling in North Africa and elsewhere. During those years he was gored by a bull and contracted various illnesses—traumatic mishaps to the confirmed hedonist and sportsman. Despair was reflected in much of Montherlant's subsequent work, until "salvation" came with research for his later novels. During World War II Montherlant again served at the front and was again wounded. Though some of his subsequent work was banned by the Nazis, toward whom his behavior remained coldly correct, Montherlant was charged by a few compatriots with defeatism and excessive fascination with power tactics—the natural reaction of an admirer of classical Romanism and Nietzschean philosophy. After the war Montherlant withdrew from politics and society, devoting his time to scholarship and writing. It was in that period that his plays appeared.

The first of them, *L'Exil,* had been written as early as 1914 though it remained unpublished until 1929. Inspired by a friend's enlistment, it has remained unproduced except for a scene staged in 1934. *Pasiphaé* (1936), a dramatic poem, was produced in 1938. It was only in 1942 with *Queen After Death,* however, that Montherlant became a playwright. The popular contemporary "bourgeois" tragedy *Fils de personne* (NO MAN'S SON, 1943)—its sequel, *Demain fera jour* (TOMORROW THE DAWN, 1949), was less successful—was followed by MALATESTA (1946), which is atypically dramatic and colorful. Montherlant's next play, *Le Maître de Santiago* (THE MASTER OF SANTIAGO, 1947), was the first of the self-styled *"autos sacramentales"* that conclude with PORT-ROYAL (1954). The second in this "Catholic trilogy" is the partly autobiographical *La Ville dont le prince est un enfant* (1951), which dramatizes Montherlant's expulsion from school. Its protagonist is an abbé who indignantly tries to stop the indiscreetly fervent if Platonic friendship of two adolescent boys he loves, who are thereupon expelled; the school's superior exposes the abbé's real motives, but suggests the possibilities of redemption, from the love of man to that of God, "that last and tremendous Love compared with which everything else is nothing." *Celles qu'on prend dans ses bras* (1950) also deals with sexual obsession, this time among five people. Further variations on spiritual and sexual themes appear in Montherlant's remaining plays: *Brocéliande* (1956); *Don Juan* (1958), a farce about the sixty-four-year-old lover whose death mask, as he finally meets Ana, adheres to and merges with his face; *Le Cardinal d'Espagne* (*The Cardinal of Spain,* 1960), and *La Guerre civile* (*The Civil War,* 1965).

Most of these plays were produced by the Comédie-Française, where Montherlant's drama became a staple. This is surprising, for not only Montherlant's manner but his matter are anomalous in modern drama. Though much of it portrays Catholic themes, his drama is not traditionally religious, like that of PAUL CLAUDEL. Furthermore, Montherlant is scornful of his audiences, flaunting all rules of consistency and making concessions neither to comfortable conventions of REALISM nor to the familiar and fashionable mid-century theatre of the ABSURD. Instead of action, long allusive and occasionally declamatory speeches portray psychological conflict. These speeches, written in a sometimes lyrical prose, contain much and often epigrammatic wisdom. They obviously excited his audiences, whose strong but opposing reactions were stimulated by an apparent conflict in Montherlant's outlook. He outraged women by denouncing them in novels and essays, yet he often portrayed them sympathetically as models of sensitivity and self-sacrifice. He opposed marriage as a byproduct of romantic love, which Montherlant scorned as much as he did women—though he was a heterosexual sensualist. Similarly paradoxical, he both exalted and damned his spent old protagonists such as Alvaro in *The Master of Santiago* and Ferrante in *Queen After Death,* who renounce the world. The agnostic Montherlant's dramatizations of the spiritual struggle are as mystifying as is his preoccupation with it. What little action there is in the plays almost invariably occurs in the resolution, in a final conversion to a mystifying—sometimes affirmative, sometimes despairing—cosmic insight.

Montherlant's plays have been published singly and in collections, and many of them have been translated. Jonathan Griffin's edition of Montherlant's *The Master of Santiago and Four Other Plays* (1951) has a critical preface and includes *Queen After Death, Malatesta, No Man's Son,* and *Tomorrow the Dawn.* Studies of his life and work are John Cruickshank's *Montherlant* (1964), John Batchelor's *Existence and Imagination, the Theatre of Henry de Montherlant* (1967), Robert B. Johnson's *Henry de Montherlant* (1968), and Lucille F. Becker's *Henry de Montherlant: A Critical Biography* (1970).

MOODY, William Vaughn (1869–1910), American dramatist, poet, scholar, and educator, was one of the first serious native dramatists. He was most successful with THE GREAT DIVIDE (1906), originally produced as *The Sabine Woman.* His second though earlier-conceived prose play, THE FAITH HEALER (1909), was not nearly as popular, though some critics have ranked it above the other play. Both are characterized by melodrama and sentimentality, and despite their frequently praised language they sound decidedly old-fashioned. Nonetheless, both plays confront and deal intelligently with weighty questions, and they do so in actions and words that are superior to anything that had hitherto been seen on American stages.

Moody's other dramatic work consists of a religious verse trilogy that celebrates the rebellion of man against an imperfect God, and his eventual unity with an evolved, more perfect divinity. While they were unproduced during Moody's lifetime and continued to remain little known thereafter, all three plays have been highly praised by Moody scholars. *The Masque of Judgment* (1900), the trilogy's first play, was envisioned by Moody as "a kind of Hebrew Götterdammerung"; it deals with Judgment Day, and its main characters are the archangels Raphael and Uriel. *The Fire-Bringer* (1904) dramatizes Prometheus's rebellion against the gods, his bringing the divine fire to Deukalion and Pyrrha after the flood, and his punishment by Zeus. Only the first act of *The Death of Eve* (1912)—Moody also wrote a narrative poem by that name and on the same theme—the last part of the trilogy, was completed; Eve, too, is portrayed as a rebel against an imperfect God: returning to Paradise with Cain after her expiatory suffering, she seeks reconciliation with a more perfect God.

Moody was born in Indiana. He attended Harvard University, where he also did graduate work and taught before he was appointed to the English faculty of the University of Chicago. He edited the works of Bunyan, Milton, Coleridge, and Scott, and wrote many lyric poems as well as two books (with Robert Morss Lovett) on English literature. In 1902 he gave up teaching in order to devote himself exclusively to writing poetry and drama—and to travel. He married shortly before his untimely death of a brain tumor.

The Poems and Plays of William Vaughn Moody (1912) were edited, in two volumes, by John M. Manly. Two book-length studies of Moody relate his biography and examine his work in detail: David D. Henry's *William Vaughn Moody: A Study* (1934) and Martin Halpern's *William Vaughn Moody* (1964); both contain extensive bibliographies.

MOON FOR THE MISBEGOTTEN, A, a play in four acts by EUGENE O'NEILL, written in 1943, produced in 1947, and published in 1952. Setting: a dilapidated farmhouse in Connecticut, September 1923.

This, O'Neill's last play, is a biography of and an elegy to his brother, James, and something like a sequel to LONG DAY'S JOURNEY INTO NIGHT. The first act is broadly farcical, and the whole play abounds in cliché situations. But there is great poignancy in the portrayal of the "misbegotten" lovers' tragic revelations, as the grotesquely built maternal virgin fathoms the emotional (soon to be followed by the physical) death of Tyrone, haunted by Oedipal furies of guilt and self-aversion. So moving is this portrayal that, according to Lawrence Langner (*The Magic Curtain*), the actors wept at the first reading, one of them commenting prophetically—for the play had catastrophic censorship and production problems—"We're *all* crying now. I guess it will be the management's time to cry later."

Josie and Phil Hogan, a twenty-eight-year-old almost freakishly oversized Irishwoman and her conniving father, affectionately banter each other about his stinginess, her notorious promiscuity, and her love for James Tyrone, Jr., their dissipated landlord. To protect their tenancy, Hogan suggests that Josie seduce Tyrone when there is "a moon in the sky to fill him with poetry and a quart of bad hootch inside of him," but Josie bitterly reflects that he prefers Broadway tarts to "an ugly cow" like herself. Tyrone and Hogan are great friends, and when he arrives, they begin exchanging the usual insults, which they relish. Then, in a highly farcical scene (related in *Long Day's Journey Into Night*), father and daughter ridicule their millionaire neighbor, who comes to complain about their trespassing hogs. At night, Hogan comes home drunk, telling Josie that Tyrone sold the farm to the millionaire. She is furious at Tyrone's duplicity and now is willing to go along with her father's plot, but when Tyrone comes she realizes that he was only riling her father about the farm. Tyrone's love for Josie soon becomes evident, but it is interlarded with profound self-loathing. In her compassion and love for him, she drops her pride and admits that she is a virgin (her boasts compensate for her unlovable self-image) and now passionately wants him. As she pulls him to her room, he is tormented by an ever-growing memory and suddenly he becomes a crude and brutal cynic. When Josie, terribly hurt, brings him to his senses, he is ready to leave: he does not want to poison her and their love. Josie gives up her passionate longing; she wishes to relieve his suffering and listens as he proceeds with his long confession and self-abasement. Unable to face losing his mother, he had resumed his heavy drinking when she fell ill. On the train from the West Coast after her death, he nightly caroused and entertained a whore in his drawing room while his mother lay in a coffin in the baggage car: "It was as if I wanted revenge—because I'd been left alone—because I knew I was lost, without any hope left." He was too drunk even to attend her funeral. Comforting him and promising him "a dawn that won't creep over dirty windowpanes but will wake in the sky like a promise of God's peace in the soul's dark sadness," Josie provides something like absolution to Tyrone and lullabies him to sleep: "God forgive me, it's a fine end to all my scheming, to sit here with the dead hugged to my breast, and the silly mug of the moon grinning down, enjoying the joke!" At dawn she is still sitting, sorrowing at his deathlike exhaustion, with Tyrone sleeping against her breast. When he awakes, he gratefully remembers the beauty of the night they spent and she knows that he must now leave—and die. Hogan returns, admitting that he had tricked her, because he hoped they would marry and both become happy. Father and daughter resume their old banter—"A ginger-haired, crooked old goat like you to be playing Cupid!"—but as the curtain falls, Josie looks tenderly and sadly down the road: "May you have your wish and die in your sleep soon, Jim, darling. May you rest forever in forgiveness and peace."

MOON IN THE YELLOW RIVER, THE, a play in three acts by DENIS JOHNSTON, published and produced in 1931. Setting: an old fort used as a dwelling in Ireland, September 1927.

The title of Johnston's best-known play comes from Ezra Pound's version of the Chinese poem sung at the second-act climax. A mixture of tragedy, farce, and melodrama, the play has sensitive characterizations of various people who face the problems of religion and industrialization.

Tausch, a kindly German directing the installation of a power plant, visits a distinguished but embittered engineer. That night various local rebels plan to blow up the power plant. "He has outraged the sacred person of our beloved mother," Ireland, they say of Tausch, who calls them "machine wreckers" and argues for progress. The plot appears to fail. The insurgents' leader sings about Li-Po, who "tried to embrace a Moon / In the Yellow River," when one of his men suddenly shoots him—to spare him the misery of jail, "the tomfoolery of law and justice and the torment they call 'Prepare to meet your God!' " Tausch does not understand. The engineer explains, "You'd always have been disturbing the waters with your machinery and drowning his moon in mud," and he refuses to prefer murder charges. The play ends with the explosion going off, after all. It also brings about the engineer's reconciliation with his daughter, whom he has hated and refused to educate because at birth her life rather than her mother's was saved, in accord with Catholic dogma.

MOON OF THE CARIBBEES, AND SIX OTHER PLAYS OF THE SEA, THE (1919), by EUGENE O'NEILL. First publication of IN THE ZONE, WHERE THE CROSS IS MADE, and THE ROPE; revised texts of THE MOON OF THE CARIBBEES, THE LONG VOYAGE HOME, and ILE; also contains BOUND EAST FOR CARDIFF. Reissued in 1940 as *The Long Voyage Home: Seven Plays of the Sea.*

MOON OF THE CARIBBEES, THE, a one-act play by EUGENE O'NEILL, published and produced in 1918. Setting: a ship deck; early twentieth century, in the years preceding World War I.

A revised text of this play, the first in the S.S. GLENCAIRN cycle, was published in THE MOON OF THE CARIBBEES, AND SIX OTHER PLAYS OF THE SEA.

On a moonlit night aboard the steamer *Glencairn* anchored off a West Indies island, native women with contraband rum visit the seamen. "A melancholy negro chant, faint and far-off, drifts, crooning, over the water" throughout the play. It brings up "beastly memories" (subject of IN THE ZONE) haunting the sailor Smitty, who takes the liquor but does not participate in the long debauchery that ends in a brawl. Smitty finally goes into the forecastle, where he can drink more and not hear the native chant, "the mood of the moonlight made audible."

MOORE, George [Augustus] (1852–1933), Irish writer, is best known for his poetry and fiction, particularly his novel *Esther Waters* (1894), which he dramatized in 1911. He also wrote a few other plays. The first of them, *The Strike at Arlingford,* was originally produced by Grein's Independent

Theatre in London in 1894. More important was Moore's work with WILLIAM BUTLER YEATS and EDWARD MARTYN. His vigorous publicity helped them establish the Irish Literary Theatre, for which he rewrote Martyn's *The Tale of a Town* as *The Bending of the Bough,* a comedy presented as the theatre's third production, in 1900. The next year it produced his *Diarmuid and Grania* (published in 1951), on which Moore collaborated with Yeats. Moore had a hand, too, in the composition of Martyn's *The Heather Field* and *Maeve.*

The son of a wealthy Member of Parliament, Moore as a young man studied art in Paris. There he met ÉMILE ZOLA, who was to influence Moore's later writing. His collaboration with Yeats ended in a quarrel, after which Moore ceased writing for the Abbey Theatre. With humor but considerable asperity he described Yeats, LADY GREGORY, and other former associates in his autobiographical trilogy, *Hail and Farewell* (1911–14).

Among book-length studies of Moore are Joseph Hone's *The Life of George Moore* (1936) and Malcolm J. Brown's *George Moore: A Reconsideration* (1956).

MORAX, René (1873–1963), Swiss director and playwright, was his country's first notable French-writing dramatist. With his brother, Jean, he in 1908 founded the Théâtre du Jorat in Mézières, near Lausanne—an open-air festival playhouse that became western Switzerland's leading theatrical center. It achieved international renown in 1921 with his *Le Roi David,* with music by Arthur Honegger. The play has been contrasted with RICHARD BEER-HOFMANN's uncompleted trilogy: both deal with the same material, but Morax's portrayal emphasizes the historical and the human more than the ideal and the heroic.

Morax and his brother wrote a popular festival play, *La Dime* (1903, also titled *Le Drame des pommes de terre*), and directed the 1905 Vine-dressers festival play at Vevey, for which they wrote a libretto. In 1908 Morax joined avant-garde playwrights and wrote a peasant drama, *Henriette.* With Honnegger he collaborated on another play for the Jorat theatre, the biblical *Judith* (1925). Among Morax's other legend plays for that theatre is his *La Servante d'Evolène* (1937), and he also wrote puppet plays and novels.

MORE STATELY MANSIONS, an uncompleted play by EUGENE O'NEILL, produced in 1962 and published in 1964. Setting: Massachusetts, 1832–41.

The fourth play in O'Neill's A TALE OF THE POSSESSORS SELF-DISPOSSESSED continues the lives of characters in A TOUCH OF THE POET. Because O'Neill had extensively revised the long draft of this play by 1943, he did not then burn it with his other scripts. Inadvertently, this unfinished work also escaped destruction later. After shortening it to three acts, KARL GIEROW produced it in his Swedish Royal Dramatic Theatre and helped prepare its publication. The title comes from Oliver Wendell Holmes's "The Chambered Nautilus" (1858).

Simon Harford, encouraged by his sensual wife, Sara, loses his "touch of the poet." He frightens his mother, Deborah, by laughing at her romantic delusions of past glory and power. He takes over his father's business and becomes a ruthless Napoleon of industry, while Sara takes over the Harford mansion, which she covets. Deborah is content to have her grandchildren and her garden retreat, with its mysterious summerhouse. But her battle with Sara over Simon continues and (with the love-hate relationships among the three principals) constitutes the major conflict of the play. Simon's and Sara's greed and lust grow monstrously: they ruin their competitors and scandalize all with their debaucheries. Then, yearning for idyllic childhood love, Simon returns to the mother he has spurned, and makes her unlock the summerhouse she had always refused to open. Sara repentantly decides to give Simon up so that he can again become a poet and write the "book that will save the world and free men from the curse of greed in them!" Deborah, feeling beaten by Sara's sacrifice, yields Simon. She goes mad, and Sara, "with a fierce, passionate, possessive tenderness," becomes Simon's mother-wife.

MORGAN, Charles [Langbridge] (1894–1958), English novelist and essayist, also wrote three dramas and a radio play (*The Confession*). Born in Kent, Morgan became a naval cadet at thirteen. In the latter part of World War I he was a military prisoner. Subsequently he attended Oxford, and after receiving his degree in 1921 he joined the staff of the London *Times.* He became assistant drama critic, and after A. B. Walkley's death succeeded him, serving as that newspaper's drama critic from 1926 to 1939. Morgan was, as he himself noted, a mystic concerned with "the conflict between the spirit and the flesh." His essays and even more his novels had a following among discriminating readers—although he was also considered pretentious. Morgan's plays were less popular.

The first of the plays, *The Flashing Stream* (1938), deals with a group of officers occupied with a scientific invention; isolated, they are joined and their lives are complicated by two women, one good and the other bad. In 1952 Morgan dramatized and produced his 1949 novel about a man's remorse and redemption, *The River Line.* It was only with THE BURNING GLASS (1953) that he achieved a measure of success as a dramatist. While it is as much of an ideological tract as the others (and is also prefaced by an explanatory essay), its plot is suspenseful—and the problem it dramatizes remains persistently relevant.

For a detailed analysis of Morgan's writings, see Henry Charles Duffin's *The Novels and Plays of Charles Morgan* (1959).

MORSELLI, Ercole Luigi (1882–1921), Italian dramatist, wrote three notable tragedies, the last of which appeared posthumously. In all of them mythic themes express his concern with contemporary problems, particularly the emptiness of the kind of sensuous life glorified by GABRIELLE D'ANNUNZIO. Most successful was Morselli's tragicomedy *Orione* (1910); its title hero, a great hunter who derides and vanquishes whatever he can, is himself killed by an insignificant scorpion. The hero of Morselli's *Glauco* (1919) leaves his happy home and his beloved, seeking glory elsewhere; he returns unfulfilled and finds that she has died for the love of him. The posthumous *Belfagor* (1930) is a dramatization of Machiavelli's story about the title character, the archdevil who manages to marry a mortal but fails to win her love: she remains faithful to her sailor sweetheart.

Born in Pesaro but raised in Florence, where he studied medicine, Morselli traveled widely to regain his health. Nonetheless, he died early of tuberculosis and enjoyed only brief glory with the success of *Orione*. A chapter on his life and work appears in Isaac Goldberg's *The Drama of Transition* (1922).

MORTIMER, John [Clifford] (1923–), English playwright, practiced law and wrote six novels before he became known in 1958 with his first play, THE DOCK BRIEF. It won the Italia Prize, made Mortimer a dramatist, and—with his other early one-acter, WHAT SHALL WE TELL CAROLINE? (1958)—has remained among his most successful works. Both illustrate the oft-quoted preface to his first play collection: Comedy is "the only thing worth writing in this despairing age, provided the comedy is truly on the side of the lonely, the neglected, the unsuccessful, and plays its part in the war against established rules and against the imposing of an arbitrary code of behaviour upon individual and unpredictable human beings" (*Three Plays,* 1958; the third play is *I Spy*). Again describing his characteristic drama, he noted that his comedy is distinctly *not* "about successful lawyers, brilliant criminals, wise schoolmasters, or families where the children can grow up without silence and without regret." But if Mortimer's drama expresses rebellion against the Establishment, it does so in conventional ways. His "lonely . . . neglected . . . unsuccessful" characters are serio-comic types recalling those of Charles Dickens. Sentimentality and the maudlin are kept at bay only by Mortimer's gift of humor and his grotesque situations.

Mortimer was born in London, attended Oxford University, and worked in documentary films during World War II. Though he spent "formative years" in that occupation, Mortimer believed that "documentary films bear as little relation to art as they do to life, existing uninterestingly between the two like the instructions you get with do-it-yourself garden furniture." It was the persistence of a radio producer that started him on writing drama, and it was over the radio and on television that much of his drama first appeared.

His humor and unusual situations are noticeable particularly in the short plays, in which Mortimer has excelled. Here he succeeds frequently in sustaining interest in the featured caricatures. In *I Spy,* a detective finally will marry his employer's victim, whom he is stalking—a woman as "lonely" and "neglected" as himself; the title work of *Lunch Hour and Other Plays* (1960), produced in 1957, depicts a noon-hour tryst that fails because the literal-minded girl insists on living out the story her would-be lover told his landlady so that they could get a room; similarly frustrated people with little lies inhabit the other pieces in the collection: *David and Broccoli, Collect Your Hand Baggage,* and *Call Me a Liar.*

Mortimer's talents function less well on a broader canvas. In *The Wrong Side of the Park* (1960), his first full-length play, a suburban matron's much-touted earlier happiness is revealed to be nothing but guilt feelings about her first husband. *Two Stars for Comfort* (1962) features a buoyant hotel proprietor who is exposed as an aging, deserted, and empty man. The plot of *The Judge* (1967), a locquacious drama, is reminiscent of Dürrenmatt's less comic THE VISIT. Mortimer's farce *Cat Among the Pigeons!* (1969) is an adaptation of *Un Fil à la patte,* a farce by GEORGES FEYDEAU, whose *La Puce à l'oreille* Mortimer translated as *A Flea in Her Ear* (1966). *Come As You Are!* (1970), a quartet of one-acters titled after their different London district settings, portrays various extramarital relationships in moods ranging from farce to the macabre. *A Voyage Round My Father* (1970) in a series of domestic episodes provides a witty and affectionate portrayal of Mortimer's parent.

Aside from being a playwright and a novelist, Mortimer was a drama critic for the *Evening Standard*. With his wife Penelope, a novelist and a critic, he wrote a travel book, *With Love and Lizards* (1957). See Mortimer's prefaces to his play collections, and John Russell Taylor's *Anger and After* (retitled *The Angry Theatre* in America, revised edition 1969).

MOSEL, Tad (1922–), American playwright, made his reputation as a television writer after he failed to achieve success Off-Broadway. But he returned to the legitimate theatre with his Pulitzer Prize-winning *All the Way Home* (1960), a dramatization of James Agee's moving posthumous autobiographical novel of Southern life, *A Death in the Family* (1957), which had won the Pulitzer Prize in 1958. Mosel was born in Ohio and studied at the Yale School of Drama.

MOTHER COURAGE AND HER CHILDREN (*Mutter Courage und ihre Kinder*), a play in twelve scenes by BERTOLT BRECHT (music by Paul Dessau), produced in 1941 and published in 1949. Setting: Sweden, Poland, and Germany; 1624–36.

One of Brecht's most frequently produced works and perhaps his masterpiece, this EPIC "chronicle play of the Thirty Years' War" is very loosely based on works by the seventeenth-century German author Hans Jakob Grimmelshausen. Brecht meant his "merchant-mother" to portray a villainous war profiteer. Instead, audiences have been moved by her maternal suffering and "little man's" pluck in enduring life's adversities and the horrors of war. Even the speech Brecht subsequently inserted at the end, after she loses her last child—"I must get back to business"—has not diminished audiences' sympathy for Mother Courage.

Scenes 1 through 3. Mother Courage (Anna Fierling), accompanied by her mute daughter, Kattrin Haupt, follows the Swedish armies in her mobile canteen, pulled by her sons, Eilif Nojocki and Swiss Cheese Fejos. All her children are by different fathers, and she received her nickname, she tells a recruiting sergeant, because "fearing commercial ruin" she braved a bombardment with her canteen: "I had no choice." Though she approves of war for the business it brings, she will not allow her sons to be recruited. But while she is momentarily occupied, Eilif is persuaded to enlist. Courage tells Kattrin, "Now you must help your brother pull the wagon." A couple of years later, haggling with an officer's cook, she is overjoyed when she accidentally meets Eilif on his big day. He is being rewarded for having appropriated the cattle of some peasants, at the risk of his life. Proudly Courage joins her brave son, who is dancing a saber dance, in the "Song of the Woman and the Soldier"—and then boxes his ears: "Didn't I teach you not to risk your life?" Three years later Courage, along with some Finnish troops, is taken prisoner. With her are Kattrin, Swiss Cheese (now an army paymaster), and a brash camp-following whore, Yvette Pottier, who sings "The Fraternization Song," which tells of her ruin by the officer's cook. This cook, accompanied by a frightened Protestant chaplain, comes to court Courage. They discuss the war, Courage agrees to help disguise the chaplain, and Kattrin innocently primps herself with Yvette's garish clothes. Swiss Cheese is hauled away; trying to escape, he refuses to betray his trust and attempts to save the regimental cashbox. Having seduced an ancient colonel, Yvette offers to lease the canteen and negotiate the purchase of Swiss Cheese's life. In a highly dramatic scene, Courage haggles over the price until it is too late: a distant roll of drums announces her son's execution. His corpse is brought in: to save Kattrin and herself, Courage now must pretend she does not know her son. As the sheet is drawn back, she looks down and shakes her head, mutely.

Scenes 4 through 8. Mother Courage prepares to lodge a complaint against injustice, as does an angry young soldier. She persuades him of the futility of "little" anger and sings a "Song of the Great Capitulation" interspersing it with comments that counsel opportunism and ironically cite success clichés. Finally aware of the futility of his anger and of ideals in this world, and unable to muster the necessary "great" (revolutionary) anger, the soldier drops his complaint—and Courage forgets about hers. Some years later, "General Tilly's victory at Magdeburg costs Mother Courage four officers' shirts," which are confiscated to bandage civilian casualties. When she worries that peace will "break out," the chaplain advises her to keep buying goods: the continuation of war will always be assured by

Mother Courage and Her Children. Helene Weigel (Brecht's wife) as Mother Courage in the Berliner Ensemble production, 1949. (Harry Croner, *Ullstein Bilderdienst,* Berlin)

kings, the emperor, and the pope. Sent to buy goods, Kattrin is attacked by soldiers. Courage consoles her, but when cannon shots mark the "historic occasion" of General Tilly's burial, she breaks out with a curse: "It's a historic moment all right—they scarred my daughter's face," and now she will never get a man. The war has made Kattrin mute ("a soldier stuck something in her mouth when she was little") and taken Courage's sons: "Damn the war!" But soon she continues, undaunted, pulling her laden wagon with Kattrin and the chaplain: "I won't have you spoil my war. They say it destroys the weak, but they can't survive in peacetime, either. Only war feeds its people better." War is a business, she concludes, "except that it's in lead rather than cheese." When peace momentarily descends, the cook returns—to the jealous annoyance of the chaplain, who calls Courage a "battlefield hyena." Yvette, now the wealthy widow of a colonel, also returns. Finally Courage's son Eilif appears briefly. He has just repeated his former heroics; but because it is now peacetime, Eilif is executed for looting.

Scenes 9 through 12. War soon resumes, and Courage, accompanied by the cook, continues her travels with the canteen wagon. In 1634, after sixteen years of devastating religious warfare, the cook decides to go home. Though business is bad and she is willing to marry him, Courage declines his proposal. She will not leave her helpless Kattrin, even after the cook's persuasive "Song of the Wise and Good" (expanded from "The

Song of Solomon" in THE THREEPENNY OPERA), accompanied by homely, practical reflections. Now Courage has only Kattrin to help pull her wagon. While Courage is in town buying supplies, Catholic troops prepare a surprise night attack on Halle. Overcome by the thought of the impending bloodbath, Kattrin climbs a peasant's roof and starts to drum a warning to the town. The kindhearted mute groans and weeps in torment as soldiers threaten her and the canteen wagon. But she does not stop her drumming and, though she is finally shot while doing it, she succeeds in alerting the town. Toward morning, Courage sings a farewell lullaby to Kattrin and pays the peasants for her burial. Hearing the departing, singing troops, she prepares to resume her travels. Bereft of her children and all alone in the world, Mother Courage hitches herself to her wagon and continues to follow the army.

MOTHER, THE (*Die Mutter*), a play in fifteen scenes by BERTOLT BRECHT (music by Hanns Eisler), published and produced in 1932. Setting: Russia, 1905–17.

Subtitled "Life of the Revolutionist Pelagea Vlassova from Tver" and freely adapted from the novel by MAXIM GORKY, this play is another of Brecht's antitheatrical, didactic works. He insisted at length (in notes to the play) that it "is a piece of antimetaphysical, materialistic, non-Aristotelian drama" requiring "EPIC" productions like the Theater am Schiffbauerdamm (Berlin) premiere, in which the lead was played by his wife, Helene Weigel. Despite Brecht's theories, Pelagea is a moving, human portrayal.

A mother bemoans the poverty that forces her to serve her son watery soup. But "what can I, Pelagea Vlassova, the widow of a worker and the mother of a worker, do?" she asks the audience. She disapproves when her son brings other revolutionaries to the apartment. The police search it, leaving her home in a shambles. Since her son is known to the police, however, she volunteers to distribute his strike leaflets. Eventually impressed with the justice of the workers' demands, she is fully persuaded of the cause when she witnesses the brutality opposing a peaceful demonstration. She becomes an active revolutionist and teaches her neighbors the principles of Marxism. This ideal becomes the bond that forever unites mother and son, "a great thing, common to many men." He escapes from Siberia and is shot, but though grief-stricken, the mother rejects her pious neighbors' consolations. Resignation to God is absurd, and she shows them how man's only hope lies in the immortal Party. During the 1917 antiwar demonstrations, Pelagea, now an old woman, is beaten up. But her faith in the workers' future is unswerving: "The victims of today are the victors of tomorrow / And *never* will be *immediately!*"

MOTHERLOVE (*Moderskärlek*), a one-act play by AUGUST STRINDBERG, published in 1893 and produced in 1909. Setting: a fisherman's cottage in a contemporary Swedish seaside resort.

This short, bitter work might be considered an epilogue to THE FATHER, while the character of the mother prefigures that of the mother in THE PELICAN.

A sensitive young actress is virtually the prisoner of her neurotically possessive mother, a common prostitute who thus avenges herself on the daughter's father. When the daughter learns the truth and is given a chance of success, however, she is too strongly conditioned and dependent to leave the gloating mother.

MOUNTAIN GIANTS, THE (*I giganti della montagna*), a three-act fragment by LUIGI PIRANDELLO, produced in 1937 and published in 1938. Setting: a contemporary Italian town at the foot of a mountain, and the mountain.

This, Pirandello's last play, is a "cosmographic drama [which] carries the essence of his philosophy," George Freedley wrote in his foreword to the English translation (1958) by Marta Abba. He did not live to finish it. "Insofar as I am able to reconstruct it from what my father told me about the plot" two nights before he died, Stefano Pirandello completed it by writing a fourth act or "moment." In Italy this SYMBOLIC part-fantasy has been produced both in its unfinished and in its four-act version.

Since their play failed with the people "in the world below," the Countess Ilse and her husband lead their seedy theatrical troupe to a villa in an almost deserted town. Its sole inhabitants are the outcast *"Scalognati,"* led by a magician; they create apparitions and pursue a life of dreams and fantasy. Feeling that they no longer need ordinary human beings, the troupe and several *Scalognati* decide to perform on the mountain before bestial giants, "the rulers of the world." These giants (who never appear in the play) are too busy to be concerned with art. But they allow the troupe to perform their play before the servants and workmen hired to carry out the giants' mighty designs. Countess Ilse needs the recognition of the rest of the world to give meaning to her performance, and starts to act. The hired help are unappreciative of poetry, and kill her. The magician understands, however, that no one is really to blame. "For it was not poetry which had been refused," Stefano Pirandello explains; "it was just that the poor, fanatical slaves of life, who today have no taste for spiritual things but who someday might very well have, had innocently killed the fanatical slaves of Art the way they would break rebellious puppets; for these slaves of Art are unable to speak to man because they have excluded themselves from life," from reality.

MOURNING BECOMES ELECTRA, a trilogy in three parts (thirteen acts) by EUGENE O'NEILL, published and produced in 1931. Setting: a New England residence and a clipper ship, 1865–66.

In his published "Working Notes" to this major play, O'Neill wrote that he had attempted to reproduce the "Greek sense of fate [in a modern play], which an intelligent audience of today, possessed by no belief in gods or supernatural retribution, could accept and be moved by." In this reinterpretation of the classic legend of Atreus, first dramatized in Aeschylus's *Oresteia,* Electra (Lavinia) becomes the agent of retribution as well as the final expiator of the family guilt, Orestes (Orin) being relegated to a more passive role. Mannon, Christine, and Brant are O'Neill's Agamemnon, Clytemnestra, and Aegisthus. A chorus of townsfolk, in Puritanical New England at the time of the Civil War, comments on the action and on the family curse. Suggestively façaded or "masked" like the characters, the setting—ugly gray walls and contrasting white-wood Greek temple portico and columns—symbolizes repressions that explain as well as motivate the tragedy. The furies haunting Orin and Lavinia are "modern psychological approximation[s]" that come from within: their pangs of conscience over the murders they committed, and over their lust and incestuous fixations, which resulted from the suppression of their healthy sexuality. Over five hours long, this play was filmed in 1947 and was made into an opera by Marvin David Levy in 1967.

Part I: "Homecoming." Act I. The Civil War is rumored to have ended, and General Ezra Mannon and his son Orin are therefore expected home soon. Before the Mannon house appear the general's attractive wife, Christine, and then, eyeing her with hatred, their daughter, Lavinia; angular, carrying herself with a wooden, military bearing, and unattractive, still she resembles her mother. There is a brief scene with the healthy and wholesome Peter Niles and his sister, Hazel, with whom Lavinia and Orin have long been romantically linked. Lavinia soon has bitter, insinuating words with Christine, having confirmed her suspicions of the mother's adultery with Adam Brant, a sea captain who is courting Lavinia. From the gardener Lavinia learns that Brant is probably the son of her father's brother, who long ago had been expelled by their father for making a servant girl pregnant and then marrying her. After the brother's death, his name had never again been mentioned in the family, and Ezra Mannon had refused to help the sick widow, leaving her to starve. Lavinia traps Brant into admitting his identity, and realizes that he has used her mother to avenge himself on her father. *Act II.* Lavinia accuses her mother of adultery; Christine admits it and reveals her loathing of Mannon since her wedding night and her hatred of him for having taken Orin to war. Lavinia insists that there must be no scandal: Christine must give up Brant, and become a dutiful wife to Lavinia's beloved father, who is not well. Though Lavinia has been cold and ruthless, she becomes disconcerted by her mother's accusations: "You wanted Adam Brant yourself! . . . You've tried to become the wife of your father and the mother of Orin!" After Lavinia leaves, Christine and Brant passionately plan their joint future and plot Mannon's murder. As cannon booms announce the war's end, Christine, who has sent Brant for poison, exults: "You'll never dare leave me now, Adam." *Act III.* Mannon comes home a week later. Having seen much death, he is free to face life and love for the first time: "I came home to surrender to you—what's inside me"—his heritage of Mannon Puritanism. He is tenderly passionate, and though Christine is full of aversion and Lavinia (fearful as well as jealous) tries to stop them, he takes his wife to the bedroom. *Act IV.* By dawn Christine has goaded Mannon with her hatred and adultery until he has a heart attack, and then she substitutes poison for his medicine. Lavinia hears his dying accusations and swears she will punish her mother.

Part II: "The Hunted." Act I. Orin, who has the Mannon look of his father and of Brant, comes home two days later, and his mother and sister start their battle for him. Christine is panicky, wondering what Lavinia really knows about her father's death and what she intends to do. *Act II.* Jealous of Brant, Orin tries to make his mother jealous of Hazel. Christine reassures Orin and then tries to disarm him against Lavinia, who, she says, is insane and will try to turn him against her. As Orin lovingly caresses his mother, Lavinia insists that he go to view his father's body, and Christine angrily tells her to keep Orin out of their fights. She recklessly dares Lavinia to reveal her secret to Orin, but then breaks down in terror and decides to warn Brant. *Act III.* Viewing Mannon's body on a bier in the study, Orin notes, "Death becomes the Mannons!" He finally starts to believe Lavinia's accusation when she reveals that Brant is Christine's lover, and frenziedly swears to kill him if this be true. In a state of near collapse, Christine begs Orin not to listen to Lavinia. Suddenly noticing the box of poison Lavinia has placed on Mannon's chest, Christine wildly implores the corpse, "Don't let her harm Adam! I am the only guilty one! Don't let Orin—!" *Act IV.* In a picturesquely eerie scene aboard Brant's ship at a Boston wharf, Christine hysterically warns her lover of their danger, and they desperately decide to leave and seek happiness. Having hunted them out, Orin and Lavinia overhear their talk from a hiding place on the deck. After Christine's departure, Orin, following Lavinia's carefully laid plans, shoots Brant; then they rifle the cabin to make it look as if it has been robbed. Orin stares at the corpse, fascinated: "By God, he does look like Father! This is like my dream. I've killed him before—over and over." *Act V.* At home the following night, Orin harshly confronts his mother and tells her that he has killed her lover; but, unable to bear her anguish, he breaks down and begs forgiveness. Lavinia orders him off: "After all that's happened, are you becoming her crybaby again?" She tells Christine that justice has now been done and that Christine may live. But when she rushes off and a pistol shot is heard, Lavinia accepts the suicide too as justice. She soothes her grief-stricken brother: "You have me, haven't you? I love you. I'll help you forget."

Part III: "The Haunted." Act I (two scenes). A year has passed, and Orin and Lavinia are returning from a long trip. Orin looks lifeless and more than ever like his father. Lavinia, looking animated and strikingly resembling her mother, reassures her brother, who is haunted by guilt for the murder and Christine's suicide: "The dead have forgotten us! We've forgotten them!" Assured of Peter's abiding love for her, Lavinia joyfully embraces him, but Orin glares at them in jealous rage. *Act II.* A month later Orin is driven by his conscience to record the family history of crimes. In a frenzy he accuses Lavinia of having discarded her mourning on their trip because she had fallen in love with and wanted various men. Increasingly morbid, he tells her, "I'm now in Father's place and you're Mother," and warns her against leaving him to marry Peter. As she breaks down weeping, he sends her out: "Don't cry. The damned don't cry." *Act III.* Orin decides that Lavinia "can't have happiness! She's got to be punished!" He finally proposes that they become lovers: "You would never dare leave me—then! You would feel as guilty then as I do! You would be as damned as I am!" Repulsed, Lavinia goads her brother to suicide: "You'd kill yourself if you weren't a coward!" First terrified, he then accepts her sentence: "You want to drive me to suicide as I drove Mother! . . . Yes! That would be justice." As she desperately clings to Peter for love and happiness, Orin shoots himself in the library. Lavinia hides Orin's family history and defiantly stares at the Mannon portraits: "Wasn't it the only way to keep your secret, too? But I'm through with you forever now. . . . I'll live in spite of you!" *Act IV.* In mourning for her brother three days later, she passionately pleads with Peter to possess her at once: "Forget sin and see that all love is beautiful." In frantic abandonment she begs Peter, "Want me! Take me, Adam!" When she becomes conscious of her slip of the tongue, she surrenders to fate: "Always the dead between! It's no good trying any more!" She dismisses Peter, orders the shutters nailed, and marches into the ancestral mansion, never to leave it again: "I'm the last Mannon. I've got to punish myself! . . . I'll live alone with the dead, and keep their secrets, and let them hound me, until the curse is paid out and the last Mannon is let die!"

MROŻEK, Sławomir (1930–   ), Polish satirist, was his country's leading playwright in the 1960's. In 1957 he made a popular one-act play out of one of the fables in his first publication, *Słoń* (*The Elephant,* 1953). It was quickly followed by *Policjanci* (THE POLICE, 1958) and by other works that made him a notable ABSURD dramatist, who pessimistically viewed life as grotesque and carried absurd situations to their insanely logical conclusions. Most of his plays are one-act satires about lonely people victimized by the overwhelming system. The best known is probably the frightening SYMBOLIC farce, TANGO (1964). It and other Mrożek works have been widely translated and produced throughout Europe; though a few have been seen in Off-Broadway theatres, they have remained little known in America.

Born in Borzęcin into a clerk's family, Mrożek studied architecture and Oriental philosophy, and attended Cracow's Academy of Fine Arts. He began his career as a journalist and then published a series of satiric essays, stories, and novels. Though he has been recognized as one of his country's most original writers, his works began to be banned in the early 1960's. Mrożek and his wife thereupon left Poland to live in Italy and then in Paris. When he denounced the invasion of Czechoslovakia in 1968, he was stripped of his Polish citizenship.

His plays are transparent satires of contemporary life in an authoritarian society. Aside from those already mentioned, he has written *Męczeństwo Piotra Oheya* (*The Martyrdom of Peter Ohey,* 1959), a tragic farce about the grotesque hunt for and sacrifice of an ordinary man; *Indyk* (*The Turkey Cock,* 1961), a satire set in a romantic kingdom whose inhabitants are impotent, cynical, and apathetic; *Karol* (*Charley* or *Charlie*) and *Striptease* (*Striptease*), two short 1961 satires, the first about an old man getting glasses so that he can recognize someone he wants to shoot, and the second about two meek gentlemen gradually stripped (by a monstrous hand) of their clothes, their dignity, and, finally, their lives; *Na pełnym morzu* (*Out at Sea,* 1961), a sardonic one-acter about three men on a raft who discuss survival and persuade the weakest among them to agree enthusiastically to save the others by letting himself be eaten; *Czarowna noc* (*The Enchanted Night,* also produced as *What a Lovely Dream*) and *Zabawa* (*Party,* also produced as *Let's Have Fun*), two clownish 1963 one-acters, the first (characterized as "a humorous NO EXIT") about a disturbing female embodiment of two bureaucrats' dreams, and the second presenting bored farmhands at pointless activities that culminate in attempted suicide; *Kynolog w rozterce* (*Kynologist in a Dilemma,* 1963), a comic opera (music by Henryk Czyż) about animal lovers; *Dom na granicy* (*Home on the Border,* 1967), an adaptation of Mrożek's comic story about a family's tribulations when an international frontier line is drawn right through the center of their house; and *Vatzlav* (*Vatzlau,* 1970), an allegorical portrayal of a shipwrecked slave's bizarre adventures as a free man in a modern capitalist society that includes characters like Genius, Justice, Genghis Khan, and Oedipus.

Police, The Martyrdom of Peter Ohey, Out at Sea, Charley, Party, and *Enchanted Night* were published in *Six Plays by Slawomir Mrozek* (1967). Others of his plays, with biographical and critical information on Mrożek, appear in individual translations.

MUNK, Kaj (1898–1944), Danish clergyman and dramatist, was the most widely performed native author in the 1930's and 1940's. Eventually overshadowed by KJELD ABELL, Munk achieved martyrdom when, after fearlessly denouncing the Nazis he had once admired, he was murdered by the Gestapo and dumped into a ditch near his parsonage in Vedersø, on the western coast of Jutland. He had been as contemptuous of the middle class as were his fellow Danish playwrights Abell and CARL ERIK SOYA, and he admired the strong-arm methods of Hitler—until he witnessed them in Germany, whereupon his admiration turned to a loathing that he expressed courageously and that was to cost him his life. Though he published sermons, essays, verse, and travel sketches, it was for his drama that Munk became famous. He is chiefly known for some eight major plays written between 1925 and his death. Only one was overtly religious: *Ordet* (THE WORD, 1932), which has been praised as his finest work. Most of his plays are on historical themes and reflect the Renaissance's gaudy, idyllic, and brutal romanticism, which Munk preferred to the fashionable modern psychological approach. His early plays feature various supermen; these reappeared later in a much-subdued form, as in his most famous historical play, NIELS EBBESEN (1942).

Kaj Harald Leininger Petersen was born in Maribo. By the time he was six his parents had died, and he adopted his foster parents' surname. He attended the University of Copenhagen, where in 1924 he was awarded his theology degree. His early "supermen" are bloody, brooding heroes like Herod, in *En Idealist* (1928; translated as *Herod the King*), his first-produced play. Professor Krater of *I Brændingen* (1929) is a satiric portrait of the Danish scholar-empiricist Georg Brandes. Munk's "supermen" include also Henry VIII (dealing with the hypocritical cant rationalizing his changing relations with Anne Boleyn), in *Cant* (1931), a Shakespearean verse tragedy; King David, in *De Udvalgte* (1933); and Benito Mussolini (in his Ethiopian venture), in *Sejren* (1936). Munk's last plays tend to focus on the "little man." Aside from *Niels Ebbesen,* these include *Han sidder ved Smeltediglen* (*He Sits at the Melting-Pot,* 1938), a play inspired by Munk's indignation at German anti-Semitism and featuring a fussy old scholar who has the courage ultimately to withstand the Nazi pressure to make him compromise his integrity; *Egelykke* (1940), a play about the religious reformer N. F. S. Grundtvig; and the posthumous one-act *Før Cannae* (*Before Cannae,* 1945), which also deals with the struggle of power and humanism. Another posthumous one-acter, *Ewalds Død* (*The Death of Ewald*), was written in 1943 and published in *The Norseman* in 1949.

In their day the plays of Munk aroused considerable and often polemical interest. However, they have not withstood the test of time very well. Munk used the stage as a pulpit from which to elaborate on the problems of divinity and humanity, and his plays are dated by their often flippant depiction of excessive romanticism, horror, and brutality. Yet there is no question of Munk's artistic zeal to make drama eschew what he considered the lifelessness of psychologically oriented "hour-long dissections," and his preference for its return to the violence of earlier times and participation in "the struggle." "Art has only one answer," Munk declared: "an affirmation of life. It must plunge in, no matter how terrifying."

His many writings include an autobiography, *Foråret så sagte kommer* (*Spring Comes So Gently,* 1942). *Niels Ebbesen* is one of the *Scandinavian Plays of the Twentieth Century* (Second Series, 1944); Alrik Gustafson's introductory essay to this volume discusses the life and works of Munk, as does R. P. Keigwin's introduction to his translation of Munk's *Five Plays* (1953): *Herod the King, The Word, Cant, He Sits at the Melting-Pot,* and *Before Cannae.*

MURDER IN THE CATHEDRAL, a verse play in two parts and an interlude by T. S. ELIOT, published and produced in 1935. Setting: Canterbury, England; December 1170.

Written for the 1935 Canterbury Festival, this short liturgical play was immediately successful. It was filmed (with Eliot himself speaking the Fourth Tempter's lines) and has been frequently revived and praised even by critics who object to its preachments. Unlike Anouilh's BECKET or Fry's CURTMANTLE, the play is focused on and objectifies the mind and conscience of Thomas à Becket during the last days and assassination of the subsequently canonized archbishop. The play's ritual characters, chorus, and starkness are in the tradition of medieval morality as well as classical Greek drama. Two striking prose passages punctuate the rich, melodious verse.

Part I. It is December 2, the day of Archbishop Thomas's return from seven years of exile in France after quarrels with his former friend, King Henry II. The women of Canterbury (the chorus) are frightened by premonitions: "Some malady is coming upon us." The priests have little faith in "temporal government" and, waiting, wonder whether the quarrel between king and archbishop is really over. As a herald reports Thomas's approach amidst cheering crowds, the women's fears grow. "Ill the wind, ill the time, uncertain the profit, certain the danger," they chant, wishing he would turn back to France. Their lives have been difficult, "Yet we have gone on living, / Living and partly living." A priest chides the women when Thomas enters. "Peace. And let them be, in their exaltation. / They speak better than they know, and beyond your understanding," Thomas begins: "They know and do not know, what it is to act or suffer." Thomas suggests the paradox of acting and suffering, both "fixed / In an eternal action, an eternal patience." Though he has foiled his enemies' plots temporarily, he predicts that the "End will be simple, sudden, God-given." But first there must be "strife with shadows." It begins at once, with four Tempters, personifications of Thomas's thoughts. The first offers a return to worldly pleasures and success: "Now that the King and you are in amity, / Clergy and laity may return to gaiety, / Mirth and sportfulness need not walk warily." Thomas easily rejects him. The

Murder in the Cathedral, Part I. Thomas (Robert Speaight) and the tempters (left to right: Guy Spaull, G. R. Schjelderup, David King-Wood, Norman Chidgey). London, 1935. (*British Theatre Museum*)

second Tempter offers return to the chancellorship. "Power is present. Holiness hereafter," he tells Thomas: "Chancellor richly rules. / . . . / To set down the great, protect the poor, / Beneath the throne of God can man do more?" The third Tempter offers leadership of the barons challenging the king. But Thomas rejects the "punier power" of the second as well as the "treacheries" of the third. Only the unexpected fourth Tempter is troublesome. Insidiously he describes "glory after death," with "pilgrims, standing in line / Before the glittering jewelled shrine" of the saint. "Seek the way of martyrdom," he advises Thomas, who cries out, "Is there no way, in my soul's sickness, / Does not lead to damnation in pride?" But as the cynical Tempter, soon joined by the others, mocks him with his own opening paradoxical words, and as the chorus and priests voice their fears, Thomas works out his resolution: "Now is my way clear, now is the meaning plain." He rejects the fourth temptation, "the greatest treason: / To do the right deed for the wrong reason"—to seek martyrdom for selfish purposes. He will serve only God, "For those who serve the greater cause may make the cause serve them, / Still doing right." He announces the presentation of "What yet remains to show you of my history" and concludes, "I shall no longer act or suffer, to the sword's end. / Now my good Angel, whom God appoints / To be my guardian, hover over the swords' points."

A prose *Interlude* consists of Thomas's Christmas morning sermon. He notes the paradox of joy and sorrow simultaneously celebrated that day for Christ's birth and Crucifixion, contrasts Christ's peace with that of the world, and describes the selfless nature of martyrdom. Then he bids his listeners remember the sermon because it may be his last one "and because it is possible that in a short time you will have yet another martyr."

Part II. Four knights rudely enter the Archbishop's Hall on December 29. They accuse Thomas, "the backstairs brat who was born in Cheapside," of pride and treason. Then they present the king's demands: to lift the excommunication Thomas has laid on rebellious bishops, and to leave England. Thomas denies their accusations and rejects the demands. Ready for martyrdom, Thomas is momentarily saved by his priests, who take him to the cathedral. But the chorus despairs while a *Dies Irae* is heard, and when the knights return, Thomas orders his priests to "Unbar the door!" Ready for death, he explains: "It is out of time that my decision is taken / If you call that decision / To which my whole being gives entire consent." The knights, now drunk, repeat their accusations, and Thomas prays. As the women hysterically chant a dirge, he is killed. When their work is completed, each of the knights steps up front and, in strikingly modern prose, they justify their act. Though their ganging up on an "underdog" seems to violate sportsmanship, they insist that they were "perfectly disinterested." They have served England by taking the first historical step toward "a just subordination of the pretensions of the Church," which has tried to set itself above the State. The last speaker notes that they were provoked by Thomas himself, who refused to save himself because he sought martyrdom: "I think, with these facts before you, you will unhesitatingly render a verdict of Suicide while of Unsound Mind. It is the only charitable verdict you can give, upon one who was, after all, a great man." After the knights leave, the priests mourn, though they are consoled with having a new saint. As a distant choir sings a *Te Deum,* the chorus reaffirms the glory of God and concludes, "Lord, have mercy upon us. / Blessed Thomas, pray for us."

MURRAY, T[homas] C[ornelius] (1873–1959), Irish dramatist, was born in County Cork, taught briefly in St. Patrick's College in Dublin, and wrote peasant drama, usually NATURALISTIC tragedy with religious and poetic overtones. His first play, *The Wheel of Fortune* (1909), was a one-acter later revised as *Sovereign Love* (1913). It was with *Birthright* (1910), a modern Cain-and-Abel tragedy, that Murray became an important Abbey Theatre playwright. Then came *Maurice Harte* (1912), which Una Ellis-Fermor (in *The Irish Dramatic Movement,* 1954) considered vastly superior to Jones's similar play, MICHAEL AND HIS LOST ANGEL. The unproduced *The Briery Gap* (1917) was followed by a one-act tragedy about poverty and greed, *Spring* (1918), and by *Aftermath* (1922), another tragedy.

Murray's best play, by general agreement, is *Autumn Fire* (1924); its plot resembles that of O'Neill's DESIRE UNDER THE ELMS, but the conflicts remain unsolved.* Murray's other peasant dramas are *The Pipe in the Fields* (1927), *The Blind Wolf* (1928), *A Flutter of Wings* (1929), *Michaelmas Eve* (1932), *A Spot in the Sun* (1938), and *Illumination* (1939). In part, perhaps, because his plot resolutions are too often unbelievable, Murray's plays have not enjoyed much subsequent popularity, although they have been highly praised by some critics.

MUSHANOKŌJI Saneatsu (1885–), Japanese painter, novelist, playwright, and nobleman. He studied at Tokyo's Imperial University and in America, and in 1918 bought real estate outside his native city to establish a Utopian village—which never materialized. Influenced by the writings of MAURICE MAETERLINCK as well as those of LEO TOLSTOI, Mushanokōji founded the *Shirakaba* magazine (1907), for which he wrote comedies and religious plays that greatly influenced contemporary Japanese youth. Among Yozan T. Iwasaki and Glenn Hughes's *New Plays from Japan* (1930) is a Mushanokōji comedy, *Aru katei* (*A Family Affair,* 1909). His religious works include a play about a monk who turns out to be less sinful but more sensible than he first seemed, *Aruhino Ikkyu* (*Monk Ikkyu,* 1913); a playlet about the Indian philosopher Daruma (*Bodhidharma,* 1924); and a play about Buddha, *Washimo Shiranai* (*I Don't Know Either,* 1914); along with a reproduction of Mushanokōji's painting of the young Buddha these were published in Umeyo Hirano's collected translations of *Buddhist Plays from Japanese Literature* (1962).

* See Matthew T. Conlin's "The Tragic Effect in *Autumn Fire* and *Desire under the Elms,*" *Modern Drama* (February 1959).

MY FAIR LADY, a musical play in two acts by ALAN JAY LERNER (music by Frederick Loewe), published and produced in 1956. Setting: London, 1912.

Directed by MOSS HART and adapted from Shaw's PYGMALION, this musical was the most successful Broadway show of its time. Its run of over twenty-seven-hundred consecutive performances had previously been exceeded only by Lindsay and Crouse's LIFE WITH FATHER and Kirkland's TOBACCO ROAD.

The musical follows much of the script by BERNARD SHAW, and uses many of his original lines. But it deletes the noncomic dialogue and action that develop Shaw's themes. Instead, deftly utilizing hints Shaw himself provided for the 1938 film version of *Pygmalion, My Fair Lady* (as its title suggests) is a romance that focuses on the Cinderella story and the sentimentality of the Pygmalion myth. This was accomplished by adding scenes that dramatize Eliza's education and transformation, by providing an Ascot race and a grand ball scene (see illustration, next page), and by making the resolution a happy, romantic one—in accord with the musical's portrayal throughout of the relationship of Higgins and Eliza.

MY HEART'S IN THE HIGHLANDS, a one-act play by WILLIAM SAROYAN, produced in 1939 and published in 1940. Setting: a shack in Fresno, California; August and November 1914.

This hour-and-a-half play, Saroyan's first stage success, was originally a short story (1926), and was subsequently dramatized as a short one-acter (1927). It was expanded into its final form for the Group Theatre. Unabashedly naïve, sentimental, nostalgic, and optimistic, the play features nine-year-old Johnny Alexander, his Armenian grandmother, and "Johnny's Father," self-proclaimed as "one of the greatest unknown poets living."

A famished and thirsty old actor appears, playing "My Heart's in the Highlands" on the trumpet. Johnny's Father invites him to stay, and Johnny persuades the kind-hearted grocer, himself almost bankrupt, to advance them further credit. Enthralled by the old man's music, the neighbors bring provisions. But the old man is soon taken back to the Old People's Home. Johnny's Father's poems are rejected, so the check he had hoped for does not materialize. Johnny steals some grapes, and the frightened family barricade the door against the law, which turns out to be only the old trumpeter,

My Fair Lady. At the grand ball, a suspicious Hungarian phonetics professor (Leo Britt) watches Eliza (Julie Andrews) dancing with Higgins (Rex Harrison). New York, 1956. (*Zodiac Photographers*)

much feebler and come to die with his friends. Though Johnny's Father is bitter about people who prefer war to poetry, he remains optimistic as the family is evicted. But as they pick up their few belongings and leave home, Johnny wonders, "I'm not mentioning any names, Pa, but something's wrong somewhere."

MYSTERY-BOUFFE (*Misteriya-buff*), "an Heroic, Epic, and Satiric Representation of Our Epoch" in six acts by VLADIMIR VLADIMIROVICH MAYAKOVSKY, published and produced in 1918. Setting: the North Pole, an Ark, Hell, Paradise, the Promised Land, etc.

This enormous pageant, the first important Soviet Russian play, was produced by Vsevolod Meyerhold on the first anniversary of the Revolution. A mixture of opera bouffe, parody of allegorical medieval mystery drama, and ideological paean, it reinterprets biblical tales in Soviet terms. In 1921 a new and better-known version, prepared by Mayakovsky and again produced by Meyerhold, introduced a more theatrical prologue and a revised epilogue based on the "International," and interpolated bitter references to the Versailles peace treaty and some of its architects.

Seven pairs of grimy workers (the "Unclean") emerge from the audience and tear down the conventional velvet curtain: "Make way for us! The land, swollen with blood, has given birth to us!..." At the North Pole survivors from various countries reveal that the world is engulfed by a flood—the Bolshevik Revolution. Lloyd George, Clemenceau, and other members of the "Clean" save themselves on an ark built by the Unclean. These are kept on the ark in cruel subjugation, first by a tsar and, when he is overthrown, by "democratic" representative Cleans. But these are merely a "tsar with a hundred mouths," the Unclean discover and throw them overboard. The Man of the Future walks the waves and invites the Unclean to an earthly paradise, which they can build themselves. In Hell the Unclean shock Beelzebub and the other devils with their accounts of earthly torments. In Paradise the Unclean reject Methuselah and other inhabitants (including the silent saints Jean Jacques Rousseau and LEO TOLSTOI), whose lives are unproductive and dull. When God comes to destroy the Unclean, they seize His thunderbolts, which they plan later to use as electric-power sources. In the Land of Fragments they work and produce, after they defeat Compromise and Confusion. The Unclean envision the joyful, beautiful, and productive land of the future, accessible only "on the wings of the machines." At its gate, the Unclean decide to enter and use the idle machines. Sickle and Hammer lead Storegoods to the Unclean, who are amazed to receive food without cost. The machines apologize for the harm they once did the Unclean: it was the fault of the fat men who usurped and drove them. Now the machines are free and eager to serve the workers. These form a ring with the machines and the tools, and all burst into a "Hymn to the Sun": "... We are the builders of the world. Chains of iron have given place to chains of loving hands. All glory be to you! Shine forth, O Sunny Commune of Ours!"

N

NAKAMURA Kichizō (1877–1941), Japanese novelist and playwright, was a major early contributor to the *Shingeki* (New Drama) movement, which he helped promote by introducing Western plays. His most lasting original success was *Kamisori* (*The Razor,* 1914), a frequently revived one-acter about a disgruntled provincial barber who cuts the throat of a prominent friend. With its depiction of personal frustrations and NATURALISTIC social protest this play, like Nakamura's other works, evidences the influence of HENRIK IBSEN.

Nakamura was born in Shimane Prefecture. While still a student at Waseda University he won fame as a novelist. Subsequently he studied in Europe and in America. In 1909 he returned to Japan, where he began his career as a playwright with *Bokushi no Ie* (1910), an exposure of religious corruption. In 1913 Nakamura became stage director of the Geijutsuza (Art Theatre) Troupe, which was to produce many of his plays. These include the historical *Ōshio Heihachirō* (1921), set in feudal times and featuring the philosopher who tried to help peasants starved by a self-seeking official, led a revolt to open the granaries, and then committed suicide; and another historical drama, the long and novelistic *Ii Tairo-no Shi* (*The Death of Ii Tairo,* 1920), dealing with the later career of the chief minister of a shogun who in 1858 helped open Japan to foreign trade and was assassinated by conservatives two years later.

The Death of Ii Tairo was published in English with an extensive introduction, as was *The Razor,* among the *Three Modern Japanese Plays* (1923) compiled by Yozan T. Iwasaki and Glenn Hughes.

NAŁKOWSKA, Zofia (1885–1954), Polish novelist, was particularly distinguished for exploring psychologically the borderline between the permissible and the criminal in a novel that won the Grand Prize of Poland in 1937, *Granica* (*The Frontier*). Not very different in subject is her play *Dzień jego powrotu* (*The Day of His Return,* 1931), which portrays a released criminal and the secret guilt among those connected with him, including the wife who intends to leave him. Nałkowska's other important stage work is *Dom kobiet* (*The House of Women,* 1930), a drama of little action but considerable suspense, achieved through the often erotic reminiscences of female tenants of various ages.

NASH [originally Nusbaum], **N. Richard** (1916–), American playwright, like PADDY CHAYEFSKY, is primarily a television writer. His only hit, *The Rainmaker* (1954), is an expanded television script that was also filmed and made into a successful musical in the tradition of Rodgers and Hammerstein's OKLAHOMA!, *110 in the Shade* (1963, music by Harvey Schmidt). The play, a "romantic comedy," is about a con man who succeeds in bringing rain to parched farmlands and love to awaken a homely "sleeping beauty," heretofore a frustrated spinster who after this encounter is able to get herself a husband—more solid if less romantic than the "rainmaker." Nash's earlier plays include *Second Best Bed* (1946), a farce about Shakespeare; and *See the Jaguar* (1952), a pretentious romantic tragedy in verse. His other plays and musicals also portray integrity corrupted and regained, like that of the "rainmaker." For the most part commercial failures, they include comedies such as *Girls of Summer* (1956) and *Keep It in the Family* (1967), and a number of musicals.

NATURALISM, a term sometimes used interchangeably with REALISM, in drama usually refers to relentless portrayals of the seamy side of life—poverty, misery, and (often sexual) sordidness. As envisioned by its earliest, scientifically oriented French practitioners and theoreticians (ÉMILE ZOLA, HENRY BECQUE, EUGÈNE BRIEUX), it documented a SLICE OF LIFE. It was a reaction against the shopworn baroque and romantic, as well as the WELL-MADE PLAY popular in the late nineteenth century. The plays of GERHART HAUPTMANN and MAXIM GORKY (particularly THE WEAVERS and THE LOWER DEPTHS) are often cited as examples of naturalist drama. But the form has persisted, with EUGENE O'NEILL (in THE ICEMAN COMETH, for example) and later writers.

Naturalism was foreshadowed by the Goncourt brothers' writings, and the term has been used in philosophy. As now defined, it began with Zola and evolved from his novels. His THÉRÈSE RAQUIN and Léon Hennique's (1832–1907) dramatization of Zola's short story *Jacques Damour* into a one-act play (which launched the Théâtre-Libre in 1887)* ushered naturalism into modern drama, and Becque's THE VULTURES became the genre's

* The Théâtre-Libre and its company, founded in Paris by the French director André Antoine (1859–1943), introduced the works of the playwrights mentioned in this entry and, though it survived for only a few years (1887–94), became the cradle of naturalism; its influence on the course of subsequent modern drama—including countermovements by JACQUES COPEAU and others—has been immense.

French prototype. In his essays on the subject, collectively entitled *Le Naturalism au théâtre* (1881), Zola adumbrated the principles of naturalism in the theatre, which reflected the rising spirit of science: a case study, an objective, clinical reproduction of emotions and interacting human beings as he envisioned them naturally to be—conditioned by their environment, their heredity, and their physical-psychological makeup. Naturalism was characterized also by intentionally "untheatrical" productions, particularly in its early days in the important experimental theatres —Antoine's Théâtre-Libre, Brahm's Freie Bühne, and Stanislavsky's Moscow Art Theatre—which popularized this kind of drama and its greatest artists, including AUGUST STRINDBERG, HENRIK IBSEN, and ANTON CHEKHOV. These strove to reproduce unadorned physical reality: cluttered settings, actors turning their backs to the audience, disorganized ("natural") talk, etc.

See Lawson A. Carter's *Zola and the Theater* (1963) and Mordecai Gorelik's *New Theatres for Old* (1940), both of which list further sources.

NED MCCOBB'S DAUGHTER, a comedy in three acts by SIDNEY HOWARD, published and produced in 1926. Setting: a restaurant and a home at a Maine ferry terminus, 1926.

This popular rural melodrama features thirty-year-old Carrie Callahan, the warmly human but shrewd daughter of an old New England sea captain. She is decent and devoted to her children, for she believes that "raisin' kids is jest 'bout the only thing on earth wuth makin' a fuss over." Taking things in her stride, she conceals her husband's criminal past. But the discovery of his thefts kills Captain McCobb, who has mortgaged his house to get the husband out of an earlier scrape. His brother, another city slicker, offers to save Carrie if she will let him use the homestead for his bootleg-liquor business. Desperate, Carrie agrees. Then she learns that the house was mortgaged to pay for her husband's love affair. She gets rid of him, and when his brother tries to use her children as blinds for his bootlegging, she outwits the city slicker and saves the day for the McCobbs.

NEMIROVICH-DANCHENKO, V[ladimir] I[vanovich] (1858–1943), Russian playwright and novelist, will always be remembered more as the cofounder and director, with Konstantin Stanislavsky, of the Moscow Art Theatre. But before their momentous meeting in 1897, Nemirovich-Danchenko was already a successful writer. As a dramatist—he wrote about a dozen plays—he was eclipsed later by ANTON CHEKHOV and MAXIM GORKY, whose success as playwrights was due largely to Nemirovich-Danchenko, one of the great directors of the tsarist as well as the Soviet governments.

Born in Ozurgety, Georgia, Nemirovich-Danchenko became a drama critic while yet a student at Moscow University. Subsequently he taught drama at the Moscow Philharmonia's training school; among his students who were to join the Moscow Art Theatre were such later theatrical luminaries as Olga Knipper (subsequently Chekhov's wife) and the great actor-producer Vsevolod Meyerhold. Nemirovich-Danchenko's first play, *Sipovnik,* which portrays a house's exterior before its "fourth wall" was removed to reveal what transpired inside it, was produced at the Maly Theatre in 1882. He remained associated with that imperial theatre for some years, directing his own plays as well as those of others. It was there that he began revitalizing the moribund Russian stage and instituting reforms that presaged his and Stanislavsky's revolution in the theatre.

V. I. Nemirovich-Danchenko (right) and Konstantin Stanislavsky. (Tass from *Sovfoto*)

Nemirovich-Danchenko's own plays were conventional hits that, with their portrayal of the futility of middle-class Russian life, presaged the theatre of the great NATURALIST playwrights he was to discover and encourage in his theatre. He presaged their drama, too, with such REALISTIC physical touches as the sprinkling of pine essence on the stage in forest scenes. His other plays include *Poslednyaya volya* (1888), a comedy; *Novoe delo* (1890), another comedy and his first major success; *Zoloto* (1894), a long one-acter which scrupulously observed the unities; and *Tsena zhizni* (1896), which won the Griboyedov Prize in a competition with, among others, Chekhov's THE SEAGULL. These and other works, as well as his life and career, are discussed in various memoirs, translated and published in English as *My Life in the Russian Theatre* (1936).

NEUMANN, Alfred (1895–1952), German novelist and playwright, specialized in historical fiction. In 1926 he dramatized his story of court intrigue, *Der Patriot* (1925), into his greatest stage success; produced in England two years later as *Such Men Are Dangerous,* it portrays the 1801 revolution and the assassination of the mad Tsar Paul I, as engineered by the Russian Governor Peter von der Pahlen. Another historical drama, *Königsmaske* (1928), deals with France after the July Revolution and features Louis Philippe as a weakling who has only the "mask" of royalty, thus betraying his own interests and forced to sacrifice his followers and abdicate in 1848. Other Neumann plays are

Frauenschuh (1929), *Haus Danieli* (1930), and *Abel* (1948), which he later made into a novel, *Viele heissen Kain* (1950).

Born in Lautenburg and educated in Berlin and Rostock, Neumann in his novels on Sweden's Queen Christina (stressing her eroticism) and the French and Italian revolutions (stressing men's struggle for power), as in his plays, presented history as unheroically symbolic of contemporary problems. When the Nazis came to power Neumann escaped to the United States, where he continued to write. He died in Switzerland.

NEW COLONY, THE (*La nuova colonia*), a "myth" in a prologue and three acts by LUIGI PIRANDELLO, published and produced in 1928. Setting: a seaport in contemporary southern Italy, and an offshore island.

Though this play has been criticized as being pro-Fascist and antiliberal, its primary sentiment is antiutopian. Pirandello appeared to despair of men's and society's ability to control their dissolute natures—despite the exalted ideal he embodied in La Spera, the transformed prostitute.

The act-long prologue depicts smugglers and other social dregs in a port tavern. Hounded by society, they decide to seek refuge on a penal island recently closed because it is slowly sinking. As the whore La Spera remarks, "You'll never sink any deeper than you are now! But there, at least, you'll sink by an act of God, not at the hands of men even worse than yourself." She and Currao, one of the outcasts, whose child she has just borne, lead the group to a new life. The innate decency of individuals now blooms as Currao rules ably and selflessly, and La Spera—ennobled into a beautiful, saintly being—gives unstintingly of herself in cooking, nursing, and caring for the community. But their harmony is threatened by ambition, greed, and lust. An evil and disaffected member of the group escapes. Soon he returns with some inhabitants from the "old civilization," who bring wine and women to capture, exploit, and wreck "the new colony." They succeed in persuading Currao to desert La Spera. She acquiesces meekly, but refuses to yield her baby, and escapes up a mountain. There La Spera evokes the forces of nature to help protect her child. Immediately the earth quakes and the island starts sinking. Only the mother and child atop the mountain are spared.

NEW YORK IDEA, THE, a play in four acts by LANGDON MITCHELL, produced in 1906 and published in 1908. Setting: New York, 1906.

This comedy of manners deals with the problem of frivolous marriage and divorce (which is what the title implies) and true love, and satirizes sophisticated social leaders. One of the best American comedies of the age, it was translated and produced in Europe. It has been frequently revived, and was favorably reviewed in *The New York Times* as late as 1963.

Cynthia, a recently divorced young society woman, prepares to marry a prominent conservative judge, whose divorced wife, something of a vampire, loves John Karslake, Cynthia's ex-husband and a sportsman. The wedding is delayed when the spirited Cynthia has second thoughts about marrying the boring judge, whose frivolous divorced wife, she fears, Karslake is about to marry. She goes to Karslake's home and is relieved to discover that her rival has married an English ladies' man. Finding that they are still in love and that their original divorce is technically invalid, Cynthia and Karslake are happy to resume their marriage.

NEW ZEALAND has had much amateur but little professional theatre other than occasional visiting troupes from abroad. Native dramatists have emerged only with the recent formation of a professional New Zealand theatre. Promising new playwrights include Allen Curnow (1911–   ), a poet praised for his *The Axe* (1949) and other verse plays; and Bruce E. G. Mason (1921–   ), a critic who produced a successful autobiographical drama, *The Pohutukawa Tree* (1960). A collection of works by earlier dramatists, who were dependent entirely on amateur and radio productions, is Eric Bradwell's *"Clay" and Other New Zealand One-Act Plays* (1936).

NEWLY-MARRIED COUPLE, THE (*De nygifte*), a play in two acts by BJØRNSTJERNE BJØRNSON, published and produced in 1865. Setting: Norway, 1860's.

Though slight and artificial, this play was immediately successful and is still performed. The first Norwegian prose drama on contemporary themes, it aroused considerable controversy, was translated into many languages, and received major productions throughout Scandinavia and beyond.

Axel Hargaut insists that he and his immature young wife move out of her possessive parents' home. A year later her confidante, by writing an anonymous novel about their lives, makes Axel and his wife understand themselves and able to have a mature marriage, safe from unhealthy emotions and a jealous family.

NICARAGUA. Dramatized Spanish and Indian folk legends started Nicaraguan theatre, and in later times its best COSTUMBRISMOS were written in verse. The country has produced a number of notable playwrights since the emergence of its major literary figure, the poet Rubén Darío (1867–1916)—who himself essayed the theatre with fair success in 1896 with the now-lost comic one-acter *Cada oveja* . . . and a tragedy about the poet *Manuel Acuña.* More important as dramatists are Hernán Robleto (1893–   ) and Pablo Antonio Cuadra (1912–   )—the former for his much-produced "customs comedy" *La rosa del paraíso* (1920) and the prizewinning comedy *El vendaval* (1925), the latter for another popular but bitter comedy written in 1937 "for strolling players on street corners, to carry a message of rebellion against the routine politics imposed by governments and revolutions" responsible for national misery and poverty, *Por los caminos van* *los campesinos* (1958). Among more recent playwrights are José de Jesús Martínez (1928–), who moved to Panama and whose works include the cynical *Caifas* (1961), which portrays the high priest Caiaphas inducing national guilt feelings to make people regain their faith; and Rolando Steiner (1935–), whose fantasies include *El ángel extraviado de Judit* (1958), a PIRANDELLian play about a man who dreams of a murder and then wakes up to find that he has actually committed one.

For studies of the Nicaraguan theatre see LATIN AMERICA.

NICHOLS, Anne (1891?–1966), American playwright, made her name with ABIE'S IRISH ROSE (1922). Though she wrote some twenty other plays and numerous vaudeville sketches, she remained memorable only for this immensely popular sentimental Irish-Jewish comedy, which was revived on Broadway as late as 1954. From the first she had sufficient faith in its ultimate success to mortgage her home to get it produced and kept open after its initially lukewarm reception. She spent the rest of her life compulsively checking up on its various revivals and adaptations.

Born in Georgia and raised in Philadelphia, Anne Nichols ran away from home to become a chorus girl. In 1915 she married an actor-producer, Henry Duffey, whom she divorced in 1924. Shortly before her death she was working on her autobiography, *Such Is Fame.*

NICHOLS, Robert M[alise] B[owyer] (1893–1944), English Georgian poet, was born on the Isle of Wight. During World War I he was a soldier-poet in France. The Lafcadio Hearn Professor of English at the Imperial University in Tokyo, Japan (1921–24), he edited the works of Chikamatsu Monzayemon, "the Japanese Shakespeare." He also wrote a few plays, including *Guilty Souls* (1922) and *Twenty Below* (1927; written with Jim Tully, 1888–1947). His importance as a dramatist rests on his coauthorship of WINGS OVER EUROPE (1928).

NIELS EBBESEN, a play in five acts by KAJ MUNK, published in 1942 and produced in 1945. Setting: medieval Denmark.

This play was a transparent attack on the Nazis, who were occupying Denmark—and prohibited the production of the play. Its title protagonist is a national hero who centuries earlier had defied other invading Germans. The best-known but the most subdued of Munk's heroic historical dramas, *Niels Ebbesen* was his last play: shortly after its appearance (it was circulated clandestinely), Munk was murdered by Nazi thugs.

Niels Ebbesen, the master of Nørreris Manor, rejects his family's and neighbors' demands that he resist Denmark's German oppressors. He quarrels with his wife and with his daughter's patriotic fiancé, and has his farmers turn in their weapons. Profoundly mindful of the grim consequences of battle, Ebbesen would rather be called "coward and traitor" than agree to violence, for, as he says, "everything that has to do with war I shun and flee from as long as I can." He shelters their chief oppressor, a brutal German count who is ill. But when the count recuperates and resumes his viciousness, a hard-drinking and frail priest who heroically withstands torture incidentally points the way for Niels Ebbesen. He goes to the tyrant's chamber and, unable to reason with him, assassinates the count. Now persuaded of the need to fight for peace, Niels Ebbesen, preparing to lead his countrymen in the battle to free Denmark, embraces his wife: "The greatest reward is to know that my children will grow up and be Danes."

NIGGER, THE, a play in three acts by EDWARD SHELDON, produced in 1909 and published in 1910. Setting: the South, 1909.

Like SINCLAIR LEWIS's much later novel *Kingsblood Royal* (1947), this play features a white man who is discovered to have Negro blood. The play's lynch talk and title—which Sheldon used to show whites' contempt of Negroes—shocked Northerners.

The governor of a Southern state refuses to give in to special-interest pressures, though this refusal will make known his just-discovered strain of Negro blood. His bride, at first revolted by the discovery, ultimately returns to him. But before the governor makes his revelation to the crowds that come to cheer him, he persuades the girl to give him up. There is much pain in the world, he tells her, "But aftah this pain's been used—fo, it *has* a use, an' a good one, too!—why, we'll get the fruits o' the whole experience, an' I reckon they'll make up fo' ev'rythin'!"

NIGHT AT AN INN, A, a one-act play by LORD DUNSANY, produced in 1916 and published in 1924. Setting: a contemporary English inn.

This popular horror play portrays a group of thieves who have stolen the ruby eye of an Indian idol. They outsmart and kill the "black" priests who have followed them. But then, as the thieves celebrate their success, the idol himself walks in. As they watch in paralyzed horror, he recoups his eye and draws the thieves to their deaths, one by one. The last to go is the leader, a "toff" who foresaw everything except this ending to the adventure.

NIGHT MUST FALL, a play in three acts and a prologue by EMLYN WILLIAMS, published and produced in 1935. Setting: Essex, England; 1930's.

This murder thriller, subsequently filmed twice, was Williams's first success as a playwright.

Dan, a baby-faced bellhop, ingratiates himself with an obnoxious elderly invalid. Her niece, simultaneously fascinated and repelled by Dan, soon realizes that he is a brutal murderer. She shields him even when he kills her aunt and is about to murder her. Caught in the nick of time, Dan insolently kisses her: "Well, I'm goin' to be hanged. . . . But they'll get their money's worth at the trial. You wait!"

NIGHT OF THE IGUANA, THE, a play in three acts by TENNESSEE WILLIAMS, produced in 1961 and published in 1962. Setting: a hotel in Mexico on a jungle-covered hilltop overlooking a beach, summer 1940.

Originally a short story and then a one-acter produced at the 1959 Spoleto Festival in Italy, this play was continuously revised until it opened on Broadway. Like THE GLASS MENAGERIE, it is a poetic mood piece about loneliness and despair, but it is NATURALISTIC and diffuse in plot. It was filmed and won the New York Drama Critics' Circle Award.

T. Lawrence Shannon, a thirty-five-year-old minister defrocked for blasphemy and for seducing a young girl, is on the verge of another crack-up. He is the tour director of a busload of Baptist ladies up in arms because he has led them off the comfortable advertised route and has slept with one of the girls in the party. Shannon brings the group to a hotel run by an aging, "affable and rapaciously lusty" widow who wants to keep Shannon there permanently. Other guests include a Nazi family and an ethereal spinster, the watercolor painter Hannah Jelkes, and her grandfather, "the oldest living and practicing poet." The sick Shannon is pursued by his young charge and the foul-mouthed widow, and by an aggressive Baptist who succeeds in having him fired. Thereupon Shannon becomes maniacal, and the widow has him tied up in a hammock. In a night-long talk, the fettered Shannon and Hannah reach out for each other and expose their innermost souls: the prim and strong but gentle spinster who has denied her passions, and the backsliding clergyman who has lost his faith and reached the end of his rope. An iguana, tied with a rope while fattened as a Mexican delicacy, symbolizes their plight. Hannah begs Shannon to cut it loose. He does so, "because God won't do it." The widow jealously drags him off for a "swim in that—liquid moonlight." As Shannon agrees to become her companion, he takes a last look at the sensitive Hannah. Accepting her fate, she looks at her old grandfather, who has just exulted at completing the poem he has been struggling over. Now he is dead.

NO EXIT (*Huis clos*), a one-act play by JEAN-PAUL SARTRE, published and produced in 1944. Setting: a locked drawing room furnished in French Second Empire style.

This long one-acter, originally published as *Les Autres* (*The Others*) and also translated as *In Camera,* became one of Sartre's best-known plays. It is a "philosophical melodrama" set in a unique kind of hell. The three people consigned to it gradually reveal their true characters and past actions as they realize that they must eternally judge each other and themselves. This is their torture, their damnation, their hell. All of them—but especially Garcin—personify Sartre's existentialist philosophy.

A noncommital valet ushers Joseph Garcin, a recently executed pacifist journalist, into a hotel room. It is a chamber for the dead, where tears and sleep are impossible and where the bell usually fails to ring. Soon two others are brought in: Inès Serrano, a lesbian post-office clerk who died of gas, and Estelle Rigault, a pretty society matron who died of pneumonia. Periodically they glimpse life on earth, where they used to torment others. Their tensions are aggravated by conflicting erotic passions. Inès, the most sadistic but perceptive of the three, understands that instead of the traditional devil they expected they are doomed to torture one another: "An economy of man-power—or devil-power, if you prefer. The same idea as in the cafeteria, where customers serve themselves." Garcin succeeds temporarily in persuading the women to work out their own salvations privately, in silence. But Estelle's vanity and Inès's perverse passion soon reactivate mutual recriminations. Garcin relates how he compelled his loving wife to serve him and his mistress coffee in bed. Inès tells how she seduced her cousin's wife, helped her make his life miserable until he was run over by a streetcar, and tormented her until the wife turned on the gas that killed them both. Estelle too confesses her rottenness: she committed adultery, murdered her illegitimate daughter, and drove her lover to suicide. Now, seeing a former lover dance with her friend, Estelle yearns "to go down to earth for just a moment and dance with him again." Inès keeps goading Garcin and importuning Estelle—who spits at her and, maddened with desire, throws herself into Garcin's arms. Inès watches coldly: "Yes, have it your own way, make love and get it over with; my turn will come." But Garcin is distracted when he hears former associates on earth despise and then forget him.

Garcin now wonders about his pacifist idealism. He relates how he escaped to avoid fighting, was caught at the border, and executed. Inès suggests that he was a coward even in facing death. Garcin begs Estelle to show her faith in his heroism, for "one person's faith would save me." When Estelle does, Inès laughs—for she knows Estelle would say anything to gratify her passion. Estelle does not deny it: "I'd love you just the same, even if you were a coward. Isn't that enough?" Disgusted, Garcin turns away. But Inès, though she tries again, is still spurned by Estelle. Furiously Garcin tries to escape them: "Anything would be better than this agony of mind, this creeping pain that gnaws and fumbles and caresses one and never hurts quite enough." He rattles the door—and (amazingly) it opens. Estelle urges Garcin to help her throw Inès out, but he refuses: "It's because of her I'm staying here." It is Inès—who knows what it is to be a coward—whom he must convince of his heroic idealism: "I couldn't leave you here, gloating over my defeat." Inès demands that he prove his "heroism" was not a dream: "It's what one does, and nothing else, that shows the stuff one's made of." When he protests that he "died too soon," that he was "not allowed time to—to do my deeds," Inès is not persuaded: "One always dies too soon—or too late. And yet one's whole life is complete at that moment, with a line drawn neatly under it, ready for the summing up. You are—your life, and nothing else." Suggesting that Garcin take his revenge on Inès, Estelle begs him to make love to her. He starts to do so, but Inès sneers at the "lovely scene: coward Garcin holding baby-killer Estelle in his manly arms!"—and she taunts him with his cowardice. Unable to continue, Garcin finally realizes that he is truly in hell: "Hell is—other people!" The frustrated Estelle tries to stab Inès—but fails, since they are all already dead. Doomed, they slump into their seats, laugh hysterically, and then look at each other. Their torments must go on, endlessly. "Well, let's continue," Garcin says.

NO MAN'S SON (*Fils de personne*), a play in four acts by HENRY DE MONTHERLANT, produced in 1943 and published in 1944. Setting: Cannes, winter 1940–41.

Originally a novel, this three-character play has been characterized as a "bourgeois tragedy." It is virtually devoid of action, but became one of Montherlant's most popular stage works. Themes already touched upon in QUEEN AFTER DEATH are here developed. They are resolved in the play's sequel, TOMORROW THE DAWN.

Georges Carrion, a successful forty-three-year-old lawyer, has evacuated to unoccupied France his former and until recently forgotten mistress, Marie Sandoval, and their fourteen-year-old son Gillou (Gilles), whom Georges has first met only recently. A mediocre woman, Marie does not mind Gillou's being like her: "My son has no need to be exceptional." But "the nation has need that its sons should be," Georges insists, increasingly dissatisfied with his boy's shortcomings. Father and son try to communicate and to express their mutual affection, but fail. Nonetheless Georges is reluctant to let them leave, as both Marie and Gillou wish to. Finally, perceiving his son's apparent indifference, Georges feels "condemned" to let him go. "I sacrificed him to the idea I have of man, she sacrificed him to the need she has of man," Georges concludes; but Gillou "alone was the one to be sacrificed. Woman's son? No, no man's son. No man's son, like the others." He sends the boy and Marie to her home in Le Havre. Just before they leave Gillou reveals that his mother has a new lover there. Gillou now wants to return to his father. But it is too late, and Georges pushes the now-affectionate boy away from him.

NO TIME FOR COMEDY, a play in three acts by S. N. BEHRMAN, published and produced in 1939. Setting: New York, 1938.

Behrman's last important original play was this sophisticated comedy, which dramatizes its author's own concern with writing comedies while World War II was breaking out. The dilemma of whether the playwright should produce slick humor or extend his artistic talents by composing profound tragedies is personified in two women—but the resolution is that of a conventional triangle.

Gaylord ("Gay") Esterbrook has made his wife, Linda, a famous actress with his drawing-room comedies. Amanda Smith, a banker's earnest young wife, persuades him to immortalize Loyalist Spain and write drama more appropriate to the seriousness of the age. Linda is jealous and fearful that Amanda will ruin Gay with her inspiration. "Sleep with him if you like, but for pity's sake don't ruin his style," she tells Amanda; "I'd rather have him write trivial comedy than shallow tragedy." Linda fails and Gay, "sick of my work, sick of myself," seems determined to do something important as the international holocaust is about to erupt. "I'm sick of the triviality, sick of ringing changes on what I've already written, sick of the futility," he decides: "If necessary, I swear to God, I want it shot out of myself." Even Amanda's crusty husband's offer to marry Linda does not console her for losing Gay—who is less eager to leave when the time comes to go to Spain with Amanda. Suddenly Linda has an idea. "Why don't you write a play about Mandy and me?" she suggests; "the builder-upper and the breaker-downer—the critical faculty versus the clinging vine—WHAT EVERY WOMAN KNOWS in reverse." Gay is increasingly fascinated with the idea, with the question of "Which wins out in the end." Amanda telephones for Gay to join her. Gay wants Linda to answer the call for him, but Linda insists that he must formulate his own resolution: "You ought to know. You've got to write it. It's the curtain for your last act, isn't it?" He lifts the receiver and agonizes over what to say. Confident of his choice, Linda watches him, "a knowing smile on her face."

NOAH (*Noé*), a play in five acts by ANDRÉ OBEY, published and produced in 1931. Setting: biblical.

This simple but poignant play is "a meditation on the allegorical, moral, and anagogical reality of the Noah story," Francis Fergusson wrote in his analysis of *Noah* in *The Idea of a Theater* (1949); it is "histrionic theater-poetry," he continued, that shows "in miniature, as it were in a colored stereoscopic view, the perpetual death and rebirth, the tragic rhythm, of human life."

Cheerfully building his ark, Noah calls out for helpful advice: "Lord . . . it's me, sorry to bother you again." He alone persists in trusting God, however difficult He is to reach. The animals aboard the ark cavort amusingly and communicate with Noah. But his sons and their women have no respect for their parents, and his wife has no faith. Atop Mount Ararat, the sons wildly run off with their women—who spit on the ark—to stake their land claims, and Noah's old wife falls asleep, too tired to face the future. Despite the apparent futility of doing good and ridding the world of evil, Noah remains faithful. He asks for God's sign that He is satisfied, too—whereupon a rainbow appears. "That's fine!" Noah concludes.

NORMAN, Frank (1931–   ), English writer hailed by some as the DAMON RUNYAN of his country, became known with *Fings Ain't Wot They Used T'Be* (music by Lionel Bart), produced by Joan Littlewood's London Theatre Workshop in 1959. Its lowlife sketches are set in Norman's own underworld milieu. The illegitimate son of a fruit peddler, Norman was first arrested at twelve. He became a burglar, was repeatedly jailed, and learned to read and write in prison. Norman has displayed a fine gift for storytelling, and his vulgarly comic drama is in the tradition of BERTOLT BRECHT and BRENDAN BEHAN. Norman's second play is also a musical, *A Kayf Up West* (1961, Cockney for "a café in the West End"); it is based on his autobiography, *Stand on Me* (1960). *Inside-out* (1969), Norman's third play, derived from his experiences in prison. An earlier autobiography was *Bang to Rights: An Account of Prison Life* (1958), and yet another autobiographical work is his novel *The Guntz* (1961).

NORTH AFRICA. In this part of the world, theatres feature principally ARAB DRAMAS, although there have also been some in French. Notable among the latter is that of Algerians such as the novelist-playwright Emmanuel Roblès (1914–), whose *Montserrat* was adapted by LILLIAN HELLMAN; Mouloud Mammeri (1917–), another novelist-playwright, who produced the revolutionary drama *Le Foehn* (1967); and Kateb Yacine (1929–), who moved to France and whose topically anticolonial *Le Cadavre encerclé* (1958), an avant-garde portrayal of the death and rebirth of a massacred Algerian, was first produced in Brussels.

For studies, see AFRICA.

NORWAY is particularly distinguished in the history of modern drama because of the work of HENRIK IBSEN, the Western world's first great modern playwright. Only BJØRNSTJERNE BJØRNSON approaches his importance in Norwegian literary history, and he does so mostly because of his nondramatic writings. Sigrid Undset, Norway's greatest twentieth-century author, did not write plays. Another Nobel Prize novelist, Knut Hamsun (1859–1952), wrote little and relatively insignificant drama: a trilogy on the life of a Nietzschean superman, *Ved rikets port* (1895), *Livets spill* (1896), and *Aftenrøde* (1898); an eight-act poetic "world drama" that has been likened to Ibsen's PEER GYNT and that features a nomad hunter, *Munken Vendt* (1902); and two romances, the Eastern history *Dronning Tamara* (1903) and the modern comedy *Livet ivold* (1910). A third and still earlier distinguished Norwegian novelist, Jonas Lie (1833–1908), had equally scant success with his few plays, which include the poetic tragedy *Faustina Strozzi* (1876) and the comedies *Lystige koner* (1894) and *Lindelin* (1897).

Like all modern Scandinavian literature, Norwegian drama received its great impetus with the work of Georg Brandes, the Danish literary historian and critic of nineteenth-century romanticism. Much of the earlier Norwegian drama was intertwined with that of Denmark, and written in Dano-Norwegian, the language of the educated classes. At the time Ibsen made his first important contributions, the only native drama of significance was that of such writers as Andreas Munch (1811–84) and Ivar Aasen (1813–96), whose musical folk play *Ervingen* (1855) achieved great popularity because of its songs. These and other Norwegian plays never achieved an importance comparable to that of the major and soon internationally acclaimed (and excoriated) works of Ibsen (and to a lesser extent of Bjørnson), although GUNNAR HEIBERG carried on Ibsen's spirit.

Major writers in other genres occasionally succeeded in the theatre. The novelist Alexander Lange Kielland (1849–1906) lightly satirized such contemporary issues as the "new woman" and changing university life in such plays as *Tre par* (*Three Couples,* 1886), *Bettys formynder* (1887), and *Professoren* (1888). The scholar, novelist, and poet Arne Garborg (1851–1924) wrote a religious verse trilogy in which the hero of *Læraren* (1896), its first play, resembles the protagonists of Ibsen's BRAND and Bjørnson's BEYOND HUMAN POWER I; the trilogy's sequels are *Den burtkomne faderen* (1899), a portrayal of egotism that is considered one of Garborg's masterpieces, and *Heimkomin son* (1908), a highly personal but less impressive work.

There were others who produced early modern drama of note. Much Norwegian drama, then and later, was nationalistic (Norway broke off with Sweden in 1905) and dealt with native themes. Hans Aanrud (1863–1953) wrote regional comedies, including the satire *Hanen* (1906). The lyric poet Nils Collett Vogt (1864–1937) also wrote psychological drama, notably *Moren* (1913) and *Therese* (1914). Hans Ernst Kinck (1865–1926) wrote penetrating mystic novels and dramas on Norwegian society and nature; verse plays about an erratic genius resembling Ibsen's Peer Gynt, *Driftekaren* (1908), and its sequel, *På rindalslægeret* (1925); and such plays about Renaissance Italy as the tragedy *Agilulf den vise* (1906, based on Boccaccio), *Den sidste gjest* (1910), *Lisabettas brødre* (1921), and others. The short-lived poet Sigbjørn Obstfelder (1866–1900) wrote a prophetic play about the danger of technology to the human spirit, *De røde dråper* (1897). Interested primarily in nature, the essayist and dramatist Nils Kjær (1870–1924) first made his name with an attack on moral relativism, *Regnskabets dag* (1902), a play that was followed by such other attacks on liberalism as *Mimosas hjemkomst* (1907), the political comedy *Det lykkelige valg* (1913), and *For træet er der håp* (1917).

The early twentieth century saw the emergence of no notable new dramatists, and it was not until the years between the two world wars that Norwegian drama began to thrive again. Novelists of the period who occasionally essayed the drama include Oskar Braaten (1881–1939), a proletarian writer who produced a popular play about Oslo factory girls, *Den store barnedåpen* (1925); Sigurd Christiansen (1891–1947), who also wrote proletarian drama (*Edmund jahr,* 1926) as well as a number of Ibsenite plays, the only successful one being *En reise i natten* (1931); the religious writer Ronald Fangen (1895–1946); and the Danish-born Aksel Sandemose (1899–1965).

The only Norwegian drama of the period between

the wars at all known outside of Scandinavia is that of the country's leading playwrights of the time, HELGE KROG and NORDAHL GRIEG; the latter inspired his countrymen during World War II, in which he lost his life. The poet Tore Ørjasæter (1886–) achieved success as a playwright with his portrayal of the famous nineteenth-century reindeer hunter *Jo Gjende* (1917) and other NATURALISTIC portrayals of simple men's quest for self-identity; he excelled in EXPRESSIONIST religious works, as in the Saint Christopher play *Christophoros* (1947) and in a modern Passion play dealing with Nazi-occupied Norway, *Den lange bryllaupsreisa* (1949). The novelist Tarjei Vesaas (1897–), while best known for his Telemark tales, also wrote SYMBOLIC plays beginning with a study of guilt and atonement, *Guds bustader* (1925), and including an expressionistic study of human impurity symbolized in a laundry, *Bleikeplassen* (1946). Though the rising menace of Nazism was frequently portrayed in Norwegian novels in the 1930's and 1940's, few dramas on the subject succeeded in production. The later, postwar theatre flourished, but it produced no new native drama of international significance. Playwrights of promise in the 1960's were Jens Bjørneboe (1920–), whose BRECHTian *Fugleelskerne* (1966) portrays contemporary German tourism with overtones that recall the earlier Nazi occupation; and Finn Carling (1926–), whose *Gitrene* (1966) is a complex drama set in a zoo and deals with animals, humans, and the divine.

Harald Beyer's *Norsk litteraturhistorie* (1952), translated as *A History of Norwegian Literature* (1956), is an extensive study of that country's writers, including dramatists.

NOTORIOUS MRS. EBBSMITH, THE, a drama in four acts by ARTHUR WING PINERO, published and produced in 1895. Setting: Venice, Italy; 1890's.

After THE SECOND MRS. TANQUERAY Pinero produced this similarly serious, more popular—though less impressive—work. "The play is bad," BERNARD SHAW wrote in his review, poking particular fun at the "bible-burning" scene, the third-act curtain that made the play something of a SUCCÈS DE SCANDALE.

Acts I and II. Agnes Ebbsmith is a young widow who was unhappily married. An idealist, she followed her father in becoming a soap-box orator against capital and marriage. She was effective but gave up preaching for nursing to keep from starving. In Rome she nursed Lucas Cleeve, an idealistic young aristocrat on the verge of political prominence. Unhappily married, he became attracted to Agnes. They joined forces, and now live and work together. She wants their union to be passionless, to help them both fight for their causes. A duke, Cleeve's cynical and profligate uncle, is sent to "save" him. He once heard "the notorious Mrs. Ebbsmith," who was also known as "Mad Agnes," preaching from her platform. Though she is "Trafalgar Squaring" at him now, Agnes recognizes some truth in his depiction of Cleeve's real and less than admirable character, and she comes to see that her attraction to him is entirely sensual. Despite her fanatic aversion to love and marriage, Agnes finds she loves Cleeve; to have "her hour" as a woman, she is willing to make herself attractive, wear the low-cut gown he bought her, and even marry him.

Acts III and IV. Friends attempt to persuade Agnes to give up her liaison and return to England with them. They press a "small leather-bound book" into her hand, but Agnes becomes increasingly agitated. "You foolish people, not to know that Hell or Heaven is here and here!" she says, pointing to the book. She throws it into the fire—and then, with "a look of fright and horror," thrusts her arm into the stove and pulls the charred book out. "My—hour—is—over," she writes Cleeve, and goes to her friends. His wife comes to beg her to return for a while, to give Cleeve the courage to go to England, preserve appearances, and save his career. But Agnes recognizes his falsity and cowardice and her own failure to be true to herself, to set an example to others, to show "how laws—laws made and laws that are natural—may be set aside or slighted; how men and women may live independent and noble lives without rule, or guidance, or sacrament." But her figure—like Cleeve's—"was made of wax—it fell awry at the first hot breath that touched it!" Now she sees only baseness and wickedness in their relationship. She sends the amazed Cleeve away with the promise that "when I have learnt to pray again, I will remember you every day of my life."

NOVELLO, Ivor (1893–1951), English actor, composer, and dramatist, was a prolific and popular producer of musical plays. Born into the Davies family of musicians—his real name was David Ivor Davies—Novello achieved phenomenal success in World War I with "Keep the Home Fires Burning." He composed other songs for musicals and wrote plays in which he usually acted the leading part. Best among his nonmusical plays are *The Rat* (1924; written with Constance Collier, 1878–1955) and *We Proudly Present* (1947). The romantic musicals with which he achieved his great success from 1935 until 1951 include *Glamorous Night* (1935), *The Dancing Years* (1939, a permanent World War II British production), *Perchance to Dream* (1945), *King's Rhapsody* (1949, in which he was starring at the time of his death), and *Gay's the Word* (1951). See Peter Noble's *Ivor Novello: Man of the Theatre* (1951).

NOWACZYŃSKI, Adolf (1876–1944), Polish journalist and playwright, wrote satires and erudite but highly unorthodox historical dramas. Many of them have grand scenic effects and are chronicles in dialogue modeled on BERNARD SHAW. They include *Tsar Dmitri* (1908); *Wielki Fryderyk* (1909), on Frederick the Great; *Sen srebrny Salomei Kohn* (1923), a typical satire; *Wojna wojnie* (1928), an Aristophanic comedy; *Wiosna narodów* (1929), a satire of the eventful year 1848 in Poland; and

Cezar i człowiek (1937), a fantastic romantic linking of Lucrezia Borgia and Copernicus.

NUDE WITH VIOLIN, "a light comedy" in three acts by NOËL COWARD, produced in 1956 and published in 1957. Setting: Paris, 1954.

This play dramatizes the revelation, following his death, that a prominent artist was a fraud—a plot similar to those of Milne's THE TRUTH ABOUT BLAYDS, Fauchois's THE LATE CHRISTOPHER BEAN, and ARNOLD BENNETT's adaptation of his own novel *Buried Alive*.

His long-deserted wife, their adult children, and the dealer who helped establish his international reputation all return from the funeral of the great painter. His valet and longtime friend, Sebastian (Sebastien Lacréole), reveals some shocking news to them. A delightfully suave, multilingual scoundrel who served in many jails, Sebastian reads them the artist's affidavit that attests to his not having been the creator of any of his masterpieces, which adorn the leading museums of the world. The cynically worded document, Sebastian remarks, "was his final gesture, a last decisive blow aimed at the parasites who, in his opinion, had betrayed the only thing he really respected in human nature, the creative instinct" he himself lacked. The real painters are a motley crew, the work of each of whom has been attributed to a particular "period" in the artist's career. One by one they now appear: former mistresses (a Russian tart parading as a princess, and a Cockney "ex-Jackson girl"), a Negro immersionist missionary, and Sebastian's illegitimate little boy. The family and the art dealer finally agree to pay the required blackmail, to avoid ridicule and the swindle's exposure, and Sebastian's son can put his last touches on the dead artist's final masterpiece, "Nude with Violin."

NUGENT, Elliott (1900–   ), American actor, director, and playwright, the son of show-business people, began appearing on the vaudeville stage when he was four, and wrote plays while a student at Ohio State University. With his actor-playwright father, John Charles Nugent (1868–1947), he authored some ten comedies, beginning with *Kempy* (1922). The most popular of them was *The Poor Nut* (1925), whose turning-of-the-worm theme provided the idea for *The Male Animal* (1940). This popular play features a once mild-mannered professor vigorously fighting for intellectual freedom and romance when an attempt is made to prevent his public reading of Vanzetti's last speech, and when his marriage is endangered by his wife's former suitor, a football player. Revived for an even longer run in 1952, at the height of McCarthyism, *The Male Animal* was a collaboration with Nugent's old friend James Thurber (1894–1961). (It was the humorist-cartoonist's only play, though in 1960 he dramatized a collection of his writings as *The Thurber Carnival*.) Nugent directed and acted in a number of Hollywood films, and starred in many Broadway hits, including *The Male Animal*.

O

OBALDIA, René de (1918–   ), Hong-Kong-born French novelist and playwright, amused and shocked theatre audiences in the 1960's with light "impromptus" such as *Génousie* (*Jenusia,* 1960; a bizarre murder mystery), *Impromptus à loisir* (*Seven Impromptus for Leisure,* 1961), *Le Satyre de la Villette* (1963), and *Du Vent dans les branches du sassafra* (*The Wind in the Sassafras Trees,* 1965), a portrayal in revue-sketch style of a Hollywood western as seen through European eyes and produced also as *Rockefeller and the Red Indians* ("Rockefeller" being one of the ranchers). Consisting of fantastic dialogue and stage effects, most of them depict human exuberance in the face of burlesqued contemporary cultural and popular fashions.

The first volume of Obaldia's translated *Plays* (1965) includes *Jenusia* and *Seven Impromptus for Leisure.*

OBEY, André (1892–   ), French dramatist, is best known for the plays he wrote for JACQUES COPEAU's company, which he joined in 1929. Most important among the works he produced there—the first to be presented by the *Compagnie des Quinze* at the Vieux-Colombier—was *Noé* (NOAH, 1931), but in the same year also appeared his *Le Viol de Lucrèce* and a nonmusical war oratorio, *La Bataille de la Marne.* The former is a dramatization of Shakespeare's *The Rape of Lucrece;* adapted by THORNTON WILDER as *Lucrece* (1932), Obey's play (with music by Deems Taylor) was produced on Broadway. Another Obey modernization of a classic tale made famous by a Shakespeare poem is *Venus et Adonis* (*Venus and Adonis,* 1932), a short but striking theatre piece.

These plays are in modern but formal language, and stylized in their employment of narrators and other PRESENTATIONAL devices. Further such dramatizations are *Don Juan* (1934), revised as *L'Homme de cendres* (1950); *Oedipe* (1948); *Lazare* (1951), the story of Lazarus; and *Une Fille pour du vent* (1952), based on the Iphigenia legends. Plays on other subjects include his collaboration with Denys Amiel (1884–   ) on *La Souriante Mme Beudet* (1921, produced in New York as *The Wife with the Smile*), a *Madame Bovary* with a happier resolution; and *Maria* (1945), a PIRANDELLian polarization of illusion and reality, and of theatre and life. Later plays include *Plus de miracles pour Noël* (1957, translated as *Frost at Midnight*), a nativity play-within-a-play. He also adapted *Les Gueux du Paradis* with its Belgian author, GASTON MARTENS.

With informative notes on Obey and the plays, *Noah* appears in John Gassner's collection *Twenty Best European Plays on the American Stage* (1963), and *Venus and Adonis* in Eric Bentley's *From the Modern Repertoire, Series Two* (1952).

OBOLER, Arch (1907–   ), American dramatist, principally wrote radio plays and film scripts. His *Night of the Auk* (1956), a science-fiction play about moon travel and atomic warfare, had intellectual and artistic pretensions (it is written in verse) but failed with Broadway audiences as well as with literary critics. Oboler was born in Chicago. His collection of *Fourteen Radio Plays* (1940) was the first of its kind ever published.

O'CASEY, Sean (1880–1964), Irish playwright, like J. M. SYNGE, the Abbey Theatre's earlier major dramatist, transformed the vernacular into rich and—especially in his later plays—poetic prose. Like his predecessor, too, O'Casey incited theatre riots with his unsentimental depiction of the Irish. A self-educated common laborer, he was in his mid-forties when his first play was produced. But he soon gained international fame; it has not diminished, despite the commercial theatres' scant interest in his later, non-REPRESENTATIONAL plays, which he—as have many of his admirers—esteemed most. O'Casey's popular reputation, however, rests on the early masterpieces, on the NATURALISTIC plays dealing with lower-class life during the wars that accompanied Irish independence, and primarily on JUNO AND THE PAYCOCK (1924) and on THE PLOUGH AND THE STARS (1926).

He was the last of thirteen children born to poor Dublin Protestants, Susan and Michael Casey. Christened John, he gaelicized his full name to Sean O'Cathasaigh when he fought for Irish freedom and, when he despaired of its attainment, anglicized the surname to O'Casey. His father, a worker for the Irish Church Mission, died when O'Casey was six, and the mother struggled to support the children who did not perish in infancy. O'Casey grew up amidst poverty and squalor. Physically frail, his eyes became diseased, causing him great pain as a child and near-blindness as an adult. His formal schooling was brief. Beaten by his teacher, the tempestuous Johnny reciprocated by smashing a ruler "on the pink, baldy, hoary oul' head of hoary oul' Slogan," as he later wrote in his autobiography. He went to work as a boy, moving from one unskilled job to another, for he refused to put up with any injustice or abuse.

Returning to the miserable tenements after his long working hours, he sought the beauty he craved. Like Ayamonn in RED ROSES FOR ME

(1942), he manifested considerable talent in painting, music, and acting. He taught himself to read and write, and became fascinated with (and influenced by) the drama of Shakespeare—and the earlier Irish-born playwright, Dion Boucicault. His activities in the Church and in the Gaelic League stimulated his interest in the biblical idiom and the Irish language. Though he became increasingly critical of the Church and the Irish Republican movement, his interest in Socialism continued for the rest of his life. He joined the Irish Transport and General Workers' Union, becoming one of the lieutenants of Jim Larkin (the famous radical union organizer) and the secretary of labor's nationalistic Irish Citizen Army, founded after the bitter 1913 strike. This background permeates his plays, and his first two books chronicle patriotic and labor insurrections: *The Story of Thomas Ashe* (1918) and *The Story of the Irish Citizen Army* (1919).

In 1918, too, O'Casey published some of his songs and, possibly, a drama. Before 1923, when his plays were first produced, he had written *The Robe of Rosheen, The Frost in the Flower, Nipped in the Bud, The Harvest Festival,* and *The Crimson in the Tri-Colour*. The first of these plays, he recalled in his autobiography, was published in a Republican newspaper.* Those O'Casey sent to the Abbey Theatre were rejected by the directors, but with increasingly warm encouragement, especially by LENNOX ROBINSON. In fact, LADY GREGORY wanted to produce *The Crimson in the Tri-Colour,* but WILLIAM BUTLER YEATS disagreed. O'Casey's next play, THE SHADOW OF A GUNMAN (1923), made it—and his reputation.

O'Casey's second play was also produced in 1923. A one-act "political phantasy," *Kathleen Listens In* is a witty satire of contemporary Ireland: representatives of various factions court the title character, a personification of Ireland, for her vote. Then, a few months after *Juno and the Paycock*, his one-act *Nannie's Night Out* was produced; it is a tragicomedy about a widowed Dublin shopkeeper, her three "oul" suitors, and the title character, a raucous but doomed young alcoholic.†

The riot caused by *The Plough and the Stars,* his next play, was the most disastrous since the production of Synge's THE PLAYBOY OF THE WESTERN WORLD almost twenty years earlier. Once again Yeats appeared onstage to castigate a howling mob of indignant Irishmen's "ever-recurring celebration of the arrival of Irish genius." But O'Casey was fed up. Like other distinguished expatriates—notably OSCAR WILDE, BERNARD SHAW, and JAMES JOYCE—the forty-six-year-old playwright left Ireland and its stifling parochialism shortly later and settled in England. There he soon met and married the twenty-three-year-old star in the London production of *The Plough and the Stars,*

Sean O'Casey. (*Irish Tourist Board*)

Eileen Reynolds Carey, a Catholic. (Her memoirs, *Sean*, appeared in 1971.) They had three children and lived in England until his death.

O'Casey's next play, THE SILVER TASSIE (1928), marks the turning point of his dramaturgy by its departure from representationalism. It also caused his break with the Abbey Theatre, for Yeats rejected the play. The ensuing debate has been widely and frequently publicized. Its practical result was injurious to both parties. O'Casey lost a permanent theatre in which to experiment; the Abbey lost its artistic and financial mainstay, and declined.

O'Casey's experimentation continued in the "morality" WITHIN THE GATES (1934). The same year he also published two unimportant but spirited one-act farces, *The End of the Beginning* and *A Pound on Demand.* But O'Casey devoted the next few years principally to nondramatic writings. These include two autobiographies: *I Knock at the Door* (1939), produced in on- and Off-Broadway stage readings seventeen years later, and *Pictures in the Hallway* (1942), dramatized in 1956 by Paul Shyre (1927–   ). The earlier *The Flying Wasp* (1937) is in a part rebuttal of James Agate, the influential London critic who had dismissed *Within the Gates* as "pretentious rubbish" but persisted in praising the contemporary drama of writers like NOËL COWARD. O'Casey's book attacks frothy popular drama with pretensions of REALISM (particularly the plays of Coward) and defends artistic experimentation. This was the dark period of depression and war, and O'Casey's "morality" plays that followed reflect their period. Two wartime proletarian (pro-Communist), anti-Fascist plays of that period have been dismissed as propaganda tracts and inferior drama: *The Star*

* It and the other unpublished, unproduced, and apparently lost apprentice works are discussed in Robert Hogan's "O'Casey's Dramatic Apprenticeship," *Modern Drama* IV: 3 (December 1961).

† These two one-acters were published in O'Casey's autobiography, *Feathers from the Green Crow* (1962).

Turns Red (1940) depicts a Christmas Eve battle between workers and storm troopers, the latter supported by priests; *Oak Leaves and Lavender* (1946)* is set in an old English mansion at the beginning of World War II, and has some effective scenes and characterizations. With considerably greater success, the themes of the first were soon redramatized in *Red Roses for Me,* in the fantasy of the second in the farcical PURPLE DUST (1940), and in COCK-A-DOODLE DANDY (1949).

O'Casey mastered new PRESENTATIONAL techniques in these plays, particularly in *Cock-a-Doodle Dandy,* his finest work in that genre. It was followed by three one-act "Irish" farces published in 1951: the tragicomic *Hall of Healing* ("a Sincerious Farce") depicts an incident in a parish dispensary for the poor; in *Bedtime Story* ("an Anatole Burlesque") a timid young clerk is robbed and thoroughly discomfited by a "gay lass" who seduces him in his lodgings; and *Time to Go* ("a Morality Comedy") portrays venal storekeepers and farmers, temporarily chastened by a miracle, but soon dismissing it as "only an halleelucination!"

In the same decade O'Casey produced two full-length plays, THE BISHOP'S BONFIRE (1955) and THE DRUMS OF FATHER NED (1959), and in 1961 appeared his last three plays. *Behind the Green Curtains,* the finest of these one-acters, follows O'Casey's preoccupations of the previous major plays. In three scenes it portrays contemporary Irish writers and artists bravely opposing the bigoted, Puritan joylessness of the priesthood and its "blessed saints, Stepaslide, Touchnrun, Dubudont, an' Goslow"—so long as the "rebels" are in secure comfort "behind the green curtain" of their patron's home; but when the Church intimidates them with socioeconomic pressures and physical brutality, their heroism falters and only a few "rebels" have the courage to uproot themselves and leave. The remaining plays treat the same themes much more lightly and briefly. In *Figuro in the Night,* an "indecent" statue incites respectable Dubliners to shocked fury, but gives joy to the women and the young. *The Moon Shines on Kylenamoe* is a good-natured farce in which a group of squabbling Irish peasants best an important English lord. It is perhaps a fitting last play: as in *Purple Dust,* an Irish spirit prevails—as it did in O'Casey himself.

His plays are distinguished for the sheer fun of his characters, the wild beauty and lusty humor of their speech and actions, their song and dance, and the sympathetic and moving portrayal of the human condition. The ironic blend of pathos and farce juxtaposes man's lofty ideals and his ignominious practices. Everywhere there is O'Casey's passionate hatred of all that negates life and its joys: war, exploitation, hypocrisy, injustice, enslavement. His satire often lashes the Church, capitalism, and Fascism. His ideals are personified by his indomitable characters (usually women), by pacifism, and by Communism. But if some of his espousals are questionable or exasperating, the ideas and feelings behind them are not. They celebrate O'Casey's love of life, vitality, and gaiety; and they express the compassion the self-styled "green crow" felt for his fellow beings.

O'Casey's drama is readily available in *The Collected Plays* (four volumes, 1949) and in various other editions. The six autobiographies are collected in the two-volume *Mirror in My House* (1956). There is a discussion of the plays as theatre in Robert Hogan's *The Experiments of Sean O'Casey* (1960). David Krause's *Sean O'Casey: The Man and His Work* (1960), Saros Cowasjee's *Sean O'Casey: The Man Behind the Plays* (1964), Gabriel Fallon's *Sean O'Casey, The Man I Knew* (1965), and essay collections edited by Sean McCann (*The World of Sean O'Casey,* 1966) and Ronald Ayling (*O'Casey: Modern Judgments Series,* 1967) allude to further studies, relevant documents, and reminiscences. *The Sean O'Casey Reader: Plays, Autobiographies, Opinions* (1968), a substantial collection edited and introduced by Brooks Atkinson, has a comprehensive bibliography.

* Subtitled "A Warld on Wallpaper," in answer to one of Yeats's famous objections to *The Silver Tassie:* "There should be no room in a play for anything that does not belong to it; the whole history of the world must be reduced to wallpaper in front of which the characters must pose and speak."

ODETS, Clifford (1906–63), American playwright, became notable overnight with a short and doctrinaire left-wing drama, WAITING FOR LEFTY (1935). Its success motivated the Group Theatre, in which Odets served his apprenticeship and his most fruitful years, to bring the play to Broadway, and to produce the revised script of an earlier-written play, AWAKE AND SING! (1935). Together with GOLDEN BOY (1937), these works made Odets the most promising American playwright of the 1930's. But though he wrote some dozen plays in his life (all but one of them produced on Broadway), his subsequent drama diminished in quantity and importance, and his once-popular plays seemed dated to post-Depression audiences. Odets recouped commercial success after World War II with THE COUNTRY GIRL (1949), and he was praised by noted critics for his last play, THE FLOWERING PEACH (1954). But he never regained his reputation of the 1930's. His drama in that decade, however, and his influence on the postwar American theatre (especially on playwrights such as ARTHUR MILLER and TENNESSEE WILLIAMS) made his work artistically as well as historically significant.

Born in Philadelphia to a poor Jewish working-class family that eventually moved to the Bronx and prospered, Odets began his career as an actor. He played with a Manhattan neighborhood company that specialized in one-act plays, then joined a cooperative group that produced plays in a church basement, recited poetry, acted in vaudeville, and worked as a radio announcer and sound-effects man. In 1925 Odets formed a company of his own and presented radio programs, which he wrote himself. Then he played stock, notably the lead in Nichols's ABIE'S IRISH ROSE. After some further work in stock and on the radio, Odets joined the Theatre Guild and eventually became a charter member (and later the star dramatist) of its offshoot, the Group Theatre (1931–40), which featured drama about social problems. Odets joined the Communist Party, but left it after eight months when he found its pressures on his playwriting artistically stifling. He started writing a number of plays, including one on Beethoven. For a while he was stymied as a playwright, however, because the Group chose to present the drama of SIDNEY KINGSLEY and confined Odets's activities to acting.

But all that changed with the success of *Waiting for Lefty*. Not only did the Group Theatre now accept the previously rejected script of *Awake and Sing!* (originally titled *I've Got the Blues*), but it also produced (together with *Lefty*) Odets's hastily written anti-Nazi piece, *Till the Day I Die* (1935). It depicts a sensitive German Communist, tortured by the Nazis to betray his comrades, who is not quite broken but is nonetheless blacklisted by the Communists and can reinstate himself only by committing suicide. The play is harrowing but it rings false, perhaps because of Odets's ignorance of the foreign setting and characters. At that time —his *annus mirabilis,* 1935—Odets headed a commission to investigate "the domination of Cuba by American financial and industrial interests." He and his companions were arrested in Havana and sent back, but their protest received publicity, and Odets was hailed for his courage. A play he wrote about this experience, however, never got beyond the first draft.

The Group Theatre next produced its by then foremost dramatist's *Paradise Lost* (1935). Similar in its setting and characters to *Awake and Sing!, Paradise Lost* is about a family beset by many horrendous disasters, though the lovable father, finally bankrupt and evicted, can retain his ideals and look toward a Paradise Regained; "Ohhh, darling, the world is in its morning," he tells his wife, "and *no man fights alone!*" After the play's commercial failure, Odets accepted a lucrative Hollywood offer. His friends accused him of "selling out" to the Establishment, and Odets atoned and purged himself, as it were, with *Golden Boy*. He helped the Group Theatre finance it, and the highly successful production enabled the Group to continue its precarious existence. Odets further aided the Group's survival with his next play, ROCKET TO THE MOON (1938). In 1939 Odets's reputation was sealed—almost literally—with the Modern Library's publication of his collected drama, *Six Plays of Clifford Odets*. (A seventh, *The Silent Partner,* was completed in 1937 but remained unproduced.) At the end of the decade Odets returned to the Group, for whom he wrote his next play, *Night Music* (1940), "a song cycle on a given theme" (homelessness). It was a commercially unsuccessful, tender play that features, among many other lonely characters, a Hollywood man and the girl he gets entangled with in New York when two trained apes he is escorting to California snatch her purse. Odets's next play, *Clash by Night* (1941), is a weak triangle drama about a marriage that collapses because of the couple's loneliness and inability to communicate.

Odets spent the following years in Hollywood, writing screenplays. The most successful of these were probably *The General Died at Dawn* (1936), *None But the Lonely Heart* (1943), and *The Sweet Smell of Success* (1957). Shortly before his death he began to write television drama, but completed only two minor works. His remaining plays were an adaptation of Simonov's THE RUSSIAN PEOPLE (1942); *The Big Knife* (1949), a sardonic attack on Hollywood that depicts a movie star who finally commits suicide because he can retain his integrity no more than could the protagonist of *Golden Boy;* the considerably more successful play with a similar setting, *The Country Girl;* and—though he enthusiastically began, but never completed, writing a number of others—his last play, *The Flowering Peach*. At the time of his death Odets was working on a musical version of *Golden Boy*.

When Odets first went to Hollywood he fell in love with and in 1937 married the film star Luise Rainer. Pursuit of independent careers soon caused a separation, and their divorce became final in 1941. Two years later he married Bette Grayson, an actress he had known since the early thirties.

The importance of Odets should not be underestimated, despite his failure to fulfill his great early promise. First of all, he transformed the slight and ephemeral AGITPROP drama into something more substantial, noteworthy, and permanent. *Waiting for Lefty* is the only work in the genre that is still read and revived, although its contemporary impact, of course, is forever lost. If much of Odets's dramas were propagandistic depictions of "exploiters" and "exploited," there is some validity in his claim that "all plays, just like all literature, are essentially propaganda." His drama reflects the influence of ANTON CHEKHOV and SEAN O'CASEY, but Odets's personality and inherent talents gave it a distinctive and American stamp. Particularly unique is Odets's memorable dramatization of the Depression era and his often lyrical depiction of the Jewish-American milieu—especially of the family unit—whose speech, mannerisms, and characterizations Odets caught so well. But, as is particularly true of his last work, Odets used his milieu for a parable of all men and of his age. Unfortunately he delayed too long in developing the creative talents that first made him famous. Only his last two plays took him beyond the 1930's type of drama he kept writing long after the age had passed.

Six Plays of Clifford Odets (1939) has an appendix, "Three Introductions by Harold Clurman." Odets's friend and the Group Theatre's director, Clurman also published *The Fervent Years* (1945; subtitled "The Story of the Group Theatre and the Thirties"), which includes reminiscences of play productions and his association with Odets. Book-length studies of Odets are R. Baird Shuman's *Clifford Odets* (1962), Edward Murray's *Clifford Odets: The Thirties and After* (1968), Michael J. Mendelsohn's *Clifford Odets: Humane*

Dramatist (1969), and Gerald Weales's *Clifford Odets—Playwright* (1971).

OELSCHLEGEL, Gerd (1926–), German dramatist, in the 1950's started writing popular NATURALISTIC plays that dramatize the kind of "objective theatre" he advocated: *Zum guten Nachbarn* (1954, also titled *Romeo und Julia 1953 in Berlin*) and *Staub auf dem Paradies* (1957).

OF MICE AND MEN, a play in three acts by JOHN STEINBECK, published and produced in 1937. Setting: the Salinas River Valley in California, the mid-1930's.

A dramatization of Steinbeck's NATURALISTIC novel, which was published the same year and which GEORGE S. KAUFMAN helped to stage, this play won the New York Drama Critics' Circle Award, was filmed in 1939, and was made into a musical in 1958.

Lennie Small, a powerful but feebleminded itinerant farm laborer, reports for work in a new job with his protective friend, George Milton. They dream of someday having a farm of their own, where Lennie would be allowed to tend to the animals. He is affectionate and loves to handle soft objects (small pets that die in his strong hands), but the menacing combination of his physical strength and mental weakness causes repeated trouble and eventual tragedy. The boss's son, a bully, is hurt in a fight with him, and the bully's flirtatious wife, impressed by Lennie's strength, starts to seduce him. Accidentally he crushes her to death, and then tries to escape. George manages to divert the mob gathered to lynch Lennie. Then he calms the huge but frightened cretin, who looks across the river, envisioning their "little place . . . with cow . . . pig . . . chickens . . . alfalfa . . . rabbits . . ." As he mumbles dreamily, George aims his pistol at the back of Lennie's head, and kills him.

OF THEE I SING, a musical play in two acts by GEORGE S. KAUFMAN and MORRIE RYSKIND (music by George Gershwin, lyrics by Ira Gershwin), produced in 1931 and published in 1932. Setting: various places in the United States during a presidential campaign in the 1920's, and Washington, D.C.

The first musical to win the Pulitzer Prize, this play has often been revived, notably by Erwin Piscator in 1949. In a manner that recalls W. S. GILBERT and Arthur Sullivan, it satirizes the charlatanism and absurdities of politics and campaigning. The same authors' sequel, *Let 'Em Eat Cake* (1933), was considerably less successful.

Handsome young John P. Wintergreen runs for President on the slogan "Put Love in the White House." He is supposed to marry the winner of a beauty contest; instead, he falls in love with and eventually marries a campaigner who makes delicious corn muffins, and he proposes to her in every state during his presidential campaign. The spurned beauty queen, a Southern belle claiming to be "the illegitimate daughter of an illegitimate son of an illegitimate nephew of Napoleon," sues Wintergreen, and is assisted by the French ambassador. After his election, President Wintergreen wins popular support with the announcement that he is about to become a father—whereupon the Supreme Court decides that the child will be twins, one of each sex. The beauty queen marries Alexander Throttlebottom, the forgotten Vice-President who keeps seeking recognition, and all ends happily with the play's "anthem," "Of Thee I Sing, Baby."

OKLAHOMA!, a musical comedy in two acts by OSCAR HAMMERSTEIN II (music by Richard Rodgers), published and produced in 1943. Setting: the Indian Territory admitted in 1907 as the State of Oklahoma, c. 1900.

Based on Riggs's GREEN GROW THE LILACS, *Oklahoma!* (originally titled *Away We Go*) was one of the most successful and longest-running American musicals of the century, and its integration of plot, ballet, and songs profoundly influenced subsequent musicals. The play is considered something of a national drama; it has represented America throughout the world and its title song was adopted as the Oklahoma state anthem. The original folk songs were supplanted with new ones that are often based on Riggs's lines—and have in turn become folk songs in their own right. Though the idiom is made more sophisticated for Broadway audiences, the plot and dialogue closely follow those of *Green Grow the Lilacs.*

OLAF LILJEKRANS, a play in three acts by HENRIK IBSEN, produced in 1857 and published (in German translation) in 1898. Setting: a mountain district in the Middle Ages.

In 1850 Ibsen wrote *Rypen i Justedal,* a fragment based on András Fáy's folktales. He revised it in 1856 into this poetic romance, whose subject is taken from "Olaf Liljekrans," one of the folk ballads in Magnus Landstad's collected *Norske Folkeviser* (1853).

Shortly before his wedding to the spirited daughter of his plebeian and hostile—but wealthy—neighbor, Count Olaf is entranced by the beautiful mountain girl Alfhild. His proud mother insists that he marry his affianced bride, and succeeds in condemning the heartbroken Alfhild to death. At the end, Alfhild is saved by and reunited with Olaf; the bride is united with her true lover, her father's page.

OLD LADY SAYS "NO!," THE, "A Romantic Play in Two Parts with Choral Interludes" by DENIS JOHNSTON, published and produced in 1929. Setting: Dublin, the 1920's and, in the mind of a contemporary actor (the Speaker), back through 1803.

This EXPRESSIONIST play with music and poetry, written in 1926 and originally titled *Shadowdance,* was returned to Johnston by the Abbey Theatre with its present title—either as an alternate, the playwright remarked, or to convey LADY GREGORY's judgment. Despite its satire, the play has been a popular one in Ireland. Replete with historical,

Oklahoma! New York, 1946. (*Culver Pictures*)

literary, and social satire, however, its topical allusions are so specially Irish that the play has had little meaning and few productions elsewhere.

An actor (or Speaker) is portraying the Irish hero Robert Emmet. In a bombastic opening (reminiscent of nineteenth-century patriotic Irish melodrama), Emmet is arrested while he bids his sweetheart farewell. The "Redcoat" who knocks him down injures the actor playing the part of Emmet, and a physician from the house tends to him. While the doctor is out looking for a blanket for him, the dazed actor imagines the various fast-moving and quickly dissolving episodes of the play. They blend the character of Emmet with early and late nineteenth-century and contemporary Irish history and society, and stress the gap between Emmet's idealism and past and present reality. At the end, the actor declaims snatches of Emmet's final speech, which is interlarded with Patrick Henry Pearse's funeral oration for O'Donovan Rossa. His eyes close as he softly finishes: "There now. Let my epitaph be written." The physican reappears, puts a finger to his lips as he looks at the audience, covers the unconscious actor with a rug, and has the curtain drawn.

OLESHA [or Olyosha], **Yuri Karlovich** (1899–1960), Russian novelist, essayist, and playwright, occupies an anomalous position in Russian literature. He was born in Elizavetgrad and raised in Odessa, and he welcomed the Bolshevik Revolution. But as its excesses persisted over the years, the artist became increasingly disturbed by what he saw and felt. The remainder of his creative life Olesha spent in anguished vacillation between his enthusiasm for the new world, and criticism of its restrictive and strangling effect on artistic expression—between admiration for the ideals and changes wrought by the Revolution, and a yearning for a return to artistic freedom and the older morality. In 1934 Olesha expressed these views movingly in a courageous and memorable speech before the First All-Union Congress of Writers: despite its profound impact on his fellow writers, Olesha was not heard of again for two decades, and his works were taken out of circulation. Somehow he survived the purges; he died in his apartment in the Soviet writers' village of Peredelkino.

The agonizing doubts about the conflict of old and new values are reflected in the short tragic farce that made Olesha famous, the novel *Zavist* (*Envy,* 1927)—and in his five plays. By far the most notable of these is *Spisok blagodeyanii* (A LIST OF ASSETS, 1931). The Hamlet-like autobiographical character of this play reappears in various guises in Olesha's other plays and fiction. *Zagovor chuvstv* (*The Conspiracy of Feelings,* 1929), a dramatization of his novel *Envy,* features a vulgar philosopher-clown who rebels against stifling restrictions and glories in the traditional bourgeois feelings prohibited by Communist materialism (personified by a salami tycoon); though unattractive, he expresses many of Olesha's true feelings. The comedy *Tri tolstyaka* (*The Three Fat Men,* 1928) is a dramatization of his adventure novel by the same name, which also was made into a ballet. More important is the short, perhaps unfinished *Chorny chelovek,* published in 1932. It depicts the struggle between a writer and the Black Man, "a cynic, a quack, a poisoner," Olesha explained—"the struggle," he added "between the idea of death in art and the idea of reconstruction of the world through creative work." His last major work, published in 1934, remained unproduced: *Strogi yunosha* (1932), originally a film script, portrays the complex love relationships of six characters who symbolize —again—the clash of old and new values.

Olesha's quest for self-realization and freedom shines through his plays. At the same time the plays reflect Olesha's struggle to decide between the two irreconcilable worlds of the old and the new. These themes recur in his plays and are symbolized by images of Hamlet, Charlie Chaplin, and Hans Christian Andersen's ugly duckling—symbols of the human and tragic quest for self-realization and dignity. Undoubtedly censorship necessitated the periodic oversimplifications and artificial resolutions that mar these plays. What is surprising is that Olesha was able—and was allowed—to present his quest as powerfully and as frankly as he did.

In 1956 an edition of Olesha's works was published in Russia. *A List of Assets* appeared in Andrew MacAndrew's collections *20th Century Russian Drama* (1963) and *Envy and Other Works of Yuri Olesha* (1967), and *The Conspiracy of Feelings* is in Bernard F. Dukore and Daniel C. Gerould's *Avant-Garde Drama* (1969), all with prefaces on Olesha. See also the relevant chapters in Gleb Struve's *Soviet Russian Literature 1917–50* (1951), Nikolai A. Gorchakov's *The Theater in Soviet Russia* (1957), Vera Alexandrova's *A History of Soviet Literature* (1963), and Edward J. Browne's *Russian Literature Since the Revolution* (revised in 1969).

OLMO, Lauro (1922–), Spanish poet and short-story writer, became known as a dramatist when his first play, *La camisa* (1961), won the National Literature Prize. He followed it with *La noticia* (*The News Item,* 1963), a one-acter in a projected series on the Spanish press, which portrays the mechanics and effects of totalitarian censorship on a group of people first indignant about a newspaper story but easily diverted with the latest ballgame scores. Later Olmo plays include the tragicomic *El cuerpo* (1965) and *La condecoración* (1965). *The News Item,* with a brief note on Olmo, appears in Michael Benedikt and George E. Wellwarth's *Modern Spanish Theatre* (1968).

ON BAILE'S STRAND, a one-act verse play by WILLIAM BUTLER YEATS, published in 1903 and produced in 1904. Setting: legendary Dundealgan, near the sea.

This is the first of Yeats's Cuchulain plays—and its premiere also launched the Abbey Theatre. The plot is partly derived from *Cuchulain of Muirthemne* (1902), the retelling of the Irish saga by LADY GREGORY, who also had a hand in the writing of this play. Two mutually dependent scoundrels, the Fool and the Blind Man, provide a prose framework that heightens the tragedy's irony.

For the sake of national peace and order, the old high king, Conchubar, demands that King Cuchulain take an oath of allegiance to him and his heirs. Conchubar's children fear the turbulent Cuchulain, who "burns the earth as if he were a fire, / And time can never touch him." Unwilling to be bridled, and bitter because he has no son of his own, Cuchulain angrily debates Conchubar. But all the other kings agree with the high king that Cuchulain must take the oath. "You've wives and children now, / And for that reason cannot follow one / That lives like a bird's flight from tree to tree," Cuchulain says, and submits his sword to the mastery of "the threshold and hearthstone." When Cuchulain concludes his oath of obedience to Conchubar, a young man arrives to challenge Cuchulain. The young man is from Scotland, whose "fierce woman" warrior Cuchulain had defeated and then loved. Cuchulain immediately feels drawn toward the young man, is reluctant to kill him, and rejects the challenge: "If I had a son / And fought with him, I should be deadly to him; / For the old fiery fountains are far off / And every day there is less heat o' the blood." Again, however, Conchubar thwarts Cuchulain's spirit. Though the hero wants the stranger's friendship, the high king now orders him to fight. Conchubar and the other kings believe Cuchulain is maddened by witchcraft, especially when the reluctant hero lays angry hands on the high king. He is compelled to obey Conchubar, supported by the other kings, all of whom were ready to fight in Cuchulain's stead. Cuchulain's battle and victory are reported by a chorus of women. It is the Fool and the Blind Man who reveal to the returning Cuchulain that the young man's mother, "a proud, pale, amorous woman," had had but "one lover, and he the only man that had overcome her in battle." The young man Cuchulain has slain was his own son. The maddened hero rushes out to kill Conchubar, "who sat up there / With your old rod of kingship, like a magpie / Nursing a stolen spoon." The Fool describes Cuchulain's rushing into the ocean and his battling the waves until he is overcome, mastered by them, and drowned. The Blind Man calls the Fool into the houses, deserted because their inhabitants are still on the beach: "The ovens will be full. We will put our hands into the ovens."

ON THE HARMFULNESS OF TOBACCO (*O vrede tabaka*), a one-act comic monologue by ANTON CHEKHOV, published in 1886 and approved by the censors for production in 1887. Setting: a contemporary lecture hall.

Chekhov kept revising this "vaudeville lecture" (translated also as *Smoking Is Bad for You*) delivered for charity, completing six different versions (1886–1903) that reveal, with progressive subtlety, the pathetic life of Marcellus Nyukhin, a henpecked elderly man who starts out to lecture on the evil of smoking but winds up delivering an extended plaint about his marital problems, and his longing to run away and "just forget."

ON THE HIGHWAY (*Na bolshoi doroge*), a dramatic study in one act by ANTON CHEKHOV, published in 1914. Setting: a contemporary Russian inn on a stormy night.

Chekhov adapted this NATURALISTIC play (also translated as *On the High Road*), a moving depiction of down-and-outers, from his story "Osenyo" ("In the Autumn," 1883). The censor vetoed its production in 1885; believing the play, because of its unallayed naturalism, to fall below the "highest moral purpose," Chekhov himself suppressed it, deleting it from his collected works. It was published and produced posthumously.

As poor pilgrims and wayfarers huddle in the inn, an alcoholic pauper pitifully begs the innkeeper for a drink. Finally he pawns a gold locket and is revealed to be a once-wealthy landowner. He was ruined by dipsomania after his wife, whom he adored, deserted him for her lover on their wedding day. All, including a thieving bully of a tramp, now take pity on the alcoholic pauper. They provide him with liquor and try to make him comfortable. When the wife accidentally arrives to seek shelter, the tramp, another victim of female betrayal, furiously tries to kill her. He fails, she leaves, and as the curtain falls the tramp breaks down and sobs, "Oh misery! Cruel misery! Have pity on me, good Christians!"

ON THE ROCKS, "A Political Comedy" in two acts by BERNARD SHAW, produced in 1933 and published in 1934. Setting: 10 Downing Street, London; 1933.

Shaw's long preface is as interesting and controversial as the play and its amused disillusionment with Western civilization, its attack on "sham democracy," and its defense of dictatorship. A brilliant and shocking and inconsistent dialectic on extermination, the preface deplores man's cruel and sadistic propensities. It advocates, on the one hand, humane and scientific extermination of those who do not pull their weight in the "social boat" and, on the other hand, tolerance for ideas, no matter how heretical or false. It contains the "Jesus-Pilate Scene," an imaginative dramatization of the trial. Pilate wants Jesus to cite "a sound reason for letting a seditious blasphemer go free"; Jesus replies that "without sedition and blasphemy the world would stand still and the Kingdom of God never be a stage nearer," and thus forces Pilate, who recognizes Jesus's "power to turn men's hearts against" Caesar's empire and laws, to execute him. But the last words are Christ's and urge tolerance of heresy: "He who does not fear you and shews you the other side is a pearl of the greatest price. . . ."

Act I. Prime Minister Sir Arthur Chavender, on the verge of a nervous collapse, rejects his police commissioner's proposal—to machine-gun unemployed demonstrators—because of its effect on the elections. Sir Arthur attempts to compose a safe speech on The Family, for "when a statesman is not talking bunk he is making trouble for himself." His squabbling children, Flavia (nineteen) and David (eighteen), come in with Lady Chavender, who affectionately tells Sir Arthur that since "the country isnt governed: it just slummocks along anyhow," he should go for a rest cure in her doctor's sanatorium. When they leave, he resumes work on his speech but is interrupted now by the Isle of Cats's labor deputation, which includes Viscount Barking, an unshaven Communist tough, and the brilliant and efficient alderwoman Aloysia Brollikins. They want to know how he intends to cope with the unemployment crisis, and he tells them that he already has done all he can: "I am in the grip of economic forces that are beyond human control." He is told to read Marx, and after they leave, he tries again to work on his speech but is interrupted when Flavia and David excitedly come to tell him that they have almost been arrested with Aloysia and Barking, whom they are now courting. Finally, a mysterious lady who turns out tc be his wife's doctor persuades him to come to her sanatorium: he suffers from "that very common English complaint, an underworked brain," and thus has "piloted England on to the rocks." Deciding to take advanced radical books with him to improve his mind, he vows to hold his own with future deputations of intellectuals.

Act II. Three months later an aghast cabinet (and other striking caricatures of contemporaries) protest the now radical Sir Arthur's nationalization and other revolutionary proposals. He soon wins over all but Sir Dexter Rightside, the foreign minister and leader of the Conservative Party in the coalition government. His near-victory is upset by the Isle of Cats's labor deputation, which refuses to accept compulsory labor. After long, amusing, and witty arguments, they warn Sir Arthur that he will lose the people's support, and walk out: "We're on the rocks, the whole lot of us." Sir Arthur is unimpressed, but Sir Dexter challenges him: "Do you think you can govern in this country without the consent of the English people?" That is precisely what he intends to do: "No country has ever been governed by the consent of the people, because the people object to be governed at all." People are sick of democracy, "they want rulers," and "they are ready to go mad with enthusiasm for any man strong enough to make them do anything," provided only that it is cruel. But Sir Arthur is defeated when Sir Dexter dissolves the coalition and walks out. Though encouraged by his friends—one of whom delivers a lengthy endorsement of Fascism—to take the leadership, Sir Arthur shrinks from acting and retires from politics. The play ends with the comic love affairs of David-Aloysia and Flavia-Barking happily resolved, as rioting crowds outside chant revolution.

ON TRIAL, a play in three acts by ELMER RICE, produced in 1914 and published in 1919. Setting: New York, 1913.

The first commercially produced play by Rice (it appeared under the name Elmer R. Reizenstein), this sensationally successful murder mystery was performed throughout the world and made into a film and a novel—though Rice himself rightly called it merely "a shrewd piece of stage carpentry." It was the first play credited with utilizing the cinema's instant-flashback technique (although the flashback had just been used the year before in Sheldon's popular ROMANCE), achieved with an easily movable "jack-knife" set that Rice himself devised. Audiences were more enthralled by the then-new technique than by the plot, which pivots on whether a killing was impulsive or coldly premeditated. The play starts and ends in a courtroom, but much of the action consists of dramatizations of the testimony. The defendant admits killing his friend and business associate when he believed him to be his wife's lover. In a surprise ending that proves his wife innocent and the killing impulsive, the husband is freed and the couple are reunited.

ONCE IN A LIFETIME, a play in three acts by GEORGE S. KAUFMAN and MOSS HART, published and produced in 1930. Setting: New York, a Pullman car, and Los Angeles; 1920's.

The first joint hit by Kaufman and Hart, this was probably the best of the many contemporary burlesques of Hollywood. It is a madcap in which three vaudevillians decide to make their fortune with the new "talkies." They go to Hollywood to teach elocution. The witless remarks of the trio's boob get him appointed as studio director, and his harebrained doings make all their fortunes—as well as that of an equally stupid female he falls in love with and catapults into stardom. Kaufman himself acted the part of a New York scriptwriter who goes mad in his lucrative but totally forgotten and ignored Hollywood niche.

ONDINE, a play in three acts by JEAN GIRAUDOUX, published and produced in 1939. Setting: a fisherman's cottage and a palace in the Middle Ages.

This is one of Giraudoux's most lyrical and appealing plays. Though charmingly fanciful and ironic, it is moving and suggestive in its observations on life and love. It is based on a frequently adapted old Germanic legend first published in La Motte-Fouqué's tale *Undine* (1811).

Act I. On a stormy night in a poor fisherman's cottage, a young knight, Hans von Wittenstein zu Wittenstein, seeks shelter. He talks of his beautiful Princess Bertha, who made it a condition of their marriage that he wander alone through the woods for a month. The old fisher couple hospitably prepare food for him when the lovely Ondine comes in. She is their adopted sixteen-year-old daughter—and a water sprite. Artlessly Ondine falls in love with Hans as soon as she sees "How beautiful he is." Though the hungry Hans seems at first more interested in eating than in love, he quickly renounces his beloved Bertha for Ondine. "I shall be the breath of your lungs. I shall be the hilt of your sword and the pummel of your saddle," Ondine tells Hans: "I shall be your tears, your laughter, and your dreams." Other water sprites warn Ondine of the fickleness of humans. But she is determined on marrying Hans and living with him—like dogfish, which, after coupling, never leave each other: "Through storm and calm they swim together, side by side, two fingers apart, as if an invisible link held them together." Her uncle, the King of the Sea, warns her, "The world of men is not your world, Ondine. It will bring you sorrow." But the deeply infatuated Ondine persists, agreeing only that if Hans ever deceives her, he must die and she will return to the water.

Act II. At the palace a welcome is prepared for the return of Hans and his bride. Entertainments are being planned by the royal chamberlain and the theatre superintendent. They are joined by the King of the Sea, who is disguised as an illusionist and dazzles the others with his supernatural powers. He evokes the future—long magic scenes that foreshadow the unfaithfulness of Hans with Bertha. Then Hans arrives with Ondine. She almost immediately throws the court into an uproar with her natural simplicity and charm. The queen understands Ondine and—like the King of the Sea—cautions her against the humanly small-souled Hans. "Don't you see, my dear, that Hans loves what is great in you only because he sees it small?" she asks. "You are the sunlight and he loves a blond; you are grace itself and he loves a madcap and you are adventure and he loves an adventure"—thus Ondine is bound eventually to lose him. Instead, however, Ondine tries to keep Hans by humbling herself before the jealous Bertha, apologizing to her, and inviting her to live with them. The "illusionist" prepares to continue his presentation of the future, but the royal chamberlain calls for an intermission.

Act III. It is the morning of Bertha and Hans's wedding. As expected, Hans deceived Ondine, who then ran away. Months later she has been caught. She is to be tried as a witch this very day. The medieval judges appear, and the semicomic trial begins. To save Hans, Ondine pretends she was unfaithful. No one is fooled, but Hans falls in love with her again. One of the witnesses is the King of the Sea, disguised as a fisherman. He testifies that Ondine abandoned her powerful race and became "human by choice." The judges condemn her to death because she "transgressed the boundaries of nature. However, the evidence indicates that in doing so she brought with her nothing but kindness and love"—and therefore she will be spared the humiliation of a public execution. According to the pact with her uncle, Hans now must die for having betrayed her. Ondine begs the King of the Sea to save him. That is impossible; but to be humane, he promises to have Hans die the same moment that Ondine will be made utterly to forget him. Hans and Ondine's tender first love scene now is repeated—but in reverse order, as he begins to die. They kiss for the last time. Then Hans drops dead, and Ondine at once loses her memory of him. The King of the Sea comes to lead her home to the water. She questions him about the handsome body lying on the floor, wondering if it cannot be brought to life. Learning that it is the body of a knight named Hans who died and cannot be revived, Ondine says, "What a pity! How I should have loved him!"

ONE DOES NOT KNOW HOW (*Non si sa come*), a play in three acts by LUIGI PIRANDELLO, published and produced in 1935. Setting: contemporary Italy.

Most of the play—which was first performed in STEFAN ZWEIG's translation, in Germany—is an anguished monologue.

Count Romeo Daddi is a man obsessed by two former actions: his boyhood slaying of another child who cruelly killed a lizard, and an adulterous episode with his friend's wife. He does not know how—"one does not know how"—they happened: in both cases he was momentarily overwhelmed by powerful, cosmic forces. Equally guilty, the wife loves her husband and does not wish to wreck their lives for what she feels was a momentary, instinctive, and uncontrollable act that was really unimportant and had best be forgotten. Romeo, however, is overwhelmed by his guilt and keeps torturing himself and those around him, including his own wife. He is driven to affront commonly practiced discretion and confesses to the wronged friend. Though he himself has lapsed occasionally, the husband is a practical man. He is outraged by the revelation and shoots Romeo, whose dying words are "That was done in the human way."

ONE-THIRD OF A NATION, a play in two acts by ARTHUR ARENT, published and produced in 1938. Setting: New York City, 1705–1938.

Produced by the Federal Theatre Project of the Works Progress Administration for a whole season in New York and soon throughout the country, this was the most successful LIVING NEWSPAPER DRAMA. It is episodic, it utilizes the genre's characteristic props to illustrate filthy living conditions, and it propagandizes for government intervention (cheap public housing) to solve social problems. A composite "Little Man" represents the ill-housed "one-third of a nation" (in President Franklin D. Roosevelt's famous phrase) through the ages.

A tenement burns, and the investigation attributes the fire and the authorities' helplessness to "whatever it was that made New York City real estate the soundest and most profitable speculation on the face of the earth." Through the ages, real-estate values and consequent shenanigans have spawned profitable slums. In 1794 Aaron Burr is bribed with land to drop a rent investigation, and rents keep soaring as the immigrant "Little Man" is cheated by the landlord and crowded into slums that breed disease. Laws are ineffective, philanthropy is inadequate, and even substandard housing is difficult to obtain. The 1937 Public Housing Bill is debated by New York's Senator Robert Wagner and his opponent, Virginia's Senator Harry Byrd. It passes, but the appropriation, dwarfed by that for the military, is woefully inadequate. "We're going to holler. And we're going to keep on hollering until they admit in Washington it's just as important to keep a man alive as it is to kill him!" Little Man's wife protests: "Can you hear me—you in Washington or Albany or wherever you are! Give me a decent place to live in! Give me a home! A home!"

ONE WAY PENDULUM, "A Farce in a New Dimension" in two acts by N. F. SIMPSON, produced in 1959 and published in 1960. Setting: a middle-class English living room, 1950's.

This madcap features the Groomkirby family, each of whose members lives a separate fantasy life. The father "earns" a living from the sixpences he feeds his own parking meters, which he then stands in front of for an hour so that he will not feel overcharged and thus lose "a customer"; he also pursues his hobbies of carpentry and law by transforming his living room into a courthouse. Kirby Groomkirby, the son who can respond only to Pavlovian whistles, trains five hundred weighing machines to sing the "Hallelujah Chorus": he plans to transport them to the North Pole, bring about a tilt of the earth's axis, and thus cause many deaths—which will enable him to indulge his passion for wearing black. There is also a professional eater hired by Mrs. Groomkirby to consume the family's leftovers, a mad aunt, and a teen-age daughter. The second act features the trial of Kirby, who is proved guilty of mass murder. "In sentencing a man for one crime, we may be putting him beyond the reach of the law in respect to those other crimes of which he might otherwise have become guilty," the judge concludes: "The law, however, is not to be cheated in this way. I shall therefore discharge you."

O'NEILL, Eugene [Gladstone] (1888–1953), America's greatest dramatist, came of wholly Irish-Catholic stock. His mother, Ella Quinlan, was born in Connecticut to immigrant parents who eventually prospered; his father, the famous actor James O'Neill, came to America when he was nine years old. Eugene, their third child (one boy died in infancy), was born in a New York hotel. His father had already become the star of *The Count of Monte Cristo* (1883), the money-making vehicle that was to frustrate his artistic development and career; his mother began taking morphine to alleviate the pains caused by Eugene's birth, and soon became an addict.

Few artists have been as overwhelmingly and relentlessly autobiographical as was Eugene O'Neill. Again and again he dramatized the intense love-hate relationships among his father, mother, brother, and himself. Most explicitly portrayed in the posthumous LONG DAY'S JOURNEY INTO NIGHT (1956, one of his major works), these relationships and individuals are mirrored in all his plays. Almost every husband or father is James O'Neill, every wife or mother, Ella; the hopelessly alcoholic brother, Jamie, is featured in A MOON FOR THE MISBEGOTTEN (1943); and, of course, O'Neill himself is most plays' sensitive and suffering protagonist.

Nursed and weaned in the theatre, O'Neill spent his early boyhood on tour with his father. He was later sent to private Catholic schools, but although his parents were devout believers, he totally rejected religion when he was fifteen. Though he remained an agnostic to his death (a solitary lapse is dramatized in DAYS WITHOUT END, 1934), O'Neill in his plays persistently expressed his agonizing quest for spiritual values. Indeed, a revealing letter on DYNAMO (1929), the most explicit dramatization of his predominant theme, expresses his conviction that all artists "must dig at the roots of the sickness" of our age: "the death of the old God and the failure of science and materialism" to furnish man with a satisfying new religion.

He entered Princeton in 1906, but, disliking college, occupied himself so exclusively with "hell-raising," drink, and debauchery that he was dropped at the end of his first year. Subsequently he educated himself in bookstores and variety halls, and worked at various jobs. Immediately after a secret marriage in 1909 to a New York girl, Kathleen Jenkins, O'Neill escaped to gold prospecting in Honduras. When he returned the next year, he did not even go to see his young wife and their infant son.* He mostly went on drunken bouts, in Argentina and New York, though he also toured with his father in *The Count of Monte Cristo* and took to the sea again, as a sailor. In 1912 he stayed in his parents' summer home in New London, Connecticut; there he briefly worked as a reporter for the New London *Telegraph,* contributing also to the poetry column. At the end of the year he had to be hospitalized for tuberculosis.

It was in the sanatorium, from which he was discharged after a few months (dramatized in THE STRAW, 1921), that he decided on his vocation and wrote (but discarded) his first play, A WIFE FOR A LIFE. He attended Professor George Pierce Baker's playwriting class (English 47) at Harvard University in 1914–15. Much of the next year he spent in New York's Greenwich Village, where he lived congenially with revolutionary radicals, criminals, and down-and-outers. In 1916 he formed his important association with The Provincetown Players, organized by GEORGE CRAM COOK and SUSAN GLASPELL.† That summer their productions on an abandoned wharf in Provincetown, Massachusetts, on Cape Cod, included THIRST (1914) and BOUND EAST FOR CARDIFF (1916), and over the next three years they produced in their Greenwich Village theatre all the other plays in THE MOON OF THE CARIBBEES collection (1919), as well as BEFORE BREAKFAST (1916), FOG (1916), *The Sniper* (1917; published in the misleadingly titled LOST PLAYS OF EUGENE O'NEILL, 1950), and THE DREAMY KID (1919). Reflecting O'Neill's seafaring days, *The Moon of the Caribbees* one-acters were something new and impressive in American drama. Largely because of these plays The Provincetown Players became the most important of the seminal "little theatre" groups, a movement that by the 1920's had made the American theatre come of age. As in O'Neill's later works, tragic irony was occasionally blunted by melodrama; but his plays, fusing NATURALISM and SYMBOLISM, contrasted vividly with the popular WELL-MADE thrillers and the romances of BRONSON HOWARD, DAVID BELASCO, and their heirs. Some of the one-acters were published in the widely read *Smart Set* magazine, one of whose editors, George Jean Nathan, later became O'Neill's close friend and wrote about him frequently and perceptively. Nathan was instrumental in getting BEYOND THE HORIZON produced on Broadway in 1920—and O'Neill immediately became America's leading playwright.

In the next fourteen years twenty-one more O'Neill plays were produced. They include some of the ones already mentioned and an impressive number of other important ones: *Exorcism* (1920, an unpublished farcical dramatization of his suicide attempt), THE EMPEROR JONES (1920), DIFF'RENT (1920), GOLD (1921), ANNA CHRISTIE (1921), THE FIRST MAN (1922), THE HAIRY APE (1922), WELDED (1924), *The Ancient Mariner* (1924; an unsuccessful dramatization of Coleridge's poem, published in 1960 and notable because it is the first play in which O'Neill used masks), ALL GOD'S CHILLUN GOT WINGS (1924), DESIRE UNDER THE ELMS (1925), THE FOUNTAIN (1925), THE GREAT GOD BROWN (1926), MARCO MILLIONS (1927), LAZARUS LAUGHED (1927), STRANGE INTERLUDE (1928), MOURNING BECOMES ELECTRA (1931), and AH, WILDERNESS! (1933).

His later plays include THE ICEMAN COMETH (1939), A TOUCH OF THE POET (1957), HUGHIE (1958), and the already noted *A Moon for the Misbegotten* and *Long Day's Journey into Night*. These and the earlier plays evidence O'Neill's versatility and genius as an innovator. While he was influenced by the Greek masters and by such moderns as HENRIK IBSEN, FRANK WEDEKIND, and (particularly) AUGUST STRINDBERG, he continually strove to represent and symbolize reality as he himself saw and felt it. Though frequently pressured, he always refused to compromise his artistic integrity for theatrical expedience and box-office success. He ceaselessly experimented—in short one-acters, in standard-length plays, and in gigantic nine- and thirteen-acters—with differing dramatic methods. O'Neill knew that in the theatre, as he told his first biographer (Barrett H. Clark), "Everything is a matter of convention. If we accept one, why not another, so long as it does what it's intended to do?" He was discussing the "asides" of the nine-act *Strange Interlude,* but this was only one device, and he found others—ranging from conventional REPRESENTATIONALISM to the avant-garde—to accomplish his purpose in other plays. Of course, not all his experiments worked. The alter ego of *Days Without End* (audible but invisible to the other characters) and the protracted laughter of *Lazarus Laughed* were among the failures. Among the many that did work were various forms of EXPRESSIONISM (most vividly used in *The Hairy Ape*), and pervasive sound effects, including foghorns (in many

*Eugene O'Neill, Jr., later a brilliant classical scholar, committed suicide in 1950. Eugene O'Neill and Kathleen Jenkins were divorced in 1912.

† Glaspell's *The Road to the Temple* (1927) is an informative memoir of the group and of O'Neill.

Eugene O'Neill in 1929. (*Theatre Collection, New York Public Library*)

of the naturalistic one-acters, *Anna Christie,* and *Long Day's Journey Into Night*) and—most notably—the tom-tom in *The Emperor Jones.* All these effectively externalize and symbolize the protagonists' internal, psychologically probed conflicts and stresses.

O'Neill's plays are characterized by theatrical craftsmanship, occasional sardonic humor, and many powerful and moving lyrical passages. His intense explorations of man's inner being and quest for values, and his portrayal of obsessive sexual and family relationships, are unusually lacerating. But the continuing response of worldwide audiences, numbering in the millions, suggests an essential truth and universality in O'Neill's perception of man's struggles against what he considered fate and environment. Even in his failures—plays flawed by bathos, verbosity, and repetition—he was a dramatist who lived up to William Wordsworth's famous definition of a poet: one who is "endowed with more lively sensibility, more enthusiasm and tenderness, who has a greater knowledge of human nature, and a more comprehensive soul, than are supposed to be common among mankind."

Between 1934 and 1946 O'Neill did not come out with any new plays, though he was working prodigiously on the plays produced in subsequent years and on two cycles: A TALE OF POSSESSORS, SELF-DISPOSSESSED, parts of which, including MORE STATELY MANSIONS (1962), appeared posthumously; and *By Way of Obit,* eight projected one-act plays of which only *Hughie* survives. In 1936 he was awarded the Nobel Prize—the first American dramatist so honored (he won the Pulitzer Prize four times). Then, in 1946, came one of his greatest works, *The Iceman Cometh,* set in the New York waterfront dive he had occupied in 1912, and characterizing the Village down-and-outers he had befriended in 1915–16. This was the last production he lived to see. His health gave way more and more to the ravaging, rare disease (resembling Parkinson's) he had suffered from all his life. After *A Moon for the Misbegotten* his tremors made further writing impossible.

From 1918–29 O'Neill was married to the writer Agnes Boulton, who bore him two children (Shane and Oona, later Mrs. Charles Chaplin). Their tempestuous relationship was chronicled in her *Part of a Long Story* (1958), and dramatized in O'Neill's already noted play *Welded.* Immediately after their divorce he married Carlotta Monterey, an actress noted for her beauty.

The three-volume New York edition, *The Plays of Eugene O'Neill* (1951), contains thirty of his fifty plays (but none of the so-called LOST PLAYS OF EUGENE O'NEILL or THIRST AND OTHER ONE-ACT PLAYS); later plays were published individually. He also copyrighted but failed to produce or publish *Bread and Butter* (1914, a tragedy), *Now I Ask You* (1917, a farce), and *Shell Shock* (1918, an antiwar one-acter).

Important biographies are Arthur and Barbara Gelb's *O'Neill* (1962) and Louis Sheaffer's *O'Neill: Son and Playwright* (1968). Also of special interest are Barrett H. Clark's *Eugene O'Neill: The Man and His Plays* (revised, 1947), which contains much source material and bears O'Neill's imprimatur; and Agnes Boulton's aforementioned reminiscences. Book-length studies of his dramas include Edwin A. Engel's *The Haunted Heroes of Eugene O'Neill* (1953), Doris V. Falk's *Eugene O'Neill and the Tragic Tension* (1958), Doris Alexander's *A Tempering of Eugene O'Neill* (1962), and John H. Raleigh's *The Plays of Eugene O'Neill* (1965). A useful comprehensive anthology—criticisms, reviews, memoirs, and an extensive bibliography—is *O'Neill and His Plays* (1961), edited by Oscar Cargill, N. Bryllion Fagin, and William J. Fisher; and John Gassner's edition of *O'Neill: A Collection of Critical Essays* (1964) provides a handy sampling of differing approaches to O'Neill's work. For the most comprehensive bibliography to date, see Jordan Y. Miller's *Eugene O'Neill and the American Critic* (1962). J. Russell Reaver's three-volume computerized *An O'Neill Concordance* (1969), though inadequate, has 280,000 references to most—but not all—of his plays.

ONLY JEALOUSY OF EMER, THE, a one-act verse play by WILLIAM BUTLER YEATS, published in 1919 and produced in 1922. Setting: a patterned screen before a wall.

This is the second of FOUR PLAYS FOR DANCERS and one of the Cuchulain plays. It also appeared as *Fighting the Waves,* a prose version produced in 1929 and published in 1934.

The unconscious Cuchulain is on his deathbed while his ghost is being enticed by the idol-like Woman of Sidh. Cuchulain's wife, Emer, and his mistress try to reawaken him. The mistress fails, though Queen Emer encourages her. To be saved from the supernatural temptress, Cuchulain begs Emer to renounce her love. Emer does so, despite her passion for him, and Cuchulain is saved. When he wakes up, he is ignorant of what has happened, and gratefully embraces his mistress.

OPEN LETTERS TO THE INTIMATE THEATRE (*Öppna brev till Intima Teatern*), essays by AUGUST STRINDBERG, published in his collected works (Stockholm, 1911–21).

These letters (written from 1907 to 1909), published together with a memorandum (*Memorandum till Intima Teatern*) and essays on various Shakespeare plays, were prompted by Strindberg's concern with stagecraft problems at the Intimate Theatre. They discuss the theory and production of THE CHAMBER PLAYS and also deal extensively with historical drama—with particular reference to his own chronicle plays and those of Goethe and Shakespeare. Strindberg wrote, "Even in the historical drama the purely human is of major interest, and history the background: the inner struggles of souls awaken more sympathy than the combat of soldiers or the storming of walls; love and hate, and torn family ties, more than treaties and speeches from the throne." This comment describes his own practice in writing historical plays. Strindberg also stressed the importance of stage NATURALISM, much as he did in his preface to MISS JULIE.

Open Letters to the Intimate Theater, translated and with a comprehensive introduction by Walter Johnson, was published in 1967. Translated excerpts appear in Evert Spinchorn and Seabury Quinn, Jr.'s translation of *The Chamber Plays* (1962).

OPTIMISTIC TRAGEDY, AN (*Optimisticheskaya tragediya*), a play in three acts and a prologue by VSEVOLOD VITALEVICH VISHNEVSKY, published and produced in 1933. Setting: a military cruiser and the Russian battlefield, 1918.

Vishnevsky's first and greatest hit, this Civil War drama has long been among the most popular Russian plays, and was filmed in 1963. It is an episodic work, focused on the idealized, ultimately martyred heroine, and unified by a narrator-chorus that also articulates the Soviet ideals dramatized by the lively action onstage.

Anarchists have taken over a battleship of the Baltic Fleet. Led by a cruel "chief" and his criminal henchman, they terrorize civilians and naval personnel. To restore order and discipline, the Party sends a commissar—a woman. When one of the sailors approaches to rape her, she shoots him. There are arguments about anarchy, and the chorus periodically proclaims the strength of the Party and deplores the "extra high percentage of traitors," as Lenin put it, at the dawn of Bolshevism. For a while the chief still tries to dominate the scene, and he secretly summons anarchist reinforcements. Eventually, as his bestiality (including a number of dramatized executions) becomes intolerable, the lady commissar has him shot. His reinforcements are overpowered and pressed into Soviet service—and they gradually become an enthusiastic part of the unit. The commissar forms the "first marine regiment of the newly created Red Army." It must defend the area against the Whites and their German reinforcements. The executed chief's former henchman fearfully escapes after stabbing the guard. The Germans thereupon succeed in surprising the regiment. Many are killed and wounded, and the commissar is captured. Stalling for time and refusing to betray an imminent attack by her comrades, the commissar is brutally tortured. The attack begins, the imprisoned Reds join in the fighting, and they win. The bleeding commissar is carried in. As she dies from the tortures inflicted on her by the Germans, she cries out, "Hold high our flag, the flag of our Idea."

ORCHARDS OF POLOVCHANSK, THE (*Polovchanskie sady*), a play in four acts by LEONID MAKSIMOVICH LEONOV, published and produced in 1938. Setting: a Soviet apple orchard in Polovchansk, the Ukraine; 1938.

This is something like a "positive" version of Chekhov's THE CHERRY ORCHARD, and was produced in England as *The Apple Orchards* (1948). It is an often-lyrical play with rounded characters, especially in its first version. For the later version, ultimately produced at the Moscow Art Theatre, Leonov transformed Pylyaev from a "superfluous man" who has made a mess of his life—the antithesis of the orchard director, Makkaveev—into a subversive agent. But even in this melodramatic guise the anti-Soviet villain, like the hero, remains three dimensional.

Adrian Timofeevich Makkaveev, the ailing director of a noted apple orchard, has five sons by his first marriage, and another boy and a daughter (Masha) by his second. The Makkaveevs have all their lives fought Russia's internal enemies—the insects threatening their productive orchard—and now gird themselves to fight its external enemies. The older sons, established in various professions, are returning for a family reunion. The joy and festivities of the family and their friends are dampened by the unexpected appearance of the long-absent Matvei Fomich Pylyaev, now the sinister wreck of a man. He was once the lover of Makkaveev's wife, a youthful indiscretion for which the generous and affectionate orchard director has long ago forgiven her. But Pylyaev's malicious and surreptitious bearing has them all on edge. When Masha's suitor appears, he is viewed suspiciously. Her prizefighter brother boxes with—and is beaten by—the suitor, who turns out to be a capable young Red Army commander. Tension is heightened, too, by the continued absence of Makkaveev's favorite son. Ultimately Pylyaev is exposed as an enemy agent, is subdued in a fight, and is turned over to the authorities. Makkaveev's beloved son, however, never appears; instead, word comes that he has died valiantly while on a secret Arctic expedition. The patriotic self-assurance and gaiety of his remaining children and Masha's suitor, "bearers of destiny" who are like "individual feathers that help the eagle soar," enable Makkaveev to bear the sorrow of his son's death. He knows his beloved orchard needs to be protected from "the devils, . . . the Japs and the Germans . . . who are crawling nearer all the time," and he exhorts his sons: "Let them break their heads against your chests." The sons return to their jobs, and Masha's suitor is recalled before his leave is up. Makkaveev notes his daughter's fortitude, the "gladness in your eyes." Masha returns after seeing her suitor off. She is wet from the rain and her eyes are closed. "What a mist there is outside," she says; and then, "Why are you all so still? I want everything and everyone to be joyful tonight. It is my day, my day. Boys—where's your music, boys?—"

ORNIFLE, OR THE DRAFT (*Ornifle, ou le courant d'air*), a comedy in four acts by JEAN ANOUILH, produced in 1955 and published in 1956. Setting: France, 1950's.

Ornifle is a famous but superficial poet, an aging, cynical Don Juan. Aristocratic ladies give him their pearls, which his skin is supposed to rejuvenate. He is threatened and "shot" by a poor young man who turns out to be his son, the product of a long-forgotten affair. Though the lad's fiancée has removed the bullet, Ornifle falls —fainting. This episode and his conviction that he has a heart condition change Ornifle. For a while he recognizes people's "souls," including his wife's, and starts to "redeem" his associates, including his materialistic friend and agent, Machetu. But when doctors find nothing wrong with his heart, Ornifle resumes his philandering. He starts to seduce his son's fiancée, and goes to meet one of his women in a hotel. Its manager calls to announce that Ornifle has had a fatal heart attack, and asks what to do with "Mr. Ornifle's body." A maiden secretary who has long lusted for Ornifle answers the telephone. As a hymn is sung offstage, the hysterical old maid drops the telephone, embraces a pillow, and repeats frantically, "Mr. Ornifle's body!"

ORPHÉE, "A Tragedy in One Act [thirteen scenes] Briefly Interrupted by an Interval" by JEAN COCTEAU, produced in 1926 and published in 1927. Setting: a strange room in legendary Thrace and Heaven.

This short, histrionic, tragicomic modernization of the Orpheus and Eurydice legend is generally acknowledged as Cocteau's finest play. Anti-illusionist and poetic, it SYMBOLICALLY presents Cocteau's concepts of poetic inspiration and the appeal of death—a magic substitute for life, and a passage through a mirror. Cocteau's fascination with the play is evidenced in his two film versions (1950 and 1959), and his preoccupation with eerie events during the preparation of the play, including the opium-evoked name Heurtebise ("wind-breaker"). The acrostic of the horse's poetic line ("*Madame Eurydice reviendra des enfers*") parallels the Rabelaisian exclamation that opens Jarry's KING UBU. A five-sentence prologue by the actor playing Orphée requests the audience to refrain from making any noise, for "we are playing at a great height, and without a safety-net."

(*1*) Orphée is interpreting a "poetic" message his pet horse is tapping out. His prosaic wife, Eurydice, is jealous of this horse and angry because it has alienated Orphée's affection. But he insists that the horse dives into and brings back from "my night" remarkably poetic sentences. "I am discovering a new world, I am living again, I am stalking the unknown," Orphée tells Eurydice. The astonishing line tapped out by the horse—"Lady Eurydice shall return from the underworld"—is "a poem of vision, a flower deep-rooted in death." And he is submitting it to Thrace's annual poetry contest. Orphée and Eurydice squabble angrily, and he breaks the window—as she does daily, in order to see the glazier, Heurtebise. (*2*) Heurtebise comes in, "bends a knee and crosses his hands over his heart." (*3*) Eurydice tells Heurtebise that she loves Orphée. To help her, Heurtebise has seen Aglaonice, one of the Bacchantes, Eurydice's former friends. Aglaonice has given Heurtebise a lump of poisoned sugar for the horse, in exchange for a compromising letter

Orphée. JEAN COCTEAU as Heurtebise. Paris, 1927. (*French Cultural Services*)

in Eurydice's possession. (*4*) Orphée returns while they talk. He takes away the chair on which Heurtebise stands, leaving the glazier suspended in midair as he continues working. Only Eurydice notices this. (*5*) When Orphée leaves she complains bitterly, "It's all very well living with a horse that talks, but a friend who floats in the air becomes of necessity an object of suspicion." She dismisses Orphée: "All mystery is my enemy. I have decided to fight it." But after she licks and seals the envelope Aglaonice had prepared for the compromising letter, she dies—for the envelope was poisoned. Heurtebise rushes out to call Orphée. (*6*) Death, a beautiful young woman in elegant evening attire, comes through the mirror with two assistants in surgeons' uniforms. She feeds the horse the poisoned sugar, and fetches Eurydice by the use of various rituals—magic motions, a whirring machine, a dove, and a watch borrowed from the audience. (*7*) Orphée rushes in, weeping at Eurydice's death: "The horse is of little consequence! I want to see Eurydice again. I want her to forgive me for having neglected and misunderstood her." Heurtebise helps him. He knows Death has forgotten her rubber gloves, and if Orphée takes them to her, she will reward him. Heurtebise shows him the way to the underworld, through the mirror: "Mirrors are the doors through which Death comes and goes. . . . You only have to watch yourself all your life in a mirror, and you'll see Death at work like bees in a glass hive." (*8a*) As Heurtebise waits for Orphée's return, a postman knocks. Heurtebise tells him to slip the letter under the door.

There is a momentary Interval.

(*8b*) The previous scene is repeated, word for word. (*9*) Orphée emerges from the mirror with Eurydice. She promises henceforth to be "a new wife to Orphée, a honeymoon wife," and he is determined to make their marriage work. Her return has been predicated on the stipulation that he not look at her—or she will disappear instantly. They sit down with Heurtebise to eat lunch, but the couple's squabbles soon resume, bitterly. Inadvertently he loses his balance and looks at her. When she disappears through the mirror, Orphée tells Heurtebise that he looked at her on purpose. He opens the letter and learns that Aglaonice has discovered the acrostic of the poetry line, has persuaded the judges that he is a fraud, and is mobilizing the Bacchantes to kill him. Despite Heurtebise's pleas, Orphée refuses to save himself. "The horse has tricked me," he says; "the words are a pretext which hides a deep and religious hatred." Ready to die and rejoin Eurydice, Orphée leaves to face the drumbeating Bacchantes, who are eager to kill him. "This [sculptor's] marble is stupid. Life is shaping me," he tells Heurtebise; "it is making a masterpiece. I must bear its blows without understanding them." His voice is heard briefly and then something is hurled into the room through the window: Orphée's head. The drumbeats become fainter. (*10*) As the severed head calls for her, Eurydice comes through the mirror. She beckons and leads Orphée's invisible body through the mirror with her. (*11*) When the police arrive, Heurtebise quickly puts Orphée's head on an empty pedestal. The police commissioner reveals that public opinion has changed now that Orphée is dead. The Bacchantes are demanding a bust of Orphée for their celebrations in his honor. As the commissioner's back is turned while he questions him, Eurydice summons Heurtebise from the mirror. He plunges into it, following her. (*12*) Subsequent questions by the commissioner are answered by the head on the pedestal. When he asks what Heurtebise's name and address are, Orphée's head replies, "Jean Cocteau" and gives his address. The police finally notice Heurtebise's disappearance, conduct a futile search, and then take the "bust" on the pedestal along with them. (*13*) Led by Heurtebise, Eurydice and Orphée arrive in Heaven. "They look at their home as if they were seeing it for the first time," smile, and sit down. Orphée recites a prayer: he thanks God for sending Heurtebise, their guardian angel; "for having saved Eurydice, because, through love, she killed the devil in the shape of a horse"; and finally, "for having saved me because I adored poetry, and thou art poetry. Amen." Eurydice pours wine for Heurtebise, who concludes, "Perhaps we can have lunch at last."

ORPHEUS DESCENDING, a play in three acts by TENNESSEE WILLIAMS, produced in 1957 and published in 1958. Setting: the general dry-goods store, with a connecting confectionery, in a small Southern town; c. 1940.

As *Battle of Angels,* Williams's first professionally produced work, this play in 1940 was angrily hooted off the stage before it reached New York. (The opening in Boston was a fiasco in which the smoke-making machine went out of control.) Williams kept revising it and, as *Orpheus Descending,* it finally reached Broadway seventeen years later. But neither the play nor the film (*The Fugitive Kind,* 1959; Williams's first screen version of any of his plays) was commercially viable. Only Off-Broadway succeeded with this, Williams's favorite play, a loose potpourri of religio-Freudian-mythological SYMBOLISM.

The handsome Val Xavier (i.e., Saviour), a now-restrained, thirty-year-old former hell-raiser wearing a snakeskin jacket and strumming a guitar, "descends" to an intrigue-ridden, bigoted town where he meets the general store's proprietress, Lady (the Virgin) Torrance. Long ago she had been bought by her vicious husband after a lover had jilted her. Only at the end of the play does she learn that her husband, now dying of cancer, was among the vigilantes who years before had "burned up and killed the old Dago," her father, for serving Negroes in his wine garden. Among the townswomen excited by Val are a corrupted young aristocrat, who tries to seduce him; the sheriff's sex-starved wife, a pious fanatic who paints her religious visions; and Lady, who is remodeling a confectionery to resemble her father's burnt wine garden. She and Val, two lonesome people who find life and strength in their love, are defeated by the malignant society about them. The sheriff mistakes Val's kindness to his deranged wife for amorous advances and orders him to leave town. When her dying husband, evil to the last, comes down with a gun, Lady interposes her body to save Val—and is shot. Her husband loudly accuses Val of the murder, and thus precipitates the lynching of Val with a blowtorch.

ORTON, Joe (1933–67), English playwright, had a promising future when, at thirty-four, he was hammered to death by his roommate. By then Orton had already attracted a coterie with his outrageous black farces, notably *Entertaining Mr. Sloane* (1964) and *Loot* (1966), both of them winners of awards. Expressing his contempt for social institutions as well as his delight in shocking people, Orton wrote plays that are wildly comic but honed with savage, Swiftian satire.

Born in Leicester, Orton early manifested his contempt for authority when he mutilated and then pasted pornographic pictures in over two hundred library books. His ensuing six-months prison sentence confirmed his conviction that a mere façade covers the hypocrisy and viciousness of the police, as well as those of the Church and most other social institutions. This conviction he soon dramatized.

His first work, *The Ruffian on the Stair,* was produced on the BBC in 1964 and as a stage play in 1967, together with *The Erpingham Camp,* under the title *Crimes of Passion*. *Entertaining Mr. Sloane* portrays a young murderer blackmailed into submissiveness by two middle-aged homosexuals; and *Loot* depicts great brutality amidst genteel dialogue: a burglar, viciously beaten by the police, after hiding his loot in his mother's coffin mutters in horror—but only because he has to bury her naked, "a Freudian nightmare." The posthumous *What the Butler Saw* (1969) satirizes psychiatrists in a characteristically fast-moving farce that has some similarities to the drama of OSCAR WILDE (whom Orton admired) and that reproduces theatrically the logic of Lewis Carroll's *Alice in Wonderland*. Here, as in his other plays, Orton presents a comic yet terrifying view of man and contemporary society.

OSBORN, Paul (1901–), American playwright, became known with *The Vinegar Tree* (1930), a play about free love; and with *On Borrowed Time* (1938), his dramatization (filmed in 1939) of Lawrence E. Watkin's whimsical tale about an old man who traps and incapacitates Death in an apple tree, causing universal misery, until his little grandson can die along with him. Although Osborn wrote other original plays, such as *Mornings at Seven* (1939), a rustic CHEKHOVian comedy of futility, his greatest hits were further dramatizations of novels. These include *The Innocent Voyage* (1943, by Richard Hughes), *A Bell for Adano* (1944, by John Hersey), *Point of No Return* (1951, by J. P. Marquand) and *The World of Suzie Wong* (1958, by Richard Mason). Osborn also wrote the film scripts of *Mme. Curie* (1943), SOUTH PACIFIC (1958), and other works.

Born in Indiana, Osborn was educated at the University of Michigan, where he taught English for a short time. He studied playwriting at Yale University with George Pierce Baker.

OSBORNE, John [James] (1929–), English playwright, achieved immediate fame with his epoch-making LOOK BACK IN ANGER, whose 1956 production has become a milestone in English drama. His play dubbed—and Osborne became the spokesman for—a new English generation of writers, the "angry young men."

Born in London, Osborne came from the lower-class background that so often provides the setting for his plays. His father was a barkeep and a commercial artist; but the boisterous "anger" that distinguishes Osborne's protagonists stems from his maternal ancestry. "Even if they did get drunk and fight, they were responding; they were not defeated," Osborne wrote of the family of his mother, a Cockney barmaid. Their very hostilities reflected their being alive, for, as Osborne saw it, "to become angry is to care." Osborne did not attend a university, but he attained a general certificate of education from Belmont College, Devonshire. Then he wrote for trade journals, and eventually drifted into the theatre. He tutored children in a touring company, and in 1948 began acting (in Sheffield).

His first play, *The Devil Inside Him* (written with Stella Linden, ? -) was produced in the provinces in 1949. Revived in 1962 (as "*Cry for Love,* by Robert Owen"), it is a melodrama about a Welsh poet who kills a girl when she charges him with the paternity of her child. The second play, *Personal Enemy* (1955), is about an American turncoat in the Korean war back home in the Midwest, victimized by his family. Unproduced and suppressed by Osborne, it was written with a Scottish fellow actor, Anthony Creighton (1923–), who also collaborated on the next play, EPITAPH FOR GEORGE DILLON (1958)—which was not produced until after Osborne had become famous with *Look Back in Anger*.

Look Back in Anger (which starred Osborne's second wife, Mary Ure, and was filmed in 1958) was produced by the English Stage Company at the Royal Court Theatre—the same house that fifty years earlier had achieved fame under the leadership of J. E. Vedrenne and HARLEY GRANVILLE-BARKER. For a while its fortunes and Osborne's grew together. *Look Back in Anger* was the third play to be produced there by George Devine, its actor-director. Osborne's playwriting enticed Laurence Olivier to act the vulgar hoofer in his next play, THE ENTERTAINER (1957). The music-hall dramaturgy of this play is carried still further in the one that followed, *The World of Paul Slickey* (1959). Subtitled "A Comedy of Manners with Music," it is a vicious and wholesale attack on practically all elements of society, on tastelessness, and on venality; its protagonist is a gossip columnist, and the plot, which consists of adulteries and a frantic struggle for a legacy, culminates in sex-changing injections.

Osborne followed this generally unsuccessful work with a BBC play, *A Subject for Scandal and Concern* (1960), produced on television in 1961; it dramatizes the life, prosecution, and conviction of George Holyoake, a Socialist lecturer who in 1842 was the last defendant in a blasphemy trial. More important and successful was Osborne's next historical play, LUTHER (1961), which was followed by *Plays for England* (1963), two one-acters produced in 1962. The first, *The Blood of the Bambergs,* portrays the marriage of a prince; killed in a crash just before the wedding, his place is assumed by a photographer who resembles him—for the photographer's mother was intimate with the prince's deceased father. The second, *Under Plain Cover,* portrays a happy, apparently "nice, ordinary" couple who act out fetishes until their marriage is destroyed by gutter journalism: exposed as brother and sister, they are separated, but eventually reunite, happy once more and resisting further intrusion by the world. INADMISSIBLE EVIDENCE (1964), Osborne's next play, was followed by *A Patriot for Me* (1965), a historical spectacle depicting the decadent Austro-Hungarian Empire, and featuring Alfred Redl, the homosexual officer who became a spy and committed suicide in 1913; *A Bond Honoured* (1966), a long one-act adaptation of a seventeenth-century religious drama, Lope de Vega's *La fianza satisfecha; Time Present* (1968), a tirade very much like his first hit, but featuring an angry young woman; *The Hotel in Amsterdam* (1968), about a film producer's six emotionally entangled employees' secret weekend together; and *West of Suez* (1971), which, like Shaw's HEARTBREAK HOUSE, portrays British social degeneration in a CHEKHOVian manner. Osborne has also written screenplays, notably the prize-winning *Tom Jones* (1963).

For a few years after his first plays appeared in London—and then throughout the world—Osborne was hailed as a new BERNARD SHAW. These claims were heard less frequently as time went on. Osborne appeared able to sustain neither the verbal fireworks nor the necessary intellectual tension. His talents in the semimusical genre, too, were questioned. To some extent such limitations were obscured by brilliant star performances such as Olivier's Archie Rice and Albert Finney's Luther. But eventually the "anger" at royalty and the Tory government that had rallied a generation was extended indiscriminately to other targets and began to grate and sound like whining. Eventually, too, the muddled dramaturgy even of Osborne's most famous play became evident. At the same time, Osborne has amply demonstrated his gifts as an articulate social satirist who can entertain and a versatile writer whose drama ranges from NATURALISM to music-hall turns and EPIC chronicles.

Osborne's plays have been published individually, and he has also published an autobiographical account in his credo "They Call it Cricket," in *Declaration* (1958), edited by Tom Maschler. For discussions of his career and drama see Simon Trussler's *The Plays of John Osborne* (1969), Martin Banham's *Osborne* (1969), and Alan Carter's *John Osborne* (1969).

OTHER SON, THE (*L'altro figlio*), a one-act comedy by LUIGI PIRANDELLO, produced in 1923 and published in 1925. Setting: a Sicilian village (Farnia) in the early 1900's.

This picturesque tragicomedy is Pirandello's dramatization of a short story he published in 1905.

A wretched old pauper wails for her two sons who, like most of the village men, have left to seek their fortune abroad. Because she spurns her remaining son, who wants to care for her, the woman is considered a nuisance and is ridiculed and deceived by the neighbors. But a visiting doctor becomes sympathetic after she tells her story: When Sicily was overrun by bandits, her husband was brutally slain; the other son was born after she had been raped by the bandits; therefore, she realizes, "it's not me, it's my blood that denies him!"

OULD, Hermon (1885–1951), English journalist and poet, wrote numerous plays that were not very popular but were praised by critics. They include *Between Sunset and Dawn* (1913) and *The Black Virgin* (1922), the latter about a homosexual affair and portraying the post-World War I defeated people of Germany, where the action is set. Ould also translated works of ERNST TOLLER and wrote books that include a study of JOHN GALSWORTHY, *Shuttle: An Autobiographical Sequence* (1945), and *The Art of the Play* (revised, 1948).

OUR BETTERS, a comedy in three acts by SOMERSET MAUGHAM, produced in 1917 and published in 1923. Setting: a drawing room in Mayfair and a morning room in Suffolk; contemporary England.

One of Maugham's most popular plays, *Our Betters* (fimed in 1933) portrays a profligate society consisting of title-seeking, wealthy Americans who hunt for husbands among the wealth-seeking English nobility. The depiction of immorality is in the spirit of Restoration comedy.

Bessie Saunders, a young American heiress, visits her sister Pearl (now Lady George Grayston) in London. Her husband's title and her sensuous old lover's wealth have helped make Pearl a power in English society. She arranges a marriage between Bessie and a young nobleman. But Bessie gradually becomes disillusioned with the totally debauched society she had found so appealing when she first arrived. Her embarrassment and shame reach their climax when she discovers Pearl *in flagrante* with the worthless young lover of her friend, a duchess twice his age and madly infatuated with the dissolute youth. The assembled company know what has happened, and Pearl upon her entrance with him (the second act curtain) coolly remarks before them all, "You damned fool, I told you it was too risky." She flatters herself back into the arms of her rich old lover, who has publicly characterized her as a slut; then, by fetching her a much-sought Italian dancing master, she regains the friendship of the duchess. Bessie is disgusted and, fearful of becoming like the others if she were to remain in that environment, breaks her engagement with the young English lord. She looks at an "exquisite spectacle—two ladies of title kissing one another," the reconciled duchess and Pearl, and leaves: "They're not worth making a fuss about. I'm sailing for America next Saturday!"

OUR THEATRES IN THE NINETIES (three volumes, 1932), by BERNARD SHAW. These still highly readable essays, written for *The Saturday Review* while he was its drama critic from January 1895 through May 1898, include Shaw's evaluations of almost all contemporary and important earlier (from Marlowe and Shakespeare to HENRIK IBSEN) dramatists as well as of the theatre of the time. Selections from the 151 essays were first published as *Dramatic Opinions and Essays* in 1906, and more recently in *Shaw's Dramatic Criticism* (1959). A book-length study is Harold Fromm's *Bernard Shaw and the Theater in the Nineties: A Study of Shaw's Dramatic Criticism* (1967).

OUR TOWN, a play in three acts by THORNTON WILDER, published and produced in 1938. Setting: "Grover's Corners," New Hampshire; 1901–13.

Our Town is an American classic and one of the most frequently performed native plays, a particular favorite of school and other amateur groups. It brought Wilder his second Pulitzer Prize and was filmed in 1940. The play depicts everyday routines and focuses on the Webb and Gibbs children's romance. Common village folk, colloquial language, and sketchy episodes evoke and reaffirm the simple values of life—at times sentimentally.* The humdrum temporal experiences, however, are invested with immense cosmic signifiance within an eternal order of nature and the divine. The play is PRESENTATIONAL: instead of scenery, there are pantomime and a few props arranged by a Stage Manager—the narrator who addresses the audience directly and introduces, interrupts, and comments on the action in which he himself periodically participates.

Act I. "Daily Life." The Stage Manager places props onstage, introduces the play, and describes Grover's Corners, a "Nice town, y'know what I mean?" It is dawn, and "There's Doc [Frank] Gibbs comin' down Main Street now" after delivering twins; and he adds, "Doc Gibbs died in 1930." The newspaper boy hurls imaginary newspapers into imaginary doorways, the milkman comes by, and Mrs. Gibbs prepares breakfast and calls down their son, George, and his little sister. Next door the Webb family begin their day as Mrs. Webb calls her daughter, Emily, and her little brother for breakfast. The Stage Manager interrupts further morning scenes and invites a State University professor to "sketch in a few details," statistics on the town's geology, meteorological conditions, population, etc. Charles Webb, editor of the town's newspaper, supplies further information. There are questions from the audience, including one on the town's interest in culture. "There ain't much," the Stage Manager replies. Daily activities continue as the children return from school. George chats about homework with Emily, who then asks her mother whether she (Emily) is pretty. "We'll have to interrupt again here. Thank you, Mrs. Webb; thank you, Emily," the Stage Manager says, and discusses various other inhabitants of the town. He intends to have a copy of this play put in a cornerstone to be buried so that posterity will know how ordinary people used to live. By the moonlight and perched on ladders simulating their respective bedroom windows, Emily helps George with his arithmetic. The church choir finishes its practice, and the women gossip about the unhappy choir director's drinking. Dr. Gibbs gently chastises George for not helping his mother with house chores, and later the Gibbs parents stroll in their garden, reviewing the day's happenings. Mr. Webb bids Emily goodnight, and goes off whistling "Blessed Be the Tie That Binds." George's sister recalls a letter addressed to Grover's Corners, its address concluding: "the Solar System; the Universe; the Mind of God. . . . And the postman brought it just the same," she says. "That's the end of the First Act, friends," the Stage Manager announces: "You can go and smoke now, those that smoke."

Act II. "Love and Marriage." The Stage Manager watches the audience return to their seats. "Three years have gone by," and he describes what has happened in the meantime and what is to follow. He enumerates Mrs. Gibbs's and Mrs. Webb's decades of tending their families, all the dinners cooked and clothes washed, and concludes by quoting Edgar Lee Masters, "one of those Middle West poets": "You've got to love life

* ALEXANDER WOOLLCOTT, a great admirer of the play, is said to have begged off commenting on the play: "I'd as soon think of endorsing the Twenty-Third Psalm!"

Our Town, Act III. At her funeral in the rain, Emily (Martha Scott) walks to the seated dead, who include Mrs. Gibbs, (Evelyn Varden), Mrs. Webb (Helen Carew), and the choir director (Philip Coolidge). New York, 1938. (*Vandamm Photo, Theatre Collection, New York Public Library*)

to have life, and you've got to have life to love life." Morning activities begin in Grover's Corners. The newsboy—he will be sent to college but then get killed, the Stage Manager remarks—delivers his papers. The Gibbs and Webb families are excited and tearful, for it is the morning of George and Emily's wedding. George asks Emily's father for advice—and is advised "never to ask advice on personal matters." The Stage Manager interrupts to show "how all this began." Time shifts back to the courtship. Coming home from school, Emily chides George for being "awful conceited and stuck up." People ought to be perfect, as are their own parents, both of them agree. Penitent, George offers to buy Emily a soda. As they sit at the drugstore counter, he decides to skip agricultural college: they were made for each other, and shyly decide to get married. The parents eventually concur, and the Stage Manager, who will play the minister, sermonizes on the gravity of marriage. The most important person is not yet here, he notes, quoting "one of the European fellas" (Shaw's preface to MISALLIANCE): "Every child born into the world is Nature's attempt to make a perfect human being." Just before the ceremony both George and Emily panic, sure that they are making a mistake. But they are calmed by their parents as the organ music starts. The ceremony concludes happily, and the couple joyously run up the auditorium aisle. "That's all the Second Act," the Stage Manager says: "Ten minutes' intermission, folks."

Act III (implied title: "Death and the Meaning of Life"). The actors bring in and arrange chairs in three rows, and sit down. "This time nine years have gone by, friends," the Stage Manager begins. It is the cemetery, it is raining, and the sitters are the dead. They include Mrs. Gibbs and the choir director, who committed suicide. Becoming philosophical as he brings the audience up to date, the Stage Manager remarks, "Everybody knows in their bones that *something* is eternal, and that something has to do with human beings." And so he introduces the dialogue of the dead, who observe and comment, as the living, protected from the rain by umbrellas, hold a funeral for Emily Webb Gibbs, who died in childbirth. Emily joins the dead and talks with them. When she discovers she can go back and relive her past, she eagerly chooses her twelfth birthday. "You not only live it; but you watch yourself living it," the Stage Manager cautions her. Time shifts back fourteen years as the town's morning routine starts. Young Emily is happy as she gets her presents, but soon she is grief-stricken. "I can't bear it. They're so young and beautiful," she says to herself. "Oh, Mama, just look at me one minute as though you really saw me," she urges Mrs. Webb, recounting all that will befall them soon: "Mama, just for a moment we're happy. Let's look at one another." But Mrs. Webb cannot hear her. Unable to stand it any longer, Emily asks to be taken back to her grave. "Oh, earth, you're too wonderful for anybody to realize you," she concludes: "Do any human beings ever realize life while they live it?—every, every minute?" The Stage Manager shakes his head: only "the saints and poets, maybe." But though the choir director dismisses the living as time-wasting slaves of passion, "ignorance and blindness," Mrs. Gibbs protests, "That ain't the whole truth and you know it." The grieving George returns to fling himself on Emily's grave, but the Stage Manager, too, is not without hope. He draws a curtain across the scene, looks at the stars "doing their old, criss-cross journeys in the sky," and winds his watch. "Hm," he concludes: "Eleven o'clock in Grover's Corners.—You get a good rest, too. Good-night."

OUTLAW, THE (*Den fredlöse*), a one-act drama by AUGUST STRINDBERG, produced in 1871 and published in 1876. Setting: a hut in medieval Iceland.

Strindberg reconstructed this play from *Blotsven,* a five-act tragedy he had written and destroyed a year earlier. *The Outlaw* is a stilted heroic romance, derivative of BJØRNSTJERNE BJØRNSON's and HENRIK IBSEN's dramatizations of Norse sagas. But it was Strindberg's first work to show promise, and sufficiently impressed King Charles XV to award him a much-needed endowment.

The proud pagan Thorfinn was to become Earl of Iceland, but because he broke his word and led plunders and massacres, he is declared an outlaw. His stoic wife is ready to die with her estranged husband. So is his affection-starved but proud daughter, who has embraced Christianity. Thorfinn, who worships only the strength that "bowed thousands of wills," angrily rejects her. His minstrel comrade makes him look into himself; he begins to waver, and fears his defeat by the new God. Won over by their self-sacrificing love after he has fallen in battle, Thorfinn kisses his wife and, with his dying breath, blesses his kneeling daughter and a kinsman crusader whom she loves, and commends all to the "Eternal—Creating—God—"

OUTWARD BOUND, a play in three acts by SUTTON VANE, produced in 1923 and published in 1924. Setting: on board a ship in the 1920's.

This fantasy about a ship cruising to eternity with an assorted group of dead passengers was filmed twice, in 1930 and as *Between Two Worlds*—in 1944.

Act I. A number of people are starting their voyage: a high-strung young drunkard, a snobbish dowager, an officious businessman, a clergyman, a cockney charwoman, two nervous young lovers, and the ship's calm and kind steward. The drunkard becomes increasingly disturbed by the peculiarity of the setting and the vagueness of their destination. At last he suspects they are all dead, and the steward admits it. Their destination is "Heaven, sir. (*Pause.*) And Hell, too. (*Pause.*) It's the same place, you see."

Act II. Over their bickerings the others begin to sense a strangeness: the blackness outside, the absence of a crew, their uncertainty about personal matters. The charwoman, whose common language appalls the dowager, reveals how she sacrificed herself to send her son to the university and enable him to become a playboy, shielding her identity all the while so he would not be shamed by her menial position. The drunkard finally makes the others aware of their true situation. "There's nothing to be done. Just go on as if nothing has happened," the steward tells them.

Act III. They wait for the Examiner. When the ship anchors, the elderly Examiner comes aboard. He is a jolly clergyman, a friend of the minister. After they reminisce, the latter is reemployed—he will share the Examiner's "digs near your work, right in the center of the parish." Then they examine the various passengers. The dowager, reprimanded as "a bad harlot," must rejoin her late husband, learn to become a good wife, and be punished by her new-found knowledge. The businessman, too, gets his comeuppance. The drunkard begs for the oblivion of death, but it is not granted him. The charwoman asks to be allowed to serve him and readily forgoes the seaside cottage awaiting her. "It's 'Eaven, that's what it is, it's 'Eaven," she exclaims as she happily runs after the drunkard—assured by the Examiner that he will never find out she is his mother. Only the lovers cannot be examined; they remain aboard and the ship sails on. Then the lovers gradually remember, with the help of the steward, that like him they are "half-ways"—suicides. As they reminisce, the boy's yearning to return to life intensifies to the point where he succeeds, and leaves. The girl weeps for him, and though the steward believes it impossible, the boy returns for a moment because of her great longing. "I've come to fetch you home, dear," he says: "We've got such a lot to do, my love. And such little time to do it in. Quick. Quick." The steward watches them go out, hand in hand.

OVERRULED, "a demonstration" in one act by BERNARD SHAW, produced in 1912 and published in 1916. Setting: the lounge of a contemporary seaside hotel.

Shaw's preface deals with sex morality and adultery, "the dullest of themes on the stage" but one that should be faced honestly; its treatment in his "farcical comedy," he argued, is "a clinical study of how the thing actually occurs."

A couple decorously making love is succeeded by a second couple—the spouses of the first; in the remainder of the play the four bewildered, conventional people discuss their behavior, agreeing finally to continue their harmless and delightful flirtations.

P

PAGNOL, Marcel [Paul] (1895–   ), French author of satiric as well as sentimental comedies, turned to film-making after completing his world-famous trilogy of a lower-middle-class Marseilles family, *Marius, Fanny,* and *César. Marius* (1929), adapted as *Sea Fever* by JOHN VAN DRUTEN and as *Marseilles* by SIDNEY HOWARD, starts the story with Fanny's aiding Marius to follow his dream and go to sea, though her mother, when she learns of their affair, demands that they get married. In *Fanny* (1931), made into an American musical (1954) by S. N. BEHRMAN and JOSHUA LOGAN, Fanny reluctantly marries an elderly suitor after telling him of her pregnancy; Marius's father, César, is equally unhappy, but gives in for the sake of his grandchild. The comic folk drama concludes with *César* (1937), which unlike the others originally appeared as a film (1933); it is years later, Fanny's husband dies, and her son seeks and finds his real father, Marius, who ultimately agrees to accept Fanny's money and marry her for the sake of their son.

Pagnol was born in Aubagne, near Marseilles. At first he planned to pursue an academic career, and he began as an English professor in southern France, and then in Paris. After editing a literary review and writing poetic dramas, Pagnol achieved some success with *Les Marchands de gloire* (*Merchants of Glory,* 1925), a play (written with Paul Nivoix, 1893–1958) that flays war profiteers. Pagnol's first great hit was *Monsieur Topaze* (*Topaze,* 1928), a satiric comedy (filmed in 1933) about a teacher who is used by crooks but manages, by employing their methods, to defeat them and thus becomes a tycoon. Another Pagnol play is *Jazz* (1926), a satire on pedantry that he rewrote in 1931 as *Phaéton.* Subsequently Pagnol adapted Shakespeare and wrote *Judas* (1955) and a few other plays, none of them successful. He devoted the rest of his career principally to writing and producing major films, notably *La Femme du boulanger* (*The Baker's Wife,* 1938) and *La Fille du puisatier* (*The Well-Digger's Daughter,* 1940). In 1946 he was elected to the French Academy, the first film maker to be thus honored.

Widely praised for their charm are Pagnol's autobiographies, which include *Le Temps des secrets* (1960).

PAKISTAN has produced little and generally undistinguished drama in either of its principal languages (Urdu and Bengali) in the early decades since partition and its independence in 1947. For its earlier drama see INDIA.

PANAMA, like PARAGUAY, was considered to be a country without any theatre at all by the River Plate Theatre Congress of 1941. Since then, however, amateur and other Panamanian theatre groups have sprung up and have begun to produce drama, the best of it dealing with post-World War II social and political problems. Notable in recent times have been the short metaphysical plays, particularly *El juicio final* (1962), of the NICARAGUAN José de Jesús Martínez (1928–   ), who resettled in Panama.

For further studies see LATIN AMERICA.

PANDORA'S BOX (*Die Büchse der Pandora*), a tragedy in a verse prologue and three acts by FRANK WEDEKIND, published in 1904 and produced in 1905. Setting: contemporary Germany, Paris, and London.

See EARTH-SPIRIT, the first part of the tragedy that ends with *Pandora's Box.* The shocking last act of this play sealed Wedekind's reputation as a "pornographer," although the play was legally cleared of obscenity charges, as he recounts in his "Foreword." He also describes the lesbian Geschwitz as the play's "tragic central figure," and Rodrigo as representing the bourgeois rabble—Wedekind's and art's chief antagonist. These ideas, too, are dramatized in a "Prologue in the Bookshop."

Prologue. A Normal Reader wishes to purchase a book from the Enterprising Publisher. To protect this reader, a Public Prosecutor attempts to suppress a Timid Author's poems, but the latter refuses to alter any of them.

Act I. After Lulu has served a year in prison, Countess Geschwitz attempts to help her escape: the countess has become a prison nurse, has infected herself and Lulu with cholera, and has been able to confuse the attending nurse with their identities. Waiting for Lulu, Rodrigo plans on taking her to London, where he expects to train her with a whip if necessary; and Alwa, who praises Geschwitz for her self-sacrifice, speculates on Lulu's suitability as a dramatic subject: "To bring about a rebirth of genuine vigorous art we should go as much as possible among men . . . whose actions are dictated by the simplest animal instincts" (as he did "in my play *Earth-Spirit,*" Wedekind wrote). Lulu manages to escape from the prison hospital, but when Rodrigo sees the worn-out "bag of gnawed bones," he is repelled and leaves. Still vain, Lulu tells Alwa that she kept dreaming "that I'd fallen into the hands of a sex-maniac," and then seduces Alwa "on the very sofa on which your father bled to death."

Act II portrays a depraved party attended by Lulu, her entourage, and all kinds of decadents in Paris. One of her lovers—the procurer Marquis Casti-Piani, who is featured in DEATH AND DEVIL—threatens to denounce Lulu as an escaped convict unless she goes to work in a fashionable Egyptian brothel. Also threatened and importuned for money by Rodrigo and others, Lulu arranges a tryst at Schigolch's between the mutually antipathetic Geschwitz and Rodrigo. Schigolch agrees to throw Rodrigo into the river after removing his golden rings if Lulu will sleep with him again. "Is that all you want? But you have a mistress," Lulu says. But the old lecher laments that his "lady-love . . . is no longer in her first youth." Lulu sends Geschwitz off after promising to be hers if she goes with Rodrigo. Then, in the general confusion, Lulu escapes just before the police come for her.

Act III. It is shortly before Christmas, in a dilapidated London attic. Dressed in rags, Lulu prepares to walk the streets. Alwa and Schigolch, who live with her, urge her to start—they need the money. After a drink Lulu goes out and the men reminisce about her. Soon Lulu brings home her first customer, and Alwa and Schigolch go into the next room while she entertains him. After he leaves the men return. "How exciting he was," Lulu says tonelessly, and prepares to go out again. Geschwitz arrives with Lulu's portrait by her first husband, which they discuss emotionally. Soon Lulu goes out again and returns with her second customer—an African prince who, when he notices the hidden Alwa, kills him, kisses Lulu, and bolts without paying. Schigolch is discouraged and departs: "She can't make a living out of love because love is her life." Geschwitz, still desperately in love with Lulu, tries to kill herself. Lulu returns with another customer, who leaves when he sees Alwa's corpse. Lulu wretchedly begs her next customer, Jack, to take her for whatever little money he may have. He attacks her, Lulu screams for help, and Geschwitz rushes in. Jack plunges a knife into her and then takes Lulu into the adjoining room. Her screams soon stop, and then "The Ripper" comes out, wipes the blood off his hands, and leaves. Geschwitz dies: "Lulu! —My angel! —Let me see you once more! —I am near you—will stay near you—in eternity! —Oh, God!—"

PANOVA, Vera Fyodorovna (1905–   ), Russian novelist, began her career as a playwright. Born in Rostov-on-Don to the family of a clerk who drowned when she was five, Panova grew up in poverty. She became a journalist, and was a war correspondent on a hospital train, an experience that resulted in her first major novel, *Sputniki* (*The Train,* 1946). Married to an engineer, she settled in Leningrad. The Stalin Prize was awarded her in 1947, 1948, and 1950. Panova decided early in her career that "the dramatic form confined" her, and therefore devoted most of her efforts to fiction.

Particularly adept in characterizations of simple and usually young people in love and vulnerable in their first confrontation with adults, Panova's plays include *Ilya Kosogor* (1939), *Metelitsa* (1941), *Devochki* (1945, about two sisters evacuated to the Urals during World War II), *Provody belykh nochei* (1960), and *Skolko let, skolko zim!* (*It's Been Ages!,* 1966). This last named play, a lyrical love drama set at an airport, appears in Franklin R. Reeve's *Contemporary Russian Drama* (1968). For a discussion of Panova's life and work, see Vera Alexandrova's *A History of Soviet Literature* (1963), which includes a bibliography.

PANTAGLEIZE, a play in three acts and an epilogue by MICHEL DE GHELDERODE, produced in 1930 and published in 1934. Setting: a European city, a day "on the morrow of one war and the eve of another."

Subtitled "a Farce to Make You Sad," *Pantagleize* features a lovable fool, a modern Everyman who demonstrates a little man's capacity for human commitment in a rapacious world. "He is bound to Parsifal by purity, and to Don Quixote by courage and holy madness," Ghelderode wrote in an "epitaph," and recalls seeing such a Chaplinesque figure in Germany, obliviously reading a book amidst machine-gun fire during the 1919 Spartacist revolts.

At six in the morning his Negro servant awakes Pantagleize, a fashion-magazine writer. It is his fortieth birthday, and he sadly concludes that destiny has slighted him: "I have neither vanity, nor pride, nor love, nor self-respect. I have nothing but my queer name, my crucial age, and an insufficient intellectual ballast, all completely out of date." He decides on the day's cliché with which

Pantagleize. The Jewess (Patricia Conolly) and Pantagleize (Ellis Rabb). New York, 1968. (*Culver Pictures*)

to greet people: "I shall say that the day is lovely"—unaware that this is the signal for the Liberals' uprising. At a café various revolutionaries, including the Negro, plot while a disguised policeman observes them. Innocently Pantagleize, at first taken for an imbecile, comes out with his cliché and thus starts the revolution. A Jewess knocks out the policeman and later rescues and embraces Pantagleize: "You have saved humanity with a phrase." He falls in love with her, readily follows her instructions, and starts on a series of wild adventures. The revolutionary Jewess is killed by the policeman while Pantagleize captures the Conservatives' treasure: he enters the state bank by telling the militia and then the cowardly commander, General Macboom, to "go to the devil"—which happens to be the day's password. Then he is acclaimed by the revolutionists, and briefly enjoys distinction at a banquet, during which—unnoticed by him—the revolutionaries one by one, are felled by the waiters. The revolution fails and leaders are brought before a War Council, tried, and executed. Pantagleize is brought in last. Though his counsel pleads that "he is the plaything of really terrible coincidences," Pantagleize too is condemned. The epilogue shows his execution. He is still oblivious to reality when the firing squad shoots him. As he falls, he thinks of the beautiful Jewess. After the officer's *coup de grâce,* the dying Pantagleize "in a voice both gruesome and childish," repeats the fateful phrase: "What—a—lovely—day!" The church clock strikes midnight, the day is over, "and the farce to make you sad is finished."

PAOLO AND FRANCESCA, a poetic tragedy in four acts by STEPHEN PHILLIPS, published in 1899 and produced in 1902. Setting: thirteenth-century Italy.

This dramatization of the fifth canto of Dante's *Divine Comedy* for a while was hailed as the beginning of a renaissance of great English poetic drama, and it is Phillips's best and best known work. Though it is slow-moving and never achieved the popularity of d'Annunzio's more passionate FRANCESCA DA RIMINI or Maeterlinck's more haunting PELLÉAS AND MÉLISANDE on the same subject, it has a lyric grandeur that echoes Elizabethan drama, and it was again praised by critics when it was revived in the 1920's. Except for the character of Lucrezia and a prose tavern interlude, Phillips followed the traditional story.

Paolo is sent for Francesca, who will be the wife of his much older brother, Giovanni Malatesta, Lord of Rimini. Occupied with military affairs, he asks his beloved brother, Paolo, to keep Francesca company. The young people are concerned only with doing their wifely and brotherly duties—but they are drawn to each other: "Unwillingly he comes a wooing: she / Unwillingly is wooed: yet shall they woo." Francesca tries to resist, but Paolo's "kiss was on her lips ere she was born." The brothers' embittered cousin, the widowed and childless Lucrezia, spies on the lovers and informs Malatesta. She repents of her betrayal too late to save Francesca, who has implored her to help. Malatesta discovers Paolo and Francesca in each other's arms, abides by the honor code, and kills them. Then he grieves for those he loved: "She takes away my breath. / I did not know the dead could have such hair. / Hide them. They look like children fast asleep."

PAOLO PAOLI, a play in twelve scenes by ARTHUR ADAMOV, published and produced in 1957. Setting: France, 1900–14.

A seven-character BRECHTian EPIC play, *Paolo Paoli* is a sardonic satire of capitalist society prior to the outbreak of World War I. Each scene opens with projections of ironically juxtaposed contemporary newspaper headlines, which underline the relation between trade (in ludicrous commodities like butterflies and feathers) and human exploitation, the penal system, the Church, international relations, and war.

The dealer Paolo Paoli gets wealthy on the rare butterflies caught by one of his hunters, an ex-convict who is in his power. His wife becomes Paolo's mistress, while Paolo's German-born wife becomes the mistress of an ostrich-feather dealer who also makes his fortune and sets her up as a milliner. Among other dealings, Paolo sends the ex-convict to hunt for butterflies in war-torn Morocco. Various intricate machinations are disrupted when he returns to France and becomes a labor agitator in the ostrich-feather factory. Its union is controlled by a churchman as greedy and power-hungry as the others, who denounce the ex-convict as a traitor just as war breaks out. Paolo alone reforms, determined at last to benefit humanity rather than have his money continue making its rounds "in the same dirty little circuit."

PAQUET, Alfons (1881–1944), German dramatist, wrote the documentary plays *Fahnen* (1923) and *Sturmflut* (1926), the first about the 1886 Chicago anarchist strike, the second (produced by Erwin Piscator with film clips) on the revolt of the German navy and Scapa Flow. Paquet's other plays include the dramatic biographies *William Penn* (1927) and *Eleonora Duse* (1929); and *Stinchen von der Krone* (1932), a tragic medieval romance about a woman's vengeance.

A post-World War I playwright, Paquet began as an EXPRESSIONIST poet, and also published exotic utopian novels.

PARAGUAY, like PANAMA, had no national theatre according to the River Plate Theatre Congress of 1941 at Montevideo. This announcement stimulated activity in succeeding decades, though some drama had indeed appeared earlier. Julio Correa (1890–1953) was the chief playwright of the short-lived Indian-language (Guaraní) theatre. The first Spanish-writing dramatist of consequence was Luis Ruffinelli (1889–   ), whose *Sorprendidos y desconocidos* (1924), which vindicates divorce, is considered the first significant Paraguayan play. The Argentine-born Arturo Alsina (1897–   ) made his name with a number of dramas derivative of HENRIK IBSEN and LUIGI PIRANDELLO. More productive and distinguished were Roque Centurión Miranda (1900–60) and Josefina Pla (1907–), a theatre director and a poetess, respectively, who wrote plays singly and in collaboration. No fewer than three of their joint efforts won distinction at the 1942 Paraguayan drama contest held in response to the aforementioned Congress, the first prize going to *Aquí no pasa nada,* their drama of a man's affection for his wife's adulterously conceived child. Notable among more recent writers is José María Rivarola Matto (1917–), a novelist whose few dramas include "a modern miracle play" about a football star, *El fin de Chipí González* (*The End of Chipi González,* 1954). It appears in Willis Knapp Jones's *Men and Angels: Three South American Comedies* (1970), and Matto's work—and that of other Paraguayan dramatists—is discussed in studies listed under LATIN AMERICA.

PARIAH (*Paria*), a one-act duologue by AUGUST STRINDBERG, produced in 1889 and published in 1890. Setting: a contemporary farmhouse in southern Sweden.

This QUART D'HEURE is a Poe-inspired free adaptation of a story by Strindberg's younger Swedish contemporary, Ola Hansson.

An outcast (Y) schemes to blackmail an archaeologist (X). Though X is guilty of an inadvertent murder, his superior intelligence foils Y, a self-effacing scoundrel.

PARIS BOUND, a play in three acts by PHILIP BARRY, produced in 1927 and published in 1929. Setting: New York, 1921–27.

The hard-pushed thesis of this sophisticated comedy, Barry's first hit, is that in an otherwise successful marriage a passing affair is not important enough to justify divorce.

Jim and Mary Hutton prepare to leave on their honeymoon after the wedding breakfast. They are deeply in love, but agree to be "sensible" about each other's possible lapses in the future—for they are modern, and they are afraid to follow in the footsteps of Jim's parents, whose lives are embittered by divorce. To oblige Mary, Jim chides a tipsy bridesmaid who is enamored of him and is making a scene. Six years later Jim and Mary have two children and are blissfully happy and more in love than ever. Discovering that once, while on a business trip, Jim had an affair with the former bridesmaid, Mary totally reverses her earlier sentiments of tolerance. "Theories are fine, before things happen," she tells Jim's father, who begs her not to throw away their happiness for "the least important element in your whole relationship. I don't mean to belittle sex," he continues, "but love is something else again, and marriage is still another thing." He chides Mary for giving in to her lower, possessive instincts by seeking a fashionable divorce—in "Paris, with the rest of the defeated sisterhood." Feeling miserable as she prepares to confront and then leave her husband, Mary follows her impulse to kiss a young composer whom she has helped—and almost surrenders herself to him, when Jim returns unexpectedly. Though he has reason to suspect her of infidelity, and though he does not know she has discovered his own, Jim refuses to let Mary explain: "There's nothing ever can affect *us,* you know—nothing in the world." His love, ebullient charm, and common sense—and Mary's realization of the unimportance of her own momentary weakness—end Mary's thoughts of divorce. Hand in hand and as happily in love as ever, they go to see their children.

PARISIAN WOMAN, THE (*La Parisienne*), a comedy in three acts by HENRY BECQUE, published and produced in 1885. Setting: an elegant Paris drawing room in the 1880's.

This amusing portrayal of a marital *ménage à trois* is a cynical SLICE OF LIFE of hypocritical society. The play created a sensation when it was first performed, but failed when it was produced again five years later. The bored and superficial yet vivacious and by no means evil or contemptible title character reappears in Becque's one-act sequel, *Veuve!* (*Widowed!,* 1897). There the just-widowed Clotilde tells her lover, Lafont, that she does not know whether her husband knew of their affair. But before he died he suggested that for her own and their children's sake she marry "their friend" if he should propose. "That's funny," Lafont replies, "I thought those things happened only in plays." The play has also been translated as *Woman of Paris.*

Act I. "Open the desk and give me that letter," Lafont jealously demands of Clotilde. They have a violent domestic scene, but Clotilde soon gets him to apologize meekly for his eternal demands to know where she has gone and whom she saw. Lafont preaches the need for respectability and exhorts her to beware of temptations. "Resist, Clotilde, resist! By remaining faithful to me, you remain respectable and honorable; the day when you deceive me—" Clotilde interrupts him, "Take care, here comes my husband." Du Mesnil cordially greets Lafont but is irritable toward Clotilde. Soon she has him, too, give in to her and regret his objection to her "disreputable" female society friends. Clotilde is solicitous about his comforts and, after he leaves, reproaches Lafont for not being sufficiently fond of her husband. She defends herself against her lover's accusations that she is reactionary. "I love order, peace, well-established principles. I want the churches to be open, if the mood takes me to make the rounds"—just like stores—and she is scandalized by his "freethinking": "I do believe that you could very pleasantly come to terms with a mistress who had no religion; how dreadful!" Promising to follow him immediately to his rooms, she succeeds in ridding herself of the uxorious lover—and then asks her maid for her nightwear: "I'm not going out again."

Act II. Lafont's endless and quarrelsome visits become tiresome to Clotilde. She sends him off just as her husband appears, ill-humored because his expected government appointment is not materializing. Thereupon Clotilde communicates with her own "disreputable" friends, the influen-

The Parisian Woman. Rehearsal photograph: Clotilde (Yvonne Gaudeau) and Du Mesnil (François Chammette), in front; Lafont (Georges Descières), the maid (Catherine Samie), and the sportsman lover (Jacques Toja), in rear. Paris, 1960. (*French Cultural Services*)

tial society where she can advantageously use her charms to assure her husband's future. She sends Du Mesnil out for the evening, blandly tells the ever-returning Lafont that his suspicions of her infidelity are justified—and breaks off their affair.

Act III. Clotilde's other affair, entered into to advance her husband's prospects, is just as peremptorily ended by her influential lover, a sportsman who is tired of Paris. She weeps briefly "and quite sincerely," she assures him, admitting that women are "weak for those who appeal to us, but we always come back to those who love us." To resist temptation and remain faithful would be best, she concludes: "Life wouldn't be very amusing or very thrilling, perhaps, but one would avoid many worries, many deceptions, and many regrets." With her husband she rejoices in his appointment, obtained through her latest liaison. When Lafont again calls on her, Clotilde (again "free") agrees to resume her relationship with him. It is the husband, Du Mesnil, who has particularly missed their friend's long absence. He attributes Lafont's jealous unhappiness over "a mistress" to Lafont's being celibate and therefore "deprived," and persists in questioning Lafont about whether or not he really was deceived. "Is there any man, even one, who would swear that his mistress has *not* deceived him?" Lafont replies doubtfully: "We're reconciled; no doubt that's what we both wanted." Clotilde urges him to have faith in women: "Trust us, Monsieur Lafont, trust us; that's the only system that succeeds with us." "It's always been mine, my love!" her husband remarks as the curtain falls.

PARKER, Louis N[apoleon] (1852–1944), English playwright, was born in France to an American father and an English mother. He studied, taught, and composed music; directed a music school; is credited with being the inventor of pageants; and wrote well over one hundred plays. The first, *A Buried Talent,* appeared in 1890, and the most famous was George Arliss's popular vehicle DISRAELI (1911). Other Parker plays include *Rosemary* (1896), *The Cardinal* (1903), and *Beauty and the Barge* (1904), on which he collaborated with W. W. Jacobs (1863–1943), whose well-known and macabre short story *The Monkey's Paw* (1902) Parker dramatized.

Much of Parker's work was hack, but some of

it has merit. Immensely active in many fields, he aptly titled his reminiscences *Several of My Lives* (1928).

PARODY, THE (*La Parodie*), a play in a prologue and twelve scenes by ARTHUR ADAMOV, published in 1950 and produced in 1952. Setting: a dance hall, a square, the street, etc.

Adamov was influenced by ANTONIN ARTAUD's theatre of CRUELTY and by Strindberg's A DREAM PLAY in this, his first play. Its title suggests its ABSURDist view of the world, for as Adamov noted, he meant to portray, "as crudely and as visibly as possible, the loneliness of man, the absence of communication." This nightmare of life is dramatized in a quasi-EXPRESSIONIST setting (space literally shrinks and timelessness is indicated by a handless clock) and unnamed main characters—one optimistic and dynamic, the other pessimistic and passive. Neither wins the vacuous girl both love. One ends in prison, the other is killed and swept into a garbage can. Others who court her include a prominent newspaperman who appears in the guise of various characters. Interchangeable couples constitute a chorus and suggest the faceless crowd.

PASO [Gil], **Alfonso** (1926–), Spanish playwright, among the most popular and prolific of his country's post-World War II writers. His works have been produced regularly, a number of them sometimes running simultaneously in Madrid's fashionable theatres. Most of Paso's well over one hundred plays completed by the end of the 1960's are extravagant comedies about ordinary people. They are amusing but sufficiently bland politically to have passed Franco's censorship—though Paso has considered himself a "tremendous rebel" against social convention. Few of his plays are known abroad, though his *El canto de la cigarra* (*Song of the Grasshopper,* 1960), a comedy about an amiable middle-aged loafer and roué, had a short Broadway run in 1967. A number of his other plays have been adapted into English by Reginald Denham (1894–): *El cielo dentro de casa* (1957, as *Blue Heaven*), *Cosas de papá y mamá* (1960, as *Oh, Mama! No, Papa!*), and *Receta para un crimen* (*Recipe for a Crime,* 1962).

Born in Madrid to an actress and a playwright of some prominence, Antonio Paso y Cano (1870–1958), Alfonso Paso was educated at the University of Madrid, where he completed a graduate degree in American history. Among his first produced plays was *Un tic-tac de reloj* (1946). His writings also include movie scenarios and popular newspaper columns.

PASSEUR, Stève [originally Étienne Morin] (1899–1966), French dramatist, born in Sedan, wrote romantic plays, mostly in the 1930's, that focus on passion and are resolved with some psychological insight. His best and a typical work, *L'Acheteuse* (1930), features a woman who uses her wealth to buy a man's love she could not win otherwise, and commits suicide when he escapes her hold. Other Passeur plays include *Les Tricheurs* (1932), *Je vivrai un grand amour* (1935), and the later *Telles sont les femmes* (1956).

PASSING OF THE THIRD FLOOR BACK, THE, a play in three acts by JEROME K. JEROME, published and produced in 1908. Setting: a boardinghouse in Bloomsbury, London; early twentieth century.

Jerome's popular pietistic drama features a mysterious man who rents a small back room in a dismal lodging house. He changes the lives of its flinty mistress and its unhappy inhabitants, making them all kinder and better people. "You are—" says a grateful boarder and starts kneeling before the preacherlike figure; but he stops her: "A fellow-lodger. Good night." The slatternly servant thanks him for showing her the beauty of life. "I also am a servant. I have my work," he says, gently kisses her, and leaves: "I came because you wanted me." As he departs into the fog, a shaft of sunlight falls on the servant's radiant face.

PASSING OF THE TORCH, THE (*La Course du flambeau*), a play in four acts by PAUL HERVIEU, published and produced in 1901. Setting: France and the Swiss mountains, early twentieth century.

Published in America as *The Trail of the Torch* (1915), with an appreciative introduction by Brander Matthews, this play made Hervieu famous. One of the characters echoes the title as he describes the Athenian torch-passing festival of "lampadephoria," which Plato and Lucretius saw as "a symbol of all the generations of the earth."

The protagonist, Sabine Revel, at first considers "filial piety which has been the inspiration of many deeds of heroism" more pressing than parental obligations. But when her daughter needs help to save her husband from bankruptcy, Sabine's filial piety is displaced by her maternal instincts. She tries to rob and then sacrifices her own mother for the sake of her girl—who finally denounces and deserts Sabine. As her mother dies in her arms, Sabine, now alone, cries out, "For my daughter I have killed my mother!"

PASSION FLOWER, THE (*La Malquerida*), a drama in three acts by JACINTO BENAVENTE, published and produced in 1913. Setting: the outskirts of a small contemporary town in Castile, Spain.

La Malquerida (the term has also been translated as "the maid of shame") was Benavente's most popular play. It is a suspenseful and searing domestic tragedy that depicts the intense, long-suppressed passions of a girl and her stepfather, a hardworking, well-to-do peasant. The hot-blooded townspeople exacerbate the struggle of the consciences of those two people and that of the equally passionate wife and mother.

Act I. Various friends and neighbors congratulate Raimunda on the engagement of her daughter, Acacia. They allude to her broken engagement with a former fiancé, her cousin Norbert. Raimunda deplores her daughter's hatred of her stepfather, Esteban; despite his kindness and generosity, Acacia has always refused to call him "father," and has "never let him kiss her even when she was a child, much less now." Raimunda attributes this attitude to Acacia's resentment of Raimunda's quick remarriage after the death of her first husband, Acacia's father. Now night is falling, the party disbands, and Esteban accompanies his guests home. Raimunda questions Acacia, and is reassured of her daughter's happiness. But a faithful old servant has disturbing presentiments, and Acacia seems agitated. She shows a friend the gifts Esteban has given her over the years, but stresses her resentment of him. Her mother is always "wrapped up in him," she complains, and she says that she is marrying only to get away from him. When her friend suggests that Acacia is still in love with Norbert, she excitedly tears up his letter. Suddenly there is a shot in the distance. Soon the townspeople bring in Acacia's betrothed—who has just been murdered in the dark by an unknown assailant. "Everyone thinks it was Norbert—so as to fill the cup of misfortune which we must drain in this house!" Raimunda remarks, and then begs the others to say the rosary for the victim: "I cannot pray. I am thinking of his mother's broken heart!"

Act II. It is some weeks later. The family has moved to an isolated farmhouse to escape the town gossip. At the trial Norbert's innocence was proved definitively. But the victim's family, still convinced of his guilt, have declared a blood feud, and the townsfolk are divided in their opinions and sympathies. Raimunda questions everyone, obsessed with solving the mystery of the murder. She attempts to persuade the victim's angry father that her kinsman Norbert is innocent. In the meantime, Esteban's servant becomes increasingly impudent; he spends much money on liquor, and while drunk is said to brag and make suspicious comments. In her determination to discover the truth, Raimunda summons Norbert. Reluctantly he tells her what the townspeople are saying: the servant was paid to kill the fiancé of Acacia, who is called *La Malquerida* because she inspires forbidden desires. The townsmen even sing a song about "The Passion flower": he who loves her will be betrayed by her unholy love. Finally Norbert admits he was forced to give up Acacia, and the dead man, who refused to do likewise, was killed "because he dared lay eyes on Acacia." Horrified, Raimunda begins to understand. She questions Acacia, who hysterically voices her hatred of "that man" Esteban. "He would eat me up with his eyes while you sat there; he followed me around the house like a cat," she reveals, and accuses Raimunda: "You have loved him so much—more than you ever loved my father! . . I wanted you to hate him as I hate him, as my father in heaven hates him!" Raimunda calls her husband, accuses him of cowardice (paying a servant to commit murder for him), and vows to protect Norbert from the victim's family, who have been called by Esteban and are now hiding outside, ready to shoot Norbert. "You are not man enough to do it yourself," she says. In a passionate denunciation she tells him to hide in the wilds like a beast, and pushes him away from her. "Now I know! You have nothing to hope for from me. Oh, I was alone with my child!—and you came," Raimunda says, pointing at Acacia; "there she stands—*La Malquerida!* . . . I am still here to guard her from you, to tell you that her father still lives in heaven—and to shoot you through the heart if you make one step to lay your hand on her!"

Act III. Norbert has been shot and wounded leaving the house, but is recuperating. Despite Raimunda's outburst, she keeps waiting for Esteban's return from the wilds to which she sent him away: "The habits of a lifetime cannot be changed in a day." She loathes him, yet still yearns for him. The old servant suggests that Acacia's initial hatred, her refusal as a little girl to treat him as a father, eventually inflamed Esteban, who is not a bad man. Shortly afterward, when Acacia reiterates her aversion, the servant suggests that "a hate like that always grows out of a great love." The haunted Esteban returns, weeping with mortification, exhaustion, and love for Raimunda. Her determination to have him suffer for his sins is mixed with passion and pity: "Dry your eyes; you have wept blood. Take a sip of water—I wish it was poison. . . . The thorns have torn your skin. You deserved knives. Let me wash you off; it makes my blood creep to look at you." Still deeply in love with his wife, Esteban admits his longing for Acacia. Raimunda decides to send the girl to a convent, then perhaps have her get married: "Later she could return and have her children, and we would be grandfather and grandmother, and grow old with them around us, and be happy once more in this house." Acacia overhears her. Furious, she threatens to denounce Esteban: "I have to take the blame, while you stay here and enjoy yourself with your husband." Raimunda is ready to forgive him now, and is frantic when Esteban prepares to give himself up. She begs Acacia, too, to forgive him: "Throw your arms about his neck. Call him father." Raimunda is horrified by what follows: "But you don't call him father. Has she fainted? Ah! Lip to lip, and you clutch her in your arms! Let go, let go!" She curses her daughter, blaming her for the tragedy. Acacia at last recognizes and faces the reality of her passion: "Kill me! It is true, it is true! He is the only man I ever loved." Raimunda is hysterical: she calls the people and denounces husband as well as daughter: "I have the murderer! Take this wicked woman, for she is not my child." When she bars his escape, Esteban shoots Raimunda, and then gives himself up. The catastrophe reconciles daughter and mother. "This man cannot harm you now. You are saved," the dying Raimunda tells Acacia; "blessed be the blood that saves, like the blood of our Lord Jesus Christ!"

PATAPHYSICS, a nonsensical philosophical system proclaimed by ALFRED JARRY and defined (in his posthumous novel *Gestes et opinions du Docteur Faustroll*) as "the science of imaginary solutions, which symbolically attributes the properties of objects, described by their virtuality to their lineaments." For their serious amusement, some of his admirers—including EUGÈNE IONESCO, BORIS VIAN, and other writers—in 1949 formed a Collège de Pataphysique, with elaborate rules and rituals. Under its auspices were published the posthumous *Le Bétrou* (1956), the most ambitious play of the vagabond poet Julien Torma (1902–33); and *Petit Théâtre* (1957), nonsense playlets by the poets René Daumal (1908–44) and Roger Gilbert-Lecomte (1907–43). The pataphysics movement was ultimately absorbed by the theatre of the ABSURD.

PATRICK, John (1910–), American dramatist, writer of film and stage plays, of which the most popular is the periodically revived Pulitzer Prize Broadway hit, THE TEAHOUSE OF THE AUGUST MOON (1953). Born in Kentucky and educated in Southern schools as well as at Harvard and Columbia universities, Patrick began his career as a scriptwriter for NBC in San Francisco. His first play, *Hell Freezes Over* (1935), failed. During World War II Patrick served with an ambulance unit in the Near East, from which experience emerged his romantic play set in a military hospital, *The Hasty Heart* (1945). It was followed by *The Story of Mary Surratt* (1947)—in which the title character (hanged as a conspirator in Lincoln's assassination) is the innocent victim of a vindictive tribunal—and other drama before he achieved his major success. Later plays such as *Everybody Loves Opal* (1962) have failed to duplicate its popularity.* Patrick has written a number of film scripts, including those of *Les Girls* (1957) and of *The Teahouse of the August Moon.*

PAUL LANGE AND TORA PARSBERG (*Paul Lange og Tora Parsberg*), a play in three acts by BJØRNSTJERNE BJØRNSON, published and produced in 1898. Setting: Norway, 1890's.

This late Bjørnson play deals with political intolerance and is based on an actual occurrence.

Paul Lange is a weak idealist, an indecisive lover, and a politician who hesitates at a crucial moment. An insensitive public as well as his friends and associates misunderstand, and he is accused of disloyalty to his ideals. The healthy and proud yet humble Tora Parsberg tries to protect Lange, and almost succeeds. But victimized by continued badgering, Lange commits suicide. Tora realizes that all society is to blame for his death. Her final outcry resembles that of Shaw's SAINT JOAN: "Oh, why should it be so, that those who are good often become martyrs? Will we never come so far that they will become our leaders?"

PEABODY, Josephine Preston [Mrs. Lionel Marks] (1874–1922), American poet and playwright, was born in Brooklyn and attended Radcliffe College. There she came under the influence of WILLIAM VAUGHN MOODY and turned from lyric poetry to eloquent, sometimes mystic verse drama. Her most accomplished play was the 1910 Stratford-on-Avon Prize winner, *The Piper* (1907), based on the Pied Piper of Hamelin legend and portraying a religious conflict between good and evil. Her other plays include a one-acter about Shakespeare and Mary Fitton, *Fortune and Men's Eyes* (1900); *Marlowe* (1901), a romantic five-act tragedy featuring the Elizabethan playwright in love with two women; *The Wolf of Gubbio* (1913), another romantic tragedy, in which the humble Saint Francis of Assisi makes the townsfolk momentarily overcome their selfishness and charms a beast into returning an infant to its heartbroken mother; and *Portrait of Mrs. W.* (1922), a prose play about the romance of Mary Wollstonecraft and William Godwin in which appear other literary notables, including the young Shelley.

The Piper was republished in Montrose J. Moses's *Representative American Dramas* (1925), which has an essay on the life and work of the playwright.

PEDESTRIAN IN THE AIR, THE (*Le Piéton de l'air*), a one-act play by EUGÈNE IONESCO, published and produced in 1963. Setting: England, 1960's.

In this long one-act play, also translated as *Stroll in the Air,* Ionesco's Chaplinesque Bérenger is a playwright visiting England with his even more prosaic wife and his imaginative daughter. In a press interview he elaborates on Ionesco's ideas about the theatre. Later, while on a walk, Bérenger joyously starts walking in the air, and then flies up even further. But high in the sky he perceives such apocalyptic horrors that his euphoria is squelched, and he returns to earth. "Why take so much trouble when we can get to the other side of the valley in a few seconds simply by crossing the bridge in an automobile?" a British journalist asks. But Bérenger does not really know why he started his poetic flight, and he cannot answer satisfactorily. "Nothing more for the moment," he concludes. (For the published version Ionesco added a final speech by the daughter: "Perhaps the fires will go out, perhaps the ice will melt, perhaps the abysses will fill themselves up, perhaps . . . the gardens . . . the gardens . . .")

PEER GYNT, a verse drama in five acts by HENRIK IBSEN, published in 1867 and produced in 1876. Setting: Norway, Morocco, Egypt, etc.; early-to-mid-nineteenth century.

This "great national poem of Norway," a lyrical and SYMBOLIC play in rhymed verse, is perhaps Ibsen's most universally appealing work. The degenerate yet lovable protagonist, the antithesis of BRAND and a satirical portrait of Ibsen's fellow Norwegians, is based on the historical-legendary Peer Gynt, whose adventures are related in Peter Christen Asbjørnsen's fairy tales. Though very popular, Ibsen's "phantasmagory" (as WILLIAM ARCHER called it) is long and difficult to perform, and Act IV is often omitted in

*A similar and even more sentimental East-West comedy hit was Leonard Spigelgass's (1908–) *A Majority of One* (1959), in which "kreplach and kindness" resolve international problems.

Peer Gynt, Act II, Scene 3. Peer (Henrik Klausen) and the mountain girls. World premiere, Christiania (Oslo), 1876. (*National Theatret archives, Oslo*)

performance. Edvard Grieg composed his famous suite for the original production of *Peer Gynt*. PAUL GREEN wrote an "American version" of the play for ANTA's New York production in 1951.

Act I. Scene 1. "Peer, you're lying!" his widowed old mother, Åse, insists when Peer Gynt, in torn and filthy clothes, brags of his hunting exploits. She reproaches him for neglecting their farm, but Peer vows that, despite his laziness and brawling, he will yet do something "really big." When Åse bemoans the wedding of a wealthy neighbor's daughter who once fancied Peer, he puts his protesting mother on the roof of their house and runs off to stop the marriage. *Scene 2.* Afraid and taunted by the others, Peer still dreams of future glory and is tempted to join the wedding festivities. *Scene 3.* At the dance, Peer is snubbed by all the girls except Solveig, a pretty stranger. When she learns that he is Peer, however, she too avoids him. He gets drunk and irritates the men with his boasts. Finally he kidnaps the bride, slings her over his shoulder, and escapes by climbing up a nearby mountain. Åse, who has come to clout Peer, watches in anger and then terror: "May God strike you down—! Be careful!"

Act II. Scene 1. Ill-tempered after having seduced the bride, Peer abandons her in the mountains and dreams of Solveig. *Scene 2.* Åse searches for her son with the family of Solveig, who has fallen in love with Peer. *Scene 3.* Peer boastfully accompanies three lusting mountain girls who are actually trolls. *Scene 4.* Later, sick of sporting and drinking, Peer wants to soar to greatness; he jumps, but strikes a rock and is knocked unconscious. *Scene 5.* Peer courts and wins the Troll King's daughter, and they ride off on her "bridal steed"—a huge pig. *Scene 6.* To marry her, Peer willingly accepts the King's demands that he become a self-sufficient troll, wear a tail, and see beauty where there is ugliness. But when Peer refuses to let his eyes be slit to help distort his view of reality, the King orders his death. Peer is saved by distant church bells, whose sound drives the trolls away. *Scene 7.* The shapeless and slimy Boyg, a ubiquitous troll monster who refuses to fight, blocks Peer's flight home; exhausted, Peer falls, but the sound of church bells and psalms again saves him: "He was too strong. There were women behind him," gasps the Boyg as it shrinks into nothing. *Scene 8.* Solveig is at Åse's farm, but runs away when Peer comes.

Act III. Scene 1. An outlaw hunted for the bride's kidnapping, Peer is building a hut in the woods. He tries to resist romanticizing reality, and with admiration watches a boy courageously hack off his finger to evade military service. *Scene 2.* The Gynts' belongings have been confiscated, but Åse blames the devil for having led her boy to cause this misery. *Scene 3.* Peer is overjoyed when Solveig, who has given up her family for him, is ready to spend her life with Peer. The Troll King's daughter, now an old hag, appears with an ugly child, the son of Peer's lecherous thoughts, and demands his love. Unable to face the pure Solveig, Peer runs away but tells Solveig to wait for him.

Scene 4. Peer visits his dying mother. He calms her fears and she dies while he tenderly tells her children's fairy tales. He kisses his dead mother, and leaves the farm and Norway.

Act IV. Scene 1. Years later in Morocco, the prosperous, middle-aged Peer tells his dinner guests how, by living for himself alone, he made his fortune in America by importing slaves and exporting Bibles and rum. *Scene 2.* Peer's fortune is stolen, but when his yacht explodes with the thieves aboard, Peer's trust in providence returns. *Scenes 3 through 13.* While the now middle-aged Solveig still waits patiently, Peer has many adventures. He is taken for the Prophet by Arabian dancing girls. He woos one of them, Anitra, and in the desert, as he dances before her—"Only in the vigor of youth / Can I be myself"—Anitra gallops off with his money belt. Having much time and little to do, Peer next decides to study the past. He goes to Egypt, where he fails to solve the riddle of the statue of Memnon and of the Sphinx. Always asserting his selfhood, Peer is finally conducted to a Cairo madhouse, where each inmate is truly himself and preoccupied with himself. There Peer is crowned Emperor and cheered: "Hail Emperor of Self!"

Act V. Scenes 1 and 2. Now a rich but lonesome old man, Peer is returning to Norway. He meets a strange passenger and, after the ship sinks, casts another man from the dinghy that can hold only one of them. *Scene 3.* Overhearing a funeral service for the boy who had chopped off his finger (Act III, Scene 1) and later lived in shame, Peer rejoices over the priest's commendation for the man's having been "himself." Peer concludes that it is in accord with the best principles to "be oneself and look after oneself / And one's own." *Scenes 4 and 5.* Peer is a legend to his countrymen, who do not recognize him. He peels an onion and finds that, like himself, it has no heart. When he sees his old hut and hears Solveig, "One who kept what the other has lost," he runs off in terror at his discovery: "Here was my Empire and my crown!" *Scenes 6 and 7.* On a moor Peer is stopped by the Button Moulder: having been neither evil nor virtuous, Peer can go to neither heaven nor hell; as waste, he must be melted down into the pool of raw material to be reshaped. Peer, afraid of oblivion, frantically begs for time to prove himself. *Scene 8.* He meets the Troll King, now an old beggar, who insists that Peer, despite his escape, has lived and prospered by the trolls' principles. *Scenes 9 and 10.* Peer begs for more time to find witnesses to attest his having been a sinner, and is turned down in his request for shelter by the Devil, dressed in a priest's cassock. Peer is about to be taken by the Button Moulder when he sees Solveig. He asks her for a testimonial of his guilt. Instead, Solveig assures him that his true self is in her love for him, which has made her life happy. The Button Moulder leaves, promising to meet Peer "at the last crossroad." As Peer buries his face in her protective arms, Solveig sings, "I will cradle you, I will guard you. / Sleep, sleep and dream."

Peg o' My Heart. Laurette Taylor as Peg. New York, 1912. (*Brown Brothers*)

PEG O' MY HEART, "a comedy of youth" in three acts by J. HARTLEY MANNERS, produced in 1912 and published in 1918. Setting: Scarborough, England; early summer, c. 1912.

Dedicated to and written as a vehicle for Manners's wife, Laurette Taylor, this sentimental piece became her greatest hit and one of the best-known and most widely produced plays of its time. With its setting shifted to the jazz age, it reappeared as *Peg* (1967), a musical by Robert Emmett (1941–) with music by John Brandon.

Act I. "The Coming of Peg." Financially ruined, the widowed Mrs. Chichester and her son and daughter get a partial bequest contingent on her taking in Peg O'Connell from New York, the daughter of Mrs. Chichester's deceased sister and an "improvident" Irishman. Peg is a beautiful but shabbily dressed eighteen-year-old lass who arrives with a parcel and her shaggy Irish terrier. She overhears a scene between Mrs. Chichester's daughter and her married suitor, is angered by Mrs. Chichester's slurs on her beloved father, and decides to return to New York: "Sure it's easier to suffer the want of food than the want of love." But Jerry, a neighbor who is smitten by her, persuades Peg to stay. Mrs. Chichester, ashamed of "the family skeleton," decides grimly, "She must be taught, and at once."

Act II. "The Rebellion of Peg." A month later the splendidly gowned Peg, when accosted by the pleasure-loving husband who has paid court to Miss Chichester, boxes his ears. The snobbish Chichesters are troubled by Peg, who is full of life, tender with her dog, and, as she confesses, has "a devil in me someplace, and every now and again he pops out." Her father used to tell her it "is the original sin in ye, and ye're not to be punished because ye can't help it." Instead, he punished himself, and Peg suggests that Mrs. Chichester do the same. Peg tries to model herself on the daughter, but they have a falling out when Peg criticizes her continuing interest in the married bounder. Jerry takes Peg out to a dance, though Peg does not have her aunt's permission. When they return, the daughter is about to run off with her would-be lover. Affectionately Peg persuades the girl to desist, and thus saves her from scandal. But Mrs. Chichester, when her daughter faints before she can confess, turns on Peg. Jerry, who is revealed to be a titled gentleman (Sir Gerald Adair), intercedes for Peg. But Peg, angry at her aunt's unfairness and shame of her, decides to go back to New York: "My father knows more about motherhood than any man in the world."

Act III. "Peg o' My Heart." Next morning, to save their income, Mrs. Chichester has her son propose to Peg. Laughingly she turns him down—as she later does the family solicitor, who also tries to save the Chichesters. Now Peg finally realizes she is an heiress and understands why she was taken in. "You got paid for abusing me?" she asks her aunt—yet generously decides to stay. But when the Chichesters' fortune is restored, she again prepares to leave. There is a thunderstorm, and Peg is frightened. She begs Jerry to "Shut it out!" He proposes to Peg, but she fears he will be ashamed of her. When he persists, Peg admits: "I love you, too, I do." In response to his question about what her father would say, she quotes a favorite line of his: "Sure, there's nothing half so sweet in life as love's young dream." And as the thunder crashes, Peg puts her head on Jerry's shoulder.

PELICAN, THE (*Pelikanen*), a play in three scenes by AUGUST STRINDBERG, published and produced in 1907. Setting: a contemporary living room.

Opus IV of THE CHAMBER PLAYS, this play launched Strindberg's Intima Teatern. With Poe-like horror it portrays the final spasms of a vampire mother who is the exact reverse of the fabled self-sacrificing pelican in the medieval bestiary.

Recently widowed, the Mother has always let her family starve and freeze while she herself ate well and kept warm. Her Son now is alcoholic and her Daughter, just married, is a sterile sleepwalker. The Mother is infatuated with her son-in-law, with whom she has possibly had an affair. She is brought near madness by his sudden cruelty, ghostlike manifestations of her wronged dead husband in his creaking rocking chair, and her stunted children's bitter reproaches of her vampiric motherhood. Finally confessing her guilt, she blames it on the ugliness of her own childhood: "It's all inherited . . . from generation to generation." Desperate, the drunken Son sets the house on fire. As "everything old and mean and evil and ugly" burns, the Mother leaps out of the window, and her children, awaiting death, embrace. At last the room gets warm and, with visions and memories of youthful happiness, the children ecstatically sink down in the flames.

PELLÉAS AND MÉLISANDE (*Pelléas et Mélisande*), a play in five acts by MAURICE MAETERLINCK, published in 1892 and produced in 1893. Setting: a castle and the surroundings in an imaginary medieval land.

This is Maeterlinck's most important work. It is an elusive, shadowy, SYMBOLIST drama whose dialogue is characterized by suggestive but mysterious repetitions and silences. Atmosphere is more important than the story, which resembles those of Tristram and Isolde and of Paolo and Francesca da Rimini (as related at the end of the fifth canto of Dante's *Inferno*). *Pelléas and Mélisande*'s later popularity was greatly enhanced by Claude Debussy's operatic score, an impressionistic masterpiece (1902).

Act I. Servants prepare to wash King Arkel's palace, but the porter jeers that they will never be able to clean it. In the forest, Prince Golaud has lost his way while hunting and comes upon a beautiful girl weeping by a spring. She is very frightened and is vague in answering questions about her origin. At the spring's bottom shimmers a golden crown that she says someone had given her; it fell while she wept, but she will not let Golaud fetch it. She reveals only her name—Mélisande—and then, being cold, she reluctantly agrees to accompany Golaud. Later, at the castle, his mother reads to the weak-eyed King Arkel, his grandfather, a letter from Golaud. In the letter, written to his younger half-brother, Pelléas, Golaud reveals that he has married Mélisande without the king's permission. Now Golaud craves forgiveness before he dares return, and the king grants it. Some time later, brought to the castle, Mélisande is depressed by the gloominess of the gardens and the forests, but Golaud's mother assures her that one gets used to it. Pelléas joins them and they watch Mélisande's ship depart. As he gives her his arm, Pelléas tells Mélisande that he intends to leave. Mélisande sadly asks: "Oh! . . . why do you go away?"

Act II. Pelléas and the mysterious child-wife Mélisande seem increasingly drawn to each other. While at an abandoned spring in the park, Mélisande plays with her wedding ring and loses it in the water. Golaud, recuperating from a hunting injury, discovers the loss, becomes suspicious, and angrily sends her and Pelléas to find the ring. Increasingly unhappy, Mélisande at a seaside grotto with Pelléas sees three sleeping old beggars—and becomes very frightened. Pelléas fails, at the castle, to obtain the king's permission to leave the kingdom.

Act III. Pelléas passes by the tower as Mélisande, combing her long golden hair at her window, is singing in the moonlight. Her tresses fall about him as she leans out, and Pelléas kisses them, though the pair still do not openly avow their love: "I have never seen such hair as thine, Mélisande! . . . It floods me to the heart! . . . and it is sweet, sweet as if it fell from heaven! . . . Thou art my prisoner tonight; all night, all night! . . ." He ties her tresses to a tree as Golaud appears. Laughing nervously, Golaud chides them: "Do not play so in the darkness. . . . What children!" Later he leads Pelléas through the eerie castle vaults, apparently intending to murder him. But Golaud desists, and instead tells Pelléas that Mélisande must not be excited: "She is perhaps with child. . . . There might be something between you. . . . Avoid her as much as possible." His jealous suspicions growing, he questions his little son by a previous marriage. He hoists the child up to observe Pelléas and Mélisande through Mélisande's window: "Are they near the bed? . . . They make no gestures? . . . They make no signs?" "No, little father," the boy cries: "Oh! oh! little father; they never close their eyes. . . . I am terribly afraid."

Act IV. Mélisande agrees to meet Pelléas, who is finally to leave the land. As she tells the king she is not unhappy, Golaud appears and suddenly flies into a rage. He seizes her hair and forces her down. After he regains his calm and leaves, Mélisande is in tears: "He does not love me any more. . . . I am not happy! . . . I am not happy!" She meets Pelléas by the park's fountain on the evening before his departure. "Thou knowest not why I must go afar. . . . Thou knowest not it is because . . ." says Pelléas—and at last they acknowledge their mutual love. They embrace passionately as Golaud appears. Desperate and ready to die, they kiss. Golaud kills Pelléas with his sword, but Mélisande, losing her courage, runs off. Golaud pursues her silently.

Act V. In the castle the servants relate how Golaud and Mélisande were found "huddled together like little children who are afraid": Golaud, wounded by his suicide attempt, and Mélisande with the infant she has just borne. She has incurred only a slight wound from his sword, but is dying—apparently of a broken heart. Golaud reaffirms his love and begs her forgiveness. But he implores Mélisande to tell him whether she loved Pelléas "with a forbidden love." "No, no; we were not guilty. —Why do you ask that?" Mélisande replies. As she fears death's dreadful cold she dies, turning toward her newborn child. Golaud desperately reiterates his innocence in her death, and King Arkel tries to console him: "She must not be disturbed. . . . The human soul is very silent. . . . The human soul likes to depart alone. . . . It suffers so timorously." He deplores the "sadness of all we see! . . . 'Twas a little being, so quiet, so fearful, and so silent. . . . 'Twas a poor little mysterious being, like everybody." And then, puzzled by the meaning of it all as he leaves with Golaud, King Arkel looks compassionately at Mélisande's infant daughter: "She must live now in her place. . . . It is the poor little one's turn. . . ."

PEMÁN, José María (1897–   ), Spanish poet and playwright, a Nationalist leader during the Spanish Civil War and esteemed by conservatives for his sometimes declamatory drama. He wrote well over fifty plays beginning with *Isoldina y Polión* (1928) and including adaptations of the ancient classics as well as patriotic, religious, and biographical drama—and even farces like *Los tres etcéteras de don Simón* (1958). Among his hits are the St. Francis Xavier play *El divino impaciente* (1933), *Metternich* (1942), and a number of invocations to his native port city of Cádiz, including *Señorita del mar* (1934). Also a lawyer and an orator, Pemán was President of the Royal Spanish Academy from 1939 to 1947.

PENZOLDT, Ernst (1892–1955), German writer, started as a poet before turning to fiction and drama. Lyricism and narrative skill characterize his plays, most of which are historical satires. The most notable among them are *Die portugalesische Schlacht* (1931), which features Sebastian, the Portuguese king who fell in his futile battle for glory in 1578, and, in the drama, is replaced by doubles to gratify hero-worshiping masses; and *So war Herr Brummel* (1933), a portrayal of English society and the dandy Beau Brummel in his associations with King George III and King George IV, until his decline, insanity, and death. In another drama, *Sand* (1931), Penzoldt debunked the martyrdom of Karl Ludwig Sand after his political assassination of the playwright August von Kotzebue in 1819. Penzoldt's other works include a comic fairy tale, *Der gläserne Storch oder Es hat alles sein Gutes* (1950).

PERETZ, Yitskhok Leybush (1852–1915), "the colossus of Yiddish literature," who led the half-century renaissance crippled by the Nazi holocaust, was born in Lublin, Poland, and died in Warsaw. Also known as the "Father of Yiddish Literature," he wrote distinguished fiction, poetry, and essays, but never achieved success as a dramatist. His best-known work, the title story ("Bontshe Shvayg") of the translated *Bontche the Silent and Other Stories* (1927), appeared in a popular Off-Broadway production, *The World of Sholom Aleichem* (1953), a group of stories dramatized by Arnold Perl (1914–   ) which was subsequently televised.

Peretz devoted much time to his plays, constantly revising them, hoping to make them hits and yet convey his ideas. A good example is his first full-length play, a Hassidic drama about a great man who tries to elevate the lives of others into ecstatic holiness: the play was originally in Hebrew prose and titled *Khurbon Bayit Tsadik*, revised in 1906 into a Yiddish version that was unsuccessfully presented in Warsaw as *Der Nisoyon*, and in a further revision into rhymed Yiddish verse published the following year as *Di Goldene Keyt*. In 1907, too, Peretz published *Klezmer* (also known as *Vos in Fidele Shtekt*), the drama of a suffering musician redeemed by his art. Occasionally praised is *Banakht Oyfn Altn Mark* (1907), an eerie spectacle in rhymed verse, and a Faustian *Walpurgisnacht* presented in terms of the ghetto. His final full-length play, *In Polish oyf der Keyt* (1908), depicts the decay of tradition-bound Judaism (the title means "chained in the synagogue vestibule") in a modern world. Peretz's only dramas to achieve any popularity were short sketches, of which *Shampanyer* (*Champagne*), *Nokh Kvureh* (*After the Funeral*), *A Frimorgn* (*Of an Early Morning*), and *Di Shvester* (*The Sisters*) appear in English. They were published in Etta Block's two volumes of *One Act Plays from the Yiddish* (1923, 1929).

My Memoirs, a translation of autobiographical accounts of his youth, was published in 1964. See also A. A. Roback's *Peretz, Psychologist of Literature* (1935); and Maurice Samuel's *Prince of the Ghetto* (1948), a biography that includes criticisms and translations of Peretz's works.

PÉREZ GALDÓS, Benito (1843–1920), a Spanish writer who has been linked with Dickens and Balzac as one of the great nineteenth-century novelists, is notable particularly for his forty-six-volume cycle on Spanish history, *Episodios nacionales*. Late in his career he turned to the theatre. *Realidad* (1892), his first play, is based on his fiction and is considered of some importance in modern Spanish theatre REALISM. He wrote a total of twenty-six plays (including dramatizations of his fiction) which reflect his novelistic artistry, the skill of his characterizations, and his sensitive probing of philosophical, moral, and psychological problems. The most notable of his plays are *La de San Quintín* (*The Duchess of San Quentin*, 1894), *Electra* (1901), and *El abuelo* (*The Grandfather*, 1904). The first is an IBSENite drama of an enlightened aristocrat who turns down a wealthy suitor to marry the young Socialist she loves. *Electra*, which caused numerous uproars in Spain and abroad because of its anticlericalism, is a SYMBOLIC treatment of progress in a plot centering on a girl who experiences doubts about convent life. *The Grandfather*, a dramatization of the novel on his favorite theme of the socially leveling power of love, has been likened to *Hamlet* and *King Lear* and deals with a nobleman's obsessive quest to discover the identity of his legitimate granddaughter, who turns out to be less noble-hearted than the natural one he had been determined to discard in order to preserve the family honor.

Pérez Galdós is now considered unimportant as a dramatist and his plays are much inferior to his novels. In the beginning of the century, however, they were greatly esteemed and frequently translated. *The Duchess of San Quentin* was anthologized in Barrett H. Clark's *Masterpieces of Modern Spanish Drama* (1917), and *Electra* in Charles A. Turrell's *Contemporary Spanish Dramatists* (1919). Extensive descriptions and synopses of Pérez Galdós's plays appear in Isaac Goldberg's *The Drama of Transition* (1922) and Frank W. Chandler's *Modern Continental Playwrights* (1931). A biographical and critical study is Hyman C. Berkowitz's *Pérez Galdós, Spanish Liberal Crusader* (1948).

PERU achieved independence in 1824 and by the end of the century some four hundred plays—romantic histories, comedies, and COSTUMBRISMOS—had been produced by one hundred and twenty Peruvians. The most prominent among them were Manuel Ascensio Segura (1805–71), "Grandfather of the Peruvian Drama"; and Carolina Freyre de Jaimes (1844–1916), the mother of BOLIVIA's distinguished poet-playwright, Ricardo Jaimes Freyre. Notable in the early twentieth century were Felipe Sassone (1884–1959), who emigrated to and worked in Spain, where the theatre was more viable; and Julio de la Paz (1888–1925), whose nationalistic *El cóndor pasa* (1916), performed with authentic Inca music, became the country's favorite play for decades. "The last romanticist," Ladislao F. Meza (1892–1925), toward the end of his short life wrote NATURALIST drama on social themes. Peru's *costumbrista* José Chioino (1898–1958), a major figure in his country's theatre, also wrote drama that showed the influence of BERNARD SHAW.

The Asociación de Artistas Aficionados (the A.A.A.) stimulated theatrical activity in the 1950's into what appeared to be a rebirth of Peruvian drama. Among more recent playwrights on the scene have been Juan Ríos (1914–), who has dramatized classical themes; Sebastián Salazar Bondy (1924–65), a highly praised writer in all genres who portrayed human anguish in much-performed existentialist drama and was hailed as the principal figure of the Peruvian theatre's renaissance; and Julio Ramón Ribeyro (1929), who interweaves local color in his very popular light domestic drama, fantasy, and satire.

Studies are listed under LATIN AMERICA.

PERZYŃSKI, Włodzimierz (1878–1930), Polish novelist and playwright, was adept at dramatizing middle-class mores. The most successful among his comedies was the still-revived *Szczęście Frania* (1909): its idealist hero is "lucky" to receive the unexpected permission to marry his sweetheart—for her parents are eager to hide the consequences of her affair with a friend. Other comedies are *Lekkomyślna siostra* (1904), a satire on middle-class money morality, and *Aszantka* (1906), on the Pygmalion theme. Perzyński's mastery of plot construction deteriorated, however, in his later plays, the best known of which were *Uśmiech losu* (1926) and *Lekarz miłości* (1928). His last play was *Dziękuję za służbę* (*Giving Notice*, 1929), a comedy about a wife who rejects an interesting suitor and stays with her family, though she is no longer loved by her husband or needed by her grown-up children.

PETER BRAUER, "a tragicomedy" in three acts by GERHART HAUPTMANN, published and produced in 1921. Setting: Berlin and a Silesian town, 1890's.

This tragicomedy was completed in 1910. Its protagonist, like that of COLLEAGUE CRAMPTON, is an unsuccessful artist. Though cheerfully self-deluded with grandeur, he is pitifully ineffectual; despite his occasional bluster, he is decent and harms no one but himself. Competitive industrial society exacerbates his failure and provides an environment that underlines the comic-serious, often farcical-tragic, admixture of the play.

The painter Peter Brauer faces prosecution for his debts. Claiming to have received an out-of-town commission, he tremulously begs money from his wife and escapes from their Berlin apartment. In a provincial inn he meets a nobleman who has him paint murals for his garden chapel. Happily Brauer sits before the chapel, drinking wine and enjoying himself. He invites his family to come and witness his success. While he is triumphantly photographed with them, the nobleman arrives with his family to view the work. Brauer's son—the only agreeable member of his family—extols the few gnomes and dwarfs Brauer has managed to finish. But the work is unsuitable and the nobleman withdraws his commission. Brauer's wife and daughter leave indignantly; the son, too weak to do more than sympathize unhappily with Brauer, finally runs after them. "Go, go! Don't worry about me, dear boy!" the weeping father says, left sitting alone and in despair.

PETER PAN, a play in five acts by JAMES M. BARRIE, produced in 1904 and published in 1928. Setting: contemporary London and the Never Land.

Subtitled "The Boy Who Would Not Grow Up," this fantasy has remained one of the most popular of all modern plays and a favorite with children and adults since its first appearance. It is produced every Christmas in London, and on Broadway it was successfully revived as a play (with music and songs by Leonard Bernstein) in 1950 and as a musical comedy in 1954. Its impressive history (including photographs, details on the composition, productions, stories, screen versions, and sequels) is chronicled in Roger L. Green's *Fifty Years of* **Peter Pan** (1954). One performance of the play in 1908 was followed by Barrie's short sequel, *When Wendy Grew Up: An Afterthought,* which was published in 1958. Though Barrie deferred publication of *Peter Pan* for over two decades, he allowed short synopses (as early as 1907) and retellings of the story by others; his own *Peter and Wendy* (1911) is a full-length novel that contains almost all the dialogue of the play. In 1912 he arranged and paid for the erection of the famous bronze statue of Peter Pan in Kensington Gardens.

Act I. The Darling family's nursemaid Nana, a Newfoundland dog, prepares the children's beds and baths. Before going out for dinner, the parents come to tuck in Wendy and her two young brothers. The mother sees a strange face at the window and Nana barks. But the grumpy father, miffed because his jokes have fallen flat, chains Nana up in the yard. No sooner are the parents gone and the children asleep than Peter Pan, dressed in autumn leaves and cobwebs, flies into the room. Guided by a light—his fairy, Tinker Bell—Peter finds his shadow, which he had lost. Wendy wakes up and sews it back on for him. Peter dances happily with it: "Look, look; oh the cleverness of me!" Though annoyed by such conceit, Wendy soon is enthralled by Peter, who ran away from home because he wants "always to be a little boy and to have fun." Now he is the captain of a group of lost little boys in the Never Land. But they need "female companionship" and, by teaching Wendy and her brothers to fly, Peter persuades them to accompany him.

Act II. At the woods and lagoon of Never Land are six cavorting boys; pirates led by Captain Jas. Hook, a villain with a hook for an arm; and Indians led by the belle of the Piccaninny tribe, Tiger Lily. Captain Hook is out to defeat the boys. He is particularly incensed against Peter, who during a fight cut off Hook's arm and threw it to a crocodile. This crocodile, wishing to finish its meal, keeps following Hook. But though the captain is scared of being surprised by the crocodile, he is always saved by the telltale ticking of an alarm clock the crocodile once swallowed. The children see Wendy flying toward them. Mistaking her for a bird, and egged on by Peter's jealous fairy, Tinker Bell, they shoot her down. But the arrow hits an acorn button Peter had given her, and only knocks her unconscious. All the boys now build a house for Wendy, and when she wakes up, she agrees to be their mother. Like a mother, she scolds them affectionately and then tells them a bedtime story. In the meantime, Peter marches outside with his drawn sword to protect his "family" from Indians and wolves.

Acts III and IV. The children have many adventures. At the Mermaids' Lagoon they try to catch mermaids, and then they rescue Tiger Lily from the Marooners' Rock, where Captain Hook has fettered her to be drowned. In a big battle the boys defeat the pirates. But to savor the adventure fully, Peter remains on the rock until the water almost covers and kills him: "To die will be an awfully big adventure." Back at their underground home, the children are now guarded by the grateful Tiger Lily and her redskins. Wendy mothers the boys, but she is unhappy because, despite her own feelings for him, Peter loves her only like a "devoted son," and she gets homesick. Suddenly Wendy has an idea: her mother will adopt all the boys. But Peter refuses to go: "I just want always to be a little boy and to have fun." He is ready to send the others off when the pirates, violating the laws of Indian warfare, basely attack and defeat the redskins above. Then Captain Hook fools the children below into thinking that the Indians have won. Innocently Peter sends them out and goes to sleep. The pirates capture the children and take them away, and Captain Hook sneaks down and drops poison into Peter's drink. To save him, Tinker Bell drinks the poison and dies. She can be brought back to life only when Peter gets the children in the theatre audience to assure her that they believe in fairies.

Act V. On the pirate ship the doomed but brave children are ready to walk the plank. By heroisms and various stratagems Peter saves them. Then comes his big battle with Hook. The captain, about to lose, cries out, "'Tis some fiend fighting me! Pan, who and what art thou?" And Peter answers,

Peter Pan, Act V. The battle of Peter Pan (Maude Adams) and Captain Hook (Ernest Lawford). New York, 1905. (*Museum of The City of New York*)

"I'm youth, I'm joy, I'm a little bird that has broken out of the egg." Defeated, Captain Hook drops into the jaws of the waiting crocodile. Back at the Darling home, the grieving parents and the nursemaid Nana rejoice when the children return. The Darlings are glad to adopt all the boys, and Wendy tries once more to seduce Peter into staying with them. When he learns that he would have to go to school, Peter declines. "No one is going to catch me, lady, and make me a man," he tells Mrs. Darling. He does not want to become solemn: "I want always to be a little boy and to have fun." He agrees to have Wendy visit him once a year, for spring cleaning "(whatever *that* may be)." A year later Wendy does so. Having grown a little older, Wendy can no longer see him quite so clearly—and she cannot see Tinker Bell at all. Wendy wishes she could hug Peter, take him "up and squdge" him, but she understands his shrinking back. Unlike her, he will never grow up. Wendy leaves and Peter happily takes out his pipes. "The Never birds and the fairies gather closer, till the roof of the little house is so thick with his admirers that some of them fall down the chimney. He plays on and on till we wake up."

PETRIFIED FOREST, THE, a play in two acts by ROBERT E. SHERWOOD, produced in 1934 and published in 1935. Setting: the lunchroom of the Black Mesa Filling Station and Bar-B-Q in the eastern Arizona desert during an autumn afternoon and evening, 1934.

This "didactic vaudeville—a melodramatic farce-with-a-moral," as Joseph Wood Krutch aptly termed it in *The American Drama Since 1918* (1957), allegorically conveys the despair common during the Depression and the rise of pre-World War II totalitarianism. Leslie Howard's portrayal of the sensitive intellectual Alan Squier and a striking performance by the then almost unknown Humphrey Bogart as Duke Mantee were filmed in 1936 and further popularized the play.

Act I. Frustrated at his "miserable little service station on the edge of nowheres," Jason Maple strongly objects to his customers' radical comments. He leaves for an American Legion meeting, resplendent in his uniform. His daughter, Gabby (Gabrielle), waits on Alan Squier, a writer hitchhiking to the West Coast. Quickly enamored of the urbane Squier, Gabby recites François Villon poems ("they get the stink of the gasoline and the hamburger out of my system") and reveals her artistic yearnings and her desire to visit France, her mother's home. Squier is searching for "something that's worth living for—or dying for." He feels hollow and disillusioned: "I belong to a vanishing race . . . the intellectuals, who thought they'd conquered Nature" but find that Nature is

The Petrified Forest, Act II. Left to right: Duke (Humphrey Bogart) and a member of his gang (Slim Thompson), the chauffeur (Ross Hertz) and the wealthy couple (Blanche Sweet and Robert Hudson), Squier (Leslie Howard), Gabby (Peggy Conklin), and Old Gramp (Charles Dow Clark). New York, 1935. (*Vandamm Photo, Theatre Collection, New York Public Library*)

reclaiming the world for "the apes." Though Gabby offers herself to him, he advises her to "yield to the ardors" of the gas station attendant, a former football star. After Squier's departure with a wealthy couple who give him a lift, Gabby is deeply aroused. She is ready to accompany the attendant, but their plans are frustrated by the arrival of the killer Duke Mantee and his gang, who are evading a national dragnet. Old Gramp, Gabby's grandfather, who dreams of the old frontier days and Billy the Kid, rejoices at the excitement of having a man of action around again; and Squier, who had to leave the wealthy couple and return, agrees, "It's pleasant to be back again—among the living."

Act II. Everyone is forced to stay in the lunchroom while Duke awaits his girl. They all sit around drinking and talking of their lives and frustrations. Squier proposes that he and Duke be buried in the nearby petrified forest. It seems to represent "the world of outmoded ideas. Platonism—patriotism—Christianity—romance—the economics of Adam Smith—they're all so many dead stumps in the desert," Squier believes; "That's where I belong—and so do you, Duke. For you're the last great apostle of rugged individualism." Feeling that he has finally found a reason to die, Squier makes out his life insurance to Gabby and then asks Duke to shoot him. Duke is impressed by Squier, and promises to oblige: "You're all right, pal. You've got good ideas. I'll try to fix it so's it won't hurt." As the sheriff's posse shoots it out with the gangsters—betrayed by Duke's girl, for whom he was waiting—Squier and Gabby have a tender love scene. Then he insists that Duke shoot him before Duke makes his getaway. Squier dies in Gabby's arms while the others excitedly describe Duke's escape. Gabby plans to bury Squier in the petrified forest, as he had asked her to do. She elegizes him with a poem by Villon:

> Thus in your field my seed of harvestry
> will thrive—
> For the fruit is like me that I set—
> God bids me tend it with good husbandry:
> This is the end for which we twain are met.

PHILADELPHIA STORY, THE, a comedy in three acts by PHILIP BARRY, published and produced in 1939. Setting: a mansion outside Philadelphia, late June 1939.

This very popular comedy was produced by the Theatre Guild, and filmed, with Katharine Hepburn, for whom Barry had created the role of Tracy. Probably his finest play, it is a comedy of manners that is not only witty and often broadly comical; it is also moving in its vindication of human tolerance and decency.

Tracy Lord, a wealthy, beautiful, and vivacious young socialite divorcée, is about to marry a handsome snob who started as a coal miner. Her precocious fifteen-year-old sister reports that C. K. Dexter Haven, Tracy's former husband, whom she divorced for "cruelty and drunkenness," is back in town. Tracy remains calm, eager to forget both him and her father, who left her mother and is having an affair in New York. To divert the society columns from this scandal, a member of the family brings a reporter and a photographer to the mansion to cover the wedding. Soon Tracy is infatuated with the reporter, a liberal and sensitive writer despite his callous exterior ("The prettiest sight in this fine, pretty world is the privileged class enjoying its privileges"). When her easygoing former husband joins her bottom-pinching uncle and the rest of the company, Tracy is further shaken in her determination to marry her successful but priggish fiancé. "She is a goddess, without patience for any kind of human imperfection," Dexter says about Tracy, "a virgin goddess" to whom he was supposed to be "a kind of high priest." He blames his drinking on her—as Tracy's father, arriving for the wedding, blames his affair on his daughter's lack of "an understanding heart." He calls her "a prig—and a perennial spinster, however many marriages." At the prewedding festivities that night, Tracy gets drunk and goes swimming in the nude with the reporter. The next morning she discovers that only the reporter's decency stopped him from taking advantage of her. Chastened and now painfully aware of her fiancé's unwavering smugness, she breaks off her marriage even as the ceremony is getting underway. Instead, she announces to the assembled guests her remarriage to Dexter. Tolerant and understanding, she feels "like a human being" instead of a queen or goddess. This new feeling, she lovingly exclaims to her father as she walks toward the altar, is heavenly.

The Philadelphia Story. Tracy (Katharine Hepburn) and the reporter (Van Heflin). Theatre Guild production, 1939. (*Brown Brothers*)

PHILANDERER, THE, "A Topical Comedy in Four Acts of the Early Eighteen-Nineties" by BERNARD SHAW, published and produced in 1898. Setting: London, 1890's.

Partly autobiographical, this is the second of Shaw's "unpleasant" plays that deal with "social horrors." Of it, Shaw wrote in his preface to PLAYS UNPLEASANT: "I have shewn the grotesque sexual compacts made between men and women under marriage laws which . . . society has outgrown but not modified, and which 'advanced' individuals are therefore forced to evade." Particularly "unpleasant" are the play's atmosphere and Julia's "typical" marriage.

Act I. Mrs. Grace Tranfield and Leonard Charteris are making love in her father's flat. Charteris admits that he has proposed to Grace, who is a widow, to end his affair with Julia Craven. Entering in a jealous rage, Julia creates a violent scene. After Grace leaves the room, Charteris reminds Julia that she claimed to be an unwomanly "woman of advanced views" who "regarded marriage as a degrading bargain," and though she storms and weeps, he refuses to marry her. As he tries to rush away, Grace's father, Joseph Cuthbertson, a somewhat pompous drama critic,* comes home with the retired Colonel Daniel Craven, who is Julia's father. Old friends who have just met again, they are surprised to discover Charteris, a frequent visitor to both their houses. Julia and Charteris trump up an explanation for their presence and Grace's absence, and, to distract Craven, who has been assured by Dr. Paramore that he will soon die of a newly discovered liver disease, Charteris and Cuthbertson urge him to join the IBSEN Club, which is open to certified unwomanly women and unmanly men.

Act II. The following day Craven meets Dr. Paramore and Cuthbertson in the library of the Ibsen Club. Charteris complains of his romantic troubles with Julia and Grace to their indignant fathers. Julia attempts to corner Charteris, but they are interrupted; after she goes out, Charteris is relieved to hear that Dr. Paramore loves Julia and will soon propose. Then Grace comes in to tell him that she loves him; but, being an Ibsenite woman, she cannot marry a man she loves so much because "it would give him a terrible advantage over me: I should be utterly in his power."

Act III. A broken Dr. Paramore staggers into the library and tells Craven that the existence of the liver disease he discovered has been disproved. He is contemptuous of Craven's bitterness about his own needless deprivations and fears because of this "disease," and protests to Charteris that not even to win Julia can he feign joy at Craven's having been spared at the expense of a scientific discovery. "The Nonconformist conscience is bad enough," Charteris remarks, "but the scientific conscience is the very devil." When Julia starts another jealous row, Grace threatens to have her expelled from the club for being a womanly woman. Suddenly, however, Julia decides to follow Dr. Paramore, who has left, and Charteris attempts to detain the others to give Paramore time to propose to her.

Act IV. In his reception room Dr. Paramore proposes to and is reluctantly accepted by the unhappy Julia, who, knowing that she is a "shallow, jealous, devilish creature," needs someone to be good to her. The others arrive, and Charteris's delight at hearing of the engagement makes Julia, who obviously still loves him, again create a scene. But Charteris makes a great show of having lost her, and, having been turned down by Grace, he resolves "to go on philandering."

* A caricature of Clement (William) Scott (1841–1904), the prominent theatre reviewer of the *Daily Telegraph* who is quoted in THE QUINTESSENCE OF IBSENISM for his intemperate attacks on Ibsen's GHOSTS. He wrote several pseudonymous plays, including translations of VICTORIEN SARDOU.

PHILIPPINES, THE, are unique among Southeast Asian nations because of their previous domination by Spain and America. Both left their imprint on Filipino drama. *Zarzuela* troupes performing slightly plotted topical, often anti-American song-and-dance revues furnished popular commercial entertainments until the 1920's, and in remote villages presented *zarzuelas* as folk drama after World War II. Distinctively Filipino was *moro-moro,* melodrama that originated in the seventeenth century and crudely depicted Christian Philippine victories over the Moors. Japan's military occupation cut the islands off from American movies during World War II and helped stimulate native theatre. Excelling as dramatists were later-prominent statesmen, foremost among them Carlos Pena Rómulo (1899–); the best of his stage works (all written in English) is the title play of his *Daughter for Sale and Other Plays* (1924), about a wealthy man whose daughters reject the rich suitors he provides for the poor ones they love and live with happily ever after.

The theatre has been flourishing in the Philippines since the middle of the century. Exclusively in the hands of amateurs, many of them enormously talented, the modern theatre has been encouraged and generously supported by wealthy Filipinos. It has produced more Western than indigenous drama, but many native playwrights have written principally in the Philippine (Tagalog) language and often on contemporary and controversial topics. Their drama has been stimulated by the Arena Theatre and its workshops, founded by the English-writing actor-director-playwright Severino Montano (1915?–); his best drama is *The Love of Leonor Rivera* (1954), a tragedy depicting the romance of the patriot José Rizal and Maria Clara (after whom a national dance was named), but Montano has also written stinging political satires.

A collection of *Short Plays of the Philippines* (1940) for students was edited by Jean G. Edades. Faubion Bowers's *Theatre in the East* (1956) has an informative chapter on Filipino drama and dance. Antonio Manuud's *Brown Heritage* collection of "Essays on Philippine Cultural Tradition and Literature" was published in Quezon City in 1967.

PHILLIPS, Stephen (1864?–1915), English poet and dramatist born near Oxford, first achieved prominence with his collection of *Poems* (1898). Its success prompted the commissioning of his best-known work, the verse tragedy PAOLO AND FRANCESCA (1899). Immediately popular in book form, its stage presentation was preceded by that of another verse tragedy, *Herod* (1900), which, like his next work, *Ulysses* (1902), was produced by Herbert Beerbohm Tree. Further plays were *The Sin of David* (1904), a dramatization of the Bathsheba story in the milieu of Cromwell's England; two potboilers, *Aylmer's Secret* (1905, a one-act prose play) and *The Bride of Lammermoor* (1908, also titled *The Last Heir*); *Nero* (1906), also produced by Tree; *Faust* (1908; written with J. Comyns Carr, 1849–1960), a "pyrotechnic pantomime"; *Pietro of Siena* (1910); three short works produced in 1913, *The King* (1912), *Iole,* and *The Adversary;* and *Armageddon* (1915), a patriotic play, and his last to be staged. Just before he died he finished *Harold,* a verse play on the Norman Conquest.

Phillips's early experience as an actor gave him a working knowledge of the stage that went well with his poetic talents. For a while Phillips was hailed as a modern harbinger of great English verse drama. But his range was restricted; his later works did not live up to this promise, and he died in relative obscurity.

PHILOSOPHER'S STONE, THE (*De vises sten*), a play in four acts by PÄR LAGERKVIST, published in 1947 and produced in 1948. Setting: a town in medieval Europe.

This conventionally structured and sometimes verbose work became one of Lagerkvist's most popular stage plays. It recalls Brecht's LIFE OF GALILEO with its medieval setting yet modern language and apprehensive attitudes about the ethics and responsibilities of scientists.

Act I. The alchemist Albertus gets money for his laboratory by prostituting his daughter, Catherine, to the prince. Albertus's pious wife is helplessly indignant as well as suspicious of his scientific studies. He justifies to Rabbi Simonides his efforts "to try to find out about the remarkable structure of God's creation, the divine truth in His work." Since we do not have the truth, God "in his wisdom has not intended it for us. Instead we grope in the darkness, and He is the only one who can lead us through it," Simonides replies: "If we attempt anything with our own power, we end up in sin and error." He is delighted that Albertus is not eager to have his (Gentile) daughter marry Simonides's son, who has loved her since childhood. When Catherine returns from the prince's house with money and fineries, Simonides leaves. His son, Jacob, a dreamer, proposes to Catherine, who soon reveals her tawdry doings to the horrified young idealist. Albertus's wife—feeling guilty for helping her husband, however reluctantly, with his impious work—tells her daughter that Albertus has sold his soul to the devil.

Act II. Years later Catherine is one of the town's prostitutes. The prince no longer gives her money, and Albertus is barely able to continue his experiments. A plague is raging, and the superstitious populace threatens a pogrom. Though his wife does not want him to receive Rabbi Simonides and his son ("they crucified Our Lord Jesus Christ . . .") when they come for their first visit in years, Albertus warmly greets his old friend. Simonides praises Albertus's continuing search for wisdom, though the alchemist seems impoverished, tired, and less confident of finding truth. They recognize the danger to them both from the ignorant populace, who attribute their troubles to Jews and truth seekers like Albertus. The latter consoles Simonides, who glories in his son's scholarly accomplishments. Catherine appears with prostitute and wastrel friends. Fearing the constable, she hysterically blames her father for her ruin. "Are you satisfied now!" she screams: "Are you satisfied with your goddamned oven, tell me how your devil's tricks are turning out . . . ," and accuses him of Satanism. When the town constable comes in to take Catherine as his whore, Jacob in a blind fury kills him.

Act III. Albertus pleads with the prince for the life of Simonides's son. The cynical prince refuses to believe Albertus's protestations that he himself is the murderer. Angrily Albertus accuses him of his daughter's debauchery, a sacrifice to the ruler's never-ending quest for power and wealth, "for all of your vain, meaningless world! You are fools! Fools and criminals!" "You sacrifice people too," the prince replies: "For a higher purpose than mine, of course. But anyway. Obviously we are both guilty of a crime." And he demonstrates to Albertus how little human life means to either of them. Though Catherine too pleads for Jacob's life, the prince remains adamant ("Should I pardon a Jew for Christ's sake?"). He imprisons Albertus for his impudence, and sadly (for he himself has never known real love) allows Catherine to see the doomed man. Though Jacob must die, he rejoices in her love and in the imminence of his return to the dream land he has always yearned for. "How happy I am not to have to live here," he says as he is led away, while outside his grieving father is mocked by the crowds: "This is the place of tears."

Act IV. Some days later the broken Albertus returns home. The execution is over, and the Jews are being expelled, a blind man tells him. Albertus's wife and daughter, who is about to join a convent, describe Jacob's public execution. As Catherine tells her mother how she longs for the convent, the Jews prepare for their banishment, and Simonides expostulates with God. "Lord, Lord, how can you let this happen!" he wails, mourning the loss of his son, which leaves him "like a ravaged old tree," and begging for death to release him from "this accursed earth which you have chosen for the unrighteous and his seed!" Then he prays for forgiveness, bids Albertus farewell, and inspires his mourning fellow Jews with confidence as he leads them out. Albertus's wife exults at the miracle of her daughter's release from worldly sinning as she departs for the convent. The two old people are left alone. Tenderly his wife strokes the exhausted Albertus, who is too fatigued to light his oven: "But tomorrow. Tomorrow I'll light it again."

PHOENIX TOO FREQUENT, A, a one-act blank-verse comedy by CHRISTOPHER FRY, published and produced in 1946. Setting: a tomb near Ephesus, in ancient Greece, at night.

Fry's first notable work dramatizes a brief sketch in Petronius's *Satyricon*. The play has been interpreted as "a debate between convention and the primitive, enduring life-force," as a study of frustrated idealism, and as a dramatization of various philosophies. But it is primarily a delightful piece of slapstick. The title comes from Martial, as quoted by Robert Burton: "To whom conferr'd a peacock's undecent, / A squirrel's harsh, a phoenix too frequent."

Young Dynamene is ready to die of grief in the tomb of her just-deceased husband. Her maid, Doto, is sharing her fate, though after two days of fasting she cannot put men out of her mind. The beautiful Dynamene remembers only her husband, "Virilius. Where is the punctual eye / And where is the cautious voice which made / Balance-sheets sound like Homer and Homer sound / Like balance-sheets?" Weeping over this "peroration of nature," she falls asleep. Enter Tegeus, a handsome young corporal guarding the corpses of six hanged men. Soon Doto agrees to share his wine, to take "one for the road," and then "another little swiggy." Hiccuping as she gets increasingly drunk and amorous, Doto amazes the idealistic Tegeus by telling him of Dynamene's wifely sacrifice: "This is privilege, to come so near / To what is undeceiving and uncorrupt / And undivided." When she awakes, Dynamene too agrees "to strengthen myself / In order to fast again; it would make me abler / For grief." But already the smell of Tegeus's wine confuses her. "When the thoughts would die, the instincts will set sail / For life," she admits, and then recalls her disciplined (if dull) husband, whose "brain was an ironing-board / For all crumpled indecision." Tegeus sees Dynamene as "a vision, a hope, a promise" of "loyalty, enduring passion, / Unrecking bravery and beauty all in one." Gradually enamored of him, Dynamene stops Tegeus when he wants to leave—to safeguard his ideal of her, to pursue his ambition, "to find / A reason for living." But after they declare their mutual love, he reasons that her husband would approve. He would say to his wife, Tegeus declares, "Repeat me in love, repeat me in life, / And let me sing in your blood for ever." Before the consummation Tegeus goes to check on his corpses, while Dynamene gets rid of Doto. Tegeus returns, terribly upset and hardly making sense: "Why should I have found / Your constancy such balm to the world and yet / Find, by the same vision, its destruction / A necessity?" During his absence one of the corpses he is supposed to be guarding has been stolen. He therefore will surely be hanged, and is determined rather to kill himself. Dynamene turns his earlier rationale on him: "Am I to live on alone, or find in life / Another source of love, in memory / Of Virilius and of you?" She finds, instead, a ready solution: her husband's corpse, to be substituted for the missing one. She assuages Tegeus's horror: "How little you can understand. I loved / His life not his death. And now we can give his death / The power of life. Not horrible: wonderful!" She concludes, "My darling, / I give you Virilius." "And all that follows," Tegeus replies, as the bibulous Doto reappears with a toast to "The master. Both the masters."

PHYSICISTS, THE (*Die Physiker*), "a comedy" in two acts by FRIEDRICH DÜRRENMATT, published and produced in 1962. Setting: the drawing room of a former villa, now a private sanatorium, c. 1961.

This is a detective thriller as well as a topical parable about a world imperiled by nuclear science. It became one of the most popular plays of Dürrenmatt, who noted his maintaining the classical unities ("necessary to keep in shape action that takes place among madmen") and pointedly furnished the kind of "reversal" Aristotle considered characteristic of the best tragedy. Though similar to Brecht's LIFE OF GALILEO in its portrayal of the morally troubled scientist, *The Physicists* differs in its despairing resolution.

Act I. As policemen examine a corpse, the head nurse forbids smoking or drinking in the drawing room. The inspector questions her about "the murderer" but is interrupted: "the poor man's ill, you know." The "assailant," one of the three patients (all physicists) housed in the villa, is called Albert Einstein "because he thinks he is Einstein." Recently a patient who thinks he is Sir Isaac Newton strangled his nurse in the same room, the inspector recalls. He now must wait before he may question the agitated Einstein, who is calming down in Room 2, playing the fiddle—or the sanatorium's director, Fräulein Doctor Mathilde von Zahnd, who accompanies him on the piano. "Newton" emerges from Room 3 dressed in eighteenth-century clothes, has a brandy and a cigarette, which, he explains, only patients may have. He remarks that his own killing of a nurse was different from Einstein's: that poor man is mad and really believes himself to be Einstein, whereas "Newton" merely pretends, knowing that he himself is Einstein. He returns to his room and then appears Dr. Zahnd, a hunchbacked spinster. She discusses her distinguished family, whose sole survivor she is, and admits that she is puzzled by the killings and had been mistaken in her diagnoses of Newton and Einstein. Though she assures the inspector that the other patient, Johan Wilhelm Möbius in Room 1, is a harmless physicist who has spent the last fifteen years at the sanatorium, she agrees to replace the nurses with male attendants. Möbius's wife comes with her three sons to bid him farewell: she has just married a missionary assigned to the Pacific area. When she weeps about being unable to pay for Möbius's continued care, Dr. Zahnd offers to keep him anyway, for "money's as thick as muck around here. . . ." Möbius is called in and is pleasant, though he appears not to remember his family. When his son expresses the intention to study physics, Möbius objects, for his own studies made everybody think him crazy "because King Solomon appears to me." The family's embarrassment is heightened when his wife introduces her new husband, and to cover it the boys play their recorders. Möbius interrupts, dashes to his room, and crouches in his overturned table to recite—as he says the king often does—"A Song of Solomon to be sung to the Cosmonauts." Then Möbius angrily sends his frightened and weeping family off. Alone with Möbius, his nurse accuses him of pretending madness. He admits he wants to forget the past, especially now that his wife is taken care of and he himself has completed his "Principles of Universal Discovery." About to be transferred, the nurse expresses her faith in his genius and sanity, and confesses that she loves him. Möbius admits he loves her, too—and therefore urges her to leave. Einstein comes in for a moment to warn her: his nurse and he also were in love—before he strangled her. Again Möbius tells his nurse to go, but she implores him to join her: she has already arranged for his release and a professional evaluation of his new scientific discoveries. With tears in his eyes, Möbius strangles her. Newton comes in, pours himself a brandy, and, after hearing Möbius's confession, remarks about the music in Room 2: "Einstein's off again. Kreisler. Humoresque."

Act II. An hour later the inspector and his policemen examine the most recent murder. Enormous new male attendants wheel in a sumptuous dinner. As the corpse is removed Möbius cries out after it. The inspector has a cigar and a drink, but cheerfully declines to arrest Möbius: because the murderers are madmen "justice is on a holiday." After he leaves, Newton comes in. Eating heartily, he confesses to Möbius his true identity. He is a Western scientist who had perceived Möbius's genius, had revealed it to the authorities, and had been hired by his country's intelligence to get into the sanatorium and abduct Möbius. Einstein comes in and reveals that he, too, is a prominent and sane scientist who had perceived Möbius's genius and had been sent by his country (in the Eastern block) to abduct Möbius. Both had had to strangle their nurses when they became suspicious, and both have been foiled because each believed the other was really a madman. For a moment they threaten to shoot each other. Then they agree to join forces and escape the sanatorium, which is being barred with new iron grilles. But Möbius refuses to join them, though he admits his discoveries make possible fantastic technical advances. Therefore he should work for their countries, his colleagues insist. "We have far-reaching, pioneering work to do" and what is important is the freedom to work, not morality—Newton says—for "whether or not humanity has the wit to follow the new trails we are blazing is its own lookout, not ours." Einstein disagrees because he thinks that as the inventors of colossal power, scientists have "the right to impose conditions" and themselves "must become power politicians." Again the agents are ready to shoot—but Möbius tells them he has destroyed the manuscripts they seek. Thereupon each urges him to start afresh in his nation. "Remuneration and accommodation could not be better," Newton offers: "The climate is murderous, but the air-conditioning is excellent." Einstein stresses the importance of power and, "in any case, without hope, all political systems are untenable." Rejecting both offers, Möbius refuses to risk the destruction of mankind. Having realized fifteen years ago that his discoveries would make it possible, he gave up family and career, and simulated insanity, for "only in the madhouse can we think our thoughts. Outside they would be dynamite." He persuades the others to stay here with him, for "today it's the duty of a genius to remain unrecognized. . . . Either we wipe ourselves out of the memory of mankind or mankind wipes itself out." Though caged, they realize that as scientists they are potential wild beasts and have no moral alternative. "Let us be mad, but wise," Newton says. "Prisoners but free," Einstein adds. "Physicists but innocent," Möbius concludes. Suddenly Doctor Zahnd enters. She has overheard and recorded their conversation and had made sure they would remain her prisoners—murderers certified as madmen. Long before, she had photostated all Möbius's papers before they were destroyed. With his scientific discoveries she has established the machinery to give her control of the world. King Solomon has appeared before her and chosen her to be his handmaiden and make her mighty, she proclaims, ready to "ransack the solar system." As she leaves for a board meeting the physicists realize that she is totally mad—and they and the whole universe are now at her mercy. "What was once thought can never be unthought," Möbius says. Resigned, the physicists return to their rooms after introducing themselves to the audience, in matter-of-fact voices, as Sir Isaac Newton, Albert Einstein—and, Möbius concludes, as Solomon: "When I no longer feared God my wisdom destroyed my wealth. Now the cities over which I ruled are dead . . . [in a] radioactive earth. . . . I am poor King Solomon."

PICHETTE, Henri (1924–), French poet and playwright, author of two allegorical verse dramas on the struggle of good and evil as well as love and hate, *Les Epiphanies* (1947) and *Nucléa* (1952). The first portrays the life and death of a poet-lover-creator; the second (written in alexandrines) attempts to convey the allegorical struggle with cacophonous music, human screams, and other vivid and assaulting sound effects. Though both are unremarkable works in the SURREALIST vein, they had distinguished Parisian productions and seemed to augur a new French poetic theatre. See Leonard C. Pronko's chapter on Pichette in *Avant-Garde* (1962).

PICNIC, a play in three acts by WILLIAM INGE, published and produced in 1953. Setting: a porch and the yard of two adjoining drab houses in a small Kansas town; Labor Day and the next morning, early 1950's.

Picnic began as a one-act character sketch of five variously frustrated women sitting on a porch. To provide a plot and a protagonist for the full-length play, Inge introduced the vagabond Hal Carter, "an exceedingly handsome, husky youth" wearing cowboy boots, whose appearance agitates and changes the women's humdrum lives. In 1962, after *Picnic*'s success as a Pulitzer Prize winner (1953) and a film (1956), Inge published *Summer Brave,* a revision with a new ending and other changes that, Inge wrote in the preface, made this play "more humorously true."

Act I. After eating the large breakfast he has requested of a kind elderly matron, Hal does her yardwork. His preening in a T-shirt, which he soon discards, upsets her neighbor, Flo Owens, a forty-year-old widow, but fascinates Flo's daughters: a precocious but homely sixteen-year-old who reads voluminously, smokes secretly, and is aggressively shy of boys; and her older sister, Madge, a very beautiful but not very bright salesgirl. Somewhat edgy from bringing up the girls by herself, Flo encourages Madge to marry her wealthy suitor. Madge confesses she feels uncomfortable with his college crowd, and is tired of being appreciated only for her looks: "Mum, what good is it to be pretty?" Joined by their boarder, a spinster schoolteacher who affects a disdain for men, and the kindly old neighbor whose own love troubles (her still-domineering mother long before had had her marriage annulled) have not soured her, Flo watches Hal. She senses his danger to her daughters. But he turns out to be an old fraternity brother of Madge's suitor—the only one who did not then sneer at the athletic-scholarship winner's boorishness and who now listens sympathetically as Hal gloats about his postcollege mishaps. Because of the friendship, Flo lets Hal join the impending picnic.

Act II. Even Madge's tomboyish sister is prettily dressed for the picnic that afternoon—because of Hal, who helps her overcome her shyness with boys. They dance to some background music, and soon others join. When Madge appears, she and Hal slowly drift toward and are attracted to each other. "It's like they were *made* to dance together, isn't it?" the neighbor remarks pleasantly. But the schoolteacher, intoxicated by a few drinks and stirred by Hal's virility, gives full vent to her repressed frustrations. First she snaps at her middle-aged "friend-boy," a local merchant. Then she snatches Hal, embarrasses him with her bawdy abandonment, and—when he resists her—excoriates him viciously: "The gutter's where you came from and the gutter's where you belong." Her suitor takes her away after this outburst, Madge's sister gets sick from the drinks she has sneaked, and Hal is left crushed, deeply hurt and humiliated. To Madge he admits the justice of the attack. His mother rejected him, he tells Madge, and had him sent to reform school. "I—I wish there was something I could say—or *do,*" Madge says sympathetically, and impulsively kisses him. Caught up by his animal vitality when he responds, she falls in his arms. He carries her into the house: "We're not goin' on no God-damn picnic."

Act III. After midnight, the schoolteacher returns from an amorous evening with her middle-aged merchant. Almost hysterical at the hopelessness of her lonely life, she insists—and then humbly begs—that he marry her. After he leaves, promising to return in the morning, Hal and Madge come out of the house. Their evening, too, was amorous—and both are self-condemnatory. But when they kiss good-bye, their passion again overcomes them. The next morning the schoolteacher's lover returns for her, and both get a "Happy Wedding" send-off. Flo worriedly asks Madge what happened and what her wealthy suitor will do now. Hal suddenly appears, bloody and disheveled, to say good-bye before hopping a train to Tulsa: he has gotten into a fight with the police, and begs Madge to escape with him. "When you hear that train pull outa town and know I'm on it, your little heart's gonna be busted, 'cause you love me," he insists when she refuses. Anguished after he leaves, Madge asks her mother, "What can you do with the love you feel?" Flo "never found out," she admits. She unhappily thinks of her daughter's lost chances with the rich boy, and listens to her neighbor defending Hal's visit: "There was a man in the house, and it seemed good." Then Madge appears with her suitcase, ready to take a bus to Tulsa and join Hal. "He'll never be able to support you. When he does have a job, he'll spend all his money on booze. After a while," the experienced Flo concludes, "there'll be other women." Madge replies, "I've thought of all those things"; but she is unable to suppress her love for Hal, and leaves. "Could anyone have stopped you?" her neighbor asks Flo. And she consoles her when the grieving mother thinks of all the things she had meant to tell Madge: "Let her learn them for herself, Flo."

PIGEON, THE, a drama in three acts by JOHN GALSWORTHY, published and produced in 1912. Setting: a contemporary English artist's studio and the street outside; Christmas Eve, New Year's Day, and April 1.

This semicomic "modern Christmas Carol" features a compassionate painter who cannot resist helping anybody in need. His casual humanity to three irreclaimable derelicts is contrasted with the theories of reformers representing the church, science, and the police, who at the end are shown to be as bankrupt as the down-and-outers. But the salvationist "pigeon," plucked by every beggar and reduced to taking cheaper lodgings where he can continue to cater to the needy, has his joke; after he tells the wastrels they can drink up his decanter, they are shocked to discover that it is not liquor: "*Tea!*... 'E's *got* us!"

PILLARS OF SOCIETY (*Samfundets støtter*), a play in four acts by HENRIK IBSEN, published and produced in 1877. Setting: a small contemporary Norwegian coastal town.

An indictment of society's sham ideals and corrupt foundations, this—though not among his better ones—was Ibsen's first major play and the first of his dramas of social criticism. The finale, in which the fraudulent, unscrupulous Consul Bernick confesses and apparently reforms, is not very convincing; but it is theatrical and highly emotional.

Though Karsten Bernick, the wealthy owner of the town's shipyard, is the respected pillar of his society, a scandal surrounds his wife's family. Many years before, her brother, Johan Tønnesen, had been seen escaping an actress's home as her husband returned. Tønnesen soon left for America, accompanied by Mrs. Bernick's stepsister, Lona Hessel. Rumor has it that he stole much of the Bernick fortune, but Bernick, after his marriage, succeeded in recouping the family business. Since the actress's death, in shame and poverty, her daughter (Dina Dorf) has been brought up in Bernick's home.

The town's puritanical leading ladies smugly discuss these and other scandals, and their own moral superiority, with the local schoolmaster, an eloquent idealist but a coward, who secretly loves Dina Dorf. Planning a dishonest business venture, Consul Bernick decides to support the building of a new seacoast railway he had hitherto opposed. Because of anticipated profits, the leading citizens now back the railway with the same piety with which they had earlier fought it. Then, having ordered his foreman to cease agitating against "progress" (new machines that are replacing workers), Bernick insists that an American ship be repaired and sent out in two days, though such haste will probably preclude its being made seaworthy and will cause it to go down with its crew. The unexpected return of Tønnesen and the unconventional, outspoken Lona Hessel agitate the company. Dina and Tønnesen fall in love; she is ready to go with him to America, where people are not "so terribly respectable and moral," when the schoolmaster brands him as her mother's seducer. Eventually the truth is revealed. Bernick has made his reputation, and has lived, on lies. It really was he who had an affair with the actress, and Tønnesen took the blame to shield him; furthermore, Bernick jilted Lona Hessel, whom he loved, for her wealthy stepsister. He needed money to save the shipyard, which had been on the verge of bankruptcy, and he therefore even spread the rumor of Tønnesen's theft—one that was never committed. Now he justifies his actions as necessary for the weal of the community, which has been supported by the shipyard and must not be disillusioned in its distinguished citizens. Lona urges him, for his own salvation, to tell the truth. When Tønnesen insists that his name be cleared so that he can marry Dina, Bernick sees to it that, before the truth comes out, Tønnesen will leave on the doomed ship. Later he is horrified to learn that his own son is a stowaway on that ship. Providentially, his son is brought back, and the ship is prevented from sailing when the foreman disobeys Bernick's orders. Badly shaken and repentant as the town honors him, Bernick publicly confesses his ruthless and dishonest manipulations. As Lona applauds this victory over himself, he rejects the town's way of life, with its former "veneer, its hypocrisy and its sham, with its pretence of respectability and its fawning." He urges the people to go home and look into their own hearts: "When we have all calmed down, it will be seen whether I have lost or gained by speaking out." Bernick finally acknowledges women's importance in the social order, and Lona remarks, "The spirit of truth and the spirit of freedom—*these* are the pillars of society."

PINERO, Sir **Arthur Wing** (1855–1934), English playwright, wrote popular farces and melodramas before he startled his contemporaries with what were considered PROBLEM PLAYS. Of his fifty dramas (thirty of them published), best remembered today are THE SECOND MRS. TANQUERAY (1893) and MID-CHANNEL (1909). Like most of Pinero's serious plays, they portray "sinning women" who are ultimately punished according to the laws of the theatre; but considering the age, these plays were daring. Like HENRY ARTHUR JONES, Pinero was one of the pioneers who brought something of the spirit of HENRIK IBSEN to English stages. BERNARD SHAW ridiculed the seriousness with which "Pinerotic themes" were taken. But he credited Pinero with the craftsmanship for which he has been frequently praised—and which in time dated his plays. Ironically, Pinero's popularity, which began in the 1880's, was doomed before World War I by his own share in elevating the drama from WELL-MADE frivolity and reestablishing it as a serious art—an accomplishment that justifies his historical importance.

Pinero was the son of a London solicitor whose father was named Pinheiro and whose ancestors were Portuguese Jews. Although he had been intended for the bar, Pinero was attracted by the theatre even as a child. He was taken out of school early and worked as an apprentice for his father, whose practice declined. But Pinero's fascination with the theatre continued, and he was inspired by Thomas Robertson's cup-and-saucer drama. Pinero wanted to act and—in his characteristically methodical manner—took elocution lessons. He also wrote plays, but they were rejected. When the opportunity presented itself, he went to Edinburgh to join a stock company. Subsequently he acted in Liverpool and then in London. He played with Sir Henry Irving's company, and his performances gained some recognition from leading actor-managers. At last, in 1877, two of his curtain raisers were produced: *£200 a Year* and *Two Can Play at That Game*. Though amusing, these remained unpublished, like other short pieces produced in the next few years: *Daisy's Escape, Hester's Mystery,* and *Bygones*.

Pinero's first produced full-length play, *The Money Spinner* (1880), was a popular, cynical comedy about cheating gamblers. It was followed by two further hits: *Imprudence* (1881), another cynical comedy about unpleasant characters; and *The Squire* (1881), a tragedy. Though in the early 1880's it was Jones's melodrama that cornered the popularity market, Pinero's box-office appeal grew rapidly. In 1882 he produced *Girls and Boys* and the next year—when he married a widowed actress he had courted since her appearance in his earliest works—he produced *The Rector, Lords and Commons,* and *The Rocket*. In 1884 appeared Pinero's *Low-Water, The Iron Master* (one of a number of English adaptations of *Le Maître de forges* [1883], the best known of the dramas of Georges Ohnet, 1848–1910), and *In Chancery*—all popular potboilers. By then he was not only a celebrity but also directed the companies that produced his plays. Feared and hated as an overbearing director who insisted on having everything done his way, Pinero was nevertheless so respected as a master technician that great actors willingly submitted themselves to his tyranny. Privately, however, Pinero was a remarkably shy and retiring man who avoided personal publicity.

Popular for his potboilers, Pinero strove for even greater acclaim. He therefore relinquished cynicism, farce, and melodrama for sentimental character comedy. The first in this new genre (and, incidentally, his first published play) made a great hit in London: *The Magistrate* (1885), a deftly manipulated plot about a woman who does not reveal her and her son's true age and thus gets into trouble with her second husband. It was followed by *Mayfair* (1885), an adaptation of *Maisons neuve* (1866) by VICTORIEN SARDOU; *The Schoolmistress* and *The Hobby-Horse,* two farces that achieved popularity in 1886; *Dandy Dick* (1887), one of his most successful farces; and *Sweet Lavender* (1888), a sentimental love story with Dickensian portraitures and psychological probings that was so great a hit that Pinero's position as the most popular London playwright of the day became firmly established.

A year after *The Weaker Sex* (1888), another comedy, Pinero had his first important success with the type of "unpleasant" play with which his name has come to be associated. The title character of *The Profligate* (1889) is a husband with "a past" whose discovery brings about the tragedy, though Pinero was persuaded to write a happy ending for the production. It was followed by *The Cabinet Minister* (1890), another farce. Then Pinero returned to writing serious plays that purported to deal with "problems." After less notable efforts in that genre—*Lady Bountiful* and *The Times* (both 1891)—and another farce (*The Amazons,* 1893), Pinero produced his most famous play, *The Second Mrs. Tanqueray*. It was followed by THE NOTORIOUS MRS. EBBSMITH (1895), *The Benefit of the Doubt* (1895, an unsuccessful attempt to combine a serious theme with comic treatment), *The Princess and the Butterfly* (1897, a light comedy), TRELAWNY OF THE "WELLS" (1898), THE GAY LORD QUEX (1899, his best comedy), IRIS (1901), *Letty* (1903, which like *Trelawny of the "Wells"* depicts class conflict), *A Wife Without a Smile* (1904, a farce that was considered vulgar), HIS HOUSE IN ORDER (1906), and his two last important works, THE THUNDERBOLT (1908) and MID-CHANNEL (1909).

Though he continued to write until he died, Pinero's career as a playwright was insignificant after 1909, the year he was knighted. His remaining plays are *Preserving Mr. Panmure* (1911), *The "Mind the Paint" Girl* and *The Widow of Wasdale Head* (both 1912), *Playgoers* (1913), *The Big Drum* (1915), *Mr. Livermore's Dream: A Lesson in Thrift* (1917), *The Freaks: An Idyll of Suburbia* and *Monica's Blue Boy* (both 1918), *Quick Work* (1919), *A Seat in the Park* and *The Enchanted Cottage* (both 1922, the latter a cynical fantasy about a wounded veteran and his homely bride), *A Private Room* (1928), *Two Plays* (*Dr. Harmer's Holidays* and *Child Man*, both published in 1930), and his last produced play, *A Cold June* (1932). He also collaborated on *The Beauty Stone,* an Arthur Sullivan operetta unsuccessfully produced in 1898.

Pinero's well-made-play formula now is painfully obvious. His dramas are too often dependent on coincidence and resolved by contrivance. Even the comedies, amusing as they sometimes are, abound in melodrama, sentimentality, and cant. His double-standard "problems" are at best suggestive, more often spurious—as Shaw quickly pointed out. Nonetheless, Pinero gave significant impetus to the development of modern drama. His craftsmanship and his shrewd gauging (and anticipation) of public taste made his plays popular. The women who are Pinero's protagonists are unadmirable and suffer the popularly approved consequences. If such dramaturgy presents Pinero in a "Victorian" hue, however, it should be noted, too, that his sympathetic and occasionally impressive depiction of "fallen women" and his use of situations shunned by earlier dramatists hastened the demise of Victorian prudery in the English theatre. And if Pinero himself lacked profundity as a thinker, his plays stimulated the drama of more original thinkers such as Shaw and prepared audiences for the more important drama to come—and thus soon dated Pinero's once-advanced plays.

Aside from the separately published Pinero plays, eight were collected in the four-volume *The Social Plays of Arthur Wing Pinero* (1917–22), edited and with introductions and prefaces by Clayton Hamilton. Hamilton Fyfe's *Sir Arthur Pinero's Plays and Players* (1930) also provides useful critical, biographical, and historical information. A balanced scholarly study is Wilbur Dwight Dunkel's *Sir Arthur Pinero: A Critical Biography With Letters* (1941), which contains a bibliography of primary and secondary works.

PING PONG (*Le Ping-Pong*), a play in two acts by ARTHUR ADAMOV, published and produced in 1955. Setting: a large city in twentieth-century France.

Martin Esslin in *The Theatre of the Absurd* (revised 1968) called this "one of the masterpieces" of the ABSURD genre. The play is episodic and often nonsensical in dialogue and action, yet predominantly NATURALISTIC in character and setting. A pinball machine symbolizes the futility of what Adamov considered contemporary civilization's perverted values—technological, political, religious, or social. The "absurdity" of men's dehumanizing preoccupation with the machine, a communal cynosure, is underlined by the senile Ping-Pong game in which Arthur and Victor finally while away their remaining time before death.

Act I. Scene 1. Arthur, a young art student, and Victor, a young medical student, are fascinated with a pinball machine, the main attraction at Mrs. Duranty's bar. They argue about the proper way to play and beat it. Sutter, the pinball company's hard-boiled collector, comes "to open up the monster" and empty out its many coins. The bigoted Mrs. Duranty sneers at a poor but talented young man, Roger, who detests the "ugly and vulgar" machines, and at those who are too cheap to play them. Annette, a pretty movie usherette who turns the heads of the men, gets fascinated with the machine as Sutter describes its conception by the Old Man (his school friend Constantine), details his many tasks for the company, and reveals that the "inventors" of improvements make the "really big money." When Annette hears that Roger had come by, she runs out after him. Alone, Arthur and Victor have an idea for improving the machine and decide to see the company's president. *Scene 2.* The Old Man (a caricature of a capitalist boss) seems delighted with an improvement that would "double enjoyment by inspiring fear." Unfortunately the invention has already been made, he tells them, though he encourages their coming to him with further ideas. Their disappointment changes to surprise when they see that Roger is the Old Man's secretary: he has decided to use the despised machines to make a living. *Scene 3.* At Mrs. Duranty's public baths the students, Sutter, and Annette are increasingly preoccupied with pinball machines. Mrs. Duranty yearns to have one for her current establishment, and Annette, eager to join the company, flirts with Sutter. Though suspicious of the Old Man, Arthur and Victor decide to try again. *Scene 4.* This time he has accepted their idea and paid them, and they use the money to buy shoes in the store where Annette now works as a salesgirl. Roger argues with her, declining to use his influence to have Mrs. Duranty's machine repaired on credit. Annette admits she is unhappy because the company is not hiring her. Players, she claims, are dissatisfied because they are uncertain about the results. Arthur and Annette thereupon excitedly devise "concrete images" of athletics and moon rockets to enliven the game and illuminate the players. *Scene 5.* As Arthur and Victor present the improvement to the Old Man, Sutter interrupts with aggressive demands for a loan. The suddenly furious Old Man rebuffs the students, insisting on "something new, something fantastic and complicated—I mean big business, women, wars, everything we love—in fact, everything we're prepared to die for." *Scene 6.* Though discouraged, the students decide to try another invention. Knowing that pinball-machine players "must be constantly disconcerted," they devise various combinations to confuse them with "different visual motifs."

Act II. Scene 1. Now a doctor and no longer in touch with Arthur, Victor is examining the complaining Mrs. Duranty. She is running a dancing school across the street from an arcade, which will soon be nationalized. The Old Man comes for her signature on a petition to keep pinball machines from "the legalized bandit who grabs the fruit of our toil." He is delighted, when he meets her, to hire Annette. But when he asks her to continue as a manicurist ("What a marvellous profession—intimate and public at the same time!") and become the company's secret agent, she angrily runs out. *Scene 2.* Reunited, Arthur, Victor, and Annette consider approaching the Old Man once more. When they see Sutter betray him, they go to visit the Old Man. *Scene 3.* Roger and Annette minister to the sick Old Man, who is delirious, thinking about the millions they need. Increasingly senile, he fondles Annette while he raves about improvements to be made in "the machine at the center of the world," crawls after Annette—and suddenly collapses, dead. *Scene 4.* Though he still despises the machines, Roger is now intrigued by them. Victor tells Annette that he has broken up with Arthur—who heretofore has courted her—and asks her to become his assistant. *Scene 5.* Lying at Mrs. Duranty's some weeks later is the corpse of Annette, who has been killed in an accident at the arcade. Sutter appears, half starved. As he walks around excitedly talking about the machines, he knocks against the furniture and Annette's corpse falls on the floor. *Scene 6.* Victor and Arthur, now white-haired septuagenarians, play Ping-Pong on a table divided into black and white squares. They argue incessantly about their lives ("I don't make as much as you do at Universal Correspondence, but then, I don't have to work as hard as you do at Universal Correspondence"), the score, and the game. Soon they decide to do without net and paddles. "Come on then, serve," Arthur laughs: "Go on, with your right hand—what does it matter?" Wildly they hit balls, leap into the air to catch them, and snicker. Victor starts panting. As he jumps for a ball he collapses. Panicky, Arthur cries out, "Victor! Victor!"

PINGET, Robert (1920–   ), Swiss-born French painter and writer, was better noted as a novelist than as a playwright. Born in Geneva, he studied and then practiced law. Subsequently he turned to art, and soon had his paintings exhibited in Paris. Thereafter he lived in England, where he wrote novels and plays in the ABSURDist tradition of his friend SAMUEL BECKETT.

Pinget's collected plays were translated in two volumes. *Three Plays,* Volume I (1963) includes *La Manivelle* (*The Old Tune,* 1960), a radio play about two reminiscing old men and a satire of language, translated into the Irish idiom by Beckett; *Ici ou ailleurs* (1961, translated as *Clope*), a dramatization of his novel about human isolation, *Clope au dossier* (1961); and *Lettre morte* (*Dead Letter,* 1959), a two-act variation on the Prodigal Son parable that features an anguished and lonely old father obsessed with a letter to his son, based on Pinget's 1959 novel *Le Fiston* and originally produced with Beckett's KRAPP'S LAST TAPE. Volume II (1967) includes *Architruc* (1961), about a lonely and irrational old king; *Autour de Mortin* (*About Mortin,* 1965), nine radio sketches; and *L'Hypothèse* (*The Hypothesis,* 1961), another portrayal of a lonely and trapped man. All of these are avant-garde tragicomedies resembling those of Beckett.

A discussion of Pinget's work appears in Martin Esslin's *The Theatre of the Absurd* (revised 1968).

PINSKI, David (1872–1959), Yiddish writer and editor, probably has had more of his plays appear in English translation than has any other Yiddish dramatist. They were also produced by the Theatre Guild, by the Provincetown Players, and by Max Reinhardt. Pinski edited Yiddish-American periodicals, and aside from essays, novels, and tales, he wrote more than sixty plays. These range remarkably in subject and type: short one-act as well as long four-act plays; NATURALISTIC, messianic, biblical, and sex dramas; allegories; and comedies. They depict not only the East European Jew but also characters and viewpoints indigenous to the mainstream of Western culture. Best known among Pinski's plays are *Di Familie Tsvi* (THE ZWIE FAMILY, 1905; also known in English as *The Last Jew*), ISAAC SHEFTEL (1907), his satiric masterpiece *Der Oytser* (THE TREASURE, 1910), and the one-acters collectively titled *Dovid Hamelakh un zayne Vayber* (KING DAVID AND HIS WIVES, 1919).

Although he spent most of his life in New York and wrote almost all his plays there, Pinski was born in Mohilev, Russia. First he was prepared for a rabbinical career. Later the family moved to Moscow, and by 1892 Pinski was studying medicine in Vienna. Then, too, he began to write—first in Russian and Hebrew, thereafter in Yiddish. In that language he soon published his first work, a short story, and founded a publication with YITSKHOK LEYBUSH PERETZ. In 1896 Pinski studied literature in Berlin, where he met many distinguished writers. Soon thereafter he was invited to join the staff of a Yiddish-American newspaper. In 1899 he went to New York, where he remained for half a century.

Pinski was a Socialist, active in the labor movement, and his earliest plays—for which he is still best remembered—portray the working classes. After the one-act *Yesurim* (1899), his first play, came the already noted *Isaac Sheftel,* which is as typical of his early naturalist drama as its protagonist is of his proletarian as well as his visionary heroes. *Di Muter* (1901) followed, and then the more important *The Zwie Family;* though it deals with Jewish themes, Pinski in his foreword stressed the universality of this "tragedy of a moribund religion, of a crumbling world-philosophy." It was the writing of this play, too, that determined Pinski's subsequent career: his preoccupation with the play kept him from attending his Columbia University doctoral examination; passing it might have launched Pinski on another career, as a professor of German literature. Then came *Gliksfargessene* (*Forgotten Souls,* 1905), a one-act depiction of a girl's self-sacrifice for her sister, followed by another one-acter and the first of his messianic plays, *Der Fremder* (*The Stranger,* 1906; also known as *Der Eybiker Yid*). Next came probably his best and most popular work, *The Treasure.*

With the searing love dramas that followed, Pinski continued to transcend the parochial. *Gabri un di Froyen* (1908), the one-act *Mit Zigerfonnen* (1908), and *Yankl der Schmid* (1910) are all dramas of passion in which the wife succeeds in reclaiming a husband enamored of another woman. Also rooted in sex—and in Western tradition—is *Miriam fun Magdelah* (1913), which is similar in treatment to Maeterlinck's MARY MAGDALENE: Pinski's Mary renounces her faith in Eros after her charms fail to seduce Christ as they had all the other holy men; won over by His teachings, she (like Maeterlinck's Mary) refuses to violate them even to purchase His rescue.

Professor Brenner (1911) and *Di Bergshtayger* (1912) echo the late drama of HENRIK IBSEN. The first dramatizes the failure of a marriage between an aged artist and his admiring young pupil, while the second, an allegorical drama, traces the ascent of various couples to a mountaintop. In one of its memorable speeches Pinski expresses characteristic attitudes. "Just to be alive is the highest happiness," his protagonist says; "we need happiness—but not the happiness of the victor who strides over the corpses of his victims. We need the inner happiness that warms and irradiates and which only goodness can confer upon us." *Der Shtumer Meshiekh* (*The Dumb Messiah,* 1911) was inspired by fourteenth-century history but is original in plot and its title character, a balked creative visionary like Isaac Sheftel. The play is another on the messianic theme, which Pinski returned to in 1936 with *Sabbatai Zevi,* the legendary character whose life SHOLEM ASCH had dramatized some decades earlier.

Among Pinski's remaining plays are *Nina Mordens Libes* (written in 1915–16), whose protagonist has been characterized as "a sort of feminine ANATOL," and *Alexander and Diogenes* (1930). Pinski's Diogenes presents his positive view of life when chided for "nay-saying" by Alexander. "It is true that I have lived in a barrel. . . . [But] I have assimilated all of nature into my being. I have acquired wisdom and knowledge in fullest measure," the ragged philosopher tells the mighty monarch, and adds, "Did you, with all your battles and bloodshed, gain more for yourself?" It is the principle of happiness adumbrated in *Di Bergshtayger,* and implied in many Pinski plays.

He resided in New York with his wife for most of his life. Shortly after the state of Israel was proclaimed, Pinski—an active and lifelong Zionist—settled there for his remaining years. Among Pinski's other plays are the one-acters published in translation (*Ten Plays,* 1920): *Der Fonograf* (*The Phonograph*), *Der Got fun dem Raykhgevorenem Volhendler* (*The God of the Newly Rich Wool Merchant*), *A Doler* (*A Dollar*), *Kalikes* (*The Cripples*), *Der Erfinder un dem Kenigs Tokhter* (*The Inventor and the King's Daughter*), *Politik* (*Diplomacy*), *Kleyne Heldn* (*Little Heroes*), *Di Sheyne None* (*The Beautiful Nun*), *Tokheykho* (*Poland—1919*), and *Der Fremder* (or *Der Eybiker Yid,* translated as *The Stranger*). The *Three Plays* (1918) are *Isaac Sheftel, The Last Jew* (*The Zwie Family*), and *The Dumb Messiah. The Treasure* was published in English in 1915, and *King David and His Wives* is in Joseph C. Landis's *The Dybbuk and Other Great Yiddish Plays* (1966). Pinski's *Dos Yiddishe Drama* (1909) is a short but important history of the Jewish theatre. See also Isaac Goldberg's *The Drama of Transition* (1922), Sol Liptzin's *The Flowering of Yiddish Literature* (1963), and Charles A. Madison's *Yiddish Literature: Its Scope and Major Writers* (1968).

Harold Pinter. (*Zodiac Photographers*)

PINTER, Harold (1930–   ), English playwright, became famous with THE CARETAKER (1960), a haunting farce-tragedy that was subsequently filmed. Like his earlier THE BIRTHDAY PARTY (1958) and his later THE HOMECOMING (1965), it evidences the influence of writers such as Franz Kafka, LUIGI PIRANDELLO, and SAMUEL BECKETT (also, as Pinter later acknowledged, that of American gangster films) more than those of his "angry" young English contemporaries. There is, it is true, a strong anti-Establishment note in his plays—and an echo of ABSURDist drama like that of EUGÈNE IONESCO. But the most striking quality of Pinter's plays is their evocation of terror. It is that quality—allied with farcical dialogue and "business"—which led reviewers aptly to dub Pinter's drama the "comedy of menace."

The son of a Portuguese-Jewish tailor in East London, Pinter attended a drama and speech school as well as the Royal Academy of Dramatic Art. Beginning to write in his teens, he produced a considerable number of poems and prose works (many in dialogue) for little magazines. As a conscientious objector he declined the call for National Service, and was twice tried and fined. In 1949 he became an actor (under the name David Baron), played repertory in Ireland and the English provinces, and started to write a novel. He wrote a play, *The Room,* in 1957 at the suggestion of a friend at Bristol University, where it was immediately produced. Both its situation and title suggest the drama soon to become associated with Pinter's work. "I started off with this picture of two people [in a room] and let them carry on from there," Pinter remarked about his first SYMBOLIC horror play. The unspecified outside menace that scares its characters, Pinter explained, "is a world bearing upon them which is frightening. I am sure it is frightening to you and me as well." The people are an old couple; the truckdriver husband goes off to work, the wife fears her shelter is threatened as a janitor and prospective new tenants appear, a blind Negro visitor (death?) brings her a message ("Your father wants you to come home"), and the husband returns and beats the Negro senseless—whereupon the wife is struck blind.

This eerie and original one-acter was followed by the less melodramatic, equally suggestive, and more amusing THE DUMB WAITER (1960). It was subsequently produced together with *The Collection* (1962, originally televised in 1961), a Pirandellian one-acter about a married couple, a possible adulterer, and a jealous homosexual. Many of Pinter's other works also were originally written for radio and television, but later staged. *A Slight Ache* (1959) was published in 1961 with *A Night Out, The Dwarfs,* and five revue sketches. It is a one-act play in which the mysterious and soundless presence of an old matchseller brings out the inner emptiness of a well-to-do writer and the inherent warmth and sensuousness of his middle-aged wife. The sinister title creatures of *The Dwarfs* (originally a novel that remained unpublished), characters in a reworking of the protagonist's unfinished novel, are in his mind, and their meaning constitutes the central mystery of the play. In *A Night Out,* a longer work, a man escapes his possessive mother, takes up with a prostitute on whom he works out Oedipal repressions and hostilities, and then returns to his mother. Similar in theme are *Night School* (1960) and later plays, many of them originally on television. In *The Lover* (1963), a bitter comedy that bears some resemblance to Genet's THE BALCONY and to JOHN OSBORNE's *Under Plain Cover,* a suburban couple lead a gratifying love life by indulging in elaborate make-believe, in which the office-worker husband returns in the afternoons pretending to be his wife's lover; communication is possible to them only through fantasy. In *Tea Party* (1965), a family play like *The Homecoming,* social and sexual insecurities topple a wealthy industrialist who marries an aristocrat but is involved with his sensuous secretary; feeling guilty he becomes blind and collapses during a family tea party when he perceives (rightly or wrongly) his wife's brother seducing both women in his very presence. *The Basement* (1967) presents a grim *ménage à trois* that culminates in the girl's two lovers' dueling over her with broken milk bottles. A lyrical double bill features multiple solitary reminiscences of old people: in *Landscapes* (1968) by a sentimental wife and her hearty but unimaginative mate; in *Silence* (1969) by a woman and two men with whom she once associated. These two plays seemed a departure by Pinter, who, however, returned to his earlier dramaturgy in *Old Times* (1971), a play about a middle-aged couple and their mysterious visitor, the wife's former girlfriend.

In Pinter's plays communication between people has well-nigh collapsed. It has given way to pathetic games, to cliché, or to sinister threat. In his later works these horrors are compounded by agonizing solipsism of characters who find it difficult to perceive, conceptualize, or articulate. Either threatening or dully responsive, their dialogue is in Cockney—or in grotesquely fanciful words. As in ANTON CHEKHOV, the frequent pauses are as important and expressive as the dialogue. Among recurring themes are the quests for security and shelter, self-identification, and verification of truth. But the philosophical implications and the social satire are presented in suspenseful yet often comic plots. Though he wrote few plays in the first decade of his creativity, Pinter soon achieved a reputation as an important dramatist of considerable power, originality, and promise.

While Pinter continued to act occasionally after his drama began to appear—and distinguished himself also as a director—he soon devoted himself principally to playwriting. Aside from radio and television drama, some of which was subsequently staged, Pinter wrote the scripts for *The Caretaker* (1963) and other films, including *The Pumpkin Eater* (1963), *The Servant* (1964), *The Quiller Memorandum* (1966), and *Accident* (1967). Book-length studies of his life and work include Arnold P. Hinchliffe's *Harold Pinter* (1968), Martin Esslin's *The Peopled Wound: The Work of Harold Pinter* (1970), and Katherine H. Burkman's *The Dramatic World of Harold Pinter* (1971).

PIRANDELLO, Luigi (1867–1936), Italy's greatest modern playwright, also wrote an impressive number of excellent short stories, novels, and poetry. In Italy he is perhaps most renowned as a short-story writer, but internationally Pirandello's fame rests on his dramas (he wrote a total of forty-four), particularly on *Sei personaggi in cerca d'autore* (SIX CHARACTERS IN SEARCH OF AN AUTHOR, 1921) and *Enrico IV* (HENRY IV, 1922). He was the most prominent practitioner of the GROTESQUE drama of disillusionment that anticipated the midcentury theatre of the ABSURD—the *teatro grottesco* whose vogue began with Chiarelli's THE MASK AND THE FACE (1916). It is characteristically Pirandellian in its tragicomic probing into the conflicts of illusion and reality, the mask and the face. With Pirandello the dramatic mixture of ludicrous pathos, fantasy, rhetoric, and cerebration achieved its most impressive form, and he has come to be recognized as one of the principal architects of the modern theatre.

He was born in Girgenti, Sicily, after the end of the Garibaldian era of rebellion. His father, Stefano Pirandello, was a wealthy sulfur-mine owner, whose fiery temperament and infidelities his wife, Caterina, endured in silent resignation. Characteristically—in an island where tempestuous emotionalism is common—his father slapped down a Mafia extortionist and was subsequently shot and wounded in an ambush.

At sixteen Pirandello started writing poetry, and

two years later, after a short and unsuccessful venture in business, he was sent to the University of Rome. He completed his studies at Bonn in 1891, obtaining his doctorate in philology for a dissertation on his native dialect. His poetry was collected and published in 1889, and there were five subsequent volumes, the last of which appeared in 1912. But Pirandello's particular genius and his bitter humor appeared to lend themselves better to prose. His first collection of stories was published in 1894.

In Rome he became immersed in a life of letters. He was vigorously opposed to GABRIELE D'ANNUNZIO, whose romantic Nietzschean cult was then at the height of fashion. At the same time, there was in Italy a strong reaction by the FUTURISTS (led by FILIPPO TOMMASO MARINETTI), who passionately opposed the nineteenth-century conventions of NATURALISM, romanticism, religion, and the idealization of women and art. Grotesque literature was a part of the futurist movement, and Pirandello was temperamentally and intellectually most attuned to it.

His marriage to Antonietta Portulano in 1894 had been contracted—as marriages then frequently were—by the parents, business associates who wanted to consolidate their wealth; the principals had not even met before the wedding was arranged. Their early years together were pleasant; they lived in comfort and had three children, the oldest of whom (Stefano Landi) was to become a fairly successful writer, and another (Fausto) an eminent painter. Then double disaster struck: the wealth that supported them was literally washed away by the 1904 floods that ruined the mines; and Antonietta, already weakened by the birth of her youngest child, fainted when she heard the news, became paralyzed, and went insane. Pirandello secured a position in Rome as a professor of Italian literature at a girls' normal school in 1904, and started drudging for his living. Antonietta's derangement and hysterical jealousies increased; she became violent, and life was a perpetual torment to her family. Virtually isolating himself from people and enduring her mad fury, Pirandello cared for her himself until, as his friends had urged him to do all along, he finally committed her to an asylum in 1918, shortly before her death. Unquestionably this life affected his later drama, throwing into sharper relief his preoccupation with the grotesque, with illusion, with madness, and with the relativity of reality.

Throughout the harrowing years of Antonietta's insanity Pirandello continued his writing. He published volume after volume of short stories; by 1916 he had also published some six novels, the most important of which is *Il fu Mattia Pascal* (*The Late Mattia Pascal,* 1904), which was subsequently filmed. But success came to him only after a long time. It was not until he turned to drama that his reputation began to grow, and it was not until the early 1920's, when *Six Characters in Search of an Author* became well known, that Pirandello achieved international fame.

He wrote three plays before World War I: *La morsa* (THE VISE, 1910), *Lumie di Sicilia* (SICILIAN LIMES, 1910), and *Il dovere del medico* (THE DOCTOR'S DUTY, 1912). These one-act plays did not create much of a stir; nor did the next, his first full-length play, *Se non cosí* (IF NOT THUS, 1915; later published as *The Rights of Others*). But Pirandello was spurred to persist by the actor Angelo Musco, who was looking for good dialect comedies. The war, which intensified Pirandello's horror of life's cruel irrationality, stimulated his dramatic genius. In the five years before he produced his popular masterpiece in 1921, he brought out fifteen plays, some written with incredible speed: *Pensaci, Giacomino!* (JUST THINK, GIACOMINO!, 1916; composed in three days), LIOLÀ (1916, in one week), *Così è (se vi pare)* (RIGHT YOU ARE [IF YOU THINK YOU ARE], 1917; six days), *Il berretto a sonagli* (CAP AND BELLS, 1917), *La giara* (THE JAR, 1917), *Il piacere dell'onestà* (THE PLEASURE OF HONESTY, 1917), *Ma non è una cosa seria* (IT IS REALLY NOT SERIOUS, 1918), *Il giuoco delle parti* (THE RULES OF THE GAME, 1918), *L'innesto* (GRAFTING, 1918), *La patente* (THE LICENSE, 1918), *L'uomo, la bestia e la virtù* (MAN, BEAST, AND VIRTUE, 1919), *Tutto per bene* (ALL FOR THE BEST, 1929), *Come prima, meglio di prima* (AS WELL AS BEFORE, BETTER THAN BEFORE, 1920), CECÈ (1920, also translated as *Chee-Chee*), and *La Signora Morlì, una e due* (SIGNORA MORLI, ONE AND TWO, 1920).

Most of these and the later plays are labeled "comedies," but Pirandello's comedy is bitter, ironic, pessimistic. It dissects man's tortured personality and psyche, and constantly dramatizes Pirandello's relativistic view of ever-changing truth, reality, and being. The revealingly titled and already noted *Right You Are (If You Think You Are)* is the most explicit statement of Pirandello's belief that knowledge can never be objective. But like the others, this play is more than metaphysics: it *dramatizes* the tragicomic implications of Pirandello's belief. The same note is sounded in other plays, and there is some justification for calling Pirandello repetitious. In almost all his plays the metaphysical agonizing is expressed by men. Pirandello's hope, sympathy, and consolation seem to lie with the instinctive love of women, often portrayed in awakened maternal feelings. Maternity is the ennobling quality of a number of his heroines, and the proverbial "where children are, there is the home" provides the resolution to a number of his plays.

Pirandello's drama has been called cerebral and overintellectualized and it is, in fact, highly charged with debate. His dialogues and monologues often become magnificently rhetorical (hence, incidentally, they lose in translation). But if Pirandello's plays are "discussion drama," the emphasis is on *drama,* drama that embodies the playwright's great flair for theatre. Pirandello was tormented by compassion for human suffering and by morbid ratiocination, but the many picturesque characters he created seethe with passions. Though discursive, his drama differs fundamentally from the work of BERNARD SHAW, that other discursive giant playwright. Shaw dealt with men's social

Luigi Pirandello in 1935. (*Edward Steichen*)

problems; he showed and preached how one should live. Pirandello, on the other hand, dramatized metaphysical problems and kept asking: What is life? What is reality? Are life and reality merely illusory?

It is in the trilogy that begins with *Six Characters in Search of an Author* that the last question receives its most poignant expression. At the end of that play, the "real" people are mere puppets before the agonizing reality of the "characters." As in the later plays of this trilogy, *Ciascuno a suo modo* (EACH IN HIS OWN WAY, 1924) and *Questa sera si recita a soggetto* (TONIGHT WE IMPROVISE, 1930), Pirandello's characteristic preoccupation is here focused on the relation between life and the theatre—significantly underlining the fact that Pirandello's dramaturgy derives from the *commedia dell'arte. Henry IV,* his next play and generally considered his greatest, is focused on madness. Other variations of Pirandello's typical themes occur in his remaining works: *All'uscita* (AT THE EXIT, 1916), *L'imbicelle* (THE IMBECILE, 1922), *Vestire gli ignudi* (TO CLOTHE THE NAKED, 1922; a major play), *L'uomo dal fiore in bocca* (THE MAN WITH THE FLOWER IN HIS MOUTH, 1923; perhaps his most moving one-act sketch), *La vita che ti diedi* (THE LIFE I GAVE YOU, 1923), *L'altro figlio* (THE OTHER SON, 1923; also translated as *The House with the Column*), *La sagra del Signore della nave* (THE FESTIVAL OF OUR LORD OF THE SHIP, 1924), *Diana e la Tuda* (DIANA AND TUDA, 1926), *L'amica delle mogli* (THE WIVES' FRIEND, 1927), BELLAVITA (1927), *Scamandro* (a minor play in five scenes, published in 1909 but not produced until 1928), *La nuova colonia* (THE NEW COLONY, 1928), *O di uno o di nessuno* (EITHER OF ONE OR OF NO ONE, 1929), *Lazzaro* (LAZARUS, 1929), *Come tu mi vuoi* (AS YOU DESIRE ME, 1936; filmed with Greta Garbo), *Trovarsi* (TO FIND ONESELF, 1932), *Quando si è qualcuno* (WHEN ONE IS SOMEBODY, 1933) *La favola del figlio cambiato* (*The Fable of the Exchanged Son,* 1934; a libretto for an opera by Francesco Malipiero), *Non si sa come* (ONE DOES NOT KNOW HOW, 1935), *Sogno* (*ma forse no*) (DREAM [BUT PERHAPS NOT], 1929; also translated as *I'm Dreaming, But Am I?*), and *I giganti della montagna* (THE MOUNTAIN GIANTS, 1937). This last play remained uncompleted, but it has been hailed as the finest of Pirandello's later *miti* (myth) plays on society, religion, motherhood, and art. Pirandello also collaborated on a number of plays in dialect—*'A Vilanza* (1917) and *Cappiddazzu paga tuttu* (1922)—with Nino Martoglio (1870–1921), who in 1903 had founded a Sicilian-dialect repertory troupe, and whom Pirandello helped with his comedy hit, *L'Aria del continente* (1915).

Pirandello was vitally concerned with the theatrical production of his works. He discovered Marta Abba, the young actress who was to star in many of his plays and with whom he was said to have been romantically linked; he modeled heroines after her, dedicated some of his plays to her, and willed nine of them to her outright. In 1925 Pirandello opened his own Teatro D'Arte (1925–28) in Rome; he worked tirelessly with his company, traveling with them on successful European and South American tours. But international fame, crowned by the 1934 Nobel Prize, did not appear to bring Pirandello happiness. The story of his later life, furthermore, is marred by his public support of Mussolini and Fascism, though the regime came to censure some of his last works as "anti-Fascist."

Pirandello's collected dramas have appeared since 1918 under the appropriately suggestive title *Maschere Nude* (*Naked Masks*). Though some have not yet been translated into English, the major plays are available; good and readily procurable collections with introductions are Eric Bentley's *Naked Masks: Five Plays** (1952), William Murray's *To Clothe the Naked and Two Other Plays*† (1962), and *Pirandello's One-Act Plays*‡ (1964).

Book-length studies of Pirandello in English include Domenico Vittorini's *The Drama of Luigi Pirandello* (1937, republished in 1957), a detailed analysis of thirty-eight plays; Walter Starkie's *Luigi Pirandello* (1926; republished in 1965 in an augmented edition which contains a bibliography, a brief biography, and an extensive survey of the Italian milieu and background of Pirandello's plays); and Oscar Büdel's *Pirandello* (1966). *Pirandello* (1967), Glauco Cambon's handy "Collection of Critical Essays," also has a bibliography. More specialized studies are Lander MacClintock's *The Age of Pirandello* (1951) and Thomas Bishop's *Pirandello and the French Theater* (1960).

PLATONOV, a play in four acts by ANTON CHEKHOV, published in 1923 and produced in 1928. Setting: an estate in a southern Russian province in the latter part of the nineteenth century.

Chekhov's earliest play was written about 1881, over forty years before it was discovered, long after his death. He destroyed his copy when the play was rejected, and all that remains is a long draft without a title. Since its publication it has been performed widely and successfully under various titles: *Without Fathers, A Play Without a Title, A Country Scandal, Don Juan in the Russian Manner,* and *That Worthless Fellow Platonov.* Though long, unwieldy, and melodramatic, it clearly evidences the characteristics of Chekhov's maturer genius.

Mikhail Platonov, the handsome and intelligent village schoolmaster, has failed to realize his high youthful expectations. Now married and a father,

**Liolà, Right You Are (If You Think You Are). Henry IV, Six Characters in Search of an Author, Each in His Own Way;* informative appendixes include Pirandello's important preface to *Six Characters in Search of an Author* as well as biographical, historical, theatrical, and bibliographical data.

† *The Rules of the Game* and *The Pleasure of Honesty.*

‡ Thirteen one-acters: *The Vise, Sicilian Limes, The Doctor's Duty, The Jar, The License, Chee-Chee, At the Exit, The Imbecile, The Man with the Flower in His Mouth, The Other Son, The Festival of Our Lord of the Ship, Bellavita,* and *I'm Dreaming, But Am I?*

he is constantly pursued by women who throw themselves at him. But he despondently blames himself for his many conquests. Irresolute like Hamlet, he constantly agonizes and philosophizes: "I've no will of my own! O God! Why am I always weak with women? . . . I am a woman's man. A pitiful Don Juan." While his simple and loving wife forgives his lapses, he succumbs to various women, including the attractive, widowed estate owner, Anna Voynitsev. But when he is drawn into an affair with Sonya, recently (and unhappily) married to the widow's stepson, Sergei, Platonov's wife leaves him and is saved from suicide only at the last moment. Platonov, too, attempts suicide, but his nerve fails him. The widow loses her estate which is auctioned off, and Sonya almost persuades Platonov to start "a new life" with her. But again he hesitates. Word comes that his wife has taken poison and, in her illness, is asking for him. He decides to go to her, and the jilted Sonya shoots him.

Noteworthy among the many fine characterizations is that of Osip, the Caliban-like estate steward who worships both the widow and Platonov's kindly wife; he attempts to kill Platonov, and is finally lynched by the peasants, whom he has cruelly exploited.

PLAYBOY OF THE WESTERN WORLD, THE, a play in three acts by J. M. SYNGE, published and produced in 1907. Setting: a contemporary country shebeen* on the coast of Mayo, Ireland; autumn.

Synge's tragicomic masterpiece has, as he implied, "several [serious] sides." The play satirizes hero worship, its effects, and its fickleness. With profound suggestiveness, it also portrays archetypal struggles and the powers of illusion. The language, Synge noted in his preface, derives from Irish peasant folk-imagination "superb and wild in reality[,] . . . fiery and magnificent, and tender." It was this poetic yet earthy language (especially the third-act allusion to female underwear) that triggered the notorious Abbey Theatre riots against the play and its supposed insult to Irishmen. Despite the courageous championing of the play by WILLIAM BUTLER YEATS, mob censorship prevented completion of the premiere, raged for a week, and spread to the United States. Synge achieved his aim to make "every speech . . . as fully flavoured as a nut or apple." As was recognized only later, he also succeeded in depicting, with immense vividness and humor, the follies of mankind. See Thomas R. Whitaker's edition of *Twentieth Century Interpretations of "The Playboy of the Western World"* (1969) and James Kilroy's *The Playboy Riots* (1970).

Act I. Pegeen Mike (Margaret Flaherty), the publican's "wild-looking but fine" daughter, is bored with her drab life. She is irritated by her cousin, a meek fool who is betrothed to her; but fearing the priest's disapproval, he refuses to remain alone with her while her father goes out

*Public house, or pub.

The Playboy of the Western World. Christy (Arthur Shields, right) with the widow (Sara Allgood) and the publican (Barry Fitzgerald). Dublin, 1930. (*Irish Tourist Board*)

drinking. When the publican jokingly tries to force him to stay, he runs off hysterically. Soon a slight, frightened, and exhausted young man—Christy Mahon—comes in. The company is intrigued with his mysterious fear of the police. After much coaxing, he confesses, "I killed my poor father[.] . . . He getting old and crusty, the way I couldn't put up with him at all." Christy explains, "I just riz the loy and let fall the edge of it on the ridge of his skull." Immediately he becomes the center of attraction and great admiration as "a daring fellow." Pegeen suggests he be hired as potboy, and her father agrees: "Bravery's a treasure in a lonesome place, and a lad would kill his father, I'm thinking, would face a foxy divil with a pitchpike on the flags of hell." Christy gains self-confidence and Pegeen becomes enamored of this "fine, handsome young fellow with a noble brow." Unaccustomed to such attention, Christy is delightedly surprised: "Is it me?" A neighboring thirty-year-old widow's designs on Christy heighten Pegeen's feelings. She gets rid of the widow, and Christy retires smugly: "Two fine women fighting for the likes of me—till I'm thinking this night wasn't I a foolish fellow not to kill my father in the years gone by."

Act II. In the morning village girls come to gawk at and idolize Christy. With growing bravado, he recounts his deed. Pegeen throws the ecstatic girls out, and irritably chastens Christy. For a while he is subdued, but then her fiancé and the widow arrive. They offer him fine clothes to give Pegeen up and go away. Strutting around vainly, Christy refuses. The desperate fiancé is scared to attack him even from the back, and finally leaves. As the widow proposes that Christy marry her, he swaggers about the mighty blow he dealt his father—and suddenly staggers back and hides in terror. Old Mahon, his head bandaged, comes looking for his pathetic weakling of a son, "an ugly young streeler with a murderous gob on him, . . . a dirty, stuttering lout." The widow misdirects the father away, laughs at his terrified son ("Well, you're the walking Playboy of the Western World, and that's the poor man you had divided to his breeches belt"), and urges him to marry her. But he refuses, though he now dreads the thought of being found out. Aspiring to win his beloved Pegeen, Christy promises to pay the widow handsomely for her help when he becomes master of the saloon. Then he runs out to compete in the village sports.

Act III. Later that day, Old Mahon returns to the saloon. From the outside cheers are heard for Christy, who is winning various competitions. The widow manages to get Old Mahon away just before "the champion Playboy of the Western World" triumphantly enters with an admiring throng. With eloquent ardor he proposes to Pegeen, "the crowning prize I'm seeking now." He anticipates "squeezing kisses on your puckered lips, till I'd feel a kind of pity for the Lord God is all ages sitting lonesome in his golden chair." Radiant and now eloquent herself, Pegeen agrees: "And to think it's me is talking sweetly, Christy Mahon, and I the fright of seven townlands for my biting tongue." She rejects her cousin—"a middling kind of a scarecrow, with no savagery or fine words in him at all"—whom Christy chases out. As Christy's happiness is crowned with the almost-sober publican's blessing, Old Mahon rushes in and starts beating his son. The disillusioned crowd soon jeers "the playboy" and Pegeen remarks contemptuously, "And to think of the coaxing glory we had given him, and he after doing nothing but hitting a soft blow and chasing northward in a sweat of fear." Desperate and his courage rising with their contempt and Pegeen's dismissal of him, Christy, followed by the crowd, grabs a spade and chases after his father. Soon he returns, and again rejects the widow's proposal: "It's Pegeen I'm seeking only, and what'd I care if you brought me a drift of chosen females, standing in their shifts itself . . ."* The crowds return appalled. Christy has again felled his father, and now they get ready to turn him over to the police. Pegeen herself throws a fettering rope around him: "A strange man is a marvel, with his mighty talk; but what's a squabble in your back-yard, and the blow of a loy, have taught me that there's a great gap between a gallous story and a dirty deed." Christy is horrified by this treachery and the thought of being executed. Writhing on the ground, he begs to be released. When Pegeen cruelly helps to torture and subdue him, Christy's spirit returns. He becomes gay as his courage wells up, and he taunts the villagers. His father crawls in—again having been only stunned—cuts him free, and prepares to leave with him. But Christy now asserts his new power also over his father, and pushes him forward. Old Mahon meekly but delightedly submits to his son's mastery, and Christy thanks the villagers who "turned me a likely gaffer in the end of all, the way I'll go romancing through a romping lifetime from this hour to the dawning of the judgment day." He leaves, and now Pegeen laments wildly, "Oh, my grief, I've lost him surely. I've lost the only Playboy of the Western World."

* It was this speech that particularly inflamed the audience and stopped the play.

PLAYING WITH FIRE (*Leka med elden*), a one-act comedy by AUGUST STRINDBERG, published in 1893 and produced in 1908. Setting: a contemporary seaside resort.

This is a comic reminiscence of Strindberg's courting of his first wife, then married to his friend. But here the husband's friend (Axel), after exchanging love vows with the wife and confronting the husband, wildly escapes and leaves the married couple to their breakfast.

PLAYLETS OF THE WAR (1919), a collection of four World War I one-acters by BERNARD SHAW: *O'Flaherty, V.C.* (1915), an amusing "recruiting pamphlet" about a disillusioned Irish hero who prefers war to home life; *The Inca of Perusalem* (1916), i.e., the pompous but intelligent German Kaiser, who discusses the war; *Augustus Does His Bit* (1917), a farce about English wartime officialdom; and *Annajanska, The Bolshevik Empress* (1918), a comic "bravura piece" about the Russian Revolution.

PLAYS PLEASANT (1898), by BERNARD SHAW; ARMS AND THE MAN, CANDIDA, THE MAN OF DESTINY, and YOU NEVER CAN TELL.

In the preface to this, the second volume of *Plays, Pleasant and Unpleasant,* which consists of these four plays, Shaw told of the circumstances of their composition; pleaded for more commercial productions, however deficient managers, actors, and audiences may be; and manifested the view that underlies his drama: "To me the tragedy and comedy of life lie in the consequences, sometimes terrible, sometimes ludicrous, of our persistent attempts to found our institutions on the ideals suggested to our imaginations by our half-satisfied passions, instead of on a genuinely scientific natural history." See also the entries on the four plays and on PLAYS UNPLEASANT.

PLAY'S THE THING, THE (*Játék a kastélyban,* literally, "play in the castle"), a comedy in three acts by FERENC MOLNÁR, published and produced in 1924. Setting: a castle on the Italian Riviera, early 1920's.

This sophisticated and very amusing work,

adapted by P. G. Wodehouse (1881–   ), was one of Molnár's Broadway hits. There are echoes of Pirandello's SIX CHARACTERS IN SEARCH OF AN AUTHOR as Turai and his collaborator discuss and experiment with their scenes. Most of the humor is in the dialogue of Turai and the castle's wry footman, and in the discomfiture of the actor, an aging Don Juan with a wife and four children, whom Turai threatens with scandal and humiliates in his play.

An elderly dramatist, Sándor Turai, is working with a collaborator and a young composer who madly loves his fiancée, an actress and singer. Turai and the young lover overhear a famous actor paying elaborate court to the not-too-reluctant fiancée, who was once his mistress. To keep the heartbroken young composer from committing suicide and to save the engagement, the cynical Turai immediately writes a play that incorporates the overheard love scene. He thus succeeds in making it appear that it was an innocent rehearsal.

PLAYS UNPLEASANT (1898), by BERNARD SHAW: WIDOWERS' HOUSES, MRS. WARREN'S PROFESSION, and THE PHILANDERER.

In the preface to this first collection of his plays and the first volume of *Plays, Pleasant and Unpleasant,* Shaw told how his "normal" view of reality made him a failure as a novelist but a success as a critic. When he felt that he began to repeat himself, he decided to publish his plays. He deplored their censorship in the theatres, but welcomed the possibility of reaching a wider audience by publishing them. A further advantage of publication, he noted, is that the dramatist, through detailed stage directions, can present the plays exactly as he envisions them and is not at the mercy of the usual poor stage productions. Finally, he explained the application of the label "Unpleasant" to each of these plays. See also the entries on these three plays and on PLAYS PLEASANT.

PLEASURE OF HONESTY, THE (*Il piacere dell'onestà*), a comedy in three acts by LUIGI PIRANDELLO, produced in 1917 and published in 1918. Setting: a town in contemporary central Italy.

As in IT IS REALLY NOT SERIOUS, this play portrays the transformation of a mock marriage (the characteristically Pirandellian "mask") into a true one (reality). Despite long, often abstract rhetorical speeches, the play is compelling. Pirandello considered it among his best.

Act I. The Marquis Fabio Colli, separated from a dissolute wife, has become Agata Renni's lover. Agata could not "resist the spontaneous impulse to show him . . . that there are women who will return your love," according to her mother, a penitent accomplice in the intrigue. Now Agata is pregnant, and to save appearances Colli and the mother, both of them conventionally moral and respectable weaklings, arrange a *pro forma* marriage. Their man is Angelo Baldovino, a strange, profligate intellectual who, embittered by life, has renounced emotion and sentiment for reason and logic. Bankrupt and considered dishonest because he has been unable to pay some trifling debts, he agrees to marry Agata—but on the condition of uncompromising honesty henceforth for all of them. As he tells Colli, "You'll have to respect not me, but the form, the form I represent: the honest husband of a respectable woman."

Act II. Baldovino adheres to the form of honesty zealously and rigorously. Agata's lover and mother had intended to get rid of him after the baby's birth, but he is incorruptible and sees through them. "You know I have this horrible beast in me, this creature I freed myself from by chaining it here, in the conditions imposed by our agreement," he tells a friend in a revealing moment: "It's in their own best interest to see that I continue to respect those conditions, as I firmly wish to do, because, once unchained, today or tomorrow, who knows where the beast will lead me, what will become of me?" He rules his home, as well as the banking firm Colli has founded for him, with great ability and unanswerable logic—gaining nothing for himself, as he remarks, but living "*deliciously* in the absolute of a pure, abstract form." He easily prevails over their artificial and superficial morality because he justifies everything by the demands of honesty. The others are confounded when Agata herself decides on the child's unfashionable baptism in church in opposition to their wishes—and in accord with Baldovino's. She persists in warding off Colli as long as Baldovino remains her husband—if only in name. Her desperate lover concocts a financial plot to trap and disgrace Baldovino, who sees through it easily, but also senses his growing love for Agata. If he were to let it flower, his life of abstract logic would end. Then "the beast" would emerge, the mask would drop. Therefore he confronts Colli with his despicable act but, in effect, agrees to leave: "The pleasure of honesty isn't worth it."

Act III. But the financiers as well as the family now find their welfare dependent on Baldovino's continued presence with them. His adamant refusal to remain is changed only when he realizes that Agata is no longer acting out of concern for appearances. She has learned to respect and love him, and now feels herself his wife in fact—and is prepared to accompany him wherever he may go and help him in whatever he may do. Then the "black blood that is full of the bitter poison of my memories" vanishes from his consciousness. "With immense joy"—the final "pleasure of honesty"—Baldovino recognizes that the idealistic mask he wore has become his human reality: the grotesque "beast" that chafed under the intellectual perfectionism and rhetoric is replaced by a loving and beloved husband.

PLEBEIANS REHEARSE THE UPRISING, THE (*Die Plebejer proben den Aufstand*), "a German tragedy" in four acts by GÜNTER GRASS, published and produced in 1966. Setting: an East Berlin theatre; June 17, 1953.

"The Boss" in the play is BERTOLT BRECHT, who rehearsed his Berliner Ensemble during the

The Plebeians Rehearse the Uprising. The Boss (Rolf Henniger) talks to the workers. Berlin, 1968. (*German Information Center*)

abortive insurrection. In a mixture of prose and poetry (some of it from *Coriolanus*, though actually Brecht rehearsed another play at the time), this controversial though commercially not very successful drama probes Brecht's paradoxical character and his failure to support freedom and justice. The play was published with Grass's extensive commentary ("The Prehistory and Post-history of the Tragedy of *Coriolanus* from Livy and Plutarch via Shakespeare down to Brecht and Myself") and a "Documentary Report" on the East Berlin events of June 16 and 17.

As The Boss rehearses the company in his adaptation of Shakespeare's *Coriolanus*, workers rioting against increased production norms appear in the theatre and ask him to draw up and publicly support their manifesto. "You're internationally known, you're, well— / A name to reckon with," they say, and an actress adds, "A few words from you will give their stammering meaning." The Boss does not turn them down directly. "I'm curious to know which will come off better in the end: nature or my theatre," he says, making notes for his *Coriolanus*, which also deals with revolution. Cynically he tells the workers that they "will not even have the courage to step on the lawn," which provokes them to trample on the setting. The proclamation he finally composes is so ambiguous that the workers angrily start to hang him and his assistant. The two talk themselves free and supply the workers with beer, after which The Boss plays back this episode, which he has taped on his recorder. But he also recognizes his betrayal of the revolt: "What did I say? It doesn't touch me. / The Holy Spirit breathed, and I mistook / It for a draft, and cried: / Who's come here to molest me?" He agrees to write a letter to the government. It is feeble and embarrassing, a "pussyfooting document," an actress remarks, that first criticizes, but then supports the government. Only the latter part will be publicized, the actress knows, and it will encourage contradictory legends about The Boss as a "cynical opportunist" and as a "home-grown idealist." But though The Boss admits feeling ashamed, he sends the letter off to save his state-supported theatre. Then he cancels his *Coriolanus* and goes to the country to rest—and write poetry. He looks at his tape recorder and realizes he is "condemned to live forever with voices in my ears. You. You. I'll tell you. Do you know what you are? You, you, you're a . . ." Leaving, he indicts all artists and intellectuals and others who cower before tyranny: "You poor babes in the woods! Bowed down with guilt, I accuse you!"

PLIEVIER, Theodor (1892–1955), German writer, was best known for his left-wing, journalistic novels, particularly for a trilogy about World War II and for *Des Kaisers Kulis* (1930), which deals with the 1918 Kiel mutiny. Made into a play in 1930, it was premiered the same night as was ERNST TOLLER's *Draw the Fires!*, which dramatizes the same events. Plievier's other play, *Haifische*, also appeared in 1930.

Born in Berlin to poor working people, the anti-Nazi Plievier fled to Russia in 1933, but returned to (American-occupied) Germany in 1947. His phenomenally popular *Stalingrad* (1946), a documentary novel about the German army's disastrous siege, was dramatized by CLAUS HUBALEK in 1961.

PLOUGH AND THE STARS, THE, a tragedy in four acts by SEAN O'CASEY, published and produced in 1926. Setting: Dublin; November 1915 and Easter Week, 1916.

The background and themes of the anti-British Easter Rebellion here portrayed are revealed in O'Casey's biographies and in his *The Story of the Irish Citizen Army* (1919). The title alludes to the flag of this army, whose plough and stars symbolize the workers' ideal and reality. The ironic tragicomedy of the dichotomy between this ideal and reality permeates the play. Turbulent, lusty, and richly orchestrated, it teems with actions and characters—all of whom constitute a "mass" hero, or, rather, antihero. The Abbey Theatre riot at the premiere, caused by patriots' objections to the portrayal of Irish lowlife (including whoring and looting) amidst the struggle for high ideals, resembled the one against Synge's THE PLAYBOY OF THE WESTERN WORLD twenty years earlier. This and JUNO AND THE PAYCOCK are usually acclaimed O'Casey's masterpieces.

Act I. In the tenement apartment of Jack Clitheroe, a bricklayer, and his attractive young wife, Nora, various people react to poverty and intimations of war (the Easter Rebellion). Clitheroe is eager to leave the tenement and be a leader in battle, while the sensitive Nora seeks beauty and romance in her home and marriage. Their relatives are a fussy laborer who likes splendid uniforms, and the young Covey, a party-line Socialist. Others are a loudmouthed yet inherently brave, sensible, and decent carpenter, Fluther Good; a hard and coarsened loyalist fruit-vendor, Bessie Burgess; and a nervous charwoman who has a consumptive child. Outside, worker demonstrators prepare a march. Inside, there is comic bickering. At the height of the arguments Nora comes in. Her peace-making is interrupted by Bessie. She tongue-lashes the frightened Nora for her complaints about singing at night when Bessie "has a few up." Clitheroe now comes home and gets rid of Bessie, and the family have dinner. Then the Clitheroes are alone. Their romantic scene ends when he is invited to join the Citizen Army and is told he has been given the command he yearns for. Nora had destroyed the notification of his appointment without telling him about it, and now implores him to stay home: "Because they've made an officer of you, you'll make a glorious cause of what you're doin', while your little red-lipp'd Nora can go on sittin' here . . ." But Clitheroe leaves his now-bitter wife. A departing regiment's chorus of "Tipperary" is heard. Bessie angrily says, "There's th' men marchin' out into th' dhread dimness o' danger, while th' lice is crawlin' about feedin' on th' fatness o' the land! But yous'll not escape from th' arrow that flieth be night, or th' sickness that wasteth be day." And the charwoman's tubercular daughter asks Nora, "Is there anybody goin', Mrs. Clitheroe, with a titther o' sense?"

Act II. Outside a pub there is a fiery meeting of the Independents. (The addresses include snatches from Padraig Pearse's proclamation of the Irish Republic.) Activities inside the pub provide ironic counterpoint and commentary. A pretty young prostitute complains about business: "They're all thinkin' of higher things than a girl's garthers." During the speeches, Fluther, the Covey, the laborer, and others come for drinks. The laborer feels inspired by the meeting. But the Covey, rejecting the prostitute's overtures, sneers, "There's only one freedom for th' workin' man: conthrol o' th' means o' production . . ." The charwoman and Bessie start arguing politics, and then insult and fight each other. While the speeches outside extol the "sanctity of bloodshed," Fluther argues with the Covey; though he maintains that "it would take something more than a thing like you to flutther a feather o' Fluther," he angrily kicks the Covey out when he insults the prostitute. Then Fluther invites her for a drink. The excited leaders vow to give their all for Ireland, and Fluther leaves happily and tipsily with the prostitute, their arms around each other and she singing a lusty, amorous song. Clitheroe's voice is heard outside, commanding units of the army.

Act III. Easter Week, 1916. In front of the Clitheroes' house the various disputants of the pub are discussing the rebellion when Fluther carries in Nora. The pregnant young wife has unsuccessfully sought her husband amidst the battle lines. She is exhausted and has been saved only by Fluther's heroism. The men fight only out of fear, she knows: "They're afraid to say they're afraid." Hysterical with worry about her husband, she deplores the war that has "dhriven away th' little happiness life had to spare for me." Bessie, watching the battle from the window, angers the others with her harangue, complaining about the disloyalty against the English as well as the cowardice of the Irish who are not fighting; and the Socialist Covey sneers about its being the wrong fight. Then, while the firing continues, the looting of stores begins, and Bessie and the charwoman argue over a pram in which they want to haul back their loot. Clitheroe returns unhurt, but one of the other leaders is dying of a stomach wound. Nora embraces her husband, begging him not to rejoin the madness outside. But he soon flings her off and leaves. The distraught wife starts losing her mind and screaming as her labor pains begin. The tenement dwellers return with their loot. Fluther is singing, too drunk to help, and the others are too scared. Saying a brief prayer, Bessie bravely departs through the bullet-ridden streets to seek a doctor for Nora.

Act IV. It is a few days later and the tenement dwellers, sheltering from the street battle, are in Bessie's attic flat. Nora has lost her premature baby and is now mad. The charwoman's consumptive child, too, is dead. With great self-sacrifice, Bessie is taking care of Nora. As the men play cards, one of the officers comes to bring news of Clitheroe's death in "a gleam of glory." But though he talks of heroism, the officer is afraid to return to the hopeless battle, which he has been able to escape only by changing into his worker's clothes. British soldiers enter. Despite their bravado, the men are taken out for custody in a church. The deranged Nora stands by the window and is saved from being shot only because Bessie interposes herself. Fatally wounded, Bessie dies singing a hymn. Artillery fire is heard outside, the rebels are wiped out, red fire flares are reflected on the window, and the English soldiers, back and relaxing over a cup of tea, join in the chorus of the soldiers heard singing offstage: "Keep the 'owme fires burning, / While your 'earts are yearning; / . . . Turn the dark cloud inside out, / Till the boys come 'owme!"

POGODIN [originally Stukalov], **Nikolai Fyodorovich** (1900–62), Russian playwright, was among the most popular and prolific Soviet dramatists of his age. Though his plays exemplify Soviet dogma and sloganeering, Pogodin was able to sustain their appeal by focusing on current events and enriching his dramatizations with tolerance toward the problems of youth and with his considerable powers of observation of common people (he excelled in crowd scenes) as well as party dignitaries. His were the first stage depictions of Lenin: *Kremlyovskie kuranti* (THE CHIMES OF THE KREMLIN, 1940), one of Pogodin's most frequently produced plays, is the second of a trilogy on the subject that opened with *Chelovek s ruzhyom* (1937). A popular Stalin Prize winner set on the eve of the Russian Revolution and caricaturing capitalists, officers, and Mensheviks, *Chelovek s ruzhyom* is an episodic play whose title protagonist ("the man with the gun") is a common soldier going to the front, but whose real heroes are the leaders he encounters, Lenin and Stalin. *Tretya pateticheskaya* (1958, produced in London twelve years later as *Lenin—The Third Pathetique*), the concluding play, deals with Lenin's death but, in accord with Soviet policies in 1958, Stalin is not even mentioned and Lenin attacks modern art in words that echo Khrushchev's pronouncements. Among Pogodin's other important earlier works are *Temp* (TEMPO, 1930), his first play, and *Aristokraty* (ARISTOCRATS, 1934).

Pogodin was born in a Cossack town on the Don, in Tambov. His parents were poor peasants, and Pogodin had little formal education. After a series of manual jobs he started to write. He became a correspondent for *Pravda* when he was twenty, and remained with that newspaper until he turned to playwriting ten years later. His other works are also characterized by zealous adherence to the Party line, and by topical settings and effective dramaturgy. They reflect Pogodin's consistent optimism about reconstruction, and they feature the new Soviet Man. He is invariably ebullient and comradely, and his private interests are the same as—or subsumed by—those of society.

Poema o topore (1931) deals with the problems depicted in his first play and culminates in the invention of a stainless-steel ax. The hero of *Moi drug* (1932) is a construction chief who overcomes the usual obstacles, a new Soviet Man who is more rounded than the protagonists of the earlier plays. *Sneg* (1932), featuring a Caucasus Mountain expedition, and *Posle bala* (1934), a mixture of farce and melodrama set on a collective farm, were followed by his popular *The Aristocrats* and *Chelovek s ruzhyom*. *Gioconda* (1938), one of his few depictions of a private life, dramatizes the story of a rest-home patient who falls in love with a woman whose smile resembles that of the Mona Lisa. It was followed by *Pyad serebryanaya* (1939), which warned of the Japanese threat at the Manchurian border; and by *Mol* (1939), whose middle-class wife, "the moth" of the title, fails to subvert the ideals of her aviator husband.

After the immensely successful *The Chimes of the Kremlin* Pogodin produced two war plays: *Moskovskie nochi* (1942), a dramatization of the siege of Moscow in the winter of 1941–42; and *Lodochnitsa* (1943), about a Soviet heroine who transports soldiers and food to besieged Stalingrad, a play that was criticized for profaning a revered subject with a "ridiculous aquatic pantomime." These were followed by *Sotvorenie mira* (*The Creation of the World*, 1946), whose title describes the rebuilding of a town totally demolished by the Nazis, while separated lovers and family survivors attempt to reunite—affectingly portrayed in accord with Party-line optimism, though Pogodin was criticized for failing to present and unmask the villains who had collaborated with the enemy; *Missuriisky vals* (1949), an anti-American propaganda play ridiculing President Truman; *Kogda lomaytsya kopya* (1953), a comedy; *Mi vtroyom poyechali na tselinu* (1955), which dramatized Premier Khrushchev's agricultural directive; and the atypical *Sonet Petrarki* (*A Petrarchan Sonnet,* 1956). This last play not only deals with personal problems—it is a love story—but it also challenges the Party's intransigence and attempts to interfere in the "Petrarchan love" of an elderly man and a younger woman. Aside from the third Lenin play, Pogodin's final works include *Malenkaya studentka* (1958) and *Albert Einstein* (1961). Pogodin tore up and completely rewrote the manuscript of this last play after a trip to the United States; originally it had reflected Pogodin's anti-American views, which were altered by his visit.

In his last years Pogodin edited *Teatr* and enhanced that periodical's artistic stature. Pogodin also wrote fiction, film scripts, and a book on theory, *O dramaturgii* (1934). Perhaps the foremost Soviet playwright—he won a Stalin Prize in 1941 and a Lenin Prize in 1959—Pogodin was little known elsewhere though a number of his plays are available in English: *Tempo* in Eugene Lyons's *Six Soviet Plays* (1934), *The Aristocrats* in Ben Blake's *Four Soviet Plays* (1937), *The Chimes of the Kremlin* in Alexander Bakshy's *Soviet Scene: Six Plays of Russian Life* (1946), and *A Petrarchan Sonnet* in Franklin D. Reeve's *Contemporary Russian Drama* (1968), all with brief notes on Pogodin. A revealing account of some of his work, particularly *The Chimes of the Kremlin,* appears in Viktor Komissarzhevsky's *Moscow Theatres* (1959), a handsome Soviet book available in English. For the opposite ideological viewpoint, see Nikolai A. Gorchakov's more scholarly account on some of Pogodin's work in *The Theater in Soviet Russia* (1957).

POLAND. Modern Polish drama was little known in the English-speaking world until very recent times. Polish fiction became world famous with the work of the Nobel Prize novelists Henryk Sienkiewicz and Władysław Stanisław Reymont. Not a single native dramatist, however, has achieved comparable international stature.

Partitioned among Russia, Prussia, and Austria until 1918, modern Poland enjoyed only brief independence—in the period between the two world wars. During World War II it was occupied by Nazi Germany, and though it became nominally independent in 1945, Poland was at once absorbed into the Soviet orbit. Nonetheless, its intellectual and artistic life has never been as monolithically conformist as that of the Soviet Union. The post-Stalin "thaw" that came in the mid-1950's and the "little revolution" (October 1956) were followed by a literary, artistic, and especially a cinematic revival which was rooted in Polish traditions as well as in the general mainstream of Western culture. Concerned with such themes as freedom, human identity, and social justice, Poland's new literature—frequently one of protest—manifested itself primarily in poetry and fiction. But some of the important new writers in those genres—particularly TADEUSZ RÓŻEWICZ (whose plays appeared also in America) and ZBIGNIEW HERBERT—distinguished themselves as dramatists, too. And though plays were always chosen and "digested" by state theatres "to meet the needs" of Polish audiences, significant new playwrights emerged in the 1960's. Especially interesting are ROMAN BRANDSTAETTER, JERZY BROSZKIEWICZ, and SŁAWOMIR MROŻEK; the last-named impressed audiences far beyond his native Poland.

The most important early modern playwright of note was Count Aleksander Fredro (1793–1876), the prolific "Polish Molière" and his country's preeminent comic playwright, whose masterpieces are the romantic *Śluby panieńskie* (*Maidens' Vows,* 1833) and *Zemsta* (*Vengeance,* 1833). Major poet-dramatists of Polish romanticism—Adam Mickiewicz (1798–1855), Juliusz Słowacki (1809–49), and Zygmunt Krasiński (1812–59)—have become influential in the development of twentieth-century Polish drama and theatre. Fredro was followed in the latter part of the century by such other comic playwrights as MICHAŁ BAŁUCKI and Józef Bliziński (1827–93), the most popular of whose dozen comedies were the still-revived social satires of the landed gentry *Pan Damazy* (*Mr. Damazy,* 1877) and *Rozbitki* (1881). Among other early modern Polish playwrights were Tadeusz Miciński (1873–1919), a lyric poet whose historical dramas include *Kniaź Potemkin* (*Count Potemkin,* 1907), a depiction of the mutiny in a half-NATURALISTIC, half-SYMBOLIC and mystic manner that employs the figures of Christ and Lucifer; and the immensely popular theatre man Kazimierz Zalewski (1849–1919), who in the 1880's and 1890's produced many long-lasting, if slight, romantic hits about fashionable society.

There was a literary resurgence in Poland during those decades near the end and at the turn of the century. STANISŁAW PRZYBYSZEWSKI was hailed as its first writer and as the "founder of Polish modernism." STANISŁAW WYSPIAŃSKI achieved a native reputation approximating that of Shakespeare in Western Europe and America. His disciples included KARL HUBERT ROSTWOROWSKI and Ludwik Hieronim Morstin (1886–1966), a neoclassic poet and essayist whose outstanding drama was the poetic *Obrana Ksantypy* (*Xanthippe,* 1938), and whose other works are a high comedy on Odysseus's return (*Penelopa,* 1945) and a sympathetic portrayal of Cleopatra (*Kleopatra,* 1956). An antithesis of Wyspiański's poetic drama is that of the iconoclastic ADOLF NOWACZYŃSKI.

Jan August Kisielewski (1876–1918) wrote a number of satires of Krakow's provincialism and its devastating effects on individuals: Przybyszewski thought Kisielewski's *W sieci* (1899) comparable to Ibsen's GHOSTS as a "great and universal symbol" of that "unhappy" age. Other notable twentieth-century drama before World War I was written by JAN KASPROWICZ, STEFAN ŻEROMSKI, TADEUSZ RITTNER, LUCJAN RYDEL, GABRIELA ZAPOLSKA, and WŁODZIMIERZ PERZYŃSKI. There were a few dramatists of note between the two world wars while Poland was independent: WITOLD GOMBROWICZ's reputation began to spread in the 1950's; JERZY SZANIAWSKI was for a while thought to have augured a renaissance that did not, in fact, materialize; ANTONI CWOJDZIŃSKI achieved popularity with his meretricious "science" plays; and ZOFIA NAŁKOWSKA was preeminent primarily as a novelist. Maria Morozowicz-Szczepkowska (1886 or 1889–), a successful 1930's author of family dramas, is remembered only for her *Sprawa Moniki* (*Dr. Monica,* 1933); this three-character (all female) play about a childless physician whose life is wrecked by her husband's infidelities was produced on Broadway in 1934 and filmed in 1935. The physicist-playwright Bruno Winawer (1883–1944), who wrote SHAVian comedies on contemporary social problems, is notable for *Księga Hioba* (*The Book of Job,* 1921), his portrayal of the post-World War I degradation of a Warsaw scientist; JOSEPH CONRAD was so intrigued with this play that he translated it into English. Perhaps the most interesting dramatist of that period—though not a very popular one—is STANISŁAW IGNACY WITKIEWICZ, that genius experimenter in the arts, whose popularity burgeoned in the 1960's.

Among early writers to be produced again after the end of World War II (during which most of Poland's theatres were destroyed) was the novelist JAROSŁAW IWASZKIEWICZ, who had made his first hit in the mid-thirties. Konstanty Ildefons Gałczyński (1905–53), a poet particularly esteemed by postwar Polish youth, wrote a number of dramatic sketches and satires. The prominent Party official LEON KRUCKOWSKI, whose masterpiece *Niemcy* (1949) was the first significant Polish dramatization of contemporary issues, excelled in SOCIALIST REALISM that was emulated by Adam Tarn (1902–) in a comparable play, *Zwykła sprawa* (1951), which depicts Americans intimidated during the contemporary period of McCarthyism. Another important writer of socialist realism is Jerzy Lutowski (1923–), a physician whose plays include *Ostry dyżur* (*The Middle of the Operation,* 1956); its protagonist must perform emergency surgery on a Party functionary who has persecuted him. The poet-novelist-playwright Marian Pankowski (1918–), who was in four German concentration camps in World War II and subsequently taught in Brussels, wrote a concentration-camp drama that also satirizes East European democracies, *Teatrowanie nad Świętym Barsczem* (1969).

Interest in Polish drama has been stimulated in recent years by the productions of the renowned Polish Laboratory Theatre and the theories of its director, Jerzy Grotowski, published in his *Towards a Poor Theatre* (1968). Translations into English of works about Polish drama, hitherto scant, have begun to appear; among them are Manfred Kridl's scholarly and comprehensive *A Survey of Polish Literature and Culture* (1956) and Czeslaw Milosz's *The History of Polish Literature* (1969).

Informative individual articles appear in *World Theatre;* a complete number (Summer 1957) is devoted to the "Theatre in Poland," and the 1962 volume (pp. 288–93) includes Andrzej Wladyslaw Kral's "The Rebirth of the Polish Drama." Edward Csato's *The Polish Theatre* (1963) is a handsome, illustrated volume that has interesting information about Polish drama as well as the theatre. Bołeslaw Taborski's *Polish Plays in English Translations: A Bibliography* (1968) includes, as well, thumbnail sketches of some eighty authors; brief synopses of all their translated plays; and a seven-page bibliography of studies in English of Polish playwrights, drama, and theatre.

POLICE, THE (*Policjanci*), a comedy in three acts by SŁAWOMIR MROŻEK, produced in 1958 and published in 1959. Setting: a mythical European kingdom.

This popular satire of the contemporary police state was also presented as *The Policemen* in England and America. Mrożek's first play, it is farcically boisterous and irreverent. Nonetheless, it was produced successfully in Poland and other East European countries.

The state's last remaining prisoner has "experienced a crisis" and abjures his subversive ideas. He insists on signing an oath of allegiance to the infant king and his uncle, the regent, and therefore must be released. The police commissioner and his sergeant despair of their jobs, for now all citizens "have gone cruelly, wildly, bestially loyal." To save the police department from utter extinction, the commissioner persuades the sergeant to become a martyr. "You're the incarnation of the police-mystique—a policeman-saint!" he says flatteringly. Then he coaches the sergeant in shouting treasonable criticisms of the state, characterizing the king as a dwarf and the regent as "a queer." Arrested and imprisoned, the sergeant gradually becomes truly subversive. He throws a bomb at a general—who escapes to the toilet and thus remains unharmed. But in the ensuing confusion everyone arrests everyone else. "The rebel in him completely awakened," the sergeant shouts, "Long Live Liberty."

POLLOCK, Channing (1880–1946), American theatre critic and dramatist, wrote over thirty plays, including farces, melodramas, musical-comedy librettos, and thesis plays. He dramatized Frank Norris's *The Pit* (1903) the year after its publication, collaborated on AVERY HOPWOOD's first drama, *Clothes* (1906), and later wrote plays that propagandized for pacifism (*The Enemy,* 1925), honesty in a capitalist society (*Mr. Moneypenny,* 1928), and other ideals. Some of these plays are allegorical, such as *The House Beautiful* (1931), in which a wife views her clerk husband as a legendary hero. As Pollock's success as a playwright diminished, he turned to lecturing and to other writings. These include the popular Fanny Brice song "My Man," and volumes of memoirs and personal philosophy like *The Adventures of a Happy Man* (1939, augmented in 1946) and *Harvest of My Years* (1943).

POOR BITOS (*Pauvre Bitos, ou le dîner de têtes*), a play in three acts by JEAN ANOUILH, published and produced in 1956. Setting: the hall of a historic Carmelite priory in a French town, 1955.

Not unlike Pirandello's HENRY IV, *Poor Bitos* (one of Anouilh's "grating" plays) merges two periods. The French subtitle is a pun; it means both "wig party" and a "dinner where heads will fall."

André Bitos is a fanatic, a wartime resistance fighter who still tracks down and prosecutes Occupation collaborators. When he was a boy supported by scholarships and his washerwoman mother, his self-righteousness and intellectual zeal had infuriated his fellow students. Avenging themselves on Bitos, now a leading "incorruptible" citizen in town, they invite him to a "*dîner de têtes*" at which all masquerade as characters of the Reign of Terror. As Robespierre, Bitos is cruelly humiliated by "Saint-Just" (his host), "Danton," "Mirabeau," and other former schoolmates, now wealthy society who resent the ruthless puritan as a "second rate" upstart. Bitos faints when he recognizes the assailant of Robespierre as one of his judicial victims. In a dream Bitos relives his life as Robespierre, rising to bloody eminence because of his poverty and suffering as a child, and still despised. "Poor Robespierre, who kills because he couldn't succeed in growing up," says "Lucile Demoulins," impersonated by a girl whose family has spurned Bitos. She warns him against accompanying his tormentors, who plan further humiliations. Quickly sobered, Bitos thanks her. But he vows vengeance—and "you are the one I shall start with." He escapes and the girl murmurs, "Poor Bitos . . ."

POOR HEINRICH (*Der arme Heinrich*), a verse drama in five acts by GERHART HAUPTMANN, published and produced in 1902. Setting: medieval Germany.

This long play, translated also as *Henry of Auë* and subtitled "a German legend," is in blank verse. It dramatizes (frequently merely narrates) a story also told in Longfellow's *Golden Legend.*

When Heinrich von Auë, a knight, is stricken with leprosy, he escapes into the wilderness mad with grief. He can be cured "If but a maiden pure and virginal / In willing faith yield herself unto a knife." Ottegebe, a peasant girl, persuades Heinrich to let her sacrifice her life for him. During his journey with her Heinrich's despairing bitterness turns to love, and at the fatal moment he saves Ottegebe from the sacrificial rack. That selfless act miraculously heals him. When Ottegebe recognizes her feelings for Heinrich as being divine, not only earthy (as she had feared), they can marry. Both are united and redeemed "in the eternal universe of love."

PORGY, a play in four acts by DOROTHY and DUBOSE HEYWARD, published and produced in 1927.

Porgy as opera. Last scene: Porgy (William Warfield, center) learns from his Catfish Row neighbors that Bess is gone. Texas State Fair Music Hall, 1952. (*Brown Brothers*)

Setting: Catfish Row (a Negro tenement district in Charleston, South Carolina) and nearby Kittiwah Island, 1920's.

A dramatization of DuBose Heyward's 1925 novel by the same name, this is a colorful and panoramic folk drama. Its many Negro spirituals suggested to George Gershwin the possibility of transforming the popular play into a folk opera. The resulting *Porgy and Bess* (1935, libretto by Ira Gershwin and DuBose Heyward) became a classic—America's outstanding and most frequently produced opera.

Act I. A group of Negroes are shooting dice. They include Crown, a powerful bully; Sporting Life, a dope peddler; and Porgy, a crippled beggar who uses a goat cart in place of his paralyzed legs. The drunken Crown fights with the crap-game winner and kills him. "Wake up an' hit it out," his girl, Bess, urges the dazed Crown: "de police'll be comin'." Homeless and penniless without Crown, the hussy Bess is denied shelter by all but Sporting Life, who wants her to be his woman now. "I ain't come to dat yet," Bess proudly tells the gay blade, and goes to Porgy, who has long loved her and does not shut his door in her face. In the room of the murdered man, the Negroes sing a dirge over his body and try to fill the collection plate for his burial. Porgy comes in with Bess. Though the others snub her, they accept Bess's donation when Porgy says the money is his. White detectives arrest a deaf old Negro as a witness of the murder. Later the slain man's widow pleads with the Negro undertaker to bury her husband, for otherwise the cadaver will be used by medical students. When the undertaker agrees to do so, the Negroes sing a joyful spiritual.

Act II. It is six months later and Bess now is Porgy's woman. She is off liquor and dope, but the other women still spurn her. A Negro lawyer persuades Porgy to "buy a divorce" from Crown for Bess. The deaf old Negro is freed with the help of a friendly white man, who warns the lawyer to stop selling phony divorces and asks Porgy not to hitch his smelly goat under the white man's window. A hovering buzzard agitates the superstitious Negroes, who quickly chase if off. Sporting Life tempts Bess with "happy dust" (cocaine), and tries to get her to accompany him to New York—but suddenly Porgy appears and, using his powerful grip, sends Sporting Life away. Bess is eager to participate in the traditional Kittiwah Island picnic, but the women still cold-shoulder her. Finally one of them relents, and Porgy happily sends Bess along. As soon as he is alone, the shadow of a buzzard the crippled Porgy cannot by himself chase off frightens him. The picnickers are leaving Kittiwah Island when Crown emerges from the palmetto jungle, where he has been hiding ever since the murder.

Bess tries to resist him, but fails. "I knows yo' ain't change'!" he tells her when Bess protests that she is now Porgy's woman and "libin' decent": "Wid yo' an' me, it always goin' be de same. See?"

Act III. A week later Bess is back in Catfish Row, sick and delirious. All realize she has met Crown. "She lobe Porgy" and knows he is good for her, a neighbor remarks: "But, ef dat nigger [Crown] come after she, dey ain't going' be nobody 'round here but Porgy an' de goat." Porgy has the delirious Bess exorcised of her "debil," and rejoices when she recuperates. Though he knows she met Crown, Porgy still loves Bess and wants her to stay with him. Bess tells Porgy she loves him, but admits worrying about Crown's influence on her: "Ef he jus' don' put dem hot han' on me, I can be good! I can 'membuh! I can be happy!" During a hurricane, the Negroes huddle together in panic. Suddenly Crown comes in. He has braved the elements and swaggers about braving God. "Gawd an' me frien'" now, he says, as the terrified Negroes sing. Insisting he will have Bess, Crown gets the others to forget their fear in a dance. Suddenly they see a capsized fishing boat. The fisherman's wife hands her infant to Bess and rushes out into the storm. Only Crown has the courage to follow her; all watch in horror, pray, and sing as the wharf crashes about them both.

Act IV. They are sure Crown is dead, and Bess is determined to remain good. God knows she now is "different inside," she says: "He wouldn't ha' gib' me Porgy if he didn't want to gib me my chance." Sporting Life alone is convinced Crown still is alive. Soon, indeed, Crown appears and stealthily enters Porgy's door. Suddenly there is a thud, and then Porgy laughs a "deep, swelling, lustful" laugh. "Yo' gots Porgy now, an' he look atter he 'oman," he tells Bess: "Yo' gots a *man* now!" Detectives seek Crown's killer, whom they believe to be his earlier victim's widow. They summon Porgy to identify the corpse. Porgy's terror mounts when Sporting Life describes how, "when de man what done um goes in dat room, Crown' wounds begin to bleed." Porgy tries to escape and is imprisoned for contempt of the court summons. He will be locked away for a year, Sporting Life assures Bess, offering her "happy dust" to "scare away de lonesome blues" and urging her to accompany him to New York. She tries to resist, but temptation in the face of Porgy's expected long imprisonment overwhelms her. A week later Porgy, his sentence served, returns from jail, loaded with gifts for Bess. His neighbors attempt to persuade him that he is better off without her: "Dat gal ain't neber had Gawd in she heart, an' de debil get um at last." But brushing aside all warnings, Porgy asks for the way to New York—and drives his goat cart north, to find his Bess.

PORT-ROYAL, a one-act play by HENRY DE MONTHERLANT, published and produced in 1954. Setting: the monastery of Port Royal, in Paris; 1664.

Originally in four unpublished and unproduced acts completed in 1942, this historical play later was rewritten and became the last of Montherlant's "*autos sacramentales.*" In his preface to this inner, psychological drama, Montherlant alluded to the stark tragedy of the Greeks and of Racine.

In two distinct actions of this full-length play, spiritual force (the Jansenite reformers) is juxtaposed with worldly power (Church and State). The twelve Jansenite nuns, led by their abbess, Angélique Arnauld, are confronted by the Archbishop of Paris and his men-at-arms. Refusing to follow the papal instructions to denounce Jansenism, and betrayed by a Judas-like fellow nun, the sisters submit to persecution by the Church and let themselves be deported from their convent.

PORTO-RICHE, Georges de (1849–1930), French dramatist and poet, wrote about a dozen plays, most of them about love. He rightly surmised that his name, if it lived at all, would be in "*l'histoire du cœur*" and for the most notable among his depictions of "the history of the heart," *Amoureuse* (THE LOVING WOMAN, 1891). It is characteristically Porto-Richean in its avoidance of the facile tricks of the WELL-MADE PLAY and in its NATURALISTIC dissection of the physiology and psychology of passion. His other works are nearly forgotten now. But this play was highly praised by (among others) the critic Francisque Sarcey and by JULES LEMAÎTRE, and was often revived. Its importance as a landmark of early modern French drama is considered second only to that of Becque's THE VULTURES.

Born in Bordeaux of Jewish-Italian extraction, Porto-Riche as a child was abnormally sensitive and felt neglected and lonesome. After extensive travels with his parents, he was sent to a boarding school. At sixteen he was apprenticed in a bank and then in his father's business. Later he studied law, but continued to indulge his literary interests. He published three slim volumes of poetry between 1872 and 1877, gave up law, and spent his time traveling and writing. His first dramas are insignificant one-acters and a romantic full-length play, *Un Drame sous Philippe II* (1875); a verse dramatization of history, the latter was not very successful. Not until he came out with *La Chance de Françoise* (*Françoise' Luck*) did he make his reputation; a subtly comic one-act study of a modern Don Juan, it was initially staged by André Antoine in 1888 at the Théâtre-Libre and frequently revived (in New York as *Lover's Luck,* 1916). Porto-Riche's next play, the poetic *L'Infidèle,* is about a *crime passionelle;* it shocked its contemporaries when first produced in 1890, but impressed critics. It was followed by Porto-Riche's masterpiece, *The Loving Woman.*

Even more esteemed by critics was *Le Passé* (1897), which in a relatively restrained manner dramatizes the love of a liar and his devoted mistress; but it failed to impress Odéon Theatre audiences, who had only two nights earlier attended the premiere of Rostand's CYRANO DE BERGERAC. After a tender middle-class comedy, *Les Malfilâtre* (1904), came the long-awaited play on which Porto-Riche had been working for fifteen years, *Le Vieil Homme*. Produced in 1911 and highly praised by Léon Blum and others (and successfully revived in 1923), this enormously long play (over four hundred printed pages) depicts a reformed roué, "the old man" whose backsliding destroys his son. Porto-Riche's remaining plays are *Zubiri* (1912), a one-act comedy; *Le Marchand d'estampes* (1917), a love drama intensified by the tragedy of war; and *Les Vrais Dieux* (1929), his last work, whose title neatly summarizes Porto-Riche's lifelong concern with "the true gods" of love, here portrayed in a classical setting. The starkly dramatized, turbulent struggles in his plays are caused by the lovers' own natures rather than by outside forces. For that reason the drama of Porto-Riche has been rightly termed a bridge between that of Racine's classicism and the later modern erotic theatre. Elected to the French Academy in 1923, Porto-Riche was probably the major influence on playwrights such as MAURICE DONNAY and HENRY BATAILLE.

Porto-Riche's plays were collected in four volumes (1898–1929). *Four Plays of the Free Theatre* (1915), which includes *Françoise' Luck*, has an informative introduction on Porto-Riche by Barrett H. Clark.

PORTUGAL,* in contrast to its Iberian neighbor, has produced little noteworthy modern drama. Derivative of the drama of SPAIN and FRANCE, the best Portuguese drama has consisted of bedroom farces and skits—and of *théâtre de fauteuil,* unproduced plays. During the long rule (1932–68) of Salazar, when strict censorship was enforced, playwrights prudently refrained from criticizing his dictatorship.

Skits are traditional in Portuguese drama and were the stock in trade of its founder and most celebrated author, Gil Vicente (1465–1536?). The foremost "modern" playwright was Almeida Garrett (1799–1854), a liberal leader who wrote romantic novels and poetry as well as plays—his masterpiece is a sixteenth-century tragedy, *Frei Luís de Sousa* (1843)—and founded a National Theatre. By the early 1970's no playwright of comparable stature had yet appeared.

Júlio Dantas (1876–1962) was one of the very few whose plays were even translated (into French and Spanish); verse dramas dealing with both history and modern Lisbon life, they include the three-monologue play *A Ceia dos Cardeais* (1902) and a deftly constructed piece for two characters, *Rosas de Todo o Ano* (1907). Poets occasionally essayed the drama, but more successful were the NATURALIST plays of Raul Brandão (1867–1930); Alfredo Cortês (1880–1946), whose big hit was *Tá-Mar* (1936); and Ramada Curto (1886–1961). Declamatory social and history plays by Marcelino Mesquita (1856–1919) were very popular at the turn of the century. Notable recent Portuguese playwrights are José Régio (1901–), whose drama is predominantly religious; Miguel Torga (1907–) and Joaquim Paço d'Arcos (1908–), better known respectively as a poet and a novelist; Luiz Francisco Rebello (1924–), a drama critic who turned from EXPRESSIONIST to social-protest drama (within the limits of state censorship) such as *Condenados à Vida* (1963); Bernardo Santareno (1924–), equally occupied with the common people in plays such as *Anunçiacão* (1962); and Luís de Sttau Monteiro (1926–), the leading Portuguese playwright of the 1960's, a repeatedly imprisoned liberal socialist whose drama was influenced by BERTOLT BRECHT's and often satirizes the military, as in *Felizmente há Luar!* (1961).

In English little has been written on Portuguese drama. Harold V. Livermore's collection of essays, *Portugal and Brazil* (1953), has bibliographies, including one on Portuguese literature in English translation.

* See also BRAZIL, whose Portuguese-language theatre in modern times began with a play on "O Judeu" (the Jew), the Brazilian playwright Antonio José da Silva (1705–39), who at eight settled in Lisbon and therefore belongs more to the literature of Portugal, where he was killed by the Inquisition.

POST OFFICE, THE (*Dakghar*), a play in two acts by RABINDRANATH TAGORE, published in 1912 and produced in 1913. Setting: a village in India, early twentieth century.

This short drama was translated and staged in European countries before it was produced in India in its Bengali original, in 1917. ANDRÉ GIDE's French version, *Amal et la lettre du roi,* was produced in 1928. WILLIAM BUTLER YEATS highly praised Tagore's most widely known play for its construction and the "emotion of gentleness and peace" conveyed by Tagore's portrayal of the delicate little boy's curiosity and yearnings.

An overly anxious physician has Amal's guardian confine the sickly boy to his room. From his window Amal longingly watches the village world. He chats with passersby: workers and officials, a group of boys to whom he gives his toys so that he may see them play nearby, and a neighbor girl who promises to bring Amal flowers. The postman idly remarks that the king himself may write Amal. The boy seizes upon this suggestion, especially after an old braggart promises to have the king apprized of Amal's wish. The boy gets weaker, but the expected letter keeps him buoyant: "I feel quite happy and don't mind being quiet and alone." His innocent faith is rewarded, for word does reach the king, who sends his physician to the village. He airs out the sickroom and Amal happily prepares for the king's visit, deciding to ask for an appointment as a royal postman. Confidently he closes his eyes and dies—as the little neighbor comes with the promised flowers and asks the doctor to "tell Amal [that she] has not forgotten him."

POTTING SHED, THE, a play in three acts by GRAHAM GREENE, published and produced in 1957. Setting: England, an autumn in the 1950's.

Like Greene's Catholic novels and THE LIVING ROOM, this is a study of faith. It is also a modernization of the Lazarus story and is partly autobiographical.

The precocious granddaughter of a dying prominent agnostic summons his son, James Callifer. He has long been estranged from his family and his wife, and his appearance now disturbs everyone. Particularly troubled are the agnostic's old doctor friend and the mother; she refuses to let Callifer see his father, who soon dies. Callifer yearns to know why all are against him, and what is wrong with him. He tries desperately to uncover the past he cannot remember, even with the aid of a psychiatrist. "You are not alive," his wife tells Callifer, and his mother refuses to answer his questions about the past. Gradually Callifer discovers the truth. It leads him to his uncle, an alcoholic priest who lost his faith and also became estranged from the family. Callifer learns that as a boy he had hanged himself in the potting shed. Dead when he was cut down, he was resurrected because of his uncle's prayer: "Take away my faith but let him live." This miracle destroyed his uncle's faith—as well as his father's faith in agnosticism. But since the famous man could not face such a loss, Callifer's mother disowned her son (a living testimonial to the miracle) for the sake of her husband.

POWER OF DARKNESS, THE (*Vlast tmy*), a drama in five acts by LEO TOLSTOI, published in 1886 and produced in 1888. Setting: a contemporary Russian village.

Tolstoi's best-known play is a NATURALISTIC dramatization of an actual event and of the plight of the Russian peasants who, though legally emancipated, are enslaved by poverty. Banned in Russia until 1895, this colorful peasant drama had its premiere in Paris. It made André Antoine's Théâtre-Libre famous, and the next year it was among the first and most influential works produced at Otto Brahm's Freie Bühne in Berlin. The dark powers of evil and ignorance, which culminate in adultery, poisoning, and infanticide, are portrayed in many richly drawn characters (particularly that of Nikita's jolly but depraved mother, Matryona) and powerful episodes. "Do not strike out a single scene or a single word!" ÉMILE ZOLA exclaimed after seeing the play; and BERNARD SHAW wrote of Nikita's redemption in the shed (V,1) and of the drunk old soldier (played by Stanislavsky in 1902) who encourages him, "I remember nothing in the whole range of drama that fascinated me more."

Act I. The thirty-two-year-old Anisya is tired of her sickly old husband, a rich farmer. She has an affair with their young farmhand, the roué Nikita, and is waiting for her husband to die so she can marry him. But she worries about Nikita's escapades. Recently he has seduced and ruined an orphan girl whom he may have to marry. Nikita tells Anisya that he cannot help it: "If women love me, I'm not to blame." His shrewd mother, Matryona, a ruthless schemer and a pious, proverb-spouting fraud, wants her son to get the farm. She reassures Anisya that she will not let her "witless old husband," Akim, force their son into marriage. Then Matryona offers her some poison and wheedles the frightened but passionate Anisya to buy and use it on her husband: "What's evil about it, pet? It'd be different if your man was in strong health, but now he just makes a bluff at being alive. He don't belong to the living." Nikita's simple and pious father insists that he marry the orphan because of "the injury done the girl, you know; she's a what d'you call it, an orphan, y'see, the girl is. And she's been injured." But when Nikita swears he is not responsible, Matryona succeeds in averting the marriage. Further, she arranges to have Nikita rehired as a farmhand for another year. Uneasy about his false oath to Akim, Nikita crosses and reassures himself: "If I married 'em all, I'd have a lot of wives." When the ruined orphan girl appears, Nikita brusquely sends her off. The farmer's half-witted daughter, Akulina (Anisya's stepdaughter), who also loves Nikita, tells him, "You wronged her. You'll wrong me the same way—you cur!" Nikita is distressed: "I love the girls like sugar; but if a fellow sins with them—there's trouble!"

Acts II and III. The farmer is near death six months later, after Anisya has given him some of the poison. But she and Matryona cannot find his money, which he intends to give his sister, whom he has just summoned. Moaning that his insides are burning, the dying man crawls into the room and begs forgiveness for his sins. Matryona discovers the money on a string around his neck, and spurs Anisya to giving him the rest of the poison. When Anisya reappears with the money, Matryona has the frightened woman give it to Nikita. Then, as neighbors arrive, Anisya begins the conventional wailing at her husband's death. Nine months pass, and Nikita and Anisya are now married. His affair with the half-witted Akulina is flourishing. But because of her passion and fear (since he has the money), Anisya is at his mercy. His father is witness to Nikita's drunken appearance with Akulina, who has made him buy her many gifts. When Anisya and Akulina quarrel bitterly, the stepdaughter accuses her of having poisoned her first husband. Nikita coldly insists that his wife be quiet or get out of the house. The father is appalled at the sordidness of Nikita's home, refuses his money, and leaves: "Your wealth's caught you in a net; in a net, you know. Ah Nikita, it's the soul that God wants!" His drunken party spoiled, Nikita weeps, "Oh, life is hard for me, awful hard!"

Act IV. It is a moonlit night the following autumn. Akulina is pregnant, but Matryona has succeeded in helping to arrange a marriage for her. As the wedding approaches, Akulina keeps to her room with "stomach pains." The baby is born in secret and Nikita, its father, begs to have it placed in a foundling home. But his wife, Anisya, and his mother, Matryona, have him dig a hole in the cellar. "You're ready to do anything nasty, but you don't know how to get rid of it," Anisya jeers, yearning to avenge herself and wanting him, too, to feel like a murderer. Piously exhorting her to

The Power of Darkness, Act V, Scene 2. Nikita (O. Komissarov) in center. Moscow Art Theatre, 1947. (*Sovfoto*)

baptize the infant, Matryona has Anisya bring it down and persuades Nikita to crush its skull with a board. He does so, but then, hysterical and ready to kill his exultant wife, Nikita rushes out: "How those little bones cracked, and how it wailed! Mother, darling, what have you done to me!" Matryona takes care of the infant's burial as Nikita drinks and stops his ears to shut out the imaginary sounds: "I've ruined my life, ruined it! What have they done to me? . . . Where shall I go!" (Tolstoi's *Variant Ending for Act IV*, the ending more frequently used in production, merely reports the infanticide: Anisya's frightened little daughter, trying to go to sleep, is comforted by an old laborer, a retired soldier. Nikita's hysterical entrance and Matryona's attempt to calm him reveal what has happened in the cellar.)

Act V. Scene 1. It is Akulina's wedding day. Haunted by his crime, Nikita tarries in the farm shed. The orphan girl he once ruined passes by. Now happily married to an elderly widower to whom she has confessed her sin, she repulses Nikita's renewed advances. She urges him to reform and tells him to join the guests, who are awaiting him. Increasingly desperate, Nikita gets ready to commit suicide. He is interrupted by his mother and his wife, both happy that everything has turned out so well. Nikita promises to follow them to the party, and then prepares to hang himself. The retired old soldier, though drunk, stops him. He tells Nikita that one should not be afraid of people, for that strengthens the devil's hand. Nikita overcomes his fears and courageously goes to the wedding. *Scene 2.* Arriving at the party, Nikita confesses his sins to the celebrants, assumes the sins of Anisya, and begs forgiveness. Old Akim rejoices at Nikita's repentance: "Speak, my son! Tell everything—you'll feel better! Confess to God, don't fear men! God! God! This is His work!" Nikita recalls how "in the very beginning, when I began to meddle with this nasty whoredom, you said to me: 'If a claw is caught, the whole bird is lost.'" (Tolstoi's epigraph to this play.) The old man ecstatically assures his son of redemption: "You have not spared yourself, He will spare you." Now Akulina, too, wants to confess. But Nikita, as he is bound and taken away, stops her: "I did it all by myself. I planned it and I did it. Lead me wherever you want to. I will say no more."

PRAGA, Marco (1862–1929), Italian playwright, at the turn of the century wrote popular NATURALISTIC drama about illicit love. Adultery, already the subject of his first hit—the one-act *L'amico* (1886)—underlines the plot of his best works: *Le vergini* (1889), *La moglie ideale* (1890), *La crisi* (1904), and *La porta chiusa* (*The Closed Door*, 1913), a star vehicle in which Eleonora Duse portrayed an anguished mother who pays for her sinful life when her adored son learns of his illegitimacy and spurns her. The "virgins" of *Le vergini* come from an immoral middle-class family that encourages its daughters to indulge their wealthy lovers; one of them penitently confesses her past and thereupon is contemptuously dropped by her self-centered fiancé—a typical Praga male. The heroine of the 1890 play is "the ideal wife" because of her ability simultaneously and without compromising herself to carry on an adulterous as well as a marital relationship, while *La crisi* portrays the anguish of a husband who is aware of his wife's infidelity but loves her too much to do anything about it or to give her up.

Praga was born in Milan, the son of a notable poet who died early of alcoholism. After a humdrum beginning as a bank accountant Praga turned to the theatre, for which he wrote until his suicide. He published ten volumes of theatre criticisms and founded the Societa degli Autori (Society of Authors). Irony as well as psychological insight characterize his plays; they focus on the moral struggles, usually of women, and eschew didacticism—and, often, sympathy. In their naturalistic-psychological stress they resemble the drama of Praga's contemporary, ROBERTO BRACCO.

PRESENTATIONAL is a term denoting dramatizations and staging methods that "present reality," as it were, by emphasizing artificiality, the illusory or theatrical nature of a play. On stage, presentational theatre is characterized by scant props and settings—or none at all; performers pantomime to simulate actions such as eating, closing doors, carrying objects, etc. The illusion of reality is minimized, and the theatrical—the presentational—is stressed. Well known presentational plays are Wilder's OUR TOWN, Williams's THE GLASS MENAGERIE, and many of BERTOLT BRECHT's plays. Antonyms: REPRESENTATIONAL, NATURALISM, REALISM.

PRETENDERS, THE (*Kongs-emnerne*), a historical play in five acts by HENRIK IBSEN, published in 1863 and produced in 1864. Setting: early thirteenth-century Norway.

"Ibsen's first real and incontrovertible masterpiece,"* this chronicle play abounds with characters and action. It is slightly marred by prolixity and overdependence on statement—rather than on dramatization—in the intriguing portrayal of Bishop Nikolas's death scene (almost the whole third act). The rivalry of the Hamlet-like Skule and the perhaps superficial but utterly self-confident and confidence-exuding Håkon is in part a dramatization of the rivalry between Ibsen and BJØRNSTJERNE BJØRNSON, though Ibsen is equally embodied in Skule's bard Jatgeir, a self-confident and effective idealist.

The chief pretenders to the Norwegian throne are Håkon Håkonsson and Earl Skule Bårdsson, respectively supported by the Birkebeiner and the Bagler factions. Håkon is elected king and marries Skule's daughter. Though he receives a third of the kingdom and is keeper of the royal seal, Skule dreams of the opportunities he has missed and of being king. Bishop Nikolas Arnesson, evil and frustrated in his lust for power, schemes to prevent either man's greatness: "No one else shall reach what *I* have failed to attain." He urges the introspective Skule to overcome his paralyzing vacillation and act as if he had self-confidence—the *ingenium,* as the Romans called it, that is the source of Håkon's strength and makes him "one of Fortune's children"—and tells him of the existence of a letter that may shed doubt on Håkon's descent. Skule keeps seeking this letter, and vows to seize the crown if Håkon proves to be illegitimate. With death imminent, Bishop Nikolas frantically orders the choir of monks to be augmented so that his soul may be saved, and attempts to gain a few more hours of life to plot for his immortality in a *perpetuum mobile* of frustrating doubt and strife between Håkon and Skule. He succeeds with Skule. Though Håkon confidently predicts that he himself will "consecrate" their country ("Norway was a *kingdom,* it shall become a *nation*"), Skule decides to fight him: "Better far to sit up there enthroned, doubting one's self, than stand down here among the common herd with doubts of him who sits above me." He breaks with Håkon and has himself crowned. Soon he is plagued by doubts of his cause and his ability to fathom "kingly thoughts." When questioned, his Icelandic bard Jatgeir urges him, "Believe in yourself and you will be saved." Only toward the end, however, when he learns of the existence of a son fathered long ago with a mistress, does he muster the determination to war against Håkon. But he is by then almost mad. Though Håkon offers to share the kingdom with him, Skule insists on his son's succession to the throne and orders Håkon's son—his own grandson—caught and killed. Håkon thus is forced to order Skule's death, though he privately urges him to flee the country. Skule sees his son corrupted by the political struggle and—even though the Ghost of Bishop Nikolas appears and once more tempts him to seize Håkon's power—he at last recognizes his doom. To save his grandson and redeem his injuries to his family and to Håkon, Skule gives himself and his son up to the mob: "I have no life work for which to live; I cannot live for Håkon's either; but I can die for it!" Before he is killed he leaves a message that acknowledges the innate justness of Håkon's regal claim, regardless of his birth. When Håkon arrives, he must step over his enemy's corpse. But he declares him to have been a misjudged mystery: "Skule Bårdsson was God's stepchild on earth; that was the mystery!"

PRICE, THE, a play in two acts by ARTHUR MILLER, published and produced in 1968. Setting: New York, 1968.

This four-character play deals literally and SYMBOLICally with Miller's favorite themes of guilt and responsibility, and features his typical family paying "the price" for past and present sins, individual and societal. Though curiously anachronistic with its IBSENite dramaturgy and its 1930's language and concerns, the play is engaging and

*James W. McFarlane's introduction to the play in *The Oxford Ibsen* (Volume II).

theatrical. Best by far is its philosophizing old furniture dealer, a Yiddish vaudeville character. The action is continuous and the Broadway production had no intermission.

Act I. Police Sergeant Victor Franz enters the cluttered attic of a Manhattan brownstone soon to be demolished. He examines the heavy old furnishings, strokes a harp, and plays an old Gallagher and Shean comedy record on the Victrola as his wife enters. She is depressed by the place and impatient for the arrival of the dealer Victor has called to dispose of its contents. They talk about Victor's imminent retirement and allude to his failure: he quit college to support his father, a businessman ruined in the Depression. Victor's brother, Walter, contributed only a few dollars a month and went on to become a famous surgeon. Now Victor has tried in vain to reach Walter, with whom he had lost contact sixteen years ago, to participate in the disposal of their dead parents' belongings. Suddenly there is loud coughing and panting from the staircase. The dealer, Gregory Solomon, an eighty-nine-year-old "phenomenon," enters in a state of near collapse, and Victor offers him a glass of water. "Water I don't need; a little blood I could use," Solomon replies. Soon recuperated, he chats and craftily withholds his estimate, for "the price of used furniture is nothing but a viewpoint"—which he explores at length. Finally he makes an offer "for everything," and Victor resignedly accepts it. As Solomon counts out the money, a well-dressed man enters. It is Walter.

Act II. An increasingly bitter confrontation between the long-estranged brothers uncovers the failures, guilts, frustrations, and fantasies of both of them. "You had a responsibility here and you walked out on it," Victor charges. "There was nothing here to betray," replies Walter, who, though successful, has had a breakdown and is divorced. He disillusions his brother by revealing the futility of Victor's sacrifice: their father exploited him, for he lived off a secret pile of money he kept hidden. "Were we really brought up to believe in one another?" Walter asks: "We were brought up to succeed, weren't we?" He suggests that they face reality—that there was never any love in their home—and concludes, "What was unbearable is not that it all fell apart, it was that there was never anything here." But if Victor has wallowed in fantasies of self-pity for his filial self-sacrifice, Walter has been guilty of the equally corrupting quest for success. Both brothers—and even Victor's wife and Solomon—have paid the price of a loveless family life and a materialistic society. At last aware of it, they depart as Solomon starts his inventory of the attic. Alone, he cannot resist playing the Victrola. The old record brings back memories and relieves Solomon's dejection. He sits down and soon smiles at and joins in the recorded laughter, "with tears in his eyes, howling helplessly to the air."

PRIESTLEY, J[ohn] B[oynton] (1894–   ), English playwright, novelist, and writer of essays and criticisms, made effective BBC broadcasts during World War II, was a political and economic reporter, and held important positions such as the United Kingdom's delegate to UNESCO. He was born in Yorkshire, educated at Cambridge, and served in the military all through World War I. His writing career began soon thereafter, and he made his name first with a novel, *The Good Companions* (1929). Later he dramatized it (1931, with EDWARD KNOBLOCK) and, like a number of his plays, it eventually was filmed.

His first hit, DANGEROUS CORNER (1932), was followed by an even greater success, the comic LABURNUM GROVE (1933). His next play was *Eden End* (1934), a nostalgic period piece, and then came such lesser works as *Duet in Floodlight* and *Cornelius* (both 1935). But with TIME AND THE CONWAYS (1937) and *I Have Been Here Before* (1937) Priestley consolidated his position as an important English playwright. Both stressed his preoccupation with time and space concepts, the philosophical strain that permeates Priestley's drama.

These plays were followed by *When We Are Married* (1938), a Yorkshire farce; *The Long Mirror* (1940), in which extrasensory perception plays a significant part in a romance; *Good Night Children* (1942), a spoof on the BBC; *They Came to a City* (1943), which attempts to cope with contemporary political problems; *Music at Night* (1944), an experimental play like his earlier JOHNSON OVER JORDAN (1939); AN INSPECTOR CALLS (1947) and *The Linden Tree* (1947), both strongly moralistic; and (in 1963) an adaptation with Iris Murdoch (1919–   ) of the latter's novel *A Severed Head.*

Priestley's plays were written for the stage, not the study, and—though he has created good stories—they play better than they read. While his drama is distinctive, it falls into various types. Plays such as *Dangerous Corner* and *An Inspector Calls* (which are among his most popular works) have a conventional and unchanging setting and dialogue meant to lull audiences and thus heighten the effect of trick endings, which underline Priestley's philosophical and didactic concerns. In plays such as *Eden End* and *The Linden Tree* Priestley strove to approximate something like ANTON CHEKHOV's evocation of atmosphere and character. *Johnson Over Jordan* and *Music at Night* evidence Priestley's interest in experimenting with new EXPRESSIONISTIC and other theatrical devices. Many critics have found him best when he is least concerned with reforming and teaching —i.e., in comic pieces such as *Laburnum Grove* and *When We Are Married,* where his gift for the portrayal of Yorkshire folk is given full range.

Collections of Priestley's thirty-odd plays appeared in successive volumes, beginning in 1948. He has also published many novels and miscellaneous other works, including *The Art of the Dramatist* (1957) and an autobiography, *Margin Released* (1962). See also Ivor J. C. Brown's *J. B. Priestley* (1957), David Hughes's *J. B. Priestley: An Informal Study of His Work*

(1958), Gareth L. Evans's *J. B. Priestley—The Dramatist* (1964), and Susan Cooper's *J. B. Priestley: Portrait of An Artist* (1970).

PRINCE D'AUREC, THE (*Le Prince d'Aurec*), a comedy in three acts by HENRI LAVEDAN, produced in 1892 and published in 1894. Setting: Paris and a French country estate, 1890's.

The title hero of Lavedan's most notable play is a decadent but proud young aristocrat. "I am a gentleman, and I do no more nor less than others to maintain my dignity as such," he tells his wealthy mother, a commoner who criticizes his irresponsible life. A Jewish baron who aspires to join exclusive clubs and seduce the aristocrat's wife loans them great sums of money, though he knows they despise Jews. When he propositions the princess, she and her husband contemptuously dismiss him: "I have even shown myself in public with you, I have ridden with you in your own carriages, and now you talk about your damned money!" With equal contempt the baron insists on being repaid and threatens to sue. The prince's wealthy mother ultimately agrees to save her son. Chastened, he vows thereafter "to live the life of an honest man and, when the time comes, die like a prince"—on the battlefield. "As would any of us," remarks another Jew, a prominent writer. Prince d'Aurec replies with great hauteur, "*Il y a la manière!*" ("There is a certain way of doing it!").

In Lavedan's sequel to the play, *Les Deux Noblesses* (*The Two Nobilities,* 1894), the Prince goes into trade and restores the family's fortunes.

PRINCE WHO LEARNED EVERYTHING OUT OF BOOKS, THE (*El príncipe que todo lo aprendió en los libros*), a fantasy in two acts by JACINTO BENAVENTE, produced in 1909 and published in 1910. Setting: a palace, open country, a hut, etc.

This comic fairy tale opened Madrid's Children's Theatre. It depicts the adventures of a young prince who judges reality by the fairy tales he has read. With his fool and his tutor, the innocent prince travels forth into the world and undergoes many allegorical but beguiling experiences with people he misjudges as fairies and ogres. Repeatedly rescued, he is never disillusioned by reality. "I have learned that it is necessary to dream beautiful things in order to do beautiful things," he says at the end, when he is saved from marrying an evil princess: "Happy are they who know how to make out of life one beautiful tale!"

PRIVATE LIVES, "an intimate comedy" in three acts by NOËL COWARD, published and produced in 1930. Setting: France, c. 1930.

A film version of this very popular comedy appeared in 1932, and it has received frequent revivals, some of them major. Coward's one-act parody, *Some Other Private Lives,* was produced in 1930 and published the following year.

Act I. Elyot Chase and his bride, Sibyl, a pretty and conventional blond, observe the beautiful view from their hotel terrace. It is their honeymoon, but Sibyl keeps harping on Elyot's first wife, whom he had divorced five years before. When they go into their rooms, Amanda Prynne appears on the

Private Lives, Act III. Victor (Laurence Olivier), Sibyl (Adrianne Allen), Elyot (NOËL COWARD), and Amanda (Gertrude Lawrence). London, 1931. (*Culver Pictures*)

adjoining terrace: she is on her honeymoon with the convential Victor—who keeps harping on *her* first marriage and is shocked by some of her views. "Very few people are completely normal really, deep down in their private lives," Amanda assures him; it is all a matter of chemistry—"That was the trouble with Elyot and me, we were like two violent acids bubbling about in a nasty little matrimonial bottle." Elyot and Amanda sit back to back on their terraces, waiting to have cocktails with their spouses, who are getting dressed for dinner. From below come the strains of a song they recognize, and as they hum it, they suddenly see each other. Though shaken by the reunion and the coincidence of honeymooning in the same hotel, they remain suave and soon leave. Then they reappear, in tandem, trying desperately to persuade their spouses to change the honeymoon plans and go to Paris. Neither Victor nor Sibyl is willing to do so, and both couples row. While their angry partners are downstairs, Elyot and Amanda chat, have a cocktail, and reminisce about the wonderful times they used to have. When the orchestra again strikes up their song they fall into each other's arms and decide to escape to Amanda's Paris flat. Returning for them, Victor and Sibyl meet; since their spouses cannot be found, they drink the remaining cocktails, with forced gaiety: "To absent friends."

Act II. A few evenings later, in her Paris flat, Amanda and Elyot are still happily reunited, more in love than ever. But as they discuss their private lives of the past few years, they become jealous, start bickering, and rake up old quarrels. They check themselves by using an agreed-upon danger signal to cool off, and then resume chatting affectionately. "Let's be superficial and pity the poor philosophers," Elyot remarks: "Let's savour the delight of the moment." But their squabbles quickly resume, get nastier, and reach a climax when the two start fighting like animals. "Beast; brute; swine; cad; beast; beast; brute; devil—" Amanda screams, and they roll on the floor in furious combat. Just then Victor and Sibyl enter.

Act III. The next morning Victor and Sibyl try to discuss matters with their spouses. Elyot and Amanda are ready to go their own ways. But putting on a cheerful front, they order coffee. Victor gets increasingly indignant and wants to punch Elyot. Amanda welcomes the idea of their fighting and pulls Sibyl out of the room. Elyot calms Victor down, persuades him that a fight over them is exactly what the women want, shocks him by refusing to remarry Amanda ("a vile tempered wicked woman"), and leaves him speechless by calling him "a rampaging gas bag." Though the women are disappointed because there has been no fight, the married couples—Elyot and Sibyl, and Victor and Amanda—soon are reconciled to some degree. All four sit down to have coffee. Then, as each defends his or her own mate and attacks the other's, Victor and Sibyl start arguing. They get increasingly more abusive: "Malicious little vixen"—"Insufferable great brute." Amanda and Elyot smile and become reconciled. And while Victor and Sibyl furiously assault each other, Elyot and Amanda pick up their suitcases and quietly go out, arm in arm.

PRIVATE TUTOR, THE (*Der Hofmeister*), a play in five acts by BERTOLT BRECHT, produced in 1950 and published in 1951. Setting: Germany after the Seven Years' War.

This modernized version of J. M. R. Lenz's 1774 *Sturm und Drang* drama has also been translated as *The Tutor*. Brecht inserted debates on love and philosophy, and stressed the plot's relevance to Nazi Germany and its timid, emasculated intellectuals.

Läuffer, a poor young schoolmaster treated as a lowly servant by his employer's family, is seduced by the daughter. After escaping her enraged family, he is once more endangered in a similar situation. He castrates himself and then becomes socially acceptable.

PROBLEM PLAYS (also known as dramas of ideas, *pièces à thèse,* or thesis plays) are dramas that subordinate timeless universal issues to contemporary social ones. Such plays may end happily or unhappily and they are often didactic, not only presenting such problems but also propagandizing for a solution. Problem plays appeared in the nineteenth century, particularly with HENRIK IBSEN and BERNARD SHAW. Ibsen espoused female emancipation and attacked contemporary marriage and divorce laws in plays such as A DOLL'S HOUSE and GHOSTS, while Shaw dealt with slums and prostitution in WIDOWERS' HOUSES and MRS. WARREN'S PROFESSION. Other notable authors of such plays were EUGÈNE BRIEUX and JOHN GALSWORTHY, who dramatized contemporary problems of education and the penal code—while JAMES M. BARRIE burlesqued all problem plays in a love-triangle lampoon, *Alice Sit-by-the-Fire* (1905). Nonetheless, they have continued to appear to the present day.

Defining and analyzing the genre, Shaw noted that dramatists necessarily depict people in conflict with two types of circumstances: institutional and noninstitutional. While the latter deals with such timeless topics as love, death, and character, the former—which provides the material of "problem plays"—deals with contemporary economic, political, legal, and other "temporal circumstances."* As some of Shaw's own and Ibsen's plays suggest, because of their authors' genius—their insight into human nature and their art—problem plays can transcend the genre and remain relevant long after the particular issues dramatized have been resolved. In fact, many plays that are not "problem plays" also deal with the contemporary, and their survival, too, depends not on their subjects but on the artistry of the depiction.

A book-length study is Ramsden Balmforth's *The Problem Play and Its Influence on Modern*

* Several essays on the subject are reprinted in E. J. West's edition of *Shaw on Theatre* (1958).

Thought and Life (1928), but the subject is discussed also in most works on modern drama.

PROCESSIONAL, a play in four acts by JOHN HOWARD LAWSON, published and produced in 1925. Setting: outskirts of a large town in the West Virginia coal fields during a strike, 1920's.

Lawson called this "a jazz symphony of American life." An EXPRESSIONISTIC play that is "essentially vaudevillesque in character," as he explained his technique, it employed vaudeville's crude and glaring backdrops, burlesque stereotypes (Jew, Negro, city slicker, etc.), brassy saxophone music, and song-and-dance routines. In many episodes the play depicts class warfare, jingoism, race prejudice, and other contemporary phenomena. While its strident vitality offended some, its New York Theatre Guild production had a respectable run. A revised version was produced by the Federal Theatre in 1937.

Act I. On the Fourth of July striking, jazz-playing miners walk by Isaac Cohen's Cut-Rate Store. His seventeen-year-old daughter, Sadie, dances with a city slicker, "a very GEORGE M. COHAN sort of newspaper man" who is chased off by her father. A "Buffalo Bill style" sheriff appears menacingly with a man in a silk hat, which is shot off; this so unnerves him that he cannot finish his patriotic speech. The journalist placates the sheriff with whiskey, and then goes off with a miner arrested as "one a' them Armenian Bolcheviks," to inspect the "pigsties an' barns" in which the miners live.

Act II. His mother and grandmother visit the jailed Dynamite Jim Flimmins, a dim-witted miner. A Negro suffering from the blues tries to break into jail as Jim breaks out and hides in a coffin. The sheriff raises an alarm for Jim, who is carried away in the coffin by the scared Negro and a miner. Some soldiers are frightened by the dark and by the angry populace. Sadie, calling herself Desdemona, strolls by with the journalist. Dynamite Jim comes out of the coffin and, after a struggle, bayonets a soldier. Horrified by his deed, he bends over the body: "I want my mammy's arms 'cause I done a black thing, oh, mammy, help me now!"

Act III. Dynamite Jim hides in his mother's basement. Sadie warns them that the soldiers are coming, and later she demonstrates how she will dance on Broadway—"I'm goin' away, gonna find a lotta men to gimme kisses an' diamonds!"—until her father spanks her. The sheriff searches the house, though Jim's mother tries to distract and then to bribe him. She admits that she has slept with soldiers to get money to save her son. Later Jim comes out of hiding, broken by the discovery that "every guy's had my mammy's arms!" Though she pleads that she did it for him and that he stay with her, Jim bitterly vows to leave—and to kill recklessly. "I'm through, I'm free now," he shouts: "Let hell loose!" As the miners fight the soldiers and the Ku Klux Klan, Sadie unsuccessfully tries to get the journalist (who turns out to be "a good middle-class man") to take her to New York. Escaping the soldiers, Jim runs into Sadie. Still bitter about his mother's promiscuity, he embraces the not-too-reluctant Sadie. "Wimmin is all bums," he says, lifting her up and taking her into the mine. The soldiers soon find and chase him. Caught on a fence by his pants, "he hangs like a flag, a human flag, with arms and legs that wave in the wind, the flag of defeat," a soldier reports as they capture him.

Act IV. Six months later Sadie, now pregnant, is living with Jim's mother. Both are captured by the Ku Klux Klan, who prepare to discipline them for their immoral behavior. "She's a Jazz kid," a Goblin says, and others agree. "It's outrageous! It's contagious!" they sway and chant: "It's contortionate! It's disreputable!" The journalist tries to rescue the women as some of the Klansmen unmask: one is Isaac Cohen, and another is the Negro—who leads the shouting KKK away. Dynamite Jim appears, blind: the KKK gouged his eyes when they started to hang him. His mother tells him Sadie "tuk the curse off you . . . she carries [it]." But Sadie is satisfied: "I carry a gravestone inside me, but I don't care; I'm a-gonna raise my kid." The man in the silk hat comes with a pardon for all the miners and grants their demands (though he will double-cross them that night); he also has a telegram from Calvin Coolidge that declares all men brothers. In a jazz ceremony the sheriff marries Sadie and Jim. All rejoice in a final procession, and Sadie, pregnant with "the future," sways and sings.

PROFESSOR BERNHARDI, a comedy in five acts by ARTHUR SCHNITZLER, published and produced in 1912. Setting: contemporary Vienna.

Schnitzler reworked this play for over a dozen years. Despite its "comedy" label, it is an occasionally subtle PROBLEM PLAY about ethics and religion. Schnitzler's background and experiences are reflected in the play's hospital setting, its depiction of anti-Semitism, and the variegated character portrayals.

Professor Bernhardi, the hospital's distinguished founder, does not wish a priest to visit a girl who is dying after an abortion. She is in a state of euphoria and unaware of her true condition, which the priest's appearance would instantly give away. "It is part of my duty to see that my patients have a happy death—as far as may be possible," he tells the priest, who, in turn, maintains that her immortal soul is more important. As they argue, the nurse who summoned the priest reveals his presence to the patient, who immediately dies. Bernhardi's being a Jew blows this minor episode up into a major public and political scandal, and unleashes anti-Semitic feelings. The differing individual reactions of the doctors (who include Bernhardi's son) manifest themselves in their attitudes toward Bernhardi. For opportunistic reasons as well as to save the hospital from ruin, many want to give in to popular indignation. They are led by the assistant director, whose scheming is abetted by Bernhardi's posture. Ironic and proud, he resigns at his board's stormy meeting: "I will not submit myself to judgment." He is tried on a charge of religious obstruction. The nurse's fraudulent testimony and his own defiance help convict him. Later, after Bernhardi has served his prison sentence, the priest admits that Bernhardi was right. But the priest reveals, in their long discussion, that though the Church censured him for his sympathetic testimony, he could not publicly express his belief that Bernhardi had acted properly: such an acknowledgment would have made his own life a lie, would have harmed "something really sacred." Though they disagree, Bernhardi and the priest are both idealists who can agree, finally, to shake hands over the "wide chasm" of their different convictions. Public opinion in the meantime has swung to Bernhardi, but he is unwilling to have his sentence reviewed. A scientist, he is concerned only with returning to work and healing the sick, and he applies for the restitution of his license. In his final confrontation with the health minister, his one-time colleague in medical school, Professor Bernhardi declines involvement in the ebb and flow of politics and expedience—even though these now favor him.

PROFESSOR TARANNE (*Le Professeur Taranne*), a play in two scenes by ARTHUR ADAMOV, published and produced in 1953. Setting: a police station and a hotel in France, c. 1950.

Adamov considered this short play, the dramatization of a dream, his most satisfactory one. Its reiterated "I am Professor Taranne" is Adamov's substitute for his real dream exclamation, "I am the author of THE PARODY!" A Kafkaesque nightmare of the ABSURD, the play does not clarify whether Taranne is a fraud or the victim of a universal conspiracy—or both.

"I am Professor Taranne," the middle-aged man accused of indecent exposure tells the police: "I'm famous, I'm respected." Refuting the charge that he took off his clothes in public, Taranne insists he is a distinguished scholar who has recently delivered notable lectures in Belgium. But various people deny his identity and a woman who seems to recognize him addresses him as "Professor Ménard," Taranne's colleague. In his hotel policemen charge Taranne with another offense—littering his beach cabin—and he again gets involved in a maze of apparent contradictions when he cannot decipher an almost blank notebook he identifies as his lecture notebook. He receives a steamship dining-room chart with his own seat marked at the captain's table—and a letter from the Belgian university, which, he tells his sister, will be another invitation and thus confirm his claims. But the letter is a denunciation of his earlier lecture and an accusation that he plagiarized from the work of his distinguished colleague, Professor Ménard. Alone, Taranne unrolls and hangs up the seating chart. It is blank. He looks at it, and then slowly starts taking off his clothes.

PROMISE, THE (*Moi bedny Marat*), a play in three acts by ALEKSEI NIKOLAEVICH ARBUZOV, published and produced in 1965. Setting: Leningrad, March 1942 through December 1959.

The title ("my poor Marat") of this bittersweet romantic comedy was changed in English and American productions to avoid confusion with Weiss's MARAT/SADE. Arbuzov's is a three-character triangle play that emphasizes social duty. It begins during the siege of Leningrad and portrays the trio's first meeting and their developing relationships as they are affected by war and peace.

Lika wants to be a doctor—a specialist—and she expresses her ideals in "the promise": "Children are born into this world to succeed where their parents failed. I promise there will be no more disease left at the end of the twentieth century." She marries a sickly poet who needs her, though she loves his friend, Marat, an imaginative engineer who builds bridges. As time goes on, Lika becomes merely a general practitioner, and her husband is a failure. Aware of it, he summons Marat and leaves his wife and friend. Lika and Marat are at last united, though their youthful hopes are gone. Marat asks fearfully: "Is living together going to be all that easy for us?" (This was the curtain line of the stage production; the printed version continues with Lika's consoling optimism about future success and happiness: "Don't be afraid, my poor Marat!")

PROPOSAL, THE (*Predlozhenie*), "a jest in one act" by ANTON CHEKHOV, published in 1888 and produced in 1889. Setting: the drawing room of a contemporary estate.

"I've scribbled a lousy little farce," Chekhov wrote a friend about this short vaudeville, "but it will go down well in the provinces." It achieved immediate success in Moscow and St. Petersburg, and was given a special performance before the tsar in 1889.

A nervous and hypochondriac landowner comes to propose to his neighbor's daughter, but starts to quarrel with her, as usual, and leaves angrily. When she discovers the purpose of his visit, she immediately has him called back, but soon they start arguing again. The father finally has them kiss, and at the curtain he shouts down their renewed bickering by ordering champagne.

PRUNELLA, OR LOVE IN A DUTCH GARDEN, a verse play in three acts by LAURENCE HOUSMAN and HARLEY GRANVILLE-BARKER, produced in 1904 and published in 1906. Setting: a Dutch garden "where it is always afternoon."

Much of this Pierrot fantasy, which was frequently revived and appeared in a four-act version in 1930, is music (originally by Joseph Moorat), dance, and masquerade.

The mummer Pierrot comes to the garden where Prunella lives in fairyland seclusion from the world. That very charming life is, however, ruled by somewhat dull Victorian proprieties. Prunella is cautioned by her three aunts, Prim, Prude, and Privacy. But when Pierrot serenades her ("Little bird in your nest, are you there, are you there?") and the statue of Love comes to life, Prunella is enchanted and follows Pierrot into the world. Behind his mask, Pierrot leads a life of fantasy and selfishness—sinister qualities personified by Scaramel (who is derived from Molière's Sganarelle, Don Juan's servant). Prunella becomes disenchanted; seeking a more fulfilling reality and truth, she leaves him. Eventually Pierrot misses her, and returns to the garden to find her again. Prunella does not at first recognize the rich stranger, who has grown older and sadder. Then the statute of Love lights up and plays its viol, and song bursts forth in the garden. Prunella will be reunited with a Pierrot redeemed and brought back to her by love.

PRZYBYSZEWSKI, Stanisław (1868–1927), Polish editor, novelist, and playwright, has been called the "founder of Polish modernism." A poet of the "naked soul" and of lust, and a proponent of "art for art's sake," Przybyszewski wrote in both Polish and German. Some of his psychological and metaphysical plays, written for Eleonora Duse and PRESENTATIONAL in form, achieved considerable success because of the actors who starred in them and because of their "demonic" STRINDBERGian prose depictions of sex and violence: *Dla szczęścia* (*For the Sake of Happiness,* 1899), *Złote runo* (1901), *Śnieg* (*Snow,* 1903), and *Topiel* (1913). Przybyszewski's powerful personality made him the center of a Kracow circle of writers and artists at the turn of the century, when he edited the revolutionary journal *Życie*. He brought giants of the modern theatre—Strindberg, HENRIK IBSEN, GERHART HAUPTMANN, and MAURICE MAETERLINCK—into native repertoires and wielded a profound artistic influence on his Polish contemporaries.

PUERTO RICO became a cultural attraction with its post-World War II festivals. Though the most famous of them were Pablo Casals's concerts, annual drama festivals sponsored by the Instituto de Cultura started in 1958 to encourage and stimulate new playwrights. The most prominent writer associated with these festivals has been RENÉ MARQUÉS, whose drama had already been seen in New York.

Until then little drama of interest had appeared in Puerto Rico though theatres were founded and plays were written in the nineteenth century. Uniquely Puerto Rican was drama about the rural farmer, or *jíbaro*. Marqués's *La carreta* (*The Ox Cart*) is the best known of such local-color plays, which began to appear in the 1850's. In 1912 a prolonged visit by the actress Virginia Fábregas inspired the writing of musical and other comedies, the most notable of the latter being *La crisis del amor* (1912) by the Spanish-born Puerto Rican José Pérez Losada (1879–1937). Another early modern native play was *El Grito de Lares* (1914), a poetic dramatization by the Spanish-educated lawyer Luis Lloréns Torres (1878–1944) of the island's first and abortive rebellion against Spain; it inspired a series of similar plays, and romantic history drama flourished in Puerto Rico for some time.

The modern national theatre was founded by Emilio S. Belaval (1903–), a lawyer and minor playwright who founded the short-lived (1938–41) but influential Areyto group of amateurs, which inspired young writers to turn to the theatre. In comedies as well as serious drama they portrayed expatriate Puerto Ricans—the *jíbaro* and others—in the United States, as well as rural problems and political and social issues. The Areyto authors include the island's distinguished poet and critic Cesáreo Rosa-Nieves (1904–), who dramatized historical and rural themes in verse; and Manuel Méndez Ballestero (1909–), also a novelist and public official, who distinguished himself particularly with the tragedy *Tiempo muerto* (1940) and whose *Encrucijada* (*Crossroads,* 1938), like *The Ox Cart,* deals with Puerto Rican immigrants in New York, whose traveling summer-theatre company performed it in 1969.

Founded in 1941 after the Areyto's demise, Teatro Universitario nurtured the next generation of dramatists. Its principal figures have been Marqués and Francisco Arriví (1915–), who studied playwriting at Columbia University and founded an experimental group that produced his fantasy drama as well as his more NATURALISTIC later work. Best among Arriví's fantasies is *Club de solteros* (1940, retitled *Una sombra menos* in its 1953 published version), the SYMBOLIC portrayal of a misogynist who launches a sex war; his naturalistic drama includes *Máscara puertorriqueña,* a trilogy on the significance of the Puerto Ricans' Negro ancestry; its middle play, *Vejigantes* (1957), launched the original Drama Festival and was hailed as Arriví's best work.

The plays produced at the yearly Instituto de Cultura festivals have been published annually (but not in English). Bibliographies are listed in the studies noted under LATIN AMERICA.

PUGET, Claude-André (1905–), French playwright of light romantic comedies, many of them about adolescence. The most popular include *La Ligne de cœur* (1931); *Les Jours heureux* (1938), adapted by ZOË AKINS as *Happy Days;* and *Le Cœur volant* (1957). Collected volumes of Puget's plays began to appear in 1943.

PULLMAN CAR HIAWATHA, a one-act play by THORNTON WILDER, published and produced in 1931. Setting: a pullman train en route from New York to Chicago, c. 1930.

This PRESENTATIONAL play (actors bring in chairs to simulate berths, etc.) anticipates OUR TOWN with its stage manager and articulate dead people, and THE SKIN OF OUR TEETH with its procession of hours representing philosophers. As the train moves through the night in its specified cosmic position, various passengers reveal themselves. Angels take away a dead wife after she unhappily bids farewell to her hometown, family, and friends, but an insane woman must still remain on earth. Finally the train arrives in Chicago, the passengers jostle out, and the scrubwomen come to clean up.

PUPPET SHOW, THE (*Balaganchik*), a one-act "fairy show" in prose and verse by ALEKSANDR ALEKSANDROVICH BLOK, published and produced in 1906. Setting: a room.

Blok's first performed drama received a notable production by V. Y. Meyerhold. It is a harlequinade, a stylized work with lyrics and dance. Blok called it a "piece of buffoonery," meant to express the immutable vitality of the world. The buffoonery obscures some of the gloomy pessimism. The focal character, a beautiful but silent Columbine, is also a symbol of the promised Russian constituion.

Columbine is courted by a sorrowful Pierrot and a romantic Harlequin. Her arrival enchants Pierrot, who sees her as his bride. But she frightens a group of asinine mystics, whose leader warns Pierrot, "Don't you see the *kosà* [meaning both "braid" and "scythe"] on her shoulder? Don't you recognize death?" Harlequin takes her away, and an absurd author appears. He complains about the way his work is being misplayed, and describes the REALISM he projected; but soon he is pulled backstage. At a masked ball three pairs of lovers exchange vows. Harlequin leaps at illusory vistas through the paper set, a clown struck with a wooden sword "bleeds" ("Help—I'm dripping with cranberry juice!"), and the figure of Death appears. As Pierrot stretches out his arms to this figure, she becomes Columbine. The author returns, the scenery flies up, and all but Pierrot disappear. He again mourns for his lost bride: "She's fallen down— / I'm very sad. You think it's funny?" And he plays a sad little tune on his little reed pipe.

PURGATORY, a one-act verse play by WILLIAM BUTLER YEATS, produced in 1938 and published in 1939. Setting: "a ruined house and a bare tree in the background."

Purgatory has elicited more commentaries than any of Yeats's other plays. Though acknowledging its "extraordinary theatrical skill," T. S. ELIOT (in "The Poetry of W. B. Yeats") described the play, one of Yeats's last works, as "not very pleasant." Concentrated in a few pages and limited to two unnamed characters, it is highly suggestive and far more complex (despite the simple plot) than his earlier purgatorial play, THE DREAMING OF THE BONES.

A coarse sixteen-year-old boy and an old man, father and son, stand before a house. Though the boy sees nothing but a gutted building, the father envisions and reveals its history. It is the anniversary of his mother's wedding night—and of his own conception. She was the daughter of the house, married its worthless stable groom, and died in childbirth. The groom eventually ruined the house and set fire to it. His sixteen-year-old son (now the old man) killed him and ran away to escape prosecution. In time he became a peddler and begot a "bastard"—the boy—"Upon a tinker's daughter in a ditch." A window lights up, and though the boy sees nothing but an empty hole in the wall, the old man sees his mother. She appears as the young girl on her wedding night, waiting for her groom's return from the public house: "This night she is no better than her man / And does not mind that he is half drunk, / She is mad about him." The old man cries out to warn his mother of the groom's touch: "If he touch he must beget / And you must bear his murderer." But she cannot hear the old man and is driven by remorse to relive that night. While the old man watches the vision of his parents, the boy tries to steal his money and run away. It scatters on the ground and they struggle for it. The boy threatens his father: "What if I killed you? You killed my grand-dad, / Because you were young and he was old. / Now I am young and you are old." Suddenly the father sees the groom at the lighted window, pouring himself a drink. The boy, too, sees the vision now and is horrified. To end his mother's purgatory, the old man kills the boy—"My father and my son on the same jack-knife!" The window darkens, but the tree suddenly stands in a "cold, sweet, glistening light." The old man associates it with his mother because he thinks she is now purified: "I killed that lad because had he grown up / He would have struck a woman's fancy, / Begot, and passed pollution on." But her purgatory continues. "Twice a murderer and all for nothing," the old man says, imploring God to "Appease / The misery of the living and the remorse of the dead."

PURPLE DUST, "a wayward comedy in three acts" by SEAN O'CASEY, published in 1940 and produced in 1944. Setting: an old Tudor mansion in contemporary Clune na Geera, Ireland.

Like Shaw's JOHN BULL'S OTHER ISLAND, this is a satire on the relations of the English and the Irish. But it is more farcical as well as lyrical, and it also spoofs pastoral yearnings and various human foibles. The two foolish London financiers' scheme of refurbishing a Tudor mansion for themselves to live in like country squires of old is harebrained. The shrewd and spirited Irish rustics hasten the scheme's and the mansion's collapse into "purple dust."

Early in the morning Basil Stoke and Cyril Poges dance with servants and the Irish mistresses they have brought from London. They are dressed in pastoral costumes, and they sing of "the pigeon's coo" and "the lark's song too." The laborers who are repairing the dilapidated old mansion watch these antics with surprised amusement. They flirt with the mistresses and try to sell the Englishmen's cattle and "entherprisin'" hens "that lay with pride an' animation." The patriotic and blustering Englishmen, though they try to rejoice in nature and re-create the manor's past glory, are increasingly upset by rural discomforts and inefficiency. The exasperated Poges, calling one of the workers a fool, must listen to an angry lecture by the proud Irishman. Stoke is thrown off his horse and the foreman rides off with his mistress—"naked and unashamed," one of the Irishmen reports. Upstairs, a worker who keeps knocking holes through the wrong part of the ceiling is anguished: "Oh, isn't it like me to be up here outa sight o' th' world, an' great things happenin'!" Calamities multiply as the Englishmen freeze in the drafty house, buy a gigantic grass roller that crashes through the wall, and get frightened by and shoot a cow in their hallway: "What an awful country to be living in! A no-man's land; a waste land; a wilderness!" An antique desk is crazily rammed through a narrow entrance by workers who do not care whether it is a "squattrocento or nottrocento." To the Englishmen, Irish tales of past glories are meaningless. "There is sweet music in the land, but not for th' deaf," a worker tells them; "there is wisdom too, but it is not in a desk it is, but out in th' hills, an' in the life of all things rovin' round, undher th' blue sky." But the Englishmen do not understand and pay no heed to his dire prophecies. Soon flood waters break into the house, and the mistresses on whom the Englishmen have foolishly made lifetime settlements go off to the rural hills with their Irish suitors. As the Englishmen escape from their ruins, Poges laments, "Would to God I were in England, now that winter's here!"

PYGMALION, a verse play in five acts by GEORG KAISER, published in 1948 and produced in 1953. Setting: legendary Thebes.

Kaiser here expressed his disillusionment through the protagonist. The second in his Greek trilogy, his last three plays, this one suggests that despite benevolent divine intervention, the artist can escape the reality of worldly emptiness only in his work.

Pygmalion has completed his statue and dreams of happiness with her on an uninhabited island. Despairing as he awakes to reality, he is stopped by Athene from taking his life. Though she knows he will be disillusioned, the goddess breathes life into the statue. This statue—Pygmalion names her Chaire—too has dreamed of their happiness on that island. But practical affairs intervene: the merchant who commissioned the statue demands his money back if he cannot have the statue. He and others assume Pygmalion is defrauding them because he now has a mistress. Pygmalion publicly "identifies" Chaire as a nobleman's respectable niece. This story, Pygmalion's second "creation," compounds his difficulties. A nobleman who bears the name Pygmalion had given out as being that of Chaire's uncle angrily denies his story, and Pygmalion is arrested with Chaire. His revelation of Chaire's true identity is taken as a joke, a search is made for the statue, and Chaire is sent to the brothel from which she presumably escaped. In his studio Pygmalion again wants to commit suicide. Again Athene intervenes, returning Chaire in her original form as a statue, and persuades Pygmalion that the statue—ideal artistic creation—cannot be mixed with worldly reality: "She cannot be both." Bitterly disillusioned, Pygmalion must seek salvation in his art, and try to understand why "Dream and Life are not supposed to unite / In one circle without beginning or end."

PYGMALION, "A Romance in Five Acts" by BERNARD SHAW, produced in 1913 and published in 1914. Setting: London, 1912.

An immediate hit at its world premiere in Vienna (in SIEGFRIED TREBITSCH's translation), and a SUCCÈS DE SCANDALE in London (1914) because of the taboo word "bloody" in Act III, *Pygmalion* has remained one of Shaw's most popular plays. For Gabriel Pascal's 1938 film version Shaw himself added speeches and entire scenes which stress the Cinderella theme; the play also was made into an enormously popular musical, Lerner and Loewe's MY FAIR LADY. In his preface to the published play Shaw noted *Pygmalion*'s didacticism—the importance of improving phonetics, a subject almost as close to Shaw's heart as the simplification of the alphabet—and cited the immense success of *Pygmalion* as proof "that great art can never be anything else" but didactic. Though the plot is a very free modern adaptation of the Pygmalion-Galatea legend, Higgins (modeled on an Oxford phonetician, Professor Henry Sweet) is a characteristically Shavian hero. Interesting discussions on the play and its London production appear in Shaw's correspondence with Mrs. Patrick Campbell (published in 1952), who played Eliza.

Act I. At the portico of St. Paul's Church in Covent Garden some people are sheltering from an evening rainstorm. Freddy Eynsford-Hill, an impoverished and helpless young gentleman, goes to find a taxi for his mother and his sister. Henry Higgins, a brilliant professor of phonetics, makes notes and comments on the dialects of the bystanders, ridiculing in particular the speech of Eliza Doolittle, a pert and dirty Cockney flower girl. Colonel Pickering, a Sanskrit expert just arrived from India to meet him, is delighted to find Higgins, who has been equally desirous of meeting Pickering. After calling Eliza a "squashed cabbage leaf" who has "no right to live" because she is an "incarnate insult" to "the language of Shakespear and Milton and The Bible," Higgins tosses her some change and leaves with Pickering. When Freddy arrives with his cab and finds his mother and sister gone, Eliza grandly takes the cab herself, flashing Higgins's change to the amused driver.

Act II. The next morning, in the laboratory of his home on Wimpole Street, Higgins demonstrates recordings of dialects and vowel sounds to Pickering. Eliza arrives and offers Higgins a shilling for speech lessons so that she can become a lady in a flower shop. He bullies and insults her, but then becomes intrigued by Pickering's bet that he could not train Eliza well enough to pass her off at the ambassador's party in six months. "I shall make a duchess of this draggletailed guttersnipe," Higgins announces, challenged by her being "so deliciously low—so horribly dirty." He bullies and tempts Eliza with candy, clothes, and the practical advantages of gentility. She finally agrees to his training regimen, and is taken off to be washed and fitted out. Throughout, Higgins has made no bones about his total unconcern with the possibility of her having any feelings worth bothering about, but he assures Pickering that no advantage will be taken of Eliza's position. His housekeeper asks

Higgins to watch his manners and language before the girl, a request that surprises and amuses Higgins, who considers himself "a shy, diffident" man. Eliza's father, the dustman Alfred Doolittle, enters. He has heard that Eliza is in Higgins's house, and, being "of the undeserving poor . . . up agen middle class morality," Doolittle wants to be paid for her so he can have a spree. Higgins is won over by the nerve, vitality, and liveliness of Doolittle's expression of his roguish philosophy. Eliza returns clean and dressed like a lady, but her speech and manners convince the gentlemanly Pickering that Higgins has "taken on a stiff job."

Act III. A few months later, to test her progress, Higgins takes Eliza to tea at one of his mother's at-homes. He has instructed Eliza to talk only of the weather and everybody's health, which she proceeds to do. With precise enunciation but in tangled syntax and gutter argot she relates how her father "kept ladling gin" down her aunt's throat; thus, though she was reported to have died of influenza, "it's my belief they done the old woman in." One of the guests, Freddy Eynsford-Hill, who thinks he remembers having met Eliza somewhere before, becomes enchanted with her. When he asks to walk her home, she departs with, "Walk! Not bloody likely. I am going in a taxi"; the oath scandalizes all but the smitten Freddy. Later Mrs. Higgins asks her son what he intends to do with Eliza once her training is completed, but Higgins is not concerned about that. Mrs. Higgins is exasperated with Higgins, who leaves with Pickering, happily planning further training and social outings for Eliza.

Act IV. Late at night, back home after the ambassador's party, Higgins is relieved that the experiment is over and he complacently accepts Pickering's congratulations on his great success with Eliza. In a fury because she is being totally ignored, Eliza finally throws his slippers at the amazed Higgins. He cannot understand her anger, ridicules her feelings, and tells her not to worry about her future: they will find someone for her to marry, or they will set her up in a flower shop. His nonchalance and insensitivity to her infuriate Eliza; bitterly sarcastic, she finally goads Higgins into losing his temper. He accuses her of ingratitude and heartlessness, and stalks out.

Act V. The next morning, not knowing that Eliza is there, Higgins and Pickering arrive at Mrs. Higgins's, greatly agitated about Eliza's having disappeared, and for no apparent reason. A splendidly attired but broken Alfred Doolittle comes in, reproaching Higgins at length for having destroyed his happiness: Higgins's recommendation, to a millionaire, of Doolittle as an original moralist has resulted in a bequest to Doolittle that has trapped him into middle-class morality and respectability. Mrs. Higgins explains to her incredulous son that Eliza's reaction to his lack of consideration the night before was justified. After his sulky promise to behave, Mrs. Higgins calls Eliza. Pointedly ignoring Higgins, who becomes increasingly more furious, Eliza thanks Pickering for having treated her like a human being and a lady, but she refuses to return to them. She finally tells Higgins that it is his indifference to her that has hurt her. Employing flattery and abuse, Higgins asks her to return and live with them as a friend, "for the fun of it." When she asks him why he went through all the trouble with her if he did not care for her, he replies: "Would the world ever have been made if its maker had been afraid of making trouble? Making life means making trouble." Seeing that Higgins will not change, she leaves after announcing that she will marry Freddy, who loves her, and will teach phonetics to support him. Higgins is convinced that Eliza will return to them and, as the curtain falls, he is smugly amused at the thought of her marrying Freddy.

In a lengthy postscript Shaw vigorously defended this nonromantic ending and finished the story: Eliza marries Freddy, for "Galatea never does quite like Pygmalion: his relation to her is too godlike to be altogether agreeable."

Q

QUARE FELLOW, THE, a "comedy-drama" in three acts by BRENDAN BEHAN, produced in 1954 and published in 1956. Setting: a prison in Dublin, Ireland, in the mid-twentieth century.

This, Behan's first play, was originally a one-act piece entitled *The Twisting of Another Rope* (an allusion to DOUGLAS HYDE's similarly titled play). Rejected by the Abbey Theatre, the play was produced by Dublin's avante-garde Pike Theatre. Its production in England two years later—and a notorious drunken appearance on television at the time (May 1956)—made Behan famous, and the play was filmed in 1963. Inspired by Behan's own experiences, it vividly portrays prison life at the time of an execution. Its gallows humor does not obscure Behan's revulsion of capital punishment. The condemned man ("the quare fellow") never appears onstage, and most of the prisoners and warders are unnamed.

Act I. A prisoner sings offstage. Then other prisoners appear. They discuss the revoking of the death sentence of a fellow convict who beat his wife to death with a silver-topped cane; but another condemned man, who killed and dismembered his brother with a meat chopper, will be hanged the next morning. Speculating on the way in which quare fellows spend their last night, the prisoners devise means to peek at and quarrel over the "mots" who hang out their washing in the adjoining women's prison. The reprieved murderer gets increasingly depressed at the thought of life imprisonment—though one of the old-timers assures him it is "a bloody sight better than death any day of the week"—and is incensed at having "a bloody sex mechanic" (a morals offender) placed in the adjoining cell. While a kindly warder, Regan, massages his rheumatic legs, the old prisoner drinks up the rubbing alcohol. An unctuous Justice Department examiner makes his periodic visit to hear prisoners' complaints. His pompousness is not ruffled even when the depressed convict tries to hang himself. The examiner asks Warder Regan, who becomes increasingly irritable as the execution hour nears, why he stays in such work. "It's a soft job, sir, between hangings," Regan replies.

Act II. That evening the prisoners wander around the partly dug grave. They place bets on a last-minute reprieve, joke, discuss the mechanics of hanging, scuffle, and admire the lavishness of the quare fellow's last supper tray. As the man takes his exercise in the adjoining yard, the chief warder tells a colleague no reprieve will come. Later the prisoners talk about Regan, whom they consider peculiar but decent. Condemned prisoners always ask him to accompany them to their execution, though "hanging seems to get on his nerves." When someone suggests that Regan opposes capital punishment, a prisoner is indignant: "My God, the man's an atheist! He should be dismissed from the public service. . . . There are still a few of us who care about the state of the country, you know." They discuss the quare fellow's vicious crime but, says a prisoner, "Sure, you'd pity him all the same. It must be awful to die at the end of a swinging rope and a black hood over his poor face." Then they argue over religion. Regan briefs a young warder who is to accompany him to the execution. He recalls the horror of his own first visit, but impresses the novice with the quare fellow's needs: "He's depending on you, and you're going to do your best for him." The hangman arrives, a likable traveling-salesman type who invites the warders for a drink and makes his preparations for a proper, efficient execution.

Act III. That night, as the execution moment nears, the excitement mounts. The prisoners communicate by tapping on the hotwater pipes, and a shifty, vicious warder, who anticipates becoming the Principal, tells a colleague they are in this job "for the three P's, boy, pay, promotion and pension, that's all that should bother civil servants like us." Regan, increasingly nervous, describes the gruesomeness of executions and bitterly tells his chief that these performances should be made public, "in Croke Park; after all, it's at the public expense and they let it go on." The hangman returns from the pub, and everything is ready, even "the hood slit to anoint him on the rope." Early in the morning the execution takes place. A prisoner reports it from his cell window. "We take you to the bottom of D. Wing," he declaims: "We're off," and the warders take off their caps. He visualizes the last few steps and the end, "His feet to the chalk line. He'll be pinioned, his feet together . . ." The hour strikes, the warders cross themselves, and there is "ferocious howling" from all the prisoners. Regan returns, reports that the new warder fainted during the execution, and tosses the executed man's letters into the grave. Some of the prisoners scramble for them, eager to sell them to the Sunday papers—"For what's a crook, only a businessman without a shop." The curtain falls as a prisoner sings about living with the female prisoners next door: "Then that old triangle / Could jingle jangle / Along the banks of the Royal Canal."

QUARTS D'HEURE, fifteen-minute dramatic pieces written by avant-garde dramatists for experimental theatres such as André Antoine's Théâtre-Libre (1887–96). Perhaps the best-known of these is Strindberg's THE STRONGER; it as well as his SIMOON and PARIAH, written for the Copenhagen experimental theatre he was trying to establish in 1888–89 and inspired by the philosophy of Nietzsche and the tales of Edgar Allan Poe, are compelling NATURALISTIC thrillers.

QUEEN AFTER DEATH (*La Reine morte*), a play in three acts by HENRY DE MONTHERLANT, published and produced in 1942. Setting: Portugal, "in the past."

Subtitled *Comment on tue les femmes* (*How to Kill Women*), this play was Montherlant's first hit and made him a major French dramatist. It was inspired by the works of Lope de Vega and other sixteenth- and seventeenth-century Spanish playwrights, and is Renaissance in plot and characters. But physical action is subordinated to the characterization of an agonizing, Hamlet-like protagonist. The elderly King Ferrante is a cross between a vulgar and a spiritual man (Montherlant wrote in his "Notes" to the play), who "seeks to be in this world without being of it; to belong without total commitment."

Act I. Brought to Portugal to marry the prince, the Infanta of Navarre (Doña Bianca) is incensed upon her arrival to find herself rejected because the prince loves Doña Inès de Castro. Angrily the Infanta complains to King Ferrante, who asks her to wait a few days, for the prince's "folly may pass." The Infanta proudly replies, "If God were willing to give me heaven itself, but wished to put it off till later, I should rather hurl myself into hell than have to wait on God's good pleasure." Ferrante reasons with his son and deplores his mediocrity as a man. He suggests finally that the prince keep Inès as his mistress but for reasons of state marry the Infanta: the Infanta would not object, for "she will have the kingdom, and the kingdom is well worth this little vexation." To Ferrante's consternation, however, the prince refuses to give up his "pleasure." Later the lovers agree they must inform the king of their secret marriage—and of Inès's pregnancy. Before the prince can summon the courage to do so, Ferrante himself arrives and demands to see Inès. Trying to get her to persuade her lover to marry the Infanta, Ferrante learns of the marriage. "He's no less a coward than a cheat and a fool," Ferrante exclaims angrily, remembering his son's evasive replies, and has him arrested: "To prison for mediocrity!"

Act II. Ferrante's counselors advise the execution of Inès "for the good of the State." The king is torn by doubts. As his prime minister persists, Ferrante sighs, "O God, never forgive him, for he knows what he is doing." After gently chiding his pages for their antics, Ferrante summons Inès. He allows her to visit the imprisoned prince, to urge him to agree to marry the Infanta if a papal dispensation may be obtained. But Ferrante himself refuses to see his son: "He makes me ashamed of myself—of having at one time believed in my love for him and of not being capable of keeping that love." Inès rejoices to see her beloved, but their tender scene is interrupted and ended by the Infanta. Perceiving the inevitable tragedy, she predicts that Inès will be executed, and asks Inès to accompany her back to Spain. She cannot understand Inès's inability to tear herself away from her beloved: all men she herself has met seemed cowards, and "no human being is worth dying for." When Inès persists, the Infanta sadly dismisses her. She gives Inès a bracelet—"a symbol of our own failure to clasp"—and, alone, looks at a distant cataract: "One must let the waters fall—"

Act III. Inès has a long interview with the somber king, who comes to like her but is angered by the Pope's refusal to grant the annulment. Morose and uncertain, Ferrante confesses to Inès that, though he has the needed courage and strength, he lacks the third kingly prerequisite: faith. His duties, his need to judge and pronounce sentence, lack reality for he feels only indifference. The shade of the Infanta warns Inès to leave at once, for the king "is throwing into you his despairing secrets, as into a tomb." Courtiers listen in the background and depart in horror as Ferrante voices his despair. Inès now reveals her pregnancy, but the thought of a grandson merely heightens Ferrante's despair: "Another spring to begin all over again, and to begin again less well!" He recalls how hope for his own son vanished as the boy became a disappointment. "Not my son," Inès is sure: "I should be capable of killing him if he did not answer to what I expect of him." Increasingly bitter, Ferrante brings Inès near despair. As he does so, however, he himself passes his "crisis of sincerity." Though moved by Inès, he regains the strength to rule—and judge. After he promises her

Queen After Death, Act III. Inès (Mony Dakmès) on her bier; Ferrante's young page (André Falcon), kneeling. Paris, 1942. (*French Cultural Services*)

safety, Inès looks up at the sky as she leaves: "There's a star that has gone out." Ferrante replies, "It will light up again elsewhere." Then he calls a captain and orders that Inès be killed at once. In agony he considers remanding his order as he awaits its execution. The moment Inès is killed on her way home, Ferrante himself collapses and dies. The subservient courtiers call for the release of the prince—now their king. They leave Ferrante and kneel before the corpse of Inès—the new king's beloved queen—brought in on a bier. Only Ferrante's young page kneels before the old King's corpse. He glances at the others, finally gets up, and joins them before Inès's bier. On the other side of the stage the dead King Ferrante lies alone.

QUEEN AND THE REBELS, THE (*La regina e gli insorti*), a play in four acts by UGO BETTI, published and produced in 1951. Setting: a large town hall in a mountain village in the "present day."

Though *The Queen and the Rebels* is one of Betti's few political plays, like the others it too portrays characteristic psychological and moral quests for self-identity.

Act I. Taken off their bus by rebel forces of the revolution, worried travelers are bullied by a military interpreter. They are detained in a search for the deposed and escaped queen. When the interpreter examines them individually, he recognizes among them his former mistress. A still-attractive prostitute, Argia had come to the rebel town searching for him. Insultingly he rejects her, unwilling to burden himself with her in his determination to survive by joining the winning side. Commissar Amos arrives with the wounded commanding general, eager to capture the queen, who, they know, is there. Argia recognizes a frightened peasant woman as the queen and excitedly calls the interpreter. "I'm worth marrying now," she whispers, anticipating her reward: "I'm a splendid match."

Act II. Agitated and blustering, the interpreter plans to have the peasant woman (the queen) shot, "grab what we can out of it," and escape with Argia. Soon the queen confesses to Argia her identity and her terror, and provides a harrowing description of the misery of her life as a fugitive who has had to buy safety even with her body. Argia takes pity on the broken woman, whose sole desire is to remain alive, and helps her escape. During the commotion that follows, Commissar Amos appears, observes Argia suspiciously, and begins to question her: "Madam: what is your name?"

Act III. Believing her to be the queen, Amos continues his questioning. Argia laughs when she realizes his mistake, and explains her haughty bearing as a practiced response to a life of humiliation: "Every time I've come away with my cheeks still burning, what scathing retorts, what tremendous, noble answers I've always imagined!" The interpreter she calls as her witness denies knowing her, and the the captured peasant woman (the real queen) commits suicide. Unable to prove her own identity, Argia rises. "Not every eye shall look to the ground," she says with proud defiance: "Yes, I am the Queen!" Delighted, the rebels begin the kangaroo court. "The revolution has decided that the Queen must die," Amos announces: "The sentence will be carried out during the course of the night."

Act IV. The firing squad is ready, but Amos offers Argia a pardon in return for a signed confession of her "illegal and dishonorable conduct" and a list of her "accomplices." With growing dignity Argia refuses. Amos describes the tortures she may be subjected to and urges her to follow her human instincts for self-preservation. Anguished, Argia demands respect "because I am—the Queen! The Queen, and destined for other things than this." Suddenly she realizes that she is no longer afraid—and that she is indeed assuming majesty: "I am as I would always have wished to be. And it would have been simple after all. It would have been enough to want to be. Palaces have nothing to do with it. It was my own fault." Amos confronts her with the queen's child and threatens to kill him. In a moment of confusion Argia is about to reveal the information, which the real queen had given her, in a futile gesture to save the child. But she has forgotten the names and, relieved, looks forward to death and the last judgment: "He will be asking what my profit has been. The only one I have had I have had this night." As she goes out to her execution Argia looks at the starry sky: "Unquestionably, this is a seat for kings, and in it we must try to live regally." Amos covers the child's ears as Argia is shot.

QUINTESSENCE OF IBSENISM, THE (1891), by BERNARD SHAW, is a lively and perceptive, though tendentious, study of HENRIK IBSEN's contribution of NATURALISM and discussion to modern drama and thought. Shaw emphasized and illustrated Ibsen's exposé of ideals and idealism with a play-by-play analysis of his major dramas. Often more descriptive and revealing of its author than its subject, the book is considered by many to be "The Quintessence of Shavianism." Shaw wrote additional prefaces to the volume's second (1913) and third (1922) editions.

R

R.U.R., a play in three acts and a prologue by KAREL ČAPEK, published in 1920 and produced in 1921. Setting: a remote island, in the future.

Like THE GOLEM of Jewish legend and Mary Shelley's Frankenstein, the creatures who populate this play personify technology gone awry and destroying humanity. The original title is English and stands for "Rossum's Universal Robots," the factory's name: the first word comes from the Czech word for "reason," the third—which introduced the word into common usage—from *robota,* Czech for "forced labor" or "drudgery." Though the play bears some affinity to Kaiser's GAS trilogy, its dramaturgy is conventionally melodramatic. Despite various improbabilities and the final thematic confusion, its science-fiction appeal made *R.U.R.* one of the most popular plays of the 1920's.

Prologue. (This comic prologue usually appears as Act I in English translations, which print the last act as an "epilogue.") Harry Domin, the factory's general manager, is dictating to a robot secretary when Helena Glory, the company president's daughter, visits the island. Because she is also young and beautiful, Domin freely discusses the factory. "The manufacture of artificial people is a secret process," but he tells the apparently curious girl its history. Long ago, "Old Rossum," a pure scientist, had discovered a substance with which he could create life. A rationalist, "he wanted to become a sort of scientific substitute for God" and tried to make ordinary humans. It was his young nephew, a practical industrial scientist, who created robots. Young Rossum believed that "man is something that feels happy, . . . wants to do a whole lot of things that are really unnecessary." But a worker is best if he is cheap, hence the robots: "Mechanically they are more perfect than we are . . . but they have no soul." Helena is appalled to discover that Domin's apparently human secretary is a manufactured robot. Proud of the factory, Domin describes the "vats for the preparation of liver, brains . . . the spinning-mill for weaving nerves and veins," etc. The similarity of humans and robots thoroughly confuses Helena. She mistakes the various factory officers for robots, identifies herself as a representative of the Humanity League, and attempts to incite them to rebellion. After being introduced, they explain the usefulness of robots, despite some of their flaws. Only Alquist, the construction engineer, sees virtue in "toil and weariness"; the others envision the proliferation of robots as hastening the arrival of the millennium. "There'll be no poverty," Domin says; "everybody will be freed from worry, and liberated from the degradation of labor. Everybody will live only to perfect himself." Alone with Helena, Domin, in his characteristically jerky, breathless manner, proposes marriage to her. All the directors are in love with her, he reveals, and he gives her five minutes to decide. They fall into each other's arms and are congratulated by Domin's returning colleagues.

Act I. Ten years later Domin and his colleagues bring Helena anniversary gifts. Domin's is a gunboat, for robot rebellions are spreading across the world. Helena's old nurse is frightened of the island's robots, who are beginning to "act up." A pious soul, she considers them heathens and sinful inventions. Helena discovers newspapers that reveal not only the extent of the international robot rebellion but also the cessation of all human births. The nurse vindictively declares this to be a divine punishment. The old engineer Alquist, too, prays for deliverance from the robots: "Enlighten Domin and all those who are astray; destroy their work, and aid mankind to return to their labors." A particularly recalcitrant robot, Radius, proclaims his hatred of humans and his desire to be master. The physician examines him and perceives in the robot emotional reactions, traces of a heart, perhaps even a soul. "People are becoming superfluous," the doctor remarks, but is surprised that it has happened so soon. Helena secretly burns the robot-manufacturing formula, hoping this will somehow avert further disaster. To her horror, Domin plans to manufacture mutually hostile and destructive "National Robots" of different colors and languages. Soon there is news of local uprisings and victories by the robots. They are reported to be distributing leaflets calling for the destruction of mankind, and are observed as they capture the gunboat, surround the house, and prepare to attack.

Act II. With their colleagues, Domin and Helena are barricaded in their apartment. Domin persists in justifying their attempt to end "the unclean and murderous drudgery" of man. But Alquist calls robot-making a crime: "Old Rossum only thought of his godless tricks, and the young one of his millions" and, Alquist adds, the "R.U.R. shareholders . . . dream of dividends." The men place an electrically charged wire outside, and this kills a number of invading robots. The doctor had tampered with the manufacturing process and now admits his guilt in the robots' action: "I was transforming them into human beings." Helena takes the blame: "I wanted him to make souls for the robots." To save the humans' lives, the business manager suggests that they sell the robots the

R. U. R., Act III. Alquist (Louis Calvert) and the robot delegation headed by Radius (John Rutherford). New York, 1922. (*Culver Pictures*)

formula of production. The men debate the morality of this proposal, but then cannot find the formula. Helena reveals that she has destroyed it: "I wanted to put an end to the factory and everything. It was so awful . . . children had stopped being born—Harry, that's awful!" Frantically the business manager goes out with company funds to negotiate for their lives, touches the electrified wire, and dies. Then the current is cut off. The robots enter and kill all but Alquist, who refuses to defend himself. "He works with his hands like the robots," Radius, the robot leader, decides: "You will build for us! You will serve us!" And then Radius proclaims the end of man and the rise of "the rule of the Robots."

Act III. A year later in the R.U.R. laboratory, Alquist desperately tries to manufacture robots for his masters. All attempts to find surviving humans have failed, and the robots are increasingly worried about their own extinction. "Only human beings can procreate—renew life, increase," Alquist reiterates. He refuses to dissect robots to study and possibly reproduce their structure, and keeps urging them to discover human beings. "We are sterile," Radius admits, but no longer machines: "terror and pain have turned us into souls." Exhausted, old Alquist falls asleep. A male and a female robot enter. They are Primus and the robot named after Helena. Their talk evidences human qualities: they have yearnings, appreciation of beauty, affection, a sense of humor. When one of them laughs, Alquist wakes up. He senses their human qualities, tests them, and discovers that the robots love each other: neither will allow him to experiment on and dissect the other, each offers himself. Though the concept of death has heretofore been meaningless to robots, these two now refuse to be killed: "We—we—belong to each other." Almost in tears, Alquist tells them, "Go, Adam, go, Eve." The humanized robots embrace and depart. Alquist picks up a Bible, declaims the verses of Genesis, and concludes joyfully, "Life will not perish."

RAIN FROM HEAVEN, a play in three acts by S. N. BEHRMAN, produced in 1934 and published in 1935. Setting: an English country house outside London, 1934.

An anti-Fascist, sophisticated "dark" comedy, this play was inspired by GERHART HAUPTMANN's rebuffing, during the Nazi regime, of his friend Alfred Kerr, the distinguished German-Jewish critic who had helped make him famous.

Lady Lael (Violet in the acting version) Wyngate, a wealthy and charming liberal, is in love with a famous American explorer hero. Among her other guests are his financier brother, a virulent anti-Communist come to England to organize a Fascist youth league; and Hugo Willens, a "one eighth" Jewish refugee music critic put into a concentration camp during the German "chromosome hunt." The pathologic capitalist, frustrated in his efforts to enlist an English newspaper tycoon in his Fascist scheme, tries to stop his brother from marrying the liberal Lael, whose guest he insults. "You think it's because you killed Christ that we fear and hate you," he tells Hugo: "No! It's because you gave birth to Lenin!" The capitalist's wife, who is in love with Hugo and jealous of Lael, accuses her of being Hugo's mistress. The naïve explorer, shocked by Lael's supposed "defilement," calls Hugo a "dirty Jew." Thereupon Lael falls in love with Hugo. But though he reciprocates her love, Hugo decides to return to Germany to fight Fascism. Lael rejects but consoles the young explorer, who is penitent over his anti-Semitic outburst: "We're all shut in behind our little fences."

RAISIN IN THE SUN, A, a play in three acts by LORRAINE HANSBERRY, published and produced in 1959. Setting: Chicago's South Side, sometime between World War II and 1959.

Winner of the New York Drama Critics' Circle Award, this portrayal of blacks who dream and yearn has been compared to Jewish and Irish family dramas such as Odets's AWAKE AND SING and O'Casey's JUNO AND THE PAYCOCK. The play's title comes from a poem by LANGSTON HUGHES: "What happens to a dream deferred? / Does it dry up / Like a raisin in the sun?"

The Younger family, cramped in a black ghetto slum apartment, eagerly await the arrival of the life-insurance check after the death of the father. Mama wants to use the money to buy a house for all of them: her son Walter Lee and his family, and her daughter, who aspires to the study of medicine. But her son, a chauffeur who dreams of being a financier like those he sees "turning deals worth millions of dollars," wants to invest the money in a liquor business. Mama makes a down payment on a house and Walter is even more frustrated when he learns his wife is pregnant again. Mama has trouble also with her daughter, a modern girl who denies God, decides not to marry a wealthy suitor, and keeps company with a visiting Nigerian student who wants to take her back to Africa with him. The Youngers are warned against moving into their new house, which is in a white suburb, and are offered the chance to sell out at a profit. Entrusted with the remaining insurance money, Walter loses everything in a business deal. Bitter and defeated, he is ready to sell out to the whites. But his family give him the strength to regain his pride and reject the offer. As the curtain falls, the Youngers move out to their new home.

RATS, THE (*Die Ratten*), a "Berlin Tragicomedy" in five acts by GERHART HAUPTMANN, published and produced in 1911. Setting: a Berlin tenement, 1880's.

Like Rice's STREET SCENE, Hauptmann's last important play (though he was to write for three-and-a-half more decades) teems with many characters and episodes. It has two concurrent, intertwining plots: Mrs. John's efforts to pass a baby off as her own and keep it when its real mother wants it back; and Hassenreuter's attempts to reestablish himself as a theatre director. (In their disputations, his daughter's suitor champions NATURALISM, of which this play itself is a significant example.) The first plot is tragic, the second comic, and both comment ironically, if indirectly, on and modify each other. The two plots are connected by their rat-infested setting, which—like that of THE RED COCK—symbolizes the degeneration of *fin de siècle* society.

Act I. In Harro Hassenreuter's studio, his cleaning woman, Mrs. John, talks to a desperate servant girl. Pregnant and abandoned by her lover, she is persuaded to let Mrs. John, whose own baby died, take her unwanted child after it is born. They are interrupted by Mrs. John's hoodlum brother; by Hassenreuter's young daughter, come for a tryst with Erich Spitta, a theology student and the family tutor; and finally by Hassenreuter himself, whose unexpected arrival sends the others into hiding. The eloquent ex-theatre director, now a dramatic coach, has come for an assignation with an actress in this tenement, which, he remarks, "cringes and creeps, moans, sighs, sweats, cries out, curses, mutters, hammers, planes, jeers, steals, drives its dark trades up and down these stairs." The lovers, in turn, are interrupted by his daughter's suitor, Spitta. While Hassenreuter talks with him, Mrs. John filches some of the wine for the servant girl's delivery. He discovers its absence when he returns; hearing the actress sing, he laughs happily: "Heavens, she's tipsy already."

Acts II and III. Mrs. John succeeds in passing the infant off as her own. Her kindly husband, Paul, a mason working out of town, rejoices, as do the neighbors. But the servant girl, her maternal feelings aroused, returns to claim the child. Mrs. John disappears. The girl, mistaking a paupered neighbor's baby for her own, steals it and creates an uproar. In the meantime, Spitta gives up theology and studies acting. He exasperates Hassenreuter by insisting on stage realism; even common folk, he says, can become tragic protagonists: "Before art as before the law all men are equal." To the conservative romanticist Hassenreuter this is incredible. He considers it symptomatic of progressive social degeneration caused by "rats who are beginning, in the field of politics, to undermine our glorious and recently united German Empire!" As in art, he claims, these rats "are gnawing at the roots of the tree of idealism." Then he becomes exasperated with another conservative, Spitta's pastor father, come to save his son from what *he* considers degenerate: the city, the theatre, and Spitta's sweetheart—Hassenreuter's daughter.

Acts IV and V. The daughter, knowing of her father's affair with the actress, stands up to him when Hassenreuter (who has just heard of his appointment to the sought-for directorship) moralizes disapprovingly about Spitta. Mrs. John returns, increasingly apprehensive. She had asked her hoodlum brother to keep the servant girl away. He arrives wearing a lilac sprig. Gradually he reveals that he murdered the girl under a lilac bush: "I got a little bit excited—an' then, well . . . that's how it come . . ." The police now search the area. As the tension mounts, Mrs. John's husband, Paul, becomes increasingly confused and upset: "Everythin's rotten here, everythin's worm eaten! Everythin's undermined by varmint an' by rats an' by mice." He wants to remove "his" baby from this environment: "Any minute the whole business might crash down into the cellar." His wife is overcome with guilt and fear, and soon the truth emerges. The baby is snatched away from her arms but she rushes out, crazed with grief. Her husband, having earlier turned against her, now frantically tries to stop her: "Mother! Stop! Hold her!" Present during this drama, Hassenreuter smugly asserts his new conviction to Spitta: "Tragedy is not confined to any class of society. I always told you that!" Outside, Mrs. John throws herself under the traffic. She is immediately killed.

RATTIGAN, Terence [Merryn] (1911–), English playwright, has produced some of the most popular comedies of his time. The first author to pass the one-thousand-consecutive-performance mark with two plays (FRENCH WITHOUT TEARS, 1936; and WHILE THE SUN SHINES, 1943), Rattigan has written such other comedy hits as LOVE IN IDLENESS (1944, titled *O Mistress Mine* in America) and THE SLEEPING PRINCE (1953). What critical reputation Rattigan has achieved, however, rests on his serious plays, particularly THE WINSLOW BOY (1946, his first departure from light comedy), THE BROWNING VERSION (1948), THE DEEP BLUE SEA (1952), SEPARATE TABLES (1954), and ROSS (1960), his "dramatic portrait" of Lawrence of Arabia.

Born in London, Rattigan attended Harrow and Oxford University. During World War II he served with the Royal Air Force. According to Rattigan's own testimony, he was always supremely confident of his gifts as a playwright. His early success with the public seemed to justify this confidence. He raised something of a journalistic furor when he announced his "preference for plays of character and narrative over plays of ideas" and blandly declared that the theatre is not a place for ideas, sentiments reiterated in the introductions to his collected plays. While his comedies are, indeed, no more than very amusing fluff, these dicta need not be taken wholly at face value. Rattigan's serious drama, if not didactic, certainly is thoughtful and demonstrates his understanding of and concern with important human problems. Though his skill in depicting these in the theatre—and his consequent popularity with fashionable audiences—would appear to add to rather than detract from the plays' quality, students of the drama have generally ignored his work. Dismissed as a mere, though first-rate craftsman, Rattigan has never been accorded his deserved stature as a dramatist.

Rattigan's other plays include *First Episode* (1934); *After the Dance* (1939); *Follow My Leader* (1940; written with Hector Bolitho, 1899–); *Flare Path* (1942), a war play that was successful in England but failed in America; *Adventure Story* (1949); *Who Is Silvia?* (1950); *Variations on a Theme* (1958), a "*La Dame aux Camélias* in twentieth-century guise"; and *A Mutual Pair* (1968), his adaptation (further elaborated as *A Bequest to the Nation,* 1970) of an earlier television play (*Nelson*) about the Admiral's last days and his relations with Emma Hamilton.

The Collected Plays of Terence Rattigan were published in three volumes (1953-64), each with an introduction by the author.

RAYNAL, Paul (1890–), French dramatist, distinguished himself in France during the period between the two world wars with modern tragedies written in the tradition of Corneille and Racine. His most popular work, *Le Tombeau sous l'Arc de Triomphe* (1924), is a three-character play that depicts a soldier's brief furlough, during which he succeeds in conveying something of his own courage and high-mindedness to his father's and his fiancée's prosaic, peace-loving lives behind the front. Raynal's first play, *Le Maître de son cœur,* portrays conflicts in the friendship of a rationalist and a sentimentalist in their love for a passionate woman; it was written in 1909 and submitted in 1913, but the war delayed its production until 1920—when it became an immediate Paris hit. Notable later Raynal plays are the "*comédie épique*" *Napoléon unique* (1936), a rounded characterization and tragic conception of the emperor's marriage to and break with Josephine; and *À souffert sous Ponce Pilate* (1939), a sympathetic portrait of a Judas, who, though disillusioned, tries to save Jesus and hangs himself when he realizes his unwitting betrayal. Despite their occasional oratory these and other Raynal dramas have been praised for their lyricism and psychological insight.

Le Tombeau sous l'Arc de Triomphe was produced in New York and published in Cecil Lewis's translation, *The Unknown Warrior,* in 1928.

REALISM is as loose a term in the drama as it is in the other arts. It refers to any attempt at reproducing verisimilitude on the stage. Since this could mean the representation of external or internal, physical or psychological or philosophical—or even political, sociological, or economic—"realities," and since these may be perceived in many different ways, the term is almost meaningless. Instead of being a *description* of anything, it is popularly used as an *evaluation,* usually an approving value judgment on the "truthfulness" of a work. For more meaningful terms with which it is often confused see NATURALISM and REPRESENTATIONAL.

RED COCK, THE (*Der rote Hahn*), a "tragicomedy" in four acts by GERHART HAUPTMANN, published and produced in 1901. Setting: a village near Berlin, 1890's.

Also known as *The Conflagration* (symbolized by a red cock in Germany), this is a sequel to THE BEAVER COAT. Mrs. Wolff's husband has died, and she is now married to a shoemaker, the procuring police spy alluded to in the earlier play. Von Wehrhahn, the growing village's magistrate, is an even more reactionary patriot and bumbler, and an increasingly militant supporter of the

Church. The sequel, less successful than the earlier play, is a mordant protest against the degeneration of *fin de siècle* industrial society.

The late Wolff's widow persuades her second husband to do as others have done: set their house on fire and collect the insurance. Her older daughter, now an unmarried mother, is pursued by the village smith as well as the constable. The younger daughter has succeeded in marrying the building speculator, who is rapidly becoming the prospering village's master. While she and her husband are in Berlin, the former Mrs. Wolff manages to have her house burned down and implicate a demented village lad. Von Wehrhahn examines the case and admonishes his audience, including the most decent character in the play, a Jewish doctor: "Degeneration is caused by lack of religion! . . . Brotherly love! The Christian spirit! Breeches down tight and have your behind flogged! Christian discipline!" At the end Mrs. Wolff justifies herself before the distraught father of the suspect: "If you don't join the scramble you're lazy, if you do you're bad.—An' everythin' we does get, we gets outta dirt. . . . An' they, they tells us: be good. But how?" Her anti-Semitic and antilabor son-in-law cynically professes democratic ideals and is able to gain the villagers' support. As the weather vane is erected on the house he has built with the fire insurance, the former Mrs. Wolff has a heart attack and dies.

RED MAGIC (*Magie rouge*), a play in three acts by MICHEL DE GHELDERODE, produced in 1934 and published in 1935. Setting: Flanders, in olden times.

This is a macabre play that, like HOP SIGNOR!, features a lustful virgin wife. But the main character here is her husband, Hieronymus, an old miser. In his cellars a clever crook tricks him out of money and wife, and murders his own accomplices. He makes Hieronymus believe himself immortal and immensely wealthy, able to buy the Pope and the Trinity. "I am like God. . . . You do not know that I am immortal, do you?" Hieronymus tells the jeering crowd, and laughs as he is dragged off to be executed.

RED MILL, THE (*A vörös malom*), "a play in three parts and many scenes" by FERENC MOLNÁR, published and produced in 1922. Setting: Hell.

Molnár referred to this elaborate spectacle, adapted as *Mima* by DAVID BELASCO, as a sentimental morality that ends as a jest. Its critical reception was mixed, but its popularity was great. The elaborate stage machinery is illustrated and explained in the March 1929 issue of *The Scientific American*.

The architect of Hell has completed the Red Mill, an enormous "man-corrupting machine" he calls the "psycho-corrupter." Before the silent Satan, his ministers, court, guards, and the many devils, "devilkins and devilets," he is ready to demonstrate its ability to make a "finished blackguard" out of a virtuous man in one hour. First such a man must be found, however. After they reject a number of inadequate specimens, the devils bring in the simple forester János, a completely pure man. In different parts of the Red Mill he is tempted by various synthetic devils. Chief among them is the beautiful Mima. Within an hour she gets him to gamble, commit blackmail and adultery, pimp, and participate in assorted other crimes. Every time János sins a bell rings, and soon it chimes almost continuously—to the great amusement of the vast infernal audience. But when János is about to murder the evil Mima, she pleads for mercy. Though she has betrayed him viciously and still lies, János forgives her. This act of mercy destroys the machine—which starts to rumble, bursts into flames, and then blows up. János awakes in his simple cottage as his beloved wife calls him for supper.

RED ROBE, THE (*La Robe rouge*), a play in four acts by EUGÈNE BRIEUX, published and produced in 1900. Setting: Mauléon, France; c. 1900.

This condemnation of the French judiciary was produced in America also as *The Letter of the Law*. It portrays the widespread intrigue for promotion (for the coveted "red robe" of a judge) that supersedes concern with justice, as well as the judiciary's obsequiousness to the press and their dependence on politicians. Despite the rhetoric and melodramatic ending, it was considered Brieux's most effective play.

Act I. The local prosecutor is eager for his long-overdue promotion. His wife years before had bought—but has had to keep packed in mothballs—the red robe he yearns to wear. Successful prosecution of a new murder case would please the ministry—which is dissatisfied with the region's few capital convictions—and thus assure his promotion. His ambitious examining magistrate, Mouzon, undertakes to discover the criminal and establish his guilt.

Act II. He finds a suspect, the Basque peasant Pierre Etchepare. Though suffering from a hangover after a riotous night, Mouzon conducts a brilliant interrogation, during which he bullies, cajoles, and entraps first a witness and then Etchepare himself. The peasant's accounts conflict, but it is nonetheless evident that he is innocent. "I can't say I did it when I didn't!" Etchepare pleads: "I almost wished I could admit I was guilty if only you'd leave me in peace." Thereupon Mouzon interrogates Etchepare's wife, Yanetta, an exemplary wife and mother. But Mouzon has unearthed an old youthful liaison and felony. By threatening to reveal her past to Etchepare and thus destroy her family life, and by suggesting that her husband's confession would result in a mere token sentence, Mouzon gets Yanetta to beg Etchepare to confess to the murder. But again convinced of her husband's innocence when he is brought in, Yanetta repudiates her deposition and defies Mouzon. "When you've forced the poor wretch to condemn himself you're delighted, like a savage would be!" she screams as Mouzon has her taken away: "Butcher! Coward! Judas! Pitiless beast! . . . The poorer one is the more wicked you are—"

Act III. During the trial a retired judge privately explains to Etchepare's old mother that while justice is indeed free, "the means of obtaining access to it are not"; the rightness of Etchepare's cause is not enough, either: "You must have the law on your side too." In a brilliant (offstage) oration the prosecutor demolishes the defense and is assured of the guilty verdict and death sentence that would guarantee his promotion. But troubled by doubts about Etchepare's guilt, his conscience compels him—despite his wife's ambitions and the presiding officials' irritation by the spoiling of a neatly settled case—to reveal his doubts to the jury, "to do my duty as an honest man."

Act IV. He thus effects Etchepare's acquittal. Court officials are unconcerned ("one must keep oneself above the little miseries of humanity") that they have ruined Etchepare's home and—with the ferreting out of his wife's past—his life. She pleads with her husband to forgive an old sin long expiated. But he casts her off as a "loose woman," unfit ever again to see her children. The prosecutor, because of his honesty, again loses the promotion. In a package deal among various politicians, it goes to Mouzon, despite his disgraceful libertinism, which has jeopardized the authorities with a scandal. Yanetta, desperate over losing home and children, confronts Mouzon. When he coldly dismisses her, she seizes his paper knife, a souvenir from the guillotining of a woman he once prosecuted. "You nearly made a criminal of an innocent man, and you force an honest woman, a mother—to become a criminal!" Yanetta cries out, and she stabs him to death.

RED ROSES FOR ME, a play in four acts by SEAN O'CASEY, published in 1942 and produced in 1943. Setting: Dublin, "a little while ago."

Like his ineffectual *The Star Turns Red,* this play is partisan. But it is an accomplished play that dispenses with the propagandistic touches that mar the earlier work, and it has been produced successfully. Though it is NATURALISTIC for the first two acts, SYMBOLISM predominates in the remaining two. The setting suggests the bitter Transport Union Strike of 1913, in which O'Casey participated, and much of the character of Ayamonn Breydon is autobiographical.

Acts I and II. Ayamonn is a young railroad-yard worker and strike leader who, his mother remarks, overdoes things by also "sketchin', readin', makin' songs, an' learnin' Shakespeare." But to Ayamonn "they are all lovely, and my life needs them all." His study of Shakespeare is interrupted by Sheila Moorneen, his Catholic sweetheart, who braves her parents' objections to a Protestant and who wants him to spend less time on the planned strike. Other visitors to his flat include fervent patriots, Catholics, and atheists who argue incessantly, and three anguished neighbors searching for their holy statue. It has been stolen by the melodeon-playing landlord, a gruff but compassionate old Protestant who secretly repaints and then replaces it. The strike becomes unavoidable, for the workers will not be able to get their shilling raise otherwise. Sheila urges Ayamonn to take the opportunity to advance himself by scabbing, for her sake. Appalled, he pushes her back: "Go to hell, girl, I have a soul to save as well as you." And "with a catch in his voice" he adds, "Oh, Sheila, you shouldn't have asked me to do this thing!"

Acts III and IV. In a street scene on the banks of the Liffey, Ayamonn evokes for the poor and miserable a glimpse of the glory that could be theirs: "Our hands shall stretch out to th' fullness of labour, / Till wondher an' beauty within thee shall reign." The setting becomes suffused with light and the transformed paupers dance ecstatically. Then Dublin darkens again. Though warned, Ayamonn, in his church, determines to attend the strike meeting. There is a pause, and soon the strikers return, escaping from the police's brutal strikebreaking. But Ayamonn has been shot during the melee. When his body is brought into the church, the people and the rector honor him as their martyr. Now recognizing his nobility, Sheila puts red roses on his chest: "Maybe he saw the shilling in th' shape of a new world." And the landlord softly sings a ballad written by Ayamonn: "A sober black shawl hides her body entirely, / Touch'd be th' sun an' th' salt spray of th' sea." The woman is Ireland. "But down in th' darkness a slim hand, so lovely, / Carries a rich bunch of red roses for me!"

REGENT, THE (*Riksföreståndaren*), a historical play in five acts by AUGUST STRINDBERG, published in 1909 and produced in 1911. Setting: Sweden, 1520–23.

This is a companion play to THE LAST KNIGHT, which, according to Strindberg's prefatory note, "serves as the saga of youth in contrast to the heavy struggle of *The Regent.*" The settings of the earlier work are used in reverse order here, and Strindberg characteristically dissects Trolle's suffering.

After the Danes' victory and bloody executions, the ruthless Archbishop Gustav Trolle was appointed regent. Now the nominal ruler of Sweden, he feels insecure so long as Gustav Vasa is alive. Vasa escapes captivity, returns to Sweden, and seizes power from the terrified Danish henchman, who runs off. Though Vasa's mother and sisters are captive hostages, the "practical idealist" chooses duty to his country first. He is elected regent and, with the support of Herman Israel, Olaus Petri, and others, ably effects Sweden's independence. Deeply grieved to hear of the death of his mother and sisters, and well aware of future difficulties, Gustav Vasa can still make the best of things when he enters Stockholm as the triumphant king: "Sweden's realm is one, and the Swedes have become their own masters! . . . Let us go to the altar of the Great Church and sing *Te Deum laudamus!*"

REHBERG, Hans (1901–63), German playwright, was the most successful dramatizer of historical themes during the Nazi regime, though his plays are devoid of propaganda. They are objective, in prose but with high intensity and quickly moving scenes. After writing plays on *Cecil Rhodes* (1932) and *Johannes Kepler* (1933), Rehberg turned to Prussian history with *Friedrich I* (1934), *Friedrich Wilhelm I* (1935), and *Der siebenjährige Krieg* (1937). These were followed by plays on Spanish history (*Die Königin Isabella,* 1938), and, with notably little success after World War II, on English history (*Heinrich VII,* 1947; *Elisabeth und Essex,* 1949), on art (*Rembrandt,* 1956), and, finally, on the playwright who had inspired Rehberg's own work, Heinrich von Kleist (*Kleist,* 1957).

REHEARSAL, THE (*La Répétition, ou l'amour puni*), a play in five acts by JEAN ANOUILH, published and produced in 1950. Setting: a French estate, 1940's.

In this bitter comedy a middle-aged count meets a young governess and falls in love for the first time in his life. During rehearsals for a play he is preparing for his ball, the count's wife and his mistress plot to break up the romance. They approach his friend Héro, who went to seed after the count, many years before, had prevented his marriage to a girl who was subsequently ruined. Héro is persuaded to seduce the count's beloved, who thereupon leaves in shame. Héro, now completely debased, courts death in a duel with the countess's foolish lover.

REHFISCH, Hans José (1891–1960), German dramatist, wrote well-constructed plays on topical themes that were produced with acclaim in Berlin theatres after World War I. His *Heimkehr* (1918) was an early hit, one of the first of many German dramas on the problems that faced returning soldiers. Rehfisch touched the same theme in his best play, *Wer weint um Juckenack?* (1924), presenting vividly depicted types in NATURALISTIC Berlin settings and atmosphere; it features a clerk who, after dreaming of his death, seeks salvation by loving his fellowmen and performing humanitarian acts, but is rewarded with perfunctory gratitude rather than reciprocal love, and dies insane. Among Rehfisch's many other plays are *Der Chauffeur Martin* (1920), which portrays a man's spiritual regeneration; *Die Erziehung durch Kolibri* (1921), a tragicomedy set in a brothel, satirizing avaricious philistines; *Nickel und die 36 Gerechten* (1925), another tragicomedy; *Duell am Lido* (1926), an EXPRESSIONIST comedy about crooks; *Der Frauenarzt* (1927), a protest against antiabortion laws; *Die Affaire Dreyfus* (1929), written with Wilhelm Herzog (1884–1960) and presented under the pseudonym René Kestner, a documentary dramatization of the famous case that features ÉMILE ZOLA; and *Brest-Litowsk* (1930), a similarly documentary work presenting tableaux based on Trotsky's memoirs. Among Rehfisch's later plays are *Das ewig Weibliche* (1951), *Lysistratas Hochzeit* (1952), and *Bumerang* (1960). Further plays appeared after his death in Switzerland, including *Verrat in Rom* (1961) and *Jenseits der Angst* (1962).

RENARD, Jules (1864–1910), French novelist and essayist, also wrote witty satiric plays. He was particularly successful with the autobiographical *Poil de carotte* (1900), which features a child drudge, portrayed by Ethel Barrymore in the 1902 American version, *Carrots;* the more sentimental *Monsieur Vernet* (1903); and *La Bigote* (1909), a return to the *Carrots* family with an even sharper satire of Renard's mother.

His complete works were published in sixteen volumes (1925–27). Book-length studies include Helen B. Coulter's *The Prose Work and Technique of Jules Renard* (1935) and Arthur J. Knodel's *Jules Renard as a Critic* (1951).

REPORT ON HERRNBURG (*Herrnburger Bericht*), a cantata in ten songs and brief commentaries by BERTOLT BRECHT (music by Paul Dessau), published and produced in 1951. Setting: a concert platform.

Written for the Communist World Youth Festival and awarded the East German National Prize First Class, this tendentious piece is based on the West German police action taken against youths returning from the 1950 festival. Brecht did not include it in his collected plays or poems, and the East German publishers did not release it for export. "The text, consisting largely of witless and abusive doggerel, is one of the low points of Brecht's literary career" (Martin Esslin, in *Brecht: The Man and His Work*): ". . . Adenauer, Adenauer, show us your hand / For thirty pieces of silver you sell our land," etc. A few song titles suggest the story: "Encounter Near Herrnburg," "The Youths Refuse to Give West German Police Their Names," "Policeman Asks Youths How They Got On in the German Democratic Republic," "Police Caution Free German Youths They Must Not Sing When Marching Through Lübeck," etc.

REPRESENTATIONAL is the more accurate term for describing what is frequently called REALISM. It refers to dramatizations and staging methods that stress the illusion (or convey the delusion) that reality is being represented onstage. Actors, for example, consume real food, turn their backs to audiences, and speak in low conversational voices. Similarly, props and settings are made scrupulously to appear like the objects represented—as, for instance, DAVID BELASCO did when he constructed the replica of a Childs restaurant for *The Governor's Lady* (1912). Antonym: PRESENTATIONAL.

RESISTIBLE RISE OF ARTURO UI, THE (*Der Aufhaltsame Aufstieg des Arturo Ui*), a "parable play" in seventeen blank-verse scenes (plus prologue and epilogue) by BERTOLT BRECHT, published in 1957 and produced in 1958. Setting: Chicago and nearby Cicero, 1929–38.

Hitler's rise to power is burlesqued as a gangster syndicate terrorizing Chicago (i.e., Germany) and Cicero (Austria). Brecht completed this long play in 1941, but it was not produced in his lifetime; since he did not prepare manuscripts for publication without making changes during production,

Brecht left this play unpublished. Later it received effective—though not generally popular—major productions that followed his "Notes," posthumously published with the play: "top-speed tempo," noisy, "on a grand scale; preferably with obvious harkbacks to the historical Elizabethan theatre." There are parodies of Shakespeare (particularly the *Richard III* wooing scene) and of Goethe's *Faust,* but Brecht noted: "Pure travesty should be avoided, and even the grotesque must be depicted with revulsion."

Amidst ragged music and noises, an announcer steps out to introduce the characters—various gangster henchmen (famous Nazi leaders), and finally "our most remarkable curiosity! / The gangster-in-chief! The infamous / Arturo Ui!" (Hitler). During an economic crisis Ui and his gangsters blackmail the gullible mayor and "sell protection" to the city's vegetable trust (as Hitler had gulled Hindenburg and the German capitalists). By murder and rapine they gradually gain complete power. Various episodes (many grimly comic) parallel such events as the Reichstag fire and the 1934 purges. At the end, crowds cheer Ui's raving oratory in Cicero. An epilogue comments that Ui almost conquered the world before he was defeated: "But boast not too early of your triumph — / The womb from which he crawled is fertile still."

RESOUNDING TINKLE, A, a one-act play by N. F. SIMPSON, produced in 1957 and published in 1958. Setting: the living room of a suburban bungalow in England, late 1950's.

Simpson's ABSURDist first play appeared in different versions, originally in two acts. Like Ionesco's THE BALD SOPRANO, it depicts a couple.

Since the elephant just sent Bro and Middie Paradock is too large for their garden, they exchange it for a snake that their neighbor found too small, and they argue about the animals' names. The Paradocks are entertained by two comedians (deleted in the shorter version), who discuss Bergson's theory of comedy with the audience. An uncle who has become a female since last seen visits the Paradocks. The visitor has "a read" in books that are sampled for refreshment, like tea. There is a radio broadcast from "the Church of the Hypothetical Imperative in Brinkfall." Prayer and Response "weep at the elastic as it stretches, . . . and rejoice that it might have been otherwise." They also give thanks for such things as woodlice, dictionaries, and drugs. "Give us light upon the nature of our knowing," Prayer intones, "for the illusions of the sane man are not the illusions of the lunatic, and the illusions of the flagellant are not the illusions of the alcoholic . . ." The author sums up the "odd evening" by noting that "the retreat from reason means precious little to anyone who has never caught up with reason in the first place. It takes a trained mind to relish a *non sequitur.*"

RESTLESS HEART (*La Sauvage*), a play in three acts by JEAN ANOUILH, published and produced in 1938. Setting: a resort café and an estate in France, 1930's.

One of Anouilh's "black" plays, *La Sauvage* was written in 1934.

Thérèse Tarde, a member of a disreputable family of café performers, is engaged to a successful musician she loves. But she is tormented by her impoverished and sordid background. After her dissolute father and her mother's lover visit her, Thérèse decides to forego a life of wealth, comfort, and happiness. "It wouldn't be any use cheating," she concludes; "there will always be a stray dog somewhere in the world who'll stop me being happy." As her beloved fiancé obliviously plays the piano in the adjoining room, she escapes, "small, and strong and lucid, to pit herself against all the sharp corners in the world."

RESURRECTION, THE, a one-act play by WILLIAM BUTLER YEATS, published in 1927 and produced in 1934. Setting: a room, shortly after the Crucifixion.

Unlike CALVARY, Yeats's other Christ drama, this is a prose play, and Jesus here remains silent.

While some of Christ's followers (a Greek, a Hebrew, and a Syrian) prepare to defend the staircase from the Dionysian celebrants outside, they debate His divinity. His figure suddenly appears. He does not speak, but the beat of his heart is audible. The hitherto skeptical Greek now understands: "God and man die each other's life, live each other's death."

RETURN OF PETER GRIMM, THE, a play in three acts by DAVID BELASCO, produced in 1911 and published in 1920. Setting: a manor in New York State, early twentieth century.

This whimsical play, whose idea was suggested by Cecil B. De Mille, in part owed its popularity to David Warfield's portrayal of the title character, a stubborn old botanist.

Peter urges his ward, Catherine Staats, to marry Frederik Grimm, the nephew he totally misjudges and counts on to perpetuate the family business. After Peter's death Frederik reveals his true character, that of a ruthless wastrel. Peter returns from the dead, visible only to the audience. But he is strangely influential on the others, as he tries to rectify his errors. Frederik turns out to be the natural father of the cook's sick grandchild. Through the boy, himself near death, Peter persuades Catherine to reject Frederik and marry the right man. Then Peter takes the dying boy with him. "If the rest of them only knew what they're missing, eh?" he asks, as the two laughingly dance off over the bridge of light that connects them with the living.

RETURN OF THE PRODIGAL, THE, a comedy in four acts by ST. JOHN HANKIN, produced in 1905 and published in 1907. Setting: Gloucestershire, early 1900's.

This amusing play ridicules social and commercial pretensions in an English village. The title character, Eustace Jackson, is a cynical young ne'er-do-well. Because his father is running for office and the prim older brother fears Eustace might win his girl, the prodigal succeeds in blackmailing them into setting him up with an allowance in London. Particularly amusing is the sharp-tongued mother of the girl.

REUNION IN VIENNA, a play in three acts by ROBERT E. SHERWOOD, produced in 1931 and published in 1932. Setting: Vienna on August 18, 1930, one hundred years after the birth of the late emperor.

Its famous stars helped make a resounding success of this MOLNÁRian comedy, which bears a particularly striking resemblance to THE GUARDSMAN. Alfred Lunt (John Barrymore in the 1933 screen version) played the banished one-time Archduke Rudolf Maximillian, now a taxi driver in Nice; Lynn Fontanne (Diana Wynyard in the film) was Elena, once his mistress and now the loyal wife of Anton Krug, Vienna's most prominent psychiatrist.

Former nobility—now wrinkled and poor wrecks—forget the present as they try to relive past glory at a celebration of the late emperor's birthday. Giving his wife the same advice he gives patients, Krug urges Elena to lay the ghost of her first romance to rest by going to the party and seeing former friends as they are now. Rudolf—as buoyant as ever—passionately demands that they relive their past for a night. As in Molnár's play, there is but the slightest ambiguity about what really occurs when Krug leaves them alone that night. Since Rudolf has eaten the kidneys, a delicacy reserved for Krug's breakfast, Elena asks the maid "to cook some more"; and when her father-in-law, a faithful old monarchist, says he has never had as much fun as last night, Elena smiles at him: "Neither have I."

RHINOCEROS (*Rhinocéros*), a play in three acts by EUGÈNE IONESCO, published and produced in 1959. Setting: a small provincial town in contemporary France.

This play, an ABSURDist allegory, made Ionesco internationally famous. Its portrayal of mass submission to bestiality was interpreted as an account of Nazi Germany, but the play's meaning is more complex and its finale is more subtle—for individualism is shown to be no less absurd than conformity. Here Bérenger, the protagonist, is slothful and less idealistic than his Parisian avatar in THE KILLER.

Act I. It is a summer Sunday and the townspeople in the square go through their mechanical routines. An unkempt and weary Bérenger meets his fastidious friend Jean in a café. Peremptorily self-righteous, Jean criticizes Bérenger's drinking, indolence, and sloppy dress: "It's a positive disgrace! I feel ashamed to be your friend." Bérenger meekly blames his drinking on the need to escape his meaningless life. "I'm not made for the work I'm doing," he docilely tells his preaching friend Jean: "Every day at the office, eight hours a day—" They are interrupted by a rhinoceros's suddenly thundering by. The townspeople express their amazement ("Well, of all things!"), comfort a frightened cat, and resume their doings. A discussion between a logician and an old gentleman counterpoints and increasingly echoes Bérenger and Jean's talk. Bérenger drinks because he is frightened by "a sort of anguish difficult to describe," he says: "I feel out of place in life, among people, and so I take to drink." At the same time the logician explains and illustrates a syllogism: "All cats die. Socrates is dead. Therefore Socrates is a cat." Bérenger tells of his love for Daisy, a girl in his office; but having neither a future nor qualifications, he feels his love is hopeless. As Jean condescendingly cheers Bérenger by instructing him in grooming and sobriety, another rhinoceros thunders by, smashing glasses and killing the cat. Daisy joins the group, excitedly discussing the damage, as Bérenger and Jean argue about the rhinoceros. The pompous Jean gets angry at Bérenger and leaves, though Bérenger is repentant and tries to placate him. The logician decides that there are two breeds of rhinoceros, with different numbers of horns. "Too upset to go to the museum," Bérenger resumes his drinking: "I'll cultivate my mind some other time."

Act II. Scene 1. In the office, Bérenger's colleagues argue about the rhinoceros. Some refuse to believe Daisy's and the newspaper's account ("in the dead cats column"). "Rhinoceros or no rhinoceros, flying saucers or no flying saucers, work must go on," the boss finally decides, and

Rhinoceros, Act II, Scene 2. The start of the transmogrification of Jean (Zero Mostel). New York 1960. (*Zodiac Photographers*)

though the argument continues for a while, the office routine begins. The wife of a worker who has failed to show up suddenly appears, breathless: "I was chased here all the way from the house by a rhinoceros." The pachyderm is soon heard below, making anguished noises and smashing the staircase. "It's my husband! . . . He's calling me," the wife now cries out: "I'm coming my darling, I'm coming!" She jumps over the landing, and rides off on his back. A doubting colleague still denies the reality of the transformation (later, he, too, turns into a rhinoceros, for "We must move with the times!"), while the boss is troubled by the necessity of replacing a lost employee. Daisy, calling the fire department for help, learns that rhinoceroses are proliferating and smashing staircases all over town. The firemen eventually arrive with ladders and rescue the office personnel. *Scene 2.* Visiting Jean's house, Bérenger is surprised to find his friend disheveled—still in bed, coughing and talking hoarsely, and becoming increasingly greener and more thick-skinned. A bump on Jean's head keeps growing as he sprints back and forth to the bathroom. He refuses Bérenger's offer to call a doctor: "I only have confidence in veterinary surgeons." As Jean's changes continue and his veins swell ("It's a sign of virility," he remarks), he rejects the solicitous Bérenger: "There's no such thing as friendship." Breathing harder and pacing the room like a caged animal, Jean approves of his colleagues' turning into rhinoceroses: nature should take the place of morals, "we must get back to primeval integrity." He snarls at Bérenger, throws off his clothes, and before Bérenger's eyes turns into a ferocious rhinoceros. Bérenger barely manages to lock him in the bathroom and, over the din of trumpeting, call for help. Rhinoceros-headed figures appear—"A whole herd of them!"—as Bérenger wrings his hands; the din grows, and the walls are about to collapse.

Act III. At home Bérenger is awaking from a nightmare, anxiously examines himself in the mirror, and has a drink. A visiting colleague assures Bérenger his appearance is unchanged, and consoles him about his friend Jean's metamorphosis. "You think that everything that happens concerns you personally; you're not the center of the universe, you know," he remarks; "why get upset over a few cases of rhinoceritis?" Disturbed, Bérenger nonetheless decides, "I must try to readjust myself," though he considers it an evil that should be attacked "at the roots." His colleague disagrees. "Leave the authorities to act as they think best," he urges, and he denies rhinoceritis's being evil: "it's just a question of personal preferences." They continue disputing over the trumpeting noises outside. Rhinoceritis is wrong, "I feel it instinctively"—Bérenger begins—but "no, that's not what I mean, it's the rhinoceros which has instinct—I feel it intuitively." Shaken when he recognizes the logician among the stomping rhinoceroses, Bérenger vows, "I'll never join up with you! Not me!" Daisy comes in with more news of the epidemic: many shops are "closed on account of transformation." Their colleague decides to join the herd: "I prefer the great universal family to the little domestic one." Daisy and Bérenger are the only humans left. They have a tender love scene, but it soon degenerates into bickering. "Oh, dear!" Bérenger realizes as Daisy weeps: "In the space of a few minutes we've gone through twenty-five years of married life." The appeal of the increasingly melodious rhinoceros noise outside becomes irresistible to Daisy. "They're beautiful," she exclaims: "They're like gods"—and she leaves to join them. Alone, Bérenger locks the windows and the doors. He vows never to become like them, but is less and less sure of himself. He hangs up some photographs of people, but they are ugly beside the increasingly beautiful rhinoceros heads. "Oh, how I wish I was like them!" Bérenger now moans, ashamed of his soft skin and the absence of a horn: "Their song is charming . . . I wish I could do it." But he cannot: "Now it's too late! Now I'll never become a rhinoceros, never, never!" He cannot bear looking at himself: "I'm so ugly! People who try to hang on to their individuality always come to a bad end!" Gradually, however, Bérenger becomes more confident: "I'm the last man left, and I'm staying that way until the end. I'm not capitulating!"

RIBEMONT-DESSAIGNES, Georges (1884–), a leading French exponent of DADAISM, wrote *Le Serin muet* (1920), a drama about a Negro who thinks he is the composer Gounod and teaches music to his mute canary, and equally bizarre but more sadistic plays such as *L'Empereur de Chine* (1921) and *Le Bourreau du Pérou* (1928). These and other works by him are discussed in his autobiography, *Déjà Jadis* (1958), and in Martin Esslin's *The Theatre of the Absurd* (revised, 1968).

RICE, Elmer [originally Elmer Leopold Reizenstein] (1892–1967), American dramatist, director, and novelist, wrote well over fifty full-length plays as well as novels, essays, and numerous short stories and one-act plays. He was so eclectic and versatile a dramatist that his plays have been studied under such diverse headings as "potboilers, dramas, thesis plays, comedies, fantasies, melodramas, parables, EXPRESSIONISTIC fables, and . . . panoramas" (Robert Hogan). Yet despite his copious and versatile output, Rice is remembered only for a few plays, principally his two masterpieces—THE ADDING MACHINE (1923) and STREET SCENE (1929)—and for such hits as ON TRIAL (1914), COUNSELLOR-AT-LAW (1931), and DREAM GIRL (1945). Though many of his plays are artistically negligible, Rice also produced enough serious drama to make him a significant—probably the first significant—modern American playwright.

He was born in New York, the son of an epileptic part-time cigar salesman. Attending the New York University Law School at night, Rice graduated cum laude in 1912, and served as a clerk in his cousin's law office. But he did not like the legal profession, which was to provide him with the raw material for many of his plays. Only a few weeks after being admitted to the New York bar (December 1913), Rice gave up law to devote himself entirely to writing. He was almost immediately—and immensely—successful. Employing the flashback technique suggested by something he had read, Rice wrote *On Trial* and was amazed to have it accepted enthusiastically by the first producer with whom he had left it, and overwhelmed by his fame shortly thereafter. The play netted the twenty-two-year-old Rice a hundred thousand dollars and made him an important man.

Rice was aware of, and frankly admitted, the "gimmicky" nature of the play. Eager to improve his craft, he studied drama at Columbia University and became active in various theatrical activities there, including directing. He changed his name to Rice and continued writing plays. Some of them were produced at the university and some on Broadway: *The Iron Cross* (1917), one of the first plays about World War I; The *Home of the Free* (1917), a gentle one-act satire of overzealous libertarianism; *A Diadem of Snow* (1918), a satiric one-acter about the just-deposed Tsar Nicholas II and his family; *For the Defense* (1919), another courtroom play; *Wake Up, Jonathan* (1921), written with HATCHER HUGHES and starring Minnie Maddern Fiske; *It Is the Law* (1922), the dramatization of an unpublished novel; and others. He also served a brief and lucrative but unsatisfying stint as a scriptwriter in Hollywood.

Back east, he produced his first major play, *The Adding Machine*. In the same vein, both in theme and expressionism, was *The Subway* (1929), though its victimized file-clerk heroine is portrayed more sympathetically than Zero. With Dorothy Parker (1893–1967), Rice wrote a satire on the boredom of suburban life, *Close Harmony* (1924), produced more successfully on tour as *The Lady Next Door*. A more interesting collaboration was with PHILIP BARRY: *Cock Robin* (1928), a comic mystery play that fared only moderately well on Broadway. Rice's stature as a distinguished dramatist was achieved in 1929 with the Pulitzer Prize play considered by many to be his best work, *Street Scene*.

Of the many other plays Rice wrote and often directed himself, relatively few are noteworthy. *See Naples and Die* (1929), an "extravagant [love] comedy" that also satirizes dictatorship, was a failure on Broadway but was later reworked into a movie. *The Left Bank* (1931), a love drama about expatriates, and the aforementioned *Counsellor-at-Law,* produced a month later, were among his most popular works. Very much less successful but considerably more controversial was *We, the People* (1933), a panoramic drama of social criticism that presents—in many episodes and characters—the deleterious effects of poverty, portrayed as caused by unscrupulous businessmen, power-hungry politicians, and a pleasure-seeking leisure class. *Judgment Day* (1934), which also had a large cast, was equally controversial and made out considerably better in England than on Broadway; loosely based on the Nazi trials following the Reichstag fire, it portrays the travesty of justice under the rule of a dictator finally shot by an honest judge—who then commits suicide. Another notable but not very successful multicharacter play, *Between Two Worlds* (1934), dramatizes the agonizing conflict of many in the 1930's who had to choose between Russian Communism and democratic American capitalism. *Not For Children* (1934), also praised by some despite its failure on the boards, is a complex play-within-a-play about the commercial theatre, whose glaring shortcomings Rice frequently deplored.

Rice was a founding member of the Playwrights' Company, which produced his later important plays. Most of these were concerned with pressing national issues: *American Landscape* (1938), an allegorical attack on isolationism; *Flight to the West* (1940), a disquisitory political melodrama set aboard a transatlantic airplane and featuring an unmasked spy, Americans of differing political convictions, a Nazi, and a liberal Jew, who gives his own life to save the Nazi; and *A New Life* (1943), which dramatically explores the desirability of bearing children in a war-torn world. Rice also produced some lighter works, principally *Two on an Island* (1939), an episodic and panoramic comedy featuring the adventures of a couple trying to make their fortune in Manhattan; and his last hit, the earlier-mentioned *Dream Girl*. Later New York productions include *The Grand Tour* (1951) and *The Winner* (1954), both dealing with money and morality, and *Cue for Passion* (1958), a psychiatric drama freely based on *Hamlet*. *Love Among the Ruins,* produced and published in 1963, was written a decade earlier; it explores the problems of adjustment to a devastated postwar world and is set, symbolically, among ruins in Lebanon.

Rice's drama reflects his deep concern with social, political, and moral issues. It frequently degenerates into melodrama, bathos, and sentimentality. But even then are evident the real talents that characterize and distinguish his best work: Rice's skill in constructing plots and in depicting large casts and different ethnic characters, and his fearlessness in employing novel theatrical devices and exploring controversial issues. Rice was among those who helped initiate the Federal Theater Project. Appointed as the head of the New York Region theatre, he produced LIVING NEWSPAPER DRAMA; when the government forbade the production of *Ethiopia* (1936), a living-newspaper critique about Mussolini's regime, Rice strongly denounced censorship and resigned. Other activities on behalf of literary and social causes include his presidency of the American Authors League; his founding of the Dramatists' Guild, whose president he became; and his service on the board of the American Civil Liberties Union. A peppery little man with a pugnacious bearing softened by a wry sense of humor, Rice was married three times. His second wife (they were divorced in 1956) was Betty Field, the young star in some of his earlier plays, for whom he wrote *Dream Girl*.

Seven Plays by Elmer Rice (1950) includes *On*

Trial, The Adding Machine, Street Scene, Counsellor-at-Law, Judgment Day, Two on an Island, and *Dream Girl.* Rice's *The Living Theatre* (1959) is a collection of essays, and *Minority Report* (1963) is his autobiography. Studies of the playwright and his work are Robert Hogan's *The Independence of Elmer Rice* (1965) and Frank Durham's *Elmer Rice* (1970).

RICHARDSON, Jack [Carter] (1935–), American playwright, like EDWARD ALBEE has distinguished himself Off-Broadway—but has failed to fulfill his promise to go on to the heights Albee soon reached. Richardson's first play, *The Prodigal* (1960), is an existentialist retelling of the Orestes legend; influenced particularly by JEAN-PAUL SARTRE's work, it has some excellent dialogue but is dramatically static. It was followed by *Gallows Humor* (1961), two sardonic tragicomedies set in a prison. Richardson's *Lorenzo* (1963), featuring a mobile acting company in Italy whose members get involved in "a small war of the Renaissance," reached Broadway, where it failed in a lavish production. His even less successful *Xmas in Las Vegas* (1965) is a tragicomedy about a compulsive gambler and his family.

Richardson was born in New York. After graduating from Columbia University he continued his studies at the University of Munich. He has also written a novel, many short stories, and drama and theatre criticisms.

RICHEPIN, Jean (1849–1926), French editor and writer, was a journalist and the author of sometimes controversial poetry and morbidly NATURALISTIC fiction and plays, both in prose and in verse. Drama was not among his most popular work. DU BARRY, for which DAVID BELASCO paid him an advance, was a failure until the American dramatist in 1901 rewrote it himself. Beginning with his first produced play, *L'Etoile* (1873; written with André Gill, 1840–85), Richepin did succeed with a number of plays, notably *Le Flibustier* (1888), *Par le glaive* (1892), and *Don Quichotte* (1905). His most popular work, *Le Chemineau* (1897), is a rustic drama.

RIDERS TO THE SEA, a one-act play by J. M. SYNGE, published in 1903 and produced in 1904. Setting: a contemporary cottage kitchen on an island off the Irish west coast.

This very short, classically stark tragedy (which resembles Heijermans's THE GOOD HOPE and inspired Brecht's SEÑORA CARRAR'S RIFLES) is among the finest one-act plays in English. Its somber tone and moving, elegiac prose universalize man's daily struggle in the face of the proximity and experience of death. The play is strongly colored by Synge's stay on the Aran islands and dramatizes his comments on a local funeral: "This grief of the keen is no personal complaint . . . but seems to contain the whole passionate rage that lurks somewhere in every native of the island." The keen reveals (he wrote in his book on Aran) "the mood of beings who feel their isolation in the face of a universe that wars on them with winds and seas."

A twenty-year-old girl bakes bread and then starts spinning at the wheel as her younger sister enters. Reassured, after her subdued question, that their mother is asleep, she pulls out a bundle. It contains the clothes of a drowned man, perhaps their missing brother. The sisters anxiously look out when the door is blown open by the rising wind. Not wanting their mother to see it, they hide the bundle just as she comes in. The mother—Maurya—is querulous and worried about her youngest son, who plans to journey to a fair. He now hurries in and asks for rope to tie his horse. Trying to stop him from leaving, Maurya says that they will need the rope if her missing son is washed up from the sea, "for it's a deep grave we'll make him." She continues, "It's a hard thing they'll be saying . . . there's no man in it to make the coffin, and I after giving a big price for the finest white boards." He does not answer her directly but remarks that he will return in a few days; though sad and quiet, he must go, for horse prices at the fair are good. "What is the price of a thousand horses against a son where there is one son only?" Maurya asks him, and cries out as he leaves, "When the black night is falling I'll have no son left me in the world." The girls persuade Maurya to follow him with the bread he forgot—and to give him her blessing. She goes out, supporting herself on his stick: "In this place it is the young men do be leaving things behind for them that do be old." Now the sisters open the bundle—and recognize their missing brother's clothes. Their voices rise in lamentation: "Isn't it a bitter thing to think of him floating that way to the far north, and no one to keen him but the black hags that do be flying on the sea?" When Maurya returns, they do not immediately tell her the bad news. But she is already distraught with "the fearfulest thing": a vision of eight dead men (her husband, his father, and her six sons) riding to the sea—and to death. She remembers how some of her drowned men "were found and some of them were not found, but they're gone now the lot of them." A cry is heard from the shore, but Maurya obliviously continues her lament of a lifetime's suffering. She tells how one of her drowned boys was brought in. At that moment the wet corpse of her youngest son is carried in, the same way. He was knocked into the sea by the horse and was washed ashore by the surf, one of the mourning women relates. As they chant their keen, a terrible resignation comes over Maurya: "They're all gone now, and there isn't anything more the sea can do to me." Her daughter, noticing that Maurya has forgotten to get nails for the coffin, remarks, "It's getting old she is, and broken." Maurya sprinkles the last holy water, and places the cup mouthdown on the table. "They're all together this time, and the end is come," she says, asking God's mercy for each of her lost men "and on the soul of every one is left living in the world." The women's keen continues and Maurya, all her men now provided with coffins or already in their graves, concludes, "What more can we want than that? No man at all can be living forever, and we must be satisfied."

RIGGS, Lynn (1899–1954), American poet and playwright, is best remembered for his first hit, GREEN GROW THE LILACS (1930)—which a dozen years later was transformed by OSCAR HAMMERSTEIN II and Richard Rodgers into one of the most popular musical comedies of all time, OKLAHOMA! A regional author who portrayed the cowboy culture of the Indian Territory—soon the state of Oklahoma—where he was born into a cattleman's family, Riggs was most accomplished as a writer of comedies. His greatest Broadway success (117 performances) was *Russet Mantle* (1936), which has many amusing caricatures, principally that of a scatterbrained mother unable to control her promiscuous daughter—who matures after her affair with a sensitive poet, for whom she abandons her conventionally prejudiced family, when she gets pregnant, "to live in a world that's *our time*."

Riggs took various odd jobs before attending the state university, where he also taught for a brief period while he was still a student. He moved to New York in 1926, where *Big Lake* was produced the following year. It was no more successful than others of his tragedies, *Sump'n Like Wings* (1928) and *The Cherokee Night* (1936). His *Roadside* (1930), a comedy written in Paris on a Guggenheim Fellowship and originally titled *Borned in Texas,* and *The Cream in the Well* (1941) fared as badly as did his remaining plays. After the end of World War II, during which he enlisted as a private and served for a year, Riggs settled in New Mexico. He published his poems and plays in a number of volumes.

RIGHT YOU ARE (IF YOU THINK YOU ARE) (*Così è [se vi pare]*), a "parable" in three acts by LUIGI PIRANDELLO, produced in 1917 and published in 1918. Setting: a small provincial capital in Italy, 1916.

This tragicomedy is Pirandello's most explicit dramatic statement of his belief in the relativity of truth, a kind of solipsism summarized in the title. Like Ibsen's THE WILD DUCK, this play depicts the beneficial powers of illusion, and the harm that is caused by meddlers (here a picturesquely characterized company) who fail to respect it. These views are repeatedly expressed by the *raisonneur* Laudisi. The play dramatizes a short story Pirandello published in 1916; the title (literally "Thus it is if it seems thus to you") has also been translated as *It* Is *So* (*If You Think So*), *And That's the Truth!,* etc.

Act I. The town councilor's wife tells her brother, Lamberto Laudisi, of her family's indignation about their new neighbor, Signora Frola. They were barred at her door by her son-in-law, Ponza, a new official who is the councilor's subordinate. She admits to Laudisi's sarcastic accusation that their "courtesy call" was really made to learn more about Ponza's unusual domestic arrangements: Why did he set his mother-in-law up in an expensive town apartment, while he lives on the top floor of a house out of town? Why is Signora Frola not allowed to visit her daughter, though she daily talks to her from the courtyard and exchanges notes with her? The town's busybodies soon join in the speculations, and the councilor returns after having complained to the prefect about Ponza's rudeness. As a result, Signora Frola herself, a "most affable little old lady who seems sad but eager to talk," arrives to apologize. Prodded by the curious gossips, she tells them that Ponza is wonderfully kind and solicitous of her; but he is so much in love with her daughter that she refrains from invading the "completeness of devotion in which his wife must live." The company, still mystified after she leaves, is given another explanation by Ponza, who also comes to apologize. A "short, thick-set, dark-complexioned man of a distinctly unprepossessing appearance," he tells them that his mother-in-law is deranged: her daughter died four years ago and he has remarried; Signora Frola's grief has given way to a madness in which she thinks that her daughter still lives and that he loves her so much that he will not allow anyone to see her. "I do my very best, in spite of the sacrifices entailed, to keep up this beneficial illusion," he tells them. Signora Frola returns soon after her son-in-law's departure to reveal the true reason for their living arrangements: Ponza was prostrated by grief when his sick wife was taken to a sanatorium; since he thought her dead and was convinced that the woman who came back was someone else, another (mock) wedding was held and he has subsequently considered her his second wife. Signora Frola leaves and the company is stunned by this contradictory but plausible account. Laudisi, who does not believe that "the truth" about people is ever ascertainable, bursts out laughing.

Act II. A search for documents to verify one story or the other proves futile, for all records were destroyed in an earthquake. Yet Laudisi maintains that this is unimportant, "for the truth is not in them but in the mind." There, he continues, the people involved have created "a world of fancy which has all the earmarks of reality itself. And in this fictitious reality they get along perfectly well, and in full accord with each other." But not satisfied with that explanation, the busybodies arrange a direct confrontation. Signora Frola seems to win, for she obviously humors Ponza in her attempt to calm him down. But no sooner has she left than Ponza apologizes for having acted like a madman. It was a pretense, he tells them, to keep up her illusion and "remedy the evil . . . you are doing to this unhappy woman—with your compassion." The company is again astounded and confused, and Laudisi again bursts out laughing: "And so, ladies and gentlemen, we learn the truth!"

Act III. The townspeople decide that Ponza's wife is the only one to resolve the confusion. The prefect himself will question her. The company tensely awaits her arrival, still speculating on whether she is Ponza's second wife or Signora Frola's daughter. Ponza is appalled to learn that his wife has been summoned, and wants to resign his job. "This is just plain persecution," he tells the prefect: "I refuse to submit to this ferocious prying into my private affairs which will end by undoing a work of love." Signora Frola, with equal compassion for Ponza, also begs that the investigation be stopped, but to no avail. Ponza's wife, heavily veiled, finally appears. She and Signora Frola throw their arms around each other. But when Ponza dashes into the room and "shrieks desperately," his wife draws herself up and tells him, "Don't be afraid! Just take her away!" He and Signora Frola walk out, affectionately holding each other up. The wife explains, "There is a misfortune here, as you see, which must stay hidden: otherwise the remedy which our compassion has found cannot avail." When they insist, she tells the "simple truth": "I am the daughter of Signora Frola—and the second wife of Signor Ponza." Asked what she is to herself, she insists, "I am nobody! . . . I am she whom you believe me to be," and leaves. "And there, my friends, you have the truth!" Laudisi defiantly tells the company: "Are you satisfied?"—and he laughs at them derisively.

RINEHART, Mary Roberts (1876–1958), the well-known American detective-story writer, also made her name in other genres, including the drama. With AVERY HOPWOOD she collaborated on four of her nine plays. The first was a popular farce, *Seven Days* (1910), but by far the most famous was their *The Bat* (1920), based on one of her first successful mystery horror stories, *The Circular Staircase* (1908). The play, in which the supposed detective is unmasked as the criminal, featured May Vokes's comic portrayal of the terrified servant girl. It was a drama that included every conceivable crime, and was "full of hokum, tricks and much unnecessary lying," Robert Benchley wrote in his *Life* (September 9, 1920) review: "But it certainly is a grand show!" Other Rinehart plays achieved nowhere near the popularity of *The Bat,* which ran on Broadway for over two years.

Mary Roberts Rinehart wrote over sixty books, including an autobiography, *My Story* (1931; revised, 1948).

RING ROUND THE MOON (*L'Invitation au château*), a comedy in five acts by JEAN ANOUILH, produced in 1947 and published in 1953. Setting: a French winter-garden in the spring, at the turn of the twentieth century.

Translated as "a charade with music" by CHRISTOPHER FRY in 1950, this spirited "comedy of errors" is one of Anouilh's *"pièces brilliantes."* It features many typical Anouilh characters, including a dowager and a poor girl cast in a social masquerade. There are various amusing plots and counterplots, and the climax is the dowager's grand ball. Wealthy twins (played by one actor) share the romantic male lead. They finally are paired off happily and properly, the cynical twin with an heiress, and the romantic one with the poor young girl.

RISE AND FALL OF THE CITY OF MAHAGONNY (*Aufstieg und Fall der Stadt Mahagonny*), an opera in twenty scenes by BERTOLT BRECHT (music by Kurt Weill), published in 1929 and produced in 1930. Setting: a deserted region, later "Mahagonny."

Brecht's verse "attempt at Epic Opera: an account of mores" is based on MAHAGONNY and lampoons the merely sensual appeal of opera. It was less successful than his EPIC THEATRE; opera audiences resented being satirized and attacked Brecht's "vile and immoral content," while Marxists attacked its "negativism."

With other fugitive crooks, the Widow Begbick founds the city of Mahagonny. There, only self-indulgent pleasures—eating, making love, fighting, drinking—are encouraged and sold. A man is deserted by his tart (Jenny Smith) and condemned for not having money. In the electric chair he understands the reason for his downfall: "the joy I bought was not joy, and freedom for money was not freedom." The city burns down, chaos reigns, and demonstrators with signs proclaiming the moral bankruptcy of their money-oriented society finally agree in despair that money "can not help a dead man, can not help us, can not help you, can not help anybody."

RISING OF THE MOON, THE, a one-act play by LADY GREGORY, produced in 1907 and published in 1909. Setting: at night on the quay of a seaport town in contemporary Ireland.

In this popular nationalistic comedy a sergeant seeks to earn the posted reward for the capture of a rebel. A ragged ballad singer reminisces and sings patriotic songs with him. Eventually the ballad singer reveals his identity as the fugitive and persuades the greedy sergeant to forego the reward and let his fellow Irishman escape.

RITTNER, Tadeusz (1873–1921), Polish playwright and novelist, was brought up in Vienna. He continued to live in Austria, where he served as an official of the Ministry of Education. Writing in both German and Polish, he produced seventeen plays, which subtly and ironically observe the comic as well as the tragic in life. Often Rittner dramatized the wastage of man's nobility—as in his best work, *Głupi Jakób* (*Stupid Jack,* 1910), a play not unlike SOMERSET MAUGHAM's novel *Of Human Bondage* (1915). Another of his important and still-revived plays is *W małym domku* (*The Little Home,* 1904), a tragedy featuring a provincial doctor's seduced wife—an IBSENite Nora manqué whose husband kills her and then, overcome by guilt, shoots himself.

Other notable Rittner plays are *Unterwegs* (*On the Way*, 1909), a modern Don Juan drama about a woman-chasing count killed by his secretary (its Polish title was, in fact, *Don Juan*);

Sommer (*Summer,* 1912), a comedy; *Wilki w nocy* (*Wolves in the Night,* 1916; also translated as *The Human Touch*), a satire of a philistine pedant, a prosecutor whose guilty past unexpectedly affects a trial and his own future; *Ogród młodości* (*The Garden of Youth,* 1917), a comic fairy tale; and *Tragedia Eumenesa* (1920), a pseudo-SHAVian comedy, set in ancient Greece and performed in America as *Tyrants* (1924), about a poet delegated to kill a tyrannical governor who turns out to be a gentle youth.

ROAD TO ROME, THE, a play in three acts by ROBERT E. SHERWOOD, published and produced in 1927. Setting: Rome and a converted temple nearby; June, 216 B.C.

Sherwood's first Broadway production, this is a sophisticated romantic comedy with strong pacifist overtones. It irreverently reinterprets history in modern terms, like Shaw's CAESAR AND CLEOPATRA (hence the deprecation of Sherwood by some as a "Shaw in short pants"). Speculating on Hannibal's failure to capture Rome when it was within his reach, Sherwood also wittily presents a Rome that resembled his view of Calvin Coolidge's America: smugly respectable, dully unimaginative, and success worshiping.

Act I. Fabius Maximus pompously tells his proud mother that he has just been elected Dictator of Rome. His young wife, Amytis, returns from her shopping. When told of Fabius's promotion, she stops talking of her purchases only to remark, "Isn't that nice." The indignant mother attributes this lack of interest to Amytis's origin: "After all, she's only a Greek." Fabius self-importantly describes the menace of Hannibal and chides Amytis for her frivolity. "I had the misfortune to be born in Athens, where gaiety is not listed among the unpardonable sins," Amytis replies, adding, "Perhaps my Athenian frivolousness is purely superficial." Both Fabius and his mother are scandalized by her request to see *Oedipus Rex,* which they consider "one of the coarsest plays ever written." Fabius lists the Roman virtues they must exemplify now that he is Dictator: "Respectability, modesty, economy, devotion to duty, reverence, chastity, and—" "Mediocrity," Amytis concludes. When he describes Hannibal's cruelty, Amytis wonders, "Is there any soldier who is otherwise?" And she shocks Fabius with her remarks at the thought of the impending Carthaginian rapine: "Is it wrong for me to admire good, old-fashioned virility in men? I certainly haven't seen any too much of it in my own life." Then she mollifies Fabius; but when Hannibal's army is reported to be ready to sack the city, Amytis decides to flee, with two faithful Sicilian slaves, rather than fall heroically beside her husband. She counsels Fabius to negotiate for peace, exhorts him not to "eat too much starchy food while I'm away," and leaves—in her new silk dress, her mother-in-law notes reprovingly.

Act II. Hannibal's headquarters is a mile off, in a commandeered temple which the Carthaginians have decorated with an Oriental opulence that contrasts vividly with "the virtuous but unimaginative simplicity of Rome." Amytis and her slaves are brought in: they have been caught as spies and must die, as Hannibal's brother, keeper of the elephants, assures them. Amytis begs a last request from Hannibal. Alone with him, she disconcerts Hannibal with her questions about why he fights. When he talks about being "divinely inspired [by Ba-al] to crush the enemies of Carthage," Amytis replies, "That was the voice of the shopkeepers in Carthage, who are afraid that Rome will interfere with their trade." Hannibal demands that she make her request. "There's a certain—a certain ceremony" before a female prisoner's death, she remarks. Though he tries to resist her, Amytis comes closer. "There's a thing called the human equation," Amytis says as she comes still closer, and it is "so much more beautiful than war." She urges him to seek life, not death—to release the human being in him. He raises his dagger—but then throws it away and takes her in his arms.

Act III. The following morning Fabius appears at the head of a Roman delegation. Hannibal tells Amytis he will spare Rome if she will go with him. But she insists that Hannibal save himself. "Rome will destroy itself," she is sure, urging that he show his strength by giving up fighting. "Every sacrifice made in the name of war is wasted," she says. "When you believe that, you'll be a great man." Hannibal's officers are incredulous and near rebellion when he agrees to forego capturing Rome. But he persuades them that his decision was caused by a divine portent—"from Tanit, the daughter of Ba-al," and he looks furtively at Amytis. He tells the smug Fabius that Amytis came to his camp to find the husband she worried about. Before leaving, Hannibal wishes happiness to Fabius, his wife, and his sons. Fabius tells Hannibal he has none. "You may have," Hannibal remarks; "and if you do, I hope that your first-born will inherit the qualities of greatness that were so evident in his father." Amytis whispers, "Hannibal! You're a great man." When he rides off, Fabius notes that Hannibal, "with all his elephants and all his men, could not subdue the high moral purpose of Rome." Amytis replies, "Virtue is rewarded—isn't it, Fabius?"—and waves to the departing Carthaginians.

ROBINSON, [Esmé Stuart] **Lennox** (1886–1958), Irish dramatist and man of letters, was intimately associated with and a major figure in the Abbey Theatre, whose "official history" he chronicled in *Ireland's Abbey Theatre: A History, 1899–1951* (1951). He managed the theatre from 1910 to 1914 and from 1919 to 1923, and remained a director there until 1956. Most of his plays (he wrote about thirty) were first produced there. Most popular were his comedies and NATURALISTIC dramas, but he also wrote notable satires and experimental plays in which he explored morals and psychology. While they have rarely been anthologized, Robinson's plays were much praised, and were produced also in England and America, and a few of them—notably THE WHITEHEADED BOY (1916) and THE

FAR-OFF HILLS (1928)—achieved considerable success. Particularly in the comedies, his drama charmingly portrays the Irish, and it proved consistently entertaining to Abbey audiences.

The son of a Church of Ireland clergyman, Robinson was born in County Cork. According to his own account he had a "meagre" education. His first play was a stark one-act tragedy, *The Clancy Name;* produced at the Abbey in 1908, it is a grim portrayal of an Irish farm woman whose son commits murder but whose name remains unsullied when he takes his crime to the grave. It was followed by three unsuccessful tragedies, *The Cross Roads* (1909) and *Harvest* (1910), and *Patriots* (1912), a PROBLEM PLAY deploring Irish political indifference. *The Dreamers* (1915) dramatizes Robert Emmet's abortive rebellion; it was more popular. This play was followed by *The Whiteheaded Boy,* and by another but less successful historical play, about Charles Stewart Parnell (who appears, confusingly, as Lucius Lenihan), *The Lost Leader* (1918).

After WILLIAM BUTLER YEATS had chosen Robinson to be the Abbey Theatre manager in 1910, Robinson was dispatched to study theatre with BERNARD SHAW in London. During Robinson's second managerial term he was most instrumental in discovering and encouraging SEAN O'CASEY. Robinson traveled widely in Ireland beginning in 1915, while he served as Organising Librarian for Carnegie Trust in Ireland; he repeatedly visited the United States, where he lectured from 1928 to 1930, and in 1956 he traveled to Communist China to celebrate Shaw's centenary.

Robinson's other plays include *Crabbed Youth and Age* (1922, a charming one-act comedy that portrays a mother who is more intriguing to young suitors than are her daughters), *The Round Table* (1922), *Never the Time and Place* (1924), *Portrait* and *The White Blackbird* (1925), *The Big House* (1926, a topical play on divided loyalties in the changing Irish order), *Give a Dog* (1927), *Ever the Twain* (1929), *All's Over Then?* (1932), *Drama at Inish* (1933; a comedy produced in America as *Is Life Worth Living?,* about a town demoralized by tragedies performed by the repertory company hired to stimulate tourist trade), *Church Street* (1934, an atypical EXPRESSIONIST tragicomedy about a dramatist in which Robinson's treatment of reality and illusion is reminiscent of LUIGI PIRANDELLO), *When Lovely Woman* (1936), *Killycreggs in Twilight* (1937, a portrayal of the gentry's decline), *Bird's Nest* (1938), *Forget-Me-Not* (1941), *Pictures in a Theatre* (1947), *The Lucky Finger* (1948, a comedy he himself produced that year at Bowling Green University while visiting the United States), and *Speed the Plough* (1952).

Robinson wrote a number of books on drama and theatre, and an autobiography, *Curtain Up* (1941). A study of his life and work is Michael J. O'Neill's *Lennox Robinson* (1964).

ROCKET TO THE MOON, a play in three acts by CLIFFORD ODETS, produced in 1938 and published in 1939. Setting: the waiting room of a dentist's office, summer 1938.

This is a NATURALISTIC portrayal of the difficulty of love in contemporary society.

Ben Stark is a kind but timid and not very successful forty-year-old dentist. His wife nags and domineers him because she is frustrated by her inability to have children. Stark falls in love with his young assistant, Cleo Singer—a lonely girl who attracts another lonely person, Stark's father-in-law, a successful and amusing old financier. Stark does not have the courage to take his "rocket to the moon": a permanent fling at joyful life. Realizing that Stark is a weakling whose wife "just twists him around her little finger, like a spit curl," Cleo finally rejects Stark's love—as well as the proposal of his father-in-law, who is too old for her. "I want a love that uses me, that needs me," Cleo says: "I want to *live* it [life]. Something has to feel real for me, more than both of you. You see? I don't ask for much."

ROLLAND, Romain [Edmé Paul Émile] (1866–1944), French writer, musicologist, and humanist, is now remembered most for his much-translated ten-volume novel about a musical genius, *Jean-Christophe* (1903–12). Attempting to supplant the boulevard theatre with a "theatre of the people" (aims elaborated in his *Le Théâtre du peuple,* 1903), he also wrote two monumental play cycles, *Tragédies de la foi* and *Tragédies de la révolution.* These expressed his idealism in often SYMBOLIC terms, dramatizing the French Revolution in broad, impartial sweeps as conflicts of individualism and social discipline, freedom and abnegation. Among the cycle plays are *Saint-Louis* (1897), Rolland's first play; *Les Loups* (*The Wolves,* 1898), originally published as *Morituri* and inspired by the Dreyfus case; *Danton* (1900), in which the title character, an idealist, is confronted by the ruthlessly dogmatic Robespierre; *Le Quatorze juillet* (*The Fourteenth of July,* 1902), a pageant; *Le Jeu de l'amour et de la mort* (*The Game of Love and Death,* 1925); and *Les Léonides* (1928), in which former revolutionaries unite against Napoleon. Other historical plays include *Robespierre* (1938), a partial rehabilitation of the previously excoriated leader.

Rolland was born at Clamecy (in Burgundy) and received a doctorate at the Sorbonne, for which he wrote a dissertation (published in 1895) on early opera. He wrote numerous monumental biographies (including one on LEO TOLSTOI, who greatly influenced him) and studies of the arts, as well as pacifist and other tracts. His various academic positions included the chair of the history of music at the Sorbonne. In 1915 he shared the Nobel Prize for literature.

An extensive listing of Rolland's works is William T. Starr's *A Critical Bibliography of the Published Writings of Romain Rolland* (1950). Among other book-length studies are STEFAN ZWEIG's *Romain Rolland: The Man and His Work* (1921).

ROMAINS, Jules [pen name of Louis Farigoule] (1885–), French novelist, poet, scientist, philosopher, and playwright, has been extraordinarily versatile and prolific. His series of twenty-seven panoramic novels ("a vision of the modern world"), *Les Hommes de bonne volonté* (*Men of Good Will,* 1932–46), and the Molière-like farce *Knock, ou le triomphe de la médecine* (DOCTOR KNOCK, 1923) brought him international acclaim. Other comedies among his nearly twenty plays were also popular, though some preferred his verse drama *Cromedeyre-le-Vieil,* which JACQUES COPEAU produced at the Vieux-Colombier in 1920. It expresses Romains's particular theory of reality, *unanimisme* (unanimism), described in the poem *La Vie unanime* (1908) and in other "gospels," and portrayed in his novel *Les Copains* (1913) and in all his fiction and drama. From individuals evolves "the design of an individuality more extensive than theirs, which is that of the group," Romains defined unanimism, and thus individualism is conditioned by and subordinated to collective thought and psychology. Unanimism has been attacked as Communistic and Fascistic—a charge apparently confirmed by Romains's brief admiration of Mussolini—and his writings were criticized as doctrinaire. But when France fell, Romains escaped and fought totalitarianism, and his works present trenchant depictions of men and society. Though he stopped writing plays in 1947, those written until then and the novels he continued to publish brought Romains popular and critical acclaim that led to many distinctions, including election in 1946 to the French Academy.

The son of a teacher, Romains was born in Saint Julien-Chapteuil (department of Haute-Loire) but moved to Paris as a young child. Taking neither to his Catholic upbringing nor (later) to military life, he joined Montmartre's circle of artists and writers. In 1904 he published his first book, a collection of poems. It was quickly followed by essays on unanimism and fiction. Barely twenty-one and now a student at the École Normale, he achieved a reputation not only in belles lettres but also in science—his first love, which, however, he relinquished for literature.

Successful as a poet and a novelist, Romains soon turned to the stage. *L'Armée dans la ville* (1911), his first play, depicts in verse a province's bloody but abortive rebellion against a well-disciplined occupation army. *Cromedeyre-le-Vieil,* "a modernised and 'unanimised' version of the Sabine legend" (P. J. Norrish), features a collective hero (the utopian village) and a strong individual leader, the dictator who also represents the village's consciousness. Romains used the characters of *Les Copains* in his comedy *Donogoo,* published as a film scenario (*Donogoo-Tonka*) in 1920 and as a play in 1930, and popular in both media; Donogoo is a fictitious town that becomes real and prosperous because of the ability of a slick operator like Dr. Knock to shape a creative community. Another charlatan from *Les Copains* is the debauched pedant in *Monsieur Le Trouhadec saisi par la débauche* (1922, a comedy produced in England as *Cupid and the Don*), who reappears in the play's sequel, *Le Mariage de M. Le Trouhadec* (1925).

Remaining notable Romains plays are *Le Dictateur* (1926), whose Socialist hero finds that power necessitates unexpected actions on his part; *Jean Le Maufranc* (1927), whose protagonist, to resist government infringement of his privacy, becomes a hypocritical churchman—a resolution changed in a revised version, *Jean Musse ou l'école de l'hypocrisie* (1930), where the protagonist as well as individual liberty are doomed because science now can detect lies; *Boën ou la possession des biens* (1931), in which a millionaire can find happiness only by sharing his wealth with the community and becoming part of it; *Grâce encore pour la terre!* (1941), a plea to save the human race, which God (the setting is Heaven) grants to all "men of good will"; and *L'An mil* (1947), his last play, in which true lovers are promised that they will be saved from the impending end of the world. Romains's other writings include *Amédée ou les messieurs en rang* (1926), a one-act comic mystery dramatizing unanimism in a shoe shop; and the script for the popular film version of the *Volpone* of STEFAN ZWEIG, whose biography Romains was to publish in 1941.

Romains's plays appeared separately and in a seven-volume collection (1924–35). Aside from *Doctor Knock* they are not readily available in English. Of the many books on Romains, P. J. Norrish's *Drama of the Group* (1958) is the most comprehensive study of Romains's drama; it has a good bibliography.

ROMANCE, a play in three acts, a prologue, and an epilogue, by EDWARD SHELDON, produced in 1913 and published in 1914. Setting: New York in 1867 and in the 1890's.

Romance. Cavallini (Doris Keane) and the rector (William Courtenay). New York, 1913. (*Culver Pictures*)

Sheldon's most popular play, *Romance* was successful all over the world. Audiences' interest was heightened by Sheldon's just-broken engagement to Doris Keane, who played the notorious Italian diva Cavallini. This was one of the first plays to use flashback, a technique that became the rage the following year with Rice's ON TRIAL.

In order to dissuade his grandson from marrying an actress, an old bishop tells him the story of his great romance. The scene shifts to the past as the bishop, then a young rector, meets the Italian singer Margherita Cavallini. Her gay life and chatter with everybody, including her pet monkey, contrast vividly with the temperament of the staid rector of St. Giles, who falls in love with her. He wants to marry her despite her sinful past, but shrinks back when she tells him of a recent affair. First he tries to save her soul, and then begs her to give herself to him for a night. But Cavallini, the good in her awakened by him, sends the young man off so she can remember him always as the rector she admired. In the epilogue, the grandson, though much moved by the story, is still determined to marry his actress. Smiling, the old bishop agrees to perform the ceremony. Then, reading a newspaper account of Cavallini's death, he plays her Victrola record of the song that first attracted him to her.

ROMANOFF AND JULIET, a comedy in three acts by PETER USTINOV, produced in 1956 and published in 1957. Setting: "The Main Square in the Capital City of the Smallest Country in Europe," 1950's.

This farce (later filmed) about Russo-American relations depicts a love story set between the hostile embassies of the two major powers. A harassed comic-opera general also parodies their national foibles and, after the lovers are united, articulates the "message" that man should strive for "the realm of sense, of gentleness, of love."

ROMULUS THE GREAT (*Romulus der Grosse*), "an unhistorical historical comedy" in four acts by FRIEDRICH DÜRRENMATT, published in 1948 and produced in 1949. Setting: the emperor's residence in Tivoli (near Rome); March 15 and 16, 476 A.D.

This humanized, freely altered history recalls those of BERNARD SHAW. In an extensive 1957 revision Dürrenmatt enhanced the heroism and dignity of his Romulus Augustulus. His "tragedy lies in the comedy of his end," Dürrenmatt wrote, for Romulus, a rationalist as well as a moralist and a would-be judge, "has the wisdom and the insight to accept his fate." In 1962 GORE VIDAL adapted the play as *Romulus.*

The enemy is approaching but Romulus is interested only in his hobby of raising chickens. He dismays his family and the court with his tired jokes, and is considered a disgrace as an emperor. But his apparent levity cloaks a twenty-year-long policy to do his duty, as he conceives it, to destroy the tyranny of Rome: "Only by becoming Emperor [and doing nothing] did I have the opportunity to liquidate the empire." He forbids his daughter's sacrificial marriage to a wealthy industrialist who could save Rome. Bravely he faces assassination as a traitor, but the conspirators ringed about him are interrupted by the barbarians' approach. Again Romulus is ready to die the next morning when the barbarian leader, Odoacer, appears. Instead of killing Romulus, however, the equally urbane Odoacer (another chicken fancier, who recognizes the danger of his power-hungry nephew) reluctantly accepts his own destiny—as Rome's last emperor accepts his. Dissolving his empire, Romulus proclaims Odoacer king. Deprived of the anticipated hero's death, Romulus is pensioned off and sadly departs for his villa.

ROOTS, a play in three acts by ARNOLD WESKER, published and produced in 1959. Setting: Norfolk, England; late 1950's.

This is generally considered the best in *The Wesker Trilogy,* which begins with CHICKEN SOUP WITH BARLEY and concludes with I'M TALKING ABOUT JERUSALEM. When it first appeared, this CHEKHOVian play established Wesker as an important new English dramatist. A portrayal of working-class futility, the play has often been associated with Osborne's LOOK BACK IN ANGER.

Act I. Beatie Bryant arrives from London to see her family before getting married. First she visits her sister and her husband, a mechanic. She tells them of Ronnie Kahn, to whom she is engaged and who is to follow her soon. Ronnie is a cook, an intellectual Socialist whom Beatie constantly quotes. She "chased him" until they became lovers, and though he persistently tries to teach her "about politics and art and all that," she is really concerned only with him: "Once we're married and I got babies I won't need to be interested in half the things I got to be interested in now." She tries to jolt her family from their rut of poverty, ignorance, and apathy. But they are skeptical of Ronnie's quoted notions and Beatie's own faith in them, and resentful of her "pushin' ideas across at us—we're alright as we are." A lusty old neighbor comes by and teases her about "hevin' yer myself for breakfast" if Ronnie does not marry her soon. Beatie gossips with her sister, cleans and rearranges the household, and, before going to sleep, tells her how Ronnie has got her to take up abstract painting.

Act II. Scenes 1 and 2. At her parents' house Beatie probes her mother about a popular song the mother likes: "How do the words affect you? Are you moved?" Mrs. Bryant replies, "Them's as good words as any," and becomes exasperated with Beatie's continued questions about the song, "Blust gal! That ent meant to be a laxative!" But Beatie realizes that she herself has inherited her mother's inarticulateness and contentment with the shoddy. "Talk and look and listen and think and ask questions," she quotes Ronnie as telling her: "But Jesus! I don't know what questions to ask or *how* to talk." The family's sometimes amusingly courageous endurance in spite of the limitations of their cliché-ridden and bored lives is demonstrated while Beatie takes a bath: word comes of the sudden death of the lusty old neighbor, and the father begrudges his family electricity and quarrels with the mother. Quoting the sayings of Ronnie, Beatie begs her folks to be on their best behavior when he comes, and berates them, "You spend your time among green fields, you grow flowers and you breathe fresh air and you got no majesty. Your mind's cluttered up with nothing and you shut out the world." Her mother is indignant: "I fed you. I clothed you. I took you out to the sea. What more d'you want?" Later Beatie tries to explain good music to her; "I aren't saying it's all squit," Mrs. Bryant says as they dance and clap hands gleefully to one of Beatie's records.

Act III. It is two weeks later, and Ronnie is expected momentarily. Beatie's father has tried unsuccessfully to hide his sickness from the farm manager, and has gotten demoted to a half-pay job. Suddenly a letter from Ronnie is delivered. He has changed his mind about marrying Beatie, and admits his ideas are "quite useless and romantic." Her family jeers at Beatie, who has been criticizing them and preaching at them about solving their problems—and now cannot even solve her own. "The apple don't fall far from the tree," the mother says. "Your daughter's bin ditched," Beatie cries, and demands that they comfort her. Despairing, Beatie realizes she is like the rest of them: "Stubborn, empty, wi' no tools for livin'. I got no roots in nothing. I come from a family o' farm labourers yet I ent got no roots—just like town people—just a mass o' nothin'." When Mrs. Bryant cannot understand her thinking that they can be bored when they have "radio and television an' that," Beatie waxes eloquent. "Education ent only books and music—it's asking questions, all the time. There are millions of us," she continues, "all taking the easiest way out. . . . We don't fight for anything, we're so mentally lazy we might as well be dead. Blust, we are dead!" Hence the success of "the slop singers and the pop writers and the film makers and women's magazines and the Sunday papers and the picture strip love stories"—all of which come easy. "The whole stinkin' commercial world insults us and we don't care a damn," she concludes; "it's our own bloody fault. We want the third-rate—we got it!" And then she stops, amazed, smiling ecstatically: "D'you hear it? Did you listen to me? I'm talking . . . I'm not quoting no more." The family sit down to eat, unmoved, but Beatie rejoices: "It does work, it's happening to me . . . I'm beginning, on my own two feet"—and "articulate at last."

ROPE, THE, a one-act play by EUGENE O'NEILL, produced in 1918 and published in 1919. Setting: a New England barn; early twentieth century, in one of the years preceding World War I.

Published in THE MOON OF THE CARIBBEES, AND SIX OTHER PLAYS OF THE SEA, this play strongly resembles O'Neill's later and more important DESIRE UNDER THE ELMS.

In his barn on the seacoast, the mad old Bible-quoting Abraham Bentley has hung up a rope for his son, Luke, who stole money and ran away, to hang himself. Bentley's daughter and her cunning, hypocritical husband scheme to get Bentley's farm and find his hidden money. Luke unexpectedly returns, humors Bentley by putting his head in the noose, and gets furious when he sees that his father is not joking when he happily and eagerly gestures that Luke really hang himself. With his brother-in-law, Luke plots to torture the miserly old man until he reveals where his money is hidden. After they leave, Bentley's little granddaughter accidentally finds the money bag, which was tied to the beam at the other end of the rope. She happily uses the shiny, flat twenty-dollar gold pieces for skipping stones, which she hurls into the ocean from the edge of the cliff as the curtain falls.

ROSE AND THE CROSS, THE (*Roza i krest*), a verse play in five acts by ALEKSANDR ALEKSANDROVICH BLOK, published in 1916. Setting: Languedoc and Brittany, early thirteenth century.

Praised as one of the greatest of Russian poetic dramas, this work resembles a medieval morality and was conceived originally as a ballet and then as an opera. It was completed as a play, rehearsed over two hundred times (1916–18) at Konstantin Stanislavksy's Moscow Art Theatre—but not, finally, produced. Romantic, lyrical, and SYMBOLIC, yet marked by disillusionment and irony, the play features a countess, who languishes in the tower in which her jealous husband has imprisoned her; and her lifelong adorer, "Sir Hapless," the castle's warden Bertran ("the head and the heart of the play," according to Blok).

Bertran finds the unknown troubadour for whom the countess pines, but the poet turns out to be an old man. After she listens to his haunting song, the countess takes a younger lover, a conceited young knight. The heartbroken Bertran is mortally wounded fighting the count's enemies. His last act is to help the young knight to climb into the chamber of his beloved countess. Dying, Bertran realizes that "The immutable law of the heart / Is that happiness and suffering are one."

ROSE BERND, a play in five acts by GERHART HAUPTMANN, published and produced in 1903. Setting: the contemporary Silesian countryside.

This NATURALISTIC drama is based on an actual perjury-infanticide trial. Though it deals with a situation common in melodrama, it does so with uncommon artistry, particularly in characterization and atmosphere. This drama, unique despite its superficial similarity to Hebbel's *Maria Magdalena* (1844), is analyzed in detail by Margaret Sinden (*Gerhart Hauptmann*).

Rose Bernd, a warm-blooded young peasant girl, tells the appealing but married middle-aged squire in whose house she has grown up that their pleasurable liaison must end. She is giving in to her widowed old father's pressure to marry a pious suitor. Soon Rose is accosted by a vicious machinist; he has discovered her affair and threatens to expose Rose unless she surrenders to his lust. Later, finding herself pregnant, she reluctantly prepares for the marriage, but the machinist's taunting threats stop her. Amidst a group of peasants, he then irritates Rose's sickly fiancé—and her equally pietistic father—with his innuendos. (Rose, it appears, had gone to beg for his silence, and he raped her.) The infuriated groom attacks him, and has one of his eyes knocked out. Old Bernd indignantly sues the machinist for slander, and Rose, increasingly guilt-ridden and bewildered, perjures herself in court. After the machinist's revealing testimony, the squire feels relieved of his guilt in her ruin and washes his hands of her. Even the squire's kindly invalid wife cannot help Rose. An old peasant brings the exhausted girl home. Shortly her father and her fiancé appear. The latter, having talked to the penitent machinist, realizes the truth and reveals it to old Bernd. The father self-righteously curses and rejects his "fallen" daughter, but the pious groom, unexpectedly generous and human, sticks with Rose: "Somehow, we'll get along. Maybe we're ready for it only now. . . . Who knows which love is stronger, happy love or unhappy love!" Increasingly hysterical, Rose tries to justify herself before the hard-hearted father, who ignores her: "I'm alive! I'm sitting here! . . . Oh Jesus, in what a small little room you're living, all of you! And you've no idea what's going on outside that room! I know what's going on! I've found out . . . in convulsions I've found out!—Everything. . . ." Raving, she confesses having strangled the baby she has just borne in the fields: "I didn't want it to live and to suffer the same tortures as me! I wanted it to stay where it belongs." As she is taken away by the police, her suitor is deeply moved: "What she must have suffered!"

ROSE TATTOO, THE, a play in three acts by TENNESSEE WILLIAMS, produced in 1950 and published in 1951. Setting: a Sicilian colony on the Gulf Coast between New Orleans and Mobile; 1947–50.

Though denigrated by some critics for its author's characteristic preoccupation with sex and violence, this is a successful and atypical slapstick comedy—a "Dionysian" paean (as Williams called it) that has had extensive runs in America and abroad and was made into a popular film. Portraying the fiery-tempered people the author came to admire in Italy, it combines an American Southern setting with Sicilian customs and superstitions—personified by the religious hysteria and heated passions of a robust peasant, Serafina.

Act I. Scene 1. Serafina Delle Rose, the local seamstress and mother of the twelve-year-old Rosa, has a plump, voluptuous body that now is tightly corseted and sheathed in rose silk. She is awaiting the homecoming of her husband, a truck driver—and dope smuggler. Immensely proud of him as her handsome nightly lover and the nephew of a baron, Serafina can hardly contain her joy, for she is carrying his second child: the rose tattoo on her husband's chest appeared on her breast on the night of conception. A thin, blond casino blackjack dealer asks Serafina to sew a silk shirt for her lover, a man "wild like a Gypsy." Their talk is interrupted by a black goat that periodically runs loose in the yard, is followed by the local witch, and causes a neighborhood commotion. *Scene 2.* It is dawn, and the neighbors, led by the priest, come to tell Serafina her husband has been killed. *Scene 3.* That noon the priest tries in vain to prohibit the "pagan idolatry" of her cremating her husband and worshiping his ashes. He also sends away the blackjack dealer, who wants to view the corpse. *Scene 4.* It is three years later, the day of Rosa's graduation. A slovenly Serafina, dressed only in a dirty slip, is beside herself. Rosa, her daughter, has tried to cut her wrists because Serafina locked her up to keep her from seeing a young sailor she had met at a school dance. Rosa complains to her teacher of Serafina's wanting Rosa "to be like her, a freak of the neighborhood." For Serafina, who lost her baby in the wild grief of her mourning, has become totally absorbed in the worship of her husband's memory and ashes, and has neglected her home and person for three years. "Mama, you look disgusting!" Rosa exclaims as she rushes away. *Scene 5.* As the hurt but aroused Serafina tries to dress for the graduation, two very common middle-aged women come for their party blouses. When Serafina is offended by their crude behavior and language ("You're sitting in the same room with Our Lady and with the blessed ashes of my husband!"), and proudly recounts her joyful lovemaking with a pure husband "that was mine—*only mine!*" they spitefully tell Serafina of her husband's adultery with the blackjack dealer. Half-crazed, Serafina chases them out. Then she implores her statue: "Che dice, Signora? *Oh, Lady! Give me a sign!*" *Scene 6.* She is still imploring two hours later, when Rosa returns with her young sailor. Though Serafina is distracted by sorrow, she makes the innocent young sailor kneel before the statue and swear "That I will respect the innocence of the daughter, Rosa, of Rosario delle Rose." Then the young couple leave for the school picnic, Serafina pitifully holding out the graduation watch she has bought Rosa—and she again turns to the statue: "Oh, Lady, give me a sign!"

Act II. Some hours later Serafina still murmurs these words. She is worn out, and there are wine stains on her slip. The priest chides her for her idolatry and her sinful pride in her love for her husband. Noting her present slovenliness, he urges her to pull herself together. Serafina berates him for allowing school dances that "ruin" girls. Then, becoming increasingly wilder, she insists he tell her whether her husband ever mentioned another woman in the confessional. She is about to attack him bodily when neighbors drag her away. As Serafina sits, half crazed and disconsolate, a stupid and mean salesman urges her to buy a useless article. He is interrupted by Alvaro Mangiacavallo, a young truck driver the salesman has gratuitously attacked on the road as a "wop." Now the salesman kicks Alvaro in the groin, and threatens to have him fired. Hurt and frustrated, Alvaro weeps in Serafina's house. Sympathetically she joins his weeping, and the two are united in their grief. Offering to sew his torn jacket, Serafina gasps when he takes it off: "Madonna Santa!—*My husband's body,* with the head of a *clown!*" She thinks Alvaro is the prayed-for sign, though he is foolish and admits to being the village idiot's grandson. Alvaro has elder dependents but—though the salesman managed at once to get him fired—he remarks that he would like "a lady a little older than me.—I don't care if she's a little too plump or not such a stylish dresser!" Serafina lends him the silk shirt the blackjack dealer never picked up, and Alvaro helps catch the goat, which has again got loose in the yard. Then, still playing the buffoon, he makes a date with Serafina for that evening. Addressing the ashes, now that she believes Alvaro to be the solicited sign, Serafina says: "Forgive me for thinking the awful lie could be true!"

Act III. Scene 1. A transformed, well-dressed Serafina sits stiffly in the parlor that evening, waiting for Alvaro. Her girdle is intolerable, so she takes it off just as Alvaro appears. Their courting is constantly jeopardized by Alvaro's bumbling, and is almost ruined when contraceptives drop out of his pocket. But his embarassment, self-abasement, and contrition are so genuine that Serafina is moved to let him stay. He admits he just that afternoon had had a rose tattoed on his chest, and helps her resolve the uncertainty of her husband's adultery. When she learns it was true, she staggers about brokenly. Alvaro gently helps her get hold of herself—and she invites him to come to her in the dark: "Now we can go on with our—conversation . . ." *Scene 2.* Before daybreak, Rosa returns with her sailor, frustrated and furious that her mother made him swear the oath he found almost impossible to keep. She vows to meet him before he sails away, and goes to sleep. *Scene 3.* After a night of love Alvaro stumbles into the living room. Rosa screams and Serafina rushes in to help attack Alvaro. In the ensuing pandemonium, they smash the urn containing the ashes. Though Serafina tries to pretend nothing has happened between her and Alvaro, Rosa is not fooled. She leaves, determined to meet her sailor in a hotel room. "How beautiful—is my daughter! Go to the boy!" Serafina says. Alvaro races out of the house half dressed, loudly proclaiming his love of Serafina before the mocking neighbors. As she did after her last conception, Serafina again feels the rose tattoo on her breast. She rushes toward Alvaro, shouting joyfully, "Vengo, vengo, amore!"

ROSENCRANTZ AND GUILDENSTERN ARE DEAD, a play in three acts by TOM STOPPARD, published and produced in 1967. Setting: Shakespeare's Elsinore Castle in Denmark, and a ship.

Originally produced in a shorter version as a "fringe event" of the 1966 Edinburgh Festival, this elusive tragicomedy is a mixture of Beckett's WAITING FOR GODOT, the drama of LUIGI PIRANDELLO, and Shakespeare's *Hamlet,* from which the

Rosencrantz and Guildenstern Are Dead. Center: Rosencrantz (Brian Murray, holding letter) and Guildenstern (John Wood); the boy player (Douglas Norwick), dressed as a queen, stands behind the barrel. New York, 1967. (*Zodiac Photographers*)

almost interchangeable protagonists are taken and in whose action they are painfully suspended.

Two Elizabethan courtiers philosophize and play endless games. Vaguely uneasy and not sure which of them is Rosencrantz and which is Guildenstern, they know only that they have been summoned to court. A Player (Shakespeare's Player King, whom the two introduced to the court), passing with his troupe, banters and haggles with them. But they are trapped "till events have played themselves out," Guildenstern tells his companion: "There's a logic at work—it's all done for you." The players act out *The Murder of Gonzago,* which includes the death of two lords who resemble the courtiers. They do not recognize themselves, though Guildenstern realizes that the Player foreknows and apparently controls the happenings: "Operating on two levels, are we?! How clever!" In a burlesque routine they try to trap Hamlet, who evades them as he drags out Polonius's corpse. Aboard the ship, the two courtiers open and discuss Claudius's letter to the English king—but do not notice Hamlet's exchanging it for another. Rosencrantz echoes his companion's anguish ("It must be your dominant personality," he answers the complaining Guildenstern), which rises after pirates attack the ship. "Nothing will be resolved without him," Guildenstern tells the Player angrily: "We need Hamlet for our release!" Then they learn of their ordained death. "To be told so little . . . to such an end—and still—finally—to be denied an explanation," Guildenstern moans, and angrily chides the Player, who, despite his knowledge does not, the courtiers think, understand what death really means—though he portrays it convincingly. Rosencrantz and Guildenstern move on to their fate, exhausted and confused, to Shakespeare's final *Hamlet* scene.

ROSMERSHOLM, a play in four acts by HENRIK IBSEN, published in 1886 and produced in 1887. Setting: a contemporary estate in western Norway.

Originally called *Hvide heste* (*White Horses,* the symbol of the past haunting the present and presaging a catastrophe), this is one of the last of the social dramas Ibsen was to write. Upon his return to Norway in 1885, he was repelled by factional excesses: "Nobility must find its way into our public life, . . . nobility of character, of mind and of will. That alone can liberate us." But beyond the resulting satiric portraits of conservatives (the fanatic Kroll) and liberals (the freethinking opportunist Mortensgård and the ineffectual Brendel) are the psychologically more rounded principals, Rosmer and the intriguing Rebecca. Their complex, gradually unfolding characters and fates symbolize a tragic incompatibility of personal nobility and social action.

Act I. The attractive Rebecca West watches Johannes Rosmer, the estate owner and a former clergyman, circle the bridge from which his wife, Beata, committed suicide. "They cling long to their dead here at Rosmersholm," she tells the housekeeper. Schoolmaster Kroll, Rosmer's old friend and brother-in-law, who has avoided the house since his sister's death, comes for a visit. An intransigent conservative, he seeks help from the contemplative Rosmer, heir of "the foremost family in the district" for two hundred years, in defending its "sacred" principles against the increasingly powerful liberal party. The friends are interrupted by the ranting Ulric Brendel, Rosmer's former tutor, still a genial radical but now a tramp. He has decided to sacrifice his ideals by sharing them with the masses—"to place my mite on the altar of liberty"—and has come to borrow money and clothes. After Brendel's departure, Rosmer reveals that he has renounced his ancestral political doctrines and religion. To oppose the growing factional hatred, he will try to ennoble people "by liberating their minds and purifying their wills," and will give his all "to create a true democracy in this land" by working with the new liberal leaders. Gentle and decent, Rosmer is upset by Kroll's acrimony and sudden personal enmity. Because of his friend Rebecca, however, Rosmer will not be all alone: "there are two of us to bear the loneliness." "Beata's very words!" Kroll bitterly remarks, and immediately repents his words.

Act II. Next morning, however, Kroll openly accuses Rosmer of being the lover of Rebecca, whom he holds responsible for Rosmer's apostasy. Furthermore, though Rosmer is sure that his wife was losing her mind, Kroll believes that Beata's death was ruthlessly caused by Rebecca, to free Rosmer for herself. Urged at least not to make his apostasy public, Rosmer insists on participating in "the battle of life." Kroll leaves angrily after the arrival of Peter Mortensgård, the coldly practical liberal leader. He is anxious to announce the important news of Rosmer's conversion—but not the politically damaging news of his religious lapse. He, too, assumes that Rosmer is having an affair with Rebecca. Now disturbed by guilty doubts and suspicions, Rosmer asks her to marry him, to confront "all the misery of the past . . . with a new and living reality." After a cry of joy Rebecca masters herself and declines his proposal. Though she will remain at Rosmersholm, she vows that, if he ever again asks her to marry him, "I go the way Beata went."

Act III. Kroll accuses Rebecca of a "cold heart" and a morality affected by her mysterious background, which may be illegitimate and incestuous. Rebecca is deeply disturbed by these possibilities, as well as by Rosmer's growing feelings of guilt for his wife's death. To restore his "happy innocence" so that he may continue his "great and splendid" life's task, she confesses her complete guilt: something of an adventuress, "I wanted to be in at the dawning of the new age, wanted to be in on everything, all the new ideas." She had sought to gain influence over him, to rouse him to leadership. To do so, she had to free him from his gloomy marriage. Making his wife think that Rebecca had had an affair and was going to have a child by Rosmer, Rebecca suggested to Beata that her death was necessary for his sake: "You are innocent. It was *I* who . . . ended by luring

Beata out on the twisted path . . . that led to the millstream." Horrified, Rosmer goes out, again allied with Kroll. Rebecca suddenly is afraid and decides to leave Rosmersholm.

Act IV. Rosmer returns before Rebecca's departure. Realizing that she has been using him, he gives up his perhaps somewhat spurious ideal of ennobling men's minds. Rebecca admits that she gradually lost her original unscrupulousness—and with it "the courage of a free mind." "A wild and uncontrollable passion" for Rosmer, as well as the spirit of Rosmersholm, finally broke her will and paralyzed her power. She insists that his "philosophy of life ennobles all right. . . . But it kills happiness." A ruined Brendel appears; ready at last to reveal his ideals, "I made the painful discovery that I was bankrupt." The liberal party leader is "lord and master of the future," having found the secret of practical success: he "never wants to do more than he *can*. Peter Mortensgård is quite capable of living his life without ideals." After Brendel leaves, Rosmer demands proof of Rebecca's love and ennoblement: she must follow in Beata's footsteps for him. When she agrees, Rosmer, who now considers himself emancipated and believes in no divine judge, goes to atone with her: "We must judge ourselves." The horrified housekeeper sees an apparition of the white horse that presages death, and screams as the lovers jump into the millstream.

ROSS, "a dramatic portrait" in two acts by TERENCE RATTIGAN, published and produced in 1960. Setting: a Royal Air Force depot near London in 1922, and the Middle East; 1916–18.

This play depicts the adventures of Lawrence of Arabia. These are presented in the framework of T. E. Lawrence's abortive 1922 attempt at anonymity as Aircraftman John Hume Ross.

ROSSO DI SAN SECONDO, Pier [Luigi] **Maria** (1887–1956), Italian dramatist, wrote in the GROTESQUE vein of LUIGI CHIARELLI and LUIGI PIRANDELLO. Of the many plays he produced from 1918 until shortly before his death, the most notable is *Marionette che passione!* (1918), which made Rosso famous; its unhappy characters are puppets of fate who in a chance meeting in a restaurant confess to each other their torments and passions. Other plays express Rosso's pessimism even more despairingly: *La bella addormentata* (1919) portrays the empty life of a prostitute who is saved by a benefactor's forcing her seducer to marry her; *La roccia e i monumenti* (1923) centers on a war veteran who learns from his former sweetheart, now unhappily married, how to construct a new existence for himself; the tragicomic *L'avventura terrestre* (1924) suggests, in the story of a pair of lonely lovers, that we cannot know even ourselves; and a host of other plays, sometimes technically daring but increasingly opaque and less successful.

Born in Sicily to a nobleman's family, Rosso was educated in Rome. He traveled widely and published many of his nondramatic works while he was abroad. They include novels, short stories, a study of Pirandello, and a number of books on film, drama, and the theatre.

ROSTAND, Edmond [Eugène Alexis] (1868–1918), French playwright, achieved early and international fame with his masterpiece, the "heroic comedy" CYRANO DE BERGERAC (1897). Exemplifying a flamboyant reaction to the NATURALIST and SYMBOLIST drama that increasingly dominated European stages at the end of the nineteenth century, Rostand resuscitated romantic verse drama and dazzled audiences with his torrential rhetoric no less than with his wit. His larger-than-life heroes, fighting the world for an ideal, nonetheless face the conflict with a wistful awareness of reality. Aside from his dramatization of the otherwise unmemorable life of the seventeenth-century soldier-poet Cyrano, Rostand succeeded with a drama about Napoleon's son, L'AIGLON (1900), still held by some critics to be Rostand's finest play. After a ten-year silence his much-heralded and elaborately produced *Chantecler* (CHANTICLEER, 1910) disappointed audiences, though it has continued to arouse claims as Rostand's most interesting play. A curious latter-day Rostand success, finally, was that of a youthful drama, *Les Romanesques* (THE FANTASTICKS, 1894).

Rostand was born in Marseilles to wealthy parents. He went to Paris to study law and was admitted to the bar, but became more interested in writing poetry than in the legal profession. In 1890 he published a volume of lyric verse that received a few favorable reviews. The same year Rostand, then twenty-two, married Rosemonde Gérard, a nineteen-year-old poetess of later distinction and the granddaughter of a Marshal of France under Napoleon. Such personal associations with national glory as well as Rostand's upbringing in southern France perhaps accentuated a natural penchant for romance and grandiloquence. He published other poetry and became increasingly attracted to the theatre, to which he was to devote most of his future efforts.

Two unpublished dramatic trifles predate his first verse collection, and the second of these, *Les Deux Pierrots* (*The Two Pierrots*), came near being produced at the Comédie-Française in 1891. His first play actually to reach the boards was *Les Romanesques,* a charming if trivial satire on romance that was to achieve enormous success in New York over half a century later as *The Fantasticks.* Though it ridicules excessive romantic attitudes, the play itself is in sharp contrast to the drab naturalism of contemporary drama, and it presages the very mixture of imaginative romanticism, declamation, wit, and wistfulness that was to characterize Rostand's major works. His next verse play, *La Princesse lointaine* (*The Princess Far Away,* 1895), an overblown paean to the ideal of love, features the twelfth-century Aquitaine troubadour Jaufre Rudel, who dies faithful to the ideal of his beloved but faithless princess and embodies the conviction that "True love's travail does the work of heaven!" Sarah Bernhardt, who played the title role, two years later starred in Rostand's *La Samaritaine* (*The Woman of Samaria,* 1897), "an Evangel in three parts." Here the triumph of ideal over physical love is dramatized in a biblical spectacle with a very human Jesus (speaking like Rostand himself) inspiring a new Magdalen (Photine) to carry His message, lead the mob to Jacob's Well, where Jesus waits, and join in the Lord's Prayer.

It was his next work, however, that elevated Rostand into the ranks of great French playwrights. *Cyrano de Bergerac,* completed while he joined ÉMILE ZOLA and others in vigorously defending Alfred Dreyfus, brought him immediate and worldwide fame. Not yet thirty, he was lionized at home. In 1900 Rostand was appointed Officer of the Legion of Honor, and three years later he became the youngest member ever elected to the French Academy—because of the literary distinction his play was considered to possess above and beyond its immense theatricality. He wrote his leading parts for great French actors such as Constant-Benoît Coquelin and Sarah Bernhardt, the latter of whom played Napoleon's weak-willed son in Rostand's next work, *L'Aiglon.* While this play did not create quite the furor of *Cyrano,* it enjoyed international success and consolidated Rostand's reputation.

Ill health at this time caused Rostand to leave his admirers in Paris and take his family into retirement to a luxurious villa in Cambo, in the southern countryside at the foot of the Pyrenees. He became interested in writing an allegorical animal drama, and spent many years working on what eventually became the third of his important plays, *Chanticleer.* The conception of the leading character, the "Gallic Cock," he worked out with Coquelin, for whom the part was created—but the elderly Coquelin died shortly before the beginning of rehearsals. The play was eagerly anticipated by a public that had not had a new Rostand drama for a decade. But though it has been praised by some critics as his most profound work, it never enjoyed the popularity of the preceding two plays. In his last years Rostand produced a verse pantomime, worked on a never-completed *Faust,* and almost finished his dramatization of another legendary character in the posthumous *La Dernière Nuit de Don Juan* (1921), which soon was adapted by the American playwright SIDNEY HOWARD as *The Last Night of Don Juan* (1925).

It is *Cyrano de Bergerac,* however, that warrants Rostand's inclusion among the great modern playwrights, though his presence in that group constitutes an anomaly. Brilliant as he was in conveying exaltation in witty yet bombastic, and rhapsodic yet wistful verse, Rostand added no new dimension to the drama. His plays are, rather, grounded in the even-then-dated tradition of heroic verse, and his plots are comparable to those of the cheap popular romances of the nineteenth century. Their phenomenal and lasting success has rested in large part on the appealing change Rostand provided to the popular but depressing naturalism and wearisome symbolism of his age. What distinguish Rostand's drama are wit and subtly conveyed pathos—an awareness of the real world confronted by idealists such as his Cyrano, a character who has much in common with Cervantes's Don Quixote. It is this mixture of the real with the romance of the heroic and ideal that accounts for both Rostand's popular and his literary achievement—for the immense theatrical success the play has enjoyed for three-quarters of a century, and for its continued appeal not only to actors and audiences but also to critics, readers, and translators. Though rhetorical excesses make Rostand's lesser plays appear absurd today, his particular genius is evident in his very best plays; they have dated less than have many of the works of superior dramatists.

At the beginning of World War I Rostand volunteered for service, but was rejected. He thereupon devoted his energies to composing popular patriotic verse. He and Rosemonde Gérard had two sons, both of whom became writers and one of whom, MAURICE ROSTAND, achieved a measure of fame. Gérard's *Edmond Rostand* (1935) is the most interesting of the biographies of her husband. In English, introductions and bibliographies in the numerous editions of *Cyrano de Bergerac* provide further information about Rostand and his work. The collected *Plays of Edmond Rostand* (translated by Henderson D. Norman) appeared in two volumes in 1921.

ROSTAND, Maurice (1891–1968), French poet and playwright, and the son of EDMOND ROSTAND, wrote verse dramas in the style of but not nearly as successful as those of his illustrious father. With his mother, the poet Rosemonde Gérard, he collaborated on *Un Bon Petit Diable* (*A Good Little Devil,* 1911), a popular fairy play about a blind girl. In *La Gloire* (1911), a tragic romance that recalls Edmond Rostand's L'AIGLON and which he considered his best play, Maurice Rostand dramatized the complex relationship of a famous father and an untalented son. Further Maurice Rostand plays were inspired by World War I and by other historical events, and include *Napoléon IV* (1928), which created a mild sensation because it seemed to blame the death of the Prince Imperial on Queen Victoria; and *Le Procès d'Oscar Wilde* (1935), a dramatization of the trials of WILDE.

ROSTWOROWSKI, Karol Hubert (1877–1938), Polish playwright, was praised as his nation's greatest pre-World War I dramatic poet. The Krakow heir of STANISŁAW WYSPIAŃSKI, Rostworowski was an antiNATURALIST proponent of "monumental" pageant theatre. Striving for elevated actions and language, Rostworowski succeeded particularly with the biblical *Judasz z Kariotu* (1912). Another noteworthy achievement was a trilogy on the expiation of a crime through three generations: *Niespodzianka* (1929), *Przeprowadzka* (1930), and *U mety* (1932); the first of these resembles ALBERT CAMUS's dramatization of a European folktale, THE MISUNDERSTANDING. Another play reminiscent of Camus is *Kajus Cezar*

Kaligula (1917). Rostworowski also experimented with EXPRESSIONISM, notably in his allegorical mystery *Filantropia* (1920). Rostworowski's further grandiose dramatic endeavors—he wrote some seventeen plays—to perpetuate the work of Wyspiański impressed some of the critics, but not the public.

ROUNDHEADS AND THE PEAKHEADS, THE (*Die Rundköpfe und die Spitzköpfe*), a play in eleven prose and blank-verse scenes and a prologue by BERTOLT BRECHT (music by Hanns Eisler), produced in 1936 and published in 1937. Setting: the city of Luma in the kingdom of Jahoo, 1930's.

A school production of this play, which Brecht labeled a "horror tale," was given in 1933, the year its publication was stopped by the Nazis. Brecht's subtitle is a pun on *Reich* (meaning "empire" as well as "wealth"): *Reich und Reich Gesellt Sich Gern* ("*Reich* and *Reich* like to fraternize"). Though it is a "parable type of non-Aristotelian drama," Brecht noted that his play is "addressed to a 'wide' public and takes greater account of purely entertainment consideration" (as does his later and similar THE RESISTIBLE RISE OF ARTURO UI). The play is loosely based on Shakespeare's *Measure for Measure.*

The viceroy despairs over Jahoo's deteriorating economy and threats by the revolutionary peasant organization, "the Sickle." He leaves after appointing as ruler Angelo Iberin (i.e., Hitler), a demagogue who, knowing that people are "little inclined to abstractions," blames all troubles on a minority—those who have peak heads. The distinction between them and round-headed people obscures the real problem—the class struggle—by cutting through all classes. Small shopkeepers soon and brutally liquidate their peak-headed competitors and, like others in the kingdom, nurse self-contradictory illusions. The middle class, the poor, and the peasant organization become self-divided and impotent.

A wealthy peak-headed landlord, Emanuel de Guzman, is denounced by a round-headed whore as her seducer. He can be saved only at the price of the virginity of his sister Isabella, a nun. The whore is paid to impersonate Isabella, while her father, Guzman's tenant, is paid to serve Guzman's term. The substitutions are discovered by the returning viceroy, who resolves the case and reinstates all the wealthy. Since "the Sickle" has been vanquished, Iberin must stop persecuting the peakheads. The viceroy has him prepare Jahoo for war against the far-off land of squareheads. The poor are again under the yoke of the wealthy, who feast at the viceroy's table. The revolutionary leaders, singing their "Sicklesong," are being hanged on his gallows.

ROUSSIN, André (1911–   ), French playwright, a successful author of a number of fashionable, witty comedies resembling—but less impressive than—those of his English contemporary TERENCE RATTIGAN. His most popular one was *La Petite Hutte* (1947), a Gallic farce set on a desert island and featuring the *ménage à trois* of husband, wife, and lover; in Nancy Mitford's (1904–   ) adaptation, *The Little Hut* played in London (1950) and New York (1953). Other Roussin hits are *Nina* (1949, about a middle-aged wife attempting to keep her young lover), *Bobosse* (1950), and *L'École des autres* (1962). His plays appear in various French collections.

ROYAL FAMILY, THE, a comedy in three acts by GEORGE S. KAUFMAN and EDNA FERBER, produced in 1927 and published in 1928. Setting: New York, 1920's.

A portrait of three generations of Cavendishes, who suggest the Barrymores ("the royal family of Broadway"), this play was produced in England as *Theatre Royal.* The lure of the stage accentuates the temperamental lives of the Cavendishes, who are dominated by Fanny, a sharp-tongued, courageous trouper. At the play's climax, the daughter bitterly denounces the theatre—and then rushes off to start her evening's stage performance.

RÓŻEWICZ, Tadeusz (1921–   ), Polish poet, established his reputation as a promising new dramatist with his first play, *Kartoteka* (*The Card Index,* 1960; also produced as *The Dossier*). A monologue by its protagonist is illustrated by satiric episodes and reflections about life in pre-World War II and Nazi-occupied Poland. Różewicz's drama is ironic, in the tradition of the theatre of the ABSURD, and it satirizes man's problems in the postwar world. *Grupa Laokoona* (*The Group of Laocoon,* 1961) metaphorically represents mankind in the throes of nihilism in episodic discussions. *Świadkowie, albo nasza mała stabilizacja* (*The Witnesses, or Things Are Almost Back to Normal,* 1962), three individually untitled plays inspired by SAMUEL BECKETT and originally written for television, were produced in New York: the first play consists of abstract metaphors; the second presents a couple discussing trivia at breakfast, while children outside torture and mutilate a cat; and in the third, two men facing in opposite directions discourse in monologues, while a dog at their feet undergoes its death paroxysms. *Śmieszny staruszek* (*The Funny Old Man,* 1964) is a "comedy" of old age and misery, and consists principally of the protagonist's self-revealing monologue. Różewicz's "other plays" collected in *The Card Index and Other Plays* (1969) are *Wyszedł z domu* (*Gone Out,* 1964; also translated as *Left Home*) and *Akt przerywany* (*The Interrupted Act,* 1964); the former depicts a happy amnesiac returning to his frustrated wife, and the latter consists of antitheatre reflections on the impossibility of writing modern drama. He also produced other semiSURREALIST sketches.

Born in a clerk's family in Radomsko, Różewicz made his name with a collection of poems, *Niepokój* (1947). He also wrote fiction and film and television scripts.

ROZOV, Victor Sergeevich (1913–   ), Russian playwright, has been most successful with *Vechno* *zhivye* (*Alive Forever,* 1956), a play on which Mikhail Kalatozov based *Letyat zhuravli* (*The Cranes Are Flying,* 1957), his internationally successful film about a wartime romance. Rozov's plays—many of which also became film scripts—usually deal with the conflict of the generations. Successful particularly in articulating the viewpoints of younger people, his plays became very popular in the Soviet Union. Among the best-known ones are *V dobry chas* (1955), about a Soviet youth who finds himself; *V poiskach radosti* (*In Search of Happiness,* 1955); *Neravny boi* (1960), whose title refers to the characteristic "unequal combat" in Rozov's plays, and whose hero is a sixteen-year-old boy; *ABVGD* (1961), which dramatizes the story of an obstreperous young man; *Pered uzhinom* (1963); and *V den svadby* (1963).

Alive Forever, with a preface and notes by Rozov, appears in Franklin D. Reeve's collection *Contemporary Russian Drama* (1968).

RUEDERER, Josef (1861–1915), German playwright, is notable for two dialect comedies that achieved considerable popularity at the turn of the century. *Die Fahnenweihe* (1895), a satire of village life, ridicules among others the corrupt postmaster, who tries to get rich with the help of one of his wife's lovers, and the priest, who participates in a lynching in which he himself becomes the victim. *Die Morgenröte* (1904) dramatizes the 1848 Munich riots, featuring beer-garden politicians as well as the dancer Lola Montez and the students who successfully opposed her viewpoints—a victory of the banal over the romantic.

Ruederer, who lived in his native Munich, also wrote grotesque short stories and novels.

RULES OF THE GAME, THE (*Il giuoco delle parti*), a comedy in three acts by LUIGI PIRANDELLO, produced in 1918 and published in 1919. Setting: a large contemporary Italian city.

The protagonist, Gala, is an embittered and characteristically Pirandellian figure, though he is masked as a witty, detached philosopher whose only pleasures are gastronomical. This is the play being rehearsed in the opening scene of SIX CHARACTERS IN SEARCH OF AN AUTHOR; there the manager tells the actor playing Gala, "You stand for reason, your wife is instinct. It's a mixing up of the parts, according to which you who act your own part become the puppet of yourself." This tragicomedy has also been translated as *Each in His Own Role* and as *Mixing It Up*.

Act I. It is a late evening and Silia is bored with her lover, Guido Venanzi. Though her husband, Leone Gala, has given her their luxurious apartment and complete freedom, she is infuriated by his calm indifference. Obsessed with him, she even suggests that Guido kill Gala. When he arrives for his daily half-hour visit, which she insists upon, Silia sends her lover to talk to him. Already feeling uncomfortable in the situation, Guido is further disconcerted by Gala's calm philosophizing. Life, he tells his wife's lover, is a game whose rules one must understand; in order to survive one must do away with all emotions—"even the lingering trace of bitterness." One must "empty" oneself and then find a counterweight, "the pivot of a concept on which you can make your stand." In that way he has "emptied" himself of his emotions for Silia, the sensual, betraying woman, and has substituted the merely formal concept of wife. His analogy (recurrent in the play) is with an egg: to avoid being splattered by it, "punch a hole in each end, and suck it out," leaving an empty shell one can play with and crush. Enraged, Silia throws an eggshell out of the window after him. Four drunk gentlemen in the street below mistake her for an immoral dancer, and her gesture for an invitation. Silia immediately makes use of the situation to do away with Gala. She locks Guido in the bedroom, sends the maid for help, and then leads the revelers on shamelessly. When the neighbors arrive, she charges the men with having insulted her. She refuses their apology: her husband must avenge her honor by dueling with one of them, a renowned swordsman. When they are alone again, Silia cuddles up to Guido.

Act II. In his strange combination study and dining room, Gala and his servant (whom he calls "Socrates") are engaged in cooking experiments. As Gala entertains the servant with "a little metaphysical conversation to whet the appetite," Guido comes to warn him. Silia herself arrives before he can reveal her plans. When Gala hears her story he fully understands, and amazes the lovers by calmly agreeing to duel. "I am trapped in my assigned role of husband. And I haven't the slightest intention of disillusioning her," he tells Guido, and turns to Silia: "I am the husband and you are the wife and he"—referring to her lover—"well, naturally he will act as my second," since his "delicate position" has prevented his emerging to defend her. Though Guido resists at first, he soon is goaded by Silia to accept; in fact, to ingratiate himself with her, he proposes excessive terms to make certain Gala will be killed. Calmly Gala assures them he knows what he is doing, and sets the time (the next morning) and place (his garden) for the duel. Silia is torn between remorse and anger at Gala's docility and indifference. Though he does not even know how to hold a sword, Gala consoles her: "I don't need to. . . . I live in a climate, my dear, where nothing can touch me, where life and death have no significance." He knows the rules of the game and he has rid himself of his strong, successive emotions of love and hate for her. Yet he admits that he still has emotions; but he prevents them from devouring him, and thus depriving him of the pleasure of life: "I never let them get away from me. I seize them, I dominate them and I nail them up."

Act III. The next morning everything is ready for the duel. His friends, the doctor, and the others arrive, but Gala is still sleeping soundly. When finally roused, he amazes everybody with his calm announcement that Guido will do the fighting: "As the husband, I, of course, had to send the challenge. He couldn't very well be expected to do that, in his somewhat unofficial capacity. But as for fighting the duel itself, that's something else." He deftly parries their accusation that he is acting monstrously: "It's the most natural thing in the world, if you understand the rules of the game." Had not Guido and Silia arranged to send him to his death? According to logic and custom, the second must act for the withdrawing principal. So Guido goes to the appointed place while Gala prepares for his breakfast. When he tells his frightened but enraged wife that she is punished now, Silia venomously says he did so at the cost of covering himself with shame. "*You* are my only shame!" he tells her, and flings her away. Hysterically she asks where her lover is and where they are fighting. Gala suggests that she watch the duel from the roof: "Wonderful view from up there." Guido is killed. The servant announces breakfast, but Gala, as if he does not hear, remains immobile.

RUMANIA, under foreign domination—Turkish, Austrian, Russian—for most of the modern period, was late in producing any literature. To date there has been little Rumanian drama of interest, and not a single playwright of international note. TRISTAN TZARA, the founder of DADAISM, emigrated to Switzerland and France, and EUGÈNE IONESCO renounced his Rumanian citizenship and language some time before he made his worldwide reputation as a French playwright.

Rumania's earliest modern dramatists were Vasile Alecsandri (1821–90) and Ion Luca Caragiale (1852–1912). Alecsandri wrote patriotic poetry and a number of light comedies, the most successful of which were *Iorgu de la Sadagura* (1844) and *Boieri şi ciocoi* (1874); his most notable plays are *Despot-vodă* (1879), a native historical drama that remained popular until midcentury, and two plays on classical themes, *Fîntîna Blanduziei* (1883) and *Ovidiu* (1885). Caragiale, Rumania's first and only important dramatist, has in recent times been praised as a critic of the bourgeoisie. Eventually the director of the National Theatre, he wrote witty sketches and satiric comedies such as the popular *O noapte furtunoasă* (*A Stormy Night,* 1879) and *O scrisoare pierdută* (*A Lost Letter,* 1883), whose title alludes to the compromising epistle a rival politician discovers during an election; and distinguished tragedies such as *Năpasta* (1890), which resembles Strindberg's THE FATHER but failed to achieve popular success.

Other playwrights and plays mentioned in specialized studies include *Manasse* (1900), a drama by Ronetti Roman (1852–1908) portraying various and changing mores in a Moldavian village; Barbu Delavrancea (pen name of Barbu Ştefănescu, 1858–1918), who wrote popular historical plays, including a tragedy about Stephen the Great, Moldavia's heroic fifteenth-century prince; Alexandru Davila (1862–1929), a director of the National Theatre, whose most successful play was a verse tragedy about fourteenth-century Wallachia, *Vlaicu Vodă* (1902); Nicolae Iorga (1871–1940), a historian and politician whose writings include plays about Dante, Molière, and Cleopatra; a writer popular for his dramatic thrillers, Haralamb G. Lecca (1873–1920); Mihail Sorbul (pen name of Mihail Smolski, 1885–1966), who wrote historical and social drama, including *Patima roşie* (1916) and *Prăpastia* (1921); Horia Furtună (1888–1952), who earned critical acclaim for his verse folk drama *Păcală* (1927); Victor Eftimiu (1889–), a poet who wrote folk plays and poetic fantasies, including *Ave Maria* (1913) and *Prometeu* (1919), and *Cocoşul negru* (*The Black Cock,* 1913); and Ion Sân-Giorgiu (1893–1950), author of *Madame Sevastita* (1936) and other plays.

Other modern playwrights include Camil Petrescu (1894–1957), notable for his theatre of ideas and psychology; the philosopher-poet Lucian Blaga (1895–1961), who wrote historcal and folklore drama, often from a psychoanalytical perspective; the short-lived author of bittersweet plays, Mihail Sebastian (1907–45); Horia Lovinescu (1918–), the leading post-World War II writer steeped in the Soviet cult of SOCIALIST REALISM; Alexandru Mirodan (1927–), whose dramas include *Celebrul 702* (1960), an anti-American satire about the California convict Caryl Chessman and his execution, which elicited international attention at the time; and Ecaterina Oproiu (1930–), a film-magazine editor who achieved success with a simple romantic drama, *Nu sînt turnul Eiffel* (1965), that eschewed socialist realism.

See E. D. Trappe's introductory essay to *Rumanian Prose and Verse* (1956), and *World Theatre* XIII:3 (1964).

RUNYON, [Alfred] Damon (1884–1946), American short-story writer and journalist, collaborated with HOWARD LINDSAY on one play: *A Slight Case of Murder* (1935). A broad comedy about beer-smuggling racketeers, it failed on Broadway but succeeded in Hollywood. Many of Runyon's slangy Broadway character stories have been filmed. A number of these were reshaped into *Guys and Dolls* (1952), a New York Drama Critics' Circle Award-winning popular musical comedy by Jo Swerling (1897–) and ABE BURROWS, with music by Frank Loesser.

RUSIÑOL, Santiago (1861–1931), Spanish-Catalonian writer and painter, was most prominent as an artist. He was successful as a playwright especially with *El místico*, translated (by the playwright Joaquín Dicenta, 1863–1917) into the Castilian from the Catalan *El mistic* (1903), which portrays the life of the great Catalonian poet-priest Jacint Verdaguer. But Rusiñol is memorable primarily because of his association with GREGORIO MARTÍNEZ SIERRA. Their comedy *Vida y dulzura* (1907) was Martínez Sierra's first produced play, and their Catalan *Aucells de pas* (1908), another comedy, became a Spanish operetta. Martínez Sierra translated into the Spanish some of Rusiñol's Catalonian novels, essays, and other plays.

RUSSELL, George William (1867–1935), or Æ, as he signed himself, was an Irish poet and an important figure in the Irish Literary Revival. WILLIAM BUTLER YEATS in *Dramatis Personae* reveals how Russell frequently suggested plots to others. He himself, however, wrote only *Deirdre* (1902), whose legend Yeats and J. M. SYNGE too dramatized. For his life and career see Herbert Howarth's *The Irish Writers 1880–1940* (1958). Una Ellis-Fermor's *The Irish Dramatic Movement* (1954) discusses his drama.

RUSSIA in modern times has produced some playwrights of major international importance. The best of them—ANTON CHEKHOV, MAXIM GORKY, and perhaps LEO TOLSTOI—wrote their famous plays in the late nineteenth and early twentieth centuries. Postrevolutionary Russia, it is true, can boast of theatrical activities that are significant both in quantity and quality, and it has also had outstanding actors, designers, and directors. But it has produced nothing comparable in drama, for Soviet censorship has stifled creativity in the arts and in literature. Most Russian playwrights have been noted primarily for their fiction and verse, and their drama, perhaps more than their work in other literary genres, has suffered from the state's insistence on SOCIALIST REALISM—that vaguely defined but rigidly applied principle which forces all writing into contemporary social, economic, and political molds, forbids "excessive" NATURALISM or FORMALISM, and has succeeded over the decades in encouraging only hack propaganda.

Ultrarestrictive censorship had hampered Russian drama as early as the seventeenth century. Nonetheless, despite their autocratic rule, the tsars initiated and supported theatrical activities, and the Russian (almost always imperial) theatre flourished in the 1800's. Among the notable dramatists of the nineteenth century, two in particular advanced the cause of naturalism: Nikolai Vasilevich Gogol (1809–52) and Aleksandr Nikolaevich Ostrovsky (1823–86). Gogol's satiric masterpiece *Revizor* (*The Inspector-General,* 1836) picturesquely depicts the pettiness and corruption of municipal government—and of all Russian officialdom. The prolific Ostrovsky delineated contemporary society, particularly in satiric comedies such as *Na vsyakogo mudretsa dovolno prostoty* (*The Diary of a Scoundrel,* 1868) and in *Groza* (*The Storm,* 1859; also translated as *The Thunderstorm*), a tragedy of religious intolerance and adultery. Both Gogol's and Ostrovsky's plays achieved lasting popularity within and beyond Russia, and directly influenced ALEKSANDR VASILEVICH SUKHOVO-KOBYLIN, whose *Krechinsky's Wedding* became popular in post-Revolution repertoires. Other notable nineteenth-century figures are Aleksei Pisemsky (1820–81), whose *Gorkaya sudbina* (*A Hard Lot,* 1859) is one of Russia's earliest peasant tragedies and a precursor of Tolstoi's THE POWER OF DARKNESS; and Ivan Turgenev (1818–83), more important as a novelist but also a classic playwright whose *Mesyats v derevne* (*A Month in the Country,* a comedy written in 1850 but not published until 1869 and produced in 1872) is a precursor of Chekhov's drama.

Their work and that of other theatre innovators brought about simpler and more REALISTIC staging and less stilted acting techniques. On a now-historic date, June 21, 1897, Konstantin Stanislavsky and V. I. NEMIROVICH-DANCHENKO met in a restaurant to confer, for fifteen consecutive hours, about ways to cure the Russian theatre's "false pathos, declamation, artificiality in acting, bad staging and décor conventions," as Stanislavsky later recalled. Most important to the history of modern drama was their determination to do something about "the insignificant repertoires of the time." The result of that momentous meeting was the founding of the Moscow Art Theatre, which made famous (and was itself made famous by the productions of) Russia's greatest modern playwrights, Chekhov and Gorky. The latter's work bridged the tsarist and Soviet eras much as did the Theatre itself, which was later named after Gorky. Stanislavsky's theories and practices of naturalism were soon to influence the modern stage and drama throughout the world, and some of his pupils, such as the Armenian Yevgeni Vakhtangov and Vsevolod Yemilevich Meyerhold, left their own unique stamp on subsequent drama. A gifted and radical innovator, Meyerhold became interested in SYMBOLISM and stylization, and produced the works of LEONID ANDREEV and VLADIMIR MAYAKOVSKY, "The Poet of the Revolution." Meyerhold used anti-REPRESENTATIONAL settings and featured AGIT-PROP troupes and LIVING NEWSPAPER brigades; but eventually he was criticized as a "formalist"—and purged. Another important early-twentieth-century innovator was Aleksandr Yakovlevich Tairov; in contradistinction to Stanislavsky's naturalistic theories, he stressed the theatrical.

Before the Moscow Art Theatre was founded in 1898, the most notable plays of the late nineteenth century were written by Leo Tolstoi, whose innate genius as a dramatist was thwarted by restrictive censorship. His cousin, Aleksei Konstantinovich Tolstoi,* wrote the play which launched the Moscow Art Theatre: *Tsar Fyodor Ivanovich,* the second of an exotic historical trilogy in blank verse. VLADIMIR SOLOVYOV also wrote plays of this type which received contemporary acclaim, as did the work of MIKHAIL ARTSYBASHEV, who became popular with his erotic-anarchistic writings. Among other notable pre-World War I dramatists were the symbolist ALEKSANDR BLOK and NIKOLAI YEVREINOV; the former's work in the theatre belongs more properly in a discussion of poetry, but Yevreinov was a playwright and dramatic theoretician of considerable originality. Other

* For further information about this writer, see under ALEKSEI NIKOLAEVICH TOLSTOI, yet another relative of the great novelist.

symbolists include Andreev and FYODOR SOLOGUB, who made more important contributions to poetry and fiction.

The effects of the 1917 Revolution were as cataclysmic in the theatre as they were in other facets of Russian life. The people Stanislavsky now played to had never before been inside a theatre, and the interaction between these new audiences and the actors brought about changes in both.* The Soviets' eagerness to wipe out all traces of prerevolutionary times would have obliterated the classics, had it not been for Lenin's cultivated friend ANATOLI LUNACHARSKY, the first Soviet Commissar of Education, who himself wrote a number of model dramatic reinterpretations of history and made an important impact on the Soviet theatre. Nonetheless, Soviet plays too often seem excessively naïve and propagandistic. They invariably portray the Civil War or World War II—fought by heroic Reds against treacherous Whites and foreigners—and the building of the Soviet utopia, commonly exemplified in "boy-meets-tractor" plots. The proletariat drama, produced by state directive for proletariat audiences, was necessarily simplistic.

Among the many playwrights who furnished this kind of fare a number stand out, either because of their professional skill or because they transcend the naïvely two-dimensional and yet remain within the bounds of the officially permissible. Among the more important propaganda playwrights were the aforementioned Mayakovsky and Yevreinov, who composed typical epic spectacles and pageants produced outdoors with casts of thousands, fireworks, simulated naval bombardments, etc. Similarly sensational were Ivanov's ARMORED TRAIN 14-69; THE CHIMES OF THE KREMLIN by the very successful NIKOLAI POGODIN, who also wrote a Lenin trilogy; and Meyerhold's production of *Rychi Kitai!* (*Roar China!*) by SERGEI TRETYAKOV. Other such writers were VLADIMIR BILL-BELOTSERKOVSKY, ANATOLI GLEVOB, VLADIMIR KIRSHON, SERGEI MIKHALKOV (who specialized in propaganda for children), ANATOLI SUROV, the TUR BROTHERS, and VSEVOLOD VISHNEVSKY. ALEKSEI ARBUZOV became known even outside Russia because of the love themes—a rarity in Soviet drama—in his otherwise orthodox plays.

World War II and the cold war that followed became frequently dramatized topics. Undoubtedly the best-known playwright who dealt with the war, in both his fiction and his drama, was KONSTANTIN SIMONOV. Others include earlier-mentioned playwrights as well as VASSILI ILENKOV, ALEKSANDR KORNEICHUK (a Ukrainian who became prominent as a writer as well as a politician), and VERA PANOVA, who became notable for not shying away from love themes. A few writers have attempted to present less stereotyped portrayals of the Soviets and their enemies. Distinguished among these attempts are Bulgakov's DAYS OF THE TURBINS

ANTON CHEKHOV and LEO TOLSTOI. (*Sovfoto*)

(1926) and *Gostinitsa Astoriya* (1957) by ALEKSANDR SHTEIN. Something comparable was achieved in the de-Stalinization drama of SAMUIL ALYOSHIN. But of greater interest are the few attempts of Russian playwrights to deal honestly with the intellectual's problems in the Soviet dictatorship. Outstanding among writers who essayed this dangerous topic are two whose important plays appeared in the 1930's, ALEKSANDR AFINOGENOV and YURI OLESHA.

Yet the best drama produced in the Soviet Union has come from writers who were either banned or miraculously evaded official detection. Foremost among these is YEVGENI SHVARTS, perhaps the most underrated Soviet playwright. He escaped liquidation only because his brilliant satires were camouflaged (however lightly) by fairy-tale plots and settings. YEVGENI LVOVICH ZAMYATIN, noted for his antiutopian novel *My* (*We*), was less successful in having his dramatic satires produced. NIKOLAI ERDMAN, another fine satirist, was purged, as was ISAAK BABEL, the short-story writer who also left two plays of considerable power. "The Russian NOËL COWARD," VALENTINE KATAEV, achieved great fame with his SQUARING THE CIRCLE; but he wrote within the confines of approved Soviet dogma, as did VASILI SHKVARKIN and ANATOLI SOFRONOV, who gained popularity with light comedies. VICTOR ROZOV, who like Arbuzov is among the more important new dramatists to emerge since Stalin's death, became internationally known when one of his plays was filmed. LEONID LEONOV, a novelist whose introspective characters reflect the influence of Dostoevsky, wrote a sensitive Soviet play which inevitably

* The effects as well as the changes are charmingly described in Stanislavsky's *Moya zhizn v iskusstve* (*My Life in Art*, 1924).

recalls Chekhov's THE CHERRY ORCHARD. The older BORIS LAVRENEV was a romanticist poet and novelist who, under both regimes, wrote about the officers' code of honor; and SAMUIL MARSHAK, a professional translator and children's writer, produced a charming folk drama.

Among more recent playwrights whose names have appeared abroad are Leonid G. Zorin (1924–), praised in his youth by Gorky, a 1961 film prize winner at the International Venice Festival, and author of some twenty plays since 1941, including the bittersweet two-character romance *Varshavskaya melodiya* (*A Warsaw Melody*, 1967); and Mikhail F. Shatrav (pseudonym of M. F. Marshak, 1932–), whose first important work, the 1967 hit *Bolsheviki* (*Tridtsatoe Avgusta*), boldly depicts early Bolshevik history: the attempt to assassinate Lenin on August 30, 1918.

Also important among recent dramatists is Aleksandr Volodin (pseudonym of Lifshyts, 1919–), who has received considerable popular acclaim for two dramas on the romantic and psychological problems of youths, *Fabrichnaya dezchonka* (1956) and *Pyat vecherov* (*Five Evenings*, 1959); but Volodin has been censured for his failure to resolve these plays in accord with socialist realism and for his criticism of various aspects of Soviet society. The novelist Aleksandr I. Solzhenitsyn's (1918–) *Olen i shalashovka* (*The Love-Girl and the Innocent*) was banned in Moscow after its 1962 dress rehearsal but published in England in 1969 and produced in the United States the following year as *A Play by Aleksandr Solzhenitsyn;* it is set in a 1945 Stalinist slave-labor camp—like the ones he himself served in and described in his fiction—has a cast of seventy, and dramatizes the romance of an idealist and a girl who argues for survival by compromising integrity.

These plays are the exception. Most Soviet drama is drab, and little of it has interested the Western world. Despite fine acting and staging, the propaganda and falseness of Prolecult ("Proletarian Culture") has made it so unappealing that few plays are even available in translation.

The following collections also provide information about Russian drama and individual playwrights: George R. Noyes's *Masterpieces of the Russian Drama* (1933), Eugene Lyons's *Six Soviet Plays* (1934), Ben Blake's *Four Soviet Plays* (1937), *Four Soviet War Plays* (1943), H. W. L. Dana's *Seven Soviet Plays* (1946), Alexander Bakshy's *Soviet Scene: Six Plays of Russian Life* (1946), Franklin D. Reeve's *An Anthology of Russian Plays* (Volume II, 1963), Andrew R. MacAndrew's *20th Century Russian Drama* (1963), Michael Glenny's *Three Soviet Plays* (1966), and Franklin D. Reeve's *Contemporary Russian Drama* (1968). There are also a few collected translations of plays by (and noted under) individual authors.

Information about Soviet drama and playwrights is difficult to come by. Rehabilitated writers are occasionally mentioned, but data about many purged figures who are not in this category remains as inaccessible as do their writings—and indeed the writings even of the "rehabilitated." The Russian entries in *The Oxford Companion to the Theatre* (1950; 2nd ed., 1957) are scandalously biased.* H. W. L. Dana's *Handbook on Soviet Drama* (1938), though dated, consists of comprehensive "Lists of Theatres, Plays, Operas, Ballets, Films and Books and Articles About Them," in the words of the subtitle. Prince D. S. Mirsky's *Contemporary Russian Literature 1881–1925* (1926) is valuable for its discussion of earlier modern playwrights. Gleb Struve's *Soviet Russian Literature 1917–50* (1951), Marc Slonim's *Soviet Russian Literature: Writers and Problems, 1917–1967* (1967), and Edward J. Brown's *Russian Literature Since the Revolution* (revised 1969) are solid scholarly studies of the subject and include invaluable bibliographies; a similar though less comprehensive work is Vera Alexandrova's *A History of Soviet Literature: 1917–1962* (1963). Nikolai A. Gorchakov's *The Theater in Soviet Russia* (1957), an expert history of the pre-Revolution and Soviet drama and theatre, examines both the Soviet enslavement of the theatre and the resistance efforts of various playwrights. Among popular accounts of the drama and theatre are Norris Houghton's *Moscow Rehearsals* (1936) and *Return Engagement* (1962), Faubion Bowers's *Broadway, U.S.S.R.* (1959), and Marc Slonim's *Russian Theater from the Empire to the Soviets* (1961).

RUSSIAN PEOPLE, THE (*Russkie lyudi*), a play in three acts by KONSTANTIN SIMONOV, published and produced in 1942. Setting: the southern front in Russia, autumn 1941.

This poignant war drama portrays the quiet heroism of a number of individualized Russians. Some of them appeared in Simonov's earlier play, *Paren iz nashego goroda* (1940), a Stalin Prize winner about a schoolteacher who grows in stature; when war comes, he—as well as others—prove equal to the grim challenge. This even more successful sequel was produced in the United States in a CLIFFORD ODETS adaptation, and in England as *The Russians.* Later Simonov was pressured by Stalinist criticism to declare that he "had not known how to raise himself above the idea of Russian patriotism . . . and had not shown what Soviet patriotism was."

Act I. The town is occupied by savage Germans, who have appointed the local doctor mayor. His wife visits her friend, the mother of Ivan Nikitich Safonov, a one-time chauffeur and now battalion leader of a besieged detachment across the river. Hidden while the women talk is Valya Anoshchenko, an attractive young scout from the detachment. At his headquarters, Safonov appoints an old tsarist soldier his chief of staff, and a poet his intelligence officer. To the relief of Safonov, who loves her, Valya returns safely from the occupied town. Another messenger, a cynical medical

* For an exposé of these entries, see Eugene Lyons's "Red Propaganda, Oxonian Style" in the August 1955 issue of *Theatre Arts.* They were modified only in the book's third edition, 1967.

assistant, returns from his mission. Though their situation becomes increasingly desperate, the fighters are prepared "to die with a purpose," for Russia. "Our little hut in Novo-Nikolaevsk used to stand on the edge of a village, near a stream with two birch trees on the bank," Valya recalls, describing what Russia means to her; "when I hear people speak of their great motherland, the two trees are all I remember." Reluctantly, Safonov must again send Valya across the river on a dangerous mission. Even then, in a tender talk, he is too shy to avow his love.

Act II. The Germans at the house of the doctor-mayor prepare a diabolical torture. Discovering that his son, a Red Army officer, has just fallen in battle, they first ask the doctor to reaffirm his loyalty to the Germans, and his regret that his son fights them. Then they spring the news of his son's death on him, and make him express his pleasure at this news. Almost hysterical with grief over her loss and her disgust with her husband, his wife poisons one of the Germans. She implicates her husband in this act, though he protests his innocence and is crazed with fear. "Hang us! Yes, oh God—hang us, hang us!" she cries as both are taken out. On the other side of the river Valya prepares to cross again and Safonov lovingly but shyly bids her farewell: "If we stay alive, I'll have a lot to say!" A traitor in their ranks attempts to subvert the detachment's efforts and corrupt the chief of staff, the former tsarist officer.

Act III. The traitor is unmasked, though his doings have probably doomed Valya and her mission. The medical assistant cheerfully prepares to go on an almost certainly fatal mission. He takes some vodka ("not for courage—it's to keep me warm") and goes out singing: "A song helps for courage." In town, Safonov's mother is to be hanged by the Germans. "I'd show your mothers what their sons have done," she tells the vicious captors before she is taken out: "And I'd say, 'See, you bitches! Look at the litters you have whelped. Look at the rats and beetles you bore! The unspeakable beasts you gave to the world!'" The captured Valya courageously resists the Germans' attempts to make her betray her comrades, and the medical assistant outsmarts the Germans and thus helps the Red Army to rescue Safonov's guerrilla detachment. Before the Germans flee, they machine-gun their prisoners, though the medical assistant saves Valya—at the cost of his own life. The Red Army, led by an old friend of Safonov, recaptures the town. Though relieved to discover Valya alive, he sorrows over his losses, including his hanged mother. His friend, the general, consoles him: "When one tree dies we must plant two others in its place." Eager to remain alive, now, Safonov determines "to live on till my own eyes shall see the very last one of those who did all this lying dead!"

RYDEL, Lucjan (1870–1918), Polish lyric poet connected with the Young Poland Movement, wrote a few plays—notably the popular *Zaczarowane koło* (1899), which combines magic with an ominous view of the human race. He also wrote a popular nativity based on folklore, *Betlejem polskie* (*Polish Bethlehem,* 1905); and a Christmas mystery and historical drama, *Zygmunt August* (1913). But he is best remembered as the subject of one of the most distinguished Polish poetic dramas, *Wesele* (*The Wedding,* 1901), by STANISŁAW WYSPIAŃSKI—one of the many guests at the grand marriage festival of Rydel (who in the play is referred to only as the Bridegroom), a professor's son, to a beautiful peasant girl.

RYSKIND, Morrie (1895–), American librettist, became known for the half-dozen musical comedies he wrote with GEORGE S. KAUFMAN. Most popular among them were OF THEE I SING (1931); *Animal Crackers* (1928), notable for the ebullient performances (soon filmed) of the Marx brothers; *Strike Up the Band* (1930) and *Let 'Em Eat Cake* (1933, the less successful sequel to *Of Thee I Sing*), both with music by George Gershwin; *Bring On the Girls* (1934); and *Louisiana Purchase* (1940), with music by Irving Berlin. His other stage works include *The Gang's All Here* (1931, written with JEROME LAWRENCE and ROBERT E. LEE).

Born in New York, Ryskind also published humorous verse and other light pieces.

S

S.S. GLENCAIRN, four one-act plays by EUGENE O'NEILL, all dealing with the seamen of the British tramp steamer *Glencairn,* and first produced together as one play in 1924. The one-acters are performed in the following order, which is the logical but inverse order of their composition: THE MOON OF THE CARIBBEES, IN THE ZONE, THE LONG VOYAGE HOME, BOUND EAST FOR CARDIFF.

SABBATAI ZEVI, a play in three acts by SHOLEM ASCH, published in 1908. Setting: Jerusalem, Poland, Cairo, and Gallipoli; the latter part of the seventeenth century.

Like DAVID PINSKI's play by the same name, Asch's is a dramatization of the strange career of the false Messiah who appeared to the Jews at a time of great tribulations. Joyfully worshiped, the overconfident Sabbatai succumbs to fleshly lust. He loses his divinity and in despair becomes an apostate to Muhammadanism. A prophet tells the wailing Jews that God will release the true Messiah only when they are ready for him. And the Jews persist in their hope that "the Messiah will come, and although he tarrieth long, yet . . . He will come!"

SACRED FLAME, THE, a play in three acts by SOMERSET MAUGHAM, published and produced in 1928. Setting: a contemporary drawing room in a house near London in June.

In his preface Maugham discussed the literary, "unnatural" dialogue of this popular crime drama, filmed in 1929 and (as *The Right to Live*) in 1935. It deals with a young cripple, paralyzed in an accident.

The cripple is betrayed by his beloved wife and his brother. Before learning of the betrayal and his wife's pregnancy, he dies in his sleep. His repressed nurse, who loved him, discovers that he had an overdose of sleeping pills. Sure of her evidence, she in effect accuses the wife of murder and demands an autopsy. The victim's gentle, mystic mother is aware of the wife's decency and the reason for the nurse's insistence. Trying to make the nurse less censorious, the mother talks of the relativity of morals. The unhappy young wife does not feel sinful: she loved her husband, who believed in the transmigration of souls. In her child, she feels, her husband, "forgiving me the wrong I did him, will live out the life that was his due" (the sacred flame). When the nurse remains adamant, the mother reveals that it was she who gave her son the fatal overdose to spare him the misery of discovering his wife's unfaithfulness. The unhappy nurse, no longer motivated by jealousy, permits the doctor to sign the natural-death certificate and keep the family's secret inviolate.

SACRIFICE (*Visarjan*), a one-act play by RABINDRANATH TAGORE, published and produced in 1890. Setting: a temple in Tippera, in ancient times.

Considered the best of his early plays, this dramatization of the novel *Rajarshi,* which he had written five years earlier, was slightly revised by Tagore in its English edition. The play portrays such a characteristic Tagore figure as an abnegating king, and conflicts of violence and nonviolence, love and hate, and humanity and religious custom. Raghupati was Tagore's most successful acting role.

The king forbids further bloody sacrifices to the Mother Goddess Kali after a little girl's sorrowful offering of her pet goat, "for a man loses his humanity when it concerns his gods." The Priest Raghupati thunders his universal call for bloodshed and counsels the rebellion of the queen, the king's brother, and his own young pupil. The apple of Raghupati's eye, that boy is torn by conflicting loyalties and sacrifices himself at Kali's altar. Raghupati thereupon denounces his earlier philosophy of murder and the Goddess of Destruction: "Look how she stands there, the silly stone —dead, dumb, blind!"

SAINT JOAN, "A Chronicle Play in Six Scenes and an Epilogue" by BERNARD SHAW, produced in 1923 and published in 1924. Setting: fifteenth-century France.

Saint Joan is one of the great plays of modern times. In a preface almost as lively and long as the play itself, Shaw surveyed previous literary treatments of Joan: "romantic poppycock" that melodramatically depicts heroes and villains, not real people. Shaw explained how his play accurately and meaningfully presents, in modern terms, the "high tragedy" of what really happened during and after "the romance of her rise" (Scenes I–III). The Church, he maintained, conducted a fairer trial than any civil court would today in a comparable case. Joan's sainthood is a technicality of Church classification; what is important is that she was a genius, that is, "a person who, seeing farther and probing deeper than other people, has a different set of ethical valuations" and the vitality to express them. She was the founder of Protestantism and of the modern state, Shaw wrote, because she thought of God and King without the intervention of Church and feudal peerage. Thus she naturally came in conflict with the authorities, who had to destroy her freedom of individual conscience so that established society could survive. The tragedy (Scenes IV–VI) lies in such an irreconcilable, perennial confrontation of the two essential but incompatible forces: social institutions and genius. The Epilogue, presenting "the comedy of the attempts of posterity to make amends," said Shaw, dramatizes an essential part of Joan's history. Bernard F. Dukore's illustrated edition of Shaw's film version, *Saint Joan, a Screenplay* (1968), has notes and an extensive introduction.

Scene I. In the castle of Vaucouleurs in 1429, a blustering squire, Captain Robert de Baudricourt, is told by his steward that he cannot have his eggs: The Maid of Lorraine, who has been waiting to see him, has cast a spell on his hens. Joan enters and announces to him, "You are to give me a horse and armor and some soldiers, and send me to the Dauphin. Those are your orders from my Lord." When the outraged Robert tells her that the divine voices she claims to hear really come from her imagination, she readily agrees, "Of course. That is how the messages of God come to us." With pertness and common sense, and with the help of Bertrand de Poulengey, a gentleman-at-arms who has been won over and inspired by the energy and faith of the "farm wench," Joan disarms Robert, who acquiesces to her request when he comes to believe that she may well put fight into the Dauphin and the troops. The steward's announcement after her departure that the hens have resumed laying eggs persuades Robert that, indeed, "she did come from God."

Scene II. The Archbishop of Rheims and La Trémouille, the commander-in-chief of the army, soon joined by young Gilles de Rais (Bluebeard) and the gruff Captain La Hire, are awaiting the Dauphin (Charles VII) in the throne room at Chinon, in Touraine. Charles—"a poor creature physically . . . accustomed to be kicked, yet incorrigible and irrepressible"—is treated with open contempt. But he insists on seeing Joan, who has impressed La Hire with her miracles. The Archbishop finally agrees; but he ridicules as too simple the proposed stratagem to have Joan spot Charles among his courtiers, in order to test her ability to perform a miracle (which he defines as any "event which creates faith"). Joan enters and at once sees through the ruse: "Coom, Bluebeard! Thou canst not fool me. Where be Dauphin?" and then spots him. She announces her mission: "I am sent to you to drive the English away from Orleans and from France, and to crown you king in the cathedral at Rheims." When she and the Dauphin are left by themselves, Joan inspires Charles with courage and, though he would rather not fight and though he is disconcerted by her always "talking about God and praying," he summons the others and announces, to La Trémouille's fury and La Hire's delight, that he has given command of the army to Joan.

Scene III. On an evening six weeks later, at the south bank of the Loire, the commander Dunois ("The Bastard of Orleans") impatiently waits for a west wind so that his rafts can sail the river and engage the English. Joan, dressed in armor, enters in a rage because her troops are still miles behind and she wants to be on the Orleans bank of the river, where she can fight the English. She urges courage and haste, but the good-natured and practical Dunois counsels patience until a favorable wind comes. As soon as Joan prays to Saint Catherine, the wind changes. Dunois, acknowledging the miracle, kneels and hands Joan his commander's baton. As brothers-in-arms, they leave for the battle.

Scene IV, the only scene in which Joan is not physically present, is the turning point from romance to tragedy. In a tent in the English camp, the Earl of Warwick (Richard de Beauchamp) and John de Stogumber, a bullnecked English chaplain, await Cauchon, the Bishop of Beauvais. When he arrives, they discuss ways of coping with Joan's heresies, her success in defeating the English, and the imminent coronation of Charles. Over the chaplain's chauvinistic interjections ("How can what an Englishman believes be heresy? It is a contradiction in terms") and indignant demands for the burning of "the witch," and despite their rivalry, Warwick and Cauchon come to terms because they recognize Joan as their "common enemy" and a threat to both their institutions: to the Church because of her increasingly popular heresy, and to feudalism because of actions "which would wreck the whole social structure." They therefore agree that her "protest of the individual soul against the interference of priest or peer," as Warwick puts it, must be silenced by their united powers, although Cauchon "will strive to the utmost" for Joan's salvation. When the chaplain is implacably concerned only with the burning of the "rebel," Cauchon blesses him: "Sancta simplicitas!"

Scene V. In the ambulatory in the cathedral of Rheims, just after Charles's coronation, Dunois tells Joan—who is bored now that the battle and the ceremonies are over—that her triumphs have made her many enemies. Joan cannot understand why people do not love her for setting "them right when they were doing all sorts of stupid things." Charles, who is followed by La Hire, is relieved to hear that Joan may go back to her father's farm. But when he talks of making a peace treaty, she terrifies him by urging that they resume the battle for Paris. Dunois predicts that Joan will be captured by the English and that no one, including himself, will try to save her. The Archbishop, who has joined the group and is nettled by what Joan calls her voices and common sense and by what he calls her pride and disobedience, predicts that she will be burned at the stake. Joan, though aware that they will no longer follow her, is confident that she has saved them and done God's work, and that she will go through the

Saint Joan, Epilogue. Sybil Thorndike as Joan. London, 1925. (*British Theatre Museum*)

fire to the hearts of the common people, who are calling for her and to whom she then goes out. The dispirited group follows her glumly and with forebodings.

Scene VI. It is two years later, at the Rouen Bishop's Court, with the Inquisition participating. Warwick, who had brought Joan to the Inquisition after her capture nine months earlier, expresses his impatience at the length of the proceedings, but the Inquisitor and Cauchon, and even the Prosecutor, Canon John D'Estivet, are determined to give the grave charge of heresy a fair and full hearing. The assessors enter; they are headed by Chaplain de Stogumber, who stupidly haggles over unimportant issues. When the Inquisitor insists on their dealing with the main issue of heresy, Brother Martin Ladvenu, a Dominican, suggests that Joan's heresy may be due to harmless simplicity—"many saints have said as much as Joan." This is answered at great length by the Inquisitor: such simplicity, he maintains, may found "a heresy that will wreck both Church and Empire," and it has to be stamped out; while they must be merciful and try to save Joan, "justice comes first." Joan is brought in. She is chained, but her vitality is unabated and she answers charges of heresy by arguing that her acts are natural, not heretical. She will readily obey the Church—if it not "bid me do anything contrary to the command I have from God." When asked whose judgment is to decide what constitutes the will of God, hers or that of the Church, she replies, "What other judgment can I judge by but my own?"—an answer that scandalizes the court and condemns her. But when she realizes that her execution is really imminent, she momentarily despairs at the apparent deception of her voices, accepts the Church's proffered mercy, and listlessly signs a recantation. Hearing that she will not be set free but will be imprisoned for life, however, she tears up the paper: "Light your fire: do you think I dread it as much as the life of a rat in a hole? My voices were right." Duly excommunicated, she is handed over to the English secular arm, to the chaplain's great joy. As she is taken out to the stake, the Inquisitor and Cauchon remain behind to contrast the illegal speed with which the English carry out the execution with the fairness of the trial and their own compassion for the girl. "It is a terrible thing to see a young and innocent creature crushed between these mighty forces, the Church and the Law," neither of which she understands, the Inquisitor remarks. After a short pause, the chaplain rushes in hysterically, penitent and sick after having witnessed the execution. Ladvenu tells of Joan's courage in facing death, and suggests that "this is not the end for her, but the beginning." The executioner renders his official report to Warwick: "Your orders have been obeyed. Her heart would not burn, my lord; but everything that was left is at the bottom of the river. You have heard the last of her." Warwick wryly replies: "The last of her? Hm! I wonder!"

Epilogue. In the royal bedchamber on a night twenty-five years later, Ladvenu mysteriously appears to announce to Charles VII (now known as "the Victorious") that Joan's sentence has just been annulled. Entering amidst sudden wind and lightning, Joan reassures the frightened Charles that she is but a vision in his dreams. Dunois appears, and then Cauchon (now dead), who reaffirms the justice and mercy of his acts, despite his later excommunication for them and the Church's desecration of his corpse. Next comes a dead soldier who had given Joan a cross at the stake, and is therefore given one day off a year from hell. As he expatiates on the jolliness of hell, Chaplain de Stogumber, now old, deaf, and half-witted, enters and tells of his redemption through Joan. The executioner and Warwick follow, the latter apologizing to the amused Joan that "the burning was purely political." Finally a clergyman, dressed in 1920 clothes ridiculed by the others, proclaims Joan's canonization. As all kneel in praise before the new saint, she asks them whether she should return to them alive. In the general consternation that follows, Charles goes back to sleep and the others make a hasty departure, after assuring her that they would act the same way again: "the heretic is always better dead," "we are not yet good enough," and "political necessities, though occasionally erroneous, are still imperative." Alone as the hour of midnight strikes, Joan prays, "O God that madest this beautiful earth, when will it be ready to receive Thy saints? How long, O Lord, how long?"

SAINT JOAN OF THE STOCKYARDS (*Die Heilige Johanna der Schlachthöfe*), a play in eleven scenes by BERTOLT BRECHT, published in 1932. Setting: Chicago stockyards, stock exchange, etc., c. 1930.

Brecht was well established in Germany by 1932 and this is esteemed among his "greatest and most characteristic works," according to Martin Esslin (*Brecht: The Man and His Work*). But political pressures kept the play off the boards: its first performance was in 1959, though an abridged version was broadcast over Berlin radio in 1932 and an amateur performance was produced by Brecht some three years later in Copenhagen. Brecht's prose and free-verse modernization of the Joan of Arc story, written in 1929–30 to commemorate the five-hundredth anniversary of her death, interprets it from a Marxist viewpoint. Derived from HAPPY END and influenced by Shaw's SAINT JOAN and MAJOR BARBARA, the play parodies classics revered by the German bourgeoisie, particularly Goethe's *Faust* and Schiller's *Die Jungfrau von Orleans*. Choruses of salvationists, workers, livestock dealers, etc., are used extensively.

Scenes 1 through 7. Lieutenant Joan Dark of the Salvation Army (here called the Black Strawhats) seeks to return God to the "dehumanized humanity" of the starving unemployed. In ruthless competition with other meatpacking tycoons, Pierpont Mauler has just closed his factory. Joan "descends to the depths" to seek out this creator of human misery, and exerts an immediate influence on his heart (characterized by a colleague as "a sensitive garbage pit"). But though he gives her money, Mauler shows her that the poor are undeserving because of their wickedness. In her "second descent into the depths," Jean observes the disloyalty, dishonesty, and other evils starvation forces upon people. Though dejected, Joan realizes that these evils are not innate to the poor but are, rather, the result of desperate need. Taking her shock troops to the stock exchange, Joan overwhelms the conscience-stricken Mauler with her fervent speeches, and persuades him to buy unwanted meat. A market crash is averted, and the poor as well as the small investors seem to have been saved by Joan. It turns out, however, that Mauler's buying was a wise speculation. As Joan continues to exert pressure on him, he agrees to buy livestock as well, and soon he controls the market. Cornered by Mauler's move, the other tycoons offer their riches to the mission of their "Sainted Joan of the Livestock Exchange," so that she will use her influence on Mauler to release the livestock. Furiously she "expels the money changers from the temple." But her mission superior, upset at the loss of the tycoons' lucrative offer, expels the "simpleton" Joan from the evangelical army. Joan vows not to return until she can do so with a truly penitent Mauler, whose riches would then be acceptable.

Scenes 8 through 11. Though unwilling to open the slaughterhouses, Mauler offers Joan a check for her army. He believes in the importance of religion: "Beat the drum for Him so that He may / Gain a foothold in the regions of misery and His / Voice may ring out in the slaughterhouses." Unwilling to be bought, Joan makes her third descent into the depths and joins the unemployed, with whom she vows to remain until Mauler reopens the slaughterhouses. As their plight becomes more desperate (and Mauler's squeeze on the exchange gradually ruins his competitors), the Communists organize a strike. Freezing in the snow before the slaughterhouses, Joan agrees to join it. But when armed strikebreakers appear, she refuses to lend her support to violence. Rather than face imprisonment like the strike leaders, Joan decides to leave: ". . . Three days' descent / Growing weaker on the third day and / Swallowed by the swamp at the end. Say: / It was too cold." Soon Joan hears voices that reproach her for betraying the strikers. Apparently ruined, Mauler again is successful in spite of himself. With the proffered blessing of the Salvation Army (in return for his financial support) Mauler revitalizes the meatpacking industry on the principle of cheap labor through perpetual unemployment. Strikers—"criminals who impiously troubled peace and order"—are jailed, and the Salvation Army organ is played joyfully. Joan is brought in, dying of pneumonia. Her last words denounce God and the class system, and exhort violence: "Only force helps where force rules, and / Only men help where there are men." But her words are purposely drowned out as she is being canonized. The chants and hosannas of the Salvation Army and the meatpacker tycoons, and then loudspeaker announcements of the collapse of the Western economy, unite in antiphonal choruses. These culminate in an ironically bathetic finale over the flag-bedecked corpse of Joan Dark, Saint Joan of the Stockyards.

ST. JOHN'S NIGHT (*Sancthansnatten*), a comedy in three acts by HENRIK IBSEN, produced in 1853 and published in 1909. Setting: the Norwegian countryside.

Ibsen later disowned this lifeless literary satire (hissed off the boards for its antinationalism) and refused to have it published. Partly a lyrical fantasy, the plot resembles that of Shakespeare's *A Midsummer Night's Dream.*

Mortals and fairy creatures are occupied in nocturnal doings that end in rearranged marriages. The innate power and truth of Norwegian folklore are not perceived by a patriotic and windy poet, Julian Paulsen. Having fallen in love with a fairy, he is pained to discover that she has a tail: "Aesthetics and nationalism fought a life and death struggle in my breast."

SAINTS AND SINNERS, a play in five acts by HENRY ARTHUR JONES, produced in 1884 and published in 1891. Setting: England, 1880's.

Jones's early hit was one of the first plays published under the 1891 American Copyright Act, whose importance is discussed in his preface. A NATURALISTIC play, it shocked audiences because it quoted the Scriptures on the stage and portrayed religious hypocrisy. The melodramatic plot features a minister, Jacob Fletcher. His saintliness provokes persecution by venal deacons and eventual expulsion, and his daughter is seduced by a villain. Jones increased the play's popularity when he substituted a happy ending for the original one, in which the daughter dies.

SALACROU, Armand (1899–   ), French playwright, sometimes rated among the most important dramatists of the century though little known in the English-speaking world. Many of his thirty-odd plays have been widely translated and successfully produced in Paris and throughout Europe. But few have appeared in England or the United States. This is especially curious because Salacrou's philosophy as well as his dramaturgy are in the mainstream of popular contemporary theatre. He articulated existentialist anguish—much as did ALBERT CAMUS and JEAN-PAUL SARTRE—with psychologically impressive characterizations and in a traditionally NATURALISTIC manner. For example, *Three Plays* (1967), the first English collection of his work, consists of a historical spectacle, *La Terre est ronde* (THE WORLD IS ROUND, 1938); a boulevard farce, *Histoire de rire* (WHEN THE MUSIC STOPS, 1939); and a domestic drama, *La Marguerite* (*Marguerite*, 1944). These conventional dramatic forms, however, were effectively modified by Salacrou to express his characteristic preoccupation with moral values (particularly sexual purity) in a civilization no longer bound by traditional religion, and with such timeless problems as reality and illusion, human solitude, and death.

The son of a pharmacist, Salacrou was born in Rouen but raised in Le Havre. As a youngster he rejected religion and founded a "Young Socialist" club. In 1917 Salacrou went to Paris, where he studied medicine and philosophy. After passing his examinations in 1920 he became a journalist and an assistant film director, and moved in avant-garde artistic circles where writers such as TRISTAN TZARA encouraged him to become a dramatist. His first produced (by Aurélien-Marie Lugné-Poë) works, the SURREALIST double bill *Tour à terre* and *Le Pont de l'Europe* (1925), did not draw audiences but did attract the attention of the experimental theatre entrepreneur Charles Dullin. He produced Salacrou's *Patchouli* (1930), which impressed Louis Jouvet but failed on the boards. Nonetheless Salacrou gave up his film job to work for Dullin. To augment a salary inadequate to support wife and children, Salacrou launched an advertising business that soon became one of the largest in the country. (In 1938 he sold it to devote all his time to writing.) He virtually abandoned poetic surrealism, and had his first success as a dramatist with a comedy, *Atlas-Hôtel* (1931).

Many of the plays that followed became artistic as well as popular successes. Existentialist in theme though diversified in theatrical mode, they include *Une Femme libre* (1934), whose title protagonist rebels against the female subservience espoused by her lover; *Les Frénétiques* (1934), portraying an archetypal film producer; *L'Inconnue d'Arras* (1935), a much-revived imaginative PIRANDELLian play, technically indebted to HERMAN TEIRLINCK, about a man who relives his whole life in the split second of his suicide following the discovery of his wife's adultery; and *Un Homme comme les autres* (1936), a naturalistic portrait of adultery less amusing but more shocking than *The World Is Round.*

Upon the outbreak of World War II Salacrou enlisted; he was soon captured, but escaped to Vichy France, where he joined the underground. After the war he became director of the Théâtre de l'Odéon, where, with Jean-Louis Barrault, he staged some of his own plays. Salacrou's postwar drama includes the already noted *Marguerite*, a haunting one-acter in which a young widow overwhelmed by her dying father-in-law's illusion guiltily rejects her lover and envisions her dead husband; *Les Fiancés du Havre* (1944), the first of a projected trilogy about three characters' daydreams; the "historic divertissement" *Le Soldat et la sorcière* (1945), a study of the Maréchal Maurice de Saxe's fatal passion for Justine Favart; *Les Nuits de la colère* (1946, produced in New York as *Nights of Wrath* and over the BBC as *Men of Wrath*), a fictionalized documentary of the French Resistance that, like the earlier *L'Inconnue d'Arras,* brilliantly distorts time and space; *L'Archipel Lenoir* (1947), a black tragicomedy about a wealthy family; *Pourquoi pas moi?* (1950), a one-act study of a girl whose daydreams unmask her employers' guilts and repressions; *Poof* (1950), a satire of modern advertising; and *Dieu le savait!* (1950), a self-styled "love story told like a detective novel" about a ninety-five-year-old woman and her ancient scoundrel lover, set in a bombed house.

Armand Salacrou. (*French Cultural Services*)

Later Salacrou productions include a dramatization of the 1910 trial of a labor agitator, *Boulevard Durand* (1961); *Comme les Chardons* (1964); and *La Dernière Rencontre* (1965).

Esteemed by great literary figures and artists of the age, Salacrou was elected to the Académie Goncourt and became president of the International Theatre Institute of UNESCO. Publication of his collected plays began in 1943, and by 1966 had reached eight volumes. His memoirs appeared in 1960 and 1966. The earlier mentioned English collection, *Three Plays by Armand Salacrou,* includes Norman Stokle's informative introduction and bibliography.

SALOMÉ, a one-act play by OSCAR WILDE, published in 1893 and produced in 1895. Setting: Herod's palace, in biblical times.

This intense, decadent, much-extolled work freely dramatizes the Gospel story of Matthew 14 and Mark 6. In its evocative SYMBOLISM it resembles the dramas of MAURICE MAETERLINCK. Wilde wrote the play in French and Lord Alfred Douglas translated it into English in a version which Wilde himself altered considerably. The play has been frequently revived and Richard Strauss used it for the libretto of his famous opera. In 1892 Sarah Bernhardt rehearsed the play in England. She and Wilde were infuriated when it was denied a license for production in London: an old law prohibited the representation of biblical characters on the stage.

"How beautiful is the Princess Salomé tonight!" exclaims a young Syrian officer. Herod Antipas, Tetrarch of Judea, is holding a feast. Like the officer, he keeps staring at Salomé. She is his niece, his wife Herodias's daughter by Herod's brother, whom he had killed in order to marry Herodias. For that reason he fears and does not kill the prophet Jokanaan (John the Baptist), who curses Herodias from the cistern in which he is imprisoned, and prophesies the coming of Christ. Salomé inveigles the love-smitten officer into having Jokanaan brought before her. She rhapsodizes sensuously over the stern and unyielding prophet. "Thy body is white like the lilies of a field that the mower hath never mowed," she says; "thy hair is like clusters of grape." And finally she begs him, "Let me kiss thy mouth." Thus preoccupied, Salomé pays no mind to the distraught Syrian officer, even when he stabs himself to death before her eyes. "I will kiss thy mouth," she insists, though the prophet denounces her before he is returned to his prison: "Daughter of an incestuous mother, be thou accursed!" Herod now begs Salomé to sit by him. Herodias is angered by his attentions to her daughter, and by his refusal to punish the prophet and hand him over to the disputing Jews. Jokanaan continues his harangue from below: "Ah, the wanton! The harlot! Ah, the daughter of Babylon with her golden eyes and her gilded eyelids! Thus saith the Lord God, Let there come up against her a multitude of men. Let the people take stones and stone her." Feeling sad, Herod suddenly begs Salomé to dance for him. When he offers her anything she might demand, "even unto the half of my kingdom," she agrees. As the moon becomes increasingly redder, Salomé dances the Dance of the Seven Veils. Then she names her price: "I would that they presently bring me in a silver charger . . . The head of Jokanaan." Though Herod fearfully offers her his precious jewels, his peacocks, half his kingdom, Salomé (supported by her delighted mother) persists in her original demand. At last Herod wearily surrenders and dispatches the executioner. Suspense mounts as no sound is heard. Then there is a noise of something falling on the ground, and soon the executioner's arm emerges from the cistern. It holds out a silver shield on which lies the severed head of the prophet. Herod hides his face, Herodias fans herself and smiles, the terrified guests kneel and pray. But Salomé ardently addresses the head. "Ah! thou wouldst not suffer me to kiss thy mouth," she says; "I will kiss it now. I will bite it with my teeth as one bites a ripe fruit." Again she rhapsodizes voluptuously. As Herod goes out, Salomé's voice continues, "I have kissed thy mouth. There was a bitter taste on thy lips. Was it the taste of blood?" A moonbeam covers her with light as Herod turns back. He motions to his soldiers: "Kill that woman!" And they quickly crush Salomé to death with their shields.

SALVATION NELL, a play in three acts by EDWARD SHELDON, produced in 1908 and published in 1967. Setting: the Cherry Hill district of New York City, early twentieth century.

Considered a milestone in the American theatre as an early Broadway hit presenting serious social problems, this play was likened to Gorky's THE LOWER DEPTHS. It was highly praised for its scenic REALISM, particularly of street life, and provided Minnie Maddern Fiske with one of her best roles.

Nell Sanders supports her wastrel lover by slaving as a scullery maid in a bar. He keeps abusing her, loses his job, gets into a fight, murders a man, and drops into a drunken stupor. In the production's climax, Nell holds her drunken lover's head in her lap for a long time, sitting silently in "rigid and weary misery." When he is sent to prison, the desperate Nell rejects the alternative of prostitution and joins the Salvation Army. She is happy there, eight years later, ready to marry a fellow worker who is willing to accept her illegitimate child. Then her lover returns, beats her when she refuses to go back to him with their child, and escapes; but afraid he has killed her, he later comes back, without having joined his burglary gang. Though she loves him, Nell still refuses to take her unreformed lover back. "Dear, I'm not blaming ye—I'm not even blamin' myself," she says, attributing their ills to environment: "We was just like heaps of others. 'Twasn't our fault a bit." Again he starts to leave angrily. Then, overhearing her stirring Salvation Army address to the crowds, he contritely returns to her: "I want ter see things as ye see them, Nelly. Won't yer learn me how?" The two are united as Nell holds out her hands: "Wait for me, Jim. I'll meet ye there [in the Hall]. I want ye to take me home."

SALZBURG GREAT THEATRE OF THE WORLD, THE (*Das Salzburger grosse Welttheater*), a one-act verse play by HUGO VON HOFMANNSTHAL, published and produced in 1922. Setting: before a palace, and later a stage.

This allegorical drama, presented like *Jedermann* (EVERYMAN) at the Salzburg Festival, is based on Calderón's Corpus Christi play *El gran teatro del mundo* (c. 1645).

In a play-within-a-play, the Master (God) asks World to stage the play of human life. Various souls (Beauty, Wisdom, Rich Man, etc.) are costumed and given their parts. Only one, the Beggar, rejects his miserable role. In angry rebellion, he raises his ax to destroy injustice and thereby destroy all order. It is God's gift of "the spark of supreme freedom," to make a moral choice, that inspires the Beggar to choose rightly and desist. He recognizes human life as a transitory "play" within a greater scheme, and retreats to a contemplative life. When Death recalls the Beggar, he appears joyfully before God, free and equal in His sight with the other souls.

SÁNCHEZ, Florencio [Antonio] (1875–1910), was the first major Spanish American dramatist. He is acclaimed as "our greatest playwright" both by his native URUGUAY and by ARGENTINA, where he produced his NATURALISTIC portrayals of rural as well as city life in GAUCHO DRAMAS of ideas, ideals, and social protest. Influenced by HERMANN SUDERMANN, they are comparable to the better European drama of the time, and though he has

The Salzburg Great Theatre of the World. Salzburg Festival, 1925. (*Ellinger*)

been dismissed by some as a minor Creole IBSEN (*"Ibsencito criollo"*), Sánchez was far in advance of earlier South American dramatists. Many of his twenty plays, including a dozen one-acters, appear in translation and are still performed.

The oldest of a nomadic family's eleven children, Sánchez was born in Montevideo. His first writings were political lampoons and skits, and he became involved in various patriotic skirmishes. After some journalism and theatre work in Buenos Aires that included a popular *zarzuela, Canallita* (*A Newspaper Boy,* 1902), Sánchez dashed off *M'hijo el dotor* (*My Son the Lawyer,* 1903). A domestic drama about an admirable old gaucho who opposes the city-educated title character's ruthless new ways and confronts him with their consequences, this, the first part of a "rural trilogy," immediately brought Sánchez fame in Argentina, Uruguay, Italy, and shortly thereafter in Japan. Even more esteemed were the remaining plays of Sánchez's trilogy, *La gringa* (*The Immigrant Girl,* 1904) and *Barranca abajo* (*Down the Gully,* 1905)—the first dramatizing the conflict of old and new in a romance of the offspring of industrious immigrants and easygoing, inefficient Creole natives; the second a sympathetic portrait of an aging gaucho who cannot accept the new ways, is abandoned by his family, and commits suicide.

These are Sánchez's best and remained his most popular full-length plays. He also wrote *sainetes* such as the nationalistic *Cédulas de San Juan* (1904, translated as *Midsummer Day Parents*), and farces such as *Mano santa* (*The Healing Hand,* 1905) and *Moneda falsa* (*Phony Money,*

1906). Other plays deal with city slums—including the one-act naturalistic tragedies *El desalojo* (*Evicted,* 1906) and *La tigra* (*The Tigress,* 1907), about a mother who can support her children only through prostitution—and middle-class family life, as in the once-acclaimed *En familia* (*The Family Circle,* 1905); a thesis play on motherhood, *Nuestros hijos* (*Our Children,* 1907); and *Los derechos de la salud* (1907), which was filmed as *Pasión imposible* (1942) and portrays a dying woman who sees herself displaced in her own home by her sister.

In 1909 Sánchez got the Uruguayan government to dispatch him to Italy, where he had achieved his first foreign success and where he vainly tried to increase his fame. He failed and died there the following year, at thirty-five, of consumption aggravated by lifelong dissipation during which he wrote all his plays at breakneck speed.

Willis Knapp Jones's translated collection of ten *Representative Plays of Florencio Sánchez* (1961) has an introduction and a bibliography. The studies listed under LATIN AMERICA all have sections on Sánchez, Isaac Goldberg's *The Drama of Transition* (1922) includes extended analyses and plot summaries, and there is a book-length work, Ruth Richardson's *Florencio Sánchez and the Argentine Theatre* (1933).

SARDOU, Victorien (1831–1908), French playwright, became the principal practitioner of the WELL-MADE PLAY in its heyday after the death of Eugène Scribe in 1861. Parisian-born, Sardou gave up his medical studies for playwriting in the early 1850's. He achieved little success until his wife's friend Virginie Déjazet, a popular actress, played in his *Les Premières Armes de Figaro* (1859).* Like other early plays, it demonstrates Sardou's debt to Scribe and his own gifts as the "supremely skillful contriver and arranger" characterized by HENRY JAMES. Sardou's first great hit, *Les Pattes de mouche* (A SCRAP OF PAPER, 1860), exemplifies the well-made play and assured Sardou's stature as the most successful fashionable playwright of his age. This play also illustrates the hackneyed superficiality and triviality characteristic of a type of drama BERNARD SHAW dubbed "Sardoodledom" —a term that, perhaps more than the well-made plays themselves, helped immortalize Sardou, who in 1887 was elected to the French Academy.

Expertly constructed, Sardou's plays include farces, comedies, melodramas, spectacles, and social dramas. ARTHUR WING PINERO adapted his *Maison Neuve* (1866) as *Mayfair* (1885), but more famous Sardou works are *Patrie!* (1869), a historic-patriotic-romantic spectacle set in Brussels during the sixteenth-century subjugation of Flanders by the Spaniards; *Dora* (1877), adapted by Clement Scott (1841–1904) and B. C. Stephenson (1839?–1906) as the long-popular *Diplomacy* (1878), which became the model for Wilde's AN IDEAL HUSBAND; and *Divorçons!* (*Let's Get a Divorce!,* 1880), an anti-divorce farce (written with Émile de Najac, 1828–89) about a bored young wife whose connubial love is rekindled when her wily middle-aged husband encourages her to divorce him and marry his young cousin, who has tried to seduce her—and thus takes the spice out of the incipient affair. Sardou also wrote satires, social-thesis drama, "crook" plays, and melodramatic vehicles for Sarah Bernhardt—notably *Fédora* (1882); *Théodora* (1884), an immensely popular spectacle; *La Tosca* (1887), which Giacomo Puccini in 1890 made into one of his great operas; *Cléopâtre* (1890; written with Émile Moreau, 1852–1922); and *La Sorcière* (*The Sorceress,* 1890), set during the Inquisition. Among his later successes are *Madame Sans-Gêne* (*Madam Devil-May-Care,* 1893, written with Moreau), a comic historical romance set at Napoleon's court and depicting the rise of a pert washerwoman, Réjane's greatest part; and Sardou's final work, *L'Affaire des poisons* (1907), a historical spectacle set in the court of Louis XIV.

Barrett H. Clark has an appreciative essay on Sardou's drama in his translation of *Patrie!* (1915). More recent translations of Sardou's plays were published in Eric Bentley's edition of *Let's Get a Divorce! and Other Plays* (1958), and in *Camille and Other Plays* (1957), which includes *A Scrap of Paper,* a bibliography, and an introduction by Stephen S. Stanton that deals revealingly with Sardou and the well-made play. A book-length study of his life and work is Jerome A. Hart's *Sardou and the Sardou Plays* (1913).

*Sardou's daughter married the playwright ROBERT DE FLERS.

SARMENT [originally Bellemère], **Jean** (1897–), French actor and playwright, portrayed lost illusions of romance with protagonists who are dissatisfied with the pettiness of their lives but not sufficiently grand to command their destinies. The first of his twenty plays, *La Couronne de carton* (1920), features a prince in mufti who is disillusioned when he realizes that people believe him only when he pretends. Similarly in *Le Mariage d'Hamlet* (1922) the Danish prince, given another chance to live (cf. Barrie's DEAR BRUTUS), returns with Ophelia and Polonius to find his new and too mundane life a travesty of his heroic former existence. *Le Pêcheur d'ombres* (*Rude Awakening,* 1921), which PETER USTINOV translated as *Fishing for Shadows* (1940) and which is vaguely reminiscent of Pirandello's HENRY IV though more IBSENite in dramaturgy, features a spurned lover who finds comfort in madness, is restored to sanity and the reality that he cannot bear—and escapes into death. Sarment's most ambitious play, *Je suis trop grand pour moi* (1924; the title could be translated as "I have delusions of grandeur"—a characteristic of most of Sarment's protagonists) is similar, but muddled by excessive characters and episodes. Some critics considered *Les Plus Beaux Yeux du monde* (1925) his best play; characteristically it contrasts the lives of two friends who strive, with varying degrees of failure, to achieve their ideals. Later Sarment plays are

Le Plancher des vaches (1932); *Le Discours des prix* (1934), the comic satire of a meek professor in a provincial university; *Madame Quinze* (1935), a dramatic rehabilitation of "the beloved, detested, timid, impudent, and lonely Louis XV"; and a fine one-act portrayal of a village stationmaster's futile dream, *Le Voyage à Biarritz* (1936).

John Palmer's *Studies in the Contemporary Theatre* (1927) has a chapter on Sarment.

SAROYAN, William (1908–), American short-story writer, novelist, and playwright. The son of Armenian immigrants, like those frequently portrayed in his works, he became famous with "The Daring Young Man on the Flying Trapeze" (1934), the title story of a collection published the same year. Saroyan's first success as a playwright came five years later with MY HEART'S IN THE HIGHLANDS (1939), and it immediately grew with his best and most popular play, THE TIME OF YOUR LIFE (1939). Though Saroyan has written many more plays, he has been unable to sustain—much less increase—his fame as a dramatist. Like his fiction, Saroyan's plays are an ebullient and formless mixture of unabashed sentiment and optimism. They made their impact primarily during the late 1930's and early 1940's—in the Depression and war age, whose mood Saroyan reflected with a sometimes cloying poignancy.

Born in Fresno, California, Saroyan spent his early childhood in an orphanage. He was as eccentric a pupil and (later) a worker as his fictional, usually autobiographical, creations. His good-natured and innocent brashness made him an unreliable worker, and he was blacklisted by the local employment bureau. An avid reader, he soon expressed in his writings his flamboyant personality—as well as his loneliness, bewilderment, and scorn of an impersonally organized and brutal, money-grubbing society. But though Saroyan's characters are depressed by their surroundings, they joyfully (often fantastically) transcend them and cultivate a natural exuberance. "Be alive" is probably Saroyan's most frequently repeated exhortation. His plays express these moods and aspirations. Poverty and cruelty are not glossed over; but his autobiographical heroes overcome them in fairy-tale fashion—as in *The Time of Your Life,* whose setting, characters, and situation resemble those of O'Neill's THE ICEMAN COMETH, but whose atmosphere and effect convey the reverse viewpoint. Even when Saroyan's heroes are killed, like the itinerant gambler of HELLO OUT THERE (1941, his best short one-acter), or evicted like the Armenian-Americans of *My Heart's in the Highlands,* their spirit soars high above that of the society about them: the downtrodden but incorruptible innocents are the ones who are really victorious.

It is not the plot that matters in these plays. Formless and almost completely plotless, like the life they attempt to represent, Saroyan's plays are clustered vignettes and routines that portray man's miseries but celebrate his inherent goodness and *joie de vivre.* This, too, is the theme in *Love's Old Sweet Song* (1940), a "part vaudeville show, part musical comedy, part autumn romance, part wrestling match, part three-alarm fire," as the *Christian Science Monitor* reviewed this characteristic Saroyan series of improvisations set in a small California town and held together by the most tenuous of plots. But in this play Saroyan failed to appeal to audiences as he had earlier. He had equally little success with *The Beautiful People* (1941), another play about an irresponsible California family that articulates Saroyan's favorite maxim: "Every life in the world is a miracle, and it's a miracle every minute each of us stays alive, and unless we know this, the experience of living is cheated of the greater part of its wonder and beauty" (Act II).

In 1942 appeared two Saroyan one-acters, *Across the Board on Tomorrow Morning* and *Talking to You,* both revived Off-Broadway in 1961; the first resembles *The Time of Your Life* but is set in a New York bar, and the second is set in a San Francisco basement. Both feature typical Saroyan innocents, but neither play was successful. Except for the above noted *Hello Out There*, most of his later plays have remained unproduced. Only a single new play appeared on Broadway since World War II, *The Cave Dwellers* (1957), which features a group of failures who seek shelter in an abandoned theatre slated for demolition; though characteristic of Saroyan and moving, it demonstrates no advance in his art. Three plays appeared in 1960 in Europe, where Saroyan has spent much of his later life: *The Paris Comedy, or The Secret of Lily; The London Comedy, or Sam the Highest Jumper of Them All;* and *Settled Out of Court* (the dramatization of a novel by Henry Cecil). The following year, *High Time Along the Wabash* was produced at Purdue University, where Saroyan was Writer-in-Residence. His *Making Money, And 19 Other Very Short Plays* was published in 1969.

Saroyan's most important other work is *The Human Comedy,* a film scenario written in 1941 and published as a novel in 1943; it is autobiographical, about a telegraph messenger (Saroyan was a messenger at the age of twelve) during World War II. During the war Saroyan served in the Signal Corps. He twice married—and divorced—Carol Marcus. *My Name is Aram* (1940) is a collection of autobiographical stories; he has also written typically discursive autobiographies such as *The Bicycle Rider in Beverly Hills* (1952), *Here Comes, There Goes, You Know Who* (1961), *Not Dying* (1963), and *I Used to Believe I Had Forever, Now I'm Not So Sure* (1968). A book-length study of his work, Howard R. Floan's *William Saroyan* (1966), includes a bibliography.

SARTRE, Jean-Paul (1905–), French philosopher, novelist, and playwright, and the leading post-World War II existentialist. His name became associated with that of ALBERT CAMUS, who was esteemed principally as a philosophical novelist. Sartre has achieved major success with his philosophy tracts as well as with some of his nearly dozen plays. *Les Mouches* (THE FLIES, 1943), *Huis Clos* (NO EXIT, 1944), and *Les Mains sales* (DIRTY HANDS, 1948) were followed by such other important if less popular dramas as *Le Diable et le bon Dieu* (THE DEVIL AND THE GOOD LORD, 1951) and *Les Séquestres d'Altona* (THE CONDEMNED OF ALTONA 1959). All of these articulate his left-wing political views and the metaphysics of a godless and meaningless universe grounded in the philosophies of Søren Kierkegaard and Martin Heidegger, and described in Sartre's renowned philosophic tract *L'Être et le néant* (*Being and Nothingness,* 1943). But Sartre's perception of an existentially absurd cosmos is balanced by a fervently ethical morality. To affirm his existence, Sartre believes, man must choose freedom and create his own conscience. It is not enough merely to philosophize and aspire. Assuming total responsibility for their acts, men must rise to heroic heights by becoming "engaged" in social and political causes—as Sartre himself did during the war and thereafter.

Sartre was born in Paris, the son of a Catholic marine engineer who died when the boy was two years old. He grew up in the home of his maternal grandfather, Schweitzer (Sartre was Albert Schweitzer's cousin), a Calvinist and a distinguished professor of German. His mother remarried when Sartre was eleven, and the family moved to the provinces, where he attended the *lycée* until he was sent back to Paris three years later. Sartre studied in Germany and at the Sorbonne, where he met and began his union (there was no formal marriage) with the celebrated philosopher-novelist Simone de Beauvoir. Like her, he became a *professeur de lycée*—in Le Havre, in Laon, and finally in Paris. He also started to publish his writings: psychological studies, the novel *La Nausée* (*Nausea,* 1938), and *Le Mur* (*The Wall,* 1939), a collection of short stories also translated as *Intimacy.* Despairing in its portrayals of life in an existentially meaningless world, Sartre's fiction created a stir that quickly brought him fame. His success enabled Sartre to give up teaching and devote full time to his writing. Upon the outbreak of World War II Sartre was drafted and served as an artillery observer on the Maginot Line. He was captured by the Germans, but was repatriated and returned to Paris, where he helped form a resistance group.

While risking his life in the French Underground Sartre also saw his great philosophical treatise through the press and completed his first significant play, *The Flies.* The horrors of the Nazi Occupation, the suffering of the French populace, and the special dangers facing those in the Resistance—all these sharpened Sartre's sense of human mortality and freedom to choose. Not surprisingly he became preoccupied with man's ability to face gruesome suffering for his beliefs, for his "engagement" in a cause. "We were brought to the point of the deepest knowledge a man can have of himself," Sartre wrote in *Situations III* (1949): "The secret of a man is not his Oedipus Complex or his inferiority complex; it is the limit of his own freedom—his capacity for standing up to torture and death." These ideas and experiences Sartre dramatized in *Morts sans sépulture* (*The Unburied Dead,* 1946; also produced as *The Victors* and as *Men Without Shadows*), a philosophic-NATURALISTIC four-act play in which captured Resistance fighters question the meaning of their suffering even as they undergo tortures that are vividly depicted onstage; their final, gratuitous execution and their Nazi tormentors' own suffering add ironic dimensions to the play's tenseness and unrelenting horror.

A different kind of horror is portrayed in Sartre's second play, *No Exit.* It was dramatized in a different manner as well. Like the first play (*The Flies*) and some later ones—the historical pageant *The Devil and the Good Lord* and the eerie *The Condemned of Altona*—*No Exit* includes a considerable amount of debate. There is more physical action in *Dirty Hands* (his most popular play), *La Putain respectueuse* (*The Respectful Prostitute,* 1946), *Kean* (1953), and *Nekrassov* (1955). *The Respectful Prostitute,* an existentialist melodrama subsequently filmed, shows how a whore is gradually made to falsely denounce a Negro as a rapist; despite its crude caricature of the American South, the play is an often-valid exposure of moral and political depravity in the United States. *Kean,* subtitled *"Désordre et génie"* ("disorder and genius"), is a witty adaptation of Alexandre Dumas's 1836 play about an amorous rivalry between Edmund Kean (before his departure for America with a young actress) and the Prince of Wales. Sartre's changes—including a spectacular *Othello* production in which the protagonist, like a PIRANDELLO hero, breaks out of character—stress Kean's ultimate acceptance of his dual nature as man and actor. As in other plays, Sartre here, too, dramatized man's need to face—and live responsibly within—his human limitations. Sartre's only comedy, *Nekrassov,* is a political farce that portrays the French authorities falling for a hoax: the "defection" of an "important Russian" to the West. An unsuccessful satire of anti-Communism, even this play articulates Sartre's existentialism—here his conviction (explicitly stressed in *No Exit*) that what matters is action, not mere intention. The play starts with the title character, a desperate swindler, trying to drown himself. But he seizes the rope thrown him by a passing tramp, gains safety, and then remonstrates, "Have you fallen so low that you no longer respect the last wish of a dying man?" The tramp replies, "You weren't a dying man." Their discussion continues: "Yes, I was, since I was going to die." "But you weren't going to die, since you're not dead." "I'm not dead because you violated my last wish." "What was it?" "The wish to die." "That wasn't your last wish . . . you were swimming. . . ."

The founder and popularizer of the most important modern school of existentialism, Sartre embraces but also transcends the despair of that philosophy of cosmic absurdity. To his vision Sartre brings human dignity by insisting that man accept the anguish of responsibility and freedom. Sartre's heroes—Orestes, Goetz, Franz, Hugo—ultimately perceive the Sartrean universe and accept their social responsibilities, thereby asserting their own as well as their fellowman's humanity and existence. Yet it is not his intellectual anguish and his philosophy alone that have made Sartre an important playwright: his heroes' tormented passage from ignorance to awareness of existentialist reality is often depicted in highly theatrical terms. Occasionally Sartre's histrionics degenerate into unabashed melodrama, and the dialogue into mere philosophical recitation. But at their best, Sartre's metaphysics are effective, not only cerebrally but also viscerally. It was Sartre's ability to create suspenseful drama that attracted theatre and movie audiences (some of his plays have been filmed, and he has also written original film scripts). The philosophic themes, however, charge his dramas with further dimensions; they make his plays meaningful and elevate them to something more than mere thrillers.

Sartre's works, including the plays and screen scenarios such as *Les Jeux sont faits* (*The Chips Are Down,* 1946) and *L'Engrenage* (*In the Mesh,* 1946), are available in English translation. So, too, is his book on JEAN GENET, *Saint Genet, comédien et martyr* (*Saint Genet: Actor and Martyr,* 1952), as revealing of both playwrights as is BERNARD SHAW's book on HENRIK IBSEN, THE QUINTESSENCE OF IBSENISM. There are many books on Sartre's life, thought, and writings. These as well as shorter works are listed in the bibliographies of such readily accessible English studies of his life and work (including the drama) as Philip Thody's *Jean-Paul Sartre: A Literary and Political Study* (1960), Maurice Cranston's *Sartre* (1962), Edith Kern's *Sartre: A Collection of Critical Essays* (1962), and Dorothy Kaufmann McCall's *The Theatre of Jean-Paul Sartre* (1969).

SASTRE, Alfonso (1926–), is one of the leading post-World War II Spanish playwrights (ANTONIO BUERO VALLEJO is the other). His drama is concerned with political problems—a "theatre of anguish," as he has called it—rather than with more conventional fantasy, which he calls the "theatre of magic." Sastre considers himself a playwright with a mission: to protest social injustices. Though influenced by the drama of HENRIK IBSEN, AUGUST STRINDBERG, LUIGI PIRANDELLO, and THORNTON WILDER, he has been most affected by the work of ARTHUR MILLER. *La cornada* (*Death Thrust,* 1960), a suspenseful (if obvious) portrayal of a frightened bullfighter, is transparently indebted to DEATH OF A SALESMAN in plot, dramaturgy, and themes. Though a less characteristic play, *Ana Kleiber* (ANNA KLEIBER, 1952)—which has been praised as Sastre's finest work—also portrays man's vain search for happiness in a corrupt society. Such an outlook naturally precluded frequent production of Sastre's works in Franco's Spain. Nonetheless well known and esteemed there, he has achieved the reputation of an underground playwright.

Originally a philosophy student (like the tormented hero of *Anna Kleiber*), Sastre in 1946 wrote a quartet of one-acters published in 1949: *Ha sonado la muerte* and *Comedia sonambula* (both written with Medardo Fraile, 1925–), *Cargamento de sueños,* and *Uranio 235.* Sastre's first notable full-length play, the antimilitarist *Escuadra hacia la muerte* (*Condemned Squad,* 1953), is set in a future world war and features a group of men awaiting an expected enemy attack. *La mordaza* (1954), an existentialist drama of passion and crime, has been likened to O'Neill's DESIRE UNDER THE ELMS: it is about a murderer who lusts after his daughter-in-law, is betrayed by her, and is killed while trying to escape. Other Sastre plays include *La sangre de Dios* (1956), *El pan de todos* (*Everybody's Bread,* 1957), the one-act *El cuervo* (1960), *En la red* (1961, about the Algerian underground movement), *Muerte en el barrio* (1961), and *Prologo patetico* (*Pathetic Prologue,* 1964); the last of these, like *Everybody's Bread,* depicts the violence accompanying social reform. His other writings include a study in which Sastre discusses his concepts of the "theatre of magic" and "theatre of anguish" as well as Miller's *Death of a Salesman, Drama y sociedad* (*Drama and Society,* 1956).

Though Sastre's drama is more deeply rooted in European and American theatre than in that of Spain, he is better known there than abroad. Selections from his *Drama and Society* as well as his *Anna Kleiber* appear in Robert W. Corrigan's *The New Theatre of Europe* (1962); *Death Thrust* is one of the *Masterpieces of the Modern Spanish Theatre* (1967), also edited by Corrigan; *Condemned Squad* is in Marion Holt's collection *The Modern Spanish Stage: Four Plays* (1970); and the earlier-banned *Guillermo Tell tiene los ojos tristes* (*Sad Are the Eyes of William Tell,* 1955), an anti-Fascist retelling of the legend that mixes medieval and modern elements, first appeared in George E. Wellwarth's *The New Wave Spanish Drama* (1970). Farris Anderson's *Alfonso Sastre* (1971) is a book-length study of his life and work.

SATIN SLIPPER, THE (*Le Soulier de satin*), a "Spanish play" in four cycles (called "Days") by PAUL CLAUDEL, published in 1924 and produced in 1943. Setting: "the world, and more specially the close of the sixteenth, unless it be the opening of the seventeenth century."

Although this enormously long and grandiose poetic drama has been likened to Dante's *Divine Comedy,* it more resembles Goethe's two-part *Faust.* It was meant for reading rather than staging, though Jean-Louis Barrault gave it a memorable premiere. In many tableaux historical personages and events of the Spanish Golden Age are freely kaleidoscoped in this mass mystery-miracle play, whose lovers' epic passions and adventures assume Catholic universality. Claudel characterized this SYMBOLIC verse play as "an incongruous mixture of buffoonery, passion, and mystery" that sums up his whole poetic and dramatic work—as well as his mystic-religious convictions. The play is subtitled "The Worst Is Not the Surest," and its epigraph is made up of a Portuguese proverb and the words of Saint Augustine: *"Deus escreve direito por linhas tortas"—"Etiam peccata"* ("God writes straight with crooked lines"—"Even sins").

First Day. Tied to the mast of a destroyed vessel amidst corpses, a dying Jesuit father reaffirms his faith in God and prays that the play's lovers, the conquistador Don Rodrigue and Doña Prouhèze (Maravilla), will be embued "with such longing as shall involve, in the deprivation of each other's presence through the daily play of circumstance, / Their primal integrity, and their very essences as God conceived them both." Prouhèze is to bring about Rodrigue's salvation. Not in love with the man to whom she is bound in holy matrimony, she is consumed by what she conceives to be a holy passion for Rodrigue—and prays to the Virgin's statue for help in her agonizing dilemma, for strength to withstand sin. Then she places her satin slipper in the statue's hands. "I give you my shoe, Virgin Mother," she says: "When I try to rush headlong into evil, let it be with halting foot!" The Spanish king appoints Rodrigue governor of America. After talking to his Chinese servant of his hopeless love for Prouhèze, Rodrigue is wounded by brigands. Prouhèze seeks him, knowing that he loves her. "To him I am not a voice," she says, but "a sword, right through his heart." She and her party barely escape a band of attacking knights.

Second Day. Rodrigue's imminent expedition to America is discussed by caballeros. Righteously trying to keep Prouhèze from sinning against their marriage, her husband sends her on a mission to secure Africa for the Church. His plan is foiled by the king. Momentarily frail, Rodrigue doubts Prouhèze. She is able to control Don Camillo, the weak villain who, too, loves and needs her for his salvation. In a torture chamber while watching both men from behind a curtain, she chooses Camillo and, upon the death of her husband, marries him. Rodrigue is humiliated and defeated in his impossible longings, but has the innate strength Camillo lacks—and leaves. Physically separated, the lovers' spirits merge as two shadows in the moonlight. Their eternal union is celebrated by the personified moon: "This sacred throbbing by which the commingling souls know each other without go-between, like father and mother at the moment of conception—that is what I serve to manifest."

Third Day. The Battle of the White Mountain is over, an announcer surveys the world's doings, and the great saints of Christianity gather in Prague. Rodrigue, now a famous conqueror, is governing America. In her dreams, Prouhèze, yearning for Rodrigue, has a long debate with her guardian angel. She objects to being bait for Rodrigue, to bring about his salvation through their self-abnegating passion; but the angel retorts that "sin, too, serves." He forecasts her death and ultimate sainthood after she redeems both Rodrigue and Camillo, sketches Rodrigue's conquests of Asia, and vanishes amid the celestial glitter of an image of the Immaculate Conception. In an agonizing talk between Camillo and Prouhèze about their marriage and their child's paternity, Camillo, after proclaiming himself a Muhammadan, recognizes Christ in his wife, and cries out for Him. At last Rodrigue and Prouhèze meet face to face. There is a terrible struggle between love and duty, expedience and honor. In complete renunciation Prouhèze gives her child to Rodrigue and chooses her fortress prison—and death. The two can never belong to each other, both of them know, if he is to be her means of sainthood and she is to be his salvation.

Fourth Day. The Armada against England is magically envisioned by the Spanish king in his floating palace. Rodrigue is to be made Viceroy of England and with much pomp is raised to the heights of public adulation. Then he is toppled from power. In his calvary, Rodrigue is scorned by mobs and brutally tormented. He bears all with great fortitude, unswerving in his faith in the ultimate liberation of God's Church. Suffering, he rises to peaks of physical and spiritual heroism. Finally he consents to be given into slavery to perform menial tasks at a convent. Led off to board his ship, he rejoices to learn that the child Prouhèze gave him is not dead as had been reported. "My child is safe!" he exclaims, secure in the knowledge that his work will be carried on. In a final appeal, a priest asks "Deliverance to all souls in prison!"

SATURDAY NIGHT (*La noche del sábado*), "a novel for the stage arranged in five tableaux" and a prologue by JACINTO BENAVENTE, published and produced in 1903. Setting: the contemporary Riviera.

This "pageant of life" features a large cast of fictitious international characters, many of them from the Italian Renaissance. It is a complex and subjective allegory on ambition, every tableau representing a dominant mood (as John Garrett Underhill noted in the preface to his translations of Benavente). The scenes of decadence and of circus life recall those of FRANK WEDEKIND. The play is among Benavente's most interesting ones and became quite popular in Spain. In 1926 it launched Eva Le Gallienne's Civic Repertory Theatre, and it has also been translated as *The Witches' Sabbath.*

Fashionable but decadent princes and adventurers discuss Imperia, once a starving model of the sculptor Leonardo, a wry idealist. The dissolute Prince Florencio took her for his mistress, but his sadism eventually repelled her. Ambitious, she is now the mistress of the weak probable successor to the throne. Her ambition is being thwarted by maternal concern for Donina, the daughter who represents her own youth to Imperia. Donina is a circus dancer in love with another performer, who, tired of her, palms her off on Florencio. Imperia is determined "to prevent another infamy," but it is Donina who kills the decadent prince in the back room of a dive frequented by pimps, prostitutes, and bored society seeking titillation. The murder is covered up by a frantic communal dance before the corpse when the police arrive. Imperia hides the body and later persuades the police and the nobles that in their own interests they must proclaim Florencio's death a suicide. Instead of pursuing her will to power, Imperia now devotes all her strength to save her daughter, Donina, who is dying. When her circus lover cynically reveals that he is there only because Imperia pays him, Donina dies. Now Imperia is willing to follow her prince to the throne, which she had given up for her daughter. "In order to realize any great object in life we must destroy reality," she says, the sole reality being "the path of our dreams toward the ideal where the souls flit about during their Witches' Sabbath"—some toward evil, "others toward good, to dwell forever there as spirits of light and love." Thus Imperia manifests, she tells Leonardo, "The spirit you gave me, as grand as your ideal!"

SATURDAY'S CHILDREN, a comedy in three acts by MAXWELL ANDERSON, published and produced in 1927. Setting: New York City, 1926.

This is an engagingly naïve comedy that depicts two "Saturday's children" of the lower middle class. As in the nursery rhyme, they must work for a living.

In love with Rims O'Neil, Bobby is persuaded by her sister to trap him into proposing. Under the everyday problems of marriage their romance sours. Bobby's father, the *raisonneur,* tells his daughter, "Marriage is no love affair. It's little old last year's love affair, my dear. It's a house and bills and dishpans and family quarrels." Rims and Bobby feel increasingly trapped in their new position, are resentful, and constantly argue about the management of their limited income. Finally, after a particularly bitter squabble, they separate. Rims returns to his card games, and Bobby returns to her secretarial job and resumes dating. But they cannot stay apart long. Rims finds her in a boardinghouse and asks her to return home. Bobby refuses: "I want my love affair back. I want hurried kisses and clandestine meetings, and a secret lover. I don't want a house. I don't want a husband. I want a lover." The hour for gentlemen callers is up and Rims leaves angrily. Bobby throws herself on her bed and weeps. Suddenly Rims returns through the fire-escape window. He has brought a padlock, which he quietly starts fitting on the door as the curtain falls: the lovers will have their clandestine tryst!

SAYERS, Dorothy [Mrs. Oswald Atherton Fleming] (1893–1957), English writer. Famous as a detective novelist and the creator of Lord Peter Wimsey, she also wrote theological essays, translations of Dante, and dramas. Her first play was a dramatization (with M. St. Clare Byrne, 1895–) of *Busman's Honeymoon* (1936), her detective novel. Becoming increasingly interested in Christian dogma, which she considered "the most exciting drama that ever staggered the imagination of man," Sayers then produced religious (usually verse) plays: *The Zeal of Thy House* (1937), *The Devil to Pay* (the 1939 Canterbury Festival Play), *Love All* (1940), *The Man Born to Be King,* (1941, a cycle of twelve radio plays on the life of Christ), *The Just Vengeance* (1946, a modern miracle play), *Four Sacred Plays* (1948), and *The Emperor Constantine: A Chronicle* (1951).

When Sayers (who also employed the pseudonym Johanna Leigh) graduated in 1915, she was among the first women to get a degree from Oxford. Her most popular works are the three volumes of *The Omnibus of Crime,* published in England as *Great Short Stories of Detection, Mystery, and Horror* (1928–34).

SCANDINAVIA has produced two founders of the modern theatre, HENRIK IBSEN and AUGUST STRINDBERG. While no other Scandinavian playwrights are nearly as important, some of them have contributed significantly to the modern theatre and have achieved reputations beyond the boundaries of their native lands. The drama of Scandinavian countries is written in different languages and has progressed in distinctive ways. Therefore it is discussed separately under the headings of DENMARK, FINLAND, ICELAND, NORWAY, and SWEDEN.

General collections of translated Scandinavian drama are Alrik Gustafson's three-volume *Scandinavian Plays of the Twentieth Century* (1944–51) and *Modern Scandinavian Plays* (1954), and editions by Evert Sprinchorn (*The Genius of the Scandinavian Theater,* 1964) and Robert W. Corrigan (*Masterpieces of the Modern Scandinavian Theatre,* 1967). Studies of Scandinavian literature including the drama are Frederika Blankner's translation and edition of *The History of the Scandinavian Literatures* (1938), H. G. Topsöe-Jensen's *Scandinavian Literature from Brandes to Our Day* (1939), and *An Introduction to Scandinavian Literature From the Earliest Time to Our Day* (1951) by Elias Bredsdorff, Brita Mortensen, and Ronald Popperwell.

SCARECROW, THE, a play in four acts by PERCY MACKAYE, published in 1908 and produced in 1909. Setting: a town in Massachusetts, late seventeenth century.

This fantasy, subtitled "The Glass of Truth, a Tragedy of the Ludicrous," is based on Nathaniel Hawthorne's story "Feathertop" (1852). Rejecting irony in favor of a conception of "the essential tragedy of the ludicrous," MacKaye noted that he changed Hawthorne's scarecrow from a ridiculous fop to a "pitiful . . . emblem of human bathos." The play was soon translated and produced in Europe, filmed (as *Puritan Passions*) in 1923, and revived in New York in 1953.

With the help of a devil, a witch creates a live scarecrow. As the fashionable but strange Lord Ravensbane she sends him to win the hand of Rachel Merton, the niece of the lover who had wronged the witch in her youth and now a puritanical judge. Ravensbane, helped by the devil, succeeds in winning Rachel. After satirical encounters with Harvard College masters and a song with a fantastic celestial accompaniment,

Ravensbane is revealed before the mirror of truth as the scarecrow he is rather than the man he strove to be. Though he tries to slay the image, the mirror never lets him forget it. The devil assures Ravensbane that all men are ridiculous and that though he has been given a soul, Ravensbane is a scarecrow whose life's breath comes from the brimstone-burning pipe he must perpetually smoke. He gets the chance to marry Rachel, but to guarantee her happiness, Ravensbane breaks his pipe, thus outwitting the devil and gaining true manhood and life through death. As he dies, Ravensbane asks whose image he sees in the glass. "Yourself, my lord—'tis the glass of truth," Rachel exclaims, amazed. Ravensbane dies exultantly, uttering the name of Rachel, whose love has helped give him dignity and a soul, and has thus made him "A man!"

SCHARY, Doré (1905–), American producer and writer, was long notable as a controversial Hollywood motion-picture producer of socially significant films. Then he made his very successful premiere as a Broadway playwright with his Franklin D. Roosevelt drama, SUNRISE AT CAMPOBELLO, first performed on January 30, 1958—the seventy-sixth anniversary of FDR's birth. Schary's later plays have been less successful; they include *Banderol* (1962); *One by One* (1964), about paraplegics; and *Brightower* (1970), about a famous author meant to suggest ERNEST HEMINGWAY. Schary has been very active in many professional activities and various Hollywood and New York productions, as well as the author of stories and articles.

SCHEHADÉ, Georges (1910–), Egyptian-born French dramatist of Lebanese parentage. Dividing his time between Paris and Beirut, where he was a professor, he has written allusively SYMBOLIC and allegorical verse plays in French. Loosely structured, they have many puppetlike characters, and usually feature a naïve, pure hero, seduced by illusions and pursuing his quest in vain. The protagonist of *Histoire de Vasco* (1956, translated as *Vasco*), the most important of Schehadé's plays, is a timid barber who is chosen for a heroic wartime task and becomes the ideal of a beautiful vagabond girl traveling with her dreamer father; she sees Vasco for the first time when his corpse lies before her, riddled with bullets. Schehadé's first play, *Monsieur Bob'le* (1951), aroused literary controversy when originally produced; it features a paradoxical but saintly village poet who disappears, sends mysterious messages that continue to direct his friends' lives, and dies on his return trip. Similarly, the hero of *La Soirée des proverbes* (1954), a poet in quest of an ideal, chooses death rather than compromise. Other Schehadé plays include *Les Violettes* (1960), *Le Voyage* (1961), and *L'Emigré de Brisbane* (1965), a PIRANDELLesque play about greed that has been compared to Dürrenmatt's THE VISIT.

Chapters on Schehadé and bibliographies may be found in Wallace Fowlie's *Dionysus in Paris* (1960), Leonard C. Pronko's *Avant-Garde* (1962), and Jacques Guicharnaud's *Modern French Theatre* (1967).

SCHISGAL, Murray (1926–), American playwright, was born in Brooklyn, served as a sailor in World War II, and upon his discharge took various odd jobs, studied and then practiced law, and later taught in East Harlem. Adept with clever character portrayals and dialogue, Schisgal first attracted attention in his native New York in 1963 with two of a quartet of one-acters (*Schrecks,* 1960) that had earlier impressed London theatregoers, *The Typists* and *The Tiger;* the first depicts the romance of two typists in a manner analogous to that of Wilder's THE LONG CHRISTMAS DINNER, while the second is about a timid clerk overwhelmed with gratitude by the married woman he tries to rape. Schisgal was nationally acclaimed in 1964 with *Luv* (1963), a triangle play—with many satiric thrusts at psychiatry, success dreams, and the avant-garde—that had failed in London before becoming a Broadway hit and a film (1967). It was followed by two one-acters produced Off-Broadway as *Fragments* (1967); a comedy about a young failure, *Jimmy Shine* (1968); and another pair of short comedies, *The Chinese* and *Dr. Fish* (1970).

SCHLAF, Johannes (1862–1941), German writer, was among the founders of his country's NATURALIST movement. Together with ARNO HOLZ he wrote *Familie Selicke,* a portrayal of the wretched family of an alcoholic bookkeeper, produced at the Freie Bühne in 1890. Hauptmann's BEFORE SUNRISE was dedicated to Schlaf and Holz, who had provided "important inspirations" with their phonetically and photographically REALISTIC *Papa Hamlet* prose sketches, published in 1889 under the pseudonym Bjarne P. Holmsen. Schlaf also wrote long impressionistic novels, and books on philosophy, religion, and the works of Walt Whitman, EMILE VERHAEREN, and MAURICE MAETERLINCK. His only other notable drama, *Meister Oelze* (1892), was praised for its naturalistic depiction of a murderer who tenaciously refuses to confess his crime even on his deathbed; it never achieved success in the theatre, though Schlaf revised it in 1908.

SCHLUCK AND JAU (*Schluck und Jau*), a comedy in six episodes by GERHART HAUPTMANN, published and produced in 1900. Setting: an ancient hunting castle and surrounding woods.

This comedy in prose and verse deals with the themes of the inductions of Shakespeare's *The Taming of the Shrew* and of Calderón's *La vida es sueño* (*Life Is a Dream*). Thoroughly original, however, it is a mixture of low comedy and romantic fantasy about an enamored young prince, a philosophizing courtier, and—most notably—a pair of archetypal ragamuffins: Schluck, a generous, lovable village clown and artistic tramp; and Jau, a Falstaffian vagabond whose truculence turns into tyranny when he becomes "prince for a day."

Despite Schluck's efforts to keep him going, Jau

collapses into a drunken stupor by the roadside just as a prince and his hunting party appear. First they are angered by the drunken tramps. Then they decide to have some fun. They imprison Schluck, and persuade Jau, upon his awakening, that he is the prince. Jau soon relishes his new life, feasts and drinks in Gargantuan proportions, and delights the court with his crude gusto. Schluck, in the meantime, happily entertains the ladies by cutting "silhouwettes." Then—being a sometime actor—he is fitted out to impersonate the deluded and blustering Jau's "wife." As the masquerade continues to amuse the prince, his courtier suggests its moral. "The less / Thou hast, the more is thine," he tells him; prince and pauper alike wander "as utter strangers through this wealthy realm / Which will endure when both of ye at length / Are mouldering dust. / . . . Our highest happiness is soap-bubbles." Life is a dream—but one must nonetheless cling to the dream in order to endure. Jau is disgusted with his simpering "wife" (Schluck) and orders "her" done away with. He becomes enamored of a widowed young lady-in-waiting. Uproarious in his vulgar solicitations, he bullies everybody: "On your bellies you gotta lie—creepin'! . . . When I wants a thing, it's gotta be done an' no whinin'! . . . If I sneeze you gotta wet your breeches out of fright!" He orders beer and whiskey: "I wanta mix my drinks!" His excesses and cruelties finally endanger the prince himself, and he is drugged and returned to the roadside. The good-natured Schluck, briefly happy with his clowning and "silhouwetting," is thrown out with Jau. The courtier tells them that they, like all people, have lived but a momentary dream: "But stretch not forth thine hands to pluck the clouds." Jau quickly accustoms himself to his former state. "Come, li'l brother," he tells Schluck, "we'll go over to the inn now an' sit down with plain people an' I'll be reel condescending, reel friendly like!" Schluck never ceases admiring his scampish mate: "Well, well, you are a devil of a fellow!"

SCHMIDTBONN [originally Schmidt], **Wilhelm** (1876–1952), German novelist, poet, and dramatist, wrote many of his plays before World War I. Originally a NATURALIST, he became a romanticist and made his name with *Mutter Landstrasse* (1901, produced by Max Reinhardt in 1904), the biblical tale of the Prodigal Son modernized by the respectable father's turning him out again to tramp on the "mother highway" of the title; later Schmidtbonn redramatized the parable more faithfully in *Der verlorene Sohn* (1912). While many of his other works similarly deal with legends, they often reflect his concern with contemporary affairs as well. They include *Der Graf von Gleichen* (1908), the oft-retold legend of the crusader who brings home a second wife, here concluding tragically when she is killed by the first wife; *Der Zorn des Achilles* (1909), in which Achilles pays with his life for his Nordic superman excesses; *Ein Kind ist vom Himmel gefallen* (1910), the tragicomedy of a burglar who settles down with the daughter of the house he came to rob; *Die Stadt der Besessenen* (1915), about the Anabaptists at Münster; *Die Passion* (1919), an adaptation of the religious French pageant *Le Mystère de la Passion* (1452); *Der Geschlagene* (1920), a moving drama about a pilot embittered after being blinded in the war, but regenerated by his wife's love; and a number of comedies, including a poetic and wistful depiction of fleeting youth, *Die Schauspieler* (1921).

Schmidtbonn, the son of a businessman, was born in Bonn and studied music and literature at various universities in Germany and Switzerland, where he spent much of his life. Also *Dramaturg* at the Düsseldorf theatre, Schmidtbonn was a very prolific author who published many volumes of verse and fiction as well as plays. An autobiographical collection of over one hundred sketches, "the fairy tale of my life," is his *An einem Strom geboren; ein Lebensbuch* (1935).

SCHNITZLER, Arthur (1862–1931), Austrian playwright and novelist, is best remembered for such once-daring works as *Reigen* (HANDS AROUND, 1900; also known as *La Ronde*), and the novella *Fräulein Else* (1924). His plays embody the gaiety and charm of Vienna at the turn of the century. But just as these were never recaptured after World War I, so Schnitzler's work—banned by the Nazis—never regained its popularity after World War II. Though many of his forty-odd plays are dated, his sympathetic yet clinical and ironic portrayal—often represented in terms of sex—of people's futile attempts to find life's meaning and forget death's proximity set the direction for much subsequent drama. Schnitzler is not likely ever to win back his great renown, but his share in the growth of modern drama cannot be ignored.

The son of a prominent physician, Schnitzler studied medicine in Vienna, where he spent most of his life, married, and died. He became a doctor in 1885 and wrote for medical reviews on such subjects as hypnotism and psychotherapy. Intuitively he discovered some of the theories Sigmund Freud was then working out. Schnitzler subsequently expressed these ideas in poetry and fiction (particularly in *Leutnant Gustl,* his 1901 novel whose stream-of-consciousness device anticipated the work of JAMES JOYCE) that began to appear in the late 1880's. His earliest works were signed "Anatol," soon the eponymous hero (but not *raisonneur*) of his first important play. With friends such as HUGO VON HOFMANNSTHAL, Schnitzler joined the antiNATURALISTIC *Jungwien* ("Young Vienna") group of romantic-decadent writers. But Schnitzler's wistful romanticism is undercut by morbidity and cynical objectivity, and his decadence is accompanied by skepticism.

His first plays (some later collected in ANATOL, 1893) were unsuccessful. They include *Das Märchen* (*The Fairy Tale,* 1891) and one-acters such as *Das Abenteuer seines Lebens* (1888) and *Alkandis Lied* (1890). *Anatol* and *Liebelei* (LIGHT-O'-LOVE, 1895) soon established his reputation. The latter features the sweet lower-class girl, the plaything of a gentleman—types (and motifs, such as a duel) characteristic of Schnitzler's plays. The one-act verse playlet *Paracelsus* (1898), featuring the Renaissance alchemist, is typical in its psychiatric probing of wifely fidelity and marital relationships. Other plays of this period are the first-noted *Hands Around, Freiwild* (*Free Game,* 1896), *Die überspannte Person* (1896), *Halbzwei* (1897), *Das Vermächtniss* (1898), and *Der Schleier der Beatrice* (*The Veil of Beatrice,* 1900), a wildly romantic five-act verse play set in Bologna at the time of the Borgias.

Of the one-acters, *Der grüne Kakadu* (THE GREEN COCKATOO, 1899) is best known. Others are *Die Gefährtin* (1899), *Die Frau mit dem Dolche* (*The Lady with the Dagger,* 1902), *Lebendige Stunden* (*Living Hours,* 1901), *Die letzten Masken* (*Last Masks,* 1902), *Sylvesternacht* (1901), and the witty *Literatur* (*Literature,* 1902), incisive portraits of love relationships among artists. Another group of one-act plays, the "puppet" trio that mordantly exposes the delusion that we master our own fates, consists of *Der Puppenspieler* (1903), *Der tapfere Kassian* (*Gallant Cassian,* 1904; made into a musical comedy by Oscar Straus in 1909), and *Zum grossen Wurstel* (1905). The remaining one-acters are *Komtesse Mizzi; oder, der Familientag* (*Countess Mizzie,* 1909), whose protagonist reluctantly marries to legitimatize her son's aristocratic origin; and *Stunde des Erkennens, Grosse Szene,* and *Das Bacchusfest* (all 1915). He wrote two pantomimes, *Die Verwandlungen des Pierrot* (1908) and *Der Schleier der Pierrette* (1910), the latter with music by Ernst von Dohnányi.

Der einsame Weg (THE LONELY WAY, 1904), one of Schnitzler's most distinguished works, exemplifies his limitations as a dramatist: static character and plot, and lack of unity. Other, less successful plays were *Zwischenspiel* (*Intermezzo,* 1905) and *Der Ruf des Lebens* (*The Call of Life,* 1906), where passions end in dissipation and crime: a girl murders her villainous father and, though conscience-stricken, follows "the call of life" and rejoins her lover. *Der junge Medardus* (1910), a historical play, is set in Vienna and features a cast of seventy-four, including Napoleon. *Das weite Land* (1911) is a tragicomedy that exposes the "vast domain" of the soul of the protagonist, a brutal philanderer. Schnitzler's last important play is the atypical, somewhat autobiographical PROFESSOR BERNHARDI (1912); like his novel *Der Weg ins Freie* (1908), it reveals Schnitzler's concern with anti-Semitism, by which he himself was victimized. The final plays are three comedies—*Fink und Fliederbush* (1917), *Die Schwestern, oder Casanova in Spa* (1919, a verse comedy), *Die Komödie der Verführung* (1924)—and two wistfully nostalgic plays, *Der Gang zum Weiher* (1925) and *Im Spiel der Sommerlüfte* (1930). The year after his death three one-acters appeared: *Anatols Grössenwahn* (*Anatol's Megalomania*), *Die Mörderin,* and *Die Gleitenden.*

These were produced by his son Heinrich, who later became a dramatics professor in California. Biographical information about Schnitzler is scant and most of his autobiographical manuscripts have remained unavailable, but some of them were published in 1968 as *Jugend in Wien* (*My Youth in Vienna*). Sol Liptzin's *Arthur Schnitzler* (1932) discusses primarily his important writings, most of which were translated. A comprehensive bibliography is Richard H. Allen's *An Annotated Arthur Schnitzler Bibliography* (1966).

SCHOLZ, Wilhelm von (1874–1969), German writer, distinguished himself in many forms of literature. He was a neoclassicist disciple of PAUL ERNST and achieved considerable success with *Der Jude von Konstanz* (1905), his play about a medieval doctor who becomes a martyr during a pogrom by reassuming the Judaism he left in order to help humanity more effectively. Scholz frequently used medieval settings and became increasingly interested in the occult. In his drama as in his other works he stressed the importance of the imagination.

The son of Bismarck's secretary of finance, Scholz was born in Berlin. There he spent much of his time, though he also lived in his Lake Constance castle and was dramatic director of Stuttgart's Court Theatre (1910–23). Later, in Berlin, he served as President of the Nazi-founded Dichterakademie. His early plays—*Der Besiegte* (1899) and *Der Gast* (1900)—are SYMBOLIST interpretations of the irrationalism of reality. Most accomplished among his later treatments of psychology and the occult are *Meroë* (1906), a poetic tragedy derivative of Hebbel's *Herodes und Mariamne* (1850) and portraying contemporary problems in quasi mythical guises; *Vertauschte Seelen* (1910), a redramatization of Tirso de Molina's Renaissance fairy tale of the "exchanged souls" of a king and a beggar; *Gefährliche Liebe* (1913), an adaptation of Choderlos de Laclos's sensational epistolary novel *Les Liaisons dangereuses* (1784); *Der Wettlauf mit dem Schatten* (1920), a PIRANDELLian conflict between a poet and his marital rival, a character in one of his novels; and *Die gläserne Frau* (1924), a dramatization of the split personality and hallucinations of a girl subconsciously enamored of a prominent physician. Later, less successful plays include *Das Säckinger Trompetenspiel* (1955). Scholz also adapted dramas of Calderón and miracle and marionette plays.

His other writings consist of volumes of poetry, short stories, novels, essays on the drama (*Gedanken zum Drama,* 1905; revised 1915), and editions of the German classics and biographies. Notable among his memoirs are *Wanderungen* (1934) and *Eine Jahrhundertwende* (1936).

SCHÖNHERR, Karl (1867–1943), Austrian playwright, was an important early modern folk dramatist. Excelling in NATURALISTIC depictions of peasant life, he particularly distinguished himself with *Glaube und Heimat* (*Faith and Fireside,* 1910) and *Der Weibsteufel* (1914). The first, a peasant tragedy set at the time of the Counter-Reformation, portrays suffering Tyrolean peasants ruthlessly driven from their homes because they refuse to return to the Catholic Church; while *Der*

Weibsteufel, a three-character sex tragedy set in a Tyrolean mountain hut, depicts a ruthless woman (the title's "female devil") getting her weak husband murdered by the young hunter who wants to become her lover and whom she also destroys. Many Schönherr plays characterize the elemental passions of peasants, but he also wrote about middle-class city life, medicine, and other topics.

Schönherr came from the Tirol. Like ARTHUR SCHNITZLER, he was a physician whose practice was overshadowed by his writing. After dabbling in fiction and poetry Schönherr discovered his métier in the drama. He polished and perfected his much-praised dramaturgical skills in frequent revisions, to which he subjected his plays even after their production and publication. His first hits were peasant tragedies such as the one-act *Die Bildschnitzer* (1900) and *Sonnwendtag* (1902), the drama of a superstitious peasant woman's struggles against modern liberalism—which he later reworked in comic form as *Die Trenkwalder* (1913). Schönherr's first important full-length play was *Erde* (1907), in which an old peasant tenaciously holding on to life smashes the coffin built for him by greedy heirs. In *Das Königreich* (1908) Schönherr dramatized a popular folktale about children who save a young prince as well as the devil who has enslaved him. *Über die Brücke* (1909; reworked as *Der Komödiant*, 1924) is an early Schönherr venture into drama of Viennese life—here the struggle between bourgeois and artist, a theme that reappears in other plays.

During World War I Schönherr wrote *Volk in Not* (1916), a patriotic play about the Tyrolean uprising led by Andreas Hofer against Napoleon. Another play about Hofer appeared in 1927, *Der Judas von Tirol*, Schönherr's revision of his early (1897) failure by the same name. A number of his plays dramatize the suffering of starvation brought about by the war, including *Die Hungerblockade* (1925, reworked into *Der Armendoktor* in 1926), and others. Drama about problems of his profession include the two-character *Es* (1922), the tragedy of a consumptive doctor powerless to continue his campaign against perpetuating the disease in later generations; and *Haben Sie zu essen, Herr Doktor?* (1930), which shows physicians deprived of their livelihood by quacks, whom gullible, superstitious people prefer. Schönherr also wrote a religious folk mystery, *Passionsspiel* (1933), which depicts Judas's betrayal from a psychological viewpoint.

Schönherr spent most of his life in Vienna and wrote until shortly before his death. His later plays, however, were not successful artistically or commercially. His plays are discussed in H. F. Garten's *Modern German Drama* (1964), whose bibliography lists German studies of Schönherr published in the 1920's.

SCHREYVOGL, Friedrich (1899–   ), Austrian dramatist, wrote many popular plays from the 1920's to the 1960's. Some of them are revuelike histories, such as *Die Flucht des Columbus* (1926). The best is *Habsburgerlegende* (1933), a revision of his *Johann Orth* (1928); it dramatizes the life of John Nepomuck Salvator, the Austrian archduke who after marrying a commoner renounced his titles in 1889 and vanished abroad, returning only as an old man to view his figure in a Viennese waxworks exhibit. Other Schreyvogl plays include *Die kluge Wienerin* (1941), a comedy set in ancient Vienna; *Eine Stunde vor Tag* (1956), dramatizing life in the theatre; *Ton und Licht* (1960), about Emperor Ferdinand Maximilian and Carlota of Mexico; and *Ich liebe eine Göttin* (1961).

SCHWEYK IN THE SECOND WORLD WAR (*Schweyk im Zweiten Weltkrieg*), a play in eight scenes (plus prelude, interludes, and postlude) by BERTOLT BRECHT (music by Hanns Eisler), published and produced in 1957. Setting: Prague and the Russian front during World War II.

Brecht completed this play around 1944, but it was not produced in his lifetime; since he did not prepare manuscripts for publication without making changes during production, Brecht left this play unpublished. Long before writing it, Brecht had participated in the adaptation of the 1928 Erwin Piscator production of Jaroslav Hašek's novel *The Good Soldier Schweik* (1920-23). Brecht saw much of himself in the figure of the legendary Schweik, some of whose characteristics are also shared by HERR PUNTILA's servant Matti and THE CAUCASIAN CHALK CIRCLE's Azdak. In this play, originally conceived as an opera with Kurt Weill, the good soldier is most comically recreated as a Prague patriot during the Nazi occupation of Czechoslovakia and a soldier impressed by the German army to fight in the Battle of Stalingrad.

Schweyk is a dog dealer who spends much time with his patriotic companions in the tavern run by an attractive widow. His friend is obsessed with food and constantly threatens to join the German forces simply in order to indulge his gluttony. With his characteristic idiocy, Schweyk makes fools of a member of the Gestapo and an SS leader, the latter of whom wants Schweyk to steal a particular dog for him. Schweyk's amusing adventures include arrest by the Gestapo, an enforced stint in the Voluntary German Labor Service, and detention in a military prison filled with malingerers. He manages to talk himself into and out of many scrapes—and at the same time to insult the Germans. For a while his name saves him from combat: "My name is Schweyk with a 'y'—if I spell myself with a simple 'i' then I have German ancestry and can be drafted." But finally he is sent to fight, "gets lost," and is seen picking up and consoling a stray dog near Stalingrad: "Don't fret, the war won't last forever, any more than the peace." In intermittent low-comic interludes, Hitler has his leaders reassure him of the "little man's" love for him. Finally the lost dictator encounters little Schweyk in the snows around Stalingrad. Schweyk tells the desperate Hitler to go to hell, and the cast, removing their masks, sing "The Moldau Song."

SCRAP OF PAPER, A (*Les Pattes de mouche;* literally, "fly tracks" or "scrawls"), a comedy in three acts by VICTORIEN SARDOU, published and produced in 1860. Setting: near Chinon, France; mid-nineteenth century.

This farce—Sardou's first major success—centers about Clarisse Vanhove's attempts to retrieve an indiscreet note written to her lover, Prosper Block, shortly before her marriage. Prosper must immediately find a wife to avoid being disinherited, and he uses the incriminating "scrap of paper" to force Clarisse to let him marry her sister—who, however, is in love with someone else. Clarisse's spirited cousin undertakes to reclaim the letter. In her battles for it she and Prosper fall in love with each other.

This slight plot hinges on the whereabouts of the note and the attempts of the various characters to snatch it and keep it from Clarisse's husband. Their frantic efforts to obtain, retain, conceal, and destroy the note illustrate the ups and downs characteristic of the WELL-MADE PLAY as Stephen S. Stanton traces them in his introduction to *Camille and Other Plays* (1957), which includes *A Scrap of Paper*. The genre's *scène à faire* is the husband's partial reading and near comprehension of the note, and the happy resolution finds the "scrap of paper" destroyed and the various sets of lovers united.

SCREENS, THE (*Les Paravents*), a play in seventeen scenes by JEAN GENET, published and produced in 1961. Setting: an open-air, four-tiered theatre with an earth platform, representing Algeria during the 1954–62 war.

This long, stylized mass drama has almost one hundred masked characters, most of them outcasts. It portrays the filth, degradation, and crime both of the colonial overlords and of the village Arabs at home, in a brothel, in the marketplace, etc. The play is titled after its props: changing screens on which settings are painted, often by the actors themselves. The play was not produced in France until 1966—when still-resentful audiences interrupted the performance. Offensive attitudes and language, as well as difficult and unconventionally ritualistic dramaturgy juxtaposing the real and the illusory, have precluded frequent production of this play.

The peasant Saïd is so poor that he can afford to marry only a woman who is so ugly that her face must be covered with a hood. She becomes his shadow while Saïd is sustained and dominated by his mother. The three of them encounter and weave through multifarious episodes of rebellion, degeneration, violence, and obscenity. From the stage's topmost tier, those who die and are murdered then observe the living. The loathsome Saïd seeks to discover "what I can say, what I can sell out on, so as to be a complete louse." Despised and reviled by the Arabs as well as the Europeans, Saïd becomes a thief and a traitor, and is imprisoned and eventually killed. But he is not admitted even into the domain of the dead, whom he rejects with an obscene exclamation. Thus nothing is left of him, though his dead mother is confident he will live on in folklore, "in a song."

SEAGULL, THE (*Chaika*), a comedy in four acts by ANTON CHEKHOV, published and produced in 1896. Setting: a contemporary Russian estate.

This, the first of his four great plays, is typical of Chekhov's lyrical, tragicomic depiction of yearning and futility. Its richness is enhanced by the SYMBOLISM articulated in the title and the *Hamlet* allusions; and in the characterizations, including those of successful artistic mediocrities such as Trigorin and Irina, whom Chekhov characterized as "a foolish, mendacious, self-admiring egoist." Though the premiere failed dismally and Chekhov decided never again to write plays, *The Seagull* was successfully produced in 1898 by the Moscow Art Theatre. Its production, by V. I. NEMIROVICH-DANCHENKO, in which Konstantin Stanislavsky acted Trigorin and Olga Knipper (later Chekhov's wife) acted Irina, established the reputation both of the newly formed group (whose symbol became a seagull) and of Chekhov as a playwright.

Act I. Konstantin Treplev (pronounced "Trepl-yov") nervously awaits the start of his private theatrical. In the lead will be Nina Zarechny, the wealthy neighbor's daughter, whom he loves. But Treplev is most concerned over his mother, the famous actress Irina Arkadina, about whom he complains to her lovable old brother. Jealous

The Seagull. Irina (Olga Knipper) and Trigorin (Konstantin Stanislavsky). Moscow, 1898. ("Tass" from *Sovfoto*)

over her affair with Boris Trigorin, a famous writer, Treplev criticizes her appearing in dead plays: "We must have new forms," Treplev insists, "and if we can't get them we'd better have nothing at all." Nina arrives, terrified about performing before the famous novelist, and especially in Treplev's "dream" play, which, she says, "has no living characters in it." Irina makes her appearance, and half-jokingly exchanges Gertrude-Hamlet speeches with her son. The curtain rises, and Nina recites Treplev's long opening oration—pretentious poetic drivel. Irina finally ridicules it and Treplev furiously stops the performance and leaves. Nina meets Trigorin, and later, when Treplev returns, a kindly doctor praises his play. After this and other discussions, the elderly doctor, himself beloved by her mother, comforts the steward's daughter, who suffers in her love for Treplev: "How nervous they all are! And so much love!"

Act II. Irina feels insulted by an outburst of the unruly steward and decides to return to Moscow with Trigorin. Though she soon changes her mind, Treplev becomes increasingly jealous and angry. He brings Nina a seagull he has killed. "It's the way I'll soon end my own life," he remarks, and complains of her growing coldness toward him since the failure of his play. He leaves bitterly when he sees Trigorin, whom Nina envies for his great success and fame. She is surprised to hear his modest opinion of himself, as he describes his writing, his love of nature, and his passion for fishing. When he sees the dead gull, he writes down an idea for a short story about a girl like Nina, "happy and free like a seagull. But by chance a man comes, sees her, and with nothing better to do, destroys her"—as the seagull has been destroyed. After he leaves, Nina, now in love with Trigorin, is entranced: "It's a dream!"

Act III. Irina and Trigorin are departing. Treplev has tried to shoot himself, but succeeded only in wounding his head. As Irina bandages it, he tells her how, "these last days, I have loved you as tenderly and fully as when I was a child. Except for you, there's nobody left me now." But when he sneers about Trigorin (whom he had challenged to a duel), the "trashy" plays in which she acts, and her miserliness, Irina angrily defends her lover and coldly lashes out at her son: "You are not fit to write even wretched vaudeville. Kiev burgher! Sponge! Beggar! Nonentity!" Miserable, he breaks into tears; she quickly apologizes and they make up. When Trigorin notices that his farewell gift from Nina has an amorous inscription, he begs Irina to postpone their departure. Thereupon Irina prostrates herself before him and soon regains her mastery over him. Then he sees Nina; they agree to meet in Moscow—and finally embrace passionately.

Act IV. It is two years later. The unhappy steward's daughter is no happier with an impecunious schoolteacher, whom she has married to forget Treplev. The uncle is quite ill, and Irina has been summoned to the estate. Painfully Treplev tells the doctor, who has just returned from a trip abroad, about Nina. Now an actress, she had become Trigorin's mistress, bore him a child that soon died, and later was cast off by both her lover and her father. Treplev has published with some success, but he despairs because his writing is still dead. To himself he admits that his failure stems not from his concern with a new form, but from his lack of purpose: a true artist, he realizes, "writes because it comes pouring out from his soul." While the others are away, Nina comes for her final leave-taking. Though occasionally distracted and disappointed with her hardships as an itinerant provincial actress, she loves her career and, through her work, is finding herself. "My soul grows stronger every day," she tells Treplev; "I have faith and it all doesn't hurt me so much, and when I think of my calling I'm not afraid of life." Treplev sadly recognizes that, while she seems to have found her way, "I have no faith, and I don't know where my calling lies." Nina leaves and Treplev worries that someone may see her. "That might upset Mother," he remarks, tears up all his manuscripts, and goes out. The others return and resume their lotto game. A shot is heard; the doctor takes Trigorin aside and quietly tells him that Treplev has just killed himself.

SECOND MAN, THE, a play in three acts by S. N. BEHRMAN, published and produced in 1927. Setting: a suite in New York, 1920's.

This "high comedy" was Behrman's first stage success. Despite tarnished wit, creaking dramaturgical machinery, and artificial characterization, its comic integrity is sustained by the consistent and untemporizing resolution of the plot.

Clark Storey frankly admits to his mistress that he is a glib second-rate writer who wants to marry her for her money. His quest for comfort is threatened by an idealistic flapper who loves him; she, in turn, is worshiped by a brilliant and wealthy—but dull—scientist. Storey tells her of "the second man" in him, "a cynical, odious person" who mocks civilization and his charming veneer, and constantly makes him face his gross self. Spurning her advances, Storey reveals, too, how he gave up idealism for profitable hackwork. To hold him she announces that she is pregnant with his baby. His mistress and the scientist leave scandalized, and the latter tries to kill Storey. But the flapper finally sees Storey for the opportunist he is, and decides to marry the scientist. Storey placates his rich mistress, who loves him though she has no illusions about him. She agrees to take him along on her cruise—and, presumably, to marry him.

SECOND MRS. TANQUERAY, THE, a play in four acts by ARTHUR WING PINERO, produced in 1893 and published in 1895. Setting: London and Surrey, England; 1890's.

Some have heralded this as the first modern English drama. Featuring "a woman with a past," it was considered so advanced that stars dared not play Paula Tanqueray. A then-unknown young actress who took the part, Mrs. Patrick Campbell,

The Second Mrs. Tanqueray, Act I. Paula (Mrs. Patrick Campbell) and Tanqueray (George Alexander). London, 1893. (*Culver Pictures*)

became famous overnight when the play unexpectedly became a hit. In his 1895 review BERNARD SHAW noted its clumsy exposition, reliance on artificial dramatic devices, and Pinero's sham originality of characterization and theme—"a work of prejudiced [conventional] observation instead of comprehension," though an effective stage piece "for the modern commercial theatre." But other reviewers praised it as a PROBLEM PLAY with complex yet lucid characterizations, and it has been frequently revived by great actresses, including Eleanora Duse and Tallulah Bankhead.

Act I. Aubrey Tanqueray, a cultivated elderly widower, surprises his friends with the announcement that he will be married the next day. He adds that it "isn't even the conventional sort of marriage likely to satisfy society." Temporarily left alone, the friends speculate about the bride's identity. When another friend, Cayley Drummle, appears, he unwittingly wounds Tanqueray with his excuse for being late: he had to console the mother of a friend who has married an adventuress and is therefore ruined socially. Tanqueray later confesses to Drummle that he proposes to do the same thing: his bride also has a past. But he refuses to accept the analogy. "To you, Cayley, all women who have been roughly treated, and who dare to survive by borrowing a little of our philosophy, are alike," he says; "I'll prove to you that it's possible to rear a life of happiness, of good repute, on a—miserable foundation." Tanqueray is momentarily shocked by Paula's improper visit, at night. The beautiful, innocent-looking girl has come to present him with a letter in which she has detailed her various adventures. Giving him the opportunity to get out of the marriage, she urges him to read it. When he burns the sealed letter, Paula admits that she would have killed herself had he behaved caddishly, as other men had. While she gets her cloak before leaving, Tanqueray reads a letter from his daughter, Ellean. With a frigid piety she inherited from her mother, Ellean had intended to become a nun. Now she has changed her mind: "I am ready to take my place by you. Dear father, will you receive me?"

Act II. Some months later, at Tanqueray's country house, Paula is irritable and bored. They have been cut by society, and Paula is jealous of his daughter, who now lives with them. "She is your saint. Saint Ellean!" she says: "There are two sorts of affection—the love for a woman you respect, and the love for the woman you—love. She gets the first from you: I never can." And she adds, "If Ellean cared for me only a little, it would be different. I shouldn't be jealous then." But the girl coldly shrinks away from her. Tanqueray and Paula eventually confide their unhappiness to Drummle, who has come for a visit. He reveals that their neighbor has repented her snubbing Paula and, furthermore, would like to take Ellean for a trip to London and Paris. Though the neighbor is courteous and sincerely contrite when she calls, Paula is vicious in her cutting replies. Later Paula angrily blames Tanqueray for "taking Ellean from me." Despite his protests, she spitefully mails an invitation to the adventuress who married and made a drunken sot of Drummle's former friend.

Act III. Three weeks later the Tanquerays are hardly on speaking terms. The adventuress and her husband are vulgar, obnoxious visitors, and they exacerbate the Tanquerays' difficulties. Paula admits to Drummle that she wishes they would leave. But she cannot get herself to speak to her husband because she is ashamed of having intercepted his daughter's letter during a fit of mad jealousy. Drummle persuades her to see Tanqueray, who is surprised by her confession—but remains gentle and kind. Paula is angered when Tanqueray cannot deny that he had agreed to his daughter's trip because Paula is not a decent companion for her. He recalls her own innocent youth to Paula and compares it with her sneering and cynicism before Ellean. Paula is overwhelmed with shame and begs for another chance with the girl. Unexpectedly Ellean suddenly appears with the neighbor. Upset because they have received no reply to their letters, they reveal Ellean's having fallen in love with a young officer she met in Paris and wants to marry. Tanqueray begs his daughter to be gentle with Paula, and goes to meet the officer, who has returned with them. In the meantime, however, the officer has slipped through the neighboring hedge to visit Ellean. She has him go out before Paula appears, and then she displays the affection Paula has craved so long. Shyly she confesses her beloved's proximity, and Paula asks to see him. When he enters they stare blankly at each other and then have Ellean go out for a moment. Desperately they debate what is to be done—for he is revealed to be one of Paula's former lovers. "[Ellean] kissed me tonight! I'd won her over!" Paula sobs, "and now —just as she's beginning to love me, to bring this on her!" She insists that he give up Ellean and that Tanqueray be told. The officer is furious and, though he does not believe she will dare to tell Tanqueray, warns her not to come between him and Ellean.

Act IV. After her vulgar guests leave, Paula tells her husband that the officer's name was among those in the letter Tanqueray burned before the marriage. "Why don't you strike me? Hit me in the face—I'd rather you did! Hurt me! hurt me!" she cries out. A note from the officer announces his returning to Paris, though he implores their help in marrying Ellean. Tanqueray tells her the marriage cannot be, but refuses to specify the nature of the officer's "dissolute life." She questions Paula and gradually reads the truth in Paula's face when she admits telling Tanqueray what she knew of his life: "What can you know? You can only speak from gossip, report, hearsay! How is it possible that you—!" She stops, stares at Paula, and backs away. "I have always known what you were," Ellean exclaims, though Paula hysterically denies it: "From the first moment I saw you I knew you were altogether unlike the good women I'd left." Ellean weakly tells her father that she no longer wishes to see her officer, and leaves. "I'm tainted through and through," Paula says, and offers to give Tanqueray his freedom: "You needn't be afraid I'd go back to—what I was. I couldn't." He suggests that they leave and forget the past, but Paula replies, "I believe the future is only the past again, entered through another gate." With growing desperation she envisions their future and her gradually waning attraction to him, and then she goes out. Tanqueray is overcome with bitterness and compassion: "Curse him! My poor, wretched wife!" Then Ellean calls her father. She tells him to go to Paula's room and then she breaks down: "I—I went to her room—to tell her I was sorry." But Paula had killed herself: "Yes—yes. So everybody will say. But I know—I helped to kill her. If I'd only been merciful!"

SECRET OF HEAVEN, THE (*Himlens hemlighet*), a one-act play by PÄR LAGERKVIST, published in 1919 and produced in 1921. Setting: a huge blue-black sphere, partly illuminated by a lightbeam.

The premiere of *The Secret of Heaven,* at AUGUST STRINDBERG's refurbished Intima Teatern, marked the first Scandinavian production of a totally EXPRESSIONIST play. Like THE DIFFICULT HOUR, it is a nightmare vision of life and death. Highly theatrical in setting and pantomime, biting and scornful, and with a minimum of dialogue, it portrays a group of pathetic, isolated creatures—a microcosm of the world. They include a helpless old woodsman (God) who never looks about him; a strutting dwarf; a "wizened little man with a skull-cap and large spectacles [who] sits on his haunches, mumbling to himself"; "an old woman with a toothless grin," picking her "dirty feet and great pigeon toes"; a powerful man in tights who eternally lops off the heads of performing dolls, miniature people whose bodies he piles up on the side; a mad girl who keeps seeking a nonexistent golden string (happiness); and a brooding young man who searches for the meaning of life.

These creatures crawl about pitifully, ignoring each other. The youth finds happiness when he sees the mad girl and falls in love with her. "You are good," he tells her: "That's why I understand you. The others are a puzzle. But you, you are so pretty." The girl is soon frightened by his strange, impassioned speech, and by his exhortations that she observe the beauties of nature and love him. "I'm mad, I'm mad! Let me go!" she cries out. The misshapen dwarf struts before her, giggling as she, preferring him to the youth, admires him: "Yes, my dear, you're handsome! —And I'm crazy as a loon. Hehehe!—" She picks up her guitar: "Now I'll play, and you shall dance. Dance, little mopsey! Dance, do you hear!" As she plays wildly and the dwarf dances for her, the desperate young man, defeated in love as well as in the cosmic quest for an answer ("What is the meaning of it?" he keeps asking, until told to "Go to hell!"), rushes off—and throws himself into the darkness. "Bless my soul, he must have gone to the bottom," the dwarf remarks. The man in tights continues lopping off heads, and the man with a skullcap laughs, "The bottom, hehe . . . The bottom . . ."

SECRET OF THE GUILD, THE (*Gillets hemlighet*), a play in four acts by AUGUST STRINDBERG, published and produced in 1880. Setting: fifteenth-century Sweden.

This early play ends happily, though it was influenced by Ibsen's THE PRETENDERS and anticipates his THE MASTER BUILDER.

A guild of masons for many years has tried to complete the Uppsala cathedral. The honest and able old architect in charge is replaced by his arrogant and dishonest rival—his own son. The tower collapses when the great bell is rung, because of the son's ineptness and ignorance of the secret of success: faith. His wife and father know that secret; she has remained steadfastly loyal, and the father remarks, "The church was built in sin and therefore it lies in ruins."

SEÑORA AMA, a comedy in three acts by JACINTO BENAVENTE, published and produced in 1908. Setting: a farmhouse in contemporary Castile, Spain.

Though virtually unknown abroad, this multi-charactered rustic drama was Benavente's own favorite.

The landowner heroine of the title, Dominica, is a woman whose husband is a Don Juan. Despite his infidelities, she remains smugly tolerant: "He enjoys himself with all women and deceives them, but I am his wife, the only one and above all the others." Impending motherhood changes her attitudes and character. Matching her husband's egotism, Dominica soon manages to bring about his marital loyalty.

SEÑORA CARRAR'S RIFLES (*Die Gewehre der Frau Carrar*), a one-act play by BERTOLT BRECHT, published and produced in 1937. Setting: an Andalusian fisherman's cottage, April 1937.

Though atypically conventional (i.e., neither EPIC nor openly didactic), this Brecht play (also produced as *The Guns of Carrar*) was intended as pro-(Spanish)-Nationalist propaganda. Reminiscent of THE MOTHER, it was inspired by Synge's RIDERS TO THE SEA.

Having lost her husband in one uprising, Teresa Carrar refuses to let her sons join the Republican army in the Civil War ravaging Spain. Her brother, a worker who has already enlisted, comes for rifles that her husband concealed before his death. She will not release them and is backed in her abhorrence of war by the arguments of a priest. Her brother attacks her neutrality, which she expects Franco's men to respect: "Not helping our fight does not mean not fighting; it means helping the rebels." Her son's corpse is brought in: he has been ruthlessly machine-gunned while fishing. "They aren't human—they are scum and must be dealt with like scum," Teresa Carrar now realizes. She releases the rifles and accompanies her younger son and her brother to battle the Fascist rebels.

SEPARATE TABLES, two one-act plays by TERENCE RATTIGAN, produced in 1954 and published in 1955. Setting: an English boardinghouse, 1950's.

Both plays have the same drab setting and lonely characters. There is a compassionate landlady, and the boarders include a harridan, a meek old widow, a lady gambler, a pensioned schoolteacher, and an unsympathetic young couple. In *Table Number Seven* a pathetic old fraud of a major is exposed and humiliated, but retains the affections of a fading wallflower. In *Table by the Window* a divorcée fearful of aging humbles herself before her former husband, the wreck of a famous politician she had ruined.

SERJEANT MUSGRAVE'S DANCE, "An Unhistorical Parable" in three acts by JOHN ARDEN, produced in 1959 and published in 1960. Setting: a mining town in northern England, a winter about 1880.

This play, though a failure in its first production, soon became widely successful (beginning with English student productions) and established Arden's reputation. Added to the gallows humor and patches of melodrama are his typical use of songs and his thematic ambiguities. In his introduction Arden called it "a REALISTIC, but not a NATURALISTIC" play. Acknowledging critics' "puzzlement," Arden suggested that the play advocates the "very hard doctrine" of "complete pacifism."

Serjeant Musgrave, a religious fanatic, and three privates arrive in a snowbound mining town. Deserters who pretend to be on a recruiting mission, they antagonize the miners, who fear them as strikebreakers. The taciturn and puritanical Musgrave treats the townsmen to beer and eventually gains a measure of acceptance. The mine owners, politicians, and clergy support the recruiters in order to keep the rebellious workers preoccupied. During the night, one of the privates is killed in a brawl over the local wench, and Musgrave has a nightmare. After the recruiting parade Musgrave wins everybody's benign attention when he starts his speech. But he creates pandemonium when he reveals his ideas and the contents of the box they brought with them: the skeleton of a former townsman, now hoisted up for all to see. The townsman was a soldier murdered by rebellious natives in one of the empire's outposts; in retaliation the British army executed five natives. Musgrave explains, "Therefore, for five of them we multiply out, *and* we find it five-and-twenty. . . . So, as I understand Logic and Logic to me is the mechanism of God—that means that today there's twenty-five persons will have to be—" executed. As a protest against murder and the horror of war, he trains the guns on his audience and prepares to shoot down twenty-five leading citizens (five for each of the murdered natives). But while Musgrave exhorts his reluctant mates to "join along with my madness," dragoons come in the nick of time; they shoot one private and arrest Musgrave and the remaining soldier as deserters. In chains, Musgrave is puzzled and despairs: "God was with me . . . God . . ." Outside, the townsfolk dance happily. "You can't cure the pox by further whoring," his mate tells Musgrave. And after a final song he remarks, "They're going to hang us up a length higher nor most apple-trees grow, Serjeant. D'you reckon we can start an orchard?"

SERVITUDE, a play in three acts by EUGENE O'NEILL, published in 1950 and produced in 1960. Setting: a study in Tarryville-on-Hudson, New York; "about ten o'clock in the evening . . . the present day," i.e., c. 1914.

Though this first full-length play by O'Neill is very amateurish and old-fashioned—for which reason O'Neill himself discarded it—it prefigures his later work with its clash of ideal and material values, its introspective male and loving-sacrificing female characters, and its concern with illusions that mask people's identities. The play was written in about 1914 and first published in LOST PLAYS OF EUGENE O'NEILL.

A wealthy stockbroker's beautiful and intelligent wife, inspired by the writings of a famous novelist-playwright, becomes an IBSENite "New Woman," and leaves her husband. She visits the author, an egotist with a simple and self-effacing wife, who unknowingly helps the others to resolve their problems by demonstrating that "Happiness is servitude.... Servitude in love, love in servitude!"

SEVEN DEADLY SINS OF THE PETTY BOURGEOIS, THE (*Die sieben Todsünden der Kleinbürger*), a ballet-cantata in seven sections by BERTOLT BRECHT (music by Kurt Weill), produced in 1933 and published in 1957. Setting: twentieth-century America.

Also known as *Anna-Anna,* this choreographed poem was translated by W. H. AUDEN and Chester Kallman in *The Tulane Drama Review* (Autumn 1961). Its first publication was on the jacket of a phonograph record, Columbia KL 5175.

The dual nature of a dancer is portrayed by two sisters, Anna 1 and Anna 2. The dancer resists her (virtuous) instincts and avoids "the seven deadly sins" of capitalist society: Pride (in her art, which would have prevented her becoming a stripper), Lust (loving the man she loves, rather than the one who pays her), Anger (at evil), etc. Therefore she succeeds, amasses wealth, and can return home to Louisiana to retire in comfort.

SEVEN KEYS TO BALDPATE, "a mysterious melodramatic farce" in a prologue, two acts, and an epilogue, by GEORGE M. COHAN; produced in 1913 and published in 1914. Setting: a deserted summer mountain resort (Baldpate Inn), winter 1913.

Based on Earl Derr Biggers's 1913 novel, this is a clever crime and suspense play-within-a-play (filmed in 1935) about an apparently motley group of crooked politicians, murderers, and reporters. At the end they are revealed as actors performing a story.

SHADOW AND SUBSTANCE, a play in four acts by PAUL VINCENT CARROLL, published and produced in 1937. Setting: the Parochial House of Ardmahone, a small town in County Louth, Ireland; 1930's.

The immediate success of this play, written in 1934, established Carroll's reputation as a leading Irish dramatist. The protagonist is Canon Skerritt, a strict scholastic and epicurean of Irish-Spanish ancestry who feels exiled in his parish and despises rural Irish "boobs." He likes only his servant Brigid, a simple Irish soul who loves both him and his enemy, a crusading young intellectual liberal. The play's distinction lies not in the slight plot but rather in the comic portrayal of rural ignorance and bigotry, and in the characterizations, especially that of the Canon and his sardonic treatment of the villagers.

Act I. The Very Reverend Thomas Canon Skerritt's servant Brigid tells the intellectual local schoolmaster, Dermot Francis O'Flingsley, that she has had a vision of the blessed Saint Brigid. She also tries—without success—to make him feel less antagonistic toward the overbearing Canon. The latter is incensed, despite Brigid's attempts to appease him, because his young niece, whom he disclaims as a relation—"a human dumpling who reeks eternally of peppermints"—has come to solict her appointment as schoolteacher. Later, his cruel irony withers his two young curates. Periodically he holds a hand to his ear and remarks, "I didn't quite catch that word," making them look foolish as they repeat some colloquial or athletic expression. And he instructs them in his conviction that "Catholicism rests on a classical, almost abstract, love of God, rather than on the frothy swirl of stirred emotionalism." Brigid begins and then, afraid, refuses to tell the Canon of her vision. He bullies her, but then gently lets her go: "You are the Canon's friend, Brigid. Let it be written of you. Let it be written of both of us."

Act II. The next day, affecting graciousness, he interviews a spinster and her nephew, who seeks a teaching appointment. But the Canon's enjoyment at exposing the fools is short-lived. First Brigid expresses her wish to leave him and become a nun. Then the curates let out their resentment against the tyranny of the Canon by venomously defacing an anonymous book that attacks Irish-Catholic intolerance. They head an indignant delegation of rural Irishmen, but the Canon puts them all in their place and forbids any action against the book. When Brigid at last tells him about her vision of Saint Brigid, the Canon orders her to reject such "tempting illusions," tries to persuade her that she is ill, and urges her to take a rest. Unhappily Brigid submits, but sobs when he leaves—and stretches her arms out to her vision.

Act III. The Canon discovers the offending book's author to be his enemy, the reforming young teacher. He decides to fire O'Flingsley and give his job to the spinster's foolish nephew. Simultaneously he gets rid of his unwanted niece by having her marry the new teacher. Brigid tries to persuade O'Flingsley, summoned to be fired, that the Canon's proud, lacerating exterior covers a truly religious soul. For a moment she watches them together, "to be sure that I loved the two of yous and could serve yous always." But though basically alike, also in recognizing and deploring Ireland's ills, the two cannot overcome their deep personal antagonism. O'Flingsley leaves in triumph when the Canon will not answer

Shadow and Substance. Brigid (Julie Haydon) and Canon Skerritt (Cedric Hardwicke). New York, 1938. (*Culver Pictures*)

him: "You loathe and detest the whole miserable fabric of things here," he tells the Canon, and points at the new teacher: "Why then do you perpetuate it through that poor spineless imbecile there beside you?"

Act IV. While the servant prepares to devote herself to Saint Brigid, the townsfolk learn that O'Flingsley authored the offensive book. When he ridicules the incensed crowds, they attack him. Brigid tries to protect O'Flingsley and is hit by a rock aimed at him. "God of mercy, do not take this, my one consolation, away from me," the Canon remorsefully begs when Brigid is carried in. He implores her to live, now willing himself to accept her vision: "I will bend for you. The Canon will bend. He will stoop. He will—believe. . . ." But she dies, her glowing faith remaining intact. Together, the Canon and O'Flingsley cover the corpse. Huskily the Canon then asks his enemy: "Do not leave me, O'Flingsley. . . . I am alone." But the teacher departs: "We must work this out" individually—their abstract, intractable virtue that cost Brigid her life. The Canon wonders, "Am I just an embittered old man—living here with shades too glorious to forget?" And then, alone, he lowers his head. "I am not well. . . ."

SHADOW OF A GUNMAN, THE, a play in two acts by SEAN O'CASEY, produced in 1923 and published in 1925. Setting: a Dublin tenement room, May 1920.

O'Casey's first produced and first full-length play is this tragicomedy about boasting cowards (like its mock hero, the wise fool Davoren) and unassuming heroes during the Irish-English terror. It is effective and eloquently expressive, though structurally flawed. Originally entitled *On the Run,* its script was accepted immediately. Only the name was changed by the Abbey Theatre, whose bankruptcy was averted by this and O'Casey's popular next play, JUNO AND THE PAYCOCK.

Act I. Amidst various interruptions, Donal Davoren keeps trying to compose a poem. His roommate, Seumas Shields, is a peddler beneath whose primitive superstition and cowardice there is amiable humor. Davoren is amused by Shields's excessive sleeping and dismisses his faith as "simply the state of being afraid that God will torture your soul in the next world as you are afraid the Black and Tans will torture your body in this." The fellow peddler whom Shields is waiting for comes by briefly to tell Shields he will be unable to work with him today, and leaves his peddler's bag. Before going to work himself, Shields is further irritated when the landlord comes for overdue rent. Alone at last, Davoren tries to complete his poem, dramatically sighing all the while: "Ah me, alas! Pain, pain ever, for ever. Like thee, Prometheus, no change, no pause, no hope. Ah, life, life, life!" Soon he is interrupted by a pretty neighbor, Minnie Powell. She romantically envisions the poet as a dangerous patriot, a "gunman on the run." Flattered, Davoren does not deny it. In fact, he boasts about his accomplishments as a terrorist—and an artist. "A pioneer in action as I am a pioneer in thought," he notes, as he embraces her. But their kiss is interrupted by a drunk patriot, and then by other tenement inhabitants, who engage him in a long, farcical scene. Before them, too, Davoren accepts the role of an insurgent Irish Republican Army (I.R.A.) hero. But he is visibly agitated by news of an ambush in which Shields's peddler friend who had come by earlier was killed. When the others leave, he kisses Minnie. "Very pretty, but very ignorant," he then remarks to himself, worrying about his pose: "But Minnie is attracted to the idea, and I am attracted to Minnie. And what danger can there be in being the shadow of a gunman?"

Act II. It is night, and Davoren is still composing his poem and sighing. Shields is sleepy, and indignant about the death of his peddler friend. His bluster—and that of Davoren about the efficacy of "the poet [who] ever strives to save the people"—dies down as he fearfully thinks he hears a tapping on the wall. Yet Shields perceives their situation. He ridicules Davoren's attachment to Minnie, "a Helen of Troy come to live in a tenement" who flatters his ego by thinking him a hero. And he bitterly characterizes the general madness about them. "Instead of counting their beads now they're countin' bullets; their Hail Marys and paternosters are burstin' bombs," he remarks; "petrol is their holy water; their Mass is a burnin' buildin'; their De Profundis is 'The Soldiers' Song,' an' their creed is, I believe in the gun almighty. . . ." Though he is a Nationalist, he stopped his activities when he heard "the gunmen blowin' about dyin' for the people, when it's the people that are dyin' for the gunmen!" He and Davoren proclaim their fearlessness, Shields because of religion and Davoren because of his philosophy. When shots are heard outside, however, both men are terrified. A neighbor worries about her absent husband, a Bible-quoting drunkard who soon returns unharmed. But as the English auxiliaries, the "Black and Tans," approach, Davoren is horrified to discover the contents of the sack Shields's dead peddler friend left earlier that day. Unknown to them, the laconic peddler was a patriot gunman, and the bag contains bombs. Minnie rushes in to tell them that the "Tans" are surrounding the house. Shields and Davoren almost collapse in terror. For love of Davoren, Minnie takes the bag up to her room. While the auxiliaries terrorize the house, the various braggarts display their cowardice. The bag is found, Minnie is dragged off, and still the roommates do nothing: "For God's sake keep quiet or somebody'll hear you," the frightened Shields tells the equally weak but penitent Davoren: "It'll be all right if she only keeps her mouth shut." The auxiliaries leave and the men resume their boasting. Suddenly an explosion is heard, and word is brought that Minnie has been shot. Shields refuses to take any blame: "She did it off her own bat—we didn't ask her to do it." But Davoren knows otherwise. "Ah me, alas! Pain, pain, pain ever, for ever!" he moans, and castigates himself: "Shame is your portion now till the silver cord is loosened and the golden bowl be broken. Oh, Davoren, Donal Davoren, poet and poltroon, poltroon and poet!" Shields maintains solemnly: "I knew something ud come of the tappin' on the wall!"

SHADOW, THE (*Ten*), a fairy tale in three acts by YEVGENI LVOVICH SHVARTS, published and produced in 1940. Setting: a mythical southern European country.

A free adaptation of Hans Christian Andersen's tale of the same title, this stylized fantasy is a brilliant social satire. Its mordant tone and depiction of human evil recall O'Casey's COCK-A-DOODLE DANDY. Nonetheless, and unlike Andersen's story, the play ends happily: the Scholar is resurrected to defeat his shadow after the betrayal. Like THE DRAGON and *The Naked King,* this play too was revived in 1962, amidst the renewed interest in Shvarts's drama; but though successful, it was not permitted to remain in Soviet repertoires.

Act I. A simple and kind visiting scholar is amazed to find apparitions in his room, which was once occupied by Hans Christian Andersen. His innkeeper's daughter, Annunziata, tells the Scholar that this is a land of fairy tales. But "many fairy tales end sadly," she warns him, and begs him to be careful. The Scholar is visited by her father, a quick-tempered man who shoots at people; by a beautiful but squint-eyed singer; and by an ambitious young newspaperman who alludes to the late king's testament. Annunziata later tells the Scholar about this testament, which instructs his daughter, the incognito princess, to marry an educated commoner. Just then a beautiful girl on the adjoining balcony intrigues and distracts the Scholar. Annunziata leaves, and the Scholar and the girl soon fall in love. When she returns to her room, the Scholar sends his shadow after the girl, to tell her he loves her. The Shadow does so, and—bereft of his shadow—the Scholar faints. As the innkeeper and the newspaperman await the doctor, they guess that the girl is the princess. Annunziata realizes the Scholar's danger: "They're not going to forgive him for being such a good man! Something's going to happen!"

Act II. Two weeks later in a park, the ruthless Prime Minister and the evil Minister of Finance—a lame old man carried by valets—furtively agree to eliminate the Scholar: the princess must not marry a naïve foreigner. An assistant—the Scholar's Shadow—comes forth and offers to help. Later, among a group of health resorters, the Scholar appears: he has grown a new shadow and is recuperating. But the doctor, dissatisfied with his progress, wishes he would learn to "look at the world through his fingers, wave his hand in disgust at everything, and possess the art of shrugging his shoulders." The Scholar, however, is preoccupied with marrying the princess, abdicating the throne, and setting a good example to people. The singer, beloved by the finance minister, warns the Scholar of danger. She tries to save him. When the minister is brought in, he proposes to her while he has his valets prop him in various poses ("extreme amazement," "extreme indignation," etc.) and finally bullies her into being his and helping to defeat the Scholar. In the meantime the Shadow, assisted by the ambitious young newspaperman and the innkeeper, plots for power and the Scholar's downfall. The Shadow worms his way into the Scholar's confidence, tricks him into signing a renunciation of the princess, and—helped by the singer, who admits she does not want to be "a virtuous, sentimental, middle-class girl"—wins the princess's love. Scheduled to marry her and become king, he quickly takes over, wins the toadying counselors' fealty, and tells the unhappy Scholar to write a surrender letter. Only Annunziata, who loves him, remains on the Scholar's side. "Maybe you'll wave your hand in disgust at all this?" she says, but adds, "I'll help you. I'm a very reliable girl, sir." The Scholar sighs, "Annunziata, what a sad fairy tale!"

Act III. The Shadow is king, and the innkeeper, now a high official, bullies the people. The newspaperman, also rewarded with a high post, helps defeat the Scholar. Annunziata is grief-stricken by the Scholar's imprisonment, and the singer, now the minister's bride, suffers from the unpleasantness. When the Scholar appears, the Shadow appoints him to a high rank, "my shadow." The Scholar, however, denounces the king as an imposter—as his shadow. Except for Annunziata, no one will support the Scholar or testify for him. He starts reciting a magic formula, and the Shadow begins to falter. But even the doctor, who is sympathetic to the Scholar, dares not help him. The Scholar thereupon is executed. At that moment the king's head, too, flies off, thus unmasking him as the Scholar's shadow. But because the Scholar is "a good man," he is magically resurrected. The princess now begs him to marry her, but the Scholar rejects her, the fawning courtiers, and corrupt society. He takes Annunziata's hand and goes off with his newfound, true love.

SHAFFER, Peter [Levin] (1926–), English dramatist, worked in New York for some years but was born in Liverpool and raised in London. He attended St. Paul's School and Cambridge University, and began writing plays when he completed his degree. His first play, *The Saltland,* deals with the Israeli civil war and appeared on television in 1955. After other, unimportant television dramas, Shaffer made his reputation with FIVE FINGER EXERCISE (1958). Soon considered an important new playwright, Shaffer repeated his success with *The Royal Hunt of the Sun* (1964), an elaborate spectacle about Pizarro's sixteenth-century conquest of the empire of Atahuallpa, the Inca of Peru.

The first of his double bill of one-acters, *The Private Ear* and *The Public Eye* (1962), depicts a sensitive clerk who entertains a young lady he idolizes, and then comes to see her for the ordinary girl she is; the second portrays an unusual detective, who reconciles an accountant with his unjustly suspected young wife. Perhaps even more popular was Shaffer's next double bill of two long one-acters, *Black Comedy* (1966), a farce, and *White Lies* (1967), a three-character play (produced in England as *White Liars*) whose style and themes echo those of *Five Finger Exercise*. His next play, *The Battle of the Shrivings* (1970), is a domestic melodrama that features a prominent, idealistic philosopher's struggle with his satanic former pupil, a famous poet.

Shaffer has also written literary criticism and detective novels, the first of which was published when he was twenty-one.

SHAIRP, [Alexander] **Mordaunt** (1887–1939), English teacher and writer, was born in Totnes, Devon. He wrote a number of plays, the most successful being THE GREEN BAY TREE (1933). A university lecturer at Oxford (where he received his own education) and London, Shairp wrote a few other plays: *The Offence* (1925), *The Phoby* (1929, a one-acter), and *The Crime at Blossoms* (1932). He also edited and wrote an introduction to the two-volume *Modern Plays in One Act* (1929, 1935).

SHAKES VERSUS SHAV, a one-act puppet play by BERNARD SHAW, produced in 1949 and published in 1950. Setting: a puppet stage.

This amusing ten-minute blank-verse puppet play was commissioned for the Malvern Festival. It is the last play completed for production by Shaw, then ninety-three years old. He dealt with two topics that had intrigued him all his life, puppetry and Shakespeare, which he discussed in his preface to the published play.

Shakes[peare] and Shav[ius] argue their respective merits and spar, knocking each other down. When Shakes asks, "Couldst write Macbeth?" Shav replies, "No need. He has been bettered / By Walter Scott's Rob Roy"—whereupon these two heroes enter and stage a battle that culminates in Rob Roy's cutting off Macbeth's head. Shav matches his HEARTBREAK HOUSE (from which appears a tableau of Captain Shotover and Ellie Dunn) against Shakes's *King Lear*. "We both are mortal. For a moment suffer / My glimmering light to shine," Shav pleads as a light appears between him and Shakes. But Shakes snuffs it out: "Out, out, brief candle!"

SHAW, [George] **Bernard** (1856–1950), Anglo-Irish dramatist and critic. The greatest playwright in the English-speaking world since Shakespeare, GBS (as he is often called) was born in Dublin of cultivated Protestant parents who had great social pretensions but little money. His father, a pensioned civil servant turned unsuccessful merchant, took to drink. His mother, from whom he received an excellent background in music, became a singing teacher, and eventually moved to London.

Though he was sent to the best theatrical and musical performances, Shaw had little formal schooling and gave that little up when he went to work at fifteen. He joined his mother in London in 1876 and by 1883 had written five novels, none of which he could get published. But he did manage considerably to extend his self-education at the British Museum, at debates, and at lectures, at one of which he was greatly impressed by Henry George. He read Marx, became a socialist, and in 1884 joined the newly founded Fabian Society, which included his friends Beatrice and Sidney Webb and H. G. Wells. His Fabian enthusiasms—reflected in his dramatic and non-dramatic writings to the end of his life (most explicitly in *The Intelligent Woman's Guide to Socialism and Capitalism,* 1928)—led him to overcome a congenital shyness and to develop into an effective reformer and socialist soapbox orator at street corners and in lecture halls.

By the 1880's he was writing extensively in various fields—Fabian tracts, book reviews for *The Pall Mall Gazette* (1885–88), and art criticisms for *The World* (1886–89)—but he first attracted general attention as the pseudonymous Corno di Bassetto, writing music criticisms for *The Star* (1888–90), and later *The World* (1890–94). Even more important, however, were his dramatic criticisms for *The Saturday Review* (1895–98), subsequently reprinted as OUR THEATRES IN THE NINETIES (1932). In these reviews and in his championing of HENRIK IBSEN, particularly in THE QUINTESSENCE OF IBSENISM (1891), Shaw called for a new drama that would reflect modern problems and outlooks as Shakespeare's drama had reflected those of the Elizabethan age. His notorious attacks on Shakespeare, whose plays he knew thoroughly and admired deeply, began as attacks on the "bardolatry" that had made Shakespeare a critically sacrosanct classical model for a stale and unviable contemporary drama. With the characteristic extravagance that almost always gained him a hearing, he announced his own vast superiority to Shakespeare, and, beginning with WIDOWERS' HOUSES (1892), he proceeded to write the kind of plays he felt were needed. Shaw wanted to reach and affect the minds of men, and he used the theatre as a vehicle of instruction. But audiences came back for more because he sugared his didactic pills with coats of extremely amusing—and refreshingly shocking—comedy.

In order to propagate his ideas further—and to increase his royalties—Shaw also geared his dramas for audiences who ordinarily do not buy and read plays. Instead of the conventionally terse and technical stage directions, he wrote substantial descriptive passages for his plays' publication in book form, thus creating the impression that they were much like the novels that people ordinarily liked to buy and read. It was his new play-*reading* public that stimulated Shaw's famous prefaces—those brilliant polemical essays, written in his clear and incisive style, that explicated plays such as SAINT JOAN (1923), elaborated upon the theme of plays such as ANDROCLES AND THE LION (1913), or simply picked up and developed a minor subject mentioned in plays such as MISALLIANCE (1910). These prefaces, like the plays that accompany them, dealt with a great variety of topics: sex, theology, sociology, politics, history, economics, biology, medicine, literature, etc. Often as important (and almost as long) as the plays themselves, they helped to gain Shaw a wider audience than any reached by previous playwrights. The work and proselyting of his foremost translator, SIEGFRIED TREBITSCH, soon made this audience international. Shaw's plays, attacking the vested interests of the Establishment and dealing in unconventional ways with topics hitherto shunned in theatres, often ran into censorship troubles—which further increased his fame and fortune, and which he exploited in some of the prefaces, particularly those of MRS. WARREN'S PROFESSION (1898) and the SHEWING-UP OF BLANCO POSNET (1909).

The plays that so often scandalized the public are characterized by an almost never-flagging vitality and humor, by extensive seriocomic discussions, and by a titillating inversion of romantic audience expectations: villains (slum landlords, brothelkeepers) turn out to be not at all villainous, and (military) heroes turn out to be very unheroic; in courtship, it is the women who do the hunting and the men who try in vain to elude them. Adhering to his firm and lifelong belief that the sole function of art is didactic, Shaw created plots and characters that made his plays, especially the early PLAYS UNPLEASANT (1898), propaganda vehicles for the reform of particular social evils. He urged the adoption of scientific attitudes (education and Fabian Socialism) to deal with the problems of society, but at the same time he ridiculed and attacked people's gullible and unquestioning worship of science, as he attacked religious "Crosstianity" and literary "bardolatry."

He espoused vegetarianism, orthographic reforms, more equitable distribution of wealth, and other causes, but the basic and most important of his beliefs was in something variously known as Creative Evolution, the Life Force, or the *élan vital.* It appears in many forms (including women's predatory reproductive instincts, dramatized particularly in MAN AND SUPERMAN, 1903), and its chief tenet is man's willful though perhaps unconscious evolution to a higher being—a Superman—in whom the mind becomes the dominant organ. Most Shavian heroes embody this characteristic Life Force and reach one of the rungs that lead to the ultimate ideal, which is dramatized in the "Don Juan in Hell" episode in *Man and Superman* and in the last part of BACK TO METHUSELAH (1921). Most Shavian heroes (Joan of Arc, Caesar, Higgins, Shotover, etc.), in short, are Shavian supermen to a greater or lesser degree. In his old age, it was this belief in the superman, coupled with Shaw's growing impatience with "sham democracy," that led to his pseudochampioning of dictatorships in such later plays as ON THE ROCKS (1933) and GENEVA (1938).

Shaw gained a sort of notoriety for the fearless expression of his caustic and highly unorthodox views, especially during the two world wars, when his attitudes appeared particularly unconventional and unpalatable. But neither disapproval nor laughter at the clownish attitudes he so often assumed—though he himself persistently emphasized that "the real joke is that I am in earnest"—precluded the public's general awareness and appreciation of his brilliance, wit, and dramatic genius, which received official recognition with the award of the Nobel Prize in 1925. Despite criticisms that they contained too much Shavian talk and propaganda, Shaw's plays have remained popular on the boards—and later as musical comedies and as films. No other plays of his age could stand and pass the test of the many and continuous worldwide "revivals" of Shaw's plays, which even in his lifetime had already attained the status of "classics" that he himself often deprecated.

In 1898 he married Charlotte Payne-Townshend, whom he outlived by some seven years. Their marriage survived his amorous and tempestuous relationships with women such as Mrs. Patrick Campbell and Ellen Terry, for whom he wrote some of his plays. These two relationships, mostly epistolary and subsequently published, provide a fascinating picture of the writers no less than of the theatre of the time.* Another valuable record of Shaw's practical and intimate involvement with the theatre is his published correspondence with the actor-director-critic HARLEY GRANVILLE-BARKER.

Shaw wrote for seventy-five years and covered almost all areas of human endeavour. His collected works run to well over thirty sizable volumes.

* Jerome Kilty (1922–   ) dramatized Shaw's correspondence with Mrs. Campbell as *Dear Liar* (1960).

Bernard Shaw at eighty-seven. (© Karsh of Ottawa. *Rapho Guillumette*)

Almost sixty of his plays appear in the American six-volume edition of the *Complete Plays with Prefaces* (1962), but these include some very minor works, such as those collected in PLAYLETS OF THE WAR (1915–18) and in TRANSLATIONS AND TOMFOOLERIES (1926). Other works of his were staged, including CHRISTOPHER ISHERWOOD'S 1969 dramatization of Shaw's satiric *The Adventures of the Black Girl in Her Search for God* (1933). Apart from the collections and plays already mentioned, the following others are particularly important: PLAYS PLEASANT (1898, consisting of ARMS AND THE MAN [1894], CANDIDA [1898], THE MAN OF DESTINY [1897], and YOU NEVER CAN TELL [1898]), THE DEVIL'S DISCIPLE (1897), CAESAR AND CLEOPATRA (1899), MAJOR BARBARA (1904), THE DOCTOR'S DILEMMA (1906), PYGMALION (1913), and HEARTBREAK HOUSE (1919).

The following dramatic works are now generally less well known: CAPTAIN BRASSBOUND'S CONVERSION (1899), JOHN BULL'S OTHER ISLAND (1904), HOW HE LIED TO HER HUSBAND (1904), GETTING MARRIED (1908), THE DARK LADY OF THE SONNETS (1910), FANNY'S FIRST PLAY (1911, Shaw's first popular success), OVERRULED (1912), GREAT CATHERINE (1913), THE APPLE CART (1929), TOO TRUE TO BE GOOD (1932), THE SIX OF CALAIS (1934), THE SIMPLETON OF THE UNEXPECTED ISLES (1935), THE MILLIONAIRESS (1936), CYMBELINE REFINISHED (1937), "IN GOOD KING CHARLES'S GOLDEN DAYS" (1939), BUOYANT BILLIONS (1948), SHAKES VERSUS SHAV (1949), and FARFETCHED FABLES (1950).

Finally, these minor dramatic works are of interest, if only because of Shaw's towering stature in the modern theatre: *The Gadfly; or, The Son of the Cardinal* (1898), a comedy adapted for stage production from Ethel Voynich's novel; two slight comic sketches, *The Interlude at the Playhouse* (1907) and *Beauty's Duty* (1913); *Village Wooing* (1934), a two-character "comediettina" in three parts that traces a female's successful snaring of her prey, a Shavian author; the political sketches *Arthur and Acetone* (1917), in which Arthur Balfour and Dr. Chaim Weizmann discuss a deal involving independence for Palestine in return for Weizmann's scientific discoveries, and *The British Party System* (1944), a dramatization from Shaw's *Everybody's Political What's What* (1944), which demonstrates the "history" of the party system with fictitious conversations among noted seventeenth- and eighteenth-century figures. Shaw's last play, written shortly before his death, was *Why She Would Not,* "a little comedy" published in 1956 that depicts a typically "vital" hero who is rejected by an heiress for much the same reason that Eliza rejects Higgins in *Pygmalion.*

Notable among the numerous collections are the standard thirty-six volume *The Works of Bernard Shaw* (1930–50); the 1965 reprint of the one-volume *The Complete Plays of Bernard Shaw* (last reissued in 1950 with fifty-one plays and a prefatory "Warning from the Author") and of the companion one-volume *Prefaces by Bernard Shaw* (1938); the six-volume American edition of *Bernard Shaw: Complete Plays with Prefaces* (1962); and *The Bodley Head Bernard Shaw: Collected Plays, With Their Prefaces,* whose first volume appeared in 1970: under the editorial supervision of Dan H. Laurence, this probably "definitive edition" when completed will include all the fugitive playlets and "dialogues," character and subject indexes, and data on each play's composition, production, and publication. Laurence is the editor, too, of Shaw's *Collected Letters,* whose first volume was published in 1965.

Of the many books written on Shaw, particular notice should be taken of G. K. Chesterton's classic *George Bernard Shaw* (1909); ST. JOHN ERVINE'S tendentious *Bernard Shaw: His Life, Work and Friends* (1956); Raymond Mander and Joe Mitchenson's *Theatrical Companion to Shaw* (1955), "A Pictorial Record of the First Performances of the Plays of G.B.S. with Synopses, Casts and Detailed Notes" (dust jacket) profusely illustrated and containing a wealth of production, publication, and other factual data; Archibald Henderson's massive standard biography, *George Bernard Shaw: Man of the Century* (1956); Eric Bentley's critical study, *Bernard Shaw* (updated edition, 1967); Martin Meisel's study of the contemporary context's relation to Shavian dramaturgy, *Shaw and the Nineteenth-Century Theater* (1963); and E. D. Bevan's *Concordance to the Plays and Prefaces of Bernard Shaw* (1971). Current bibliographies are the *Shaw Review*'s annual "A Continuing Checklist of Shaviana."

SHAW, Irwin (1913–), American short-story writer, novelist, and playwright. His best-remembered drama is his first produced work, the one-act BURY THE DEAD (1936), though the run of his melodramatic comedy, THE GENTLE PEOPLE (1939), featuring movie stars, enjoyed a greater popular success. Ironically the two plays propound opposing viewpoints: pacifism, and the need to confront the Fascist menace with force. But both plays express Shaw's idealism, his faith in individual decency in a generally hostile world, and his American-Jewish urban roots.

Born in New York City, Shaw attended Brooklyn College. He graduated in 1934 after overcoming a failure in calculus that forced him temporarily to give up his studies for various odd jobs. After finishing his degree he became a radio scriptwriter, described as a depressing occupation in his story "Main Currents of American Thought" (1939). Shaw wrote other but unsuccessful plays, and then went to Hollywood, where he worked on screenplays. At the conclusion of World War II, in which he served as a soldier, he became drama critic for the *New Republic* and wrote and adapted more plays. These include *Sons and Soldiers* (1944), a philosophical-psychological study of maternity and war; *The Assassin* (1945), on Admiral Darlan's murder in Algiers; and *A Choice of Wars* (1967), a pacifist curtain raiser. He reached considerably more fame with a World War II novel, *The Young Lions* (1948); his 1956 novel *Lucy Crown* was made into a play (under the same title) by Jean-Pierre Aumont (1911–).

Shaw's fiction collections include *Sailor Off the Bremen* (1939) and *Mixed Company* (1950), which contains stories from earlier collections.

SHELDON, Edward [Brewster] (1886–1946), American playwright, achieved great popularity early in life with SALVATION NELL (1908)—his first production, written while he was still attending George Pierce Baker's 47 Workshop—THE NIGGER (1909), THE BOSS (1911), ROMANCE (1913), and other plays. Since Sheldon's writing demonstrated an amazing knowledge and understanding of life for so young a man, much was expected of him. Yet he did not finally develop into a great playwright. In 1923 Sheldon was crippled by a progressive paralysis that soon blinded him. But though he remained totally bedridden for the rest of his life, Sheldon continued to exert considerable influence on the New York theatre. He became an almost legendary focus of noted theatre and literary figures. They flocked to his bedside to consult him, attracted by Sheldon's tremendous charm, intelligence, and sympathy.

Born in Chicago, Sheldon graduated from Harvard University in 1907. Immediately successful with his first play, Sheldon went on to produce hit after hit. While his plays have dated considerably over the years and would strike present-day audiences as sentimental and melodramatic, Sheldon helped bring seriousness and social insight to the theatre of the early twentieth century. He also displayed in his drama the qualities that later attracted his many friends: sympathy for human aspirations, of the lowly as well as the great.

Other Sheldon plays include such romances as *The Princess Zim-Zim* (1911), whose title protagonist is a Coney Island snake charmer in love with a millionaire; *The High Road* (1912), a character study of a farm drudge who marries a governor about to be elected President of the United States; *The Garden of Paradise* (1914), a dramatization of Hans Christian Andersen's story "The Little Mermaid"; *The Song of Songs* (1914), a dramatization of *Das hohe Lied*, a novel by HERMANN SUDERMANN; *The Jest* (1919), an adaptation of SEM BENELLI's blank-verse melodrama; *Bewitched* (1924), a postwar romance set in France, written with SIDNEY HOWARD; *Lulu Belle* (1926), a sordid melodrama about a Negro prostitute's degeneration, written with CHARLES MACARTHUR—whose brother had married Sheldon's sister; and three plays written with Margaret Ayer Barnes (1886–1967): a dramatization Sheldon suggested (and helped complete) of Edith Wharton's *The Age of Innocence* (1928), the comedy *Jenny* (1929), and *Dishonored Lady* (1930), a gory crime drama based on a nineteenth-century murder case. There were many further, unacknowledged collaborations in as well as play doctoring on the work of others, who visited Sheldon's sickroom in the decades that followed.

An extensive account of this man's unique and rich life is Eric Wollencott Barnes's *The Man Who Lived Twice: the Biography of Edward Sheldon* (1956).

SHEPPEY, a play in three acts by SOMERSET MAUGHAM, published and produced in 1933. Setting: contemporary England.

Maugham aptly labeled *Sheppey* a "sardonic comedy." It was his last play: audiences' puzzlement about the fantasy in the third act convinced him that he had lost touch with the public. It is a powerful play, biting yet amusing in its comedy, relentless in its indictment of conventional everyday Christianity, and moving in the morality at the end. Maugham's biographer (Richard A. Cordell) considered it possibly his "most underrated" play, and SEAN O'CASEY called it a masterpiece.

Act I. Sheppey (Joseph Miller) is a jovial, middle-aged barber nicknamed after his birthplace and favorite locale, the Isle of Sheppey. Popular but "a bit of a character," Sheppey amazes his colleagues with his ability to sell hair lotion to customers. As he works away cheerfully, he remarks on his natural luck. Recently he had witnessed a pauper's trial and imprisonment for theft, and the experience had shaken him. He deplores the hardships of the poor, but the others in the shop express different views. The poor have only themselves to blame and in this life, the manicurist remarks, it is "everyone for himself." Just then comes word that Sheppey has won a sizable lottery prize. Imperturbably he continues his tasks, refusing to speak to his wife on the telephone during working hours even on this important occasion: "When I'm at 'ome I'm at 'er beck and call, within reason, you know, but when I'm at the shop I'm me own master, as far as she's concerned." A reporter comes to interview him and then, when the day's work is done, Sheppey gets champagne for them all to celebrate his luck. He returns with the bottle and, to the consternation of the others, with a seedy streetwalker he has befriended. After a little celebrating Sheppey gets very ill. The streetwalker helps him get home in a taxi.

Act II. It is a week later, at Sheppey's home. His daughter, Florrie, madly in love with a conceited young schoolteacher, is looking forward to a honeymoon on Sheppey's lottery winnings. So is her ambitious fiancé, Ernie (Ernest) Turner. "With my brains and your beauty we can do anything," he tells Florrie and explains that a trip is an investment "to train ourselves so that when the opportunity comes we shall be ready to take it." The proprietor of Sheppey's barbershop offers him a full partnership. This is something Sheppey has long wished for, but to the bewilderment of his family he turns it down: he is going to follow the Gospels and give his money to the poor. Ernie joins Florrie in trying to dissuade Sheppey, but he remains adamant. Increasingly miffed by the humiliating thought of marrying the daughter of a mad laborer ("If I have a father-in-law who lives like Jesus of course I shall look a fool"), Ernie argues that a mere barber isn't one to set examples to others. "Why not?" Sheppey asks: "Jesus was only a carpenter, wasn't he?" Florrie is shocked: "Who ever heard of anyone wanting to live like Jesus at this time of day? I think it's just blasphemous." When Sheppey brings the streetwalker and a thief home to shelter them, his distressed family call a doctor. He, too, suspects that Sheppey is losing his mind, Florrie sobs ("What a humiliation for people in our position!"), and Sheppey's kindly wife deplores the fact that winning the lottery did not bring them peace and happiness.

Act III. Distraught at losing Ernie, Florrie can confide even in the streetwalker: "After the first shock, I mean you being an immoral woman and me being virtuous, I can't see you're any different from anybody else." When her mother tells her that Sheppey's sanity is being examined by a specialist, Florrie, anxious to save the money, keeps praying, "O God, make them say he's potty." But Sheppey's wife is moved by her husband's goodness and is determined to support him if he is judged sane. Ernie is sure that that is impossible: "Sanity means doing what everybody else does, and thinking what everybody else thinks. That's the whole foundation of democracy." The streetwalker and the thief sheltered by Sheppey begin to yearn for their old life, and leave. Sheppey is adjudged insane. "A sane man is not going to give all his money away to the poor," the doctor remarks: "A sane man takes money from the poor." And he agrees with a colleague's diagnosis "that philanthropy in general could always be ascribed to repressed homosexuality." Mrs. Miller admits being puzzled by Sheppey: "It seems so funny for a good man to become religious." Not knowing that he will be certified and committed, Sheppey turns down the doctor's suggestion that he go to a sanatorium for a rest; instead, he sells the doctor a bottle of hair restorer. But he feels very tired, and when his wife goes out to get him some kippers, he takes a nap. In his imagination the streetwalker appears. She soon is transformed into the figure of Death, and gently takes Sheppey out. When his family return, they find Sheppey dead in his chair. His wife looks at him, relieved he has been spared being committed as a lunatic: "He always said 'e was born lucky. He's died lucky too."

SHERRIFF, R[obert] C[edrick] (1896–   ), English dramatist, wrote his country's most popular antiwar play, as well as other drama and a number of novels. Born in Surrey, he was educated at Oxford and had barely started his career in an insurance company when World War I broke out. He rose to a captaincy at the age of twenty-one, like his famous hero Stanhope. Then he returned to the insurance business. For a number of years he wrote plays—*Profit and Loss* (1923), *Mr. Bridie's Finger* (1926), and others—for amateur productions. Asked for a drama with an all-male cast, he re-created and reevoked the horror of his wartime experiences in JOURNEY'S END (1928).

When MAURICE BROWNE produced it professionally after the London Stage Society's solitary performance, Sherriff immediately became famous and wealthy. It was played throughout the world and translated into most European languages. But though Sherriff continued to write drama in subsequent decades, he never equaled his first success. His other plays include a village comedy, *Badger's Green* (1930); *Windfall* (1933); *St. Helena* (1935; written with Jeanne de Casalis, 1897–1966), a deglamorized depiction of Napoleon in his final years; *Miss Mabel* (1948); *Home at Seven* (1950), the portrayal of an amnesiac; *The White Carnation* (1953); *The Long Sunset* (1955); *The Telescope* (1957); and *A Shred of Evidence* (1960). While some of these had renowned productions, none was a hit. Among his subsequent successes were a novel, *The Fortnight in September* (1931), and a number of screenplays—notably those of James Hilton's novel *Goodbye, Mr. Chips* (1936), F. L. Green's novel *Odd Man Out* (1945), and SOMERSET MAUGHAM'S tales *Quartet* (1948) and *Trio* (1950). Sheriff also wrote an autobiography, *No Leading Lady* (1968).

SHERWOOD, Robert E[mmet] (1896–1955), American writer, was most famous for his fifteen dramas—particularly for IDIOT'S DELIGHT (1936), ABE LINCOLN IN ILLINOIS (1938), and THERE SHALL BE NO NIGHT (1940)—and for his important study of *Roosevelt and Hopkins* (1948). Each of these works won Sherwood a Pulitzer Prize, and his political, social, and professional activities gained him further distinction. Sherwood also wrote some thirty film scripts, including not only those for his own plays—most of which were screened—but also such hits as *The Scarlet Pimpernel* (1935), *The Ghost Goes West* (1936), the dramatization of Daphne du Maurier's *Rebecca* (1940), and the award-winning *The Best Years of Our Lives* (1946). As a dramatist, his reputation rests on the above-noted plays and other hits such as THE ROAD TO ROME (1927), REUNION IN VIENNA (1931), and THE PETRIFIED FOREST (1934). The first was influenced by BERNARD SHAW, the second by FERENC MOLNÁR, and the third by the whole school of Western melodrama. Nonetheless they all have Sherwood's characteristic stamp and they demonstrate his versatility as a playwright. Sherwood excelled in comedy and history drama, but was equally at home with satire, low comedy, romance, sentiment, melodrama, and tragedy. His plays, however melodramatic or comic, are ideological and hortatory: early ones preach pacifism, later ones warfare against evils that have menaced democracy—slavery in Lincoln's time, and Fascist world domination in the 1930's and 1940's. Yet the best of Sherwood's plays retain their vitality, although the immediate issues have been resolved.

Born in New Rochelle, New York, Sherwood at the age of two was moved to Manhattan, where he soon was to indulge his love for the theatre. He came by his talents naturally. His mother was a painter and illustrator as well as a housewife. His father, from whom Sherwood inherited both his great height (six feet seven inches) and his penchant for satire, was a successful broker who, as a Harvard student, had founded *The Lampoon*, which Sherwood, too, edited during his college days. He took young Sherwood to the theatre when he was yet in kindergarten, and both parents encouraged his juvenile writings. At Harvard, which Sherwood entered in 1914, he was not only magazine editor and contributor but also a playwright: his *A White Elephant* was produced by the university's Hasty Pudding Club in 1916, and *Barnum Was Right,* whose production had been canceled because of America's entry into the war, was produced there in 1919.

Sherwood's academic achievements were less notable, and he left Harvard in 1917 to enter the war (he was awarded his B.A. in 1918). Rejected for American military service because of his height, Sherwood joined the Canadian Black Watch Regiment. His fervent pacifism dated from the war, during which he was gassed and wounded. He was afflicted for life with a recurrent facial neuritis that was so excruciating that it made the otherwise witty and warm Sherwood appear dour. Upon his release from the hospital, Sherwood became a movie critic for *Vanity Fair,* a position he soon resigned to protest Dorothy Parker's dismissal. In 1920 Sherwood joined the old *Life,* where he distinguished himself until 1928 with his penetrating film reviews. By 1922 he had completed his first drama intended for professional production, *The Dawn Man;* he quickly discarded it as "dreadful" and gave up playwriting. But a few years later he was inspired to try again when he witnessed the success of Anderson and Stallings's WHAT PRICE GLORY? The success of his history-debunking antiwar comedy about his schoolboy hero, Hannibal (*The Road to Rome*), enabled him thereafter to devote full time to the drama.

The plays that immediately followed were, by and large, undistinguished. *The Love Nest* (1927), Sherwood's dramatization of Ring Lardner's story about the alcoholic wife of a movie magnate, had the shortest of runs. *The Queen's Husband* (1928) was somewhat more successful, particularly on the road and in England and Canada, and it was filmed as *The Royal Bed* (1931); set in "a mythical and anonymous kingdom . . . in the North Sea," it is a romance of intrigue and melodrama about a henpecked king who finally asserts himself. Sherwood made little headway in 1930 with *Waterloo Bridge,* a sentimental duologue between a naïve Canadian soldier and a London streetwalker who fall in love; and with *This Is New York,* a comedy whose melodramatic plot deals with the suicide of a bootlegger's mistress and whose cast includes a pompous western Senator who hates New York, his D.A.R. wife, and their unconforming daughter. *Marching As to War,* a frequently revised play about the Crusaders, was announced in succeeding seasons until 1930, but ultimately remained unproduced.

With his next plays Sherwood justified his earlier promise and consolidated his position as a leading dramatist of his age. Following in quick order during the years 1931 to 1940 were the aforementioned *Reunion in Vienna, The Petrified Forest, Idiot's Delight, Abe Lincoln in Illinois,* and *There Shall be No Night.* They appeared with great stars of the stage and screen (notably Alfred Lunt and Lynn Fontanne, who played many leading Sherwood parts), and were invariably filmed. Another success was Sherwood's 1935 adaptation of JACQUES DEVAL's comedy *Tovaritch.* A SUCCÈS D'ESTIME with which Sherwood was long preoccupied, *Acropolis* (1933), opened in London, was repeatedly and unsuccessfully reworked, and finally remained unproduced in New York; it is an antiwar play in which appear Socrates, Cleon, Phidias, Anaxagoras, and Aspasia, the beloved hetaera of Phidias and subsequently Pericles's wife. Though Sherwood did other distinguished work thereafter, his last plays were failures. *The Rugged Path* (1945) features a perplexed postwar idealist who chooses the "rugged path" of battle (the quotation is from the Keats poem cited in the first scene of *Abe Lincoln in Illinois*) to ensure a better world; even its popular star (Spencer Tracy) could not rescue the play. *Miss Liberty* (1949), a musical, was a collaboration with MOSS HART and Irving Berlin. That same year Sherwood also did the final "carpentry" on the play *Second Threshold* (1951) of his recently deceased friend PHILIP BARRY. Sherwood's last play, the posthumous *Small War on Murray Hill* (1957), is a pale echo of his first hit; the setting is New York during the War of Independence, and the warrior seduced from battle is General Sir William Howe.

Sherwood's principal attributes as a dramatist were—apart from his talents in creating plot, characters, and dialogue—his wit and earnestness. The published versions of his plays—like those of Shaw—are accompanied by comprehensive essays to elucidate the playwright's didactic intentions, which were overlooked by audiences who relished the entertainment but ignored the message. Like his friend Barry, Sherwood was torn between writing comedy and serious drama—although he was considerably more successful than Barry in his serious efforts. The antiwar plays (mostly comedies) are more impervious to the ravages of time than those that espoused the justification of war, and *There Shall Be No Night* is the most dated of his important plays. Between it and *The Petrified Forest* came his best dramas, *Idiot's Delight* and *Abe Lincoln in Illinois;* both were written when Sherwood was least certain of his ideological commitment, between the time of his intransigent pacifism and his zealous support of the embattled enemies of Communist Russia and Nazi Germany. Some of Sherwood's plays are trivial and others are equally unlikely to survive for long. But these two works stand at the head of those that exemplify his genuine artistry—his wit, his capacity to entertain and move and simultaneously depict, in particular situations and characters, truths that are universal and timeless.

Sherwood's first marriage, to an actress who must have provided Sherwood with something of a model for his Mary Todd Lincoln, ended ignominiously; subsequently he married the divorced wife of MARC CONNELLY, a union that proved happy and lasting. In 1937 Sherwood became president of the Dramatists' Guild and a founding member of the Playwrights' Producing Company;

in 1940 he was elected president of the American National Theatre and Academy (ANTA). His admiration and support of President Roosevelt eventually led to Sherwood's appointment as a special assistant to the Secretaries of War (1940) and the Navy (1945), as director of the Overseas Branch of the Office of War Information (1942), and to the inner council of the President, some of whose most notable speeches he helped to write. It was this association that sparked Sherwood's interest and qualified him for writing what his biographer once called his greatest drama, the "intimate history" of *Roosevelt and Hopkins*.

John Mason Brown did not live to finish the concluding volume of his definitive biography and comprehensive study of Sherwood's work, *The Worlds of Robert E. Sherwood: Mirror to His Times 1896–1939* (1965), which appeared posthumously as *The Ordeal of a Playwright: Robert E. Sherwood and the Challenge of War* (1970). More modest are R. Baird Shuman's *Robert E. Sherwood* (1964), which focuses on individual plays; and Walter J. Meserve's introduction to the man and his writings, *Robert E. Sherwood: Reluctant Moralist* (1970).

SHEWING-UP OF BLANCO POSNET, THE, "A Sermon in Crude Melodrama" in one act by BERNARD SHAW, produced in 1909 and published in 1911. Setting: "a territory of the United States of America," probably in the nineteenth century.

"This religious tract in dramatic form," in many ways reminiscent of THE DEVIL'S DISCIPLE, was banned, and Shaw wrote a long preface for it on censorship; he dealt specifically and entertainingly with the 1909 Parliament hearings on the subject, published in a Blue Book (and containing the testimony of Shaw and many other eminent men), of which he gave a summary. The play was first produced by LADY GREGORY and WILLIAM BUTLER YEATS at Dublin's Abbey Theatre.

The badman Blanco Posnet is brought into a small-town courthouse, accused of having stolen the sheriff's horse from Elder Daniels that morning. The hypocritical Elder turns out to be Blanco's brother, who has turned from drinking to selling liquor, because "what keeps America today the purest of the nations is that when she's not working she's too drunk to hear the voice of the tempter." Blanco angers the hostile townspeople, who are ready to hang him, with his stinging contempt, but insists that, since he was not caught with the horse, a witness must be found. The town prostitute, Feemy Evans, is about to swear that she saw him on the horse, when a woman comes in and reveals that a man gave her the horse so that she could get her dying child to a doctor. To save Blanco from hanging she refuses to identify him, but Feemy finds she now cannot testify against Blanco, and the sheriff, also softened, releases him. Blanco preaches a sermon (which caused the play's censorship) on God's perhaps silly but "greater game" having defeated their sensible but "rotten game" of a bad life. However, he has lost his "rotten feel," and invites everybody for a drink.

SHIELS, George (1886–1949), Irish dramatist, was (with SEAN O'CASEY and BRINSLEY MACNAMARA) one of the "new pillars who supported the [Abbey] Theatre" between 1918 and 1924, according to the account of LENNOX ROBINSON. He also refers to Shiels as "the Thomas Moore of the Irish Theatre," because of his poetic dialogue. Beginning with a one-act farce, *Bedmates* (1921), Shiels wrote about two dozen plays, some of which have been repeatedly revived. Originally farcical or warmhearted, they became increasingly more thoughtful and wry —and masterful.

Shiels was born and educated in Ballymoney, County Antrim (Northern Ireland). He spent some of his youth in Canada, where he was involved in a railway accident that crippled him for life. Returning to Ireland, he remained confined in his country home and began to write, first articles and short stories, and then the plays that made him famous.

Notable among these are *Paul Twyning* (1922), his first real success; *Professor Tim* (1925), one of the most popular plays in Ireland, portraying the return of a hero from America and his unmasking before his relatives as a drunken failure; *The New Gossoon* (1930), a much-praised comedy that features a radical youth (the "gossoon") tempered by a girl who embodies his ideals as well as the wisdom of his ineffectual elders, against whom he rebels; *Passing Day* (1936), one of Shiels's few tragedies, which has been revived often; *The Rugged Path* (1940), a drama of anarchy, law enforcement, and informing that became the Abbey's first long run (twelve weeks); and *The Summit* (1941), *The Rugged Path*'s sequel, in which the community learns that lawlessness is an anachronism and that authority must be respected.

For contemporary accounts of Shiels's plays see Robert Hogan and Michael J. O'Neill's edition of *Joseph Holloway's Abbey Theatre* (1967) and the three-volume *Joseph Holloway's Irish Theatre* (1968–70).

SHKVARKIN, Vasili Vasilevich (1893–), Russian playwright, made his fortune with a farce about two engineering students and the girl both love, *Chuzhoi rebyonok* (1933). His first play, *Glukhoe tsarstvovanie* (1925), protrays revolutionary struggles at the beginning of the nineteenth century, and he wrote a number of little-known comedies and vaudevillian satires. *Chuzhoi rebyonok* appears (as *Father Unknown*) in Alexander Bakshy's collection *Soviet Scene: Six Plays of Russian Life* (1946), which has some notes on Shkvarkin. See also *Soviet Theaters 1917–1941* (1954), edited by Martha Bradshaw, and Peter Yershov's *Comedy in the Soviet Theater* (1956).

SHOEMAKER'S PRODIGIOUS WIFE, THE (*La zapatera prodigiosa*), "a violent farce in two acts" by FEDERICO GARCÍA LORCA, published and produced in 1930. Setting: contemporary Andalusia.

This popular *commedia dell'arte*-like farce was inspired by a folk ballad. Light and amusing, much of it is ballet, music, and spectacle. But it anticipates themes that dominate García Lorca's later tragedies.

Even before the Author finishes his prologue, the irrepressible young shoemaker's wife (*la zapatera*) tries to burst onstage. She is a romantic daydreamer who is frustrated with and tired of her dull old husband. Her flirting and bad-tempered impudence finally drive him away. Then she must cope with the lecherous advances of customers in the shoeshop, which she has converted into a tavern, and with the village gossip. Remaining completely honorable, she romanticizes her absent husband. He returns, disguised as a traveling puppet-show player. When he discovers her virtuous constancy, he reveals himself and they are reconciled in a happy ending. But immediately she starts again: "Gallows-bird, rascal!" and complains—though now she is only mock serious —"How unfortunate I am with this man that God has given me!"

SHOLEM ALEICHEM [Solomon Rabinowitsch] (1859–1916), the great Yiddish humorist, has been called "the Jewish Mark Twain" as well as "the Grandson of Yiddish Literature." His tales have been successfully dramatized by others, and he himself wrote not only essays, stories, and novels, but also numerous plays. He was a major force in the Yiddish theatre, where many of his works—particularly his one-act sketches—have been staged. His *nom de plume* (the Yiddish greeting "Peace be with you") became most widely known in the theatre with the American musical *Fiddler on the Roof* (1964), Joseph Stein's (1912–) adaptation (music by Jerry Bock) of Sholem Aleichem's many stories about Tevye, a comic Yiddish Everyman; they were earlier dramatized by Sholem Aleichem as *Tevye, The Dairy-Man* (produced in 1919). The Off-Broadway and television success, Arnold Perl's *The World of Sholom Aleichem* (1953), is a dramatization of short stories of which only one is by Sholem Aleichem.

He was born in Pereyaslav, Russia. At the time he began writing the tales for which he is famous, he edited a literary annual, and speculated disastrously—experiencing the business mishaps of his quixotic *Luftmentshen* in "Tevye" and other stories. In 1906 he came to the United States, then went to lecture in Europe, and returned to New York in 1914. He died there, and is buried in Brooklyn.

Sholem Aleichem's most popular play was *Dos Groyse Gevins* (1915, translated as *Two Hundred Thousand*), a comedy about a tailor who is mistakenly notified of a lottery prize, fawned upon by fair-weather friends, and then happily returns to his tailoring. His other plays include *Tsezeyt un Tseshpreyt* (1903); *Samuel Posternak* (1907); *Shver tsu zayn a Yid* (*It's Hard to Be a Jew,* 1914), and one-acters such as *A Doktor!* (translated as *She Must Marry a Doctor,* in I. Goldberg's *Six Plays of the Yiddish Theatre,* 1916), a good example of his vaudevilles. Other plays include the one-act *Der Get* (1887), *Mazel Tov* (1889), and his dramatizations of his own novels and stories such as *Stempenyu* (1905) and *Der Oysvurf* (1907).

Few of his plays are readily available, but many of Sholem Aleichem's essays and stories have appeared in English, including *Tevye's Daughters* (1949) and *Stories and Satires* (1959). His uncompleted autobiography, *Funem Yarid,* was translated as *The Great Fair: Scenes From My Childhood* (1955). See also Maurice Samuel's *The World of Sholom Aleichem* (1943), and Marie Waife-Goldberg's *My Father, Sholom Aleichem* (1968).

SHOW-OFF, THE, "A Transcript of Life" in three acts by GEORGE KELLY, published and produced in 1924. Setting: Philadelphia, early 1920's.

This very successful comedy originally appeared as *Poor Aubrey,* a vaudeville sketch frequently performed in the early 1920's. Filmed in 1926, 1934, and again in 1947, the play became a minor American classic on television and in 1950 and 1967 Broadway revivals. It features a cheerfully blustering loudmouth, a mixture of comic fool and folk hero. He is juxtaposed with his spiritless, prosaic in-laws—a satire of another American type.

Act I. The Fishers dread the regular evening appearance of their daughter Amy's absurd suitor, Aubrey Piper. He is a noisy and pompous clerk who is ridiculed by others for his pretensions, but Amy adores him and enjoys his banality. "The pride of old West Philly," as he calls himself, laughs boisterously when he appears—a toupeed dandy with a carnation in his buttonhole. Mrs. Fisher keeps listening at the keyhole, and her husband angrily goes to bed. By midnight, after persistent raucous talk and laughter, Aubrey finally leaves. Mrs. Fisher warns Amy that "this clown" will not be able to support her, but this only makes her the more determined to marry him.

Act II. Half a year later and married, Aubrey is in debt and on the verge of being homeless. Just as windy as ever, he has borrowed money from Amy's married sister. "Give the growing boy a chance," he exhorts Mrs. Fisher when she lectures him on his irresponsible ways; "Rome was not built in a day." Amy is subdued, but no less adoring of him. Her father has a stroke. As the family prepare to go to the hospital, Aubrey reappears. He has just wrecked a borrowed car, has run into a policeman, and has been bailed out by his brother-in-law. But his spirits are undaunted as he blusters about "shaking up" the police department and grandly regrets he is unable to drive the family to the hospital. After they leave, he lovingly reassures Amy about his impending trial. Then he tells a visitor about "his" house and how, after he got married, he had his wife's family move in with him. When word comes that Fisher has died, Aubrey looks down at the tip of his cigar. "Your Mother'll have you and me to comfort her now," he says—and suggests that Amy persuade her mother to let them move in. "The Kid from West Philly," as he now calls himself, always told the old man to quit work, Aubrey now remembers. "Sic transit gloria mundi," he remarks—an old saying from the French, he explains to Amy, that means "We're here to-day, and gone tomorrow."

Act III. Fined heavily, Aubrey is again bailed out by Amy's married sister. She too once despised him, but now sees in him virtues her own responsible but cold and silent husband lacks. Though Aubrey is phony, he has vitality and loves Amy. She persuades her mother to let him move in, and then lectures him sternly. But Aubrey is irrepressible. When Amy's young brother announces happily that his chemical discovery has been bought for $100,000, Aubrey says, with self-satisfaction: "So we put it over!" And he had, in fact, gone to the firm, which had originally offered $50,000. As "head of the house," Aubrey told them he would not let them cheat the boy, "that I refused to allow you to negotiate further—unless they doubled the advance, market it at their expense, and one half the net—*sign* on the dotted line" (Aubrey's favorite expression). Mrs. Fisher regrets they did not know Aubrey and call his bluff. Aubrey swaggers, "I beat them to it; I called theirs first." Amy exclaims: "Aubrey, you're wonderful!" "A little bit of bluff goes a long way sometimes, Amy," Aubrey remarks, as his wife worshipfully gazes at him.

SHTEIN, Aleksandr Petrovich (1906–), Russian dramatist and short-story and film-script writer, also worked as a correspondent and newspaper editor. His early plays include a collaboration with the TUR BROTHERS, *Utopiya* (1930), as well as *Zakon chesti* (1948); *Flag admirala* (1949); *Personalnoe delo* (1954), among the first plays to suggest negativism in a hero and shortcomings in the Communist Party; and *Prolog*, a dramatization, staged in 1955 and filmed the following year, of Stalin's part in the 1905 revolution.

Shtein was willing to explore topics considered dangerous in Soviet Russia. Nonetheless well established there at midcentury, his most successful play was *Gostinitsa Astoriya,* the hit of the 1957–58 Moscow season. Set in Leningrad during the 1942–43 siege, it portrays many human—rather than stereotyped—characters, the most important of whom was unjustly imprisoned during the purges of the late 1930's; his wife remarried but, he tells a suffering friend who has abandoned the Party, "I did not lose my faith in this country, or even in Communism." Later popular Shtein plays include *Vesennie skripki* (1959). For an account of Shtein, particularly of *Gostinitsa Astoriya,* see Faubion Bowers's *Broadway, U.S.S.R.* (1959).

SHVARTS, Yevgeni Lvovich (1896?–1958), Russian editor, story writer, and dramatist, was only moderately popular during his lifetime. It was after his death that he became celebrated among intellectuals both in Russia and abroad. A brilliant wit, Shvarts was something of an anomaly among Soviet playwrights, one of the few whose works are free of Marxist cant—and criticize the essence of the authoritarian state. Though they are not exactly anti-Communist, his satires are patently aimed at all encroachments on human liberty and integrity, all totalitarianism. Particularly such a work as his superb *Ten* (THE SHADOW, 1940) seems to depict not only the Stalin state but also to prophesy de-Stalinization and the rise of subsequent regimes. Like his other important play, *Drakon* (THE DRAGON, 1943), it is cast in the form of the fairy-tale drama introduced by LUDWIG FULDA—as are most of Shvarts's plays. Their incisive satire of contemporary societies like that of Nazi Germany and Soviet Russia is apparent even in the adaptations of classic fairy tales—so much so that many of them were promptly banned, sometimes even before the premiere, and few were published during his lifetime.

A man as well noted for his cleverness and humor as for his kindness and decency, Shvarts was the son of two medical students whose professional careers were cut short by their revolutionary activities. They were banished from Russia's major cities, and wandered in various obscure towns. Shvarts himself, however, was allowed to pursue his law studies at Moscow University, which he entered in 1913. But he was drawn to the stage, first as an actor, then as a writer. Eventually he gave up law, joined the Leningrad Children's Publishing House, and wrote fairy tales, novels, film scripts (including that of *Don Quixote*)—and plays.

One of his first plays, *Undervud* (1929), has a contemporary setting, features an Underwood typewriter, and contains the fairy-tale elements characteristic of Shvarts's best drama. It was followed by *Klad* (1931); *Priklyuchenya Gogenshtaufena* (1934), another satiric fantasy; *Goly korol* (*The Naked King,* completed in 1934 but unproduced until 1960), an adaptation of Hans Christian Andersen's "The Emperor's New Clothes," with added satiric thrusts; *Krasnaya shapochka* (1937), a dramatization of "Little Red Riding Hood"; *Snezhnaya koroleva* (*The Snow Queen,* 1938), another adaptation of Andersen and the work that made Shvarts famous, became a standard play in the Russian repertoire, and was subsequently adapted (and published) for production in England and America; *Zolushka* (*Cinderella,* 1947), made into a film script; *Pervoklasnitsa* (1947); *Dva Klena* (1953), a children's play; *Povest o molodykh suprugakh* (1955), a portrayal of marital adjustment in contemporary Russia; and *Obyknovennoe chudo* (1956).

What distinguishes these plays and particularly the most notable ones among them (*The Shadow* and *The Dragon*) is a wonderful fusion of fantasy, theatricality, comedy, wit, and satire—all immensely entertaining and amusing. At the same time they are deeply earnest, yet devoid of preachiness. The taxing exigencies of a state-controlled culture seem not to have compromised Shvarts's artistic and intellectual integrity. The medium of the fairy tale, which he so often utilized, enabled him to express—with relative impunity—sentiments one hardly ever finds in Soviet drama. Though some of his work was banned in Stalin's time, Nikolai P. Akimov, the renowned director of Leningrad's Comic Theatre, was able to stage his most important plays a few times before they were ordered off the boards. An intrepid Shvarts enthusiast, it was Akimov who again staged these plays in the 1960's and had much to do with Shvarts's growing posthumous reputation.

Kukolny gorod, a collection of Shvarts's plays for the puppet theatre, was published in 1959 and included *Skazka o poteryannom vremeni* (*A Tale of Stolen Time*). His other plays appeared (many for the first time) in a 1960 collection of fairy tales, novellas, and plays; though the small edition of four thousand was sold out by noon of publication day, it was not reprinted. Little information about Shvarts and only a few of his plays are available in English. F. D. Reeve's *An Anthology of Russian Plays,* Volume II (1963), includes *The Shadow;* his *Contemporary Russian Drama* (1968) includes *The Naked King;* and *The Dragon* appears in Michael Glenny's edition of *Three Soviet Plays* (1966); all these have brief comments on Shvarts.

SICILIAN LIMES (*Lumí di Sicilia*), a one-act play by LUIGI PIRANDELLO, produced in 1910 and published in 1911. Setting: an anteroom of the salon of a fashionable contemporary home in a north Italian city.

Sicilian Limes and THE VISE, produced together, were Pirandello's first plays. *Sicilian Limes* is the dramatization of a short story he had published in 1900.

Micuccio Bonavino, a peasant band musician, arrives at a successful singer's home. He is the one who discovered the girl's voice and sold his land to send her to a conservatory. Deeply in love, they had decided to marry once she made her name. Now the simple, decent rustic talks with her impudent servants and then with her mother, a plain and affectionate woman despite her sophisticated environment. They reminisce as they wait for the singer, who is entertaining fashionable company at a raucous party in the adjoining salon. Finally she comes, for one moment only, to greet Micuccio casually. He is shocked and stupefied by her immodest, flashy dress. The mother's remark that the girl is now unworthy of him makes him realize fully how modern city life and success have changed her. He has brought a momento all the way from their native village, a sack of "beautiful Sicilian limes." Now he wants to hurl them at the dandies. Then, angrily telling the singer not to "touch them! Don't you even look at them!" he gives the limes to her mother, and leaves.

SIEGFRIED, a play in four acts by JEAN GIRAUDOUX, published and produced in 1928. Setting: Siegfried's official residence in Germany and a frontier railway station, 1920's.

Giraudoux's first play is this dramatization of *Siegfried et le Limousin* (1922), his allegorical novel of postwar France and Germany. The dramatization went through many revisions (later ones prepared with Louis Jouvet), some of which have been published. Personal and political emotions are deftly fused in the soul-searching of the amnesiac Siegfried and the two women who struggle for him. The play was immediately successful.

In the 1914–18 war, an unidentified soldier had been saved on the battlefield by a German nurse, Eva. Now he is the popular liberal leader of Germany, Siegfried, and Eva is his devoted supporter. Neither he nor anyone around him knows anything of his past. But his opponent, rightly suspecting Siegfried to be a Frenchman reported lost in action, plots against him and discovers and summons his fiancée, Geneviève Prat. Though Siegfried's political and military backers as well as Eva attempt to foil her, Geneviève eventually reveals his origin to him. At their moving confrontation, in his presence, the women battle for Siegfried. Eva pleads for the sake of Germany, whose hope Siegfried is. Geneviève claims "the unseen web of that memory" that constitutes his past. It is a terrible choice, one Geneviève herself characterizes as being " between a splendid life that is not his own and a void that is." At the fall of the third-act curtain, the agonized Siegfried asks, "What can be the choice of a blind man?" At a frontier railroad station, amidst the comic petty concerns of customs officials, Siegfried appears. He has chosen to give up fame and glory, but hopes to reconcile the "two fates chance gave me." France and Germany, he says to the leaders who make a last attempt to get him to return, similarly must learn to reconcile their differences. Geneviève has secretly followed him. As he crosses his native frontier she can bring herself to call him by the name she swore never to use: "Siegfried, I love you."

SIFTON, Paul (1898–　　), American playwright, attacked Henry Ford and the assembly-line system in an early play, *The Belt* (1927). His *1931*—(1931), a partly EXPRESSIONIST protest play written with his wife, Claire (1897–　　), merges a portrait of mass unemployment with that of an American Everyman as degraded by unemployment as his girl is by prostitution; "I've got a right to live!" the worker cries out; "I've got a right to work! Whaddeys say?" Sifton wrote other but less notable social-protest dramas (some with his wife) in the 1930's.

SIGNORA MORLI, ONE AND TWO (*La Signora Morlì, una e due*), a play in three acts by LUIGI PIRANDELLO, produced in 1920 and published in 1922. Setting: contemporary Florence and Rome.

This serious comedy resembles AS WELL AS BEFORE, BETTER THAN BEFORE and Shaw's CANDIDA in plot, though—ironically—the personalities of husband and lover are reversed. Later this play was revised as *Due in una* (*Two in One*). It portrays the single power of maternal love that eventually subsumes two amorous passions of a dual personality.

Years before, Evelina Morli's young husband had deserted her and their baby son. Then a staid lawyer fell in love with her, and they lived happily as man and wife for fourteen years, eventually having a child of their own, a girl. whereas

Evelina was lighthearted and gay with her carefree husband, she is serious and responsible with her lover. Now her husband Ferrante returns from America to reclaim his son. The boy is glad to go and live with his father in Rome, but both soon miss Evelina. They trick her into visiting them, and the once-joyous love of husband and wife soon is rekindled. Evelina's feelings are torn between husband and lover, to each of whom she bore a child. Her dilemma is heightened when her daughter falls ill, and she returns to Florence. Now husband and lover both claim Evelina; yet, as she tells them, "I cannot divide myself, half there, half here." Each man cares more for her than for his child. "You are men, only men. I am a mother," Evelina tells them. Her love for the men is in her—and their—children. Eventually Evelina makes the difficult moral—though superficially improper—choice. Even though her romantic husband is the more attractive man and her legal mate, he had forfeited his rights by abandoning her. She chooses to remain the wife—in all but the legal sense—of the man who gave her a home, her staid and proper lover.

SIGURD THE BASTARD (*Sigurd Slembe*), a dramatic trilogy by BJØRNSTJERNE BJØRNSON, published in 1862. Setting: Norway and Scotland, 1122–39.

Parts of this long trilogy, Bjørnson's finest history drama, have been staged from time to time, and launched Norway's National Theatre in 1899. Influenced by Shakespeare and Schiller (particularly the latter's *Wallenstein* trilogy), it has been likened to Ibsen's THE PRETENDERS. Like Ibsen's Skule, Sigurd (the epithet has been translated also as "ill-disposed" or "worthless"), too, fails in his driving ambition to gain a throne to which his claims are questionable. Though Ibsen excelled in characterization, Bjørnson demonstrated fine historical insight and created impressive crowd scenes. Except in the lyrical first play, the portrayals follow the saga accounts.

Part I: Sigurd's First Flight (*Sigurds første flugt*), a one-act play in blank verse, is set in Stavanger, Norway, in 1122. The twenty-year-old Sigurd prays to Saint Olav, begging to discover his father's identity. Tora, Sigurd's mother, confesses that he is the illegitimate son of King Magnus III (Magnus Barfod), her sister's husband. After a passionate outburst and a vow to insist on his royal succession, Sigurd bids farewell to his mother and goes on a Crusade.

Part II: Sigurd's Second Flight (*Sigurds annen flugt*), a three-act prose play, is set in Caithness and in Orfjara (Orphir) in the Orkney Islands, Scotland, five years later. In the service of the weak Earl of Caithness, Harald (a Hamlet-like figure), Sigurd causes death and ruin among the noble families because of his ambitions. Sigurd is so appalled by the horrors for which he has been responsible ("I am the restless one who brings but evil in return for good") that he goes on another Crusade, though he and Harald's niece Audhild are deeply in love.

Part III: Sigurd's Homecoming (*Sigurds hjemkomst*), a five-act prose play, is set in Norway during the years 1136 to 1139. Sigurd returns to Stavanger, seeking the recognition of his half-brother, King Harald Gille. Though the weak monarch is willing to grant it, his courtiers arrest Sigurd and plan to kill him. Sigurd escapes and plans vengeance. He kills the king and heads a revolt, which is doomed. Shortly before going to his certain defeat and cruel death, he bids farewell to his mother, now a penitent nun. He begs to hear "the Crusader's Song. I may joyfully go hence after that." Then he rests his head on his mother's breast.

SILVER BOX, THE, a comedy in three acts by JOHN GALSWORTHY, produced in 1906 and published in 1909. Setting: London, 1906.

Though this is Galsworthy's first play, he had already written novels for some ten years. The play, successful when first produced, is a NATURALISTIC portrayal of social injustice. Its ironic label ("comedy") applies only to the smug remarks of the young man's stupid mother.

A wealthy young man and an unemployed pauper steal a purse and a silver cigarette box while drunk. Because of his father's money and position, the young man leaves court unscathed. Sentenced to prison, the indignant pauper shouts, "It's *'is money* got *'im* off—*Justice!*" His destitute wife humbly appeals to the young man's father, whose charwoman she once was. But he refuses his help shamefacedly and hurries out.

SILVER CORD, THE, a comedy in three acts by SIDNEY HOWARD, published and produced in 1926. Setting: an eastern American city, 1926.

This blatant indictment of possessive motherhood features a neurotic woman who sublimates her frustrated romantic emotions in her sons. The "comedy," as Howard labeled it, was characterized by one of the critics, who likened it to Strindberg's THE FATHER, as "a workaday counterpart to Strindberg's lunatic grandeur."

Act I. Mrs. Phelps is subtly rude to her new daughter-in-law, Christina, a biologist her son David met and married in Europe. Greeting him with joyous excitement, she hardly notices Christina—or her other son, Robert, and his fiancée. Mrs. Phelps claims that she needs David, and decides that it is best for him to practice architecture at her home. To subvert Christina's intention to settle in New York, where both she and David have been offered promising positions, Mrs. Phelps enlists the assistance of Robert, whom she also asks to give up his fiancée. The weak Robert succumbs to his mother's blandishments and kisses her. At cocktails, Christina's announcement of her pregnancy so upsets Mrs. Phelps that she spills her drink.

Act II. Mrs. Phelps is surly about the pregnancy and persists in trying to keep Christina and David apart. When Robert breaks his engagement, his fiancée gets hysterical. Mrs. Phelps rips out the telephone and prevents her leaving the house and causing a scandal. Later, in David's old bedroom, Mrs. Phelps appears in her negligee. "The bond between mother and son is the strongest bond on earth," she tells him, eager to get him to give up his plans to go to New York. She reappears after overhearing David and Robert talking. "Are my two beaux quarreling? Jealous, jealous Robin!" she admonishes her younger son, and she pleads for their consideration of her "weak heart." She pouts, stomps out angrily, and returns, her face tearstained. Thus she persuades David to settle down at home. Christina exposes his mother's doings to David. "Our marriage and your architecture were suffering from the same thing," she tells him: "Your mother keeps you." David tries to convince Christina that he cannot leave his mother. Mrs. Phelps returns, and David again falls under her spell. Robert's fiancée, while running away, slips into a pond and almost drowns. Robert and David rush off to save her, though Mrs. Phelps tries to call them back, afraid they will catch pneumonia.

Act III. Mrs. Phelps plans to take Robert to Europe—and tries to persuade David to accompany them. Christina, in the meantime, is determined to leave the house at once and see "whether David is going on from this point as your son or as my husband." Presenting herself "as a sort of scientific Nemesis," she frankly unveils Mrs. Phelps's obsession and despicable actions, while her sons stand by. When Mrs. Phelps advances her claims of noble motherhood, Christina remains unimpressed. "An embryological accident is no grounds for honor," she remarks, and repeats Robert's fiancée's earlier remark about children. "Have 'em. Love 'em. And then leave 'em be." Characterizing Mrs. Phelps's life as sterile, Christina adds, "You belong to a type that's very common in this country, Mrs. Phelps—a type of self-centered, self-pitying, son-devouring tigress, with unmentionable proclivities suppressed on the side"—a form of cannibalism. Mrs. Phelps tries to defend herself, recounting her self-sacrifice after a bad marriage: "I didn't live without romance. I found it . . . where you say it doesn't belong . . . in motherhood." When David decides to stay with his mother, Christina leaves bitterly: "Remember me, won't you, on Mother's Day!" Realizing how trapped he has been by his mother all his life, David follows Christina after all—and is saved. Robert, however, kneels by his mother, "engulfed forever."

SILVER TASSIE, THE, a tragicomedy in four acts by SEAN O'CASEY, published in 1928 and produced in 1929. Setting: Dublin and France during World War I.

Though he had championed O'Casey's THE PLOUGH AND THE STARS, WILLIAM BUTLER YEATS rejected this play for production at the Abbey Theatre. Yeats and O'Casey's unresolved controversy over the play's merits has been frequently reprinted. A bitter antiwar drama, the play is experimental: Acts I, III, and IV are a mixture of NATURALISM, farce, and musical comedy; Act II is wholly EXPRESSIONISTIC.

Act I. Sylvester Heegan and his friend, another old dockworker, comically and exuberantly resist the "distempering piety" of Susie Monican, an attractive but prim hell-fire-and-damnation fanatic. She loves Heegan's son, Harry; but he loves another, "so she hides her rage an' loss in the love of a scorchin' Gospel," Heegan explains. Harry is a soldier on leave and a local hero whose exploits the "oul' butties" recount. They are interrupted by a neighbor's wife, who is escaping a beating from her husband, another soldier on leave. He soon appears, and the old braggarts quickly hide. Harry Heegan then comes in with his admirers. He bears the silver tassie he has again won for his football club by scoring the winning goal. Amidst boisterous celebrations and much singing, the hero and his girl kiss, and drink out of the silver tassie. Then the celebrating soldiers are persuaded to return to battle, and Heegan's mother is relieved that they have gotten to the boat in time.

Act II. In the war zone—amidst the ruins of a monastery—a life-size crucifix, a figure of the Virgin, and a cannon dominate the setting. A crouching soldier intones the parody of a prayer, and sullen soldiers chant their anguish: "Cold and wet and tir'd. . . . Why 's 'e 'ere, why 's 'e 'ere—that's wot 'e wants to know!" And the choral reply is, "We're here because we're here, because we're here, because we're here!" A pompous civilian official callously surveys the scene with an equally pompous staff officer. The wounded and mutilated are carried by, the soldiers chant their despair, and war and church ritual alternate in antiphonal songs and chants. "To the guns," the soldiers repeat, as an enemy breakthrough is announced. The soldiers' guns flash rhythmically—and soundlessly.

Act III. In a hospital ward, the men of Act I recuperate from their wounds. The old dockworkers are not seriously hurt, and their antic miseries provide much comedy. But Harry Heegan, shot in the spine, is lifeless from the waist down. Bitterly he threatens to "make my chair a Juggernaut, and wheel it over the neck and spine of every daffodil that looks at me, and strew them dead to manifest the mercy of God and the justice of man!" The evangelistic Susie now is an insensitive nurse, attracted to an equally hardened surgeon. Heegan's sweetheart, not interested in a cripple, takes up with his friend, who saved him and thus became a war hero. As the Sisters of the ward sing the *Salve Regina* offstage, the agonized Heegan cries, "God of the miracles, give a poor devil a chance, give a poor devil a chance!"

Act IV. There is a dance at the football club where Heegan once gloried in his victories. His former sweetheart is disconcerted by his "wheeling after us" and spoiling her fun with his friend. Susan and her surgeon, too, are dancing, and the old dockers provide amusement with their capers. Heegan demands a drink out of the silver tassie, and then smashes it to the ground. Bitterly he castigates his fickle sweetheart and his friend, insulting both until the friend hits him. A blinded soldier takes Heegan home. "The Lord hath given and man hath taken away!" Heegan says, and the blind man answers, "Blessed be the name of the Lord!" After they are gone, Susie insists nothing can be done. War brings woe, "but we, who have come through the fire unharmed, must go on living." The dance resumes. "It's a terrible pity Harry was too weak to stay an' sing his song," the blinded soldier's wife concludes; "for there's nothing I love more than the ukelele's tinkle, tinkle in the night-time."

SIMON, Neil (1927–), American playwright, has been immensely successful first as a television writer and then as the author of the musical *Promises, Promises* (1968) and bromidic comedies, beginning with *Come Blow Your Horn* (1961), a Jewish-family farce characteristically set in his native New York. Simon's later hits include *Barefoot in the Park* (1963), which depicts the tribulations of newlyweds; *The Odd Couple* (1965), portraying the housekeeping and other trials of two recently divorced men; *Plaza Suite* (1968), three sketches of marriage and adultery; *The Last of the Red Hot Lovers* (1969), dramatizing three abortive adulterous flings of a middle-aged New Yorker; and *The Gingerbread Lady* (1970), an earnest depiction of a fading singing star who is subject to nymphomania and alcoholism.

SIMONOV, Konstantin Mikhailovich (1915–), Russian poet, novelist, and playwright, became the Soviets' most prominent writer during World War II. Particularly impressive were his front-line dispatches, some of which reappeared in expanded form in his world-famous novel about the Battle of Stalingrad, *Dni i nochi* (*Days and Nights,* 1944). His best-known play is *Russkie lyudi* (THE RUSSIAN PEOPLE, 1942; also translated as *The Russians*). He wrote about a dozen other plays, including the comedy *Tak i budet* (AND SO IT WILL BE, 1944; produced also as *The Whole World Over*), as well as volumes of poetry and fiction. Translated into some forty languages, his most popular works were filmed in the Soviet Union. In 1942 Simonov became the editor of *Novy Mir,* the Russian journal in which he published Vladimir Dudintsev's controversial novel *Ne chlebom yedinym* (*Not by Bread Alone,* 1956).

The son of an army officer who was reported lost (presumably killed) in World War I, Simonov was born in Petrograd (Leningrad). He attended elementary school at Saratov on the Volga and became a factory mechanic in Moscow at the age of seventeen. He continued his studies in the evening and graduated from the Gorky Institute of Literature in 1938. That year, too, was published his first poem, *Pavel Chorny,* which (like Pogodin's ARISTOCRATS) celebrated the construction of the White Sea–Baltic Canal. Most of Simonov's subsequent writing, in all genres, deals with patriotic themes.

Simonov's first play, *Istoriya odnoi lyubvi* (1940), features a taciturn Arctic explorer, Bearskin (originally the play's title), whose wife and wealthy friend fall in love while he is occupied in a Mongolian border incident. Though love dramas were relatively rare in Russia at the time, Simonov's attitude, as revealed in the dialogue ("People are dying out there and you talk of love!") was conventional enough. This play was not particularly successful, but the next one (*Paren iz nashego goroda*), which appeared a month later, was widely praised and became the basis of Simonov's most famous play, *The Russian People.* Russia had by then been invaded by the Nazis, and Simonov, serving at the front, distinguished himself as a war correspondent for *Krasnaya Zvezda* (*Red Star*). He also wrote love poetry, verses for his wife, and ballads, collected in *S toboi i bez tebya* (*With and Without You,* 1944). "Zhdi menya" ("Wait for Me"), one of his poems, expresses the sentiment that some woman at home waits for every soldier; Simonov turned it into a popular song and, in 1942, enlarged upon the poem in a play with the same title and portraying a captured aviator whose confidence in his wife gives him the strength to fight his way home, where all but his wife had given him up for dead.

At the end of the war, Simonov's travels with the Red Army that was liberating Eastern Europe from the Germans became the basis of *Pod kashtanami Pragi* (1945), which stresses the friendship of peoples. Soon after the war, however, Simonov's drama started to reflect the growing estrangement of the Allies. *Russki vopros* (*The Russian Question,* 1946) presents the Soviet view of the conflict between the Western and the Communist blocs. Later plays are *Dym otechestva* (1947), a dramatic expression of hope for an improved postwar life, panned by the critics; *Chuzhaya ten* (1949), another anti-Western play, in which a great Soviet discovery is perverted into an extermination weapon by American scientists; and *Dobroe imya* (1953), a comedy about old and new concepts about Russia.

The winner of five Stalin Prizes and many other honors, Simonov was a deputy of the Supreme Soviet (1946–50), and was elected a deputy of the RSFSR of the Supreme Soviet in 1955. The following year his approval and publication of Dudintsev's work was censured, and Simonov's subsequent self-criticism was deemed inadequate. In 1957 he lost his editorship of *Novy Mir,* and he was not mentioned publicly in Russia thereafter. In 1962, however, his *Chetvyorty,* an anti-nuclear-war play set somewhere in the menacing West, was produced successfully in Moscow and Leningrad.

The four-volume *Ot Tschornoga do Parencova morya* (1941–45), a collection of Simonov's essays and fiction, was translated as *No Quarter* (1943). *The Russian People* (as *The Russians*) appears in *Four Soviet War Plays* (1944).

SIMOOM (*Samum*), a one-act play by AUGUST STRINDBERG, published in 1890 and produced in 1892. Setting: the inside of an Algerian shrine in the 1880's.

This QUART D'HEURE is a thriller inspired by Poe: a fanatic Arab girl, "stronger than the simoom" raging outside and aided by her lover, avenges herself by killing a French officer through hypnosis.

SIMPLETON OF THE UNEXPECTED ISLES, THE, a play in a prologue and two acts by BERNARD SHAW, produced in 1935 and published in 1936. Setting: a tropical island, the future.

The "Preface on Days of Judgment" is an abridged rehash of Shaw's preface to ON THE ROCKS, whose principles are here applied to "Judgment Day" and this drama, where the angel's "inquiry is not whether you believe in Tweedledum or Tweedledee but whether you are a social asset or a social nuisance." As for the four beautiful offspring, "who embody all the artistic, romantic, and military ideals of our cultural suburbs," Shaw noted that "they cease to exist like the useless and predatory people: it becomes apparent that they never did exist."

An Oriental priest and priestess and two Occidental couples on the Unexpected Isles perform a communal eugenic experiment: "a biological blend of the flesh and spirit of the west with the flesh and spirit of the east." They produce four children, beautiful beings with cultivated artistic but no moral consciousness. In time the two girls fall in love with and marry—thus continuing the experiment—the visiting simpleton Iddy (short for "idiot"), a clergyman kidnaped by pirates who wanted "to make people believe that they were respectable." When England hears of the polygamy it is scandalized and sends out its fleet—and then secedes from the Empire. An angel now comes down and announces Judgment Day: "The lives which have no use, no meaning, no purpose, will fade out. You will have to justify your existence or perish." He flies off, and soon reports come from all over the world, first of the appearance of angels, and then of the disappearance of people, particularly doctors and politicians. One of the girls disappears while in Iddy's arms; the other offspring also disappear, and even their names are forgotten (Iddy remembers them as "Love, Pride, Heroism and Empire"). As the Westerners quickly take up various tasks to justify their existence and avoid being "weeded out," the Oriental priest and priestess decide that they "must continue to strive for more knowledge and more power," that they need each other, and that "life needs us both."

SIMPSON, N[orman] F[rederick] (1919–), English playwright, first became known with A RESOUNDING TINKLE (1957), a comic fantasy that won the *Observer* play contest and revealed a kinship with the ABSURDist protest drama of predecessors such as ALFRED JARRY and EUGÈNE IONESCO. Like Simpson's next full-length play, ONE WAY PENDULUM (1959), it presents a middle-class setting and apparently mad people. But the madness is that of society—as satirized by Simpson. His plays also satirize the human logic that Simpson appears to flaunt. He has a logic of his own, grounded in Lewis Carroll's *Alice in Wonderland* and the comic operas of W. S. GILBERT and Arthur Sullivan. The result has been found hilarious by English audiences (*One Way Pendulum* has often been produced in repertory), and critics have commended Simpson's social and philosophical lampooning.

Simpson was born in London, worked in a bank, served in the Intelligence Corps during World War II, and then became an adult-education lecturer.

Simpson's plays (except for *One Way Pendulum*) were first collected in *The Hole and Other Plays and Sketches* (1964). Its one-act title play (1958) is set in a road into which was dug a hole wherein various passers-by see and interpret their differing visions of sports, a prison, an aquarium, etc.; here Simpson satirized lopsided thinking and such specific matters as religious ritual (the Trinity is parodied in an apostrophe to the aquarium). This collection also includes a short version of *A Resounding Tinkle* and a number of other brief farces: *The Form* (1961, depicting a job interview), *Gladly Otherwise* (1959), *Oh* (1960), and *One Blast and Have Done* (1960). A later full-length play is *The Cresta Run* (1965), which deals with counter-espionage. John Russell Taylor's *Anger and After* (retitled *The Angry Theatre* in America, revised edition 1969), Martin Esslin's *The Theatre of the Absurd* (revised edition 1968), and George E. Wellwarth's *The Theater of Protest and Paradox* (1964) deal in part with Simpson's work.

SION, Georges S. (1913–), Belgian playwright, had his first popular success with *La Matrone d'Ephèse* (1942), a bubbling comedy based on a story by Petronius. More weighty is *Charles le Téméraire* (1944), a fifteenth-century chronicle play about Charles the Bold's wars against the French and the Swiss over Lorraine. Other Sion plays are *La Princesse de Chine* (1951), an adaptation of Carlo Gozzi's *Turandot* (1762); *Le Voyageur de Forceloup* (1951), a mystical exploration of suffering; *La Malle de Pamela* (1955), a return to his earlier, light style; and translations from Shakespeare.

SIR BENGT'S WIFE (*Herr Bengts hustru*), a historical play in five acts by AUGUST STRINDBERG, published and produced in 1882. Setting: sixteenth-century Sweden.

Despite its medieval and historical setting, this play is a domestic drama concerned with nineteenth-century ideas. Though similar in plot to Ibsen's A DOLL'S HOUSE, Strindberg's very different attitudes placed him in the antifeminist—and anti-IBSEN—camp.

Sir Bengt, a knight, saves Margit from going to a convent and marries her. Their blissful happiness is broken by economic difficulties that Bengt has concealed from his romantic wife, who believes herself neglected by her husband. Ensuing quarrels culminate in Bengt's raising his hand against her. She leaves him and goes to the convent, where she is advised of a better place to practice her Christian virtues: at home, with her family. Still rebellious, she takes poison, but is saved by a timely antidote. Her proximity to death helps her to return to Bengt, who admits having hated her and wanting to kill her for deserting him and their child. Now he asks her, "Do you believe in the power of love over an evil will?" And Margit, now reconciled with her husband, replies, "I believe!"

SIWERTZ, Sigfrid (1882–), Swedish novelist, poet, and playwright, was one of the most flamboyant native writers of his generation. His early commitment to *fin de siècle* aesthetics and Bergsonian optimism was modified by the repercussions of the horrors of World War I that he witnessed in Sweden. These are reflected in the most successful and effective of his novels, *Selambs* (1920, translated as *Downstream*), a family chronicle of evil. Siwertz's drama, however, is urbane and deftly (if superficially) treats popular contemporary issues. Appearing in the 1930's, the most popular of his plays were *Jag har varit en tjuv* (1931), *En hederlig man* (1933), *Ett brott* (1933), and *Spel på havet* (1938).

SIX CHARACTERS IN SEARCH OF AN AUTHOR (*Sei personaggi in cerca d'autore*), a play in three acts by LUIGI PIRANDELLO, published and produced in 1921. Setting: the stage of a contemporary theatre.

HENRY IV and *Six Characters in Search of an Author* are Pirandello's best known works and his finest dramatizations of the conflicts of reality and illusion. The latter, "a play in the making" inspired by a short story he published in 1913, is the more popular one. In the guise of a play-within-a-play, this brilliant, highly influential tragicomedy explores the complexities of human nature and conduct, of thought, and of art and life. Pirandello considered this play the first "of a trilogy of the theatre in the theatre" (the others are EACH IN HIS OWN WAY and TONIGHT WE IMPROVISE); i.e., plays in which the theatre itself (drama, actors, spectators, etc.) is involved in the conflicts. Here the conflicts are not only between the theatre people and the "fictitious" characters but also within each of the two groups. In a revealing preface, written after the play had made him world-famous, Pirandello analyzed it and described his intention: to dramatize the creative process rather than the characters' story.

Act I. An unimaginative, irascible Manager starts rehearsing his actors in Pirandello's THE RULES OF THE GAME, a play they all find ridiculous. Suddenly six "characters" appear on the stage. They are led by a fifty-year-old Father and his beautiful eighteen-year-old Stepdaughter. All six are "in search of an author" for their story, which also features the downcast Mother, in widow's weeds; the supercilious twenty-two-year-old Son, who is contemptuous of the Father and indifferent to the Mother; the timid fourteen-year-old Boy; and a Child, the Boy's four-year-old sister. After creating them, their author had failed to put them into a work of art, and they are now compelled to seek life by enacting their drama. Before the incredulous Manager and his troupe, the Father insists that they are not mad: life appears in many forms, and "Nature uses the instrument of human fantasy in order to pursue her high creative purpose." Despite their jeering, the Manager and his actors become intrigued with the characters (and the Stepdaughter's provocative song and dance) and the sordid story they now reveal. The Father, a pale, fattish man with clear and piercing eyes, is an intellectual who married the Mother, a simple and uneducated woman, to balance the "complicated torments of my spirit." But husband and wife were unhappy, and he sent their Son to be reared in the country. Then, urged on by his "demon of experience" and sensing their mutual love, the Father forced his wife to make her home with his humble clerk. The story continues amidst questions by the theatrical troupe (whose leading man ogles the impudent Stepdaughter, despite the leading lady's jealous anger) and the other characters' different viewpoints about the Father's lofty version of what happened. Eventually the Mother and the clerk had three children: the Stepdaughter, the Boy, and the Child. For a while the Father—his life now empty though his Son was again living in his house—watched over them, bringing gifts to the Stepdaughter as she grew older. Then the family moved away, not to return until after the clerk's death (hence the Mother's mourning) years later. The poverty-stricken Mother became a seamstress for Madame Pace, a dressmaker whose shop was also a brothel. There the Stepdaughter was about to entertain a client when the Mother appeared and with a shriek of horror identified him as the Father. He then took the whole family into his home, where the strained relationships were aggravated by the legitimate Son's resentment of the intruders. It is the climactic brothel confrontation, however, that Father and Stepdaughter yearn to act out. To the Father, this scene reveals "a fleeting, shameful moment" of life in which he should not have been observed. The reality of that moment should not be fixed upon him forever: every man falls victim to his weak flesh, "only to rise . . . again, afterwards, with a great eagerness to reestablish one's dignity, as if it were a tombstone to place on the grave of one's shame." To the Stepdaughter, "all these [are] intellectual complications [that] make me sick, disgust me—all this philosophy that uncovers the beast in man, and then seeks to save him, excuse him"—and she feels revolted by the Father's remorse. The Manager is at last persuaded that there may be a successful play in their story. He invites the characters to his office to help him sketch out the scenes.

Act II. As the Manager prepares to stage the brothel scene, the Mother desperately begs the Son to overcome his cruel disdain. The Father and the Stepdaughter are dissatisfied with the setting and the actors' false attempts to recreate reality. But soon the characters all begin enacting their story. Madame Pace herself arrives at the proper moment—a reality, the Father notes when the troupe accuse him of trickery, "which comes to

Six Characters in Search of an Author. Left to right: Son (Paul Guilfoyle), Little Girl (Bebe Gilbert), Boy (Buddy Proctor), Mother (Doris Rankin), Stepdaughter (Eleanor Phelps), Father (Eugene Powers), Leading man (L'Estrange Millman), Manager (Walter Connolly). Madame Pace (Ina Rorke); other actors of the company are grouped at right. New York 1931. (*Vandamm Photo, Theatre Collection, New York Public Library*)

birth attracted and formed by the magic of the stage itself, which has indeed more right to live here than you, since it is much truer than you." Even while they argue, however, the scene continues. As the brothel's client, the Father offers to buy the Stepdaughter a new hat; she declines, pointing to her black dress: she is in mourning. Now the actors try to act the same scene, but the characters cannot contain their laughter at the imitation. The Stepdaughter insists that they use the words actually spoken: "'Ah well,' he said, 'then let's take off this little frock.'" The Manager objects on the grounds of theatrical expedience: "Acting is our business here. Truth up to a certain point, but no further." Angrily the Stepdaughter replies, "What you want to do is to piece together a little romantic sentimental scene out of my disgust, out of all the reasons, each more cruel and viler than the other, why I am what I am." The Mother, too, insists on the truth and confuses the Manager by maintaining that their story is still taking place: "It happens all the time. My torment isn't a pretended one." And the Father, pointing at the Stepdaughter, agrees: "The eternal moment! She is here to catch me, fix me, and hold me eternally in the stocks for that one fleeting and shameful moment of my life." She recalls stepping behind a screen and, "with these fingers tingling with shame," unhooking her dress; as she rests her head on the Father's shoulder and puts her arms around him, the Mother appears. She shrieks as she sees and separates them: "No! My daughter, my daughter! You brute! you brute! She is my daughter!" The Manager is delighted: "Fine! fine! Damned good! And then, of course—curtain!" A stage technician mistakes the remark for an order, and drops the curtain. This annoys the Manager, who, however, is pleased by "his" play: "Effect certain! That's the right ending. I'll guarantee the first act at any rate."

Act III. The Manager now prepares his second act. The characters again protest against his manner of creating "the illusion of reality," and again confuse him by insisting that this illusion is, in fact, their only existence. "Ours is an immutable reality," the Father tells him; "your reality is a mere transitory and fleeting illusion" that changes from day to day, and is therefore less true than that of the characters. The Manager becomes exasperated with the Father's eternal philosophizing; it reminds him "of a certain author whom I heartily detest . . . although I have unfortunately bound myself to put on one of his works." He arranges the characters in a garden scene, and again they quickly step into their story, which they have already revealed. The Father again suffers the agony of the Mother's discovering him with the Stepdaughter, and the Stepdaughter arrogantly loathes him and the sneering Son. The latter is resentful and angry; he goes to the garden reluctantly, followed by his unhappy, rejected Mother. There the Boy is hiding with a gun. When his little sister, the Child, falls in the fountain and drowns, the Boy shoots himself. The Mother runs to him, crying in terror, and some of the actors help carry him out. He is dead, though a few actors claim the whole thing is only pretense. "Pretense? Reality, sir, reality!" the Father exclaims "with a terrible cry," and then goes out after the Stepdaughter, Mother, and Son. The confused Manager curses about the entire affair: "I've lost a whole day over these people, a whole day!" He ends the rehearsal and dismisses the actors and stagehands. When the theatre is darkened, he calls for a light "so I can get out of here!" As by mistake, the background is illuminated with a green light, and behind the black cloth appear the shadows of the Father, Mother, Stepdaughter, and Son. When the Manager sees them, he runs out in terror.

SIX OF CALAIS, THE, a one-act play by BERNARD SHAW, produced in 1934 and published in 1936. Setting: Calais, 1347.

A mixture of heroics, pathos, and bawdy farce, this "is an acting piece" only and "has no moral whatever," Shaw noted in his preface. Inspired by Rodin's sculpture "The Burghers of Calais," Shaw based his play on an historical incident narrated by "that absurd old snob Froissart," as Kaiser did his THE CITIZENS OF CALAIS.

Before the walls of besieged Calais, Edward III is ready to hang six of its leading citizens, including Eustache de Saint-Pièrre. His pregnant queen beguiles and browbeats the henpecked Edward until he weeps, snarls, and finally sets the shivering hostages free.

SKIN GAME, THE, a tragicomedy in three acts by JOHN GALSWORTHY, published and produced in 1920. Setting: a contemporary English country estate and surroundings.

In this once-popular play the crude "gloveless" fight—"the skin game"—between the unscrupulous nouveau-riche Hornblower and the proud aristocrat Hillcrist is over land. To preserve the traditional from the "man with a future," the country gentleman is reduced to dishonorable tactics. He realizes at the end that, though he has won, his gentility is bankrupt because "it can't stand fire." The play's apt motto is "Who touches pitch shall be defiled."

SKIN OF OUR TEETH, THE, a play in three acts by THORNTON WILDER, published and produced in 1942. Setting: Excelsior, New Jersey, and the Atlantic City Boardwalk; throughout human history.

In both structure and theme this raucous, allegorical fantasy was influenced by JAMES JOYCE's *Finnegans Wake,* by nineteenth-century domestic comedy, and by EXPRESSIONIST and EPIC theatre. It features the suburban Antrobus (a variation on the Greek for *man*) family and Sabina, their saucy maid and an archetypal (Lilith-like) temptress, portrayed by an actress who periodically stops the action to complain about the play. It is a kaleidoscopic dramatization of (and an expression of faith in) man's indestructibility; he survives "by the skin of his teeth," despite the malignancy of nature and of man himself, through the Ice Age, the Flood, and modern war. Time is telescoped through the juxtaposition of biblical figures and bathing beauties, a talking dinosaur and singing telegrams. Though its critical reception was mixed, this unorthodox play won the Pulitzer Prize; subsequently it achieved great popular as well as critical success, and has received major revivals (in 1955 and 1961) in America and abroad.

Act I. An announcer reports an ice movement that is causing unprecedented weather for August. He introduces George Antrobus, a pillar of the suburban community and the inventor of the wheel and the alphabet; and he congratulates "this typical American family on its enterprise." Their blond, overrouged maid, Sabina, appears. "Oh, oh, oh! Six o'clock and the master not home yet," she worries. She dusts the room—whereupon parts of the setting move and disappear—explains the daily routine, and describes the family: the typical middle-class mother and daughter, and the son, Henry (formerly named Cain), a "clean-cut American boy" who killed his brother with a rock. Sabina repeats a cue; when nothing happens, she angrily decides to quit. "I hate this play," says the actress, who took the part of Sabina in desperation after two years without work, and "I don't understand a single word of it." When the stage manager persuades her to continue, she tells Mrs. Antrobus that she milked the mammoth; but though it is so cold that "the dogs are sticking to the sidewalks," she let the fire go out. Mr. Antrobus, we learn, brought her home from the Sabine hills, raped her, and gave her a life of luxury. But eventually the mistress was sent to the kitchen and the wife regained dominance. Now Sabina gives her notice as a boy delivers a singing telegram from Antrobus. Soon Antrobus himself blusters in with his wheel. While Sabina tells the audience to ignore the play, Antrobus reveals the imminent end of the world. Over Mrs. Antrobus's protests he invites in some seedy refugees—Moses, a judge; Homer, a blind beggar; and the Muse sisters—who gather about the fire, recite, and sing. Outside, Henry, who already sports Cain's mark, kills another boy. "He's only four thousand years old," his protective mother wails, but Antrobus furiously starts stamping out the fire: "We'll not try to live." Eventually the others cajole him to resume his faith in mankind, and the fire is rebuilt. As ushers start bringing up chairs from the auditorium to feed the fire, Sabina calls on the audience to help: "Pass up your chairs, everybody. Save the human race."

Act II. Antrobus has been elected President of the Ancient and Honorable Order of Mammals, Subdivision Humans, which is meeting in Atlantic City at its six hundred thousandth Annual Convention. In his acceptance speech Antrobus counsels the members to "Enjoy Yourselves." Mrs. Antrobus, in a rambling talk to the convention, reveals that she is celebrating their five thousandth wedding anniversary. On the boardwalk, amidst sideshows and conventioneers' merriment, Sabina appears in a silk bathing suit. Antrobus has picked her winner of the beauty contest, and she is determined to marry him. She lures him into her beach cabana, and (though the actress who plays her again balks at speaking her lines) persuades him to give up his wife. His daughter flounces in with red stockings, Henry (Cain) hits a Negro boy with a stone, and Antrobus informs his wife of his decision to leave her. But Mrs. Antrobus calmly gets Antrobus to stay with her—for the Deluge about to flood the world compels the family, Sabina, and the animal pairs to enter the ark. "They're safe," says a boardwalk fortune-teller: "A new world to make,—think it over!"

Act III. It is just after a great war. Much of the population has been wiped out, but the Antrobus family have survived. Sabina emerges, dressed as a

Napoleonic camp follower. The play is interrupted: a shortage of actors forces the stage manager to rehearse a procession (it is meant to provide "poetic effect," he explains) in which "hours" represent and quote great philosophers, portrayed by the theatre house staff. The play continues. Henry (Cain) has risen to prominence on the enemy side, and returns more evil than ever and ready to kill his father. When Antrobus comes in, their dispute gets so bitter that the play is stopped, and the actors portraying Henry and Antrobus express their personal and emotional involvement in their parts. Antrobus admits he would rather battle Henry than "build up a peacetime with you in the middle of it." However, his will to life is soon rekindled. "The most important thing of all," he says, is "the desire to begin again." Sabina, after calming Henry, returns with her feather duster—as in Act I. She surrenders the beef cubes she hoarded during the war, asking to keep only enough with which to buy her way to the movies—which keep her sane. Antrobus returns to his books. He knows "living is struggle" and good must constantly be fought for: "All I ask is the chance to build new worlds and God has always given us that." The philosopher procession passes by again. Sabina comes in. "Oh, oh, oh. Six o'clock and the master not home yet," she says—as she did at the start of the play. Then she turns to the audience. "We have to go on for ages and ages yet," she tells them: "The end of this play isn't written yet. Mr. and Mrs. Antrobus! Their heads are full of plans and they're as confident as the first day they began,—and they told me to tell you: good night."

SKLAR, George (1908–), American writer, did his most notable work as the author of leftist protest drama in the 1930's. With ALBERT MALTZ he produced conventionally NATURALISTIC plays interspersed with Marxist slogans. Their *Merry-Go-Round* (1932), an unsuccessfully censored Broadway play, is about corrupt police who protect influential killers and brutalize innocent victims; *Peace on Earth* (1933), their pacifist play that launched the Theatre Union, features a liberal professor converted to Marxism, framed on a murder charge, and hanged. The most successful of Sklar's plays was *Stevedore* (1934), a militant protest drama about Negro persecution written with Paul Peters (1906–). It features an outspoken Negro stevedore who is falsely accused of rape, pursued by a lynch mob, and shot; but with the aid of his white comrades in the Communist union, the Negro community wins the fight against the mob. Sklar's shrill social-action type of drama seemed very dated by the time he produced *And People All Around* (1966), a bitter dramatization of the 1964 murder of three civil-rights workers in Mississippi. Sklar has also written Hollywood film scripts and numerous novels.

SLEEP OF PRISONERS, A, a blank-verse one-act play by CHRISTOPHER FRY, published and produced in 1951. Setting: a contemporary church, in an enemy country, used as a makeshift military prison.

A modern Passion play with antiwar sentiments, *A Sleep of Prisoners* has been produced in churches on both sides of the Atlantic. In England it was hailed as Fry's best work, but it achieved less success in America. Most of the action consists of Old Testament sequences—individual dreams that, Fry noted, finally become "a state of thought entered into by all the sleeping men, as though . . . they shared, for a few moments of the night, their sleeping life also."

Of four English soldiers locked up for the night, David King is particularly on edge. He yells that his friend Peter Able drives him "potty" playing the organ, and he then leaps up to the pulpit and chokes him almost to death. They are separated, and David soon feels repentant. "How d'you feel now, Pete?" he asks, unlacing his boots. "Beautiful," Peter mumbles, and falls asleep. The others soon follow his example. They dream of the squabble, which becomes transformed into episodes suggested by their church environment. As Cain, David again assaults his friend, now the biblical Abel. A corporal, as Joab, is commanded by David (now King David) to kill Peter (now Absalom). Next David appears as Abraham, ready to sacrifice Peter, who is now his son, Isaac. In the last dream humanity's problems are mirrored in the Nebuchadnezzar story of Shadrac, Meshac, and Abednego—the "three blind mice of Gotham" cast into the furnace: "If the fire had been hotter / Their tales would have been shorter." Then the four soldiers wake up "In a sort of a universe and a bit of a fix." The oldest comments, "It began to feel like the end of the world / With all your bunks giving up their dead." Finally the prisoners lie down again; the church clock strikes, and the sound of a bugle is heard from the distance.

SLEEPING CLERGYMAN, A, a play in two acts by JAMES BRIDIE, published and produced in 1933. Setting: Glasgow, 1930's and the past.

Like THE ANATOMIST, this play depicts ruthless but creative energy and devotion to science. Here, however, it is portrayed over a span of three generations, and within a framework that unifies the play's ten scenes. Revelations about the family and its descendants are made in discussions among relaxing club members, one of whom is the title's clergyman, who sleeps throughout and is symbolic of God. First to be enacted is the story of the family's progenitor, a poor and ill medical student experimenting on himself and rejecting his benefactor's sister, whom he has seduced: "I'm going to fight without any long-haired, soft-skinned, piping-voiced bag of whims and vapours hanging round my neck." He dies shortly thereafter, and the next episodes portray his ruthless bastard, a beautiful female who poisons her lover when he interferes with her plans to marry a better man. Finally, her twin offspring are portrayed as benefactors of mankind. Ultimately, good has thus sprung out of evil.

SLEEPING PRINCE, THE, "an occasional fairy tale" in two acts by TERENCE RATTIGAN, produced in 1953 and published in 1954. Setting: the Royal Suite of the Carpathian Legation in London, during the coronation of George V in 1911.

In this delightful romp Laurence Olivier played the Prince Regent of Carpathia, who fails to seduce an American chorus girl, played by Vivien Leigh (and by Marilyn Monroe in the film version, *The Prince and the Showgirl,* 1957). She falls in love with him and helps resolve political troubles with his royal father. At last he loses his heart to her and offers to make her his mistress for life. She declines, but promises to come to Carpathia when her show ends its run.

SLICE OF LIFE, a translation of the French *tranche de vie,* a phrase coined by JEAN JULLIEN. It refers to the drama of NATURALISM that means to depict an episode or part of life naturally —without artificial plotting—and "scientifically," as ÉMILE ZOLA put it. Such drama was to demonstrate that life is conditioned solely by physiological and psychological factors. See the entries on NATURALISM and on Zola's THÉRÈSE RAQUIN.

SMITH, Winchell (1871–1933), American playwright, began his career as an actor. Later, in the first years of the century, he made his mark as a producer (with Arnold Daly) of BERNARD SHAW's drama. Then he turned to playwriting, sometimes in collaborations to which Smith contributed the broad Yankee comic situations and caricatured personifications in which he excelled. In 1906 he and Byron Ongley (? –1915) wrote a long-popular dramatization of George Barr McCutcheon's comic novel about an unexpected inheritance, *Brewster's Millions* (1902). *The Fortune Hunter* (1909), another Smith success, featured small-town types—and the first notable appearance of John Barrymore. *Turn to the Right* (1916), a farce written with John E. Hazzard (1881–1935), bears some resemblance in plot to Anouilh's THIEVES' CARNIVAL. But unquestionably Smith's greatest hit was LIGHTNIN' (1918, written with FRANK BACON), whose 1,291 consecutive performances, beginning in 1918, broke all previous Broadway records. None of Smith's later comedies is noteworthy, although he was tremendously successful (also as a play doctor) and died a millionaire.

SMUG CITIZENS, THE (*Meshchane*), a play in three acts by MAXIM GORKY, published and produced in 1902. Setting: a provincial town in Russia, 1902.

Gorky produced his first play (it has also appeared in English as *The Philistines, The Petty Bourgeois,* and *The Courageous One*) when he was already a famous writer. Though the Russian censors deleted such lines as "He who works is the master," it still created an uproar which is described in the memoirs of V. I. NEMIROVICH-DANCHENKO. Gorky himself was dissatisfied with this play, which came out the same year as THE LOWER DEPTHS, his masterpiece. The more CHEKHOVIAN *The Smug Citizens,* while weaker, is interesting historically (also because Nil is the first staged ideal hero of the Soviets): it became a favorite with Soviet audiences, and also proved theatrically successful in an Off-Broadway revival over half a century after its premiere.

The self-complacent and well-to-do Vasili Vasilevich Bezsemenov is a petty tyrant in his middle-class household. He is constantly angered, and as tedious as the rest of his family: his browbeaten wife, a son expelled from the university for radicalism, and a daughter, a spinster schoolteacher who expresses their attitudes of life: "It's dull and dreary and monotonous. Life is just a big, muddy river—and one gets so bored with it one doesn't even care enough to wonder why it flows." Their lack of spirit and direction is contrasted with the cheerful vitality and courage of various boarders and visitors. These include a prison official's vivacious young widow, who prefers convicts to the smug townsmen; Bezsemenov's foster son Nil, a young worker who is unintellectual but glories in living; and a choir singer who characterizes Bezsemenov as "an ideal Philistine." "You embody insipidness so completely," he tells him; "you embody that power which conquers even heroes and entire lives." When Nil decides to marry a poor but animated seamstress rather than Bezsemenov's daughter, the latter tries to kill herself by swallowing poison. The "smug citizen's" son has the intellect but lacks the spirit to stand up to his father; however, he may be saved by the young widow, who wants to marry him. At the end, Bezsemenov as usual proclaims his paternal martyrdom, while his wife wails, "What have we done that our children have punished us like this?" The daughter collapses over the piano, whose crashing discordant notes gradually die out.

SNOB, THE (*Der Snob*), a play in three acts by CARL STERNHEIM, published and produced in 1914. Setting: Germany before 1914.

The title character of this sequel to THE UNDERPANTS, which also appeared as *A Place in the World,* is the Maskes' son, Christian. Shortly before his rise to the presidency of a large corporation, he dismisses the mistress who taught him manners and bearing. To avoid another embarrassment, the discovery of his low origin, Christian pays his parents to leave the country while he successfully courts his titled partner's daughter. Then, when it becomes advantageous to introduce them, Christian summons his parents back to Germany. On his wedding night, Christian tells his bride a doctored version of the lost underpants: A vicomte saw his mother and fell in love with her about nine months before he was born, Christian says—but refuses to continue, for "there is also a son's respect for his mother," who has just died. "Blessed Adulteress!" the bride exclaims as she joyfully sinks into Christian's arms: "My dearest lord and master!"

The fortunes of the Maske family conclude in *1913* (1915). Christian is an elderly, titled munitions tycoon now, and has two worthless sons and a ruthless daughter with whom he struggles for domination. He foils her armaments deal but, realizing that their social order and civilization are doomed, he prophesies, "After us, the collapse!" He dies, and his degenerate children perform a *danse macabre* around his corpse.

SOCIALIST REALISM, the "basic method" of Soviet art and literature, was promulgated by Stalin, MAXIM GORKY, and the Party dictator for ideology in the arts, Andrei Aleksandrovich Zhdanov. Negating the possibility of individual creativity and extolling Lenin's demand for the "partyness of literature," socialist realism became compulsory with the establishment of the Union of Soviet Writers in 1932. Zhdanov defined socialist realism as the style necessary to the "truthful" depiction of life: "Not lifelessly, not just as 'objective reality,' but . . . in its revolutionary development." To do so the writer must be "an engineer of human minds," Zhdanov continued in his address before the Writers Union First Pan-Soviet Congress; "truthfulness and historical concreteness of artistic depiction must be combined with the task of ideological remolding and re-education of the toiling people in the spirit of Socialism."

Russian drama since the Revolution necessarily has adhered to this style, which is distinguished from ordinary REALISM by (1) its reflection of socialist concepts, (2) its being optimistic and positive, (3) its anticipation of socialist "tomorrows" instead of bourgeois utopias, and (4) its substitution—for the romanticism of early post-revolutionary writers—of a greater objectivity and humanism, to be reflected in the depiction of heroes. The translation of Zhdanov's speech is reprinted in H. G. Scott's edition of *Problems of Soviet Literature: Reports and Speeches at the First Writers' Congress* (1935). See also Gleb Struve's *Soviet Russian Literature 1917–50* (1951) and Edward J. Brown's *Russian Literature Since the Revolution* (revised 1969).

SODOM AND GOMORRAH (*Sodome et Gomorrhe*), a play in two acts and a prologue by JEAN GIRAUDOUX, published and produced in 1943. Setting: a country house outside Sodom and Gomorrah, in biblical times.

This is a stark, intense philosophical discourse, unrelieved by humor: an archangel delivers God's ultimatum to destroy the two cities unless one happy couple is found. Lia (the main character) and Jean are said to be such a couple, but the play reveals the contrary. They argue incessantly: Jean wants an ordinary wife, but Lia is a bitter, disillusioned intellectual who seeks perfection. Their bickerings are juxtaposed with those of another couple, equally unfulfilled. Believing themselves to be mismated, the couples exchange partners. In the meantime, the fearful inhabitants of the doomed cities turn to Samson and Delilah; but they are also unsuitable—a smugly deceitful wife and an uxorious husband. Lia and Jean's exchanges prove unsatisfying; they return to each other and resume arguing. Too selfish to avert it, they await the apocalypse. It occurs with the men and the women standing in separate groups. As they and the world are reduced to ashes, Lia and Jean's voices can still be heard. "Death was not enough," an angel remarks; "the quarrel goes on and on . . . and on. . . ."

SOFRONOV, Anatoli Vladimirovich (1911–), Russian poet and playwright, editor of the mass-circulation magazine *Ogonyok,* and author of light comedies and other drama that became popular in the Soviet repertoire. Sofronov's plays include *Milion za ulybku* (*Million for a Smile,* 1955; produced in London in 1967), *Dengi* (1956), *Stryapuha* (1959, his first hit), and *Gibel bogov* (1961). These are comedies interspersed with Sofronov's songs, and they are uniformly sympathetic to youth. Sofronov's most notorious play was *Karera Beketova* (1949), a portrayal of the humiliation of a cosmopolitan scholar and one of the works written in response to Andrei Aleksandrovich Zhdanov's (and the Central Committee's) anti-Western campaign. But despite its orthodoxy, the play was criticized. It is discussed in detail in Peter Yershov's *Comedy in the Soviet Theater* (1956).

SOLDIER TANAKA (*Der Soldat Tanaka*), a play in three acts by GEORG KAISER, published and produced in 1940. Setting: modern Japan.

This play is more bitterly antiwar than THE CITIZENS OF CALAIS. A social drama, it is a commentary on Nazi Germany, whence Kaiser had exiled himself—and on its perhaps even more ruthlessly autocratic Asian ally.

Visiting home on leave, Private Tanaka is surprised by his lavish reception despite rice-crop failures and consequent famine. He is told that his parents, eager to honor their warrior, have apprenticed his sister to a rich farmer. Accidentally he discovers her in a brothel, into which, she reveals, the desperate parents had to sell her to pay their war taxes. He kills her as well as her client, a brutish noncommissioned officer. Court-martialed and sentenced to death, Tanaka can save his life by pleading for the Emperor's pardon. Though heretofore he has been unquestioning in his loyalty to Emperor and State, he now rebels. Indignantly he tells the court how his sister was sold into prostitution to pay taxes for military debts: "Rice sometimes fails to grow—taxes always grow." And he concludes, "The Emperor should beg my pardon!" Having asserted his human dignity, Tanaka is executed.

SOLDIERS (*Soldaten*), a verse play in a prologue, three acts, and an epilogue by ROLF HOCHHUTH, published and produced in 1967. Setting: Coventry, a ship, a London bedroom, and a Buckinghamshire garden; 1943 and 1964.

Like THE DEPUTY, this very long and controversial work—subtitled *Nekrolog auf Genf* ("an obituary for Geneva")—is more interesting for its topic and more admirable for its moralistic fervor than for its dramaturgy. It is a play-within-a-play that depicts Winston Churchill as causing the death of General Wladyslaw Sikorski, head of the Polish government-in-exile, and provoking the Luftwaffe Blitz so he can retaliate with English terror bombings, "Vietnam style." The portrait of the British leader is ambivalent, worshipful as well as condemning. Production by Britain's National Theatre was banned, but elsewhere the play was produced in necessarily cut—but not necessarily censored—versions.

Prologue. In Coventry's cathedral a theatre director ("Everyman"), guilt-ridden by his participation in wartime bombings and eager to reform the Geneva Convention, rehearses his play about Churchill:

Acts I through III. On a battleship en route to Scapa Flow, Churchill debates mass terror bombings with his advisers and decides to approve them, in deference to his Russian allies. He discusses the future of Poland with his friend and ally Sikorski and realizes that this "very picturesque and knightly figure" may pose a threat to the Churchill-Stalin alliance—in part because of Sikorski's insistence that the Red Cross investigate the Katin murder of four thousand officers, attributed to the Nazis but committed by the Russians. From his bedside Churchill is conducting the war with General Sir Alan Brooke, and eventually decides to have Sikorski killed in a plane crash off Gibraltar. In the garden at Chequers later, discussing the morality of terror bombing with Bishop Bell of Chichester, the most influential and outspoken opponent of mass bombing, Churchill is informed of Sikorski's death. When the bishop notes that the Polish leader was Churchill's friend, the Prime Minister replies, "Men may be linked in friendship. / Nations are linked only by interests." Although ultimately shaken, he concludes to his incredulous associates, who are appalled by the betrayal of Sikorski, "Soldiers must die, / but by their death—they nourish / the nation that gave them birth."

Epilogue. "Greatness has its own dimensions," the director remarks, and when asked if Churchill really killed Sikorski, he replies, "If he thought it necessary, yes. / If not, no." A telegram is delivered and he announces, "The play has been banned in England."

SOLOGUB [pen name of Teternikov], **Fyodor Kuzmich** (1863–1927), Russian SYMBOLIST poet, novelist, and playwright, was born in St. Petersburg, the son of a shoemaker. "The greatest and most refined poet of the first generation of Symbolists," as Prince Mirsky called him, he made his reputation with *Melki bes* (*The Little Demon*), a novel about evil people in a province, completed in 1902 and first published serially (1905–07). Mirsky described Sologub's "strange genius" of portraying "Manichæan Idealism" and his "peculiar 'complex,'" which delighted in depicting the cruel and in humiliating the beautiful.

Sologub's plays share these characteristics—with an added measure of eroticism. As a dramatist, Sologub strove "to impose the order of beauty upon the chaos of nature," a process that invariably led to the protagonist's doom. The subjects of Sologub's plays, produced by Vsevolod Meyerhold with stylized settings, go back to classical and medieval times and eschew the present. (Sologub became disillusioned after the 1905 revolution and remained politically aloof thereafter.) His first play, *Dar mudrych pchol* (1907), reinterprets the legend of Laodamia, whose lover falls in the Trojan War and whose father destroys his statue ("Life melts like wax in the hot breath of Aphrodite" is the final choral chant). *Pobeda smerti* (1907), which has a medieval setting and is something of a pageant, was followed by the better-known *Vanka Klyuchnik i Pazh Zhean* (1909). This is an ironic contrast, in alternating scenes, of two seductions: the graceful one of a medieval French lady by her husband's page, and the coarse one of a contemporary Russian wife by the butler.

For Sologub's life and work see the relevant sections in D. S. Mirsky's *Contemporary Russian Literature 1881–1925* (1926).

SOLÓRZANO, Carlos (1922–   ), Guatemalan-born Mexican playwright, was praised as "a true and original dramatic talent" by his friend ALBERT CAMUS and by others as one of the great postwar American dramatists. Artistic director of Mexico's National University Theatre, he has published books on Mexican drama and theatre, and began his own career as a playwright with *Doña Beatriz* (1952), a portrayal of Beatriz de la Cueva, "The Luckless" wife of the sixteenth-century conquistador Pedro de Alvarado, as she succumbs to religious fanaticism and hatred of Indians because of her marital anguish. Solórzano continued to dramatize his humanism in *El hechicero* (1954), a stylized tragedy whose magician, Merlin, is a philosopher striving for the ideals of peace and goodness; and in *Las manos de Dios* (*God's Hands,* 1957), an agonizing tragedy that allegorizes the defeat of the Devil (a handsome youth who stands for goodness) by a priest (evil) who nonetheless fails to win the soul of the village girl, the prize for which they strive. Later one-acters further dramatize such themes in Solórzano's characteristically intellectual yet nonsimplistic and highly theatrical style.

In the 1960's Solórzano compiled and annotated a number of collections of modern LATIN AMERICAN plays and wrote an important history, *Teatro latinoamericano del siglo XX* (1961). A study of Solórzano is Frank Dauster's "The Drama of Carlos Solórzano," *Modern Drama* VII:1 (1964).

SOLOVYOV, Vladimir Aleksandrovich (1907–   ), Russian poet and playwright, was born in Sumy, a Ukrainian town situated between Kharkov and Kiev. His earliest published writing consisted of poetry, but soon he turned to drama. *My Olonetskie,* his first play, was staged in 1930, and depicts the lives of foundry workers. His next play, *Lichnaya zhizn* (1934), is in verse and achieved considerable popularity; it deals with the individual's rights in a collective society. *Semeinaya khronika* (1938), a play about Stakhanovite workers who discover their brother to be an enemy of the Soviets, was followed by Solovyov's masterpiece, *Feldmarshal Kutuzov* (*Field Marshal Kutuzov,* 1939). A monumental verse history play, it appeared shortly before the Nazi invasion of Russia, won the Stalin Prize, and was widely performed for years; it was filmed as *Kutuzov* (1944) and produced in America as *1812* (its original title was *A.D. 1812*). The play's hero is not so much Prince Mikhail Illarionovich Kutuzov, the general who helped defeat Napoleon (who also appears in the play), but rather the common and oppressed peasants, who fight only for love of their fatherland.

Solovyov's later dramas include *Front* (1941), a patriotic war play; *Veliki Gosudar* (1945), a whitewashing of Ivan the Terrible and, under the guise of a historical drama, a panegyric to Stalin as a great military and political leader; *Doroga pobedy* (1946), another war play in verse, featuring a heroic and indomitable officer captured by the Germans; *Myortvy kapital* (1956); and *Gibel poeta* (1962). Solovyov has also translated Rostand's CYRANO DE BERGERAC, dramatized stories of Dostoevsky and ANTON CHEKHOV, and has written film scripts. He and NIKOLAI POGODIN were among the first playwrights whose drama departed from civil-war themes.

Field Marshal Kutuzov appears in *Seven Soviet Plays* (1946) with a prefatory essay on Solovyov. *A Solovyov Anthology,* edited by S. L. Frank with a select bibliography, was published in 1950.

SORGE, Reinhard Johannes (1892–1916), German poet and dramatist, is notable principally for his first work, *Der Bettler* (THE BEGGAR, 1912). It was influential from the moment of its publication in 1912, though it remained unproduced for five years. Since the play brought EXPRESSIONISM to the German theatre, Sorge's name is significant in the annals of modern drama despite his failure to create any other drama of special distinction.

Sorge's life is dramatized in his autobiographical *The Beggar*. Born in Berlin of French-Protestant ancestry, he moved to Jena with his family in 1909 after the death of his father, whose mind had been deranged for many years. Sorge was influenced by the poetry of the German neoromanticists and the philosophy of Nietzsche. *The Beggar* came at the midpoint of Sorge's career, for it reflects Nietzsche's influence as well as the beginning of Sorge's liberation from it: the Poet is a Superman but also a humble "beggar" who subordinates personal ambitions to social betterment. Early in 1911, shortly before the composition of this play, Sorge met his future wife. In a transformed and idealized manner he dramatized this meeting in the story of the Poet and the Girl. Shortly afterward Sorge underwent a religious crisis. In 1913 he and his wife converted to Catholicism (Sorge at the same time added "Johannes" to his name) when they went to Rome, following his winning of the Kleist Prize upon the recommendation of the poet Richard Dehmel. About this time he also met the other distinguished poets he had admired for some time, Stefan George and Rainer Maria Rilke. In 1915 he entered the army, and he fell in Flanders a year later, in July 1916.

The play on which his reputation rests has failed to withstand the test of time and now appears naïve, full of bombast and bathos. The ecstatic quest for spiritual fulfillment and beauty embodied in its autobiographical Poet-Beggar was dramatized by Sorge in more explicitly religious terms in three mysteries collected as *Metanoeite* (1915); in the biblical *König David* (1916), and in his posthumous drama: *Gericht über Zarathustra* (1921), a play on Nietzsche and his best-known book; and *Der Sieg des Christos* (1922), one-acters on, respectively, Saint Francis and Luther. Sorge also published poetry and wrote essays, many of which, like other plays of his, have remained unpublished.

Of his drama, a truncated version of *The Beggar* appears in *An Anthology of German Expressionist Drama* (1963), edited by Walter H. Sokel. German studies of Sorge are noted in Richard Samuel and R. Hinton Thomas's *Expressionism in German Life, Literature and the Theatre (1919–1924)* (1939), which has a chapter on Sorge.

SOUMAGNE, Henri (1891–1951), Belgian playwright, is notable principally for *L'Autre Messie* (1923), a religious farce produced by Aurélien-Marie Lugné-Poë in Paris. Set in a run-down Warsaw saloon and full of topical allusions, it features a group of Jews arguing about the existence of God and culminates in a bizarre boxing match to decide whether God exists; the one who denies Him loses and, after a debate about His identity, the loser is proclaimed God. Soumagne's anti-Semitic attitudes in this play were repeated in his favorite work, *Madame Marie* (1928), a "mystery" that depicts Christ's Passion and attributes Judas's betrayal to Matthew's machinations. Other Soumagne plays include *Bas-Noyard* (1924), a farce on popular elections; *Les Danseurs de Gigue* (1925), a PIRANDELLian speculation on an individual's inhabiting two separate bodies; *Terminus* (1927), a mystic comedy about the fear of death; and, finally, a number of dramatizations of court scenes and trials, all of them appearing in the 1940's—the best of them, *Le Seigneur de Bury* (1946), about a nobleman's attempt to inherit an estate by nicotine-poisoning his brother-in-law.

Born to a middle-class Catholic family of Walloon origin, Soumagne was educated in Brussels's Jesuit college and the university. He received a law degree and became a barrister. A blasphemous mystic whose highly theatrical but unconventional drama shocked audiences in Belgium and other European countries, Soumagne started to write plays while a prisoner of war. His life and work are discussed in Vernon Mallinson's *Modern Belgian Literature 1830–1960* (1966).

SOUPAULT, Philippe (1897–   ), French poet and novelist, began his career as a DADAIST and SURREALIST, collaborating with ANDRÉ BRETON in the "automatic writing" of plays such as *Les Champs magnétiques* (1920) and *S'il vous plaît* (IF YOU PLEASE, 1920). Subsequently Soupault gave up avant-garde writing for lyrical novels and, eventually, literary and political criticism. He published his memoirs, *Histoire d'un blanc* (1927) and, after his wartime imprisonment by the Vichy government, *Le Temps des assassins* (*Age of Assassins*, 1945).

SOUTH AFRICA has produced literature in English, in Afrikaans, and in the vernacular. It consists mostly of prose (especially short stories) and poetry because tours by major British troupes have discouraged playwriting by the natives. Though English-language and Afrikaans theatres have entertained white audiences for centuries, the Boers were the first to produce drama in South Africa, notably *Die Wildeboudjie* (*The Quarter of Venison*, 1941) by F. S. Steyn (1913–53). DORIS LESSING has been the only prominent South African author of European descent to become a playwright, though some of Alan Paton's fiction has been dramatized.

An upsurge of native drama began in the 1950's. Its most important product was the racially mixed theatre of Athol Fugard (1932–　　), a controversial white writer whose plays were also produced abroad: the antiapartheid *The Blood Knot* (1961), about two brothers, one black, the other white; an intense but nonracial two-character domestic drama, *Hello and Goodbye* (1967); and *Boesman and Lena* (1970), a three-character drama about a half-breed white South Africans classify as "colored." In the 1960's, apartheid soon stymied this lively growth of native drama. Leading playwrights went into exile or were banned. Among the former are the revolutionary Negroes Alfred Hutchinson (1924–　　), grandson of a Swazi chief and author of *The Rain-Killers* (1964); and Lewis Nkosi (1936–　　), whose *The Rhythm of Violence* (1964) bears comparison with Arden's SERJEANT MUSGRAVE'S DANCE.

Hutchinson's and Nkosi's plays were republished in Fredric M. Litto's *Plays from Black Africa* (1968), which has an introduction and notes. *Curtain Up! The Story of Cape Theatre* (1951) is a three-hundred-year chronicle by the once-prominent playwright and music critic Olga Racster (1875–1955). Other studies are noted under AFRICA.

SOUTH PACIFIC, a musical play in two acts by OSCAR HAMMERSTEIN II and JOSHUA LOGAN (with music by Richard Rodgers), published and produced in 1949. Setting: two islands in the South Pacific during World War II.

Immensely successful all over the world, this is a Pulitzer Prize dramatization of two of James A. Michener's *Tales of the South Pacific* (1947): "Our Heroine," featuring the wartime romance of a sophisticated elderly French planter and a naïve Army nurse from Arkansas; and "Fo' Dollah," the MADAME BUTTERFLY romance of a Tonganese girl and a United States Army lieutenant that became the musical's subplot. Of great appeal were the exotic wartime setting and characters, the bittersweet romance hampered by personal as well as racial problems, and songs such as "I'm Gonna Wash That Man Right outa My Hair," "I'm in Love with a Wonderful Guy," "Some Enchanted Evening," "Bali Ha'i," and others.

SOYA, Carl Erik (1896–　　), Danish author born in Copenhagen, was in his time the *enfant terrible* of Scandinavian dramatists. Relentlessly satirizing middle-class values, he ruffled audiences' sensibilities with vulgar language and Freudian symbols and themes. Soya's drama is notable more for its vivacious and salty dialogue and for its topics than for its ideas, though his later works have been likened to those of HENRIK IBSEN.

The cynical *Parasitterne* (1929) is a grim, NATURALISTIC social satire that met with little success—as did the Freudian *Hvem er jeg?* (1931) and *Lord Nelson* (1934), and satires like *Chas* (1938) and *Min høje hat* (1939), in which Soya features himself as a visiting professor who fulfills the dreams of various members of a disaffected middle-class family. Soya made his mark with a popular trilogy (subsequently a tetralogy) of unresolved PROBLEM PLAYS about justice: *Brudstykker af et mønster* (1940), *To tråde* (*Two Threads*, 1943), and *Tredive års henstand* (1944); later he added a farcical epilogue with alternate resolutions, *Frit valg* (1948). He wrote a few plays about the German occupation and a highly theatrical antiwar comedy, *Løve med korset* (1950); it employs cinematic devices and other props and features an angel of peace and three "doctors" who try to determine the cause of his sickness (i.e., of war): a materialist, a psychologist, and a romanticist. Yet another of his plays is an adaptation of the Orpheus legend, *Petersen i dødsriget* (1957).

Soya, the son of an art professor and the author of detective stories and newspaper articles, also published semiautobiographical psychological novels, *Min farmors hus* (*My Grandmother's House*, 1943) and *Sytten* (*Seventeen*, 1953–54). *Two Threads* appears, with comments on Soya, in Elias Bredsdorff's edition of *Contemporary Danish Plays* (1955). For further discussion of his work see P. M. Mitchell's *A History of Danish Literature* (1957).

SOYINKA, Wole (1934–　　), Nigerian novelist, poet, and dramatist, was the first African writer of international repute. He has been likened to J. M. SYNGE—and the Elizabethans—for his use of lusty poetry to reinvigorate English-language plays in which tribal customs and bushmen appear in a dramaturgical mixture of the native and the European. His works were produced by Soyinka-founded Nigerian theatre companies, notably the 1960 Masks and the Orisun Players. Particularly successful were THE LION AND THE JEWEL (1963) and THE TRIALS OF BROTHER JERO (1964), two of the ten plays Soyinka had finished by 1967, when he was arrested by his government for attempting to help end the Nigerian-Biafran civil war. He remained in prison two years, most of the time in solitary confinement.

Born in Isara, Ijebu Ramo, to a family of the large Yoruba tribe, Soyinka attended the University of Ibadan, whose school of drama he later headed. In 1954 Soyinka visited England. He attended the University of Leeds and was a play reader in London. In 1960 he returned to Nigeria to lecture at various universities and to produce his plays. These are based on Yoruba myth, religion, and poetry; but they express modern themes in contemporary African settings, though they employ traditional masks, drums, and dance. Vibrant and full of gusto and humor, Soyinka's plays nonetheless explore the darkness of men's hearts. Old as well as new values are satirized by Soyinka, and his themes deal with the scapegoat, with man as a killer, and with the return of the savage old gods as well as the Messiah.

The Strong Breed, one of Soyinka's *Five Plays* (1964), parallels the Christian Passion tale in a terrifying jungle hunt (with flashbacks reminiscent of O'Neill's THE EMPEROR JONES) and the ritual sacrifice of a native intellectual torn in his commitments between tribal custom and modern social progress. Other plays in the *Five Plays* collection are *The Swamp Dwellers,* a drama of anger at apparently senseless crop destructions and man's loss of faith; and *A Dance of the Forests,* a complex SYMBOLIC play produced in 1960 at the Nigerian Independence celebration and featuring numerous characters, including a dead couple and a "carver" thrown together in the woods among spirits.

Later Soyinka plays are *The Road* (1965), a prize winner that is something of an African WAITING FOR GODOT; and *Kongi's Harvest* (1967), a highly theatrical and poetic, if not always lucid, mixture of the plots and themes of *The Trials of Brother Jero* and *The Strong Breed.* Following his release from prison at the end of the civil war, Soyinka visited the United States, where he helped stage his *Madmen and Specialists* (1970), a play he described as dealing with "the betrayal of vocation for the attraction of power in one form or another."

Wole Soyinka, 1970. (*Vernon L. Smith* from "Scope")

Soyinka's plays have been published and discussed extensively in all modern literature and theatre studies of Nigeria and WEST AFRICA.

SPAIN. Spanish drama* became the country's least distinguished form of literature after the Golden Age of Lope de Vega, Tirso de Molina, and Calderón. Its phenomenal decline has been attributed to debased and commercial tastes; to excellent dramatic surrogates such as flamenco, bullfights, and religious processions; and to the economic, social, and especially the political environment. Members of the Falangist Party killed Spain's most distinguished modern dramatist, FEDERICO GARCÍA LORCA,† and the repressive totalitarian censorship of Franco's regime that was to rule long after the Civil War (1936–39) alienated many others, including the highly esteemed JACINTO GRAU and ALEJANDRO CASONA (the first contender for García Lorca's preeminence), who spent their productive years in exile. Among significant recent playwrights, ANTONIO BUERO VALLEJO and ALFONSO SASTRE have been rarely produced in Spain and their reputations have remained principally "underground," while FERNANDO ARRABAL totally severed native ties and became a French-writing Parisian.

Distinctive features of Spanish drama are its ritual, its poetic language, and its portrayals of explosive passions—sexual as well as religious. The Don Juan legend is recurrently revived by Spanish playwrights, and each November 2 to cap off visits to the cemeteries on All Saints' Day there are performances of the hackneyed but ever-popular José Zorrilla (1817–93) version, *Don Juan Tenorio* (1844).

The first important modern Spanish playwright was JOSÉ ECHEGARAY, who was soon followed by a second Nobel Prize laureate, JACINTO BENAVENTE. The latter, as incredibly prolific as his classical predecessors and some modern Spaniards, was one of the principal figures of the so-called Generation of 1898. Spain had been deeply shaken by its defeat by the United States that year, and the movement brought about a turning point in Spanish life as well as in its literature. Institutions were founded where later-influential artists and writers (including García Lorca and RAFAEL ALBERTI, who subsequently went into exile) experimented with SYMBOLISM, SURREALISM, DADA, and other forms.

* See also LATIN AMERICA.

† Spanish surnames frequently are composites of both parents' names.

Other major writers of the Generation of 1898—notably the philosopher-poet MIGUEL DE UNAMUNO, the flamboyant poet-novelist RAMÓN MARÍA DEL VALLE-INCLÁN, and the novelist-essayist Azorín (José Martínez Ruiz, 1873–1967), whose surrealist as well as other dramas have remained little known—played a lesser role in Spain's theatrical life. So, too, did important figures not principally associated with either the Generation of 1898 or the drama, such as the major novelist BENITO PÉREZ GALDÓS and the artist SANTIAGO RUSIÑOL, who is remembered as a dramatist because of his association with the equally versatile but much more important GREGORIO MARTÍNEZ SIERRA. The latter's gentle and optimistic drama had great popular appeal, though it was the Andalusian ÁLVAREZ QUINTERO brothers who excelled in folk drama, particularly in *sainetes,* as the short, usually comic one-acters are called. Another master of unpretentious short popular dramatic forms—known as the *género chico*—was Carlos Arniches y Barrera (1866–1943), a greatly favored author of over two hundred *sainetes* and *zarzuelas* (comedies in which music, singing, and dancing alternate with dialogue). One of the most notable *zarzuelas* is *La verbena de la Paloma* (1894) by the prolific librettist Ricardo de la Vega (1839–1910). Also popular in the Spanish theatre has been puppetry, occasionally and differently employed by Rusiñol, Valle-Inclán, Benavente, García Lorca, and others.

NATURALISM and thesis drama in the early modern Spanish theatre was best represented by Echegaray's disciple Joaquín Dicenta (1863–1917); his *Juan José* (1895) depicts the brutalization of a decent laborer, while *El lobo* (1913) portrays the regeneration of a criminal. The Catalonian poet Ángel Guimerá (1849–1924) also wrote naturalist plays in Catalan and Castilian, including *Terra Baixa* (1896, translated as *Marta of the Lowlands*), a violent sex drama culminating in a laborer's murder of his boss, who has been trying to renew a former intimacy with the laborer's wife; and *La pecadora* (1902, translated as *Daniela*), about a lady who returns wealthy but sick to her native village, where envy and cruelty hasten her death. The Castilian poet Eduardo Marquina (1879–1946) wrote lavishly produced declamatory verse drama on historical themes, most successfully on the final days of Spain's occupation of the Netherlands, *En Flandes se ha puesto el sol* (1910); and *Cuando florezcan los rosales* (*When the Roses Bloom Again,* 1913), a drama about a selfless woman who relinquishes her man to the sick friend who also loves him, but then finds happiness with a devoted old admirer.

Praised as the finest Spanish historical drama of the nineteenth century was the poet Gaspar Núñez de Arce's (1834–1903) *El haz de leña* (1872), which focuses on the mysterious death of the crown prince Don Carlos. Though more notable as lyric poets, the Machado brothers, Manuel (1874–1947) and Antonio (1875–1939), also collaborated on historical and other verse drama, the most successful being *La Lola se va a los puertos* (1930). Manuel Linares Rivas (1867–1938) wrote moral satires of human frailties and tackled social and political problems; his masterpiece is *La garra* (*The Claw,* 1914), the tragedy of a man destroyed by reactionaries because he obtained a divorce. The classical scholar Pedro Muñoz Seca (1881–1936) wrote many popular *astracanadas*—clever intrigues that deal with the grotesque and utilize puns—such as *La venganza de don Mendo* (1918). Now forgotten but once significant as a playwright was the novelist Eduardo Zamacois (1876–1954), whose *Los reyes pasan* (*The Passing of the Magi,* 1912), a sentimental one-acter about an unhappy widow who runs off to her lover, is featured in Charles A. Turrell's anthology (see below).

The second modern period of Spanish literature, including drama, has been heralded as a new golden age. This period started shortly before the fall of Primo de Rivera's dictatorship in 1930. Beginning in the following year, the short-lived Republican regime sponsored two traveling theatre companies to educate the unlettered rural masses with productions of Golden Age drama and, to organize and direct these troupes, appointed two promising modern writers—García Lorca and Casona. The dramatic creativity of both these writers was inspired and affected by these appointments. During the same decade JARDIEL PONCELA became notable for his popular light drama, and the patriot JOSÉ MARÍA PEMÁN was praised for his histories and his adaptations of the classics. Franco's rise to power aborted the domestic careers of many promising writers, and significant Spanish drama therefore was written abroad, in France and Latin America. To the major exiled figures already mentioned may be added other, if less important, names in the theatre: the poet Pedro Salinas (1891–1951), who produced works in all genres, wrote thirteen plays that were collected in 1957; and the artist Pablo Picasso (1881–   ), who created decor and designs for many French productions,* himself wrote a couple of surrealist fantasies, of which the later-produced *Le Désir attrapé par la queue* (*Desire Caught by the Tail*) was banned as "salacious" after a public reading in 1944 by the artist, ALBERT CAMUS, JEAN-PAUL SARTRE, and others. In Spain itself, Víctor Ruiz Iriarte (1912–   ), a journalist and prolific playwright whose first hit was *El landó de seis caballos* (1950), placed his naturalistic and romantic plots in settings of poetic fantasy. Other playwrights who are notable because of their tremendous popularity and occasional success in having their works produced abroad include JOSÉ LÓPEZ RUBIO, MIGUEL MIHURA, JOAQUÍN CALVO SOTELO, and ALFONSO PASO. Though they claimed to convey serious and critical themes, theirs is by and large boulevard fare. More promising is the drama of JOSÉ-MARÍA BELLIDO and LAURO OLMO, whose work first attracted attention in the 1960's. Others who became known in that decade—though their plays more often than not were banned in Spain and first appeared abroad—

* See Douglas Cooper's handsomely illustrated monograph, *Picasso's Theatre* (1968).

are José Ruibal (1925–), whose cabaret pieces include extended satirical skits such as *El asno* (*The Jackass,* 1970) and *El hombre y la mosca* (*The Man and the Fly,* 1970); and Antonio Martínez Ballesteros (1929–), whose cynical allegories are set in mythical places: *En el país de Jauja* (*The Best of All Possible Worlds,* 1966; a satire of dictatorships) and *El héroe* (*The Hero,* 1970; on the futility of heroism).

Aside from the works of Benavente and García Lorca, few modern Spanish plays are readily accessible in English. There are a number of collections, including Barrett H. Clark's *Masterpieces of Modern Spanish Drama* (1917), Charles A. Turrell's *Contemporary Spanish Dramatists* (1919), Angel Flores's *Spanish Drama* (1962), Robert W. Corrigan's *Masterpieces of the Modern Spanish Theatre* (1967), Michael Benedikt and George E. Wellwarth's *Modern Spanish Theatre* (1968), Wellwarth's *The New Wave Spanish Drama* (1970), and Marion Holt's *The Modern Spanish Stage: Four Plays* (1970). Their introductions and bibliographies may be supplemented with such works as Richard E. Chandler and Kessel Schwartz's *A New History of Spanish Literature* (1961); and Robert O'Brien's annotated bibliography, *Spanish Plays in English Translation* (1963).

SPENDER, Stephen (1909–), known principally as an English poet, associated with W. H. AUDEN and other poets. He wrote one notable play, TRIAL OF A JUDGE (1938). Other works include translations of FRANK WEDEKIND and of ERNST TOLLER's last play, *Pastor Hall* (1939); and Spender's autobiography, *World Within World* (1951).

SPEWACK, Bella [Cohen] (1899–) and **Sam[uel]** (1899–1971), American dramatist-collaborators born in Hungary and Russia, respectively, and married in 1922. At a very early age both emigrated to the United States with their parents. They became journalists, Mrs. Spewack assisting her husband when he was a foreign correspondent in the 1920's. In that decade they began writing comedies, and they became famous with the Hollywood satire *Boy Meets Girl* (1935), whose two prankster screenwriters are caricatures of the irreverent BEN HECHT and CHARLES MACARTHUR. *Leave It to Me* (1938), another popular collaboration, was a satiric musical (music by Cole Porter) based on the Spewacks' earlier play on their experiences in Moscow, *Clear All Wires* (1932); it introduced Mary Martin (singing "My Heart Belongs to Daddy") to Broadway. Aside from over a dozen plays, the Spewacks wrote film and television scripts, and during World War II Sam Spewack headed the OWI's Bureau of Motion Pictures. Popular postwar collaborations include a modern play-within-a-play musical adaptation of Shakespeare's *The Taming of the Shrew, Kiss Me, Kate* (1948, again with Porter); and *My Three Angels* (1953), a murder comedy based on Albert Husson's (1912–) Paris hit, *La Cuisine des anges* (1952). Both wrote fiction, and Sam Spewack did a number of plays by himself—notably *Under the Sycamore Tree* (1952). But the best Spewack work is their jointly produced comic and satiric drama.

SPREADING THE NEWS, a one-act play by LADY GREGORY, produced in 1904 and published in 1909. Setting: the outskirts of a contemporary Irish village fair.

Lady Gregory's first comic peasant drama concluded the opening bill (it began with Yeats's ON BAILE'S STRAND) of the Abbey Theatre. Originally conceived as a tragedy, this farce has been frequently revived.

Bartley Fallon is a henpecked and lugubrious little man who is convinced that "if there's ever any misfortune coming to this world, it's on myself it pitches." He goes to return a pitchfork to a neighbor, and village gossip soon has it that Fallon has murdered the neighbor for love of the neighbor's wife. A pompous new magistrate gets his chance to muddle the case further. He arrests Fallon, whose wife tears into her meek "villain." Even the appearance of the "dead" neighbor fails to clear up the mistake or to satisfy the magistrate, who arrests both men. As they are taken away, Fallon tragically predicts that in their cell his neighbor's handcuffs will be removed, "and murder will be done that time surely!"

SPRING'S AWAKENING (*Frühlings Erwachen*), a "tragedy of childhood" in three acts by FRANK WEDEKIND, published in 1891 and produced in 1906. Setting: contemporary Germany.

Wedekind's first important and most popular play—long banned as obscene, it made him famous and engendered many imitations when finally produced by Max Reinhardt—depicts the sexual awakening of adolescents. Their troubled confusion is aggravated by the stupid prudery of their elders, who are responsible for the ensuing tragedies. The play consists of short, episodic, and occasionally fragmentary and stylized scenes. The children's lyrical, emotionally heightened language contrasts with that of their farcically imbecilic schoolmasters and evasive, primly narrowminded parents.

Act I. "Why have you made my frock so long, Mother?" fourteen-year-old Wendla Bergmann asks, and is told that the "penitential garment," as the girl calls it, must keep her warm. The parents of her schoolmates are even stricter, which intensifies the pressure of schoolwork. Particularly disturbed are Moritz Stiefel—a poor student who worries about the effect his failure would have on his parents—and his friend, Melchior Gabor. Both feel their self-asserting manhood. The more erudite Melchior tries to explain, and suggests "a cozy chat about reproduction"; but Moritz must study for examinations and cannot let himself be distracted: "To swot successfully I must be as stolid as an ox." Amongst themselves, the girls, like the boys, puzzle about sex and decide they will bring up their own children more liberally. One sunny afternoon Melchior and Wendla happen to meet in the woods, and soon are troubled by their emotions. When she chides Melchior for kissing her, he protests: "You must see that I'm controlling myself. . . . Why are you so ungenerous with your riches! You can trust me to make no movement that will frighten you! But before you go, tell me just this one thing—when will I see you again, you fortune's favorite?" Wendla replies, "When I come after you, that's when you'll see me again."*

Act II. Melchior's mother gently rebukes him for reading Goethe's *Faust*. Later Moritz explains: "Your Mama means the business with Gretchen." The boys discuss the long essay on sex that Melchior has written for Moritz, who is exhausted by his studies. Wendla's mother, in the meantime, tells the girl that the stork has just visited her sister. When the mother laughs at Wendla's naïve questions, the girl reveals she has not "the slightest idea how it all comes about," and begs her mother to explain. Making a supreme effort, she haltingly tries: "In order to have a child—one must love the man—to whom one is married" with a love "one can't describe," in a way that "you at your age are incapable of loving. —Now you know." One night Wendla visits Melchior in a hayloft. "I've come after you," she keeps on repeating, and weakly tries to resist him: "People love each other—if they kiss—don't, don't!" Overcome by uncontrollable feelings, they embrace as Melchior assures her, "There's no such thing as *love!* It's all egoism, self-seeking!" Moritz learns that he has failed the examinations, cannot get money to leave home, and despairs when he thinks of his parents. By the banks of a river a former schoolmate turned prostitute tries to seduce him. Moritz sends her away—"For that one needs a clear head and a carefree heart. But it's a pity—a pity to have missed such an opportunity"—and weeps as he prepares to commit suicide: "*This child of fortune, child of the sunshine! This prostitute, on my way of sorrows!* —Oh!—Oh! . . . Now I shan't go home any more."

Act III. The schoolmasters ostensibly debate the expulsion of Melchior. His essay for Moritz, "The Facts of Propagation," has abetted the high-school "suicide epidemic." In a farcical scene, "Monkeyfat," "Brokenbones," and other teachers spend most of the time deciding not to open a window in the stuffy room, for "the prevailing atmosphere leaves nothing to be desired." Though Melchior tries to defend his scientific essay, he is summarily expelled. Moritz's father is encouraged by a smug minister and hypocritical relatives to disown his son at the funeral. After they leave, the prostitute comes by with a friend. She has removed the pistol with which Moritz blew off his head ("His brains were hanging in the willowtrees round about"). After prolonged consideration, Melchior's self-righteous father persuades the mother to send their son to a reformatory: "The boy will at last learn to desire what is *good* rather than what is *interesting*, to conduct himself with reference to the law rather than to his own natural inclinations." Wendla dies after an abortion her mother has forced on the still-naïve girl, who could not believe she was pregnant ("I'm not married!"). She cries out, "Oh, Mother, why didn't you tell me everything?" Melchior escapes from the monstrous reformatory and appears at Wendla's grave on a winter night. The ghost of Moritz, carrying his head under his arm, tries to persuade his boyhood friend to join him in death. But a "Muffled Gentleman"—the author, representing Life—reveals the hypocrisy of bourgeois behavior and the superiority of life over death. He shows Melchior the way, gives him strength, and leads him to life. Moritz's ghost remains alone, ready to "lie down on my back, warm myself with putrefaction, and smile—"

* In Wedekind's original version, instead of the kiss, Wendla begs Melchior to beat her with a switch, harder and harder. He does so, then madly pummels her with his fists until she screams, and finally, "sobbing pitifully," he runs off.

SQUARING THE CIRCLE (*Kvadratura kruga*), "a jest in three acts" by VALENTIN PETROVICH KATAEV, published and produced in 1928. Setting: a room in a municipalized Moscow tenement in the late 1920's.

Kataev's best-known play, *Squaring the Circle* resembles Coward's PRIVATE LIVES and has been performed throughout the world. Western translations stress his satire of paradoxes and excesses in the Soviet Party line. But though it is a sportive farce about Communist life, Kataev reaffirms the ideals of its Komsomol (Communist Youth League) protagonists, whose problems are accentuated—and made more comic—by the Moscow housing shortage.

Act I. Without informing each other, Komsomol roommates Vasya and Avram get married. First appears the serious Vasya with his bride, Lyudmila. A flirtatious girl eager to establish a domicile, Lyudmila is shocked to discover that they will have to share the room with Vasya's friend. She drags Vasya away from his homemade radio. "Pussy—do you love me?" she asks him, and demands that he kiss her "on my teeny-weeny nose." Then she rushes off for things to make the room more cozy. The bride of the more frivolous roommate, Avram, arrives. A serious Komsomol, Tonya is only mildly surprised that she and her new husband will have to share the room with Vasya, her former boyfriend. Quickly she settles down to study her Communist books. Just as Vasya has had trouble adjusting to the "bourgeois" Lyudmila, the comfort-loving Avram has trouble adjusting to his no-nonsense bride. He rationalizes their compatibility: "Class consciousness, a common political platform, labor solidarity." The roommates finally confess their marriages. "Just another concession to the petty bourgeoisie and to the prosperous peasantry," Avram admits. They agree to divide their quarters by drawing a chalk line across the room. Each couple then settles on its side. Vasya looks over at Tonya, longingly, and together the two soon start a Communist student song. Jealous, Lyudmila becomes more possessive. "Vasyuk, darling, tell your pussykin 'Meow!' Right away, say 'Meow'!" she insists. Annoyed, Vasya barks out, "Meow!"

Act II. The divided room now consists of two distinct parts. Lyudmila's is very homey, while Tonya's is bleak and empty—for her money goes for books. Vasya gets increasingly irritated with Lyudmila, who keeps wanting to exchange kisses on their "teeny-weeny noses" and tries to feed him milk and make him "your wifie's roly-poly little boy." "I'm drowning in this petty bourgeois swamp," he finally exclaims: "kiss your own damn nose!" and he runs out. The hungry Avram has "a real 100% medieval family scene" with Tonya, who angrily leaves. Avram tiptoes into the other side to steal some food. His clumsiness amuses Lyudmila, who has been quietly weeping for Vasya. Soon she feeds the more congenial Avram, and flirts with and babies him. They rationalize their kissing, and go out together. Vasya and Tonya return to the empty room, and their mutual attraction, too, grows. They consider marrying. "Will it be the right thing to do from the point of view of Communist family morality?" Tonya asks, and then sadly decides in the negative: "We shall have to surrender our personal well-being in the interest of general social well-being." Vasya replies, "How unpleasant"—but their feelings overwhelm them. An older comrade appears just as they embrace. Naturally he assumes that they are the married couple, and when Avram reappears amorously with Lyudmila, the comedy of errors is heightened. "Go on kissing, kids, go on kissing. This can't hurt the Revolution," the old Bolshevik remarks. He is joined by an athletic poet and a group of youngsters, come to celebrate the double wedding.

Act III. Alone after the celebration, Lyudmila and Avram sadly agree they cannot marry: it would hurt their doting spouses too much. "It is wrong in principle to build personal family happiness on a foundation of the domestic unhappiness of other comrades," Avram concludes, and leaves. Vasya is astounded by his wife's newly acquired (from Avram) Party-line language. Each wants to get rid of—without hurting the feelings of—the other. The same situation arises between Avram and Tonya, who finally leaves and sends Avram a farewell letter. Avram dances with joy, but when Vasya hears of Tonya's departure, he turns on his roommate. "You lousy little bourgeois!" he calls Avram, who calls Vasya "a renegade and an opportunist." The wise and experienced old Bolshevik finally straightens out matters. Both couples argue, fight, and try to rationalize their behavior on ideological grounds. "Don't be an overclever parrot," he tells the sloganeering Avram, and agrees to divorce and remarry them with their proper mates. The poet recites new verses, and the old Bolshevik tells the lovers to "love one another and don't play the fool. It can't hurt the Revolution." Vasya turns on his homemade radio to a confusion of station noises. "By radio we met, and by radio we wed, and by radio we got a pretty baby Red," a gay voice sings; other voices intone, "Love, superstition and other bourgeois prejudices . . . Workers of the world . . ." And a Red Army song blares forth.

SQUIRE, Sir **J[ohn] C[ollings]** (1884–1958), English writer, is memorable as a leading poet of the Georgian school, editor-in-chief of the English Men of Letters series, and many volumes of essays, literary criticism, history, biography, and travelogues. Sir John (who published much of his work under the name J. C. Squire) was also a skillful parodist, and his *Collected Parodies* (1921) include many on repertory drama. Though he himself produced only a single unimportant play, the one-act comedy *The Clown of Stratford* (1922), he is notable as a dramatist because he coauthored (with JOHN LLOYD BALDERSTON) a once-popular and still-intriguing play, BERKELEY SQUARE (1926).

STAGE DOOR, a play in three acts by EDNA FERBER and GEORGE S. KAUFMAN, published and produced in 1936. Setting: the Footlights Club for young actresses, contemporary New York City.

This amusing, sentimental play depicts the tribulations of a group of budding actresses. They include a girl who commits suicide when she fails to make a living on Broadway, and a second-rate actress with a pretty face who goes to Hollywood and becomes a great star. The plot focuses on Terry Randall, who refuses to compromise by going to Hollywood; her more equivocal boyfriend, a left-wing playwright become scriptwriter, "one of those fellows [who] started out on a soapbox and ended up in a swimming pool"; and a famous movie director, a former theatre man who finally rejects Hollywood and gives Terry the leading part in his Broadway production.

STALLINGS, Laurence (1894–1968), American playwright and novelist, is most notable for his collaboration with MAXWELL ANDERSON on WHAT PRICE GLORY? (1924). It was Stallings who was so impressed by his fellow journalist's first play (WHITE DESERT) that he helped have it produced. Their joint masterpiece was followed the next year (1925) by two further collaborations about swashbucklers, *First Flight* and *The Buccanneer;* the first features young Andrew Jackson, the second Sir Henry Morgan. He succeeded with neither of these plays, nor with a few he wrote by himself at the time.

Stallings was born in Georgia. A marine during World War I, he lost a leg in combat and was as embittered about war as his famous collaborator. He became a New York journalist and critic, wrote novels, edited a best-selling photographic account of *The First World War* (1933), and wrote many operatic and screen scenarios, including that of ERNEST HEMINGWAY's *A Farewell to Arms* (1930). Stallings returned to journalism to serve as a foreign correspondent in the Ethiopian war in 1935.

His collaborations with Anderson were published as *Three American Plays* (1926). A good account of his life is his autobiographical novel, *Plumes* (1924).

STATE OF SIEGE (*L'État de siège*), a play in three parts by ALBERT CAMUS, published and produced in 1948. Setting: modern Cádiz, Spain.

This declamatory, operatic spectacle is not an adaptation of *The Plague,* despite the dictator's name. As Camus also noted in his preface, it is a didactic allegory.

The Plague, a fat and dour uniformed man accompanied by his female secretary, Death, easily takes over the city from its despicable government. He puts the nihilistic drunk Nada in charge of a siege of terror and death. A courageous medical student, Diego, resists the tyranny. His faith and sacrifice of his own life save his sweetheart and return life and freedom to the city.

STATE OF THE UNION, a comedy in three acts by HOWARD LINDSAY and RUSSEL CROUSE, produced in 1945 and published in 1946. Setting: contemporary Washington, Detroit, and New York.

This amusing political satire mentioned real persons and was altered daily to fit the news. A popular Pulitzer Prize winner, it portrays a successful industrialist (like the 1940 Republican candidate Wendell Willkie) being groomed for the presidential nomination. His success is threatened by rivalry between his estranged wife and his scheming mistress, and even more by his own honesty. He refuses to temporize, to give in to the many pressures and agree to the necessary shady deals—and forgoes the nomination. But though he quits the race, "I'm not out of politics. Nobody can afford to be out of politics," he tells his wife, promising to stump the land, to bring "the people" into politics and give them honest answers. The sentimentally contrived ending suggests that "the state of the union" as well as his personal happiness are secure when he takes his reconciled wife in his arms and assures her, "We've got something great to work for!"

STEFFEN, Albert (1884–1963), Swiss writer and philosopher, in 1925 became the leader of the mystic Christian anthroposophist sect, whose teachings he dramatized in *Das Viergetier* (1924) and *Hieram und Salomo* (1927). The latter, a play about Solomon and Queen Sheba, is the last in a biblical trilogy whose other parts are *Barnabas* (1949) and *Das Todeserlebnis des Manes* (1934), a drama about the founder of the Manichaeans, Mani. In this as in other plays, such as *Auszug aus Ägypten* (1916) and *Alexanders Wandlung* (1953), Steffen expressed spiritual values in the manner of LEO TOLSTOI and PAUL ERNST. Among the finest of Steffen's sixteen dramas are *Friedenstragödie* (1936), which portrays Woodrow Wilson's postwar career in a tragedy of pure idealism; and *Pestalozzi* (1939), whose humanitarian title hero, the first great exponent of universal education, becomes Steffen's real victor in Alexander I and Napoleon's conflict for world domination. Though he was a major figure in prewar Swiss literature, few of Steffen's seventy-odd works, including novels and poetry, are available abroad. For a study in English, see Ruth J. Hofrichter's *Three Poets and Reality* (1942).

STEIN, Gertrude (1874-1946), American writer and Paris literary-salon hostess for her country's "lost generation" (notably ERNEST HEMINGWAY, though there were innumerable other writers), to whom she assigned that label, and other artists and writers from all over the world. Among her publications are many plays. The first of them, *It Happened a Play,* was written in 1913 and portrays a dinner party (according to her autobiography, *The Autobiography of Alice B. Toklas,* 1933). It was revived as *What Happened,* a HAPPENING classic, and won an Obie Award in 1964. This and her other plays were conceived as "static in form" and written in her usual apparently plotless, discursive, "nonobjective prose" style. Many of them belong to the DADAIST movement. YES IS FOR A VERY YOUNG MAN (1946), one of her last works, had a respectable run in a 1948 Princeton Players production. Her *In Circles* playlet, "a circular play" about a group of friends in a French garden, became a successful avant-garde musical Off-Broadway in 1967. Other dramatic work by Gertrude Stein consists of opera librettos (with music by Virgil Thompson), notably *Four Saints in Three Acts* (1934) and *The Mother of Us All* (1947), a lyrical portrayal of a host of characters headed by Susan B. Anthony; and the posthumous volume of playlets, poems, and essays made into a revue, *Gertrude Stein's First Reader* (1969).

Stein's plays are collected in *Operas and Plays* (1932) and in *Last Operas and Plays* (1949). The latter's introduction by Carl Van Vechten has extensive bibliographical and historical information on her drama. See also the *Autobiography* and John Malcolm Brinnin's biographical-critical study, *The Third Rose: Gertrude Stein and Her World* (1959).

STEINBECK, John [Ernst] (1902–68), American Nobel Prize novelist, successfully dramatized (with GEORGE S. KAUFMAN doing the staging) his OF MICE AND MEN immediately upon its publication in 1937. He wrote only a couple of other dramas: *The Moon is Down* (1942), an anti-Nazi play simultaneously published as a novel (like *Of Mice and Men*); and *Burning Bright* (1950). The latter features a sterile man who discovers and learns to accept the fact that in order to give him the child he desires his wife has taken a lover; Steinbeck called it a "play-novelette," i.e., "a play that is easy to read or a short novel that can be played simply by lifting out the dialogue." In 1938 JACK KIRKLAND dramatized Steinbeck's humorous episodic novel about California *paisanos* (Mexican-American peasants), *Tortilla Flat. Pipe Dream* (1955, music by Richard Rodgers) is OSCAR HAMMERSTEIN II's dramatization of Steinbeck's novel about Cannery Row, *Sweet Thursday* (1954). Some of Steinbeck's other fiction also was dramatized and filmed. In addition, Steinbeck wrote a number of screen dramas, including *Viva Zapata!* (1952).

STERNHEIM, [William Adolf] **Carl** (1878–1942), German playwright, novelist, and critic, was an early EXPRESSIONIST and is best remembered for his comedy *Die Hose* (THE UNDERPANTS, 1911). It is the first of a cycle that continues with *Der Snob* (THE SNOB, 1913) and nine other plays collectively published in 1922 as *Aus dem bürgerlichen Heldenleben* (*Scenes from the Heroic Life of the Middle Class*). In clipped, "telegraphic" language only slightly exaggerating that of overbearing Prussians and Berliners, Sternheim attacked the burghers—the common men whose immorality, philistinism, and smug egotism were to dominate society and help bring about World War I and the social upheavals that followed. Sternheim's terse style anticipated that of GEORG KAISER and was influenced by FRANK WEDEKIND, whose plays also stress man's animal nature. But Sternheim was less concerned with eroticism than with flailing the morality of the middle class. His perspective and manner have been likened to those of Molière—and of the artist George Grosz.

The son of a Jewish banker, Sternheim was born in Leipzig. He studied at a number of universities, traveled, was married twice (the second time to Wedekind's daughter, Pamela), and lived in various German and other European cities. His early plays are minor romantic works such as *Don Juan* (1909), a verse tragedy that was hissed off the stage in 1912. With his next play, *The Underpants*, Sternheim found his true subject and theme, characteristic style—and popularity. It and its two sequels (*The Snob* and *1913*, 1915) constitute a trilogy about a petty official's family that, by the time of the war, has risen to great industrial power. Other comedies in the eleven-play cycle are *Bürger Schippel* (1913, translated as *Paul Schippel*), a once-popular play about a laborer who is accepted by society only for his useful tenor voice, mistakes that acceptance and aspires to marry an aristocrat, haughtily refuses to marry her to legitimatize the consequences of her affair with a prince, and is finally accepted as an equal when he wins a duel against a challenger who is as scared of it as is Schippel. He reappears as a wealthy industrialist in *Tabula rasa* (1916), a satire of radical labor leaders who become Sternheim's characteristically smug burghers. Another successful comedy was *Die Kassette* (*The Strongbox*, 1911), a Molière-like farce about a professor whose passions are transformed into avarice for a wealthy relative's moneybox, which he takes to bed instead of his attractive wife; he eagerly sacrifices her, along with his daughter—though the fortune, ironically, has already been secretly willed to the Church. The last comedy of the cycle is *Das Fossil* (*The Fossil*, 1923), a satire of the Prussian military caste.

After the war Sternheim's popularity declined and his plays became insignificant. They were adaptations of Molière and the fiction of Flaubert and others, including *Die Marquise von Arcis* (1919, translated as *The Mask of Virtue*), based on Diderot's tale of a noblewoman's vengeance on her lover; and *Manon Lescaut* (1921), based on the Abbé A. F. Prévott's semiautobiographical novel (1732). Original plays include *Der Nebbich* (1922), another satire of a social climber; *Oskar Wilde, sein Drama* (1923); *Die Schule von Uznach* (1926), a satire of modern dance; *J. P. Morgan* (1930), a comedy about American life; and *Aut Caesar aut nihil*, an unpublished satire on Nazism written in 1931. His best early plays, however, with their pungent ridicule of middle-class morality and the common man who increasingly characterized postwar society, received major revivals in Germany after World War II.

Sternheim also published books of political and literary criticism, novels, and memoirs. *Scenes from the Heroic Life of the Middle Class* (1970) is a collection of five plays translated by M. A. L. Brown and others: *The Fossil, 1913, Paul Schippel, The Underpants* (or *The Bloomers*), and *The Snob;* the last two as well as *The Strongbox* have also appeared in other anthologies. Volume II of Alex Natan's edition of *German Men of Letters* (1963) and H. F. Garten's *Modern German Drama* (1964) have sections on Sternheim and bibliographies.

STOPPARD [originally Straussler], **Tom** (1937), English playwright, became notable in 1967 with his first play, ROSENCRANTZ AND GUILDENSTERN ARE DEAD. Stoppard was born in Czechoslovakia, the son of a physician killed by the Nazis. The rest of the family escaped to the Far East—Stoppard went to school in Darjeeling, India—and, after his mother married a British officer, they went to England. There Stoppard attended preparatory school, where he wrote film and drama criticisms. He began his career as a journalist, and soon produced radio and television drama. He won minor prizes for them and then went to Berlin, where his hit play first appeared in an embryonic, one-act burlesque version. Later Stoppard dramas include *The Real Inspector Hound* (1967), a play-within-a-play about two critics watching a thriller; *Enter a Free Man* (1968), a not very successfully refurbished television comedy that was likened to Miller's DEATH OF A SALESMAN and that features a dreamer who resigns himself to mundane reality; and *After Magritte* (1970), an ABSURDist one-acter about a bickering husband and wife questioned by a demented policeman about a robbery.

Stoppard has been strongly influenced by the theatre of the absurd. Though later plays have so far not shown much development or originality, all his works have clever and amusing dialogue, and evidence considerable ingenuity and technical virtuosity.

STORM, THE (*Oväder*), a play in three scenes by AUGUST STRINDBERG, published and produced in 1907. Setting: façade and interior of a modern house.

This drama, Opus I of THE CHAMBER PLAYS, has also been translated as *Storm Weather*. The passing storm symbolizes the Gentleman's momentarily reawakened, painful passions. Settling his accounts, the aging Strindberg wrote Harriet Bosse, his young third wife from whom he had recently been divorced, that in this autobiographical play "I tried to write you and [our child] out of my heart."

"Are you almost finished?" his brother asks the old Gentleman, a recluse cared for by a young cousin. It is a sultry late-summer evening, and he soon comes out of the apartment to which he has been rooted for ten years by memories of his divorced wife and their daughter. The Gentleman's old-age tranquillity (and his chess playing) is disturbed by the noisy new tenants above him. These turn out to be his former wife, Gerda, and her second husband, who beats her, uses her daughter as bait in their gambling place, and is deserting her for a younger woman. As a storm rages, Gerda's presence and the rehashing of their past shatter "the image in my memory—she erased all the beauty I had hidden." He can now face her—and coldly reject the distressed and penitent Gerda's offer to return to him: "No thanks! I don't want you." And he pities "poor Gerda" when she sneers at his kinswoman: "Jealous of my servant—that *really* restores me!" But he helps rescue their daughter from Gerda's adventurer husband and sighs contentedly when he hears of Gerda's departure with their daughter. The storm ends and the Gentleman, now purged of painful memories, peacefully watches the lamplighter: "The first street lamp—now autumn is here! That's our season, old chaps! It begins to get dark, but understanding comes and shines with its dark light, so we don't get lost. . . . And this fall I'm moving out of 'The Quiet House!'"

STRAMM, August (1874–1915), German poet and dramatist, wrote so-called *Schreidramen* ("screamplays"), EXPRESSIONIST works characterized by pantomime interspersed with explosions of ecstatic exclamations. *Sancta Susanna* (1913), a one-acter produced (1918) with music by Paul Hindemith, modernizes the tale of the distraught nun who, after nakedly embracing a figure of Christ that comes to life, is stoned by the other nuns. *Kräfte* (1915), another violent portrayal of a remorseful woman, is also a drama of passions and horror—and expletive dialogue: one of its longest speeches ("he touched me") is the wife's deceitful confession to her husband that results in a fatal duel; then she forces her girl friend to kiss the dead man, slices off the girl's cheeks and lips, throws them to the dogs, and commits suicide. *Das Erwachen* (*Awakening,* 1915), also about lust and murder, is again in Stramm's telegraphic style, resembling that of the silent films.

Born in Münster to a Catholic mother and a Protestant father who, respectively, intended him to enter the priesthood and the civil service, Stramm studied at various universities and was awarded a Ph.D. in 1909. His poetry is as extreme as his drama—the balance of which consists of a few short sketches—in its mainly monosyllabic ejaculations. When *Sancta Susanna* was published in the periodical *Der Sturm,* Stramm became the leader of an extremist circle of expressionists, the *Sturmgruppe*. Commissioned in the reserve corps in World War I, Stramm fell on the Eastern front.

Awakening was published with an introduction in James M. Ritchie and Hugh F. Garten's *Seven Expressionist Plays: Kokoschka to Barlach* (1968).

STRANGE INTERLUDE, a play in nine acts by EUGENE O'NEILL, published and produced in 1928. Setting: New England and New York after World War I.

This is one of O'Neill's most experimental and successful plays. Its primary innovations are its length and interior monologues, introspective asides that are as numerous and important as the conventional speeches. The play takes almost six hours to perform and is usually given with an hour's dinner intermission at the end of Part I (Act V). The asides, heard by the audience but not by the other characters, voice private, sometimes almost subconscious, thoughts. Furnishing ironic and highly theatrical counterpoint (with the asides of another character or with the "regular" speeches by the same or another character), the asides themselves constitute much of the "drama" and round the characters. The most important of these is Nina, who embodies the manifold and antithetical attributes of Woman. Her love, needs, and vitality mold the lives of all who come in contact with her. In this play O'Neill touches on many themes, including his favorite one of man's loss of religion and his disaffection with science. It should be noted that despite his heavy use of Freudian psychology, O'Neill here expresses his rejection of science (particularly through Darrell).

Act I. Charles Marsden, an old-maidish and mother-fixated novelist, visits Professor Henry Leeds in his library. He loves Leeds's daughter, Nina, who treats "dear old Charlie" with condescending filial love. Nina's fiancé, Gordon, a sports idol and then a war ace, was killed in battle. Now she bitterly resents her father for having prevented their "impractical" marriage and caused her "cowardly" puritan scruples: "Gordon never possessed me! I'm still Gordon's silly virgin! . . . And now I am lonely and not pregnant with anything at all, but—but loathing." Leeds admits that jealousy played a part in his objection to a quick marriage, and at Nina's insistence that she must expiate by becoming a nurse in a crippled soldiers' hospital, he finally agrees to her departure.

Act II. Still resentful when she returns a year later, Nina cannot feel grief at her father's death. With her are the ineffectual Sam Evans, who worships Nina as well as Gordon's memory, and Dr. Edmund ("Ned") Darrell, who rigidly subordinates his emotions to scientific objectivity. Darrell tells Marsden that Nina has attempted to expiate through rampant promiscuity with crippled soldiers. To save her, he prescribes marriage to the wholesome Evans, which will give her the "normal outlets" she needs. Though hardened, Nina sadly confesses to Marsden, whom she now looks upon as a father, and asks him to punish her for her foolishness. She tells him how she has failed: "It's horribly hard to give anything, and frightful to receive!" Torn between love and loathing, Marsden assumes her father's tone and tells her to marry Evans.

Act III. Nina does marry Evans. Some months later, with Nina rejoicing in her pregnancy, they visit Evans's mother. In a heartrending talk, she persuades Nina that, because of congenital insanity in the Evans family (of which Sam is unaware), the baby must not be born. After detailing the suffering she herself had undergone, Mrs. Evans urges Nina to breed with a "healthy male" without Sam's knowledge. "Being happy, that's the nearest we can ever come to knowing what's good! . . . You've got to have a healthy baby—sometime—so's you can both be happy! It's your rightful duty!"

Act IV. Some months after the abortion, Evans is unsuccessfully writing ads in Leeds's library. Helping Nina with her biography of Gordon, Marsden worries about his ailing mother. Nina tells the visiting Darrell what had happened, and accuses him of having "aided and abetted God the Father in making this mess." Darrell, who is repressing his desire for her, is mesmerized by Nina to prescribe himself "scientifically" as the disinterested "healthy male," and Nina triumphantly thinks, "I shall be happy! . . . I shall make my husband happy!"

Act V. Nina once again rejoices in pregnancy ("I am a mother . . . God is a Mother"), but unexpectedly the scientific prescription has also produced love. Darrell fights it and tells Nina, "You're simply letting your romantic imagination run away with you—as you did once before with Gordon Shaw!" Realizing that he has jealously mentioned Gordon because he does love her, she insists on telling Evans and divorcing him, though it may drive him to insanity or death. But Darrell escapes her possessive love and leaves for Europe, after telling Evans—who thereupon kneels in thanksgiving—that they will have a child. Deciding that she must now stay with Evans, Nina still thinks in anguish of the afternoons with her lost lover.

Act VI. A year later, Marsden is aged by grief over his mother's death, and Nina is proud of her little boy, Gordon, and of Evans, who adores the child and has become self-confident and successful since his birth. Jealous when she learns that Darrell is philandering in Europe, Nina is soon reassured by his return. Drawn back to her and no longer caring about Evans or his own career, Darrell wants Nina and his child. Though she is happy to get her lover back and promises never to let him leave her again, she refuses to disillusion Evans and rob him of "his" child and happiness. Angry but helplessly in her power, Darrell sits by her with Evans and Marsden. Nina is triumphant. "My three men! . . . I feel their desires converge in me! . . . husband! . . . lover! . . . father! " she says in an aside: "And the fourth man! . . . little man! . . . little Gordon! . . . he is mine too! . . . that makes it perfect! . . . only I better knock wood . . . before God the Father hears my happiness!"

Act VII. It is Gordon's eleventh birthday. He loves Evans but resents Darrell, whom he senses as a rival. Like Marsden, Darrell has become wealthy backing Evans's business. He has given up medicine for a biology station in the West Indies, and has become bitter over the years. Though she still loves him, Nina finds his visits too long and difficult. Gordon and Darrell quarrel, and then Gordon happens to see him kissing Nina. Furious, he smashes the sailboat Darrell has given him for a present. After Darrell's departure, Gordon happily talks of being a hero some day like Gordon Shaw, but sensing his mother's thoughts and lies about Darrell to Evans and himself, he leaves the room resentfully. Nina is nettled into hatefulness by Evans's smug, self-confident masculinity: "Oh, Mother God, grant I may some day tell this fool the truth!"

Act VIII. Aboard a motor cruiser ten years later, the family watch Gordon row in the big Navy race. Nina, now highly neurotic, fulminates with bitter jealousy against Gordon's fiancée, Madeline Arnold. Determined to break the match, she is foiled by Darrell, who refuses ever again to meddle with human lives. In her desperation she confesses their long affair and Gordon's paternity to Marsden, who loves and forgives her. Evans, rejoicing in the excitement of Gordon's victory that the boy is "a dead ringer" for his namesake and not "a poor boob" like himself, suddenly is felled by a stroke. Darrell grieves, but Marsden, though ashamed, exultantly thinks, "I will not have long to wait now!"

Act IX. Some months later, after Evans's death, Gordon argues with Darrell. As Nina gets hysterical at the grotesque situation, the son slaps his father. They soon make up and Nina is able at last to send Gordon off to marry Madeline, never to know that Darrell is his father. His plane passes over them, and Nina feels old and ready "to bleach in peace." With their love now cold, she rejects Darrell, who gives up "the cry for happiness" and prays "to be resigned to be an atom." At the end of the short interlude that is life, she agrees to marry Marsden: "Yes, our lives are merely strange dark interludes in the electrical display of God the Father!" She falls asleep, weary but content, on the shoulder of "dear old Charlie . . . who, passed beyond desire, has all the luck at last!"

STRAW, THE, a play in three acts by EUGENE O'NEILL, published and produced in 1921. Setting: a home in Connecticut and a nearby tuberculosis sanatorium, early 1920's.

Its sanatorium setting (based on O'Neill's experiences and including a dramatic weighing scene in which the patients fearfully await judgment of their curability), and perhaps its maudlin sentimentality, made this play a failure. Its resolution is strongly affirmative, though somewhat ambiguous.

Eileen Carmody, overworked with caring for her selfish and drunken widower father and his other children, becomes seriously ill and must go to a tuberculosis sanatorium. There she meets Stephen Murray, a cynical newspaperman with whom she falls in love. She inspires and helps him to write stories that ultimately become successful, and he comforts her when she is disillusioned with her selfish family and fiancé. When Murray is released four months later, Eileen surreptitiously meets him outside the sanatorium and tells him of her love. Deeply moved, he can only stammer and silently curse "in impotent rage at himself and at Fate" for being unable to reciprocate her love. Eileen understands and, broken after his departure, loses hope and the will to live. Murray, in the meantime, has found that away from her influence his creativity is waning. When he visits her four months later, the sympathetic infirmary superintendent tells him that, to give Eileen happiness and keep her alive a little longer, he must say he loves her. Out of friendship and gratitude he tells her the lie, but her joy is so great that it overwhelms him and makes the lie a truth and his own life meaningful: "I suddenly saw—how beautiful and sweet and good she is—how I couldn't bear the thought of life without her." At the same moment, however, he also realizes in horror that she is doomed to die soon. When he blames the superintendent—"Why did you give me a hopeless hope?"—she replies, "Isn't all life just that—when you think of it? But there must be something back of it—some promise of fulfillment—somehow—somewhere—in the spirit of hope itself." Murray clutches at the straw of that hope of defeating death: "You'll see! I'll make Eileen get well, I tell you! Happiness will cure! Love is stronger than—." Giving himself to Eileen, he tells her of his need for her to nurse him back to health, and she radiantly and solicitously plans their new life together.

STREET SCENE, a play in three acts by ELMER RICE, published and produced in 1929. Setting: exterior of a New York tenement, 1920's.

Like Hauptmann's THE RATS, this grimly humorous work vividly depicts (and indicts) city slum life. The romance and the melodramatic plot—a *crime passionel*—are overshadowed by the picturesque NATURALISTIC tenement setting and the portrayal of the life routines of some fifty characters, including many ethnic types. A Pulitzer Prize winner, it was transformed by Rice and LANGSTON HUGHES into a musical (1947, music by Kurt Weill). The history of the play, as well as the author's difficulty in finding a producer for it (the script was rejected again and again), is detailed in Rice's *The Living Theatre* (1959) and *Minority Report* (1963).

Act I. On a stifling June night various tenement dwellers chat, gossip, and argue. Among them are the Irish Maurrants: Frank (a surly stagehand) and his wife, Anna, and their young son and their twenty-year-old daughter, Rose, an office worker; the Jewish Kaplans: Abraham (an old Marxist who insists revolution will solve all problems), and his schoolteacher daughter and his son, Sam, a prelaw honor student; a jovial Italian music teacher and his plump German wife; a snide busybody and her husband, and their vulgar daughter and their ruffian cabdriver son; a deserted wife and her two children who live on charity and are about to be evicted ("I tella you da whola troub'," the Italian remarks good-naturedly, "she's a don' gotta nobody to sleepa wit'"); and the Swedish janitor and his wife. Scandalized by Anna

Street Scene, Act I. The Swedish janitor (John M. Qualen, left) watches Rose (Erin O'Brien Moore) and a neighbor (T. H. Manning) stop Frank Maurrant (Robert Kelley) from assaulting Abraham Kaplan (Leo Bulgakov), who is sitting at the window with his schoolteacher daughter (Anna Kostant); at right are the Italian music teacher (George Humbert), his wife (Eleanor Wesselhoeft), and the busybody (Beulah Bondi). New York, 1929. (*White Collection, New York Public Library*)

Maurrant's affair with a married milk-company collector and anticipating trouble should Maurrant discover it, various tenants also disapprovingly discuss the romance of her daughter, Rose, and their Jewish neighbor's son, Sam. Maurrant enters, chides his family, aggressively insists on strict, old-fashioned standards, and makes slurring comments about the old Jew and threatens to beat him up. Rose appears with her wealthy, married office manager who offers to take her out of her sordid environment and set her up in an apartment. Later, after protecting Rose from the cabdriver, who roughs him up, the intellectual Sam has a tender love scene with the Irish girl. City and night noises are punctuated by labor-pain screams from a woman in the tenement.

Act II. At daybreak tenement life resumes. Rose asks Mrs. Maurrant, who has been up most of the night helping in her neighbor's delivery, whether their lives might not improve if they were to buy a house in the suburbs. The mother, a warm and kind woman yearning for affection and happiness, obliquely seeks to justify herself before Rose for her adultery: "What's the good of being alive, if you can't get a little something out of life?" Sam's sister tells Rose to "marry with your own kind" and let Sam concentrate on his studies. After Rose leaves, Maurrant returns unexpectedly and surprises his wife and her lover. He shoots them both, and escapes. The excited crowd watch as Rose appears when the dying Mrs. Maurrant is taken out on a stretcher.

Act III. Later that day Maurrant is caught. He sobs penitently as he bids Rose farewell, and asks her to take care of her young brother. Having declined her wealthy admirer's offer, Rose also declines, at least for the present, the marriage proposal of Sam, who is willing to give up law school for her. It will not work out, she tells him; poverty would bring them both unhappiness. When Sam declares that they belong to each other, she rejects such love and attributes her family's unhappiness to it. "I don't think people ought to belong to anybody but themselves," Rose says: "[Father and Mother] were always depending on somebody else for what they ought to have had inside themselves." Sam leaves heartbroken, and Rose prepares to make a new home for herself and her brother, away from the city slum. The snide busybody, resuming her gossip, is sure Rose will turn out like her mother: "She's got a gentleman friend, that I guess ain't hangin' around for nothin'. I seen him late last night, and this afternoon, when I come home from the police—" As children offstage sing "The Farmer in the Dell," a shabby couple ring to inquire about the newly vacated apartment, and a sailor strolls across the stage, his arms around two girls.

STREETCAR NAMED DESIRE, A, a play in eleven scenes by TENNESSEE WILLIAMS, published and produced in 1947. Setting: the French Quarter of New Orleans, late 1940's.

Williams's most popular play, *A Streetcar Named Desire* has been produced all over the world, filmed, and awarded important prizes. It evolved from early one-acters, and features a typical Williams character: the faded Southern belle who lives in illusions of the past. Blanche's disintegration constitutes, on the one hand, a clinical case. On the other hand, Blanche represents culture, beauty, and sensitivity—a decadent civilization that has been displaced by the crude, brutal, cynical practicality personified by Stanley. Williams's ambivalence about both characters—and both worlds—enriches but at times muddles the drama. Though suspenseful and grimly NATURALISTIC, the play is also SYMBOLIC, poetic—and comic.

Scene 1. On a May evening, Stanley Kowalski passes his run-down apartment. "Hey, there! Stella, Baby!" he bellows at his laughing wife, throws her a package of meat, and goes bowling. Stella soon follows him. Blanche DuBois, a neurasthenic, mothlike woman carrying a valise and incongruously dressed as if for a summer tea, looks in shocked disbelief at the address: "They told me to take a streetcar named Desire, and then transfer to one called Cemeteries and ride six blocks and get off at—Elysian Fields!" Identifying herself to a neighbor as Stella's sister, Blanche nervously pours herself a whiskey and quickly replaces the bottle as her sister enters. "Stella, oh, Stella, Stella! Stella for Star!" she exclaims, begging her sister not to look at her "till I've bathed and rested! And turn that over-light off!" Feverishly hysterical, she asks Stella for a drink, explains how she quit schoolteaching because of a nervous breakdown, and seeks reassurance about her looks. When Blanche, in a frenzied outburst, recounts having been left alone to bear the bankruptcy of their Belle Reve estate while Stella was "in bed with your Polack!" Stella goes out in tears. Stanley appears, greets Blanche brusquely ("You going to shack up here?"), comments on the depleted liquor bottle, and questions her about her first husband. "The boy—the boy died," Blanche says: "I'm afraid I'm—going to be sick!" *Scene 2.* Shortly before Stanley's poker night at home Blanche is singing in the bathtub. Stanley gets angry as Stella recounts the loss of the estate. "We have the Napoleonic code according to which what belongs to the wife belongs to the husband and vice versa," he announces. He pulls Blanche's clothes and imitation jewelry out of her trunk, wondering how she could afford them on a teacher's salary, and decides to have them appraised by knowledgeable acquaintances. Blanche appears from her bath, airily flirting with Stanley as she dresses. Roughly Stanley questions her about the lost estate and snatches her papers. They detail her ancestors' squandering of the property "for their epic fornications," Blanche says, and, learning that Stella is pregnant, goes out to embrace her sister. "Maybe he's what we need to mix with our blood now that we've lost Belle Reve," Blanche says, and reassures her about Stanley and herself before going out for the evening: "We thrashed it out." *Scene 3.* The poker game is still on when the sisters return. Blanche is interested in one of the players,

Mitch (Harold Mitchell), a shy, clumsy man who lives with his mother. Genteelly she lies about her age, and shades the light bulb with a colored lantern. Then Blanche turns on the radio, waltzing romantically as Mitch watches with delight. Furious at her interruption of his poker game, Stanley hurls the radio out of the window and strikes the protesting Stella. Then men subdue Stanley, and Blanche takes Stella upstairs to stay with a neighbor. But soon Stanley bellows "like a baying hound" for her. Tear-stained, Stella returns. They approach each other with "low, animal moans," and Stanley carries Stella into the flat. *Scene 4*. The next morning, as Stella lies on her bed in an "almost narcotized tranquility," Blanche hysterically comes to comfort her. She is appalled to find Stella perfectly content, with no inclination to escape her "brutal" husband: "There are things that happen between a man and a woman in the dark—that sort of make everything else seem—unimportant." Calling it simply "brutal desire" (like the streetcar's name), Blanche lashes out at Stanley as a "sub-human . . . survivor of the stone age! Bearing the raw meat home from the kill in the jungle!" Recounting mankind's progress and pleading for art and human tenderness, she implores Stella, *"Don't hang back with the brutes!"* Stanley, who has overheard all this, comes in. In full view of Blanche Stella embraces him fiercely—as he grins at Blanche.

Scene 5. Blanche is writing a letter to a millionaire admirer, she tells Stella. Stanley comes to question Blanche: a friend of his thinks he met her at a disreputable hotel in the town of Laurel. Though she tries to laugh it off as a mistake, she worriedly asks later whether Stella has "heard any—unkind—gossip about me." Tensely she is waiting for Mitch, whom she yearns to marry—in order to solve her problems. Alone and drinking, she kisses a newsboy who has come to collect his money—and then sends him off: "It would be nice to keep you, but I've got to be good—and keep my hands off children." *Scene 6*. Coming home late that night, Blanche—nervous and coyly prim—chides Mitch for his advances. Mitch says he has talked of her to his mother. Blanche tells him the story of her first marriage: she discovered her beloved young husband to be a homosexual, and rejected him with disgust at a dance; he rushed out and shot himself—hence she (and the audience) periodically hears polka music ending with a shot. Telling her that she needs someone just as much as he (a lonely mother's boy) does, Mitch takes her in his arms and proposes. Blanche sobs gratefully, "Sometimes—there's God—so quickly!"

Scene 7. On a mid-September afternoon Stella is setting a birthday table for Blanche, who is taking a bath. Stanley comes in with verified reports of Blanche's past: her promiscuity was so outrageous that she was evicted from the disreputable Laurel hotel, and she was discharged from her school for seducing a pupil. Stanley tells Stella he has revealed these things to his friend Mitch, who will not be coming to the birthday party. When Blanche appears from her bath, she senses something amiss, but Stella denies it. *Scene 8*. Some time later the three finish a dismal birthday supper, with Mitch's chair conspicuously empty. Stanley explodes at being called a "Polack," and hurls the dishes to the floor. But alone with Stella, he comforts her. "It's gonna be all right after she goes and after you've had the baby," he assures Stella; then they can have "them nights we had together" again. He gives Blanche "a little birthday remembrance": a bus ticket back to Laurel. When Stella accuses him of being cruel to Blanche—who used to be "tender and trusting" until "people like you abused her, and forced her to change"—Stanley talks of their own happiness after Stella left her estate: "I pulled you down off them columns and how you loved it, having them colored lights going!"—until Blanche came, "Hoity-toity, describing me as an ape." Stella's labor pains begin, and Stanley takes her to the hospital. *Scene 9*. Later that evening Mitch comes in, disheveled and half drunk. He rips the paper lantern off the light bulb to see Blanche "good and plain." She admits to Stanley's accusations, for after her husband's suicide, "intimacies with strangers was all I seemed able to fill my empty heart with." Panicky, she came here, and thought that, since both needed someone, they could help each other. Angrily Mitch fumbles for her, wanting "what I been missing all summer." But when Blanche asks him to marry her, Mitch declares her "not clean enough to bring in the house with my mother." Blanche screams at him to get out. *Scene 10*. Some hours later Stanley returns from the hospital. Blanche tells him that she has been invited on a cruise with an old admirer, and that Mitch had come begging for her forgiveness. Stanley jeers at her lies and she

A Streetcar Named Desire, Scene 10. Stanley (Marlon Brando) and Blanche (Jessica Tandy). New York, 1947. (*Eileen Darby* from "Graphic House")

hysterically tries to telephone "Shep Huntleigh." Later Stanley comes out of the bathroom, dressed in gaudy silk pajamas. "Let me get by you," Blanche demands. As she nervously insists he go back yet further and not try to interfere with her, Stanley remarks, "Come to think of it—maybe you wouldn't be bad to—interfere with." Blanche smashes a bottle and threatens him with its broken top. Thereupon Stanley catches her wrist and carries her to the bed: "We've had this date with each other from the beginning!" *Scene 11.* Some weeks later, Stanley is playing poker as Stella tells her neighbor about the arrangements made for Blanche's commitment: "I couldn't believe her story and go on living with Stanley." Blanche comes from her bath, asking if there have been any calls for her, and preparing to leave with her wealthy admirer. A doctor and a matron come. "That man isn't Shep Huntleigh," Blanche whispers in fright, and then battles the matron. The doctor intervenes and gently supports her. "Whoever you are—I have always depended on the kindness of strangers," Blanche says, taking his arm and walking out with him. Stella sobs as Stanley comes over and comforts her sensually. The piano "blues" are heard from the adjoining bar and one of the poker players announces, "This game is seven-card stud."

STRIFE, a drama in three acts by JOHN GALSWORTHY, published and produced in 1909. Setting: near the Tin Plate Works at the English-Welsh border on a contemporary February afternoon.

This is Galsworthy's first important drama, and it established his reputation as a playwright. Its depiction of a struggle between labor and capital is balanced and restrained, unlike that of Hauptmann's THE WEAVERS, to which the play has been compared. Probably Galsworthy's most objective drama, its sympathy is equally divided between the two chief antagonists, whose unbending nature suggests the classic hubris, and their followers, who yearn for compromise.

Act I. After six months of the Tin Works strike and considerable loss to shareholders and suffering to starving workers, the directors are willing to negotiate a compromise. But the aged chairman and founder of the Works, John Anthony, disagrees. "I've always fought them; I've never been beaten yet," he insists: "Better go to the devil than give in!" Because of a few excessive demands, the trade union has withdrawn its support of the strikers. But its representative seeks to negotiate a settlement if both sides agree to reasonable concessions. The workers' delegation, like the board of directors, is ready to compromise. But their leader, David Roberts, silences his men and is as implacable as Anthony. The struggle between the groups centers on these two leaders, neither of whom will yield anything. "There can be only one master," Anthony tells Roberts, who replies, "Then, be Gad, it'll be us." Later Anthony refuses various pleas, even his daughter's, to relent a little before the desperate workers: "What sort of mercy do you suppose you'd get if no one stood between you and the continual demands of labour?"

Act II. Scene 1. In Roberts's cottage, his consumptive and starving wife, Annie, defends her husband's firmness to the other women, who, like their husbands, are increasingly unwilling to continue the strike. Though Annie knows they are risking total defeat, she remarks, "Roberts says a working man's life is all a gamble, from the time 'e's born to the time 'e dies." She returns food given her by Anthony's daughter, who sympathetically came to visit her. Roberts is gentle with Annie, but unaware of the seriousness of her illness. *Scene 2.* At the strikers' meeting, the union representative asks the men to agree to a settlement. Roberts is beginning to lose control as more men turn against his leadership. He mounts the rostrum and exhorts them passionately, lashing out against the "white-faced, stony-hearted monster" that is capitalism: "'Tis not for this little moment of time we're fighting, not for ourselves, our own little bodies, and their wants, 'tis for all those that come after throughout all time." He almost has them persuaded when he receives word that his wife is dying. Unable to continue his oration, he leaves the hall, and the workers agree to let the union negotiate for them.

Act III. Internal strife threatens Anthony as it has Roberts. But again he refuses to heed his daughter's pleas: "You think with your gloved hands you can cure the trouble of the century?" Now word comes that Annie Roberts has died, and the board, including his own son, presses Anthony to cease starving the women and children. When the directors move for a settlement, Anthony for the last time exhorts them to persist: "It is for us to lead and to determine what is to be done, and to do it without fear or favour"—neither to labor nor to the shareholders; "I am thinking of the future of this country, threatened with the black waters of confusion, threatened with mob government, threatened with what I cannot see." Before the vote he warns them that if they yield to pressure, "you will never make a stand again! You will have to fly like curs before the whips of your own men." But the motion for settlement carries—and Anthony resigns. The men enter and the union's compromise terms are soon signed. Roberts looks at Anthony incredulously—and suddenly understands: "So—they've done us both down, Mr. Anthony?" The chairman agrees: "Both broken men, my friend Roberts!" As Anthony leaves, Roberts's expression "changes from hostility to wonder," and the two enemies silently express their respect for each other. Sorry for the widowed Roberts, the union representative remarks, "A woman dead; and the two best men both broken!" And the company secretary, noticing that the compromise terms are identical to the ones suggested before the strike, adds, "All this—and—and what for?" The union official replies grimly, "That's where the fun comes in!"

STRINDBERG, [Johan] **August** (1849–1912), Sweden's—and one of the modern world's—greatest and most prolific dramatists, is also distinguished for his other writings, particularly fiction, poetry, autobiography, criticism, and philosophy. Further, he was accomplished in painting, sinology, and science. He wrote a total of some seventy plays (including dramatic fragments) which range from histories (some considered by many to be as good as Shakespeare's best), through nineteenth-century NATURALISM, folk drama and fantasy, and finally to a SYMBOLISM and SURREALISM that were ahead of his age—and still may be ahead of ours. His variegated dramaturgy defies easy categorizing and summary. At the same time, it is distinctive, and it is consistently autobiographical—more so than the work of any other major dramatist before EUGENE O'NEILL. Strindberg suffered from the emotional cataclysms that characterize and are amply reflected in his plays and that many Swedish scholars believed to have been "schizophrenia of the paranoid type." Most often outgrowths of his love-hate feelings toward women (especially toward the first of his three wives), these upheavals inspired his most distinguished literary productions.

They also inspired a characteristic depiction of "sex duels" that gained him the reputation of a mad misogynist—a "bedeviled Viking" and "psychopathic Don Quixote of the bedroom." Further, they obscured the master playwright and, as James Huneker predicted as early as 1905 (in *Iconoclasts*), "will not make him popular in America, a land peopled with gynolatrists." (The most abusive attack from respectable quarters, however, came from England almost sixty years later, in F. L. Lucas's *Ibsen and Strindberg*.) Yet Strindberg's stature is secure and has been acknowledged by other giant playwrights. Reciprocating his dislike, HENRIK IBSEN nonetheless kept Strindberg's photograph on his desk and predicted, "There is one who will be greater than I." O'Neill frankly acknowledged Strindberg's enormous influence on his own work; SEAN O'CASEY considered him the greatest of all modern playwrights; BERNARD SHAW at least once echoed this judgment, and, with Strindberg in mind, used his Nobel Prize money to encourage translations from the Swedish. Strindberg's continued effect on modern drama, increasingly perceptible since midcentury developments, can hardly be exaggerated.

He was fourth of the twelve children of Ulrica Eleonora and Carl Oscar Strindberg, who got married shortly before his birth in Stockholm. His father, educated and of good family, was a shipping agent. However, he was in financial difficulties when he married his mistress, a servant who died before she reached forty. Strindberg was influenced by both parents, but sensitively stressed his being "the son of a servant." He received next to no help from his father (remarried shortly after his mother's death in 1862), who had little sympathy for his temperamental son when he left home in 1867 to attend the University at Uppsala. Strindberg's studies were not very successful.

Nor was he successful in his brief careers as a schoolteacher, a medical student, and an actor. But his failure as an actor, in 1869, provided the stimulus for his first play: in hopeless despair, he took opium and when he awoke he visualized, as in a dream, a whole play. Writing in feverish haste, he completed the play and four days later sent to Stockholm's Dramatic Theatre, where he had just washed out as an actor, the manuscript of a two-act comedy, *En namnsdagsgåva*. Rejected by the management and no longer extant, it was apparently based on a story Strindberg had just read. But it dramatized a personal fantasy: a father's inducing the reconciliation of a son with his stepmother.

August Strindberg and Siri von Essen, 1886. (*August Strindberg Drottningsholms Teatermuseum*)

Though he did considerable writing in the next few years, Strindberg underwent hardship and suffering from poverty, mental depression, fears of insanity, youthful debaucheries, and much soul searching. An omnivorous reader, he was at the time greatly influenced by Georg Brandes and by Ibsen's BRAND; he believed in Unitarianism, advocated political reforms, and joined Runa, a small literary club. For a brief period his poverty was relieved by a royal stipend for *Den fredlöse* (THE OUTLAW, 1871). Other early works at the time gained him neither money nor reputation: *Fritänkaren* (THE FREETHINKER, 1870; his first published play), *I Rom* (IN ROME, 1870; his first produced play), HERMIONE (1871), *Anno fyrtioåtta* (*Anno 48*, a comedy published in 1881), and *Mäster Olof* (MASTER OLOF, 1886; eventually one of his most popular works). These early plays, and others he immediately destroyed (including one on Jesus, an elaborate refutation of Christianity), were based on history, religion, and saga. He earned a pittance—but some acclaim—as a journalist, and in 1874 he was appointed to a coveted minor post at the Royal Library.

It was at that time that he met a woman who was to affect his whole life and work profoundly. Siri von Essen, the wife of a Captain of the Guards, soon reciprocated Strindberg's violent passion. An ambitious actress, she divorced her husband and married Strindberg in 1877, shortly before the birth of the first of their three children. Their tempestuous marriage lasted until 1891, and stimulated the writing of his two most famous naturalistic dramas, *Fadren* (THE FATHER, 1887) and *Fröken Julie* (MISS JULIE, 1888). Other plays written during that middle period of his creative career give further insights into Strindberg's agonies and life with Siri. The earlier works—*Gillets hemlighet* (THE SECRET OF THE GUILD, 1880), *Lycko-Pers resa* (LUCKY PEHR'S JOURNEY, 1882), and *Herr Bengts hustru* (SIR BENGT'S WIFE, 1882)—reflect the atmosphere of their early years of marriage, happy despite occasional bitterness. Many of the works that followed—particularly *Kamraterna* (COMRADES, 1888) and *Fordringsägare* (CREDITORS, 1889)—dramatize the couple's jealous and torturous sex duels. *Bandet* (THE BOND, 1893) is remarkable for its searing depiction of Strindberg's divorce proceedings. His tormented yearning for his children, whom he lost to Siri, is reflected particularly in *Himmelrikets nycklar* (THE KEYS OF HEAVEN, 1892), *Inför döden* (FACING DEATH, 1893), and *Moderskärlek* (MOTHERLOVE, 1893). Somewhat less grim is Strindberg's 1889 dramatization of his second novel, *Hemsöborna* (*The People of Hemsö*, 1887), which portrays an ambitious farmhand's achievements in an isolated Swedish fishing community; he marries a wealthy widow despite her son's opposition, but eventually corrupted, he is disinherited and defeated. Other plays written during this period include *Höstslusk* (*Autumn-Splash,* a parody published in 1884), *Paria* (PARIAH, 1889), *Den starkare* (THE STRONGER, 1889; the most masterful of his short one-act plays), *Samun* (SIMOOM, 1890), *Debet och kredit* (DEBIT AND CREDIT, 1893), *Första varningen* (THE FIRST WARNING, 1893), and *Leka med elden* (PLAYING WITH FIRE, 1893). A short-story collection, *Giftas* (*Married*), created a legal sensation in 1884, and a series of autobiographical novels revealed more of Strindberg's life; the most popular of them were *Tjänstekvinnans son* (*The Son of a Servant*, 1886), *I röda rummet* (*In The Red Room,* 1886), and *En dåres försvarstal* (*The Defense of a Fool*, 1887). Of particular significance, however, was the later *Inferno* (1897).

It describes the last phase of Strindberg's "Inferno Crisis," an almost complete breakdown that began after the devastating divorce from Siri. It was accompanied by quasi-scientific and religious preoccupations and hallucinations. Strindberg's spiritual crisis was exacerbated by paranoid convictions that supernatural powers instigated his torments. He immersed himself in reading (Swedenborg, Nietzsche, and religious works—all of which influenced his later plays), painting, and zealous experimentations in alchemy. Briefly he committed himself for treatment; but he soon fled, believing that the doctor intended to murder him.

The major part of that crisis began in 1894. The previous year Strindberg had married a young journalist, Frida Uhl. They had one child and the marriage, though in many ways similar to Strindberg's first, was brief. Their divorce became final in 1897. That year Strindberg emerged from his "Inferno Crisis"—and began dramatizing it in *Til Damaskus* (TO DAMASCUS, 1898–1904), which also portrays his second marriage. *To Damascus* is a baffling work that eschewed the ZOLAesque naturalism of his earlier plays for a new form that is partly EXPRESSIONISTIC. It marks the beginning of Strindberg's last creative phase, for none of the dramas that followed *The Bond* is naturalistic, though scenes of that type—and sex duels—occur in even his most surrealist plays.

These later works also reflect Strindberg's increasing preoccupation with occultism and religion, his struggles against—and yearnings for chastening by—God. His concern with expiation predominates in his best-known later plays: *Brott och Brott* (CRIMES AND CRIMES, 1899), *Påsk* (EASTER, 1901), and *Spöksonaten* (THE GHOST SONATA, 1907). And it is ever-present in the others. Even the later history plays do not escape autobiographical perspective, from Strindberg's obvious self-portrayal in the somber *Carl XII* (CHARLES XII, 1901) to the subtler, charmingly witty GUSTAV III (1903). The other of his twenty-one history plays—also practically unknown in the English-speaking world, despite the excellence of many of them—written in this later period are *Folkungasagan* (THE FOLKUNG SAGA, 1899), GUSTAV VASA (1899, his greatest historical drama), ERIC XIV (1899), GUSTAV ADOLF (1900), ENGELBREKT (1901), KRISTINA (1903), *Näktergalen in Wittenberg* (*The Nightingale in Wittenberg,* 1904; a dramatic biography of Martin Luther), *Sistæ riddaren* (THE LAST KNIGHT, 1909), *Riksföreståndaren* (THE REGENT, 1909), and *Bjälbo-Jarlen* (THE EARL OF BJÄLBO, 1909).

Better known among Strindberg's later works are *Dödsdansen* (THE DANCE OF DEATH, 1901) and *Ett drömpsel* (A DREAM PLAY, 1902), both written in 1901. That year Strindberg, then fifty-two, married for a third time. His union with the twenty-three-year-old actress Harriet Bosse, however, was doomed to quick failure. It was legally dissolved in 1904, though his wife had left with their only child the previous year. Other plays of this last period are ADVENT (1899); *Kaspers Fet-Tisdag* (*Casper's Shrove Tuesday,* 1901; a Punch-and-Judy trifle); *Midsommar* (MIDSUMMER, 1901); *Kronbruden* (THE CROWN-BRIDE, 1902) and *Svanevit* (SWANWHITE, 1902), both influenced by MAURICE MAETERLINCK; *Abu Casems tofflor* (*Abu Casem's Slippers,* 1908), a comic fairy play; *Genom öknar till arfland* (*Through Deserts to Ancestral Lands,* 1918), a biblical drama written in 1903 and also known as *Moses; Lammet och vilddjuret* (*The Lamb and the Beast,* 1918), a play written in 1903 and featuring the Roman emperors Caligula, Claudius, and Nero, but focused on the *Christ* who never appears on stage but gives the play this other title; *Hellas* (1918), a play written in 1903 and also known as *Socrates,* depicting the protagonist and his circle; and a number of fragments, including one scene of the projected *Holländarn*

(THE DUTCHMAN, 1902) and the prologue and one scene of a projected verse saga, *Starkodder skald* (*Starkad the Skald,* 1906).

Strindberg's last play was *Stora londsvägen* (THE GREAT HIGHWAY, 1909). His most important late work, however, was for the Intima Teatern he helped found. This small Stockholm art theatre (1907–10), which produced twenty-four of his plays, gave Strindberg his final creative stimulus. He became concerned with production matters and wrote *Kammarspel* (THE CHAMBER PLAYS*) and the important essays on dramatic theory and criticism published as *Öppna brev till Intima Teatern* (OPEN LETTERS TO THE INTIMATE THEATRE, 1911–21). At the Intima Teatern, too, the elderly Strindberg met and fell in love with a nineteen-year-old actress to whom he became engaged. He moved to an apartment in her house, where he was looked after by her family. But the marriage never took place, and she and her family left. Strindberg remained alone in this residence—"The Blue Tower," as he called it—where he was soon to die, painfully, of stomach cancer.

There is not yet a complete collected English edition of Strindberg's plays. They are not even all available in English, though this gap is gradually being filled by many excellent modern translations of individual plays, including Michael Meyer's *The Plays of Strindberg,* the first volume of which appeared in 1964. Special mention should also be made of Walter Johnson's translations of the major history plays (1955 ff.), the first scholarly English editions of Strindberg's drama.

Strindberg's above-mentioned autobiographies have been translated but there are relatively few biographical and critical works in English. Martin Lamm's pioneering two-volume Swedish biography, *August Strindberg* (revised 1948), was translated and extensively annotated by Harry G. Carlson in 1971. Other studies are Carl E. W. L. Dahlström's *Strindberg's Dramatic Expressionism* (1930); Elizabeth Sprigge's biography, *The Strange Life of August Strindberg* (1949); Brita M. E. Mortensen and Brian W. Downs's *Strindberg: An Introduction to His Life and Work* (1949); Borge G. Madsen's *Strindberg's Naturalistic Theatre* (1962); Franklin S. Klaf's *Strindberg: the Origin of Psychology in Modern Drama* (1963); Walter Johnson's comprehensive study of the histories, *Strindberg and the Historical Drama* (1963); Maurice Valency's *The Flower and the Castle* (1963); and Chapter 8 (and its bibliography) of Alrik Gustafson's *A History of Swedish Literature* (1961). These books and the Strindberg issue of *Modern Drama,* V:3 (December 1962) all contain extensive bibliographies.

STRONG, Austin (1881–1951), American playwright, is notable primarily for *The Drums of Oude* (1906), a well-known one-act melodrama whose offstage drumbeats suggested the device to EUGENE O'NEILL for THE EMPEROR JONES. A skillful playwright, Strong also wrote *Seventh Heaven* (1920), a romantic melodrama that became a popular Helen Menken vehicle, and other works. His best-known play appears in the Modern Library collection of *One-Act Plays* (1943) and in Strong's *The Drums of Oude—and Other One Act Plays* (1926).

STRONGER, THE (*Den starkare*), a "scene" by AUGUST STRINDBERG, produced in 1889 and published in 1890. Setting: a contemporary café on Christmas Eve.

This brilliant monologue is the best known among the QUARTS D'HEURE Strindberg wrote for the experimental theatre he was trying to establish in Copenhagen and for the Théâtre Libre. His estranged wife, Siri, first played Mrs. X. It was made into an opera (1952, by Hugo Weisgall), and it inspired another dramatic monologue, O'Neill's BEFORE BREAKFAST.

The loquacious Mrs. X, an actress on her way home with Christmas parcels for her husband and children, meets Y, another actress. Gradually X becomes aware of the fact that Y, coldly silent and proud, used to be her husband's mistress. Now X sees how, after Y rejected him, she adopted all Y's ways to please her husband: "Your soul crept into mine, like a worm into an apple." But suddenly she realizes that, with her family and home, she is the stronger: "You never received anything from *me* while *you gave* something to me! . . . You find it hard to bend, to humble yourself—and so you broke like a dry reed—and I survived! . . . And thank you for teaching my husband how to love! Now I am going home—to love him!"

STURGES, Preston (1898–1959), American playwright and movie director, was born in Chicago, adopted at the age of three, and educated in Europe. He began his career in his mother's cosmetics business, where he invented such items as a "kissproof lipstick." Later he became a stage manager and a dramatist. Of his half-dozen plays, the most notable is *Strictly Dishonorable* (1929), an irreverent comedy of manners set in a Manhattan speakeasy, and portraying an Italian singer's winning a gentle Southern girl away from her stuffy fiancé. In Hollywood, Sturges wrote and produced distinguished films, including an Academy Award winner, *The Great McGinty* (1940).

SUCCÈS DE SCANDALE is a term used to label work that achieves fame or success (or both) because it scandalizes audiences. Among plays of this type are KING UBU, whose opening expletive caused an uproar and made ALFRED JARRY famous; Shaw's PYGMALION, whose initial popularity was due in large measure to Eliza's use of the then-taboo word *bloody*; and Hochhuth's THE DEPUTY, whose controversial portrayal of Pope Pius XII raised an international storm of unprecedented intensity.

SUCCÈS D'ESTIME, a play that is praised by critics but fails commercially, e.g., Herne's MARGARET FLEMING and Mayer's CHILDREN OF DARKNESS.

* Aside from *The Ghost Sonata,* these consist of *Oväder* (THE STORM, 1907), *Brända tomten* (THE BURNT HOUSE, 1907), *Pelikanen* (THE PELICAN, 1907), *Svarta handsken* (THE BLACK GLOVE, 1909), and the posthumous fragment *Toten-Insel, eller, Hades* (ISLE OF THE DEAD, 1918).

SUDDENLY LAST SUMMER, a one-act play in four scenes by TENNESSEE WILLIAMS, published and produced in 1958. Setting: a mansion in the Garden District of New Orleans, 1936.

This very successful *tour de force* was published and produced Off-Broadway in a double bill, *Garden District.* Its curtain raiser was a one-acter from the 27 WAGONS FULL OF COTTON collection, *Something Unspoken. Suddenly Last Summer,* a catharsis of Williams's psychoanalysis, was his most shocking play to date. But its treatment of perversions and cannibalism is restrained, even poetic: there is little action, the dramatic tension stemming from Catharine's long narrative. The sensational film version by GORE VIDAL, however, featured snake-pit and other violent scenes merely suggested in the play.

In a fantastic jungle garden of carnivorous plants, the aging Mrs. Violet Venable explains to a young doctor why she wants a frontal lobotomy performed on her institutionalized niece, Catharine Holly. Witnessing the death of Mrs. Venable's son, Sebastian, on a Mediterranean island unhinged Catharine, whose "obscenities and babblings" now are jeopardizing Sebastian's reputation. Each summer for twenty-five years he had traveled with his mother—once to an island where they observed carnivorous birds devouring newly hatched turtles—and wrote one poem. But the previous summer Mrs. Venable had had a stroke and Catharine accompanied him. When Catharine appears with her attendant, her mother and brother try to persuade her to retract her story so they can inherit Sebastian's legacy. Catharine replies, "It's a true story of our time and the world we live in." The doctor administers a truth serum, and Catharine narrates the lengthy tale of her summer with Cousin Sebastian. He was a corrupted idealist, a sybarite homosexual poet who "suddenly last summer" changed. He gave up his poetry and fastidiousness, and frequented a public beach. Catharine realized he was using her as he had formerly used his mother ("we all use each other and that's what we think of as love"): to procure young men for him. But when the group of starving island youths got out of hand, Sebastian became frightened and tried to escape. They followed him "up the steep white street in the sun that was like a great white bone of a giant beast that had caught on fire in the sky!" Catharine ran for help. When she returned she found his mutilated, partly devoured body "that looked like a big white-paper-wrapped bunch of red roses." Mrs. Venable screams, *"State asylum, cut this hideous story out of her brain!"* But the doctor wonders.

SUDERMANN, Hermann (1857–1928), German playwright and novelist, achieved considerable fame in the last decade of the nineteenth century with over three dozen NATURALIST dramas, most notably with *Heimat* (MAGDA, 1893). They resemble the PROBLEM PLAYS of GERHART HAUPTMANN, ÉMILE ZOLA, and HENRIK IBSEN, since they deal with social conflicts (between parents and children, provinces and the city, etc.). But Sudermann did not really explore issues. His were essentially derivative of the WELL-MADE PLAYS of VICTORIEN SARDOU and others, and they became hits because of their skillfully constructed climaxes and strong parts, such as that of Magda, which was acted by celebrated contemporary stars throughout Europe. Sudermann's stature was eroded by the vitriolic contempt of Alfred Kerr and other critics, who continued to expose deficiencies such as the paucity of his plays' "ideas," the poetic bombast and sentimental claptrap with which ideas were evaded, and Sudermann's dependence on excessive contrivance and cheap theatrical effects. These qualities, however, gained Sudermann's plays a popularity that the social drama of major writers such as Ibsen never could achieve.

The son of a Mennonite brewer of Dutch origin and the stepfather of ROLF LAUCKNER, Sudermann was born in an East Prussian province near the Lithuanian-Russian border that became the setting and whose ruling Junker class became the subjects of many of his later works. Though his family was relatively poor, Sudermann was university educated, first in Prussia and then in Berlin, where he was to remain most of his life. After concluding his studies Sudermann did some tutoring, edited a small journal, and wrote short stories and novels. A collection of his short stories was published in 1886, and the following year appeared his first novel, *Frau Sorge.* Neither book attracted much notice, nor did a second published novel. But two years later Sudermann achieved instant fame with his first play, *Die Ehre* (*Honor,* 1889). A social-protest drama about the double standard of honor for the rich and the poor, it features, in divided contrasting settings, a young man who challenges his wealthy employer's son to a duel for seducing his sister, and is turned down because he is a social inferior. Like the later *Magda* and *Das Glück im Winkel* (THE VALE OF CONTENT, 1895), *Honor* exploits characteristic devices of the well-made play beneath the façade of a social-problem play.

So, too, do the plays that followed in quick succession until the end of the century, and they, too, enjoyed immediate and great success. The most notable among them are his second (but less popular) play, *Sodoms Ende* (1890, translated as *A Man and His Picture*), another contrast of the wealthy and the poor, focusing on an artist who gets entangled with Berlin society women and becomes increasingly corrupted by the city; *Schmetterlingsschlacht* (*The Battle of the Butterflies,* 1894), in which a civil servant's widow tries to arrange a lucrative marriage for one of her three daughters; *Morituri* (1896), a cycle of one-acters, the most successful of them (*Fritzchen*) portraying a young officer and his parents on the evening before his fatal duel, and another (*Teja*) a history play featuring the sixth-century king of the Goths, Teias; *Johannes* (*John the Baptist,* 1898), another modern dramatization of history and legend, focusing on the degeneration of a villainous Herodias and a hedonistic Salomé; *Die drei Reiherfedern* (1899), a verse drama based on medieval romance; *Es lebe das Leben* (*The Joy of Living,* 1901), an internationally popular variation on *Magda* gilded with adultery and political intrigue, and resolved when the "woman with a past" poisons herself (toasting the joy of life) to save her former lover, whose son seals his doom by remarking, "A man of honor would be more eager to give his life than the husband would be to take it"; and *Johannisfeuer* (*The Fires of St. John,* 1900; also translated as *St. John's Fire*), a fantasy set in East Prussia during a midsummer-night saturnalia that resolves the conflict of heathen passion and Christian morality.

The opposition of critics elicited increasingly bitter counterattacks by Sudermann. But he was unable to repeat his early successes, though he continued to try, with plays such as *Sturmgeselle Sokrates* (1903), a political comedy; *Stein unter Steinen* (1905), portraying an ex-convict's rehabilitation with the help of his girl and a friend; *Strandkinder* (1909), a historical drama about the battle of two pagan brothers raised as slaves; *Der Bettler von Syrakus* (1911), based on the war between Syracuse and Carthage; *Die gutgeschnittene Ecke* (1915), an attack on pre-World War I materialism revived with some success after 1918; and *Das deutsche Schicksal* (1921), a patriotic trilogy about postwar German society. His last play was *Der Hasenfellhändler* (1925). A posthumous drama about returning military prisoners and a woman's choice between lover and fiancé, *Die Entscheidung der Lissa Hart* (1932), had appeared in 1923 as *Wie die Träumenden;* it attracted some attention and very briefly reestablished Sudermann's German reputation as a notable playwright. Soon his obvious shortcomings, however, permanently relegated him to the ranks of minor dramatists. Even his best plays failed to withstand the test of time, and today they appear totally dated with their counterfeit naturalism, artificiality, sentimentality, fustian, and utter humorlessness.

Because his later plays failed to attract audiences, Sudermann returned to his prose writing. He achieved success with *Litauische Geschichten* (1917; tales about East Prussian life translated as *The Excursion to Tilsit,* 1930), and a number of novels; the last of them, *Purzelchen,* was published the year of his death and translated two years later as *The Dance of Youth.*

Though many of Sudermann's plays appeared in English, and *Magda* and *The Vale of Content* were anthologized, few are readily available today. Kerr's attacks on Sudermann's drama were collected in the first volume of the critic's *Das neue Drama* (1904). Sudermann's autobiography is *Das Bilderbuch meiner Jugend* (1922, translated as *Book of My Youth*). Volume II of Alex Natan's edition of *German Men of Letters* (1963) and H. F. Garten's *Modern German Drama* (1964) have sections on Sudermann and bibliographies.

SUICIDE PROHIBITED IN SPRINGTIME (*Prohibido suicidarse en primavera*), a play in three acts by ALEJANDRO CASONA, produced in 1937(?) and published in 1940. Setting: a "spiritual sanatorium" in the Spanish mountains, early 1930's.

Reminiscent of Barry's HOTEL UNIVERSE in its tone and episodic psychodramas, this is a typical Casona play: wistful and whimsical, dealing with love and suicide and, most of all, attempts to escape harsh reality through illusion, but the ultimate finding of happiness by facing up to one's problems.

In a home based "on the philosophic and esthetic cult of death," everything is made inviting to help the inmates carry out their intended suicides: perfumed deadly gases, Werther Gardens with hanging nooses, lakes for drowning, etc. This pleasurable ease, however, frustrates the "heroic sense of death" for, as the institution's mysterious director explains, "a warm desire for life" takes hold of the would-be suicides who at present comprise: "Disillusioned lovers, 8. Skin diseases, 2. Aimless lives, 4. Economic disaster [and assorted] drug addicts," and a clerk who imagines himself to be the lover of a famous opera singer, whom he rejects when she proves overwhelming in the flesh. A slender plot is provided by the chance appearance of a blissfully happy couple, both journalists, who learn the importance of fantasy and themselves become involved in suffering and ultimate redemption.

SUKHOVO-KOBYLIN, Aleksandr Vasilevich (1817–1903), Russian dramatist, wrote only a trilogy and is best remembered for its partly autobiographical first play, *Svadba Krechinskogo* (*Krechinsky's Wedding*), originally produced in 1855. An aristocratic Moscow ladies' man, Sukhovo-Kobylin was tried after the 1850 murder of his mistress, in a case that dragged on for some seven years. Written in prison, *Krechinsky's Wedding*—influenced by the satiric drama of his friend Gogol—features a nobleman who sells a fake diamond but is saved when his fiancée takes the blame. Krechinsky disappears, and the trilogy's second play, *Delo* (*The Case,* written in 1862 and produced in 1882), features the trial of the fiancée; it is a devastating attack on Russian bureaucracy and justice, reminiscent (together with the next play) of Dickens's 1852–53 novel *Bleak House. Smert Tarelkina* (*The Death of Tarelkin*), the trilogy's final play, was written in 1868 and produced in 1900. Here both principal characters have disappeared; the play is a grotesque farce about the struggle of two officials, one of whom pretends to be dead in order to confuse his superior, whose incriminating papers he has and wants to use for blackmail.

Sukhovo-Kobylin's satire of tsarist Russian decadence and corruption caused his plays to be banned. Staged by Michael Chekhov and Vsevolod Meyerhold, they were very popular after the Revolution, and became part of the Soviet repertoire. Sukhovo-Kobylin himself, overwhelmed by the murder and its aftermath, and exhausted by his struggles against censorship, moved to France, where he died. Harold B. Segel translated and wrote an informative introduction to *The Trilogy of Alexander Sukhovo-Kobylin: Krechinsky's Wedding, The Case, The Death of Tarelkin* (1969).

SUMMER AND SMOKE, a play in a prologue and two parts by TENNESSEE WILLIAMS, produced in

1947 and published in 1948. Setting: Glorious Hill, Mississippi; c. 1900–1916.

Successful in its original theatre-in-the-round production in Dallas and in a 1952 Off-Broadway revival, and a favorite with little-theatre groups, this play failed on Broadway. It appeared there the year after A STREETCAR NAMED DESIRE, and most critics compared it unfavorably with that play. *Summer and Smoke* suffers from excessive SYMBOLISM and abstract characterization. Like O'Neill's ALL GOD'S CHILLUN GOT WINGS, it is fleetingly episodic, and portrays lovers separated by an unbridgeable gulf. But Williams presents an oversimplified dichotomy of spirit (*alma* is Spanish for "soul") and flesh. The play was republished in 1965 together with Williams's "radically different [revised] version," *The Eccentricities of a Nightingale*.

Before the town park's fountain statue of the Angel of Eternity two children discuss their already different views of life. Alma Winemiller is the introverted daughter of a minister, and John Buchanan, Jr., is a doctor's wild son. Her father's puritanism and her mother's insanity accentuate Alma's development into a nervous spinster, while John, though a brilliant medical student, becomes dissolute. Periodic attempts to communicate their reciprocal love falter before their totally different natures. "Some women," Alma says, "bring their souls" to love. But John sees no soul on his anatomy chart: he does note a brain and stomach, which hunger for truth and food, and "the sex which is hungry for love because it is sometimes lonesome." By the time John and Alma accept each other's way of thinking, it is too late. John marries another girl, and the rejected Alma goes to the fountain, where she picks up a young traveling salesman.

SUMMER OF THE SEVENTEENTH DOLL, a play in three acts by RAY LAWLER, produced in 1956 and published in 1957. Setting: a cottage in Carlton (a Melbourne suburb), Australia; December 1952 to January 1953.

This was the first internationally successful Australian play. The winner of a competition and produced by the newly formed Elizabethan Theatre Trust, it strongly influenced native drama, and then appeared in London's West End and on New York's Broadway, and was filmed. The play is conventionally structured and contains patches of sentimentality. But it has local color, and it effectively depicts a doomed frontier spirit—and human disillusionment.

Act I. For sixteen years Barney Ibbot and Roo Webber have come with presents (always including a kewpie doll) and spent their five-month "lay-off" from Queensland sugar-cane cutting with their steadies, two bar girls. This year Olive Leech has found a substitute for the other girl, who finally got married. She tries to express to the skeptical new woman, a righteous widow, the "heaven" these unconventional summers with their "kings" (as compared with the "soft city blokes") mean to her: "Not just playin' around and spending' a lot of money, but a time for livin'." Perpetuating his reputation as a great lover, Barney tries to win over the newcomer. He also reveals that his friend's prowess was successfully challenged by a younger cutter; thereupon the humiliated Roo ran off for the rest of the season, and is broke.

Act II. Roo breaks their custom and takes a job during the lay-off. The visit is gloomy, and the newcomer, though she has succumbed to Barney's charm, fails to perceive the glamor of the life Olive described. When the good-natured but stupid Barney tries to reconcile his friend with their cane-field mates, Roo makes Barney admit his protective lie—that Roo was beaten because he had an injured back. He was perfectly well, he tells the women, and reveals Barney's late attempts—and failures—to be a ladies' man: "It's about time they knew what they was dealin' with, anyway, a couple lousy no-hopers!" There is a violent fight between the friends, and in the melee the seventeenth kewpie doll is damaged.

Act III. "You're too old for it any more," Olive's wizened old mother later tells the confused Roo. "Chasin' wimmen" and "bein' top dog," she adds, "that's all very fine and a lot of fun while it lasts, but last is one thing it just don't do." Olive is heartbroken by the failure of this lay-off and her friend's inability to understand the romance of her life. Roo decides to keep his job and stay with her—and asks Olive to marry him. Incredulous, the submissive, adoring woman rejects conventional security. "I want what I had before," she cries hysterically, pounding Roo's chest and weeping, "You give it back to me—give me back what you've taken." Roo realizes the past is dead:

Summer of the Seventeenth Doll. Barney (RAY LAWLER, examining the kewpie doll), Roo (Lloyd Berrell), and Olive (June Jago). Melbourne, 1960. (*Australian News and Information Office*)

"This is the dust we're in and we're gunna walk through it like everyone else for the rest of our lives!" Alone and bewildered by her rejection, he smashes the doll and then breaks down. Barney comes in, pats him on the shoulder, and leads him to the door as they leave for good: "Come on, Roo. Come on, boy."

SUNKEN BELL, THE (*Die versunkene Glocke*), a verse "fairy-tale drama" in five acts by GERHART HAUPTMANN, produced in 1896 and published in 1897. Setting: Germany, mountains and a village below.

This work established Hauptmann's reputation as a poetic dramatist. Except for THE WEAVERS, it remained his most successful play for years. Its fairy folklore, like that of Shakespeare's *A Midsummer Night's Dream,* delighted people, and its romantic-mystic SYMBOLISM was particularly fashionable at the turn of the century. In form and mood it resembles Shakespeare's *The Tempest,* Ibsen's PEER GYNT, and the plays of MAURICE MAETERLINCK; its allegory and theme—the conflict between family responsibilities and artistic aspirations—are not unlike those of Ibsen's THE MASTER BUILDER; and in subject it suggests autobiographical yearnings dramatized in other Hauptmann plays, notably in LONELY LIVES. Despite these many kinships, Hauptmann's first total departure from stage NATURALISM is a wholly original fantasy.

Act I. A woodsprite tells the golden-locked nymph Rautendelein how he toppled a big new bell down into a lake. It was meant to sound from atop a mountain chapel; its unhappy maker, the bell-founder Heinrich, desperately dropped after it. Now he staggers up lost and exhausted, and soon faints. When he awakes, Rautendelein gives him water; she tells him that he collapsed because he is "not used to mountain ways. Your home / Lies in the vale below, where mortals dwell." Quickly enamored of her, Heinrich begs her to stay: "Release me from this cruel earth, / Whereunto the hour nails me, as to a cross." She draws a protective magic circle around him; but when his earthly companions seek him, a witch releases him to the villagers. The fairies perform a joyous dance; but Rautendelein now discovers sadness and an unknown moisture—tears. Though warned by an elemental spirit, she yearns to go "to the world—of men!"

Act II. In his home in the valley, Heinrich's wife and little children await his return. Deathly ill, the bell-founder is carried in. His adoring wife cannot understand his despairing over the sunken bell, "A work—so highly prized, so free from flaw" that when it rang all marveled: "The Master's bell sings as the angels sing." But it "was for the valley—not the mountain-top!" Heinrich now knows. And he is no longer satisfied in the valley: "Since on the peak I stood, / All that I am has longed to rise, and rise, / Cleaving the mists, until it touched the skies!" When his wife is out, Rautendelein, "all mood and impulse," comes in; she charms him with her magic and releases him for a free life on the mountain heights.

Act III. In the mountains, Heinrich works, loves, and lives joyfully with his Rautendelein: "She serves him like a slave, by night and day, / . . . He makes her rings, and chains, and braeelets rare." He also makes bells for the sprites, but they are resentful of the new master, "A bastard thing, half brute, half God— / The pride of earth—to heaven a clod." The townsfolk, led by the vicar, come to summon Heinrich down to duty. Heinrich refuses; he wants nothing to do with the "murderous chains of worldly interest," and he describes the new temple he is building in happy worship of the sun. When the vicar chides him for blasphemy and irresponsibility toward his weeping, deserted wife and children, Heinrich is torn by conflicting emotions. Yet, he asks, "Should he whose hand is as the eagle's claw / Stroke a sick child's wet cheek?" The vicar finally leaves, after warning him, "That bell shall toll again! Then think of me!"

Act IV. Now Heinrich is at his anvil. His assisting dwarfs begin lapsing in their obedience, and the spirits taunt him: "Death is the burden of that lost bell!" Fearfully he seeks encouragement from Rautendelein, who tries to protect him. The villagers return to destroy Heinrich's heathen work, but he repulses them. Kissing Rautendelein, he muses about his being "A stranger and at home down there—so up here / A stranger and at home." His despair begins when his children appear with an urn that contains their mother's tears; it reaches its high point when he learns of her suicide in the lake, where the sunken bell now begins tolling, louder and louder. Distraught, he curses Rautendelein, himself, and his work—and rushes away to the village.

Act V. Rautendelein goes to her sprite lover. He describes how Heinrich's drowned wife sought for her mate by ringing the sunken bell with her dead hand. Heinrich, now an outcast from below, reappears looking for Rautendelein. When he discovers that he can no longer have his life on the mountain, he seeks death. The old witch tells him, "He who has flown so high, / Into the very Light, as thou hast flown, / Must perish, if he once fall back to earth!" She offers him magic potions to see Rautendelein once more—but then he must die. Gladly he takes them. Rautendelein appears and, as dawn breaks, Heinrich perishes in her arms—ecstatically: "High up: Sun-bells' chimes! / The Sun . . . The Sun appears! —Night is long."

SUNRISE AT CAMPOBELLO, a play in three acts by DORÉ SCHARY, published and produced in 1958. Setting: Campobello, New Brunswick (Canada), and New York City; 1921–24.

This biographical Broadway hit features Franklin D. Roosevelt overcoming the frustrations of his crippling disease. The future president is struck down by polio as he is vacationing with his family in their Campobello summer home. He is cared for by his wife, Eleanor, and by his mother. The elderly and autocratic Mrs. Sara Delano Roosevelt wants him to settle down as an aristocrat at Hyde Park, but Louis McHenry Howe insists Roosevelt pursue his political destiny, and helps him do so.

Patiently and with faith and humor, the paralyzed man overcomes his fears and insecurities, wins independence from his mother, and with the support of Eleanor ("Cousin—wife—dearest") resumes his political career. Finally, at Madison Square Garden, crowds tensely watch and wait as Roosevelt—without help—walks the fateful steps. As he gets to the lectern, ready to make his nomination speech for Al Smith, the "happy warrior," the band plays and the crowds wildly cheer.

SUNSET (*Zakat*), a play in eight scenes by ISAAK BABEL, published and produced in 1928, Setting: Odessa, 1913.

A great popular success when first produced at the Moscow Art Theatre, *Sunset* was soon banned for failing to reflect the aims of the Revolution. The terse dialogue and Russo-Jewish settings are in the unique and incomparable Babel style, though the lowlife characters—including the gangster Benya Krik of the *Odessa Tales*—have an affinity with Brecht's THE THREEPENNY OPERA, and the tragicomic father-son conflict is analogous to that of Synge's THE PLAYBOY OF THE WESTERN WORLD.

Scene 1. The matchmaker brings a rich merchant for Mendel Krik's daughter, an old maid. The powerful old head of a carting business, Krik brutally (but wordlessly) rejects the match. Thereupon his daughter gets hysterical, and his son Lyovka, a hussar on leave, mutters imprecations. *Scene 2.* Tactiturn old Krik is stupefied when his other son, Benya ("a flashy young man of 26"), dares to enter the parental bedroom at night and confront him. *Scene 3.* Mendel Krik intends to run off with a young girl with whom he has fallen in love. In a tavern, her drunken mother bargains with him. *Scene 4.* Later Krik returns home with the girl, who chatters as she undresses (while the enraptured old man watches wordlessly), before she embraces him. *Scene 5.* It is during the synagogue service, while he arranges a robbery with an accomplice, that Benya learns about his father's impending desertion with the girl. *Scene 6.* He and his brother, Lyovka, confront their father and try to thrash the old man. In the fight, Mendel Krik is stronger than his boys, but Benya fells him with a pistol blow on the head. *Scene 7.* Now the ruthless Benya takes over the carting business. Old Krik is ready to leave with his girl, who, the bibulous mother informs him, is pregnant. But when he sees Benya, Mendel Krik cowers before his son: "Don't hit me, Benchik." "They've killed the falcon!" the amazed old sot exclaims, while the matchmaker mournfully likens Krik to the aged King David. *Scene 8.* Ready to marry off their sister to the rich merchant, the Krik brothers invite guests to a Jewish feast. "I want Sabbath to be Sabbath. I want us to be as good as other people. I want to walk with my feet down and my head up," Benya the gangster declares, and Lyovka says, "After all, Papa, you've had your fun." Making up with their father, Jewish Odessa's one-time strong man, redeems both sons in the guests' eyes, and the foolish and garrulous old rabbi rejoices at old Mendel Krik's finally returning to the fold: "He wanted to warm himself in the sun all his life long, he wanted to remain all his life long on the spot where mid-day had found him. But God has policemen on every street, and Mendel had sons in his house." They drink a toast when he concludes, "Day is day, and evening is evening. All is as it should be."

SUPERVIELLE, Jules (1884–1960), French poet, novelist, and playwright, was born to a French family in Montevideo, Uruguay. Principally a novelist and a poet, he was expected to become the successor of PAUL CLAUDEL. But Supervielle did not produce the hoped-for major poetic drama: most of his plays, though occasionally featuring verse passages, are in prose and excel primarily in narrative suspense. Among Supervielle's plays are *La Belle au bois* (1931), a synthesis of three fairy tales (*Puss-in-Boots, Blue Beard,* and *The Sleeping Beauty*); *Bolivar* (1936), a historical pageant on the life of the South American liberator; *Shéhérazade* (1948), another fairy fantasy; and dramatizations of his fiction, notably the 1926 novel *Le Voleur d'enfants* (1948).

Joseph Chiari's *The Contemporary French Theatre* (1958) has a chapter on Supervielle.

SUPPRESSED DESIRES, a comedy in two episodes by SUSAN GLASPELL, in collaboration with GEORGE CRAM COOK, produced in 1915 and published in 1916. Setting: a Greenwich Village (New York City) studio apartment, c. 1915.

This amusing spoof of overzealous psychiatry has been frequently produced by amateurs around the world.

A wife insists on "analyzing" her husband and her sister. Since she believes that suppressing the unconscious is deleterious to sanity, she urges them to see her psychiatrist. The latter discovers the husband's "suppressed desires" for freedom, and the sister's for the husband. Thereupon the wife decides that "psychoanalysis doesn't say you have to *gratify* every suppressed desire"—and tearfully agrees to give up forever her interest in it.

SUROV, Anatoli Alekseevich (1910–   ), Russian author of undistinguished propaganda drama, rose to preeminence after World War II. He won Stalin Prizes for such plays as *Zelyonaya ulitsa* (1948), which deals with Soviet railroad production norms; *Nezadachlivy galantereishchik* (1948), a satiric portrayal of President Truman, the title's "ill-starred" or "mad" haberdasher who is likened to Hitler; and *Rassvet nad Moskvoi* (1950), an attack on conservatives, personified by a textile factory directress who is ultimately reeducated to more progressive ideas and methods—a topic Surov dramatized repeatedly. For a discussion of his work, see Nikolai A. Gorchakov's *The Theater in Soviet Russia* (1957).

SURREALISM, a movement in literature and the arts, flourished in the 1920's and 1930's. It strove to depict and yet transcend reality by pursuing the form of dreams, the irrational, and the unconscious. The movement was antiREALISTIC, and sprang from psychoanalysis, romanticism, and DADAISM. Less common in drama than in painting, poetry, and fiction, surrealism was foreshadowed by Jarry's KING UBU, Strindberg's TO DAMASCUS and A DREAM PLAY, and Apollinaire's THE BREASTS OF TIRESIAS. It was in Apollinaire's "*drame surréaliste*" that the term was first used. In his prologue and preface to the play Apollinaire stressed his opposition to photographic realism, and his aim to depict reality by imaginatively transmuting it: "When man wanted to imitate walking he created the wheel, which does not resemble a leg. In the same way he has created surrealism unconsciously."

But it was ANDRÉ BRETON who founded surrealism. His various manifestos, starting in 1924, proclaimed the individual's refusal to be restricted by the limitation of reality, and called for an imaginative evocation of the dream world. Surrealism was to be created by automatic writing and other nonintellectual efforts, though this principle later became modified. ANTONIN ARTAUD and ROGER VITRAC produced surrealist drama in their Théâtre Alfred-Jarry, founded in 1927, and French surrealism continued during and beyond World War II. Gradually it spread across the Atlantic, got involved in political and Marxist squabbles, and became absorbed into the mainstream of Western drama. Its traces are apparent in Wilder's THE SKIN OF OUR TEETH, the theatres of the ABSURD and of CRUELTY, and elsewhere.

Distinctive dramas of surrealism from ALFRED JARRY to EUGÈNE IONESCO (including *The Breasts of Tiresias* and an early attempt at collaborative automatic playwriting, Breton and Soupault's IF YOU PLEASE) are collected in Michael Benedikt and George E. Wellwarth's *Modern French Theatre: The Avant-Garde, Dada, and Surrealism* (1964); its informative introduction refers to other studies on the subject, including those of Breton.

SUTRO, Alfred (1863–1933), English playwright, translated and thus introduced almost all the works of his friend MAURICE MAETERLINCK to England. Later characterized as a "minor ARTHUR WING PINERO" or HENRY ARTHUR JONES, Sutro—the grandson of a German rabbi—was a very fashionable Edwardian playwright. His first produced work was *The Chili Widow* (1896), an adaptation (with Arthur Bourchier, 1863–1927) of Alexandre Bisson's *Monsieur le Directeur* (1895). Sutro's most popular drama, *The Walls of Jericho* (1904), features an Australian backwoodsman who has made a fortune, has joined London society, gets fed up with its frivolity, and takes his English wife back to rural Australia after he "brings down the walls" with his indignant denunciations of Belgravia's "brainless, indecent" Smart Set. Sutro came out with at least one play per season. *Mollentrave on Women* (1905) and *The Perfect Lover* (1905, a sentimental drama) were followed by *The Fascinating Mr. Vanderveldt* (1906) and *John Glayde's Honour* (1907), whose ambitious protagonist discovers that his neglected wife has found solace with an artist. Other Sutro plays are *The Barrier* (1907), *The Builder of Bridges* (1908), *The Choice* (1919), and *Living Together* (1929), his last produced play. His autobiography, *Celebrities and Simple Souls,* was published a few days after his death.

SWAN SONG (*Lebedinnaya pesnya*), a "study" in one act by ANTON CHEKHOV, published in 1887 and produced in 1888. Setting: an empty stage of a contemporary provincial theatre late at night.

This, the earliest of Chekhov's "vaudeville" pieces, is the dramatization of his short story "Kalkhas" (1886).

A lonesome old actor, having gotten drunk after his performance, awakes in the empty theatre. With mixed pathos and farce he complains of his life. Though he was much acclaimed, the girl he loved would not marry the actor she adored because he would not give up his socially unaccepable profession. But after reciting Shakespeare with an old prompter he is consoled. "Where there's art and genius, there's no old age, or loneliness, or sickness, and death itself is robbed of half its terror," he exclaims tearfully, and then struts off as he continues reciting Shakespeare.

SWAN, THE (*A hattyú*), a play in three acts by FERENC MOLNÁR, published and produced in 1918. Setting: the royal castle in a mythical European kingdom, early twentieth century.

This bittersweet romantic comedy was Molnár's first post-World War I play. A popular work, it won him the cross of the French Legion of Honor.

An absurd princess is eager to effect a match between her beautiful daughter, Alexandra, and a visiting prince. When Princess Alexandra's charms fail to entice this self-centered prince, the mother suggests she make him jealous. Princess Alexandra thereupon flirts with her brothers' young tutor, but the flirtation gets out of control and the couple soon avow their mutual love. Aided by her worldly-wise uncle, however, Princess Alexandra averts a scandal and gives up the idyll. She agrees to marry the now-aroused prince, though she can feel only friendship and respect for him. His mother reminds her of her royal obligations and of her father's calling her his swan. Being a swan means "gliding proudly, majestically, where the moon gleams on the mirror of the water, gliding always in the purple radiance and never coming ashore," she tells her son's half-reluctant bride: "For when a swan walks, my daughter, when she waddles up the bank, then she painfully resembles another bird. . . . Natural history teaches that the swan is nothing but an aristocratic duck."

SWANWHITE (*Svanevit*), a fairy play in three acts by AUGUST STRINDBERG, published in 1902 and produced in 1908. Setting: a medieval castle.

An engagement present to his third wife, Harriet Bosse (from whom, however, he was divorced by the time the play was produced), *Swanwhite* was inspired by MAURICE MAETERLINCK's first play, *La Princesse Maleine* (1889). Strindberg discusses its story—his own "in imagination. A springtime in the winter"—in OPEN LETTERS TO THE INTIMATE

THEATRE. Sibelius composed his incidental music to the play in 1908.

Swanwhite is mistreated by her wicked stepmother, particularly after her father, the duke, leaves for war. She falls in love with a prince sent by the king, to whom she was betrothed at birth. The stepmother, eager to have the prince wed her own (and homely) daughter, uses magic in her attempts to foil the lovers, and a gardener succeeds in sowing ugly discord between them. Yet their love (and magic intercession by, among others, the spirit of Swanwhite's dead mother) eventually turns all evil to good. The king, a lustful drunkard, is shamed and charmed by the lovers; even the stepmother, hateful because she lost the lover of her youth, changes to an agent of goodness when Swanwhite's pious love saves her from the duke's fury. After being banished from Swanwhite's presence, the prince had aged and was drowned. But love and Swanwhite's faith restore his life and youth. "I believe. I will. I pray," Swanwhite says, and whispers the three stages of her will (mind, heart, and soul) to him. He awakens, and as the lovers embrace, all kneel and the music swells to its climax.

SWEDEN. Swedish drama* was virtually unknown before AUGUST STRINDBERG. In the eighteenth century, playwrights were much encouraged by King Gustav III, "the father of the Swedish stage," himself a playwright, and the title hero of one of Strindberg's historical dramas. The National Theatre was founded during his reign, but despite the resulting flurry of cultural activity, Swedish drama long remained derivative and insignificant.

In the late nineteenth century the stimulus of Strindberg and Scandinavia's other great playwright, the Norwegian HENRIK IBSEN, brought about the first notable Swedish drama. It took a while for Strindberg's unconventional works to achieve prominence and respectability with native audiences but in time, of course, it was Strindberg who became Sweden's best-known dramatist—and one of the seminal figures in modern Western drama. Yet there are later Swedish playwrights who have enjoyed much success in Scandinavia and the remainder of Europe, particularly PÄR LAGERKVIST, HJALMAR BERGMAN, and (to a lesser extent) the short-lived STIG DAGERMAN. Like the dramatists of earlier centuries as well as Strindberg, all of these, it is interesting to note, were writers who excelled also in other literary genres. Among such early modern authors, the novelist Gustaf af Geijerstam (1858–1909), for example, was active in the "Young Sweden" group that in the 1880's attempted to "modernize" literature; his many works include a number of popular peasant farces, fairy-tale dramas, and other theatre pieces. Hjalmar Söderberg (1869–1941), a master of the short story, also produced a few novels and such plays as *Gertrud* (1906), one of his maturest works and a devastating drama on the illusion of love, whose cynicism is emblazoned on the title-page epigraph: "I believe in the lust of the flesh and the incurable loneliness of the soul."

In 1907 the young director August Falck founded the experimental Intima Teatern for and with the aged Strindberg, to produce not only Strindberg's unconventional drama but also that of others. As a result a number of new playwrights became established in Sweden at the turn of the century and in the years before World War I. Most prominent among these were TOR HEDBERG, PER HALLSTRÖM, and Ernst Didring (1868–1931). The last-named was one of the few Swedish playwrights who confined his writings almost entirely to the drama; the acclaim he achieved for his *Elna Hall* (1917), however, was short-lived, and he died practically unknown.

The plays of Lagerkvist and Bergman began to appear soon after the end of World War I. Though the direct heirs of Strindberg, these major Swedish writers worked in distinctively original ways that, in turn, both stimulated and influenced the playwrights who followed. Flourishing dramatists between the two world wars were RAGNAR JOSEPHSON, SIGFRIED SIWERTZ, and RUDOLF VÄRLUND. Notable, too, in the theatre during that period were HERBERT GREVENIUS, KARL RAGNAR GIEROW, and the novelist VILHELM MOBERG, all of whom continued doing important work in the decades following World War II. Gierow, who had begun as a verse dramatist, became an influential director and was responsible for the preparation and world premieres of some of EUGENE O'NEILL's posthumous drama.

The Swedish theatre, then, has remained significant in the Western mainstream in which Strindberg so memorably placed it. In later times its importance has been greater, perhaps because of film personalities such as Ingmar Bergman (1918–), himself a very minor dramatist (most successful with his one-act *Trämulning,* 1955; the basis of his 1956 film *The Seventh Seal*) but a major director whose contributions to the theatre have been as prominent as his contributions to the movies. (In this latter medium Sweden has, of course, produced such world-renowned actresses as Greta Garbo and Ingrid Bergman, also a distinguished stage actress.) As is true for the drama of other Western countries, Swedish drama is as variegated as are its authors, and it does not lend itself to summary characterization. Like the plays of other countries that are widely produced in Sweden, native comic and tragic drama includes much dross. Yet aside from the already-cited playwrights, younger new voices began to be heard in the Swedish theatre in the years following World War II.

The most notable of these are Björn-Erik Höijer (1907–), Werner Aspenström (1918–), and the lyric poet Lars Forssell (1928–). Höijer, a writer typical of the early postwar years in his interest in psychological problems and in man's quest for ethical and spiritual values, produced fiction as well as drama that features his native milieu of the Malmberg mining region, just above the Arctic Circle; the most notable among his

*For other drama written in Swedish, see FINLAND.

plays is *Isak Juntti hade många söner* (1954), which, despite its melodrama, effectively portrays inhuman religious fanaticism. Aspenström, a poet as well as a playwright, wrote a drama on the poet's function in society (*Poeten och kejsaren,* 1956) and short ABSURD plays: science fiction fantasies such as *Det eviga* (1959) and *Spindlarna* (1966); the "apes" of the first play use tape recorder and projector to reconstruct an image of a collapsed world, while the "spiders" of the second play are men who settle on the moon after the earth's destruction. Forssell's first plays were a reinterpretation of the Alcestis myth, *Kröningen* (*The Coronation,* 1956), and three charades published as *Prototyper* (1961), the most notable of which (*Charlie MacDeath*), a philosophical debate between a ventriloquist and the dummy with whom he exchanges places, was the curtain raiser to Forssell's *Mary Lou* (1962), an interpretation of America's World War II traitress "Axis Sally" as a lonely neurotic in a play that established him as a dramatist; Forssell's reputation was enhanced by *Söndagspromenaden* (*The Sunday Promenade,* 1963), a play that features the disengaged modern hero as a grocer who tries to transcend his drab life and absurd cosmos, and by a historical drama, *Kristina* (1968), that invited immediate favorable comparison with Strindberg's KRISTINA.

A very comprehensive study in English of Sweden's dramatic literature is Alrik Gustafson's *A History of Swedish Literature* (1961), which has extensive annotated bibliographies. *World Theatre* IV: 2 (Spring 1955) and the *Tulane Drama Review* VI: 2 (November 1961) are both devoted entirely to the theatre of Sweden; they include essays, bibliographies, and the first publication in English of a number of Swedish plays. *Swedish Theatre* (1968) consists of essays by Niklas Brunius and others, and includes a complete bibliography of Swedish dramas in translation.

SWEDENHIELMS, THE (*Swedenhielms*), a comedy in four acts by HJALMAR BERGMAN, published and produced in 1925. Setting: Stockholm, a spring in the 1920's.

Bergman made his reputation as a dramatist with this distinguished and very popular domestic comedy, produced in America as *The Nobel Prize* and in England as *The Family First*. Particularly successful among its good-natured caricatures are those of two old-fashioned Swedish types: the exuberant, eccentric, and paternal Rolf Swedenhielm, who voices rigid concepts of honor; and his dour but zealous housekeeper and sister-in-law, Marta Boman, whose actions provide the plot's final twist. The satire of human foibles is at times sentimental and moralistic, though Bergman does not judge his characters.

Act I. Rolf Swedenhielm, Junior, an engineer, is chagrined because his father apparently has not won the Nobel Prize—and the much-needed money that comes with it. Ill-humored, he calls his sister, a vivacious actress, a "performing ape." Their young flight-officer brother, in the meantime, orders a huge breakfast from Boman, the ever-busy housekeeper who indulges his whims though she rudely ignores the rest of the family. As the brothers shamefacedly tell each other how they have been reduced to borrowing money, an incompetent young journalist comes to interview the Nobel Prize loser. After explaining his own contribution to his father's work, young Rolf Swedenhielm wants to send the bungling reporter away—though the others in the household (including even the laconic Boman) are eager to get into the papers. A letter from their father is brought in. It was written when the old man felt depressed, and his family fear he has committed suicide. But as they weep and worry, the zestful old man appears. "Now I'm happy, devilishly happy," he tells them, bellowing affectionately at each of his children, at Boman, and even at the confused reporter. Though he is broke, he orders Boman to cease her persistent housecleaning and get up an elaborate lunch. Her refusal does not dampen Swedenhielm's spirit. "Satan's hag!" he exclaims; "Boman, I defy you"—and he takes his family out for lunch: "There's always a penny or so left over for a bottle of champagne."

Act II. When they return, Boman has the curtains and rugs removed for general housecleaning. The flight-officer son unhappily decides that because of their poverty he must break off his match with the heiress he loves. But the spirited girl has no intention of giving him up. While they alternately argue and embrace, old Swedenhielm pretends to be asleep. Later he urges her to give his boy up. He glories in his son's "sense of honor" as he envisions his own future (speaking of himself in the third person), without fame, fortune, and happiness. "But not honor. He carried that between his hands . . . and did not let go of it," Swedenhielm declaims: "You [people] turned him into an unsuccessful genius, into an idiot, a fool. But a happy fool, right up to his death. Honor and joy cannot be separated"—though he castigates himself for leaving his children poor. Just as his sons start telling him about the money they have borrowed, their "usurer" appears. At the same time news comes that Swedenhielm has, indeed, won the Nobel Prize after all. The old man is overjoyed. He recognizes and greets the moneylender as his foster brother, and introduces him to Boman. "With her brooms and pails she has driven me at a gallop through half a century, she has mislaid my papers, disturbed me in my work, she has turned my happiness sour and my sorrow rancid," he recounts, citing her "three functions in life: to nag, to rub, and to scrub. She is life's personified prose," Swedenhielm continues: "she is silent, oppressive poverty. She is soul-destroying misery." The old housekeeper thinks Swedenhielm is losing his mind as he finally orders her and her buckets out: "I have got the Nobel Prize and I do not intend to be browbeaten any longer."

Act III. He and the moneylender review their youth while the brothers fearfully wait outside, their sister rehearses her play, and the simple-minded reporter returns for another story. Swedenhielm reiterates his strict sense of morality to the moneylender, who bitterly recalls an old punishment. When Swedenhielm remains adamant ("one does not compromise in matters of probity"), he is confronted with his sons' promissory notes—two of which are forgeries of his signature. Believing his beloved younger son guilty, Swedenhielm is overwhelmed with grief and horror at his "soiled reputation." Boman reports his room and bed ready, and he slowly walks off, a bent and beaten old man.

Act IV. The Nobel Prize ceremony is about to start. Swedenhielm's family await him, worried about his unhappiness. He quickly loses his temper when he appears, and slaps his younger son: "I cannot accept any public honors whatever, small or great. If a man has not even been able to make honorable men of his own sons, nothing else can be of much value." Thereupon Boman confesses it was she who forged the notes—to provide the family with the luxuries they demanded. "Put me in the cell!" she insists, as she bitterly recounts how the equipment for their experiments and their demands for food, drink, and clothes had to be paid for somehow. Old Swedenhielm is relieved to discover his son's innocence. "You are very ugly," he tells Boman, putting his cheek against hers: "But no woman has ever made me so happy as you—today—" He leaves to accept his Nobel Prize, confident that Boman—"Wonderful old lady!"—will obey his instructions to receive the "usurer" with honor. "Well, well, now they're off," Boman mutters. Then she happily waits for the moneylender, preparing her strong cane, and ready to administer to him a physical equivalent of the tongue-lashing she has just given the Swedenhielm family: "Now he can come, that fellow."

SWEENEY AGONISTES, a verse playlet by T. S. ELIOT, published in 1932 and produced in 1933. Setting: a contemporary London flat.

Eliot's first dramatic work (its original title was *Wanna Go Home, Baby?*), *Sweeney Agonistes* is subtitled "Fragments of an Aristophanic Melodrama" and consists of an incomplete "Prologue" (1926) and "Agon" (1927). Later Eliot wrote a concluding prose scene, published in Hallie Flanagan's *Dynamo* (1943). Syncopated poetic rhythms and vulgar language portray a social wasteland, parody exotic romance, and suggest the sinister, which is heightened by the "apeneck" Sweeney of Eliot's poems.

In their flat, two girls discuss boyfriends. Then they cut cards and draw—a coffin. Later they are visited by men, including Americans who find London too frivolous. Another guest, Sweeney, proposes to take one of the girls to a cannibal-crocodile island where there would be only "Birth, and copulation, and death. / I've been born, and once is enough." After the minstrel-singing of love songs ("Under the bamboo" and "My little island girl"), Sweeney tells of (confesses?) a brutal but undiscovered murder. Yet he reiterates the girls' conviction that "somebody's gotta pay the rent." They all chant, "And you wait for a knock and the turning of a lock for you know the hangman's waiting for you. / And perhaps you're alive / And perhaps you're dead," and they laugh—and there is an ominous knock.

SWEET BIRD OF YOUTH, a play in three acts by TENNESSEE WILLIAMS, published and produced in 1959. Setting: a Gulf Coast town on a modern Easter Sunday.

An early version of this play (originally the one-act *The Enemy: Time,* published in 1959) was produced in Florida in 1956. Williams revised the play in 1961, when it was hailed by Broadway audiences and newspaper reviewers. It is marred not only by excesses of plot, sex, and violence, but also by stereotyped portrayals and a lack of unity. The dramatic potential of the gigolo's relation with the aging actress remains unrealized, but what is successful is her sympathetic characterization.

Act I. Chance Wayne, handsome but dissipated in his late twenties, wakes up in a St. Cloud hotel bedroom next to the "Princess," the former movie star Alexandra (or Ariadne) del Lago, whose servant-prostitute he is. The Princess gasps for her oxygen mask, liquor, and hashish to face the day. She is terrified by her comeback attempt, a new film whose premiere showed the ravages of her age and, she dimly recalls, was a nightmare. She and Chance use each other in their battle against lost youth. Chance has brought her back to his home town to stage a talent contest that he would win with his girl, the daughter of the local political boss. When Chance bumbles an attempt to blackmail her, the Princess ridicules but feels closer to him: "When monster meets monster, one monster has to give way, AND IT WILL NEVER BE ME." She needs him for sexual oblivion, and stipulates her terms. Only through lovemaking can she forget the horror of time and failure, and find "dependable distraction so when I say now, because I need that distraction, it has to be now, not later."

Act II. The local boss, a study of malignancy, has sworn to have Chance castrated. Some years ago the boy had infected his daughter, and the operation that followed sterilized her. Over a huge television screen he delivers a "Voice of God" harangue on protecting white Southern womanhood, his white-gowned daughter forced to stand beside him. A heckler is savagely beaten up by the boss's goons.

Act III. The Princess learns that her comeback was a great success. Saved by her art, she nonetheless realizes she is still at the mercy of time, and offers to take Chance back with her. But Chance, defeated by his own weakness as well as by time, stoically awaits the mob coming to castrate him. "I don't ask for your pity, but just for your understanding—not even that—no," he tells the audience: "Just for your recognition of me in you, and the enemy, time, in us all."

SWITZERLAND during both world wars was a refuge for many of the German and French dramatists who were subsequently to become influential in their home countries. DADAISM originated in Zurich's cabarets and helped to inspire subsequent European drama, including major BERTOLT BRECHT plays, some of which had their world premieres in Switzerland. After Brecht, the most prominent writers for the German-speaking theatre were two Swiss novelist-playwrights, MAX FRISCH and FRIEDRICH DÜRRENMATT. FRITZ HOCHWÄLDER, though an Austrian by birth, is often considered as a Swiss since most of his work has been done in Switzerland, where his major plays first appeared. Otherwise Swiss drama has remained of little importance and virtually unknown. The population of Switzerland is multilingual, but since much of its literature is in German, it is often thought of as part of Germany's literature. Yet Swiss culture and geography affect its authors, whose works bear a distinctively native stamp. Furthermore, Swiss drama appears not only in German but also in French and Italian—and in various Swiss dialects.

Among the earliest and most popular kind of native plays was the *Tellspiel*, which dramatize the exploits of the legendary fourteenth-century Swiss hero as early as 1512. *Tell* (1920) by Paul Schoeck (1882–1952) is less romantic than the best-known in the genre, Schiller's *Wilhelm Tell* (1804), which is to this day produced outdoors with the whole countryside as its setting. Among Switzerland's open-air theatres the Jorat in Mézières became notable because of its productions of *Le Roi David* (1921) by RENÉ MORAX and the composer Arthur Honneger. More recent playwrights for such theatres were the director Oskar Eberle (1902–56) and Cäsar von Arx (1895–1949), both of whom also wrote dialect drama. Eberle in the 1930's produced avant-garde works as well as *Das luzerner Passionsspiel* (1934), a Thomas More drama (*Der heilige Kanzler,* 1936), and religious carnival plays, including a dialect version of Hofmannsthal's EVERYMAN, *Jedema* (1940). Von Arx wrote folk and legend plays such as *Schweizer Legendenspiele* (1919) and *Die rot Schwizerin* (1921), comedies (*Vogel friss oder stirb,* 1932), and historical-religious and commemorative works such as *Brüder in Christo* (1947), *Das Solothurner Gedenkspiel* (1949), and *Das Bundesfeierspiel* (1941), a festival play revived in 1955 at Vevey in a huge open-air theatre especially built for it. The painter-novelist Albert J. Welti (1894–1965) wrote dialect and pageant drama as well as historical plays on religious figures: *Servet in Genf* (1930), dramatizing the tragic end of Miguel Serveto, who was burned in 1553 as a heretic at the insistence of Calvin, here portrayed as relenting too late to save the famous Spanish physician; and *Hiob der Sieger* (1955), on Kepler's attempts to save his mother from a similar fate.

The reputation of the mystic ALBERT STEFFEN extended beyond Switzerland. Less known abroad are the plays of the poet Robert Faesi (1883–); they range from verse treatments of the classics such as *Odysseus und Nausikaa* (1911) and a church festival play about the frequently dramatized story of the burghers of Calais, *Das Opferspiel* (1925), to the more delicate ARTHUR SCHNITZLER type of comedy, *Die offenen Türen* (1911), and to broad satire of contemporary pomposities, *Leerlauf* (1929). More conventional is the drama of Felix Moeschlin (1882–) and Herbert Meier (1928–). Moeschlin wrote comedies, notably *Revolution des Herzens* (1918), produced at the Mézières theatre and portraying the passion of an artist who pursues his idealized beloved but declines her passion when he realizes she is not the embodiment of purity he envisioned. Meier, who became notable after World War II, had also written comedies: *Kolondji* (1948, about Africa), *Kaiser Jovian* (1951, a Roman comedy), and others; his most notable play is the lyric and symbolic *Die Barke von Gawdos* (1954), which with much action but little dialogue portrays a man's conflict between his love for a girl and the desire to avenge his own father's murder by killing her father.

Much of Switzerland's renown in modern times has come from its geographic position, which made it a haven during both world wars. It remained unstifled by wartime or other kinds of censorship and therefore continued to flourish as a cosmopolitan center. Adolphe Appia, the founder of modern stage lighting and scenic design, was Switzerland's most distinguished citizen of the theatre.

Swiss histories and guidebooks in English allude briefly to native drama and playwrights. More comprehensive specific information may be found in the general studies listed under GERMANY.

SYLVANUS, Erwin (1917–), German playwright, attracted attention with his *Korczak und die Kinder* (1957, translated as *Dr. Korczak and the Children*). A bitter protest (like those of ROLF HOCHHUTH and PETER WEISS) against the quick and easy forgetting of World War II horrors, it is a PIRANDELLian play-within-a-play in which a group of actors performing the historical events gradually become involved—as Sylvanus hoped the audience would, too—in the guilt of the Nazi murder of sixty-five Polish-Jewish children and Janusz Korczak, who chose to share their fate.

Sylvanus, the descendant of an old Silesian family, was born in Westphalia. His horror at man's brutality is expressed also in his other plays, including *Der rote Buddha* (1961), a dramatization of human cruelties from eighteenth-century Paris to twentieth-century Hiroshima.

Dr. Korczak and the Children appears in Michael Benedikt and George E. Wellwarth's *Postwar German Theatre* (1967).

SYMBOLISM is a term used in a special as well as in a general sense. Specifically, it designates a literary movement that began in France in the 1880's with Stéphane Mallarmé, Paul Valéry, and other poets. They used objects and concrete phenomena, including the sounds employed in their verse, not to communicate ideas to the reader but, rather, to evoke the emotions and associations (the "esoteric affinities") of the writer. Such symbolism shares with SURREALISM a dreamlike quality, as in the drama of MAURICE MAETERLINCK and WILLIAM BUTLER YEATS, two of the purest well-known modern symbolist playwrights, and in a Wagnerian play admired by these and other writers, Villiers de L'Isle-Adam's (1838–89) long poetic drama of lovers seeking fulfillment in death, *Axël* (1890).

In its general sense, symbolism denotes one of the ways in which dramatists convey ideas and themes. It appears in a play's physical objects (setting, props), sometimes also in the plot, characters, actions, speeches, mood, and atmosphere. Symbols begin with such objective concepts as Oswald's syphilis in Ibsen's GHOSTS, ANTON CHEKHOV's cherry orchard, and SAMUEL BECKETT's Godot. But such "symbols" may well represent a cluster of meanings, only partly expressible and perhaps as infinite and inexhaustible in their suggestiveness as Hamlet's vacillation, and sometimes allusive even to their creator; as ARMAND SALACROU said: "In all our writings there is that which one calls the part of God (or the part of the devil), which makes the author, when he is working well, say more than he realizes. One pulls on a rope, and the bell rings."* Symbols proliferate in all plays. Simply by their presence, without regard to their aesthetic effect and the total context, they are no more indicative of a play's excellence or failure than is the mere presence of plot, characters, and dialogue.

An alphabetical listing that elucidates the meaning and sources of recurrent symbols in the arts and literature is J. E. Cirlot's *A Dictionary of Symbols* (1962). Haskell M. Block's *Mallarmé and the Symbolist Drama* (1963) and Anna Balakian's *The Symbolist Movement* (1967) are general studies of the subject; specific discussions may be found in virtually all works on the modern drama and on individual playwrights.

SYNGE,† J[ohn] M[illington] (1871–1909), was modern Ireland's first great playwright. He died before he reached his thirty-eighth birthday, and his dramatic legacy consists of only six plays. Yet he stood in the vanguard of the Celtic revival, one of the leaders of the Irish renaissance. WILLIAM BUTLER YEATS, who played a significant part in Synge's career, was the leading poet of the movement, and was himself the author of important dramas. But Synge was the famous—to many, at the time, infamous—playwright who transformed and immortalized the Irish folk vernacular into glorious poetic yet earthy prose. His work made him one of the modern world's major—and the greatest of the early Abbey Theatre—dramatists.

Little in his Protestant, landed-gentry background suggested such a future for Synge. He was born in Rathfarnham (now a Dublin suburb), the youngest of five children whose father, a barrister, died the following year. His mother reared her children by her strict evangelical convictions. Frail and frequently ill, Synge attended school irregularly. He intensively studied natural science, and then music. In 1888 he entered Trinity College, where he became interested in Hebrew and Irish, and in Irish antiquities. To his mother's deep sorrow, he would not share the family's pietism; agnostic, he finally dropped all pretense of religious conformity. He pursued his musical studies, and in 1891 gave a violin concert that was well reviewed in the newspapers. His mother's opposition to the "folly of wasting all his time" on music foreshadowed her later attitude toward his plays, not one of which she ever went to see.

He graduated from Trinity College with a pass (or "gentleman's") degree in 1892, and soon left Ireland. In the *Wanderjahre* that followed, he traveled in Germany, Italy, and France, where he studied at the Sorbonne. He read widely, wrote poetry and reviews, briefly joined the Irish League (in Paris), and had an unhappy love affair. He also worked on a play about an Irish landlord who marries one of his cottagers' daughters. (In a later version, he falls in love with a nun—but neither play ever appeared in public.) Most significant to his development as a dramatist, however, was his encounter with Yeats. In his preface to Synge's THE WELL OF THE SAINTS (1905), Yeats described their 1896 meeting; he recalls telling Synge to leave Paris and return to Ireland, specifically the Aran islands: "Live there as if you were one of the people themselves; express a life that has never found expression." Synge followed this advice, and achieved miraculous results. Life in those barren islands off the west coast of Ireland (depicted in his book on *The Aran Islands*, 1907) provided material for the plots, characterizations, and language of his plays. His work, as Yeats later noted, suddenly flowered into artistic maturity.

J. M. Synge, from a 1905 drawing by John B. Yeats. (*National Library of Ireland*)

* In a letter to Paul Hahn, published in the *Educational Theatre Journal*, III:1 (March 1951).

† Pronounced "sing"; "You singe a cat, you sing Synge," as a visitor was admonished during an episode related in LENNOX ROBINSON's "Pictures in a Theatre," reprinted in *Ireland's Abbey Theatre: A History 1899–1951* (1951).

After his first trip to the Aran islands, in 1898, Synge returned to live amidst the harsh, primitive struggles for existence there. In the decade or so that was left Synge, he wrote the plays on which his reputation rests: IN THE SHADOW OF THE GLEN (1903), RIDERS TO THE SEA (1903, perhaps the finest one-act play in English), the already cited *The Well of the Saints,* THE PLAYBOY OF THE WESTERN WORLD (1907, his masterpiece), THE TINKER'S WEDDING (1908), and DEIRDRE OF THE SORROWS (1910), which he did not live to finish. All of these plays are in Synge's characteristic prose, stimulated by the "superb and wild" folk idiom derived from Gaelic and Elizabethan English. ("All art," Synge wrote in his revealing preface to *The Playboy of the Western World,* "is a collaboration.") All of them also testify to Synge's gifts of dramatic characterization and action. His plays are for the most part peopled by simple folk: peasants, vagrants, beggars, tinkers, publicans, and the like.

Except for *Riders to the Sea*, Synge's plays are characterized by robust humor. As he noted in his prefaces to *The Tinker's Wedding* and *The Playboy of the Western World*—and indeed demonstrated in his plays—he disliked the ponderous didacticism of German and IBSENite PROBLEM PLAYS, and the ZOLAesque portrayal of NATURALISM "in joyless and pallid works." Drama, Synge wrote, "does not teach or prove anything"; when it tries, it soon becomes old-fashioned. Hence he stressed the importance of humor, the quality most needful to "nourish the imagination." Though he championed REALISM, it was its zest that he emphasized, "the rich joy found only in what is superb and wild in reality." His humor, like all true humor, however, is basically serious. Synge probed into universal human attitudes and relationships. He depicted the tension between reality and illusion, and man's quest (or failure) to realize and savor his brief life to its fullest—though it be at the expense of comfort and security. Even the one work that is unremitting in tragic intensity (*Riders to the Sea*) deals with these subjects but it focuses on the ever-looming presence of death, a presence that is only somewhat less intense in the other plays. Synge's preoccupation with such themes (the more poignant because of the brevity of his own life), however, is expressed in an exhilarating, "audacious, joyous, ironical" manner, as Yeats characterized it.

It was this manner—so different from his personal mildness—that evoked the ire of Irish mobs against his finest work, *The Playboy of the Western World.* It was the same manner, however, that impressed his fellow artists in the Irish Literary Revival—Yeats, LADY GREGORY, GEORGE WILLIAM RUSSELL (Æ), GEORGE MOORE, and others. And it is this manner, finally, that makes his plays the world masterpieces they are. It gives them their unique poetic-prose blend of tragedy and comedy (and farce), realism and romantic fantasy.

Though Synge spent his summers in the Aran islands until 1902, he lived in Paris the rest of the year. Then he moved to Dublin, where he wrote his plays and took an increasingly active part in the Irish National Theatre Society. It produced his first play, *In the Shadow of the Glen,* in 1903. During his few remaining years, he wrote and worked at the Abbey Theatre, which was founded in 1904. In 1906 he fell in love with and became engaged to Molly Allgood; she appeared (under her stage name, Maire O'Neill) as the original Pegeen (in *The Playboy of the Western World*) and Deirdre, and also acted in Synge's other plays. Recurrent outbreaks of his illness (lymphatic sarcoma, or Hodgkin's disease), of which he was soon to die, prevented their marriage.

The Works of John M. Synge were first published in four volumes in 1910, but this edition has been superseded by the annotated four-volume *Collected Works: Poems* (1962, edited by Robin Skelton), *Prose* (1966, edited by Alan Price), and the two-volume *Plays* (1970, edited by Ann Saddlemyer). The plays also have appeared in many separate reprints and anthologies. The standard biography is David H. Greene and Edward M. Stephens's *J. M. Synge, 1871–1909* (1959); it has a bibliography of Synge's published works, including his contributions to periodicals. Comprehensive studies of Synge's plays are Alan Price's *Synge and Anglo-Irish Drama* (1961) and Robin Skelton's *The Writings of J. M. Synge* (1971). Particularly noteworthy comments on Synge occur in the *Autobiographies* (1955) and *Essays and Introductions* (1961) of Yeats.

SZANIAWSKI, Jerzy (1886–1966), Polish playwright and short-story writer, for some years was considered "the dean of Polish dramatists." An experimenter who dramatized the conflicts of reality and dreams and tried to revive SYMBOLIST drama, Szaniawski expressed the brutality of modern life—often in terms of the artist's attempt to adjust to "the mob." Perhaps most successful was his *Ptak* (1923), whose hero tries to bring joy to a small, stuffy town by releasing an exotic bird. Szaniawski dramatized his ideas even more explicitly in *Dwa teatry* (1946); here various concepts of the theatre are discussed, and the "Little Mirror Theatre" (REPRESENTATIONALISM) is contrasted with the more imaginative "Theatre of Dreams" (PRESENTATIONALISM) and illustrated in a couple of one-acters, identical except for their alternative endings: *Matka* (*Mother*) and *Powódź* (*The Flood*). Other notable plays are *Adwokat i róże* (*The Lawyer and the Roses,* 1929), a "serious comedy" in which a celebrated lawyer defends a culprit though the latter is out to steal the most precious of his "roses," the lawyer's wife; and *Most* (*The Bridge,* 1933), a psychological fantasy about an old man who secretly destroys a bridge to preserve his mode of life, but then risks and loses everything to help his son.

The high hopes placed in Szaniawski did not finally materialize. In 1951 he fell into official disgrace, and retired. In 1958, however, a collection of his plays was published. Some of them have been translated, though they are not readily available.

T

TAGORE, Sir **Rabindranath** (1861–1941), Hindu poet and philosopher, was the first world-renowned modern playwright in India—and indeed in all of Asia. Fusing indigenous Indian folk and literary Western theatre, Tagore wrote over forty plays, most of them short and lyrical. They are permeated with mysticism and recall the romantic Western drama of the late nineteenth and early twentieth centuries, particularly MAURICE MAETERLINCK's and HUGO VON HOFMANNSTHAL's. Typical are *Visarjan* (SACRIFICE, 1890) and CHANDALIKA (1933), notable among, respectively, Tagore's early and late plays. *Dakghar* (THE POST OFFICE, 1912), an atypically simple, nonmystic playlet, was widely produced in Europe at about the time Tagore's stature was acknowledged as well as enhanced with the 1913 Nobel Prize. Two years later he was knighted.

Tagore was born in Calcutta to a Bengali family already prominent in the arts, literature, and religious reform—in all of which Tagore was to achieve great distinction. After studying law in England he established in Bolpur the Santiniketan ("abode of peace") that was to become his famous international institute. There and in his worldwide travels Tagore lectured on Oriental philosophy and his faith in man's oneness with God. This was a leading theme of his talks and correspondence with the greatest thinkers of the time, and of his essays, fiction, and poetry. It is explicitly dramatized in *Chandalika* and other plays.

Also a gifted performer who starred in his own works and trained his students to act in them, Tagore at sixteen played the lead in a comedy by his brother, and a few years later in his own *Valmiki Pratibha* (*The Genius of Valmiki,* 1881), an early musical drama—Tagore was also a composer, as well as a painter—about the robber-turned-saint author of the Hindu Sanskrit epic, the *Ramayana*. Tagore's first notable play was *Prakritir Pratishodh* (*Nature's Revenge*, 1884; also translated as *Sanyasi, or the Ascetic*), a verse sketch about a hermit who soliloquizes about the joys of infinity until a girl brings him back "into the bondage of human affections"—another central concept of Tagore's philosophy. Other early plays are dramatizations of the Hindu Sanskrit epic *Mahabharata,* such as the tales of *Karna and Kunti* (1899) and *Chitrangada* (1892, translated as *Chitra*), which in a lyrical spring mood relates the romance of a warrior-princess who falls in love, temporarily is granted beauty to win her hero, and after satiating his passion wins him permanently in her own plain form; *Raja o Rani* (*The King and the Queen,* 1889), a Shakespearean blank-verse drama about a king whose excessive passion for his wife

Rabindranath Tagore in 1916. (*Culver Pictures*)

causes domestic and national tragedy; and *Malini* (1890), whose shadowy princess focuses conflicts between Hindu orthodoxy and compassionate universal love. Tagore's other early works include cosmopolitan farce-comedies: *Baikunther Khata* (1891), about a writer who bores people with his manuscript; *Goray Galad* (1892, translated as *Radically Wrong*), about the love and marriage of sophisticated young couples; and *Chira Kumar Sabha* (*The Bachelor's Club,* 1904), spoofing the problems of womanless males.

Tagore's later plays are usually in prose and weighted with SYMBOLISM. Many are about an elusive, tyrannical king: in the sometimes obscure *Raja* (1910, translated as *The King of the Dark Chamber*), he speaks to the people out of the dark; invisibly in *Mukta-dhara* (1922, translated also as *Free Current* and *The Waterfall*) he tries to enslave neighboring peoples by diverting the river that nourishes their crops, but is defeated by a prince who gives his life to destroy the dam and save the community; in *Rakta-Karabi* (1925, translated as *Red Oleanders*) he pitilessly drives his subjects to mine gold for him until a dauntless youth protests and—though executed—triggers rebellion. In *Natir Puja* (1926), the Buddha "worship of the dancing girl" defies the royal ban, but the victim's willing self-sacrifice (by beheading) shocks the king and his queen into converting to Buddhism. Tagore also wrote a play-within-a-play fantasy, *Phalguni* (1916, translated as *The Cycle of Spring*), in which an aging king is entertained by a minstrel's drama about urchins who expose Old Man Winter as Spring.

Most of Tagore's plays are mystic, brief, and sketchy—and baffling to Westerners. Like WILLIAM BUTLER YEATS, with whom he had much in common and who admired his work, Tagore is more important—even in his drama—as a poet. Like Yeats too, however, Tagore became a major influence in restoring modern folk theatre by reviving, evolving, and popularizing native myths. Long after his death he remained the only widely known modern Eastern playwright abroad.

Sometimes translated from the original Bengali by Tagore himself, his plays are generally available in English (though usually in much-altered form) individually and in anthologies. Eight of them appear in *The Collected Poems and Plays of Rabindranath Tagore* (1936), and three appear in Amiya Chakravarty's *A Tagore Reader* (1961). There are numerous studies of his work, the first comprehensive one of the plays being Edward Thompson's *Rabindranath Tagore Poet and Dramatist* (revised edition, 1948). Biographies include Krishna Kripalani's *Rabindranath Tagore* (1962), which has a bibliography of translations.

TALE OF POSSESSORS, SELF-DISPOSSESSED, A, EUGENE O'NEILL's projected cycle of nine (?) plays dramatizing the history of the United States from 1775 to the 1920's through the story of an Irish-American family, told with a stress on the destructive effects of greed. The titles (some of them provisional) of the plays are: 1. *The Greed of the Meek,* which opens on Evan Harford's Massachusetts farm on a spring morning in 1775; 2. *Or Give Us Death;* 3. A TOUCH OF THE POET; 4. MORE STATELY MANSIONS; 5. *The Calm of Capricorn;* 6. *The Earth's the Limit;* 7. *Nothing Lost But Honor;* 8. *The Man on Iron Horseback;* 9. *Hair of the Dog.* O'Neill worked on them from 1934 to 1943, and had almost completed the first six. But in his last illness he destroyed the manuscripts of all except the third and fourth, which appeared posthumously. An extensive two-part work (also destroyed and variously entitled *The Life of Bessie Bowen* and *The Career of Bessie Bolan*), covering the period from the 1890's to 1928 and dealing in part with the motorcar-industry boom, was apparently not a part of the cycle.

TANGO, a play in three acts by SŁAWOMIR MROŻEK, published in 1964 and produced in 1965. Setting: a contemporary Polish home.

One of Mrożek's most distinguished plays, *Tango* is a grotesque but terrifying tragicomedy. It quickly became a modern Polish classic and was popular in Scandinavia and on the Continent. But 1966 London audiences were confused by the concluding allegorical portrayal of totalitarianism. Conventional family attitudes are reversed in this play: the elders are freethinking YOU CAN'T TAKE IT WITH YOU Bohemians, dissipated and revolutionary, while the son is a conservative who yearns to impose respectability and moral righteousness. He insists on an old-fashioned wedding to his reluctant cousin, who is content merely to sleep with him, and he is stymied in his efforts to reform his family, whose antics constitute the major part of the comedy. His mother's lover, a moronic bounder, kills him. In the climactic resolution, his strange uncle (a glib sentimentalist, and hitherto the son's only ally) and the moron dance a tango over his corpse.

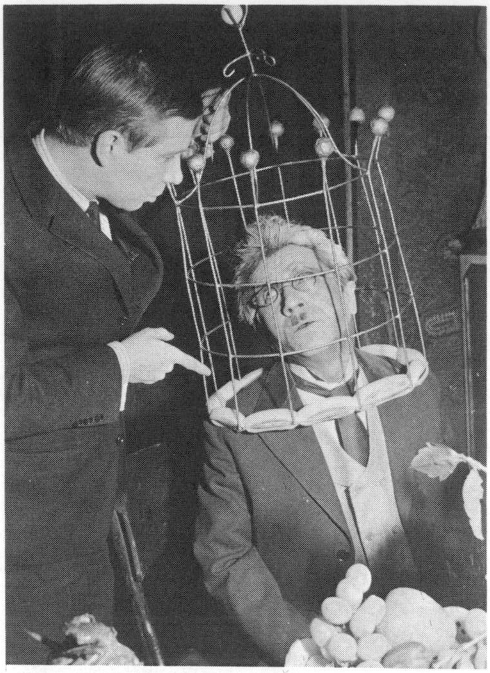

Tango. The son (Michal Szewczyk) and the uncle (Czeslaw Przbyla). Lodz, 1966. (*Eastfoto*)

TARDIEU, Jean (1903–), French poet and playwright, was a precursor of the theatre of the ABSURD. Before World War II he achieved a reputation as a lyric poet. He became director of the French radio and television network's experimental workshop in 1947 and began to write dramatic sketches, which were published in two volumes in 1955 and 1960. These are one-acters, pioneering works that bridge the poetic drama of writers such as GEORGES SCHEHADÉ and, in their concern with mechanization and the breakdown of communication and traditional values, the absurdist drama of writers such as EUGÈNE IONESCO, ARTHUR ADAMOV, and JEAN GENET.

Qui est là? (*Who Goes There?,* 1949), for example, resembles Ionesco's THE BALD SOPRANO as *La Politesse inutile* (*Courtesy Doesn't Pay,* 1950) does Ionesco's THE LESSON. To a lesser degree *La Serrure* (1955) recalls Genet's THE BALCONY and *Le Meuble* (1955), Adamov's PING PONG, while

Faust et Yorick (*Faust and Yorick*, 1955), not unlike Wilder's THE LONG CHRISTMAS DINNER, merges time sequences. *Un Geste pour un autre* (*One Way for Another*, 1955) is a short spoof on etiquette. Among Tardieu's most effective plays is the Kafkaesque *Le Guichet* (*The Information Bureau*, 1955; also translated as *The Enquiry Office*), in which a timid questioner is rigorously cross-examined about his life by a train official who finally consults a horoscope and announces that the questioner will shortly be killed—which he is as soon as he leaves the office. There is striking experimentation with language in *Les Amants du Métro* (*The Underground Lovers*, 1960), "a comic ballet without dance and music"; these arts, however, are conveyed by the speech of the lovers and the other subway riders. Similar Tardieu "poems for acting" are sketches such as *L'A.B.C. de notre vie* (1960), which articulates a day's events through indistinct but poetically suggestive murmurings and dictionary recitations. In *Une Voix sans personne* a voice evokes the past while the stage remains empty; it was produced in 1956 with Tardieu's more conventional drama, *Les Temps du verbe, ou le pouvoir de la parole*, a play about the ambiguity of time, which is said simply to be determined by the use of tenses: its protagonist lives in the past and is discovered upon his death to be a person who died long ago.

"A playwright's playwright," Tardieu is notable for his influence on avant-gardists of the 1950's and 1960's. *The Underground Lovers and Other Experimental Plays* (1968), the first translated collection, consists of a dozen Tardieu plays as well as a preface by him and an introduction by the translator, Colin Duckworth. There are chapters on Tardieu in Leonard C. Pronko's *Avant-Garde* (1962), George E. Wellwarth's *The Theater of Protest and Paradox* (1964), and Martin Esslin's *The Theatre of the Absurd* (revised 1968).

TARKINGTON, [Newton] **Booth** (1869–1946), American novelist, also wrote some twenty-five plays, many of them with HARRY LEON WILSON. Their biggest hit was *The Man from Home* (1907), a sentimental-patriotic comedy about a simple but honest American saving his ward from marriage to an undesirable European nobleman ("I wouldn't trade our State Insane Asylum for the worst ruined ruin in Europe"). Tarkington also collaborated on plays with Julian Street (1879–1947)—notably on *The Country Cousin* (1916)—and he dramatized some of his own novels, including *Monsieur Beaucaire* (1900). Tarkington is best remembered, however, for his entertaining if shallow fiction, much of which has been dramatized and filmed. The most famous of his forty-odd novels were *Seventeen* (1916), featuring a lovelorn adolescent and dramatized in 1918 by Hugh H. Stange (1894–   ) and Stannard Mears (? –); *The Magnificent Ambersons* (1918); *Alice Adams* (1921); and a series about another adolescent, beginning with *Penrod* (1914).

A comprehensive study is James Woodress's *Booth Tarkington: Gentleman from Indiana* (1955).

TASTE OF HONEY, A, a play in two acts by SHELAGH DELANEY, produced in 1958 and published in 1959. Setting: Salford, Lancashire; 1958.

Partly a music-hall piece and partly NATURALISTIC, this play, written when Delaney was eighteen, quickly became popular and was filmed in 1961. It portrays the adolescent Jo(sephine), who wonders, "I really do live at the same time as myself, don't I?" She banters resentfully—but without real anger or communication—with her mother, Helen, a "semi-whore" who suddenly leaves her and marries one of her customers. (When he thinks of giving Helen an engagement ring, Jo remarks, "I should have thought their courtship had passed the stage of symbolism.") Jo finds temporary solace with a Negro sailor and becomes pregnant. The sailor disappears, and a gentle young homosexual moves in and takes care of her. Then Helen's marriage breaks up. She returns to the flat and throws out Jo's "pansified little freak." Shocked to learn that the baby will be half-Negro, Helen runs out for a drink. She promises to return and take care of Jo and the baby, and suggests: "Put it on the stage and call it Blackbird."

TEA AND SYMPATHY, a play in three acts by ROBERT ANDERSON, published and produced in 1953. Setting: a boys' preparatory school in New England, early 1950's.

Anderson's first Broadway play, like Hellman's THE CHILDREN'S HOUR, is about homosexuality and gained additional significance because of its indirect attack on the political witch-hunting that flourished at the time. A sentimental play with stereotyped characterizations, it has become a stock company favorite.

Because eighteen-year-old Tom Lee is a sensitive boy who is interested in art, his manliness is suspected by his fellow students, his father ("Why isn't my boy a regular fellow?"), and particularly by his gruff housemaster, Bill Reynolds, whose vindictiveness is heightened by his tender wife Laura's partiality to the lonely boy. Unsuccessfully Laura tries to do more than her job of "giving him tea and sympathy," by trying to persuade his roommate "how easy it is to smear a person." In desperation Tom visits the local tart to prove his manhood, but he is repulsed by her and fails. This "confirms" his "queerness" to himself and the others. Angry at the maliciousness of her husband, Laura decides to leave him—and not because of "this fairy," as he sneers, for "this boy is more of a man than you are. . . . Manliness is also tenderness, gentleness, consideration." She counters his sanctimoniousness by revealing Reynolds's own repressed homosexuality: "You persecute in him the thing you fear in yourself." Then she goes to Tom's room and consoles the desperate boy, who has tried to commit suicide. Laura assures him that he is virile and slowly unbuttons her blouse. She guides his hands gently as the curtain falls: "Years from now . . . when you talk about this . . . and you will . . . be kind."

TEAHOUSE OF THE AUGUST MOON, THE, a play in three acts by JOHN PATRICK, produced in 1953 and published in 1954. Setting: Okinawa, just after the end of World War II (c. 1946).

This popular comedy (based on the 1951 novel by Vern Sneider) won both the Pulitzer Prize and the New York Drama Critics' Circle Award, and Patrick rewrote it in 1970 as a musical called *Lovely Ladies, Kind Gentlemen* (music and lyrics by Stan Freeman and Franklin Underwood). It is played somewhat in the manner of the Chinese theatre.

An ageless Okinawan interpreter presents and projects the story of America's Occupation and democratization of an Okinawan village. Eastern folk wisdom and tradition clash amusingly with American mores and industrial know-how. A colonel receives as a present the geisha girl Lotus Blossom, for whom he builds the teahouse the villagers have yearned for, and the distillery that makes them prosperous. During the colonel's birthday celebration at the teahouse—which is climaxed by an Oriental wrestling match—the commanding officer suddenly appears ("What in the name of the Occupation is going on here?") and furiously orders an end to the colonel's unorthodox Occupation methods. The colonel is saved when Washington, impressed by his reports, orders that his methods be studied for application everywhere. The interpreter finishes the story, and tells the "lovely ladies" and "kind gentlemen" of the audience to "go home to ponder" the eternal truths.

TEIRLINCK, Herman (1879–1967), Belgian novelist and playwright, experimented with EXPRESSIONISM and brought it to the popular Flemish-language theatre. Using multimedia devices, he adapted film techniques for the stage, and his first play was significantly titled *Der Vertraagde Film* (1922), i.e., "slow-motion picture." In a manner foreshadowing ARMAND SALACROU's *L'Inconnue d'Arras* (1935), it portrays, in the instant preceding unconsciousness, the lives of lovers who are committing suicide by drowning, claw at each other as they change their minds and try to save themselves, and separate forever after they are rescued. Other experimental Teirlinck drama includes *Ik Dien* (1924), a spectacle about the medieval Flemish Beatrijs legend; and *De Man Zonder Lijf* (1935), an allegory in the tradition of *Everyman* and Maeterlinck's THE BLUE BIRD. His last drama, *De Ekster op de Galg* (1937), was more conventional, though it featured simultaneous sets; it is a character study of an old man who realizes he has not lived his life fully and tries, disastrously, to make up for lost opportunities with an adulterous affair. After this play Teirlinck returned to writing novels. An account of his work appears in SUZANNE LILAR's *The Belgian Theatre Since 1890* (3rd edition, 1962).

TEMPO (*Temp*), a play in four acts by NIKOLAI FYODOROVICH POGODIN, published and produced in 1930. Setting: "a remote section of the U.S.S.R. which is being newly industrialized; first year of the Five-Year Plan, 1928–29."

More of a hortatory documentary than a conventional play, this popular Soviet drama, Pogodin's first, features the then-uncompleted Stalingrad tractor plant. Like *Time, Forward!* by VALENTIN KATAEV, it depicts the transformation of peasants into proletarians who are spurred to increase their work speed. The play's characters include an American industrialist (an amiable caricature of a Detroiter who has helped in the plant construction) who is appalled at the slovenliness of the Russians. Fervent Communists, attempting to equal and surpass American industrial speed "norms," are temporarily impeded by the inexperienced peasants-turned-workers and by anti-Soviet saboteurs. But they finally succeed magnificently, to the amazement of the American and the gratification of the plant director: "On one sixth of the globe, in pain and joy, a Socialist world is being born."

TENTH MAN, THE, a play in three acts by PADDY CHAYEFSKY, produced in 1959 and published in 1960. Setting: an orthodox synagogue in the 1950's.

A contemporary Americanized analogue to Anski's THE DYBBUK, this romantic melodrama deplores modern intellectual cynicism. Such cynicism is personified in a young lawyer, who tells the girl who loves him that "I simply do not believe anybody loves anyone." The girl is possessed by a dybbuk. In the play's climactic scene the dybbuk is exorcised by a chanting cabalist and the blowing of the ram's horn. It is not the girl but the lawyer who collapses with a scream—exorcised of the dybbuk of cynicism. Now the lawyer has a reason for living: he has gained "the ability to love." An old Jew rejoices over the "miracle," but another is doubtful: "He still doesn't believe in God. He simply wants to love." The old men who are present resume their disputations: "And when you stop and think about it, gentlemen, is there any difference? Let us make a supposition . . ."

THAILAND (formerly Siam) has had one of the more developed of Asian theatres. The popularity of its classic *lakon* dance-drama was challenged at the turn of the century by *likay,* an episodic spoken drama with dance and music, on ancient as well as modern themes, like the Laotian *mohlam luang* produced in northern Thailand. *Likay,* a common (often crude) folk entertainment most popular in the 1920's and 1930's, has been used by the government in the 1960's and early 1970's to indoctrinate troops with anti-Communist propaganda. A new type of *lakon,* analogous to turn-of-the-century Western musical comedy, appeared briefly after World War II; romantic and melodramatic, it featured heroic gods and kings. All these genres have included JATAKAS. Shadow and puppet plays, as well as the classic *khon* (masked pantomimes), have also continued to remain popular in Thailand.

A specialized account is Dhanit Yupho's *The*

Khon and Lakon: Dance Dramas Presented by the Department of Fine Arts (1963), published in Bangkok. Faubion Bowers's *Theatre in the East* (1956) and James R. Brandon's *Theatre in Southeast Asia* (1967) have sections on Thailand and bibliographies.

THEATRE OF THE SOUL, THE (*V kulisach dushi*), "a monodrama in one act" by NIKOLAI NIKOLAEVICH YEVREINOV, published and produced in 1912. Setting: "the soul in the period of half a second," a large throbbing heart, and a nervous system represented as a jangling telephone.

The most notable example of Yevreinov's theories, this short and bizarre (but *not* DADAIST) play created a mild sensation when it was produced in London in 1915. Its characters are the projections and the "entities" of the professor in whose soul the action takes place: the rational "entity" (M1), the emotional (M2), and the subliminal (M3).

The professor learnedly explains and illustrates these concepts before a blackboard, upon which he draws a large human heart. Then the play starts. M1, bespectacled and soberly dressed, tries to talk M2, dressed as an artist, out of deserting his able wife and children for a fascinating chanteuse. The wife and the singer appear—each in two characters, the projections of M1 and M2: M1's wife is gentle and loving, M2's is a "slovenly bourgeoise." M1's singer is an ugly hag, M2's is ravishing. While they debate and fight, M3, dressed as a traveler, slumbers. Finally M2 strangles M1, is rejected by his chanteuse, and shoots himself. Ribbons of blood come out of the heart. The eternal soul must resume its wandering. "This is Everyone's Town. You have to get out here, sir. You change here," a porter tells M3. M3 stretches and follows the porter, yawning.

THÉÂTRE TOTAL is a concept of theatrical production as the *director's* creation. The dramatist's script is but one of the many elements of the director's final product, of no greater importance than costumes, lights, music, movement, etc. JEAN COCTEAU made a unique contribution to this synthesis of the arts, and a notable exponent of *Théâtre Total* was Jean-Louis Barrault at the Comédie-Française and elsewhere in the 1940's and 1950's. An example of such a production is Claudel's THE BOOK OF CHRISTOPHER COLUMBUS.

THERE SHALL BE NO NIGHT, a play in seven scenes by ROBERT E. SHERWOOD, published and produced in 1940. Setting: Finland, 1938-40.

In this Pulitzer Prize winner Sherwood attempted to end America's "suicidal isolationism" and shame her into joining the fighting democracies of World War II. Sherwood's earlier pacifism here gives way to the view that "the time comes when you've bloody well got to fight." The time is during Finland's invasion by Russia and, soon, Nazi Germany. Sherwood's spokesman is Dr. Kaarlo Valkonen, a Nobel Prize neurologist who quotes Jung's finding that "there is no coming to consciousness without pain." The doctor and his son die on the battlefield; his American wife, Miranda, preparing to defend their home against the invading hordes, presumably will die soon. A propaganda play with much speechifying, it was moving in a popular production starring Alfred Lunt and Lynn Fontanne. With only slight changes, it became a hit in England two years later—when it dramatized the Italian invasion of Greece.

THÉRÈSE RAQUIN, a drama in four acts by ÉMILE ZOLA, published and produced in 1873. Setting: a Paris bedroom, 1860's.

In staging his 1867 novel (also called *Thérèse*), Zola consciously ushered NATURALISM into modern drama. He aimed to depict the case history of "a strong man and an unsatisfied woman, to seek in them the beast, to see nothing but the beast, to throw them into a violent drama and note scrupulously the sensations and acts of these creatures." In this SLICE OF LIFE, Zola wrote in the play's famous preface, his manifesto for the new drama, "I have simply done on two living bodies the work which surgeons do on corpses." The play was a failure with contemporary audiences, who were shocked by its sordidness. In periodic revivals (including the 1944 production in England entitled *Guilty*), however, audiences have found the play compelling despite its final melodrama.

Acts I and II. Laurent is painting the portrait of his friend Camille Raquin, a foolish, sickly clerk. Madame Raquin dotes on her son, but Thérèse, his wife, is sullen. Though Laurent and Thérèse seem antagonistic, they freely and passionately embrace as soon as they are alone. The three young people arrange a boat ride, and friends and neighbors come by for their weekly game of dominoes. Their gossip about a crime crystallizes Laurent and Thérèse's determination to achieve happiness. A year later Madame Raquin and Thérèse are in mourning. Gradually the story of Camille's death is recounted. Though Laurent and Thérèse killed him, their account of the outing persuaded Madame Raquin that they risked their lives trying to save her son from drowning when the boat capsized. Encouraged by friends and neighbors, the grateful mother herself suggests to an apparently reluctant Laurent and Thérèse that they marry. "Longing to make you [the mother] happy," they finally agree: "It is our duty."

Acts III and IV. On the wedding night happiness seems within reach at last. But crime has corroded Laurent and Thérèse, and instead of love and joy they find horror. The memory of Camille destroys them. "We're not in love any longer. We have killed love," Thérèse tells Laurent when they cannot overcome their terror with idle talk. Attracted by their cries, Madame Raquin comes in while Laurent, mesmerized by Camille's portrait, exclaims: "There he is—just as when we threw him into the river." The discovery of her son's murder immediately brings about a stroke that paralyzes Madame Raquin. Only her eyes remain terribly alive, and thereafter she watches the criminals' gradual breakdown. During their friends' visit, Madame Raquin suddenly regains the use of one hand. She begins spelling out a message, but stops before the crucial word, "murder." When the company leaves, the terrified lovers' mutual recriminations increase. "It was you who killed him," Thérèse reiterates, and Laurent blames her: "Twice you've made me act like a wild beast. . . . From adultery you led me to murder." Surreptitiously Laurent prepares poison and Thérèse picks up a knife—and simultaneously they discover one another's murderous plans: "Oh, Laurent, we loved each other so much—and now we have come to this—" Just then Madame Raquin regains her physical powers. She rises from her chair and tells them why she did not reveal their murder to the company: "Human justice would be too swift. . . . I want to watch you pay for your crime, here, in this room where you robbed me of my happiness." She rejects their plea for pity, and refuses even to turn them over to justice. The desperate couple judge themselves. Quickly they seize the bottle of poison and empty it. As they collapse at her feet, Madame Raquin sits down slowly as she whispers: "Dead! dead!"

THEY KNEW WHAT THEY WANTED, a play in three acts by SIDNEY HOWARD, produced in 1924 and published in 1925. Setting: a farmhouse in the Napa Valley vineyards of California, early 1920's.

Howard's first hit, this play has been called a modernization of the Paolo-Francesca and Tristram-Isolde themes. Its resolution is unconventional for a "sinning woman" drama, and its morality was challenged. But, like such analogous works as O'Neill's ANNA CHRISTIE and the Quintero brothers' MALVALOCA, *They Knew What They Wanted* is not a PROBLEM PLAY. Believable, unheroic character portrayals, an accurate depiction of the local as well as the individual idiom, buoyant theatricality and humor, a provocative plot—all these helped to make and keep the play successful. It won the Pulitzer Prize and was revived in major productions, filmed, and adapted into *The Most Happy Fella* (1956), a popular musical by Frank Loesser (1910–69).

Act I. Tony, a prosperous bootlegging winegrower ("Ees not for pro'ibish' God mak' dees country. Ees for growin' da grape!"), nervously drives off to meet his bride, Amy, a lovely waitress he once admired from afar in San Francisco and then courted by mail. Afraid of her rejection, the middle-aged Italian has sent her a photograph of his handsome young assistant and friend, Joe, a footloose Wobbly whom he treats like a son. Amy arrives at the farmhouse and shyly opens her heart to Joe, whom she mistakes for Tony. The misunderstanding is not cleared up until Tony is brought in, badly injured in a car accident, but full of love and still determined to have the wedding that night. Amy is terribly upset when she discovers that *he* is Tony: "Of all the dirty, low-down

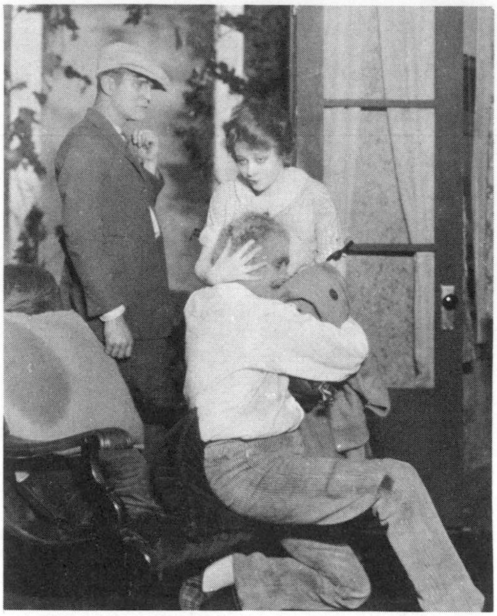

They Knew What They Wanted, Act III. Joe (Glenn Anders), Amy (Pauline Lord), and Tony (Richard Bennett). New York, 1924. (*Culver Pictures*)

tricks that was every played on a girl!" But broke, lonely, and yearning for security, she finally decides to stay: "I'm here and I might as well stick. I guess he ain't so bad, at that."

Act II. At the wedding "festa" that evening, Tony feels worse about having tricked Amy than about his broken limbs. Madly in love with her, Tony overwhelms Amy with kindness and generous gifts, but is upset by her spiteful antagonism toward Joe. The festivities and a comic dispute between a doctor and a priest break the tension. Later, Tony timidly asks Amy not to "be mad with Tony for bein' so crazy-wild with love," and rhapsodizes her: "You come in da house like da pink flower dat sit on de window sill. W'en you come da whole world is like da inside da wine cup." Amy is touched by his appealing qualities, and decides to nurse him herself in the months ahead. Preparing for her night's vigil she meets Joe, who has also intended to watch over the drugged patient. Amy continues to bait Joe, who asks her to be good to Tony—"a nut an' a wop an' all that, but he's just the best old fella I ever knew." The day's excitement and girl's resentful unhappiness finally explode—in the release of their suppressed passions.

Act III. It is three months later. Tony, Joe, and the priest argue about prohibition, the I.W.W., and capitalism. Amy and Joe have not met alone since the wedding night, but now the doctor reveals that Amy is pregnant. Having come to appreciate Tony deeply—and to love him—Amy is humiliated and brokenhearted. Reluctantly she agrees to leave with the equally penitent Joe. First, however, she confesses to her husband: "I love you, Tony! . . . I been straight all my life! Only that one night."

After raging in fury and weeping in despair, Tony cheers up. He decides to keep Amy, who he knows "is wantin' stay here nice an' safe in dees fine house with Tony," and the baby he yearns to have for an heir. "Ees good sense! Ees w'at is evrabody wantin' here! You an' Joe an' me!" he tells them: "We tellin' evrabody he's Tony's baby. Den evrabody say Tony is so goddam young an' strong he's break both his leg' an' havin' baby just da same!" And Tony concludes, "What you done was mistake in da head, not in da heart. . . . Mistake in da head is no matter." Amy and Tony embrace, and agree with Joe's conclusion as he cheerfully leaves to roam again with the Wobblies: all three have got what they wanted; "I guess there ain't none of us got any kick comin', at that."

THIEF, THE (*Le Voleur*), a play in three acts by HENRY BERNSTEIN, produced in 1906 and published in 1907. Setting: a country house near Paris, early twentieth century.

This thriller with didactic overtones became Bernstein's greatest success both in France and abroad. Its high point is the tense and Gallically bold second-act marital duologue in which cross-examination and confession are accompanied by discovery.

Richard Voysin and his wife, Marie Louise, can barely control their passion for each other while visiting a longtime business associate. Another guest, a detective hired to investigate a series of domestic thefts, uncovers the criminal: the host's nineteen-year-old son. Puzzled by his confession, Voysin tries, in his own room, to duplicate the boy's alleged manner of forcing a drawer. Marie Louise becomes increasingly frightened as he discovers large sums of hidden money. Although she uses all her feminine wiles, she fails to entice her beloved husband to bed. Finally she admits stealing the money, but only "because I adored you; I wanted to be beautiful to please you." Pressed further, Marie Louise reveals that the boy took the blame because, after she flirted with him, he fell in love with her. Voysin is maddened by jealousy, but ultimately comes to see his wife's innocence. "We men teach our wives only one duty: that of pleasing! When they are desirable, desired, then it is we who triumph," he explains to his host: "I have unconsciously encouraged her into coquetry." The couple are reconciled, and Marie Louise bids farewell to the sobbing, lovesick boy: "You will soon laugh to think that you ever had any idea of dying for a miserable little creature like me!"

THIEVES' CARNIVAL (*Le Bal des voleurs*), a play in four acts by JEAN ANOUILH, published and produced in 1938. Setting: the public gardens and a villa in a contemporary French spa (Vichy).

Anouilh wrote this stylized, sprightly Gallic farce six years before its successful production. Later he included it in his "rose" volume of plays.

Acts I and II. A couple is embracing as a clarinetist plays. Although punchdrunk with passion, the lover surreptitiously appraises the girl's rings. He is one of three thieves, soon revealed to each other behind their disguises. They plan to rob Lady Hurf, a rich old woman occupying a villa with her senile friend and two nieces. One of these is the charming young widow just embraced by the thief. The thieves are envied by two decadent adventurers, a father and son also interested in the nieces' fortune. Lady Hurf sees through all the disguises. But she is "as bored as a piece of old carpet" and "in the mood for a gigantic piece of folly." When the trio come disguised as Spanish grandees, she invites them to her villa. The youngest thief, Gustave, and a niece, Juliette, fall in love. The young widow—the other niece—no longer finds appealing the thief she had embraced earlier; despite the many disguises he now assumes, he is unable to reproduce the image that first attracted her.

Acts III and IV. While the others are at a carnival, Gustave fetters Juliette as he ransacks the villa. But their love for each other prevails: he releases her, they embrace, and she becomes his assistant thief. When the company returns, the decadent adventurers are mistaken as the burglars and are arrested. Sadly Lady Hurf lets the real criminals go after letting them know that they have not fooled her. The charming widow dismisses her lover, who has at last succeeded in reconstructing the right disguise, for he no longer appeals to her. Just then Gustave staggers in, carrying his loot and Juliette. "I want him for my lover, since you will never let him be my husband," Juliette cries as they embrace. Lady Hurf is moved by their love, but cannot see any hope for its fulfillment because of their different backgrounds. Only when her senile friend claims Gustave as his long-lost son is the lovers' happiness assured. Lady Hurf and the young widow, however, must be "alone again, like bobbing corks. It's only for those who have played it with all the zest of youth that the comedy is a success, and only then because they were playing their youth, a thing which succeeds always," Lady Hurf says; "they were not even conscious of the comedy." As the ubiquitous clarinetist plays his finale, "the characters come in through all the doors, dancing and exchanging beards."

THINGSPIEL, pageant drama established by the Nazis in the 1930's and derived from ancient Germanic festivals at a *Thing*, or place. Produced at open-air theatres (*Thingplätze*) before masses of people, these community dramas with choruses and semichoruses glorified the ideals of the National Socialist state and expressed "the monumental and heroic will of the age." One of the *Thingspiel's* chief works was Richard Euringer's (1891–) EXPRESSIONISTIC *Deutsche Passion 1933* (1933), a virtually official Nazi "Passion play" celebration of the emergence of the Third Reich after the defeat of an "Evil Spirit" embodying Marxists, intellectuals, and war profiteers. Other celebrated *Thingspiele* were written by KURT HEYNICKE and EBERHARD WOLFGANG MÖLLER.

THIRST, a one-act play by EUGENE O'NEILL, published in 1914 and produced in 1916. Setting: a raft, early twentieth century.

This short melodrama became the title work of THIRST AND OTHER ONE-ACT PLAYS. With O'Neill playing the Negro, it was the second of his plays to be produced.

On a life raft, a dancer, a gentleman, and a Negro sailor are dying of thirst. After failing to seduce the Negro into giving them water she believes he is hiding, the dancer goes mad and dies. The Negro is ready to plunge his knife into the body ("We shall eat. We shall drink"), but the horrified gentleman pushes her corpse into the shark-infested ocean; furiously attacking the gentleman, the Negro is pulled off the raft with his victim, as "the sun glares down like a great angry eye of God."

THIRST AND OTHER ONE-ACT PLAYS, the first publication of EUGENE O'NEILL's plays. This collection was published in 1914 by The Gorham Press of Boston as one of the American Dramatists Series, with the author's name given as Eugene G. O'Neill. O'Neill prevented the republication of the five plays in this now-rare book, subsidized by the playwright's father. But when the copyright expired, they were republished posthumously, together with LOST PLAYS OF EUGENE O'NEILL, as *Ten "Lost" Plays* (1964). Aside from the title play, the volume contains THE WEB, WARNINGS, FOG (the most impressive work), and *Recklessness*, a melodrama in which a husband avenges himself by causing the death of his wife and her lover.

THOMA, Ludwig (1867–1921), German novelist and playwright, was a satiric NATURALIST. Best known among his drama was *Moral* (*Morality,* 1908), produced in America also under its original title. It is a satire of small-town hypocrisy exposed in the comic confusions following the police's discovery of a list of the local brothel's customers —including the pillars of society who are members of a Union for Moral Uplift. A versatile author, Thoma wrote other plays that also were quite popular and include *Die Lokalbahn* (1902), a satire of philistines; *Erster Klasse* (1910), a farce in dialect; *Lottchens Geburtstag* (1911), a comic twist on Wedekind's SPRING'S AWAKENING that features a group of youngsters who—to the consternation of their solemn fathers—are all-too-well-informed on the facts of life; and *Magdalena* (1912), a study of social problems dramatized in the tragedy of a "falling woman" whose love life gradually is affected by mercenary considerations.

Born in Oberammergau and starting his career as a lawyer, Thoma moved to Munich to become, in 1899, the coeditor of *Simplicissimus,* which had been founded by FRANK WEDEKIND. Like his drama, Thoma's fiction masterfully portrays the Bavarian peasant and the small-town life he knew so well. It also reveals Thoma's keen powers of observation and his social consciousness, both in his comedy and in his tragedy—as in *Andreas Vöst* (1905), his bitter tale of a farmer's destruction by the injustice and hypocrisy of the clergy.

THOMAS, Augustus (1857–1934), American dramatist, wrote about sixty plays, almost all of them on native themes and many of them hits. He was considered "the Dean of American Playwrights" after the death of BRONSON HOWARD in 1908, but few of his plays, once noted for their architectonic skill and attempts at truthful delineations of minor characters, are still remembered. One of his best works is a melodrama that thrilled contemporary audiences with its hypnotism, THE WITCHING HOUR (1907). Before then, Thomas had made a reputation with romantic and racy "regional" plays such as *Alabama* (1891), his first success, which stresses reconciliation between North and South; *In Mizzoura* (1893), a rural comedy written for Nat Goodwin; and similar pieces named after particular localities. *Oliver Goldsmith* (1899) is a biographical play about the eighteenth-century playwright, poet, and novelist, and portrays such contemporary figures as David Garrick, James Boswell, Samuel Johnson, and Edmund Burke. Later Thomas established a reputation for "idea" plays: *As a Man Thinks* (1911) explores a common problem, concluding (in the words of the *raisonneur*) that "there is a double standard of morality because upon the golden basis of woman's virtue rests the welfare of the world"; while *The Copperhead* (1918) features a spy who surrenders personal happiness upon the exhortation of President Lincoln to "give up sumpin' more'n life" for his country.

Thomas was born in St. Louis, Missouri. He started to work as a page in the state and then the federal House of Representatives, and at various odd jobs. His father opened a theatre during the Civil War, and the boy was deeply impressed by the prominent actors he met at home. Mainly self-educated, he started acting and writing plays. Though he studied law, he was more interested in the amateur theatrical groups he joined. For them he dramatized Frances Hodgson Burnett's novel *Editha's Burglar* (1888) into a sketch that eventually became the four-act *The Burglar* (1889), a long-popular vehicle for Maurice Barrymore. Thomas also was a journalist and a cartoonist, manager of the famous actress Julia Marlowe, and an advance agent for a prominent mind reader—an experience that provided him with material for *The Witching Hour*. He published an illustrated autobiography, *The Print of My Remembrance* (1922).

THOMAS, Brandon (1856–1914), English actor and playwright, is remembered for one work, CHARLEY'S AUNT (1892). Born in Liverpool and originally trained to be an engineer, he acted in many plays and wrote over a dozen comedies. They were as inane but nowhere nearly so successful as *Charley's Aunt*.

THOMAS, Dylan [Marlais] (1914–1953), British poet, was born in Swansea, Wales, and died in

New York City. His richly lyrical poetry, steeped in Welsh lore, grew in popularity after his death. So did his fiction—particularly *Portrait of the Artist as a Young Dog* (1940) and *Adventures in the Skin Trade* (1955)—and his dramatic work, UNDER MILK WOOD (1954). Thomas also wrote documentary film and radio scripts, some of them collected in *Quite Early One Morning* (1954), whose title story inspired *Under Milk Wood.* Separately published were *The Doctor and the Devils* (1953), a film scenario (based on a story by Donald Taylor) about the famous body-snatching and murder case involving Dr. Robert Knox, previously dramatized in Bridie's THE ANATOMIST; an incomplete film script of Maurice O'Sullivan's *Twenty-Years A-Growing* (1964); and one sequence of an unfinished script, *Me and My Bike* (1965). *The Collected Poems* appeared in 1952. Many books—as well as a play, *Dylan* (1964), by SYDNEY MICHAELS—have been written about the work and the short, tempestuous, and finally tragic life of Thomas. His last years, during which time his play appeared, are chronicled in John Malcolm Brinnin's authoritative *Dylan Thomas in America* (1955). Notable, too, is the narrative of his widow, Caitlin Thomas's *Leftover Life to Kill* (1957).

THOMPSON, Denman (1833–1911), American actor and playwright, is notable for one play: *The Old Homestead* (1886), a sentimental rural drama based on *Joshua Whitcomb* (1875), a variety sketch written with (perhaps by) George W. Ryer (1845–1902). Thompson extended the sketch into four acts and himself played Joshua, the homely old farmer of this immensely popular play, for well over twenty years, until his death. Thompson did not achieve success with other roles or with his other, now forgotten, plays.

THREE DAUGHTERS OF M. DUPONT, THE (*Les Trois Filles de M. Dupont*), a comedy in four acts by EUGÈNE BRIEUX, published and produced in 1897. Setting: the French provinces, 1890's.

This bitter attack on marriages contracted solely for a dowry and other economic considerations was translated by ST. JOHN HANKIN and is one of the *Three Plays by Brieux* (1911) introduced in a long and laudatory preface by BERNARD SHAW.

The printer Dupont's two older daughters are a prosperous Parisian courtesan and a religious spinster barely helping to support herself at home. Ashamed of both and placing his hopes in Julie, his youngest daughter, Dupont shrewdly negotiates a marriage with an equally shrewd family who can bring much business to the print shop and whose son expects a big inheritance. Dupont persuades Julie to accept the young man though she does not love him and considers "a marriage that is a mere business partnership horrible." Her marriage does, indeed, soon deteriorate. The sensitive girl is frustrated by her husband, a voluptuary to whom a wife is a sex object and a housekeeper—and whose inheritance fails to materialize. A bequest made to the older sisters is eagerly sought by Julie's husband as well as by her father. While jockeying for the money the two families become increasingly bitter; each is disappointed in its expectations and considers itself cheated by the other. Relations between Julie and her husband also worsen. Though to her "children mean happiness, . . . the one thing worth living for," he decides they will not have any because they cannot afford them, and brutally insists on his rights as her lover—and master. Julie thereupon decides to leave him and support herself. Her sisters try to dissuade her. The spinster describes the demeaning hardships of earning a living, while the courtesan disillusions Julie about advantages lovers might have over even an imperious husband. Now more understanding of each other's problems, the three sisters realize they are all trapped. "Ah, my children, everything comes right when once you make up your mind to be like the rest of the world," Dupont blandly remarks when the couple are reconciled. "I dreamed of something better," Julie replies, returning to her loathsome husband though determined nonetheless to take a lover: "But it seems it was impossible."

THREE PLAYS FOR PURITANS (1901), BERNARD SHAW'S THE DEVIL'S DISCIPLE, CAESAR AND CLEOPATRA, and CAPTAIN BRASSBOUND'S CONVERSION.

In the preface to the volume Shaw discussed the deplorable state of English drama, which he had observed as drama critic for *The Saturday Review* from 1895 to 1898. Attempting to please everybody and succeeding only in being dull, this drama featured stage sensuousness and piety that were unreal, and romanticized and deified—i.e., falsified—both sex and religion. "The pleasures of the senses I can sympathize with and share; but the substitution of sensuous ecstasy for intellectual activity and honesty is the very devil"; hence Shaw's call to puritans, and the necessity for prefaces to explain his new type of drama. The last and perhaps best known section of the preface, "Better Than Shakespear?," deals with *Caesar and Cleopatra*.

THREE SISTERS, THE (*Tri sestry*), a drama in four acts by ANTON CHEKHOV, published and produced in 1901. Setting: a house in a contemporary provincial Russian town.

This major tragicomedy is replete with characters, conflicts, apparently random talk, and little action. Despite its complexity and NATURALISM, the basic pattern is starkly classical. All is focused on the main action and theme: man's frustrated attempts to escape the pain and tedium of life, expressed in the reiterated yearning to go "to Moscow." The dialogue (philosophizing on existence, complaints about boredom and irritations, dreams of life and work), though REPRESENTATIONAL, is often reminiscent of the Greek chorus; the opening scene, for example, approximates the strophe and antistrophe. Comedy and tragedy, irony, naturalism, and SYMBOLISM—all these coalesce, especially in the cathartic finale.

Act I. Irina, the youngest of the three Prozorov sisters, is radiant on her twentieth birthday. Masha, unhappily married to a kindly but pedantic and foolish schoolmaster, is ill humored. The oldest sister, Olga (twenty-eight), a schoolteacher, talks sadly of their dead father, a general who was sent with his brigade from Moscow to the province eleven years ago. Like her sisters, Olga has "such a longing to get back home to Moscow!" "It's nonsense"—according to a stray snatch from another conversation, behind the ballroom columns, between an elderly army doctor and a young officer, Baron Tuzenbakh, who loves Irina. The baron predicts a mighty storm that will soon improve life: "It's going to blow away all this idleness and indifference, the prejudice against work, this rot of boredom that our society is suffering from." The new battery commander, Colonel Aleksandr Vershinin, joins the party. When the sisters hear that he is from Moscow, they excitedly talk of the city and proudly introduce him to their brother, who is studying to be a professor. Masha deplores the uselessness of their learning and culture, but Vershinin remonstrates vehemently: people like the sisters will leave their impact and others will become like them, he insists: "So, in two or three hundred years life on this old earth of ours will have become marvellously beautiful." The feast begins. Masha deplores her "damnable, intolerable life," and, apologizing for a boorish friend, Baron Tuzenbakh makes love to Irina. Her brother's beloved, Natasha, a local girl without taste or manners, feels out of place among the cultivated, and rushes off; the brother runs after her and kisses her passionately: "My precious, my sweet, my innocent girl, please—I want you to marry me!"

Act II. Some eighteen months have passed. Married to Natasha, the brother has lost his ambitions and, lonesome and bored with the coarse and predatory Natasha, he has taken to gambling. Also unhappy in his marriage, to a neurotic woman to whom he feels tied because of his two daughters, Vershinin declares his love to Masha. He and the baron agree that life is difficult, but they console themselves by philosophizing about happiness in later centuries. Vershinin assures the sensitive Masha that being in Moscow would not improve matters: "We're not happy and we can't be happy: we only want happiness." Their love scene is interrupted when word comes of his wife's latest suicide attempt. Irina feels that she is aging, and she is tired of her dull job in a telegraph office. Baron Tuzenbakh's boorish friend tries to make love to her; rejected, he vows to kill any successful rival. Olga, exhausted after substituting for the headmistress and unhappy because of her brother's gambling losses, goes to bed. Natasha, who had at the last minute canceled the sisters' party for that evening because—she claims—her baby is unwell, goes for an evening drive with a former suitor. Alone, Irina longingly yearns for "Moscow! Moscow! Moscow!"

Act III. Late one night two years later, a large fire is raging in town. As Olga collects clothes

The Three Sisters. The doctor (Edmund Gwenn), Irina (Gertrude Musgrove), Olga (Judith Anderson), Masha (Katharine Cornell). New York, 1942. (*Culver Pictures*)

for the homeless, Natasha, in a temper, expels the old family servant and bullies Olga. The doctor, upset because he mistreated a case, has got drunk; he smashes a clock and bitterly jeers at everybody's ignoring Natasha's scandalous affair. Vershinin is still optimistic about the future. He and Masha are deeply in love, but she is disgusted with her brother for having mortgaged the house, and with her husband for his fatuous love. The baron has resigned his commission and begs Irina, "Let's go away and work together!" When she weeps at life's passing her by, Olga advises her to marry him, even if she is not in love. Masha confesses her love for Vershinin to her sisters; their brother insists, pathetically, on defending his wife, and then tearfully admits having mortgaged their home. Later, as Masha's husband seeks her and the doctor drunkenly knocks below, Irina tells Olga, "I'll agree to marry the Baron, if only we can go to Moscow!"

Act IV. The battery is leaving the province and the officers bid the sisters farewell in their garden. The brother is pushing a pram with Natasha's second child asleep in it; when the doctor advises him to leave her, the husband, acknowledging Natasha's vulgarity, replies in simple but terrifying words: "A wife is a wife. . . ." Irina is to marry Baron Tuzenbakh the next day and depart with him, but she worries about an altercation he has had with his rude friend. Olga, having become headmistress, cannot now go to Moscow. Masha bids Vershinin farewell and then weeps while her husband attempts to console her: "My dear, sweet Masha. You're my wife, and I'm happy in spite of everything." Natasha sees a misplaced fork, and rushes into the house, shrieking at a maid. A shot is heard, and then the doctor arrives to announce that the baron has been killed by his friend in a duel. The three sisters huddle together: "We must go on living," Masha says. Irina agrees: "I'll go on working and working!" Olga, listening to the band music of the departing battery, sees the possibility of a happier future: "Maybe, if we wait a little longer, we shall find out why we live, why we suffer." Their brother pushes the pram; the band music grows fainter; the old doctor, as usual reading his newspaper, mutters, "What does it matter? Nothing matters!"; but Olga keeps wondering: "If only we knew, if only we knew!"

THREEPENNY OPERA, THE (*Die Dreigroschenoper*), a play in three acts by BERTOLT BRECHT (music by Kurt Weill), produced in 1928 and published in 1929. Setting: Soho, London; late nineteenth century.

This play (or ballad opera) immediately catapulted Brecht as well as Weill to international fame. It is a free, anticapitalist adaptation of John Gay's *The Beggar's Opera* (1728), with nineteen songs, some of them by François Villon and Rudyard Kipling. Like the art of George Grosz, the play caustically reflects and summarizes an era of European culture. Brecht's most popular work, it has been filmed, and translated and performed in many countries; it was successfully revived in the 1950's in an English version by MARC BLITZSTEIN. Despite the play's conventional division into acts (each with three scenes), Brecht's "Notes" to it deal with the founding of the EPIC THEATRE. The movie script Brecht wrote for the play was rejected, but it formed the basis for *Der Dreigroschenroman* (*The Threepenny Novel,* 1934), his very loose Marxist adaptation of, and glossary to, the play.

Act I. The "Mackie the Knife" overture is sung in the marketplace while "beggars are begging, thieves thieving, and whores whoring." In his wardrobe room, Jonathan Jeremiah Peachum, chief of the beggars, is surrounded by signs with biblical exhortations. He confides his business philosophy to the audience: "I must find something new to exploit pity." After disciplining a would-be beggar before costuming and setting him up in trade, Peachum is chagrined to learn that his daughter, Polly, is out. That "heap of sensuality," he fears, has eloped with the robber Macheath, "Mackie the Knife." In a song with his wife, Celia, he deplores the foolishness and danger of love. In the meantime, his daughter, Polly, celebrates her wedding to Mackie in a stable. His gang of thieving cutthroats transform it into a Victorian living room, and bring Macheath gifts. They sing and sup, Macheath periodically bullies and berates them, and Polly entertains the company with a ballad, "Jenny the Pirate's Bride." Suddenly London's Police Chief Brown ("Tiger Brown") appears. But he is in his private capacity —as Macheath's childhood friend and protector.

The Threepenny Opera, Act II. Macheath (Harald Paulsen) and the whores, Jenny (Lotte Lenya) third from left. Berlin, 1928. (*German Information Center*)

They sing of their former army life together and reaffirm their warm (and mutually profitable) friendship. Alone, Mackie and Polly embrace—for "now sentimentality must have its moment, else man is nothing but a workhorse." At home Polly confesses her marriage. Her angered parents plan to denounce Macheath, and then the Peachums sing the act's finale: Because of poverty, men cannot be good; virtue inevitably backfires, Peachum insists, "The world is poor and man is base / I'm sad to say this states the case."

Act II. Polly warns Mackie of her parents' plans. Compelled to flee, he appoints her the new leader of his gang. The lovers tearfully part after Mackie promises to remain faithful. Mrs. Peachum (in "The Ballad of Sexual Bondage") assures Jenny Smith, whom she has bribed to betray Macheath, that he will follow his bourgeois habits and visit her in the brothel. And he does just that. Settled contentedly among the whores, he sings of his former life with his favorite, Jenny—and soon is arrested. In prison, Police Chief Brown weeps as he is being ignored by Macheath, who thus punishes his friend and then wistfully sings "The Ballad of Comfort." Brown's daughter, Lucy, visits Mackie, and soon Polly arrives. The women wrangle in their "Jealousy Duet," each claiming Mackie as her husband. Later Lucy helps Mackie escape. By threatening to mar the impending coronation with his disgusting beggar hordes, thus ruining the police chief, Peachum persuades Tiger Brown to recapture Macheath. The cause of evil is the subject of the act's finale. Stepping forth with his betrayer, Jenny, Macheath remarks, "Eats first, morals after" (Brecht's perhaps most famous line) and the chorus concludes, "So, gentlemen, you must concede to me: / Men live by foul misdeeds exclusively."

Act III. As Peachum plots to disorganize the coronation, Jenny reports that Macheath has returned to the brothel. When Tiger Brown arrives, Peachum convinces him of the hopelessness of trying to avert a beggars' demonstration by his arrest. Only hanging Macheath will avert it, and he informs the unhappy police chief of his friend's whereabouts. Jenny (in "The Song of Solomon") catalogues the futility of greatness—in wisdom, in beauty, in heroism—even in voluptuousness, which soon will fell Mackie. After a brief talk between Lucy and Polly, Macheath is seen in his death cell. Desperately he tries to raise money to effect his escape, but every plan fails. He sings a ballad in which he begs forgiveness from all men. Polly and Lucy are ready to stand by their husband's side in his last moments; the execution is about to begin. Suddenly Peachum announces a surprise ending: at least in opera, mercy may occasionally prevail over justice. And so, a mounted messenger arrives with the Queen's pardon for Macheath, his elevation to the nobility, and a lifetime pension. "Mounted royal messengers rarely come to save those who retaliate for their injustice. Therefore one should not be too ready to oppose inequity," Peachum remarks, and leads a final chorale to that effect: ". . . Remember the darkness and the icy cold / Of this worldly vale of misery and woe."

THUNDERBOLT, THE, "An Episode in the History of a Provincial Family" in four acts by ARTHUR WING PINERO, produced in 1908 and published in 1909. Setting: the Midlands, England; early 1900's.

This depiction of provincial pettiness and greed is a much-praised early example of a mass protagonist. The sardonic portrayals transcend the trite plot of a lost will.

With their husbands and wives, the Mortimores gather in the house of their deceased brother, the family's black sheep. The would-be heirs' expectations are frustrated by "the thunderbolt"—the discovery that his fortune has been willed to an illegitimate daughter.

TIDINGS BROUGHT TO MARY, THE (*L'Annonce faite à Marie*), "a mystery" in four acts and a prologue by PAUL CLAUDEL, published and produced in 1912. Setting: Combernon, a large farm in the Monsanvierge archdiocese in Champagne; early fifteenth century.

Claudel's best-known work, this verse play has been performed in many countries and praised as a (if not *the*) masterpiece of religious-poetic drama. It is an epic biblical pageant, set in medieval France, that deals with the dichotomy of worldly and spiritual love. In a SYMBOLIC portrayal of an Immaculate Conception, its saintly, self-abnegating protagonist resuscitates a dead child, and she elevates and purifies all those around her—even the evil sister who ultimately murders her. The play kept evolving in Claudel's mind for many years and exists in three distinct versions; of the two earlier ones, both titled *La Jeune Fille Violaine,* the first was published in 1892.

Prologue. The architect Pierre de Craon, already mounted, prepares to leave the Combernon barn shortly before dawn. He is stopped by the vivacious eighteen-year-old Violaine. "Halt, my lord cavalier! Dismount!" she laughs: "Is that the way one leaves the house, like a thief without an honest greeting to the ladies?" He begs her forgiveness for the attempt he once made to rape her, for which he was punished the very next day: "I discovered in my side the horrible scourge"—leprosy. Only the bishop's dispensation keeps it secret and Pierre free. As the bells toll in the distance, they recite the Angelus. "I am at peace with you," says the innocent Violaine, who long ago forgave Pierre. Radiant in the love for her betrothed, Jacques Hury, she exclaims, "Ah, how beautiful the world is, and how happy I am!" She feels tender compassion for the unhappy Pierre, and, as an offering for the cathedral he is about to build, presents him with her gold ring. Imploring him to cast out hatred from his heart, Violaine tells Pierre to make himself worthy of God and of the flame consuming him. As he departs, tears come to her eyes; full of compassion for his hopeless love for her and for his dreadful disease, Violaine kisses the

The Tidings Brought to Mary. Vercors (Stanley Howlett) and his wife (Helen Westley) New York, 1922. (*Theatre Collection, New York Public Library*)

leper on the lips. Mara, her younger sister, who has just entered unseen, watches in amazement.

Act I. At home the sisters' old father, Anne Vercors, tells their mother of his decision to make a pilgrimage to Jerusalem. The old woman tries to dissuade him from jeopardizing their happiness. "That is it," he replies; "we are too happy, / And the others are not happy enough." Deeply troubled by the division within both France and Christianity, Vercors insists on this act of devotion to express his gratitude for his and his ancestors' good fortunes. He turns over his lands and paternal authority to Jacques, whom—in the absence of a male heir—they have raised like a son and to whom Vercors now betrothes Violaine. Her hateful sister, Mara, always jealous of the preference shown the beautiful and good Violaine, vows to commit suicide unless the marriage is called off. In a long, affecting scene Vercors, before finishing the meal, takes leave of his family and servants. Gently he removes the tearful Violaine's embracing arms—"What is it, little lamb? / You have exchanged a husband for thy father!"—and goes out.

Act II. Her unhappy mother tells Mara that Violaine must marry Jacques as the father commanded. Mara angrily tells Jacques of Violaine's kissing Pierre, but he refuses to believe her. There is a long love scene between Jacques and Violaine, gorgeously attired in the ritualist Monsanvierge dress. "O Jacques! Tell me again that you think me beautiful!" she requests. Professing her own great love for him, Violaine cautions Jacques, "There cannot be justice between us two! but only faith and charity." Increasingly alarmed by her talk, Jacques realizes hers "is not a woman's dress, but the robe of one who offers the sacrifice at the altar," and begs her, before she goes on: "There are enough angels to serve the mass in heaven! / Have pity on me, who am only a man without wings." He reaffirms his great love, whereupon Violaine slits her gown and reveals her secret: the hideous mark of leprosy now upon her. "Infamous reprobate, / infamous in your soul and in your flesh!" Jacques curses her, now believing her sister's accusation that Violaine sinned with Pierre, "that measled pig of yours." She refuses to defend herself, forcing Jacques to draw his own conclusions and make his choice. Unable to trust her or to perceive the spirit beyond the body, he tells Violaine to go that very night to the outcast leper refuge. Dressed in black, Violaine then takes leave of her sorrowing mother and of Mara, to whom she gives all her belongings, including her gowns—"Ah, ah! my poor wedding-dress that was so pretty!"

Act III. In a forest on Christmas Eve eight years later, workers are building a road for the coronation of the Dauphin by Joan of Arc. Mara, carrying a bundle, is seeking the leper woman (Violaine) living nearby. Sounding her wooden rattle, the blind leper appears and picks up a piece of bread contemptuously thrown her by a worker. Mara follows her into her cave. "It is easy to be a saint when leprosy helps us," she bitterly remarks to the pious, uncomplaining Violaine, and tells of her marriage to Jacques. Knowing her own heart to be pure, Violaine bears the loss of Jacques with the same pious resignation with which she bears her terrible affliction. "Our happiness is great," Mara tells her, commenting on her marriage: "But yours is greater, with God." Soon, however, Mara reveals her deep sorrow: the bundle she carries is her baby daughter who has just died, while Jacques was away. "Accept, submit," Violaine counsels her sister. But the despairing Mara, thrusting the corpse into Violaine's arms, implores her to bring it to life: "Ah! figure-of-two, ah, heart-of-a-sheep! Ah, if I had access to your God as you have!" In agony, Violaine maintains: "I swear and I protest before God that I am not a saint!" She asks Mara to read the Christmas service, "the First Lesson of each of the three Nocturnes." As Mara recites the biblical verses, voices of angels from heaven make themselves audible to Violaine. Suddenly she cries out and puts her hand to the corpse under her cloak. A miracle is accomplished: the infant comes to life. "It is Christmas Day, when all joy is born," Violaine tells Mara: "And for us, too—a little child is born to us!" Mara jubilantly picks up her living child, but suddenly exclaims, "Violaine! / What does this mean? Its eyes were black, / And now they are blue like yours." Violaine does not reply and Mara continues, "And what is this drop of milk I see on its lips?"

Act IV. Later, at home, Pierre—miraculously cured after Violaine's kiss—carries in the dying Violaine, whom he found almost totally buried in a sandpit. She reveals to Jacques that she never sinned with Pierre: "If you had believed in me, / Who knows but what you might have cured me?" Jacques still loves her and is anguished at losing her again, now that he knows of her innocence. Violaine relates to him "the great mystery" of his child's rebirth, and then begs him not to pursue her murderer—Mara, who pushed her into the pit and then emptied a truckload of sand over her. Dying, Violaine anticipates their reunion in heaven: "When you see the great door creak and move, / I shall be on the other side and you will find me waiting." When Vercors returns from his pilgrimage, Mara confesses the murder of her sister. Now she grieves for her and weeps in her despairing love for Jacques: "What could I do to defend myself, I who am not beautiful, nor agreeable, a poor woman who can only give pain? / That is why I killed her in my despair!" The sorrowing father asks Jacques to forgive her, and he does. Vercors now has no further earthly goods, and his daughter and wife are dead; but though Joan of Arc has been burned at the stake, he feels that religious and political schisms are ending. As Pierre talks of his new church, Vercors decides to visit it. He realizes what his daughter Violaine exemplified. "Is the object of life only to live? Will the feet of God's children be fastened to this wretched earth?" he asks, and then concludes that "it is not to live, but to die, and not to hew the cross, but to mount upon it, and to give all that we have, laughing!" They bless the memory

Time and the Conways. Mrs. Conway (Sybil Thorndike) with Kay (Jessica Tandy, left) and her other children (Hazel Terry, Joan Henley, Godfrey Kenton, Christopher Quest, and Mary Jones). New York, 1938. (*New York Public Library, Picture Collection*)

of the saintly Violaine, the sun sets, and the Angelus rings. [In the 1948 stage variant for this act, Mara is more bitter and Pierre does not appear; instead, Vercors brings home his daughter's body.]

TIME AND THE CONWAYS, a play in three acts by J. B. PRIESTLEY, published and produced in 1937. Setting: a villa in an English manufacturing town, 1919 and 1937.

Like Lenormand's TIME IS A DREAM, this play deals with life, time, and fate. But though wistful, it is more optimistic—and theatrical.

Acts I and III depict the widowed Mrs. Conway and her six children at Kay's twenty-first birthday party. The family play happily and chat about the future, confident of achieving their various grand ambitions. Then Kay, who hopes to be a famous novelist, has a vision (Act II): It is almost twenty years later; she is a plodding journalist, and except for the youngest, who was to have been a great star but died long ago, all the Conways lead unhappy lives; only Alan, who never was ambitious, is still content as a clerk, and persuades Kay that their misery now does not undo the happiness they had when they were younger: "Time doesn't destroy anything. It merely moves us on." When the scene returns to the 1919 birthday party, Kay has a dim memory of her vision of their future and of Alan's consolation as he quotes a verse from Blake: "Man was made for joy and woe; / And when this we rightly know, / Safely through the world we go."

TIME IS A DREAM (*Le Temps est un songe*), a play in six scenes by HENRI-RENÉ LENORMAND, published in 1918 and produced in 1919. Setting: an old estate in Utrecht, Holland; early twentieth century.

This tragedy articulates the relationships of life, time, and fate more despairingly and philosophically—but less theatrically—than does Priestley's TIME AND THE CONWAYS.

Romée Cremers thinks she has just seen a man drowning in the estate's lake. Later she realizes that it was a vision and, when he returns from a long stay in the East, that it was her fiancé's face she saw in the lake. Nervous and troubled by her hints and questions, he remarks that all men are "prisoners of time," that "one may know the future, but one can't change it." Romée becomes increasingly apprehensive as the lake changes in accord with her earlier vision. Perceiving her fiancé's imminent death, Romée becomes convinced that by her obsession with the vision she is causing it: "It is I who put the idea into his mind—it is I who sent him to his death." With the help of his sister she tries to circumvent fate and leave with him—but fails. She learns that he has gone out "towards the lake," looks out the window—and collapses in horror.

TIME OF YOUR LIFE, THE, a play in five acts by WILLIAM SAROYAN, published and produced in 1939. Setting: a San Francisco waterfront honky-tonk, October 1939.

This is Saroyan's best and most popular play. His first to win both the Pulitzer Prize (which he declined) and the Drama Critics' Circle Award, it was a success on tour, on Broadway, in revivals (1955 and 1969), and on television (1958). It is quintessentially Saroyan, sharing the attributes of MY HEART'S IN THE HIGHLANDS. Equally formless, as well as haphazard in act divisions, it is a mood piece with many colorful characters and "routines" and a scant melodramatic plot—all combined into an expression of contemporary native discontents and fears, and at the same time a paean to the country's youth and the American dream. "In the time of your life, live—" the preface begins, "so that in that good time there shall be no ugliness or death for yourself or for any life your life touches."

Act I. Joe, a well-dressed and gentle young loafer with a heart of gold, sits at his accustomed place, sipping champagne and thinking. He buys all the newsboy's papers, and after glancing at the headline throws them away. A dour harmonica-playing Arab looks at them, shakes his head, and makes his usual comment: "No foundation. All the way down the line." A young "marble-game maniac" plays the pinball machine, and "The Missouri Waltz" blares from the jukebox. The play begins. Joe summons Tom, a big and handsome dumb innocent and Joe's "admirer, disciple, errand boy, stooge, and friend." He sends the mystified Tom out to buy toys just as a newcomer appears: the ethereal streetwalker Kitty Duval, whom Tom instantly adores. Joe invites her to sit with him, though the proprietor gruffly calls her "a two-dollar whore." Quickly softening in Joe's presence, Kitty dreams of a romantic past. A shallow young man telephones his beloved and swears he will kill himself for her. A would-be comedian and a half-starved Negro boy apply for jobs. Tom returns with the toys. When Joe sees how he moons over Kitty, he gives Tom five dollars, tells him to dance with her, and then watches them go to her room. The appearance of the villainous vice-squad chief immediately creates disharmony and tension in the place, and the proprietor angrily tells him to leave. Then he hires the comedian—as a dancer—and the Negro boy—as a pianist. "What's she mean, calling me a dentist?" he mutters, remembering Kitty's reply to his insult: "I wouldn't hurt anybody, let alone a tooth."

Act II. A little later, Joe flirts with a beautiful customer. He tells her why he always drinks: "Because I don't like to be gypped. Because I don't like to be dead most of the time." If one does not drink, Joe philosophizes, one just thinks and waits, and life is "dull, dead, boring, empty, and murderous. Minutes on the clock, *not time of living*." While the habitués go through their usual routines, a policeman who hates his job comes in with his friend, an intelligent longshoreman, who looks at the comedian's dance and remarks, "It's awful, but it's honest and ambitious, like everything else in this great country." Tom comes down to tell Joe that Kitty is crying about her past. When

The Time of Your Life, Act I. In center, Kitty (Julie Haydon) and the comedian-dancer (Gene Kelly); at right, Tom (Edward Andrews), standing, and Joe (Eddie Dowling), sitting. New York, 1940. (*Vandamm Photo, Theatre Collection, New York Public Library*)

Tom asks whether Joe believes her story "about being in burlesque," he replies: "I believe dreams sooner than statistics." An old-time trapper they call "Kit Carson" comes in and tells wild tales of the West. Joe, the only one to believe him, amazes Tom by getting up from his table for once—to help console the crying Kitty.

Act III. In Kitty's room (barely suggested within the bar's setting) Joe cheers her up with the toys and urges Tom to love her. The big, hulking Tom almost beats up her friendly former client in his eagerness to "protect the innocence in her which is in so much danger when Tom isn't near."

Act IV. Later, the Negro boy plays and the comedian dances and the Arab and the others are in their accustomed places. The proprietor, on the telephone, protests the vice-squad chief's appearance. The shallow young man's girl, a nurse embittered by all she sees, believes "love is impossible in this world" of dying, but agrees to escape with him for a night to "a cheap hotel" where they can dream—before their problems and the coming war will be with them again, in the morning. The longshoreman and the cop return, the latter feeling more trapped than ever.

Act V. In the evening the habitués are joined by a slumming wealthy couple. Joe reveals how he suffers because he once made money—i.e., "like everybody else," "stole" it and "hurt people to get it." Now he loafs, to exchange the "social conscience" for a "Christian conscience." The pinball-machine player finally defeats the machine, which lights up wildly and wins him six nickels. Joe and Tom have a gum-chewing contest; then Joe gets Tom a truckdriver's job, and persuades Kitty to marry him. The vice-squad chief returns, sadistically makes Kitty do a striptease, and beats up the Negro boy and "Kit Carson" when they protest. The proprietor angrily kicks him out. On the street, he is shot by "Kit Carson," who returns and somberly begins another story: "I shot a man once. In San Francisco. Shot him two times. In 1939, I think it was." Joe "looks at him with great admiration and affection." Then he departs, as the habitués fondly wave good-bye. The pinball machine "goes into its beautiful American routine again: flag, lights, and music."

TINKER'S WEDDING, THE, a comedy in two acts by J. M. SYNGE, published in 1908 and produced in 1909. Setting: a contemporary Irish village roadside at night and the following morning.

This, the least popular of Synge's six plays, may well be the first one he wrote. He began working on it in 1902, kept returning to it, eventually expanded it from one to two acts, and finally had it published. It was never performed during his life; Abbey productions were out of the question because of the unsympathetic portrayal of the priest and the climax, in which he is tossed into a sack. Despite its reputation, the play is significant; it is characteristic of Synge in theme, language and earthy humor. Its brief preface contains Synge's frequently quoted criticism of HENRIK IBSEN and the work of other contemporary playwrights, "too often stocked with the drugs of many seedy problems."

The tinkers Sarah Casey and Michael Byrne have lived contentedly for years with his cheerful, usually drunk mother. Sarah, "the Beauty of Ballinacree," suddenly has unnatural, "queer thoughts" for a tinker: she wants to be respectably married. She talks a censorious yet pleasure-loving priest into marrying her and the grimly reluctant Michael in the morning for a reduced fee and a tin can. That night, however, the mother exchanges the can for liquor. The priest refuses to perform the ceremony and angrily threatens to inform the police of the tinkers' thefts. Provoked, the three of them overpower and gag him, and tie him in a sack. Only when he promises not to inform on them do they release him. After his behavior Sarah has lost her yen for Christian respectability: "It'll be a long day till I go making talk of marriage or the like of that." As soon as he is set free, the "old villain," as the mother indignantly calls the priest, loudly utters maledictions over them. "Run for your lives," they shout, rushing out hurriedly and "leaving the Priest master of the situation."

TO CLOTHE THE NAKED (*Vestire gli ignudi*), "a comedy" in three acts by LUIGI PIRANDELLO, produced in 1922 and published in 1923. Setting: Rome, 1922.

The gradual and retrospective exposition of this drama, like that of HENRY IV, creates a few initial difficulties. But the play—often appearing under the title *Naked*—is esteemed as one of Pirandello's finest. Its protagonist, Ersilia, evokes great sympathy in her pathetic, almost tragic quest for illusion to clothe the real and loathesome essence of life.

Act I. A beautiful but haggard girl, Ersilia Drei, comes from the hospital to the home of Ludovico Nota, a well-known, elderly writer. She was formerly nursemaid at the Smyrian consul's home, where she met and fell in love with a visiting young naval officer. When she learned that he had become engaged to someone else, she took poison. Expecting to die, she told her story to a reporter. It created a sensation when it was published, and deeply stirred the public. Nota saw in it possibilities for a novel and offered Ersilia his home. Though sympathetic, he cannot hide his satisfaction as she admits how accurately, with his writer's imagination, he has visualized her story—including her night before the suicide attempt when, broke and desperate, she offered herself to the first stranger: "Ah, how rightly I guessed it all, all of it! And then the loathing, the horror at the failure of this last sordid attempt—perfect! Perfect!" The street noises become louder as an ugly accident takes place below. Then Ersilia continues talking of her despair at being unwanted, at having nothing but "a servant's dress, faded and worn, that you hang each night from a nail." She learns with horror that the newspaper article mentioned Consul Grotti and the baby that had fallen to its death. She is particularly bitter about the consul's wife, who seemed to trap Ersilia with the young naval officer, "leaving me there alone—on purpose—in that garden, drunk on the perfume of that night." It was after the child's death that she had fired Ersilia. Then Ersilia sought the naval officer, learned of his betrayal, and tried to end her life. Now she yearns for Nota to write her story: "If just once I could be something! . . . And now I think I have a right at least to live in the story you'll make out of it—which will be beautiful, so beautiful . . ." Their talk is interrupted by the return of the landlady, who at first was crudely insulting and contemptuous to the girl. She has just discovered Ersilia to be the girl over whose newspaper story she had wept, and her attitude is completely changed. News of the arrival of Consul Grotti, who demands the story's retraction, so overpowers Ersilia that the landlady must put her to bed. Then the naval officer, Franco Laspiga, comes in. After reading the story, his fiancée broke their engagement; overwhelmed by Ersilia's great love for him, Laspiga has come "to throw myself at her feet, to beg her forgiveness. . . . The whole world is full of the harm I've done! I have to make it up to her!" But unaccountably she refuses even to see him. When the men leave, Ersilia, desperate with the fear of being hounded by Laspiga and the consul, wants to run away. The landlady affectionately persuades the weak girl to stay; Ersilia stares wildly as she hears the raucous noises outside, on the street.

Act II. Next morning, the sentimental landlady tells Nota that Ersilia is weak, helpless, and tormented, "like one of these mangy little dogs you see in the streets with all the other dogs after it!" Nota, however, is exasperated by the unexpected complications. When Laspiga returns, fervently to beg her to marry him, Ersilia coldly rejects him. She reveals her shameful prostitution before she took poison, and insists that Laspiga and she are both different people now. She no longer loves him—in fact, she never loved him. Ersilia admits she lied, trying always—and failing—to make her life meaningful. Now Consul Grotti appears. His agonizing interview with Ersilia strips more romantic masks from her story. Grotti angrily castigates Ersilia for jeopardizing his career with her lies. The actual truth is that Grotti was her lover. Ersilia claims he took advantage of her after Laspiga's departure: "You took me when I was helpless, burning from the fire he lit in my flesh." Grotti furiously replies, "You bitch! You were just leading me on!" Their lust directly caused the neglect and accidental death of the consul's child, and Grotti's wife, discovering the situation, fired Ersilia. But after these recriminations Grotti's passions reawaken. He begs Ersilia, "Oh, God, let's cling together in our despair." Remembering the child whose death they caused, Ersilia screams hysterically and throws Grotti out.

Act III. The interview between Grotti and Ersilia was overheard, and the landlady is again outraged about "the slut." So is Laspiga, though Nota reminds him that he is hardly in a position to complain about betrayed love. In fact, Nota is amused by "the comedy of a lie laid bare"—the reactions of both the landlady and Laspiga. But the writer, too, is puzzled by Ersilia's deathbed lie that she was dying for Laspiga. Consul Grotti soon returns, and a bitter argument between him and Laspiga reveals how the men—including Nota—mask their selfish actions with idealistic veils no less than has Ersilia. She suddenly appears, having taken another, this time fatal, dose of poison. "We all want to make a good impression," she explains in accounting for her lies. Overcome with self-loathing, she can hardly pronounce the words: "The more horrible we are, the more beautiful we want to seem, that's all. Oh, God, yes—to hide our nakedness in decent clothing, that's all." She never realized her wish "to make some sort of impression on anyone. It was always torn away from me by all the dogs—the dogs who waited for me everywhere, in every street—no dress that wasn't immediately soiled by all the filth of the streets." All she wanted was a beautiful "dress" to die in. But she cannot even have that: "This corpse died naked."

TO DAMASCUS, PART I (*Till Damaskus, första delen*), a play in five acts by AUGUST STRINDBERG, published in 1898 and produced in 1900. Setting: street corner, etc., 1890's.

"A drama that completely frustrates any attempt to assign it to any known category" (C. Dahlström, *Strindberg's Dramatic Expressionism*), the SYMBOLIC and highly experimental *To Damascus* trilogy may perhaps be described as EXPRESSIONIST dream—or nightmare—drama with NATURALISTIC overtones.* The trilogy is an autobiography of Strindberg in his Inferno period and depicts his psychological and spiritual agonies. He modeled the Unknown (*den Okände*) on himself, and used the combined personalities of his first wife, Siri, and his second wife, Frida Uhl, for the Lady (called "Ingeborg" by her family and "Eve" by the Unknown). Part I is the trilogy's most frequently performed play. The settings of its seventeen scenes are symmetrically repeated (first and last, second and next-to-last, etc.), except for the apical ninth (convent) scene. Strindberg chose Harriet Bosse, a young actress and soon his third wife, to create the part of the Lady.

Acts I and II. At a street corner, the Unknown hesitates about the direction he should take. He stops the passing Lady—"It's you! I almost knew you'd come"—and begs her to stay with him. Waiting for the post office to open, he reviews his life. Later he is frightened by a friendly Beggar, who resembles him. He refuses to accompany the Lady to church, talks with a group of mourners, is expelled from a café, and, afraid of his mail, forgoes the post office. Then he woos the Lady, who seems to have been sent for the purification of his soul. As if compelled by a higher power to join the Unknown, she decides to leave her husband, a doctor whom she calls a "werewolf." Together they journey, first to the Doctor's house. There the Unknown is frightened by the madman Caesar, who resembles him. The Doctor, whom the Unknown had wronged long before, is a sinister figure. But he submits to his wife's elopement. In a hotel room the Unknown and the Lady find their dreams of freedom turned into horrible realities. Everywhere reminded of their past guilt, they deplore their tribulations and poverty and find "this honeymoon's becoming a pilgrimage!" A brief idyll by the sea ends when expected funds fail to materialize. Ready to suffer further, the Unknown must reluctantly follow the Lady to her parental home. They walk the road, bewailing their beggary. In a ravine, despising money, the Unknown hurls away his last copper. In the parental kitchen, the religious Mother grudgingly welcomes the Unknown.

Act III. But the Mother is her son-in-law's enemy. In the Rose Room she causes trouble by making her daughter break her promise and read his book. Having "eaten of the tree of knowledge" of her husband, the Lady confronts the Unknown with his evil. He finally leaves the house. Three months later, he is recuperating in a convent. He had been found in a ravine, unconscious after an apparently terrible struggle. In his delirium he has confessed to horrid sins. Now, in the spectral company of past crimes and victims, and while a requiem is heard from the chapel, the Confessor reads the Curse of Deuteronomy over him. The Unknown leaves to seek medical help and revisit the earlier "stations." Back in the Rose Room, he tells the now less-vindictive Mother that his conversion is beginning: "There are forces which, till now, I've not believed in." But he still stubbornly intends to stand up to God.

Acts IV and V. Later at night, the Mother and the Unknown resume their discussion in the kitchen. The Mother finally tells him, "You have left Jerusalem and are on the road to Damascus. Go back the same way you came. Erect a cross at every station, and stay at the seventh." He seeks his wife through the ravine and on the road, where the Beggar reappears and horrifies him by echoing his own thoughts: "Saul! Saul! Why persecutest thou Me?" He finally meets the Lady by the sea and they resume their journey back together. In the hotel room, he decides to risk being committed to a mental institution, and visits the Doctor. There he seeks punishment and forgiveness, but is granted only the first. Back at their street corner, the Lady persuades the Unknown to pick up his letter. It contains money—all their tribulations have been for nought! Changed, he is ready to hide their shame and misery in the mountains. Before they leave, the Lady asks him to accompany her to church. He agrees to pass through that way, but will not stay. She suggests that he may stay: "In there you shall hear new songs." "Perhaps!" he concludes, following her to the church door, as she beckons: "Come!"

TO DAMASCUS, PART II (*Till Damaskus, andra delen*), a play in four acts by AUGUST STRINDBERG, published in 1898 and produced in 1916. Setting: house, banquet hall, prison, etc., 1890's.

The banquet scene in Act III is the high point of this play, which develops the themes of the trilogy's first part.

The Mother tells the Confessor about the suffering of the now-pregnant Lady and the Unknown, who plague each other. The Lady humiliates the Unknown, intercepts his mail, and frustrates his scientific work. He is further tormented by the

* The title alludes to the journey that culminated in the conversion of Saul the Christ-Hater into Paul the Apostle. A detailed analysis of the trilogy—"Strindberg's best drama"—appears in F. L. Lucas's *Ibsen and Strindberg* (1962), an otherwise vitriolic denunciation of Strindberg's work.

Confessor and by the mad Caesar. The werewolf Doctor, whose despair at the loss of his wife is growing, reappears to torture both of them. But the Unknown continues his experiments for making gold, "to paralyze the present order, to disrupt it." He is called from his laboratory as the Lady's labor begins, but the Mother embitters him by insisting that he is not the child's father, and he runs away. A lavish banquet is in progress to honor him as the great scientist who has made gold. But even while the Unknown is eulogized by a frock-coated professor, funeral music is heard, the golden goblets become tin, and the company are magically transformed into tramps and whores. The hall becomes a dive, and the Unknown is a charlatan who is unable to pay the banquet bill and therefore is taken to prison. The Lady is still in labor and the Unknown now wonders, at her bedside, whether he dreamed the banquet. A daughter is born, but afraid of becoming attached to her and feeling damned, the Unknown departs. Now he is seen at his most degraded. But then Caesar commits suicide and the Doctor, also mad, is ready to do likewise. Saved from despair by the Beggar, the Unknown returns to the Lady. There, the Confessor (revealed as her former lover) helps him to master his pride and cynicism. Though he abuses the enchanting Lady and his child, the Unknown simultaneously agrees to accompany the Confessor to the convent: "Come, priest, before I change my mind."

TO DAMASCUS, PART III (*Till Damaskus, tredje delen*), a play in four acts by AUGUST STRINDBERG, published in 1904 and produced in 1916. Setting: a mountain monastery and vicinity.

In the end of the trilogy, written some years later, the Unknown's decision becomes final. The lyrical love scenes portray Strindberg's third marriage.

The still-questioning Unknown is instructed by the Confessor, who leads him toward the monastery. The fulfillment of his one desire—to see his oldest daughter—becomes a disappointment. By a river and awaiting the ferry, he meets the Lady. Her baby has died and, having suffered and now purged of his evil as well as hers, she appears young and beautiful—and maternal. The Unknown decides to make another try at life. He reweds her and for a few days the lovers are rapturous in their mountain cottage. But soon happiness gives way to boredom, then hatred, and finally parting. The brief visit of his first wife and more probing dialogues with a ubiquitous Tempter serve merely to hasten his way to the monastery. In the face of worldly error, deception, and contradiction, amply illustrated to the Unknown, a wise divine counsels "Humanity and Resignation." Now exhausted, the Unknown is ready for the symbolic death before his new monastic life. He is wrapped in a bier cloth as the Confessor and the chorus chant their blessing: "May he rest in peace! Amen!"

TO FIND ONESELF (*Trovarsi*), a play in three acts by LUIGI PIRANDELLO, published and produced in 1932. Setting: contemporary Italy.

The heroine is a superior being modeled on—and written to be acted by—Marta Abba. Donata Genzi seeks to find her identity (*"trovarsi"* means "to find oneself"). The play, also translated as *She Wanted to Find Herself*, touches on the conflict of marriage and career. But its primary conflict, as explicitly presented here as in DIANA AND TUDA, is that of art and life.

The famous acress Donata Genzi is visiting a friend's Riviera villa. There two writers discuss life: one believes that knowledge comes by instinct and experience, the other (Pirandello's mouthpiece) believes in imagination. Donata holds to the latter viewpoint: "I am each time as my role wants me to be, with the greatest sincerity." This view has preempted her personal life, she suddenly realizes; never being herself has kept her from living fully. While still overwhelmed by that discovery, she meets Elj Nielsen, a young artist who lives by instinct and whose creed is spontaneity: "Only what is sudden is beautiful for me—what does not seem true—the continuous surprise that overtakes us. If I look closely at something and think of it, I am lost." He saves Donata from a capsized sailboat during a storm, and they soon fall in love. But their idyll is threatened when she discovers that her lovemaking duplicates her stage gestures. Returning to the theatre, Donata suffers during the early acts of the play: "It is worse, worse to have a life of your own." But suddenly she finds herself: "Freedom was mine. I forgot everything. I felt myself taken, carried away." In her art, and through love, Donata has found that she "possessed life again and so full, so full, and so easy—in such complete intoxication of happiness, that everything glowed, burned, lived, and grew with me." After the performance she rushes to tell Elj, but finds him gone. He has returned to his sailboat, horrified by the public display of her intimate gestures. Donata finally realizes she can live only in re-creating great lives, not in living herself: "When we perform an act, it is not our whole being which performs it, all life which is in us—but only what we are in that moment—and yet that act, once accomplished, immediately imprisons us—stops us with obligations and responsibilities, in that given way and in no other, irreparably." At the curtain, her private room is gradually transformed into a stage setting.

TOBACCO ROAD, a play in three acts by JACK KIRKLAND, produced in 1933 and published in 1934. Setting: a farm situated on a tobacco road in the Georgia back country, early 1930's.

In this dramatization of Erskine Caldwell's 1932 novel of a degenerate sharecropper family, only Jeeter (originally played by Henry Hull) is a fully realized character. The play was a tremendous SUCCÈS DE SCANDALE, the comic portrayal of tragic horror making it an early modern example of "black humor." Considered repulsive as well as obscene, it became the second longest-running drama on Broadway (its 3,182 performances had been topped only by Lindsay and Crouse's LIFE

Tobacco Road. Pearl (Reneice Behan), Jeeter (James Barton), and his wife (Margaret Wycherly). New York, 1934. (*Brown Brothers*)

WITH FATHER), and it was filmed (1941) and frequently revived, once with an all-Negro cast.

Act I. Jeeter Lester and his starving family live in a squalid shack. "Stop chunkin' that ball against that there old house," he admonishes his sixteen-year-old son, Dude. "Aw, go to hell, you dried-up old clod," Dude replies. Jeeter whines about the boy's lack of respect, and thinks about planting a crop. Dude jeers at this futile plan and sadistically predicts that Jeeter—like his dead father—will be buried in the corn crib and have his face chewed up by rats. Then Dude jeers at his sick mother, who yearns only for a new dress to be buried in, and at Jeeter's groveling old mother, who later dies in the fields—whereupon Jeeter remarks, casually, that he will "go out and look around [for her] one of these days." His eighteen-year-old daughter, Ellie May, cannot find a man because she has a repulsive harelip, and Jeeter's remaining fifteen children have left home and are no longer heard from—except for Pearl, his beautiful fourteen-year-old daughter. Jeeter sold her for seven dollars, and her husband, Lov Bensey, a thirty-year-old "cracker" laborer at the railroad coal chute, now comes to complain about her not speaking—or sleeping—with him. He rejects Jeeter's offer to talk to her in return for Lov's bag of turnips, which the starving family eye yearningly. When the sex-starved Ellie May distracts Lov by wriggling up and getting Lov to fondle her, Jeeter steals the turnips and runs off. Later, a portly middle-aged woman evangelist, while praying, is smitten with Dude and starts petting him. When he hears that the land owner is returning from a trip, Jeeter is confident of obtaining credit to start growing a new, large crop. In preparation, he gets ready to burn off the broom sedge.

Act II. Next morning the buxom evangelist returns, reporting that God told her to "marry Dude the first thing." Dude is reluctant until she promises to buy him a new car. Lov comes to report that Pearl has run away: he must have her back. As soon as he is gone, she appears and rushes to her mother. When Jeeter tries to get Pearl to return to Lov, his wife protects the girl and casually informs Jeeter that he is not the father. "By God and by Jesus! Do you know what you're saying, woman?" Jeeter exclaims. But he is not angry, merely curious. Then, while they are off to steal some food, Lov comes to speak with Pearl. Just then Jeeter and his wife return, and the latter, again protecting her daughter, beats Lov with a stick. Since Lov needs a woman, Jeeter suggests he take Ellie May—who immediately starts wriggling and giggling. But Lov complains about her "ugly-looking face," whereupon the girl starts beating up her pretty sister. Dude returns with his evangelist, merrily blowing the horn of his new car, which he has already dented by running into a wagon and killing its Negro driver. The evangelist herself conducts their marriage ceremony, and immediately drags him into the house. As the Lesters try to peek in, the landowner arrives with a bank official. He has lost his land to the bank, he explains, and Jeeter must move. Heatedly Jeeter argues against the bank's taking away his land, and feels saved when the bank agrees to rent the land to him. Rescuing Dude from his amorous new wife, Jeeter sends him to the adjoining county, to get the rent money from the most reliable of his many sons.

Act III. At dawn Jeeter wonders why Dude is not yet back. Lov comes to offer Jeeter a large piece of salt pork and money if he will persuade Pearl to return to him. But her mother refuses to allow it. Just as Jeeter tells his wife that they will not use the anticipated money to take Pearl to live in the city—"I was born here on the land, and by God and by Jesus that's where I'll die"—Dude returns with his bride and the almost totally wrecked new car. He tells how the "reliable" son insultingly refused to give a cent for his parents. The evangelist will not lend Jeeter the car to haul his wood to town so he can earn the money needed for the rent. Desperate, Jeeter seizes Pearl and sends for Lov—knowing that he will be paid well for her. As she tries to save the girl, Jeeter's wife is run over by her son. ("I guess the wheels ran over her," Dude blandly reports.) Dying, she bites Jeeter's hand, thus enabling Pearl to run off. "You shouldn't have done that," Jeeter murmurs to himself. He sends the delighted hare-lipped Ellie May to keep house for Lov, and falls asleep. A rotted shingle falls from the dilapidated porch.

TOBIAS AND THE ANGEL, a play in three acts by JAMES BRIDIE, produced in 1930 and published in 1931. Setting: Mesopotamia and northern Persia before the reign of Ahasuerus.

This dramatization of the Apocryphal Book of Tobit became a popular repertory piece.

The generous blind old Tobit and his family are living in a Nineveh slum when the Archangel Raphael comes to bring them gifts. He takes them on a journey, during which the charming and witty central episodes of the play occur. Raphael transforms the shy and gauche son, Tobias, into a confident, dashing youth, as well as a lover and a human benefactor. The devil is defeated, the family finally becomes wealthy, Tobias gets a wife, and Tobit's sight is miraculously restored.

TOLLER, Ernst (1893–1939), German playwright, was a leading EXPRESSIONIST who became best known abroad for his *Masse-Mensch* (MASSES AND MAN, 1921) and other revolutionary plays, such as *Die Maschinenstürmer* (THE MACHINE-WRECKERS, 1922) and *Hoppla, wir leben!* (HOPPLA! SUCH IS LIFE!, 1927). In these, in HINKEMANN (1922, also translated as *Brockenbrow*), and in his remaining plays, Toller reiterated his opposition to war and to the decadent, materialistic society that had brought it about—as it later brought about Fascism. Strident in his dramatization of political and social evils, Toller presented heroic martyrs who work for and proclaim a utopia of human brotherhood and love—idealists who, especially in later plays such as *Hoppla! Such Is Life!*, increasingly despair over world events and, like Toller himself, finally commit suicide.

Born to a Jewish family in Posen, Prussia, Toller studied law at Grenoble. At the outbreak of World War I he returned to volunteer for service in the German army, but completely lost his nationalistic fervor after seeing front-line action. Invalided and discharged in 1916, he resumed his studies at Heidelberg. Soon he became active as a left-wing pacifist and was imprisoned. In 1919 he was sentenced to a five-year term for participating in the Munich Communist uprising that year and for his position (Commissar of Education) in the short-lived *Bayerische Räterepublik* (the "Bavarian Soviet Republic"). It was while Toller was in prison that he wrote his first plays, beginning with *Die Wandlung* (*Transfiguration*, 1919). In thirteen *Stationen* (or tableaux), this NATURALISTIC and expressionistic prose and verse play transmutes Toller's experiences into the drama of a sensitive patriot who leaves his dull life and middle-class family to enlist in the war; as in *Masses and Man*, alternate scenes portray external events and the protagonist's subconscious, the horrors of war and the protagonist's growth as a humanitarian idealist who calls for revolution, exhorting the masses "to beat [soldiers'] swords into ploughshares" and "march forward in the light of day!" This first play was followed by the similar *Masses and Man* and *The Machine-Wreckers*, and by *Der entfesselte Wotan* (1923), a satiric portrait of the early Hitler, here an unsuccessful barber, a rabble-rouser who dreams of national glory, is arrested, and prepares to write his memoirs in prison.

Hinkemann and *Hoppla! Such Is Life!* evidence Toller's progressive disillusionment. *Feuer aus den Kesseln* (*Draw the Fires!* 1930), his last drama about German political history during the time of World War I, is naturalistic; it portrays the 1916–17 Kiel naval mutiny that preceded the November 1918 Revolution, and features historical figures, including Karl Liebknecht and Admiral von Scheer. *Die blinde Göttin* (*The Blind Goddess*, 1932; adapted by DENIS JOHNSTON in 1936 as *Blind Man's Buff*) dramatizes a famous contemporary case in which two lovers, wrongfully convicted of murder though exonerated some years later, are nonetheless broken by the inhuman judicial system alluded to in the title. With HERMANN KESTEN Toller wrote a drama about the founder of Christian Science, *Mary Baker Eddy* (1934), produced in London under its translated original title, *Wunder in Amerika* (*Miracle in America*). Other Toller plays are *Bourgeois bleibt Bourgeois* (1929, written with WALTER HASENCLEVER) and *No More Peace!* (1937), with lyrics adapted by W. H. AUDEN. Toller's last play, *Pastor Hall* (1939), portrays a clergyman courageously sustaining his faith despite Gestapo persecution; originally published in English in a translation by STEPHEN SPENDER, it is a dramatization of the life of Pastor Martin Niemöller.

Even Toller's best plays are flawed by such typical excesses of expressionism as crude characterization and similarly melodramatic actions. They created a sensation in imaginative German productions and they succeeded in American and English theatres more than did the works of GEORG KAISER and other German expressionists because, it has been suggested, they were more adaptable to translation. Toller's later plays, written as Germany became increasingly Nazified and the world progressed inexorably to the catastrophe of a second world war, are more despairing and artistically less impressive. All Toller's dramas play down party-line sloganeering; instead, they stress his ideals of humanitarian socialism—universal peace, brotherhood, and love. They are "social dramas and tragedies," he wrote in the introduction to his *Seven Plays* (1935): "They bear witness to human suffering, and to fine yet vain struggles to vanquish this suffering." Articulating his concept of tragedy, Toller continued: "For only unnecessary suffering can be vanquished, the suffering which arises out of the unreason of humanity, out of an inadequate social system. There must always remain a residue of suffering, the lonely suffering imposed upon mankind by life and death. And only this residue is necessary and inevitable, is the tragic element of life and of life's symbolizer, art."

When Hitler came to power, Toller fled Germany and moved first to England and then to America. Though he lectured and was active in Spanish Civil War causes, he was overcome by despair and committed suicide in a New York hotel room. Aside from his drama, he left volumes of expressionist poetry composed in prison, notably *Das Schwalbenbuch* (*The Swallow-Book*, 1924), and an autobiography, *Eine Jugend in Deutschland* (1933; translated as *I Was a German*, 1934).

The *Seven Plays* (1935) are *Transfigura-*

tion, Masses and Man, The Machine-Wreckers, Hinkemann, Hoppla! Such Is Life!, The Blind Goddess, and *Draw the Fires!;* the volume includes an eighth play, *Mary Baker Eddy.* A booklet on his life and work is William A. Willibrand's *Ernst Toller, Product of Two Revolutions* (1941), and a comprehensive bibliography is John M. Spalek's *Ernst Toller and His Critics* (1968).

TOLSTOI, Count **Aleksei Nikolaevich** (1883–1945), Russian novelist and playwright, through his mother (a Turgenev by birth) was related distantly to LEO TOLSTOI.* Like his great ancestor, Aleksei Tolstoi was less important for his plays than for his many novels, particularly the *Khozhdenie po mukam* trilogy (1920-41; translated as *The Road to Calvary* in 1946, and as *Ordeal* in 1953), and for *Pyotr Pervy* (1929-34), a three-part epic novel set in seventeenth- and eighteenth-century Russia and published in English as *Peter the Great* (1936) and *Peter the First* (1959). Tolstoi made dramatic versions of this novel (*Peter I,* 1930; and others) and a very popular screenplay. In these dramatizations the portrayal of Peter is less that of the novel's admirable genius who changed and westernized Russia: gradually Tolstoi interpreted the past more in terms of the present, making Peter something like a forerunner of Lenin. Of Tolstoi's forty-two plays, however, the most important is *Ivan Grozny* a two-part "dramatic tale" about Ivan the Terrible: *Oryol i orlitsa* (1942) and *Trudnye gody* (1943). These are more obvious reinterpretations in Soviet terms of sixteenth-century Russian history, an apologia for the tsar ("that great and passionate Russian character," Tolstoi wrote in his autobiography), who is represented, like Peter, as a forger of the future Soviet Union—and an analogue to Stalin.

Tolstoi had an aristocratic upbringing, and published his first works under the imperial regime. He supported the Whites and emigrated to Germany after the October Revolution, but returned in 1923. Though he was first viewed suspiciously by the Soviets, he eventually became one of their most able supporters and practitioners of SOCIALIST REALISM. His novel *Khleb* (*Bread,* 1937) reinterpreted the defense of Tsaritsyn (Stalingrad, later Volgograd) against the Whites, and helped establish the Stalin personality cult by glorifying the leader's role and "exposing" Trotsky's supposed treason and stupidity.

Tolstoi's first post-Revolution play deals with the often-dramatized theme of Danton's death, *Smert Dantona* (1919). It was followed, later the same year, by *Lyubov—kniga zolotaya,* a love story set at the court of Catherine the Great. Other early plays are *Bunt mashin* (1924), an adaptation of Čapek's R.U.R.; *Aelita* (1924), a Russian science-fiction drama; *Zagovor imperatritsy* (1925; written with P. E. Shchegolev, 1877–1931), about Rasputin; *Izgnanie bludnogo besa* (1925); *Azef* (1925), about a spy in the 1905 revolution; *Chudesa v reshete* (1926); *Fabrika molodosti* (1927), a farce on rejuvenation; and similar trifles. Other late plays are *Put k pobede* (1939), on the Soviet Revolution and Germany's interference; and *Khozhdenie po mukam* (1939), satirizing Nazi mythologies. It was in these later plays (including *Ivan Grozny*) that Tolstoi inspired Russians with Soviet ideals and love for Stalin. His portrayals of earlier Russian battles against foreign invaders gave heart to a people suffering from the Nazi holocaust, and encouraged unity and national pride.

Tolstoi's best-known nondramatic works are generally available in English but his plays are not. Informative comments on Tolstoi appear in Vera Alexandrova's *A History of Soviet Literature* (1963) and in Edward J. Brown's *Russian Literature Since the Revolution* (revised 1969).

* Another writer-relation was Leo Tolstoi's cousin Count Aleksei Konstantinovich Tolstoi (1817–75), a poet, novelist, and playwright. His major dramatic work is an exotic historical blank-verse trilogy: *Smert Ivana Groznogo* (*The Death of Ivan the Terrible,* 1866), a subject very differently treated later by Aleksei Nikolaevich Tolstoi; *Tsar Fyodor Ivanovich* (1868), long banned for its unsympathetic portrayals of the weak tsar (though Tolstoi was a friend of Aleksandr II, and idealized feudal Russia), Ivan the Terrible's son and Boris Godunov's brother-in-law and predecessor, but the first work produced by Konstantin Stanislavsky and VLADIMIR NEMIROVICH-DANCHENKO in their Moscow Art Theatre (1898); and *Tsar Boris* (1870), a dramatization resembling, but inferior to, Pushkin's *Boris Godunov* (1825).

TOLSTOI,* Count **Leo** [Lev Nikolaevich] (1828–1910), Russian writer and philosopher, is one of the great figures in world literature. He is best known for his novels and novellas, and achieved fame also with his autobiographies and works on philosophy, religion, and aesthetics. Only a small part of his writing was devoted to the drama: nine plays and some brief dramatic fragments. Most of the plays were written comparatively late in life, when Tolstoi had already achieved fame in other fields. Yet two of his plays establish Tolstoi's prominence as a dramatist: *Vlast tmy* (THE POWER OF DARKNESS, 1866) and the posthumous *I svet vo tmye svetit* (THE LIGHT SHINES IN DARKNESS, 1911). All of his plays, aside from their intrinsic interest, reveal his potential in that genre. But the prevailing censorship proved discouraging to Tolstoi, and deprived the world of further dramatic masterpieces and a playwright of the highest order.

Count Tolstoi came from a wealthy and noble family. He was born on their estate at Yasnaya Polyana, near Tula. Though his parents died early he received the university education and training of a nobleman. He joined the army in the Caucasus in 1851 and participated in the Crimean War. While he spent much of his youth in dissipating pleasures, he established his literary reputation with volumes of autobiographical stories as early as the 1850's, when he was already active as a social reformer. He opened schools to educate peasants, traveled in Europe to study modern educational and industrial practices, and upon his return to Yasnaya

* Illustration on page 665.

Polyana in 1861 freed his serfs before the Emancipation Act was proclaimed. The next year he married Sofia Bers, a physician's daughter. She bore him thirteen children, and he lived with her at Yasnaya Polyana for the next eighteen years. During that time Tolstoi published the novels that made him world famous. In 1876 began his conversion to idealistic Christianity and his faith was in physical toil, nonresistance to evil, pacifism, love, and simplicity. It gained prominence in his numerous writings and was put into practice when Tolstoi joined his peasants, dressing like them and working in the fields with them. Many people became his disciples, some being persecuted for their pacifism. He tried to give up his property and break with his wife, who loved him but rejected his theories. In conflict with his family as well as with the government, Tolstoi was finally excommunicated by the Greek Orthodox Church for his novel *Voskresenie* (*Resurrection,* 1899–1901), written after he supported a sect of pacifist dissenters. He died at the small Astapovo railroad station (later renamed the Leo Tolstoi Station) while escaping from home for the last time, accompanied by one of his daughters.

Soon after his marriage Tolstoi wrote two comedies, neither of which was published until 1928: *Zarazhyonnoe semeistvo* (*A Contaminated Family,* also translated as *The Progressives*), denied production in 1864; and *Nigilist* (*The Nihilist*), privately performed in 1866. Tolstoi did not seriously resume playwriting until 1886, when he published *Pervy vinokur* (*The First Distiller*), a comic temperance fantasy dramatizing "The Imp and the Crust," one of his *Twenty-Three Tales.* More important is the play published later that year but banned by the Russian censor, his great *The Power of Darkness.* It was followed by his popular comedy *Plody prosveshcheniya* (THE FRUITS OF ENLIGHTENMENT, 1889). This was the last play to appear during Tolstoi's lifetime; the publications of all his other plays were posthumous.

The most important of these are *Zhivoi trup* (THE LIVE CORPSE, 1911; also known as *Redemption*) and *The Light Shines in Darkness,* the autobiographical play many consider to be his finest. *Ot nei vse kachestva* (*The Cause of It All,* 1912), another temperance playlet, features the kind of worker who became popular with the Soviets. These and the previously mentioned plays evidence Tolstoi's remarkable mastery of a medium he did not really begin to work in until his late fifties. Rich in characterization and plot, they portray his deep knowledge of peasants and their lives. Tolstoi's plays are usually classified as grimly NATURALISTIC, and they unabashedly preach, for Tolstoi considered didacticism his principal aim as a playwright. But they also abound with humor that is often earthy as well as subtle, though his religious quest and ideals permeate all his plays, as they do his other works.

Among Tolstoi's remaining dramatic work are four extant fragments written about 1856: *Svobodnaya lyubov, Dyadyushkino blagoslovenie, Dvoryanskoe semeistvo,* and *Prakticheski chelovek.* Three of his sketches were published posthumously: the unfinished *Aggey* (1926) and *Detskaya mudrost* (*The Wisdom of Children,* 1911), and a brief four-acter set in third-century Syria, *Pyotr khlebnik* (*Peter the Boarder,* 1918). His last dramatic work, *Ot nei vse kachestva,* a didactic farce on temperance that Tolstoi wrote for a peasant performance shortly before his death, was produced in 1912. Novels such as *Voina i mir* (*War and Peace,* 1865–69), *Anna Karenina* (1875–77), and *Resurrection* have been made into popular plays.

Louise and Aylmer Maude translated six of Tolstoi's plays in 1923 for "The World's Classics." The latter's two-volume biography (1930), Ernest J. Simmons's *Leo Tolstoy* (1946) and *Introduction to Tolstoy's Writings* (1968), Henri Troyat's *Tolstoy* (1968), and R. F. Christian's *Tolstoy: A Critical Introduction* (1969) are outstanding among the innumerable major studies of Tolstoi and his work.

TOMORROW THE DAWN (*Demain il fera jour*), a play in three acts by HENRY DE MONTHERLANT, published and produced in 1949. Setting: Paris, 1944.

In this sequel to NO MAN'S SON, "nothing remains of Georges' love for his son," Montherlant wrote in his "Note" to the play; "in 1941 he sacrificed his son to an ideal. In 1944 he sacrifices him to his own fear. And it is the same man."

Gillou, now seventeen and still mediocre and uninspiring to his father, wants to join the Resistance. Bickering with him and Marie, Georges at first refuses to let him do so. Then he changes his mind, for it would be convenient for Georges, who may after the war be accused of collaboration, to have a martyred son. Gillou goes out on his first Resistance assignment—and is immediately killed.

TO-NIGHT AT 8:30, a series of one-act plays by NOËL COWARD, published and produced in 1935–36. Setting: England in the 1930's and (in one play) in 1860.

Coward wrote these ten pieces, which portray declining Western civilization, "as acting, singing, and dancing vehicles for Gertrude Lawrence and myself." *Star Chamber* was produced only once and remained unpublished. The other plays were grouped in various combinations to make up three different shows on succeeding evenings, and also appeared as *To-night at 7:30* and (in matinees) *To-day at 2:30.* A number of the plays have been filmed, notably Coward's expanded adaptation of *Still Life* as *Brief Encounter* (1945).

In *We Were Dancing,* a comedy in two scenes, a couple fall in love at a dance and spend the night persuading her husband to let her go to Australia with her lover. At dawn the magic is gone; bored, she leaves the lover.

The Astonished Heart is a more profound play in six scenes (Scenes 2 through 5 in flashbacks). It portrays the tempestuous and overwhelming love affair of a psychiatrist and his wife's friend. When they break up after a final quarrel, the psychiatrist throws himself out of the window. At the beginning of the play he is dying in an adjoining room, asking for her. In the last scene she arrives, sees him, and reports his last words. Mistaking her for his wife, he said, "I'm not submerged any more," repeated the wife's name "again—and then—then he died."

"Red Peppers" is a comic interlude with music: it features a quarreling husband-and-wife vaudeville team.

Hands Across the Sea, a light comedy, is a witty and popular portrayal of a scatterbrained London society woman who mistakes two of her guests for a couple who had entertained her during a recent tour in the Far East.

Fumed Oak, "an unpleasant comedy" in two scenes, "is based on the good old 'Worm will turn' theme" (Coward). It portrays a Cockney family in their dirty fumed-oak apartment. The husband is at last fed up with his nagging mother-in-law, sloppy and bad-tempered wife, and perpetually sniveling daughter. He takes some money he has saved and, when they try to stop him, squelches the women. Then he leaves, to see the world and start life anew.

Shadow Play, a musical fantasy, portrays a couple who are about to get divorced. In the imagination of the wife, who has taken an overdose of sleeping pills, they relive the happiness of their early years together. Her memories reunite and reconcile the couple.

Family Album, a comedy (with music) Coward labeled "a sly satire on Victorian hypocrisy," takes place in a Kent house in 1860. The family read their deceased father's will. Their piety evaporates as their drinks take effect. "To hell with Papa!" says the daughter who nursed him: "He was cruel to Mama, he was unkind to us, he was profligate and pompous, and, worse still, he was mean." She has destroyed a later will that disinherited them in favor of his mistresses and a memorial to himself. But the old butler, the only witness, retreats into deafness when asked if her assertion is true: "I shall never be able to hear that particular question." The family give him a drink, wind up the music box, and dance around him.

Ways and Means, a comedy in three scenes, portrays an impecunious couple whose difficulties are solved when their host on the the fashionable Côte d'Azur is robbed by a friendly chauffeur who shares the loot with them.

Still Life, a play in five scenes, is the most compelling in the series. In five episodes set in a railway-station refreshment room and with the comic background activities of its personnel, two married people meet, fall in love, have a few furtive moments of happiness and agonies of guilt, and finally part. Ironically, their farewells are cruelly spoiled by a garrulous friend who happens to pass by.

TONIGHT WE IMPROVISE (*Questa sera si recita a soggetto*), a play in three acts by LUIGI PIRANDELLO, published and produced in 1930. Setting: the theatre and a town in contemporary Sicily.

This is the last play in the trilogy that begins with SIX CHARACTERS IN SEARCH OF AN AUTHOR. "A play within a play," it is based on a short story Pirandello published in 1912. Again the action occurs on various levels as reality and illusion merge and the actors transcend the limitations of a theatrical production. They rebel against a fussy director when they actually become the characters of the play.

Before *Act I* starts, noises from behind the curtain confuse the audience. Suddenly a small man rushes down the center aisle. It is Doctor Hinkfuss, the director. Amidst interruptions from the audience, Hinkfuss announces that he will dramatize a Pirandello short story. After a long and philosophical lecture on the immutability of art and the flux of life, Hinkfuss explains the Sicilian setting and introduces the characters: a mother (Signora Ignazia), a father, and their four "plump, pretty, sentimental, lively and warm-blooded" daughters. The leading man —the play's aviator, Rico Verri—objects to being introduced by his real name: "I have contracted with you to improvise tonight, by speaking whatever words may spring—spring—from the part I play, accompanied by spontaneous action and with every gesture in place." The other actors similarly step out of their parts as the story unfolds, over "the annoyance and restraint of a circumscribed setting" and Hinkfuss's efforts to extract theatrical effects. Coming from Naples, the family scandalizes the Sicilian town. The mother throws gay parties for her daughters and nearby airforce officers, and intimidates her husband, an ineffectual man in love with a lugubrious chanteuse. After Hinkfuss arranges an elaborate procession, the scene shifts to a cabaret, where the father is the butt of ridicule. His overbearing wife and the daughters with their officers pass by on their way to a theatre. They argue with the cabaret customers, and Signora Ignazia sends her husband home. The stage is rearranged and a movie begins. Signora Ignazia and her party noisily settle in a theatre box among the audience, who complain about the disturbance. Hinkfuss announces the end of the act and invites the audience to follow Signora Ignazia and her party to "witness the scandal which these charming people are about to cause in the lobby"; those remaining in their seats are invited to observe the scenery changes.

Act II. Variously grouped, the actors continue the play in the theatre lobby. Three of the daughters and their officers discuss the father's infatuation with the chanteuse. Simultaneously, Signora Ignazia loudly complains about the malicious townsfolk, and Verri jealously castigates Mommina, the eldest of the girls, for her family's scandalous behavior. In the meantime, Hinkfuss creates striking settings on the stage. As the audience returns, he reviews with them what has happened in the lobby, and then calls for the next act.

Act III. At a party, Signora Ignazia is suffering from a toothache. To relieve it, her daughters prepare a fanciful prayer ritual. Then, unwilling to give in to her pain, Signora Ignazia persuades Mommina, the daughter with the finest voice, to join the others in singing *Il Trovatore*. They are interrupted by Verri, who violently stops the festivities. Suddenly he steps out of character to complain about the propriety of a line. As the actors argue with Hinkfuss, the father appears. He finds his entrance spoiled because of the arguments, yet he is completely identified with the character he portrays. As he deplores his inability to die according to the script, he does in fact succeed, and drops dead. Hinkfuss applauds the effect, and sets the stage for the next scene. But the actors resent his interferences, his failure to respect their spontaneous performance after he "let loose life in us with all its passion and all its madness." Hinkfuss protests and claims the demands of the theatre, but the actors throw him out. "You can't play with passion," they tell him; "the birth of life is something that no one can control!" The leading lady is made up into an older, worn-out Mommina. Now married to Verri, who keeps her imprisoned, her suffering is intensified by his raging jealousy as he imagines her remembering pleasures with other men. Madly he tears at her until Mommina shouts for help and sinks down, exhausted, by her two little children. Thinking of her now-famous sister on tour in *Il Trovatore,* Mommina starts to sing the opera. But her heart breaks, and she collapses and dies. Her family appear, and Hinkfuss joins them, delighted at the "splendid tableau. . . . In this place, if there is need of obedience to the rules of art, there is also need of me" to "predetermine and regulate" the actors' work, Hinkfuss smugly concludes. It is up to him to take the author's lines and "give them life for a moment."

TOO TRUE TO BE GOOD, "A Political Extravaganza" in three acts by BERNARD SHAW, produced in 1932 and published in 1934. Setting: England and a mountainous country, 1930's.

Though in part witty and wise, and peopled with amusing characters, the play is somewhat formless and not always clear. In his preface Shaw explained that its "main gist and moral" is that our social system is "cruel to the rich," and dealt with government and religion, whose teachings the sergeant and the rascally windbag Aubrey find difficult to reconcile with reality. Private Meek is a portrait based on Lawrence of Arabia.

By the bedside of a wealthy Patient (Miss Mopply), a Monster Microbe, invisible to the Patient and her mother, wretchedly complains to the doctor that he has been infected by the Patient. After Mrs. Mopply and the doctor leave, the nurse (Sweetie, a burglar's moll) is joined by the burglar, Aubrey Bagot, a wartime ace and former clergyman. The Patient kicks him in the solar plexus, but then falls in love with him. The persuasive Aubrey suggests that she free herself from sickly wealth and respectability, and do what she likes. She agrees to steal her own necklace, use its proceeds for a spree, and have Aubrey kidnap her to a romantic country. They next appear on a beach in a mountainous country, Sweetie as a countess and the Patient as her native servant. Though he has received ransom money for the kidnapped Patient from Mrs. Mopply, the commanding Colonel Tallboys will not encourage criminality by paying it out. He is repeatedly exasperated by the sloppy but efficient Private Meek, who noisily buzzes around on his motorcycle and runs everything. When Meek repels a native attack, Tallboys decides to leave the command of the British expedition to him and to devote himself to his hobby of painting. After having reveled in her new freedom and in the "miracles of the universe," the Patient is miserable because she has nothing sensible to do. The bored Sweetie attempts to seduce a Bible-reading sergeant, who bewilders her by wanting "to explore her mind as well as her body." They are interrupted by Aubrey's father; he is disappointed in his burglar son (brought up as a "Godfearing atheist") and in Einstein, who destroyed Newton's universe and the father's convictions. The Patient's mother arrives and badgers Tallboys until he strikes her with his umbrella. The play ends as Sweetie decides to marry the sergeant, Tallboys is awarded the order of Knight Commander of the Bath for Meek's work, and Aubrey delivers a long and eloquent sermon during which the others steal away. Asserting that though the Patient will "found an unladylike sisterhood with her mother as cook-housekeeper" and that though all are really "falling endlessly and hopelessly through a void in which they can find no footing," Aubrey admits that he must go on preaching even if he has "nothing to say."

TOTHEROH, Dan (1894-   ), American playwright, became known with *White Birds* (1925), a tragic psychological drama about a reform-school boy who is beaten to death and an orphan girl who commits suicide. Interested also in western themes —Totheroh was born in California, at whose university he became a theatre director—he followed this play with *Distant Drums* (1932), a case study of a neurotic female traveling in a covered wagon. Totheroh gave similar dramatic treatment to the Brontë sisters in *Moor Born* (1934). His other plays include *Mother Lode* (1934), a drama of early California, written with the poet George O'Neil (1898–1940); and *Live Life Again* (1943), a *Hamlet*-like play transposed to a Nebraska farm. Totheroh also composed and produced outdoor pageants, published a collection of *One-Act Plays for Everyone* (1931), and wrote film scripts (including that of *The Count of Monte Cristo,* 1933) and a number of novels.

TOUCH OF THE POET, A, a play in four acts by EUGENE O'NEILL, published and produced in 1957. Setting: a tavern outside Boston; July 27, 1828.

O'Neill wrote this posthumous play in 1939–40 and copyrighted it as an unpublished dramatic composition in 1946. Like MORE STATELY MANSIONS, it is part of A TALE OF POSSESSORS, SELF-DISPOSSESSED.

The aristocratically raised son of an Irish "thieving shebeen keeper" turned wealthy, Cornelius ("Con") Melody disgraced himself after a valorous military career. He emigrated to America, where he is now a destitute tavernkeeper. Snubbed by Yankee aristocrats and hated by the Irish because of his contempt for them, the handsome Melody lives in a dream world where he is still the refined major, haughtily recites Byron before a mirror, and rides his thoroughbred mare. These indulgences have impoverished him and worn out his wife, Nora, whom he browbeats for her coarse Irish ways and looks. But she forgives and worships him, begs tradesmen for credit, and does menial work to support his pretensions. Sara, the daughter in whom are combined his aristocratic and Nora's peasant characteristics, is torn between pride and bitter hatred of her father, and they fight each other viciously. On his annual celebration of the Battle of Talavera, in which Cornelius distinguished himself with Wellington, Sara swears that this is the last time she will play waitress to him and his sponging cronies, and decides to marry Simon Harford, a Yankee capitalist's son now lying sick upstairs (he is never seen onstage). Nora comments on the "touch av the poet in him," and warns Sara of her pride, which will "kape you from ivir givin' all of yourself, and that's what love is." When Sara refuses to become a slave like her mother, Nora exultantly tells her, "There's no slavery in it when you love!" and then begs her not to "take the pride of my love from me, Sara, for without it what am I at all but an ugly, fat woman gettin' old and sick!" Melody, playing the seductive charmer, soon is made a fool of by Simon's beautiful mother, Deborah, and is later humiliated with a cash offer sent by Simon's father to prevent his son's marriage to a lowly barkeep's daughter. Off to avenge this insult like a gentleman of old—with a duel—Melody is beaten instead in a vulgar police brawl (observed by Simon's mother) and then bailed out of prison by the father. Thoroughly mortified and disillusioned, Melody gives up his proud dreams and ridicules his former pretensions of being a Byronic "lord wid a touch av the poet." He reverts to his Irish brogue, and melodramatically shoots his beloved mare, the symbol of what used to be the aristocratic major: "He's dead now, and his last bit av lyin' pride is murthered and stinkin'." Melody is broken, but in the meantime, to assure his marrying her, Sara has seduced Simon. In giving herself to love, however, she has also learned to understand her mother's love: "I knew tonight the truth of what you said this morning, that a woman can forgive whatever the man she loves could do and still love him, because it was through him she found the love in herself; that, in one way, he doesn't count at all, because it's love, your own love, you love in him, and to keep that your pride will do anything." Melody half-playfully slaps Sara when she attempts to stop his going to carouse as an equal with the "Irish scum," and she weeps for the death of her father's pride and illusions. As the curtain falls, Nora, moved by the thought of Melody's returning love for herself, teasingly comforts Sara: "Shame on you to cry when you have love. What would the young lad think of you?"

TOWER, THE (*Der Turm*), a tragedy in five acts by HUGO VON HOFMANNSTHAL, published in 1925 and produced in 1928. Setting: seventeenth-century Poland.

This adaptation of Calderón's *La vida es sueño* (*Life is a Dream*, 1673), Hofmannsthal's most ambitious drama, occupied him for many years. Its first version, the trochaic *Das Leben ein Traum* (the translation of Calderón's title), appeared in 1902; the final prose version appeared in 1927. Increasingly, Hofmannsthal transformed the original plot into a parable of twentieth-century perplexities.

From infancy Sigismund has been imprisoned in a tower by his father, King Basilius, who seeks to forestall a prophecy that the prince would eventually overpower him. Caged and partly brutalized, Sigismund also feels spiritually tormented by his identity. At last the prison governor, scheming for power, persuades King Basilius to acknowledge and receive his son. Confronting his despotic father, Sigismund rebels indignantly. He is subdued and King Basilius orders his execution. The order triggers rebellion against Basilius by various warring factions, including mobs incited by a would-be dictator. They force Basilius to abdicate, make Sigismund king, and attempt to use him. Saintlike, Sigismund strives in vain for order and justice. Anarchy and brutality prevail in the struggles for power. Victimized on the throne as he was in the tower, the messianic Sigismund refuses to compromise his integrity. When the crowds outside clamor for him ("Do not leave us!"), he appears at the window. Immediately he is felled by a shot. Sigismund dies reaffirming faith and hope: "Bear witness, I was here, though no one knew me."

TOYS IN THE ATTIC, a play in three acts by LILLIAN HELLMAN, published and produced in 1960. Setting: New Orleans, two summer days in the late 1950's.

This is a sometimes confused drama about decaying Southern whites.

Two spinster sisters, one them incestuously possessive of her recently married brother, are upset by his sudden and mysterious wealth. Unable to stand the thought of his independence of them, the possessive sister causes him to be outsmarted, beaten up, and robbed of all his money. Thus he is again dependent, and she happily prepares to pamper him once more. Among other characters are his deranged young wife and her bizarre, aristocratic mother, who lives with a gentlemanly Negro.

TRAGEDIAN IN SPITE OF HIMSELF, A (*Tragik ponevole*), "a jest in one act" by ANTON CHEKHOV, published and approved by the censor for production in 1889. Setting: a contemporary St. Petersburg apartment.

A dramatization of Chekhov's short story "Odin iz mnogikh" ("One of Many," 1887), this farce has also been translated as *A Tragic Role* and as *Summer in the Country*.

A civil servant, loaded with parcels, begs his friend for a pistol. He details his troubles as a summer commuter from the country. Daily he is burdened with errands for his wife and the neighbors, and he suffers further hardships upon his return at night. When the friend asks him to do an errand for him in the country, the commuter goes berserk.

TRAGEDY OF NAN, THE, a play in three acts by JOHN MASEFIELD, published and produced in 1908. Setting: Broad Oak on the Severn, Gloucestershire; 1810.

Masefield's most popular prose play is in the rustic dialect of country folk. Except for the unfortunate heroine, her weak uncle, and the mad old Gaffer, these folk are presented as a thoroughly contemptible lot.

Nan Hardwick's father was hanged for sheep stealing. Now she lives as a charity case with her uncle and his mean, hypocritical wife, mistreated and resented as a "gallus-bird." Her aunt also fears that Dick Gurvil, a prospective husband for her daughter, will prefer Nan. Cruel taunting finally drives Nan to hysteria. Then the daughter worms her way into Nan's confidence and discovers that Nan is, indeed, "soft on Dick." At a party Nan and Dick avow their love for each other. Dick puts a rose in Nan's hair, kisses her, and asks her to be his wife. He will not let Nan tell him about her father, and she gives in: "If you love me, Dick —O, my love! Us together! Us needn't fear what they say." But by financial threats and ridiculing Dick's plans "to marry a girl whose dad was 'ung at Glorster, like the thief 'e was," Nan's aunt gets him to choose her daughter instead. Gaffer Pearce, a mad old fiddler who furnishes the party's music, mirrors Nan's emotions. He mourns for his long-dead wife, reminisces ecstatically, and talks of the river's roaring waters. "The tide be comin' for some on us," Gaffer tells Nan; the fishermen's nets will have "strange fish out of the sea." Then a government official proclaims "a sad miscarriage of justice": another man has just confessed to the theft for which Nan's father was hanged. He gives her a bag of gold as compensation, and rushes out to his coach. Nan remembers her father: "That voice of his'n was choked out with a cord"—and for that "I get little yellow round things." The smugness of the parson, the greed of the relatives (who make immediate plans of their own for the gold), and the viciousness of her cousin exacerbate Nan's suffering. When Dick returns to her and reveals himself to be a hypocritical mercenary, Nan grabs a pastry knife and kills this unworthy man to whom she had given her heart. The mad Gaffer claps his hands and babbles of her beauty, of that of his dead wife ("my white vlower"), and of the rising tide. And Nan walks out to drown herself, "a strange fish in the nets to-morrow."

TRANSLATIONS AND TOMFOOLERIES (1926), a collection of seven plays by BERNARD SHAW. Though these trifles "may disgust the admirers of my more pretentious work," Shaw noted in his preface to the volume, "tomfoolery is as classic as tragedy." The plays are JITTA'S ATONEMENT, THE ADMIRABLE BASHVILLE, and five one-acters: *Passion, Poison, and Petrifaction; or The Fatal Gazogene* (1905), a zany burlesque melodrama; *Press Cuttings* (1909), "a topical sketch" about a suffragette who defeats—and marries—the prime minister; *The Fascinating Foundling* (1909), a farce about foundlings mated by the lord chancellor; *The Music Cure* (1914), "a piece of nonsense" about a "female Paderewski" and a youth on the verge of a nervous breakdown; and *The Glimpse of Reality* (1926), a fifteenth-century "tragietta" about a courageous Italian nobleman.

TRAVELER WITHOUT LUGGAGE (*Le Voyageur sans bagage*), a play in five scenes by JEAN ANOUILH, published and produced in 1937. Setting: a French country house, 1930's.

This early work, one of the "black plays," was Anouilh's first hit. While the plot, with its amnesiac protagonist, recalls Giraudoux's SIEGFRIED, Anouilh's is a suspense drama that is resolved in a very different manner.

Gaston lost his memory while at the front, and has spent the following eighteen years in institutions. Because of his accumulated pension, blood claims have been advanced by many families. The wealthiest of these, which he now meets, appears to be the true one. The putative mother and the brother with his young wife, as well as the servants, are sure Gaston is theirs. Gradually he discovers his revolting past: he was a cruel boy who wantonly tortured animals, crippled his best friend in a row over a seduced maid, and became the lover of his brother's wife. Gaston is so appalled by his discoveries that he decides "to deny my past and the people in this house, including myself." He rejects the importuning claimants, particularly his sister-in-law and former mistress, who wants him back, and instead accepts a family whose only remaining member and heir is a child.

TREADWELL, Sophie (1890–1970), American journalist and playwright, became known for an experimental play, MACHINAL (1928). Of Spanish and English ancestry, Treadwell was born in Stockton, California, and was raised in the San Joaquin Valley by her parents, pioneer California settlers. In 1910 she married a later-prominent sportswriter and columnist, William O. McGeehan. She became the first accredited woman correspondent for an American newspaper, *The San Francisco Bulletin,* in World War I, and covered the Carranza revolution in Mexico for *The New York Tribune*. A graduate of the University of California, she was encouraged to write plays by the then-retired actress Helen Modjeska, with whom she studied acting and whose memoirs Treadwell helped to write.

Her first produced play was *Gringo* (1922), a Mexican-American melodrama. In *Hope for a Harvest* (1941), a social-protest play, she attacked man's enterprise in building machinery rather than human character; a conventionally structured drama, it was successfully produced in various cities, but failed when the Theatre Guild brought it to New York. Her other plays are also nonexperimental. They include *Ladies Leave* (1929), a satire about bored wives who leave their husbands for their psychoanalysts; and *Plumes in the Dust* (1936), a dramatization of the life of Edgar Allen Poe. She also published a novel about exurbanites and their transgressions, *One Fierce Hour and Sweet* (1959).

TREASURE, THE (*Der Oytser*), a drama in four acts by DAVID PINSKI, published and produced in 1910. Setting: a contemporary provincial Russian gravedigger's house and the adjoining cemetery, on the Ninth of Av (the Jewish fast-day commemorating the destruction of Jerusalem) and the following day.

This comedy (written in 1906) first carried Pinski's name beyond the Yiddish theatre. Initially produced in German by Max Reinhardt, it was the first Pinski play published in English (1915), and it was produced by the Theatre Guild in 1920. Its farcical plot and comic—yet NATURALISTICally drawn—individual and collective portraits depict men's quest for happiness, a quest that—as the fantasy ending suggests—is not necessarily an avaricious evil.

Acts I and II. Tille's half-wit brother finds some gold coins when he buries his dog. He gives them to Tille, who refuses to turn them over to her ever-lamenting mother or to the gravedigger Khone, her father. Instead, she rejoices at the thought of realizing her fondest dreams: to dress in fineries and catch a handsome husband. Money makes her feel wonderful—"like a new human being in a new skin." Her brother has forgotten where he buried his pet, but Tille is sure he will find the spot and the remaining treasure. Though it is a holy day, she runs out to purchase fancy clothes and jewelry, and the town soon buzzes with excitement. Khone becomes increasingly worried as the congregation and the town's elite congratulate and question him. He argues with Tille, who will not give him the money she has left. "What can you lose?" she asks her distraught father, who ridicules his "millionaire" daughter's fancy notions when the half-wit still fails to find the treasure spot. Now come various fawning visitors. Tille eggs on the leading marriage broker, who has always avoided the poor Khone household, to send for the handsome, rich groom she craves. The town's capitalist threatens a lawsuit, and the president of the congregation makes his claims. Khone and his wailing wife go out to dig for the treasure. But though it may never be found, Tille is still enraptured: "Ah, at least for one day I've been a millionaire!"

Acts III and IV. Afraid of what Tille's doings may cost him, Khone avoids callers by feigning illness. Representatives of The Society for Providing Poor Maidens with a Dowry and other organizations come to solicit funds for their worthy causes, and even try to steal money from the bedridden gravedigger. The capitalist and the president of the congregation, too, return with their demands. Since he is thought to be a millionaire, Khone's job is given to someone else. Khone desperately tells them exactly what happened, that his demented son found a few sovereigns, but forgot where. The whole town now rushes to the cemetery, digging around for the treasure and desecrating the graves while doing so. Suddenly Tille's demented brother remembers the spot: a holy man's burial place. It contains no more gold, but before Khone reveals it, he manages to get back his job. When the disappointed crowds leave, Tille laughs—"What have I to be ashamed of? Let *them* be ashamed!"—and happily remembers that "for one day at least I was a millionaire lady." And she reveals that she has banked the remaining "treasure": "It's not a great deal, to be sure, but enough to catch a man with—a very modest one and perhaps not so very modest after all. I'm such a celebrity in the town now and I have such a fine trousseau—" When the cemetery is empty, the souls of the disturbed dead appear. "Money—money—money . . . and that is life!" they laugh. "And yet it must lead to something. Surely there must be a goal," they speculate. "Only God knows that. . . . And man must learn what it is," the spirits conclude: "And that will be man's greatest victory."

TREBITSCH, Siegfried (1869–1956), Austrian playwright, novelist, and most important, translator of BERNARD SHAW's plays (nine volumes, 1911–40). These remarkable translations, used for performances—many of them world premieres of Shaw plays—wherever German was spoken, raised and spread Shaw's fame and made him a fortune.

Trebitsch's own novels and plays were overshadowed by his monumental labors for the greater man, although some of Trebitsch's plays were independently successful: *Gefährliche Jahre* (1908), *Ein Muttersohn* (1911), *Kaiser Diocletian* (1922), and others. His best-known play is *Frau Gitta's Sühne* (1920), which, as a token of his friendship and gratitude, Shaw translated (and prefaced with a tribute to Trebitsch) as JITTA'S ATONEMENT (1923). Further accounts of their relationship appear in Trebitsch's *Chronik eines Lebens* (*Chronicle of a Life,* 1951).

TRELAWNY OF THE "WELLS," a play in four acts by ARHUR WING PINERO, published and produced in 1898. Setting: England, early 1860's.

This sentimental comedy is notable for its tribute to Pinero's precursor, Thomas W. Robertson (in the character of Tom Wrench). Its portrayal of backstage life abetted its long popularity.

Rose Trelawny is bored by her fiancé's fashionably dull family, who despise her actor friends as gypsies. She returns to act at the "Wells" and eventually is reunited with her lover, whose grandfather provides the money needed to produce a new play Tom Wrench has written for her.

TRENYOV, Konstantin Andreevich (1878?–1945), Russian playwright, was most successful with his popular *Lyubov Yarovaya* (1926), produced in a revised version at the Moscow Art Theatre in 1937 and subsequently the winner of a Stalin Prize. Like his other drama, this is a propaganda play, set at the end of the Civil War; the title heroine, a schoolteacher, is a revolutionary who finally chooses to denouce her husband, a White Guard. *Pugachovshchina* (1925), which features the famous outlaw Emilian Pugachov (the peasant rebellion leader during the reign of Catherine the Great), "is one of the best examples of Soviet falsifications of history," according to Nikolai A. Gorchakov's *The Theater in Soviet Russia* (1957). Trenyov's other plays include *Zhena* (1928), a comedy about marriage in Soviet Russia; *Opyt* (1930), depicting the murder of a scientist by religious fanatics; *Yasny lug* (1931), dramatizing the advantages of collective farming; *Gimnazisty* (1935); and *Na beregu nevy* (1937), portraying Lenin just before the Revolution. *Lyubov Yarovaya* is reprinted in Alexander Bakshy's collection, *Soviet Scene: Six Plays of Russian Life* (1946), which includes a brief essay on Trenyov.

TRETYAKOV, Sergei Mikhailovich (1892–1939?), Russian poet, literary theoretician, and playwright, was among those purged in the late 1930's. He became famous with his *Rychi Kitai!* (*Roar China!*), which was produced with great success by Vsevolod Meyerhold in 1926, and then throughout Europe and by the New York Theatre Guild (1930). It is a crude anti-imperialist propaganda play based on an actual event, the 1924 coolie uprising after a British gunboat captain killed Chinese boatmen on the Yangtze River. ("These are the facts," Tretyakov wrote in his preface; "I have hardly had to change anything.")

Tretyakov was born in Riga and studied law at the University of Moscow. He became interested in the Far East during the Revolution, and joined his friend VLADIMIR MAYAKOVSKY's group of FUTURIST poets. In 1922–23 he worked with Sergei Eisenstein, then the Prolecult Theatre director, and he wrote a number of adaptations as well as two original plays, *Slushai Moskva* and *Protivogazy* (both 1924); these are characteristic Communist propaganda plays, set in Germany. In 1924 Tretyakov left for Peking, where he became Literary Professor at the National University. It was then that he wrote his best-known play. His last play is a eugenics comedy, *Khochu rebyonka* (1929). He also wrote a number of film scripts.

The English translation of *Roar China!* was published twice in 1931, and the English production changed the gunboat into a French one. The translation is prefaced by H. W. L. Dana's short essay on the life and work of Tretyakov.

TRIAL OF A JUDGE, a verse tragedy in five acts by STEPHEN SPENDER, published and produced in 1938. Setting: a palace of justice and prison cells.

This is a poetic allegory about an unnamed judge. The setting suggests Germany in the early 1930's, and the plot suggests the Nazi terror. Though haunting, the play was not commercially viable.

A judge is forced to reverse the death sentence of Fascists guilty of murder and to condemn Communists for a lesser crime. Himself condemned by the Fascists, the judge dies, rhapsodizing his avoidance of force. But this attitude has brought Fascism to power, "For, in refusing to use [force], his like secretly destroyed / The sources of their own power, their over-ripeness held out a breast / At which the blonde monster, which would destroy them, fed." To the accompaniment of symbolic drum taps, a chorus of doomed Red prisoners whispers, "We shall find peace."

TRIAL OF LUCULLUS, THE (*Das Verhör des Lukullus*), a radio play in fourteen short verse sections by BERTOLT BRECHT, published and produced in 1940. Setting: Rome in the first century B.C., and the nether world.

Brecht adapted this play into an opera, *Die Verurteilung des Lukullus* (*The Condemnation of Lucullus,* music by Paul Dessau—by Roger Sessions for the English version), published and produced in 1951. At first there were few changes, but angered Communist authorities persuaded Brecht to alter the pacifist text to express justification for some wars (see Martin Esslin, *Brecht: The Man and His Work*). At the end, Lucullus is condemned: "May he disappear into nothingness."

After the colorful funeral procession of General Lucullus, he is tried in the nether regions. The great victories on which he prides himself are shown to be nothing but murder and carnage. His only acknowledged virtue turns out to be a weakness—his importation of an Asian cherry tree, a *living,* beautiful trophy to his career. But it does not justify his bloody deeds, and the tribunal retires to consider its decision.

TRIALS OF BROTHER JERO, THE, a play in five scenes by WOLE SOYINKA, published in 1964 and produced in 1967. Setting: contemporary Lagos.

Soyinka's first play to reach worldwide audiences, this is a farce that satirizes religious humbug in the person of Jero (Jeroboam), a lusty self-proclaimed "beach divine."

In an opening soliloquy Jero expounds his philosophy, recalls the good old days when prophets won beaches "by getting women penitents to shake their bosoms in spiritual ecstasy," deplores the difficulty of finding new converts now that "they all prefer High Life [and television] to the rhythm of celestial hymns," and concludes that one experience—which will now be dramatized—"shook me quite a bit, but . . . the Lord protects his own. . . ." The virago from whom he has purchased an ornate velvet cloak hounds Jero for payment. She appears with and berates her husband, Jero's assistant. Unaware of this sale, he has long sought his master's permission to beat up his troublesome wife. Now Jero grants it so he himself may be rid of her. The assistant discovers this reason and routs Jero. But in a final twist Jero turns his ignominious retreat into a miracle and reaffirms his "divinity" to a gullible new victim, who prostrates himself before Jero and in "rapt awe" whispers, "Master!"

TRIFLES, a one-act play by SUSAN GLASPELL, published and produced in 1916. Setting: the kitchen of an abandoned Midwest farmhouse, c. 1916.

Susan Glaspell later rewrote this suspenseful drama as a short story, "Jury of Her Peers." One of the early productions of the Provincetown Players, it became her most frequently performed play, and it is still popular with amateur companies. Neatly constructed and replete with local color and REALISTIC details, it features two women.

The sheriff's wife and the neighbor of a strangled farmer discover among household trifles the evidence, while sheriff and county attorney look all over for it, that would convict the victim's widow. As the two women tensely reconstruct events, they portray the suspect's personality and lonesome life with a hard, cruel husband. Feeling guilty because they failed to stand by and help her, the women finally decide that though murder is "an awful thing," the farmer's wife was justified. They conceal the evidence from the dense officials—who have smugly scoffed at the women's "worrying over trifles."

TROJAN WAR WILL NOT TAKE PLACE, THE (*La Guerre de Troie n'aura pas lieu*), a play in two acts by JEAN GIRAUDOUX, published and produced in 1935. Setting: ancient Troy.

CHRISTOPHER FRY's well-known translation of this play, one of Giraudoux's major works, is titled *Tiger at the Gates.* The play wittily probes serious problems whose topical relevance was clear to pre- (and then post-) World War II audiences. The setting follows Greek legend, but the plot is wholly original; so are the characterizations, particularly those of Helen and of Hector, Giraudoux's noble spokesman.

Act I. "There's not going to be a Trojan War," Andromache believes. Her returning husband, Hector, promised the last war would be their final one; besides, Paris and Helen are no longer in love, and the girl can therefore be given back to the Greek ambassadors, who are expected momentarily. But Cassandra disagrees: she recognizes two eternal "great stupidities," those of men and those of the elements. Now Cassandra sees destiny crouching before the War Gates like a sleepy tiger, prodded by militant spirits in Troy. Hector, sickened by war, is determined to preserve peace and yield Helen to the Greeks. But his brother Paris does not want to give her up. Neither does their father, Priam, and he is supported by the Trojans—particularly by a mathematician and by

The Trojan War Will Not Take Place, produced as *Tiger at the Gates.* Paris (Leo Ciceri), Cassandra (Leueen McGrath), Hector (Michael Redgrave). New York, 1955. (*Zodiac Photographers*)

a patriotic poetaster—who are bewitched by Helen's beauty. At last Hector persuades Priam and Paris to let Helen herself decide. Though Helen is concerned only with her own pleasures, Hector succeeds in persuading her, too, and she agrees to return to her husband. The priests, however, send word of their opposition to closing the War Gates: the gods would consider it an affront to their honor.

Act II. Before the War Gates the old Trojans—the politicians, the superpatriots, and the sophists—come to urge war. Hector argues eloquently for peace. War, he says when asked to deliver an oration for the fallen Trojan soldiers, is "the most sordid, hypocritical way of making all men equal." The Greeks arrive, no less bellicose than the Trojans. Hector goes to all lengths to avoid war, allowing himself to be insulted and even slapped by Ajax. When Hector also agrees to yield Helen, the wily Ulysses insists that she must be as pure as when she left Greece. The Trojans contradict their leader Hector's assurances that she is. But the gods now rule that the issue of war or peace must be decided between Ulysses and Hector alone. In their portentous private talk both leaders agree that they do not want war; "but I'm less sure whether war may not want us," Ulysses says. He knows that of all women, Helen has "the shallowest brain, the hardest heart, the narrowest understanding of sex." Yet he agrees to take her back. In doing so, he realizes that he challenges destiny, which created Helen and seems to make war inevitable. Yet "I'm quite willing to join issue with fate," he tells Hector; "I've more than enough eloquence to convince a husband of his wife's virtue." All depends on his success in returning to the Greek ship before his or Hector's people can instigate hostilities. As Ulysses approaches his destination, the drunken Ajax appears. His pawing of Andromache is about to provoke Hector's blows when Ajax moves off. Peace seems assured. Then the fanatic poetaster bursts in, enraged at such "cowardice." He calls the Trojans to arms, inciting them to sing his war song. Hector strikes him down, determined that "the war isn't going to happen." But with his dying breath the poetaster, to fan the war flames, shouts out that it was Ajax the Greek who killed him. The absurdities of chance and human nature prevail. The War Gates slowly open, Helen is revealed kissing young Troilus, and the poetaster is dead. "And now the Grecian poet will have his word," Cassandra says.

TRUTH ABOUT BLAYDS, THE, a play in three acts by A. A. MILNE, produced in 1921 and published in 1922. Setting: London, early 1920's.

Despite its amusing satire, this play is more serious than most of Milne's other drama. It resembles Coward's NUDE WITH VIOLIN, Fauchois's THE LATE CHRISTOPHER BEAN, and ARNOLD BENNETT's adaptation of his own novel, *Buried Alive*. Milne's title character, Oliver Blayds, is a much-revered ninety-year-old poet, the last of the great Victorians.

Shortly before Blayds dies he tells his youngest daughter, Isobel, that he has defrauded the world: his poems were really written by Jenkins, an unknown friend who died when they were both young. Blayds's appalled family debate what is to be done. Isobel, who gave up love and marriage, and wasted her life in nursing her "genius" father, is determined to expose the fraud publicly and redeem the real poet. The others, including a son-in-law who was Blayds's secretary and is writing his biography, are worried about the money they will lose by the exposure. Their financial fears are relieved by the discovery that young Jenkins made his friend Blayds his heir before he died. Gradually they persuade themselves that Blayds's deathbed confession was a hallucination. In any case, it is the poetry that matters, they decide, not the author, whose true identity can never be established now. "It's no good. You can't start another miserable Shakespeare-Bacon controversy. Hadn't we better just leave him with the poetry?" remarks the critic whom Isobel had loved long before, and suggests her determination to act may be due to her pent-up resentment. He persuades her to marry him, and the family are delighted when "she believes" their interpretation. "It is our duty to tell the *whole* truth about that great man," his biographer decides; he will record Blayds's "chivalrous attempt to assist his friend," and to assign the authorship of Blayds's only original—and, incidentally, his only unsuccessful—collection to Jenkins: "And so that is how the story will be handed down."

TRUTH, THE, a comedy in four acts by CLYDE FITCH, produced in 1906 and published in 1907. Setting: New York and Baltimore, early twentieth century.

Though a failure in America, this play has been praised highly by critics. It was a success abroad and gave Fitch an international reputation. The play resembles his THE GIRL WITH THE GREEN EYES.

Like her father, Becky is a congenital liar. Her husband, Tom Warder, cannot understand this shortcoming, thinks she has been unfaithful rather than merely flirtatious, and leaves her. She seeks refuge with her father, who wires Warder that Becky is dying. The landlady, who wants to marry Becky's father, reveals the deception. Warder is about to return to New York, utterly disgusted with his wife. But at the last moment Becky tells him the truth, and Warder forgives her. "We don't love people because they are perfect," he says; "we love them because they are themselves."

TS'AO YÜ [pen name of Wan Chia-Pao] (1905–   ), modern China's first great playwright, began his career as an actor, starring as Nora in Ibsen's A DOLL'S HOUSE. He became famous in 1934 with *Lei Yü* (*Thunder and Rain,* also translated as *Thunderstorm*), a tragedy that was immediately published, toured throughout China, and was still produced in (politically) revised form in the 1960's; influenced by O'Neill's MOURNING BECOMES ELECTRA and its Aeschylean source, yet very Chinese in characters, customs, and actions, this grim portrayal of feudal breakdown traces incestuous and other relationships among seven characters who go insane or perish by suicide or accidental death. Ts'ao Yü's reputation was consolidated with his next two tragedies: *Jih Ch'u* (*The Sunrise,* 1935), a drama that won China's annual literary prize and deals with sex and a dishonest speculator's conflict with a group of decent laborers between 1931 and 1935 ("during the reactionary rule of the Kuomintang," according to the 1960 Peking Foreign Languages Press edition notes to the play); and *Yuan Yeh* (*The Prairie,* 1937), a turbulent drama of passion and vengeance in which two families are destroyed. Ts'ao Yü's other important plays are *Pei Ching Jen* (*Peking Man,* 1940?), an optimistic drama about man's ultimate victory over the destructive forces of civilization; *Chia* (*Family,* 1941?), a four-generation chronicle dramatization of a notable Chinese novel about the disintegration of the old society and the triumph of the new; and *T'o Pien* (*Metamorphosis,* 1941?), a war propaganda drama whose protagonist personifies China at the time of Japan's attack. After a private showing Chiang Kai-shek ordered its production amplified to clarify the play's political import.

Ts'ao Yü was born in Chien-Kiang, Hupei. When in high school he was already active in experimental drama and theatre groups. At Tsinghua University he studied Western literature, and then he became a lecturer at Chungking's National Academy of Drama, and a film-maker. During the troubled era before the fall of the Kuomintang and after a visit to the United States prompted by the State Department's invitation (1946), he lapsed for five years into what he called a "silence of despair," but he then returned to teaching, at Shanghai's Experimental Dramatic School, and to writing. His silence as a playwright was broken with *Ming lang ti tien* (*Bright Skies,* 1956). According to the 1960 translation note, this play shows how doctors at Peking's Medical College embark on service to the people: they shake off their subservience to and expose the Americans who founded their college and then became imperialist agents by waging germ warfare against Korea. This and his later plays on ancient history lack the power of the plays Ts'ao Yü wrote before he joined the "Great Proletarian Cultural Revolution."

Thunder and Rain with Ts'ao Yü's prefatory essay appeared in the *T'ien Hsia Monthly,* October 1936 through February 1937, as well as in *Three Famous Chinese Plays* (1946?). It and his other plays are discussed in Faubian Bowers's *Theatre in the East* (1956) and in Walter J. and Ruth I. Meserve's "Ts'ao Yu: Dramatist in Communist China" (*Comparative Drama* II:2, 1968), and, from a different perspective, in the prefaces to the Peking translations.

TSUBOUCHI Shōyō [originally Yūzō] (1859–1935), Japanese scholar, academician, director, and playwright, was a pioneer of his country's modern theatre and drama, and one of its most prolific and versatile writers. He was the first to acquaint Japan with the masterpieces of Western drama by translating and producing the works of Shakespeare. In 1888 he set out to reform the native theatre, and by 1906 he had brought about the *Shingeki,* or New Theatre, by founding the Bungei Kyōkai (Literary and Art Association), which soon produced Western drama. His *Wagakuni no Shigeki* (1893) became the standard work on Japanese theatre history. In 1894 appeared the first of his many historical plays, *Kiri Hitoha,* a tragedy that portrays the decline and fall of a noble family. Publishing extensive theoretical studies on the drama, Tsubouchi analyzed his own works and constructed a poetics of the historical and then of the dance and musical drama that he wrote next. It is a transplantation of European opera that, like his historical tragedy, amalgamated classical Nipponese with Western conventions. The first and most important of Tsubouchi's musical dramas was the legendary *Shinkyoku Urashima,* an opulent romantic fantasy about the princess of an underwater kingdom; written in 1904 and analyzed by Tsubouchi himself the following year, it was staged in part in 1907 and then abridged by Tsubouchi for wider production, which it enjoyed only in the next (Taisho) era. In that same genre Tsubouchi wrote numerous other works, many of them pantomimes. An immense influence on later Japanese playwrights, Tsubouchi introduced classic Occidental plays and REALISTIC theatre conventions (including women performers) to Japan, thus literally setting the stage for Japan's modern drama.

Tsubouchi was born in Ōta and attended the Aichi English (finishing) school and Kaisei Kō, the predecessor of Tokyo University. Appointed to a professorship, he became famous first as a novelist, in 1885. Among his many accomplishments was the founding of the subsequently important Theatre Museum at Waseda University. Tsubouchi's voluminous writings and extensive theatre activities are discussed in V. H. Viglielmo's translation of Okazaki Yoshie's *Japanese Literature in the Meiji Era* (1955).

TUR BROTHERS, Leonid Davidovich (1905–61) and **Pyotr Davidovich** (1907–   ), Russian playwrights, collaborated with various other writers in a series of popular plays, most of them "thrillers" about anti-Soviet villains. Among their early successes was *Zemlya i nebo* (1932), featuring an astronomer whose observatory is surrounded by Interventionists. *Vostochny batalyon* (*The Eastern Battalion,* 1935) was a plagiarized wartime propaganda play whose outlandish history is related in *Soviet Theaters 1917–1941* (1954), edited by Martha Bradshaw. The Tur Brothers collaborated with ALEKSANDR SHTEIN on *Utopiya* (1930), but their most successful collaboration was with Lev Romanovich Sheinin (1905–67), a detective-story writer and former coroner and N.K.V.D. official. Their first great hit was *Ochnaya stavka* (*The Showdown,* 1938), a play about the arrest of Nazi spies, filmed in Russia and produced in New York

(1939). Their other joint works with Sheinin include *Generalny konsul* (1939), whose consul general of the title combats pro-Fascist émigrés; *Chrezvychainy zakon* (1943); *Poyedinok* (1944); and *Osobnyak v pereulke,* which was published in 1962 but had been produced before 1956.

Their *Dym otechestva* (*Smoke of the Fatherland,* 1942), a play about a kulak who joins the Nazi invaders in a futile effort to regain his land, appears, with prefatory comments on Sheinin and the Tur Brothers, in H. W. L. Dana's collection of *Seven Soviet Plays* (1946).

TURKEY is renowned for its *karagöz* (puppet) and *hayal-i zill* or *kukla* (shadow) shows, *orta oyunu* (an open-air *commedia dell'arte* type of drama), and *meddah* (story-telling mimics), all of them popular with natives and visitors.* Under the impact of modern Western civilization, however, they have increasingly given way to modern drama. The generally accepted date of its beginning is 1859, the publication year of a one-act satire of conventionally contracted marriages, *Şair evlenmesi,* by the Western-oriented poet, journalist, and playwright Ibrahim Şinasi (1826–71). Because of government suppression, especially during the reign of Abdülhamit II (1876–1908), Turkey's early modern drama was long in developing. Nonetheless, many plays were written in the 1870's and 1880's. They were mainly patriotic dramas or situation comedies, the latter being principally concerned with local customs and manners. The patriotic works of the period were generally tragedies which drew their plots mainly from Turkish history and legends, but reflected a peculiar mixture of French neoclassical and romantic influence.

The most popular early modern playwrights are Namık Kemal (1840–88), a reformer arrested and banished for his patriotic drama *Vatan yahut Silistre* (1872), which created a sensation and was subsequently banned only to be produced clandestinely; Ahmet Mithat Efendi (1844–1912), a novelist and journalist whose social drama challenged superstition and customs such as polygamy; Recaizade Mahmut Ekrem (1847–1913), a poet and novelist whose melodramas include the popular folktale of *Afife/Anjelik* (1872); and the leading modern poet Abdülhak Hamit (1852–1937), who from 1875 until shortly before his death produced declamatory verse plays derivative of Shakespeare and the French neoclassicists.

The early modern period was characterized by the introduction of some Western drama into the Turkish theatre. From the 1890's on, increasing censorship made it impossible for the theatrical troupes to operate until the revolution of the Young Turks in 1908, which inspired the growth of nationalistic literature. Playwriting was greatly stimulated in 1914 by André Antoine, who came from his Théâtre-Libre in Paris to found Istanbul's Municipal Theatre and Drama School. Among the many playwrights producing popular work during that period were Musahipzade Celâl (1870–1959), who wrote a historical tragedy but excelled particularly in writing comedies and musicals that have much local color; Ibnürrefik Ahmet Nuri [Sekizinci] (1874–1935), whose dramas included adaptations of Western works as well as vaudevilles; and Cevat Fehmi Başkut (1905–), a journalist who wrote many light comedies, the most popular of which, *Paydos* (1948), was revived in the 1960's.

The development of modern drama, briefly impeded by World War I, was accelerated when Turkey became a republic in 1923. Since then the Turkish theatre has flourished, particularly under Muhsin Ertuğrul, the head and artistic director of the Istanbul Municipal Theatre in the years 1927–47 and 1959–65. Turkish plays deal with perennially popular topics: triangles, romance, marriage, and other topics that reflect audiences' interest in social reform, personal integrity, the generation gap, the role of Turkish women, city versus small-town life, kismet, dreams and psychoanalysis, and history and legend. Among notable later playwrights are Reşat Nuri Güntekin (1886–1956), who dramatized his own novels and wrote original comedies and sentimental plays; and Nazım Hikmet Ran (1901–63), a revolutionary poet who escaped to Russia in 1951 after winning the Moscow Peace Prize and wrote folk plays, a dramatization of Joseph's struggle with Pharaoh as a strike play against the labor-exploiting monarch, SURREALISTIC political farce, and comedies. The poet Ahmet Kutsi Tecer (1901–67) is notable for his sometimes comic SLICE OF LIFE verse drama about an Istanbul coffeehouse area, *Köşebaşı* (*The Neighborhood,* 1947), the first Turkish play to be produced in America (at the University of Wisconsin, 1952).

In most recent times Turkish theatre as well as drama has developed considerably. With the opening of many new theatres and the formation of road companies that bring their fares to the villages, the theatre industry has thrived. The drama, too, has taken new directions: subject matter derived from international and cosmopolitan as well as local sources has made plays more varied, with increasing numbers of farces and popular political satires. Among the more recent successful playwrights are Nazım Kurşunlu (1911–), who has written entertaining social-protest dramas; Aziz Nesin (1915–), author of comedies, including *Bir şey yap Met* (*Do Something, Met,* 1964), which has been produced abroad; Haldun Taner (1916–), whose big hit, *Keşanlı Ali destanı* (1962), features a small-time crook; Necati Cumalı (1921–), who has dramatized folklore in popular farces such as *Nalınlar* (1962); Orhan Asena (1921–), among whose popular plays is *Hürrem Sultan* (1959); Refik Erduran (1928–), who has attempted to bring people together with drama meant to appeal to the masses as well as to intellectuals; Hidayet Sayın (1929–), a physician and social crusader, especially for the education of the masses; Adalet Ağaoğlu (1929–), who from her female view-

* Nicholas N. Martinovitch's *The Turkish Theatre* (1933) is a book-length description with illustrations of these forms.

point daringly portrayed women's repression in the controversial comedy *Evcilik oyunu* (1964); Güngör Dilmen (1930–), whose dramas include *Midas'ın kulakları* (1965); Turgut Özakman (1930–), whose plays depict urban problems; and Güner Sümer (1936–), also an actor and director, who as a playwright consciously follows the model of ANTON CHEKHOV.

Turkish drama is not readily available in English translation, but these and other playwrights and their works are described in Metin And's comprehensive *A History of Theatre and Popular Entertainment in Turkey* (1963–64).

TWELVE-POUND LOOK, THE, a one-act comedy by JAMES M. BARRIE, produced in 1910 and published in 1914. Setting: contemporary London.

This popular and frequently revived playlet depicts a bumptious businessman about to be knighted. Accidentally he meets his first wife, now a typist. She reveals that she left him, not for another man, but because she could not stand his smug quest for success. She waited until she could earn twelve pounds to buy a typewriter, and then ran off and became a worker. He is momentarily piqued by her failure to admire him, and his morning is soon spoiled again. His intimidated second wife, noticing how contented and alive the typist looked, asks if typewriters are expensive. Briefly, he senses in her, too, "the twelve-pound look."

27 WAGONS FULL OF COTTON AND OTHER ONE-ACT PLAYS (1946, 1953), a collection of eleven (thirteen in the later edition) plays by TENNESSEE WILLIAMS. Some of these are sketches for the major plays. Among the one-acters are the duologue *Something Unspoken* (the curtain-raiser for SUDDENLY LAST SUMMER), a mood piece of loneliness, portraying the love-hate relationship of an aggressive, socially prominent spinster and her long-time, dependent secretary, a widow; *Lord Byron's Love Letter,* a wistful tale (made into an opera by Raffaello de Banfield in 1955) of old women eking out a pitiful living in New Orleans by displaying the letter of the title; and the book's title play (produced on Broadway in 1955), a bawdy portrayal of the mean and selfish owner of a cotton gin who gratifies his monstrously fat, immature, and indolent wife's masochistic-erotic cravings, burns down a rival cotton gin, and, as he processes the additional twenty-seven wagons of cotton, has the wife entertain the arson's victim—who gets his vengeance by brutally raping the compliant wife. Williams reworked and combined this play with another one-acter about the same couple, *The Long Stay Cut Short; or, The Unsatisfactory Supper* (published in Margaret Mayorga's *The Best One Act Plays of 1945* and in Williams's *American Blues,* 1948); together and enlarged, these two one-acters became a popular film, *Baby Doll* (1956).

TWILIGHT or *crepuscolari* drama, like that of the almost identical *intimisti* school, are subdued and dreamy early twentieth-century Italian plays that reflect disillusionment with sensuality and pleasure. The movement was a reaction to both GABRIELE D'ANNUNZIO and World War I, and, like VERISM and the theatre of the GROTESQUE, a manifestation of the serious new Italian drama. Its major practitioners were FAUSTO MARIA MARTINI and Cesare Vico Lodovici (1885–), a translator of Shakespeare and the author of ANTON CHEKHOV-inspired drama such as *L'Incrinatura o Isa dove vai?* (1937).

TZARA, Tristan (1896–1963), Franco-Rumanian poet and playwright, was a major founder of DADAISM in Zürich in 1916, where he had migrated from his native Rumania at the start of World War I. Eventually he moved to Paris, where he remained the movement's chief spokesman and theoretician. Among his extant dada plays is *La Cœur à gaz* (THE GAS HEART, 1920). His various pronouncement on dadaism were published in *Sept Manifestes dada* (1924).

U

ULRICH VON LICHTENSTEIN, a comedy in four acts by GERHART HAUPTMANN, published and produced in 1939. Setting: thirteenth-century Italy.

This is a rhymed-verse dramatization of a medieval legend: Ulrich, a capering nobleman who lusts for his young niece as well as the duchess whom she serves, eventually is tricked to bed with his own wife during a masked ball.

UNAMUNO [y Jugo], **Miguel de** (1864–1936), Spain's distinguished philosopher-poet-novelist, was also a dramatist. His dozen plays were meant to be—and most of them actually were—staged. Nonetheless, Unamuno's accomplishments as a dramatist were minor, both artistically and commercially. The most popular of his works to appear on the boards was an adaptation (1925; by Julio de Hoyos, 1882–) of one of Unamuno's *Tres novelas ejemplares* (1920), *Nada menos que todo un hombre*—the story of an almost superhumanly willful man defeated only by death. Unamuno's stage works include the adaptation of another novella (*Tulio Montalbán y Julio Macedo,* 1920), featuring a split personality, *Sombras de sueño* (1930); modernizations and adaptations of the classics, *Fedra* (1918) and Seneca's *Medea* (1933); *La esfinge* (1909); *La difunta* (*The Dead Wife,* 1910), a *sainete; La venda* (1921), which deals with problems of faith; *El pasado que vuelve* (1923), which traces a family through four generations; two plays on loneliness and frustrated maternity, *Raquel encadenada* (1926) and the posthumous *Soledad* (written in 1929, produced in 1953); *El otro* (1932), on the Cain-Abel theme; and a PIRANDELLian Don Juan play written in 1929, *El Hermano Juan o el mundo es teatro.*

UNATTAINABLE, THE, a farce in three acts by SOMERSET MAUGHAM, produced in 1916 and published in 1923. Setting: a contemporary Regent's Park drawing room on an early summer day.

This play was originally produced as *Caroline* and successfully revived in midcentury.

Thirty-five-year-old Caroline Ashley has long been separated from her husband. When word comes of his death in Nairobi, her meddlesome friends naturally expect Caroline to marry the middle-aged lawyer she loves, her suitor for the past ten years. But though pressured, neither really wants to give up comfort and romance for marriage. Miffed to discover his reluctance to marry her, Caroline proposes to a younger suitor. This one becomes miserable at the thought of exchanging a passion that is hopeless—and therefore most gratifying—for marriage. Unhappy that no man wants to marry her and troubled by approaching middle age, Caroline proposes to her urbane elderly doctor. He resolves her problems by publicly proclaiming her husband's death report erroneous. Again safely "unattainable" and therefore appealing to men, Caroline is happy. "I am young. I am beautiful. I am desired," she exclaims, and the lawyer embraces her: "Caroline, I adore you."

UNCLE VANYA (*Dyadya Vanya*), "Country Life Scenes in Four Acts" by ANTON CHEKHOV, published in 1897 and produced in 1898. Setting: a contemporary Russian estate.

Chekhov incorporated major sections of THE WOOD DEMON verbatim into this revision of the older drama. His changes and cuts, however, sharpened the diffused original into a play that Chekhov could rightly call entirely new. These changes, including the new ending substituted for Vanya's suicide, illustrate Chekhov's growing mastery of playwriting and make this one of his major works. Sergei Rachmaninov orchestrated Sonya's concluding speech of the play.

Act I. The arrival of Aleksandr Serebryakov, an old retired art professor, and his beautiful young wife, Yelena, upsets the estate's routine. Ivan Voinitsky—Uncle Vanya—the gentle and hard-working brother of the professor's first wife, runs her estate with his kind and simple niece, Sonya, Serebryakov's daughter. But now Vanya is disillusioned with the scholarly brother-in-law he has worked so hard for and used to admire, and sees him for what he really is: a conceited "dried mackerel," a pedant who can only chew over other people's thoughts. Sonya loves the idealistic if disillusioned Mikhail Astrov (the "wood demon" of the earlier play), an overworked doctor who becomes enamored of Yelena—as does Vanya.

Act II. Suffering from gout and disappointment —"I want to live, I love success, I love fame, applause," he admits—Serebryakov exhausts everyone with his selfish demands. Yelena rebuffs the advances of Vanya, who feels old and regrets not having married her when he knew her ten years before. Sonya indirectly confesses her love to Astrov, who, however, does not grasp her true meaning. Then she at last becomes friendly with Yelena, who assures her that she did not marry Sonya's father for gain: "I was infatuated with him as a learned and famous man," a feeling she mistook for love. Now she is bored and unhappy. Led on by Sonya's praise of Astrov, who "heals the sick and plants woodlands," she enthusiastically expatiates on his virtues. After this harmonious talk Yelena yearns to play the piano. But the professor, in another room, is irritated by music and does not allow it.

Act III. Unhappy because she is not beautiful, Sonya agrees to have Yelena find out whether Astrov loves her. Yelena's interrogation confirms his indifference to Sonya. But Astrov suddenly sees through Yelena. "You darling bird of prey," he exclaims, "you must have victims!" He has given up work since her arrival in order to be near her, he admits, "and this you like hugely!" He takes her in his arms, but Vanya's entrance interrupts the embrace. Later, Serebryakov holds a family meeting to announce his plans: he wants to sell the estate so that he can afford to live in town. Vanya is appalled by the thought of losing his and Sonya's home, the estate he has managed for beggarly wages and without thanks for twenty-five years. "All our thoughts and feelings belonged to you alone. . . . My life is lost to me! I am talented, intelligent, brave," he continues in near hysterics: "Had I lived a normal life, there might have come out of me a Schopenhauer, a Dostoevsky." After he rushes out, the others succeed in persuading Serebryakov to go and make it up with Vanya. A shot is heard, and Serebryakov runs in, followed by Vanya, who shoots at—and misses—him again. Vanya drops down in despair as Yelena cries out, "Take me away, kill me, but . . . I cannot stay here, cannot!"

Act IV. Astrov wistfully kisses Yelena farewell; he sees the necessity of their parting: "Everyone who worked here . . . had to drop work and for the entire summer they occupied themselves with your husband's gout and you. Both of you—he and you—infected us with your idleness." Astrov leaves to resume his work, and Vanya, who had contemplated suicide, sadly returns to the accounts he and Sonya have neglected so long. Though her life, too, has been ruined, Sonya courageously comforts Vanya in a moving final speech: "What can we do? We must go on living! . . . We'll patiently bear the trials fate sends us; we'll work for others." And after death, she devoutly concludes, "we shall be happy and will look back tenderly with a smile on these misfortunes we have now—and we shall rest!"

UNDER MILK WOOD, "a play for voices" by DYLAN THOMAS, published and produced in 1954. Setting: night dreams and a contemporary spring day in the coastal town of Llareggub, Wales.

Parts of this lyrical "radio play," written for the BBC but subsequently (1957) produced on Broadway,* were published as "Llareggub, a Piece for Radio Perhaps" (1952) and given a concert reading (with Thomas himself taking several of the parts) in 1953. It grew out of a short story, "Quite Early One Morning," and was completed a few weeks before his death. Gossamer and full of life and gaiety, *Under Milk Wood* begins with dream vignettes (not unlike those of Wilder's OUR TOWN) of the villagers. Continuity is provided by two narrators, the first of whom opens the play.

"To begin at the beginning: It is Spring, moonless night in the small town . . ." A blind old sea captain's dreams and evocations of his drowned shipmates are followed by those of a dressmaker and her lover. A twice-widowed jade dreams of her husbands, who "dust the parlour and spray the canary," "put on rubber gloves and search the peke for fleas." The village awakens and there follow episodes of children at play, love affairs, and village gossip. At last night falls, "a breeze from the creased water sighs the streets close under Milk waking Wood" and, the narrator concludes, "the suddenly wind-shaken wood springs awake for the second dark time this one Spring day."

* For a book-length history of the play and analyses of textual variants in its eleven extant versions, see Douglas Cleverdon's *The Growth of Milk Wood* (1969).

UNDERPANTS, THE (*Die Hose*), a comedy in four acts by CARL STERNHEIM, published and produced in 1911. Setting: a town in Germany, c. 1910.

Also translated as *A Pair of Drawers* and as *The Bloomers,* the then-shocking title of the play had to be changed for the premiere. As *Der Riese* ("the giant") it launched *Aus dem bürgerlichen Heldenleben* (*Scenes from the Heroic Life of the Middle Class*), a cycle of comedies satirizing the hypocrisy of bourgeois life. Clipped, early-EXPRESSIONIST language reflects the cliché mentality of its middle-class characters. The fortunes of the Maske family are continued in the play's sequels.†

Theobald Maske, a petty official, castigates Luise, his attractive young wife. While watching a procession, she disgraced them by losing her bloomers on the crowded street. The public mishap attracted two men: a sickly barber and a raving poet. To be near her, each man rents a furnished room from Maske. Luise repulses the advances of the barber, but indulging her daydreams, the bored wife eagerly responds to the poet. Afraid of real emotion, however, the poet escapes to his room and idealizes his love by composing a poem about it. His self-confidence is shaken by Luise's husband. In a session with his boarders, Maske smugly proclaims his philistine ignorance and his lack of interest in books, which are merely "the opinions of other people." Considering his life anything but "empty and tragic," as the poet maintains, Maske admits indulging "without inhibitions in my inclinations." The poet, an admirer of Nietzsche, regains his equanimity by idealizing a prostitute. Maske rents the poet's room to a new boarder, and fleeces the broken-down barber, a romantic Wagner enthusiast. "The giant" common man of the future, the vulgar Maske is successful even in love. While Luise goes to church, he brings passion to the spinster who comes by with Luise's new bloomers. Seducing her, he remarks that "I do such things very much in secret. And not often, though with great pleasure." Luise returns from church,

† See THE SNOB.

reconciled to dull domesticity. Complacently Maske tells her that now, because of the money he has made from his boarders attracted by her mishap, "I can give you a child." He settles down with his newspaper as Luise cooks dinner and mechanically answers his comments on world happenings, which he finds "repulsive."

UNITED STATES. Modern drama and theatre developed in this country much later than elsewhere in the Western world, not only because the American nation was late in coming into being but also because no matter how fiercely cherished their newly won political independence, Americans continued to feel dependent culturally upon England and western Europe throughout much of the nineteenth century. Before the Civil War, native drama had no artistic stature: the only literarily significant play was a romantic verse tragedy on a much-dramatized theme, George Henry Boker's *Francesca da Rimini* (1855). Indigenous themes and characters appeared rarely: principally in "Indian" drama, in a few comedies (the best of which was Anna Cora Mowatt's *Fashion,* 1845), and in two long-popular melodramas, W. H. Smith's *The Drunkard* (1844) and George L. Aiken's *Uncle Tom's Cabin* (1852). Immediately following the Civil War—by which time HENRIK IBSEN's great early drama had already appeared—the actor Joseph Jefferson toured his *Rip Van Winkle,* a popular vehicle until he died in 1905. Much of the later nineteenth-century American theatre consisted of such inanely amusing, melodramatic, or romantic star vehicles, including those of DENMAN THOMPSON and the adaptation of Alexander Dumas's *The Count of Monte Cristo* (1883) by the actors Charles Fechter (1824–79) and James O'Neill (1846–1920), the father of America's first major playwright, EUGENE O'NEILL.

It was only with O'Neill, after World War I, that native drama first achieved international or even national stature. America had no *fin de siècle* art movement similar to the Théâtre-Libre, the Freie Bühne, the Moscow Art Theatre, or England's Independent Theatre. Insofar as was possible in a vast and decentralized nation, America's post-Civil War theatre before O'Neill was dominated in turn by three dramatist-managers: the Irish-born Dion Boucicault (1822–90), whose distinctively American melodramas (his career was divided between England and the United States) include long-time hits such as *The Poor of New York* (1857) and *The Octoroon* (1859); AUGUSTIN DALY, who is remembered for his *Under the Gaslight* (1867) and his internationally famous company; and DAVID BELASCO, whose collaborations with JOHN LUTHER LONG furnished librettos for popular Giacomo Puccini operas. Among late-nineteenth-century hits, particularly notable are Frank H. Murdoch's (1843–72) frontier melodrama *Davy Crockett* (1872); stock favorites such as Bartley Campbell's (1843–88) *My Partner* (1879) and *The White Slave* (1882); the farces of EDWARD HARRIGAN (of the Harrigan and Hart team), CHARLES H. HOYT, and GEORGE ADE; Edward M. Alfriend (1843–1901) and A. C. Wheeler's (1835–1903) detective thriller *The Great Diamond Robbery* (1895); and the work of WILLIAM GILLETTE and of CLYDE FITCH, who was the most popular turn-of-the-century playwright. Despite some successful farces, WILLIAM DEAN HOWELLS failed as a serious playwright (even in collaboration with Mark Twain), as did HENRY JAMES and JAMES A. HERNE, who reaped his fortune with a potboiler. Esteemed as important writers were BRONSON HOWARD, AUGUSTUS THOMAS, and WILLIAM VAUGHN MOODY, who for a while seemed destined to be America's first great playwright. Many of these dramatists did feature distinctively native types and themes, but they failed to transcend pedestrian writing that adhered to pat formulas and audience expectations. However advanced their scenic REALISM, these writers eschewed comparably "realistic" depictions of people and social problems.

The twentieth century did not usher in such a new and long-overdue drama. The popular plays were those of GEORGE M. COHAN and GEORGE BROADHURST; tear-jerking melodrama such as Lillian Mortimer's (? –1946) *No Mother to Guide Her* (1904), Manners's PEG O' MY HEART (1912), Jean Webster's (1877–1916) *Daddy Long-Legs* (1914), and Catherine Chisholm Cushing's (? –1952) *Pollyana* (1916), the dramatization of Eleanor H. Porter's novel; bedroom farces such as Salisbury Fields (? – ?) and Margaret Mayo's (d. 1951) *Twin Beds* (1914) and James Montgomery's (1882–1966) *Nothing But the Truth* (1916), which resembles Cohan's SEVEN KEYS TO BALDPATE; crime melodrama (with which ELMER RICE gained his first fame, at this time) such as Bayard Veiller's (1869–1943) *Within the Law* (1912) and *The Thirteenth Chair* (1916); and EUGENE WALTER's PROBLEM PLAYS. More interesting were comedies such as Mitchell's THE NEW YORK IDEA, George C. Hazelton (1868–1921) and J. Harry Benrimo's (1875–1942) poetic romance *The Yellow Jacket* (1912), Eleanor Gates's (1876–1951) dramatic fairy tale *The Poor Little Rich Girl* (1913), and the plays of EDWARD SHELDON, RACHEL CROTHERS, JOSEPHINE PRESTON PEABODY, and PERCY MACKAYE, who dealt with artistic as well as with personal and social problems. It was not, however, until the founding of the Provincetown Players, the Washington Square Players, and the Theatre Guild in the second decade of the century—and the work of actor-director-dramatists such as GEORGE CRAM COOK, SUSAN GLASPELL, LAWRENCE LANGNER, and PHILIP MOELLER—that America entered the mainstream of modern drama.

These groups produced new native writers—most notably O'Neill—and they brought the works of great European playwrights to America. It is difficult to overestimate their influence, though they existed apart from the commercial Broadway theatre. Like the 47 Workshop of Professor George Pierce Baker at Harvard, and other university projects, these groups made native drama viable and artistically respectable. Beginning with BEYOND THE HORIZON in 1920, O'Neill's plays changed from

The Wharf Theatre in Provincetown, Massachusetts. The plays of EUGENE O'NEILL were launched in this converted Cape Cod fishhouse by the Provincetown Players in 1916. (*Brown Brothers*)

Greenwich Village SUCCÈS D'ESTIME to commercial Broadway hits. Though Nichols's ABIE'S IRISH ROSE was one of the age's greatest successes, other Broadway hits surpassed the artificial and superficial drama of earlier times, tailor-made merely to demonstrate comforting but questionable moral truisms about individuals and society. In addition to romantic fantasies such as Balderston and Squire's BERKELEY SQUARE, the melodrama of AUSTIN STRONG and EDWARD CHODOROV, the horseplay of Bacon and Smith's LIGHTNIN' and of that longtime sex queen MAE WEST, the 1920's saw the emergence not only of O'Neill but also of PHILIP BARRY, GEORGE KELLY, MARC CONNELLY, OWEN DAVIS, JAMES FORBES, ZOË AKINS, SOPHIE TREADWELL, MARTIN FLAVIN, PRESTON STURGES, DAN TOTHEROH, EDWIN JUSTUS MAYER, and the dramatists who in the next decade united as The Playwrights' Company to produce high-standard drama: MAXWELL ANDERSON, S. N. BEHRMAN, SIDNEY HOWARD, Rice, and ROBERT E. SHERWOOD.

LILLIAN HELLMAN was the first new talent to emerge in the 1930's, and soon the Theatre Union, the Group Theatre (an offshoot of the Theatre Guild), and the WPA's Federal Theatre Project produced AGITPROP and other protest dramas by left-wing playwrights—including another important writer, CLIFFORD ODETS. MICHAEL GOLD and the Lithuanian-born Emjo Basshe (1898–1939) had organized, as early as 1926, the New Playwrights group, which included JOHN HOWARD LAWSON and JOHN DOS PASSOS. *Pins and Needles* (1937), a long-running and periodically refurbished labor union revue with music and satirical lyrics by Harold Rome and sketches by a group including MARC BLITZSTEIN and ARTHUR ARENT, was put on by labor's I.L.G.W.U. players. Others who wrote for such groups included PAUL SIFTON, E. P. CONKLE, ALBERT BEIN, JOHN WEXLEY, ROBERT ARDREY, ALBERT MALTZ, and GEORGE SKLAR. Some of them later succeeded with different kinds of drama; yet, however limited their activities, the left-wing movement is historically significant for the purpose and vigor it brought to the American theatre.

Within another restrictive setting was the equally vital emerging verse drama—by Anglo-Americans such as T. S. ELIOT and W. H. AUDEN as well as by native playwrights such as Anderson (who had become famous with WHAT PRICE GLORY?, a rowdy war play written with LAURENCE STALLINGS) and poets such as EDNA ST. VINCENT MILLAY, E. E. CUMMINGS, ROBINSON JEFFERS, and ARCHIBALD MACLEISH. More popular theatrical distractions just before World War II were the plays of PAUL OSBORN; Samson Raphaelson's (1899–   ) *Accent on Youth* (1934), a comedy about a playwright and the theatre; William Joyce Cowen (1888?–1964) and his wife's (Lenore Coffee, ? – ?) *Family Portrait* (1939), an unusual drama in which Jesus never appears though the impact of his life and death on his family is vividly portrayed; Victor Wolfson's (1910–   ) *Excursion* (1937), a sentimental play about people's temptation to avoid reality by going to a magic island while crossing on a Harlem-Coney Island ferry; and the madcap *Hellzapoppin* (1938), a long-running revue by Ole Olsen (1892–1963) and Chic Johnson (1891–1962).

The critics EDMUND WILSON, CHANNING POLLOCK, and ALEXANDER WOOLLCOTT; novelists such as THEODORE DREISER, THOMAS WOLFE, GERTRUDE STEIN, and F. Scott Fitzgerald (1896–1940), who wrote the satiric drama *The Vegetable* (1923); the short-story writers DAMON RUNYON, WILLIAM CARLOS WILLIAMS, and CONRAD AIKEN; and the humorist Ring Lardner (1885–1933), who wrote dramatic sketches and a loose adaptation (with GEORGE S. KAUFMAN) of his "Some Like Them Cold" (1921), *June Moon* (1924)—all these were not very successful as playwrights. But one of the greatest hits of all times was Kirkland's 1933 adaptation of Caldwell's novel TOBACCO ROAD, and novelists and short-story writers who did succeed as playwrights include ZONA GALE, ROSE FRANKEN, EDNA FERBER, JESSE LYNCH WILLIAMS (author of the first Pulitzer Prize play), SINCLAIR LEWIS, JOHN STEINBECK, and WILLIAM SAROYAN. The philosopher Ayn Rand's (1905–) *The Night of January 16* (1935) was a hit mystery drama; John O'Hara (1905–70) published some unproduced plays and wrote the libretto for *Pal Joey* (1940), the Richard Rodgers and Lorenz Hart hit musical based on O'Hara's collection of stories about "a tap-dancing heel"; and Louis O. Coxe (1918–) and Robert Chapman (1919–) made a notable dramatization of Herman Melville's 1891 novella, *Billy Budd* (1950). The novelist Bruce Jay Friedman (1930–) achieved popular success with a stage farce (*Scuba Duba,* 1967) and critical esteem with a comic religious allegory (*Steambath,* 1970), but Norman Mailer (1923–) with *The Deer Park* (1967) and Joseph Heller (1923–) with *We Bombed in New Haven* (1968) were less adept at converting their novelistic aptitudes to the drama. Other novelists who wrote for the stage include CARSON MCCULLERS, ERNEST HEMINGWAY, JULIEN GREEN, ROBERT PENN WARREN, WILLIAM FAULKNER, TRUMAN CAPOTE, HERMAN WOUK, and Saul Bellow (1915–), whose *The Last Analysis* reached Broadway in 1964. The well-known humorist and cartoonist Jules Feiffer (1929–) wrote a number of comedies, notably *Little Murders* (1967).

Though leg shows and frothy comedies continued to attract large audiences, so too did the plays of the serious dramatists cited above—and others, major writers such as THORNTON WILDER and lesser playwrights such as SIDNEY KINGSLEY, ARTHUR KOBER, and CLARE BOOTHE. Some regional authors (LULA VOLLMER, DOROTHY and DUBOSE HEYWARD, HATCHER HUGHES, and LYNN RIGGS) were produced on Broadway, and the pageant drama of MacKaye, PAUL GREEN, and KERMIT HUNTER attracted mass audiences in the South and elsewhere. Popular drama was produced by collaborators such as BEN HECHT and CHARLES MACARTHUR, GEORGE ABBOTT and PHILIP DUNNING (and JOHN CECIL HOLM and others), novelists BOOTH TARKINGTON and HARRY LEON WILSON, AVERY HOPWOOD and MARY ROBERTS RINEHART, Kaufman and MOSS HART (and others), JEROME LAWRENCE and ROBERT E. LEE, JEROME CHODOROV and JOSEPH FIELDS, ELLIOT NUGENT and the humorist James Thurber (1894–1961), and John Murray (1906–) and Allen Boretz (1900–), whose 1937 farce hit *Room Service,* set in a seedy Times Square hotel and featuring a preposterous assortment of characters, was revived on Broadway in 1953 and 1970, and filmed twice (with the Marx Brothers in 1938 and as the musical *Step Lively* in 1944).

The popular World War II and postwar fare was comedy and musicals. JOSHUA LOGAN's dramatization of *Mister Roberts* (1948) became one of the most successful comedies about the war. Other comedies were those of BELLA and SAM SPEWACK, MARY COYLE CHASE's invisible-rabbit play *Harvey,* GARSON KANIN's *Born Yesterday,* and such long-running hits as Lindsay and Crouse's LIFE WITH FATHER and JOSEPH O. KESSELRING's *Arsenic and Old Lace.* EMMET LAVERY, previously an author of religious drama, succeeded with a biographical play, as WILLIAM W. HAINES did with his World War II drama. Musicals, America's most distinctive contribution to Western drama, developed from the crude spectacle of Charles M. Barras's (1820?–73) *The Black Crook* (1866), traditionally cited as the genre's first work, into the hits of OSCAR HAMMERSTEIN II, MORRIE RYSKIND, HOWARD DIETZ, ABE BURROWS, ALAN JAY LERNER, Betty Comden (1919–) and Adolph Green (1918–)—a team notable for such hits as *On the Town* (1944, music by Leonard Bernstein) and *Applause* (1970, music by Charles Strouse)—and their many collaborators. Rodgers and Hammerstein's OKLAHOMA! set new standards for these increasingly lavish musicals, which integrated drama with music and choreography.

The most impressive dramatists to emerge in the 1940's were ARTHUR MILLER and TENNESSEE WILLIAMS, whose work long continued to arouse interest. Miller's DEATH OF A SALESMAN became a controversial modern classic, while Williams's drama, too, left its impact on many later playwrights, including some who appeared in the next decade: WILLIAM INGE, ROBERT ANDERSON, and ARTHUR LAURENTS. O'Neill's reputation grew here and abroad; and the Hacketts' dramatization of THE DIARY OF ANNE FRANK stirred audiences throughout the world. Such playwrights of the 1950's as JOSEPH KRAMM, N. RICHARD NASH, JOHN PATRICK, DORÉ SCHARY, and GORE VIDAL are notable for their popularity rather than for any more lasting contributions to the drama—as are Meyer Levin (1905–) for his 1957 dramatization of his *Compulsion,* a novel about the Loeb-Leopold case of the 1920's; Meredith Willson (1902–) for his long-running musical *The Music Man* (1957), the sentimental treatment of a small-town con man; Morton Wishengrad (1914-63) for his sex and psychiatry drama about a guilt-ridden mother and her deformed child, *The Rope Dancers* (1959); and the perennial crop of harmless erotic comedies by writers such as NEIL SIMON; George Axelrod (1922–), whose hits include *The Seven Year Itch* (1953) and *Will Success Spoil*

Rock Hunter? (1955); and Jean Kerr (1923–), the wife of the drama critic Walter Kerr (1913-), with whom she wrote the musical *Goldilocks* (1958), and whose greatest success was *Mary, Mary* (1961).

Broadway inherited from the radio and television industries writers such as ARCH OBOLER and PADDY CHAYEFSKY. But of greater interest in the 1960's were such Off- and Off-Off-Broadway movements as HAPPENINGS, guerrilla theatre (renascent AGITPROP), and the "Living Theatre" group that redramatized such work as *Frankenstein* and *Antigone* to elicit audience participation in communal social protest. Issues shunned by Broadway were presented in other New York areas, often in the lofts, cafés, and small theatres of Greenwich Village. From the Village cafés came JEAN-CLAUDE VAN ITALLIE, the first internationally successful Off-Off-Broadway playwright; Lanford Wilson (1938–), the most traditional of the group and the first to have his collected plays published (*Balm in Gilead and Other Plays,* 1965); and Sam Shepard (1943–), once considered Off-Off-Broadway's "dean" and notable for his anti-Establishment *Chicago* (1965) and other one-act satires, as well as for his full-length *Operation Sidewinder* (1969), a "comic strip" social-protest play featuring a sacred Hopi Indian rattlesnake that is also a computer created by a mad Air Force scientist.

Other new Off-Broadway playwrights and plays became widely known: LIONEL ABEL and his dramatizations of legend and the Bible; ARTHUR KOPIT and his zany drama; *In White America* (1963), a documentary of Negro life in the United States, by the Princeton historian Martin B. Duberman (1930–); *Hogan's Goat* (1965), a study of an ambitious politician in the Brooklyn of 1890 by another professor, Harvard's William Alfred (1922–); Barbara Garson's (1942–) *MacBird* (1967), a vicious plague-on-both-your-houses satire, in the form of a *Macbeth* parody on President Lyndon Johnson and the Kennedy brothers, and one of the first of many propaganda pieces attacking the Vietnamese war; Rochelle Owens's (1936–) *Futz!* (1967), a depiction of violence and corruption in a hillbilly community incensed by a simpleminded farmer's love affair with his sow; Israel Horovitz's (1939–) *The Indian Wants the Bronx* (1968), in which a foreigner is assaulted by bored New York toughs; Paul Foster's (1932?–) *Tom Paine* (1968), a vigorous experimental ensemble production in which the revolutionist is depicted as an alcoholic, unheroic, real-life analogue to 1960's revolutionists; Mart Crowley's (1936–) very successful tragicomic drama of a group of New York homosexuals, *The Boys in the Band* (1968); and Paul Zindel's (1937–) acclaimed *The Effects of Gamma Rays on Man-in-the-Moon Marigolds* (1964), a play strikingly similar to Williams's THE GLASS MENAGERIE, and whose 1970 Off-Broadway revival won the 1971 Pulitzer Prize.

Some of the great hit musicals of the decade were Isobel Lennart's (? –) *Funny Girl* (1964, music by Jule Styne) about the life of Fanny Brice; Joseph Stein's (1912–) adaptation of SHOLEM ALEICHEM stories, *Fiddler on the Roof* (1964, music by Jerry Bock), which in 1971 set a new record for Broadway's longest running musical; Michael Stewart's (1929–) adaptation of Wilder's THE MATCHMAKER as *Hello, Dolly!* (1965, music by Jerry Herman); Dale Wasserman's (1917–) adaptation of his television play about Cervantes and Don Quixote, *Man of La Mancha* (1965, music by Mitch Leigh); and Lawrence and Lee's adaptation of their earlier dramatization of Patrick Dennis's 1955 farcical novel, *Auntie Mame,* as *Mame* (1966, music by Herman).

Important Off-Broadway musicals were New York's longest-running play—on *and* off Broadway—Tom Jones's (1928–) 1960 adaptation (with music by Harvey Schmidt) of Rostand's THE FANTASTICKS; and Gerome Ragni (1943–) and James Rado's (1940–) "American Tribal-Love Rock Musical" *Hair* (1967, music by Galt MacDermot), whose pandemonium, nudity, obscene language, and anti-Establishment sentiments shocked audiences and which, after the cast of youngsters moved it to Broadway the following year, became a major national and international hit. Symptomatic of new trends was *Oh! Calcutta!* (1969), nudist and other explicit sex sketches by famous contributors including SAMUEL BECKETT, Tennessee Williams, and Kenneth Tynan (1927–), the British drama critic who devised and assembled this "evening of civilized erotic stimulation."

The most important and successful dramatist in the 1960's was EDWARD ALBEE, who graduated from Off-Broadway to national and international fame. Other playwrights who became known during the decade include JACK RICHARDSON, TAD MOSEL, SIDNEY MICHAELS, WILLIAM HANLEY, MURRAY SCHISGAL, WILLIAM GIBSON, FRANK GILROY, and the distinguished poet ROBERT LOWELL. JACK GELBER shocked with THE CONNECTION, his play on a theme (narcotics addiction) that Michael V. Gazzo (1923–) had tackled the previous decade in *A Hatful of Rain* (1955); Henry Denker (1912–), author of the first notable play about the Korean War, *Time Limit!* (1956; written with Ralph Berkey, 1912–), produced dramas about Freud (*A Far Country,* 1961) and Marilyn Monroe (*Venus at Large,* 1962); J. P. DONLEAVY dramatized some of his fiction; James Goldman (1927–) wrote a play about England's Henry II (*The Lion in Winter,* 1966); and Howard Sackler (1928?–) became notable for *The Great White Hope* (1968), a powerful episodic spectacle based on the career of the first Negro world heavyweight champion, Jack Johnson, and the whites' hateful campaign to destroy him and regain the crown.

Negro playwrights and black drama started to become important in the late 1960's. Earlier, white playwrights like O'Neill, Connelly, and Green occasionally had featured blacks; the Heywards' PORGY (1927) became a modern classic as George Gershwin's folk opera, *Porgy and Bess* (1935); and Philip Yordan's (1914–) NATURALISTIC *Anna Lucasta* (1944) was Broadway's first serious hit about Northern urban Negro life. The earliest black playwright whose works were widely produced was LANGSTON HUGHES, and Negro drama was stimulated in the late 1950's and the early 1960's by the productions of LORRAINE HANSBERRY, JAMES BALDWIN, and Ossie Davis (1917–), whose *Purlie Victorious* (1961)—which Peter Udell (1934–) and others made into the musical *Purlie* (1970, music by Gary Geld)—is a slapstick satire on race relations that features a stereotype Negro preacher and trickster. It was with the work of LEROI JONES in the 1960's, however, that black revolutionary drama established its identity. "Black playwrights" were heard from in growing numbers, and their works started to be widely produced in New York and elsewhere in the United States and abroad. Among them are Adrienne Kennedy (1931–), whose *Funnyhouse of a Negro* (1964), an experimental one-acter that dramatizes a sensitive student's nightmares, won the 1964 Obie Distinguished Play Award; Ed Bullins (1935–), who made his reputation with the short "tragicomedy" *The Electronic Nigger* (an assimilated black instructor conducting a college course) in 1968, the year he became editor of the newly founded *Black Theatre* magazine and playwright in residence at The New Lafayette Theatre; Douglas Turner Ward (1931–), an actor who became a notable playwright in 1966 when his first works, the satiric short comedies *Happy Ending* and *Day of Absence,* won the Vernon Rice Drama and the Obie awards, and who was instrumental in launching the Negro Ensemble Company in 1968; Lonne Elder III (1933–), whose first work, *Ceremonies in Dark Old Men* (1969), a highly praised drama about the disintegration and lawlessness of a Harlem family, was the first major production of the Negro Ensemble Company; and Charles Gordone (1925–), who has been hailed as an important new American playwright for his "Black-black comedy" *No Place to Be Somebody* (1969), a violent yet witty "saloon drama" that deals imaginatively with racial as well as personal problems, and that became the first Off-Broadway play to win a Pulitzer Prize.*

Collections and studies of American drama are innumerable; only a few can be cited here, but most of these have extensive bibliographies. For the period through the 1920's the most detailed chronicle is Arthur H. Quinn's two-volume *A History of the American Drama from the Civil War to the Present Day* (revised, 1936). Alan S. Downer's *Fifty Years of American Drama 1900–1950* (1951) and Walter J. Meserve's *An Outline History of American Drama* (1965) are concise surveys. An interesting account, with many contemporary reviews, is Barnard Hewitt's *Theatre U.S.A. 1665–1957* (1959). Critical surveys dealing with more recent drama include Gerald Weales's *American Drama Since World War II* (1962) and *The Jumping-Off Place: American Drama in the 1960's* (1969), and Allan Lewis's *American Plays and Playwrights of the Contemporary Theatre* (revised, 1970). For the period between the two world wars, Joseph Wood Krutch's *The American Drama Since 1918* (revised, 1957) is particularly informative. In addition to the works cited in individual entries, there are many studies of specialized topics, including Harold Clurman's *The Fervent Years: The Story of the Group Theatre and the Thirties* (revised, 1957); Cecil M. Smith's *Musical Comedy in America* (1950) and David Ewen's *The Complete Book of the American Musical Theater* (revised, 1970); John L. Toohey's illustrated *A History of the Pulitzer Prize Plays* (1967); W. David Sievers's *Freud on Broadway* (1955); Casper Nannes's *Politics in the American Drama* (1960); and Loften Mitchell's *Black Drama: The Story of the American Negro in the Theater* (1967) and Doris E. Abramson's *Negro Playwrights in the American Theatre: 1925–1959* (1969).

Helen H. Palmer and Jane A. Dyson's *American Drama Criticism* (1967) is a bibliography of reviews and criticisms of individual plays for the years 1890–1965; and an invaluable continuing and up-to-date history is provided in the annual *Best Plays* volumes, beginning with the first "Burns Mantle Yearbook," *The Best Plays of 1919–20,* and containing synopses of each season's new plays and a wealth of other material.

* Anthologies of the works of these and other playwrights, with historical, critical, and bibliographical material, began to be published in the late 1960's: William Couch, Jr.'s *New Black Playwrights* (1968), Bullins's *New Plays from the Black Theatre* (1969), and Clinton F. Oliver's *Contemporary Black Drama from "A Raisin in the Sun" to "No Place to Be Somebody"* (1971).

UNKNOWN, THE, a play in three acts by SOMERSET MAUGHAM, published and produced in 1920. Setting: a village in Kent at the end of World War I.

This is the dramatization of an idea Maugham used in an early novel, *The Hero* (1901). Much of the play is devoted to polemical expressions of orthodox religious and agnostic views. The villagers' differing convictions are exacerbated by the miseries of the war. Audiences were shocked by an anguished character's question: "Who is going to forgive God?"

A returning war hero appalls his pious old parents and his fiancée by the loss of his childhood faith. The father, momentarily frightened by the sudden imminence of his death, regains his own belief and comfort at a final Communion. Hoping for a similar transformation in the son, his fiancée tricks him into going to Communion. The trick does not work, and the lovers, hopelessly at odds, part forever.

UNRUH, Fritz von (1885–1970), German novelist, poet, and playwright, was a leading EXPRESSIONIST of the World War I period. He was likened to the romanticist Heinrich von Kleist, from whose military and patriotic values he gradually broke away. Idealistic and lyrical, Unruh's works had a lesser impact than did those of GEORG KAISER and other contemporary expressionists, and he was little known in the English-speaking world. Yet he wrote nearly a dozen plays that in their day enjoyed considerable esteem.

The son of a Prussian general, Unruh also became an officer. His first play, *Offiziere* (1911), was one of the great hits of prewar Germany and received a notable production by Max Reinhardt. In the tradition of Kleist's romanticism, it portrays peacetime officers who yearn for the excitement of war and proclaim the ideals of duty and loyalty. It was followed by *Louis Ferdinand Prinz von Preussen* (1913), which again expressed traditional heroic sentiments (here voiced by Frederick the Great's nephew) but in more lyrical and idealistic ways. Unruh found military life increasingly incompatible with his beliefs and literary bent. He resigned his commission, but was called back to fight in World War I.

It was then that he started to use the new expressionist style with which his name is associated. His greatest artistic success was *Ein Geschlecht* (1917), an abstract, poetic, one-act Aeschylean family portrayal set in a graveyard: the mother bears responsibility, guilt, and sorrow for bringing her sons into a world of suffering; their various acts of violence reflect this world, but their and their mother's death presages a better world. *Platz* (1920), a sequel, portrays this better, postwar world in less abstract terms, and culminates in a man's choice of the woman who symbolizes the love on which any future order must be based.

Later Unruh plays include *Heinrich aus Andernach* (1925), a festival play that celebrates peace and evokes the spirit of the unknown soldier; *Bonaparte* (1927), a history play that appeared in English and predicted the advent of German dictatorship; and comedies such as *Phaea* (1930), about the film industry, and *Zero* (1932), about gambling. His remaining works were less successful. They include another history play, *Charlotte Corday* (1936); and comedies such as *Bismark oder Warum steht der Soldat da?* (1955), which is set in St. Petersburg, where Bismarck served in 1859.

When the Nazis came to power, Unruh declined their offer to make him the national poet. Instead, he emigrated and spent the World War II years in the United States. He returned to Germany after the war. But though he continued to write, he never reestablished his preeminence.

His works include travel books, novels, poems, and an autobiography, *Des Sohn des Generals* (1957). Among the few works that were translated is a pacifist narrative written in 1916 during the battle over Verdun, *Opfergang* (*The Way of Sacrifice,* 1918). His life and work are discussed in W. F. Mainland's essay on Unruh in Volume II of Alex Natan's *German Men of Letters* (1964).

UNTO THESE HILLS, "a drama of the Cherokee" in two acts by KERMIT HUNTER, produced in 1950 and published in 1951. Setting: the Great Smokies; Washington, D.C.; Georgia; and Alabama; 1811–1842.

Like Green's THE LOST COLONY, this is a vast "symphonic" pageant drama annually presented outdoors for summer visitors at the Mountainside Theatre in Cherokee, North Carolina. It features the Shawnee chief Tecumseh, sundry Cherokee chiefs, and notable whites including Hernando de Soto (in the prologue), Sam Houston, Daniel Webster, and President William Henry Harrison.

The Cherokee Indians struggle against the white men's hostile reluctance to let them remain in their homes and to grant them citizenship. Chief Junaluska saves Andrew Jackson's life, but various promises to the Cherokees are nonetheless broken treacherously. The Cherokees' calamitous forced trek to Oklahoma (the Trail of Tears) costs the lives of thousands. But Christian fortitude and patience enable the courageous tribe, led by its venerated chiefs, to endure. "I will lift up mine eyes unto the hills," the narrator concludes when Junaluska rejoices over the birth of a great chief's grandchild who "will someday be an American citizen." For that is "the way of peace," without regard to a man's skin color. "This, then, was the dream of the Cherokee. This, then, is America!"

URUGUAY is relatively new and small among LATIN AMERICAN nations, and its theatre sometimes is discussed jointly with ARGENTINA's in studies of the River Plate area. Both countries claim as their own South America's greatest playwright, FLORENCIO SÁNCHEZ, as well as the origin of GAUCHO DRAMA, which marks the beginning of the real popularity of Uruguay's theatre and remains significant there to this day. The country's next important dramatist was ERNESTO HERRERA, the successor of Sánchez and, according to some, his equal. Other writers of the early modern period are more identified with nineteenth-century romanticism, and their leading figure in Uruguay was Samuel Blixen (1868–1911). Victor Pérez Petit (1871–1947) distinguished himself with many often-sentimental plays—most of them written in Argentina—including PROBLEM PLAYS, gaucho plays, and comedies. Among other notable playwrights are the Paraguay-born Otto Miguel Cione (1875–1945), who lived mostly in Buenos Aires but became a citizen of Uruguay and wrote well-constructed plays ranging from gaucho to drama of ideas; Carlos Mauricio Pacheco (1881–1924), who also spent much time in Argentina and wrote some seventy *sainetes criollos;* and Vicente Martínez Cuitiño (1887–), a much-traveled theatre man, some of whose Sánchez-inspired tragedies—which include the 1922 prize-winner *Malón blanco, El espectador o la cuarta realidad* (1928), and *Diamantes quebrados* (1934)—were directed by JACINTO BENAVENTE and provided star vehicles for South American and Spanish actors.

A number of Uruguayan diplomats and politicians also became playwrights. These include the prolific Edmundo Bianchi (1888–), whose plays won national prizes in the 1930's and 1940's; Justino Zavala Muñiz (1898–), the author of novels and NATURALIST tragedies; and Juan León Bengoa (1895–), a lawyer whose drama often deals with historical themes and whose *La patria en armas* (1950) was particularly successful. Among dramatists who gained recognition in midcentury were Fernán Silva Valdés (1887–), a notable poet in the 1920's who emerged as a dramatist with the portrayal of the gaucho minstrel *Santos Vega* (1952) and with other history and legend as well as modern plays; and Héctor Plaza Noblía (1924–), whose somewhat static cerebral drama includes *Alcestes o la risa de Apolo* (1955), in which the protagonist evades reality by creating an imaginary statue of Apollo.

Uruguayan drama and playwrights are discussed in the studies listed under LATIN AMERICA.

USIGLI, Rodolfo (1905–), Mexican poet, critic, theatre director, diplomat, and one of the midcentury's major Latin American dramatists. His plays are often experimental and controversial, ranging from social and political satire to psychological analysis and historical drama. They have appeared abroad more than those of other Spanish-American playwrights, and his *Corona de sombra* (*Crown of Shadows,* 1947) elicited the admiration of BERNARD SHAW. Considered Usigli's masterpiece, it is an antihistorical treatment of a favorite Mexican subject, the relationship of the Emperor Maximilian and the Empress Carlotta (the title refers to the latter's sixty-year madness following Maximilian's execution by Juárez), set in the year of the empress's death (1927) and portrayed in flashbacks.

Usigli's theatre career started when he was yet a child. First to be staged were his translations; his original works met resistance, though one of the earliest, *El niño y la niebla* (1936), a Scribean melodrama on hereditary madness, interlaced with Mexican politics, had record-breaking runs in the 1950's and was filmed. After studying drama in the United States Usigli wrote a tragedy analogous to Pirandello's HENRY IV, *El gesticulador* (*The Gesticulator,* 1937), about a professor who impersonates and then identifies with a revolutionary and is felled by his hero's assassin; considered politically offensive, this play remained unproduced until 1947. *La familia cena en casa* (1943) is a Shavian PROBLEM PLAY *manqué,* suffering from Usigli's penchant for sentimentality. More successful were the later-filmed *Otra primavera* (*Another Spring,* 1938), portraying an old man considered mad but saved by his wife's pretense of insanity; and *Juno es una muchacha* (1952), about a prostitute.

The plays of Usigli were published with prefaces analogous to those of Shaw's, whom he admired. Usigli abandoned his successful career as a dramatist to teach playwriting and help train actors and thus continued materially to elevate Mexico's theatre until he joined the foreign service in 1944.

An excerpt from *Crown of Shadows* appears in Willis Knapp Jones's *Spanish-American Literature in Translation* (1963), and Usigli's drama is discussed also in the studies listed under LATIN AMERICA.

USTINOV, Peter [Alexander] (1921–), English actor, cartoonist, writer, director, film-maker, and playwright, is perhaps better known as a performer and a flamboyant film and theatre personality than as a dramatist. A prolific writer, he is best at sophisticated and witty political satires such as his two very successful plays, THE LOVE OF FOUR COLONELS (1951) and ROMANOFF AND JULIET (1956).

Ustinov's antecedents, though confusingly many (primarily Russian, French, and German), were not English and his nationality was a matter of chance. His journalist father was assigned to London by a German news agency shortly before his artist-wife bore their son. Ustinov grew up in London, attending Westminster School and then the London Theatre Studio. He made his first stage appearance in 1938, and the following year began to play in some of his own sketches and "Diversions," which gained Ustinov critical recognition in 1940: *The Bishop of Limpopoland,* on an old clergyman's boring tales of South African conversions; and *Madame Liselotte Beethoven-Finck,* about an Austrian *Lieder* singer "of horrid appearance and piercing voice." He translated JEAN SARMENT's *Le Pêcheur d'ombres* (1921) as *Fishing for Shadows* (1940) and continued acting until he was inducted into the British army. During his 1942–46 stint his assignments included scriptwriting for a military film unit. After his discharge from the army Ustinov, by then noted as a promising playwright, won further praise as an actor.

His first play, *The House of Regrets,* was publicly praised by James Agate before it was produced in 1942; it is a tragicomic sketch on Russian expatriates in London. The following year appeared *Blow Your Own Trumpet,* a comedy that failed. It was followed by *The Banbury Nose* (1944), a Bennett and Knoblock's "MILESTONES in reverse" that reestablished Ustinov's reputation as a dramatist. His other plays include *The Tragedy of Good Intentions* (1945), a play about the Crusades; *The Indifferent Shepherd* (1948), dealing with a clergyman; *Frenzy* (1948), an adaptation of a Swedish film script by Ingmar Bergen; *The Man in the Raincoat* (1949); *The Moment of Truth* (1951), a SYMBOLIC satire of politics and the military that recalls the fall of France and is in part derived from *King Lear; High Balcony* (1952); *No Sign of the Dove* (1953), a comedy vaguely echoing the Noah legend; *The Empty Chair* (1956); *Paris Not So Gay* (1958), about Paris and Helen; *Photo Finish* (1962), "An Adventure in Biography" about a successful eighty-year-old writer who confronts his various younger selves; *The Unknown Soldier and His Wife* (1967), a light antiwar entertainment whose title characters are prototypes in a series of wars ranging from Roman times through the 1960's; and *Halfway Up the Tree* (1967), a comedy about the generation gap.

Collections of his plays (with introductions by Ustinov) are *Plays About People* (1950), which contains *The Tragedy of Good Intentions, Blow Your Own Trumpet,* and *The Indifferent Shepherd;* and *Five Plays* (1965): *Romanoff and Juliet, The Moment of Truth, The Love of Four Colonels, No Sign of the Dove,* and *Beyond,* a one-act tragicomic sketch of three old men, produced in 1943. Many of these—as well as his fiction and other publications, stage and film appearances, and film scripts—are discussed in Geoffrey Willans's biography, *Peter Ustinov* (1957).

V

VALE OF CONTENT, THE (*Das Glück im Winkel*), a drama in three acts by HERMANN SUDERMANN, produced in 1895 and published in 1896. Setting: a small district seat in North Germany, 1895.

This play, set in Sudermann's native East Prussia, resembles Ibsen's THE LADY FROM THE SEA.

An impoverished and chaste noblewoman, Elizabeth, has married the much older and widowed Georg Wiedemann, a disillusioned but dedicated school principal with three children, and makes them a happy family life. They are visited by a childhood friend and her husband, Freiherr Alfred von Roecknitz, a self-proclaimed "devil of a chap" with a lifelong insatiable lust: "I demand women—I need women—I can't live without women." He pursues the chaste Elizabeth, whom he knew and desired before and who now, in a weak moment, admits she married Wiedemann because she feared she might become unable to conquer her passion for Roecknitz. To have her near him, he makes Wiedemann an attractive offer to work on his estate, and then insists that Elizabeth give in to their passion. Elizabeth steals out of the house to drown herself, but Wiedemann stops her. "I've thrown myself upon his neck, in your own house," she says, confessing why she married Wiedemann: "You were done with your youth, but I was not. In me all was still on fire . . . I was full to the brim of longing." But as she did not deceive him, Wiedemann can understand and forgive. Loving her as much as ever, he consoles her: "The desires will become more still—the longing will go to sleep—every one must resign one's self—even the happiest—And who knows but then there'll be once more some happiness in this old nook of ours." His young wife looks at him with new love: "It seems as if I saw you tonight for the first time."

VALLE-INCLÁN, Ramón María del [originally Ramón del Valle y Peña] (1866–1936), Spanish novelist, poet, essayist, and playwright, was a major figure of the Generation of '98. Likened to GABRIELE D'ANNUNZIO because of his sensual decadence as well as his personal flamboyance, Valle-Inclán was known principally for his fiction. But he also wrote over two dozen plays, some of them more accurately characterized as "dialogued novels." Praised particularly for his brilliant use of language, Valle-Inclán epitomized *fin-de-siècle* aestheticism in Spain with a unique art that he termed *comedia bárbara* ("savage comedy") and ESPERPENTO. Though he subtitled some of his plays with these terms, both characterize others of his plays—such as *Divinas palabras* (DIVINE WORDS, 1820), his first to appear in an English collection during the 1960's, when Valle-Inclán's works began to enjoy a belated revival.

He was born in Villanueva de Arosa, Pontevdra, Galicia, in northwest Spain—the still-primitive and superstitious region that furnishes the settings for much of his drama. Early in life he became a legend with his long beard and hair, picturesque dress, and the romantic tales he cultivated to explain the loss of his arm—in a café brawl with a critic. He married an actress in 1907, practiced law, traveled to Mexico, and at various times supported himself with teaching, journalism, cattle ranching, and theatre management. Much of his life he spent in Madrid, where he was involved in politics and imprisoned (1929) by the Primo de Rivera government. Under the Republic he ran for office and was appointed a museum director and the Curator of National Art.

Valle-Inclán's style underwent major changes from the time he published his first book in 1894: initially morbid and sensual, he ultimately turned to satirizing the popular and the historic. Yet he always reveled in the use of language and style. In his prose no less than his poetry he experimented with the unusual in vocabulary and diction. His plays illustrate this fascination as well as his love of the grotesque, the exotic, the sensual, and the degenerate. Though rooted in the Spanish tradition and given to dramatizing native folk themes, Valle-Inclán became an original precursor of the midcentury ABSURD and other avant-garde movements.

His novelistic *comedias bárbara* trilogy dramatizing the story of the *hidalgo* Don Juan Manuel de Montenegro and his brutal family in a medieval setting of barbarism and lust consists of *Águila de blasón* (1907), *Romance de lobos* (1908), and *Cara de plata* (1922). The plays he labeled *esperpento* are *Luces de Bohemia* (*Lights of Bohemia,* 1920), which in many tableaux depicts the ugliness and brutality of city life as experienced by a poor blind poet who is cheated, manhandled, and dies, though he first rises above his anguish, and is regenerated; as well as *Los cuernos de don Friolera* (1921), *Las galas del difunto* (1930), and *La hija del capitán* (1930). Among his other dramas are the one-act *Comedia de ensueño* (*The Dream Comedy,* 1903), the NATURALIST portrayal of "intimate life episodes" *El yermo de las almas* (1908), the verse play *Cuento de abril* (1910), the sophisticated children's farce *Farsa infantil de la cabeza del dragón* (*The Dragon's Head,* 1910), the verse "pastoral tragedy" on his favorite theme of the

Carlist wars *Voces de gesta* (1911), the grotesque satiric farce *La Marquesa Rosalinda* (1912), the sinister naturalistic tragedy *El embrujado* (1913), and the satire of Isabel II's court, *Farsa y licencia de la reina castiza* (1920). Important in his work (as in MICHEL DE GHELDERODE's) is the use of puppets, and he wrote a number of "melodramas for marionettes" (*La rosa de papel* and *La cabeza del Bautista,* both 1924) and *"autos* for silhouettes" (*Ligazón* and *Sacrilegio,* both 1927).

Divine Words, with a short preface on Valle-Inclán, appears in Michael Benedikt and George E. Wellwarth's *Modern Spanish Theatre* (1968). The first comprehensive introductions in English to his life and work were Anthony N. Zahareas's collection of sixty-three essays (about half of them in Spanish), *Ramón del Valle-Inclán: An Appraisal of His Life and Works* (1968); and Ricardo Gullón's edition of the *Valle-Inclán Centennial Studies* (1968).

VALLEY FORGE, a play in three acts by MAXWELL ANDERSON, published and produced in 1934. Setting: Pennsylvania, 1778.

This prose-and-verse history portrays a frequently discouraged George Washington, whose quest for national independence and freedom falters in the face of apparently hopeless odds. The play's idealism is balanced with NATURALISTIC depictions of the army's suffering during the famous "winter of despair."

Washington's army is freezing and starving at Valley Forge. Confronted with further desertions, Washington tells the men, "This is your fight more than mine"; their fight is for a dream that may be premature, he admits, "and may never come true" at all. At a splendid ball in Sir William Howe's Philadelphia headquarters, the gallant English commander sends Mary Philipse Morris, now married but still regretful about having once spurned Washington's love, to persuade Washington to give up the hopeless fight. He does not tell Mary that he has intercepted France's offer of assistance to the Continental army, an offer that will win their war if Washington persists. In the meantime, Washington asks his commanders whether they should attempt to hold out until spring and brave continued suffering, mass desertions, and the Continental Congress's insultingly flimsy support. Though admittedly "close to faltering," Washington is encouraged by his men (including the Marquis de Lafayette) to persist. He wearily rejects Mary's message—and her invitation to a romantic interlude. As his troops courageously bear their hardships, inspecting government commissioners arrive. Washington soon discovers the Continental Congress's chief concern: trade profits. When he hears of its double-crossing him with peace negotiations, he furiously boots out the commissioners. Though he now despairs, Washington vows to control the peace terms himself. He starts negotiating with Howe. But the soldiers, embued with Washington's earlier spirit, are appalled by thoughts of surrender. Spurred by their faith, Washington tells Howe, "I am servant / to these men in the rags of homespun. They've heard from me / this proposition of the king's, and they / refuse it flatly. This war, to your brief misfortune, / is not mine to end, but theirs." Though their situation looks grim, Washington's faith in the "dream that men / shall bear no burdens save of their own choosing" is restored: "It's destined to win, this dream, / weak though we are. Even if we should fail, / it's destined to win!"

VAN DE VELDE, Anton [Gerard Jozef] (1895–), Belgian playwright, was an important contributor to the Flemish theatre. In his first play, the SYMBOLIC *De Zonderlinge Gast* (1924), a farmer's daughter is gradually captivated by and goes with the title's "strange guest," Death. The religious *Christoffel* (1924) is similarly symbolic but more humorous. Most praised were van de Velde's *Tyl I* (1925) and *Tyl II* (1930), patriotic propaganda pieces characterized by passion and grossness and simultaneously distinguished for their tenderness and wit. Esteemed for his sense of fantasy and humor as well as his intelligence, van de Velde also wrote a play on student life, *Hans Worst* (1938), and some children's drama.

VAN DRUTEN, John [William] (1901 1957), Anglo-American playwright, was born in London, studied law and legal history at London University, and subsequently taught these subjects at University College in Wales. A periodic visitor to the United States, Van Druten settled there in the 1930's and was naturalized in 1944. He is best known for comedies such as I REMEMBER MAMA (1944), BELL, BOOK AND CANDLE (1949), and *The Voice of the Turtle* (1943), a long-running romantic comedy about a soldier on leave. But Van Druten also wrote serious plays, notably I AM A CAMERA (1951), an adaptation of the CHRISTOPHER ISHERWOOD stories. And it was with a serious study of school life and adolescence, *Young Woodley* (1925), that Van Druten first made his reputation as a dramatist; denied a licence in England, this play originally was staged in the United States and published in England as a novel.

Some of Van Druten's plays were filmed, and he himself staged many of them—as well as those of others. Light but intelligent, popular, entertaining, and occasionally quite penetrating, Van Druten's other plays are *The Return Half* (1924), *Chance Acquaintance* (1927), *Diversion* (1928), *The Return of the Soldier* (1928, an adaptation of Rebecca West's novel), *After All* (1929), *London Wall* (1931), *Sea Fever* (1931; an adaptation of MARCEL PAGNOL's *Marius,* written with Auriol Lee, 1881–1941), *There's Always Juliet* (1931; a comedy about the first love of an Englishwoman and an American, also published as a novel), *Hollywood Holiday* (1931, written with BENN W. LEVY), *Somebody Knows* (1932), *Behold, We Live* (1932), *The Distaff Side* (1933, "a comedy of women"), *Flowers of the Forest* (1934), *Most of the Game* (1935), *Gertie Maude* (1937), *Leave Her to Heaven* (1940, a murder drama), *Old Acquaintance* (1940), *Solitaire* (1942, an adaptation of a novel by Edwin Corle),

The Damask Cheek (1942; a period comedy written with Lloyd Morris [1893–1954] and set in New York at the turn of the century), *The Mermaid's Singing* (1945, a comedy that first appeared as *Home Ground*), *The Druid Circle* (1947; originally *Professor White,* another venture into the serious), and *Make Way for Lucia* (1948, a comedy based on E. F. Benson's novels).

Van Druten also wrote several novels and autobiographies. Among the latter are *The Way to the Present* (1938), *The Playwright at Work* (1953), and *The Widening Circle* (1957).

VAN ITALLIE, Jean-Claude (1936–), American playwright, became known in 1966 with *America Hurrah* (1965), a scathing parody of life in the United States. In the most devastating of its three sequences (originally performed by itself as *America Hurrah*) a proprietress describes her motel while two grotesque dummies silently scribble obscene graffiti on its walls, tear the place apart, and finally dismember the speaker. Premiered at Café La Mama in Greenwich Village, it was the first Off-Off-Broadway play to become a hit Off-Broadway and abroad. His next full-length play, the equally avant-garde and largely mimed "ceremony" *The Serpent* (1968), written in collaboration with The Open Theater group, juxtaposes events from Genesis and modern times.

Van Itallie was born in Belgium. He grew up in Long Island and graduated from Harvard University in 1958.

VANE, Sutton [originally Vane Sutton-Vane] (1888–1963), English actor and dramatist, made his name with a single play, OUTWARD BOUND (1923). He was shell-shocked early in World War I and then returned to France to perform with an entertainment troupe behind the lines. Although Vane wrote some ten plays, only *Outward Bound* was successful; originally he financed and helped to stage it himself because commercial producers considered it too odd for them. (*Fear No More* [1946], written by his wife, Diana Hamilton [1897–1951], and CONRAD AIKEN, is a similar drama.) Vane's other plays include *Falling Leaves* (1924); *Overture* (1925); *I'll Tell You a Story* (1925); *Man Overboard* (1931), which traces the course of a river that SYMBOLICALLY represents man; and two plays set in a London pub, *Time, Gentlemen, Please* and *Marine Parade* (both 1935).

VÄRLUND, Rudolf (1900–45), Swedish novelist and playwright, expressed his proletarian sympathies in boldly experimental fiction and drama about contemporary problems. His most successful work as a playwright was influenced by the German EXPRESSIONISM of the 1920's and consists of tragedies: *Vägen till Kanaan* (1932); *Den heliga familjen* (1932), a working-class drama set amidst the struggles of the labor movement; and *U 39* (1939), a psychological study of people in a submarine disaster. Värlund also wrote folk comedy, most notably the bucolic *Sångare* (1933).

VASSA ZHELEZNOVA, a play in three acts by MAXIM GORKY, published in 1910 and produced in 1911. Setting: a wealthy contemporary home in a Russian province.

This is a melodrama, abounding in violence and depravity, about a strife-torn merchant family. It is an excellent example of early twentieth-century NATURALISM, almost a parody of the style. Gorky altered and republished the play in 1936, stressing its "social significance" and toning down the maternal suffering. In the first version (one of the translated *Seven Plays of Maxim Gorky*), the mother sends her crippled son to a monastery after he murders his wife's lover, who is his uncle. Though not above committing crimes for the sake of her family business, Vassa is conscious of sin: "I've done much evil—I've sinned—against worthless people, it's true; all the same—you feel sorry for them after you've bested them." And she suffers: "After all, I'm human—I've done such a thing to my son—my own flesh and blood." In the later, even more melodramatic version of 1936, she commits greater crimes for the sake of the business, and a revolutionary worker, one of her daughters-in-law, becomes the play's heroine.

VAUTHIER, Jean (1910–), French avant-garde playwright, became known in 1956 when Jean-Louis Barrault produced his *Le Personnage combattant* (1955). In what is a monodrama until the end, he portrayed a successful aging writer who attempts to recapture his youthful integrity amidst the objects and noises of the dilapidated hotel room where he started writing; he fails and is destroyed at last by a brutal homosexual hotel employee.

Vauthier's other drama is equally stark, its few characters' agonizing introspection and savage sexual battles reminiscent of Sartre's NO EXIT and Strindberg's THE DANCE OF DEATH. But Vauthier's drama is distinguished by his juxtaposition of the poetic and the colloquial in sometimes grotesque and SYMBOLIC "verbal ballets." Vauthier's other plays include an adaptation of Machiavelli's *La Mandragola* as *La Nouvelle Mandragore* (1952); *Capitaine Bada* (1952), parodically depicting the lifelong quest for the ineffable and the inner struggles of a poet and his sex duels with his flighty wife—a clownish relationship whose continuation in the afterlife Vauthier dramatized in a sequel, *Badadesque* (1965); and *Les Prodiges* (1958), another depiction of sex duels, about a romanticist who finds religious solace after his shallow and murderous mistress leaves him.

Chapters on Vauthier appear in Leonard C. Pronko's *Avant-Garde* (1962) and in Jacques Guicharnaud's *Modern French Theatre* (1967).

VELAND, a verse tragedy in three acts by GERHART HAUPTMANN, published and produced in 1925. Setting: the Sheep Island of antiquity.

Hauptmann took almost three decades to complete this Sophoclean drama, which is based on the Norse *Edda* legends.

Veland, a horrible monster artisan with supernatural powers, is subdued and maimed by the king. In revenge, he kills the king's sons and seduces his daughter. At a gruesome banquet Veland graphically reveals his actions to the king and then flies away on wings he has fashioned for himself.

VENEZUELA after a slow beginning produced some hundred native plays in the last half of the nineteenth century. In the twentieth century a number of significant playwrights appeared on the scene, encouraged by Venezuelan presidents, who were themselves drama buffs, and by various theatre festivals. Eduardo Calcaño (1831–1904) became "the founder of the modern theatre" of Venezuela with his historical drama about a female revolutionary, *Policarpa Salavarrieta* (1891). A pungent "satire in verse against Caudillism," *La República de Caín* (1936), was one of the plays of the politician and scholar Julio Planchart (1885–1948). Leopoldo Ayala Michelena (1897–) was Venezuela's most popular playwright at the time of World War I; his later *Almas descarnadas* (1950), which deals with a father's exposure of his son's selfishness, was selected for Venezuela's 1959 Theatre Festival as his "most representative" play. The novelist-playwright Ramón Díaz Sánchez (1903–) created a furor with his drama on the conflicts of traditional and modern Venezuela, *La casa* (1956, also produced as *Bajo estos aleros*). Often played was *El hombre que se fue* (1938), a social comedy by the Spanish-born Luis Peraza (1908–), whose best work is *Mala siembra* (1940), another comedy that also dramatizes his plea for progressive education.

Among more recent writers, Rafael Angel Díaz Sosa (1926–), a poet educated in the United States and better known as Rafael Pineda, has won prizes for a number of plays, including the violent *Los conjurados* (1950). Venezuela's playwright best known abroad is the diplomat, journalist, and poet Aquiles Certad (1914–); his amusing works have been popular in Buenos Aires, particularly his *Lo que faltaba a Eva* (1943), a high comedy whose title character's "lacks" include two left toes as well as the ability to thrill one suitor and firmly decline the offers of another; and *Cuando quedamos trece* (1944), a drama about a superstitious couple puzzled by the crash of an airplane supposed to bear the husband, who was really out on a fling with his mistress. Also notable are Román Chalbaud (1924–), who became notorious after his plays were criticized on the grounds of politics as well as obscenity; and Isaac Chocrón (1932–), who has been acclaimed for his portrayals of men's inability to communicate and the "inferno" of those incapable of love, as in *El quinto infierno* (1961).

For bibliography see under LATIN AMERICA.

VENUS OBSERVED, a blank-verse play in three acts by CHRISTOPHER FRY, published in 1949 and produced in 1950. Setting: a castle in Stellmere Park, England; the 1940's.

Commissioned by Laurence Olivier after the success of Fry's THE LADY'S NOT FOR BURNING, this is a sophisticated autumnal comedy in the same spirit and style as the earlier play.

The aging Duke of Altair prepares to resign himself to monogamy. He has invited to his castle three beautiful women, former mistresses. While he observes Venus during a solar eclipse, his son is to choose among them, giving an apple (Paris-like) to his mother-to-be. When he is about to do so, the emerging sun's rays fall on a new arrival—Perpetua, the estate agent's lovely daughter. The Duke snatches the apple and proffers it to her, but she pulls out a pistol and shatters it. Later her father urges Perpetua to marry the Duke: as a father-in-law he is not likely to be prosecuted by the Duke, whom he has robbed for years. At a tryst after the enamored Duke instructs Perpetua in archery, she is ready to accept him, when he reveals that he has always known about her father's thievery—and never intended to do anything about it. Perpetua thereupon admits that, despite the Duke's charm, it is a younger man—his son—whom she loves. Just then the castle bursts into flames. It has been set afire by a disappointed former mistress, the only one who really loves the Duke and therefore resents not being chosen. After they are saved from the observatory, the Duke suavely decides to marry her when she completes her prison term for arson. He gives up Perpetua, gracefully accepting his decline. Wrapped in blankets, he sits outside the burned palace with his dishonest bailiff—two rascals in "a unison of ageing."

VERA; OR, THE NIHILISTS, a drama in four acts and a prologue by OSCAR WILDE, privately printed in 1880 and produced in 1883. Setting: Russia, 1795 and 1800.

Wilde's first play was scheduled for production in 1881 because of its topicality after Tsar Aleksandr II's assassination early that year. But he withdrew it, probably in deference to his friendship for the Prince of Wales, who was related to the tsars. The play is sympathetic to the revolutionaries, although the emphasis is on personal conflicts. It is a puerile melodrama, interlarded with fantastic anachronisms and Wildean witticisms spoken by Russia's evil prime minister and others.

Vera, an innkeeper's daughter, joins the Nihilists to avenge her condemned brother. She becomes one of the most feared revolutionaries, but falls in love with the young tsar she is to assassinate. Instead, she stabs herself, and dies in his arms.

VERGA, Giovanni (1840–1922), Italian novelist and playwright, belonged to the VERIST school. He achieved international fame with Pietro Mascagni's opera version (1890) of his *Cavalleria rusticana* (1884), a one-act dramatization of an earlier-published Verga story of the love, adultery, and jealousy of four peasants. This tragedy (one of a number of his works translated by D. H. LAWRENCE) is typical of Verga's writings in its depiction of ferocious passions in rural Sicily, and its despair has been likened to that in the novels of THOMAS HARDY. Thus *In portineria* (1885) portrays a pitiful round robin of unreciprocated love (as in Chekhov's THE SEAGULL), while *La lupa* (1896) and the one-act *La caccia al lupo* (1901) portray the animalistic passions of, respectively, a husband who hatchets his amorous mother-in-law (the title's "she-wolf") and a wife who becomes so enraged by her lover's cowardice when they are discovered that she cheers her husband on to kill him. Among Verga's other notable plays is *Dal tuo al mio* (1903), which depicts the class struggle in the marriage of a worker and a mine-owner's daughter.

Verga was born in Catania. He started his career by writing fiction, and became famous as the author of the novel *I Malavoglia* (1881, translated as *The House by the Medlar Tree*). Though he was principally a writer of stories (some of which he later dramatized) and only a minor playwright, his NATURALISM has a poetic quality rare in such drama and he helped pave the way for the work of LUIGI PIRANDELLO and UGO BETTI.

The collected plays of Verga were published in 1952. They are discussed in Isaac Goldberg's *The Drama of Transition* (1922).

VERHAEREN, Émile (1855–1916), Belgian poet, wrote a number of verse plays, notably *Les Aubes* (*The Dawn,* 1898) and *Le Cloître* (*The Cloister,* 1900). The former, the last work of a trilogy whose earlier parts are sociological poems, depicts urban-rural conflicts and presages a millenium of universal brotherhood and peace. *The Cloister* portrays a monk's masochistic self-denunciation and his consequent ruin when he becomes prior—and the probable ruin of the rebellious monks and their order, symbolically all of society. Verhaeren's other poetic drama reinterprets the reign of *Philippe II* (1904) as that of a morally diseased king and kingdom; and the story of *Hélène de Sparte* (*Helen of Sparta,* 1912) as a tragedy triggered by the incestuous love of Helen's brother Castor, who kills Menelaus and is in turn killed by Electra.

A major European SYMBOLIST poet, known as the Belgian Walt Whitman, Verhaeren was killed in a train-station accident. Among book-length studies of his life and work is the English translation of STEFAN ZWEIG's *Emile Verhaeren* (1914).

VERISM (*Verismo*), a movement in the early twentieth-century Italian theatre that is analogous to the NATURALISM of ÉMILE ZOLA. It portrayed the humble and their brute passions in a manner that stressed the movement's emphasis on representing reality, no matter how ugly or sordid, without any embellishment. Principal exponents of verism were GIUSEPPE GIACOSA and GIOVANNI VERGA, and its theorist was the Sicilian dialect playwright Luigi Capuana (1839–1915).

VERNEUIL, Louis [originally Louis Jacques Marie Collin du Bocage] (1893–1952), French actor, director, and playwright, was notable for his many light sex and other comedies. Some of them were performed by Sarah Bernhardt, who was his grandmother-in-law (he was also the son-in-law of GEORGES FEYDEAU). By 1940 over sixty of Verneuil's plays had been produced in Paris. Praised for their dexterously constructed intrigue as well as for their depiction of contemporary manners, many of them were translated and a number became Broadway hits, particularly *Mademoiselle ma mère* (1920, as *Oh Mama*), *Pile ou face* (1924, adapted by ZOË AKINS as *First Love*), and *Le Mariage de maman* (1925, as *Matrimony Pfd.*).

Just before the fall of Paris in 1940 Verneuil moved to the United States. There he wrote film scripts as well as plays, and in 1950 directed his first play to be written in English, the Broadway comedy hit about a retired Washington senator, *Affairs of State*. Another comedy written in English is *Love and Let Love* (1952). Verneuil also wrote a biography of Sarah Bernhardt and a book of memoirs, *Rideau à neuf heures* (*Curtain at Nine,* 1945).

VIAN, Boris (1920–59), French writer, had a remarkable career as novelist, poet, critic, translator, and playwright—as well as engineer, pornographer, jazz trumpeter, singer, actor, and artist. His few satiric experimental plays on war and death achieved some notoriety and a growing posthumous reputation. The first, the "paramilitary vaudeville" *L'Equarrissage pour tous* (1950, translated as *Knackery for All* as well as *The Knacker's ABC*), portrays the eccentric family of a knacker (a dealer and slaughterer of old horses) on June 6, 1944, the day of the Allied landing at Arromanches; after some grotesque and ribald doings their house blows up and the few survivors murder each other to the strains of the "Marseillaise." Vian's posthumous *Les Bâtisseurs d'empire, ou Le Schmurz* (*The Empire Builders,* 1959), probably his most notable play, can be produced "as farce, but also as national tragedy, as REALISTIC drama, or as allegory," according to Vian, and it "should embarrass the spectator." It features an ever-diminishing family who (while beating the silent, misshapen, semi-human Schmurz, whom they do not appear to see) flee a terrifying noise by climbing to ever-smaller apartments; finally only the father remains, in a tiny attic room he cannot leave, and he dies at the approach of the noise. Other Vian plays are *Le Dernier des métiers* (1950) and a sardonic antiwar play produced in 1965, *Le Goûter des généraux* (*The Generals' Tea-Party*), whose meticulously planning generals discover they have forgotten to choose an enemy and kill themselves in an uproarious collective game of Russian roulette.

Vian, who became a PATAPHYSICIAN and an important Parisian figure among artistic Bohemians, studied and practiced engineering for the government and in industry. The variety of his occupations was as extraordinary as the mass of his literary accomplishments. Aside from the four plays, he wrote three opera librettos, nine novels and as many ballet scenarios, three volumes of poetry and many short stories, almost one hundred cabaret skits, four hundred songs (which he himself sang in Paris nightclubs), twenty major translations (of AUGUST STRINDBERG, General Omar N.

Bradley, and others), and almost nine thousand articles. In his short life—he died at thirty-nine of a heart attack—he also produced sketches, paintings, and a patent for an elastic wheel.

Vian's plays have been translated; they are discussed in Jacques Guicharnaud's *Modern French Theatre* (1967) and in Martin Esslin's *The Theatre of the Absurd* (revised 1968).

VICTIMS OF DUTY (*Victimes du devoir*), a one-act "pseudo-drama" by EUGÈNE IONESCO, produced in 1953 and published in 1954. Setting: "a petit bourgeois interior."

This is an allusive philosophical-psychological thriller, a dramatic inquiry into the nature of drama, and a theatricalization of the brutal absurdity of existence.

Choubert tells his wife, Madeleine, that plays are nothing more than realistic thrillers. "Every play's an investigation brought to a successful conclusion," he maintains: "Might as well give the game away at the start." They invite a passing Detective, whose gentleness soon turns to ferocity. To discover the proper spelling of the name of a man he is investigating, the Detective makes Choubert go into his subconscious. For most of the play Choubert thereupon wanders around the room, and crouches under and climbs on top of furniture. He sinks below and rises above sound and sight barriers, while his wife changes into a seductress, an old woman, the Detective's mistress, and Choubert's mother. "To plug the holes in his memory," Choubert is brutally stuffed with bread ("Chew! Swallow!") by the Detective, who is supplied with endless cups of coffee by Madeleine. A bearded poet propounds theories of non-Aristotelian drama—though he sees no point in further writing ("We've got Ionesco and Ionesco, that's enough!") and though the conventional Detective and Madeleine neither understand nor approve of such "ABSURD" drama. The poet finally knifes the Detective, who dies with the excuse that he is "a victim of duty" and the shout: "Long live the white race!" Now the poet stuffs Choubert with bread, and Madeleine helps him: "We're all victims of duty!" As the curtain falls, an enigmatic lady who has sat aside joins in as all order each other to "Chew! Swallow! Chew! Swallow!"

VICTORIA REGINA, a play in three acts by LAURENCE HOUSMAN, published and produced in 1935. Setting: various castles in England and Scotland, 1837–97.

Originally ten among Housman's fifty-four one-acters depicting different phases of the life of a willful yet romantic Queen Victoria, the play was banned in England because of its personal portrayal of royalty. Its New York success (with Helen Hayes) was repeated in England two years later, when the play was licensed on the centenary of Victoria's accession.

Act I. "The Six O'Clock Call, 1837": Young Victoria is notified that the king is dead; the new queen's first wish is for a bedroom of her own.

Victoria Regina. Helen Hayes in the title part. New York, 1935. (*Vandamm Photo, Theatre Collection, New York Public Library*)

"Suitable Suitors, 1838": Victoria tells her prime minister of the qualifications her future husband must have; alone, she kisses the portrait of Prince Albert, though the prime minister considers him an ineligible prospect. *"Woman Proposes, 15th October 1839":* At Windsor Castle, Victoria in defiance of their father's wish chooses Albert over his brother. *"Morning Glory, 11th February 1840":* At dawn after their wedding, Victoria delightedly watches Albert shave, "revelling in wifely submission."

Act II. "A Good Lesson!, 1842": Albert tames Victoria, who was furious when he refused to obey her peremptory summons. *"Under Fire, 30th May 1842"* depicts Albert and Victoria's love and heroism during an attempted assassination. *"The Rose and the Thorn, 1846":* Victoria is in a jealous rage, then has the grace to apologize, and weeps as she and Albert make up. *"Intervention, 30th November 1861":* The sick Albert helps Victoria during an international crisis, and then collapses.

Act III. "'The Queen! God Bless Her!', 1877": Vacationing in the Highlands, the widowed Victoria chats with a comic Scotsman, then has a moving political-personal interview with Disraeli, and, alone, weeps for Albert. *"Happy and Glorious, 20th June 1897,"* the Diamond Jubilee celebration at Buckingham Palace: Old Queen Victoria, in a wheelchair, is cheered by international royalty and by her subjects. As she is wheeled away, gratified by her triumph, she says, "Albert! Ah! if only you could have been here!"

VIDAL, Gore (1925–), American novelist and playwright, has succeeded with a number of light satires, principally with *Visit to a Small Planet* (1957), a farce about a man from outer space.

The Best Man (1960) and *Weekend* (1968), more serious comedies, deal with the maneuverings of presidential aspirants in an election year. Vidal adapted Dürrenmatt's ROMULUS THE GREAT as *Romulus* (1962), and has written screenplays (including that of Williams's SUDDENLY LAST SUMMER), television drama, and many novels. A book-length study of his life and work is Ray Lewis White's *Gore Vidal* (1968).

VIETNAM had a theatre as long ago as the Middle Ages. Its classic *hat cheo* (satirical folk plays) and *hat boi* (a type of opera) genres in the early twentieth century were modified into the *cai luong,* serious spectacles with dialogue, singing, music, and dance derived from Chinese opera and fiction, whose sociohistorical themes were adapted into modern Vietnamese settings. Though its vogue peaked in the 1930's, *cai luong* has remained the most popular stage entertainment through the present. The other modern Vietnamese theatre genre, *kich,* was derived from the French; it is one-act REPRESENTATIONAL drama on contemporary subjects, produced without music or song. Professional *cai luong* as well as *kich* troupes have performed all across Vietnam and over the Vietnamese radio. During the 1960's and 1970's fighting, classic *hat cheo* was widely produced as propaganda in North Vietnam, but the divisions and ravages of war stultified native cultural developments there as well as in South Vietnam.

Song Ban's *The Vietnamese Theatre* (Hanoi, 1960) describes some of this drama. A more generally accessible study is Faubion Bowers's *Theatre in the East* (1956).

VIEW FROM THE BRIDGE, A, a play in two acts by ARTHUR MILLER, published and produced in 1955. Setting: a Brooklyn waterfront tenement, 1950's.

Produced (unsuccessfully) with A MEMORY OF TWO MONDAYS, this was originally a sparse one-act classical tragedy; Miller discussed his modernization of the Greek genre in "On Social Plays," his preface to this version. It is the two-act revision for the successful London production (1956, published in 1957), however, that has been widely performed and was published in the *Collected Plays.* In it, Miller recast verse passages into prose, enlarged the roles of the women, and elevated the character of Eddie—the incestuous informer who is self-deluded, like Willy Loman in DEATH OF A SALESMAN, but dies to save his name, like John Proctor in THE CRUCIBLE. The setting is skeletal, and the lawyer-narrator provides the detached "view from the [Brooklyn] bridge." The play was made into a widely performed Italian opera by Renzo Rossellini (libretto by Gerardo Guerrieri), *Uno sguardo dal ponte* (1961).

Act I. An Italian-born lawyer strolls into his office. He tells the audience about the neighborhood and about a longshoreman, Eddie Carbone—who enters his apartment as the office spotlight fades. Eddie is greeted affectionately by his young niece, Catherine, whom he has brought up and lovingly chides for "walkin' wavy! I don't like the looks they're givin' you in the candy store." Eddie only reluctantly agrees to Catherine's accepting a job. Afraid to let her leave him, he cautions her, "Most people ain't people." As Eddie watches her go to the kitchen, the lawyer remarks, "He was as good a man as he had to be in a life that was hard and even." Now arrive his wife's cousins, illegal immigrants ("submarines") from Italy. Marco is a strong and steady man eager to work and send money to his impoverished family, while Rodolpho is a handsome blond youngster, full of jokes and song. Catherine is drawn to him, and Eddie gets increasingly irritated. The simple Eddie now has "a destiny," the narrator remarks. Eddie waits for Catherine and Rodolpho to come home from the movies. "He's like a weird," Eddie says resentfully, complaining about Rodolpho's singing and blond hair: "For that character I didn't bring her up." But his wife, anxious about his preoccupation with Catherine, wonders, "When am I gonna be a wife again, Eddie? . . . It's almost three months . . ." When the youngsters come home, Eddie warns Catherine that Rodolpho wants to marry her only to become an American citizen—"the oldest racket in the country." Catherine weeps, and Eddie's wife, warning her about walking around in a slip and chatting with Eddie "when he's shavin' in his underwear," tells her she is "a grown woman" now and must lead her own life. Eddie visits the lawyer, who remarks, "His eyes were like tunnels; my first thought was that he had committed a crime." But the lawyer realizes it is passion, and tells Eddie there is no way to stop the marriage to this "blond guy" who sings high notes and designs dresses. Warning him about "too much love for the niece," the lawyer says Eddie can do nothing: except for Rodolpho's immigration, everything is legal—and normal. Eddie is furious. At home, he chaffs Marco about extra kids he may find upon his return to Italy. When Rodolpho says sex customs are stricter in Italy, Eddie warns him, "It ain't so free here either, Rodolpho, like you think." As Eddie baits him, Catherine angrily puts on a record and asks Rodolpho to dance. Eddie insists on giving him a boxing lesson—and "playfully" staggers him with a blow. Marco thereupon challenges Eddie to lift a chair by the leg with one hand. Eddie fails, but Marco raises the chair over Eddie's head, menacingly—and then smiles.

Act II. For the first time Rodolpho is alone in the house with Catherine. He gets angry when he realizes her suggestions about living in Italy after they get married have been prompted by Eddie. When Catherine weeps ("[Eddie] was always the sweetest guy to me"), Rodolpho gently leads her to the bedroom. Half drunk, Eddie comes in—and orders Rodolpho out of the house. Catherine is determined to leave, too, but suddenly Eddie kisses her passionately. When Rodolpho pulls him away, Eddie pins his arms back and derisively kisses him. "You see?" he tells Catherine, "he ain't right." Then Eddie goes out and calls the Immigration Bureau. By the time he returns, the brothers have moved upstairs with other illegal immigrants. The officers appear almost immediately and arrest all the "submarines." As Marco is taken away, he spits in Eddie's face. Before the neighbors, he charges Eddie with being an informer: "That one stole the food from my children!" Denying it, Eddie appeals to his neighbors—who walk away. In prison, Marco must promise not to continue the vendetta and kill Eddie if he is to be paroled for the wedding of Rodolpho and Catherine. "Only God makes justice," the lawyer repeats, and grudgingly Marco gives the promise. At home Eddie tries to prevent his wife's attending Catherine's wedding. Rodolpho wants to make up, but Eddie pulls his hand away. His wife bluntly warns him about Catherine: "You can never have her." When Marco comes in, Eddie demands that he retract his accusation. "Wipin' the neighborhood with my name like a dirty rag! I want my name, Marco," he insists, and then hurls himself at Marco: "Come on, liar, you know what you done!" Marco strikes him on the neck: "Animal! You go on your knees to me!" Eddie lunges at him with a knife. Marco twists his arm and presses it—with the knife—into Eddie, who falls to his knees and dies in his wife's arms. (In the original version, Eddie dies at his niece's feet with the words "Catherine—Why?") "Most of the time now we settle for half," the lawyer says, "but the truth is holy, and even as I know how wrong he was, and his death useless, I tremble, for I confess that something perversely pure calls to me from his memory . . . for he allowed himself to be wholly known." The lawyer concludes, "And yet, it is better to settle for half, it must be! And so I mourn him—I admit it—with a certain . . . alarm."

VIKINGS AT HELGELAND, THE (*Hærmændene på Helgeland*), a play in four acts by HENRIK IBSEN, published and produced in 1858. Setting: Helgeland, Norway; tenth century.

A nationalistic heroic play, it is based, as Ibsen noted in his preface to its German edition (1876), "on the various surviving Icelandic Family Sagas, in which the larger-than-life conditions and events of the *Nibelungenlied* and the *Volsungasaga* are . . . very often reduced to more human dimensions." In this symbolic representation of powerful elemental passions, Hjørdis is a Brunhild who embodies the Viking ideal of strength—and also foreshadows later heroines such as HEDDA GABLER and the wife of JOHN GABRIEL BORKMAN.

The legendary hero Sigurd and his friend Gunnar are married, respectively, to Dagny and her foster sister, Hjørdis. Sigurd reveals to his wife, Dagny, that it was really he who had performed the heroic feat (killing a fierce white bear) that made Gunnar famous and won him Hjørdis, who had demanded it as the price for her hand. Though Sigurd had then spent the night with her, his sword lay between them, and Hjørdis was not aware of his true identity—which has remained a secret to all but Gunnar. At a great banquet, Hjørdis's vicious taunts finally cause the gentle Dagny to reveal the secret. Hjørdis almost succeeds in getting the husband she despises to murder his friend, and she plunges Dagny into despair by persuading her that she is an unsuitably timid wife who has brought her husband only unhappiness and shame. Sigurd reveals to Hjørdis the "wretched web the Fates have spun around us": not having known of her love for him (which she only now confesses), he had sacrificed his love for her to his friendship for Gunnar. But Hjørdis blames Sigurd himself: "A man can give all things to his faithful friend," she declares, "except the woman he loves. For if he does that, he breaks the secret web of Fate, and two lives are wrecked." She urges that they free themselves from their "miserable" mates and seek their destiny together: "No, not as your wife, Sigurd, but as a Valkyrie is how I will come—firing your blood to battle and to great deeds, standing by your side as the sword-blows fall. . . . And when your funeral song is sung, it shall tell of Sigurd and Hjørdis together!" But Sigurd refuses to act dishonorably toward Dagny. Determined to be unified with him in the abode of fallen heroes, Hjørdis shoots Sigurd with a bow she had strung with her own hair. He dies—but foils her plans with his revelation that he had some time before embraced Christianity. Now unwilling to go with the riders she had summoned to take her and Sigurd to Åsgard, the home of the gods, she tries to escape by throwing herself into the sea from a cliff. When Gunnar and his child arrive, they are terrified to see a vision of her in the clouds and "hear the sound of 'Åsgårdsreiden' in the air—the last ride of the dead on their way to Valhalla."

Another important figure in the play is Hjørdis's foster father, the Icelandic chieftain Ørnulf. She brings tragedy to him by causing the death of his last and favorite son. Persuaded by Dagny to compose a funeral song that is later to be recorded in runes, Ørnulf is able at last to overcome his despair.

VILDRAC [originally Messager], **Charles** (1882–), French poet and playwright, was best known for his *Le Paquebot Tenacity* (*S.S. Tenacity*, 1919) and *Michel Auclair* (1921), both adapted by SIDNEY HOWARD. The first, a major production of JACQUES COPEAU's Vieux Colombier and a popular play in the 1920's, depicts the opposing destinies of two friends in a manner that despite its sea and seaport settings recalls the situation and tone of another play of the same year, O'Neill's BEYOND THE HORIZON. The title character of *Michel Auclair,* a love drama produced also by the Provincetown Players, becomes the savior of the woman he forgave for leaving him for the scamp to whom she is married. Other Vildrac dramas that combine lyricism with psychological insight are *Madame Béliard* (1925), set in a dyeing shop and characterized as a modernization of Racine's *Bérénice; La Brouille* (1930), depicting the quarrels of an idealist and a realist; and *L'Air du temps* (1938), a portrayal in domestic terms of the chaos and evil then engulfing Europe.

The brother-in-law of GEORGES DUHAMEL, with whom he wrote *Notes sur la technique poétique*

(1911) and founded an experimental community-living house for artists in 1906–07, Vildrac was active in the French Resistance during World War II. Collections of Vildrac's *Plays* appeared in 1942 and 1948.

VISE, THE (*La morsa*), a one-act play by LUIGI PIRANDELLO, produced in 1910 and published in 1914. Setting: a contemporary provincial home.

The Vise and SICILIAN LIMES, produced together, were Pirandello's first plays. *The Vise* was published in an earlier version as *L'epilogo* (1898).

Andrea Fabbri eloped with Giulia and later, to atone for his rashness, worked hard to become successful. Feeling neglected, Giulia has deceived Andrea with his friend. Now her frightened lover tells her how he has been tortured by Andrea's hints that he has discovered their affair. Andrea soon comes to tighten "the vise" by tormenting Giulia in the same manner. She breaks down, unable to deny her guilt, and Andrea orders her from the house. Begging him to keep her shame from their children, Giulia rushes out and shoots herself.

VISHNEVSKY, Vsevolod Vitalevich (1900–51), Russian dramatist, wrote one of the most popular of all Soviet plays, *Optimisticheskaya tragediya* (AN OPTIMISTIC TRAGEDY, 1933)—his only notable work. A former sailor and a cavalry machine-gunner during the Revolution, he first became known with short stories based on his military experiences. He also wrote a number of film scenarios, and he is considered a classic playwright in the Soviet Union. A fanatic Communist, he became deeply embroiled in a political-literary dispute in the 1930's, when he defended JAMES JOYCE against Soviet charges of "decadence."

His first play, *Pervaya konnaya* (1930), is an episodic drama featuring a collective hero and a common tsarist soldier who rises to his full potential when he joins the Red Army. His next play, *Posledni i reshitelny* (1931), deals with the eventual war (the "final and decisive" battle alluded to in the title) against capitalism, and, like *An Optimistic Tragedy,* has impressive crowd scenes and features sailors; it created considerable resentment because of its gloom and the author's title, a quotation from the sacred "Internationale." Vishnevsky's other plays include *Na zapade boi* (1933), which dramatizes the growing spread of Fascism; *U sten Leningrada* (1944), which deals with the heroic defense of that city; and *Nezabyvayemy 1919-y* (1949), which features Stalin as Lenin's indispensable companion: the curtain falls as Stalin telephones Lenin the news that he has just quelled the Kronstadt rebellion of 1921, and thus saved the Revolution. For this distortion of history Vishnevsky was awarded the Stalin Prize First Class.

Vishnevsky's selected works were published in 1950, and *An Optimistic Tragedy* was published in English in Ben Blake's *Four Soviet Plays* (1937). His work is discussed in Gleb Struve's *Soviet Russian Literature 1917–50* (1951) and in Nikolai A. Gorchakov's *The Theater in Soviet Russia* (1957).

VISIONS OF SIMONE MACHARD, THE (*Die Gesichte der Simone Machard*), a play in four parts by BERTOLT BRECHT (with LION FEUCHTWANGER*), published in 1956 and produced in 1957. Setting: a small town (St. Martin) in central France, June 1940.

Completed in 1943, this play is among a number of Joan of Arc dramas by Brecht. The play's NATURALISTIC depiction of wartime France and the lyrical depiction of Simone's visions are continuously fused. Brecht's masterful use of language ranges from harsh official cliché to fragile poetic fantasy.

Simone Machard, "a small, half-grown girl," is a servant in the town's "hostellerie" at the time of the German army's advance. In four dreams and daydreams, her external life intertwines with the story of Joan of Arc, which Simone is reading. She sees her brother, a front-line soldier, as an angel urging her to save France, and the people around her as various historical figures connected with Joan. In the panic of the Germans' approach, her selfish employer tries to save his food stores and equipment; Simone/Joan causes them to be distributed to needy refugees. During the Occupation, Simone/Joan saves France's honor by setting fire to black-market gasoline that collaborators plan to sell the German army. She is declared "sick" by her practical masters, who commit her to a cruel mental asylum run by nuns. But as she is taken away, her example is already inspiring the downtrodden refugees to action.

VISIT, THE (*Der Besuch der alten Dame*; literally, "the visit of the old lady"), "a tragic comedy" in three acts by FRIEDRICH DÜRRENMATT, published and produced in 1956. Setting: Güllen, "at the present time."

This macabre work made Dürrenmatt world-famous. His note to the play, whose repeatedly dissolving and changing scenes are set in a mythical Swiss town, disclaims allegorical intentions but associates the gruesome if comic Claire with classic figures such as Medea. SYMBOLISM and ritual are implicit in Alfred Ill's attainment of tragic stature and, as the parodic verse epilogue emphasizes, in his fellow townsmen's becoming polluted rather than purged when they make him the scapegoat of microcosmic Güllen. In the popular American production (1958), Claire's role was softened and her relationship with Ill (renamed Anton Schill) was romanticized. Dürrenmatt adapted his play into the libretto for Gottfried von Einem's opera in 1971.

Act I. As trains speed by dilapidated Güllen, its inhabitants remember how celebrities once used to visit there. Eagerly they await the arrival of Claire Zachanassian, formerly a local girl and now a philanthropic multimillionairess—and their great hope. They prepare a festive reception with the

* Brecht's collaboration with Feuchtwanger—who also reworked the play into a novel, *Simone*—is described the latter's "Zur Entstehungsgeschichte des Stückes 'Simone,'" *Schauspiel, 9* (Frankfurt, 1956–57).

help of the only person who remembers her, her childhood lover, Alfred Ill, a shopkeeper. "We've got to do this cleverly, use psychology," he remarks, assured because of his new importance of becoming Güllen's next mayor. An express train suddenly screeches to a halt. Out steps Claire, who had pulled the train's emergency cord. She is a grotesquely dressed sixty-three-year-old redhead with an impassive face but an air of grace, and she is followed by her seventh husband, a young playboy equipped with fishing gear, and an eighty-year-old butler wearing dark glasses. The indignant conductor is placated by Claire's immense bribe, is told to "take the train away," and departs obsequiously. Then Claire overcomes Ill's embarrassment by recalling their happy past. Confidently Ill whispers to a friend, "See, I don't have to worry about *her* now!" When he remarks that he is still her "black panther," as she used to call him, Claire replies: "Nonsense, you're fat now—and gray and a souse." The hurriedly improvised reception ceremonies are drowned out by passing trains as Claire alternately amuses and embarrasses people with her bizarre and ghoulish comments. Then she is carried off in her sedan chair by two convicts she had bought in America. She is followed by two castrated blind old men who chant short phrases and by servants carrying an empty coffin and a caged black panther. The scene changes as the townspeople marvel at her affluence. Noting that Ill called her "my bewitched little wildcat," they are confident he will elicit a substantial donation for the town from Claire, though they admit she is weird, "like a Greek goddess of fate." Again the scene shifts as Claire, after exploring the town, visits with Ill the forest where they recall their old haunts and their love. Claire smokes a cigar as Ill assures her that his not marrying her had made Claire wealthy: with him she would have languished and been as bored and poor as he is. As he pats her leg she notes that it is artificial—as is the "soft little hand" he starts to kiss and as are many of her other limbs. A plane crash killed everybody else, but only mutilated Claire, who is indestructible—a phrase echoed by her blind old eunuchs. The scene changes to a festive luncheon, where Claire announces her stupendous gift of a billion—but offered with a condition. Her butler explains: he was the Güllen judge who long ago had exonerated Ill in Claire's paternity suit when Ill bribed two men to commit perjury. The judgment drove the poor pregnant girl out of town in disgrace and to prostitution, and caused the eventual death of their child. Later she married a wealthy old brothel customer. Then Claire tracked down the two false witnesses and, as the blind old eunuchs now chant, had them "castrated and blinded." In return for her billion Claire now wants

The Visit, Act I: Claire (Lynn Fontanne) makes her offer and Ill (Alfred Lunt) begs for mercy; her butler (John Wyse) and the mayor (Eric Porter) look on. New York, 1958. (*Vandamm Photo, Theatre Collection, New York Public Library*)

"someone [to] kill Alfred Ill." "But you can't demand that," Ill cries out; "it happened long ago! It's long since forgotten." Claire has forgotten nothing, however, and insists on justice. Güllen's mayor declines her offer "in the name of humanity," and the crowds applaud him wildly, for "we'd rather be poor than heathen murderers." Unperturbed, Claire replies, "I can wait."

Act II. In his shop Ill confidently chats with his family. Periodically Claire is seen in the background: she has sent her playboy away and breakfasts with a handsome young film star, her eighth husband. Poor and hitherto frugal customers recklessly purchase Ill's best merchandise on credit. Suddenly realizing how they expect to get the money to pay for it, he rushes out and vainly seeks help from the police, the mayor, and the pastor—all of whom are similarly making credit purchases. In the background Claire is seen chatting, smoking cigars, and drinking whiskey. The mayor tells Ill that he is morally unfit to become his successor, and the pastor implores Ill to escape and not tempt the townspeople. These are now hunting Claire's black panther, who has escaped. Shots are heard, and Ill collapses. The panther is reported killed in front of Ill's shop, and Claire orders a funeral march. Ill appears at the railway station, carrying an old valise and ready to leave Güllen. The townspeople crowd around and intimidate him. As the train departs without him, Ill breaks down: "I am lost."

Act III. Claire has just married her ninth husband, a brilliant young scientist. The townspeople beg her to buy Güllen's industries and thus help extricate them from their debts. She reveals that she had long ago bought all the now-idle factories and lands—and deliberately impoverished Güllen to accomplish her vengeance: "The world made me into a whore; now I make the world into a brothel." In Ill's refurbished shop his wife and offspring appear, sumptuously dressed in new clothes. As Ill paces endlessly upstairs, his family and the townsmen worry that he may reveal things to the reporters and photographers who are arriving in Güllen from all over the world. The town's conscience-stricken teacher almost tells them the truth, but is silenced—even by Ill himself—though the teacher warns Ill that he will be killed: "The poverty is too bitter, the temptation is too great." The mayor announces the town council's imminent vote on Claire's offer. He hands Ill a pistol, suggesting that "for the sake of your friends" and family he spare them from making a decision. "You may kill me if you like," Ill replies, promising neither to protest nor to defend himself and recalling the agony he has undergone while watching the town go on purchasing sprees in anticipation of his murder: "But I won't do your job for you either." For the last time Ill and Claire meet in the woods. That night he will be condemned and "a useless life will thus come to an end," Ill says. Claire tells him how her love, instead of dying, "turned into . . . something evil [that] . . . reached out for your life." She will transport his corpse to Capri and bury him near her villa, overlooking the Mediterranean. The scene shifts to the town meeting. Because of the reporters the council discusses Claire's offer in vague terms, and Ill agrees to abide by the decision "made for his sake." The vote is called. Indicating acceptance, everybody gradually raises his hand, at last even the teacher—on moral grounds, they reiterate: not for the money, but to reestablish justice. Ill's execution is to be at once. Now unafraid, he tells the pastor to pray not for him but for Güllen, and asks for a last cigarette. Then Ill is rudely pulled to his feet. Slowly he steps amidst the menacing men, who close about him. When they move back, Ill lies on the floor. The doctor examines him: "Heart failure." The mayor's declaration, "He died of joy," is picked up by the crowds and the reporters outside. Claire has the corpse brought before her, looks at it, and orders it placed in the coffin. Then she summons the mayor and hands him a piece of paper: "The check." The scene shifts to the railway station. A chorus chants of Güllen's joyful wealth and implores its divine preservation. Claire is borne to the train in her sedan chair. She is followed by servants carrying the coffin.

VITRAC, Roger (1899–1952), French SURREALIST poet and playwright who with TRISTAN TZARA helped found DADAISM. He and ANTONIN ARTAUD were expelled from ANDRÉ BRETON's inner circle for planning to produce avant-garde drama commercially—which Artaud and Vitrac did after founding the Théâtre ALFRED-JARRY in 1927. The opening program included Vitrac's *Les Mystères de l'amour* (*The Mysteries of Love*), perhaps a product of automatic writing that, in its concern with language, anticipates the theatre of the ABSURD; it portrays two lovers' vicious hallucinations in which appear (among others) Benito Mussolini and Lloyd George, who saws off heads and stashes away bits of corpses. Vitrac's *Victor ou les enfants au pouvoir* (1928), which was revived by JEAN ANOUILH in 1962, is less surrealistic but more preoccupied with the banality of language and the theatre, both of which it parodies; Vitrac's most important play, it is a bitter drawing-room farce about a stupid, middle-class family, featuring a monstrously adult nine-year-old boy who dies of a stroke and whose parents commit suicide after the father's adultery with the mother of his equally monstrous six-year-old girlfriend. Vitrac's later plays, though still partly surrealist, are more conventional. They include *Le Coup de Trafalgar* (1934), dramatizing Paris life during World War I; *Le Loup-garou* (1940), a comedy set in a fashionable lunatic asylum; and the more extravagantly surrealist farce *Le Sabre de mon père* (1951).

The Mysteries of Love was published, with prefatory comments, in Michael Benedikt and George E. Wellwarth's *Modern French Theatre* (1964).

VOLLMER, Lula (1898–1955), American playwright, wrote folk drama set in the North Carolina mountain region where she grew up. Her biggest hit, produced after she had become a box-office clerk in New York, was *Sun-Up* (1923); it features an illiterate woman who loses her husband to the (incomprehensible to her) law and her son in the faraway World War. *The Shame Woman* (1923), another successful folk tragedy set in the North Carolina mountains, also features a maternal victim of fate; she goes to the scaffold, after killing her former seducer to save the memory of her adopted daughter—another one of his victims.

Vollmer wrote other, less notable plays. *Sun-Up* is reprinted in Arthur H. Quinn's *Representative American Plays* (1938), with an informative essay on Lula Vollmer.

VOLLMOELLER, Karl Gustav (1878–1948), German SYMBOLIST poet and dramatist, was a disciple of HUGO VON HOFMANNSTHAL and MAURICE MAETERLINCK. Like the latter in *Soeur Béatrice,* Vollmoeller too dramatized the medieval legend of the runaway nun whose place is assumed by the Virgin—in *Das Mirakel* (*The Miracle,* 1912), a pantomime-spectacle that brought him international renown when Max Reinhardt produced it. Vollmoeller's other plays are also poetic and romantic, sometimes bordering on decadence. The climax of the Renaissance drama that first made him famous, *Catharina, Gräfin von Armagnac, und ihre beiden Liebhaber* (1903), has the heroine—as in Wilde's SALOMÉ—addressing and kissing the severed head of her poet-lover.

The son of a wealthy Stuttgart manufacturer, Vollmoeller studied the classics in various European universities, and traveled most of his life. Though a successful writer in Germany, his influence on the Austrian theatre was more profound because of his membership in the poet Stefan George's circle, to which Hofmannsthal too had belonged. In his later works Vollmoeller relied more on spectacle than on dialogue—as in *The Miracle* and in the Oriental show *Assüs, Fitne und Sumurud* (1904). His other plays include *Der deutsche Graf* (1906), a didactic portrayal of Casanova; adaptations of Aeschylus's *Oresteia* (1908) and Gozzi's eighteenth-century drama *Turandot* (1911); and the theatrical popular success *Wieland* (1911), probably the first play ever written about an aviator. One of Vollmoeller's last works is a variation on MAX DREYER's *Das Tal des Lebens,* the comedy *Cocktail* (1930). Vollmoeller also published volumes of collected verse, much of it as baroque as his drama.

VORTEX, THE, a play in three acts by NOËL COWARD, produced in 1924 and published in 1925. Setting: London and an English country house, the 1920's.

The success of this witty tragedy of manners established Coward, who played the part of Nicky, as a playwright as well as an actor. It was also his first play produced in New York.

Florence Lancaster, a wealthy woman making her daily rounds in the fashionably effete society of hypocrites, craves perpetual adoration and youth. Her son, Nicky, a dandified, dope-addicted pianist, returns from Paris with his fiancée. She turns out to be the former mistress of Florence's most recent young lover, and during a party at the Lancaster country house the two fall in love again. The cast-off Florence goes into a rage of jealousy. Nicky confesses his own despair and forces his mother to admit and face the degeneracy of their lives. Only thus can they change and perhaps salvage something: "We swirl about in a vortex of beastliness. This is a chance—don't you see—to realize the truth—our only chance."

VOYSEY INHERITANCE, THE, a play in five acts by HARLEY GRANVILLE-BARKER, produced in 1905 and published in 1909. Setting: London, early twentieth century.

Revised and republished in 1913 and again in 1934, this play dramatizes John Ruskin's indictment of capitalism. It also depicts the maturation of young Voysey.

Edward Voysey discovers that the family's investment firm, his "inheritance," achieved its wealth through his father's dishonest manipulations of clients' funds. The father justifies his conduct as necessary and inherited, in turn, from his own father. He urges Edward to take over, carry on, and prevent detection and public exposure. "You've lived a quiet humdrum life up to now, with your books and your philosophy and your agnosticism and your ethics . . . and you've never before been brought face to face with any really vital question," he tells his shocked and revolted son. Edward Voysey eventually decides to take over and make restitution. The father dies, and Voysey is confronted with the pristine idealism of a brother (who wants work to be creative rather than merely remunerative) and exposure by a defrauded client. Though Voysey is finally more knowledgeable and sophisticated, the end is left unresolved. He may yet be prosecuted and imprisoned; and despite their understanding, it is not clear whether he will marry the girl who stands by him.

VULTURES, THE (*Les Corbeaux*), a drama in four acts by HENRY BECQUE, published and produced in 1882. Setting: Paris, c. 1880.

For five years managers refused to stage this "bible of the dramatic realists" (as James Huneker called it in *Iconoclasts*) and attempted to change its text to make the play conform to the formats of the then fashionable PROBLEM and WELL-MADE PLAYS. Ultimately this prototype of French NATURALISTIC drama, also translated as *The Crows* and as *The Ravens,* was produced as Becque had written it—and made him famous. Because of its portrayal of the ruthless and rapacious exploitation of the helpless, the play has frequently been compared to Hellman's THE LITTLE FOXES. Though *The Vultures* is considered Becque's masterpiece, old-fashioned heavy-handedness—particularly a long and sentimental first act—makes it more dated than THE WOMAN OF PARIS.

Act I. Vigneron, a hard-working elderly manufacturer, spends a tender, affectionate evening with his three daughters, his son, and his wife. She recounts Vigneron's working his way up to become the partner of Teissier, a former small banker the family dislike. After Vigneron reluctantly leaves to do more work, Mrs. Vigneron makes final preparations for their dinner party. The first guest is a social-climbing and avaricious widow whose son is engaged to Blanche, the youngest of the Vigneron girls. The women discuss dowry arrangements and Teissier, the partner who has never before been a guest of the Vignerons. The other guests arrive: old Teissier, an unpolished man with "the eyes of a fox and the face of a monkey"; the partners' lawyer, whom Teissier privately cautions against excessive unscrupulousness; and a music teacher who encourages the second daughter to pursue an artistic career. As Vigneron's ingrate son mimics his father, the old manufacturer is brought in on a stretcher—killed by a sudden stroke.

Act II. A month has passed. Teissier has reluctantly sent the grieving Mrs. Vigneron money she had requested, but now informs her of her late husband's many supposed debts and urges her to sell her share of the factory to repay them. The partner's deceit infuriates Mrs. Vigneron. Marie, the oldest and homeliest but most practical daughter, negotiates with the detested partner. Later she warns her sister Blanche about their impending ruin: it may stop her planned wedding. Blanche proclaims her and her fiancé's eternal love—but even "if he should prove to be the vilest creature in the world, I should still have to marry him." The lawyer, supporting Teissier against the helpless Vignerons, seems to confirm their ruin. As they detail the bankruptcy of Vigneron's estate others come with fraudulent claims for unpaid bills. Mrs. Vigneron persists in refusing to sell—but weeps impotently before the mounting bills.

Act III. When Mrs. Vigneron attempts to order her affairs by hiring someone else, her unscrupulous lawyer tightens his hold and urges her to sell immediately. The once-friendly music teacher, seeing the family destitute, forgets their kindnesses to him and deserts them. But Teissier is becoming attached to Marie. He suggests that she ignore her family and take care of herself—"That's the way I should feel"—and move in with him: "Perhaps later on I'll see about marriage." Indignantly Marie refuses and returns his banknotes. The mother of Blanche's fiancé cancels the wedding now that the Vignerons are unable to provide the dowry. She remains unmoved by Blanche's entreaties ("Is it necessary for both of you to sacrifice your whole lives for the sake of a slip?") and when Blanche, increasingly desperate, loses her temper, she dismisses Blanche as "a fallen woman." Equally desperate before her self-proclaimed creditors, Mrs. Vigneron submits to selling her share of the factory. "I should like to keep what belongs to me," the widow says, "but the first thing is to save my children."

Act IV. The Vignerons now live in shabby quarters. "When businessmen get into a house where a person has just died, you may as well say: 'Here come the vultures,'" their loyal old servant remarks: "They don't leave anything they can carry away." Mrs. Vigneron has turned gray; Blanche is hopelessly insane; and the second daughter, bluntly disillusioned about her artistic talents by the music teacher ("If you're respectable, you'll be esteemed without being helped; if you're not, you'll be helped without being esteemed"), considers becoming a streetwalker. When the lawyer brings a marriage proposal from Teissier, Marie decides to sacrifice herself for her family. Teissier's fortune was not made honorably, the lawyer admits—"Whose is?"—but Teissier will be a good husband. "You had to give way to the law of the strongest" but "today this law has shifted in your favor" because Teissier wants Marie, the lawyer tells the Vignerons. He is helping to draw up an advantageous marriage contract because the situation has changed: "You've got the trumps. Play 'em!" He advises them to insist on immediate half ownership of all Teissier's possessions: "Then all you would have to do would be to pray that time [his death] would not be too long deferred." Soon another tradesman arrives with a claim. Teissier summarily dismisses him and turns to Marie. "Child, since your father died you've been surrounded by a lot of scoundrels," the old partner piously tells his bride: "Let's go and join your family."

W

WAITING FOR GODOT (*En attendant Godot*), a "tragicomedy" in two acts by SAMUEL BECKETT, published in 1952 and produced in 1953. Setting: a country road and a tree, on two successive evenings.

This immensely popular though mystifying play quickly made Beckett world famous. A modern classic of the ABSURD, it has been translated into many languages, the English version being Beckett's own.* SYMBOLIC and teeming with classic and biblical allusions, the play combines philosophy and vaudeville; an aptly paraphrased comment by JEAN ANOUILH describes it as a "music-hall sketch of Cartesian man performed by Chaplinesque clowns." Much of the dialogue is stichomythic and repetitive, with one of the characters apparently describing the play itself: "Nothing happens, nobody comes, nobody goes, it's awful!" The protagonist tramps waiting for the Godot who never appears, Vladimir and Estragon, who call each other Didi and Gogo and assume yet other names, in part represent mind and body. Ruby Cohn's *Casebook on Waiting for Godot* (1967) consists of an extensive collection of studies of this play and a bibliography.

Act I. Estragon tries unsuccessfully to take his boot off. Exhausted, he gives up and tries again as Vladimir comes in. "Nothing to be done," Estragon says, hopelessly, and Vladimir agrees. He too keeps trying "everything," gives up, and then resumes the struggle. After the friends have greeted each other, Estragon tells how he spent last night in a ditch, beaten up—as usual—probably by "the same lot." Vladimir inspects his bowler hat and Estragon, when he gets it off, inspects his boot. They should repent, Vladimir proposes. "What?" Estragon asks, and when Vladimir declines "to go into the details" he asks, "Our being born?" Vladimir laughs and then worries about discrepancies among the Gospel narrations. When Estragon wants to leave, Vladimir reminds him, "We're waiting for Godot." They persuade themselves this is the appointed place—"He said by the tree," and this leafless willow is the only tree around. Must they return tomorrow if Godot does not come? Were they here yesterday? They argue about these things and Estragon, unsure about the day, falls asleep. Later he tries to tell his dream to Vladimir, who refuses to listen. They quarrel, make up, and, to pass the time, think of hanging themselves. But since the tree's bough is too weak to hold them, they decide to wait for Godot. In the meantime they wonder about what they had wanted from him, and about the conditional nature of his reply. "Where do we come in?" Estragon asks, and Vladimir replies, "On our hands and knees." When he is hungry, Estragon gets a carrot from Vladimir. "Funny, the more you eat the worse it gets," he remarks, but Vladimir reacts differently: "I get used to the muck as I go along." Suddenly there is a terrible cry. Lucky comes in, a rope around his neck, driven by Pozzo, who holds the rope. Lucky carries a heavy bag and supplies for Pozzo. The latter cracks a whip and abuses Lucky, who crashes to the ground. For a while Estragon wonders whether Pozzo is Godot (whose name he keeps forgetting). Pozzo condescends to the tramps and brutally orders Lucky to set up his picnic. Estragon and Vladimir speculate on Lucky's deplorable appearance and position, solicit Pozzo's cast-off chicken bones, and deprecate his treatment of Lucky. Why does not the mute slave put down his bags, they want to know. Pozzo sprays his throat with a vaporizer, demands everyone's attention, and explains that Lucky behaves as he does because he wants to keep his position—"Such is his miserable scheme. As though I were short of slaves!" Pozzo intends to sell him, but when Lucky starts crying and Estragon goes to comfort him, Lucky kicks him viciously. Furious, Estragon spits on him. Pozzo orders Lucky to remove his hat (all four wear bowlers), which reveals Lucky's white hair, and then Pozzo breaks down at the thought of how badly Lucky treats him. Vladimir is appalled at Lucky: "How dare you! It's abominable! Such a good master! Crucify him like that! After so many years! Really!" They suggest that Lucky entertain them, and Pozzo has him dance. Then, telling him to put on his hat ("he can't think without his hat"), he orders Lucky to think. Lucky starts a very long tirade: "Given the existence as uttered forth in the public works of Puncher and Wattmann of a personal God quaquaquaqua with white beard quaquaquaqua outside time . . ." until the others, after trying to stop him, finally throw themselves on him and silence him. "There's an end to his thinking!" Pozzo remarks, kicks him ("Up pig!"), and asks the tramps to hold Lucky up. When Pozzo complains of the smell, Estragon explains, "He [Vladimir] has stinking breath and I have stinking feet." Finally Pozzo and Lucky depart, and Vladimir is glad that they have helped to pass the time. The tramps resume their wait when a boy comes with a message: "Mr. Godot told me to tell you he won't come this evening but surely to-morrow." He goes out, and night suddenly

* A sequel by Miodrag Bulatović appeared in 1966; see page 849.

falls. Estragon leaves his boots, and decides to go barefooted ("Christ did"). They promise to bring a piece of rope tomorrow to hang themselves with, reminisce about Estragon's throwing himself into the Rhone when they were grape harvesting, and wonder if they might not do better separately. Then they agree that it is not worthwhile to separate now. "Well, shall we go?" Estragon asks, and Vladimir replies, "Yes, let's go." Neither moves as the curtain falls.

Act II. The next evening Vladimir appears in the same spot and sings an endlessly repetitive ballad. Estragon comes in, but rebuffs Vladimir's welcoming embrace. He has been beaten up once more by "them," and suggests that he and Vladimir may be better off alone. They start waiting for Godot again, though Estragon has already forgotten the events of the previous evening and does not even recognize the spot. As they try to pass the time they discover that the bare tree now has some leaves. A pair of boots lie where Estragon had left his, but he claims they are not the same. When he wants to leave, Vladimir reminds him that they are waiting for Godot. He gives Estragon a radish when he complains of hunger, but because it is not pink, Estragon returns it. He puts on the boots and goes to sleep. Vladimir covers him with his own coat and keeps warm by exercising. Suddenly Estragon wakes up with a start, and Vladimir calms him. Then they see Lucky's hat. Vladimir tries it on, gives his own to Estragon, and a prolonged three-way hat-swapping routine ensues. It ends with Vladimir's taking Lucky's hat and discarding his own. They play at being Pozzo and Lucky, get frightened when they think they hear "them" coming, curse each other, and then play at abusing each other, Estragon winning with the epithet "Crritic!" They make up, and try to pass the time by doing exercises. Suddenly Lucky and Pozzo reappear, crashing and falling before them. Pozzo is now blind. He asks for help and is, they realize, at their mercy. They debate how they can use him. Now that they can act, Vladimir insists, they should. They know what they are doing: "Waiting for Godot to come. . . . We have kept our appointment and that's an end to that. We are not saints, but we have kept our appointment. How many people can boast as much?" When Pozzo offers them two hundred francs, they try to help him. But they stumble—and Estragon soon falls asleep. Finally they manage to get up, and try to rouse Pozzo. They call him, also by the names Abel and Cain, and since he answers, Estragon concludes Pozzo is "all humanity." When they get Pozzo up he does not recognize them. He asks for his "menial." Estragon kicks Lucky, but hurts his foot doing so. "Oh, the brute!" he moans. Pozzo prepares to leave again with Lucky, who is now dumb. Since when? What does time matter, Pozzo says angrily, "One day he went dumb, one day I went blind, one day we'll go deaf, one day we were born, one day we shall die.... They give birth astride of a grave, the light gleams an instant, then it's night once more." He jerks the rope and moves on. Estragon too wants to leave, but they must wait

Waiting for Godot. Estragon (Bert Lahr) and Vladimir (E. G. Marshall, right). New York, 1956. (*George Karger* from "Pix")

for Godot. He falls asleep and the boy comes again. He denies being the same boy who came yesterday. His message from Mr. Godot is that "he won't come this evening"; but he will come tomorrow, "without fail." Vladimir questions him about Godot. "He does nothing, Sir," the boy says of Godot; and he has a beard, "I think it's white." Very agitated, Vladimir says, "Tell him . . . tell him you saw me. . . . You're sure you saw me, you won't come and tell me to-morrow that you never saw me!" The boy runs off. Suddenly night falls. Estragon wakes up. He wants to leave, never to return, but Vladimir says of Godot, "He'd punish us." Estragon suggests that they hang themselves on the tree. Since they have no rope, they try Estragon's belt. But it breaks. Thereupon they decide to come tomorrow with some rope. "We'll hang ourselves tomorrow," Vladimir says, "unless Godot comes," in which case "we'll be saved." He tells Estragon to pull up his trousers. "What?" "Pull on your trousers." "You want me to pull off my trousers?" "Pull ON your trousers." Now Estragon realizes that the trousers are down. "True," he says, and pulls them up. Vladimir asks, "Well? Shall we go?" Estragon replies, "Yes, let's go." Neither moves as the curtain falls.

WAITING FOR LEFTY, a one-act play by CLIFFORD ODETS, published and produced in 1935. Setting: a platform occupied by six or seven seated strike-committee men; workers planted among the audience complete the effect of an auditorium during a union meeting in 1935.

Odets's first notable work was this history-making one-hour play, inspired by New York's 1934 taxicab drivers' strike. It is an episodic drama rooted in AGITPROP, especially in its catalogue of various capitalist evils and in its hortatory finale. Written in three days for a contest sponsored by the left-wing New Theatre League, it won and was produced on January 5, 1935, at a special benefit performance which electrified the audience. Soon the play was moved to Broadway, where the Group Theatre produced it (with the author playing the part of the Jewish doctor) on a double bill with Odets's anti-Nazi work, *Till the Day I Die*. In the final form the episodes within the framework of this frequently banned one-acter were transposed to alternate between those featuring workers and professionals. The "Lab Assistant Episode" replaced the original "V. The Young Actor," whose starving protagonist, rejected for a job by a ruthless Broadway producer preoccupied with hospital reports about his ailing dog, is exhorted by the office stenographer to read *The Communist Manifesto* and become "MILITANT!"

Harry Fatt, the corpulent and porcine union leader, finishes his address to the taxicab drivers (the audience), while a toothpick-chewing gunman lolls against the proscenium. "All we workers got a good man behind us now," Fatt says, referring to President Roosevelt and urging them not to strike, despite the low wages: "That's why the times ain't ripe for a strike." Voices from the audience shout their disagreement, and ask for Lefty Costello, their militant strike-committee chairman. "It ain't my fault Lefty took a run-out powder," Fatt retorts. He castigates the hecklers as "damn reds" and urges the workers to go home to their "hot suppers." But "sure," he says when they jeer and he is forced to give in to their demands to let the committeemen on the platform speak: "Let's hear what the red boys gotta say!" One of them, Joe Mitchell, gets up. "I ain't a red boy one bit!" he remarks; "[we are] the black and blue boys," because "we been kicked around so long we're black and blue from head to toes." As for "hot suppers . . ." The houselights fade and a spotlight illuminates the part of the stage where his speech explaining why they must strike is dramatized.

I. "Joe and Edna." As Joe comes home from work his wife, Edna, stands sullenly in their bare apartment. The furniture has been repossessed, and Edna is desperate. "I wish I was a kid again and didn't have to think about the next minute," Joe remarks. Edna angrily urges him to strike, but Joe says they cannot rush "the guys at the top," the union racketeers, who would shoot them. If the workers are that cowardly, Edna remarks, "let them all be ground to hamburger!" She threatens to leave him and the starving children and go to her old boyfriend unless he stands up to the boss, who is "giving your kids that fancy disease called the rickets. He's making a jelly-fish outa you and putting wrinkles in my face," and "throwing me into [the boyfriend's] lap." When Joe accuses her of "talking like a red," she says, "I don't know what that means. But when a man knocks you down you get up and kiss his fist! You gutless piece of baloney." And she urges him to "get those hack boys together" and fight. Inspired, Joe runs out. As the lights come up again Joe finishes his speech: "You guys know this stuff better than me. We gotta walk out!"

II. "Lab Assistant Episode." Another committeeman, a laboratory assistant, is offered a promotion by his industrialist boss. He is to work under a distinguished chemist—and regularly send confidential reports (i.e., spy) on his work: the preparation of poison gas. "If big business went sentimental over human life there wouldn't be big business of any sort," he remarks when the assistant mentions war casualties, and he appeals to the young man's patriotism. He would dig ditches before doing such work, the assistant says. "That's a big job for foreigners," the industrialist remarks. "But sneaking—and making poison gas—that's for Americans?" asks the assistant. When the industrialist cheerfully concludes, "No hard feelings?" the assistant floors him with a punch in the face: "Plenty of hard feelings! Enough to want to bust you and all your kind square in the mouth."

III. "The Young Hack and His Girl." In another episode, a committeeman and his girl friend discuss the three years of their courtship, in which "we never even had a room to sit in somewhere." Her family objects to him—because he will not be able to support her on a cabby's income. "Don't you see I want something else out of life," she tells her brother, who wants her to continue working to help support their mother; "I want romance, love, babies." But the cabdriver, though he loves her dearly, realizes "the cards is stacked against you." His own brother has joined the navy, where "they'll teach [him] to point the guns the wrong way" (i.e., at other, foreign workers, instead of at native capitalists). He thinks her family is right to oppose their marriage: "If we can't climb higher than this together—we better stay apart." They try to joke, but soon she starts weeping; the cabby falls on his knees and buries his face in her lap.

IV. "Labor Spy Episode." "You don't know how we work for you," Fatt tells the workers, and he calls on a man who, Fatt says, participated in an unsuccessful strike elsewhere and "got knocked down like the rest—and blacklisted after they went back." This man confirms Fatt's statements and his opinion that "the time ain't ripe." "That's a company spy," a heckler calls from the auditorium. "You'll prove all this or I'll bust you in every hack outfit in town!" Fatt threatens. The heckler finally reveals that "HE'S MY OWN LOUSY BROTHER!!" And then adds, "Too bad you didn't know about this, Fatt!"

V. "Interne Episode." A brilliant Jewish intern with seniority, another strike-committee man, is dismissed just before an important operation on a charity case. His place is taken by a senator's nephew who is "incompetent as hell." Amazed at the anti-Semitism despite the Jews on the hospital's

Waiting for Lefty. The call to "STRIKE!" Elia Kazan (center) as one of the workers. New York, 1935. (*Culver Pictures*)

board, the intern is told by his doctor friend, "Doesn't seem to be much difference between wealthy Jews and rich Gentiles. Cut from the same piece!" And since he has been overruled by politicians and the board, and cannot keep the Jewish intern, the doctor adds bitterly, "The men who know their jobs don't run anything here [in America], except the motormen on trolley cars." The patient dies under the incompetent doctor's knife. "I wanted to go to Russia," the intern says, thinking of "the wonderful opportunity to do good work in their socialized medicine." But "our work's here—America!" he decides: "Get some job to keep alive—maybe drive a cab." He raises his clenched fist: "Fight! Maybe get killed, but goddamn! We'll go ahead!"

The stage lights go on, and another committeeman addresses the workers and condemns union leadership. Fatt and the gunman try to stop him. But the other committeemen protect him, and he angrily calls for a strike. "This is your life and mine! It's skull and bones every incha the road! Christ, we're dyin' by inches," he continues, "for the debutant-ees to have their sweet comin' out parties in the Ritz! . . . with our blood." He calls on all workers to fight: "These slick slobs stand here telling us about bogeymen. That's a new one for the kids—the reds is bogeymen! But the man who got me food in 1932, he called me Comrade!" And he exhorts them, "What are we waiting for. . . . Don't wait for Lefty! He might never come." Just then word reaches the meeting that Lefty has been found—dead, shot by company goons. The committeeman angrily shouts for action: "HELLO AMERICA! HELLO. WE'RE STORMBIRDS OF THE WORKING-CLASS, WORKERS OF THE WORLD. . . . We'll die for what is right! put fruit trees where our ashes are!" When he questions the audience, they shout, "STRIKE!" He demands, "LOUDER!" And they shout again, "STRIKE!" Joined by others, he once more demands, "AGAIN!" The whole auditorium shouts its reply: "STRIKE, STRIKE, STRIKE!!!"

WALSER, Martin (1927–), German novelist and playwright, became notable in the 1960's with *Der Abstecher* (*The Detour,* 1961), a romantic comedy; *Eiche und Angora* (1962, translated as *The Rabbit Race*), a satiric indictment of Nazi "fellow travelers" and German philistines, personified by a simpleminded rabbit breeder who is unmanned in a concentration camp and cheerfully lets himself be institutionalized; and *Der schwarze Schwan* (1964), a similarly satiric but more tragic work about Germany's guilt, featuring a disturbed young man who exposes the shabby pasts of collaborating physicians.

WALTER, Eugene (1874–1941), American playwright born in Cleveland, Ohio. He wrote over a dozen skillfully constructed and successful melodramas, the most notable being THE EASIEST WAY (1908), a once-controversial portrayal of a "fallen" woman. Like the plays of ARTHUR WING PINERO,

Walter's plays are well-contrived thrillers that at their best appear to be (and sometimes come close to being) PROBLEM PLAYS about the conflict between human nature and morality. His best and most popular other works include his first play, *Serjeant James* (1902), which dramatizes some of Walter's experiences as a cavalryman in the Spanish-American War; *The Undertow* (1907), which deals with politics, the railroads, and the newspaper profession, in which Walter began his career; *Paid in Full* (1908), which depicts a strong "moral" woman ready to sacrifice her "virtue" for her weak and erring husband; and *Fine Feathers* (1912), which studies the morality of a courageous weakling who commits suicide when his dishonesty is revealed. Walter also adapted two popular American adventure novels by John Fox, Jr., *The Trail of the Lonesome Pine* (1908), in 1911, and *The Little Shepherd of Kingdom Come* (1903), in 1916; wrote many film scripts; and published a collection of his lectures on dramaturgy, *How to Write a Play* (1925).

WALTZ OF THE TOREADORS, THE (*La Valse des toréadors*), a play in five acts by JEAN ANOUILH, published and produced in 1952. Setting: France, c. 1910.

General Saint-Pé and his maniacal wife, Emily, like the play's setting and mood, are the same characters as those of ARDÈLE. Particularly effective is the brutal fourth-act confrontation between those two characters.

Act I. As General Saint-Pé is working in his study, his wife rails at him from the adjoining room: "Where were you just now in your head? With what woman? In which kitchen, tumbling Heaven knows what drab." He dictates his memoirs but is interrupted by his gawky daughters, who want new dresses. "My God, aren't they ugly," complains the General, a connoisseur. Soon he is interrupted by his friend, his wife's doctor, who attributes her paralysis to psychological causes. Finally comes Mlle. Ghislaine de Ste.-Euverte, whom the General has loved chastely for seventeen years. They reminisce passionately about their first meeting at a ball, when they danced the "Waltz of the Toreadors." Then she reveals evidence of his wife's infidelity—love letters to the doctor. Now Ghislaine sees no reason for waiting any longer to consummate their love.

Act II. The outraged General challenges his friend to a duel. But the doctor persuades him that the letters were never mailed and that he ought to stop his jealousy, leave his wife, and marry his beloved. General Saint-Pé goes to his wife's room, which he finds empty save for a note: having overheard the talk, she has rushed out to end her life. He runs after her and Ghislaine, sure he still loves the wife, decides to kill herself. But the pistol she has kept seventeen years to defend her virginity no longer functions. So Ghislaine throws herself out of the window—and lands on the young secretary rocking in a hammock. Awakening from her faint, Ghislaine mistakes the secretary for her beloved General, and demands that he kiss her. The General carries in his unconscious wife, who soon also awakens and demands to be kissed.

Act III. While the women are resting, the General confesses boredom and loneliness despite his philandering: "It is my terror of living which sends me scampering after them." He has loved only Ghislaine, but has been unwilling to desert his invalid wife. Then, while his daughters fight over the secretary, whom both love, Saint-Pé flirts with their dressmaker. Later the secretary proclaims his love for Ghislaine. The General laughs at the boy and then gives him cynical advice about life. When he admits that happiness should be seized in one's youth, the boy goes to Ghislaine.

Act IV. In her room, the wife berates the General: "You pig, you satyr, you lascivious goat!" When he accuses her of infidelity she rebukes him for rifling her desk, and feigns a heart attack. Then she demands his love: "Why don't you bite me all over like a young terrier any more?" The embarrassed General replies, "Dammit, Madam, young terriers grow into old ones. . . . Besides, I've lost my teeth." Again she castigates him for his philandering, blames him for ruining her career as a singer, and then taunts him with her own adulteries, which began with an officer she met at the same ball where he met Ghislaine. Their reproaches and hatred reach a climax as the wife admits she has feigned paralysis to hold him: "I love you because you are mine, my object, my thing, my hold-all, my garbage bin—" Madly she jumps off her bed, pursues him and insists on dancing the "Waltz of the Toreadors" with him. At last, shouting "Phantasmagoria!!" he grips her by the throat.

Act V. The doctor assures the General that his wife is all right now. Though they soon return, his lovesick daughters run off, leaving a suicide note. The secretary and Ghislaine announce that they have become lovers and Saint-Pé furiously plans to stop their marriage. The secretary is not of age, but he is revealed to be the General's own illegitimate son, and takes Ghislaine away. The General is left alone. A new maid appears. As his wife shouts a warning from the adjoining room, General Saint-Pé goes for a stroll in the moonlit garden, his arm around the girl's waist: "It's nicer like this, don't you think? Not that it means anything, but still, one feels less lonely, in the dark." And the curtain falls as they go out, "an absurd couple."

WARNINGS, a one-act play by EUGENE O'NEILL, published in 1914. Setting: a contemporary flat in the Bronx (New York) and the wireless room of a ship.

Originally published in THIRST AND OTHER ONE-ACT PLAYS, this short, early piece is in two scenes, the first of them a SLICE OF LIFE.

In order to keep his job and the income desperately needed by his family, a wife persuades her wireless-operator husband not to report his oncoming deafness to his employers. In a second scene, aboard a sinking transatlantic liner, deafness has overtaken him and, realizing his responsibility for the ship's disaster, he shoots himself.

WARREN, Robert Penn (1905–), American poet, novelist, and critic, adapted his *All the King's Men* (1964), a novel about a Southern demagogue modeled on Huey Long, into an Academy Award-winning film and into a stylized play. It appeared in a workshop production by Erwin Piscator in 1948, and in a revised Off-Broadway version in 1959. Warren's dramatized version of his *Brother to Dragons* (1953), a verse tale about President Jefferson's confrontation with his nephew's torture-murder of a black slave, was produced in 1968.

WARRIOR'S BARROW, THE (*Kjæmpehøjen*), a one-act dramatic poem by HENRIK IBSEN, produced in 1850 and published in 1854. Setting: an island off Sicily, "shortly before the introduction of Christianity into Norway."

A revision of an even earlier piece, this play (like CATILINE) is pseudonymous and in blank verse, and was influenced by the Danish poet Adam Oehlenschläger.

King Gandalf appears with other Norwegian Vikings to exact revenge. He falls in love with an old recluse's foster daughter, who at last sails back with him. The recluse is revealed as Gandalf's father, a magnanimous Christian convert who remains on the island near his "throne": the warrior's barrow in which he buried his sword and armor.

WASTE, a play in four acts by HARLEY GRANVILLE-BARKER, produced in 1907 and published in 1909. Setting: Hertfordshire and London, early twentieth century.

This once highly praised drama (banned from public performance because of the abortion), which reappeared in a second version in 1926, is loosely based on the careers of two statesmen ruined by the scandal of adultery, Sir Charles Dilke and Charles Stewart Parnell.

When his affair becomes public, Henry Trebell faces professional ruin. The possibility of his entering the Cabinet is examined by various politicians, and Trebell himself questions his—or anyone's—fitness to be a statesman: "We're an adulterous and sterile generation. Why should you cry out at a proof now and then of what's always in the hearts of most of us?" he asks his chief political antagonist. His mistress's revelation of her pregnancy and the abortion that culminates in her death affect and are juxtaposed with Trebell's presentation of his Disestablishment Bill, and cause a political uproar. His reputation destroyed and his policy defeated, Trebell commits suicide. His young secretary cries in anguish "at the waste of a good man. Look at the work undone . . . think of it! Who is to do it! Oh . . . the waste . . . !"

WAYWARD SAINT, THE, a satirical comedy in three acts by PAUL VINCENT CARROLL, published and produced in 1955. Setting: Kilkevin, a little village near the Northern Irish border, 1950's.

A wild romp replete with magical doings, this play features an elderly canon vaguely modeled on Francis of Assisi.

Canon Daniel McCooey has the reputation of a saint: he communicates with birds and is believed to have restored a dead child to life. His bishop, finding saints a "confounded nuisance," has sent him to this retreat, run by a grim housekeeper. All kinds of doings transpire when Satan's emissary, in the guise of a worldly nobleman, moves in with his retinue and tries to win the canon's soul. At the end Canon Daniel is about to be vanquished by this evil force. But the virtue of a neighbor girl saves him, and an escaped circus lion domesticated by the canon eats the satanic being. The bishop returns to send Canon Daniel to the Pope, to be examined for sainthood. As the curtain falls, they argue. "You're going to Rome, Daniel," the bishop orders, and the Canon refuses: "Not a solitary foot."

WEAVERS, THE (*Die Weber*), "a play of the 1840's" in five acts by GERHART HAUPTMANN, published in 1892 and produced in 1893. Setting: three Silesian mountain towns, 1840's.

This NATURALISTIC masterpiece brought Hauptmann international fame. Its powerful depiction of the workers' hunger and oppression, which finally explode into abortive riots, had inflammatory effects that Hauptmann perhaps did not intend to create: the play was banned by the government and exploited by the Social Democrats. It is a "mass drama" with a collective hero, but there are many individualized characters. Despite a slender plot, the action is intensely—if unconventionally—dynamic. The panoramic scenes are unified by the unremitting picture of misery and by the repetition of the weavers' "Bloody Justice" song, a *leitmotif* of the play. Also published under the Silesian-dialect title, *Die Waber,* the play is based on an actual uprising in 1844. Hauptmann's great portrayal of human degradation and suffering, still topical in the 1890's, has also been found so in the twentieth century.

Act I. At Dreissiger's textile plant, emaciated weavers tensely wait for the inspection of webs they have been weaving at home. The pitiful wages for their work are doled out and further lowered by the arrogant staff, who ruthlessly reject the starving but submissive workers' individual pleas. As Old Baumert, a worker, tells of having killed his dog to save his family from starvation, the only weaver to speak out fearlessly is discharged and blacklisted. The manufacturer Dreissiger becomes annoyed when a small child, sent by his sick family to deliver their work, faints of hunger. Blustering, he orders his staff to accept no further webs brought by children, expatiates on the irresponsibility of weaver parents, and complains about the hard life of a factory owner. The weavers meekly accept his opinions. As he leaves, he tells them of his willingness to risk hiring additional hundreds of weavers who are currently unemployed. He quickly escapes when individual weavers implore his help; his manager further reduces their pay, and the miserable weavers start grumbling.

Act II. At Old Baumert's shack, his crippled

The Weavers, Act II. Old Baumert (Fritz Richard, center), his emaciated daughters (Selma Scholz and Rose Müller, right), their hoary landlord (Carl Wallauer), Jäger (Wilhelm Dieterle, sitting on chair), and Old Baumert's wife (Paula Eberty, extreme right). Berlin, 1921. (*Ullstein Bilderdienst, Berlin*)

aged wife is spooling as her emaciated daughters, idiot son, and starving grandson crouch nearby. They talk to an equally destitute neighbor who has just about reached the end of her rope. The hoary landlord comes in, and then Old Baumert, holding under his arm a package—the little dog he has killed to save them from starvation. Accompanying him is Moritz Jäger, formerly a local weaver but now a soldier. He is well fed and has money; he has also been around and—as he passes his bottle—tells them how manufacturers live: "They don't hardly know what to do with all their wealth and arrogance." Soon Old Baumert, his stomach unaccustomed to meat, throws up the dog he has just eaten, and weeps in rage: "Ya finally get something good, and ya can't even hold it down!" As their angry indignation against the exploiters grows, Jäger reads them the "Bloody Justice" song: ". . . Here bloody justice thrives . . . Men are slowly tortured . . . A curse will be your payment . . ." Deeply stirred, and enraged against Dreissiger, the weavers begin thinking of rebellion: "We won't take it no more, come what may!"

Act III. At the local tavern, a traveling salesman is ogling the innkeeper's daughter. When he expresses his surprise at the elaborate funeral of a poor weaver, he is told that the clergy encourage poor people's going into debt to increase the funeral offertory. The entrance of a forester triggers the weavers' resentment against dated feudal restrictions that add to their misery. The salesman interrupts his philandering to remark that government inspectors have found reports of local poverty greatly exaggerated; but an old ragpicker furiously describes the gruesome situation that the inspectors, fearful of muddying their shoes, never bother to go to see. Jäger comes in with a group of weavers and treats them to drinks, and their excitement mounts. When a policeman prohibits singing of the "Bloody Justice" song, their anger explodes. Singing it, they go off to Dreissiger to demand a raise. The old ragpicker remarks, "Ah, every man has his dream."

Act IV. At a social gathering in Dreissiger's house, a pastor chastizes the manufacturer's family tutor for defending the agitating weavers. "A keeper of souls must not concern himself with bellies," he tells the young theology student. Their host comes in, and fires the tutor when he repeats his defense of the weavers. But the riots have now reached Dreissiger's house. Jäger is brought in by the police, and disconcerts the others with his impertinent defiance—even toward the pastor, who tells him to "be a good Christian": "I'm a Quaker now, Pastor; I don't believe in anything anymore." He is taken out, but soon Dreissiger's manager comes in breathless and fearful for his life. The rioting weavers have freed Jäger, have beaten up the police, and are rushing the house. The pastor goes out to talk to them, and is quickly overcome. Terrified, Dreissiger and his family escape. After a few moments, the weavers break into the empty room. First they are silent, but gradually their timidity gives way to anger. They heap threats on the absent manufacturer and his manager, and plan to wreck the factory and go on to others, where there are "steam-power looms." At the curtain, all of them—even the more conservative older weavers—are smashing up Dreissiger's luxurious home.

Act V. In a poor weaver's room the next morning, the family (Old Hilse, his blind wife, and their son and his wife) are finishing their prayers. Old Hilse is incredulous and then appalled to hear of the riots. When his little grandchild comes in with a spoon found in front of Dreissiger's home, Old Hilse is furious and has his son go off to return it. His daughter-in-law screams hysterically against those who have caused her children's death of starvation, and jeers at the weavers, "milksops who'd run away in fright." Old Hilse, however, would not dream of joining the riot, and remains unshakable in his pious belief in Judgment Day. Victorious weavers come in with booty and food from one of the factories, but Hilse will accept nothing, and ridicules their dream of the changed and better life that is coming. Now the militia is approaching, and Hilse's son is torn between his father's pietism and his wife's rebellious militancy. When the shooting starts and she fights in the front ranks, he rushes out to battle. Though warned to seek cover, Old Hilse sits down at the window and starts weaving: "Not me! Not if ya all go bats. Here my Heavenly Father put me. Right, Mother? Here we'll stay sittin' and doin' what's our duty!" A volley of shots is heard, and he falls down as his grandchild excitedly rushes in to report on the battle's progress. She sees him crumpled up and, frightened, calls upon him repeatedly. So does his blind old wife: "C'mon, Old Man, say something. Yer scarin' me."

WEB, THE, a one-act play by EUGENE O'NEILL, published in 1914. Setting: contemporary Lower East Side New York.

This play was written in 1913 and published in THIRST AND OTHER ONE-ACT PLAYS. Refusing to publish A WIFE FOR A LIFE, which he had written earlier in the same year, O'Neill claimed *The Web* as his first play. Although a melodramatic minor one, it presents prototypes of characters and themes he was to develop later.

In the bedroom of a squalid tenement, the dying consumptive prostitute Rose Thomas, who cannot reform because the respectable society that "got me where I am . . . won't let yuh do it," is bullied and beaten by her "protector." He shoots a fugitive bandit (equally trapped by life) who had wanted to help Rose and had fallen in love with her, and manages to implicate her in the murder. Before policemen lead the coughing Rose away, they take her baby and are shocked by the profanity of her cry: "Gawd! Gawd! Why d'yuh hate me so?" Victims in "the web" of circumstances and social forces over which they had no control, Rose and the bandit have nonetheless been held responsible and punished by a hypocritical society. "It's a bum game all round," Rose concludes.

WEDDING, THE (*Svadba*), a one-act play by ANTON CHEKHOV, passed by the censor for production in 1889 and published in 1890. Setting: a room in a contemporary second-class restaurant.

Chekhov's dramatization of his short story "Svadba s generalom" ("A Wedding with a General," 1884) portrays wedding festivities marred by various farcical squabbles and misunderstandings among the family and guests, including a "general" who turns out to be a superannuated captain of a small ship.

WEDEKIND, [Benjamin] **Frank[lin]** (1864–1918), German dramatist and actor, probably influenced modern German playwrights more than any of his contemporaries, including GERHART HAUPTMANN. Wedekind's dramatization of sex elicited popular indignation, and his plays were banned by the Kaiser as well as the Nazis. But he was vigorously championed by literary and theatre people—and by moral reformers. Today Wedekind is virtually forgotten—despite the power of his best plays, his sensational personal history (for apparently he lived the kind of life he espoused), and his importance as a precursor of EXPRESSIONISM and other postNATURALISTIC drama.

Though born in Germany, Wedekind was technically an American. His father, a German political radical and an adventurer, was a physician who practiced in America for a time, was naturalized, and married a young Hungarian actress before returning to Germany. Eventually the family moved to Switzerland; there Wedekind grew up with his sister, a later famous diva. Their father sent Wedekind to Munich to study law; when he decided to become a writer instead, there were bitter family arguments, which he related to Hauptmann, who based THE FEAST OF RECONCILIATION on the story. Already opposed to Hauptmann's naturalistic dramaturgy, Wedekind thereupon caricatured him in an early play, *Kinder und Narren* (1891), as a poet snooping for material among sexually repressed boarding-school girls.

Wedekind started as a journalist, and took various writing and secretarial jobs. He drifted toward circuses and variety halls—a lifelong association reflected in his plays. With Tilly, who was to become his wife and costar, he gave public readings of HENRIK IBSEN's and his own works, and sang ballads in cabarets—like BERTOLT BRECHT, whose works (and history) bear some resemblance to Wedekind's. In 1890 he settled in Munich for a short while, and began writing the plays that made him famous: *Frühlings Erwachen* (SPRING'S AWAKENING, 1891), the "Lulu plays" *Erdgeist* (EARTH SPIRIT, 1895) and *Die Büchse der Pandora* (PANDORA'S BOX, 1904), *Der Kammersänger* (THE COURT SINGER, 1897; also known as *The Tenor*), *Der Marquis von Keith* (THE MARQUIS OF KEITH, 1900), *König Nicolo, oder so ist das Leben* (KING NICOLO, OR SUCH IS LIFE, 1902), *Hidala, oder Karl Hetmann, der Zwerg-Riese* (HIDALLA, OR KARL

Frank Wedekind. (*Culver Pictures*)

HETMAN, THE GIANT MIDGET, 1904), and *Tod und Teufel* (DEATH AND DEVIL, 1905; sometimes considered one of the "Lulu plays"). Less important early works are *Der Schnellmaler, oder Kunst und Mammon* (1889); *Fritz Schwigerling,* a farce (completed in 1892 and published as *Der Liebestrank,* 1899) about the variety theatre he loved and one of its stars whom he admired; *Die Kaiserin von Neufundland* (1897), a pantomime; and *Das Sonnenspektrum* (*The Solar Spectrum*), a projected four-act play about a prostitute in a bordello, beginning with her initiation in "Der Liebesgarten," the only part Wedekind completed (in 1894).*

Wedekind was one of the founders and the editor of *Simplizissimus,* the well-known satirical journal. In Paris he met AUGUST STRINDBERG (with whose wife Frida he had a tempestuous affair after her break with Strindberg) and Willy Grétor, whom he immortalized as the Marquis of Keith. Frequently acting in his own plays, Wedekind escaped by way of the stage door after one performance to avoid arrest for satirizing the Kaiser. Eventually he returned and served his sentence. But though he achieved popularity with Max Reinhardt's production of *Spring's Awakening,* which spawned a host of "adolescent" and "school" plays (including those of ARNO HOLZ, MAX DREYER, OTTO ERNST, and LUDWIG THOMA), it was short lived. The public soon became indignant with Wedekind's revolutionary ideas and dramaturgy.

His contempt of philistine society with its venality and hypocrisies was as offensive as his attitudes on sex and his dramaturgy, which were ahead of their age. Many considered him a "pornographer," and Hauptmann characterized the Lulu plays as "excreta." Striving to release men from the stifling and injurious sex secrecy that he considered symptomatic of modern immorality, Wedekind portrayed antisocial—i.e., antibourgeois—behavior as heroic: his criminals and prostitutes are the admirable members of the human menagerie. He celebrated the body as having "a soul of its own" and, in a manner suggestive of Nietzsche, sang of the superman—of great human strength and beauty.

Similarly, Wedekind's dramaturgy is garish and fragmentary, recalling that of Georg Büchner. Its staccato dialogue prefigured the expressionism of GEORG KAISER, ERNST TOLLER, and others, though it depicts individuals rather than the mass. And if the didacticism and cabaret elements prefigure Brecht's drama, the sex duels recall Strindberg's—though Wedekind's victor is usually the male, physically (Jack the Ripper vanquishes Lulu) as well as morally.

Despite their GRAND GUIGNOL and occasional absurdity, some of Wedekind's plays are still powerful, highly theatrical, and surprisingly undated. In other plays, however, he increasingly reverted to self-pity and self-justification. The later works, though highly autobiographical, are of little more than historical interest: *Musik* (1908), "a picture of morals in four scenes"; *Die Zensur* (1908), a diatribe against censorship; *Rabbi Esra* (written about 1908, published in 1924), a dramatization of a story by him; *Oaha* (1908), a four-act Till Eulenspiegel comedy; *Der Stein der Weisen* (1909); *Schloss Wetterstein* (*Castle Wetterstein,* 1910), another prostitution drama, whose heroine strongly resembles Lulu; *Franziska* (1912), "a modern mystery play" in prose and verse, with choruses—a Faust drama whose female protagonist makes a pact enabling her to lead a sensual life, passes through experiences analogous to those in Goethe's drama, and finally cheats her Mephistorake by getting pregnant and retiring to a rustic, maternal idyll; *Simson, oder Scham und Eifersucht* (1913), dramatizing the biblical tale of Samson and Delilah; *Bismarck* (1916), a patriotic historical play; *Überfürchtenichts* (1916); and *Herakles* (1917), a depiction of Hercules as a superman burdened with a curse.

Wedekind also wrote poetry, fiction, and essays defending and proclaiming his ideas on sex and morals. His reputation, however, rests primarily on his nearly thirty published plays, to which he tended to give alternative titles. The most important of these have been translated and anthologized—notably in Carl R. Mueller's edition of *The Lulu Plays* (1967) and in *Five Tragedies of Sex*†

* It appears, with notes and an outline of the whole projected work, in the *Tulane Drama Review* IV:1 (1959).

† Cotranslated by STEPHEN SPENDER: *Spring's Awakening, Earth Spirit, Pandora's Box, Death and Devil,* and *Castle Wetterstein.*

(1952), which has an introduction by LION FEUCHTWANGER. A full-length study is Sol Gittleman's *Frank Wedekind* (1969).

WEISENBORN, Günther (1902–), German writer, is known as a left-wing critic, poet, and novelist no less than as a playwright. A disciple of BERTOLT BRECHT, he wrote pacifist drama in the 1920's and—following his exile, anti-Fascist activities, and imprisonment—continued his writing and theatre work after World War II. His best-known play, *Die Illegalen* (1945), dramatizes the wartime uprising and execution of Munich students; but the play is also based on Weisenborn's other eventful experiences.

He was born in the Rhineland, studied medicine, and went to Berlin in 1928. When the Nazis came to power and banned his works in 1933 he went to Argentina to be a farmer, and then became a journalist in New York. In 1937 he returned to Germany, where he joined the underground opposition to the Nazis until he was caught in 1942 and sent to various concentration camps. Upon his release in 1945 he became the mayor of Luckau; in 1951 he was appointed *Dramaturg* of Berlin's Hebbel Theatre.

Weisenborn's writings reflect his socialist bias; usually satiric, they criticize such evils as war and social injustice. His plays deal with history, revolution, pacifism, and social reconstruction. Early plays were AGITPROP works like *U-Boot S4* (1928) and *SOS, oder die Arbeiter von Jersey* (1929). His 1930's plays, some of which appeared pseudonymously, include *Die Neuberin* (1935) and a drama about the bacteriologist Robert Koch, *Die guten Feinde* (1936). While in prison, Weisenborn wrote *Babel* (1945). His first postwar plays were the earlier-mentioned *Die Illegalen* and *Ballade vom Eulenspiegel, vom Federle und von der dicken Pompanne* (1949), in which he associates the folk hero with the rebel cause in the Peasant War. Later Weisenborn works include *Das Spiel vom Thomaskantor* (1950), *Die Familie von Nevada* (1958, about atom bomb tests), *Göttinger Kantate* (1958, another anti-atom-bomb work, this time in the form of an oratorio), and *15 Schnüre Geld* (1959, based on an old Chinese play by Chu Su Chen).

In these and in his dozen or so other plays Weisenborn strove to express his concept of the theatre as "a place where humanity can talk with itself," articulate the "inner voice of the people," and manifest its principal attribute, that of always being "a place of change."

WEISS, Peter (1916–), German-born playwright, novelist, and film producer, began his career as a painter. After his phenomenal success with the long-titled drama that became known simply as MARAT/SADE (1964), Weiss confined himself principally to playwriting. *Die Ermittlung* (THE INVESTIGATION, 1965), his oratorio on Auschwitz, and other later works are more explicitly political in their protest. However, they have aroused less interest—or controversy.

Weiss was born in Nowawes, near Berlin, the son of a Swiss woman and her Czechoslovakian husband, whose nationality and citizenship Weiss automatically assumed at birth. He was brought up in his mother's Christian rather than his father's Jewish faith, and attended school in Nowawes and Berlin before leaving Germany in 1934, shortly following the advent of Nazism. After studying at the Art Academy in Prague, Weiss moved to Switzerland and in 1939 he emigrated to Sweden. There he was to spend much of his life with his wife, Gunilla Palmstierna, an artist who designed the costumes for his plays. In Sweden Weiss gave up painting and began to publish novels and to direct documentary and experimental films that achieved limited renown and were shown overseas —notably *Hallucinations* (1953), a six-minute series of erotic tableaux; and *The Mirage* (1958), a full-length Kafkaesque depiction of a starving man's fantasies.

Weiss turned to drama with *Der Turm* (*The Tower,* 1962), a phantasmagoric one-act allegory about an escape artist who returns to perform in the tower and, amidst disembodied memories of the past, for the last time bursts his bonds—"the rope that dangles from him now like an umbilical cord." Weiss's next play, *Nacht mit Gästen,* was his first to be produced; appearing in Berlin in 1963, it too is a one-acter and it portrays puppetlike figures who commit murders in a Punch-and-Judy setting and mood. It was with the work that followed, *Marat/Sade,* that Weiss became internationally known. *The Investigation,* despite its harrowing effect, did not attract such mass audiences, though it too was produced in many countries.

Weiss continued to dramatize his indignation about cruelty and injustice with equal ardor if less success in the plays that followed. *Gesang vom Lusitanischen Popanz* (*Song of the Lusitanian Bogey,* 1967; translated also as *The Lusitanian Bogey*), a "political musical" with dance, portrays the exploitation of Angola and Mozambique from the time of the first Portuguese explorers until the Africans' abortive revolt in March, 1961. *Viet Nam Diskurs* (*Vietnam Discourse,* 1968; translated also as *Discourse on the Progress of the Prolonged War of Liberation in Vietnam, etc.*), a tendentious two-part documentary without music, traces the history of Vietnamese occupations from 500 B.C. to Dien Bien Phu and then to 1968, and includes characters like Winston Churchill, Cardinal Spellman, and Presidents Eisenhower, Kennedy, and Johnson; its unabridged title (like that of *Marat/Sade*) summarizes the plot: "Discourse About the Background and Course of the Long-Lasting Fight for Freedom in Vietnam as an Example for the Necessity of an Armed Struggle of the Suppressed Against the Suppressors as Well as About the Attempt of the United States of America to Eradicate the Foundation of the Revolution." *Wie dem Herrn Mockinpott das Leiden ausgetrieben wird* (1968) deals with serious issues farcically and culminates with its Chaplinesque hero's complaining to a God sitting on a toilet-throne. Weiss returned to political themes with *Trotzki im Exil* (1970), an anti-Soviet depiction of Trotsky's exile; and with *Hölderlin* (1971)—Weiss's first major work since *Marat/Sade*—presenting the poet as a revolutionary who simulates madness and reveals his secret writings upon learning from young Karl Marx that his enemies Goethe and Schiller have died.

Though *Marat/Sade* appeared to take drama into new directions, it was readily identified by critics as a synthesis of such earlier styles as the theatre of CRUELTY; the drama of Georg Büchner (1813–37), BERTOLT BRECHT, and SAMUEL BECKETT; and the philosophies of JEAN-PAUL SARTRE and the novelist Franz Kafka. Weiss's later works, however, resemble the sociopolitical avant-garde theatre of the 1920's and 1930's. "Every word I write is political," Weiss has declared, adding that "writing for me is an outlet for my opinions as well as my fantasy." Though he became a Swedish citizen—despite his rejection of nationalism—he has continued to write in German. Most of his plays are in free verse.

Early autobiographical novels by Weiss appeared in English as the one-volume *Exile* (1968).

WELDED, a play in three acts by EUGENE O'NEILL, published and produced in 1924. Setting: New York, early twentieth century.

Stilted in language and overly histrionic in its love-hate sex duels, this unsuccessful autobiographical play was strongly influenced by AUGUST STRINDBERG.

Eleanor and Michael Cape, a playwright and an actress, are passionately in love. But egotism, pride, and jealous need for self-expression and fulfillment constantly torture their love and drive them to battle. Eleanor regards Michael's matrimonial ideal for them as being too high and therefore inhuman. The appearance of an old friend triggers bitter recriminations about the past and jealous suspicions about the present. They rush out, determined to kill their love for each other. But neither can do this. At the crucial moment in the friend's house, Eleanor sees a vision of Michael, and she concludes that "My love for him is my own, not his! That he can never possess! It's *my* own. It's *my* life!" Michael learns stoicism from a prostitute: "To learn to love life—to accept it and be exalted—that's the one faith left to us!" Back at home later at night, they start their agonizing self-analysis again: "Thinking explains. It eliminates the unexplainable—by which we live," says the husband, to which the wife warningly adds, "By which we love. Sssh!" Finally, though they recognize that "we'll torture and tear, and clutch for each other's souls!—fight—fail and hate again—but!—fail *with pride*—with joy!" They recognize also that they are "welded" to each other. Triumphantly they achieve their union in mystic love: Eleanor awaits him with outstretched arms, and "as their hands touch they form together one cross. Then their arms go about each other and their lips meet."

WELL-MADE PLAY (or *pièce bien faite*), a usually pejorative term, refers to shallow, nonliterary but theatrical drama (farce or intrigue with serious social overtones) that sacrifices the pretense of any kind of REALISM for mechanical and arbitrarily contrived patterns of plot structure and suspense. The well-made play customarily is predicated on a withheld secret and focused on a trivial object, climaxed by a *scène à faire* (or "obligatory scene") in which the secret is revealed and resolved happily for the hero. It was originated and popularized by the prolific French dramatist Augustin Eugène Scribe (1791–1861), and dominated the later nineteenth-century theatres of Europe and America. Especially notable among Scribe's many disciples are Eugène Labiche (1815–87), the author of innumerable popular farces, and VICTORIEN SARDOU. The latter's success elicited BERNARD SHAW's derisive label of "Sardoodledom" to characterize the triviality and meretriciousness of non-IBSENite and pre-Shavian drama.

The structure and parts of the well-made play are exemplified by Bernstein's THE THIEF and Sardou's A SCRAP OF PAPER, and they are described in WILLIAM ARCHER's *Playmaking, A Manual of Craftsmanship* (1928). See also Stephen S. Stanton's introduction to *Camille and Other Plays* (1957), which has a bibliography on the well-made play; and John Russell Taylor's *The Rise and Fall of the Well-Made Play* (1967), a more subjective assessment with separate chapters on HENRY ARTHUR JONES, ARTHUR WING PINERO, Shaw, OSCAR WILDE, SOMERSET MAUGHAM, HARLEY GRANVILLE-BARKER, JOHN GALSWORTHY, FREDERICK LONSDALE, NOËL COWARD, and TERENCE RATTIGAN.

WELL OF THE SAINTS, THE, a play in three acts by J. M. SYNGE, published and produced in 1905. Setting: rural east Ireland, "one or more centuries ago."

This is the first of Synge's full-length plays. It had a generally cool reception and has remained one of his less popular plays, though it has had its particular admirers, including GEORGE MOORE. Based on a familiar folklore theme, it is a caustic satire of illusion as well as reality.

Act I. Martin Doul and his wife, Mary, are blind, weather-beaten, ugly old beggars. Sitting by the roadside, however, they are happy with the world, which they believe to be beautiful like themselves. The villagers encourage their delusion and the couple complacently dismiss as jealousy occasional malicious hints of the truth. The village smith announces the arrival of a saint (a wandering friar) with miraculous water from a holy well, and they rejoice at the prospect of finally seeing each other. When the Saint restores his sight, Martin rapturously praises the beauty of various girls whom he mistakes for his wife. He is crushed and speechless when he identifies Mary; she is equally bitter about him: "I'm thinking it's a poor thing when the Lord God gives you sight and puts the like of that man in your way." Miserable and totally disillusioned, they ridicule and threaten to hit each other. The Saint separates them: "May the Lord who has given you sight send a little sense into your heads, the way it won't be on your two selves you'll be looking—on two pitiful sinners of the earth—but on the splendour of the Spirit of God."

Act II. Now separated from Mary and half-heartedly doing odd jobs for the smith, Martin is intensely aware of the world's horrible ugliness. He sees loveliness only in the cruel girl engaged to the smith. Even her ridicule of him as "a little, old, shabby stump of a man" does not dampen his passion, for he thinks she embodies the beauty and happiness he is seeking. She denounces him, and completes his shame by revealing his "dreams" and yearnings to Mary. Blindness again threatens Martin, and he cries frantically, "Is it the darkness of thunder is coming?" When he seizes Mary's arm, she hits his face with an empty sack. He is ridiculed and cast away by his wife, the girl, and the smith, who threatens to beat him. In agony, Martin prays for and envisions a hereafter where he can watch the smith and his girl "on a high bed, and they screeching . . . twisting and roaring out" for all eternity: "It won't be hell to me, I'm thinking, but the like of heaven itself."

Act III. Mary, also blind again, returns to the roadside, lonely and bitter. Martin soon joins her, equally dejected. Eventually, however, their mutual jibes stimulate their imaginations. Mary weaves new fantasies about her looks: "A beautiful white-haired woman is a grand thing to see." Admiring her and already accepting her new self-portrait, Martin thinks of resuming their former relationship: "But I'll never rest easy, thinking you're a grey beautiful woman, and myself a pitiful show." Suddenly he has a solution: he will grow a beard, "a beautiful, long, white, silken, streamy beard, you wouldn't see the like of in the eastern world." Mary agrees cheerfully: "We're a great pair, surely, and it's great times we'll have yet." Their happiness is threatened by the returning Saint, who wants to restore their sight again. They resist what they now consider a fearful menace. Martin eloquently describes the ugly realities he has seen, and asks to be allowed to remain blind—and happy. The Saint, however, stresses the great goodness and beauty of God's world, and insists on curing them. Martin dashes the holy water to the ground, rejecting the Saint's religious (as well as the villagers' practical) views: "It's a good right ourselves have to be sitting blind, hearing a soft wind turning round the little leaves of the spring and feeling the sun, and we not tormenting our souls with the sight of the grey days, and the holy men, and the dirty feet is trampling the world." Cast out by the scandalized villagers, Mary and Martin leave to seek a place whose ugliness and villainy they at least do not know about. The Saint, ready to perform the smith's wedding, leads the villagers to church.

WERFEL, Franz (1890–1945), Austrian writer, was famous for his novels, principally for *Die vierzig Tage des Musa Dagh* (*The Forty Days of Musa Dagh,* 1933). He was notable also for his poetry and for a number of plays, especially, in the English-speaking world, for the horror-inspiring *Bocksgesang* (GOAT SONG, 1921) and for his last work, the amusingly autobiographical *Jacobowsky und der Oberst* (JACOBOWSKY AND THE COLONEL, 1944). In the United States, his novelistic tribute to the saint of Lourdes, *Das Lied von Bernadette* (*The Song of Bernadette,* 1941), was filmed as well as made into a play in 1946, by Jean (1923–) and Walter Kerr (1913–); while the Hungarian László Bus-Fekete (1898–) and Mary Helen Fay (? –) in 1944 dramatized another of his novels, *Der veruntreute Himmel* (*Embezzled Heaven,* 1938). In German-speaking countries Werfel was esteemed as a dramatist for his literary treatments of history and legend.

Born in Prague, then part of the Austrian Empire, Werfel was provided with an excellent education by his wealthy father, a businessman. Subsequently Werfel made his reputation and lived in Austria until the Nazi Anschluss drove him out in 1938. As dramatized in his last play, Werfel escaped to Paris and, after its fall, to America, where he was to spend the remainder of his life. He began his career as an EXPRESSIONIST poet, publishing his first verse collection in 1911. It was followed by other books of poems and by a free adaptation of Euripides's *The Trojan Women, Die Troerinnen* (1915), the contemporary relevance of whose "shrill cries of dying individualism" Werfel stressed in his preface and underlined in the text. Though this play, which greatly impressed its audiences, characterized Werfel as a revolutionary pacifist, he served in the Austrian army during World War I. It was then that he met the widow of the composer Gustav Mahler, Alma Maria Schindler, whom he eventually married. He died in California.

After World War I Werfel came out with his ambitious verse trilogy *Spiegelmensch* (1920); influenced by the Faust legend as well as by Ibsen's PEER GYNT (and parodied by KARL KRAUS), it is a magic portrayal of the title's "mirror man" as an evil *Doppelgänger* of the protagonist, who ultimately triumphs over temptations, abjures his transgression—and thus wins redemption. *Goat Song,* Werfel's sensation-causing next play, was followed by *Schweiger* (1922), which, like the trilogy, portrays a schizoid personality: a respectable citizen who under psychoanalysis recalls a terrible crime, attempts to atone for it, becomes involved in various contemporary political struggles, breaks down, and commits suicide.

Most of Werfel's remaining plays are historical: *Juarez und Maximilian* (*Juarez and Maximilian,* 1924), an idealist-pacifist characterization of the Austrian archduke crowned Emperor of Mexico in 1864 and killed three years later by political realities embodied in Juárez, who never appears on stage; *Paulus unter den Juden* (*Paul Among the Jews,* 1926), a dramatization of early Christianity's emancipation from its Jewish roots; *Das Reich Gottes in Böhmen* (1930), a portrayal of the fifteenth-century Austrian Hussites, whose bestiality destroys the ideals and humanitarianism of their leader, Andrew Rokop; *Der Weg der Verheissung* (*The Eternal Road*, 1935), a verse pageant (spectacularly produced by Max Reinhardt in New York) dramatizing biblical accounts of the suffering of the Jews; *In einer Nacht* (1937), a less than successful depiction of a dead man's soul returning to earth to communicate with the living; and Werfel's last and, atypically, comic play, *Jacobowsky and the Colonel*.

Like his novels, Werfel's dramas are grounded in the tradition of German romanticism as well as in the expressionism of his poetry. In his plays Werfel lyrically and SYMBOLICally explored his own affinities with his Jewish antecedents as well as with Catholic mysticism—though he never joined the Church. Werfel's style changed over the years, ranging from lyric expressionism to variations of NATURALISM. But he remained consistent in dramatizing his ideals of human brotherhood and the need for spiritual redemption. As he expressed his philosophy in the preface to his first play, *Die Troerinnen*: "There is an essential tragedy in the world, a break, an original sin, wherein all participate, and from which the understanding soul suffers most."

Nearly all Werfel's plays were translated. But they are not as readily available as are the novels, nor has their appeal been nearly as durable. The original Theatre Guild productions are described in Lawrence Langner's *The Magic Curtain* (1951). Lore B. Foltin's edition of essays, *Franz Werfel, 1890–1945* (1950), has a bibliography.

WESKER, Arnold (1932–), English dramatist, gained his reputation with ROOTS (1959) and with CHIPS WITH EVERYTHING (1962). The former became part of *The Wesker Trilogy* (the others in this NATURALISTIC trilogy are CHICKEN SOUP WITH BARLEY [1958] and I'M TALKING ABOUT JERUSALEM [1960]), which was restaged at the London Court Theatre in 1960. Each of these three plays is complete in itself, but all characterize the English working class (especially Wesker's Jewish milieu in London's East End) in the welfare state. Following along the "angry" trail that had been blazed a few years earlier by JOHN OSBORNE, Wesker was considered one of the leading new English dramatists of the 1960's. When he was only thirty-three and had produced but five plays, a book about him (by Ribalow) was published—and Wesker had already for some time been the subject of many articles and book chapters.

The son of East European immigrants (both of them tailors), Wesker was born in London and was evacuated during the war years (1939–45), which he spent with foster parents in England and Wales. He attended Jewish and elementary schools as well as the commercial Upton House School in London's East End, and joined the Young Communist League and, later, the Zionist Youth Movement. Apprenticed at odd jobs until 1950, he then served two years with the Royal Air Force, where he did some acting. Subsequently he studied at the London School of Film Technique. After more manual jobs, he became a professional cook—in London and then in Paris. The first play of what was to become his trilogy appeared in 1958. As a promising young playwright, he was awarded a grant by the Arts Council of Great Britain, and (still in the same year) he married a former waitress. In 1959 an earlier play, *The Kitchen*, was produced; a losing entry in a 1957 competition, it was filmed, and revived (in substantially expanded form) in 1961. It is a slight melodrama set in a restaurant kitchen (whose employees' many nationalities underline the play's microcosmic significance), an allegory of life featuring, as John Russell Taylor aptly summarized it in *Anger and After* (1962), "illicit love among the ladies, a knife fight, a scalding, a miscarriage, and a climactic smash-up."

Their Very Own and Golden City (1966) was received with less enthusiasm, though it won the first Marzotto Prize for European drama. Again Wesker depicted his search for a new Jerusalem (socialism), this time in terms of a young architect's abortive attempts (throughout, the refrain is "Defeat doesn't matter") to build beautiful cities owned by their beautiful worker-inhabitants; as he gets older, he learns the disillusioning lesson that the unionists who were to support it do not really believe in socialism, and it is the Tory industrialists who finally accomplish the feat. In this play are mirrored Wesker's own efforts to bring culture to British workers through Centre 42, the project he launched in 1960 with DORIS LESSING, SHELAGH DELANY, and others, and headed until 1971. His *The Four Seasons* (1965) is an introspective depiction of two young failures (the only characters in the play) who have left their own spouses and spend a year together in a futile romance that leads to no solution of their problems. *The Friends* (1970) too depicts the failures, personal as well as business, of a group of working-class youths who try to make new lives for themselves. Wesker also wrote *Pools*, a short story published in 1958 and presented by BBC television in 1963; and *The Menace*, a television play published in 1963.

Wesker's left-wing social commitment (he was sentenced to jail in 1961 after Ban-the-Bomb demonstrations) and his individualistic idealism (the final long speech in *Roots* is often cited as its most fervent articulation) have occasionally militated against theatrical success: a tendency to preach—as in the last part of the trilogy—has alienated audiences. Principally Wesker has made drama the platform for his message of brotherhood for strife-torn humanity and the quest for more fulfilling individual lives. His early plays also reveal a carelessness in plot construction, and a hesitancy about the direction he intended to take as a dramatist. Wesker's biggest accomplishment with these early plays apparently was his familiarizing a middle-class audience (to whom, despite his attempts with Centre 42, these plays most appealed) with the lives of the lower working class.

The Wesker Trilogy appeared as a collection in 1960, and the other plays have been published separately. *Fears of Fragmentation* (1970) consists of sometimes autobiographical essays and lectures on drama, theatre, and society. Harold U. Ribalow's *Arnold Wesker* (1965) is a comprehensive study of Wesker's early work and thought; it includes a biographical sketch and extensive bibliographies.

WEST AFRICA has teemed with theatrical activity, especially in Nigeria since that country became independent in 1960. A notable drama school was established at the University of Ibadan in Nigeria, and there are other university drama programs in Ghana and the Ivory Coast. Africa's first important playwrights were the Nigerians WOLE SOYINKA and J. P. CLARK. Their plays and other Nigerian drama in English, the most important in Africa, is a synthesis of many native and foreign influences, yet remarkably original and experimental. Folk opera is most popular in Nigeria. Its leading creator, Hubert Ogunde (1916–), started his successful career with *The Strike* (1945) and then toured and appeared on television with his troupe—whose actresses he was able to retain by the simple expedient of marrying all of them himself. In his and Soyinka's companies other leading Nigerians started their careers. Duro Ladipo (1932?–), a composer of short folk operas that explore Yoruba history dramatically, had a major hit in Berlin with *Oba Koso* (1963), one of his *Three Yoruba Plays* (1964); and in *Moremi* (1967), portraying a historical parallel to Judith and Holofernes. Obotunde Ijimere's (1930–) *The Imprisonment of Obatala and Other Plays* (1966) includes *Eda,* Hofmannsthal's EVERYMAN transformed into Yoruba reincarnation terms; and *Woyengi,* a dramatization of the Ijaw Creation; yet another Yoruba history play is his *Born with the Fire on His Head* (1967). Also notable among Nigerian playwrights are the physician James Ene Henshaw (1924–), the most popular of whose many one-acters is the 1952 prize-winning folk comedy *The Jewels of the Shrine;* and Wale Ogunyemi (1939–), who has written satirical sketches and *The Scheme* (1967), a verse drama about the stoning of a prophetess.

There are English-language playwrights in other West African countries, including Sierra Leone and Ghana. Efua Theodora Sutherland (1924–), head of the Ghana Drama Studio, has written poems, stories, and plays, including the tragedy *Edufa* (1964). In Cameroon, Guillaume Oyono-Mbia (1939–) has written French plays, including a comic intrigue with music and dance, *Trois prétendents . . . un mari* (*Three Suitors, One Husband,* 1964), which has been produced abroad.

Aside from individual playwrights' collections there are Ulli Beier's *Three Nigerian Plays* (1967): Ladipo's *Moremi,* Ogunyemi's *The Scheme,* and Ijimere's *Born with the Fire on His Head;* and Fredric M. Litto's *Plays from Black Africa* (1968), including those of Clark, Henshaw, and Sutherland. These anthologies include discussions of West African drama and biographies of the playwrights represented. Oladele Taiwo's *An Introduction to West African Literature* (1967) has a chapter on Nigerian drama; Margaret Laurence's *Long Drums and Cannons: Nigerian Dramatists and Novelists 1952–1966* (1968) includes bibliographies. See also works noted under AFRICA.

Mae West in *Diamond Lil* (with J. Merrill Holmes and Ernest Anderson). New York, 1928. (*Culver Pictures*)

WEST, Mae (1893–), American actress and author, is best remembered as a comic sex symbol and "the tired businessman's bosom friend" in once-shocking pictures—and for her many sayings ("Come up and see me sometime," "Beulah, peel me a grape," etc.) and her swagger, which added superb self-parody to her sexual enticement. What is less well remembered is that Mae West wrote many of her own scripts, some of them adaptations of novels she herself authored. Her most notable play is *Diamond Lil* (1928), a lurid Bowery saloon drama she adapted into the film *She Done Him Wrong* (1933) in which she played the title role of a heavily jeweled, provocative, and much fought-over mistress of a white-slave trader. Other plays she wrote include her first hit, *Sex* (1926), a suggestive, fast-moving drama in which she played a waterfront prostitute and for which she was jailed; *The Drag* (1927), a study of homosexuality closed by censors before it reached New York but rewritten by her for Broadway as *The Pleasure Man* (1928); and *Sextet* (1961). Her books include an autobiography whose title quotes a punchline from *Diamond Lil: Goodness Had Nothing to Do with It* (1959).

WEXLEY, John (1907–), American writer of leftist social-protest plays in the 1930's, was particularly successful with *The Last Mile* (1930), an attack on capital punishment and a plea for prison reform; *They Shall Not Die* (1934), a defense of the victims of the notorious 1931 Scottsboro (Alabama) Negro boys' rape case also dramatized by LANGSTON HUGHES; and *Running Dogs* (1938), a portrayal of Chinese Communist intraparty struggles before the 1931 Japanese invasion.

WHAT EVERY WOMAN KNOWS, a comedy in four acts by JAMES M. BARRIE, produced in 1908 and published in 1918. Setting: contemporary Scotland and England.

This popular play has been periodically revived and filmed twice (1921 and 1934). The heroine, Maggie, is an antithesis of the predatory women of BERNARD SHAW, though she too gets her man—because of her self-effacing love, goodness, and wisdom. Obscure women with such qualities, Barrie implies in this humorous if sentimental play, stand behind and are responsible for the success of great men.

Act I. Like their widowed father, her bachelor brothers adore Maggie Wylie. But they wish someone would marry the plain girl, "for though Maggie is undersized she has a passion for romance." Maggie conceals many fine attributes behind her old-fashioned curls, her love of poetry, and her knitting. Yet she sadly remarks on her lack of charm, it is "a sort of bloom on a woman. If you have it, you don't need to have anything else; and if you don't have it, it doesn't much matter what else you have." That night they surprise a "burglar." He is John Shand, a poor young railway porter. Also an ambitious university student, he has broken into the house to use its library. The shrewd Scotsmen persuade the able and confident but humorless Shand ("I never laughed in my life") to sign a pact. They will pay for his law studies if he agrees to marry Maggie when he is established. The spinster honestly admits that her family has misrepresented her: actually, she has never had an offer, and she is twenty-six, not twenty-five. But Shand wants to accomplish great things, needs the money to do so, and therefore still agrees. When he leaves, her brother mutters, "It was very noble of her to tell him she's twenty-six. But I thought she was twenty-seven."

Act II. It is Shand's great day six years later as he wins his first election to Parliament. He is unaware of Maggie's help in his work. Now in love with him, she suggests that "one needs a sense of humour to be fond of me." When she sees how charmed he is by a beautiful if empty-headed noblewoman, she offers to release him. Shand has many failings, not the least of which is his conceited refusal to be aware of them. As her brother remarks, "there are few more impressive sights in the world than a Scotsman on the make." Nonetheless, Shand honorably announces his betrothal to Maggie to his cheering constituents.

Act III. The wife's unobtrusive guidance and "editing" of his speeches, as is obvious to others but not to Shand himself, soon get him to the top. But he is in love with the foolish noblewoman. Maggie realizes this and finally must act. True to her promise not to be a typical wife, she arranges for him to spend some weeks with his beloved in a country house owned by a French Comtesse, Maggie's friend, before they get a divorce.

Act IV. The expected happens. Always together, the lovers soon tire of each other. Furthermore, the simpering beauty fails to inspire Shand as expected. In fact, the speech he composes while in her company, although competent, is disappointing and his future suddenly seems less promising. When Maggie arrives with her retyped "copy" of his first draft, however, the old sparkle is there. Finally Shand realizes how important Maggie is to his career, and he no longer wants her to leave him. "It's nothing unusual I have done," she tells him: "Every man who is high up loves to think that he has done it all himself; and the wife smiles, and lets it go at that. It's our only joke. Every woman knows that." But if he would only have a sense of humor! If he could only learn to laugh! She shows him how, and he tries hard. Is what every woman knows that "the first woman was made not out of one of Adam's ribs but out of his funny-bone"? And at last he starts laughing, for the first time in his life. Maggie wins again—and Shand is saved.

WHAT PRICE GLORY?, a play in three acts by MAXWELL ANDERSON and LAURENCE STALLINGS, produced in 1924 and published in 1926. Setting: near and at the battlefront in France, 1918.

This deft mixture of NATURALISM, comedy, and romance took Broadway by storm; it was filmed in 1926, 1936, and again in 1952, and there were a number of film sequels in the 1920's and 1930's. It is noteworthy that Flagg and Quirt are swashbuckling heroes, yet not motivated by patriotic ideals; similarly, war is portrayed unromantically, yet this is not an antiwar play. Its theatrically unorthodox psychology and earthy language, at the time especially shocking, advanced the cause of stage REALISM.

Act I. Scene 1. In a French farmhouse converted into company headquarters, three corporals are discussing women. Then Captain Flagg gets ready to go to Paris, and consoles his attractive local tart, the innkeeper's daughter, Charmaine de la Cognac. First Sergeant Quirt, another veteran U.S. Marine, comes to prepare Flagg's "shambling bunch of hams" for combat. Flagg and Quirt are lifelong rivals who respect but always fight and insult each other. Flagg leaves Quirt in command, threatening to break him if he drinks. After Flagg's departure, Quirt meets the crying Charmaine and comforts her: "Well, baby, you better stick to me, and you'll have another papa." When he knocks out a drunken marine, Charmaine smiles and embraces her new hero. *Scene 2.* Flagg returns a week later, having been jailed after a drunken fight with a military policeman. Charmaine's father charges the Americans with corrupting the morals of *"ma fleur délicate,"* and demands money and a son-in-law. As Quirt taunts Flagg, the latter gets his revenge: "I'm going to marry you to Charmaine. . . . We're

What Price Glory?, Act I, Scene 2. Flagg (Louis Wolheim), Charmaine (Leyla Georgie), Quirt (William Boyd), and (at right) Charmaine's father (Luis Alberni). New York, 1924. (*Culver Pictures*)

going to let you hold the bag!" The company is suddenly ordered into battle, however, and Quirt, now indispensable to Flagg, escapes marriage and allotment deductions from his pay. They cheerfully bid Charmaine farewell, and leave. Charmaine tries but is unable to seduce the one remaining marine, an elderly sergeant.

Act II. In the wine cellar of a town at the front, the horrors of war are revealed. The embattled men talk of the slaughter outside as casualties are brought in. Overwhelmed by his men's suffering, one of the officers hysterically describes a German sniper bleeding to death in a tree, "crying *'Kamerad! Kamerad!'* Just like a big crippled whippoorwill. What price glory now?" Flagg comforts him, with surprising gentleness. Overwhelmed by their desperate position, he bitterly greets some newly arrived lieutenants. Quirt is slightly wounded, and rejoices at the thought of returning "to my little skookum lady," Charmaine. Angry and anxious to get the leave promised as a reward for the capture of an enemy officer, Flagg finds one and brings him in. As the curtain falls, he compassionately soothes a dying marine.

Act III. Quirt has escaped from the hospital. He arrives at Charmaine's, and is soon followed by Flagg. They drink and resume their old arguments. Flagg proposes to settle their fight over Charmaine in a game of blackjack: "The man that wins gets a gun, and the man that loses gets a head start. Everybody wins, see? One gets the girl and the other gets the chance to stay in bed the rest of this war." Quirt loses, but manages to escape unharmed. Unexpectedly the company is ordered back to the front immediately. Drunk and exhausted, Flagg first demurs, but then obeys orders, however reluctantly: "There's something rotten about this profession of arms, some kind of damned religion connected with it that you can't shake." After he leaves Charmaine, Quirt appears. He has been hiding upstairs, but when he hears the orders, he too obeys. He kisses Charmaine goodbye and staggers out: "What a lot of God damn fools it takes to make a war! Hey, Flagg, wait for baby!"

WHAT SHALL WE TELL CAROLINE?, a play in two scenes by JOHN MORTIMER, published and produced in 1958. Setting: Coldsands (on the Norfolk coast of England), March 1958.

The departure upon her eighteenth birthday of the title character of this comedy unmasks the pathetic truth about the *ménage à trois* of the adults in the play—a pretense providing all three with illusions that make their drab lives bearable.

The assistant to the headmaster of a boys' boarding school for eighteen years has paid court to the headmaster's wife. He accompanies himself on a ukulele and boasts about his youthful romantic escapades, while the headmaster shouts angrily at both of them. Throughout this period, the daughter (Caroline) has remained mute. The frustrations and boredom of the three adults come out as they talk of life to the silent Caroline. After her sudden ability to speak and her departure for a job in London, the headmaster is insulted upon hearing that the teacher does not love his wife and wants to stop paying court to her. She needs the attention of another man, he insists, just as he needs to express his love by shouting at and quarreling about her. It all started with a joke eighteen years before, the teacher recalls, "and now, it seems, I've got to live on that joke forever." And so he starts with another lurid tale about his youth, gazes lovingly at the wife, plays his ukulele, and sings to her. The headmaster shouts as he crashes his fist on the desk: "Stop singing to my wife! Take your greedy eyes off her!"

WHEN ONE IS SOMEBODY (*Quando si è qualcuno*), a play in three acts by LUIGI PIRANDELLO, published and produced in 1933. Setting: contemporary Italy.

The perhaps autobiographically conceived protagonist of this part-fantasy is a distinguished writer. Fame has crushed his real self into a public mask under which he suffers. His public image destroys the individual, even his name: his speeches and actions are indicated by three asterisks (***), which suggest his fixed, stellar position; other characters address him as "Maestro." Pirandello created the role of Veroccia for Marta Abba.

The famous elderly poet *** has been rejuvenated by and has fallen in love with his nephew's beautiful young sister-in-law, Veroccia. She has discovered and brought out in him hidden life and youth. His vibrant new poetry, inspired by Veroccia, is published under the pseudonym Délago, reputed to be a young Italian poet living in America. "Délago" becomes the rage of Italy's youth and his reputation threatens to depose ***'s literary leadership. *** dreams of escaping with Veroccia, of giving up the eternal torment of being "just a statue," unable "to give in for a moment to what you think and feel!" always having "to writhe with the pain that is within you": "There I am, motionless, forever!" When his wife and children—themselves satellite puppets of his renown—come for him, his torment grows: he must decide between the image of the elderly celebrity and the life of Veroccia's young Délago. The pressures of his family, his publisher, and the cabinet minister who prepares to have *** publicly honored are coupled with ***'s own realization that he can no longer actually be the youthful man he feels himself to be. His stately white locks, which Veroccia has cut off, grow back, and he again becomes the official monument. In his musty, churchlike study, Dante, Ariosto, and other writers emerge from their picture frames to gesticulate in their traditional poses. *** publicly exposes "Délago's" book as a hoax. Deeply wounded by his repudiation, Veroccia approaches *** one last time: "I gave myself to you without reservations and you did not have the courage to take me, to take the life I wanted to give you, because you suffered from not having any life and not even being able to hope to have one. You received that gift of life from me and then you let them call it all a joke. Coward! Coward! Coward!" Only after she leaves can *** express the "almost obscene shame of feeling a young and hot-blooded heart within an old body," unable to change: "My dear, you took my last living moment." Now he must live and suffer as his public image. In an elaborate ceremony Italy gratefully confers the title of Count on him. The ceremony resembles a funeral and the cabinet minister's speech a eulogy. *** moves like an automaton, and his brief speech appears as an epigraph etched on the wall even as he talks. Later he sits down, alone; the stone seat "is slowly raised up with *** in his customary rigid position, now the statue of himself."

WHEN THE MUSIC STOPS (*Histoire de rire*), a play in three acts by ARMAND SALACROU, produced in 1939 and published in 1940. Setting: Paris and a resort hotel, 1930's.

Despite many farcical situations and dialogue and a superficial resemblance to boulevard comedies like Coward's PRIVATE LIVES, this is an existentialist drama (also produced as *No Laughing Matter*) of moral ambiguity in an era when, as one character says, "religion means nothing" and "the only morality left to [our wives] is 'love,' the most uncertain, most imprecise word in the human vocabulary." Everything, therefore, becomes *histoire de rire* (a joke).

A prosperous young businessman about to run off with a married woman is appalled to learn that his best friend's wife is running off with a lover. Each adultery has differing effects on its participants. Most of them cannot forgo making moral judgments about others and cannot come to terms with themselves and with reality. To overcome

When the Music Stops. Left to right: Yves Nobert, Danielle Delorme, and Pierre Dux. Paris, 1945. (*French Cultural Services*)

everyday drabness, they choose promiscuity, admittedly "false happiness," or misogyny. When the wives get bored with their lovers and return to their husbands, one of the lovers commits suicide. Only one of the characters is able to accept the limitations of life. "If you're not frightened by death as it approaches," he remarks, "you become aware of having grown in stature, of a certain dignity." The others sadly discover that adultery, "their great love—was just a big joke." One of the wives concludes, "A big joke? How sad."

WHEN THE NEW WINE BLOOMS (*Når den ny vin blomstrer*), a play in three acts by BJØRNSTJERNE BJØRNSON, published and produced in 1909. Setting: a spacious Norwegian home, early twentieth century.

Bjørnson's last play, almost a reply to Ibsen's WHEN WE DEAD AWAKEN and a reversal of the problem in Bjørnson's own LOVE AND GEOGRAPHY, reaffirms family solidarity. The Kierkegaard saying that provides the title ends: "then the old wine ferments."

Arvik's household is disrupted by the bustle of his daughters' amours and by his wife, a "new woman" who takes herself and her activities with the young people very seriously. Arvik finally refuses to submit any longer to the neglect caused by her independence. He almost leaves the family he has always provided for—something his wife seems conveniently to forget. But catastrophe is averted when she comes to her senses. "It is frightful how exaggerated I am—and the children have that from me," she admits—and she embraces her husband.

WHEN WE DEAD AWAKEN (*Når vi døde vågner*), "a dramatic epilogue" in three acts by HENRIK IBSEN, published in 1899 and produced in 1900. Setting: resorts and a mountain top, contemporary Norway.

Some critics (including WILLIAM ARCHER and Edmund Gosse) thought Ibsen's last play, with its shadowy characterizations and confusing plot, a product of Ibsen's dotage. Others—most notably BERNARD SHAW and JAMES JOYCE—praised it as a stunning self-portrait of the artist, and as a play that advanced the possibilities of poetic SYMBOLISM. While Rubek resembles JOHN GABRIEL BORKMAN and MASTER BUILDER Solness, he ends like the earlier BRAND—in an icy mountain avalanche, and in divine exaltation.

Act I. An elderly sculptor, Professor Arnold Rubek, married the childlike young Maja four years ago. Rubek became world famous with his masterpiece, "The Day of Resurrection," but lately has been able to sculpt only a few portraits. These amuse him because his patrons fail to perceive the animals represented in their likenesses. Having returned from their travels, Rubek and Maja, now discontented with each other, are at a seacoast resort. Other guests are the crude, bearbaiting Squire Ulfheim, and a strange lady and her deaconess. While Maja goes off with the boastful Ulfheim, Rubek talks with the lady—Irene von Satow, the model who had inspired his masterpiece, their "child." Having yearned for love and motherhood, she blames him for his self-control, his having kept her an unprofaned ideal for the sake of his art. After leaving him, she posed in music halls, ruined men, and finally went mad: "But now, slowly, I am beginning to rise from the dead." Maja returns, and readily obtains Rubek's permission to accompany Ulfheim to the mountains. Irene concludes that Rubek has wronged her—and himself: "I gave you my soul—young and alive. And left myself empty—without any soul! That's why I died, Arnold."

Act II. At a mountain resort, Maja feels repelled by, yet attracted to the ugly Ulfheim (Shaw called these two uncultivated "stone age" people), and Rubek admits his stultifying boredom with her. Terming art "empty, hollow, and meaningless," he wants Irene, who alone has the key to his "locked casket of visions." Since Maja now has plans of her own, she cheerfully suggests that Irene live with them. Throwing petals into a stream with Irene, Rubek confesses he has changed his masterpiece, their "child": he shifted the original solitary ideal figure, awakening to light and glory, from the center; then he added realistic, beastlike humans; and finally he put into the foreground "a man weighted down by guilt" and the hellish knowledge that he can never succeed. (These changes symbolize Ibsen's early, middle, and last dramas.) Almost ready to kill him with her poised knife, Irene scorns his penitent self-indulgence: "You were only an artist, not a man"—a poet, "a word that condones all sins." She refuses to try and resurrect their former lives, and still smarts at his final words after she had stripped her being for him: "This has been an inspiring episode in my life!" But when Maja, singing a song of freedom, goes up the mountain with Ulfheim, Rubek and Irene agree to do the same that night—though it is now too late to retrieve the life they have missed. "When we dead awaken," as Irene says, "we find that we have never lived."

Act III. On a stormy mountain crest, Maja and Ulfheim decide to "stitch their tattered lives together," to go down and find safety and life in his castle below. Rubek and Irene decide to go to the dangerous top. She had not knifed him after his confession, she reveals, because she realized that he too is already dead. "Then let us two dead people live life to the full for a brief moment," Rubek exclaims passionately. Irene accompanies him ecstatically to the "promised mountain top, . . . into the light, where glory shines." As Maja's happy freedom song is heard from below, a glacial avalanche from above buries Rubek and Irene. The deaconess, whose ready straitjacket Irene had dreaded, makes the sign of the cross: *"Pax vobiscum!"*

WHERE THE CROSS IS MADE, a one-act play by EUGENE O'NEILL, produced in 1918 and published in 1919. Setting: a lookout post atop a California coast house in one of the years preceding World War I.

This early version of the final act of GOLD was published in THE MOON OF THE CARIBBEES, AND SIX OTHER PLAYS. It differs from the later play in the following particulars:

Over Sue's objection, Nat, here the protagonist, gets ready to commit their father to preserve his own sanity, and to save the house from foreclosure and sell it for a good price. The phantom crew with the treasure chests actually appear onstage, though they are visible only to the Captain and the now equally mad Nat. The play ends with Nat's triumphantly extracting from his dead father's fist the map on which the treasure is indicated "where the cross is made," as Sue, heartbroken, tries to recall him to sanity.

WHILE THE SUN SHINES, a comedy in three acts by TERENCE RATTIGAN, produced in 1943 and published in 1944. Setting: London, 1943.

In this popular comedy an American Army Air Force officer falls in love with a Women's Auxiliary Air Force corporal. She turns out to be a roguish duke's daughter and the fiancée of his host, a wealthy earl whose naval incompetence keeps him in the rank of a common sailor. After much bedlam that also involves a Free French officer and a lovable tart, the earl and the WAAF are reunited.

WHITE COCKADE, THE, a play in three acts by LADY GREGORY, produced in 1905 and published in 1912. Setting: Ireland, 1690.

J. M. SYNGE said that this short tragicomedy "made the writing of historical drama again possible," and WILLIAM BUTLER YEATS called it "merry and beautiful." It is a humorous dramatization of the same folk legend which DOUGLAS HYDE made into *Rig Seumas,* a Gaelic play translated by Lady Gregory as *King James* (1903). Much of the action takes place in a Duncannon inn whose proprietress is a proverb- and cliché-spouting opportunist.

After the Battle of the Boyne, cowardly King James II escapes in a wine barrel to save his skin. His brave General Patrick Sarsfield, the Earl of Lucan, is a foil to this unworthy ruler whose weakness betrays Ireland. Ultimately the supporters of the Stuart line (identified by a white cockade) are variously ruined by James's failure. Only Sarsfield buckles his sword, loyal though the cause is lost. Says a mad old lady who has dreamed of the restoration of the Stuarts: "Fighting for a dead king!—ha! ha! ha! Poor Patrick Sarsfield is very, very mad!"

WHITE DESERT, a play in a prologue and four acts by MAXWELL ANDERSON, produced in 1923. Setting: nineteenth-century North Dakota, winter.

Anderson's unpublished first play is in blank verse. It tells the story of a scoundrel just arrived in Dakota's snowy "white desert" with his loyal young bride. His nasty-minded jealousy and abuse eventually goad her to seduce a neighboring homesteader. When she penitently confesses, her husband shoots her.

WHITE SAVIOR, THE (*Der weisse Heiland*), a "dramatic fantasy" in eleven scenes by GERHART HAUPTMANN, published and produced in 1920. Setting: Mexico, sixteenth century.

In this verse play Hauptmann's sympathies went to the defeated Mexican natives and their mystic ruler; however, the Spanish leaders are not all portrayed as villainous stereotypes.

King Montezuma welcomes Hernando Cortes as the "white savior" promised in ancient Aztec prophecies. Despite the Spaniards' bloody plunderings, Montezuma—like Cortes's apostate native mistress—naïvely believes: "Sons of the sun they needs must be. / And what's more, they are our friends." Too late do their murderous greed and ruthless attempts to convert the "savages" to Christianity open Montezuma's eyes. His son is killed, he himself is imprisoned, and—during Cortes's brief absence—his subjects are butchered at their religious festival. Bitterly Montezuma looks at the crucifix shown him: "He betrayed my lands for me. / He betrayed my God for me. / He betrayed me, me myself!" He blames himself for having been "a poor blind leader" who mistook heartless and soulless demons for divine supermen. The Mexicans at last revolt against their oppressors, and though Cortes threatens him with torture and death, Montezuma refuses to stop them. The Spaniards forcibly expose Montezuma to his people—who now stone him. Cortes and his followers try to save the dying Montezuma's soul with the sacraments. Regaining consciousness, he violently tears off his bandages and rejects and curses "This white brood who desecrate / The bosom of our mother earth / With filth and abomination!"

WHITE STEED, THE, a comedy in three acts by PAUL VINCENT CARROLL, published and produced in 1939. Setting: Lorcan, a seaside village in County Louth, Ireland; 1930's.

Rated by some as superior to SHADOW AND SUBSTANCE, which it resembles, this play was refused production at the Abbey Theatre in 1938 because of its portrayal of fascistic clericalism. The plot and title allude to the Irish folk legend quoted by Nora in the second act.

Act I. Canon Matt Lavelle is a wise and benevolent but eccentric old man who has become paralyzed. A young priest, Father Shaughnessy, is sent to administer the parish. Militantly efficient, he immediately riles the old canon by setting up a Vigilance Committee and discharging the library assistant, Nora Fintry, a spirited lass recently back from England, for going with a boy: "And what the hell does he want her to go with, an elephant?" The "mathematically-minded" Shaughnessy lectures the canon on the moral laxness of his parish: the library contains "Dean Swift's filth, BERNARD SHAW's blasphemous humor, AE's [GEORGE WILLIAM RUSSELL's] pantheistic cant, and the ravings of a humbug called HENRIK IBSEN"; further, there have been forced marriages and other evidence of "spiritual carelessness." Though the canon ascribes these to inevitable "human weakness" and defends the decency of his people, Shaughnessy is determined "to work in close conjunction with the Civil Law and . . . make full use of the new law in the Constitution against public impropriety." The canon angrily defends himself: "I may be blind in one eye and my fur is a bit tore with the furze and whins, but I know the dark well enough to round up me sheep and take them home." But Shaughnessy proceeds with his Vigilance Committee meeting, castigates Nora, who refuses to truckle to him or to allow her father to do so, and coerces Denis Dillon, the young schoolmaster, into giving up his non-Catholic girl friend.

Act II. Fortified by liquor, Dillon comes to Nora's house. He deplores his cowardice, for he yearns always to be as brave as he is after he has had a few drinks. It is then that he writes notes signed "The Man Without Fear," one of which is soon discovered: a scurrilous missive directed against a vigilante. Shaughnessy chides Nora for laughing at it, and angers the town's inspector by insisting that the police support his illegal search-and-seizure tactics. When Nora, alone with Dillon, again expresses her contempt of his cowardice, Dillon likens her dreams of old Ireland to his own drinking: both give them courage. Nora declares that she hates "all things black and little"—Ireland as she sees it now—and recounts her childhood fascination with the legend of the goddess Niam: "And when she looked on Ossian and saw how wise and tender he was and how beautiful and strong, she felt herself filled with a great love for him and longingly and with quiet hands, she drew the folds of her robe of gold more closely to her and made room for him behind her on the back of the white steed"; so long as he remained with the goddess, he partook of her power and eluded human pettiness. Dillon begs Nora to give him similar strength: "Don't send me away out where I will be a little black man again, weeding the clerical garden. Lift me on your white steed, Nora." Half drunk with frustrated anger, they smash the china cups she abhors—and then embrace passionately.

Act III. The police inspector insists on protecting Nora's secular rights. "You stick to your pulpit, and I'll stick to my barracks," he tells Shaughnessy; "what are they, after all, but the two strait-jackets of human nature!" Nora defends her "defiance" as "the struggle of a spirit to escape standardization and to preserve its integrity and humanity." Father Shaughnessy and the canon quarrel. "What have you achieved!" the canon ridicules the priest: "You have only succeeded in dragging into the light the things we old codgers grow in the dark in Ireland." The young priest prepares to have the canon sent away, and there is a clash between the police and the vigilantes. The canon refuses to be taken away. He locks himself up and prays that the Virgin restore the use of his limbs. To the amazement of all and the consternation of Shaughnessy, the canon suddenly is able to walk. He quells the rioting mob, and again takes charge of his parish in his own inimitable way—wheedling, blustering, taking little bribes of vegetables and milk, but giving his parishioners what they need and keeping them happy. Dillon may have back his appointment as schoolmaster, but the canon insists he be married. Nora refuses: "I have no pity, Denis, for a man who wants to live on in servitude. I have been born out of warriors, poets, saints, and heroes; and am I to bear children to a servant?" She knows that, for the security of a job, he will be the wily canon's tool. Suddenly Dillon realizes that he must give up comfort and forge a road of his own. He throws up the job and apologizes to the canon as he runs out to follow Nora. "Och, your grannie. Stop asking people to forgive you and begin telling them to go to blazes," the canon tells him. Alone, he sits down and looks at the picture of the Virgin: "Well, Holy Mother, we're used to these little mountain storms, but sure, the mountains remain. So we needn't be afraid, need we now?"

WHITEHEADED BOY, THE, a comedy in three acts by LENNOX ROBINSON, produced in 1916 and published in 1921. Setting: a village in contemporary Ireland.

Robinson's best and most popular play is this amusing trifle about a group of likable but addleheaded Irish. Their pet, Denis Geohegan, is sent to study medicine. He fails his examinations, returns home, marries the postmaster's daughter, and again becomes the family's "whiteheaded boy."

WHITING, John (1917–63), English playwright, captivated the public only with THE DEVILS (1961), his free adaptation of an ALDOUS HUXLEY novel. His other plays were ignored by audiences, panned by most critics—and extolled by a few distinguished producers and actors. It was their enthusiasm that had prompted the Royal Shakespeare Company to commission his one successful play.

Whiting was born in Salisbury, attended the Royal Academy of Dramatic Art, became an actor, served in World War II, and then returned to acting. His first important play was *Saint's Day* (1951), which won an award and was savagely dismissed by critics; a violent but allusively allegorical drama of an old poet persuaded to attend a dinner party in his honor, it depicts the social alienation and self-destruction of intellectuals and artists. *A Penny for a Song* (1951), Whiting's first staged play, is a comic fantasy set in Dorset during the Napoleonic wars. *Marching Song* (1954), an internalized but suspenseful drama about political ethics, also deals with self-destruction—and regeneration; its protagonist is a general who must choose between suicide and public disgrace: with the help of a young girl he discovers himself and finds life in death, while his mistress is saved from death in life.

Despite their sex and violence, Whiting's plays were caviar to the general public. They fell outside the stream of contemporary English drama: Whiting's social protest (unlike that of JOHN

OSBORNE and the other "angry young men") was dissipated by his literary art—and yet his drama was prose, not part of the poetic "revival" that T. S. ELIOT and CHRISTOPHER FRY were thought to be inaugurating. Financially unsuccessful as a dramatist for most of his creative life, Whiting turned to screenwriting (his last completed work was a film script about the life of SEAN O'CASEY). His promise as an important playwright grew with the popularity of *The Devils,* and then was cut short when he died of cancer.

Whiting's other works include *Conditions of Agreement,* his first play, which he suppressed and later rewrote for television as *A Walk in the Desert* (1960); *The Gates of Summer* (1956), a comedy; and *No Why* (1961), a one-acter that depicts a child's suicide. He also translated some plays of JEAN ANOUILH and wrote theatre criticisms and other articles, collected in the posthumous *John Whiting on Theatre* (1966) and *The Art of the Dramatist* (1970).

The Plays of John Whiting (1957), with a preface by the author, contains *Saint's Day, A Penny for a Song,* and *Marching Song.* Ronald Hayman edited the two-volume *The Collected Plays of John Whiting* (1969) and wrote the first comprehensive study of his life and work, *John Whiting* (1969).

WHO'S AFRAID OF VIRGINIA WOOLF?, a play in three acts by EDWARD ALBEE, published and produced in 1962. Setting: the living room of a house on a small New England college campus before dawn on a Sunday morning, c. 1960.

Albee's first full-length play (later a major film) created an international sensation. When it was denied the Pulitzer Prize—the only important award it missed—two judges resigned and no prize at all was given that year. The searing drama of a mutually destructive sex duel in the tradition of Strindberg's THE DANCE OF DEATH, Albee's play has much sadistic humor and SYMBOLISM. There are other conflicts among the two impotent academes—a humanist historian and a technician scientist—and their barren wives. Sterility and lust, reality and illusion, personal failure and mock religious ceremony—these are the "Fun and Games" (Act I) of the play. Act II is called "Walpurgisnacht" and Act III is "The Exorcism"—the play's original title. Its nonsense title alludes to the English novelist and is sung to the tune of "Who's Afraid of the Big, Bad Wolf?"

Act I. It is 2 A.M. and the buxom and boisterous Martha (fifty-two) is coming home with her husband, George (forty-six), a history professor. "Jes*us* . . . H. Christ," she laughs loudly. When George tries to quiet her, she gets irritated: "What a cluck you are . . . What a dump." They argue about the movie that line comes from, and George grumbles about the Saturday night parties given by her father, the college president. Martha calls for a drink and informs George that she has invited home a couple "Daddy said we should be nice to." When George sulks, Martha sings "Who's afraid of Virginia Woolf," which went over big at the party. They quarrel over Martha's wanting another drink and "a big sloppy kiss," and George warns her not to "start in on the bit about the kid" before their guests. She explodes, "SCREW YOU!"—just as the couple enter. They are Nick, a strapping blond youth, and his wife, Honey, a mousy blond who giggles when she asks for a brandy. George starts needling the younger man, a new instructor who is no match for George's wit. As the guests politely praise the party and Martha's father, George complains about being married to the president's daughter—though Martha sneers, "*Some* men would give their right arm for the chance." While the wives are out, George again razzes Nick, who angrily threatens to leave. When George learns that Nick is a biologist, he complains about scientists' "rearranging" genes. George is defensive about not being chairman of the history department and mysterious about having children. Nick says that he and Honey will postpone having children until they are settled. Honey returns and upsets George with the announcement that Martha has told her about their son, whose twenty-first birthday is tomorrow. Soon Martha comes back, voluptuously dressed. She flirts with Nick and sneers at George's academic and athletic failures. George aims a shotgun at her—which shoots a large Chinese parasol. Pleased by the joke, Martha pulls George's hand to her breast. "Oh-ho! That's what you're after, is it?" George exclaims, moving away. Furious, she curses him and sidles up to Nick. Again George accuses him of plotting with other biologists to create "superb and sublime" but undistinguishable test-tube men. Eventually "culture and races" will vanish, he adds, and humorless "ants" like Nick "will take over the world." Honey, drunk and shocked by the increasingly obscene talk, asks about Martha's son. Though Martha is reluctant to discuss him, George keeps egging her on until Martha suggests he is unsure of the boy's paternity. Indignant, George denies this. Martha tells her guests about her past how she admired and adored her father, and how she came to "fall for" and marry George. When she again alludes to his failures, George angrily warns her to shut up: "You've already sprung a leak about you-know-what . . . our *son.*" But when she keeps talking, he drowns her out with the "Virginia Woolf" song. Honey, getting sick, runs to the bathroom and Nick goes after her. Martha follows them after looking contemptuously at George: "Jesus!"

Act II. Nick returns, again telling George he does not like to get "involved" in their marital squabbles. Though mocked by George, he soon relates that he married Honey because she had "a hysterical pregnancy." They laugh, and George tells about a friend who thirty years ago had shot his mother, killed his father in a car accident, and ended up in an asylum. Then Nick admits he married Honey for her money—inherited from her father, a crooked preacher. Martha's money, George says, came from her stepmother, "a *good* witch [who] married the white mouse . . . with the tiny red eyes"—Martha's college-president father

Who's Afraid of Virginia Woolf? Left to right: Nick (George Grizzard), George (Arthur Hill), Honey (Melinda Dillon), Martha (Uta Hagen). New York, 1962. (*Zodiac Photographers*)

—and died almost immediately. But "your story's a lot nicer," George concludes, "about your pumped-up little wife, and your father-in-law who was a priest." Smugly Nick, a "historical inevitability," tells how he plans to take charge of the college by "plow[ing] a few pertinent wives." George suggests that he start with Martha. She comes back and accuses George of making Honey sick—as he did their son. As they argue viciously, Honey, who has also returned, asks for more brandy and suggests that they dance. George puts on a Beethoven record. "All right, kiddies," he says: "choose up and hit the sack." The drunken Honey dances solo, and Martha puts on other music to which Martha and Nick undulate. As they do so and George warns her to stop talking, Martha relates how her father prevented George from publishing his book—about a boy who killed his parents. Furious, George throttles her until Nick tears him away. The next game should be "Get the Guests," George remarks when they finish "Humiliate the Host"—and he proceeds to tell what he has just learned of Nick's marriage. Horrified by her husband's betrayal, Honey rushes to the bathroom, sick again, and Nick vows to avenge himself: he no longer is scared at the thought of the next game George had suggested, "Hump the Hostess." While he is out for a moment, checking after Honey, Martha and George angrily lash out at each other. George goes for some ice, and Martha starts seducing Nick. George returns, announces that Honey is asleep on the bathroom floor and "sucking her thumb," and cheerfully sits down to read. "The son of a bitch is going to read a book!" Martha exclaims incredulously, and as George tells her and Nick to amuse themselves, they embrace. When George remains indifferent, Nick remarks, "You're disgusting." George laughs: "Because *you're* going to hump Martha, *I'm* disgusting?" After they leave, George hurls his book at the chimes, whose ringing brings in Honey. Still half asleep and drunk, she whimpers, "I . . . don't . . . want . . . any . . . children. I'm afraid! I don't want to be hurt. . . . PLEASE!" Now George understands why she has no children: "How do you make your secret little murders stud-boy doesn't know about, hunh?" When Honey snaps fully awake, George tells her the ringing chimes announced the death of their son. He laughs softly—and cries—as he envisions telling it to his wife: "Can you hear me, Martha? Our boy is dead."

Act III. Martha comes into the empty living room, talking to herself. She whines at being "abandoned," and talks to a picture of "Daddy White-Mouse," who has red eyes "because you cry all the time"—just as she does. When Nick appears, Martha sneers at his inadequacy "in some departments," accusing him of being a flop like all the others, "a bunch of boozed-up . . . impotent lunk-heads." Only George has ever made her happy, she says, and contemptuously sends Nick to answer the doorbell. It is George, carrying a bunch of flowers. After arguing with each other, Martha and George gang up on Nick. "I know the game," George tells him: "You don't make it in the sack, you're a houseboy." He throws flowers at Martha, tells Nick to bring in Honey, and though Martha pleads with him, insists on a last game. He slaps Martha and pulls her hair until she is angry enough to battle again, and announces the game: "Bringing up baby." He prompts Martha to describe their child's growing up, and then starts contradicting her. They argue about the reason for their boy's unhappiness, and when their quarrel reaches its climax, George intones the requiem mass. Then he tells Martha of the son's death—in a car accident identical to that of his friend thirty years before. Furiously Martha yells, "I WILL NOT LET YOU DECIDE THESE THINGS!" But George declares he had the right to kill the son, for "you broke our rule, baby. You mentioned him . . . you mentioned him to somebody else." Gradually Nick understands that the son is illusory: they never had a child. "We couldn't," they both admit. Thereupon Nick and Honey say good-bye and leave. Sadly and quietly Martha asks George whether he had to do what he did. "It was . . . time," George says; "it will be better." Gently he puts his hand on her shoulder and sings, softly, "Who's afraid of Virginia Woolf?" He nods as Martha replies, "I . . . am . . . George. . . . I . . . am. . . ."

WHY MARRY?, a comedy in three acts by JESSE LYNCH WILLIAMS, published in 1914 and produced in 1917. Setting: a country house, c. 1914.

This SHAVian comedy about the institution of marriage is notable because in 1918 it won the first Pulitzer Prize ever awarded. Originally a novel, *And So They Were Married* (1914), and produced by amateurs under that title, the play became successful professionally with Nat C. Goodwin playing the *raisonneur* judge, Uncle Everett.

At a weekend party various guests manifest the shortcomings of marriage and such other societal evils as the disproportionate rewards obtained by practitioners of various occupations. A young scientist—who is very low on society's salary scale—is admired by his assistant, Helen, who defends him as a courageous lifesaver before her brother, a businessman who dismisses him as a "mollycoddle germ-killer." As contemptuous of convention as is the scientist, Helen intends to accompany the scientist to Europe without marrying him, though she loves him. But Uncle Everett amusingly tricks them into a mutual avowal of their love and their conviction that "in the sight of God" they are married—and in his official capacity as a judge thereupon pronounces them man and wife. "All you've said of marriage is true. There is only one thing worse—and that is what you tried to do," he tells them, delighted that "respectability" is saved this time. And he laughs as he asks them what they will do about his action: "Separate and get divorced?"

WIDOWERS' HOUSES, "An Original Didactic Realistic Play" in three acts by BERNARD SHAW, published and produced in 1892. Setting: Germany and England in the 1880's.

His first play, *Widowers' Houses* is one of Shaw's three "unpleasant" plays that deal with the "social horrors" of slum housing—which still exist nearly a century later. In this work, he wrote in his preface to PLAYS UNPLEASANT, "I have shewn middle class respectability and younger son gentility fattening on the poverty of the slum as flies fatten on filth. That is not a pleasant theme." Shaw began the play in 1885 in collaboration with WILLIAM ARCHER, but Archer laid it aside and repudiated it when he saw Shaw's dialogue and plans for the plot: Archer had conceived of the play as a sentimental comedy.

Act I. In the garden restaurant of a Remagen hotel on the Rhine, buoyant young Dr. Harry Trench and his middle-aged travel companion, the pompous William de Burgh Cockane, meet the imposing and domineering Mr. Sartorius, whose daughter, Blanche, had been seeing Trench clandestinely. Left alone with the sharp-tongued girl, Trench finally works up the nerve to propose to her. When Sartorius returns, he agrees to the marriage if Trench can present evidence guaranteeing Blanche's full acceptance by his aristocratic family. Commissioned by Trench to draft the necessary letters to his family for him, the curious Cockane is told by Sartorius, somewhat aggressively, that he is prosperous but self-made. His income, like Trench's, is derived from London real estate, and he will leave his fortune to his expensively educated daughter.

Act II. A month later in his villa in Surbiton, Surrey, Sartorius discharges his servile agent, Lickcheese, for spending a few shillings to repair a dangerous staircase in one of his tenements. Trench comes with Cockane to present the family's letters, which express delight at Trench's coming marriage. While Sartorius is out to tell Blanche the good news, Lickcheese reveals to Trench and Cockane the source of Sartorius's wealth: starving paupers in run-down slum tenements. Horrified, Trench tells Blanche that he has resolved not to take any of Sartorius's money. Refusing to live in poverty and not knowing the reason for Trench's decision, Blanche finally loses her temper and breaks off the engagement. Sartorius attempts to patch up the quarrel, and finally informs Trench that Trench's own income derives from the same source. Though sickened by this information, he now agrees to accept Sartorius's money. Blanche is still in a temper, however, and begs her father to send Trench away. The match is broken, and Trench and Cockane indignantly leave the house.

Act III. On an evening four months later in Sartorius's London residence, the now-wealthy Lickcheese appears. He suggests that Sartorius join him in one of his new schemes: to buy out and improve slums in an area he knows to be slated for demolition. He has invited Trench, the mortgagee whose consent must be obtained, to the house. Blanche, who has been pining for Trench, now learns what her father's business really is. A "coarsened and sullen" Trench arrives and understands the proposition: "the dirtier a place is the more rent you get; and the decenter it is, the more compensation you get. So we're to give up dirt and go in for decency"; but he says that he cannot afford to take the financial risk involved. Left alone, he lovingly gazes at a portrait of Blanche, who enters unobserved. When he notices her, she breaks out in a torrent of abuse that he eventually recognizes as erotic, "undisguised animal excitement." As they embrace, Trench announces that he will join Lickcheese and Sartorius in their scheme.

WIFE FOR A LIFE, A, a one-act play by EUGENE O'NEILL, published in 1950. Setting: a gold-mining camp in the Arizona desert, c. 1913.

O'Neill repudiated this, his earliest play, which he wrote in 1913. Declining his father's offer to perform it and refusing to allow its publication (its unauthorized printing in THE LOST PLAYS OF EUGENE O'NEILL was possible because of the copyright expiration), he claimed the later-written THE WEB as his first play. *A Wife for a Life,* which he called his worst play and the only one he ever wrote with an eye on the box office, is a melodramatic vaudeville sketch that dispenses only with the genre's conventional villain.

An elderly goldminer in Arizona, seeking to find and kill his young wife's lover, discovers him to be the friend to whom he owes his life. As the young man innocently goes off to marry the now-free woman (her husband not having returned for a year), the older man blesses both and sadly concludes, "Greater love hath no man than this that he giveth his wife for his friend."

WILD DUCK, THE (*Vildanden*), a play in five acts by HENRIK IBSEN, published in 1884 and produced in 1885. Setting: contemporary Norway.

A wild duck symbolizes various characters in Ibsen's NATURALISTIC tragicomedy, which has intrigued writers almost as much as *Hamlet*. (Ibsen predicted that critics would "find plenty to quarrel about, plenty to interpret.") It is concerned, as Ibsen frequently was, with the conflicts of ideals and reality. Unlike Gorky's Luka in THE LOWER DEPTHS but like O'Neill's salesman in THE ICEMAN COMETH, Gregers Werle calamitously attacks illusions ("life-lies"), particularly those of the idle poseur Hjalmar. In the integrity-obsessed neurotic who relentlessly enforces the "claim of the ideal," Ibsen caricatured himself and his youthful battles for truth. There are also in this play strong traces of Ibsen's father, in Old Ekdal, and of Ibsen's beloved sister, Hedvig. Sources and analyses are assembled in Dounia B. Christiani's edition of *The Wild Duck* (1968).

Act I. Håkon Werle, an elderly industrialist, is giving a dinner party for the homecoming of his son, Gregers. Gregers's friend, the photographer Hjalmar Ekdal, is shy and uncomfortable among the wealthy guests. A brief appearance by Old Ekdal embarrasses Hjalmar, who pretends not to recognize his father shuffling by with some copy work charitably given him by Werle. The background of their families is revealed in Gregers's conversations with Hjalmar and later with his father, whom Gregers loathes for his unscrupulousness. The Ekdals were ruined because Old Ekdal, Werle's former business partner, was imprisoned for Werle's swindles. Hjalmar tells the incredulous Gregers of Werle's help, which had enabled him to marry Gina. He smugly notes that she has become "cultured through her daily contact with me," although she had been only a housekeeper for Werle. What Hjalmar does not know is that she had been Werle's mistress as well. Gregers is indignant at the thought of Hjalmar's living in a house "built on a lie." He sneers at his father's intention to remarry, rejects an appeal to stay and become his business partner, and again leaves home: "For now at last I see an objective I can live for."

Act II. At Hjalmar's studio (where the remainder of the play takes place), his prosaic and loving wife, Gina, and their fourteen-year-old daughter, Hedvig, cheerfully await Hjalmar's return. He comes home gushing over his "poor, white-haired, old father" and swaggers before his admiring family about the impressive figure he had cut at Werle's party. Instead of the delicacy from the dinner he had promised Hedvig and then forgot, he gives her the menu. He relishes his family's affectionate fuss over him, though he ostentatiously insists he does not need "life's little pleasures"; soon he will work "till I'm fit to drop." Sentimentally playing a song on his flute, he breaks off to rejoice in his blissful family life. Gregers comes to visit the friend he has always heroworshiped, and starts probing into his domestic affairs. He learns about the converted family loft, which is an illusory forest where Hjalmar and Old Ekdal, formerly an active woodsman, happily "hunt" caged poultry, rabbits, and pigeons. The pride of the roost is Hedvig's wild duck, shot by Werle, retrieved by his dog, and given to the Ekdals. Full of self-hatred, Gregers wishes he were a dog—"the sort that goes in after wild ducks when they dive down and bite on to the weeds and tangle in the mud." Though the practical Gina is reluctant, he insists on renting the Ekdals' spare room, and moves in at once.

Act III. The next morning, Hjalmar listlessly retouches pictures. Gina, who thinks him too good for it, really does the photography work—and supports the family. Soon he is off to play in the imaginary forest, leaving the retouching to Hedvig, who adores him and who is going blind from an inherited disease. She tells Gregers of her "mysterious," once-free duck, saved from "the briny deep." This poetic expression, used by both Hedvig and Gregers, establishes a bond between them. Hjalmar later expatiates on "the tragedy of the House of Ekdal" and his "life's work" on a remarkable invention he will yet finish. Some day it will restore the fortune and honor of his "silver-haired" father. (On other occasions, "the humble inventor's only reward" is to be a secure future for his beloved daughter, or else for his widowed

The Wild Duck, Act III. Left to right: Old Ekdal (Henrik Börseth), Hedvig (Evy Engelsborg), Hjalmar (Stein Grieg Halvorsen), Dr. Relling (Borseth Rasmussen), Gina (Ella Hval), a neighbor (Tryve Larsen), Gregers (Olaf Havrevold). Oslo 1953. (*Norwegian Embassy Information Service*)

"helpmate.") Gregers admires him, but insists that the idle dreamer must be pulled up from the illusory depths he has sought, like the wild duck, though Hjalmar tells him that "in my house people never talk to me about unpleasant things." Werle warns his son against meddling, while Dr. Relling, the *raisonneur* who deplores Gregers's "inflamed scruples," and Gina, who has always considered Gregers "a queer fish," warn Hjalmar against listening to him. But intent on revealing "the situation as it is" and freeing Hjalmar from "lies and deceit," Gregers takes him for a long walk.

Act IV. Hjalmar returns after the walk, melodramatically refuses his dinner, and upsets Hedvig by wishing he could wring the neck of the wild duck Werle gave them. He confronts Gina with her past. She frankly admits it, but disappoints Hjalmar by refusing to acknowledge "suffering agonies of worry and remorse" over the years: "What with running the house and everything," she had almost forgotten the past. Gregers officiously views the results of his efforts "to lay the foundation of a true marriage" as Hjalmar tragically announces that "everything's over and done with now." Learning that Werle is going blind and has left Old Ekdal a pension that is to revert to Hedvig, Hjalmar suspiciously questions Gina. When she tells him that she cannot guarantee Hedvig's paternity, Hjalmar wildly repudiates the by-now hysterical child and rushes out of the house. Gregers suggests secretly to Hedvig that she sacrifice the wild duck so that Hjalmar will come back to her.

Act V. Relling argues with Gregers about "ideals." "We've got a plain word that's good enough," Relling remarks: "Lies." What helps the Ekdals survive are "life-lies," illusions. Relling concludes: "Take the life-lie away from the average man and straight away you take away his happiness." Hjalmar returns, unable to tear himself away from the indispensable comforts provided by Gina. He goes through the motions of leaving, to wander "from house to house seeking shelter for my father and myself," when a shot is heard. Hedvig has killed, not the wild duck, but herself. Hjalmar cries out affectedly, and as the corpse is taken away, Relling predicts his maudlin self-pity in future speeches about "the child so untimely torn from a loving father's heart." Gregers insists he will continue pursuing ideals, but the doctor remarks, "Oh, life would be fairly tolerable if only we'd be spared these blasted bill collectors who come around pestering us paupers with the claim of the ideal."

WILDE, Oscar [Fingal O'Flahertie Wills] (1854–1900), is commonly remembered as an Irish-born English wit, a dramatist, a dandy, and a principal figure in a notorious scandal. But he also wrote some remarkable poetry, fiction, criticism, and philosophy; and as BERNARD SHAW pointed out, his greatness as a personality and as a

Oscar Wilde in 1893. (*Culver Pictures*)

conversationalist and raconteur cannot be reproduced. Wilde left but seven complete plays, and in only two of them—SALOMÉ (1893) and THE IMPORTANCE OF BEING EARNEST (1895)—did his dramatic genius flower. Yet they suffice to account for the widely held belief that Wilde was the greatest and "the most individual British dramatist between Shakespeare and Shaw" (Hesketh Pearson).

Born in Dublin, he was the second son of Sir William Robert Wills Wilde, a distinguished ear-and-eye surgeon, and Jane Francesca Elgee, a poetess, novelist, and Irish patriot who before her marriage wrote inflammatory tracts under the name of Speranza. She wanted a daughter (later she had one), and for several years dressed Oscar like a girl. He attended school in Enniskillen and then Trinity College in Dublin, where he distinguished himself as a student. In 1874 he won the highest award in classics and a scholarship to Magdalen College, Oxford. There he was profoundly influenced by the aesthetic theories of two dons, Walter Pater and John Ruskin. Following his father's death in 1876, Wilde used his small inheritance to travel in Italy and Greece. This trip inspired much of his early poetry, as well as his lifelong ideal of pagan beauty and hedonism. Lady Wilde had moved to London after her husband's death, and in her salon young Wilde met prominent and fashionable people like James McNeill Whistler. He finished Oxford triumphantly, winning the most coveted poetry award, the Newdigate Prize, for *Ravenna;* as was customary, the university published the winning poem in book form.

Now Wilde set himself up in London as a self-proclaimed art critic and a "Professor of Aesthetics," preaching the gospel of "art for art's sake." He extravagantly courted the famous beauty Lillie Langtry (he was also to charm such other actresses as Helena Modjeska, Mary Anderson, and Sarah Bernhardt), and his ostentatious affectation of unconventionality in dress and manner and his wit soon established his reputation. It was heightened by satires about him and the aesthetic movement in *Punch,* and by the public's identification of Wilde with Bunthorne in W. S. GILBERT and Arthur Sullivan's *Patience* ("Though the Philistines may jostle, you will rank as an apostle in the high æsthetic band, / If you walk down Piccadilly with a poppy or a lily in your mediæval hand"). In 1880 he published his first play, VERA, and soon began writing his second play, the equally inferior THE DUCHESS OF PADUA (1883); his first collection of *Poems* appeared the following year.

"I have nothing to declare except my genius," he announced to the customs officials when he arrived in New York in 1882. His declining finances had prompted his American lecture tour, which Richard D'Oyly Carte encouraged to publicize *Patience.* During this eventful tour Wilde's legend grew. In America he met leading literary and artistic figures, as he did in Paris in 1883. The following year he married a prominent Dublin barrister's daughter, Constance Mary Lloyd, with whom he had been in love for some years. They made their home in London, and Wilde was happy for a while. But his expenses, heightened by his extravagance and the birth of his sons, Cyril and Vyvyan [Holland], eventually became a heavy burden.

For his children he wrote *The Happy Prince and Other Tales* (1888); two years later appeared his famous novel *The Picture of Dorian Gray,* and the following year the philosophical and critical essays in *Intentions* and *The Soul of Man Under Socialism.* During that time his dissipation increased; he also became more aware of his homosexual propensities, and yielded to—and brazenly flaunted—them. Wilde's downfall was brought about by his relationship with the young poet Lord Alfred Douglas. When Douglas's father, the Marquis of Queensberry, publicly accused him of sexual perversions, Wilde sued him for slander. In the sensational 1895 trials, Wilde's charge collapsed and he was himself tried, convicted on morals charges, and sentenced to two years at hard labor. After his release he settled in France for the few years left him, a broken man. Haunted by his prison memories, Wilde wrote his most famous poem, *The Ballad of Reading Gaol* (1898). He died of syphilis in a cheap Paris hotel room. The day before his death he converted to Catholicism, a step he had contemplated taking ever since his college days.

It was in the three years preceding the trial that Wilde produced the works on which his reputation as a playwright rests. LADY WINDERMERE'S FAN (1892), A WOMAN OF NO IMPORTANCE (1893), and AN IDEAL HUSBAND (1895)—all immediate and brilliant successes—are comic PROBLEM PLAYS. Despite their nineteenth-century brand of sentimentality and melodrama, they depict moral problems with sensitivity and sparkling repartee. Wilde's distinctive wit pervades all, and especially the third of these plays: flashing epigrammatic paradoxes and puns, and use of such comic devices as inverted clichés and anticlimax. His masterpiece is *The Importance of Being Earnest,* one of the most brilliant comedies in the English language, which dispenses with problems and manifests a farcical elegance that camouflages the underlying satire. This comedy and *Salomé,* the short and powerful prose lyric drama that epitomizes his relation to aesthetic decadence, substantiate at least the first part of Wilde's famous claim: "I took the drama, the most objective form known to art, and made of it as personal a mode of expression as the lyric or the sonnet; at the same time, widened its range and enriched its characterization" (*De Profundis,* 1905; written in prison).

Wilde left two posthumous dramatic fragments, both very short. *La Sainte Courtisane, or, The Woman Covered with Jewels* is an almost-completed lyrical drama whose finished manuscript he lost shortly before his death. *A Florentine Tragedy* is a blank-verse play whose manuscript was stolen during the ransacking of Wilde's home at the time of the trials; he later tried to rewrite it, but only the fragment remains. Frank Harris (1856–1931) developed a Wilde scenario into the four-act play *Mr. and Mrs. Daventry,* successfully produced in 1900 and published in 1956 with an informative introduction by H. Montgomery Hyde.

Wilde's plays have been frequently reprinted. There are numerous biographies, including dramatic ones such as the younger ROSTAND's *Le Procès d'Oscar Wilde* (1935), Leslie and Sewell Stokes's *Oscar Wilde* (1938), Fred Gaines's *Wilde!* (1967), and Norman Holland's *Years of the Locusts* (1968). Many of the biographies are sensational and unreliable, including Frank Harris's *Oscar Wilde: His Life and Confessions* (1916), republished in 1960 with Shaw's *Memories of Oscar Wilde.* Among other notable studies are Frances Winwar's *Oscar Wilde and the Yellow Nineties* (1940), Hesketh Pearson's *Oscar Wilde, His Life and Wit* (1946), Edouard Roditi's *Oscar Wilde* (1947), J. E. Agate's *Oscar Wilde and the Theatre* (1947), and ST. JOHN ERVINE's *Oscar Wilde* (1951). Many of these works have selected bibliographies, the most complete being the book-length bibliography published by the William Andrews Clark Memorial Library of Los Angeles, which houses the best collection of Wilde's books and manuscripts. Special note, too, should be made of Wilde's *Letters* (1962, edited by Rupert Hart-Davis) and of *Oscar Wilde, a Pictorial Biography* (1960), a collection of photographs and commentaries by Wilde's son, Vyvyan Holland.

WILDENBRUCH, Ernst von (1845–1909), German writer, linked the classic Schiller drama with emerging NATURALISM. His great early successes were the patriotic blank-verse dramas *Die Karolinger* (1881), about the quarrels of Charlemagne's grandsons at the time of Louis the Pious; and *Die Quitzows* (1888), portraying the struggle of the Pomeranian and the Berlin nobles. Other histories include *Harold* (1882), a tragedy on the Norman Conquest; the double drama *Heinrich und Heinrichs Geschlecht* (1895), the first (translated as *King Henry*) dealing with the humiliation of Henry IV of Germany by Pope Gregory at Canossa, and the second featuring his son, Henry V; *Die Rabensteinerin* (1907, translated as *Barseba of Rabenstein*), portraying the passion of an Augsburg patrician for the gun-toting daughter of a robber baron; and *Christoph Marlow* (1884), a dramatization of the life and death of the English playwright. Wildenbruch's masterful handling of crowd scenes and dialogue, as well as his colorful common folk, account for the great popularity of these historical plays. To remain abreast of changing literary fashions, Wildenbruch subsequently produced naturalistic plays. The most successful of these were *Die Haubenlerche* (1890) and *Meister Balzer* (1892); the first portrays a working girl who rejects wealthier suitors to marry a laborer, and the second deals with an artisan's struggle against the encroaching factories.

Born in Beirut, Syria, Wildenbruch was the offspring of the Prussian diplomat son of Prince Louis Ferdinand. He grew up in Athens and Istanbul, was commissioned a Lieutenant of the Guards, and served in the Foreign Office in Berlin after marrying Carl Maria von Weber's granddaughter. A widely esteemed writer proud of his national heritage, he published volumes of verse, stories, and novels that include the partly autobiographical *Schwester-Seele* (1894). A book-length study is E. A. Morgan's dissertation, *Wildenbruch as a Naturalist* (1930).

WILDER, Thornton [Niven] (1897–), American novelist and playwright, became famous with *The Bridge of San Luis Rey* (1927), a still-popular best seller that won him the first of his three Pulitzer Prizes. As early as 1915 he had begun to write drama, some of which was subsequently published, and in 1926 he had his first full-length play professionally produced. It was not until 1938, however, that he made his mark as a dramatist—with his best-known work, OUR TOWN (1938). He has written only two other successful full-length plays, THE SKIN OF OUR TEETH (1942) and THE MATCHMAKER (1954; subsequently made into *Hello, Dolly!*), and some one-acters frequently produced by school and community theatre groups. Wilder's considerable reputation as a playwright rests on these few works. In form they are highly theatrical, experimental, and eclectic (as are his novels); but the language is as homespun as the attitudes that are expressed. Such traditionalism accounts for Wilder's general popularity; it is his striking dramaturgy that has made him one of the important playwrights of his age.

He was born in Madison, Wisconsin. In 1906 his father, a newspaper editor, was appointed to the Hong Kong, and subsequently the Shanghai, consulate. Thus Wilder spent some of his childhood in the Orient, though his experiences were confined to foreign-colony schools. Eventually he returned to America, and he finished high school in California. He attended Oberlin College and then Yale University. After his enlistment in the Coast Artillery in World War I (he enlisted in the Army Air Force in World War II) he completed his B.A., in 1920. In that year *Yale Literary Magazine* concluded serial publication of his first full-length play, *The Trumpet Shall Sound*. In 1926 the American Laboratory Theatre produced this insignificant undergraduate effort, an allegory about a housemaster (God) who returns from a journey and rewards his servants according to their deserts.

After Yale Wilder went to Rome on a fellowship and studied archaeology at the American Academy there. Upon his return in 1921 he taught French at a New Jersey preparatory school for four years, and completed his master's degree (in French) at Princeton University. Wilder made his home in Hamden, Connecticut, and also did much of his writing at the MacDowell Colony, outside a little hillside town in New Hampshire. With his sister Isabel he toured Europe after the success of *The Bridge of San Luis Rey*, spending much of his time in theatres, whose productions he reviewed for *Theatre Arts Monthly*. Wilder was particularly interested in studying PRESENTATIONAL drama, with which he had already experimented in his short works and which he was to develop in his most distinguished full-length plays.

Between 1915 and 1927 Wilder wrote some forty three-minute dramatic sketches, sixteen of which he published in 1928 as *The Angel That Troubled the Waters and Other Plays*. These are three-character religious or philosophical parables, some dealing with biblical and religious figures (Christ, Satan, Saint Francis), others with composers and writers (Mozart, HENRIK IBSEN, Shelley), and still others with fictitious characters. In 1931 Wilder published what were to become his most popular one-acters in THE LONG CHRISTMAS DINNER *and Other Plays in One Act*. The title play as well as PULLMAN CAR HIAWATHA and THE HAPPY JOURNEY TO TRENTON AND CAMDEN all have a narrator, telescoped time, allegorical processions—dramatic devices Wilder developed further in his major plays; the three minor comic sketches in the collection are *Queens of France, Love and How to Cure It,* and *Such Things Only Happen in Books,* the last of which Wilder himself deleted from the 1963 reprint of the collection. His best-selling novel brought him many lecture invitations, including an appointment at the University of Chicago, where he taught literature (one semester a year) from 1930 to 1936. In New Hampshire during these years he wrote further novels, which, however, failed to duplicate his earlier success.

Turning again to drama, Wilder was first produced on Broadway with *Lucrece* (1932), a translation of ANDRÉ OBEY's poetic play *Le Viol de Lucrèce* (*The Rape of Lucrece*). A failure despite a distinguished production starring Katharine Cornell, it brought about Wilder's professionally important friendship with various actors, producers, and writers like ALEXANDER WOOLLCOTT and EDWARD SHELDON. Wilder's translation of Ibsen's A DOLL'S HOUSE opened on Broadway in late 1937, less than two months before his masterpiece, *Our Town*.

Later in 1938 his second Broadway play, *The Merchant of Yonkers,* proved less successful; the most conventionally structured of his plays, it was subsequently revised as *The Matchmaker*. During the war Wilder's reputation as a dramatist grew with *The Skin of Our Teeth,* despite a much-publicized plagiary charge by JAMES JOYCE scholars.* After World War II he repeated his popular success as a novelist with *The Ides of March* (1948), his fifth novel. He continued writing, lecturing, and traveling, but (aside from *The Matchmaker*) produced few important works. In 1950–51 he was the Charles Eliot Norton Professor of Poetry at Harvard, and he published his lectures on American writers and his researches on the early Spanish drama. His other plays include a translation of Sartre's THE VICTORS and an original and very loose adaptation of Euripides's *Alcestis, The Alcestiad* (retitled *A Life in the Sun*). Produced at the 1955 Edinburgh Festival, it was harshly reviewed and was not brought to or published in the United States. Wilder prepared a libretto of this play (as he did for *The Long Christmas Dinner*); the opera *Die Alkestiade* (music by Louise Talma) was produced in Germany in 1962. At that time Wilder began a double play-cycle of fourteen one-acters meant to summarize his art and philosophy. The first part of the cycle was to depict the seven ages of man, the second the seven deadly sins. Three of the plays were presented in 1962 on a single bill, *Plays for Bleecker Street: Infancy, Childhood,* and *Someone from Assisi* (a sermon that features Saint Francis in a fictionalized episode). But Wilder abandoned the cycle to write a novel, *The Eighth Day* (1967).

In his plays Wilder has attempted to present universal—often cosmic—ideas. These are personified by simple, homespun characters like the Stage Manager, or allegorical characters like Mr. Antrobus (Wilder himself occasionally acted both roles). His often wistful portrayals of the triumph of good over evil, of the essential dignity of man, and the virtue of simple pleasures and emotions may seem trite, and they are occasionally superficial, sentimental, and arch. At the same time, Wilder's drama is impressive in its theatrical vitality, and it is notable for the new artistic life it brought to the American drama of the 1930's, which for the most part was restricted to NATURALISTIC protest plays and conventional Broadway fluff. Going to classical and Oriental traditions that stressed the artifact, the illusory nature of the theatre, Wilder at the same time was influenced by contemporary literary and theatrical innovations, notably those of Joyce, and GERTRUDE STEIN, ANTON CHEKHOV, and LUIGI

* In the preface to his major *Three Plays* (1957) Wilder readily acknowledged his indebtedness to *Finnegans Wake*. "I should be very happy if, in the future, some author should feel similarly indebted to any work of mine," he wrote: "Literature has always more resembled a torch race than a furious dispute among heirs."

PIRANDELLO. Though by no means always of comparable stature, Wilder's works nonetheless are significant for their originality and their effect on subsequent presentational drama in America and abroad as, for example, on the work of MAX FRISCH. And their popularity has made at least some of them classics during his own lifetime.

Wilder's important plays were gathered in the earlier-mentioned collections, whose prefaces summarize Wilder's ideas about drama, literature, and life. (Another important essay is his oft-reprinted "Some Thoughts On Playwriting," 1941.) *The Long Christmas Dinner and Other Plays in One Act* was republished in 1963, with an introduction and critical bibliography by John Gassner. MICHAEL GOLD excoriated Wilder's work in a controversial *New Republic* article in 1930. Book-length studies of Wilder and his work include Rex Burbank's *Thornton Wilder* (1961), Malcolm Goldstein's *The Art of Thornton Wilder* (1965), and Donald Haberman's *The Plays of Thornton Wilder* (1967), all of which have bibliographies.

WILDGANS, Anton (1881–1932), Austrian poet and author of middle-class verse tragedies that linked Austro-German NATURALISM and EXPRESSIONISM. His most successful play was *Armut* (1914), in which a poverty-stricken invalid cannot be saved from death by his daughter, who offers to sell her body, or by his son, who hurls poetic accusations at cold-hearted humanity. Nearly as popular in Viennese theatres were *Liebe* (1916), in which Wildgans dramatized the death of a couple's love (once sexual ardor is gone) as universal suffering; and *Dies Irae* (1918), in which popular expressionist themes are anticipated in the suicide of such a couple's unwanted adolescent and in his friend's bombastic attack on "Those who engender man / Not for the sake of man."

The son of a cabinet minister, the Vienna-born Wildgans had a bitter childhood. He studied law, but was able to devote his life to literature and the theatre when his poetry made him financially independent. His first stage success was *In Ewigkeit Amen!* (1913), a courtroom one-acter about a sadistic judge and his morally superior victim. Later Wildgans started a biblical trilogy of which he completed only *Kain* (1920), a "mythical poem" whose title character's murder of Abel foreshadows man's inhumanity. For a couple of years in the early 1920's and again shortly before Hitler's rise Wildgans directed the important Vienna Burgtheater. Despite his stage hits, Wildgans is now remembered mainly for his poetry.

WILLIAMS, Charles [Walter Stansby] (1886–1945), English writer, is best known for his literary and theological essays, his poetry (particularly his cycles on Arthurian myth), and his novels, among which *Descent into Hell* (1937) was presumably Eliot's source for THE COCKTAIL PARTY. A devout Anglo-Catholic, he wrote religious verse drama for performance by church groups. The best of his fifteen plays probably are *Thomas Cranmer of Canterbury,* produced at the 1936 Canterbury Festival, and *The House of the Octopus* (1945), his last full-length drama.

John Heath-Stubbs's introduction to the *Collected Plays* (1963) discusses Williams as a dramatist. See also *Essays Presented to Charles Williams* (1947), by C. S. Lewis, DOROTHY SAYERS, and others.

WILLIAMS,* [George] Emlyn (1905–   ), British actor and director, was also Wales's first successful dramatist. His most notable plays, all written in English, are a murder thriller, NIGHT MUST FALL (1935), and the autobiographical THE CORN IS GREEN (1938). Williams's drama is eminently theatrical and readable. But it is somewhat shallow, sentimental, and dependent on melodramatic effects. These shortcomings are obviated by Williams's charm, intelligence, and moral integrity —qualities he has demonstrated also as a director and an actor, on both stage and screen.

The son of a stoker and a housemaid, who ran the village pub, Williams was born in Flintshire, North Wales. As a boy he spoke only Welsh, but with the help of a teacher whom he later immortalized as Miss Moffat he became fluent in a number of languages. He was educated in Switzerland and, like the hero of *The Corn Is Green,* at seventeen won a scholarship to Oxford, where he subsequently took his M.A. It was at Oxford that he became fascinated with the theatre. He began acting in 1927 and became known four years later, when he starred in *A Murder Has Been Arranged,* a play that he had both written and directed. But it was with the impersonation of his psychopathic, baby-faced murderer Dan in *Night Must Fall* that he became famous both as an actor and a playwright. Three years later Williams's reputation became international with *The Corn Is Green.*

He has also acted in most of his other plays and adaptations. These include *Glamour* (1928); *Full Moon* (1929); *Port Said* (1931); his adaptation from the French of Fauchois's THE LATE CHRISTOPHER BEAN (1932, and set in Wales); *Vessels Departing* (1933); *Spring 1600* (1934), an unsuccessful comedy about Shakespeare's leading actor, Richard Burbage (revised in 1945 and made into a musical in 1969); *He Was Born Gay* (1937), an expensive failure about Louis XVII, the "lost dauphin"; *The Light of Heart* (1940), the story of an alcoholic actor, performed in New York as *Yesterday's Magic; The Morning Star* (1941), a portrayal of England's resistance to the *Luftwaffe*'s Blitz; *A Month in the Country* (1943), an adaptation of Turgenev; *The Druid's Rest* (1944), set in Wales—with much of the dialogue written in Welsh; *Trespass* (1947); *Accolade* (1950); *Someone Waiting* (1953); and *Beth* (1958). Williams has also created successful one-man entertainments like *Charles Dickens* (reading selections of Dickens's works, 1951) and *Bleak House* (1952); and readings from the short stories of his fellow Welshman, *Dylan Thomas Growing Up* (1955). His other work includes the writing and directing of—and acting

* Illustration on page 201.

in—*The Last Days of Dolwyn* (1949, in America titled *The Woman of Dolwyn*), a film that portrays the extinction of a Welsh mining town.

Williams's *The Collected Plays* (Volume I), with the author's introduction, was published in 1961; it contains *Night Must Fall, He Was Born Gay, The Corn Is Green,* and *The Light of Heart.* Other plays were published separately. An autobiography, *George* (1962), covers the early years of his life. See also Richard Findlater's *Emlyn Williams* (1956).

WILLIAMS, Jesse Lynch (1871–1929), American journalist, short-story writer, and novelist, is memorable as a playwright for his popular SHAVian comedy WHY MARRY? (1914), the first winner of the then just-established Pulitzer Prize. In the early years of the twentieth century, Williams was second only to LANGDON MITCHELL as a satiric American playwright. All his dramas deal with serious subjects, but in an amusing manner.

Born in Sterling, Illinois, and a graduate of Princeton University (1892), where he helped write revues, Williams began his career as a journalist and a writer of entertaining novels and short stories. Some of them are about Princeton, others about his experiences as a reporter for the New York *Sun.* In 1906 he dramatized one of his newspaper tales as *The Stolen Story,* a thriller he immediately reworked as a novel, *The Day Dreamer.*

Williams's later plays include another adaptation of a novel (*Remating Time*) into *Why Not?* (1922), "a comedy of conventions" satirizing the absurdity of divorce laws, here illustrated with two mismated couples who would be best off exchanging partners (the resolution remains inconclusive, however); and *Lovely Lady* (1925), a satire about the relations of parents and children.

WILLIAMS, Tennessee [Thomas Lanier] (1911–), American dramatist, became one of his country's leading playwrights (ARTHUR MILLER was the other) in the 1940's and 1950's, after the appearance of THE GLASS MENAGERIE (1944) and A STREETCAR NAMED DESIRE (1947). In succeeding years Williams's reputation spread far beyond those of other contemporary dramatists: stars and motion-picture companies were attracted by and filmed most of his plays, which are notable for their strong parts and exciting plots. Excessive emphasis on violence, sex, and SYMBOLISM frequently mars these plays. But however sensational his writing, Williams has striven for and often achieved "theatre poetry" in his depiction of fear, suffering, and loneliness. At their best, his dramas are lyrical works of originality and power.

A Southerner, Williams (in the late 1930's he adopted his college nickname "Tennessee," where he had spent some of his youth) was born in Mississippi. His father, a salesman for a shoe company, did much traveling, and the family for a while lived with Williams's maternal grandfather, a clergyman. When he was promoted to sales manager in 1918, Williams's father moved his family to St. Louis. Living together did not work out well and there was much friction because of the exuberant, domineering man—a stingy and coarse tippler, according to Williams's mother. Young Tom, shy and a hypochondriac after acute diphtheria, which for years paralyzed his legs and affected his kidneys, hated St. Louis. His father ridiculed his reading and writing (he called Tom "Miss Nancy"), and after he failed ROTC in his third year at the University of Missouri, took him out of college to clerk for a shoe company. Williams loathed his work, and found his escape in writing (most of the night) and going to the movies. After three years he broke down, recuperated in Memphis at his grandparents' home, and then worked his way through Washington University and the University of Iowa, where he received his degree in 1938.

Williams's family life (he himself has remained unmarried) is strongly reflected in his plays. His first success (*The Glass Menagerie*) portrays the St. Louis period and his introverted sister, Rose, whose mental breakdown and lifelong commitment to an institution filled Williams with anguished guilt. His parents appear in various guises in many of Williams's plays. Other influences of Williams's youth on his writing were his preoccupations with loneliness, with the need to communicate, with overstimulated fantasy that leaned toward the bizarre, and—a reaction against his puritanical maternal upbringing in the rectory—with sex.

Williams wrote stories and poems even before he entered college. Some of his early plays were produced by university and summer-theatre groups. The first of them, *Cairo! Shanghai! Bombay!,* is a farce about sailors on shore leave, produced in 1935. The next year he won a local drama contest, and until 1938 he wrote plays for The Mummers, a St. Louis theatre group. Unlike his later drama, which focuses on individual rather than social problems, they are NATURALISTIC protest plays. The most successful among them, *Candles to the Sun* (1936), deals with suffering Alabama coal miners. *The Fugitive Kind* (1937) is a play about St. Louis's skid row that was roundly damned; its title was later used for the 1959 film version of ORPHEUS DESCENDING (1957). In 1939 Williams won New York's Group Theatre citation for three one-acters collectively titled *American Blues* and published in 1948 in the larger collection by that name.

The citation brought him to the notice of Audrey Wood, the agent who helped Williams reach and retain his important position. He received a scholarship to the New School for Social Research's playwriting seminar given by John Gassner, who persuaded the Theatre Guild to produce Williams's *Battle of Angels* (later rewritten as *Orpheus Descending*). It had an abortive pre-Broadway run, but Williams, drifting in New Orleans, Florida, and Mexico, continued to write plays and stories. Back in New York he led a Bohemian life in Greenwich Village, and completed a potboiler with Donald Windham (1920–), *You Touched Me!*—a romanticized dramatization of D. H. LAWRENCE's story by the

Tennessee Williams, 1956. (©Karsh of Ottawa. *Rapho Guillumette*)

same name. (It reached Broadway in 1945, after Williams had become famous.) Wood got him a lucrative screenwriter's job in Hollywood; there his synopsis for a projected film was rejected and Williams, after leaving the studio, converted it into *The Glass Menagerie*.

His reputation became firmly established with *Streetcar*, his next play. Thereafter Williams produced hit after hit: SUMMER AND SMOKE (1947), a disappointment on Broadway, but a success Off-Broadway; THE ROSE TATTOO (1950), inspired by a trip to Rome, perhaps his finest comedy, featuring the first of a number of Latin heroines; CAMINO REAL (1953), a venture into EXPRESSIONISM that became another Broadway disappointment to succeed Off-Broadway; CAT ON A HOT TIN ROOF (1955), the most popular play since *Streetcar* and, like that play, a Pulitzer Prize winner; the revision of *Battle of Angels* into *Orpheus Descending;* two hits, SUDDENLY LAST SUMMER (1958) and SWEET BIRD OF YOUTH (1959); *Period of Adjustment* (1960), a Broadway-tailored comedy about newly-weds; and THE NIGHT OF THE IGUANA (1961), another critical as well as popular success.

Later plays have fared less well. *The Milk Train Doesn't Stop Here Anymore* (1963), originally a one-acter presented at the Spoleto Festival, within a few months received two different Broadway productions; a Kabuki-inspired allegory about an evil old libertine actress and a handsome Christ figure who teaches her to accept death, it failed in all three versions, but was resurrected as *Boom!* (1968), a lavish film written by Williams. *The Mutilated* and *The Gnädiges Fräulein*, which collectively appeared as *Slapstick Tragedy* (1965), also failed. Audiences were perplexed by *The Two Character Play* (1967), a PIRANDELLian horror play-within-a-play about a brother and sister, actors who have been deserted by their company and alone perform—or may in fact actually live—a mad and incestuous brother-sister act. Somewhat more successful was *The Seven Descents of Myrtle* (1968), published as *Kingdom of Earth* and filmed as *Last of the Mobile Hot-Shots* (1970), a three-character tragicomedy about an impotent transvestite who is dying and the sensitive showgirl he marries to spite and cheat his virile, part-Negro half-brother out of their decayed Delta home; typical Williams characters, one of them (the victorious stud) expresses the author's faith in the flesh before he causes the heroine's final "descent" by making her his whore: "There's nothing in this whole kingdom of Earth to compare with what's able to happen between a man and a woman." *In the Bar of a Tokyo Hotel* (1969) features the middle-aged neurotic wife of a famous ailing painter—a transparently autobiographical figure; he attempts to discover new art forms, breaks down, and dies as his lonely and promiscuous wife, yearning for freedom, flirts with the hotel barman and walks the streets.

Williams's dramaturgy has not changed perceptibly over the decades. He has used similar types in play after play: fragile and neurotic Southern women like Blanche; lusty women like the Princess and Serafina; incredibly handsome and/or virile youths, some of them savage studs like Stanley Kowalski, others hell-raisers turned mystics, like Val; and dreamers like Tom Wingfield. Williams's plots tend to be lurid, featuring violence and perversions that range from priapism and homosexuality to cannibalism. But however sensational, such grotesqueries are not expressed merely for their own sakes or for popular appeal. Williams portrays the dark world that he has seen, and his plays probe his protagonists' psyches and his own preoccupations: illusion and reality, art and sensitivity being destroyed by brutality and ugly industrialism and practicality, human failure and loneliness, men's faltering attempts to communicate with one another, the strife of spirit and flesh, and (as Williams himself has aged) the menace of time.

Lawrence has been Williams's greatest literary influence, and probably the earliest (in *The Glass Menagerie* Williams portrays the mother's indignation at Tom's reading the "diseased" and "insane Mr. Lawrence"). Williams coauthored the already-noted dramatization of a Lawrence story, and after visiting his widow in 1940, Williams wrote a one-act play about his idol: *I Rise in Flame, Cried the Phoenix* (1951) depicts the Lawrences' violent love-hate relationship shortly before and at the time of the writer's death. Other literary influences on Williams are perceptible to a lesser degree in his drama; they include AUGUST STRINDBERG, FEDERICO GARCÍA LORCA, ANTON CHEKHOV, and the poet Hart Crane.

A prolific if generally unpublished poet, Williams in his plays has written lyrical dialogue that abounds (like his many stage props) in symbolism. He attempts—not always successfully—to create a mood by integrating evocative language, setting, sound effects, lighting, props, and costumes. In lengthy "production notes" and stage directions he specifies the PRESENTATIONAL means he sometimes employs—particularly skeletal settings that merely suggest reality, as well as lighting and music—necessary to the desired mood. His efforts to create poetic theatre exemplify Williams's unique strengths as well as his weaknesses: when they are overdone—as is often the case—they appear grotesque and tasteless. Yet his seriousness as an artist is manifested in the pains he has taken with his dramas. All of them had their germ in a short story, sketch, or one-act play; he has repeatedly rewritten—sometimes even after plays have succeeded on Broadway—and republished them in revised versions. Curiously enough, however, despite all this effort, and despite his development as a craftsman, he has failed to grow artistically. Williams's best works are still his early hits. However impressive technically and seductive theatrically, his later works for the most part merely rehash earlier character types, themes, and moods.

Williams's one-acters were collected in 27 WAGONS FULL OF COTTON AND OTHER ONE-ACT PLAYS (1946) and in *American Blues: Five Short Plays* (1948). The latter includes *The Unsatisfactory Supper* (also titled *The Long Stay Cut Short*)—which with the earlier collection's title play became Williams's popular screenplay *Baby Doll* (1956)—and *Moony's Kid Don't Cry,* a characteristic sketch of a young man trapped by family responsibilities and industrialization. It appeared in Margaret Mayorga's *The Best One Act Plays of 1941*—a series that repeatedly featured Williams plays before he became famous. Many of the later stories and plays appeared in *Esquire* magazine. Williams has also published collections of poems and short stories, and a novel (filmed in 1961), *The Roman Spring of Mrs. Stone* (1950).

Biographies of Williams include his mother's memoirs, Edwina Dakin Williams's *Remember Me to Tom* (1963), which contains many Williams letters; and Maxwell Gilbert's *Tennessee Williams and Friends* (1965). Book-length studies (most of them containing bibliographies) include Signi L. Falk's *Tennessee Williams* (1961), Benjamin Nelson's *Tennessee Williams: The Man and His Works* (1961), Nancy M. Tischler's *Tennessee Williams: Rebellious Puritan* (1961), and Esther M. Jackson's *The Broken World of Tennessee Williams* (1965).

WILLIAMS, William Carlos (1883–1963), American physician and author, wrote in all genres but became best known as a poet. After some now-lost verse drama, Williams wrote prose plays collected in *Many Loves and Other Plays* (1961). The episodic title work is unified by a framework depicting a young playwright's production of three short plays that present various types of love, and was produced in repertory Off-Broadway in 1959. Others are *A Dream of Love* (1949), a play about an adulterous physician, with which Williams hoped in vain to conquer Broadway; *Tituba's Children,* a play (completed in 1950) on the same theme and with some of the same characters as Miller's THE CRUCIBLE; *The Cure* (1960), a play about a nurse and her patient; and an opera libretto about George Washington, *The First President* (1936). Only *Many Loves* enjoyed a successful production.

WILSON, Edmund (1895–), American essayist and critic of major distinction, has also worked in other literary genres. The most notable of his collected *Five Plays* (1954), *The Little Blue Light,* was first published in 1950 and ran briefly in New York the following year; a satiric intellectual morality play, it portrays man's struggle against political and other powers and his near defeat by a fantastic "little blue light," which is triggered by human feelings. The title play of *The Duke of Palermo and Other Plays* (1969) is a broad but incisive satire of academe and features a parody of Elizabethan drama; the other plays are *Osbert's Career, or The Poet's Progress,* "a comic strip" composed over a forty-year period and dealing with the increasing sterility and violence in American life; and *Dr. McGrath,* a one-act satire of virulent anti-Communism.

WILSON, Harry Leon (1867–1939), American comic novelist and essayist. His most enduring novels are *Ruggles of Red Gap* (1915) and *Merton of the Movies* (1922). The former, featuring a British butler transplanted to America, was immediately adapted into a musical comedy by Harrison Rhodes (1871–1929, music by Sigmund Romberg), and filmed a number of times; *Merton of the Movies,* a Hollywood satire, also was filmed and turned into a popular comic drama by MARC CONNELLY and GEORGE S. KAUFMAN. Wilson collaborated on some eleven plays with BOOTH TARKINGTON, most successfully on *The Man from Home* (1907), which ran for almost six years.

WINGLESS VICTORY, THE, a play in three acts by MAXWELL ANDERSON, published and produced in 1936. Setting: Salem, 1800.

This is a verse drama of miscegenation, puritanical intolerance, and cupidity.

Nathaniel McQueston returns home after many years, flaunting his wealth ("I am . . . a bacon-bringer of a fairly engaging sort") and his black wife and children. His disagreeable, pious family are shocked; but they need his money, and therefore ungraciously put up with Oparre, a Malayan princess turned Christian. The townspeople soon get Nathaniel's wealth by borrowing and trickery. He is totally at their mercy when they find out he stole his ship, formerly *The Wingless Victory*. Their and his family's contemptuous hatred of the superior Oparre finally contaminates his love, and he agrees to send her away. After castigating "all these white frightened faces" and their "Christ and his beggar's doctrine," Oparre returns to the ship. There she poisons herself and her children, and when Nathaniel returns to her penitently it is too late.

WINGS OVER EUROPE, "a dramatic extravaganza on a pressing theme" in three acts by ROBERT M. B. NICHOLS and MAURICE BROWNE, produced in 1928 and published in 1929. Setting: the Cabinet Council Room at 10 Downing Street, London; "to-morrow morning."

This atom-bomb play is compelling no less for its prophetic intensity (seventeen years before the then-fantastic assumptions were realized in fact) than for its characterizations of various Cabinet ministers as they face Lightfoot's ultimatum. The play's gripping suspense is only slightly diminished by occasional stage rhetoric, by the idealistic scientist's incredible arrogance and conceit—and by the authors' mistaken assumption that scientists would behave differently than other human beings.

Act I. The Prime Minister introduces his nephew, Francis Lightfoot, a brilliant scientist, to his most distinguished minister, Evelyn Arthur. Lightfoot expresses his admiration of Shelley. "Our only romantic poet with scientific leanings," Arthur remarks—and is amazed at Lightfoot's resemblance to Shelley. When the Cabinet assembles, the Prime Minister presents his nephew—a genius extolled by Albert Einstein and about to win the Nobel Prize at twenty-five. Lightfoot's elaborate prefatory explanation of the structure of the universe as well as his pleas for humanity are cut short by the genial Lord Privy Seal, a sportsman who begs him, "Be a good feller: have mercy on a lot of old codgers: cut the cackle an' come to the hosses." "Gentlemen," Lightfoot finally reveals excitedly, "I can control . . . the energy . . . in the atom." They are skeptical of and impatient with his idealistic dreams, which are to be realized by his control of matter. "Well, perhaps you'll listen to this," Lightfoot explains; "so far as matter is concerned, what I will to be, will be, and what I will not to be, will not be." Exultantly he presents them with an opportunity to serve civilization, "to build a House for Man." Promising to prove his power with a scientific demonstration, he leaves confidently. Some ministers are doubtful, but Arthur is not: "It would be better for that poor young man and for the world had he never been born."

Act II. Appalled by the demonstration ("Detonatin' that lump o' sugar an' leavin' a crater as big as St. Paul's"), the ministers vote to ask Lightfoot to destroy his discovery and reveal it to no one. But if Lightfoot should refuse? In that case, tnough the Prime Minister is reluctant, the Cabinet decides to arrest and confine him. Lightfoot indignantly refuses their demand. Arthur envisions the destructive effect of his invention, but Lightfoot envisions its limitless benefits. Arthur attempts to persuade Lightfoot that the humanity he talks of never even heard of, much less cares about, Shelley and Lightfoot's other idols. A laborer, a socialist, and a civil servant are brought in from the street; though the test is amusing, it is indecisive. Lightfoot sneers about the Cabinet's integrity and, in impassioned responses, various ministers reveal an idealism that, however, has to adjust to reality. "Damn it, boy, the mass of mankind is still unimaginably ignorant. One must do what one can," says the President of the Board of Education. Lightfoot answers, "Rubbish! One must do what one can't. That's why I tackled the atom." He is most disgusted by the War Minister, the only one to abstain from the vote—because "with this weapon the Americans an' ourselves could be cock o' the walk an' teach all other peoples on the globe where they got off." Once more Lightfoot urges the ministers to meet their responsibility: "Mastery over matter. At last, Man is free to enlarge the Kingdom of the Spirit." Threatened with arrest, Lightfoot jeers at and insults the Cabinet. He has made airtight preparations: "Understand this: either, by *noon* to-morrow, you will be prepared to formulate, under my supervision, a constructive program satisfactory to *me,* or at *one o'clock to-morrow* England ends." A prior accident's befalling him would automatically detonate the explosion. Arthur begs him, "Don't be so hard. Forgive Man for being what he is." Lightfoot replies, "My hardness will make Man what he might be. . . . I will raise Man, though it be upon a cross, and crown him, though it will be with thorns."

Act III. The next day the ministers capitulate. They are amazed when a haggard Lightfoot despairingly submits his own capitulation. The world is not ready for "the decision between Right and Wrong." Bitterly he concludes, "Man has not yet sufficiently evolved to face life, nor I to decide whether I have the right to force Man to face it." And he adds, to the horror of the ministers, "I, who gave Man his opportunity, am about to take it away." The world will be destroyed in fifteen minutes. While he is out in the park feeding the swans, the minutes tick away. The ministers react with varying degrees of courage and hysteria. When Arthur is reproved for reading Benedetto Croce "in the face of the futility of everything," he replies, "And what else is philosophy for, if not to reconcile us to that futility?" The Prime Minister silently watches his beloved granddaughter playing in the garden, periodically checks the clock, and stops some of his ministers' vicious squabbling: "We have seven minutes left. . . . Give thanks for the beauty and bravery that have been on earth; failing that, at least preserve man's dignity by silence." Suddenly the war minister realizes that the control mechanism must be on Lightfoot's person. He persuades his colleagues that, for the sake of their and the whole world's survival, Lightfoot must be shot. But as he returns from the park, Lightfoot is accidentally run over by a lorry.* He is brought in, the clock strikes twelve, and he dies an instant before he can move the fateful dial. But as the ministers rejoice, a message arrives. "The Guild of United Brain-Workers of the World" has discovered and made atom bombs, and is now summoning world leaders to Geneva. Already airplanes containing atom bombs are flying "over the capitals of every civilized country"

*In the original Theatre Guild production, instead of being run over by a lorry Lightfoot was shot by the War Minister.

to enforce the summons. "Nature doesn't often give us a second chance," Arthur remarks, and the Prime Minister asks his Cabinet, "Gentlemen, those wings even now sound over Europe. Are we with them or against them?" Puckishly taking Lightfoot's mechanism along, Arthur leaves for Geneva. In a final tableau, the ministers assume two attitudes. Some are "expectant of calamity," others raise their hands "as if to welcome a supreme hope. The roar of aeroplanes fills the entire theater."

WINSLOW BOY, THE, a play in four acts by TERENCE RATTIGAN, published and produced in 1946. Setting: London, shortly before World War I.

This is a dramatization (filmed in 1949) of an actual case—George Archer-Shee's dismissal from the Royal Naval Academy for petty thievery, and his father's struggle to establish the boy's innocence. It is a hortatory play about democracy; despite its domestic setting it conveys the excitement of courtroom drama.

Ronnie Winslow, a frightened thirteen-year-old, comes home. Accused of stealing a five-shilling postal order, he has been expelled from the Royal Naval College. After assuring himself that the boy is innocent, his father, Arthur, tries to have the case reexamined, but is rebuffed by the Admiralty. Finally he interests England's most prominent attorney in this minor case. Apparently heartless and supercilious, the attorney grills Ronnie unmercifully and infuriates the Winslows. Then he blandly takes on the case. For two years Arthur Winslow spares no efforts to clear his boy. He loses his health and money, taking his older son out of Oxford when he can no longer afford the cost. The case attracts much attention, and the family becomes a laughingstock to some for challenging the national government and preoccupying it with a piddling case. Ronnie is settled in another school, and Mrs. Winslow begs her husband to stop: "The cost may be out of all proportions." Winslow, however, is concerned with righting the injustice, whatever the cost. He weakens when his daughter, Catherine, a suffragette and a trade unionist, loses her fiancé because of the case. But though she is aging and is eager to marry, Catherine herself approves of continuing the fight: "People should know that a Government Department has ignored a fundamental human right and that it should be forced to acknowledge it," she tells her departing fiancé: "If ever the time comes that the House of Commons has so much on its mind that it can't find time to discuss a Ronnie Winslow and his bally postal order, this country will be a far poorer place than it is now." She is suspicious of the attorney, whom she considers a reactionary opportunist. Then she learns that he took their case at considerable personal sacrifice. Finally he wins it, and the Winslows are informed of the jubilant and emotional courtroom scenes. Catherine realizes that though he mistrusts emotion, the attorney really believes in the formal phrase, "Let Right be done." Before these spokesmen for Labour and Conservatism part as understanding friends ("No party has a monopoly of concern for individual liberty"), Ronnie comes in. He had gone to a show while the verdict on his case was announced.

WINTER BALLAD, A (*Winterballade*), a blank-verse tragedy in seven scenes by GERHART HAUPTMANN, published and produced in 1917. Setting: a winter in sixteenth-century Sweden.

This study of crime and expiation was inspired by Selma Lagerlöf's novel, *Herr Arnes penningar* (*Herr Arne's Hoard,* 1904).

Along with two other Scottish mercenaries, Sir Archie robs and murders an old pastor and his family. He becomes obsessed with his guilt and imagines that Elsalil, another child, is the pastor's granddaughter, whom he stabbed while she clung to him. Elsalil escaped being murdered, but she has become deranged by the tragedy and falls in love with Sir Archie. Jealous of being taken for the dead girl, she bites his hand to persuade him of her reality. In Sir Archie's fantasies the two girls merge, becoming betrayer as well as betrayed. Insanely he hurls objects at the imaginary "she-cur" he sees on the ice—and indeed, Elsalil is later found dead there. His fellow murderers urge him to escape to Scotland with them, but Sir Archie nobly refuses—whereupon, he falls dead. The pastor's son, come to avenge his father, recognizes that Sir Archie's "tremendous 'No'" to his companions' urgings signified the birth of his soul: "Amen, Amen! / Here lies a conqueror . . . here lies / a man redeemed, friends!—and where is my foe?!"

WINTERSET, a verse play in three acts by MAXWELL ANDERSON, published and produced in 1935. Setting: contemporary tenements and an alley at a riverbank in Manhattan under a bridge, winter.

Many critics consider this play to be Anderson's greatest work, though some have characterized it as a sentimental melodrama in pedestrian verse. *Winterset* is an imaginative sequel to the Sacco-Vanzetti case, which Anderson had dramatized in GODS OF THE LIGHTNING. Here, however, private grief and social protest are not presented as propaganda: the conflicts of vengeance, justice, faith, truth, and love are universalized. Themes of *Romeo and Juliet, Hamlet,* and *King Lear* are modernized in powerful characterizations, highly theatrical atmosphere and action, and intellectually keen as well as often affecting blank verse. In "Poetry in the Theater," his preface to the play, Anderson noted the novelty of basing poetic drama on a contemporary situation. Calling the theatre "essentially a cathedral of the spirit, devoted to the exaltation of men," and attributing the greatness of classic tragedy to its poetry (the supreme "language of emotion"), Anderson believed that poetry can best furnish the theatre's intrinsic "power to weld and determine what the [human] race dreams into what the race will become."

Act I. Scene 1. Recently released from a long

Winterset, Act I, Scene 3. Mio (Burgess Meredith) and Miriamne (Margo); at left, Trock (Eduardo Ciannelli) giving instructions to his henchman (Harold Johnsrud). New York, 1935. (*Vandamm Photo, Theatre Collection, New York Public Library*)

prison term, the gangster Trock Estrella knows he is dying of tuberculosis. He bitterly curses humanity, and aggressively tells his henchman that he will get even if attempts are made to imprison him again on new evidence. *Scene 2.* He visits the cellar apartment of Esdras, a philosophizing old Jew, and his children, Garth (a violinist) and the pretty fifteen-year-old Miriamne. Garth is conscience-stricken and fearful of Trock's threats. He knows Trock is guilty of the crime for which the innocent radical Romagna was executed. A professor's researches now may well reopen the case, for they have uncovered Garth as a material witness who never testified. Trock warns him to remain silent and stay put. Miriamne is appalled to learn of her brother's secret and guilty knowledge, but old Esdras attempts to console his son. "Till it's known you bear no guilt at all," he says: "Only what men can see / exists in that shadow" that is life. When Miriamne says that she would prefer death to lying, Esdras wearily says: "Because you're young. . . . [That's] the only reason." *Scene 3.* After a short street-life interlude, the remaining principals appear in response to the new developments in the Romagna case: Gaunt, who was the presiding judge at the trial, and Mio (Bartolomeo Romagna), the victim's seventeen-year-old son. Gaunt has finally lost his sanity after thirteen years of self-recriminations, and Mio has grown up to be a bitter youth obsessed with the injustice done his father. Both Gaunt and Mio seek Garth—the distraught judge, to reassure himself that his testimony would have made no difference in the final verdict; the son, to expose the evidence of his father's innocence: "I've got to find out who did it / and make them see it till it scalds their eyes / and make them admit it till their tongues are blistered / with saying how black they lied!" The tenement dwellers and some passersby amuse themselves with music and dancing in the street until a policeman stops the festivities. In the meantime, Mio and Miriamne meet and immediately fall in love. The raving judge is sheltered by old Esdras, but Trock intends to have him killed; when his henchman refuses to commit the murder, Trock has the henchman shot and thrown into the river.

Act II. At Esdras's, Judge Gaunt and Mio soon confront each other. Fearful of Trock and eager to protect himself, Garth denies to Mio that he has evidence or knowledge of the crime. Though tortured with guilt, Gaunt gradually makes Mio doubt himself and his father's innocence. Mio's desperation grows when he learns that Miriamne is the sister of the man who will not clear his father's name. But when Trock arrives to abduct the judge, the truth unexpectedly comes out: Trock's henchman is not yet dead; as a storm rages outside, he comes in to revenge himself, and Trock, momentarily terrified by the apparent ghost, reveals Romagna's innocence in an eerie mock trial. Gaunt defends his prejudiced judging on the grounds of "the common good [that is] worth more / than small injustice." Any judge, he says, would "let the record stand, / let one man die. For justice, in the main, / is governed by opinion. Communities / will have what they will have, and it's quite as well, / after all, to be rid of anarchists." When policemen come in, Mio wants to report the crime. He starts by sending them after Trock's henchman, who lies dead in the hall. But to protect her brother, Miriamne persuades Mio to forfeit his opportunity and pretend he was joking. His revenge blunted, Mio is bitter and goes out: "You might have picked / some other stranger to dance with!"

Act III. As Trock's gunmen wait to ambush Mio outside and old Esdras futilely seeks help, Miriamne begs Mio's forgiveness for betraying him. Though his friend comes by, Mio does not reveal his plight and thus fails to seize his last chance for help: "I've lost / my taste for revenge if it falls on you," he then tells Miriamne; "I think I'm waking / from a long trauma of hate and fear and death / that's hemmed me from my birth—and glimpse a life / to be lived in hope—but it's young in me yet, I can't / get free, or forgive! But teach me how to live / and forget to hate!" When Miriamne says that his father would have forgiven, Mio is persuaded. Yet he feels that it is too late: "I came here seeking / light in darkness, running from the dawn, / and stumbled on a morning." The gunmen cut Mio down as he tries to make his escape. Heartbroken and guilt-ridden, Miriamne also seeks their fire. She is fatally wounded and crawls to die beside Mio. Old Esdras delivers the valedictory over their corpses: "Forgive the ancient evil of the earth / that brought you here. . . . / This is the glory of earth-born men and women, / not to cringe, never to yield, but standing, / take defeat implacable and defiant, / die unsubmitting. I wish that I'd died so, / long ago." Then he and Garth carry out the bodies of the young lovers.

WISTERIA TREES, THE, a play in three acts by JOSHUA LOGAN, published and produced in 1950. Setting: a Louisiana wisteria plantation at the end of the nineteenth century.

Successfully produced on Broadway, this is an adaptation of Chekhov's THE CHERRY ORCHARD. Some critics felt that Logan romanticized and vulgarized Chekhov's subtle astringency, while others praised *The Wisteria Trees* as a moving new American drama. The plot is virtually identical with Chekhov's, though transplanted to a post-Civil War American setting with native characters: a Southern aristocratic family and its Negro servants.

WITCHING HOUR, THE, a play in four acts by AUGUSTUS THOMAS, produced in 1907 and published in 1916. Setting: Louisville, Kentucky, and Washington, D.C.; 1907.

This once-popular melodrama deals with the then newly topical and exciting subject of mental telepathy and hypnotism.

At Jack Brookfield's gambling place, Helen Whipple's son kills a man who teases him with a scarf pin that displays a cat's eye, to which he has "inherited a compulsive aversion." Helen appeals to a Supreme Court Justice who once loved her mother. Jack Brookfield, in the meantime, recognizing his telepathic powers, uses them to get Helen's son acquitted by implicating the district attorney in the assassination of the governor-elect. Brookfield successfully hypnotizes the infuriated district attorney, who has come to shoot him: "You can't shoot—that gun—you can't even hold it." Later Brookfield tells Helen, whom he courted in vain for many years, that he had thought of the assassination before it happened. Since he thus himself unwittingly may have suggested the crime, Brookfield will try to save the district attorney. He turns to Helen, whom he still loves, and asks for her help. She gives him her hand: "You've made your fight, Jack, and you've won."

WITCH'S RIDE (*Hexenritt*), a one-act "satyric drama" by GERHART HAUPTMANN, produced in 1929 and published in 1930. Setting: contemporary ruins of a Swedish castle.

This play was published and produced with THE BLACK MASK under the joint title *Spuk* (*Spectre*).

A Swedish explorer and his Berlin friend spend a night in a haunted island castle. In their sleep they see specters of former residents: a female Bluebeard—also referred to as Astarte and Venus—and her seven husbands, all of them now brooms.

WITHIN THE GATES, "a morality in four scenes" by SEAN O'CASEY, published in 1933 and produced in 1934. Setting: a park on a spring morning, summer noon, autumn evening, and winter night.

This is an EXPRESSIONIST parable. The play has been only moderately successful in production, but O'Casey himself highly esteemed it and critical opinion remains divided. The play is complex and teems with symbolic characters who chant, sing, and dance. They include a young whore, a bishop who is discovered to be her natural father, her atheist stepfather, a dreamer (or poet), an evangelist, nursemaids, a gardener, various passersby, and a crowd of down-and-outers.

The slight plot transpires "within the gates" of a park resembling London's Hyde Park and symbolizing the modern world with its ugliness and inherent beauty. It deals with the whore's efforts to be saved. Conventional Christianity, atheism, and capitalism are bankrupt, unable to save her. It is the dreamer's affirmative and joyful poetic vision and the bishop's eventual humility that bring her final salvation. She dies receiving the blessing of the bishop, who helps guide her hand in the sign of the cross, after she dances with the dreamer, who gives her courage and happiness.

WITKIEWICZ [nicknamed Witkacy], **Stanisław Ignacy** (1885–1939), Polish novelist and playwright who committed suicide when Poland fell, was the son of a prominent painter and art critic. Something of a dilettante genius, Witkiewicz was also a painter, a poet, and a theoretician of "pure form." To achieve it, he subordinated rigorous dramatic construction to his metaphysical ideas and to free association. In over two dozen plays and various novels he attempted to demonstrate the weirdness of human existence. Witkiewicz's plays are experimental, often comic and SURREALIST, and always fantastic. He was hailed as a precursor of the ABSURDist theatre and was frequently produced in the 1960's when many of his plays first appeared.

They include *Kurka wodna* (*The Water Hen,* 1922), in which a fantastic world ultimately explodes while some elderly men continue their card playing; *Wariat i zakonnica* (*The Madman and the Nun,* 1923), in which allegorical figures representing science and religion rule a prison-lunatic asylum which represents the world that liberates itself through violence and nudity; *Oni* (*They,* 1962), a farce composed in 1920, depicting mechanized totalitarianism destroying man and art; *Szalona lokomotywa* (*The Crazy Locomotive,* 1962), a futuristic spectacle composed in 1923; *Matka* (*The Mother,* 1962), an "unsavory" portrayal of society's perversions, composed in 1924, which satirizes modern drama, parodies Ibsen's GHOSTS and Strindberg's THE GHOST SONATA, and exemplifies Witkiewicz's own style; and *Szewcy* (*The Shoemakers,* 1948), an orgiastic portrayal of the end of Western civilization, composed in 1934. These six works appear with extensive critical, biographical, and bibliographical material about Witkiewicz in Daniel C. Gerould and C. S. Durer's edition of *The Madman and the Nun and Other Plays* (1968).

WITTLINGER, Karl (1922–), German playwright, in the 1950's started producing popular comedies: *Kennen Sie die Milchstrasse?* (*Do You Know the Milky Way?,* 1955), a two-character drama in cabaret style, set in a mental institution where a psychiatrist impersonates people involved in the life of his patient, a World War II veteran; *Kinder des Schattens* (1957); and *Lazarus* (1958). His *Seelenwanderung* (1963) is a flippant BRECHTian modernization of the Faust legend; it features a postwar German burgher who achieves social success with the money he receives for pawning his soul, which is eventually put up for auction.

WIVES' FRIEND, THE (*L'amica delle mogli*), a comedy in three acts by LUIGI PIRANDELLO, published and produced in 1927. Setting: Rome, 1927.

Pirandello dedicated this play—the dramatization of a short story he published in 1894—to Marta Abba, its original star. The heroine bears her name and is characterized as a superior woman in looks, personality, and intelligence—although one Pirandello scholar (Landor MacClintock) considers her "an absurd prig, utterly lacking in common sense and tact, whose interference in the affairs of her ex-suitors eminently justifies her tragic end." The play has been hailed by many critics, who have variously interpreted it as a drama of passion and crime, a comedy of modern corruption, and "the tragedy of one who is doomed to loneliness by the loftiness of her nature" (Domenico Vittorini).

The lives of four young couples are dominated by the spell of Marta's beauty, serenity, and intelligence. She has helped the husbands' courting, has furnished the brides' apartments, and becomes the wives' intimate friend, adviser, and confidante. Marta lives only for her friends. Herself unmarried, she objects to woman's conventional role as nothing but man's sensual object. Apparently the men—who do not admit their love for her even to themselves—were too timid when faced by her perfection to propose to her. Now they hold her up as a model their humanly inferior wives cannot possibly emulate. One of the husbands, jealous when he perceives that Marta might at last marry one of the other three men, whose wife is dying, concocts a diabolical plan. He tortures the couple as well as Marta with thoughts none has dared bring into consciousness, and he finally murders the man. Marta, now changed, sends away all her friends: "Leave me. I wish to remain alone, alone, alone." When told that this seems to be her destiny, she replies, "Do you really think that is a punishment?"

WOLF, Friedrich (1888–1953), German playwright, was among the leading left-wing revolutionary propagandists after World War I. Though he began as an EXPRESSIONIST, Wolf, unlike BERTOLT BRECHT and ERNST TOLLER, was most successful with REPRESENTATIONAL drama—notably with *Die Matrosen von Cattaro* (*The Sailors of Cattaro,* 1930) and *Dr. Mamlocks Ausweg* (1935), which won international fame as *Professor Mamlock.* The first, a stock proletarian theatre piece about the Austro-Hungarian naval mutiny that broke out shortly before the end of the war, portrays the heroic ringleaders going to their execution proclaiming that "This is not the end, this is only the beginning." *Professor Mamlock,* which was made into a widely shown Soviet film, has autobiographical overtones in its tragedy of a Jew victimized by Nazi terror: a prominent surgeon, Mamlock is driven from his profession and commits suicide.

Wolf's earliest play, *Mohammed,* was written in 1917. Next came his *Das bist du* (1918), a love tragedy. Also expressionistic are the plays that immediately followed, including *Der Unbedingte* (1919) and *Tamar* (1921), about the wife of Er (Genesis 38). By 1923 Wolf had turned to NATURALISM, and the next year, with a depiction of the 1514 Württemberg peasant revolt in *Der arme Konrad* (1924), he openly proclaimed his revolutionary message. *Kolonne Hund* (1927) continued along those lines with the portrayal of a Communist swamp reclamation scheme, while *Cyankali* (1929), the tragedy of a young girl, protests antiabortion laws. Another major Wolf play, *Tai Yang erwacht* (1931), dramatizes a 1927 uprising led by a working girl against Shanghai capitalists and became an epic Communist-propaganda production under the direction of Erwin Piscator.

This was Wolf's last play to be written in Germany, for the Nazis drove him into exile. He spent the next years writing topical dramas, including *Floridsdorf* (1935), about the 1934 rebellion of Viennese workers; *Beaumarchais* (1946), about the tragedy of another fighter for freedom, the eighteenth-century playwright who was unable to support the Revolution his comedies helped bring about; and *Patrioten* (1946), about the French

Resistance. After World War II ended in 1945 Wolf settled in East Germany. Of little distinction, his last plays include *Bürgermeister Anna* (written in 1950) and a biographical drama about the radical religious leader who preached for the establishment of a godly communist state and was executed in 1525, *Thomas Münzer* (1953). Like Brecht, Wolf declined as a productive writer when he came to live in the social order he himself had always advocated. Shortly before he died he remarked, "I must reproach myself for having abandoned for the first time, after more than thirty years of work on the German stage, the fight against bureaucracy, apathy, and stupidity." The quotation appears in the section on Wolf in H. F. Garten's *Modern German Drama* (1964), which has a bibliography of English translations.

WOLFE, Thomas (1900–38), American novelist, originally wanted to be a playwright. He went to Harvard University to attend George Pierce Baker's Workshop 47, and Baker for some years had serious hopes for him. Thousands of pages of Wolfe's dramatic manuscripts and typescripts are extant, and six of his plays (four of them one-acters) were published. But Wolfe failed to get them produced professionally, and soon dismissed his ambitions to be a dramatist.

All Wolfe's plays were written in his apprenticeship years (1918–26). Professor Frederick Koch's Carolina Playmakers produced two of his one-acters in 1918, *The Third Night* and *The Return of Buck Gavin.* Both of them are slight melodramas, as is *The Mountains,* produced by Harvard's Workshop in 1921 and published in 1970. In 1923 Harvard also produced Wolfe's full-length *Welcome to Our City,* a drama of "real estate, greed, and racial prejudice." The Theatre Guild briefly considered it and Wolfe's most notable drama, *Mannerhouse.* Finally the Guild rejected both plays, but *Mannerhouse* was published in 1948 and received major professional productions throughout Germany in 1956. A mordant satire of patriotism in war—with characters modeled on Polonius, Ophelia, and Hamlet—*Mannerhouse* dramatizes the decline and fall of a Southern family during the Civil War. The romantic but bitter and disillusioned hero fights in the war, in which he does not believe; then, Samson-like, he pulls down the manor built by his ancestor (portrayed in a prologue) after his dying father (a general) sells it to an upstart. Wolfe's own criticisms of this youthful play and its derivations appear in Chapter LXII of *Of Time and The River* (1935). This novel also portrays Professor Baker (as Hatcher), and was dramatized at Baylor University in 1958. But the most notable dramatization of Wolfe's monumental tetralogy is Ketti Frings's (? –) Pulitzer Prize-winning *Look Homeward, Angel* (1957), which to some Broadway reviewers recalled O'Neill's LONG DAY'S JOURNEY INTO NIGHT.

Elizabeth Nowell's *Thomas Wolfe: A Biography* (1960) and B. R. McElderry's "Thomas Wolfe: Dramatist" (*Modern Drama* VI:1, 1963) have further details on Wolfe's plays.

WOMAN OF NO IMPORTANCE, A, a drama in four acts by OSCAR WILDE, produced in 1893 and published in 1894. Setting: The Shires (in the English country), 1893.

Wilde was as witty and successful with this play as with LADY WINDERMERE'S FAN. He confounded those who had criticized the earlier work for having too little action, by asserting that in the first act of this play, "There is absolutely no action at all. It is a perfect act." *A Woman of No Importance* too is serious in theme and, even more than the earlier play, Victorian in situation and sentimentality. It is also epigrammatic, and it abounds in minor characters with amusing idiosyncrasies.

Lord Illingworth, a successful diplomat, meets young Gerald Arbuthnot, likes him, and offers to make him his secretary. Illingworth is a dandy and an opportunist who lives by the precept that "nothing succeeds like excess." Soon it turns out that Arbuthnot is Illingworth's illegitimate son. Long ago, he had left the mother because he thought her "a woman of no importance." Now "Mrs." Arbuthnot, whose life has been ruined by Illingworth, begs her son not to take the position. When Illingworth molests the boy's wealthy American fiancée, a zealous upholder of virtue for women *and* men, Arbuthnot is ready to kill him. Then his mother reveals their relationship. In profound agony, she refuses her beloved son's demand that she force the scoundrel to make her an honest woman and marry her. At the end, she is persuaded to make her home with Arbuthnot and his bride, turns down Illingworth's proposal, strikes his face when he insults her, and dismisses him as "a man of no importance."

WOOD DEMON, THE (*Leshi*), a comedy in four acts by ANTON CHEKHOV, produced in 1889 and published in 1923. Setting: nineteenth-century Russia.

This, Chekhov's first attempt to dramatize life "realistically" (and lyrically), as he himself noted, "flopped and bust." He refused to have the play performed again or published, but later, after mastering his art, he reworked the script into a notable major play, UNCLE VANYA.

Georgi Voinitsky is disillusioned with the distinguished Aleksandr Serebryakov, a retired professor. Serebryakov's first wife was the sister of Voinitsky, who now is in love with the ailing and self-centered old scholar's second wife, the young and beautiful Yelena. A neighboring landowner, the idealistic Mikhail Khrushchov (the Wood Demon), loves Sonya, Serebryakov's daughter by his first wife. Khrushchov is obsessed with the importance of preserving natural resources, particularly his beloved woods, from man's increasing destructiveness. Most of the play's action deals (not very lucidly) with the Khrushchov-Sonya romance, which is complicated by a boorish rival; with the rumor that Yelena is Voinitsky's mistress, and the attempts of another villainous boor to seduce her; and with the selfish complacency of Serebryakov, a pedant who can only rehash other people's views. When Serebryakov attempts to gain control of the estate, the gentle Voinitsky finally loses his temper. He realizes the futility of his own life, devoted to paying off the mortgage and managing the estate, which should rightly go to Sonya; and accuses Serebryakov, who has never paid him adequately or even thanked him, of being a selfish fraud. Voinitsky leaves, and a few minutes later shoots himself. His suicide is instrumental in reforming various villains (including the professor) and in resolving happily various romances, including that of Sonya and the Wood Demon.

WOOLLCOTT, Alexander [Humphreys] (1887–1943), American journalist, drama critic, and radio broadcaster, is best remembered for his witty essays. Viciously insulting and yet sentimental, he also became the butt of others' wit. He appears as a character in EDNA FERBER's *Show Boat,* but he is most notably portrayed in Kaufman and Hart's THE MAN WHO CAME TO DINNER. Delighted with rather than offended by the portrait, Woollcott himself played Sheridan Whiteside on tour. He did other occasional acting, and wrote two plays in collaboration with GEORGE S. KAUFMAN: *The Channel Road* (1929), based on de Maupassant's "Boule de Suif" ("Tallow Ball" or "Ball of Fat," 1880); and *The Dark Tower* (1933), a melodrama about a sadist who hypnotizes his wife and is murdered by her brother. Neither play was very successful.

His many collections include *While Rome Burns* (1934) and *The Portable Woollcott* (1946). For his biography, see Samuel Hopkins Adams's *A. Woollcott: His Life and His World* (1945) and Edwin P. Hoy's *Alexander Woollcott: The Man Who Came to Dinner* (1968).

WORD, THE (*Ordet*), a "legend of today" in four acts by KAJ MUNK, published and produced in 1932. Setting: a Danish village, two December days in the 1920's.

Written in 1925 and originally staged as *I Begyndelsen var Ordet* (*In the Beginning Was the Word*), this modern miracle play has been praised as Munk's best and was turned into a monumental film by Carl-Theodor Dreyer in 1954. Though a rejoinder to Bjørnson's BEYOND HUMAN POWER I, Munk's drama has more NATURALISTIC and often amusing portrayals than ideological disputation.

The elderly yeoman farmer Mikkel Borgen belongs to the Lutheran State Church's quasi-rational Grundtvigian sect. Therefore he opposes a match between his youngest son and the daughter of a pietistic neighbor who belongs to a Fundamentalist sect. But Borgen is nonetheless insulted and angry when the neighbor, too, rejects the marriage (both men fear that their offspring will succumb to the other's religion): "You stifle me—blaspheme against my God, the manifold God of light and life, with your Dismal Jimmy faces and your longing for death and your tommyrot about conversion." Borgen's oldest son, Young Mikkel, believes only in love for his wife. When she suddenly becomes ill the pietistic neighbor calls it a divine miracle meant to reform Borgen—who thereupon clouts him and rushes home. Young Mikkel's wife soon dies. Borgen's remaining son, who years earlier became mentally deranged after his Christ-like attempts to resurrect his dead fiancée failed, now castigates his family as well as their pompous physician and equally ridiculous pastor for their unchristian skepticism. "I tell you —all things are possible to him that believeth," he insists, and prays before his sister-in-law's coffin: "Give me the Word—the Word that Christ brought down to us from heaven—the creative, quickening Word of life. . . . I say to you—woman, arise!" Resurrected, she opens her eyes. The pastor dismisses the miracle as "a physical impossibility" while the doctor derisively demands the abolition of "amateur death-certificates." But the miracle reconciles old Borgen with his neighbor, and both rejoice with Young Mikkel in his wife's restoration to "Life!"

WORDS UPON THE WINDOW-PANE, THE, a one-act play by WILLIAM BUTLER YEATS, produced in 1930 and published in 1934. Setting: a room in a modern Dublin lodging house.

This is an effective REPRESENTATIONAL dramatization of a séance that reenacts the affairs of Jonathan Swift and the women who loved him, Stella (Esther Johnson) and Vanessa (Hester Vanhomrigh).

In rooms long ago visited by Stella, a séance is about to begin. One of the participants is writing a thesis on Swift. He recognizes words carved on the windowpane as lines from Stella's birthday poem to Swift, and discusses Swift's tragic life with the spiritualist society's president. Despite the comically grotesque doubts of some of the spiritualists, the medium evokes two scenes with Swift. In the first, Vanessa avows her love for Swift; but fearful of transmitting his incipient madness, he rejects procreation because he wants to "leave to posterity nothing but his intellect." After his mad despair, there is a calmer scene in which he is comforted by Stella's Platonic love. The spiritualists consider the séance a failure, and the thesis writer is convinced that the medium is merely an accomplished actress and Swift scholar. But she insists that she saw only a "dirty old man . . . his face covered with boils," with one of his eyes diseased: "it stood out from his face like a hen's egg." Alone, the exhausted medium prepares herself a cup of tea. She falls into a trance once more and speaks, again in his voice, the words of the insane Swift: "Perish the day on which I was born!"

WORKHOUSE WARD, THE, a one-act comedy by LADY GREGORY, produced in 1908 and published in 1909. Setting: a ward in Cloon Workhouse, early twentieth century.

This was originally a Gaellic play by DOUGLAS HYDE, *Teach na mBocht,* translated by Lady Gregory as *The Poorhouse,* published in 1903 and produced in 1905. Her subsequent revision, *The Workhouse Ward,* has been praised as one of the finest short one-act comedies in the English language.

Two sick old paupers on their beds have been lifelong antagonists who cannot stop quarreling. The widowed sister of one of them offers to take him home. The other pauper dreads his enemy's leaving: "To be lying here and no conversible person in it would be the abomination of misery!" But she refuses to let herself be talked into taking him along, and the brother, who also cannot imagine life without his sparring partner, declines her invitation: "Let you go so, as you are so unnatural and so disobliging, and look for some man of your own, God help him!" No sooner is she gone when the disputes and insults resume. "My curse and the curse of the four and twenty men upon you!" says one, and the other replies: "That the worm may chew you from skin to marrow bone!" At the curtain, the old men are angrily hurling their pillows and other belongings at each other.

WORLD IS ROUND, THE (*La Terre est ronde*), a play in three acts by ARMAND SALACROU, published and produced in 1938. Setting: Florence, 1492–98.

The Florentian theocracy of Savonarola is here depicted in a world about to lose its position in the center of the universe. The spectacle of Florence's populace, the French invaders, the worldly amorality of the Borgias' papal court, and the Fascist child militia of Savonarola—all these satirize events of the twentieth century, contrast with the ascetic "black monk," and underline conflicts of flesh and spirit, rampant immorality and militant puritanism, faith and reason, human suffering and cosmic insignificance. Fictional characters in part duplicate historical actions, while Savonarola himself is seen only sporadically—alone as he vainly seeks a sign from God and soliloquizes an anguish resembling that of Camus's CALIGULA.

A rich wool-merchant indulges his carnality but strictly enforces puritanism for his daughters. One of them goes to Rome to become the mistress of a cardinal and the Pope's confidante, while the other daughter disillusions her beloved's concepts of purity by seducing him. The young idealist thereupon abandons her and follows Brother Girolamo Savonarola. During the terror reign of the "black monk" the idealist destroys her marriage to ensure her "purity." Ultimately he enters the fire ordeal, incited by the other daughter, in the place of Savonarola. After disdaining the proffered cardinal's hat because it would imply recognition of the criticized Pope's greater power, the ascetic Savonarola is bitterly disillusioned by God's failure to manifest Himself to him. Unwilling to give the mob the demanded ordeal miracle, Savonarola, following a night of torture, welcomes death. "Must I live yet another day among men?" he asks the executioner who prepares to hang him the next day. And Savonarola concludes with a vision of cosmic nihilism: "All is comedy and the comedy is over."

WOUK, Herman (1915–), American writer, dramatized parts of his popular novel *The Caine Mutiny* (1951) into the 1954 Broadway hit *The Caine Mutiny Court Martial.* A courtroom drama produced on a bare stage and without a curtain, it depicts the gradual disintegration of the psychopathic captain and the Jewish lawyer's final about-face and defense of military leadership. Wouk's novels and inspirational books have continued to be best sellers, but his few other plays, including a spy thriller about an atomic scientist, *The Traitor* (1949), have failed.

WURZEL-FLUMMERY, a one-act comedy by A. A. MILNE, produced in 1917 and published in 1920. Setting: a London townhouse on "a June day before the war."

Milne's short first play was originally written in three acts, was produced in two acts, and was finally published in one-act form. It is a farce in which rival politicians accept an inheritance conditional on their both adopting the absurd name "Wurzel-Flummery."

WYSPIAŃSKI, Stanisław (1869–1907), Polish painter, musician, and poet, has been called the "creator of modern Polish drama" (Manfred Kridl). He was an artistic genius who turned to the theatre only in the last decade of his life. Immensely popular in his own time, he was one of the first practitioners of the "pure theatre" of Edward Gordon Craig and Adolphe Appia. In his drama Wyspiański integrated elements of Greek classicism, Elizabethan tragedy, Polish romantic drama, and Polish folk spectacle, particularly the *szopka,* a form of Nativity puppet theatre.

Wyspiański's best and most successful play, *Wesele* (*The Wedding,* 1901),* dramatizes the marriage of his friend LUCJAN RYDEL to a peasant girl from a village near Kracow. A devastating satire of contemporary society as well as a warning against the potential evil of romanticism, the play evokes a poetic MAETERLINCKian atmosphere: under the influence of the mood and the alcohol, guests move about like puppets and express thoughts and ideals that contrast ironically with their lethargic, weak, and flawed personalities. These themes are further explored in *Wyzwolenie* (1903), an intellectual, PIRANDELLian comedy set in a Kracow theatre and something of a sequel to *The Wedding;* it features Konrad, the protagonist of Adam Mickiewicz's classic verse drama *Dziady* (1832).

A number of Wyspiański's plays are based on Polish history and legend. These include *Legenda* (1897, revised in 1904), a medieval story portrayed with Wagnerian underwater scenery; two distinguished plays on the abortive November 1830 uprising: the hortatory patriotic piece *Warszawianka* (1898) and *Noc listopadowa* (1904), in which Greek gods join the battle of historic characters;

*On April 12, 1962, it was privately produced in New York by the Institute for Advanced Studies in the Theatre Arts; the unpublished translation was by Floryan Sobienioski and Hesketh Pearson.

Legion (1900), a fantasy about the legion founded in Italy in 1848 by Mickiewicz; and *Bolesław Smiały* (1903) and *Skałka* (1905), both set in medieval Poland (the first dramatizes the twelfth-century conflict between King Bolesław II and Bishop Stanisław Szczepanowski).

Many of Wyspiański's plays are original dramatizations of Greek mythology. These include *Meleager* (1898), *Protesilas i Laodamia* (*Protesilaus and Laodamia*, 1899), *Achilleis* (1903, a pessimistic dramatization of Homer's text), and *Powrót Odyssa (The Return of Odysseus*, 1907). *Klątwa* (1899), while dealing with contemporary Polish life, is in the classical mood. *Akropolis* (1904), set in a Kracow cathedral,* creates an even greater synthesis of past and present by bringing to life the cathedral's Homeric and biblical statues; it ends with the resurrection of Christ and of Poland. Wyspiański's last play, *Sędziowie* (1907), like *Klątwa,* is a modern drama written in the style of classical tragedy.

Wyspiański's plays are still important in Poland, though his tremendous turn-of-the-century popularity has waned. *Meleager* and *Protesilas i Laodamia* appeared in English in 1933, and *The Return of Odysseus* in 1966. All the plays are discussed at some length in Manfred Kridl's *A Survey of Polish Literature and Culture* (1956) and in Czeslaw Milosz's *The History of Polish Literature* (1969), both of which have bibliographies. Sections of *The Wedding* are reprinted (but only in the original Polish) in Kridl's *An Anthology of Polish Literature* (1957), which has considerable editorial material.

*In the Auschwitz concentration camp in Jerzy Grotowski's 1960's revival.

Y

YEATS, William Butler (1865–1939), Irish poet and dramatist. As with T. S. ELIOT, Yeats's great fame rests on his poetry, not his drama. But his importance in launching the Irish Dramatic Movement and the careers of J. M. SYNGE and SEAN O'CASEY is indisputable. Yeats himself wrote over thirty dramas, almost all of them short one-acters in verse. They are usually esteemed as poetry—and rejected as plays. Often they are criticized as being sentimental, obscure, esoteric, literary, and antitheatrical. Some of these qualities indeed characterize Yeats's drama, which is avowedly anti-NATURALISTIC and seeks basic—not surface—truths. At the same time, his plays are more viable as theatre than is generally supposed. Yeats noted, "I wished through the drama, through a commingling of verse and dance, through singing that was also speech, through what I called the applied arts of literature, to plunge it back into social life." To a remarkable degree he succeeded, not only in mastering the art of stagecraft in his own plays, but in revitalizing and repopularizing poetic dramaturgy in the English-speaking world.

Yeats was the oldest of the four children of John Butler Yeats, a prominent artist. Born at Sandymount (near Dublin), he was sent to school in England but spent his vacations in Sligo (western Ireland) with his maternal grandparents. Though a Protestant, Yeats was early attracted to occultism, which permeates his writings. His *A Vision* (1925), which describes his personal mythology, is an interesting key to his ideas and work. In England in the 1880's he met BERNARD SHAW, OSCAR WILDE, and other writers, but was more influenced by theosophy, SYMBOLIST poetry, and Irish mythology. In those years he published *The Island of Statues* (1885) and *Mosada* (1886); both are dramatic poems, but neither is included in his *Collected Plays.*

It was in the next decade that his work in the theatre began to flourish. In 1892 he published his first play, THE COUNTESS CATHLEEN; two years later his THE LAND OF HEART'S DESIRE was produced in England. With LADY GREGORY (soon his codirector at the Abbey Theatre and collaborator on a number of his plays*) and EDWARD MARTYN Yeats in 1899 founded the Irish Literary Theatre, which in 1902 was reorganized as the Irish National Theatre Society. It opened on May 8, 1899, with *The Countess Cathleen.* Together with GEORGE MOORE, who assisted the original founders of the Theatre, Yeats wrote *Diarmuid and Grania* (produced in 1901 but not published until 1951). He also produced the popular CATHLEEN NI HOULIHAN (1902) and *The Pot of Broth* (1902), a light one-act peasant comedy. These early plays are based on Irish legend and mythology; except for the comedy, they are romantic fantasies with nationalistic sentiments. Audiences were puzzled and bored by the symbolic *The Shadowy Waters* (1900), a lyrical one-act play in which a pirate magically achieves ideal love with a captured queen. This play, like THE HOUR-GLASS (1903) and a number of others, also appears in an acting version, and Yeats frequently rewrote it, as he did most of his plays. Yeats subsequently repudiated *Where There Is Nothing* (1902), a relatively long mystic play written with DOUGLAS HYDE and Lady Gregory; it depicts a Christian fanatic who rebels against institutionalized religion and life, both victimized by civilization. For his *Collected Plays* Yeats substituted the more restrained and coherent *The Unicorn from the Stars* (1907). *The King's Threshold* (1903) is an episodic verse drama about an Irish poet who is dismissed by his king and protests by starving himself to death.

In 1904 Yeats's theatre society moved into a concert hall on Abbey Street. On its stage first appeared the works of some of the greatest of modern playwrights, and it became the cradle of modern poetic drama in English. Without Yeats the theatre would probably not have been founded, and it certainly could not have survived its early years. He refused to court popularity by pandering to expedience and philistinism. Instead, he worked indomitably to refine audiences' tastes. As one of the Abbey's directors, he fearlessly defended the masterpieces of Synge and O'Casey when audiences rioted at their premieres. Artistic experimentation was much more demanding on audiences (though less controversial) in Yeats's own, particularly the later, symbolist, drama. FOUR PLAYS FOR DANCERS (1921) and many of the other plays are derived from Oriental, especially classical Japanese No, drama in which his secretary, Ezra Pound, had interested Yeats.† These later plays externalize action stylistically and allusively with poetry, masks, dance, music, gesture, and choral narrative. The settings are stark and symbolic: almost bare stages with patterned screens or cloths ritualistically folded and unfolded. In these plays Yeats

* *Cathleen ni Houlihan, Deirdre, The Hour-Glass* (prose version), *King Oedipus, The King's Threshold, On Baile's Strand, The Pot of Broth, The Unicorn from the Stars,* and *Where There Is Nothing.*

†See Hiro Ishibashi, *Yeats and the Noh: Types of Japanese Beauty and Their Reflection in Yeats's Plays* (Dolmen Press Yeats Centenary Papers, 1966).

William Butler Yeats. (*Irish Tourist Board*)

harnesses language and other histrionic devices to examine—often to celebrate—love, art, and life. Myth and legend, metaphysics, romance, and farce are intermingled with his poetry and rich, evocative prose.

Yeats's plays were regularly produced at the Abbey Theatre, which was launched (on December 27, 1904) with ON BAILE'S STRAND (1903), the first of Yeats's plays about Cuchulain, the hero of the Ulster Cycle of Irish legend. The other Cuchulain plays are THE GREEN HELMET (1910; originally *The Golden Helmet*, 1908), AT THE HAWK'S WELL (1916), THE ONLY JEALOUSY OF EMER (1919), and THE DEATH OF CUCHULAIN (1939). Yeats also published and produced DEIRDRE (1906); *The Player Queen* (1919), a symbolic farce stressing his mask philosophy of the "antithetical self" and depicting a cruel beauty who banishes her unfaithful, drunken poet-husband and becomes the queen; THE DREAMING OF THE BONES (1919); CALVARY (1921); *The Cat and the Moon* (1924), a fantasy and a dance play in which two crippled beggars must choose between cure and blessedness; two translations of Sophocles, *King Oedipus* (1926; perhaps his most frequently produced drama, which he began writing with Lady Gregory in 1905) and *Oedipus at Colonus* (1927); THE RESURRECTION (1927); *Fighting the Waves* (1929, a prose version of *The Only Jealousy of Emer*); THE WORDS UPON THE WINDOW-PANE (1930), a play about Swift; THE KING OF THE GREAT CLOCK TOWER (1934) and its alternate version, *A Full Moon in March;* THE HERNE'S EGG (1938); PURGATORY (1938), his most frequently discussed play; and the already mentioned last of the Cuchulain plays (*The Death of Cuchulain*), which Yeats barely finished before his death.

Yeats was long in love with Maud Gonne, an Irish actress and patriot who inspired his plays as well as his poetry, but married an Englishwoman, who bore him two children. In 1922 he was invited to join the Irish Senate, and the following year he was awarded the Nobel Prize for literature. Yeats died in France, but after the war his body was returned to Ireland, where—after a state funeral—he was buried, according to the wishes expressed in a famous poem, "Under Ben Bulben" (1938).

The definitive collection of the complete plays, *The Variorum Edition of the Plays of W. B. Yeats* (1966), edited by Russell K. Alspach, has a wealth of editorial aids, including a record of all revisions and a bibliography. The enlarged edition of *The Collected Plays of W. B. Yeats* was published in 1952. *The Autobiography of William Butler Yeats* (1958) is a collection of his memoirs that includes portraits of Synge, Wilde, Moore, and others. Joseph Hone's *W. B. Yeats, 1865–1939* (1943) and Richard Ellmann's *Yeats: The Man and the Mask* (1948) are comprehensive biographies; Peter Ure's *Yeats the Playwright* (1963), Helen Hennessy Vendler's *Yeats's VISION and the Later Plays*

(1963), Leonard E. Nathan's *The Tragic Drama of William Butler Yeats* (1965), David R. Clark's *Yeats and the Theatre of Desolate Reality* (1965), and John Rees Moore's *Masks of Love and Death: Yeats as Dramatist* (1971) study his dramaturgy; George Brandon Saul's *Prolegomena to the Study of Yeats's Plays* (1958) gives detailed textual and bibliographical information about every Yeats play.

YEGOR BULYCHOV AND THE OTHERS (*Yegor Bulychov i drugie*), a play in three acts by MAXIM GORKY, published and produced in 1932. Setting: a provincial Russian town just before and at the beginning of the March Revolution, 1917.

Gorky's best play after THE LOWER DEPTHS, this is the first of an uncompleted trilogy that was to dramatize bourgeois decay and the Revolution in a provincial setting. It is an effective character study of its towering protagonist and a Russian classic like its sequel, DOSTIGAEV AND THE OTHERS.

Yegor Bulychov, a merchant, is dying of cancer. A powerful and zestful man who has acquired great wealth, the shrewd Bulychov is openly contemptuous of his corrupt, predatory milieu—including his well-bred wife, his daughter ("a weasel"), and her conniving husband. But however superior, he is a product of this milieu, which, like his own body, symbolizes the dying order. His family are waiting to inherit his money; and his wife's sister (an abbess), rival merchants like Dostigaev, a priest, and others intrigue for wealth and power during the chaos of military defeat and a toppling regime. Bulychov is close only to his illegitimate daughter, the fiery Shura; his spirited godson, Yakov Laptev, who is suspected of revolutionary activities; and his longtime servant and mistress. Contemporary superstitions are dramatized by faith healers summoned to cure Bulychov. One of them attributes all disease to "bad air in the stomach," which he blows out by playing a tuba. Bulychov unmasks these frauds and ridicules the rapacious priest, who reminds him that man is made of dust: "You inspire and bless—and what a hell of a mess! ... I don't feel like paying God. ... Dust, but you're greedy for everything—" And he tells Shura, "You see—those priests, tsars, governors—what the hell do I need them for? ... Good people are as rare as—counterfeit coins." When the family bring an "exorcist" to drive away the devil (and frighten Bulychov to death), Shura finally has the "holy man" thrown out. Bulychov's cunning partner and rival, Dostigaev, leaves with his wife: "Bulychov looks very bad to me. And there's the demonstration going on right now—we must join it." Bulychov calls out as he is dying, "Thy kingdom—what kingdom? Nothing but beasts! ... Everybody has to die? Why? Well, let others die. Why should I?" Shura opens the window and calls him to watch the demonstrating crowds sing the Revolutionists' song heard from the street. Bulychov collapses: "What's that? A requiem mass—again a requiem. ... Oh, Shura—"

YELLOW JACK, "a history" play in four scenes by SIDNEY HOWARD, published and produced in 1934. Setting: London, Cuba, and West Africa; 1900–27.

This documentary, based on Paul de Kruif's biography of Major Walter Reed in *Microbe Hunters* (1926), dramatizes the struggle to discover the cause of and develop a vaccine against yellow fever. In flashbacks, *Yellow Jack* recounts the tribulations of the doctors and soldiers in the face of the infectious disease and the opposition to their research by narrow-minded conservatives.

YERMA, "a tragic poem in three acts and six scenes" by FEDERICO GARCÍA LORCA, produced in 1934 and published in 1937. Setting: contemporary rural Spain.

Yerma's name literally means "barren" or "sterile." Like the other "rural tragedies" (BLOOD WEDDING and THE HOUSE OF BERNARDA ALBA), but with greater focus on a single figure, it portrays an unfulfilled woman. García Lorca's brother noted that MIGUEL DE UNAMUNO said of *Yerma,* "This is the play I wish I had written."

Act I. Yerma awakes from her dream about a child. Though she embraces her husband, Juan, her ardor is for a baby. Juan, on the other hand, laboring ceaselessly to make his land profitable, loves her body and is not concerned with having children. Yerma sings a lullaby to an imaginary baby, and then becomes very excited when she learns of a friend's pregnancy. She feels her blood will "turn to poison" if she herself does not conceive soon. A lusty old neighbor woman frankly tells Yerma that her barrenness is rooted in her failure to enjoy sex. To Yerma's "God help me" she replies that it is not God but men who will help her, "though there should be a God, even if a tiny one, to send his lightning against those men of rotted seed who make puddles out of the happiness of the fields." Yerma talks with other, more lighthearted and happy women, and with a shepherd to whom she is strongly attracted. Juan chides her and sends her home: he himself will work on his land all night.

Act II. At their work, washerwomen sing, debate Yerma's obsessive wish for a child, and reveal that Juan has brought home his sisters to watch over her and preserve the family's honor. Juan and Yerma become increasingly bitter toward each other; he castigates her for brooding over a child, and refuses to let her go out. Under the watchful eyes of Juan's sisters, her friend visits with her baby—but grows alarmed by Yerma's obsession with the fertility all about her. The shepherd, bought out by the industrious Juan, takes his leave. He is unable to answer Yerma's anguished questions—and her code of honor forbids her taking him as a lover, just as it represses her pleasure when she is in her husband's arms. But despite Juan's prohibition, she escapes to visit a sorceress.

Act III. In the cemetery, after a midnight prayer for a child, Yerma admits that Juan is good and hard-working; but he does not want children, and therefore, she says, "he doesn't give them to me. I don't love him; I don't love him, and yet he's my only salvation. By honor and by blood." Juan suddenly appears, furious at being publicly disgraced by her absence at night. Yerma protests that she is innocent: she has done nothing wrong. She beseeches him yet again—"It's your blood and help I want"—but he casts her off. Bitter and resigned, Yerma leaves: "It's one thing to wish with one's head and another for the body—cursed be the body!—not to respond." She will fight no more. At a fertility rite in a mountain hermitage, Yerma rejects having children with another man: "Where would that leave my honor?" When told that "when one's thirsty, one's grateful for water," Yerma replies, "Mine is a sorrow already beyond the flesh." But Juan has been spying on her and now appears. He admits he is happy without children, wanting only her love. As Juan embraces her, Yerma finally and completely fathoms the hopelessness of her yearning. In frenzied passion she chokes him to death and with him she kills all her hopes for a child. "Barren, barren, but sure . . . and alone," she says; "I've killed my son. I myself have killed my son!"

YES IS FOR A VERY YOUNG MAN, a play in two acts by GERTRUDE STEIN, produced in 1946 and published in 1948. Setting: France, June 1940 to August 25, 1944.

This short work (originally titled *In Savoy*) was the first of Gertrude Stein's plays to be produced without music—and in public; its premiere was at the Pasadena Playhouse. It is set in German-occupied France and attempts to recapture the American Civil War atmosphere among families with divided loyalties that she had heard about as a child. Written in her unique prose style, it is a play not of rounded characters but of various types who represent different reactions to the Occupation.

A self-centered young wife accepts the Occupation but yearns for material improvements; her husband secretly works for the Underground; an American spinster (modeled on CLARE BOOTHE) resists passively; and the Underground fighter's brother, infatuated with the spinster, finally rejects his shallow sister-in-law and the spinster's maternal protectiveness, and joins his brother in the Underground. At the Liberation these people and others are satisfied with returning to prewar peace—except for the brother-in-law, who realizes the war is not over. "For me it is just beginning, yes is for a very young man," he tells the spinster. "I won't have time to think so I won't think about you and the quays of Paris and the roast chickens . . . no I won't have time to think. Goodbye," he concludes, and goes off to continue fighting.

YEVREINOV [or Evreinov], **Nikolai Nikolaevich** (1879–1953), Russian playwright and director, was an opponent of REPRESENTATIONAL drama. In 1909, influenced by modern psychology and anticipating some of the plays of LUIGI PIRANDELLO, he constructed an elaborate theory of "monodrama," described in his three-volume *Teatr dlya sebya* (*The Theatre for One's Self,* 1915–17),* and illustrated in his best-known play, *V kulisach dushi* (THE THEATRE OF THE SOUL, 1912). The essence of his theory is that the spectator can fully perceive only one character in each play. The multifarious projections and ever-changing perspectives of this one figure are Yevreinov's subject. "Only one acting character is possible," Yevreinov believed; "in the strict meaning of the word only one subject of action is thinkable."

Yevreinov was interested in the theatre from early childhood. Born in Moscow, the gifted and versatile boy studied music with Rimsky-Korsakov, and law at St. Petersburg. He wrote and produced a play when he was seven, and he was active also as a painter, a historian, a philosopher, and in other capacities. Yevreinov wrote plays for his law academy's drama circle, acted, and began his professional playwriting in earnest after the Revolution. *Krasivy despot* (THE BEAUTIFUL DESPOT, 1906) was his first important play. In 1908 he became Meyerhold's successor at Moscow's Kommissarzhevskaya theatre (where he directed a notable production of Wilde's SALOMÉ); subsequently he founded and directed the "Gay Theatre for Grown-Up Children" in Petrograd and the "Crooked Looking-Glass" theatre in St. Petersburg, where his most notable play was first produced.

While Yevreinov wrote many plays, as well as operas and operettas, only a few are available in English, among them his own favorites, *The Beautiful Despot* and *Vesyolaya smert* (A MERRY DEATH, 1909). His *Samoe glavnoe* (*The Chief Thing,* 1921) was produced by the New York Theatre Guild in 1926; its title stands for illusion, which a comforter uses successfully to console a group of down-and-outers. Yevreinov wrote about twenty other plays, including the early *Proiskhozhdenie schastya* (1902), an episode about gravediggers; *Dr. Savin* (1903); *Styopik i Manyurotchka* (1905), a one-act comedy; *Bubushka* (1907); *Takaya zhenshchina* (1908); *Predstavlenie lyubvi* (1910), his first monodrama; *Shkola etualei* (1911), about a director's interviews of aspiring actresses; *Chetvyortaya stena* (1915), which ridicules theatre REALISM and contains a parody of *Faust;* and *Radio-potselui* (1926), an erotic melodrama.

It was in his nonmonodramatic works that Yevreinov seems to have done best. His theories and his practice of a flamboyant theatricality, which strove to transcend NATURALISM, were on the whole unsuccessful, and his experiments and ideas did not fit into the SOCIALIST REALISM espoused by the Soviets. He supported their Revolution at first, and in 1920 staged the gigantic patriotic pageant *Vzyatie zimnego dvortsa* in the Winter Palace Square, using eight thousand actors and salvos from the historical cruiser *Aurora* to reenact the Bolshevik capture of the

*Condensed and revised for the one-volume translation, *The Theatre in Life* (1927).

Winter Palace. From 1925 until his death nearly thirty years later he lived in France, where his writings included works about the theatre and dramatic theories, but no notable plays.

A Merry Death is one of the *Five Russian Plays* (1916) translated by C. E. Bechhofer. The "Russia" chapter of Isaac Goldberg's *The Drama of Transition* (1922) is devoted exclusively to Yevreinov and contains references to other studies.

YIDDISH DRAMA, like Hebrew drama before ISRAEL achieved statehood, has no national boundaries. Most of it, however, originated in Eastern Europe. The plays were not uncommonly translated back and forth from Yiddish to Hebrew, and were also occasionally published in Russian, Polish, or German. Among the important modern Yiddish playwrights was the triumvirate of the founders of Yiddish literature—MENDELE MOKHER SFORIM (its Grandfather), YITSKHOK LEYBUSH PERETZ (its Father), and SHOLEM ALEICHEM (its Grandson)—as well as ABRAHAM GOLDFADEN, JACOB GORDIN, PERETZ HIRSHBEIN, DAVID PINSKI, H. LEIVICK, S. ANSKI, OSSIP DYMOV, and SHOLEM ASCH. Many of them eventually emigrated to America.

Yiddish drama is too variegated in subject and form to be easily characterized. However, much of it utilizes Jewish legend and history, and the messianic theme recurs frequently. Serious as well as comic plays are set in the *shtetls* (the small home towns of East European Jewry), the European ghettos, or the large Western centers of Jewish immigration. The plays are steeped in the Ashkenazic, rarely the Sephardic, attitudes of the inhabitants of such settings.

Though the Yiddish theatre is a relatively modern phenomenon, its drama is rooted in tradition. From the ninth or tenth century, popular entertainments were commonly put on to celebrate the Feast of Purim. Improvised one-act Purim *Shpiln* (or plays) depicted Haman's defeat by Ahasuerus's queen (as described in the Book of Esther), the story of Joseph and his brothers, and other biblical tales. Another form of popular entertainment was presented in wine taverns. There, so-called *"Broder Zinger,"* itinerant Jewish performers who were also costumed impersonators and monologists, amused people after their day's work. It was such performances—the *commedia dell' arte* type of improvisations like the Purim *Shpiln*—that in Jassy, Rumania, inspired Goldfaden to present his first show in early October 1876. This was the birth of the Yiddish theatre.

Goldfaden was also influenced by the Jewish opposition to traditional Hasidic ways, which was called the *Haskalah* (Enlightenment). Its earliest dramatist was Solomon Ettinger (1800–56), a Polish doctor in whose *Serkele* (written c. 1825) Goldfaden, while a rabbinical student in 1862, played the leading role, the title's virago. This was one of the first Yiddish plays. (It was published in 1861, and also influenced Gordin's *Mirele Efros,* 1898.) Another significant pre-Goldfaden play is *Di Vaybershe Kniplekh* (1874), an anti-Hasidic comedy by Ludwig Levinsohn (1842–1904). The popularity of the drama of Goldfaden and—in Odessa—that of Joseph Lerner (1849?–1907), particularly his adaptation of Karl Gutzkow's (1811–78) historical tragedy *Uriel Acosta* (1847), alarmed the Russian government, which was sensitive to any popular movements, especially Jewish ones. It therefore banned all Yiddish drama in 1883—a ban that was not lifted until 1904. As increasingly bloody pogroms, too, broke out, Goldfaden and his followers migrated westward, many of them eventually settling in the United States.

While most of Goldfaden's drama was trivial fare for the masses, at least a few of his operettas (produced in the United States by Boris Thomashefsky) had some merit. This cannot be said for the work of his most successful disciples, who dominated the scene for years and made no bones about the exclusively commercial purpose of their shows: JOSEPH LATEINER, MOSHE HURWITZ, and the novelist Abraham Shomer (Nahum Meier Shaikevitch, 1849–1905). It was Gordin who brought literary and artistic integrity to the Yiddish theatre, and his work made possible that of other able dramatists. Notable among these were Leon Kobrin (1873–1946), the author of *Minna* (with Gordin, 1899), *Children of Nature* (1912, based on his tale *Yankl Boyleh*), and *Riverside Drive* (1927), and the translator of ISRAEL ZANGWILL, Goethe, and Shakespeare;* and Z. Libin (pseudonym of Israel Hurwitz, 1872–1955), the most successful of whose fifty plays was *Gebrokhene Hertser* (1903), filmed with Leila Lee and Maurice Schwartz in 1920. Like Gordin, these playwrights excelled in NATURALISTIC, social-protest drama, often set in New York's Jewish immigrant milieu. Other playwrights usually set their dramas in the *shtetls.*

Ayzik Meyer Devenishski (1878–1919) was a long-imprisoned political agitator in Russia who in his brief life wrote (under the pen name Vayter) poetic-SYMBOLIST plays like *Far Tog* (1907) and *Der Shtumer* (1912). A Polish-Yiddish playwright of interest was Felix (Fishel) Bimko (1890–1965), whose *Ganovim* (1919) is a sordid, naturalistic drama that has been called a Yiddish LOWER DEPTHS and bears some resemblance to that Gorky play as well as to Asch's GOD OF VENGEANCE; he also wrote symbolist plays (*Dembes* and *Farsunkene Veltn*) and comedies (*Feter, Men Ken Aykh* and *America Ganef*), all of which appeared in 1922. Other Yiddish playwrights include Chone Gottesfeld (1890–1964), a writer of domestic comedies, of which *Raykhe Kabtsonim* (1922) was the most successful; Harry Sackler (1883–   ), the author of legendary and historical drama in Yiddish, in Hebrew, and in English; a number of Polish-Yiddish playwrights who perished in the Polish ghetto: Mark Arnstein (1878–1943), Jacob Preger (1887–1943), and Alter

* See Kobrin's *Memoirs of a Dramatist* (1925).

Katzizne (1885–1943); Aaron Zeitlin (1898–), whose comic folktales *Wise Men of Helm* (1933) have been dramatized in English; Peretz Markish (1895–1952), whose plays were frequently produced on Soviet-Yiddish stages; Ezekiel Dobrushin (1883–1953), a playwright who also adapted Goldfaden's plays and dramatized the tales of Mendele Mokher Sforim and Sholem Aleichem; the popular novelist I. J. Singer (1893–1944), who wrote and immediately dramatized his *The Family Carnovsky* (1943), while Maurice Schwartz (1889–1960) successfully adapted Singer's novel *Yoshe Kalb* (1932) in 1932 and his *The Brothers Ashkenazi* (1936) in 1937; Aaron Kushnirov (1892–1949), who, like Leivick, dramatized the martyrdom of *Hirsh Lekert* (1928); and William Siegel (1893–1966), who wrote over one hundred and fifty plays, mostly comedies like *The Great Moment* (1927) and *Di Farkoyfte Kale* (1917), better known by its later title, *Der Shikker* (*The Drunkard*), and still internationally produced.

After Gordin's death, the Yiddish theatre in America went into a temporary decline. In Russia it rose to new heights soon after productions were legalized in 1904. It was then that the Yiddish art drama began to flourish with the work of the outstanding Yiddish dramatists Peretz, Sholem Aleichem, Pinski, Asch, Hirshbein, and later Anski and Leivick. After World War I, Moscow's State Yiddish Theatre was established; its original director was Alexander Granovsky, and Marc Chagall painted its murals. Earlier, The Hirshbein Troupe had brought Yiddish drama to the Russian provinces, and had indirectly exported it throughout the Western world. This troupe was followed in 1916 by the Vilna Troupe of David Hermann, some of whose members were to join New York groups. In America, the Folksbine (founded in 1915) and Artef (1928–37), an experimental Yiddish art theatre directed by Benno Schneider of the original Habima group, produced Yiddish drama. But the leading figure was Maurice Schwartz—famous as an actor as well as a director—who in 1918 founded New York's Yiddish Art Theater and until 1950 was the most important American producer of Yiddish drama.

After the closing of this theatre, Yiddish drama remained stillborn for some time. Like all drama, it has been repeatedly declared moribund. In his *History of Yiddish Literature in the Nineteenth Century* (1899), Leo Wiener expressed such a belief. Then came the golden age of Pinski and Hirshbein, and THE DYBBUK, THE GOLEM, and *God of Vengeance*—the plays which became famous internationally. The Nazi holocaust that followed well-nigh obliterated East European Jewry and the *shtetl*. Since World War II, however, the Jewish ethos has assumed major importance in the modern drama of Western nations, but it has become increasingly assimilated. Probably this ethos will continue to be expressed, as it has been in recent decades, in the tongues of all the countries in which Jewish dramatists write.

Collections of Yiddish drama in translation include Isaac Goldberg's two volumes of *Six Plays of the Yiddish Theater* (1916, 1918), Etta Block's two volumes of *One Act Plays from the Yiddish* (1923, 1925), and Joseph C. Landis's *The Dybbuk and Other Great Yiddish Plays* (1966). Sol Liptzin's *The Flowering of Yiddish Literature* (1963) and Charles A. Madison's *Yiddish Literature: Its Scope and Major Writers* (1968) contain excellent chapters on individual writers and comprehensive bibliographies. Detailed discussions of individual plays and playwrights appear in Isaac Goldberg's *The Drama of Transition* (1922) and in A. A. Roback's *The Story of Yiddish Literature* (1940). Hutchins Hapgood's *The Spirit of the Ghetto* (1902) is informative about the turn-of-the-century Yiddish theatre. Useful for its bibliography, production lists, and photographs is David S. Lifson's *The Yiddish Theater in America* (1965). Louis Lipsky's *Tales of the Yiddish Rialto* (1962), as the subtitle states, are fictionalized "Reminiscences of Playwrights and Players in New York's Jewish Theatre in the Early 1900's," a topic also explored in Ronald Sanders's *The Downtown Jews* (1969).

YOU CAN'T TAKE IT WITH YOU, a play in three acts by GEORGE S. KAUFMAN and MOSS HART, produced in 1936 and published in 1937. Setting: New York City, 1930's.

This comedy has proved to be the most lastingly successful of the collaborators' works. It won the Pulitzer Prize, became notable also as a film (1938), and was successfully revived in the 1960's.

Grandpa (Martin Vanderhof) presides over a household where the prime interest is "living," where "you do as you like, and no questions asked." It is a madhouse: Grandpa attends Columbia University convocations; his daughter, Penelope Sycamore, is engrossed in playwriting; her husband manufactures fireworks in the basement with an iceman; and their elder daughter is a would-be ballet dancer who constantly stands on her toes. "Confidentially, she stinks," remarks her Russian instructor, a habitué of the household, which also includes a Negro cook, her boyfriend, and a former Russian princess but now a waitress. Penelope's younger daughter has somehow "escaped the tinge of mild insanity" of her eccentric family, whom she nonetheless loves. But she is enamored of her boss's son, and calamity ensues when his stuffy family come for dinner. The romance almost founders, but is saved when Grandpa converts the boss to his philosophy: "Life is simple and kind of beautiful if you let it come to you."

YOU NEVER CAN TELL, a comedy in four acts by BERNARD SHAW, published and produced in 1898. Setting: Devon, August 1896.

Shaw noted in his preface to PLAYS PLEASANT that he wrote this play for the managers who wanted a comedy with the "brilliancy" of ARMS AND THE MAN "tempered" to fashionable tastes. Successfully revived from time to time and considered by some critics to be one of Shaw's finest works, it wittily dramatizes themes later developed in MAN AND SUPERMAN.

Act I. At a seaside resort, Valentine extracts a tooth from his first patient, the voluble Dolly, who has just arrived with her family from Madeira. Her equally voluble twin brother, Philip, appears, and at once they invite the dentist to lunch. They are joined by their mother, the famous Mrs. Clandon, authoress of social-reform treatises; and by their elder sister, Gloria, who is her mother's haughty disciple and with whom Valentine promptly falls in love. Though pressed, Mrs. Clandon refuses to tell her children who their father is, and she leaves. Valentine's landlord, the ill-tempered Fergus Crampton, wants a tooth pulled; betting his six-weeks' rent arrears that he can extract the tooth without Crampton's feeling it, Valentine pulls the tooth after he dexterously uses the anesthetic Crampton had refused.

Act II. At lunch on the hotel terrace, Mrs. Clandon has her solicitor tell her children about their father, from whom she had separated eighteen years ago because of his cruelty. Their dismay at discovering that he is Crampton is somewhat allayed when they hear that Crampton is wealthy. When he arrives to have lunch with Valentine, Crampton is greatly upset by the unexpected meeting with his family. The luncheon party threatens repeatedly to blow up, and is saved only by William, the "perfect waiter" who diplomatically smoothes everyone's feelings and tells them of his son, a distinguished Queen's Counsel. After lunch, Gloria infuriates Crampton with her cold rationality, but is herself completely thrown off her defenses by Valentine's "sensible and scientific" lovemaking.

Act III. The wild-spirited twins explain to Mrs. Clandon that Gloria's emotional behavior is due to her having fallen in love. Valentine tells Mrs. Clandon that he has won Gloria by using "thoroughly modern" scientific methods in the "duel of sex," but when the "emancipated" Gloria hears that he has loved other women, she furiously rejects him. The solicitor, reporting that Crampton is demanding custody of the twins, observes that though Crampton is uncouth he is a kind man who has been unfairly dealt with in the separation deed, and he gets Mrs. Clandon to agree to arbitration by an eminent visiting Q.C.

Act IV. That evening, during a masked ball, the Q.C., who turns out to be the waiter's son, expertly brings about a friendly reconciliation. It appears that Gloria too has had a number of love affairs; this shocks and enrages Valentine, but also opens the way to their reconciliation and engagement. As all dance away, Valentine, "the defeated Duellist of Sex," ruefully observes that he feels like "a married man already." The perfect waiter comforts him about marriage: though his wife, like Gloria, "was of a commanding and masterful disposition," many marriages turn out very well: "I'd do it again, I assure you. You never can tell, sir."

YUGOSLAVIA. Yugoslav drama, like Yugoslav history, reflects the three different cultures—Croatian, Slovenian, and Serbian—which were joined in 1918.

Croatian drama was predominantly historical. Typical were the plays of Eugenii Kumičić (1850–1904), for example the tragic *Petar Zriniski* (1901); and Ante Tresić-Pavičić (1867–1949), who dramatized similar themes in his plays on *Herod* (1910) and *Cato of Utica* (1911). The leading Croatian dramatist of his age was the Yugoslav patriot Ivo Vojnović (1857–1929), who was also a poet and a novelist. At first he wrote SYMBOLIC fantasies; his *Lazarevo Vaskrsenje* (*The Resurrection of Lazarus,* 1913) is a moving play, but the historical *Dubrovačka trilogija* (*A Trilogy of Dubrovnik,* 1902) is generally considered his finest drama. Other playwrights whose work came before the establishment of the Yugoslav state were Srđan Tucić (1873–1940), a religious-symbolist writer whose plays include *Golgotha* (1913); and Milan Ogrizović (1877–1923), another symbolist, whose plays include *Smrt Cara Dioklecijana* (1913) and yet another treatment of the historical Zriniski theme, *Pogibija Zrinskog i Frankopana* (1921).

Romanticism characterized early modern Serbian drama. Djura Jakšić (1832–78) wrote poetic plays on native history, while Laza Kostić (1841–1910), employing similar themes, wrote ballad dramas. Later in the century came more popular playwrights, whose forte was comedy and drama of intrigue, while dramaturgy in the new century received its impetus from folk comedies by a number of now-forgotten writers. The leading Serbian playwright was Branislav Nušić (1864–1938), much of whose drama appeared in the nineteenth century; a keen and popular satirist, his comedies include *Put oko Sveta* (1910) and *Gospodja ministarka* (1927), and he also wrote a tragedy, *Pokojnik* (1936), on political denunciation. The Belgrade-born Aleksandar (Mica) Popović (1929–) won prizes with his play about sharpers and their victim, *Krmeći kas* (*Swine's Gallop,* 1966), and notice abroad with his comedy about an operator, *Razvojni Put Bore šnajdera* (*The Progress of Bora, the Tailor,* 1967); a late and innovative dramatist of the ABSURD and the most popular recent Serbian playwright, Popović produced such other widely performed tragicomedies as *Smrtonosna motoristika* (*Deadly Motorism,* 1967), *Kape dole* (*Hats Off!,* 1968), and *Druga vrata levo* (*Second Door Left,* 1969).

Slovenian drama frequently treated the theme of the Styrian House of Celje's last great representative, Count Ulrich, and other histories. The first great Slovenian playwright was Josip Jurčič (1844–81), who wrote a romantic tragedy on the tenth-century Germanic chieftain *Tugomer* (1876) as well as an unfinished play on the House of Celje, *Veronika Deseniška,* produced posthumously in 1892. Later Slovenian playwrights came under the influence of HENRIK IBSEN: Josip Stritar (1836–1923) in his *Klara* (1880), Josip Vošnjak (1834–1911) in his *Doktor Dragan* (1894), and Anton Medved (1869–1910), formerly a romantic playwright, in a whole series of Ibsenite dramas. Ivan Cankar (1876–1918), the great Slovenian dramatist, poet, and novelist, also was influenced by Ibsen as well as by GERHART HAUPTMANN and by the Czech playwright Jaroslav Hilbert (1871–1936). Cankar's especially notable dramas are *Za narodov blagor* (1901), which features a man of reason who opposes Pan-Slavic sentimentality and political corruption; *Pohujšanje v dolini šentflorjanski* (1908), a farce that satirizes intellectuals; *Hlapci* (1910), a drama on the same theme; and *Lepa Vida* (1912), a lyric romance based on a popular ballad. Other playwrights of the time were Kristan Etbin (1867–1953), who wrote social dramas, and Alojz Kraigher (1877–1959), who wrote an influential Freudian play, *Školjka* (1911).

Most of the prominent dramatists whose works appeared in the independent state of Yugoslavia were Croats. Aside from the distinguished MIROSLAV KRLEŽA and the already-noted Vojnović, a most important southern Slavic writer, Croatian culture contributed Josip Kosor (1879 1961), "the Croatian GORKY," whose concern with the abstractions of good and evil is manifested in plays like *Požar strasti* (*Passion's Furnace,* 1912), *Žena* (*The Woman,* 1920), *Nepobjediva ladja* (*The Invincible Ship,* 1921), and *Pomirenje* (*Reconciliation,* 1926); Slavko Kolar (1891–1964), whose comic-NATURALIST dramas include *Sedmorica u Podrumu* (1948); and Josip Kulundžič (1899–   ), a prolific playwright famous for *Ponoc* (1921), who was known as the "anti-PIRANDELLO." More important modern Croatians, however, have been the already noted Krleža and Marjan Matkovic (1915–   ), the latter a prolific essayist and adapter of foreign plays for the radio; his most successful work, a play cycle about man's loneliness and despair, began with *Vašar Snova* (1958) and *Ranjena Ptica* (1965). Two Serbian Yugoslavs of note were Dušan Nikolajević (1885–1961) and Ranko Mladenović (1893–1943); the former's semifarcical "modern mystery" *Volga, Volga* (1927) features Dostoevsky confronting Lenin "on the borders of Europe and Russia," whereas Mladenović wrote social satires like *Strah od Vernosti* (*Fear of Truth,* 1937). Slovenes who became prominent as Yugoslavians include Cvetko Golar (1879–1965), who wrote popular comedies; Fran Saleški Finžgar (1871–1962), who wrote peasant drama; a number of playwrights, notably Stanko Majcen (1888–   ) and Bratko Kreft (1905–   ), whose plays deal with social problems; Pavel Golia (1887–1959), who became popular with his children's plays; Oton Župančič (1878–1949), a poet, and Anton Novačan (1887–1951), who, in their respective plays *Veronika Deseniška* (1924) and *Herman Celjski* (1928), redramatized the popular Slovenian theme of the House of Celje; and Rado Murnik (1870–1932), who achieved lasting success with a comedy, *Napoleonov samovar* (1898).

The Montenegrin novelist Miodrag Bulatović (1930–   ) created a minor furor with his interesting but rambling sequel to Beckett's WAITING FOR GODOT, *Godo je došao* (*Godot Has Come,* 1966); its three acts portray continued waiting (as in Beckett's play), the arrival of Godot (a baker bearing the staff of life but rejected by the tramps as the wrong Godot), and an exchange of places between Pozzo and Lucky (who turns out to be an equally vicious tyrant).

Even though some of the Yugoslav plays have been produced in English, they are not readily available. Accounts of the more recent drama appear occasionally in literary and theatre journals.

Z

ZAMYATIN, Yevgeni Ivanovich (1884–1937), Russian author, excelled in the writing of short stories and novels. His antiutopian novel *My* (*We,* written in 1920, published abroad in 1924), which made his name internationally known though it did not appear in Russia, is a frightening precursor of ALDOUS HUXLEY's *Brave New World* (1932) and George Orwell's *1984* (1949). Aside from fiction, Zamyatin also wrote essays—as well as five plays, one of which was quite popular for a few seasons. His work was gradually banned, however, as Zamyatin's unconforming and uncompromising attitudes increasingly irritated the Soviet authorities.

Born in Lebedyan, a town in Central Russia, Zamyatin studied engineering in St. Petersburg. As a student, he was for a time an active member of the Bolshevik faction of the revolutionary movement. He began to write before the Revolution, but his best work did not appear until the 1920's. On a government mission in England during World War I, Zamyatin returned to Russia eagerly during the Revolution. But by 1924 he wrote, "I was . . . a Bolshevik (now I am not)." He became an increasingly powerful influence on young Russian writers (a group of whom in 1921 became known as the "Serapion Brothers"), but his satire on conformity, the servility of fellow artists, and Soviet totalitarianism soon made the publication of his works impossible. With the help of a courageous letter he wrote Stalin, and with the intervention of MAXIM GORKY, Zamyatin and his wife were allowed in 1932 to emigrate to Paris, where he spent the remainder of his life. His last years were marked by privation and loneliness, especially because he refused to join the émigré community. Zamyatin was among the few writers not rehabilitated during the post-Stalin "thaw."

His first play, *Ogni sv. Dominika* (*The Fires of St. Dominic,* 1923), a historical drama about Spain during the Inquisition, covertly satirizes the Cheka (OGPU's predecessor). Zamyatin's most popular play, *Blokha* (*The Flea,* 1925), appeared at about the same time; it is a farce in the *commedia dell'arte* tradition and based on a story by Nikolai Leskov, "Levsha" (1881, translated as "The Lefthanded Smith"), itself an adaptation of the folktale about a Russian master smith of such surpassing skill that he was able to shoe the tiny steel flea which the English smiths had constructed. *Obshchestvo pochotnykh zvonarei* (*The Society of Honorary Bell-Ringers,* 1926) is Zamyatin's free dramatization of his "Ostrovityane" ("The Islanders," 1917), a satiric story about English bourgeois life. A romantic comedy which satirizes Soviet manners, *Afrikansky gost* (*African Guest*), has remained unproduced since its completion in 1930 and was first published in New York in 1963. Zamyatin's final play was *Attila,* a tragedy about the Scythian ruler's love for a royal captive who kills Attila on their wedding night; following Gorky's high praise of the play in 1928, it was rehearsed for production but ultimately banned because of Zamyatin's fall from Soviet grace, and remained unpublished until 1950. These plays, like Zamyatin's other writings, show influences as divergent as those of Dostoevsky, Gogol, ALEKSANDR BLOK, and the English novelist H. G. Wells.

Mirra Ginsburg's translation of these as *The Collected Plays,* to be published in 1972, has informative introductions. Zamyatin's fiction and other works, though unavailable in Russia, are also available in English translation. David R. Richard's *Zamyatin* (1962) and Alex M. Shane's *The Life and Works of Evgenij Zamjatin* (1968) are studies of the man and his writings.

ZANGWILL, Israel (1864–1926), English writer, became famous with *Children of the Ghetto* (1892), *The King of Schnorrers* (1894), and other novels set in London's Jewish ghetto. He also wrote poetry and essays, and was active as a "Zionist, Territorialist, pacifist, polemicist, suffragist, and member of other sundry quasi-political movements" (Maurice Wohlgelernter). Zangwill wrote sixteen plays (some of them adaptations of his novels and short stories), primarily on Jewish themes; the most popular is entitled THE MELTING-POT (1908), an epithet thereupon used to describe America. Another successful play was his comedy *Merely Mary Ann* (1921), originally a short story (1893). His first plays, *The Great Demonstration* and *Six Persons,* both short, were produced in London in 1892. The 1899 dramatization of his most famous novel (*Children of the Ghetto*) was followed by *The Moment of Death, or the Never, Never Land,* a one-act tragedy produced in New York in 1900. *The Revolted Daughter,* a comedy, appeared the following year. Zangwill also wrote a trilogy of antiwar plays set in the Balkans: *The War God* (1911), *The Cockpit* (1920), and *The Forcing House* (1922); and two plays on religion: *The Next Religion* (1912), which was banned for its "heretical" advocacy of a new and liberal international theology; and *Plaster Saints* (1915), a comedy that criticizes loveless and pusillanimous religion. Apart from two unpublished plays, his works include the dramatization of his political Boer War novel,

Israel Zangwill in 1904. (*Culver Pictures*)

The Mantle of Elijah (1900); a comedy, *Nurse Marjorie* (1906); *Too Much Money* (1925), a farce produced in 1918; and his last and not very successful work, *We Moderns,* a comedy satirizing Freudianism and other "new" contemporary ideas, which was produced in 1924 with Helen Hayes in one of her earliest starring roles.

Zangwill was born in London, the son of an orthodox immigrant who became a countryside peddler. Educated at the Jews' Free School and at London University, Zangwill married a Gentile, and became one of the most distinguished interpreters of ghetto life and transmitters of Yiddish tales to non-Jews. He was Theodor Herzl's first English disciple, but later headed the Territorialist movement and also advocated the American "melting pot" as a haven for persecuted and homeless Jews. Passionately concerned with art, theology, pacifism, and politics, Zangwill frequently expressed conflicting emotions and ideas. He became a controversial figure, violently attacked by leading Jews for his "Watchman, What of the Night?" (1923), an address to the American Jewish Congress, in which he pronounced political Zionism dead. But Zangwill's personal, intellectual, and artistic integrity remained unquestioned.

Among recent biographies is Joseph Leftwich's *Israel Zangwill* (1957); a comprehensive study of his work and thought is Maurice Wohlgelernter's *Israel Zangwill* (1964), which contains extensive bibliographies.

ZAPOLSKA [pseudonym of Piotrowska], **Gabriela** (1860–1921), Polish playwright, first became famous as an actress. Her NATURALISTIC dramas, which have been revived frequently, deal with Jewish and other topics like the theatre and actresses, marriage and infidelity, and bourgeois morality. Most popular among her plays has been *Moralność Pani Dulskiej* (*The Morals of Mrs. Dulska,* 1907), a tragic farce of manners about a betrayed virgin; its title character became the Polish eponym for the ruthless bourgeois of elastic morality. Others include tragicomedies on lower-class figures like the poor Jewish shopkeepers *Małka Szwarcenkopf* (1897) and *Jojne Firułkes* (1899), and "the red-kneed housemaid" *Kaśka Kariatyda* (1899); *W Dąbrowa Górniczej* (*In Dabrowa Gornicza,* 1897), another play on proletarian life; *Panna Maliczewska* (*A Miss What's Her Name,* 1910), which is set in a theatre milieu and depicts a married man's sexual exploitation of a poor girl; *Ich czworo* (1912), about marital problems; and a romantic comedy about a marital quadrangle, *Skiz* (1909, translated as *The Secret of Skiz*).

Gabriela Zapolska was a radiant *fin de siècle* personality. While an actress, she played in André Antoine's Théâtre-Libre in Paris as well as in its Polish counterpart, the Red Theatre. She is also variously known as Śniezkowa (her name during her first, very unhappy marriage), as Janowska (after her second marriage), and as Józef Masków, a pseudonym.

ŻEROMSKI, Stefan (1864–1925), Polish novelist and dramatist, was primarily noted for his fiction. Because of his powerful depiction of social injustice and suffering, he became something of a national conscience in the first two decades of the century. Żeromski's drama for the most part supplements his many short stories and novels. His earliest works in that genre were, in fact, "reading plays" meant more for the study than the stage. Nonetheless, *Sułkowski* (1909), a tragedy about one of Napoleon's adjutants, who also was to become the subject of a play by ROMAN BRANDSTAETTER, was successfully produced in the 1960's. But another historical closet drama —this one about the 1905 revolution—*Róża* (1909), fared less well. Żeromski turned seriously to the theatre only in the last few years of his life, and then produced his best and most popular play, *Uciekła mi przepióreczka* (1924),* a comedy about a self-sacrificing idealist, a scientist who falls in love with one of the village teachers who attend his lectures, and then sacrifices his reputation for the sake of a cause.

Other notable plays are *Ponad śnieg bielszy się stanę* (1920), a social melodrama; the posthumous *Grzech* (Żeromski's first play, written in 1897 but not discovered for half a century), adapted by LEON KRUCZKOWSKI with a new last act for the lost original and successfully staged in 1951; and *Turoń* (1923), a grimly tragic epilogue to Żeromski's important novel *Popioły* (*Ashes,* 1904), based on the 1846 Insurrection.

For Żeromski's life and an analysis of his

* Literally, "my little quail has fled," a quotation from a native proverb; the play was translated as *Breaking the Spell.*

fiction see Manfred Kridl's *A Survey of Polish Literature and Culture* (1956) and Czeslaw Milosz's *The History of Polish Literature* (1969); his plays are discussed (in English) in Marta Piwińska's "Stefan Żeromski Dramas" in the journal *Le Théâtre en Pologne* (February 1964).

ZOLA, Émile [Édouard Charles Antoine] (1840–1902), French writer, is remembered primarily for his novels and criticisms, and for the part he played in the Dreyfus Affair. For a time he was the most popular and controversial writer in France. In 1871 he launched his twenty *Rougon-Macquart* novels on the "natural and social history of a family under the Second Empire," a series that was to rival Balzac's *Comédie humaine*. With *L'Assommoir* (1877) Zola made his fortune, and his fame grew with novels like *Nana* (1880) and *Germinal* (1885).

The son of a Frenchwoman and an Italian engineer who died soon after Zola's birth in Paris, he grew up in great poverty, in Aix. He was unable to complete his education, and became a clerk in a publishing house. Eventually his own articles and novels began to appear and soon brought him fame. He attracted considerable attention with THÉRÈSE RAQUIN (1867), the novel he dramatized in 1873 to launch NATURALISM in the theatre. He was always interested in drama, although that side of his career is little remembered now. His polemical theatre criticisms stressed the need to rejuvenate the stage, to replace the contemporary shopworn drama with works reflecting Zola's idealism of science. He was fanatic in his insistence on representing the scientific "truths" of heredity and environment, of the "dissecting" of "real life," usually that of the lower middle class. In practice, this often meant the depiction of the seamy and the sordid in a SLICE OF LIFE. At the same time, naturalism provided a stimulus to liberate the stage from stagnant conventions of romanticism and the trivial but popular WELL-MADE PLAY. Zola's work—foreshadowed by that of the Goncourt Brothers—established naturalism, which became a vital and lasting force despite its shortcomings and excesses. His work, along with that of HENRY BECQUE, also established André Antoine's Théâtre-Libre—launched in 1887 with Léon Hennique's (1851–1935) one-act dramatization of Zola's then-published short story on the Enoch Arden theme, "Jacques Damour"—and gave a forum to the production of plays by writers like HENRIK IBSEN. Thus, Zola's influence on the development of modern drama was considerable.

Despite this influence and his distinction as a novelist, Zola's drama is relatively insignificant. He wrote but a few plays and opera librettos, and occasionally collaborated on the many dramatizations of his fiction—most notably with William B. Busnach (1832–1907) on *L'Assommoir* (1879), the most popular staging of any of his works. The best and historically most important of Zola's plays, however, is the already-noted *Thérèse Raquin*. Earlier he had written *Madeleine*, a three-act tragedy of a woman with a past; it was turned down by producers in 1866, rewritten as a novel (*La Honte* and retitled *Madeleine Ferat*, 1868), and given only one performance, in 1889. A three-act satiric farce about greed, *Les Héritiers Rabourdin* (1874) also had but little success, and his next farce, *Le Bouton de rose* (1878), fared even worse. His last play, *Renée*, a five-act drama based on the Phèdre-type triangle culled from Zola's novel *La Curée* (1872), ran for thirty-eight performances in 1887. *L'Enfant-Roi*, a lyrical comedy, appeared posthumously, in 1905. Zola's librettos include *Messidor* (1897), *L'Ouragan* (1901), and three that first appeared posthumously in 1921: *Lazare, Violaine la chevelue,* and *Sylvanire ou Paris en amour;* unlike his naturalistic plays, these librettos are SYMBOLIC and lyrical.

Zola's plays were collected in the posthumous *Poèmes lyriques* (1921) and in two of the fifty volumes of his complete works (1927–29). Of his plays only *Thérèse Raquin* is readily available in English. His important preface to this play, a manifesto for naturalist drama, appears in Toby Cole's collection of essays, *Playwrights on Playwriting* (1960). A comprehensive study of Zola's theatrical and dramatic work is Lawson A. Carter's *Zola and the Theater* (1963); it contains a brief biography and an extensive bibliography. See also the entry on NATURALISM.

ZOO STORY, THE, a one-act play by EDWARD ALBEE, produced in 1959 and published in 1960. Setting: New York's Central Park on a Sunday afternoon, c. 1958.

Albee's first play is a SYMBOLIC duologue in the ABSURDist tradition. It dramatizes such characteristic Albee themes as Western man's sterility and his failure to become involved and communicate with fellow humans.

A self-acknowledged "permanent transient" returning from the zoo accosts a successful "square" reading on a park bench. Surprising similarities in their otherwise very different lives emerge from the conversation, insolently pursued by the drifter. He tells a long story about his struggles with the vicious dog owned by his lusting landlady. Then he provokes the solid citizen into a fight, slapping him at each "fight": "You fight, you miserable bastard; fight for that bench; fight for your parakeets; fight for your cats, fight for your two daughters; fight for your wife; fight for your manhood, you pathetic little vegetable"—and spitting in his face he sneers, "You couldn't even get your wife with a male child." Throwing him a knife, the "transient" promptly impales himself on it and urges the horrified respectable citizen to run off. He does, and the dying man scornfully half mimics and half supplicates: "Oh . . . my . . . God."

ZUCKMAYER, Carl [or Karl] (1896–), German playwright, though hailed by many as the successor of GERHART HAUPTMANN, has remained relatively unknown in the English-speaking world —despite the fact that as a refugee from Nazi

Germany he lived in the United States for six years. Here he wrote *Des Teufels General* (THE DEVIL'S GENERAL, 1946), which became the most popular German play about the Nazi war machine. Its success was equaled only by that of *Der Hauptmann von Köpenick* (THE CAPTAIN OF KÖPENICK, 1930), which had first brought Zuckmayer international acclaim. Many of his remaining plays have been frequently revived and filmed. Almost all of them are conventionally REPRESENTATIONAL, despite Zuckmayer's early literary radicalism. His folk satire and treatment of social problems are traditional and constitute a direct link with the older German drama, particularly with Hauptmann's. In 1952 Zuckmayer acknowledged his admiration and debt to his predecessor by adapting *Herbert Engelmann,* a moving antiwar play Hauptmann had written but discarded twenty-eight years earlier (in 1924). After World War II, Zuckmayer's work revitalized the West German theatre, and he remained its leading dramatist for nearly two decades.

Zuckmayer was born in the Rhineland village of Nackenheim, where his father owned a small bottling factory. When he was four the family moved to nearby Mainz, where he attended school until the outbreak of World War I. Volunteering immediately, Zuckmayer served with distinction and won many decorations for his front-line valor. During his four-year service Zuckmayer started to write and publish verse that mirrored the chaotic times. After the war he studied at the universities of Frankfurt and Heidelberg. He joined Bohemian literary and artistic circles, wrote poetry, fiction, and dramatic sketches, and eked out a precarious existence by working as a miner, as the editor of a revolutionary review, and even as a dope peddler. Until 1924 Zuckmayer continued to lead a miserable life of deprivation, which brought him to the brink of despair while he tried to succeed as a writer. Increasingly interested in drama, Zuckmayer took odd jobs in theatres in the provinces and then in Vienna and in Berlin.

His first play, *Kreuzweg,* was produced at the Berlin State Theatre in 1920. A shrill fantasy derivative of the popular EXPRESSIONIST theatre of the age, it closed after three performances. His adaptation of Terence's *Eunuchus* in 1923 was judged obscene and the production was closed by the police. *Pankraz erwacht* (1925, also known as *Kiktahan oder die Hinterwäldler*), a Wild West melodrama, had only a single performance. But Zuckmayer's fortunes were already changing. In 1924 he was employed by Max Reinhardt as a play reader and an assistant producer (as was BERTOLT BRECHT), and in late 1925 Zuckmayer became famous with *Der fröhliche Weinberg* (THE HAPPY VINEYARD).

His next play, *Schinderhannes* (1927), successfully dramatized the life of a notorious German Robin Hood in the age of Napoleon. It was followed by *Katharina Knie* (1928), a play about rope dancers in a traveling circus; *Kakadu Kakada* (1930), a children's play; *The Captain of Köpenick,* his masterpiece; *Der Schelm von Bergen* (1934), a free and highly theatrical dramatization of the medieval Rhenish legend about an executioner and his son, who ultimately marries an empress; and *Bellman* (1938), a sometimes-autobiographical portrayal of the eighteenth-century Swedish vagabond bard and later court poet Carl Michael Bellman, revised in 1953 as *Ulla Winblad*—the name of his mistress, who marries a nobleman but returns to her minstrel as he is dying.

Bellman was being rehearsed in Austria, where Zuckmayer had settled after the Nazis came to power, when Hitler's armies occupied that country. His belongings confiscated by the Gestapo, Zuckmayer fled to Switzerland and ultimately to the United States. From 1940 to 1946 he worked in Hollywood, in New York (where he taught playwriting at the New School for Social Research), and in his Vermont villa. There he composed his second major success, *The Devil's General,* which premiered in Switzerland. Shortly thereafter, on completing an assignment in Europe, he resettled in Switzerland. His controversial *The Devil's General* gave rise to many public and university debates in which Zuckmayer frequently participated.

Zuckmayer's later drama continued—but with less success—to explore the conflicts of individual and social integrity. *Der Gesang im Feuerofen* (1950) is set in occupied France on the Swiss border during a Christmas, and portrays Resistance fighters betrayed by their comrade and thereupon burned to death by the Germans. *Das kalte Licht* (1954), like *The Devil's General,* is based on an actual case (that of the atom bomb spy Dr. Klaus Fuchs) and features a similarly haunted protagonist, here a misguided idealist; it also became controversial, but is marred by excessive diffusiveness and prolixity. Yet at its best, Zuckmayer's drama teems with life, song, and humor. He excels in portraying even minor characters with considerable individuality, and in creating episodes which are not only important to the plot but delightful in themselves.

Other postwar work include another history play, *Barbara Blomberg* (1949), a dramatization of the life of the mistress of Charles V of the Holy Roman Empire, who was the mother of the illegitimate Don Juan, John of Austria; and *Die Uhr schlägt eins* (1961) an IBSENite family tragedy of affluent postwar Germans caught up in contemporary world affairs. Zuckmayer adapted a number of American works, including Anderson and Stallings's WHAT PRICE GLORY? (as *Rivalen,* 1929) and ERNEST HEMINGWAY'S 1929 novel *A Farewell to Arms* (as *Kat,* 1931). He also wrote the scripts of major films, notably the Marlene Dietrich-Emil Jannings hit *Der blaue Engel* (*The Blue Angel,* 1929; based on HEINRICH MANN'S novel *Professor Unrat*) and the Charles Laughton *Rembrandt* (1936). Though they were less popular than his plays, Zuckmayer was also distinguished as author of novels like *Salwàre oder Die Magdalena von Bozen* (1936, published in English as *The Moons Ride Over*), volumes of poetry, and miscellaneous prose works.

His autobiographies include *Second Wind* (1940), originally published in English; and *Als wärs ein Stück von mir* (*A Part of Myself,* 1966), an even more vivid portrait of himself, of Berlin in the 1920's, and of numerous luminaries in his artistic and intellectual milieu. See also H. F. Garten's *Modern German Drama* (1964), which has a section on Zuckmayer and a bibliography.

ZWEIG, Arnold (1887–1968), German writer (not related to STEFAN ZWEIG), was principally a novelist, although he also wrote some half-dozen plays. International renown came to him after the publication of his *Der Streit um den Sergeanten Grischa* (*The Case of Sergeant Grischa,* 1927), a suspenseful antiwar novel in a series based on Zweig's combat experiences, and on his play *Das Spiel vom Sergeanten Grischa* (written in 1921 and produced in 1930). In this and in his other works Zweig dramatized his concern with social problems and human suffering. He was also interested in psychology, and became a close friend of Sigmund Freud.

Zweig was born into a middle-class Jewish family in Silesia, and first made his name with *Die Novellen um Claudia* (1912, translated as *Claudia*), tales about an oversensitive girl. After dramatizing the biblical story of *Abigail und Nabal* (1913), Zweig achieved success as a playwright with *Ritualmord in Ungarn* (1914), a Kleist Prize "Jewish tragedy" about human misery, revised in 1919 as *Die Sendung Semaels* and produced by Max Reinhardt. *Die Umkehr des Abtrünnigen* (1925), a play about the breakdown of a violently anti-Semitic but himself partly-Jewish nobleman who is feared for the pogroms he has instigated, was followed by a historical drama, *Bonaparte in Jaffa* (1939); another history play, *Austreibung 1744, oder Das Weihnachtswunder* (1946), portrays Maria Theresa and Frederick the Great. Zweig is remembered best, however, for his drama and novel on Grischa Paprotkin, a mistaken-identity victim of the Prussian military, which is portrayed with characterizations that range from the lowliest private to the Kaiser himself; Grischa is tried, condemned, and executed despite his proven innocence. The work inspired a spate of antiwar novels like Erich Maria Remarque's *Im Western nichts Neues* (*All Quiet on the Western Front,* 1928).

Virtually blind from injuries he suffered in World War I, Zweig in 1933 was exiled by the Nazis from Berlin, where he had spent much of his life. He soon settled in Haifa, but though a long-time Zionist, he was unable to accommodate himself to the strife that eventuated in the establishment of the state of Israel. In 1948 he returned to East Berlin, where he continued to engage actively in literary activities, serving as President of the Academy of Arts from 1949 to 1952. For his antiwar writings he was awarded the Lenin Peace Prize in 1958.

ZWEIG, Stefan (1881–1942), Austrian writer (no relation to ARNOLD ZWEIG), achieved his greatest popularity with historical novels and biographies, but also published verse, essays, and dramas. His most popular plays were *Jeremias* (*Jeremiah,* 1917) and *Volpone* (1926), a widely performed adaptation of Ben Jonson's seventeenth-century "humours" comedy that was made into a popular film by Zweig's friend and biographer, JULES ROMAINS. A different kind of Jonson adaptation by Zweig was the libretto for Richard Strauss's opera *Die Schweigsame Frau* (*The Silent Woman,* 1935), based on *Epicœne, or The Silent Woman* (1609). Zweig also translated plays of ROMAIN ROLLAND (the subject of one of his biographies) and others, including those of LUIGI PIRANDELLO and of Zweig's close friends Romains and ÉMILE VERHAEREN, about whom he wrote a number of books. Intimately associated with many of the great writers of the age, Zweig, who was of patrician Jewish ancestry, matured during the *Jungwien* period when HUGO VON HOFMANNSTHAL and ARTHUR SCHNITZLER dominated Austrian letters.

Like many other cultivated intellectuals, Zweig was profoundly shaken by World War I, which inspired his principal stage work, *Jeremiah.* In nine poetic scenes spanning the start of the Assyrian war and the destruction of Jerusalem, it articulates Zweig's own feelings in the prophet's eloquent protests ("But I say unto you, people of Jerusalem, war is a wild and wicked beast, he eats the flesh from the strong and sucks the marrow from the mighty ones . . ."); Jeremiah is mocked and imprisoned, and upon his release bitterly accuses but ultimately comforts the people as he envisions the bliss of redemption and universal brotherhood made possible through military defeat.

Tersites (1907), Zweig's first stage work, is also a dramatic poem; it contrasts the misshapen title hero with the handsome and powerful but morally inferior Achilles. Zweig's other plays are *Das Haus am Meer* (1911), a domestic verse tragedy; *Der verwandelte Komödiant* (1912), a short drama about a dynamic actor; *Legende eines Lebens* (1919), dealing with the suppressed son of a great man and exposing the reality behind his legend; and *Das Lamm des Armen* (*The Lamb of the Poor,* 1929), a panoramic work, produced in a number of countries, that portrays Napoleon destroying a lowly subordinate by capriciously seducing his wife.

These later plays achieved some success because of Zweig's fame as a novelist and a biographer. However, he did not feel at ease in the theatre. After the advent of Hitlerism Zweig had to escape from Austria, which disheartened him, as did the inevitability of a second world war. He divorced his wife when he fell in love with his ailing young secretary; eventually he married her but, feeling too old and tired to start life anew in exile, he committed suicide with her in Brazil.

The translated biography by his first wife, Friderike Zweig's *Stefan Zweig* (1946), has a chapter on his drama; Zweig's autobiography, *Die Welt von Gestern* (*The World of Yesterday,* 1943), includes a bibliography of all his works. His life and work are discussed in W. I. Lucas's essay on Zweig in Volume II of Alex Natan's *German Men of Letters* (1963), which also has a bibliography.

ZWIE FAMILY, THE (*Di Familie Tsvi*), a tragedy in four acts by DAVID PINSKI, published and produced in 1905. Setting: "Place: The exile. Time: A bitter one for Jews."

In his foreword, Pinski called this hortatory play, which also appeared in English as *The Last Jew,* "the tragedy of a moribund religion, of a crumbling world-philosophy." Stimulated by the recent Kishinev pogrom, Pinski was so engrossed in completing the play that he forwent his 1904 doctoral examination at Columbia University. The drama was frequently smuggled into tsarist Russia and produced there.

"The last Jew" is Reb Moyshe, a religious idealist and the oldest of the Zwie family. His son, more interested in worldly affairs, pays only lip service to Jewish ideals. His three grandsons have inherited Reb Moyshe's idealism—but of different kinds: Zionism, Socialism, and assimilation. When the bloody pogrom breaks out, Reb Moyshe goes to his synagogue to protect the Holy Scrolls. The others protect their own individual interests, and the community at large ignores his pleas for help. Defending the Scroll by himself, Moyshe is struck by one of the rocks hurled into the synagogue, and dies—just as the grandsons enter, at the head of a Jewish people's militia come to help him. "Dead! The old order has departed. And—now—?" a grandson asks. His arrival suggests that the "last Jew" is not, after all, the last.

Character Index

Character Index

This is an index of all the characters named in the play entries as well as in the plays discussed in biographical, national, and other entries, as noted under "Arrangement of Contents," page xiii. Alphabetization is by name, not title: Bismarck, Otto von (*not* Von Bismarck, Otto); Elizabeth I, Queen (*not* Queen Elizabeth I); Hook, Captain (*not* Captain Hook); Joan, Saint (*not* Saint Joan); Juan, Don (*not* Don Juan).

D

F

G

I

J

L

General Index

General Index

As noted under "Arrangement of Contents" (page xiii), this is a comprehensive index of: (1) modern **plays** and other dramatic works (but *not* films) and their alternate titles; (2) nineteenth- and twentieth-century **playwrights**, including their variant name forms; (3) **countries** and other geographical areas; and (4) modern dramatic **terms.** SMALL CAPITALS denote subjects that have separate entries. Foreign plays that do *not* have separate entries are indexed under their original titles or, if translated, under their English titles only. For method of alphabetizing, see pages xv–xvi.

B

H